A DICTIONARY of IRAQI ARABIC

ENGLISH – ARABIC

Beverly E. Clarity, Karl Stowasser, and Ronald G. Wolfe, Editors

ARABIC – ENGLISH

D. R. Woodhead and Wayne Beene, Editors

Georgetown University Press
Washington, D.C.

Georgetown University Press, Washington, D.C.

Printed in the United States of America

10 9 8 7 6 5 4 3 2 1 2003

This book is printed on acid-free recycled paper meeting
the requirements of the American National Standard
for Permanence in Paper for Printed Library Materials.

Library of Congress Cataloging-in-Publication Data

A dictionary of Iraqi Arabic.
p. cm. – (Georgetown classics in Arabic language and linguistics)
Consists of two previously published dictionaries.
Includes bibliographical references.
Contents: English-Arabic / Beverly E. Clarity, Karl Stowasser, and Ronald G. Wolfe, editors – Arabic-English / D.R. Woodhead and Wayne Beene, editors.
ISBN 0-87840-136-9 (pbk. : alk. paper)
1. English language—Dictionaries—Arabic. 2. Arabic language—Dialects—Iraq—Dictionaries. I. Series.

PJ6826.D53 2003
492.7′321—dc21

2003045211

CONTENTS

Georgetown Classics in Arabic Language and Linguistics

Karin C. Ryding and Margaret Nydell, series editors

For some time, Georgetown University Press has been interested in making available its seminal publications in Arabic language and linguistics that have gone out of print. Some of the most meticulous and creative scholarship of the last century was devoted to the analysis of Arabic language and to producing detailed reference works and textbooks of the highest quality. Although some of the material is dated in terms of theoretical approaches, the content and methodology of the books considered for the reprint series is still valid and, in some cases, unsurpassed.

With global awareness now refocused on the Arab world, and with renewed interest in Arab culture, society, and political life, it is essential to provide easy access to classic reference materials, such as dictionaries and reference grammars, and to language teaching materials. The components of this series have been chosen for their quality of research and scholarship, and have been updated with new bibliographies and an introduction to provide readers with resources for further study.

Georgetown University Press hereby hopes to serve the growing national and international need for reference works on Arabic language and culture, as well as to provide access to quality textbooks and audiovisual resources for teaching Arabic language in its written and spoken forms.

Books in the Georgetown Classics in Arabic Language and Linguistic series

Arabic Language Handbook
Mary Catherine Bateson

A Basic Course in Moroccan Arabic
Richard S. Harrell with Mohammed Abu-Talib and William S. Carroll

A Dictionary of Iraqi Arabic: English–Arabic, Arabic–English
B. E. Clarity, Karl Stowasser, and Ronald G. Wolfe; and D. R. Woodhead and Wayne Beene, editors

Arabic Research at Georgetown University

In the thirty-eight years since the original publication of *A Dictionary of Iraqi Arabic: English–Arabic*, the world of research in Arabic theoretical linguistics has expanded, but the production of quality professional textbooks in colloquial Arabic has remained limited. Despite the passage of years, the Richard Slade Harrell Arabic Series has consistently been in demand from Georgetown University Press because of the quality of research that went into its composition, the solid theoretical foundations for its methodology, and the comprehensive coverage of regional Arabic speech communities.

The Arabic Department at Georgetown University (now Department of Arabic Language, Literature and Linguistics) recognizes the need to sustain the tradition of research and publication in Arabic dialects and has continued dialectology field research and textbook production, most notably with Margaret (Omar) Nydell's *Syrian Arabic Video Course*, a three-year research project funded by Center for the Advancement of Language Learning from 1991 to 1994. Currently, we are engaged in a four-year dialectology research project aimed at producing "conversion" courses to assist learners of Modern Standard Arabic in converting their knowledge and skills of written Arabic to proficiency in selected Arabic dialects. This project is part of a grant administered by the National Capital Language Resource Center under the directorship of James E. Alatis and Anna Chamot.

We pay tribute to the tradition initiated and led by Richard Harrell, the founder of this series, and of the original Arabic Research Program at Georgetown University. His scholarship and creative energy set a standard in the field and yielded an unprecedented and as yet unsurpassed series of, as he put it, "practical tools for the increasing number of Americans whose lives bring them into contact with the Arab world." We hope that this series of reprints and our continuing efforts in applied Arabic dialectology research will yield a new crop of linguistic resources for Arabic language study.

For more information about the Department of Arabic Language, Literature and Linguistics at Georgetown University, its course offerings, its degree programs, and its research agenda, see our website at www.georgetown.edu/departments/arabic.

Karin C. Ryding
Sultan Qaboos bin Said Professor of Arabic
Georgetown University

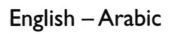

English – Arabic

My personal contribution in

the compilation of this dictionary

is dedicated to

my mother and her two close friends,

"Eileen" and "Cleo."

R. G. W.

Foreword

I was delighted to receive Georgetown University Press's invitation to write an introduction to the reprinting of *A Dictionary of Iraqi Arabic: English–Arabic.* This dictionary, specifically designed for an English speaker acquiring Arabic as a second language, remains a key resource for anyone learning the colloquial speech of Iraq. In format and arrangement, it follows Hans Wehr's *Dictionary of Modern Written Arabic.* Its distinguishing feature is that, in most cases, illustrative sentences are provided to show how individual word entries are used in context and to reinforce the user's acquisition of colloquial Iraqi. Emphasis is placed on the educated speech patterns of educated residents of Baghdad, in particular. While this dictionary will also prove useful in other major Iraqi urban areas, Basra and Mosul, for example, the user should not be surprised to find some variation there in vocabulary and phonetics. Two other important Iraqi dialect tools to be used in conjunction with this volume were produced at Georgetown University during the 1960s: Dr. Wallace M. Erwin's *Short Reference Grammar of Iraqi Arabic* and the companion volume to this one, *A Dictionary of Iraqi Arabic: Arabic–English,* edited by Daniel R. Woodhead and Wayne Beene.

Georgetown's Arabic dictionaries have both withstood the test of time and inspired similar volumes on a greater scale. The most notable example is the comprehensive 1000-page *Dictionary of Egyptian Arabic,* published in 1987 by El-Said Badawi and the late Martin Hinds, for whom my coeditor, the late Karl Stowasser, served as consulting lexicographer. It follows the identical approach of employing romanized transliteration and illustrating lexical items in sentences first used for Iraqi Arabic dictionaries at Georgetown.

On a personal note, I wish to acknowledge some deeply felt and long overdue debts. Nearly thirty-nine years have passed since the night of February 27, 1964, when I completed the last round of corrections to the galley proofs of this dictionary. I remember it as clearly as yesterday and for a truly wonderful reason—just a few hours later my daughter Kirstin was born and became the first new member of our family. I was in my fourth year of undergraduate Arabic study at Georgetown.

The U.S. Air Force had sent me, an airman just out of high school, to Georgetown University in January 1958 to take a thirty-nine–week intensive course in Egyptian Arabic. Richard S. Harrell, who headed the Arabic Department and the Arabic Research Program that produced this series of grammars and dictionaries, had joined the university faculty in September 1957 and administered the courses being taught there. He was twenty-eight and held a Harvard doctorate in linguistics, and I found him truly inspiring! He had engaged Laila Tewfik, a Georgetown Master's degree candidate in economics, and George Selim, newly arrived from Alexandria, Egypt, to teach the Egyptian course from mimeographed sheets that subsequently became another book in this series: *Lessons in Colloquial Egyptian Arabic.* I am deeply indebted to both of them for the love of Arabic I discovered while they were my teachers. They became lifelong friends and colleagues.

During those thirty-nine weeks, Dr. Harrell visited the classroom at least weekly to explain grammar points and monitor class progress. Reflecting on this period, I remember how much I looked forward to those weekly visits, both for the knowledge he conveyed and for the example of excellence he represented. In early 1961, six months before I was to be discharged from the Air Force, I wrote to Dr. Harrell to say that I wished to return to Georgetown to pursue a degree in Arabic but lacked the means to do so. He cleared my admission, arranged for loans and a scholarship, and hired me as a research assistant to work on this dictionary. No undergraduate student of Arabic has ever been so fortunate.

Spring 1964 was Harrell's last semester teaching Arabic and linguistics. His sudden death in Cairo the following November at thirty-five, during a sabbatical for a Fulbright fellowship, left those who knew and marveled at his brilliance and accomplishments in a state of profound shock and disbelief. His was a tremendous loss for the Georgetown community, and the impact of his death on the future course of Arabic language study and research was certainly even greater in its adversity.

Georgetown University published a memorial volume in 1967 titled *Linguistic Studies in Memory of Richard Slade Harrell*. The volume's editor, Don Graham Stuart, summarized Harrell's approach to life and his impact on students and colleagues alike.

> "[Richard Harrell] delighted in learning, and he also delighted in teaching. To acquire knowledge, to order it, to add to it his own judgments and insights, and to transmit it all to others—these were his talents and these were his joys. He was that rarest of teachers, one capable of communicating not facts alone, not interpretation alone, but the very love of learning itself. Student, scholar, teacher, author, he will be remembered not only in these written works which he created, but in the atmosphere of intensity, enthusiasm, and general excellence which surrounded all his actions, and which for years to come will remain to refresh and inspire the lives of all who knew him."

Stuart's tribute remains as brilliantly keen and insightful today as was the educator it describes during his brief lifetime.

How I wish Richard Harrell were still around to provide his guidance! The world of Arabic linguists would be a very different, and better, place. Finally, I wish to express my great appreciation to Georgetown University Press for providing me with the chance to put my gratitude on record.

Ronald G. Wolfe, Ph.D., Arabic
October 2002

The Arabic Research Program
Institute of Languages and Linguistics
Georgetown University

The Arabic Research Program was established in June of 1960 as a contract between Georgetown University and the United States Office of Education under the provisions of the Language Development Program of the National Defense Education Act.

The first two years of the research program, 1960–1962 (contract number SAE-8706), were devoted to the production of six books, a reference grammar, and a conversational English–Arabic dictionary in the cultivated spoken forms of Moroccan, Syrian, and Iraqi Arabic. The second two years of the research program, 1962–1964 (contract number OE-2-14-029), call for the further production of Arabic–English dictionaries in each of the three varieties of Arabic mentioned above, as well as comprehensive basic courses in the Moroccan and Iraqi varieties.

The eleven books of this series, of which the present volume is one, are designed to serve as practical tools for the increasing number of Americans whose lives bring them into contact with the Arab world. The dictionaries, the reference grammars, and the basic courses are oriented toward the educated American who is a layman in linguistic matters. Although it is hoped that the scientific linguistic and the specialist in Arabic dialectology will find these books both of interest and of use, matters of purely scientific and theoretical importance have not been directly treated as such, and specialized scientific terminology has been avoided as much as possible.

As is usual, the authors or editors of the individual books bear final scholarly responsibility for the contents, but there has been a large amount of informal cooperation in our work. Criticism, consultation, and discussion have gone on constantly among the senior professional members of the staff. The contribution of more junior research assistants, both Arab and American, is also not to be underestimated. Their painstaking assembling and ordering of raw data, often in manners requiring considerable creative intelligence, has been the necessary prerequisite for further progress.

Staff work has been especially important in the preparation of the dictionaries. Although the contributing staff members are named on the title page of the individual dictionaries, special mention must be made of Karl Stowasser's work. His lexicographical experience, acquired in his work on the English version of Professor Wehr's *Arabisches Wörterbuch für die Schriftsprache der Gegenwart* (Hans Wehr, *A Dictionary of Modern Written Arabic*, ed. J. Milton Cowan (Ithaca, N.Y.: Cornell University Press, 1961)), along with his thorough knowledge of Arabic, has been critically important for all our lexicographical work, covering the entire range from typography to substantive entries in the dictionaries.

In most cases the books prepared by the Arabic Research Program are the first of their kind in English, and, in some cases, the first in any language. The preparation of them has been a rewarding experience. It is hoped that the public use of them will be equally so. The undersigned, on behalf of the entire staff, would like to ask the same indulgence of the reader as Samuel Johnson requested in his first English dictionary: To remember that although much has been left out, much has been included.

Richard S. Harrell
Associate Professor of Linguistics
Georgetown University

Director
Arabic Research Program

Preface

The compilation of this dictionary was begun in the summer of 1960 by Thomas B. Irving of the University of Minnesota, with the assistance of Munir Malayka of Baghdad, Iraq. Unfortunately, Dr. Irving was not able to see the dictionary through to its completion, and, for a variety of technical reasons, the mass of material which he had so conscientiously and diligently collected had largely to be abandoned.

The re-editing and completion of the work was undertaken by B. E. Clarity, formerly of the linguistics department of the Arabian-American Oil Company and now professor at Beloit College, Beloit, Wisconsin. The work was then given a final revision by Ronald G. Wolfe under the editorial supervision of Karl Stowasser. The compilation of the dictionary was the work of many diligent hands and minds. Mr. Clarity's chief assistants, in addition to Ronald Wolfe, were Dan Woodhead, Munir Malayka, Husein Mustafa, and Faysal Al-Khalaf. Contributions were also made by Majid Damah, Basil Al-Bustani, Hasan Al-Hashimi, Jerome Hoffman, and Thomas Fox.

The long task of reading the proofs, both galley and page, was undertaken by Ronald Wolfe.

R. S. H.
Washington, D.C.
February 1964

Editors' Introduction

This dictionary is based, in format, on the English–German section of the bilingual German and English *Dictionary of Everyday Usage*.[1] The aim of this work has been to present, for the first time, a dictionary for English speakers containing the basic vocabulary of the Iraqi dialect. Technical terms have been largely avoided. The usage is primarily that of Muslim speakers from Baghdad, but some southern Iraqi usage is also included. The illustrative English sentences are based on everyday conversational usage with a deliberate avoidance of literary style. In a few cases somewhat awkward English constructions have been resorted to in order to give a clearer picture of Iraqi sentence structure.

The transcription system is identical to that of Wallace M. Erwin's *A Short Reference Grammar of Iraqi Arabic*,[2] which should be consulted for further treatment of Iraqi phonology.

The consonants are as follows:

ʾ — glottal stop; not a distinctive feature of English, but similar to the variant for English *t* in *button* or *bottle*.

b — voiced bilabial stop; similar to English *b* as in *bake*.

p — voiceless bilabial stop; similar to English *p* as in *pole*.

t — voiceless dental stop; similar to English *t* as in *take*.

θ — voiceless interdental spirant; similar to English *th* as in *thank*.

j — voiced palatal affricate; similar to English *j* as in *jail*.

č — voiceless palatal affricate; similar to English *ch* as in *cheese*.

ح — voiceless pharyngeal spirant; no English equivalent, but same as Classical Arabic ح.

x — voiceless velar spirant; no English equivalent but similar to *ch* as in German *Bach*.

d — voiced dental stop; similar to English *d* as in *desk*.

δ — voiced interdental spirant; similar to English *th* as in *than*.

r — alveolar flat, generally voiced; unlike English *r*, but similar to the *t* or *d* flap of English *Betty* or *body*.

z — voiced dental spirant; similar to English *z* as in *zeal*.

s — voiceless dental spirant; similar to English *s* as in *seen*.

š — voiceless palatal spirant; similar to English *sh* as in *sheep*.

ṣ — voiceless dental spirant, emphatic; no equivalent in English.

δ̣ — voiceless interdental spirant, emphatic; no equivalent in English.

ṭ — voiceless dental stop, emphatic; no equivalent in English.

ع — voiced pharyngeal spirant; no equivalent in English, but same as Classical Arabic ع.

ġ — voiced velar spirant; no equivalent in English, but similar to some occurrences of French *r*.

f — voiceless labio-dental spirant; similar to English *f* as in *fan*.

q — voiceless post-velar stop; no equivalent in English.

k — voiceless velar stop; similar to English *k* as in *kick*.

g — voiced velar stop; similar to English *g* as in *get*.

l — voiced alveo-dental lateral; unlike most English *l*'s, but similar to *l* as in *million*.

m — voiced bilabial nasal; similar to English *m* as in *meat*.

n — voiced dental nasal; similar to English *n* as in *neat*.

h — voiceless glottal spirant; similar to English *h* as in *home*.

The semivowels are as follows:

w — voiced high back rounded semivowel; similar to English *w* as in *way*.

y — voiced high front unrounded semivowel; similar to English *y* as in *yell*.

The short vowels are as follows:

a — short line central vowel; the quality of this vowel varies with its environment and is similar to the English *a* as in *father*, or a sound between the vowels of *father* and *fought*, or *bet* and *bat*.

i — short high front unrounded vowel; the quality of this vowel varies with its environment and is similar to the English *i* as in *machine*, *bit*, or the English *e* as in *sister*.

o — short mid back rounded vowel; similar to the first part of the diphthong in English *boat*.

µ — short high back rounded vowel; the quality of this vowel varies with its environment, and is similar to the vowel of English *boot*, or to a sound between the vowels of *bull* and *ball*, or to the vowel sound of English *book*.

The long vowels are as follows:

aa — long low central vowel; this vowel, when not next to an emphatic, is between the vowels of English *had* and *hod*, but longer. Next to an emphatic, it ranges between the vowel of English *hod* and *haul*.

ee — long mid front unrounded vowel; this vowel is between the vowel sounds of English *fez* and *phase*, or else has diphthong quality, the first part being like the sound of *eat*, the second like the sound of *let*.

ii — long high front unfounded vowel; similar to the *i* of English as in *machine*.

oo — long mid back rounded vowel; this vowel, when not next to an emphatic, has the quality of the first element in the diphthong of English *chose*, or if next to an emphatic, it is similar to the vowel of English *ball*.

uu — long high back rounded vowel; if next to an emphatic, it is between the vowel of *choose* and the first element of the diphthong of *chose* in English, otherwise it is similar to the vowel of English *choose*.

A dot beneath a letter other than the three aforementioned emphatics (ṣ, δ̣, ṭ) indicates that the letter is also emphatic. As a general rule, the assimilation of a radical to a preceding or following consonant has not been shown. The notable expectation is that partial assimilation as to emphasis (velarization) is shown. For example *ṭṣiir* "you become" and *ṣṭubar* "he was patient."

English homonyms are treated in the same main entry. The Arabic equivalent of an English entry is usually followed by a contextual example that is designed to illustrate and define its semantic range or syntactic behavior, or both. Several Arabic equivalents separated by commas are interchangeable within these confines. An English entry that has no word-for-word equivalent in Arabic is followed by a colon and one or more contextual examples that demonstrate paraphrasitic possibilities. A double asterisk (**) preceding an English sentence or Arabic phrase signals idiomatic rendering.

An Arabic noun is regularly followed by its sound and/or broken plural, the former in abbreviation (*-a*, *-iyya*, or *-iin*, *-iyyiin*, or *-aat*). The adjectives are given in masculine form with only broken plurals being indicated. An asterisk following an adjective ending in <u>*-i*</u> indicates that it follows this pattern: feminine *-iyya*; plural *-iyyiin*, *-iyyaat*.

An Arabic verb is quoted in the conventional third person singular (masculine) of the perfect. It is followed by parentheses containing the stem vowel of the imperfect and the verbal noun or nouns. If the verb has a passive voice it will be indicated by the proper prefix, *n-* or *t-*, following the closed parentheses. Following the passive form prefix appears the obligatory prepositional complement, if there is one; e.g., *ƹtiraf b-* "to admit," *ƹtimad ƹala* "to trust," whereas free prepositional complements are relegated to the illustrative sentences for demonstration.

A noun may occur in a verb entry either before or after the preposition. A tilde (˜) following a noun indicates that the noun is the object of the verb and takes the possessive pronominal suffix agreeing with the subject-doer of the verb: *daar (i) baal˜ ƹala* "to tend" becomes *daar baal<u>a</u> ƹaj-jihhaal* "He tended the children."

In a certain number of instances where the English verb is expressed in Arabic by a compound of verb plus noun, a hyphen (-) is placed after the noun to indicate annexion: *šaaf (u) manδ̣ar-* "to view" becomes *šaaf manδ̣ar il-zaadiθ* "He viewed the accident."

Elsewhere, the use of the hyphen in a compound of verb plus noun indicates that the noun is the subject of the Arabic verb and takes a pronominal suffix corresponding to the subject of the equivalent English sentence: *ġaabat (i) rooƺ-* "to faint" becomes *ġaabat rooƺ<u>a</u>* "He fainted."

The abbreviations used are as follows:

coll. – collective
f. – feminine
m. – masculine
pl. – plural

The editors wish to express their appreciation to Georgetown University for providing an academic home during the compiling of this dictionary, and, above all, to the authors of the National Defense Education Act and its administrators in the Department of Health, Education, and Welfare, who made possible for us its undertaking.

B. E. C.
K. S.
R. G. W.

Washington, D.C.
February 1964

Notes

1. *German-English English-German Dictionary of Everyday Usage*, ed. By J. Alan Pfeffer (New York: Henry Holt and Company). Although the content of this dictionary is, in strictly legal terms, public domain since it was prepared as a part of the American war effort in World War II, we wish to express our thanks to the publishers for raising no copyright objections to our use of the material.

2. *A Short Reference Grammar of Iraqi Arabic*, by Wallace M. Erwin (Institute of Languages and Linguistics, Georgetown University, Arabic Series, 4). Washington, D. C., Georgetown University Press, 1964.

A

a - 1. (no equivalent). Do you have a stamp and an envelope? *Ɛindak ṭaabiƐ w-ẓaruf?* **2.** *fadd.* There is a man at the door. *ʔaku fadd rijjaal bil-baab.* **3.** *l-.* These eggs are fifty fils a dozen. *hal-beeẓ id-darzan ib-xamsiin filis.*

to **abbreviate** - *xtiṣar (i xtiṣaar).* The British Broadcasting Corporation is abbreviated B.B.C. *maṣlaẓat il-ʔiδaaƐa l-bariiṭaaniyya muxtaṣara ʔila "bii bii sii".*

ability - *qaabliyya* pl. *-aat, qtidaar.* I don't doubt his ability. *ma-ašukk ib-qaabliita.*

able - *miqtidir, kafu* pl. *ʔakiffaaʔ.* I'm sure he's an able officer. *ʔaani mitʔakkid huwwa ẓaabuṭ kafu.*
to be able - *gidar (a maqdira, qudra).* Will you be able to come? *raẓ-tigdar tiji?*

aboard - *Ɛala.* We went aboard the boat an hour before it sailed. *ṣƐadna Ɛal-markab saaƐa gabuḷ-ma miša.*
**all aboard! (ship) *kullkum ṣiƐdu Ɛal-markab.* (train) *kullkum rukbu bil-qiṭaar.*

to **abolish** - *liġa (i ʔilġaaʔ) n-.* When was slavery abolished in the United States? *šwakt inliġat il-Ɛubuudiyya b-amriika?*

abortion - *taṭriiẓ* pl. *-aat.* Abortion is against the law. *t-taṭriiẓ ẓidd il-qaanuun.*
to perform an abortion on - *ṭarraẓ (i taṭriiẓ) t-.* He was arrested for performing an abortion on a young girl. *twaqqaf li-ʔan ṭarraẓ ibnayya ẓġayyra.*

about - 1. *ẓawaali, taqriiban.* There were about thirty people present. *čaan ʔaku ẓawaali tlaaθiin waaẓid.* -- It's about the same. *taqriiban nafs iš-šii.* **2.** *Ɛala wašak.* Lunch is about ready. *l-ġada Ɛala wašak yiẓẓar.* -- He was about to leave when the phone rang. *čaan Ɛala wašak yiṭlaƐ min dagg it-talafoon.* **3.** *Ɛan, Ɛala.* They were talking about the war. *čaanaw yiẓčuun Ɛann il-ẓarub.* **4.** *b-.* My husband is very particular about his food. *rajli hwaaya diqdaaqi b-ʔakla.*
**It's about time you got here. *ma-yaḷḷa Ɛaad!* or *ween ẓalleet?*
what ... about - *Ɛala weeš.* What are you talking about? *ʔinta Ɛala weeš da-tiẓči?* or *ʔinta š-da-tiẓči?*
what about - *š-raʔyak, š-itguul.* What about this one? *š-raʔyak ib-haaδa?* or *šloonak bii?*
to be about - 1. *Ɛala weeš.* What's it all about? *Ɛala weeš haaδa kulla?* or *š-ṣaar?* or *š-aku?* **2.** *Ɛala.* It's about the money he owes me. *haay Ɛal-ifluus il-ʔaṭlubh-iyyaa.* **3.** *čaan yriid.* I was about to send for you. *činit da-ariid adizz Ɛaleek.* **4.** *Ɛala wašak.* She was about to burst into tears. *čaanat Ɛala wašak tibči.*

above - 1. *foog.* He is above average height. *ṭuula foog il-muƐaddal.* **2.** *bis-saabiq.* As already mentioned above. *miθil-ma nδikar bis-saabiq.*
above all - *wil-ʔahamm, la-siyyama, Ɛala l-axaṣṣ, xuṣuuṣan.* Above all, remember to be on time. *wil-ʔahamm, iδδakkar laazim itkuun Ɛal-wakit.* or *la-siyyama, la-titʔaxxar.*
to be above - *(čaan) ʔaƐla min, ʔarfaƐ min, foog.* She's above such petty things. *hiyya ʔarfaƐ min hal-ʔašyaaʔ iṭ-ṭafiifa.* -- He's above suspicion. *huwwa foog iš-šubhaat.*

abroad - *xaarij.* Are you going abroad this summer? *ʔinta msaafir lil-xaarij haṣ-ṣeef?* -- He lives abroad. *huwwa yƐiiš bil-xaarij.* -- At home and abroad ... *bil-waṭan w-bil-xaarij ...*

abrupt - 1. *yaabis.* He has a very abrupt manner. *Ɛinda ʔaxlaaqa hwaaya yaabsa.* **2.** *fujaaʔi*.* We noticed an abrupt change in his attitude. *laaẓaẓna taġayyur fujaaʔi b-mawqifa.*

abruptly - *b-jafaaf.* He treated me rather abruptly. *Ɛaamalni b-jafaaf.*

absence - *ġiyaab.* No one noticed his absence. *maẓẓad laaẓaẓ ġiyaaba ʔaslan.*

absent - *ġaayib.* Three members were absent because of illness. *tlaθ ʔaƐẓaaʔ čaanaw ġaaybiin ib-sabab il-maraẓ.*

absent-minded - *fikr- šaarid, daalġači.* He's very absent-minded. *haaδa kulliš fikra šaarid* or *huwwa kulliš daalġači.*

absolute - 1. *xaaliṣ, ṣirf, maẓẓ.* That's the absolute truth. *haaδa ṣ-ṣudug il-xaaliṣ.* -- That's an absolute fact. *haδiič l-ẓaqiiqa l-maẓẓa.* **2.** *muṭlaq.* The dictator exercised absolute power. *d-diktatoor maaras ṣulṭa muṭlaqa.*

absolutely - *qaṭƐan.* He's absolutely right. *l-ẓaqq wiyyaa qaṭƐan.*

to **absorb - 1.** *maṣṣ (u maṣṣ) n-.* The sponge absorbed the water quickly. *l-isfanja maṣṣat il-maay bil-Ɛajal.* **2.** *hiẓam (u haẓum) n-.* You can't absorb all that material in a single lesson. *ma-tigdar tuhẓum kull hal-maƐluumaat ib-fadd daris.*

to **be absorbed** - *nhimak (i nhimaak).* He was so absorbed in his book, he didn't hear me come in. *čaan hal-gadd minhimik bil-iqraaya ma-ẓass biyya min xaššeet.*

to **abuse - 1.** *ʔasaaʔ (i ʔisaaʔa) n- l-istiƐmaal.* He's abusing his authority. *da-ysiiʔ istiƐmaal ṣuluṭṭa.* **2.** *ʔasaaʔ (i ʔisaaʔa) n- l-muƐaamala.* He abuses his wife. *huwwa ysiiʔ muƐaamalat marta.*

academic - 1. *diraasi*.* The academic year. *s-sana d-diraasiyya.* **2.** *naẓari*.* This is an academic matter. *haaδi qaẓiyya naẓariyya.*

academy - *majmaƐ* pl. *majaamiƐ.* Scientific academy. *majmaƐ Ɛilmi.*

accelerator - *ʔaksaleeta.* The accelerator's broken. *l-ʔaksaleeta maksuura.*

accent - 1. *lakna, lahja.* He speaks with a German accent. *yiẓči b-lakna ʔaḷmaaniyya.* **2.** *tašdiid* pl. *-aat.* Where is the accent in this word? *ween it-tašdiid ib-hal-kilma?*

to **accept** - *qibal (a qubuul) n-.* Are you going to accept that position? *raẓ-tiqbal haδiič il-waẓiifa?*

access - 1. *stiƐmaal.* Access to the files is restricted to supervisors. *stiƐmaal il-faaylaat maqṣuur Ɛal-mulaaẓiẓiin.* **2.** *maxraj* pl. *maxaarij.* Iraq has access to the sea through the Shatt-al-Arab. *l-Ɛiraaq Ɛinda maxraj lil-baẓar Ɛan ṭariiq šaṭṭ il-Ɛarab.*
to have access to - 1. (things) *gidar (a) yistaƐmil.* He has access to the files. *huwwa yigdar yistaƐmil il-ʔiẓbaaraat.* **2.** (persons) *gidar (a) yitwaṣṣal.* She has access to the minister of interior. *tigdar titwaṣṣal il-waziir id-daaxiliyya.*

accident - *ẓaadiθa* pl. *ẓawaadiθ, qadar* pl. *ʔaqdaar.* When did the accident happen? *šwakit ṣaarat il-ẓaadiθa?*
by accident - 1. *biṣ-ṣidfa.* I found it out by accident. *ktišafitha biṣ-ṣidfa.* **2.** *min keef-.* That didn't happen by accident. *haδiič ma-ṣaarat min keefha.*

accidentally - 1. *bila taƐammud.* I dropped the plate accidentally. *waqqaƐt il-maaƐuun bila taƐammud.* **2.** *ṣidfatan.* I accidentally learned the truth. *Ɛiraft iṣ-ṣudug ṣidfatan.*

to **accommodate** - **We can accommodate three more people. *nigdar inhayyiʔ makaan l-itlaθ ašxaaṣ baƐad* or *Ɛidna makaan l-itlaaθa baƐad.*

accommodating - *xaduum.* The manager was very accommodating. *l-mudiir čaan kulliš xaduum.*

accompaniment - *Ɛazif.* Who's going to play the accompaniment? *minu raẓ-yquum bil-Ɛazif?*

to **accompany - 1.** *raafaq (i muraafaqa), ṣaaẓab (i muṣaaẓaba).* He accompanied her on the lute. *huwwa raafaqha Ɛal-Ɛuud.* -- I played the lute and Ali accompanied me on the flute. *ʔaani daggeet Ɛuud* *w-εali ṣaazabni εan-naay.* 2. *raaζ (u) wiyya.* We'll accompany you to Damascus. *nruuζ wiyyaak liš-šaam.*

to **accomplish** - 1. *xallaṣ (i taxliiṣ) t-, kammal (i takmiil) t-.* He accomplished what he set out to do. *xallaṣ iš-šii l-bida bii* or *kammal il-raad ysawwii.* 2. *ṭallaε (i ṭaṭliiε) t-.* For one day he accomplished quite a lot. *ṭallaε ihwaaya šuġul ib-fadd yoom.* 3. *ζaqqaq (i taζqiiq) t-.* He's accomplished a good deal in his life. *ζaqqaq ihwaaya ġaayaat ib-ζayaata.* 4. *twaṣṣal (a tawaṣṣul).* Did you accomplish anything in Washington? *twaṣṣalit iš-šii b-waašintin?*

accomplished - *maahir.* He's an accomplished musician. *huwwa muusiiqi maahir.*

**Mission accomplished. *l-maṭluub ṣaar* or *l-ġaraδ̣ itζaqqaq.*

accomplishment - 1. *ṣaniiεa* pl. *ṣanaayiε.* His mother was proud of his accomplishments. *ʔumma čaanat faxuura b-ṣanaayεa.* 2. *εamal* pl. *ʔaεmaal.* Really, that was no small accomplishment. *ṣudug, čaan εamal muu šaqa.*

accord - 1. *ttifaaq.* They acted in complete accord with him. *tṣarrifaw b-ittifaaq kaamil wiyyaa.* 2. *keef-.* He did it of his own accord. *sawwaaha min keefa.*

in **accordance with** - *ζasab, b-muujib.* In accordance with your request we are sending you three more copies. *ζasab ṭalabak ʔiζna daazzii-lak itlaθ nusax baεad.*

accordingly - 1. *εala hal-ʔasaas.* I acted accordingly. *tṣarrafit εala hal-ʔasaas.* 2. *binaaʔan εalee.* Accordingly, I wrote him a check for the full amount. *binaaʔan εalee, kitabit-la čakk bil-mablaġ kulla.*

according to - *ζasab.* Everything was carried out according to instructions. *kullši tnaffaδ ζasab it-taεliimaat.*

account - 1. *ζsaab* pl. *-aat.* I have an account in this bank. *εindi ζsaab ib-hal-ṗang.* 2. *taqriir* pl. *taqaariir, waṣuf* pl. *ʔawṣaaf.* His account of the accident isn't clear. *taqriira εal-ζaadiθa muu waaδ̣iζ* or *waṣfa lil-ζaadiθa muu waaδ̣iζ.*

on account of - *εala ʔasaas, b-sabab.* The game was postponed on account of rain. *l-liεib itʔajjal ib-sabab il-muṭar.*

on no account - *b-ʔay ζaal, mahma ṣaar.* On no account must you open this drawer. *ʔinta ma-laazim itfukk hal-mijarr ib-ʔay ζaal* or *ma-laazim itfukk hal-mijarr mahma ṣaar.*

to call to account - *ζaasab (i muζaasaba) t-.* I'll call him to account. *raζ-aζaasba.*

to give an account of - *bayyan (i tabyiin) t-.* You have to give me an account of every penny you spend. *laazim itbayyin-li kull filis il-tuṣurfa ween yiruuζ.*

**Give me an account of what happened. *ζčii-li illi ṣaar* or *ʔooṣif-li illi ṣaar.*

to take into account - *ʔaxaδ ib-naδ̣ar il-iεtibaar.* You have to take all the facts into account. *laazim taaxuδ kull il-ζaqaayiq ib-naδ̣ar il-iεtibaar.*

to account for - 1. *εallal (i taεliil) t-.* How do you account for that? *šloon itεallil haaδa?* 2. *barrar (i tabriir).* You'll have to account for your actions. *laazim itbarrir aεmaalak.*

to be **accountable for** - *tζaasab (a taζaasub) εan.* You alone will be accountable for the materials. *ʔinta waζdak raζ-titζaasab εan hal-mawaadd.*

accountant - *muζaasib* pl. *-iin.*

accurate - 1. *daqiiq.* She's very accurate in her work. *hiyya kulliš daqiiqa b-šuġulha.* 2. *maδ̣buuṭ.* Is that watch accurate? *has-saaεa maδ̣buuṭa?*

accurately - *biδ̣-δ̣abuṭ, b-ṣuura maδ̣buuṭa, b-diqqa.* She figured it out accurately. *ζisbatha biδ̣-δ̣abuṭ.*

to **accuse** - *tiham (i ttihaam) n-.* You can't accuse me of being lazy. *ma-tigdar tithimni bil-kasal.* -- He was accused of theft. *ntiham ib-booga.*

accustomed - *mitεawwid εala.* She's not accustomed to that. *hiyya ma-mitεawwda εala haaδa.*

to get accustomed to - *tεawwad (a taεawwud) εala.* He can't get accustomed to the strict discipline. *huwwa ma-yigdar yitεawwad εan-niδ̣aam id-daqiiq.*

ace - *ʔaas* pl. *-aat, billi* pl. *-iyyaat.* He has all four aces. *huwwa εinda l-ʔarbaε ʔaasaat.*

to **ache** - *wijaε (a wujaε).* My ear aches. *ʔiδni toojaεni.*

to **achieve** - *ζaqqaq (i taζqiiq) t-.* He achieved his purpose. *ζaqqaq maraama.*

acid - 1. *ζaamuδ̣* pl. *ζawaamiδ̣.* Bring me that bottle of acid. *jiib-li δaak baṭl il-ζaamuδ̣.* 2. *laaδiε.* He made a few acid remarks. *εallaq šwayyat taεliiqaat laaδεa.*

to **acknowledge** - *εtiraf (i εtiraaf).* We acknowledge receipt of your letter dated ... *niεtirif b-istilaam maktuubak il-muʔarrax ...*

acknowledged - *muεtaraf.* He is an acknowledged expert. *huwwa xabiir muεtaraf bii.*

acorn - *balluuṭa* pl. *-aat* coll. *balluuṭ.*

to **acquaint** - *ʔaṭlaε (i ʔiṭlaaε) εala, εarraf (u taεriif) b-.* First I want to acquaint you with the facts of the case. *ʔawwalan ʔariid ʔaṭliεak εala ζaqaayiq il-qaδ̣iyya.*

to acquaint oneself - *tεarraf (a taεarruf), ṭṭilaε (i ṭṭilaaε).* It'll take me a week to acquaint myself with all the problems. *yinraad-li sbuuε ζatta ʔatεarraf εala kull il-mašaakil.*

to get acquainted with - *tεarraf (a taεarruf) εala.* You two should get acquainted with each other. *laazim ʔintu l-iθneen titεarrfuun εala baεaδ̣kum.*

acquaintance - 1. *waaζid min il-maεaarif.* He's an old acquaintance of mine. *huwwa waaζid min maεaarfi l-εittag.* 2. *maεrifa.* I am pleased to make your acquaintance. *ʔaani farζaan ib-maεriftak.*

to **acquire** - 1. *ζaṣṣal (i ζuṣuul) t- εala.* We acquired the house when our uncle died. *ζaṣṣalna εal-beet min maat εammna.* 2. *ktisab (i ktisaab).* He's acquired considerable skill in tennis. *ktisab ihwaaya mahaara bit-tanis.*

to **acquit** - *barra (i tabriya) t-.* The judge acquitted him. *l-ζaakim barraa.*

across - *b-ṣoob il-laax.* The station is across the river. *l-maζaṭṭa b-ṣoob il-laax imniš-šaṭṭ.*

across the street - *ġbaal.* He lives across the street from us. *huwwa yiskun igbaalna.*

to go across - *εubar (u εubuur) n-.* Let's go across the bridge. *xal-niεbur ij-jisir.*

**This bus goes right across town. *hal-ṗaaṣ yijtaaz il-wlaaya εala ṭuul.*

act - 1. *εamal* pl. *ʔaεmaal, fiεil* pl. *ʔafεaal.* That wasn't a selfish act. *haaδa ma-čaan εamal ʔanaani.* 2. *faṣil* pl. *fuṣuul.* I don't want to miss the first act. *ma-ariid yfuutni l-faṣl il-ʔawwal.*

**Don't put on an act! *la-titṣannaε!*

to act - 1. *tṣarraf (a taṣarruf).* He's been acting like a child. *čaan yitṣarraf miθl iz-zaεṭuuṭ.* 2. *maθθal (i tamθiil) t-.* She's going to act in that new play. *raζ-itmaθθil ib-δiič it-tamθiiliyya j-jidiida.*

to act on - *ttixaδ (i ttixaaδ) ijraaʔ b-.* They're going to act on our proposal tomorrow. *raaζ yittaxδuun ijraaʔ b-iqtiraaζna baačir.*

action - 1. *ζawaadiθ.* The action of the novel takes place in Turkey. *ζawaadiθ il-quṣṣa tijri b-turkiya.* 2. *ʔijraaʔ* pl. *-aat.* This situation requires firm action. *hal-waδ̣iε yitṭallab ijraaʔ ζaazim.* 3. *taṣarruf* pl. *-aat.* His actions are hard to understand. *taṣarrufaata ṣaεub tinfihim.*

in action - *bil-maεraka.* He was killed in action. *nkital bil-maεraka.*

to bring action against - *qaam (i ʔiqaama) n- daεwa εala.* They will bring action against him. *raζ-yqiimuun εalee daεwa.*

to take action - *ʔaxaδ (u ʔaxiδ) n- ʔijraaʔ.* Has any action been taken on my case? *nʔixaδ ʔay ijraaʔ ib-qaδ̣iiti?*

active - 1. *εaamil.* Are you an active member? *ʔinta εuδ̣u εaamil?* 2. *našiiṭ.* He's still very active for his age. *baεda kulliš našiiṭ bin-nisba l-εumra.* 3. *faεεaal.* He has always been very active in our club. *huwwa čaan w-la-yzaal kulliš faεεaal ib-naadiina.*

activity - 1. *našaaṭ.* He had to give up all physical activity for a while. *δ̣ṭarr yitruk kull našaaṭ jismi fadd mudda.* 2. *ζaraka* pl. *-aat.* There's not much activity around here on Sunday. *ma-aku hwaaya ζaraka hnaa yoom il-aζζad.* 3. *εamal* pl. *ʔaεmaal.* She

engages in a lot of social activity. *tištirik b-ihwaaya ʔaεmaal ijtimaaεiyya.*
feverish activity – *xabṣa* pl. *xabaṣaat.* What's all that feverish activity over there? *šinu hal-xabṣa hnaak?*

actor – *mumaθθil* pl. *-iin.*

actress – *mumaθθila* pl. *-aat.*

actual – **1.** *ħaqiiqi*, fiεli*.* The actual reason was something entirely different. *s-sabab il-ħaqiiqi čaan fadd šii yixtilif tamaaman.* **2.** *ʔaṣli*.* She works here, but her actual office is on the second floor. *hiyya tištuğuḷ ihnaa laakin muħall šuğuḷha l-ʔaṣli biṭ-ṭaabiq iθ-θaani.*

actually – **1.** *ħaqiiqatan, fiεlan, ṣudug.* Do you actually believe that story? *ʔinta ṣudug tiεtiqid ib-haδiič l-ičaaya?* **2.** *ṣaħiiħ.* Did he actually write this letter? *ṣaħiiħ kitab hal-maktuub?*

acute – **1.** *ħaadd.* He has acute dysentery. *εinda dazantari ħaadd.* -- This triangle has two acute angles. *hal-muθallaθ bii zaawiiteen ħaadda.* **2.** *šadiid.* If the pain becomes acute, call the doctor. *ʔiδa ṣaar il-ʔalam šadiid xaabur iṭ-ṭabiib.* **3.** *qawi*.* Dogs have an acute sense of smell. *l-iclaab εidha ħaassat šamm qawiyya.*

ad – *ʔiεlaan* pl. *-aat.* I'd like to put in an ad. *ʔariid anšur iεlaan.*

to **adapt** – **1.** *tkayyaf (a takayyuf).* She adapts easily to new social situations. *hiyya titkayyaf ib-suhuula εala l-ħaala l-ijtimaaεiyya j-jidiida.* **2.** *tlaaʔam (a talaaʔum).* This method will adapt well to my purposes. *haṭ-ṭariiqa titlaaʔam zeen wiyya ʔağraaδ̣i.* **3.** *kayyaf (i takyiif) t-.* He adapts himself easily. *huwwa ykayyif nafsa b-suhuula.*

to **add** – **1.** *zaad (i zyaada).* You'll have to add some sugar. *yinraad-lak itziid išwayyat šakar.* **2.** *δ̣aaf (i ʔiδ̣aafa) n-.* I've nothing to add to that. *ma-εindi sii ʔaδ̣iif il-haaδa.* **3.** *jimaε (a jamiε) n-.* Add up these figures. *ʔijmaε hal-arqaam.*
to add up to – *ṣaar (i).* How much will the bill add up to? *šgadd raħ-iṭṣiir il-qaaʔima?*

addition – **1.** *jamiε.* Is my addition correct? *jamεi ṣaħiiħ?* **2.** *mulħaq* pl. *-aat.* They're building an addition on that building. *da-yibnuun mulħaq il-haaδi l-binaaya.* **3.** *ziyaada.* The addition of turpentine will thin the paint. *ziyaadt it-tarbantiin raħ-itxaffif iṣ-ṣubuğ.*
in addition – *čmaal-, foog-.* In addition he asked for ten dollars. *čmaala ṭulab εašir doolaaraat.*
in addition to – *bil-iδ̣aafa εala.* In addition to his fixed salary he gets commissions. *bil-iδ̣aafa εala maεaaša yaaxuδ qoomisyoon.*

additional – **1.** *ʔiδ̣aafi*.* He gave me an additional amount for incidentals. *nṭaani fadd mablağ iδ̣aafi l-maṣaariif naθriyya.* **2.** *ʔazyad.* An additional dollar gives you better quality. *fadd doolaar azyad yinṭiik nooε ʔaħsan.*

address – **1.** *εinwaan* pl. *εanaawiin.* Send these books to this address. *dizz hal-kutub li-haaδa l-εinwaan.* **2.** *xiṭaab* pl. *-aat.* The President delivered an important address. *r-raʔiis ʔalqa xiṭaab muhimm.*
to address – **1.** *εanwan (i) t-.* Address this letter to the manager. *εanwin haaδa l-maktuub lil-mudiir.* **2.** *xaaṭab (u muxaaṭaba).* How shall I address him? *šloon axaaṭba?* **3.** *wajjah (i tawjiih) t-.* I would like to address a question to the speaker. *ʔaħibb awajjih suʔaal lil-mutakallim.*

adhesive tape – *šariiṭ lizzeeg.*

adjective – *ṣifa* pl. *-aat.*

to **adjoin** – **1.** *ħadd (i).* My garden adjoins his. *ħadiiqti tħidd ħadiiqta.* **2.** *jaawar (i mujaawara).* Their garage adjoins the house. *garaajhum yjaawir il-beet.*

to **adjourn** – *faδ̣δ̣ (u faδ̣δ̣) n-.* He adjourned the meeting. *huwwa faδ̣δ̣ il-ijtimaaε.*

to **adjust** – **1.** *δ̣ubaṭ (u δ̣abuṭ) n-.* The mechanic adjusted the carburetor. *l-miikaaniiki δ̣ubaṭ il-kaabreeta.* **2.** *ṣaħħaħ (i taṣħiiħ) t-.* The manager will adjust your bill. *l-mudiir raħ-ysaħħiħ qaaʔimtak.* **3.** *εaddal (i taεdiil) t-.* She adjusted her clothing. *εaddilat ihduumha.* **4.** *kayyaf (i takyiif) t-.* I can't adjust myself to the climate here. *ma-agdar akayyif nafsi l-haj-jaww.*

adjustable – *mitħarrik.* Is this seat adjustable? *haaδa l-maqεad mitħarrik?*

to **administer** – **1.** *daar (i ʔidaara) n-.* Who's administering his estate? *minu da-ydiir tarikaata?* **2.** *sawwa (i).* He showed us how he administers artificial respiration. *raawaana šloon ysawwi tanaffus iṣṭinaaεi.*

administration – *ʔidaara* pl. *-aat.*

admiral – *ʔamiiraal* pl. *-aat, -iyya.*

admiration – *ʔiεjaab.* He got the admiration of all his friends. *naal iεjaab kull aṣdiqaaʔa.*

to **admire** – *kaan muεjab b-.* I admire her beauty. *ʔaani muεjab ib-jamaalha.*
**I admire your patience. *yiεjibni ṣabrak.*

admission – **1.** *duxuul.* How much is the admission? *beeš id-duxuul?* **2.** *qubuul.* I have an appointment with the Director of Admissions. *εindi mawεid wiyya mudiir il-qubuul.* **3.** *εtiraaf* pl. *-aat.* His admission proved my innocence. *εtiraafa ʔaθbat baraaʔti.*

admission charge – *ʔujrat duxuul.* There's no admission charge. *ma-aku ʔujrat duxuul.*

to **admit** – **1.** *daxxal (i tadxiil) t-, xaššaš (i taxšiiš) t-.* Give this card to the doorman and he'll admit you. *ʔinṭi hal-kart lil-bawwaab w-huwwa ydaxxlak.* **2.** *qibal (a qubuul) n-.* We can't admit this type of student. *ma-nigdar niqbal hiiči tilmiiδ.* **3.** *qarr (u ʔiqraar) b-.* The accused finally admitted his guilt. *l-muttaham axiiran qarr ib-δanba.* **4.** *εtiraf (i εtiraaf).* I admit I was wrong. *ʔaεtirif činit ğalṭaan.*

to **adopt** – **1.** *tbanna (a tabanni).* My friend has adopted a small boy. *ṣadiiqi tbanna walad iṣğayyir.* **2.** *εtinaq (i εtinaaq).* They adopted Islam toward the end of the first century. *εtinqaw il-ʔislaam ib-ʔawaaxir il-qarn il-ʔawwal.* **3.** *ttixaδ (i ttixaaδ).* They adopted the measure unanimously. *ttixδaw il-qaraar bil-ʔijmaaε.* **4.** *ttibaε (i ttibaaε).* Better results could be obtained if we adopted this method. *nitwaṣṣal ʔila nataaʔij ʔaħsan ʔiδa ttibaεna haṭ-ṭariiqa.*

adult – *čibiir* pl. *kbaar.* There was milk for the children and coffee for the adults. *čaan aku ħaliib liṣ-ṣiğaar w-gahwa lil-ikbaar.*

advance – **1.** *taqaddum, taraqqi.* Great advances have been made in medicine during the last few years. *hwaaya taqaddum ṣaar biṭ-ṭibb bis-siniin il-ʔaxiira.* **2.** *sulfa* pl. *sulaf.* Can you give me an advance? *tigdar tinṭiini sulfa?*
in advance – *li-giddaam.* Let me know in advance if you're coming. *ʔixbirni li-giddaam ʔiδa raħ-tiji.*
to advance – **1.** *traqqa (a taraqqi).* He advanced rapidly in the company. *traqqa bil-εajal biš-šarika.* **2.** *raffaε (i tarfiiε) t-.* They just advanced him to assistant manager. *tawwhum raffiεoo ʔila muεaawin mudiir.* — He was advanced to chief clerk. *traffaε ʔila raʔiis kuttaab.* **3.** *qaddam (i taqdiim) t-.* They advanced the date of the lecture. *qaddmaw taariix il-muħaaδ̣ara.* **4.** *tqaddam (a taqaddum).* Our army advanced twenty miles. *jeešna tqaddam εišriin miil.* **5.** *sallaf (i tasliif).* The bank advanced him one thousand dinars. *l-bang sallafa ʔalif diinaar.*

advantage – *faaʔida* pl. *fawaaʔid.* This method has advantages and disadvantages. *haṭ-ṭariiqa biiha fawaaʔid w-εiyuub.*
an advantage over – *ʔafδ̣aliyya εala.* Your technical education gives you an advantage over me. *θaqaaftak il-fanniyya tinṭiik ʔafδ̣aliyya εalayya.*
to one's advantage – *l-maṣlaħat ʔaħħad.* This is to your advantage. *haaδa l-maṣlaħtak.*
to take advantage of – **1.** *ntihaz (i ntihaaz).* He takes advantage of every opportunity. *yintihiz kull furṣa.* **2.** *stiğall (i stiğlaal).* Don't let people

take advantage of you. *la-txalli n-naas yistiġilluuk.*

advantageous - *mufiid, naafiɛ.*

adventure - *muxaaṭara* pl. *-aat, mujaazafa* pl. *-aat, muġaamara* pl. *-aat.*

adverb - *ð̣aruf* pl. *ð̣uruuf.*

to **advertise** - *ɛilan (i ʔiɛlaan) n-.* The store advertised a sale. *l-maxzan ɛilan tanziilaat.*

advertisement - *ʔiɛlaan* pl. *-aat.*

advertising - *diɛaaya, ʔiɛlaan.* Our company spends a lot on advertising. *šarikatna tuṣruf ihwaaya ɛad-diɛaaya.*

advice - *naṣiiʐa.* My advice is that you leave immediately. *naṣiiʐti ʔan itruuʐ ʐaalan.*
to ask advice - *stašaar (i stišaara), ṭilab (u) naṣiiʐa.* I asked his advice. *stišarta* or *ṭlabit naṣiiʐta.*
to give advice - *niṣaʐ (a) n-, ʔinṭa (i naṭi) naṣiiʐa.* It is hard to give advice in this matter. *ṣaɛub waaʐid yinṣaʐ ib-hal-mawð̣uuɛ* or *ṣaɛub waaʐid yinṭi naṣiiʐa b-hal-mawð̣uuɛ.*

advisable - 1. *l-ʔaɛqal.* I think it's advisable for you to stay home today. *ʔašuuf il-ʔaɛqal tibqa bil-beet il-yoom.* 2. *mustaʐsan.* Would that be an advisable step to take? *tiɛtiqid hal-xaṭwa mustaʐsana?*

to **advise** - *niṣaʐ (a) n-, šaar (i) n- ɛala.* What do you advise me to do? *š-tinṣaʐni ʔasawwi?*

adviser - 1. Legal adviser. *mušaawir ɛadli.* 2. Political adviser. *mustašaar siyaasi.* 3. Student adviser. *muršid.*

advisory - *stišaari*.*

aerial - *ʔeeryal* pl. *-aat.* The aerial on the radio isn't connected. *l-ʔeeryal maal ir-raadyo ma-mittiṣil.*

aerial warfare - *ʐarub jawwiyya.*

affair - 1. *ʔamur* pl. *ʔumuur.* I don't meddle in his affairs. *ma-atdaxxal ib-ʔumuura.* 2. *šuġuḷ* pl. *ʔašġaal.* That's your affair. *haaða šuġḷak ʔinta.* 3. *šaʔin* pl. *šuʔuun.* He handled the affairs of the company badly. *daar šuʔuun iš-šarika b-ṣuura mxarubṭa.* 4. *munaasaba* pl. *-aat.* Her party was a real nice affair. *ʐaflatha čaanat munaasaba ḷaṭiifa jiddan.* 5. *ɛalaaqa* pl. *-aat.* The cook had an affair with the chauffeur. *ṭ-ṭabbaaxa ṣaar ɛidha ɛalaaqa (ġaraamiyya) wiyya s-saayiq.*

to **affect** - 1. *ʔaθθar (i taʔθiir) ɛala.* That damp climate affected his health. *haðaak it-ṭaqis ir-raṭib ʔaθθar ɛala ṣiʐʐta.* 2. *tð̣aahar (a tað̣aahur).* He has affected an Egyptian accent. *yitð̣aahar ɛinda lakna miṣriyya.*
to be affected - *tʔaθθar (a taʔaθθur) b-.* His vision was affected by his illness. *nað̣ara tʔaθθar ib-marað̣a.*

affected - 1. *mitṣanniɛ.* She's terribly affected. *hiyya kulliš mitṣanniɛa.* 2. *mitkallif.* Is his style in writing always that affected? *ʔisluuba bil-kitaaba daaʔiman hiiči mitkallif?*

to **afford** - *tmakkan (a tamakkun).* We can't afford to buy a car. *ma-nitmakkan ništiri sayyaara* or ***ma-ʔilna qaabliyyat sayyaara.*
**I can't afford that much. *haaða ġaali ɛalayya.*
**You can afford to laugh. *ʐaqqak tið̣ʐak* or *ʔið̣ʐak, leeš laa.*

Afghanistan - *ʔafġaanistaan.*

to be **afraid** - *xiša (a xišya).* I'm afraid its going to rain. *ʔaxša raʐ-tumṭur.*
to be afraid of - *xaaf (a xoof) n- min.* He's not afraid of anyone. *ma-yxaaf min ʔaʐʐad.*

Africa - *ʔafriiqya.*

African - *ʔafriiqi** pl. *-iyyiin.*

after - 1. *baɛad.* Can you call me after supper? *tigdar itxaaburni baɛd il-ɛaša?* 2. *wara.* He arrived after me. *wiṣal waraaya.* 3. *ɛala.* Day after day, his health is improving. *yoom ɛala yoom ṣiʐʐta da-titʐassan.* — He named his son after his grandfather. *samma ʔibna ɛala ʔisim jidda.* 4. *ɛala ʔaθar.* After the death of my father, I had to quit school. *ɛala ʔaθar wafaat ʔabuuya ð̣ṭarreet abaṭṭil imnil-madrasa.*
after all - 1. *mahma ykuun.* Why shouldn't I help him? After all, he's my friend. *luweeš ma-asaaɛda? mahma ykuun huwwa ṣadiiqi.* 2. *taaliiha.* You are right, after all. *taaliiha l-ʐaqq wiyyaak.*
after this - *minnaa w-ġaadi.* After this, please let us know in advance. *minnaa w-ġaadi ʔinṭiina xabar li-ġiddaam.*
to be after - *dawwar (u tadwiir) ɛala.* The police have been after him for two weeks. *š-šurṭa da-tdawwur ɛalee min muddat isbuuɛeen.*

afternoon - *ɛaṣriyya* pl. *-aat.* I would like to see you one afternoon. *yiɛjibni ʔašuufak fadd ɛaṣriyya.*
in the afternoon - *baɛd ið̣-ð̣uhur, wara ð̣-ð̣uhur, l-ɛaṣir.* I never drink coffee in the afternoon. *ʔaani ʔabad ma-ašrab gahwa wara ð̣-ð̣uhur.*
this afternoon - *l-yoom il-ɛaṣir.* Can you come this afternoon. *tigdar tiji il-yoom il-ɛaṣir?*

afterwards - *baɛdeen.* We ate dinner and went to a movie afterwards. *tġaddeena w-baɛdeen riʐna lis-siinama.*

again - 1. *marra lux, marrt il-lux, marra θaanya.* I'll tell him again. *raʐ-agul-la marra lux.* 2. *min jiht il-lux.* Again, we should study the other proposal, too. *min jiht il-lux, hamm laazim nidrus il-iqtiraaʐ iθ-θaani.* 3. *baɛad.* He never made that mistake again. *huwwa ma-sawwa ðiič il-ġalṭa baɛad.*
again and again - *marra wara marra, yaama w-yaama.* I warned him again and again. *ʐaððarta marra wara marra.*
over and over again - *marraat ihwaaya.* He tried over and over again. *huwwa ʐaawal marraat ihwaaya.*
then again - *ḥammeen.* But then again, that's not always true. *laakin ḥammeen, haaða muu daaʔiman ṣaʐiiʐ.*

against - 1. *b-ṣaff.* Move this table over against the wall. *ʐuṭṭ hal-meez ib-ṣaff il-ʐaayiṭ.* 2. *ð̣idd.* We had to swim against the current. *ð̣ṭarreena nisbaʐ ð̣idd il-maay.* — He voted against me. *huwwa ṣawwaṭ ð̣iddi.* 3. *ɛala.* He was leaning against the house. *čaan mintiči ɛal-beet.*
as against - *muqaabil.* Fifty ships went through the canal as against thirty five last month. *xamsiin safiina marrat imnil-qanaal muqaabil xamsa w-θlaaθiin biš-šahr il-faat.*

age - 1. *ɛumur, sinn.* He's about my age. *huwwa taqriiban ib-ɛumri* or *huwwa taqriiban ib-sinni.* 2. *ɛaṣir.* This is the atomic age. *haaða ɛaṣr ið-ðarra.*
in ages - *min zamaan.* We haven't seen them in ages. *ma-šifnaahum min zamaan.*
of age - *baaliġ sinn ir-rušud.* He'll come of age next year. *raʐ-yibluġ sinn ir-rušud is-sana j-jaaya.*
old age - *kubur.* He died of old age. *maat imnil-kubur.*
to age - 1. *šayyab (i).* He's aged a great deal lately. *šayyab ihwaaya bil-ʔayyaam il-ʔaxiira.* 2. *ɛattaq (i taɛtiiq) t-.* The brewery aged the beer ninety days. *maɛmal il-biira ɛattaq il-biira tisɛiin yoom.* 3. *tɛattaq (a).* They left the wine to age for a number of years. *xallaw iš-šaraab yitɛattaq čam sana.*

agency - 1. *wakaala.* Our company has an agency in Beirut. *šarikatna ɛidha wakaala b-beeruut.* 2. *daaʔira* pl. *dawaaʔir.* Government agencies submit their budgets this month. *dawaaʔir il-ʐukuuma yqaddimuun miizaaniyyaathum haš-šahar.*

agent - 1. *wakiil* pl. *wukalaaʔ.* Your agent called on me yesterday. *wakiilak jaani l-baarʐa.* 2. *ɛamiil* pl. *ɛumalaaʔ.* He is said to be a communist agent. *l-šaayiɛ ɛanna huwwa ɛamiil šiyuuɛi.* 3. *mumaθθil* pl. *-iin.* The insurance company sent its agent to the accident site. *šarikat it-taʔmiin dazzat wakiilha l-mukaan il-ʐaadiθ.* 4. *sirri* pl. *-iyyiin.* I think he's a police agent. *ʔaɛtiqid huwwa sirri mniš-šurṭa.* 5. *ɛaamil* pl. *ɛawaamil.* This is a strong chemical agent. *haaða ɛaamil kiimyaawi faɛɛaal.*

to aggravate – 1. *zahhag (i tzihhig, tazhiig) t-.* His bragging really aggravated me. *t-tabajjuz maala zahhagni hwaaya.* 2. *ʔazzam (i taʔziim) t-.* The border incident aggravated the situation. *zaadiθ il-zuduud ʔazzam il-waḍiε.* 3. *zayyad (i tazyiid) t-.* Scratching will aggravate the inflammation. *l-zakk raz-yzayyid il-iltihaab.*

aggravation – 1. *ʔizεaaj* pl. *-aat.* Her nagging is a source of constant aggravation. *ʔilzaazha maṣdar izεaaj mustamirr.* 2. *taʔazzum, tadahwur.* Any aggravation of the situation may lead to war. *ʔay taʔazzum bil-zaala yimkin yʔaddi ʔila zarub.*

ago – *gabuḷ.* I was there two months ago. *čint ihnaak gabuḷ šahreen.*

a while ago – *gabuḷ mudda.* He left a while ago. *raaz gabuḷ mudda.*

agony – *tmurmur, εaδaab.* I can't bear this agony. *ma-agdar atzammal hat-tumurmur.*

to agree – 1. *ttifaq (i ttifaaq).* Their opinions never agree. *ʔaraaʔhum ʔabad ma-tittifiq.* 2. *waafaq (i muwaafaqa) εala.* He agreed to buy the radio. *waafaq εala ʔan yištiri r-raadyo.*

to agree on – *ttifaq (i ttifaaq) εala.* We've agreed on everything. *ʔizna ttifaqna εala kullši.*

to agree to – *waafaq (u muwaafaqa) εala.* Do you agree to these terms? *twaafuq εala haš-šuruuṭ?*

to agree with – 1. *ttifaq (i ttifaaq) wiyya.* Do you agree with me? *tittifiq wiyyaaya?* 2. *laaʔam (i mulaaʔama) t-, waalam (i muwaalama) t-.* This weather doesn't agree with me at all. *haj-jaww ma-ywaalimni ʔabadan.*

agreeable – 1. *samiz.* She has an agreeable disposition. *εidha fadd ṭabuε samiz.* 2. *maqbuul.* These terms are not agreeable. *haš-šuruuṭ ma-maqbuula.*

to be agreeable – *waafaq (u muwaafaqa).* Is he agreeable to that? *huwwa ywaafuq εala haaδa?*

agreement – 1. *ttifaaqiyya* pl. *-aat.* The agreement has to be ratified by Parliament. *l-ittifaaqiyya laazim tiṭṣaddaq min majlis il-umma.* 2. *ttifaaq* pl. *-aat.* The contract was extended by mutual agreement. *l-muqaawala tmaddidat b-ittifaaq iṭ-ṭarafeen.*

to be in agreement – *ttifaq (i ttifaaq).* This is definitely not in agreement with the original terms of the contract. *haaδa qaṭεiyyan ma-yittifiq wiyya šuruuṭ il-muqaawala l-ʔaṣliyya.* — Are you in agreement with me? *ʔinta mittifiq wiyyaaya?*

to come to an agreement – *wuṣal (a wuṣuul) ʔila ttifaaq.* We came to an agreement on that point. *wuṣalna ʔila ttifaaq zawil haδiič in-nuqṭa.*

agricultural – *ziraaεi*.*

agriculture – *ziraaεa.* Inquire at the Department of Agriculture. *ʔisʔal ib-wizaart iz-ziraaεa.* — There isn't much agriculture in this region. *ma-aku hwaaya ziraaεa b-hal-manṭiqa.*

ahead – 1. *mitqaddim.* He's ahead of everybody in his studies. *huwwa mitqaddim εala l-kull ib-diraasta.* — I'm way ahead in my work. *ʔaani hwaaya mitqaddim ib-šuġli.* 2. *gabuḷ.* Are you next? No, he's ahead of me. *hassa siraak? laa, huwwa gabḷi.* 3. *saabiq, ġaaḷub.* My horse was ahead during the race. *zṣaani čaan ġaaḷub wakt is-sibaaq.* 4. *giddaam, ʔamaam.* The soldiers marched ahead of the sailors in the parade. *j-jinuud mišaw giddaam il-bazzaara bil-istiεraaḍ.*

straight ahead – *gubaḷ, εadil.* Go straight ahead. *fuut gubaḷ.*

to get ahead – *tqaddam (a taqaddum).* He doesn't seem to get ahead. *ma-da-ybayyin εalee yitqaddam.*

to go ahead – 1. *miša (i) b-faal~.* Just go ahead, don't mind me. *ʔimši b-faalak. ma-εleek minni.* 2. *raaz (u) gabuḷ.* You go ahead, I'll follow you later. *ruuz gabḷi, ʔaani ʔaliʒgak baεdeen.* 3. *stimarr (i stimraar), daawam (u mudaawama).* Just go ahead with your work, don't let me stop you. *stimirr ib-šuġlak, la-txalliini ʔaεaṭṭlak.*

**Go ahead and take it! *tfaḍḍaḷ ʔuxuδa.*

**Go ahead and tell him. *yaḷḷa, gul-la* or *ma-yxaalif, gul-la.*

aid – 1. *ʔisεaaf* pl. *-aat.* I gave him first aid. *sawweet-la ʔisεaaf ʔawwali.* 2. *musaaεada.* That country received quite a bit of economic aid. *had-dawla stilmat kammiyya kbiira mnil-musaaεadaat il-iqtiṣaadiyya.*

to aid – *saaεad (i musaaεada) t-, εaawan (i muεaawana) t-.* Can I aid you in any way? *ʔagdar asaaεdak ib-ʔay ṭariiqa?*

aide – 1. *muraafiq.* The British general and his aide went to Iraq. *l-janaraal il-bariiṭaani w-muraafqa raazaw lil-εiraaq.* 2. *muεaawin* pl. *-iin, musaaεid* pl. *-iin.* The minister consulted his top aides. *l-waziir istašaar ʔakbar muεaawinii.*

ailing – *mariiḍ, wajεaan.* She's always ailing. *hiyya εala ṭuul mariiḍa.*

aim – 1. *ġaaya* pl. *-aat, maqṣad* pl. *maqaaṣid, ġaraḍ* pl. *ʔaġraaḍ, hadaf* pl. *ʔahdaaf.* His aim is to become a good doctor. *ġaayta yṣiir ṭabiib zeen.* 2. *niišaan* pl. *nyaašiin.* He took careful aim and fired. *ʔaxaδ niišaan zeen w-ḍirab.*

to aim – 1. *neešan (i).* He aimed at a rabbit. *neešan εala ʔarnab.* 2. *nuwa (i niyya).* What do you aim to do this afternoon? *š-tinwi tsawwi hal-εaṣriyya?* 3. *wajjah (i tawjiih) t-.* He aimed an insult at me. *wajjah masabba ʔili.*

**You're aiming too high! *ʔinta da-tuḍrub bil-εaali* or *j-janna ʔagrab* or *da-tuṭlub muṭar.*

air – 1. *hawa.* The air in this room is bad. *l-hawa b-hal-ġurfa muu zeen.* 2. *jaww.* The meeting was surrounded by an air of mystery. *l-ijtimaaε čaan muzaaṭ ib-jaww ġaamuḍ.* 3. *jawwi*.* Send us a letter by air mail. *dizz-inna maktuub bil-bariid ij-jawwi.*

**He's continually putting on airs. *huwwa daaʔiman yiṭḍaahar εala ġeer zaqiiqta.*

to be on the air – *δaaε (i ʔiδaaεa).* The president will be on the air this evening. *r-raʔiis raz-yδiiε hal-leela.*

to air – 1. *hawwa (i tahwiya) t-.* Would you please air the room while I'm out? *ʔarjuuk hawwi l-ġurfa lamma ʔakuun barra.* 2. *šarr (u šarr) n-.* I have to air the blanket this morning. *laazim ašurr il-baṭṭaaniyya haṣ-ṣubuz.*

**Don't air your personal problems in public. *la-tiṭliε in-naas εala mašaaklak iš-šaxṣiyya.*

air base – *qaaεida* (pl. *qawaaεid*) *jawwiyya.*

aircraft carrier – *zaamilat ṭaaʔiraat.*

airfield – *maṭaar* pl. *-aat.* Let's meet at the airfield. *xalli nitlaaga bil-maṭaar.*

air force – *quwwa* (pl. *-aat*) *jawwiyya.*

air line – *xuṭuuṭ jawwiyya, šarikat ṭayaraan.*

air mail – *bariid jawwi.* Send the package by air mail. *dizz ir-ruzma bil-bariid ij-jawwi.*

airplane – *ṭiyyaara* pl. *-aat.* How long does it take by airplane? *šgadd yṭawwul biṭ-ṭiyyaara?*

airport – *maṭaar* pl. *-aat.*

air raid – *ġaara* (pl. *-aat*) *jawwiyya.*

air sick – **He gets air sick every time he flies. *tiliεma ṣ-ṣufra kull-ma yṭiir.*

aisle – *mamša* pl. *mamaaši, mamarr* pl. *-aat.* He had to stand in the aisle. *ḍṭarr yoogaf bil-mamša.*

ajar – *mafkuuk šwayya.* The door was ajar. *l-baab čaanat mafkuuka šwayya.*

alarm – 1. *jaraṣ ʔinδaar.* Who turned in the alarm? *minu dagg jaraṣ il-ʔinδaar?* 2. *xoof.* She was full of alarm. *čaanat kullha xoof.* 3. *munabbih* pl. *-aat.* Set the alarm for six. *ʔunṣub il-munabbih εas-saaεa sitta.*

to alarm – 1. *xarraε (i taxriiε) t-, fazzaz (i tafziiz) t-.* Her screams alarmed the whole building. *εyaaṭha xarraε kull il-binaaya.* 2. *šawwaš (i tašwiiš) t-.* The news report alarmed

me. *n-našra l-ixbaariyya šawwišatni.*
to be alarmed - *xtiraε(i).* Don't be alarmed! *la-tixtiriε.*
alarm clock - *saaεa* (pl. *-aat*) *munabbiha.* I bought myself a new alarm clock yesterday. *štireet-li saaεa munabbiha jidiida l-baarḥa.*
album - *ʔalboom* pl. *-aat.* He gave me a photograph album. *nṭaani ʔalboom taṣaawiir.*
alcohol - *kuḥuul, spiirtu.* The medicine has alcohol in it. *d-dawa bii kuḥuul.* -- She started the fire with alcohol. *šiεalat in-naar bil-ispiirtu.*
Aleppo - *ḥalab.*
alert - **1.** *mityaqqiδ̣, mitnabbih.* He's an alert fellow. *huwwa fadd waaḥid mityaqqiδ̣.*
on alert - *taḥt il-ʔinδaar.* The defense minister put the army on alert. *waziir id-difaaε xalla j-jeeš taḥt il-ʔinδaar.*
to be on the alert - *twaqqaε (a tawaqquε), tḥaδ̣δ̣ar (a taḥaδ̣δ̣ur).* Be on the alert for a call from me. *twaqqaε nidaaʔ minni.*
to alert - *ḥaδ̣δ̣ar (i taḥδ̣iir) t-.* They alerted us about the coming of a storm. *ḥaδ̣δ̣iroona b-majiiʔ εaaṣifa.*
Alexandria - *l-iskandariyya.*
Algeria - *l-jazaaʔir.*
Algerian - *jazaaʔiri**.
Algiers - *madiinat il-jazaaʔir.*
alien - (m.) *muqiim ʔajnabi* pl. *muqiimiin ʔajaanib.* (f.) *muqiima ʔajnabiyya* pl. *muqiimaat ʔajnaabiyyaat.*
alike - **1.** *fadd šikil, fadd šii.* These tables are all alike. *hal-imyuuza kullha fadd šikil.* **2.** *suwa.* We treat all customers alike. *ʔiḥna nεaamil kull il-maεaamiil suwa.*
alive - **1.** *ḥayy, εadil, ṭayyib.* This fish is still alive. *has-simča li-hassa ḥayya.*
**The atmosphere was alive with tension. *j-jaww čaan mašḥuun bit-tawattur.*
**This marsh is alive with snakes. *hal-hoor kulla ḥayaaya.*
to be alive with - *εajj (i).* The pantry is alive with ants. *l-kilar yεijj bin-namil.*
to keep alive - **1.** *δ̣all (a) ṭayyib.* It's a wonder they kept alive. *l-muεjiza δ̣allaw ṭayybiin.* **2.** *buqa (a baqaaʔ) εaayiš.* How can you keep alive on this salary? *šloon tigdar tibqa εaayiš ib-hal-maεaaš?* **3.** *xalla (i) εaayiš.* The doctor kept him alive for two weeks. *ṭ-ṭabiib xallaa εaayiš isbuuεeen.*
all - **1.** *kull.* Did you all go? *kullkum riḥtu?* -- This will upset all my plans. *haaδa raḥ-yxarbuṭ kull mašaariiεi.* -- The bread's all gone. *l-xubuz kulla xilaṣ.* **2.** *ṭuul.* I've been waiting all day. *ṣaar-li da-antiδ̣ir ṭuul in-nahaar.* **3.** *jamiiε.* He took a vote of all the officers. *ʔaxaδ aṣwaat jamiiε iδ̣-δ̣abbaaṭ.*
**That's all. *haaδa huwwa.*
**If that's all there is to it, I'll do it. *ʔiδa b-has-suhuula, raḥ-asawwiiha* or *ʔiδa hiiči sahla, raḥ-asawwiiha.*
**The captain's all for starting now. *l-qabṭaan yfaδ̣δ̣il nibdi hassa.*
**He isn't all there. *huwwa mašxuuṭ.*
all along - *εala ṭuul, daaʔiman.* We've suspected him all along. *ʔiḥna εala ṭuul činna nšukk bii.*
all hours - *ʔay wakit.* He comes home to lunch at all hours. *yiji lil-beet yitġadda ʔay wakit čaan.*
all in - *talfaan.* The kids are all in from playing. *j-jahhaal talfaaniin imnil-liεib.*
all in all - *šii εala šii.* All in all, the movie was good. *šii εala šii, l-filim čaan zeen.*
all of a sudden - *εala ġafla.* All of a sudden it got dark. *ṣaarat δ̣alma εala ġafla.*
all over - *kull makaan.* They came from all over. *ʔijaw min kull makaan.* -- He traveled all over the country. *saafar il-kull makaan bil-balad.* **2.** *kull.* He trembled all over from fright. *rijaf kulla mnil-xoof.* -- He has pimples all over his face *εinda danaabil ib-kull wijja.* **3.** *min jidiid.* You have to do it all over. *laazim itsawwiiha min jidiid.*
**He came back after the war was all over. *rijaε baεad-ma ntihat il-ḥarub.*
all right - **1.** *tamaam, maaši.* Is everything all right? *kullši maaši?* or *kullši tamaam?* -- I'd like to go, all right, but it's impossible. *tamaam ariid aruuḥ, bass haaδa mustaḥiil.* -- He knows why, all right. *huwwa tamaam yuεruf luweeš* or *huwwa zeen yuεruf luweeš.* **2.** *ṭayyib, zeen.* All right, I'll do it. *ṭayyib, raḥ-asawwiiha* or *zeen, raḥ-asawwiiha.*
**Is that all right with you? *ma-εindak maaniε?*
all set - *ḥaaδ̣ir, mitḥaδ̣δ̣ir.* We were all set to leave. *činna mitḥaδ̣δ̣riin inruuḥ.*
all the better - *baεad aḥsan.* If that is so, all the better. *loo hiiči, baεad aḥsan.*
all the same - **1.** *fadd šii, nafs iš-šii.* That's all the same to me. *kullha fadd šii bin-nisba ʔili.* **2.** *walaw, maεa haaδa, εala kull ḥaal.* All the same, you didn't have to do it. *walaw, ma-čaan laazim itsawwiiha.*
all the time - *εala ṭuul, daaʔiman, kull wakit.* She's complaining all the time. *hiyya kull wakit titšakka.*
all told - *šii εala šii.* All told, he's not a bad fellow. *šii εala šii, huwwa xooš walad.*
above all - *εala l-ʔaxaṣṣ, ʔahamm šii.* Above all, don't get discouraged. *εala l-ʔaxaṣṣ la-tiftar εaziimtak.*
at all - *ʔabad, ʔabadan, bil-marra, ʔaṣlan.* He has no patience at all. *maa εinda ṣabur ʔabadan.*
in all - *kull bil-kull.* How many are there in all? *šgadd ʔaku kull bil-kull?*
Allah - *ʔaḷḷa.*
alley - *darbuuna* pl. *daraabiin, εagid* pl. *εguud.*
alliance - *ḥilif* pl. *ʔaḥlaaf.* The two countries formed an alliance. *d-dawilteen šakklaw ḥilif.*
to **allow** - **1.** *simaḥ (a samaaḥ) n-.* He won't allow that. *ma-yismaḥ ib-haaδa.* -- He doesn't allow himself a minute's rest. *ma-yismaḥ in-nafsa wala daqiiqa raaḥa.* **2.** *ḥisab (i ḥsaab) n-.* How much will you allow me for my old car? *beeš raḥ-tiḥsib sayyaarti l-εatiiga?* **3.** *xalla (i) t-.* How much should I allow for traveling expenses? *šgadd laazim axalli l-maṣaariif is-safar?* **4.** *raxxaṣ (a tarxiiṣ) t-.* They're not allowed to sell beer after midnight. *ma-mraxxaṣiin ybiiεuun biira baεad nuṣṣ il-leel.*
allowance - **1.** *xarjiyya* pl. *-aat.* Do you give your son an allowance? *tinṭi l-ʔibnak xarjiyya?* **2.** *muxaṣṣaṣaat.* In addition to the regular salary, there is a cost of living allowance. *bil-ʔiδ̣aafa ʔila r-raatib il-iεtiyaadi ʔaku muxaṣṣaṣaat ġalaaʔ il-maεiiša.*
to make allowance for - *ḥisab (i) ḥsaab l-.* You've got to make allowance for his inexperience. *laazim tiḥsib iḥsaab il-qillat xibirta.*
ally - *ḥaliif* pl. *ḥulafaaʔ.* They are our allies. *humma ḥulafaaʔna.*
to ally oneself - *tḥaalaf (a taḥaaluf).* They allied themselves with a neighboring country. *tḥaalfaw wiyya fadd dawla mujaawira.*
almond - *looza* pl. *-aat* coll. *looz.*
almost - **1.** *taqriiban.* I'm almost finished. *ʔaani taqriiban xallaṣit.* **2.** *εala wašak.* We were almost ready to surrender. *činna εala wašak insallim.* **3.** *ʔilla šwayya.* The glass almost broke when I dropped it. *l-iglaaṣ inkisar ʔilla šwayya min waggaεta.*
alms - *ṣadaqa* pl. *-aat.*
alone - **1.** *waḥid.* Do you live alone? *tiskun waḥdak?* **2.** *bass.* You alone can help me. *bass ʔinta tigdar itsaaεidni.*
all alone - *waḥiid.* He seems to be all alone in the world. *ybayyin waḥiid bid-dinya.*
to leave alone - *jaaz (u) n- min, εaaf (u).* Leave the radio alone! *juuz imnir-raadyo* or *εuuf ir-raadyo.*
along - **1.** *wiyya.* Do you want to come along with me? *triid tiji wiyyaaya?* -- How much baggage should I take along. *šgadd ġaraaδ̣ laazim aaxuδ wiyyaaya.* **2.** *b-muḥaaδaat, wiyya.* We walked along the railroad tracks. *mšeena b-muḥaaδaat siččat il-qiṭaar.* **3.** *εala ṭuul, b-jaanib, b-ṣaff.* We have flowers planted along the walk. *εidna ʔawraad mazruuεa εala ṭuul il-mamša.* **4.** *b-ṣaff, wiyya.* He parked his car along the wall. *waggaf sayyaarta b-ṣaff il-ḥaayiṭ.* **5.** *ḥibla.* My wife is four months along. *marti ʔarbaεt išhur ḥibla.*
all along - **1.** *daaʔiman.* I said so all along. *činit daaʔiman aguul haaδa.* **2.** *εala ṭuul.* We saw rabbits all along the road. *šifna ʔaraanib εala ṭuul iṭ-ṭariiq.*
alphabet - *ʔaliif baaʔ, ʔaliif bee.*
alphabetical - *ḥasab il-ʔaliif bee.*
already - **1.** *gabuḷ.* Haven't you been through this line already? *ʔinta ma-činit ib-has-sira gabuḷ?* **2.** *no equivalent.* They had already left when we arrived. *čaanaw raayḥiin lamma wṣalna.* I've eaten already. *ʔaani maakil.* -- It's already time to eat. *ṣaar wakt il-ʔakil.* -- So you'll already be there by the time I arrive? *laεad raḥ-itkuun ihnaak ib-wakt*

il-ʔoosal?

also - *hamm, hammeen, ʔayδan.* We also discussed the test. *w-hammeen ibzaθna l-imtizaan.*

altar - *mizraab* pl. *mazaariib* (mosque), *maδbaz* pl. *maδaabiz* (church or temple).

to **alter** - *baddal (i tabdiil) t- b-, ġayyar (i taġyiir) t- b-, Ɛaddal (i taƐdiil) t-, ṣallaz (i taṣliiz) t-.* The tailor is going to alter my suit. *l-xayyaaṭ raz-ybaddil ib-qaaṭi.*

alteration - *taƐdiil* pl. *-aat, tabdiil* pl. *-aat, taġyiir* pl. *-aat, taṣliiz* pl. *-aat.* The alterations are free. *t-taƐdiilaat ib-balaaš.* -- We'll have to make a few alterations in the text of the speech. *laazim insawwi šwayya taġyiiraat ib-naṣṣ il-xiṭaab.*

alternative - **1.** *xiyaar.* They left us no alternative. *ma-tirkoo-nna xiyaar.* **2.** *čaara.* You'll have to go. There's no alternative. *laazim itruuz. ma-aku čaara.* **3.** *ġeer.* I don't see any alternative solution. *ma-da-ašuuf ġeer zall.*

although - *walaw.* I'll be there, although I have very little time. *raz-akuun ihnaak, walaw wakti kulliš δayyiq.*

altitude - *rtifaaƐ* pl. *-aat, Ɛilu.* The plane was flying at a very high altitude. *ṭ-ṭiyyaara čaanat ṭaayra Ɛala rtifaaƐ Ɛaali.*

altogether - **1.** *šii Ɛala šii, kull bil-kull, bil-majmuuƐ.* Altogether there are thirty books. *kull bil-kull ʔaku θlaaθiin iktaab.* **2.** *b-ṣuura Ɛaamma.* Altogether, this plan is good. *b-ṣuura Ɛaamma hal-xuṭṭa zeena.* **3.** *bil-marra, fadd marra.* These prices are altogether too high. *hal-ʔasƐaar Ɛaalya bil-marra.* **4.** *tamaaman.* You're altogether right. *ʔinta ṣaziiz tamaaman.*

aluminum - *faafoon, ʔaliminyoom.*

always - *daaʔiman, Ɛala ṭuul.* I'm always at home. *ʔaani daaʔiman bil-beet.* -- She's always been rich. *hiyya čaanat zangiina Ɛala ṭuul* or ***ṭuul Ɛumurha čaanat zangiina.*

amateur - *haawi* pl. *huwaat.* For an amateur he paints quite well. *ka-haawi yirsim kulliš zeen.*

to **amaze** - *Ɛajjab (i taƐjiib) t-.* He amazed us with his magic tricks. *Ɛajjabna b-ʔalƐaaba s-sizriyya.*

to be amazed - *staġrab (i stiġraab).* I was amazed at his lack of concern. *staġrabit min Ɛadam ihtimaama.*

amazing - *Ɛajiib, mudhiš.*

ambassador - *safiir* pl. *sufaraaʔ.*

amber - *kahrab.*

ambergris - *Ɛanbar.*

ambiguous - *ġaamiδ.*

ambiguity - *ġumuuδ.*

ambition - *ṭumuuz.* He has no ambition. *ma-Ɛinda ṭumuuz.*

ambitious - *ṭamuuz.*

ambulance - *sayyaarat ʔisƐaaf.* This man is hurt! Call an ambulance! *har-rijjaal mitƐawwir! xaabur Ɛala sayyaarat ʔisƐaaf!*

ambush - *kamiin* pl. *-aat.* They set up an ambush for him. *niṣboo-la kamiin.*

to be ambushed - *wigaƐ (a wuguuƐ) b-kamiin.* The patrol was ambushed outside the village. *d-dawriyya wigƐat ib-kamiin xaarij il-qarya.*

**They ambushed the caravan. *hijmaw Ɛal-qaafila Ɛala ġafla.*

America - *ʔameerka, ʔamriika.*

American - *ʔameerki,* ʔamriiki,* ʔamriikaani** pl. *ʔamriikaan.*

Amman - *Ɛammaan.*

ammunition - *Ɛitaad, δaxiira, muuna.*

amnesia - *daaʔ in-nisyaan, maraδ in-nisyaan.*

amnesty - *Ɛafu Ɛaamm.*

among - **1.** *been.* You're among friends. *ʔinta been ʔaṣdiqaaʔ.* -- Look among the papers! *baawiƐ been il-waraq.* -- **2.** *beenaat, been.* We decided it among ourselves. *qarrarna beenaatna.* -- There were many nice people among them. *čaan ʔaku beenaathum xooš awaadim ihwaaya.* **3.** *min.* He's popular among most of the people. *huwwa mazbuub min akθar in-naas.* **4.** *Ɛala.* Pass the leaflets out among the crowd. *wazziƐ il-manaašiir Ɛal-zaaδriin.* **5.** *wiyya, been, b-nuṣṣ.* He lived four years among the Bedouins. *Ɛaaš ʔarbaƐ isniin wiyya l-badu.*

among other things - *min jumlat il-ʔašyaaʔ, min δimn il-ʔašyaaʔ.* Among other things he collects stamps. *min jumlat il-ʔašyaaʔ yjammiƐ ṭawaabiƐ.*

amount - **1.** *mablaġ* pl. *mabaaliġ.* Write a check for the full amount. *ʔiktib čakk bil-mablaġ kulla.* **2.** *kammiyya* pl. *-aat, miqdaar* pl. *miqaadiir.* We bought a large amount of coffee. *štireena kammiyya kabiira mnil-gahwa.* **3.** *majmuuƐ* pl. *majaamiiƐ.* Add up these numbers and tell me the amount. *ʔijmaƐ hal-ʔarqaam w-gul-li bil-majmuuƐ.*

to amount to - **1.** *sawwa (i), ṣaar (i).* How much does the bill amount to? *šgadd itsawwi l-qaaʔima?* **2.** *suwa (a).* He doesn't amount to much. *huwwa ma-yiswa šii.*

to **amputate** - *bitar (i batir) n-, gaṣṣ (u gaṣṣ) n-, giṭaƐ (a gatiƐ) n-.* The doctor amputated his leg. *ṭ-ṭabiib bitar rijla.*

amulet - *ziriz* pl. *zuruuz.*

to **amuse** - **1.** *wannas (i) t-.* That amuses me very much. *haaδa ywannisni hwaaya.* **2.** *lahha (i) t-, salla (i tasliya) t-.* He amuses himself by reading. *ylahhi nafsa bil-iqraaya.* **3.** *δazzak (i taδziik) t-.* The comedian amused the audience. *l-hazali δazzak il-zaaδriin.*

amusement - *tasliya, lahu, winsa.* He paints for amusement only. *yirsim lit-tasliya faqaṭ.*

amusement tax - *δariibat malaahi.*

amusing - *mumtiƐ.* I read an amusing article in the paper today. *qreet maqaal mumtiƐ bij-jariida l-yoom.*

anarchist - *fawδawi* pl. *-iyyiin.*

anarchy - *fawδawiyya.*

analogous - *mšaabih, mmaaθil.*

analogy - *tamaaθul, tašaabuh.*

analysis - *tazliil* pl. *-aat.* They made a chemical analysis during class. *sawwaw tazliil kiimyaawi wakt id-daris.*

to **analyze** - *zallal (i tazliil) t-.* First of all, analyze the problem. *ʔawwal šii, zallil il-muškila.*

anatomical - *tašriizi*.*

anatomy - **1.** *Ɛilm it-tašriiz.* He studies anatomy at Cairo University. *yidrus Ɛilm it-tašriiz ib-jaamiƐat il-qaahira.* **2.** *tarkiib jismi.* We dissected the rabbit and studied its anatomy. *šarrazna l-ʔarnab w-dirasna tarkiiba j-jismi.*

ancestor - *jidd* pl. *ʔajdaad, salaf* pl. *ʔaslaaf.*

anchor - *ʔangar* pl. *ʔanaagir.* The boat lost its anchor in the storm. *δaaƐ ʔangar il-markab bil-Ɛaaṣifa.*

**Our boat lay at anchor in the harbor. *markabna čaan raasi bil-miinaaʔ.*

to drop anchor - *δabb (i δabb) n- ʔangar.* The ship dropped anchor in the bay. *l-baaxira δabbat ʔangar bil-xaliij.*

to weigh anchor - *šaal (i šeel) n- il-ʔangar, rufaƐ (a rafuƐ) n- il-ʔangar, jarr (u jarr) n- il-ʔangar.* We weighed anchor after the storm passed. *šilna l-ʔangar baƐad-ma marrat il-Ɛaaṣifa.*

to anchor - **1.** *risa (i rasu) n-.* They anchored the ship out in the bay. *risaw il-baaxira bil-xaliij.* **2.** *θabbat (i taθbiit) t-.* They anchored the telephone pole in cement. *θabbitaw Ɛamuud it-talafoon bič-čibeentu.*

**He stood there as if he were anchored to the spot. *wugaf Ɛabaalak imbasmar ib-mukaana.*

ancient - **1.** *qadiim* pl. *qudamaaʔ.* This is the palace of the ancient kings of Babylon. *haaδa qaṣir miluuk baabil il-qudamaaʔ.* **2.** *qadiim, Ɛatiig.* Why did you invest so much money in that ancient building? *leeš zaṭṭeet halgadd ifluus Ɛala δiič il-binaaya l-Ɛatiiga?* -- I'm very much interested in ancient statues. *ʔaani kulliš muulaƐ bit-tamaaθiil il-qadiima.*

and - *w-.* They sell books and stationery. *ybiiƐuun kutub w-qirṭaasiyya.*

and so forth (or **on**) - *w-ma ʔašbah,* or *w-ʔila ʔaaxirihi.* I need paper, ink, and so forth. *ʔariid waraq, Ɛibir, w-ma ʔašbah.*

anesthetic - *banj.*

angel - *malak, malaak* pl. *malaaʔika.*

anger - *ġaδab, zaƐal.* In his anger, he said a lot of things he didn't mean. *b-ġaδaba, gaal ihwaaya ʔašyaaʔ ma-yiqṣudha.*

to anger - **1.** *ziƐal (a zaƐal), ġiδab (a ġaδab).* He doesn't anger easily. *ma-yizƐal bil-Ɛajal.* **2.** *zaƐƐal (i tazƐiil) t-, ʔaġδab (i ʔiġδaab).* His remarks angered me. *zčaayaata zaƐƐalatni.*

angle - **1.** *zaawiya* pl. *zawaaya.* Measure each angle of the triangle. *qiis kull zaawiya min zawaaya l-muθallaθ.* **2.** *wijih* pl. *wujuuh, naaziya* pl. *nawaazi.* We considered the matter from all angles. *bzaθna l-mawδuuƐ min kull il-wujuuh.* --

angry - *zaƐlaan, ġaδbaan.* I haven't seen him angry very often. *ma-šifta zaƐlaan ʔilla qaliil.*

to be angry - *ziƐal (a zaƐil), ġiδab (a ġaδab).* Please don't be angry with me! *ʔarjuuk la-tizƐal*

minni. -- Are you angry at him? *ʔinta zaɛlaan ɛalee?* or *ʔinta ġaḍbaan ɛalee?*
to make angry - *zaɛɛal (i tazɛiil), gaḍḍab (i taġḍiib).* That remark must have made him very angry. *hal-mulaaẓaḍa laazim ihwaaya zaɛɛlata.*

animal - *ẓaywaan* pl. *-aat.* Don't feed the animals. *la-tʔakkil il-ẓaywaanaat.*

Ankara - *ʔanqara.*

ankle - *mafṣal qadam.*

anniversary - *ðikra sanawiyya.* The bank is celebrating the anniversary of its foundation. *l-þang da-yiẓtifil ib-ðikraa s-sanawiyya l-taʔsiisa.*

to **announce** - **1.** *ðaaɛ (i ʔiðaaɛa).* They announced the results on the radio. *ðaaɛaw in-nataaʔij bir-raadyo.* **2.** *ɛilan (i ʔiɛlaan).* They announced their engagement last night. *ɛilnaw xuṭbathum il-baarẓa bil-leel.*

announcement - **1.** *bayaan* pl. *-aat.* The government issued an announcement on their new policy. *l-ẓukuuma ʔaṣdirat bayaan ɛan siyaasatha j-jidiida.* **2.** *ʔiɛlaan* pl. *-aat.* An announcement of their engagement was in the paper last night. *ʔiɛlaan xuṭbathum čaan bij-jariida l-baarẓa bil-leel.*

announcer - *muðiiɛ* pl. *-iin.* The announcer has a pleasant voice. *l-muðiiɛ ɛinda ṣooṭ ẓilu.*

to **annoy** - *ziɛaj (i ʔizɛaaj) n-, ʔazɛaj (i ʔizɛaaj), ḍawwaj (i taḍwiij) t-.* He annoyed me all morning. *ʔazɛajni ṭuul iṣ-ṣubuẓ.*
to get annoyed - *nziɛaj (i ʔinziɛaaj), ḍaaj (u ḍawajaan).* I got very annoyed at her. *nziɛajit minha hwaaya.*

annoying - *muzɛij.* That's very annoying. *haaða kulliš muzɛij.*

another - **1.** *laax* (f.) *lux* (pl.) *luxra, θaani* (f.) *θaanya.* Give me another cup of coffee please. *nṭiini finjaan gahwa laax rajaaʔan.* **2.** *ġeer, θaani.* Show me another pattern. *raawiini ġeer tufṣaal.* **3.** *baɛad.* I don't want to hear another word about it. *ma-ard asmaɛ čilma baɛad ɛanha.*
one another - **1.** *waaẓid ɛal-laax.* We depend on one another. *niɛtimid waaẓid ɛal-laax.* **2.** *waaẓid wiyya l-laax.* Those two are always fighting with one another. *hal-iθneen yitɛaarkuun waaẓid wiyya l-laax ɛala ṭuul.* **3.** *waaẓid bil-laax.* They don't trust one another. *ma-yθiquun waaẓid bil-laax.*

answer - **1.** *jawaab* pl. *ʔajwiba.* I'm waiting for an answer to my letter. *da-antiðir jawaab il-maktuubi.* **2.** *ẓall* pl. *ẓluul.* How did you arrive at this answer? *šloon itwaṣṣalit il-hal-ẓall.*
to answer - *jaawab (i mujaawaba) t-, radd (i radd) n-.* He answered my question without any hesitation. *jaawab ɛala ʔasʔilti biduun taraddud.*

ant - *namla* pl. *-aat* coll. *namil.*

antelope - *ġazaal* pl. *ġizlaan.*

antenna - *ʔeeryal* pl. *-aat.*

anthem - *našiid* pl. *ʔanaašiid.* They played the national anthem before the game started. *ɛizfaw in-našiid il-waṭani gabuḷ-ma yibdaʔ il-liɛib.*

antic - *tahriij* pl. *-aat.* His antics were very amusing. *tahriijaata čaanat ihwaaya tḍaẓẓik.*

to **anticipate** - *twaqqaɛ (a tawaqquɛ).* The attendance was larger than we had anticipated. *l-ẓaaḍriin čaanaw ʔazyad min-ma twaqqaɛna.*

antidote - *duwa (ḍidd it-tasammum).* What is the antidote for arsenic poisoning? *šinu d-duwa ḍidd it-tasammum imniz-zarniix?*

Antioch - *ʔanṭaakya.*

antique - **1.** *ɛantiik.* He bought a very expensive antique watch. *štira saaɛa ɛantiika kulliš ġaalya.* **2.** *qadiim.* We visited some antique ruins yesterday. *zirna baɛaḍ il-ʔaaθaar il-qadiima l-baarẓa.*

anxiety - *qalaq.*

anxious - *qaliq.* We spent several anxious minutes waiting for their return. *gḍeena ɛiddat daqaayiq qalqa b-intiðaar rujuuɛhum.*
to be anxious - **1.** *mitẓammis, muštaaq.* I'm anxious to see the new book. *ʔaani mitẓammis ašuuf l-iktaab ij-jidiid.* **2.** *qaliq.* He's very anxious about his future. *huwwa qaliq ɛala mustaqbala.*

anxiously - *b-ištiyaaq.* They waited anxiously about an hour until the news came in. *ḍallaw yintaḍruun b-ištiyaaq ẓawaali saaɛa ʔila ʔan wuṣlat l-axbaar.*

any - **1.** *ʔay.* Did you find any books there? *ligeet ʔay kutub ihnaak?* -- Any mechanic can fix that. *ʔay miikaaniiki yigdar yṣalliẓ haaða.* **2.** *šii.* Don't eat any of it. *la-taakul šii minna.*
not .... any - *ma- .... kull, ma- .... ʔay.* There isn't any bread. *ma-aku kull xubuz.*

anybody - **1.** *ʔaẓẓad.* Was anybody at home? *čaan ʔaẓẓad bil-beet?* **2.** *ʔay waaẓid.* Anybody can do that. *ʔay waaẓid yigdar ysawwi haaða.*
**If he's anybody at all in this town, I'd know him. *law čaan šaxṣiyya b-hal-balad, la-čaan ɛirafta.*
**We can't take just anybody. *ma-nigdar inɛayyin yaahu č-čaan.*

anyhow - *ɛala ʔay ẓaal, ɛala kull ẓaal.* I would have gone anyhow. *ʔaani čaan riẓit, ɛala kull ẓaal.*

anyone - *ʔaẓẓad, ʔay waaẓid.* If anyone needs help, send him to me. *ʔiða ʔaẓẓad yiẓtaaj musaaɛada dizza ɛalayya.* -- Anyone can do that. *ʔay waaẓid yigdar ysawwi haaða.*

anything - *ʔay šii, fadd šii, šii.* Is there anything for me here? *ʔaku ʔay šii ʔili hnaa?* -- Did he say anything? *gaal šii?* or *gaal fadd šii?*
**I wouldn't do that for anything. *ma-asawwi haaða mahma čaan.*
**I was anything but pleased with his work. *ma-činit mirtaaẓ min ɛamala ʔabadan.*
anything but - *kullši bass.* You can do anything but that. *tigdar itsawwi kullši bass haaða.*

anyway - *ɛala kull ẓaal.* She didn't want to come anyway. *ma-raadat tiji ɛala kull ẓaal.* -- I didn't go anyway. *ma-riẓit ɛala kull ẓaal.*

anywhere - **1.** *fadd mukaan, fadd maẓall.* Are you going anywhere today? *raayiẓ fadd mukaan il-yoom?* **2.** *ween-ma.* Anywhere you look there's dust. *ween-ma tbaawiɛ ʔaku ɛajaaj.*
not ... anywhere - *ma ... ʔay makaan, ma ... ʔay maẓall.* I couldn't find him anywhere. *ma-gidarit ʔalgaa b-ʔay mukaan.*
**That won't get you anywhere. *haaði ma-raẓ-itwaṣṣlak il-fadd natiija.*

apart - **1.** *mfaṣṣix.* Is my watch still apart? *saaɛati li-hassa mfaṣṣixa?* **2.** *miftiriq.* They were apart for two weeks. *čaanaw miftirqiin il-muddat isbuuɛeen.* **3.** *minfaṣil.* They've been living apart since their quarrel. *čaanaw ɛaayšiin minfaṣliin min wakt iɛraakhum.* **4.** *ɛala ẓida.* Let's consider each argument apart from the others. *xal-nunḍur ib-kull ẓijja ɛala ẓida ɛan il-ẓijaj il-uxra.*
**The two buses will leave five minutes apart. *l-þaaṣeen yiṭlaɛuun xamas daqaayiq waaẓid wara l-laax.*
apart from this - *ma-ɛada haay.* Apart from this, he's a good man. *ma-ɛada haay, huwwa xooš rijjaal.*

apartment - *šiqqa* pl. *siqaq, ʔaþartmaan* pl. *-aat.* We're looking for an apartment. *da-ndawwir ɛala šiqqa.*

apartment house - *ɛimaara* (pl. *-aat*) *lis-sukna.* They're building an apartment house on our street. *da-yibnuun ɛimaara lis-sukna b-šaariɛna.*

ape - *šaadi* pl. *šwaadi, qird* pl. *qiruud.* We saw an ape at the zoo. *šifna fadd šaadi b-ẓadiiqt il-ẓaywaanaat.*

apiece - *kull waaẓid, kullman.* My brother and I earned six dollars apiece. *ʔaani w-axuuya ẓaṣṣalna kull waaẓid sitt doolaaraat.*

to **apologize** - *ṭilab (u ṭalab) il-ɛafu, ɛtiðar (i ɛtiðaar), tɛaððar (a taɛaðður).* I apologize. *ʔaṭlub il-ɛafu* or *ʔaani ʔaɛtiðir.*
to apologize to - *tɛaððar (a) min, ʔila, ɛtiðar (i) min, ʔila.* Did you apologize to her? *ɛtiðarit ʔilha?*

apology - *ɛtiðaar* pl. *-aat, taɛaðður* pl. *-aat.*

apostrophe - *ɛalaamat* (pl. *-aat*) *ixtiṣaar, ɛalaamat* (pl. *-aat*) *iḍaafa.*

apostle - *rasuul* pl. *rusul, ẓawaari* pl. *-iyyiin.*

apostolic - *rasuuli*.* Could you direct me to the Apostolic Legation? *tigdar iddalliini ɛal-qaṣaada r-rasuuliyya.*

apparatus - *jihaaz* pl. *ʔajhiza.*

apparent - *mbayyin, ðaahir, waaḍiẓ.* It's apparent that he didn't understand the question. *mbayyin ma-ftiham is-suʔaal.*

apparently - *ɛala-ma yiðhar, ẓasab-ma yiðhar.* He has apparently changed his mind. *ɛala-ma yiðhar ġayyar fikra.*

appeal - **1.** *stiʔnaaf* pl. *-aat.* The appeal was denied. *l-istiʔnaaf irrufaḍ.* **2.** *ṭalab* pl. *-aat.* The United Nations got many appeals for help this year. *l-ʔumam il-muttaẓida stilmat ɛiddat ṭalabaat musaaɛada has-sana.* **3.** *jaaðibiyya.* She's got a lot of sex appeal. *ɛidha jaaðibiyya jinsiyya hwaaya.*
to appeal - **1.** *ɛijab (i ʔiɛjaab).* It doesn't appeal to me. *ma-tiɛjibni.* **2.** *twassal (a tawassul).* He appealed to the president to pardon his son. *twassal imnir-raʔiis yiɛfi ɛan*

ʔibna. 3. *staʔnaf (i stiʔnaaf).* The lawyer decided to appeal the case. *l-muḥaami qarrar yistaʔnif id-daεwa.* 4. *stanjad (i stinjaad), stiğaaθ (i stiğaaθa).* During the flood, the country appealed for help from the neighboring countries. *b-wakt il-fayað̣aan, il-balad istanjad musaaεada mnil-bilaad il-mujaawira.*

to **appear** - 1. *bayyan (i tbiyyin) t-.* He appeared at the last moment. *bayyan ib-ʔaaxir laḥð̣a.* 2. *ṭilaε (a ṭuluuε) n-.* This paper appears every Thursday. *haj-jariida tiṭlaε kull xamiis.* 3. *ð̣ihar (a ð̣uhuur) n-.* A ship appeared on the horizon. *fadd sifiina ð̣ihrat εal-ʔufuq.*

appearance - 1. *ð̣uhuur* pl. *ð̣awaahir.* It's his first appearance on the stage. *haaða ʔawwal ð̣uhuura εal-masraḥ.* 2. *mað̣har* pl. *mað̣aahir.* You have to pay more attention to your appearance. *laazim tihtamm ib-mað̣harak ʔazyad.* -- Appearances are deceiving. *l-mað̣aahir xaddaaεa.*

appendicitis - *ltihaab il-muṣraan l-aεwar, ltihaab iz-zaaʔida d-duudiyya.*

appendix - 1. *z-zaaʔida d-duudiyya, l-maṣraan l-aεwar.* They took his appendix out when he was five years old. *gaṣṣoo-la z-zaaʔida d-duudiyya min čaan εumra xams isniin.* 2. *mulḥaq* pl. *mulaaḥiq.* Perhaps it's in the appendix. *yimkin haaða bil-mulḥaq.*

appetite - 1. *šahiyya* pl. *-aat.* Our boy has a good appetite. *ʔibinna εinda šahiyya zeena.* 2. *rağba* pl. *-aat.* He has a tremendous appetite for knowledge. *εinda hwaaya rağba bil-εilim.*

appetizer - *mušahhi* pl. *-yaat.*

appetizing - *musahhi*.*

to **applaude** - *ṣaffag (u taṣfiig, tṣuffug) t-.* We applauded heartily. *ṣaffagna min kull galubna.*

applause - *taṣfiig, tṣuffug.* They met him with applause. *staqbiloo bit-taṣfiig.*

apple - *tiffaaḥa* pl. *-aat* coll. *tiffaaḥ.*

appliance - *jihaaz* pl. *ʔajhiza.* We carry all kinds of electrical appliances. *nitεaaṭa jamiiε il-ʔajhiza l-kahrabaaʔiyya.* -- This place sells household appliances. *hal-maḥall ybiiε ʔajhiza beetiyya.*

application - 1. *stimaara* pl. *-aat.* Fill in this application and forward it to the university. *ʔimli hal-istimaara w-dizzha lij-jaamiεa.* 2. *εariið̣a* pl. *εaraayið̣.* He forwarded his application to the manager. *qaddam εariið̣ta lil-mudiir.* 3. *taṭbiiq* pl. *-aat.* The application of his theory wasn't practical. *taṭbiiq nað̣ariita ma-čaan εamali.* 4. *ṭalab* pl. *-aat.* His application was rejected. *ṭalaba nrufað̣.* 5. *qaaṭ* pl. *qooṭ, ṭabaqa* pl. *-aat.* You'll have to give it another application after this coat dries. *laazim tuð̣rubha qaaṭ laax baεad-ma yeebis hal-qaaṭ.*

to **apply** - 1. *qaddam (i taqdiim) t-.* I'd like to apply for the job. *ʔaḥibb aqaddim εal-wað̣iifa.* 2. *ṭabbaq (i taṭbiiq) t-.* You've applied this rule incorrectly. *ṭabbaqit hal-qaaεida ğalaṭ.* 3. *ḥaṭṭ (u ḥaṭṭ) n-, staεmal (i stiεmaal).* Apply a hot compress every two hours. *ḥuṭṭ ð̣amaada ḥaarra kull saaεteen.* -- I had to apply all my strength. *ð̣ṭarreet aḥuṭṭ kull quuti.* 4. *ṭilab (u ṭalab) n-.* My father applied for a loan. *ʔabuuya ṭilab deen.* 5. *ḥaṭṭ (u ḥaṭṭ) n-, xalla (i txilli) t-.* She applied another coat of polish to her fingernails. *ḥaṭṭat qaaṭ ṣubuğ θaani εala ʔað̣aafirha.* 6. *šimal (i šumuul) n-, nṭubaq (u nṭibaaq) εala, sira (i saryaan).* This order applies to everybody. *hal-ʔamur yišmil il-kull.*

to apply oneself - *biðal (i baðil) n- jahid.* He's smart but he doesn't apply himself. *huwwa šaaṭir laakin ma-yibðil jahda.*

to **appoint** - *εayyan (i taεyiin) t-.* The ministry appointed five new engineers. *l-wuzaara εayyinat xamis muhandisiin jiddad.*

appointment - 1. *taεyiin* pl. *-aat.* Congratulations on your appointment. *t-tahaani εala taεyiinak.* 2. *mawεid* pl. *mawaaεiid.* I had to cancel all appointments for tomorrow. *ð̣ṭarreet algi kull il-mawaaεiid maal baačir.* -- I have an appointment with him. *εindi mawεid wiyyaa.*

to make an appointment - *twaaεad (a twaaεud).* I made an appointment with Ali for five-o-clock. *twaaεadit wiyya εali s-saaεa xamsa.*

appraisal - *taqdiir* pl. *-aat, taθmiin* pl. *-aat.* A careful appraisal of the property showed that ... *taqdiir il-muluk ib-ṣuura daqiiqa bayyan ʔan ...*

to **appraise** - 1. *ḥallal (i taḥliil) t-.* We want you to appraise the situation and give us your opinion. *nriidak itḥallil il-wað̣iε w-tinṭiina raʔyak.* 2. *qaddar (i taqdiir) t-, θamman (i taθmiin) t-.* A broker's coming to appraise the house. *fadd dallaal raḥ-yiji yqaddir il-beet.*

to **appreciate** - 1. *čaan (u) mimtann, mamnuun.* I would appreciate it, if you could come. *ʔakuun mamnuun ʔiða tigdar tiji.* 2. *qaddar (i taqdiir) t-.* She doesn't appreciate what we've done for her. *ma-da-tqaddir illi sawweena-lh-iyyaa.* -- He doesn't appreciate good music. *ma-yqaddir il-muusiiqa r-raaqya.* 3. *εiraf (u) n-.* I quite appreciate that it can't be done overnight. *ʔaεruf zeen haaða ma-yimkin yixlaṣ ib-fadd yoom.*

appreciation - *taqdiir* pl. *-aat.* I don't expect any appreciation. *ma-atwaqqaε ʔay taqdiir.* -- She has no appreciation for art. *ma-εidha taqdiir lil-fann.*

appreciative - *mamnuun.* He doesn't seem very appreciative. *ybayyin εalee muu mamnuun.*

apprentice - *ṣaaniε* pl. *ṣunnaaε (taḥt it-tadriib), εaamil* pl. *εummaal (taḥt it-tadriib).*

approach - 1. *madxal* pl. *madaaxil.* They're repairing the approaches to the bridge. *da-yṣalluḥuun madaaxil ij-jisir.* 2. *ṭariiqa* pl. *ṭuruq.* Am I using the right approach? *da-astaεmil iṭ-ṭariiqa ṣ-ṣaḥiiḥa?*

to approach - 1. *tqarrab (a taqarrub).* They approached the enemy's camp cautiously. *tqarrbaw min muεaskar il-εaduww ib-ḥaðar.* 2. *faataḥ (i mufaataḥa) t-.* I'm going to approach my boss about a raise. *raḥ-afattiḥ ir-raʔiis maali bit-tarfiiε.* 3. *εaalaj (i muεaalaja) t-.* How would you approach the problem? *sloon itεaalij il-muškila?*

appropriate - *munaasib, mlaaʔim, laayig.* This gift is very appropriate. *haaði l-hadiyya kulliš munaasiba.*

to appropriate - 1. *stawla (i stiilaaʔ).* My son has appropriated all my ties. *ʔibni stawla εala kull ʔarbiṭti.* 2. *xaṣṣaṣ (i taxṣiiṣ) t-.* The city has appropriated fifty thousand dinars to build a new library. *l-baladiyya xaṣṣiṣat xamsiin ʔalif diinaar il-binaayat maktaba jdiida.*

approval - *muwaafaqa, muṣaadaqa.* You'll have to get his approval on it. *laazim taaxuð muwaafaqta εaleeha.*

**This color will not meet her approval. *ma-raḥ-itwaafiq εala hal-loon.*

on approval - *εala šarṭ il-muwaafaqa.* They sent me the book on approval. *dazzoo-li l-iktaab εala šarṭ il-muwaafaqa.*

to **approve** - 1. *waafaq (u muwaafaqa) t-.* Do you approve of my suggestion? *twaafuq εala qtiraaḥi?* -- He doesn't approve of his son staying out late at night. *ma-ywaafuq εala ʔibna yitʔaxxar bil-leel.* 2. *ṣaadaq (i muṣaadaqa) t-, waafaq (u muwaafaqa) t-.* The president approved the housing project. *r-raʔiis ṣaadaq εala mašruuε il-ʔiskaan.* -- The National Assembly approved the new constitution. *l-majlis il-waṭani ṣaadaq εala d-dustuur ij-jidiid.*

approvingly - *b-istiḥsaan.* She nodded her head approvingly. *hazzat raasha b-istiḥsaan.*

approximate - *taqriibi*.* The approximate speed of the new planes is six-hundred miles an hour. *s-surεa t-taqriibiyya liṭ-ṭiyyaaraat ij-jidiida sitt miit miil bis-saaεa.*

approximately - *ḥawaali, taqriiban.* He left approximately a month ago. *saafar gabuḷ šahar taqriiban.*

apricot - *mišimšaaya* pl. *-aat* coll. *mišmiš.*

April - *niisaan.*

apron - *ṣadriyya* pl. *-aat, ṣadaari.*

apt - 1. *munaasib, b-makaana.* That was a very apt remark. *haaði čaanat mulaaḥað̣a kulliš munaasiba.* 2. *muḥtamal.* I'm apt to be out when you call. *muḥtamal akuun barra lamma txaabur.* 3. *mnil-mitwaqqaε.* When he's drunk, he's apt to do anything. *lamma ykuun sakraan, imnil-mitwaqqaε ysawwi ʔay šii.* 4. *yjuuz.* It's apt to be two o'clock before we get home. *yjuuz itkuun is-saaεa θinteen gabuḷ-ma noosal il-beet.*

**He is an apt pupil. *yilguṭ bil-εajil.*

Aqaba - *l-εaqaba.*

Arab - *εarabi** pl. *εarab.*

arabesque - 1. *zuxruf.* He's very good at arabesque. *huwwa kulliš zeen biz-zuxruf.* 2. *zuxrufi*.* There's a beautiful arabesque engraving on the wall. *ʔaku naqiš zuxrufi jamiil εal-ḥaayiṭ.*

Arab League - *j-jaamiεa l-εarabiyya.*

Arabian Peninsula - *j-jaziira l-εarabiyya.*

Arabian Sea - *l-baḥr il-εarabi.*

Arabic - *εarabi, l-luğa l-εarabiyya.*

Arabist - *mustašriq* pl. *-iin.*
Aramaic - *l-luğa l-ʔaaraamiyya.*
arch - *ṭaag* pl. *ṭuug.* That bridge has a tremendous arch. *haδaak ij-jisir bii fadd ṭaag ḍaxim.*
fallen arches - *flaatfuut, ʔaqdaam musaṭṭaḥa.* He has fallen arches. *Ɛinda flaatfuut.*
to arch - *ḥina (i ḥinaaʔ) n-.* The cat arched it's back. *l-bazzuuna ḥinat ḍaharha.*
arched - *mṭawwag.* The church's ceiling is arched. *sagf il-kaniisa mṭawwag.*
architect - *muhandis miƐmaari* pl. *muhandisiin miƐmaariyyiin.*
architecture - *handasa miƐmaariyya.*
area - **1.** *manṭiqa* pl. *manaaṭiq.* The area around Baghdad is densely populated. *l-manṭiqa ḥawaali bağdaad kulliš mizdaḥma bis-sukkaan.* **2.** *masaaḥa* pl. *-aat.* The area of the city is four square miles. *masaaḥt il-madiina ʔarbaƐ ʔamyaal murabbaƐa.*
Argentina - *l-ʔarjantiin.*
to **argue** - *jaadal (i mujaadala, jadal) t-, naaqaš (i munaaqaša, niqaaš) t-, ḥaajaj (i muḥaajaja) t-.* Don't argue with me. *la-tjaadilni.* -- I won't argue that point. *ma-ʔajaadil Ɛala han-nuqṭa.* -- That's something that can't be argued. *haaδa fadd šii ma-yitjaadal bii.*
to argue (with someone) - *tjaadal (a tajaadul), tḥaajaj (a taḥaajuj), tnaaqaš (a tanaaquš).* He'll argue with anyone about anything. *yitjaadil wiyya ʔay šaxiṣ Ɛala ʔay šii kaan.* -- They argue all the time. *yitjaadluun Ɛala ṭuul.*
argument - **1.** *ḥijja* pl. *ḥijaj.* They presented very convincing arguments. *qaddimaw ḥijaj kulliš muqniƐa.* **2.** *xilaaf* pl. *-aat, nizaaƐ.* It was just a small argument. *čaan fadd xilaaf baṣiiṭ.* **3.** *lağwa* pl. *-aat, lağaawi.* We had a violent argument. *ṣaarat beenaatna lağwa.*
to **arise** - **1.** *ḍihar (a ḍuhuur).* The problem arose some time ago. *l-muškila ḍihrat gabuḷ mudda.* **2.** *giƐad (u guƐuud) n-.* I arose at six this morning. *giƐadit iṣ-ṣubuḥ saaƐa sitta.* **3.** *gaam (u goom).* He arose from his chair and left the room. *gaam imnil-kursi maala w-tirak il-ğurfa.* **4.** *sinaḥ (a sinuuḥ).* As soon as the opportunity arises ... *ʔawwal-ma tisnaḥ il-furṣa ...*
arithmetic - *ḥisaab.*
arm - **1.** *δraaƐ* pl. *ʔaδruƐ.* He broke his arm. *kisar iδraaƐa.* **2.** *yadda* pl. *-aat.* The arms on this chair are too low. *yaddaat hal-iskamli kulliš naaṣya.* **3.** *slaaḥ* pl. *ʔasliḥa.* All arms have to be turned over to the police. *kull il-asliḥa laazim titsallam liš-šurṭa.*
underarm - *ʔubuṭ* pl. *ʔubaaṭ.*
under arms - *taḥt is-silaaḥ.* All ablebodied men were under arms. *kull ir-rijaal il-muqtadriin čaanaw taḥt is-silaaḥ.*
to be up in arms - *haaj (i hayajaan).* Everybody was up in arms. *kull waaḥid čaan haayij.*
to arm - *sallaḥ (i tasliiḥ) t-.* The company armed its guards. *š-šarika salliḥat ḥurraasha.*
to be armed - *tsallaḥ (a tsilliḥ).* The policeman is always armed with a revolver. *š-šurṭi daaʔiman yitsallaḥ ib-musaddas.* -- The gang is armed. *l-Ɛiṣaaba mitsallḥa.*
armchair - *kursi ʔabu yaddaat* pl. *karaasi ʔummahaat yaddaat.*
armistice - *hudna* pl. *-aat.*
armor - **1.** *diriƐ* pl. *druuƐ.* These shells can't penetrate the heavy armor of a battleship. *hal-qanaabil ma-tixtiriq dirƐ il-baarija l-ḥarbiyya.* **2.** *muṣaffaḥa* pl. *-aat.* Armor doesn't operate well in this mountainous terrain. *l-muṣaffaḥaat ma-tištuğul zeen ib-hal-manṭiqa j-jabaliyya.*
armored - *mṣaffaḥ.* Those tanks are heavily armored. *haaδi d-dabbaabaat imṣaffaḥa kulliš.*
army - *jeeš* pl. *jyuuš.* Did you serve in the army or the navy? *xidamit bij-jeeš loo bil-baḥriyya?*
around - **1.** *qariib.* He lives right around here. *yiskun qariib min ihnaa.* **2.** *ḥawaali.* I have around twenty dinars. *Ɛindi ḥawaali Ɛišriin diinaar.* **3.** *daayir.* He tied the rope around the barrel. *laff il-ḥabal daayir il-barmiil.* **4.** *b-.* There are some good movies around town this week. *ʔaku fadd ʔaflaam zeena bil-wlaaya hal-isbuuƐ.*
**Is there anybody around? *ʔaku ʔaḥḥad ihnaa?*
**The racetrack is a half mile around. *farrat is-saaḥa nuṣṣ miil.*
to **arouse** - **1.** *fazzaz (i tafziiz, tfizziz) t-.* A barking dog aroused me in the middle of the night. *fadd čalib yinbaḥ fazzazni b-nuṣṣ il-leel.* **2.** *ʔaθaar (i ʔiθaara) n-.* Her strange behavior aroused my suspicion. *taṣarrufha l-ğariib ʔaθaar šakki.* **3.** *waƐƐa (i twiƐƐi) t-.* What time shall I arouse you? *s-saaƐa beeš awaƐƐiik?*
arrack - *Ɛaraq.*
to **arrange** - **1.** *ṣaffaṭ (u taṣfiiṭ) t-, rattab (i tartiib) t-.* Who arranged the books? *minu ṣaffaṭ il-kutub?* **2.** *rattab (i tartiib) t-.* They arranged the room in two hours. *rattibaw il-ğurfa b-saaƐteen.* **3.** *dastar (i ddistir) t-, dabbar (i tadbiir) t-, rattab (i tartiib) t-.* I arranged with the guard to smuggle cigarettes to the prisoners. *dastaritha wiyya l-ḥaaris ḥatta yxaššiš jigaayir lil-masaajiin.*
arrangement - *tartiib* pl. *-aat, tadbiir* pl. *tadaabiir, ddistir.* How do you like this arrangement? *yƐijbak hat-tartiib?*
arrest - *ʔilqaaʔ qabuḍ.* The arrest was made at his home. *ʔilqaaʔ il-qabuḍ ṣaar ib-beeta.*
under arrest - *mawquuf, mwaqqaf.* He's been under arrest for two days. *čaan imwaqqaf yoomeen.*
to hold under arrest - *waqqaf (i tawqiif) t-.* They held him under arrest at the police station. *waqqufoo b-markaz iš-šurṭa.*
to arrest - *qubaḍ (u qabuḍ) n- Ɛala.* They arrested him and released him on bail. *qubḍaw Ɛalee w-fakkoo b-kafaala.*
arrival - *wuṣuul.* His arrival caused a lot of enthusiasm. *wuṣuula sabbab ḥamaas ihwaaya.*
to **arrive** - **1.** *wuṣal (a wuṣuul).* When did the train arrive? *šwakit wuṣal il-qiṭaar?* **2.** *twaṣṣal (a tawaṣṣul).* Did they arrive at a decision? *twaṣṣalaw il-fadd qaraar?* **3.** *nwilad (i).* The baby arrived at three this morning. *ṭ-ṭifil inwilad is-saaƐa tlaaθa ṣ-ṣubuḥ.*
arrow - **1.** *sahim* pl. *ʔashum.* The arrow points north. *s-sahim yʔaššir liš-šimaal.* **2.** *nišaaba* pl. *-aat* coll. *nišaab.* He killed the rabbit with an arrow. *qital il-ʔarnab ib-nišaaba.*
arsenic - *zarniix.*
art - *fann.* He knows a lot about art. *yuƐruf ihwaaya Ɛan il-fann.* -- There's an art to it. *yriid-ilha fadd fann.*
work of art - *qiṭƐa* (pl. *qiṭaƐ*) *fanniyya.* This building contains many works of art. *hal-binaaya tiḥwi qiṭaƐ fanniyya hwaaya.*
art gallery - *matḥaf* (pl. *mataaḥif*) *finuun.*
arthritis - *ltihaab il-mafaaṣil.*
article - **1.** *maqaal, maqaala* pl. *-aat.* There was a good article about it in the newspaper. *čaan ʔaku maqaal zeen Ɛanna bij-jariida.* **2.** *maadda* pl. *mawaadd.* Please read article three of the constitution. *rajaaʔan iqra l-maadda θ-θaalθa mnid-dastuur.* **3.** *šii* pl. *ʔašyaaʔ, maadda* pl. *mawaadd.* Many valuable articles were stolen. *hwaaya ʔašyaaʔ θamiina nbaagat.*
definite article - *ʔadaat it-taƐriif.*
artificial - *ṣṭinaaƐi*.* Are those flowers artificial? *hal-warid iṣṭinaaƐi?* -- She has an artificial smile. *Ɛidha btisaama ṣṭinaaƐiyya.*
artillery - *madfaƐiyya.*
artist - *fannaan* pl. *-iin.* He is a famous artist. *huwwa fannaan mašhuur.*
as - **1.** *Ɛala-ma.* Leave it as it is. *xalliiha Ɛala-ma hiyya.* **2.** *miθil-ma.* Do as you please. *sawwi miθil-ma yƐijbak.* -- Everything stands as it was. *kullši baaqi miθil-ma čaan.* **3.** *Ɛala, ḥasab.* He's late, as usual. *huwwa mitʔaxxir, ḥasb il-Ɛaada.* **4.** *maadaam, li-ʔan.* As he is leaving tomorrow, we must hurry. *maadaam huwwa maaši baačir, laazim nistaƐjil.* **5.** *w-.* Did you see anyone as you came in? *šifit ʔaḥḥad w-inta daaxil.* **6.** *ka-, miθil.* I think of him as a brother. *ʔaƐtabra ka-ʔax.* -- He used his coat as a pillow. *staƐmal sitirta ka-mxadda.* **7.** *b-.* His house is as big as ours. *beeta b-kubur beetna.*
**I work as a clerk for them. *ʔaštuğul kaatib Ɛidhum.*
**I regard it as important. *ʔaƐtabra muhimm.*
as far as - **1.** *l-ḥadd.* The train goes as far as Nasriyya. *l-qiṭaar yruuḥ il-ḥadd in-naṣriyya.* **2.** *ḥasab-ma, Ɛala-ma.* As far as I can see, he's right. *ḥasab-ma ašuuf, huwwa ṣaḥiiḥ.* **3.** *Ɛala madd.* The fields extend as far as you can see. *l-mazaariƐ timtadd Ɛala madd il-baṣar.*
as far as he's concerned - *bin-nisba ʔila, min naaḥiit~.* As far as he's concerned it's all right. *bin-nisba ʔila, zeena.*

as for - *ʔamma, min ṭaraf, bin-nisba l-, min naẓiit~.* As for him, it's all right. *ʔamma huwwa, ma-ɛinda maaniɛ.*

as if - *ɛabaalak, ka-ʔan.* He acts as if he were the director himself. *da-yiṭṣarraf ɛabaalak il-mudiir nafsa.*

as soon as - *ʔawwal-ma, ẓaal-ma.* Let me know as soon as you get here. *xabburni ʔawwal-ma tooṣal ihnaa.*

as yet - *l-ẓadd al-ʔaan, li-hassa, lil-ʔaan, baɛad.* Nothing has happened as yet. *ma-ṣaar šii l-ẓadd al-ʔaan.*

asbestos - *ʔazbast, spasto.*

ascetic - *mitzahhid, mitnassik.*

asceticism - *tanassuk, tazahhud.*

to **be ashamed** - **1.** *xijal (a xajal).* Don't be ashamed of this job. *la-tixjal min haš-šuġuḷ.* **2.** *xtiza (i xizi).* He's not ashamed of anything. *ma-yixtizi min ʔay šii.* **3.** *staẓa (i mistaẓa).* He was ashamed to show his grades to his father. *staẓa yraawi darajaata l-ʔabuu.*

ash can - *tanakat* (pl. *-aat*) *zibil.*

ashes - *rumaad.*

ashore - *lil-barr, lis-saaẓil.* We weren't allowed to go ashore. *ma-čaan masmuuẓ-inna ninzil lil-barr.*

ashtray - *ṭabla* pl. *-aat, nuffaaḍa* pl. *-aat.*

Asia Minor - *ʔaasya ṣ-ṣuġra.*

aside - *ɛala ṣafẓa, ɛala jiha.* I have to put a little money aside for the trip. *laazim axalli šwayya fluus ɛala ṣafẓa lis-safra.*

aside from - **1.** *b-ġaḍḍ in-naḍar ɛan.* Aside from the paint, it's a good car. *b-ġaḍḍ in-naḍar ɛan iṣ-ṣubuġ hiyya xooš sayyaara.* **2.** *ma-ɛada.* Aside from that, I have nothing else to add. *ma-ɛada haaḍa, ma-ɛindi šii ʔaḍiifa.*

to **ask** - **1.** *siʔal (a suʔaal) n-.* I'll ask him right away. *raẓ-ʔasʔala ẓaalan.* — Ask at the ticket office in the railroad station. *ʔisʔal ib-šibbaač beeɛ it-taḍaakir ib-maẓaṭṭat il-qiṭaar.* **2.** *ṭilab (u ṭalab) n-.* He asked for help. *ṭilab musaaɛada.* **3.** *ṭilab (u ṭalab) n-, raad (i reed) n-.* How much did he ask for washing the car? *šgadd ṭilab ɛala ġasḷ is-sayyaara?*

asleep - **1.** *naayim.* I must have been asleep. *laazim činit naayim.* **2.** *xadraan, mnammil.* My leg's asleep. *rijli xadraana.*

to fall asleep - *ġufa (i ġafu).* I fell asleep about three o'clock. *ġufeet ẓawaali is-saaɛa θlaaθa.*

aspect - **1.** *naaẓiya* pl. *nawaaẓi.* We studied the problem from every aspect. *dirasna l-muškila min kull nawaaẓiiha.* **2.** *maḍhar* pl. *maḍaahir.* This is one of the aspects of Iraqi life. *haaḍa maḍhar min maḍaahir il-ẓiyaat il-ɛiraaqiyya.*

asphalt - *giir, zifit, ʔasfalt.*

aspirin - *ʔaspiriina* pl. *-aat* coll. *ʔaspiriin.*

ass - *zmaal* pl. *zmaayiḷ, zmaar* pl. *zamiir.*

to **assassinate** - *ġtaal (a ġtiyaal).* His former friends assassinated him. *ʔaṣdiqaaʔa s-saabqiin iġtaaloo.*

assault - **1.** *hujuum* pl. *-aat.* The assault on the island began at five o'clock. *l-hujuum ɛaj-jaziira btidat is-saaɛa xamsa.* **2.** *taɛaddi.* He was charged with assault. *ntiham bit-taɛaddi.*

to assault - **1.** *tɛadda (a taɛaddi).* That man assaulted me. *tɛadda ɛalayya ḍaak ir-rijjaal.* **2.** *hijam (i hujuum) n- ɛala, haajam (i muhaajama).* They assaulted the enemy position with everything they had. *hijmaw ɛala mawqiɛ il-ɛadu b-kull-ma ɛidhum.*

to **assemble** - **1.** *tjammaɛ (a tajammuɛ), ltamm (a ltimaam).* The pupils assembled in the auditorium. *t-talaamiiḍ itjammɛaw bil-qaaɛa.* **2.** *jtimaɛ (i jtimaaɛ), tjammaɛ (a tajammuɛ).* The lawyers will assemble to discuss the case tomorrow morning. *l-muẓaamiin raẓ-yijtamɛuun il-baẓθ il-qaḍiyya bukra iṣ-ṣubuẓ.* **3.** *jimaɛ (a jamiɛ) n-.* You'll have to give me enough time to assemble the information. *laazim tinṭiini wakit kaafi ẓatta ʔajmaɛ il-maɛluumaat.* **4.** *rakkab (u tarkiib) t-.* He assembles airplane engines. *yrakkub makaayin ṭayyaaraat.*

assembly - **1.** *jamaaɛa* pl. *-aat, ẓašid* pl. *ẓušuud, jamhuur* pl. *jamaahiir.* He spoke before a large assembly of lawyers. *xiṭab giddaam jamaaɛa čbiira mnil-muẓaamiin.* **2.** *jamɛiyya* pl. *-aat.* The General Assembly of the United Nations rejected the proposal. *j-jamɛiyya l-ɛaamma lil-ʔumam il-muttaẓida rufḍat il-iqtiraaẓ.* **3.** *qisim* pl. *ʔaqsaam, juzuʔ* pl. *ʔajzaaʔ.* We'll have to remove this entire assembly. *laazim inšiil hal-qisim kulla.*

assembly line - *xaṭṭ tarkiib, xaṭṭ tajmiiɛ.* I work on the assembly line in an automobile factory. *ʔaštuġul ib-xaṭṭ it-tarkiib maal maɛmal is-sayyaaraat.*

to **assign** - **1.** *ɛayyan (i taɛyiin) t-, niṭa (i naṭi) n-.* The teacher assigned us a composition. *l-muɛallim inṭaana ʔinšaaʔ.* **2.** *xaṣṣaṣ (i taxṣiiṣ) t-, ɛayyan (i taɛyiin) t-.* He assigned two men to guard the prisoner. *xaṣṣaṣ rajjaaleen il-ẓiraasat il-masjuun.*

assignment - **1.** *waḍiifa* pl. *waḍaayif, waajib* pl. *-aat.* Our teacher gave us a difficult assignment. *muɛallimna nṭaana waajib ṣaɛub.* **2.** *šaġla* pl. *-aat, waḍiifa* pl. *waḍaayif, muhimma* pl. *mahaamm.* The boss gave me an interesting assignment. *l-mudiir inṭaani fadd šaġla laṭiifa.* **3.** *tawziiɛ* pl. *-aat, taɛyiin* pl. *-aat, taqsiim* pl. *-aat.* The assignment of jobs only took ten minutes. *tawziiɛ il-ašġaal ʔaxaḍ ɛašir daqaaʔiq.*

to **assist** - *saaɛad (i musaaɛada), ɛaawan (i muɛaawana).* Who assisted you? *minu ɛaawanak?*

assistance - *musaaɛada* pl. *-aat, muɛaawana* pl. *-aat.* He did it without any assistance. *sawwaaha b-layya musaaɛada.*

assistant - *musaaɛid* pl. *-iin, muɛaawin* pl. *-iin.*

associate - *zamiil* pl. *zumalaaʔ, rafiiq* pl. *rufaqaaʔ* He's been my associate for many years. *ṣaar-la zamiili sniin ihwaaya.*

associate judge - *naaʔib ẓaakim* pl. *nuwwaab ẓukkaam.*

associate member - *ɛaḍu musaanid* pl. *ʔaɛḍaaʔ musaanidiin.*

associate professor - *ʔustaaḍ musaaɛid* pl. *ʔasaatiḍa musaaɛidiin.*

to associate - **1.** *xaalaṭ (i muxaalaṭa), xtilaṭ (i xtilaaṭ) wiyya, ɛaašar (i ɛušra, muɛaašara), tɛaašar (a taɛaašur).* He doesn't like to associate with them. *ma-yɛijba yxaaliṭhum.* **2.** *rabaṭ (u rabuṭ) ɛalaaqa.* I always associate big cars with rich people. *ʔaani daaʔiman ʔarbuṭ ɛalaaqa been is-sayyaaraat ič-čibiira wiz-zanaagiin.*

**He was associated with them for ten years. *čaanat ʔila ɛalaaqa wiyyaahum min ɛašr isniin.*

association - **1.** *jamɛiyya* pl. *-aat.* I don't think I'll join the association. *ma-aɛtiqid raẓ-aštirik bij-jamɛiyya.* **2.** *ɛalaaqa* pl. *-aat.* I wouldn't ever make that particular association. *ʔaani ʔabad ma-asawwi ḍiič il-ɛalaaqa l-xaaṣṣa.*

assorted - *mšakkal, mnawwaɛ.* I want one kilo of assorted chocolates. *ʔariid keelu čukleet imšakkal.*

assortment - *taškiila* pl. *-aat.* They've got a large assortment of ties. *ɛidhum taškiila čbiira mnil-ʔarbiṭa.*

to **assume** - **1.** *twaqqaɛ (a tawaqquɛ), qaddar (i taqdiir).* I assume that he'll be there too. *ʔatwaqqaɛ raẓ-ykuun ihnaak ʔayḍan.* -- I assume the price will be less than twenty dinars. *ʔaqaddir is-siɛir ykuun ʔaqall min ɛišreen diinaar.* **2.** *tẓammal (a taẓammul).* I can't assume any responsibility for what happened. *ma-agdar atẓammal ʔay masʔuuliyya ɛan illi ṣaar.* **3.** *tḍaahar (a taḍaahur).* Don't assume such an air of innocence! *l-tiṭḍaahar ib-salaamt in-niyya.* **4.** *furaḍ (u faraḍ) n-.* For example, let's assume birds can't fly. *maθalan, xalli nufruḍ iṭ-ṭiyuur ma-tigdar iṭṭiir.*

assurance - *taɛahhud* pl. *-aat, taʔkiid* pl. *-aat.* He gave me his assurance that he'd pay. *nṭaani taɛahhud raẓ-yidfaɛ.*

to **assure** - *ʔakkad (i taʔkiid) t-, tɛahhad (a taɛahhud).* He assured us that he would be there. *ʔakkad-inna raẓ-ykuun ihnaak.*

asthma - *tanag nifas, ḍiig nifas, rabu.*

at - **1.** *b-.* I'll wait for you at the entrance. *raẓ-anṭaḍrak bil-baab.* -- I did it at his request. *sawweetha b-raġubta* or *sawweetha ẓasab raġubta.* -- The children are at school. *l-ʔaṭfaal bil-madrasa.* -- It happened at night. *ṣaarat bil-leel.* -- He came at three o'clock. *ʔija biθ-θilaaθa* or *jaa s-saaɛa biθ-θilaaθa* or *jaa s-saaɛa θlaaθa.* **2.** *ɛind, ɛid.* We were at the tailor's. *činna ɛind il-xayyaaṭ.* -- I met him at the dentist's. *qaabalta ɛid ṭabiib il-ʔasnaan.* **3.** *min.* I was astonished at the size of the city. *ndihašit min kubr il-wlaaya.* **4.** *ʔila.* We haven't arrived at a decision yet. *ma-twaṣṣalna ʔila fadd qaraar il-ẓadd il-ʔaan.* **5.** *ɛala.* He aimed at the target. *neešan ɛal-hadaf.* **6.** *ɛala, min.* Don't get angry at me. *la-tizɛal ɛalayya* or *la-tizɛal minni.*

at all - *ʔabad, ʔabadan, ʔaṣlan, bil-marra.* I haven't got any money at all. *ma-Eindi fluus ʔabadan* or *ʔabad ma-Eindi ʔay ifluus.*

at all costs - *b-ʔay θaman.* We must get it at all costs. *laazim naaxδa b-ʔay θaman.*

at first - *bil-bidaaya, bil-ʔawwal, ʔawwalan.* At first we didn't like the town. *bil-bidaaya ma-ẓabbeena l-wlaaya.*

at last - *ʔaxiiran, bit-taali, taaliiha.* He came at last. *ʔaxiiran jaa.*

at least - 1. *Eal-ʔaqall.* There were at least a hundred people present. *čaanaw Eal-ʔaqall miit waaẓid ẓaaδriin.* 2. *ʔaqallan.* At least, mention my name to him. *ʔaqallan, ʔiδkur-la ʔismi.*

at most - *ʔakθar šii.* At most the bill will come to twenty dinars. *ʔakθar šii raẓ-itwaṣṣil il-qaaʔima il-Eišriin diinaar.*

at once - 1. *ẓaalan, hassa.* Do it at once. *sawwiiha ẓaalan.* 2. *b-fadd wakit, b-fadd marra.* I can't do everything at once. *ma-agdar asawwi kullši b-fadd marra.*

at that - *b-haš-šikil, Eind hal-ẓadd, Eala-ma huwwa.* Let's leave it at that. *xal-niturka b-haš-šikil.*

at times - *dooraat, ʔaẓyaanan, noobaat, marraat.* At times I'm doubtful. *dooraat ʔašukk.*

at will - *miθil-ma yriid, ẓasab-ma yriid, b-keef˜.* They come and go at will. *yirẓuun w-yijuun miθil-ma yirduun* or ***yisraẓuun w-yimraẓuun.*

atheism - *ʔilẓaad.*

atheist - *mulẓid* pl. *-iin.*

athlete - *riyaaδi* pl. *-iyyiin.*

athletic - *riyaaδi*.*

athletics - *riyaaδa.*

Atlantic - *l-muẓiiṭ il-ʔaṭlasi, ʔaṭlanṭiiki, ʔaṭlanṭi.*

atlas - *ʔaṭlas* pl. *ʔaṭaalis.* We're going to take the atlas with us on the trip. *raẓ-naaxuδ il-ʔaṭlas wiyyaana bis-safra.*

atmosphere - *jaww.* The atmosphere contains oxygen. *j-jaww yiẓtiwi Eala ʔaksiijiin.* — We work in a very nice atmosphere. *ništuġul ib-jaww kulliš zeen.*

atmospheric - *jawwi*.*

atom - *δarra* pl. *aat.* We live in the age of the atom. *nEiiš ib-Eaṣr iδ-δarra.*

atomic - *δarri*.*

atrocity - *jariima* pl. *jaraaʔim.* The enemy committed many atrocities during the war. *l-Eadu rtikab jaraaʔim ihwaaya ʔaθnaaʔ il-ẓarub.*

to **attach** - 1. *šakkal (i taskiil) t-.* Please attach the envelope to the letter with a pin. *rajaaʔan šakkil iδ-δaruf bil-maktuub ib-dambuus.* 2. *rufaq (i ʔirfaaq) n-.* Don't forget to attach a picture with your application. *la-tinsa tirfiq ṣuura b-Eariiδtak.* 3. *ẓijaz (i ẓajiz) n-.* We can attach his salary if he doesn't pay up. *nigdar niẓjiz raatba ʔiδa ma-yidfaE.* 4. *Eallaq (i taEliiq) t-.* You attach too much importance to money. *tEalliq ʔahammiyya hwaaya Eal-ifluus.*

to be attached to - *tEallaq (a taEalluq) b-.* I've become attached to this child. *ʔaani tEallaqit ib-haṭ-ṭifil* or *ṣirit mitEalliq ib-haṭ-ṭifil.*

attaché - *mulẓaq* pl. *-iin.*

attached - *miltiẓiq.* He's attached to the embassy. *huwwa miltiẓiq bis-safaara.*

attachments - 1. *mulẓaq* pl. *-aat.* I bought a vacuum cleaner with all its attachments. *štireet muknaasa kahrabaaʔiyya wiyya kull mulẓaqaatha.* 2. *muraffaq* pl. *-aat.* There are five attachments to the letter. *ʔaku xamas muraffaqaat wiyya l-maktuub.*

attack - *hajma* pl. *-aat* coll. *hujuum.* The attack was beaten back. *l-hajma nraddat.*

to attack - 1. *hijam (i hajuum) n-.* They attacked the castle in the middle of the night. *hijmaw Eal-qalEa b-nuṣṣ il-leel.* 2. *haajam (i muhaajama) t-.* He attacked them in the newspaper. *haajmoohum bij-jariida.* 3. *tnaawal (i tanaawul).* Let's attack this problem from a slightly different angle. *xalli nitnaawil hal-muškila min jiha tixtilif išwayya.*

heart attack - *sakta (*pl. *-aat) qalbiyya.* He died from a heart attack. *maat bis-sakta l-qalbiyya.*

attempt - *muẓaawala* pl. *-aat.* At least make an attempt! *Eal-ʔaqall sawwi fadd muẓaawala.*

to attempt - *ẓaawal (i muẓaawala) t-.* Don't attempt to do too much at one time. *la-tẓaawil itsawwi ʔašyaaʔ ihwaaya b-fadd wakit.*

to **attend** - 1. *ẓiδar (a ẓuδuur) n-.* Did you attend the meeting? *ẓiδart il-ijtimaaE?* 2. *daawam (u mudaawama) t-.* I attended business school. *daawamit ib-madrasat tijaara.* 3. *raajaE (i muraajaEa) t-, Eaalaj (muEaalaja) t-.* What doctor attended you? *yaa ṭabiib raajaEak?*

to attend to - *baašar (i mubaašara), Eaalaj (i Eilaaj, muEaalaja) t-.* I still have some things to attend to. *baEad Eindi baEaδ il-ʔašyaaʔ laazim ʔabaaširha.*

attendance - *ẓuδuur.* Attendance is compulsory. *l-ẓuδuur ʔijbaari.*

attention - *ntibaah.* I tried to attract his attention. *ẓaawalit ʔajlib intibaaha.*

to call attention - *lifat (i lafit) n- in-naδar.* I've called attention to that repeatedly. *lifatit in-naδar iδ-δaak Eiddat marraat.*

to pay attention - *ntibah (i ntibaah), daar (i doora) baal˜.* Please pay attention! *ʔintibih min faδlak.*

attentively - *b-intibaah.* The children listened attentively. *j-jahhaal itṣannṭaw b-intibaah.*

attitude - 1. *waδiE* pl. *ʔawδaaE.* I don't like his attitude in class. *ma-yiEjibni waδEa bis-ṣaff.* 2. *mawqif* pl. *mawaaqif, wajhat* (pl. *-aat) naδar.* I don't understand your attitude towards religion. *ma-da-aftihim mawqifak imnid-diin.*

attorney - *muẓaami* pl. *-iin.* Who's your attorney? *minu muẓaamiik?*

to **attract** - 1. *jaab (i jeeb) n-.* What's attracting the flies here? *š-da-yjiib iδ-δabbaan ihnaa?* 2. *jiδab (i jaδib) n-.* Magnets attract nails. *l-maġaaniṭ tijδib il-ibsaamiir.* 3. *jilab (i jalib) n-.* Be quiet! You're attracting attention. *ʔiskut, da-tijlib in-naδar.*

attraction - 1. *jaaδibiyya* pl. *-aat.* The attraction of the moon causes the tides. *jaaδibiyyat il-gumar ysabbib il-madd wij-jazir.* 2. *muġri* pl. *-iyyaat.* What's the big attraction around this town? *šinu l-muġri b-hal-wlaaya?*

attractive - 1. *jaδδaab.* She is very attractive. *hiyya kulliš jaδδaaba.* 2. *muġri.* He made me a very attractive offer. *Eiraδ Ealayya fadd Eariδ kulliš muġri.*

auction - *mazaad* pl. *-aat.*

audience - *l-ẓaaδriin.* The audience was enthusiastic. *l-ẓaaδriin čaanaw mitẓammsiin.*

August - *ʔaab.*

aunt - (paternal) *Eamma* pl. *-aat,* (maternal) *xaala* pl. *-aat.*

Austria - *n-namsa.*

Austrian - *namsaawi** pl. *-iyyiin.*

authentic - 1. *ẓaqiiqi*.* He wrote an authentic account of the war. *kitab waṣuf ẓaqiiqi lil-ẓarub.* 2. *ʔaṣli*, ẓaqiiqi*.* This is an authentic Babylonian vase. *haaδi mizhariyya baabiliyya ʔaṣliyya.*

author - 1. *muʔallif* pl. *-iin.* He always wanted to be an author. *daaʔiman čaan yriid yṣiir muʔallif.* 2. *ṣaaẓib* pl. *ʔaṣẓaab.* The prime minister is the author of the plan. *raʔiis il-wuzaraaʔ ṣaaẓib hal-xiṭṭa.*

authorities - *ṣulṭaat, maraajiE.* The local authorities condemned the building. *ṣ-ṣulṭaat il-maẓalliyya ʔumrat ib-hadm il-binaaya.*

authority - 1. *ṣalaaẓiyya* pl. *-aat, taxwiil* pl. *-aat.* He has no authority to sign the check. *ma-Einda ṣalaaẓiyya ywaqqiE iṣ-ṣakk.* -- Do you have the authority to sign this contract for him? *Eindak taxwiil itwaqqiE Eanna hal-Eaqid?* 2. *ṣulṭa* pl. *-aat.* The police have no authority over diplomats. *š-šurta ma-Eidha ṣulṭa Ead-diblumaasiyyiin.* 3. *ẓujja* pl. *ẓujaj.* He's an authority on the Koran. *huwwa ẓujja bil-qurʔaan.*

to **authorize** - *xawwal (i taxwiil) t-.* Who authorized you to spend that money? *minu xawwalak tuṣruf hal-ifluus?*

authorized - *mxawwal* pl. *-iin.* He's authorized to sign the receipts. *huwwa mxawwal ywaqqiE il-wuṣuulaat.*

automatic - 1. *musaddas* pl. *-aat, warwar* pl. *waraawir.* Officers carry automatics. *δ-δubbaaṭ šaayliin musaddasaat.* 2. *ʔootoomaatiiki*.* Is this an automatic pump? *hal-maδaxxa ʔootoomaatiikiyya?*

automatically - *b-ṣuura tilqaaʔiyya, b-ṣuura ʔootoomaatiikiyya, b-layya šuEuur.* He picked up the phone automatically. *šaal it-talafoon ib-ṣuura tilqaaʔiyya.*

automobile - *sayyaara* pl. *-aat.*

autopsy - *tašriiẓ* pl. *-aat.*

autumn - *xariif.* I hope to stay through the autumn. *ʔatʔammal ʔabqa n-nihaayat il-xariif.*

available - 1. *mawjuud.* They used all available

cars. *staɛmilaw kull is-sayaaraat il-mawjuuda.* -- Is this pen available in red? *hal-qalam il-paandaan mawjuud ɛala ʔaẓmar?* 2. *jawwa l-ʔiid.* I have two houses available. *ɛindi beeteen jawwa l-ʔiid.* 3. *faariġ.* When will the director be available? *šwakit il-mudiir ykuun faariġ?* 4. *maysuur, mityassir.* Vegetables are available in the market. *l-muxaððraat mityassira bis-suug.*

avenue - *šaariɛ* pl. *šawaariɛ.*

average - **1.** *muɛaddal* pl. *-aat.* He has a good average in school. *ɛinda xooš muɛaddal bil-madrasa.* 2. *mustawa ɛtiyaadi.* He's of average intelligence. *mustawa ðakaaʔa ɛtiyaadi.*

on the average - *b-muɛaddal.* I go to the movies on the average of once a week. *ʔaruuẓ lis-siinama b-muɛaddal marra bil-isbuuɛ.*

to average - *ṭallaɛ (i taṭliiɛ) muɛaddal.* He averages sixty dollars a week. *ytalliɛ muɛaddal sittiin doolaar bil-isbuuɛ.*

to **avoid** - *tẓaaša (a tẓaaši), tjannab (i tajannub).* Why is he avoiding me? *luweeš da-yitẓaašaani?*

to **await** - *ntiðar (i ntiðaar), traqqab (a taraqqub), twaqqaɛ (a tawaqquɛ).* They were ordered to await the signal. *jaahum ʔamur yintaðruun il-ʔišaara.*

awake - *ṣaaẓi, gaaɛid.* Are you awake? *ʔinta ṣaaẓi?*

to awake - *ṣaẓa (i ṣaẓu), giɛad (u gaɛid), faaq (i feeq).* I awoke at seven o'clock. *gɛadit is-saaɛa sabɛa.*

to **awaken** - *qaɛɛad (i tqiɛɛid) t-, ṣaẓẓa (i tṣaẓẓi) t-, fayyaq (i tfiyyiq) t-.* A noise awakened me. *fadd ẓiss ṣaẓẓaani.*

aware - **1.** *ɛaarif, daari, ɛinda xabar.* I'm aware of the difficulties involved in the subject. *ʔaani ɛaarif biṣ-ṣuɛuubaat id-daaxla bil-mawðuuɛ.* -- He's not aware of his brother's death yet. *li-hassa ma-ɛinda xabar ib-mootat axuu.* 2. *ẓaass.* He was aware of movements behind him. *čaan ẓaass ib-ẓarakaat waraa.*

away - *ġaayib.* Have you been away? *činit ġaayib?*

to be away - *ġaab (i ġiyaab).* He was away from school for a week. *ġaab ɛan il-madrasa l-muddat isbuuɛ.*

**The station is far away from our house. *l-maẓaṭṭa kulliš ibɛiida min beetna.*

**Park the car away from the house. *waggif is-sayyaara bɛiid ɛann il-beet.*

awful - **1.** *faðiiɛ.* It was an awful accident. *čaan ẓaadiθ faðiiɛ.* 2. *qabiiẓ.* That coat is awful. *has-sitra qabiiẓa.* 3. *wakiẓ.* The kids have been awful today. *j-jahhaal čaanaw wakẓiin il-yoom.*

**It's been an awful day. *čaan yoom ʔaswad.*

awfully - *kulliš, hwaaya.* I'm awfully tired. *ʔaani kulliš taɛbaan.*

awhile - *fatra, šwayya.* He was here awhile this afternoon. *čaan ihnaa fadd fatra il-yoom il-ɛasir.* -- I want to think about it awhile. *ʔariid afakkir biiha šwayya.*

awkward - **1.** *mxarbaṭ.* Why is he so awkward in everything he does? *luweeš huwwa hiiči mxarbaṭ ib-kullši l-ysawwii?* 2. *muẓrij.* It was an awkward situation. *čaanat fadd waðɛiyya muẓrija.*

awning - *šamsiyya* pl. *-aat, šamaasi.*

axe - *faas* pl. *fuus, faasa* pl. *-aat.*

axis - *miẓwar* pl. *maẓaawir.* The world turns on its axis once a day. *l-ʔarð itduur ẓawil miẓwarha marra bil-yoom.*

axle - *ʔaksil* pl. *-aat.* The axle is broken. *l-ʔaksil maksuur.*

B

baby - **1.** *ṭifil* pl. *ʔaṭfaal.* The baby is crying. *ṭ-ṭifil da-yibči.* They treat me like a baby. *yɛaamluuni miθil ṭifil.* 2. *jaahil* pl. *jihhaal.* My sons are still babies. *wildi baɛadhum jihhaal.*

to baby - *dallal (i tadliil).* You baby your children more than necessary. *ʔinta tdallil jihhaalak akθar imnil-laazim.*

to baby oneself - *daara (i mudaaraa) nafis~.* He babies himself very much. *huwwa ydaari nafsa kulliš ihwaaya.*

baby carriage - *ɛarabaana maal jaahil* pl. *ɛarabaayin maal jihhaal.*

bachelor - *ʔaɛzab* pl. *ɛuzzaab.* My older brother is still a bachelor. *ʔaxuuya č-čibiir baɛda ʔaɛzab.*

back - **1.** *ðahar* pl. *ðhuur.* He was lying on his back. *čaan minjiṭil ɛala ðahra.* -- This chair has a high back. *hal-iskamli ðahra ɛaali.* -- My back aches. *ðahri yoojaɛni.* 2. *warraani*.* The back rooms are dark. *l-gubab il-warraaniyya ðalma.*

**They did it behind my back. *sawwaaha bala ẓissi.*

**He walked back and forth in the room. *ðall yruuẓ w-yiji bil-gubba.*

in back - *li-wara.* I prefer to sit in back. *ʔafaððil agɛud li-wara.*

in back of - *wara.* There's a garden in back of the house. *ʔaku ẓadiiqa wara l-beet.* — I wonder who is in back of this plan? *ɛajaba minu wara hal-mašruuɛ?*

in the back of - *b-ʔaaxir.* You'll find it in the back of the book. *raẓ-tilgaaha b-ʔaaxir il-iktaab.*

**I have had it in the back of my mind to tell you for a long time. *haay ṣaar-ilha mudda ib-fikri ʔariid ʔagul-lak-iyyaaha.*

to be back - *rijaɛ (a rujuuɛ).* He isn't back yet. *li-hassa baɛad ma-rijaɛ.*

to come back - *rijaɛ (a rujuuɛ).* When is he coming back? *šwakit raẓ-yirjaɛ?*

to go back - *rijaɛ (a rujuuɛ).* When are you going back to Basra? *šwakit raẓ-tirjaɛ lil-baṣra?*

to go back over - *raajaɛ (i muraajaɛa).* He went back over his work in order to find his mistakes. *raajaɛ šuġla ẓatta yilgi ġaliṭṭa.*

to step back - **1.** *rijaɛ (a rujuuɛ) li-wara.* Step back a bit. *ʔirjaɛ šwayya li-wara.* 2. *twaxxar (a tawaxxur).* Please step back out of the way. *baḷḷa twaxxar ɛan iṭ-ṭariiq.*

to back - *ʔayyad (i taʔyiid) t-.* All parties are backing him. *kull il-aẓzaab itʔayyda.*

to back down - *traajaɛ (a taraajuɛ).* He finally backed down and admitted his error. *ʔaxiiran itraajaɛ w-iɛtiraf ib-ġaliṭṭa.*

to back up - *rijaɛ (a) li-wara.* 1. I still can't back up. *ʔaani baɛadni ma-agdar arjaɛ li-wara.* 2. *saanad (i musaanada).* He backs me up in all my decisions. *ysaanidni ib-kull qaraaraati.* 3. *rajjaɛ (i tarjiiɛ, trajjaɛ) li-wara.* Back up your car a little. *rajjiɛ sayyaartak li-wara šwayya.*

backbone - **1.** *ɛamuud faqari* pl. *ʔaɛmida faqariyya.* They performed an operation on her backbone. *sawwaw ɛamaliyya bil-ɛamuud il-faqari maalha.* 2. *jurʔa.* If only he had a little backbone he'd tell her to shut up. *loo čaan ɛinda šwayyat jurʔa čaan gall-ilha "yeezi ɛaad".*

background - **1.** *gaaɛiyya* pl. *-aat.* The cloth has a black background with white dots. *l-igmaaš gaaɛiita sooda w-imnaggaṭ b-abyað.* 2. *xibra.* We want someone with a wide background for this job. *nriid waaẓid ɛinda xibra waasɛa l-hal-waðiifa.*

in the background - *biṣ-ṣufuuf il-xalfiyya.* His father remained in the background throughout the elections. *ʔabuu ðall ib-ṣufuuf il-xalfiyya xilaal il-intixaabaat* or *ʔabuu ma-bayyan nafsa xilaal il-intixaabaat.*

back talk - *jasaara, tajaasur.* I won't listen to any back talk. *ma-raẓ-asmaɛ ib-ʔay tajaasur.*

backward - **1.** *mitʔaxxir.* The people there are very backward. *n-naas ihnaak ihwaaya mitʔaxxiriin.* 2. *baliid.* Her son is a bit backward. *ʔibinha šwayya baliid.*

backward(s) - **1.** *li-wara.* He fell backwards. *wugaɛ li-wara.* 2. *bil-magluub.* You've got that sweater on backwards. *ʔinta laabis hal-ibluuz bil-magluub.*

**He knows the lesson backwards and forwards. *yuɛruf id-daris čilma ɛala čilma.*

bad - **1.** *baṭṭaal, muu zeen, sayyiʔ.* He has a bad reputation. *ɛinda sumɛa muu zeena.* 2. *qawi.* I have a bad cold today. *ɛindi fadd našla qawiyya l-yoom.* 3. *baʔs b-.* That is not a bad idea. *haaði fikra la-ba's biiha.* 4. *ma- ... zeen.* He has bad eyes. *ɛyuuna ma-tšuuf zeen* or ****naðara ðaɛiif.* I feel bad today. *ʔaani muu zeen hal-yoom* or ****ma-ali xulug il-yoom.* 5. *šeen.* We have to take the good with the bad. *laazim nirða biz-zeen w-iš-šeen.*

**His business is going from bad to worse. *šuğla da-yitdahwar.*

too bad - 1. *mu?sif.* That's too bad! *haaδa šii mu?sif.* **2.** *maεa l-asaf.* Too bad that you couldn't come. *maεa l-?asaf ?inta ma-gdarit tiji.*

to feel bad - *t?aθθar (a ta?aθθur).* Now he feels very bad about what happened. *huwwa hassa kulliš mit?aθθir imn illi jira.*

bag - 1. *čiis* pl. *čyaas.* Put these apples in a bag. *ẓuṭṭ hat-tiffaaẓ ib-čiis.* **2.** *janṭa* pl. *jinaṭ.* She took some change out of her bag. *ṭallεat išwayya xurda min janṭatha.* -- Where can I check my bag? *ween agdar a?ammin janṭati?* **3.** *guuniyya* pl. *gwaani, čiis* pl. *čyaas.* Have them put the bags of rice in the truck. *xalliihum yẓuṭṭuun igwaani it-timman bil-loori.*

**He has the money and I'm left holding the bag. *huwwa yiδrub bid-dijaaj w-aani ?atlagga l-εajaaj* or *n-naas taakul bit-tamur w-aani n-nuwaaya ẓiṣṣati.*

**They moved in on us, bag and baggage. *?ijaw kullhum fadd nooba w-giεdaw εala gluubna.*

baggage - *ğaraaδ.* I want to send my baggage on ahead. *?ariid adizz ğaraaδi li-giddaam.*

bail - *kafaala.* The court fixed his bail at two thousand dinars. *l-maẓkama qarrirat ?an itkuun kafaalta b-?alfeen diinaar.*

to put up bail - *kifal (a kafaala) n-.* Who is going to put up bail for him? *minu raẓ-yikfala?*

to bail out - 1. *ğiraf (u ğaruf) n-.* We used our helmets to bail the water out of the boat. *staεmalna xuwaδna ẓatta nuğruf il-maay imnil-balam.* **2.** *ṭufar (u ṭafur).* I had to bail out of my plane at an elevation of five thousand feet. *?aani njabarit ?aṭfur min ṭiyyaarti min εilu xamist aalaaf gadam.*

bait - *ṭuεum.* He put bait on the hook so he could catch himself a fish. *xalla ṭuεum biš-šuṣṣ ẓatta yṣiid-la simča.*

to **bake - 1.** *xubaz (u xabuz) n-.* My mother baked bread yesterday. *?ummi xubzat il-baarẓa.* **2.** *sawwa (i) bil-firin.* She baked the baklava in the oven. *sawwat il-baqlaawa bil-firin.*

baker - *xabbaaz* pl. *-iin, xabaabiiz, čurukči* pl. *-iyya.* This baker has good bread. *hal-xabbaaz εinda xooš xubuz.*

bakery - *maxbaz* pl. *maxaabiz, firin* pl. *?afraan.* The bakery is around the corner. *l-maxbaz ib-looft iš-šaariε.*

baking powder - *beekin pawdar.*

baking soda - *sooda maal keek, beekin sooda, soodat xubuz.*

balance - 1. *miizaan* pl. *myaaziin.* The jeweler put the bracelets on the balance and weighed them. *ṣ-ṣaayiğ ẓaṭṭ il-iswaaraat bil-miizaan w-wuzanhum.* **2.** *muwaazana.* I lost my balance. *xtallat muwaazanti.* **3.** *baaqi.* Pay one-third down and the balance in monthly installments. *?inti θilθ il-qiima li-giddaam wil-baaqi b-?aqsaaṭ šahriyya.*

**His life hung in the balance. *tεallag been il-ẓayaat wil-moot.*

to balance - 1. *waazan (i muwaazana) t-.* Can you balance a stick on your forehead? *tigdar itwaazin εuuda εala guṣṣtak?* -- Our bookkeeper balances his books at the end of each month. *muẓaasibna ywaazin dafaatra b-nihaayat kull šahar.* **2.** *ṭaabag (u muṭaabaga).* Does the account balance? *l-iẓsaab da-yṭaabug?*

balcony - 1. *balkoon* pl. *-aat.* I have an apartment with a balcony. *εindi šiqqa biiha balkoon.* **2.** *galari* pl. *-yaat.* We had seats in the first balcony. *čaan εidna maqaaεid ib-?awwal galari.*

bald - *?aṣlaε* pl. *ṣalεiin.* He was bald at thirty. *čaan ?aṣlaε biθ-θilaaθiin.*

bald spot - *ṣalεa* pl. *-aat.* He has a small bald spot. *εinda ṣalεa ṣgayyra.*

ball - 1. *ṭooba, kura.* They played ball all afternoon. *liεbaw ṭooba l-εaṣir kulla.* **2.** *kabbuuba* pl. *-aat, kubbaaba* pl. *-aat.* I'd like a ball of white wool. *?ariid kabbuubat ṣuuf abyaδ.* **3.** *ṭooba* pl. *-aat, ṭuwab; kura* pl. *-aat.* He butted the ball with his head. *nigar iṭ-ṭooba b-raasa.*

balled up - 1. *mxarbaṭ.* I found everything all balled up. *ligeet kullši mxarbaṭ.* **2.** *mirtibik.* He was all balled up. *čaan kulliš mirtibik.*

balloon - *baaloon* pl. *-aat, nuffaaxa* pl. *-aat.*

ballot - *waragat* (pl. *?awraag) intixaab.* Have all the ballots been counted? *kull awraag il-intixaab inεaddat?*

secret ballot - *ntixaab sirri.*

ballroom - *qaaεa* (pl. *-aat) maal rigiṣ.*

Baltic Sea - *baẓr il-balṭiiq.*

bamboo - *xayzaraan.*

to **ban -** *minaε (a maniε) n-.* The government has banned the sale of narcotics. *l-ẓukuuma minεat beeε il-muxaddiraat.*

banana - *mooza* pl. *-aat* coll. *mooz.*

band - 1. *jooq* pl. *?ajwaaq.* The band played dance music all evening. *j-jooq dagg muusiiqat rigiṣ ṭuul il-leel.* **2.** *šariiṭ* pl. *šaraayiṭ.* The Christians tie a black band on their arm in mourning. *l-masiiẓiyyiin yšidduun šariiṭ ?aswad εala ?iidhum lil-ẓuzin.* **3.** *εiṣaaba* pl. *-aat.* The police caught the leader of the bank of smugglers. *š-šurṭa lizmat ra?iis εiṣaabat il-muharribiin.* **4.** *mawja* pl. *-aat.* You can get that station on the 25 meter band. *tigdar itẓaṣṣil hal-maẓaṭṭa εala mawja xamsa w-εišriin.*

bandage - *laffaaf* pl. *-aat.* Don't undo the bandage. *la-tfukk il-laffaaf.*

to bandage - *laff (i) ib-laffaaf.* You'd better bandage the cut at once. *?aẓsan-lak itliff ij-jariẓ ib-laffaaf hassa.*

bandit - *ẓaraami* pl. *-iyya, sallaab* pl. *-a.*

bang - *ṭagga* pl. *-aat.* The loud bang startled her. *ṭ-ṭagga l-εaalya jafflatha.*

to bang - *δirab (u δarub).* He banged his shoe on the table. *δirab qundarta εal-meez.*

to **banish - 1.** *?abεad (i ?ibεaad).* They banished the troublemakers from the capital for two years. *?abεidaw il-mušaağibiin imnil-εaaṣima l-muddat santeen.* **2.** *nifa (i nafi) n-.* They banished the party leaders from the country. *nifaw zuεamaa? il-ẓizib imnil-bilaad.*

banister - *mẓajjar* pl. *-aat.* Hold on to the banister. *?ilzam l-imẓajjar.*

bank - 1. *bang* pl. *bunuug.* I keep my money in the bank. *?aani ?aδumm ifluusi bil-bang.* **2.** *šaaṭi* pl. *šwaaṭi.* He swam to the nearby bank. *sibaẓ liš-šaaṭi l-giriib.*

to bank on - 1. *εtimad (i εtimaad) εala.* You can bank on that. *tigdar tiεtimid εala δaak.*

banker - *ṣarraaf* pl. *ṣraariif.*

bank note - *nooṭ* pl. *nwaaṭ.*

bankrupt - 1. *miflis, minkisir.* He is bankrupt. *huwwa miflis.* **2.** *kasir.* The company went bankrupt. *š-šarika ṭilεat kasir.*

to go bankrupt - *filas (a ?iflaas), nkisar (i nkisaar).* He went bankrupt. *filas.*

bankruptcy - *?iflaas, kasir.* The firm had to announce its bankruptcy. *š-šarika njubrat tiεlin iflaasha.*

banner - *beeraq* pl. *byaariq, εalam* pl. *εlaam.*

banquet - *εaziima* pl. *εazaayim, ẓafla* pl. *-aat.*

to **baptize -** *εammad (i taεmiid) t-.* He baptized him in the Jordan River. *εammada b-nahr il-?ardun.*

bar - 1. *qaalab* pl. *qwaalib.* Here's a bar of soap. *haak haaδa qaalab ṣaabuun.* **2.** *šiiš* pl. *šyaaš.* We are going to need more iron bars to finish this foundation. *raẓ-niẓtaaj baεad šiiš ẓatta nṣalliẓ hal-?asaas.* **3.** *baar* pl. *-aat.* Let's meet in the bar in an hour. *xal-nitlaaga bil-baar baεad saaεa.* -- Let's have a drink at the bar. *xal-nišrab-inna fadd šii bil-baar.* **4.** *mayxaana* pl. *-aat.* There was a fight in this cheap bar last night. *ṣaarat εarka b-haay il-mayxaana l-baarẓa bil-leel.* **5.** *faaṣla* pl. *-aat.* He played a few bars of the tune. *dagg čam faaṣla mnin-nağma.* **6.** *naqaabat il-muẓaamiin.* When were you admitted to the bar? *šwakit inqibalit b-naqaabat il-muẓaamiin?* **7.** *jazra* pl. *-aat.* Let's swim out to the bar. *xal-nisbaẓ lij-jazra.*

to bar - 1. *sadd (i sadd) n-.* He forgot to bar the stable door. *nisa ysidd baab iṭ-ṭoola.* **2.** *minaε (a maniε) n-.* They posted soldiers at the entrances to bar people from entering. *ẓaṭṭaw junuud bil-madaaxil ẓatta yimnaεuun in-naas imnid-dixuul.*

barbed wire - *silk šaa?ik* pl. *?aslaak šaa?ika.*

barber - *mzayyin* pl. *mzaayna, ẓallaaq* pl. *-iin.* Is there a good barber in town? *?aku mzayyin zeen bil-wlaaya?*

barber shop - *ṣaaloon* (pl. *-aat) ẓilaaqa, dukkaan* (pl. *dakaakiin) imzayyin.*

bare - 1. *mṣallax* pl. *mṣaaliix, εaryaan* pl. *-iin.* Little kids are always swimming bare. *l-wulid iṣ-ṣiğaar daa?iman yisbaẓuun mṣaaliix.* **2.** *mkaššaf.* Don't go out in the sun with your head bare. *la-tiṭlaε barra biš-šamis imkaššaf ir-raas.* **3.** *xaali.* I looked in the cupboard and found the shelves were bare. *baawaεit bid-diilaab w-ligeet* *ir-rufuuf čaanat xaalya.* -- These are the bare facts. *haaδi hiyya l-ʒaqaayiq xaalya min kull rituuš.*

to bare - 1. *kaššaf (i tkiššif) t-.* The nurse told me to bare my right arm. *l-mumarriδa gaalat-li ʔakaššif iδraaƐi l-yamiin.* **2.** *tfarraƐ (a tafarruƐ).* The men bared their heads when the flag passed. *r-riyaajiil itfarrƐaw min marr il-Ɛalam.*

barefoot - *ʒaafi* pl. *ʒiffaay.* Children, don't play barefoot. *ġġaar, la-tilƐabuun ʒiffaay.*

barely - 1. *duub, yaaduub.* He's barely ten. *huwwa duub Ɛašr isniin.* -- I barely had time to finish the book. *l-wakt il-čaan Ɛindi yaaduub kaffa ʔaxalliṣ l-iktaab.* **2.** *bil-kaad.* He barely managed it. *bil-kaad dabbarha.*

bargain - 1. *šarwa* pl. *-aat.* This book was a good bargain. *hal-iktaab čaan xooš šarwa.* **2.** *ṣafqa* pl. *-aat.* That's just part of the bargain. *δaak fadd qisim imniṣ-ṣafqa.* **3.** *ttifaaq* pl. *-aat.* According to our bargain you were to pay half. *ʒasb ittifaaqna čaan laazim tidfaƐ in-nuṣṣ.*

**All right, it's a bargain! *zeen, ṣaar!* or *zeen, mwaafiq!*

to bargain - 1. *tƐaamal (a Ɛimla).* She bargains for hours with the shopkeepers. *titƐaamal saaƐaat wiyya d-dukkančiyya.* **2.** *faawaδ (i mufaawaδa).* The workmen are bargaining with their employer for a raise. *l-Ɛummaal da-yfaawδuun mustaxdimhum ʒawil ziyaada bil-ʔujuur.*

**He got more than he bargained for. *ʒaṣṣal ʔakθar min-ma twaqqaƐ.*

bark - 1. *gišra* pl. *gšuur.* The eucalyptus trees have a thin bark. *ʔašjaar il-yuukaaliptus ʔilha gišra xafiifa.* **2.** *nabʒa* pl. *-aat.* The dog's bark is worse than his bite. *nabʒat ič-čalib ʔangas min Ɛaδδta.*

to bark - *nibaʒ (a nbaaʒ), Ɛawwa (i tƐuwwi).* The dog barked loudly. *č-čalib Ɛawwa b-ṣooṭ Ɛaali.*

barley - *šƐiir.*

barometer - *baroomatir* pl. *-aat.*

barrack(s) - *θakana* pl. *-aat, muƐaskar* pl. *-aat.* Our barracks were built of concrete. *θakanatna mabniyya b-simant.*

barrel - 1. *barmiil* pl. *baraamiil.* We used up a whole barrel of oil. *staƐmalna barmiil kaamil imnid-dihan.* **2.** *sabaṭaana* pl. *-aat.* Show the boy how to clean the barrel of his gun. *raawi l-walad išloon ynaδδuf sabaṭaanat bundiqiita.*

barren - 1. *qaaʒil.* Except for a strip along the river, all the land is barren. *b-istiθnaaʔ wuṣla muʒaaδiya lin-nahar, kull il-ʔaraaδi qaaʒla.* **2.** *Ɛaaqir.* He divorced his wife because she is barren. *ṭallag marta li-ʔanha Ɛaaqir.*

barricade - *maaniƐ* pl. *mawaaniƐ.* The rebels set up barricades in the streets. *θ-θuwwaar niṣbaw mawaaniƐ biš-šawaariƐ.*

to barricade - *sadd (i sadd) n-, giṭaƐ (a gaṭiƐ) n-.* They barricaded all the roads into the area. *saddaw kull iṭ-ṭuruq l-itfuut lil-manṭiqa.*

base - 1. *qaaƐida* pl. *qawaaƐid.* The base of the statue was still standing. *qaaƐidat it-timθaal čaanat baƐadha baaqya.* -- The planes returned to their base. *ṭ-ṭiyyaaraat rijƐat il-qaaƐidatha.* **2.** *ʔasaas* pl. *-aat.* The water pipe passes under the base. *buuri l-ṃaay yfuut jawwa l-ʔasaas.*

**Paint the bathroom walls with an oil-base paint. *ʔuṣbuġ ʒiiṭaan il-ʒammaam ib-dihin.*

to base - 1. *bina (i binaaʔ) n-.* On what do you base your figures? *Ɛala-weeš ibneet iʒsaabak?* **2.** *sawwa (i taswiya) markaz.* The company decided to base its operations in Basra. *š-šarika qarrirat itsawwi markazha bil-baṣra.*

basement - *sirdaab* pl. *saraadiib.*

bashful - *xajuul.* She is very bashful. *hiyya fadd wiʒda kulliš xajuula.*

to be bashful - 1. *xijal (a xajal), stiʒa (i stiʒaaʔ).* She is bashful with people. *tistiʒi mnin-naas.* -- Don't be bashful, ask him. *la-tixjal, ʔisʔala.*

basic - *raʔiisi*, ʔasaasi*, jawhari*.* He earns enough money for his basic needs. *yʒaṣṣil ifluus itkaffi ʒaajaata r-raʔiisiyya.* -- The argument came up because of a basic difference of opinion. *n-niqaaš ṣaar ib-sabab xilaaf raʔiisi bir-raʔi.*

basically - *jawhariyyan.* There is nothing basically wrong with your idea. *fikirtak ma-biiha Ɛeeb jawhariyyan.*

basil - *riiʒaan* pl. *riyaaʒiin.*

basin - 1. *njaana* pl. *-aat.* Please bring me a basin of warm water. *ʔarjuuk jiib-li njaana ṃaay daafi.* **2.** *ʒooδ* pl. *ʔaʒwaaδ, waadi* pl. *wudyaan.* The basin of the Tigris and Euphrates is the most fertile in Iraq. *ʒooδ nahr dijla wil-furaat ʔaxṣab ʔarδ bil-Ɛiraaq.*

basis - *ʔasaas* pl. *ʔusus.* We can't continue on this basis. *ma-nigdar nistimirr Ɛala hal-ʔasaas.*

basket - *salla* pl. *-aat, slaal.* Put the clothes in the basket. *ʒuṭṭ l-ihduum bis-salla.*

basketball - *kurat is-salla, baaskitbool.*

to baste - 1. *kawwak (u tkuwwuk, takwiik) t-.* It's better to baste the hem first. *ʔawwal loo tkawwuk iṭ-ṭawya ʔaʒsan.* **2.** *saaqa (i musaaqaa).* Baste the chicken with the oil from time to time while it's cooking. *saaqi d-dijaaja bid-dihin min ʒiin il-ʔaaxar lamma tinṭubux.*

bat - 1. *xaffaaš* (pl. *xafaafiiš*) *il-leel, xaššaaf il-leel.* I'm afraid of bats. *ʔaani ʔaxaaf min xafaafiiš il-leel.*

to bat - *δirab (u), ṭaffar (u).* He batted the ball over the fence. *δirab iṭ-ṭooba l-xaarij is-siyaaj.*

**He really went to bat for me. *ṣudug wugaf-li.*

**He told his story without batting an eye. *ʒiča ʒčaayta bala-ma titruf-la Ɛeen.*

batch - 1. *xabṭa* pl. *-aat.* This batch of cement won't be enough. *hal-xabṭa mnič-čimantu ma-raʒ-itkaffi.* **2.** *jooga* pl. *-aat.* The second batch of pilgrims will arrive tomorrow. *j-jooga θ-θaanya mnil-ʒijjaaj raʒ-toosal baačir.* **3.** *tannuur* pl. *-aat, tanaaniir.* How many batches of bread do you bake a day? *čam tannuur xubuz tuxbuz bil-yoom?* **4.** *baṭin* pl. *bṭuun.* This is the biggest batch of kittens our cat has ever had. *haay ʔakbar baṭin jaabata bazzuunatna.*

bath - *ʒammaam* pl. *-aat.* I'd like to take a hot bath. *da-ariid aaxuδ ʒammaam ʒaarr.* Have you a room with bath? *Ɛindak ġurfa biiha ʒammaam?*

to bathe - 1. *ġisal (i ġasil) n-.* Bathe the baby in lukewarm water. *ʔiġsil iṭ-ṭifil ib-ṃaay daafi.* -- We usually bathe at the public bathhouse. *ʔiʒna Ɛaadatan niġsil bil-ʒammaam il-Ɛumuumi.* **2.** *sibaʒ (a sibiʒ) n-.* We went bathing in the river almost every day. *sibaʒna biš-šaṭṭ taqriiban kull yoom.*

bathhouse - 1. *ʒammaam Ɛaamm* pl. *-aat Ɛaamma.* There are many public bathhouses in the city. *ʔaku hwaaya ʒammaamaat Ɛaamma bil-wlaaya.* **2.** *manzaƐ* pl. *manaaziƐ.* There is a bathhouse at the beach where we can change our clothes. *ʔaku manzaƐ bil-masbaʒ nigdar ninzaƐ ihduumna bii.*

bathing suit - *maayo* pl. *-waat* (for women), *čiswa* pl. *čisaw* (for men).

bathrobe - *roob* pl. *-aat, burnuṣ* pl. *baraaniṣ.*

bathroom - *ʒammaam* pl. *-aat.* I'm looking for the toilet not the bathroom. *da-adawwur Ɛal-mirʒaaδ muu l-ʒammaam.*

bath towel - *manšafa* pl. *manaašif.*

bathtub - *baanyo* pl. *-waat.*

batter - *Ɛajiina* pl. *-aat.* Is the batter for the cake mixed? *l-Ɛajiina maal il-keek maxbuuṭa?*

to batter in - *kassar (i ṭaksiir) t-.* The firemen battered in the door and saved the man. *rijaal il-ʔiṭfaaʔ kassraw il-baab w-xallṣaw ir-rijjaal.*

battered-up - *mhaššam.* He bought a battered-up old car. *štira sayyaara Ɛatiiga mhaššama.*

battery - *paatri* pl. *-iyyaat.* My car has to have a new battery. *sayyaarti yinraad-ilha paatri jdiid.*

battle - *maƐraka* pl. *maƐaarik.*

battlefield - *saaʒat il-maƐraka, miidaan* pl. *mayaadiin.*

battle ship - *baarija* pl. *bawaarij.*

to bawl - *ṣirax (u ṣraax), Ɛayyaṭ (i Ɛyaaṭ).* The child has been bawling for an hour. *ṭ-ṭifil ṣaar-la saaƐa da-yuṣrux.*

to bawl out - *razzal (i tarziil, trizzil) t-.* Why did he bawl you out? *luweeš razzalak?*

bay - *xaliij* pl. *xiljaan.* There's a steamship anchored out in the bay. *ʔaku baaxira raasiya bil-xaliij.*

bayonet - *sungi* pl. *sanaagi, ʒarba* pl. *-aat, ʒraab.*

to be - 1. *čaan (ykuun koon).* Are you planning to be there? *b-niitak itkuun ihnaak?* -- When will you be at home? *šwakit raʒ-itkuun bil-beet?* -- Where have you been? *ween činit?* -- I was planning to go with you. *činit naawi ʔaruuʒ wiyyaak.* -- I wasn't at home when you phoned me. *ma-činit bil-beet min xaabaritni.* -- He had climbed that hill when he was a child. *čaan mitsalliq hat-tall min čaan jaahil.* -- When I got to the office, he was about to leave. *lamma wuṣalt id-daaʔira, čaan da-yiṭlaƐ.* -- His children were playing with ours. *jihhaala čaanaw da-yilƐabuun wiyya jihhaalna.* **2.** *ṣaar (i ṣayra).*

Be good while I'm away, children. *yaa jhaal, ṣiiru εiqqaal ib-ġiyaabi.* — Don't be rude! *la-tṣiir xašin!* — He wants to be an engineer. *yriid yṣiir muhandis.* — How much is it going to be? *šgadd raḥ-yṣiir?* — Would it be all right if we used this room? *yṣiir nistaεmil hal-ġurfa?* — How much will that be? *šgadd ṣaar?* — If that were true, we'd all be rich. *loo haaδa ṣudug, čaan kullna ṣirna zanaagiin.* — He has been climbing that hill everyday for years. *ṣaar-la sniin yitsallaq δaak it-tall kull yoom.* — He had already been there a month when he resigned. *čaan ṣaar-la šahar ihnaak min qarrar yistiqiil.* **3.** (no equivalent). How much is this? *haaδa beeš?* — The man is a merchant. *r-rijjaal huwwa taajir* or *r-rijjaal fadd waaḥid taajir.* — His name is Salih. *ʔisma ṣaaliḥ.* — They are all company employees. *kullhum mustaxdamiin biš-šarika.* — He is ill. *huwwa mariiδ̣.* He seems to be ill. *ybayyin (huwwa) mariiδ̣.* — The children are playing in the street. *j-jihaal da-yilεabuun bid-darub.* If I were you, I'd forget the whole thing. *loo ʔaani b-makaanak, ʔansa kullši.*

there is, are – *ʔaku.* There are five men at the door. *ʔaku xams iryaajiil bil-baab.*

there isn't, aren't – *ma-aku.* There isn't anyone at home. *ma-aku ʔaḥḥad bil-beet.*

there was, were – *čaan ʔaku.* There were many people ahead of me. *čaan aku hwaaya naas gabḷi.*

there wasn't, weren't – *ma-čaan aku.* There wasn't anyone at the door. *ma-čaan aku ʔaḥḥad bil-baab.*

beach – *balaaj* pl. *-aat.* We built a fire on the beach. *šεalna naar εal-balaaj.*

bead – **1.** *xirza* pl. *xiraz.* How many beads are there on this string? *čam xirza ʔaku b-hal-xeeṭ?* **2.** *ḥabba* pl. *-aat.* Beads of sweat covered his forehead. *ḥabbaat il-εarag ġaṭṭat gușṣta.*

beads – *glaada* pl. *-aat, glaayid.* She lost her beads on the way home from the party. *δ̣ayyεat iglaadatha b-ṭariiqha lil-beet imnil-ḥafla.*

prayer beads – *sibḥa* pl. *sibaḥ.* I never saw him without his prayer beads in his hand. *ʔabad ma-šifta min ġeer sibḥa b-ʔiida.*

beam – **1.** *jisir* pl. *jsuura.* The roof was supported by strong beams. *s-saguf čaan masnuud b-ijsuura qawiyya.* **2.** *šeelmaana* pl. *-aat* coll. *šeelmaan.* The warehouse has a framework of steel beams. *l-maxzan haykala min šeelmaan.* **3.** *šuεaaε* pl. *ʔašiεεa.* Throw a beam of light on it. *wajjih šuεaaε δ̣uwa εalee.*

to beam – **1.** *ʔašraq (u ʔišraaq).* Her face beams every time he talks to her. *yišruq wijihha kull-ma yiḥči wiyyaaha.* **2.** *šaεε (i ʔisεaaε).* The face of the pious man beams with light. *wučč ir-rijjaal iṣ-ṣaaliḥ yšiεε nuur.* **3.** *wajjah (i tawjiih).* This program is being beamed to the Middle East. *hal-manhaj imwajjah ʔila š-šarq il-ʔawṣaṭ.*

beans – *faaṣuuliyya.*

broad beans – *baagillaaya* pl. *-aat* coll. *baagilla.*

bear – *dibb* pl. *dibaba.* Are there any bears in this forest? *ʔaku dibaba b-hal-ġaaba?*

to bear – **1.** *tḥammal (a taḥammul).* I can't bear the suspense any longer. *ma-agdar atḥammal hal-ġumuuδ̣ baεad.* He has to bear all the responsibility himself. *huwwa waḥda laazim yitḥammal kull il-masʔuuliyya.* **2.** *šaal (i šeel) n-.* This date tree didn't bear last year. *han-naxla ma-šaalat is-sana l-faatat.* **3.** *wilad (i wilaad) n-.* She bore her first child when she was eighteen. *wildat ʔawwal ṭifilha min čaan εumurha θmanṭaεaš.*

to bear down – **1.** *daas (u doos) n-.* Don't bear down so hard on the pencil, it might break. *la-tduus εal-qalam ḥeel, tara yinkisir.* **2.** *twajjah (i).* The car bore down upon us at a terrible speed. *s-sayyaara twajjhat εaleena b-surεa haaʔla.* **3.** *δ̣iġaṭ (u δ̣aġiṭ) n-.* The boss is beginning to bear down on us more everyday. *l-mudiir gaam yuδ̣ġuṭ εaleena ʔakθar yoom εala yoom.*

to bear fruit – *ʔaθmar (i ʔiθmaar).* The apricot trees did not bear much fruit this year. *ʔašjaar il-mišmiš ma-ʔaθmirat has-sana.* After many years, his efforts finally bore fruit. *baεad ihwaaya sniin, juhuuda ʔaxiiran ʔaθmirat.*

bearable – *mumkin iḥtimaala.* It is bearable for a while, but not continually. *haaδa mumkin iḥtimaala fatra bass muu εala ṭuul.*

to be bearable – *nṭaaq (a ntaaqa), nḥimal (i nḥimaal).* The heat is still bearable. *l-ḥarr baεda yinḥimil.*

beard – *liḥya* pl. *liḥa.* He has a long beard. *huwwa mṭawwil-la liḥya.* — I'm letting my beard grow. *da-arabbi liḥiiti.*

bearing – *beerin* pl. *-aat.* This motor needs new bearings. *hal-makiina yinraad-ilha beerinaat jidiida.*

to get one's bearing – *εayyan (i taεyiin) t- mawqiεʼ.* First let's get our bearings. *xalli ʔawwil inεayyin mawqiεna.*

to have bearing on – *ʔila εalaaqa b-.* What bearing does that have on what we're doing? *haaδaak š-ila εalaaqa biš-šii d-da-nsawwii.*

beast – **1.** *daabba* pl. *dawaabb.* The horse, the donkey and the mule are beasts of burden. *l-ḥṣaan wuz-zumaaḷ wil-baġaḷ dawaabb.* **2.** *ḥaywaan* pl. *-aat, ḥwaawiin.* He paced up and down in the room like a caged beast. *raaḥ w-jaa bil-ġurfa miθl il-ḥaywaan il-maḥṣuur.*

beat – **1.** *nabuδ̣.* His heartbeat has become stronger. *nabuδ̣ gaḷba ṣaar ʔaqwa.* **2.** *dagga* pl. *-aat, δ̣arba* pl. *-aat.* Count the heartbeats. *ʔiḥsib daggaat il-gaḷub.*

to beat – **1.** *δ̣irab (u δ̣arub) n-, buṣaṭ (u baṣiṭ) n-.* If you keep on throwing stones at my car, I'll beat you up. *ʔiδa tδ̣all itδibb iḥjaar εala sayyaarti, tara ʔabuṣṭak.* **2.** *dagg (u dagg) n-.* If you want to beat your drum, go outside. *ʔiδa triid itdugg ṭablak, ʔiṭlaε barra.* — Her heart was beating wildly from fear. *gaḷubha čaan da-ydugg ḥeel imnil-xoof.* **3.** *ṭirag (u ṭarig) n-.* Beat two eggs. *ʔuṭrug beeδ̣teen.* **4.** *ġiḷab (u ġuḷub) n-.* We beat them in today's game. *ʔiḥna ġḷabnaahum bil-liεib il-yoom.* **5.** *sibaq (i sabiq) n-.* He beats me to work every day. *yisbiqni liš-šuġuḷ kull yoom.*

to beat down – *gaṣṣ (u gaṣṣ) n-.* I was able to beat down the price 10 Dinars. *gdarit ʔaguṣṣ εašr idnaaniir mnis-siεir.*

to beat in – *xubaṭ (u xabuṭ) n-, mizaj (i mazij) n-.* Beat the eggs into the mixture. *ʔuxubṭi l-beeδ̣ ib-hal-xaliiṭ.*

to beat off – *ṭarrad (i ṭarid) t-.* I beat off the dogs with a club. *ṭarradit l-ičlaab ib-tuuθiyya.*

to beat up – *buṣaṭ (u baṣiṭ) n-, δ̣irab (u δ̣arub) n-, kital (i katil) n-.* They beat him up. *buṣṭoo.* **Beat it! *walli!*

beautician – *ʔaxiṣṣaaʔi* (pl. *-iyyiin*) *bit-tajmiil.*

beautiful – **1.** *ḥilu, jamiil, badiiε.* What a beautiful day! *šloon nahaar ḥilu!* The bride is a beautiful girl. *l-εaruus ibnayya ḥilwa.* **2.** *badaaεa, mumtaaz.* He did a beautiful job on that. *sawwa šaġla badaaεa b-haaδa.*

beautifully – *kulliš zeen.* Your daughter sews beautifully. *bintak itxayyiṭ kulliš zeen.*

to **beautify** – *jammal (i tajmiil) t-.* The plans for beautifying the city are almost finished. *l-xiṭaṭ il-tajmiil il-madiina εala wašak titihayyaʔ.*

beauty – **1.** *jamaal.* They stood there a long time enjoying the beauty of the sunset. *wugfaw ihnaak mudda ṭuwiila yitmattaεuun ib-jamaal il-ġuruub.* **2.** *badaaεa, falla.* She's a real beauty! *hiyya badaaεa* or *hiyya ṣudug falla.* — The fish we caught were beauties. *s-simač iṣ-ṣidna čaan falla.*

beauty parlor – *ṣaaloon* (pl. *-aat*) *tajmiil.*

became – see become.

because – *li-ʔan, b-sabab.* He didn't come because he was sick. *ma-jaa li-ʔan čaan mariiδ̣.* I didn't buy it because the price wasn't agreeable to me. *ma-štireeta li-ʔan is-siεir ma-waafaqni.*

because of – **1.** *li-ʔan, b-sabab.* Ali, I'm going to be late because of you. *ya εali, ʔaani raḥ-atʔaxxar ib-sababak.* **2.** *εala muud, l-xaaṭir.* I did it because of her. *sawweeta εala muudha.* — I don't want you to do it just because of me. *ma-ariidak itsawwiiha bass il-xaaṭiri.*

to **become** – *ṣaar (i), ʔaṣbaḥ (a).* What became of them? *š-ṣaar minhum?* or *ween ʔaṣbiḥaw?* What has become of my purse? *jizdaani ween ṣaar?* It has become a matter of ''pull''. *l-qaδ̣iyya ʔaṣbaḥat waaṣṭa.*

to be **becoming** – *laag (u) l-.* That color is very becoming to you. *hal-loon ihwaaya yluug-lič.*

bed – **1.** *fraaš* pl. *furiš.* I want a room with two beds. *ʔariid ġurfa biiha fraašeen.* — My bed hasn't been made. *fraaši ma-msawwa.* **2.** *sariir* pl. *sraayir.* The government is building a new hospital with 80 beds. *l-ḥukuuma da-tibni mustašfa jidiid bii θmaaniin sariir.* **3.** *čarpaaya* pl. *-aat.* Where was this bed (stead) made? *hač-čarpaaya ween maεmuula?* **4.** *jiwwa* pl. *jiwaw.* I want you to weed the rose beds today. *ʔariidak tišlaε il-ḥašiiš min jiwaw il-warid il-yoom.* **5.** *gaaεiyya* pl. *-aat.* Put the

box in the middle of the truck bed. *zuṭṭ iṣ-ṣanduug ib-nuṣṣ gaaԑiit il-loori.*
**He must have gotten up on the wrong side of the bed today. *huwwa ma-adri b-wijj man imṣabbuz hal-yoom.*
to go to bed - *naam (a, noom).* I went to bed late. *nimit mitʔaxxir.*
to put to bed - *nawwam (u tanwiim) t-, nayyam (i tanwiim) t-.* Tell the nurse to put the children to bed early. *guul lil-murabbiya tnayyim ij-jihhaal min wakit.*
to stay in bed - *buqa (a) bil-ifraaš, ḍall (a) bil-ifraaš.* He still has to stay in bed. *baԑda laazim yibqa bil-ifraaš.*

bed bug - *baggat l-ifraaš.*
bed clothes - *čaraačif.*
bedding - *l-furiš wič-čaraačif.* Air the bedding today. *hawwi l-furiš wič-čaraačif hal-yoom.*
Bedouin - *badwi** pl. *-iyyiin* coll. *badu.*
bed pan - *qiԑԑaada* pl. *-aat.*
bed rock - *ṭ-ṭabaqa ṣ-ṣaxriyya.*
bed room - *ġurfat* (pl. *ġuraf*) *noom, gubbat* (pl. *gubab, gbaab*) *noom.*
bedspread - *čarčaf* pl. *čaraačif, ġiṭa maal ifraaš.*
bedstead - *sariir* pl. *sraayir* (wooden), *čarpaaya* pl. *-aat* (metal).
bee - *nazla* pl. *nazal, zanbuur* pl. *zanaabiir.*
beech tree - *zaan.*
beef - *lazam hooš.* Do you like beef? *tzibb lazm il-hooš?*
beehive - *kuurat* (pl. *kuwar*) *nazal, kuurat* (pl. *kuwar*) *zanaabiir.*
been - see be.
beer - *biira.* I'd like a glass of beer, please. *ʔariid fadd iglaaṣ biira, rajaaʔan.*
beet - *šwandara* pl. *-aat* coll. *šwandar.*
beetle - *xunfusaana* pl. *-aat* coll. *xunfusaan.* The beetles have eaten all the leaves. *l-xunfusaan ʔaklaw kull waraq iš-šajar.*
before - *gabuḷ.* I'll be there before two o'clock. *raz-akuun ihnaak gabḷ is-saaԑa θneen.* -- The telegram should be there before evening. *l-barqiyya laazim tooṣal ihnaak gabḷ il-miġrub.* -- Call me up before you come. *xaaburni gabuḷ-ma tiji.*
**Business before pleasure. *š-šuġul gabḷ il-liԑib.*
before long - 1. *baԑd išwayya.* Before long he'll be able to help you. *raz-yigdar yԑaawnak baԑd išwayya.* 2. *ḍall išwayya.* Before long the money we've been saving will come to a hundred dinars. *ḍall išwayya l-fluus il-da-nlimmha ṭṣiir miit diinaar.*
never ... before - *ma- ... gabuḷ ʔabad, b-ԑumr~ ma-.* I've never been there before. *ʔaani ma-raayiz l-ihnaak gabuḷ ʔabad* or -- *b-ԑumri ma-riẓit l-ihnaak.*
the day before - 1. *gabḷ ib-yoom.* It had rained the day before. *muṭrat gabḷ ib-yoom.* 2. *l-yoom is-saabiq l-.* I didn't get my passport until the day before I left. *ma-zaṣṣalit paaṣpoorti lil-yoom is-saabiq is-safari.*
the day before yesterday - *ʔawwal il-baarza.* He was here the day before yesterday. *čaan ihnaa ʔawwal il-baarza.*
beforehand - *li-giddaam.* I knew it beforehand. *ʔaani ԑrafitha li-giddaam.*
to beg - 1. *jadda (i jidya).* He spends most of his day begging in the market. *yigḍi muԑḍam yooma yjaddi bis-suug.* 2. *twassal (a twissil, tawassul) b-.* The children begged their father for some money. *l-ʔaṭfaal itwasslaw b-abuuhum ԑala čam filis.* -- They begged us to help them. *twasslaw biina nsaaԑidhum.*
beggar - 1. *mgaddi* pl. *mgaadi, mjaddi* pl. *mjaadi.* There's a beggar at the door. *ʔaku mjaddi bil-baab.*
**Beggars can't be choosers. *laazim nirḍa bil-maqsuum* or *l-buṭar muu zeen.*
to begin - 1. *bida (i badwa, bidaaya) n-.* When did you begin working in your present job? *šwakit bideet tištuġul ib-waḍiiftak ij-jidiida?* 2. *ballaš (i tabliiš) t-.* The oil company has begun drilling. *šarikt in-nafuṭ ballšat bil-zafur.* -- As soon as they met on the street, they began to curse one another. *min itlaagaw biš-šaariԑ ballšaw yšattmuun waazid ԑal-laax.* 3. *gaam (u qiyaam).* All at once, the donkey began to bray. *fujʔatan, l-izmaal gaam yjooԑir.*
to begin with - *ʔawwalan, gabuḷ kullši.* To begin with, we haven't got enough money. *ʔawwalan, ma-ԑidna fluus kaafya.*
beginner - *mubtadiʔ* pl. *-iin.* He's still a beginner. *baԑda mubtadiʔ.*
beginning - *bidaaya.* The box office remains open until 10 minutes after the beginning of the film. *mazall il-biṭaaqaat yibqa maftuuz ԑašir daqaayiq baԑad bidaayt il-filim.*
to **begrudge** - *zisad (i zasad).* Why should he begrudge me my job? *leeš yizsidni ԑala waḍiifti?* -- I don't begrudge him his success, he deserves it. *ma-azisda ԑala najaaza, huwwa yistaziqqa.*
on **behalf of** - *bin-niyaaba ԑan.* I want to thank you on behalf of our organization. *ʔazibb ʔaškurak bin-niyaaba ԑan muʔassasatna.*
to **behave** - 1. *ṭṣarraf (a taṣarruf).* He doesn't know how to behave. *ma-yuԑruf šloon yiṭṣarraf.* 2. *tʔaddab (a taʔaddub), zassan (i tazsiin) t-siluuk~.* Behave yourself! *tʔaddab, zassin siluukak!* or *ṣiir xooš walad!*
behind - *wara.* There's a garage behind the house. *ʔaku garaaj wara l-beet.* -- The attack came from behind. *ʔija l-hujuum min wara.*
to be behind - 1. *tʔaxxar (a tʔuxxur).* My watch is always ten minutes behind. *saaԑati daaʔiman mitʔaxxra ԑašir daqaayiq.* 2. *ʔayyad (i taʔyiid) t-.* All the people are behind the president of the republic. *kull in-naas yʔayyiduun raʔiis ij-jamhuuriyya.* 3. *wara.* Who's behind this project? *minu wara hal-mašruuԑ?*
to fall behind - *tʔaxxar (a tʔuxxur).* He has fallen behind in his work. *huwwa mitʔaxxir ib-šuġla.*
to leave behind - 1. *tirak (u tarik) n-.* We had to leave our trunk behind. *ḍṭarreena nitruk ṣanduugna.* 2. *xalla (i).* We left the dog behind to watch the house. *xalleena č-čalib ydiir baala ԑal-beet.*
belch - *taryuuԑa* pl. *-aat.*
to belch - *ttaryaԑ (a ttiryiԑ).* He ate radishes and began belching a lot. *ʔakal fijil w-gaam yittaryaԑ ihwaaya.*
Belgian - *baljiiki** pl. *-iyyiin.*
Belgium - *baljiika.*
belief - 1. *ʔiimaan.* My belief in him was seriously shaken. *ʔiimaani bii ḍiԑaf kulliš ihwaaya.* 2. *ԑtiqaad.* Belief in superstitions is wide-spread among illiterates. *l-iԑtiqaad bil-xaraafaat šaayiԑ been il-ʔummiyyiin.*
to **believe** - 1. *ṣaddag (i taṣdiig) t-.* Don't believe anything he says. *la-tṣaddig ʔay sii l-yguula.* 2. *ԑtiqad (i ԑtiqaad).* I don't believe he did it. *ʔaani ma-aԑtiqid huwwa sawwaaha.*
to believe in - *ʔaaman (i) b-.* Do you believe in his sincerity? *inta tʔaamin b-ixḷaaṣa?*
bell - *jaraṣ* pl. *jraaṣ.* The bell doesn't work. *j-jaraṣ ma-yištuġul.*
belligerent - 1. *mušaakis* pl. *-iin.* He is always belligerent and rude to the people that work with him. *huwwa daaʔiman mušaakis w-xašin wiyya n-naas il-yištaġluun wiyyaa.* 2. *mitzaarub* pl. *-iin.* They have arranged a truce between the two belligerent nations. *dabbiraw hudna been id-dawilteen il-mitzaarubteen.* 3. *mitxaaṣum* pl. *-iin.* The leaders of both the belligerent parties have been arrested. *zuԑamaaʔ il-fariiqeen il-mitxaaṣmeen twaqqfaw.*
bellows - 1. *minfaax* pl. *manaafiix.* Where can I buy a pair of bellows? *ween ʔagdar ʔaštiri minfaax?* 2. *jraab.* The bellows on my camera is ripped. Can you fix it? *l-ijraab maal kaameerti mašguug, tigdar itṣallza?*
belly - 1. *baṭin* pl. *bṭuun.* This strap goes around the horse's belly. *has-seer yiltaff ԑala baṭn il-izṣaan.* -- The plane made a forced landing and slid two hundred meters on its belly. *ṭ-ṭiyyaara nizlat nizuul iḍṭiraari w-zizfat ԑala baṭinha miiteen matir.* 2. *kariš* pl. *kruuš.* He has a very big belly. *ԑinda kariš čibiir.*
to **belong to** - 1. *ԑaad (u) l-.* This building belongs to the oil company. *hal-ibnaaya tԑuud iš-šarikt in-nafuṭ.* 2. *xaṣṣ (u).* These files belong to the Personnel Section. *hal-faaylaat itxuṣṣ šuԑbat iḍ-ḍaatiyya.* 3. *maal.* Who does this car belong to? *has-sayyaara maal man?* 4. *(čaan) ԑuḍu b-.* He also belongs to the club. *huwwa hamm ԑuḍu bin-naadi.*
below - 1. *jawwa.* The temperature here seldom gets below zero. *darajt il-zaraara hnaa naadir tinzil jawwa ṣ-ṣifir.* 2. *tazat.* The Dead Sea is below sea-level. *l-bazr il-mayyit tazat mustawa l-bazar.*
belt - 1. *zzaam* pl. *zizim.* Do you wear a belt? *tilbas izzaam?* 2. *gaayiš* pl. *-aat.* My pump needs a new belt. *makiinti yird-ilha gaayiš jidiid.*
**He's got a few under his belt. *širab-la čam*

peek.
**That's hitting below the belt. *haaδi naδaala.*

bench - *maṣṭaba* pl. *-aat, maṣaaṭib.* The benches were just painted. *l-maṣṭabaat tawwha maṣbuuġa.*

bend - *loofa* pl. *-aat, lawya* pl. *-aat.* We can cross the river at the bend. *nigdar nuƐbur iš-šaṭṭ bil-loofa.*
to bend - **1.** *Ɛuwaj (u Ɛawij) n-, luwa (i lawi) n-.* He bent the wire. *Ɛuwaj is-siim.* **2.** *maal (i mayl, mayalaan).* The tree bends when the wind blows. *š-šajara tmiil min yhibb il-hawa.* **3.** *ẓina (i ẓani) n-.* Bend your head forward. *ʔiẓni raasak li-giddaam.*
**We must bend every effort. *laazim nibδil kull majhuud.*
to bend down - *naṣṣa (i tanṣiya) t-.* I can't bend down. *ʔaani ma-agdar anaṣṣi.*

beneath - **1.** *jawwa.* He was buried beneath the tree. *huwwa ndifan jawwa š-šajara.* -- I put it beneath all the other papers. *xalleetha jawwa kull il-ʔawraaq il-luxra.* **2.** *ʔanzal min.* That's beneath his level. *haδiič ʔanzal min mustawaa.*

benefactor - *naṣiir* pl. *nuṣaraaʔ, Ɛaδiid* pl. *Ɛuδadaaʔ.* He was both a friend and a benefactor to me. *čaan-li ṣadiiq w-Ɛaδiid.*

beneficial - *mufiid* pl. *-iin, naafiƐ* pl. *-iin.* The new treatment has proved very beneficial to my back. *l-Ɛilaaj ij-jidiid ʔaθbat kawna jiddan mufiid iδ-δahri.*

beneficiary - *mustafiid* pl. *-iin.* He made me the beneficiary of his life insurance policy. *sawwaani l-mustafiid min Ɛagd il-taʔmiin Ɛala ẓayaata.*

benefit - *faaʔida* pl. *fawaaʔid.* I don't expect to get any benefit out of it. *ma-atwaqqaƐ ʔaẓaṣṣil ʔay faaʔida minha.*
to benefit - *faad (i faaʔida) n-.* The trip did not benefit us much. *s-safra ma-faadatna hwaaya.*

bent - **1.** *minẓini.* He is bent with age. *huwwa minẓini mnil-kubur.* **2.** *ʔaƐwaj.* The nail is bent. *l-bismaar ʔaƐwaj.* **3.** *maayil.* The tree is bent from the force of the wind. *š-šajara maayla min quwwat il-hawa.* **4.** *mitqawwis, mqawwas.* His leg is bent this way because he had rickets when he was young. *rijla mqawwsa hiiči li-ʔan ṣaar bii maraδ il-kisaaẓ min čaan jaahil.*
bent out of shape - *mitƐawwij, maƐwuuj, mƐawwaj.* The pan is all bent out of shape. *j-jidir kulla mitƐawwij.*

berry - no generic equivalent. see specific kinds.

berth - *manaam* pl. *-aat, fraaš* pl. *furiš.* I couldn't get a berth in the late train. *ma-gdarit ʔaẓaṣṣil Ɛala manaam bil-qiṭaar il-ʔaxiir.*
**Whenever I see her I try to give her a wide berth. *kull-ma ʔašuufha ʔaẓaawil atjannabha.*

beside - **1.** *yamm.* Please put this trunk beside the other one. *ʔarjuuk ẓuṭṭ haṣ-ṣanduuq yamm iṣ-ṣanduuq il-laax.* -- Who's that standing beside your father? *minu δaak il-waaguf yamm ʔabuuk?*
**That's beside the point. *haaδi waẓẓad.*
to be beside oneself - *txabbaḷ (a txubbuḷ, xbaal).* He was beside himself when I heard the news. *txabbaḷ ixbaal min simaƐ il-xabar.* He was beside himself with rage. *čaan mitxabbuḷ imnil-ġaδab.* -- She was beside herself with grief. *čaanat mitxabbḷa mnil-ẓiẓin.*

besides - **1.** *bil-ʔiδaafa ʔila.* Besides his being a large landowner, he has a soap factory. *bil-ʔiδaafa ʔila kawna muzaariƐ Ɛinda maƐmal ṣaabuun.* **2.** *Ɛalaawa Ɛala.* He's a good worker, and besides, everybody likes him. *huwwa šaaġuul w-Ɛalaawa Ɛala δaak kull waaẓid yẓibba.* **3.** *čmaala.* And besides, he is not related to me. *w-ičmaala, huwwa muu garaaybi.* **4.** *foog.* Besides his wages, he gets tips. *foog ʔujuura yẓaṣṣil baxšiiš.*

best - **1.** *ʔaẓsan.* We don't want anything but the best. *ʔiẓna ma-nriid ġeer il-ʔaẓsan.* -- I work best in the morning. *ṣ-ṣubuẓ ʔaẓsan wakit ʔagdar ʔaštaġuḷ bii.* -- I think this is the best way. *ʔaƐtiqid haaδi ʔaẓsan ṭariiqa.* **2.** *ʔaƐazz.* He's my best friend. *huwwa ʔaƐazz ʔaṣdiqaaʔi.* **3.** *ʔazyad sii.* I like your hair best this way. *šaƐrič yiƐjibni hiiči ʔazyad šii.*
**Perhaps it's all for the best. *belki biiha l-xeer.*
at best - *mahma ykuun, š-ma ykuun.* At best, potatoes are a very poor substitute for rice. *mahma tkuun, il-puteeta muu xooš bidal lit-timman.*
to get the best of - **1.** *qašmar (u qašmara) t-.* We have to be careful that he doesn't get the best of us. *laazim indiir baanna ẓatta la-yqašmurna.* **2.** *ġiḷab (u ġuḷub).* I think we got the best of this bargain. *ʔaƐtiqid ġiḷabna b-haṣ-ṣafqa.*
**This cold will get the best of me. *hal-našla ma-raẓ-itxalli biyya ẓeel.*
to make the best of - *riδa (a raδi) b-.* We don't like our new apartment, but we'll have to make the best of it. *ma-tiƐjibna šiqqatna j-jidiida laakin laazim nirδa biiha.*

bet - *rahan* pl. *ruhuun.* When are you going to pay me the bet? *šwakit raẓ-tidfaƐ-li r-rahan?*
**That's your best bet. *haδaak ʔaẓsan šii ʔilak.*
to bet - **1.** *traahan (a taraahun) Ɛala.* Want to bet? *titraahan?* **2.** *raahan (i muraahana).* I'll bet you haven't seen anything like this before. *ʔaraahnak ʔinta ma-šaayif šii miθil haaδa gabuḷ.*
to bet on - *liƐab (a liƐib) n- Ɛala, traahan (a) Ɛala.* I bet five dinars on the black horse. *ʔaani ʔalƐab xams idnaaniir Ɛal-iẓṣaan il-aswad.*

to **betray** - **1.** *xaan (u xiyaana) n-.* He betrayed his best friend. *xaan ʔaẓsan ʔaṣdiqaaʔa.* **2.** *xayyab (i taxyiib).* She betrayed my confidence. *hiyya xayybat θiqti.*

better - **1.** *ʔaẓsan.* Don't you have a better room? *ma-Ɛindak ġurfa ʔaẓsan?* -- They got better after they had practiced a little. *ṣaaraw ʔaẓsan baƐad-ma tmarrnaw šwayya.* -- Do you feel better? *tišƐur ʔaẓsan?* -- We'd better go before it rains. *ʔaẓsan-inna nruuẓ gabuḷ-ma tumṭur.* -- You'd better go. *ʔaẓsan-lak loo truuẓ.*
to be better off - **1.** *ʔaẓsan l-.* We'll be better off if we move to another house. *ʔaẓsan-inna ʔiδa nitẓawwal il-ġeer beet.* **2.** *(čaan) ʔaẓsan.* We used to be better off before the war. *ẓaalatna čaanat ʔaẓsan gabḷ il-ẓarub.* -- We'd have been better off without his help. *čaan ʔaẓsan-inna bila musaaƐada minna.*
to get the better of - *ġiḷab (u ġuḷub) n-.* He tried to get the better of you. *raad yġuḷbak.*

between - **1.** *been.* We'll meet between six and seven. *raẓ-nitlaaga been is-sitta wis-sabƐa.* **2.** *beenaat, been.* This is just between you and me. *haaδi beeni w-beenak.* -- Just between us it's his own fault. *l-ẓači beenaatna, tara ṣuuča.*
**Honest people are few and far between. *l-xooš awaadim qaliiliin w-naadir yiltiguun.*

beverage - **1.** (alcoholic) *mašruub* pl. *-aat.* **2.** (non-alcoholic) *muraṭṭibaat.*

to **beware of** - *tqayyad (a taqayyud) min.* Beware of him! *tqayyad minna!* **2.** *daar (i deer) baal min.* Beware of pickpockets! *diir baalak min δarraabiin ij-jiyuub.*

to **bewilder** - *tẓayyar (a taẓayyur).* I was completely bewildered. *tẓayyarit tamaaman.*

beyond - **1.** *ġaadi.* The house is beyond the river. *l-beet ġaadi mniš - šaṭṭ.* **2.** *wara.* The house is right beyond the hospital. *l-beet wara l-mustašfa tamaaman.* **3.** *ʔakθar min, foog.* We are living beyond our means. *da-nuṣruf ʔakθar min ṭaaqatna.* - Our neighbors are living beyond their means. *jiiraanna da-yƐiišuun foog mustawaahum.*
**He is beyond help. *ma-ṭṣiir-la čaara.*
to go beyond - *faaq (u).* That goes beyond my authority. *haaδa yfuuq ṣuluṭṭi.*

biased - *mitẓayyiz, muġriδ.* He is very biased. *huwwa kulliš mitẓayyiz.*

Bible - *l-kitaab il-muqaddas.*

bicarbonate of soda - *kaarboonaat.*

bicycle - *paaysikil* pl. *-aat, darraaja* pl. *-aat.* My bicycle needs fixing. *l-paaysikil maali yirraad-la taṣliiẓ.*

bid - *Ɛaṭaaʔ* pl. *-aat.* All the bids for the new building must be in by the fifteenth of the month. *kull il-Ɛaṭaaʔaat lil-binaaya j-jidiida laazim itkuun ihnaa gabḷ ixmuṣṭaƐaš biš-šahar.*
to bid - *zaayad (i muzaayada).* He bid ten dinars for the rug. *zaayad Ɛašr idnaaniir Ɛas-sijjaada.*

big - *čbiir* pl. *kbaar.* The live in a big house. *ysuknuun ib-beet ičbiir.* -- Her father is a big lawyer. *ʔabuuha muẓaami čbiir.* -- He talks big. *yiẓči kbaar.*
**He's a big shot now. *ṣaar šaxṣiyya hassa.*

bill - **1.** *qaaʔima* pl. *qawaaʔim.* We have to pay this bill today. *laazim nidfaƐ hal-qaaʔima l-yoom.* **2.** *nooṭ* pl. *nwaaṭ.* Give me some small bills, please. *ʔarjuuk inṭiini nwaaṭ iṣġayyra.* **3.** *laaʔiẓa* pl. *lawaaʔiẓ.* The bill was passed. *l-laaʔiẓa ṭṣaddqat.* **4.** *mungaar* pl. *manaagiir.* Storks have long bills. *l-lagaalig Ɛidha manaagiir iṭwiila.* **5.** *ʔiƐlaan* pl. *-aat.* Posting bills is forbidden here. *laṣq il-ʔiƐlaanaat mamnuuƐ ihnaa.*

to fill the bill - *wufa (i wafaa?) bil-maraam.* I don't think that these will fill the bill. *ma-aδunn haδoola yoofuun bil-maraam.*

to foot the bill - *difaƐ (a dafiƐ) l-iʒsaab.* Who's going to foot the bill for all this? *minu raʒ-yidfaƐ kull haaδa l-iʒsaab?*

to bill - *dazz (i) qaa?ima.* Bill me for the account. *dizz-li qaa?ima bil-iʒsaab.*

billboard - *loozat* (pl. *-aat*) *iƐlaan.*

billfold - *jizdaan* pl. *jizaadiin.*

billiards - *bilyaard.* Let's play a game of billiards. *xal-nilƐab fadd geem bilyaard.*

billion - *bilyoon* pl. *balaayiin.* That runs into billions. *haaδa yooṣal ?ila balaayiin.*

to **bind** - **1.** *jallad (i tajliid) t-.* Can you bind these magazines for me? *tigdar itjallid-li hal-majallaat?* **2.** *ʒiṣar (i ʒaṣir).* This coat binds a little under the arms. Can you let it out? *has-sitra tiʒṣirni šwayya jawwa l-?ubuṭ. tigdar itkabburha?* **3.** *lizam (i).* Your signature binds you to fulfill the contract on time. *tawqiiƐak ylizmak ib-?injaaz il-Ɛaqid Ɛal-wakit.* **4.** *šadd (i sadd), rubaṭ (u rabuṭ).* The police bound the thief's hands with his handkerchief. *š-šurṭa šaddaw ?iideen il-ʒaraami b-čaffiita.* -- Put glue on both surfaces and bind them together tightly with wire. *ʒuṭṭ ğira Ɛaṣ-ṣafiʒteen w-šiddhum suwa b-teel ʒeel.*

to bind up - *δammad (i taδmiid).* Bind up his wounds and give him two aspirins with some water. *δammid ijruuʒa w-inṭii ?aspiriinteen wiyya šwayya maay.*

binder - **1.** *mujallid* pl. *-iin.* The newspapers are at the binder's. *j-jaraayid Ɛind il-mujallid.* **2.** *maʒfaδa* pl. *maʒaafiδ.* You'd better buy a binder for those loose papers. *?aʒsan loo tištiri maʒfaδa l-hal-?awraaq il-mafluula.*

bindery - *maʒall* (pl. *-aat*) *tajliid il-kutub.*

binding - *tajliid* pl. *-aat.* The binding is damaged. *t-tajliid talfaan.*

to be binding - *(čaan) mulzim.* This contract is binding on both parties. *hal-Ɛaqid mulzim Ɛaṭ-ṭarafeen.*

binoculars - *doorbiin* pl. *-aat, naaδuur* pl. *nawaaδiir.*

bird - *ṭeer* pl. *ṭyuur.* What kind of bird is this? *šinu nooƐ haṭ-ṭeer?*

**A bird in the hand is worth two in the bush. *Ɛaṣfuur bil-?iid ?aʒsan min Ɛašra Ɛaš-šajara.* -- **He killed two birds with one stone. *δirab Ɛaṣfuureen b-iʒjaara.*

birth - **1.** *miilaad* pl. *mawaaliid, wilaada* pl. *-aat.* They announced the birth of their son. *Ɛilnaw miilaad ?ibinhum.* **2.** *wilaada, jeebuuba.* This time it was an easy birth. *hal-marra l-wilaada čaanat sahla.*

by birth - *bil-wilaada.* Are you an American by birth? *?inta ?amriiki bil-wilaada?*

date of birth - *taariix il-wilaada.* You forgot to put down your date of birth? *niseet itʒuṭṭ taariix wilaadtak.*

place of birth - *maʒall il-wilaada.* My place of birth is Bagdad. *maʒall wilaadti bağdaad.*

birth control - *taʒdiid in-nasil.*

birthday - *Ɛiid miilaad.* We are celebrating our son's birthday today. *da-niʒtifil ib-Ɛiid miilaad ?ibinna l-yoom.*

birthday party - *ʒaflat Ɛiid il-miilaad.* My wife is giving a birthday party tomorrow for our daughter. Can you come? *marti da-tsawwi ʒaflat Ɛiid miilaad il-binitna baačir, tigdar tiji?*

birth rate - *nisbat il-wilaada.* The government is concerned about the rapid rise in the birth rate. *l-ʒukuuma maqluuqa mniz-ziyaada č-čibiira b-nisbat il-wilaada.*

bishop - **1.** *maṭraan* pl. *maṭaarna.* His uncle is a bishop. *Ɛamma maṭraan.* **2.** *fiil* pl. *fyaal.* You've already lost one bishop and the game has just begun. *nkital Ɛindak fiil wil-liƐib tawwa bida.*

bit - **1.** *lijaam* pl. *-aat.* The horse's mouth has been injured by the bit. *ʒalg il-iʒsaan majruuʒ imnil-lijaam.* **2.** *šwayya.* The tea is a bit strong. *č-čaay šwayya ṭoox.* -- I'm sorry but you'll have to wait a bit longer. *mit?assif laakin laazim tintiδir baƐad išwayya.* **3.** *nitfa* pl. *nitaf.* There's a bit of lint on your coat. *?aku nitfat guṭin Ɛala sitirtak.*

**That's going a bit too far. *θaxxanitha.*

**That doesn't make a bit of difference. *ma-yhimm ?abadan.*

bit by bit - *šwayya šwayya.* We learned the story bit by bit. *Ɛirafna l-iʒčaaya šwayya šwayya.*

not a bit - *wala šwayya, ?abadan, wala wuṣla.* There's not a bit left. *maa baaqi wala šwayya.* -- There isn't a bit of bread in the house. *ma-aku wala wuṣlat xubuz bil-beet.* --

bite - **1.** *Ɛaδδa* pl. *-aat.* The bite itches. *l-Ɛaδδa tʒukk.* -- He took a bite out of the apple. *?axaδ-la fadd Ɛaδδa mnit-tiffaaʒa.* **2.** *wuṣla* pl. *wuṣal.* We haven't a bite left. *ma-buga Ɛidna wala wuṣla.* **3.** *lugma* pl. *lugam.* Won't you have a bite with us? *ma-taakul-lak fadd lugma wiyyaana?*

to bite - **1.** *Ɛaδδ (a Ɛaδδ) n-.* Will the dog bite? *č-čalib yƐaδδ?* **2.** *nigar (u nagir).* The fish are biting well today. *s-simač da-yungur zeen hal-yoom.*

**I tried twice but he didn't bite. *niṣabit-la fuxx marrteen laakin ma-wugaƐ* or *δabbeet-la ṭuƐum marrteen laakin ma-nṣaad.*

biting - *gaṣṣ (u gaṣṣ).* It's a biting wind. *haaδa fadd hawa yguṣṣ.*

bitter - **1.** That tastes bitter. *δaak ṭaƐma murr.* -- He has had some bitter experiences. *marr ib-tajaarub murra.* **2.** *qaasi, šadiid.* It was bitter cold. *čaan il-barid qaasi.* **3.** *laduud* pl. *?aliddaa?.* They are bitter enemies. *humma ?aƐdaa? ?aliddaa?.*

**They fought to the bitter end. *ʒaarbaw lil-moot.*

bitterly - *b-ʒurga, b-?alam, b-maraara.* He complained to me bitterly. *tšakkaa-li b-ʒurga.*

black - **1.** (m) *?aswad* (f) *sooda* pl. *suud.* His hair is black. *šaƐra ?aswad.* **2.** *zunji** pl. *zunuuj.* He has become a leader of the black people. *ṣaayir zaƐiim iz-zunuuj.*

to turn black - *swadd (a).* The sky turned black before the storm. *d-dinya swaddat gabḷ il-Ɛaaṣifa.*

black bird - *zarzuur* pl. *zaraaziir.*

blackboard - *ṣabbuura* pl. *-aat, lawʒa* pl. *-aat.* Write it on the blackboard. *kitba Ɛaṣ-ṣabbuura.*

to **blacken** - *sawwad (i taswiid) t-.* The smoke from the fire blackened the ceiling. *d-duxxaan imnin-naar sawwad is-saguf.*

black market - *s-suuq is-sawdaa?.*

blackness - *sawaad.*

blackout - *taƐtiim* pl. *-aat.* The army is going to carry out a trial blackout tomorrow. *j-jeeš raʒ-yquum ib-tamriin taƐtiim baačir.*

to black out - *Ɛattam (i taƐtiim) t-.* The government has decided to blackout the city for ten minutes. *l-ʒukuuma qarrirat itƐattim il-madiina l-muddat Ɛašir daqaayiq.*

Black sea - *l-baʒr il-?aswad.*

blacksmith - *ʒaddaad* pl. *-iin.*

bladder - *maθaana* pl. *-aat.*

blade - *muus* pl. *mwaas, mwaasa; raas ʒaadd* pl. *ruus ʒaadda.* I need a knife with two blades. *?aʒtaaj siččiina ?umm raaseen.* -- These blades don't fit my razor. *hal-imwaas ma-yirhamuun Ɛala makiinat iz-ziyaan maalti.*

blame - **1.** *mas?uuliyya* pl. *-aat.* He took the blame for their mistake. *?axaδ mas?uuliyyat ğalṭathum Ɛala nafsa.* **2.** *loom.* Don't put the blame on me! *la-tδibb il-loom Ɛalayya.*

to blame - *laam (u loom) n-, bila (i balwa) n-.* Don't blame me. *la-tibliini ?ili.* -- Under these circumstances I could hardly blame her. *b-hal-ʒaala kulliš ṣaƐub ?agdar ?aluumha.* -- This child can't be blamed for anything. *haaδa ṭifil ma-yinlaam Ɛala šii.*

to be to blame for - *čaan muṣwič b-.* Who's to blame for the collision? *minu l-muṣwič bil-iṣṭidaam?*

blank - **1.** *stimaara* pl. *-aat.* Would you help me to fill out this blank form? *tigdar itsaaƐidni b-taris hal-istimaara?* **2.** *faraağ* pl. *-aat.* Fill in all blanks. *ʒašši kull il-faraağaat.* **3.** (m) *?abyaδ* (f) *beeδa* pl. *biiδ.* The envelope contained only a blank sheet of paper. *δ-δaruf ma-bii ğeer warqa beeδa.* **4.** *xaali.* Did you notice her blank expression? *laaʒaδit išloon wujihha xaali min kull taƐbiir?*

**My mind is a complete blank. *fikri waaguf tamaaman.*

blanket - **1.** *baṭṭaaniyya* pl. *-aat.* Take another blanket and you won't be cold any more. *?uxuδ baṭṭaaniyya lux w-baƐad ma-tubrad.* **2.** *šaamil.* He made a blanket statement which satisfied no one. *ṣarraʒ taṣriiʒ šaamil ma-raδδa ?aʒʒad.*

to blanket - *ğaṭṭa (i tğiṭṭi, tağṭiya).* A thick fog blanketed the airfield. *δubaab kaθiif ğaṭṭa l-maṭaar.*

blast - *nfijaar* pl. *-aat.* You can hear the blast for miles. *tigdar tismaƐ l-infijaar min biƐid ?amyaal.*

full blast - *leel-nahaar, b-kull ṭaaqa.* The plant is going full blast. *l-maƐmal da-yištuğul* *leel-nahaar.*

to blast - 1. *fajjar (i tfijjir, tafjiir) t-.* They're blasting a tunnel. *da-yfajjruun nafag.* 2. *nisaf (i nasif) n-.* The guerrillas blasted the bridge last night. *l-fidaaʔiyyin nisfaw ij-jisir il-baarza bil-leel.*

blaze - 1. *zariiq* pl. *zaraayiq.* The blaze destroyed a whole block. *l-zariiq dammar kull il-manṭiqa lli-been iš-šaarƐeen.* 2. *naar* pl. *niiraan.* Come and warm your hands over the blaze. *taƐaal w-daffi ʔiideek Ɛan-naar.*

to blaze (up) - *ltihab (i ltihaab).* Don't put kerosene in the brazier or the fire will blaze up. *la-tzuṭṭ nafuṭ bil-manqal tara n-naar tiltihib.*

blazing - *laafiz.* We had to stand for half an hour in the blazing sun. *ðṭarreena noogaf zawaali nuṣṣ saaƐa jawwa š-šams il-laafza.*

to **bleach - 1.** *kišaf (i kašif).* The wash is bleaching in the sun. *l-ihduum da-tikšif biš-šamis.*

to **bleed -** *nizaf (i nazif).* My nose is bleeding. *xašmi da-yinzif.*

to bleed to death - *maat (u moot) mnin-naziif.* He nearly bled to death. *maat imnin-naziif ʔilla šwayya.*

blend - *xabṭa* pl. *-aat, xaliiṭ, maziij.* I make the blend I smoke myself. *ʔaani ʔasawwi l-xabṭa l-adaxxinha b-iidi.*

to **bless -** *baarak (i mubaaraka) t-.* May God bless you! *baarak aḷḷaa fiik!*

blessing - *baraka* pl. *-aat, razma* pl. *-aat.* It was really a blessing that she came. *jayyatha čaanat fadd razma min ʔaḷḷa.* -- Go with my blessing! *ruuz bil-baraka.*

blew - see blow.

blind - 1. *qiim* pl. *-aat.* Shall I pull up the blinds? *ʔaṣaƐƐid il-qiimaat?* 2. (m) *ʔaƐmi* (f) *Ɛamya* pl. *Ɛimyaan, baṣiir* pl. *-iin.* This building is a home for the blind. *hal-binaaya hiyya daar lil-Ɛimyaan.* -- We helped the blind man across the street. *Ɛaawanna r-rijjaal il-ʔaƐmi zatta yuƐbur iš-šaariƐ.* 3. *ġaafil.* I'm not blind to her faults. *ʔaani muu ġaafil Ɛan ġalṭaatha.*

blind (in one eye) - (m) *ʔaƐwar* (f) *Ɛoora* pl. *Ɛuur.* He's been blind in one eye from birth. *čaan ʔaƐwar imnil-wilaada.*

to go blind - *Ɛima (a Ɛama).* I hope he's not going to go blind. *ʔatʔammal huwwa ma-yiƐma.*

to blind - *Ɛima (i Ɛami) n-.* The sun is blinding me. *š-šamis da-tiƐmiini.*

blind alley - *darbuuna* (pl. *daraabiin*) *ma-tiṭlaƐ.* I drove into a blind alley and had to back all the way out. *xaššeet ib-darbuuna ma-tiṭlaƐ w-iðṭarreet ʔarjaƐ baak.*

to **blink - 1.** *rimaš (i ramiš).* He blinked his eyes when I turned the light on. *rimaš Ɛeena min šiƐalt ið-ðuwa.* 2. *šiƐal w-ṭaffa (i-i).* Blink your lights to attract his attention. *ʔišƐil w-ṭaffi l-laayt maalak zatta tijlib intibaaha.*

blister - *buṭbaaṭa* pl. *-aat, buṭaabiiṭ.* He has a blister on his foot. *Ɛinda buṭbaaṭa b-rijla.*

blizzard - *Ɛaaṣifa* (pl. *Ɛawaaṣif*) *θaljiyya.* This is the worst blizzard we've had in ten years. *haaði ʔarzal Ɛaaṣifa θaljiyya marrat Ɛaleena b-xilaal Ɛašr isniin.*

bloc - *kutla* pl. *kutal.* There are a number of political blocs in Parliament. *ʔaku Ɛiddat kutal siyaasiyya bil-barlamaan.*

block - 1. *qiṭƐa* pl. *qiṭaƐ.* What do you plan to do with these blocks of wood? *š-raz-itsawwi b-hal-qiṭaƐ xišab?* 2. *mukaƐƐab* pl. *-aat.* Jamil, put your blocks away. *jamiil, ðumm il-mukaƐƐabaat maaltak.* 3. *šaariƐ* pl. *šawaariƐ.* Walk three blocks and then turn right. *ʔimši tlaθ šawaariƐ w-baƐdeen duur lil-yimna.*

**The fire destroyed the whole block. *l-zariiq dammar kull il-ibnaayaat been haš-šawaariƐ il-ʔarbaƐa.*

to block - 1. *sadd (i sadd) n-, qiṭaƐ (a qaṭiƐ) n-.* The road is blocked. *ṭ-ṭariiq masduud.* 2. *zaṭṭ (u) n- b-qaalab.* I'd like to have my old hat blocked. *ʔariid šafiqti l-Ɛatiiga tinzaṭṭ ib-qaalab.*

blond - (m) *ʔašgar* (f) *šagra* pl. *šugur.* She has blond hair. *Ɛidha šaƐar ʔašgar.*

blonde - *šagra* pl. *-aat.* Who's that good-looking blonde over there? *minu haðiič iš-šagra l-zilwa hnaak?*

blood - *damm* pl. *dmuum, dimaaʔ.* The doctor took a sample of my blood. *d-diktoor ʔaxað numuuðaj min dammi.* -- She fainted at the sight of all the blood on the floor. *xirbat min šaafat l-idmuum bil-gaaƐ.*

**Blood is thicker than water. *ʔaani w-ʔaxuuya Ɛala bin Ɛammi w-ʔaani w-bin Ɛammi Ɛala l-ġariib.*

in cold blood - *bala razma.* They were murdered in cold blood. *nqitlaw bala razma.*

**He shot them in cold blood. *rimaahum bir-riṣaaṣ wala Ɛinda bil-qeed.*

blood poisoning - *tasammum id-damm.*

blood pressure - *ðaġiṭ damm.* He has high blood pressure. *Ɛinda ðaġiṭ damm Ɛaali.*

blood shed - *ʔiraaqat id-dimaaʔ.* We must avoid bloodshed at all costs. *laazim nitjaada ʔiraaqat id-dimaaʔ ib-ʔay θaman.*

blood shot - *mizmarr.* His eyes are bloodshot from loss of sleep. *Ɛyuuna mizmarra min qillat in-noom.*

blood stain - *lakkat* (pl. *-aat*) *damm.* The bloodstains on my shirt will not come out. *lakkaat id-damm Ɛala θoobi ma-tiṭlaƐ.*

blood type - *nooƐ* (pl. *ʔanwaaƐ*) *damm.*

bloody - 1. *mdamma.* His handkerchief was all bloody. *čaffiita čaanat kullha mdammaaya.* 2. *damawi**.* Did you hear the rumors about the bloody battle between the tribes. *smaƐt il-ʔišaaƐaat Ɛan il-maƐraka d-damawiyya been il-Ɛašaayir.*

bloom - 1. *warda* pl. *-aat* coll. *warid.* She picked the choicest blooms in the garden for us. *guṭṭat-ilna ʔazsan warid il-bil-bistaan.* 2. *šarix* He died in the bloom of his youth. *maat ib-šarix šabaaba.*

in bloom - *mwarrad.* The apricot trees are now in bloom. *ʔašjaar il-mišmiš hassa mwarrda.*

to bloom - *warrad (i tawriid).* My roses didn't bloom well last year. *l-warid maali ma-warrad zeen is-sana l-faatat.*

blossom - 1. *warda* pl. *-aat* coll. *warid.* The blossoms are falling off the pomegranate bushes. *l-warid da-yoogaƐ min šajart ir-rummaan.* 2. *(citrus) qiddaaz.* The scent from the orange blossoms filled the whole garden. *riizt il-qiddaaz tirsat il-zadiiqa.*

to blossom - *warrad (i tawriid).* The carnations will start to blossom next week. *l-iqrinfil raz-yibdi ywarrid isbuuƐ ij-jaay.*

blot - *lakka* pl. *-aat.* The page is full of blots. *ṣ-ṣafza kullha lakkaat.*

to blot - *naššaf (i tanšiif) t-.* Blot the signature before you fold the letter. *naššif il-ʔimðaaʔ gabuḷ-ma tiṭwi l-maktuub.*

to blot out - *sadd (i sadd).* The trees blot out the view. *l-ʔašjaar itsidd il-manðar.*

to blot up - *naššaf (i tanšiif).* Blot up the ink with a blotter. *naššif il-zibir bin-niššeef.*

blotch - *ṭugƐa* pl. *ṭugaƐ.* What caused these red blotches on your face? *š-sabbab haṭ-ṭugaƐ il-zamra b-wiččak?*

blotter - *niššeefa* pl. *-aat* coll. *niššeef, niššaafa* pl. *-aat* coll. *niššaaf.* Quick, give me a blotter! *nṭiini niššeef bil-Ɛajal!*

blotting paper - *waraqa* (pl. *-aat*) *niššaaf* coll. *waraq niššaaf.* I'd like three sheets of blotting paper. *ʔariid itlaθ waraqaat niššaaf.*

blow - *ðarba* pl. *-aat.* That was a hard blow. *ðiič čaanat fadd ðarba qawiyya.* -- That blow struck home. *ðiič ið-ðarba jatti b-makaanha* or ***had-dagga ṣirbat bid-damaar.*

to blow - 1. *habb (i habb).* The wind is blowing from the North. *l-hawa da-yhibb imniš-šimaal.* 2. *gaḅḅ (u gaḅḅ).* Last night a severe sandstorm blew in on Baghdad. *l-baarza gaḅḅat Ɛajja qawiyya Ɛala baġdaad.* 3. *dagg (u dagg).* When do they blow taps? *šwakit ydugguun buuq in-noom?* 4. *dagg (u dagg), ṭawwaṭ (u ṭṭuwwuṭ) t-.* Blow the horn three times. *dugg il-hoorin itlaθ daggaat.* 5. *ṣoofar (i mṣoofra) t-.* The umpire blew his whistle three times. *l-zakam ṣoofar ib-ṣaafirta tlaθ marraat.* 6. *nufax (u nafux).* Blow on the coffee, if you want to cool it. *ʔunfux Ɛal-gahwa ʔiða triid itbarridha.*

to blow away - 1. *ṭaar (i).* The paper blew away. *l-warga ṭaarat.* 2. *ṭayyar (i ṭṭiyyir).* The wind blew the papers away. *l-hawa ṭayyar il-waraq.*

to blow one's nose - *muxaṭ (u maxiṭ).* I have to blow my nose. *laazim ʔamxuṭ.*

to blow out - 1. *ṭaffa (i taṭfiya).* Take a deep breath and blow out the candle. *ʔuxuð nafas ṭuwiil w-ṭaffi š-šamƐa.* 2. *ṭagg (u ṭagg).* The old tire blew out. *t-taayar il-Ɛatiig ṭagg.* 3. *fakk (u) bil-hawa.* Blow out the clogged tube. *fukk il-buuri* *l-masduud b-waaṣiṭṭ il-hawa.* **4.** *ḥirag (i ḥarig).* Be careful you don't blow out the fuse. *diir baalak la-tḥrig l-ifyuuz.*

to blow over - 1. *hida (a hiduuʔ).* The storm will blow over soon. *l-ʕaaṣifa raḥ-tihda baʕad išwayya.* **2.** *burad (a).* Her anger will soon blow over. *ġaḍabha raḥ-yibrad baʕad išwayya.*

to blow up - 1. *nfijar (i nfijaar).* The powder plant blew up. *maʕmal il-baaruud infijar.* **2.** *nisaf (i nasif).* The enemy blew up all the bridges. *l-ʕadu nisaf kull ij-jisuur.* **3.** *nufax (u nafux).* Blow up the balloons for the children. *ʔinfux in-nuffaaxaat lij-jihhaal.*

blowout - *p̣ančar* pl. *p̣anaačir.* We had a blowout on the way home. *b-ṭariiqna lil-beet ṣaar ʕidna p̣ančar.*

blue - 1. (m) *ʔazrag* (f) *zarga* pl. *zurug.* She has beautiful blue eyes. *ʕidha ʕyuun zurug ḥilwa.* **2.** *maqhuur.* She looks blue this morning. *ybayyin ʕaleeha maqhuura hwaaya l-yoom.*

**He arrived out of the blue. *nizal ʕaleena mnis-sima.*

to get the blues - *nqubaḍ (u nqibaaḍ).* I get the blues when it rains. *ʔanqubuḍ min timṭur* or *nafsi tinqubuḍ min timṭur.*

to turn blue - *zragg (a).* Your face has turned blue with cold. *wiččak izragg imnil-barid.*

blueing - *čuwiit.*

blueness - *zaraag.*

blue print - *xariiṭa* pl. *xaraayiṭ, taṣmiim* pl. *taṣaamiim.* Show him how to read the blueprint. *raawii šloon yiqra l-xariiṭa.*

bluff - 1. *juruf ʕaali* pl. *jruuf ʕaalya.* He's building his house on a bluff overlooking the river. *da-yibni beeta ʕala juruf ʕaali yṭill ʕaš-šaṭṭ.* **2.** *qašmara, balfa* pl. *-aat.* That's only a bluff. *haaδi muu ʔakθar min fadd balfa.*

to bluff - 1. *qašmar (u qašmara) t-.* He's only bluffing. *haaδa da-yqašmur.* **2.** *bilaf (i balif) n-.* When he took another card, I knew he was bluffing. *min ʔaxaδ warqat il-lux ʕirafit da-yiblif.*

**If I were you, I'd have called his bluff. *loo čint ib-makaanak, čaan xalleeta yikšif liʕibta.*

blunder - *ġalṭa* pl. *-aat.* I made an awful blunder. *ʔaani sawweet fadd ġalṭa faḍiiʕa.*

blunt - (m) *ʔaʕmi* (f) *ʕamya.* This knife is too blunt. *has-siččiina kulliš ʕamya.*

**Said is awfully blunt. *saʕiid yṭugg il-iḥčaaya ib-wučč il-waaḥid.*

bluntly - **He told me the truth very bluntly. *ṭagg il-ḥaqiiqa b-wučči.*

to **blush -** *ḥmarr (a ḥmiraar).* She blushes easily. *hiyya tiḥmarr bil-ʕajal.*

board - 1. *looḥa* pl. *-aat, lwaaḥ* coll. *looḥ.* We need some large boards. *niḥtaaj čam looḥa čbiira.* -- Write it on the board. *kitba ʕal-looḥa.* **2.** *ʔakil.* My board costs me more than my room. *ʔakli ykallifni ʔazyad min ʔiijaari.*

on board (ship) - *bil-markab.* There was a famous actress on board ship with us. *čaan ʔaku mumaθθila mašhuura bil-markab wiyyaana.*

on board (train) - *bil-qiṭaar.* Is everybody on board the train? *l-kull rikbaw bil-qiṭaar?*

room and board - *ġurfa maʕa ʔakil.* How much do you pay for room and board? *šgadd tidfaʕ ʕann il-ġurfa maʕa l-ʔakil?*

to board - 1. *ʔakal (u) b-ifluus.* I would like to arrange to board with an Iraqi family. *ʔariid ʔasawwi tartiib wiyya ʕaaʔila ʕiraaqiyya ḥatta ʔaakul ʕidhum b-ifluus.* **2.** *rikab (u rukub) n-.* We boarded the train in Washington. *rikabna l-qiṭaar ib-waašinṭin.*

boarder - **Do you take in boarders? *ʕidkum tartiib in-naas yaakluun ib-beetkum b-ifluus?*

board of health - *daaʔirt iṣ-ṣiḥḥa.*

to **boast - 1.** *tbajjaḥ (a tabajjuḥ).* Stop boasting! *ma-yeezi titbajjaḥ!* **2.** *tbaaha (a tabaahi).* He is always boasting about how much influence his family has. *ʕala ṭuul yitbaaha b-nufuuδ ʕaaʔilta.*

boat - 1. *balam* pl. *blaam.* We went fishing in his boat. *riḥna nṣiid simač bil-balam maala.* **2.** *markab* pl. *maraakub, baaxira* pl. *bawaaxir.* This boat goes to Australia. *hal-markab yruuḥ il-ʔusturaalya.*

**We're all in the same boat. *kullna fil-hawa sawa.*

bobby pin - *firkeeta* pl. *-aat, maaša* (pl. *-aat*) *maal šaʕir.*

body - 1. *jisim* pl. *ʔajsaam, jasad* pl. *ʔajsaad.* He has a rash on his body. *ʕinda šira b-jisma.* -- There are solid, liquid, and gaseous bodies. *ʔaku ʔajsaam ṣalba, w-saaʔla w-ġaaziyya.* **2.** *lašša* pl. *-aat, jiθθa* pl. *jiθaθ.* The body of the dog is still lying in the middle of the road. *laššt ič-čalib baʕadha maδbuuba b-nuṣṣ iš-šaariʕ.* -- The body was cremated. *j-jiθθa nḥirgat.*

**They barely manage to keep body and soul together. *ma-ʕidhum ʕaša leela.*

in a body - *b-jooga, b-jamaaʕa.* They left the hall in a body. *ṭilʕaw imnil-qaaʕa b-joogathum.*

bodyguard - *ḥaaris* pl. *ḥurraas.*

to **bog down - 1.** *ṭumas (u ṭamuṣ) n-.* The car bogged down in the mud. *s-sayyaara ṭumṣat biṭ-ṭiin.* **2.** *ṭammas (u ṭṭummus) t-.* This illness bogged me down financially. *hal-maraḍ ṭammasni bid-deen.*

boil - 1. *dimbila* pl. *dnaabil.* He has a boil on his neck. *ʕinda dimbila b-rugubta.* **2.** (Baghdad boil). *ʔuxut* pl. *xawaat.* That round scar on his face is a Baghdad boil. *han-nadba l-imdawwra b-wučča ʔuxut.*

to boil - 1. *faar (u fawaraan), ġila (i ġalayaan) n-.* The water is boiling. *l-ṃaay da-yfuur.* **2.** *fawwar (u tafwiir, tfuwwur) t-.* Boil the water before you give it to the baby. *fawwr il-ṃaay gaḅuḷ-ma tinṭii lij-jaahil.* -- Boil the vegetables in salted water. *fawwr il-xuḍrawaat ib-ṃaay w-miliḥ.* **3.** *silag (i salig) n-.* Please boil the eggs two minutes. *baḷḷa ʔislig il-beeḍ daqiiqteen.*

to boil with rage - *gila mnil-ġaḍab.* He was boiling with rage. *čaan da-yigli mnil-ġaḍab* or ***čaan ṣaayir naar.*

boiler - *booylar* pl. *-aat, qazaan* pl. *-aat.* The boiler exploded. *ṭagg il-booylar.*

bold - *jasir* pl. *-iin, jariʔ* pl. *-iin.* That was a bold statement. *haaδa taṣriiḥ jariʔ.*

bolt - 1. *burgi* pl. *baraaġi.* This nut doesn't fit the bolt. *haṣ-ṣammuuna ma-tirham ʕal-burġi.* **2.** *ṭool* pl. *twaal.* There are only ten yards of material left in this bolt. *buqat bass ʕašir yardaat iqmaaš ib-haṭ-ṭool.* **3.** *lisaan* pl. *-aat, lisin; ṣiqqaaṭa* pl. *-aat.* Did you push the bolt shut? *saddeet il-lisaan.* **4.** *ṣaaʕiqa* pl. *ṣawaaʕiq.* The news came like a bolt from the blue. *δiič il-ʔaxbaar nizlat miθl iṣ-ṣaaʕiqa.*

to bolt - 1. *ḥaṭṭ (u) ṣiqqaaṭa b-.* You forgot to bolt the garage door. *ʔinta niseet itḥuṭṭ iṣ-ṣiqqaaṭa b-baab il-garaaj.* **2.** *šadd (i šadd), rakkab (i).* Bolt the plate onto the work bench. *šidd ir-raaṣṭa ʕat-tizgaa.* **3.** *jimaḥ (a jmuuḥ).* Suddenly the horse shied and bolted. *ʕala ġafḷa jifal l-iḥṣaan w-jimaḥ.*

bomb - *qumbula* pl. *qanaabil, ḅamḅa* pl. *-aat.* The whole district has been destroyed by bombs. *l-manṭiqa kullha čaanat imdammra bil-qanaabil.*

to bomb - *qiṣaf (u qaṣuf) n-.* The planes bombed the factory again during the night. *ṭ-ṭiyyaaraat quṣfat il-maʕmal marra lux bil-leel.*

bomber - *qaaṣifa* pl. *-aat.* The Air Force is using a new type of long-range bomber. *l-quwwa j-jawwiyya da-tistaʕmil nooʕ jidiid imnil-qaaṣifaat biʕiidt il-madad.*

bond - 1. *sanad* pl. *-aat.* He invested all his money in stocks and bonds. *kull ifluusa šaġġalha bil-ʔashum wis-sanadaat.* **2.** *raabiṭa* pl. *rawaabuṭ.* There's a firm bond between the two friends. *ʔaku fadd raabiṭa qawiyya been iṣ-ṣadiiqeen.*

bone - *ʕaḍma* pl. *-aat, ʕaḍum* pl. *ʕḍaam.* Give the dog a bone. *nṭii lič-čalib fadd ʕaḍma.* -- He's nothing but skin and bones. *huwwa bass jild w-ʕaḍum.* -- This fish has an awful lot of bones. *has-simča malyaana ʕḍaam.*

**He made no bones about his intentions. *huwwa ma-ḥaawal ysawwi šii jawwa l-ʕabaa.*

**I feel chilled to the bone. *da-aḥiss jimdat iʕḍaami.*

bonfire - *naar* pl. *niiraan.*

bonnet - *klaaw* pl. *-aat.*

bonus - *ʕlaawa* pl. *-aat, minḥa* pl. *minaḥ.* The employees here get a bonus at the end of each year. *l-mustaxdamiin ihnaa yaaxδuun iʕlaawa b-nihaayat kull sana.*

book - *ktaab* pl. *kutub.* Did you like the book? *ʕijabak l-iktaab?*

bookbindery - *maḥall* (pl. *-aat*) *tajliid il-kutub.*

bookcase - *diilaab* pl. *dwaaliib, maktaba* pl. *-aat.* Close the bookcase. *sidd id-diilaab maal il-kutub* or *sidd baab il-maktaba.*

book end - *sannaada* (pl. *-aat*) *maal kutub.*

bookkeeper - *muḥaasib* pl. *-iin.*

bookkeeping - *muḥaasaba, masik dafaatir.*

booklet - *kurraasa* pl. *-aat.*
bookstore - *maktaba* pl. *-aat.* Were you in this bookstore? *ʔinta xaašš ib-hal-maktaba?*
boom - **1.** *dawya* pl. *-aat.* You can hear the boom of the cannon. *tigdar tismaε dawyat il-madfaε.* **2.** *wakt in-niεma, wakt il-xeer.* He made all his money in the boom during the war. *ħaṣṣal kull ifluusa b-wakt in-niεma ʔaθnaaʔ il-ħarub.* -- How do you explain this sudden boom? *šloon itfassir hal-xeer iṣ-ṣaar εala ġafla?*
 to boom - **1.** *laεlaε (i laεlaεa), duwa (i dawi).* He has a booming voice. *εinda ṣoot ylaεliε.* **2.** *raaj (u rawaaj), zdihar (i zdihaar).* Our business is booming now. *šuġulna hassa raayij.*
to **boost** - *ṣaεεad (i taṣεiid) t-.* The drought has boosted the prices of wheat. *qillat il-muṭar ṣaεεidat ʔasεaar il-ħunṭa.*
boot - **1.** *juzma* pl. *juzam.* When I go fishing I wear high boots. *lamma aruuħ iṣ-ṣeed is-simač ʔalbas juzma.* **2.** *puṣṭaal* pl. *paṣaaṭiil.* Soldiers wear black boots. *j-jinuud yilbasuun paṣaaṭiil suud.*
 to boot - *cmaala, εlaawa.* He paid me for my work and gave me five dinars to boot. *difaε-li ħaqqi w-inṭaani xams idnaaniir ičmaala.*
 to boot - *čallaq (i tačliiq) t-.* They booted him out of the coffee house. *čalliqoo mnil-gahwa.*
bootblack - *ṣabbaaġ* (pl. *ṣabaabiiġ*) *qanaadir.*
booth - **1.** *maħall* pl. *-aat.* There were many display booths at the fair. *čaan aku hwaaya maħallaat εariδ̣ bil-maεraδ̣.* **2.** *maqṣuura* pl. *-aat.* I'm calling from a phone booth. *da-axaabur min maqṣuurat talafoon.*
border - **1.** *ħiduud* (pl.). When do we reach the border? *šwakit nooṣal lil-ħiduud?* **2.** *ħaašya* pl. *ħawaaši.* The border of this rug is getting worn. *ħaašyat haz-zuuliyya saayfa.*
 to be bordered by - *nħadd (a), (čaan) maħduud b-.* Holland is bordered on the south by Belgium. *hoolanda maħduuda mnij-jinuub ib-baljiika.*
 to border on - *kaad (a) yooṣal l-.* That borders on the ridiculous. *haaδa ykaad yooṣal il-darajt is-saxaafa.*
border line - **1.** *ħiduud.* The border line of my property is marked by a row of trees. *ħiduud mulki mεayyan ib-qaṭar ʔašjaar.* **2.** *bayna bayn.* That is a border line case. *hal-qaδ̣iyya bayna bayn.*
to **bore** - **1.** *ziraf (u zuruf) n-.* We'll have to bore a hole through the wall. *ʔiħna laazim nizruf zuruf bil-ħaayiṭ.* **2.** *δ̣awwaj (i tδ̣uwwuj, taδ̣wiij) t-.* His speech bored me. *l-ħadiiθ maala δ̣awwajni.*
to be **bored** - *mall (i malal) n-, δ̣aaj (u δ̣ooj, δ̣awajaan).* I'm bored of always seeing the same faces. *malleet min šoofat nafs il-wujuuh.*
boredom - *δ̣uwaaja.* I almost died of boredom. *mitit imniδ̣-δ̣uwaaja ʔilla šwayya.*
boric acid - *ħaamiδ̣ il-booriik.*
to be **born** - *nwilad (i), jaa (i jayya) lid-dinya, mawluud.* Where were you born? *ʔinta ween inwiladit?* -- She was born blind. *jatti lid-dinya εamya.* -- My grandfather was born in Basra. *ʔabu jiddi nwilad bil-baṣra.*
to **borrow** - *tdaayan (a), ṭilab (u ṭalab).* She borrowed the book from him. *ṭulbat minna l-iktaab.*
bosom - *ṣadir* pl. *ṣduur.*
 **They are bosom pals. *δoola ʔaṣdiqaaʔ ṭoox.*
boss - **1.** *raʔiis* pl. *ruʔasaaʔ.* Do you know my boss? *tuεruf ir-raʔiis maali?* **2.** *l-kull bil-kull.* Talk to his wife, she's the boss. *ʔiħči wiyya marta hiyya l-kull bil-kull.*
 **Who wouldn't want to be his own boss? *minu ma-yriid yṣiir malik nafsa?*
 to boss (around) - *tʔammar (a taʔammur).* Who gave him the right to boss me around? *minu nṭaa sulṭa yitʔammar εalayya?*
to **botch up** - *xarbaṭ (u xarbaṭa) t-.* Your workman botched the job up and you'll have to repair it. *ṣaanεak xarbaṭ iš-šaġla w-inta laazim itṣalliħha.*
both - *θ-θineen.* Both brothers are in the navy. *l-ʔuxwa θ-θineen bil-baħriyya.* -- We both visited him. *ʔiħna θneenna zirnaa.* -- I like to do both equally well. *yiεjibni ʔasawwi θ-θineen ib-duun tafδ̣iil.*
bother - **1.** *kuluufa* pl. *-aat.* It's no bother at all. I'm always at your service. *ma-aku ʔay kuluufa, ʔaani daaʔiman bil-xidma.* **2.** *dooxat raas.* Getting ready for the holiday is a big bother. *l-istiεdaad lil-εiid dooxat raas čibiira.* -- His constant questions are getting to be a bother. *ʔasʔilta l-mitkarrira ṣaarat dooxat raas.* **3.** *maġaθθa.* This job is all bother and strain with no profit in it. *haš-šaġla ma-biiha ġeer il-maġaθθa w-šilεaan il-galub w-maa min waraaha faaʔida.* **4.** *ʔizεaaj.* Pardon the bother, but I have to see you. *ʔarju l-maεδira εan ʔizεaajak, laakin laazim ʔašuufak.*
 to bother - **1.** *ziεaj (i ʔizεaaj) n-.* Please don't bother me! *ʔarjuuk la-tizεijni.* -- Does my cigarette smoke bother you? *d-duxxaan maal jigaarti da-yziεjak?* -- Does the cough bother you much? *l-gaħħa da-tziεjak ihwaaya?* **2.** *dawwax (u tduwwux, tadwiix) t- raas.* I really hate to bother you. *ʔaani bil-ħaqiiqa ma-ard adawwux raasak.* -- I can't bother with that. *ma-agdar adawwux raasi b-δiič.* **3.** *ġaθθ (u ġaθθ) n-.* What's bothering you? *šinu l-ġaaθθak?* or *ʔinta min eeš maġθuuθ?* or *š-da-yġuθθak?* **4.** *ʔannab (i taʔniib), εaδδab (i taεδiib).* His conscience bothered him. *δ̣amiira ʔannaba.*
 to bother oneself - *tkallaf (a takalluf).* Please don't bother yourself on my account. *ʔarjuuk la-titkallaf εala muudi.*
bottle - *buṭil* pl. *bṭuula, šiiša* pl. *šiyaš.* Shall I get a few bottles of beer? *tirduun ʔajiib čam buṭil biira?* -- I'd like a bottle of ink. *ʔariid šiišat ħibir.*
bottle neck - **1.** *εaqaba* pl. *-aat.* The only bottle neck on Rashid Street is the Mirjan mosque. *l-εaqaba l-waħiida b-saariε ir-rašiid hiyya jaamiε mirjaan.* **2.** *εarqala* pl. *εaraaqiil.* The main bottle neck in the Post Office is the sorting section *l-εarqala r-raʔiisiyya b-daaʔirt il-bariid, šuεbat it-tafriiq.*
bottom - **1.** *čaεab* pl. *čεuub.* He found it at the bottom of the trunk. *ligaa b-čaεb iṣ-ṣanduug.* -- Bottoms up! - *čaεb ʔabyaδ̣!* **2.** *ʔasaas* pl. *ʔusus.* We have to get to the bottom of this affair. *ʔiħna laazim nuεruf ʔasaas hal-qaδ̣iyya.* **3.** *ʔaεmaaq.* I thank you from the bottom of my heart. *ʔaškurak min ʔaεmaaq galbi.* **4.** *jawwaani*.* Your shirts are in the bottom drawer. *θyaabak bil-imjarr il-jawwaani.*
 from top to bottom - **1.** *min foog li-jawwa.* They searched the house from top to bottom. *dawwraw il-beet min foog li-jawwa.* **2.** *mnir-raas lič-čaεab.* The policeman searched me from top to bottom. *š-šurṭi fattašni mnir-raas lič-čaεab.*
 to reach rock bottom - *wuṣal (a) il-ʔasfal darak.* We've reached rock bottom! Things can't get worse. *wṣalna l-ʔasfal darak! l-ħaala ma-mumkin itṣiir ʔatεas.*
 to touch bottom - *gayyaš (i geeš).* Can you touch bottom here? *tigdar itgayyiš ihnaa.* -- The boat has touched bottom. *l-balam gayyaš.*
to **bounce** - **1.** *gumaz (u gamuz).* This ball doesn't bounce. *haṭ-ṭooba ma-tugmuz.* **2.** *gammaz (u tagmiiz, tgummuz) t-.* He bounced the ball. *huwwa gammaz iṭ-ṭooba.*
 to get (or be) bounced - *nṭirad (i).* He was bounced yesterday. *nṭirad il-baarħa.*
bound - **1.** *mčattaf.* We found the man bound with a sheet. *liqeena r-rijjaal imčattaf ib-čarčaf.* **2.** *mjallad.* I bought a book bound in red leather. *štireet iktaab imjallad ib-jilid ʔaħmar.* **3.** *mirtibiṭ.* I am bound by contract to finish this building in two months. *ʔaani mirtibiṭ ib-εaqid ʔaxalliṣ hal-ibnaaya b-šahreen.*
 to be bound (for) - *twajjah (i) ʔila.* That boat is bound for America. *hal-markab mitwajjih ʔila ʔamriika.*
 **She's bound to be late. *tara raħ-titʔaxxar min kull budd.*
 **It was bound to happen sooner or later. *haaδa ʔawwal w-taali ma-čaan minna mafarr.*
boundary - *ħadd* pl. *ħiduud.* There is no boundary separating his property and mine. *ma-aku ħadd faaṣil been mulka w-mulki.*
to be **bounded by** - *(čaan) maħduud b-.* Germany is bounded on the south by Switzerland. *ʔalmaanya maħduuda mnij-jinuub b-iswiisra.*
boundless - *ma-la ħadd.* He has boundless self-confidence. *θiqta b-nafsa ma-lha ħadd.*
bounds - *ħadd* pl. *ħiduud.* His greed knows no bounds. *ṭamaεa ma-la ħadd.*
 out of bounds - **1.** *foog ħadd.* The price he is asking is way out of bounds. *s-siεr il-da-yṭulba foog kull ħadd.* **2.** *ʔaawt.* The ball went out of bounds. *ṭ-ṭooba ṭilεat aawt.*
 within the bounds - *δ̣imin ħiduud.* I don't care what you do so long as you stay within the bounds of decency. *ma-adiir baal iš-ma-tsawwi ṭuul-ma*

tibqa ðimin zįduud in-nazaaha.

bouquet - *šadda* pl. *-aat*, *baaga* pl. *-aat*. Where did you get that beautiful bouquet of roses? *mneel-lak haš-šaddat il-warid il-zilwa?*

bow - **1.** *ṣadir* pl. *ṣduur*. I like to stand at the bow of the ship. *yiĉjibni ʔoogaf ib-ṣadr il-markab.* **2.** *zanya* pl. *-aat*. He greeted me with a polite bow of the head. *zayyaani b-zanyat raas muʔaddaba.*

to bow - **1.** *nzina (i)*. He bowed and left the stage. *nzina w-tirak il-masraz.* **2.** *zina (i zani) n-*. He bowed his head in shame. *zina raasa mnil-xajal.* **3.** *xiðaĉ (a xuðuuĉ)*. He bowed to his father's wishes. *xiðaĉ il-raġbat abuu.*

bow - **1.** *qaws* pl. *ʔaqwaas*, *gooz* pl. *gwaaza*. Boys like to play with bows and arrows. *l-wilid yzibbuun yliĉbuun bil-gooz win-niššaab.* **2.** *qurdeela* pl. *-aat*. She had a pretty bow in her hair. *čaanat laabsa qurdeela zilwa b-šaĉarha.* **3.** *qaws* pl. *ʔaqwaas*. The violinist is tightening the strings of his bow. *l-kamanjaati da-yðubb ixyuuṭ il-qaws maala.* **4.** *ĉawaaj* pl. *-aat*. This pole has a bow in it. Find me a straight one. *hal-ĉamuud bii ĉawaaj. ʔilqii-li waazid ĉadil.* **5.** *yadda* pl. *-aat*. Can you adjust the bows of my glasses? *tiqdar itĉaddil-li yaddaat manðarti?*

bowl - *minčaasa* pl. *-aat*, *manaačiis*, *ṭaasa* pl. *-aat*. Put these apples into a bowl. *zuṭṭ hat-tiffaazaat ib-fadd minčaasa.*

to bowl over - *ṣiĉaq (a) n-*. I was bowled over when I heard the news. *nṣiĉaqit min simiĉt il-xabar.*

bowlegged - (m) *ʔaĉwaj* (f) *ĉooja* pl. *ĉuuj; mqawwas*. He's bowlegged. *rijla ĉooja* or *rijla mqawwsa.*

bow tie - *warda* pl. *-aat*. Teach me how to tie a bow tie. *ĉallimni šloon ašidd warda.*

box - **1.** *ṣanduug* pl. *ṣnaadiig*, *quuṭiyya* pl. *qwaaṭi*. Shall I put the shoes in a box? *ʔazuṭṭ il-qundira b-quuṭiyya?* -- I have another box of cigars. *ĉindi quuṭiyya lux ičruud.* -- Would you drop this letter in the box for me? *tigdar itðibb-li hal-maktuub ib-ṣanduug il-bariid?* **2.** *looj* pl. *-aat*, *lwaaj*, *maqṣuura* pl. *-aat*. All boxes are sold out for the play. *kull il-loojaat maal ir-ruwaaya mabyuuĉa.*

to box - *laakam (i mulaakama)*, *tlaakam (a talaakum)*. Would you like to box? *tzibb titlaakam?*

boxer - **1.** *mulaakim* pl. *-iin*. He has become a famous boxer. *ṣaar mulaakim šahiir.* **2.** *čalib* (pl. *člaab*) *booksar*. My brother brought back a boxer from England. *ʔaxuuya jaab wiyyaa čalib booksar min ʔingiltara.*

box office - *mazall* (pl. *-aat*) *biṭaaqaat*. The box office is open from ten to four. *mazall il-biṭaaqaat maftuuz imnil-ĉašra lil-ʔarbaĉa.*

boy - **1.** *walad* pl. *wulid*. This boy is Ali's son. *hal-walad ibin ĉali.* **2.** *ṣaaniĉ* pl. *ṣinnaaĉ*. I'll have the boy deliver them. *raz-axalli ṣ-ṣaaniĉ yjiib-ilkum-iyyaahum.*

**Boy, what a night! *yaa yaaba šloon leela!*

boycott - *muqaaṭaĉa* pl. *-aat*. The boycott was lifted. *nšaalat il-muqaaṭaĉa.*

to boycott - *qaaṭaĉ (i muqaaṭaĉa) t-*. We should boycott foreign products. *laazim inqaaṭiĉ il-maṣnuuĉaat il-ʔajnabiyya.*

boy scout - *kaššaaf* pl. *kaššaafa*. They have asked the Boy Scouts to take part in the parade. *ṭilbaw imnil-kaššaafa yištarkuun bil-istiĉraað.*

boy's school - *madrasa* (pl. *madaaris*) *maal wulid*. That's a boy's school. *haðiič madrasa maal wulid.*

brace - **1.** *mašadd* pl. *-aat*. He's still wearing a brace on his left leg. *huwwa baĉda laabis mašadd ĉala rijla l-yisra.* **2.** *masnad* pl. *masaanid*. This chair needs four braces to hold it firm. *ʔhal-kursi yinraad-la ʔarbaĉ masaanid itlizma.* **3.** *mizraf* pl. *mazaaruf*, *bariina* pl. *baraayin*. Get a brace and bit and drill the holes in this board where I have marked. *jiib mizraf w-sawwi zruuf ib-hal-looza bil-makaanaat il-ʔaššaritha.*

to brace - *qawwa (i taqwiya)*. Brace the corners with wooden cross-pieces. *qawwi z-zuwaaya b-xišbaat ĉurðaaniyya.*

to brace oneself - **1.** *tzaððar (a tazaðður)*. Brace yourself, here they come. *tzaððar, tara ʔijaw.* **2.** *ðabb (i ðabb) n- nafs~*. They both braced themselves against the door and didn't let anyone in. *θneenhum ðabbaw nafishum wara l-baab w-ma-xallaw ʔazzad yxušš.*

to brace oneself up - *našnaš (i) t-*. I need a shot to brace me up. *ʔariid-li fadd peek zatta ʔanašniš.*

**Brace up! *šidd zeelak!* or *tšajjaĉ!*

to be **braced** - *nsinad (i)*. The wall will need to be braced in two places. *l-zaayiṭ yinraad-la yinsinid ib-mukaaneen.*

bracelet - *swaar* pl. *-aat*. I've lost my bracelet. *ðayyaĉt iswaari.*

bracket - **1.** *ĉikis* pl. *ĉkuus*. One of the brackets for the shelf has come loose. *waazid min iĉkuus ir-raff mašluuĉ.* **2.** *qaws* pl. *ʔaqwaas*. Put the foreign words in brackets. *zuṭṭ il-kalimaat il-ʔajnabiyya been qawseen.* **3.** *fiʔa* pl. *-aat*. My last raise put me in a higher income-tax bracket. *tarfiiĉi l-ʔaxiir zaṭṭni b-fiʔa maal ðariibt id-daxal ʔaĉla.*

to **brag** - **1.** *tbajjaz (a tabajjuz)*. Does he always brag that way? *huwwa daaʔiman yitbajjaz haš-šikil?* **2.** *tbaaha (a tabaahi)*. Don't brag so much about your ancestors. *la-titbaaha hal-gadd ib-ʔajdaadak.*

braid - **1.** *gṣiiba* pl. *giṣaayib*, *ðufiira* pl. *ðufaayir*. I admire her thick braids. *ʔaani muĉjab ib-giṣaayibha l-mitiina.* **2.** *šariiṭ* pl. *šaraayiṭ*. The doorman was wearing a uniform ornamented with gold braid. *l-bawwaab čaan laabis badla mzarkaša b-šaraayiṭ ðahab.*

to braid - *ðufar (u ðafur) n-*. Her mother braids her hair for her. *ʔummha tuðfur-ilha šaĉarha.*

brain - *muxx* pl. *mxaax*, *damaaġ* pl. *ʔadmiġa*. The bullet penetrated his brain. *r-riṣaaṣa xaššat ib-damaaġa.* -- He hasn't a brain in his head. *ma-ĉinda muxx* or *haaða muxx sizz.*

to rack one's brain - *šaġġal (i tašġiil) fikr~*, *dawwax (u tadwiix) raas~*. There's no use racking your brains over it. *ma-zaaja tšaġġil fikrak ihwaaya biiha.*

to brain - *kisar (i kasir) n- raas*. If you do that again I'll brain you. *ʔaksir raasak ʔiða tsawwiiha marra lux.*

brake - *breek* pl. *-aat*. The brake doesn't work. *l-ibreek ma-yištuġul.*

to put on the brakes - *lizam (a) breek*. I tried to put on the brakes, but I didn't make it. *ʔaani zaawalit ʔalzam ibreek laakin ma-lazzagit.*

branch - **1.** *ġuṣin* pl. *ġṣuun*, *ʔaġṣaan*. The wind broke off several branches. *l-hawa kisar čam ġuṣin.* **2.** *fariĉ* pl. *fruuĉ*. Our firm has a branch in Mosul. *šarikatna ĉidha fariĉ bil- mooṣil.* -- The bank has two branches in town. *l-bang ĉinda farĉeen bil-wlaaya.*

to branch - *tfarraĉ (a tafarruĉ)*. The road branches off here. *ṭ-ṭariiq yitfarraĉ ihnaa.*

brand - **1.** *maarka* pl. *-aat*. What brand of cigarettes do you smoke? *ʔay maarkat jigaayir ʔinta tdaxxin?* **2.** *nooĉ* pl. *ʔanwaaĉ*, *ṣinif* pl. *ʔaṣnaaf*. We carry all the best brands of tea. *ĉidna kull il-ʔaṣnaaf iz-zeena mnič-čaay.* **3.** *damġa* pl. *-aat*, *ṭamġa* pl. *-aat*, *waṣum* pl. *wṣaam*. We recognized our cattle from the brand mark. *ĉirafna baqarna mniṭ-ṭamġa.*

to brand - **1.** *wuṣam (i waṣum) n-*. He was branded as a traitor. *nwuṣam bij-jaasuusiyya.* **2.** *dumaġ (u damuġ) n-*, *tumaġ (u tumuġ) n-*. Have they finished branding the new horses yet? *xallṣaw ydamġuun l-izṣuuna j-jidiida loo baĉad?*

brand-new - *bil-kaaġad*. It's still brand-new. *baĉda bil-kaaġad.*

brandy - *braandi*.

brass - **1.** *prinj* (for castings). The mortar is cast from brass. *l-haawan maṣbuub min iprinj.* **2.** *ṣifir*. Some of our kitchen pans are of sheet brass. *qisim min ij-jiduur ib-muṭbaxna min ṣifir.* **3.** *ð-ðubbaaṭ*. All the high brass were present. *kaaffat kibaar ið-ðubbaaṭ čaanaw zaaðriin.*

brassiere - *zixma* pl. *zixam*.

brat - *malĉuun* pl. *malaaĉiin*. He's a nasty brat. *haaða fadd malĉuun zafir.*

brave - *šujaaĉ* pl. *šujĉaan*. The brave die but one death. *š-šujĉaan ymuutuun moota wizda.*

bravery - *šajaaĉa*.

brawl - *ĉarka* pl. *-aat*. Those two taxi-drivers started the brawl. *has-suwwaaq it-taaksi l-iθneen bidaw il-ĉarka.*

to brawl - *tĉaarak (a ĉraak)*. Those people were always brawling and disturbing the whole neighborhood. *haðoola čaanaw daaʔiman yitĉaarkuun w-yizĉijuun kull il-imzalla.* -- That man and his wife are always brawling with each other. *har-rijjaal w-marta daaʔiman yitĉaarkuun waazid wiyya l-laax.*

bread - **1.** *xubza* pl. *-aat* coll. *xubuz*. Our baker makes the best bread in town. *xabbaazna ysawwi ʔazsan xubuz bil-wlaaya.* **2.** (Flat rounds of bread) *gurṣa* pl. *guraṣ*. Give me six loaves of Arab flat bread. *nṭiini sitt guraṣ.* **3.** (Small raised loaves) *ṣammuuna* pl. *-aat* coll. *ṣammuun.* May I have another half bread roll, please. *ʔarjuuk inṭiini nuṣṣ ṣammuuna ɛwaaẓa.* -- Divide the bread into four pieces. *qassim iṣ-ṣammuuna ʔila ʔarbaɛ wuṣal.* -- You had better buy three extra bread rolls for dinner tonight. *laazim tištiri tlaθ ṣammuunaat lil-ɛaša hal-leela.*

breadth - *ɛuruḍ, ttisaaɛ.*

break - **1.** *kasir* pl. *ksuur.* They are trying to find the break in the water main. *da-yẓaawluun yilguun il-kasir bil-ʔabbi.* **2.** *nqiṭaaɛ* pl. *-aat.* A break in relations between the two countries can no longer be avoided. *nqiṭaaɛ il-ɛalaaqaat been il-baladeen la-budd minna.* **3.** *faṭir* pl. *fṭuur.* Germs enter the body through a break in the skin. *l-mikroobaat itxušš ib-jismak min faṭir bij-jilid.* **4.** *raaẓa* pl. *-aat.* Take a short break before you start the next job. *ʔuxuḍ-lak fadd raaẓa qṣayyra gabuḷ-ma tbaašir ib-waḍiiftak ij-jidiida.* -- Whenever they want a break, give it to them. *kull-ma yriiduun raaẓa ʔinṭiihum-iyyaa.* **5.** *furṣa* pl. *furaṣ.* We have an hour break for lunch. *ɛidna furṣa saaɛa wiẓda lil-ġada.* **6.** *ẓaḍḍ.* He's had a lot of bad breaks in his life. *ṣaadafa hwaaya suuʔ ẓaḍḍ ib-ẓayaata.*

**That's a tough break! *šloon ẓaḍḍ naẓis!*

to give someone a break - **1.** *niṭa (i) furṣa.* Give me a break. *nṭiini furṣa.* **2.** *tsaahal (a) wiyya.* I'll give you a break this time but don't do it again. *hal-marra raẓ-atsaahal wiyyaak, laakin la-tsawwiiha baɛad.*

to break - **1.** *kisar (i kasir) n-.* I broke my leg. *ksarit rijli.* -- My watch is broken. *saaɛti maksuura.* -- The boys broke the window pane. *l-wilid kisraw j-jaama maal iš-šibbaač.* -- He won't break his word. *huwwa ma-yiksir čilimta.* **2.** *fuṣax (u faṣix) n-.* She broke her engagement. *hiyya fuṣxat xuṭbatha.* **3.** *niṭa (i).* We'll have to break the news to him gently. *laazim ninṭii l-xabar b-luṭuf.* **4.** *giṭaɛ (a gaṭiɛ) n-.* He broke the string on the package. *giṭaɛ xeeṭ ir-ruzma.* -- He broke a string on his violin. *giṭaɛ watar ib-kamanjta.* -- The wires are broken. *l-waayaraat magṭuuɛa.* **5.** *ngiṭaɛ (i ngiṭaaɛ).* The string broke. *l-xeeṭ ingiṭaɛ.* **6.** *xaalaf (i muxaalafa).* He has broken the law. *huwwa xaalaf il-qaanuun.* **7.** *jawwaz (i tajwiiz).* I'll break him of that habit. *raẓ-ajawwza min hal-ɛaada.*

to break down - **1.** *xirab (a xaraab).* The machine broke down this morning. *l-makiina xurbat hal-yoom iṣ-ṣubuẓ.* **2.** *twaqqaf (a tawaqquf), tɛaṭṭal (a taɛaṭṭul).* The internal organization of the country broke down near the end of the war. *t-tanḍiimaat id-daaxiliyya lil-mamlaka twaqqfat qurub nihaayt il-ẓarub.* **3.** *fiqad (u fuqdaan) ṣayṭara ɛala ɛawaaṭif~.* He broke down when he heard the news. *fiqad iṣ-ṣayṭara ɛala ɛawaaṭfa min simaɛ il-xabar.*

to break in - **1.** *darrab (u tadriib).* I'll have to break in another beginner. *ʔaani raẓ-aḍṭarr adarrub waaẓid laax jidiid ɛaš-šuġuḷ.* **2.** *nizal (i nuzuul) ɛala, siṭa (i saṭu) n- ɛala.* Last night thieves broke in our neighbor's house. *ẓaraamiyya nizlaw ɛala beet ij-jiiraan il-baarẓa bil-leel.* **3.** *kisar (i kasir).* They lost the key and had to break in the door. *ḍayyɛaw il-miftaaẓ w-iḍṭarraw ykisruun il-baab.*

to break off - **1.** *giṭaɛ (a gaṭiɛ) n-.* They have broken off relations with our country. *giṭɛaw ɛalaaqaathum wiyya dawlatna.* **2.** *nkisar (i nkisaar).* Then, the branch broke off. *t-taali, nkisar il-ġuṣin.*

to break oneself - *jaaz (u jooz).* I broke myself of that habit long ago. *jizit min hal-ɛaada min zimaan.*

to break out - **1.** *nhizam (i haziima).* He broke out of prison. *nhizam imnis-sijin.* **2.** *ḍihar (a ḍuhuur).* The plague has broken out in the south. *mariḍ iṭ-ṭaaɛuun ḍihar bij-jinuub.* **3.** *nišab (i nušuub), bida (i btidaaʔ).* The fire broke out towards midnight. *nišab il-ẓariiq gabuḷ nuṣṣ il-leel b-išwayya.* **4.** (with measles) *ẓaṣṣab (u taẓṣiib).* My oldest boy broke out with measles this morning. *ʔibni č-čibiir ẓaṣṣab hal-yoom iṣ-ṣubuẓ.* **5.** (with small pox) *jaddar (i tajdiir).* If you have broken out with small pox when you were young, you won't do so again. *ʔiḍa jaddarit min činit jaahil, ma-raẓ-itjaddir baɛad.*

to break up - **1.** *farraq (i tafriiq, tfirriq), faḍḍ (u faḍḍ) n-.* The police broke up the demonstration. *š-šurṭa farriqaw il-muḍaahara.* -- The party broke up early. *l-ẓafla faḍḍat min wakit.* -- The police came and broke up the fight. *š-šurṭa ʔijaw w-faḍḍaw il-ɛarka.* **2.** *tfarraq (a).* We broke up about midnight. *tfarraqna ẓawaali nuṣṣ il-leel.* **3.** *nkisar (i nkisaar).* The cold spell is about to break up. *mawjat il-barid raẓ-tinkisir.*

**Break it up! *bass ɛaad!* or *yeezi ɛaad!* or *fuḍḍuuha!*

breakdown - **1.** *ɛaṭal, ɛawaara, xalaal.* The breakdown happened about five miles outside of town. *l-ɛaṭal ṣaar ẓawaali xams amyaal xaarij il-balad.* **2.** *ngiṭaaɛ* pl. *-aat, fašal.* We must avoid a breakdown in the negotiations at all costs. *laazim nitẓaaša fašal il-mufaawaḍaat ib-ʔay θaman.*

nervous breakdown - *nhiyaar ɛaṣabi.* She had a nervous breakdown. *ṣaar ɛidha inhiyaar ɛaṣabi.*

breakfast - *riyuug, fṭuur.* I always have an egg for breakfast. *ʔaani daaʔiman ʔaakul-li fadd beeḍa lir-riyuug.*

to give (someone his) breakfast - *rayyag (i).* His mother gave him his breakfast. *ʔumma rayyigata.*

to have breakfast - *trayyag (a), fuṭar (u fuṭuur).* Have you had your breakfast yet? *trayyagit loo baɛad?*

breast - *nahid* pl. *nhuud, dees* pl. *dyuus, ṣadir* pl. *ṣduur.*

breath - *nafas* pl. *ʔanfaas.* Hold your breath. *ʔigṭaɛ nafasak.*

to be out of breath - *nihag (a).* I'm completely out of breath. *da-anhag imnit-taɛab.*

to catch one's breath - *jarr (u) nafas, ʔaxaḍ (u) nafas.* I have to catch my breath first. *xalli šwayya ʔajurr nafasi ʔawwal.*

to **breathe** - *tnaffas (a tanaffus).* He's breathing regularly. *da-yitnaffas b-intiḍaam.*

**Don't breathe a word of this to anyone. *la-tṭalliɛ haay min ẓalqak.*

**He is breathing his last. *da-yɛaalij* or or *da-yilfuḍ ʔanfaasa.*

**I'll breathe again when I'm done with this job. *min ʔaxalliṣ haš-šaġla yinzaaẓ kaabuus ɛan ṣadri.*

to **breed** - **1.** *waalad (i muwaalada).* My uncle breeds horses. *ɛammi ywaalid il-xeel.* **2.** *twaalad (a tawaalud).* Rabbits breed faster than many animals. *l-ʔaraanib titwaalad ʔasraɛ min ihwaaya mnil-ẓaywaanaat.*

breeze - *nasmat* (pl. *-aat*) *hawa, hawa ṭayyib.* At night we got a cool breeze from the lake. *bil-leel habbat ɛaleena nasma barda mnil-buẓeera.* -- There's not a breeze stirring. *ma-aku wa-laa nasmat hawa titẓarrak* or *l-hawa waaguf tamaaman.*

to **brew** - *xammar (u taxmiir, txummur) t-.* We brew our own beer. *ʔiẓna nxammur biiratna b-iidna.*

brewery - *maɛmal* (pl. *maɛaamil*) *biira.* Bavaria is known for its good breweries. *baavaarya mašhuura b-maɛaamil biiratha.*

bribe - *rašwa* pl. *-aat, rašaawi.* He was caught accepting a bribe. *nlizam da-yaaxuḍ rašwa.*

to bribe - *riša (i rašwa) n-.* You can't bribe him. *ma-tigdar tiršii.*

brick - *ṭaabuuga* pl. *-aat* coll. *ṭaabuug.* Their house is built of yellow brick. *beethum mabni b-ṭaabuug.*

mud brick - *libna* pl. *-aat* coll. *libin.* The farmer and his sons are making mud bricks. *l-fallaaẓ w-wilda da-ysawwuun libin.*

bricklayer - *banna* pl. *bnaani.* He's a bricklayer. *huwwa banna.*

bride - *ɛaruus* pl. *ɛaraayis.*

bridegroom - *ɛaruus* pl. *ɛirsaan.*

bridge - **1.** *jisir* pl. *jsuur.* There's a bridge across the river a mile from here. *ɛala biɛid miil minnaa ʔaku jisir ɛan-nahar.* -- The dentist is making a new bridge for me. *ṭabiib il-ʔasnaan da-ysawwii-li jisir jidiid.* **2.** *maẓall qiyaada, ġurfat* (pl. *ġuraf*) *qiyaada.* Can you see the captain on the bridge? *da-tšuuf ir-rubbaan waaguf ib-ġurfat il-qiyaada?* **3.** *brij.* Do you play bridge? *ʔinta tilɛab brij?*

**He burned his bridges behind him. *ma-xallaa-la xaṭṭ rajɛa.*

to bridge - *bina (i) jisir.* There is some talk of bridging the river at a point near our village. *ʔaku ẓači raẓ-yibnuun jisir ɛaš-šaṭṭ yamm qaryatna.*

bridle - *risan* pl. *risin.*

brief - **1.** *qṣayyir, qaṣiir.* He paid me a brief visit before he left. *zaarni zyaara qṣiira gabuḷ-ma saafar.* **2.** *muxtaṣar.* His speech was brief and helpful. *xiṭaaba čaan muxtaṣar w-mufiid.*

in brief - *b-ixtiṣaar, muxtaṣar mufiid.* In brief, our plan is this. *muxtaṣar mufiid, haaḍa manhajna.*

to brief - *nawwar (u tanwiir), zawwad (i tazwiid) t-*. Our leader briefed us on every detail of the operation. *qaa?idna nawwarna ɛan kull tafaaṣiil il-ɛamaliyya.* -- Tuesday you will be briefed with the final information. *yoom iθ-θalaaθaa? raẓ-titzawwduun bil-maɛluumaat in-nihaa?iyya.*

to be brief - *xtiṣar (i xtiṣaar)*. Please be brief. *xtiṣir, min faḍlak.*

brief case - *junṭa* (pl. *-aat*) *maal kutub.*

briefing - *tawziid bil-maɛluumaat.* The briefing session lasted more than an hour. *jalsat it-tazwiid bil-maɛluumaat istamarrat ?akθar min saaɛa.*

bright - **1.** *wahhaaj.* I like a bright fire. *tiɛjibni n-naar il-wahhaaja.* **2.** *zaahi.* She likes to wear bright colors. *yiɛjibha tilbas ?alwaan zaahya.* **3.** *ðaki.* He's a bright boy. *huwwa walad ðaki.* **4.** *ẓaṣiif.* That was a bright idea. *haay čaanat fikra ẓaṣiifa.*

**She's always bright and cheerful. *ɛala ṭuul ɛaṣaafiirha ṭaayra w-bašuuša.*

bright and early - *ġubša.* We're going to start out bright and early. *raẓ-niṭlaɛ min ġubša* or *raẓ-inġabbuš.*

brilliant - **1.** *ṣaarix.* You can tell his paintings by the brilliant colors. *tigdar tuɛruf irsuuma mnil-?alwaan ṣ-ṣaarxa lli yistaɛmilha.* **2.** *baariɛ.* He's a brilliant speaker. *huwwa fadd xaṭiib baariɛ.* **3.** *ðaki.* He's the most brilliant man I know. *huwwa ?aðka waaẓid ?aɛurfa.*

brim - **1.** *raas* pl. *ruus.* The glass is filled to the brim. *l-iglaaṣ matruus lir-raas.* **2.** *ẓaašya* pl. *ẓawaaši.* The brim of your hat will protect your face and neck from the sun. *ẓaašyat šafiqtak raẓ-tuẓfuḍ wiččak w-rugubtak imniš-šamis.*

to **bring** - *jaab (i jeeb) n-*. Bring me a glass of water. *jiib-li fadd iglaaṣ maay.* -- Won't you please bring me the other folder? *ma-tjiib-li l-malaffa l-lux, min faðlak?* -- He brought the children a present. *jaab fadd hadiyya lil-?aṭfaal.*

to bring about - *?antaj (i ?intaaj), sabbab (i tasbiib).* The depression brought about a change in living standards. *l-kasaad ?antaj tabaddul ib-mustawa l-ẓayaat.*

to bring along - *jaab (i) wiyya.* Bring your children along. *jiib il-jihhaal wiyyaak.*

to bring back - *rajjaɛ (i trijjiɛ, tarjiiɛ) t-*. Please bring the book back. *?arjuuk rajjiɛ l-iktaab.*

to bring down - *nazzal (i tnizzil, tanziil) t-*. I also brought down the big box. *hamm nazzalit iṣ-ṣanduug ič-čibiir.*

to bring in - **1.** *jaab (i).* The dance brought in a hundred dollars. *ẓaflat ir-rigiṣ jaabat miit doolaar.* **2.** *daxxal (i tadxiil), xaššaš (i taxšiiš).* Bring the boxes in the house. *xaššiš iṣ-ṣanaadiig bil-beet.*

to bring out - **1.** *ṭallaɛ (i taṭliiɛ).* Bring out the chairs and put them on the terrace. *ṭalliɛ il-karaasi w-ẓuṭṭhum biṭ-ṭarma.* -- They're bringing out a new edition of my book. *raẓ-yṭallɛuun ṭabɛa jdiida min iktaabi.* **2.** *ɛiraḍ (i ɛariḍ) n-*. He brought out his point convincingly. *huwwa ɛiraḍ ra?ya b-ṭariiqa muqniɛa.*

to bring to - *ṣaẓẓa (i taṣẓiya).* Cold water will bring him to. *l-maay l-baarid yṣaẓẓii.*

to bring to bear - *staɛmal (i stiɛmaal).* He brought all his influence to bear. *staɛmal kull nufuuða.*

to bring up - **1.** *rabba (i tarbiya).* Her aunt brought her up. *ɛammatha rabbatha.* **2.** *ṣaɛɛad (i taṣɛiid).* Bring up my coat when you come. *ṣaɛɛid sitirti min tiṣɛad.* **3.** *θaar (i ?iθaara).* I'll bring it up at the next meeting. *raẓ-aθiirha bij-jalsa j-jaaya.*

brisk - **There is a brisk wind blowing today. *l-hawa da-yilɛab il-yoom.*

briskly - *b-našaaṭ.* He walks very briskly for such an old man. *yimši kulliš ib-našaaṭ il-waaẓid šaayib miθla.*

bristle - *šaɛra* pl. *-aat* coll. *šaɛar.* The bristles of this brush are beginning to fall out. *šaɛar hal-firča bida yoogaɛ.*

British - *bariiṭaani** pl. *-iyyiin.*

brittle - *hašš.*

broad - *ɛariið.* He has broad shoulders. *čtaafa ɛariiða.*

**It happened in broad daylight. *ṣaarat ib-raabiɛt in-nahaar.*

**That's as broad as it's long. *kullha yak ẓasaab* or *mneem-ma tijiiha siwa.*

broadcast - *?iðaaɛa* pl. *-aat.* Did you listen to the broadcast? *smaɛt il-?iðaaɛa?*

to broadcast - **1.** *ðaaɛ (i ?iðaaɛa) n-*. They will broadcast directly from London. *raẓ-yðiiɛuun min landan ra?san.* -- If you tell her, she'll broadcast it all over the neighborhood. *?iða tgul-lha tara tðiiɛ-ilk-iyyaa b-kull il-maẓalla.* **2.** *nišar (u našir) n-*. I wouldn't broadcast it if I were you. *ma-anšurha, loo b-makaanak.*

broadcloth - *čoox* pl. *čwaax.* I bought a good piece of broadcloth today. *štireet qiṭɛa čoox zeena l-yoom.*

broad-minded - *ṣadra raẓib.* She's a very broad-minded person. *ṣadirha raẓib ihwaaya.*

brochure - *kurraasa* pl. *-aat.* There is a very interesting brochure on that subject. *?aku kurraasa mumtiɛa ɛan hal-mawðuuɛ.*

to **broil** - *šuwa (i šawi) n-*. Broil the chicken on a skewer. *?išwi d-dijaaja b-šiiš.*

broke - *miflis* pl. *mafaaliis.* I was broke at that time and couldn't afford to buy it. *činit miflis ðaak il-wakit w-ma-gdarit aštirii.*

to go broke - **1.** *filas (i ?iflaas), ?aflas (i).* Ali went broke again. *ɛali hamm ?aflas.* **2.** *nkisar (i).* The merchant is about to go broke. *it-taajir ɛala wašak yinkisir.*

broker - *dallaal* pl. *-iin.* If you want to sell your house quickly, get a broker. *?iða triid itbiiɛ beetak ib-saaɛ, šuuf-lak dallaal.*

customs broker - *mṭalliɛči* pl. *-iyya.* Can you find me a customs broker to take on this job? *tigdar tilgii-li mṭalliɛči yaaxuð haay ɛala ɛaatqa?*

bronchitis - *ltihaab il-qaṣabaat.* Your boy has a bad case of bronchitis. *?ibnak ɛinda ltihaab qaṣabaat šadiid.*

bronze - *brunz.*

brooch - *brooš* pl. *-aat.* I'd like to buy a nice brooch for my wife. *?ariid ?aštiri brooš ẓilu l-marti.*

brood - *fruux, fraariij.* The hen and her brood come when you call her. *d-dijaaja w-fruuxha yijuun min itṣiiẓha.*

to brood - **1.** *nġamm (a ġamm), nhamm (a hamm).* Don't brood about it; try and forget it. *la-tinġamm ɛala muud haaða, ẓaawil tinsaa.* **2.** *(čaan) maġmuum, (čaan) mahmuum.* What are you brooding about? *leeš maġmuum?* or *?inta leeš mahmuum?*

brooder - *makiinat* (pl. *makaayin*) *tafriix.* If I can find a small brooder I'm going to hatch my own chickens. *?iða ?algi makiinat tafriix iṣġayyra raẓ-afaggis dijaaji b-nafsi.*

brook - *majra* pl. *majaari, saagya* pl. *swaagi.* The brook dries up in the summer. *yjiff il-majra biṣ-ṣeef* or *s-saagya teebas biṣ-ṣeef.*

broom - **1.** *makinsa, muknaasa* pl. *makaanis.* Get the broom and sweep the floor. *jiib il-muknaasa w-iknus il-gaaɛ.*

broth - *maay laẓam.* Drink a little of this chicken broth; it will do you good. *?išrab išwayya min hal-mayy dijaaj, ynifɛak.*

brothel - *karxaana* pl. *-aat, kallačiyya* pl. *-aat.* The club turned out to be nothing but a brothel. *n-naadi ṭilaɛ bil-ẓaqiiqa karxaana.*

brother - *?ax* pl. *?uxwaan, ?uxwa.* Have you a brother? *ɛindak ?ax?* -- I bought it from Hasso Bros. *štireeta min ẓassu xwaan.*

brotherhood - *?uxuwwa.* His speech was all about brotherhood and pan-Arabism. *xiṭaaba kulla čaan ɛann il-?uxuwwa wil-ɛuruuba.*

brother-in-law - **1.** *nisiib* pl. *nisbaan, rajil uxut* pl. *riyaajiil xawaat.* **2.** (wife's sister's husband). *ɛadiil* pl. *ɛidlaan.*

brow - *guṣṣa* pl. *guṣaṣ.* He wiped the sweat off his brow. *misaẓ il-ɛarag min guṣṣta.*

brown - **1.** *bunni*, qahwaa?i*, ?asmar* pl. *sumur.* Her hair and eyes are brown. *loon šaɛarha w-iɛyuunha bunni.*

to brown - **1.** *ẓmarr (i).* Leave the meat in the oven until it browns. *xalli l-laẓam bil-firin ?ila ?an yiẓmarr.* **2.** *ẓimas (i ẓamis).* First brown the onions in a little fat. *?awwal ?iẓmis il-buṣal b-išwayya dihin.*

to **browse** - *tfarraj (a tafarruj).* I love to browse for books in a good book store. *yiɛjibni ?atfarraj ɛal-kutub ib-maktaba zeena.*

brucellosis - *l-ẓumma l-maalṭiyya.*

bruise - *raḍḍa* pl. *-aat.* He had a bruise on his left foot. *čaan ɛinda raḍḍa b-rijila l-yisra.*

to bruise - *raḍḍ (u raḍḍ) n-*. The boy bruised his

knee. *l-walad raḍḍ rukubta.*
brunette - *samra* pl. *sumur.*
brunt - *šidda.* The infantry bore the brunt of the attack. *šiddat il-hujuum wugaɛ ɛal-mušaat.*
brush - *firča* pl. *firač, pirča* pl. *pirač.* You can use this brush for your shoes. *tigdar tistaɛmil hal-firča l-qanaadrak.* -- Who left the brush in the paint? *minu tirak il-firča biṣ-ṣubuġ?*
to brush - *farrač (i tfirrič) t-, parrač (i tpirrič) t-.* I brush my hair every evening. *ʔaani ʔafarrič šaɛri kull leela.* -- I have to brush my teeth. *laazim ʔafarrič isnuuni.*
to brush aside - *tjaahal (a tajaahul).* He brushed my protests aside. *tjaahal iʒtijaajaati.*
to brush up on - *raajaɛ (i muraajaɛa).* I'm brushing up on German. *da-araajiɛ il-luġa l-ʔalmaaniyya.*
brush off - *dafɛa.* She gave me the brush off. *nṭatni dafɛa* or *ligat-li ʒijja.*
to brush off - *farrač (i tafriič) t-.* Brush off your overcoat. *farrič miɛṭafak* or *farrič qappuuṭak.*
brutal - *waʒši*, faḍḍ* pl. *ʔafḍaaḍ, šaris* pl. *-iin.*
brute - *waʒiš* pl. *wuʒuuš, šaris* pl. *-iin.* He's a brute. *huwwa šaris.*
brute strength - *quwwat ðiraaɛ.* We raised the car by brute strength. *ṭallaɛna s-sayyaara b-quwwat iðraaɛaatna.*
bubble - *buqbaaqa* pl. *-aat, buqaabiiq; fuqaaɛa* pl. *-aat.* You can see the bubbles rise to the surface of the water. *tigdar itšuuf il-buqbaaqaat da-tiṭlaɛ foog il-maay.*
to bubble - *baqbaq (u baqbaqa).* The water is beginning to bubble. *l-maay bida ybaqbuq.*
to **buck** - *qaawam (u muqaawama).* We had to buck the current all the way. *ḍṭarreena nqaawum it-tayyaar ṭuul il-masaafa.*
bucket - *ṣaṭla* pl. *-aat, ṣṭuul.*
buckle - *bziim* pl. *-aat.* I lost the buckle of my leather belt. *ḍayyaɛit l-ibziim maal iʒzaami.*
to buckle - **1.** *šadd (i šadd) n-.* I can't buckle the strap. *ma-ʔagdar ʔašidd is-seer.* -- I can't buckle my belt. *ma-agdar ašidd iʒzaami.* **2.** *ṭallaɛ (i) baṭin.* The wall buckled. *l-ʒaayiṭ ṭallaɛ baṭin.* **3.** *tɛawwaj (a tɛuwwuj).* The linoleum buckled from the heat. *l-imšammaɛ itɛawwaj imnil-ʒarr.* **4.** *nɛuwaj (i).* The beams buckled from the weight of roof. *š-šeelmaan inɛuwaj min θugl is-saguf.*
**It's about time we buckled down to work. *ṣaar il-wakit ʒatta nšidd ʒeelna liš-šuġuḷ* or *ṣaar il-wakit ʒatta nðibb nafisna ɛaš-šuġuḷ.*
bud - **1.** (flower) *jumbuda* pl. *janaabid* coll. *jumbud.* The cold killed all the buds. *l-barid kital kull ij-jumbud.* **2.** (new growth) *burɛum* pl. *baraaɛum.* In spring, buds appear on the trees, *bir-rabiiɛ il-baraaɛum tiṭlaɛ bil-ʔašjaar.*
**The uprising was nipped in the bud. *l-ɛiṣyaan inqiḍa ɛalee w-huwwa bil-mahad.*
to bud out - *ṭagṭag (i ṭagṭaga).* The new cuttings are budding out. *l-iqlaam ij-jidiida da-ṭṭagṭig.*
budding - *naaši?* pl. *-iin.* He's a budding author. *huwwa fadd muʔallif naašiʔ.*
to **budge** - *zaʒzaʒ (i zaʒzaʒa).* I couldn't budge it. *ma-gdarit ʔazaʒziʒha.*
budget - *miizaaniyya* pl. *-aat.* Our budget doesn't allow that. *miizaaniyyatna ma-titʒammal haðaak.* -- This is not in this year's budget. *haaða ma-daaxil ib-miizaaniyyat has-sana.*
to budget - *waazan (i muwaazana) t-.* You'll have to budget your expenses with your salary. *ʔinta laazim itwaazin maṣrafak wiyya raaṭbak.*
to **buff** - *ṣiqal (u ṣaqil).* They buff the trays to give them a high polish. *yṣiqluun iṣ-ṣuwaani ʒatta tṣiir biiha lamɛa.*
buffalo - (water buffalo) *jaamuus* pl. *jawaamiis.*
buffet - *buufya* pl. *-aat, buufee* pl. *-yaat.* The dishes are in the buffet. *l-imwaaɛiin bil-buufya.*
bug - **1.** *ʒašara* pl. *-aat.* This spray is good for all kinds of bugs. *had-duwa mufiid ḍidd kull il-ʒašaraat.* **2.** *bagga* pl. *-aat* coll. *bagg.* The leaves were covered with bugs. *l-ʔawraaq čaanat imġaṭṭaaya bil-bagg.* **3.** *gaariṣ, bagg.* I couldn't sleep because of bed bugs. *ma-gdart anaam ib-sabab il-gaariṣ.* **4.** *barġaša* pl. *-aat* coll. *barġaš.* At night on the river the flying bugs give you a lot of trouble. *bil-leel yamm iš-šaṭṭ il-barġaš yḍawwj il-waaʒid.*
bugle - *buuq* pl. *ʔabwaaq.*
to **build** - *bina (i binaaʔ) n-, ɛammar (u taɛmiir) t-.* Our neighbor is building a new house. *jaarna da-yibni beet jidiid.* -- The company is going to build houses for its employees. *š-šarika raʒ-itɛammur ibyuut il-ɛummaalha.*
to build in - *bina (i) bil-ʒaayiṭ.* I'm going to build in bookcases here. *raʒ-abni hnaa maktaba bil-ʒaayiṭ.*
to build on - *ḍaaf (i ʔiḍaafa) n-.* We're going to build on a new wing to the hospital. *raʒ-inḍiif janaaʒ jidiid lil-mustašfa.*
to build up - *namma (i tanmiya) t-, kabbar (u takbiir) t-.* He built up the business. *nammaa liš-šuġuḷ* or *kabbar il-maṣlaʒa.*
building - *binaaya* pl. *-aat, ɛimaara* pl. *-aat.* Both offices are in one building. *d-daaʔirteen ib-fadd binaaya.* -- They're going to build a ten story building on this piece of ground. *raʒ-yibnuun ɛimaara biiha ɛašir ṭawaabiq ɛala hal-qiṭɛat il-ʔarḍ.*
bulb - **1.** *gloob* pl. *-aat.* This bulb is burnt out. *hal-igloob maʒruug.* **2.** *buṣla* pl. *-aat, ʔabṣaal,* coll. *buṣaḷ.* I have some Dutch bulbs in my garden. *ɛindi ʔabsaal hoolandiyya b-ʒadiiqti.*
bulge - *ntifaax* pl. *-aat.* What's that bulge in your pocket? *šinu hal-intifaax ib-jeebak?*
to bulge - **1.** *ṭallaɛ (i) baṭin.* The wall is bulging dangerously. *l-ʒaayiṭ imṭalliɛ baṭin ib-ṣuura muxṭira.* **2.** *ntufax (u ntifaax).* Their stomachs were bulging with so much food. *baṭinhum intufxat imnil-ʔakil.*
bulging - *manfuux, waarum.* His briefcase was bulging with papers. *januṭṭa čaanat manfuuxa bil-ʔawraaq.*
bulk - **1.** *muɛḍam.* The bulk of my salary goes for rent and food. *muɛḍam maɛaaši yruuʒ lil-ʔajar wil-ʔakil.* **2.** *bil-wazin, falla.* Buying bulk tea is cheaper than packaged tea. *širaaʔ ič-čaay bil-wazin ʔarxaṣ min čaay l-iqwaaṭi.*
in bulk - *bij-jumla.* We buy dates in the bulk and package them ourselves. *ništiri tamur bij-jumla w-inɛallba b-nafisna.*
bulky - *čibiir* pl. *kbaar.* The sofa is too bulky to go through the door. *l-qanafa kulliš čibiira ma-tfuut imnil-baab.*
bull - *θoor* pl. *θiiraan.*
to **bulldoze (level)** - **1.** *siʒag (a saʒig).* First of all, we have to bulldoze all this rock and gravel level. *ʔawwalan laazim nisʒag haṣ-ṣaxar wil-ʒaṣu kulla.* **2.** *waxxar (i) bil-buldoozar.* Bulldoze them out of the way. *waxxirhum imniṭ-ṭariiq bil-buldoozar.*
bulldozer - *buldoozar* pl. *-aat.* The contractor is in the market for a new bulldozer. *l-qunṭarči da-yriid yištiri buldoozar jidiid.*
bullet - *riṣaaṣa* pl. *-aat* coll. *riṣaaṣ.* The bullet lodged in his shoulder. *r-riṣaaṣa staqarrat ib-čitfa.*
bully - *ʔašqiyaaʔ* pl. *-iyya.* He is the bully of the school. *huwwa ʔašqiyaaʔ il-madrasa.*
to bully - *baaɛ (i beeɛ) šaqaawa.* They are complaining about him bullying the smaller children. *da-yitšakkuun minna li-ʔan da-ybiiɛ šaqaawa ɛaj-jihaal.*
bum - *mhatlaf* pl. *-iin, ɛaaṭil* pl. *-iin.*
bump - **1.** *ɛinjurra* pl. *-aat, ɛanaajiir.* Where did you get that bump on your head? *mneen jattak ðiič il-ɛinjurra b-raasak?* **2.** *ɛukra* pl. *ɛukar, ṭaṣṣa* pl. *-aat.* The car went over a bump. *s-sayyaara ṭaṣṣat ib-ɛukra.*
to bump (into) - **1.** *ɛiθar (a ɛuθuur) n-.* He bumped into a chair in the dark. *ɛiθar b-iskamli biḍ-ḍalma.* **2.** *ṣaadaf (i muṣaadafa) t-.* Guess who I bumped into yesterday. *ʔiʒzir il-man ṣaadafit il-baarʒa.*
bumper - *daɛɛaamiyya* pl. *-aat.* He bent the bumper when he ran into me. *ɛuwaj id-daɛɛaamiyya lamma diɛamni.*
bumpy - *(bii) ṭaṣṣaat.* We drove for about an hour over a bumpy road. *siqna ʒawaali saaɛa b-darub kulla ṭaṣṣaat.*
bunch - *baaga* pl. *-aat, šadda* pl. *-aat, ḍabba* pl. *-aat.* Let me have a bunch of radishes, please. *balla nṭiini fadd baaga fijil.*
bundle - **1.** *rabṭa* pl. *-aat, buqča* pl. *buqač.* Is that bundle too heavy for you? *hal-buqča θagiila ɛaleek?* **2.** *ḍabba* pl. *-aat.* I want two bundles of iron rods. *ʔariid ḍabbteen šiiš.* **3.** *šadda* pl. *-aat, laffa* pl. *-aat.* I gave him a bundle of newspapers. *nṭeeta šaddat jaraayid.*
to **bungle** - *laaṣ (u looṣ).* It was a delicate job and he bungled it. *čaanat fadd šaġla daqiiqa w-huwwa laaṣha.*
to **bunk (with)** - *baat (a).* If you don't have a place to sleep, you can bunk with us. *ʔiða ma-ɛindak makaan itnaam bii, tigdar itbaat ɛidna.*

burden - **1.** *θugul.* I don't want to be a burden to you. *ma-ariid ʔaṣiir θugul ɛaleek.* **2.** *mašaqqa* pl. *-aat, taɛab.* Most of the burden of bringing up the children fell on the mother. *ʔakθar mašaqqat tarbiyat il-ʔaṭfaal wuqɛat ib-raas il-ʔumm.* **The burden of proof lies with the complaintant. *l-bayyina ɛal-muddaɛi* or *l-muddaɛi laazim yiθbit.*
to burden - *kallaf (i takliif) t-, ḥammal (i taḥmiil) t-.* I don't want to burden you with my troubles. *ʔaani ma-ariid ʔakallifak ib-masaakli.* -- She is burdened with a lot of responsibilities. *mḥammla masʔuuliyyaat ihwaaya.*

bureau - **1.** *diilaab* pl. *dawaaliib, kuntoor* pl. *kanaatiir.* The bottom drawer of the bureau is stuck. *l-imjarr ij-jawwaani maal diilaab l-ihduum ɛaaṣi.* **2.** *daaʔira* pl. *dawaaʔir.* Bureau of Vital Statistics. *daaʔirat il-ʔiḥṣaaʔ.*

burglar - *ḥaraami* pl. *-iyya, liṣṣ* pl. *liṣuuṣ.*

burglary - *booqa* pl. *-aat, sariqa* pl. *-aat, saṭu, ḥaadiθat saṭu.* When was the burglary committed? *šwakit ṣaarat il-booqa?*

burial - *dafin, dafna* pl. *-aat.*

burn - *ḥarig* pl. *ḥruug, čawya* pl. *-aat.* This is a serious burn. *haaδa ḥarig xaṭiir.*
to burn - **1.** *ḥirag (i ḥarig) n-.* Have the boy burn the papers. *xalli l-farraaš yiḥrig il-ʔawraaq.* **2.** *ḥtirag (i ḥtiraag), štiɛal (i štiɛaal).* This wood burns well. *hal-ḥaṭab yiḥtirig zeen.* **3.** *čuwa (i čawi) n-.* Don't touch the iron; it will burn your fingers. *la-ṭṭuxx il-uuti; tara yičwi ʔaṣaabɛak.* **4.** *čawwa (i tčuwwi) t.* The sand is so hot it burns the feet. *r-ramul hal-gadd ḥaarr yčawwi r-rijil.*
**I'm burning with curiosity. *ʔaani mayyit imnil-fuδuul.*
**He's burnt his bridges behind him. *giṭaɛ kull ʔamal lir-rajɛa* or *ma-xallaa-la xaṭṭ rajɛa.*
**He has money to burn. *ɛinda fluus miθil iz-zibil.*
**The building has burned down to the ground. *l-ibnaaya dammarha n-naar* or *n-naar sawwat l-ibnaaya qaaɛ ṣafṣaf.*
to get burned - *nčuwa (i).* I got burned on the iron. *nčuweet bil-ʔuuti.*
to burn oneself - *nčuwa (i).* I burned myself once already and I don't want to do it again. *nčuweet marra w-ma-ariid ančuwi marra lux.*
to burn out - *ḥtirag (i ḥtiraag).* This bulb burned out. *hal-igluub iḥtirag.*
to burn up - *ḥtirag (i ḥtiraag).* His books burned up in the fire. *kutba ḥtirgat bil-ḥariiq.*
to be burnt up - *tgarδam (a tgurδum).* He's burnt up because he can't come along. *da-yitgarδam li-ʔan ma-yigdar yiji wiyyaana.*

burning hot - *miθl in-naar.* The soup is burning hot. *š-šoorba miθl in-naar.*

burr - *šooka* pl. *-aat* coll. *šook.* The sheep's wool was filled with burrs. *l-ġanam ṣuufhum čaan malyaan šook.*

to **burst** - *nfijar (i nfijaar), ṭagg (u ṭagg) n-, nkisar (i nkisaar).* The water pipe burst. *buuri l-mayy infijar.* -- She's bursting with curiosity. *raḥ-iṭṭugg imnil-fuδuul.* -- Last year the dam burst. *s-sana l-faatat inkisar is-sadd.*
to burst into - **1.** *čifat (i čafit) n- l-.* He burst into the room. *čifat lil-gubba.* **2.** *ṭagg (u ṭagg) n-.* She burst into tears. *ṭaggat idmuuɛha.* -- **3.** *gaam(u).* He burst into loud laughter. *gaam yqahqih.* -- She burst into crying. *gaamat tibči.*
to burst out - *ṭagg (u ṭagg) min.* The rice is bursting out through the seams of the bag. *t-timman ṭagg imnil-guuniyya.*

to **bury** - **1.** *difan (i dafin) n-.* We buried her yesterday. *difannaaha l-baarḥa.* **2.** *ṭumar (u ṭumur) n-.* He buried my application under the rest of the papers on purpose. *ṭumar ɛariiδti jawwa baaqi l-ʔawraaq ɛamdan.*

bus - *paaṣ* pl. *-aat.* Would you rather go by bus? *tfaδδil itruuḥ bil-paaṣ?* -- There's a bus every ten minutes. *yfuut paaṣ kull ɛašir daqaayiq.*

bush - **1.** *daġla* pl. *-aat* coll. *daġla.* He hid behind a bush. *xital wara d-daġla.* **2.** *zariɛ.* He is hiding in the bushes. *huwwa xaatil wara z-zariɛ.*
to beat around the bush - *laff (i) w-daar (u).* Don't keep on beating around the bush. *la-tδill itliff w-itduur.*

bushel - (no equivalent).

business - **1.** *tijaara* pl- *-aat.* They're selling their business. *da-yṣaffuun tijaarathum.* **2.** *šuġuḷ.* Business is flourishing. *š-šuġuḷ maaši* or *s-suug zeen.* That's none of your business. *haaδa muu šuġlak* or ***haaδa ma-yxuṣṣak* or ***ʔinta maa lak daxal.* -- What business is he in? *šinu šuġḷa?* or *š-yištiġuḷ?* -- You have no business around here. *ʔinta maa ʔilak šuġuḷ ihnaa.* -- Mind your own business. *la-titdaaxal* or *ɛaleek ib-šuġlak.* **3.** *šaġla, masʔala, qaδiyya.* Let's settle this business right away. *xal-infuδδ haš-šaġla ḥaalan.* **4.** *šaʔin* pl. *šiʔuun.* Don't meddle in other people's business. *la-titdaaxal ib-šiʔuun ġeerak.*
**What business is it of yours. *ʔinta yaahu maaltak?*
**Business comes before pleasure. *j-jadd qabl il-liɛib.*
on business - *b-šuġuḷ* I have to see him on business. *laazim ʔašuufa b-šuġuḷ.*
to go into business for oneself - *štiġal (u) ɛala ḥsaab~.* They have gone into business for themselves. *gaamaw yištaġḷuun ɛala ḥsaabhum.* -- Going into business for oneself requires a lot of capital. *š-šuġuḷ ɛala ḥsaab il-waaḥid yinraad-la hwaaya raasmaal.*

businessman - *rajul* (pl. *rijaal*) *ʔaɛmaal.* He's a successful businessman. *huwwa fadd rajuḷ ʔaɛmaal naajiḥ.*

bust - **1.** *timθaal niṣfi* pl. *tamaaθiil niṣfiyya.* The sculptor is doing a bust of Ahmad. *n-naḥḥaat da-ysawwi timθaal niṣfi l-ʔaḥmad.* **2.** *ṣadir* pl. *ṣduur.* The blouse is a little too tight across the bust. *hal-ibluuz išwayya δayyig min yamm iṣ-ṣadir.*

busy - **1.** *mašġuuḷ* pl. *-iin.* I'm even too busy to read the paper. *ma-agdar ʔaqra j-jariida halgadd-ma mašġuuḷ.* -- We're very busy at the office. *bid-daaʔira ʔiḥna hwaaya mašġuuḷiin* or ***ma-nigdar inḥukk raasna bid-daaʔira mniš-šuġuḷ.* -- The line's busy. *l-xaṭṭ mašġuuḷ.* **2.** *bii ḥaraka.* They live on a busy street. *ysiknuun ib-šaariɛ bii ḥaraka w-šuġuḷ.*

but - **1.** *bass, laakin.* We can go with you, but we'll have to come back early. *nigdar inruuḥ wiyyaak bass laazim nirjaɛ min wakit.* -- But you'll admit she's pretty. *bass ʔinta tiɛtirif hiyya ḥilwa.* -- But you know that I can't go. *laakin ʔinta tidri ʔaani ma-agdar ʔaruuḥ.* -- I didn't mean you but your friend. *ʔaani ma-ɛneetak inta laakin ɛineet ṣadiiqak.* **2.** *ġeer.* Nobody was there but me. *ma-čaan aku ʔaḥḥad ihnaak ġeeri.* **3.** *ʔilla.* All but one escaped. *l-kull xilṣaw ʔilla waaḥid.* -- Nothing but lies! *ma-aku ʔilla č-čiδib!* -- Now nothing but an operation can save him. *hassa ma-txaḷḷṣa ʔilla ɛamaliyya.*
**I was anything but pleased with it. *ʔaani wala raaδi bii ʔabadan.*
but then - *laakin ɛaad.* The suit is expensive, but then it fits well. *l-qaaṭ ġaali, laakin ɛaad tugɛud ɛalayya zeen.*

butcher - *gaṣṣaab* pl. *-iin, giṣaaṣiib.* I always buy the meat at the same butcher's. *ʔaani daaʔiman aštiri l-laḥam min nafs il-gaṣṣaab.*

butcher shop - *dukkaan gaṣṣaab* pl. *dukaakiin gaṣaaṣiib.*

butt - **1.** *miqbaδ* pl. *maqaabiδ.* Take the gun by the butt. *ʔilzam il-bunduqiyya mnil-miqbaδ.* **2.** *guṭuf* pl. *gṭuuf.* The ash tray is full of butts. *n-nuffaaḍa matruusa gṭuuf.* **3.** *maδḥaka.* Doesn't he realize that he's the butt of their jokes? *haaδa ma-da-yḥiss huwwa ṣaayir maδḥaka maalhum?*
to butt - *niṭaḥ (a naṭiḥ) n-.* The goat kept butting his head against the fence. *ṣ-ṣaxla δallat tinṭaḥ bil-imḥajjar.*
to butt in - **1.** *tdaxxal (a tadaxxul).* This is none of your business, so don't butt in! *haaδa muu šuġlak, fa-la titdaxxal.* **2.** *nabb (i nabb) n- ɛala.* Every time we talk, her little brother butts in with a question. *kull-ma niḥči ynibb ʔaxuuha l-iṣġayyir ɛaleena b-fadd suʔaal.*
to butt together - **1.** *raawas (i muraawasa) t-.* Butt the two boards together. *raawis il-looḥteen.* **2.** *ṭubag (u ṭabug) n- suwa.* Butt the desks together this way. *ʔuṭbug il-meezaat suwa hiiči.*

butter - *zibid.* Let me have a pound of butter, please. *ntiini paawan zibid min faδlak.*
to butter - *ḥaṭṭ (u) zibid.* Shall I butter your bread? *triid aḥuṭṭ-lak zibid ɛal-xubuz?*

butterfly - *faraaša* pl. *-aat* coll. *faraaš.*

button - **1.** *dugma* pl. *digam.* She sewed the button on for me. *xayyṭat-li d-dugma.* **2.** *zirr* pl. *zraar.* You have to press the button. *laazim itduus iz-zirr.*
to button (up) - *daggam (u tduggum) t-.* Button up your overcoat. *daggum qappuuṭak.*

buttonhole - *beet dugma* pl. *byuut dugam, zuruf dugma* pl. *zruuf dugam.* This buttonhole needs fixing. *beet id-dugma haaδa yirraad-la taṣliiζ.*
buy - *šarwa* pl. *-aat.* That's a good buy. *haaδi šarwa tiswa.*
to buy - *štira (i šira) n-.* What did you buy at Ali's shop? *š-ištireet min dukkaan εali?*
to buy a ticket - *gaṣṣ (u) biṭaaqa, giṭaε (a) biṭaaqa, štira (i) biṭaaqa.* Buy me a ticket too. *ʔili hamm guṣṣ-li biṭaaqa.* -- Did you buy the theater tickets? *giṭaεit il-biṭaaqaat lir-ruwaaya?*
to buy into - *štira (i) ʔashum b-.* I'm thinking of buying into that company. *da-ʔafakkir aštiri ʔashum ib-haš-šarika.*
to buy up - *lamm (i lamm) n-.* That monopolist bought up all the sugar in the market. *hal-muζtakir lamm kull iš-šakar il-bis-suug.*
buzz - **1.** *ṭaniin.* The buzz of the mosquito kept me awake. *ṭaniin il-bagga ma-xallaani ʔanaam.* **2.** *wašwaša.* A buzz of voices filled the courtroom. *ṣaarat fadd wašwaša b-qaaεat il-maζkama.*
to buzz - *ṭanṭan (i ṭanṭana).* The bee buzzes. *n-naζla tṭanṭin.*
buzzer - *jaraṣ* pl. *jraaṣ.* Push the buzzer. *dugg ij-jaraṣ.*
by - **1.** *qariib min.* The house stands close by the river. *l-beet mabni qariib min iš-šaṭṭ.* **2.** *yamm, b-jaanib.* He went by me without saying a word. *faat min yammi bala-ma yguul wala čilma.* **3.** *b-.* The club has been closed by order of the police. *nsadd in-naadi b-ʔamur imniš-šurṭa.* -- That horse won by a length. *δaak l-iζṣaan ġilab b-ṭuul waaζid.* -- We came by car. *jeena b-sayyaara.* -- He'll be back by five o'clock. *raζ-yirjaε bil-xamsa* or *raζ-yirjaε saaεa xamsa.* -- The table is four feet by six. *l-meez kubra ʔarbaεa fuutaat ib-sitta.* **4.** *b-, εala.* She can't work by artificial light. *ma-tigdar tištuġul b-δuwa ṣṭinaaεi.* **5.** *b-waaṣṭa, b-.* I'll send it to you by mail. *raζ-adizz-lak-iyyaaha b-waaṣṭat il-bariid.*
**This book was written by a Frenchman. *haaδa l-iktaab il-waaζid fransi.*
**Little by little he fought his way through the crowd. *šwayya šwayya šagg-la ṭariiq min been in-naas.*
**I got the story out of him word by word. *čilma čilma ṭallaεit l-iζčaaya min ζalga.*
**That's done by machine. *haaδa šuġuḷ makiina.*
by and by - **1.** *bit-tadriij.* You'll get used to it by and by. *raζ-titεallam εaleeha bit-tadriij.* **2.** *baεd išwayya.* He told me he'd let me know by and by. *gal-li yinṭiini xabar baεd išwayya.*
by and large - *εal-εumuum.* By and large, the results were satisfactory. *εal-εumuum, in-nataayij čaanat zeena.*
by far - *b-ihwaaya.* This is by far the best hotel in town. *haaδa ʔaζsan ʔuuteel bil-wlaaya b-ihwaaya.*
by name - *bil-ʔisim.* I just know him by name. *ʔaani ʔaεurfa bass bil-ʔisim.*
by oneself - *waζζad-, b-nafis-.* He did that by himself. *huwwa sawwaaha waζζda* or *sawwaaha b-nafsa.*
by sight - *biš-šikil.* I know him only by sight. *ʔaani ʔaεurfa biš-šikil.*
by that - **1.** *min haaδa.* What do you understand by that? *š-tifhim min haaδa?* **2.** *b-haaδa.* What do you mean by that? *š-tiεni b-haaδa?*
by the hour - *bis-saaεa.* Do you know of a place where they rent boats by the hour? *tuεruf makaan yʔajjiruun bii blaam bis-saaεa?*
by the way - *bil-munaasaba.* By the way, I met a friend of yours yesterday. *bil-munaasaba, ṣaadafit waaζid min ʔaṣdiqaaʔak il-baarζa.*
by way of - *εala ṭariiq.* Are you going to Europe by way of Beirut? *ʔinta raayiζ il-ʔooruppa εala ṭariiq beeruut?*
day by day - *yoom wara yoom, yoom εala yoom.* Day by day his condition improves. *yoom wara yoom ζaalta da-titζassan.*
one by one - *waaζid wara waaζid, waaζid wara l-laax, waaζid waaζid.* One by one they left the room. *waaζid wara l-laax ṭilεaw imnil-ġurfa.*
bylaw - *niδaam* pl. *ʔanδima.* The bylaws of the society are available from the secretary. *niδaam ij-jamεiyya yitζaṣṣal imnis-sikirteer.*

C

cab - *taksi* pl. *-iyyaat, sayyaarat* (pl. *-aat*) *ʔujra.*
cabbage - *lahaana.* Cabbage is hard to digest. *l-lahaana ṣaεub tinhuδum.*
cabin - **1.** *kapra* pl. *-aat.* We have a cabin in the mountains. *εidna kapra bij-jibal.* **2.** *qamaara* pl. *-aat, kabiina* pl. *-aat.* Would you please tell me which deck my cabin is on? *gul-li, min faδlak, ib-ʔay daraja l-qamaara maalti?*
cabinet - **1.** *diilaab* pl. *dwaaliib.* We keep our good dishes in a small cabinet. *nδumm immaaεiinna z-zeena b-diilaab iṣġayyir.* **2.** *wazaara.* The cabinet met with the President of the Republic yesterday. *l-baarζa jtimaε il-wazaara wiyya raʔiis ij-jamhuuriyya.*
cabinet maker - *ṣaaniε* (pl. *ṣunnaaε*) *moobiilyaat.*
cable - **1.** *silk* pl. *ʔaslaak.* The cables support the bridge. *l-ʔaslaak laazimta lij-jisir.* Can the cable be laid within ten days? *mumkin tinnuṣub il-ʔaslaak ib-xilaal εaširt iyyaam?* **2.** *barqiyya* pl. *-aat.* I want to send a cable to New York. *ʔariid adizz barqiyya li-nyu yoork.*
to cable - *ʔabraq (i ʔibraaq).* Cable immediately when you arrive. *ʔibruq barqiyya ʔawwal-ma tooṣal.*
cadet - *tilmiiδ ζarbi* pl. *talaamiiδ ζarbiyyiin.*
cafe - *gahwa* pl. *gahaawi, maqha* pl. *maqaahi.*
cage - *qafaṣ* pl. *qfaaṣ.* The room is just like a cage. *l-ġurfa εabaalak qafaṣ.*
cake - **1.** *keeka* pl. *-aat* coll. *keek.* I'd like cake with my coffee. *ʔariid keek wiyya gahuuti.* **2.** *qaalab* pl. *qwaalib.* Can you bring me a cake of soap and a towel? *tigdar itjiib-li fadd qaalab ṣaabuun w-xaawli?*
calamity - *nakba* pl. *-aat, kaariθa* pl. *kawaariθ, faajiεa* pl. *fawaajiε.*
calcium - *kaalisyoom.*
to **calculate** - **1.** *ζisab (i ζisaab) n-.* It was difficult to calculate the costs. *čaan ṣaεub il-waaζid yiζsib il-kulfa.* **2.** *qaddar (i taqdiir) t-.* Let's call in an expert to calculate the extent of the damage. *xalli njiib xabiir ζatta yqaddir mada δ-δarar.*
calculated - *maζsuub.* This is a calculated risk. *haaδi mujaazafa maζsuub-ilha ζsaab.*
calculating - *nafεi*, maṣlaζi*.* She's a shrewd calculating woman. *haay fadd mara daahya nafεiyya.*
calculating machine - *ʔaalat* (pl. *-aat*) *ζaasiba.*
calendar - **1.** *taqwiim* pl. *taqaawiim, ruznaama* pl. *-aat.* I've noted it on my calendar. *ʔaani ʔaššaritha bit-taqwiim maali.* **2.** *manhaj* pl. *manaahij, birnaamij* pl. *baraamij.* What events are on the calendar this month? *šaku faεaaliyyaat bil-manhaj haš-šahar?*
calf - **1.** *εijil* pl. *εjuul.* Cows and calves were grazing in the field. *l-ihwaayiš wil-iεjuul čaanaw da-yirεuun bil-marεa.* -- That bag is made of genuine calf. *haj-janṭa msawwaaya min jilid εijil ʔaṣli.* **2.** *karša* pl. *-aat.* The bullet struck him in the calf of his leg. *r-riṣaaṣa ṣaabata b-karšat rijla.*
caliph - *xaliifa* pl. *xulafaaʔ.*
caliphate - *xilaafa* pl. *-aat.*
call - **1.** *nidaaʔ* pl. *-aat, muxaabara* pl. *-aat.* Were there any calls for me? *čaan ʔaku ʔili nidaaʔaat?* -- How much was the call? *šgadd kallaf in-nidaaʔ?* **2.** *daεwa.* He was the first to answer the call to arms. *čaan ʔawwal man labba d-daεwa lij-jihaad.*
**I thought I heard a call for help. *ʔaεtiqid simaεit waaζid yistanjid.*
to call - **1.** *ṣaaζ (i syaaζ) n-, naada (i nidaaʔ).* I called him but he didn't hear me. *ṣiζit εalee laakin ma-simaεni.* -- Shall I call you a cab? *ʔaṣiiζ-lak taksi?* **2.** *xaabar (u muxaabara) t-.* You can call me any time at my office. *tigdar itxaaburni lid-daaʔira šwakit-ma triid.* **3.** *dazz (i dazz) n- εala.* Call a doctor! *dizz εala ṭabiib!* **4.** *samma (i tasmiya) t-.* What do you call this in Arabic? *š-itsammi haaδa bil-εarabi?* -- Let's call him Ali. *xalli nsammii εali.*
to call attention to - *jilab (i jalb) n- intibaah*

l-, nabbah (i tanbiih) t- Ɛala. I called his
attention to it. *jilabt intibaaha ʔilha or nabbahta*
Ɛalee.

to call down - *zaff (i zaff) n-.* My boss called
me down for being late. *raʔissi zaffni li-ʔan*
ʔatʔaxxar

to call for - 1. *marr (u muruur) n- Ɛala, jaa*
(i majiiʔ) Ɛala. Will you call for me at the hotel?
tigdar itmurr Ɛalayya bil-ʔuuteel? 2. *raaz (u rooz)*
Ɛala. I have to call for my laundry. *laazim ʔaruuz*
Ɛala hduumi Ɛind il-makwi. 3. *stadƐa (i stidƐaaʔ),*
haaδi tistadƐi ztifaal. 4. *nraad (a) l-.* That calls
for a drink. *haaδa yinraad-la peek.* 5. *ṭilab*
(u ṭalab) n-. The president called for a vote on the
matter. *r-raʔiis ṭilab it-taṣwiit Ɛal-mawδuuƐ.*
6. *qarrar (i taqriir) t-.* The director has called
for a rehearsal for four o'clock. *l-muxrij qarrar*
ysawwi tamriin saaƐa ʔarbaƐa. 7. *Ɛayyan (i taƐyiin)*
t-. He called the conference for Monday, the fourth.
Ɛayyan wakt il-muʔtamar yoom iθ-θineen ʔarbaƐa
biš-šahar.

to call in - *lamm (i lamm) n-.* All old notes are
being called in. *kull il-ʔawraaq in-naqdiyya*
l-Ɛatiiga da-tinlamm.
Call him in. *ʔuṭluba or dizz Ɛalee or ṣiiza.*
We had to call in a specialist. *δṭarreena*
nistišiir ixtiṣaaṣi or čaan laazim nuṭlub raʔi
xtiṣaaṣi.

to call off - *ʔalġa (i ʔilġaaʔ) n-.* Today's
broadcast was called off for technical reasons.
ʔiδaaƐat il-yoom inliġat il-ʔasbaab fanniyya.

to call on - 1. *zaar (u zyaara) n-, jaa (i majiiʔ).*
We'll call on you next Sunday. *raz-inzuurak yoom*
il-ʔazzad ij-jaay or raz-nijiik yoom il-ʔazzad
ij-jaay. -- Our agent will call on you tomorrow.
wakiilna raz-yijiik baačir. 2. *stanjad (i stinjaad).*
You can call on me for help in case of necessity.
tigdar tistanjid biyya Ɛind iδ-δuruura.

to call out - 1. *ṭilab (u ṭalab) n-.* They had to
call out the firemen to put out the fire. *δṭarraw*
yṭulbuun il-ʔiṭfaaʔiyya zatta yṭaffuun in-naar.
2. *naada (i nidaaʔ) t-.* The demonstrators began to
call out his name with enthusiasm. *l-mutaδaahriin*
qaamaw ynaaduun ʔisma b-zamaas. 3. *Ɛilan (i ʔiƐlaan)*
n-. The conductor calls out all the stops. *j-jaabi*
yiƐlin ʔisim kull il-mazaṭṭaaṭ. 4. *ṣaaz (i ṣiyaaz)*
n-. They stopped in front of the door and called
out my name. *wugfaw giddaam il-baab w-ṣaazaw ʔismi.*

to call together - *lamm (i lamm) n- siwa, jimaƐ*
(a jamiƐ) n-. He called all of us together in his
office. *lammna kullna siwa b-ġurufta.*

to call (up) - 1. *xaabar (u muxaabara).* I'll
call you up tomorrow. *ʔaani raz-axaabrak baačir.*
2. *diƐa (i daƐwa) n-.* I heard they are calling up
year group 1944 for duty. *simaƐit raz-yidƐuun*
mawaaliid ʔalf w-tisiƐ miyya w-ʔarbaƐa w-ʔarbaƐiin
il-xidmat il-Ɛalam.

caller - 1. *zaaʔir pl. zuwwaar, xuṭṭaar pl. xṭaaṭiir.*
I'm expecting a gentleman caller this afternoon.
da-antiδir fadd rijjaal xuṭṭaar il-yoom il-Ɛaṣir.
2. *muraajiƐ pl. -iin.* Did I have any callers while
I was out of the office? *ʔijooni muraajiƐiin*
lil-maktab min činit ṭaaliƐ?

calling card - *kaart šaxṣi pl. -aat šaxṣiyya, biṭaaqa pl.*
-aat.

callus - *bismaar pl. bsaamiir.* I got calluses on my
hand from digging. *ṭilaƐ-li bismaar ib-ʔiidi*
mnil-zafur.

calm - 1. *saakin, haadiʔ.* The sea is calm again.
l-bazar saakin marra lux. 2. *haadiʔ.* He remained
calm and in control of the situation. *biqa haadiʔ*
w-imṣayṭir Ɛal-waδiƐ.

to keep calm - *ztifaδ (u ztifaaδ) b-huduuʔ~.*
Keep calm, everybody. *ztafδu b-huduuʔkum kullkum.*

to calm - *hadda (i tahdiʔa) t-, barrad (i tabriid)*
t-. We tried to calm the frighten animals.
zaawalna nhaddi l-zaywaanaat ij-jaafla.

to calm down - 1. *haffat (i tahfiit) t-.* Try to
calm him down. *zaawul ithaffta.* 2. *hifat (i hafit),*
hida? (a huduuʔ) n-. It took her some time to calm
down. *nraad-ilha mudda zatta tihfit. --* The wind has
calmed down. *l-hawa hifat or l-hawa wugaf or hidaʔ*
il-hawa.

to calm oneself - *ṭawwal (i taṭwiil) baal~,*
sakkan (i taskiin) ruuz~, barrad (i) nafis~,
hadda (i) nafis~, hidaʔ (a huduuʔ). Calm yourself!
ṭawwul baalak! or ʔihdaʔ!

calmly - *b-huduuʔ, b-buruud.* She took the news calmly.
ʔaxδat il-xabar ib-huduuʔ.

camel - *jimal pl. jimaal, biƐiir pl. biƐraan.*

camel dung - *baƐra pl. -aat coll. baƐar, baƐruura pl.*
-aat coll. baƐruur.

camel litter - *hawdaj pl. hawaadij.*

camera - *kaamira pl. -aat, makiinat (pl. makaayin)*
rasim.

camouflage - *tamwiih.*

to camouflage - *mawwah (i tamwiih) t-.*

camp - 1. *muƐaskar pl. -aat.* At what camp did you
get your training? *b-yaa muƐaskar itdarrabit?*
2. *muxayyam pl. -aat.* The boy scout camp is going
to be in the north. *l-kaššaafa raz-ykuun*
muxayyamhum biš-šimaal.

to camp - 1. *xayyam (i taxyiim).* We camped in
the woods. *xayyamna bil-ġaabaat.* 2. *Ɛaskar*
(i tƐiskir). The division camped a mile outside
the city. *l-firqa Ɛaskirat Ɛala buƐud miil*
imnil-wlaaya.

campaign - *zamla pl. -aat.* He took part in the
African campaign. *štirak bil-zamla l-ʔafriiqiyya.*
His election campaign lasted three months. *l-zamla*
l-intixaabiyya maalta ṭawwilat iθlatt išhur.

to campaign - *qaam (u) b-zamla.* He campaigned to
get himself elected to the presidency. *qaam*
ib-zamla l-ġarδ intixaaba lir-riyaasa.

camphor - *kaafuur.*

can - *quuṭiyya pl. qwaaṭi, Ɛilba pl. Ɛilab.* Give me a
can of green peas. *nṭiini quuṭiyya bazaalya xaδra.*

can - 1. *gidar (a maqdira) n-, tmakkan*
(a tamakkun), ʔamkan (i ʔimkaan), sṭaṭaaƐ
(i stiṭaaƐa). Can you speak English? *tigdar tizči*
ngiliizi? or *b-ʔimkaanak tizči ngiliizi? --* Could I
look at it, please. *ʔagdar ʔašuufha min faδlak? --*
She could be wrong. *yimkin ġalṭaana. --* Can't that
be simplified? *ma-yimkin tabṣiiṭ haaδa? --* Can't
you delay this a few hours. *ma-mumkin itƐaṭṭil*
haaδa čam saaƐa. -- He did everything he could.
sawwa kull-ma čaan b-imkaana. -- He could have come.
čaan ib-ʔimkaana yiji. -- If you can bring me the
book tomorrow, I'll appreciate it. *ʔiδa titmakkan*
itjiib-li l-iktaab baačir iṣ-ṣubz ʔakuun mamnuun.
2. *yjuuz.* He could have said that. *yjuuz gaala*
l-haaδa.
**I can't say yet whether I'll run for election or
not.** *l-hassa ma-aƐruf baƐad ʔiδa raz-atqaddam*
lil-intixaab loo laa.

to can - *Ɛallab (i taƐliib) t-.* This factory is
set up to process and can all kinds of vegetables.
hal-maƐmal munšaʔ il-tahyiiʔat w-taƐliib anwaaƐ
il-muxaδδaraat.

canal - 1. *qanaal pl. -aat, qanaat pl. ʔaqniya,*
qanawaat. We came by way of the Suez Canal. *jeena*
Ɛala ṭariiq qanaal is-suweez. 2. *saagya pl. swaagi,*
saajya pl. swaaji, turƐa pl. turaƐ. We'll have to
dig a canal here to drain the land. *laazim nuzfur*
saajya hnaa l-bazl il-ʔaruδ.

canary - *kanaari pl. -iyya.*

to cancel - 1. *ʔalġa (i ʔilġaaʔ) n-, baṭṭal (i tabṭiil,*
tbuṭṭil) t-. They have cancelled the order.
ʔalġaw l-ʔamur. -- I'd like to cancel my newspaper
subscription. *ʔazibb alġi štiraaki bij-jariida. --*
I had to cancel my doctor's appointment. *δṭarreet*
alġi mawƐidi wiyya ṭ-ṭabiib. -- The meeting was
canceled. *l-ijtimaaƐ inliġa.* 2. *ṣaqqaṭ*
(i taṣqiiṭ) t-. He cancelled the rest of my debt.
ṣaqqaṭ il-baaqi min deena Ɛalayya. -- These postage
stamps are canceled. *haṭ-ṭawaabiƐ il-bariidiyya*
mṣaqqaṭa.

cancer - *saraṭaan.* They discovered too late that he
had cancer. *ligaw Ɛinda saraṭaan baƐad-ma faat*
il-wakit.

candid - *ṣariiz.*

candidacy - *taršiiz.*

candidate - *muraššaz pl. -iin.* Our party isn't
putting up a candidate. *zizibna ma-raz-yraššiz*
muraššaz. -- We have three candidates for the
position. *Ɛidna tlaθ muraššaziin lil-waδiifa.*

candle - *šamƐa pl. šmuuƐ.* We had to light a candle.
δṭarreena nišƐil šamƐa.

candlestick - *šamiƐdaan pl. -aat.*

candy - *šakraaya pl. -aat coll. šakaraat.*

chocolate candy - *čukleetaaya pl. -aat coll.*
čukleet.

to candy - *šakkar (i taskiir) t-.* He brought us
a box of candied fruits. *jaab-inna quuṭiyya*
fawaakih imšakkira.

cane - 1. *guṣba pl. -aat coll. guṣab.* The marsh
dwellers build their houses of cane. *sukkaan*
il-ahwaar yibnuun ibyuuthum min guṣab. 2. *Ɛuučiyya*

pl. *-aat, ℇawaači.* Ever since I broke my leg I have been walking with a cane. *min wakit-ma nkisrat rijli gimit amši ℇal-ℇuučiyya.* 3. *baaṣṭoon* pl. *-aat.* He only carries the cane for show. *huwwa šaayil il-baaṣṭoon lil-kašxa bass.* 4. *ℇaṣa* pl. *ℇiṣi.* The blind man feels his way with the cane. *l-ʔaℇmi yitzassas ṭariiqa bil-ℇaṣa.*

canned goods - *muℇallabaat.* Canned goods can be kept a long time. *muℇallabaat il-ʔaṭℇima tinzufuδ mudda ṭawiila.*

cannibal - *ʔaakil* (pl. *ʔakilat*) *lazam il-bašar.*

cannon - *madfaℇ* pl. *madaafiℇ, ṭoob* pl. *ṭwaab.*

can opener - *fattaaza* pl. *-aat.*

cantaloupe - *baṭṭiixa* pl. *-aat* coll. *baṭṭiix.*

canteen - 1. *maṭṭaara* pl. *-aat.* Did you fill your canteen? *trast il-maṭṭaara maaltak?* 2. *kaantiin* pl. *-aat.* The soldiers are waiting for the canteen to open. *j-junuud yintaδruun il-kaantiin yfattiz.*

canvas - 1. *čunfaaṣ, junfaaṣ.* My gym shoes are made of canvas. *qundart il-riyaaδa maalti msawwaaya min čunfaaṣ.* 2. *kittaan* pl. *-aat.* This picture is painted on canvas. *haṣ-ṣuura marsuuma ℇala kittaan.*

to **canvass** - 1. *marr (u muruur) n- ℇala.* They asked me to canvass the whole group to get their opinions. *ṭilbaw minni ʔamurr ℇala kull ij-jamaaℇa w-astaṭliℇ ʔaraaʔhum.* 2. *jass (i jass) nabuδ.* Before we change anything, let's canvass the group. *gabuḷ-ma nġayyir šii, xalli njiss nabδ ij-jamaaℇa.*

cap - 1. *ℇaraqčiin* pl. *-aat, klaaw* pl. *-aat.* He's wearing a small cap under his head cloth. *laabis ℇaraqčiin jawwa ġuṭurta.* 2. *raas* pl. *ruus.* I've lost the cap to my fountain pen. *δayyaℇit ir-raas maal qalam il-zibir maali.* 3. *ġiṭa* pl. *ġuṭaayaat, qabaġ* pl. *-aat.* Put the cap back on the bottle. *rajjiℇ qabaġ il-buṭil ib-makaana.* 4. *talbiisa* pl. *-aat.* The cap is cutting my gums. *t-talbiisa da-tijraz laθθti.* 5. *kaap* pl. *-aat.* The jockey's cap fell off during the race. *wugaℇ il-kaap maal il-jaaki ʔaθnaaʔ is-sibaaq.*

to cap - 1. *labbas (i talbiis) t-.* This tooth needs capping. *has-sinn yinraad-la talbiis.* 2. *qabbaġ (i tqubbuġ, taqbiiġ) t-.* They cap the bottles with metal caps. *yqabbuġuun l-ibṭuula b-qabaġaat maℇdan.*

capability - *maqdira.*

capable - *miqtidir, qaadir.* She's a very capable person. *hiyya fadd wazda kulliš miqtadra.* -- He's capable of anything. *huwwa qaadir ℇala kullši* or ****yitlaℇ min ʔiida kullši.*

capacity - 1. *siℇa* pl. *-aat.* The tank has a capacity of one hundred gallons. *siℇat it-taanki miit gaḷin.* 2. *sifa* pl. *-aat.* I am here in my capacity as guardian. *ʔaani hnaa b-ṣifati waṣi.* 3. *ṭaaqa* pl. *-aat.* It is already working up to full capacity. *min hassa da-tištuġul kull ṭaaqatha.*

**The tank is full to capacity. *t-taanki malyaan lir-raas* or *t-taanki matruus il-ʔamaana.*

cape - *raas* pl. *ruus.* The Cape of Good Hope. *raas ir-rijaaʔ iṣ-ṣaaliz.*

capital - 1. *ℇaaṣima* pl. *ℇawaaṣim.* Have you ever been in the capital? *b-ℇumrak raayiz lil-ℇaaṣima?* 2. *raasmaal.* How much capital do you need to start your business? *šgadd tiztaaj raasmaal zatta tibdi šuġḷak?* 3. *maal* pl. *ʔamwaal.* His capital is invested abroad. *ʔamwaala mustaθmara bil-xaarij.* 4. *zaruf čibiir* pl. *zuruuf čibiira.* When you write English, begin every sentence with a capital. *min tiktib bil-ingiliizi ʔibdi kull jumla b-zaruf ičbiir.* 5. *ṣarmaaya* pl. *-aat.* Ahmed is going to provide me with a capital of ID 1,000 to open a shop. *ʔazmad raz-yintiini ṣarmaaya ʔalif diinaar afattiz biiha dukkaan.*

capitalist - *raʔismaali* pl. *-iyyiin.*

capitalism - *raʔismaaliyya.*

capitalistic - *raʔismaali*.*

to **capitalize** - *staġall (i stiġlaal).* We are planning to capitalize on the situation. *b-niyyatna nistiġill il-waδiℇ.*

capital offense - *jinaaya* pl. *-aat.*

capital punishment - *ℇuquubat il-ʔiℇdaam.*

capon - *diič maxṣi* pl. *dyuuč maxṣiyya.*

capricious - *hawaaʔi*, sweeℇati*.*

**She is capricious. *saaℇaatha muu suwa.*

capsule - *zillaaja* pl. *-aat* coll. *zillaaj, gullaaja* pl. *-aat* coll. *gullaaj, kabsuula* pl. *-aat* coll. *kabsuul.*

captain - *qabṭaan* pl. *-iyya, raʔiis* pl. *ruʔasaaʔ.* The captain was the last to leave the sinking ship. *l-qabṭaan čaan ʔaaxir man tirak is-sifiina l-ġargaana.* -- The captain was taken prisoner with his entire company. *r-raʔiis itʔassar, huwwa wil-fawj maala kulla.* -- Who's the captain of the team? *minu raʔiis il-fariiq?*

to **captivate** - *ʔisar (yiʔsar ʔasir) n-.* She captivated us all with her charm and good looks. *ʔisratna kullna b-fitnatha w-jamaalha.*

captive - 1. *ʔasiir* pl. *ʔasra.* The captives are arriving from the front in large numbers. *l-ʔasra da-yooṣluun imnij-jabha b-ʔaℇdaad čibiira.* -- The captive tiger hasn't eaten for two days. *n-nimr il-ʔasiir ṣaar-la yoomeen ma-ʔakal.* 2. *rahiina* pl. *rahaayin.* He was held captive by the band until his family paid the ransom. *buqa rahiina ℇind il-ℇiṣaaba ʔila ʔan ℇaaʔilta difℇaw il-xaawa.* 3. *maszuur* pl. *-iin.* He held his audience captive with his tales of adventure. *tirak is-saamℇiin maszuuriin ib-qiṣaṣ muġaamaraata.*

captivity - *ʔasir.*

to **capture** - 1. *ʔassar (i tʔissir, taʔsiir) t-.* They captured a general and his entire staff. *ʔassraw janaraaḷ w-kull ʔarkaan zarba.* 2. *stawla (i stiilaaʔ).* Our armies have captured two cities. *jeešna stawla ℇala madiinteen.* 3. *ʔaxaδ (u ʔaxiδ) n-.* We captured the town without a shot being fired. *ʔaxaδna l-madiina bila ʔiṭlaaq naar.*

car - 1. *sayyaara* pl. *-aat.* Would you like to ride in my car? *yℇijbak tirkab ib-sayyaarti?* 2. *faargoon* pl. *-aat, faraagiin.* Two cars went off the track. *faargooneen ṭilℇat imnis-sičča.*

carafe - *saraazi, saraaziyya* pl. *-aat.* Get the carafe of water out of the refrigerator. *jiib saraazi l-maay imniθ-θillaaja.*

carat - *qiiraaṭ* pl. *-aat, qaraariiṭ; zabba* pl. *-aat.* These earrings are made of eighteen carat gold. *hat-taraači δahabha θmunṭaℇaš qiiraaṭ.*

caravan - *karwaan* pl. *karaawiin, qaafila* pl. *qawaafil.*

caravansary - *xaan* pl. *-aat.*

carbon - *kaarboon.*

carbon paper - *waraq* (pl. *ʔawraaq*) *karboon.* I need some new carbon paper. *ʔaztaaj šwayya waraq kaarboon ijdiid.*

carburetor - *kaabreeta* pl. *-aat.*

card - 1. *waraqa* pl. *ʔawraaq* coll. *waraq.* They played cards all evening. *liℇbaw waraq ṭuul il-leel.* 2. *biṭaaqa* pl. *-aat.* They have a fine selection of greeting cards in that shop. *ℇidhum majmuuℇa badiiℇa min biṭaaqaat tahaani b-δaak il-maxzan.* -- He sent me a card from Beirut. *ʔarsal-li biṭaaqa min beeruut.* 3. *kaart* pl. *-aat.* He left me his card with his telephone number. *tirak-li kaarta maℇa raqam talafoona.*

**He's quite a card! *huwwa fadd nimra xaaṣṣa!*

to card - 1. *mišaṭ (i mašiṭ) n.* The women spent the whole day carding the wool. *n-nisaaʔ giδaw kull in-nahaar ymištuun iṣ-ṣuuf.* 2. *nidaf (i nadif) n-.* The cotton in this mattress needs carding. *l-guṭin maal haaδa l-ifraaš yinraad-la nadif.*

cardboard - *mqawwaa* pl. *-aat* coll. *mqawwa.* Put a piece of cardboard in between. *zuṭṭ fadd imqawwaaya bin-nuṣṣ.* -- Put them in a cardboard box. *zuṭṭhum ib-ṣanduug imqawwa.*

cardomom - *heel.* Don't put too much cardomom in the tea. *la-tzuṭṭ heel ihwaaya bič-čaay.*

care - 1. *mdaaraa.* Regular care of the teeth is important. *mdaaraat l-isnuun b-intiδaam muhimm jiddan.* 2. *ℇinaaya.* He's under the doctor's care. *huwwa tazat ℇinaayat iṭ-ṭabiib.* 3. *ʔamaana.* May I leave these documents in your care. *ʔagdar axalli hal-mustanadaat ib-ʔamaantak?*

in care of - *b-waaṣṭat, ℇala ℇinwaan.* Send me the letter care of Ahmed Husayn. *dizz-li l-maktuub ℇala ℇinwaan azmad izseen.*

to take care - 1. *htamm (a htimaam).* I took care to mention everything. *htammeet ʔaδkur kullši.* 2. *tzaaša (a tazaaši).* I took care not to mention anything. *tzaašeet aδkur ʔay sii.*

to take care of - 1. *daar (i deer) n- baal~.* The maids work is to take care of the children. *l-xaadma šuġulha deer baalha ℇaj-jihhaal.* -- Take care of my money for me. *diir baalak ℇala fluusi.* 2. *sawwa (i taswiya) t-, xallaṣ (i taxliiṣ) t-.* I still have a few things to take care of. *ʔaani baℇad ℇindi baℇδ il-ʔašyaaʔ laazim asawwiiha.* 3. *ℇtina (i ℇtinaaʔ) b-, zaafaδ (i muzaafaδa) t-.* He takes care of his clothes. *yiℇtini b-ihduuma.*

**That takes care of that. *xilsaṭ wis-salaam* or *hal-muškila nzallat* or *haaδa ntiha ʔamra* or *šii ysidd šii.*

**Good-by; take care of yourself. *fiimaanilla,*

ʔaḷḷa wyaak! or *fiimaanillaa, ʔamaant aḷḷa εala nafsak!*

to care - 1. *maal (i meel) l-.* I don't care much for movies. *ma-amiil ihwaaya lis-siinama.* **2.** *daar (i deer) n- baal.* Who cares? *minu ydiir baal?*

**What do I care? *w-aani š-aεlayya?*

**I don't care what he thinks. *ma-yhimmni huwwa š-yiftikir.*

**For all I care, you can go wherever you like. *wala yhimmni, tigdar itruuʒ ween-ma yεijbak.*

**I don't care to go to the movies tonight. *ma-yiεjibni ʔaruuʒ lis-siinama hal-leela.*

to care for - 1. *εtina (i εtinaaʔ) b-, tiεab (a taεab, taεbaan) εala.* This garden is well cared for. *hal-ʒadiiqa miεtiniin biiha hwaaya* or *hal-ʒadiiqa taεbaaniin εaleeha hwaaya.* **2.** *daar (i deer) n- baal~, daara (i mudaaraa).* My sister is caring for the children today. *ʔuxti da-tdiir baalha εal-ʔaṭfaal hal-yoom.* **3.** *ʒabb (i ʒubb).* Do you care for her? *tʒibbha?*

**Would you care for gravy on the meat? *yεijbak marag εala l-laʒam?*

to be cared for - *čaan matεuub εala, ndaar (a) baal εala.* The children are well cared for. *l-ʔaṭfaal ihwaaya matεuub εaleehum.*

career - 1. *mihna* pl. *mihan.* Her career is more important for her than her marriage. *mihnatha ʔahamm-ilha mniz-zawaaj.* -- He made medicine his career. *ttixaδ iṭ-ṭibb mihna ʔila.* **2.** *siira* pl. *siyar.* I have been following his career with great interest. *da-atεaqqab siirta b-ihtimaam šadiid.* **3.** *maslak* pl. *masaalik.* He spent his life in this career. *qiδa εumra b-hal-maslak.* **4.** *maslaki*.* He is a career diplomat. *huwwa dabloomaasi maslaki.*

carefree - *εadam mubaalaat.* He leads a carefree life. *yεiiš εiišat εadam mubaalaat.*

careful - 1. *daqiiq.* He's a very careful person. *huwwa šaxiṣ kulliš daqiiq.* **2.** *ʒaδir, mitʒaδδir.* He is very careful about how he invests his money. *huwwa kulliš ʒaδir b-istiθmaar ifluusa.*

to be careful - 1. *daar (i deer) n- baal~.* Be careful not to break this vase. *diir baalak la-truuʒ tiksir hal-mazhariyya.* **2.** *čaan ʒariiṣ.* I was careful not to mention anything. *kunit ʒariiṣ la-ajiib δikir fadd šii.*

carefully - 1. *b-εinaaya.* They lifted the stretcher carefully. *šaalaw is-sadya b-εinaaya.* **2.** *b-diqqa.* Check the figures carefully. *ʔifʒaṣ il-ʔarqaam ib-diqqa.* **3.** *b-ʒaδar.* He drives carefully. *ysuug is-sayyaara b-ʒaδar.*

careless - *muhmil.* She's become careless lately. *ṣaayra muhmil bil-ʔayyaam il-ʔaxiira.*

**He's careless with his money. *ma-ydiir baala εala fluusa.*

cargo - *ʒumuula* pl. *-aat, šaʒna* pl. *-aat.*

carnation - *qranfila* pl. *-aat* coll. *qranfil.*

carpenter - *najjaar* pl. *-iin, najaajiir.*

carpet - *zuuliyya* pl. *zwaali, sijjaada* pl. *sijjaad.* This is a nice carpet. *haz-zuuliyya ʒilwa* or *haaδi xoos sijjaada.*

to have someone on the carpet - *razzal (i razaala) t-, wabbax (i tawbiix) t-.* The boss had him on the carpet again this morning. *l-mudiir razzala l-yoom iṣ-ṣubuʒ marra lux.*

to carpet - *furaš (u fariš) n- b-sijjaad, ġaṭṭa (i taġṭiya) t- b-sijjaad.* All the stairs were carpeted. *kull id-darjaat čaanat mafruuša b-sijjaad.*

carrot - *jizra* pl. *-aat* coll. *jizar.*

to **carry - 1.** *šaal (i šeel) n-.* He'll carry your bags for you. *huwwa raʒ-yšiil-lak ij-junaṭ.* **2.** *ʒimal (i ʒamil) n-.* This truck carries five tons. *hal-loori yiʒmil xamis aṭnaan.* **3.** *baaε (i beeε) n-.* Do you carry men's shirts? *tbiiε iθyaab maal iryaajiil?* **4.** *niqal (u naqil) n-.* Mosquitoes carry malaria. *l-bagg yinqul il-malaarya.* **5.** *faaz (u fooz) n-.* He carried the election with an overwhelming majority, *faaz bil-intixaabaat ib-ʔakθariyya saaʒiqa.* **6.** *niṭa (i naṭi) bid-deen.* The grocer agreed to carry us until I get another job. *l-baggaal waafag yinṭiina bid-deen ʒatta algi šuġul.* **7.** *qibal (a qubuul) n-.* The motion was carried. *l-iqtiraaʒ inqibal.*

**This crime carries the death penalty. *haaδi l-jariima εaleeha εuquubt il-ʔiεdaam.*

**The captain carries himself well. *r-raʔiis šamurta ʒilwa.*

**Isn't that carrying things a little too far? *muu θixnat εaad?*

to carry away - 1. *jiraf (u jaruf) n-.* The flood carried the house away. *l-fayaδaan jiraf il-beet.* **2.** *ṭirab (u ṭarab) n-.* The music carried me away. *l-moosiiqa ṭirbatni.* **3.** *hazz (i hazz) n- εawaaṭif, siʒar (a saʒir) n-.* The crowd was carried away by the eloquence of the speaker. *j-jamhuur inhazzat εawaaṭfa b-faṣaaʒat il-xaṭiib.* **4.** *ʔaxaδ (u ʔaxiδ) n-.* He was carried away by the idea. *nʔixaδ bil-fikra.*

to carry on - *waaṣal (i muwaaṣala) t-.* His son carries on his business. *ʔibna da-ywaaṣil tijaarta.*

to carry out - 1. *naffaδ (i tanfiiδ) t-.* We'll try to carry out your plan. *raʒ-inʒaawil innaffiδ il-xiṭṭa maaltak.* **2.** *ṭallaε (i taṭliiε, ṭṭilliε) t-.* Carry out the garbage. *ṭalliε iz-zibil barra.*

to carry weight - *(čaan) ʔila wazin, (čaan) ʔila ʔahammiyya.* His opinion carries great weight. *raʔya ʔila wazin čibiir.*

cart - *εarabaana* pl. *εarabaayin.* The cart was so loaded that he could hardly push it. *l-εarabaana čaanat mašʒuuna ʔila daraja ʔan čaan bil-kaad yidfaεha.*

to cart - *ʒimal (i ʒamil) n-.* The sand has to be carted away. *r-ramul laazim yinʒimil minnaa.*

cartridge - 1. *fišga* pl. *fišag, ṭalqa* pl. *-aat.* Three shots remained in the revolver. *buqat bil-musaddas itlaθ ṭalqaat.* **2.** *ʔigna* pl. *-aat.* I want to change the cartridge on my recordplayer. *ʔariid abaddil il-ʔigna maal foonooġraafi.*

to **carve - 1.** *niqaš (u naqiš) n-.* This is the man who carved the teak doors of the mosque. *haaδa r-rajil ʔilli niqaš ʔabwaab iṣ-ṣaaj maal il-masjid.* **2.** *niʒat (a naʒit) n-.* The Assyrians used to carve winged bulls from stone. *l-ʔaašuuriyyiin iεtaadaw yinʒatuun θiiraan imjannaʒa mniṣ-ṣaxar.* **3.** *gaṣgaṣ (i tigiṣgiṣ) t-.* Will you carve the turkey? *tʒibb itgaṣgiṣ il-εališiiš?* **4.** *ʒufar (u ʒafur) n-.* He carved his name on the trunk of the tree. *ʒufar ʔisma εala jiδε iš-šajara.*

case - 1. *ṣanduug* pl. *ṣnaadiig.* Leave the bottles in the case. *xalli l-ibṭuula biṣ-ṣanduug.* **2.** *beet* pl. *byuut, quuṭiyya* pl. *qwaaṭi.* I need a new case for my glasses. *ʔaʒtaaj beet jidiid lil-manaaδir maalti.* **3.** *ʔiṣaaba* pl. *-aat.* There were five new cases of malaria. *čaan aku xamis ʔiṣaabaat jidiida bil-malaarya.* **4.** *qaδiyya* pl. *qδaaya, ʒaadiθ* pl. *ʒwaadiθ.* I read about the case in the newspaper. *qreet εan il-qaδiyya bij-jariida.* -- He presented his case well. *εiraδ qaδiita εariδ zeen.* **5.** *daεwa* pl. *-aat, daεaawi.* He's lost his case. *huwwa xiṣar daεuuta.* **6.** *ʒaala* pl. *-aat.* That being the case... *ṭaal-ma l-ʒaala hiiči...*

**The doctor is out on a case. *ṭ-ṭabiib raaʒ yšuuf mariiδ.*

in any case - *εala kull ʒaal, mahma kaan.* I'll call in any case. *ʔaani ʔaxaabur εala kull ʒaal.*

in case - *ʔiδa.* Wait for me in case I'm late. *stanδirni ʔiδa tʔaxxarit.*

in case of - *b-ʒaalat.* In case of fire, use the emergency exit. *staεmil baab iṭ-ṭawaari b-ʒaalat il-ʒariiq.*

cash - 1. *naqid.* I have no cash with me. *ma-εindi naqid wiyyaaya* or *ma-šaayil ifluus.* **2.** *naqdi*, naqdan.* I'll pay cash. *raʒ-adfaε naqdi.* -- We sell only for cash. *ʔiʒna ma-nbiiε ġeer naqdi* or *nbiiε bass bin-naqdi.*

to cash - *ṣarraf (u taṣriif) t-.* Can you cash a check for me? *tigdar itṣarruf-li čakk?*

cashier - *ṣarraaf* pl. *-iin, ṣraariif, ʔamiin* (pl. *ʔumanaaʔ*) *ṣanduuq.*

cashmere - *kašmiir.* I bought my sister a cashmere sweater. *štireet il-ʔuxti bluuz kašmiir.*

casket - *taabuut* pl. *twaabiit.* Six of his best friends carried his casket. *sitta min ʔaʒsan ʔaṣdiqaaʔa šaalaw taabuuta.*

cast - 1. *majmuuεa* pl. *-aat, hayʔa* pl. *-aat.* The new play has an excellent cast of actors. *t-tamθiiliyya j-jidiida biiha xooš majmuuεat mumaθθiliin.* **2.** *qaalab* pl. *qwaalib.* How long will you have to wear the cast? *šgadd laazim tilbas il-qaalab?*

to cast - 1. *ṣabb (u ṣabb) n-.* The statue will be cast in bronze. *t-timθaal raʒ-yinṣabb min ibrunz.* **2.** *niṭa (i naṭi).* I cast my vote for the majority party nominee. *nṭeet ṣooti l-muraššaʒ ʒizb il-ʔakθariyya.*

**The die is cast. *quδiya l-ʔamr.*

to cast anchor - *risa (i rasu) n-, δabb (i δabb) n- ʔangar.* We cast anchor at dawn. *δabbeena ʔangar wiyya l-fajir.* -- The ship cast anchor. *l-baaxira* *risat.*

castle - *qalƐa* pl. *qilaaƐ*. Have you seen the old castle? *šift il-qalƐa l-qadiima?* -- I'm taking the pawn with the castle. *raẓ-aktul ij-jundi bil-qalƐa.*

castor oil - *dihn il-xirwiƐ.*

casual - *Ɛaabir, ṭaari?, ṣaṭẓi*, Ɛaraḏi**. It was nothing more than a casual remark. *ma-čaanat ?azyad min mulaaẓaḏa Ɛaabira.* -- He's only a casual acquaintance. *?aƐurfa bass maƐrifa ṣaṭẓiyya.*

to be casual about - *ma-htamm (a) b-, ma-?axaδ (u) iƐtibaar l-.* I wish I could be as casual about it as he is. *yaa reet agdar aṣiir miθla w-ma-aaxuδ lil-mawḏuuƐ ihwaaya Ɛtibaar.*

casually - **1.** *Ɛaraḏan, ṣidfatan.* He said it to me quite casually. *gaal-li-yyaaha Ɛaraḏan.* **2.** *ṣaṭẓiyyan, b-ṣuura ṣaṭẓiyya.* I only know him casually. *?aƐurfa b-ṣuura ṣaṭẓiyya.*

casualties - *?iṣaabaat, xasaa?ir.* Our casualties in Africa were small. *xasaa?irna b-?afriiqya čaanat qaliila.*

cat - **1.** *bazzuun* pl. *bzaaziin, hirr* pl. *hruura.* Our cat had kittens yesterday. *bazzuunatna jaabat ifruux il-baarẓa.* **2.** *qiṭṭ* pl. *qiṭaṭ.* When the cat's away, the mice will play. *ġaab il-qiṭṭ, ?ilƐab yaa faar.*

catalogue - *kataloog* pl. *-aat.* The sample clothes patterns in this catalogue are better. *namaaδij tafṣiil il-malaabis ib-hal-kataloog ?aẓsan.* -- Why don't you arrange your (card) catalogue alphabetically? *leeš ma-trattbuun il-kataloog ẓasab il-ẓuruuf il-?abjadiyya?*

catastrophe - *kaariθa* pl. *kawaariθ, nakba* pl. *-aat.*

catch - **1.** *zuqfaala* pl. *-aat, quful* pl. *qfaala.* The catch on the camera is broken. *z-zuqfaala maal il-kaameera maksuura.* **2.** *ṣeeda* pl. *-aat.* Ten fish is a good catch. *Ɛašir simčaat xooš ṣeeda.* -- That girl is a good catch. *hal-ibnayya xooš ṣeeda.* **3.** *ẓiila* pl. *ẓiyal, liƐba* pl. *laƐab.* There must be a catch to it. *laazim biiha liƐba.*

to catch - **1.** *ṣaad (i ṣeed) n-.* We caught a lot of fish. *ṣidna simič ihwaaya.* **2.** *ligaf (u laguf) n-.* Here, catch it! *yaḷḷa, ?ilgufha!* **3.** *laẓẓag (i talẓiig) t- b-.* I have to catch a train at five o'clock. *laazim alaẓẓig ib-qiṭaar is-saaƐa xamsa.* **4.** *lizam (a lazim) n-.* I caught him at it. *?aani lzamta biiha.* -- They caught him red-handed. *lizmoo mitlabbis bij-jariima.* -- They caught him before he could get over the border. *lizmoo gabuḷ-ma yigdar yuƐbur il-ẓiduud.* **5.** *qibaḏ (u qabuḏ) n- Ɛala, kumaš (u kamuš) n-.* The police caught the thief. *š-šurṭa qibḏaw Ɛala l-ẓaraami.* **6.** *?axaδ (u ?axiδ) n-.* The lock doesn't catch well. *l-qifil ma-da-yaaxuδ zeen.* **7.** *simaƐ (a samiƐ) n-.* I didn't catch his name. *ma-smaƐit ?isma zeen.* **8.** *šakkal (i taškiil) t-.* My coat caught on a nail. *sitirti šakklat ib-fadd bismaar.* **9.** *ẓiṣar (i ẓaṣir) n-.* I've caught my finger in the door. *?iṣibƐi nẓiṣar bil-baab.*

to catch cold - *nnišal (i), ?axaδ (u ?axiδ) barid.* You'll catch cold. *?inta raẓ-tinnišil.*

to catch fire - **1.** *štiƐal (i stiƐaal), ẓtirag (i ẓirag).* The wood is so dry that it will catch fire quickly. *l-xišab halgadd-ma yaabis yištiƐil ib-saaƐ.* **2.** *Ɛtilag (i).* The wood didn't catch fire. *l-ẓaṭab ma-Ɛtilag.*

to catch hold - *lizam (a lazim) n-.* Catch hold of the other end. *?ilzam min ṣafẓat il-lux.*

to catch on - **1.** *diraj (u darij).* That song caught on very quickly. *hal-?uġniya dirjat bil-Ɛajal.* **2.** *ligaf (u laguf) n-, ftiham (i ftihaam).* He catches on quickly. *yilgufha bil-Ɛajal.* -- She immediately caught on to the idea. *hiyya bil-Ɛajal iftihmatha lil-fikra.*

to catch the eye - *lifat (i lafit) n- naḏar, jilab (i jalib) n- naḏar.* The neckties in the window caught my eye. *l-?arbiṭa biš-šibbaač liftat naḏari.*

to catch the measles - *ẓaṣṣab (u tẓiṣṣib) t-, ?axaδ (u ?axiδ) n- il-ẓaṣba, nṣaab (a) bil-ẓaṣba.* I caught the measles from him. *?axaδit il-ẓaṣba minna.*

to catch up - **1.** *laẓẓag (i tliẓẓig).* Try to catch up in your work. *ẓaawil itlaẓẓig ib-šuġḷak.* -- Go ahead, I'll catch up with you. *ruuẓ, Ɛuud ?aani alaẓẓig biik.* **2.** *Ɛawwaḏ (i taƐwiiḏ) t-.* I have to catch up on my sleep. *laazim aƐawwiḏ Ɛan noomi.*

catching - *muƐdi.* Measles are catching. *l-ẓaṣba muƐdiya.*

caterpillar - *duudat* (pl. *-aat* coll. *duud*) *qazz.*

cathedral - *kaatidraa?iyya* pl. *-aat.*

cattle - *mawaaši, hawaayiš, baqar.* They raise fine cattle in this part of the country. *yrabbuun xooš mawaaši b-hal-qisim imnil-balad.*

to get **caught** - **1.** *wugaf (a waguf, wuguuf).* A fish bone got caught in his throat. *Ɛaḏmat simač wugfat ib-lahaata.* **2.** *nlizam (i lazim).* I got caught in a shower on the way home. *nlizamit ib-maṭra b-ṭariiqi lil-beet.* -- Don't get caught! *la-txalli nafsak tillizim* or *la-txalli nafsak tinkumuš.*

cauliflower - *qarnaabiiṭ.*

cause - *sabab* pl. *?asbaab, ġaaya* pl. *-aat.* What is the cause of the delay? *šinu sabab it-ta?xiir?* -- He died for a good cause. *huwwa maat ib-sabiil ġaaya šariifa.*

to cause - *sabbab (i tasbiib) t-.* What caused the accident? *š-sabbab il-ẓaadiθ?* -- He causes her a lot of grief. *huwwa ysabbib-ilha hwaaya qahar.*

caution - *ẓaδar, taẓδiir, ẓtiyaaṭ, ẓtiraas.* Caution in this work is just as important as speed. *l-ẓaδar ib-haaδa š-šuġuḷ muhimm miθil ?ahammiyyat is-surƐa.*

cautious - *mitẓaδδir, miẓtiris, mintibih.* He's very cautious. *huwwa kulliš mitẓaδδir.*

cave - *kahaf* pl. *khuuf, maġaara* pl. *-aat, maġaayir.* We hid in a cave. *?iẓna xtalna b-fadd kahaf.*

to cave in - *ṭubag (u ṭabug).* I'm afraid the house is going to cave in. *da-axaaf il-beet raẓ-yiṭbug.*

cavity - *ẓafur* pl. *ẓfuur.* I have a cavity in this tooth. *Ɛindi ẓafur ib-has-sinn.*

to **cease** - **1.** *kaff (u kaff) n-.* The company has decided to cease publication of its monthly magazine. *š-šarika qarrirat itkuff Ɛan našir majallatha š-šahriyya.*

cease-fire - *waqf iṭlaaq in-naar.* A cease-fire is expected before midnight. *waqf iṭlaaq in-naar muntaḏar gabuḷ nuṣṣ il-leel.*

cedar - *?arza* pl. *-aat* coll. *?ariz.*

ceiling - **1.** *saguf* pl. *sguuf.* The ceiling is painted white. *s-saguf maṣbuuġ ib-?abyaḏ.* **2.** *ẓadd ?aqṣa.* We shouldn't exceed the ceiling the government has set. *laazim ma-nitjaawaz il-ẓadd il-?aqṣa ?illi Ɛayynata l-ẓukuuma.*

to **celebrate** - *ẓtifal (i ẓtifaal).* We're celebrating his birthday tomorrow. *raẓ-niẓtifil ib-Ɛiid miilaada baačir.*

celebration - *ẓtifaal* pl. *-aat.* The celebration took place yesterday. *l-iẓtifaal ṣaar il-baarẓa.*

cell - **1.** *zinzaana* pl. *-aat.* Take the prisoner to his cell. *waddi l-maẓbuus il-zinzaanta.* **2.** *xaliyya* pl. *xalaaya, ẓjayra* pl. *-aat.* We were able to observe the structure of the cells under the microscope. *tmakkanna nšuuf tarkiib il-xalaaya taẓt il-mijhar.* **3.** *xaliyya* pl. *xalaaya.* The cell is the basic unit in the organization of the party. *l-xaliyya hiyya l-wuẓda l-?asaasiyya l-munaḏḏamat il-ẓizib.*

cellar - *sirdaab* pl. *saraadiib.*

cement - *simint, čbintu, čmintu.* Put more sand than cement in the mixture next time. *ẓuṭṭ ramuḷ ?azyad imnis-simant bil-xabṭa marra lux.*

to cement - *ṣabb (u ṣabb) n- b-ičbintu, bina (i binaa?) n- b-ičbintu.* Are you going to cement the basement floor or leave it dirt? *raẓ-itṣubb qaaƐ is-sirdaab bil-čibintu loo txalliiha traab?* -- Are you going to cement it? *raẓ-tibniih ib-čibintu?*

cemetery - *maqbara* pl. *maqaabur.*

censor - *raqiib* pl. *ruqabaa?.*

to censor - *raaqab (i muraaqaba, riqaaba) t-.* During the state of emergency the government will censor all letters leaving the country. *b-ẓaalat iṭ-ṭawaari? il-ẓukuuma raẓ-itraaqib kull il-makaatiib il-mursala xaarij il-bilaad.*

censorship - *muraaqaba, riqaaba.* The censorship has been lifted. *nrufiƐat ir-riqaaba.*

census - *?iẓṣaa?.*

cent - **1.** *sant* pl. *-aat.* There are a hundred cents in a dollar. *d-doolaar bii miit sant.* **2.** *filis* pl. *fluus.* I haven't a cent in change. *ma-Ɛindi wala filis xurda.* -- He doesn't have a cent. *ma-Ɛinda filis* or *huwwa miflis.* -- I wouldn't give a cent for it. *ma-aštiriiha b-filis.*

**I'm almost down to my last cent. *?aani taqriiban iflasit.*

**Do you have to put in your two cents worth? *šinu hal-laġwa l-faarġa?* or *yaƐni laazim itδibbha l-had-durra?*

center - **1.** *nuṣṣ* pl. *nṣaaṣ, wasaṭ* pl. *?awsaaṭ.* The table is standing in the center of the room. *l-meez manṣuub ib-nuṣṣ il-ġurfa.* -- He lives in the center

of the town. *yiskun ib-nuṣṣ il-wlaaya.* 2. *markaz* pl. *maraakiz.* She's the center of attention. *hiyya markaz ihtimaam il-kull.*
to center - *rakkaz (i tarkiiz, trikkiz) t-.* Center the slide under the lens. *rakkiz is-slaayd taḥt il-εadasa.* -- All his thoughts were centered on her. *kull afkaara čaanat mitrakkza εaleeha.*
centigrade - *miʔawi*.* The temperature today is 20° centigrade. *l-ḥaraara l-yoom εišriin miʔawiyya.*
centimeter - *saantiimatir* pl. *-aat.*
centrally - *wasaṭi*, markazi*, bil-wasaṭ.* The hotel is centrally located. *l-ʔuuteel ṣaayir ib-maḥall wasaṭi.*
century - *qirin* pl. *quruun.*
ceremony - *ḥtifaal* pl. *-aat.* The ceremony will take place in the Embassy. *l-iḥtifaal raḥ-yijri bis-safaara.*
certain - 1. *muḥaqqaq, muʔakkad.* He's certain to pass the exam. *najaaḥa bil-imtiḥaan fadd šii muʔakkad.* 2. *mitʔakkid.* I am certain that I signed the papers myself. *ʔaani mitʔakkid waqqaεt il-ʔawraaq ib-nafsi.* 3. *muεayyan.* I mean certain people I'd rather not name. *ʔaεni ʔašxaaṣ muεayyaniin ma-ariid ajiib ʔasmaaʔhum.* 4. *baεaδ̣.* There are certain things I want to discuss with you. *ʔaku baεδ̣ ašyaaʔ ʔariid ʔabḥaθha wiyyaak.* 5. *ʔakiid, muqarrar.* The date is certain but the time hasn't been set yet. *l-mawεid ʔakiid laakin is-saaεa ma-tεayynat baεad.*
certainly - 1. *bit-taʔkiid.* She's certainly right. *hiyya bit-taʔkiid ṣaḥiiḥa.* 2. *maεluum, ṭabεan, yaqiin.* Why, certainly! *maεluum!* -- He's certainly coming. *yaqiin raḥ-yiji.*
certificate - *šahaada* pl. *-aat, taqriir* pl. *-aat.* He needs a doctor's certificate. *yiḥtaaj šahaada ṭibbiyya.* -- Submit a copy of your birth certificate with the other papers. *qaddim nusxa min šahaadat wilaadtak wiyya baqiit il-ʔawraaq.* -- Do you have a Certificate of Good Conduct? *εindak šahaadat ḥusn is-suluuk?*
certified - 1. *qaanuuni*.* He is a certified public accountant. *huwwa muḥaasib qaanuuni.* 2. *muṣaddaq.* This is a certified copy. *haay nusxa muṣaddaqa.*
to **certify** - 1. *šihad (a šahaada) n-.* He says he will certify that they were all present at the time. *yguul raḥ-yišhad bi-ʔan kullhum čaanaw ḥaaδ̣riin δ̣aak il-wakit.* 2. *ṣaddaq (i taṣdiiq) t- εala.* A notary public has to certify the signature. *kaatib εadil laazim yṣaddiq εat-tawqiiε.*
chain - 1. *maεδ̣ad* pl. *maεaaδ̣id.* She wears a golden chain. *tilbas maεδ̣ad δahab.* 2. *zanjiil* pl. *zanaajiil.* Do you have a chain I can use to tow the car? *εindak zanjiil agdar astaεmila l-saḥb is-sayyaara?* 3. *silsila* pl. *salaasil.* This firm operates a chain of food stores. *haš-šarika tdiir silsilat maxaazin il-beeε il-maʔkuulaat.*
to chain - *zanjal (i zanjala) t-, rubaṭ (u rabuṭ) n- b-zanjiil.* They chained the prisoners together. *zanjilaw il-masaajiin waaḥid bil-laax.*
chair - 1. *kursi* pl. *karaasi, skamli* pl. *-iyaat.* Please sit down in this chair. *ʔarjuuk ʔugεud εala hal-kursi.* 2. *qultuġ* pl. *-aat.* Sit in the upholstered chair. *ʔugεud εal-qultuġ* or *ʔugεud εal-kursi l-baṭṭiixa.*
chalk - *tabaašiir.* How many sticks of chalk are in the box? *čam qaalab tabaašiir ʔaku bil-quuṭiyya.*
**Chalk that up to experience. *qayyidha xibra lil-mustaqbal.*
challenge - *taḥaddi* pl. *-iyaat.* Our team accepted their challenge. *fariiqna qibal taḥaddiihum.*
to challenge - *tḥadda (a taḥaddi).* I challenge the winner. *ʔaani ʔatḥadda l-ġaalub.*
chambermaid - *xaadma* pl. *-aat.*
chamber of commerce - *ġurfat* (pl. *ġuraf*) *tijaara.*
chamber pot - *qaεεaada* pl. *-aat.*
champagne - *šampaanya* pl. *-aat.*
champion - *baṭal* pl. *ʔabṭaal.*
championship - *buṭuula.* They're wrestling for the championship. *da-yitṣaarεuun εala l-buṭuula.*
chance - 1. *furṣa* pl. *furaṣ.* Give me a chance. *nṭiini fadd furṣa.* -- I had a chance to go to the ruins of Babel. *ṣaar εindi fadd furṣa ʔaruuḥ il-xaraaʔib baabil.* 2. *ʔamal* pl. *ʔaamaal.* Is there any chance of catching the train. *ʔaku ʔamal inlaḥḥig bil-qiṭaar?* -- Not a chance. *ma-biiha ʔamal.* 3. *yaanaṣiib.* Won't you buy a chance? *triid tištiri yaanaṣiib?*
by chance - *ṣidfatan, biṣ-ṣidfa.* I met him by chance. *laageeta biṣ-ṣidfa.*
to take a chance - *xaaṭar (i muxaatara) t-, jaazaf (i mujaazafa).* Let's take a chance on it. *xalli nxaaṭir biiha.*
to chance - *xaaṭar (i muxaaṭara) t-, jaazaf (i mujaazafa).* I'll chance it. *raḥ-axaaṭir bii* or *raḥ-ajarrub ḥaδ̣δ̣i.*
chandelier - *θurayya* pl. *-aat.*
change - 1. *taġyiir* pl. *-aat, tabdiil* pl. *-aat.* Have there been any changes in my absence? *ʔay taġyiiraat ṣaarat ʔaθnaaʔ ġiyaabi?* -- You need a change of air. *yinraad-lak šwayya taġyiir hawa.* -- I'm for a change in the present administration. *ʔaani min muʔayyidiin taġyiir in-niδ̣aam il-ḥaali.* 2. *xurda* pl. *-awaat.* Have you any change ? *εindak xurda?*
for a change - *lit-tabdiil, lit-taġyiir.* For a change I'd like to go to the movies tonight. *lit-tabdiil yiεjibni ʔaruuḥ lis-siinama hal-leela.*
to change - 1. *ṣarraf (u taṣriif) t-.* Can you change a dinar for me? *tigdar itṣarruf-li diinaar?* 2. *ġayyar (i taġyiir) t-.* We may have to change our plans. *ʔaku ḥtimaal niδ̣ṭarr inġayyir manhajna.* 3. *tġayyar (a taġayyur).* The weather is going to change. *ṭ-ṭaqis raḥ-yitġayyar.* -- You won't believe when you see him how much he has changed. *ma-tṣaddig min itšuufa šgadd mitġayyir.* Nothing has changed. -- *ma-tġayyar šii.* 4. *baddal (i tabdiil, tbiddil) t-.* Can you wait until I change my clothes? *tigdar tintiδ̣ir ʔila ʔan ʔabaddil ihduumi?* -- I haven't changed my mind. *ma-baddalit fikri.* -- You'll have to change your tone if you want to talk to me. *ʔiδa triid tiḥči wiyyaaya laazim itbaddil lahijtak.* -- We have to change trains at the next station. *laazim inbaddil il-qiṭaar bil-maḥaṭṭa j-jaaya* or *laazim inġayyir il-qiṭaar bil-maḥaṭṭa j-jaaya.* 5. *tbaddal (a tabaddul).* The management of this hotel has changed hands a number of times. *ʔidaarat hal-ʔuteel itbaddlat čam marra.* 6. *ḥawwal (i taḥwiil, taḥawwul) t- ʔila.* Our plan is to change this hotel into a hospital. *xiṭṭatna ʔan inḥawwil hal-ʔuteel ʔila mustašfa.* 7. *tḥawwal (i taḥwiil, taḥawwul).* This store has changed hands often. *had-dukkaan itḥawwal min ʔiid il-ʔiid.* 8. *ngilab (i ngilaab).* She has changed from an ugly girl into a real beauty. *ngulbat min bašεa ʔila ʔaaya bij-jamaal.*
changeable - 1. *mitġayyir.* The weather is very changeable at this time of year. *l-hawa mitġayyir ihwaaya haaδa l-wakit imnis-sana.* 2. *mitqallib.* She has a changeable disposition. *εidha ṭabuε mitqallib.*
channel - 1. *majra* pl. *majaari, qanaat* pl. *qanawaat.* The two lakes are joined by a narrow channel. *l-buḥayraat iθ-θinteen mittaṣla b-majra δ̣ayyig.* -- The application will have to go through proper channels. *l-εariiδ̣a laazim taaxuδ majraaha l-ʔuṣuuli.* 2. *qanaal* pl. *-aat.* We crossed the English Channel in the storm. *εubarna l-qanaal il-ingiliizi ʔaθnaaʔ il-εaaṣifa.* 3. *maḥaṭṭa* pl. *-aat.* How many channels can you get on your television set? *čam maḥaṭṭa tigdar itḥaṣṣil ib-talafizyoonak?*
to channel - *wajjah (i tawjiih) t-.* I'm trying to help him channel his efforts into useful activities. *da-aḥaawil ʔasaaεda ywajjih jihuuda ʔila ʔaεmaal mufiida.*
to **chant** - 1. *waδδan (i tawδiin) t-, ʔaδδan (i taʔδiin) t-.* We hear the muezzin chanting from the minaret every morning. *nismaε il-muwaδδin ywaδδin imnil-manaara kull yoom iṣ-ṣubuḥ.* 2. *jawwad (i tajwiid) t-.* We are learning to chant the Koran in religion class. *da-nitεallam tajwiid il-qurʔaan ib-dars id-diin.* 3. *rattal (i tartiil) t-.* He chants the passages from the Koran at the Friday service. *yrattil ʔaayaat il-qurʔaan ib-ṣalaat ij-jumεa.*
chaos - *fawδ̣a, hoosa.*
chaotic - *fawδ̣awi*.*
to **chap** - 1. *maššag (i tmiššig) t.* The wind chapped my face today. *l-hawa maššag wičči l-yoom.* 2. *faṭṭar (i tafṭiir) t-.* My lips are chapped. *šfaafi mfaṭṭira.*
chapter - 1. *faṣil* pl. *fṣuul.* Did you read the last chapter of this book? *qreet il-faṣl il-ʔaxiir min hal-iktaab?* 2. *juzuʔ* pl. *ʔajzaaʔ.* That's a closed chapter in my life. *haaδa juzuʔ mintihi min ḥayaati.* 3. *ṣuura* pl. *ṣuwar.* The Koran is divided into 114 chapters. *l-qurʔaan imqassam ʔila miyya w-ʔarbaṭaεaš ṣuura.*
character - 1. *xuluq* pl. *ʔaxlaaq.* I've misjudged his character. *ʔaxṭaaʔit ib-ḥukmi εala ʔaxlaaqa.* -- Your son has character. *ʔibnak εinda xuluq.* 2. *šaxṣiyya*

pl. *-aat*. How many characters are there in the play? *čam šaxṣiyya ʔaku bir-ruwaaya?* 3. *ṣuura* pl. *-aat*. This man is a familiar character here. *har-rijjaal ṣuura maʔluufa hnaa.* 4. *ʔintiika* pl. *-aat*, *Єantiika* pl. *-aat*. He's quite a character. *haaδa ṣudug Єantiika.* 5. *ramiz* pl. *rumuuz*. He is trying to decipher the cuneiform characters on the stone. *da-yzaawil zall ir-rumuuz il-mismaariyya Єala ṣ-ṣaxar.*

characteristic - 1. *ṣifa* pl. *-aat*. He has many good characteristics. *Єinda hwaaya ṣifaat zeena.* 2. *miiza* pl. *-aat*, *mazaaya*. That's characteristic of our times. *haaδi miizat haz-zamaan.* 3. *xaaṣṣiyya* pl. *xawaaṣṣ*. One of the characteristics of salt is its solubility. *ʔizda xawaaṣṣ il-miliz qaabliita liδ-δawabaan.*

charcoal - *fazma* pl. *-aat* coll. *fazam*.

charge - 1. *kulfa* pl. *kulaf*, *ʔujra* pl. *ʔujuur*. What is the charge for shortening trousers? *šgadd kulfat tagṣiir il-panṭiruun?* 2. *tuhma* pl. *tuham*. What are the charges against this man? *šinu t-tuham δidd har-rijjaal?* 3. *quwwa* pl. *-aat*. The charge of dynamite is sufficient to destroy the whole building. *quwwat id-dinaameet kaafya l-hadim il-binaaya kullha.*

free of charge - *balaaš, majjaanan, biduun rusuum.* We'll mail it to you free of charge. *raz-indizz-lak-iyyaaha bil-bariid majjaanan.*

in charge - *masʔuul*. Who's in charge of this section? *minu masʔuul Єan haš-šuЄba?*

to take charge - *twalla (a tawalli) r-riʔaasa, traʔʔas (a taraʔʔus).* He's taking charge of the new branch. *raz-yitwalla riʔaasat iš-šuЄba j-jidiida.*

to charge - 1. *saam (u soom) n-*. This merchant charges twice what the others do. *hat-taajir ysuum δiЄf il-baaqiin.* 2. *kallaf (i takliif) t-, ʔaxaδ (u ʔaxiδ) min, Єala.* How much are you going to charge me for the stitching? *šgadd raz-itkallifni Єala l-xiyaaṭa?* 3. *šihan (a šahin) n-*. We can charge your battery for you for a dirham. *nigdar nišhan-lak il-baaṭri b-dirham.* 4. *hijam (i hujuum) n- Єala.* The mounted police charged the crowd of demonstrators. *š-šurṭa l-xayyaala hijmaw Єal-mutaδaahiriin.* 5. *zisab (i zsaab) n- Єala, qayyad (i taqyiid) t- b-izsaab.* You have charged me for something I never got. *zisabit Єalayya siЄir šii maa maaxδa.* -- **I'd like to charge it, please. *zuṭṭa Єala l-izsaab, rajaaʔan.* 6. *ttiham (i ttihaam), tiham (i tahim) n-*. They charged him with theft. *ttihmoo bis-sariqa.*

charitable - 1. *xeeri**. She is a member of several charitable organizations. *hiyya Єuδwa b-jamЄiyyaat xeeriyya mutaЄaddida.* 2. *muzsin* pl. *-iin*. He is a charitable man; loves to do good. *huwwa muzsin, muzibb il-Єamal il-xeer.*

charity - 1. *xeer, l-barr wil-ʔizsaan.* He gives all his money to charity. *yinṭi fluusa kullha lil-xeer.* 2. *ṣadaqa* pl. *-aat*, *ʔizsaan*. She's too proud to accept charity. *haay tistankif tiqbal ṣadaqa.* **Charity begins at home. *l-ʔaqrabuun ʔawla bil-maЄruuf.*

charm - 1. *sizir, fitna.* She has a lot of charm. *Єidha fadd sizir qawi.* 2. *ziriz* pl. *zuruuz*, *dillaaЄa* pl. *-aat*. He always carries a charm against the evil eye. *yšiil ziriz daaʔiman δidd il-Єeen.*

to charm - *sizar (a sizir) n-, fitan (i fatin) n-*. She charmed us with her wit and pleasant personality. *sizratna b-δaraafatha w-šaxṣiyyatha l-laṭiifa.*

charming - *saazir, fattaan.* His sister is a very charming person. *ʔuxta kulliš fattaan.*

charter - *miiθaaq* pl. *mawaaθiiq*. He took part in drawing up the United Nations' charter. *ʔištirak ib-waδiЄ miiθaaq il-ʔumum il-muttazida.*

to charter - *staʔjar (i stiʔjaar).* Our group is going to charter a bus for the trip. *jamaaЄatna raz-tistaʔjir paaṣ lis-safra.*

chase - 1. *muṭaarada* pl. *-aat*. A wild chase began. *fadd muṭaarada Єaniifa bidat.* 2. *taЄqiib, qtifaaʔ.* The chase led them thru the market and down to the shore. *t-taЄqiib qaadhum lis-suuq w-lis-saazil.*

to chase - 1. *lizaq (a laziq) n-*. Before he was married he used to chase the girls all the time. *gabul-ma yitzawwaj čaan yilzag il-banaat Єala ṭuul.* 2. *loozag (i tloozig).* Their dog is always chasing our cat. *čalibhum Єala ṭuul yloozig bazzuunatna.*

to chase around - *daar (u door), ftarr (a ftiraar).* My son chases around with a pretty wild crowd. *ʔibni da-yduur wiyya fadd jamaaЄa wikkaz.*

to chase away - *kašš (i kašš) n-*. Chase the birds away from the tomato vines. *kišš iṭ-ṭiyuur min xuδrat iṭ-ṭamaaṭa.*

to chase down - *tЄaqqab (a taЄaqqub).* I spent three days chasing down that reference. *qiδeet itlaθt iyyaam atЄaqqab hal-marjaЄ.*

to chase out - *ṭarrad (i taṭriid) t-*. I chased him out of the house. *ṭarradta mnil-beet.*

chassis - *šaaṣi* pl. *-yaat*.

chaste - *Єafiif, ṭaahir.*

chastity - *Єiffa, ṭuhur.*

chat - *zači*. We had a nice chat. *jira beenna zači laṭiif.*

to chat - *soolaf (i tsoolif) t-*. We spent a very pleasant hour chatting with each other. *giδeena saaЄa laṭiifa nsoolif.*

chatter - *θarθara, laġwa.* Stop that foolish chatter. *baṭṭil haθ-θarθara.*

to chatter - 1. *θarθar (i θarθara), liġa (i laġwa).* They chatter incessantly. *yilġuun Єala ṭuul.* 2. *ṣṭakk (a), ṭagṭag (i).* My teeth are chattering. *snuuni da-tiṣṭakk* or *snuuni da-tṭagṭig.*

chatterbox - *θarθaar* pl. *-iin*.

chauffeur - *saayiq* pl. *suwwaaq, dreewil* pl. *-iyya*.

cheap - 1. *rixiiṣ* pl. *rxaaṣ*. Fruit is cheap this year. *l-fawaakih rixiiṣa has-sana.* -- He offered it to me cheap. *Єiraδha Єalayya b-siЄir rixiiṣ* or *nṭaani-yyaaha rixiiṣ.* 2. *ma-yiswa.* That's cheap stuff. *haaδa šii ma-yiswa.* 3. *waaṭi.* Her manners are cheap. *ʔaxlaaqha waaṭya.* 4. *mubtaδal.* She looks cheap in those clothes. *tbayyin Єabaalak mubtaδala b-hal-ihduum.* 5. *danii*ʔ. He played a cheap trick on me. *sawwa biyya ziila daniiʔa.* 6. *waδiiЄ.* She is a cheap, vulgar woman. *haay fadd wazda waδiiЄa.* 7. *duuni**. These goods are cheap quality. *hal-baδaayiЄ duuniyya.* -- He ruined his feet from wearing cheap shoes. *Єidam rijla min libs il-qanaadir id-duuniyya.*

**His openhandedness made me feel cheap. *karama xajjilatni.*

cheat - *ġaššaaš* pl. *-iin*. They all know he's a cheat. *kullhum yЄurfuun huwwa fadd waazid ġaššaaš.*

to cheat - 1. *ġašš (u ġišš) n-*. Be careful you don't get cheated. *diir baalak la-tinġašš.* -- He always cheats at cards. *daaʔiman yġušš ib-liЄib il-ʔawraaq.* 2. *sawwa (i taswiya) qoopya.* He's always cheating at exams. *daaʔiman ysawwi qoopya bil-imtizaanaat.* 3. *xaan (u xiyaana).* His wife is cheating on him. *zoojta da-txuuna.* 4. *zaaġal (i zuġul) wiyya.* I know he's cheating me but I can't prove it. *da-aЄruf da-yzaaġil wiyyaaya laakin ma-agdar aθibta.* 5. *qašmar (i qašmara) t-, laflaf (i laflafa).* He cheated him out of all his money. *qašmara w-axaδ kull ifluusa* or *laflaf kull ifluusa.*

check - 1. *čakk* pl. *-aat*, *ṣakk* pl. *ṣukuuk*. I'll send you a check tomorrow. *Єuud adizz-lak čakk baačir.* 2. *waṣil* pl. *wṣuulaat*. Give your baggage check to the porter. *ʔinṭi l-waṣil maal ġaraaδak lil-zammaal.* Here's your hat check, sir. *sayyid, tfaδδal waṣl iš-šafqa maaltak.* 3. *ʔišaara* pl. *-aat*, *Єalaama* pl. *-aat*. Put a check before the name of each one as he reports in. *zuṭṭ ʔišaara giddaam ʔisim kull waazid min yiji.* 4. *zsaab* pl. *-aat*. Waiter, the check please. *booy, l-izsaab min faδlak.*

in check - *makšuuš*. Your king is in check. *l-malik maalak makšuuš.*

to keep in check - *δubaṭ (u δabuṭ) n-*. I'm no longer able to keep him in check. *ma-agdar aδubṭa baЄad.*

to check - 1. *ʔamman (i taʔmiin) t-, waddaЄ (i tawdiiЄ) t-*. Check your hat and coat here. *ʔammin šafuqtak w-qappuuṭak ihnaa.* 2. *ʔamman (i taʔmiin) t-*. Can I check this suitcase at the station? *ʔagdar aʔammin haj-junṭa bil-mazaṭṭa?* 3. *ʔaššar (i taʔšiir) t-*. Check the items you want. *ʔaššir il-ʔašyaaʔ li-triidha.* 4. *čayyak (i tačyiik) t-, fuzaṣ (a faziṣ) n-*. Please check the oil. *ʔarjuuk ifzaṣ id-dihin.* 5. *fattaš (i taftiiš) t-*. They will check your passports at the border. *raz-yfattišuun paaṣpoortaatkum bil-ziduud.* 6. *daqqaq (i tadqiiq) t-*. Will you please check the bill once more? *ʔarjuuk ma-tdaqqiq l-izsaab marra lux?* 7. *raaqab (i muraaqaba) t-*. We have been asked to check on the water table levels at all seasons of the year. *nṭilab min Єidna nraaqib mustawa l-maay ib-kull fuṣuul is-sana.* -- We are required to check on each man's daily output. *maṭluub minna nraaqib išgadd* *kull waazid yṭalliE bil-yoom.* 8. *raajaE* (*i muraajaEa*) *t-*. Check with me again before you go. *raajiEni marrt il-lux gabuḷ-ma truuz.* 9. *kašš* (*i kašš*) *n-*. You gave me a chance to check your king. *nṭeetni furṣa ʔakušš il-malik maalak.*

to check in – 1. *sajjal* (*i tasjiil*) *t-*. They checked in at the hotel at 2 P.M. *sajjlaw bil-ʔuteel saaEa biθ-θinteen.* 2. *ziδar* (*a zuδuur*). What time do we have to check in? *šwakit laazim nizδar?*

to check off – *ʔaššar* (*i taʔšiir*) *t-*. Check them off as you go. *ʔašširhum w-inta maaši.*

to check out – *ġaadar* (*i muġaadara*), *tirak* (*u tarik*). What time did he check out of the hotel? *šwakit ġaadar il-ʔuteel?*

to check over – *fuzaṣ* (*a faziṣ*) *n-*. Check over the list and see if we can use any of the items. *ʔifzaṣ il-qaaʔima w-šuuf ʔiδa niztaaj šii min hal-mawaadd.*

to check through – *dazz* (*i dazz*) *n- l-*, *waṣṣal* (*i tawṣiil*) *t-*. I want this baggage checked through Mosul. *ʔariid hal-ġaraaδ tindazz lil-muuṣil.*

to check up – 1. *daqqaq* (*i tadqiiq*) *t-*. We had better check up on the accuracy of his accounts. *l-ʔazsan indaqqiq ṣizzat zisaabaata.* 2. *zaqqaq* (*i tazqiiq*) *t-*, *staElam* (*i stiElaam*). Did you check up on him? *zaqqaqit Eanna?* or *sawweet tazqiiq Eanna* or *staElamit Eanna.* 3. *tzaqqaq* (*a tazaqquq*). We have to check up on his statements. *laazim nitzaqqaq min kalaama.*

to check with – *ttifaq* (*i ttifaaq*) *wiyya*, *ṭaabaq* (*i muṭaabaqa*) *t-*. That checks with what he told me. *haaδa yittifiq wiyya lli gal-li-yyaa.*

check book – *daftar* (pl. *dafaatir*) *čakkaat.*

check point – *nuqṭat* (pl. *nuqaṭ*) *taftiiš*, *markaz* (pl. *maraakiz*) *taftiiš.*

check room – *ġurfat* (pl. *ġuraf*) *taEliiq il-ihduum.*

check-up – *faziṣ*, *kašif.* You should see your doctor for a general check-up once a year. *laazim itruuz lit-ṭabiib zatta ysawwii-lak faziṣ Eaamm marra bis-sana.*

cheek – *xadd* pl. *xuduud.* My cheek is all swollen. *xaddi kulla mwarrum.*

cheer – *hitaaf* pl. *-aat.* We heard the cheers from quite a distance. *smaEna l-hitaaf min masaafa bEiida.* -- Three cheers for our team. *θlaθ hitaafaat il-fariiqna.*

**They gave him a cheer. *hitfoo-la.*

to cheer – 1. *hitaf* (*i hitaaf*) *n-*. The crowd cheered. *j-jamaahiir hitfat.* -- The crowd cheered the speaker. *l-mujtamEiin hitfaw lil-xaṭiib.*

to cheer up – 1. *farraz* (*i tafriiz*) *t-*, *sarr* (*i*). The news cheered her up. *l-ʔaxbaar farrizatha.* 2. *tšajjaE* (*a tašajjuE*). Cheer up, he'll be back soon. *tšajjaE, huwwa raz-yirjaE qariiban.*

cheerful – *farzaan*, *fariz*, *mitwannis.* He's very cheerful today. *huwwa kulliš farzaan il-yoom.* -- Isn't this a cheerful room. *baḷḷa muu hal-gubba kulliš farzaʔ.*

cheese – *jibin* pl. *ʔajbaan.* What kind of cheese do you have? *yaa nooE jibin Eindak?*

chef – *baaštabbaax* pl. *-iin.*

chemical – *kiimyaawi*.* He's working in a chemical laboratory. *huwwa yištuġuḷ ib-fadd muxtabar kiimyaawi.*

chemist – *kiimyaaʔi* pl. *-yyiin*, *kiimyaawi* pl. *-yyiin.*

cherry – *karaza* pl. *-aat*, coll. *karaz.* These are good cherries. *haaδa xooš karaz.*

chess – *šiṭranj.* Do you know how to play chess? *tuEruf tilEab šiṭranj?*

chess set – *šiṭranj* pl. *-aat.* All the chess sets are in use. *kull iš-šiṭranjaat da-tilEab.*

chest – 1. *ṣadir* pl. *ṣduur.* He has a broad chest. *Einda ṣadir Eariiδ.* -- That's a load off my chest. *haaδa čaan fadd zimil w-inzaaz Ean ṣadri.* 2. *ṣanduug* pl. *ṣanaadiig.* Put the tools in the chest. *zuṭṭ il-ʔadawaat biṣ-ṣanduug.* 3. *diilaab* pl. *dwaaliib.* She bought a beautiful chest of drawers. *štirat diilaab ʔabu mjarraat zilu.*

chestnut – 1. *kistaanaaya* pl. *-aat* coll. *kistaana.* Let's buy some roasted chestnuts. *xal-ništiri šwayya kistaana mzammṣa.* 2. *kastanaaʔi*.* Her hair is chestnut. *šaEarha kastanaaʔi.*

chestnut tree – *šajarat il-kistaana.*

to **chew –** *Eilač* (*i Ealič*) *n-*, *Eilas* (*i Ealis*) *n-*, *muṣaġ* (*u maṣiġ*) *n-*. Chew your food well. *ʔiElis ʔaklak zeen.*

chewing gum – *Eilič.* How many sticks of chewing gum are there in the package? *čam qiṭEat Eilič ʔaku bil-paakeet?*

chic – *šiik*, *ʔaniiq.*

chicken – *dijaaja* pl. *-aat* coll. *dijaaj.* We're having chicken for dinner. *Eašaana dijaaj.*

chicken pox – *jidri maay.*

chick peas – *zummuṣ*, *lablabi.*

chief – 1. *raʔiis* pl. *ruʔasaaʔ.* Who's the chief of the division? *minu raʔiis il-qisim?* 2. *mudiir* pl. *mudaraaʔ.* Where's the office of the Chief of Police? *ween daaʔirat mudiir iš-šurṭa?* 3. *baaš.* He has worked in our office as chief clerk for five years. *ṣaar-la xams isniin yištuġuḷ baaš kaatib ib-daaʔiratna.* 4. *ʔawwal.* He is chief legal advisor to the company. *huwwa l-mušaawir il-qaanuuni l-ʔawwal liš-šarika.* 5. *raʔiisi*.* These are the chief reasons why we should accept the plan. *haay il-ʔasbaab ir-raʔiisiyya lli tijEalna niqbal il-xiṭṭa.* -- What are the chief exports of Iraq? *šinu ṣaadiraat il-Eiraaq ir-raʔiisiyya?*

child – *jaahil* pl. *jihaal*, *juhhaal*, *ṭifil* pl. *ʔaṭfaal*, *ṣġayyir* pl. *ṣġaar.* They took the child along on a trip. *ʔaxδaw ij-jaahil wiyyaahum ib-safra.* -- Next year we have budgeted more money for child welfare. *s-sana j-jaaya xaṣṣaṣna fluus ʔazyad il-riEaayt il-ʔaṭfaal.* -- I've been used to it ever since I was a child. *haaδi mitEallim Ealeeha min ʔaani ṣġayyir.*

childhood – *ṭufuula*, *ṣuġur*, *juhul.* I spent part of my childhood in the country. *gδeet qisim min ṭufuulti bir-riif.* -- In his childhood he didn't have much contact with other children. *b-juhla ma-ṣaar Einda hwaaya ttiṣaal ib-baqiit il-ʔaṭfaal.*

childish – 1. *zaEṭuuṭ* pl. *zaEaaṭiiṭ.* He is very childish in his demands. *huwwa kulliš zaEṭuuṭ ib-ṭalabaata.* 2. *mazEaṭa* pl. *-aat.* This is childish. *haay mazEaṭa.* -- The whole thing was childish. *l-masʔala čaanat mazEaṭa.* 3. *ṣibyaani*.* What you did was childish. *Eamalak čaan ṣibyaani.*

to act childish – *tzaEṭaṭ* (*a tziEṭiṭ*), *ṣaar zaEṭuuṭ.* Don't act so childish; you're old enough to know better. *la-tṣiir zaEṭuuṭ hal-gadd; ʔinta čibiir w-tiftihim.*

chill – 1. *barid.* I've got a chill. *ʔaani maaxiδ barid.* 2. *qašEariira.* Suddenly I felt a chill. *Eala ġafḷa šiEarit ib-qašEariira.*

to chill – *barrad* (*i tabriid*) *t-*. Chill them before you serve them. *barridha gabuḷ-ma tqaddimha.*

**I'm chilled to the bone. *l-barid yabbas Eaδaami.*

chilly – 1. *baarid.* It's chilly outside. *baarda barra.* -- They received us in a chilly manner. *staqbiloona stiqbaal baarid.* 2. *bardaan.* I'm chilly. *ʔaani bardaan.*

chimney – 1. *madxana* pl. *madaaxin.* They are repairing the chimney. *da-yṣallzooha lil-madxana.* 2. *šiiša* pl. *šiyaš.* Where's the chimney for the lamp? *ween iš-šiiša maal il-faanuus?*

chimpanzee – *šimbaanzi* pl. *-yaat.*

chin – *zinič* pl. *znuuč*, *δiqin* pl. *δiquun.* He has a protruding chin. *Einda zinič baariz.*

**Chin up! *tšajjaE* or *šidd zeelak.*

China – *ṣ-ṣiin.* He lived in China for a long time. *Eaaš biṣ-ṣiin mudda ṭwiila.*

china – *faxfuuri*, *farfuuri.* We got this set of china as a wedding present. *haṭ-ṭaxm il-faxfuuri jaana hadiyyat zawaaj.*

Chinese – *ṣiini** pl. *-iyyiin.* The owner of this store is a Chinese. *ṣaazib hal-mazall ṣiini.* I got a Chinese vase. *zaṣṣalit Eala mazhariyya ṣiiniyya.*

chip – 1. *θilma* pl. *θilam.* There is a chip out of the plate. *ʔaku θilma ṭaayra mnil-maaEuun.* 2. *šugfa* pl. *šugaf.* Fill in the spaces between the stones with chips. *ʔitris il-faraaġaat been iṭ-ṭaabuug ib-šugaf.* 3. *fiiša* pl. *-aat*, *fiyaš.* When the game finished, I had three white chips left. *min xilaṣ il-liEib čaan baEad Eindi tlaθ fiyaš beeδa.* 4. *njaara*, *šugfa* pl. *šugaf.* The carpenter left the floor littered with chips. *n-najjaar Eaaf il-gaaE matruusa njaara.* -- Where did this chip of wood come from? *haš-šugfat il-xišab imneen jatti?*

**He always has a chip on his shoulder. *haaδa ydawwur zirša.*

to chip – 1. *θilam* (*i θalim*) *n-*, *gaššaṭ* (*i tagšiiṭ*) *t-*. Be careful you don't chip the dishes when you wash them. *diir baalak la-tiθlim il-imwaaEiin min tiġsilha.* -- The rim of this glass is chipped; bring me another. *zaašyat hal-iglaaṣ maθluuma; jiib-li ġeera.* -- The edge of the table is chipped. *zaašiit il-meez magšuuṭa.* 2. *nijar* (*u najir*) *n-*. This man can chip the bricks in any shape you want. *har-rajjaal yigdar yinjur iṭ-ṭaabuug ib-ʔay sikil*

triida. **3.** *tgaššaṭ (a tgiššiṭ).* The paint is beginning to chip. *ṣ-ṣubuġ bida yitgaššaṭ.*
to **chirp** - *zaqzaq (i zaqzaqa).* A little bird was chirping at the window and woke me up. *ṭeer iṣġayyir čaan yzaqziq biš-šibbaač w-gaʕʕadni.*
chisel - *minqaar* pl. *manaaqiir.*
  to chisel - *zufar (u zafur) n-.* Have them chisel the name on the stone in both languages. *xalliihum yzafruun il-ʔism bil-zajar bil-luġteen.*
chocolate - *čukleet.* Is this chocolate bitter or sweet? *hač-čukleet murr loo zilu?* -- I want to buy a box of chocolate. *ʔariid aštiri fadd quuṭiyya čukleet.*
choice - **1.** *xtiyaar* pl. *-aat, xiyaar* pl. *-aat.* I had no other choice. *ma-čaan ʕindi ġeer ixtiyaar.* -- If I had a choice, I'd do it. *loo b-iidi xiyaar, sawweeta.* **2.** *taškiila.* They have a wide choice of colors to choose from. *ʕidhum taškiila čibiira mnil-ʔalwaan tixtaar minha.* **3.** *mumtaaz.* These are choice cuts of meat. *haaδi wuṣal mumtaaza mnil-lazam.* **4.** *muxtaar, mistanga.* He has a choice but small collection of books. *ʕinda majmuuʕa muxtaara wa-loo ṣġayyra mnil-kutub.*
choir - *kooras* pl. *-aat.* He sings in a choir in the church. *yġanni b-kooras bil-kaniisa.*
choke - *čook.* The choke doesn't work. *č-čook ma-da-yuštuġul.*
  to choke - **1.** *xinag (i xanig) n-.* I could choke you. *min widdi ʔaxungak.* -- The collar is choking me. *l-yaaxa xaangatni.* **2.** *xtinag (i xtinaag).* I nearly choked on a fishbone. *xtinagit ib-ʕaδm is-simča ʔilla šwayya.*
  to choke back - *minaʕ (a maniʕ) n-, zişar (i zaşir) n-, δubaṭ (u δabuṭ) n-.* She choked back her tears. *minʕat dumuuʕha.*
  to choke up - *sadd (u sadd) n-.* The stovepipe is choked up. *buuri d-duxxaan masduud.*
cholera - *hayδa, kuleera.*
to **choose** - *ntixab (i ntixaab), stanga (i), xtaar (a xtiyaar).* The editors chose the book of the month for their readers. *l-muzarririin ixtaaraw kitaab iš-šahar il-qurraaʔhum.* -- Choose the oranges you want. *ʔistangi l-purtiqaalaat li-triidha.* -- They chose him as candidate for the party. *ntixboo muraššaz ʕann il-zizib.*
choosy - *diqdaaqi*.* There's no need to be so choosy. *ma-aku zaaja ṭṣiir hal-gadd diqdaaqi.*
to **chop** - *faššag (i tafšiig, tfiššig) t-, kassar (i taksiir) t-.* Did you chop some wood? *faššagit šwayyat zatab?*
  to chop down - *gaṣṣ (u gaṣṣ) n-.* They chopped the dead tree down. *gaṣṣooha liš-šajara l-mayyta.*
  to chop off - *gaṣṣ (u gaṣṣ) n-, gitaʕ (a gaṭiʕ) n-.* Be careful you don't chop your finger off. *diir baalak la-tguṣṣ iṣibʕak.*
  to chop up - **1.** *θarram (i tθurrum) t-, θiram (u θarum) n-.* Chop the meat up fine. *θarrim il-lazam naaʕim.* -- This dish calls for chopped meat. *haṭ-ṭabxa yinraad-ilha lazam maθruum.* **2.** *gaṣgaṣ (i tgiṣgiṣ) t-.* Have the butcher chop up the meat for you. *xalli l-gaṣṣaab ygaṣgiṣ-lak il-lazam.*
chops - **1.** *qulbaaṣṭi.* I'd like the lamb chops with vegetables and rice. *yiʕjibni l-gulbaaṣṭi wiyya xuδra w-timman.* **2.** *čaap.* Can you cut me some lamb chops? *tigdar itguṣṣ-li šwayyat čaap?* **3.** *buuz.* The dog licked his chops. *č-čalib lizas buuza.*
  to lick one's chops - *maṭṭag (i tamṭiig) t-.* The food he makes makes you lick your chops. *l-ʔakl il-ysawwii yxalli l-waazid ymaṭṭig.*
Christ - *l-masiiz.*
Christian - *masiizi** pl. *-iyyiin, naṣraani** pl. *naṣaara.* He's a member of the Young Men's Christian Association. *huwwa ʕuδu b-jamʕiyyat iš-šubbaan il-masiiziyyiin.*
Christianity - *l-masiiziyya.*
Christmas - *ʕiid il-miilaad, krismis.* Christmas comes on a Wednesday this year. *ʕiid il-miilaad has-sana raz-yoogaʕ yoom ʔarbaʕa.*
chromium - *kroom.*
chronic - *muzmin.* He has a chronic disease. *ʕinda maraδ muzmin.*
to **chuckle** - *δizak (a δazik) wazd~, santaawi.* He chuckles whenever he thinks of it. *yiδzak wazda kull-ma tiji b-baala.*
church - **1.** *kaniisa* pl. *kanaayis.* Is there a Catholic church here? *ʔaku kaniisa kaaθoolikiyya hnaa?* **2.** *ṭaaʔifa* pl. *ṭawaaʔif.* What church do you belong to? *min ʔay ṭaaʔifa ʔinta?* or *šinu diinak?*
cider - *ʕaṣiir tiffaaz.*
cigar - *siigaar* pl. *-aat, čarid* pl. *čruud.*
cigarette - *jigaara* pl. *jigaayir.* Have a cigarette *tfaδδal fadd jigaara.*
cigarette case - *quuṭiyyat (pl. qwaaṭi) jigaayir.* I've lost my cigarette case. *ʔaani δayyaʕit quuṭiit ij-jigaayir maalti.*
cigarette lighter - *qiddaaza* pl. *-aat.*
cinch - **1.** *seer* pl. *syuur.* The saddle is loose; tighten the cinch. *s-sarij raaxi; δubb is-seer.* **2.** *muʔakkada.* That's a cinch. *haay muʔakkada.*
cinder - *fazma (pl. -aat) mazruuga,* coll. *fazam mazruug.* What are they doing with this big pile of cinders? *š-ysawwuun ib-hal-koom ič-čibiir imnil-fazam il-mazruug?* -- I've got a cinder in my eye. *xaššat fazma ṣġayyra b-ʕeeni.*
cinnamon - *daarsiin.*
circle - **1.** *daaʔira* pl. *dawaaʔir.* Draw the circle with a compass. *ʔirsim id-daaʔira b-purgaal.* **2.** *zalaqa* pl. *-aat.* He has a wide circle of friends. *ʕinda fadd zalaqa čbiira mnil-ʔaṣdiqaaʔ.* **3.** *waṣaṭ* pl. *ʔawṣaaṭ.* They are well-known in diplomatic circles. *δoola maʕruufiin zeen bil-ʔawṣaaṭ id-dibloomaasiyya.*
  to circle - **1.** *ftarr (a farr), zaam (u zoom) n-.* The airplane is circling over the town. *ṭ-ṭayyaara da-tiftarr foog il-wlaaya.* **2.** *daar (u dawaraan) n-, ftarr (a farr).* The moon circles around the earth. *l-gumar yduur zawl il-ʔarδ.*
circular - **1.** *daaʔiri*.* Apply the polish with a circular movement. *ʔuδrub il-pooliš ib-zarakaat daaʔiriyya.* **2.** *mdawwar.* A circular staircase leads to the top of the minaret. *fadd daraj imdawwar yquud il-qummat il-manaara.* **3.** *manšuur* pl. *manaašiir.* We need some boys to distribute circulars. *niztaaj čam walad il-tawziiʕ il-manaašiir.*
to **circulate** - *daar (u dawaraan) n-.* Cold water circulates through these pipes constantly. *l-maay il-baarid yduur ib-hal-buuriyyaat ʕala ṭuul.* -- There's a strange rumor circulating. *ʔaku fadd ʔišaaʕa ġariiba daayra.*
circulation - **1.** *dawaraan.* His blood circulation is not too good. *dawaraan damma muu kulliš zeen.* **2.** *tawziiʕ, ntišaar.* Our paper has a circulation of a hundred and fifty thousand. *tawziiʕ ij-jariida maalatna ywaṣṣil ila miyya w-xamsiin ʔalf.* **3.** *tadaawul.* The government has put new bills into circulation. *l-zukuuma nazlat nwaaṭ jidiida bit-tadaawul.*
circumference - *muziiṭ* pl. *-aat.* How do you get the circumference of the circle? *šloon iṭṭalliʕ muziiṭ id-daaʔira?*
circumstances - **1.** *δaruf* pl. *δuruuf.* Under these circumstances I can't blame her. *tazat haδ-δuruuf ma-agdar aluumha.* **2.** *ʔazwaal, ʔumuur.* He's in very good circumstances. *ʔazwaala zeena* or *ʔumuura maašya.*
circus - *sarkiis* pl. *-aat.*
citation - *stišhaad* pl. *-aat.* His speech is full of citations from the Koran. *xiṭaaba zaafil b-istišhaadaat imnil-qurʔaan.*
to **cite** - *stašhad (i stišhaad) b-.* Cite the passage exactly as the author wrote it. *ʔistašhid bil-maqṭaʕ tamaaman miθil-ma kitaba l-muʔallif.*
citizen - *muwaaṭin* pl. *iin.* Fellow citizens, choose your candidate carefully. *ʔayyuha l-muwaaṭiniin, ʔintaxbu muraššazkum ib-diqqa.*
  **I am an Iraqi citizen. *ʔaani ʕiraaqi.*
citizenship - *jinsiyya* pl. *-aat.* I have Iraqi citizenship. *ʕindi jinsiyya ʕiraaqiyya.*
city - **1.** *madiina* pl. *mudun, wlaaya* pl. *-aat.* How far is the nearest city from here? *šgadd tibʕid ʔaqrab madiina minnaa?* **2.** *baladi*.* She is in the City Hospital. *hiyya bil-mustašfa l-baladi.*
city dweller - *saakin (pl. sukkaan) mudin, zaδari* pl. *zaδar.* He is a city dweller and doesn't know much about agriculture. *huwwa min sukkaan il-mudin w-ma-yuʕruf ihwaaya ʕann iz-ziraaʕa.* -- The bedouins and the city dwellers do not get on well together. *l-badu wil-zaδar ma-yitraahmuun.*
city hall - *saraay* pl. *-aat.*
city life - *zayaat il-madiina.* She is not accustomed to city life. *ma-mitʕawwda ʕala zayaat il-madiina.*
civil - **1.** *naazik, muʔaddab.* At least he was civil to us. *hamm-zeen čaan naazik wiyyaana.* **2.** *madani*.* This is the concern of the civil authorities. *haaδi min ixtiṣaaṣ is-sulṭaat il-madaniyya.* **3.** *ʔahli*.* The difficulty almost led to civil war. *l-muškila*

taqriiban ˀaddat ila ẓarub ˀahliyya.
civil code - *l-qaanuun il-madani.*
civilian - *madani** pl. *-iyyiin.* There were civilians and soldiers in the crowd. *čaan ˀaku madaniyyiin w-ʕaskariyyiin been ij-jamhuur.* -- Was he wearing civilian clothes? *čaan laabis ihduum madaniyya?* or *čaan laabis suwiil?* -- He used to work as a teacher in civilian life. *čaan yištuğul muʕallim ˀaθnaaˀ ẓayaata l-madaniyya.*
civilization - *madaniyya* pl. *-aat, ẓaḍaara* pl. *-aat.* The Babylonians had an advanced civilization. *l-baabiliyyiin čaan ʕidhum ẓaḍaara mitqaddma.*
to **civilize** - *maddan (i tamdiin) t-, ẓaḍḍar (i taẓḍiir) t-.* They were unable to civilize them. They remain savages. *ma-gidraw ymaddinuuhum. buqaw mitwaẓẓišiin.*
civilized - *mitmaddin, mitẓaḍḍir.*
civil service - *xidma madaniyya.*
claim - **1.** *ddiʕaaˀ* pl. *-aat.* You must submit your claim within ten days. *laazim itqaddim iddiʕaaˀak xilaal ʕaširt iyyaam.* -- I don't believe his claim that he won the lottery. *ma-aṣaddig iddiʕaaˀa ˀinnahu rubaẓ il-yaanaṣiib.* **2.** *ẓaqq* pl. *ẓuquuq.* I have no claim to that. *maa ʕindi ẓaqq biiha.*
to claim - **1.** *ṭaalab (i muṭaalaba) t- b-.* I claim my share. *ˀaani ˀaṭaalib ib-ẓuṣṣti.* -- Where do I claim my baggage? *ween aṭaalib b-ijnaaṭi?* **2.** *ddaʕa (i ddiʕaaˀ).* She claims to know the man. *hiyya tiddiʕi taʕurfa lir-rijjaal.*
to **clap** - *ṣaffag (u taṣfiig, ṭṣuffug).* He clapped to summon the waiter. *ṣaffag ẓatta yṣiiẓ il-booy.*
to **clarify** - *waḍḍaẓ (i tawḍiiẓ) t-, fassar (i tafsiir) t-.* We have asked you to come in and clarify a few points for us. *ṭilabnaak tiji ẓatta twaḍḍiẓ-ilna čam nuqṭa.*
clash - **1.** *štibaak* pl. *-aat.* He was wounded in a clash on the border. *njiraẓ b-ištibaak ʕal-ẓiduud.* **2.** *taṣaadum* pl. *-aat, muṣaadama* pl. *-aat.* The real source of the trouble is a clash of personalities. *s-sabab il-ẓaqiiqi lil-muškila huwwa t-taṣaadum biš-šaxṣiyyaat.*
to clash - **1.** *ṭṣaadam (a taṣaadum).* Government troops clashed briefly with rebel forces yesterday. *quwwaat il-ẓukuuma ṭṣaadmat il-baarẓa l-mudda qaṣiira wiyya quwwaat iθ-θuwwaar.* **2.** *ṭḍaarab (a taḍaarub).* The interests of the two parties clashed over the question of government subsidies. *maṣaaliẓ il-ẓizbeen itḍaarbat ẓawl il-musaaʕadaat il-ẓukuumiyya.* -- These two colors clash with each other unpleasantly. *hal-looneen yitḍaarbuun waaẓid wiyya l-laax ib-ṣuura maa ẓilwa.*
clasp - **1.** *qabḍa* pl. *-aat.* He has a firm handclasp. *ʕinda qabḍat ˀiid qawwiyya.* **2.** *ṭubbaaga* pl. *-aat.* Can you fix the clasp on my purse? *tigdar itṣalliẓ iṭ-ṭubbaaga maal junuṭṭi.* **3.** *čillaab* pl. *člaaliib, šakkaala* pl. *-aat.* Hook the clasp on my necklace please. *šakkil ič-čillaab maal igḷaadti rajaaˀan.*
to clasp - *lizam (a lazim) n-.* They walked down the street clasping hands. *tmaššaw biš-šaariʕ laazmiin waaẓid ˀiid il-laax.*
class - **1.** *ṣinif* pl. *ṣunuuf, ˀaṣnaaf.* Arrange the items according to their classes. *rattib il-mawaadd ẓasab ˀaṣnaafha.* **2.** *daris* pl. *druus.* You're going to be late for class. *raẓ-titˀaxxar ʕala d-daris.* -- There are no classes on Friday. *ma-aku druus yoom ij-jumʕa.* **3.** *ṣaff* pl. *ṣfuuf.* Our class is going on a field trip tomorrow. *ṣaffna raẓ-yiṭlaʕ safra baačir.* **4.** *ṭabaqa* pl. *-aat.* He is popular with all classes of society. *maẓbuub min kull iṭ-ṭabaqaat il-ijtimaaʕiyya.* -- This word is not used by the educated classes. *hal-kalima ma-mustaʕmala min qibal iṭ-ṭabaqaat il-muθaqqafa.* **5.** *wajba* pl. *-aat, dafʕa* pl. *-aat.* We are all alumni of the class of 1934. *kullna min xirriijiin wajbat ˀalf w-tisiʕmiyya w-ˀarbaʕ w-itlaaθiin.* **6.** *daraja* pl. *-aat.* You'll find the first class coaches ahead just behind the engine. *tilgi ʕarabaat id-daraja l-ˀuula li-giddaam mubaašaratan wara l-makiina.* **7.** *ṭiraaz* pl. *ˀaṭriza.* He is a first class politician. *huwwa siyaasi mniṭ-ṭiraaz il-ˀawwal.*
classical - **1.** *klaasiiki**. He prefers classical music to jazz. *yfaḍḍil il-moosiiqa l-iklaasiikiyya ʕala j-jaaz.* **2.** *faṣiiẓ.* He is making good progress in his study of classical Arabic. *da-yitqaddam zeen ib-diraasta lil-luğa l-ʕarabiyya l-faṣiiẓa.* **3.** *taqliidi**. This is a classical example of Eastern architecture. *haaḍa fadd maθal taqliidi lil-handasa š-šarqiyya.*
classification - *taṣniif.*
classified - **1.** *mubawwab.* I found the car advertised in the classified ad section of the newspaper. *ligeet is-sayyaara maʕluun ʕanha b-ṣafẓat il-iʕlaanaat il-mubawwaba mnij-jariida.* **2.** *sirri**. These papers are all classified. *hal-ˀawraaq kullha sirriyya.*
to **classify** - *ṣannaf (i taṣniif) t-, bawwab (i tabwiib) t-.* The remaining items are hard to classify. *l-mawaadd il-baaqya yiṣʕab taṣniifha.*
classroom - *ṣaff* pl. *ṣfuuf.* The teacher is still in the classroom. *l-muʕallim baʕda biṣ-ṣaff.*
clatter - **1.** *ṭagṭaga.* The clatter of dishes in the kitchen disturbs the guests. *ṭagṭagat l-imwaaʕiin bil-maṭbax tizʕij il-xuṭṭaar.* **2.** *ṭargaʕa.* We heard the clatter of the wagon wheels as he went through the alley. *simaʕna ṭargaʕat ičruux il-ʕarabaana min marr bil-ʕagid.* **3.** *ṭarbaga.* We awakened to the clatter of horses' hooves on the pavement. *giʕadna ʕala ẓiss ṭarbagat ẓawaafir il-xeel biš-šaariʕ.*
to clatter - *ṭargaʕ (i ṭargaʕa).* She clattered down the stairs in her clogs. *nizlat id-daraj w-qubqaabha yṭargiʕ.*
clause - *band* pl. *bnuud, šarṭ* pl. *šruuṭ.* I won't sign the contract if it has that clause in it. *ma-amḍi l-ʕaqid ˀida bii hal-band.*
claw - **1.** *maxlab* pl. *maxaalib.* The hawk had a mouse in his claws. *ṣ-ṣigar laazim ijreedi b-maxaalba.* **2.** *ḍifir* pl. *ˀaḍaafir.* The cat has sharp claws. *l-bazzuuna ʕidha ˀaḍaafir ẓaadda.*
clay - *ṭiin* pl. *ˀaṭyaan.* Is this clay good for pottery? *haṭ-ṭiin zeen lil-ikwaaza?* -- The floor is made of clay pounded hard. *l-gaaʕiyya msawwaaya min ṭiin madčuuč.*
clean - **1.** *naḍiif* pl. *nḍaaf.* This plate is not clean. *hal-maaʕuun muu naḍiif.* **2.** *baṣiiṭ.* I like the clean lines of that building. *yiʕjibni t-taṣmiim il-baṣiiṭ maal ḍiič il-ibnaaya.*
**Wipe the pane clean. *naḍḍuf ij-jaama zeen.*
to clean - **1.** *naḍḍaf (u tanḍiif) t-.* Has the maid cleaned the room yet? *l-xaadma naḍḍfat il-ğurfa loo baʕad?* -- Please clean the chicken for me. *ˀarjuuk naḍḍuf-li d-dijaaja.* -- Where can I have my clothes cleaned? *ween agdar awaddi hduumi lit-tanḍiif?* -- We still have to clean the windows. *baʕad laazim innaḍḍuf iš-šibaabiič.* **2.** *ʕazzal (i taʕziil) t-.* We gave the house a thorough cleaning today. *ʕazzalna l-beet taʕziila zeena l-yoom.*
**He cleaned house in the poker game last night. *l-baarẓa bil-leel šaal kull il-gaaʕ bil-ḍookar.*
to clean out - **1.** *farrağ (i tafriiğ) t-.* This drawer has to be cleaned out. *hal-imjarr laazim yitfarrağ.* **2.** *ˀaxaḍ il-ˀaku wil-maaku min.* They cleaned me out all right. *ˀaxḍaw minni l-ˀaku wil-maaku* or **ḍirboo-li jyuubi ˀuuti.*
to clean up - **1.** *ğassal (i tağsiil) t-.* I'd like to clean up before dinner. *ˀariid ağaṣṣil gabḷ il-ʕaša.* **2.** *naḍḍaf (u tanḍiif) t-.* When are you going to clean up this mess on your desk? *šwakit raẓ-itnaḍḍuf hal-xarbaṭa min ʕala meezak?*
cleaner - **1.** *munaḍḍif* pl. *-aat.* This cleaner will remove all the spots. *hal-munaḍḍif raẓ-yrawwiẓ kull il-lakkaat.* **2.** *mukawwi, makwi.* Do you know a good cleaners in this area? *tuʕruf fadd makwi zeen ib-hal-manṭiqa?*
cleaning - *tanḍiif, taʕziil.* The house needs a good cleaning. *l-beet yinraad-la tanḍiif zeen.*
cleaning plant - *maẓall* (pl. *-aat*) *kawi.* They have their own cleaning plant. *ʕidhum maẓall kawi xaaṣṣ biihum.*
cleaning woman - *ṣaanʕa* pl. *-aat.* Where can I find a good cleaning woman? *ween ˀagdar ˀalgi fadd ṣaanʕa?*
cleanser - *munaḍḍif* pl. *-aat.* This cleanser cleans pans well. *hal-munaḍḍif ynaḍḍif il-ijduur tanḍiif zeen.*
clear - **1.** *ṣaafi.* The water is deep and clear. *l-maay ğamiij w-ṣaafi.* -- Try to keep a clear head. *ẓaawil itxalli fikrak ṣaafi.* **2.** *waaḍiẓ.* His voice was very clear over the radio. *ṣoota čaan kulliš waaḍiẓ bir-raadyo.* **3.** *ṣaẓu, mṣaẓẓi.* We have had clear weather all week. *čaan ij-jaww ʕidna ṣaẓu ṭuul il-ˀisbuuʕ.* **4.** *ḍaahir.* It is clear from the letter that he isn't satisfied. *ḍaahir min maktuuba ˀinna muu raaḍi.* **5.** *maftuuẓ, masluuk.* Is the road clear up ahead? *ṭ-ṭariiq giddaam maftuuẓ?* **6.** *mirtaaẓ.* My conscious is clear. *ḍamiira mirtaaẓ.* **7.** *bari* pl. *ˀabriyaaˀ.* We're going to release you; you're in the clear. *raẓ-inhiddak, ˀinta bari.*
to clear - **1.** *ṣiẓa (a ṣaẓu).* The sky is beginning to clear. *s-sima bidat tiṣẓa.* **2.** *naḍḍaf (u tanḍiif)*

t-. We've finished eating; you may clear the table now. *xallaṣna l-ʔakal hassa tigdar itnaḍ̇ḋuf il-meez.* 3. *fakk (u fakk) n-*. These drops will clear your head and sinuses. *hal-qaṭra tfukk raasak w-ijyuubak il-ʔanfiyya.* 4. *ɛubar (u ɛubuur) n- foog, faat (u foot) n- foog.* The plane just barely cleared the tree tops as it took off. *ṭ-ṭiyyaara bil-kaad ɛubrat foog ruus il-ʔašjaar min ṭaarat.* 5. *barra (i tabriya) t-*. The court cleared him of the charges against him. *l-maẓkama barrata mnit-tuham iḍ̇-ḋidda.* 6. *xallaṣ (i taxliiṣ) t-*. Look and see if I'm going to clear that car. *baawiɛ-li w-šuuf ʔiḋa ʔaxalliṣ min has-sayyaara.* 7. *ʔaxla (i ʔixlaaʔ).* Clear the court room. *ʔixlu qaaɛt il-maẓkama.* 8. *ṭilaɛ (a tuluuɛ).* Your residence permit will take a week or two to clear. *ʔiqaamtak raẓ-taaxuḋ isbuuɛ loo sbuuɛeen ẓatta tiṭlaɛ.* 9. *marr (u marr) n-*. It took us an hour to clear customs. *ʔaxḋatna saaɛa ẓatta nmurr bil-kumrug.*

to clear away - *šaal (i šeel) n-*. Tell her to clear away the dishes. *gul-lha xalli tšiili l-imwaaɛiin.*

to clear off - *šaal (i šeel) n- min.* Clear this stuff off your table. *šiil hal-ʔašyaaʔ min ɛala meezak.*

to clear one's throat - *tnaẓnaẓ (a naẓnaẓa).* He cleared his throat before he entered the room. *tnaẓnaẓ gabul-ma yxušš lil-gubba.*

to clear out - 1. *farraġ (i tafriiġ) t-*. I'll clear out this closet so you can hang your clothes in it. *raẓ-afarriġ hal-diilaab ẓatta tigdar itɛallig ihduumak biiha.* 2. *šilaɛ (a šaliɛ).* He cleared out in the middle of the night. *šilaɛ ib-nuṣṣ il-leel* or *******šammaɛ il-xeeṭ ib-nuṣṣ il-leel.*

to clear up - 1. *ṣaẓẓa (i), ṣifa (a ṣafaaʔ).* The weather has cleared up and the rain has stopped. *ṣaẓẓat id-dinya wil-muṭar baṭṭal.* 2. *ṣifa (a ṣafaaʔ).* The dust storm is over; the weather has cleared up. *raaẓat il-ɛajja; ṣifa j-jaww.* 3. *waḍ̇ḋaẓ (i tawḍ̇iiẓ) t-, fassar (i tafsiir) t-.* Several points remain to be cleared up. *ɛiddat nuqaṭ baɛad yinraad-ilha tawḍ̇iiẓ.*

clearance - 1. *majaal pl. -aat.* I don't think there is enough clearance here for the truck to turn around. *ma-aɛtiqid ʔaku majaal kaafi lil-loori ydeewur ihnaa.* 2. *muwaafaqa pl. -aat, muṣaadaqa pl. -aat.* Foreigners have to get clearance from the proper authorities to work in Iraq. *l-ʔajaanib laazim yaaxḋuun muwaafaqat iṣ-ṣulṭaat il-muxtaṣṣa lil-ɛamal bil-ɛiraaq.*

clearly - *b-wuḋuuẓ, b-ṣuura waaḋẓa.* Please speak more clearly. *ʔarjuuk itkallim ib-wuḋuuẓ ʔakθar.*

clergy - *ʔikliirus.*

clerical - *kitaabi*.* I am looking for a clerical job. *da-adawwir-li fadd šaġla kitaabiyya.*

clerk - *kaatib pl. kuttaab.* He's a clerk in a big office. *huwwa kaatib ib-daaʔira čbiira.*

clever - 1. *ḋaki, faṭin.* He's a clever fellow. *huwwa fadd waaẓid ḋaki.* 2. *maahir, ẓaaḋiq.* He's a very clever tailor. *huwwa fadd xayyaaṭ kulliš maahir.* 3. *labiq.* He's a clever speaker. *huwwa fadd xaṭiib labiq.* 4. *šaaṭir, ẓaaḋiq, faahim.* He's a clever business man. *huwwa fadd rajul ʔaɛmaal šaaṭir.*

click - *ṭagga pl. -aat.* I heard the click of the lock. *smaɛit ṭaggat il-keeluun.*

to click - 1. *ṭagg (u ṭagg) n-*. He clicked his heels and saluted me. *ṭagg-li salaam.* 2. *ṭagṭag (i ṭagṭaga).* I heard her heels clicking as she came toward me down the hall. *smaɛit ɛaɛab qundaratha ṭṭagṭig min jatt mittajha ɛalayya bil-mamarr.* 3. *nijaẓ (a najaaẓ).* The show clicked from the first night on. *t-tamθiiliyya nijẓat min ʔawwal leela.* *******Everything clicked beautifully. *kullši miša miθl is-saaɛa.*

client - *maɛmiil pl. mɛaamiil, muraajiɛ pl. -iin.*

cliff - *juruf pl. jruuf.*

climate - 1. *manaax.* The climate here is not suitable for planting coconut. *hnaa l-manaax ma-ylaaʔim zariɛ joos il-hind.* 2. *jaww pl. ʔajwaaʔ.* The political climate is favorable for his return to power. *j-jaww is-siyaasi ysaaɛid ɛala rijuuɛa lil-ẓukum.*

climax - 1. *ḋarwa pl. -aat.* The climax of the excitement came when the president appeared on the balcony. *ḋarwat il-ẓamaas ṣaar lamma r-raʔiis ḋihar bil-baalqoon.* 2. *ʔawj.* Islamic art reached a climax in the era of Haroun Al-Rashid. *l-fann il-ʔislaami wuṣal ʔila ʔawja b-ɛahad haaruun ir-rašiid.*

climb - *ṣaɛda, tasalluq.* You'll find the climb difficult. *raẓ-itšuuf iṣ-ṣaɛda ṣaɛba.*

to climb - 1. *ṣiɛad (a ṣiɛuud) n-*. She can't climb the stairs anymore due to old age. *ma-tigdar tiṣɛad id-darab baɛad imnil-kubur.* -- They climb the date palms about five times a year. *yiṣɛaduun ɛala n-naxal zawaali xamis marraat bis-sana.* 2. *tšalbah (a tšilbih, šalbaha).* The children enjoy climbing on the fence. *j-jihaal yẓibbuun it-tišilbih ɛal-imzajjar.* 3. *ɛalla (i), rtifaɛ (i rtifaaɛ).* The jet planes climb rapidly after take-off. *ṭ-ṭiyyaaraat ij-jatt itɛalli b-surɛa baɛad-ma ṭṭiir.*

to climb down - *niẓal (i niẓuul) n-*. The cat is afraid to climb down the tree. *l-bazzuuna txaaf tinẓil imniš-šajara.*

to climb up - *ṣiɛad (a ṣiɛuud).* I climbed up on the rock first and then helped the rest of them up. *ṣiɛadit foog iṣ-ṣaxra ʔawwal w-saaɛadit il-baaqiin ɛaṣ-ṣaɛda.*

to cling - 1. *čallab (i tačliib).* The child is clinging to its mother. *j-jaahil imɛallib ib-ʔumma.* 2. *lizag (a laziġ) n-*. My shirt was clinging to my back with sweat. *θoobi čaan laaziġ ɛala ḋahri mnil-ɛaraġ.*

clinic - *ɛiyaada pl. -aat.* You can get a blood analysis at the clinic. *tigdar itsawwi taẓliil damm bil-ɛiyaada.* -- This hospital has an out-patient clinic. *hal-mustašfa biiha ɛiyaada xaarijiyya.*

clip - 1. *danbuus pl. danaabiis.* She put a golden clip on her dress. *šakklat danbuus ḋahab ɛala nafnuufha.* 2. *klips pl. -aat, šikkaala pl. -aat.* Please give me a box of paper clips. *ʔarjuuk inṭiini paakeet iklips.* 3. *mišiṭ pl. mšuuṭ, mšaaṭ.* Can you show me how to put the clip in the rifle? *tigdar itraawiini šloon azuṭṭ il-mišiṭ bil-bunduqiyya?*

to clip - 1. *gaṣṣ (u gaṣṣ) n-*. Don't clip my hair too short. *la-tguṣṣ šaɛri kulliš igṣayyir.* -- I clipped this article out of the magazine. *gaṣṣeet hal-maqaala mnil-majalla.* 2. *garṭaf (u garṭafa) t-*. The gardener clipped the hedges. *l-bistanči garṭaf is-siyaaj.* 3. *šakkal (i taškiil) t-*. Clip these papers together. *šakkil hal-awraaq suwa.*

clipping - *quṣaaṣa pl. -aat.* He showed me some clippings from the local newspapers. *raawaani čam quṣaaṣa mnij-jaraayid il-maẓalliyya.*

cloak - 1. *ɛaba pl.-ɛibi.* The sheikh's cloak is made of pure camel wool. *l-ɛaba maal is-seex min wubar xaaliṣ.* 2. *ɛabaaya pl. -aat.* Only her face was visible in the cloak. *bass wučča čaan imbayyin imnil-ɛabaaya.*

to cloak - *sitar (u satir) n-*. He is using his social position to cloak his membership in the secret organization. *da-yistiġill markaza l-ijtimaaɛi ẓatta yistir ɛuḋwiita bij-jamɛiyya s-sirriyya.*

clock - *saaɛa pl. -aat.* We set our clock by the radio. *nuḋbuṭ saaɛatna ɛar-raadyo.*

to clock - *lizam (a lazim) wakit, waqqat (i tawqiit) t-*. Will you clock me for the hundred-meter run? *tilzam-li wakit ir-rikḋ il-miit matir? -- Clock the workers and see how much work they put out a day. *waqqit hal-ɛummaal w-šuuf išgadd yṭalliɛuun šuġul bil-yoom.*

to clog - 1. *sadd (i sadd) n-*. The pipes are clogged. *l-ibwaari masduuda.* 2. *sadsad (i tsidsid) t-*. The holes in the strainer are clogged up. *ɛuyuun l-maṣfi msadsida.*

clogs - *qubqaab pl. qabaaqiib.* She wears clogs instead of sandals. *tilbas qubqaab badal in-naɛaal.*

close - 1. *ẓamiim pl. -iin.* We are close friends. *ʔiẓna ʔaṣdiqaaʔ ẓamiimiin.* 2. *giriib, qariib.* The hotel is close to the station. *l-ʔuteel qariib imnil-maẓaṭṭa.* -- This is close to what I had in mind. *haaḋa giriib imniš-šii l-čaan ib-baali.* -- He is one of my closest friends. *huwwa min ʔaqrab ʔaṣdiqaaʔi.* -- The car drove up very close. *s-sayyaara wugfat kulliš qariib.* 3. *yamm.* We sat close together. *giɛadna waaẓid yamm il-laax.* 4. *qurub, gurub.* We use to live close to each other. *činna niskun qurub baɛaḋna.* 5. *maẓuur, waxim.* The air is very close in this room. *l-hawa kulliš maẓuur ib-hal-qubba.* 6. *zeen.* Pay close attention. *diir baalak zeen.* 7. *ḋaʔiil.* He won the election by a close margin of the vote. *ribaz il-intixaab ib-fariq ḋaʔiil bil-aṣwaat.* 8. *daqiiq.* This problem needs close study. *hal-muškila tiẓtaaj diraasa daqiiqa.* 9. *naaɛim.* The barber gave me a close shave this morning. *l-imzayyin zayyan-li wučči naaɛim il-yoom iṣ-ṣubuẓ.* *******He had a close call. *xilaṣ b-iɛjuuba.*

close by – *b-qurub.* Is there a restaurant close by? *ʔaku maṭɛam ib-hal-qurub?*
close – *nihaaya, ʔaaxir.* I'll see you at the close of the meeting. *ʔašuufak ib-nihaayt il-ijtimaaɛ.*
to close – **1.** *sadd (i sadd) n-.* Please close the door. *min faδ̣lak, sidd il-baab.* — The museum is closed Sundays. *l-matȥaf yinsadd ʔayyaam il-ʔaȥȥad.* **2.** *ġilag (u ġalig) n-, sadd (i sadd) n-.* The road is closed. *ṭ-ṭariiq maġluug.* **3.** *ɛaȥȥal (i taɛȥiil) t-.* They close at six. *yɛaȥȥluun bis-sitta.* **4.** *xitam (i xitaam) n-.* They closed the program with the national anthem. *xitmaw il-manhaj bin-našiid il-waṭani.* **5.** *ġammaδ (u tġummuδ) t-.* Close your eyes and go to sleep! *ġammuδ ɛuyuunak w-naam!*
to close one's eyes – *tɛaama (a taɛaami).* Don't close your eyes to the facts. *la-titɛaama ɛann il-ȥaqaayiq.*
closely – *b-diqqa.* Look at it closely. *baawuɛha b-diqqa.*
closet – *diilaab* pl. *dwaaliib, xazaana* pl. *xazaayin.* Her closet is full of new clothes. *diilaabha matruus ihduum jidiida.*
close up – **1.** *ṣuura (pl. ṣuwar) muqarraba.* Have you seen the close-ups we took of the baby. *šift iṣ-ṣuwar l-muqarraba l-ʔaxaδnaaha lij-jaahil.* **2.** *min giriib, ɛan qurub.* From close up it looks different. *min giriib itbayyin ġeer šikil.*
cloth – **1.** *qmaaš* pl. *-aat, ʔaqmiša.* In the cloth market you find cloth for dresses, shirts, and pajamas. *b-suug l-iqmaašaat tilgi qmaaš maal nafaaniif, w-iθyaab, w-beejaamaat.* — The book has a cloth binding. *ġilaaf l-iktaab min iqmaaš.* **2.** *xirga* pl. *xirag.* Use a clean cloth for the dusting. *ʔistaɛmil xirga nδ̣iifa lit-tanδ̣iif.*
**He made the story up out of whole cloth. *xilaq l-iȥčaaya min baṭna* or ***xilaq l-iȥčaaya min jawwa l-gaaɛ.*
to clothe – *kisa (i ʔiksaaʔ) n-.* The Red Crescent feeds and clothes the poor from its funds. *l-hilaal il-ʔaȥmar yiṭɛum w-yiksi l-fuqaraaʔ min mawaarda.*
clothes – *hduum, malaabis.* I want these clothes cleaned and pressed. *ʔariid hal-ihduum titnaδ̣δ̣af w-tinδ̣urub ʔuuti.*
clothes hanger – *tiɛlaaga* pl. *-aat.*
clothes hook – *ɛillaaga* pl. *-aat.* We need a few more clothes hooks to hang up the clothes. *niȥtaaj baɛad fadd čam ɛillaaga l-taɛliig l-ihduum.*
clothesline – *ȥabil* (pl. *ȥbaal*) *šarr il-ihduum.*
clothespin – *qirraaṣa* pl. *-aat.* What has become of the clothespins? *š-ṣaar imnil-qirraaṣaat?*
clothes rack – *šimmaaɛa* pl. *-aat.* There's a clothes rack in the hall. *ʔaku šimmaaɛa bil-mamarr.*
clothing – *malaabis, hduum.*
cloud – *ġeema* pl. *ġyuum* coll. *ġeem.* The sun has disappeared behind the clouds. *š-šamis ixtifat wara l-ġeem.*
**He always has his head in the clouds. *haaδa daalġači* or *haaδa dallaaġ.*
to cloud up – *ġayyam (i taġyiim).* Just after we started the sky clouded up. *baɛad-ma bdeena b-šwayya ġayymat id-dinya.*
cloudy – *mġayyim.*
clover – *barsiim.*
club – **1.** *doonki* pl. *-iyyaat.* The policeman had to use his club. *š-šurṭi njubar yistaɛmil doonkiyya.* **2.** *migwaar* pl. *migaawiir, klung* pl. *-aat.* They fought with clubs and sickles. *tɛaarkaw bil-migaawiir wil-manaajil.* **3.** *naadi* pl. *nwaadi.* Are you a member of the club? *ʔinta ɛuδ̣u bin-naadi?* **4.** *sinak.* I played the ace of clubs. *δabbeet il-billi s-sinak.*
to club – *δ̣irab (u δ̣arub) n- bil-migwaar.* The man was clubbed. *r-rijjaal inδ̣irab bil-migwaar.*
clue – **1.** *ʔišaara* pl. *-aat.* Can you give me a clue? *tigdar tinṭiini fadd ʔišaara?* **2.** *daliil* pl. *ʔadilla.* The police found no clues. *š-šurṭa ma-ligaw ʔay daliil.*
clumsy – **1.** *mxarbaṭ.* That's a clumsy sentence. *haaδi jumla mxarbuṭa.* **2.** *θgiil.* He's as clumsy as a bear. *huwwa θgiil miθil id-dibb.*
clutch – **1.** *klač* pl. *-aat.* Push in the clutch. *duus ɛal-iklač.* **2.** *qabδ̣a.* He fell into the clutches of some gangsters. *wugaɛ ib-qabδ̣at čam ʔašqiyaaʔ.*
**He had him in his clutches. *xallaa jawwa ɛbaaṭa.*
to clutch – **1.** *ɛiṣar (i ɛaṣir) n-, čallab (i tačliib) t- b-.* The child clutched my hand. *ṭ-ṭifil ɛiṣar iidi.* **2.** *madd (i madd) n- ʔiid~.* He clutched at the rope but he wasn't able to get ahold of it. *madd iida ɛal-ȥabil laakin ma-gidar ykumša.*

coach – **1.** *ɛarabaana* pl. *ɛarabaayin, fargoon* pl. *-aat.* The train consists of the engine and four coaches. *l-qiṭaar yitʔallif min makiina w-ʔarbaɛ fargoonaat.* **2.** *mudarrib* pl. *-iin.* He's the best coach in this school. *huwwa ʔaȥsan mudarrib ib-hal-madrasa.*
to coach – **1.** *darrab (i tadriib) t-.* He coaches the soccer team. *ydarrib firqat kuurat il-qadam.* **2.** *ɛallam (i taɛliim) t-.* Students in the back of the room began coaching him when he was asked a question. *ṭ-ṭullaab ib-ʔaxiir il-ġurfa bidaw yɛallmuu lamma nsiʔal suʔaal.*
coal – *faȥma* pl. *-aat* coll. *faȥam.* We have to order coal. *laazim nuṭlub faȥam.*
coal bin – *maxzan* (pl. *maxaazin*) *faȥam.*
coarse – *xašin.* This material is very coarse. *hal-uqmaaš kulliš xašin.* — He's a very coarse person. *huwwa fadd waaȥid kulliš xašin.*
coast – *saaȥil* pl. *sawaaȥil.* We approached the coast at night. *tqarrabna mnis-saaȥil bil-leel.*
to coast – *tdahdar (a tdihdir).* We coasted for three hundred meters. *tdahdarna tlaθ miit matir.*
coast guard – *xafar is-sawaaȥil.*
coat – **1.** *qappuuṭ* pl. *-aat, miɛṭaf* pl. *maɛaaṭif.* You can't go out without a coat in this weather. *ma-tigdar titlaɛ iblayya qappuuṭ ib-haj-jaww.* **2.** *sitra* pl. *sitar.* The pants are fine but the coat's too tight. *l-panṭaruun maδ̣buuṭ laakin is-sitra kulliš δ̣ayyga.* **3.** *qaaṭ* pl. *quuṭ.* This house needs another coat of paint. *hal-beet yinraad-la qaaṭ subuġ θaani.*
coated – *mġaṭṭa.* The car was coated with mud. *s-sayyaara čaanat imġaṭṭaaya biṭ-ṭiin.*
coat hanger – *tiɛlaaga* pl. *-aat.*
cobweb – *ɛišš ɛankabuut, beet ɛankabuut, xyuuṭ ɛankabuut.*
cockroach – *ṣurṣur* pl. *ṣaraaṣir, ṣarṣuur* pl. *ṣaraaṣiir, bint* (pl. *banaat*) *murdaan.*
cocktail – *kookteel* pl. *-aat.*
cocoa – *kakaaw.*
coconut – *joozat* (pl. *-aat*) *hind,* coll. *jooz hind.*
code – **1.** *rumuuz, ʔišaaraat.* They sent the telegram in Morse code. *dazzaw il-barqiyya b-rumuuz moors.* **2.** *šafra.* They tried to decipher the code. *ȥaawlaw yfassiruun iš-šafra.*
code of ethics – *qawaaɛid ʔadabiyya.*
code of Hammurabi – *šariiɛat ȥamuraabi.*
code of morals – *qawaaɛid ʔaxlaaqiyya.*
coffee – *gahwa.* The coffee is freshly roasted. *l-gahwa stawha tȥammṣat.*
coffee pot – *dalla* (pl. *-aat, dlaal*) *maal gahwa.*
coffin – *taabuut* pl. *twaabiit.*
cog – *sinn* pl. *snuun.* One of the cogs is broken off this gear. *waaȥid imn-isnuun had-dišli maksuur.*
cognac – *koonyaak.*
coil – *laffa* pl. *-aat.* You'll have to buy a coil of wire. *laazim tištiri laffat waayar.*
ignition coil – *kooyil* pl. *-aat.*
to coil – *ltaff (a ltifaaf).* The snake coiled around the man's arm. *l-ȥayya ltaffat ȥawl iδ̣raaɛ ir-rajjaal.*
to coil up – *laff (i laff) n-.* He coiled up the wire. *laff is-siim.*
coin – *ɛumla* pl. *-aat.* He collects old gold coins. *yjammiɛ ɛumla δahabiyya qadiima.*
to coin – **1.** *δ̣urab (a δ̣arub) n-.* This money was coined in Belgium. *hal-ɛumla nδ̣urbat ib-baljiika.* **2.** *xilaq (i xaliq) n-.* Scientists are coining new words every day. *l-ɛulamaaʔ da-yxilquun kalimaat ijdiida kull yoom.*
coincidence – *ṣudfa* pl. *ṣudaf.* What a strange coincidence! *šloon ṣudfa ġariiba!*
coke – *faȥam il-kuuk.* We use coke for heating. *nistaɛmil faȥam il-kuuk lit-tadfiʔa.*
cold – **1.** *barid.* I can't stand this cold. *ma-agdar atȥammal hal-barid.* **2.** *bardaan.* I'm cold. *ʔaani bardaan.* **3.** *barid, našla, zukaam.* He has a bad cold. *ɛinda našla qawiyya.* **4.** *baarid.* It was a cold night. *čaanat leela baarda.*
**The blow knocked him cold. *δ̣-δ̣arba ʔafqidat šuɛuura.*
to collaborate – **1.** *tɛaawan (a taɛaawun).* She collaborated with the enemy. *tɛaawnat wiyya l-ɛadu.* **2.** *štirak (i štiraak), tɛaawan (a taɛaawun).* Two teams of scientists collaborated in the experiment. *firiqteen imnil-ɛulamaaʔ ištirkat ib-ɛamal it-tajruba.*
to collapse – **1.** *nhaar (a nhiyaar), nhidam (i nhidaam), tdahwar (a tadahwur).* The bridge suddenly collapsed. *j-jisir inhaar ɛala ġafla.* **2.** *wugaɛ (a wguuɛ),*

xirab (a). He collapsed in the middle of the street. *wugaƐ ib-nuṣṣ ij-jaadda.*

collar - *yaaxa* pl. *-aat.* Do you want your collars starched or not? *triid yaaxaatak imnaššaaya loo laa?*

collar bone - *Ɛaẓm* (pl. *Ɛẓaam*) *ṭurquwa.*

to **collect** - **1.** *jimaƐ (a jamiƐ) n-, jammaƐ (i tajmiiƐ) t-, lamm (i lamm) n-.* I collect stamps. *ʔajammiƐ ṭawaabiƐ.* -- Give me a chance to collect my thoughts. *nṭiini majaal ʔajmaƐ fikri.* **2.** *ltamm (a ltimaam).* People collected in the square. *n-naas iltammaw bis-saaza.*

collected - **1.** *ẓaabuṭ il-aƐṣaab.* In spite of the danger, he remained calm and collected. *b-raġm il-xaṭar, buqa haadiʔ w-ẓaabuṭ aƐṣaaba.* **2.** *majmuuƐ.* I bought the collected works of Taha Hussein. *štireet il-muʔallafaat il-majmuuƐa li-ṭaaha zseen.*

collection - *majmuuƐa, majaamiiƐ.* The library has a famous collection of books on America. *l-maktaba biiha majmuuƐa mašhuura mnil-kutub Ɛan ʔamriika.*

**What time is the last mail collection? *šwakit ʔaaxir marra yinlamm il-bariid?*

**They took up a collection for the beggar. *jimƐaw ifluus lil-faqiir.*

college - *kulliyya* pl. *-aat.*

to **collide** - *ṣṭidam (i ṣṭidaam), tṣaadam (a taṣaadum).* The cars collided at the intersection. *s-sayyaaraat itṣaadmat ib-mafraq iṭ-ṭariiq.*

collision - *taṣaadum* pl. *-aat, ṣṭidaam* pl. *-aat.*

colloquial - *Ɛammi*, jilfi*.* How do I say this in the colloquial language? *šloon aguul haay bil-luġa l-Ɛammiyya?*

cologne - *riiza, qaloonya.*

colon - **1.** *nuquṭṭeen.* Use a comma instead of a colon. *ʔistaƐmil faariza badal nuquṭṭeen.* **2.** *kooloon* pl. *-aat.* Your colon is in an inflammed condition. *l-kooloon maalak miltihib.*

colonel - *Ɛaqiid* pl. *Ɛuqadaaʔ.*

to **colonize** - *staƐmar (i stiƐmaar).* They colonized the island. *staƐmiraw ij-jaziira.*

colony - *mustaƐmara* pl. *-aat.* We were a colony until two years ago. *činna mustaƐmara ʔila gabuḷ santeen.* -- There's a colony of ants in our back yard. *ʔaku mustaƐmarat namil ib-zadiiqatna.* **2.** *jaaliya.* The majority of the American colony lives in this district. *ʔakθariyyat il-jaaliya l-ʔamiirkiyya tiskun ib-hal-manṭiqa.*

color - *loon* pl. *ʔalwaan.* I don't like any of these colors. *ma-azibb ʔay loon min hal-ʔalwaan.* -- The team wore its school colors. *l-fariiq libas loon madrasta.*

to color - *lawwan (i talwiin) t-.* She colored some pictures. *lawwinat čam ṣuura.*

colored - **1.** *mulawwan* pl. *-iin.* Several colored families live near here. *Ɛiddat Ɛawaaʔil imnil-mulawwiniin itƐiiš qariib min ihnaa.* -- Do you have any colored handkerchiefs? *Ɛindak ʔay icfaafi mlawwna?* **2.** *maṣbuuġ.* His ideas are colored by Communism. *ʔaaraaʔa maṣbuuġa biš-šuyuuƐiyya.*

color-blindness - *Ɛama l-ʔalwaan.*

colt - *muhur* pl. *muhuur.*

column - **1.** *Ɛamuud* pl. *ʔaƐmida, Ɛawaamiid.* You can recognize the house by its white columns. *tigdar tuƐruf il-beet imnil-Ɛawaamiid il-biiẓ il-bii.* -- Write your name in the right-hand column. *ʔiktib ismak bil-Ɛamuud illi Ɛal-yimna.* **2.** *ṭaabuur* pl. *ṭwaabiir, ratil* pl. *ʔartaal.* Four columns of soldiers marched down the road. *ʔarbaƐ artaal imnij-jinuud mišat bis-saariƐ.* -- I believe she's a member of the fifth column. *ʔaƐtiqid hiyya mnir-ratl il-xaamis.*

comb - **1.** *mišiṭ* pl. *mšaaṭ.* Where can I buy a comb? *mneen agdar aštiri mišiṭ?* **2.** *xaliyya* pl. *xalaaya.* The comb is full of honey. *l-xaliyya malyaana Ɛasal.*

to comb - *maššaṭ (i tamšiiṭ, tmiššiṭ) t-.* Did your mother comb your hair? *ʔummak maššiṭat saƐrak?* -- The police combed the whole city. *š-šurṭa maššṭooha lil-wlaaya kullha.*

combination - *jamiƐ.* How do you like the combination of red and gray? *šloon yƐijbak ij-jamiƐ been il-ʔazmar wir-rumaadi?*

**We are the only ones who know the combination to the safe. *ʔizna l-waziidiin illi nuƐruf tartiib rumuuz fatz il-qaaṣa.*

to come - **1.** *jaa (i majiiʔ).* When does he come to town? *šwakit yiji lil-wlaaya?* -- Joking comes natural to him. *t-tankiit yijii b-ṣuura ṭabiiƐiyya.* -- This cloth comes only in two colors. *hal-iqmaaš ma-yiji ġeer ib-looneen.* **2.** *ṣaadaf (i muṣaadafa), tṣaadaf (a taṣaaduf).* My birthday comes on a Monday this year. *Ɛiid miilaadi yṣaadif has-sana yoom il-iθneen.* **3.** *taƐaal.* Come here a minute, Nizar. *taƐaal fadd daqiiqa, nazaar.* -- Hey boys, come over here! *yaa ʔawlaad, taƐaalu!*

**I don't know whether I'm coming or going. *ma-da-aƐruf iš-da-asawwi.*

**Come now, I'm not that foolish. *bass Ɛaad, ʔaani mu l-had-daraja ġabi.*

to come about - *jira (i majra), ṣaar (i ṣeer).* How did all this come about? *šloon jira haaδa kulla?*

to come across - **1.** *Ɛubar (u Ɛabur) n-.* He had to come across the bridge to visit us. *ẓṭarr yuƐbur ij-jisir zatta yzuurna.* **2.** *liga (i lagi) n-.* I accidentally came across my friend's name in this book. *lgeet ʔisim ṣadiiqi b-hal-iktaab biṣ-ṣidfa.*

**He's the wisest man I've ever come across. *huwwa ʔaƐqal šaxiṣ šifta.*

to come after (or for) - *jaa (i majiiʔ) Ɛala.* I've come after my passport. *jeet Ɛala paaspoorti.*

to come along - *miša (i maši).* How's your work coming along? *šloon da-yimsi suġlak?*

to come apart - *tfaṣṣax (a tafaṣṣux), tfallaš (a tfilliš).* This chair is coming apart. *hal-kursi da-yitfaṣṣax.*

to come around - *Ɛaawad (i muƐaawada).* The beggar comes around to us every Friday. *l-imjaddi yƐaawidna kull yoom jimƐa.*

to come back - **1.** *rijaƐ (a rujuuƐ).* They're coming back tomorrow. *yirjaƐuun baačir.*

to come by - **1.** *marr (u muruur) min.* He's coming by here this afternoon. *raz-ymurr minnaa l-yoom il-Ɛaṣir.* **2.** *dabbar (u tadbiir) t-.* How did he come by all that money? *šloon dabbar kull hal-ifluus?*

to come down - **1.** *nizal (i nuzuul).* Can you come down a moment? *tigdar tinzil fadd lazẓa?* **2.** *xaffaẓ (u taxfiiẓ, txuffuẓ) t-, nazzal (i tanziil, tnizzil) t-.* We can't come down a bit on this price. *ma-nigdar inxaffuẓ has-siƐir wala filis.* **3.** *nṣaab (a ʔiṣaaba).* He came down with a bad cold. *nṣaab ib-fadd našla qawiyya.*

to come in - **1.** *dixal (u duxuul), xašš (u xašš).* Please come in. *ʔarjuuk idxul* or *rajaaʔan xušš.* **2.** *wuṣal (a wuṣuul).* What time does the train come in? *šwakit yooṣal il-qiṭaar?* **3.** *jaa (i majiiʔ).* Requests for help are coming in daily. *ṭalabaat il-musaaƐada da-tiji yoomiyyan.*

to come in handy - *faad (i faaʔida), nifaƐ (a nafiƐ).* It'll come in very handy to you later. *raz-itfiidak baƐdeen.*

to come off - **1.** *nšilaƐ (i).* One leg of the table has come off. *wizda min rijleen il-meez inšilƐat.* **2.** *ngiṭaƐ (i ngiṭaaƐ).* The button has come off. *d-dugma ngiṭƐat.* **3.** *gaam (u goom), nzakk (a).* The color comes off these gloves. *ṣ-ṣubuġ da-yguum min hač-čifuuf.* **4.** *ṭilaƐ (ṭuluuƐ).* The play came off real well. *t-tamθiiliyya ṭilƐat zeena.*

to come out - **1.** *ṭilaƐ (a ṭuluuƐ).* Are you going to come out to the farm with us? *raz-tiṭlaƐ wiyyaana lil-mazraƐa?* -- The ink spot won't come out of this shirt. *buqƐat il-zibir ma-tiṭlaƐ min haθ-θoob.* -- Who came out on top in the fight? *minu ṭilaƐ ġaaḷub bil-mulaakama?* or *minu ġiḷab bil-mulaakama?* or *minu faaz bil-mulaakama?* **2.** *ẓihar (a ẓuhuur), ʔija (i majiiʔ), ṭilaƐ (a ṭuluuƐ).* Their product came out on the market a month ago. *mantuujhum ẓihar bis-suug gabuḷ šahar.* **3.** *bayyan (i tbiyyin) t-.* The truth finally came out. *l-zaqiiqa bayyinat bit-taali.* **4.** *ẓihar (a ẓuhuur), bayyan (i tbiyyin).* The president came out in favor of high taxes. *r-raʔiis ẓihar yfaẓẓil iẓ-ẓaraaʔib il-Ɛaalya.*

to come over - **1.** *ʔija (i majiiʔ).* Some friends are coming over to see us this evening. *baƐẓ il-ʔaṣdiqaaʔ raz-yjuun Ɛidna hal-leela.* **2.** *ṣiƐad (a ṣuƐuud), faaẓ (i feeẓ).* The water's starting to come over the curb. *l-mayy bida yiṣƐad Ɛala zaaffat ir-raṣiif.* **3.** *Ɛubar (u Ɛabur) n-.* They came over the bridge on their way to town. *Ɛubraw ij-jisir ib-ṭariiqhum lil-madiina.*

**I don't know what's come over him. *ma-adri š-bii.*

to come through - **1.** *marr (u muruur) n- b-.* Did you come through the woods on your way here? *marreet bil-ġaaba b-ṭariiqak l-ihnaa.* -- He came through the operation safely. *marr bil-Ɛamaliyya b-salaama.* **2.** *xaaẓ (u xooẓ) n- b-, marr (u muruur) n- b-.* He had to come through mud to get here. *ẓṭarr yxuuẓ* *ib-ṭiin ḥatta yooṣal l-ihnaa.*

to come to - 1. *waṣṣal (i twiṣṣil).* The bill comes to two dollars. *l-qaaʔima twaṣṣil doolaareen.* 2. *ṣiḥa (i ṣaḥu).* After a few minutes she came to. *ṣiḥat baεad fadd čam daqiiqa.* 3. *ṣaar (i ṣeer).* Who knows what all this will come to? *minu yidri š-raḥ-yṣiir?* 4. *ʔija, jaa (i majiiʔ) b-.* Her name doesn't come to me right now. *ʔisimha ma-yiji b-baali hassa.*

to come true - *tḥaqqaq (a taḥaqquq).* Her dream came true. *tḥaqqaq ḥilimha.*

to come up - 1. *ṭilaε (a ṭuluuε).* The diver came up after three minutes under water. *l-ġawwaaṣ ṭilaε li-foog baεad-ma čaan iθlaθ daqaayiq taḥt il-ṃayy.* -- The wheat is beginning to come up. *l-ḥunṭa bida tiṭlaε.* 2. *ð̣ihar (a ð̣uhuur).* This problem comes up every day. *hal-muškila tið̣har kull yoom.* 3. *ṣaar (i ṣeer).* A thunderstorm is coming up. *raḥ-itṣiir εaaṣifa.* 4. *ṣiεad (a ṣuεuud, ṣaεid).* Can you come up for a minute? *tigdar tiṣεad il-fadd daqiiqa?* 5. *jaab (i jeeb) n-.* If you can come up with a better idea, go right ahead. *ʔiða tigdar itjiib fikra ʔaḥsan, itfað̣ð̣al.*

to come upon - 1. *twaṣṣal (a tawaṣṣul) l-.* I came upon the solution by accident. *twaṣṣalit lil-ḥall biṣ-ṣidfa.* 2. *ʔija, jaa (i majiiʔ) εala.* We came upon a man lying in the street. *jeena εala rijjaal waagiε biš-šaariε.*

to come up to - *ṭaabaq (i muṭaabaqa), nṭubaq (u nṭibaaq) εala.* The new bridge didn't come up to government specifications. *j-jisir ij-jidiid ma-ṭaabaq muwaaṣafaat il-ḥukuuma.*

comedy - *ruwaaya (pl. -aat) hazaliyya.* Did you like the comedy? *εijbatak ir-ruwaaya l-hazaliyya?*

comet - *muðannab* pl. *-aat.*

comfort - *wasiilat* (pl. *wasaaʔil*) *raaḥa.* This hotel has all the comforts you can ask for. *hal-funduq bii jamiiε wasaaʔil ir-raaḥa lli tuṭlubha.*

to comfort - *εazza (i taεziya).* We went to comfort her after her son died. *riḥna nεazziiha baεad-ma maat ibinha.*

comfortable - 1. *muriiḥ.* This chair is very comfortable. *hal-kursi kulliš muriiḥ.* 2. *mirtaaḥ.* I don't feel very comfortable. *ʔaani ma-mirtaaḥ.*

to make oneself comfortable - *stiraaḥ (i stiraaḥa).* Sit down and make yourself comfortable. *ʔugεud w-istiriiḥ* or *ʔugεud w-xuð raaḥtak.*

comical - *hazali*, fukaahi*, muð̣ḥik.* The movie was very comical. *l-filim čaan kulliš hazali.*

comma - *faariza* pl. *fawaariz.*

command - 1. *ʔamur* pl. *ʔawaamir.* Why wasn't my command carried out? *leeš ma-tnaffað ʔamri?* 2. *ṣayṭara.* He has an excellent command of English. *εinda ṣayṭara taamma εal-luġa l-ingiliiziyya.*

in command - *ʔaamir.* Who's in command of these soldiers? *minu ʔaamir hal-jinuud?*

to command - 1. *ʔumar (u ʔamur).* He commanded the soldiers to return. *ʔumar ij-junuud bir-rujuuε.* 2. *jilab (i jalib) n-.* He commands respect everywhere he goes. *yijlib iḥtiraam ween-ma yruuḥ.* 3. *qaad (u qiyaada) n-.* My father commands the Fifth Army. *ʔabuuya yquud ij-jeeš il-xaamis.*

to command a view - *ṭall (u ʔiṭlaal), ʔašraf (i ʔišraaf).* Our house commands a view of the entire lake. *beetna yṭull εal-buḥeera kullha.*

commander - *qaaʔid* pl. *quwwaad.* He's been appointed commander of the Fourteenth Army. *huwwa tεayyan qaaʔid lij-jeeš ir-raabiε εašar.*

to **commend** - 1. *midaḥ (a madiḥ) n-, ḥimad (i ḥamid) n-.* He commended the soldiers for their bravery in the battle. *midaḥ ij-junuud il-basaalathum bil-maεraka.* 2. *sallam (i tasliim) t-.* He commended his soul to God. *sallam rooḥa l-ʔaḷḷa.*

comment - *taεliiq* pl. *-aat, mulaaḥað̣a* pl. *-aat.* Did he have any comments on the subject? *čaanat εinda taεliiqaat εal-mawð̣uuε?*

to comment - *εallaq (i taεliiq) t-.* The editor commented on the president's visit. *l-muḥarrir εallaq εala ziyaarat ir-raʔiis.*

commercial - *tijaari*.* He's well known in commercial circles. *huwwa zeen maεruuf bil-ʔawsaaṭ it-tijaariyya.*

to **commit** - 1. *rtikab (i rtikaab).* Who committed the crime? *minu rtikab ij-jariima?* 2. *daxxal (i tadxiil).* They committed her to a mental hospital. *daxxlooha b-mustašfa l-ʔamraað̣ il-εaqliyya.*

to commit one's self - *tεahhad (a taεahhud), ltizam (i ltizaam).* The president refused to commit himself. *r-raʔiis rufað̣ yitεahhad.*

to commit suicide - *ntiḥar (i ntiḥaar).* He committed suicide last week. *ntiḥar bil-ʔisbuuε il-maað̣i.*

committee - *lujna* pl. *lijaan.*

common - 1. *šaayiε.* Some French words are in common use in the Lebanese dialect. *baεað̣ ič-čilam il-fransiyya šaayεat il-istiεmaal bil-lahja l-lubnaaniyya.* 2. *muštarak.* We have common goals. *εidna ġaayaat muštaraka.* 3. *εaammi* pl. *εawaamm.* The common people don't care about politics. *l-εawaamm ma-yihtammuun bis-siyaasa.*

common knowledge - *l-maεruuf εan.* It is common knowledge that he lies. *l-maεruuf εanna huwwa yičðib.*

common market - *suuq muštarak.*

commotion - *haraj w-maraj.* There was a terrific commotion in the street. *čaan ʔaku haraj w-maraj biš-šaariε.*

to **communicate** - 1. *ttiṣal (i ttiṣaal).* We communicate with them daily by radio. *nittiṣil biihum yoomiyyan bir-raadyo.* 2. *tfaaham (a tafaahum).* They have difficulty communicating because of a language problem. *b-ṣuεuuba yitfaahmuun ib-sabab muškilt il-luġa.*

communication - 1. *muwaaṣalaat.* He works in the communication branch. *da-yištuġul ib-qism il-muwaaṣalaat.* 2. *muraasala* pl. *-aat.* We received their communication a week ago. *stilamna muraasalathum gabḷ isbuuε.*

Communism - *šiyuuεiyya.*

Communist - *šiyuuεi** pl. *-iyyiin.*

community - *wlaaya* pl. *-aat.* He lives in a small community about four miles from Baghdad. *yεiiš b-wlaaya ṣġayyra ḥawaali ʔarbaε imyaal min baġdaad.*

compact - 1. *quuṭiyyat* (pl. *-aat*) *p̣oodra.* She bought a new compact. *štireet quuṭiyyat p̣oodra jdiida.* 2. *maḥšuuk, marṣuuṣ.* That's a very compact package. *har-ruzma maḥšuuka ḥašik.*

company - 1. *fawj* pl. *ʔafwaaj.* I served in his company. *xidamit bil-fawj maala.* 2. *šarika* pl. *-aat.* What company do you represent? *ʔay šarika tmaθθilha?* 3. *xiṭṭaar, ð̣uyuuf.* We are expecting company this evening. *nitwaqqaε xiṭṭaar hal-leela.* 4. *jamaaεa, ʔaṣdiqaaʔ, rifjaan.* A man is known by the company he keeps. *r-rajul maεruuf imnij-jamaaεa lli yimši wiyyaahum.* 5. *rafiiq* pl. *rufaqaaʔ, rifiij* pl. *rifjaan.* I find him very good company. *šifta kulliš xooš rafiiq.*

**Keep me company for a while. *ʔubqa wiyyaaya fadd išwaaya.*

comparatively - *nisbiyyan.* The test was comparatively easy. *l-ixtibaar čaan nisbiyyan saahil.*

to **compare** - *qaaran (i muqaarana) t- been.* We compared the two methods. *qaaranna been iṭ-ṭariiqteen.*

comparison - *muqaarana* pl. *-aat.* Can you make another comparison between the two? *tigdar itsawwi muqaarana ʔuxra been il-iθneen?*

**There is no comparison between the two. *ween haaða min ðaak?* or *haaða ween w-ðaak ween?*

compartment - 1. *maqṣuura* pl. *-aat.* All compartments in this car are crowded with people. *kull il-maqṣuuraat ib-hal-εaraba mizdaḥma bin-naas.* 2. *xaana* pl. *-aat, beet* pl. *-byuut.* The drawer has compartments for knives, forks, and spoons. *j-jaraar bii xaanaat lis-sičaačiin wič-čaṭalaat wil-xawaašiig.*

compass - 1. *booṣla* pl. *-aat.* Without the compass we would have been lost. *loo maa l-booṣla čaan ð̣iεna.* 2. *p̣urgaaḷ* pl. *p̣araagiiḷ.* I can draw a circle without a compass. *ʔagdar ʔarsim daaʔira blayya p̣urgaaḷ.*

to **compel** - *jubar (u jabur) n-, ð̣ṭarr (a ð̣ṭiraar).* The accident compelled us to leave a day early. *l-ḥaadiθ jubarna nitruk yoom gabuḷ.*

compensation - *taεwiið̣* pl. *-aat.* I demand full compensation. *ʔaṭaalub ib-taεwiið̣ kaamil.*

to **compete** - 1. *tnaafas (a tanaafus), tsaabaq (a tasaabuq).* The two teams are competing for the silver cup. *l-firiqteen yitnaafsuun εal-kaʔs il-fuð̣ð̣i.* 2. *naafas (i munaafasa), zaaḥam (i muzaaḥama).* I won't ever be able to compete with him in the exams. *ma-raḥ-agdar ʔanaafsa bil-imtiḥaanaat.*

competent - *muqtidir, kafu.*

competition - *munaafasa, muzaaḥama.* Competition is necessary in business. *l-munaafasa ð̣aruuriyya bil-ḥayaat it-tijaariyya.*

competitor - *munaafis* pl. *-iin, muzaaḥim* pl. *-iin.* Our competitor's product is no good. *ʔintaaj munaafisna muu zeen.*

to **compile** - *jammaε (i tjimmiε) t-.* He's compiling

material for his new book. *da-yjammiε mawaadd l-iktaaba j-jidiid.*

to **complain** - *štika (i tšikki), tšakka (a tšikki).* She complains of severe pains. *da-tištiki min wujaε šadiid.* 2. *tðammar (a taðammur), štika (i tšikki), tšakka (a tšikki).* He complains about his work. *da-yitðammar min šuġla.*

complaint - 1. *šakwa* pl. *šakaawi, šakaaya* pl. *-aat.* Do you have any complaints? *εindak ʔay šakwa?* 2. *daεwa* pl. *daεaawi.* I filed a complaint with the police after the assault took place. *sajjalit daεwa εind iš-šurṭa baεad-ma ṣaar il-iεtidaaʔ.*

complete - *kaamil.* This volume makes my collection complete. *haj-juzuʔ ysawwi majmuuεati kaamla.* 2. *tamaam, bil-marra.* He's a complete fool. *huwwa ʔaħmaq tamaam.*

to complete - *kammal (i tkimmil) t-, xaḷḷaṣ (i txiḷḷiṣ) t-, tammam (i ttimmim) t-, ʔanha (i ʔinhaaʔ) n-.* We'll complete the arrangements for the trip tomorrow. *raħ-inkammil it-tartiibaat lis-safra bukra.*

completely - 1. *tamaaman.* He convinced me completely. *ʔaqnaεni tamaaman.* 2. *bil-marra.* You're completely wrong. *ʔinta ġalṭaan bil-marra.*

complexion - *bušra* pl. *-aat.* He has a very dark complexion. *l-bušra maalta kulliš samra.*

to **complicate** - *εaqqad (i taεqiid).* Don't complicate matters any more than they are. *la-tεaqqid il-ʔumuur ʔakθar mim-ma hiyya.*

complicated - *mεaqqad.*

compliment - 1. *madiħ, θanaaʔ* pl. *-aat.* Thanks for the compliment. *ʔaškurak εala l-madiħ.* 2. *taħiyya* pl. *-aat.* Please accept this gift with the compliments of the company. *rajaaʔan itqabbal hal-hadiyya maεa taħiyyat iš-šarika.*

to compliment - *midaħ (a madiħ) n-, ʔaθna (i θanaaʔ) n- εala.* He complimented me on my cooking. *midaħni εala ṭabxi* or *ʔaθna εalayya b-ṭabxi.*

to **comply** - 1. *labba (i talbiya) t-.* We regret that we cannot comply with your request. *ʔaasfiin ma-nigdar inlabbi ṭalabak.* 2. *tjaawab (a tajaawub), ṭaaε (i ʔiṭaaεa).* He refused to comply with the rules of the university. *rufaḍ yṭiiε qawaaniin ij-jaamiεa* or *rufaḍ yitjaawab wiyya qawaaniin ij-jaamiεa.*

to **compose** - 1. *ʔallaf (i taʔliif) t-.* He composed a piece of music for the occasion. *ʔallaf qiṭεa muusiiqiyya lil-munaasaba.* -- This sentence is composed of a subject and a predicate. *haj-jumla titʔallaf min mubtadaʔ w-xabar.* 2. *ḍubaṭ (u ḍabuṭ), hadda? (i thiddiʔ, tahdiʔa).* Just try to compose yourself a bit. *ħaawil tiḍbuṭ nafsak išwayya.*

composed - 1. *ḍaabut in-nafis, haadiʔ, mṣaytir εala n-nafis.* He remained composed during the whole trial. *buqa ḍaabuṭ nafsa ṭuul il-muħaakama.* 2. *mitkawwin.* This fabric is composed of rayon and silk. *hal-iqmaaš mitkawwin min riiyoon w-ħariir.*

composition - 1. *taʔliif* pl. *taʔaaliif.* The orchestra is going to play his compositions tonight. *l-firqa l-muusiiqiyya raħ-tiεzif taʔaaliifa hal-leela.* 2. *murakkabaat, mukawwinaat.* The composition of this rock isn't known. *murakkabaat haṣ-ṣaxra muu maεruufa.* 3. *ʔinšaaʔ* pl. *-aat.* Have you done your English composition? *sawweet ʔinšaaʔak il-ingiliizi?*

compress - *ḍamaada* pl. *-aat, kammaada* pl. *-aat.* A cold compress will relieve the pain. *ḍamaada barda raħ-itxaffuf il-wujaε.*

to compress - *ḍiġaṭ (u ḍaġiṭ) n-.* It is difficult to compress water. *mniṣ-ṣaεub tuḍġuṭ il-ṃayy.*

compromise - *taraaḍi.* The problem cannot be solved but by compromise. *l-masʔala ma-tinħall ʔilla bit-taraaḍi.*

to compromise - 1. *traaḍa (i taraaḍi), tsaahal (a tasaahul), saawa (i musaawaa).* They don't want to compromise. *ma-yirduun yitraaḍuun.* 2. *εarraḍ (i taεriiḍ) t- lil-xaṭar.* You have compromised the security of our country. *εarraḍit salaamat baladna lil-xaṭar.*

comrade - *rafiiq* pl. *rufaqaaʔ, rifaaq; zamiil* pl. *zumalaaʔ.*

to **conceal** - *ḍamm (u ḍamm) n-, ʔaxfa (i ʔixfaaʔ) n-.* He concealed himself behind a tree. *ḍamm nafsa wara fadd šijara.* -- He attempted to conceal the truth from the judge. *ħaawal yixfi l-ħaqiiqa εan il-ħaakim.*

conceited - *mitkabbur, maġruur, šaayif in-nafis.* Those girls are all very conceited. *hal-banaat kuḷḷhin mitkabburaat.*

conceivable - *mumkin ʔidraak.* A few years ago a trip to the moon wasn't even conceivable. *gabuḷ εam sana is-safar lil-gumar ma-čaan mumkin ʔidraaka.*

to **conceive** - *tṣawwar (a taṣawwur).* I can't conceive of her doing such a thing. *ma-yimkin ʔatṣawwarha tsawwi hiiči šii.*

concentrate - *murakkaz.* Mix one can of orange juice concentrate with three cans of water. *ʔixluṭ quuṭiyyat εaṣiir purṭaqaal murakkaz wiyya tlaθ qawaaṭi ṃayy.*

to concentrate - 1. *ħaššad (i taħšiid, tħiššid) t-.* The commanders concentrated the armies at the base of the hill. *l-quwwaad ħaššdaw ij-juyuuš jawwa j-jibal.* 2. *rakkaz (i tarkiiz) t-.* We're going to concentrate on pronunciation today. *raħ-inrakkiz εat-talaffuḍ il-yoom.* -- The textile industry is concentrated in the North. *ṣinaaεat in-nasiij mitrakkza biš-šimaal.*

concern - 1. *šarika* pl. *-aat.* How long have you been with this concern? *šgadd ṣaar-lak ib-haš-šarika?* 2. *daεwa* pl. *daεaawi, šuġuḷ* pl. *ʔašġaal.* She said it was no concern of mine. *gaalat ma-ʔili daεwa biiha.* 3. *qalaq.* There's no reason for concern. *ma-aku daaεi lil-qalaq.*

to concern - *xaṣṣ (u), hamm (i hamm).* This bulletin concerns everyone in this office. *hal-manšuur yhimm kull waaħid ib-had-daaʔira.*

to be concerned - *htamm (i htimaam), qilaq (a qaliq).* She gets very concerned over the smallest thing. *da-tihtamm ihwaaya εala ʔaqall šii.* -- The police are concerned with this increase in crime. *š-šurṭa mihtamma b-hiδiyaad ij-jaraaʔim haaδi.*

as far as one's concerned - *bin-nisba ʔila, min naaħiya~, min yamm.* As far as I'm concerned you can do as you like. *bin-nisba ʔili tigdar itsawwi š-ma-triid.*

concerning - *b-xuṣuuṣ.* Nothing was said concerning the vacation. *ma-ngaal šii b-xuṣuuṣ il-εuṭla.*

to **conclude** - 1. *ʔanha (i ʔinhaaʔ), xitam (i xatim) n-, faḍḍ (u faḍḍ) n-.* They concluded the meeting yesterday afternoon. *ʔanhaw l-ijtimaaε il-baarħa l-εaṣir.* 2. *εiqad (i εaqid) n-, ʔabram (i ʔibraam) n-.* The two countries concluded the trade agreement two days ago. *l-baladeen εiqdaw l-ittifaaqiyya t-tijaariyya gabuḷ yoomeen.* 3. *stantaj (i stintaaj).* What do you conclude from his remark? *š-tistantij min mulaaħaḍ̣ta?*

conclusion - 1. *natiija* pl. *nataaʔij, stintaaj* pl. *-aat.* What conclusions did you draw from the debate? *šinu n-nataaʔij illi stalxaṣitha mnil-munaaqaša?* 2. *xitaam.* In conclusion, I should like to state that .... *w-bil-xitaam, ʔaħibb ʔan ʔabayyin ʔinna ....*

concrete - 1. *kankiriit, kankari.* The bridge is built of concrete. *j-jisir mabni b-kankari.* 2. *maḍbuuṭ, qawi.* Give me a concrete example. *nṭiini fadd maθal maḍbuuṭ.*

to **condemn** - 1. *ħikam (u ħukum) n-.* The judge condemned him to death. *l-ħaakim ħikama bil-ʔiεdaam.* 2. *ðamm (i ðamm) n-.* They condemned him for his actions. *ðammoo l-ʔaεmaala.* 3. *ʔumar (u ʔamur) n- b-hadim.* The municipality condemned the old building. *l-baladiyya ʔumrat ib-hadm il-binaaya l-qadiima.*

condition - 1. *ħaala* pl. *aat, ʔaħwaal.* The house was in good condition. *l-beet čaan ib-ħaala zeena.* 2. *šariṭ* pl. *šuruuṭ.* I'll accept the offer on one condition. *raħ-aqbal il-εariḍ ib-šarṭ waaħid.*

conduct - *siluuk, siira* pl. *siyar.* Your conduct is disgraceful. *siluukak šaaʔin.*

to conduct - 1. *qaad (u qiyaada) n-.* Who's conducting the orchestra tonight? *minu da-yquud il-firqa ḷ-muusiiqiyya hal-leela?* 2. *dawwar (i tadwiir), farrar (i tafriir, tfirrir), dalla (i ddilli).* The guide conducted us around the ruins. *d-daliil dawwarna been il-ʔaaθaar.* 3. *waṣṣal (i tawṣiil) t-.* Metal conducts heat better than wood. *l-maεdan ywaṣṣil il-ħaraara ʔaħsan imnil-xišab.* 4. *daar (i ʔidaara) n-.* He conducts his work very well. *da-ydiir ʔašġaala kulliš zeen.*

to conduct oneself - *silak (u siluuk), tṣarraf (a taṣarruf).* She conducts herself like a lady. *tisluk siluuk is-sayyida.*

conductor - 1. *mufattiš* pl. *-iin, tiiti* pl. *-iyyaat.* Did the conductor punch your ticket? *l-mufattiš giraḍ it-tikit maalak?* 2. *muuṣila* pl. *-aat.* Silver is a good conductor of electricity. *l-fuḍḍa muuṣila zeena lil-kahrabaaʔiyya.* 3. *qaaʔid* pl. *quwwaad.* Who is the conductor of the orchestra? *minu qaaʔid* *il-firqa l-muusiiqiyyaʔ*

cone - *maxruuṭ* pl. *maxaariiṭ*. The vase was made in the shape of a cone. *l-mizhariyya čaanat maεmuula b-šikil maxruuṭ*.

conference - **1.** *jtimaaε* pl. *-aat*. He had a conference with the doctor. *čaan εinda jtimaaε wiyya ṭ-ṭabiib*. **2.** *muʔtamar* pl. *-aat*. He wrote an article on the disarmament conference. *kitab maqaal εan muʔtamar nazε is-silaaƶ*. **3.** *mudaawala* pl. *-aat*. After a short conference with my wife, I agreed to buy the car. *baεad mudaawala qaṣiira wiyya zawijti waafaqit aštiri s-sayyaara*.

to **confess** - *εtiraf (i εtiraaf), qaar (u qaar) n-*. The defendant confessed. *l-muttaham iεtiraf*.

confession - *εtiraaf* pl. *-aat, ʔiqraar* pl. *-aat*. The criminal made a full confession. *l-mujrim iεtiraf iεtiraaf kaamil*.

confidence - *θiqa*. I have confidence in him. *εindi θiqa bii*.

confident - *waaθiq, mitʔakkid, mitqayyin*. I'm confident that everything will turn out all right. *ʔaani waaθiq kullši raƶ-yṣiir ƶasb il-ʔuṣuul*.

confidential - *sirri**. This letter is confidential. *hal-maktuub sirri*.

confidentially - *ƶaači beenaat-, b-ṣuura sirriyya*. Confidentially, I don't like that proposal. *ƶaači beenaatna ma-yiεjibni hal-iqtiraaƶ*.

to **confirm** - **1.** *ʔayyad (i taʔyiid, tʔiyyid) t-, ʔakkad (i taʔkiid, tʔikkid) t-*. The president confirmed the news report. *r-raʔiis ʔayyad našrat il-ʔaxbaar*. -- You'll have to confirm the reservation tomorrow. *laazim itʔakkid il-ƶajiz iṣ-ṣubuƶ*. **2.** *θabbat (i taθbiit, tθibbit)*. That confirms my faith in him. *haaða yθabbit ʔiimaani bii*.

conflict - **1.** *nizaaε* pl. *-aat, taṣaadum* pl. *-aat, εraak*. Four men were killed in the border conflict. *ʔarbaε riyaajiil inkitlaw ib-nizaaε il-ƶuduud*. **2.** *ṣiraaε, nizaaε* pl. *aat*. It's the eternal conflict between good and evil. *huwwa ṣ-ṣiraaε il-ʔabadi been il-xeer wiš-šarr*. **3.** *tanaaquð̣* pl. *-aat, taεaaruð̣* pl. *-aat*. Because of the conflict between the two reports another committee went to investigate the matter. *b-sabab it-tanaaquð̣ been it-taqriireen lujna lux raaƶat titƶarra εan il-qað̣iyya*.

to conflict - **1.** *tεaarað̣ (a taεaaruð̣)*. Will this appointment conflict with your schedule? *hal-mawεid raƶ-yitεaarað̣ wiyya manhajakʔ* **2.** *tεaarað̣ (a taεaaruð̣), tnaaqað̣ (a tanaaquð̣)*. His philosophy conflicts with the basic tenets of Islam. *falsafta titεaarað̣ wiyya mabaadiʔ il-ʔislaam il-ʔasaasiyya*.

to **confuse** - **1.** *xarbaṭ (u txurbuṭ) t-, ʔarbak (i ʔirbaak) n-, ƶayyar (i tƶiyyir) t-*. The map confused me. *l-xariiṭa xarbuṭatni*. -- The problem confused me. *l-muškila ƶayyiratni*. **2.** *štibah (i štibaah) b-*. He must have confused me with someone else. *laazim ištibah biyya b-šaxiṣ ʔaaxar*.

confusion - **1.** *rtibaak*. That will cause a lot of confusion. *haaði raƶ-itsabbib irtibaak ihwaaya*. **2.** *xabṣa* pl. *-aat, hoosa* pl. *-aat, harja* pl. *-aat*. He escaped in the confusion. *nhijam bil-xabṣa*.

to **congratulate** - *hanna (i thinni, tahniya) t-, baarak (i mubaaraka) t-*. We congratulated him on his success. *hanneenaa b-najaaƶa*.

congratulations - *tahaani, mabruuk, εal-baaraka*. Congratulations on your appointment! *tahaaniina εala taεyiinak!*

congress - *majlis* pl. *majaalis*.

to **connect** - **1.** *waṣṣal (i twiṣṣil, tawṣiil) t-*. A short hallway connects our offices. *mamarr qaṣiir ywaṣṣil dawaaʔirna baεað̣ha b-baεað̣*. -- Have they connected the telephone for you yet? *waṣṣloo-lak it-talafoon loo baεadʔ* **2.** *rubaṭ (u rabuṭ) n-, waṣṣal (i twiṣṣil, tawṣiil) t-*. Connect these wires to the battery. *ʔurbuṭ hal-waayaraat bil-paatri*. **3.** *rubaṭ (u rabuṭ) n-*. The police have connected the crime to two men who were seen in the area. *s-surṭa rubṭat ij-jariima b-rijjaaleen inšaafaw bil-manṭiqa*.

connection - **1.** *ttiṣaal* pl. *-aat*. I can't hear you very well. There must be a bad connection. *ma-agdar asimεak zeen. laazim ʔaku ttiṣaal muu zeen*. **2.** *εalaaqa* pl. *-aat*. He has very good connections with the government. *εinda kulliš xooš εalaaqaat wiyya l-ƶukuuma*. **3.** *munaasaba* pl. *-aat, εalaaqa* pl. *-aat*. In what connection did he mention it? *b-ʔay munaasaba ðikarhaʔ* **4.** *ṣila* pl. *-aat, εalaaqa* pl. *-aat*. There's no connect between the two. *ma-aku ṣila been l-iθneen*.

to **conquer** - **1.** *fitaƶ (a fatiƶ) n-*. He wanted to conquer the whole world. *raad yiftaƶ il-εaalam kulla*. **2.** *qihar (a qahir) n-*. Scientists have conquered polio. *l-εulamaaʔ qihraw marað̣ šalal il-ʔaṭfaal*.

conquest - *fatiƶ* pl. *fituuƶaat*.

conscience - *ð̣amiir* pl. *ð̣amaaʔir, wujdaan* pl. *-aat*. I have a clear conscience. *ð̣amiiri mirtaaƶ*.

conscientious - *mujidd*. He's a conscientious student. *huwwa ṭaalib mujidd*.

conscious - *ƶaasis, waaεi, ṣaaƶi*. You can talk to him now. He's conscious. *tigdar itƶaačii hassa. huwwa ƶaasis*.

consent - *rið̣a, muwaafaqa, qubuul*. This was done without my consent. *haaði ṣaarat biduun rið̣aaya*.

to consent - *waafaq (i muwaafaqa), qibal (a qubuul), rið̣a (a rið̣a)*. He consented to stay. *waafaq yibqa*.

consequence - *εaaqiba* pl. *εawaaqib, natiija* pl. *nataaʔij*. I'm afraid of the consequences. *ʔaani xaayif imnil-εawaaqib*.

consequently - *wa-εaleehi, binaaʔan εala ðaalik, bin-natiija*.

conservative - **1.** *muƶaafið̣*. He's a very conservative politician. *huwwa siyaasi muƶaafið̣ kulliš*. **2.** *miqtiṣid*. You'll have to be more conservative with your allowance. *laazim itkuun miqtiṣid akθar ib-muxaṣṣaṣaatak*.

to **consider** - **1.** *εtubar (u εtibaar), ƶisab (i ƶsaab) n-*. I consider him an able chemist. *ʔaεtabra kiimyaawi qadiir*. **2.** *nið̣ar (u nað̣ar) n- b-*. We're still considering your request. *li-hassa da-nunð̣ur ib-ṭalabak*.

considerable - *ð̣axim, muƶtaram*. Building this house cost me a considerable sum of money. *binaaʔ hal-beet kallafni mablaġ ð̣axim* or ***binaaʔ hal-beet kallafni mablaġ laa baʔis bii*.

considerate - *muqaddir, munṣif*. My boss is very considerate. *raʔiisi fadd waaƶid muqaddir*.

consideration - **1.** *nað̣ar*. We have three plans under consideration. *εidna tlaθ mašaariiε taƶt in-nað̣ar*. **2.** *εtibaar*. He hasn't any consideration for anybody. *ma-εinda εtibaar il-kull ʔaƶƶad*.

consignment - *wadiiεa, ʔamaana*. He took the goods on consignment. *ʔaxað il-bið̣aaεa bil-ʔamaana*.

to **consist of** - *štimal (i štimaal) εala, trakkab (a tarakkub) min, ƶuwa (i ƶawi) εala*. The meal consisted of fish, vegetables, and coffee. *l-wajba štimlat εala simač w-xuð̣rawaat w-gahwa*.

consistent - *muttifiq, mulaaʔim*. His ideas are consistent with those of his party. *ʔafkaara muttafqa maεa ʔafkaar ƶizba*.

to **consolidate** - *waƶƶad (i tawƶiid, twiƶƶid) t-*. The two presidents consolidated the two oil companies. *r-raʔiiseen waƶƶidaw šarikteen in-nafuṭ*.

conspiracy - *muʔaamara, taʔaamur*.

constant - **1.** *mistimirr, daaʔimi**. This constant noise is making me nervous. *haṣ-ṣoot il-mistimirr da-ysawwiini εaṣabi*. **2.** *mitkarrir, mistimirr, daaʔimi**. These constant trips to the doctor are costing me money. *haz-ziyaaraat il-mitkarrira liṭ-ṭabiib da-yitkallafni fluus*. **3.** *θaabit*. Wheat prices have remained constant for two months. *ʔasεaar il-ƶunṭa buqat θaabta šahreen*. **4.** *nisba (pl. nisab) θaabita*. If you know the constant you can solve the problem. *loo tuεruf in-nisba θ-θaabita tigdar itƶill il-masʔala*.

constantly - *b-istimraar, εala ṭuul, daaʔiman*. The The telephone rang constantly. *t-talifoon dagg b-istimraar*.

constellation - *majmuuεat (pl. -aat) nujuum*.

constitution - **1.** *dastuur* pl. *dasaatiir*. Our freedom is guaranteed by the constitution. *ƶurriyyatna mað̣muuna bid-dastuur*. **2.** *bunya* pl. *-aat*. He has a very strong constitution. *εinda bunya kulliš qawiyya*.

to **construct** - *bina (i binaaʔ) n-*. We're going to construct a new hotel here. *raƶ-nibni fadd funduq jidiid ihnaa*.

construction - *binaaʔ*. The construction of this dam will take five years. *binaaʔ has-sadd raƶ-yṭawwil xams isniin*. -- My father works for a construction company. *ʔabuuya da-yištuġul ʔila šarikat il-binaaʔ*.

consul - *qunṣul* pl. *qanaaṣil*.

consulate - *qunṣuliyya*. Were you at the American consulate? *činit bil-qunṣuliyya l-ʔamriikiyyaʔ*

to **consult** - *stišaar (i stišaara)*. You should have consulted us. *čaan laazim tistišiirna*.

to **consume** - *stahlak (i stihlaak), ṣiraf (u ṣaruf) n-*. My car consumes a lot of gas. *sayyaarti tistahlik ihwaaya banziin*.

consumption - **1.** *stihlaak*. Consumption has gone up fifty per cent. *l-istihlaak zaad xamsiin bil-miyya.* 2. *sill.* He has consumption. *Ɛinda sill.*

contact - **1.** *ttiṣaal* pl. *-aat.* He's never had any contact with foreigners. *ʔabad ma-čaan Ɛinda ʔay ittiṣaal wiyya l-ʔajaanib.* **2.** *Ɛalaaqa* pl. *-aat.* I've made several new contacts. *sawweet Ɛiddat Ɛalaaqaat jidiida.*

to come into contact with - *mass (i mass) n-.* By accident, his hand came into contact with a bare electric wire. *biṣ-ṣudfa ʔiida massat silik kahrabaaʔi Ɛaari.*

to contact - *ttiṣal (i ttiṣaal) b-.* I'll contact you as soon as I arrive. *raz-attiṣil biik ʔawwal-ma ʔooṣal.*

contagious - *muƐdi.*

to **contain** - **1.** *zuwa (i zawi), ztiwa (i ztiwaaʔ) Ɛala.* That trunk contains clothing. *haṣ-ṣanduug yizwi hduum* or ***haṣ-ṣanduug bii hduum.* **2.** *lizam (a lazim), ḍubaṭ (u ḍabuṭ).* Don't get excited! Try to contain yourself. *la-tinxubuṣ. zaawil tilzam nafsak.*

contempt - *stixfaaf, zdiraaʔ.*

content - **1.** *muqdaar* pl. *maqaadiir.* The alcoholic content is very low. *muqdaar il-kuhuul kulliš qaliil.* **2.** *qaaniƐ, raaḍi.* He was content with what we offered him. *čaan qaaniƐ b-illi Ɛraḍnaa Ɛalee.*

contents - *muztawayaat.* Dissolve the contents of this package in one glass of water. *ðawwub muztawayaat hal-paakeet ib-fadd iglaaṣ maay.*

table of contents - *fihras* pl. *fahaaris.*

contest - *sibaaq* pl. *-aat, musaabaqa* pl. *-aat, munaafasa* pl. *-aat.* Who won the contest? *minu faaz bil-musaabaqa?*

to contest - *ṭaƐan (a ṭaƐan) n-.* They're contesting the validity of the will. *da-yṭiƐnuun ib-ṣizzat il-waṣiyya.*

continent - *qaarra* pl. *-aat.*

continual - *mistimirr, mitwaaṣil.* This continual arguing is annoying me. *haj-jidaal il-mistimirr da-yizƐijni.*

continually - *daaʔiman, b-istimraar, Ɛala ṭuul.* The line is continuaaly busy. *l-xaṭṭ mašġuul daaʔiman.*

to **continue** - **1.** *stamarr (i stimraar) b-, daawam (i dawaam, mudaawama), waaṣal (i muwaaṣala).* Let's continue with our work. *xaali nistimirr ib-šuġulna.* **2.** *waaṣal (i muwaaṣala).* We'll continue our discussion tomorrow. *raz-inwaaṣil munaaqašatna baačir.* **3.** *ḍall (u ḍall), stamarr (i stimraar).* His condition continued to be the same. *zaalta ḍallat Ɛala-ma hiyya.*

continuously - *b-istimraar, daaʔiman, Ɛala ṭuul.* The phone has been ringing continuously. *t-talifoon da-ydugg b-istimraar.*

contract - *muqaawala* pl. *-aat, qunṭaraat, Ɛaqid* pl. *Ɛuquud.* I refuse to sign that contract. *ʔarfuḍ awaqqiƐ hal-Ɛaqid.*

to contract - **1.** *tqallaṣ (a taqalluṣ).* Which metal contracts the most? Iron or copper? *ʔay maƐdan yitqallaṣ ʔakθar? l-zadiid loo n-nuzaas?* **2.** *tqaawal (a taqaawul), sawwa (i tsiwwi) qanṭaraat.* They've contracted to build the building in five months. *tqaawlaw yibnuun il-Ɛimaara b-xamist išhur.* **3.** *ʔaxað (u ʔaxið) n-.* I contracted pneumonia. *ʔaxaðit nimoonya.*

contractor - *qunṭarči* pl. *-iyya, muqaawil* pl. *-iin.*

to **contradict** - *Ɛaaraḍ (i muƐaaraḍa), naaqaḍ (i munaaqaḍa).* Don't contradict me! *la-tƐaariḍni.*

contradictory - *mitnaaqiḍ, mitxaalif.* We heard the most contradictory reports on it. *smaƐna Ɛanha taqaariir kulliš mitnaaqḍa.*

contrary - **1.** *Ɛnaadi*.* She's very contrary. *hiyya kulliš iƐnaadiyya.* **2.** *b-Ɛakis, b-xilaaf, ḍidd.* Contrary to what we expected he passed the exam. *b-Ɛakis-ma twaqqaƐna nijaz bil-imtizaan.* **3.** *muxaalif, muƐaakis.* That's contrary to our agreement. *haaða muxaalif l-ittifaaqna.*

on the contrary - *bil-Ɛakis.* On the contrary, nothing could be worse. *bil-Ɛakis, ma-aku ʔatƐas minna.*

contrast - *xtilaaf* pl. *-aat, tabaayun.* There's a big contrast between the two brothers. *ʔaku xtilaaf čibiir been il-ʔuxwa l-iθneen.*

to contrast - *bayyan (i tbiyyin) t- xtilaaf.* He contrasted the programs of the two parties. *bayyan il-ixtilaaf been manaahij il-zizbeen.*

to **contribute** - **1.** *tbarraƐ (a tabarruƐ) b-.* I contributed five dinars to the Red Cross. *tbarraƐit ib-xams idnaaniir liṣ-ṣaliib il-ʔazmar.* **2.** *saaƐad (i musaaƐada).* The interference of the police just contributed to the confusion. *tadaxxul iš-šurṭa bass saaƐad Ɛal-irtibaak.* **3.** *qaddam (i tqiddim, taqdiim) t-.* He's continually contributing articles to the daily newspaper. *daaʔiman da-yqaddim maqaalaat lij-jariida l-yoomiyya.*

contribution - *tabarruƐ* pl. *-aat, musaaƐada* pl. *-aat.* We received your contribution yesterday. *stilamna tabarruƐak il-baarza.*

control - **1.** *sayṭara, ḍabuṭ.* He lost control of the car. *fuqad is-sayṭara Ɛala s-sayyaara.* **2.** *muraaqaba.* The control tower is at the north end of the runway. *murj il-muraaqaba ṣaayir bit-ṭaraf iš-šimaali mnil-madraj.* **3.** *sulṭa, sayṭara.* The police have no control over diplomats. *š-šurṭa ma-Ɛidha sulṭa Ɛad-dibloomaasiyyiin.* **4.** *qiyaada.* Let me take over control for a while. *xalliini ʔastilim il-qiyaada šwayya.* -- The co-pilot took over the controls. *muƐaawin iṭ-ṭayyaar istilam ʔaalaat il-qiyaada.*

to control - *ḍubaṭ (u ḍabuṭ) n-, sayṭar (i tsayṭar) t-.* The teacher couldn't control the class. *l-muƐallim ma-gidar yuḍbuṭ iṣ-ṣaff.*

convenience - *wasiilat* (pl. *wasaaʔil) raaza.* Our apartment has every modern convenience. *šiqqatna biiha kull wasaaʔil ir-raaza l-zadiiθa.*

**Call me at your earliest convenience. *xaaburni b-ʔawwal wakit ynaasbak.*

convenient - *munaasib, mulaaʔim, muriiz.* Will five o'clock be convenient for you? *s-saaƐa xamsa raz-itkuun munaasiba lak?*

conveniently - *b-ṣuura mulaaʔima, b-ṣuura munaasiba.* The telephone is conveniently located so everybody can reach it. *t-talifoon mazṭuuṭ ib-ṣuura mulaaʔima zatta kull waazid yigdar yooṣal-la.*

convent - *deer* (pl. *ʔadyira) lir-raahibaat.*

convention - **1.** *muʔtamar* pl. *-aat.* Were you at the convention last year? *činit bil-muʔtamar is-sana l-faatat?* **2.** *Ɛurf, Ɛaada.* Everything he does is according to convention. *kullši ysawwii zasb il-Ɛurf.*

conventional - *mutƐaaraf Ɛalee, muƐtaad Ɛalee.* I prefe: the conventional methods. *ʔafaḍḍil iṭ-ṭuruq il-mutƐaaraf Ɛaleeha.*

conversation - *mukaalama* pl. *-aat, zači, zadiiθ* pl. *ʔazaadiiθ.* Our telephone conversation lasted an hour. *mukaalamatna t-talifooniyya ṭawwilat saaƐa.*

convert - **1.** *mitnaṣṣir* pl. *-iin.* His wife became a Christian convert. *zawijta ṣaarat mitnaṣṣira.* -- **2.** *mistaslim* pl. *-iin.* There are many converts to Islam living here. *ʔaku mistasilmiin ihwaaya yƐiišuun ihnaa.* **3.** *mithawwid* pl. *-iin.* This man is a convert to Judaism. *har-rijjaal mithawwid.*

to convert - **1.** *baddal (i tbiddil, tabdiil) t-, zawwal (i tazwiil, tziwwil) t-.* Where can I convert these dollars into dinars? *ween ʔagdar abaddil had-doolaaraat ila danaaniir?* **2.** *zawwal (i tazwiil, tziwwil) t-, gilab (u galub) n-.* This experiment converts starch into sugar. *hat-tajruba tzawwil in-niša ʔila šakar.* -- He converted his house into a restaurant. *zawwal beeta ʔila maṭƐam.* **3.** *gilab (u galub) n-.* You cannot convert this atheist to any religion. *ma-tigdar tuglub hal-mulzid il-ʔay diin.*

convict - *mudaan* pl. *-iin, mazkuum Ɛalee* (pl. *-hum).* Three convicts escaped. *tlaθ mazkuum Ɛaleehum hirbaw.*

to convict - *ʔadaan (i ʔidaana).* The judge convicted him of murder. *l-zaakim ʔadaana b-jariimat il-qatil.*

to **convince** - *qannaƐ (i tqinniƐ, taqniiƐ) t-, ʔaqnaƐ (i ʔiqnaaƐ).* You can't convince me. *ma-tigdar itqanniƐni.*

cook - *ṭabbaax* pl. *-iin.* She a very good cook. *hiyya ṭabbaaxa kulliš zeena.*

**Too many cooks spoil the broth. *s-safiina, ʔiða kiθraw imlaaliizha, tiġrag.*

to cook - *ṭubax (u ṭabux) n-.* We don't have time to cook tonight. *ma-Ɛidna wakit niṭbux hal-leela.*

cookie - *kleečaaya* pl. *-aat* coll. *kleeča.* I brought you some cookies. *jibit-lak šwayya kleeča.*

cool - **1.** *baarid.* The weather is cool here, especially at night. *d-dinya baarda hnaa, xuṣuuṣan bil-leel.* -- Bring me some cool water. *jiib-li šwayya mayy baarid.* **2.** *haadiʔ, baarid.* I tried to keep cool after the accident. *zaawalit abqa haadiʔ baƐd il-zaadiθ.*

to cool - **1.** *burad (a buruud).* Don't let the soup cool too long. *la-txalli š-šoorba tubrad ihwaaya.* **2.** *hidaʔ (a huduuʔ), burad (a buruud).* Leave him alone. He'll cool off after a while. *xallii wazda. raz-yihdaʔ baƐd išwayya.* **3.** *barrad* *(i tbirrid, tabriid) t-.* The air conditioner cools the entire house. *l-mukayyifa tbarrid il-beet kulla.* **4.** *haddaʔ (i tahdiʔa, thiddiʔ) t-, barrad (i tabriid, tbirrid) t-.* Try to cool him down a bit. *ʒaawil ithaddiʔa šwayya.*

coop - *beet* pl. *byuut.* Clean out the chicken coop. *nað̣ð̣uf beet id-dijaaj.*

to coop up - *ʒibas (i ʒabis) n-, ʒiṣar (i ʒaṣir) n-.* I cooped the children up in the house this morning for being naughty. *ʒbasit ij-jihhaal iṣ-ṣubuʒ bil-beet li-ʔan čaanaw yʔaððuun.*

to **co-operate** - *tεaawan (a taεaawun).* I wish they would co-operate with us more. *ʔatmanna yitεaawnuun wiyyaana ʔakθar.*

co-operation - *taεaawun.* Can we count on your co-operation? *nigdar niεtimid εala taεaawnak?*

copper - *ṣifir, nʒaas.*

Copt - *qabṭi* pl. *ʔaqbaaṭ.*

copy - **1.** *nusxa* pl. *nusax, ṣuura* pl. *ṣuwar.* I made a copy of the letter. *sawweet nusxa mnil-maktuub.* **2.** *nusxa* pl. *nusax.* Do you have a copy of this morning's paper? *εindak nusxa mnij-jariida ṣ-ṣabaaʒiyya maalt il-yoom.*

to copy - **1.** *niqal (u naqil) n-.* Copy these two sentences off the blackboard. *ʔiniqlu haj-jumalteen imniṣ-ṣabbuura.* **2.** *sawwa (i taswiya, tsiwwi) qooḅya.* The teacher gave him a zero in the examination because he copied. *l-muεallim niṭaa ṣifir bil-imtiʒaan li-ʔanna sawwa qooḅya.* **3.** *qallad (i tqillid, taqliid) t-.* He copies his father in everything. *yqallid ʔabuu b-kullši.*

coral - *marjaan.* I'd like to buy a coral necklace. *ʔariid aštiri glaada marjaan.*

cord - **1.** *xeeṭ* pl. *xyuuṭ.* My son doesn't have enough cord to fly his kite. *ʔibni ma-εinda xeeṭ kaafi yṭayyir iṭ-ṭiyyaara bii.* **2.** *waayar* pl. *-aat.* We'll have to get a new cord for the iron. *laazim injiib waayar jidiid lil-ʔuuti.*

cordial - *ʒaarr, qalbi*.* The host gave us a cordial welcome. *l-imεazzib istaqbalna stiqbaal ʒaarr.*

cork - *tabbaduur* pl. *-aat, filliina* pl. *-aat.* The cork fell into the bottle. *t-tabbaduur wugaε bil-buṭil.*

to cork - *sadd (i sadd) n- bit-tabbaduur.* Don't forget to cork the bottle. *la-tinsa tsadd il-buṭil bit-tabbaduur.*

corkscrew - *burġi* pl. *baraaġi.*

corn - **1.** *ʔiðra.* He doesn't grow much corn. *ma-yizraε ʔiðra hwaaya.* **2.** *bismaar* pl. *bisaamiir.* Doctor, this corn on my foot is bothering me. *daktoor, hal-bismaar li-b-rijli da-yoojaεni.*

corn bread - *xubuz ʔiðra.*

corner - **1.** *rukun* pl. *ʔarkaan.* The man stood by the corner of the building. *r-rajul wugaf yamm rukn il-ibnaaya.* **2.** *zwiyya* pl. *-aat.* Put the books in the corner. *ʒuṭṭ il-kutub biz-zuwiyya.*

to corner - *ʒiṣar (i ʒaṣir) n-.* I cornered him this morning and demanded my money. *ʒiṣarta ṣ-ṣubuʒ w-itlabit ifluusi.*

corn flour - *ṭʒiin ʔiðra.*

corporal - *naayib εariif* pl. *nuwwaab εurafaaʔ.*

corpse - *jiθθa* pl. *jiθaθ.*

corral - *ziriiba* pl. *zaraayib.*

correct - *ṣaʒiiʒ, tamaam, mað̣buuṭ.* Is this the correct address? *haaða l-εinwaan iṣ-ṣaʒiiʒ.*

to correct - **1.** *ṣaʒʒaʒ (i taṣʒiiʒ, tṣiʒʒiʒ) t-, ṣallaʒ (i taṣliiʒ, tṣilliʒ) t-.* Please correct the mistakes in my French. *ʔarjuuk ṣaʒʒiʒ ʔaġlaaṭi bil-ifransi.* **2.** *ð̣ubaṭ (u ð̣abuṭ) n-, εaddal (i taεdiil, tεiddil) t-, ṣaʒʒaʒ (i) t-, ṣallaʒ (i)* These glasses will correct your vision. *hal-manaað̣ir raʒ-tuð̣buṭ nað̣arak.*

correction - *taṣʒiiʒ* pl. *-aat, taṣliiʒ* pl. *-aat, taεdiil* pl. *-aat, ð̣abuṭ.* Please make the necessary corrections. *ʔarjuuk sawwi it-taṣʒiiʒaat il-laazma.*

to **correspond** - **1.** *ṭaabaq (u muṭaabaqa) t-.* The translation does not correspond with the original. *t-tarjuma ma-tṭaabuq il-ʔaṣil.* **2.** *traasal (a taraasul), tkaatab (a takaatub).* We've been corresponding for six years. *ṣaar-inna sitta sniin nitraasal.*

correspondence - *muraasala* pl. *-aat, mukaataba* pl. *-aat.* My job is answering the correspondence. *šuġli ʔajiib εal-muraasalaat.*

correspondent - *muraasil* pl. *-iin.* He's a correspondent for the Times. *huwwa muraasil jariidat it-taaymz.*

corridor - *mamša* pl. *mamaaši, dihliiz* pl. *dahaaliiz, mamarr* pl. *-aat, mjaaz* pl. *-aat.*

corrugated - *mεarraj.*

cosmetic - *masʒuuq* pl. *masaaʒiiq.* She uses a lot of cosmetics. *da-tistaεmil masaaʒiiq ihwaaya.*

cost - **1.** *takliif* pl. *takaaliif, kulfa* pl. *-aat.* He was forced to sell everything at less than cost. *njubar ybiiε kullši b-ʔaqall imnit-takliif.* -- The cost of living is rising. *kulfat il-maεiiša da-tirtifiε.* **2.** *qiima* pl. *qiyam, siεir* pl. *ʔasεaar, θaman* pl. *ʔaθmaan, takliif* pl. *takaaliif, kulfa* pl. *kulaf.* The cost of this item on the market is twenty dinars. *qiimat haš-šii bis-suug εišriin diinaar.*

at any cost - *b-ʔay θaman, mahma ykuun iθ-θaman.* He wants it at any cost. *yriidha b-ʔay θaman.*

to cost - *kallaf (i takliif).* How much do these shoes cost? *hal-qundara šgadd itkallif?* -- The battle cost the enemy the loss of many lives. *l-maεraka kallifat il-εadu xasaaʔir ihwaaya bil-ʔarwaaʒ.*

costly - *ġaali.* She uses very costly perfume. *da-tistaεmil riiʒa ġaalya hwaaya.*

costume - *zayy* pl. *ʔazyaaʔ, libis.* The dancer wore a beautiful costume. *r-raaqiṣa libsat zayy ʒilu.*

cot - *čarpaaya (pl. -aat) safariyya, siriir safari* pl. *saraayir safariyya.*

cottage cheese - *liban imnaššaf.* Give me a half kilo of cottage cheese. *nṭiini nuṣṣ kiilu liban imnaššaf.*

cotton - *guṭin.* Bring me a piece of cotton. *jiib-li fadd wuṣlat guṭin.* -- I'd like to buy a pair of cotton socks. *ʔariid aštiri fadd zooj ijwaariib guṭin.*

couch - *qanafa* pl. *-aat.*

cough - *gaʒʒa* pl. *-aat.* Do you have something that's good for a cough? *εindak šii zeen lil-gaʒʒa?*

to cough - *gaʒʒ (u gaʒʒ).* The baby coughed all night. *ṭ-ṭifil gaʒʒ ṭuul il-leel.*

could - see under can.

council - *majlis* pl. *majaalis.*

councilman - *εuð̣u (pl. ʔaεð̣aaʔ) majlis.*

counsel - **1.** *naṣiiʒa* pl. *naṣaayiʒ, mašuura* pl. *-aat, stišaara* pl. *-aat.* Let me give you some good counsel. *xalli ʔanṭiik fadd naṣiiʒa zeena.* **2.** *muʒaami* pl. *-iin.* The counsel for the defense arrived late. *muʒaami d-difaaε wuṣal mitʔaxxir.*

count - **1.** *tiεdaad* pl. *-aat, εadd, ʒsaab* pl. *-aat.* The count has not been taken yet. *t-tiεdaad ma-ṣaar baεad.* **2.** *koont* pl. *-aat.* She married a count. *tzawwjat koont.*

to count - *ʒisab (i ʒsaab) n-, εadd (i tiεdaad, εadd) n-.* Please count your change. *ʔarjuuk iʒsib il-xurda maaltak.*

to count on - *εtimad (i εtimaad) εala, wiθaq (i θiqa) n- b-.* You can not count on him at all. *ma-tigdar tiεtimid εalee bil-marra.*

counter - **1.** *kaawntir* pl. *-aat.* Your package is on the counter. *r-ruzma maaltak εal-kaawntir.* **2.** *ð̣idd.* This is counter to our beliefs. *haaða ð̣idd muεtaqadaatna.*

counterfeit - **1.** *mzayyaf, qalib.* This money is counterfeit. *hal-ifluus imzayyifa.* **2.** *mzawwar.* This signature is counterfeit. *hat-tawqiiε imzawwar.*

to counterfeit - *zayyaf (i tazyiif, tziyyif) t-, zawwar (i tazwiir, tziwwir) t-.* He counterfeited one thousand dinars. *zayyaf ʔalif diinaar.*

countess - *koonteesa* pl. *-aat.*

country - **1.** *balad* pl. *buldaan, blaad, quṭur* pl. *ʔaqṭaar, dawla* pl. *duwal.* I've seen many countries. *šifit buldaan ihwaaya.* **2.** *riif* pl. *ʔaryaaf.* We spent our vacation in the country. *gð̣eena εuṭlatna bir-riif.* **3.** *manṭiqa* pl. *manaaṭiq.* The country around Baghdad is agricultural. *l-manṭiqa ʒawaali baġdaad ziraaεiyya.*

couple: A young couple sat in front of us in the movie. *fadd šaabb w-šaabba giεdaw giddaamna bis-siinama.* -- I'm living with an elderly couple. *ʔaani saakin wiyya fadd šaayib w-εajuuz.*

a couple of - *fadd* and foll. noun in dual. I bought a couple of ties. *štireet fadd rabuṭṭeen.* -- Hand me a couple of nails. *naawušni fadd bismaareen.* -- He was here a couple of days ago. *čaan ihnaa gabuḷ fadd yoomeen.*

to couple - *šakkal (i taškiil, tšikkil).* They coupled the coach to the train. *šakkilaw il-fargoon bil-qiṭaar.*

coupling - *ṣammuuna* pl. *-aat.* They connected the two pipes with a rubber coupling. *rubṭaw il-buuriyyeen ib-ṣammuuna laastiik.*

coupon - *kooḅoon* pl. *-aat.*

courage - *šajaaεa, jurʔa.* Don't lose your courage. *la-tufqud šajaaεtak.*

course – 1. *ttijaah* pl. *-aat,* *ţariiq* pl. *ţuruq.* The plane is holding a straight course. *t-ţiyyaara laaƶma ttijaah ɛadil.* **2.** *ttijaah* pl. *-aat,* *majra* pl. *majaari.* The river changed its course. *n-nahar ġayyar ittijaaha.* **3.** *daris* pl. *druus.* How many courses did you take? *čam daris axaδit?* **4.** *ţariiqa* pl. *ţuruq,* *xuţţa* pl. *xuţaţ,* *sabiil* pl. *subul.* Tell me the course of action you're going to follow. *gul-li ţariiqt il-ɛamal il-raz-titbaɛha.* **5.** *saaƶa* pl. *-aat.* It takes almost a half hour to walk around the course. *ţţawwil ƶawaali nuşş saaɛa maši ƶawl is-saaƶa.* **6.** *dafɛa* pl. *-aat.* They served the meal in three courses. *qaddimaw l-ʔakil ɛala tlaθ dafɛaat.*

in due course – *b-wakitha.* We will notify you in due course. *raz-inxabbrak ib-wakitha.*

in the course – *b-xilaal,* *ʔaθnaaʔ.* He got two promotions in the course of one year. *ƶaşşal ɛala tarfiiɛeen ib-xilaal sana wiƶda.*

of course – *ţabɛan,* *biţ-ţabuɛ.* Of course I know what you mean! *ţabɛan,* *ʔaɛruf iš-tuqşud.*

court – 1. *maƶkama* pl. *maƶaakim.* I'll see you in court tomorrow. *raz-ašuufak bil-maƶkama baačir.* **2.** *saaƶa* pl. *-aat.* The tennis court is still wet. *saaƶt it-tinis baɛadha raţba.* **3.** *ƶooš* pl. *ƶawaaš,* *saaƶa* pl. *-aat.* The maid is washing the clothes in the court. *l-xaddaama da-tiġsil l-ihduum bil-ƶooš.* **4.** *ƶaašiya.* The king entered the game with his court. *l-malik ƶiƶar is-sibaaq wiyya ƶaašiita.*

to court – *tqarrab (a taqarrub) ila,* *tƶabbab (a taƶabbub) ila.* He tried to court her several times. *ƶaawal yitqarrab ilha ɛiddat marraat.*

courteous – *mujaamil.* Try to be courteous while they're here. *ƶaawil itkuun mujaamil lamma ykuunuun ihnaa.*

courtesy – *mujaamala.* You should learn some courtesy. *laaƶim titɛallam šwayya mujaamala.*

courtroom – *qaaɛat* (pl. *-aat*) *maƶkama.*

cousin: father's brother's son, *ʔibin* (pl. *wulid*) *ɛamm;* father's brother's daughter, *bint* (pl. *banaat*) *ɛamm;* father's sister's son, *ʔibin* (pl. *wulid*) *ɛamma;* father's sister's daughter, *bint* (pl. *banaat*) *ɛamma;* mother's brother's son, *ʔibin* (pl. *wulid*) *xaaḷ;* mother's brother's daughter, *bint* (pl. *banaat*) *xaaḷ;* mother's sister's son, *ʔibin* (pl. *wulid*) *xaaḷa;* mother's sister's daughter, *bint* (pl. *banaat*) *xaaḷa.*

cover – 1. *ġaţa* pl. *ġaţaayaat,* *čarčaf* pl. *čaraačif.* The cover to this chair is dirty. *ġaţa hal-kursi waşix.* **2.** *qabaġ* pl. *-aat,* *ġaţa* pl. *ġaţaayaat.* Where is the cover for this box? *ween qabaġ hal-quuţiyya?* **3.** *ġlaaf* pl. *-aat.* Who tore the cover off this book? *minu šaggag iġlaaf hal-iktaab?* **4.** *malja?* pl. *malaaji?.* Deer don't have good cover in this area. *l-ġizlaan ma-ɛidha malja? ƶeen ib-hal-manţiqa.* **5.** *lƶaaf* pl. *liƶif,* *liƶfaan;* *ġaţa* pl. *ġaţaayaat.* Fatma, take the covers off the bed. *faaţma, šiili l-liƶif imnil-ifraaš.*

to cover – 1. *ġaţţa (i taġţiya, tġiţţi) t-.* We covered the ground with a blanket. *ġaţţeena l-gaaɛ ib-baţţaaniyya.* **2.** *ġaţţa (i),* *kaffa (i tkiffi) t-.* Will fifty dollars cover your expenses? *xamsiin doolaar itġaţţi maşaariifak?* **3.** *ġaţţa (i),* *δamδam (u ţδumδum), ţamţam (u ţţumţum).* She's always covering for her friend. *hiyya daaʔiman itġaţţi l-şadiiqatha.* **4.** *šimal (i šumuul) n-.* I believe that covers everything. *ʔaɛtiqid haaδa yišmil kullši.* **5.** *qiţaɛ (a qaţiɛ) n-.* We covered the distance in four hours. *qţaɛna l-masaafa b-ʔarbaɛ saaɛaat.* **6.** *şallaţ (i taşliiţ, ţşilliţ) t- ɛala.* He covered us with a revolver. *şallaţ ɛaleena l-musaddas.*

**Is your house covered by insurance? *beetak imʔamman ɛalee? or beetak imşoogar?*

cow – *baqara* pl. *-aat* coll. *baqar,* *haayša* pl. *hwaayiš* coll. *hooš.* The cows were milked this morning. *l-ihwaayiš inƶilbaw haş-şubuƶ.*

coward – *jabaan* pl. *jubanaaʔ,* *xawwaaf* pl. *-iin.* Don't be such a coward! *la-ţşiir haš-šikil jabaan.*

cozy – *mčaknam.* I like this room because it's cozy. *ʔaƶabb hal-ġurfa li-ʔanha mčaknima.*

crab – 1. *ʔabu j-jinneeb.* We saw four crabs at the seashore. *šifna ʔarbaɛ ʔabu j-jinneeb ɛala saaƶil il-baƶar.* **2.** *niqnaaqi* pl. *-iyyiin.* He's an old crab. *huwwa fadd waaƶid niqnaaqi.*

crab lice – *gamuḷ šiɛra.*

to crab – *naqnaq (i tniqniq).* Stop crabbing. *bass ɛaad itnaqniq.*

crack – 1. *faţir* pl. *fţuur,* *faliɛ* pl. *fluuɛ,* *šagg* pl. *šguug.* The crack in the dam is getting larger. *l-faţir il-bis-sadd da-yikbar.* **2.** *ţagga* pl. *-aat.*

I think I heard the crack of a rifle. *ʔaδunn ismaɛit ţagga maal bunduqiyya.* **3.** *tahakkum* pl. *-aat.* That crack was very appropriate. *hat-tahakkum čaan kulliš ib-maƶalla.* **4.** *maahir.* He's a crack shot. *huwwa raami maahir.*

**We got up at the crack of dawn. *gɛadna wiyya ţarrat il-fajir.*

to crack – 1. *fuţar (u faţir) n-.* I've cracked the crystal of my watch. *fţarit ij-jaama maal saaɛti.* **2.** *kassar (i taksiir, tkissir) t-.* Who's going to crack the nuts? *minu raz-ykassir ij-jooƶ?* **3.** *ƶall (i ƶall) n-.* The police finally cracked the code. *š-šurţa ʔaxiiran ƶallat rumuuƶ iš-šafra.* **4.** *ţagg (u ţagg) n-.* He cracked the whip several times. *ţagg il-qamči ɛiddat marraat.* -- Crack another bottle of wine for the guests. *ţugg buţil šaraab θaani liδ-δuyuuf.* **5.** *ţagţag (i ţţigtig) t-.* He's always cracking his knuckles. *huwwa daaʔiman yţagţig işaabiiɛa.*

**He didn't crack a smile. *wala btisam.*

to crack jokes – *nakkat (i tankiit, tnikkit).* He's always cracking jokes. *huwwa daaʔiman ynakkit.*

to crack open – *filaɛ (a faliɛ) n-.* He dropped the watermelon and cracked it open. *waggaɛ ir-raggiyya w-filaɛha.*

to crack up – 1. *txabbaḷ (a txubbuḷ, xbaaḷ).* He cracked up under the strain. *txabbaḷ imnil-ʔijhaad.* **2.** *ƶaţţam (i taƶţiim) t-.* He cracked up his car three weeks ago. *ƶaţţam sayyaarta gabuḷ itlaθ asaabiiɛ.*

cradle – *mahad* pl. *mhaad,* *kaaruuk* pl. *kwaariik.*

craft – *mihna* pl. *mihan,* *šaġla* pl. *-aat,* *şanɛa* pl. *-aat.* Rugmaking is a difficult craft. *ɛamal iz-ƶuwaali mihna şaɛba.*

to cram – 1. *ƶišak (i ƶašik) n-,* *ƶišar (i ƶašir) n-,* *ƶişar (u ƶaşir) n-.* He crammed everything into one trunk. *ƶišak kullši b-şanduug waaƶid.* **2.** *ƶašša (i taƶšiya, tƶišši) t- δihin~.* I started cramming the night before the exam. *bdeet aƶašši δihni bil-leela l-gabḷ il-imtiƶaan.*

cramp – *ʔabu š-širgeeḷ,* *ʔabu š-širgeet,* *tašannuj* pl. *-aat.* I have a cramp in my leg. *ɛindi ʔabu š-širgeeḷ ib-rijli.*

crane – 1. *ġarnuuq* pl. *ġaraaniiq.* We saw a flock of cranes in the marsh. *šifna majmuuɛa mnil-ġaraaniiq bil-hoor.* **2.** *sling* pl. *-aat.* They're using a crane to destroy the house. *da-yistaɛmiluun isling il-tafliiš il-beet.*

crank – 1. *hindir* pl. *-aat.* We have to use the crank to start the car. *laaƶim nistaɛmil il-hindir ƶatta nšaġġil is-sayyaara.* **2.** *yadda* pl. *-aat.* The window crank is rusty and won't turn. *yaddat iš-šibbaač imƶanjira w-ma-tinfarr.*

cranky – *niqnaaqi** pl. *-iyyiin.* Why are you so cranky this morning? *ʔinta leeš hiiči niqnaaqi haş-şubuƶ?*

crash – 1. *ştidaam* pl. *-aat,* *taşaadum* pl. *-aat,* *şadma* pl. *-aat.* Was anyone hurt in the crash? *ʔaƶƶad itʔaδδa bil-iştidaam?* **2.** *şoot* pl. *ʔaşwaat,* *ƶiss* pl. *ƶsuus.* We heard a crash when the tree fell. *smaɛna ƶiss lamma š-šijra wugɛat.*

to crash – *ştidam (i ştidaam) b-,* *şidam (i şadim) n-.* The car crashed into the wall. *s-sayyaara ştidmat bil-ƶaayiţ.*

crate – *qufaş* pl. *qfaaş.* I bought a crate of oranges. *štireet qufaş purtaqaal.*

to crawl – 1. *ƶizaf (a ƶaƶif).* The dog crawled under the table. *č-čalib ƶizaf jawwa l-meez.* **2.** *ƶiba (i ƶabi),* *ƶizaf (a ƶaƶif).* Her child is beginning to crawl. *ţifilha bida yiƶbi.* **3.** *diba (i dabi).* An ant was crawling on my hand. *fadd namla čaanat tidbi ɛala ʔiidi.*

crazy – 1. *majnuun* pl. *majaaniin,* *mxabbaḷ* pl. *mxaabiiḷ.* They put him in the hospital because he was crazy. *daxxloo l-mustašfa li-ʔan čaan majnuun.* **2.** *mitxabbuḷ* pl. *-iin,* *majnuun* pl. *majaaniin.* He's crazy about that girl. *huwwa mitxabbuḷ ɛala δiič il-ibnayya.* **3.** *saxiif.* That's a crazy idea. It'll never work. *haay fikra saxiifa. ma-ţşiir ʔabadan.*

to creak – *jaġjaġ (i juġjuġ, jaġjaġa).* The wooden stairs are creaking. *d-daraaj il-xišab da-yjaġjiġ.*

cream – 1. *kriim.* You'll have to buy the cream canned. *laaƶim tištiri l-ikriim imɛallab.* **2.** *dihin* pl. *dhuunaat,* *kriim.* This cream is good for the complexion. *had-dihin ƶeen lil-bašara.* **3.** *ƶaliibi**. The color of the walls is cream. *loon il-ƶayaaţiin ƶaliibi.*

**These students are the cream of the crop. *hat-ţullaab humma l-ɛiina.*

Devonshire cream (clotted) - *geemar.*
crease - *kasra* pl. *-aat.* The rain took the crease out of my pants. *l-muṭar rawwaz kasrat il-panṭuruun maali.*
to **create** - **1.** *xilaq (i xaliq) n-, kawwan (i takwiin, tkiwwin) t-.* God created the world. *ʔaḷḷa xilaq il-ɛaalam.* **2.** *ʔazdaθ (i ʔizdaaθ) n-, xilaq (i xaliq) n-, ʔawjad (i ʔiijaad) n-.* We have to create a position for him. *laazim nizdiθ-la waḍiifa.*
creature - *maxluuq* pl. *-aat, kaaʔin* pl. *-aat.* He wrote a story about the creatures in the forest. *kitab quṣṣa ɛan maxluuqaat il-ġaaba.*
credentials - *waθaaʔiq, ʔawraaq il-iɛtimaad, mustanadaat.*
credible - **1.** *ṣaadiq.* He's a credible witness. *huwwa šaahid ṣaadiq.* **2.** *mṣaddag.* His story wasn't credible. *zčaayta ma-čaanat imṣaddiga.*
credit - **1.** *deen* pl. *dyuun, zsaab* pl. *-aat.* We can buy the furniture on credit. *nigdar ništiri l-ʔaθaaθ bid-deen.* **2.** *mafxara* pl. *mafaaxir, faxar, faḍil* pl. *ʔafḍaal.* The credit for his success goes to his teacher. *b-najaaza yɛuud il-faxar il-muɛallim maala.* -- He's a credit to his profession. *huwwa fadd mafxara l-mihinta.* **3.** *ɛtimaad* pl. *-aat.* They don't have enough credit to import this many cars. *ma-ɛidhum iɛtimaad kaafi l-istiiraad halgadd sayyaaraat.*
to credit - **1.** *ʔaḍaaf (i ʔiḍaafa) n-, zisab (i zsaab) n-.* We're going to credit this amount to your account. *raz-inḍiif hal-mablaġ ɛala zsaabak.* **2.** *niṭa (i naṭi) n- faḍil.* They credited him with saving her life. *niṭoo l-faḍil b-inqaaδ zayaatha.*
creditor - *daaʔin* pl. *dayyaana.*
to **creep** - **1.** *zizaf (a zazif).* My son is always creeping around the house. *ʔibni daaʔiman yizzaf bil-beet.* **2.** *kazbar (u tkizbur) t.* That movie made my skin creep. *δaak il-film xalla jildi ykazbur.*
crescent - *hlaal* pl. *ʔahilla.* The star and crescent is a symbol of Islam. *n-najma wil-hilaal ramz il-ʔislaam.*
the Fertile Crescent - *l-hilaal il-xaṣiib.*
the Red Crescent - *l-hilaal il-ʔazmar.*
crew - **1.** *jamaaɛa* pl. *-aat, firqa* pl. *firaq.* The entire crew drowned when the ship sank. *jamaaɛt il-bazzaara kullhum ġirgaw lamma l-markab ġirag.* **2.** *mallaaziin.* The plane's crew consists of five persons. *mallaaziin it-taaʔira ɛadadhum xamsa.* **3.** *jooga* pl. *-aat.* The foreman divided his workmen into three crews with a special job for each. *l-ʔuṣṭa qassam il-ɛammaala ʔila tlaθ joogaat; kull jooga ʔilha šuġuḷ xaaṣṣ.*
crib - **1.** *maɛlaf* pl. *maɛaalif.* Did you put hay in the crib? *zaṭṭeet it-tibin bil-maɛlaf?* **2.** *kaaruuk* pl. *kwaariik, mahad* pl. *mhaad.* Don't take him out of the crib. *la-tšiila mnil-kaaruuk.*
cricket - *ṣurṣur* pl. *ṣaraaṣiir.*
crime - *jariima* pl. *jaraaʔim.* He committed several crimes. *rtikab ɛiddat jaraaʔim.*
criminal - **1.** *mujrim* pl. *-iin.* He's a well-known criminal. *huwwa fadd mujrim mašhuur.* **2.** *jinaaʔi*.* He's studying criminal law. *huwwa da-yidrus il-qaanuun ij-jinaaʔi.*
cripple - *muqɛad* pl. *-iin, mgarram* pl. *-iin, ṣigaṭ* pl. *ṣigaṭ.* It is hard for cripples to get a job. *l-muqɛadiin ṣaɛub ɛaleehum yzaṣṣluun ɛala šuġuḷ.*
to cripple - *garram (u tgurrum) t-, ṣaggaṭ (i taṣgiiṭ) t-.* He was crippled in an automobile accident. *tṣaggaṭ ib-zaadiθ sayyaara.*
crippled - *muqɛad* pl. *-iin, mgarram* pl. *-iin, ṣigaṭ* pl. *ṣigaṭ.* They're going to open a school for crippled children. *raz-yiftazuun madrasa lil-ʔaṭfaal il-muqɛadiin.*
crisis - **1.** *ʔazma* pl. *-aat.* The country is facing an economic crisis in the near future. *l-balad da-yjaabih ʔazma qtiṣaadiyya bil-mustaqbal il-qariib.* **2.** *šidda* pl. *šadaaʔid.* The patient passed the crisis safely. *l-mariiḍ marr biš-šidda b-salaama.*
crisp - **1.** *mgassib* pl. *-iin, mjassib* pl. *-iin.* The bread is fresh and crisp. *l-xubuz taaza w-imgassib.* **2.** *hašš.* This cucumber is crisp, not wilted. *hal-ixyaara hašša, muu δabla.*
**The air is a bit crisp tonight. *l-hawa bii garṣat barid il-leela.*
critic - *naaqid* pl. *nuqqaad.* Did you read the movie critic's article before you saw the film? *qreet maqaal in-naaqid is-sinamaaʔi gabuḷ-ma šift il-filim?*
critical - **1.** *muntaqid.* He is sharply critical of social conventions. *huwwa muntaqid laaδiɛ lil-ʔawḍaaɛ il-ijtimaaɛiyya.* **2.** *xaṭiir, xaṭir.* His condition is critical. *zaalta xaṭra.*
criticism - *ntiqaad* pl. *-aat, naqid.* He can't stand criticism. *huwwa ma-yitzammal intiqaad.* -- She has nothing to offer but criticism. *maa ɛidha ġeer il-intiqaad.*
to **criticize** - *ntiqad (i ntiqaad), ɛayyab (i tɛiyyib) t-.* They severely criticized him. *ntiqdoo ntiqaad murr.* -- She criticizes the way I dress. *hiyya tɛayyib ɛala libsi.*
to **crochet** - *zaak (u ziyaaka) n-.* His mother crocheted a pair of slipper tops for him. *ʔumma zaakat-la zooj iklaaš.*
crock - *bastuuga* pl. *basaatiig.* When you go to the market buy a crock of pickles. *lamma truuz lis-suug štiri bastuugat ṭurši.*
crockery - *faxxaar.* This is made of crockery. *haaδa maɛmuul imnil-faxxaar.*
crocodile - *timsaaz* pl. *tamaasiiz.*
crocus - *zaɛufraan.*
crook - **1.** *ɛoočiyya* pl. *-aat, ɛaṣaaya* pl. *-aat.* The shepherd struck the lamb with his crook. *r-raaɛi ḍurab iṭ-ṭili bil-ɛoočiyya.* **2.** *mqurbaaz* pl. *-iyya, -iin; muztaal* pl. *-iin, ġaššaaš* pl. *-iin.* He's a crook. *huwwa mqurbaaz.*
crooked - **1.** *ʔaɛwaj, maɛwuuj, mɛawwaj.* This pin is crooked. *had-danbuus maɛwuuj.* **2.** *mqurbaaz* pl. *-iyya, -iin; muztaal* pl. *-iin, ġaššaaš* pl. *-iin.* All the merchants in this street are crooked. *kull it-tijjaar ib-has-suug imqurbaaziyya.*
crop - **1.** *zaaṣil* pl. *zaaṣil, mazṣuul* pl. *mazaaṣiil.* The farmers expect a good crop this year. *l-fallaaziin yitwaqqɛuun zaaṣil zeen has-sana.* **2.** *zooṣla* pl. *zawaaṣil.* The chickens are so full their crops are almost touching the ground. *d-dijaaj šabɛaan ʔila daraja zawaaṣla qariiban itdugg il-gaaɛ.*
to crop up - *ḍihar (a ḍuhuur).* Many new problems are sure to crop up. *mašaakil jidiida hwaaya mnil-muʔakkad tiḍhar.*
cross - **1.** *ṣaliib* pl. *ṣulbaan.* Do you see the church with the big cross on the steeple? *tšuuf il-kaniisa lli ɛala burujha ṣaliib čibiir?* -- The central office of the International Red Cross is in Geneva. *d-daaʔira l-markaziyya l-jamɛiyyat iṣ-ṣaliib il-ʔazmar il-ɛaalamiyya maqarrha b-janeef.* **2.** *mḍarrab.* The mule is a cross between a horse and a donkey. *l-baġal imḍarrab been il-izṣaan wil-izmaar.*
to cross - *ɛubar (u ɛubuur) n-.* Cross at the intersection of the street. *ʔuɛbur min raas iš-šaariɛ.* -- When do we cross the border? *šwakit nuɛbur il-zuduud?* **2.** *tqaaṭaɛ (a taqaaṭuɛ) wiyya.* Rashid St. crosses Amin St. at Amin Sq. *šaariɛ ir-rašiid yitqaaṭaɛ wiyya šaariɛ il-ʔamiin ib-saazt il-ʔamiin.*
**Cross your heart! *twajjah ɛal-qibla w-izlif!*
to cross out - *šiṭab (u šaṭub) n-, čazz (i čazz) n-.* Cross out the items you don't want. *ʔisṭub il-mawaadd illi ma-triidha.*
to **crossbreed** - *ḍarrab (i taḍriib) t-.* On this farm they crossbreed varieties of sheep with each other. *b-hal-mazraɛa yḍarrbuun ʔanwaaɛ il-ʔaġnaam maɛa baɛaḍha.*
cross-eyed - m. *ʔazwal* pl. *zool, zooliin,* f. *zoola* pl. *-aat.* She's cross-eyed. *hiyya zoola.*
crossing - **1.** *mafraq* pl. *mafaariq.* There's no traffic light at this crossing. *ma-aku ḍuwa maal muruur ib-hal-mafraq.* **2.** *ɛubuur.* How far are we from the crossing point. *šgadd nibɛid ɛan nugṭat il-ɛubuur?* **3.** *ɛibra* pl. *-aat.* On the ferry they charge ten fils for each crossing. *bil-ɛabbaara yaaxδuun ɛašr ifluus ɛan kull ɛibra.*
cross section - *maqṭaɛ* pl. *maqaaṭiɛ.*
crosswise - *bil-ɛuruḍ.* Cut this cucumber crosswise. *guṣṣ hal-ixyaara bil-ɛuruḍ.*
crossword puzzle - *l-kalimaat il-mutaqaaṭiɛa.*
to **crouch** - *naṣṣa (i tniṣṣi) nafs~.* He crouched down behind the table so I couldn't see him. *huwwa naṣṣa nafsa wara l-meez zatta ma-ašuufa.*
crow - *ġraab* pl. *ġirbaan, zaaġ* pl. *-aat.* The black and white crows are bigger than the black crows. *l-ġirbaan ʔakbar imniz-zaaġ.*
to crow - *ɛooɛa (i tɛooɛi), ṣaaz (i ṣyaaz).* I woke up when the rooster crowed. *gɛadt imnin-noom lamma d-diič ɛooɛa.*
crowbar - *hiim* pl. *hyaama.*
crowd - **1.** *zdizaam* pl. *-aat, jamhuur* pl. *jamaahiir.* Have you seen the crowd in front of the theater? *šift il-izdizaam ib-baab is-siinama?* -- There was a

small crowd standing at the bus stop. *čaan aku jamhuur iṣġayyir mawjuud ib-mawqif il-paaṣ.* 2. *jamaaᶓa* pl. *-aat.* He goes around with a bad crowd. *yruuẓ wiyya jamaaᶓa muu zeena.*
to crowd - 1. *zdiẓam (i zdiẓaam), ndiẓas (i ndiẓaas).* We all crowded into the bus. *kullatna zdiẓamna bil-paaṣ.* 2. *ẓišak (a ẓašik) n-, ẓišar (u ẓašir) n-.* I don't think you can crowd another thing in there. *ma-aᶓtiqid tigdar tiẓšik šii laax ihnaak.*
crowded - *muzdaẓim.* The bus was crowded, as usual. *l-paaṣ čaan muzdaẓim kal-ᶓaada.*
crowded to capacity - *mqappuṭ.* The hall was crowded to capacity. *l-qaaᶓa čaanat imqappṭa.*
crown - *taaj* pl. *tiijaan, tuuj.* He wore a gold crown. *libas taaj ðahabi.*
to crown - *tawwaj (i tatwiij) t-.* They crowned him king in 1925. *tawwijoo malik sanat alf w-tisiᶓmiyya w-xamsa w-ᶓišriin.*
crown prince - *waliyy* (pl. *ʔawliyaaʔ*) *ᶓahid.*
to **crucify** - *ṣilab (u ṣalub) n-.* The Romans used to crucify their prisoners. *r-ruumaaniyyiin čaanaw yṣilbuun masaajiinhum.*
crude - 1. *xašin, faðð.* He's a rather crude person. *huwwa fadd waaẓid xašin.* 2. *xaam.* These barrels contain crude oil. *hal-baraamiil biiha nafuṭ xaam.*
cruel - *qaasi* pl. *-iin, qusaat.* Why are you this cruel? *ʔinta luweeš hiiči qaasi?*
cruelty - *qasaawa.*
cruiser - *ṭarraad* pl. *-aat.* My brother is assigned to a cruiser. *ʔaxuuya mᶓayyan ib-ṭarraad.*
crumb - *ftaata* pl. *-aat* coll. *ftaat.* He left bread crumbs on the table. *tirak iftaat xubuz ᶓal-meez.*
to crumb - *fattat (i taftiit, tfittit) t-.* Crumb the bread and mix it with the meat. *fattit il-xubuz w-xubṭa wiyya l-laẓam.*
to **crush - 1.** *fuᶓaṣ (u faᶓuṣ) n-.* You're crushing my hat. *ʔinta da-tufᶓuṣ šafuqti.* 2. *siẓag (a saẓig) n-.* The army remained loyal and crushed the insurrection. *j-jeeš buqa muxliṣ w-siẓag it-tamarrud.* -- He crushed out the cigarette with his foot. *siẓag ij-jigaara b-rijla.* 3. *jiraš (u jariš) n-.* When are you going to crush the wheat? *šwakit raẓ-tijruš il-ẓunṭa?* 4. *kassar (i taksiir, tkissir) t-.* This machine crushes the rocks. *hal-makiina tkassir iṣ-ṣuxuur.* 5. *ṣidam (i ṣadim) n-.* The news crushed him. *ṣidama l-xabar.*
crust - *gišra* pl. *-aat.* I can't eat the crust. *ma-agdar aakul il-gišra.* -- The thickness of the earth's crust is several miles. *gišrat il-ʔaruð simukha ᶓiddat ʔamyaal.*
crutch - *ᶓikkaaza* pl. *-aat.* He has to walk on crutches. *laazim yimši ᶓala ᶓikkaazaat.*
cry - 1. *ṣeeẓa* pl. *-aat, ᶓeeṭa* pl. *-aat, ṣarxa* pl. *-aat.* We heard a loud cry and went to investigate. *smaᶓna ṣeeẓa ᶓaalya w-riẓna nitẓarra.* 2. *bačya* pl. *-aat.* She'll feel better after a good cry. *raẓ-tirtaaẓ baᶓad fadd bačya zeena.*
to cry - 1. *biča (i biča, bači).* The baby was crying for its mother. *ṭ-ṭifil čaan yibči ᶓala ʔumma.* 2. *ṣaaẓ (i ṣyaaẓ).* I heard an animal crying in the forest. *smaᶓit ẓaywaan yṣiiẓ bil-ġaaba.*
to cry out - *ṣirax (a ṣraax), ᶓaaṭ (i ᶓyaaṭ), ṣaaẓ (i ṣyaaẓ).* He cried out from the pain. *ṣirax imnil-ʔalam.*
to cry to oneself - *naaẓ (u nooẓ).* We saw her at her son's grave crying to herself. *šifnaaha ᶓala gabur ʔibinha tnuuẓ.*
crystal - 1. *balluura* pl. *-aat* coll. *balluur.* We studied salt crystals under the microscope. *drasna balluuraat il-miliẓ taẓt il-mikriskoop.* -- I broke the last piece of crystal that I had. *ksarit ʔaaxir qiṭᶓa mnil-balluur illi ᶓindi.* -- They bought a crystal chandelier for the reception room. *štiraw iθrayya balluur il-ġurfat il-istiqbaal.* 2. *jaama* pl. *-aat.* I need a new crystal for my watch. *ʔaẓtaaj jaama jdiida s-saaᶓti.*
cube - *mukaᶓᶓab* pl. *-aat.* Draw a cube on the blackboard. *ʔirsim mukaᶓᶓab ᶓaṣ-ṣabbuura.*
cucumber - *xyaara* pl. *-aat* coll. *xyaar.*
to **cuddle - 1.** *ẓiðan (u ẓaðin) n-.* The mother cuddled her children. *l-ʔumm ẓiðnat jahhaalha.* 2. *tlaflaf (a tliflif).* The children cuddled up in their blankets. *l-ʔaṭfaal itlafilfaw ib-baṭṭaaniyyaathum.*
cue - 1. *ʔišaara* pl. *-aat.* I'll give you the cue to start talking. *raẓ-anṭiik ʔišaart il-ibtidaaʔ bil-kalaam.* 2. *ᶓaṣa* pl. *ᶓiṣi, kyuu* pl. *-aat.* He hit his friend on the head with a billiard cue. *ðurab ṣadiiqa ᶓala raasa b-ᶓaṣa bilyaard.*
cuff - *ṭawya* pl. *-aat, kaffa* pl. *-aat, θanya* pl. *-aat.* I tore my pants cuff. *šaggeet ṭawyat il-panṭaroon maali.*
on the cuff - *bid-deen.* Can you put it on the cuff until tomorrow? *tigdar tiẓsibha bid-deen il-baačir?*
cuff link - *dugmat* (pl. *digam*) *irdaan.* I lost one of my cuff links. *ðayyaᶓit wiẓda min digam irdaani.*
culprit - *muðnib* pl. *-iin.* They found the culprit. *ligaw il-muðnib.*
cultural - *θaqaafi*.* He is Iraq's cultural attache. *huwwa mulẓaq iθ-θaqaafi maal il-ᶓiraaq.*
culture - 1. *ẓaðaara* pl. *-aat.* He's a specialist in ancient Greek culture. *huwwa muxtaṣṣ ib-ẓaðaarat il-yunaan il-qadiim.* 2. *θaqaafa.* He is a man of high culture. *huwwa ṣaaẓib θaqaafa ᶓaalya.* 3. *zariᶓ* pl. *zruuᶓ.* He is studying microbe culture. *da-yidrus zariᶓ il-mikroobaat.*
cultured - *mhaððab, mθaqqaf.* She's a cultured woman. *hiyya fadd wiẓda mhaððba.*
culvert - *burbux* pl. *baraabix.*
cuneiform - *mismaari*.*
cunning - *muraawiġ, ẓayyaal, šeeṭaan, makkaar.* The fox is a very cunning animal. *θ-θaᶓlab fadd ẓaywaan muraawiġ ihwaaya.*
cup - 1. *finjaan* pl. *fnaajiin.* He drank three cups of coffee. *širab iθlaθ ifnaajiin gahwa.* 2. *kuub* pl. *kwaaba.* I asked our neighbors for a cup of sugar. *ṭlabit min jiiraanna kuub šakar.* 3. *kaʔis* pl. *kuʔuus.* Who won the cup? *minu ẓaṣṣal ᶓal-kaʔis?*
cupboard - *diilaab* (pl. *dwaaliib*) *imwaaᶓiin.*
curb - 1. *raṣiif* pl. *-aat.* I stood on the curb watching the parade. *wgafit ᶓar-raṣiif atfarraj ᶓal-istiᶓraað.* 2. *taqyiid* pl. *-aat.* The government put a curb on emigration. *l-ẓukuuma xallat taqyiid ᶓal-hijra.*
to curb - 1. *qayyad (i taqyiid, tqiyyid) t-.* The government has begun curbing foreign imports. *l-ẓukuuma btidat itqayyid il-istiiraadaat il-xaarijiyya.* 2. *ðubaṭ (u ðabuṭ) n-.* You have to try to curb your temper. *laazim itẓaawil tuðbuṭ ʔaᶓṣaabak.*
cure - *duwa* pl. *ʔadwiya, ᶓilaaj* pl. *-aat.* There is no cure for cancer. *ma-aku duwa liṣ-ṣaraṭaan.*
to cure - 1. *ṭayyab (i ṭṭiyyib) t-, šaafa (i šifaaʔ) t-.* The doctors cured his deafness. *d-dakaatra ṭayyibaw iṭ-ṭaraš maala.* 2. *xammar (u taxmiir, txummur) t-.* They cure the tobacco in these warehouses. *yxammruun it-titin ib-hal-maxaazin.*
curfew - *maniᶓ tajawwul.*
curiosity - 1. *ẓubb istiṭlaaᶓ.* She aroused my curiosity. *ʔaθaarat ẓubb istiṭlaaᶓi.* 2. *ġariib* pl. *ġaraayib.* He brought with him some curiosities from India. *jaab wiyyaa ġaraayib imnil-hind.*
curious - 1. *muẓibb lil-istiṭlaaᶓ.* Don't be so curious. *la-tṣiir hal-gadd muẓibb lil-istiṭlaaᶓ.* 2. *ġariib.* This is a very curious situation. *haaði fadd waðᶓiyya ġariiba kulliš.*
curl - *tajᶓiid* pl. *-aat, kaᶓkuula* pl. *-aat.* Her hair is all curls. *šaᶓarha kulla tajᶓiidaat.*
to curl - *jaᶓᶓad (i tajᶓiid) t-, kaᶓkal (i tkiᶓkil) t-.* Fatma, who curled your hair? *faaṭma, minu jaᶓᶓad šaᶓarič?*
to curl up - *lamlam (i tlimlim) nafs~, tlamlam (a tlimlim).* The dog curled up and went to sleep. *č-čalib itlamlam w-naam.*
currency - *naqid* pl. *nuquud, ᶓumla* pl. *-aat.* Their currency is made in this country. *nuquudhum maᶓmuula b-hal-balad.*
current - 1. *tayyaar* pl. *-aat.* The current is very swift here. *t-tayyaar kulliš sariiᶓ ihnaa.* -- The electric current has been turned off. *nqiṭaᶓ it-tayyaar il-kahrabaaʔi.* 2. *jaari, ẓaali*.* The bill for the current month is attached. *l-qaaʔima maal iš-šahr ij-jaari murfaqa.* 3. *daarij.* Wearing of the fez was current in Baghdad before the First World War. *libs il-fiina čaan daarij ib-baġdaad gabuļ il-ẓarb il-ᶓaalamiyya l-ʔuula.*
curse - *šattuuma* pl. *-aat, štaayim; laᶓna* pl. *-aat, naᶓla* pl. *-aat, šatma* pl. *-aat, masabba* pl. *-aat.* I don't want to hear another curse out of you. *ma-ard asmaᶓ šattuuma lux minnak.*
to curse - *šattam (i tšittim) t-, sabb (i sabb) n-, šitam (i šatim) n-.* He cursed him for his slow driving. *šattam ᶓalee s-siyaaqta l-baṭiiʔa.*
curtain - *parda* pl. *-aat, sitaar* pl. *sitaaʔir.*
curtain rod - *šiiš* (pl. *šyaaš*) *parda.*
curve - *munᶓaṭaf* pl. *-aat, loofa* pl. *-aat.* This road

has a lot of curves. *hat-tariiq bii loofaat ihwaaya.*
to curve - *daar (u dawaraan), laaf (u loof), nԑitaf (u nԑitaaf).* The road curves to the right. *t-tariiq yduur lil-yamiin.*
cushion - *kušin* pl. *-aat, mxadda* pl. *mxaadiid, mindar* pl. *manaadir, maqԑad* pl. *maqaaԑid.*
cuspidor - *mibṣaqa* pl. *mabaaṣiq.*
custody - *tawqiif, zajiz.* They took him into custody. *ʔaxδoo lit-tawqiif.*
custom - **1.** *ԑaada* pl. *-aat.* This is an old Iraqi custom. *haaδi ԑaada ԑiraaqiyya qadiima.* **2.** *tunṣaa.* His cars are all custom-made. *kull sayyaaraata maԑmuula tuuṣaa.*
customary - *zasb il-ԑaada, zasb il-ԑuruf, ԑtiyaadi*.*
customer - *maԑmiil* pl. *maԑaamiil, zabuun* pl. *zabaayin.* He's my best customer. *huwwa ʔazsan maԑmiil ԑindi.*
customs - **1.** *gumrug* pl. *gamaarig.* Do we have to pay customs on this? *laazim nidfaԑ gumrug ԑala haay?* **2.** *gumrugi*.* We had to go through a customs inspection when we arrived. *lamma wṣalna čaan laazim inmurr ib-taftiiš gumrugi.*
cut - **1.** *jariz* pl. *jruuz.* The cut is nearly healed. *j-jariz indimal taqriiban.* **2.** *taxfiiδ* pl. *-aat, tanziil* pl. *-aat, taqliil* pl. *-aat, tangiiṣ* pl. *-aat.* He had to take a cut in his salary. *δṭarr yiqbal taxfiiδ ib-raatba.* **3.** *tifṣaal* pl. *-aat, tafṣiil* pl. *-aat.* I don't like the cut of this coat. *ma-yiԑjibni tifṣaal has-sitra.* **4.** *zuṣṣa* pl. *zuṣaṣ.* You'll get your cut after everything is sold. *raz-taaxuδ zuṣṣtak baԑad-ma kullši yinbaaԑ.* **5.** *ġiyaab* pl. *-aat, ngiṭaaԑ* pl. *-aat.* He gave me a cut for being a quarter of an hour late for class. *sajjal ԑalayya ġiyaab li-ʔann itʔaxxarit rubuԑ saaԑa ԑan id-daris.* **6.** *wuṣla* pl. *wuṣal, qiṭԑa* pl. *qiṭaԑ.* Give me a good cut of beef. *nṭiini wuṣlat lazam hooš zeena.*
cut rate - *siԑir muxaffaδ.* He bought it cut-rate. *štiraaha b-siԑir muxaffaδ.*
to cut - **1.** *gaṣṣ (u gaṣṣ) n-, jiraz (a jariz) n-.* I cut my finger. *jrazit iṣibԑi.* -- That remark cut him a great deal. *hal-mulaazaδa jirzata kθiir.* **2.** *gaṣṣ (u gaṣṣ) n-.* Will you cut the watermelon please? *baḷḷa ma-tguṣṣ ir-raggiyya rajaaʔan?* -- Would you cut the cards please? *baḷḷa ma-tguṣṣ il-waraq rajaaʔan?* **3.** *xaffaδ (u taxfiiδ, txuffuδ) t-, nazzal (i tanziil, tnizzil) t-, qallal (i taqliil, tqillil) t-, naggaṣ (i tangiiṣ, tniggiṣ) t-.* They've cut the prices on winter clothes. *xaffiδaw il-ʔasԑaar lil-malaabis iš-šitwiyya.* **4.** *ġaab (i ġiyaab), ngiṭaԑ (ngiṭaaԑ).* He cut class three days in a row. *ġaab ԑan iṣ-ṣaff itlatt iyyaam mitwaalya.* **5.** *xaffaf (i taxfiif, txiffif) t-.* Cut the paint with a gallon of turpentine. *xaffif iṣ-ṣubug ib-galin tarpantiin.* **6.** *ṭallaԑ (i ṭṭilliԑ) t-.* Our son is beginning to cut his teeth. *ʔibinna btida yṭalliԑ isnuun.*
to cut across - *gaṣṣ (u gaṣṣ) n-, ԑubar (u ԑabur) n-.* We cut across the orange grove on our way home. *gaṣṣeena bistaan il-purtaqaal ib-jayyatna lil-beet.*
to cut back - *xaffaδ (i), nazzal (i), naggaṣ (i), qallal (i).* They've cut back production fifty percent. *xaffiδaw il-ʔintaaj xamsiin bil-miyya.*
to cut in - *tdaxxal (a tadaxxul).* He's always cutting in when we're having a discussion. *huwwa daaʔiman yitdaxxal lamma tkuun ԑidna munaaqaša.*
to cut off - **1.** *qiṭaԑ (a qaṭiԑ) n-.* They cut off his allowance. *qiṭԑaw muxaṣṣaṣaata.* -- The police cut off the roads leading to town. *š-šurṭa qiṭԑat iṭ-ṭuruq il-muʔaddiya lil-wlaaya.* -- The company cut off the electricity. *š-šarika qiṭԑat il-kahrabaaʔ.* **2.** *bitar (i batir) n-, gaṣṣ (u gaṣṣ) n-.* He cut off the dog's tail. *bitar δeel ič-čalib.*
to cut out - **1.** *baṭṭal (i tabṭiil) min.* Cut out that running around the house. *baṭṭilu min har-rakuδ bil-beet.* **2.** *gaṣṣ (u).* The censor cut two sentences out of the letter. *r-raqiib qaṣṣ jumulteen imnil-maktuub.* **3.** *yeezi ԑaad, bass ԑaad.* Cut it out! Stop making that noise. *yeezi ԑaad! baṭṭilu min hal-lagwa.*
**He's not cut out to be a teacher. *huwwa muu maal muԑallim* or *huwwa muu wijih muԑallim.*
to cut up - *gaṣgaṣ (i tgiṣgiṣ) t-, gaṭṭaԑ (i tgiṭṭiԑ) t-.* Cut up the carrots in small pieces. *gaṣgiṣ il-jizar wuṣal iṣġaar.*
cute - *laṭiif, zabbuub.* She's a very cute girl. *hiyya fadd ibnayya hwaaya zabbuuba.* -- He told a cute story. *ziča quṣṣa laṭiifa.*
cycle - *dawra* pl. *-aat.* This machine completes it's cycle in five minutes. *hal-makiina tkammil dawratha b-xamas daqaayiq.*
cylinder - **1.** *silindar* pl. *-aat.* This engine has six cylinders. *hal-makiina biiha sitt silindaraat.* **2.** *ṣṭuwaana* pl. *-aat.* The volume of a cylinder is equal to multiplying the area of the base times its height. *zajm il-iṣṭuwaana ysaawi δarb masaazat il-qaaԑida bil-irtifaaԑ.*
cymbal - *ṭaas* pl. *ṭuus.*
Cypriot - *qubruṣi** pl. *-iyyiin.*
Cyprus - *qubruṣ.*
czar - *qayṣar* pl. *qayaaṣira.*

D

dad - *yaaba, yaab, baaba.* Dad, can I use the car? *yaab, ʔagdar astaԑmil is-sayyaara?*
daddy - *baaba.* Is your daddy home? *baaba bil-beet?*
daffodil - *narjisa* pl. *-aat* coll. *narjis.*
dagger - *xanjar* pl. *xanaajir.*
daily - **1.** *bil-yoom, kull yoom.* The mail is delivered twice daily. *l-bariid yitwazzaԑ marrteen bil-yoom.* **2.** *yoomi*.* The daily rate is three dollars. *l-ʔujra l-yoomiyya tlaθ doolaaraat.*
dairy - **1.** *maԑmal (pl. maԑaamil) ʔalbaan.* I bought the butter at the dairy. *štireet iz-zibda min maԑmal il-ʔalbaan.* **2.** *ʔalbaan.* My uncle has a dairy farm. *ԑammi ԑinda mazraԑat ʔalbaan.*
dam - *sadd* pl. *suduud.* The dam is broken. *s-sadd maksuur.*
damage - *δarar* pl. *ʔaδraar, talaf* pl. *-iyyaat.* How much damage took place? *šgadd ṣaar δarar?*
to damage - *tilaf (i talif).* The storm damaged the roof. *l-ԑaaṣifa tilfat iṣ-ṣaṭiz.*
damages - *taԑwiiδaat.* He had to pay damages. *δṭaar yidfaԑ taԑwiiδaat.*
Damascene - *dimišqi** pl. *-iyyiin, šaami** pl. *-iyyiin, šwaam.*
Damascus - *dimašq, š-šaam.*
damn - *malԑuun.* Throw that damn cat out! *ṭalliԑ hal-bazzuuna l-malԑuuna barra!*
**I don't give a damn what he says. *zčaayta w-qundarti.*
to damn - **1.** *liԑan (a laԑin) n-.* Damn him! *ʔaḷḷa yilԑana!* **2.** *liԑan (a laԑin) n- maδhab, niԑal (a naԑil) n- maδhab, šiԑal (a šaԑil) n- diin.* She damned me up and down for running over her cat. *niԑlat maδhabi li-ʔan disit bazzuunatha b-sayyaarti.* -- I'll be damned if I'll do it! *ʔanniԑil ʔiδa asawwiiha!*
damned - *malԑuun, manԑuul.*
damp - *raṭib, naadi.* Everything gets damp in the cellar. *kullši yṣiir raṭib bis-sirdaab.*
dampness - *ruṭuuba, nida.*
dance - **1.** *rigṣa* pl. *-aat.* May I have the next dance? *tismazii-li bir-rigṣa j-jaaya?* **2.** *zaflat (pl. -aat) rigiṣ.* Are you going to the dance? *raz-itruuz il-zaflat ir-rigiṣ?*
to dance - *rigaṣ (u rigaṣ).* They danced until midnight. *rigṣaw ʔila nuṣṣ il-leel.*
dancer - *raaqiṣa* pl. *-aat.* They have a good dancer at the Select Night Club. *ԑidhum raaqiṣa zeena b-malha salakt.*
**He's a good dancer. *yirguṣ zeen.*
danger - *xaṭar.* The doctor says she is out of danger now. *t-tabiib gaal il-xaṭar zaal ԑanha hassa.* -- Caution! Danger! *ntibih lil-xaṭar!*
in danger of - *muԑarraδ.* He's in danger of losing his job. *huwwa muԑarraδ il-fuqdaan waδiifta.*
dangerous - *muxṭir.* Is swimming here dangerous? *s-sibiz ihnaa muxṭir?*
to **dare** - *jiraʔ (a jurʔa), jisar (u jisaara).* I didn't dare leave the baby alone. *ma-jraʔit atruk iṭ-ṭifil wazda.* -- How dare you open my mail? *šloon tijsur tiftaz bariidi?*

dark - 1. *δ̣alma.* The road is hard to find in the dark. *ṭ-ṭariiq ṣaɛub yinligi biδ̣-δ̣alma.* **2.** *δ̣alaam.* Don't keep me in the dark this way. *la-titrukni b-δ̣alaam hiici.* **3.** *ṭoox.* I want a darker color. *ʔariid loon ʔaṭwax.* **4.** *ʔasmar* pl. *sumur.* She is quite dark. *hiyya samra kulliš.*
  to get dark - *δ̣lamm (a δ̣alaam).* In summer it gets dark late. *biṣ-ṣeef tiδ̣lamm faayit wakit.*
darling - 1. *mdallal* pl. *-iin.* He's his mother's pampered darling. *huwwa mdallal maal ʔumma.* **2.** *ʒabiib.* What's the matter, darling? *š-biik, ʒabiibi?*
  **What a darling child! *šloon jaahil yinʒaṭṭ bil-gaḷub!*
to **darn -** *xayyaṭ (i xyaaṭa).* Did you darn my socks? *xayyaṭṭii-li jwaariibi?*
  **I'll be darned if it isn't Jalil! *ʔaguṣṣ ʔiidi ʔiδa haaδa muu jaliil.*
dash - 1. *xaṭṭ* pl. *xuṭuuṭ, šuxuṭ* pl. *šxuuṭ.* Put a dash after the first word. *ʒuṭṭ xaṭṭ baɛd il-kalima il-ʔuula.* **2.** *ʒabba* pl. *-aat.* All it needs is a dash of salt. *ma-yinraad-la ġeer ʒabbat miliʒ.* **3.** *rikiδ̣.* Who won the hundred meter dash? *minu ġilab ib-rikδ̣ il-miit matir.*
  to dash - 1. *rašš (u rašš), δabb (i δabb).* He came to when I dashed some water in his face. *raddat ruuʒa lamma raššeet šwayya ṃaay ɛala wujja.* **2.** *ṭufar (u ṭafur).* He grabbed his hat and made a dash for the door. *ligaf šafuqta w-ṭufar ṭafur bil-baab.*
  to dash off - *ɛallag (i taɛliig).* He dashed off before I could answer. *ɛallag, gabuḷ-ma ʔajaawba.*
dashboard - *dašbuul* pl. *-aat.*
date - 1. *tamra* pl. *-aat* coll. *tamur.* How much is a kilo of dates? *beeš kiilu t-tamur.* **2.** *taariix* pl. *tawaariix.* What's the date today? *šinu taariix il-yoom?* or *******l-yoom išgadd biš-šahar?* **3.** *mawɛid* pl. *mawaaɛiid.* I have a date for lunch today. *ɛindi mawɛid lil-ġada hal-yoom.* **4.** *yoom* pl. *ʔayyaam.* You set the date. *ʔinta ɛayyin il-yoom.*
  to date - *li-hassa, ʔila l-ʔaan.* We haven't heard from him to date. *ma-smaɛna minna li-hassa.*
  to date - *ʔarrax (i taʔriix) t-.* The letter is dated June 6. *l-maktuub imʔarrax ib-sitta ʒaʒayraan.*
  to date from - *rijaɛ (a rujuuɛ) it-taariix ʔila.* The oldest house in town dates from the 17th century. *ʔaɛtag beet bil-madiina yirjaɛ taariixa ʔila l-qarn is-saabiɛ ɛašar.*
date palm - *naxla* pl. *-aat* coll. *naxal.*
daughter - *bitt, bint* pl. *banaat.*
daughter-in-law - *čanna* pl. *-aat, čnaayin.*
dawn - *fajir.* We had to get up at dawn. *δ̣ṭarreena nigɛud imnil-fajir.*
  to dawn - 1. *ṣabbaʒ (i taṣbiiʒ).* The day dawned, clear and sunny. *ṣabbaʒ in-nahaar ṣaaʒi w-mišmis.* **2.** *wuδ̣aʒ (a wuδ̣uuʒ) l-, ʔadrak (i ʔidraak).* It finally dawned on me what he meant. *ʔaxiiran wuδ̣aʒ-li qaṣda* or *ʔaxiiran ʔadrakit iš-ɛina.*
day - 1. *yoom* pl. *ʔayyaam.* I haven't seen him since that day. *ma-šifta min δaak il-yoom.* -- I'll drop by your house some day. *raʒ-amurr il-beetkum fadd yoom imnil-ʔayyaam.* -- One of these days you'll be sorry. *raʒ-tindam fadd yoom.* **2.** *nahaar* pl. *-aat.* He's been sleeping all day. *ṣaar-la naayim ṭuul in-nahaar.*
  **Let's call it a day! *ṗaaydoos!*
  a day - *bil-yoom.* Take three pills a day. *ʔiblaɛ itlaθ ʒabbaat bil-yoom.*
  by the day - 1. *yoom baɛad yoom, yoom ɛala yoom.* It gets more difficult by the day. *da-yṣiir ʔaṣɛab yoom ɛala yoom.* **2.** *ɛala ʔasaas il-ʔayyaam, kull yoom ib-yooma.* You can rent this room by the day. *tiġdar itʔajjir hal-ġurfa ɛala ʔasaas il-ʔayyaam.*
  day after day - *yoom wara yoom.* Day after day he tells us the same old story. *yoom wara yoom yɛiid w-yiṣqul ib-nafs il-quṣṣa.*
  day by day - *yoom ɛala yoom, yoom baɛad yoom, yoom wara yoom.* Day by day his condition is improving. *yoom ɛala yoom ʒaalta da-titʒassan.*
  day off - *ɛuṭla* pl. *ɛuṭal.* Tuesday is my day off. *ɛuṭilti yoom iθ-θilaaθaa.*
  every day - *kull yoom.* He works every day except Friday. *yištugul kull yoom ma-ɛada yoom ij-jumɛa.*
daybreak - *fajir.* We're leaving at daybreak. *raʒ-insaafir il-fajir.*
to **daze -** *dawwax (u), siṭar(u saṭir) n-.* The explosion dazed him. *l-infijaar dawwaxa.*
dazed - *daayix, maṣṭuur.* He seemed completely dazed. *čaan imbayyin ɛalee daayix tamaaman.*
dead - 1. *mayyit* pl. *mawta, ʔamwaat.* They buried their dead. *difnaw mawtaahum.* -- The meeting was pretty dead. *j-jalsa čaanat mayyta* or *j-jalsa ma-čaan biiha ʒayaat.* **2.** *tamaaman.* I'm dead tired. *ʔaani taɛbaan tamaaman.* -- I'm dead certain I put it there. *ʔaani mitʔakkid tamaaman xalleetha hnaak.*
  **The fire is dead. *n-naar xumdat.*
dead-end - *ma-bii ṭalɛa, ma-yiṭlaɛ.* This is a dead-end street. *haaδa šaariɛ ma-yiṭlaɛ.*
deadly - *qaatil, qattaal, mumiit.* This poison is deadly. *has-samm qaatil.*
deaf - m. *ʔaṭraš* pl. *ṭaršiin,* f. *ṭarša* pl. *-aat, -iin.* He's completely deaf. *huwwa ʔaṭraš tamaaman.*
to **deafen -** *ṭarraš (i taṭriiš).* That noise is deafening. *haṣ-ṣoot yṭarriš.*
deal - 1. *ṣafqa* pl. *-aat.* He made a lot of money on that deal. *sawwa xooš ifluus ib-haṣ-ṣafqa.* **2.** *ʒuṣṣa* pl. *ʒuṣaṣ.* All I want is a fair deal. *kull-ma ʔariida huwwa ʒuṣṣa ɛaadla.* **3.** *tawziiɛ* pl. *-aat.* Whose deal is it now? *door man hassa bit-tawziiɛ?* or *minu ywazziɛ waraq?* **4.** *dagga.* That's a good deal! *haay xooš dagga!*
  **They gave him a raw deal. *ɛaamloo muu xooš* or *ġumṭaw ʒaqqa.*
  a good deal - *ihwaaya.* There's a good deal to be done yet. *ʔaku baɛad ihwaaya yirraad-la msaawaa.*
  to deal - *wazzaɛ (i tawziiɛ) t-, qassam (i taqsiim) t-, farrag (i tafriig) t-.* Who dealt the cards? *minu wazzaɛ il-waraq?*
  to deal with - 1. *tɛaamal (a taɛaamul) maɛa, wiyya.* He dealt fairly with me. *tɛaamal wiyyaaya b-ɛadil.* -- He deals directly with the company. *yitɛaamal maɛa š-šarika raʔsan.* **2.** *tɛallaq (a taɛalluq) b-.* The book deals with labor problems. *l-iktaab yitɛallaq ib-mašaakil il-ɛummaal.*
  **This problem has been dealt with. *hal-muškila nbiʒθat w-xilṣat.*
dealer - 1. *taajir* pl. *tijjaar.* He's a dealer in Persian rugs. *huwwa taajir bis-sijjaad il-ɛajmi.* **2.** *bayyaaɛ* pl. *-iin.* There's a used car dealer near our house. *ʔaku bayyaaɛ sayyaaraat mustaɛmila yamm beetna.*
dear - 1. *ɛaziiz.* His sister is very dear to him. *ʔuxta kulliš ɛaziiza ɛalee.* **2.** *ġaali.* Everything in the market is very dear these days. *kullši bis-suug kulliš ġaali hal-ʔayyaam.*
  oh dear - *ʔaax yaaḅa.* Oh dear, we'll be late again. *ʔaax yaaba! raʒ-inkuun mitʔaxxriin marra lux!*
dearly - *ġaali.* He had to pay dearly for his mistake. *δ̣ṭarr yidfaɛ ġaali ɛala galiṭṭa.*
death - 1. *moot* pl. *ʔamwaat, wafaat, wafiyya* pl. *-aat.* His death was announced in the newspapers. *moota nɛilan bij-jaraayid.* **2.** *ʔiɛdaam.* This crime carries the death penalty. *hal-jariima tiṭδ̣amman ɛuquubat il-ʔiɛdaam.*
  **You'll catch your death of cold. *raʒ-yṣiibak barid ymawwtak.*
  **He'll be the death of me yet. *raʒ-yimawwitni waḷḷa.*
  **Don't work yourself to death. *la-tihlik nafsak imniš-šuġuḷ.*
  **He's in the throes of death. *gaɛad ynaaziɛ.*
debate - *munaaqaša* pl. *-aat.* The debate lasted for hours. *l-munaaqaša daamat ɛiddat saaɛaat.*
  to debate - *naaqaš (i munaaqaša).* The students debated the subject among themselves. *ṭ-ṭullaab naaqšaw il-mawδ̣uuɛ beenaathum.* — The question was debated for a long time. *s-suʔaal ṭawwlat manaaqašta mudda ṭwiila.*
  to debate with oneself - *daanaš (i mudaanaša) in-nafis.* I debated with myself whether or not to go. *daanašit nafsi ʔaruuʒ loo laa.*
debt - *deen* pl. *dyuun.* This payment settles your debt. *had-dafɛa tinhi deenak.*
  in debt - 1. *madyuun.* Is he still in debt? *huwwa baɛda madyuun.* **2.** *bid-deen.* He's up to his ears in debt. *huwwa ṭaamus bid-deen.*
debtor - *madyuun* pl. *-iin.*
decade - *ɛaqid* pl. *ɛuquud.*
decay - *nʒilaal.* Some means must be found to prevent any further decay in our economic system. *fadd wasiila laazim tinligi l-maniɛ ʔayy inʒilaal ʔaaxar ib-niδ̣aamna l-iqtiṣaadi.*
  to decay - 1. *xaas (i xees, xayasaan).* The vegetables decayed rapidly in the heat. *l-xuδ̣rawaat xaasat bil-ɛajal min ʒaraart ij-jaww.* **2.** *sawwas (i taswiis) t-.* The tooth decayed. *s-sinn sawwas.*
decayed - 1. *xaayis.* Throw all the decayed vegetables

into the garbage can. *δibb kull il-xuδrawaat il-xaaysa b-tanakt iz-zibil.* 2. *mitsawwis, msawwis.* The tooth is decayed and I'll have to pull it. *s-sinn imsawwis w-laazim ʔašlaεa.* 3. *mitfassix.* The body was so decayed that it could not be identified. *j-juθθa halgadd-ma mitfassxa maa mumkin it-taεarruf εala hawiyyat ṣaaẓibha.*

deceit - *ġišš, muxaatala, xidaaε, qašmara.*

deceitful - *muxaadiε.* She is a lying, deceitful woman. *haay fadd mara čaδδaaba w-muxaadiεa.*

to **deceive** - 1. *ġašš (i ġašš) n-, xidaε (a xidaaε) n-, qašmar (u qašmara).* Appearances are deceiving. *l-maḍaahir tixdaε.* -- He deceived us. *ġaššna.* 2. *xaan (u xiyaana), xidaε (a xidaaε) n-.* His wife is deceiving him. *zawijta da-txuuna.*

December - *kaanuun il-ʔawwal.*

decency - *ʔadab, liyaaqa.* He didn't even have the decency to thank me. *ma-kaan εinda ẓatta ʔadab kaafi yiškurni.*

decent - 1. *muẓtaram, muʔaddab.* He's a decent fellow. *huwwa fadd waaẓid muẓtaram.* -- He lives a decent life. *yεiiš εiiša muẓtarama.* 2. *šariif.* He did the decent thing and married her. *sawwa šii šariif w-itzawwajha.* 3. *zeen.* I make a decent living from this job. *haš-šaġla twaffir-li εiiša zeena.*

to **decide** - *qarrar (i taqriir) t-.* I decided to stay. *qarrarit ʔabqa.* -- What did you decide on? *š-qarrarit?*

decided - *θaabit, ẓatman.* His height gave him a decided advantage in the flight. *ṭuula nṭaa ʔafḍaliyya ẓatman bil-εarka.*

decidedly - *ẓatman, ʔakiid.* He is decidedly worried about the examination. *ẓatman huwwa qaliq imnil-imtiẓaan.*

decision - 1. *qaraar* pl. *-aat.* At last he has come to a decision. *w-ʔaxiiran wuṣal ʔila qaraar.* 2. *ẓukum* pl. *ʔaẓkaam.* The judge hasn't come to his decision yet. *l-ẓaakim ma-wuṣal ʔila ẓukma baεad.*

deck - 1. *saṭiẓ* (pl. *suṭuuẓ*) *baaxira.* Is he in his cabin or on the deck? *huwwa b-maqṣuurta loo εala saṭẓ il-baaxira.* 2. *dasta* pl. *-aat, šadda* pl. *-aat.* Let's take a new deck of cards. *xan-naaxuδ dastat waraq jidiida.*

to deck out - *zayyan (i tazyiin) t-, zarwaq (u zarwaqa) t-.* The city was all decked out with lights. *l-madiina čaanat mzayyna bil-ʔaḍwiya.*

declaration - 1. *taṣriiẓa* pl. *-aat.* He presented his customs declaration to the customs inspector. *qaddam taṣriiẓta l-gumrugiyya l-mufattiš il-gumrug.* 2. *ʔiεlaan* pl. *-aat, ʔišhaar* pl. *-aat.* He broadcasted the declaration of war over the radio. *δaaε ʔiεlaan il-ẓarub bir-raadyo.*

to **declare** - 1. *ʔaεlan (i ʔiεlaan).* They declared war on us. *ʔaεlinaw εaleena ẓarub.* 2. *qaddam (i taqdiim) taṣriiẓa b-.* Do I have to declare the tobacco at the customs? *laazim aqaddim taṣriiẓa bit-tibig bil-gumrug?*

decline - 1. *tanaaguṣ.* The decline in new cases of cancer continued this month. *t-tanaaguṣ bil-iṣaabaat ij-jidiida biṣ-ṣaraṭaan istamarr haš-šahar.* 2. *tadahwur.* The empire's decline continued for several years. *tadahuur il-imparaaṭooriyya stamarr εiddat isniin.*

to decline - 1. *nẓaṭṭ (a nẓiṭaaṭ).* His health has declined over the past year. *ṣiẓẓta nẓaṭṭat xilaal is-sana il-maaḍiya.* 2. *tnaagaṣ (a tanaaguṣ).* Club membership has declined recently. *ʔuḍwiyyat in-naadi tnaagṣat muʔaxxaran.* 3. *rifaḍ (u rafuḍ) n-.* They had to decline his invitation. *ḍṭarraw yrufḍuun daεuuta.*

to **decorate** - 1. *ṣannaε (i taṣniiε) t-.* The baker decorated the cake for our party. *baayiε il-keek ṣannaε il-keeka l-ẓaflatna.* 2. *zayyan (i tazyiin) t-.* They decorated the school for graduation. *zayyinaw il-madrasa l-ẓaflat it-taxarruj.* 3. *zaxraf (u zaxrafa) t-.* The walls of the mosque are decorated. *ẓiiṭaan ij-jaamiε mzaxrafa.*

decoration - 1. *ziina* pl. *-aat.* The government is putting up decorations in the street for Republic Day. *l-ẓukuuma da-tẓuṭṭ ziina biš-šawaariε il-εiid ij-jamhuuriyya.* 2. *wisaam* pl. *ʔawsima.* What did they give him the decoration for? *εala weeš inṭoo l-wisaam?*

decrease - *nxifaaḍ* pl. *-aat, nuqṣaan.* Statistics show a decrease in the death rate in the last few years. *l-ʔiẓṣaaʔiyyaat itbayyin inxifaaḍ ib-εadad il-wafiyyaat bis-siniin il-ʔaxiira.*

decree - *marsuum* pl. *maraasiim.* The decree goes into effect tomorrow. *l-marsuum yitnaffaδ min baačir.*

to decree - *ṣaddar (i taṣdiir) marsuum b-.* The government decreed a holiday. *l-ẓukuuma ṣaddirat marsuum ib-ʔiẓdaaθ εuṭla.*

to **deduct** - *xiṣam (u xaṣum), staqṭaε (i stiqṭaaε).* Deduct ten per cent. *ʔixṣum εašra bil-miyya.*

deed - 1. *ẓijja* pl. *ẓijaj.* The deed to the house is at the lawyer's. *ẓijjat il-beet εind il-muẓaami.* 2. *εamal* pl. *ʔaεmaal.* There are good deeds and bad deeds. *ʔaku ʔaεmaal il-xeer w-ʔaεmaal iš-šarr.*

to deed - *sajjal (i tasjiil) b-isim, kitab (i kitaaba) b-isim.* My father has deeded the house to me. *ʔabuuya kitab il-beet b-ismi.*

deep - *εamiiq, ġamiij.* This subject is too deep for me. *hal-mawḍuuε kulliš εamiiq bin-nisba ʔili.* **The lake is ten feet deep. *l-buẓayra ġumijha εašir ʔaqdaam.*

deeply - *kulliš, hwaaya.* He was deeply affected by their story. *čaan kulliš mitʔaθθir ib-quṣṣathum.*

defeat - *haziima, nkisaar.* The enemy suffered a crushing defeat. *l-εadu qaasaw haziima saaẓiqa.*

to **defeat** - 1. *ġilab (u ġulub) n-.* He defeated three candidates and got a seat in parliament. *ġilab itlaθ muraššaẓiin w-ẓaṣṣal in-niyaaba.* 2. *rifaḍ (u rafuḍ) n-.* The motion was defeated. *l-iqtiraaẓ inrifaḍ.*

defect - *εeeb* pl. *εuyuub.* There's a natural defect in this cloth. *ʔaku εeeb ʔaṣli b-hal-iqmaaš.*

defective - *bii εeeb, bii xalal.* The radio is defective; either exchange it or give me my money back. *r-raadyo bii εeeb; ʔamma tbaddla loo tinṭiini fluusi.*

to **defend** - *daafaε (i difaaε) εan.* They decided not to defend the town. *qarriraw ʔan ma-ydaafεuun εan il-madiina.* -- There's no need to defend yourself. *ma-aku ẓaaja tdaafiε εan nafsak* or ***ma-aku majaal tiεtiδir.*

defense - *difaaε.* The defense was weak. *d-difaaε čaan ḍaεiif.* -- He works for the Ministry of Defense. *yištuġul ib-wizaart id-difaaε.*

to **define** - 1. *ẓaddad (i taẓdiid) t- maεna, εarraf (u taεriif) t- maεna.* Can you define the word "democracy"? *tiġdar itẓaddid maεna kalimat "dimooqraaṭiyya"?* 2. *εayyan (i taεyiin) t-.* The boundaries were defined by the treaty. *l-ẓuduud itεayyinat bil-muεaahada.*

definite - *muẓaddad, muεayyan.* Do you have any definite plan? *εindak ʔay xuṭṭa muεayyna?*

definitely - *bit-taʔkiid, ʔakiid.* I'm definitely coming. *ʔaani jaay bit-taʔkiid.*

to **defy** - *tẓadda (a taẓaddi).* The opposition defied the government to find a solution to the problem. *l-muεaaraḍa tẓaddat il-ẓukuuma ʔan yilguun ẓall lil-muškila.*

degree - 1. *daraja* pl. *-aat.* Last night the temperature dropped ten degrees. *l-baarẓa bil-leel inxufḍat darajat il-ẓaraara εašir darajaat.* 2. *šahaada* pl. *-aat.* I got my degree last year. *ʔaxaδit šahaadti bis-sana l-faatat.*

delay - *taʔxiir.* What's causing the delay? *šinu lli msabbib it-taʔxiir?*

to delay - 1. *ʔaxxar (i taʔxiir) t-, εaṭṭal (i taεṭiil) t-, εawwag (i taεwiig) t-.* I was delayed on the way. *ʔaani tεawwagit biṭ-ṭariiq.* 2. *ʔajjal (i taʔjiil) t-, ʔaxxar (i taʔxiir) t-.* We're going to delay the trip for a week. *raẓ-inʔajjil is-safra l-muddat isbuuε.*

delegate - *manduub* pl. *-iin.* The delegates will arrive tomorrow. *l-manduubiin raẓ-yooṣluun baačir.*

delegation - *wafid* pl. *wufuud, baεθa* pl. *-aat.* The delegation arrived yesterday. *l-wafid wuṣal il-baarẓa.*

deliberate - *mutaεammad, maqṣuud.* That was a deliberate insult. *haay čaanat ʔihaana maqṣuuda.*

deliberately - *εan qaṣid, εan εamid, qaṣṭani*.* I don't think he did it deliberately. *ma-aεtiqid sawwaaha εan qaṣid.*

delicate - 1. *ḍaεiif, naazik.* Her health is very delicate. *ṣiẓẓatha kulliš ḍaεiifa.* 2. *muẓrij.* That's a delicate question. *haaδa suʔaal muẓrij.* 3. *daqiiq.* Repairing watches is a delicate job. *taṣliiẓ is-saaεaat šaġla daqiiqa.* 4. *ẓassaas.* That's a delicate instrument. *haay ʔaala ẓassaasa.*

delicious - *laδiiδ.* This is delicious candy. *haaδi ẓalawiyyaat laδiiδa.*

delighted - *masruur, farẓaan, mkayyif.* I was delighted to see him. *činit farẓaan ib-šoofta.*

delightful - *laṭiif, badiiε, raaʔiε.* It was a delightful evening. *čaanat is-sahra laṭiifa.*

to **deliver** - **1.** *sallam (i tasliim) t-, waṣṣal (i tawṣiil) t-.* We'll deliver it to you tomorrow. *raz-insallmak-iyyaaha baačir.* -- Please deliver these packages to my house. *ʔarjuuk waṣṣil har-rizam il-beeti.* **2.** *wazzaƐ (i tawziiƐ) t-.* How often is the mail delivered here? *čam marra yitwazzaƐ il-bariid ihnaa?* **3.** *wallad (i tawliid) t-.* The doctor only charged 5 dinars to deliver the baby. *ṭ-ṭabiib ʔaxaδ xams idnaaniir bass il-tawliid iṭ-ṭifil.*

delivery - **1.** *tasliim* pl. *-aat.* I'll pay you on delivery. *ʔadfaƐ-lak Ɛind it-tasliim.* **2.** *tawziiƐ.* There's no mail delivery today. *ma-aku tawziiƐ bariid il-yoom.*

demand - *ṭalab* pl. *-aat.* There's a big demand for fresh fruit. *ʔaku hwaaya ṭalab Ɛala l-fawaakih it-taaza.* -- The library can't supply the demand for books. *l-maktaba ma-tigdar toofi ṭ-ṭalab Ɛal-kutub.* -- Their demands never cease. *ṭalabaathum ma-tixlaṣ.*

**This job makes heavy demands on my time. *haay iš-šağla maaxδa waqti kulla.*

in demand - *maṭluub, Ɛalee ṭalab.* This model is very much in demand and is sold out. *haaδa l-muudeel Ɛalee ṭalab ihwaaya w-nifaδ.*

to demand - *ṭilab (u ṭalub), ṭaalab (u muṭaalaba).* He's demanding more money. *da-yiṭlub ifluus ʔakθar.*

democracy - *dimuuqraaṭiyya.*

democratic - *dimuuqraaṭi**.

to **demolish** - *haddam (i tahdiim) t-.* The workers demolished the building. *l-Ɛummaal haddimaw il-binaaya.*

demon - *jinni* pl. *jinuun* coll. *jinn.*

to **demonstrate** - **1.** *raawa (i truuwi), bayyan (i tabyiin).* Now I'm going to demonstrate to you how the machine works. *hassa raz-araawiikum išloon tištuğul il-makiina.* **2.** *tẓaahar (a taẓaahur).* There is a group of students demonstrating in front of the embassy. *ʔaku jamaaƐa mniṭ-ṭullaab da-yitẓaahruun giddaam is-safaara.*

demonstration - *muẓaahara* pl. *-aat.* There was a demonstration in the street yesterday. *čaan aku muẓaahara biš-šaariƐ il-baarza.*

den - **1.** *mağaara* pl. *-aat.* There's a fox den over there. *ʔaku mağaara maal θaƐlab ihnaak.* **2.** *Ɛariin* pl. *Ɛurun.* We found a lion's den, but the lion wasn't there. *ligeena Ɛariin ʔasad, laakin il-ʔasad ma-čaan ihnaak.*

denial - *ʔinkaar.* Nobody believed his denial of the charge. *mazzad ṣaddag inkaara lit-tuhma.*

dense - **1.** *kaθiif.* We drove through a dense fog. *siqna b-ẓabaab kaθiif.* **2.** *baliid* pl. *-iin, buladaaʔ; ğabi* pl. *ʔağbiyaaʔ.* Most of the time he's very dense. *b-ʔakθar il-zaalaat huwwa hwaaya baliid.*

dent - *ṭaƐja* pl. *-aat, daƐma* pl. *-aat.* There's a new dent in the fender of my car. *ʔaku ṭaƐja jdiida bil-čaamullуğ maal sayyaarti.*

to dent - *ṭiƐaj (a ṭaƐij) n-, diƐam (a daƐim).* The bumper was badly dented. *d-daƐƐaamiyya čaanat maṭƐuuja ṭaƐja qawwiyya.*

dentist - *ṭabiib (*pl. *ʔaṭibbaaʔ) ʔasnaan.* Is there a good dentist around here? *ʔaku ṭabiib ʔasnaan zeen ihnaa?*

to **deny** - **1.** *nikar (u ʔinkaar).* He denies having been a member of that party. *yinkur kawna Ɛuδu b-hal-zizib.* **2.** *rifaẓ (u rafuẓ) n-.* I couldn't deny him such a small favor. *ma-gdarit arfuẓ-la maƐruuf ṣğayyir miθil haaδa.*

to **depart from** - **1.** *xiraj (u xuruuj) Ɛala.* You're not allowed to depart from standard procedure. *maa masmuuz-lak tuxruj Ɛala niẓaam il-muttabaƐ.* **2.** *ğaadar (i muğaadara), tirak (u tarik).* The train departed from the station at six o'clock. *l-qiṭaar tirak il-mazaṭṭa s-saaƐa sitta.*

department - **1.** *qisim* pl. *ʔaqsaam.* Which department does he work in. *b-ʔay qisim yištuğul?* **2.** *wizaara* pl. *-aat.* This is a matter for the Department of State. *haay masʔala itxuṣṣ wizaarat il-xaarijiyya.*

departure - *safar.* The departure is scheduled for three o'clock. *s-safar itqarrar is-saaƐa tlaaθa.*

to **depend** - **1.** *Ɛtimad (i Ɛtimaad).* Can I depend on him? *ʔagdar aƐtimid Ɛalee?* **2.** *twaqqaf (a tawaqquf).* That depends on the circumstances. *haaδi titwaqqaf Ɛaẓ-ẓuruuf.*

dependent - *mittikil, miƐtimid.* I'm financially dependent on him. *maaliyyan ʔaani mittikil Ɛalee.*

**How many dependents do you have? *čam waazid itƐiil?*

to **deport** - *ʔabƐad (i ʔibƐaad) n-, saffar (i tasfiir).* They deported him. *ʔabƐidoo.*

to **depose** - *xilaƐ (a xaliƐ) n-, Ɛizal (i Ɛazil) n-Ɛan.* They want to depose the king. *yirduun yxilƐuun il-malik.*

deposit - **1.** *taʔmiin* pl. *-aat, Ɛarabuun* pl. *-aat.* We'll lay it aside for you, if you leave a deposit. *niztufuẓ-lak biiha ʔiδa tzuṭṭ Ɛarabuun.* -- I had to pay five fils deposit for the bottle. *ẓṭarreet adfaƐ xams ifluus taʔmiinaat Ɛal-buṭil.* **2.** *rawaasib.* They've just discovered a rich deposit of iron in the north. *hassa ktišfaw rawaasib ğaniyya maal l-zadiid biš-šimaal.*

to deposit - *waddaƐ (i tawdiiƐ), ʔawdaƐ (i ʔiidaaƐ).* I'm going to deposit some money in the bank. *raz-awaddiƐ išwayya fluus bil-þang.*

to **depress** - *qubaẓ (u qabuẓ) nafis, zizan (i zuzin).* His letters always depress me. *makaatiiba tuqbuẓ nafsi daaʔiman.*

depressed - *kaʔiib, zaziin.* He's been very depressed lately. *huwwa kulliš kaʔiib bil-ʔayyaam il-ʔaxiira.*

depressing - *muqbiẓ lin-nafis.*

depression - **1.** *kasaad.* We lost all our money in the depression. *xsarna kull ifluusna bil-kasaad.* **2.** *hamm, ğamm, zuzin.* No one can bring him out of his depression. *mazzad yigdar yfarrij Ɛan hamma.*

to **deprive** - *ziram (u zirmaan) n-.* I wouldn't want to deprive you of your cigarettes. *ma-ariid azarmak min jigaayrak.* -- They were deprived of all their rights. *nzirmaw min kull zuquuqhum.*

depth - *Ɛumuq* pl. *ʔaƐmaaq, ğumij* pl. *ğmuuj.* The depth of the lake has never been measured. *Ɛumuq hal-buzayra ʔabadan ma-yinqaas.*

deputy - *naaʔib* pl. *nuwwaab.* He's the deputy from our district. *huwwa n-naaʔib min manṭiqatna.*

chamber of deputies - *majlis (*pl. *majaalis) nuwwaab.*

to **derail** - *ʔaxraj (i ʔixraaj) Ɛan il-xaṭṭ.* The saboteurs derailed the train. *l-muxarribiin ʔaxrijaw il-qiṭaar Ɛan il-xaṭṭ.*

derrick - **1.** *burij* pl. *bruuj, ʔabraaj.* They left the derrick up after they struck oil. *tirkaw il-burij ib-mazalla baƐad-ma xiraj in-nafuṭ.* **2.** *slink* pl. *-aat.* They set up a derrick on the dock to unload boat cargo. *nuṣbaw islink Ɛar-raṣiif zatta yfarriğuun zumuulat is-sifiina.*

dervish - *daarwiiš* pl. *daraawiiš.*

to **descend** - **1.** *nizal (i nuzuul), hubaṭ (u hubuuṭ), nzidar (i nzidaar).* I'd never have thought she'd descend so low. *ʔabadan ma-tṣawwaritha tinzil il-hal-mustawa.* -- He's descended from a prominent family. *huwwa minzidir min Ɛaaʔila Ɛariiqa.* **2.** *nizal (i).* His relatives descended on him. *garaayba nizlaw Ɛalee.*

descendent - *δurriyya* pl. *-aat, saliil* pl. *sulaala.* This is a picture of Abu Khalil with all his descendents. *haay ṣuurat ʔabu xaliil wiyya kull δurriita.*

to **describe** - *wuṣaf (u waṣuf).* He described it accurately. *wṣafha b-ẓabuṭ.*

description - *waṣuf* pl. *ʔawṣaaf.* Can you give me a detailed description? *tigdar tinṭiini waṣuf tafṣiili?*

desert - *ṣazraaʔ* pl. *ṣazaari.* They crossed the desert in twenty days. *qiṭƐaw iṣ-ṣazraaʔ ib-Ɛisriin yoom.*

to desert - **1.** *tirak (u tarik).* Don't desert me now! *la-titrukni hassa!* **2.** *hijar (u hajir, hijraan), Ɛaaf (u Ɛoof).* He deserted his wife and children. *hijar zawijta w-ʔawlaada.* **3.** *hirab (u harab, huruub), farr (u farr, firaar).* The soldiers deserted in droves. *j-junuud hirbaw ib-ʔaƐdaad.*

deserted - *mahjuur.* After a long march they came to a deserted village. *baƐad mašya ṭwiila wuṣlaw ʔila qarya mahjuura.*

to **deserve** - *stazaqq (i stizqaaq), staahal (i).* Such a good worker deserves higher pay. *miθla waazid šaağuul yistaziqq raatib ʔaƐla.*

design - **1.** *taṣmiim* pl. *taṣaamiim, taxṭiiṭ* pl. *-aat.* He is working on the design for a new house. *da-yištuğuḷ ib-taṣmiim beet jidiid.* **2.** *naqiš* pl. *nuquuš, rasim* pl. *rusuum.* The tablecloth has a simple design. *n-naqiš illi Ɛala ğaṭa l-meez basiiṭ.*

to design - *ṣammam (i taṣmiim), faṣṣal (i tafṣiil).* She designs her own clothes. *hiyya tṣammim ihduumha b-iideeha.*

desirable - **1.** *marğuub bii.* A change would be very desirable now. *t-tağyiir fadd šii kulliš marğuub bii hassa.* **2.** *marğuub.* This is a very desirable neighborhood for a hotel. *haay manṭiqa marğuuba* *il-binaa? findiq biiha.*

desire - *rağba* pl. *-aat.* My desires are easily satisfied. *rağbaati mumkin titzaqqaq ib-suhuula.*

desk - *meez* pl. *-aat, myuuza, minǒada* pl. *manaaǒid.* This desk is too small for me. *hal-meez kulliš işğayyir ʕalayya.*

information desk - *maktab* (pl. *makaatib*) *istiʕlaamaat.* Ask at the information desk over there. *?is?al ib-maktab l-istiʕlaamaat.*

desolate - *muuziš.* This must be a desolate place in winter. *haaǒa laazim ykuun makaan muuziš biš-šita.*

despair - *ya?is, qunuuṭ.* She was about to commit suicide in her despair. *raadat tintizir min ya?isha.*

desperate - *yaa?is, m?ayyis, may?uus min, mistaktil, bila ?amal.* She's in a desperate situation. *zaalatha yaa?sa.* -- The situation's desperate. *l-waǒiʕ may?uus minna.*

to **despise** - *ztiqar (i ztiqaar).* I despise that man. *?aani ?aztiqir haaǒa r-rajjaal.*

dessert - *zalaa, zalawiyyaat.* You forgot to bring the dessert. *niseet itjiib il-zalawiyyaat.*

destination - *zadd.* My destination is Baghdad. *?aani zaddi l-bağdaad.*

destiny - *maṣiir* pl. *maṣaa?ir.*

to **destroy** - 1. *tilaf (i talif) n-.* All my papers were destroyed in the fire. *kull ?awraaqi ntilfat bil-zariiq.* 2. *dammar (u tadmiir) t-, xarrab (u taxriib) t-.* The earthquake destroyed a third of the town. *z-zilzaal dammar θilθ il-madiina.*

destroyer - *mudammira* pl. *-aat.*

destruction - *taxriib, damaar.* The fire caused a lot of destruction. *n-naar sabbibat ihwaaya damaar.*

detail - *tafṣiil* pl. *-aat, tafaaṣiil.* Today's paper gives more details. *jariidat il-yoom biiha tafaaṣiil ?akθar.*

in detail - *bit-tafṣiil.* He described the incident in detail. *wuṣaf il-zaadiθ bit-tafṣiil.*

detailed - *mfaṣṣal.* He gave me a detailed report. *qaddam-li taqriir imfaṣṣal.*

to **detain** - *zijaz (i zajiz) n-.* The police detained him for questioning. *š-šurṭa zijzata lit-tazqiiq.* 2. *?axxar (i ta?xiir) t-.* Authorities detained the plane a half hour to look for a bomb. *ṣ-ṣulṭaat ?axxirat iṭ-ṭiyyaara nuṣṣ saaʕa lil-baziθ ʕan il-qumbula.*

determination - *taṣmiim, ʕazim.* He showed definite determination. *huwwa bayyan ʕazim ?akiid.*

determined - *muṣammim, muṣirr.* She's determined to have her way. *hiyya mṣammima ʕala ?an itsawwi lli triida* or *hiyya muṣirra ʕala ra?iiha.*

to **detour** - *laaf (u loof), ltaaf (a ltifaaf), ltaff (a ltifaaf).* Rashid St. is closed at the Defence building and we had to detour by way of Waziria St. *šaariʕ ir-rašiid masduud yamm id-difaaʕ w-iǒṭarreena nluuf ʕala šaariʕ il-waziiriyya.*

deuce - *θneen, ?abu-θneen.* He held three deuces and two kings. *čaan ʕinda tlaθ iθneenaat w-šaaybeen.*

to **develop** - 1. *ġisal (i ġasil) n-.* Could you develop this film for me? *mumkin tiġsil-li hal-filim?* 2. *ṭṭawwar (a taṭawwur).* The situation's developed a lot in the last week. *l-mawgif ihwaaya ṭṭawwar bil-isbuuʕ il-?axiir.* 3. *ʕammar (i taʕmiir) t-, zassan (i tazsiin) t-.* The government is developing this area. *l-zukuuma da-tʕammir hal-manṭiqa.*

development - 1. *taṭawwur* pl. *-aat.* Do you know anything about the latest developments? *tuʕruf ?ay šii ʕan ?aaxir it-taṭawwuraat?* 2. *?iʕmaar.* The development plan requires more money. *xiṭṭat il-?iʕmaar tiztaaj ?ila fluus ?akθar.*

device - 1. *tadbiir* pl. *tadaabiir, xiṭṭa* pl. *xiṭaṭ.* That's an ingenious device for getting his approval. *haaǒi fadd tadbiir baariʕ l-istizṣaal muwaafaqta.* 2. *jihaaz* pl. *?ajhiza.* He invented a device to peel potatoes. *xtiraʕ jihaaz il-tagšiir il-puteeta.*

devil - *šeeṭaan* pl. *šayaaṭiin, ?ibliis* pl. *?abaaliis, ?abaalisa.*

to **devote** - 1. *karras (i tkirris, takriis), xaṣṣaṣ (i txiṣṣiṣ, taxṣiiṣ).* He devoted all his spare time to study. *karras kull wakit faraağa lid-diraasa.* 2. *wihab (i wahib) n-.* He devoted his life to science. *wihab zayaata lil-ʕilim.*

to be devoted - *barr (u birr).* He's very devoted to his mother. *huwwa kulliš baarr ib-?umma.*

dew - *nida.*

diabetes - *maraǒ is-sukkar.*

diagonal - *munzarif, qiraaj.* Now draw a diagonal line. *hassa ?irsim xaṭṭ munzarif.*

diagonally - *qiraaj.* You have to park diagonally here. *laazim itṣuff is-sayyaara qiraaj ihnaa.*

dial - *quruṣ* pl. *?aqraaṣ.* The dial on the telephone is broken. *qurṣ it-talifoon maksuur.* -- The dial on my watch is dirty. *qurṣ saaʕti waṣix.*

to dial - *farr (u farr) n- numra, daar (u deer) n- numra.* She dialed the wrong number. *farrat in-nimra l-ġalaṭ.*

dialect - *lahja* pl. *-aat.* Many dialects are spoken here. *hwaaya lahjaat tinziči hnaa.*

diameter - *quṭur daa?ira* pl. *?aqṭaar dawaa?ir.*

diamond - 1. *?almaasa* pl. *-aat* coll. *?almaas.* This ring has four diamonds. *hal-mihbas bii ?arbaʕ ?almaasaat.* 2. *maʕiin* pl. *-aat.* The new traffic signs are diamond-shaped. *?išaaraat il-muruur ij-jidiida ʕala šikil il-maʕiin.* 3. *dinaari**. I've got a diamond flush. *ʕindi flooš dinaari* or *ʕindi flooš baqlaawa.*

diarrhea - *?ishaal.*

dice - see under **die**.

to **dictate** - 1. *?amla (i ?imlaa?), malla (i ?imlaa?).* He's dictating a letter. *huwwa da-yimli maktuub.* -- He's dictating a letter to his secretary. *da-ymalli kitaab ʕas-sikirtaara maalta.* 2. *t?ammar (a ta?ammur).* I can't stand anyone dictating to me! *?aani ma-aqbal waazid yit?ammar ʕalayya.*

dictation - *?imlaa?.* I gave my class a dictation today. *nṭeet ṣaffi ?imlaa? il-yoom.*

dictator - *diktaatoor* pl. *-iyyiin.*

dictatorial - *diktaatoori**.

dictatorship - *diktaatooriyya.*

die - 1. *qaalab* pl. *qawaalib.* The die for that part is broken. *qaalab hal-?aala maksuur.* 2. *zaar* pl. *-aat.* They play chuck-a-luck with three dice. *yilʕabuun lagaw b-iθlaθ zaaraat.*

**The die is cast. *quǒiya l-?amr.*

to die - 1. *maat (u moot), twaffa (a tawiffi, wafaat).* He died today at two o'clock. *twaffa l-yoom saaʕa θinteen.* 2. *ǒibal (a ǒabil).* The tree is dying. *š-šajara da-tiǒbal.* 3. *nṭufa (i nṭufaa?), ṭaffa (i ṭṭiffi) t-.* The motor died. *l-makiina nṭufat.*

**I'm dying to find out what he said. *mazruug bass ?ariid aʕruf huwwa š-gaal.*

to die away - *tlaaša (a talaaši).* The noise of the train died away in the distance. *tlaaša ṣoot il-qiṭaar lamman ibtiʕad.*

to die down - *xumad (i xamud), nṭufa (i).* We let the fire die down. *trakna n-naar tixmid* or *trakna n-naar tinṭufi wazidha.* -- The excitement will die down in a few days. *hal-hiyaaj raz-yixmid ib-kam yoom.*

to die laughing - *ṭagg (u ṭagg) imniǒ-ǒizik, maat (u moot) imniǒ-ǒizik.* I just about died laughing when I heard that. *ṭaggeet imniǒ-ǒizik min ismaʕitha.*

to die off - *ǒmazall (i ǒmizlaal).* The older generation is dying off. *j-jiil il-qadiim gaʕad yiǒmazill.*

diet - 1. *rajiim.* I have to go on a diet. *laazim asawwi rajiim.* 2. *?akil.* For weeks our diet consisted of nothing but fish. *xilaal ʕiddat asaabiiʕ ?akilna ma-čaan ġeer simač.*

to diet - *sawwa (i taswiya) rajiim.* I've been dieting for a month, but I still haven't lost any weight. *?aani msawwi rajiim ṣaar-li šahar w-ma-fqadit šii min wazni.*

to **differ** - 1. *xtilaf (i xtilaaf).* They differ in every respect. *yixtalfuun ib-kullši.* -- I beg to differ with you. *?aani ?axtilif wiyyaak* or *?aani ma-awaafqak.* 2. *tǒaarab (a taǒaarub).* Opinions differ on this topic. *l-?aaraa? mitǒaarba b-hal-mawǒuuʕ.*

difference - 1. *xtilaaf* pl. *-aat, fariq* pl. *furuuq.* Can you show me the difference? *tigdar itbayyin-li l-fariq?* — It makes no difference when you come. *ma-aku fariq išwakit-ma tiji.* 2. *xilaaf* pl. *-aat.* They ironed out their differences. *ṣaffaw xilaafaathum.*

to make a difference - *firaq (u fariq).* Does it make any difference to you if I write in pencil? *tifruq-lak ?iǒa ?aktib ib-qalam riṣaaṣ?*

different - 1. *muxtalif.* The brothers are very different. *l-?uxwa kulliš mixtalfiin.* 2. *mitǒaarub, mitbaayin.* The two ideas are different. *l-fikirteen mitbaayna.* 3. *ġeer, ?aaxar.* That's a different matter. *haaǒa ġeer mawǒuuʕ* or *haay mas?ala tixtilif.*

differently - *ġeer šikil, b-šikil ?aaxar, b-šikil muxtalif.* I think differently about it. *?aani ?anǒur-ilha ġeer šikil.*

difficult - **1.** *ṣaεub.* It's difficult to understand what he means. *ṣaεub tifham iš-yaεni.* -- That's a difficult assignment. *haaδi muhimma ṣaεba.* **2.** *mitṣaεεub.* He's difficult (to deal with). *huwwa mitṣaεεub.*

difficulty - *ṣuεuub* pl. *-aat, ṣiεaab.* He overcame the difficulties. *tġallab εala ṣ-ṣuεuubaat.*

to **dig** - *ħufar (u ħafur) n-.* Dig the hole a little deeper. *ʔiħfur il-ħufra šwayya ʔaġmaj.*

to dig up - *nibaš (i nabiš) n-.* The dog dug up a bone he had buried in the ground. *č-čalib nibaš εaḍum čaan daafna bil-gaaε.*

**Dig up the rose bush. *ʔiħfur daayir εirg il-warid w-ṭallεa.*

to **digest** - *hiḍam (u haḍum) n-.* Nuts are hard for us to digest. *č-čarazaat ṣaεub εaleena nihḍumha.*

digestion - *haḍum.*

dignified - *waquur.* His father was a dignified old gentlemen. *ʔabuu čaan fadd šeex waquur.*

dim - *miεtim, xaafit, ḍaεiif.* I couldn't see anything in the dim light. *ma-gdarit ašuuf šii biḍ-ḍuwa l-miεtim.*

to dim - *xaffaḍ (i taxfiiḍ) t-.* Dim your lights! *xaffiḍ ḍawaak!*

dimple - *raṣεa* pl. *-aat.* She has a nice dimple. *εidha raṣεa ħilwa.*

dinar - *diinaar* pl. *danaaniir.*

to **dine** - *tεašša (a taεašši).* They're dining with us tonight. *da-yitεaššuun wyaana hal-leela.* -- We dine out occasionally. *ʔiħna ʔaħyaanan nitεašša barra.*

dining room - *ġurfat* (pl. *ġuraf*) *ʔakil, ġurfat* (pl. *ġuraf*) *ṭaεaam.* Bring another chair into the dining room. *jiib kursi laax il-ġurfat il-ʔakil.*

dinner - **1.** *εaša* pl. *-aayaat.* Dinner is ready. *l-εaša jaahiz.* **2.** *εaziima* pl. *εazaayim.* We're giving a dinner in his honor. *raħ-insawwi εaziima εala šarafa.*

to have dinner - *tεašša (a taεašši).* We have dinner at six o'clock every day. *nitεašša s-saaεa sitta yoomiyya.*

dip - **1.** *ħadra* pl. *-aat, nazla* pl. *-aat.* There's a dip in the road ahead of us. *ʔaku ħadra biṭ-ṭariiq giddaamna.* **2.** *ġaṭṭa* pl. *-aat, ṭamsa* pl. *-aat.* There's nothing like a dip in the river to refresh you on a hot day. *ma-aku miθil il-ġaṭṭa biš-šaṭṭ tiniεšak ib-yoom ħaarr.*

to dip - *ṭammas (u ṭṭummus, taṭmiis).* I dipped my finger into the water. *ṭammasit ʔiṣbaεi bil-maay.*

direct - **1.** *mubaašir.* There is no direct route. *ma-aku ṭariiq mubaašir* or ***ma-aku ṭariiq yiṭlaε raʔsan.* **2.** *tamaaman.* It's the direct opposite of what we expected. *hiyya εakis-ma twaqqaεna tamaaman.*

to direct - **1.** *ʔumar (u ʔamur).* He directed us to follow the old regulations. *ʔumarna ʔan nitbaε it-taεliimaat il-qadiima.* **2.** *wajjah (i tawjiih).* A policeman is directing the traffic. *šurṭi da-ywajjih il-muruur.* **3.** *dalla (i tdilli).* Can you direct me to the post office? *tigdar itdalliini εala markaz il-bariid.* **4.** *xarraj (i taxriij), ʔaxraj (i ʔixraaj).* Who is directing the play? *minu da-yxarrij it-tamθiiliyya?*

direct current - *tayyaar mubaašir, diisi.*

direction - **1.** *jiha* pl. *-aat, ttijaah* pl. *-aat.* Which direction did he go? *l-ʔay jiha raaħ?* **2.** *ʔiršaad* pl. *-aat.* His directions are clear. *ʔiršaadaata waaḍħa.* **3.** *ʔidaara, ʔišraaf.* They have made great progress under his direction. *xiṭaw xaṭwaat waasεa taħat ʔišraafa* or *ħaqqiqaw taqaddum kabiir taħat ʔidaarta.* **4.** *taεliim* pl. *-aat.* The government issued directions concerning the election. *l-ħukuuma ʔaṣdirat taεliimaat titεallaq bil-intixaabaat.*

directly - *mubaašaratan, raʔsan.* Let's go directly to the hotel. *xalli nruuħ lil-ʔuteel raʔsan.* -- Our house is directly opposite the store. *beetna muqaabil il-maxzan mubaašaratan.*

dirham - *dirhim* pl. *daraahim.*

dirt - **1.** *traab* pl. *ʔatriba.* How many trucks of dirt do we need to fill this in? *čam loori traab niħtaaj il-dafin haay?* **2.** *zimiij.* The dirt in the flower pots should be replaced this year. *z-zimiij b-isnaadiin il-warid laazim yitbaddal has-sana.* **3.** *wuṣax.* There is some dirt on your shirt. *ʔaku šwayya wuṣax ib-θoobak.*

dirt-cheap - *ʔaxu l-balaaš, ʔuxt il-balaaš.* I bought the car dirt-cheap. *štireet is-sayyaara ʔuxt il-balaaš.*

dirty - **1.** *waṣix.* The floor is dirty. *l-gaaε waṣxa.* **2.** *baδiiʔ.* Most of his stories are pretty dirty. *muεḍam quṣaṣa baδiiʔa.* **3.** *daniiʔ, ħaqiir.* He played a dirty trick on us. *sawwa biina nukta daniiʔa.*

**He gave us a dirty look. *niḍarna b-izdiraaʔ* or *baawaεna b-iħtiqaar.*

**That is a dirty lie. *haay čiδba qadra.*

to dirty - *waṣṣax (i tawṣiix, twiṣṣix).* Don't dirty the carpet with your muddy shoes. *la-twaṣṣix iz-zuuliyya b-qundartak l-imṭayyna.*

disability - *εajiz.* He can't play soccer because of a disability. *ma-yigdar yilεab kurat il-qadam ib-sabab il-εajiz.*

to **disable** - *sawwa (i) εajiz.* The auto accident disabled him. *ħaadiθ is-sayyaara sawwaa εajiz.*

to be disabled - *nṣaab (a) ib-εajiz.* The soldier was permanently disabled. *j-jundi nṣaab ib-εajiz daaʔim.*

disadvantage - *maḍaar.* You'll have to weigh the advantages and disadvantages before you decide. *laazim itwaazin been il-maḍaar wil-manaafiε gabul-ma tqarrir.*

to **disagree** - **1.** *xtilaf (i xtilaaf).* I disagree with you. *ʔaani ʔaxtilif wiyyaak.* **2.** *xaalaf (i muxaalafa).* I disagree with the method. *ʔaani ʔaxaalif iṭ-ṭariiqa* or *ʔaani ma-aʔayyid haṭ-ṭariiqa.* **3.** *ma-waalam (i muwaalama).* Melons disagree with me. *l-baṭṭiix ma-ywaalimni* or ***ʔaani muu ṣuħba wiyya l-baṭṭiix.*

to **disappear** - *xtifa (i xtifaaʔ).* He disappeared in the crowd. *xtifa bil-xabṣa.* **2.** *tlaaša (a talaaši).* The river disappears in the desert. *n-nahar yitlaaša biṣ-ṣaħraaʔ.*

to **disappoint** - *xaab (i xayabaan) ʔamal.* I was very much disappointed. *xaab ʔamali hwaaya.*

disappointment - *xeebat* (pl. *-aat*) *ʔamal.* It was a great disappointment. *čaanat xeebat ʔamal čibiira.*

to **disapprove** - *stankar (i stinkaar).* He disapproves of our plans. *yistankir xuṭaṭna.*

to **disarm** - *jarrad (i tajriid) t- mnis-silaaħ.* They disarmed the prisoners immediately. *jarridaw il-ʔasra mnis-silaaħ bil-ħaal.*

disarmament - *nazε is-silaaħ.*

disaster - *nakba* pl. *-aat, kaariθa* pl. *kawaariθ, muṣiiba* pl. *maṣaayib.* The airplane crash was a great disaster. *suquuṭ iṭ-ṭiyyaara čaan kaariθa čibiira.*

disastrous - *murwiε, muriiε.* The collision was disastrous. *t-taṣaadum čaan kulliš murwiε.*

discharge - *tasriiħ* pl. *-aat.* Your discharge is in November. *tasriiħak ib-tišriin iθ-θaani.*

to discharge - **1.** *fuṣal (u faṣul) n-, ṭirad (u ṭarid) n-.* The company discharged him for his carelessness. *š-šarika fuṣlata il-ʔihmaala.* **2.** *sarraħ (i tasriiħ) t-.* You're going to be discharged when the war ends. *raħ-titsarraħuun lamma tintihi l-ħarub.* **3.** *xallaṣ (i taxliiṣ), ʔanha (i ʔinhaaʔ), ʔadda (i tʔiddi).* He discharges his responsibilities promptly. *yxalliṣ waajibaata b-surεa.* **4.** *farraġ (i tafriiġ) t-, nazzal (i tanziil) t-.* The ship discharged its cargo on the dock. *s-safiina farrġat šuħnatha εar-raṣiif.* **5.** *ḍiεaf (a ḍuεuf).* Turn off the lights, don't discharge the battery. *ṭuffi l-uḍwiya, la-tiḍεif il-baatri.* **6.** *ṭilaε (a ṭuluuε).* The hospital discharged him after 10 days. *l-mustašfa ṭilεata baεad εaširt iyyaam.*

discipline - *ḍabuṭ, ṭaaεa, niḍaam.* The teacher can't maintain discipline in class. *l-ʔustaaδ ma-yigdar yħaafuḍ εaḍ-ḍabuṭ ib-ṣaffa.*

to discipline - *jaaza (i mujaazaa).* The lieutenant disciplined his troops for disobediance. *l-mulaazim jaaza j-jinuud il-εadam ṭaaεathum.*

to **disclose** - *kišaf (i kašif) εan, ʔaḍhar (i ʔiḍhaar).* The investigation disclosed new facts. *t-taħqiiq kišaf εan ħaqaayiq jidiida.*

to **disconnect** - *fiṣal (i faṣil) n-.* If we disconnect these two wires the lights will go out. *ʔiδa fiṣalna hal-waayreen tinṭufi l-ʔuḍwiya.*

discontented - *ma-raaḍi.* He's discontented in his present job. *huwwa ma-raaḍi b-šuġla l-ħaaliyya.*

to **discontinue** - *baṭṭal (i), waggaf (i), qiṭaε (a qaṭiε) n-.* We're going to discontinue mail service in this area. *raħ-inbaṭṭil xidmat il-bariid ib-hal-manṭiqa.*

discount - *xaṣum.* Can you get a discount on these books? *tigdar itħaṣṣil xaṣum εala hal-kutub?*

to **discourage** - *θabbaṭ (i taθbiiṭ) t- εaziima.* He did his best to discourage me from going. *ħaawal kullši ħatta yθabbuṭ εaziimti w-ma-aruuħ.* -- He gets discouraged easily. *yitθabbaṭ εaziimta b-suhuula.*

discouraging - *muθabbiṭ lil-ɛazim, ġeer mušajjiɛ.* The results are discouraging. *n-nataa?ij muθabbiṭa lil-ɛazim.*
to **discover** - *ktišaf (i ktišaaf).* Columbus discovered America. *kaloombis iktišaf ?amriika.*
discovery - *ktišaaf* pl. *-aat.* He made an important discovery in science. *ʒaqqaq iktišaaf muhimm bil-ɛilim.*
to **discuss** - *naaqaš (i munaaqaša), biʒaθ (a baʒiθ).* They discussed the subject from all sides. *naaqišaw il-mawḍuuɛ min kull in-nawaaʒi.* -- Discuss the matter with him. *?ibʒaθ il-mawḍuuɛ wiyyaa.*
discussion - *munaaqaša* pl. *-aat, baʒiθ.*
disease - *maraḍ* pl. *?amraaḍ.* This disease is contagious. *haaδa l-maraḍ muɛdi.*
to **disfigure** - *šawwah (i tašwiih) t-.* The injury disfigured his face. *j-jariʒ šawwah wujja.*
disgrace - *ɛaar, xizi, faḍiiʒa* pl. *faḍaayiʒ.* He brought disgrace on his family. *jaab il-xizi l-ɛaa?ilta.*
  to disgrace - *fuḍaʒ (a faḍiiʒa) n-.* She disgraced her family. *fuḍʒat ɛaa?ilatha.*
to **disguise** - *nakkar (i tankiir, tnikkir) t-.* He disguised himself to avoid capture. *tnakkar ʒatta yitjannab il-qabuḍ ɛalee.*
disguised - *mitnakkir.* Haroun al-Rashid had the habit of walking in the streets of Baghdad disguised as a merchant. *haaruun ir-rašiid čaanat ɛaadta yimši b-šawaariɛ baġdaad mitnakkir ka-taajir.*
disgust - *šmi?zaaz, taqazzuz.* He turned away in disgust. *daar wujja b-išmi?zaaz.*
  to disgust - *qazzaz (i taqziiz) t- nafis.* His conduct disgusts me. *taṣarrufaata tqazziz nafsi.*
  to be disgusted - *šmi?azz (i šmi?zaaz), tqazzaz (a taqazzuz).* I was disgusted by his conduct. *šmi?azzeet min taṣarrufaata.*
  **I'm disgusted with everything. *?aani baz?aan min kullši* or *ṭaafra ruuʒi min kullši.*
dish - **1.** *maaɛuun* pl. *mwaaɛiin, ṣaʒan* pl. *ṣuʒuun.* He dropped the dish. *waggaɛ il-maaɛuun.* -- I'd like a dish of ice cream. *?ariid maaɛuun doondirma.* **2.** *loon* (pl. *?alwaan*) *?akil.* I have a recipe for a new dish. *ɛindi waṣfa l-loon jidiid imnil-?akil.*
dishonest - *ġeer šariif, ġaššaaš, muu šariif.*
to **disinfect** - *ɛaqqam (i taɛqiim) t-, ṭahhar (i taṭhiir) t-.* Did you disinfect the wound? *ɛaqqamta lij-jariʒ?*
disinfectant - *muṭahhir, muɛaqqim.* I need a disinfectant. *?aʒtaaj muṭahhir.*
to **disinherit** - *ʒiram (a ʒirmaan) imnil-?iriθ.* His father threatened to disinherit him. *?abuu haddada b-ʒirmaana mnil-?iriθ.*
to **disintegrate** - *tʒallal (a taʒallul).* The empire disintegrated. *l-impiraaṭooriyya tʒallilat.*
dislike - *nufuur, karaaha, ɛadam maʒabba.* I couldn't conceal my dislike for him. *ma-gdarit aktim nufuuri minna.*
  to dislike - *ma-ʒabb (i ʒabb), nufar (u nafur) min.* I dislike that fellow. *ma-aʒibb haaδa r-rajjaal.*
to **dislocate** - *xilaɛ (a xaliɛ) n-.* He dislocated his shoulder. *xilaɛ čitfa.*
disloyal - *ġeer muxliṣ, xaayin.*
dismal - *ka?iib.* It's a dismal day today. *hal-yoom ka?iib* or **hal-yoom yuqbuḍ iṣ-ṣadir.*
to **dismiss** - **1.** *ṭirad (i ṭarid).* She was dismissed after two weeks. *nṭiradat wara sbuuɛeen.* **2.** *rufaḍ (u rafuḍ) n-.* The court dismissed the complaint. *l-maʒkama rufḍat iš-šakwa.* **3.** *ṣiraf (u ṣaruf) n-.* He dismissed the soldiers after an hour's drill. *ṣiraf ij-jinuud baɛad tadriib saaɛa.*
dispensary - *mustawṣif* pl. *-aat.*
display - *waajiha* pl. *-aat.* Have you seen the beautiful displays in the shops on Rashid St.? *šifit waajihaat il-maxaazin il-ʒilwa b-šaariɛ ir-rašiid?*
  on display - *maɛruuḍ.* The statute is on display at the museum. *t-timθaal maɛruuḍ bil-matʒaf.*
  to display - **1.** *raawa (i muraawaat), bayyan (i tabyiin), ?aḍhar (i ?iḍhaar).* He displayed great courage. *bayyan šajaaɛa faa?iqa.* -- There's no need to display your ignorance. *ma-aku ʒaaja tiḍhir jahlak.* **2.** *ɛiraḍ (u ɛariḍ) n-.* You can't display your fruit on the side walks of a main street. *ma-tigdar tuɛruḍ fawaakhak ɛar-raṣiif ib-šaariɛ ɛaamm.* **3.** *xalla (i txilli, taxliya), rifaɛ (a rafiɛ).* All the houses displayed flags. *kull il-ibyuut xallat iɛlaam.*
disposal - *?amur.* I'm at your disposal. *?aani taʒat ?amrak.* **2.** *taṣriif.* There's no garbage disposal plant in this village. *ma-aku maʒall taṣriif il-miyaah il-qaḍra b-hal-qarya.*
  **They agreed to put a car at my disposal. *waafqaw yxalluun sayyaara jawwa ?iidi.*
to **dispose** - *txallaṣ (a taxalluṣ).* They will leave as soon as they dispose of their furniture. *raʒ-yturkuun ?awwal-ma yitxallṣuun min ?aθaaθhum.*
disposition - *ṭabuɛ.* He has a poor disposition. *ṭabɛa muu zeen.*
to **disregard** - **1.** *himal (i ?ihmaal) n-.* If I were in your place, I'd disregard the letter. *loo b-makaanak, ahimla lil-maktuub.* **2.** *tġaaδa (a tġaaδi) ɛan.* We can't disregard his objections. *ma-nigdar nitġaaδa ɛan iɛtiraaḍaata.*
to **disrupt** - *giṭaɛ (a gaṭiɛ) n-.* Communications were disrupted by the storm. *l-muwaaṣilaat ingiṭɛat imnil-ɛaaṣifa.*
dissatisfied - *muu raaḍi.* You look dissatisfied. *ybayyin ɛaleek muu raaḍi.*
to **dissipate** - **1.** *baddad (i tabdiid) t-.* He dissipated his entire fortune. *baddad kull θaruuta.* **2.** *nqišaɛ (i nqišaaɛ).* We'd better wait until the fog dissipates a bit. *?aʒsan nintiḍir ?ila ?an yinqišiɛ iḍ-ḍabaab išwayya.*
  **He leads a dissipated life. *huwwa mušrif bil-malaδδaat.*
to **dissolve** - **1.** *δaab (u δawabaan), tʒallal (a taʒallul).* Salt dissolves in water. *l-miliʒ yδuub bil-ṃaay.* **2.** *δawwab (i taδwiib).* Dissolve the tablet in a glass of water. *δawwib il-quruṣ b-iglaaṣ ṃaay.*
distance - **1.** *masaafa* pl. *-aat, buɛad* pl. *?abɛaad.* The distance between Baghdad and Najaf is about 180 kilometers. *l-masaafa been baġdaad win-najaf ʒawaali miyya w-θmaaniin kiiloomatir.* **2.** *masaafa, biɛiid.* You can see the tower from a distance. *tigdar itšuuf il-burij min biɛiid.*
  to keep one's distance - *lizam (a lazim) ʒadd~, ḍibat (u ḍabut) ʒadd~.* He knows how to keep his distance. *yuɛruf ween yilzam ʒadda.*
distant - *min biɛiid.* She's a distant relative of mine. *hiyya garaaybi min ibɛiid.*
distinct - *waaḍiʒ, mbayyin, ḍaahir.* There's a distinct difference between the two. *?aku xtilaaf waaḍiʒ been il-?iθneen.*
distinctly - *b-wuḍuuʒ.* I told him distinctly not to come. *?aani fahhamta b-kull wuḍuuʒ ?an ma-yiji.*
to **distinguish** - **1.** *farzan (i tfirzin), mayyaz (i tamyiiz) t-.* I couldn't distinguish the features of his face in the dark. *ma-gdarit afarzin malaamiʒ wujja biḍ-ḍalma.* -- I could hardly distinguish one from the other. *b-ṣuɛuuba gdarit amayyiz ɛan baɛaḍhum.* **2.** *mayyaz (i tamyiiz), farraq (i tafriiq).* Can you distinguish between the two? *tigdar itfarriq been il-iθneen?* **3.** *?abraz (i ?ibraaz).* He distinguished himself by his courage. *?abraz nafsa b-šajaaɛta.* -- He's a distinguished soldier and statesman. *huwwa jundi w-rajul dawla baariz.*
distress - **1.** *šidda, ḍiiq.* The Red Crescent did everything possible to relieve the distress. *jamɛiyyat il-hilaal il-?aʒmar sawwat kull-ma mumkin lit-taxfiif imniš-šidda.* — The ship was in distress. *l-baaxira čaanat ib-ḍiiq.* **2.** *ġamm.* He caused his mother much distress. *sabbab il-?umma hwaaya ġamm.*
to **distribute** - *wazzaɛ (i tawziiɛ) t-, qassam (i taqsiim) t-.* The profits were evenly distributed. *l-?arbaaʒ itqassimat bit-tasaawi.*
district - **1.** *manṭiqa* pl. *manaaṭiq, naaʒiya* pl. *nawaaʒi.* This is a very poor district. *haaδi manṭiqa kulliš faqiira.* **2.** *qisim* pl. *?aqsaam, manṭiqa* pl. *manaaṭiq.* The city is divided into ten districts. *l-madiina mqassma ?ila ɛašir ?aqsaam.*
to **distrust** - *ma-wiθaq (i) b-.* I distrust him. *?aani ma-aθiq bii.*
to **disturb** - **1.** *?azɛaj (i ?izɛaaj), šawwaš (i tašwiiš).* Don't disturb the others! *la-tizɛij il-?aaxariin.* **2.** *qilaq (i qaliq).* The news disturbed me. *l-?axbaar qilqatni.* **3.** *xarbaṭ (u txurbuṭ).* Someone has disturbed my papers. *waaʒid xarbaṭ ?awraaqi.*
ditch - *saaqya* pl. *swaaqi.* The car got stuck in the ditch. *s-sayyaara ṭumsat bis-saaqya.*
to **dive** - **1.** *δabb (i δabb) zarig.* Do you know how to dive? *tuɛruf išloon itδibb zarig?* **2.** *ġaaṣ (u ġooṣ).* They dive for pearls in Kuwait. *yġuuṣuun min ?ajil il-lu?lu? bil-kuweet.*
diver - *ġawwaaṣ* pl. *-iin.* They hired a diver to inspect the wreck of the ship. *sta?jiraw ġawwaaṣ*

il-faʒiʂ ʒiʈaam is-safiina.
**He's a good diver. huwwa yðibb ʒarig ʒeen.

to **divide** - 1. qisam (i qasim) n-, qassam (i taqsiim) t-. Divide the total by four. ʔiqsim il-majmuuɛ ɛala ʔarbaɛa. -- The book is divided into two parts. l-iktaab minqisim ʔila qismeen. -- Divide the group into two teams. qassim ij-jamaaɛa ʔila fariiqeen. 2. tfarraɛ (a tafarruɛ), tfarraq (a tafarruq). The road divides at the end of the village. ʈ-ʈariiq yitfarraɛ ib-ʈaraf il-qarya. 3. qaasam (i muqaasama). I divide the profits between me and my partner. ʔaani ʔaqaasim il-ʔarbaaʒ beeni w-been šariiki.

division - 1. qisim pl. ʔaqsaam. He works in another division. yištuġuḷ ib-qisim laax. 2. firqa pl. firaq. Ten divisions were destroyed. ɛašir firaq itdammrat. 3. qisma, taqsiim. When are you going to learn division? šwakit raz-titɛallam l-qisma?

divorce - ʈalaag. She's suing for divorce. gaayma b-daɛwat ʈalaag.
  to **divorce** - ʈallag (i ʈaʈliig, ʈʈillig) t-. It's been several years since he divorced his wife. ʂaar-la ɛiddat sanawaat min ʈallag marta.

divorced - mʈallag. She's divorced. hiyya mʈallga.
**He's divorced. huwwa čaan mitʒawwaj w-ʈallag.

dizzy - daayix. I feel dizzy. ʔaani daayix or **ʔašɛur ib-dooxa.

to **do** - 1. sawwa (i taswiya), ɛamal (i ɛamal). Let him do it by himself. xalli ysawwiiha b-nafsa. -- What are we going to do now? š-raz-insawwi hassa? -- Do it the way I do. sawwiiha biʈ-ʈariiqa lli ʔasawwii. -- I don't do things like that. ʔaani ma-asawwi hiiči ʔašyaaʔ. 2. qaam (u qiyaam) b-, sawwa (i). He can't do this work because he has a hernia. ma-yigdar yquum ib-haš-šuġul li-ʔan ɛinda fatiq. -- Can I do anything for you? ʔagdar aquum-lak ib-ʔay xidma? 3. kaffa (i kifaaya). This meat will have to do for four people. hal-lazam laazim ykaffi l-ʔarbaɛ ʔašxaaʂ. -- That will do for now. haaða ykaffi hassa. 4. ʂilaz (a ʂalaaz), nifaɛ (a nafiɛ), faad (i faaʔida). This screwdriver won't do. had-darnafiis ma-yiʂlaz. 5. giða (i gaði). He did five years in jail. giða xams isniin bis-sijin. 6. xaʂʂ (u). That has nothing to do with the matter. haaða ma-yxuʂʂ il-mawðuuɛ or **haaða maa ʔila ɛalaaqa bil-mawðuuɛ. 7. ʈallaɛ (i ʈaʈliiɛ). This car won't do more than forty miles per hour. has-sayyaara ma-ʈʈaliiɛ ġeer ʔarbaɛiin miil bis-saaɛa. 8. rattab (i tartiib). It takes her an hour to do her hair. yinraad-ilha saaɛa ʒatta trattib šaɛarha. 9. miša (i maši). Your son is doing well in school this year. ʔibnak maaši ʒeen bil-madrasa has-sana. -- My tomato plants are doing well. ʈ-ʈamaaʈa maalti maašya ʒeen.
  **He wears his hat just the way I do. yilbas šafuqta tamaaman biš-šikil miθil-ma ʔalbasha ʔaani.
  to **do away with** - txallaʂ (a taxalluʂ) min. They want to do away with most of the redtape. da-yriiduun yitxallʂuun min ʔakθar il-ruutiiniyyaat.
  to **do good** - 1. ʔazsan (i ʔizsaan), ɛamal (i ɛamal) xeer. Our neighbor was well-known for his piety and doing good. jaarna čaan mašhuur bit-taqwa wil-ʔizsaan. 2. faad (i faaʔida). Complaining won't do you much good. š-šakwa ma-raz-itfiidak ihwaaya. -- If you take a vacation, it will do you lots of good. loo taaxuð ɛuʈla, tfiidak ihwaaya.
  to **do harm** - 1. ðarr (ʔiðraar). Rerouting the traffic to the new street has done much harm to my business. taġyiir il-muruur liš-šaariɛ ij-jidiid ðarr šuġli hwaaya. 2. ʔaðða (i ʔiiðaaʔ). His interference in our work has done us more harm than good. tadaxxula b-šuġuḷna ʔaððaana ʔakθar min-ma faadna.
  to **do in** - kital (u katil) n-. They did him in. kitloo. -- Working in this heat has done me in. š-šuġuḷ ib-hal-zarr kitalni.
  to **do one's best** - biðal (i baðil) jahid~. I'll do my best to finish it on time. raz-abðil jahdi ʒatta ʔaxaḷḷuʂha ɛal-wakit.
  to **do out of** - sawwa (i) b-. He did me out of all my money. sawwaaha biyya w-ʔaxað kull ifluusi.
  to **do without** - staġna (i stiġnaaʔ) ɛan. Can you do without this pencil for a while? tigdar tistaġni ɛan hal-qalam il-fadd faʈra?

dock - raʂiif (pl. ʔarʂifat) miinaaʔ. I nearly fell off the dock. wugaɛit min raʂiif il-miinaaʔ ʔilla šwayya.
  to **dock** - 1. wačča (i tuwičči, toočiya). Where

do most of the tugboats dock? ween itwačči ʔakθar il-maaʈooraat ib-baġdaad? 2. risa (i rasu) n-. The ship will dock at Baʂra at seven o'clock. l-baaxira raz-tirsi bil-baʂra saaɛa sabɛa. 3. staqʈaɛ (i stiqʈaaɛ) min. I was late 15 minutes, but they docked me an hour's wages. ʔaani činit mit.ʔaxxir bass rubuɛ saaɛa laakin istaqʈiɛaw minni ʔujrat saaɛa.

doctor - ʈabiib pl. ʔaʈibbaaʔ, daktoor pl. dakaatra. Please send for a doctor. dizz ɛala ʈabiib, min faðlak.
  to **doctor** - ʈabbab (i taʈbiib), daawa (i mudaawaat). We doctored him ourselves. ʈabbabnaa b-nafisna.

doctorate - diktoora pl. -aat. He has a doctorate. ɛinda diktoora.

document - waθiiqa pl. waθaayiq, mustanad pl. -aat. Do you have all the documents? ɛindak kull il-waθaayiq?

dodge - ziila pl. ziyal, liɛba pl. -aat. What dodge has he thought of now? ʔay ziila fakkar biiha hassa?
  to **dodge** - 1. zaaġ (u zooġ), tjannab (a tajannub, tjinnib). If I hadn't dodged, he would have hit me. loo ma-azuuġ minna, čaan ðirabni. 2. tmaḷḷaʂ (a tamaḷḷuʂ, tmiḷḷiʂ). He tried to dodge the question. zaawal yitmaḷḷaʂ imnis-suʔaal.

dog - čalib pl. člaab, kalib pl. kilaab. Take that dog out of here! waxxir hač-čalib minnaa!
  **He's going to the dogs. da-ydammir nafsa b-iida.

dog-eared - maθni. The pages are all dog-eared. ʂ-ʂafʒaat kullha maθniyya.

dogma - ɛaqiida pl. ɛaqaaʔid.

dogmatic - mitɛaʂʂub ib-ʔafkaar~. Our Arabic teacher is very dogmatic. mudarris il-ɛarabi maalna mutɛaʂʂub ib-ʔafkaara kulliš.

doll - laɛɛaaba pl. -aat. She likes to play with dolls. yiɛjibha tilɛab bil-laɛɛaabaat.

dollar - doolaar pl. -aat, duulaar pl. -aat.

domestic - 1. beeti*. She is studying to be a Domestic Science teacher. da-tidrus ʒatta tʂuun mudarrisa lil-funuun il-beetiyya. 2. maʒalli*, waʈani*. These are all domestic products. haaði kullha muntajaat waʈaniyya. 3. beet. It is hard to find domestic help these days. yiʂɛab tilgi xaddaamiin beet hal-ʔayyaam.

domesticated - ʔahli*, daajin. The chicken is a domesticated animal. d-dijaaj imnil-zaywaanaat il-ʔahliyya.

to **donate** - tbarraɛ (a tabarruɛ) b-. I donated two dinars to the Red Crescent. tbarraɛit ib-diinaareen lil-hilaal il-ʔazmar.

donation - tabarruɛ pl. -aat. Donations are welcome. baab it-tabarruɛaat maftuuz.

done - 1. msawwa, mxallaʂ, xalʂaan. All my lessons are done. waðaayfi kullha msawwaaya. 2. laaziq, mistiwi. In ten minutes the meat will be done. b-xilaal ɛašir daqaayiq il-lazam raz-ykuun laaziq.
  done in - halkaan, manhuuk. I'm done in from working in this weather. ʔaani halkaan imniš-šuġuḷ ib-haj-jaww.
  to **be done for** - ntiha (i ntihaaʔ) ʔamur. If the boss finds this out I'm done for. ʔiða ʒaʂʂ biiha ir-raʔiis, ʔintiha ʔamri. -- These tires are done for. hat-taayiraat mintihi ʔamurha.

donkey - zmaaḷ pl. zʲaayil, zmaar pl. zamiir.

door - baab pl. ʔabwaab, biibaan. Please open the door. ʔarjuuk fukk il-baab.

doorbell - jaraʂ (pl. ʔajraʂ) baab.

doorknob - yaddat (pl. -aat) baab, qabðat (pl. -aat) baab.

doorman - bawwaab pl. -iin.

doorway - madxal pl. madaaxil. Please don't stand in the doorway! rijaaʔan la-toogaf bil-madxal.

dope - muxaddir pl. -aat. He uses dope. yistaɛmil muxaddiraat.

dormitory - radha pl. -aat.

dose - jarɛa pl. -aat. That's too big a dose for a child. haj-jarɛa kulliš čibiira liʈ-ʈifil. -- Take it in small doses. ʔuxuðha b-jarɛaat iʂġayyra.

dossier - ʔiðbaara pl. -aat, malaffa pl. -aat, faayil pl. -aat. Let me see Ali's dossier. xalliini ʔašuuf ʔiðbaarat ɛali.

dot - nuqʈa pl. nuqaʈ. Wear your dress with the blue dots. libsi l-badla ʔumm in-nuqaʈ iz-zarga. -- Add three dots. zuʈʈ itlaθ nuqaʈ.
  on the dot - 1. bið-ðabuʈ. I'll see you at three on the dot. raz-ašuufak saaɛa tlaaθa bið-ðabuʈ. 2. ɛal-mawɛid, ɛal-wakit, bil-wakit. He came right on the dot. ʔija ɛal-wakit.

double - *dabil, ḍuʿuf.* We got paid double today. *stilamna ḍuʿuf raatib il-yoom.* -- Bring me a double portion of ice cream. *jiib-li dabil doondirma.* -- It's double the size of mine. *haaḏi ḍuʿf il-ḥajim maali.*
**He could be your double. *huwwa ṣuura ṭabq il-ʔaṣil minnak.*
to double - *ḍaaʿaf (u muḍaaʿafa).* He doubled his capital in two years. *ḍaaʿaf raasmaala b-santeen.*
double-breasted - *ʔabu siraween.* He wore a double-breasted suit. *libas qaaṭ ʔabu siraween.*
doubles - *zawji, θneen-iθneen.* Let's play doubles. *xal-nilʿab zawji.*
doubt - *šakk* pl. *šukuuk.* Do you have any doubts? *ʿindak ʔay šakk?* -- Without a doubt he's the best man for the job. *biduun šakk huwwa ʔaḥsan waaḥid liš-šaġla.*
in doubt - *maškuuk b-.* The result is still in doubt. *n-natiija baʿadha maškuuk biiha.*
to doubt - *šakk (u šakk).* I doubt that the story is true. *ʔašukk ʔan ykuun il-quṣṣa ṣaḥiiḥa.* -- I don't doubt it in the least. *ʔaani ʔabadan ma-ašukk biiha.*
doubtful - **1.** *maškuuk b-.* It is doubtful if he'll get well. *maškuuk bii ʔan yṭiib.* **2.** *šaakik b-.* I'm still doubtful about it. *ʔaani baʿadni šaakik biiha* or ***baʿad ʿindi šakk biiha.*
dough - *ʿajiin.* He put the dough in the oven. *xalla l-ʿajiin bil-firin.*
down - **1.** *riiš naʿim.* This pillow is filled with down. *hal-imxadda mḥaššaaya riiš naʿim.* **2.** *zaġab.* The chick is covered with down. *farx id-dijaaja mgaṭṭa biz-zaġab.* **3.** *jawwa.* Did you look down there? *baawaʿit jawwa hnaak?*
**Down with imperialism! *yasquṭ il-istiʿmaar!*
to down - *waggaʿ (i tawgiiʿ) t-.* I downed the duck with one shot. *waggaʿt il-baṭṭa b-fadd ṭalqa.*
downgrade - *nḥidaar.* The road has a steep downgrade. *ṭ-ṭariiq bii nḥidaar šadiid.*
downhearted - *maqhuur, ḥaziin.* He looks downhearted. *ybayyin ʿalee maqhuur.*
downhill - *minḥidir.* From here on the road is downhill all the way. *minnaa w-hiiči ṭ-ṭariiq minḥidir ʿala ṭuul.*
down payment - *muqaddam, ʿarabuun* pl. *-aat.* How much of a down payment can you make? *šgadd tigdar tilfaʿ muqaddam?*
downpour - *zaxx.* We were caught in the downpour. *lizmatna z-zaxx.*
downstairs - *jawwa.* I'll be waiting downstairs. *raḥ-antiḏir jawwa.*
**He tripped and fell downstairs. *ʿiθar w-wugaʿ imnid-daraj.*
downtown - **Let's go downtown. *xal-ninzil lil-wlaaya* or *xal-inruuḥ lis-suug.* **He's downtown right now. *huwwa bis-suug hassa.*
dowry - *ḥagg.* How much dowry did he pay her? *šgadd difaʿ-ilha ḥagg?*
to **doze** - *ʔaxaḏ (u) ġaffa, ġafwa, ġafya.* I've just been dozing. *bass činit maaxiḏ ġaffa.*
to doze off - *ġifa (i ġafi).* He dozed off after supper. *ġifa wara l-ʿaša.*
dozen - *darzan* pl. *daraazin.* Please give me a dozen eggs. *balla nṭiini darzan beeḏ.*
draft - **1.** *tayyaar* (pl. *-aat*) *hawa.* I can't stand the draft in this room. *ma-agdar atḥammal tayyaar il-hawa b-hal-ġurfa.* -- The fire went out because there wasn't enough draft. *xumdat in-naar li-ʔan ma-čaan aku tayyaar hawa kaafi.* **2.** *miftaaḥ* (pl. *mafaatiiḥ*) *hawa.* Did you open the draft on the heater? *fakkeet miftaaḥ il-hawa biṣ-ṣooba?* **3.** *miswadda* pl. *-aat.* The first draft is ready. *l-miswadda l-ʔuula ḥaaḏra.* **4.** *tajniid.* You have to report to the draft officer. *laazim itraajiʿ ḍaabuṭ it-tajniid.*
to draft - *ʔaxaḏ (u ʔaxiḏ) lij-jundiyya, jannad (i tajniid).* They drafted him last month. *ʔaxḏoo lij-jundiyya biš-šahr il-faat.*
to **drag** - **1.** *siḥal (a saḥil) n-.* I had to drag the trunk into the house myself. *ḏṭarreet ʔasḥal iṣ-ṣanduug lil-beet ib-nafsi.* -- Your coat is dragging on the floor. *qappuuṭak da-yisḥal bil-gaaʿ.* **2.** *marr (u marr) ib-buṭuʔ.* Time drags when you don't have anything to do. *l-wakit ymurr ib-buṭuʔ lumman maa ʿindak šii tsawwii.* **3.** *jarr (u jarr).* He could hardly drag himself to work. *bil-moot yaḷḷa yjurr nafsa liš-šuġuḷ.*
to drag on - *maṭmaṭ (u maṭmaṭa).* The meeting dragged on for three hours. *l-ijtimaaʿ maṭmaṭ itlaθ saaʿaat.*
dragon - *tinniin* pl. *tanaaniin.*
drain - *balluuʿa* pl. *balaaliiʿ.* The drain is stopped up again. *l-balluuʿa nsaddat marra lux.*
to drain - *farraġ (i tafriiġ) t-.* They drained the swimming pool only yesterday. *bass il-baarḥa farrġaw ṃaay il-masbaḥ.*
to drain off - *tṣarraf (a taṣarruf).* The water doesn't drain off quickly. *l-ṃayy ma-da-yitṣarraf ib-surʿa.*
drastic - *ṣaarim, šadiid.* The government took drastic measures. *l-ḥukuuma ttixḏat ʔijraaʔaat ṣaarima.*
to **draw** - **1.** *risam (i rasim) n-.* He likes to draw pictures of animals. *yḥibb yirsim ṣuwar ḥaywanaat.* **2.** *siḥab (a saḥib) n-.* He drew the winning number in the lottery. *siḥab ir-raqam ir-raabiḥ bil-yaanaṣiib.* **3.** *jiḏab (i jaḏib) n-.* The concert is sure to draw a big crowd. *ʔakiid il-ḥafla l-mawsiiqiyya raḥ-tijḏib jamhuur kabiir.* **4.** *ṭabb (u ṭabb).* The train is just drawing into the station. *l-qiṭaar hassa da-yṭubb lil-maḥaṭṭa.* **5.** *jarr (u jarr) n-, ḥišar (u ḥašir) n-.* I was drawn into this argument against my will. *nḥišarit il-hal-mujaadala ḍidd raġubti.*
to draw conclusions - *stantaj (i stintaaj), staxliṣ (i stixlaaṣ).* Draw whatever conclusions you want to. *stantij iš-ma triid.*
to draw in - **1.** *jarr (u jarr) n-.* Draw in your breath. *jurr in-nafis.* **2.** *qallaṣ (i tqulluṣ, taqliiṣ).* Draw in your stomach. *qalliṣ baṭnak.*
to draw out - **1.** *siḥab (a saḥib) n-.* I'll have to draw out fifty dinars from the bank. *laazim asḥab xamsiin diinaar imnil-ḅang.* **2.** *stadraj (i stidraaj).* See if you can draw him out. *jarrub tistadrij.*
to draw up - *wuḍaʿ (a waḍiʿ) n-.* Who drew up the plan for your house. *minu wuḍaʿ xuṭṭat beetak?* -- I'm going to draw up the report. *ʔaani raḥ-ooḍaʿ it-taqriir.*
drawer - *mjarr* pl. *-aat, dirij* pl. *druuj.* You'll find it in the top drawer. *tilgii bil-imjarr il-foogaani.*
drawn - *manhuuk.* His face looks drawn. *ybayyin ʿala wijja manhuuk.*
dread - *xoof, xišya.* I have a dread of doctors. *ʿindi xoof imnil-ʔaṭibbaaʔ.*
to dread - *xaaf (a xoof), xiša (a xaši).* I dread the dark. *ʔaxaaf imniḏ-ḏilma.*
dreadful - *faḏiiʿ, muriiʿ.* She wears dreadful clothes. *tilbas ihduum faḏiiʿa.* -- That was a dreadful accident. *haaḏi čaanat ḥaadiθa muriiʿa.*
dream - *ḥilim* pl. *ʔaḥlaam.* I had a strange dream last night. *šifit ḥilim ġariib leelt il-baarḥa.*
to dream - *ḥilam (a ḥalim).* Last night I dreamed that I was home. *ḥilamit ʔaani činit ib-beeti l-baarḥa bil-leel.*
**I wouldn't dream of doing it. *ma-aṭṣawwar aguum biiha ḥatta b-manaami.*
dreary - *kaʔiib.* It was an awfully dreary day. *caan fadd nahaar kulliš kaʔiib.*
dredge - *ḥaffaara* pl. *-aat.* The dredge is being repaired right now. *l-ḥaffaara da-titṣallaḥ hassa.*
to dredge - *kira (i kari) n-.* After the flood they had to dredge the river. *baʿad il-fayaḏaan iḏṭarraw yikruun in-nahar.*
dress - *nafnuuf* pl. *nafaaniif.* She wants to buy a new dress. *triid tištiri nafnuuf jidiid.*
to dress - **1.** *libas (a libis) n-.* I'll dress quickly. *raḥ-albas bil-ʿajal.* -- He's always well-dressed. *daaʔiman laabis zeen* or *daaʔiman yilbas zeen.* **2.** *labbas (i talbiis).* Mother is dressing the baby. *ʔummi da-tlabbis iṭ-ṭifil.* **3.** *ḍammad (i taḍmiid).* Did you dress the wound? *ḍammadt ij-jariḥ?*
to dress up - *kišax (a kašix).* Look at him, all dressed up. *šuufa šloon kaašix.*
dresser - **1.** *diilaab, duulaab* pl. *dwaaliib.* The handkerchiefs are in the dresser. *č-čifaafi bid-diilaab.* **2.** *muḍammid* pl. *-iin.* The doctor looked at my injuries and told the dresser to treat them. *ṭ-ṭabiib kišaf ʿaj-juruuḥ maalti w-xalla l-muḍammid yʿaalijha.*
dressing - *ḍammaad* pl. *-aat, šdaad* pl. *-aat, lfaaf* pl. *-aat.* The nurse changes his dressings every morning. *l-mumarriḏa tbaddil ḍammaadaata kull yoom iṣ-ṣubuḥ.*
dressing gown - *burnuṣ* pl. *baraaniṣ, roob* pl. *-aat.*
dressing table - *meez* (pl. *-aat*) *itwaaleet.*
dressmaker - *xayyaaṭa* pl. *-aat.*
dried - *yaabis.* Buy me a kilo of dried beans.

štirii-li keelu faaṣuuliyya yaabsa.
to **drift** - *sayyas (i tasyiis).* They cut the motor and let the boat drift. *waggifaw il-muzarrik w-xallaw il-maaṭoor ysayyis.*
drill - **1.** *mizraf* pl. *mazaarif.* The mechanic needs another drill. *l-miikaaniiki yiztaaj mizraf laax.* -- I just bought a new set of drills. *hassa štireet ṭaxum jidiid mazaarif.* **2.** *tamriin* pl. *tamaariin.* There are two drills on this rule on the fifth page. *ʔaku tamaariin iθneen Ɛala hal-qaaƐida biṣ-ṣafza l-xaamsa.* **3.** *tadriib* pl. *-aat.* I was late for drill today and they gave me extra duty. *tʔaxxarit Ɛan it-tadriib il-yoom w-inṭooni waajib iδaafi.*
to drill - **1.** *ziraf (u zaruf) n-, sawwa (i taswiya) zuruf.* Drill a hole in the beam. *sawwi zuruf biš-šeelmaana.* **2.** *zufar (u zafur) n-.* The dentist had to drill the tooth. *ṭabiib il-ʔasnaan iδṭarr yizfur is-sinn.* **3.** *zaffaδ (i tazfiiδ).* The teacher drilled us in the multiplication table. *l-muƐallim zaffaδna jadwil iδ-δarub.* **4.** *marran (i tamriin) t-, darrab (i tadriib) t-.* The soldiers drill every day. *j-jinuud yitmarranuun kull yoom.*
drink - **1.** *mašruub* pl. *-aat.* Lemonade is a refreshing summer drink. *l-leemuunaat mašruub ṣeefi munƐiš.* -- What kind of drinks have you got? *yaa nooƐ imnil-mašruubaat Ɛindak?* **2.** *jurƐa* pl. *-aat, juraƐ, gumuƐ* pl. *gmuuƐ.* He's choking, give him a drink of water. *da-yixtinig, ʔinṭii jurƐat maay.* **3.** *šwayya.* May I have a drink of water. *tismaz-li b-išwayyat mayy.*
to drink - *širab (a šurub) n-.* Drink plenty of water! *ʔišrab ihwaaya mayy!* -- Let's drink to your return. *xal-nišrab Ɛala šaraf rujuuƐak.*
to **drip** - **1.** *nigaṭ (u naguṭ).* Let it drip dry. *xallii yinguṭ lamma yinšif.* **2.** *naggaṭ (i tniggut).* The faucet is dripping. *l-zanafiyya da-tnaggiṭ.*
drive - *zamla* pl. *-aat.* We raised five thousand dollars in the last drive. *jimaƐna xamist aalaaf diinaar bil-zamla l-ʔaxiira.*
**We took a drive. *ṭlaƐna bis-sayyaara.*
to drive - **1.** *saaq (u siyaaqa) n-.* Can you drive a truck? *tigdar itsuuq loori?* **2.** *saag (u siyaaga) n-.* Drive the sheep to the pasture. *suug il-ġanam lil-marƐa.* **3.** *difaƐ (a dafiƐ) n-.* Hunger drove him to stealing. *j-juuƐ difaƐa lil-boog.* **4.** *zaθθ (i zaθθ).* The foreman drives his workers continually. *raʔiis il-Ɛummaal yziθθ Ɛummaala Ɛal-Ɛamal b-istimraar.* **5.** *dagg (u dagg) n-.* Drive the nail into the wall. *dugg il-bismaar bil-zaayiṭ.*
**What are you driving at? *š-tuqṣud?* or *š-tiƐni?*
to drive away - *ṭirad (u ṭarid) n-, biƐad (u baƐid) n-.* Drive the dog away. *ʔibƐad ič-čalib.*
to drive crazy - *xaββal (u txuββul) t-.* You'll drive me crazy. *raz-itxaββulni.*
to drive off - *zaad (i zeed) n- Ɛan.* The boat was driven off its course by the wind. *l-markab inzaad Ɛan ittijaaha b-sabab ir-riyaaz.*
driver - **1.** *saayiq* pl. *suwwaaq.* He's a good driver. *huwwa xooš saayiq.* **2.** *Ɛarabanči* pl. *-iyya.* The driver lost control of his horses. *l-Ɛarabanči fuqad is-sayṭara Ɛala xyuula.*
driving license - *ʔijaazat* (pl. *-aat*) *siyaaqa.* Let me see your driving license. *xalli ʔašuuf ʔijaazat siyaaqtak.*
to **drizzle** - *naθθ (i naθθ), naff (i naff).* It's been drizzling all day. *ṣaar-ilha tniθθ in-nahaar kulla.*
to **droop** - *δuwa (i δawi), δibal (a δabil).* The flowers are beginning to droop. *l-warid bida yiδbal.* -- The flower is drooping. *l-warid δaawi.*
drooping - *mhaddil, raaxi.* He has drooping shoulders. *čtaafa mhaddila.*
drop - *qaṭra* pl. *-aat, nuqṭa* pl. *-aat.* Put three drops in a glass of water. *zuṭṭ itlaθ qaṭraat b-iglaaṣ mayy.*
to drop - *wugaƐ (a wuguuƐ).* The box dropped out of the window. *ṣ-ṣanduug wugƐat imniš-šibbaač.* -- Some of them dropped from exhaustion. *baƐaδhum wugƐaw imnit-taƐab.* **2.** *waggaƐ (i tawgiiƐ) t-.* You dropped something. *waggaƐit šii.* **3.** *nizal (i nuzuul), nxufaδ (u nxifaaδ).* The temperature dropped very rapidly. *darajat il-zaraara nizlat ib-surƐa.* **4.** *tirak (u tarik) n-, himal (i ʔihmaal) n-.* Let's drop the subject. *xal-nitruk il-mawδuuƐ.* **5.** *nazzal (i tanziil) t-.* Please drop me at the corner. *rajaaʔan nazzilni bil-loofa.* **6.** *ṭirad (u ṭarid) n-, ṭilaƐ (a ṭuluuƐ) n-.* I'll be dropped from the club. *raz-anṭarid imnin-naadi.* **7.** *δabb (i δabb) n-.* Please drop this card in the mail box. *rajaaʔan δibb hal-kaart ib-ṣanduug il-bariid.*
to drop a hint - *lammaz (i talmiiz).* She dropped a hint to me that she wanted to go. *lammzat-li hiyya triid itruuz.*
to drop in - *marr (u marr).* Drop in sometime. *murr fadd yoom.*
drought - *jafaaf.* The drought hurt the crop very much. *j-jafaaf ihwaaya ʔaδδa l-zaaṣil.*
drove - **1.** *qaṭiiƐ* pl. *qiṭƐaan.* We waited for the drove of sheep to pass. *ntiδarna zatta ymurr qaṭiiƐ il-ġanam.* **2.** *jamaaƐa* pl. *-aat.* People came in droves. *n-naas ʔijaw ib-jamaaƐaat.*
to **drown** - **1.** *ġirag (a ġarig).* He drowned in the river. *ġirag biš-šaṭṭ.* **2.** *ġarrag (i taġriig).* She had to drown the kittens. *δṭarrat itġarrig l-ibzaaziin l-iṣġaar.*
to drown out - *ṭiġa (i ṭaġi, ṭuġiyaan) Ɛala.* The noise drowned out his remarks. *l-hoosa ṭiġat Ɛala ṣoota.*
drowsy - *naƐsaan.* I feel drowsy. *da-aziss naƐsaan.*
drug - **1.** *duwa* pl. *ʔadwiya.* This drug is sold only on prescription. *had-duwa ma-yinbaaƐ ʔilla b-waṣfa.* **2.** *muxaddir* pl. *-aat.* He became addicted to drugs. *ṣaar mudmin Ɛal-muxaddiraat.*
drugstore - *ṣaydaliyya* pl. *-aat.* Where is the nearest drugstore? *ween ʔaqrab ṣaydaliyya?*
drum - **1.** *ṭabul* pl. *ṭubuul, dumbug* pl. *danaabug.* Can you here sound of the drums? *tigdar tismaƐ ziss iṭ-ṭubuul?* **2.** *barmiil* pl. *baraamiil, þiiþ* pl. *þyaaþ.* They unloaded six drums of kerosene. *farrġaw sitt baraamiil nafuṭ.*
to drum - *dagg (u dagg).* Please stop drumming on the table. *baṭṭa bass Ɛaad itdugg Ɛal-meez.*
drunk - *sakraan* pl. *sakaara.* Was that drunk annoying you? *čaan da-yziƐjič has-sakraan?* -- He's dead drunk; if you pull on him, he won't feel a thing. *sakraan ṭiina; ʔiδa tjurra ma-yziss.*
to get drunk - *sikar (a sukur).* He got drunk at her birthday party. *sikar ib-zaflat Ɛiid miilaadha.*
dry - **1.** *naašif, yaabis, jaaff.* Is the wash dry yet? *l-ġasiil naašif loo baƐad?* -- My throat is dry. *zarduumi yaabis.* or *riigi naašif.* -- The well is dry. *l-biir naašfa.* **2.** *jaaff.* It has been a dry summer. *čaan ṣeef jaaff.* -- The lecture was so dry, I walked out. *ʔaani ṭlaƐit min wakit li-ʔan il-muzaaδara čaanat kullis jaaffa.* **3.** *yaabis.* Let's gather some dry wood. *xalli nijmaƐ išwayya zaṭab yaabis.*
to dry - **1.** *yibas (a yibaas), nišaf (a našif), jaff (i jafaaf).* The paint dries in five hours. *ṣ-ṣubuġ yinšaf ib-xamis saaƐaat.* **2.** *naššaf (i tanšiif).* Who's going to dry the dishes? *minu raz-ynaššif l-imwaaƐiin?* -- Dry yourself well. *naššif nafsak zeen.*
to dry up - *jaff (i jafaaf), yibas (a yibaas), nišaf (a našif).* Every summer this stream dries up. *kull ṣeef hal-majra yinšaf.*
dry cleaner - *mukawwi* pl. *-iin.* I sent your gray suit to the dry cleaner. *dazzeet qaaṭak ir-rumaadi lil-mukawwi.*
dual - *muθanna, θunaaʔi*.*
duck - *baṭṭa* pl. *-aat* coll. *baṭṭ.* We're having roast duck for dinner. *Ɛašaana lazam baṭṭ mišwi.*
to duck - **1.** *naṣṣa (i tnuṣṣi, tanṣiya), zina (i zani) n-, giṭaf (i gaṭif).* He ducked his head. *naṣṣa raasa.* **2.** *ġiṭaṣ (u ġaṭiṣ), ġaṭṭ (u ġaṭṭ).* The duck ducked under the water. *l-baṭṭa ġiṭṣat bil-mayy.* **3.** *ġaṭṭaṣ (i tġiṭṭiṣ, taġṭiiṣ), ġaṭṭaṭ (i tġiṭṭiṭ).* He ducked his brother's head under the water. *ġaṭṭaṭ raas ʔaxuu bil-mayy.*
due - *zaqq* pl. *zuquuq.* That's his due. *haaδa zaqqa.*
**He's due to arrive at ten. *muntaδar wuṣuula saaƐa Ɛašra.*
due to - *b-sabab, b-natiija.* Due to an oversight, she wasn't invitated. *ma-nƐizmat ib-sabab sahu.* -- That was due to a mistake. *ṣaar ib-natiijat ġalṭa.*
to be due - *stazaqq (i stizqaaq).* The rent is due next Monday. *l-ʔiijaar mistiziqq iθ-θineen ij-jaay.*
duel - *ṣiraaƐ, mubaaraza.*
dues - *badalaat.* I pay membership dues every month. *ʔaani ʔadfaƐ badalaat il-ištiraak kull šahar.*
dull - **1.** *ʔaƐmi, Ɛimyaan* pl. *Ɛimi.* This knife is dull. *has-siččiina Ɛamya.* **2.** *baliid* pl. *buladaaʔ.* He's terribly dull. *huwwa kulliš baliid.* **3.** *θaqiil.* I feel a dull pain in my side. *ʔašƐur ib-wajaƐ θaqiil ib-ṣafuzti.* **4.** *šaazib.* She likes dull colors. *tiƐjibha l-ʔalwaan iš-šaazba.*
dumb - **1.** *ʔaxras* pl. *xarsiin.* He's deaf and dumb. *huwwa ʔaṭraš w-ʔaxras.* **2.** *ġabi, baliid, dimaaġsizz.*

He's too dumb to notice. *hal-ġabi ma-ylaaḥiδ̣.*
to strike dumb - *δihal (i δahil) n-, lijam (i lajim) n-.* We were struck dumb when we heard the news. *nδihalna lamman simaεna l-xabar.*
dumbfounded - *maδhuul.* I was dumfounded when I heard it. *ṣirit maδhuul lumman simaεit biiha.*
dump - *mazbala* pl. *mazaabil.* Where's the dump? *ween il-mazbala?*
**Their house is an awful dump. *beethum kulliš imxarbaṭ.*
down in the dumps - *maqbuuδ̣ in-nafis.* I've been down in the dumps all day. *činit maqbuuδ̣ in-nafis ṭuul in-nahaar* or ***nafsi čaanat maqbuuδ̣a ṭuul in-nahaar.*
to dump - *δabb (i δabb) n-.* Don't dump the sand in front of the door. *la-tδibb ir-ramul giddaam il-baab.* -- Don't dump the coffee grounds in the sink. *la-tδibb it-tilif maal il-gahwa b-ḥalg il-maġsal.*
dumpy - *mdaḥdaḥ.* She has a dumpy figure. *εidha jisim imdaḥdaḥ.*
dune - *kaθiib* pl. *kuθbaan.* The sand dunes extend for miles. *kuθbaan ir-ramul timtadd il-biεiid ʔamyaal.*
dung - *dimin.* Do you use chemical fertilizer or dung in your garden? *tistaεmil samaad kiimyaawi loo dimin ib-ḥadiiqtak?*
duplicate - *nusxa* pl. *nusax.* You need a duplicate of your birth certificate. *tiḥtaaj nusxa š-šihaadat miilaadak.*
to duplicate - *stansax (i stinsaax).* I'll have the secretary duplicate them for you. *raḥ-axalli s-sikirteera tistansixhum ʔilak.*
duplication - *zdiwaaj* pl. *-aat.* We must avoid duplication in the work. *laazim nitḥaaša l-izdiwaaj biš-šuġuḷ.*
to be **durable** - *daawam (u dawaam).* These tires are cheap but they are not durable. *hat-taayaraat irxiiṣa laakin ma-tdaawum.*
during - *ʔaθnaaʔ, xilaal.* I met him during the war. *εirafta xilaal il-ḥarub.*
dust - *ġubaar, traab, εajaaj.* There's a heavy layer of dust on the table. *ʔaku ṭabaqa θixiina mnil-ġubaar εal-meez.*
to dust - **1.** *naffaδ̣ (u tanfiiδ̣) imnil-εajaaj.* Please dust my desk. *ʔarjuuk naffuδ̣ meezi mnil-εajaaj.* **2.** *rašš (u rašš).* They dusted a chemical substance on the cotton fields by plane. *raššaw mawaadd kiimyaawiyya εala ḥuquul il-guṭin imnit-ṭayyaara.*
dust storm - *εajaaj* pl. *-aat.*
Dutch - *hoolandi** pl. *-iyyiin.*
duty - **1.** *waajib* pl. *-aat.* It was his duty to support his parents. *ʔaṣbaḥ min waajba ʔan yεiil ʔumma w-abuu.* -- Answering the phone is one of my duties. *l-ʔijaaba εat-talifoon min waajibaati.* -- I'm on duty all night. *ʔaani bil-waajib ṭuul il-leel* or *ʔaani xafaara ṭuul il-leel.* **2.** *gumrug, rsuum gumrugiyya.* I paid 300 dinars duty on it. *difaεit itlaθ miit diinaar gumrug εalee.*
dwarf - *gurri* pl. *-iyya.*
to **dwell** - **1.** *εaaš (i εeeš) n-.* The Bedouins dwell in the desert most of the year. *l-badu yεiišuun bil-barr miεδ̣am is-sana.* **2.** *stimarr (i stimraar).* There's no point in dwelling on this subject any longer. *ma-aku daaεi nistimirr bil-mawδ̣uuε ʔakθar.*
dye - *ṣubuġ* pl. *ʔaṣbaaġ.* Please get me a package of blue dye. *ʔarjuuk jiib-li paakeet ṣubuġ ʔazrag.*
to dye - *ṣubaġ (u ṣubuġ).* I dyed my blue dress with black dye. *ṣbaġit nafnuufi l-ʔazrag ib-ṣubuġ ʔaswad.*
dynamic - *našiṭ, ḥarik.* He's a dynamic businessman. *huwwa rajul ʔaεmaal našiṭ.*
dysentery - *dizantari.*

E

each - **1.** *kull.* Each one of us received a pack of cigarettes. *kull waaḥid min εidna ʔaxaδ paakeet jigaayir.* -- He comes here each week. *yiji hnaa kull isbuuε.* -- Give one to each child. *ʔinṭi waḥda l-kull jaahil.* **2.** *waaḥid.* These apples are ten fils each. *hat-tiffaaḥ wiḥda b-εašr ifluus.*
each and every one - *jamiiε.* You can count on each and every one of us. *tigdar tiεtimid εala jamiiεna.*
each other - **1.** *waaḥid il-laax, baεaδ̣hum baεaδ̣.* They see each other every day. *yšuufuun waaḥid il-laax kull yoom.* -- They have nothing to do with each other. *ma-lhum lizuum waaḥid bil-laax.* **2.** (sometimes expressed in sixth form of verb). They've been writing to each other for a year. *čaanaw yitraasluun il-muddat sana.* -- They're not not talking to each other. *ma-yitḥaačuun.*
eager - *muštaaq, mitšawwiq.* I am eager to meet your friend. *ʔaani muštaaq atεarraf ib-ṣadiiqak.*
eagle - *nisir* pl. *nisuur.*
ear - **1.** *ʔiδin* pl. *ʔaδaan, ʔiiδaan* pl. *-aat.* She's deaf in her right ear. *ʔiδinha l-yimna ṭarša.* -- I have no ear for music. *ma-εindi ʔiδin mawsiiqiyya.* **2.** *εarnuuṣ* pl. *εaraaniiṣ.* Make popcorn out of these ears of corn. *sawwi šaamiyya min εaraaniiṣ il-ʔiδra haaδi.* **3.** *sunbula* pl. *sanaabil.* This ear of wheat has fifty grains on it. *has-sunbult il-ḥunṭa biiha xamsiin ḥabba.*
**He's up to his ears in debt. *ṭaamus bid-deen ʔila raasa.*
earlier - *gabuḷ.* Come earlier than usual. *taεaal gabḷ il-muεtaad.*
earliest - **1.** *ʔawwal* pl. *ʔawaaʔil.* The earliest immigrants came from Europe. *ʔawaaʔil il-muhaajiriin ʔijaw min ʔooruppa.* **2.** *ʔaqdam.* He is one of the earliest advocates of this idea. *huwwa min ʔaqdam duεaat hal-fikra.*
early - **1.** *min wakit, εala wakit.* Please wake me up early. *ʔarjuuk gaεεidni min wakit.* **2.** *εaajil, sariiε.* We expect an early reply. *nitwaqqaε jawaab εaajil.* **3.** *mubakkir.* She got married at an early age. *tzawwjat ib-εumur mubakkir.*
**He will arrive early next month. *raḥ-yooṣal ib-ʔawaaʔil iš-šahr ij-jaay.*
to **earmark** - *xaṣṣaṣ (i taxṣiiṣ) t-.* We earmarked two million dinars for the new bridge. *xaṣṣaṣna milyooneen diinaar lij-jisir ij-jidiid.*
to **earn** - **1.** *ḥaṣṣal (i taḥṣiil) t-, ṭallaε (i taṭliiε) t-.* How much do you earn a week? *šgadd itḥaṣṣil bil-isbuuε?* -- She earns her living as a dressmaker. *tṭalliε εiišatha mnil-ixyaaṭa.* **2.** *ktisab (i ktisaab).* He earned his reputation the hard way. *ktisab šuhurta b-šaqq il-ʔanfus.* **3.** *kisab (i kasib) n-.* His conduct earned him universal respect. *taṣarrufaata kisbat-la ḥtiraam ij-jamiiε.*
earnings - *maḥṣuul* pl. *maḥaaṣiil, maksab* pl. *makaasib.*
earrings - *tirčiyya* pl. *taraači.* She bought a new pair of earrings. *štirat zooj taraači jidiida.*
earth - **1.** *dinya, εaalam, ʔarδ̣.* Nothing on earth can save him. *ma-aku šii bid-dinya yxallṣa.* **2.** *ʔarδ̣.* The earth is a sphere. *l-ʔarδ̣ kurawiyya.* **3.** *traab.* This ditch has to be filled with earth. *han-nugra laazim tindifin b-itraab.*
**There is nothing like it on the face of the earth. *haaδa ma-aku minna εala wajh il-baṣiiṭa.*
**He is very down to earth. *haaδa kulliš waaqiεi.*
earthquake - *zilzaal* pl. *zalaazil.* The earthquake destroyed twenty houses. *z-zilzaal dammar εišriin beet.*
ease - *suhuula, baṣaaṭa.* Did you notice the ease with which he does things? *laaḥaδ̣it išloon ysawwi l-ʔašyaaʔ ib-suhuula?*
at ease - *mirtaaḥ.* I never feel quite at ease when I'm with her. *ʔabadan ma-ʔašεur mirtaaḥ min ʔakuun wiyyaaha.*
**At ease! *stariiḥ!*
to ease - **1.** *xaffaf (u taxfiif) t-.* This medicine will ease the pain. *had-duwa yxaffuf il-wujaε.* **2.** *hawwan (i tahwiin) t-.* Nothing will ease my grief. *ma-aku šii yhawwin qahri.*
**We have to ease the box through the narrow door. *laazim infawwit iṣ-ṣanduug εala keefna mnil-baab iδ̣-δ̣ayyig.*
to ease up - *xaff (u xiffa), qall (i qilla).* The pressure is beginning to ease up. *δ̣-δ̣agiṭ bida yxuff.*
easily - *b-suhuula, b-baṣaaṭa.* He did it easily. *sawwaaha b-suhuula.* -- This can easily be believed. *haay tiṭṣaddag ib-suhuula.*
east - **1.** *šarq.* The arrow points east. *s-sahim yʔaššir liš-šarq.* **2.** *šarji.* It's an east wind.

l-hawa šarji.
the Far East - *š-šarq il-ʔaqṣa.*
the Middle East - *š-šarq il-ʔawṣaṭ.*
the Near East - *š-šarq il-ʔadna.*
Easter - *ɛiid il-qiyaama, ɛiid il-fuṣiz.* Easter comes early this year. *ɛiid il-qiyaama yiji min wakit has-sana.*
eastern - *šarqi**. I know the eastern part very well. *ʔaɛruf il-qism iš-šarqi kulliš zeen.*
easy - 1. *sahil, baṣiiṭ.* That was an easy question. *δaak čaan suʔaal sahil.*
**Take it easy, don't get mad. *ɛala keefak, la-tizɛal* or *yawaaš, la-tizɛal.*
easy-going - *mitsaahil.* He's an easy-gcing fellow. *huwwa fadd waazid mitsaahil.*
to **eat** - 1. *ʔakal (u ʔakil) n-.* I haven't eaten a thing in two days. *ṣaar-li yoomeen ma-akalit šii.* -- He walked in just as we sat down to eat. *ṭabb min giɛadna naakul.* 2. *ziraf (u zaruf).* The acid ate three holes in my pants. *l-zaamuδ ziraf itlaθ izruuf bil-panṭaroon maali.*
to eat out - 1. *ʔakal (u), ziraf (u).* Rust ate out the bottom of the pan. *z-zinjaar ʔakal čaɛb ij-jidir.* 2. *ʔakal (u) barra.* Why don't we eat out tonight? *leeš ma-naakul barra hal-leela?*
echo - *ṣada* pl. *ʔaṣdaaʔ.* If you listen you can hear the echo. *ʔiδa titṣannaṭ tigdar tismaɛ iṣ-ṣada.*
to echo - 1. *niṭa (i) ṣada.* The sound of the shot echoed through the hills. *ṣoot iṭ-ṭalqa niṭa ṣada been il-itlaal.* 2. *raddad (i tardiid).* Stop echoing every word he says. *bass ɛaad itraddid kull čilma yguulha.*
eclipse - 1. *xusuuf* pl. *-aat.* There will be a partial lunar eclipse tomorrow night. *raz-yṣiir xusuuf juzʔi baačir bil-leel.* 2. *kusuuf* pl. *-aat.* We watched the solar eclipse from the top of the building. *šifna l-kusuuf min ṣaṭz il-ibnaaya.*
to eclipse - *ṭiġa (a ṭuġyaan) ɛala.* She eclipsed everybody else at the party. *ṭiġat ɛala kull il-baaqyaat bil-zafla.*
to be eclipsed - 1. *xisaf (i xusuuf).* The moon will be eclipsed tonight. *l-gumar raz-yixsif hal-leela.* 2. *kisaf (i kusuuf).* Don't forget that the sun will be eclipsed this afternoon. *la-tinsa š-šamis raz-tiksif hal-ɛaṣriyya.*
economic - *qtiṣaadi**. Their economic situation is improving. *zaalathum il-iqtiṣaadiyya da-titzassan.*
economical - 1. *muqtaṣid, mudabbir.* She's a very economical woman. *haay fadd mara kulliš muqtaṣida.* 2. *qtiṣaadi**. This car is very economical. *has-sayyaara kulliš iqtiṣaadiyya.*
economics - *qtiṣaad.* He's studying economics. *da-yidrus iqtiṣaad.*
to **economize** - *qtiṣad (i qtiṣaad).* She economizes in household expenditures. *hiyya tiqtiṣid ib-maṣaariif il-beet.*
edge - 1. *ṭaraf* pl. *ʔaṭraaf.* He lives at the edge of town. *yiskun ib-ṭaraf il-wlaaya.* 2. *zaašya* pl. *zawaaši.* Don't put the glass real close to the edge. *la-tzuṭṭ l-iglaaṣ kulliš giriib lil-zaašya.* 3. *zadd* pl. *zduud.* The knife's edge is dull. *zadd is-siččiina ʔaɛmi.* 4. *ʔafδaliyya.* He has the edge on me. *ʔila l-ʔafδaliyya ɛalayya.*
on edge - *miztadd.* She's on edge today. *hiyya miztadda l-yoom.*
edible - *ṣaaliz lil-ʔakil.* Is this edible? *haaδa ṣaaliz lil-ʔakil?*
to **edit** - *zarrar (i tazriir) t-.* He has been editing this magazine for several years. *ṣaar-la ɛiddat isniin yzarrir hal-majalla.*
edition - *ṭabɛa* pl. *-aat, ɛadad,* pl. *ʔaɛdaad.* Have you seen the new edition of his book? *šift iṭ-ṭabɛa j-jidiida min iktaaba?*
editor - *muzarrir* pl. *-iin.* My brother has just become editor of our local newspaper. *ʔaxuuya stawwa ṣaar muzarrir jariidatna l-mazalliyya.*
editorial - *maqaal iftitaazi* pl. *maqaalaat iftitaaziyya.* Did you read the editorial? *qireet il-maqaal il-iftitaazi?*
editor-in-chief - *raʔiis (pl. ruʔasaaʔ) tazriir.* You have to see the editor-in-chief about this. *laazim itraajiɛ raʔiis it-tazriir zawil haaδa.*
to **educate** - 1. *ɛallam (i taɛliim) t-.* We have to educate our children to tolerance. *laazim inɛallim ʔaṭfaalna ɛat-tasaamuz.* 2. *θaqqaf (i taθqiif) t-, ɛallam (i).* We need many more teachers to educate the masses. *niztaaj ihwaaya baɛad muɛallimiin il-taθqiif ʔabnaaʔ iš-šaɛab.*
educated - *mθaqqaf* pl. *-iin, mitɛallim* pl. *-iin.* He's an educated person. *haaδa šaxiṣ imθaqqaf.*
education - 1. *θaqaafa, taɛliim.* Her parents neglected her education. *ʔahalha himlaw θaqaafatha.* 2. *diraasa, taɛliim, tazṣiil, θaqaafa.* I completed my education in England. *kammalit diraasti b-ingiltara.* 3. *tarbiya.* He has an M.A. in education. *ɛinda maajisteer bit-tarbiya.*
ministry of education - *wizaarat il-maɛaarif.*
educational - *diraasi**. The new law provides many educational opportunities. *l-qaanuun ij-jidiid yhayyiʔ furaṣ diraasiyya hwaaya.*
effect - 1. *taʔθiir* pl. *-aat.* His appeal produced the desired effect. *stiġaaθta ʔantijat it-taʔθiir il-marġuub.* 2. *mafɛuul.* The effect of this medicine is not what I would like it to be. *mafɛuul had-duwa muu miθil-ma ʔariida.* 3. *taδaahur.* He does it for effect. *ysawwiiha l-ġaraδ it-taδaahur.* 4. *musabbab* pl. *-aat.* This is a cause, not an effect. *haaδa sabab, muu musabbab.*
to go into effect - *sira (i sarayaan) mafɛuul.* This law will go into effect next month. *hal-qaanuun raz-yisri mafɛuula š-šahr ij-jaay.*
to have an effect - *ʔaθθar (i taʔθiir).* Scolding has no effect on him. *t-tarziil ma-yʔaθθir bii.*
to take effect - *sira (i) mafɛuul.* This injection is beginning to take effect. *l-ʔubra bida yisri mafɛuulha.*
to effect - *sawwa (i taswiya) t-, ʔajra (i ʔijraaʔ), zaqqaq (i tazqiiq) t-.* He effected the change without difficulty. *sawwa t-taġyiir bila ṣuɛuuba.*
effective - 1. *muʔaθθir.* They produced a very effective new weapon. *ʔantijaw silaaz jidiid kulliš muʔaθθir.* 2. *faɛɛaal.* The committee was very effective in handling the dispute. *l-lujna čaanat kulliš faɛɛaala b-muɛaalajat in-nizaaɛ.* 3. *mafɛuul.* These pills have proved to be very effective. *hal-zubuub θibat mafɛuulha qawi.* 4. *ɛtibaaran min.* Effective Monday, we'll go on summer time. *ɛtibaaran min yoom iθ-θineen raz-nistaɛmil it-tawqiit iṣ-ṣeefi.*
efficiency - *kafaaʔa, qtidaar.* We all admire his efficiency. *kullna nqaddir kafaaʔta.*
efficient - *kafuʔ* pl. *ʔakiffaaʔ, muqtadir* pl. *-iin.* He's very efficient. *haaδa kulliš kafuʔ.*
effort - 1. *juhud* pl. *juhuud, majhuud* pl. *-aat.* All his efforts were in vain. *kull juhuuda raazat ɛabaθ.* 2. *masɛa* pl. *masaaɛi.* I wouldn't have got the job without your efforts. *ma-čaan zaṣṣalt il-waδiifa blayya masaaɛiik.* 3. *taɛab* pl. *ʔatɛaab.* That isn't worth the effort. *haaδa ma-yiswa t-taɛab.*
**We spared no effort to make the program a success. *biδalna l-ġaali wir-rixiiṣ zatta nijɛal l-mašruuɛ naajiz.*
to make an effort - *siɛa (a saɛi), jtihad (i jtihaad), biδal (i baδil) masɛa.* I will make a real effort to get you the job. *raz-asɛa min ṣudug zatta azaṣṣil-lak il-waδiifa.*
egg - *beeδa* pl. *-aat* coll. *beeδ.* How much is a dozen eggs? *beeš darzan il-beeδ?*
**Don't put all your eggs in one basket. *la-tikšif kull ʔawraaqak* or *daaʔiman xallii-lak xaṭṭ rajɛa.*
eggplant - *beetinjaana* pl. *-aat* coll. *beetinjaan.*
Egypt - *miṣir.*
Egyptian - *miṣri** pl. *-iyyiin.*
eight - 1. *θmaanya.* It's eight o'clock. *s-saaɛa θmaanya.* 2. *θman.* He has eight children. *ɛinda θman ʔaṭfaal.*
eighteen - *θmunṭaɛaš.*
eighteenth - *θ-θmunṭaɛaš.* That's the eighteenth time he hasn't come to work this month. *haay il-marra θ-θumunṭaɛaš ma-ʔija liš-šuġuḷ haš-šahar.*
eighth - 1. *θumun.* He could only get an eighth of a pound of butter. *gidar yaaxuδ θumun paawan zibid bass.* 2. *θaamin.* That is his eighth book. *haaδa ktaaba θ-θaamin.*
eightieth - *θ-θimaaniin.* They celebrated his eightieth birthday. *ztiflaw ɛiid miilaada θ-θimaaniin.*
eighty - *θmaaniin.*
either - 1. *fadd waazid min θineen.* Does either of these roads lead to Baghdad? *ʔaku fadd ṭariiq min haθ-θineen yruuz il-baġdaad.* 2. *ʔay waazid imniθ-θineen.* Either (one) is correct. *ʔay waazid imniθ-θineen ṣaziiz.* 3. *-een.* There are trees on either side of the road. *ʔaku ʔašjaar ɛala jihteen iš-šaariɛ.* 4. *ʔamma, loo.* I leave either tonight or tomorrow morning. *ʔasaafir ʔamma l-yoom ʔaw baačir iṣ-ṣubuz* or *ʔasaafir loo l-yoom loo baačir iṣ-ṣubuz.* 5. *hamm.* He doesn't know it either. *huwwa hamm ma-yuɛrufha.*

elaborate - *mufaṣṣal.* He gave us an elaborate description of it. *nṭaana waṣuf mufaṣṣal ɛanha.*
to elaborate - *faṣṣal (i tfiṣṣil, tafṣiil), waδδaz (i twiδδiz, tawδiiz) ʔakθar.* Can you elaborate upon your decision? *tigdar itwaδδiz taqriirak ʔakθar?*
elastic - **1.** *laastiig.* Do you need any elastic for the blouse? *tiztaajiin ʔay laastiig lil-ibluuz?* **2.** *marin.* This metal is very elastic. *hal-maɛdan kulliš marin.*
elbow - *ɛikis* pl. *ɛukuus.* I banged my elbow. *ḍirabit ɛiksi.*
to elbow - **1.** *šagg (u šagg) b-ɛikis~.* She elbowed her way through the crowd. *šaggat ṭariiqha b-ɛikisha bil-xabṣa.* **2.** *naġġ (u naġġ) b-ɛikis~.* He shut up after she elbowed him in his ribs. *sikat baɛad-ma naġġata b-ɛikisha b-iḍluuɛa.*
to **elect** - *ntixab (i ntixaab).* Whom did they elect president? *ʔilman intixbaw raʔiis?*
election - *ntixaab* pl. *-aat.*
electric - *kahrabaaʔi*.* Where can I plug in my electric razor? *ʔaku ṗlaak ʔašakkil bii makiinat iz-ziyaan il-kahrabaaʔiyya maalti?*
electric bulb - *gloob* pl. *-aat.*
electrician - *ʔabu* (pl. *ʔahil) kahrabaaʔ.*
electricity - *kahrabaaʔ.* The electricity's been cut off! *l-kahrabaaʔ ingiṭaɛ!*
electron - *ʔalakitroon* pl. *-aat.*
electronic - *ʔalakitrooni*.*
elegant - *ʔaniiq.*
element - **1.** *ɛunṣur* pl. *ɛanaaṣir.* What are the elements of water? *šinu hiyya ɛanaaṣir il-ṃaay?* — This group constitutes the important element of the population. *haj-jamaaɛa tkawwan il-ɛunṣur il-muhimm bil-majmuuɛ.* **2.** *muziiṭ* pl. *-aat.* He's out of his element. *huwwa muu b-muziiṭa l-mulaaʔim.*
elementary - **1.** *ʔasaasi*.* Practice is elementary to learning any language. *t-tamriin šii ʔasaasi l-taɛallum ʔay luġa.* **2.** *ʔawwali*, btidaaʔi*.* I studied in an elementary school in Baghdad. *drasit ib-madrasa btidaaʔiyya b-baġdaad.*
elephant - *fiil* pl. *fyaal, fyaala.*
elevation - *rtifaaɛ.* The elevation of this village is six hundred meters above sea level. *rtifaaɛ hal-qarya ɛan mustawa l-bazar sitt miit matir.*
elevator - **1.** *maṣɛad* pl. *maṣaaɛid.* Let's take the elevator. *xalli naaxuδ il-maṣɛad.* **2.** *maxzan* pl. *maxaazin.* How much wheat does this elevator hold? *šgadd hal-maxzan yilzam imnil-zunṭa?*
eleven - *daɛaš, hdaɛaš.* I had to fill out eleven forms. *čaan laazim amli hdaɛaš istimaara.*
eleventh - *d-daɛaš, l-ihdaɛaš.* Take the tenth book and give me the eleventh. *ʔuxuδ il-iktaab il-ɛaašir w-inṭiini il-ihdaɛaš.*
to **eliminate** - **1.** *zaal (i ʔizaala), miza (i mazu, mazi).* The robbers eliminated all traces of the crime. *l-zaraamiyya zaalaw kull ʔaaθaar ij-jariima.* **2.** *ṣaqqaṭ (u tṣuqquṭ taṣqiiṭ) t-.* They eliminated him in the third race. *ṣaqqṭoo b-θaaliθ musaabaqa.* **3.** *ziδaf (i zaδif) n-.* His name was eliminated from the candidate list. *ʔisma nziδaf min qaaʔimat il-muraššaziin.* **4.** *ʔalġa (i ʔilġaaʔ) n-.* They finally eliminated taxes. *bil-ʔaxiir alġaw iḍ-ḍaraayib.*
eloquence - *balaaġa.*
else - **1.** *baɛad, ʔaaxar.* What else can we do? *š-nigdar insawwi baɛad?* — Do you want something else? *triid šii ʔaaxar?* **2.** *laax, baaqi.* I'll take everything else. *raz-aaxuδ kullši laax.*
or else - *tara.* Hurry, or else we'll be late. *bil-ɛajil, tara raz-nitʔaxxar.*
elsewhere - *mazall ʔaaxar, ġeer mukaan.* If you don't like it here, we can go elsewhere. *ʔiδa ma-yɛijbak hal-mazall nigdar inruuz il-mazall ʔaaxar.*
embargo - *maniɛ.* The government issued an embargo on all goods to that island. *l-zukuuma ṣaddirat maniɛ ɛala jamiiɛ il-baḍaayiɛ itruuz il-haj-jaziira.*
to **embarrass** - *xajjal (i txijjil, taxjiil) t-, faššal (i tafšiil) t-.* That child is always embarrassing me in front of people. *haṭ-ṭifil daaʔiman yxajjilni giddaam in-naas.*
embarrassed - *xajlaan, fašlaan.* I was terribly embarrassed. *činit xajlaan il-daraja muzɛija.*
embarrassing - *mxajjil, mfaššil.* It was an embarrassing situation. *čaanat fadd waḍɛiyya mxajjila.*
embassy - *safaara* pl. *-aat.* Where is the American Embassy? *ween is-safaara l-ʔamriikiyya?*
to **embezzle** - *xtilas (i xtilaas).* How much has he embezzled? *šgadd ixtilas?*
to **embrace** - **1.** *ziḍan (i zaḍin).* He embraced his mother tenderly. *ziḍan ʔumma b-zanaan.* **2.** *ḍamm (u ḍamm) n-.* Islam embraces people from many various nationalities. *l-ʔislaam yḍumm naas min muxtalif iš-šuɛuub.*
emerald - *zmurrada* pl. *-aat* coll. *zmurrad.*
to **emerge** - **1.** *ṭilaɛ (a ṭuluuɛ), xiraj (u xuruuj).* He emerged from the meeting smiling. *ṭilaɛ imnil-ijtimaaɛ w-wujha yibtisim.* **2.** *biraz (i buruuz).* He emerged as one of the leaders of the party. *biraz ka-ʔazzad zuɛamaaʔ il-zizib.* **3.** *niša? (i naši?), ḍahar (a ḍuhuur).* These facts emerged from the study of the problem. *hal-zaqaayiq nišʔat min diraasat il-muškila.* **4.** *bizaġ (a bizuuġ).* The sun emerged from behind the hills. *bizġat iš-šamis min wara j-jibaal.*
emergency - **1.** *ṭaariʔa* pl. *ṭawaariʔ.* A state of emergency was declared. *zaalat iṭ-ṭawaariʔ inɛilnat.* **2.** *ḍṭiraari*, mustaɛjal.* This is an emergency case. *haaδi zaala ḍṭiraariyya.* **3.** *ḍaruura.* In case of emergency call the doctor. *ɛind iḍ-ḍaruura xaabur iṭ-ṭabiib.*
emergency brake - *handibreek* pl. *-aat.*
emergency exit - *baab* (pl. *bwaab) ṭawaariʔ.*
emigrant - *muhaajir* pl. *-iin.* Lebanese emigrants have settled all over the world. *l-muhaajiriin il-lubnaaniyyiin istawṭinaw ib-kull makaan bil-ɛaalam.*
to **emigrate** - *haajar (i muhaajara).* In recent years many people have emigrated from Europe. *bis-siniin il-ʔaxiira hwaaya naas haajraw min ʔawruṗṗa.*
eminent - *baariz.*
emir - *ʔamiir* pl. *ʔumaraaʔ.*
emotion - *ɛaaṭifa* pl. *ɛawaaṭif, šuɛuur.* He couldn't hide his emotion. *ma-gidar yixfi ɛaaṭifta.*
emperor - *ʔimbiraaṭoor* pl. *-iin.*
emphasis - *ʔahammiyya, taʔkiid.*
to **emphasize** - *ʔakkad (i taʔkiid) t-.* He emphasized the need for more teachers. *ʔakkad il-zaaja ʔila muɛallimiin ʔakθar.*
emphatically - *b-šidda, b-taʔkiid.* I'll have to deny that emphatically. *raz-aḍṭarr ʔanfi haδaak ib-šidda.*
empire - *ʔimbiraaṭooriyya* pl. *-aat.*
to **employ** - *staxdam (i stixdaam), šaġġal (i tšiġġil, tašġiil) t-.* This factory employs a thousand workers. *hal-maɛmal yistaxdim ʔalif ɛaamil.*
**Where are you employed? *ʔinta ween tištuġul?*
employee - *mustaxdam* pl. *-iin, muwaḍḍaf* pl. *-iin.*
employer - *mustaxdim* pl. *-iin.*
employment - **1.** *šuġuḷ.* What kind of employment did you finally get? *taaliiha šinu nooɛ iš-šuġuḷ illi zaṣṣalta?* **2.** *stixdaam.* The employment of children is forbidden by law. *stixdaam iṣ-ṣiġaar mamnuuɛ qaanuunan.*
empty - *faariġ, xaali.* Do you have an empty box? *ɛindak fadd ṣanduug faariġ?* — He made empty threats. *haddad tahdiidaat faarġa.*
to empty - **1.** *farraġ (i tfurriġ, tafriiġ) t-, ʔaxla (i ʔixlaaʔ) n-.* Please empty this tank. *rajaaʔan farriġ hat-tanki.* **2.** *xila (i ʔixlaaʔ).* The hall emptied in five minutes. *l-qaaɛa xilat ib-xamis daqaayiq.* **3.** *ṣabb (u ṣabb).* This river empties into the ocean. *han-nahar yṣubb bil-muziiṭ.*
to **enable** - *makkan (i tmikkin) t-, ʔahhal (i tʔihhil) t-.* This experience will enable you to get a good position. *hat-tajruba la-budd itmakkinak imnil-zuṣuul ɛala waḍiifa zeena.*
to **enact** - *sann (i sann) n-.* This law was enacted in 1920. *hal-qaanuun insann ib-sanat ʔalf w-tisiɛmiyya w-ɛišriin.*
to **enclose** - *rifaq (i ʔirfaaq) n-.* I've enclosed herewith the newspaper clippings you wanted. *rfaqit ṭayyan quṣaaṣaat ij-jaraayid ir-riditha.* — The sum due you is enclosed herewith. *l-mablaġ il-maṭluub bii ʔilak murfaq ṭayyan.*
to **encourage** - *šajjaɛ (i tašjiiɛ) t-.* He encouraged me to stick it out. *huwwa šajjaɛni ɛal-ʔiṣraar ɛaleeha.*
encouragement - *tašjiiɛ.*
to **encroach** - *ɛtida (i ɛtidaaʔ), tjaawaz (a tajaawuz).* That would be encroaching upon his rights. *δaak ykuun iɛtidaaʔ ɛala zuquuqa.*
encyclopedia - *daaʔirat* (pl. *dawaaʔir) maɛaarif, ʔinsikloopiidya* pl. *-aat, mawsuuɛa* pl. *-aat.*
end - **1.** *ʔaaxir* pl. *ʔawaaxir, nihaaya* pl. *-aat.* I'll pay you the balance at the end of the month. *raz-adfaɛ-lak il-baaqi b-ʔaaxir iš-šahar.* **2.** *nihaaya* pl. *-aat.* Tie the two ends together. *ʔurbuṭ in-nihaayteen suwa.* — That is the end of the program. *haaδi nihaayat il-barnaamij.* **3.** *ġaaya*

pl. *-aat.* He believes that the end justifies the means. *yiεtiqid ʔinna l-ġaaya tbarrir il-waasṭa.*
4. *ẓadd.* Can't you put an end to these squabbles? *ma-tigdar itẓuṭṭ ẓadd il-han-nizaaε?*
**He scolded a bit and that was the end of it. *rabrab išwayya w-intiha l-mawḍuuε.*
**Except for a few loose ends, everything is done. *kullši kimal ma-εada baεḍ il-ʔašyaaʔ il-basiiṭa.*
to end - 1. *ʔanha (i ʔinhaaʔ) n-, xaḷḷaṣ (i txiḷḷiṣ) t-.* He ended his speech with a quotation from the Koran. *ʔanha muẓaaḍarta b-ʔaaya qurʔaaniyya.* 2. *xilaṣ (a xalaaṣ), ntiha (i ntihaaʔ).* Won't this back-biting ever end? *hal-qaal w-qiil ma-raẓ-yixlaṣ ʔabad?*
endeavor - *masεa* pl. *masaaεi.* He did not succeed in his endeavor. *ma-nijaẓ ib-masεaa.*
to **endorse** - 1. *jayyar (i tajyiir) t-, ḍahhar (i taḍhiir) t-.* Endorse the check, please. *jayyir ič-čakk rajaaʔan.* 2. *ʔayyad (i taʔyiid) t-.* He endorsed my program. *ʔayyad barnaamiji.*
to **endure** - *tẓammal (a taẓammul).* She endured the grief quietly. *tẓammlat il-faajiεa b-kull huduuʔ.*
enema - *ẓuqna* pl. *ẓuqan.*
enemy - *εadu* pl. *ʔaεdaaʔ.*
energy - 1. *ẓayawiyya, našaaṭ.* He's full of energy. *haaḍa malyaan ẓayawiyya* or *kulla ẓayawiyya.* 2. *ṭaaqa.* I read a book on atomic energy. *qreet iktaab εan iṭ-ṭaaqa ḍ-ḍarriyya.*
to **enforce** - *ṭabbaq (u taṭbiiq) t-, naffaḍ (i tanfiiḍ) t-.* This law has never been strictly enforced. *hal-qaanuun ʔabadan ma-ṭṭabbaq biḍ-ḍabuṭ.*
to **engage** - 1. *staxdam (i stixdaam).* We've just engaged a new maid. *hastawwna staxdamna xaadma jdiida.* 2. *tεaaqad (a taεaaqud) wiyya.* We engaged him for two concerts. *tεaaqadna wiyyaa b-ẓafilteen mawsiiqiyya.* 3. *tdaxxal (a tadaxxul).* I don't engage in politics. *ʔaani ma-atdaxxal bis-siyaasa.* 4. *ṣaadam (i muṣaadama).* They engaged the enemy on the hill. *ṣaadmaw il-ʔaεdaaʔ εat-tall.*
engaged - 1. *maxṭuub.* How long have they been engaged? *šgadd ṣaar-ilhum maxṭuubiin?* 2. *mašġuul.* I'm presently engaged in research. *ʔaani hassa mašġuul ib-baẓiθ.*
engagement - 1. *mawεid* pl. *mawaaεid.* I have an engagement this evening. *εindi mawεid hal-masa.* 2. *xuṭba* pl. *-aat, xuṭab.* They announced her engagement. *ʔaεlinaw xuṭbatha.*
engine - *makiina* pl. *makaayin.* You left the engine running. *ʔinta xalleet il-makiina tištuġul.* — This train has two engines. *hal-qiṭaar bii makiinteen.* — The factory is equipped with electric machines. *l-maεmal imjahhaz bil-makaayin il-kahrabaaʔiyya.*
engineer - 1. *muhandis* pl. *-iin.* I've asked the engineer to draw a new set of plans. *ṭlabit imnil-muhandis ʔan yirsim majmuuεa jdiida mnil-muxaṭṭaṭaat.* 2. *saayiq* (pl. *suwwaaq*) *qiṭaar.* The engineer stopped the train. *saayiq il-qiṭaar waggaf il-qiṭaar.* 3. *makiinači* pl. *-iin, -iyya.* The engineer says there's something wrong with the boiler. *l-makiinači gaal ʔaku fadd εaṭub bil-marjal.*
to engineer - *naḍḍam (u tanḍiim, tnuḍḍum) t-.* Who engineered this plan? *minu naḍḍam hal-xuṭṭa?*
engineering - *handasa.*
English - 1. *ʔingiliizi.* He speaks English very well. *yiẓči ʔingiliizi kulliš zeen.* 2. *ʔingiliizi*.* That's an old English custom. *haaḍi εaada ʔingiliiziyya qadiima.* -- 3. *ʔingiliizi* pl. *ʔingiliiz.* The English fight well. *l-ʔingliiz yẓaarbuun zeen.*
to **engrave** - 1. *ẓufar (u ẓafur) n-.* My name is engraved on my watch. *ʔismi maẓfuur εala saaεti.* 2. *niqaš (u naquš) n-.* What is this design engraved on the sword? *šinu han-naqaš manquuš εala s-seef?*
to **enjoy** - 1. *tmattaε (a tamattuε) b-.* He's enjoying his life. *huwwa mitmattiε ib-ẓayaata.* -- He's enjoying excellent health. *yitmattaε ib-ṣiẓẓa mumtaaza.*
to enjoy oneself - *twannas (a tawannus).* Did you enjoy yourself at the dance? *twannasit bir-rigiṣ?*
enjoyment - *tamattuε, laḍḍa.*
to **enlarge** - 1. *kabbar (u tkubbur) t-.* Do you enlarge pictures? *ʔinta tkabbur ṣuwar?* 2. *wassaε (i tawsiiε, twissiε) t-, kabbar (u tkubbur) t-.* We're going to have to enlarge this room. *laazim inwassiε hal-ġurfa.*
enlargement - *ṣuura* (pl. *ṣuwar*) *mukabbara.* How many enlargements do you want? *čam ṣuura mukabbara triid?*
to **enlist** - *ṭṭawwaε (taṭawwuε).* He enlisted in the navy two days ago. *ṭṭawwaε ib-silk il-baẓriyya gabuḷ yoomeen.*
enormous - *ḍaxim, haaʔil, jasiim, εaḍiim.* That's an enormous project. *haaḍa fadd mašruuε ḍaxim.* -- He spent enormous amounts of money on this building. *difaε mabaaliġ εaḍiima b-hal-binaaya.*
enormously - *b-daraja εaḍiima, b-ḍaxaama, b-ṣuura kabiira.* The need for raw materials has grown enormously. *l-ẓaaja lil-mawaadd il-ʔawwaliyya zdaadat ib-daraja εaḍiima.*
enough - *kifaaya, kaafi.* Have you had enough to eat? *ʔakalit kifaaya?* -- Do you have enough money? *εindak ifluus kaafya?*
**Would you be kind enough to open the window? *tismaẓ tiftaẓ iš-šabbaač?*
to be enough - *kaffa (i tkiffi).* Will that be enough? *haaḍa ykaffi?*
to have enough - *šibaε (a šibiε), tkaffa (a tkiffi).* I've had enough of that talk. *šbaεit min hal-ẓači.*
to **enroll** - 1. *sajjal (i tasjiil) t-.* I'm going to enroll my son in first grade. *ʔaani raẓ-asajjil ibni biṣ-ṣaff il-ʔawwal.* 2. *tsajjal (a tasajjul).* He's going to enroll in night school. *raẓ-yitsajjal ib-madrasa masaaʔiyya.*
enslavement - *stiεbaad.*
to **enter** - 1. *xašš (u xašš), dixal (u duxuul), ṭabb (u ṭabb).* Everyone rose when the guest of honor entered. *kull waaẓid gaam min xašš ḍeef iš-šaraf.* 2. *daxxal (i tdixxil) t-.* Enter these names in the list. *daxxil hal-ʔasmaaʔ bil-qaaʔima.*
enterprise - *mašruuε* pl. *mašaariiε.* The enterprise was successful. *l-mašruuε nijaẓ.*
enterprising - *muntij.* He's the most enterprising one in the company. *huwwa ʔakθar waaẓid muntij biš-šarika.*
to **entertain** - *wannas (i twunnis) t-.* He entertained the guests with his amusing stories. *wannas il-xiṭṭaar ib-quṣaṣa j-jaḍḍaaba.*
**They entertain a great deal. *humma ysawwuun ihwaaya εazaayim.*
entertainment - 1. *tasliya.* Who's going to provide the program of entertainment? *minu raẓ-yqaddim manhaj it-tasliya?* 2. *lahu.* What do you do for entertainment around here? *šaku wasaaʔil lahu b-hal-manṭiqa?*
enthusiasm - *ẓamaas.* He didn't show any enthusiasm. *ma-raawa ʔay ẓamaas.*
enthusiastic - *mitẓammis.* I'm quite enthusiastic about it. *ʔaani kulliš mitẓammis il-haay.*
entire - *kull, kaamil, jamiiε.* The entire amount has to be paid in cash. *kull il-mablaġ laazim yindifiε naqdan.* --
**The entire evening was wasted. *ḍaaεat εalayya l-leela b-kaamilha.*
entirely - 1. *tamaaman.* You're entirely right. *ʔinta muẓiqq tamaaman.* 2. *kulliyyan, bil-kulliyya.* These two things are entirely different. *haš-šiyyeen mixtalfiin kulliyyan.*
entrance - *madxal* pl. *madaaxil, baab* pl. *bwaab.*
entry - 1. *tanziil* pl. *-aat.* The last entry in the account was five dinars. *ʔaaxir tanziil bil-ẓsaab čaan xams idnaaniir.* 2. *duxuul.* Entry into this room is not allowed. *d-duxuul il-hal-ġurfa mamnuuε.*
envelope - *ḍaruf* pl. *ḍruuf.* I need an envelope for the letter. *ʔaẓtaaj ḍaruf lil-maktuub.*
environment - *biiʔa* pl. *-aat, muẓiiṭ* pl. *-aat.* He was raised in a poor environment. *trabba b-biiʔa muu zeena.*
envoy - *manduub* pl. *-iin, mumaθθil dawli* pl. *mumaθθiliin dawliyyiin.*
envy - 1. *ġiira, ẓasad.* He was green with envy. *da-ymuut min ġiirta.* 2. *maẓsuud.* You'll be the envy of all your friends. *raẓ-itkuun maẓsuud min kull ʔaṣdiqaaʔak.*
to envy - *ẓisad (i ẓasad) n-, ġaar (a ġiira) n- min.* I envy you! *ʔaani ʔaẓisdak!*
epidemic - *wabaaʔ* pl. *ʔawbiʔa.* An epidemic has broken out among the cattle. *fadd wabaaʔ intišar been il-maašiya.*
epilepsy - *ṣaraε.*
epoch - *door* pl. *ʔadwaar.*
epsom salts - *milẓ ifringi.*
equal - *mitsaawi.* Cut this bread into three equal parts. *guṣṣ haṣ-ṣammuuna ʔila tlaθ ʔaqsaam mitsaawiya.* 2. *kafuʔ* pl. *ʔakfaaʔ.* I don't think I'm equal to that job. *ma-aεtiqid ʔaani kafuʔ il-hal-εamal.*
to equal - 1. *εaadal (i muεaadala), tεaadal*

(*a taEaadul*) *wiyya*. It will be hard to equal him. *mniṣ-ṣuEuuba titEaadal wiyyaa*. **2.** *saawa* (*i musaawaa*). Five plus five equals ten. *xamsa zaa?idan xamsa ysaawi Eašara*.

equality - *musaawaat*. I'm a believer in equality among men. *?aani mu?min bil-musaawaat been in-naas*.

equally - **1.** *bit-tasaawi*. The two books are equally important. *l-iktaabeen muhimma bit-tasaawi*. **2.** *b-gadd*. I liked his first play equally well. *zabbeet tamθiiliita l-?uula b-gadd haay*.

equation - *muEaadala* pl. *-aat*.

equator - *xaṭṭ* (pl. *xṭuuṭ*) *istiwaa?*.

equilibrium - *tawaazun, muwaazana*.

to **equip** - *jahhaz* (*i tajhiiz*) *t-*, *hayya?* (*i tahyi?a*) *t-*. Our planes are equipped with the latest instruments. *ṭayyaaraatna mujahhaza b-?azdaθ il-wasaa?il*.

equipment - **1.** *?adawaat*. They make welding equipment. *ysawwuun ?adawaat il-liziim*. **2.** *lawaazim, garaaḍ*. He put the hunting equipment in the trunk of the car. *xalla lawaazim iṣ-ṣeed ib-ṣanduug is-sayyaara*.

equivalent - *muEaadil, musaawi, mukaafi?*.

era - *Eaṣir* pl. *Euṣuur*.

to **erase** - *misaz* (*a masiz*) *n-*, *miza* (*i mazi*) *n-*. He erased the signature. *misaz il-?imḍaa?*. -- Will you please erase the board? *?arjuuk ?imsaz is-sabbuura?*

eraser - **1.** *missaaza* pl. *-aat*, *mazzaaya* pl. *-aat*. I bought two pencils and an eraser. *štireet qalameen w-missaaza*. **2.** *missaaza* pl. *-aat*. We need some chalk and an eraser. *niztaaj išwayya tabaašiir w-fadd missaaza*.

to **erect** - *bina* (*i binaa?*) *n-*. Who erected this building? *minu bina hal-ibnaaya?*

erosion - *ta?aakul*.

to **err** - *ġilaṭ* (*a ġalaaṭ*).

errand - *šaġla* pl. *-aat*. I have a few errands I want to do. *Eindi čam šaġla ?ariid asawwiiha*.

erroneous - *maġluuṭ*. The information he gave us was erroneous. *l-maEluumaat lli nṭaana-yyaaha čaanat maġluuṭa*.

error - *ġalṭa* pl. *-aat*, *?aġlaaṭ*. I made four errors on the exam. *ġlaṭit ?arbaE ġalṭaat bil-imtizaan*.

escape - **1.** *huruub, haziima* pl. *hazaayim*. The prisoners' escape was cleverly planned. *huruub il-imsaajiin čaan imdabbar ib-mahaara*. **2.** *taxalluṣ*. We had a narrow escape. *txalluṣna čaan ib-?iEjuuba*.

to escape - **1.** *hirab* (*a huruub*), *nhizam* (*i nhizaam*). Two prisoners have escaped from the penitentiary. *masjuuneen inhizmaw imnis-sijin*. **2.** *raaz* (*u rawaaz*) *min baal*. Her face is familiar but her name escapes me. *wujihha muu ġariib laakin ?isimha raaz min baali*. **3.** *xilaṣ* (*a xalaaṣ*) *min*, *faat* (*u foot*). Nothing escapes her. *ma-aku fadd šii yixlaṣ minha* or *ma-yfuutha šii*. **4.** *txallaṣ* (*a taxalluṣ*) *min*, *xallaṣ* (*i txilliṣ*) *min*. That's the third time he's escaped punishment. *haay il-marra θ-θaalθa xallaṣ biiha mnil-Eiqaab*.

especially - *la-siyyama, b-ṣuura xaaṣṣa, xuṣuuṣan*. She's been trying especially hard lately. *da-tzaawil jahidha la-siyyama bil-mudda l-?axiira*. -- She's especially interested in sports. *hiyya mihtamma bir-riyaaḍa b-ṣuura xaaṣṣa*.

espionage - *tajassus, jaasuusiyya*.

essay - *maqaala* pl. *-aat*, *?inšaa?* pl. *-aat*.

essence - **1.** *jawhar* pl. *jawaahir*. What was the essence of his lecture? *šinu čaan jawhar zadiiθa?* **2.** *Eaṭir* pl. *Euṭuur, riiza* pl. *riiz*. This contains essence of roses. *haay tiztiwi Eaṭir il-warid*.

essential - *?asaasi**, *ḍaruuri**, *jawhari**. Fresh vegetables are essential to good health. *l-xuḍrawaat iṭ-ṭariyya šii ?asaasi liṣ-ṣizza z-zeena*.

essentials - *?usus*. You can learn the essentials in an hour. *tigdar titEallam il-?usus ib-saaEa wizda*.

to **establish** - **1.** *?assas* (*i ta?siis*) *t-*, *?anša?* (*i ?inšaa?*) *n-*. This firm was established in 1905. *haš-šarika t?assisat ib-sana ?alf w-tisiEmiyya w-xamsa*. **2.** *θibat* (*i θabaat*) *n-*. This is an established rule. *haay qaaEida θaabta*. **3.** *qarrar* (*i taqriir*) *t-*. Contrary to regulations established in the law. *xilaafan lit-taEliimaat il-muqarrara bil-qaanuun*. **4.** *ḍirab* (*u ḍarub*). He established a new record. *ḍirab raqam qiyaasi jidiid*.

establishment - *mu?assasa* pl. *-aat*, *munši?a* pl. *-aat*.

estate - *muluk* pl. *?amlaak*. His entire estate went to his eldest son. *kull mulka raaz il-?ibna č-čibiir*.

real estate - *Eiqaar* pl. *-aat*.

esteem - *ztiraam*.

estimate - **1.** *taqdiir* pl. *-aat*. My estimate was absolutely accurate. *taqdiiri čaan maḍbuuṭ tamaaman*. **2.** *siEir taqdiiri* pl. *?asEaar taqdiiriyya*. The painter made us an estimate. *ṣ-ṣabbaaġ inṭaana fadd siEir taqdiiri*.

to estimate - *qaddar* (*i taqdiir*) *t-*, *xamman* (*i taxmiin*) *t-*. The flood damage was estimated at a million dinars. *ḍarar il-fayaḍaan itqaddar ib-milyoon diinaar*.

et cetera - *?ila ?aaxirihi*.

eternal - *?azali**, *?abadi**, *xaalid*. The Imam spoke on eternal life. *l-?imaam ziča Ean il-zayaat il-?abadiyya*.

ether - *?aθiir*.

Ethiopia - *l-zabaša*.

Ethiopian - **1.** *zabaši* pl. *-iyyiin*, *?azbaaš*. Four Ethiopians visited our town today. *?arbaE ?azbaaš zaaraw madiinatna l-yoom*. **2.** *zabaši**. I'd like to learn the Ethiopian language. *yiEjibni ?atEallam il-luġa l-zabašiyya*.

etiquette - *?uṣuul, ?adaab*.

Euphrates - *l-furaat*.

Europe - *?ooruppa*.

European - *?ooruppi** pl. *-iyyiin*.

to **evacuate** - *?axla* (*i ?ixlaa?*) *n-*. We have to evacuate the town or else we'll be killed. *laazim nixli l-madiina w-?illa ninkitil*.

evacuation - *?ixlaa?*.

to **evade** - *tharrab* (*a taharrub*), *tmallaṣ* (*a tamalluṣ*). She evaded the question. *tharrbat imnis-su?aal*.

to **evaluate** - *Eaadal* (*i muEaadala*). The college evaluated my diploma and accepted me. *l-kulliyya Eaadlat šihaadti w-qiblatni*.

to **evaporate** - *tbaxxar* (*a tabaxxur*), *ṭaar* (*i ṭeeraan*). The alcohol has all evaporated. *l-kuzuul kulla tbaxxar*.

even - **1.** *zawji**. Two, four, and six are even numbers. *θneen w-arbaEa w-sitta ?arqaam zawjiyya*. **2.** *haadi?*. He has an even disposition. *Einda ṭabuE haadi?*. **3.** *Eadil*. I have an even dozen left. *buqa Eindi darzan Eadil*. **4.** *zatta*. Even a layman can understand that. *zatta š-šaxṣ il-mu-muxtaṣṣ yigdar yiftihimha l-haay*. -- Not even he knows the truth. *zatta huwwa ma-yuEruf il-zaqiiqa*. -- That's even better. *haaḍi zatta baEad ?azsan*.

even now - *zatta baEad hassa*. Even now I can't convince him. *zatta baEad hassa ma-agdar aqinEa*.

even so - *maEa haaḍa*. Even so I can't agree with you. *maEa haaḍa ?aani ma-attifiq wiyyaak*.

even though - *walaw*. Even though he succeeds in everything, he's not satisfied. *walaw yinjaz ib-kullši huwwa ma-raaḍi*.

not even - *zatta ma-*. I couldn't even see him. *?aani zatta ma-gdart ašuufa*.

to be even - *twaafa* (*a tawaafi*), *tpaawak* (*a tapaawuk*). He took his money from me and we were even. *?axaḍ ifluusa minni w-twaafeena*.

to get even - *tpaawak* (*a tapaawuk*), *?axaḍ* (*u*) *zeel~*. Just you wait! I'll get even with you! *?uṣbur-li šwayya!* *?atpaawuk wiyyaak!* or *?usbur-li šwayya! raz-aaxuḍ zeeli minnak!*

to even up - *Eaadal* (*i muEaadala*). Your team is stronger than ours. Let's even them up before we play. *firqatkum ?aqwa min firqatna. xalli nEaadilhum gabuḷ-ma nilEab*.

evening - *masaa?, masa* pl. *?umsiyaat, leela* pl. *lyaali*. The evenings here are cool. *l-?umsiyaat ihna baarda*. -- Good evening! *masaa? il-xeer!* -- We take a walk every evening. *nitmašša kull leela*.

evenly - *bit-tasaawi, bit-taEaadul*. The paint isn't spread evenly. *ṣ-ṣubuġ ma-mitwazziE bit-tasaawi*. -- Divide the apples evenly among you. *qismu t-tiffaaz beenaatkum bit-tasaawi*.

event - **1.** *zadaθ* pl. *?azdaaθ, zaadiθa* pl. *zawaadiθ*. It was the most important event of the year. *čaanat ?ahamm zadaθ bis-sana*. **2.** *zaal* pl. *?azwaal*. I'll be there in any event. *raz-akuun ihnaak Eala ?ay zaal*. **3.** *zaala* pl. *-aat*. In the event of an accident, call the police. *b-zaalat wuquuE zaadiθa, ?ixbir iš-šurṭa*.

eventually - *?axiiran, bil-?axiir*.

ever - *?abad, ?abadan* (with negative). Haven't you ever been in the United States? *?inta ?abad ma-raayiz lil-wilaayaat il-muttazida?* -- Don't ever do this again. *la-tsawwi haaḍa marra θaaniya ?abadan*.

**Who ever heard of such a thing! *minu saamiE ib-hiiči šii!*

ever since - *min, min wakit*. Ever since the

accident I've had pains in my leg. *min wakt il-ʒaadiθ buqa* ʕ*indi* ʔ*alam ib-rijli.* --
hardly ever - *naadiran, mnin-naadir.* I hardly ever have a headache. *naadiran yoojaʕni raasi.*
every - *kull.* He comes here every week. *huwwa yiji hnaa kull isbuuʕ.* -- Give every child one. ʔ*inṭi wiʒda l-kull ṭifil.* -- It rains every time we want to go out. *kull marra nriid niṭlaʕ tumṭur id-dinya.*
every now and then - *been kull mudda w-mudda.*
• He takes a drink every now and then. *yaaxuδ-la fadd peek been kull mudda w-mudda.*
every other - *been- w-, kull -een.* They have meat every other day. *yaakluun laʒam been yoom w-yoom* or *yaakluun laʒam kull yoomeen.*
everybody - *kull waaʒid, kull in-naas.* Everybody has to do his duty. *kull waaʒid laazim yquum ib-waajba.* -- I told it to everybody. *gilitha l-kull in-naas.*
everybody else - *kull il-*ʔ*aaxariin, kull il-baaqiin.* I have no objection if everybody else is agreed. ʔ*aani ma-*ʕ*indi maaniʕ* ʔ*iδa kull il-*ʔ*aaxariin imwaafqiin.*
everything - *kullši.* He's mixed up everything. *xarbaṭ kullši.*
everywhere - *b-kull makaan.* I've looked everywhere for that book. *dawwarit* ʕ*ala δaak il-iktaab ib-kull makaan.*
to **evict** - *ṭallaʕ (i taṭliiʕ) t-.* The landlord evicted them from the house. *ṣaaʒb il-muluk ṭallaʕhum imnil-beet.*
evidence - *bayyna* pl. *-aat, burhaan* pl. *baraahiin, ʒijja* pl. *ʒijaj, daliil* pl. ʔ*adilla.* He was convicted on the basis of false evidence. *nʒikam istinaadan* ʕ*ala bayynaat kaaδiba.*
evident - *ḍaahir, waaḍiʒ.* It was evident that she was sick. *čaan waaḍiʒ hiyya mariiḍa.*
evil - **1.** *šarr* pl. *šuruur,* ʔ*ašraar.* He chose the lesser of the two evils. *xtaar* ʔ*ahwan iš-šarreen.* **2.** *sayyi*ʔ. He has evil intention. ʕ*inda qaṣid sayyi*ʔ.
evolution - *taṭawwur, rtiqaa*ʔ.
ewe - *naʕja* pl. *-aat.*
exact - *ṭabq il-*ʔ*aṣil, tamaam.* Is this an exact copy? *haaδi nusxa ṭabq il-*ʔ*aṣil?*
**Write down the exact amount. ʔ*iktib il-mablaġ biḍ-ḍabuṭ.*
exactly - *tamaaman, biḍ-ḍabuṭ, maḍbuuṭ.* That is exactly the same. *haaδi miθilha biḍ-ḍabuṭ.* -- That wasn't exactly nice of you. *haδiič čaanat muu ʒilwa tamaaman minnak.*
to **exaggerate** - *baalaġ (i mubaalaġa) t-, hawwal (i tahwiil) t-, ḍaxxam (u taḍxiim) t-, ġaala (i muġaalaat) t-.* You're exaggerating as usual. ʔ*inta da-tbaaliġ ʒasb il-*ʔ*uṣuul.*
exaggeration - *tahwiil, mubaalaġa, muġaalaat, taḍxiim.* There's no need for exaggeration. *ma-aku ʒaaja l-hat-tahwiil.*
exam - *mtiʒaan* pl. *-aat.*
examination - **1.** *mtiʒaan* pl. *-aat.* The examination was easy. *l-imtiʒaan čaan sahil.* **2.** *faʒiṣ* pl. *fuʒuuṣ.* What did the examination show? *š-ṭilaʕ bil-faʒiṣ?* **3.** *stijwaab* pl. *-aat.* The examination of the witnesses lasted two hours. *stijwaab iš-šuhuud ṭawwal saaʕteen.*
to **examine** - **1.** *fuʒaṣ (a faʒiṣ) n-.* The doctor examined me thoroughly. *ṭ-ṭabiib fuʒaṣni faʒiṣ daqiiq.* **2.** *stajwab (i stijwaab).* The witnesses haven't been examined yet. *li-hassa baʕad ma-stajwibaw iš-šuhuud.* **3.** *daqqaq (i tadqiiq).* I'm here to examine the books. ʔ*aani hnaa da-adaqqiq id-dafaatir.* **4.** *mtiʒan (i mtiʒaan), xtibar (i xtibaar).* He examined me in geography first. *mtiʒanni bij-juġraafiya bil-*ʔ*awwal.*
example - **1.** *maθal* pl. ʔ*amθaal.* Give me an example. *nṭiini maθal.* **2.** *qudwa* pl. *-aat, miθaal* pl. ʔ*amθaal.* You should take him as an example in studying. *laazim tittaxδa qudwa bid-diraasa.* **3.** ʕ*ibra* pl. ʕ*ibar, miθaal* pl. ʔ*amθaal.* The government punished him so he'd be an example to others. *l-ʒukuuma* ʕ*aaqbata ʒatta ykuun* ʕ*ibra l-ġeera.*
for example - *maθalan,* ʕ*ala sabiil il-miθaal, bil-maθal.* Let's take Russia, for example ... *xalli naaxuδ ruusya maθalan ...*
excavation - **1.** *ʒafur.* When will the excavation for the new houses begin? *šwakit raʒ-yibdi ʒafr il-*ʔ*asaasaat lil-ibyuut ij-jidiida?* **2.** *ʒafriyya* pl. *-aat, tanqiib* pl. *-aat.* Excavations in Iraq uncovered many relics of the past. *l-ʒafriyyaat bil-*ʕ*iraaq kišfat* ʕ*an muxallafaat* ʔ*aθariyya kaθiira* ʕ*an il-maaḍi.*

to **exceed** - **1.** *zaad (i ziyaada)* ʕ*ala,* ʕ*an.* The country's imports exceed the exports. *l-waaridaat bil-balad da-tziid* ʕ*an iṣ-ṣaadiraat.* **2.** *tjaawaz (a tajaawuz).* They caught him exceeding the speed limit. *lizmoo mitjaawaz il-ʒadd il-*ʔ*aqṣa lis-surʕa.* **3.** *faaq (u fooq), zaad (i ziyaada)* ʕ*ala.* The enemy's strength exceeded ours. *quwwat il-*ʕ*adu faaqat quwwatna.*
exceedingly - *kulliš.* She's exceedingly beautiful. *hiyya ʒilwa kulliš.*
to **excel** - **1.** *faaq (u fawq) n-, tfawwaq (a tafawwuq)* ʕ*ala.* He excelled them all. *faaqhum kullhum.* **2.** *biraʕ (a baraaʕa) b-, biraz (i buruuz) b-.* He excelled in sports. *biraʕ bir-riyaaḍa.*
excellency - *maʕaali.* I'd like to present my brother to your excellency. ʔ*aʒibb aqaddim il-maʕaaliikum* ʔ*axuuya.*
excellent - *mumtaaz, baariʕ, falla.* He's an excellent tennis player. *huwwa laaʕib tanis mumtaaz.*
except - *ma-*ʕ*ada,* ʔ*illa, ġeer, b-istiθnaa*ʔ. Everyone believed it except him. *l-kull iʕtiqdaw biiha ma-*ʕ*adaa.* -- I like the book except for one chapter. ʔ*aʒibb il-iktaab b-istiθnaa*ʔ *faṣil waaʒid.*
exception - *stiθnaa*ʔ pl. *-aat.* We make no exceptions. *ma-*ʕ*idna stiθnaa*ʔ*aat* or *ma-nistaθni* ʔ*aʒʒad.*
excerpt - *maqṭaʕ* pl. *maqaaṭiʕ.* He read me an excerpt from the new book. *qiraa-li maqṭaʕ imnil-iktaab il-ijdiid.*
excess - *zaayid.* Pour off the excess fat. *diir id-dihin iz-zaayid.*
to excess - *b-*ʔ*ifraaṭ.* I drink sometimes, but not to excess. ʔ*aani* ʔ*aʒyaanan ašrab, laakin muu b-*ʔ*ifraaṭ.*
excessive - *faadiʒ, baaʒiḍ.* Their charges are excessive. ʔ*ujuurhum faadʒa.* -- They've been making excessive profits. *čaanaw da-yʒaqqiquun* ʔ*arbaaʒ faadiʒa.*
exchange - **1.** *tabaadul.* We've arranged for an exchange of prisoners. *tdabbarna mas*ʔ*alat tabaadul il-*ʔ*asra.* **2.** *baddaala* pl. *-aat.* The rebels have captured the telephone exchange. *θ-θuwwaar stawlaw* ʕ*ala baddaalat it-talafoon.*
rate of exchange - *siʕir il-*ʕ*umla.* What's the rate of exchange today? *šinu siʕir il-*ʕ*umla l-yoom?*
stock exchange - *boorṣa.* Where's the stock exchange? *ween il-boorṣa?*
to exchange - **1.** *baddal (i tabdiil) t-.* I want to exchange this book for another one. ʔ*ariid abaddil hal-iktaab wiyya waaʒid laax.* **2.** *tbaadal (a tabaadul).* The ministers met to exchange views. *l-wuzaraa*ʔ *ijtimʕaw yitbaadal wujhaat in-naḍar.*
to **excite** - **1.** *hayyaj (i tahyiij) t-.* The way she walks excites me. *ṭariiqat mašiiha thayyijni.* **2.** *ʒammas (i ʒamaas) t-.* His speech excited the people. *xiṭaaba ʒammas in-naas.*
to get excited - **1.** *ʒimaq (a ʒamaaqa), ṣaar (i)* ʕ*aṣabi, haaj (i hayajaan).* Don't get excited, I'll do it later on. *la-tiʒmaq, raʒ-asawwiiha baʕdeen.* **2.** *thayyaj (a tahayyuj).* Don't get excited dear, we've got all night. *la-tithayyaj* ʕ*aziizi, l-leel kulla* ʔ*ilna.* **3.** *ḍṭirab (i ḍṭiraab).* He got excited when he saw the enemy. *ḍṭirab min šaaf il-*ʕ*adu.* **4.** *tʒammas (a taʒammus).* The crowd got excited and stormed the embassy. *j-jamaahiir itʒammisat w-haajimat is-safaara.* -- I'm so excited about the elections. ʔ*aani kulliš mitʒammis bil-intixaabaat.*
exclamation mark - ʕ*alaamat taʕajjub.*
to **exclude** - *staθna (i stiθnaa*ʔ*).* Our club rules exclude women. *qawaaʕid naadiina tistaθni in-niswaan.*
exclusive - **1.** *ma-*ʕ*ada.* Your bill comes to 50 dinars exclusive of tax. *qaa*ʔ*imtak itsawwi xamsiin diinaar ma-*ʕ*ada ḍariiba.* **2.** *muṭlaq.* We have exclusive rights to this invention. ʕ*idna ʒaqq muṭlaq ib-hal-ixtiraaʕ.* **3.** *xaaṣṣ.* This is quite an exclusive club. *haaδa naadi kulliš xaaṣṣ.*
excuse - **1.** ʕ*uδur* pl. ʔ*aʕδaar.* That's no excuse! *haaδa muu* ʕ*uδur!* **2.** *mubarrir* pl. *-aat.* There's no excuse for this. *ma-aku mubarrir il-haay.*
to excuse - *simaʒ (a samiʒ) l-.* Excuse my broken Arabic. ʔ*ismaʒ-li b-luġat il-*ʕ*arabiyya l-imkassira.* **2.** ʕ*ifa (i* ʕ*afi,* ʔ*iʕfaa*ʔ*) n-.* They excused him from military service. ʕ*ifoo mnil-xidma l-*ʕ*askariyya.*
to **execute** - **1.** ʕ*idam (i* ʔ*iʕdaam) n-.* The government executed the murderer at daybreak. *l-ʒukuuma* ʕ*idmat il-qaatil il-fajir.* **2.** *naffaδ (i tanfiiδ) t-.* They executed his orders promptly. *naffiδaw* ʔ*awaamra ʒaalan.*
execution - **1.** ʔ*iʕdaam* pl. *-aat.* When will his execution take place? *šwakit raʒ-yijri l-*ʔ*iʕdaam*

bii? 2. *tanfiið.* When do you expect to put the plan into execution? *šwakit tit?ammal itẓuṭṭ il-xiṭṭa mawṭiε it-tanfiið?*

executive – *?idaari*, tanfiiði*.* The executive branch has been given wide powers. *ṣ-ṣulṭa l-?idaariyya nniṭat ṣulṭaat waasεa.*

to exempt – 1. *εifa (i εafi) n–.* I've been exempted from the exam. *nεifeet imnil–imtiẓaan.* 2. *staθna (i stiθnaa?), εifa (i).* The government exempted army officers from paying the new tax. *l–ẓukuuma staθnat ḍubbaat ij–jeeš min dafε iḍ–ḍaraayib ij–jidiida.*

exercise – 1. *tamriin* pl. *tamaariin.* The tenth exercise is difficult. *t–tamriin il–εaašir ṣaεub.* 2. *riyaaḍa.* Walking is good exercise. *l–maši xooš riyaaḍa.*

to exercise – 1. *rayyaḍ (i taryiiḍ) t–.* I exercise the horse every day. *?arayyiḍ il–iẓṣaan kull yoom.* 2. *trayyaḍ (a tarayyuḍ).* You have to exercise every morning. *laazim titrayyaḍ kull yoom iṣ–ṣubuẓ.* 3. *maaras (i mumaarasa) t–.* He exercised his authority to end the strike. *maaras ṣulṭaata il–?inhaa? il–?iḍraab.*

to exert – 1. *jihad (i ?ijhaad, jahid).* He never exerts himself. *ma–yijhid nafsa ?abadan.* 2. *firaḍ (u fariḍ) n–.* That group exerts considerable influence on the party's decisions. *haj–jimaaεa tufruḍ ta?θiir kabiir εala qaraaraat il–ẓiẓib.*

to exhaust – 1. *stanfaḍ (i stinfaaḍ).* I've exhausted all possibilities. *stanfaḍit kull il–iẓtimaalaat.* 2. *xaḷḷaṣ (i taxḷiiṣ) t–.* We've almost exhausted our ammunition. *εala wašak inxaḷḷiṣ εiṭaadna.* 3. *stanẓaf (i stinẓaaf).* The oil reserves in this area are exhausted. *ẓtiyaaṭ in–nafuṭ ib–hal–manṭiqa mustanẓaf.* 4. *nihak (i ?inhaak) n–.* Traveling eight hours by train is exhausting. *safrat iθman saaεaat bil–qiṭaar tinhik.*

exhaustion – *?iεyaa?.* The runner dropped from exhaustion. *r–raakuuḍ wugaε imnil–?iεyaa?.*

exhaust pipe – *gzooz* pl. *–aat.* The exhaust pipe is broken. *l–igzooz maksuur.*

exhibit – *maεraḍ* pl. *maεaariḍ.* Did you see the science exhibit? *šift il–maεraḍ il–εilmi?*

to exhibit – 1. *raawa (i muraawa?a).* His wife loves to exhibit her jewelry. *marta yiεjibha traawi mujawharaatha.* 2. *?aḍhar (i ?iḍhaar).* He exhibited great courage in the battle. *?aḍhar šajaaεa faa?iqa bil–maεraka.* 3. *εiraḍ (u εariḍ) n–.* The Russians exhibited their new farm machinery at the fair. *r–ruus εirḍaw ?aalaathum iẓ–ẓiraaεiyya ij–jidiida bil–maεraḍ.*

exhibition – *maεraḍ* pl. *maεaariḍ.*

exile – *manfa* pl. *manaafi.* He is in exile. *huwwa bil–manfa.* 2. *manfi* pl. *–iyyiin.* I met several exiles in Beirut. *ltigeet wiyya εiddat manfiyyiin ib–beeruut.*

to exist – 1. *wujad (a wijuud) n–.* As far as I'm concerned, Israel doesn't exist. *bin–nisba ?ili, ?israa?iil ḡeer mawjuuda.* 2. *εaaš (i εeeš).* How does he manage to exist on that amount of money? *šloon yigdar yεiiš εala hal–mablaḡ?*

existence – 1. *εiiša* pl. *–aat.* He's leading a miserable existence. *da–yεiiš εiisa taεṣa.* 2. *wujuud.* He's not even aware of my existence. *wala yidri b–wujuudi.* 3. *baqaa?.* The professor explained the theory of the struggle for existence. *l–?ustaaḍ širaẓ naḍariyyat iṣ–ṣiraaε min ?ajl il–baqaa?.*

in existence – 1. *mawjuud.* This business has been in existence for fifty years. *haš–šaḡla ṣaar–ilha mawjuuda xamsiin sana.* 2. *bil–wujuud.* There is no such thing in existence. *ma–aku hiiči šii bil–wujuud.*

exit – *baab* (pl. *biibaan) ṭalεa, maxraj* pl. *maxaarij.* I can't find the exit! *ma–agdar ?algi baab iṭ–ṭalεa.*

to expand – *wassaε (i tawsiiε) t–.* They're planning to expand the communications network. *gaεad yooḍaεuun xiṭṭa it–tawsiiε šabakat il–muwaaṣalaat.*

expansion – *tawassuε.* Expansion of trade is beneficial to the country. *tawassuε it–tijaara mufiid lil–balad.*

to expect – 1. *twaqqaε (a tawaqquε), t?ammal (a ta?ammul).* I expect him at three o'clock. *?atwaqqaεa saaεa tlaaθa. –– Does he expect a tip? haaða yit?ammal baxšiiš?* 2. *ntiḍar (i ntiḍaar), t?ammal (a), twaqqaε (a).* You can't expect that of him. *ma–mumkin tintiḍir haaði minna.*

expectation – *tawaqquε.* Contrary to my expectations, the experiment succeeded. *ḍidd tawaqquεi, t–tajruba nijẓat.*

expedition – *biεθa* pl. *–aat.* He's a member of the archaeological expedition. *huwwa εuḍu bil–biεθa l–?aθariyya.*

to expel – *ṭirad (u ṭarid) n–.* The boy was expelled from school. *l–walad inṭirad imnil–madrasa.*

expenditure – *maṣruuf* pl. *–aat, maṣaariif.* Government expenditures will decrease this year. *maṣruufaat il–ẓukuuma raẓ–itqill has–sana.*

expense – *maṣraf* pl. *maṣaariif, nafaqa* pl. *–aat.* I can't afford the expense. *ma–atẓammal hal–maṣraf.*

at the expense of – *εala ẓsaab, εala nafaqa.* He made the trip at the expense of the company. *gaam bis–safra εala ẓsaab iš–šarika.*

expensive – 1. *ḡaali.* This house is very expensive. *hal–beet kulliš ḡaali.* 2. *θamiin, ḡaali.* He was wearing a very expensive watch. *čaan laabis saaεa θamiina jiddan.*

experience – 1. *xibra.* Do you have any experience in these matters? *εindak ?ay xibra b–hal–?umuur?* 2. *tajruba* pl. *tajaarub.* I had a strange experience last night. *marrat εalayya tajruba ḡariiba l–baarẓa bil–leel.*

to experience – *marr (u marr) b–.* I never experienced anything like it before. *ma–marreet ib–šii miθil haaða gabuḷ.*

experienced – 1. *mujarrib.* He's an experienced mechanic. *huwwa mujarrib miikaaniiki.* 2. *muẓannak, mujarrib.* He's an experienced politician. *haaða siyaasi muẓannak.*

experiment – *tajruba* pl. *tajaarub.* The experiment was successful. *t–tajruba čaanat naajẓa.*

to experiment – 1. *sawwa (i) tajruba.* The scientist is experimenting with rabbits. *l–εaalim da–ysawwi tajaarub εal–?araanib.* 2. *jarrab (u tajriib) t–.* The artist experimented with a new technique. *l–fannaan jarrab ṭariiqa jdiida.*

experimental – *tajrubi*.* This medicine is still in the experimental stage. *had–duwa baεda biṭ–ṭawr it–tajrubi.*

expert – 1. *xabiir* pl. *xubaraa?.* The experts declared the document a forgery. *l–xubaraa? ṣarriẓaw ?inna l–waθiiqa muẓawwara.* 2. *maahir, xabiir.* He's an expert salesman. *haaða bayyaaε maahir.*

to expire – *xilṣat (tixlaṣ) muddat–, ntiha(i) mafεuul–.* His visa expired last week. *l–viiza maalta xilṣat muddatha l–isbuuε il–faat or l–viiza maalta ntiha mafεuulha l–isbuuε il–faat.*

to explain – *fassar (i tafsiir) t–, širaẓ (a šariẓ) n–.* I explained it to him. *fassart–ilh–iyyaa.*

explanation – *tafsiir, šariẓ.* His explanation wasn't very clear. *tafsiira ma–čaan kulliš waaḍiẓ.*

explicit – *waaḍiẓ, jali*.* We gave her explicit instructions. *nṭeenaaha taεliimaat waaḍẓa.*

to explode – 1. *nfijar (i nfijaar).* A shell exploded near our house. *fadd qumbula nfijrat yamm beetna.* 2. *fajjar (i tafjiir) t–.* The government exploded an atomic bomb. *l–ẓukuuma fajjirat qumbula ðarriyya.*

exploit – 1. *ma?θara* pl. *ma?aaθir, mafxara* pl. *mafaaxir.* He never stops talking about his exploits. *ma–yiεjaz imnil–ẓači εan–ma?aaθra.* 2. *šeeṭana.* He doesn't talk about his exploits with women. *ma–yjiib ṭaari šeeṭanta wiyya n–niswaan.*

to exploit – *staḡall (i stiḡlaal).* He exploits his workers. *yistiḡill εummaala. ––* You've just begun to exploit the country's resources. *tawwkum bideetu tistiḡilluun mawaarid id–dawla.*

to explore – 1. *ktišaf (i ktišaaf).* Sections of the Rub al Khali haven't been explored yet. *baεḍ ajzaa? ir–rubε il–xaali baεadha ma–muktašafa.* 2. *biẓaθ (a baẓiθ) n–.* We explored all the possibilities of understanding. *biẓaθna jamiiε iẓtimaalaat it–tafaahum.*

explorer – *muktašif* pl. *–iin, raa?id* pl. *ruwwaad.*

explosion – *nfijaar* pl. *–aat.* The explosion was heard for miles. *l–infijaar čaan yinsimiε εala buεd amyaal.*

export – *taṣdiir.* The government has stopped the export of wheat. *l–ẓukuuma waggfat taṣdiir il–ẓunṭa.*

exports – *ṣaadiraat.* This year our exports exceeded our imports. *has–sana ṣaadiraatna ẓaadat εala stiiraadaatna.*

to export – *ṣaddar (i taṣdiir) t–.* Germany exports lenses. *?almaanya ṭṣaddir εadasaat.*

exporter – *muṣaddir* pl. *–iin.*

to expose – 1. *εiraḍ (i εariḍ) n–, εarraḍ (i taεriiḍ) t–.* How long did you expose the shot? *šgadd εiraḍt iṣ–ṣuura liṭ–ḍuwa?* –– He's constantly exposed to danger. *huwwa muεarraḍ lil–xaṭar daa?iman.* 2. *fuḍaẓ (a faḍiẓ) n–, šinaε (a šaniε).* He was exposed as a spy. *nfuḍaẓ ka–jaasuus.* 3. *kišaf (i kašif) n–, ṭallaε (i taṭliiε).* She exposed her navel before

the crowd. *kišfat ṣurratha giddaam ij-jamaahiir.*
exposure - *taεarruð̣.* He died from exposure to the sun. *maat imnit-taεarruð̣ liš-šamis.*
express - **1.** *ʔiksipras.* I went to Basra by the express. *riḥit lil-baṣra bil-ʔiksipras.* **2.** *ṣariiḥ.* It was his express wish. *haaði čaanat raġubta ṣ-ṣariiḥa.* **3.** *muεayyan.* The tool was bought for this express purpose. *hal-ʔaala nširat il-hal-ġarað̣ il-muεayyan.*
to express - **1.** *εabbar (u taεbiir) t- εan, ʔabda (i ʔibdaaʔ).* He expressed his opinion freely. *εabbar εan raʔya b-ḥurriyya.* **2.** *ʔaεrab (i ʔiεraab) εan.* Did he express any wish? *ma-ʔaεrab εan ʔay raġba?* **3.** *bayyan (i tabyiin) t-.* He expressed his concern about the situation. *bayyan qalaqa ḥawl il-ḥaala.*
expression - **1.** *taεbiir* pl. *-aat.* There's no better expression for it. *ma-ʔilha ʔaḥsan min hat-taεbiir.* **2.** *malaamiḥ, taεbiir.* I can tell by the expression on your face that you don't like it. *ʔagdar aεruf min malaamiḥ wujjak ʔanna ma-yεijbak.*
expressive - *muεabbir.* She has very expressive eyes. *εidha εyuun kulliš muεabbira.*
expressly - *ṣaraaḥatan.* The law expressly says ... *l-qaanuun ynuṣṣ ṣaraaḥatan εala ...*
expulsion - *ṭarid.* We threatened him with expulsion from the party. *haddadnaa biṭ-ṭarid imnil-ḥizib.*
exquisite - *raaʔiε.* She has exquisite features. *εidha malaamiḥ raaʔiεa.*
extemporaneous - *rtijaali*, murtajal.* The minister gave an extemporaneous speech. *l-waziir ʔalqa xiṭaab irtijaali.*
to **extend** - **1.** *mtadd (a mtidaad).* The dunes extend for miles. *r-rawaabi timtadd il-buεud ʔamyaal.* **2.** *madd (i madd) n-.* He extended a helping hand to me. *madd-li yadd il-musaaεada.* **3.** *maddad (i tamdiid) t-.* I'd like to extend this visa. *ʔaḥibb amaddid hal-viiza.* **4.** *qaddam (i taqdiim) t-.* We'd like to extend our sincere congratulations. *nwidd ʔan inqaddim tahaaniina l-qalbiyya.*
extended - *ṭuwiil.* He remained in the hospital for an extended period. *buqa bil-mustašfa mudda ṭuwiila.*
extension - **1.** *tamdiid* pl. *-aat.* He gave me another week's extension. *nṭaani tamdiid l-muddat isbuuε laax.* -- The extension of the new road to Mosul will be finished next year. *tamdiid iṭ-ṭariiq ij-jidiid lil-mooṣil raḥ-yikmal is-sana j-jaaya.* **2.** *fariε* pl. *furuuε.* We need two more extensions for our telephone. *niḥtaaj farεeen baεad lit-talafoon maalna.*
extension cord - *waayir sayyaar* pl. *waayraat sayyaara.*
extensive - *waasiε.* He was given extensive powers. *nniṭa ṣulṭaat waasεa.*
extent - **1.** *daraja, ḥadd.* To a certain extent, he's responsible for the disaster. *ʔila daraja muεayyana, huwwa masʔuul εan il-kaariθa.* **2.** The extent of his influence is still not known. *mada nufuuða baεad ma-maεruuf.*
**He resembles his father to some extent. *yišbah ʔabuu baεð̣ iš-šabah.*
exterior - **1.** *xaariji*, barraani*.* This is an exterior view of the house. *haaða manðar xaariji lil-beet.*
to **exterminate** - *qið̣a (i qað̣aaʔ) n- εala, staʔṣal (i stiʔṣaal).* We hired a man to exterminate the termites. *šaġġalna rijjaal ḥatta yiqð̣i εal-ʔarð̣a.*
external - *xaariji*.* This medicine is for external use only. *had-duwa lil-istiεmaal il-xaariji faqaṭ.*
extinct - *munqarið̣.* The dinosaur is an extinct animal. *d-daynaṣoor ḥaywaan munqarið̣.*

to **extinguish** - *ṭaffa (i taṭfiya) t-.* The fire department extinguished the fire. *daaʔirt il-ʔiṭfaaʔ ṭaffat il-ḥariiq.*
extra - **1.** *zaayid, ʔið̣aafi*.* Do you have a few extra pencils? *εindak čam qalam zaayid?* **2.** *jiddan.* These are extra large eggs. *hal-beeð̣ ikbaar jiddan.*
extract - *xulaaṣa* pl. *-aat.* Give me a bottle of lemon extract. *nṭiini šiiša min xulaaṣt il-leemuun.*
to extract - **1.** *šilaε (a šaliε) n-.* The dentist extracted two of my teeth. *ṭabiib il-ʔasnaan šilaε iθneen min isnuuni.* **2.** *staxlaṣ (i stixlaaṣ).* He has a factory for extracting aluminum from its ore. *εinda maεmal l-istixlaaṣ il-ʔalaminyoom min maaddta l-xaam.*
extradition - *tasliim il-mujrimiin.* We have extradition agreements with many countries. *εidna muεaahadaat tasliim il-mujrimiin wiyya hwaaya duwal.*
extraordinary - **1.** *ġeer iεtiyaadi*.* Only an extraordinary person could do that. *bass fadd šaxiṣ ġeer iεtiyaadi yigdar ysawwi haaða.* -- The president is given extraordinary powers in time of war. *r-raʔiis yinniṭi ṣulṭaat ġeer iεtiyaadiyya b-wakt il-ḥarub.* **2.** *foog il-εaada.* The cabinet will have an extraordinary session tomorrow. *l-wuzaara raḥ-tiεqud ijtimaaε foog il-εaada baačir.* **3.** *xaariq.* That's something really extraordinary. *haaða fadd šii ṣudug xaariq.*
extravagant - *muṣrif* pl. *-iin, mubaððir* pl. *-iin.* She's very extravagant. *haay kulliš muṣrifa.*
extreme - **1.** *šadiid.* We had to resort to extreme measures. *ð̣ṭarreena niljaʔ ʔila ʔijraaʔaat šadiida.* **2.** *miṭṭarrif.* He is an extreme nationalist. *haaða waṭani miṭṭarrif.*
extremely - *lil-ġaaya, jiddan, hwaaya, kulliš.* This news is extremely sad. *hal-xabar muḥzin lil-ġaaya.* -- I am extremely surprised. *ʔaani mindihiš jiddan.*
eye - **1.** *εeen* pl. *εyuun.* On a clear day you can see the town from here with the naked eye. *b-yoom ṣaḥu tigdar itšuuf il-madiina minnaa bil-εeen il-mujarrada.* -- I've had my eye on that for a long time. *ṣaar-li mudda ṭuwiila ḥaaṭṭ εeeni εala haaða.* -- Keep your eye on the children while I'm out. *ḥuṭṭ εeenak εaj-jihhaal min aṭlaε.* **2.** *xurum* pl. *xruum.* The eye of this needle is very small. *xurum hal-ʔubra kulliš iṣġayyir.* **3.** *nað̣ar.* I've been trying to catch your eye for a half hour. *ṣaar-li nuṣṣ saaεa da-aḥaawil ʔalfit nað̣arak.* -- All are equal in the eyes of the law. *l-kull mitsaawiin ib-nað̣ar il-qaanuun.*

**He's lowered himself in her eyes. *wugaε min εeenha.*
to eye - *baawaε (i mbaawaεa) εala.* He eyed the chocolate longingly. *baawaε εač-čukleet ib-šahya.*
eyebrow - *ḥaajib* pl. *ḥwaajib.* He has thick eyebrows. *εinda ḥwaajib θixiina.*
eyedrops - *qaṭra* pl. *-aat.* Use these eyedrops three times a day. *staεmil hal-qaṭra θlaθ marraat bil-yoom.*
eyeglasses - *manð̣ara, manaað̣ir* pl. *manaað̣ir, εweenaat.* Do you wear eyeglasses? *tilbas manaað̣ir?*
eyelash - *rimiš* pl. *rmuuš, hadab* pl. *ʔahdaab.* You have pretty black eyelashes. *εindič irmuuš sooda ḥilwa.*
eyelid - *jifin* pl. *jfuun.* She's wearing eyeshadow on her eyelids. *hiyya xaalla kuḥul εala jfuunha.*
eyesight - *baṣar, nað̣ar.* You have weak eyesight. *baṣarak ð̣aεiif.*

F

fabric - *qmaaš.* My wife bought some fabric to make a new jacket. *marti štirat iqmaaš ḥatta txayyiṭ sitra.*
face - **1.** *wujih* pl. *wjuuh.* If I'd been in your place, I'd have told him to his face. *loo b-makaanak, čaan gitt-la b-wujha.* -- She slammed the door in my face. *saddat il-baab ib-wujhi.* **2.** *ð̣aahir.* On the face of it, it looks like a good proposition. *ḥasb ið̣-ð̣aahir, ybayyin xooš iqtiraaḥ.*
at face value - *b-mað̣aahir xaarijiyya.* She takes everything at face value. *taaxuð kullši b-mað̣aahirha l-xaarijiyya.*

to face - **1.** *waajah (i muwaajaha) t-.* Let's face the facts. *xalli nwaajih il-ḥaqaayiq.* -- I can't face him. *ma-agdar awaajha.* -- Face the wall. *waajih il-ḥaayiṭ.* **2.** *ttijah (i ttijaah), waajah (i).* Our windows face south. *šbaabiična tittijih lij-jinuub.*
**The building is faced with red brick. *waajhat il-ibnaaya mabniyya b-ṭaabuug ʔaḥmar.*
facing - *gbaal, mwaajih, muqaabil.* He lives in the house facing the theater. *yiskun bil-beet li-gbaal is-siinama.*
fact - *ḥaqiiqa* pl. *ḥaqaayiq, waaqiε* pl. *waqaayiε.* That's a well-known fact. *haðiič ḥaqiiqa kulliš*

maεruufa. --
**He has a matter-of-fact way about him. *huwwa rajul waaqεi.*

factor - *εaamil* pl. *εawaamil.* That's an important factor. *haaδa fadd εaamil muhimm.*

factory - *maεmal* pl. *maεaamil, maṣnaε* pl. *maṣaaniε.* He's working in a factory. *huwwa da-yištuġul ib-maεmal.*

factual - *waaqεi**. His reports are always factual. *taqaariira daaʔiman waaqεiyya.*

to **fade** - 1. *kišaf (i kašif).* My socks faded in the wash. *jwaariibi kišfat bil-ġasil.* -- The wallpaper is all faded. *kull ʔawraaq il-ḥyaaṭiin loonha kišaf.* 2. *δibal (i δubuul).* These roses faded very quickly. *hal-warid δibal kulliš bil-εajal.* 3. *tlaaša (a talaaši).* The music faded in the distance. *l-mawsiiqa tlaašat min biεiid.*

to **fail** - 1. *fišal (a fašal).* His experiment failed. *tajrubta fišlat.* -- All our efforts failed. *kull muḥaawalaatna fišlat.* 2. *ṣiqaṭ (u ṣuquuṭ) b-, risab (i rusuub) b-.* Five students failed in geometry. *xamis talaamiiδ ṣiqṭaw bil-handasa.* 3. *xaan (u xiyaana) n-.* If my eyes don't fail me, that's him. *haaδa huwwa ʔiδa ma-txuunni εeeni.* 4. *ḍiεaf (a ḍuεuf).* His eyesight is failing. *naḍara da-yiḍεaf.*
**I won't fail you. *ma-axayyib ḍannak.*
don't fail ... - *la-ykuun ma-...* Don't fail to see that picture. *la-ykuun ma-tšuuf hal-filim.*
without fail - *min kull budd, ḥatman.* I'll be there without fail. *ʔaani raḥ-akuun ihnaak min kull budd.*

failure - 1. *fašal.* The failure of the experiment was due to carelessness. *fašal it-tajruba čaan sababa l-ʔihmaal.* 2. *faašil.* As a businessman he was a complete failure. *ka-rajul ʔaεmaal kaan faašil tamaaman.* 3. *sakta.* He died of heart failure. *maat ib-sakta qalbiyya.*

faint - 1. *ḍaεiif, xaafit.* I heard a faint noise. *smaεit ḥiss xaafit.* -- There's only a faint hope left. *ma-buqa ġeer ʔamal kulliš ḍaεiif.* 2. *daayix.* I feel faint. *ʔaḥiss daayix.*
**I haven't the faintest idea. *ma-εindi ʔaqall fikra.*
to faint - *ġaabat (tġiib) rooḥ-, ġima (i ʔiġmaaʔ) εala.* She fainted with fright. *ġaabat rooḥha mnil-xoof* or *ġima εaleeha mnil-xoof.*

fair - 1. *maεraḍ* pl. *maεaariḍ.* Are you going to the Damasaus International Fair? *ʔinta raayiḥ il-maεraḍ dimašq id-dawli?* 2. *muεtadil, munaasib.* That's a fair price. *haaδa siεir muεtadil.* 3. *ṣaaḥi.* Tomorrow the weather will be fair and cool. *baačir ij-jaww raḥ-ykuun ṣaaḥi w-šwayya barid.* 4. *ʔašgar* pl. *šugur.* She has blue eyes and fair hair. *εidha εyuun zurug w-šaεar ʔašgar.* 5. *mitwaṣṣiṭ.* The work is only fair. *š-šuġuḷ mitwaṣṣiṭ.*
**That wouldn't be fair! *haδaak ma-ykuun ʔinṣaaf!*

fairy tale - *qiṣṣa (pl. quṣaṣ) xaraafiyya.*

faith - 1. *diin* pl. *ʔadyaan.* I don't know what his faith is. *ma-aεruf diina šinu.* 2. *θiqa.* I lost faith in him. *ʔaani fqadit θiqti bii.*

faithful - *muxliṣ.* He's faithful to his wife. *huwwa muxliṣ il-zawijta.* -- She's very faithful in her work. *hiyya kulliš muxliṣa b-šuġuḷha.*

fake - *muqallad, mzayyaf, kaaδib.* This picture is a fake. *haṣ-ṣuura muqallada.* -- He's not a real doctor, he's a fake. *huwwa muu ṭabiib ḥaqiiqi, huwwa mzayyaf.*
to fake - 1. *zayyaf (i tziyyif, tazyiif) t-, qallad (i taqliid, tqillid) t-.* The documents are faked. *l-waθaayiq muzayyfa.* 2. *tḍaahar (a taḍaahur) b-.* He faked poverty. *tḍaahar bil-fuqur.*

fall - 1. *wagεa* pl. *-aat.* He hasn't recovered from his fall yet. *baεad li-hassa ma-ṣiḥa min wagiεta.* 2. *suquuṭ.* What do you know about the fall of the Roman Empire? *š-tuεruf εan suquuṭ id-dawla r-roomaaniyya?* 3. *xariif.* I'll be back next fall. *ʔaani raḥ-arjaε il-xariif ij-jaay.*
to fall - 1. *wugaε (a wuguuε).* He fell from the ladder. *huwwa wugaε imnid-daraj.* 2. *siqaṭ (u suquuṭ).* How did the Roman Empire fall? *šloon siqṭat id-dawla r-roomaaniyya?*
to fall apart - 1. *tkassar (a tkissir, taksiir), tfaṣṣax (a tfuṣṣux, tafṣiix).* The chair is already falling apart. *l-kursi min hassa da-yitkassar.* 2. *wugaε (a wuguuε), tfallaš (a tafalluš).* That old house is falling apart. *haδaak il-beet il-εatiig da-yoogaε.*
to fall asleep - *ġufa (i ġafu).* I fell asleep. *ʔaani ġufeet.*
to fall back on - *ltija (i ltijaaʔ) l-, lijaʔ (a ʔiljaaʔ) n- ʔila.* We can always fall back on what we've saved. *ʔiḥna daaʔiman nigdar niltiji l-illi waffarnaa.*
to fall behind - *tʔaxxar (a taʔaxxur).* We fell behind in the rent. *ʔiḥna tʔaxxarna εan dafε il-ʔajaar.*
to fall for - *nxidaε (i nxidaaε) b-.* I fell for his story. *nxidaεit b-iḥčaayta.*
to fall off - 1. *wugaε (a wuguuε).* The lid fell off. *l-qabaġ wugaε.* 2. *nizal (i nuzuul).* Receipts have been falling off lately. *l-waarid da-yinzil hal-ʔayyaam il-ʔaxiira.*
to fall through - *fišal (a fašal).* The plans for the trip fell through. *manaahij is-safra fišlat.*

fallen arches - *flaatfuut.*

false - 1. *ġalaṭ, xaṭaʔ, kaaδib.* Is this true or false? *haaδa ṣaḥiiḥ loo ġalaṭ?* 2. *εaari**, *mustaεaar.* Many people have false teeth. *hwaaya naas εidhum isnuun εaariyya.*

familiar - 1. *miṭṭiliε.* I'm not familiar with that. *ʔaani ma-miṭṭiliε εala haay.* 2. *maʔluuf.* Soldiers are a familiar sight these days. *tšuuf jinuud fadd šii maʔluuf hal-ʔayyaam.* 3. *maεruuf.* It's good to see a familiar person. *zeen waaḥid yšuuf fadd šaxiṣ maεruuf.*

family - 1. *εaaʔila* pl. *εawaaʔil, ʔahal* pl. *ʔahaali, ʔusra* pl. *ʔusar.* Did you notify his family? *ʔaxbarit εaaʔilta?* 2. *faṣiila* pl. *faṣaaʔil.* Is this animal of the cat family? *hal-ḥaywaan min faṣiilat il-qiṭṭ?*

famine - *majaaεa* pl. *-aat, qaḥaṭ.* Many people died during the famine. *hwaaya naas maataw ʔaθnaaʔ il-majaaεa.*

famous - *mašhuur, maεruuf.* His book made him famous. *kitaaba sawwaa mašhuur.*
to become famous - *štihar (i štihaar).* The restaurant became famous in a short time. *l-maṭεam ištihar b-mudda qaṣiira.*
to make famous - *šihar (i šuhra).* Her records made her famous. *ṣṭiwaanaatha šihratha.*

fan - 1. *panka* pl. *-aat, mirwaḥa* pl. *maraawiḥ.* Turn on the fan. *šaġġil il-panka.* 2. *mhaffa* pl. *mahaafiif.* Hand each one of the guests a fan. *ʔinṭi mhaffa l-kull waaḥid imnil-xuṭṭaar.*

fancy - 1. *hawa* pl. *ʔahwaaʔ, meel* pl. *myuul, walaε.* It's just a passing fancy with her. *haaδa fadd hawa wakti jaa b-raasha.* 2. *faxim, ʔaniiq.* She doesn't like fancy clothes. *ma-tiεjibha l-malaabis il-faxma.*
**Don't you look fancy! *ʔamma kaašix tamaaman!*

fantastic - *xayaali**, *taṣawwuri**.

far - 1. *biεiid* pl. *biεaad.* People came from far and near. *n-naas ʔijaw min giriib w-min biεiid.* -- That's not far wrong. *haaδa muu biεiid εan il-ḥaqiiqa.* -- I'm far from satisfied with your work. *ʔaani biεiid εan ir-riḍa εan šuġuḷak.* 2. *li-bεiid.* Don't go far. *la-truuḥ li-bεiid.*
**This joke has gone far enough. *hal-mahzala tεaddat ḥuduudha.*
as far as - 1. *l-ḥadd.* We walked together as far as the R.R. station. *mišeena suwa l-ḥadd maḥaṭṭat il-qiṭaar.* -- As far as it goes, your idea is good. *l-ḥadd, fikirtak zeena.* 2. *ḥasab-ma.* As far as I can see, his papers are o.k. *ḥasab-ma ašuuf, ʔawraaqa zeena.*
by far - *b-ihwaaya.* This is the best book by far I have read this year. *hal-iktaab b-ihwaaya ʔaḥsan iktaab qareeta has-sana.*
so far - *li-hassa, l-hal-ḥadd.* So far, you've been pretty lucky. *li-hassa, ʔinta činit kulliš maḥḍuuḍ.*

farce - *mahzala* pl. *mahaazil.* The elections were a farce. *l-intixaabaat čaanat mahaazil.*

fare - *ʔujra* pl. *ʔujar.* How much is the fare? *šgadd il-ʔujra?*

Far East - *š-šarq il-ʔaqṣa.*

farewell - *tawdiiε, wadaaε.* They gave him a farewell party. *sawwoo-la ḥaflat tawdiiε.*

farm - *mazraεa* pl. *mazaariε.* The village is surrounded by farms. *l-qarya muḥaaṭa bil-mazaariε.*
to farm - *ziraε (a ziraaεa) n-.* My sons and I can farm the land by ourselves. *ʔaani w-wuldi nigdar nizraε hal-gaaε waḥḥadna.*

farmer - *zarraaε* pl. *zurraaε, muzaariε* pl. *-iin.* Most of the farmers have already harvested their crops. *ʔakθar iz-zurraaε ḥiṣdaw il-ḥaaṣil maalhum.*

farming - *ziraaεa.* There isn't much farming in this region. *ma-aku ziraaεa hwaaya b-hal-manṭiqa.*

farther - *ʔabɛad.* You'll have to walk a little farther. *laazim timši šwayya ʔabɛad.*
to **fascinate** - *fitan (i fatin) n-, siʒar (a saʒir) n-, jiδab (i jaδib) n-.* The entire audience was fascinated by his story. *kull il-ʒaaδriin insiʒraw b-iʒcaayta.*
fascinating - *jaδδaab, fattaan, musʒir.* This is a fascinating book. *haaδa ktaab jaδδaab.*
fashion - **1.** *mooda* pl. *-aat.* Is that the latest fashion? *haaδa ʔaaxir moodaʔ* **2.** *ṭariiqa* pl. *ṭuruq, ṭaraaz* pl. *-aat, šikil* pl. *ʔaškaal, namaṭ* pl. *ʔanmaaṭ.* I want you to do it in this fashion. *ʔaʒibbak itsawwiiha ɛala haṭ-ṭariiqa.* **3.** *ʔisluub* pl. *ʔasaaliib.* He tries to write after the fashion of Manfaluti. *yʒaawil yqallid ʔisluub il-manfaluuṭi.*
fashionable - *daarij, mooda.* It is fashionable now for Iraqi women to wear western clothing. *daarij ib-hal-wakit il-imrayya l-ɛiraaqiyya tilbas malaabis ġarbiyya.*
fast - **1.** *ṣiyaam, ṣoom.* Ramadan is the month of the fast. *ramaδaan šahr iṣ-ṣiyaam.* **2.** *bil-ɛajal, b-surɛa, sariiɛ.* Don't talk so fast. *la-tiʒči hal-gadd bil-ɛajal.* **3.** *faasiq.* He travels in fast company. *huwwa yimši wiyya jamaaɛa faasqiin.* **4.** *θaabit.* Are these colors fast? *hal-ʔalwaan θaabtaʔ* -- In this case you can't make hard and fast rules. *b-hal-ʒaala ma-tigdar itʒuṭṭ qawaaɛid θaabta.* **5.** *saabiq, raakiδ.* My watch is ten minutes fast. *saaɛti saabqa ɛašir daqaayiq.* **6.** *mustaġriq.* I was fast asleep. *ʔaani činit mustaġriq ib-noomi.*
  to fast - *ṣaam (u ṣoom).* I'm fasting. *ʔaani ṣaayim.*
to **fasten** - *šadd (i šadd) n-, rubaṭ (u rabuṭ) n-.* Where can I fasten the string? *ween ʔagdar ašidd il-xeeṭʔ*
fat - **1.** *šaʒam.* This meat has very much fat on it. *hal-laʒam bii kulliš ihwaaya šaʒam.* **2.** *dihiin.* The meat is too fat. *l-laʒam kulliš dihiin.* **3.** *simiin* pl. *smaan.* He's gotten fat. *huwwa ṣaayir simiin.*
fatal - *qattaal, mumiit.* The blow was fatal. *δ-δarba čaanat qattaala.*
fate - *qaδaaʔ w-qadar, qisma, baxat.*
father - *ʔabu, ʔab* pl. *ʔaabaaʔ, ʔabbahaat; waalid.* He has no father. *ma-ɛinda ʔab.* -- The father was killed, but the mother is still alive. *l-ʔabb inkital laakin il-ʔumm baɛadha ṭayyba.* -- How's your father? *šloon ʔabuukʔ*
father-in-law - *ʔabu z-zawj, ʔabu z-zawja.* His father-in-law is a merchant. *ʔabu zawijta taajir.*
faucet - *ʒanafiyya* pl. *-aat; mzambila, mzammila* pl. *-aat.* The faucet is dripping. *l-ʒanafiyya da-tnaggiṭ.*
fault - **1.** *ɛeeb* pl. *ɛyuub.* We all have our faults. *kullna ɛidna ɛyuub.* **2.** *ġalṭa* pl. *-aat, ʔaġlaaṭ; xaṭaʔ* pl. *-aat.* It's not his fault. *hiyya muu ġaliṭṭa.*
  to find fault - *ntiqad (i ntiqaad).* You're always finding fault. *ʔinta ɛala ṭuul tintiqid* or *******ʔinta ɛala ṭuul da-tṭalliɛ min galbak ʒači.*
faulty - **1.** *xaṭaʔ, muxṭiʔ, maġluuṭ.* That's faulty thinking. *haaδa tafkiir xaṭaʔ.* **2.** *b- ɛeeb.* This machine is faulty. *hal-makiina biiha ɛeeb.*
favor - **1.** *jamiil* pl. *-aat, ʔiʒsaan* pl. *-aat, faδil* pl. *ʔafδaal, maɛruuf, minniyya* pl. *-aat.* I want you to do me a favor. *ʔariidak itsawwii-li fadd jamiil.* **2.** *jaanib, maṣlaʒa.* She spoke in my favor. *ʒičat min jaanbi.*
  in favor of - *b-jaanib.* I'm in favor of immediate action. *ʔaani b-jaanib fikrat il-ibtidaaʔ ʒaalan.*
  to favor - *faδδal (i tafδiil) t-.* He favors the youngest child. *huwwa yfaδδil il-ʔibn il-ʔaṣġar.*
favorable - **1.** *mulaaʔim, mnaasib.* He bought the house on very favorable terms. *štira l-beet ib-šuruuṭ kulliš mulaaʔima.* **2.** *mwaati.* I'm only waiting for a favorable opportunity. *ʔaani bass da-antiδir il-furṣa l-imwaatiya.*
favorite - *mufaδδal, maʒbuub.* This is my favorite book. *haaδa ktaabi l-mufaδδal.* -- This book is a great favorite with children. *hal-iktaab ihwaaya maʒbuub imnil-ʔaṭfaal.*
fear - *xoof* pl. *maxaawuf.* He doesn't know the meaning of fear. *ma-yuɛruf maɛna l-xoof.* -- Your fears are unfounded. *maxaawfak ma-ʔilha ʔasaas.*
  for fear of - *xoofan min ʔan.* He took a taxi for fear of missing the train. *ʔaxaδ taaksi xoofan min ʔan yfuuta l-qiṭaar.*
  to fear - *xaaf (a xoof) n- min.* He doesn't fear death. *ma-yxaaf imnil-moot.*
fearful - **1.** *xaayif.* Mother is so fearful about my health. *ʔummi kulliš xaayfa ɛala ṣiʒʒti.* **2.** *muxiif, yxawwuf.* That's a fearful wound you have. *haaδa jariʒ yxawwuf ɛindak.*
feat - *ɛamal ɛaδiim* pl. *ʔaɛmaal ɛaδiima.* That was quite a feat. *δaak čaan fadd ɛamal ɛaδiim.*
feather - *riiša* pl. *-aat* coll. *riiš.* The feathers are coming out of the pillow. *r-riiš da-yiṭlaɛ imnil-imxadda.* -- This hat is light as a feather. *haš-šafqa xafiifa miθl ir-riiša.*
feature - *naaʒiya* pl. *nawaaʒi.* This plan has many good features. *hal-mašruuɛ bii ɛiddat nawaaʒi zeena.* ******When does the main feature begin? *šwakit yibdi il-ʔasaaṣiʔ*
features - *taqaaṭiiɛ.* Her facial features are beautiful. *taqaaṭiiɛ wijihha ʒilwa.*
February - *šbaaṭ.*
fee - *ʔujra* pl. *ʔujuur.* The doctor's fee was thirty dinars. *ʔujuur iṭ-ṭabiib čaanat itlaaθiin diinaar.*
feeble - *δaɛiif* pl. *δuɛafaaʔ, ɛaajiz* pl. *-iin, ɛajaza.* My grandmother is very feeble. *jiddti kulliš δaɛiifa.*
feed - **1.** *luguṭ.* Did you tell them to bring the feed for the chickens? *gilt-ilhum yjiibuun il-luguṭ lid-dijaajʔ* **2.** *ɛalaf.* Did you tell them to bring the feed for the cows? *gilt-ilhum yjiibuun il-ɛalaf lil-hawaayišʔ*
  to feed - *ṭaɛɛam (u tṭuɛɛum) t-, wakkal (i twikkil).* She's feeding the chickens. *hiyya da-tṭaɛɛum id-dijaaj.*
  to be fed up with - *δaaj (u δooj) min, bizaɛ (a bazaɛ) min.* I'm fed up with this whole business. *ʔaani δijit min haš-šaġla kullha.*
to **feel** - **1.** *jass (i jass) n-.* The doctor felt my pulse. *ṭ-ṭabiib jass nabδi.* **2.** *šiɛar (u šuɛuur), ʒass (i ʒass).* He doesn't feel well. *huwwa ma-da-yišɛur zeen.* -- He feels very strongly against women drinking. *kulliš yišɛur δidd širb in-niswaan lil-mašruubaat.* -- All of a sudden I felt a sharp pain in my back. *ɛala ġafla šiɛarit ib-ʔalam ʒaadd ib-δahri.* **3.** *kamkaš (i tkumkiš), tʒassas (a tʒissis).* He felt his way to the window. *huwwa kamkaš ṭariiqa liš-šibbaač.*
  to feel about - *šiɛar (u šuɛuur) b-.* How do you feel about this matter? *ʔinta š-tišɛur ib-hal-qaδiyyaʔ* or *******š-raʔyak ib-hal-mawδuuɛʔ*
  to feel for - *tʔaθθar (a taʔaθθur) ɛala, nkisar (i nkisaar) galub- ɛala.* I really feel for you. *ʔaani ṣudug atʔaθθar ɛala ʒaalak.*
  to feel out - *tʒassas (a taʒassus) ʒaalat-.* I'll feel him out and let you know. *ʔaani raʒ-atʒassas ʒaalta w-agul-lak.*
feeling - **1.** *ʔiʒsaas.* I have no feeling in my right arm. *ʔiidi l-yimna ma-biiha kull ʔiʒsaas.* **2.** *šuɛuur.* I really didn't mean to hurt your feelings. *ma-čaan qaṣdi ʔajraʒ šuɛuurak ʔabadan.*
fellow - *ʔinsaan* pl. *naas, šaxiṣ* pl. *ʔašxaaṣ.* He's a nice fellow. *huwwa fadd ʔinsaan ṭayyib.* -- How many fellows were there? *čam šaxiṣ čaan ʔaku hnaakʔ* ******Poor fellow! *miskiin!*
felt - *čoox.*
female - *niθya* pl. *niθaaya.* Is this cat a male or a female? *hal-bazzuuna faʒal loo niθyaʔ*
feminine - *muʔannaθ.* This word is feminine in Arabic. *hal-kalima muʔannaθa bil-ɛarabi.*
fence - *siyaaj* pl. *-aat, ʒaajiz* pl. *ʒawaajiz.* There's a hole in the fence. *ʔaku zuruf bis-siyaaj.*
  to fence - *tbaaraz (a tabaaruz), liɛab (a liɛib) saas.* Do you know how to fence? *tuɛruf išloon titbaarazʔ*
  to fence in - *sayyaj (i tsiyyij) t-.* We fenced in the orchard. *sayyajna l-bistaan.*
to **ferment** - *txammar (a taxmiir).* The wine is fermenting. *š-šaraab da-yitxammar.*
fertile - *xaṣib.* The soil here is very fertile. *t-turba hnaa kulliš xaṣba.* -- He has a very fertile imagination. *ɛinda xayaal xaṣib.*
to **fertilize** - **1.** *sammad (i tasmiid) t-.* We fertilize the garden twice a year. *nsammid il-ʒadiiqa marrteen bis-sana.* **2.** *laqqaʒ (i talqiiʒ) t-.* The female fish lays the eggs somewhere, and the male comes along and fertilizes them. *s-simča n-niθya txalli l-beeδ ib-mukaan wil-faʒal yiji ylaqqiʒa.*
fertilizer - **1.** *smaad.* I'd advise you to use a chemical fertilizer. *ʔanṣiʒak tistaɛmil ismaad kiimyaawi.* **2.** *dimin, smaad.* Your shoes are covered with fertilizer. *qundartak kullha mġaṭṭaaya b-dimin.*
to **fester** - *tqayyaʒ (a tqiyyiʒ).* Is the wound still festering? *j-jariʒ baɛda mitqayyiʒʔ*

festival - *ztifaal* pl. *-aat, mahrajaan* pl. *-aat.* The festival was cancelled at the last minute. *il-iztifaal inliğa b-ʔaaxir lazδa.*
festive - *mufriz, mubhij.*
festivity - *ztifaal* pl. *-aat.*
to fetch - *jaab (i jeeba) n-.* Fetch me the newspaper. *jiib-li j-jariida.*
fever - **1.** *ṣxuuna, zumma.* Do you have any fever? *ɛindak iṣxuuna?* **2.** *zaraara.* They were all in a fever of excitement. *kullhum čaanaw ib-zaraarat il-hayajaan.*
feverish - *mṣaxxin, mazmuum.* He's feverish. *jisma mṣaxxin.*
**Why all the feverish activity over there? *luweeš kull hal-iδṭiraabaat ihnaak?*
feverishly - *b-zaraara, b-našaaṭ, b-jidd.* They're working feverishly on the new project. *da-yištağluun ib-zaraara bil-mašruuɛ ij-jidiid.*
few - **1.** *šwayya, qaliil.* Few people come to see us in the summer. *šwayya naas yjuun yzuuruuna biṣ-ṣeef.*-- Good people are few and far between. *l-xooš awaadim qaliiliin w-ṣaɛub yiltiguun.* **2.** *čam.* May I ask a few questions? *mumkin ʔasʔal fadd čam suʔaal?* or *mumkin ʔasʔal šwayyat ʔasʔila?* -- We go to see him every few days. *ʔizna nruuz inšuufa kull čam yoom.*
quite a few - *ɛadad la-baʔis bii.* Quite a few people were present. *ɛadad la-baʔis bii mnin-naas čaanaw zaaδriin.*
fiance - *xaṭiib* pl. *xuṭbaan.* Give my regards to your fiance. *sallimii-li ɛala xaṭiibič.*
fiancee - *xaṭiiba* pl. *-aat.* My fiancee writes me every day. *xaṭiibti tiktib-li kull yoom.*
fickle - *hawaaʔi*, mitqallib.* She's a very fickle person. *hiyya fadd wazda kulliš hawaaʔiyya.*
fiddle - *kamanja* pl. *-aat.* Quit scratching on that fiddle. *bass ɛaad itwaṣwuṣ ib-hal-kamanja.*
**He's not satisfied playing second fiddle to anyone. *huwwa ma-yirδa yquum ib-ɛamal θaanawi.*
to fiddle - *liɛab (a liɛib).* Don't keep on fiddling with the radio! *la-tδill tilɛab bir-raadyo!*
to fiddle away - *daɛfas (i tdiɛfis).* He fiddled away the whole day doing absolutely nothing. *δall ydaɛfis ṭuul il-yoom w-kullši ma-sawwa.*
field - **1.** *zaqil* pl. *zuquul.* We walked across the fields. *mišeena bil-zuquul.* **2.** *saaza* pl. *-aat.* The teams are coming onto the field. *l-firaq raz-tinzil lis-saaza.* **3.** *xtiṣaaṣ.* He's the best man in his field. *huwwa ʔazsan waazid b-ixtiṣaaṣa.*
fierce - **1.** *zaadd.* He have me a fierce look. *niδarni fadd naδra zaadda.* **2.** *šaris.* The lion is a fierce animal. *l-ʔasad zaywaan šaris.* **3.** *šadiid.* The heat's fierce today. *l-zaraara šadiida hal-yoom.*
fiery - *naari*.* He made a fiery speech. *ʔalqa xiṭaab naari.*
fifteen - *xumuṣṭaɛaš.*
fifteenth - *l-xumuṣṭaɛaš.* This is my fifteenth car. *haay sayyaarti l-xumuṣṭaɛaš.*
fifth - **1.** *xumus.* I got only a fifth of the money. *ʔaxaδit bass xums il-ifluus.* **2.** *xaamis.* This is my fifth car. *haay sayyaarti l-xaamsa.*
fifties - *xamsiinaat.* He's in his fifties. *huwwa bil-xamsiinaat.*
fiftieth - *l-xumuṣṭaɛaš.* This is my fifteenth car. day. *l-ɛiid intiha bil-yoom il-xamsiin.*
fifty - *xamsiin.* I gave him fifty dinars. *nṭeeta xamsiin diinaar.*
fifty-fifty - *xamsiin bil-miyya, nuṣṣ w-nuṣṣ.* I'll go fifty-fifty with you on the expenses. *raz-ašaarkak xamsiin bil-miyya mnil-maṣruufaat.*
fight - **1.** *mukaafaza* pl. *-aat, kifaaz* pl. *-aat.* He played an important part in the fight against tuberculosis. *huwwa liɛab door muhimm ib-mukaafazt is-sill.* **2.** *maɛraka* pl. *maɛaarik.* It was a fight to the finish. *čaanat fadd maɛraka lil-moot* or ***stamaataw bil-qitaal.* **3.** *ɛarka* pl. *-aat, maɛraka* pl. *maɛaarik, mbaaṣaṭ.* When the police arrived the fight was already over. *min wuṣlaw iš-šurṭa l-ɛarka caanat xalṣaana.* **4.** *mulaakama* pl. *-aat.* Were you at the fight last night? *činit bil-mulaakama l-baarza bil-leel?* **5.** *muqaawama.* He hasn't any fight left in him. *baɛad ma-buqa ɛinda ʔay muqaawama.*
**He had a flight with his wife. *tɛaarak wiyya marta.*
to fight - **1.** *zaarab (i muzaaraba).* They fought bravely in World War II. *zaarbaw ib-šajaaɛa bil-zarb il-ɛaalamiyya θ-θaanya.* **2.** *qaawam (u muqaawama) t-.* You've got to fight that habit. *ʔinta laazim itqaawum hal-ɛaada.* -- I'm going to fight this suit to the end. *raz-aqaawum had-daɛwa lil-ʔaaxir.* **3.** *tɛaarak (a ɛarka).* Have you two been fighting again? *hamm itɛaarakta marra lux?*
**Let them fight it out by themselves. *xalliihum yinjaazuun biiha b-nafishum.*
figure - **1.** *raqam* pl. *ʔarqaam.* Add up these figures. *ʔijmaɛ hal-ʔarqaam.* **2.** *kasim* pl. *ʔaksaam, jisim* pl. *ʔajsaam.* She has a nice figure. *ɛidha kasim zilu.* **3.** *šikil* pl. *ʔaškaal.* Figure seven in the book shows you the parts of the locomotive engine. *š-šikil raqam sabɛa bil-iktaab yraawiik ʔajzaaʔ makiint il-qiṭaar.* **4.** *šaxṣiyya* pl. *-aat.* He's a mighty important figure in this town. *huwwa fadd šaxṣiyya kulliš muhimma b-hal-madiina.*
**Are you good at figures? *ʔinta zeen bil-ʔizsaab?*
to figure - *qaddar (i taqdiir) t-.* I figure it's about five-thirty. *ʔaqaddir is-saaɛa bil-xamsa w-nuṣṣ.*
**The way I figure, it will cost about twenty dinars. *b-izsaabi hiyya tkallif zawaali ɛišriin diinaar.*
to figure on - *zisab (i zsaab) n- izsaab.* We didn't figure on having company. *ma-zsabna zsaab yijiina xiṭṭaar.*
to figure out - **1.** *zall (i zall) n-.* Can you figure out this problem? *tigdar itzill hal-muškila?* **2.** *zisab (i zsaab) n-.* Figure out how much it will cost. *ʔizsib išgadd raz-itkallif.* **3.** *fiham (a fahim) n-, ftiham (i fahim).* Can you figure out what he means? *tigdar tifham iš-yuqṣud?* **4.** *zizar (i zazir) n-.* I can't figure you out. *ma-agdar azizrak.*
to figure up - **1.** *zisab (i zsaab) n-.* Figure up how much I owe you. *ʔizsib išgadd ʔaani madyuun ʔilak.* -- Did you figure up the first column? *zsabt il-ɛamuud il-ʔawwal?* **2.** *waṣṣal (i tawṣiil).* The bill figures up to a hundred dollars. *l-qaaʔima twaṣṣil ʔila miit doolaar.*
file - **1.** *mubrad* pl. *mabaarid.* You need a finer file than that. *tiztaaj mubrad ʔanɛam min haaδa.* **2.** *malaffa* pl. *-aat, ʔiδbaara* pl. *-aat, faayil* pl. *-aat.* File the report in the Iraqi Oil Company file. *ʔizfuδ it-taqriir ib-malaffat šarikat in-nafṭ il-ɛiraaqiyya.* **3.** *mizfaδa* pl. *mazaafiδ, duulaab* pl. *dwaaliib.* Isn't her address in the file? *ma-mawjuud ɛinwaanha bil-mizfaδa?* **4.** *sira* pl. *siraayaat, siraawaat; xaṭṭ* pl. *xṭuuṭ.* Line up in single file! *ṣṭaffu bis-sira waazid!*
on file - *mazfuuδ.* Do we have his application on file? *ɛariiδta mazfuuδa ɛidna?*
to file - **1.** *burad (u burid) n-.* I have to file this down first. *laazim ʔabrud haaδa ʔawwal.* **2.** *zufaδ (u zafuδ) n-.* The letters have not yet been filed. *l-makaatiib baɛad li-hassa ma-nzufδat.* **3.** *qaddam (i taqdiim) t-.* I filed my application today. *qaddamit ṭalabi hal-yoom.*
filing cabinet - *duulaab* pl. *dwaaliib.*
fill - **I've had my fill of it. *wuṣlat il-xašmi.*
to fill - **1.** *tiras (u taris) n-, mila (i mali) n-.* Fill this bottle with water. *ʔitrus hal-buṭil maay.* -- The hall was filled to capacity. *l-qaaɛa čaanat matruusa tamaaman.* **2.** *šiğal (i ʔišğaal), mila (i).* The position has been filled. *l-waδiifa nšiğlat.* **3.** *ʔaxaδ (u ʔaxiδ) n-, tiras (u taris) n-.* The sofa just about fills half the room. *l-qanafa taqriiban taaxuδ nuṣṣ il-ğurfa.* **4.** *zašša (i tazšiya) t-.* This tooth will have to be filled. *has-sinn laazim yitzašša.* **5.** *jahhaz (i tajhiiz) t-.* The order hasn't been filled yet. *ṭ-ṭalabiyya baɛadha ma-tjahhzat.* **6.** *difan (i dafin) n-.* We filled the ditch in an hour. *difanna n-nugra b-saaɛa.*
to fill in - **1.** *difan (i dafin) n-.* The ditch has been filled in. *ndifnat in-nugra.* **2.** *mila (i mali) n-, tiras (u taris) n-.* Fill in all the blanks. *ʔimli kull il-faraağaat.*
**Fill your name in here. *ʔiktib ʔismak ihnaa.*
**I'm just filling in here temporarily. *ʔaani bass da-aquum bil-ɛamal ib-ṣuura muwaqqata.*
to fill up - **1.** *tiras (u taris) n-, mila (i mali) n-.* He filled up the glasses. *tiras il-iglaaṣaat.* -- Fill 'er up! *ʔitrisha!* **2.** *ntiras (i), nmila (i).* The theater was slowly filling up. *s-siinama čaanat da-tintiris išwayya šwayya.*
filling - **1.** *zašwa.* I've lost a filling from my tooth. *wugɛat il-zašwa maal sinni.* **2.** *zašu.* The cookie filling is walnuts and sugar. *l-zašu maal il-ikleeča jooz w-šakar.*
film - **1.** *ṭabaqa* pl. *-aat.* A thin film of oil formed on the water. *ṭabaqa xafiifa mnid-dihin tkawwnat ɛal-*

maay. 2. *filim* pl. *ʔaflaam.* I don't like funny films. *ma-aẓibb il-ʔaflaam il-hazaliyya.* -- I have to get another roll of film. *laazim ʔaštiri filim laax.*
to film - *ṣawwar (i taṣwiir) t-, ʔaxaδ (u ʔaxiδ) n- rasim.* They filmed the entire ceremony. *ṣawwraw kull il-iẓtifaal.*
filter - 1. *maṣfi* pl. *maṣaafi.* The water comes from the river and goes through the filter. *l-maay yiji mnin-nahar w-yidxul bil-maṣfi.* **2.** *ʔumm guṭna, mzabban.* I bought a pack of filter cigarettes. *štireet paakeet jigaayir ʔumm guṭna.*
to filter - *ṣaffa (i taṣfiya) t-.* The water will have to be filtered. *l-maay laazim yitṣaffa.*
final - 1. *nihaaʔi*.* How did you make out on your final exam? *šloon sawweet bil-imtiẓaan in-nihaaʔi?* **2.** *qaṭʕi*, nihaaʔi*.* Is this your final decision? *haaδa qaraarak in-nihaaʔi?* **3.** *ʔaxiir, xitaami*.* This is the final lecture. *haaδi l-muẓaaδara l-ʔaxiira.* **4.** *mtiẓaan nihaaʔi* pl. *mtiẓaanaat nihaaʔiyya.* I passed the final. *nijaẓit bil-imtiẓaan in-nihaaʔi.* **5.** *sibaaq nihaaʔi* pl. *sibaaqaat nihaaʔiyya, liʕib nihaaʔi* pl. *ʔalʕaab nihaaʔiyya.* The finals are being played tomorrow. *s-sibaaqaat in-nihaaʔiyya raẓ-itṣiir baačir.*
finally - 1. *ʔaxiiran, bil-ʔaxiir.* He finally yielded. *ʔaxiiran ʔaδʕan.* **2.** *taali-ma-taali, taaliiha.* So they finally got married. *laʕad taali-ma-taali tzawwjaw.*
financial - *maali*.* Our financial situation is improving. *waδiʕna l-maali da-yitẓassan.*
find - *ligya* pl. *-aat.* This book is a real find. *hal-iktaab ṣudug ligya.*
to find - 1. *liga (i lagi) n-.* I found this pencil in the street. *ligeet hal-qalam biš-šaariʕ.* -- I can never find my way around here. *ʔaani mustaẓiil ʔalgi darbi hnaa.* **2.** *wujad (i wujuud) n-.* I found him at home. *wujadta bil-beet.*
to find out - 1. *šaaf (u šoof).* Let's go out and find out what is going on. *xal-niṭlaʕ barra w-inšuuf šaku.* **2.** *ktišaf (i ktišaaf), ʕiraf (u maʕrifa).* I found out he doesn't speak English. *ktišafit ʔanna ma-yiẓči ngiliizi.*
fine - 1. *ġaraama* pl. *-aat.* He had to pay a fine. *δṭarr yidfaʕ ġaraama.* **2.** *naaʕim.* Strain it through a fine piece of cloth. *ṣaffii b-wuṣlat iqmaaš naaʕma.* **3.** *xooš, zeen.* That's a fine car you've got. *xooš sayyaara ʕindak* or *sayyaartak zeena.* **4.** *ʕaal, zeen, ṭayyib.* That's fine! *ʕaal.* **5.** *daqiiq.* That's too fine a distinction. *haaδa tafriiq kulliš daqiiq.* **6.** *luṭuf.* That was mighty fine of him. *haaδa čaan luṭuf kabiir minna.* **7.** *rifiiʕ.* I'd like a fountain pen with a fine point. *ʔariid paandaan sillaayta rifiiʕa.* **8.** *zeen.* Thanks, I'm feeling fine. *šukran, ʔaani zeen.*
to fine - *ġarram (i taġriim) t-, jazza (i jazaaʔ) t-.* The judge fined him half a dinar. *l-ẓaakim ġarrama nuṣṣ diinaar.*
finger - *ʔiṣbiʕ* pl. *ʔaṣaabiʕ.* I cut my little finger. *jiraẓit ʔiṣibʕi l-iṣġayyir.*
**He let the opportunity slip through his fingers. *δayyaʕ il-furṣa min ʔiida.*
**Keep your fingers crossed. *twakkal ʕal-aḷḷa.*
forefinger - *sabbaaba* pl. *-aat.*
little finger - *xunṣur* pl. *xanaaṣir.*
middle finger - *ʔiṣbiʕ* (pl. *ʔasaabiʕ*) *wuṣṭa.*
ring finger - *bunṣur* pl. *banaaṣir.*
finger print - *ṭabʕat ʔiṣbiʕ* pl. *ṭabʕaat ʔaṣaabiʕ.* Have you taken his fingerprints? *ʔaxaδit ṭabʕaat ʔaṣaabʕa?*
finish - 1. *nihaaya* pl. *-aat, ʔaxiir.* I read the book from start to finish. *qireet l-iktaab imnil-bidaaya lin-nihaaya.* -- It was a fight to the finish. *čaanat maʕraka lil-ʔaxiir.* **2.** *ṣubuġ.* You're rubbing off the finish of the car. *da-tjalliġ ṣubġ is-sayyaara.*
to finish - *xallaṣ (i taxliiṣ), kammal (i takmiil).* Have you finished washing the car? *xaḷḷaṣit ġasl is-sayyaara?* — I couldn't even finish my coffee. *ẓatta ma-gdarit akammil gahuuti.*
**If he does it once more, he'll be finished. *ʔiδa sawwaaha marra lux yintihi ʔamra.*
fire - 1. *naar* pl. *niiraan.* Has the fire gone out? *n-naar inṭufat?* — We were under fire all day. *činna taẓt in-naar ṭuul il-yoom.* **2.** *ẓariiq* pl. *ẓaraayiq, ẓariijiyya* pl. *-aat.* The fire damaged the building. *l-ẓariiq dammar il-binaaya.*
to be on fire - *ẓtirag (i ẓtiraag), štiʕal (i štiʕaal).* The house is on fire. *l-beet da-yiẓtirig.*
to catch fire - *ʔaxaδ (u ʔaxiδ) naar.* The hay caught fire. *t-tibin ʔaxaδ naar.*
to set on fire - *ẓirag (i ẓarig) n-.* He set the car on fire. *ẓirag is-sayyaara.*
to fire - 1. *rima (i rami), ʔaṭlaq (i ʔiṭlaaq) naar.* He fired two shots. *rima ramiiteen* or *ʔaṭlaq naar marrteen.* **2.** *δurab (u δarub).* He fired the gun twice. *δurab il-bunduqiyya marrteen.* **3.** *ṭallaʕ (i taṭliiʕ) t-, ṭirad (u ṭarid) n-, lazzam (i talziim) t- baab, fuṣal (i faṣil) n-.* I fired my driver when he wrecked the car. *ṭallaʕt is-saayiq maali min diʕam is-sayyaara* or *lazzamt is-saayiq il-baab min diʕam is-sayyaara.* -- We are going to fire five workers. *raẓ-nuṭrud xamis ʕummaal.*
fire department - *daaʔirt ʔiṭfaaʔ, ʔiṭfaaʔiyya.* Call the fire department. *xaabur daaʔirt il-ʔiṭfaaʔ.*
fire extinguisher - *ʔaalat* (pl. *-aat*) *ʔiṭfaaʔ il-ẓariiq.*
fireman - *ʔiṭfaaʔči* pl. *-iyya.*
fireplace - *šoomiina* pl. *-aat.*
fireproof - *δidd in-naar.* The walls are fireproof. *l-ẓiiṭaan δidd in-naar.*
firm - 1. *šarika* pl. *-aat.* What firm do you represent? *ʔay šarika ʔinta tmaθθil?* **2.** *raasix, waṭiid, θaabit.* I have a firm belief in God. *ʕindi ʔiimaan raasix ib-ʔaḷḷa.* **3.** *ṣalib, qawi*.* The ground is firm here. *l-gaaʕ ṣalba hnaa.* **4.** *qaaṭiʕ.* We have a firm agreement with your company to supply our paper needs. *ʕidna ttifaaq qaaṭiʕ wiyya šarikatkum il-tajhiizna b-kull ẓaajaatna mnil-waraq.*
firmly - *b-ṣuura jaazima.* I'm firmly convinced that she is innocent. *ʔaani miqtiniʕ ib-ṣuura jaazima ʔanha bariiʔa.*
first - 1. (m) *ʔawwal* (f) *ʔuula.* It's the first house on the left. *huwwa ʔawwal beet ʕal-yisra.* -- She's the first woman to become a minister. *hiyya ʔawwal mara ṣaarat waziira* or *hiyya l-mara l-ʔuula lli ṣaarat waziira.* -- I get paid on the first of the month. *ʔaaxuδ raatib ib-ʔawwal iš-šahar.* **2.** *gabuḷ, ʔawwal.* The doctor will see the women first. *d-diktoor raẓ-yšuuf in-nisaaʔ gabuḷ.* **3.** *ʔawwalan.* First let me ask you a question. *ʔawwalan xalli ʔasʔalak suʔaal.* **4.** *ʔawwali*.* They gave him first aid. *sawwoo-la ʔisʕaaf ʔawwali.*
at first - *bil-ʔawwal.* I didn't believe it at first. *ma-ṣaddagitha bil-ʔawwal.*
first of all - *gabuḷ kullši, ʔawwalan.* First of all, you misunderstood me. *gabuḷ kullši, ʔinta ma-ftihamitni.*
first-class - 1. *daraja ʔuula.* I always travel first-class. *ʔaani daaʔiman asaafir bid-daraja l-ʔuula.* **2.** *faaxir, mumtaaz.* It's a first-class job. *haay šaġḷa faaxra.*
fish - *simča* pl. *-aat* coll. *simač.* Do you like fish? *tẓibb is-simač?*
to fish - 1. *ṣaad (i ṣeed) simač.* Do you want to go fishing? *triid itruuẓ itṣiid simač?* **2.** *dawwar (u tduwwur), xamm (u xamm).* He fished in his pocket for ten fils. *dawwar ib-jeeba ʕala ʕašr ifluus.*
fishbone - *ʕaδum* (pl. *ʕδaam*) *simač.* A fishbone caught in his throat. *ʕaδum simač wugaf ib-zarduuma.*
fisherman - *sammaač* pl. *-iin, ṣayyaad* (pl. *-iin*) *simač.*
fish glue - *ġira.*
fist - *qabδat* (pl. *-aat*) *ʔiid.* He shook his fist at me. *hazz qabδat ʔiida b-wučči.*
fit - *nooba.* Every time I mention it, he has a fit of anger. *kull-ma ʔaδkurha ṭṣiiba noobat ġaδab.*
**This suit isn't a good fit. *hal-qaaṭ ma-gaaʕid zeen.*
to be fit - 1. *laag (u liyaaga).* Is he fit for this kind of work? *huwwa laayig il-han-nooʕ šuġuḷ?* **2.** *ṣilaẓ (a ṣalaaẓ).* This meat isn't fit to eat. *hal-laẓam muu ṣaaliẓ lil-ʔakil.*
to fit - 1. *riham (a rahum).* These shoes don't fit me. *hal-ẓiδaaʔ ma-yirham ʕalayya.* **2.** *rahham (u tarhiim) t-.* Can you fit these rings to the pistons? *tigdar itrahhum har-ringaat ʕal-pasaatin?*
to fit together - *ṭṭaabaq (a muṭaabaqa).* These parts don't fit together. *hal-qiṭaʕ ma-tiṭṭaabaq.*
fitting - 1. *praawa* pl. *-aat.* When will the suit be ready for a fitting? *šwakit ykuun il-qaaṭ ẓaaδir lil-ipraawa.* **2.** *mnaasib.* Let's wait for a more fitting time. *xal-nintiδir ʔila wakit imnaasib ʔakθar.*
five - 1. *xamis.* I bought it for five dinars. *štireeta b-xams idnaaniir.* -- There are five starlings on the tree. *ʔaku xams izraaziir ʕaš-šijra.* **2.** *xamist.* His salary is five thousand dinars a year. *raatba xamist aalaaf diinaar bis-sana.* -- I spent five days on my uncle's farm. *gδeet xamist*

iyyaam ib-mazraƐat Ɛammi. 3. *xamsa.* Take five of them and leave the rest. *ʔuxuδ xamsa minha w-xalli l-baaqi.* -- Take the five from here and add it to this number. *ʔuxuδ il-xamsa minnaa w-ḍiifha Ɛala har-raqum.*

fix - *warṭa* pl. *-aat.* He's in a terrible fix. *waaqiƐ ib-warṭa čibiira.*

to fix - 1. *zaddad (i tazdiid) t-.* The price was fixed at ten dinars. *s-siƐir itzaddad ib-Ɛašr idnaaniir.* 2. *Ɛaddal (i taƐdiil) t-.* Fix your tie. *Ɛaddil booyinbaaġak.* 3. *ṣallaz (i taṣliiz) t-.* Can you fix the typewriter for me? *tigdar itṣalliz-li ʔaalat iṭ-ṭaabiƐa.* 4. *sawwa (i taswiya) t-, hayyaʔ (i tahyiʔa) t-.* I have to fix supper now. *laazim ʔasawwi l-Ɛaša hassa.*

flag - *Ɛalam* pl. *ʔaƐlaam.* The colors of the American flag are red, white, and blue. *ʔalwaan il-Ɛalam il-ʔamiirki ʔazmar, w-abyaḍ, w-azraq.*

flake - *nidfa* pl. *nidaf.* The snow is falling in big flakes. *θ-θalij da-yinzil ib-nidaf ikbaar.*

flames - *šuƐla, lahab.* The whole house was in flames. *l-beet kulla čaan ṣaayir šuƐla.*

flare - *nuur kaššaaf* pl. *ʔanwaar kassaafa.* They fired flares so it would be known where they were. *ʔaṭliqaw ʔanwaar kaššaafa zatta yinƐarfuun ween.*

to flare up - 1. *ḍṭiram (i ḍṭiraam).* The fire flared up when I poured some gasoline on it. *n-naar iḍṭirmat min čabbeet Ɛaleeha šwayya baanziin.* 2. *θaar (u θawra).* He flares up at the slightest provocation. *haaδa yθuur min ʔaqall zirša.*

flash - 1. *lamaƐaan.* Did you see the flash of lightning? *šifit lamaƐaan il-bariq?* 2. *lazḍa.* It was all over in a flash. *kullši xilaṣ ib-lazḍa* or *kullši xilaṣ miθil il-barq.*

to flash - 1. *limaƐ (a lamaƐaan).* His eyes flashed with anger. *Ɛyuuna limƐat imnil-ġaḍab.* 2. *xiṭar (u xuṭraan).* Many thoughts flashed through my mind. *hwaaya ʔafkaar xiṭrat Ɛala baali.* 3. *šiƐal (i šaƐil) n-.* He flashed the light in my face. *šiƐal iḍ-ḍuwa b-wučči.* 4. *xiṭaf (u xaṭuf).* The bird flashed by the window. *ṭ-ṭeer xiṭaf min yamm iš-šibbaač.*

flashlight - *toorič* pl. *-aat.* Can you lend me your flashlight? *tigdar itƐiirni t-toorič maalak?*

flat - 1. *šaqqa* pl. *šiqaq.* I just moved into a new flat. *stawwni tzawwalit ʔila šaqqa jidiida.* 2. *pančar* pl. *panaačir.* On the way back we had a flat. *b-ṭariiq rajƐatna ṣaar Ɛidna pančar.* 3. *minbaṣiṭ, mabṣuuṭ, mustawi.* The country around Baghdad is flat. *l-ʔaraaḍi zawil baġdaad minbaṣṭa.* 4. *faahi, bila ṭaƐam.* The soup is flat. *š-šoorba faahya.* 5. *baat, qaaṭiƐ.* His answer was a flat ''no''. *jawaaba čaan nafi baat.* 6. *mfalṭaz.* He has a flat nose. *Ɛinda xašim imfalṭaz.*

flat feet - *flaatfuut.* He has flat feet. *Ɛinda flaatfuut.*

flat iron - *ʔuuti* pl. *-iyyaat.*

to **flatten** - 1. *waggaƐ (i twiggiƐ).* He flattened him with one punch. *waggaƐa b-boox waazid.* 2. *ṭabbag (u ṭṭubbug) t-.* Flatten the cardboard boxes and stack them on the shelf. *ṭabbug iṣ-ṣinaadiig il-imqawwa w-ṣaffuṭha Ɛar-raazuuna.*
**He stepped on my hat and flattened it. *daas Ɛala šafuqti w-sawwaaha wiyya l-gaaƐ.*

to **flatter** - *tmallaq (a tamalluq) l-.* He tried to flatter me. *zaawal yitmallaq-li.*

to flatter oneself - *tbaaha (a tabaahi).* He flatters himself that he's a good judge of character. *yitbaaha b-kawna yigdar yizzir ʔaṭbaaƐ in-naas.*

flattery - *malaq, tamalluq.* Flattery won't get you anywhere. *l-malaq ma-yfiidak.*

flavor - *ṭaƐam.* The coffee has lost all its flavor. *l-gahwa ma-buqa biiha ṭaƐam.*

flight - 1. *qaaṭ* pl. *quuṭ, ṭaabiq* pl. *ṭawaabiq.* How many more flights do we have to climb? *čam qaaṭ baƐad laazim niṣƐad?* 2. *ṭayaraan.* The flight to Rome took an hour. *ṭ-ṭayaraan ila rooma ṭawwal saaƐa.*
**There are four flights a day to Mecca. *ʔaku ʔarbaƐ ṭayyaaraat yṭiir yoomiyya ʔila makka.*

to **fling** - *šumar (u šamur) n-, δabb (i δabb) n-.* He flung his jacket on a chair and rushed to the telephone. *šumar sitirta Ɛala skamli w-rikaḍ Ɛat-talafoon.*

to **flirt** - 1. *ġaazal (i muġaazala) t-.* She flirts with every man she meets. *haay itġaazil ʔay rijjaal itlaagii* or *titġaazal wiyya ʔay rijjaal itlaagii.*
**I've been flirting with this idea for a long time. *hal-fikra ṣaar-ilha mudda tdaaƐib Ɛaqli.*

float - 1. *Ɛawwaama* pl. *-aat.* Let's swim to the float. *xal-nisbaz lil-Ɛawwaama.* 2. *ṭawwaafa* pl. *-aat.* When the float starts bobbing around, you know there's a fish on the hook. *min gaamat titzarrak iṭ-ṭawwaafa Ɛrafit aku simča biš-šuṣṣ.*

to float - 1. *ṭaaf (u ṭoof), Ɛaam (u Ɛoom).* What is that floating on the water? *šinu δaak iṭ-ṭaayif Ɛal-mayy?* 2. *sayyas (i tasyiis).* They floated a raft loaded with watermelons down to Baghdad. *sayysaw kalak imzammal raggi ʔila baġdaad.* -- The logs were floated down the river. *jδuuƐ il-ʔašjaar itsayysat biš-šaṭṭ.*

flock - 1. *qaṭiiƐ* pl. *qiṭƐaan.* They followed him like a flock of sheep. *tibƐoo miθil qaṭiiƐ ġanam.* 2. *sirib* pl. *ʔasraab.* We saw a flock of birds flying south. *šifna sirib iṭyuur ṭaayir lij-jinuub.*

to flock - *tgaaṭar (a tagaaṭur).* The children flocked into the circus. *l-ʔaṭfaal itgaaṭraw Ɛas-sarkis.*
**People came flocking to hear him. *n-naas ʔijaw joogaat joogaat zatta yismaƐuu.*

flood - *fayaḍaan* pl. *-aat.* Many perished in the flood. *hwaaya maataw bil-fayaḍaan.*

to flood - 1. *faaḍ (i fayaḍaan).* The river floods every year. *š-šaṭṭ yfiiḍ kull sana.* 2. *ġirag (a ġarag).* The whole street was flooded. *š-šaariƐ kulla ġirag.* 3. *ġarrag (i taġriig).* The rain water flooded the basement. *maay il-muṭar ġarrag is-sirdaab.* -- They flooded the market with Egyptian cigarettes. *ġarrigaw is-suug ib-jigaayir miṣriyya.*

floor - 1. *gaaƐ* pl. *giiƐaan.* My glasses fell on the floor. *manaaḍri wugƐat bil-gaaƐ.* 2. *ṭaabiq* pl. *ṭawaabiq.* I live on the second floor. *ʔaskun biṭ-ṭaabiq iθ-θaani.* 3. *zaqq il-kalaam.* May I have the floor, Mr. Chairman? *yaa zaḍrat ir-raʔiis, ʔagdar ʔaaxuδ zaqq il-kalaam?*

flop - *faašil* pl. *-iin.* He's a flop as a singer. *haaδa faašil ka-muġaani.*

to flop - 1. *δabb (i δabb) nafis~.* She flopped into a chair. *δabbat nafisha Ɛala kursi.* 2. *fišal (a fašil).* The play flopped. *r-ruwaaya fišlat.* 3. *lubaṭ (u labuṭ).* The fish flopped around on the bottom of the boat. *s-simča lubṭat ib-gaaƐiit il-balam.*

flour - *ṭiziin.* I want a sack of flour. *ʔariid čiis ṭiziin.*

to **flourish** - *zdihar (i zdihaar).* A highly developed civilization flourished here 2,000 years ago. *fadd zaḍaara mitqaddma jiddan izdihrat ihnaa gabuḷ ʔalfeen sana.*

flourishing - *muzdahir.* We had a flourishing trade with Syria. *čaanat Ɛidna tijaara muzdahra wiyya suurya.*

flow - *wuruud.* The flow of food supplies was cut. *ngiṭaƐ wuruud il-mawaadd il-ġiδaaʔiyya.*

to flow - 1. *jira (i jarayaan).* The Tigris flows from north to south. *nahar dijla yijri mniš-šimaal lij-jinuub.* 2. *ṣabb (u ṣabb).* The Shatt al-Arab flows into the Persian Gulf. *šaṭṭ il-Ɛarab yṣubb bil-xaliij il-faarisi.*

flower - *warda* pl. *-aat* coll. *warid.* He took some flowers to a sick friend. *wadda šwayya warid il-fadd ṣadiiq mariiḍ.*

flu - *ʔanfluwanza.* Our whole family had the flu. *kull Ɛaaʔilatna ṣaar biihum ʔanfluwanza.*

to **fluctuate** - 1. *tqallab (a taqallub).* Prices fluctuate. *l-ʔasƐaar titqallab.* 2. *tδabδab (a taδabδub, δabδaba).* The gas gauge began to fluctuate. *geej il-baanziin bida yitδabδab.*

fluently - *b-ṭalaaga.* He speaks Persian fluently. *yizči faarsi b-ṭalaaga.*

fluid - 1. *saaʔil* pl. *sawaaʔil.* You should drink more water to replace your body fluids. *laazim tišrab mayy ʔazyad zatta tƐawwuḍ sawaaʔil jismak.* 2. *maayiƐ.* I watched them pour the fluid metal into the mold. *raaqabithum ydiiruun il-maƐdam il-maayiƐ bil-qaalab.*

flush - 1. *flašš* pl. *-aat.* He always beats me with a flush. *Ɛala ṭuul da-yiġlubni bil-iflašš.* 2. *wiyya.* The shelf is built flush with the wall. *r-raazuuna mabniya wiyya l-zaayit.*

to flush - 1. *zmarr (a zmiraar).* His face flushed with anger. *wičča zmarr imnil-ġaḍab.* 2. *šayyaš (i tašyiiš) t-.* We'll have to flush your radiator. *laazim inšayyiš ir-raadeeta maalak.*
**Don't forget to flush the toilet. *la-tinsa tjurr is-siifoon.*

fly - *δibbaana* pl. *-aat* coll. *δibbaan.* The flies around here are terrible. *δ-δibbaan ihnaa muzƐij.*

to fly - 1. *ṭaar (i ṭayaraan).* The birds are flying south. *ṭ-ṭuyuur da-yṭiiruun lij-jinuub.* -- We're flying to Paris tomorrow. *raẓ-inṭiir il-paariis baačir.* **3.** *ṭayyar (i taṭyiir) t-.* Can you fly a plane? *tigdar iṭṭayyir ṭiyyaara?* **4.** *ʔaxað (u) ib-ṭiyyaara, wadda (i) ib-ṭiyyaara.* The child was flown to a hospital. *ṭ-ṭifil innixað lil-mustašfa b-ṭiyyaara.* **5.** *rufaƐ (a rafuƐ) n-.* The ship was flying the Indian flag. *l-baaxira čaanat raafƐa l-Ɛalam il-hindi.*

flyer - *ṭayyaar* pl. *-iin.* He's a famous flyer. *haaða fadd ṭayyaar mašhuur.*

foam - 1. *waġaf.* There's more foam than beer. *ʔaku waġaf akθar min il-biira.* **2.** *zabad.* The water below the falls was covered with foam. *l-maay jawwa š-šallaal čaan imġaṭṭa biz-zabad.*

to foam - *zabbad (i tzibbid).* He was foaming at the mouth. *ẓalga čaan yzabbid.*

to **focus - 1.** *ðibaṭ (u ðabuṭ) n-.* Focus the camera at 50 feet. *ʔiðbuṭ il-kaamira Ɛala xamsiin qadam.* **2.** *rakkaz (i tarkiiz).* Try to focus your eyes on this dot. *ẓaawil itrakkiz iƐyuunak Ɛala han-nuqṭa.*

fog - *ðubaab.* A dense fog shut out the view. *ðubaab kaθiif sadd il-manðar.*

fold - 1. *θanya* pl. *-aat.* The curtains are faded at the folds. *l-pardaat kaašfa mniθ-θanyaat.* **2.** *ṭayya* pl. *-aat.* He hid the knife in the folds of his clothes. *ðamm is-siččiina b-ṭayyaat ihduuma.*

to fold - *ṭawwa (i taṭwiya) t-, ṭabbag (u taṭbiig) t-, ṭiwa (i ṭawi) n-.* Help me fold the blanket. *saaƐidni ʔaṭawwi l-baṭṭaaniyya.*

to fold one's arms - *tčattaf (a tačattuf).* He folded his arms. *tčattaf.*

to fold up - *fišal (a fašil).* His business folded up last year. *šaġilta fišlat is-sana l-faatat.*

folder - *malaffa* pl. *-aat.* The copies are in the blue folder. *n-nusax bil-malaffa z-zarga.*

folks - 1. *waaldeen.* How are your folks? *šloon waaldeek?* **2.** *rabuƐ, jamaaƐa.* Let's go, folks! *xalli nruuẓ, yaa rabuƐ!*

to **follow - 1.** *lizag (a lazig) n-, tibaƐ (a tabiƐ).* You lead the way and we'll follow you. *ʔinta tqaddam w-iẓna nilẓagak.* **2.** *tƐaqqab (a taƐaqqub).* Somebody's following us. *fadd waaẓid da-yitƐaqqabna.* **3.** *tibaƐ (a) n-.* Follow these instructions exactly. *ʔitbaƐ hat-taƐliimaat ib-diqqa.* -- He's following in his father's footsteps and becoming a doctor. *da-yitbaƐ xaṭawaat ʔabuu w-da-yṣiir ṭabiib.* **4.** *Ɛiqab (i Ɛaqib) n-, tibaƐ (a tabiƐ) n-.* Rain followed the hot weather. *j-jaww il-ẓaarr Ɛiqaba muṭar.* **5.** *ttabbaƐ (a tatabbuƐ).* Have you been following the news lately? *ʔinta mittabbiƐ il-ʔaxbaar hal-ʔayyaam?* -- I couldn't follow his explanation. *ma-gdarit attabbaƐ it-tafsiir maala* or *ma-gdarit afham tafsiira.*

**From this fact it follows that... *yubna Ɛala hal-ẓaqiiqa ʔanna ...*

as follows - *ka-ma yali.* The letter reads as follows ... *l-maktuub yiqra ka-ma yali ...*

follower - *taabiƐ* pl. *ʔatbaaƐ, naṣiir* pl. *ʔanṣaar.* He's one of the party's most faithful followers. *haaða waaẓid min ʔaxlaṣ ʔatbaaƐ il-ẓizib.*

following - 1. *taali.* The following day it rained. *muṭrat bil-yoom it-taali.* -- I need the following items. *ʔaẓtaaj il-ʔašyaaʔ it-taaliya.* **2.** *baƐad.* Following the party we went to his house. *baƐad il-ẓafla riẓna l-beeta.*

**He has a very large following. *Ɛinda ʔatbaaƐ ihwaaya.*

fond - 1. *muulaƐ.* We're fond of music. *ʔiẓna muulaƐiin bil-mawsiiqa* or ***Ɛidna walaƐ bil-mawsiiqa.* -- She's fond of children. *hiyya muulaƐa bil-ʔaṭfaal* or ***hiyya tẓibb il-ʔaṭfaal.* **2.** *mitƐalliq.* Our boy is very fond of you. *ʔibinna hwaaya mitƐalliq biik.*

to become fond of - *tƐallaq (a taƐalluq) b-.* The children became very fond of their teacher. *j-jihhaal itƐallqaw kulliš ib-muƐallimathum.*

food - 1. *ʔakil.* The food is excellent in this restaurant. *l-ʔakil mumtaaz ib-hal-maṭƐam.* **2.** *maʔuuna.* Food got scarcer day after day. *l-maʔuuna qallat yoom wara yoom.*

**This will give you food for thought. *haaða yinṭiik maadda lit-tafkiir.*

foodstuff - *mawaadd ġiðaaʔiyya.* We've got to increase our production of foodstuff. *laazim inzayyid intaajna mnil-mawaadd il-ġiðaaʔiyya.*

fool - *ġabi* pl. *ʔaġbiyaaʔ, ʔaẓmaq* pl. *ẓumuq.* He's a fool if he believes that story. *huwwa ġabi ʔiða yṣaddig hal-iẓčaaya.*

**He's nobody's fool. *maẓẓad yigdar yiðẓak Ɛalee* or *haaða ma-yitqašmar.*

to fool - 1. *tšaaqa (a tašaaqi).* I was only fooling. *činit bass da-atšaaqa.* **2.** *qašmar (u qašmara).* You can't fool me. *ma-tigdar itqašmurni.* **3.** *liƐab (a laƐib) n-, naġbaš (u naġbaša) t-.* Don't fool with the radio while I'm gone. *la-tilƐab bir-raadyo min ʔaani ṭaaliƐ.*

to fool around - *taxxam (i tatxiim) t-.* I just fooled around all afternoon. *taxxamit il-Ɛaṣriyya kullha.*

foolish - *saxiif.* Don't be foolish! *la-tṣiir saxiif.*

foot - 1. *rijil* pl. *-een.* The shoe is tight on my foot. *l-qundara ðayyga Ɛala rijli.* **2.** *qadam* pl. *ʔaqdaam, fuut* pl. *-aat.* He's over six feet tall. *ṭuula foog sitt aqdaam.* **3.** *čaƐab.* They camped at the foot of the mountain. *xayymaw ib-čaƐb ij-jibal.*

**It'll take a month to get back on our feet after the fire. *yinraad-ilna šahar ẓatta nistaƐdil baƐd il-ẓariiq.*

**They'll keep on until you put your foot down. *raẓ-yðalluun ysawwuuha ʔila ʔan itraawiihum Ɛeen ẓamra.*

**I really put my foot in it that time! *jilaṭitha xooš jalṭa han-nooba!*

on foot - *bir-rijil, maši.* We had to cover the rest of the distance on foot. *ðṭarreena nigṭaƐ baaqi l-masaafa bir-rijil.*

on one's feet - *waaguf Ɛala ẓeel~.* He's on his feet all day long. *haaða waaguf Ɛala ẓeela ṭuul in-nahaar.*

footprint - *ʔaθar qadam* pl. *ʔaaθaar ʔaqdaam.* We followed the footprints. *tbaƐna ʔaaθaar il-ʔaqdaam.*

for - 1. *ka-.* For an American, he speaks Arabic well. *ka-waaẓid ʔamriikaani, yiẓči Ɛarabi zeen.* -- What do you use for firewood? *š-tistaƐmil ka-ẓaṭab lin-naar?* **2.** *l-.* He married her for her money. *tzawwajha l-fluusha.* Aspirin is good for headaches. *l-ʔaspiriin zeen il-wujaƐ ir-raas.* -- They continued talking about it for several days. *ðallaw yiẓčuun biiha l-Ɛiddat ʔayyaam.* -- Take this fifty fils for some breakfast. *ʔuxuð hal-xamsiin filis ir-ruyuugak.* **3.** *b-.* You can buy this table for a dinar. *tigdar tištiri hal-meez ib-diinaar.* -- An eye for an eye, and a tooth for a tooth. *l-Ɛeen bil-Ɛeen, wis-sinn bis-sinn.* **4.** *ʔila.* I've got some letters for you. *ʔaku ʔilak čam maktuub Ɛindi.* **5.** *Ɛan, Ɛala.* Did anyone ask for me? *ʔaẓẓad siʔal Ɛanni?* **6.** *l-, min.* I haven't heard from him for a long time. *ma-smaƐit minna l-mudda ṭuwiila.* -- They laughed at him for his stupidness. *ðiẓkaw Ɛalee min saxaafta.*

**I've been wearing this coat for three years. *ṣaar-li tlaθ isniin da-albas hal-qappuuṭ.*

for heaven's sake - *l-xaaṭir ʔaḷḷa, yaa mƐawwad.* For heaven's sake, stop! *l-xaaṭir ʔaḷḷa, bass Ɛaad!*

what ... for - 1. *l-ʔay šii.* What's that good for? *l-ʔay šii haaða yinfaƐ?* **2.** *leeš, luweeš.* What did you do that for? *leeš sawweet haaða?*

force - 1. *quwwa* pl. *-aat.* We had to use force. *ðṭarreena nistaƐmil il-quwwa.* -- How large is the Baghdad police force? *šgadd quwwat iš-šurṭa b-baġdaad.* -- The land and sea forces are under the command of one commander. *l-quwwaat il-barriyya wil-quwwaat il-baẓriyya taẓat ʔimrat qaaʔid waaẓid.* **2.** *šidda.* The storm hasn't reached its full force yet. *l-Ɛaaṣifa ma-wuṣlat šiddatha baƐad.* **3.** *ẓukum.* She does it from force of habit. *tsawwiiha b-ẓukm il-Ɛaada.*

in force - *naafið, jaari l-mafƐuul.* Is that law still in force? *hal-qaanuun baƐda naafið?*

in full force - *b-kaamil Ɛadad-.* The family turned out in full force. *l-Ɛaaʔila ʔijat ib-kaamil Ɛadadha.*

to force - *jubar (u ʔijbaar) n-, ʔakrah (i ʔikraah), riġam (u ʔirġaam), ðṭarr (a ðṭiraar), ġuṣab (u ġaṣub).* You can't force me to sign. *ma-tigdar tijburni ʔamði.* -- You can't force these things; we'll just have to wait. *ma-tigdar itsawwi hal-ʔašyaaʔ ġaṣban, laazim nintiðir.* -- We'll have to force our way in. *laazim nidxul bil-ʔikraah.*

forced - *ðṭiraari*.* The plane made a forced landing in the desert. *ṭ-ṭiyyaara nizlat nizuul iðṭiraari.*

forecast - *nubuuʔa* pl. *-aat.* His forecast didn't turn out. *nubuuʔta ma-tẓaqqiqat.*

to forecast - *tnabbaʔ (a tanabbuʔ) b-.* They forecast cooler weather. *tnabbʔaw ib-jaww ʔabrad.*

forehead - *guṣṣa* pl. *guṣaṣ, jabha* pl. *-aat.*

foreign - *ʔajnabi*, blaadi*, maal iḃlaad.* That's a foreign make. *haay šuġuḷ ʔajnabi.*
foreigner - *ʔajnabi* pl. *ʔajaanib.* Before the war many foreigners came here. *gabḷ il-ɂarb ihwaaya ʔajaanib ʔijaw ihnaa.*
forest - *ġaaba* pl. *-aat.*
forever - *lil-ʔabad.* I'm afraid I'll be stuck in this place forever. *ʔaxša raɂ-aḏṭarr ʔabqa b-hal-makaan lil-ʔabad.*
to **forget** - *nisa (a nasi, nisyaan) n-.* She has forgotten everything. *hiyya nisat kullši.*
to **forgive** - *saamaɂ (i musaamaɂa), ɛifa (i ɛafi) ɛan, ġtifar (i ġtifaar) l-.* He'll never forgive you for that. *ʔabadan ma-ysaamɂak ɛala haaḏa.*
fork - 1. *čaṭal* pl. *-aat.* Could you hand me a knife and fork? *tigdar tinṭiini siččiina w-čaṭal?* 2. *mafraq* pl. *mafaariq, muftaraq* pl. *-aat.* When we get to the fork, you take the right road, and I'll take the road on the left. *lamma niji lil-mafraq, ʔinta ʔuxuḏ ṭariiq il-yamiin, w-ʔaani ʔaaxuḏ ṭariiq il-yisaar.*
to fork - *tšaɛɛab (a tašaɛɛub), ftiraq (i ftiraaq).* The road forks beyond the village. *ṭ-ṭariiq yitšaɛɛab min wara l-qarya.*
form - 1. *šikil* pl. *ʔaškaal.* The sculptor uses many new forms. *n-naɂɂaat yistaɛmil ihwaaya ʔaškaal jidiida.* 2. *ṣiiġa* pl. *-aat, šikil* pl. *ʔaškaal.* Can you put your question in a different form? *tigdar itṣiiġ suʔaalak ib-ġeer ṣiiġa?* 3. *qaalab* pl. *qwaalib.* They built a form to pour the concrete into. *sawwaw qaalab ɂatta yṣubbuun ič-čimantu bii.* 4. *stimaara* pl. *-aat.* You'll have to fill out this form. *laazim timli hal-istimaara.* 5. *šikli*.* It's only a matter of form, but you'll have to do it. *haaḏa fadd šii šikli, bass laazim itsawwii.*
to form - 1. *šakkal (i taškiil) t-, ʔallaf (i taʔliif) t-.* He formed a new cabinet. *šakkal wizaara jidiida.* 2. *kawwan (i takwiin) t-.* I haven't formed an opinion yet. *baɛad ma-kawwanit raʔi li-hassa.*
formal - *rasmi*.* You needn't be that formal. *ma-aku ɂaaja tṣiir hal-gadd rasmi.*
formalities - *šakliyyaat, rasmiyyaat.* She's very careful to observe the formalities. *tdiir baalha ɂatta ma-tiṭlaɛ ɛan iš-šakliyyaat.*
former - *saabiq.* The former owner has retired. *l-maalik is-saabiq itqaaɛad.*
formerly - *saabiqan.* This was formerly the business section. *saabiqan haaḏi čaanat il-manṭiqa t-tijaariyya.*
fort - *ɂuṣin* pl. *ɂuṣuun.* There's an old fort on the hill. *ʔaku fadd ɂuṣin qadiim ɛat-tall.*
fortieth - *l-ʔarbaɛiin.* That's the fortieth day he's refused to eat meat. *haaḏa l-yoom il-ʔarbaɛiin il-muḏrib bii ɛan ʔakl il-laɂam.*
to **fortify** - *ɂaṣṣan (i taɂṣiin) t-.* The island was fortified. *j-jaziira čaanat muɂaṣṣana.*
fortress - *qalɛa* pl. *qilaaɛ, ɂuṣin* pl. *ɂuṣuun.*
fortunate - 1. *saɛiid.* That was a fortunate occurrence. *haaḏi čaanat ṣidfa saɛiida.* 2. *maɂḏuuḏ.* He was fortunate to get a bargain like that. *čaan maɂḏuuḏ lil-ɂuṣuul ɛala šarwa miθil haay.*
fortunately - *l-ɂusn il-ɂaḏḏ.* Fortunately, I got there in time. *l-ɂusn il-ɂaḏḏ, wuṣalit ihnaak ɛal-wakit.*
fortune - 1. *θarwa* pl. *-aat.* She inherited a large fortune. *wurθat θarwa ṭaaʔila.* 2. *ɂaḏḏ* pl. *ɂḏuuḏ.* I had the good fortune to meet her the other day. *čaan ɂaḏḏ saɛiid ʔan atɛarraf ɛaleeha ḏaak il-yoom.* 3. *faal.* She told my fortune. *fitɂat-li faal.*
fortune teller - *fattaaɂ* (pl. *-iin*) *faal.*
forty - *ʔarbaɛiin.*
forward - 1. *ʔila l-ʔamaam.* Forward, march! *ʔila l-ʔamaam, sirr!* 2. *li-giddaam.* They sent four men forward to investigate. *dazzaw ʔarbaɛ riyaajiil li-giddaam yitɂarruun.* 3. *hjuum.* They have two good forwards on their soccer team. *ɛidhum ʔiθneen ihjuum mumtaaziin ib-fariiq kurat il-qadam maalhum.* 4. *mitjaasir* pl. *-iin.* They beat him up because he was so forward with girls. *busṭoo li-ʔan čaan kulliš mitjaasir ɛal-banaat.*
to forward - *dazz (i dazz) n-.* Your mail will be forwarded to your new address. *bariidak raɂ-yindazz ʔila ɛinwaanak ij-jidiid.*
foul - 1. *faawul* pl. *-aat.* Touching the ball with your hand in soccer is a foul. *ṭaxxat iṭ-ṭooba bil-ʔiid faawul ib-kurat il-qadam.* 2. *ġaadir, qaḏir.* That was a foul blow. *haay čaanat ḏarba ġaadra.* 3. *jaayif.* Where does that foul smell come from? *har-riiɂa j-jaayfa mneen tiji?* 4. *fšaar.* He uses foul language a lot. *yiɂči kalaam ifšaar ihwaaya* or *yfaššir ihwaaya.*
to **found** - *ʔassas (i taʔsiis) t-.* When was the club founded? *swakit in-naadi tʔassas?*
foundation - 1. *ʔasaas* pl. *-aat.* The flood damaged the foundations of the building. *l-fayaḏaan dammar ʔasaasaat il-binaaya.* -- Your remarks are completely without foundation. *taɛliiqaatak ma-ʔilha ʔasaas.* 2. *muʔassasa* pl. *-aat.* They're setting up a charitable foundation. *da-yʔassisuun muʔassasa xeeriyya.*
fountain - *šadirwaan* pl. *-aat.* There's a fountain in in the square. *ʔaku šadirwaan bis-saaɂa.*
fountain pen - *paandaan* pl. *-aat, qalam* (pl. *ʔaqlaam*) *ɂibir.* I'll have to fill my fountain pen. *laazim ʔatrus paandaani.*
four - 1. *ʔarbaɛ.* I bought it for four fils. *štireeta b-ʔarbaɛ ifluus.* -- We took four girls to the movie. *ʔaxaḏna ʔarbaɛ banaat lis-siinama.* 2. *ʔarbaɛa.* Hold four of these in your hand. *ʔilɂam ʔarbaɛa minhum ib-iidak.* -- Multiply this number by four. *ʔuḏrub har-raqum ib-ʔarbaɛa.* 3. *ʔarbaɛt.* He has to take the medicine four times a day. *laazim yišrab id-duwa ʔarbaɛt awqaat bil-yoom.* -- He stayed with us four days. *buqa ɛidna ʔarbaɛt iyyaam.*
fourteen - *ʔarbaaṭaɛaš.*
fourteenth - *raabiɛ ɛašar, l-ʔarbaaṭaɛaš.*
fourth - 1. *rubuɛ* pl. *ʔarbaaɛ.* Only one fourth of the students were paying attention. *bass rubuɛ iṭ-ṭullaab čaanaw daayiriin baalhum.* 2. *raabiɛ.* He died on May fourth. *maat bir-raabiɛ min ʔayyaar.*
fox - *θaɛlab* pl. *θaɛaalib.* A fox is killing our chickens. *fadd θaɛlab da-yuktul dijaajna.*
fraction - 1. *kasir* pl. *ksuur.* Leave out the fractions and just give me the round numbers. *ʔutruk l-iksuur w-inṭiini bass il-ʔarqaam iṣ-ṣaɂiiɂa.* 2. *juzuʔ* pl. *ʔajzaaʔ.* He got only a fraction of his father's fortune. *ɂaṣṣal ɛala bass juzuʔ min θarwat ʔabuu.*
fracture - *kasir* pl. *kusuur.* The fracture is healing slowly. *l-kasir da-yilɂam ib-buṭuʔ.*
to fracture - *kisar (i kasir) n-.* He fell off the bicycle and fractured a bone. *wugaɛ imnil-paaysikil w-kisar waaɂid min iɛḏaama.*
frame - 1. *ʔiṭaar* pl. *-aat, čarčuuba* pl. *čaraačiib.* I'd like to have a frame for this picture. *ʔariid ʔiṭaar il-haṣ-ṣuura.* 2. *haykal* pl. *hayaakil.* The frame of the hut is wood. *l-haykal maal il-kuux xišab.* 3. *bunya* pl. *-aat.* He has a heavy frame. *ɛinda bunya xašna.* 4. *ɂaala* pl. *-aat.* He's not in a very good frame of mind; better ask him later. *hassa huwwa muu b-xooš ɂaala fikriyya; ʔisʔala baɛdeen.*
to frame - *čarčab (i čarčaba) t-.* I'll have the picture framed. *raɂ-ačarčib iṣ-ṣuura.*
**They framed him. *ḏabbaw iṣ-ṣuuč ib-rugubta.*
France - *fraansa.*
frank - *ṣariiɂ.* Be frank with me. *kuun ṣariiɂ wiyyaaya.*
frankly - *b-ṣaraaɂa.* Frankly, I don't know. *b-ṣaraaɂa, ma-aɛruf.*
frantic - *jinuuni*.* He made frantic efforts to free himself. *sawwa muɂaawalaat jinuuniyya ɂatta yxaḷḷis nafsa.*
freckles - *namaš.*
free - 1. *ɂurr* pl. *ʔaɂraar.* He's a free man again. *huwwa ɂurr min jidiid.* -- You're free to go at any time. *ʔinta ɂurr itruuɂ išwakit-ma triid.* 2. *faariġ.* Will you be free tomorrow? *raɂ-itkuun faariġ baačir?* 3. *balaaš, majjaanan.* I got it free. *ʔaxaḏitha balaaš.* 4. *majjaani*, balaaš.* The admission to the play is free tonight. *d-duxuul lir-ruwaaya l-leela majjaani.* 5. *ṣaxi* pl. *ʔaṣxiyaaʔ.* He's free with his money. *huwwa ṣaxi b-ifluusa.*
**He has a free and easy way about him. *yɂiiṭ nafsa b-jaww ma-bii takalluf.*
to free - 1. *ʔaṭlaq (u ʔiṭlaaq) siraaɂ-.* They freed the prisoners. *ʔaṭliqaw siraaɂ il-masaajiin.* 2. *ɂarrar (i taɂriir) t-.* Our army freed the city from the invaders. *jeešna ɂarrar il-madiina mnil-ġuzaat.* 3. *xallaṣ (i txilliṣ).* They tried for a half hour, but were unable to free the car from the mud. *tɂaawlaw nuṣṣ saaɛa w-ma-gidraw yxalliṣuun is-sayyaara mniṭ-ṭiin.*
freedom - *ɂurriyya.*
freely - 1. *b-ṣaraaɂa.* He admitted freely that he took it. *ɛtiraf ib-ṣaraaɂa ʔinna ʔaxaḏha.* 2. *b-ɂurriyya.* You can speak freely. *tigdar tiɂči b-ɂurriitak.* 3. *b-saxaaʔ.* He spends his

money freely. *yiṣruf ifluusa b-saxaaʔ.*

to **freeze** - **1.** *jimad (i jamid) n-.* The water in the pitcher froze during the night. *l-ṃaay jimad bid-doolka ʔaθnaaʔ il-leel.* -- He froze to death. *jimad imnil-barid w-maat.* **2.** *jammad (i tajmiid) t-.* They're building a plant to freeze food. *da-yibnuun maƐmal il-tajmiid il-ʔaṭƐima.* -- The government has frozen all foreign accounts. *l-ɀukuuma jammidat kull il-iɀsaabaat il-ʔajnabiyya.* **3.** *θallaj (i taθliij) t-.* We'll freeze this winter if we don't get a better heater. *raɀ-inθallij haš-šita ʔiδa ma-ništiri ṣooba ʔaɀsan.* -- My feet are frozen. *rijlayya mθallija.*

freight - **1.** *šaɀin.* Including freight and insurance the car will cost a thousand dinars. *wiyya š-šaɀin wit-taʔmiin is-sayyaara raɀ-itkallif ʔalif diinaar.* **2.** *ʔujrat šaɀin.* How much is the freight on this trunk? *šgadd ʔujrat iš-šaɀin Ɛala haṣ-ṣanduug?* **3.** *ɀimil.* He owns a freight company. *yimlik šarikat ɀimil.*

freight car - *Ɛarabat* (pl. *-aat*) *ɀimil.*

freighter - *baaxirat* (pl. *bawaaxir*) *ɀimil.*

French - **1.** *fransi, fransaawi.* He speaks very good French. *yitkallam ifransi kulliš zeen.* **2.** *fransi*.* Do you like French wines? *yƐijbak iš-šaraab il-ifransi?*

Frenchman - *fransi* pl. *-iyyiin.* Our neighbor is a Frenchman. *jiiraanna fransi.*

frequently - *ġaaliban.* I see him frequently. *ʔašuufa ġaaliban.*

fresh - **1.** *taaza.* Are these eggs fresh? *hal-beeδ taaza?* **2.** *naqi*.* Let's go out for some fresh air. *xalli niṭlaƐ ništamm hawa naqi.* **3.** *Ɛaδib.* The well water turned out to be fresh. *ṭilaƐ ṃayy il-biir Ɛaδib.* **4.** *waqiɀ, wakiɀ.* I can't stand that fresh kid. *ma-aqdar atɀammal hal-walad il-waqiɀ.*

friction - **1.** *ɀtikaak.* Oiling the wheel would cut down the friction. *tadhiin ič-čarix yqallil il-iɀtikaak.* **2.** *tawattur.* There's friction between the two countries. *ʔaku tawattur been id-dawulteen.*

Friday - *jimƐa* pl. *jimaƐ.*

friend - *ṣadiiq* pl. *ʔaṣdiqaaʔ, ṣaaɀib* pl. *ʔaṣɀaab.* Are we friends again? *hassa rjaƐna ʔaṣdiqaaʔ?*
  to make friends - *tṣaadaq (a taṣaaduq).* He makes friends easily. *haaδa yitṣaadaq b-suhuula.*

friendly - *widdi*.* We came to a friendly agreement. *wuṣalna ʔila ttifaaq widdi.* -- The argument was settled in a friendly way. *l-xilaaf inɀall ib-ṭariiqa widdiyya* or *l-xilaaf inɀall widdiyyan.*

friendship - *ṣadaaqa* pl. *-aat, ṣuɀba.* Our friendship lasted forty years. *ṣadaaqatna daamat ʔarbaƐiin sana.*

fright - *xoof.* You gave me an awful fright. *xawwafitni xooš xoof.*

to **frighten** - *xawwaf (u taxwiif) t-.* You can't frighten me! *ma-tigdar itxawwufni!*
  to be frightened - *xaaf (a xoof).* Don't be frightened. *la-txaaf.*

frog - *Ɛagruuga* pl. *-aat, Ɛagaariig* coll. *Ɛagruug.*

from - **1.** *min.* He just received a check from his father. *huwwa hastawwa stilam ṣakk min ʔabuu.* **2.** *Ɛan, min.* I live ten miles from the city. *ʔaskun ib-biƐid Ɛašir ʔamyaal Ɛan il-madiina.*
  from now on - *minnaa w-hiiči, minnaa w-ġaadi.* From now on I'll be on time. *minnaa w-hiiči raɀ-akuun Ɛal-wakit.*
  where ... from - *mneen.* Where are you from? *meen ʔinta?* or ***ʔinta min ʔay balad?*

front - **1.** *waajiha* pl. *-aat.* The front of the house is painted white. *waajihat il-beet maṣbuuġa ʔabyaδ.* **2.** *jabha* pl. *-aat.* Were you at the front during the war? *činit bij-jabha ʔaθnaaʔ il-ɀarub?* **3.** *ʔawwal.* The table of contents is in the front of the book. *jadwal il-muɀtawiyyat ib-ʔawwal l-iktaab.* **4.** *ʔamaami*.* We had seats in the front row. *maqaaƐidna čaanat bis-sira l-ʔamaami.*
  in front - **1.** *giddaam.* Let's meet in front of the post office. *xal-niltigi giddaam daaʔirt il-bariid.* **2.** *li-giddaam.* He always sits in front. *haaδa daaʔiman yugƐud li-giddaam.* **3.** *ʔamaam, giddaam.* The officer is marching in front of his men. *δ-δaabuṭ yimši ʔamaam jinuuda.*

to **frown** - *Ɛabbas (i taƐbiis) t-.* Why is he frowning? *leeš imƐabbis?*

fruit - *faakiha* pl. *fawaakih.* Do you have any fresh fruit? *Ɛindak faakiha taaza?*
  to bear fruit - *ʔaθmar (u ʔiθmaar).* This tree doesn't bear fruit. *haš-šajara ma-tiθmur.*

to **fry** - **1.** *gaḷḷa (i tagḷiya).* Shall I fry the fish? *triid agaḷḷi s-simač?* **2.** *tgaḷḷa (a tagaḷḷi).* The meat is frying now. *l-laɀam da-yitgaḷḷa.*

fuel - **1.** *wuquud.* We use coal, wood, and oil as fuels here. *nistaƐmil il-faɀam wil-xišab win-nafuṭ ka-wuquud ihnaa.* **2.** *baanziin.* Their fuel ran out over the desert. *baanziinhum xilaṣ foog iṣ-ṣaɀraaʔ.*

to **fulfill** - **1.** *ɀaqqaq (i taɀqiiq) t-.* Her wishes were all fulfilled. *raġbaatha kullha tɀaqqiqat.* **2.** *qaam (u qiyaam) b-.* We couldn't fulfill the terms of the contract. *ma-gidarna nquum ib-šuruuṭ il-Ɛaqid.*

full - **1.** *malyaan, matruus.* Is the kettle full? *l-kitli malyaan?* -- The book is full of mistakes. *l-iktaab matruus ġalaṭ.* **2.** *kaamil.* I paid the full amount. *difaƐt il-mablaġ kaamil.* -- Are you working full time now? *da-tištuġuḷ dawaam kaamil hassa?* **3.** *šabƐaan.* I'm full. *ʔaani šabƐaan.*
  in full - *b-kaamil-.* I paid the bill in full. *dfaƐit il-qaaʔima b-kaamilha.*

fully - **1.** *tamaaman.* Are you fully aware of what is going on? *ʔinta da-tuƐruf tamaaman iš-da-yṣiir?* **2.** *b-ṣuura kaamla.* He described it fully. *wuṣafha b-ṣuura kaamla.* **3.** *maa la-yqill Ɛan.* There were fully 200 people at the reception. *čaan ʔaku maa la-yqill Ɛan il-miiteen šaxiṣ bil-ɀafla.*

fume - *ġaaz* pl. *-aat.* The escaping fumes were poisonous. *l-ġaazaat iṭ-ṭaalƐa čaanat saamma.*

fun - *winsa.* Fishing is a lot of fun. *ṣeed is-simač kulliš winsa.*
  to make fun of - *qašmar (u qašmara) t-, δiɀak (a δiɀik) n- Ɛala.* Are you making fun of me? *da-tqašmurni?*

function - **1.** *šuġuḷ* pl. *ʔašġaaḷ.* What's his function in the office? *šinu šuġḷa bid-daaʔira?* **2.** *munaasaba* pl. *-aat.* I saw him at one of the functions at the embassy. *šifta b-ʔiɀda l-munaasabaat bis-safaara.*
  to function - *štiġaḷ (u štiġaal).* The radio doesn't function properly. *r-raadyo ma-da-yištuġuḷ zeen.*

fund - **1.** *δaxiira* pl. *-aat.* He has an inexhaustible fund of jokes. *Ɛinda δaxiira ma-tixlaṣ min in-nukat.* **2.** *Ɛtimaad* pl. *-aat.* The government established a fund to care for the poor. *l-ɀukuuma fitɀat iƐtimaad liṣ-ṣarif Ɛal-fuqaraaʔ.*
  funds - *ʔamwaal.* He misappropriated public funds. *ʔasaaʔ istiƐmaal il-ʔamwaal il-Ɛaamma.*

fundamental - *jawhari*, ʔasaasi*.* That's a fundamental difference. *haaδa xtilaaf jawhari.*

funeral - *janaaza* pl. *jnaayiz.* I'm going to his funeral. *raɀ-aruuɀ ij-janaazta.*

funnel - **1.** *raɀaati* pl. *-iyyaat, miɀgaan* pl. *maɀaagiin.* The funnel is too big for the bottle. *r-raɀaati kulliš čibiir Ɛal-buṭil.*

funny - **1.** *muδɀik.* That story is very funny. *hal-quṣṣa kulliš muδɀika.* **2.** *hazali*.* He's a very funny actor. *haaδa mumaθθil kulliš hazali.* **3.** *ġariib.* Funny, I can't find my pen. *ġariib, ma-da-agdar algi paandaani.*

funny bone - *damaar* (pl. *-aat*) *Ɛikis.* He hit me on the funny bone. *δirabni Ɛala damaar Ɛiksi.*

fur - *faru.* Most fur comes from Canada and Russia. *ʔakθar il-faru yiji min kanada w-ruusya.*

furious - *θaayir, haayij.* My boss was furious when I arrived late. *raʔiisi čaan θaayir min wuṣalit mitʔaxxir.*

furnace - *firin* pl. *ʔafraan.*

to **furnish** - **1.** *ʔaθθaθ (i taʔθiiθ) t-.* I rented a furnished house. *ʔajjarit beet imʔaθθaθ.* **2.** *jahhaz (i tajhiiz) t-.* The management will furnish you with everything you need. *l-ʔidaara raɀ-itjahhzak ib-kull-ma tiɀtaaj.* **3.** *jaab (i jeeb) n-, qaddam (i taqdiim) t-.* Can you furnish proof? *tigdar itjiib daliil?*

furniture - *ʔaθaaθ.*

further - **1.** *baƐad, ʔakθar, ʔaaxar.* Do you need any further information? *tiɀtaaj maƐluumaat baƐad?* or *tiɀtaaj maƐluumaat ʔuxra?* **2.** *ʔaaxar.* I'm closing my store until further notice. *raɀ-asidd il-maxzan maali ʔila ʔišƐaar ʔaaxar.* **3.** *ʔabƐad.* He threw the rock further than me. *δurab il-iɀjaara ʔabƐad minni.*

furthermore - *bil-ʔiδaafa ʔila haaδa.* Furthermore he's not a member. *bil-ʔiδaafa ʔila haaδa, huwwa muu Ɛuδu.*

fuse - **1.** *fyuuz* pl. *-aat.* The fuse blew out. *ṭagg il-ifyuuz.* **2.** *fitiila* pl. *fitaayil.* He lit the fuse and ran. *šiƐal il-fitiila w-rikaδ.*

fuss - *δajja* pl. *-aat.* Don't make such a fuss over

him. *la-tsawwi hiiči ḍajja zawla.*

to fuss - *liεab (a liεib) n-.* He's always fussing with his tie. *εala ṭuul yilεab ib-booyinbaaġa.*

fussy - *nazis.* He's very fussy about his food. *huwwa kulliš nazis bil-ʔakil.*

future - **1.** *mustaqbal.* This job has no future. *haš-šaġla ma-biiha mustaqbal.* **2.** *muqbil.* He introduced his future son-in-law to us. *qaddam-ilna nisiiba l-muqbil.*

G

Gabriel - *jubraaʔiil.*

gag - **1.** *kammaama* pl. *-aat.* Take the gag out of his mouth. *ṭalliε il-kammaama min zalga.* **2.** *nukta* pl. *nukaat.* There are a few good gags in the movie. *ʔaku šwayyat xooš nukaat bil-filim.*

to gag - **1.** *kammam (i takmiim, tkimmim) t-.* They gagged him with a handkerchief. *kammimoo b-čiffiyya.* **2.** *thawwaε (a thuwwuε).* I got sick and began to gag. *nafsi gaamat tilεab w-gumt athawwaε.*

gain - *ribiz* pl. *ʔarbaaz.* This table shows our net gain for the year. *haj-jadwal ybayyin ribizna ṣ-ṣaafi lis-sana.*

to gain - **1.** *kisab (i kasib) n-, zaṣṣal (i tazṣiil) t-, ktisab (i ktisaab).* What did he gain by that? *š-zaṣṣal min haay?* -- He gained my confidence. *ktisab θiqati.* **2.** *rubaz (a ribiz) n-, kisab (i) n-, zaṣṣal (i) t-.* I gained ten dollars in the card game. *rbazit εašir doolaaraat ib-liεb il-waraq.* **3.** *zaad (i ziyaada).* I weighed myself and realized that I had gained four pounds. *wzanit nafsi w-šifit ʔanni zidit ʔarbaε paawnaat.* **4.** *tqaddam (a taqaddum), tgarrab (a tagarrub).* Can't you drive any faster? The car behind us is gaining on us. *ma-tigdar itsuug ʔasraε? s-sayyaara l-waraana da-titqaddam minna.* **5.** *θabbat (i taθbiit, tθibbit).* He tried to climb the hill, but he couldn't gain a footing. *zaawal yiṣεad it-tall laakin ma-gidar yθabbit qadama.*

galaxy - *majarra* pl. *-aat.*

gale - *εaaṣifa* pl. *εawaaṣif.* The gale caused great damage. *l-εaaṣifa sabbibat ʔaḍraar baliiġa.*

gall - *jasaara.* He's got an awful lot of gall. *εinda jasaara hwaaya.*

gall bladder - *maraara* pl. *-aat.*

gallery - *galari* pl. *-iyyaat.* Our seats are in the back of the gallery. *karaasiina b-ʔaaxir il-galari.*

gallon - *galin* pl. *-aat.* The American gallon isn't exactly four liters. *l-galin il-ʔamriiki muu ʔarbaε latraat tamaam.*

gallows - *mašnaqa* pl. *mašaaniq, ṣallaaba* pl. *-aat.* They erected a gallows in the center of town. *niṣbaw mašnaqa b-nuṣṣ il-wlaaya.*

galosh - *čazma* pl. *čizam.*

to **galvanize** - *ġalwan (i tġilwin, ġalwana) t-.* This factory galvanizes metals. *hal-maεmal yġalwin il-maεaadin.* -- This pail is galvanized. *haṣ-ṣaṭal imġalwan.*

gamble - *muqaamara* pl. *-aat.* It was a pure gamble, but we had to risk it. *čaanat fadd muqaamara ʔakiida laakin iṣṭarreena njaazif.*

to gamble - **1.** *liεab (a liεib) iqmaar, qaamar (i muqaamara).* They gambled all night. *liεbaw iqmaar ṭuul il-leel.* **2.** *jaazaf (i mujaazafa).* He was gambling with his life. *čaan da-yjaazif ib-zayaata.*

to gamble away - *xiṣar (a xaṣaara) bil-iqmaar.* He gambled his whole salary away. *xiṣar raatba kulla bil-iqmaar.*

gambling - *qmaar.* He spends all his money gambling. *yiṣruf kull ifluusa bil-iqmaar.*

game - **1.** *liεba* pl. *liεab, ʔalεaab.* We bought a game for our son. *štireena fadd liεba l-ʔibinna.* **2.** *liεba* pl. *-aat, daas* pl. *duus.* The children played a game of hopscotch. *j-jahhaal liεbaw liεbat tuukiyya.* **3.** *liεba* pl. *-aat, liεab, geem* pl. *-aat, šooṭ* pl. *ʔašwaaṭ.* The referee called the end of the game. *l-zakam εilan nihaayat il-liεba.* **4.** *ṣeed.* There's a lot of game in this area. *ʔaku ṣeed ihwaaya b-hal-manṭiqa.* **5.** *wujaε.* I've got a game leg. *εindi wujaε rijil.* **6.** *mistiεidd, zaaḍir.* I'm game for anything. *ʔaani mistiεidd il-ʔay šii.*

**I can see through his game. *εaaruf kull malaaεiiba.*

gang - **1.** *εiṣaaba* pl. *-aat.* The head of the gang was a notorious criminal. *raʔiis il-εiṣaaba čaan fadd mujrim maεruuf.* **2.** *jamaaεa* pl. *-aat.* He runs around with a good gang. *da-yimši wiyya xooš jamaaεa.* **3.** *jamaaεa* pl. *-aat, zumra* pl. *zumar.* He runs around with a bad gang. *da-yimši wiyya zumra muu zeena.* **4.** *jooga* pl. *-aat.* We saw a gang of workmen with shovels in the back of the truck. *šifna joogat εummaal wiyyaahum karakaat ib-ʔaaxir il-loori.*

gangrene - *gangariin.*

gap - **1.** *fatza* pl. *-aat.* They're building a road through the mountain gap. *da-yibnuun ṭariiq bil-fatza lli been ij-jibaleen.* **2.** *θaġra* pl. *-aat.* Our infantry opened a wide gap in the enemy's lines. *mušaatna fatzaw θaġra waasεa b-xuṭuuṭ il-εadu.* **3.** *faraaġ.* Your transfer will leave a gap in this office. *naqlak raz-yitruk faraaġ ib-had-daaʔira.* **4.** *naqiṣ.* There's a large gap in his education. *ʔaku naqiṣ kabiir ib-θaqaafta.*

garage - *garaaj* pl. *-aat.*

garbage - *zibil, zbaala.*

garden - **1.** *zadiiqa* pl. *zadaayiq.* These flowers are from our garden. *hal-warid imnil-zadiiqa maalatna.* **2.** *janna* pl. *janaaʔin.* Garden of Eden. *jannat εadan.* -- Hanging Gardens of Babylon. *janaaʔin baabil il-muεallaqa.*

gargle - *ġarġara.* Water and salt is a good gargle. *l-mayy wil-miliz xooš ġarġara.*

to gargle - *tġarġar (a tġirġir).* You have to gargle three times a day. *laazim titġarġar iθlaθ marraat bil-yoom.*

garlic - *θuum.*

garment - *hidim, hduum, malaabis.*

to **garnish** - *zarwag (i tzirwig) t-.* The cook garnished the fish with parsley and lemon. *ṭ-ṭabbaax zarwag is-simča b-ikrafus w-nuumi zaamuḍ.*

garter - *ʔaaṣqi* pl. *-iyyaat.*

gas - **1.** *ġaaz* pl. *-aat.* We use gas for cooking. *nistaεmil il-ġaaz liṭ-ṭabux.* -- Cabbage always gives me gas. *l-lahhaana twallid εindi ġaazaat daaʔiman.* -- The dentist uses an anesthetic gas. *ṭabiib il-ʔasnaan yistaεmil ġaaz muxaddir.* **2.** *paanziin.* He had enough gas for ten miles. *čaan εinda paanziin ykaffi l-εašr amyaal.*

to gas - **1.** *sammam (i tasmiim, tsimmim) t- bil-ġaaz, xinag (u xanig) n- bil-ġaaz.* They gassed their prisoners during the war. *sammamaw masaajiinhum bil-ġaaz xilaal il-zarub.* **2.** *xalla (i txilli) t- paanziin b-.* I gassed the car on my way to work. *xalleet paanziin bis-sayyaara b-ṭariiqi liš-šuġuḷ.*

gasket - *gaazgeeta* pl. *-aat* coll. *gaazgeet.*

gasoline - *paanziin.*

gasoline station - *mazaṭṭat* (pl. *-aat*) *paanziin.*

to **gasp** - *lihaθ (a lahiθ).* We were gasping when we reached the top of the hill. *činna nilhaθ min wuṣalna r-raas it-tall.*

gastric - *maεidi*.*

gate - **1.** *baab* (pl. *biibaan*) *xaarijiyya, baab* (pl. *biibaan*) *barraaniyya.* Who opened the gate? *minu fitaz il-baab il-xaarijiyya?* **2.** *daxaḷ.* The manager is counting the gate now. *l-mudiir da-yizsib id-daxaḷ hassa.*

to **gather** - **1.** *jimaε (a jamiε) n-, lamm (i lamm) n-.* The children gathered firewood. *l-ʔaṭfaal jimεaw zaṭab.* **2.** *ltamm (a ltimaam), tjammaε (a tajammuε).* Many people gathered in front of the platform. *naas ihwaaya ltammaw giddaam il-manaṣṣa.* **3.** *stantaj (i stintaaj), fiham (a fahim) n-.* From what you say, I gather that you don't like him. *min illi tguula ʔastantij ʔinta ma-tzibba.* **4.** *stajmaε (i stijmaaε).* The patient gathered strength after the operation. *l-mariiḍ istajmaε quwaa baεad il-εamaliyya.*

gauge - **1.** *geej* pl. *-aat, miqyaas* pl. *maqaayiis.* The gasoline gauge isn't working. *l-geej maal il-paanziin ma-da-yištuġul.* -- Bring me a guage so I can measure these wires. *jiib-li fadd miqyaas zatta aqiis hal-waayraat.* **2.** *mitin.* I want a roll of wire in this gauge. *ʔariid laffat waayar ib-hal-mitin.* **3.** *εiyaar* pl. *-aat.* He hunts with a twelve gauge shotgun. *yṣiid ib-bunduqiyya Ɛiyaar iθnaƐaš.*

to gauge - 1. *qaas (i qiyaas) n-.* This gauges the thickness. *haaδa yqiis is-sumuk.* **2.** *qaddar (i taqdiir) t-.* I would gauge the distance to be two hundred meters. *ʔaqaddir il-masaafa miiteen matir.*

gauze - *gooz.*

gavel - *maṭraqa* pl. *-aat.*

gay - *mibtihij, farzaan.* The children were gay. *j-jahhaal čaanaw mibtihijiin.*

gazelle - *ġazaal* pl. *ġizlaan.*

gear - 1. *dišli'* pl. *-iyyaat.* I broke a tooth off the gear. *ksarit sinn imnid-dišli.* **2.** *geer.* Shift into second gear. *baddil il-geer Ɛaθ-θineen.* **3.** *ġaraaḍ.* We put the fishing gear in the trunk of my car. *xalleena ġaraaḍ ṣeed is-simač ib-ṣanduug sayyaarti.* **4.** *ʔaalaat.* Fix the steering gear. *ṣalliz ʔaalaat is-sikkaan.*

gelatin - *jalaatiin.*

to **geld** - *xiṣa (i xaṣi) n-.* The army gelds all its horses. *j-jeeš yixṣi kull il-xeel maala.*

gem - *jawhara* pl. *jawaahir.* These gems are invaluable. *haj-jawaahir ma-titθamman.*

general - 1. *Ɛaamm.* Have you heard anything about the general elections? *smaƐit ʔay šii Ɛan il-intixaabaat il-Ɛaamma?* **2.** *Ɛumuumi*.* They gave him a general anesthetic. *nṭoo banj Ɛumuumi.* **3.** *jiniraal* pl. *-aat* (not applied to Arab officer of that rank). They nominated the general to the presidency of the republic. *raššizaw ij-jiniraal ir-riʔaast ij-jamhuuriyya.* **4.** (= four-star general, Iraqi Army). *Ɛamiid* pl. *Ɛumadaaʔ* He was promoted general. *raffiƐoo Ɛamiid.*

in general - *b-ṣuura Ɛaamma, Ɛal-Ɛumuum.* In general, things are all right. *b-ṣuura Ɛaamma, l-ʔazwaal zeena.*

brigadier general - *zaƐiim* pl. *zuƐamaaʔ.*

lieutenant general - *fariiq* pl. *furaqaaʔ.*

major general - *ʔamiir liwaaʔ* pl. *ʔumaraaʔ ʔalwiya.*

general delivery - *šibbaač il-bariid.* Send the letter to me in care of general delivery. *dizz-li l-maktuub ib-waaṣṭat šibbaač il-bariid.*

generally - *b-ṣuura Ɛaamma, Ɛal-Ɛumuum.* He's generally here before eight. *huwwa Ɛal-Ɛumuum ihnaa qabḷ iθ-θimaanya.*

generation - *jiil* pl. *ʔajyaal.* His family has been in America for four generations. *Ɛaaʔilta ṣaar-ilha ʔarbaƐ ajyaal ib-ʔamriika.*

generous - *kariim* pl. *kuramaaʔ, ṣaxi* pl. *ʔaṣxiyaaʔ, barmaki* pl. *-iyya.* Don't be so generous! *la-tkuun hal-gadd barmaki!*

genius - 1. *nubuuġ, Ɛabqariyya.* That man has genius. *δaak ir-rijjaal Ɛinda Ɛabqariyya.* **2.** *naabiġa* pl. *nawaabiġ, Ɛabqari* pl. *Ɛabaaqira.* He's a genius in mathematics. *huwwa naabiġa bir-riyaaḍiyyaat.*

gentle - 1. *laṭiif.* A gentle breeze was coming from the sea. *nasiim laṭiif čaan da-yiji mnil-bazar.* **2.** *wadiiƐ, haadiʔ.* This horse is very gentle. *hal-izṣaan kulliš wadiiƐ.*

gentleman - 1. *sayyid* pl. *saada.* Will you see what this gentleman wants, please? *baḷḷa ma-tšuuf has-sayyid š-yriid?* -- Ladies and gentlemen. *sayyidaati w-saadati.* **2.** *rijjaal* pl. *ryaajiil.* There are two gentlemen outside waiting for you. *ʔaku rijjaaleen da-yintaḍruuk barra.*

gently - 1. *yawaaš, Ɛala keef-.* He knocked gently on the door. *dagg il-baab Ɛala keefa.* **2.** *yawaaš, Ɛala keef-, b-luṭuf.* You'll have to treat him gently. *laazim itƐaamla b-luṭuf.*

genuine - *ʔaṣli*.* This suitcase is genuine leather. *hal-junṭa jilid ʔaṣli.*

geography - *juġraafiya.*

geometry - *handasa.*

germ - *jarθuum* pl. *jaraaθiim.* Don't eat that! It's full of germs. *la-taakul haay. kullha jaraaθiim.*

German - 1. *ʔalmaani* pl. *-iyyiin, ʔalmaan.* Are there many Germans here? *ʔaku hwaaya ʔalmaan ihnaa?* **2.** *ʔalmaani.* He speaks German. *yitkallam ʔalmaani.* **3.** *ʔalmaani*.* I bought a German watch. *štireet saaƐa ʔalmaaniyya.*

Germany - *ʔalmaanya.*

gesture - *ʔišaara* pl. *-aat.* His gestures are very expressive. *ʔišaaraata kulliš muƐabbira.*

to **get - 1.** *stilam (i stilaam).* When did you get my letter? *šwakit istilamit maktuubi?* **2.** *zaṣṣal (i tzṣṣil, zuṣuul) t-.* We can get apples cheaper here. *nigdar inzaṣṣil it-tiffaaz ib-ʔarxaṣ ihnaa.* -- Try to get him on the telephone. *zaawil itzaṣṣila bit-talifoon.* **3.** *dabbar (u tadbiir, tdubbur) t-, zaṣṣal (i) t-.* Can you get me another copy? *tigdar itdabbur-li nusxa lux?* **4.** *ʔaxaδ (u ʔaxaδ) n-, zaṣṣal (i) t-.* He got the highest grade in the class. *ʔaxaδ ʔaƐla daraja biṣ-ṣaff.* **5.** *xalla (i txilli).* Can you get him to go there? *tigdar itxallii yruuz l-ihnaak?* -- Get him to do it for you. *xallii ysawwi-lk-iyyaaha.* **6.** *jaab (i jeeba) n-.* Go get my hat. *ruuz jiib šafuqti.* **7.** *waṣṣal (i twiṣṣil).* Can you get this message to him? *tigdar itwaṣṣil-la hal-xabar?* **8.** *wuṣal (a wuṣuul), jaa (i majiiʔ).* We got to Baghdad the next day. *wuṣalna l-baġdaad θaani yoom.* **9.** *ṣaar (i).* Do you think he'll get well again? *tiƐtiqid raz-yṣiir zeen marra lux?*

**Do you get the idea? *tšuuf išloon?*

**He got sentenced to a year in jail. *nzikam sana zabis.*

**He got hit in the mouth. *nḍurab ib-zalga.*

**He got hurt in the accident. *tƐawwar bil-zaadiθ.*

**He is getting treated at the hospital. *da-yitƐaalaj bil-mustašfa.*

**His face got real red. *wičča zmarr kulliš.*

**The grass is getting green. *l-zašiiš da-yixḍarr.*

**He got drunk. *sikar.*

**He went to get a drink of water. *raz-yišrab jurƐat ṃayy.*

**I got four hours sleep. *nimit ʔarbaƐ saaƐaat.*

**His lying really gets me. I hate it. *čiδba yxabbuḷni. ʔamuut minna.*

**I got to bed early, but I couldn't sleep. *ntirazit bil-ifraaš min wakit laakin ma-gdart anaam.*

**We get twenty miles to the gallon in our new car. *nṭalliƐ Ɛišriin miil bil-gaḷin ib-sayyaaratna j-jidiida.*

**Get lost! *walli!*

**You beat me three games in a row, but I'll get even tomorrow night. *ġiḷabitni tlaθ liƐbaat wazda wara l-lux, raz-atḍaawak wiyyaak baačir bil-leel.*

**I'll get even with him for the death of my brother. *raz-antiqim minna Ɛala mootat axuuya.*

to get about - *daar (u door) b-, ftarr (a farr) b-.* He gets about the house in a wheelchair. *yduur bil-beet ib-kursi ʔabu čruux.* -- A rumor got about that he was going to resign. *fadd ʔišaaƐa daarat bi-ʔanna raz-yistiqiil.*

to get across - 1. *fahham (i tafhiim) t-.* I wasn't able to get the idea across to him. *ma-gdart afahhima l-fikra.* **2.** *Ɛubar (u Ɛabur) n-.* I got across the river in a boat. *Ɛbarit iš-šaṭṭ ib-balam.*

to get ahead - *tqaddam (a taqaddum).* He'll never get ahead in business with that attitude. *wala raz-yitqaddam bit-tijaara b-hal-waḍiƐ.*

to get a glimpse of - *limaz (a lamiz) n-.* I got a glimpse of a man wearing a red shirt. *limazit rijjaal laabis θoob ʔazmar.*

to get along - 1. *dabbar (u tadbiir) ʔamur~.* We get along on very little money. *ndabbur ʔamurna. b-išwayya fluus.* **2.** *twaalam (a tawaalum), tlaaʔam (a talaaʔum).* We get along well with each other. *nitwaalam zeen waazid wiyya l-laax.* **3.** *miša (i maši), raaz (u rawaaz).* I'll have to be getting along now. *laazim ʔamši hassa.* **4.** *tqaddam (a taqaddum).* He's getting along in years. *da-yitqaddam bil-Ɛumur.*

**How are you getting along? *šloon ʔazwaalak?* or *šloon da-timši?*

to get around - 1. *ztaal (a ztiyaal), tmaḷḷaṣ (a tamaḷḷuṣ).* They tried to get around the tax regulations. *zaawilaw yiztaaluun Ɛala niḍaam iḍ-ḍaraayib.* **2.** *tjawwal (a tajawwul), jaal (u tajwaal).* As president, naturally he gets around a lot. *b-ṣifta raʔiis, ṭabƐan yitjawwal ihwaaya.* **3.** *ntišar (i ntišaar).* The story got around quickly. *l-izčaaya ntišrat bil-Ɛajal.* **4.** *ftarr (a farr), daar (u door).* She can't get around the house very easily. *ma-tigdar itduur bil-beet bis-suhuula.*

to get at - 1. *zaṣṣal (i tazṣiil) t-, twaṣṣal (a tawaṣṣul).* His family won't let him get at the money that's in his name in the bank. *ʔahla ma-yxalluu yzaṣṣil l-ifluus illi b-isma bil-bang.* -- We didn't get at the real reason. *ma-twaṣṣalna lis-sabab il-zaqiiqi.* **2.** *naaš (u nooš) n-.* I can't get at the bolt from here. *ma-agdar anuuš il-burġi minnaa.*

to get away - 1. *tmaḷḷaṣ (a tamaḷḷuṣ).* I'm sorry but I couldn't get away. *ʔaasif bass ma-gdarit atmaḷḷaṣ.* **2.** *nhizam (i haziima, nhizaam), hirab (u harab), filat (i falit).* The criminal got away. *l-mujrim inhizam.* **3.** *waxxar (i tawxiir, twixxir) t-.* Get the children away from the stove. *waxxir* *ij-jahhaal imniṭ-ṭabbaax.* **4.** *tirak (u tarik) n-, nhizam (i haziima, nhizaam).* I want to get away from town for a few days. *ʔard atruk l-wlaaya muddat čam yoom.*

**You won't get away with it. *haay ma-tfuut-lak.*

to get back - 1. *rijaε (a rujuuε).* When did you get back? *šwakit rijaεit?* -- I have to get these books back before noon. *laazim arajjiε hal-kutub gabḷ iḍ-ḍuhur.* **2.** *starjaε (i stirjaaε), rajjaε (i tarjiiε, trijjiε).* I want to get my money back. *ʔariid astarjiε ifluusi.*

3. *ntiqam (i ntiqaam) min.* He got me back for fighting with his brother. *ntiqam minni l-iεraaki wiyya ʔaxuu.*

to get behind - 1. *saanad (i musaanada).* The industrialists are getting behind him for the presidency. *rijjaal iṣ-ṣinaaεa da-ysaanduu lir-riʔaasa.* **2.** *tʔaxxar (a taʔaxxur).* We've started to get behind in our work. *bdeena nitʔaxxar ib-šuguḷna.*

to get by - 1. *dabbar (u tadbiir) nafis~.* I get by on thirty dinars a month. *ʔadabbur nafsi b-itlaθiin diinaar biš-šahar.* **2.** *xallaṣ (i taxliiṣ, txilliṣ) min.* How did you get by the guard? *šloon xallaṣit imnil-ḥaaris?*

to get in - 1. *dixal (u duxuul) n-, xašš (u xašš) n-.* How did you get in the house? *šloon dixalit bil-beet?* **2.** *wuṣal (a wuṣuul), ṭabb (u ṭabb).* What time did the train get in? *šwakit ṭabb il-qiṭaar?* **3.** *xaššaš (i taxšiiš) t-, fawwat (i tafwiit) t-, daxxal (i tadxiil) t-.* Get the clothes in before it rains. *xaššiš il-ihduum gabuḷ-ma tumṭur.*

**I'd like to get in a game of tennis before it rains. *ʔard alεab fadd liεbat tanis gabuḷ-ma tumṭur.*

to get off - 1. *nizal (i nuzuul) min.* I'll get off the train at the next station. *raḥ-anzil imnil-qiṭaar bil-maḥaṭṭa j-jaaya.* **2.** *δabb (i δabb) n-.* He got off a couple of funny jokes. *δabb nukutteen muḍḥika* or *δabb-la nukutteen muḍḥika.* **3.** *šaal (i šeel) n- εan.* Get your elbows off the table. *šiil iεkuusak εann il-meez.* **4.** *nizaε (a naziε) n-.* Get your clothes off and take a bath. *ʔinzaε ihduumak w-xuδ ḥammaam.* **5.** *xilaṣ (a xalaaṣ).* He got off with a light sentence. *xilaṣ ib-εuquuba baṣiiṭa.*

**The team got off to a bad start. *l-fariiq bida bidaaya muu zeena.*

**He told the boss where to get off and left. *farraġ simma bil-mudiir w-ṭilaε.*

to get on - 1. *ṣiεad (a ṣuεuud) n-, rikab (a rukuub) n-.* These passengers got on in Kirkuk. *har-rukkaab ṣiεadaw ib-karkuuk.* **2.** *libas (a libis) n-.* Help me get my coat on. *saaεidni ʔalbas qappuuṭi.* **3.** *stimarr (i stimraar).* Get on with your work. Don't mind me. *stimirr ib-šuġḷak. la-tdiir-li baal.*

to get out - 1. *ṭilaε (a ṭuluuε) n-.* I got out of the office at five. *ṭilaεit imnid-daaʔira bil-xamsa.* -- We must not let this news get out. *ma-laazim inxalli hal-xabar yiṭlaε.* **2.** *ṭallaε (i taṭliiε) t-.* Get this beggar out of the store. *ṭalliε hal-imjaddi mnid-dukkaan.* **3.** *xilaṣ (a xalaaṣ), xallaṣ (i taxliiṣ, txallaṣ).* He got out of it by paying a fine. *xilaṣ minha b-dafiε ġaraama.* **4.** *waxxar (i tawxiir), twaxxar (a tawaxxur).* Get out of my way! *waxxir min darbi!* **5.** *ḥaṣṣal (i taḥṣiil) t-.* You can't get much out of him. *ma-tigdar itḥaṣṣil minna šii.* **6.** *ḥaṣṣal (i taḥṣiil) t-, rubaḥ (a ribiḥ) n-.* How much did you get out of this deal? *šgadd ḥaṣṣalit ib-haṣ-ṣafqa.* **7.** *nizal (i nizuul).* I'll have to get out at the next stop. *laazim anzil bil-mawqif ij-jaay.*

**How much can I get out of this camera? *hal-kaamira šgadd raḥ-atjiib-li?*

to get over - 1. *txallaṣ (a taxalluṣ) min.* I had a cold, but I'm getting over it now. *čaanat εindi našla laakin da-atxallaṣ minha hassa.* **2.** *ṭallaε (i taṭliiε) min fikir~.* He still hasn't gotten over his wife's death. *baεda ma-ṭallaε moot marta min fikra.* **3.** *tnaḥḥa (a tanaḥḥi), twaxxar (a tawaxxur).* Get over a little. Let me sit down. *tnaḥḥa šwayya, xalli ʔagεud.*

to get rid of - *txallaṣ (a taxalluṣ) min.* How can I get rid of him? *šloon agdar atxallaṣ minna?*

to get through - 1. *ntiha (i ntihaaʔ), xallaṣ (i txilliṣ).* Can you get through in two hours? *tigdar itxalliṣ ib-saaεteen?* **2.** *faat (u foot) min, marr (u marr, muruur) min.* You can't get through here. *ma-tigdar itfuut minnaa.*

to get together - 1. *tlaaga (a tlaagi), jtimaε (i jtimaaε).* Let's get together during lunch. *xal-nitlaaga wakt il-ġada.* **2.** *ttifaq (i ttifaaq).* We weren't able to get together on a good solution. *ma-gdarna nittifiq εala ḥall zeen.*

to get up - 1. *gaam (u goom), giεad (u gaεda).* I get up at six every morning. *ʔaani ʔagεud yoomiyya s-saaεa sitta ṣ-ṣubuḥ.* **2.** *gaεεad (i tgiεεid) t-, fazzaz (i tfizziz) t-.* Would you get me up in the morning, please? *baḷḷa ma-tgaεεidni ṣ-ṣubuḥ rajaaʔan?* **3.** *ṣiεad (a ṣaεid) n-.* We had a hard time getting up the hill. *laaqeena ṣuεuuba b-ṣaεdat ij-jibil.*

ghost - *rooḥ* pl. *ʔarwaaḥ, šabaḥ* pl. *ʔašbaaḥ.* I don't believe in ghosts. *ma-aεtiqid bil-ʔarwaaḥ.* -- He read a story about the Holy Ghost. *qira quṣṣa εan ir-rooḥ il-qudus.* -- He hasn't a ghost of a chance in this matter. *ma-ʔila wala šabaḥ ʔamal ib-hal-qaḍiyya.*

ghoul - *ġuul* pl. *ġiilaan.*

giant - *εimlaaq* pl. *εamaaliqa.* Compared to me, he's a giant. *bin-nisba ʔili, huwwa εimlaaq.*

Gibraltar - *jabal ṭaariq.*

gift - 1. *hadiyya* pl. *hadaaya.* Thank you for your nice gift. *ʔaškurak εala hadiyytak il-laṭiifa.* **2.** *mawhiba* pl. *mawaahib.* He has a gift for drawing. *εinda mawhiba bir-rasim.*

gifted - *mawhuub, mulham.* He's a gifted boy. *huwwa walad mawhuub.*

to **giggle -** *karkar (i tkirkir).* The girls kept on giggling. *l-banaat ḍallaw ykarkiruun.*

ginger - *skanjabiil.*

giraffe - *zuraafa* pl. *-aat.*

girder - *šeelmaana* pl. *-aat* coll. *šeelmaan.* They reinforced the roof with girders. *qawwaw is-saguf ib-šeelmaan.*

girdle - *koorsee* pl. *koorsaat.* She went in to buy a girdle. *dixlat tištiri koorsee.*

girl - *bint* pl. *banaat, bnayya* pl. *-aat.* That girl is nice. *hal-bint laṭiifa.*

girlfriend - *ṣadiiqa* pl. *-aat.* She went to the movie with her girlfriends. *raaḥat lis-siinama wiyya ṣadiiqaatha.*

to **give - 1.** *niṭa (i naṭi) n-.* Please give me the letter. *ʔarjuuk inṭiini l-maktuub.* -- I'll give you five dollars for it. *raḥ-anṭiik biiha xamas doolaaraat.* **2.** *wihab (i wahib) n-, niṭa (i) n-.* The king gave a car to the foreign minister in recognition of his service. *l-malik wihab sayyaara l-waziir il-xaarijiyya ka-εtiraaf ib-xadamaata.* **3.** *niṭa (i) n-, tbarraε (a tabarruε) b-.* We gave money to the poor. *nṭeena fluus lil-fuqra.* **4.** *ballaġ (i tabliiġ, ʔiblaaġ) t-.* Give him my regards. *balliġa taḥiyyaati.* **5.** *sabbab (i tasbiib, tsibbib) l-.* This noise gives me a headache. *haṣ-ṣoot ysabbib-li wujaε raas.* -- This fellow gives me a lot of trouble. *haš-šaxaṣ da-ysabbib-li hwaaya mašaakil.* **6.** *ʔalqa (i ʔilqaaʔ) n-, qaddam (i taqdiim) t-.* Who's giving the speech this evening? *minu raḥ-yilqi l-xiṭaab hal-masa?* **7.** *tḥalḥal (a taḥalḥul).* The window's stuck; it won't give. *š-šibbaač imšakkil, ma-yitḥalḥal.*

to give away - *fiša (i ʔifšaaʔ) n-, baaḥ (u booḥ) n- b-.* Don't give away my secret! *la-tifši sirri!*

to give back - *rajjaε (i tarjiiε) t- l-, radd (i radd) n- l-.* Please give me back my pen. *rajjiε-li qalam il-ḥibir maali min faḍlak.*

to give in - *ʔaδεan (a ʔiδεaan).* Don't give in to your son every time he asks for something. *la-tiδεan il-ʔibnak kull wakit yuṭlub minnak šii.*

to give off - *niṭa (i naṭi) n-, biεaθ (a baεiθ) n-.* This flower gives off a strange odor. *hal-warid da-yinṭi riiḥa ġariiba.*

to give out - 1. *wazzaε (i tawziiε, twazzaε) t-.* Who's giving out the candy? *minu da-ywazziε il-ḥalawiyyaat?* **2.** *xilaṣ (a xalaaṣ).* My supply of ink is giving out. *l-ḥibir il-mawjuud εindi da-yixlaṣ.*

to give up - 1. *baṭṭal (i tbiṭṭil), tirak (u tarik) n-.* I'm going to give up smoking. *raḥ-abaṭṭil it-tadxiin.* **2.** *sallam (i tasliim, tsillim).* The police gave him twenty-four hours to give up. *š-šurṭa nṭoo muhla ʔarbaεa w-εišriin saaεa ḥatta ysallim.* **3.** *ʔayyas (i tʔiyyis).* After ten days searching for him, we gave up. *baεad εaširt iyyaam indawwir εalee, ʔayyasna.*

to give way - *nxisaf (i nxisaaf), xisaf (i xasif).* While he was walking the ground gave way, and he fell in a big hole. *lamma čaan yimši nxisfat bii l-gaaε w-wugaε ib-nugra čbiira.*

given - *muεayyan, muḥaddad.* I have to finish it in a

given time. *laazim axalliṣha b-xilaal wakit muεayyan.*

gizzard - *ʒooṣla* pl. *ʒawaaṣil.* Faisal likes to eat chicken gizzards. *fayṣal yʒibb yaakul ʒawaaṣil dijaaj.*

glad - **1.** *farʒaan* pl. *-iin.* The children were glad to see us. *l-ʔaṭfaal čaanaw farʒaaniin yšuufuuna.* **2.** *min suruur-, ysurr-.* I'll be glad to help you. *min suruuri ʔasaaεdak.*

gladly - *b-kull suruur, b-mamnuuniyya.* Would you do me a favor? Gladly! *ʔakallfak ib-fadd šii tsawwii? b-kull suruur!*

glance - *naḍ̣ra* pl. *aat.* At a glance I knew something was wrong. *b-naḍ̣ra wiʒda εrafit čaan aku fadd šii muu tamaam.*

to glance - *baawaε (i mubaawaεa).* I glanced at my watch. *baawaεit ib-saaεti.*

to glance off - *nʒiraf (i nʒiraaf).* The bullet hit a rock and glanced off. *ṭ-ṭalqa ḍ̣urbat iṣ-ṣaxra w-inʒirfat.*

gland - *ġudda* pl. *ġudad.*

glare - **1.** *lamaεaan, bariiq.* The glare hurts my eyes. *l-lamaεaan yʔaḍ̣ḍ̣i εyuuni.* **2.** *xazra* pl. *-aat.* He gave me a glare when I entered. *xizarni xazra lamma dxalit.*

to glare - **1.** *ṣiṭaε (a ṣaṭiε), limaε (a lamaεaan).* The sunlight glared off the surface of the water. *ḍ̣uwa š-šamis ṣiṭaε min wijh il-ṃayy.* **2.** *xanzar (i txinzir), xizar (i xazir).* Why are you glaring at me like that? *luweeš da-txanzir εalayya haš-šikil?*

glaring - *lammaaε, ṣaaṭiε.* How can you work in that glaring light? *šloon tigdar tištuġul ib-haḍ̣-ḍ̣uwa ṣ-ṣaaṭiε?*

glass - **1.** *gziiz, zujaaj.* This pitcher is made of glass. *had-doolka min igziiz.* **2.** *glaaṣ* pl. *-aat.* Bring me a glass of water. *jiib-li fadd iglaaṣ ṃayy.* **3.** *zujaaji**. Some acids must be kept in glass containers. *baεaḍ̣ il-ʒawaamiḍ̣ laazim tinʒufuḍ̣ ib-ʔawεiya zujaajiyya.*

glasses - *manḍ̣ara, manaaḍ̣ir* pl. *manaaḍ̣ir.* I can't read without glasses. *ma-agdar aqra bila manaaḍ̣ir.*

gleam - *bariiq, lamaεaan.* There was a gleam in his eye. *čaan ʔaku bariiq ib-εeena.*

to gleam - *limaε (a lamaεaan), birag (i barig).* The floor was gleaming. *l-gaaε čaanat da-tibrig.*

glider - *ṭayyaara (pl. -aat) širaaεiyya.*

glisten - *tlaʔlaʔ (a talaʔluʔ), tʔallaq (a taʔalluq), limaε (a lamaεaan), šaεε (i šuεaaε).* The stars were glistening in the sky. *n-nijuum čaanat titlaʔlaʔ bis-sima.*

globe - *kura (pl. -aat) ʔarḍ̣iyya.* The teacher brought a globe to class for our geography lesson. *l-muεallim jaab kura ʔarḍ̣iyya l-dars ij-juġraafiya maalna.*

gloomy - **1.** *mdalhim.* Yesterday was a gloomy day. *l-baarʒa čaanat id-dinya mdalihma.* **2.** *mdalhim, kaʔiib.* He's always gloomy. *huwwa daaʔiman imdalhim* or ***huwwa daaʔiman gaalub wijja.*

glorious - **1.** *raaʔiε, badiiε, faaxir, laṭiif.* We spent a glorious day at the fair. *gḍ̣eena yoom raaʔiε bil-ṃaεraḍ̣.* **2.** *majiid.* Yesterday was a glorious day in the history of the country. *l-baarʒa čaan yoom majiid ib-taariix il-balad.*

glory - *majid, εaḍ̣ama.* He spoke on the glory of our ancestors. *ʒiča εan majd ajdaadna.*

glove - *čaff* pl. *čfuuf.* I bought a pair of gloves yesterday. *štireet zooj ičfuuf il-baarʒa.*

**This suit fits him like a glove. *hal-badla raahma εalee miθl il-miʒbas.*

glove compartment - *čakmača* pl. *-aat.*

glue - *ṣamuġ, šriis.* I bought a bottle of glue. *štireet šiišat ṣamuġ.*

to glue - *lizag (i lazig) n-, ṣammaġ (i tṣummuġ) t-.* He glued the two boards together. *lizag il-looʒteen suwa.*

**She stood glued to the spot. *wugfat imbasumra.*

glutton - *šarih* pl. *-iin, nahim* pl. *-iin.* Don't be such a glutton. *la-tkuun hal-gadd šarih.*

**He's a glutton for punishment. *huwwa miθl ič-čalib il-yʒibb daamġa.*

to **gnash** - *gazgaz (i tgizgiz).* He gnashed his teeth. *gazgaz isnuuna.*

to **gnaw** - **1.** *giraḍ̣ (u gariḍ̣) n- b-.* A mouse was gnawing at the rope. *fadd faara čaanat tigruḍ̣ bil-ʒabil.* **2.** *garmaṭ (u tgurmuṭ) t- b-.* The dog gnawed the bone. *č-čalib garmaṭ bil-εaḍ̣um.*

to **go** - **1.** *raaʒ (u rooʒa) n-.* I go to the movies once a week. *ʔaruuʒ lis-siinama marra bil-isbuuε.* **2.** *raaʒ (u rooʒa) n-, miša (i maši) n-.* This train goes to Baghdad. *hal-qiṭaar yruuʒ il-baġdaad.* **3.** *miša (i) n-.* The car goes sixty miles an hour. *s-sayyaara timši sittiin miil bis-saaεa.* -- Red doesn't go with yellow. *l-aʒmar ma-yimši wiyya l-aṣfar.* **4.** *štiġal (u štiġaal), miša (i).* This engine won't go on poor gas. *hal-makiina ma-tištuġul ib-baanziin duuni.* **5.** *miša (i), ʔija (i majiiʔ).* The first line of the poem goes this way. *ʔawwal beet imnil-qaṣiida yimši haš-šikil.* **6.** *jara (i jarayaan), miša(i), ṣaar (i ṣeera).* Whatever he says goes. *lli yguula yijri.* **7.** *buqa (a baqaaʔ).* They went without food for three days. *buqaw iblayya ʔakil itlatt iyyaam.*

to go ahead - **1.** *tfaḍ̣ḍ̣al (a).* Go ahead and eat. *tfaḍ̣ḍ̣al ʔukul.* **2.** *stamarr (i stimraar), raaʒ (u) ib-faal~.* I'll just go ahead with what I'm doing. *ʔaani raʒ-astimirr biš-šii lli da-asawwii* or *ʔaani raʒ-aruuʒ ib-faali biš-šii lli da-asawwii.*

to go at - **1.** *jaa (i majiiʔ).* You're not going at it the right way. *ʔinta ma-da-tijiiha mniṭ-ṭariiq iṣ-ṣaʒiiʒ.* **2.** *raaʒ (u rooʒa) εala, hijam (i hujuum) εala.* He went at the man with a knife. *hijam εar-rijjaal bis-siččiina.*

to go back - *rijaε (a rujuuε).* She went back to the house. *rijεat lil-beet.* -- This style of architecture in Spain goes back to the time of the Arabs in Andalusia. *haṭ-ṭiraaz maal il-binaaʔ b-aṣbaanya yirjaε il-zamaan il-εarab bil-ʔandalus.*

to go back on - *traajaε (a taraajuε) εan.* I never go back on my word. *ma-atraajaε εan kalimti.*

to go by - **1.** *marr (u muruur) n-, faat (u foota) n-.* Are you going by the grocer's on you're way to work? *raʒ-itmurr εal-baggaal ib-ṭariiqak liš-šuġul?* **2.** *miša (i maši) n- εala, tibaε (a tabiε) n-.* Don't go by this map. *la-timši εala hal-xariiṭa.* **3.** *staεmal (i stiεmaal).* He goes by an assumed name. *yistaεmil ʔisim mustaεaar.*

to go down - **1.** *nizal (i nuzuul).* Prices are going down. *l-ʔasεaar da-tinzil.* **2.** *ġaab (i ġeeba).* The sun is going down. *š-šamis da-tġiib.*

to go in - **1.** *dixal (u duxuul) n-, xašš (u xašš) n-.* They went in at four o'clock. *dixlaw is-saaεa ʔarbaεa.* **2.** *štirak (i štiraak), tšaarak (a tašaaruk).* Would you like to go in with me on this transaction? *yεijbak tištirik wiyyaaya b-haṣ-ṣafqa?*

to go in for - *htamm (a htimaam) b-, εind- raġba.* I don't go in for sports. *ma-εindi raġba bir-riyaaḍ̣a.*

to go into - *dixal (u duxuul) n- b-, xašš (u xašš) n- b-.* He went into politics. *dixal bis-siyaasa.*

to go off - **1.** *θaar (u θoora).* The bomb went off. *l-qumbula θaarat.* **2.** *xitam (i xitaam) n-.* We go off the air at ten in the evening. *nixtim il-ʔiḍ̣aaεa s-saaεa εašra masaaʔan.*

to go on - **1.** *stimarr (i stimraar).* This can't go on any longer. *haay ma-mumkin tistimirr baεad ʔakθar.* **2.** *nεilag (i nεilaag).* The light went on. *ḍ̣-ḍ̣uwa nεilag.*

**Go on! I don't believe that. *yeezi εaad! ma-aṣaddig haaḍ̣a.*

to go out - **1.** *nṭufa (i nṭifaaʔ).* The candle just went out. *hassa nṭufat iš-šamεa.* **2.** *ṭilaε (a ṭalεa).* He just went out. *hastawwa ṭilaε.* **3.** *zaal (u zawaal).* The use of the horse and buggy went out with the advent of the automobile. *stiεmaal il-iʒṣaan wil-εarabaana zaal ib-majiiʔ is-sayyaara.*

to go over - **1.** *raajaε (i muraajaεa) t-.* Let's go over the details once more. *xalli nraajiε it-tafaaṣiil marra lux.* **2.** *miša (i maši).* It was a good product, but it didn't go over. *čaanat xooš biḍ̣aaεa laakin ma-mišat.* **3.** *εubar (u εabur) n-.* We didn't go over the bridge. *ma-εubarna j-jisir.*

to go through - **1.** *εubar (u εabur, εubuur) n-.* He went through the red light. *εubar iḍ̣-ḍ̣uwa l-ʔaʒmar.* **2.** *marr (u marr, muruur) b-.* That poor woman has gone through a lot of hardships. *hal-mara l-maskiina marrat ib-maṣaayib ihwaaya.*

to go through with - *sawwa (i tsiwwi) t-, naffaḍ̣ (i tanfiiḍ̣, tniffiḍ̣) t-.* Did you go through with your plan? *naffaḍ̣it xiṭṭak?*

to go under - *ġaaṣ (u ġooṣ) n-.* He went under and drowned. *ġaaṣ w-ġirag.*

to go up - **1.** *ṣiεad (a ṣaεid) n-.* We watched him going up the mountain. *baawaεna εalee yiṣεad ij-jibal.* **2.** *ṣiεad (a), rtifaε (i rtifaaε).* The price of meat is going up. *siεr il-laʒam da-yirtifiε.*

to go with - **1.** *riham (a rahum) wiyya, miša (i maši) wiyya.* This tie doesn't go with the suit. *har-ribaaṭ ma-yirham wiyya l-qaaṭ.* **2.** *tibaε* *(a tabiε)*. The trip and all that went with it cost me a hundred dinars. *s-safra w-maa yitbaεha kallfatni miit diinaar.*

goal - 1. *hadaf* pl. *ʔahdaaf, ğaraδ* pl. *ʔağraaδ, maqṣad* pl. *maqaaṣid.* He has set himself a very high goal. *ħaṭṭ giddaama fadd hadaf εaali.* **2.** *gooḷ* pl. *gwaaḷ, hadaf* pl. *ʔahdaaf.* Our team made three goals in the first half. *fariiqna sawwa itlaθ igwaaḷ biš-šooṭ il-ʔawwal.*

goat - 1. *ṣaxal* pl. *ṣxuul, εanza* pl. *-aat* coll. *εanz.* He raises goats. *yrabbi ṣxuul.* **2.** *δaħiyya* pl. *δaħaaya.* He's always the goat. *huwwa daaʔiman iδ-δaħiyya.*

**Don't let him get your goat. *la-txallii yğuθθak.*

goatee - *liħya* (pl. *liħa*) *kuusa.* He has a goatee. *εinda liħya kuusa.*

God - ʔaḷḷaah, ʔillaah. God forbid. *la-samaħ aḷḷaah.* -- In the name of God, the Merciful, the Compassionate. *b-ism illaah ir-raħmaan ir-raħiim.* -- God willing. *ʔin šaaʔ aḷḷaah.*

god - *ʔilaah* pl. *ʔaaliha.* They worship false gods. *yεibduun il-ʔaaliha.*

goggles - *manaaδir, manδara* pl. *manaaδir.*

going - 1. *daarij, maaši, jaari.* The going rate on the dinar is two dollars and eighty cents. *s-siεir id-daarij lid-diinaar huwwa doolaareen w-iθmaaniin sant.* **2.** *maaši.* They have a going concern. *εidhum šarika maašya.*

going to - *raħ-.* I'm going to bake a cake. *ʔaani raħ-aṭbux keek.*

goiter - *taδaxxum il-ğudda d-daraqiyya.*

gold - 1. *δahab.* Is that real gold? *haaδa δahab ħaqiiqi?* **2.** *δahabi*.* They awarded him a gold medal. *hidoo-la madaalya δahabiyya.*

goldsmith - *ṣaayiğ* pl. *ṣiyyaağ.*

golf - *goolf.*

gonorrhea - *sayalaan, ganooriya.*

good - 1. *faaʔida* pl. *fawaaʔid, maṣlaħa* pl. *maṣaaliħ.* I did that for your own good. *sawweet haaδa l-maṣlaħtak.* **2.** *xeer.* He doesn't know the difference between good and evil. *ma-yiεrif il-fariq been il-xeer wiš-šarr.* **3.** *zeen, yimši.* This coupon is good for ten days. *hal-koopoon zeen il-muddat εaširt iyyaam* or *hal-koopoon yimši l-muddat εaširt iyyaam.* **4.** *zeen, xooš.* He does good work. *ysawwi xooš šuğuḷ* or *ysawwi šuğuḷ zeen.* **5.** *xooš, zeen, ṭayyib.* The weather isn't good today. *j-jaww muu ṭayyib il-yoom.* -- He did me a good turn yesterday. *sawwaa-li fadd xooš dagga l-baarħa.* -- He's from a good family. *huwwa min εaaʔila ṭayyba.* **6.** *ṣaaliħ.* He's a good Moslem. *huwwa muslim ṣaaliħ.* **7.** *bil-qaliil.* There's a good dozen eggs in the refrigerator. *ʔaku bil-qaliil darzan beeδ biθ-θallaaja.* **8.** *εaaqil* pl. *εuqqaal, zeen* pl. *-iin.* The children were good all day. *l-ʔaṭfaal čaanaw εuqqaal ṭuul il-yoom.*

**One good turn deserves another. *zeeniyya b-zeeniyya.*

**If you ask him to do something, it's as good as done. *ʔiδa tuṭlub minna ysawwi šii, ħisba ṣaar.*

a good deal - *hwaaya.* He spent a good deal of time in Baghdad. *giδa wakit ihwaaya b-bağdaad.*

a good many - *xooš εadad min, εadad zeen min.* There are a good many foreigners in the hotel. *ʔaku xooš εadad imnil-ʔajaanib bil-ʔuteel.*

a good while - *mudda ṭwiila.* I haven't seen him for a good while. *ma-šifta min mudda ṭwiila.*

for good - *nihaaʔiyyan, bil-marra.* I've given up smoking for good. *qṭaεit it-tadxiin nihaaʔiyyan.*

good and - *kulliš.* Make the tea good and strong. *sawwi č-čaay kulliš ṭoox.*

Good Friday - *j-jumεa l-εaδiima, j-jumεa l-ħaziina.*

not good enough for - 1. *muu maal.* These shoes aren't good enough for school. *hal-ħiδaaʔ muu maal madrasa.* **2.** *muu maal, muu gadd.* This girl's not good enough for him. *hal-bint muu gadda.*

to be good - 1. *εiqal (a).* Both of you be good when the guests arrive. *ʔintu l-iθneen εuqlu min yijuun il-xiṭṭaar.* **2.** *ṣilaħ (a ṣalaaħ).* This clay is good for making bricks. *haṭ-ṭiin yiṣlaħ il-εamal iṭ-ṭaabuug.*

to do good - *faad (i faaʔida).* The vacation did him good. *l-εuṭla faadata.*

to make good - 1. *sawwa (i tsiwwi) zeen.* I'm sure he'll make good in the city. *ʔaani mitʔakkid raħ-ysawwi zeen bil-madiina.* **2.** *waffa (i) b-, wufa (i wafi).* He made good his promise. *waffa b-waεda.*

good-bye - *maεa s-salaama, f-iimaan illaah.*

to say good-bye - *waddaε (i tawdiiε).* We said good-bye to him at the airport. *waddaεnaa bil-maṭaar.*

good-for-nothing - *talaf, ma-yiswa šii.* Your brother is a good-for-nothing! *ʔaxuuč ma-yiswa šii!*

good-looking - *jaδδaab, ħilu.* She's a good-looking girl. *hiyya bnayya ħilwa.*

good-natured - *ħabbuub, ʔaxlaaqa laṭiifa, xooš ṭabuε.* He's good-natured. *huwwa εinda xooš ṭabuε.*

goodness - *xeer, ṭiib, zeeniyya.* She's full of goodness. *kuulha ṭiib.*

goods - *biδaaεa* pl. *baδaayiε.* We import many goods from abroad. *nistawrid baδaayiε ihwaaya mnil-xaarij.*

goose - *wazza* pl. *-aat* coll. *wazz.* We ate a goose for dinner. *ʔakalna wazza bil-εaša.*

**The police are going to cook his goose. *š-šurṭa raħ-itšuuf šuğuḷha wiyyaa.*

gorgeous - *badiiε, zaahi, raayiε.* It was a gorgeous day. *čaan fadd nahaar badiiε.*

gorilla - *ğurilla* pl. *-aat.*

gospel - *ʔinjiil* pl. *ʔanaajiil.* He memorized the four gospels. *ħufaδ il-ʔanaajiil il-ʔarbaεa.*

gossip - *ħači εan-naas, ħači wara n-naas.* She likes to hear gossip. *yiεjibha tismaε il-ħači εan-naas.*

to gossip - *ħiča (i ħači) wara n-naas, qišab (i qašib).* She's always gossiping. *hiyya daaʔiman tiħči wara n-naas.*

got - *εind.* He's got a nice house. *εinda xooš beet.*

got to - *laazim.* I've got to leave now. *laazim aruuħ hassa.*

gourd - *qarεa* pl. *-aat* coll. *qaraε.* The colocynth is a variety of gourd. *l-ħanδal nooε imnil-qaraε.*

to **govern - 1.** *ħikam (u ħukum) n-.* He governed the country well. *huwwa ħikam il-balad zeen.* **2.** *δubaṭ (u δabuṭ) n-.* This invention governs the heat of the room. *hal-ixtiraaε yuδbuṭ ħaraarat il-ğurfa.*

government - *ħukuuma* pl. *-aat.* Who heads the new government? *minu yirʔas il-ħukuuma j-jidiida?*

governor - 1. *ħaakim* pl. *ħukkaam.* I read an article on the governor of New York State. *qireet maqaal εan ħaakim wlaayat inyuu yoork.* **2.** *mutṣarrif* pl. *-iin.* The governor of Basra province visited Syria. *mutṣarrif liwaaʔ ib-baṣra zaar suurya.*

gown - 1. *dišdaaša* pl. *dišaadiiš.* The boy put the tail of his gown in his mouth and ran. *l-walad xalla δyaal dišdaašta b-ħalga w-rikaδ.* **2.** *roob* pl. *ʔarwaab.* The students wore black gowns for graduation. *ṭ-ṭullaab libsaw ʔarwaab sooda l-ħaflat it-taxarruj.*

evening gown - *swaaree* pl. *-iyyaat.*

to **grab - 1.** *lizam (a lazim) n-, ligaf (u laguf) n-.* The police grabbed the thief in the market. *š-šurṭa lizmat il-ħaraami bis-suug.* **2.** *tnaawaš (a tanaawuš), ligaf (u laguf) n-.* He grabbed a bottle off the shelf. *tnaawaš fadd buṭil imnir-raff.* **3.** *himaš (i hamiš) n-.* Don't grab. You'll get your share. *la-tihmiš raħ-taaxuδ ħuṣṣtak.*

grace - 1. *rašaaqa, xiffa.* She walks with grace. *timši b-rašaaqa.* **2.** *widd.* He wants to get into her good graces. *yriid yiksib widdha.*

to say grace - *samma (i tasmiya).* Say grace before you eat! *sammu gabuḷ-ma taakul!*

grade - 1. *daraja* pl. *-aat.* He received the highest grades in the class. *ħaṣṣal εala ʔaεla darajaat biṣ-ṣaff.* **2.** *ṣaff* pl. *ṣfuuf.* What grade is your son in? *b-yaa ṣaff ʔibnak?* **3.** *ṣinif.* Do you have a better grade of wool than this? *εindak ṣinif ṣuuf ʔaħsan min haaδa?* **4.** *nħidaar* pl. *-aat, εalwa* pl. *-aat.* The truck couldn't climb the grade. *l-loori ma-gidar yiṣεad il-inħidaar.*

**He'll never make the grade. *mustaħiil yigdar ydabburha.*

to grade - 1. *ṣannaf (i tṣinnif, taṣniif) t-.* We grade potatoes according to size. *nṣannif il-puteeta ħasab il-kubur.* **2.** *εaddal (i tεiddil, taεdiil) t-.* They're grading the road. *yεaddiluun iṭ-ṭariiq.*

gradual - *tadriiji*.* I noticed a gradual improvement. *laaħaδit taqaddum tadriiji.*

gradually - *bit-tadriij.* He's gradually getting better. *da-yitħassan bit-tadriij.*

graduate - 1. *xirriij* pl. *-iin, mitxarrij* pl. *-iin.* Most of the graduates of our university have good positions. *ʔakθar il-xirriijiin min jaamiεatna εidhum waδaayif zeena.* **2.** *εaali.* He is doing graduate study in America. *da-yidrus diraasa εaalya b-ʔamiirka.*

to graduate - *xarraj (i taxriij, txirrij) t-.* Our university graduates four hundred students per year. *jaamiεatna txarrij ʔarbaε miit ṭaalib bis-sana.*

to be graduated - *tdarraj (a tadarruj).* Taxes are

graduated according to income. *δ̣-δ̣araayib titdarraj ʒasb id-daxal.*

grain - 1. *ʒabba* pl. *ʒabaabi.* A few grains of salt were on the table. *šwayyat ʒabaabi miliʒ čaanat εal-meez.* **2.** *ʒabb* pl. *ʒubuub.* Canada exports meat and grain. *kanada tṣaddir il-luʒuum wil-ʒubuub.* **3.** *ṭabuε.* That goes against my grain. *haaδa δ̣idd ṭabεi.* **4.** *δarra.* There isn't a grain of truth in the story. *ma-aku δarra min ʒaqiiqa b-hal-quṣṣa.* **5.** *εuruug il-xišab.* Don't plane against the grain. *la-trandij δ̣idd iεruug il-xišab.*

gram - *ġraam* pl. *-aat.* Give me four grams of saffron. *nṭiini ʔarbaε iġraamaat zuεufraan.*

grammar - 1. *qawaaεid, naʒu.* I never studied Arabic grammar. *ʔaani ʔabad ma-drasit qawaaεid il-luġa l-εarabiyya.* **2.** *ktaab* (pl. *kutub*) *qawaaεid.* Do you have a good grammar for beginners? *εindak iktaab qawaaεid zeen lil-mubtadiʔiin?*

grand - 1. *čibiir.* The dance will take place in the grand ballroom. *ʒaflat ir-riqiṣ raʒ-iṭṣiir bil-qaaεa č-čibiira.* **2.** *kulli*, εaamm.* The grand total comes to three hundred and seventeen. *l-majmuuε il-kulli ywaṣṣil iθlaθ miyya w-isbaεtaεaš.* **3.** *εaδ̣iim, mumtaaz.* We saw grand scenery on our way to Europe. *šifna manaaδ̣ir εaδ̣iima b-ṭariiqna l-ʔooruppa.* -- That's a grand idea. *haaδi fikra εaδ̣iima.*

granddaughter - *ʒafiida* pl. *-aat.*

grandfather - *jidd* pl. *jduud, ʔajdaad.*

grandmother - *jiddiyya* pl. *-aat, biibi* pl. *-iyyaat.*

grandson - *ʒafiid* pl. *ʔaʒfaad.*

grant - *manʒa* pl. *minaʒ.* He received a grant for further study from the government. *stilam imnil-ʒukuuma manʒa lil-istimraar bid-diraasa.*

to grant - 1. *minaʒ (a maniʒ) n-.* They granted us the entire amount. *minʒoona l-mablaġ ib-kaamla.* **2.** *εtiraf (i εtiraaf), sallam (i tsillim, tasliim).* I grant that I was wrong. *ʔaani ʔaεtirif ib-ʔanni činit ġalṭaan.*

granted - 1. *mamnuuʒ.* The money which was orginally granted has been spent. *l-ifluus illi čaanat bil-ʔaṣil mamnuuʒa nṣirfat.* **2.** *min il-maqbuul, min il-imsallim.* Granted that your philosophy is correct, but its application is difficult. *min il-maqbuul ʔan falsaftak ṣaʒiiʒa, laakin taṭbiiqha ṣaεub.*

to take for granted - 1. *ftiraδ̣ (i ftiraaδ̣), ʒisab (i ʒasib).* I took it for granted that he'd be there. *ftiraδ̣it raʒ-ykuun ihnaak.* **2.** *stiġall (i stiġlaal).* We were friends until he started taking me for granted. *činna ʔaṣdiqaaʔ ʔila ʔan bida yistiġillni.*

grape - *εinba* pl. *-aat* coll. *εinab.*

grapefruit - *sindiyya* pl. *-aat* coll. *sindi.*

graph - *rasim bayaani* pl. *rusuum bayaaniyya, xaṭṭ bayaani* pl. *xuṭuuṭ bayaaniyya.*

to **grasp - 1.** *čallab (i tčillib, tačliib) t- b-, lizam (a lazim) n-, kumaš (u kamuš) n-, ligaf (u laguf) n-.* She grasped the rope with both hands. *čallbat bil-ʒabil b-iideenha θ-θinteen.* **2.** *fiṭan (a faṭin) n- εala, fiham (a fahim) n-.* Do you grasp what I mean? *da-tufṭun εal-illi da-aguula?*

grass - 1. *θayyil.* Did you cut the grass? *gaṣṣeet iθ-θayyil?* **2.** *ʒašiiš.* The farmer cut some grass and gave it to the cow. *l-fallaaʒ gaṣṣ ʒašiiš w-inṭaa lil-haayša.* **3.** *εišib.* The sheep are grazing on grass in the desert. *l-ġanam da-tirεa bil-εišib bil-barr.*

grasshopper - *jaraada* pl. *-aat* coll. *jaraad.*

grate - *šibča* pl. *-aat.* The easiest way to cook the meat is to put a grate on three stones. *ʔashal ṭariiqa ṭ-ṭabx il-laʒam hiyya ʔann itxalli š-šibča εala tlaθ iʒjaaraat.*

to grate - 1. *ʒakk (u ʒakk) ib-randa.* Grate the carrots when you have time. *ʒukki j-jizar bir-randa lamma ykuun εindič wakit.* **2.** *kazbar (u tkuzbur) jilid-.* The scratching of chalk on a blackboard grates on me. *šaxṭat it-tabaasiir εas-sabbuura tkazbur jildi.*

grateful - *mimtann, šaakir, mitšakkir.* I'm grateful to you for your help. *ʔaani mimtann ʔilak εala musaaεadtak.*

to **gratify** - *raδ̣δ̣a (i tarδ̣iya, triδ̣δ̣i), šabbaε (i tašbiiε, tšibbiε).* He gratified her every wish. *šabbaε kull raġba min raġbaatha.*

gratifying - *murδ̣i.* Your grades this semester are very gratifying. *darajaatak hal-faṣil kulliš murδ̣iya.*

gratitude - *mtinaan, šukur, εtiraaf bij-jamiil.* I don't know how to express my gratitude. *ma-da-aεruf šloon aεbur εan imtinaani.*

grave - 1. *gabur* pl. *gbuur.* The coffin was lowered into the grave. *t-taabuut itnazzal bil-gabur.* **2.** *sayyiʔ.* His condition is grave. *ʒaalta sayyiʔa.* **3.** *faδ̣iiε.* That's a grave mistake. *δiič fadd ġalṭa faδ̣iiεa.* **4.** *waxiim.* Children's playing with matches brings grave consequences. *liεb il-ʔaṭfaal biš-šixxaaṭ yjiib εawaaqib waxiima.*

gravel - *ʒaṣu.* The path is covered with gravel. *ṭ-ṭariiq imġaṭṭa bil-ʒaṣu.*

gravestone - *marmara* pl. *-aat.*

graveyard - *maqbara* pl. *maqaabir.*

gravity - *jaaδibiyya.*

gravy - *marga, marag.* Do you want only gravy on the rice? *triid marga xaalya foog it-timman?*

gray - 1. *riṣaaṣi, rumaadi.* Gray and red go together well. *r-rumaadi wil-ʔaʒmar yitwaalmuun zeen.* -- **2.** *riṣaaṣi*, rumaadi*.* He always wears gray suits. *daaʔiman yilbas badlaat rumaadiyya.*

to **graze - 1.** *riεa (a raεi).* The sheep grazed in the fields. *l-ġanam riεa bil-ʒuquul.* **2.** *gišaṭ (a gašiṭ) n-, xidaš (i xadiš) n-.* The bullet grazed his shoulder. *r-riṣaaṣa gišṭat čitfa.*

grease - 1. *dihin* pl. *duhuun, šaʒam, dasam.* Don't leave the grease in the pan. *la-titruk id-dihin biṭ-ṭaawa.* **2.** *griiz.* Do you need any grease for your car? *tiʒtaaj ʔay igriiz is-sayyaartak?*

to grease - 1. *dahhan (i tdihhin, tadhiin) t-.* Grease the pan before you put the meat in. *dahhin iṭ-ṭaawa gabuḷ-ma txalli l-laʒam.* **2.** *šaʒʒam (i tašʒiim, tšiʒʒim) t-.* Our best mechanic greased your car. *ʔaʒsan il-miikaaniikiyyiin maalna šaʒʒam sayyaartak.*

greasy - 1. *mdahhan, dasim.* The dishes are still greasy. *l-immaaεiin baεadha mdahhna.* **2.** *dihiin, dasim.* You eat a lot of greasy foods. *taakul ihwaaya ʔakil dihiin.*

great - 1. *εaδ̣iim* pl. *εuδ̣amaaʔ, kabiir* pl. *kubbaar, kubaraaʔ.* He's one of the greats of contemporary poetry. *huwwa min εuδ̣amaaʔ iš-šiεir il-muεaaṣir.* **2.** *εaδ̣iim, kabiir.* She's a great singer. *hiyya muġanniya εaδ̣iima.* -- That's a great idea. *haaδi fikra εaδ̣iima.* **3.** *kabiir, εaδ̣iim, baliiġ, jasiim.* The war did great damage. *l-ʒarb aʒdaθat ʔaδ̣raar kabiira.* **4.** *jasiim, kabiir, εaδ̣iim.* He's in great danger. *huwwa b-xaṭar jasiim.* **5.** *baliiġ, kabiir.* His father's death left a great mark on him. *wafaat ʔabuu tirkat ʔaθar baliiġ bii.* **6.** *kabiir, hwaaya.* He was in great pain. *čaan εinda ʔalam ihwaaya.* **7.** *hwaaya, kulliš.* They live in a great big house. *ysiknuun ib-beet kulliš ičbiir.*

Great Britain - *briiṭaanya l-εuδ̣ma.*

greatly - *b-ṣuura kabiira, b-ṣuura εaδ̣iima.* She exaggerated greatly. *baalġat ib-ṣuura kabiira.*

Greece - *l-yunaan.*

greedy - 1. *nahim* pl. *-iin, šarih* pl. *-iin.* He's very greedy when we sit down to eat. *huwwa kulliš nahim lamma nugεud naakul.* **2.** *tammaaε, jašiε.* He's a greedy merchant. *huwwa taajir tammaaε.*

Greek - 1. *yunaani* pl. *-iyyiin.* His father is a Greek. *ʔabuu yunaani.* **2.** *yunaani.* He speaks Greek. *yiʒči yunaani.* **3.** *yunaani*.* Do you like Greek wines? *yεijbak šaraab yunaani?*

green - *ʔaxδ̣ar* f. *xuδ̣ra* pl. *xuδ̣ur.* The Iraqi flag is black, white, and green with red and yellow in the middle. *l-εalam il-εiraaqi ʔaswad w-abyaδ̣ w-axδ̣ar wiyya ʔaʒmar w-aṣfar bin-nuṣṣ.*

to turn green - *xδ̣arr (a xδ̣iraar).* The grass turns green in the spring. *l-εišib yixδ̣arr bir-rabiiε.*

**He's still green at this work. *baεda lʒeemi b-haš-šuġuḷ.*

greens - *xuδ̣ra.* You should eat some greens everyday. *laazim taakul išwayya xuδ̣ra kull yoom.*

to **greet** - *sallam (i tasliim, tsillim) εala, ʒayya (i taʒiyya).* He greeted him with a wave of the hand. *sallam εalee b-iida.* **2.** *staqbal (i stiqbaal).* They greeted him with applause. *staqbiloo bit-taṣfiig.*

greeting - *taʒiyya* pl. *-aat, stiqbaal* pl. *-aat, salaam* pl. *-aat.* We never expected such a warm greeting. *ʔabadan ma-twaqqaεna hiič taʒiyya ʒaarra.*

grenade - *qumbula* (pl. *qanaabil*) *yadawiyya.*

grief - *ʒuzun, ġamm, ʒasra.* She couldn't conceal her grief. *ma-gidrat tixfi ʒuzunha.*

grill - *šibča* pl. *-aat.* I don't like the grill on your new car. *ma-aʒibb šibčat sayyaartak ij-jidiida.* -- Take the meat off the grill as soon as it's done. *šiil il-laʒam imniš-šibča bass-ma yistiwi.*

to grill - 1. *šuwa (i šawi) n- εaš-šibča.* They grilled the meat in the garden. *šuwaw il-laʒam*

εaš-šibča bil-ḥadiiqa. 2. *ṭawwal (i taṭwiil) ib-ʔasʔilat~.* The police grilled the prisoner for hours. *š-šurṭa ṭawwilat ib-ʔasʔilatha l-maḥbuus il-εiddat saaεaat.*
grim - *mεabbas.* His face was grim. *čaan wijja mεabbas.*
grin - *btisaama waafḥa.* There was a grin on his face. *čaan ʔaku btisaama waafḥa εala wujja.*
to grin - *kaššar (i tkiššir).* He grinned at me. *kaššar εalayya.*
grind - 1. *ṭaḥin* pl. *-aat.* I bought a medium grind of coffee. *štireet gaḥwa maṭḥuuna ṭaḥin waṣiṭ.* 2. *šidda* pl. *-aat, šadaaʔid.* It was a long grind, but we made it. *čaanat fadd šidda ṭwiila laakin dabbarnaaha.*
to grind - 1. *ṭiḥan (a ṭaḥin) n-, jiraš (i jariš) n-.* We saw the miller grinding flour. *šifna ṭ-ṭaḥḥaan yiṭḥan iṭ-ṭaḥiin.* 2. *čirax (a čarix) n-.* He ground the meat for hamburger. *čirax il-laḥam lil-kabaab.* -- How much does he charge to grind knives? *šgadd yaaxuð εala čarx is-sičaačiin?* -- He keeps on grinding out one novel after the other. *ḍall yičrax ib-har-ruwaayaat waḥda wara l-lux.* 3. *giraṭ (u gariṭ) b-.* He grinds his teeth in his sleep. *yigruṭ b-isnuuna b-nooma.*
grip - 1. *lazma, qabḍa, maska.* He has a strong grip. *εinda fadd qabḍa qawiyya.* 2. *yadda* pl. *-aat.* I can't carry it. It doesn't have a grip. *ma-agdar ašiilha. ma-biiha yadda.* 3. *junṭa* pl. *junaṭ.* Where can I check my grip? *ween agdar aʔammin junitṭi?* 4. *lazma.* I can carry the trunk if I can get a grip. *ʔagdar ašiil iṣ-ṣanduug ʔiða bii lazma.*
to grip - *lizam (a lazim) n-, kumaš (u kamiš) n-.* He gripped her arm tightly. *kumaš ʔiidha b-quwa.*
gripe - *tašakki* pl. *-iyyaat.* Don't tell me your gripes. *la-tgul-li b-tašakkiyyaatak.*
to gripe - *tšakka (a tašakki, tšikki).* He gripes about everything. *yitšakka min kullši.*
gripping - *muʔaθθir.* It was a very gripping film. *čaan filim muʔaθθir kulliš.*
grit - 1. *ḥaṣu.* Chicken gizzards are full of grit. *ḥawaaṣil id-dijaaj matruusa ḥaṣu.* 2. *εaẓim* pl. *εaẓaaʔim.* That boy has grit. *hal-walad εinda εaẓim.*
to grit - *gaẓgaẓ (i tgiẓgiẓ) b-.* He gritted his teeth and set to work. *gaẓgaẓ b-isnuuna w-bida yištuġul.*
groan - *winiin, taʔawwuh* pl. *-aat.* We heard his groans all night. *smaεna winiina ṭuul il-leel.*
to groan - *wann (i wniin), tʔawwah (a taʔawwuh).* The sick man was groaning. *l-mariiḍ čaan ywinn.*
grocer - *baggaal* pl. *bgaagiil.* Our grocer sells nice apples. *baggaalna ybiiε xooš tiffaaḥ.*
groceries - *miswaag.* Would you deliver these groceries to our house? *ma-twaddi hal-miswaag il-beetna?*
grocery store - *dukkaan* (pl. *dkaakiin*) *ibgaala.*
groom - 1. *εirriis* pl. *εirsaan.* That man's the father of the groom. *har-rijjaal ʔabu l-εirriis.* 2. *saayis* pl. *siyyaas.* The groom is walking the horse. *s-saayis da-ymašši l-iḥṣaan.*
to groom - *handam (i handama) t-.* He grooms himself nicely. *yhandim nafsa zeen.* -- Her children are always well-groomed. *ʔaṭfaalha daaʔiman imhandimiin.*
groove - *ḥazz* pl. *ḥzuuz.* We watched the carpenter chisel a groove in the board. *tfarrajna εan-najjaar yiḥfur ḥazz bil-xišba.*
to **grope** - *tlammas (a tlimmis), tḥassas (a tḥissis).* He groped for the switch in the dark. *tlammas is-suwiič biḍ-ḍilma.*
gross - 1. *glooṣ* pl. *-aat.* These are sold in grosses only. *haay tinbaaε bil-iglooṣaat bass.* 2. *faḍiiε.* That was a gross mistake. *ðiič čaanat fadd ġalṭa faḍiiεa.* 3. *xaliiε.* He told us a gross story. *ḥičaa-nna quṣṣa xaliiεa.* 4. *majmuuε εaamm.* How much was your gross income? *šgadd čaan majmuuε id-daxal il-εaamm maalak?*
grouchy - *magluub il-wijih, mġayyim.* He's always grouchy. *huwwa daaʔiman magluub il-wijih.*
ground - 1. *gaaε* pl. *giiεaan, ʔariḍ* pl. *ʔaraaḍi.* Leave it on the ground. *xalliiha εal-gaaε.* -- The ground in this area is not fit for agriculture. *l-gaaε ihnaa muu ṣaalḥa liz-ziraaεa.* 2. *saaḥa* pl. *-aat.* This palace has beautiful grounds. *hal-qaṣir bii saaḥaat jamiila.* 3. *mukaan* pl. *-aat, ʔamaakin; maḥall* pl. *-aat.* Are there any good fishing grounds near here? *ʔaku ʔamaakin iṣ-ṣeed is-simič qariib minnaa?* 4. *ʔarḍi* pl. *-iyyaat.* Connect the ground to the radio. *šidd il-ʔarḍi bir-raadyo.* 5. *ʔasaas* pl. *ʔusus.* On what grounds did you jail him? *εala ʔay ʔasaas isjantuu?* 6. *tilif.* Don't put the coffee grounds down the drain. *la-txalli t-tilif maal il-gahwa bil-balluuεa.* 7. *ʔarḍi*.* The dining room is on the ground floor. *qaaεat iṭ-ṭaεaam biṭ-ṭaabiq il-ʔarḍi.*
to ground - 1. *šakkal (i taškiil, tšikkil) t-ʔarḍi.* You have to ground the battery before you use it. *laaẓim itšakkil ʔarḍi l-paaṭri gabuḷ-ma tistaεmila.* 2. *minaε (a maniε) n- min iṭ-ṭayaraan.* The Aviation Commission grounded four pilots this month. *lajnat iṭ-ṭayaraan minεat ʔarbaε ṭayyaariin imniṭ-ṭayaraan haš-šahar.*
to ground out - *sarrab (i tasriib, tsirrib) t-kahrabaaʔ.* He grounded out the circuit with a screwdriver. *sarrab il-kahrabaaʔ imnil-ittiṣaal ib-darnafiis.*
group - *jamaaεa* pl. *-aat, jooga* pl. *-aat.* The class was divided into three groups. *ṣ-ṣaff čaan imqassam ʔila θlaθ jamaaεaat.*
to group - 1. *qassam (i taqsiim) t- ʔila jamaaεaat.* Group the children according to age. *qassim il-ʔaṭfaal ʔila jamaaεaat ḥasb il-εumur.* 2. *tjammaε (a tajammuε), ltamm (a ltimaam).* The students grouped around the teacher to see the experiment. *ṭ-ṭullaab itjammiεaw ḥawl il-muεallim ḥatta yšuufuun it-tajruba.*
grove - *bistaan* pl. *basaatiin.* He's working in an orange grove. *yištuġul ib-bistaan purtaqaal.*
to **grow** - 1. *nima (i nami).* Cactus grows in the desert. *ṣ-ṣubbeer yinmi bil-barr.* 2. *nima (i nami), kubar (a kubur).* Your boy has certainly grown a lot. *ʔibnak bila šakk kubar ihwaaya.* 3. *ṣaar (i ṣeer).* His financial condition grew worse. *ḥaalta l-maaliyya ṣaarat ʔatεas.* 4. *ziraε (a ziriε) n-.* He grows flowers in the garden. *yizraε warid bil-ḥadiiqa.*
to grow up - *ruba (a riba).* My friend grew up in Najef. *ṣadiiqi ruba bin-najaf.*
growl - *hamhama* pl. *-aat.* The dog's growl scared the children. *hamhamt ič-čalib xawwifat ij-jahhaal.*
to growl - *hamham (i thimhim).* The dog began growling before it barked. *č-čalib bida yhamhim gabuḷ-ma nibaḥ.*
grown-up - 1. *čibiir, kabiir* pl. *kbaar.* The admission price for grown-ups is fifty fils. *ʔujrat id-duxuul lil-ikbaar xamsiin filis.* 2. *kabraan, čibiir.* She has a grown up daughter. *εidha bnayya kabraana.*
growth - *numuww.* He spoke on economic growth. *tkallam εan in-numuww il-iqtiṣaadi.* -- They say smoking stunts the growth. *yguuluun it-tadxiin yʔaxxir in-numuww.* **He has two day's growth. *liḥiita maal yoomeen.*
grudge - *ḥaqid* pl. *ʔaḥqaad, ḍaġiina* pl. *ḍaġaaʔin.* Forget your grudges and be friends. *ʔinsu l-ʔaḥqaad w-ṣiiru ʔaṣdiqaaʔ.*
grudgingly - *b-imtiεaaḍ.* He gave in grudgingly. *staslam b-imtiεaaḍ.*
gruesome - *faḍiiε.* The scene of the automobile accident was a gruesome sight. *manḍar ḥaadiθ is-sayyaara čaan manḍar faḍiiε* or ***manḍar ḥaadiθ is-sayyaara čaan manḍar taqšaεirr minna l-ʔabdaan.*
gruff - *xašin, ġaliiḍ, faḍḍ.* He has a gruff voice. *εinda ṣoot xašin.*
to **grumble** - *damdam (i tdimdim).* He grumbles every-time we ask him for help. *ydamdim kull-ma nuṭlub minna musaaεada.*
guarantee - *ḍamaan* pl. *-aat, ṣoogarta* pl. *-aat, taʔmiin* pl. *-aat.* This watch has a five year guarantee. *has-saaεa biiha xamas isniin ḍamaan.* 2. *ḍamaan* pl. *-aat.* What guarantee do I have that he'll pay me? *šinu ḍ-ḍamaan huwwa raḥ-yidfaε-li.*
to guarantee - 1. *ḍuman (u ḍamaan) n-, kifal (i kafaala) n-.* We guarantee our product for a year. *nuḍmun ʔintaajna l-sana wiḥda.* 2. *ḍuman (u ḍamaan) n-, ṣoogar (i tṣoogir) t-.* I can't guarantee that he'll be here tomorrow. *ma-agdar aṣoogir raḥ-ykuun ihnaa baačir.*
guard - 1. *ḥaaris* pl. *ḥurraas.* The guard didn't let me enter. *l-ḥaaris ma-xallaani ʔaxušš.* 2. *muraafiq* pl. *-iin.* The king got off the plane with his personal guards. *l-malik nizal imniṭ-ṭayyaara maεa muraafiqiina l-xaaṣṣiin.* 3. *ḥaami* pl. *-iin.* The army is the country's guard against enemy attack. *j-jeeš ḥaami l-waṭan min hujuum il-ʔaεdaaʔ.*
to guard - 1. *ḥiras (i ḥiraasa) n-, ḥima (i ḥami) n-.* The army is guarding the town. *j-jeeš da-yiḥris il-balad.* 2. *ḥima (i ḥami) n-.* This toothpaste guards the teeth against decay. *hal-maεjuun yiḥmi*

l-ʔasnaan imnit-taʔakkul.
to be on one's guard - *ztiras (i ztiraas).* You have to be on your guard with her. *laazim tiztiris minha.*
guardian - *waṣi* pl. *waṣaat.* He was appointed guardian of his brother's son. *čaan mitƐayyin waṣi Ɛala ʔibin ʔaxuu.*
guess - *taxmiin* pl. *-aat, taqdiir* pl. *-aat, zazir.* That wasn't right, but it's a good guess. *haaða ma-čaan ṣaziiz, laakin xooš taxmiin.*
to guess - **1.** *zizar (i zazir) n-, xamman (i taxmiin) t-, qaddar (i taqdiir) t-.* Guess how much money I've got in my pocket. *ʔizzir išgadd Ɛindi fluus ib-jeebi.* **2.** *ðann (u ðann) n-.* I guess he's sick. *ʔaðunna huwwa mariið.*
guest - *xuṭṭaar* pl. *xṭaaṭiir* coll. *xuṭṭaar, ðeef* pl. *ðyuuf.* Our guests ate all our food. *xuṭṭaarna ʔaklaw kull ʔakilna.*
guide - **1.** *daliil* pl. *ʔadillaaʔ.* Our guide showed us the things in the museum. *d-daliil maalna farrajna Ɛal-ʔašyaaʔ il-mawjuuda bil-matzaf.* **2.** *daliil* pl. *-aat.* All the theatres are listed in the guide. *kull is-siinamaat imsajjla bid-daliil.*
to guide - **1.** *dalla (i tdilli) t-,. ʔaršad (i ʔiršaad).* Mister can you direct us to this address? *s-sayyid, tigdar itdalliina Ɛala hal-Ɛinwaan?* **2.** *dawwar (i tadwiir) t-, farrar (i tafriir, tfirrir) t-.* She guided us around the ruins. *dawwaratna been il-ʔaaθaar.*
guilt - *ðanib, jurum.* He admitted his guilt. *Ɛtiraf ib-ðanba.*
guilty - *muðnib.* The judge found him not guilty. *l-zaakim wujada ġeer muðnib.*
guitar - *qiiθaara* pl. *-aat.*
gulf - **1.** *xaliij* pl. *xiljaan.* We swam in the Persian Gulf. *sbazna bil-xaliij il-faarisi.* **2.** *huwwa Ɛamiiqa.* There's a gulf between us. *ʔaku huwwa Ɛamiiqa beenaatna.*
gull - *nƐeeja* pl. *-aat* coll. *nƐeej, bƐeeja* pl. *-aat* coll. *bƐeej.* The sea gulls followed our ship. *nƐeej il-mayy tibaƐ markabna.*
gum - **1.** *laθθa* pl. *-aat.* This toothpaste is good for the gums. *hal-maƐjuun xoos lil-laθθa.* **2.** *Ɛilič* pl. *Ɛluuč.* Do you have some gum? *Ɛindak šwayyat Ɛilič?* **3.** *ṣamuġ.* We import gum arabic from the Sudan. *nistawrid iṣ-ṣamuġ il-Ɛarabi mnis-suudaan.*
to gum - *lizag (i lazig) n-, ṣammaġ (u tṣummuġ) t-.* Did you gum the labels? *lzagt il-biṭaaqaat?*
gun - **1.** *bunduqiyya* pl. *-aat, banaadiq* coll. *banaadiq, tufga* pl. *tufag.* The soldiers were carrying their guns in the parade. *j-jinuud čaanaw šaayliin banaadiqhum bil-istiƐraað.* **2.** *ṭalqa* pl. *-aat.* They fired a twenty-one gun salute for the visiting king. *ðirbaw waazid w-Ɛišriin ṭalqa taziyya lil-malik iz-zaaʔir.*
**Don't jump the gun! *la-titsarraƐ bil-ʔumuur!*
**They gunned him down. *waggƐoo bil-banaadiq.*
gunpowder - *baaruud.*
gust - *zabba* pl. *-aat.* A gust of wind blew the boy's cap off. *zabbat hawa waggƐat Ɛaraqčiin il-walad.*
gutter - *saagya* pl. *swaagi, majra* pl. *majaari.* My cigarettes fell in the gutter. *jigaarti wugƐat bil-majra.*
**His mind's in the gutter. *yizči fasaad.*
guy - *walad* pl. *wilid.* He's a good guy. *huwwa xooš walad.*
gym - **1.** *qaaƐat* (pl. *-aat*) *riyaaða.* The party will be in the gym. *l-zafla raz-itkuun ib-qaaƐat ir-riyaaða.* **2.** *riyaaða.* We have gym three times a week. *Ɛidna riyaaða tlaθ marraat bil-isbuuƐ.*
to **gyp** - *ġašš (u ġišš) n-, ġulab (u ġalub) n-.* He gypped me. *ġaššni.*
gypsy - *kaawli* pl. *-iyya, ġajari* pl. *-iyya.* That woman is a gypsy. *hal-mara kaawliyya.*

H

habit - **1.** *Ɛaada* pl. *-aat.* That's a bad habit. *haaði Ɛaada muu zeena.* **2.** *hduum.* Have you seen my riding habit? *šifit ihduum ir-rukuub maalti?*
to get into the habit of - *tƐawwad (a taƐwiid) Ɛala.* I got into the habit of smoking at college. *tƐawwadit Ɛat-tadxiin min činit bil-kulliyya.*
haggard - *mamṣuuṣ.* He looks very haggard. *ybayyin Ɛalee mamṣuuṣ kulliš.*
hail - *zaaluuba* pl. *-aat* coll. *zaaluub.* That's hail, not rain. *haaða zaaluub, muu muṭar.*
to hail - **1.** *ðabb (i ðabb) zaaluub.* It's hailing, not raining. *da-tðibb zaaluub, ma-da-tumṭur.* **2.** *ṣaaz (i ṣiiz) n-.* The doorman hailed a passing cab. *l-bawwaab ṣaaz taaksi faayit.* **3.** *razzab (i tarziib, truzzub) t- b-.* The critics hailed it as the best play of the year. *n-nuqqaad razzibaw biiha b-iƐtibaarha ʔazsan tamθiiliyya has-sana.* **4.** *zayya (i tziyyi) t-.* The crowd hailed him as he entered the city. *j-jumuuƐ zayyoo min dixal il-madiina.*
hair - *šaƐra* pl. *-aat* coll. *šaƐar.* What color is her hair? *šinu loon šaƐarha?*
**He's always getting into people's hair. *daaʔiman yitdaaxal b-šuʔuun il-ʔaaxariin.*
haircut - *ziyaan* pl. *-aat, ziyaan* (pl. *-aat*) *raas.* Where'd you get that funny haircut? *ween zayyanit hal-izyaan il-muðzik?*
to get a haircut - *zayyan (i tziyyin) t- šaƐar~.* I have to get a haircut. *laazim azayyin šaƐri.*
hair-dresser - *zallaaq* (pl. *-iin*) *tajmiil.*
half - *nuṣṣ* pl. *nṣaaṣ.* I'll give him half of my share. *raz-antii nuṣṣ zuṣṣti.* -- I got it for half price at a sale. *štireetha b-nuṣṣ qiima bit-tanziilaat.* -- We'll be there at half past eight. *nkuun ihnaak s-saaƐa θmaanya w-nuṣṣ.*
halfway - **1.** *muu kaamil.* Halfway measures will not suffice. *ʔijraaʔaat muu kaamla muu kaafya.* **2.** *b-nuṣṣ iṭ-ṭariiq.* We ran out of gas halfway to town. *xilaṣ il-baanziin ib-nuṣṣ iṭ-ṭariiq lil-madiina.*
**I'm willing to meet him halfway. *ʔaani mustaƐidd atsaahal wiyyaa.*
hall - **1.** *mamarr* pl. *-aat.* Mr. Ani lives at that end of the hall. *s-sayyid Ɛaani yiskun ib-ðiič ij-jiha min il-mamarr.* **2.** *mijaaz* pl. *-aat.* We need a new rug for our hall. *niztaaj zuuliyya jidiida lil-imjaaz.* **3.** *qaaƐa* pl. *-aat.* He gave his speech in a large hall. *ʔalqa xiṭaaba b-qaaƐa čbiira.*
halt - *tawaqquf.* There's been a halt in steel production. *ṣaar tawaqquf b-ʔintaaj il-zadiid.*
to halt - **1.** *wugaf (a wuguuf).* Halt! Who's there? *ʔoogaf, minu hnaak?* **2.** *waggaf (u twugguf) t-.* He halted the soldiers in front of the barracks. *waggaf ij-jinuud ʔamaam iθ-θakana.*
halting - *mitraddid.* He spoke in a halting voice. *ziča b-ṣoot mitraddid.*
ham - *lazam xanziir.* Would you like some ham for breakfast? *triid išwayya lazam xanziir lir-riyuug?*
hammer - **1.** *čaakuuč* pl. *čwaakiič.* Please hand me the hammer. *min faðlak, naawišni č-čaakuuč.* **2.** *miṭraqa* pl. *maṭaariq.* The students were carrying a flag with a picture of a hammer and sickle on it. *ṭ-ṭullaab čaanaw šaayliin Ɛalam bii ṣuurat miṭraqa w-minjal.*
to hammer - **1.** *dagg (u dagg), dagdag (i tdigdig).* Our neighbor has been hammering all day long. *jaarna ṭuul in-nahaar čaan da-ydigguun.* -- Hammer this nail in please. *dugg hal-bismaar rajaaʔan.* **2.** *raṣṣax (i tarṣiix).* He hammered the rules into me. *raṣṣax it-taƐliimaat Ɛindi.*
hand - **1.** *ʔiid* pl. *ʔiidteen, ʔiideen.* Where can I wash my hands? *ween ʔagdar aġsil ʔiidi?* -- My hand was very strong. I had three queens. *ʔiidi čaanat qawiyya. čaan Ɛindi tlaθ qizaz.* -- He asked for her hand from her father. *ṭulab iidha min ʔabuuha.* -- The matter is not in my hands. *l-qaðiyya muu b-iidi.* -- Just keep your hands off that! *waxxir ʔiidak min haay!* -- This job has to be done by hand. *haš-šuġuḷ laazim yṣiir bil-ʔiid.* **2.** *yad, ʔiid.* He must have had a hand in that. *laazim čaan ʔila yad biiha.* -- **3.** *miil* pl. *ʔamyaal, myaala; Ɛagrab* pl. *Ɛagaarib.* The minute hand doesn't work. *miil id-daqaaʔiq ma-yištuġul.* **4.** *jiha.* On the other hand, he wants it finished. *w-min jiha lux, yriidha tixlaṣ.* **5.** *yadawi*.* He wanted to blow up the factory with a hand grenade. *raad yinsif il-maƐmal ib-qumbula yadawiyya.*

**I can't lay my hands on it right now. *ma-agdar azaşşilha hassa.*

on hand - *jawwa l-ˀiid, zaaδir, mawjuud.* We haven't that size on hand. *ma-ɛidna hal-zajim jawwa l-ˀiid.*

to hand - *niṭa (i naṭi) n-, naawaš (u munaawaša) t-.* Please hand me that pencil. *baḷḷa nṭiini hal-qalam.*

to hand in - *sallam (i tsillim) t-.* I'm going to hand in my application tomorrow. *raz-aruuz baačir ˀasallim ɛariiδti.*

to hand out - *wazzaɛ (i tawziiɛ) t-, farrag (i tafriig) t-.* Hand these tickets out! *wazziɛ hal-biṭaaqaat!*

handbag - *janṭat* (pl. *-aat, junaṭ*) *ˀiid.*

hand brake - *handibreek* pl. *-aat.*

handcuff - *kalabča* pl. *-aat.* Here every policeman carries a pair of handcuffs. *kull šurṭi hnaa yšiil kalabča wiyyaa.*

to handcuff - *kalbač (i tkilbič) t-.* They handcuffed the prisoners. *kalbičaw l-masaajiin.*

hand drill - *mizraf yadawi* pl. *mazaaruf yadawiyya.*

handful - *čaff* pl. *čfuuf.* He took a handful of nuts. *ˀaxaδ fadd čaff čarazaat.*

handkerchief - *čaffiyya* pl. *-aat, čfaafi.*

handle - **1.** *yadda* pl. *-aat.* My suitcase needs a new handle. *yinraad ij-janiṭṭi yadda jidiida.* **2.** *ɛurwa* pl. *ɛaraawi.* The handle of this teapot is broken. *hal-quuri ɛuruuta maksuura.*

**At the slightest occasion he flies off the handle. *yθuur min ˀadna šii.*

to handle - **1.** *ɛaamal (i muɛaamala).* He knows how to handle people. *yuɛruf išloon yɛaamil in-naas.* **2.** *lizam (a lazim) n-.* Look at it all you want, but don't handle it. *baawiɛ ɛaleeha šgadd-ma triid, bass la-tilzamha.* **3.** *tɛaaṭa (a taɛaaṭi) b-.* We don't handle that commodity. *ma-nitɛaaṭa b-has-silɛa.* **4.** *δubaṭ (u δabuṭ) n-.* I can't handle him anymore. *baɛad ma-agdar ˀaδubṭa.* **6.** *dabbar (u tadbiir) t-.* I simply can't handle all the work by myself. *mnil-waaδiz ˀaani ma-agdar adabbur kull iš-šuğuḷ wazdi.* **7.** *staɛmal (i stiɛmaal).* Do you know how to handle a revolver? *tuɛruf išloon tistaɛmil musaddas?*

**Handle that glass with care. *diir baalak ɛala haj-jaama!*

handmade - *šuğuḷ ˀiid.* That's all handmade. *haaδa kulla šuğuḷ ˀiid.*

handsome - *wasiim.* He's a handsome man. *huwwa rajul wasiim.*

**That's a handsome sum of money. *haaδa xooš mablağ imnil-maal.*

handwriting - *kitaaba, xaṭṭ iid.* His handwriting is illegible. *kitaabta ma-tinqiri.*

handy - **1.** *mufiid.* This potato peeler is very handy. *hal-gaššaara maal il-puteeta mufiida.* **2.** *maahir.* He's a very handy fellow in everything. *huwwa waazid maahir ib-kullši.* **3.** *jawwa ˀiid.* Have you got a pencil handy? *jawwa ˀiidak qalam?*

to come in handy - *faad (i faaˀida).* A knowledge of typing will come in handy to you some day. *taɛallum iṭ-ṭaabiɛa yfiidak fadd yoom.*

**The extra money comes in very handy. *l-ifluus il-ˀiδaafiyya ˀilha makaan mufiid min tiji.*

to **hang** - **1.** *šinaq (u šaniq) n-, ṣilab (u ṣalub) n-.* He was hanged yesterday. *l-baarza nšinaq.* **2.** *ɛallag (i taɛliig) t-.* Can't you hang the picture a little higher? *ma-tigdar itɛallig iṣ-ṣuura šwayya ˀaɛla?* -- Where can I hang my coat? *ween aɛallig sitirti?* **3.** *tɛallag (a taɛallug).* He hung from the limb and started swinging. *tɛallag bil-ğuṣun w-gaam yitmarjaz.* **4.** *dandal (i tdindil).* Why are you hanging your head? *leeš imdandil raasak?*

**His life hung by a thread. *zayaata čaanat waagfa ɛala šaɛra.*

to hang around - *raabaṭ (u muraabaṭa).* He's always hanging around the tavern. *ɛala-ṭuul imraabuṭ bil-mayxaana.*

to hang on - *lizam (a lazim) n-.* I hung on with all my strength. *ˀaani lizamit ib-kull quuti.*

to hang onto - **1.** *lizam (a) n-, čallab (i tčillib) t-.* I hung onto the dog as long as I could. *lizamit ič-čalib ṭuul-ma gidarit.* **2.** *baqqa (i tbiqqi) t-.* I'll hang on to the stock until its price goes up again. *raz-abaqqi l-ˀashum ˀila ˀan yirtifiɛ siɛirha.* **3.** *xalla (i txilli) t- ɛind~.* Hang onto this money for me. *xallii-li hal-ifluus ɛindak.*

to hang out - **1.** *šarr (u šarr) n-, ɛallag (i taɛliig) t-.* Did you hang the wash out? *šarreeti l-ihduum barra?* **2.** *dandal (i tdindil) t-.* The rope is hanging out the window. *l-zabil imdandal imniš-šibbaač.*

to hang up - *ɛallag (i taɛliig) t-.* Hang up your hat and coat. *ɛallig šafuqtak w-sitirtak.*

**He got angry and hung up on me. *ziɛal ɛalayya w-sadd it-talafoon ib-wujhi.*

hangar - *garaaj* (pl. *-aat*) *ṭayyaaraat.*

hanger - *tiɛlaaga* pl. *-aat.* Put your coat on a hangar. *xalli sitirtak ɛat-tiɛlaaga.*

hangover - *xmaariyya.* Take yourself a shot to get rid of the hangover. *ˀuxuδ-lak fadd peek zatta tiksir il-ixmaariyya.*

to **happen** - **1.** *zidaθ (i zuduuθ), ṣaar (i ṣeer), wuqaɛ (a wuquuɛ).* When did that happen? *šwakit zidθat?* -- What happened to the typewriter? Did someone use it? *š-ṣaayir biṭ-ṭaabiɛa? ˀazzad istaɛmalha?* **2.** *ṣaadaf (i taṣaaduf).* I don't happen to agree with you this time. *ṣaadaf ˀan ma-ˀattifiq wiyyaak hal-marra.* -- He doesn't happen to be here. *ṣaadaf ˀan ma-ykuun ihnaa.*

**Everything happens to me. *kull il-bala da-yinzil ɛala raasi.*

happily - **1.** *b-saɛaada.* They are spending their married life happily. *da-yigδuun zayaathum iz-zawjiyya b-saɛaada.* **2.** *b-suruur, b-faraz.* She does her work happily. *tsawwi šuğuḷha b-suruur.*

happiness - *saɛaada, suruur, faraz.*

happy - *saɛiid, farzaan, masruur.* I'm very happy you won. *ˀaani saɛiid li-ˀannak irbazit.*

**Happy New Year! *kull ɛaam w-intum ib-xeer!*

**Happy birthday! *ɛiid milaadak saɛiid!*

harbor - *miinaaˀ* pl. *mawaani, marfaˀ* pl. *maraafiˀ.*

hard - **1.** *qawi**. I can't sleep on a hard mattress. *ma-agdar ˀanaam ɛala fraaš qawi.* -- His death was a hard blow to us. *wafaata čaanat ṣadma qawiyya ɛaleena.* **2.** *yaabis.* The bread is hard as a rock. *l-xubuz yaabis miθl il-izjaara.* **3.** *mujidd.* He's a hard worker. *huwwa ɛaamil mujidd.* **4.** *ṣaɛub.* It's hard for me to climb stairs. *ṣaɛub ɛalayya ˀaṣɛad id-daraj.* -- Those were hard times. *čaanat ˀawqaat ṣaɛba.* -- He's a hard man to get along with. *huwwa rajul ṣaɛub titfaaham wiyyaa.* **5.** *b-jidd.* He worked hard all day. *štiğal ib-jidd ṭuul il-yoom.* **6.** *b-quwwa, zeel.* It was raining hard when he left. *čaanat tumṭur ib-quwwa lamman ṭilaɛ.* -- He hit him on the head hard. *δuraba ɛala raasa zeel.* **7.** *jaamid, qawi**. This ice cream is extremely hard. It can't be cut even with a knife. *had-doondirma jaamda kulliš, ma-tingaṣṣ zatta bis-siččiina.*

hard and fast - *θaabit.* In this case you can't make hard and fast rules. *b-hal-zaala ma-tigdar itzuṭṭ qawaaɛid θaabta.*

hard of hearing - *samiɛ θigiil.* He's hard of hearing. *samɛa θigiil.*

to be hard up for - *ztaaj (a ztiyaaj).* He's always hard up for money. *huwwa ɛala-ṭuul yiztaaj ifluus.*

to try hard - *zaawal (i muzaawala) t- jahd~, jtihad (i jtihaad).* He tried hard to do it right. *zaawal kull jahda zatta ysawwiiha zeen.*

to **harden** - *tṣallab (a taṣallub), jimad (a jamid), sakk (u sakk).* How long will it take the cement to harden? *šgadd yirraad liš-šibintu zatta yitṣallab?*

hardly - **1.** *b-ṣuɛuuba, mniṣ-ṣaɛub.* I hardly believe that. *b-ṣuɛuuba ˀaṣaddigha.*

You can hardly expect me to believe that. *la-titṣawwar raz-aṣaddig δaak ib-suhuula.* **2. *bil-kaad.* He had hardly begun to speak when ... *bil-kaad bida yizči lamman ...*

hardly ever - *mnin-naadir, naadiran.* I hardly ever go out. *mnin-naadir aṭlaɛ barra.*

harm - *δarar, ˀaδiyya.* You can never undo the harm you've done. *ma-tigdar itziil iδ-δarar illi sawweeta.* -- No harm done! *ma-zidaθ ˀay δarar!*

to harm - *δarr (u δarar) n-, ˀaδδa (i tˀiδδi) t-.* A vacation wouldn't harm you. *l-ɛuṭla ma-raz-itδurrak.* -- This dry weather has harmed the crops a lot. *haj-jaww ij-jaaff ˀaδδa z-ziriɛ ihwaaya.*

harmful - *muδirr, muˀδi.* This drought is harmful for the crops. *hal-mazal muδirr liz-ziriɛ.*

harmonica - *haarmooniika* pl. *-aat.*

harmony - **1.** *nsijaam.* There was perfect harmony between the two. *čaan aku nsijaam kaamil been iθ-θineen.* -- This song has beautiful harmony. *hal-uğniya biiha nsijaam laṭiif.* **2.** *mitnaasiq, mittifiq, mitlaaˀim.* His plans are in complete harmony with mine. *mašaariiɛa kulliš mitnaasqa wiyya maalti.*

harness - *ɛidda* pl. *ɛidad.* I just bought a new

harness for my horse. *hastawwni štireet ɛidda l-iẓṣaani.*

to harness - **1.** *sarraj (i tsirrij) t-.* Has he harnessed the horses? *sarraj il-xeel?* **2.** *staxdam (i stixdaam).* Man is attempting to harness atomic energy. *l-ʔinsaan da-yẓaawil yistaxdim iṭ-ṭaaqa δ-δarriyya.*

harp - *qiiθaar, qiiθaara* pl. *-aat.*

to harp - *dagg (u dagg) n-.* Stop harping on the same subject. *bass-ɛaad itdugg ɛala nafs il-mawδuuɛ.*

harsh - **1.** *qaasi.* Those are harsh terms. *haay šuruuṭ qaasya.* **2.** *muxaddiš.* This soap contains no harsh ingredients. *ma-aku ɛanaaṣir muxaddiša b-haṣ-ṣaabuun.*

harvest - *maẓṣuul.* We had a good harvest. *maẓṣuulna čaan zeen.*

to harvest - *ẓiṣad (i ẓaṣid) n-.* When you harvest the wheat around here? *šwakit tiẓiṣduun il-ẓunṭa b-hal-manṭiqa?*

haste - *ɛajala, surɛa.*

**Haste makes waste. *l-ɛajala mniš-šeeṭaan.*

hastily - *b-ɛajala, b-surɛa.* They took leave hastily. *ṭilɛaw ib-ɛajala.*

hasty - *b-surɛa, mitsarriɛ.* You mustn't make hasty decisions. *ma-laazim tittixiδ qaraaraat ib-surɛa.*

**I wouldn't be hasty about it, if I were you. *loo b-makaanak ma-astaɛjil biiha.*

hat - *šafqa* pl. *-aat, birneeṭa* pl. *-aat.*

to **hatch** - *faggas (i tafgiis).* The hen sits on the eggs until they hatch. *d-dijaaja tguff ɛal-beeδ ẓatta yfaggis.*

hatchet - *balṭa* pl. *-aat.*

hate - *kuruh, buġuδ.* His dislike gradually turned into hate. *bit-tadriij ɛadam maẓabbta tẓawwlat ʔila kuruh.*

to hate - *kirah (a kuruh) n-.* I hate people who are selfish. *ʔakrah in-naas il-ʔanaaniyyiin.*

hatred - *karaaha, buġuδ, karaahiyya.*

haul - **1.** *ṣeed.* The fishermen had a good haul today. *ṣayyaadiin is-simač ṭallɛaw xooš ṣeed hal-yoom.* **2.** *ẓimil* pl. *ẓumuula.* This haul is too big for the truck. *hal-ẓimil kulliš čabiir ɛal-loori.*

**It's a long haul from here to Bagdad. *masaafa ṭawiila minnaa l-baġdaad.*

to haul - **1.** *jarr (u jarr) n-, siẓab (a saẓib) n-.* The horses were unable to haul the heavy load. *l-xeel ma-gidrat itjurr il-ẓiml iθ-θigiil.* -- They hauled me out of bed at six this morning. *jarrooni mnil-ifraaš saaɛa sitta l-yoom iṣ-ṣubuẓ.*

**He hauled off as if he meant to hit me. *traajaɛ w-tẓaffaz ɛabaalak čaan yriid yiδrubni.*

to haul down - *nazzal (i tanziil) t-.* Has the flag been hauled down yet? *l-ɛalam itnazzal loo baɛad?*

to **have**: no verbal equivalent, paraphrased with prepositions: **1.** *ɛind, wiyya.* I have two tickets for the theater. *ɛindi biṭaaqteen lit-tamθiiliyya.* -- Do you have a pencil you can lend me? *ɛindak qalam tigdar itɛiirni?* -- Who had the book last? *minu ʔaaxir waaẓid čaan ɛinda l-iktaab?* -- He has a heart disease. *ɛinda maraδ qalb.* -- I have a headache. *wiyyaaya wujaɛ raas.* -- Do you have the key? *wiyyaak il-miftaaẓ?* **2.** *ʔil-, b-.* The room has three windows. *l-ġubba ʔilha tlaθ išbaabiič.* -- The argument has no end. *l-mujaadala ma-biiha nihaaya.* -- The streets have no sidewalks. *š-šawaariɛ ma-biiha ʔarṣifa.* **3.** *ɛind, ʔil-.* He has a very uncouth uncle. *ʔila ɛamm kullis ʔadabsizz.* -- She has beautiful eyes. *ɛidha ɛyuun ẓilwa.* -- You have a talent for music. *ʔilak mawhiba bil-mawsiiqa.* **4.** *xalla (i txilli).* Have him wash my car. *xallii yiġsil sayyaarti.*

**Have you had a haircut today? *zayyanit hal-yoom?*

**Has he done his job well? *sawwa šuġla zeen?*

**How long have you been in Baghdad? *šgadd ṣaar-lak ib-baġdaad?*

**How long have you been waiting for me? *šgadd ṣaar-lak tintiδirni?*

**I've been standing here for two hours. *ṣaar-li waaguf ihnaa saaɛteen.*

**I'm having my teeth treated. *da-adaawi snaani.*

**We're having a house built. *da-nibni beet.*

**I'll have to have my appendix out. *laazim asawwi ɛamaliyyat il-muṣraan il-ʔaɛwar.*

**Good stockings are simply not to be had. *j-juwaariib iz-zeen mustaẓiil tinligi ɛind ʔaẓẓad.*

**Please have a seat. *tfaδδal, istariiẓ!*

**He has it in for you. *huwwa δammha ʔilak.*

**Let's have the knife! *nṭiini s-siččiin!*

**What did she have on? *š-čaanat laabsa?*

**Wouldn't it be better to have it out with him right now? *muu ʔaẓsan loo txalluṣha wiyyaa hassa?*

I had better, you had better, etc. - *ʔaẓsan-li, ʔaẓsal-li, ʔaẓsan-lak,* etc. You'd better do it right away. *ʔaẓsal-lak sawwiiha hassa.*

to have to: (present and future) **1.** *laazim, ɛal-, waajib ɛal-.* I have to go get my wife. *laazim ʔaruuẓ ʔajiib zawijti.* -- We'll have to throw a party for these people. *laazim insawwi ẓafla l-haj-jamaaɛa.* **2.** *δṭarr (a δṭiraar), njubar (i njibaar).* I had to leave early. *δṭarreet ʔaruuẓ min-wakit.* -- They had to fire him. *δṭarraw yfuṣluu.*

**You have to have new shoes. *laazmak qundara jidiida.*

not to have to - *ma-aku ẓaaja, muu δaruuri, ma-aku lzuum, ma-laazim.* You don't have to go. *ma-aku ẓaaja truuẓ.* -- You won't have to sign again. *ma-aku lzuum timδi marra lux.* -- You didn't have to shout like that. *ma-čaan laazim itṣayyiẓ hiiči.*

hawk - *ṣagur* pl. *ṣguur.*

hay - *tibin.* The hay isn't dry yet. *t-tibin baɛda maa yaabis li-hassa.*

**It's time to hit the hay. *ṣaar wakt in-noom!*

**Let's make hay while the sun shines. *xalli nistiġill il-furṣa gabul-ma tfuut.*

hay fever - *ẓumma l-qašš.*

haystack - *beedar* (pl. *biyaadir*) *tibin.*

hazard - *xaṭar* pl. *ʔaxṭaar, muxaaṭara* pl. *-aat.* Factory workers are exposed to hazards very much. *ɛummaal il-maɛaamil muɛarraδiin lil-ʔaxṭaar kaθiira.*

hazelnut - *findiqa* pl. *-aat* coll. *findiq, bunduga* pl. *-aat* coll. *bundug.*

hazy - **1.** *mġawwaš.* It's rather hazy today. *ɛal-ʔakθar id-dinya mġawwša l-yoom.* **2.** *mubham.* Your ideas are hazy. *ʔafkaarak mubhama.*

he - *huwwa.* He's very glad. *huwwa kulliš masruur.* -- He came yesterday. *(huwwa) jaa l-baarẓa.*

head - **1.** *raas* pl. *ruus.* My head hurts. *raasi yoojaɛni.* -- Lettuce is ten fils a head. *raas il-xass ib-ɛašr ifluus.* -- I need nails with larger heads. *ʔaẓtaaj ibsaamiir raasha ʔakbar.* -- I can't make head nor tail of the story. *ma-da-agdar algi l-hal-quṣṣa laa raas wala ʔasaas.* -- He sold five head of cattle. *baaɛ xamis ruus hooš.* -- Begin at the head of the page. *ʔibdi min raas iṣ-ṣafẓa.* -- The mayor rode at the head of the procession. *raʔiis il-baladiyya miša ɛala raas il-mawkib.* **2.** *ɛaqil* pl. *ɛuquul.* He has a good head for arithmetic. *ɛinda xooš ɛaqil bil-iẓsaabaat.* **3.** *raʔiis* pl. *ruʔasaaʔ.* He's the head of the gang. *huwwa raʔiis il-ɛiṣaaba.* **4.** *rabb* pl. *ʔarbaab.* He's the head of the family. *huwwa rabb il-ɛaaʔila.* **5.** *ṣadir.* We were sitting at the head of the table. *čiina gaaɛdiin ib-ṣadr il-meez.*

**That's over my head. *ʔaani ʔaṭraš biz-zaffa.*

**You hit the nail on the head. *ʔinta lgafitha.*

**My friend is head over heels in love. *ṣadiiqi waagiɛ bil-ġuraam.*

**That may cost him his head. *haaδi mumkin itkallfa ẓayaata.*

**Heads or tails? *ṭurra loo kitba?* or *šiir loo xaṭṭ?*

**I can't keep everything in my head. *ma-agdar atδakkar kullši.*

**The man is positively out of his head. *har-rijjaal ɛaqla muu b-raasa.*

**I don't want to go over his head. *ma-ariid aruuẓ l-illi ʔaɛla minna.*

**Things had to come to a head sooner or later. *l-ʔašyaaʔ laazim fadd yoom tooṣal ẓaddha.*

**Everyone kept his head. *kull waaẓid ẓaafaδ ɛala ttizaana.*

to head - **1.** *riʔas (a riʔaasa).* He hopes to head the department some day. *yitʔammal yirʔas il-qisim fadd yoom.* **2.** *wajjah (i tawjiih) t-.* He headed the car at me to murder me. *wajjah is-sayyaara ɛalayya ẓatta ymawwitni.* **3.** *tfawwaq (a tafawwuq) ɛala.* My boy heads his class at school. *ʔibni mitfawwiq ɛala ṭullaab ṣaffa bil-madrasa.* **4.** *ttijah (i ttijaah), raaẓ (u).* They're heading for Bagdad. *humma mittajhiin ʔila baġdaad.* -- Where are you headed? *li-ween mittijih?* or *li-ween raayiẓ?*

**You're heading in the wrong direction. *ʔinta maaxiδ ittijaah ġalaṭ.*

**His name heads the list of candidates. *ʔisma b-raas qaaʔimat il-muraššaẓiin.*

headache - **1.** *wijaɛ* (pl. *-aat*) *raas, ṣudaaɛ.* I've a

bad headache. *ɛindi wijaɛ raas šadiid.* -- This problem is really a headache. *hal-muškila ħaqiiqatan wijaɛ raas.*
**The noise gives me a headache. *l-laġwa da-twajjiɛ raasi.*

headdress - *libaas raas.*

heading - *ttijaah* pl. *-aat.* The plane took a new heading. *ṭ-ṭayyaara ʔaxδat ittijaah ijdiid.*

headlight - *laayt* pl. *-aat.*

headline - *ɛinwaan* pl. *ɛanaawiin.* What are the headlines in today's paper? *šinu l-ɛanaawiin maal jariidat il-yoom?*

headlong - *ɛala raas.* He plunged headlong into the river. *čayyat biš-šaṭṭ ɛala raasa.*

headquarters - 1. *markaz* (pl. *maraakiz*) *qiyaada, maqarr* (pl. *-aat*) *qiyaada.* This officer was attached to headquarters. *haδ-δaabuṭ čaan mirtibuṭ ib-markaz il-qiyaada.* 2. *markaz ɛaamm* pl. *maraakiz ɛaamma, maqarr ɛaamm* pl. *maqarraat ɛaamma.* For further information, apply to party headquarters. *lil-ħuṣuul ɛala maɛluumaat ʔakθar qaddim ṭalab lil-maqarr il-ɛaamm lil-ħizib.*

headwaiter - *raʔiis* (pl. *ruʔasaaʔ*) *booyaat.*

to make **headway** - *tqaddam* (*a taqaddum*). We made headway slowly in the sand. *tqaddamna b-buṭuʔ bir-ramal.*

head wind - *riiħ imɛaakis* pl. *riyaaħ imɛaaksa.* We had strong head winds all the way. *ṣaadfatna riyaaħ imɛaaksa qawiyya ṭuul iṭ-ṭariiq.*

to **heal** - 1. *liħam* (*a laħim*) *n-.* The treatment is healing the wound successfully. *l-muɛaalaja da-tilħam ij-jariħ kulliš zeen.* 2. *nliħam* (*i nliħaam*). The wound isn't healing properly. *j-jariħ ma-da-yinliħim zeen.*

health - 1. *ṣiħħa.* How's his health? *šloon ṣiħħta?* 2. *ṣiħħi**. He's working on a new health project. *da-yištuġul ib-mašruuɛ ṣiħħi jdiid.*

healthy - *ṣiħħi**. This isn't a healthy climate. *haj-jaww muu ṣiħħi.*
**She looks very healthy. *mbayyna ɛaleeha ṣ-ṣiħħa.*

heap - *kooma* pl. *-aat.* What's this heap of sand for? *luweeš hal-kooma maal ir-ramal?*
to heap - *kawwam* (*u tkuwwum*) *t-, kaddas* (*i takdiis*) *t-.* The table was heaped with all kinds of food. *ʔalwaan il-ʔakil čaanat imkawwma ɛal-meez.*

to **hear** - *simaɛ* (*a samiɛ*) *n-.* I didn't hear anything. *ma-simaɛit ʔay šii.* -- I won't hear of it! *ma-ariid asmaɛha.* -- Well then, I'll expect to hear from you. *zeen ʔiδan, ʔatwaqqaɛ asmaɛ minnak.*
**You can't hear yourself in this noise. *min hal-laġwa ma-yinsimiɛ šii.*

hearing - 1. *muraafaɛa* pl. *-aat.* The hearing was set for June sixth. *tɛayyan yoom il-muraafaɛa sitta ħzayraan.* 2. *samiɛ.* His hearing is very poor. *samɛa kulliš δaɛiif.*
to lose one's hearing - *ṭrašš* (*a ṭrišaaš*). When did he lose his hearing? *šwakit iṭrašš?*

hearse - *ɛarabaanat* (pl. *ɛarabaayin*) *jinaaza, sayyaarat* (pl. *-aat*) *jinaaza.*

heart - 1. *qalb* pl. *quluub, galub* pl. *gluub.* His heart is weak. *qalba δaɛiif.* -- It breaks my heart to let him go. *šii yfaṭṭir il-galub ʔan axalli yruuħ.* -- I didn't have the heart to tell him. *galbi ma-nṭaani ʔaguul-la.* 2. *ġeeb.* I learned the poem by heart. *ħfuδṭ il-qaṣiida ɛal-ġeeb.* 3. *ħaqiiqa* pl. *ħaqaayiq, ʔasaas* pl. *ʔusus.* I want to get to the heart of this matter. *ʔariid atwaṣṣal ʔila ħaqiiqat hal-mawδuuɛ.*
**I haven't got the heart to do it. *galbi ma-yinṭiini ʔasawwiiha.*
**Cross my heart! I didn't do it! *ʔaqsim b-illaah il-ɛaδiim, ma-sawweetha.*
**He's a man after my own heart. *huwwa fadd waaħid ḥayya miθil ḥayyi.*
**Don't lose heart! *la-tifqid šajaaɛtak!*
**At heart he's really a good fellow. *jawhara zeen.*
hearts - *kuuba.* Hearts are highest. *l-kuuba ʔaɛla šii.*
to take to heart - *ʔaxaδ* (*u ʔaxiδ*) *n- ib-jidd.* He's taking it very much to heart. *huwwa maaxiδha kulliš ib-jidd.*

heart attack - *sakta* (pl. *-aat*) *qalbiyya* (fatal), *nawba* (pl. *-aat*) *qalbiyya.*

heartily - 1. *b-šahiyya, b-raġba.* We ate heartily. *ʔakalna b-šahiyya.* 2. *min kull galub-.* We laughed heartily. *δħakna min kull galubna.*

hearty - *dasim.* We had a hearty meal. *ʔakanna ʔakla dasma* or *ʔakanna b-šahiyya.*
**He's hale and hearty in spite of his age. *matruus ṣiħħa b-raġum sinna* or *kulla ṣiħħa b-raġum sinna.*

heat - 1. *ħaraara, ṣuxuuna.* I can't stand the heat. *ma-agdar atħammal il-ħaraara.* -- The stove doesn't give enough heat. *ṣ-ṣooba ma-tinṭi ħaraara kaafya.* 2. *šooṭ* pl. *ʔašwaaṭ.* My horse won the first heat. *ħṣaani ġulub biš-šooṭ il-ʔawwal.*
**It happened in the heat of the battle. *ṣaarat min čaanat il-maɛraka ħaamya.*
in heat - *mithayyija.* Our cat's in heat. *bazzuunatna mithayyija.*
to heat - 1. *daffa* (*i tdiffi*) *t-.* The room is well heated. *l-ġurfa mdaffaaya zeen.* 2. *ħima* (*a ħami*). The living-room radiator doesn't heat up. *ṣoobat ġurfat il-gaɛda ma-da-tiħma.* -- It'll be five minutes before the iron heats up. *l-ʔuuti yinraad-la xamis daqaayiq ħatta yiħma.* 3. *ħima* (*i*) *n-, saxxan* (*i tsixxin*) *t-.* I'll have to heat up some water first. *ʔawwal laazim aħmi šwayya ḥaay.*

heater - *ṣooba* pl. *-aat, madfaʔa* pl. *-aat, madaafiʔ.*

heat-resistant - *muqaawum lil-ħaraara.* Is that glass heat-resistant? *haz-zujaaj muqaawum lil-ħaraara?*

heaven - *janna.* When the good man dies he goes to heaven. *r-rajul iṣ-ṣaaliħ min ymuut yruuħ lij-janna.*
**She was in seventh heaven. *čaanat fi-ʔawj is-saɛaada.*
**For heaven's sake, stop that noise! *daxiil ʔaḷḷa baṭṭil hal-ħiss!* or *yaa mɛawwad, baṭṭil hal-laġwa!*
**Only heaven knows how often I've tried. *bass ʔaḷḷa yidri čam marra ħaawalit.*

heavy - 1. *θigiil* pl. *θgaal.* Is that box too heavy for you? *haṣ-ṣanduug kulliš θigiil ɛaleek?* -- I can't take heavy food. *ma-agdar aakul šii θigiil.* 2. *čbiir, kabiir* pl. *kbaar.* He had to pay a heavy fine. *δṭarr yidfaɛ ġaraama čabiira.* 3. *qawi**, *šadiid.* We can't leave in that heavy rain. *ma-nigdar inruuħ b-hal-muṭar il-qawi.*
**He's a heavy drinker. *huwwa sikkiir.*

Hebrew - 1. *ɛibri**, *ɛibraani**. Do you know the Hebrew alphabet? *tuɛruf il-ħuruuf il-ɛibriyya?* 2. *ɛibriyya, ɛibri.* Do you speak Hebrew? *titkallam bil-ɛibriyya?*

hedge - *siyaaj* (pl. *-aat*) *yaas.*

heel - *čaɛab* pl. *čɛuub.* I have a blister on my heel of my foot. *ɛindi buṭbaaṭa b-čaɛab rijli.* -- These shoes need new heels. *hal-qundara tiħtaaj čaɛab jidiid.*

hegira - *hijra.*

height - 1. *rtifaaɛ* pl. *-aat.* How do you determine the height of a triangle? *šloon itɛayyin irtifaaɛ il-muθallaθ?* 2. *ʔooj.* He was then at the height of his power. *b-δaak il-wakit čaan ib-ʔooj quuta.* 3. *ġaaya* pl. *-aat.* That's the height of stupidity. *haaδi ġaayat il-ġabaaʔ.*

heir - *wariiθ, waariθ* pl. *waraθa.* He's the sole heir. *huwwa l-waariθ il-waħiid.*

hell - *jahannam, jaħiim.* He died and went to hell. *maat w-raaħ ij-jahannam.*

hello - *halaw.* Hello, operator! You've cut me off. *halaw, maʔmuurat il-baddaala, qiṭaɛti l-xaṭṭ ɛanni.*

helmet - *xuuδa* pl. *xuwaδ.*

help - *musaaɛada, muɛaawana, maɛuuna.* Do you need any help? *tiħtaaj ʔay musaaɛada?*
**It's difficult to get help these days. *ṣaɛub tilgi ʔaħħad yɛaawinak hal-ʔayyaam.*
**Help! *y-ahl ir-raħam!*
to help - 1. *saaɛad* (*i musaaɛada*) *t-, ɛaawan* (*i muɛaawana*) *t-, ɛaan* (*i ɛoon*). Please help me. *min faδlak saaɛidni.* 2. *saaɛad* (*i musaaɛada*) *t-.* She helps us out on Sunday. *hiyya tsaaɛidna biš-šuġuḷ yoom il-ʔaħħad.*
**I can't help it, but that's my opinion. *š-ʔasawwi, or la-tluumni, haaδa raʔyi.*
**I couldn't help but see it. *ma-gdarit ʔilla ʔašuufha.*
**Sorry, that can't be helped. *mitʔassif, ma-mumkin titġayyar.*
to help oneself - *tfaδδal* (*a tafaδδul*). Please help yourself! *tfaδδal!*

helper - *ṣaaniɛ* pl. *ṣinnaaɛ.* He has two helpers. *ɛinda ṣaanɛeen.*

helpful - 1. *xaduum.* She's always very helpful. *hiyya daaʔiman kulliš xaduuma.* 2. *mufiid.* You've given me a very helpful hint. *nṭeetni fadd ʔišaara kulliš mufiida.*

helping - *taris maaɛuun.* I had two helpings. *ʔakalit taris maaɛuuneen.*

helpless - *ɛaajiz* pl. *-iin, ɛajaza.* A baby is helpless. *ṭ-ṭifil ɛaajiz ɛan kullši.*

hem - ẓaašya pl. ẓawaaši. I want to let out the hem. *ˀariid afukk il-ẓaašya.*
to hem - *kaff (u kaff) n-.* Mother, hem this skirt for me. *yoom kuffii-li t-tannuura.*
to hem in - *ẓiṣar (i ẓaṣir) n-, ẓaaṭ (u ẓooṭ) n-.* The house is hemmed between two tall buildings. *l-beet maẓṣuur been binaayteen ἑaalya.*
hen - *dijaaja* pl. *-aat,* coll. *dijaaj.*
her - *-ha.* I saw her last week. *šifitha bil-isbuuἑ il-maaḍi.* -- That was very nice of her. *haaδi čaanat kulliš ẓilwa minha.* -- This is her house. *haaδa beetha.*
herb - *ἑišib* pl. *ˀaἑšaab.* In Iraq they still use herbs as remedies. *bil-ἑiraaq baἑadhum yistaἑmiluun il-ˀaἑšaab ka-ˀadwiya.*
herd - *qaṭiiἑ* pl. *quṭἑaan.* Who owns this herd? *minu ṣaaẓib hal-qaṭiiἑ?*
to herd - *ẓišar (i ẓašir) n-, jimaἑ (a jamiἑ) n-.* They herded us all in to a small room. *ẓišroona kullna b-fadd ġurfa ṣġayyra.*
here - *hnaa, hnaaya.* We can't stay here. *ma-nigdar nibqa hnaa.* -- Let's cross the street (from) here. *xal-nuἑbur iš-šaariἑ minnaa.* -- The papers here say nothing about the accident. *j-jaraayid ihnaa ma-tiktib ˀay šii ἑan il-ẓaadiθa.*
**Here's the book. *haaδa l-iktaab* or *haak il-iktaab.*
**Here's to you! *l-ṣiẓẓtak* or *l-naxbak!*
hereafter - 1. *missa ġaadi, baἑdeen.* Hereafter I'll be more alert. *missa ġaadi akuun mintibih ˀazyad.* 2. *l-ˀaaxra.* Some people believe in the hereafter. *baἑaḍ in-naas yiἑtiqduun. bil-ˀaaxra.*
hernia - *fatig* (pl. *ftuug*) *riiẓ.*
hero - *baṭal* pl. *ˀabṭaal.*
heroic - *buṭuuli*.*
hers - (m.) *maalha,* (f.) *maalatha.* My hat is bigger than hers. *šafuqti ˀakbar min maalatha.*
**A friend of hers told me. *ṣadiiq min ˀaṣdiqaaˀha gaal-li.*
herself - *nafisha, ruuẓha.* She fell on the stairs and hurt herself. *wugἑat ἑad-daraj w-ˀaδδat nafisha* or *wugἑat ἑad-daraj w-tˀaδδat.* -- She did it by herself. *hiyya sawwatha b-nafisha.*
**She's not herself today. *hiyya muu ἑala baἑaḍha hal-yoom.*
to **hesitate** - *traddad (a taraddud).* He hesitated a moment before he answered. *traddad fadd laẓδa gabuḷ-ma jaawab.* -- Don't hesitate to call if you need me. *la-titraddad itxaaburni ˀiδa tiẓtaajni.*
hesitation - *taraddud.* He answered without hesitation. *jaawab ibduun taraddud.*
hiccup - *šihheega* pl. *-aat, šahga* pl. *-aat.* I have the hiccups again. *hamm jatni š-šihheega.*
hide - *jilid* pl. *jiluud.* These hides still have to be tanned. *haj-jiluud laazim baἑad tindibiġ.*
to hide - 1. *ḍamm (u ḍamm) n-, xifa (i xafi) n-, xaffa (i txiffi) t-.* He hid the money in the drawer. *ḍamm il-ifluus bil-imjarr.* 2. *xifa (i xafi) n-.* The trees hide the view. *l-ˀašjaar tixfi l-manḍar.* 3. *xital (i xatil).* Let's hide in the garage. *xalli nixtil bil-garaaj.*
hideous - 1. *bašiἑ.* That's a hideous face you have! *šloon wujih bašiἑ ἑindak!* 2. *qabiiẓ.* Where did you buy that hideous hat? *mneen ištireeti haš-šafqa l-qabiiẓa?*
hieroglyphics - *l-hiirooġliifiyya.*
high - 1. *mustawa (mnil-irtifaaἑ).* Prices have reached a new high. *l-ˀasἑaar wuṣlat ˀila mustawa jidiid imnil-irtifaaἑ.* 2. *ἑaali.* I have a high opinion of him. *raˀyi bii kulliš ἑaali.* -- The airplane is too high to see. *ṭ-ṭayyaara kulliš ἑaalya ma-tinšaaf.* 3. *ṭaab.* Now shift into high gear. *hassa ẓuṭṭha ἑala ṭaab giir.*
**That building is eight stories high. *hal-ibnaaya rtifaaἑha θman ṭabaqaat.*
highlight - *ˀahamm munaasaba* pl. *-aat.* Our party was the highlight of the season. *ẓaflatna čaanat ˀahamm munaasaba bis-sana.*
highly - 1. *kulliš.* She seemed highly pleased. *ḍiharat kulliš mamnuuna.* 2. *b-kull xeer.* He spoke very highly of him. *jaab δikra b-kull xeer.*
high school - *madrasa* (pl. *madaaris*) *θaanawiyya.*
high tide - *madd.* Let's wait till high tide. *xalli nintiḍir lamman yṣiir il-madd.*
highway - *ṭariiq* pl. *ṭuruq.* The highway between Baghdad and Najef is completely paved. *ṭ-ṭariiq been baġdaad win-najaf kulla mballaṭ.*
hike - *safra* (pl. *-aat*) *maši; mašya.* Let's go on a hike! *xalli nitlaἑ safra maši* or *xalli nsawwi mašiya.*
to hike - *miša (i maši).* We hiked five miles. *mišeena xams amyaal.*
hill - *tall* pl. *tlaal.* What's on the other side of the hill? *š-aku bij-jiha θ-θaanya mnit-tall?*
him - *-a.* I've seen him. *šifta.*
himself - *nafsa, ruuẓa.* He hurt himself badly. *ˀaδδa nafsa kulliš* or *tˀaδδa kulliš.* -- Did he do it by himself? *huwwa b-nafsa sawwaaha?*
**He's quite beside himself. *ma-yidri b-nafsa.*
**He's himself again. *rijaἑ il-ẓaalta ṭ-ṭabiiἑiyya.*
**He's not himself today. *haaδa muu ἑala baἑḍa l-yoom.*
to **hinder** - *ἑawwag (u taἑwiig) t-.* You're hindering me in my work. *ˀinta tἑawwugni b-šuġḷi.*
hinge - *nurmaada* pl. *-aat.* One of the hinges of the door is broken. *wiẓda min nurmaadaat il-baab maksuura.*
to hinge - *twaqqaf (a tawaqquf).* Everything hinges on his decisions. *kullši yitwaqqaf ἑala qaraara.*
hint - 1. *ˀišaara* pl. *-aat, talmiiẓa* pl. *-aat, tanwiiha* pl. *-aat.* Can't you give me a hint? *ma-tigdar tinṭiini fadd ˀišaara?*
**There's just a hint of mint in this drink. *ˀaku riiẓat niἑnaaἑ bil-mašruub.*
to hint - *ˀaššar (i tˀiššir) t-, lammaẓ (i tlimmiẓ, talmiiẓ) t-, nawwah (i tanwiih) t-.* He hinted that something was up. *ˀaššar bi-ˀan ˀaku fadd šii.*
hip - *wirik* pl. *ˀawraak.*
hire - *ˀujra, kari.* We have boats for hire. *ἑidna blaam lil-ˀujra.*
to hire - 1. *ˀajjar (i tˀijjir, taˀjiir) t-, kira (i kari) n-.* We hired the boat for the whole day. *ˀajjarna l-balam lil-yoom kulla.* 2. *ˀajjar (i tˀijjir, taˀjiir) t-, šaġġal (i tašġiil) t-, staxdam (i stixdaam).* We have to hire some people. *laazim inˀajjir baἑaḍ in-naas.*
his - *-a,* (m.) *maala,* (f.) *maalta.* Have you got his address? *ἑindak ἑinwaana?* -- This car is his. *haaδi s-sayyaara maalta.*
**I met a friend of his. *qaabalit waaẓid min ˀaṣdiqaaˀa.*
hiss - *faẓiiẓ, fiẓiiẓ, nafxa* pl. *-aat.* I heard the hiss of a snake. *simaἑit faẓiiẓ ẓayya.*
to hiss - *nifax (u nafux), faẓẓ (i fiẓiiẓ).* Snakes hiss. *l-ẓayyaat tinfux.*
historian - *muˀarrix* pl. *-iin.*
historic - *taariixi*.*
history - *taariix.* Have you studied European history? *dirasit taariix ˀooruppi?* -- That picture has quite a history. *haṣ-ṣuura ˀilha taariix.*
hit - *ˀiṣaaba* pl. *-aat, ḍarba* pl. *-aat.* There are two hits in the bull's-eye. *ˀaku ˀiṣaabteen ib-markaz il-hadif.*
**His song became a hit over night. *ġannuuta nšiharat ib-yoom w-leela.*
to hit - 1. *ḍirab (u ḍarub) n-.* The ball hit the door. *l-kura ḍurbat il-baab.* -- Who hit you? *minu ḍirabak?* 2. *ṣidam (i ṣadim) n-.* The news hit me hard. *l-ˀaxbaar ṣidmatni ṣadma ḍaniifa.* 3. *ṣidam (i), ḍirab (u).* The car hit him and broke his leg. *s-sayyaara ṣidmata w-kisrat rijla.* 4. *ṭaxx (u ṭaxx) n-, ḍurab (u).* I hit my knee against the door. *ṭaxxeet rukubti bil-baab.*
to hit it off - *tlaaˀam (a talaaˀum).* They hit it off pretty well after they met. *tlaaˀmaw kulliš zeen baἑad-ma ltiqaw.*
**How did you hit on the right answer? *šloon jaa j-jawaab?*
hitch - *taἑqiid.* Everything came off without a hitch. *kullši čaan ibduun taἑqiid.* -- That's where the hitch comes in! *hnaa maṣdar it-taἑqiid!*
**I'm sure there's a hitch somewhere. *ˀaani mitˀakkid aku fadd liἑba b-haš-šii.*
to hitch - *rubaṭ (u rabuṭ) n-.* Hitch your horse to the post. *ˀurbuṭ iẓṣaanak bil-ἑamuud.* 2. *šakkal (i tšikkil), čallab (i tčillib).* Did you hitch the horses to the wagon yet? *šakkalit il-xeel bil-ἑarabaana loo-baἑad?*
hive - *xaliyya* pl. *-aat.* We have six hives of honey bees. *ἑidna sitt xaliyyaat maal zanaabiir il-ἑasal.*
hives - *šira, šaraἑ.* I've got hives. *ἑindi šira.*
to **hoard** - *xizan (i xazin) n-.* They're hoarding sugar. *da-yxiznuun šakar.*

hoarse – mabʐuuʐ. He's hoarse today. ṣoota mabʐuuʐ il-yoom.

hobby – huwaaya, walaɛ. His latest hobby is collecting stamps. huwaayta l-ʔaxiira jamɛ iṭ-ṭawaabiɛ.

hog – xanʐiir pl. xanaaʐiir. He raises hogs. huwwa yrabbi xanaaʐiir.
   **Don't be such a hog! la-tkuun šariḥ!

to hold – 1. šaal (i šeel) n-. She's holding the baby in her arms. šaayla j-jaahil b-iidha. 2. lizam (a lazim) n-. That knot will hold. hal-ɛugda tilzam. -- Hold your tongue! ʔilzam ilsaanak or sidd ʐalgak! -- The room holds twenty people. l-ġurfa tilzam ɛišriin šaxiṣ. 3. kumaš (a kamiš) n-, lizam (a). Hold him! ʔukumšal 4. sawwa (i tsuwwi) t-, qaam (u qiyaam) n-. When shall we hold the election? šwakit nsawwi l-intixaab? 5. ɛind-. He holds a high position. ɛinda markaz ɛaali. 6. ɛiqad (u ɛaqid) n-, ɛigad (u ɛagid) n-. The meetings are held once a week. l-ijtimaaɛaat tinɛiqid marra bil-isbuuɛ. 7. ṭṭabbaq (a ṭṭubbuq). This rule doesn't hold in every case. hal-ʔamur ma-yiṭṭabbaq ɛala kull ḥaala. 8. jiðab (i jaðib) n-. That speaker knows how to hold his audience. hal-xaṭiib yuɛruf išloon yijðib il-mustamiɛiin.
   to hold back – minaɛ (a maniɛ) n-, lizam (a lazim) n-. I wanted to go, but he held me back. ʔaani ridit aruuz, bass huwwa minaɛni.
   to hold on – ntiðar (i ntiðaar). Can you hold on for a minute? tigdar tintiðir fadd daqiiqa?
   to hold on to – 1. čallab (i tačliib, tčillib) t-, b-, lizam (a lazim) n-, kumaš (a kamiš) n-. Hold on to me. čallib biyya. 2. zaafað (u muzaafaða) t-, ɛala, ztifað (u ztifaað) b-. Can you hold on to that job just a little longer? tigdar itzaafuð ɛala ðiič iš-šaġla l-mudda šwayya ʔaṭwal?
   to hold out – qaawam (u muqaawama). We would have held out for months if we had had enough food. loo čaan ɛidna ʔakil kaafi čaan qaawamna ʔašhur.
   to hold over – maddad (i tmiddid) t-. The movie was held over for another week. tmaddad ɛarð il-filim ʔila sbuuɛ laax.
   to hold up – 1. ɛaṭṭal (i tɛiṭṭil, taɛṭiil) t-, ʔaxxar (i tʔixxir, taʔxiir) t-. You're holding me up. ʔinta da-tɛaṭṭilni. 2. qaawam (u muqaawama) t-. Will these shoes hold up? hal-qanaadir itqaawim? 3. silab (i salib) n-. Two men held me up yesterday. salbooni θneen il-baarza.
   to get hold of – 1. liga (i lagi) n-. Where can I get hold of him? ween ʔagdar algii? 2. lizam (a lazim). Stop crying. Get hold of yourself. baṭṭil il-bači. ʔilzam nafsak.

holdup – tasliib pl. -aat. He had nothing to do with the holdup. ma-ʔila daxal bit-tasliib.
   **What's the holdup? šinu-lli mɛaṭṭilna?

hole – 1. zuruf pl. zruuf. There is a hole in his pants. ʔaku zuruf ib-panṭuruuna. 2. zufra pl. zufar. Who dug that hole? minu zifar ðiič il-zufra?
   **He lives in a dingy hole. yiskun ib-makaan raziil.
   **I'm five dinars in the hole. ɛindi xams idnaaniir ɛajiz.

holiday – ɛuṭla pl. ɛuṭal.

Holland – hoolanda.

hollow – 1. mjawwaf. These walls seem to be hollow. hal-izyaaṭiin itbayyin imjawwfa. 2. mamṣuuṣ. Her cheeks are hollow. xduudha mamṣuuṣa.

holy – muqaddas.

home – 1. beet pl. byuut. My home is in Baghdad. beetna b-baġdaad. -- We're building a new home. da-nibni beet ijdiid. -- Make yourself at home. l-beet beetak or ɛtubur haaða.beetak. 2. balad pl. buldaan; bilaad; waṭan. Where's your home? (country) ween baladak? 3. daaxil. At home and abroad ... bid-daaxil wil-xaarij ...

homeless – bduun maʔwa. Thousands of people were made homeless by the flood. ʔaalaaf in-naas ṣaaraw ibduun maʔwa mnil-fayaðaan.

homemade – šuġuḷ beet. This is homemade jelly. haaði mrabba šuġuḷ beet.

to be homesick – zann (i zaniin). I'm homesick for my country. ʔaani da-ʔazinn il-waṭani.

home town – balda, madiina, wlaaya. He's from my home town. huwwa min baldti.

homework – waajib beeti pl. waajibaat beetiyya; waðiifa (pl. waðaayif) beetiyya. Have you done all your homework? sawweet kull waajibaatak il-beetiyya?

honest – mustaqiim, ʔamiin. Do you think he's honest? tiftikir huwwa mustaqiim? -- He has an honest face.

ybayyin ɛala wujha ʔamiin.
   **An honest man is as good as his word. r-rajul iš-šariif gool w-fiɛil.

honestly – 1. ṣidug, b-šarafi, fil-zaqiiqa, zaqiiqatan. I was honestly surprised. ṣidug ʔaani činit mitɛajjib. 2. b-ṣaraaza. Honestly, I don't know what to do with you. b-ṣaraaza ma-adri š-raz-asawwi wiyyaak.

honesty – stiqaama, ʔamaana. There's no question about his honesty. ma-aku šakk b-istiqaamta. -- Honesty is the best policy. l-ʔamaana ʔazsan ṭariiq.

to honk – ṭawwaṭ (u ṭṭuwwuṭ), dagg (u dagg) n-. Honk three times, and I'll come down. ṭawwuṭ itlaθ marraat w-ʔaani ʔanzil.

honor – šaraf. It's an honor to be elected. mniš-šaraf waazid yuntaxab. -- On my honor! b-šarafi! -- We gave a banquet in his honor. sawweena daɛwa ɛala šarafa or sawweena daɛwa takriiman ʔila.
   to honor – 1. šarraf (i tširruf) t-, karram (u takriim) t-. I feel very much honored. ʔaani ašɛur kulliš mukarram. 2. qibal (a qabuul) n-. We can't honor this check. ma-nigdar niqbal hač-čakk.

hood – 1. ġiṭa, ġuṭa (pl. ġuṭaayaat, ġuṭaawaat) raas. This raincoat has a hood attached to it. hal-imšammaɛ imšakkal bii ġiṭa raas. 2. ṭanid. Lift up the hood and check the car's oil. šiil il-ṭanid w-ʔuftaṣ dihin il-sayyaara.

hoof – zaafir pl. zawaafir. There's a nail in our horse's hoof. ʔaku bismaar ib-zaafir izṣaanna.
   **We had to hoof it. ṭṭarreena nduggha maši.
   cloven hoof – ðilif pl. ʔaðlaaf.

hook – 1. tiɛlaaga pl. -aat. Hang your coat on the hook. ɛallig sitirtak bit-tiɛlaaga. 2. čillaab pl. člaaliib, čingaal pl. čanaagiil. We need a new hook for the crane. nriid čillaab jidiid lis-silink. 3. šuṣṣ pl. šṣuuṣ. What kind of hook are you using to fish? yaa nooɛ šuṣṣ da-tistaɛmil ib-ṣeed is-simač?
   **He intends to get rich, by hook or by crook. yriid ysiir zangiin b-ʔay wasiila.
   to hook – 1. ṣaad (i ṣeed) n-. How many fish did you hook? čam simča ṣidit? 2. čangaḷ (i tčingiḷ), šakkal (i tšikkil), čallab (i tčillib). Help me hook this chain. saaɛidni ʔačangiḷ haṣ-sanjiil. 3. ligaf (u laguf) n-. She finally hooked him. ʔaxiiran hiyya lugfata.
   to hook up – šakkal (i tšikkil) t-. I haven't hooked up the new radio yet. li-hassa baɛad ma-šakkalt ir-raadyo.

hop – ṭafra pl. -aat, gamza pl. -aat. It's just a short hop by plane. biṭ-ṭayyaara kullha ṭafra.
   to hop – gumaz (u gumuz), ṭufar (u ṭafur). She hopped with joy. gumzat imnil-faraz.
   to hop around – gammaz (u tgummuz), ṭaffar (u ṭṭuffur). He was hopping around on one leg. čaan da-ygammiz ɛala fadd rijil.

hope – ʔamal pl. ʔaamaal. Don't give up hope. la-tigṭaɛ il-ʔamal.
   to hope – tmanna (a tamanni), tʔammal (a taʔammul). She had hoped to see you. čaanat titmanna tšuufak.
   **I hope you didn't catch cold. nšaaḷḷa ma-axaðit barid.

hopeful – ɛind- ʔamal, mitʔammil. I am hopeful. ɛindi ʔamal.

hopeless – mayʔuus min-. The situation is completely hopeless. l-zaala kulliš mayʔuus minha.

horizon – ʔufuq pl. ʔaafaaq.

horizontal – ʔufuqi*.

horn – 1. girin pl. gruun. That cow's horn is broken. girin ðiič il-haayša maksuur. 2. hoorin pl. -aat. Blow your horn next time! dugg il-hoorin maalak il-marra j-jaaya! 3. buug pl. ʔabwaag. Can you play this horn? tigdar itdugg hal-buug?

hornet – zambuur pl. zanaabiir.

horrible – faðiiɛ. It was a horrible sight. čaan manðar faðiiɛ.

horrid – muzɛij, kariih.

horrors – faðaaɛa pl. -aat. The horrors of war are indescribable. faðaaɛaat il-zarb ma-tinwuṣuf.

horse – (m.) zṣaan pl. zuṣan, coll. xeel, (f.) faras pl. fruusa, coll. xeel.
   **A team of wild horses couldn't drag me there. ma-ʔaruuz ihnaak loo tjurrni b-ɛarabaana.
   **You shouldn't look a gift horse in the mouth. l-hadiyya muu b-θamanha.

horse race – sibaaq il-xeel, reesiz.

hose – 1. buuri (pl. bwaari) laastiig, ṣoonda pl.

-*aat*. The hose is still in the garden. *buuri l-laastiig baƐda bil-ʒadiiqa.* **2.** *jwaariib.* We just got a new shipment of women's hose. *hastawwna stilamna šaʒnat ijwaariib nisaaʔiyya jidiida.*
hospital - *mustašfa* pl. -*ayaat, quṣṭaxaana* pl. -*aat, xastaxaana* pl. -*aat, xastaxaayin.*
hospitality - *karam, ʒusun ðiyaafa.*
host - *muðayyif* pl. -*iin, ṣaaʒib* (pl. *ʔaṣʒaab*) *id-daƐwa.* He's a wonderful host. *huwwa kulliš xooš muðayyif.*
hostess - *muðayyifa* pl. -*aat.* She's a charming hostess. *hiyya muðayyifa kulliš laṭiifa.* -- She works as a hostess with Iraqi Airlines. *tištuġul muðayyifa bil-xuṭuuṭ ij-jawwiyya l-Ɛiraaqiyya.*
hot - **1.** *ʒaarr.* Do you have hot water? *Ɛindak ṃaay ʒaarr?* -- This mustard sure is hot. *hal-xardal ṣudug ʒaarr.* **2.** *ʒaadd.* He has a hot temper. *Ɛinda ṭabuƐ ʒaadd.* **3.** *qawi**. The scent is still hot. *riiʒat iṣ-ṣeed la-tazaal qawiyya.*
  **I made it hot for him. *nṭeeta daris ma-yinsaa.*
  **I haven't had a hot meal in three days. *ṣaar-li tlaθt iyyaam ma-maakil ṭabux.*
  **We were hot on his trail. *činna da-ntibƐa blayya kalal.*
hotel - *ʔuteel* pl. -*aat, findiq* pl. *fanaadiq.*
hour - **1.** *saaƐa* pl. -*aat.* I'll be back in an hour. *raʒ-arjaƐ baƐad saaƐa.* -- I'm taking nine hours a week in night school. *ʔaani maaxið tisiƐ saaƐaat bil-isbuuƐ bil-madrasa l-masaaʔiyya.* **2.** *dawaam.* See me after hours. *šuufni wara d-dawaam.* -- My hours are from nine to five. *dawaami mnis-saaƐa tisƐa lis-saaƐa xamsa.*
  at all hours - *b-ʔay wakit, kull wakit.* I can be reached at all hours. *bil-imkaan l-ittiṣaal biyya b-ʔay wakit.*
hour hand - *miil* pl. *myaal, Ɛaqrab* pl. *Ɛaqaarib.*
house - **1.** *beet* pl. *byuut, daar* pl. *duur.* I want to rent a house. *ʔariid aʔajjir beet.* **2.** *majlis* pl. *majaalis.* Both houses will meet in joint session tomorrow. *l-majliseen raʒ-yijtamƐuun ib-jalsa muštaraka baačir.*
  **The house was sold out. *kull it-tikitaat inbaaƐat.*
  to house - *nazzal (i tnizzil) t-, sakkan (i tsikkin, taskiin) t-.* Where are we going to house the visitors? *ween raʒ-innazzil iz-zuwwaar?*
household - *ʔahl il-beet.* We have something for the whole household. *Ɛidna ʔašyaaʔ il-kull ʔahl il-beet.*
housemaid - *xaadma* pl. -*aat, ṣaanƐa* pl. -*aat.*
housework - *šuġl il-beet.*
how - *šloon, keef.* How shall I do it? *šloon asawwiiha?* -- He'll show you how. *raʒ-yraawiik šloon.* -- How do you do? *šloonak?* or *šloon ʔaʒwaalak?*
  **My name's Ahmad - How do you do? *ʔismi ʔaʒmad - tšarrafna.*
  **That's a fine how-do-you-do! *yaa fattaaʒ, yaa razzaaq!*
  how come - *šloon, šinu s-sabab, luweeš.* How come you're still here? *šloon ʔinta baƐdak ihnaa?*
  how many - *čam, šgadd.* How many oranges shall I take? *čam purtaqaala ʔaaxuð?* or *šgadd purtaqaal ʔaaxuð?*
  how much - **1.** *šgadd.* How much did he pay? *šgadd difaƐ?* **2.** *beeš, šgadd.* How much is this? *haay beeš?*
however - *laakin maƐa ðaalik, bass.* I'd like to do it, however I have no time. *yiƐjibni ʔasawwiiha, laakin maƐa ðaalik ma-Ɛindi wakit.*
howl - *Ɛawi.* I thought I heard the howl of a wolf. *ftikarit simaƐit Ɛawi ðiib.*
  to howl - **1.** *Ɛawwa (i tƐuwwi).* The dog has been howling all night. *č-čalib ṣaar-la da-yƐawwi ṭuul il-leel.* **2.** *ṭagg (u ṭagg).* The audience howled with laughter. *l-mitfarrjin ṭaggaw imniš-ðiʒik.*
to **huddle** - *ltamm (a ltimaam), tzaaʒam (a tazaaʒum).* They huddled in a corner. *ltammaw ib-fadd izwiyya.* -- The sheep huddled close together. *l-ġanam iltammaw waaʒid yamm il-lax.*
hug - *ʒaðna* pl. -*aat.* She gave him a big hug. *ʒiðnata fadd ʒaðna zeena.*
  to hug - **1.** *ʒiðan (i ʒaðin).* She hugged her mother tightly. *ʒiðnat ʔummha b-quwwa.* **2.** *laazam (i mulaazama).* Our boat hugged the coastline all the way. *markabna laazam is-saaʒil ṭuul iṭ-ṭariiq.*
huge - *ðaxim* pl. -*iin* or *ðxaam.* The elephant is a huge animal. *l-fiil ʒayawaan ðaxim.*
hum - *ṭaniin.* What's that strange hum? *šinu haṭ-ṭaniin il-ġariib?*
  to hum - **1.** *hamham (i thimhim).* What's that tune you're humming? *yaa laʒin da-thamhim?* **2.** *wann (i waniin), wanwan (i twinwin).* This top won't hum. *hal-muṣraƐ ma-da-ywinn.* **3.** *ṭann (i ṭaniin), ṭanṭan (i tṭinṭin).* My ears are humming. *ʔiðni da-ṭṭinn.*
  **Things are always humming at this corner. *haz-zuwiyya daaʔiman biiha ʒaraka.*
human - **1.** *bašari**. Is this a human eye? *haay Ɛeen basariyya?* **2.** *bašar, bani ʔaadam.* I'm only human. *ʔaani bass bašar.*
humble - *mitwaaðiƐ.* Abraham Lincoln grew up in humble circumstances. *braahaam linkoolin nišaʔ ib-ðuruuf mitwaaðƐa.* -- In the beginning he acted very humble. *ʔawwal marra čaan mutawaaðiƐ ib-taṣarrufa.*
humidity - *ruṭuuba.*
to **humiliate** - *ðall (i ðall) n-, ʒaqqar (i taʒqiir) t-.* Poverty humiliated me in front of a lot of people. *l-fugur ðallni giddaam naas ihwaaya.*
humor - **1.** *mazaaj, keef.* Are you in a good humor today? *mazaajak zeen hal-yoom?* **2.** *tankiit, fakaah.* The humor in this magazine is very biting. *t-tankiit ib-hal-majalla kulliš laaðiƐ.*
humorous - **1.** *muðʒik.* He told a very humorous joke. *ʒica nukta kulliš muðʒika.* **2.** *fakih, hazali**. He's a very humorous man. *haaða fadd rijjaal kulliš fakih.*
hunch - *šuƐuur daaxili.* I have a hunch that something is wrong there. *Ɛindi fadd šuƐuur daaxili ʔaku šii muu tamaam ihnaak.*
hunchback - **1.** *ʒidba* pl. *ʒidab.* One has a hunchback. *waaʒid Ɛinda ʒidba.* **2.** (m.) *ʔaʒdab* pl. *ʒadbiin,* (f.) *ʒadba* pl. -*aat.* She's a hunchback. *hiyya ʒadba.*
hunched up - *mʒoodib, mʒaddib.* Your back hurts because you're sitting all hunched up. *ðahrak da-yoojƐak li-ʔan ʔinta mʒoodib ib-gaƐidtak.*
hundred - **1.** *miyya.* About a hundred people were present. *ʒawaali miit waaʒid čaanaw ʒaaðriin.* **2.** *miyya* pl. -*aat.* Hundreds of people were present. *miyyaat in-naas čaanaw ʒaaðriin.*
Hungarian - **1.** *majari**. He owns a Hungarian ship. *yimluk baaxira majariyya.* **2.** *majari* pl. -*iyyiin.* The Hungarians left at twelve. *l-majariyyiin raaʒaw is-saaƐa θnaƐaš.* **3.** *majari.* He speaks Hungarian very well. *yiʒči majari kulliš zeen.*
Hungary - *l-majar.*
hunger - *juuƐ.* I nearly died of hunger. *mitit imnij-juuƐ ʔilla šwayya.*
hungry - *juuƐaan* pl. -*iin, jwaaƐa.* He has to feed ten hungry stomachs. *laazim yṭaƐƐim Ɛašir ibṭuun juuƐaana.* -- We didn't go hungry. *ma-ðalleena jwaaƐa.*
to **hunt** - *ṣaad (i ṣeed) n-, tṣayyad (a taṣayyud).* They're hunting rabbits. *da-yṣiiduun ʔaraanib.* -- We're going hunting tomorrow. *baačir raʒ-nitṣayyad.*
  to hunt for - *dawwar (u tduwwur) t- Ɛala.* We were hunting for an apartment. *činna da-ndawwur Ɛala šiqqa.* -- Help me hunt for my shoes. *saaƐidni ʔadawwur Ɛala qundarti.*
  to hunt up - *ligaf (u laguf) n-, liga (i lagi) n-.* How many did you hunt up? *čam waaʒid ligafit?*
hunter - *ṣayyaad* pl. -*iin.*
hunting license - *ʔijaazat* (pl. -*aat*) *ṣeed.*
hurry - *Ɛajala.* There's no hurry. *ma-aku Ɛajala.*
  in a hurry - *mistaƐjil.* I'm in a big hurry. *ʔaani kulliš mistaƐjil.*
  to hurry - **1.** *staƐjal (i stiƐjaal).* Don't hurry! *la-tistaƐjil!* -- Hurry up! *ʔisriƐ!* or *staƐjil!* **2.** *Ɛajjal (i taƐjiil).* Don't hurry me! *la-tƐajjilni!* or *la-txalliini ʔastaƐjil!*
to **hurt** - **1.** *wujaƐ (a wujaƐ), ʔallam (i ʔalam), ʔaðða (i tʔiðði).* My arm hurts. *ʔiidi toojaƐni.* **2.** *Ɛawwar (i tƐuwwur) t-, jiraʒ (a jariʒ) n-.* Where are you hurt? *ween mitƐawwar?* -- I didn't mean to hurt your feelings. *ma-ridit ajraʒ šuƐuurak.* **3.** *ʔallam (i ʔalam) t-, ʔaðða (i ʔaða) t-.* She's easily hurt. *hiyya titʔallam min ʔaqall šii.* **4.** *ʔaðða (i tʔiðði) t-, ðarr (u ðarr) n-.* This will hurt business. *haay raʒ-itʔaðði s-suug.*
  **Will it hurt if I'm late? *raʒ-yṣiir ðarar ʔiða ʔaani ʔatʔaxxar?*
husband - *zooj* pl. *ʔazwaaj, rajil* pl. *rjuula.*
to **hush up** - **1.** *ṭamṭam (u tṭumṭum) t-.* The scandal was quickly hushed up. *l-faðiiʒa bil-Ɛajal iṭṭamṭumat.* **2.** *sakkat (i tsikkit) t-.* Try to hush up the child. *ʒaawli tsakkiti j-jaahil.*
husky - **1.** *jaθiiθ* pl. -*iin, jθaaθ.* He's quite husky. *huwwa kulliš jaθiiθ.* **2.** *xašin.* His voice is husky. *ṣooṭa xašin.*
hut - *kuux* pl. *kwaax, čardaaġ* pl. *čaraadiiġ.*
hyena - *ðabuƐ* pl. *ðbaaƐ.*

I

I - *ʔaani.* I'm cold. *ʔaani bardaan.* -- If I ask him, he'll do it. *ʔiδa ʔaani agul-la, ysawwiiha.*
ice - *θalij.* Put some ice in the glasses. *xalli θalij bil-iglaaṣaat.*
ice box - *ṣanduug* (pl. *sanaadiig*) *θalij, θallaaja* pl. *-aat.*
ice cream - *doondirma.* A dish of ice cream, please. *baḷḷa, fadd maaɛuun doondirma.*
iced - *mθallaj.* Do you serve iced tea here? *ɛidkum čaay imθallaj ihnaa?*
icy - *baarid miθl iθ-θalij, kulliš baarid.* The water is icy cold. *l-ṃaay baarid miθl iθ-θalij.*
idea - *fikra* pl. That's a good idea! *haay xooš fikra.* -- I haven't the faintest idea what he wants. *ma-ɛindi ʔay fikra ɛan iš-šii lli-yriid.*
**What gives you that idea? *š-da-yxalliik itfakkir haš-šikil?*
**Who gave you the bright idea? *haaδa minu lli-nṭaak hal-ɛaqil?*
**I couldn't get used to the idea. *ma-gdarit atɛawwad nafsi ɛal-haš-šii.*
**Of all the ideas! *min duun kull il-ʔašyaaʔ!*
**She has big ideas. *hiyya ṭamuuza.*
**That's the idea! *hassa tamaam!*
**The idea! *hiiči!*
ideal - **1.** *l-maθal il-ʔaɛla.* Our ideal is freedom and independence for all people. *maθalna l-ʔaɛla l-zurriyya wil-istiqlaal il-kull iš-šuɛuub.* **2.** *qudwa* pl. *-aat.* He's my ideal. *huwwa quduuti.* **3.** *miθaali*.* This is an ideal place for swimming. *haaδa makaan miθaali lis-sibiz.*
idealism - *miθaaliyya.*
idealist - *miθaali* pl. *-iyyiin.*
idealistic - *miθaali*.*
identical - *fadd šikil, mitšaabih.* The two copies are identical. *han-nusuxteen fadd šikil tamaaman.* -- The two girls are wearing identical dresses. *l-binteen laabsaat infaaniif fadd šikil tamaaman.*
identification card - *hawiyya* pl. *-aat.*
to **identify** - **1.** *ɛiraf (u ɛaruf) n-.* The police identified him by his fingerprints. *š-šurṭa ɛurfoo min ṭabɛat aṣaabɛa.* **2.** *ɛarraf (u).* Everyone must stand up and identify himself. *kull waazid laazim yoogaf w-yɛarruf nafsa.*
**I don't want to identify myself with them. *ma-ariid yinqirin ʔismi wiyyaahum.*
identity - *hawiyya.* The police don't know the identity of the dead man. *š-šurṭa ma-yɛurfuun hawiyyat il-mayyit.*
**The police still do not know the identity of the thief. *š-šurṭa li-hassa baɛad ma-yɛurfuun minu l-zaraami.*
ideology - *maδhab* pl. *maδaahib.* He won't support their political ideology. *ma-yʔayyid maδhabhum is-siyaasi.*
idiot - *hibil, ʔablah* pl. *buluh.*
idle - **1.** *ɛaaṭil.* He is an idle fellow. *huwwa fadd waazid ɛaaṭil.* **2.** *faariġ.* That's just idle talk. *haaδa zači faariġ.* **3.** *baṭṭaal, ɛaaṭil.* He's been idle for some time. *ṣaar-la mudda baṭṭaal.*
**The factory's been idle for years. *l-maɛmal ma-da-yištuġuḷ ṣaar-la sniin.*
**This machine is idle, we can use it. *hal-makiina mazzad da-yšaġġilha, nigdar nistaɛmilha.*
**Her tongue is never idle. *lsaanha la-yčill wala yitɛab.*
**Let the motor idle. *xalli l-makiina tištuġul* or ***la-ṭṭaffi l-makiina.*
idol - *ṣanam* pl. *ʔaṣnaam.* Worshipping idols is forbidden. *ɛibaadat il-ʔaṣnaam zaraam.*
if - *ʔiδa, loo.* If anyone asks for me, say I'll be right back. *ʔiδa ʔazzad siʔal ɛalayya, gul-la hassa yirjaɛ.* -- I don't know if he'll come or not. *ma-adri ʔiδa raz-yiji loo laa.* -- I'll go even if it rains. *ʔaruuz zatta loo tumṭur.* -- He talks as if he had been there. *yizči ɛabaalak loo huwwa čaan ihnaak.*
ignorance - **1.** *ġabaawa, ġabaaʔ, jahal.* I've never seen such ignorance. *baɛad ib-ɛumri ma-šaayif hiiči ġabaawa.* **2.** *jahal.* Ignorance of the law is no excuse. *j-jahal bil-qaanuun muu ɛuδur.*
ignorant - *ġabi* pl. *ʔaġbiyaaʔ, jaahil* pl. *juhalaaʔ.* She's such an ignorant person. *hiyya fadd mara ġabiyya.*
to **ignore** - *tjaahal (a tajaahul).* I would ignore his remark if I were you. *loo b-makaanak atjaahal izčaayta.* -- I ignored him. *tjaahalta* or ***ma-dirit-la baal.*
ill - *mariiḍ.* He was very ill. *čaan kulliš mariiḍ.*
**He can ill afford to quit his job now. *ma-yzammal waḍɛa ybaṭṭil min šuġḷa hassa.*
**He's ill at ease in such company. *huwwa ma-yirtaaz wiyya hiiči jamaaɛa.*
illegal - *ġeer qaanuuni*, muu qaanuuni*.* This illegal action will be opposed by all responsible governments. *haaδa l-ɛamal ġeer il-qaanuuni tɛaarḍa kull il-zukuumaat il-masʔuula.*
illegitimate - *ġeer šarɛi*.* He's an illegitimate child. *huwwa walad ġeer šarɛi.*
illiteracy - *ʔuṃṃiyya.* The illiteracy rate is high here. *mustawa l-ʔuṃṃiyya ɛaali hnaa.*
illiterate - *ʔuṃṃi* pl. *-iyyiin.* The people of this village are all illiterate. *ʔahil hal-qarya kullhum ʔuṃṃiyyiin.*
illness - *maraḍ* pl. *ʔamraaḍ.*
to **illustrate** - **1.** *waḍḍaz (i tawḍiiz) b-ṣuwar.* The book is illustrated. *l-iktaab imwaḍḍaz ib-ṣuwar.* **2.** *širaz (a šariz) n-, waḍḍaz (i).* I can illustrate this best by an example. *ʔagdar ʔašraz haaδa ʔazsan ib-fadd miθaal.*
illustration - **1.** *ṣuura* pl. *ṣuwar.* The catalogue has many illustrations. *l-katalook bii ṣuwar ihwaaya.* **2.** *šikil* pl. *ʔaškaal.* Look at illustration no. 10, on page 115. *šuuf iš-šikil raqam ɛašra, ṣafza miyya w-ixmuṣṭaɛaš.*
ill will - *karah.* His insults caused a lot of ill will. *ʔihaanaata sabbabat karah in-naas ʔila.*
image - **1.** *ṣuura* pl. *-aat.* The image I have of him is that of an old man. *ṣuurta l-maṭbuuɛa b-fikri maal waazid šaayib.* -- She's the image of her mother. *hiyya ṣuura min ʔummha.* **2.** *šikil* pl. *ʔaškaal, škuul.* She examined her image in the mirror. *baawɛat šikilha bil-imraaya.*
imaginable - *mumkin taṣawwur-.* He tried everything imaginable. *zaawal kullši mumkin taṣawwura.* -- That's hardly imaginable! *haaδa šii ma-mumkin taṣawwura!* or ***haaδa šii ma-yxušš bil-ɛaqil!*
imaginary - *xayaali*.* Juha is an imaginary character. *juzza fadd saxṣiyya xayaaliyya.*
**Children sometimes live in an imaginary world. *j-jahhaal dooraat yɛiišuun ib-dunya l-xayaal.*
imagination - *xayaal.* That's pure imagination! *haaδa xayaal ṣirf.* -- She has a fertile imagination. *ɛidha xayaal xaṣib.*
to **imagine** - **1.** *tṣawwar (a taṣawwur).* I can't imagine what you mean. *ma-ʔaqdar aṭṣawwar iš-da-tuqṣud.* -- I imagine so. *ʔaṭṣawwar haš-šikil* or ***ʔaḍinn!* **2.** *txayyal (a taxayyul).* You're only imagining things. *ʔinta bass da-titxayyal ʔašyaaʔ ma-mawjuuda.*
to **imitate** - *qallad (i taqliid) t-.* He can imitate my voice. *yigdar yqallid ṣooti.*
imitation - **1.** *taqliid.* The Japanese put out a poor imitation of this lighter. *l-yaabaaniyyiin ṭalɛaw fadd taqliid muu zeen il-hal-qiddaaza.* **2.** *ṣṭinaaɛi*, čaδδaabi*.* This pocketbook is made of imitation leather. *haj-janṭa maɛmuula min jilid iṣṭinaaɛi.* -- This necklace is made of imitation pearls. *hal-igḷaada msawwaaya min liilu čaδδaabi.*
immature - *muu naaḍij.* His actions are immature for his age. *taṣarrufaata muu naaḍja bin-nisba l-ɛumra.*
immediate - *mubaašir.* Ahmad is my immediate superior. *ʔazmad raʔiisi l-mubaašir.*
**There's no school in the immediate neighborhood. *ma-aku madrasa yammna mubaašaratan.*
**This amount will take care of your immediate needs. *hal-mablaġ ykaffi lit-tiztaajak hassa.*
immediately - *mubaašaratan, zaalan.* Immediately afterwards I heard a scream. *mubaašaratan waraaha smaɛit fadd ɛeeṭa.* -- I'll go there immediately. *raz-aruuz ihnaak zaalan.*
immense - *ḍaxum, haaʔil.* They have an immense

living room. *Eidhum ṣaaloon ḍaxum.* -- They stored immense quantities of meat. *xiznaw kammiyyaat haa?ila mnil-lazam.*

immigrant - *muhaajir* pl. *-iin.* About one thousand immigrants enter the country every year. *zawaali ?alif muhaajir yduxluun il-balad kull sana.*

immigration - *hujra.* The Immigration Office is in that building. *daa?irt il-hujra b-hal-binaaya.*

immoral - 1. *duuni*, naamarbuuṭi*.* That is an immoral act. *haaða Eamal duuni.* 2. *munzaṭṭ, duuni*.* This man is immoral. *har-rijjaal munzaṭṭ* or ***har-rijjaal ma-Einda qiyam ?axlaaqiyya.*

immortal - *xaalid.* Mutanabbi is an immortal Arabic poet. *l-mutanabbi fadd šaaEir Earabi xaalid.*

immunity - 1. *manaaEa.* Do you have immunity to smallpox? *Eindak manaaEa ḍidd ij-jidri?* 2. *zaṣaana.* All ambassadors have diplomatic immunity. *kull is-sufaraa? Eidhum zaṣaana dibloomaasiyya.*

impartial - *munṣif, Eaadil, zaqqaani*.* I'll try to be impartial. *raz-azaawil akuun munṣif.*

impatient - *ma-Eind- ṣabur.* He is very impatient. *haaða kulliš ma-Einda ṣabur.* -- Don't be so impatient! *la-tkuun hal-gadd ma-Eindak ṣabur!*

imperative - 1. *fiEl ?amur.* "*?iktib*" is the imperative of "*kitab*"? *?iktib hiyya fiEl il-?amur maal kitab.* 2. *?ijbaari*.* It is imperative for all students to attend the meeting. *l-zuḍuur bil-ijtimaaE ?ijbaari Eala kull it-talaamiið.*

imperialism - *stiEmaar.* Imperialism is on the decline. *l-istiEmaar ib-ṭariiqa liz-zawaal.*

impersonal - *ġeer šaxṣi*.* I always keep my relations with the staff impersonal. *daa?iman axalli Ealaaqaati wiyya l-muwaððafiin ġeer šaxṣiyya.*

to **imply** - *ḍḍamman (a).* His statement implied he was in favor of the plan. *kalaama ḍḍamman imwaafaqta Eal-xiṭṭa.*

impolite - 1. *muu mhaððab.* She is very impolite. *hiyya kulliš muu mhaððaba.* -- Why are you so impolite? *leeš hiiči ?inta muu mhaððab?* 2. *xašin.* That was very impolite of him. *haay čaanat kulliš xašna minna.*

import - *stiiraad.* The government encourages the import of raw materials. *l-zukuuma tšajjiE istiiraad il-mawaadd il-xaam.*

to import - *stawrad (i stiiraad).* Iraq imports a lot of Australian cheese. *l-Eiraaq yistawrid ihwaaya jibin ?ustiraali.*

importance - *?ahammiyya.* You attach too much importance to the problem. *?inta hwaaya txalli ?ahammiyya lil-mas?ala.* -- That's of no importance. *haaða ma-?ila ?ahammiyya.*

important - *muhimm.* I want to see you about an important matter. *?ariid ašuufak ib-qaḍiyya muhimma.* -- He was the most important man in town. *huwwa čaan ahamm rajul bil-madiina.*

imports - *waaridaat, mustawradaat.* Our imports still exceed our exports. *waaridaatna baEadha tziid Eala ṣaadiraatna.*

to **impose on** - 1. *staġall (i stiġlaal).* He's imposing on your good nature. *huwwa yistiġill ṭiibat axlaaqak.* 2. *furaḍ (u faruḍ).* Don't let them impose their will on you. *la-txalliihum yfurḍuun Ealeek miθil-ma yirduun.*

imposing - *raa?i.* That's certainly an imposing building. *haaði zaqiiqa binaaya raa?ya.*

imposition - *zazma* pl. *-aat, takliif* pl. *-aat.* If it's not an imposition, could you give me a ride? *?iða ma-aku zazma Ealeek mumkin itwaṣṣilni?*

impossible - *mustaziil.* Why is it impossible? *luweeš haaða mustaziil?*

**That man is absolutely impossible! *haš-šaxiṣ ?abadan ma-yinzimil!*

to **impress** - *?aθθar (i ta?θiir) t-.* That doesn't impress me. *haaði ma-t?aθθirni.*

impression - 1. *ta?θiir* pl. *-aat.* He made a good impression on me. *čaan ta?θiira Ealayya zeen.* 2. *naḍra, ntibaaE.* I got a bad impression of him. *?axaðit Eanna naḍra muu zeena.* -- He tries to give the impression that he's a good fellow. *yzaawil yinṭi l-inṭibaaE ?inna xooš rijaal.*

under the impression - *Eabaal-.* I was under the impression that he wanted to go. *Eabaali raad yruuz.*

impressionism - *nṭibaaEiyya.*

to **imprison** - *zibas (i zabis) n-, sijan (i sajin) n-.* The men were imprisoned for two months. *r-riyaajiil čaanaw mazbuusiin li-muddat šahreen.*

to **improve** - 1. *zassan (i tazsiin) t-.* I don't know how we can improve our product. *ma-?adri šloon mumkin inzassin intaajna.* 2. *tzassan (a tazassun).* His condition has improved. *ṣizzta tzassnat.* -- Ahmad is improving in school. *?azmad da-yitzassan bil-madrasa.*

improvement - 1. *tazassun* pl. *-aat.* I don't see any improvement in her condition. *ma-da-ašuuf ?ay tazassun ib-zaalatha.* 2. *tazsiin* pl. *-aat.* We're making some improvements in the house. *da-nsawwi baEḍ it-tazsiinaat bil-beet.*

**That's no improvement over our former method. *ma-jaab ay šii jdiid Ean ṭariiqatna s-saabiqa.*

impudence - *ṣalaafa, waqaaza.* Such impudence! *hiiči ṣalaafa!* or *?amma waqaaza!*

impulse - 1. *ndifaaE.* You've got to control your impulses. *laazim tiḍbuṭ indifaaEak.* 2. *daafiE* pl. *dawaafiE, baaEiθ* pl. *bawaaEiθ.* I had an impulse to give the beggar a dinar. *zasseet ib-fadd daafiE anṭi diinaar lil-faqiir.*

impulsive - *mindafiE.* She is a very impulsive person. *hiyya kulliš mindafEa.*

in - 1. *b-.* There's no heater in my room. *ma-aku sooba b-ġurufti.* -- He's in Najaf now. *hassa huwwa bin-najaf.* -- He's the smartest student in the entire class. *huwwa ?aðka ṭaalib biṣ-ṣaff kulla.* -- Say it in English. *guulha bil-ingiliizi.* -- That in itself isn't important. *hiyya b-zadd ðaata muu muhimma.* -- If I were in your place, I would've gone. *loo činit ib-mazallak, čaan rizit.* -- Did it happen in the daytime or at night? *zidθat bin-nahaar loo bil-leel?* -- I can finish it in a week. *?agdar axalliṣha b-isbuuE.* -- Write in ink. *?iktib bil-zibir.* 2. *baEad.* I'll be back in three days. *raz-arjaE baEad itlaθt iyyaam.* -- I'll pay you in two weeks. *raz-adfaE-lak baEad ?usbuuEeen.* 3. *mawjuud.* He's not in. *huwwa muu mawjuud.* 4. *waaṣṭa* pl. *-aat.* He has an in at the Ministry of the Interior. *Einda waaṣṭa b-wizaart id-daaxiliyya.*

**He was the only one at the party in tails. *huwwa čaan il-waziid bil-zafla laabis ifraak.*

**Sift the flour before you put the water in. *?unxul it-taziin gabul-ma txalli-la mayy.*

**Padded shoulders aren't in any more. *s-sitar ib-čattaafiyyaat muu moodat hal-wakit* or *s-sitar ib-čattaafiyyaat iṣmazallat.*

**Are you in on it with them, too? *?inta hamm mištirik wiyyaahum?*

**He has it in for you. *huwwa ðaamil-lak-iyyaaha.*

**He knows all the ins and outs. *yuEruf il-?aku wil-maaku* or *yuEruf xitlaatha.*

**He's in good with the boss. *Eilaaqta zeena bil-mudiir.*

**Now we're in for it! *?akalnaaha!*

all in - *taEbaan kulliš, hwaaya taEbaan, mayyit imnit-taEab.* I'm all in. *?aani taEbaan kulliš.*

inauguration: The inauguration of the President will be next January. *l-iztifaal ib-tanṣiib ir-ra?iis raz-ykuun ib-kaanuun iθ-θaani j-jaay.*

incense - *bxuur.*

incentive - *zaafiz* pl. *zawaafiz.* It's hard to work without an incentive. *ṣaEub tištuġul biduun wujuud zaafiz.*

inch - *?inj* pl. *-aat.* Bring me a three-inch nail. *jiib-li bismaar ṭuula tlaθ ?injaat.*

**He came within an inch of being run over. *huwwa taqriiban raad inqital.*

**He's every inch a soldier. *huwwa jundi b-maEna l-kalima.*

incident - *zaadiθ* pl. *zawaadiθ.* There've been several border incidents lately. *ṣaarat Eiddat zawaadiθ Eal-zuduud bil-mudda l-?axiira.* -- They crossed the river without incident. *Eubraw in-nahar bala-ma yṣiir zaadiθ.*

incidentally - 1. *Earaḍan.* He just said it incidentally. *gaal-ha Earaḍan.* 2. *bil-munaasaba.* Incidentally, I saw our friend Ali the other day. *bil-munaasaba, šifit ṣaazibna Eali ðaak il-yoom.*

incinerator - *mizraqa* pl. *mazaariq.*

incline - *munzadar.* I climbed the incline. *ṣEadt il-munzadar.*

to incline - *maal (i mayil).* The minaret inclines to the right. *l-manaara maayla lil-yimna.*

inclined - 1. *mayyaal.* I'm inclined to believe him. *?aani mayyaal ?ila taṣdiiqa.* 2. *maayil.* Water naturally flows down an inclined surface. *l-maay Eaadatan yinzidir Eal-?arḍ il-maayla.*

to **include** - 1. *ztiwa (i) Eala.* The dictionary doesn't include technical expressions. *l-qaamuus*

ma-yiʒtiwi *Eala ṣṭilaaʒaat fanniyya.* 2. *daxxal (i tadxiil) t-.* Include this in my bill. *daxxil haaδi ṣimn iʒsaabi.*
included - 1. *wiyya.* The room is five dinars, service included. *ʔiijaar il-ġurfa xams idnaaniir wiyya l-xidma.* 2. *b-ṣimn.* Were you included in the group that was promoted? *činit ib-ṣimn ij-jamaaEa l-itraffEaw?*
including - *b-ṣimn-, wiyya.* He earns thirty dollars, including tips. *huwwa yṭalliE itlaaθiin doolaar, ib-ṣiminha l-baxšiiš.*
income - *waarid* pl. *-aat, daxal* pl. *madxuulaat.* How much of an income does he have? *šġadd il-waarid maala?*
incompetent - *muu kafu.* The ambassador is incompetent. *s-safiir muu kafu.*
incomplete - *muu kaamil, naagiṣ.* The details of the report are incomplete. *tafaaṣiil it-taqriir muu kaamla.*
inconceivable - *muu maEquul, ma-yšiila l-Eaqil.* It's inconceivable that he'd do anything like that. *muu maEquul ysawwi hiiči šii.*
inconclusive - *muu muqniE, muu qaaṭiE.* The evidence so far is inconclusive. *l-ʔadilla li-hassa muu muqniEa.*
inconvenience - *ʔizEaaj.* The trip caused us a lot of inconvenience. *s-safra sabbibat-inna hwaaya ʔizEaaj.*
to inconvenience - *θaqqal (i taθqiil) Eala, ʔazEaj (i ʔizEaaj).* I don't want to inconvenience you. *ma-ariid aθaqqil Ealeek.*
inconvenient - *muu mulaaʔim.* He visited us at a very inconvenient time. *zaarna b-fadd wakit ʔabad muu mulaaʔim.* -- It will be inconvenient to go to the market today. *l-yoom muu hal-gadd mulaaʔim lir-rooʒa lis-suug.*
incorrect - *muu ṣaʒiiʒ, ġalaṭ.* Some of what he said was incorrect. *baEaδ illi gaala muu ṣaʒiiʒ.*
increase - *ziyaada* pl. *-aat, rtifaaE* pl. *-aat.* Statistics show a considerable increase in population. *l-ʔiʒṣaaʔaat itbayyin ziyaada kabiira bin-nufuus.*
on the increase - *b-irtifaaE.* The birth rate is on the increase. *nisbat il-wilaada b-irtifaaE.*
to increase - 1. *zayyad (i tazyiid) t-, kaθθar (i takθiir) t-.* You have to increase your output. *laazim itzayyid il-ʔintaaj.* 2. *zaad (i ziyaada) n-.* The population increased tremendously. *zaadat in-nufuus ib-nisba kabiira.*
incredible: **She told an incredible story. *ʒičat iʒčaaya ma-yšiilha l-Eaqil.*
indecent - *baδiiʔ.* His language is indecent. *luġata baδiiʔa.*
indeed - 1. *ʒaqiiqatan.* That's very good indeed! *haay ʒaqiiqatan kulliš zeena.* 2. *ṣidug.* Indeed? *ṣidug?*
indefinite - *ma-mEayyan, ma-maʒduud.* We'll be staying for an indefinite period. *raʒ-nibqa ʔila mudda ma-mEayyna.*
independence - *stiqlaal.* In these days, all African people want independence. *b-hal-ʔayyaam, kull iš-šuEuub il-ʔafriiqiyya triid istiqlaal.*
**He insists on complete independence in his work. *yṣirr Eala ʔan maʒʒad ʔabad yitdaxxal ib-šuġla.*
independent - 1. *mustaqill, mistiqill.* Lebanon is an independent state. *lubnaan balad mustaqill.* 2. *ma-mirtibuṭ.* She's independent of her family. *hiyya ma-mirtabṭa b-Eaaʔilatha.* 3. *miEtimid Eala nafs-.* He's been independent ever since he was sixteen. *čaan miEtimid Eala nafsa min Eumra siṭṭaEaš sana.*
index - *fihrast* pl. *fahaaris.* Look for the name in the index. *dawwur il-ʔisim bil-fihrast.*
index finger - *sabbaaba* pl. *-aat.*
India - *l-hind.*
Indian - 1. *hindi* pl. *hnuud.* Not all Indians are Hindus. *muu kull il-ihnuud hindoos.* 2. *hindi ʔaʒmar* pl. *hnuud ʒumur.* The original inhabitants of America were the Indians. *sukkaan ʔamriika l-ʔaṣliyyiin humma l-ihnuud il-ʒumur.* 3. *hindi*.* The Indian delegation arrived yesterday. *l-wafd il-hindi wuṣal il-baarʒa.*
Indian Ocean - *l-muʒiiṭ il-hindi.*
to **indicate -** *dall (u dall) n- Eala, bayyan (i tabyiin) t-.* His statement indicates that he's serious about the decision. *ʒčaayta tdull Eala ʔinnahu jiddi b-hal-qaraar.*
indication - *daliil* pl. *dalaaʔil.* Did she give you any indication that she liked you? *bayynat-lak ʔay daliil Eala ʒubbha?*
Indies - *jazaaʔir il-hind.*
indifference - *Eadam ihtimaam.* He showed complete indifference in the matter. *bayyan fadd Eadam ihtimaam kulli b-hal-mawṣuuE.*
indifferent - *laaʔubaali.* Don't be so indifferent. *la-tkuun hal-gadd laaʔubaali.*
**Why are you so indifferent to her? *leeš hal-gadd ma-tdiir-ilha baal?* or *leeš ma-tihtamm biiha?*
indigestion - *suuʔ haṣum.* I have indigestion. *Eindi suuʔ haṣum.*
indignant - *saaxiṭ.* He was indignant at the unfair treatment. *čaan saaxiṭ Eal-muEaamala s-sayyiʔa.*
indiscreet - 1. *ma-mitʒaffuṣ.* Your remark was very indiscreet. *ʔinta ma-činit mitʒaffuṣ ib-δiič l-iʒčaaya.* 2. *ma-mitbaṣṣir.* We feel you were indiscreet in your decision. *ʔiʒna niEtiqid inta ma-činit mitbaṣṣir ib-qaraarak.*
individual - 1. *šaxiṣ* pl. *ʔašxaaṣ, waaʒid.* He's a peculiar individual. *huwwa fadd šaxiṣ ʔaEmaala ġariiba.* 2. *farid* pl. *ʔafraad.* The communists don't respect the rights of the individual. *š-šuyuuEiyyiin ma-yihtammuun ib-ʒuquuq il-farid.* 3. *xaaṣṣ.* We each have our individual taste. *kull waaʒid minnina ʔila δawqa l-xaaṣṣ bii.*
**The individual can do nothing. *ʔiid wiʒda ma-tṣaffug.*
individually - 1. *waaʒid waaʒid.* I wish to speak to the students individually. *ʔard aʒči wiyya kull tilmiiδ waaʒid waaʒid.* 2. *kull waaʒid waʒda.* They came individually to the station. *ʔijaw lil-maʒaṭṭa kull waaʒid waʒda.*
Indonesia - *ʔandooniisya.*
Indonesian - *ʔandooniisi** pl. *-iyyiin.* He's an Indonesian. *huwwa ʔandooniisi.*
indoors - *jawwa, b-daaxil.* You'd better stay indoors today. *ʔaʒsan loo tibqa jawwa l-yoom.* -- If it rains the concert will be held indoors. *l-ʒafla l-moosiiqiyya tṣiir ib-daaxil il-qaaEa ʔiδa tumṭur id-dinya.*
industrial - *ṣinaaEi*.* They are setting up industrial centers all over the UAR. *humma gaaEid yibnuun maraakiz ṣinaaEiyya b-kull ʔanʒaaʔ ij-jamhuuriyya l-Earabiyya l-muttaʒida.*
industrialist - *ṣinaaEi* pl. *-iyyiin.* He's a famous industrialist. *huwwa ṣinaaEi mašhuur.*
industrialization - *taṣniiE.* The industrialization of Egypt is making considerable progress. *t-taṣniiE ib-maṣir gaaEid yitqaddam ib-surEa.*
industry - *ṣinaaEa* pl. *-aat.* Many industries were developed after the war. *hwaaya ṣinaaEaat iṭṭawwrat baEad il-ʒarb.*
inevitable - *ʒatmi*, laa budd min-, ma-mumkin tafaadi-.* This was an inevitable result. *haay čaanat natiija ʒatmiyya.* -- An argument with him is inevitable now. *t-talaaġ wiyyaa ma-mumkin tafaadii hassa.*
inexpensive - *rxiiṣ, muu ġaali.* I bought an inexpensive watch. *štireet saaEa rxiiṣa.*
infant - *raṣiiE* pl. *riṣaE.*
infantile - *maal ijhaal, ṣibaani*.* His actions are quite infantile. *taṣarrufaata baEadha maal ijhaal.*
infantile paralysis - *šalal.* He has infantile paralysis. *huwwa muṣaab biš-šalal.*
infantry - *mušaat.*
to **infect -** *ʒammal (i taʒmiil).* The dirt will infect that wound. *l-waṣaaxa tʒammil ij-jariʒ.*
to be infected - *ʒammal (i), ltihab (i ltihaab).* The wound is infected. *j-jariʒ imʒammil.*
infection - 1. *maraṣ* pl. *ʔamraaṣ, Eadwa.* Is there any way to keep that infection from spreading to the rest of the people? *hal ʔaku ṭariiqa txalli haaδa l-maraṣ ma-yintišir ʔila baaqi n-naas?* 2. *ltihaab* pl. *-aat.* This medicine will get rid of the infection. *haaδa d-duwa raʒ-yiqṣi Eal-iltihaab.*
infectious - *muEdi.* He has a very infectious disease. *maraṣa kulliš muEdi.*
inferior - 1. *waaṭi.* How can you tell that it's an inferior quality? *šloon tuEruf haaδa min nooE waaṭi?* 2. *ʔaqall nooEiyya.* This material is inferior to that. *haaδi l-maadda ʔaqall nooEiyya mnil-lux.*
**He is doing inferior work. *šuġla muu zeen.*
inferiority complex - *murakkab naqis.* She has an inferiority complex. *Eidha murakkab naqis.*
infidel - *kaafir* pl. *kuffaar.*
infidelity - *xiyaana.* Marital infidelity is a sin. *l-xiyaana z-zawjiyya ʒaraam.*
**He suspects his wife of infidelity. *huwwa yṣunn ʔinna zawijta xaaʔina.*
infinite - *ma-ʔil- nihaaya, ma-ʔil- ʒadd.* She has infinite patience. *Eidha xuluq ma-ʔila nihaaya.*

to be **inflamed** - *ltihab (i ltihaab).* My eye is inflamed. *Eeeni miltahba.*
inflammable - *qaabil lil-iltihaab.* Don't smoke here. The gas is inflammable. *la-tdaxxin ihnaa. l-paanziin qaabil lil-iltihaab.*
inflammation - *ltihaab.* The inflammation is going down. *l-iltihaab da-yqill.*
influence - **1.** *ta?θiir, nufuuδ.* He has no influence whatsoever. *ma-Einda ?ay ta?θiir.* **2.** *nufuuδ.* The people resist outside influence in the country. *š-šaEab yqaawum in-nufuuδ il-?ajnabi b-balada.*
**He was driving under the influence. *čaan ysuuq w-huwwa sakraan.*
to influence - *?aθθar (i ta?θiir) Eala.* I'm not trying to influence you. *ma-da-azaawil a?aθθir Ealeek.* -- He is trying to influence her in his favor *yzaawil it-ta?θiir Ealeeha l-ṣaalza.*
influential: **He's an influential man. *huwwa Einda ta?θiir čibiir. huwwa ṣaazib nufuuδ waasiE.*
influenza - *?ifluwanza.*
to **inform** - *xabbar (i taxbiir) t-, gaal (u gool) n-.* Keep me informed of your decisions. *xabburni b-kull qaraar tittaxδuu.*
**He's unusually well informed. *Einda Eilim ib-kull il-?axbaar.* or *Einda ṭṭilaaE waasiE.*
informant - *muxbir.* We got the news from a reliable informant. *zaṣṣalna Eal-?axbaar min muxbir mawθuuq bii.*
information - **1.** *maEluumaat, ?axbaar.* I can't give you any information about this case. *ma-agdar anṭiik ?ay maEluumaat titEallaq bil-qaδiyya.* **2.** *stiElaamaat.* Where's the information desk, please? *min faδlak, ween maktab il-istiElaamaat?*
infraction - *muxaalafa* pl. *-aat.* We'll charge a fine for any infraction of the rules. *raz-naδaE ġaraama Eala kull muxaalafa lit-taElimaat.*
ingenious - *baariE.* Your idea is very ingenious. *Eamma fikirtak baariE.*
to **inhabit** - *sikan (u sakan).* The Rualla tribe inhabits the northern portion of the Arabian Peninsula. *qabiilat irwaḷa siknat il-qism iš-šamaali mnij-jaziira l-Earabiyya.* -- This area was not inhabited until two years ago. *hal-manṭiqa ma-čaanat maskuuna ?illa muddat santeen.*
inhabitant - *saakin* pl. *sukkaan.* All the inhabitants of the island are fishermen. *sukkaan ij-jaziira kullhum ṣayyaadiin simač.* -- In 1960 Baghdad had a million inhabitants. *b-sanat ?alf w-tisiE miyya w-sittiin sukkaan baġdaad čaanaw milyoon.*
to **inhale** - **1.** *?axaδ (u) nafas.* The doctor told me to inhale. *ṭ-ṭabiib gal-li ?uxuδ nafas.* **2.** *bilaE (a baliE) id-duxxaan.* She's just learning to smoke, but she doesn't inhale. *hastawwha tEallmat tišrab jigaayir bass ma-tiblaE id-duxxaan.*
to **inherit** - *staaraθ (i stiiraaθ), wuraθ (a wariθ) n-.* I inherited the ring from my mother. *staaraθit il-mizbas min ?ummi.*
inheritance - *wuriθ, miiraaθ.* My uncle left me a small inheritance. *Eammi xaḷḷaf-li fadd išwayya wuriθ.*
inhuman - *wazši*.* The terrorists used inhuman methods against the populace. *l-?irhaabiyyiin istaEmal ?asaaliib wazšiyya δidd is-sukkaan.*
initial - *?awwali*, bidaa?i*.* The project is still in its initial stages. *l-mašruuE baEda b-maraazla l-?awwaliyya.*
initially - *mabda?iyyan, ?awwalan, bil-?awwal.* Initially, the government is going to appropriate one million dinars. *mabda?iyyan, il-zukuuma raz-itxaṣṣiṣ milyoon diinaar.*
initiative - *himma.* That engineer doesn't have much initiative. *hal-muhandis ma-Einda hal-gadd himma.*
**Someone has to take the initiative so the others will follow. *fadd azzad laazim yibdi zatta l-baaqiin ytibEuu.*
to **inject** - **1.** *biEaθ (a baEiθ) n-.* The change injected new life into the project. *t-taġyiir biEaθ zayaat ijdiida bil-mašruuE.* **2.** *δurab (u δarub) ?ubrat-.* They injected penicillin in his hip. *δurboo ?ubrat pansiliin ib-wirka.*
injection - *?ubra* pl. *?ubar.* Are you getting injections for diabetes? *da-taaxuδ ?ubar maal šakar?*
to **injure** - *jiraz (a jariz) n-.* How many people were injured in the accident? *šgadd naas injirzaw bil-zaadiθa?*
injury - *jariz* pl. *jruuz.* His injuries were not serious. *jruuza ma-čaanat xaṭra.*
ink - *zibir.* I need ink for my fountain pen. *?aztaaj zibir il-qalam il-paandaan maali.*
to ink - *xalla(i) zibir Eala.* Don't ink the pad too heavily. *la-txalli hwaaya zibir Eal-iṣṭampa.*
inlaid - *mṭaEEam.* That box has a cover inlaid with ivory. *qabaġ il-quuṭiyya mṭaEEam ib-Eaaj.*
inner - *daaxli*, jawwaani*.* The inner door is locked. *l-baab id-daaxli maqfuul.*
innocence - *baraa?a.* How did he prove his innocence? *šloon θibat baraa?ta?*
innocent - **1.** *barii?* pl. *?abriyaa?.* He's innocent of this charge. *huwwa barii? min hat-tuhma.* **2.** *baṣiiṭ.* He's as innocent as a new-born babe. *huwwa baṣiiṭ miθl iṭ-ṭifil.* **3.** *b-zusun niyya.* It was just an innocent remark. *čaanat mulaazaδa b-zusun niyya.*
innovation - *btikaar* pl. *-aat.* The minister introduced many innovations in his department. *l-waziir qaddam Eiddat ibtikaaraat il-taṭbiiqha b-daa?irta.*
to **inoculate** - *ṭaEEam(i taṭEiim) t-.* I haven't been inoculated against yellow fever yet. *ma-ṭṭaEEamit baEad δidd il-zimma ṣ-ṣafraa?.*
inoculation - *taṭEiim* pl. *-aat.*
to **inquire** - *staElam (i stiElaam), stafsar (i stifsaar).* I'll inquire about it. *raz-astaElim Eanha.*
inquiry - **1.** *tazqiiq.* An inquiry revealed that ... *t-tazqiiq bayyan Eala ?inna ...* **2.** *stifsaar* pl. *-aat, stiElaam* pl. *-aat.* We had a lot of inquiries about this subject. *Eidna hwaaya stifsaaraat Ean haaδa l-mawδuuE.*
insane - *majnuun* pl. *majaaniin, mxaḅḅaḷ* pl. *-iin.* That man is insane. *haaδa r-rajul majnuun.*
insane asylum - *mustašfa l-imjaaniin.* When did they release him from the insane asylum? *yamta fakkoo min mustašfa l-imjaaniin?*
inscription - *kitaaba mazfuura, kitaaba manquuša.* Can you read this inscription? *tigdar tiqra hal-kitaaba l-mazfuura?*
insect - *zašara* pl. *-aat.* Insects are a problem here. *l-zašaraat fadd muškila hnaa.*
insecticide - *qaatil zašaraat.*
to **insert** - *dimaj (i damij).* Insert this sentence in the beginning of your report. *?idmij haj-jumla b-bidaayat taqriirak.*
inside - **1.** *daaxil.* May I see the inside of the house? *?agdar ašuuf daaxil il-beet?* **2.** *bid-daaxil.* He left it inside. *tirakha bid-daaxil.* **3.** *b-xilaal, b-δimin.* Inside of five minutes the theater was empty. *b-xilaal xamis daqaayiq ṣaarat is-siinama faarġa.* **4.** *daaxili*.* Could you please give us an inside room? *mumkin min faδlak tinṭiina ġurfa daaxiliyya?*
inside out - **1.** *bil-gufa, bil-magluub.* He has his sweater on inside out. *laabis ibluuza bil-gufa.* **2.** *šibir šibir, tamaaman.* He knows the town inside out. *yuEruf il-madiina šibir šibir.* -- He knows his business inside out. *xaatim maṣlazta tamaaman.*
to come (or go) inside - *dixal (u duxuul), xašš (u xašš), ṭabb (u ṭabb).* Why don't you come inside? *leeš ma-tidxul?*
insight - *?idraak, fahim.* He showed great insight in handling economic problems. *bayyan ?idraak waasiE b-muEaalajat il-mašaakil l-iqtiṣaadiyya.*
insignia - *Ealaama* pl. *-aat, Ealaayim; ?išaara* pl. *-aat.* The cavalry's insignia is crossed rifles. *Ealaamat il-xayyaala bunduqiiteen mitqaaṭEa.*
insignificant - *ṭafiif, taafih, muu muhimm.* The difference is insignificant. *l-ixtilaaf ṭafiif.*
to **insinuate** - *lammaz (i talmiiz) t-.* He insinuated that the prime minister was taking bribes. *lammaz Eala ?an ra?iis il-wuzaraa? čaan yaaxuδ rašwa.*
insinuation - *taščiim, talmiiz* pl. *-aat.* Those insinuations are out of place. *hat-taščiim ?abad muu b-mazalla.*
to **insist** - **1.** *ṣarr (i ?iṣraar) n-.* Why do you insist on going? *luweeš iṭṣirr Ear-rooza?* **2.** *lazz (i ?ilzaaz, lazz).* Don't insist if she doesn't want to go. *la-tlizz ?iδa hiyya ma-triid itruuz.*
insistent - *lazuuz.* This beggar is very insistent. *hal-imgaddi kulliš lazuuz.*
insolence - *ṣalaafa.* Children, I don't want any more insolence from you. *wilid, bass Eaad ṣalaafa.*
insolent - *ṣalif.* He's an insolent fellow. *huwwa fadd waazid kulliš ṣalif.*
insomnia - *?araq.* I have insomnia these days. *da-yṣiir Eindi ?araq hal-?ayyaam.*
to **inspect** - *fattaš (i taftiiš) t-.* They inspected the baggage carefully. *fattšaw ij-junaṭ kulliš zeen.*
inspection - *taftiiš* pl. *-aat.* Our baggage is ready

for inspection. *jinaṭna ʒaaṣra lit-taftiiš.*
inspector - *mufattiš* pl. *-iin.*
inspiration - *waʒi, ʔilʒaam.* A good poet can't write without inspiration. *š-šaaƐir iz-zeen ma-yigdar yunṣum bala ma-yijii l-waʒi.*
to **inspire** - *ʔawʒa, wuʒa (i ʔiiʒaaʔ) n-.* His calm manner inspires confidence. *huduuʔa yuuʒi biθ-θiqa.*
to **install** - *niṣab (u naṣub) n-.* A telephone will be installed tomorrow. *baačir raʒ-yinnuṣub talafoon.*
installation - **1.** *naṣub.* Telephone installation costs 15 pounds. *naṣub talafoon ykallif ixmuṣṭaƐaš diinaar.* **2.** *munšaʔaat, muʔassasa* pl. *-aat.* He was collecting intelligence on military and industrial installations. *čaan da-yijmaƐ maƐluumaat Ɛan il-munšaʔaat iṣ-ṣinaaƐiyya wil-Ɛaskariyya.*
installment - **1.** *qisim mitsalsil* pl. *ʔaqsaam mitsalsila.* The novel is appearing in installments. *r-ruwaaya da-tiṭlaƐ Ɛala ʔaqsaam mitsalsila.* **2.** *qisiṭ* pl. *ʔaqsaaṭ.* You can pay it in five installments. *tigdar tidfaƐha b-xams aqsaaṭ.*
on installments - *bit-taqsiiṭ, bil-ʔaqsaaṭ.* We bought the furniture on installments. *štireena l-ʔaθaaθ bit-taqsiiṭ.*
to pay in installments - *qassaṭ (i taqsiiṭ).* I'll pay you the amount in installments. *Ɛuud aqassiṭ-lak il-mablaġ.*
instance - **1.** *maθal* pl. *ʔamθaal.* This is another instance of his carelessness. *haaδa maθal laax Ɛala Ɛadam ihtimaama.* **2.** *ʒaala* pl. *-aat, marra* pl. *-aat.* In this instance you're wrong. *b-hal-ʒaala ʔinta ġalṭaan.*
for instance - *maθalan.* There are quite a few possibilities, for instance ... *ʔaku Ɛiddat iʒtimaalaat, maθalan ...*
instant - *laʒδa* pl. *-aat.* Let me know the instant he arrives. *xburni bil-laʒδa lli yooṣal biiha.* -- He was gone in an instant. *xtifa b-laʒδa wiʒda.*
instantly - *ʒaalan, fawran.* He came instantly when I called. *jaa ʒaalan min ṣiʒʒta.*
instead - *badaal, badalan min, b-makaan, Ɛiwaδan Ɛan.* What do you want instead of it? *š-itriid badaala?* -- He gave me tangerines instead of oranges. *nṭaani laalingi b-bidaal il-purtaqaal.* -- Why don't you do something instead of complaining all the time? *luweeš ma-tsawwi šii badalan min ʔan titšakka Ɛala ṭuul?* -- Can you go instead of me? *tigdar itruuʒ Ɛiwaδan Ɛanni?*
to **instigate** - *ʒarraδ (i taʒriiδ).* He instigated the strike. *huwwa lli ʒarraδ Ɛal-iδraab.*
instigator - *muʒarriδ* pl. *-iin.*
instinct - *fiṭra, ġariiza.* Women love children by instinct. *n-niswaan yʒibbuun l-aṭfaal bil-fiṭra.*
institute - *maƐhad* pl. *maƐaahid.* I'm studying at the Scientific Institute. *ʔaani adrus bil-maƐhad il-Ɛilmi.*
institution - *maƐhad* pl. *maƐaahid.* It's a state institution. *haaδa maƐhad ʒukuumi.*
instruction - *muʒaaδaraat.* Professor Ahmed will give instruction in Arabic. *l-ʔustaaδ ʔaʒmad raʒ-yilqi muʒaaδaraat bil-luġa l-Ɛarabiyya.*
instructions - *taƐliimaat.* The head nurse will give you instructions. *raʔiisat il-mumarriδaat raʒ-tinṭiik it-taƐliimaat.*
instructive - *tawjiihi**. The lecture was very instructive. *l-muʒaaδara čaanat kulliš tawjiihiyya.*
instrument - *ʔaala* pl. *-aat.* Lay out the instruments for the operation. *ʒaδδiri l-ʔaalaat lil-Ɛamaliyya.* -- Do you play a musical instrument? *tigdar itdugg Ɛala ʔaala mawsiiqiyya?*
to **insulate** - *Ɛizal (i Ɛazil) n-.* Wrap the tape around the wire to insulate it. *liff it-teep Ɛal-waayir ʒatta tƐizla.* -- We'll have to insulate the heating pipes. *laazim niƐzil bwaari l-ʒaraara.*
insulated - *maƐzuul.* A well insulated wire won't give you a shock. *l-waayir il-maƐzuul zeen ma-yintil.*
insulator - *Ɛaazil* pl. *Ɛawaazil, maadda* (pl. *mawaadd*) *Ɛaazila.*
insult - *ʔihaana* pl. *-aat.* I consider that an insult. *ʔaƐtuburha ʔihaana.*
to insult - *ʔahaan (i ʔihaana) n-.* You've insulted him. *ʔinta ʔahanta.*
insurance - *taʔmiin* pl. *-aat.* You can sign the insurance policy tomorrow. *tigdar itwaqqiƐ Ɛaqd it-taʔmiin baačir.*
to **insure** - *ʔamman (i taʔmiin) t- Ɛala.* I have insured my house for 5,000 dinars. *ʔammanit Ɛala beeti b-mablaġ xamist aalaaf diinaar.*
intellectual - **1.** *muθaqqaf* pl. *-iin, Ɛaaqil* pl. *Ɛuqalaaʔ.* Many intellectuals read this magazine. *hwaaya muθaqqafiin yiqruun haaδi l-majalla.* **2.** *fikri*, δihni*, Ɛaqli**. There's an intellectual bond between them. *ʔaku beenhum irtibaaṭ fikri.* -- She's not interested in intellectual matters. *hiyya ma-Ɛidha raġba bil-ʔumuur il-fikriyya.*
intelligence - **1.** *majhuud fikri, majhuud Ɛaqli.* The exam requires a lot of intelligence. *l-imtiʒaan yirraad-la hwaaya majhuud fikri.* **2.** *stixbaaraat.* He works in the intelligence service. *huwwa yištuġuḷ ib-daaʔirat l-istixbaaraat.*
intelligent - *δaki**. She's very intelligent. *hiyya kulliš δakiyya.*
to **intend** - *nuwa (i nawi, niyya).* What do you intend to do? *š-tinwi tsawwi?* or *šinu niyytak?* -- I intend to go to Basra in April. *naawi ʔaruuʒ lil-baṣra b-niisaan.*
intended - *maqṣuud.* That remark was intended for him. *haay il-mulaaʒaδa čaanat maqṣuuda ʔila.* **This merchandise is intended for Spain. *haay il-biδaaƐa maqṣuud biiha truuʒ l-ispaanya.* or *hal-biδaaƐa manwi ʔirsaalha l-ispaanya.*
intense - *qawi*, šadiid.* I couldn't stand the intense heat. *ma-gdarit atʒammal il-ʒaraara l-qawiyya.*
intensity - *šidda, quwwa.* I was amazed at the intensity of her anger. *tƐajjabit min šiddat ġaδabha.*
intensive - **1.** *qawi*, šadiid.* The government is conducting an intensive campaign to stamp out prostitution. *l-ʒukuuma da-tsawwi ʒamla qawiyya ʒatta tiqδi Ɛal-biġaaʔ.* **2.** *kaθiif.* They're using intensive cultivation to increase their crops. *gaaƐid yistaƐmiluun iz-ziraaƐa l-kaθiifa ʒatta yʒiiduun maʒaaṣiilhum.*
intention - *niyya, qaṣid.* Was that really your intention? *ṣidug haaδi čaanat niitak?*
intentional - *Ɛamdi**. That was an intentional killing. *δaak čaan qatil Ɛamdi.*
intentionally - *Ɛamdan.* I did it intentionally. *sawweetha Ɛamdan.*
intently - *b-intibaah.* They were listening intently. *čaanaw da-ysimƐuun b-intibaah.*
to **intercept** - *ltiqaṭ (i ltiqaaṭ).* We intercepted a a message from the enemy's headquarters. *ltiqaṭna risaala min markaz il-ʔaƐdaaʔ.*
intercourse - **1.** *ttiṣaal jinsi, jimaaƐ.* Have you had intercourse with her? *ṣaar Ɛindak ittiṣaal jinsi wiyyaaha?* **2.** *Ɛalaaqaat.* We never had any social intercourse with that family. *ʔabad ma-ṣaar Ɛidna Ɛalaaqaat ijtimaaƐiyya wiyya δiič il-Ɛaaʔila.*
to have intercourse - *jaamaƐ (i jimaaƐ).* The doctor forbade him to have intercourse. *d-duktoor minaƐa min ij-jimaaƐ.*
interest - **1.** *htimaam.* He shows a special interest in it. *yibdi htimaam xaaṣṣ biiha.* **2.** *maṣlaʒa* pl. *maṣaaliʒ.* This is in your own interest. *haay il-maṣlaʒtak.* **3.** *huwaaya* pl. *-aat.* He has many interests. *Ɛinda hwaaya huwaayaat.* **4.** *walaƐ.* He has a great interest in stamp collecting. *Ɛinda hwaaya walaƐ ib-jamƐ iṭ-ṭawaabiƐ.* **5.** *faaʔida, faayiz.* How much interest does the bank pay? *šgadd faaʔida yinṭi il-bang?* **6.** *ʒuṣṣa.* Do you have an interest in the business? *Ɛindak ʒuṣṣa biš-šuġuḷ?*
to interest - **1.** *jiδab (i jaδib).* She doesn't interest me at all. *hiyya ma-tijδibni ʔabad.* **2.** *raġġab (u targiib).* Can't you interest him in that? *ma-tigdar itraġġba biiha?*
interested - **1.** *muulaƐ, Ɛind- raġba.* I'm interested in sports. *ʔaani muulaƐ bil-ʔalƐaab ir-riyaaδiyya.* **2.** *mihtamm, Ɛind- raġba.* I'm interested in these studies. *ʔaani mihtamm ib-hiiči diraasaat.* -- He's more interested in science than art. *mihtamm bil-Ɛiluum ʔakθar imnil-finuun.* **3.** *Ɛind- waahis.* I'm not interested in going. *ma-Ɛindi waahis aruuʒ.* **4.** *Ɛind- ġaaya.* He's only interested in her money. *ma-Ɛinda ġaaya ġeer ifluusha.*
interesting - *mumtiƐ.* That's an interesting article. *haaδi maqaala mumtiƐa.*
**What are the most interesting places to visit in Baghdad? *šinu hiyya ʔalṭaf il-maʒallaat illi yumkin waaʒid yʒuurha b-baġdaad.*
to **interfere** - **1.** *Ɛaaq (i ʔiƐaaqa).* He'll leave on Sunday if nothing interferes. *ysaafir il-ʔaʒʒad ʔiδa ma-yƐiiqa fadd šii.* **2.** *tdaxxal (a tadaxxul).* Don't interfere in other people's affairs! *la-titdaxxal ib-šuġuḷ ġeerak!* -- You're interfering with my work. *ʔinta da-titdaxxal ib-šuġḷi.*
interference - *wašwaša, tadaxxul.* We can't hear that station because there's so much interference in the

air. *ma-nigdar nismaε hal-maζaṭṭa li-ʔan ʔaku hwaaya wašwaša bij-jaww.*
interior - 1. *daaxil, jawwa.* The interior of their house is very beautiful. *daaxil beethum kulliš ζilu.* or *beethum min jawwa kulliš ζilu.* 2. *daaxili*, jawwaani*.* The interior walls are covered with cracks. *l-iζyaaṭiin id-daaxiliyya kullha mfaṭṭra.* 3. *daaxiliyya.* The Ministry of the Interior is on the river. *wizaarat id-daaxiliyya εaš-šaṭṭ.*
intermission - *fatra* pl. *-aat.* I was in the foyer during the intermission. *ʔaθnaaʔ il-fatra činit biṣ-ṣaaloon.*
internal - 1. *daaxili*.* The internal affairs of the country are in bad shape. *ʔaζwaal il-balad id-daaxiliyya muu zeena.* 2. *daaxili*, baaṭini*.* He died of internal injuries. *maat natiijat juruuζ daaxiliyya.*
international - *dawli*.* Do you think the International Bank will underwrite this loan? *titṣawwar ʔinna l-bank id-dawli raζ-yiδmin hal-qarδ?*
to **interpret** - 1. *fassar (i tafsiir) t-.* You can interpret it this way, too. *mumkin itfassirha b-haṭ-ṭariiqa hamm.* 2. *tarjam (i tarjama).* When the ambassador spoke with the king, he interpreted. *min čaan is-safiir yiζči wiyya l-malik huwwa čaan ytarjim.*
interpreter - *mutarjim* pl. *-iin, turjamaan* pl. *-iyya.* I acted as interpreter. *qumt ib-εamal mutarjim.*
to **interrupt** - 1. *qaaṭaε (i muqaaṭaεa).* Don't interrupt me all the time. *la-tqaaṭiεni daaʔiman.* 2. *sabbab (i) taεṭiil.* Am I interrupting? *ʔaani da-asabbib taεṭiil?*
interruption - *muδaayaqa* pl. *-aat, muqaaṭaεa* pl. *-aat.* I can't concentrate on my work with all these interruptions. *ma-agdar arakkiz εala šuġli min kuθrat il-muδaayaqaat.*
intersection - *taqaaṭuε* pl. *-aat.* The accident occurred at the intersection. *l-ζaadiθ ζiṣal εind taqaaṭuε iṭ-ṭuruq.*
interval - 1. *stiraaζa, tawaqquf.* After a short interval we continued on our trip. *baεad istiraaζa qaṣiira kammalna safratna.* 2. *masaafa* pl. *-aat.* The trees are set at close intervals. *l-ašjaar mazruuεa εala masaafaat mitqaarba.* 3. *fatra* pl. *-aat.* The bombs are set to go off at five-minute intervals. *l-qanaabil imwaqqata tinfijir ib-fatraat xamas daqaayiq.*
to **intervene** - *tdaxxal (i tadaxxul), twaṣṣaṭ*
to **intervene** - *tdaxxal (i tadaxxul), twaṣṣaṭ (i tawaṣṣuṭ).* It won't do any good to intervene in their quarrel. *ma-aku faayda min tadaxxulak beenaathum.*
intervention - *tadaxxul, tawaṣṣuṭ.* Both sides would welcome U.N. intervention in the dispute. *ṭ-ṭarafeen yraaζibuun tadaxxul hayʔat il-ʔumam il-muttaζida bin-nizaaε.*
interview - *muqaabala* pl. *-aat.* The reporter asked for an interview with the minister. *l-muraasil ṭilab muqaabalat il-waziir.*
 to interview - *qaabal (i muqaabala).* The reporter interviewed the minister. *l-muraasil qaabal il-waziir.*
intestines - *ʔamεaaʔ.* The doctor removed a part of his intestines. *d-daktoor šaal wuṣla min ʔamεaaʔa.*
intimate - *ṣamiimi*.* We're intimate friends. *ʔiζna ʔaṣdiqaaʔ ṣamiimiyyiin.* or ***ʔiζna ʔaṣdiqaaʔ kulliš.*
into - 1. *b-.* Put it into the box. *xalliiha biṣ-ṣanduuq.* -- Get into the car. *ʔidxul bis-sayyaara.* -- We have to take that into account, too. *haay hamm laazim inζuṭṭha bil-iζsaab.* 2. *l-.* Can you translate this into English? *tigdar ittarjum haay lil-ingliizi?*
 **Can these boards be made into something useful? *hal-looζaat yimkin yitsawwa minha šii yfiid?* or *hal-looζaat yimkin titζawwal ʔila šii mufiid?*
 **Those kids are always into everything. *haj-jihhaal yšaεbiθuun ib-kullši.*
intolerance - *ʔadam it-tasaamuζ.*
intolerant - *mitεaṣṣub.* That man is very intolerant. *haaδa r-rijjaal mitεaṣṣub kulliš.*
intoxicant - *musakkir* pl. *-aat.* The sale of intoxicants to minors is prohibited. *beeε il-musakkiraat il-ġeer il-baalġiin mamnuuε.*
intoxicated - *xadraan, sakraan.* I'm a little intoxicated tonight. *ʔaani šwayya xadraan il-leela.*
intoxicating - *musakkir.* This wine is very intoxicating. *haš-šaraab kulliš musakkir.*
to **introduce** - 1. *εarraf (u taεriif) t-, qaddam (i taqdiim) t-.* I'd like to introduce you to my father. *ʔaζibb aεarrfak εala ʔabuuya.* 2. *ʔadxal (i ʔidxaal), daxxal (i tadxiil) t-.* He introduced a number of changes in his government's policy. *huwwa ʔadxal baεδ it-taεdiilaat εala siyaast il-ζukuuma.* 3. *qaddam (i taqdiim) t-.* They introduced new proposals in the legislature. *qaddamaw iqtiraaζaat jidiida lil-barlamaan.*
introduction - *muqaddima* pl. *-aat.* It's mentioned in the introduction. *maδkuura bil-muqaddima.*
intrusion - *taṭafful.* Sorry for the intrusion, sir, but we've just been invaded. *ʔaδruuna mnit-taṭafful, ʔustaaδ, laakin hassa nhijam εaleena.*
intuition - *badiiha, badaaha.* You'll just have to use your intuition. *ma-εaleek ʔilla ʔan tistaεmil badaahtak.*
to **invade** - *ġiza (i ġazu) n-.* Napoleon tried to invade England. *naapilyoon ζaawal yiġzi ʔingiltara.*
invalid - 1. *εaajiz* pl. *-iin.* For many years my grandmother has been an invalid. *jiddiiti ṣaar-ilha εiddat sanawaat εaajiz.* 2. *baaṭil, ġeer šarεi*.* A will without a signature is invalid. *l-waṣiyya baaṭla biduun ʔimδaaʔ.*
invasion - *ġazwa* pl. *-aat.* The invasion has failed. *l-ġazwa fišlat.*
to **invent** - 1. *xtiraε (i xtiraaε).* Every day they invent something new. *kull yoom yixtarεuun šii jdiid.* 2. *xtilaq (i xtilaaq).* Did you invent that story? *ʔinta xtilaqit hal-quṣṣa?*
invention - *xtiraaε* pl. *-aat.*
inventor - *muxtariε* pl. *-iin.*
inventory - *jarid.* Our shop takes inventory each year. *ʔiζna nsawwi jarid kull sana.*
to **invest** - *staθmar (a stiθmaar), šaġġal (i tašġiil).* He invested his money in real estate. *huwwa staθmar ifluusa bil-εiqaar.*
to **investigate** - *ζaqqaq (i taζqiiq) t- b-.* They're investigating the case. *da-yζaqqiquun bil-qaδiyya.*
investigation - *taζqiiq* pl. *-aat.* An investigation has been ordered by the court. *l-maζkama ʔumrat ib-ijraaʔ taζqiiq.*
investment - *makaan istiθmaar.* What is the best financial investment nowadays? *sinu ʔaζsan makaan l-istiθmaar l-ifluus hal-ʔayyaam?*
investor - *mustaθmir* pl. *-iin.* We need more investors. *yinraad-inna mustaθmiriin baεad.*
invisible - *ġeer manδuur.* Carbon monoxide is an invisible gas. *ʔawwal ʔooksiid il-kaarboon ġaaz ġeer manδuur.*
invitation - *daεwa* pl. *-aat, εaziima* pl. *εazaayim.* Many thanks for your kind invitation. *ʔaškurak εala daεuutak.*
to **invite** - *εizam (i εaziima) n-, diεa (u daεwa) n-.* Who did you invite to the party? *ʔilman iεzamit lil-ζafla?* -- He invited me to lunch. *εizamni εal-ġada.*
inviting - 1. *mušahhi.* The food looks very inviting. *l-ʔakil manδara mušahhi.* 2. *muġri.* This low price is very inviting. *has-siεir ir-raxiiṣ kulliš muġri.*
 **The sea looks inviting today. *l-baζar yiġri εas-sibiζ hal-yoom.*
to **involve** - 1. *ʔašrak (i ʔišraak).* He involved me in the crime, and I wasn't even there! *ʔašrakni bij-jariima, w-ʔaani ζatta ma-činit ihnaak!* 2. *ṭṭallab (a taṭallub).* The trip involved a lot of expense. *s-safra ṭṭallibat ihwaaya maṣaariif.*
 **The work involves a certain amount of risk. *š-šaġla biiha xaṭuura.*
involved - *mεaqqad.* That's a very involved process. *haaδa ʔijraaʔ kulliš imεaqqad.*
 to get involved - *ζaṭṭ (u ζaṭṭ) nafs~.* I don't want to get involved in this. *ma-ard aζuṭṭ nafsi b-haay.*
iodine - 1. *yood.* We studied iodine in class today. *drasna l-yood ib-ṣaffna l-yoom.* 2. *tantaryook, yood.* Put a little iodine on the wound so it doesn't swell up. *xalli šwayyat tantaryook εaj-jariζ ζatta ma-yooram.*
Iran - *ʔiiraan.*
Iranian - *ʔiiraani** pl. *-iyyiin, εajmi** pl. *εajam, faarisi** pl. *-iyyiin, furs.* She's an Iranian. *hiyya ʔiiraaniyya.*
Iraq - *l-εiraaq.* Baghdad is the capital of Iraq. *baġdaad hiyya εaaṣimat il-εiraaq.*
Iraqi - 1. *εiraaqi* pl. *-iyyiin.* Are there many Iraqis here? *ʔaku hwaaya εiraaqiyyiin ihnaa?* 2. *εiraaqi*.* Iraqi industry is advancing. *ṣ-ṣinaaεa l-εiraaqiyya da-titqaddam.*
irksome - *muzεij.* He still has to cope with many irksome problems. *baεad εinda hwaaya mašaakil*

muzεija.

iron - 1. *ḥadiid.* You have to be made of iron to stand all that. *laazim itkuun min ḥadiid ḥatta tigdar titḥammal kull haaδa.* -- They're putting an iron gate up at the entrance way. *da-yḥuṭṭuun baab ḥadiid il-baab il-ḥadiiqa.* **2.** *ʔuuti* pl. *-iyyaat.* Is the iron still hot? *l-ʔuuti baεda ḥaarr?* **3.** *qawi*.* He has an iron will. *εinda ʔiraada qawiyya.*

cast iron - *ʔaahiin.* This drainpipe is made of cast iron. *hal-buuri min ʔaahiin.*

to iron - *kuwa (i kawi) n-, ḍirab (u ḍarub) n- ʔuuti.* Did you iron my shirt? *kweeti θoobi?*

to iron out - *tsaawa (a tasaawi), ṭṣaffa (a taṣaffi).* There are still a few things to be ironed out. *baεd aku baεḍ il-ʔašyaaʔ laazim titsaawa.*

Iron Curtain - *s-sitaar il-ḥadiidi.*

ironical - *min mahzalat il-aqdaar.* This turn of events is ironical. *min mahzalat il-aqdaar ʔan yṣiir hiiči šii.*

ironing board - *meez* (pl. *-aat*) *maal ʔuuti.*

irony - *εunuf, ṣaraama.* He's prone to using irony. *huwwa mayyaal ʔila stiεmaal il-εunuf.*

irrational - *ġeer mittizin.* His statements are irrational. *kalaama ġeer mittizin.*

irregular - 1. *ġeer muntaḍam, ġeer munaḍḍam.* The awarding of contracts was irregular. *ʔaḥkaam il-εuquud čaanat ġeer muntaḍma.* **2.** *ġeer niḍaami*.* We were attacked by irregular forces. *haajmatna quwwaat ġeer niḍaamiyya.*

irregularity - *talaaεub* pl. *-aat.* Some irregularities were discovered in his accounts. *nliga talaaεub b-iḥsaabaata.*

irrelevant - *ma-ʔila εilaaqa.* This question is irrelevant to the case. *haaδa suʔaal ma-ʔila εilaaqa bil-qaḍiyya.*

irresponsible - *ma-εind- masʔuuliyya.* That child is irresponsible. *haṭ-ṭifil ma-εinda masʔuuliyya.*

to **irrigate -** *ruwa (i rawi) n-, siga (i sagi) n-.* We're going to irrigate this field next year. *raḥ-nirwi haaδa l-ḥaqil s-sana l-qaadima.*

irrigation - *sagi, rawi.* We couldn't raise anything on this land without irrigation. *ma-nigdar innammi šii εala hal-gaaε bila sagi.*

irritable - *minfiεil, εaṣabi.* He was very irritable this morning. *čaan kulliš minfiεil il-yoom iṣ-ṣubuḥ.*

to **irritate - 1.** *ʔaθaar (i ʔiθaara), ʔazεaj (i ʔizεaaj).* His remark irritated me. *εibaarta ʔaθaaratni.* **2.** *hayyaj (i tahyiij) t-.* This soap doesn't irritate the skin. *haay iṣ-ṣaabuuna ma-thayyij ij-jilid.*

Islam - *l-ʔislaam.*

Islamic - *ʔislaami*.* We're studying Islamic history. *ʔiḥna nidrus it-taariix il-ʔislaami.*

island - *jaziira* pl. *jazaaʔir, juzur.* I just came from the island of Cyprus. *hassa jeet min jaziirat qubruṣ.*

to **isolate -** *εizal (i εazil) n-.* The sick children were isolated. *l-ʔaṭfaal il-marḍa čaanaw maεzuuliin.*

isolated - *mafṣuul, maεzuul.* They live in a house isolated from the village. *humma yεiišuun ib-beet mafṣuul εan il-qarya.*

Israel - *ʔisraaʔiil.*

Israeli - *ʔisraaʔiili*.*

issue - 1. *εadad* pl. *ʔaεdaad.* I haven't read the last issue. *ma-qreet il-εadad il-ʔaxiir.* **2.** *mawḍuuε* pl. *mawaaḍiiε.* This question will be an important issue in the coming elections. *has-suʔaal raḥ-ykuun mawḍuuε muhimm bil-intixaabaat ij-jaaya.* -- I don't want to make an issue of it. *ma-ariid asawwiiha mawḍuuε baḥiθ.*

to issue - *ṣaddar (i taṣdiir) t-.* Where did they issue the passports? *ween ṣaddraw jawaazaat is-safar?*

it - 1. *huwwa* (or) *hiyya* (respectively). Which is my book? Oh, that's it. *yaahu ktaabi? haδaak huwwa.* -- Where is my hat? Here it is! *ween šafuqti? hiyyaatha!* **2.** *-a* (or) *-ha* (respectively). I can't do it. *ma-ʔagdar asawwiiha.* -- I knew it! *εirafitha.* -- I can't give you the money today. I forgot it. *ma-ʔagdar anṭiik l-ifluus il-yoom niseetha.*

**Who's ''it''? Ali's ''it''. Run before he tags you! *bii-man? b-εali. ʔirkuḍ gabuḷ-ma ygiisak!*

**It's cold outside. *barra baarda.*

**It's raining. *gaaεid tumṭur.*

**It's lovely today. *l-yoom kulliš badiiε.*

**It doesn't matter. *ma-thimm* or *ma-yhimm.*

**It doesn't make any difference. *ma-tifruq.*

**He's had it! *wuṣal ḥadda.*

itch - *ḥakka.* I've got an itch. *εindi ḥakka.*

to itch - *ḥakk (u ḥakk) n-.* The wound itches. *j-jariḥ da-yḥukkni.* -- I itch all over. *kull jismi da-yḥukkni.*

**I'm itching to get started. *ʔaani kulliš muštaaq abdi.*

item - 1. *šii* pl. *ʔašyaaʔ.* We don't carry that item. *ma-εidna haš-šii.* **2.** *mawḍuuε* pl. *mawaaḍiiε.* Did you see the item in the paper? *šift il-mawḍuuε bij-jariida?* **3.** *faqara* pl. *-aat.* How many items are on that bill? *čam faqara b-hal-qaaʔima?*

to **itemize -** *ṣannaf (i taṣniif) t-.* Itemize all your expenses. *ṣannif kull maṣaariifak.*

itself - 1. *nafis-.* The child hurt itself. *j-jaahil εawwar nafsa.* -- The car itself isn't damaged, but the driver was injured. *s-sayyaara nafisha ma-tʔaδδat, laakin is-saayiq injiraḥ.* **2.** *waḥid-.* The house itself is worth that. *l-beet waḥda yiswa hal-gadd.*

**That speaks for itself. *haay ma-yinraad-ilha ḥači.*

by itself - *min keef-.* This door closes by itself. *hal-baab yinsadd min keefa.*

in itself - *b-ḥadd δaat-.* The plan in itself is good. *l-mašruuε ib-ḥadd δaata zeen.*

ivory - *εaaj.* The knife handle is ivory. *ʔiid is-siččiina min εaaj.*

J

to **jab -** *naġġ (u naġġ) n-.* He jabbed me with the pencil. *naġġni bil-qalam.*

jack - 1. *jagg* pl. *-aat.* I left the jack in the garage. *trakt ij-jagg bil-garaaj.* **2.** *walad* pl. *wulid, bajaġ* pl. *-aat.* I've got three jacks. *εindi tlaθ wulid.*

**You look as if you had hit the jackpot. *ybayyin jaaya d-dinya wiyyaak.*

to jack up - 1. *šaal (i šeel) b-jagg.* You'll have to jack up the car. *laazim itšiil is-sayyaara b-jagg.* **2.** *rifaε (a rafuε) n-, zayyad (i tazyiid) t-.* They've jacked up the price again. *rifεaw is-siεir marra θaanya.*

jackal - *waawi* pl. *-iyya.*

jackass - *zmaaḷ* pl. *zmaayiḷ, ḥmaar* pl. *ḥamiir.*

jacket - 1. *sitra* pl. *sitar, čaakeet* pl. *-aat.* You can wear that jacket with flannel slacks. *tigdar tilbas has-sitra εala panṭaroon faaneela.* **2.** *gišir* pl. *gšuur.* I boiled the potatoes in their jackets. *slagt il-puteeta b-igšuurha.* **3.** *ġlaaf* pl. *-aat.* The jacket of the book is all torn. *l-iġlaaf maal l-iktaab kulla mšaggag.*

jackknife - *čaaquuča* pl. *-aat, siččiina* pl. *sčaačiin.*

jail - *sijin* pl. *sujuun, ḥabis.* He was sentenced to six months in jail. *nḥikam sitt išhur bis-sijin.*

to jail - *ḥibas (i ḥabis) n-, sijan (i sijin) n-.* He was jailed for theft. *nḥibas li-ʔan baag.*

jalopy - *sayyaara* (pl. *-aat*) *palašqa.* He bought an old jalopy. *štira-la jadd sayyaara palašqa.*

jam - 1. *mrabba* pl. *-yaat.* I prefer homemade jam. *ʔafaḍḍil imrabba maal beet.* **2.** *ḍiiq.* I'm in an awful jam. *ʔaani b-ḍiiq šadiid.*

traffic jam - *muškilat izdiḥaam.* The police untangled the traffic jam. *šurṭa l-muruur ḥallaw muškilat l-izdiḥaam.*

to jam - 1. *šawwaš (i tašwiiš) εala.* Somebody is jamming our broadcast. *waaḥid da-yšawwiš εala ʔiδaaεatna.* **2.** *ḥiṣar (i ḥaṣir) n-.* He jammed his finger in the door. *ḥiṣar ʔiṣibεa bil-baab.* **3.** *εiṣa (i).* The drawer jammed when I tried to open it. *l-imjarr εiṣa lamma ridit ʔafitḥa.* **4.** *jayyam (i tajyiim) t-, šakkal (i taškiil) t-.* The gears are jammed. *l-geer imjayyim.* **5.** *zdiḥam (i zdiḥaam) n-.* The elevator was jammed with people. *l-maṣεad čaan muzdaḥim bin-naas.*

janitor - *farraaš* pl. *-iin, fraariiš; bawwaab* pl. *-iin.*

The janitor cleaned the windows last night. *l-farraaš naḍḍaf l-išbaabiik il-ƀaarʒa ƀil-ƀeel.*
January - *kaanuun iθ-θaani.*
Japan - *yaabaan.*
Japanese - **1.** *yaabaani* pl. *-iyyiin.* He's a Japanese. *huwwa yaabaani.* **2.** *yaabaani**. I bought a beautiful Japanese radio. *stireet raadyo yaabaani ʒilu.*
jar - *šiiša* pl. *šiyaaš, šiyaš.* I want a jar of jam. *ʔariid šiišat imraḅḅa.*
to jar - *hazz (i hazz) n-, xaḍḍ (u xaḍḍ) n-.* Don't jar the table when you sit down. *la-thizz il-meez min tigƐud.*
jasmine - *yaasmiin.* The jasmine is a common flower in Iraq. *l-yaasmiin warid šaayiƐ ƀil-Ɛiraaq.*
jaundice - *marḍ iṣ-ṣufaar, ʔabu ṣ-ṣufra, ṣ-ṣafar.*
jaw - *fačč* pl. *fčuuč.* He broke his jaw. *kisar fačča.*
jawbone - *Ɛaḍum* (pl. *Ɛḍaam*) *fačč.* Samson killed a whole lot of guys with an ass's jawbone. *šamšuun qital naas ihwaaya b-Ɛaḍum fačč maal iʒmaar.*
jealous - *ġayyaar.* She's jealous because you have a new coat. *hiyya ġayyaara li-ʔan Ɛindič qappuuṭ jidiid.*
to be jealous - *ġaar (a).* He became jealous of me because I've got a car. *ġaar minni li-ʔan Ɛindi sayyaara.*
jealousy - *ġiira.* I'm dying of jealousy since he got the new position. *l-ġiira gaaƐid itmawwitni, min ʔaxaδ waḍiifta j-jidiida.*
jeep - *sayyaara* (pl. *-aat*) *jiib.*
to **jeer** - *sixar (a suxriyya).* The audience jeered at the singer. *l-mutafarrijiin sixraw imnil-muġanni.*
jelly - *mraḅḅa.* I want rolls and jelly. *ʔariid sammuun w-mraḅḅa.*
to **jeopardize** - *Ɛarraḍ (i taƐriiḍ) t- lil-xaṭar.* The incident jeopardized his future. *l-ʒaadiθ Ɛarraḍ mustaqbala lil-xaṭar.*
jeopardy - *xaṭar.* He put his own life in jeopardy. *Ɛarraḍ ʒayaata lil-xaṭar.*

jerboa - *jarbuuƐ* pl. *jaraabiiƐ.*
Jericho - *ʔariiʒa.*
jerk - *rajja* pl. *-aat.* The train stopped with a jerk. *l-qiṭaar wugaf ib-rajja.*
to jerk - *Ɛatt (i Ɛatt) n-, nitaš (i natiš) n-.* She jerked the book out of his hand. *Ɛattat l-iktaab min ʔiida.*
jerry-built - *binaaʔ šallaali.* Those houses are jerry-built. *haay l-ibyuut binaaʔha šallaali.*
Jerusalem - *l-qudus.*
Jesus - *Ɛiisa.*
jet - *naffaaθa.* We took a jet plane from Paris to Beirut. *ʔaxaδna ṭiyyaara naffaaθa min ḅaariis ʔila beeruut.*
jet-black - *(ʔaswad) miθl il-faʒam, ʔaswad ṭoox.* Her hair is jet-black. *šaƐarha miθl il-faʒam.*
Jew - *yahuudi* pl. *-iyyiin.* She is a Jew. *hiyya yahuudiyya.*
jewel - **1.** *jawhara* pl. *-aat, jawaahir* coll. *jawhar.* The dancer had a jewel in her navel. *r-raaqiṣa ʒaaṭṭa jawhara b-ṣurratha.* **2.** *ʒajra* pl. *-aat, ʔaʒjaar* coll. *ʒajar.* My watch has seventeen jewels. *saaƐati biiha ṣḅaaṭaƐaš ʒajar.*
jewels - *jawaahir, mujawharaat.* She pawned her jewels. *rihnat jawaahirha.*
jeweler - *ṣaayiġ* pl. *ṣiyyaaġ, jawharči* pl. *-iyya.* I'm looking for a jeweler to fix my ring. *da-adawwur-li fadd ṣaayiġ yṣalliʒ il-miʒbas maali.*
jewelry - *mujawharaat.* Did you see her jewelry? *šifit mujawharaatha?*
Jewish - *yhuudi**.
to **jibe** - *nṭubaq (u nṭibaaq).* This doesn't jibe with what I saw. *haay ma-tinṭubuq Ɛala lli šifta ʔaani.*
Jidda - *jidda.*
jiffy - *laʒḍa* pl. *-aat.* It'll only take a jiffy. *ma-taaxuδ ġeer fadd laʒḍa.*
to **jiggle** - *xaδδ (u xaδδ) n-, ʒazz (i ʒazz) n-.* Stop jiggling the table. *ƀass Ɛaad itxuδδ il-meez.*
to **jilt** - *xidaƐ (a xadiƐ) n-.* His fiancee jilted him. *xaṭiibta xidƐata.*
jitters - *hawas, hwaas.* He's got the jitters. *Ɛinda hawas.*
job - *šaġla* pl. *-aat* coll. *šuġul; Ɛamal.* I'm looking for a job. *da-adawwur Ɛala šuġuḷ.* -- It wasn't an easy job to persuade her. *ʔiqnaaƐha ma-čaan fadd Ɛamal sahil.* — I've got several jobs to do today. *Ɛindi Ɛiddat šaġlaat asawwiiha l-yoom.* -- It isn't my job to tell him that. *ʔaani muu šuġḷi ʔagul-la haay.*
jockey - *jaaki* pl. *-iyya.*

to **join** - **1.** *nḍamm (a nḍimaam) l-, ntima (i ntimaaʔ) l-, štirak (i štiraak) b-.* When did he join the party? *šwakit inḍamm lil-ʒizib?* **2.** *nḍamm (i), ntima (i), ltiʒaq (i ltiʒaaq).* I'm joining the Army. *raʒ-anḍamm lij-jeeš.* **3.** *šakkal (i taškiil) t-.* Would you like to join us? *triid itšakkil wiyyaana?* **4.** *rakkab (u tarkiib) t-, šakkal (i).* How do you join these two parts? *šloon itrakkub haaδool il-qismeen?* **5.** *ttiṣal (u ttiṣaal) b-.* Where does this road join the main road? *ween haaδa ṭ-ṭariiq yittiṣil biṭ-ṭariiq ir-raʔiisi?* **6.** *šaarak (i mušaaraka), stirak (i štiraak).* Everybody joined in the singing. *l-kull šaarkaw bil-ġina.* **7.** *waʒʒad (i tawʒiid) t-.* Let's join forces. *xalli nwaʒʒid juhuudna.*
joint - **1.** *mafṣal* pl. *mafaaṣil.* All my joints ache. *kull mafaaṣli toojaƐni.* **2.** *muštarak.* The land is their joint property. *l-ʔaraaḍi muštaraka beenaathum.*
out of joint - *mafṣuux, maxluuƐ.* My knee's out of joint. *rukubti mafṣuuxa.*
to throw out of joint - *xilaƐ (a xaliƐ) n-, fiṣax (i faṣix).* I threw my shoulder out of joint. *xilaƐit čitfi.*
joke - **1.** *nukta* pl. *nukaat.* I've heard that joke before. *ʔaani smaƐit han-nukta gabuḷ.* -- I played a joke on him. *sawweet bii nukta.* or ***qašmarit Ɛalee.* -- He tried to make a joke of the whole thing. *ʒaawal yigḷub il-mawḍuuƐ ʔila nukta.* **2.** *šaqa.* That's carrying the joke too far. *ṭawwaxitha biš-šaqa.* or *riʒit biš-šaqa zaayid.* -- He can't take a joke. *ma-yitʒammal šaqa.*
to joke - *tšaaqa (a šaqa).* This time I'm not joking. *hal-marra ma-da-atšaaqa.* -- All joking aside, are you really going? *ʔitruk iš-šaqa hassa, ṣudug ʔinta raayiʒ?*

to tell jokes - *nakkat (i tankiit).* He's always telling jokes. *huwwa ynakkit Ɛala ṭuul.*
jolly - *mariʒ* pl. *-iin, bašuuš* pl. *-iin.* He's always jolly. *huwwa daaʔiman mariʒ.*
jolt - *rajja* pl. *-aat.* The car stopped with a sudden jolt. *s-sayyaara wugfat ib-rajja mufaajʔa.*
to jolt - **1.** *rajj (i rajj) n-.* The explosion jolted the whole house. *l-infijaar rajj il-ƀeet kulla.* **2.** *hazz (i hazz) n-.* The news jolted us. *l-axbaar hazzatna.*
Jordan - *l-ʔardun, l-ʔurdun.* I'm going to Jordan tomorrow. *ʔaani raayiʒ lil-ʔardun baačir.*
Jordanian - **1.** *ʔarduni* pl. *-iyyiin.* Many Jordanians live in Kuwait. *hwaaya ʔarduniyyiin yƐiišuun bil-kuweet.* **2.** *ʔarduni**. The Jordanian embassy was bombed last night. *s-sifaara l-ʔarduniyya nnisfat il-baarʒa bil-leel.*
to **jostle** - *difaƐ (a dafiƐ) n-.* He jostled me as he went by. *huwwa difaƐni min marr min yammi.*
to **jot down** - *qayyad (i taqyiid) t-.* I jotted her telephone number down. *qayyadit raqam it-talafoon maalha.*
journalist - *ṣuʒufi* pl. *-iyyiin.*
journey - *riʒla* pl. *-aat, safra* pl. *-aat.*
jovial - *mariʒ, bašuuš.* There is a jovial fellow! *huwwa kulliš mariʒ!*
joy - *faraʒ* pl. *ʔafraaʒ.* Her eyes were beaming with joy. *Ɛyuunha čaanat tilmaƐ imnil-faraʒ.*
joyful - *saarr, mufriʒ.* It was a joyful occasion. *čaanat munaasaba saarra.*
Judaism - *d-diyaana l-yahuudiyya.*
judge - **1.** *ʒaakim* pl. *ʒukkaam, qaaḍi* pl. *quḍaat.* When is the judge going to pass sentence? *šwakit il-ʒaakim raʒ-yinṭuq bil-ʒukum.* -- The judge ruled that the divorce was valid. *l-qaaḍi Ɛtubar iṭ-ṭalaaq ṣaʒiiʒ.* **2.** *ʒakam* pl. *-iyya, ʒaakim* pl. *ʒukkaam.* The judges awarded his picture the first prize. *l-ʒakamiyya inṭoo j-jaaʔiza l-ʔuula Ɛala ṣuurta.* -- The judge said the ball fell outside. *l-ʒakam gaal iṭ-ṭooba ṭilƐat xaarij.*
**You be the judge of that! *ʔinta qarrir!*
**He's as sober as a judge. *huwwa kulliš ṣaaʒi.*
**She's not a good judge of human nature. *ma-tigdar tuʒkum Ɛala ṭabiiƐat in-naas.*
to judge - **1.** *ʒikam (u ʒukum) n- Ɛala.* Don't judge him too harshly. *la-tuʒkum Ɛalee bil-muuzeen.* **2.** *qaas (i qiyaas), ʒikam (u ʒakim) n- Ɛala.* Never judge others by yourself. *la-tqiis in-naas Ɛala nafsak.* or *la-tuʒkum Ɛan-naas ʒasab iƐtiqaadak bass.*
**To judge by his face he isn't very enthusiastic. *min wujja mbayyin ma-mitʒammis.*
judgment - **1.** *taqdiir.* You can rely on his judgment.

tigdar tiƐtimid Ɛala taqdiira. 2. ʒukma pl. ʔaʒkaam, qaraar pl. -aat. The president of the court will hand down his judgment today. raʔiis il-maʒkama raʒ-yiṣdur ʒukma l-yoom. -- Don't make snap judgments. la-tuṣdir ʔaʒkaam sariiƐa. — He showed good judgment. kaan qaraara ʒakiim. 3. raʔi pl. ʔaaraaʔ. In my judgment you're doing the wrong thing. b-raʔyi ʔinta gaaƐid itsawwi ġalaṭ.

judicial - qaanuuni*. Judicial procedures are very involved. l-ʔijraaʔaat il-qaanuuniyya kulliš muƐaqqada.

judicious - muwaffaq. He made a judicious selection. čaan ixtiyaara muwaffaq.

jug - jarra pl. -aat. The women carried water jugs on their heads. n-niswaan šaalaw jarraat il-mayy Ɛala ruushum.

juice - Ɛaṣiir. I'd like a glass of orange juice, please. ʔariid iglaaṣ Ɛaṣiir purtaqaal, min faḍlak.

juicy - rayyaan, malyaan mayy. These oranges are very juicy. hal-purtuqaalaat kulliš rayyaana.

July - tammuuz.

jump - 1. qafza pl. -aat, ṭafra pl. -aat. His jump broke the national record. qafizta kisrat ir-raqam il-waṭani. 2. gamza pl. -aat. With one jump he was over the wall. b-gamza wiʒda Ɛubar il-ʒaayiṭ.

**You don't want him to get the jump on you, do you? ma-triida ysibqak, tamaam?

to jump - 1. ṭufar (u ṭafur), gumaz (u gamuz). How high can you jump? šgadd Ɛilu tigdar tuṭfur? -- He jumped off the bus before it stopped. gumaz imnil-paaṣ gabuḷ-ma yoogaf. 2. giḷab (u gaḷub), Ɛibar (u Ɛabur). We jumped pages seven to twelve. gḷabna min ṣafʒa sabƐa ʔila θnaƐaš. 3. fazz (i tafziiz). He jumped when he heard the noise. fazz min simaƐ iṣ-ṣooṭ.

**He jumped at the offer. qibal il-Ɛariḍ raʔsan. or qibal il-Ɛariḍ ib-lahfa.

**Don't jump to conclusions about things. la-tuʒkum ib-surƐa Ɛal-ʔašyaaʔ.

**The train jumped the track. l-qiṭaar ṭilaƐ imnil-xaṭṭ.

**He can go jump in the lake! xalli yḍibb nafsa biš-šaṭṭ!

to jump around - gammaz (u tgummuz, tagmiiz). Stop jumping around. yikfi Ɛaad itgammuz.

junction - taqaaṭuƐ il-xuṭuuṭ.

June - ʒuzeeraan.

jungle - ġaaba pl. -aat. He was lost in the African jungle. ḍaaƐ ib-ġaabaat ʔafriiqiya.

junior: **She's a junior in college. hiyya ṭaaliba b-ṣaff θaaliθ bil-kulliyya.

junk - 1. qalaaqiil. We'll have to clean the junk out of the storeroom. laazim innaḍḍuf il-qalaaqiil imnil-maxzan. 2. ġaraaḍ. Where did you get that junk? mneen jibit haay il-ġaraaḍ?

to junk - wadda (i twiddi) lis-sikraab. I'm afraid I'll just have to junk that car. ʔaani xaayif aḍṭarr awaddi s-sayyaara lis-sikraab.

jurisdiction - xtiṣaaṣ. The matter's outside my jurisdiction. l-qaḍiyya xaarij ixtiṣaaṣi.

jurist - faqiih pl. fuqahaaʔ.

jury - muʒallifiin.

just - 1. Ɛaadil. That's a just punishment. haaḍi Ɛuquuba Ɛaadila. 2. mustaqiim, Ɛaadil. He is a just man. huwwa rajul mustaqiim. 3. hassa, hastaww-. I just arrived. hassa wuṣalit. or hastawwni wuṣalit. 4. biḍ-ḍabuṭ, tamaaman. That's just the word I meant. haay hiyya l-kalima illi ʔariidha biḍ-ḍabuṭ. -- That's just what I wanted. haaḍa tamaaman miθil-ma ridit. or **haaḍa lli ridta! -- He's just like his father. huwwa biḍ-ḍabuṭ miθil ʔabuu. -- He is just as lazy as his brother. huwwa kaslaan miθl axuu biḍ-ḍabuṭ. -- It was just the other way around. hiyya čaanat tamaaman bil-Ɛakis. -- That takes just as long. haay taaxuḍ nafs il-wakit biḍ-ḍabuṭ. -- Just what do you mean? š-tiƐni biḍ-ḍabuṭ? 5. tamaaman. The table was just covered with dust. l-meez čaan imġaṭṭa bit-tiraab tamaaman. 6. mujarrad, bass. He's just a little boy. huwwa mujarrad ṭifil. -- I just said one word, and he got mad. gilit čilma wiʒda bass w-ziƐal. — I just want one glass of water. ʔariid igḷaas waaʒid mayy bass. 7. duub. You just made it to class on time. duub wuṣalit liṣ-ṣaff Ɛal-wakit. 8. Ɛal-ʒaaffa, duub. You just passed the exam. ʔinta nijaʒit bil-imtiʒaan Ɛal-ʒaaffa.

**That's just the way it is! l-ʔumuur hiiči maašya!

**There's just nothing you can do about it. kullši ma-tigdar itsawwi.

**Just a minute! fadd daqiiqa!

**Just what did you mean by that crack? š-tuqṣud ib-haay il-mulaaḍaḍa?

**Just for that I won't do it. l-has-sabab ʔaani ma-asawwiiha.

just right - Ɛal-maraam. The water is just right. l-mayy Ɛal-maraam. -- My coffee's just right. gahuuti Ɛal-maraam.

justice - nṣaaf, Ɛadaala. Don't expect justice from him. la-titwaqqaƐ ʔay inṣaaf minna.

to do justice - niṣaf (i naṣif) n-, Ɛidal (i Ɛadil) n-. You're not doing him justice. ʔinta ma-da-tinṣif wiyyaa.

**The picture doesn't do you justice. ṣ-ṣuura ma-tišbahak tamaaman. or ṣ-ṣuura muu ʒilwa miθlak.

justifiable - ʔila mubarrir. I think this expenditure is justifiable. ʔaƐtiqid hal-maṣruuf ʔila mubarrir.

justified - muʒiqq. I think you were perfectly justified in doing that. ʔaḍunn innak činit kulliš muʒiqq ib-Ɛamalak. — You were perfectly justified in asking for more pay. činit tamaaman muʒiqq ib-ṭalabak ib-ziyaadat raatbak.

to **justify** - barrar (i tabriir) t-. She tried to justify her actions. ʒaawalat itbarrir ʔaƐmaalha.

K

Kaaba - l-kaƐba.

kangaroo - kanġar pl. kanaaġir.

keen - 1. ʒaadd. He has a keen mind. huwwa ʒaadd iḍ-ḍakaaʔ. — His sense of smell is keen. ʒaassat iš-šamm maalta ʒaadda. -- This knife has a keen edge. ʒaašyat has-siččiina ʒaadda. 2. mitʒammis pl. -iin. I'm not so keen on that. ʔaani muu kulliš mitʒammis ilha. or **ma-Ɛindi walaƐ bii.

to **keep** - 1. ʒtifaḍ (u ʒtifaaḍ) b-. May I keep this picture? ʔagdar aʒtufuḍ ib-haay iṣ-ṣuura? -- If the team wins three times in a row, they get to keep the cup. l-firqa ʔiḍa tuġlub itlaθ marraat mitataalya tigdar tiʒtufuḍ bil-kaʔis. -- He keeps the company's books. huwwa yiʒtifiḍ ib-sijilaat iš-šarika. 2. biqa (a baqi), ḍall (i ḍall). The policeman asked us to keep moving. š-šurṭi ṭilab min Ɛidna ʔan nibqa maašiin. -- He kept talking all the time. ḍall yiʒči l-wakit kulla. -- Keep calm! ʔibqu haadʔiin. or ʔihdaʔu. -- Can't you keep quiet? ma-tigdar iṭḍill saakit? or ma-tigdar tiskut? -- He's keeping me company. huwwa yibqa wiyyaaya. — This milk won't keep till tomorrow. hal-ʒaliib ma-yitʒammal yibqa l-baačir. 3. xalla (i taxliya, txilli). Sorry to have kept you waiting. mitʔassif li-ʔan xalleetak tintiḍir. -- Keep to the right. xalliik Ɛal-yimna. or ʔibqa Ɛal-yimna. -- Keep me posted. xalliini Ɛala Ɛilim Ɛala ṭuul. -- Keep that in mind! xalliiha b-fikrak! 4. ḍamm (u ḍamm) n-, ʒtifaḍ (i ʒtifaaḍ) b-, ʒufaḍ (u ʒafuḍ). Please keep this for me. min faḍlak ḍumm-li-yyaaha. or rajaaʔan iʒtifiḍ-li biiha. 5. Ɛaṭṭal (i taƐṭiil) t-. I won't keep you very long. ma-raʒ-aƐaṭṭlak ihwaaya. 6. ḍamm(u), kitam (i katim), xabba (i taxbiya, txibbi). Can you keep a secret? tigdar iṭḍumm sirr? -- He kept his real intentions from me for quite a while. xabba qaṣda l-ʒaqiiqi mudda ṭuwiila Ɛanni. 7. baqqa (i tabqiya) t-, ʒtifaḍ (i ʒtifaaḍ), xalla (i txilli). Shall I keep your dinner warm? triidni abaqqi b-ʔaklak ʒaarr? 8. ḍibaṭ (u ḍabuṭ). Does your watch keep good time? saaƐtak tiḍbuṭ il-wakit zeen? -- Keep your temper! ʔuḍbuṭ aƐṣaabak. or **haddi nafsak. 9. wufa (i wafaaʔ, wufa). I rely on you to keep your word. ʔaani ʔaƐtimid Ɛaleek ʔan toofi b-waƐdak. 10. rabba (i tarbiya). We've been keeping chickens for the last three years. ṣaar-inna nrabbi dijaaj il-muddat itlaθ isniin. 11. daar (i ʔidaara) ʔumuur. She keeps house for her uncle. hiyya tdiir ʔumuur beet Ɛammha.

**Everytime we kick him out, he keeps coming back.

kull-ma nṭurda yirjaƐ.
**His wife just found out he's been keeping a mistress. *marta hassa Ɛurfat Ɛinda Ɛašiiqa.*
to keep away - 1. *btiƐad (i btiƐaad).* Keep away from that radio! *btiƐid Ɛan haaδa r-raadyo!* **2.** *biƐad (i ʔibƐaad).* Keep the children away from the fire. *ʔibƐid ij-jihhaal Ɛan in-naar.*
to keep from - 1. *minaƐ (a maniƐ) n- min.* Nobody can keep you from going there. *maẓẓad yigdar yimnaƐak min ʔan itruuẓ ihnaak.* **2.** *baṭṭal (i tabṭiil) min, btiƐad (i btiƐaad) Ɛan.* He can't keep from drinking. *ma-yigdar ybaṭṭil imniš-šurub.*
**to keep off - ** *btiƐad (i btiƐaad) Ɛan, waxxar (i tawxiir) min.* Keep off the grass! *btiƐid Ɛan il-θayyal!* -- Keep your hands off that car! *waxxir ʔiidak min has-sayyaara!* or *la-txalli ʔiidak Ɛala has-sayyaara!*
**to keep on - ** *ḍall (i ḍall), buqa (a baqaaʔ), stamarr (i stimraar) b-.* We kept on walking. *ḍalleena nimši.* -- Keep on trying. *stamirr bil-muẓaawala.* -- Keep right on talking. *stamirr bil-kalaam.*
to keep out - 1. *minaƐ (a maniƐ).* Ordinary glass keeps out utraviolet rays. *z-zujaaj il-Ɛaadi yimnaƐ il-ʔašiƐƐa maa wara l-banafsajiyya.* -- This isn't a beautiful raincoat, but in any event, it keeps out the rain. *haaδa muu qappuuṭ muṭar laṭiif, laakin Ɛala kull ẓaal, yimnaƐ il-muṭar.* **2.** *btiƐad (i btiƐaad) Ɛan.* Keep out of my garden! *btiƐid Ɛan ẓadiiqti!* -- It's his affair. You'd better keep out of it! *haaδa šuġla. ʔaẓsan-lak ibtiƐid Ɛanna!* **3.** *biƐad (i ʔibƐaad).* I'll try to keep him out of trouble. *raẓ-aẓaawil abiƐda Ɛan il-mašaakil.* -- Keep him out of my way! *ʔibiƐda Ɛan ṭariiqi.*
to keep up - 1. *stimarr (i stimraar) Ɛala.* Keep it up and see where it gets you! *stamirr Ɛaleeha w-šuuf išloon raẓ-titʔaδδa!* **2.** *ẓaafaḍ (u muẓaafuḍa) Ɛala.* How much does it cost you per month to keep up your car? *šgadd ykallifak biš-šahar ẓatta tẓaafuḍ Ɛala sayyaartak?* **3.** *biqa (a baqaaʔ) Ɛala.* Keep up the good work. *ʔibqa Ɛala šuġlak iz-zeen.* **4.** *laẓẓag (i talẓiig) t- b-.* I can't keep up with you when you dictate so fast. *ma-agdar ʔalaẓẓig biik min timli Ɛalayya b-surƐa.* -- It's hard for me to keep up with the others in the class. *yiṣƐab Ɛalayya alaẓẓig bil-ʔaaxariin biṣ-ṣaff.* -- I can't keep up with my work. *ma-da-agdar alaẓẓig axaḷḷiṣ šuġḷi.*
keepsake - *tiδkaar* pl. *-aat.* She gave him her ring as a keepsake. *nṭata miẓbasha ka-tiδkaar.*
kernel - *ẓabbaaya* pl. *-aat* coll. *ẓabb; ẓabba* pl. *-aat* coll. *ẓabb.*
kerosene - *nafuṭ ʔabyaḍ.*
kettle - *quuri* pl. *quwaari, kitli* pl. *-iyyaat.* The water in the kettle is boiling. *l-maay da-yigḷi bil-quuri.*
**That's a pretty kettle of fish! *haaδa mawqif muzƐij!* or *hiyya leeṣa!* or *ṣaayra xabiiṣa!*
key - 1. *miftaaẓ* pl. *mafaatiiẓ.* I've lost the key to my room. *ḍayyaƐit miftaaẓ ġurufti.* -- That was the key to the mystery. *haaδa čaan miftaaẓ il-lagiz.* **2.** *ẓaruf* pl. *ẓuruuf.* One of the keys on my typewriter gets stuck. *waaẓid min ẓuruuf it-taabiƐa maalti yšakkil.* **3.** *muhimm.* He holds a key position in the government. *huwwa Ɛinda markaz muhimm bil-ẓukuuma.* **4.** *daliil, ʔiiḍaaẓ.* The key to the map is in the right-hand corner. *daliil il-xariiṭa biz-zuwiyya l-yimna.*
**off key - ** *našaaz.* Who's singing off key? *minu da-yġanni našaaz?*
keyhole - *beet* (pl. *byuut*) *miftaaẓ.*
khaki - *xaaki.* This merchant doesn't sell anything but khaki. *hat-taajir ma-ybiiƐ ġeer xaaki.*
Khartoum - *xarṭuum.*
kick - 1. *čillaaq* pl. *člaaliiq, dafra* pl. *-aat.* I felt like giving him a good hard kick. *Ɛijabni aḍurba čillaaq qawi.* **2.** *rafsa* pl. *-aat, zagṭa* pl. *-aat, dafra* pl. *-aat.* The horse's kick broke his leg. *rafsat l-iẓṣaan kisrat rijla.* **3.** *radda* pl. *-aat.* The kick of a rifle can break your collar bone. *raddat il-bunduqiyya yimkin tiksir Ɛaḍm it-turquwa maalak.* **4.** *walaƐ, waahis.* He gets a big kick out of sports. *Ɛinda walaƐ bir-riyaaḍa.*
to kick - 1. *ḍirab (u ḍarib) n-.* Kick the ball! *ʔiḍrub it-tooba!* **2.** *rifas (u rafus) n-.* I hope this horse doesn't kick. *ʔinšaaḷḷa haaδa l-iẓṣaan ma-yirfus.* **3.** *tšakka (a tašakki).* He kicks about everything. *yitšakka min kullši.*
**I can't kick. *Ɛal-aḷḷah!*
**to kick out - ** *ṭirad (u ṭarid) n-.* I nearly kicked him out of the house. *taqriiban ṭiradta mnil-beet.*
kicks - *wansa.* What do you do for kicks around here? *š-itsawwi lil-wansa b-hal-manṭiqa?*
kid - 1. *jadi* pl. *jidyaan.* The goat had two kids. *l-maƐza Ɛidha jadyeen.* **2.** *walad* pl. *ʔawlaad, wilid; ṭifil* pl. *ʔaṭfaal, jaahil* pl. *jihhaal.* We'll feed the kids first. *nṭaƐƐum il-wilid gabuḷ.* -- Don't act like a kid! *la-titṣarraf miθl il-ʔaṭfaal.* **3.** *jilid maƐaz.* I bought some kid gloves. *štireet ičfuuf jilid maƐaz.*
**You have to handle her with kid gloves. *laazim itƐaamilha b-riqqa.*
**to kid - ** *tšaaqa (a tašaaqi), mizaẓ (a maziẓ), tmaazaẓ (a maziẓ).* I'm only kidding. *ʔaani da-atšaaqa.*
to **kidnap -** *xiṭaf (u xaṭuf) n-.* He kidnapped his sweetheart from her family. *xiṭaf ẓabiibta min ʔahilha.*
kidney - *kilya* pl. *-aat.* He's having trouble with his kidneys. *kilyaata toojƐa.* **2.** *čilwa* pl. *čalaawi.* We have kidneys for supper. *Ɛidna čalaawi lil-Ɛaša l-yoom.*
kill - *qatil, katil.* The wolves closed in on the sheep for the kill. *δ-δiyaab ṭubgaw Ɛal-xaruuf il-qatla.* **2.** *fariisa* pl. *-aat, faraayis.* The lion returned to its kill the next day. *l-ʔasad rijaƐ il-fariista bil-yoom iθ-θaani.*
to kill - 1. *kital (u katil) n-, qital (u qatil) n-.* Be careful with that car, or you'll kill somebody. *diir baalak min has-sayyaara, la-truuẓ tuktul ʔaẓẓad.* -- Her son was killed in action. *ʔibinha nqital bil-maƐraka.* **2.** *ṭaffa (i taṭfiya).* Be careful, or you'll kill the engine. *diir baalak, la-truuẓ iṭṭaffi l-makiina.* **3.** *qiḍa (i qaḍi) n- Ɛala.* I'll give you something to kill the pain. *ʔanṭiik duwa ẓatta yiqḍi Ɛal-ʔalam.* **4.** *kital (i katil), ḍayyaƐ (i tḍiyyiƐ).* We played cards to kill time. *lƐabna waraq ẓatta niktil wakit.*
**I killed two birds with one stone. *ḍrabit Ɛaṣfuureen ib-ẓajar waaẓid.*
killer - *qaatil* pl. *-iin, qatala.* The killer escaped. *l-qaatil hirab.*
killing - *qatil, katil.* We're trying to stop this useless killing. *nẓaawil inwagguf haaδa l-qatil illi ma-bii natiija.*
kilogram - *keelu* pl. *uwaat.* Give me three kilograms of sugar, please. *nṭiini tlaθ keeluwaat šakar, min faḍlak.*
kilometer - *kiilumatir* pl. *-aat.* Our car does more than a hundred kilometers an hour. *sayyaaratna ṭṭalliƐ ʔakθar min miit kiilumatir bis-saaƐa.*
kind - 1. *nooƐ* pl. *ʔanwaaƐ, jins* pl. *ʔajnaas.* This building is the only one of its kind. *haay il-binaaya hiyya l-waẓiida min nooƐha.* -- We have only two kinds of coffee. *Ɛidna nooƐeen bass imnil-gahwa.* -- What kind of car is that? *šinu nooƐ has-sayyaara?* **2.** *laṭiif.* She is a very kind person. *hiyya šaxṣiyya laṭiifa.* -- That was a kind thing to do. *haaδa čaan šii laṭiif ʔan itsawwi.*
**Would you be so kind as to mail this letter for me? *ʔiδa tismaẓ itdizz haaδa l-maktuub bil-bariid.*
**kind of - ** *b-nawƐ min.* I felt kind of sorry for him. *šiƐarit ib-nooƐ imnil-ʔasaf ittijaaha.*
kindergarten - *rawḍat aṭfaal.*
to **kindle -** *šiƐal (i šaƐil) n-.* Were you able to kindle a fire? *gidarit tišƐil in-naar?*
kindling - *Ɛuwad.* We could not find kindling to start a fire. *ma-gdarna nilgi Ɛuwad nišƐil biiha naar.*
kindly - 1. *šafuuq.* Her grandmother is a kindly old lady. *jiddiyatha mrayya šafuuqa.* **2.** *b-luṭuf.* She received us kindly. *staqbilatna b-luṭuf.* **3.** *rajaaʔan, min faḍlak.* Kindly stop when your time is up. *rajaaʔan ʔoogaf min yintihi l-wakit.* -- Kindly mind your own business! *min faḍlak, la-titdaxxal.*
kindness - *faḍil* pl. *ʔafḍaal, luṭuf* pl. *ʔalṭaaf.* I appreciate your kindness. *ʔaqaddir faḍlak.*
king - 1. *malik* pl. *muluuk.* Their king died two weeks ago. *malikhum maat min muddat usbuuƐeen.* **2.** *šaayib* pl. *šiyyaab, daaġli* pl. *-iyyaat.* I've got three kings. *Ɛindi tlaθ šiyyaab.*
kingdom - *mamlaka* pl. *mamaalik.* The Kingdom of Jordan was created after the First World War. *mamlakat il-ʔardun itʔassasat baƐad il-ẓarb il-Ɛaalamiyya l-ʔuula.*
kinship - *qaraaba, garaaba.* Kinship ties are very important among the Arabs. *ṣilat il-qaraaba muhimma jiddan Ɛind il-Ɛarab.*

Kirkuk - *karkuuk.*
kiss - *boosa* pl. *-aat, qubla* pl. *-aat.* Give me a kiss. *nṭiini boosa!*
to kiss - *baas (u boos) n-.* He kissed him on both checks. *baasa min ixduuda.*
kitchen - *maṭbax* pl. *maṭaabux.* Do you mind if we eat in the kitchen? *εindak maaniε ʔiδa naakul bil-maṭbax?*
kitchenware - *ʔadawaat ṭabax.* This store sells kitchenware. *haaδa l-maxzan ybiiε ʔadawaat ṭabax.*
kite - *ṭiyyaara* pl. *-aat.* The boys are out flying kites. *l-wilid da-yṭayyiruun ṭiyyaaraat.*
**Aw, go fly a kite! *ruuḥ dawwur-lak šaġḷa!*
kitten - *farix* (pl. *fruux) bazzuuna.* Our cat has some little kittens. *bazzuunatna εidha fruux iṣġaar.*
knack - **1.** *mahaara.* He has a knack for photography. *εinda mahaara ʔaxδ it-taṣaawiir.* **2.** *sirr.* Now I've got the knack of it. *hassa εraft is-sirr.*
knapsack - *ḥaqiiba* pl. *ḥaqaaʔib.* The boy scouts carried their food in knapsacks. *l-kaššaafa ḥimlaw ʔakilhum ib-ḥaqaaʔib εala δ̣aharhum.*
to **knead** - *εijan (i εajin) n-.* You have to knead the dough thoroughly. *laazim tiεjin il-εajiin zeen.*
knee - *rukba* pl. *-aat, rikab.* My knee hurts. *rukubti toojaεni.*
kneecap - *ṣaabuunat* (pl. *-aat) rijil.*
kneel - **1.** *burak (u baruk).* The camel knelt while they tied the load on. *j-jimal burak lamma kaanaw yšidduun il-ḥimil εalee.* **2.** *θina (i θani) rukbat~.* The soldiers knelt and fired. *j-jinuud θinaw rukbaathum w-ʔaṭlaqaw in-naar.*
knife - *siččiin* pl. *sačaačiin.* He cut himself with a knife. *jiraḥ nafsa bis-siččiin.*
knight - *faras* pl. *-aat.* I'll take the pawn with the knight. *raḥ-aaxuδ ij-jundi bil-faras.*
to **knit** - **1.** *ḥaak (u ḥook, ḥiyaaka) n-.* Did you knit these gloves, Mary? *ḥikti č-čufuuf, maryam?* **2.** *liḥam (a ltiḥaam), ltiḥam (i ltiḥaam).* It took a long time for the bone to knit. *l-εaδ̣am ʔaxaδ wakit hwaaya ḥatta liḥam.*
knitting - *ḥyaaka.* Did you notice where she left her knitting? *šifit ween xallat iḥyaakatha?*
knob - **1.** *zirr* pl. *zraar, dugma* pl. *dugam.* The maid broke one of the knobs off the radio. *l-xaadma kisrat waaḥid min izraar ir-raadyo.* **2.** *yadda* pl. *-aat.* The door knob still has to be polished. *yaddat il-baab yinraad-ilha talmiiε.*
knock - *dagg.* Did you hear the knock at the door? *simaεit id-dagg εal-baab?*
**Can you find the knock in the engine? *tigdar itšuuf leeš il-makiina tdugg?*
to knock - **1.** *dagg (u dagg).* Someone's knocking at the door. *waaḥid da-ydugg εal-baab.* -- Please knock before you come in. *min faḍlak, dugg il-baab gabuḷ-ma tidxul.* -- When I drive uphill the engine knocks. *min aṣεad εat-tall, il-makiina tdugg.* **2.** *ntiqad (i ntiqaad), ḥiča (i ḥači) εala.* He's always knocking American capitalism. *haaδa daaʔiman yintiqid ir-raasmaaliyya l-ʔameerkiyya.* **3.** *waggaε (i tawgiiε) t-.* I knocked the knife out of his hand. *waggaεit is-saččiina min ʔiida.*
to knock around - *daar (u dawaraan).* He's knocked around all over the world. *huwwa daayir id-dinya kullha.*
**She's been knocked around a lot. *šaafat ṣuεuubaat ihwaaya b-ḥayaatha.*
to knock down - *waggaε (i tawgiiε) t-.* He knocked him down with his fist. *waggaεa b-ḍarbat jimεa.* -- Be careful not to knock anything down. *diir baalak la-twaggiε šii.*
to knock off - **1.** *waggaε (i tawgiiε) t-, ṭayyar (i taṭyiir) t-.* He nearly knocked my hat off of my head. *taqriiban waggaε iš-šafqa min raasi.* **2.** *xiṣam (i xaṣum), nazzal (i tanziil).* He knocked off ten dinars from the bill. *xiṣam εašr idnaaniir imnil-qaaʔima.* **3.** *xaḷḷaṣ (i taxliiṣ) t-.* We knocked off work at 6 o'clock. *xaḷḷaṣna š-šuġuḷ saaεa sitta.*
**I'll knock your block off! *ʔaḍurbak ḍarba tiksir raasak!*
**All right, knock it off! *zeen hassa, baṭṭlu!* or *zeen hassa, bass εaad!*
to knock out - **1.** *dammar (u tadmiir) t-.* The bomb knocked out the radio station. *l-qumbula dammirat maḥaṭṭat l-ʔiδaaεa.* **2.** *qiḍa (i) εala.* He hit him hard and knocked him out. *ḍuraba ḍarba qawiyya w-qiḍa εalee.*
to knock over - **1.** *giḷab (u gaḷub) n-.* Who knocked the pail over? *minu giḷab iṣ-ṣaṭil?* **2.** *waggaε (i tawgiiε) t-.* You almost knocked me over. *taqriiban waggaεitni.*
knocker - *daggaaga* pl. *-aat.* The knocker on our door needs fixing. *daggaagat baabna yinraad-ilha taṣliiḥ.*
knot - **1.** *εugda* pl. *εugad.* Can you untie this knot? *tigdar itfukk haay il-εugda?* -- The board is full of knots. *l-looḥa malyaana εugad.* **2.** *εuqda* pl. *-aat, booṣa* pl. *-aat.* The ship's speed is fifteen knots. *s-safiina surεatha xumuṣṭaεaš εuqda.*
to knot - **1.** *εigad (u εagid) n-.* Shall I knot the string? *triid aεgud il-xeeṭ?* **2.** *šadd (i šadd) n-, εiqad (i εaqid) n-.* You have to knot the two ends together. *laazim itšidd iṭ-ṭarafeen suwa.*
knotted - **1.** *mεaggad.* The string is all knotted. *l-xeeṭ kulla mεaggad.* or ***l-xeeṭ kulla εugad.* **2.** *mšannaṭ.* The calf muscle in my leg is all knotted up. *paačat rijli mšanniṭa.*
knotty - *ṣaεub, εawiiṣ.* That's a knotty problem. *haaδi muškila ṣaεba.*
to **know** - *εiraf (u maεrifa) n-.* Do you know his address? *tuεruf εinwaana?* -- Do you know Arabic? *tuεruf εarabi?* -- I don't know how to drive a car. *ma-ʔaεruf asuuq sayyaara.* -- Do you know anything about farming? *tuεruf šii εan iz-ziraaεa?* **2.** *dira (i dari) n-, εiraf (u εarif) n-.* I know he's ill. *ʔadri huwwa mariiḍ.*
to let someone know - *xabbar (u ʔixbaar).* I'll let you know tomorrow. *ʔaxabbrak baačir.*
well-known - *mašhuur, maεruuf.* He's a well-known author. *huwwa muʔallif mašhuur.*
know-how - *maεrifa, xibra.* He hasn't the kind of know-how that would qualify him for this job. *ma-εinda l-maεrifa l-kaafiya ḥatta tʔahhila l-haay iš-šaġḷa.*
knowingly - *εan qaṣid.* He wouldn't knowingly cheat us. *ma-yixdaεna εan qaṣid.*
**She looked at him knowingly. *niḍ̣rat-la naḍ̣ra biiha maεna.*
knowledge - *maεrifa, εilim.* His knowledge of Arabic is poor. *maεrifta bil-εarabi qaliila.* -- To my knowledge he's not there. *ḥasab εilmi huwwa muu hnaak.*
**He likes to display his knowledge. *yḥibb yraawi nafsa faahim.*
**Answer to the best of your knowledge. *jaawub šgadd-ma tuεruf.*
knowledgeable: **He's quite knowledgeable on Iraqi history. *maεrifta waasεa b-taariix il-εiraaq.*
known - *maεruuf.* That's a known fact. *haay ḥaqiiqa maεruufa.*
knuckle - *mafṣal* pl. *mafaaṣil.* I skinned the knuckles of my right hand. *jilaxit mafṣal ʔiidi l-yimna.*
**He sat in the coffee shop cracking his knuckles. *giεad bil-gahwa yṭagṭig b-aṣaabεa.*
**You'd better knuckle down and work. *ʔaḥsan-lak loo tibdi tištuġuḷ.*
kohl - *kuḥul.*
Kurd - *kurdi* pl. *ʔakraad.* Most of the Kurds are Muslims. *muεḍ̣am il-ʔakraad muslimiin.*
Kuwait - *l-kuweet.*

L

label - *εalaama* pl. *-aat, maarka* pl. *-aat, leebil* pl. *-aat.* There's no label on this bottle. *ma-aku εalaama εala hal-buṭil.*
to label - *εallam (i tεillim).* Please label those jars for me. *min faḍlak εallim-li haš-šiyaš.*
labor - **1.** *šuġuḷ* pl. *ʔašġaal, εamal* pl. *ʔaεmaal.* Labor alone will cost three hundred dinars. *š-šuġuḷ waḥda ykallif itlaθ miit diinaar.* -- He was sentenced to five years at hard labor. *nḥikam εalee xamis sanawaat bil-ʔašġaal iš-šaaqa.* **2.** *kadd, majhuud.* This task involves a great deal of labor and perseverance. *haš-šaġḷa tiḥtaaj ʔila kadd w-muθaabara.* -- All our labor has been in vain. *kull majhuudna ḍaaε.* **3.** *l-εummaal.* Labor will

never agree to that proposal. *l-ɛummaal ʔabadan ma-ywaafquun ɛala hal-iqtiraaẓ.*
to be in labor - *ṭilgat (a ṭalig).* She was in labor nine hours. *ṣallat tiṭlag tisiɛ saaɛaat.*
laboratory - *muxtabar* pl. *-aat.*
laborer - *ɛaamil* pl. *ɛummaal.*
lace - **1.** *danteel.* I'd like five meters of that lace. *ʔariid xamis amtaar min had-danteel.* **2.** *qiiṭaan* pl. *qyaaṭiin.* I need a pair of shoe laces. *ʔaẓtaaj zooj qiiṭaan il-qundarti.*
to lace - *rakkab (u) qiyaaṭiin.* Wait till I lace my shoes. *ʔintiṣir ʔila ʔan arakkub il-qiyaaṭiin maal qundarti.*
lack - **1.** *naqiṣ.* There's a lack of experts. *ʔaku naqiṣ bil-xubaraaʔ.* **2.** *ɛadam.* He was acquitted for lack of evidence. *firjaw ɛanna l-ɛadam wujuud ʔadilla.* or *ʔaṭliqaw saraaẓa l-ɛadam il-ʔadilla.* -- For lack of anything else to do I went to the movies. *riẓit lis-siinama l-ɛadam wujuud ʔay šii laax asawwii.*
to lack - *niqaṣ (u niqṣaan), ɛaaz (u ɛooz).* Many conveniences are lacking in this hotel. *hal-findiq tinuqṣa hwaaya wasaaʔil raaẓa.* -- I didn't lack anything there. *ma-ɛaazni šii hnaak.*
lad - *walad* pl. *wulid, ṣabi* pl. *ṣabyaan.*
ladder - *daraj* pl. *daraaj.*
ladle - *čamča* pl. *-aat.*
lady - **1.** *mrayya* pl. *-aat, mara* pl. *niswaan, ẓurma* pl. *-aat.* Is that lady his mother? *hal-imrayya ʔumma?* **2.** *sayyida* pl. *-aat.* Ladies and Gentlemen! *sayyidaati w-saadati!* -- Where's the ladies' room? *ween ġurfat is-sayyidaat?*
**We've never had a lady president. *ma-ṣaarat ɛidna raʔiisa ʔabadan.*
to **lag** - *tʔaxxar (a taʔaxxur), txallaf (a taxalluf).* He's always lagging behind the others. *daaʔiman mitʔaxxir ɛan il-baqiyya.*
lake - *buẓayra* pl. *-aat.* We went bathing in the lake. *riẓna nisbaẓ bil-buẓayra.*
lamb - **1.** *ṭili* pl. *ṭilyaan.* Our ewe gave birth to a lamb yesterday. *naɛjatna jaabat ṭili il-baarẓa.* **2.** *laẓam ġanam.* Beef is cheaper than lamb. *laẓm il-hooš ʔarxaṣ min laẓm il-ġanam.* **3.** *quuzi.* Bring me a dish of lamb and rice. *jiib-li maaɛuun quuzi ɛala timman.*
lame - **1.** (m.) *ʔaɛraj* pl. *ɛarjiin,* (f.) *ɛarja* pl. *-aat.* He seems to be lame. *ybayyin ʔaɛraj.* -- He has a lame leg. *ɛinda rijil ɛarja.* **2.** *waahi.* That's a lame excuse. *haay ẓijja waahya.*
lamp - *ḷampa* pl. *-aat.*
lamp shade - *šamsiyya* pl. *-aat.*
lance - *rumuẓ* pl. *rmaaẓ.* His lance broke when he was fighting with it. *nkisar ir-rumuẓ min čaan yẓaarib bii.*
to lance - *fijar (i fajir), ṣurab (u ṣarub) naštar.* The doctor lanced the boil. *ṭ-ṭabiib fijar il-ẓabbaaya.*
land - **1.** *ʔarṣ, gaaɛ, barr.* We were glad to see land again. *firaẓna b-šooft il-ʔarṣ marra lux.* **2.** *ʔarṣ, gaaɛ.* The land here is very fertile. *l-ʔarṣ ihnaa kulliš xaṣba.* **3.** *ʔarṣ* pl. *ʔaraaṣi.* I have a lot of land near Baghdad. *ɛindi ʔaraaṣi hwaaya yamm baġdaad.*
to land - **1.** *nazzal (i tanziil) t-.* He had to land his plane in the desert. *ṣṭarr ynazzil ṭiyyaarta biṣ-ṣaẓraaʔ.* **2.** *nizal (i nzuul).* The plane landed without trouble. *ṭ-ṭiyyaara nizlat bila mašaakil.* **3.** *ṭallaɛ (i ṭṭilliɛ) imnil-ṃayy.* I spent a quarter of an hour before I could land the fish. *ṣrafit rubuɛ saaɛa ẓatta gdarit aṭalliɛ is-simač imnil-ṃayy.* **4.** *nṣabb (a).* He landed in jail for fighting. *nṣabb bis-sijin li-ʔan čaan yitɛaarak.* -- **We nearly landed in jail. *riẓna lil-ẓabis ʔilla šwayya.* **5.** *ẓaṣṣal (i ẓuṣuul) ɛala.* I landed a job after a week of interviews. *ẓaṣṣalit ɛala šuġuḷ baɛad muqaabalaat muddat isbuuɛ.*
landing - **1.** *nizuul.* They lowered the plane's wheels preparing for the landing. *nazzlaw čuruux iṭ-ṭayyaara stiɛdaadan lin-nizuul.* **2.** *ʔinzaal* pl. *-aat.* The landing took place at dawn. *l-ʔinzaal jira wakt il-fajir.*
landlord - *ṣaaẓib* (pl. *ʔaṣẓaab*) *muluk.*
landmark: **The monument is a landmark in this area. *n-naṣub fadd ɛalaama mumayyiza b-hal-manṭiqa.*
landowner - *ṣaaẓib muluk* pl. *ʔaṣẓaab ʔamlaak.* The big landowners are usually conservatives. *kibaar aṣẓaab il-ʔamlaak ɛaadatan muẓaafiṣiin.*
landslide - **1.** *nhiyaar* pl. *-aat.* The road through the mountains was blocked by a landslide. *ṭariiq ij-jibal čaan masduud ib-sabab inhiyaar.* **2.** *ʔaġlabiyya saaẓiqa.* He won the election by a landslide. *faaz bil-intixaab ib-ʔaġlabiyya saaẓiqa.*
lane - *darub* pl. *druub.* Follow this lane to the main road. *ʔitbaɛ had-darub ʔila ṭ-ṭariiq ir-raʔiisi.*
language - **1.** *luġa* pl. *-aat.* He knows several languages. *yuɛruf ɛiddat luġaat.* **2.** *lahja.* He used strong language in dealing with them. *staɛmal lahja šadiida b-muɛaamalta wiyyaahum.*
lantern - **1.** *faanuus* pl. *fawaaniis.* Walk in front of me with the lantern so I can see the path. *ʔimši bil-faanuus giddaami ẓatta ašuuf iṭ-ṭariiq.* **2.** *looks* pl. *-aat.* I need a new mantle for my coleman lantern. *ʔaẓtaaj fatiila jdiida lil-looks maali.*
lap - **1.** *ẓuṣin, ẓijir.* She put the baby in her lap. *ẓaṭṭat iṭ-ṭifil b-ẓuṣinha.* **2.** *dawra* pl. *-aat, farra* pl. *-aat.* He was in the lead by five yards in the first lap. *čaan bil-muqaddima xams amtaar bid-dawra l-ʔuula.*
to lap - *ṭubag (u ṭabug) n-.* Lap the boards one over the other so the roof won't leak. *ʔuṭbug il-looẓaat wiẓda ɛal-lux ẓatta s-saguf ma-yxurr.*
to lap up - *liṭaɛ (a laṭiɛ).* The cats lapped up the milk. *l-bazaaziin liṭɛat il-ẓaliib.*
lapel - *gaḷba* pl. *-aat, yaaxat sitra* pl. *yaaxaat sitar.*
to **lapse** - *buṭal (a buṭlaan), xilaṣ (a xaliṣ), ntiha (i ntihaaʔ).* If I don't pay this premium my insurance policy will lapse. *ʔiṣa ma-adfaɛ hal-qisiṭ taʔmiini yibṭal.*
lard - *šaẓam xanziir.*
large - **1.** *čibiir, kabiir, waasiɛ.* This room isn't large enough. *hal-ġurfa muu čbiira kaafi* or ***hal-ġurfa kuburha muu kaafi.* -- The mouth of this jar is large enough for me to put my hand in. *ẓalig hat-tunga maa waasiɛ ib-zeeθ ʔagdar afawwut iidi bii.* **2.** *čbiir, kabiir.* That's the largest table in the house. *haaṣa ʔakbar meez bil-beet.* -- He's a large importer from the Middle East. *huwwa mustawrid kabiir imniš-šarq il-ʔawṣaṭ.*
at large - *ẓurr.* The thief is still at large. *l-ẓaraami baɛda ẓurr.*
largely - *bil-ʔakθar.* Our company is made up largely of volunteers. *firqatna mitkawwina bil-ʔakθar min mutaṭawwiɛiin.*
large-scale - *niṭaaq waasiɛ.* The city is studying a large-scale building program. *l-baladiyya da-tidrus manhaj ʔinšaaʔ ʔabniya ɛala niṭaaq waasiɛ.*
lark - *qumbura* pl. *-aat.*
laryngitis - *ltihaab il-ẓunjara.*
lash - *qamči* pl. *-iyyaat, jalda* pl. *-aat, zooba* pl. *-aat.* They gave him forty lashes for stealing a loaf of bread. *ṣurboo ʔarbaɛiin qamči li-ʔan baag gurṣat xubuz.*
last - **1.** *ʔaaxir.* She spent her last cent on that dress. *ṣurfat ʔaaxir filis ɛidha ɛala han-nafnuuf.* -- She was the last to leave. *hiyya ʔaaxir wiẓda tirkat.* **2.** *ʔaxiir, maaṣi.* Last year I was in Europe. *s-sana l-maaṣya činit ib-ʔooruppa.* or ***l-ɛaam činit ib-ʔooruppa.* **3.** *ʔaxiir.* The last thing he said was that he didn't want to come. *ʔaxiir šii gaala čaan ma-yriid yiji.* -- He came in last in the race. *čaan il-ʔaxiir bis-sibaaq.* **4.** *bil-ʔaxiir.* He came last. *jaa bil-ʔaxiir.* or *jaa ʔaaxir waaẓid.*
at last - *ʔaxiiran.* Here we are at last! *wuṣalna ʔaxiiran!*
last night - *l-baarẓa bil-leel.* Did you sleep well last night? *nimit zeen il-baarẓa bil-leel?*
last year - *l-ɛaam.* Last year I spent the summer in Lebanon. *l-ɛaam giṣeet iṣ-ṣeef ib-lubnaan.*
to last - **1.** *daam (u dawaam), ṭawwal (i ṭṭuwwul, taṭwiil).* The war lasted six years. *l-ẓarb daamat sitt isniin.* -- I'm afraid this good weather won't last long. *xaayif ʔan haj-jaww il-ẓilu ma-yṭawwil ihwaaya.* **2.** *qaawam (u muqaawama).* This suit didn't last at all. *hal-badla ma-qaawmat ʔabadan.* -- Do you think you can last another mile? *tiɛtiqid tigdar itqaawum miil ḷaax?* **3.** *kaffa (i tkiffi).* I don't think my money will last till the end of the month. *ma-aṭṣawwar ifluusi tkaffi l-ʔaaxir iš-šahar.*
lasting - *daaʔim.* Let's hope for a lasting peace. *xalliina niʔmal ib-salaam daaʔim.*
Latakia - *l-laaṣiqiyya.*
latch - *ṣiqqaaṭa* pl. *-aat, ziḷgaaṭa* pl. *-aat, mizlaaj* pl. *mzaaliij.*
late - **1.** *ʔaxiir.* The late news is broadcast at ten o'clock. *l-ʔaxbaar il-ʔaxiira tinṣaaɛ is-saaɛa ɛašara.* **2.** *marẓuum.* Your late father was a friend of mine. *l-marẓuum abuuk čaan ṣadiiqi.* **3.** *saabiq.*

The late government encouraged exporting. *l-ḥukuuma s-saabiqa šajjiεat it-taṣdiir.* **4.** *mitʔaxxir.* You're late again! *ʔinta mitʔaxxir marra lux.* -- This installment is four days late. *hal-qusiṭ mitʔaxxir ʔarbaεt iyyaam.*
**He is in his late fifties. *εumra qariib imnis-sittiin.*
late afternoon - *l-εaṣir.* I'll be home late in the afternoon. *raḥ-akuun bil-beet il-εaṣir.*
late morning - *ḍ-ḍaḥa l-εaali.* He comes to work late in the morning. *ḍ-ḍaḥa l-εaali yaḷḷa yiji liš-šuġuḷ.*
lately - *bil-mudda l-ʔaxiira.* I haven't been feeling so well lately. *ma-da-ašεur zeen bil-mudda l-ʔaxiira.*
later - 1. *baεdeen.* You'll find out later. *raḥ-tuεruf baεdeen.* **2.** *baεad.* One day later a letter came. *w-baεad yoom jaa maktuub.*
latest - *ʔaaxir.* What's the latest news? *šinu ʔaaxir il-axbaar?* -- That's the latest style. *haay ʔaaxir mooda.*
lathe - *čarix* pl. *čruux, mixraṭa* pl. *maxaariṭ.*
lather - *waġfa* pl. *-aat* coll. *waġaf, raġwa* pl. *-aat.* Put a little soap lather on so you can shave well. *xalli šwayya waġaf ṣaabuun ḥatta tiḥliq zeen.*
to lather - *riġa (u raġwa), waġġaf (u twuġġuf).* This soap doesn't lather well. *haṣ-ṣaabuun ma-yirġu zeen.*
Latin - 1. *laatiini*.* The language of the Latin American countries is either Spanish or Portugese. *duwal ʔameerka l-laatiiniyya luġatha ʔimma spaaniyya ʔaw purtuġaaliyya.* **2.** *l-laatiiniyya.* Latin is a dead language. *l-laatiiniyya luġa mayyta.*
latitude - *xaṭṭ* (pl. *xuṭuuṭ*) *εariḍ.* It's position is at 40 degrees north latitude. *haay mawqiεha εala xaṭṭ εariḍ ʔarbaεiin šimaalan.*
lattice - *xišab imšabbač.* The balcony is hidden by a lattice. *l-balkoon mastuur ib-xišab mšabbač.*
laugh - *ḍiḥka* pl. *-aat.* He has an unusual laugh. *εinda ḍiḥka ġeer εaadiyya.*
to laugh - *ḍiḥak (a ḍaḥik).* Everybody laughed at him. *l-kull ḍiḥkaw εalee.* -- We laughed up our sleeves at his pronunciation. *ḍiḥakna b-εibbna εala talaffuḍa.*
**That's no laughing matter. *haaδa muu šaqa.*
laughingstock - *maḍḥaka, masxara.* His gullibility made him a laughingstock in front of everybody. *taṣdiiga b-kullši sawwaa maḍḥaka giddaam in-naas.*
laughter - *ḍiḥik.* We heard loud laughter behind us. *smaεna ḍiḥik εaali waraana.*
launch - *maaṭoor* pl. *-aat.* We went down the river in his launch. *nḥidarna bin-nahar ib-maaṭoora.*
to launch - 1. *nizal (i nuzuul) n- lil-ṃaay.* Another ship was launched on Monday. *sifiina lux innizlat lil-ṃaay yoom il-iθneen.* **2.** *ʔaṭlaq (i ʔiṭlaaq).* I hear they launched a new satellite. *simaεit ʔaṭliqaw kawkab iṣṭinaaεi jidiid.* **3.** *šann (i šann) n-.* The press launched a fierce attack against the Prime Minister. *ṣ-ṣaḥaafa šannat hujuum εaniif εala raʔiis il-wuzaraaʔ.* **4.** *ftitaḥ (i ftitaaḥ).* They launched the program for fighting illiteracy by holding a convention in Baghdad. *ftitḥaw mašruuε mukaafaḥat il-ʔuṃṃiyya b-εaqid muʔtamar ib-baġdaad.*
to **launder** - *ġisal (i ġasil) n-, xisal (i xasil) n-.* My landlady launders my clothes for me. *ʔumm il-beet tiġsil-li hduumi.*
laundress - *ġassaala* pl. *-aat.* We have a laundress who comes to the house. *εidna ġassaala tijiina lil-beet.*
laundry - 1. *makwi.* Where's the nearest laundry? *ween ʔaqrab makwi?* **2.** *ġasiil.* My laundry just came back. *ġasiili hassa jaa.*
laurel - *ġaar.* This soap has laurel oil in it. *haṣ-ṣaabuun bii zeet il-ġaar.*
lavatory - *mirḥaaḍ* pl. *maraaḥiiḍ, xaḷwa* pl. *xaḷaawi, ʔadabxaana* pl. *-aat, ʔadabxaayin; beet* (pl. *byuut*) *ṃayy.*
lavish - *b-ʔifraaṭ.* They gave him lavish praise. *midḥoo b-ʔifraaṭ.*
law - 1. *qaanuun* pl. *qawaaniin.* That's against the law. *haay ḍidd il-qaanuun.* -- He's studying law. *da-yidrus qaanuun.* -- According to the law of nature, the strong devour the weak. *ḥasab qaanuun iṭ-ṭabiiεa l-qawi yaakul iḍ-ḍaεiif.* -- Those people are very law abiding. *haaδool in-naas yiltazmuun bil-qaanuun.* **2.** *ḥukum* pl. *ʔaḥkaam.* The government is going to do away with martial law. *l-ḥukuuma raḥ-itšiil il-ḥukm il-εurfi.*
by law - *qaanuunan, b-ḥukm il-qaanuun.* That's prohibited by law! *haaδa mamnuuε qaanuunan!*
canon law - *šariiε* pl. *šaraayiε.* Islamic law provides that a woman's inheritance is half that of a man. *š-šariiεa l-ʔislaamiyya tnuṣṣ εala ʔan ḥaqq il-marʔa bil-ʔiriθ nuṣṣ ḥaqq ir-rajul.*
lawn - *θayyal, θayyil.* The lawn still has to be sprinkled. *θ-θayyal baεda laazim yinrašš.*
law school - *kulliyyat* (pl. *-aat*) *il-ḥuquuq.*
lawsuit - *daεwa* pl. *-aat, daεaawi.* Did Adnan win the lawsuit? *εadnaan rubaḥ id-daεwa?*
lawyer - *muḥaami* pl. *-iin.*
lax - 1. *mitmaahil, mithaawin.* He's rather lax in his work. *huwwa šwayya mitmaahil ib-šuġḷa.* **2.** *layyin, mitsaahil, mitmaahil, mithaawin.* She's always been much too lax with her children. *daaʔiman layyna wiyya ʔaṭfaalha.*
laxative - *mushil* pl. *-aat, musahhil* pl. *-aat.*
laxity - *tahaawan.* He was accused of laxity in his work. *ttihmoo b-tahaawuna b-šuġḷa.*
to **lay - 1.** *xalla (i txilli) t-, ḥaṭṭ (u ḥaṭṭ) n-.* Lay the book on the table. *xalli l-iktaab εal-meez.* -- He laid aside 50 dinars for emergencies. *xalla xamsiin diinaar εala ṣafḥa lil-iḥtiyaaṭ.* **2.** *bina (i binaaʔ).* The workmen were laying tile on the ground floor. *l-εummaal čaanaw yibnuun kaaši εaṭ-ṭaabiq il-ʔawwal.* or *l-εummaal caanaw yṭabbuguun iṭ-ṭaabiq il-ʔawwal ib-kaaši.* **3.** *δabb (i δabb) n-, xalla (i), ḥaṭṭ (u).* Don't lay the blame on me. *la-tδibb il-loom εalayya.* **4.** *baaḍ (i).* The hen laid four eggs. *d-dijaaja baaḍat ʔarbaεa beeḍaat.* **5.** *bayyaḍ (i tabyiiḍ, tbiyyiḍ) t-.* Our hens are laying well. *dijaajna zeen da-ybayyiḍ.* **6.** *traahan (a taraahun).* I'll lay ten to one that he does it. *ʔatraahan εašra l-waaḥid huwwa raḥ-ysawwiiha.* **7.** *nayyam (i tniyyim) t-, ṭiraḥ (a ṭariḥ) n-.* Lay the barrel on its side. *nayyim il-barmiil εala ṣafuḥta.*
**He's certainly laying it on thick! *hwaaya da-yθaxxinha!*
to lay claim to - *ddiεa (i ddiεaaʔ) b-.* A distant relative laid claim to the estate. *fadd waaḥid ʔila qaraaba biεiida ddiεa ḥaqq bil-muluk.*
to lay down - 1. *jiṭal (i jaṭil) n-.* Lay him down gently. *jiṭla εala keefak.* **2.** *tirak (u tarik) n-, δabb (i δabb) n-.* They were ready to lay down their arms. *čaanaw mustaεiddiin yitrukuun islaaḥhum.* **3.** *wuḍaε (a waḍiε) n-.* Let me lay down the rules for the game. *xalli ʔaani ʔooḍaε qawaaεid il-liεba.*
to lay for - *xital (i xatil) l-, traṣṣad (a taraṣṣud) l-.* They laid for him at the corner. *xitloo-la biz-zuwiyya.*
to lay off - *staġna (i stignaaʔ) εan, baṭṭal (i tabṭiil).* We have to lay off some workers. *laazim nistaġni εan baεḍ il-εummaal.* -- You're going to have to lay off the drinking for awhile! *laazim itbaṭṭil imniš-širib fadd mudda!*
to lay out - 1. *ṣiraf (u ṣarif).* How much did you lay out for the party? *šgadd ṣirafit lil-ḥafla?* **2.** *ḥaddad (i taḥdiid), xaṭṭaṭ (i taxṭiiṭ).* Lay out the dimensions before you start digging. *ḥaddad il-ʔabεaad qabil-ma tibdi tiḥfur.* **3.** *εiraḍ (i εariḍ) n-.* The chairman laid out his plans for the future. *mudiir il-majlis εiraḍ xiṭṭata lil-mustaqbal.*
to lay waste - *dumar (u damur) n-.* The whole region was laid waste by the storm. *l-manṭiqa kullha ndumrat bil-εaaṣifa.*
layer - *ṭabaqa* pl. *-aat.* Everything was covered with a thick layer of sand. *kullši čaan imġaṭṭa b-ṭabaqa θxiina mnir-ramuḷ.*
layman - *šaxuṣ εaadi* pl. *ʔašxaaṣ εaadiyyiin.* The layman wouldn't be interested in this book. *š-šaxs il-εaadi ma-yihtamm ib-hal-iktaab.*
lazier - *ʔaksal.* They say he's lazier than me. *yguuluun huwwa ʔaksal minni.*
laziness - *kasal.*
lazy - *kaslaan.* Don't be so lazy! *la-tṣiir hal-gadd kaslaan!*
lead - *riṣaaṣ.* Is this made of lead? *haaδi maṣnuuεa min riṣaaṣ?* -- Do you have some lead for my pencil? *εindak riṣaaṣ lil-qalam maali?*
lead - 1. *dawr raʔiisi* pl. *ʔadwaar raʔiisiyya.* Who's playing the lead? *minu da-yquum bid-dawr ir-raʔiisi?* **2.** *daliil* pl. *ʔadilla.* The police had a number of leads on the case. *caan εind iš-šurṭa baεḍ il-ʔadilla mutaεallqa bil-qaḍiyya.* **3.** *muqaddima.* He was in the lead by five yards in the first lap. *čaan bil-muqaddima ib-xamis yaardaat bil-farra*

l-ʔuula. -- When the army entered the town the tanks were in the lead. *lamma j-jeeš dixal il-madiina čaanat id-dabbaabaat bil-muqaddima.* -- **The first hour he had a five-mile lead on us. *bis-saaεa l-ʔuula čaan ġaalubna xams amyaal.*

to lead - 1. *qaad (u qiyaada).* The lieutenant led his men to the top of the hill. *l-mulaazim qaad junuuda ʔila foog it-tall.* **2.** *tfawwaq (a tafawwuq) εala, tqaddam (a taqaddum) εala.* Ahmed leads his class in arithmetic. *ʔaẓmad mitfawwuq εala ṭullaab ṣaffa bil-ẓisaab.* **3.** *gaad (u good) n-.* He led the child across the street. *gaad ij-jaahil w-εabbara š-šaariε.* **4.** *tqaddam (a taqaddum) εala.* Iraq leads the all countries in the production of dates. *l-εiraaq yitqaddam εala jamiiε id-duwal ib-ʔintaaj it-tamur.*

to lead the way - *tqaddam (a taqaddum).* I'll lead the way and you follow. *ʔaani raẓ-atqaddam w-ʔinta tbaεni.*

to lead to - 1. *ʔadda (i).* Where will all this lead to? *haaδa ween raẓ-yʔaddi?* -- Where does this road lead to? *ween yʔaddi haṭ-ṭariiq?* **2.** *sabbab (i tasbiib), ʔadda (i) ʔila.* Drink led to his downfall. *š-šurub sabbab xaraaba.* -- The information you gave us led to his arrest. *l-maεluumaat l-inṭeetna-yyaaha ʔaddat ʔila tawqiifa.*

to lead up to - *qiṣad (u qaṣid).* What do you think he was leading up to? *l-ʔay šii tiεtiqid čaan qaaṣid?* -- That's just what I was leading up to. *haaδa illi činit aquṣda biδ-δabuṭ.*

leader - 1. *zaεiim* pl. *zuεamaaʔ.* The leaders of all parties were present. *zuεamaaʔ kull il-ʔaẓzaab čaanaw ẓaaδriin.* **2.** *raʔiis* pl. *ruʔasaaʔ.* Who is the leader of the group? *minu raʔiis ij-jamεiyya?* -- I know the band leader. *ʔaεruf raʔiis il-firqa l-mawsiiqiyya.*

leading - *baariz, kabiir.* He's one of the leading scientists in his field. *haaδa waaẓid min abraz il-εulamaaʔ ib-farεa.* -- This is the leading newspaper in Baghdad. *haaδi ʔakbar jariida b-baġdaad.*

leaf - 1. *warga* pl. *warag.* In the fall the leaves turn brown. *bil-xariif il-warag yinguḷub loona qahwaaʔi.* -- If you add an additional leaf to the spring it'll bear a heavier weight. *ʔiδa txalli warga lux εas-sipring yitẓammal wazin ʔakθar.* **2.** *ṣaẓiifa.* He promised to turn over a new leaf. *wuεad yiftaẓ ṣaẓiifa jidiida b-ẓayaata.*

to leaf through - *gallab (u tagliib) t- b-.* I'm only leafing through the book. *bass da-agaḷḷub bil-iktaab.*

leaflet - *manšuur* pl. *manaašiir.*

league - 1. *jaamiεa* pl. *-aat.* The Arab League has its headquarters in Cairo. *j-jaamiεa l-εarabiyya markazha bil-qaahira.* **2.** *ttiẓaad* pl. *-aat.* The soccer league's having a dinner today. *ttiẓaad kurat il-qadam imsawwi daεwat εaša l-yoom.*

leak: **There's a leak in the boat. *ʔaku mukaan bil-balam yṭalliε ṃayy.*

to leak - 1. *ṭallaε (i ṭṭilliε) ṃayy, nadda (i tniddi).* The boat is leaking. *l-balam da-yṭalliε ṃayy.* **2.** *xarr (u xarr).* This pot leaks. *haj-jidir yxurr.* -- The faucet is leaking. *l-ẓanafiyya da-txurr.* **3.** *tsarrab (a tasarrub).* The story leaked out somehow. *l-quṣṣa tsarrubat b-ṣuura mniṣ-ṣuwar.* -- All the water is leaking out. *l-ṃayy kulla da-yitsarrab li-barra.*

lean - 1. *širiẓ.* Do you want lean meat or some with fat on it? *triid laẓam širiẓ loo bii šaẓam?* **2.** *maẓal, qaẓaṭ.* It was a lean year for farmers. *čaanat sanat maẓal lil-fallaaẓiin.* **3.** *naẓiif, haziil.* He's a lean man. *huwwa rajul naẓiif.*

to lean - 1. *maal (i meel, mayalaan), dannag (i ddinnig).* Don't lean out of the window. *la-tmiil imniš-šibbaak.* **2.** *maal (i).* He leans toward the right in polities. *ymiil naẓu l-yamiin bis-siyaasa.* **3.** *maal (i), mayyal (i tamyiil) jism~.* She leaned over the balcony and looked to see who was knocking. *maalat imnil-baalkoon ẓatta tšuuf minu čaan ydugg il-baab.* **4.** *tačča (i tticči), riča (i rači) n-, sinad (i sanid) n-.* Don't lean your chair against the wall. *la-tirči kursiyyak εal-ẓaayiṭ.* **5.** *stinad (i stinaad), ntiča (i).* There's nothing to lean against. *ma-aku šii tistinid εalee.* -- May I lean on your arm? *ʔagdar astinid εala δraaεak?* -- She leaned on the railing. *ntičat εal-imẓajjar.* **6.** *nẓina (i nẓinaaʔ), maal (i).* If you lean forward you can see him. *ʔiδa nẓineet li-giddaam tigdar itšuufa.*

leap - *ṭafra* pl. *-aat, gamza* pl. *-aat.* He cleared the ditch with one leap. *εubar is-saagya b-ṭafra wiẓda.*

to leap - *gumaz (u gamuz).* He leaped out of bed at the noise. *gumaz min ifraaša min simaε iṣ-ṣooṭ.*

leap year - *sana kabiisa.*

to **learn - 1.** *tεallam (i taεallum).* He hasn't learned a thing. *ma-tεallam šii.* **2.** *εiraf (u maεrifa).* He learned the truth too late. *εiraf il-ẓaqiiqa baεad fawaat il-wakit.*

to learn by heart - *ẓufaδ (u ẓafuδ) εala gaḷb~, εal-ġeeb.* She learned the poem by heart. *ẓufδat il-qaṣiida εala gaḷubha.*

lease - *εaqid* (pl. *εuquud*) *ʔiijaar.* We had to sign a lease for one year. *δṭarreena nwaqqiε εaqid iijaar il-muddat sana.*

to lease - 1. *staʔjar (i stiʔjaar).* Did you lease an apartment yet? *stiʔjarit šiqqa loo baεad?* **2.** *ʔajjar (i taʔjiir) t-.* The landlord doesn't want to lease the apartment. *ṣaaẓib il-muluk ma-yriid yʔajjir iš-šuqqa.*

least - *ʔaqall.* That's the least of my worries. *haay ʔaqall mašaakli.* -- She deserves it least of all. *hiyya tistaahilha ʔaqall il-kull.* -- That's the least you could do for him. *haaδa ʔaqall-ma mumkin itsawwii tijaaha.*

at least - *εal-ʔaqall.* These shoes cost at least two dinars. *hal-ʔaẓδiya kallfat εal-ʔaqall diinaareen.* -- At least you might have written to me. *εal-aqall čaan kitabit-li.*

not in the least - *ma- ... ʔabadan, ma- ... ʔabad.* It doesn't bother me in the least. *ma-thimmni ʔabadan.* -- It wouldn't surprise me in the least if ... *ma-astaġrub ʔabad ʔiδa ...*

leather - *jilid* pl. *jluud.* The meat is tough as leather. *l-laẓam qawi miθl ij-jilid.*

leave - *ʔijaaza* pl. *-aat.* He's taken a three months' leave. *ʔaxaδ ʔijaaza tlaθt išhur.*

to leave - 1. *tirak (u tarik) n-, raaẓ (u), εaaf (u εoof) n-, miša (i maši).* I have to leave now. *laazim ʔatruk hassa.* or *laazim aεuufkum hassa.* -- I'm leaving for good. *raẓ-atruk nihaaʔiyyan.* -- The train leaves at two-thirty. *l-qiṭaar yitruk s-saaεa θinteen w-nuṣṣ.* **2.** *saafar (i safar), tirak, miša, raaẓ.* My father left yesterday for Europe. *ʔabuuya saafar il-ʔooruppa l-baarẓa.* **3.** *xalla (i txilli) t-, tirak (u).* He left his food on the plate. *xalla ʔakla bil-maaεuun.* -- Where did you leave your suitcase? *ween xalleet jinuṭṭak?* -- My brother got all the money, and left me out in the cold. *ʔaxuuya ʔaxaδ kull il-ifluus w-xallaani aṣaffug ʔiid ib-ʔiid.* -- Leave it to me! *xalliiha εalayya.* -- When he died he left eight grand-children. *min maat tirak iθman ʔaẓfaad.* -- He left word that he would be back soon. *xalla xabar ʔanna raẓ-yirjaε baεd išwayya.*

**Are there any tickets left for tonight's performance? *buqat ʔay biṭaaqaat il-ẓaflat il-leela?*

**Eight from fifteen leaves seven. *θmaanya min xumuṣṭaεaš yibqa sabεa.*

**Where does that leave me? *ʔaani š-raẓ-ykuun maṣiiri?*

to leave out - *fawwat (i tafwiit, tfuwwut) t-, ẓiδaf (i ẓaδif) n-.* When you copy it, don't leave anything out. *min tinqulha, la-tfawwit šii.*

Lebanese - 1. *lubnaani* pl. *-iyyiin.* Most of the Lebanese know how to speak French. *ʔakθar il-lubnaaniyyiin yεurfuun yiẓčuun fransi.* **2.** *labnaani*.* I visited the Lebanese capital twice last summer. *zirit il-εaaṣima l-labnaaniyya marrteen biṣ-ṣeef il-maaδi.*

Lebanon - *lubnaan.*

lecture - *muẓaaδara* pl. *-aat.* It was an interesting lecture. *čaanat muẓaaδara laṭiifa.*

to lecture - *ʔalqa (i ʔilqaaʔ) muẓaaδara, ẓaaδar (i muẓaaδara).* He's lecturing on international trade. *da-yilqi muẓaaδara εan it-tijaara d-dawliyya.* -- He lectures on zoology at the university. *yẓaaδir ib-εilm il-ẓaywaan bij-jaamiεa.* -- He always lectures us when we're late. *daaʔiman yilqi εaleena muẓaaδara min inkuun mitʔaxxriin.* -- Don't lecture me! *la-tilqi b-raasi muẓaaδara!*

lecturer - *muẓaaδir* pl. *-iin.*

ledge - *ẓaašya* pl. *ẓawaaši.* The bird hopped onto the ledge of the window. *ṭ-ṭeer gumaz il-ẓaašyat iš-šibbaač.*

ledger: (bookkeeping) *daftar* (pl. *dafaatir*) *ẓisaab.*

leek - *kurraaθ.*

left - (m.) *yisaar, ʔaysar* (f.) *yisra.* Take the other bag in your left hand. *šiil ij-junṭa l-lux b-iidak il-yisra.* -- We had seats at the left of the stage. *maqaaƐidna čaanat Ɛala yisaar il-masraẓ.* -- I sat on the speaker's left. *ġƐadit Ɛala yisaar il-xaṭiib.* -- Turn left at the next corner. *luuf Ɛal-yisra biš-šaariƐ ij-jaay.*

left-handed - *yisraawi* pl. *-iyyiin.* He's left-handed. *huwwa yisraawi.*

leftist - *yisaari* pl. *-iyyiin.* He always was a leftist. *daaʔiman čaan yisaari.*

leg - **1.** *rijil* pl. *rijleen, rijleenaat.* I have a pain in my right leg. *Ɛindi ʔalam ib-rijli l-yimna.* -- The table leg's broken. *rijl il-meez maksuura.* -- The left pant leg is torn. *rijil panṭaruun il-yisra mamzuuga.* **2.** *marẓala* pl. *maraaẓil.* We're now on the last leg of our trip. *ʔiẓna hassa b-ʔaaxir marẓala min safratna.* **3.** *fuxuδ* pl. *fxaaδ.* Give me a small leg of lamb. *nṭiini fuxuδ ġanam iṣġayyir.* -- **They say he's on his last legs. *yguuluun ʔamra taqriiban mintihi.*
**Stop pulling my leg. *bass Ɛaad titšaaqa.*

legal - *qaanuuni*.* That's perfectly legal. *haaδa tamaaman qaanuuni.* -- He's our legal adviser. *huwwa mustašaarna l-qaanuuni.*

legality - *l-qaanuuniyya.*

legation - *mufawwaṣiyya* pl. *-aat.* Where is the Swiss legation? *ween il-mufawwaṣiyya is-suwiisriyya?*

legend - *ʔusṭuura* pl. *ʔasaaṭiir.* The origin of the legend is unknown. *manšaʔ il-ʔusṭuura ġeer maƐluum.*

legible - *waaṣiẓ.* His handwriting is hardly legible. *kitaabta muu waaṣẓa.* or *kitaabta ma-tinqiri b-suhuula.*

legion - **1.** *firqa* pl. *firaq.* The Foreign Legion's mostly mercenaries. *l-firqa l-ʔajnabiyya muƐṣamha yitkawwan min murtazaqa.* **2.** *faylaq* pl. *fayaaliq, jeeš* pl. *jyuuš.* The Arab Legion's conducting exercises near the border of occupied Palestine. *l-faylaq il-Ɛarabi da-yquum ib-tamaariin Ɛala ẓiduud falasṭiin il-muẓtalla.*

legislation - *tasriiƐ.*

legislator - *mušarriƐ* pl. *-iin.*

legislature - *musarriƐiin, sulṭa tašriiƐiyya.*

legitimate - **1.** *šarƐi*.* He is the legitimate heir. *huwwa l-wariiθ iš-šarƐi.* -- Are all her children legitimate? *kull wulidha sarƐiyyiin?* **2.** *ṣaẓiiẓ.* Those conclusions are not legitimate. *haay il-istintaajaat muu ṣaẓiiẓa.*

leisure - *faraaġ.* This job doesn't leave me much leisure. *haš-šaġla ma-titruk-li faraaġ kaafi.* -- Do it at your leisure. *sawwiiha b-faraaġak.*

lemon - *nuumiyya* (pl. *-aat*) *ẓaamṣa* coll. *nuumi ẓaamuṣ.* Go buy some lemons. *ruuẓ ištiri šwayya nuumi ẓaamuṣ.*

lemonade - *šarbat nuumi ẓaamuṣ.*

lemon juice - *Ɛaṣiir nuumi ẓaamuṣ.*

lemon tea - *čaay ẓaamuṣ, ẓaamuṣ, čaay nuumi baṣra.*

to **lend** - **1.** *Ɛaar* (*i ʔiƐaara*). Can you lend me this book? *tigdar itƐiirni hal-iktaab?* **2.** *daayan* (*i mudaayan*) *t-, Ɛaar* (*i*). Would you lend me ten dinars? *tigdar itdaayinni Ɛašr idnaaniir?*
**Lend me a hand, will you? *saaƐidni šwayya?* or *baḷḷa ʔiidak išwayya?*

length - **1.** *ṭuul* pl. *ʔaṭwaal.* Let's measure the length of the room. *xalli nqiis ṭuul il-ġurfa.* -- He stretched full length on the bed. *tmaddad ib-ṭuula Ɛat-taxit.* **2.** *fatra* pl. *-aat, mudda* pl. *-aat.* He can do a lot of work in a short length of time. *yigdar ysawwi ʔašyaaʔ ihwaaya b-fatrat wakit qaṣiira.* **3.** *wuṣla* pl. *wuṣal.* We need a short length of pipe so the faucet will reach. *yirraad-inna wuṣlat buuri ṣġayyra ẓatta l-ẓanafiyya twaṣṣil.*
**I went to great lengths to get a passport for you. *tƐabit ihwaaya ẓatta xallaṣit-lak il-paaspoort.*
at length - *biṭ-ṭafṣiil.* They discussed the plan at length. *biẓθaw il-xiṭṭa biṭ-ṭafṣiil.*

to **lengthen** - *ṭawwal* (*i taṭwiil*) *t-.* These trousers have to be lengthened. *hal-panṭaroon laazim yiṭṭawwal.*

lengthwise - *biṭ-ṭuul.* Cut the material lengthwise. *guṣṣ il-iqmaaš biṭ-ṭuul.*

lengthy - *muṭawwal.* He made a lengthy speech. *xiṭab xuṭba muṭawwala.*

lenient - *layyin, mitsaahil.* You're too lenient with him. *ʔinta kulliš layyin wiyyaa.*

lens - *Ɛadasa* pl. *-aat.* Your camera has a good lens. *l-kaameera maaltak biiha xooš Ɛadasa.*

lentil - *Ɛadasa* pl. *-aat* coll. *Ɛadas.* Add some lentils to the soup. *ṣiif išwayya Ɛadas biš-šoorba.*

leopard - *nimir imnaqqaṭ* pl. *nmuur imnaqqaṭa, fahad* pl. *fhuud.*

leper - *majδuum* pl. *-iin.*

leprosy - *marṣ ij-juδaam.*

lesbian - *saẓẓaaqiyya* pl. *-aat.*

less - **1.** *ʔaqall.* I have less money with me than I thought. *Ɛindi fluus ʔaqall min-ma Ɛtiqadit.* **2.** *naaqiṣ.* The price is 10 dinars, less the discount. *s-siƐir Ɛašr idnaaniir naaqiṣ il-xaṣum.* -- Five less three leaves two. *xamsa naaqiṣ itlaaθa yibqa θneen.*

lesson - **1.** *daris* pl. *duruus.* Translate lesson five for tomorrow. *tarjum id-dars il-xaamis il-baačir.* -- I'll have to do my lessons first. *laazim asawwi druusi ʔawwal.* -- She gives Spanish lessons. *tinṭi druus bil-iṣpaani.* **2.** *Ɛibra* pl. *Ɛibar, daris* pl. *duruus.* Let that be a lesson to you. *xalli haaδa ykuun Ɛibra ʔilak.* -- I hope you've learned a good lesson from that. *ʔinsaaḷḷa ʔaxaδit xooš daris min haay.*

let - *natt, šabaka.* That serve was a let. Take two more serves. *haṣ-ṣarba čaanat natt. ʔuxuδ-lak baƐad ṣarubteen.*
let alone - *b-ġaṣṣ in-naδar Ɛan.* He can't even read Arabic, let alone speak it. *ma-yuƐruf yiqraʔ Ɛarabi, b-ġaṣṣ in-naδar Ɛan il-ẓači.*
let's - *xalli, xal-, yaḷḷa.* Let's go home. *xalli nruuẓ lil-beet.* -- Let's not leave the party until twelve o'clock. *xal-ma-nitruk il-ẓafla ẓatta s-saaƐa θnaƐaš.*
to let - **1.** *xalla* (*i txilli*) *t-, simaẓ* (*a samiẓ*) *n- l-.* He wouldn't let me do it. *ma-xallaani asawwiiha.* -- This time I'll let it go. *hal-marra raẓ-axalliiha tfuut.* or *hal-marra raẓ-asmaẓ-lak.* -- Don't let anybody in. *la-txalli ʔaẓẓad yfuut.* -- He wouldn't let me out. *ma-xallaani aṭlaƐ.* -- Will the customs officials let us pass? *Ɛajaban muwaṣṣafiin il-gumrug raẓ-yismaẓuu-lna bil-muruur?* -- I can't let his statement stand. *ma-axalli kalaama yruuẓ ib-faala.* -- Please let me have the menu. *ʔismaẓ-li b-qaaʔimat il-ʔakil.* or ***nṭiini qaaʔimat il-ʔakil rajaaʔan.* -- Can you let me have five dinars until I get paid? *tigdar tismaẓ-li b-xams idnaaniir ʔila ʔan ʔaaxuδ raatbi?* **2.** *tirak* (*u tarik*), *xalla* (*i txilli*). Can't you let me alone for five minutes? *ma-tigdar titrukni waẓdi xamis daqaayiq?*
**Have you rooms to let? *Ɛindak ġuraf lil-ʔiijaar?*
**I really let him have it! *nṭeeta ẓagga b-ʔiida.*
to let down - **1.** *nazzal* (*i tanziil*) *t-.* Please let down the store front. *baḷḷa ma-tnazzil il-kabangaat.* **2.** *xayyab* (*i txiyyib*) His son has let him down badly. *ʔibna xayyab ʔamala kulliš.* -- He let me down when I needed him. *xayyabni min iẓtijit ʔila.* or *Ɛaafni min iẓtijit ʔila.* **3.** *tmaahal* (*a tamaahul*) He's beginning to let down in his work. *bida yitmaahal ib-šuġḷa.*
to let go of - *hadd* (*i hadd*) *n-, ẓall* (*i ẓall*) *n-.* Don't let go of the rope. *la-thidd il-ẓabil.*
to let in on - *fiša* (*i faši*). Did you let him in on the secret, too? *fišeet-la is-sirr hammeena?*
to let off - **1.** *nazzal* (*i tanziil*) *t-.* Please let me off at the next stop. *nazzilni bil-mawaṭṭa j-jaaya, min faṣlak.* **2.** *saamaẓ* (*i musaamaẓa*) *t-.* I'll let you off easy this time. *raẓ-asaamẓak hal-marra.*
to let on - *bayyan* (*i tabyiin*) *Ɛala nafs-, xalla* (*i taxliya*) *ybayyin Ɛalee.* He didn't let on that he knew anything about it. *ma-bayyan Ɛala nafsa ʔinnahu yuƐruf šii Ɛanha.*
to let out - **1.** *farraġ* (*i tafriiġ*) *t-.* Let the water out of the sink. *farriġ il-mayy imnil-maġsala.* **2.** *Ɛarraṣ* (*i taƐriiṣ*) *t-.* I told the tailor to let out the waist. *gitt-la l-xayyaaṭ yƐarriṣ il-xaṣir.*
to let up - *xaff* (*u xaff*). The storm has let up. *l-Ɛaaṣifa xaffat.*

letdown - *xeebat* (pl. *-aat*) *ʔamal.* The failure of our plan was a big letdown. *fašal mašruuƐna čaan xeebat ʔamal ičbiira.*

letter - *maktuub* pl. *makaatiib, risaala* pl. *risaaʔil.* Are there any letters for me? *ʔaku ʔay makaatiib ʔili?* -- I want to send an airmail letter. *ʔariid abƐaθ risaala bil-bariid ij-jawwi.* **2.** *ẓaruf* pl. *ẓuruuf.* The word has five letters. *l-kalima biiha xams iẓruuf.* **3.** *naṣṣ* pl. *niṣuuṣ.* He sticks to the letter of the law. *yitqayyad ib-niṣuuṣ il-qaanuun.*

letter carrier - *ʔabu l-bariid, saaƐi* (pl. *suƐaat*) *bariid.*

lettuce - *xass.*

letup - ngiṭaaε, fakka. It's been raining without any letup all day. ṣaar-ilha tumṭur biduun ingiṭaaε il-yoom kulla.

level - **1.** mustawa pl. -ayaat. His work isn't up to the usual level. šuġḷa muu bil-mustawa l-iεtiyaadi. -- The Dead Sea is below sea level. l-baʒr il-mayyit taʒit mustawa il-baʒar. -- The bookcase is level with the table. l-maktaba b-mustawa l-meez. -- The water level this year is very low. mustawa l-maay has-sana kulliš waaṭi. **2.** ṣanif pl. ʔaṣnaaf, daraja pl. -aat. There are five salary levels in our office. ʔaku xamis ʔaṣnaaf lir-rawaatib ib-daaʔiratna. **3.** gubbaan pl. -aat. Have you a level handy to check the tiles? ʔaku jawwa ʔiidak gubbaan ʒatta niḍbuṭ il-kaaši? **4.** mustawi, εadil. Is the country level or hilly? l-manṭiqa mustawiya loo jabaliyya?
**He did his level best. sawwa l-yigdar εalee.
**He always keeps a level head. daaʔiman ḍaabuṭ ʔaεṣaaba.
**Is he on the level? huwwa ṣaadiq?
to level - **1.** sawwa (i taswiya) t-, εaddal (i taεdiil) t-. The ground has to be leveled. l-gaaε yinraad-ilha taswiya. -- The artillery fire leveled the town to the ground. ḍarub il-madfaεiyya sawwa l-madiina wiyya l-gaaε. **2.** wajjah (i tawjiih). He leveled a number of insults at the president. wajjah εiddat ištaayim lir-raʔiis. -- He leveled the gun at me and threatened to fire. wajjah il-bunduqiyya εalayya w-haddadni b-ʔiṭlaaq in-naar.
to level off - staεdal (i stiεdaal), εtidal (i εtidaal). The plane leveled off at 10,000 feet. ṭ-ṭiyyaara staεdilat εal-irtifaaε εaširt aalaaf qadam.

lever - εatala pl. -aat.

to **levy** - firaḍ (u faruḍ) n-, xalla (i taxliya) t-. The government will levy a tax on gasoline. l-ʒukuuma raʒ-itfruḍ ḍariiba εala l-baanziin.

lewd - xalaaεi*. She did a lewd dance. gaamat ib-raqṣa xalaaεiyya.

liable - **1.** masʔuul. You will be liable for any damages. raʒ-itkuun masʔuul εan kull ḍarar. **2.** muʒtamal. You're liable to catch cold if you're not careful. muʒtamal taaxuδ barid ʔiδa ma-tdiir baalak.
**He's liable to forget! muʒtamal yinsa.

liability - deen pl. dyuun. His liabilities exceed his assets. dyuuna ʔakθar min-ma yimluk.

liaison officer - ḍaabuṭ (pl. ḍubbaaṭ) ittiṣaal.

liar - kaδδaab pl. -iin, čaδδaab pl. -iin.

libel - tašhiir, ṭaεin. This report is pure libel. haaδa t-taqriir kulla tašhiir.

liberal - **1.** mitʒarrir. He has liberal views. εinda ʔaaraaʔ mitʒarrira. -- He's a liberal. huwwa mitʒarrir. **2.** saxi*, kariim. She's very liberal with her money. hiyya kulliš saxiyya b-ifluusha.

to **liberate** - ʒarrar (i taʒriir) t-, εitag (i εatig) n-. He liberated his slaves. ʒarrar εabiida.

liberty - ʒurriyya. We are all fighting for liberty. kullna ndaafiε ib-sabiil il-ʒurriyya.
**He takes too many liberties for his position. yitεadda ʒiduud waḍiifta.
at liberty - ʒurr. You're at liberty to say what you wish. ʔinta ʒurr, tigdar itguul iš-ma triid.

librarian - ʔamiin (pl. ʔumanaaʔ) maktaba.

library - maktaba pl. -aat.

Libya - liibya.

Libyan - **1.** liibi pl. -iyyiin. There are three Libyans in my office. ʔaku tlaθ liibiyyiin ib-daaʔirti. **2.** liibi*. Where can I buy a Libyan newspaper? ween agdar aštiri jariida liibiyya?

license - ʔijaaza pl. -aat. You need a license to open a restaurant. tiʒtaaj ʔijaaza ʒatta tiftaʒ maṭεam. -- You cannot drive without a license. ma-tigdar itsuug bila ʔijaaza.
to license - ʔajaaz (i ʔijaaza). They licensed him to practice medicine in Iraq. ʔajaazoo l-mumaarasat iṭ-ṭibb bil-εiraaq.

licensed - mujaaz. He's a licensed pharmacist. huwwa ṣaaydali mujaaz.

license plate - quṭεa pl. quṭaε. My car's license plates are dirty. quṭaε sayyaarti waṣxa.

lick - laṭεa pl. -aat. Let him have a lick of your ice cream. xalli yaaxuδ laṭεa mnid-doondirma maaltak.
to lick - **1.** liʒas (a laʒis) n-, liṭaε (a laṭiε) n-. Just look at the cat licking her kitten. šuuf il-baʒʒuuna da-tilʒas wulidha. **2.** ḍirab (u ḍarub) n-, buṣaṭ (u baṣuṭ) n-. I'm going to lick you if you don't stop. tara raʒ-aḍurbak ʔiδa ma-tbaṭṭil. **3.** warram (i tawriim) t-, ġiḷab (u ġaḷub) n-. I can still lick you! baεadni ʔagdar awarrmak! -- All right, I'm licked. ʔaεtirif ʔaani nġiḷabit.

licking - basṭa pl. -aat. What you need is a good licking. t-tiʒtaaja basṭa naašfa.

licorice - εirg is-suus.

lid - ġiṭa pl. ʔaġṭiya, ġiṭyaat. Put the lid back on the pot. rajjiε il-ġiṭa εal-jidir.

lie - ciδba pl. -aat coll. čiδib, kiδba pl. -aat coll. kiδib. Everything he says is a lie! kullši yguula čiδib!
to lie - **1.** kiδab (i kiδib), čiδab (i čiδib). There's no doubt that he's lying. ma-aku šakk huwwa da-yikδib. **2.** tmaddad (a tamaddud). He is lying on the couch. huwwa mitmaddid εal-qanafa. **3.** Most of the town lies on the right side of the river. muεḍam il-madiina waaqiε εaj-jiha l-yimna mnin-nahar.
**The book is lying on the table. l-iktaab εal-meez.
to lie down - tmaddad (a tamaddud), njiṭal (i njiṭaal). I want to lie down for a few minutes. ʔariid ʔatmaddad čam daqiiqa.
**He's lying down on the job. ma-δaabb nafsa εaš-šuġuḷ.

lieutenant - mulaazim pl. -iin.

lieutenant colonel - muqaddam pl. -iin.

life - **1.** ʒayaat. It was a matter of life or death. čaanat masʔalat ʒayaat ʔaw moot. -- The night life in this town is dull. l-ʒayaat il-leeliyya b-hal-balad jaamda. -- He lost his life in an accident. fuqad ʒayaata b-ʒaadiθ. -- Such a life! l-ʒayaat hiiči, or haay hiyya l-ʒayaat, or **haay hiyya d-dinya. **2.** quṣṣat (pl. quṣaṣ) ʒayaat. He's writing a life of the President. da-yiktib quṣṣat ʒayaat ir-raʔiis. **3.** ʒayawiyya. She's full of life. kullha ʒayawiyya. **4.** ruuʒ. He was the life of the party. huwwa čaan ruuʒ il-ʒafla. -- I can't for the life of me remember where I put it. loo taaxuδ ruuʒi ma-agdar atδakkar ween ʒaṭṭeetha, or waḷḷaahi raʒ-atxabbaḷ ma-agdar atδakkar ween ʒaṭṭeetha. **5.** ʔaʒyaaʔ. We visited an exhibition of marine life. zirna maεraḍ il-ʔaʒyaaʔ il-maaʔiyya. **6.** muʔabbad. He was sentenced to life imprisonment. nʒikam εalee bis-sijin il-muʔabbad.
**This bulb has a life of six hundred hours. hal-igloob yduum sitt miit saaεa.
**There he stood as big as life. wugaf ihnaak waaḍiʒ miθil iš-šamis.
**You can bet your life on that. ʔakiid! or bit-taʔkiid.

life belt - ʒizaam (pl. -aat, ʔaʒzima) najaat.

lifeboat - zawraq (pl. zawaariq) najaat, qaarib (pl. qawaarib) najaat.

life insurance - taʔmiin εal-ʒayaat.

lifetime - εumur. A thing like that happens only once in a lifetime. miθil haš-šii yṣiir marra bil-εumur bass.

lift - maṣεad pl. maṣaaεid, sansoor pl. -aat. Let's take the lift to the fifth floor. xan-naaxuδ il-maṣεad liṭ-ṭaabiq il-xaamis.
**A glass of tea in the afternoon gives me a lift. stikaan čaay il-εaṣir yinεišni. or stikaan čaay il-εaṣir ygaεεid raasi.
**Can I give you a lift? ʔagdar awaṣṣlak?
to lift - **1.** šaal (i šeel) n-. He lifted the baby out of the cradle. šaal iṭ-ṭifil imnil-kaaruuk. **2.** rifaε (a rafuε). The good news lifted our spirits. l-ʔaxbaar iz-zeena rifεat maεnawiyyaatna. **3.** rifaε (a rafuε) n-, šaal (i šeel) n-. After two weeks the ban was lifted. baεad isbuuεeen il-maniε inrifaε. **4.** zaal (u zawaal). Toward noon the fog lifted. zaal iḍ-ḍubaab ʒawaali ḍ-ḍuhur.
**I won't lift a finger for him no matter what. waḷḷa ma-asaaεda loo kullši yṣiir.

light - **1.** ḍuwa pl. -aayaat, ʔaḍwiya. The light is too glaring. ḍ-ḍuwa kulliš ṣaaṭiε. -- The lights of the town came on one by one. ʔaḍwiyat il-madiina štiεlat waaʒid baεd il-laax. -- Don't cross until the light changes to green. la-tuεbur gabuḷ-ma yitbaddal iḍ-ḍuwa ʔila ʔaxḍar. **2.** šixxaaṭa, naar. Do you have a light? εindak šixxaaṭa? **3.** ḍaawi, ḍuwi*. It's staying light much longer. d-dinya tibqa ḍaawya mudda ʔaṭwal. **4.** ʔabyaḍ, kaašif. She has a light complexion. loon wujihha ʔabyaḍ. **5.** faatiʒ, kaašif. She prefers light colors. tfaḍḍil il-ʔalwaan il-faatʒa. -- I want a light blue hat. ʔariid šafqa maawiyya faatiʒ. **6.** xafiif. Why don't you take your light coat? leeš ma-taaxuδ paaltuwwak il-xafiif? -- There was a light rain today. ṣaarat maṭra xafiifa l-yoom. -- I had a light breakfast today. ryuugi čaan xafiif il-yoom. --

**He's very light-fingered. *ʔiida ṭuwiila.*
**He's at last seen the light. *w-ʔaaxiiran iktišaf il-ζaqiiqa.*
to bring to light - *ʔaḍhar (i ʔiḍhaar).* The investigation brought many new facts to light. *t-taζqiiq ʔaḍhar ζaqaaʔiq ijdiida.*
to come to light - *ḍihar (a ḍuhuur).* A number of problems came to light during our research. *baεaḍ il-mašaakil ḍihrat ʔaθnaaʔ baζiθna.*
to light - *šiεal (i šaεil) n-.* Wait till I light the fire. *ʔintiḍir ζatta ʔašεil in-naar.* — Light a match. *ʔišεil šixxaaṭa.* 2. *warraθ (i tawriiθ) t-, šiεal (i šaεil) n-.* I want to light my pipe first. *ʔariid awarriθ il-paayip maali ʔawwal.* — Is your cigarette still lit? *jigaartak baεadha mwarrθa?* 3. *ḍawwa (i taḍwiya) t-.* The hall was brightly lighted. *l-qaaεa čaanat imḍawwaaya zeen.* — The street is poorly lighted. *š-šaariε taḍwiita muu zeena.*
to light up - *limaε (a lamiε).* The children's eyes lit up. *εyuun il-ʔaṭfaal limεat.*
lightbulb - *gloob* pl. *-aat.*
to **lighten** - 1. *birag (i barig), wumaḍ (a wamiiḍ)* It's thundering and lightening. *da-tirεid w-tibrig.* 2. *xaffaf (i taxfiif), kišaf (i kašif).* Add a little white paint to lighten the color. *xalli šwayya booya beeḍa ζatta txaffif il-loon.* 3. *xaffaf (i), nazzal (i tanziil).* If you don't lighten the weight, the tires will blow out. *ʔiḍa ma-txaffif il-wazin tara t-taayiraat itdugg.*
lighthouse - *fanaar* pl. *-aat, manaara* pl. *-aat.*
lighting - *ʔiḍaaʔa, taḍwiya.* The lighting is bad here. *l-ʔiḍaaʔa muu zeena hnaa.*
lightning - 1. *ṣaaεiqa* pl. *ṣawaaεiq.* Lightning struck the church steeple. *ṣ-ṣaaεiqa nizlat εala burj il-kaniisa.* 2. *barq.* There's thunder and lightning. *ʔaku barq w-raεad.*
like - 1. *miθil.* You're just like my sister. *ʔinti biḍ-ḍabuṭ miθil ʔuxti.* — He ran like mad. *rikaḍ miθl il-majnuun.* — There's nothing like traveling! *ma-aku šii miθil is-safar!* 2. *miθil-ma.* She's just like I pictured her. *hiyya biḍ-ḍabuṭ miθil-ma tṣawwaritha.*
**That's more like it! *haaḍa ʔaqrab ʔila!* or *hassa ʔaζsan!*
**That's just like him. *haay daggaata.* or *haay εamaayla.*
**Did you ever see the likes of it? *šaayif šabiih ʔila?* — What's the weather like today? *šloon ij-jaww il-yoom?*
**Like father, like son. *ʔibn il-wazz εawwaam.*
**I don't feel like dancing. *ma-εindi raġba lir-riguṣ.*
**It looks like rain. *tbayyin raζ-tumṭur.*
like this, like that - 1. *hiiči.* It's not like that at all. *muu hiiči ʔabadan.* — Ordinarily, we do it like this. *εaadatan hiiči nsawwiiha.* 2. *miθil haaḍa.* I want something like this. *ʔariid šii miθil haaḍa.*
to like - 1. *ζabb (i ζubb) n-.* I don't like cats. *ma-aζibb il-ibzaaziin.* or ***ma-tiεjibni l-ibzaaziin.* — He never liked to do it. *ʔabadan ma-ζabb ysawwiiha* or ***ma-yεijba ysawwiiha.* — Would you like another cup of coffee? *tζibb finjaan gahwa laax?* or ***yεijbak finjaan gahwa laax?* 2. *šaaf (u).* How do you like this town? *š-itšuuf hal-madiina?*
likelihood - *ζtimaal* pl. *-aat.* There is a great likelihood that he'll come. *ʔaku ζtimaal kabiir huwwa raζ-yiji.*
in all likelihood - *εala l-ʔarjaζ.* In all likelihood he'll get the job. *εala l-ʔarjaζ huwwa raζ-yaaxuḍ iš-šaġla.*
likely - *muζtamal.* That's more likely. *haaḍa muζtamal ʔakθar.*
lilac - *leelaaqi**. She bought a lilac blouse. *štirat ibluuz leelaaqi.*
lily - *zanbaqa* pl. *zanaabiq* coll. *zanbaq.*
lily-of-the-valley - *sawsana* pl. *-aat* coll. *sawsan.*
limb - *fariε* pl. *furuuε.* He sawed off a limb from the tree. *gaṣṣ fariε imniš-šajara.*
lime - *kilis.* The soil doesn't contain enough lime. *t-turba ma-biiha kilis kaafi.*
limestone - *ζajar il-kilis, ζajar jiiri.*
limit - *ζadd* pl. *ζuduud.* There's a limit to everything. *ʔaku ζadd il-kullši.* **I've reached the limit of my patience. *nifaḍ ṣabri.*
**The speed limit is thirty-five miles an hour. *s-surεa l-masmuuζa xamsa w-tlaaθiin miil bis-saaεa.*
to limit - *ζaddad (i taζdiid) t-, ζiṣar (u ζaṣir) n-.* Please limit your talk to three minutes. *min faḍlak ζaddid kalaamak l-itlaθ daqaayiq.*
limited - *maζduud.* Our time is limited. *wakitna maζduud.*
limp - 1. *raaxi, raxi**. He has a limp handshake. *ʔiida raaxya min yṣaafuζ.* 2. *εaraj.* He has a slight limp when he walks. *bii šwayya εaraj min yimši.* **His arm hung limp. *ʔiida haddilat.*
to limp - *εiraj (i εarij), gizal (i gazil).* He limps noticeably. *huwwa da-yiεrij ib-ṣuura mbayyna.*
linden - *zeezafuun.*
line - 1. *xaṭṭ* pl. *xuṭuuṭ.* Draw a line between these two points. *ʔirsim xaṭṭ been han-nuquṭṭeen.* — There's heavy traffic on that line. *ʔaku zdiζaam εala hal-xaṭṭ.* — There's a new air lines company serving Baghdad. *ʔaku šarikat xuṭuuṭ jawwiyya jdiida tmurr ib-baġdaad.* 2. *ṣaff* pl. *ṣfuuf, xaṭṭ* pl. *xuṭuuṭ, sira* pl. *-aawaat.* There's a long line of cars ahead of us. *ʔaku ṣaff iṭwiil imnis-sayyaaraat giddaanma.* — Keep in line! *ʔibqa bis-sira!* 3. *ṣaṭir* pl. *ṣṭuur.* I still have a few lines to write. *baεad-li čam ṣaṭir laazim aktibha.* 4. *xaṭṭ* pl. *xuṭuuṭ, tajεiid* pl. *-aat, tajaaεiid.* There are deep lines in his face. *ʔaku xuṭuuṭ εamiiqa b-wučča.* 5. *ṣanif* pl. *ʔaṣnaaf, nooε* pl. *ʔanwaaε.* He handles three lines of shirts. *huwwa ybiiε itlaθ ʔaṣnaaf imniθ-θiyaab.* 6. *ζabil* pl. *ζbaal* The wash is still hung out on the line. *l-ihduum baεadha mašruura εal-ζabil.*
**Boy, does he have a smooth line! *ʔamma εinda ṭariiqat balif εajiiba!*
**It's along the line of what we discussed. *titmaaša wiyya l-mawḍuuε illi biζaθnaa.*
**Drop me a line. *ʔiktib-li čam kalima.* or *εala l-ʔaqall iktib-li salaam.*
**He was killed in the line of duty. *nkital min čaan yʔaddi waajba.*
**What line is he in? *šinu šuġla?*
**That's not in my line. *haay muu saġilti.* or *haaḍa muu xtiṣaaṣi.*
to keep in line - *ḍibaṭ (u ḍabuṭ) n-.* I can't keep the soldiers in line any more. *baεad ma-agdar aḍbuṭ ij-jinuud.*
to line - *baṭṭan (i tabṭiin) t-.* The jacket is lined with nylon. *s-sitra mbaṭṭina b-naayloon.*
to line up - *ṣṭaff (a ṣṭfaaf).* Have the boys line up in the hall. *xalli l-wilid yiṣṭaffuun bil-qaaεa.* — People lined up all along the streets to watch the parade. *n-naas iṣṭaffaw εala ṭuul iš-šawaariε ζatta yitfarrjuun εal-istiεraaḍ.*
linen - 1. *kittaan.* This tablecloth is made of linen. *ġiṭa l-meez maṣnuuε min kittaan.* 2. *čaraačif.* The linen is changed every week. *č-čaraačif titbaddal kull isbuuε.*
liner - *baaxira* pl. *-aat.* We took a liner to Europe. *ʔaxaḍna baaxira ʔila ʔooruppa.*
to **linger** - *biqa (i baqaaʔ).* We'd better not linger around here. *ʔaζsan ma-nibqa hnaa.*
linguist - *luġawi* pl. *-iyyiin.*
linguistic - *luġawi**.
linguistics - *l-luġawiyyaat.*
lining - *bṭaana* pl. *-aat.* My coat needs a new lining. *sitirti tiζtaaj ibṭaana jidiida.*
link - *ζalaqa* pl. *-aat.* One link of my watch chain is broken. *fadd ζalaqa min zanjiil saaεati maksuura.*
to link - *ribaṭ (u rabuṭ) n-.* You have to link the two ends of the chain. *laazim tirbuṭ iz-zanjiil imniṭ-ṭarafeen.* — How can you link me with the crime? *šloon tirbuṭni bij-jariima?*
lint - *nifaaya.* Lint from the fabrics collects under the furniture. *nifaayt il-iqmaaš da-titjammaε jawwa l-ʔaθaaθ.*
lion - *ʔasad* pl. *ʔusuud, sabiε* pl. *sbaaε.*
lion cub - *šibil* pl. *ʔašbaal.*
lioness - *labwa* pl. *-aat.*
lip - 1. *šiffa* pl. *-aat, šifaayif, šfaaf.* I bit my lip. *εaḍḍeet šiffti.* 2. *jasaara.* I don't want anymore lip from you! *ma-ariid minnak jasaara baεad.*
lipstick - *ζamrat šafaayif.*
liquid - *saaʔil* pl. *sawaaʔil.* He's only allowed to drink liquids. *bass masmuuζ-la yišrab sawaaʔil.* — Do you have liquid soap? *εindak ṣaabuun saaʔil?*
to **liquidate** - *ṣaffa (i taṣfiya) t-.* The company had to be liquidated to pay off its debts. *š-šarika tṣaffat ζatta tidfaε idyuunha.*
**His political opponents had him liquidated. *xuṣuuma s-siyaasiyyiin txallṣaw minna.*
liquor - *mašruub* pl. *-aat.* He doesn't touch liquor. *ma-yišrab mašruub.*
lira - *leera* pl. *-aat.*

lisp - *laθġa.* She speaks with a lisp. *hiyya tiẓči b-laθġa.*

to lisp - *liθaġ (i laθiġ).* Her youngest son lisps when he talks. *ʔibinha ṣ-ṣiġayyir yilθiġ min yiẓči.*

list - *qaaʔima* pl. *qawaaʔim.* His name is not on the list. *ʔisma muu bil-qaaʔima.*

to list - 1. *sajjal (i tasjiil) t-.* This item isn't listed. *haay il-faqara ma-msajjala.* 2. *maal (i meel).* The ship is listing to port. *s-safiina maayla Ɛala jaanibha l-aysar.*

to listen - 1. *ʔaṣġa (ʔiṣġaaʔ), stimaƐ (stimaaƐ).* They listened intently. *ʔaṣġaw b-ihtimaam.* -- She'll listen to reason. *tiṣġi lil-ẓači l-maƐquul.* 2. *simaƐ (a samiƐ) n-.* Now listen! *ʔismaƐ!* -- Listen! Somebody's coming. *ʔismaƐ, waaẓid da-yiji.*

to listen in - *ṭṣannaṭ (a taṣannuṭ)* Somebody must be listening in. *waaẓid laazim ykuun da-yiṭṣannaṭ.*

to listen to - *simaƐ (a samiƐ) n-, stimaƐ (i stimaaƐ) l-.* I like to listen to classical music. *ʔaẓibb asmaƐ moosiiqa klaasiikiyya.* -- Why didn't you listen to me? *leeš ma-smaƐit kalaami?*

listener - *mustamiƐ* pl. *-iin.*

liter - *litir* pl. *-aat.* Olive oil is sold by the liter, sir. *zeet iz-zeetuun inbaaƐ bil-litraat ʔustaað.*

literal - *ẓarfi**. This is a literal translation. *haay tarjuma ẓarfiyya.*

literally - *ẓarfiyyan.* Please translate this literally. *ʔarjuuk, tarjumha ẓarfiyyan.* -- They took the order literally. *ṭabbuqaw il-ʔamur ẓarfiyyan.*

literature - 1. *ʔadab* pl. *ʔaadaab.* Have you read a great deal of Arabic literature? *qireet ihwaaya mnil-ʔadab il-Ɛarabi.* 2. *muʔallafaat.* The ministry has sent out a lot of literature on the topic. *l-wizaara ʔaṣdirat ihwaaya muʔallafaat bil-mawḍuuƐ.*

litter - 1. *wuṣax, qaḍaara.* The alley is full of litter. *d-darbuuna malyaana wuṣax.* 2. *naqqaala* pl. *-aat, sadya* pl. *-aat.* They carried him out on a litter. *šaaloo bin-naqqaala.* 3. *dafƐa* pl. *-aat.* The cat just had a litter of kittens. *l-bazzuuna hassa jaabat dafƐa mnil-ibzaaziin l-iṣġaar.*

to litter - *waṣṣax (i tawṣiix) t-.* Don't litter the road with trash. *la-twaṣṣix iṭ-ṭariiq bil-izbaala.*

little - 1. *ṣġayyir* pl. *ṣġaar.* She has a little girl. *Ɛidha bnayya ṣġayyra.* -- We need a little table in this room. *niẓtaaj meez iṣġayyir ib-hal-gubba.* 2. *šwayya.* I have a little money. *Ɛindi šwayya fluus.* -- I can speak a little French. *ʔagdar ʔaẓči šwayya fransi.* 3. *qaliil, ðaʔiil.* It's of little importance. *ʔahammiyyatha qaliila.*

**He's little better than a thief. *huwwa tlatt irbaaƐ ẓaraami.*

**That's of little value to me. *ma-ʔila qiima bin-nisba ʔili.*

in a little while - *baƐd išwayya.* I'll come back in a little while. *raẓ-arjaƐ baƐd išwayya.*

little by little - *tadriijiyyan.* Little by little he calmed down. *hida tadriijiyyan.*

live: **I bought some live fish. *štireet simač baƐda yilbuṭ.* **Careful, that's a live wire. *diir baalak, hal-waayir yintil.*

to live - 1. *Ɛaaš (i Ɛeeš).* He lived a happy life. *Ɛaaš ẓayaat saƐiida.* -- Before the war I lived in France. *gabḷ il-ẓarb Ɛišit b-ifransa.* -- Live and learn! *Ɛiiš w-šuuf!* -- The people on this island live on nothing but fish. *sukkaan haj-jaziira yƐiišuun bass Ɛas-simač.* -- I couldn't live on so little. *ma-agdar ʔaƐiiš ib-hal-muqdaar.* 2. *sikan (u sukna, sakin), Ɛaaš (i Ɛees).* Does anyone live in this house? *ʔaku ʔaẓẓad yiskun ib-hal-beet?*

**He has barely enough to live on. *huwwa duub ykaffi Ɛiišta.* or *huwwa bil-kaad ysidd Ɛiišta.*

**He always worked hard and never really lived. *buqa ykidd ṭuul ẓayaata laakin ma-thanna b-Ɛiišta.*

**She won't live out the winter. *ma-raẓ-iṭṭawwil ir-rabiiƐ.*

to live up to - *tmassak (a tamassuk) b-.* They didn't live up to the terms of the contract. *ma-tmassikaw b-šuruuṭ il-Ɛaqid.*

**He didn't live up to my expectation. *ma-ṣaar miθil-ma twaqqaƐit.*

live coal - *jamra* pl. *-aat* coll. *jamur.* There are still live coals in the brazier. *ʔaku baƐad jamur bil-manqala.*

lively 1. *našiṭ.* He's a lively boy. *huwwa walad našiṭ.* 2. *šayyiq.* We had a lively conversation. *ṣaar beenaatna munaaqaša šayyiqa.*

**Step lively! *ẓarrik nafsak!*

liver - *kabda* pl. *kabid.* Do you care for liver? *yƐijbak il-kabid.*

livestock - *maašiya* pl. *mawaaši.* We can't get feed for our livestock. *ma-nigdar indabbur Ɛalaf lil-maašiya maalatna.*

living - 1. *Ɛiiša, maƐiiša.* Living is awfully expensive here. *l-Ɛiiša kulliš ġaalya hnaa.* -- Living conditions are very bad. *ḍuruuf il-maƐiiša kulliš muu zeena.* -- He'll have to earn his own living. *laazim ydabbur maƐiišta b-nafsa.* 2. *ẓayy.* Arabic is a living language. *l-luġa l-Ɛarabiyya luġa ẓayya.* 3. *ṭibq il-ʔaṣil.* He's the living image of his father. *huwwa ṣuura ṭibq il-ʔaṣil min ʔabuu.* 4. *ṭayyib, Ɛaayiš.* I don't know whether he's still living. *ma-adri ʔiða čaan baƐda ṭayyib.* -- Is your grandmother still living? *jiddiitak baƐadha Ɛaayša?*

living room - *ġurfat* (pl. *ġuraf*) *gaƐda.*

lizard - *breeƐṣi* pl. *-iyya, ḍabb, ʔabu breeṣ.*

load - *ẓimil* pl. *ʔaẓmaal, ẓmuulaat.* The load is too heavy for him. *l-ẓimil kulliš iθgiil Ɛalee.* -- I ordered a load of sand. *waṣṣeet Ɛala ẓimil ramul.* -- It took a load off my mind. *nzaaẓ ẓiml ičbiir Ɛan čitfi.*

**He has loads of money. *Ɛinda fluus bil-koom.*

to load - 1. *ẓammal (i taẓmiil) t-.* Load the cases on the truck. *ẓammil iṣ-ṣanaadiig bil-loori.* -- The cargo is just being loaded. *l-biḍaaƐa hassa da-titẓammal.* 2. *ẓašša (i taẓšiya) t-, Ɛabba (i tƐibbi) t-.* He loaded the gun. *ẓašša l-bunduqiyya.* 3. *rakkab (u tarkiib) t-.* Do you know how to load film in a camera? *tuƐruf išloon itrakkub filim bil-kaamira?* 4. *kawwam (i takwiim) t-.* We're loaded with work. *š-šuġuḷ mkawwam Ɛaleena.*

loaf - *ṣammuunat* (pl. *-aat*) *loof.* Please give me three loaves of bread. *baḷḷa nṭiini tlaθ ṣammuunaat xubuz loof.*

to loaf - *tkaasal (a takaasul).* He was loafing on the job. *čaan yitkaasal ib-šuġḷa.*

loafer - 1. *čata* pl. *-awaat.* He's a loafer. *huwwa čata.* 2. *ẓiðaaʔ qabaġli.* Have you seen my other loafer? *šifit takk ẓiðaaʔi l-qabaġli l-laax?*

loam - *ġaryan.*

loan - *sulfa* pl. *-aat* coll. *sulaf, qariḍ* pl. *quruuḍ.* I'd like to get a loan from the bank. *ʔariid ʔaaxuð sulfa mnil-bank.*

to loan - 1. *daayan (i mudaayana), dayyan (i ddiyyin).* She loaned him 250 fils. *daaynata miiteen w-xamsiin filis.* 2. *Ɛaar (i ʔiƐaara).* He loaned me an interesting book. *Ɛaarni ktaab laṭiif.*

loan shark - *muraabi* pl. *-iin.*

lobby - *madxal* pl. *madaaxil.* I'll meet you in the lobby after the movie. *ʔasuufak bil-madxal baƐd il-filim.*

local - 1. *maẓalli**. The local papers say nothing about the accident. *ṣ-ṣuẓuf il-maẓalliyya ma-tiðkur šii Ɛan il-ẓaadiθ.* -- He wasn't familiar with local conditions. *ma-čaan Ɛinda maƐrifa biḍ-ḍuruuf il-maẓalliyya.* 2. *daaxili**. How much is a local call? *šgadd itkallif il-mukaalama d-daaxiliyya?* 3. *mawḍiƐi** A local anesthetic will do. *banj mawḍiƐi yikfi.*

to locate - 1. *Ɛayyan (i taƐyiin) t- mawqiƐ-.* I couldn't locate him. *ma-gdarit ʔaƐayyin mawqiƐa.* 2. *ẓaddad (i taẓdiid) t- maẓall-, Ɛayyan (i taƐyiin) t- maẓall-.* I can't locate the trouble. *ma-agdar aẓaddid maẓall il-xalal.*

located - *waaqiƐ.* Where is your new store located? *ween waaqiƐ maxzanak l-ijdiid?*

location - *mawqiƐ* pl. *mawaaqiƐ.* The location of the hotel is ideal. *mawqiƐ il-findiq mumtaaz.*

lock - *quful* pl. *qfaal.* The lock needs oiling. *l-quful yiẓtaaj tadhiin.*

to lock - 1. *qufal (u qaful) n-.* Don't forget to lock the door when you leave. *la-tinsa tuqful il-baab min tiṭlaƐ.* -- I'm locked out. *nqufal il-baab Ɛalayya.* 2. *šakkal (i taškiil) t-.* The bumpers of the two cars were locked together. *daƐƐaamiyyaat is-sayyaarteen šakkilat ib-baƐaḍha.*

to lock up - *ẓibas (i ẓabis) n-.* He was locked up. *huwwa čaan maẓbuus.*

locker - *ṣanduug* pl. *ṣnaadiig.* I left my racquet in the locker. *tirakit ir-rikit maali biṣ-ṣanduug.*

lockjaw - *guzaaz.*

locksmith - *ʔabu qfaal.* Do you know of a good locksmith near here? *tuƐruf ʔabu qfaal zeen qariib minnaa?*

locomotive - *makiinat* (ph. *makaayin*) *qiṭaar.*

locust - *jarraada* pl. *-aat* coll. *jarraad.*

lodge - 1. *kapra* pl. *-aat, kuux* pl. *kwaax.* We have a hunting lodge in the north. *ɛidna kaprat ṣeed biš-šimaal.* 2. *maẓfal* pl. *maẓaafil.* Is there a Masonic lodge in Baghdaad? *ʔaku maẓfal maasooni b-baġdaad?*

to lodge - 1. *ẓišag (i ẓašig) n-.* A piece of wood is lodged in the machine. *ʔaku wuṣlat xišab maẓšuuga bil-makiina.* 2. *qaddam (i taqdiim) t-.* He lodged a complaint with the police. *qaddam šakwa liš-šurṭa.*

log - *jiδiɛ* (pl. *jδuuɛ*) *šajara.* The people put a log across the road to stop traffic. *n-naas xallaw jiδiɛ iš-šajara biš-šaariɛ ẓatta ywaggfuun is-sayyaaraat.*

**He sat there like a bump on a log. *giɛad ihnaak miθl iṣ-ṣanam* or *giɛad ihnaak miθl il-ʔaṭraš biz-zaffa.*

**I slept like a log. *nimit miθil l-iẓjaara.* or *nimit miθl il-looẓ.* or *nimit miθil il-mayyit.*

logic - *manṭiq.* Your logic is faulty. *manṭiqak ġeer maɛquul.*

logical - *manṭiqi*.*

logically - *manṭiqiyyan*

lone - *waẓiid.* He was the lone surviver. *čaan il-waẓiid ʔilli nijaẓ.*

lonely - *muuẓiš.* This place is quite lonely in winter. *hal-maẓall kulliš muuẓiš biš-šita.*

lonesome - *b-wiẓda.* She feels very lonesome. *tišɛur ib-wiẓda.*

to be lonesome for - *šiɛar (u šuɛuur) ib-wiẓša ʔil-* I'm very lonesome for you. *ʔašɛur ib-wiẓša ʔilak.*

long - 1. *ṭuwiil* pl. *ṭwaal.* We had to make a long detour. *δṭarreena nsawwi farra ṭwiila.* -- It's a long way to the top of the mountain. *ṭ-ṭariiq ṭuwiil ʔila qummat ij-jibal.* — He got there a long time after we did. *wuṣal baɛad ma-jiʔna b-mudda ṭwiila.* 2. *hwaaya.* Did you stay long at the party? *buqeet ihwaaya bil-ẓafla?*

**The room is twenty feet long. *l-ġurfa ṭuulha ɛišriin qadam.*

**How long is it? *šgadd ṭuula?*

**The child cried all night long. *ṭ-ṭifil biča ṭuul il-leel.*

**How long will it take? *šjadd yiṭṭawwal?* or *šgadd taaxuδ wakit?*

**So long! *maɛa s-salaama.*

**Everything will work out in the long run. *bil-mada l-baɛiid il-ʔumuur raẓ-titẓassan.*

long ago - *min zamaan, min mudda ṭwiila.* I knew that long ago. *ɛirafitha min zamaan.*

as long as 1. *šgadd-ma.* You can keep it as long as you wish. *tigdar itxalliiha ɛindak išgadd-ma triid.* 2. *madaam, maadaam.* It doesn't bother me as long as the work gets done. *ma-yhimmni madaam iš-šuġuḷ da-yimši.* — As long as you're here, you might as well have dinner with us. *madaam inta hnaa, δall itɛašša wiyyaana.*

to long - *štaaq (a štiyaaq), ẓann (i ẓaniin).* I'm longing to see my mother and father again. *mištaaq ašuuf ʔummi w-ʔabuuya marra lux.* --She's longing for a man. *tištaaq ir-rijjaal.* — He's longing for home. *da-yẓinn il-ʔahla.*

long-distance call - *muxaabara* (pl.-*aat*) *xaarijiyya.* Please, I'd like to make a long-distance call. *min faδlič, ʔariid asawwi muxaabara xaarijiyya.*

longer - 1. *ʔaṭwal.* This table is longer than that one. *hal-meez ʔaṭwal min δaaka.* 2. *ʔakθar, mudda ʔaṭwal.* He wanted to stay longer, but I was sleepy. *raad yibqa ʔakθar, bass ʔaani činit naɛsaan.* 3. *ʔakθar, ʔazyad.* I can't stand it any longer. *ma-agdar atẓammalha ʔakθar.*

longshoreman - *ɛaamil* (pl. *ɛummaal*) *šaẓin.*

look - *naδra* pl. -*aat.* You can see with one look that the town is dirty. *b-naδra wiẓda tigdar tuɛruf il-madiina waṣxa.*

**He gave her an angry look. *baawaɛ ɛaleeha b-zaɛal.*

**Take a good look! *lak, baawiɛ zeen!*

to look - 1. *tfarraj (a tafarruj).* I enjoy looking at pictures. *ʔaẓibb ʔatfarraj ɛaṣ-ṣuwar.* 2. *baawaɛ (i mubaawaɛa).* She looked at me when I came into the room. *baawɛat ɛalayya min fitit lil-ġurfa.* — Don't look now but the president just came in. *la-tbaawiɛ, ir-raʔiis hassa dixal.* -- She didn't so much as look at me. *ẓatta mbaawaɛa ma-baawaɛatni.* 3. *baawaɛ (i mubaawaɛa), šaaf (u šoof).* — Look, a falling star! *baawiɛ! ʔaku najma da-toogaɛ.* — May I look at Ahmad's file? *ʔagdar ašuuf malaffat aẓmad.* 4. *bayyan (i tabyiin).* You look well. *mbayyin ɛaleek ṣiẓẓtak zeena.* — It looks like rain. *tbayyin raẓ-tumṭur.*

to look after - *daar (i deera) baal˜.* Do you have someone to look after the child? *ɛindak ʔaẓẓad ydiir baala ɛaṭ-ṭifil?* -- Looking after this kid is no picnic. *deert il-baal ɛala haj-jaahil muu šaqa.*

to look down on - *ẓtiqar (i ẓtiqaar).* You mustn't look down on people just because they're poor. *ma-laazim tiẓtiqir in-naas li-ʔanhum fuqaraaʔ.*

**She looks down her nose at everyone. *šaayfa nafisha* or *šaayla xašimha ɛan-naas.*

to look for - *dawwar (u tadwiir) ɛala.* We're looking for rooms. *da-ndawwur ɛala ġuraf.* -- He's always looking for trouble. *huwwa daaʔiman ydawwur ɛala mašaakil.*

to look forward to - 1. *ntiδar (i ntiδaar).* We're looking forward to our vacation impatiently. *da-nintiδir ɛuṭlatna yoom yoom.* -- We're looking forward to the nineteenth of May when you're going to get married. *da-nintiδir yoom itsaaṭaɛaš maayis illi raẓ-titzawwaj bii.* 2. *štaaq (a štiyaaq).* I'm looking forward to seeing you. *ʔaani muštaaq ašuufak.*

to look into - *biẓaθ (a baẓiθ) n-.* We'll have to look into the matter. *laazim nibẓaθ il-mawδuuɛ.*

to look on - 1. *baawaɛ (i mubaawaɛa), tfarraj (a tafarruj).* I was just looking on. *činit bass da-abaawiɛ.* 2. *ɛtibar (u ɛtibaar).* They looked on her as a stranger. *ɛtibrooha ġariiba ɛanhum.*

to look out - 1. *daar (i deera) baal˜.* Look out! *diir baalak!* 2. *ʔašraf (i ʔišraaf), ṭall (i ṭall)* The big window looks out on the garden. *š-šibbaak ič-čibiir yišrif ɛala l-ẓadiiqa.*

to look over - *šaaf (u šoof)* Will you look over these papers? *tismaẓ itšuuf hal-ʔawraaq?*

to look up - 1. *šaal (i šeel) raas˜.* He didn't even look up when I called him. *ẓatta raasa ma-šaala min ṣiẓit-la.* 2. *niδar (u naδar) b-iẓtiraam.* She looks up to him. *tunδur-la b-iẓtiraam.* 3. *dawwar (u tadwiir) t- ɛala.* I have to look up this word in a dictionary. *laazim adawwur ɛala hal-kalima bil-qaamuus.* 4. *tẓassan (a taẓassun).* Things are beginning to look up. *l-ʔumuur bidat titẓassan.*

**Look me up some time, won't you? *zuurni fadd yoom.*

lookout - 1. *raqiib* pl. *ruqabaaʔ* A lookout was placed on every hill. *ẓaṭṭaw raqiib ɛala raas kull tall.* 2. *masʔuuliyya, šaġla.* It's your lookout now. *haay masʔuuliitak.*

to be on the lookout for - *xalla (i) ɛeen˜ ɛala.* Be on the lookout for a black '59 Cadillac license number 354. *xalli ɛeenak ɛala sayyaara kaadiilaak sooda, moodeel tisɛa w-xamsiin, raqam qiṭɛatha tiaθ miyya w-ʔarbaɛa w-xamsiin.*

looks - *maδhar* pl. *maδaahir.* To judge by his looks, he's a criminal. *min maδhara, ybayyin ɛalee mujrim.*

**From the looks of things it may take much longer than we thought. *ɛala-ma yiδhar, il-masʔala raẓ-taaxuδ ʔakθar min-ma δanneena.*

loom - *nool* pl. *nuwaal.*

loop - *ẓalaqa* pl. -*aat.* Run the rope through this loop. *fawwit il-ẓabil min hal-ẓalaqa.*

to loop - *laff (i laff).* He looped the rope over the post. *laff il-ẓabil ɛal-ɛamuud.*

loophole - *majaal* (pl. -*aat*) *lit-tamalluṣ.* Many loopholes have been left in this law. *ʔaku hwaaya majaalaat lil-tamalluṣ ib-hal-qaanuun.*

loose - 1. *raaxi.* The button is loose. *d-dugma raaxya.* 2. *mahduud, maẓluul.* Do you ever let the dog loose? *txalluun ič-čalib mahduud?* 3. *faasid.* She has loose morals. *ʔaxlaaqha faasda.*

**He must have a screw loose! *laazim ykuun mašxuuṭ* or *laazim ɛinda xeeṭ.*

**She has a loose tongue. *ma-ṭδumm iẓčaaya.*

to turn loose - *hadd (i hadd) n-.* Don't turn the dog loose! *la-thidd ič-čalib!*

to **loosen** - *raxxa (i tarxiya) t-.* Can you loosen this screw? *tigdar itraxxi hal-burġi?* -- I want to loosen my shoelaces. *ʔariid araxxi qiiṭaan qundarti.*

loot - *ġaniima, booga.* The thieves hid the loot in a tree. *l-ẓaraamiyya δammaw il-ġaniima biš-šajara.*

to loot - *nihab (i nahib) n-, silab (salib) n-.* The enemy looted the town. *l-ɛadu nihab il-madiina.*

lopsided - *ɛooja.* The picture's lopsided. *ṣ-ṣuura ɛooja.*

to **lose - 1.** *δayyaɛ (i taδyiiɛ) t-, fiqad (u faqid) n-.* I lost my pencil again. *δayyaɛit qalami marra lux.* — I lost track of them after the war. *δayyaɛit ʔaθarhum baɛad il-ẓarb.* — I've lost all my strength, since I got sick. *δayyaɛit kull quuti min itmarraδit.* — Don't lose your way! *la-tδayyiɛ ṭariiqak!* 2.

xisar (a xasaara) n-, fiqad (u faqid) n-. He lost his entire fortune during the war. *xisar kull θaruuta ʔaθnaaʔ il-ʒarb.* -- I'm afraid he'll lose the game. *xaayif ykuun yixṣar il-liεba.* 3. *fiqad (u faqid) n-.* After a few steps he lost his balance. *čam xuṭwa w-fiqad tawaazna.* -- He lost his life in the fire. *fuqad ʒayaata bil-ʒariiq.* -- He loses his temper easily. *yifqud ʔaεṣaaba bil-εajil.* -- They lost their son in the war. *fiqdaw ibinhum bil-ʒarb.* 4. *qaṣṣar (i taqṣiir), ʔaxxar (i taʔxiir).* My watch loses three minutes a day. *saaεti tqaṣṣir itlaθ daqaayiq bil-yoom.* 5. *tilaf (i talif) n-.* My things were lost in the fire. *ġaraaδi ntilfat bil-ʒariiq* or *ġaraaδi raaʒat bil-ʒariiq.*

**I lost a part of what he said. *faatni baεδ illi gaala.*

**I'm losing my hair. *šaεri da-yoogaε.*

to lose face - *ṣaxxam (i taṣxiim) wijih~, sawwad (i taswiid) wijih~.* He lost face when he couldn't come through on his promise. *ṣaxxam wičča min ma-gidar yoofi b-waεda.*

loser - *xasraan* pl. *-iin.* He was the loser. *huwwa čaan il-xasraan.*

**He's a real loser. *ʒaasibta waagfa.*

losing - *xaasir.* They are fighting a losing battle. *daaxiliin maεraka xaasra.*

loss - 1. *xasaara* pl. *xasaaʔir.* They suffered heavy losses. *tkabbidaw xasaaʔir jasiima.* -- I sold the house at a loss. *biεt il-beet ib-xasaara.* 2. *faqid, fuqdaan.* She is griefstricken at the loss of her husband. *hiyya ʒaziina εala faqid zawujha.*

**He's never at a loss for an excuse. *ma-yiṣεab εalee εuδur.* or *εuδra b-raas ilsaana.*

**She's never at a loss for an answer. *ma-yiεṣa εaleeha jawaab.*

**I'm at a loss to explain his absence. *εiṣa εalayya ʔaεruf ġiyaaba.*

lost - *nafquud, δaayiε.* I'm going to run an ad about my lost watch. *raʒ-anšur ʔiεlaan εan saaεati l-mafquuda.*

to be lost - *δaaε (i δiyaaε).* My shirt was lost in the laundry. *θoobi δaaε εind il-mukawwi.* -- I hope nothing is lost in the moving. *ʔinšaaḷḷa ma-yδiiε šii bit-taʒwiil.*

**Since his wife's death he's completely lost. *txarbaṭ min maatat zawujta.*

**He was lost in thought. *čaan δaarub daalġa.*

**I'm lost when it comes to mathematics. *yδiiε εalayya l-ʒsaab min tiji yamm ir-riyaaδiyyaat.*

lot - 1. *qaṭεat* (pl. *quṭaε*) *ʔarδ.* How big is your lot? *šgadd kubur quṭεat il-ʔariδ maaltak.* 2. *l-maktuub-l.* I don't envy his lot. *ma-aʒisda εal-maktuub-la.* 3. *dafεa* pl. *-aat.* I'll send the books in three separate lots. *raʒ-adizz il-kutub εala tlaθ dafεaat.* 4. *qurεa.* Let's draw lots. *xalli nsawwi qurεa.*

**He's a bad lot. *huwwa duuni,* or *huwwa muu xooš walad.*

a lot - *hwaaya, kθiir.* I ate a lot. *ʔakalit ihwaaya.* -- We like him a lot. *nʒibba hwaaya.* -- I still have a lot of work. *baεad εindi hwaaya šuġuḷ.* -- She's a lot better than people think. *hiyya hwaaya ʔaʒsan min-ma n-naas yδinnuun.*

lots of - *hwaaya, kθiir.* She has lots of money. *εidha hwaaya fluus.* -- We had lots of fun at the dance. *hwaaya twannasna bir-rigiṣ-*

loud - 1. *εaali.* She has a loud, unpleasant voice. *εidha ṣoot εaali muzεij.* 2. *barraaq.* I don't like loud colors. *ma-aʒibb il-ʔalwaan il-barraaqa.*

loud-speaker - *sammaaεa* pl. *-aat, mukabbir* (pl. *-aat*) *ṣoot.*

lounge - *ġurfat* (pl. *ġuraf*) *l-istiraaʒa.* We had coffee in the lounge. *šrabna gahwa b-ġurfat l-istiraaʒa.*

to lounge around - *tfattal (a tafattul).* I like to lounge around the house on holidays. *ʔaʒibb atfattal bil-beet bil-εuṭla.*

louse - *gamḷa* pl. *-aat* coll. *gamul.*

love - *ʒubb.* Love is blind. *l-ʒubb ʔaεma.* -- He must be in love. *laazim ykunn waagiε bil-ʒubb.* or **laazim da-yʒibb.*

**You can't get it for love or money. *ma-mumkin titʒaṣṣal mahma kaan.*

to love - *ʒabb (i ʒubb) n-.* He loves her very much. *huwwa yʒibbha hwaaya.* -- I love apples. *ʔaʒibb it-tiffaaʒ.* -- I love to dance. *ʔaʒibb arguṣ.*

**Would you like a cup of coffee? - I'd love one! *yεijbak finjaan gahwa? ʔii, waḷḷa b-makaana!*

lovely - *badiiε, laṭiif.* They have a lovely home. *εidhum beet badiiε.*

loving - *muʒibb.* This is my loving wife. *haay zoojti l-muʒibba.*

low - 1. *naaṣi, waaṭi.* Do you want shoes with high or low heels? *triidiin ʒiδaaʔ čaεab εaali loo naaṣi?.*-- That plane is flying too low. *haṭ-ṭayyaara da-ṭṭiir kulliš naaṣi.* 2. *waaṭi, δaεiif, naazil.* He always gets low marks. *daaʔiman yʒaṣṣil εala darajaat waaṭya.* -- His pulse is low. *nabδa waaṭi.* -- She spoke in a low voice. *tkallmat ib-ṣawṭ waaṭi.* -- You have very low blood pressure. *δaġṭak kulliš waaṭi.* 3. *maεquuč.* I feel very low today. *ʔaani šwayya maεquuč il-yoom.* 4. *waaʒid.* Put the car in low. *xalli s-sayyaara εal-waaʒid.* 5. *ʒaqaara, danaaʔa.* That was low of him. *caanat ʒaqaara minna.*

**He made a low bow. *nʒina hwaaya.*

**The sun is quite low already. *š-šamis taqriiban raʒ-itġiib.*

**I have a low opinion of him. *raʔyi muu zeen bii.*

**Our funds are getting low. *raṣiidna da-yinxufuδ.*

lower - 1. *ʔanṣa, ʔawṭa.* This chair is lower than that one. *hal-kursi ʔanṣa mnil-laax.* 2. *jawwaani*.* Put it on the lower shelf. *ʒuṭṭha bir-raff ij-jawwaani.*

to lower - 1. *nazzal (i tanziil) t-.* Lower the lifeboats. *nazzil zawaariq in-najaat.* -- He lowered himself in their eyes. *nazzal nafsa b-εeenhum.* -- They will lower the price some day. *raʒ-ynizzluun is-siεir fadd yoom.* 2. *naṣṣa (i tanṣiya) t-, waṭṭa (i tawṭiya) t-.* He lowered his voice when he saw her come in. *naṣṣa ṣooṭa min šaafha tidxul.*

loyal - 1. *muxliṣ* pl. *-iin.* He has always been loyal to the government. *daaʔiman čaan muxliṣ lil-ʒukuuma.* 2. *wafi* pl. *ʔawfiya, muxliṣ* pl. *-iin.* You couldn't have a more loyal friend. *ma-tilgi ṣadiiq ʔawfa minna.* -- I've always been a loyal friend, haven't I? *daaʔiman činit-lak ṣadiiq wafi, muu?*

loyalty - *ʔixlaaṣ.* Nobody questioned his loyalty to the government. *maʒʒad šakk ib-ʔixlaaṣa lil-ʒukuuma.* -- You can depend on his loyalty. *tigdar tiεtimid εala ʔixlaaṣa.*

lubricant - *dihin tašʒiim*

to **lubricate** - *šaʒʒam (i tašʒiim) t-.* Please lubricate the car. *min faḍlak šaʒʒim is-sayyaara.*

lubrication - *tašʒiim*

luck - 1. *ʒaδδ.* My luck has changed. *ʒaδδi staεdal.* 2. *tawfiiq, ʒaδδ.* I wish you all the luck in the world. *ʔatmannaa-lak kull it-tawfiiq.* -- Now you try your luck! *hassa ʔinta jarrub ʒaδδak.*

Good luck! *muwaffaq inšaaḷḷah!* or *ʒaδδ saεiid.*

luckily - *min ʒusn il-ʒaδδ.* Luckily, he doesn't bite. *min ʒusn il-ʒaδδ ma-yεaδδ.*

lucky 1. *saεiid.* It was a lucky coincidence. *čaanat ṣidfa saεiida.* 2. *maʒδuuδ.* You can consider yourself lucky. *tigdar tiεtibur nafsak maʒδuuδ* -- You're a lucky fellow. *ʔinta waaʒid maʒδuuδ.*

luggage - *junaṭ.* We stowed our luggage on the back seat of the car. *xalleena junaṭna bil-maqεad il-xalfi bis-sayyaara.*

lukewarm - 1. *daafi, faatir.* Take a lukewarm bath. *ʔuxuδ ʒammaam daafi.* 2. *ma-mihtamm.* He's very lukewarm about your plan. *huwwa ma-mihtamm il-mašruuεak.*

lull - **We went out during the lull in the storm. *ṭlaεna min xaffat il-εaaṣifa.*

to lull to sleep - *nawwam (i tanwiim) t-.* Her singing lulled the boy sleep. *ġinaaha nawwam iṭ-ṭifil.*

lullaby - *leeluwwa* pl. *-aat.*

lumber - *xišab.* How much lumber will be needed for the book shelves? *šgadd xišab tiʒtaaj l-irfuuf il-kutub.*

luminous - *fisfoori*.* Has your watch got a luminous dial? *saaεtak biiha myaal fisfooriyya?*

lump - 1. *kutla* pl. *-aat.* What are you going to do with that lump of clay? *š-raʒ-itsawwi b-kutlat iṭ-ṭiin haay?* 2. *waram* pl. *wruum.* He has a big lump on his forehead. *ʔaku waram ib-guṣṣṭa.* 3. *qaalab* pl. *qwaalib, fuṣṣ* pl. *fṣuuṣ.* I take only one lump (of sugar) in my coffee. *ʔaani ʔaaxuδ qaalab waaʒid il-gahuuti.*

lump sugar - *qand.*

lumpy - 1. *mfaṣṣaṣ.* The sugar is lumpy. *š-šakar imfaṣṣaṣ.* 2. *mεaggad.* This pillow is very lumpy. *hal-imxadda mεaggida.*

lunar - *qamari*.* The Moslem holidays follow the lunar calendar. *l-εuṭal l-islaamiyya titbaε it-taqwiim il-qamari.*

lunatic - *mxabbaḷ* pl. *maxaabiiḷ, majnuun* pl. *majaaniin.* He's acting like a lunatic. *da-yitṣarraf miθl il-imxabbaḷ.*

lunch - *ġada* pl. *-aayaat.* It's time for lunch. *ṣaar wakt il-ġada.*
to lunch - *tġadda (a ġada).* Will you lunch with me? *titġadda wiyyaaya?*
lung - *riʔa* pl. *-aat.* His left lung is infected. *riʔata l-yiṣra muṣaaba.*
**The boy yelled at the top of his lungs. *l-walad ẹaaṭ ib-ẹilu ẓissa.*
to **lurk** - *xital (i xatil).* We found him lurking in an alley. *šifnaa xaatil bid-darbuuna.*
lute - *ẹuud* pl. *ẹawaad.* The lute is out of tune. *l-ẹuud ma-manṣuub.*
luxury - 1. *taraf.* They lived in unbelievable luxury. *ẹaašaw b-taraf faḍiiẹ.* 2. *faxim.* They're building a luxury hotel. *da-yibnuun findiq faxim.*
luxuries - *kamaaliyyaat.* They're raising the tax on luxuries. *da-yzayyduun iḍ-ḍariiba ẹal-kamaaliyyaat.*
lying - *kiδib, čiδib.* Lying won't get you anywhere. *l-kiδib ma-yfiidak.*
lyre - *qiiθaara* pl. *-aat.*

M

machine - *makiina* pl. *makaayin, ʔaala* pl. *-aat.* The machine is working again. *l-makiina gaamat tištuġuḷ marra lux.*
machine gun - *raššaaša, raššaas* pl. *-aat, maṭrilooz* pl. *-aat.*
machinery - *makaayin, ʔaalaat.*
mad - 1. *majnuun* pl. *majaaniin, mxabbaḷ* pl. *mxaabiiḷ.* He is a little mad and unpredictable. *haaδa šwayya majnuun w-ma-tigdar tuẹruf iš-yiṭlaẹ minna.* -- He drove like mad. *saaq miθl il-imxabbaḷ.* 2. *mačluub.* He was bitten by a mad dog. *ẹaḍḍa čalib mačluub.* 3. *zaẹlaan, ġaḍbaan.* What are you mad about? *ẹala weeš zaẹlaan?* or *š-imzaẹẹlak?* or *ʔeeš biik zaẹlaan?*
to drive mad - *jannan (i tjinnin) t-, xabbaḷ (u txubbuḷ) t-.* The heat is driving me mad. *l-ẓarr raẓ-yjanninni.*
to be mad about - *txabbaḷ (a txubbuḷ) ẹala.* She's mad about him. *hiyya mitxabbḷa ẹalee.* -- My boy is mad about ice cream. *ʔibni yitxabbaḷ ẹad-doondirma.*
to be mad at - *ziẹal (a zaẹal) n- ẹala, min.* She's mad at me again. *ziẹlat ẹalayya marra lux,* or *hiyya hamm zaẹlaana ẹalayya.*
madam - *xaatuun* pl. *xwaatiin, sayyida* pl. *-aat.* Is somebody waiting on you, Madam? *xaatuun, ʔaẓẓad faḍḍ šuġḷič?*
madman - *majnuun* pl. *majaaniin, mxabbaḷ* pl. *mxaabiiḷ.*
magazine - *majalla* pl. *-aat.* Where can I buy the magazine? *mneen ʔagdar ʔaštiri l-majalla?*
magnificent - *faaxir, nafiis, mumtaaz.*
to **magnify** - *kabbar (u takubbur) t-.* This lens magnifies six times. *hal-ẹadasa tkabbur sitt marraat.*
magnifying glass - *mukabbira* pl. *-aat.* You can only see it with a magnifying glass. *ma-tigdar itšuufha ʔilla b-mukabbira.*
maid - *xaddaama* pl. *-aat, xaadma* pl. *-aat.* We let our maid go. *baṭṭalna xaddaamatna.*
old maid - *ẹaanis* pl. *ẹawaanis, ẹizba* pl. *-aat.* She acts like an old maid. *titṣarraf ẹabaalak fadd wazda ẹaanis.* -- **She died an old maid. *maatat ibnayya.*
mail - *bariid* pl. *burud, maktuub* pl. *makaatiib.* The mail is delivered at four o'clock. *l-bariid yitwazzaẹ saaẹa ʔarbaẹa.* -- Is there any mail for me? *ʔaku makaatiib ʔili?*
mails - *bariid, muwaaṣalaat bariidiyya.* The storm held up the mails. *l-ẹaaṣifa ẹaṭṭilat il-muwaaṣalaat il-bariidiyya.*
to mail - *dazz(i)n- bil-bariid.* Did you mail the package? *ʔinta dazzeet ir-ruzma bil-bariid?* -- Please mail the letter for me. *ʔarjuuk dizz-li l-maktuub bil-bariid.* or *ʔarjuuk δibb-li l-maktuub bil-bariid.*
mailbox - *ṣanduug (pl. ṣanaadiig) bariid.*
mailman - *muwazziẹ (pl. -iin) bariid.*
main - 1. *ʔabbi* pl. *-iyyaat.* The main has burst. *l-ʔabbi ṭagg.* 2. *ʔasaasi*, raʔiisi*.* That's one of our main problems. *haδiič wazda min mašaakilna l-ʔasaasiyya.* -- Did you inquire at the main office? *siʔalit bid-daaʔira r-raʔiisiyya?* -- You've forgotten the main thing. *nseet iš-šii l-ʔasaasi.*
in the main - *ẹala l-ẹumuum, bil-ẹumuum, ġaaliban.* The discussion revolved in the main around two questions. *l-munaaqaša daarat ẹala l-ẹumuum zawl masʔalteen.* -- I agree with him in the main. *ʔaani ġaaliban ʔattifiq wiyyaa.*
mainly - *ẹala l-ʔakθar.* He comes mainly on Tuesdays. *ẹala l-ʔakθar yiji ʔayyaam l-iθlaaθaa.*
to **maintain** - 1. *ṣarr (i ʔiṣraar) n- ẹala.* He maintains that he was there. *huwwa yṣirr ẹala ʔinna čaan ihnaak.* 2. *ẓtifaḍ (u ẓtifaaḍ) b-.* They have moved to Karrada, but they have decided to maintain their house in Fadhil. *ntiqlaw lil-karraada laakin qarriraw yiẓtafḍ ib-beethum il-ẹatiig bil-faḍil.*
maintenance - *ṣiyaana.*
major - 1. *raʔiis awwal* pl. *ruʔasaaʔ awwaliin.* Has anyone seen the major? *ʔaẓẓad šaaf ir-raʔiis il-ʔawwal?* 2. *mawḍuuẹ raʔiisi* pl. *mawaaḍiiẹ raʔiisiyya.* What's your major? *šinu mawḍuuẹak ir-raʔiisi?* 3. *ʔakθar, ʔakbar, ʔaẹḍam.* The major part of my income goes for rent. *l-qism il-ʔakbar min daxli yruuẓ lil-ʔiijaar.*
majority - *ʔakθariyya, ʔaġlabiyya.* The majority was against it. *l-ʔakθariyya ẹarrḍat il-mawḍuuẹ.* -- The majority of the students were sick. *ʔaġlabiyyat it-talaamiiz čaanaw wajẹaaniin.*
make - *maarka* pl. *-aat, nooẹ* pl. *ʔanwaaẹ.* What make is your radio? *r-raadyo maalak yaa maarka?* or **r-raadyo maalak šuġuḷ man?*
to make - 1. *sawwa (i tsiwwi) t-, ẹimal (a ẹamal) n-.* He made a big mistake. *sawwa ġalṭa čbiira.* 2. *ṣinaẹ (a ṣaniẹ) n-, ẹimal (a ẹamal) n-, sawwa (i tsiwwi) t-.* This factory makes bottles. *hal-maẹmal da-yiṣnaẹ ibṭaala.* 3. *sawwa (i tsiwwi) t-.* They made him president. *sawwoo raʔiis.* -- How much do you make a week? *šgadd itsawwi bil-isbuuẹ?* -- You'll have to make a few changes. *laazim itsawwi šwayya tabdiilaat.* 4. *xalla (i txilli) t-.* Onions make my eyes water. *l-buṣal yxalli ẹyuuni tidmaẹ.* 5. *ṣaar (i ṣeera).* He'd really make a good king. *huwwa ẓaqiiqatan yṣiir xooš malik.* 6. *lazzag (i tlizzig) b-.* Do you think we'll make the train? *tiẹtiqid raẓ-inlazzig bil-qiṭaar?* 7. *dabbar (u tadbiir, ddubbur).* How does he make his living? *šloon ydabbur ẹiišta?*
**He made a fool of himself in front of the people. *rtikab ẓamaaqa giddaam in-naas.*
to make a choice - *xtaar (a xtiyaar).* You have to make a choice. *laazim tixtaar.*
to make off with - *baag (u boog) n-.* They made off with our car. *baagaw sayyaaratna.*
to make out - 1. *farzan (i tfirzin) t-.* Can you make out the date on the postmark? *tigdar itfarzin it-taariix ẹala ṭamgat il-bariid?* 2. *mila (i mali) n-.* Have you made out the application blank? *mleet il-ẹariiḍa?* 3. *sawwa (i tsiwwi).* How did you make out in the exam yesterday? *šloon sawweet bil-imtiẓaan il-baarẓa?*
to make time - *siraẹ (i ʔisraaẹ).* We can make time if we take the other road. *nigdar nisriẹ ʔiδa ʔaxaδna ṭ-ṭariiq iθ-θaani.*
to make up - 1. *sawwa (i tsiwwi) t-.* Make up a list of all the things you need. *sawwi qaaʔima b-kull il-ʔašyaaʔ illi tiẓtaajha.* 2. *xilaq (i xaliq) n-.* He made up a story about his absence. *xilaq quṣṣa ẹan ġiyaaba.* 3. *tṣaalaẓ (a taṣaaluẓ).* They've made up again. *tṣaalẓaw marra lux.* 4. *ẹawwaḍ (u taẹwiiḍ, tẹuwwuḍ)* You can make up the hours you didn't work yesterday, today. *tigdar itẹawwuḍ is-saaẹaat illi ma-štaġlitha il-baarẓa, l-yoom.*
makeshift - *rtijaali*.* This is just a makeshift arrangement. *haaδa fadd tartiib irtijaali.*
make-up - *zwaaga.* Shall I put a little more make-up on? *ʔaẓuṭṭ izwaaga šwayya ʔazyad?*
**She uses an awful lot of make-up. *titzawwag akθar imnil-laazim.*
makings - *qaabliyya* pl. *-aat.* The boy has the makings of an actor. *l-walad ẹinda qaabliyya yṣiir*

mumaθθil.
male - *δakar* pl. *δkuur, faḥal* pl. *fḥuul.* Is that dog a male or female? *hač-čalib faḥal loo niθya?*
male nurse - *muδammid* pl. *-iin.*
malicious - *ḥaquud, xabiiθ, masmuum.* That was a malicious remark. *haδiič čaanat fadd iḥčaaya masmuuma.*
malt - *šiɛiir imnaggaɛ.*
Malta - *maalṭa.*
man - **1.** *rijjaal* pl. *riyaajiil, rajul* pl. *rijaal, zlima* pl. *zilim.* Who's that man? *minu har-rijjaal?* -- He's not the man for it. *haaδa muu zlimatha.* or ***ma-yiṭlaɛ min ḥaggha.* -- What does the man in the street say about it? *š-yguul ɛanha rajul iš-šaariɛ?* -- Tell the men to unload the furniture from the truck. *gul lir-riyaajiil xalli yfarrġuun il-ʔaθaaθ min il-loori.* **2.** *ʔinsaan.* Man used to live in caves. *l-ʔinsaan čaan yɛiiš bil-kuhuuf.*
**One officer and four men volunteered. *ḍaabuṭ waaḥid w-ʔarbaɛ junuud iṭṭawwɛaw.*
to **manage** - **1.** *daar (i dawaraan) n-.* Who manages the estate? *minu ydiir il-muqaaṭaɛa?* -- He managed the store for six years. *daar il-maxzan sitt isniin.* **2.** *dabbar (u tadbiir, tdubbur) t-.* How did you manage to get the tickets? *šloon dabbarit il-biṭaaqaat?* -- Can you manage on your salary? *tigdar itdabbur nafsak ib-raatbak?* or ***tigdar itɛiiš ɛala maɛaašak?* -- We have to manage very carefully on our small salary. *laazim indabbur umuurna zeen ḥatta nɛiiš ɛala raatibna l-qaliil.* **3.** *ḍubaṭ (u ḍabuṭ) n-.* I can't manage the children. *ma-agdar aḍbuṭ ɛala j-jihaal.* **4.** *dastar (i dastara) t-, rattab (i tartiib) t-.* Wasn't that cleverly managed? *ma-čaanat δiič imdastara b-mahaara?*
management - *ʔidaara* pl. *-aat.* Complain to the management! *štiki ɛind il-ʔidaara!*
manager - **1.** *mudiir* pl. *mudaraaʔ.* Where is the manager? *ween il-mudiir?* **2.** *mudabbir.* His wife is a good manager. *marta mudabbira tamaaman.*
mankind - *j-jins il-bašari, l-bašar, l-ʔinsaan.*
manner - *ṭariiqa* pl. *ṭuruq, ʔisluub* pl. *ʔasaaliib.* I liked the manner in which he went about the job. *ɛijbatni ṭariiqta biš-šuġuḷ.*
manners - *ʔadab, ʔaxlaaq.* She has no manners. *maa ɛidha ʔadab.*
to **manufacture** - *ṣinaɛ (a ṣunuɛ) n-, ɛimal (a ɛamal) n-.* What do they manufacture here? *š-yṣinɛuun ihnaa?*
manufacturer - *ṣaaḥib maṣnaɛ* pl. *ʔaṣḥaab maṣaaniɛ, muntij* pl. *-iin.*
manure - *samaad* pl. *ʔasmida.*
many - *hwaaya, mitɛaddid, ɛadiid, kiθiir.* I have many reasons. *ɛindi hwaaya ʔasbaab.* -- Many a person has been fooled by that. *hwaaya naas itqašmuraw bii.*
how many - *šgadd, čam.* How many tickets do you want? *šgadd itriid biṭaaqaat?*
map - *xariiṭa* pl. *xaraayiṭ.* I want a map of Asia. *ʔariid xariiṭa maal ʔaasya.* --Is it possible to get a road map of Iraq? *mumkin taḥṣiil xariiṭa l-ṭuruq il-ɛiraaq?*
to map - *xaṭṭaṭ (i taxṭiiṭ) t-.* The mapping of this area will be finished in a week. *taxṭiiṭ hal-manṭiqa yixlaṣ baɛd isbuuɛ.*
to map out - *ɛayyan (i taɛyiin) t-.* Have you mapped out your route yet? *ɛayyanit ṭariiq safarak loo baɛad?*
maple - *sfandiyaan.*
marble - **1.** *marmar, ruxaam.* The statue is made of marble. *t-timθaal imsawwa min marmar.* **2.** *duɛbulla* pl. *-aat, daɛaabil* coll. *duɛbul.* I used to play marbles, too. *ʔaani hamm činit ʔalɛab duɛbul.*
March - *ʔaaδaar, maart.* I plan to stay here until March. *niiti ʔabqa hnaa ʔila ʔaaδaar.*
march - **1.** *mašya* pl. *-aat, masiir, masiira.* We still have a long march ahead of us. *baɛad giddaamna mašya ṭwiila.* **2.** *maarš* pl. *-aat, moosiiqa masiir.* The band began with a march. *j-jawq bida b-maarš.*
to march - *miša (i miši) n-, ziḥaf (a zaḥif) n-.* Did you see the soldiers marching? *šift ij-jinuud da-yimšuun?*
mare - *faras* pl. *ʔafraas.*
margin - **1.** *haamiš* pl. *hwaamiš, ḥaašya* pl. *ḥawaaši.* Leave a wide margin on the left side. *ʔitruk haamiš ɛariiḍ bij-jiha l-yisra.* **2.** *ḥadd* pl. *ḥduud.* We're operating on a very small margin of profit. *da-ništuġuḷ ɛala ḥadd ḍaʔiil imnir-ribiḥ.* **3.** *ḥtiyaaṭi.* I'm allowing a margin for incidental expenses. *ʔaani ḥaaṭiṭ iḥtiyaaṭi lin-naθriyyaat.* **4.** *fariq* pl. *fruuq.* We won by a narrow margin. *ġilabna b-fariq qaliil.*
mark - **1.** *ɛalaama* pl. *-aat.* Make a mark next to the names of those present. *ḥuṭṭ ɛalaama yamm ʔasmaaʔ il-ʔašxaaṣ il-ḥaaḍriin.* **2.** *daraja* pl. *-aat.* He always gets good marks in mathematics. *huwwa daaʔiman yaaxuδ darajaat zeena bil-ḥisaab.* **3.** *ʔaθar* pl. *ʔaaθaar.* He left his mark in the world. *tirak-la ʔaθar bid-dinya.*
You hit the mark that time. *ʔinta ṣibt il-hadaf δiič il-marra.* or ***ḥčaaytak čaanat ɛal-jariḥ.*
**I don't feel quite up to the mark today. *ʔaani muu ɛala baɛḍi hal-yoom.*
**Where did you get those black and blue marks? *mneen jattak hal-kadmaat wir-raḍḍaat?*
to mark - **1.** *ʔaššar (i taʔšiir) t-.* I've marked the important parts of the article. *ʔaššarit il-ʔaqsaam il-muhimma mnil-maqaala.* -- I marked the date red on the calendar. *ʔaššarit ɛal-yoom ib-qalam ʔaḥmar bit-taqwiim.* **2.** *ɛallam (i taɛliim) t-.* The road is well marked. *ṭ-ṭariiq zeen imɛallam.* **3.** *ḥaṭṭ (u) b-baal~.* Mark my word. *ḥuṭṭ iḥčaayti b-baalak.* **4.** *ḥaṭṭ (u) ʔism~ ɛala.* Have you marked your laundry? *ḥaṭṭeet ʔismak ɛala hduumak it-tinġisil?* **5.** *ṣallaḥ (i taṣliiḥ) t-.* When will you mark our examination papers? *šwakit itṣalliḥ ʔawraaq l-imtiḥaan maalatna?*
to mark down - **1.** *sajjal (i tasjiil) t-, qayyad (i taqyiid) t-.* I've marked down the things I want. *sajjalt il-ʔašyaaʔ il-ʔariidha.* -- Mark down my address. *qayyid ɛinwaani.* **2.** *raxxaṣ (i trixxiṣ) t-.* They have marked the coats down from 20 to 15 dinars. *raxxṣaw il-maɛaaṭif min ɛišriin ʔila xmuṣṭaɛaš diinaar.*
market - *suug* pl. *swaag.* Everything is cheaper at the market. *kullši ʔarxaṣ bis-suug.* -- A new market is being built here. *suug jidiid da-yinbini hnaa.* -- They bought it on the black market. *ištirooha bis-suuq is-sawdaaʔ.*
**There is no market here for cars. *s-sayyaaraat maa ɛaleeha raġba hnaa.*
to be in the market for - *dawwar (u tadwiir) ɛala, raad (i) yištiri.* Are you in the market for a good car? *da-triid tištiri sayyaara zeena?* -- She's still in the market (for a husband). *baɛadha da-tdawwur ɛala rijjaal.* or ***baɛadha da-tintiḍir xaṭiib.*
to market - *nazzal (i tanziil) t- lil-beeɛ, ɛiraḍ (i ɛariḍ) n- lil-beeɛ, baaɛ (i beeɛ) n-.* The farmers market their produce in town. *l-fallaaḥiin ynazzluun mantuujaathum lil-beeɛ bil-wlaaya.*
to do **marketing** - *tsawwag (a miswaag).* She does her marketing in the morning. *hiyya titsawwag iṣ-ṣubuḥ.*
marriage - *zawaaj.* She has a daughter from her first marriage. *ɛidha bnayya min zawaajha l-ʔawwal.* -- Before her marriage she worked in an office. *gabuḷ zawaajha čaanat tištuġuḷ ib-daaʔira.*
married - *mitzawwij* pl. *-iin.*
to **marry** - **1.** *zawwaj (i tazwiij) t-.* They married their daughter to her first cousin. *zawwjaw binithum l-ibin ɛammha.* **2.** *tzawwaj (tazawwuj).* Is she going to marry him? *raḥ-titzawwaja?* -- Were you married in the courthouse or at home? *ʔinta tzawwajit bil-maḥkama loo bil-beet?* **3.** *ɛiqad (i) zawaaj.* Who married you? *minu ɛiqad zawaajkum?*
marvelous - *badiiɛ, ɛaal, ɛajiib.*
marsh - *mustanqaɛ* pl. *-aat, hoor* pl. *ʔahwaar.*
marshal - *maaršaal* pl. *-iyya, mušiir* pl. *-iin.*
masculine - *muδakkar.* ''Window'' is a masculine noun while ''door'' is feminine. *š-šibbaač ʔisim muδakkar wil-baab ʔisim muʔannaθ.*
to **mash** - *hiras (i haris) n-.* I want to mash the potatoes. *ʔariid ahris il-puteeta.*
mass - **1.** *jumhuur* pl. *jamaahiir.* He has the masses with him. *ɛinda j-jamaahiir wiyyaa.* **2.** *kammiyya* pl. *-aat.* He's collected a mass of material about it. *jimaɛ kammiyya čibiira ɛan il-mawḍuuɛ.*
mass production - *ʔintaaj bij-jumla.* We're not geared to mass production. *ʔiḥna ma-mithayyʔiin lil-ʔintaaj bij-jumla.*
master - *sayyid* pl. *saada.* No man can serve two masters. *ma-aku ʔaḥḥad yigdar yixdim saada θneen.* -- He is master of the situation. *huwwa sayyid il-mawqif.* or ***huwwa msayṭir ɛal-mawqif.*
to master - *ttiqan (i ttiqaan).* He mastered English in a relatively short time. *ttiqan il-ʔingiliizi b-mudda qaṣiira nisbiyyan.*

masterpiece - **1.** *fariida* pl. *faraaʔid.* His poem is one of the masterpieces of Arabic literature. *qaṣiidta min faraaʔid il-ʔadab il-εarabi.* **2.** *tuʒfa* pl. *tuʒaf.* The Iraqi Museum contains a number of masterpieces of Sumerian art. *l-matʒaf il-εiraaqi bii εiddat tuʒaf min il-fann is-soomari.*

match - **1.** *εuudat šixxaaṭ, šixxaaṭa* pl. *šixxaaṭ.* Give me a box of matches, please. *rajaaʔan inṭiini quṭiyya maal šixxaaṭ.* **2.** *musaabaqa* pl. *-aat.* Who won the match? *minu ġilab il-musaabaqa?* **3.** *nidd.* He's a match for anybody. *huwwa nidd il-kull waaʒid.* -- I'm no match for him. *ʔaani muu nidd ʔila.* or ***ʔaani muu min wazna.* or ***maa εindi qaabliita.*

to be a match - *traaham (a taraahum), twaalam (a tawaalum).* These colors aren't a good match. *hal-ʔalwaan ma-titraaham.*

to match - **1.** *ṭaabag (u muṭaabaga).* This rug matches the other one in size exactly. *haz-zuuliyya ṭṭaabug il-lux bil-kubur tamaaman.* **2.** *zaaʒam (i muzaaʒama).* No one can match our prices. *maʒʒad yigdar yzaaʒimna b-ʔasεaarna.* **3.** *waašag (i muwaašaga) t-.* You'll never be able to match this color. *ma-raʒ-tigdar itwaašig hal-loon ʔabadan.*

**I'll match you for the coffee. *xall-insawwi ṭurra kitba εal-gahwa.*

material - **1.** *maadda* pl. *mawaadd.* We use only the best materials. *ʔiʒna bass nistaεmil aʒsan il-mawaadd.* **2.** *maεluumaat.* He's collecting material for a book. *huwwa da-yijmaε maεluumaat il-fadd iktaab.* **3.** *qmaaš* pl. *ʔaqmiša.* Can you wash this material? *hal-iqmaaš yinġisil?* **4.** *maaddi** She's only interested in material things. *hiyya bass mihtamma bil-ʔašyaaʔ il-maaddiyya.* **5.** *jawhari** There is no material difference between the two. *ma-aku xtilaaf jawhari been l-iθneen.*

matter - **1.** *qaḍiyya* pl. *qaḍaaya, mawḍuuε* pl. *mawaaḍiiε.* I'll look into the matter. *ʔaani raʒ-anḍur bil-qaḍiyya.* -- This is no laughing matter. *haay muu qaḍiyyat šaqa.* -- What's the matter? *šinu l-qaḍiyya?* **2.** *masʔala* pl. *masaaʔil.* It's a matter of life and death. *haay masʔalat ʒayaat w-moot.* -- It's not a matter of price. *muu masʔalat siεir.*

**Something's the matter with his lungs. *riʔta biiha šii.*

**What's the matter with you? *š-biik?*

**That doesn't matter. *ma-yxaalif* or *ma-yhimm.*

as a matter of course - *b-ṭabiiεt il-ʒaal.* We did it as a matter of course. *sawweenaa b-ṭabiiεt il-ʒaal.*

as a matter of fact - *bil-ʒaqiiqa, bil-waaqiε.* As a matter of fact I wasn't there. *bil-ʒaqiiqa ʔaani ma-činit ihnaak.*

for that matter - *bin-nisba l-hal-mawḍuuε.* For that matter he can stay where he is. *bin-nisba l-hal-mawḍuuε yigdar yibqa b-muʒalla.*

matter-of-fact - *waaqiεi*, εamali*.* He's a very matter-of-fact person. *huwwa fadd šaxiṣ kulliš waaqiεi.*

no matter how - *šloon-ma.* No matter how we distribute them, there won't be enough for everyone. *šloon-ma nqassimhum, ma-raʒ-ykuun ʔaku kaafi l-kull waaʒid.*

no matter how much - *šgadd-ma.* No matter how much you rush me, it won't get done any sooner. *šgadd-ma txalliini ʔastaεjil, ma-raʒ-tixlaṣ ib-saaε.*

no matter what - **1.** *loo š-ma, š-ma, loo kull-ma, ma-yxaalif.* We're going no matter what you say. *loo š-ma tguul ʔinta, ʔiʒna raʒ-inruuʒ.* **2.** *š-ma.* No matter what I do, it doesn't please him. *š-ma ʔasawwi, ma-yεijba.*

matters - **1.** *ʔumuur.* You're only making matters worse. *ʔinta bass da-tεaqqid il-umuur.* **2.** *ʔašyaaʔ* You take matters too seriously. *ʔinta taaxuδ il-ʔašyaaʔ ib-jidd ʔakθar imnil-laazim.*

matting - **1.** (light) *ʒaṣiir* pl. *ʒiṣraan.* We're going to cover the floor with matting for the summer. *raʒ-nufruš il-gaaε ib-ʒiṣraan εaṣ-ṣeef.* **2.** (heavy) *baariyya* pl. *bwaari.* We need some matting to make a partition here. *yirraad-inna čam baariyya ʒatta nsawwi ʒaajiz ihnaa.*

mattress - *doošag* pl. *dwaašig.*

mature - *naaḍij.* The boy is very mature for his age. *l-walad kulliš naaḍij bin-nisba l-εumra.*

maximum - *l-ʒadd il-ʔaεla l-, ʔaqṣa.* The maximum salary for this position is eighty dinars a month. *l-ʒadd il-ʔaεla l-raatib hal-waḍiifa θmaaniin diinaar biš-šahar.* -- The maximum penalty for this crime is ten years in prison. *ʔaqṣa εuquuba l-haj-jariima hiyya εašr isniin ʒabis.*

**I'm willing to pay twenty dinars, but that's the maximum. *ʔaani mistiεidd adfaε εišriin diinaar, laakin haaδa ʔaʒyad šii.*

May - *maayis, ʔayyaar.*

may - **1.** *mumkin.* May I keep this pencil? *mumkin ʔaʒtufuḍ ib-hal-qalam?* or ***tismaʒ-li ʔaʒtufuḍ ib-hal-qalam.* -- May I have the next game? *mumkin ʔalεab il-liεba j-jaaya?* -- May I meet with you at five o'clock? *mumkin ʔaji ʔawaajhak saaεa xamsa?* -- **May I offer you a cup of coffee? *ʔagdar aqaddim-lak fadd finjaan gahwa?* **2.** *mumkin, yimkin, yjuuz.* That may be so. *yimkin hiiči.* -- I may be able to come. *ʔaani yimkin ʔagdar aji.* **3.** *rubba-ma, muʒtamal, yimkin, mumkin.* I may have said it. *rubba-ma ʔaani gilitha.*

**Be that as it may... *wa-loo haaδa hiici...*

maybe - *yimkin, mumkin, muʒtamal, rubba-ma.* Maybe he's not at home. *yimkin muu bil-beet.*

meadow - *marεa* pl. *maraaεi, giṣiil.* I want to rent some meadow land for my horse. *ʔariid aʔajjir qiṭεat giṣiil l-iʒṣaani.*

meager - *qaliil, ḍaʔiil, ṭafiif.* The results were meager. *n-nataaʔij čaanat qaliila.*

meal - *ʔakla* pl. *-aat, wajba* pl. *-aat.* Three meals a day aren't enough for him. *ma-tkaffii tlaθ ʔaklaat bil-yoom.* -- I haven't eaten a decent meal in weeks. *ṣaar-li čam isbuuε ma-maakil wajba biiha xeer.*

mean - **1.** *xissa* pl. *xisas.* It was mean of him to treat you like that. *čaanat xissa minna yεaamlak haš-šikil.* **2.** *xasiis, laʔiim.* That's a mean trick. *haδiič fadd ʒiila xasiisa.* **3.** *waḍiiε.* He says very mean things to me. *ygul-li ʔašyaaʔ kullis waḍiiεa.* **4.** *muuδi* pl. *-iyya, wakiiʒ* pl. *wukkaʒ.* Those mean boys in the street are teasing me. *hal-wulid il-muuδiyya bid-darub da-yḍawwjuuni.* **5.** *šaris.* Our neighbors have a mean dog. *jiiraanna εidhum čalib šaris.*

**He plays mean. *ybiiε naδaala.*

to **mean** - **1.** *εina (i maεna) n-, qiṣad (u qaṣid) n-, nuwa (i niyya) n-.* What do you mean by that? *š-tiεni b-haay?* -- You mean to say you saw everything? *yaεni ʔinta šifit kullši?* -- I didn't mean any harm. *ʔaani ma-qṣadit ʔay ʔaδiyya.* -- What do you mean to do? *š-tinwi tsawwi?* **2.** *hamm (i).* It means a lot to me to see him tonight. *yhimmni kulliš ʔašuufa hal-leela.* **3.** *čaan (ykuun) qaṣid-.* I meant to call, but I forgot. *čaan qaṣdi ʔaxaabur laakin niseet.*

**His friendship means a lot to me. *ṣadaaqta εaziiza εalayya.*

**That remark was meant for you. *hal-mulaaʒaḍaat ʔinta nεineet biiha.*

**Is the book meant for me? *l-maqṣuud ib-hal-iktaab ʔan ʔaaxδa ʔaani?* or *yaεni haaδa l-iktaab ʔili?*

meaning - *maεna* pl. *maεaani.* This word has several meanings. *hal-kilma ʔilha εiddat maεaani.* -- What's the meaning of this? *šinu maεna haay?*

means - **1.** *wasiila* pl. *wasaaʔil.* It was just a means to an end. *ma-čaanat ġeer wasiila l-fadd ġaaya.* -- He doesn't have the means to do it. *maa εinda l-wasaaʔil ʒatta ysawwiiha.* **2.** *qaabliyya* pl. *-aat.* He lives beyond his means. *yuṣruf ʔakθar min qaabliita.*

**She married a man of means. *tzawwjat rijjaal ʔaḷḷa mfaḍḍil εalee.*

by all means - **1.** *min kull la-budd.* By all means take the job. *min kull la-budd, ʔiqbal hal-waḍiifa.* **2.** *maεluum.* Could I have the book now? By all means! *tismaʒ-li bil-iktaab hassa? maεluum!*

by means of - *b-waaṣṭat.* -- You can regulate it by means of a screw. *tigdar itnaḍḍimha b-waaṣṭat burġi.*

by no means - *ʔabadan muu, muṭlaqan muu.* He's by no means stupid. *huwwa ʔabadan muu ġabi.*

meanwhile - *b-hal-ʔaθnaaʔ, xilaal hal-fatra.*

measles - *ʒaṣba.*

measly - *mšaʒʒaṭ.* He can't get along on his measly salary. *ma-yigdar ydabbur ʔamra b-hal-maεaaš il-imšaʒʒaṭ.*

measure - **1.** *miqyaas* pl. *maqaayiis.* A table of

weights and measures. *jadwal bil-ʔawzaan wil-maqaayiis.* **2.** *qiyaas* pl. *-aat.* What is his waist measure? *šinu qiyaas xiṣra?* **3.** *čeela* pl. *-aat, keela* pl. *-aat.* How much is popcorn by the measure? *beeš čeelt iš-šaamiyya?* **4.** *ʔijraaʔ* pl. *-aat.* We'll have to take strong measures. *laazim nittixið ʔijraaʔaat zaazima.* **5.** *wazin* pl. *ʔawzaan.* This word is on the measure ''Faεlaan''. *hal-kalima εala wazin ''faεlaan''.*

to measure - 1. *qaas (i qiyaas) n-.* Measure the height of the window exactly. *qiis irtifaaε iš-šibbaač bið-ðabuṭ.* -- We'll have to measure the room before we buy the rug. *laazim inqiis il-ġurfa gabuḷ-ma ništiri s-sijjaada.* **2.** *čaal (i čeel) n-.* He measured out two measures of watermelon seeds and put them in a bag. *čaal čeelteen zabb raggi w-zaṭṭa b-čiis.*

measurement - *qiyaas* pl. *-aat.* Are these measurements correct? *hal-qiyaasaat ṣaziiza?* -- Did the tailor take your measurements? *l-xayyaaṭ ʔaxað qiyaasaatak?*

meat - *lazam* pl. *luzuum.* Do you have any meat today? *εindak lazam hal-yoom?*

mechanic - *miikaaniiki* pl. *-iyyiin, fiitarči* pl. *-iyya.*

mechanical - *miikaaniiki**

medal - *wisaam* pl. *ʔawsima, madaalya* pl. *-aat.*

to **meddle** - *tdaxxal (a tadaxxul), tdaaxal (a tadaaxul).* He likes to meddle in other people's business. *huwwa yεijba yitdaxxal ib-šuʔuun in-naas.*

medical - *ṭibbi** I'm under medical treatment. *ʔaani tazt il-εilaaj iṭ-ṭibbi.* or *ʔaani tazt it-tadaawi.* -- Look it up in the medical dictionary. *ṭalliεha bil-qaamuus iṭ-ṭibbi.*

medicine - 1. *duwa* pl. *ʔadwiya.* This medicine tastes bitter. *had-duwa ṭaεma murr.* -- Have you taken your medicine yet? *ʔaxaðit id-duwa maalak loo baεad.* **2.** *ṭibb.* My daughter is studying medicine. *binti da-tidrus ṭibb.*

Mediterranean sea - *l-bazr il-ʔabyað il-mutawaṣṣiṭ, l-bazr il-mutawaṣṣiṭ.*

medium - 1. *mitwaṣṣiṭ, muεtadil.* He's of medium height. *ṭuula mitwaṣṣiṭ.* **2.** *εan-nuṣṣ.* I like my steak medium-broiled. *ʔariid l-isteek maali mašwi εan-nuṣṣ.*

**It's hard to find a happy medium. *mniṣ-ṣaεub tilgi zall waṣaṭ.*

medium-sized - *mitwaṣṣiṭ.* It's a medium-sized task. *hiyya fadd šaġla mitwaṣṣṭa.*

to **meet - 1.** *jtimaε (i jtimaaε).* The committee is going to meet at Ahmad's house. *l-lujna raz-tijtimiε ib-beet ʔazmad.* **2.** *tlaaqa (i talaaqi), ltiqa (i ltiqaaʔ).* Let's meet at the coffee shop at six o'clock. *xal-nitlaaqa bil-qahwa saaεa sitta.* **3.** *waajah (i muwaajaha) t-, ṣaadaf (i muṣaadafa) t-, laaga (i mulaagaa) t-.* Did you meet him on the street? *waajahta biš-šaariε?.* **4.** *qaabal (i muqaabala) t-, tlagga (a talaggi), staqbal (i stiqbaal).* He met us with a smile. *qaabalna b-ibtisaama.* -- Will you please meet them at the train station? *baḷḷa ma-truuz titlaggaahum ib-muzaṭṭat il-qiṭaar?* **5.** *tεarraf (a taεarruf) b-.* I met him at a party last night. *tεarrafit bii b-zafla l-baarza bil-leel.* -- I'm interested in meeting some artists. *yiεjibni ʔatεarraf εala baεð il-fannaaniin.* **6.** *twaṣṣal (a).* The two ends of the wire don't meet. *nihaayteen it-teel ma-yitwaṣṣaluun.* **7.** *ttifaq (i ttifaaq).* We hope this pipe will meet with your specifications. *nitʔammal hal-buuriyyaat tittifiq wiyya mawaaṣafatkum.* **8.** *waffa (i tawfiya) b-.* They couldn't meet their obligations. *ma-gidraw ywaffuun b-iltizaamaathum.* **9.** *sadd (i sadd).* I can barely meet my expenses. *bil-kaad ʔagdar asidd maṣaariifi.* **10.** *zaqqaq (i tazqiiq) t-.* My demands are easily met. *tazqiiq ṭalabaati muu ṣaεub.*

**I'll be glad to meet you halfway. *maa εindi maaniε insawwi taswiya beenaatna.*

**Pleased to meet you. *ʔatšarraf.* or *tšarrafna.*

to meet with - *ziṣal (a zuṣuul) εala.* I think this will meet with your approval. *ʔaεtiqid haaða š-šii raz-yizṣal εala riðaaʔak.*

meeting - 1. *jtimaaε* pl. *-aat, jalsa* pl. *-aat.* There were five hundred people at the meeting. *čaan ʔaku xamis miit šaxiṣ bil-ijtimaaε.* -- The committee meeting lasted two hours. *jalsat il-lujna stamarrat saaεteen.* **2.** *muqaabala* pl. *-aat.* I arranged for a meeting of the two. *rattabit fadd muqaabala beenaathum.*

melody - *naġma* pl. *-aat, lazan* pl. *ʔalzaan.*

to **melt - 1.** *ðaab (u ðawabaan), maaε (u mawaεaan).* The ice is all melted. *θ-θalij kulla ðaab.* **2.** *mawwaε (i tamwiiε) t-.* Melt the butter. *mawwiε iz-zibid.*

member - *εuðu* pl. *ʔaεðaaʔ* Are you a member of this club? *ʔinta εuðu b-han-naadi?* -- We'll have to amputate the injured member. *laazim nigṭaε il-εuðu l-muṣaab.*

membership - *εuðwiyya* pl. *-aat.* Our membership is down to less than one hundred. *l-εuðwiyya εidna nizlat ʔila ʔaqall min miyya.*

memory - 1. *ðaakira.* My memory is not what it used to be. *ðaakirti muu miθil-ma čaanat.* **2.** *ðikra* pl. *-ayaat.* I have pleasant memories of this town. *εindi ðikrayaat zilwa b-hal-madiina.*

menace - *xaṭar* pl. *ʔaxṭaar.* He's a menace to society. *huwwa xaṭar εal-mujtamaε.* -- The menace of atomic war occupies everyone's mind. *xaṭar il-zarb ið-ðarriyya šaaġil baal kull in-naas.*

to **mend - 1.** *raaf (u rwaaf) n-, xayyaṭ (i xyaaṭ, txiyyiṭ) t-.* When will you mend my jacket? *yamta raz-itruuf sitirti?* **2.** *lizam (a lazim) n-.* Have the tinsmith mend the crack in this pan. *xalli t-tanakči yilzam il-faṭir bij-jidir.* -- The broken bone will take some time to mend. *l-εaðum il-maksuur yriid-la mudda zatta yilzam.* **3.** *zassan (i tazsiin) t-.* You'll have to mend your ways. *laazim itzassin ʔaxlaaqak.* or **laazim tiεqal.*

to **mention** - *ðikar (u ðikir) n-.* He didn't mention the price. *ma-ðikar is-siεir.* or *ma-jaab ṭaari s-siεir.* -- I heard his name mentioned. *smaεit isma nðikar.* -- I would also like to mention... *hamm ʔazibb ʔaðkur ʔan...*

**Thank you very much. Don't mention it. *ʔaškurak jiddan. mamnuun.* or *l-εafu.*

**That's not worth mentioning. *ma-tistiziqq ið-ðikir.* or *haaða muu šii.*

menu - *qaaʔimat (pl. qawaaʔim) ʔakil.*

merchandise - *biðaaεa* pl. *baðaayiε, silεa* pl. *silaε.* The merchandise arrived in good order. *l-biðaaεa wuṣlat ib-zaala zeena.*

merchant - *taajir* pl. *tijjaar.*

merchant marine - *ʔisṭool tijaari.*

mercury - 1. (quicksilver) *zeebag.* **2.** (mercuric chloride) *sleemaani.* **3.** (planet) *εuṭaarid.*

mercy - *razma* pl. *-aat, raʔfa* pl. *-aat.* He pleaded for mercy. *ṭilab ir-razma.* -- He has no mercy. *maa εinda razma.*

mere - *bass, mujarrad.* The mere thought of it disturbs me. *mujarrad it-tafkiir biiha yizεijni.* -- She's a mere child; too young to get married. *hiyya mujarrad ṭifla, muu b-sinn iz-zawaaj.*

merely - *faqaṭ, laa ġeer.* I was merely joking. *čaan qaṣdi n-nukta, laa ġeer.*

merit - *qiima* pl. *qiyam.* There is little of merit in his book. *ʔaku qiima qaliila l-kitaaba.*

to merit - *staahal (i), stazaqq (i stizqaaq), stawjab (i).* I think he merits a raise. *ʔaεtiqid yistaahil tarfiiε.*

merry - *mariz.*

mess - 1. *xarbaṭa* pl. *-aat, hoosa* pl. *-aat.* Did you see the mess the painters left? *šift il-xarbaṭa l-xallooha ṣ-ṣabbaaġiin waraahum.* -- I can't find anything in this mess. *ma-agdar ʔalgi ʔay šii b-hal-hoosa.* **2.** *wurṭa* pl. *wuraṭ.* You certainly got yourself into a nice mess! *laakin ʔinta ṣidug imwaggiε nafsak ib-fadd wurṭa mlabilba.* **3.** *qaaεat* (pl. *-aat*) *ṭaεaam.* I'm invited to dinner at the officer's mess. *ʔaani madεu lil-ʔakil ib-qaaεat ṭaεaam ið-ðubbaaṭ.*

**The house is an awful mess. *l-beet waaguf ṭuul.* or *l-beet kulliš imxarbaṭ.*

to mess - 1. *štirak (i štiraak) bil-ʔakil.* You will mess with the officers during your tour of duty here. *raz-tištirik wiyya ð-ðubbaat bil-ʔakil muddat iltizaaqak ihnaa.* **2.** *liεab (a liεib) n-.* Don't mess with the radio! *la-tilεab bir-raadyo!*

to mess up - 1. *waṣṣax (i twiṣṣix) t-.* Don't mess up the floor with your wet feet. *la-twaṣṣix il-gaaε ib-rijlak l-imballila.* **2.** *xarbaṭ (i xarbaṭa) t-.* Who messed up the papers on my desk? *minu xarbaṭ il-ʔawraaq εala meezi?*

message - *xabar* pl. *ʔaxbaar, risaala* pl. *rasaaʔil, maktuub* pl. *makaatiib.* Did anyone leave a message for me? *ʔazzad tirak-li xabar?* -- Could you take a message for him? *ʔagdar azuṭṭ-la xabar εindak?* -- Did you give him the message? *ballaġta r-risaala?*

messenger - 1. *muwazziε* (pl. *-iin*) *barq.* The telegraph office employs ten messengers. *daa?irt il-barq tistaxdim Eašir muwazziEiin.* 2. *farraaš* pl. *-iin, faraariiš.* The messenger from the Director's office wants to speak to you. *farraaš il-mudiir yriid ykallmak.* 3. *taariš* pl. *tawaariiš.* A messenger came from the village to invite us to the wedding. *jaana taariš imnil-qarya zatta yiEzimna Eal-Eiris.*

metal - *maEdan* pl. *maEaadin.*

method - *tariiqa* pl. *turuq, ?isluub* pl. *?asaaliib.* He's discovered a new method. *ktišaf tariiqa jidiida.*

middle - 1. *nuşş* pl. *nşaaş.* I'm leaving the middle of next week. *?aani raayiz ib-nuşş il-?isbuuE ij-jaay.* 2. *mitwaşşit.* He's a man of middle height. *huwwa fadd rijjaal mitwaşşit it-tuul.* 3. *waşat, nuşş.* He was standing in the middle of the room. *čaan waaguf ib-waşat il-ġurfa.* -- The man fell in the middle of the street. *r-rijjal wugaE ib-nuşş iš-šaariE.* 4. *waştaani*.* Open the middle window. *fukk iš-šibbaač il-waştaani.* 5. *?aθnaa?.* He got up in the middle of the session and walked out. *gaam ib-?aθnaa? ij-jalsa w-tilaE barra.*

**I'm in the middle of packing. *?aani maxbuuş da-alimm ġaraaδi.*

**He's in his middle forties. *Eumra been il-?arbaEiin wil-xamsiin.*

middle-aged - *mutwaşşit bil-Eumur.* She's a middle-aged woman. *hiyya fadd wazda mutwaşşta bil-Eumur.*

Middle Ages - *l-quruun il-wuşta.*

Middle East - *š-šarz il-?awşat.*

midnight - *nuşş il-leel.* It was past midnight when we fell asleep. *čaanat baEad nuşş il-leel lumman iġfeena.*

might - 1. *quwwa.* Might makes right, as they say. *l-zaqq lil-quwwa, miθil-ma yguuluun.* 2. *Eaδama* pl. *-aat.* The might of the Babylonian kings will never be forgotten. *Eaδamat il-miluuk il-baabiliyyiin ?abadan ma-tinnisi.*

mighty - 1. *Eaδiim, haa?il.* He got together a mighty force and stormed the city. *jimaE quwwa Eaδiima w-inqaδδ Eal-madiina.* 2. *qawi*, šadiid.* A mighty wind destroyed their crops. *fadd riiz qawwiyya dammirat zaaşlaathum.* 3. *kulliš.* He's done mighty little work today. *huwwa tallaE kulliš šwayya šuġul hal-yoom.*

mild - 1. *muEtadil.* This is a mild climate. *haaδa jaww muEtadil.* 2. *latiif.* The sun is mild today. *š-šamis latiifa l-yoom.* 3. *baarid.* Do you have a mild tobacco. *Eindak titin baarid.* 4. *δaEiif, xafiif.* He suffered a mild heart attack last winter. *şaarat Einda nawba qalbiyya δaEiifa š-šita l-faat.*

mile - *miil* pl. *?amyaal.* It's three miles from here. *hiyya b-biEid itlaθ amyaal minnaa.*

military - *Easkari*.* They have military discipline. *Eidhum δabut Easkari.*

milk - *zaliib.* The milk has turned sour. *l-zaliib zammaδ.*

**There's no use crying over spilt milk. *l-faat maat.*

to milk - *zilab (i zalib) n-.* Do you know how to milk a cow? *tuEruf išloon tizlib baqara?* -- They tried to milk him of his money. *zaawlaw yzilbuun kull ifluusa minna.*

mill - 1. *taazuuna* pl. *tawaaziin, maEmal* pl. *maEaamil.* When are you going to take the grain to the mill? *šwakit raz-taaxuδ il-zubuub lit-taazuuna?* 2. *maEmal* pl. *maEaamil.* We ordered the paper straight from the mill. *tlabna l-waraq ra?san imnil-maEmal.*

miller - *tazzaan* pl. *-iin.*

million - *milyoon* pl. *malaayiin.* New York has seven and half million inhabitants. *nyuuyoork biiha sabiE malaayiin w-nuşş imnis-sukkaan.* -- I've got a million things to do before dinner. *laazim asawwi milyoon šii gabl il-Eaša.*

mind - 1. *fikir* pl. *?afkaar.* He had a very keen mind. *čaan Einda fikir kulliš zaadd.* -- He doesn't know his own mind. *ma-yistiqirr Eala fikir.* -- I have something else in mind. *Eindi ġeer šii b-fikri.* 2. *baal.* Keep your mind on your work. *diir baalak Eala šuġlak.* or *?izşir fikrik ib-šuġlak.* -- What's on your mind? *šaku Eala baalak?* or **š-da-tfakkir?* 3. *δihin* pl. *?aδhaan.* The thought went through my mind that I had seen him before. *l-fikra marrat ib-δihni ?aani šifta gabul.* 4. *Eaqliyya* pl. *-aat.* He has a good mind. *Eaqliita zeena.* 5. *ra?i* pl. *?aaraa?.* To my mind she's the right person for the job. *b-ra?yi ?aani hiyya š-šaxiş il-mulaa?im liš-šaġla.*

**You can't be in your right mind. *haaδa zači maal waazid Eaaqil?* or *?inta xarfaan?*

**My mind is not clear on what happened. *ma-?aEruf biδ-δabut iš-şaar.*

**I have a good mind to tell him so. *Eaqli yigtaE agul-la.*

to call to mind - *δakkar (i taδkiir, tδikkir) t- b-.* That calls to mind a story I know. *haay tδakkir ib-fadd quşşa ?aErufha.*

to make up one's mind - *staqarr (i stiqraar) Eala qaraar.* We'll have to make up our minds shortly. *laazim nistaqirr Eala qaraar baEad fatra qaşiira.*

to set one's mind on - *şammam (i taşmiim).* She has her mind set on going shopping today. *hiyya şammimat itruuz titsawwag il-yoom.*

to mind - *daar (i dayaraan) baal~.* Don't mind what he says. *la-tdiir baalak l-ill-yguula.* -- Who's going to mind the baby? *minu raz-ydiir baala Eaj-jaahil?* -- My son doesn't mind me anymore. *?ibni baEad ma-ydiir-li baal.* -- Mind your own business. *diir baalak Eala šuġlak.* or ***ma-Ealeek min šuġul ġeerak.*

**I hope you don't mind me leaving now. *?aani ?at?ammal maa Eindak maaniE ?iδa ?aruuz hassa.*

**I don't mind going alone. *maa Eindi maaniE ?aruuz wazdi.*

**I don't mind the hot weather anymore. *tEallamit Eaj-jaww il-zaarr.*

mine - 1. *manjam* pl. *manaajim.* Who owns this mine? *minu yimlik hal-manjam?* 2. *luġum* pl. *?alġaam.* Their ship ran into a mine. *δaaxirathum iştidmat ib-luġum.*

to mine - 1. *tallaE (i tatliiE) t-.* How much coal did they mine in May? *šgadd fazam tallEaw imnil-manjam xilaal maayis?* 2. *ligam (u lagum) n-.* The roads are mined. *t-turuq malġuuma.*

miner- *Eaamil (pl. Eummaal) manjam.* The miners live near the mine. *Eummaal il-manjam ysiknuun yamma.*

mine sweeper - *kaasizat (pl. -aat) ?alġaam.*

minimum - *?aqall, zadd ?adna.* What's the minimum? *šinu ?aqall šii.* -- The minimum wage is three dinars a week. *?aqall ?ujra θlaθ dinaaniir bil-?isbuuE.*

minister - 1. *qass* pl. *qasasa.* Our church has a new minister. *kaniisatna biiha qass jidiid.* 2. *waziir* pl. *wuzaraa?.* Three ministers have resigned. *tlaθ wuzaraa? istaqaalaw.* -- He was appointed minister to Portugal. *tEayyan waziir mufawwaδ bil-purtaġaal.*

minor - 1. *başiit, tafiif, taafih.* I made only minor changes. *bass sawweet tabdiilaat başiita.* -- That's a minor matter. *haaδa fadd šii taafih.* 2. *qaaşir* pl. *-iin, quşşaar.* As long as the boy is a minor, his uncle will be his guardian. *madaam il-walad qaaşir, Eamma raz-yibqa waşi Ealee.*

minority - *?aqalliyya.* We were in the miniority. *činna mnil-?aqalliyya.*

minute - *daqiiq, şġayyir.* It was so minute it could hardly be seen. *hal-gadd-ma şġayyra bil-kaad tinšaaf.* -- I have checked the most minute detail. *raajaEit zatta ?adaqq it-tafaaşiil.*

minute - 1. *daqiiqa* pl. *daqaayiq.* I'll be back in five minutes. *raz-arjaE xilaal xamis daqaayiq.* -- I'll drop in for a minute. *raz-amurr fadd daqiiqa.* 2. *lazδa* pl. *-aat.* Just a minute, please. *fadd lazδa, min faδlak.*

**I'll call you the minute I know. *raz-axaabrak ?awwal-ma yşiir Eindi xabar.*

minutes - *mazδar* pl. *mazaaδir.* The secretary will read the minutes of the last meeting. *s-sikirteer raz-yiqra mazδar ij-jalsa s-saabiqa.*

miracle - *muEjiza* pl. *-aat.*

mirror - *mraaya* pl. *-aat.* Look at yourself in the mirror. *šuuf nafsak bil-imraaya.*

miscarriage - *?ijhaaδ, tariz.* She had a miscarriage. *şaar Eidha ?ijhaaδ.* or ***hiyya tirzat.*

mischief - *?aδiyya* pl. *-aat.* That boy is always up to some mischief. *hal-walad daa?iman wara l-?aδiyya.*

miser - *šaziiz* pl. *-iin, baxiil* pl. *buxalaa?.*

miserable - 1. *taEiis* pl. *tuEasaa?, baa?is* pl. *bu?asaa?, miskiin* pl. *masaakiin.* I feel miserable today. *?ašEur taEiis hal-yoom.* or ***talfaan hal-yoom.* or ***nafsi maqbuuδa.* -- She makes life miserable for him. *da-tsawwi zayaata taEiisa.* or ***da-tnaqqiş Eiišta.* or ***da-tmarmur zayaata.* 2. *mhalhal.* They live in a miserable shack. *ysiknuun ib-fadd kuux imhalhal.* or ***saakniin ib-beet miθl il-xaraaba.* 3. *kasiif.* What miserable weather! *šloon jaww kasiif!*

misery - *taEaasa, šaqaa?, bu?s, δanak.* They lived in utter misery. *Eaašaw ib-taEaasa.*

misfortune - *muṣiiba* pl. *maṣaayib, nakba.* It won't be a great misfortune if you don't get it. *yaɛni ma-raħ-iṭṣiir fadd muṣiiba ʔiða ma-tigdar itħaṣṣla.*
to **misjudge** - *xitaʔ (i xataʔ) n- bil-ħukum.* We mustn't misjudge the seriousness of the situation. *ma-laazim nixtiʔ bil-ħukum ɛala xuṭuurat il-ħaala.*-- You misjudge him. *ʔinta xitaʔit bil-ħukum ɛalee.*
to **mislead** - *xidaɛ (a xudaaɛ) n-.* This advertisement misleads the reader. *hal-ʔiɛlaan yixdaɛ il-qaariʔ.*
misleading - *xaddaaɛ.* The description is misleading. *l-wuṣuf xaddaaɛ.*
misprint - *ġalaṭ maṭbaɛi* pl. *ʔaġlaaṭ maṭbaɛiyya, ġalṭa* (pl. *-aat*) *maṭbaɛiyya.*
miss - **1.** *ʔaanisa* pl. *-aat.* How do you do, Miss Suad? *šloon keefič, ʔaanisa suɛaad?* **2.** *xaṭya* pl. *-aat.* You have two hits and three misses. *ɛindak ʔiṣaabteen w-itlaθ xaṭyaat.*
**A miss is as good as a mile. *l-ġalṭa ġalṭa w-law ib-gadd iš-šaɛra.*
to miss - **1.** *xiṭa (i xaṭi) n-.* You missed the target. *xiṭeet il-hadaf.* -- Our house is so easy to find you can't miss it. *beetna yinligi b-suhuula, ma-tigdar taxṭii.* -- He missed hitting me by a hair. *ð̣arubta xiṭatni b-šaɛra.* **2.** *tfaawat (a tafaawut) wiyya.* I missed him at the station. *tfaawatit wiyyaa bil-maħaṭṭa.* **3.** *stawħaš (i stiwħaaš) l-* I'll miss you terribly. *raħ-astawħiš-lak kulliš ihwaaya.* or **makaanak raħ-ybayyin.*
**Don't miss this picture. *la-tfuutak hal-filim.*
**Do you think I'll miss my train? *tiɛtiqid raħ-yfuutni l-qiṭaarʔ.*
**You haven't missed a thing. *ma-faatak fadd šii muhimm.*
**You missed the point of my story. *faatak maġza ħčaayti.*
missing - *ð̣aayiɛ.* The child has been missing for three days. *ṭ-ṭifil ṣaar-la tlaθt iyyaam ð̣aayiɛ.*
mist - *ð̣ubaab xafiif.*
mistake - **1.** *ġalaṭ* pl. *ʔaġlaaṭ, ġalṭa* pl. *-aat.* How did you make such a mistake? *šloon ġalaṭit hiiči ġalṭa.* -- Sorry, I took it by mistake. *ʔaasif ʔaxaðitha bil-ġalaṭ.* -- There must be some mistake. *laazim ʔaku fadd šii ġalaṭ.* **2.** *ṣuuč.* Sorry, my mistake. *mitʔassif, ṣuuči.* or *ʔaasif, haay ġaliṭṭi.*
to make a mistake - *štibah (i štibaah).* Make no mistake, this is a serious matter. *la-tištibih, il-mawð̣uuɛ jiddi.*
to mistake - **1.** *fiham (a fahim) ġalaṭ, ʔasaaʔ (i ʔisaaʔa) fihim-.* I mistook his intention. *fihamit niita ġalaṭ.* -- Please don't mistake me. *ʔarjuuk la-tsiiʔ fihmi.* **2.** *štibah (i štibaah) b-* Sorry, I mistook you for someone else. *ʔaasif, ištibahit biik ib-šaxiṣ ʔaaxar.*
mistaken - **1.** *ġalṭaan, xaaṭiʔ.* That's a mistaken belief. *haaða ɛtiqaad ġalṭaan.* -- There you're mistaken. *ʔinta ġalṭaan ib-ðiiči.* **2.** *xaṭaʔ b-* It was a case of mistaken identity. *čaanat qað̣iyyat xaṭaʔ bit-taʕriif.*
to **mistreat** - *ʔasaaʔ (i ʔisaaʔa) n- muɛaamala-.* The servant mistreated the children. *l-xaadim ʔasaaʔ muɛaamalat ij-jihhaal.*
mistress - **1.** *ṣaaħiba* pl. *-aat, sayyida* pl. *-aat.* The dog didn't recognize his mistress. *č-čalib ma-ɛiraf ṣaaħibta.* **2.** *ɛašiiqa* pl. *-aat, rfiija* pl. *-aat.* She's his mistress. *hiyya rfiijta.*
to **mix** - **1.** *xubaṭ (u xabuṭ) n-.* I mixed yellow and red. *xbaṭit ʔaṣfar w-aħmar.* -- Mix the paint well before you use it. *ʔuxbuṭ iṣ-ṣubuġ zeen gabuḷ-ma tistaɛmila.* **2.** *traaham (a taraahum).* Pickles and milk don't mix. *ṭ-ṭurši wil-ħaliib ma-yitraahmuun.* **3.** *txaalaṭ (a taxaaluṭ), xtilaṭ (i xtilaaṭ).* We don't mix much with our neighbors. *ʔiħna ma-nitxaalaṭ ihwaaya wiyya jwaariinna.* **4.** *daxxal (i tadxiil, tdixxil) nafis˜.* She likes to mix in other people's business. *hiyya yiɛjibha tdaxxil nafisha b-šuġuḷ in-naas.*
to mix in - *tdaaxal (a tadaaxul), tdaxxal (a tadaxxul).* Don't mix in, this is none of your business. *la-titdaaxal, haaða muu šuġlak.* --
to mix up - **1.** *xarbaṭ (u xarbaṭa, txurbuṭ) t-.* Don't mix up the cards. *la-txarbuṭ il-biṭaaqaat.* **2.** *šawwaš (i tašwiiš)t-, ʔarbak (i ʔirbaak) n-.* Don't mix me up. *la-tšawwišni.* **3.** *daxxal (i tadxiil tdixxil) t-.* Don't mix me up in your argument. *la-tdaxxilni b-jadalkum.*
mixed up - **1.** *hoosa* pl. *-aat.* Your work is all mixed up. *šuġlak hoosa.* **2.** *mitxarbuṭ, mirtibik.* I'm so mixed up I don't know what I'm doing. *ʔaani hal-gadd-ma mitxarbuṭ ma-da-ʔaɛruf iš-da-asawwi.*
mixture - *maziij* pl. *-aat, xaliiṭ* pl. *-aat.*
mix-up - *xarbaṭa* pl. *-aat, xaraabiiṭ.* There was an awful mix-up. *ṣaarat fadd xarbaṭa fað̣iiɛa.*
to **moan** - *wann (i wann).* I could hear him moaning in the next room. *gdarit asimɛa ywinn ib-ġurfat il-lux.*
mob - **1.** *ġawġaaʔ.* The mob almost lynched him. *l-ġawġaaʔ taqriiban ɛalliqoo.* **2.** *jamaaɛa* pl. *-aat.* There's a mob of people waiting for you. *ʔaku fadd jamaaɛa b-intið̣aarak.*
to mob - **1.** *hijam (i hujuum) ɛala.* The girls mobbed him for his autograph. *l-banaat hijmaw ɛalee b-ṭalab tawqiiɛa.* **2.** *tkaddas (a takaddus) ɛala.* People mob the stores before the holiday. *l-maxaazin titkaddas ɛaleeha n-naas gabḷ il-ɛiid.*
model - **1.** *namuuðaj* pl. *namaaðij.* He's working on the model of a bridge. *huwwa da-ysawwi namuuðaj il-fadd jisir.* **2.** *muudeel* pl. *-aat.* This is the latest model. *haaði ʔaaxir muudeel.* **3.** *ɛaarið̣a* pl. *-aat.* She is a clothes model in a fashionable dress shop. *hiyya ɛaariḍat ʔazyaaʔ ib-maxzan ɛaṣri.* **4.** *miθaal* pl. *muθul, qidwa* pl. *-aat.* They took him as a model. *ttixðoo ka-qidwa.* **5.** *miθaali*, namuuðaji*.* She's a model wife. *hiyya zawja miθaaliyya.*
to model - **1.** *ɛirað̣ (u ɛarið̣) n-.* She models women's clothing. *tiɛrudˌ ʔazyaaʔ nisaaʔiyya.* **2.** *tšakkal (i).* The boy has begun to model himself after his hero. *l-walad bida yitšakkal ib-šikil baṭala.*
moderate - *muɛtadil, mutwaṣṣiṭ.* He has moderate political views. *ʔafkaara s-siyaasiyya muɛtadla.*
modern - *ħadiiθ, ɛaṣri*, ɛal-mooda.* She has a modern kitchen. *ɛidha fadd maṭbax ɛaṣri.*
modest - *muħtašim, mutwaað̣iɛ.* She's a very modest person. *hiyya fadd waħda kulliš muħtašma.* -- The king is modest. *l-maalik mitwaað̣iɛ.*
moist - *raṭib, nadi, naadi, mballal.*
to **moisten** - *ballal (i tabliil, tbillil) t-.* Moisten the stamp. *ballil iṭ-ṭaabiɛ.*
moisture - *rṭuuba, nida.*
mold - **1.** *ɛfuuna.* There was a layer of mold on the cheese. *čaan ʔaku ṭabaqa mnil-iɛfuuna ɛaj-jibin.* **2.** *qaalab* pl. *qwaalib.* You can use this mold for the pudding. *tigdar tistaɛmil hal-qaalab lil-puding.*
to mold - **1.** *ɛaffan (i taɛfiin) t-.* If you leave the cheese here it will mold. *ʔiða titruk ij-jibin ihnaa yɛaffin.* **2.** *kayyaf (i takyiif) t-, šakkal (i taškiil) t-.* Mold the clay with your hands. *kayyif iṭ-ṭiin ib-iidak.*
moldy - *mɛaffin, mitɛaffin.* The bread is moldy. *l-xubuz imɛaffin.*
mole - **1.** *xuld* pl. *ħaywaanaat xuld.* We've a mole in our garden. *ɛidna fadd xuld ib-ħadiiqatna.* **2.** *šaama* pl. *-aat.* He has a large mole on his cheek. *ɛinda šaama čbiira ɛala xadda.*
molecule - *juzayʔa* pl. *-aat.*
moment - *laħð̣a* pl. *-aat.* Wait a moment. *ntið̣ir laħð̣a.*
at a moment's notice - *b-ʔay laħð̣a.* Be ready to leave at a moment's notice. *kuun ħaað̣ir itġaadir b-ʔay laħð̣a.*
at the moment - *b-hal-wakit, b-hal-laħð̣a.* At the moment I can't give you any further information. *b-hal-wakit ma-agdar anṭiik ʔay maɛluumaat ʔakθar.*
in a moment - *b-xilaal laħð̣a, baɛad laħð̣a.* I'll give you your change in a moment. *ʔanṭiik baqiyyat ifluusak ib-xilaal laħð̣a.*
monastery - *deer* pl. *ʔadyira.*
Monday - *yoom iθ-θineen.*
money - *fluus.* Do you take American money? *tiqbal ifluus ʔamriikiyya?*
**He has money to burn. *ɛinda fluus miθl iz-zibal.*
**You can't get that for love or money. *guwwa mruwwa ma-titħaṣṣal.*
money order - *ħawaala (pl. -aat) maaliyya.*
monk - *raahib* pl. *ruhbaan.*
monkey - *šaadi* pl. *šwaadi, qird* pl. *quruud.*
monopoly - *ħtikaar.*
monotonous - **The work here is monotonous but the salary is good. *š-šuġuḷ ihnaa yimši ɛala fadd namaṭ laakin ir-raatib zeen.*
monster - *ġuul* pl. *ʔaġwaal, siɛluwwa* pl. *-aat.*
month - *šahar* pl. *ʔašhur.* He came last month. *ʔija b-šahar il-faat.*
monthly - **1.** *šahri*.* He writes for a monthly magazine. *huwwa yiktib ib-majalla šahriyya.* -- You can pay the amount in monthly installments. *tigdar tidfaɛ il-mablaġ ib-ʔaqsaaṭ šahriyya.* **2.** *šahriyyan.* He comes to Baghdad monthly. *yiji l-baġdaad*

šahriyyan.
**You can make a monthly payment of five dinars. *tigdar tidfaє xams idnaaniir biš-šahar.*

monument – *naṣub tiðkaari.* pl. *ʔanṣiba tiðkaariyya.*

mood – **1.** *mizaaj* pl. *ʔamzija.* He's in a good mood today. *mizaaja zeen il-yoom.* **2.** *wahas, xulug.* I'm not in the mood for that. *ʔaani maa єindi wahas l-haay.*

moody – *maqhuur.*

moon – *gumar* pl. *ʔaqmaar.* There's a ring around the moon tonight. *ʔaku ḥalqa daayir madaayir il-gumar hal-leela.*

full moon – *badir* pl. *bduur.* Is there a full moon tonight? *l-gumar badir hal-leela?*

mop – *mimsaḥa* pl. *-aat.* Take a wet mop. *ʔuxuð fadd mimsaḥa mballila.*

to mop – *misaḥ (a masiḥ) n-.* Did you mop the floor? *misaḥt il-gaaє?* -- He mopped his forehead. *misaḥ guṣṣta.*

to mop up – *qiða (i qaðaaʔ) n- єala.* The government forces mopped up the remnant of the rebels. *l-ḥukuuma qiðat єala ʔaaxir baqaaya θ-θuwwaar.*

moral – **1.** *magza, ḥikma* pl. *ḥikam.* And the moral of the story is... *w-magza l-quṣṣa huwwa...* **2.** *ʔadabi** *ʔaxlaaqi**. Children have a moral obligation to support their parents. *l-ʔabnaaʔ єaleehum masʔuuliyya ʔadabiyya yєiiluun il-waalideen.*

morals – *ʔaxlaaq.* He has no morals at all. *maa єinda ʔaxlaaq ʔabadan.* or ***huwwa ʔaxlaaqsizz.* -- She's a woman of low morals. *hiyya mara ʔaxlaaqha waaṭya.*

morale – *r-ruuḥ il-maєnawiyya, l-maєnawiyya.* The morale of the troops was excellent. *maєnawiyyat ij-jinuud čaanat mumtaaza.*

morality – *nazaaha.* We do not question the morality of his actions. *ma-nšukk ib-nazaahat ʔaєmaala.*

more – *ʔakθar, ʔazyad.* He is asking for more money. *da-yriid ifluus ʔakθar.* or ***da-yriid ifluus baєad.* -- He has more money than he needs. *єinda ʔakθar ifluus min-ma yiḥtaaj.* -- That's more likely. *haðiič muḥtamala ʔakθar.* -- He got more and more involved in the matter. *twarraṭ bil-mawðuuє ʔakθar fa-ʔakθar.* -- The price will be a little more. *raḥ-yṣiir is-siєr išwayya ʔazyad.*
**What's more? I don't believe him. *wil-ʔakθar min haaða, ʔaani ma-aṣaddig bii.*

more or less – *šii єala šii, nawєan-ma.* I believe that report is more or less true. *ʔaєtiqid hat-taqriir šii єala šii ṣaḥiiḥ.*

once more – *marra lux.* Try once more. *jarrub marra lux.*

some more – *baєad.* Won't you have some more soup? *ma-triid baєad šoorba?*

the more... the more – *kull-ma... kull-ma.* The more money they get, the more they want. *kull-ma yḥaṣṣluun єala fluus kull-ma yirduun baєad.* -- The more I see him, the more I like him. *kull-ma ʔašuufa, kull-ma ʔaḥibba ʔazyad.*
**The more I give him, the more he wants. *šgadd-ma ʔanṭii yriid baєad ʔazyad.* or *єeena ma-tišbaє.*

moreover – *w-єalaawatan єala ðaalik.*

morning – *ṣubuḥ, ṣabaaḥ* pl. *-aat.* He works from morning till night. *yištugul imniṣ-ṣubuḥ lil-leel.*

in the morning – *ṣ-ṣubuḥ.* She's only here in the morning. *hiyya hnaa bass iṣ-ṣubuḥ.* -- We stayed up till one in the morning. *siharna lis-saaєa waḥda ṣ-ṣubuḥ.*

this morning – *l-yoom iṣ-ṣubuḥ.* There was a lot to do this morning. *čaan ʔaku hwaaya šugul il-yoom iṣ-ṣubuḥ.*

mortal – **1.** *zaaʔil* pl. *-iin.* We are mortal and God is immortal. *ʔiḥna zaaʔiliin w-ʔaḷḷa daaʔim.*
2. *bašari* pl. *-iyyiin* coll. *bašar.* That isn't for ordinary mortals. *haaða fawq mustawa l-bašar.*

mortality – **1.** *wufiyyaat.* Infant mortality here is still a serious problem. *wufiyyaat il-ʔaṭfaal ihnaa li-hassa muškila čibiira.* **2.** *fanaaʔ.* It is difficult for human beings to accept the idea of their mortality. *l-bašar yiṣєab єaleehum qubuul fikrat fanaaʔhum.*

mortar – **1.** *muuna.* Mortar is made from sand and slaked lime. *l-muuna msawwaaya mnir-ramuḷ wij-juṣṣ.*
2. *haawan* pl. *hawaawiin.* Pound the coffee beans in a mortar. *dugg il-bunn ib-haawan.*

mortgage – *rahan* pl. *ruhuun.* The interest on the mortgage is due. *l-faayiz єar-rahan istaḥaqq.*

to mortgage – *rihan (i rahan) n-.* He had to mortgage his house. *ðṭarr yirhin beeta.*

Moslem – *mislim* pl. *-iin.*

mosquito – *bagga* pl. *-aat.* coll. *bagg.* We were all bitten up by the mosquitos. *ʔakalna l-bagg kullatna.*

moss – *ṭuḥlub.*

most – **1.** *ʔakθar-ma, ʔaqṣa-ma.* That's the most I can pay. *haaða ʔakθar-ma ʔagdar adfaєa.* **2.** *muєðam, ʔakθar.* Most of the day I'm at the office. *ʔaani bid-daaʔira muєðam in-nahaar.* -- Most people went home early. *ʔakθar in-naas raaḥaw lil-beet min wakit.* -- He's on the road most of the time. *huwwa msaafir ʔakθar il-ʔawqaat.* -- Who did most of the work? *minu ṭallaє ʔakθar iš-šuguḷ?* **3.** *kulliš.* The talk was most interesting. *l-ḥadiiθ čaan kulliš mumtiє.*
**We'd better make the most of our time. *ʔaḥsan-inna nḥaawil nistifiid wakitna ʔakθar-ma yimkin.*

at the most – *єal-ʔakθar.* At the most it's worth ten dinars. *єal-ʔakθar yiswa єašir danaaniir.*

mostly – *єala l-ʔaglab, єala l-ʔakθar.* He's mostly right. *huwwa ṣaḥiiḥ єal-ʔaglab.* -- The audience consisted mostly of women. *l-ḥaaðriin čaanaw єala l-ʔakθar niswaan.*

moth – *єiθθa* pl. *-aat* coll. *єiθθ.*

moth ball – *duєbullat* (pl. *-aat*) *naftaaliin.*

moth-eaten – *maєθuuθ.*

mother – *ʔumm* pl. *ʔummahaat, waalda* pl. *-aat.* She takes care of us like a mother. *tdiir baalha єaleena єabaalak ʔummna.*

to mother – *daara (i mdaaraa) t- miθl il-ʔumm.* She mothers him all the time. *tdaarii miθil il-ʔumm єala-ṭuul.*

mother-in-law – **1.** *ḥamaat* pl. *ḥamawaat.* My mother-in-law is living with us. *ḥamaati saakna wiyyaana.*
2. *mart* (pl. *niswaan*) *il-єamm.* The bride and her mother-in-law never get along. *l-єaruusa w-mart il-єamm ma-yitraahmuun.*

mother tongue – *luga* (pl. *-aat*) *ʔaṣliyya.* What is your mother tongue? *šinu lugatak il-ʔaṣliyya?*

motion – **1.** *ḥaraka* pl. *-aat.* All of her motions are graceful. *kull ḥarakaatha rašiiqa.* **2.** *qtiraaḥ* pl. *-aat.* I'd like to make a motion. *ʔariid aqaddim iqtiraaḥ.*

to motion – *ʔaššar (i taʔšiir), ʔooma (i ʔoomaaʔ, ʔiimaaʔ).* He motioned the taxi to stop. *ʔaššar lit-taaksi ḥatta yoogaf.* -- He motioned me to come. *ʔoomaa-li ʔaji.*

motionless – **1.** *bila ḥaraka.* The patient slept motionless all night. *l-mariið naam bila ḥaraka ṭuul il-leel.* **2.** *jaamid.* I stayed in my place motionless with fear until it was clear there was no snake. *biqeet jaamid ib-makaani mnil-xoof ʔila ʔan itbayyan-li ma-čaan ʔaku ḥayya.* **3.** *raakid.* The surface of the water was motionless. *saṭḥ il-maay čaan raakid.* **4.** *waaquf.* The air is motionless. *l-hawa waaquf.*

motion picture – *filim* pl. *ʔaflaam.*

to motivate – *ḥaθθ (i ḥaθθ) n-.* We are trying to find some way to motivate our son to study. *da-ndawwir єala ṭariiqa nḥiθθ biiha ʔibinna єala d-diraasa.*

motivation – *ḥaθθ.* The motivation of the employees in their work is a part of the duties of the Personnel Section. *ḥaθθ il-mustaxdamiin єaš-šuguḷ min waajibaat šuєbat ið-ðaatiyya.*

motive – *daafiє* pl. *dawaafiє, baaєiθ* pl. *bawaaєiθ.* What is the motive behind the crime? *šinu d-daafiє lij-jariima?* -- My motives are strictly honorable. *bawaaєθi jiddan šariifa.*

motor – *maaṭoor* pl. *-aat, makiina* pl. *makaayin.* I let the motor run. *xalleet l-maaṭoor yištuguḷ.*

motorcycle – *maatoorsikil* pl. *-aat.*

to mount – **1.** *rikab (a rukuub) n-.* He mounted his horse and rode off. *rikab iḥṣaana w-raaḥ.*
2. *ṣiєad (a ṣuєuud) n-, ṭilaє (a ṭuluuє) n-.* They mounted the steps slowly. *ṣiєdaw id-daraj yawaaš yawaaš.* **3.** *niṣab (u naṣub) n-, rakkab (i tarkiib) t-.* The machine will be mounted on concrete blocks. *l-makiina raḥ-tinnuṣub єala qawaalib konkiriit.* -- I'd like to have this picture mounted and framed. *ʔariid haṣ-ṣuura titrakkab w-titčarčab.* -- Can you mount this stone in a ring for me? *tigdar itrakkub hal-ḥajar ib-maḥbas ʔiliyya?*

mountain – *jibal* pl. *jibaal.* How high is the mountain? *šgadd єulu ðaak ij-jibal?* -- We're going to spend a month in the mountains. *raḥ-nigði šahar bij-jibaal.*
**Don't make a mountain out of a molehill. *la-tsawwi mnil-ḥabba gubba.*

mountainous – *jabali**

mounted police – *šurṭi xayyaal* pl. *šurṭa xayyaala,*

swaari pl. *-iyya.* He's a member of the mounted police corps. *huwwa b-silk iš-šurṭa l-xayyaala.*
to **mourn** - *biča (i bači) ʕala.* The widow is still mourning the death of her husband ten years ago. *l-ʔarmala baʕadha tibči ʕala zoojha l-maat qabuḷ ʕašir isniin.*
mourning - *ʕaza.* The mourning period is seven days. *muddat il-ʕaza sabiʕt iyyaam.*
in mourning - (m.) *mitʕazzi* pl. *-iin,* (f.) *mitʕazzaaya* pl. *-aat.* She's in mourning because of her brother's death. *hiyya mitʕazzaaya b-sabab moot ʔaxuuha.*
mouse - *faara* pl. *-aat* coll. *faar.*
mouth - **1.** *ɀalig* pl. *ɀluug.* I've got a bad taste in my mouth. *ɀalgi ṭaʕma muu ṭayyib.* -- The story passed from mouth to mouth. *l-iɀčaaya ntiqlat min ɀalig il-ɀalig.* **2.** *maṣabb* pl. *-aat.* Qurna is at the mouth of the Shatt al-Arab. *l-qurna ṣaayra ʕala maṣabb šaṭṭ il-ʕarab.* **3.** *madxal* pl. *madaaxil, baab* pl. *biibaan.* The dog stopped at the mouth of the cave. *č-čalib wugaf ib-baab il-kahif.*
**They live from hand to mouth. *duub ygidruun ysidduun ramaqhum.*
**Don't look a gift horse in the mouth. *la-tiʕtiriḍ ʕal-hadiyya š-ma čaan nawuʕha.* or *l-hadiyya muu b-θaminha.*
mouth wash - *ġasiil ɀalig.*
move - **1.** *ɀaraka* pl. *-aat.* Every move I make hurts. *kull ɀaraka ʔasawwiiha tʔaððiini.* **2.** *door* pl. *ʔadwaar.* It's your move. *hassa doorak.* or **ʔ*ilak il-liʕab.* **3.** *xaṭwa* pl. *-aat.* He can't make a move without asking his wife. *ma-yigdar yixṭi xaṭwa blayya ma-yguul il-marta.*
to be on the move - **1.** *riɀal (a raɀiil).* The Bedouins are always on the move. *l-badu daaʔiman yirɀaluun.* **2.** *tnaqqal (a tanaqqul).* He never lives in one town for long; he's always on the move. *ma-yiθbit fadd wlaaya, ʕala ṭuul yitnaqqal.*
**My boy can't sit still; he's always on the move. *ʔibni ma-yugʕud raaɀa; ʕabaalak maakuuk.*
to move - **1,** *ɀarrak (i taɀriik, tɀirrik) t-.* She can't move her foot. *ma-tigdar itɀarrik rijilha.* -- You'll have to move your car. *laazim itɀarrik sayyaartak.* **2.** *tɀarrak (a taɀarruk).* I can't move. *ma-agdar atɀarrak.* -- Don't move, or I'll shoot. *la-titɀarrak, tara ʔarmiik.* **3.** *ntiqal (i ntiqaal), tɀawwal (a taɀawwul).* Do you know where they are moving to? *tuʕruf li-ween da-yintaqluun?* **4.** *qtiraɀ (i qtiraaɀ).* I move we adjourn the session. *ʔaani ʔaqtiriɀ inʔajjil ij-jalsa.* **5.** *ʔaθaar (i ʔiθaara) ɀanaan-.* She moved me with her tears. *ʔaθaarat ɀanaani b-dimuuʕha.* **6.** *liʕab (a laʕib).* It's your play. I just moved. *haaða doorak. ʔaani hassa lʕabit.* **7.** *giḷab (u gaḷub) n-.* We moved heaven and earth to get it. *gḷabna d-dinya ɀatta gdarna nɀaṣṣilha.*
**They move in the best circles. *mittaṣliin ib-ʔaɀsan jamaaʕaat.*
**I was moved to tears. *bičeet imnit-taʔaθθur.*
to move along - *miša (i maši), tɀarrak (a taɀarruk).* Things are finally moving along now. *l-ʔumuur ʔaxiiran bidat timši šwayya.*
to move away - **1.** *ntiqal (i ntiqaal), tɀawwal (a taɀawwul).* They moved away a long time ago. *ṣaar-ilhum ihwaaya min intiqlaw minnaa.* or *tɀawwlaw min zimaan.* **2.** *waxxar (i twixxir) t-.* Move the table away, please. *waxxir il-meez, min faḍlak.*
to move on - *miša (i maši), tɀarrak(a).* Move on! *yaḷḷa, imši!*
to be moved - *tʔaθθar (a taʔaθθur).* I was deeply moved. *tʔaθθarit kulliš.* or **nkisar xaaṭri kulliš.*
movement - **1.** *ɀaraka* pl. *-aat.* They watched his movements closely. *raaqbaw ɀarakaata b-diqqa.* -- He never belonged to any political movement. *ma-ntima b-ʔay ɀaraka siyaasiyya.* **2.** *faṣil* pl. *fṣuul.* That theme is from the second movement of the Fifth Symphony. *hal-laɀan imnil-faṣl iθ-θaani mnis-simfooniyya l-xaamsa.* **3.** *makiina* pl. *makaayin.* I checked your watch; the movement is dirty. *fuɀaṣit saaʕtak; il-makiina waṣxa.*
movie - *filim* pl. *ʔaflaam.* Is there a good movie playing tonight? *ʔaku filim zeen da-yištuġul hal-leela?*
movies - *siinama* pl. *-aat.* We rarely go to the movies. *ʔiɀna naadiran inruuɀ lis-siinama.*
to **mow** - *gaṣṣ (u gaṣṣ) n-.* I'm mowing the lawn. *da-aguṣṣ iθ-θayyil.*
Mr. - *sayyid* pl. *saada.* Could I speak to Mr. Mounir? *ʔagdar akallim is-sayyid muniir?*
Mrs. - *sayyida* pl. *-aat.* Address the letter to Mrs. Ali Sheesh. *ʕinwin ir-risaala ʔila s-sayyida ʕali šiiš.*
much - *hwaaya, kaθiir.* I haven't much time. *maa ʕindi hwaaya wakit.* -- I feel much better today. *ʔašʕur ihwaaya ʔaɀsan hal-yoom.*
how much - *šgadd.* How much will it cost me? *šgadd raɀ-itkallifni?* or *beeš raɀ-iṭṣiir ʕalayya?*
that much - **1.** *hal-miqdaar.* I think that much will be enough for you. *ʔaʕtiqid hal-miqdaar ykaffiik.* **2.** *hal-gadd.* I didn't know you liked it that much. *ma-činit ʔadri tɀabba hal-gadd.* -- I can tell you that much. *ʔagdar agul-lak hal-gadd.*
very much - *kulliš ihwaaya, jiddan, jaziil.* We didn't like it very much. *ma-ʕijbatna kulliš ihwaaya.* -- Thank you very much. *šukran jaziilan.* or *ʔaškurak jiddan.*
mucus - **1.** (nasal) *mxaaṭ.* **2.** (bronchial) *balġam.*
mucus membrane - *ġišaaʔ muxaaṭi* pl. *ʔaġšiya muxaaṭiyya.*
mud - *ṭiin, waɀal.* The car got stuck in the mud. *s-sayyaara ʕiṣat biṭ-ṭiin.*
muddy - **1.** *mṭayyan, mwaɀɀal.* Your shoes are muddy. *qundartak imṭayyna.* **2.** *xaabuṭ.* This water is muddy. *hal-maay xaabuṭ.*
muggy - *waxim.* It's awfully muggy today. *d-dinya kulliš waxma l-yoom.*
mule - *baġal* pl. *bġaal.*
multiplication table - *jadwal* (pl. *jadaawil*) *iḍ-ḍarb.*
to **multiply** - **1.** *ḍirab (u ḍarub) n-.* Multiply three by four! *ʔuḍrub itlaaθa b-arbaʕa!* **2.** *tkaaθar (a takaaθur).* Rabbits multiply quickly. *l-ʔaraanib titkaaθar ib-surʕa.*
to **mumble** - *tamtam (i ttimtim, tamtama).* He is always mumbling. *huwwa ʕala ṭuul da-ytamtim.*
mumps - *nukaaf.*
municipal - *baladi*.*
municipality - *baladiyya* pl. *-aat.*
murder - *ɀaadiθ* (pl. *ɀawaadiθ*) *qatil, katil.* The murder was not discovered until a few days later. *ɀaadiθ il-qatil ma-nkišaf ʔilla baʕad muruur ʕiddat ʔayyaam.*
to murder - **1.** *kital (u katil) n-.* He was accused of having murdered his wife. *huwwa ntiham ib-katil marta.* **2.** *laaṣ (u looṣ) n-.* She murdered that song. *laaṣat hal-ġaniyya.*
murderer - *qaatil* pl. *qatala.*
muscle - *ʕaḍala* pl. *-aat.* All my muscles hurt. *ʕaḍalaati kullha toojaʕni.*
museum - *matɀaf* pl. *mataaɀif.* I've seen the museum. *ʔaani šaayfa lil-matɀaf.*
mushroom - *fṭirra* pl. *-aat.* coll. *fṭirr.* Are these mushrooms poisonous? *hal-ifṭirr saamm?*
music - **1.** *moosiiqa.* Where's the music coming from? *mneen da-tiji hal-moosiiqa?* **2.** *nooṭa* pl. *-aat.* I didn't bring my music with me. *ma-jibt in-nooṭa maalti wiyyaaya.*
musical - *moosiiqi*.*
musical instrument - *ʔaala* (pl. *-aat*) *moosiiqiyya.* Do you play any musical instrument? *ʔinta tdugg fadd ʔaala moosiiqiyya?*
musician - *moosiiqaar* pl. *-iyya.*
must - **1.** *lizuum.* There is no such thing as must. *ma-aku fadd šii ʔisma lizuum.* **2.** *laazim.* He must be sick. *huwwa laazim mariiḍ.* -- You must never forget that. *laazim ʔabad ma-tinsaa.* or *ma-laazim tinsa haaða ʔabadan.* **3.** *waajib ʕala.* You must pray five times a day. *waajib ʕaleek iṭṣalli xamis marraat bil-yoom.*
mustache - *šaarib* pl. *šwaarib.*
mustard - *xardal.*
to **mutilate** - *šawwah (i tašwiih) t-.* The machine mutilated his hand. *l-makiina šawwhat ʔiida.* -- The police found the body badly mutilated. *š-šurṭa ligaw ij-juθθa mušawwaha kulliš.*
mutiny - *ʕiṣyaan* pl. *-aat.*
to **mutter** - *tamtam (i ttimtim, tamtama).* He muttered something to himself. *tamtam ib-fadd šii beena w-been nafsa.*
mutton - *laɀam ġanam.*
mutual - **1.** *mutabaadal.* This treaty provides for mutual aid in case of war. *hal-muʕaahada tnuṣṣ ʕala fadd taʕaawun mutabaadal ib-ɀaalat il-ɀarb.* **2.** *muštarak.* The two prime ministers issued a mutual statement. *raʔiiseen il-wuzaraaʔ ṭallʕaw bayaan muštarak.*
**He's a mutual friend of ours. *huwwa ṣadiiq iṭ-ṭarafeen.* or *huwwa ṣadiiqna θneenna.*

muzzle - **1.** *kammaama* pl. *-aat.* Dogs are not allowed on the street without muzzles. *mamnuuƐ tark ič-čilaab biš-šaariƐ bila kammaamaat.* **2.** *fawha* pl. *-aat.* Don't point the muzzle of the gun at anyone. *la-tneešin fawhat il-bunduqiyya Ɛala ʔaẓẓad.*
to muzzle - *kammam (i takmiim) t-.* That dog ought to be muzzled. *hač-čalib laazim yitkammam.* -- The press is muzzled. *ʔafwaah iṣ-ṣuẓuf imkammima.*
mysterious - *ġaamiḍ, mubham.*
mystery - **1.** *laġiz* pl. *ʔalġaaz.* How they stole it is still a mystery. *šloon baagoo li-hassa laġiz.* **2.** *ġumuuḍ.* The meeting is surrounded with mystery. *l-ijtimaaƐ muẓaaṭ bil-ġumuuḍ.*
mystery story - *quṣṣa (pl. quṣaṣ) pooliisiyya.* I like to read mystery stories. *yiƐjibni ʔaqra quṣaṣ pooliisiyya.*

N

nag - **1.** *kidiiš* pl. *kidaayiš.* He put all his money on that nag. *xalla kull ifluusa b-hal-kidiiš.* **2.** *niqnaaqiyya* pl. *-aat.* His wife's a real nag. *marta niqnaaqiyya tamaam.*
to nag - *naqnaq (i tniqniq).* Her husband got sick of her nagging. *zawijha ḍaaj imn itniqniqha.*
nail - **1.** *bismaar* pl. *bsaamiir.* Don't hammer the nail in too far. *la-tdugg il-bismaar kulliš zaayid.* **2.** *ʔiḍfir* pl. *ʔaḍaafir.* She painted her nails red. *ṣubġat ʔaḍaafirha b-ʔaẓmar.*
**You hit the nail on the head. *jibitha b-mukaanha.*
to nail - *basmar (i tbismir) t-.* Please nail the board to the wall. *min faḍlak basmir il-xišba bil-ẓaayiṭ.*
**It's difficult to nail him down to anything. *ma-yinṭi lazma.*
naked - **1.** *mṣallax* pl. *mṣaaliix, Ɛaryaan* pl. *-iin.* They took a picture of their son naked. *ʔaxðaw ṣuurat ṭifihum imṣallax.* **2.** *mujarrad.* You can see the satellite with the naked eye. *tigdar itšuuf il-qamar il-iṣṭinaaƐi bil-Ɛeen il-mujarrada.*
name - **1.** *ʔisim* pl. *ʔasmaaʔ, ʔasaami.* I've heard of his name before. *ʔaani saamiƐ b-isma gabuḷ.* -- Please give me your full name; your first name, your father's first name and your family name. *ʔarjuuk inṭiini ʔismak il-kaamil, ʔismak, ʔism abuuk, w-laqabak.* **2.** *šuhra* pl. *-aat, ʔisim* pl. *ʔasmaaʔ, ʔasaami; sumƐa* pl. *-aat.* He made a good name for himself in industry. *sawwaa-la xooš isim biṣ-ṣinaaƐa.*
to name - **1.** *samma (i tasmiya, tsimmi) t-.* They named their son Ali Sheesh. *sammaw ʔibinhum Ɛali šiiš.* **2.** *Ɛadd (i Ɛadd) n-, samma (i tasmiya, tsimmi) t-.* Can you name all the planets? *tigdar itƐidd kull il-kawaakib is-sayyaara?* **3.** *Ɛayyan (i taƐyiin) t-.* The president named his ministry yesterday. *r-raʔiis Ɛayyan wizaarta l-baarẓa.*
namely - *w-huwwa, w-hiyya, yaƐni.* I have only one wish, namely, that we leave soon. *Ɛindi raġba wiẓda, w-hiyya nruuẓ qariiban.*
nap - **1.** *ġafwa* pl. *-aat.* I took a short nap after lunch. *ʔaxaðit ġafwa ṣġayyra baƐad il-ġada.* **2.** *xamla* pl. *-aat.* The nap's all worn off this rug. *l-xamla kullha maẓkuuka min haz-zuuliyya.*
to nap - *ġufa (i ġafu).* The baby napped all afternoon. *ṭ-ṭifil ġufa ṭuul il-Ɛaṣir.*
**The inspectors caught us napping. *l-mufattišiin lizmoona Ɛala ġafla.*
napkin - *čaffiyya* pl. *čfaafi.*
narcotics - *muxaddiraat.*
narghile - *nargiila* pl. *-aat, ġarša* pl. *-aat.*
narrow - **1.** *ḍayyig.* This is a narrow street. *haaða šaariƐ ḍayyig.* -- His opinions on education are very narrow. *ʔaraaʔa bit-taƐliim kullis ḍayyga.* **2.** *ḍayyiq, qaliil.* Our company's margin of profit is very narrow. *majaal ribiẓ šarikatna kulliš ḍayyiq.*
**I had a narrow escape. *njeet ib-qeed šaƐra minha.* or *xḷaṣit b-iƐjuuba.*
narrows - *maḍiiq* pl. *maḍaayiq.* We watched the ship pass through the narrows. *šifna l-baaxira tmurr bil-maḍiiq.*
to narrow - **1.** *ḍaaq (i ḍiiq).* The road narrows a mile from here. *ṭ-ṭariiq yḍiiq masaafat miil imn ihnaa.* **2.** *ḍayyaq (i taḍyiiq, tḍiyyiq) t-.* The government is narrowing the road instead of widening it. *l-ẓukuuma da-tḍayyiq iṭ-ṭariiq badal-ma twassiƐa.*
to narrow down - *ẓiṣar (u ẓaṣir) n-.* We narrowed down the suspicion to three men. *ẓṣarna t-tuhma b-iθlaθ riyaajiil.*
nasty - **1.** *qabiiẓ.* Spitting on the floor is a nasty habit. *t-tafil Ɛal-gaaƐ Ɛaada qabiiẓa.* **2.** *malƐuun, qabiiẓ.* Don't be so nasty! *la-tṣiir hal-gadd malƐuun!* **3.** *kasiif.* London has nasty weather. *landan biiha jaww kasiif.*
nation - *balad* pl. *bilaad, buldaan; ʔumma* pl. *ʔumam.* The entire nation mourned his death. *l-balad kullha ẓiznaw Ɛala moota.*
national - **1.** *waṭani*.* Can you sing the national anthem? *tigdar tiqra n-našiid il-waṭani?* **2.** *muwaaṭin* pl. *-iin.* We hired four Egyptian nationals. *šaġġalna ʔarbaƐ muwaaṭiniin miṣriyyiin.*
nationalism - **1.** *qawmiyya.* He gave a speech on Arab nationalism. *ʔalqa xiṭaab Ɛan il-qawmiyya l-Ɛarabiyya.* **2.** *waṭaniyya.* He's one of the advocates of Iraqi nationalism. *huwwa waaẓid imnil-munaaṣiriin lil-waṭaniyya l-Ɛiraaqiyya.*
nationality - *jinsiyya.*
native - **1.** *ahil* pl. *ʔahaali.* The natives of the island were very nice. *ʔahaali j-jaziira čaanaw kulliš ṭayybiin.* -- He's a native of Najaf. *huwwa min ʔahl in-najaf.* or ***huwwa najafi.* **2.** *ʔaṣli*.* His native language is Arabic. *luġata l-ʔaṣliyya Ɛarabiyya.* **3.** *waṭani*.* They attended the festival in their native costumes. *ẓiḍraw il-mahrajaan ib-malaabishum il-waṭaniyya.*
**Potatoes are native to America. *l-puteeta ʔaṣilha min ʔameerka.*
natural - *ṭabiiƐi*.* We visited a natural cave south of the town. *zirna fadd kahaf ṭabiiƐi januub il-balda.* -- The fruit in this picture looks natural. *l-faakiha b-haṣ-ṣuura tbayyin ṭabiiƐiyya.* -- The use of natural rubber is declining. *stiƐmaal il-maṭṭaaṭ iṭ-ṭabiiƐi da-yqill.*
naturally - *ṭabƐan, biṭ-ṭabuƐ.* Naturally she's a little afraid. *ṭabƐan hiyya xaayfa šwayya.*
nature - **1.** *ṭabiiƐa.* My girl friend enjoys the beauty of nature. *ṣadiiqti titmattaƐ ib-jamaal iṭ-ṭabiiƐa.* -- I can't tell you anything about the nature of my work. *ma-agdar agul-lak ʔay šii Ɛan ṭabiiƐat šuġḷi.* **2.** *ṭabuƐ, xulug, ṭabiiƐa.* He has a very good nature. *Ɛinda xooš ṭabuƐ.* **3.** *fiṭra.* He's an artist by nature. *huwwa fannaan bil-fiṭra.* **4.** *qabiil.* I enjoy doing things of this nature. *ʔartaaẓ min Ɛamal ʔašyaaʔ min hal-qabiil.*
nature lover - *Ɛaašiq (pl. Ɛuššaaq) ṭabiiƐa.*
naughty - *wakiiẓ, wakiẓ.* You've been very naughty today. *činit kulliš wakiiẓ il-yoom.*
nauseated - **I feel nauseated. *ʔašƐur nafsi da-tilƐab.*
naval - *baẓri*.* He studied at the naval academy. *diras bil-kulliyya l-baẓriyya.*
navel - *ṣurra* pl. *ṣurar.*
navy blue - *ʔaẓrag ṭoox.* I bought a navy blue suit. *štireet qaaṭ ʔaẓrag ṭoox.*
near - *giriib min, qariib min, b-qurub.* The ball landed near us. *ṭ-ṭooba wugƐat qariib minna.* -- That's a little nearer to the truth. *haaða šwayya ʔaqrab liṣ-ṣidug.*
to near - *girab (a gurub) min.* The semester is nearing its end. *l-faṣl id-diraasi yigrab min intihaaʔa.* -- We neared the city about five o'clock. *girabna mnil-madiina ẓawaali s-saaƐa xamsa.*
nearby - *Ɛan qurub.* The children stood nearby watching the fire. *l-aṭfaal wugfaw Ɛan qurub yitfarrjuun Ɛal-ẓariiq.*
Near East - *š-šarq il-ʔadna.*
nearly - *Ɛala wašak, bit-taqriib, taqriiban.* She's nearly twenty years old. *Ɛumurha Ɛala wašak itkuun Ɛišriin sana.*
neat - **1.** *ʔaniiq, mhandam.* She always looks very neat. *hiyya daaʔiman tiḍhar kulliš ʔaniiqa.*

2. *naðiif*. He turns out neat work. *da-yṭalliɛ šuġuļ naðiif*. 3. *mrattab*. His desk is always neat. *meeza daa?iman imrattab*.

necessary - 1. *laazim, luzuum*. He eats more than is necessary. *yaakul ?akθar imnil-luzuum*. 2. *ðaruuri*, laazim*. I'll stay if it's absolutely necessary. *raz-abqa ?iða kulliš ðaruuri*.

necessity - 1. *ðaruura, zaaja, ztiyaaj, luzuum*. There's no necessity for it. *ma-aku ðaruura ?ilha*. -- Necessity is the mother of invention. *l-zaaja ?umm il-ixtiraaɛ*. 2. *ztiyaaj* pl. *-aat, zaaja* pl. *-aat*. My necessities are few. *ztiyaajaati qaliila*.

neck - *rugba* pl. *rugab*. Wrap the scarf around your neck. *liff il-laffaaf ɛala rugubtak*. -- The bottle has a very narrow neck. *l-buṭil rugubta kulliš ðayyga*.

necklace - *glaada* pl. *glaayid*.

neckline - *fatzat ṣadir*.

necktie - *booyinbaaġ, bayinbaaġ* pl. *-aat, ribaaṭ* pl *?arbiṭa*.

nectarine - *xooxa* (pl. *-aat*) *imrakkuba* coll. *xoox imrakkab*.

need - 1. *zaaja* pl. *-aat, zawaayij; ztiyaaj* pl. *-aat*. There is a need for a better hospital here. *?aku zaaja ?ila mustašfa ?azsan ihnaa*. 2. *ðiiq*. You're certainly a friend in need. *?inta zaqiiqatan ṣadiiq ɛind iḍ-ḍiiq*.

needs - *mutaṭallibaat, zaajaat, ztiyaajaat, zawaayij*. My salary just covers our needs. *raatbi ykaffi mutaṭallibaatna bass*.

if need be - *?iða qtiðat il-zaaja, ɛind il-luzuum, ɛind il-zaaja, ?in lizam il-zaal*. I'll go myself if need be. *?aruuz ib-nafsi ?iða qtiðat il-zaaja*.

in need of - *b-zaaja ?ila*. He's badly in need of a vacation. *huwwa kulliš ib-zaaja ?ila ɛuṭla*.

to need - *ztaaj (a ztiyaaj)*. I need a new coat. *?aztaaj sitra jdiida*.

**I need to leave at five o'clock. *laazim aruuz is-saaɛa xamsa*.

needle - 1. *?ubra* pl. *?ubar*. Bring me a needle so I can sew on this button. *jiib-li fadd ?ubra zatta ?axayyiṭ had-dugma*. -- The phonograph needle is worn out. *?ubrat il-funnuġraaf saayfa*. 2. *muxyaṭ* pl. *maxaayiṭ*. The upholsterer uses a curved needle in his work. *d-doošamči yistaɛmil muxyaṭ maɛwuuj ib-šuġļa*.

needy - *muztaaj* pl. *-iin, faqiir* pl. *fuqaraa?*. He donated money to the needy. *tbarraɛ b-ifluus lil-muztaajiin*.

negative - 1. *jaama* pl. *-aat*. Make four prints from this negative. *?iṭbaɛ ?arbaɛ ṣuwar ɛala haj-jaama*. 2. *saalib*. Hook this wire to the negative terminal of the battery. *?urbuṭ hal-waayir bil-quṭb is-saalib maal il-paaṭri*. 3. *nafi*. Put this sentence in the negative. *zawwil haj-jumla ?ila n-nafi*.

neglect - *?ihmaal*. They fired him due to his neglect. *fuṣloo ɛala ?ihmaala*.

to neglect - *himal (i ?ihmaal)*. Don't neglect to water the plants. *la-tihmil tisgi z-zariɛ*.

to **negotiate** - *tfaawað (a tafaawuð) ɛala*. They're negotiating a peace treaty. ~~*da-yitfaawðuun*~~ *ɛala ttifaaqiyyat is-salaam*.

negotiation - *mufaawaða* pl. *-aat*. The negotiations lasted a week. *l-mufaawaðaat ṭawwlat isbuuɛ*.

Negress - *ɛabda* pl. *-aat*.

Negro - *ɛabid* pl. *ɛabiid*.

neighbor - *jaar* pl. *jiiraan, jiiraan* pl. *jwaariin*. My neighbor visited me this morning. *jiiraani zaarni haṣ-ṣubuz*.

neighborhood - 1. *jiiraan, jwaariin*. The whole neighborhood was there. *kull ij-jiiraan čaanaw ihnaak*. 2. *ṭaraf* pl. *?aṭraaf, mazalla* pl. *-aat*. We live in a good neighborhood. *niskun ib-mazalla zeena*. -- We talked for an hour in the neighborhood coffee shop. *zičeena saaɛa b-gahwat iṭ-ṭaraf*.

in the neighborhood of - *b-zuduud*. Your bill will run in the neighborhood of five hundred dinars. *l-qaa?ima maaltak raz-itwaṣṣil ib-zuduud il-xamis miit diinaar*.

neighboring - *mujaawir*. The neighboring village was flooded. *l-qariya l-mujaawra čaanat ġargaana*.

neither - *wala*. Neither one of the two was there. *wala waazid imnil-iθneen čaan ihnaak*.

neither ...nor - *laa... wala*. This word is neither Turkish nor Persian. *hač-čilma laa turkiyya wala faarsiyya*.

nephew - 1. (fraternal) *?ibin (pl. wulid) ?ax*. 2. (sororal) *?ibin (pl. wulid) ?uxt*.

nerve - 1. *ɛaṣab* pl. *?aɛṣaab*. That noise is getting on my nerves. *haṣ-ṣoot da-ydugg ib-?aɛṣaabi*. -- Instead of removing the tooth, he deadened the nerves around it. *badal-ma yišlaɛ is-sinn, kital il-?aɛṣaab illi zawla*. 2. *jasaara, ɛeen*. You mean you've got the nerve to ask such a question? *?amma ɛindak jasaara tis?alni hiič su?aal*.

nervous - *ɛaṣabi**. The last few days I've been very nervous. *l-?ayyaam il-?axiira činit kulliš ɛaṣabi*. -- His mother had a nervous breakdown last year. *?ummha ṣaar ɛidha nhiyaar ɛaṣabi s-sana l-faatat*.

nest - *ɛišš* pl. *ɛšuuš*.

net - 1. *šibča* pl. *šibač*. He caught a lot of fish in his net. *ṣaad simač ihwaaya b-šibičta*. -- He jumped over the tennis net. *ṭufar foog sibčat it-tanis*. 2. *ṣaafi*. The net weight is a kilo and a half. *l-wazn iṣ-ṣaafi kiilo w-nuṣṣ*.

mosquito net - *kulla* pl. *kulal*.

to net - *rubaz (a ribiz)*. We netted four hundred dollars. *rbazna ?arbaɛ miit doolaar*.

The Netherlands - *l-?araaði l-munxafiða*.

neutral - 1. *muzaayid* pl. *-iin*. He prefers to remain a neutral. *yfaððil yubqa muzaayid*. 2. *booš*. He left the car in neutral. *xalla s-sayyaara ɛal-booš*. 3. *ziyaadi*, muzaayid*. He fled to a neutral country. *nhizam ?ila balad ziyaadi*. 4. *mutɛaadil*. He changed the acid into a neutral solution. *ġayyar il-zaamuð ?ila mazluul mutɛaadil*.

neutrality - *ziyaad*. What's your opinion on neutrality? *šinu hiyya fikirtak ɛan il-ziyaad?* -- The policy of the government is one of positive neutrality? *šinu hiyya fikirtak ɛan il-ziyaad? -- ?ijaabi*.

never - 1. *?abadan*. I've never seen Najef. *ma-šaayif in-najaf ?abadan*. 2. *?abadan, qaṭɛan*. Never do that again. *la-tsawwi hiiči šii marra lux ?abadan*.

**Never mind, I'll buy you another. *la-tdiir baal, raz-aštirii-lak waazid laax*.

**Never mind, let it go for now. *ɛiifha, xalliiha hassa*.

**Never mind, I'll do it myself. *ma-yxaalif, asawwiiha b-nafsi*.

nevertheless - *maɛa ðaalik, bir-raġum min ðaalik*. Nevertheless, I still can't believe it. *maɛa ðaalik, ?aani ma-mumkin aṣaddig biiha*.

new - 1. *jidiid*. Are these shoes new? *hal-qanaadir jidiida?* -- What's new today? *šaku šii jidiid il-yoom?* 2. *taaza, jidiid*. Is there any new news about it? *?aku ?axbaar taaza ɛanha l-yoom?*

**I feel like a new man. *da-?ašɛur ɛabaalak maxluuq min jidiid*.

new moon - *hlaal* pl. *?ahilla*. The new moon will be visible either tomorrow or the day after. *l-ihlaal raz-yhill loo baačir loo ɛugba*.

news - *xabar* pl. *?axbaar, naba?* pl. *?anbaa?*. Did you hear the news on the radio this morning? *smaɛit il-?axbaar bir-raadyo l-yoom iṣ-ṣubuz?* -- We'll have to break the news to him gently. *laazim ingul-la l-xabar ib-luṭuf*. -- That isn't news to me. *haaða muu xabar jidiid ɛalayya*.

newspaper - *jariida* pl. *jaraayid*.

newsreel - *?axbaar siinamaa?iyya*. I missed the newsreel last night. *ma-lzagit l-?axbaar is-siinamaa?iyya l-baarza bil-leel*.

new year - *raas is-sana*.

next - 1. *jaay, taali*. We're coming to Baghdad next month. *jaayiin il-baġdaad iš-šahar ij-jaay*. -- Next time do it right! *l-marra j-jaaya sawwiiha zeen!* -- It's your turn next. *l-jaaya noobtak*. 2. *wara, baɛad*. I'm next after you. *?aani waraak*. 3. *baɛdeen*. What shall I do next? *baɛdeen is-raz-asawwi?* 4. *θaani*. The next day he got sick. *l-yoom iθ-θaani tmarrað*. or ***l-yoom l-baɛda tmarrað*.

next door to - *b-ṣaff*. The tailor lives next door to us. *l-xayyaaṭ yiskun ib-ṣaffna*. -- We live next door to the school. *niskun ib-ṣaff il-madrasa*.

next to - *yamm, b-ṣaff*. Sit down next to me. *?ugɛud yammi*.

nib - *sillaaya* pl. *-aat, riiša* pl. *riyaš*.

to **nibble** - *garmaṭ (u tgurmuṭ) t-*. Some mouse has been nibbling on this cheese. *fadd faara čaanat itgarmuṭ ib-haj-jibin*.

nice - *laṭiif, zeen, xooš, zilu*. She had on a

nice dress. *čaanat laabsa fistaan laṭiif.* -- Our doctor has a nice way with his patients. *ṭabiibna muεaamalta zeena wiyya l-marḍa.* -- He's a nice polite little boy. *huwwa fadd walad laṭiif w-mˀaddab.* -- That wasn't very nice of him to say that. *ma-čaanat ḥilwa minna yguulha.* -- Did you have a nice time? *gḍeet xooš wakit?* or **twannasit?* --The room is nice and warm. *hal-ġurfa zeena w-daafya.*

nicely - *tamaam, zeen, xooš.* Our daughter has learned to sew nicely. *bittna tεallimat itxayyiṭ zeen.*
 **This will do nicely. *haaδa yˀaddi l-ġaraḍ.*

nickname - *laqab* pl. *ˀalqaab.*

niece - **1.** (fraternal) *bint* (pl. *banaat*) *ˀax.* **2.** (sororal) *bint* (pl. *banaat*) *ˀuxt.*

night - *leela* pl. *-aat, layaali.* He only stayed with us one night. *buqa wiyyaana fadd leela wiḥda.*
 **Good night! *tiṣbaḥ εala xeer!*

night club - *malha* pl. *malaahi.* She sings in the night clubs. *hiyya tġanni bil-malaahi.*

nightgown - **1.** *dišdaaša* (pl. *dišaadiiš*) *noom.* My father prefers a nightgown to pajamas. *ˀabuuya yfaḍḍil id-dišdaaša εal-bijaama.* **2.** *θoob* (pl. *θyaab*) *noom.* I bought my wife a nylon nightgown. *štireet iz-zawijti θoob noom naayloon.*

nightingale - *bilbil* pl. *balaabil.*

night watchman - *ḥaaris leeli* pl. *ḥurraas leeliyyiin, naaṭuur* pl. *nuwaaṭiir, čarxači* pl. *-iyya, peeṣwaan* pl. *-iyya.*

nine - **1.** *tisεa.* The train leaves at nine o'clock. *l-qiṭaar yiṭlaε saaεa tisεa.* **2.** *tisiεt.* I lived there for nine months. *sikanit ihnaak tisiεt išhur.* **3.** *tisiε.* The atmosphere will be full of radioactivity in another nine years. *j-jaww raḥ-ykuun bii ˀišεaaε δarri baεad tisε isniin.*

nineteen - *tṣaaṭaεaš.*

nineteenth - *l-itṣaaṭaεaš.* This is the nineteenth of the month. *haaδa l-yoom il-itṣaaṭaεaš imniš-šahar.*

ninetieth - *t-tisεiin.*

ninety - *tisεiin.*

ninth - **1.** *taasiε.* This is the ninth of the month. *haaδa l-yoom it-taasiε imniš-šahar.* **2.** *tusuε* pl. *ˀatsaaε.* Subtract two ninths from five ninths. *ˀiṭraḥ tusεeen min xams atsaaε.*

nip - **1.** *εaḍḍa* pl. *-aat.* The dog took a good nip of my leg. *č-čalib ˀaxaδ xooš εaḍḍa min rijli.* **2.** *maṣṣa* pl. *-aat.* He took himself a good nip out of the bottle. *ˀaxaδ-la xooš maṣṣa mnil-buṭil.*

nippy - **1.** *bii garṣat barid.* The air is nippy this morning. *l-hawa bii garṣat barid haṣ-ṣubuḥ.* **2.** *ḥaadd.* This is a nippy cheese. *haj-jibin ṭaεma ḥaadd.*

nitrogen - *niitroojiin.*

no - **1.** *laa.* Answer me, yes or no. *jaawubni, ˀii loo laa.* -- Do you always have to say no? *ma-tguul ġeer laa?* **2.** *muu.* This pen is no good. *hal-qalam muu zeen.*
 **This screwdriver is no good for this job. *had-darnafiis ma-yfiid il-haš-šuġuḷ.*
 **This bicycle is no good anymore. *hal-paaysikil ma-bii faaˀida baεad.*
 **He has no money. *ma-εinda fluus.*
 **No smoking! *t-tadxiin mamnuuε!*
 **There are no more seats. *ma-aku maqaaεid baεad.*
 **No sooner did we arrive than the telephone rang. *wiyya-ma wṣalna dagg it-talifoon.*
 **I have no doubt of it whatsoever. *ma-εindi kull šakk biiha ˀabadan.*

noble - *nabiil* pl. *nubalaaˀ.* That was very noble of you. *haaδa čaan εamal nabiil minnak.*

nobleman - *nabiil* pl. *nubalaaˀ, šariif* pl. *ˀašraaf, šurafaaˀ.*

nobody - **1.** (imp.) *laḥḥad, wala waaḥid.* Nobody may leave this room. *laḥḥad yiṭlaε imnil-ġurfa.* **2.** *maḥḥad, wala waaḥid.* Nobody saw us, I'm sure. *maḥḥad šaafna, ˀaani mitˀakkid.* -- Nobody came to the party at all. *wala waaḥid jaa lil-ḥafla ˀabadan.*

nod - *hazzat* (pl. *-aat*) *raas.* He greeted us with a nod. *sallam εaleena b-hazzat raas.*
 to nod - **1.** *hazz* (*i hazz*) *n-.* She nodded her head yes. *hazzat raasha qaabla.* **2.** *ġaffa* (*i tġiffi*). He began to nod over his book. *gaam yġaffi εala ktaaba.*
 to nod to - **1.** *ˀaššar* (*i taˀšiir, tˀiššir*) *l- b-raas~.* The teacher nodded to me to go on reading. *l-muεallim ˀaššar-li b-raasa ˀastimirr bil-qiraaˀa.* **2.** *sallam* (*i salaam*) *εala b-raas~.* She nodded to me as she passed. *sallimat εalayya b-raasha lamma marrat.*

noise - **1.** *ḍajiij, ṣoot.* The noise of the traffic keeps me awake at night. *ḍajiij il-muruur yxalliini gaaεid ṭuul il-leel.* **2.** *ḥiss* pl. *ḥsuus.* I heard a noise downstairs, and I went down to investigate. *smaεit fadd ḥiss jawwa w-nizilt id-daraj ˀašuuf šaku.* **3.** *laġwa* pl. *-aat, ḍawḍaaˀ.* The noise of the crowd at the auction gave me a headache. *laġwat in-naas bil-mazaad dawwxat raasi.*

to nominate - *raššaḥ* (*i taršiiḥ*) *t-.* He's going to nominate himself for the member from the third district in Baghdad. *raḥ-yraššiḥ nafsa naaˀib εan il-manṭiqa θ-θaaliθa b-baġdaad.*

noncommissioned officer - *ḍaabuṭ* (pl. *ḍubbaaṭ*) *ṣaff.*

none - *maḥḥad, wala waaḥid.* None of my friends could help me. *maḥḥad min ˀaṣdiqaaˀi gidar ysaaεidni.* -- None of the women know anything about it. *wala waḥda mnin-niswaan tuεruf šii εanna.*
 **That's none of your business! *haaδa muu šuġḷak!*

nonsense - *kalaam faariġ, ḥači xaruṭ.* Now you're talking nonsense. *hassa da-tiḥči kalaam faariġ.* or *hassa ḥačyak xaruṭ.*

noodles - *šaεriyya.*

noon - *ḍuhur.* It wasn't as hot at noon today as it was yesterday noon. *ma-čaanat ḥaarra l-yoom iḍ-ḍuhur miθil-ma čaanat il-baarḥa ḍ-ḍuhur.*

nor - *w-laa.* I haven't seen it nor do I want to see it. *ma-šifta w-laa ˀariid ˀašuufa.*

normal - *εtiyaadi**.* His temperature is normal. *darajat ḥaraarta εtiyaadiyya.*

normally - *εtiyaadiyyan, ḥasab il-εaada.*

north - *šimaal.* The wind is coming from the north. *l-hawa jaay imniš-šimaal.* -- Mosul is north of Baghdad. *l-mooṣil ib-šimaal baġdaad.*

northern - *šimaali**.* You can find snow in the northern part of Iraq. *tigdar tilgi θiluuj bil-qism iš-šimaali mnil-εiraaq.*

Norway - *n-narwiij.*

Norwegian - *narwiiji** pl. *-iyyiin.*

nose - **1.** *xašim* pl. *xšuum.* He can't breathe through his nose because of the operation. *ma-yigdar yitnaffas min xašma b-sabab il-εamaliyya.* **2.** *muqaddama* pl. *-aat.* There was a fire in the nose of the aircraft. *čaan ˀaku ḥariiq ib-muqaddamat iṭ-ṭayyaara.*
 **He sticks his nose into everything. *ydaxxil nafsa b-kullši.*

nostril - *manxar* pl. *manaaxir.*

not - **1.** *muu.* He is not a man. *huwwa muu rajjaal.* **2.** *ma-* He did not come. *huwwa ma-ˀija.* **3.** *la-* Do not go. *la-truuḥ.*
 not at all - **1.** *muu kulliš.* I'm not at all sure. *ˀaani muu kulliš mitˀakkid.* **2.** *ma... ˀabadan, muu... ˀabadan.* They're not at all happy in their new home. *humma muu farḥaaniin ib-beethum ij-jidiid ˀabadan.* **3.** *l-εafu.* Thank you very much. Not at all. *ˀaškurak ihwaaya. l-εafu.*

to notarize - *ṣaddaq* (*i taṣdiiq*) *t-.* I have a friend that can notarize this document. *εindi ṣadiiq yigdar yṣaddiq hal-waraqa.*

notary public - *kaatib εadil* pl. *kuttaab εadil, kuttaab εuduul.*

notch - *θalma* pl. *-aat.* There's a notch on the edge of the table. *ˀaku θalma εala ḥaaffat il-meez.*
 to notch - *θilam* (*i θalim*) *n-.* He notched the ruler with his knife. *θilam il-maṣṭara b-siččiinta.*

note - **1.** *waraqa* pl. *-aat.* He left a note on the table and went out. *tirak waraqa εal-meez w-ṭilaε.* **2.** *nooṭa* pl. *-aat.* Try to sing this note. *ḥaawil itganni han-nooṭa.* **3.** *mulaaḥaḍa* pl. *-aat.* The teacher wrote several notes on the margin of my paper. *l-muεallim kitab εiddat mulaaḥaḍaat εala haamiš waraqti.* **4.** *εalaama* pl. *εalaaˀim, ˀaθar* pl. *ˀaaθaar.* There was a note of fear in his voice. *čaan ˀaku ˀaθar xoof ib-ṣoota.* **5.** *kumpiyaala* pl. *-aat.* He gave me a note for the balance. *nṭaani kumpiyaala εala baqiyyat il-ifluus.*
 notes - *ruˀuus aqlaam.* I didn't take notes in class today. *ma-ˀaxaδit ruˀuus aqlaam biṣ-ṣaff il-yoom.*
 of note - *maεruuf, malḥuuḍ.* He's written three books of note. *kitab iθlaθ kutub maεruufa.*
 to note - **1.** *δikar* (*u δikir*) *n-, nawwah* (*i tanwiih*) *t-.* He noted our assistance in a letter to the manager. *δikar musaaεadatna b-kitaab*

lil-mudiir. 2. *laaḥað̣ (i mulaaḥað̣a) t-.* Note the beautiful carving. *laaḥið̣ in-naqš ij-jamiil.*
notebook - *daftar* pl. *dafaatir.*
nothing - 1. *ma-aku, laa šii.* Something is better than nothing. *šii ʔaḥsan min laa šii.* 2. *ma-... šii.* We did nothing all afternoon. *ma-sawweena šii ṭuul il-εaṣir.*
 for nothing - *b-balaaš, majjaanan.* He gave me this shirt for nothing. *nṭaani haθ-θoob ib-balaaš.*
notice - 1. *ʔiεlaan* pl. *-aat.* Did you read the notice on the bulletin board? *qreet il-ʔiεlaan εal-looḥa?* 2. *ʔišεaar* pl. *-aat.* They fired him without notice. *ṭallεoo mniš-šuġuḷ biduun ʔišεaar.* 3. *xabar.* You'll have to give notice a month before you move. *laazim tinṭi xabar gabuḷ šahar min wakit-ma titḥawwal.*
 **I don't know how it escaped my notice. *ma-adri šloon faatat εalayya.*
 to notice - 1. *laaḥað̣ (i mulaaḥað̣a) t-, ntibah (i ntibaah).* Did you notice if he was in his office or not? *laaḥað̣it iδa kaan ib-daaʔirta loo laa?* 2. *laaḥað̣ (i mulaaḥað̣a) t-.* Everybody noticed his tie. *kull waaḥid laaḥað̣ irbaaṭa.*
to **notify** - *ballaġ (i tabliiġ, tbilliġ) t-, xabbar (u txubbur) t-, ʔaεlam (i ʔiεlaam) n-.* Notify me when you arrive. *xabburni lamma tooṣal.*
notion - 1. *meel* pl. *miyuul.* I had a notion to stay home today. *čaan εindi meel ʔabqa bil-beet il-yoom.* 2. *fikra* pl. *fikir.* I haven't any notion what he wants. *ma-εindi ʔay fikra š-yriid.*
notorious - *mašhuur.* He's a notorious criminal. *huwwa mujrim mašhuur.*
noun - *ʔisim* pl. *ʔasmaaʔ.*
nourishing - *muġaδδi.* We ate a nourishing breakfast. *ʔakalna riyuug muġaδδi.*
nourishment - *ġiδaaʔ, quut, taġδiya.* He needs more nourishment. *yriid-la ġiδaaʔ ʔakθar.*
novel - 1. *ruwaaya* pl. *-aat, quṣṣa* pl. *quṣaṣ.* I read a good novel last night. *qreet xooš ruwaaya l-baarḥa bil-leel.* 2. *jidiid.* That's a novel idea. *haaδi fikra jidiida.*
November - *tišriin iθ-θaani.*
now - *hassa, l-ʔaan.* I have to go now. *laazim ʔaruuḥ hassa.*
 by now - *hassa, l-ʔaan.* He should have been here by now. *laazim ykuun hassa hnaa.*
 from now on - *min hassa w-jaay, minnaa w-raayiḥ, minnaa w-hiič.* From now on I'll keep quiet. *minnaa w-hiič raḥ-askut.*
 just now - *hastaww-, hassa, l-ʔaan.* I talked to him just now. *hastawwni ḥčeet wiyyaa.*
 now and then - *been ḥeen w-ʔaaxar, been mudda w-mudda, been fatra w-fatra, ʔaḥyaanan.* I hear from him now and then. *ʔasmaε minna been ḥeen w-ʔaaxar.*
 up to now - *l-ḥadd il-ʔaan, li-hassa.* I haven't been sick up to now. *ma-tmarrað̣it il-ḥadd il-ʔaan.*
nowadays - *hal-ʔayyaam.* Nowadays, every house has television. *hal-ʔayyaam kull beet bii talafizyoon.*
nowhere - *ma-... b-ʔay mukaan.* He's nowhere to be seen. *ma-yinšaaf ib-ʔay mukaan.*

nozzle - *raas* pl. *ruus.* The hose needs a new nozzle. *ṣ-ṣoonda yriid-ilha raas jidiid.*
nuclear energy - *ṭ-ṭaaqa n-nawawiyya.*
nucleus - *nawaat* pl. *nuwaayaat* coll. *nuwa.*
nude - *mṣallax* pl. *-iin, mṣaaliix; εaryaan* pl. *-iin, εraaya.*
nudge - *naġġa* pl. *-aat.* He gave me a nudge when she walked by. *nṭaani naġġa lamma marrat.*
 to nudge - *naġġ (u naġġ) n-.* Don't nudge me! *la-tnuġġni.*
nuisance - *ð̣awaaj, ð̣awajaan.* Neckties are a nuisance. *l-ʔarbiṭa ð̣awajaan.*
numb - 1. *xadraan.* My fingers are numb from the cold. *ʔaṣaabεi xadraana mnil-barid.* 2. *mitxaddir, xadraan.* I feel completely numb. *ʔašεur kull jismi mitxaddir.*
 to numb - *xaddar (i taxdiir) t-.* The blow numbed my shoulder. *ð̣-ð̣arba xaddrat čitfi.*
number - 1. *raqam* pl. *ʔarqaam, numra* pl. *numar.* What's your house number? *šgadd raqam beetkum?* — Did you write down the number? *ktabit ir-raqam?* 2. *εadad* pl. *ʔaεdaad.* A number of cars are still available at reduced prices. *εadad imnis-sayyaaraat baεda mawjuud ib-ʔasεaar muxaffað̣a.* 3. *εidda.* He's been imprisoned a number of times. *nsijan εiddat marraat.*
 **I've got his number. *ʔaεruf duwaa.*
 to number - *raqqam (u truqqum, tarqiim), nammar (u tnummur) t-.* Number the boxes from one to ten. *raqqum il-εilab min waaḥid ila εašra.*
 **His days are numbered. *ʔayyaama maεduuda.*

numeral - *raqam* pl. *ʔarqaam.*
nun - *raahiba* pl. *-aat.*
nurse - 1. *mumarriḍa* pl. *-aat.* The patient needs a nurse. *l-mariið̣ yiḥtaaj mumarrið̣a.* 2. *murabbiya* pl. *-aat.* The children are out in the park with their nurse. *j-jahhaal barra bil-ḥadiiqa wiyya murabbiyathum.*
 wet nurse - *daaya* pl. *-aat.*
 to nurse - 1. *rið̣aε (a rað̣iε) n-.* They brought a woman to nurse the baby. *jaabaw mara tirð̣aε ij-jaahil.* 2. *εtina (i εtinaaʔ) b-.* He's nursing his broken leg. *da-yiεtini b-rijla l-maksuura.*
nursery - 1. *rawð̣a* pl. *-aat.* I take my child to the nursery at eight o'clock every day. *ʔaaxuδ ibni lir-rawð̣a s-saaεa θmaanya kull yoom.* 2. *maštal* pl. *mašaatil.* I bought these flowers at the nursery. *štireet hal-warid imnil-maštal.*

nut - 1. *čaraza* pl. *-aat* coll. *čaraz; karaza* pl. *-aat* coll. *karaz.* This shop sells all kinds of nuts. *hal-baggaal ybiiε jamiiε ʔanwaaε ič-čarazaat.* 2. *ṣammuuna* pl. *-aat.* This nut doesn't fit the bolt. *haṣ-ṣammuuna ma-tirham εal-burġi.* 3. *mxabbaḷ* pl. *-iin, mxaabiiḷ.* He's a real nut. *huwwa mxabbaḷ tamaam.*
nut cracker - *kassaarat* (pl. *-aat*) *jooz.*
nutmeg - *joozbawwa.*
nylon - *naayloon.* He bought nylon socks. *štira jwaariib naayloon.*

O

oak - *balluuṭ.*
oar - *mijdaaf* pl. *majaadiif.* The oars are in the boat. *l-majaadiif bil-balam.*
oasis - *waaḥa* pl. *-aat.*
oats - *hurṭumaan.* They plant a lot of oats here. *hwaaya yziriεuun hurṭumaan ihnaa.*
obedience - *ṭaaεa.*
obedient - *ṭaayiε, muṭiiε.*
to **obey** - *ṭaaε (i ṭaaεa) n-, xið̣aε (a xað̣iε) n-.* He doesn't obey me. *huwwa ma-yṭiiεni.* — I can't obey that order. *ma-agdar aṭiiε hal-ʔamur.*
object - 1. *šii* pl. *ʔašyaaʔ, ḥaaja* pl. *-aat.* He was struck on the head with a heavy object. *nð̣irab εala raasa b-šii θigiil.* 2. *qaṣid, maqṣad* pl. *maqaaṣid.* What is the object of that? *šinu l-qaṣid min δaak?*
to **object** - *εtirað̣ (i εtiraað̣), maanaε (i mumaanaεa).* I don't know why you object to it. *ma-aεruf leeš da-tiεtirið̣ εaleeha.* — **I hope you don't object to my smoking. *ʔatʔammal ma-εindak maaniε ʔiδa ʔadaxxin.*
objection - *εtiraað̣* pl. *-aat, maaniε* pl. *mawaaniε.* He didn't raise any objection. *ma-ʔaθaar ʔay iεtiraað̣.* — Is there any objection? *ʔaku ʔay maaniε?*

objectionable - *ma-maqbuul.*
objective - *hadaf* pl. *ʔahdaaf.* We reached our objective. *wuṣalna hadafna.*
obligated - *mamnuun, mumtann.* We're very much obligated to you. *ʔiḥna mamnuuniin ihwaaya minnak.*
obligation - *waajib* pl. *-aat, ltizaam* pl. *-aat, rtibaaṭ* pl. *-aat.* He can't meet his obligations. *ma-yigdar ywaffi ltizaamaata.*
 **We're under no obligation to him. *ʔiḥna muu marbuuṭiin bii.*
obligatory - *ʔijbaari*.* Military service is obligatory. *l-xidma bij-jeeš ijbaariyya.*
to **oblige** - *jubar (u ʔijbaar).* His illness obliged him to leave school for a year. *marað̣ta jubrata yitruk il-madrasa l-sana wiḥda.*
 to be obliged - *ð̣ṭarr (a ð̣ṭiraar), njubar (u njibaar).* I was obliged to take shelter in a cave. *ð̣ṭarreet altiji bil-kahaf.*
obscene - *baδiiʔ.*
observance - *ḥtifaal, ḥtiraam.* The parade is a part of the observance of Army Day. *l-istiεraað̣ qisim imnil-iḥtifaal ib-yoom ij-jeeš.*
observant - *mulaaḥið̣.* He is observant and has a good

mind. *huwwa fadd waaḥid mulaaḥiδ w-εaaqil.*

observation - 1. *muεaayana.* He entered the hospital for observation. *dixal il-mustašfa lil-muεaayana.* 2. *mulaaḥaδa* pl. *-aat.* In his speech he made a number of acute observations on the political situation. *b-xiṭaaba sawwa εiddat mulaaḥaδaat ḥaadda εan il-ḥaala s-siyaasiyya.*

observatory - *marṣad jawwi* pl. *maraaṣid jawwiyya.*

to **observe** - 1. *laaḥaδ (i mulaaḥaδa).* Did you observe the reaction she had? *laaḥaδit radd il-fiεil iṣ-ṣaar εidha?* 2. *raaεa (i muraaεaat).* Which holidays do you observe in Iraq? *yaa εuṭal itraaεuun bil-εiraaq?* -- All employees here are expected to observe the regulations. *kull il-mustaxdamiin ihnaa mafruuδ biihum yraaεuun it-taεliimaat.*

obstacle - *εaqaba* pl. *-aat, maaniε* pl. *mawaaniε.* He had to overcome many obstacles before he was successful. *δṭarr yitġallab εala hwaaya εaqabaat gabuḷ-ma yitwaffaq.*

obstinate - *εaniid* pl. *-iin, εanuud* pl. *-iin.* It won't do you any good to be obstinate about it. *ma-yfiidak iṭṣiir εaniid ib-hal-xuṣuuṣ.*

to **obtain** - *ḥaṣṣal (i taḥṣiil) t-.* He obtained all of his education abroad. *ḥaṣṣal kull taεliima l-εaali bil-xaarij.*

obvious - *waaδiḥ, δaahir, mbayyin.* It's obvious that he doesn't want to do it. *mnil-waaδiḥ ʔanna ma-yriid ysawwiiha.* -- His annoyance is obvious from his voice. *nziεaaja mbayyin min ṣoota.*

obviously - *mnil-waaδiḥ, mniδ-δaahir.* She was obviously wrong. *mnil-waaδiḥ čaanat ġalṭaana.*

occasion - *munaasaba* pl. *-aat.* A dress like this can be worn for any occasion. *fistaan miθil haaδa yinlibis ib-kull munaasaba.* -- What's the occasion? *šinu l-munaasaba?*

occasionally - *ʔaḥyaanan.* Except for a trip to Basra occasionally, I never leave Baghdad. *ma-εada safra lil-baṣra ʔaḥyaanan, ʔabad ma-aṭlaε min baġdaad.*

occupation - 1. *šuġuḷ* pl. *ʔašġaal, mihna* pl. *mihan.* What's your occupation? *šinu šuġḷak?* 2. *ḥtilaal.* Where were you during the occupation? *ween činiit ib-zaman il-iḥtilaal?*

occupied - *muḥtall.* He is a refugee from occupied Palestine. *haaδa laajiʔ min falasṭiin il-muḥtalla.*

to **occupy** - 1. *ḥtall (a ḥtilaal).* The Turks occupied the town first. *l-ʔatraak iḥtallaw il-madiina bil-ʔawwal.* 2. *sikan (u sukna) n-.* The house hasn't been occupied for years. *l-beet ma-nsikan min isniin.* 3. *šiġal (i ʔišġaal) n-.* Studying occupies all my time. *d-diraasa da-tišġil kull waqti.* -- The boss is occupied at the moment. *r-raʔiis mašġuul hassa.*

to **occur** - 1. *ṣaar (i), ḥidaθ (i ḥuduuθ), wugaε (a waguε).* When did the accident occur? *šwakit ṣaar il-ḥaadiθ?* 2. *ʔija (i).* The name occurred twice in the same chapter. *ʔija l-ism marrteen ib-nafs il-faṣil.* 3. *xiṭar (u xuṭuur).* That would never have occurred to me. *δaak wala čaan yixṭur εala baali.* 4. *tbaadar (a tabaadur).* Suddenly it occurred to me that I forgot to lock the door. *fujʔatan itbaadar-li ʔanni niseet ʔaqful il-baab.*

ocean - *muḥiiṭ* pl. *-aat.* The U.S.A. lies between two oceans. *l-wilaayaat il-muttaḥida waaqεa been muḥiiṭeen.*

o'clock - *saaεa.* The train leaves at seven o'clock. *l-qiṭaar yitruk saaεa sabεa.*

October - *tišriin il-ʔawwal.*

oculist - *ṭabiib* (pl. *ʔaṭibbaaʔ*) *iεyuun.*

odd - 1. *šaaδδ* pl. *-iin, ġariib* pl. *-iin.* He's a very odd person. *huwwa fadd waaḥid šaaδδ.* 2. *tak.* Haven't you seen an odd glove anywhere? *ma-šifit tak čaff ib-fadd makaan?* 3. *fardi*.* Pick an odd number. *ʔixṭaar raqam fardi.* 4. *w-ksuur.* It cost me thirty-odd dinars. *kallifatni tlaaθiin diinaar w-ksuur.* 5. *mitfarriġ.* He does all the odd jobs around the house. *huwwa ysawwi kull il-ʔašġaal il-mitfarrġa bil-beet.* 6. *mxaalaf.* We only have a few odd pairs left. *εidna bass fadd čam zooj imxaalfa buqat.*

odor - *riiḥa* pl. *riyaḥ, rawaayiḥ.* What is that bad odor I smell? *šinu har-riiḥa j-jaayfa lli qaaεid aštammha.*

of - 1. *min.* I have a complete edition of his works. *εindi nusxa kaamla min muʔallafaata.* -- The watch is of gold. *s-saaεa min δahab.* 2. *maal.* The roof of our house is very high. *ṣ-ṣaṭiḥ maal beetna kulliš εaali.*

**Could I have a glass of water, please? *ʔagdar ʔaaxuδ glaaṣ maay rajaaʔan.*

**He's a manager of a big store. *huwwa mudiir maxzan čibiir.*

off - *min.* This thing has been off the market for a year. *haš-šii mixtifi mnis-suug min sana.* or *haš-šii ṣaar-la sana mnis-suug.* -- There's a button off your jacket. *ʔaku dugma waagiε min sitirtak.*

**The post office isn't far off. *daaʔirat il-bariid muu kulliš biεiida.*

**Our maid is off today. *xaadmatna εidha εuṭla l-yoom.* or *xaadmatna ma-da-tištuġul il-yoom.*

**He's a little off. *huwwa šwayya εinda xyuuṭ.* or *šwayya εaqla laaεib.*

**He was off in a flash. *ġaab miθl il-barq.*

**They aren't so badly off. *humma muu kulliš miḥtaajiin.*

**They are very well off. *humma kullis ġanaagiin.*

**The ship anchored three miles off shore. *l-baaxira δabbat ʔangar itlaθ ʔamyaal εan is-saaḥil.*

**June is still three months off. *baεad itlaθt išhur il-ḥuzeeraan.* or *ḥuzeeraan baεad-la tlaθt išhur yaḷḷa yiji.*

**His figures are way off. *ḥsaabaata kullha ġaḷaṭ.*

**This is an off year for wheat. *haay muu xooš sana lil-ḥunṭa.*

**I'm going to take a week off soon. *raḥ-aaxuδ isbuuε εuṭla qariiban.*

**This thing has been off the market for a year. *naš-šii mixtifi mnis-suug min sana.* or *haš-šii ṣaar-la sana mnis-suug.*

**There's a button off your jacket. *ʔaku dugma waagiε min sitirtak.*

**Hands off! *waxxir iidak min haay!*

**They've broken off relations. *qiṭεaw εalaaqaathum.*

**The branch broke off. *nkisar il-ġuṣin.*

**One leg of the table has come off. *nšilεat rijil imnil-meez.*

**Ladies are requested to take their hats off. *maṭluub imnim-niswaan yšiiluun šafaqaathum.*

**When does the plane take off? *šwakit iṭṭiir iṭ-ṭayyaara?*

off and on - *ʔaḥyaanan, marraat.* She works off and on. *hiyya tištuġul ʔaḥyaanan.*

to **offend** - *ʔasaaʔ (i ʔisaaʔa) ʔila.* I hope I didn't offend you. *inšaḷḷa ma-ʔasaʔit ʔilak.*

offense - 1. *ʔisaaʔa* pl. *-aat.* I didn't mean any offense. *ma-qṣadit ʔay ʔisaaʔa.* 2. *muxaalafa* pl. *-aat.* Is this your first offense? *haaδi ʔawwal muxaalafa ʔilak?*

to take offense - *staaʔ (a stiyaaʔ), tkaddar (a takaddur).* He took offense at my remark. *staaʔ min mulaaḥaδti.*

offensive - 1. *musiiʔ.* His behavior was offensive to the local people. *taṣarrufa čaan musiiʔ lis-sukkaan il-maḥalliyyiin.* 2. *makruuh, kariih.* It has an offensive odor. *biiha riiḥa kariiha.*

offer - *εariδ* pl. *εuruuδ.* He made me a good offer. *sawwaa-li xooš εariδ.*

to offer - 1. *qaddam (i taqdiim) t-.* May I offer you a cup of coffee? *ʔagdar aqaddim-lak finjaan gahwa?* 2. *εiraδ (i εariδ) n-.* He offered me a hundred dinars for it. *εiraδ εalayya miit diinaar biiha.* 3. *tbarraε (a tabarruε), εiraδ (i εariδ).* My brother-in-law offered to help me paint the house. *nisiibi tbarraε yεaawinni b-ṣubġ il-beet.* 4. *bayyan (i tabyiin) t-.* Didn't they offer any resistance? *ma-bayynaw ʔay muqaawama?*

offhand - *b-ṣuura murtajala.* I can't tell you offhand. *ma-agdar agul-lak ib-ṣuura murtajala.*

**He treated me in an offhand manner. *ma-qaddarni.* or *εaamalni buruud.*

office - 1. *maktab* pl. *makaatib, daaʔira* pl. *dawaaʔir.* You can see me in my office. *tigdar itšuufni b-maktabi.*-- The offices close at five o'clock. *d-dawaaʔir tinsadd is-saaεa xamsa.* 2. *markaz* pl. *maraakiz, manṣib* pl. *manaaṣib.* He has a high office in the government. *εinda markaz εaali bil-ḥukuuma.*

**The whole office was invited. *kull il-muwaδδafiin čaanaw madεuwwiin.*

officer - 1. *δaabuṭ* pl. *δubbaaṭ.* He was an officer during the last war. *čaan δaabuṭ bil-ḥarb il-ʔaxiir.* 2. *šurṭi* pl. *šurṭa.* Ask the officer how we get to the station. *ʔisʔal iš-šurṭi šloon nooṣal lil-maḥaṭṭa.* 3. *εuδu* (pl. *ʔaεδaaʔ*) *ʔidaara.* Are you an officer of this club? *ʔinta min ʔaεδaaʔ ʔidaarat n-naadi?*

official - 1. *maʔmuur* pl. *-iin.* The customs official who examined my bags was very thorough. *maʔmuur il-gumrug illi fuḥaṣ junaṭi čaan kulliš daqiiq.*

2. *muwaδδaf* pl. *-iin.* He's a State Department official. *huwwa muwaδδaf min wizaart il-xaarijiyya.* 3. *rasmi**. He is here on official business. *huwwa hnaa b-šuġuḷ rasmi.*
officially - *rasmiyyan.* It was announced officially. *nEilnat rasmiyyan.*
often - **1.** *hwaaya, kaθiir.* Do you see him often? *tšuufa hwaaya?* -- He is absent often. *haaδa yġiib kaθiir.* **2.** *ġaaliban, ġaaliban-ma.* He often spends his afternoons with us. *ġaaliban-ma yigδi Eaṣriyyaata wiyyaana.*
how often - **1.** *čam marra.* How often do you go to the movies in a month? *čam marra truuz lis-siinama biš-šahar?* **2.** *yaa-ma.* How often I have wished that I had gone to college. *yaa-ma ʔatmanna loo daaxil kulliyya.*
to **ogle** - *baṣbaṣ (i baṣbaṣa) t- l-.* The boys stand in front of the school and ogle the girls as they come out. *l-wulid yoogfuun giddaam il-madrasa w-ybaṣbiṣuun lil-banaat min yṭilEuun.*
oil - **1.** *nafuṭ, zeet.* Oil is the most important export in Iraq. *n-nafuṭ ʔahamm ṣaadiraat il-Eiraaq.* -- We need some oil for the stove. *niztaaj nafuṭ liṭ-ṭabbaax.* **2.** *dihin* pl. *duhuun.* Vegetable oil is often used for cooking. *d-dihn in-nabaati hwaaya mustaEmal liṭ-ṭabux.* **3.** *zeet* pl. *zyuut.* I really prefer olive oil on the salad. *ʔaani bil-zaqiiqa ʔafaδδil zeet iz-zeetuun Eaz-zalaaṭa.*
to oil - *dahhan (i tadhiin) t-.* The sewing machine needs to be oiled. *makiint il-ixyaaṭa yird-ilha titdahhan.*
oilcake- *kisba* pl. *kisab.* Our water buffalo lives on oilcakes. *jaamuusna yEiiš Eal-kisba.*
oilcan - *yaaġdaan* pl. *-aat.*
oilcloth - *qmaaš imšammaE* pl. *ʔaqmiša mšammEa.*
ointment - *malzam* pl. *malaazim, dihin* pl. *duhuun.*
O.K. - **1.** *muwaafaqa, muṣaadaqa, qubuul.* I need his O.K. *ʔaztaaj muwaafaqta.* **2.** *zeen.* Everything is O.K. now. *hassa kullši zeen.*
**I'll go along, if it's O.K. with you. *ʔaruuz wiyyaak, ʔiδa ma-Eindak maaniE.*
to O.K. - *waafaq (u muwaafaqa), ṣaadaq (i muṣaadaqa).* He has to O.K. it first. *laazim ywaafuq Ealeeha ʔawwal.*
old - **1.** *Eatiig, qadiim.* I gave all my old clothes to the poor. *nṭeet kull ihduumi l-Eatiiga lil-fuqaraaʔ.* -- Is this an old model? *haay nooEha qadiima?* **2.** *čibiir* pl. *kbaar.* He's pretty old. *huwwa kulliš čibiir.*
**How old are you? *šgadd Eumrak?*
old man - *šaayib* pl. *šiyyaab.* My uncle is an old man, but he is still very active. *Eammi šaayib laakin la-yzaal kulliš našiiṭ.*
old woman - *Eajuuz, Eajuuza* pl. *Eajaayiz.* She's an old woman now. *hassa hiyya Eajuuz.*
old-fashioned - **1.** *rajEi*, mitEaṣṣub.* She's very old-fashioned in her ideas. *hiyya kulliš rajEiyya b-ʔafkaarha.* **2.** *min ṭiraaz qadiim.* His clothes are old-fashioned, but of good quality. *malaabsa min ṭiraaz qadiim laakin min nooEiyya zeena.*
to **omit** - *ziδaf (i zaδif) n-.* Omit that word. *ʔizδif hač-čilma.*
on - **1.** *Eala.* He sat on the speaker's left. *giEad Eala yisaar il-xaṭiib.* -- The drinks are on the house. *š-šurub Eala zsaab il-mazall.* **2.** *Eala, foog.* Put it on the table. *xalliiha Eal-meez.* **3.** *b-.* On what day? *b-ʔay yoom?* -- Do you sell on credit? *tbiiE ib-ʔaqṣaaṭ?* -- I live on Rashid St. *ʔaskun ib-šaariE ir-rašiid.* -- Who's on the team? *minu bil-firqa?* -- What's on the radio today? *šaku bir-raadyo l-yoom?* **4.** *Ean.* His lecture was on Arab solidarity. *muzaaδarta čaanat Ean it-taδaamun il-Earabi.*
**Are you open on Friday? *tfattiz ij-jumEa?*
**Is the gas on? *l-ġaaz mašEuul?*
and so on - *w-ʔila ʔaaxirihi.* I need paper, ink, and so on. *ʔaztaaj waraq, zibir w-ʔila ʔaaxirihi.*
once - **1.** *marra wizda, fadd marra, marra.* I've seen him only once. *šifta marra wizda bass.* -- He feeds the dog once a day. *yṭaEEum ič-čalib marra bil-yoom.* **2.** *fadd yoom.* This was once the business section. *fadd yoom haaδa čaan il-markaz it-tijaari.*
at once - **1.** *suwa, marra wizda, fadd marra.* Everything came at once. *kullši ʔija marra wizda.* **2.** *zaalan, b-saaE, sariiEan.* Come at once. *b-saaE taEaal.*
once in a while - *baEδ il-ʔazyaan, ʔazaanan, dooraat.* Once in a while I like a good glass of cold buttermilk. *baEδ il-ʔazyaan ʔazibb fadd iglaaṣ liban baarid.*
one - **1.** (m.) *waazid* (f.) *wazda.* Count from one to a hundred. *Eidd imnil-waazid lil-miyya.* -- One or two will be enough. *waazid ʔaw iθneen kaafi.* -- It's almost one o'clock. *s-saaEa zawaali l-wazda.* -- One never knows. *l-waazid iš-midrii.* -- One of us can buy the tickets. *waazid minnina yigdar yištiri l-biṭaaqaat.* **2.** *fadd, waazid.* I have one question I want to ask. *Eindi fadd suʔaal ʔariid ʔasʔala.* **3.** (m.) *ʔabu* (f.) *ʔumm.* The one with the cover is the best box for our purpose. *ʔabu l-ġiṭa ʔazsan ṣanduug il-ġaraδna.* or ***lli bil-ġiṭa ʔazsan ṣanduug il-ġaraδna.* -- The one with the top down is my car. *ʔumm it-tanta n-naazla s-sayyaara maalti.*
**I prefer the more expensive one. *ʔafaδδil il-ʔaġla.*
**Take that one. *ʔuxuδ haδaak.*
**One of these days, I'll be back. *fadd yoom imnil-ʔayyaam ʔarjaE.*
**On the one hand he wants it finished, on the other hand he doesn't give us the material. *min jiha yriidha tixlaṣ w-min jiha ma-da-yinṭiina l-mawaadd.*
one another - *waazid il-laax.* They like one another. *yzibbuun waazid il-laax.*
one at a time - *waazid waazid.* Let them in one at a time. *xaššišhum waazid waazid.*
onion - *buṣla* pl. *-aat* coll. *buṣal.*
only - **1.** *bass.* I was going to buy it, only he told me not to. *čaan ištireetha bass huwwa gal-li laa.* -- This is only for you. *haaδi bass ʔilak.* **2.** *waziid.* He's our only child. *huwwa ʔibinna l-waziid.*
open - **1.** *maftuuz, mafkuuk.* He may have come in through an open window. *yjuuz dixal min šibbaač maftuuz.* -- The dining room is not open yet. *ġurfat il-ʔakil maa maftuuza li-hassa.* **2.** *šaaġir.* Is the job still open? *l-waδiifa baEadha šaaġra?* **3.** *maftuug.* The shoulder seam of your jacket is open. *xyaaṭ čitif sitirtak maftuug.* **4.** *ṭaliq.* He's in the open air all day long. *huwwa bil-hawa iṭ-ṭaliq ṭuul il-yoom.*
to open - **1.** *fitaz (a fatiz) n-, fakk (u fakk) n-.* Open the door please. *ʔiftaz il-baab, min faδlak.* -- They opened an account at the bank. *fitzaw izsaab bil-bang.* **2.** *fattaz (i taftiiz).* We open every day at 9 A.M. *nfattiz saaEa tisEa ṣ-ṣubuz kull yoom.* **3.** *šaqq (u šaqq) n-.* The government is going to open a new highway through the mountains. *l-zukuuma raz-itšuqq ṭariiq jidiid yixtiriq ij-jibaal.* -- The police opened a way through the crowd for us. *š-šurṭa šaqqoo-nna ṭariiq been ij-jamaahiir.* **4.** *bida (i bidaaya) n-.* When does hunting season open? *šwakit yibdi mawsim iṣ-ṣeed?* **5.** *nfitaz (i nfitaaz).* The door opens easily now. *l-baab hassa da-yinfitiz ib-suhuula.*
**He's always open to reasonable suggestions. *huwwa daaʔiman yiqbal iqtiraazaat maEquula.*
to open onto - *ṭilaE (a ṭaliE) Eala.* Our room opens onto a balcony. *ġurfatna tiṭlaE Eala baalkoon.*
to open up - *fakk (u fakk) n-, fitaz (a fatiz) n-.* Open up the package. *fukk ir-ruzma.* -- Can you open up the safe? *tigdar itfukk il-qaaṣa?*
opening - **1.** *fatza* pl. *-aat.* The opening isn't big enough. *l-fatza muu čibiira kifaaya.* **2.** *bidaaya.* We missed the opening of his speech. *ma-lazzagna Eala bidaayat xiṭaaba.* **3.** *ftitaaz* pl. *-aat.* Were you at the opening of the exhibition? *činit b-iftitaaz il-maEraδ?* **4.** *šaaġir* pl. *šawaaġir.* We'll call you as soon as we have an opening. *nxaabrak ʔawwal-ma yṣiir Eidna šaaġir.*
opera - *ʔoopra* pl. *-aat.*
opera house - *daar* (pl. *duur*) *ʔoopra.*
to **operate** - **1.** *šaġġal (i tašġiil) t-.* How do you operate this machine? *šloon itšaġġil hal-makiina?* **2.** *štiġal (u štiġaal).* This machine operates on electricity. *hal-makiina tištuġul bil-kahrabaaʔ.* **3.** *sawwa (i taswiya) Eamaliyya.* The doctor says he'll have to operate on her. *d-daktoor gaal laazim ysawwii-lha l-Eamaliyya.*
operation - **1.** *Eamaliyya* pl. *-aat.* This is her third operation. *haay θaaliθ Eamaliyya ʔilha.* **2.** *zaraka* pl. *-aat.* One machine does the whole process in a single operation. *makiina wazda tquum ib-kull il-Eamaliyya b-zaraka wazda.* **3.** *stiEmaal.* They just put this line into operation. *hassa xallaw hal-xaṭṭ bil-istiEmaal.*
opinion - *raʔi* pl. *ʔaaraaʔ, fikir* pl. *ʔafkaar.* I have a very high opinion of him. *fikirti Eanna*

kulliš zeena. -- What's your opinion? *šinu ra?yak?* -- We'll have to get the opinion of an expert. *laazim naaxuδ ra?i xabiir.* --

opponent - *muεaariδ* pl. *-iin, munaafis* pl. *-iin, xaṣum* pl. *xṣuum.* He's a dangerous opponent. *huwwa munaafis xaṭir.*

opportunity - *furṣa* pl. *furaṣ.* When will you have an opportunity to see him? *šwakit yṣiir εindak furṣa tšuufa?* -- This is a big opportunity for you. *haay furṣa čbiira ?ilak.*

to **oppose** - **1.** *εaaraδ (i muεaaraδa).* He's the one who opposed your admission to the club. *huwwa lli εaaraδ intimaa?ak lin-naadi.* **2.** *naafas (i munaafasa).* He opposed me in the last election. *naafasni bil-intixaabaat il-?axiira.*

opposite - **1.** *muqaabil, gbaal.* We live opposite the library. *niskun igbaal il-maktaba.* **2.** *muεaakis, muxaalif, εakis.* He came from the opposite direction. *?ija mnij-jiha l-muεaakisa.* -- This is just the opposite of what I meant. *haaδa tamaaman muxaalif il-ma εneeta.* or *haaδa tamaaman εaks il-εineeta.*

opposition - *muεaaraδa* pl. *-aat.* The proposal met with unexpected opposition. *l-iqtiraaz waajah muεaaraδa ġeer mutawaqqaεa.*

to **oppress** - *ṭiġa (i ṭuġyaan) n- εala.* They oppressed the poor and the weak. *ṭiġaw εala l-fuqaraa? wiδ-δuεafaa?.*

oppressive - *mδaayiq, mustabidd.* The heat's oppressive today. *l-zarr il-yoom imδaayiq.*

optician - *naδδaaraati* pl. *-iyya, ṣaazib* (pl. *?aṣzaab*) *naδδaaraat.*

optimism - *tafaa?ul.*

optimist - *mitfaa?il* pl. *-iin.*

optimistic - *mitfaa?il.* Don't be so optimistic. *la-tkuun hal-gadd mitfaa?il.*

or - *loo, ?aw.* He's coming today or tomorrow. *huwwa jaay il-yoom loo baačir.*

oral - *šafahi*, šafawi*.* She passed the oral examination. *nijzat bil-imtizaan iš-šafahi.*

orally - *šafahiyyan, šafawiyyan.*

orange - **1.** *purtaqaala* pl. *-aat,* coll. *purtaqaal.* How much are the oranges? *beeš il-purtaqaal?* **2.** *purtaqaali*.* Her dress was orange and white. *nafnuufha čaan purtaqaali w-?abyaδ.*

orange juice - *šarbat purtaqaal, εaṣiir purtaqaal.*

orchard - *bistaan* pl. *basaatiin.*

orchestra - *firqa* (pl. *firaq*) *mawsiiqiyya, jooq mawsiiqi* pl. *?ajwaaq mawsiiqiyya.*

order - **1.** *?amur* pl. *?awaamir.* I'm just obeying orders. *?aani bass da-aṭiiε il-?awaamir.* **2.** *ṭalab* pl. *-aat.* Waiter, I'd like to change my order. *booy, ?ariid ?abaddil iṭ-ṭalab maali.* **3.** *tartiib* pl. *-aat.* Please put these cards in order. *min faδlak xalli hal-biṭaaqaat zasab it-tartiib.* **4.** *niδaam* pl. *-aat.* The police restored order quickly. *š-šurṭa staεaadat in-niδaam ib-surεa.*

**I disposed of it in short order. *dabbaritha bil-εajal.*

in order - **1.** *b-mazall.* Your remark is quite in order. *mulaazaδtak ib-mazallha tamaaman.* **2.** *mrattab, mnaδδam.* I'd like to see your room in order just once. *b-wuddi ?ašuuf ġuraftak imrattaba wa-law marra.* **3.** *kaamil.* His papers are in order. *?awraaqa kaamla.* **4.** *zasab.* Line up in order of height. *ṣṭaffu zasab iṭ-ṭuul.*

in order to - *zatta.* I've come from Amara in order to see you. *jaay imnil-iεmaara zatta ?ašuufak.*

made to order - **1.** *tufṣaal, tuuṣaa.* All his suits are made to order. *kull quuṭa tufṣaal.* **2.** *tuuṣaa.* Did you buy your furniture ready-made or is it made to order? *štireet ?aθaaθak zaaδra loo tuuṣaa?*

out of order - *xarbaan.* The fan is out of order. *l-paanka xarbaana.*

to order - **1.** *?umar (u ?amur) n- b-.* He ordered their arrest. *?umar ib-tawqiifhum.* **2.** *ṭilab (u ṭalib) n-.* Order the taxi for six o'clock. *?uṭulba lit-taksi yiji saaεa sitta.* **3.** *waṣṣa (i tawṣiya).* I ordered a new set of tires for the car. *waṣṣeet εala ṭaxum taayaraat jidiid lis-sayyaara.*

to order around - *t?ammar (a ta?ammur) εala.* Don't order me around! *la-tit?ammar εalayya!*

ordinary - *εtiyaadi*, εaadi*.* He's just an ordinary mechanic. *huwwa miikaaniiki εtiyaadi.*

ore: **He brought in a piece of copper ore for analysis. *jaab qiṭεa min nuzaas xaam lit-tazliil.*

organ - *εuδu* pl. *?aεδaa?.* Our lesson in Health today was on the genital organs. *darasna b-εilm iṣ-ṣizza l-yoom čaan εann il-?aεδaa? it-tanaasuliyya.*

organization - **1.** *tanδiim* pl. *-aat, tartiib* pl. *-aat.* The material is good, but the organization is poor. *l-maadda zeena laakin it-tanδiim muu zeen.* **2.** *munaδδama* pl. *-aat.* He is a member of our organization. *huwwa εuδu b-munaδδamatna.*

to **organize** - *naδδam (i tanδiim) t-, rattab (i tartiib) t-.* They have asked me to organize the election campaign for them. *ṭulbaw minni ?anaδδim-ilhum zamlat il-intixaabaat.* -- We'll call you up as soon as we get ourselves organized. *nxaabrak ?awwal-ma nrattib ?umuurna.*

**All the employees in our plant are organized. *kull il-εummaal ib-maṣnaεna minδammiin lin-naqaaba.*

Orient - *š-šarq.*

oriental - *šarqi*.*

origin - **1.** *?aṣil* pl. *?uṣuul.* Darwin named his book 'The Origin of the Species'. *daarwin samma ktaaba "?aṣl il-?anwaaε."* **2.** *?asaas* pl. *?usus.* I'm trying to get at the origin of the trouble between them. *?azaawil atwaṣṣal ?ila ?asaas il-miškila beenhum.* **3.** *tazarruk.* We will pay your way back to your point of origin. *raz-nidfaε-lak nafaqaat ir-rujuuε zatta nuqṭat tazarrukak.* **4.** *manša?* pl. *manaaši?.* All importers must submit a certificate of origin for their goods. *kull il-mistawridiin laazim ybirzuun šahaadaat manša? il-baδaa?iεhum.* **5.** *maṣdar* pl. *maṣaadir.* What is the origin of this information? *hal-?axbaar maṣdarha mneen?*

original - **1.** *?aṣli*.* The original plan was altogether different. *l-mašruuε il-?aṣli čaan mixtilif tamaaman εan haay.* **2.** *mubtakir, mubtadi?.* This architect has original ideas. *hal-muhandis in-naaši? εinda ?afkaar mubtakira.*

originally - *?awwalan, ?aṣlan, bil-?aṣil.* Originally he wanted to be a doctor. *bil-?awwal raad yṣiir ṭabiib.*

to **originate** - **1.** *ṣidar (u ṣuduur), niša? (a nišuu?).* Where did this rumor originate? *hal-išaaεa mneen ṣidrat?* **2.** *tzarrak (a tazarrak).* Where does this train originate? *hal-qiṭaar imneen yitzarrak?*

orphan - *yatiim* pl. *?aytaam.*

orphanage - *maytam* pl. *mayaatim, daar* (pl. *duur*) *?aytaam, maεhad* (pl. *maεaahid*) *?aytaam.*

ostrich - *naεaama* pl. *-aat* coll. *naεaam.*

other - **1.** (m.) *?aaxar* (f.) *?uxra* pl. *?aaxariin, θaani* pl. *-iin.* All the others got a raise but me. *kull il-?aaxariin itraffεaw ?illa ?aani.* **2.** (m.) *laax* (f.) *lux, θaani.* Take the other car, I'm going to wash this one. *?uxδ is-sayyaara l-lux, raz-?aġsilha l-haay.* -- I can't tell one from another. *ma-da-aεruf waazid imnil-laax.* **3.** *baaqi* pl. *-iin.* Put six on the shelf and leave the others in the box. *zuṭṭ sitta εar-raff w-itruk il-baaqiin biṣ-ṣanduug.*

**I saw your friend the other day. *δaak il-yoom šifit ṣadiiqak.*

**Send me someone or other, it doesn't matter who. *dizz-li yaahu l-čaan, ma-yhimm.*

**We have to get it done on time somehow or other. *laazim inxallṣa εal-wakit ib-ṭariiqa-ma.*

every other - *been ... w-.* Our poker group meets every other week. *jamaaεt il-pookar maalatna tijtimiε been isbuuε w-isbuuε.*

otherwise - **1.** *ma-εada.* Otherwise, I'm satisfied with him. *ma-εada haay, ?aani raaδi wiyyaa.* **2.** *laεad.* What would you do otherwise? *laεad šii tsawwi?* **3.** *w-?illa.* I have to return the book today, otherwise I'll have to pay a fine. *laazim ?arajjiε l-iktaab il-yoom w-?illa laazim ?adfaε ġaraama.*

ought - *yinbiġi.* I ought to tell him but it's hard to. *yinbiġi ?agul-la laakin yiṣεab εalayya.*

ounce - *?oons* pl. *-aat.*

our - *-na;* (m.) *maalna* (f.) *maalatna* (with preceding definite noun). Their house is larger than our house. *beethum ?akbar min beetna.*

ours - (m.) *maalna* (f.) *maalatna.* This book is ours. *hal-iktaab maalna.*

ourselves - *nafisna, ?anfusna.* We're just hurting ourselves. *?izna da-n?aδδi nafisna bass.*

to **oust** - *?aqṣa (i ?iqṣaa?).* Their main purpose is to oust the prime minister from his office. *ġaraδhum ir-ra?iisi yiqṣuun ra?iis il-wuzaraa? min waδiifta.*

out - *barra.* They were out when we called them.

čaanaw barra min xaabarnaahum.

**The lights are out. δ̣-δ̣uwa maṭfi.

**Straw hats are out of fashion. šafqaat il-xuṣṣ raayħa moodatha.

out of - 1. min. He did it out of spite. sawwaaha min ħiqid. 2. bila, blayya. She's out of work. hiyya blayya šuġuḷ. 3. xaarij. I'm from out of town. ʔaani min xaarij il-madiina.

**That's out of the question. haaδa maa mumkin.

**We're out of bread. l-xubiz xaḷṣaan.

**I have been out of work for two months. ṣaar-li šahreen baṭṭaal.

**You're out of step. mašyak ma-muntaδ̣am.

outbreak - 1. nušuub, ndilaaƐ. We left Europe a little before the outbreak of the war. trakna ʔooruppa šwayya gabuḷ nušuub il-ħarub. 2. δ̣uhuur. There's an outbreak of cholera in that district. ʔaku δ̣uhuur maraδ̣ il-kooleera b-hal-manṭiqa.

outfit - 1. lawaazim. We bought our son a complete Scout outfit for his birthday. štireena lawaazim kaššaafa kaamla l-ʔibinna l-yoom Ɛiid miilaada. 2. malaabis. She bought her wedding outfit in Paris. štirat malaabis Ɛirisha b-paariis. 3. waħda pl. -aat. Corporal Muhammad was transferred to another outfit. naaʔib il-Ɛariif imħammad inniqal il-ġeer waħda. 4. jamaaƐa pl. -aat. I wouldn't work for such an outfit. ma-aštuġul il-hiiči jamaaƐa.

to outfit - jahhaz (i tajhiiz) t-. You'll be able to outfit your expedition in Mosul. b-ʔimkaankum itjahhizuun baƐθatkum imnil-muuṣiḷ.

to **outgrow** - kubar (a kabur) Ɛala. The children have outgrown their clothes. j-jahaal kubraw Ɛala hduumhum.

outlet - 1. manfaδ pl. manaafiδ, maxraj pl. maxaarij. The lake has two outlets. l-buħayra biiha manfaδeen. -- Our company is looking for new outlets. šarikatna tdawwur manaafiδ taṣriif jidiida. -- Children have to have an outlet for their energies. j-jahaal laazim ykuun Ɛidhum manfaδ in-našaaṭhum. 2. nuqṭa pl. nuqaṭ, sookeet pl. -aat. We need another electrical outlet in this room. niħtaaj nuqṭa kahrabaaʔiyya θaanya b-hal-ġurfa.

outline - 1. malmaħ pl. malaamiħ. We learned to recognize the planes from their outlines. tƐallamna nmayyiz iṭ-ṭayyaaraat min malaamiħha. 2. ruus aqlaam. Did you make an outline of what you're going to say yet? sawweet ruus aqlaam l-illi tguula, loo baƐad?

outlook - 1. tabaašiir. The outlook for the future isn't very bright. tabaašiir il-mustaqbal ma-tbayyin zeena. 2. naδ̣ra pl. -aat. His outlook on life is narrow. naδ̣irta lil-ħayaat δ̣ayyqa.

to **outnumber** - faaq (u) bil-Ɛadad. In that class the girls outnumber the boys. b-δaak iṣ-ṣaff il-banaat yfuuquun il-wulid bil-Ɛadad.

out-of-the-way - minƐizil. Our house is on an out-of-the-way street. beetna Ɛala šaariƐ minƐizil.

outpost - markaz (pl. maraakiz) ʔamaami, nuqṭa (pl. nuqaṭ) ʔamaamiyya.

outrage - ʔisaaʔa pl. -aat. This is an outrage to my personal dignity. haaδi ʔisaaʔa l-karaamti š-šaxṣiyya.

to outrage - ʔasaaʔ (i ʔisaaʔa) l-. His behavior outraged the whole community. taṣarrufa ʔasaaʔ lil-mujtamaƐ kulla.

outrageous - muhawwil. Don't buy anything there; he charges outrageous prices. la-tištiri ʔay šii hnaak; haaδa yuṭlub ʔasƐaar muhawwila.

outright - muṭbaq. That's an outright lie. haaδa čiδib muṭbaq.

outside - 1. barra, xaarij. He's outside. huwwa barra. -- He lives outside the city. yiskun xaarij il-madiina. 2. barraani*. You left the outside door open. xalleet il-baab il-barraani maftuuħ.

outsider - xaariji pl. -iyyiin, barraani pl. -iyyiin. We don't permit outsiders to attend our meetings. ma-nismaħ lil-xaarijiyyiin yiħδ̣aruun ijtimaaƐaatna.

outskirts - ʔaṭraaf. Many people have orchards on the outskirts of the city. naas ihwaaya Ɛidhum basaatiin ib-ʔaṭraaf il-madiina.

outstanding - 1. baariz. He's an outstanding scholar. huwwa Ɛaalim baariz. 2. mubdiƐ. He's an outstanding performer on the lute. haaδa Ɛaazif mubdiƐ Ɛal-Ɛuud. 3. mawquuf. We still have a number of outstanding bills to collect. Ɛidna baƐad Ɛadad imnil-qawaaʔim il-mawquufa.

oven - 1. tannuur pl. tanaaniir. Our neighbor's wife has an oven, and she sells the bread she bakes. marit jiiraanna Ɛidha tannuur w-itbiiƐ il-xubuz il-tixubza. 2. firin pl. fruun. Baking the fish at home is a lot of bother; let's send it to the neighborhood oven. ṭabx is-simač bil-beet dooxa; xall indizza lil-firin maal iṭ-ṭaraf.

over - 1. foog, fooq. My room is over the kitchen. ġurufti foog il-maṭbax. -- I don't know exactly, but over a hundred at least. ma-aƐruf biδ̣-δ̣abuṭ, laakin Ɛal-ʔaqall foog il-miyya. 2. Ɛala. Don't pull the cover over your head. la-tjurr il-ġiṭa Ɛala raasak. 3. ʔakθar min. That village is over a mile away. δiič il-qarya tibƐid ʔakθar min miil waaħid.

**The water is over your head there. ma-raħ-itgayyiš ihnaak.

**Let's go over the details once more. xalli nraajiƐ it-tafṣiilaat marra θaanya.

all over - b-kull makaan. I've looked all over, but I can't find it. dawwarit ib-kull mukaan laakin ma-da-agdar ʔalgaaha.

over again - marra θaanya. Do it over again. sawwiiha marra θaanya. or **Ɛiidha!

over and over again - Ɛiddat marraat. He asked the same question over and over again. siʔal nafs is-suʔaal Ɛiddat marraat.

over there - hnaak. What's that over there? šinu δaak l-ihnaak.

to get over - xallaṣ (i taxliiṣ) t- min. I got over my cold in a week. xallaṣit imnin-našla b-isbuuƐ.

overcoat - qappuuṭ pl. qapaapiiṭ.

to **overcome** - 1. tġallab (a taġallub) Ɛala. She had many difficulties to overcome. čaan Ɛidha hwaaya ṣuƐuubaat titġallab Ɛaleeha. -- She was overcome with grief. čaan mitġallib Ɛaleeha l-ħuzun. 2. qiδ̣a (i qaδ̣aaʔ) Ɛala. The gas almost overcame me. čaan qiδ̣a Ɛalayya l-ġaaz.

to **overdo** - 1. laħħ (i laħħ). It doesn't hurt to eat fatty meat, but don't overdo it. ma-yxaalif taakul ʔakil dasim, bass la-tliħħ. 2. kaθθar (i takθiir). I like spices, but our cook overdoes it. tiƐjibni l-ibhaaraat laakin ṭabbaaxna da-ykaθθir minha.

to **overflow** - ṭufaħ (a ṭafuħ), faaδ̣ (i feeδ̣). Don't put so much water in the glass; it will overflow. la-txalli ṃayy ihwaaya bil-iglaaṣ w-ʔilla yiṭfaħ.

overfull - ṭaafiħ.

to **overlook** - 1. ġufaḷ (u ġafuḷ) Ɛan. I must have overlooked it. laazim ʔaani ġfalit Ɛanha. 2. tġaaδa (a taġaaδi) Ɛan. I'll overlook your mistakes this time, but don't do it again. raħ-atġaada Ɛan ʔaġlaaṭak hal-marra laakin la-tƐiidha marra θaanya. 3. ʔašraf (i ʔišraaf), ṭall (i ʔiṭlaal), ṣayṭar (i ṣayṭara). My window overlooks the garden. šibbaač ġurufti yišrif Ɛal-ħadiiqa.

overnight - leela. He got rich overnight. ṣaar zangiin ib-leela.

to stay overnight - baat (a beetuuta). I'm going to stay overnight in Najaf. raħ-abaat ib-najaf.

oversight - sahu, ġafla. That must have been an oversight. laazim haaδa sahu.

to oversleep: **I overslept this morning. ʔaxaδni n-noom il-yoom iṣ-ṣubuħ.

overthrow - nqilaab pl. -aat. The foreign correspondents predicted the overthrow a month ago. l-muraasiliin il-ʔajaanib itnabbiʔaw bil-inqilaab gabuḷ šahar.

to overthrow - giḷab (u gaḷub) n-. They overthrew the government. gilbaw niδ̣aam il-ħukum.

overtime - ʔiδ̣aafi*. I had to work 2 hrs. overtime last night. δ̣ṭarreet aštuġul saaƐteen ʔiδ̣aafiyya l-baarħa bil-leel. -- Beginning next month our office will be on an overtime basis. Ɛtibaaran imniš-šahr il-qaadim daaʔiratna raħ-itquum ib-ʔaƐmaal ʔiδ̣aafiyya.

to owe: **How much do I owe you? šgadd tiṭlubni? or šgadd ʔaani madyuun ʔilak? or šgadd ʔaani maṭluub-lak? or šgadd ʔilak Ɛalayya? -- **You still owe me 20 dinars. ʔinta la-zilit maṭluub-li Ɛišriin diinaar or ʔinta la-zilit madyuun-li Ɛišriin diinaar. -- **I owe a lot of money. ʔaani mindaan ifluus ihwaaya.

owl - buuma pl. buwam.

own - Ɛuhda, masʔuuliyya. From here on, your on your own. minnaa w-hiiči, ʔinta Ɛala Ɛuhudtak. or minnaa w-faayit, inta w-nafsak. -- As soon as you are familiar with the filing system here, you'll be on your own. ħaal-ma tlimm ib-niδ̣aam il-faaylaat ihnaa, raħ-itkuun Ɛala masʔuuliitak. -- He's been on his own ever since he was sixteen. min čaan Ɛumra siṭṭaƐaš sana ṣaar masʔuul Ɛan nafsa.

**I have my own room. Ɛindi ġurfa ʔili waħdi.

**Are these your own things? *haay ʔašyaaʔ mulkak ʔinta?*
to own – *milak (u muluk) n–.* He owns a house. *huwwa yimluk fadd beet.*

owner – *ṣaaḥib* pl. *ʔaṣḥaab, maalik* pl. *mullaak.* Who is the owner of the store? *minu ṣaaḥib had-dukkaan?*

ownership – *milkiyya* pl. *-aat.* You'll have to pay me in full before I transfer the ownership into your name. *laazim tidfaƐ-li kull il-mablaġ gabuḷ-ma ʔanqul il-milkiyya b-ismak.*
ox – *θoor* pl. *θiiraan.*
oxygen – *ʔooksijiin.*
oyster – *maḥḥaara* pl. *-aat* coll. *maḥḥaar.*

P

pace – **1.** *xaṭwa* pl. *-aat.* Take a pace forward. *tqaddam xaṭwa li-giddaam.* **2.** *surƐa.* This worker sets the pace for the others on the job. *hal-Ɛaamil yḥaddid surƐat iš-šuġuḷ lil-ʔaaxariin.*
to keep pace with – *jaara (i mujaaraat).* I can't keep pace with him at work. *ma-agdar ajaarii biš-šuġuḷ.*
to pace off – *qaas (i qees) n– bil-xaṭwaat.* Pace off a hundred feet. *qiis bil-xaṭwaat miit qadam.*
to pace up and down – *txaṭṭa (a taxaṭṭi), tmašša (a tamašši).* He paced up and down the room. *ḍall yitxaṭṭa bil-ġurfa.*
Pacific Ocean – *l-muḥiiṭ il-haadi.*
pack – **1.** *qaṭiiƐ* pl. *qiṭƐaan.* They went at the food like a pack of hungry wolves. *nizlaw Ɛal-ʔakil miθil qaṭiiƐ imniδ-δiyaab ij-juuƐaana.* **2.** *ḥimil* pl. *ḥmuul.* The donkeys were loaded with heavy packs. *z-zumaayiḷ čaanat imḥammila ḥmuul iθgaal.* **3.** *dasta* pl. *-aat.* Where is that new pack of cards? *ween dastat il-waraq ij-jidiida?*
**That's a pack of lies! *haaδa čiδb ib-čiδib!* or *haaδa kulla šeelmaan!*
to pack – **1.** *lamm (i lamm).* Have you packed your stuff yet? *lammeet ġaraaḍak loo baƐad?* or ***ḥaḍḍart ij-junṭa maaltak?* **2.** *ḥišak (i ḥašik) n–.* They packed more people into that little room. *ḥiškaw baƐad naas ib-δiič il-ġurfa ṣ-ṣiġayyra.* **3.** *diḥas (a daḥis) n–.* The doctor packed cotton in my ear. *ṭ-ṭabiib diḥas guṭin b-iδni.* **4.** *dačč (i dačč) n–.* Don't pack the clothes into the suitcase tightly. *la-tdičč l-ihduum bij-junṭa dačč.*
to pack up – *lamm (i lamm) n–.* He packed up his things and left. *lamm kull ġaraaḍa w-raaḥ.*
package – **1.** *ruzma* pl. *ruzam.* The mailman brought a package for you. *muwazziƐ il-bariid jaab-lak ruzma.* **2.** *paakeet* pl. *-aat.* Do you sell the coffee in the bulk or in packages? *tbiiƐ il-gahwa fraaṭa loo p-paakeetaat?*
packed – **1.** *mqaṗṗuṭ, matruus.* The bus was packed this morning. *l-paaṣ čaan imqaṗṗuṭ iṣ-ṣubuḥ.* **2.** *malyaan, matruus.* The store was packed with people. *l-maxzan čaan malyaan naas.* **3.** *mƐallab.* This fish is packed in Norway. *has-simač imƐallab bin-narwiij.*
**My things are all packed. *ġaraaḍi ḥaaḍra bij-junṭa.*
**Are these sardines packed in olive oil? *has-saardiin ib-dihin zeet?*
pack-horse – *kidiiš* pl. *kidšaan.*
pack-saddle – *jilaal* pl. *-aat.*
pact – *miiθaaq* pl. *mawaaθiiq.*
pad – **1.** *čibna* pl. *-aat, čiban.* I need a pad to put my typewriter on. *ʔaḥtaaj čibna ʔaḥuṭṭ Ɛaleeha ṭ-ṭaabiƐa maalti.* **2.** *mindar* pl. *manaadir.* Who took my chair pad? *minu ʔaxaδ mindar il-kursi maali?* **3.** *ṣṭampa* pl. *-aat.* I have the stamp, but I can't find the pad. *l-xatam hiyyaata, laakin ma-da-ʔalgi l-iṣṭampa.* **4.** *daftar* pl. *dafaatir.* Bring me one or two pads of note paper. *jiib-li daftar ʔaw daftareen waraq miswadda.* **5.** *kattaafiyya* pl. *-aat.* I had the tailor take the pads out of the shoulders of this jacket. *xalleet il-xayyaaṭ yṭalliƐ il-kattaafiyyaat min ičtaafaat has-sitra.*
to pad – *ḥašša (i tḥišši) t–.* I want the shoulders padded. *ʔariid l-ičtaafaat titḥašša.*
padding – *ḥašwa.*
padlock – *quful* pl. *qfaal, ʔaqfaala.*
page – *ṣafḥa* pl. *-aat, ṣaḥiifa* pl. *ṣaḥaayif.* The book is two hundred pages long. *l-iktaab bii miiteen ṣafḥa.*
pail – *ṣaṭil* pl. *ṣṭuul, ṣaṭla* pl. *-aat.* Get a pail of water! *jiib ṣaṭil ṃaay!*
pain – *ʔalam* pl. *ʔaalaam, wujaƐ* pl. *ʔawjaaƐ.* I feel a sharp pain in my back. *da-aḥiss fadd wujaƐ šadiid ib-ḍahri.*
to take pains – *ʔajhad (i ʔijhaad) nafis~, daqqaq (i tadqiiq) t–.* She takes great pains with her work. *tijhid nafisha kulliš ib-šuġuḷha.*
to pain – *ʔallam (i taʔliim) t–.* It pains me to have to say this but ... *yiʔlimni ʔan laazim aguul haaδa laakin ...*
painful – **1.** *ʔaliim, muʔlim.* That was a painful experience. *haay čaanat fadd tajruba ʔaliima.* **2.** *muzƐija, faḍiiƐa.* Our progress was painfully slow. *taqaddumna čaan baṭiiʔ ʔila daraja muzƐija.*
**It is painful to watch him. *manḍara yiksir il-galub.*
**Was the extraction of the tooth painful? *šalƐ is-sinn ʔaδδaak?* or *šalƐ is-sinn wujaƐak?*
paint – *ṣubuġ* pl. *ʔaṣbaaġ, booya* pl. *-aat.* The paint isn't dry yet. *ṣ-ṣubuġ baƐda ma-yaabis.*
to paint – **1.** *ṣubaġ (u ṣubuġ) n–.* What color are you going to paint the house? *yaa loon raḥ-tuṣbuġ il-beet?* **2.** *risam (i rasim) n–.* She paints in oils. *tirsim biz-zeet.*
paint brush – *firča* pl. *firač.*
painter – **1.** *ṣabbaaġ* pl. *-iin, ṣbaabiiġ.* The painters will finish the kitchen tomorrow. *ṣ-ṣabbaaġiin raḥ-yxallṣuun il-muṭbax baačir.* **2.** *rassaam* pl. *-iin.* He is a famous painter. *haaδa rassaam mašhuur.*
painting – **1.** *lawḥa* pl. *-aat, ṣuura* pl. *ṣuwar.* This is a beautiful painting. *haaδi lawḥa badiiƐa.* **2.** *rasim.* I'm especially interested in Persian painting. *ʔaani mihtamm ib-ṣuura xaaṣṣa b-fann ir-rasim il-ʔiiraani.* **3.** *ṣubuġ.* Painting the house was hard. *ṣubġ il-beet čaan ṣaƐub.*
pair – *zooj* pl. *zwaaj, ʔazwaaj.* I bought myself a pair of gloves. *štireet-li zooj ičfuuf.*
**I bought a new pair of scissors. *štireet imgaṣṣ jidiid.*
pajamas – *beejaama* pl. *-aat.*
pal – *rafiiq* pl. *rufqaan, ṣaaḥib* pl. *ʔaṣḥaab.* You're a real pal. *ʔinta ḥaqiiqatan xooš rafiiq.*
to pal around – *tṣaaḥab (a taṣaaḥub), tƐaašar (a taƐaašur).* They've palled around for years. *tṣaaḥbaw muddat isniin.* or *ṣaar-ilhum mitƐaašriin muddat isniin.*
palace – *qaṣir* pl. *qṣuur.*
palate – *sagif ḥalig* pl. *sguuf iḥluug.*
pale – **1.** *ʔaṣfar, šaaḥib.* Why are you so pale? *š-biik hiiči ʔaṣfar?* **2.** *faatiḥ, ʔaačuġ.* She had on a pale blue dress. *čaanat laabsa nafnuuf ʔazrag faatiḥ.*
to turn pale – *ṣfarr (a), šiḥab (a šuḥuub), mtiqaƐ (i mtiqaaƐ).* When he heard that, he turned pale. *min simaƐha, ṣfarr loona.*
Palestine – *falaṣṭiin.*
Palestinian – *falaṣṭiini** pl. *-iyyiin.*
palm – **1.** *čaff* pl. *čfuuf.* My palm is all calloused. *čaffi kulla mbasmir.* **2.** *naxḷa* pl. *-aat* coll. *naxaḷ.* We have four palm trees in our garden. *Ɛidna ʔarbaƐ naxḷaat ib-ḥadiiqatna.* **3.** *šajarat* (pl. *-aat* coll. *šajar) jooz hind.* We don't grow any coconut palms here. *ma-nizraƐ šajar jooz hind ihnaa.*
palm shoot – *fisiila* pl. *fisaayil.*
palpitation – *xafaqaan.*
pamphlet – *kurraasa* pl. *-aat.*
pan – **1.** *jidir* pl. *jduur, jduura.* I need a bigger pan for the rice. *ʔaḥtaaj jidir ʔakbar lit-timman.* **2.** *ṭaawa* pl. *-aat.* Use this pan for the eggs. *staƐmil haṭ-ṭaawa lil-beeḍ.*
to pan out badly – *fišal (a fašal), xaab (i xayba).* My scheme panned out badly. *xuṭṭṭi fišlat.*
to pan out well – *nijaḥ (a najaaḥ).* My scheme panned out well. *xuṭṭṭi nijḥat.*
pane – *jaama* pl. *-aat* coll. *jaam.* The storm blew in several panes. *l-Ɛaaṣifa kisrat Ɛiddat jaamaat.*
panel – **1.** *ḥalaqa* pl. *-aat.* A panel of well-known educators discussed the problem on TV. *ḥalaqa min mašaahiir il-murabbiin biḥθaw il-muškila bit-talafizyoon.* **2.** *hayʔa* pl. *-aat.* A panel of

three experts will study this problem. *hay?a min itlaθ xubaraa? raz-tudrus il-muškila.*
panic - *δuεur, ruεub.*
pansy - *ward iṣ-ṣuura.*
to **pant** - *lihaθ (a lahiθ).* He came panting up the stairs. *ṣiεad id-daraj da-yilhaθ.*
pants - **1.** *panṭaruun* pl. *-aat, panaaṭiir.* My pants have to be pressed. *laazim panṭaruuni yinḍurub ?uuti.* **2.** *širwaal* pl. *šaraawiil.* You can tell he's a Kurd from his baggy pants. *tigdar tiεurfa kurdi min širwaala.*
paper - **1.** *waraqa* pl. *-aat, ?awraaq* coll. *waraq, kaağada* pl. *-aat, kwaağid,* coll. *kaağad.* Do you have a sheet of paper? *εindak fadd ṭabqa waraq?* -- Some important papers are missing. *baεδ il-?awraaq il-muhimma ḍaayεa.* **2.** *jariida* pl. *jaraayid.* Where is today's paper? *ween jariidt il-yoom?*
paper weight - *θiggaala* pl. *-aat.*
parachute - *parašuut* pl. *-aat, maḍalla* pl. *-aat.*
parade - *stiεraaḍ* pl. *-aat.* Did you see the parade yesterday? *šift il-istiεraaḍ il-baarza?*
paradise - *janna, firdaws.*
paragraph - *faqara* pl. *-aat.* This is the beginning of a new paragraph. *haaδi bidaayat faqara jidiida.*
parallel - *muwaazi, muzaaδi.* Draw a parallel to this line. *?irsim muwaazi l-hal-xaṭṭ.* -- The road runs parallel to the river. *ṭ-ṭariiq muzaaδi lin-nahar.*
paralysis - *šalal, faalaj.*
to **paralyze** - *šall (i šalal) n-.* This disease sometimes paralyses the victim's legs. *hal-maraḍ ?azyaanan yšill rijleen il-muṣaab.*
paralyzed - **1.** *mašluul* pl. *-iin, minšall* pl. *-iin.* He is completely paralyzed. *haaδa mašluul tamaaman.* -- She has been paralyzed ever since she had that stroke. *hiyya minšalla min ṣaabat δiič iṣ-ṣadma.* **2.** (m.) *?aεḍab* pl. *-iin,* (f.) *εaḍba* pl. *-aat.* He has a paralyzed hand. *εinda ?iid εaḍba.* **3.** *mgarram* pl. *-iin.* He can't walk because he is paralyzed. *ma-yigdar yimši li-?an imgarram.* **4.** *mεaṭṭal.* Communications were completely paralyzed. *l-muwaaṣalaat čaanat imεaṭṭla tamaaman.*
paramount - *εaḍiim, kabiir.* That's of paramount importance. *haaδa εaḍiim il-?ahammiyya.*
parapet - *suur* pl. *?aswaar.* Stay behind the parapet or you'll get killed. *?ibqa wara s-suur w-?illa tinqitil.*
parasite - *ṭufayli* pl. *-iyyaat.*
parasitical - *mitṭaffil.*
parasol - *šamsiyya* pl. *-aat.*
parcel - *ruzma* pl. *ruzam, laffa* pl. *-aat.* You forgot your parcels. *?inta niseet ruzamak.*
**I'll send it by parcel post. *raz-?adizzha ruzma bil-bariid.*
**Where is the parcel post window? *ween šibbaak ir-ruzam?*
pardon - *marzama* pl. *-aat.* His pardon was refused. *nrufḍat marzamta.*
**I beg your pardon, I did'nt mean to step on your foot. *l-εafu, ma-qṣadit aduus εala rijlak.*
to pardon - **1.** *εifa (i εafu) n- εan.* He pardoned me this time. *εifa εanni hal-marra.* **2.** *ğufar (u) n-.* God will pardon my sins. *?aḷḷa raz-yuğfur iδnuubi.*
**Pardon me, I didn't hear what you said. *εafwan, ma-smaεit iš-gilit.*
**Pardon me, when does the movie begin? *?ismaz-li, šwakit yibdi l-filim?*
to **pare** - **1.** *gaššar (i tagšiir, tgiššir) t-.* Pare the potatoes and put them in a pan of cold water. *gaššri l-puteeta w-zuṭṭiiha b-jidir maay baarid.* **2.** *gaṣṣ (u gaṣṣ) n-.* You should be more careful when you pare your nails. *laazim itdiir baalak ?azyad min itguṣṣ iḍaafrak.* **3.** *qallal (i taqliil) t-.* You'll have to pare down your estimates, or else they'll turn down the budget. *laazim itqallil taxmiinaatak w-illa yrufḍuun il-miizaaniyya.*
parentage - *?aṣil.* She is of good parentage. *haaδi ?aṣilha zeen.*
parenthesis - *qaws* pl. *?aqwaas.* Put the word between parentheses. *zuṭṭ ič-čilma been qawseen.*
parents - *waalideen, ?abaween.* Respect for one's parents is a virtue. *ztiraam il-waalideen faḍiila.* -- May God keep your parents! *?aḷḷa yxalli waaldeek.*
**Both my parents are still living. *?ummi w-?abuuya θneenhum baεadhum ṭayybiin.*
parish - *?abrašiyya* pl. *-aat.*
park - *zadiiqa* pl. *zadaayiq.* There is a beautiful public park in the center of the city. *?aku zadiiqa εaamma laṭiifa b-nuṣṣ il-wlaaya.*
to park - *waggaf (u tawgiif), parrak (i tpirrik).* You can park your car here. *tigdar itwagguf sayyaartak ihnaa.*
parking - *wuguuf.* Car parking is prohibited here. *wuguuf is-sayyaaraat mamnuuε ihnaa.*
parking place - *mawqif* pl. *mawaaqif.* There's a parking place for cars behind the building. *?aku mawqif lis-sayyaaraat wara l-ibnaaya.*
Parliament - *barlamaan* pl. *-aat, majlis* (pl. *majaalis*) *?umma.*
parlor - *ğurfat* (pl. *ğuruf*) *xuṭṭaar, ğurfat* (pl. *ğuruf*) *istiqbaal.*
to **parole** - **He was paroled. *nfakk w-itxalla tazt il-muraaqaba.*
parrot - *biibimattu* pl. *-uwaat, babağaa?* pl. *-aat.*
parsley - *krafus, maεdinoos, jaεfari.*
part - **1.** *juzu?* pl. *?ajzaa?, qism* pl. *?aqsaam.* That part of the work isn't finished yet. *haj-juzu? imniš-šuğuḷ baεad ma-xilaṣ.* -- This little screw is a very important part of the machine. *hal-burği l-iṣğayyir fadd juzu? kulliš muhimm imnil-makiina.* -- Can you get spare parts for your bicycle? *tigdar tilgi ?ajzaa? iztiyaaṭiyya lil-paaysikil maalak?* -- The fence is part wood and part stone. *l-zaajiz qisim xišab w-qisim zajar.* **2.** *dawr* pl. *?adwaar.* He played the part of a king in the play. *maθθal dawr malik bit-tamθiiliyya.* **3.** *manṭiqa* pl. *manaaṭiq, naaziya* pl. *?anzaa?, nawaazi; ṭaraf* pl. *?aṭraaf.* What part of the city are you from? *?inta min yaa manṭiqa mnil-wlaaya.* -- **I haven't traveled much in these parts. *?aani ma-msaafir ihwaaya b-hal-manṭiqa.*
**For my part I have no objection. *min jihti, ma-εindi maaniε.*
for the most part - *εal-?akθar, εal-?ağlab.* His company is made up, for the most part, of volunteers. *zaḍiirta mitkawwna εal-?akθar min miṭṭawwεiin.* -- For the most part, the weather has been nice this summer. *εal-?ağlab iṭ-ṭaqis čaan laṭiif haṣ-ṣeef.*
in part - *nawεan maa, b-baεḍ, b-qisim min.* I agree with you in part. *?aani ?attifiq wiyyaak nawεan maa.*
on the part of - *min jaanib, min qibal.* We regret any discrimination against a minority on the part of a government official. *ni?saf il-?ay tafriqa ḍidd il-?aqalliyya min jaanib ?ay muwaḍḍaf zukuumi.*
to take part in - *štirak (i štiraak) b-, saaham (i musaahama).* Are you going to take part in the discussion? *raz-tištirik bil-munaaqaša?*
to take the part of - *lizam (a lazim) n- jaanib.* He always takes his brother's part. *daa?iman yilzam jaanib ?axuu.*
to part - **1.** *ftiraq (i ftiraaq).* They parted as friends. *ftirqaw ka-?aṣdiqaa?.* **2.** *tfaarag (a tafaarug).* Let's part here. *xalli nitfaarag ihnaa.* **3.** *waxxar (i twuxxur, tawxiir) t-.* She parted the curtains and looked out. *waxxirat il-pardaat w-baawεat li-barra.* **4.** *furag (u farig) n-.* He parts his hair on the left side. *yufrug šaεra εal-yisra.*
to part with - *txalla (a txalli) εan.* I wouldn't part with that book for any price. *ma-?atxalla εan δaak il-iktaab ib-?ay θaman.*
partial - **1.** *mitzayyiz, muğriḍ.* He tries not to be partial. *yzaawil ?an ma-ykuun mitzayyiz.* **2.** *juz?i** This is only a partial solution. *haaδa fadd zall juz?i bass.*
to be partial to - **1.** *zaaba (i muzaabaa).* He's always been partial to his youngest daughter. *daa?iman yzaabi binta ṣ-ṣiğayyra.* **2.** *faḍḍal (i tafḍiil) t-.* He's partial to blondes. *yfaḍḍil iš-šugur.*
partiality - *muzaabaat.* The other employees resent the partiality in his recommendations for advancements. *baqiit il-mustaxdamiin istankiraw il-muzaabaat ib-tawṣiyaata lit-tarfiiε.*
partially - *nawεan maa, juz?iyyan.* You are partially right. *?inta ṣaziiz nawεan maa.* -- It's partially finished. *xalṣaana juz?iyyan.*
to **participate** - *štirak (i štiraak), šaarak (i mušaaraka), saaham (i musaahama).* They have invited us to participate in the project. *diεoona ništirik bil-mašruuε.*
participation - *stiraak, mušaaraka, musaahama.*
participle: (active) *?isim faaεil,* (passive) *?isim mafεuul.*
particle - *δarra* pl. *-aat, zabba* pl. *-aat.* There isn't a particle of truth in that story. *ma-aku δarra mnil-zaqiiqa b-hal-quṣṣa.* -- The inflammation is from a particle of dirt on the eyeball. *l-iltihaab min δarrat wuṣax εala kurat il-εeen.*

particular - 1. *tafṣiil* pl. *tafaaṣiil.* For further particulars write to the publishers. *lil-ḥuṣuul ʕat-tafaaṣiil ʔakθar, ʔiktib lin-našir.* -- My wife will give you all the particulars. *marti tinṭiik kull it-tafaaṣiil.* **2.** *xaaṣṣ.* Our city has its own particular problems. *madiinatna ʕidha mašaakilha l-xaaṣṣa biiha.* **3.** *muʕayyan.* For no particular reason, he stopped visiting us. *baṭṭal yzuurna bduun sabab muʕayyan.* **4.** *muqarrab* pl. *-iin.* He is no particular friend of mine. *haaδa muu fadd ṣadiiq muqarrab ʔili.* **5.** *diqdaaqi* pl. *-iyyiin.* My husband is very particular about his food. *zooji kulliš diqdaaqi b-ʔakla.* **6.** *biδ-δaat.* This particular dress costs more. *hal-badla biδ-δaat itkallif ʔakθar.*

in particular - 1. *b-ṣuura xaaṣṣa, ʕala l-xuṣuuṣ.* I remember one man in particular. *ʔatδakkar fadd rijjaal ib-ṣuura xaaṣṣa.* **2.** *ʕala wajh it-taʕyiin.* Are you looking for anything in particular? *da-tdawwur ʕala fadd šii ʕala wajh it-taʕyiin?*

particularly - *b-ṣuura xaaṣṣa.* He is particularly interested in science. *huwwa mihtamm ib-ṣuura xaaṣṣa bil-ʕiluum.*

partition - 1. *ḥaajiz* pl. *ḥawaajiz.* We are going to put in a partition here. *raḥ-inḥuṭṭ ḥaajiz ihnaa.* **2.** *taqsiim.* The partition of Palestine took place as a result of a decision taken by the United Nations. *taqsiim falasṭiin jira ʕala ʔaθar qaraar ittixδata l-ʔumam il-muttaḥida.* **3.** *nqisaam.* The disagreement caused the partition of the party. *l-xilaaf sabbab inqisaam il-ḥizib.*

partly - *juzʔiyyan, baʕḍan.* The book is only partly finished as yet. *l-iktaab xalṣaan juzʔiyyan bass il-ḥadd il-ʔaan.*

partner - 1. *šariik* pl. *šurakaaʔ.* My business partner is coming back tomorrow. *šariiki biš-šuġuḷ raajiʕ baačir.* **2.** *ṣaaḥib* pl. *ʔaṣḥaab.* My partner and I have been winning every game. *ʔaani w-ṣaaḥbi da-nirbaḥ kull liʕba.*

partridge - *qabač.* I bought a pair of partridges. *štireet zooj iṭyuur qabač.*

part-time - *nuṣṣ dawaam.* Do you have any part-time work in this office? *ʔaku waḍiifa nuṣṣ dawaam ib-hal-maktab?*

party - 1. *ḥizib* pl. *ʔaḥzaab.* What political party do you belong to? *ʔinta l-yaa ḥizib siyaasi mintimi?* **2.** *ṭaraf* pl. *ʔaṭraaf, jaanib* pl. *jawaanib.* Neither of the two parties appeared at the trial. *ṭ-ṭarafeen ma-ḥiḍraw bil-muḥaakama.* -- Both parties agreed to the terms. *j-jaanibeen waafqaw ʕaš-šuruuṭ.* **3.** *ḥafla* pl. *-aat.* She likes to give big parties. *yiʕjibha tqiim ḥaflaat faxma.* **4.** *ʕaziima* pl. *ʕazaayim.* Good-night; it was a lovely dinner party. *tiṣbaḥuun ʕala-xeer; ʕaziimatkum čaanat mumtaaza.*

**I won't be a party to that. *ʔaani ma-aḥuṭṭ nafsi b-haay.*

party line - 1. *xaṭṭ muštarak* pl. *xuṭuuṭ muštaraka.* Our telephone is on a party line. *talafoonna ʕala xaṭṭ muštarak.* **2.** *manhaj ḥizib.* The party leader called upon all members to hold to the party line. *raʔiis il-ḥizib diʕa kull il-ʔaʕḍaaʔ lit-tamassuk ib-manhaj il-ḥizib.*

pass - 1. *mamarr* pl. *-aat.* The pass is covered with snow in winter. *l-mamarr yinṭumar biθ-θalij biš-šita.* **2.** *biṭaaqat* (pl. *-aat*) *muruur.* You'll need a pass to get through the gate. *tiḥtaaj biṭaaqat muruur yaḷḷa tigdar itfuut imnil-madxal.* **3.** *maʔδuuniyya* pl. *-aat.* He has a weekend pass. *ʕinda maʔδuuniyya b-nihaayat hal-isbuuʕ.*

to pass - 1. *marr (u muruur) b-.* I pass this bank building every day. *ʔamurr ib-binaayat hal-bang kull yoom.* -- The play finally passed the censor. *t-tamθiiliyya ʔaxiiran marrat bir-raqiib.* **2.** *marrar (i tamriir) t-, ʕabbar (u taʕbiir) t-.* They passed the buckets from hand to hand. *marriraw iṣ-ṣuṭuul min ʔiid il-ʔiid.* **3.** *faat (u fawt) n- min.* The train passes here at three o'clock. *l-qiṭaar yfuut minnaa s-saaʕa tlaaθa.* **4.** *ṭilaʕ (a ṭuluuʕ) n-, ġilab (u ġulub) n-.* Pass that car! *ʔiṭlaʕ δiič is-sayyaara!* **5.** *qaḍḍa (i taqḍiya) t-.* He passed most of the time reading. *qaḍḍa ʔakθar il-wakit bil-qaraaʔa.* **6.** *muḍa (i muḍi).* The days pass quickly when you're busy. *l-ʔayyaam timḍi b-surʕa min waaḥid ykuun mašġuul.* **7.** *nijaḥ (a najaaḥ) b-, ʕubar (u ʕubuur).* Did you pass the examination? *nijaḥit bil-imtiḥaan?* **8.** *ʕubar (u ʕabur), marr (u muruur) b-.* You passed through a red light. *ʕbarit ḍuwa ʔaḥmar.* **9.** *ntiqal (i ntiqaal).* The farm passes from father to son. *l-mazraʕa tintiqil imnil-ʔab lil-ʔibin.* **10.** *mašša (i tamšiya) t-.* The censor refused to pass the film. *r-raqiib rufaḍ ymašši l-filim.* **11.** *naawaš (u munaawaša).* Will you please pass me the bread? *ma-tnaawušni l-xubuz min faḍlak?* **12.** *ṣaddaq (i taṣdiiq) t-.* The House of Representatives passed the bill unanimously. *majlis in-nuwwaab ṣaddaq il-laaʔiḥa bil-ʔijmaaʕ.* **13.** *ṣaaḥ (i ṣeeḥ) paaṣ.* It's your turn; I passed. *hassa doorak; ʔaani ṣiḥit paaṣ.*

to pass around - 1. *dawwar (u tadwiir) t-, farrar (u tafriir) t-.* They passed around cookies. *dawwiraw l-ikleeča ʕal-kull.* **2.** *ṭašš (u ṭašš) n-, nišar (u našir) n-.* Pass the word around so that everyone hears. *ṭušš l-iḥčaaya ḥatta l-kull ysimʕuun.* **We passed around the hat to help him pay his hospital bill. *jimaʕnaa-la fluus ḥatta nsaaʕda yidfaʕ maṣaariif il-mustašfa.*

to pass away - *twaffa (a), maat (u moot).* Her mother passed away last week. *ʔummha twaffat isbuuʕ il-faat.*

to pass by - *marr (u muruur) min yamm, b-.* He passed right by me without seeing me. *marr min yammi tamaaman w-ma-šaafni.*

to pass judgment on - *ḥikam (u ḥukum) n- ʕala.* Don't pass judgment on him too quickly. *la-tuḥkum ʕalee kulliš bil-ʕajal.*

to pass off - 1. *fawwat (u tafwiit) t-, marrar (i tamriir) t-.* He tried to pass off an imitation as the original. *ḥaawal yfawwut šii mzayyif ka-šii ḥaqiiqi.* **2.** *ʕabbar (u taʕbiir).* He tried to pass himself off as an officer. *ḥaawal yʕabbur nafsa ka-ḍaabuṭ.*

to pass on - *waṣṣal (i tawṣiil), ʔafša (i ʔifšaaʔ).* Don't pass this on to anyone. *la-twaṣṣil haay l-aḥḥad.*

to pass out - **Several people passed out from the heat. *ʕiddat ʔašxaaṣ ġaabat ruuḥhum imnil-ḥarr.* **They passed out from drinking too much. *fuqdaw waʕiihum min kuθrat iš-šurub.*

to pass sentence - *ʔaṣdar (u ʔiṣdaar) ḥukum.* The court will pass sentence today. *l-maḥkama raḥ-tuṣdur ḥukum il-yoom.*

to pass through - 1. *marr (u muruur) min, faat (u foot) min.* You can't pass through there. *ma-tigdar itmurr minnaak.* **2.** *fawwat (i tafwiit) t-.* Pass the rope through here. *fawwit il-ḥabil minnaa.*

to pass up - 1. *fawwat (i tafwiit), ḍayyaʕ (i taḍyiiʕ).* You ought not to pass up an opportunity like that. *ma-laazim itfawwit hiiči furṣa.* **2.** *naawaš (u munaa waša) t-.* Pass your papers up to the front row. *naawšu ʔawraaqkum lis-sira l-ʔamaami.*

passable - *maqbuul.* The work is passable. *š-šuġuḷ maqbuul.*

passage - 1. *mamarr* pl. *-aat.* We had to go through a dark passage. *ḍṭarreena nisluk mamarr muḍlim.* **2.** *maqṭaʕ* pl. *maqaaṭiʕ.* He read us several passages from his book. *qiraa-lna ʕiddat maqaaṭiʕ minn iktaaba.* **3.** *ʕabra* pl. *-aat.* The passage across the river by boat takes a half hour. *ʕabrat in-nahar bil-balam taaxuδ nuṣṣ saaʕa.*

passenger - 1. *raakib* pl. *rukkaab, ʕibri* pl. *-iyya.* The bus holds thirty passengers. *l-paaṣ yilzam itlaaθiin raakib bass.* **2.** *musaafir* pl. *-iin.* The passengers must go through customs. *l-musaafiriin laazim ymurruun bil-gumrug.*

passer-by - *ʕaabir* (pl. *-iin*) *sabiil, maarr* pl. *-iin.* Some passer-by must have picked it up. *laazim ʔaxaδha fadd ʕaabir sabiil.*

passing - 1. *wafaat, moot.* The whole nation mourned his passing. *l-ʔumma kullha ḥiznat ʕala wafaata.* **2.** *ʕaabir, zaaʔil, waqti*.* It's just a passing fancy. *haaδa fadd walaʕ ʕaabir.* **3.** *najaaḥ.* I got passing grades in all my subjects. *ḥaṣṣalit darajaat najaaḥ ib-kull idruusi.* **4.** *muruur, ṭuluuʕ.* Passing on the right is dangerous. *l-muruur ʕal-yamiin xaṭar.* **5.** *ʕubuur.* After passing through the sand, you'll hit a hard surface. *baʕd il-ʕubuur imnir-ramul, raḥ-itṣaadif gaaʕ qawiyya.*

passion - 1. *walaʕ, wahas.* He has a passion for music. *ʕinda walaʕ bil-mawsiiqa.* **2.** *ʕaaṭifa* pl. *ʕawaaṭif.* You should try to control your passions better. *laazim itḥaawil itṣayṭir ʕala ʕawaaṭfak ʔakθar.*

passionate - *ʕaaṭifi*.* She has a very passionate nature. *hiyya ʕaaṭifiyya.*

passive - 1. *majhuul.* Change this sentence to the passive voice. *ḥawwil haj-jumla ʔila ṣiiġat il-majhuul.* **2.** *salbi*.* Passive resistance is a

peaceful but effective weapon. *l-muqaawama
s-salbiyya ṭariiqa salmiyya w-laakinha silaaz
naffaaδ.*
  **He is a passive spectator. *haaδa mitfarrij
maa-la daxal.*

Passover – *Ɛiid il-fuṣẓ.*

past – 1. *maaδi* pl. *mawaaδi.* The police uncovered
some suspicious activities in his past. *š-šurṭa
ktišfat ʔaƐmaal mašbuuha b-maaδiyya.* — That's a
thing of the past. *haaδa fadd šii bil-maaδi.* or
**haaδa šaar taariix.* 2. *faayit.* Where were you
this past week? *ween činit bil-isbuuƐ il-faayit?*
3. *mitjaawiz.* I am past that stage. *ʔaani
mitjaawiz hal-marẓala.*
  **It's five minutes past twelve. *s-saaƐa θnaaƐaš
w-xamsa.*
  **It's way past my bedtime. *faat wakit noomi
b-ihwaaya.*
  **The worst part of the trip is past. *ʔaswaʔ qisim
imnis-safra faat.*
  **He walked past me. *faat min yammi.*
  in the past – *gabuḷ, bil-maaδi, bis-saabiq.* That
has often happened in the past. *haay zidθat ihwaaya
gabuḷ.*

paste – *ṣamuḡ, širiis.* Where did you put the paste
jar? *ween zaṭṭeet šiišt iṣ-ṣamuḡ?*
  to paste – *lizag (i lazig) n-, lazzag (i talziig)
t-.* Paste these labels on the boxes. *ʔilzig
hal-Ɛalaamaat Ɛaṣ-ṣanaadiig.*

pastime – *tasliya, lahu.* What is your favorite
pastime? *šinu hiyya tasliitak il-mazbuuba?*

pastry – *zalawiyyaat.*

pastry shop – *mazall* (pl. *-aat*) *zalawiyyaat.*

pasture – *marƐa* pl. *maraaƐi.* Are the cows still in
the pasture? *l-baqaraat baƐadhum bil-marƐa?*

pat – *ṭabṭaba* pl. *-aat.* I got a congratulatory pat on
the shoulder. *zaṣṣalit ṭabṭubat Ɛafaarim Ɛala čitfi.*
  to pat – *ṭabṭab (u ṭabṭaba) t-.* He patted him
encouragingly on the shoulder. *ṭabṭab Ɛala čitfa
b-tašjiiƐ.* — He patted the dog. *ṭabṭab-la
lič-čalib.*

patch – 1. *rugƐa* pl. *rugaƐ.* I'll have to put a
patch on it. *laazim azuṭṭ rugƐa.* 2. *qiṭƐa* pl.
qiṭaƐ, wuṣla pl. *wuṣal.* He raises alfalfa and rents
out patches of it to people who have horses. *yizraƐ
jatt w-yʔajjir qiṭaƐ minna lin-naas il-Ɛidhum xeel.*
3. *lazga* pl. *-aat.* He had a patch over his eye for
days. *zaṭṭ lazga Ɛala Ɛeena ʔayyaam.*
  to patch – *raggaƐ (i targiiƐ).* Mother had to
patch my trousers. *ʔummi ṣṭarrat itraggiƐ panṭarooni.*
  to patch up – *faδδ (u faδδ) n-.* Have they patched
up their quarrel yet? *faδδaw il-xilaaf beenaathum
loo baƐad?*

patchwork – *talziig, talṭiiš.*

patent – *baraaʔa* pl. *-aat.* I have applied for a patent
to protect my rights on my new invention. *qaddamit
ṭalab Ɛala baraaʔa lil-muzaafuδa Ɛala zuquuqi
bil-ixtiraƐ maali.*
  to patent – *sajjal (i tasjiil) t-.* You ought to
patent your process. *laazim itsajjil ṭariiqtak.*

path – 1. *darub* pl. *druub.* A narrow path leads to
the river. *fadd darub δayyiq yʔaddi ʔila n-nahar.*
2. *sabiil* pl. *subul.* He put many obstacles in my
path. *zaṭṭ ihwaaya Ɛaqabaat ib-sabiili.*

patience – *ṣabur.* I lost my patience. *nifaδ ṣabri.*

patient – 1. *mariiδ* pl. *marδa, wajƐaan* pl. *wjaaƐa.*
How's the patient today? *šloon il-mariiδ il-yoom?*
2. *ṣabuur, ṭuwiil.* He is a very patient man.
huwwa kulliš ṣabuur. or *haaδa kulliš ṭuwiil.*

patriarch – *baṭriiq* pl. *baṭaariqa.*

patriot – *waṭani* pl. *-iyyiin.*

patriotism – *waṭaniyya.*

patrol – *dawriyya* pl. *-aat.* We sent a patrol out to
reconnoiter. *dazzeena dawriyya lil-istiṭlaaƐ.* —
Ali went out on patrol. *Ɛali ṭilaƐ dawriyya.*
  to patrol – *ṭaaf (u ṭawafaan).* An armored police
car patrols the streets all night. *sayyaarat šurṭa
musallaza ṭṭuuf iš-šawaariƐ ṭuul il-leel.*

pattern – 1. *naqiš* pl. *nquuš.* This rug has a nice
pattern. *haz-zuuliyya naqiša laṭiif.* 2. *faṣaal*
pl. *-aat.* Where did you get the pattern for your
new dress? *ween ligeeti l-faṣaal il-badaltič
ij-jidiida?* 3. *šaakila* pl. *-aat, ṭiraaz* pl. *-aat.*
All his thefts are on this pattern. *kull sariqaata
Ɛala haṭ-ṭiraaz.*

pause – *waqfa* pl. *-aat, sakta* pl. *-aat, tawaqquf* pl.
-aat. After a short pause the speaker continued.
l-xaṭiib istimarr baƐad waqfa qaṣiira.
  to pause – *twaggaf (a twugguf).* He paused in his
work to greet us as we entered. *twaggaf Ɛan šuḡla

zatta ysallim Ɛaleena min daxalna.

to pave – 1. *ballaṭ (i tabliiṭ).* They are paving
this street. *da-yballiṭuun haš-šaariƐ.* 2. *mahhad
(i tamhiid) t-.* Their efforts paved the way for
independence. *majhuudhum mahhad iṭ-ṭariiq
lil-istiqlaal.*

pavement – *tabliiṭ* pl. *-aat, tamhiid* pl. *-aat,
ʔarδiyya* pl. *-aat.* The pavement is very narrow
here. *t-tabliiṭ ihnaa kulliš δayyig.*

paw – *ʔiid* pl. *-een, -eenaat, rijil* pl. *-een, -eenaat.*
The dog has hurt his paw. *č-čalib Ɛawwar ʔiida.*

pawn – 1. *liƐba* pl. *-aat, liƐab.* We are tired of
being nothing but a pawn in their political schemes.
Ɛijazna ʔizna bass liƐba b-xuṭaṭhum is-siyaasiyya.
2. *jundi* pl. *junuud.* You have lost another pawn.
xsarit jundi laax.
  to pawn – *rihan (a rahan) n-.* I had to pawn my
watch. *δṭarreet ʔarhan saaƐti.*

pawnshop – *mazall* (pl. *-aat*) *ruhuunaat.*

pawn ticket – *waṣil* (pl. *wuṣuulaat*) *rahan.*

pay – *raatib* pl. *rawaatib, maƐaaš* pl. *-aat.* How is
the pay on your new job? *šloon ir-raatib ib-šuḡḷak
ij-jidiid?*
  to pay – 1. *difaƐ (a dafiƐ) n-.* How much did you
pay for your car? *šgadd difaƐit ib-sayyaartak?* —
I would like to pay my bill. *ʔariid adfaƐ qaaʔimti.*
2. *gaam (u qiyaam) b-.* He paid all the expenses.
gaam ib-kull il-maṣaariif.
  **That doesn't pay. *maa min waraaha faayda.* or
š-šaḡla ma-tiswa. or *haay ma-ṭṭaƐƐum xubuz.*
  **You couldn't pay me to do that. *loo tinṭiini
fluus id-dinya ma-asawwiiha.*
  to pay attention – *daar (i deer, dayaraan) baal~,
ntibah (i ntibaah).* The pupils didn't pay attention
today at all. *t-talaamiiδ ma-daaraw baalhum il-yoom
ʔabad.* — Pay no attention to him. *la-tdiir-la baal.*
or **ma-Ɛleek minna.*
  to pay a visit – *zaar (u ziyaara), raaz (u rooz)
xuṭṭaar Ɛala.* I must pay him a visit. *laazim
azuura.* — Let's pay our new neighbors a visit.
xalli nruuz xuṭṭaar Ɛala jiiraanna j-jiddad.
  to pay back – 1. *waffa (i tawfiya).* I'll pay you
back the dinar on Monday. *ʔawaffii-lak id-diinaar
yoom iθ-θineen.* 2. *rajjaƐ (i tarjiiƐ) t-.* When
are you going to pay me back what you owe me?
šwakit raz-itrajjiƐ-li deeni?
  to pay down – *difaƐ (a dafiƐ) Ɛarabuun.* They
require you to pay one-third down and the rest in
monthly installments. *yriiduuk tidfaƐ θulθ il-mablaḡ
Ɛarabuun wil-baaqi b-ʔaqṣaaṭ šahriyya.*
  to pay for – *difaƐ (a dafiƐ) n- b-, Ɛala.* How much
did you pay for the car? *šgadd difaƐit bis-sayyaara?*
— He said he would pay for the rest of us. *qaal
raz-yidfaƐ Ɛaleena kullna.*
  **I paid dearly for my mistakes. *ḡaliṭṭi kallfatni
ḡaali.*
  to pay for itself – *ṭallaƐ (i taṭliiƐ) t- fluus~.*
This machine will pay for itself in five months.
hal-makiina raz-iṭṭalliƐ ifluusha b-xamist išhur.
  to pay off – 1. *waffa (i tawfiya), saddad
(i tasdiid).* He paid off his debts. *waffa kull
idyuuna.* 2. *sadd (i sadd) n- zsaab.* He sold the
farm and paid off the help. *baaƐ il-mazraƐa w-sadd
izsaab il-Ɛummaal.*
  to pay out – 1. *širaf (u ṣaruf) n-.* We paid out
more than we took in today. *l-yoom širafna ʔakθar
min dixaḷna.* 2. *raxxa (i tarxiya) t-.* Pay out the
rope slowly. *raxxi l-zabil Ɛala keefak.*
  to pay up – 1. *waffa (i tawfiya) t-, saddad
(i tasdiid) t-.* In a month I'll have it all paid up.
b-xilaal šahar raz-awaffiiha kullha. 2. *ʔadda
(i taʔdiya) t-.* I paid up all my debts on payday.
ʔaddeet kull idyuuni yoom il-maƐaaš.

payment – 1. *dafiƐ.* Prompt payment is requested.
r-rajaaʔ id-dafiƐ ib-surƐa. 2. *qisiṭ* pl. *ʔaqṣaaṭ,
dafƐa* pl. *-aat.* I have two more payments on my car.
buqaa-li qisṭeen Ɛala sayyaarti. — I paid up the
debt in three payments. *sawweet id-deen itlaθ
dafƐaat.*

pea – *bazaalyaaya* pl. *-aat* coll. *bazaalya.*

peace – 1. *salaam, silm.* The whole world wants peace.
kull id-dinya triid is-salaam. 2. *ʔamin.* The police
are doing all they can to maintain peace. *š-šurṭa
da-ysawwuun kull-ma yigdaruun lil-muzaafaḍa Ɛala
l-ʔamin.* 3. *huduuʔ.* If only I could work in peace!
loo bass ʔagdar ʔaštiḡuḷ ib-huduuʔ!
  **He doesn't give me any peace. *ma-yxalli baali
yirtaaz.*
  **I'm doing it just to keep the peace. *ʔaani

da-asawwiiha čifyaan šarr.
**Leave me in peace! *fukk yaaxa minni!* or *juuz Ɛanni!* or *Ɛuufni!*
to make peace - *ṣaalaz (i muṣaalaza) t-.* He tried to make peace between them. *zaawal yṣaaliz beenhum.*
peaceful - **1.** *haadi?.* Everything is so peaceful around here. *kullši šgadd haadi? ihnaa.* **2.** *musaalim* pl. *-iin.* He is very peaceful. *haaδa kulliš musaalim.* **3.** *silmi**. There is no peaceful solution to this problem. *ma-aku zall silmi l-hal-muškila.*
peach - *xooxa* pl. *-aat* coll. *xoox.* These peaches are very juicy. *hal-xoox kulliš rayyaan.*
peacock - *ṭaawuus* pl. *ṭwaawiis.*
peak - **1.** *qumma* pl. *qumam.* We climbed to the peak of the mountains. *tsallaqna l-qummat ij-jibal.* **2.** *?awj, δarwa.* He was then at the peak of his power. *kaan ib-?awj quuta b-δaak il-wakit.*
peanut - *fistiqat* (pl. *-aat*) *Ɛabiid* coll. *fistiq Ɛabiid.*
pear - *Ɛarmuuṭa* pl. *-aat* coll. *Ɛarmuuṭ.* How much is a kilo of pears? *beeš il-kiilo l-Ɛarmuuṭ?*
pearl - *liiluwwa* pl. *-aat* coll. *liilu.*
peasant - **1.** *fallaaz* pl. *-iin, flaaliiz.* The peasant took some tomatoes to market. *l-fallaaz nazzal ṭamaaṭa lis-suuq.* **2.** *mƐeedi* pl. *miƐdaan.* You peasant, why don't you learn some manners? *?ay mƐeedi, leeš ma-titƐallam išwayya ?uṣuul?*
pebble - *zaṣwa* pl. *-aat* coll. *zaṣu.* The path is covered with pebbles. *l-mamarr imġaṭṭa bil-zaṣu.*
peck - *nagra* pl. *-aat.* Give me another peach, some bird took a peck out of this one. *?inṭiini ġeer xooxa, haay fadd ṭeer maaxiδ-la nagra minha.*
to peck - *nigar (u nagir) n-, naggar (i tangiir) t-.* The birds are pecking at the fruit again; chase them away. *l-iṭyuur hamm da-ynaggiruun bil-faakiha; ruuz kiššhum.*
peculiar - **1.** *ġariib, šaaδδ.* He's a peculiar fellow. *huwwa fadd waazid ġariib.* -- The incident was hushed up under peculiar circumstances. *l-zaadiθa tlaġmuṭat ib-ṣuruuf šaaδδa.* **2.** *xaaṣṣ.* This style turban is peculiar to the people in the north. *haš-šikil laffa xaaṣṣa b-?ahl iš-šimaal.*
peculiarity - *xaaṣṣiyya* pl. *-aat, xawaaṣṣ.* They are easy to identify from certain peculiarities in their speech. *mnis-sihuula tiƐrufhum min xawaaṣṣ muƐayyana b-začiihum.*
pedal - **1.** *paaydaar* pl. *-aat.* One of the pedals on this bicycle is longer than the other. *waazid imnil-paaydaaraat ib-hal-paaysikil ?aṭwal imnil-laax.* **2.** *rijil* pl. *rijleen.* Does your sewing machine have a pedal or do you operate by hand? *makiint il-ixyaaṭa maaltič maal rijil loo maal iid?* **3.** *doosa* pl. *-aat.* My foot slipped off the pedal. *rijli zilgat imnid-doosa.*
to pedal - *ṣirab (u ṣarub) paaydaar.* His legs are still too short to pedal a bicycle. *rijlee baƐadha kulliš igṣayyra l-ṣarb il-paaydaar.*
to **peddle** - *dawwar (u tduwwur) b-.* The farmer sent his son to peddle tomatoes in this neighborhood. *l-fallaaz dazz ibna ydawwur bit-ṭamaaṭa b-hal-imzalla.*
peddler - *dawwaar* pl. *-iin.*
pedestrian - *maarr* pl. *-iin, maarra; maaši* pl. *mušaat.* Drivers must watch out for pedestrians crossing the street. *s-suwwaaq laazim yintibhuun Ɛal-maarriin il-da-yiƐburuun iš-šaariƐ.*
pediatrician - *ṭabiib* (pl. *?aṭibbaa?*) *?aṭfaal.*
pedigree - *?aṣil* pl. *?aaṣaal, nasab* pl. *?ansaab.* This horse's pedigree goes back for fifty years. *hal-izṣaan ?aṣla yirjaƐ il-xamsiin sana.*
pedigreed - *?aṣiil.*
peel - *gišir* pl. *gšuur.* These oranges have a thick peel. *hal-purtaqaal bii qišir θixiin.*
to peel - *gaššar (i tgiššir) t-.* I have to peel the potatoes. *laazim ?agaššir il-puteeta.* -- My skin is peeling. *jildi da-ygaššir.*
to peel off - *tgaššaṭ (a).* The whitewash is peeling off the ceiling. *l-ibyaaṣ da-yitgaššaṭ imnis-saguf.*
peep - **1.** *waṣwaṣa* pl. *-aat.* The peeps of the baby chicks made their mother run over to them. *waṣwaṣaat ifruux id-dijaaj xallat ?ummhum turkuṣ Ɛaleehum.* **2.** *ṭagga* pl. *-aat.* I don't want to hear another peep out of you. *ma-ariid ?asmaƐ wala ṭagga baƐad.* **3.** *naṣra* pl. *-aat.* Take a peep into the room. *?ilqi naṣra bil-ġurfa.*
to peep - **1.** *waṣwaṣ (u waṣwaṣa).* The baby chicks are peeping because their mother left them. *fruux id-dijaaj da-ywaṣwuṣuun li-?an ?ummhum qaamat min Ɛaleehum.* **2.** *baawaƐ (u mbaawaƐa), dazzag (i tadziig).* He peeped through the hole in the fence. *baawaƐ min zurf is-siyaaj.*
peeved - *zaƐlaan.* She was peeved about the remark you made. *čaanat zaƐlaana Ɛal-izčaaya lli zičeetha.*
peg - **1.** *watad* pl. *?awtaad.* He tripped over a tent peg and fell. *Ɛiθar ib-watad čaadir w-wugaƐ.* **2.** *Ɛuuda* pl. *Ɛuwad, xišba* pl. *xišab.* There are some pegs on the wall to hang your clothes on. *?aku Ɛuwad bil-zaayiṭ xaaṭir itƐallig ihduumak biiha.*
pelican - *?abu jraab* pl. *ṭyuur ?abu jraab; bajaƐa* pl. *-aat* coll. *bajaƐ.*
pelvis - *zawṣ* pl. *?azwaaṣ.*
pen - **1.** *sillaaya* pl. *-aat.* This pen scratches. *has-sillaaya da-tšaxxiṭ.* **2.** *paandaan* pl. *-aat, qalam* (pl. *?aqlaam*) *zibir.* This is an expensive fountain pen. *haaδa paandaan ġaali.* **3.** *zariiba* pl. *zaraayib.* We'll have to build a pen for the sheep. *laazim nibni zariiba lil-ġanam.*
penal code - *qaanuun il-Ɛuquubaat.*
penalty - *Ɛuquuba* pl. *-aat, jazaa?* pl. *-aat.* The penalty is ten years' imprisonment. *l-Ɛuquuba Ɛašr isniin zabis.*
pencil - *qalam* pl. *qlaam.* Give me that pencil, please. *nṭiini δaak il-qalam, min faṣlak.*
pending - **1.** *rahn.* They have cancelled all permits, pending further investigation. *liġaw kull il-?ijaazaat, rahn it-tazqiiqaat il-?iṣaafiyya.* **2.** *muƐallaq.* The matter is still pending. *hal-qaṣiyya baƐadha muƐallaqa.* or ***hal-qaṣiyya baƐad ma-mabtuut biiha.*
pendulum - *raqqaaṣ* pl. *-aat.*
to **penetrate** - **1.** *xtiraq (i xtiraaq).* The enemy tanks penetrated our lines. *dabbaabaat il-Ɛadu xtirqat xuṭuuṭna.* **2.** *tġalġal (a taġalġul).* The Locust Control Expedition penetrated deep into the desert. *firqat mukaafazat ij-jaraad itġalġilat biṣ-ṣazraa?.*
peninsula - *šibih jaziira* pl. *?ašbaah juzur.*
penitentiary - *sijin* pl. *sijuun.*
penknife - *čaaquuča* pl. *-aat, čawaaqiič; siččiinat* (pl. *sačaačiin*) *jeeb.*
penname - *?isim mustaƐaar* pl. *?asmaa?, ?asaami mustaƐaara.*
penny - *beeza, filis.* I'm broke, I haven't got a penny. *?aani miflis; maa Ɛindi beeza.*
pension - *taqaaƐud.* He gets a pension from the government. *yaaxuδ taqaaƐud imnil-zukuuma.*
to pension - *zaal (i ?izaala) n- Ɛat-taqaaƐud.* He was pensioned last year. *nzaal Ɛat-taqaaƐud is-sana l-faatat.*
people - **1.** *naas.* What will people say? *s-raz-yguuluun in-naas?* **2.** *šaƐab* pl. *šuƐuub.* The government always sounds out the opinion of the people in serious matters. *l-zukuuma daa?iman titzassas ra?y iš-šaƐab zawl il-?umuur il-xaṭiira.* **3.** *qawm* pl. *?aqwaam.* The Babylonians were a people who built up a powerful kingdom in ancient times. *l-baabiliyyiin qawm binaw mamlaka qawwiyya bil-Ɛuṣuur il-qadiima.* **4.** *Ɛaalam.* Were there many people at the meeting? *čaan ?aku Ɛaalam ihwaaya bil-ijtimaaƐ?* **5.** *?ahal.* I want you to meet my people. *?ariidak titƐarraf Ɛala ?ahli.* **6.** *šaxiṣ* pl. *?ašxaaṣ.* I only knew a few people at the party. *Ɛirafit čam šaxiṣ bass bil-zafla.*
pep - *zayawiyya, našaaṭ.* Where do you get your pep? *minneen jattak hal-zayawiyya?* -- He's full of pep today. *huwwa l-yoom matruus našaaṭ.*
to pep up - *naššaṭ (i tanšiiṭ) t-.* I need something to pep me up. *?aztaaj fadd šii ynaššiṭni.*
pepper - **1.** *filfil.* Pass me the pepper, please. *naawušni l-filfil, min faṣlak.* **2.** *filfila* pl. *-aat* coll. *filfil.* See if you can find some nice peppers in the market. *šuuf ?iδa tigdar tilgi čam filfila zeena bis-suug.*
peppermint - *niƐnaaƐ.*
per - **1.** *b-.* How much do you sell the oranges for per dozen? *šloon itbiiƐ il-purtiqaal bid-darzan?* -- He makes sixty dinars per month. *yṭalliƐ sittiin diinaar biš-šahar.* **2.** *Ɛala, Ɛan.* They charge two dinars per person. *yaaxδuun diinaareen Ɛala kull nafar.*
**We paid fifty cents per person. *dfaƐna xamsiin filis kull waazid.*
per cent - *bil-miyya.* The cost of living has risen ten per cent. *kulfat il-maƐiiša rtifƐat Ɛašra bil-miyya.* -- Our bank pays two percent interest. *l-bang maalna yidfaƐ faa?ida θneen bil-miyya.* -- We'll each share fifty percent of the profits. *raz-nitqaasam il-mazṣuul kull man bil-miyya xamsiin.*
percentage - *nisba* (pl. *nisab*) *mi?awiyya.*

perennial - **1.** *ɛaayil.* These plants are perennial. *han-nabaataat ɛaayla.* or ***han-nabaataat itɛiil.* **2.** *muzmin.* He is a perennial candidate for the House of Representatives. *haaδa fadd muraššaɛ muzmin lin-niyaaba.*

perfect - **1.** *kaamil.* Nothing is perfect. *ma-aku šii kaamil.* **2.** *tamaam.* This is perfect nonsense. *haay laġwa tamaam.* **3.** *maδbuuṭ, tamaam.* He speaks perfect French. *yiɛči fransi maδbuuṭ.* **4.** *muɛkam, maδbuuṭ, mutqan.* Their plan was perfect. *xiṭṭathum čaanat muɛkama.* -- This process is not perfect yet. *haṭ-ṭariiqa baɛadha muu mutqana.*

to perfect - **The method hasn't been perfected yet. *ṭ-ṭariiqa baɛad li-hassa ma-wuṣlat darajat il-kamaal.*

perfection - *kamaal.*

perfectly - **1.** *tamaaman.* He was perfectly satisfied. *čaan raaδi tamaaman.* **2.** *biδ-δabuṭ, b-ʔitqaan, ɛal-maδbuuṭ.* He did it perfectly the first time. *ʔawwal marra sawwaaha biδ-δabuṭ.* **3.** *kulliš.* I know him perfectly well. *ʔaɛurfa kulliš zeen.*

to **perform** - **1.** *sawwa (i taswiya) t-, qaam (u qiyaam) b-.* Who performed the operation? *minu sawwa l-ɛamaliyya?* -- The acrobats performed the most difficult feats. *l-pahlawaaniyya qaamaw ib-ʔaxṭar il-ɛarakaat.* **2.** *ʔadda (i taʔdiya) t-.* He performed his duty. *ʔadda waajba.* **3.** *maθθal (i tamθiil).* This group of players has been performing this play for two years. *haj-jamaaɛa l-mumaθθiliin ymaθθiluun har-ruwaaya muddat santeen.*

performance - **1.** *ɛariδ.* Did you like the performance of the dancing troupe? *ɛijabak ɛariδ hal-firqa r-raaqiṣ?* **2.** *tamθiiliyya* pl. *-aat.* What time does the performance begin? *šwakit tibdi t-tamθiiliyya?*

perfume - *riiɛa* pl. *riyaɛ.*

to perfume - *ɛaṭṭar (i taɛṭiir) t-.* She perfumes her handkerchiefs. *tɛaṭṭir ičfaafiiha.*

perhaps - **1.** *rubbama, yimkin.* Perhaps I'll come to the meeting. *rubbama ʔaji lil-ijtimaaɛ.* **2.** *balki, yimkin, yjuuz.* Perhaps he is sick. *balki mariiδ.*

period - **1.** *mudda* pl. *mudad.* He worked here for a short period. *štiġal ihnaa mudda qaṣiira.* **2.** *fatra* pl. *-aat.* This is an important period in our history. *haay fatra muhimma b-taariixna.* **3.** *nuqṭa* pl. *nuqaṭ.* You forgot to put a period here. *niseet itɛuṭṭ nuqṭa hnaa.* **4.** *daris* pl. *druus.* I have the third period free. *ɛindi faraaġ bid-dars iθ-θaaliθ.* **5.** *ɛaada.* Doctor, my period is late this month. *daktoor, ɛaadti tʔaxxrat haš-šahar.*

period of grace - *muhla.* The period of grace expires on the tenth. *l-muhla tixlaṣ yoom ɛašra biš-šahar.*

periodical - *dawri*.* He suffered periodical setbacks. *ɛaana naksaat dawriyya.* -- I subscribe to a number of periodical magazines. *ʔaani mištirik ib-ɛadad imnil-majallaat id-dawriyya.*

perjury - *šahaadat zuur.* She committed perjury. *šihdat šahaadat zuur.*

permanent - **1.** *parmanaant.* I need a permanent. *šaɛri yirraad-la parmanaant.* **2.** *daaʔimi*, θaabit.* I have no permanent address. *ma-ɛindi ɛinwaan θaabit.* -- This is a permanent job. *haaδa šuġuḷ daaʔimi.*

permission - *ruxṣa, ʔiδin.* Did you get his permission? *ʔaxaδit ruxṣa minna?*

to ask permission - *starxaṣ (i stirxaaṣ).* He asked permission of his supervisor to leave an hour early. *starxaṣ min il-mulaaɛiδ maala yiṭlaɛ saaɛa gabḷ id-dawaam.*

permit - *ʔijaaza* pl. *-aat.* You need a permit before you can start building. *tiɛtaaj ʔijaaza gabuḷ-ma tballiš bil-binaaʔ.*

to permit - **1.** *simaɛ (a simaaɛ) n- l-, niṭa (i) ruxṣa.* I can't permit that. *ma-asmaɛ il-hiiči šii.* **2.** *raxxaṣ (i tarxiiṣ) t-.* My supervisor permitted me to leave early. *l-mulaaɛiδ maali raxxaṣni ʔaṭlaɛ ɛala wakit.*

permitted - *masmuuɛ l-, mraxxaṣ.* No one is permitted to enter this building. *maɛɛad masmuuɛ-la yidxul hal-binaaya.* -- Is smoking permitted? *masmuuɛ it-tadxiin?*

perpendicular - *ɛamuudi*.*

to **perpetuate** - *xallad (i taxliid) t-.* This deed will perpetuate his name in history. *hal-ɛamal raɛ-yxallid ʔisma bit-taariix.*

to **perplex** - *ɛayyar (i taɛyiir) t-.* His lack of interest in his studies perplexes me. *qillat ihtimaama b-druusa tɛayyirni.*

perplexing - *mɛayyir.* This is a very perplexing problem. *haay fadd muškila kulliš imɛayyira.*

perplexity - *ɛiira.* I was in such a state of perplexity I didn't know what to do. *činit ib-fadd šikil ɛiira ma-ɛrafit š-asawwi.*

per se - *b-ɛaδδaat-.* It's not worth much per se, but it has sentimental value. *ma-tiswa šii b-ɛaδδaata laakin il-ʔasbaab ɛaaṭifiyya.*

to **persecute** - *δṭihad (i δṭihaad).* He imagines people are persecuting him. *yitṣawwar in-naas da-yiδṭahduu.*

persecution - *δṭihaad.* He suffers from a persecution complex. *mibtili b-ɛuqdat iδṭihaad.*

to **persevere** - *waaδab (i muwaaδaba), daawam (i tadwiim).* If you persevere in your efforts, you might get the promotion. *ʔiδa twaaδub ɛala juhuudak yimkin itɛaṣṣil it-tarfiiɛ.*

Persia - *ʔiiraan, bilaad il-furs.*

Persian - **1.** *faarsi** pl. *furs, ɛajami** pl. *-iyyiin, ʔiiraani** pl. *-iyyiin.* He's a Persian. *huwwa faarsi.* **2.** *faarsi.* Translate that into Persian. *tarjam haaδi lil-faarsi.*

to **persist** - **1.** *laɛɛ (i ʔilɛaaɛ, laɛɛ) n-, lajj (i lajj) n-.* The boy persisted with his questions until the old man got angry. *l-walad laɛɛ ib-ʔasʔilta ʔila ʔan ir-rijjaal iš-šaayib ġiδab.* **2.** *daam (u dawaam), ṭawwal (i taṭwiil).* The effects of the disease persisted a long time. *nataaʔij il-maraδ daamat mudda ṭuwiila.* **3.** *tmaada (a tamaadi).* He persisted in lying. *tmaada bil-kiδib.*

persistent - **1.** *muṣirr.* He is persistent in his efforts to obtain a higher education. *muṣirr ɛala juhuuda lil-ɛuṣuul ɛala θaqaafa ɛaalya.* **2.** *mθaabir.* Your son doesn't learn quickly, but he is very persistent. *ʔibnak ma-yitɛallam ib-surɛa, laakin huwwa kulliš imθaabir.*

person - **1.** *šaxiṣ* pl. *ʔašxaaṣ.* He is the same person. *huwwa nafs iš-šaxiṣ.* **2.** *ʔaadmi* pl. *ʔawaadim, ʔinsaan* pl. *naas.* He is a nice person. *haaδa xooš ʔaadmi.* or *huwwa ʔinsaan ṭayyib.* **3.** *nafar* pl. *ʔanfaar.* We have place for two more persons. *ɛidna makaan in-nafareen baɛad.* **4.** (m.) *waaɛid* (f.) *waɛda.* She's a nice person. *hiyya fadd waɛda laṭiifa.*

**What sort of a person is he? *huwwa šinu min šii?*

in person - *biδ-δaat, šaxṣiyyan, b-nafs-.* Please deliver this to him in person. *ʔarjuuk sallim-la haay biδ-δaat.*

personal - **1.** *saxṣi*.* He asks too many personal questions. *yisʔal ihwaaya ʔasʔila šaxṣiyya.* -- He would like to discuss a personal matter with you. *da-yriid yiɛči wiyyaak ɛala fadd mawδuuɛ šaxṣi.* **2.** *xaaṣṣ, xuṣuuṣi*.* These are my personal belongings. *haay ġaraaδi l-xaaṣṣa.*

personality - *šaxṣiyya* pl. *-aat.* She has a loveable personality. *ɛidha šaxṣiyya maɛbuuba.*

personally - *šaxṣiyyan.* I'd like to speak to him personally. *ʔariid aɛči wiyyaa šaxṣiyyan.* -- Personally I don't like him. *šaxṣiyyan ʔaani ma-ʔamiil ʔila.*

personnel - **1.** *muwaδδafiin, mustaxdamiin.* We don't have enough personnel. *ma-ɛidna muwaδδafiin kaafiin.* **2.** *δaatiyya.* He's the director of the personnel section. *haaδa mudiir qism iδ-δaatiyya.*

perspiration - *ɛarag.*

to **perspire** - *ɛirag (a ɛarag).* I perspire a lot at night. *ʔaɛrag ihwaaya bil-leel.*

to **persuade** - *qannaɛ (i taqniiɛ), ʔaqnaɛ (i ʔiqnaaɛ).* He persuaded me to go. *qannaɛni ʔaruuɛ.*

persuasion - *taqniiɛ, ʔiqnaaɛ.* We had to use persuasion to get him to agree. *staɛmalna l-ʔiqnaaɛ ɛatta nxallii ywaafuq.*

pertinent - *ɛaaʔid.* I don't think these facts are pertinent to the case. *ma-aδinn hal-waqaaʔiɛ ɛaaʔida lil-qaδiyya.*

perversion - *nɛiraaf.* Sexual perversion can be treated. *l-inɛiraaf ij-jinsi yimkin yitɛaalaj.*

pervert - *minɛirif* pl. *-iin.* A sexual pervert approached me on the street. *ndagg biyya fadd waaɛid minɛirif jinsiyyan biš-šaariɛ.*

to pervert - *ʔafsad (i ʔifsaad).* He was accused of perverting the youth. *ntiham ib-ʔifsaad iš-šabaab.*

pessimism - *tašaaʔum.*

pessimist - *mitšaaʔim.*

to be **pessimistic** - *tšaaʔam (a tašaaʔum).* Don't be pessimistic. *la-titšaaʔam.*

pest - **1.** *bala.* The sparrows have become a pest in the orchard. *l-ɛaṣaafiir ṣaayra bala bil-ɛadiiqa.*

2. *zašara* pl. *-aat.* The government has begun a campaign against insect pests. *l-zikuuma šaanna zamla Eal-zašaraat.*
to **pester** - *bazzaE (i tbizziE) t-.* He pestered me to death with his questions. *bazzaEni b-?as?ilta.*
pestle - *?iid* (pl. *?ideen) haawan.*
pet - 1. *zaywaan ?aliif* pl. *zaywaanaat ?aliifa.* We're not allowed to keep pets in our apartments. *maa masmuuz inrabbi zaywaanaat ?aliifa b-binaayatna.* 2. (m.) *walad imdallal* pl. *wulid imdallaliin;* (f.) *bitt, bnayya mdallala* pl. *banaat imdallalaat.* She's her mother's pet. *hiyya l-ibnayya l-mdallila Eid ?ummha.*
to pet - *massad (i tamsiid) t- l-.* Don't pet the dog! *la-tmassid-la lič-čalib.*
petition - *Eariiδa* pl. *Earaayiδ, Earδazaal* pl. *-aat, maδbaṭa* pl. *maδaabuṭ.* Why don't you get up a petition? *leeš ma-tqaddim Eariiδa?*
to petition - *qaddam (i taqdiim) Eariiδa.* The villagers petitioned the central government for a new school building. *?ahl il-qura qaddimaw Eariiδa lil-zukuuma il-markaziyya li-?ajal binaaya jadiida lil-madrasa.*
petitioner - *mustadEi* pl. *-iin.*
petroleum - *nafuṭ.*
petty - 1. *ṭafiif, zahiid.* This is a petty sum. *haaδa mablaġ ṭafiif.* 2. *taafih.* I'm tired of these petty objections. *yikfi hal-iEtiraaδaat hat-taafha.*
petty expenses - *naθriyyaat.*
pharaoh - *firEoon* pl. *faraaEiin.*
pharmacist - *ṣaydali* pl. *ṣayaadila.*
pharmacy - *ṣaydaliyya* pl. *-aat.*
phase - *marzala* pl. *maraazil, ṭawr* pl. *?aṭwaar.* The second phase of the project will begin next month. *l-marzala θ-θaanya mnil-mašruuE raz-tibdi š-šahr ij-jaay.*
Ph. D. - *diktooraa.* He has a Ph. D. in economics. *Einda diktooraa bil-iqtiṣaad.*
phenomenon - *δaahira* pl. *δawaahir.* This is a strange phenomenon. *haay δaahira ġariiba.*
phenomenal - *xaariq.* He has a phenomenal memory. *Einda δaakira xaariqa.*
philanthropic - 1. *xayri*, birri*.* Philanthropic societies provide the schools for orphans with food and clothing. *j-jamEiyyaat il-xayriyya tzawwid madaaris il-?aytaam bil-?akil wil-hiduum.* 2. *?insaani*.* That's not a very philanthropic idea. *hal-fikra muu fikra ?insaaniyya kulliš.*
philanthropist - *rajul muzsin* pl. *rijaal, riyaajiil muzsiniin.*
philanthropy - *zubb il-?insaaniyya, Eamal* (pl. *?aEmaal) ?izsaan, xeer.*
philologist - *luġawi* pl. *-iyyiin.*
philology - *Eilm il-luġaat.*
philosopher - *faylasuuf* pl. *falaasifa.*
philosophic - *falsafi*.*
philosophy - *falsafa.*
phone - *talafoon* pl. *-aat.* You're wanted on the phone. *da-yriiduuk Eat-talafoon.*
to phone - *talfan (i ttilfin) l-, xaabar (i muxaabara).* I'll phone you after lunch. *raz-atalfin-lak baEd il-ġada.*
phonograph - *gramafoon* pl. *-aat, funuġraaf* pl. *-aat.*
phony - 1. *mlaffaq.* That story is phony. *hal-qiṣṣa mlaffaqa.* 2. *daEi, muddaEi.* The guy is a phony. *haaδa waazid muddaEi.*
phosphorus - *fusfoor.*
photograph - *rasim* pl. *rsuum, ṣuura* pl. *ṣuwar, taṣwiir* pl. *taṣaawiir.* Where can I have a passport photograph taken? *ween ?agdar ?aaxuδ rasim maal paaṣpoort.*
to photograph - *?axaδ (u ?axiδ) ṣuura.* Have you photographed the statue? *?axaδit ṣuurat it-timθaal?*
photographer - *muṣawwir* pl. *-iin, rassaam* pl. *-iin.*
phrase - *Eibaara* pl. *-aat, qawl* pl. *?aqwaal.* This phrase is not a complete sentence. *hal-Eibaara muu jumla kaamla.*
to phrase - 1. *Eabbar (i taEbiir) Ean-.* Can you phrase it in a better way? *tigdar itEabbur Eanha b-ṭariiqa ?azsan?* 2. *ṣaaġ (u ṣiyaaġa) n-.* He phrased his speech so as to appeal to the masses. *ṣaaġ xiṭaaba b-ṣuura t?aθθir bij-jamaahiir.*
physical - 1. *jismi*, badani*, jismaani*.* Avoid every form of physical exertion. *tzaaša ?ay irhaaq jismi.* 2. *ṭabiiEi*.* This contradicts all physical laws. *haaδa ynaaqiδ kull il-qawaaniin iṭ-ṭabiiEiyya.*
physical education - *riyaaδa, r-riyaaδa l-badaniyya.*
physical exercise - *riyaaδa, tamriin.*
physician - *daktoor* pl. *dakaatra, ṭabiib* pl. *?aṭibbaa?.*
physicist - *fiizyaa?i* pl. *-iyyiin, fiizyaawi* pl. *-iyyiin.*
physics - *fiizya, fiizyaa?.* He is studying physics. *da-yidrus fiizya.*
physiology - *faslaja.*
physique - *bunya* pl. *-aat, qalaafa* pl. *-aat.* He has a nice physique. *Einda xooš bunya.*
pianist - *Eaazif* (pl. *-iin) piyaano.*
piano - *pyaano* pl. *pyaanwaat.*
pick - 1. *qazma* pl. *-aat.* The men were carrying picks and shovels. *l-Eummaal čaanaw šaayliin qazmaat w-karakaat.* 2. *riiša* pl. *riyaš* coll. *riiš.* The pick for my lute broke. *r-riiša maal Euudi nkisrat.* 3. *xiira.* This is the pick of the lot. *haaδa xiirat il-mawjuud.* 4. *xiyaar.* I have three apples; take your pick. *Eindi θlaθ tiffaazaat; ?ilak il-xiyaar.* 5. *nuxba* pl. *nuxab, zubda.* These men are the pick of the army. *haj-jinuud nuxbat ij-jeeš.*
to pick - 1. *zuwa (i zawi) n-.* When are you going to pick the fruit? *šwakit raz-tazwi il-meewa?* 2. *xtaar (a xtiyaar) stanga (i stingaa?).* You certainly picked a nice time for an argument. *bila šakk ?inta xtaareet il-wakit il-munaasib lil-mujaadala.* 3. *nagnag (i tnignig) b-.* Don't pick at your food! *la-tnagnig ib-?aklak!* 4. *naġbaš (u naġbaša) b-.* Don't pick your teeth! *la-tnaġbuš b-isnuunak.* 5. *nagbar (u tnugbur) b-.* Don't pick your nose! *la-tnagbur ib-xašmak!* 6. *fašš (i fašš) n-.* Someone must have picked this lock. *fadd ?azzad laazim fašš hal-qufal.*
**They picked him to pieces. *šarroo Eal-zabil.* or *tnaawšoo.*
**I have a bone to pick with you. *Eindi zsaab ?ariid ?aṣaffii wiyyaak.*
**Are you trying to pick a quarrel with me? *?inta da-tdawwur-lak zirša wiyyaaya?*
to pick on - *šadd (i šadd) duub~ wiyya.* He's been picking on me all day. *šaadd duuba wiyyaaya n-nahaar kulla.*
to pick out - *xtaar (a xtiyaar), stanga (i stingaa?).* He picked out a very nice gift for his wife. *xtaar hadiyya kulliš zilwa l-zawijta.*
to pick up - 1. *šaal (i šeel) n-.* Please pick up the paper from the floor. *baḷḷa ma-tšiil ij-jariida mnil-gaaE.* -- The bus stopped here to pick up passengers. *l-paaṣ wugaf ihnaa zatta yšiil rukkaab.* 2. *ligaṭ (u lagiṭ) n-.* I picked up quite a bit of Italian on my trip. *ligaṭit miqdaar la-ba?s bii mnil-zači l-?iiṭaali b-safurti.* 3. *lizam (a lazim) n-, kumaš (u kamuš) n-.* The police picked up several suspects. *š-šurṭa lizmaw baEδ il-muštabih biihum.* 4. *ktisab (a ktisaab).* The train gradually picked up speed. *l-qiṭaar iktisab surEa tadriijiyyan.*
pickle - *ṭuršiyya* pl. *-aat,* coll. *ṭurši* pl. *ṭaraaši.* Do you have any pickles? *Eindak ṭurši?*
**He's in a pretty pickle now. *huwwa mitwarriṭ hassa.* or *huwwa waagiE ib-ma?zaq hassa.*
to pickle - *čibas (i čabis), kammax (u tkummux).* Did you pickle the turnips I brought you? *čibasti š-šalġam illi jibta ?ilič?*
pickled - *mxallal.* Buy a bowl of pickled beets. *štirii-li kaasa šuwandar imxallal.*
pick pocket - *naššaal* pl. *-iin, ṣarraab* (pl. *-iin) jeeb.*
picnic - *nuzha* pl. *-aat.*
picture - 1. *ṣuura* pl. *ṣuwar, rasim* pl. *rusuum.* They have some beautiful pictures for sale. *Eidhum baEδ iṣ-ṣuwar il-badiiEa lil-beeE.* -- This is my picture when I was in the army. *haaδa rasmi min činit bij-jeeš.* 2. *filim* pl. *?aflaam.* Was the picture good? *l-filim čaan zeen?* 3. *fikra* pl. *?afkaar.* I have to get a clear picture of it first. *laazim yṣiir Eindi fikra waaδza Eanna ?awwal.*
to give a picture of - *ṣawwar (u taṣwiir).* He gave you a false picture of it. *ṣawwar-lak-iyyaaha ġalaṭ.*
to picture - 1. *ṣawwar (u taṣwiir) t-.* This novel pictures life a thousand years ago. *har-ruwaaya tṣawwur il-zayaat gabuḷ ?alif sana.* 2. *tṣawwar (a taṣawwur).* I pictured it differently. *tṣawwaritha ġeer šikil.*
pictures - *siinama, ?aflaam.* She has been in pictures since she was a child. *tiṭlaE bis-siinama min hiyya baEadha ṭifla.*
piece - 1. *wuṣla* pl. *wuṣal.* May I take a piece of the watermelon. *?agdar ?aaxuδ wuṣla mnir-raggi?* -- Sew these two pieces together. *xayyṭi hal-wuṣilteen suwa.* 2. *qiṭEa* pl. *qiṭaE.* Get a piece of wire and fasten them together. *jiib qiṭEa*

min is-silk w-urbuṭhum suwa. **3.** *maqṭuuεa* pl. *maqaaṭiiε.* What is the name of the piece the orchestra is playing? *š-ism hal-maqṭuuεa l-da-tiεzifha l-firqa?*
**I gave him a good piece of my mind! *zaffeeta!* or *wabbaxta zeen!*
to fall to pieces - *tfaṣṣax (a tafaṣṣux).* The book is falling to pieces. *l-iktaab itfaṣṣax.* or **l-iktaab ṣaar wuṣla-wuṣla.*
to go to pieces - **1.** *nhaar (a nhiyaar).* She went completely to pieces. *nhaarat tamaaman.* **2.** *tfallaš (a tafalluš).* Sooner or later their business is bound to go to pieces. *ʔawwal w-taali tijaarathum laazim titfallaš.*
to tear to pieces - *šaggag (i tšiggig), maḷḷax (i tmiḷḷix).* The dog tore my shoe to pieces. *č-čalib maḷḷax qundarti.*
piece work - *bil-qiṭεa, bil-wiζda.* They work piece work. *yištuġluun bil-qiṭεa.*
pier - **1.** *dinga* pl. *dinag.* The bridge rests on four piers. *j-jisir murakkab εala ʔarbaε dinag.* **2.** *raṣiif* pl. *ʔarṣifa.* We were standing on the harbor's pier waiting for the boat. *čiina waagfiin εala raṣiif il-miinaaʔ da-nintiðir il-markab.*
to **pierce** - *nigab (u nagub) n-, ziraf (u zaruf) n-.* Bullets can not pierce this armored plate. *ʔirṣaaṣ ma-yigdar yingub hal-ζadiid il-mudarraε.*
pig - *xanziir* pl. *xanaaziir.*
pigeon - *ζamaama* pl. *-aat* coll. *ζamaam.*
wild pigeon - *ṭwaarni* pl. *-iyya.*
pigeonhole - *xaana* pl. *-aat.* You'll find it in one of the pigeon holes of the desk. *tilgiiha b-waζda min xaanaat il-meez.*
to pigeonhole - *nayyam (i tniyyim).* Apparently they have pigeonholed our request. *yiðhar nayyimaw iṭ-ṭalab maalna.*
pigeon house - *burij* pl. *braaj, bruuj.*
pigheaded - *εnaadi* pl. *-iyya, εanuud* pl. *-iin.* He is so pigheaded that he won't even listen to my explanation. *haaða hal-gadd iεnaadi ζatta ma-yismaε iš-šariζ maali.*
pile - **1.** *koom, kooma* pl. *kwaam.* Leave space between the piles of sand and gravel. *xalli masaafa been ikwaam ir-ramul wil-ζaṣu.* -- This pile of letters needs to be answered. *haay kooma mnil-makaatiib yinraad-ilha jawaab.* **2.** *θarwa* pl. *-aat.* He made his pile during the war. *jimaε θaruuta bil-ζarub.*
to pile - **1.** *kawwam (u takwiim) t-, kaddas (i takdiis) t-.* Pile the bricks next to the wall. *kawwum iṭ-ṭaabuug yamm il-ζaayiṭ.* **2.** *diζas (a daζis) n-.* We piled all the suitcases into the trunk of the car. *diζasna kull ij-junaṭ ib-ṣanduug is-sayyaara.* **3.** *ndiζas (i ndiζaas).* We all piled into one car. *kullna ndiζasna b-fadd sayyaara.*
to pile up - *traakam (a taraakum).* My debts are piling up. *dyuuni da-titraakam.*
piles - *buwaasiir.* He was operated on in the hospital for piles. *sawwoo-la εamaliyyat buwaasiir bil-mustašfa.*
pilgrim - *ζajji* pl. *ζijjaaj.*
pilgrimage - *ζajj.*
pill - *ζabba* pl. *ζabaabi* coll. *ζubuub.*
pillar - *εamuud* pl. *ʔaεmida, εawaamiid; dalag* pl. *-aat; dinga* pl. *dinag.* A large pillar blocked my view of the stage. *fadd εamuud ičbiir sadd manðar il masraζ min giddaami.*
pillow - *mxadda* pl. *mxaadiid.*
pillowcase - *beet imxadda* pl. *byuut imxaadiid.*
pilot - **1.** *rubbaan* pl. *rabaabina, qabṭaan* pl. *qabaaṭina.* The ship is waiting for the pilot. *l-baaxira da-tintiðir ir-rubbaan.* **2.** *ṭayyaar* pl. *-iin.* He is an Air Force pilot. *huwwa ṭayyaar bil-quwwa j-jawwiyya.*
pimple - **1.** *zungiṭa* pl. *zanaagiṭ.* Her face is full of pimples. *wujihha mṭallaε zanaagiṭ.* **2.** *ζabba* pl. *ζubuub* coll. *ζabb.* When he grew up he got rid of his adolescent pimples. *min kubar xallaṣ min ζabb iš-šabaab.*
pin - *danbuus* pl. *danaabiis.* She stuck herself with a pin. *čakkat nafisha b-danbuus.* -- She wore a silver pin. *libsat danbuus fuððа.*
**I was on pins and needles. *činit εala ʔaζarr imnij-jamur.* or *činit gaaʔid εala naar.*
hairpin - *furkeeta* pl. *-aat.*
to pin - **1.** *dambas (i tdimbis).* Pin your hankerchief to your coat. *dambis ič-čiffiyya b-sitirtak.* **2.** *εiṣa (a εaṣi).* The two men were pinned under the car. *r-rijjaaleen εiṣaw jawwa s-sayyaara.*
to pin down - *lizam (a lazim).* We couldn't pin him down to anything definite. *ma-gdarna nilzama b-šii ʔakiid.*
to pin on - **1.** *šakkal (i tšikkil), εallag (i tεillig).* I'll pin it on for you. *ʔaani ʔašakkil-lak-iyyaaha.* -- She pinned a flower on her dress. *šakkilat warda εala badlatha.* **2.** *θabbat (i taθbiit) t-.* The police pinned the crime on him. *š-šurṭa θabbitat ij-jariima εalee.*
to pin up - **1.** *šakkal (i tšikkil) li-foog, εallag (i tεillig) li-foog.* Let me pin up the hem first. *xalli ʔawwal ʔašakkil il-ζaašya li-foog.* **2.** *farkat (i tfurkit) t-.* She pinned up her hair. *farkitat šaεarha.* or *ζaaṭṭa furkeeta ib-šaεarha.*
pinch - **1.** *nitfa* pl. *nitaf, rašša* pl. *-aat.* Add a pinch of salt to the soup. *ðiif fadd nitfa miliζ εaš-šoorba.* **2.** *garṣa* pl. *-aat.* The boy gave his little sister a good pinch. *l-walad giraṣ ʔuxta ṣ-ṣiġayyra garṣa qawiyya.*
in a pinch - *εind ið-ðuruura, b-wakt ið-ðiiq.* In a pinch it will do. *εind ið-ðuruura haay itsidd il-ζaaja.* -- You can always count on him in a pinch. *b-imkaanak daaʔiman tigdar tiεtimid εalee b-wakt ið-ðiiq.*
to pinch - **1.** *giraṣ (u gariṣ) n-, garraṣ (i tagriiṣ) t-.* Don't pinch! *la-tigruṣ!* -- The door pinched my finger. *l-baab girṣat iṣibεi.* **2.** *ðayyag (i taðyiig) t- εala, ʔaðða (i taʔðiya) t-.* Where does the shoe pinch your foot? *minneen il-qundara da-tðayyig εala rijlak.*
pine - *ṣnoobara* pl. *-aat* coll. *ṣnoobar.* These pine trees are almost fifty years old. *ʔašjaar l-iṣnoobar haay εumurha ζwaali xamsiin sana.*
pineapple - *ʔananaas.*
pine wood - *xišab čaam.*
pink - **1.** *wardi**. She was wearing a pink dress. *čaanat laabsa nafnuuf wardi.* **2.** *qranfila* (pl. *-aat) wardiyya* coll. *qranfil wardi.* We had pinks in this place last year. *čaan εidna b-hal-maζall qranfil wardi s-sana l-maaðiya.*
pious - *middayyin* pl. *-iin, taqi* pl. *ʔatqiyaaʔ, ṣaaliζ* pl *-iin.* He is a very pious man. *huwwa rajjaal middayyin ihwaaya.*
pipe - **1.** *buuri* pl. *bwaari, ʔinbuub* pl. *ʔanaabiib.* The pipe has burst. *l-buuri ṭagg.* -- The oil pipe line runs from Kirkuk to Tripoli. *ʔanaabiib in-nafuṭ timtadd min kirkuuk ʔila ṭaraabluṣ.* **2.** *ṗaayṗ* pl. *-aat.* He smokes a pipe. *ydaxxin ṗaayṗ.*
to pipe - **We pipe our water from a spring. *naaxuð il-ṃaay bil-buwaari mnil-εeen.*
piracy - *qarṣana.*
pirate - *qurṣaan* pl. *qaraaṣina.*
pistachio - *fistiqa* pl. *-aat* coll. *fistiq.*
pistol - *musaddas* pl. *-aat, warwar* pl. *waraawur.*
piston - *ṗistin* pl. *-aat, ṗasaatin.*
pit - **1.** *manjam* pl. *manaajim.* No one was in the pit when the explosion occurred. *maζζad čaan bil-manjam min ṣaar l-infijaar.* **2.** *nuwaaya* pl. *-aat* coll. *niwa.* The boy swallowed an olive pit. *l-walad bilaε nuwaayat zeetuun.*
pitch - **1.** *zifit.* What's the difference between pitch and tar? *šinu l-farig been iz-zifit wil-giir?* **2.** *ðarba* pl. *-aat, šamra* pl. *-aat.* That was a good pitch. *haaði čaanat xooš ðarba.* **3.** *ζaalik, daamis.* It was pitch dark when we came home. *čaan ðalam daamis lumman jeena lil-beet.*
to pitch - **1.** *nuṣab (u naṣub) n-.* Where shall we pitch the tent? *ween ninṣub il-xeema?* **2.** *šumar (u šamur) n-.* Pitch it out of the window. *šmurha mniš-šibbaak.*
to pitch in - *tšallah (a tašalluh), šammar (u tašmiir) εann is-saaεid.* We pitched in and helped him. *tšallahna w-nizalna nεaawna.*
pitcher - *doolka* pl. *-aat.* Please get me a pitcher of water. *baḷḷa jiib-li doolka ṃaay.*
pitiable - *murθi.* He is in a pitiable condition. *ζaalta murθiya.* or **ζaalta yinriθii-lha.*
pitiful - *muʔlim, ʔaliim.* That was a pitiful sight. *ðaak čaan fadd manðar muʔlim.*
pity - **1.** *šafaqa.* I don't want your pity. *ma-ariid šafaqtak.* **2.** *ζasaafa.* It's a pity you can't come. *ζasaafa ma-tigdar tiji.* **3.** *ζeef.* It's a pity he is only seventeen, otherwise I could have employed him. *yaa ζeef εumra ṣbaaṭaεaš, w-ʔilla čaan šaġġaḷta.*
**She took pity on him. *gaḷubha nkisar εalee.*
to pity - *šifaq (i šafaqa) n- εala, riθa (i raθaaʔ) n- l-.* She doesn't want anyone to pity her.

ma-triid aḥḥad yišfiq εaleeha. -- I pity them. *ʔarθi l-ḥaalhum.*

place - *maḥall* pl. *-aat, makaan* pl. *-aat.* Please put it back in the same place. *ʔarjuuk rajjiεha b-nafs il-maḥall.* -- If I were in his place I wouldn't have done it. *loo b-makaana, ma-čaan sawweetha.* -- Do you know a good place to eat? *tuεruf fadd makaan zeen waaḥid yaakul bii?* -- Do you know the place where we stopped reading? *tuεruf il-maḥall il-wuṣalnaa bil-qiraaya?* -- What is the name of this place? *š-isim hal-maḥall?* -- How many places did you set at the table? *kam maḥall ḥaδ̣δ̣arit εal-meez?*
**Somebody ought to put him in his place. *fadd aḥḥad laazim ywaggfa εind ḥadda.*
**His heart is in the right place. *xooš ʔaadmi.* or *ʔadmi ṭayyib.* or *qaḷba naδ̣iif.*
in place of - *badaal, εiwaδ̣.* May I have another book in place of this one? *tismaḥ tinṭiini kitaab laax badaal haaδa?*
in the first place - *ʔawwalan, gabuḷ kullši.* In the first place, we can't leave until tomorrow. *gabuḷ kullši, ʔiḥna ma-nigdar niṭlaε ʔilla baačir.*
to place - **1.** *ḥaṭṭ, (u ḥaṭṭ) n-, wuδ̣aε (a waδ̣iε) n-, xalla (i txilli) t-.* Place the table next to the window. *ḥuṭṭ il-meeḥ ib-ṣaff iš-šibbaak.* **2.** *xalla (i) t-.* Place the guest of honor next to the host. *xalli δ̣eef iš-šaraf yamm ʔabu d-daεwa.* **3.** *εayyan (i taεyiin) t-.* We have placed all of our graduates. *εayyanna kull il-mitxarrjiin min εidna* or **ligeena l-kull il-mitxarrjiin šuğuḷ.* **4.** *wajjah (i tawjiih) t-.* A charge was placed against him. *fadd tuhma twajjihat δ̣idda.* **5.** *ʔalqa (i ʔilqaaʔ).* He placed the responsibility for the damage on the proper man. *ʔalqa masʔuuliyyat it-talaf εala l-faaεil il-ḥaqiiqi.* **6.** *tδakkar (a taδakkur).* I've met him before, but I can't place him. *ʔaani mlaagii gabuḷ, bass ma-ʔatδakkar minu huwwa.*

plague - *ṭaaεuun* pl. *ṭwaaεiin.*

plain - **1.** *sahil* pl. *suhuul.* There is a wide plain between the two mountain ranges. *ʔaku sahil waasiε been silsilteen ij-jibaal.* **2.** *baṣiiṭ* pl. *-iin, buṣaṭaaʔ.* They are plain people. *humma naas buṣaṭaaʔ.* -- We have a plain home. *εiddna beet baṣiiṭ.* **3.** *εtiyaadi*.* She is a plain-looking woman, but very intelligent. *haay waḥda malaamiḥha εtiyaadiyya, laakin kulliš δakiyya.* **4.** *waaδ̣iḥ. δ̣aahir.* It is quite plain that he is after her money.
**It is as plain as the nose on your face. *waaδ̣ḥa miθil εeen iš-šamis.*
**The ship now is in plain view. *l-baaxira hassa mbayyna.*
**I told him the plain truth. *git-la l-ḥaqiiqa miθil-ma hiyya.*

plan - **1.** *xariiṭa* pl. *xaraayiṭ, muxaṭṭaṭ* pl. *-aat, taṣmiim* pl. *taṣaamiim.* The plan for the new house is ready. *l-xariiṭa maal il-beet ij-jidiid ḥaaδ̣ra.* **2.** *xiṭṭa* pl. *xuṭaṭ, tadbiir* pl. *tadaabiir.* Have you made any plans yet for the future? *fakkarit ib-ʔay xuṭaṭ lil-mustaqbal loo baεad?* -- This is an excellent plan. *haaδa fadd tadbiir mumtaaz.* **3.** *mašruuε* pl. *mašaariiε.* They have great plans for beautifying the city. *εidhum mašaariiε δ̣aδ̣iima t-tajmiil il-madiina.* **4.** *manhaj* pl. *manaahij.* What are your plans for tomorrow? *šinu manhajak baačir?*
to plan - **1.** *rattab (i tartiib) t-, dabbar (u tadbiir) t-.* Our trip was carefully planned. *safratna čaanat kulliš zeena mrattba.* **2.** *naδ̣δ̣am (u tanδ̣iim) t-.* He doesn't know how to plan his time. *ma-yuεruf išloon ynaδ̣δ̣um wakta.* **3.** *sawwa (i) xariiṭa.* Who planned your house? *minu sawwa l-xariiṭa maal beetak?* **4.** *ṣammam (i taṣmiim) t-.* Who planned your garden for you? *minu ṣammam-lak il-ḥadiiqa maaltak?* **5.** *nuwa (i niyya) n-.* Where do you plan to spend the summer? *ween tinwi tigδ̣i ṣ-ṣeef?* **6.** *ḥisab (i ḥsaab) n- ḥsaab~, dabbar (u tadbiir) t- ʔamr~.* On the salary I get, I have to plan very carefully. *bir-raatib illi ʔastilma, ʔaani muδ̣ṭarr ʔaḥsib iḥsaabi b-digga.*
to plan on - *εtimad (i εtimaad) εala.* You'd better not plan on it. *ʔaḥsan-lak la-tiεtimid εalee.*

plane - **1.** *mustawa* pl. *-ayaat.* The discussion was not on a very high plane. *l-munaaqaša ma-čaanat εala mustawa kulliš εaali.* **2.** *randaj* pl. *ranaadij.* I borrowed a plane from the carpenter. *ṭlabit randaj imnin-najjaar.* **3.** *ṭiyyaara* pl. *-aat.* What sort of plane is this? *haṭ-ṭiyyaara min ʔay nooε?* **4.** *mustawi.* I studied plane geometry for two years. *drasit il-handasa l-mustawiya santeen.*
to plane - *ṣaffa (i tṣiffi) t-, δ̣irab (u δ̣arib) n- randaj, saawa (i taswiya) t-.* These boards have to be planed. *hal-looḥaat laazim tiṭṣaffa.*
to plane down - *randaj (i trindij) t-, saawa (i musaawaat) t-.* We'll have to plane the door down. We'll have to plane the door down. *laazim išwayya nrandij il-baab.*

planet - *kawkab sayyaar* pl. *kawaakib sayyaara.*

planned - *marsuum.* We'll carry out the project as planned. *raḥ-innaffiδ il-xuṭṭa miθil-ma marsuuma.*

plant - **1.** *nabaat* pl. *-aat, zariε.* What kind of plants are they? *humma min ʔay nooε imnin-nabaataat.* -- I water the plants every day. *ʔasgi z-zariε kull yoom.* **2.** *maεmal* pl. *maεaamil, maṣnaε* pl. *maṣaaniε.* The manager showed me around the plant. *l-ṃudiir farrajni εal-maεmal.*
to plant - **1.** *ziraε (a zariε) n-.* We planted flowers in our garden. *zraεna warid ib-ḥadiiqatna.* **2.** *šičax (i šačix) n-, rakkaz (i tarkiiz) t-.* The boy scouts planted the flag in the sand and put up their tents around it. *l-kaššaafa šičxaw il-εalam bir-ramuḷ w-nuṣbaw xayaamhum daayir daayra.* **3.** *xaššaš (i taxšiiš) t-, daxxal (i tadxiil, ʔidxaal) t-.* The teacher planted bad ideas in the students' minds. *l-muεallim xaššaš ib-εuquul iṭ-ṭullaab ʔaaraaʔ muu zeena.*
**They planted mines in the road to protect their retreat. *ʔalġimaw iṭ-ṭariiq ḥatta yiḥmuun taraajiεhum.*

plaster - **1.** *bayaaδ̣, juṣṣ.* The plaster on the wall is all cracked. *l-ibyaaδ̣ εal-ḥaayiṭ kulla mfaṭṭar.* **2.** *lazga* pl. *-aat.* The nurse applied a mustard plaster to my back. *l-mumarriδ̣a ḥaṭṭat lazgat xardal εala δ̣ahri.* **3.** *jiṗs.* Her arm is still in a plaster cast. *ʔiidha baεadha b-qaalab jiṗs.* -- This figure is made of plaster of Paris. *hat-timθaal imsawwa min jiṗs.*
to plaster - *bayyaδ̣ (i tibyaaδ̣) t-.* Have they finished plastering the walls yet? *xallṣaw tibyaaδ̣ il-iḥyaaṭiin loo baεad.*

plastic - *ṗlastik.*

plastic surgery - *jiraaḥat it-tajmiil.*

plate - **1.** *maaεuun* pl. *mwaaεiin.* There's a crack in the plate. *ʔaku faṭir bil-maaεuun.* **2.** *šikil* pl. *ʔaškaal.* The illustration is on Plate Three. *t-tawδ̣iiḥ εala šikil raqam itlaaθa.* **3.** *looḥa* pl. *-aat.* It's very difficult to get plates for this camera. *kulliš ṣaεub tinligi looḥaat il-hal-kaamira.* **4.** *ṭaxum* pl. *ṭxuum.* I didn't know she wore a plate. *ma-činit adri tilbas ṭaxum.* **5.** *ṗleeta* pl. *-aat.* The floor of the tank is one single plate. *gaaε taanki l-ṃaay iṗleeta wiḥda.*
to plate - *labbas (i talbiis) t-.* They make these knives of steel and then plate them with silver. *ysawwuun has-sičaačiin min fuulaaδ w-baεdeen ylabbisuuha bil-fuδ̣δ̣a.*

platform - **1.** *raṣiif* pl. *ʔarṣifa.* Let's meet on the railway platform. *xal-nitlaaga εala raṣiif il-maḥaṭṭa.* **2.** *dačča* pl. *-aat.* Back up the truck to the loading platform. *rajjiε it-tirak maalak il-daččat il-ḥimil.* **3.** *manaṣṣa* pl. *-aat.* There is a platform for the speaker in the front part of the room. *ʔaku manaṣṣa lil-xaṭiib bij-jiha l-ʔamaamiyya bil-ġurfa.* **4.** *masraḥ* pl. *masaariḥ, marsaḥ* pl. *maraasiḥ.* The speakers were all seated on the platform. *l-xuṭabaaʔ kaanaw qaaεdiin εal-masraḥ.*

platoon - *faṣiil* pl. *faṣaaʔil.*

platter - *balam* pl. *blaam.* The platter won't hold the whole melon. *l-balam ma-yilzam kull ir-raggiyya.*

plausible - *maεquul.* His explanation is plausible but I don't agree with him. *ʔiiδ̣aaḥaata maεquula bass ma-attifiq wiyyaa.*

play - **1.** *liεib.* The children are completely absorbed in their play. *l-ʔaṭfaal miltihiin bil-liεib tamaaman.* **2.** *tamθiiliyya* pl. *-aat.* I heard an amusing play on the radio in spoken Iraqi. *smaεit tamθiiliyya muδ̣ḥika bir-raadyo b-ḥači εiraaqi.* **3.** *masraḥiyya* pl. *-aat.* That company is going to perform three plays of Shakespeare this week. *hal-firqa raḥ-itquum ib-tamθiil iθlaθ masraḥiyyaat šakspiir hal-isbuuε.* **4.** *riwaaya* pl. *-aat.* We don't often get to see plays by professional actors here. *ma-da-yṣaadif inšuuf riwaayaat min qibal mumaθθiliin muḥtarifiin ihnaa.* **5.** *malεab.* The steering wheel has too much play. *s-sukkaan bii hwaaya malεab.*
to play - **1.** *liεab (a laεib) n-.* The children are playing in the garden. *j-jihaal da-yliεbuun*

bil-ḥadiiqa. -- We played for money. liεabna εala fluus. 2. dagg (i dagg) n-, εizaf (i εazif) n-. He plays the violin very well. ydugg kamanja kulliš zeen. 3. qaam (u qiyaam) ib-door, maθθal (i tamθiil) t-. Who is playing the lead? minu da-yquum ib-door il-baṭal? 4. štiġal (u šuġul), nεiraḍ (i εariḍ). What film is playing tonight? yaa filim da-yištiġul hal-leela? 5. δabb (i δabb) n-. He played his highest card. δabb ʔaεla waraqa b-iida. 6. sawwa (i taswiya). He played a joke on me. sawwa biyya nukta.

to play a role - 1. maθθal (i tamθiil) t-. They asked me to play the role of the Juliet in the play ṭilbaw minni ʔamaθθil juuleet bil-masraḥiyya. 2. liεab (a laεib) door. He played an important role in the negotiations. liεab door muhimm bil-mufaawaḍaat.

to play around - 1. ḍayyaε (i taḍyiiε) wakit. You've been playing around long enough. yikfi baεad itḍayyiε waktak. 2. εibaθ (a εabiθ), liεab (a laεib). Stop playing around with the radio. bass εaad, la-tiεbaθ bir-raadyo.

to play fair - ʔanṣaf (i ʔinṣaaf). He didn't play fair with me. ma-ʔanṣaf wiyyaaya.

to play up - ʔaḍhar (i ʔiḍhaar). He played up her good qualities. ʔaḍhar ṣifaatha z-zeena.

player - 1. laεuub pl. luwaaεiib. One of the players got hurt during the game. waaḥid imnil-luwaaεiib itʔaδδa ʔaθnaaʔ il-liεib. 2. mumaθθil pl. -iin. There was a party for the players after the play. caanat ḥafla lil-mumaθθiliin baεd it-tamθiil.

playground - malεab pl. malaaεib.

playing card - warqa pl. -aat.

plea - 1. ltimaas pl. -aat, rajaaʔ pl. -aat. He ignored my plea. ma-daar baal l-iltimaasi. 2. tawassul pl. -aat. All my pleas were in vain. kull tawassulaati raaḥat εabaθ.

to **plead** - 1. twassal (a tawassul), ltimas (i ltimaas), rija (u rajaaʔ). She pleaded with him to stay. twassalat bii yibqa. 2. traafaε (a taraafuε). I have retained the best lawyer in town to plead my case. liẓamit ʔaḥsam muḥaami bil-wlaaya ḥatta yitraafaε ib-daεuuti.

**Do you plead guilty? ʔinta muδnib ʔam laa?

pleasant - 1. laṭiif pl. -iin, luṭafaaʔ. She's a pleasant person. hiyya fadd waḥda laṭiifa. 2. mubhij. We spent a rather pleasant evening there. gḍeena hnaak fadd leela mubhija nawεan-ma. 3. saεiid. Good-bye! Have a pleasant trip! maεa s-salaama! ʔatmannaa-lak safra saεiida! 4. saarr. What a pleasant surprise! haay šloon mufaajaʔa saarra!

**It isn't pleasant for me to have to do this. yuʔsifni ʔan ʔaḍṭarr asawwiiha. or ma-yhuun εalayya ʔasawwiiha.

please - rajaaʔan, baḷḷa, luṭfan, min faḍlak, ʔarjuuk. Please shut the door. rajaaʔan sidd il-baab.

to please - 1. εijab (i ʔiεjaab) n-. How does this hat please you? šloon tiεijbak haš-šafqa? -- Do as you please. sawwi lli yεijbak. or **b-keefak. 2. ʔarḍa (i ʔirḍaaʔ). He's hard to please. huwwa fadd waaḥid ṣaεub ʔirḍaaʔa. 3. raḍḍa (i tarḍiya, triḍḍi) t-. You can't please the whole world. ma-tigdar itraḍḍi kull il-εaalam. 4. sarr (i suruur) n-. Your letter pleased me very much. maktuubak sarrni hwaaya.

to be pleased - kayyaf (i tkiyyif), nsarr (a nsiraar). He was pleased with it. kayyaf biiha.

pleasing - 1. laṭiif. He has a pleasing personality. εinda šaxṣiyya laṭiifa. 2. ḥilu. She has a pleasing voice. εidha ṣooṭ ḥilu.

pleasure - 1. laδδa pl. -aat. I get a lot of pleasure out of the work. ʔašεur ib-laδδa biš-šuġuḷ. or **ʔaltaδδ biš-šuġuḷ. 2. mitεa pl. mitaε. Watching him swim was a real pleasure. šoofta yisbaḥ čaanat mitεa lil-εeen. 3. lahu, haẓal. Business before pleasure. š-šuġuḷ gabḷ il-lahu. 4. suruur. We accepted their invitation to dinner with great pleasure. qibalna εaziimathum εal-εaša b-kull suruur.

**The pleasure is all mine. ʔaani l-mamnuun.

pleat - kasra pl. -aat, θanya pl. -aat. Do you want the dress with or without pleats? triidiin il-badla biiha kasraat loo laa?

to pleat - kassar (i tkissir) t-, θanna (i tθinni) t-. Are you going to pleat the skirt or leave it straight? ʔinti raayḥa tθanniin it-tannuura loo txalliiha εadla.

plebiscite - stiftaaʔ pl. -aat.

pledge - εahad pl. εuhuud. He didn't keep his pledge. ma-wufa b-εahda.

to pledge - 1. ʔaxaδ (u ʔaxiδ) εahad min. He pledged me to secrecy. ʔaxaδ εahad minni bil-kutmaan. 2. tεahhad (a taεahhud). I pledged to vote for him in the election. tεahhadit ʔanṭii ṣooṭi bil-intixaab.

plentiful - waafir, ġaziir, mabδuul.

plenty - 1. hwaaya, kθiir. You have plenty of time. εindak ihwaaya wakit. -- You have to get plenty of sleep. laaẓim itnaam ikθiir. 2. mitwaffir, hwaaya, kθiir. There is plenty of rice in the market. t-timman mitwaffir bis-suug.

pleurisy - δaat ij-janb.

pliable - layyin.

pliers - čillaabteen pl. -aat, ṗlaayis pl. -aat.

plight - waḍiε pl. ʔawḍaaε. We are aware of their plight and will do everything we can to help them. ʔiḥna nidri waḍiεhum w-raḥ-insawwi kull-ma nigdar εalee ḥatta nεaawinhum.

plot - 1. muʔaamara pl. -aat, dasiisa pl. dasaayis. The plot was discovered in time. l-muʔaamara nkišfat bil-waqt il-munaasib. 2. qiṭεa pl. qiṭaε, wuṣla pl. wuṣal. We bought a plot of land near the river. štireena qiṭεat gaaε εan-nahar. 3. silsila (pl. -aat) ḥawaadiθ. The story has an interesting plot. l-quṣṣa silsilat ḥawaadiθha mumtiεa.

plot of land (leased) - εaraṣa pl. -aat.

to plot - tʔaamar (a taʔaamur). They plotted against the government. tʔaamraw ḍidd il-ḥukuuma.

plow - miḥraaθ pl. maḥaariiθ. You need a heavier plow. tiḥtaaj miḥraaθ ʔaθgal.

to plow - ḥiraθ (i ḥariθ) n-, kirab (u karub, karaab) n-. I'll need all day to plow this field. ʔaḥtaaj ṭuul in-nahaar ḥatta ʔaḥriθ hal-ḥaqil.

to **pluck** - nitaf (i natif) n-. Did you pluck the chicken yet? ntafitha lid-dijaaja loo baεad?

plug - 1. qabaġ pl. -aat, saddaad pl. -aat. The sink needs a new plug. l-muṣlux yirraad-la qabaġ jidiid. 2. ṗlakk pl. -aat. Your car needs a new set of plugs. sayyaartak yinraad-ilha ṭaxum ṗlakkaat jidiid.

to plug - sadd (i sadd) n-. Plug the hole. sidd iz-ziruf. -- The pipe is plugged. l-buuri masduud.

to plug in - šakkal (i taškiil, tšikkil) ṗlakk. Plug in the fan. šakkil il-ṗlakk maal il-imhaffa.

plum - εinjaaṣa pl. -aat coll. εinjaaṣ.

plumber - ʔabu (pl. ʔahal) buuriyyaat.

plumb line - šaahuul pl. šwaahiil.

plump - matruus, θixiin. She is a little on the plump side. haay išwayya matruusa.

to **plunge** - 1. ġaṭṭ (u ġaṭṭ), ġiṭaṣ (u ġaṭiṣ). He plunged into the water. ġaṭṭ bil-ṃaay. -- When he heard the boy shouting in the river, he plunged in after him and pulled him out. min simaε il-walad da-yṣayyiḥ bin-nahar, ġiṭaṣ εalee w-jarra. 2. čayyat (i tčiyyit). He plunged into the burning house. čayyat bil-beet id-da-yiḥtirig. 3. ġaṭṭaṣ (i tġiṭṭiṣ). He plunged his hand into the cold water. ġaṭṭaṣ ʔiida bil-ṃaay il-baarid.

plural - jamiε pl. jumuuε. What is the plural of ''beet''? šinu jamiε "beet"?

broken plural - jamiε taksiir.

sound plural - jamiε saalim.

plus - zaayid, w-. Four plus three is seven. ʔarbaεa zaayid itlaaθa ysawwi sabεa.

plywood - xišab imεaakas.

pneumonia - δaat ir-riʔa.

pocket - jeeb pl. jyuub. Put this in your pocket. ḥuṭṭ haay ib-jeebak.

to pocket - ḍirab (u ḍarib) εala, laff (i laff). His partner pocketed all the profits. šariika ḍirab εalee kull il-ʔarbaaḥ.

pocketbook - 1. janṭat (pl. jinaṭ) ʔiid. The thief stole the pocketbook from the woman and ran away. l-ḥaraami baag janṭat il-ʔiid mnil-imrayya w-inhiẓam. 2. jizdaan pl. jizaadiin. He took out his pocketbook and gave me some change. ṭallaε jizdaana w-inṭaani xurda.

pocketknife - čaaquuča pl. čawaaqiič. May I borrow your pocketknife? ʔagdar aṭlub ič-čaaquuča maaltak?

podium - manaṣṣa pl. -aat. The conductor stepped up onto the podium. raʔiis il-firqa l-mawsiiqiyya ṣiεad εal-manaṣṣa.

poem - qaṣiida pl. qaṣaayid. This book contains all his poems. hal-iktaab yiḥwi kull qaṣaayda.

poet - šaaεir pl. šuεaraaʔ.

poetry - šiεir pl. ʔašεaar. My brother writes beautiful poetry. ʔaxuuya yinḍum šiεir badiiε.

point - 1. *nabbuula* pl. *-aat.* I broke the point of my pencil. *kisarit nabbuult il-qalam maali.* **2.** *raas* pl. *ruus, ṭaraf* pl. *ʔaṭraaf.* I broke the point of my knife. *kisarit raas is-siččiina maalti.* **3.** *nuqṭa* pl. *nuqaṭ.* Our team scored 23 points. *fariiqna sajjal itlaaθa w-εišriin nuqṭa.* -- We have gone over the contract point by point. *dirasna l-εaqid nuqṭa nuqṭa.* -- Women are his weak point. *n-nisaaʔ nuqṭat iδ̣-δ̣uεuf εinda.* **4.** *l-maqṣuud, beet il-qaṣiid, qaṣid.* You missed the point. *faatak il-maqṣuud.* or *faatak beet il-qaṣiid.* **5.** *mawδ̣uuε* pl. *mawaaδ̣iiε.* That is beside the point. *haaδa xaarij il-mawδ̣uuε.* **6.** *ʒadd* pl. *ʒduud.* I can understand it up to a certain point. *ʔagdar aftihimha ʔila ʒadd muεayyan.* **7.** *naaʒiya* pl. *nawaaʒi, maziyya* pl. *mazaaya.* He has good points, too. *εinda nawaaʒi* or *bii mazaaya.* **8.** *muujib.* There is no point in getting there before they open the doors. *ma-aku muujib inkuun ihnaak gabuḷ-ma yiftaʒuun il-baab.* **9.** *markaz* pl. *maraakiz.* The police set up their strong point at the entrance to the city. *š-šurṭa ʒaṭṭaw markaz quwwathum ib-madxal il-madiina.*
**Come to the point and stop beating about the bush. *guul il-ʒaqiiqa w-la-tδ̣ull tithazzam.*

on the point of - *εala wašak.* We were on the point of leaving when company arrived. *činna εala wašak da-niṭlaε min joona xuṭṭaar.*

point of view - 1. *wajhat* (pl. *-aat*) *naδ̣ar.* Our points of view differ. *wajhaat naδ̣arna tixtilif.* **2.** *jiha* pl. *-aat, naaʒiya* pl. *nawaaʒiyya.* From this point of view he's right. *min haj-jiha huwwa muʒiqq.*

to the point - *biṣ-ṣamiim, muṣiib.* His comments are always to the point. *taεliiqaata daaʔiman biṣ-ṣamiim.*

to make a point of - *ʒaṭṭ (u ʒaṭṭ) εal-baal~.* Make a point to be on time. *ʒuṭṭ εala baalak itkuun εal-wakit.*

to point - 1. *šaar (i ʔišaara) n-, ʔaššar (i taʔšiir) t-.* The arrow points north. *s-sahim yšiir liš-šimaal.* -- Point to the man you mean. *ʔaššir εar-rijjaal illi tiεnii.* -- Point out the place you told me about. *ʔaššir εal-makaan illi git-li εanna.* **2.** *dall (i tdilli) n-, dalla (i tdilli) t-.* All the signs point towards a cold winter. *kull il-maδ̣aahir itdill εala šita baarid.* **3.** *wajjah (i tawjiih) t-.* Don't point the gun at me! *la-twajjih il-bunduqiyya εalayya!*

pointed - 1. *mnabbal, ʒaadd.* Be careful with that pointed stick. *diir baalak min hal-εaṣaaya l-imnabbla.* **2.** *ʒaadd.* She's always making pointed remarks. *hiyya daaʔiman itεalliq taεliiqaat ʒaadda.*

poise - *razaana, ttizaan.* She never loses her poise. *ʔabadan ma-tifqud razaanta.*

poised - *raziin.* She is very poised for her age. *kulliš raziina bin-nisba l-εumurha.*

poison - 1. *simm, samm* pl. *smuum.* Don't touch it, it's a poison. *la-ṭṭuxxa, haaδa simm.* **2.** *saamm.* They're using poison gases in their war against the royalists. *yistaεmiluun ġaazaat saamma b-ʒarubhum δ̣idd il-malakiyyiin.*

to poison - 1. *samm (i samm) n-.* Our dog has been poisoned. *čalibna nsamm.* **2.** *sammam (i tasmiim) t-.* Our dog got poisoned from eating rotten meat. *čalibna tsammam min ʔakal laʒam jaayif.*

poisonous - *saamm, musimm.*

to **poke -** *naġġ (u naġġ) n-.* He'll wake up if you poke him. *yigεud ʔiδa tnuġġa.*

poker - *ṗookar.* Do you know how to play poker? *tuεruf tilεab ṗookar?*

polar - *quṭbi*.* This is a polar bear. *haaδa dibb quṭbi.*

pole - 1. *mardi* pl. *maraadi.* The water was so shallow they had to use the pole to push the boat. *l-ṃaay čaan kulliš δ̣aʒil iδ̣ṭarraw yistaεmiluun il-mardi l-dafε il-balam.* **2.** *εamuud* pl. *εawaamiid, ʔaεmida.* The car hit a telephone pole. *s-sayyaara δ̣urbat εamuud talafoon.* **3.** *zaana* pl. *-aat.* The pole broke just as he went over the bar. *nkisrat iz-zaana min da-yugmuz foog il-εaariδ̣a.* **4.** *quṭub* pl. *ʔaqṭaab.* How cold does it get at the poles? *šgadd iṭṣiir baarda bil-quṭbeen?*

to pole - *mašša (i tmišši) bil-mardi.* In the marshes they pole the boats from one place to another. *bil-ʔahwaar ymaššuun il-mašaaʒiif bil-mardi min mukaan il-mukaan.*

police - *šurṭa.*

to police - *xufar (u xafar) n-.* The streets are well-policed. *š-šawaariε zeen maxfuura.*

police blotter - *sijil waqaaʔiε iš-šurṭa.*

policeman - *šurṭi* pl. *šurṭa.*

police station - 1. *markaz* (pl. *maraakiz*) *šurṭa.* Where is the nearest police station? *ween ʔaqrab markaz šurṭa?* **2.** *maxfar* (pl. *maxaafir*) *šurṭa.* There is a police station halfway between the two villages. *ʔaku maxfar iš-šurṭa b-nuṣṣ iṭ-ṭariiq illi been il-qariiteen.*

policy - *siyaasa* pl. *-aat.* I make it a policy to be on time. *min siyaasti ʔan ʔakuun εal-wakit.* -- We can't support his policy. *ma-nigdar inʔayyid siyaasta.* **2.** *εaqid* pl. *εuquud.* Don't let your life-insurance policy lapse. *la-txalli εaqd it-taʔmiin maalak itfuut muddta.*

polish - 1. *ṣubuġ* pl. *ʔaṣbaaġ.* I need some brown polish for my new shoes. *ʔaʒtaaj išwayya ṣubuġ qahwaaʔi l-ʒiδaaʔi j-jidiid.* **2.** *ṣaqil, tahδiib.* He needs a little more polish. *yiʒtaaj išwayya ṣaqil baεad.*

to polish - 1. *lammaε (i talmiiε) t-, ṣiqal (i ṣaqil) n-.* I haven't polished the furniture yet. *baεad ma-lammaεit il-ʔaθaaθ.* -- The silver needs polishing. *l-fuδ̣δ̣iyyaat tiʒtaaj talmiiε.* **2.** *ṣubaġ (u ṣabuġ) n-.* I didn't have time to polish my shoes. *ma-ṣaar εindi wakit ʔaṣbuġ qundarti.*

polite - *mujaamil, muʔaddab.* He's not very polite. *huwwa muu mujaamil kulliš.*

political - *siyaasi*.* Do you belong to any political party? *ʔinta mintimi l-ʔay ʒizib siyaasi?*

politician - *siyaasi* pl. *-iyyiin.*

politics - *siyaasa.* I'm not interested in politics. *s-siyaasa muu šuġḷi.* or *s-siyaasi ma-thimmni.*

pollen - *ṭaliε.*

to **pollinate -** *laggaʒ (i talgiiʒ) t-.* Date palms are pollinated by hand. *n-naxal yitlaggaʒ bil-ʔiid.*

polls - *markaz intixaabi* pl. *maraakiz intixaabiyya.*

to **pollute -** *lawwaθ (i talwiiθ) t-, naggas (i tangiis) t-.* First we must find what is polluting the water in the well. *ʔawwalan laazim inšuuf šinu lli da-ylawwiθ il-ṃaay bil-ḅiir.*

polygamy - *taεaddud iz-zawjaat.*

pomegranate - *rummaana* pl. *-aat* coll. *rummaan.*

pond - *burka* pl. *burak, buʒayra* (pl. *-aat*) *ṣġayyra.*

pool - 1. *burka* pl. *burak.* The police found him lying in a pool of blood. *š-šurṭa ligata majṭuul ib-burkat damm.* **2.** *ʒooδ̣* pl. *ʒwaaδ̣.* The new pool has improved the appearance of our garden. *l-ʒooδ̣ ij-jidiid ʒassan manδ̣ar ʒadiiqatna.* **3.** *ṗuul, bilyaard.* Do you play pool? *tilεab ṗuul?*

swimming pool - *ʒooδ̣* (pl. *ʔaʒwaaδ̣*) *sibaaʒa, masbaʒ* pl. *masaabiʒ.* They have a very large swimming pool. *εidhum ʒooδ̣ sibaaʒa čbiir.*

poor - 1. *faqiir* pl. *fuqaraaʔ, fuqra, fuqaara.* He is well-known for his generosity to the poor. *huwwa kulliš maεruuf ib-karama εal-fuqaraaʔ.* -- Many poor people live in this neighborhood. *hwaaya naas fuqra yεiišuun ib-hal-manṭiqa.* **2.** *miskiin* pl. *masaakiin; xaṭiyya.* The poor fellow is blind. *l-miskiin ʔaεma.* **3.** *duuni*.* This is poor soil for raising wheat. *haaδi turba duuniyya l-ziraaεat il-ʒunṭa.* **4.** *δ̣aεiif* pl. *δ̣iεaaf.* He's very poor in arithmetic. *huwwa kulliš δ̣aεiif bil-ʒisaab.* **5.** *rakiik* pl. *rkaak.* That was a poor article in today's paper. *δiič čaanat fadd maqaala rakiika b-jariidat il-yoom.*

poorly - **She was poorly dressed. *libisha mbahdal.* -- **The book is poorly written. *l-kitaab rakiik.* -- **His business was doing so poorly he has decided to sell out. *šuġḷa čaan muu zeen ʔila daraja qarrar yṣaffii.*

to do poorly - *tdahwar (a tduhwur).* He's doing poorly after the operation. *ṣiʒʒta tdahwurat wara l-εamaliyya.*

to **pop - 1.** *ṭagg (u ṭagg).* The balloon popped. *n-nuffaaxa ṭaggat.* **2.** *ṭagṭag (i ṭagṭaga).* Come listen; the corn's popping! *taεaal ismaε; l-ʔiδra da-ṭṭagṭig!*

Pope - *ṗaaṗa, ḅaaba.*

poppy - *xišxaaša* pl. *-aat* coll. *xišxaaš.*

popular - 1. *šaεbi*.* They played only popular songs. *qaddimaw ʔaġaani šaεbiyya bass.* **2.** *maʒbuub.* He's very popular with the masses. *huwwa kulliš maʒbuub imnij-jamaahiir.* **3.** *šaayiε, daarij.* That's a popular notion, but it's wrong. *haaδa fadd raʔi šaayiε laakin ġalaṭ.*
**It's a very popular restaurant. *haaδa fadd maṭεam εalee hwaaya rijil.*

populated - *ʔaahil, maʔhuul, maskuun.* This area is

not populated. *hal-manṭiqa maa maʔhuula.*

population – *sukkaan, nifuus.* The population has doubled in the last twenty years. *tðaaƐaf Ɛadad is-sukkaan bil-Ɛišriin sana l-ʔaxiira.*

porcelain – *ṣiini*.* We gave her a tea set of fine porcelain. *nṭiinaaha ṭaxum maal čaay imniṣ-ṣiini l-faaxir.*

porch – *ṭarma* pl. *-aat, ṭaraami.*

porcupine – *gunfuð* pl. *ganaafuð.*

pore – *masaama* pl. *-aat, masaam.* The dust got into the pores and caused inflammation. *l-Ɛajaaj xašš bil-masaamaat w-sabbab iltihaab.*

pork – *laẓam xanẓiir.*

port – *miinaaʔ* pl. *mawaani.* The ship is at anchor in the port. *l-baaxira ðaabba ʔangar bil-miinaaʔ.*

portable – *safari*.* I want to buy a portable typewriter. *ʔariid ʔaštiri ʔaalat ṭaabiƐa safariyya.*

porter – *ẓammaal* pl. *-iin, ẓmaamiil.* Can I call you a porter? *ʔagdar ʔaṣiiẓ-lak ẓammaal?*

portion – **1.** *qisim* pl. *ʔaqsaam, juziʔ* pl. *ʔajzaaʔ.* A large portion of the city was destroyed by fire. *qisim čibiir imnil-madiina tdammar bin-naar.* **2.** *wuṣla* pl. *wuṣal, qiṭƐa* pl. *qiṭaƐ.* Just give me a small portion of meat and a vegetable. *bass inṭiini wuṣla ṣġayyra mnil-laẓam w-fadd xuðra.*

Portugal – *burtuġaal.*

Portugese – *burtuġaali** pl. *-iyyiin.*

pose – *waðƐiyya* pl. *-aat.* Let's try another pose to make sure we have a good picture. *xalli njarrub waðƐiyya lux ẓatta nitʔakkad iṣ-ṣuura zeena.*

to pose – *ʔaxað (u ʔaxið) waðƐiyya.* They posed for the photographer in front of the fountain. *ʔaxðaw waðƐiyya lil-muṣawwir giddaam il-naafuura.* -- The photographer posed me like this. *l-muṣawwir xallaani ʔaaxuð hiič waðƐiyya.*

to pose a question – *ʔaθaar (i ʔiθaara) suʔaal.* I'll pose the questions, and you answer them. *ʔaani ʔaθiir il-ʔasʔila w-inta jaawubha.*

position – **1.** *waðiƐ* pl. *ʔawðaaƐ, waðƐiyya* pl. *-aat.* I'm not in a position to pay right now. *ʔaani muu b-waðiƐ ʔagdar adfaƐ hassa.* **2.** *mawqif* pl. *mawaaqif.* This places me in a very difficult position. *haay itẓuṭṭni b-mawqif ẓarij.* -- What is your position on this subject? *šinu mawqifak ib-hal-mawðuuƐ?* **3.** *markaz* pl. *maraakiz, maqaam* pl. *-aat.* A man in your position has to be careful of his appearance. *rajul ib-maqaamak laazim yihtamm ihwaaya b-maðhara.* -- He was accused of using his position as director for his own personal interests. *ntiham b-istiġlaal markaza ka-mudiir il-muṣlaẓta l-xaaṣṣa.* -- Our army has abandoned the forward positions. *jeešna txalla Ɛan il-maraakiz il-ʔamaamiyya.* **4.** *waðiifa* pl. *waðaayif, manṣab* pl. *manaaṣib.* He has a good position with a wholesale house. *Ɛinda waðiifa kulliš zeena b-maẓall beeƐ bij-jumla.*

positive – **1.** *mitʔakkid.* I'm positive that he was there. *ʔaani mitʔakkid huwwa čaan ihnaak.* **2.** *ʔiijaabi*.* The Arab policy is one of positive neutrality in world affairs. *siyaasat il-Ɛarab hiyya l-ẓiyaad il-ʔiijaabi biš-šuʔuun il-Ɛaalamiyya.* **3.** *bil-ʔiijaab.* I expect a positive answer. *ʔatwaqqaƐ jawaab bil-ʔiijaab.*

positively – **1.** *bit-taʔkiid.* Do you know it positively? *tuƐrufa bit-taʔkiid?* **2.** *ẓaqiiqatan.* This is positively awful. *haay ẓaqiiqatan faðiiƐa.* -- The way she talks is positively vulgar. *ʔamma ẓaqiiqatan tiẓči b-ʔadabsizz luġiyya.*

to **possess** – *milak (i muluk) n-, mtilak (i mtilaak).* That's all I possess. *haaða kull-ma ʔamlik.*

**What possessed you to do that? *š-jaak w-sawweet haay?*

possession – *ẓiyaaza, mulkiyya.* How long has that been in your possession? *šgadd ṣaar-ilha b-ẓiyaaztak?*

**They lost all their possessions. *fuqdaw kull-ma yimilkuun* or *fuqdaw kull il-čaan Ɛidhum* or *xiṣraw il-ʔaku wil-maaku.*

to take possession – *stilam (i stilaam), ʔaxað (u ʔaxið) ẓiyaaza.* The new owner hasn't taken possession of the house yet. *l-maalik ij-jidiid baƐad ma-stilam il-beet.*

possibility – *ẓtimaal* pl. *-aat.* I see no other possibility. *ma-ašuuf ʔaku ʔay iẓtimaal ʔaaxar.*

possible – *mumkin.* Call me, if possible. *xaaburni, ʔiða mumkin.* or *xaaburni, ʔiða b-imkaanak.*

possibly – *mumkin, min il-mumkin.* Could you possibly call me? *mumkin itxaaburni?*

post – **1.** *Ɛamuud* pl. *Ɛawaamiid, ʔaƐmida.* We need new posts for our fence. *niẓtaaj Ɛawaamiid jidiida lil-imẓajjar maalna.* **2.** *mawqiƐ* pl. *mawaaqiƐ, mawðiƐ* pl. *mawaaðiƐ.* A good soldier never deserts his post. *j-jundi z-zeen mustaẓiil yitruk mawðiƐa.* **3.** *mukaan* pl. *-aat, ʔamaakin.* This ambassador has served in numerous posts. *has-safiir xidam ib-ʔamaakin mutaƐaddida.*

to post – **1.** *waggaf (u twugguf) t-, ẓaṭṭ (u ẓaṭṭ) n-.* Post two men at each exit. *wagguf rijjaaleen ib-kull maẓall xuruuj.* **2.** *Ɛallag (i taƐliig) t-.* Post the sign on the wall. *Ɛallig il-ʔiƐlaan Ɛal-ẓaayiṭ.* -- The order has been posted since yesterday. *l-qaraar ṣaar-la mƐallag imnil-baarẓa.*

postage – **1.** *ʔujrat (pl. ʔujuur) bariid.* How much is the postage on a registered letter? *šgadd ʔujrat il-bariid Ɛala maktuub musajjal?* -- There is postage due on this letter. *hal-maktuub ʔujurta naaqṣa.* **2.** *ṭawaabiƐ.* The letter didn't have enough postage. *l-maktuub ma-čaan Ɛalee ṭawaabiƐ kaafya.*

postal rate – *ʔujrat (pl. ʔujuur) bariid; rasim (pl. rusuum) bariid.*

post card – *poost kaard* pl. *-aat, biṭaaqa* pl. *-aat, kaart* pl. *-aat.* Did you get my post card? *stilamt il-biṭaaqa maalti?*

to be **posted** – *ṭṭilaƐ (i ṭṭilaaƐ).* He's pretty well posted. *haaða muṭṭaliƐ zeen.* -- Keep me posted! *xalliini Ɛala ṭṭilaaƐ.* or *xalliini Ɛala mustamirr.* or *xalliini Ɛala Ɛilim.*

poster – *ʔiƐlaan (pl. -aat) diƐaaya.*

postman – *poosṭači* pl. *-iyya; muwazziƐ (pl. -iin) bariid.*

postmark – *xatim (pl. ʔaxtaam) bariid; ṭamġa* pl. *-aat.* The postmark is illegible. *xatm il-bariid ma-yinqiri.*

to postmark – *xitam (i xatim) n-, ṭumaġ (u ṭamuġ) n-, ṣaqqaṭ (i taṣqiiṭ) t-.* The letter was postmarked May fifteenth. *l-maktuub maxtuum xumuṣṭaƐaš maayis.*

post office – *daaʔirat (pl. dawaaʔir) bariid, poosṭa* pl. *-aat.* We have five post offices. *Ɛidna xamis dawaaʔir bariid.* -- The post office is open from nine to six. *l-poosṭa maftuuẓa mnit-tisƐa lis-sitta.*

post-office box – *ṣanduuq (pl. ṣanaadiiq) bariid.*

to **postpone** – *ʔajjal (i taʔjiil) t-, ʔaxxar (i taʔxiir) t-, Ɛawwag (i taƐwiig) t-.* I can't postpone the appointment. *ma-aqdar aʔajjil il-mawƐid.*

posture – *wagfa* pl. *-aat.* She has poor posture. *wagfatha ma-ẓilwa.*

pot – *jidir* pl. *jduur.* There is a pot of soup on the stove. *ʔaku jidir šoorba Ɛaṭ-ṭabbaax.*

potato – *puteetaaya* pl. *-aat* coll. *puteeta.*

potential – **1.** *muẓtamal.* We must consider him a potential enemy. *laazim niƐtabra Ɛadu muẓtamal.* **2.** *qudrat ʔintaaj.* The industrial potential of our country is enormous. *qudrat il-ʔintaaj iṣ-ṣinaaƐiyya d-dawlatna haaʔila.* **3.** *kaamin.* Water has great potential power. *l-maay bii quwwa kaamina haaʔla.* **4.** *stiƐdaad, qaabliyya.* He has the potential to become a good engineer. *Ɛinda qaabliyya ʔan yiṣbaẓ muhandis mumtaaz.*

potentiality – *ʔimkaaniyya.*

potter – *faxxaar* pl. *-iin, kawwaaz* pl. *-iin.*

pottery – *xazaf.*

poultry – *ṭiyuur daajina.*

pound – *paawan* pl. *-aat.* The metric pound is a bit more than the American pound. *l-paawan il-matri šwayya ʔazyad imnil-paawan il-ʔamriiki.* How much is the English pound in American money? *šgadd yiswa l-paawan il-ʔingiliizi bif-filuus il-ʔamriiki?*

**An ounce of prevention is worth a pound of cure. *dirham wiqaaya xayrun min qinṭaar Ɛilaaj.*

to pound – **1.** *dagg (u dagg) n-.* We pounded on the door for five minutes before they heard us. *daggeena Ɛal-baab muddat xamis daqaayiq gabuḷ-ma samƐoona.* -- I wish our upstairs neighbors wouldn't pound kubba at seven in the morning. *ʔatmanna loo ðoola l-gaaƐdiin foogaana ma-ydugguun kubba saaƐa sabƐa ṣ-ṣubuẓ.* **2.** *xufaq (u xafaqaan), dagg (u dagg).* His heart was pounding with anxiety. *galba čaan da-yuxfuq imnil-qalaq.*

to **pour** – **1.** *ṣabb (u ṣabb) n-, daar (i deer).* Please pour me a cup of coffee. *ʔarjuuk ṣubb-li fadd kuub gahwa.* **2.** *tdaffaq (a tadaffuq).* The water was pouring out of the faucet. *l-maay čaan da-yitdaffaq imnil-buuri.* **3.** *zaxx (u zaxx).* It's pouring out. *da-tzuxx barra.*

**The crowd was just then pouring out of the theater. *j-jamaahiir čaanaw da-yṭilƐuun* *imnis-siinama fadd ṭalεa.*

to pour off – *čabb (i čabb) n- min.* Pour the water off of the rice. *čibb il-ṃaay imnit-timman.*

to pour out – **1.** *čabb (i čabb) n-.* Pour out the water and fill the glass with milk. *čibb il-ṃaay w-itrus il-iglaaṣ bil-ʒaliib.* **2.** *šika (i šakwa).* She poured out her troubles to me. *šikat-li hmuumha.*

poverty – *fuqur, εooz.* He is living in great poverty. *da-yεiiš ib-fuqur mudqaε.*

poverty-stricken – *faqiir* pl. *fuqaraaʔ, fuqra fuqaara.*

powder – **1.** *poodra.* You've got too much powder on your nose. *ʔaku hwaaya poodra εala xašmič.* **2.** *masʒuuq* pl. *masaaʒiiq.* What is that white powder in this bag? *šinu hal-masʒuuq il-ʔabyað̣ ib-hač-čiis?* **3.** *baaruud.* There is enough powder here to blow up the whole town. *ʔaku hnaa baaruud kaafi l-nasf il-madiina b-kaamilha.*

to powder – **1.** *siʒan (a saʒin) n-.* The pharmacist powdered some tablets and put the powder in capsules. *ṣ-ṣaydali siʒan čam ʒabbaaya w-xalla l-masʒuuq bil-kapsuulaat.* **2.** *ʒaṭṭ (u ʒaṭṭ) n- poodra εala.* She powdered her nose. *ʒaṭṭat poodra εala xašimha.*

power – **1.** *quwwa* pl. *-aat, ṭaaqa* pl. *-aat.* The machine is operated by electrical power. *l-makiina tištuğuḷ bil-quwwa l-kahrabaʔiyya.* -- The power has been turned off. *l-quwwa ngiṭεat.* -- The purchasing power is improving. *l-quwwa š-širaaʔiyya da-titʒassan.* **2.** *stiṭaaεa, ʔimkaan, quwwa, ṭaaqa.* I will do everything in my power. *raʒ-asawwi kull-ma b-istiṭaaεti.* or ***raʒ-asawwi kull-ma yiṭlaε min ʔiidi.* **3.** *ṣalaaʒiyya* pl. *-aat.* Parliament has complete power in this matter. *l-barlamaan εinda ṣalaaʒiyya taamma b-hal-mawð̣uuε.* **4.** *ʒukum.* How long has this party been in power? *hal-ʒizib išgadd ṣaar-la bil-ʒukum?* **5.** *ṣayṭara.* He lost all power on his followers. *fuqad kull ṣayṭara εala ʔatbaaεa.* **6.** *ṣulṭa, nufuuð.* He wields a lot of power. *εinda nufuuð čibiir.*

to come into power – *ʔija (i majiiʔ) lil-ʒukum.* When did the Republicans come into power? *j-jumhuuriyyiin šwakit ʔijaw lil-ʒukum?*

powerful – *qawi** pl. *-iyyiin, ʔaqwiyaaʔ.* He has a powerful voice. *εinda ṣawṭ qawi.*

powerless – **I'm sorry, but I'm powerless in this matter. *mitʔassif laakin maa b-ʔiidi šii b-hal-qað̣iyya.*

practical – *εamali*.* That isn't very practical. *haay muu kulliš εamaliyya.*

practically – **1.** *b-ṣuura εamaliyya, εamaliyyan.* You have to look at things practically. *laazim tinð̣ur lil-ʔumuur ib-ṣuura εamaliyya.* **2.** *taqriiban.* We're practically there. *taqriiban wuṣalna.*

practice – **1.** *tamriin.* I need more practice. *ʔaʒtaaj tamriin baεad.* -- Practice makes perfect. *t-tamriin ywaṣṣil lil-ittiqaan.* **2.** *εaada* pl. *-aat.* I've made it a practice to get to work on time. *ṣaarat εaada εindi ʔaruuʒ lid-daaʔira εal-wakit.* **3.** *taṣarruf* pl. *-aat.* They complained of his dictatorial practices. *štikaw min taṣarrufaata d-diktaatooriyya.*

**Dr. Ali has a wide practice. *d-diktoor εali εinda myraajiεiin ihwaaya.*

in practice – *εamaliyyan, bil-εamal, bit-taṭbiiq.* It is easy in theory, but difficult in practice. *hiyya sahla nað̣ariyyan laakin ṣaεba εamaliyyan.* -- He put his theory into practice. *wuð̣aε nað̣ariita mawð̣aε it-taṭbiiq.*

to practice – **1.** *tdarrab (a tadarrub), tmarran (a tamarrun).* He's practicing on the piano. *da-yitdarrab εal-ipyaano.* **2.** *maaras (i mumaarasa), zaawal (i muzaawala).* How long has he been practicing medicine? *šgadd ṣaar-la ymaaris iṭ-ṭibb?* **3.** *ṭabbaq (i taṭbiiq).* I wish he would practice what he preaches. *yaa reet yṭabbuq illi yguula.*

praise – *madiʒ, θanaaʔ.* The praise went to his head. *l-madiʒ kabbar raasa.*

to praise – **1.** *midaʒ (a madiʒ), ʔaθna (i θanaaʔ) εala.* Everybody praises his work. *j-jamiiε yiθnuun εala šuğḷa.* **2.** *ʒimad (i ʒamid) n- b-.* I don't want to praise myself, but. . . *ma-ariid ʔaʒmid ib-nafsi, laakin. . .* --

**He praised her to the skies. *ṣaεεadha lis-samawaat.*

prank – *nukta* pl. *nukat, ʒiila* pl. *ʒiyal.* That's a silly prank. *haay mukta saxiifa.* -- They played a prank on me. *sawwaw biyya nukta.*

to **pray** – **1.** *ṣalla (i ṣalaat).* Moslems are expected to pray five times a day. *mafruuð̣ bil-muslimiin yṣalluun xams awqaat bil-yoom.* **2.** *diεa (i duεaaʔ) n-.* I'll pray for you. *raʒ-ʔadεii-lak.*

prayer – *ṣalaa, ṣalaat* pl. *ṣalawaat; daεwa* pl. *-aat, duεaaʔ* pl. *ʔadεiya.*

to **preach** – **1.** *wuεað̣ (a waεið̣) n-.* I heard him preach at the mosque in the month of Ramadhan. *simaεta yooεað̣ bij-jaamiε ib-šahar ramað̣aan.* **2.** *baššar (i tabšiir) t- b-.* The prophet first preached the Islamic religion to the people of Mecca. *r-rasuul baššar bid-diyaana l-ʔislaamiyya l-ʔahil makka bil-ʔawwal.*

preacher – *waaεið̣* pl. *wuεεaað̣, xaṭiib* pl. *xuṭabaaʔ.*

precaution – *ʒtiyaaṭ* pl. *-aat.* You should take better precautions against fire. *laazim tittixið iʒtiyaaṭaat ʔaʒsan ð̣idd in-naar.*

to **precede** – *sibaq (i sabiq) n-.* A strange silence preceded the storm. *huduuʔ ġariib sibaq il-εaaṣifa.*

to give **precedence** – *badda (i tbiddi) t-, qaddam (i taqdiim) t-.* I gave him precedence over myself. *baddeeta εala nafsi.*

precedent – *saabiqa* pl. *sawaabiq.* This will constitute a dangerous precedent. *haaða yšakkil saabiqa xaṭra.*

precepts – *furuuð̣, taεaaliim.* He follows the precepts of Islam implicitly. *yittibiε furuuð̣ il-ʔislaam ib-ʒaðaafiirha.*

precious – **1.** *θamiin, nafiis.* He gave me a very precious gift. *nṭaani hadiyya kulliš θamiina.* **2.** *ġaali, εaziiz.* Your friendship is precious to me. *ṣadaaqtak ġaalya εindi.* **3.** *kariim.* Emeralds are precious stones. *z-zumurrad ʒajar kariim.*

precipitation – **1.** *suquuṭ il-muṭar.* What's the average annual precipitation in this area? *šgadd muεaddal suquuṭ l-muṭar is-sanawi b-hal-manṭiqa?* **2.** *raasib.* What's this white precipitation in this bottle? *šinu har-raasib il-ʔabyað̣ ib-hal-buṭul?* **3.** *tarassub.* When precipitation is over take it off the fire. *baεad-ma yikmil it-tarassub šiila min in-naar.*

precise – **1.** *daqiiq.* He is very precise in his work. *huwwa kulliš daqiiq ib-šuğḷa.* **2.** *bið̣-ð̣abuṭ.* Those were his precise words. *haay čaanat kalimaata bið̣-ð̣abuṭ.*

precisely – **1.** *b-ṣuura daqiiqa.* Translate this precisely. *tarjum haaða b-ṣuura daqiiqa.* **2.** *bið̣-ð̣abuṭ.* That is precisely what I had in mind. *haaða bið̣-ð̣abuṭ nafs iš-šii l-čaan εala baaḷi.*

precision – **1.** *diqqa, ð̣abuṭ.* The measurements must be taken with precision. *l-qiyaasaat laazim tinnixið ib-diqqa.* **2.** *daqiiq.* This company specializes in the manufacturing of precision instruments. *haš-šarika mitxaṣṣiṣa b-ṣunε il-ʔaalaat id-daqiiqa.*

predecessor – *salaf* pl. *ʔaslaaf.*

predestination – *qaðaaʔ w-qadar.*

to **predict** – *tnabbaʔ (a tanabbuʔ) b-, tkahhan (a takahhun) b-.* He predicted this. *tnabbaʔ ib-haaða.*

prediction – *nubuuʔa* pl. *-aat.*

predominant – *ġaalib.* Red is the predominant color for cars this year. *l-ʔaʒmar huwwa l-loon il-ġaalib ib-sayyaaraat has-sana.*

preface – *muqaddima* pl. *-aat.*

to **prefer** – *fað̣ð̣al (i tafð̣iil) t-.* I prefer the brand I've been using. *ʔafað̣ð̣il in-nawε illi da-astaεmila.* -- I prefer brunettes to blondes. *ʔafað̣ð̣il is-sumur εaš-šuqur.*

preference – *ʔafð̣aliyya* pl. *-aat, ʔaqdamiyya* pl. *-aat.* I don't give preference to anyone. *ma-anṭi ʔafð̣aliyya l-ʔaʒʒad.*

**I have no preference. *ma-aku fariq.* or *kulla siwa.* or *ma-tufruq εindi.*

pregnancy – *ʒabal* pl. *-aat, ʒbaala* pl. *-aat.* How many pregnancies have you had? *čam iʒbaala ṣaarat εindič?* or ***čam baṭin jibti?*

pregnant – *ʒibla, ʒaamil.*

to become pregnant – *ʒibal (a ʒabil).* She became pregnant a year after we were married. *ʒiblat baεad sana min itzawwajna.*

prejudice – **1.** *taʒayyuz* pl. *-aat, taʒazzub* pl. *-aat.* So far as I can see he hasn't any prejudices at all. *ʒasib-ma ʔašuuf maa εinda ʔay taʒayyuzaat ʔabadan.* **2.** *taεaṣṣub.* Prejudice and ignorance are hard to combat. *t-taεaṣṣub wij-jahil ṣaεub itʒaarubhum.*

prejudiced – **1.** *mitʒayyiz* pl. *-iin, mitʒazzib* pl. *-iin.* The judge is obviously prejudiced in the case. *l-qaað̣i mnil-waað̣iʒ mitʒayyiz bid-daεwa.* **2.** *mitεaṣṣib* pl. *-iin.* He is prejudiced against the new ways. *huwwa mitEaṣṣib ṣidd it-taqaaliid il-ʒadiiθa.*

preliminary - *tamhiidi**, *btidaaʔi**. This is just a preliminary investigation. *haaδa bass taʒqiiq tamhiidi.*

premature - *gabuḷ ʔawaan-.* I am afraid that step was premature. *ʔaxša hal-xaṭwa čaanat gabuḷ ʔawaanha.*

premier - **1.** *raʔiis* (pl. *ruʔasaaʔ*) *wuzaraaʔ.* The Premier is scheduled to speak to Parliament tomorrow. *l-muqarrar yuxṭub raʔiis il-wuzaraaʔ bil-barlamaan baačir.* **2.** *ʒafla* (pl. *-aat*) *ftitaaʒiyya.* We attended the premier of the film in a body. *ʒiṣarna l-ʒafla l-iftitaaʒiyya lil-filim ib-limmatna.*

premium - *qiṣiṭ* pl. *ʔaqṣaaṭ.* I have to pay the premium on the insurance policy. *laazim ʔadfaE il-qiṣiṭ maal Eaqd it-taʔmiin.*

preparation - **1.** *taʒṣiir* pl. *-aat, stiEdaad* pl. *-aat.* The preparations for the trip took us a week. *l-istiEdaadaat lis-safra ṭawwilat Eidna sbuuE.* -- The plans are still in a state of preparation. *l-xiṭaṭ baEadha b-door it-taʒṣiir.* **2.** *tahayyuʔ, taʔahhub, taʒṣiir, stiEdaad.* War preparation consumes a large part of the budget. *t-tahayyuʔ lil-ʒarub yistahlik qisim kabiir imnil-miizaaniyya.*

to **prepare** - **1.** *ʒaṣṣar (i taʒṣiir) t-, staEadd (i stiEdaad).* Did you prepare for tomorrow's exam? *staEaddeet lil-imtiʒaan maal baačir.* **2.** *hayyaʔ (i tahiyyiʔ).* Have the nurse prepare the patient for the operation. *xalli l-mumarriṣa thayyiʔ il-mariiṣ lil-Eamaliyya.* -- You had better prepare him for the shock first. *gabuḷ kullši ʔaʒsan-lak ithayyiʔa liṣ-ṣadma.* -- Prepare for the worst. *hayyiʔ nafsak il-ʔaswaʔ il-iʒtimaalaat.*

prepared - **1.** *ʒaaṣir* pl. *-iin, mistiEidd* pl. *-iin.* We are prepared to do whatever you suggest. *ʔiʒna ʒaaṣriin insawwi lli tiqtarʒa.* **2.** *jaahiz, ʒaaṣir.* The papers are all prepared except for the signature. *l-ʔawraaq kullha jaahza maa Eada t-tawqiiE.*

preposition - *ʒaruf* (pl. *ʒuruuf*) *jarr.*

to **prescribe** - *wuṣaf (i waṣuf) n-.* The doctor prescribed these pills for me. *ṭ-ṭabiib wuṣaf-li hal-ʒubuub.*

prescription - *waṣfa* pl. *-aat, raačeeta* pl. *-aat.*

presence - **1.** *ʒuṣuur.* The document has to be signed in your presence. *l-waθiiqa laazim titwaqqaE ib-ʒuṣuurak.* **2.** *wujuud.* They resented the presence of the foreign army strongly. *Eaarṣaw wujuud ij-jeeš il-ʔajnabi b-šidda.*

presence of mind - *surEat xaaṭir-.* I admire your presence of mind. *tiEjibni surEat xaaṭrak.*

present - **1.** *hadiyya* pl. *hadaaya.* Did you give him a present for his birthday? *nṭeeta hadiyya b-munaasabat Eiid miilaada.* **2.** *ʒaaṣir.* We live in the present, not in the past. *ʔiʒna nEiiš bil-ʒaaṣir muu bil-maaṣi.* **3.** *mawjuud* pl. *-iin, ʒaaṣir* pl. *-iin.* All of his friends were present. *kull ʔaṣdiqaaʔa čaanaw mawjuudiin.* **4.** *ʒaali**. In my present position I can't do anything else. *b-waṣEi l-ʒaali ma-agdar asawwi ʔay šii ʔaaxar.*

at present - *ʒaaliyyan, bil-waqt il-ʒaali.* They aren't working at present. *ma-yištağluun ʒaaliyyan.*

for the present - *l-hassa, l-ʔaan, muwaqqatan.* That will be enough for the present. *haay tikfi l-hassa.* -- We are out of pencils for the present. *l-iqlaam xalṣaana muwaqqatan.*

to present - **1.** *qaddam (i taqdiim) t-.* The ambassador is going to present his credentials tomorrow. *s-safiir raʒ-yqaddim ʔawraaq iEtimaada baačir.* **2.** *ṭallaE (i taṭliiE), xilaq (u xaliq).* Each case presents new difficulties. *kull qaṣiyya Eala ʒida ṭṭalliE mašaakil jidiida.* **3.** *Eiraṣ (u Eariṣ) n-.* Why don't you present the facts as they are? *leeš ma-tiEruṣ il-ʒaqaayiq miθil-ma hiyya.*

to present with - *hida (i ʔihdaaʔ) n-.* The company presented him with a gold watch. *š-šarika hidata saaEa δahab.*

to **preserve** - **1.** *ʒaafaṣ (i muʒaafaṣa), ṣaan (u ṣiyaana) n-.* I did this in order to preserve my dignity. *sawweet haaδa ʒatta ʔaʒaafuṣ Eala karaamti.* **2.** *ʔabqa (i ʔibqaaʔ).* We are trying to preserve what is left. *da-nʒaawil il-ʔibqaaʔ Eal-baqiyya l-baaqya.* **3.** *ʒufaṣ (u ʒafuṣ) n-.* The refrigerator will preserve the meat until we can use it. *θ-θallaaja tuʒfuṣ il-laʒam ʔila ʔan nigdar nistaEmila.*

preserved - **1.** *maʒfuuṣ.* The specimens are preserved in formaldehyde solution in the laboratory. *n-namaaδij maʒfuuṣa b-maʒluul il-formaldahaayd bil-muxtabar.* **2.** *mʒaafuṣ Eala.* The house is well-preserved. *l-beet imʒaafuṣ Ealee zeen.*

preserves - *mrabba* pl. *-ayaat.*

to **preside** - *traʔʔas (a taraʔʔus).* Ali presided over the meeting. *Eali traʔʔas ij-jalsa.*

president - **1.** *raʔiis* pl. *ruʔasaaʔ.* He has been appointed president of the board of directors. *tEayyan raʔiis il-majlis il-ʔidaara.* -- The President of the republic announced the formation of a new cabinet. *raʔiis ij-jamhuriyya ʔaElan taškiil wuzaara jidiida.* **2.** *muʒaafiṣ* pl. *-iin.* He was president of the Central Bank. *čaan muʒaafiṣ il-bang il-markazi.*

press - **1.** *ṣaʒaafa.* Will the press be admitted to the conference? *raʒ-yusmaʒ liṣ-ṣaʒaafa tiʒṣar il-muʔtamar?* **2.** *maṭbaEa* pl. *maṭaabuE.* The manuscript is ready to go to press. *l-mibyaṣṣa jaahza truuʒ lil-maṭbaEa.* **3.** *makbas* pl. *makaabis.* Can you operate a date press? *tigdar itšağğul makbas tumuur?* **4.** *miEṣaara* pl. *-aat.* I operate this fruit-juicing press. *ʔaani ʔašağğil hal-miEṣaara maal fawaakih.*

**The film had a good press. *l-filim inmidaʒ bij-jaraayid.*

in the press - *taʒt iṭ-ṭabuE.* The book is still in the press. *l-iktaab baEda taʒt iṭ-ṭabuE.*

to press - **1.** *ṣurab (u ṣarub) n- ʔuuti.* They pressed my suit nicely. *ṣurab il-qaaṭ maali xooš ʔuuti.* **2.** *daas (u doos) n-.* Press the button. *duus iz-zirr.* **3.** *Eaṣṣar (i taEṣiir) t-.* They pressed the grapes and fermented them. *Eaṣṣiraw il-Einab w-xammiroo.* **4.** *kibas (i kabis) n-, čibas (i čabis) n-.* This is where the cured dates are pressed and packaged. *haaδa l-makaan illi ykibsuun bii t-tamur w-yʒuṭṭuu bil-ṗaakeetaat.* **5.** *ṣayyaq (i taṣyiiq) Eala.* His creditors are pressing him. *d-dayyaana da-yṣayyquun Ealee.* **6.** *laʒʒ (i ʔilʒaaʒ) b-.* I wouldn't press the matter any further, if I were you. *loo b-makaanak ma-aliʒʒ bil-mawṣuuE baEad.* **7.** *ṣiğaṭ (u ṣağiṭ) Eala.* The party is pressing the President to appoint him to the Commission. *l-ʒizib da-yuṣğuṭ Eala r-raʔiis ʒatta yEayyina bil-hayʔa.*

to press together - *daas (u doos) n-, raṣṣ (u raṣṣ) n-.* Press the peppers together tightly so you can get them all in the pot. *duus il-filfil ib-quwwa ʒatta tigdar itdaxxil kullhum bij-jarra.*

presser - *ʔuutači* pl. *-iyya.* I worked as a presser for five years. *štiğalit ʔuutači l-muddat xams isniin.*

pressing - *mustaEjal.* I have a pressing engagement. *Eindi mawEid mustaEjal.*

pressure - *ṣağiṭ.* We work under constant pressure. *ništuğuḷ taʒat ṣağiṭ mustamirr.*

to put pressure on - *ṣiğaṭ (u ṣağiṭ) n- Eala, laʒʒ (i ʔilʒaaʒ).* We'll have to put pressure on him. *laazim inliʒʒ Ealee.*

prestige - *maqaam, hayba, makaana.* He has great prestige. *Einda maqaam Eaali.*

to **presume** - *tṣawwar (a taṣawwur), ṣann (u ṣann).* I presume he is at home. *ʔaṭṣawwar huwwa bil-beet.*

to **pretend** - **1.** *ddiEa (i ddiEaaʔ), ziEam (i zaEim).* He pretended that he was a doctor. *ddiEa ʔanna ṭabiib.* **2.** *tṣaahar (a taṣaahur).* He's just pretending! *haaδa da-yiṭṣaahar!*

**He pretended not to know a thing about it. *sawwa nafsa ma-yuEruf ʔay šii Eanha.*

pretense - **1.** *ddiEaaʔ* pl. *-aat.* His pretense fooled no one. *ddiEaaʔa ma-xidaE ʔaʒʒad.* **2.** *ʒiila* pl. *ʒiyal, taṣaahur* pl. *-aat.* His illness is only a pretense. *maraṣa ma-huwwa ʔilla ʒiila.*

pretext - *Euδur* pl. *ʔaEδaar, ʒijja* pl. *ʒijaj.* He's just looking for a pretext. *huwwa da-ydawwur-la fadd Euδur.*

pretty - **1.** *ʒilu.* She's a very pretty girl. *hiyya fadd ibnayya kulliš ʒilwa.* **2.** *xooš.* That's a pretty mess! *ʔamma haay xooš xarbaṭa.* **3.** *laa baʔis b-.* It tastes pretty good. *ṭaEamha laa baʔis bii.*

**He's sitting pretty. *haaδa mayya biṣ-ṣadir.*

pretty much - *taqriiban.* He eats pretty much everything. *yaakul kullši taqriiban.* -- It's pretty much the same. *hiyya nafs iš-šii taqriiban.*

to **prevail** - **1.** *jira (i jari), miša (i maši).* This custom still prevails. *hal-Eaada baEadha maašya.* **2.** *saad (u siyaada).* This opinion prevails at the moment. *har-raʔi ysuud bil-waqt il-ʒaaṣir.*

to prevail over - *tğallab (a tağallub) Eala.* The opinion of the majority prevailed over the desires of the minority. *raʔi l-ʔakθariyya tğallab Eala*

raġbaat il-ʔaqalliyya.
    to prevail upon – qannaɛ (i taqniiɛ) t-. Can't we prevail upon you to come along? ma-raz-nigdar inqanniɛak tiji wiyyaana?
to prevent – minaɛ (a maniɛ) n-. The police prevented the crowd from entering. š-šurṭa minɛaw in-naas imnid-dixuul.
preventive – wiqaaʔi*. My son has decided to specialize in preventive medicine. ʔibni qarrar yitxaṣṣaṣ biṭ-ṭibb il-wiqaaʔi.
previous – saabiq, maaḍi. I met him on a previous visit. tɛarrafit bii b-ziyaara saabqa. -- He has no previous experience in that field. ma-ɛinda xibra saabiqa b-hal-miidaan.
previously – saabiqan, min gabuḷ.
prey – ġaniima pl. ġanaayim. He is an easy prey for dishonest schemers. haaḏa ġaniima baarda b-iid il-zayyaaliin.
price – 1. siɛir pl. ʔasɛaar. The prices are very high here. l-ʔasɛaar kulliš mirtafɛa hnaa. 2. θaman pl. ʔaθmaan. I wouldn't do that for any price. ma-asawwi haaḏa mahma kaan iθ-θaman.
    **I want it regardless of price. ʔariida mahma kallaf.
    to price – 1. saɛɛar (i tasɛiir) t-, saam (u soom) n-. This merchant prices his goods too high for me. hat-taajir ysaɛɛir baṣaayɛa kulliš ġaali ɛalayya. 2. ɛaamal (i muɛaamala) ɛala. I priced this radio in several stores. ɛaamalit ɛala har-raadyo b-ɛiddat mazallaat.
to prick – čakk (u čakk) n-, niġaz (u naġiz) n-. I pricked my finger with a pin. čakkeet ʔiṣibɛi b-danbuus.
    to prick up – šantar (i šantara). The horse pricked up his ears. l-izṣaan šantar ʔiiḏaana.
prickly heat – zaṣaf.
pride – 1. ɛizza. Don't you have any pride in yourself? maa ɛindak ʔay ɛizzat nafis? -- It is a matter of national pride. haay masʔalat ɛizza qawmiyya. 2. faxar. He is the pride of his school. haaḏa faxar madrasta. 3. ʔanafa, kibriyaaʔ. His pride is unbearable. kibriyaaʔa ma-tinzimil.
    to take pride – ftixar (i ftixaar), ɛtazz (a ɛtizaaz). He takes great pride in his work. huwwa hwaaya yiɛtazz ib-šuġla.
    to pride oneself on – tbaaha (a tabaahi) b-. She prides herself on her good cooking. titbaaha b-ṭabixha z-zeen.
priest – qass, qissiis pl. -iin, qasaawusa, qissaan; xuuri pl. -iyya, xawaarna.
priesthood – kahanuut. He is going to enter the priesthood. raz-yidxul il-kahanuut.
primarily – bil-ʔaṣil, bid-daraja l-ʔuula, ʔawwalan ʔaṣliyyan. I am primarily a clerk, but I work as a driver. ʔaani bil-ʔaṣil kaatib w-laakin ʔaštuġuḷ ka-saayiq. -- This is primarily a matter for the court. haay bid-daraja l-ʔuula šuġḷat il-mazkama.
primary – 1. raʔiisi*, ʔasaasi*. His primary objective is profit. hadafa r-raʔiisi huwwa r-ribiz. 2. ʔawwali*. The primary elections will be held next month. l-intixaabaat il-ʔawwaliyya raz-itṣiir iš-šahr ij-jaay. 3. btidaaʔi*. He hasn't even completed primary school. huwwa ma-kammal zatta l-madrasa l-ibtidaaʔiyya.
prime – 1. mumtaaz, faaxir, xooš. This butcher sells only prime meat. hal-gaṣṣaab ybiiɛ lazam mumtaaz bass. 2. ɛizz, zahra. He died in the prime of life. maat ib-zahrat il-ɛumur.
prime minister – raʔiis (pl. ruʔasaaʔ) wuzaraaʔ.
primitive – bidaaʔi*. Primitive societies lived on hunting. l-mujtamaɛaat il-bidaaʔiyya ɛaašat ɛaṣ-ṣeed. -- The gufa is a primitive type of water transportation. l-guffa nawɛ bidaaʔi min il-muwaaṣalaat il-maaʔiyya.
primus stove – preemis pl. -aat.
prince – ʔamiir pl. ʔumaraaʔ.
princess – ʔamiira pl. -aat.
principal – 1. mudiir pl. mudaraaʔ. The principal called the teachers into his office. l-mudiir jimaɛ il-muɛallimiin ib-ġurufta. 2. mablaġ ʔaṣli pl. mabaaliġ ʔaṣliyya. Have you paid anything on the principal? dfaɛit šii mnil-mablaġ il-ʔaṣli. 3. ʔasaasi, raʔiisi*. The principal cause of the delay is lack of money. s-sabab ir-raʔiisi lit-taʔxiir huwwa ɛadam wujuud il-ifluus.
principality – ʔimaara pl. -aat. We have a branch office in the principality of Bahrein. ɛidna daaʔira farɛiyya b-ʔimaarat il-bazreen.

principle – 1. qaaɛida pl. qawaaɛid. I make it a principle to save some money every month. sawweetha qaaɛida ʔawaffur fadd mablaġ kull šahar. 2. mabdaʔ pl. mabaadiʔ. He is a man of principles. haaḏa waaziz zaazib mabdaʔ.
    a matter of principle – ka-mabdaʔ, ka-qaaɛida. I don't do such things as a matter of principle. ka-mabdaʔ, ma-asawwi hiiči ʔašyaaʔ.
print – 1. ṭabuɛ. The print in this book is too small. ṭ-ṭabuɛ ib-hal-iktaab kulliš naaɛim. 2. baṣma pl. -aat, ṭabɛa pl. -aat. The prints left by his fingers were found on the doorknob. baṣmaat ʔaṣaabɛa nligat ɛala yaddat il-baab. 3. ʔaθar pl. ʔaaθaar. It was easy to follow his footprints in the sand. čaan imnis-suhuula taɛaqqub ʔaaθaar ʔaqdaama ɛar-ramul. 4. nusxa pl. nusax. How many prints shall I make of each picture? kam nusxa ʔaṭalliɛ min kull ṣuura. 5. rasim maṭbuuɛ pl. rusuum maṭbuuɛa. The museum has a fine collection of prints. l-matzaf bii xooš majmuuɛa mnir-rusuum il-maṭbuuɛa. 6. mnaqqaš. You always look good in a print. ʔinti daaʔiman tiṭlaɛiin zilwa b-nafnuuf imnaqqaš.
    to print – ṭubaɛ (a ṭabuɛ) n-. We can print them for you for twenty fils per page. nigdar niṭbaɛ-lak-iyyaahum ib-ɛišriin filis iṣ-ṣaziifa. -- The letter was printed in yesterday's paper. l-maktuub inṭubaɛ ib-jariidat il-baarza.
    **Print your name. ʔiktib ismak ib-zuruuf minfaṣla.
printed matter – maṭbuuɛaat. What are the postage rates for printed matter? šgadd il-ʔujra il-bariidiyya ɛal-maṭbuuɛaat.
printer – ṭabbaaɛ pl. -iin.
print shop – maṭbaɛa pl. maṭaabiɛ.
prior – 1. gabuḷ. Prior to the war the cost of living was much lower. gabḷ il-zarub takaaliif il-maɛiiša čaanat ihwaaya ʔaqall. 2. saabiq. Have you had any prior experience in this type of work? ɛindak xibra saabqa b-han-nooɛ šuġuḷ.
priority – 1. ʔasbaqiyya, ʔafḍaliyya. This job has priority over the others. haš-šaġla ʔilha ʔasbaqiyya ɛal-baaqi. 2. tawjiib. It is our policy to give priority to regular customers. tawjiib il-miɛaamiil il-ɛittag min siyaasatna.
prism – manšuur pl. manaašiir.
prison – 1. sijin pl. sujuun. The prison is heavily guarded. s-sijin ɛalee ziraasa qawiyya. 2. zabis. The court sentenced him to five years in prison. l-mazkama zukmat ɛalee bil-zabis xams isniin.
prisoner – sajiin pl. sujanaaʔ, masjuun pl. masaajiin, mazbuus pl. mazaabiis. A prisoner has just escaped. fadd sajiin hastawwa nhizam.
    prisoner of war – ʔasiir pl. ʔusaraaʔ, ʔasra.
    to take prisoner – ʔassar (i taʔsiir) t-. We took the wounded soldier prisoner. ʔassarna j-jundi l-majruuz.
private – 1. jundi pl. junuud. I was a private in the second world war. činit jundi bil-zarub il-ɛaalamiyya θ-θaanya. 2. xaaṣṣ. This is my private property. haaḏa mulki l-xaaṣṣ. 3. xuṣuuṣi*, xaaṣṣ. Do you have a single room with a private bath? ɛindak ġurfa biiha zammaam xuṣuuṣi?
    in private – ɛala nfiraad. I'd like to talk to you in private. ʔard azči wiyyaak ɛala nfiraad.
privates – ɛawra pl. -aat. Do not expose your privates under any circumstances. la-tikšif ɛawurtak ib-ʔay zaal min l-azwaal.
privation – zirmaan.
privilege – 1. mtiyaaz pl. -aat. He was deprived of all privileges. nziram min kull il-imtiyaazaat. 2. zaqq pl. zuquuq. If you want to leave, it's your privilege. ʔiḏa triid itruuz, haaḏa zaqqak.
    **It would be a privilege to do this for you. ʔakuun mamnuun ʔaquum-lak ib-hal-xidma. or ysurrni ʔasawwi-lak haaḏa.
prize – jaaʔiza pl. jawaaʔiz. Who won the first prize? minu ribaz ij-jaaʔiza l-ʔuula?
probability – ztimaal pl. -aat. That is well within the bounds of probability. haaḏa jiddan ḍimin niṭaaq il-iztimaal.
probable – muztamal. It might be possible, but it is not very probable. haay mumkina bass muu kulliš muztamala.
probably – mnil-muztamal. You'll probably meet him on the train. mnil-muztamal raz-itlaagii bil-qiṭaar.
    most probably – ʔaġlab iḏ-ḏann. Most probably he is the one that should be blamed for it. ʔaġlab iḏ-ḏann huwwa lli laazim yinlaam ɛaleeha.

probation - *tajruba.* He is still on probation. *baɛda tazt it-tajruba.*
problem - **1.** *muškila* pl. *mašaakil.* We all have our problems. *kullatna ɛidna mašaakilna.* -- That's your problem. *haaδi muškila txuṣṣak ʔinta.* **2.** *masʔala* pl. *masaaʔil.* I couldn't solve the second problem. *ma-gdart azill il-masʔala θ-θaanya.*
problematical - *muškil.*
procedure - **1.** *ʔuṣuul.* What is the usual procedure? *šinu l-ʔuṣuul il-muttabaɛa?* **2.** *ʔijraaʔ* pl. *-aat.* The procedures for terminating the services of an employee are in this directive. *l-ʔijraaʔaat il-ʔinhaaʔ xadamaat muwaδδaf mawjuuda b-han-niδaam.*
to **proceed** - **1.** *stamarr (i stimraar), miša (i maši).* They have decided to proceed according to the original plan. *ṣammimaw ɛala ʔan yistimirruun zasb il-xiṭṭa l-marsuuma.* -- Then he proceeded to talk about the differences in the two dialects. *baɛad δaalik istamarr yizči ɛan il-xilaaf bil-lahijteen.* **2.** *daawam (i dawaam).* We stopped the car to look at the view and then proceeded on our way. *waggafna s-sayyaara l-mušaahadat il-manδar w-baɛdeen daawamna b-seerna.* **3.** *kammal (i takmiil) t-.* Let's proceed with the class. *xalli nkammil id-daris.*
proceeding - *ʔijraaʔ* pl. *-aat.* I watched the proceedings with great interest. *laazaδit seer il-ʔijraaʔaat ib-šooq ɛaδiim.*
proceeds - *waaridaat, ʔiiraad.* The proceeds will go to charity. *l-waaridaat itruuz lil-xayraat.*
process - **1.** *ṭariiqa* pl. *ṭuruq.* Our engineers have developed a new process. *muhandisiinna ṭallɛaw ṭariiqa jidiida.* **2.** *ɛamaliyya* pl. *-aat, muɛaamala* pl. *-aat.* That will be a long drawn-out process. *haay raz-itkuun ɛamaliyya ṭuwiila.*
to process - *ṣaffa (i taṣfiya) t-.* This refinery can process enough oil to cover our internal gasoline needs. *hal-maṣfa yistaṭiiɛ yṣaffi kammiyyat nafuṭ itsidd zaajatna d-daaxiliyya mnil-banziin.* **The consulate is going to process your visa. *l-qunṣuliyya raz-tijri muɛaamalat il-viiza maaltak.*
procession - **1.** *mawkib* pl. *mawaakib.* The procession of the President and his official guest will pass through this street. *mawkib ir-raʔiis w-ḍeefa r-rasmi raz-ymurr min haš-šaariɛ.* **2.** *zaffa* pl. *-aat.* The wedding procession will leave from the restaurant at seven o'clock. *z-zaffa raz-tiṭlaɛ imnil-maṭɛam saaɛa sabɛa.* **3.** *janaaza* pl. *-aat.* All of his old friends walked in his funeral procession. *kull ʔaṣdiqaaʔa l-ɛittaq mišaw ib-janaazta.*
to **proclaim** - *ʔaɛlan (i ʔiɛlaan).* They proclaimed the 14th of July a holiday. *ʔaɛlinaw yoom ʔarbaṭaɛaš tammuuz ɛuṭla.*
proclamation - *ʔiɛlaan* pl. *-aat, balaaġ* pl. *-aat.*
to **procure** - *zaṣṣal (i tazṣiil) t-.* They hired me to procure fresh vegetables and meat for them from local sources. *staxdimooni zatta ʔazaṣṣil-ilhum xuδrawaat w-lazam taaza mnil-maṣaadir il-mazalliyya.*
produce - *mazṣuul* pl. *-aat, mazaaṣiil.* The farmers sell their produce on market day. *l-fallaziin ybiiɛuun mazṣuulaathum ib-yoom il-gaɛda.*
to produce - **1.** *ʔantaj (i ʔintaaj).* We don't produce enough grain to cover our needs. *ma-nintij zubuub kaafya tsidd zaajatna.* **2.** *ṭallaɛ (i taṭliiɛ) t-.* How many cars do they produce a month? *čam sayyaara yṭallɛuun biš-šahar.* **3.** *ʔabraz (i ʔibraaz).* Can you produce any written proof? *tigdar tibriz fadd daliil xaṭṭi?*
product - *mantuuj* pl. *-aat.* This company is getting ready to put a new product on the market. *haš-šarika da-tistiɛidd il-tanziil mantuuj jidiid lis-suug.*
production - *ʔintaaj* pl. *-aat.*
productive - *muntij, muθmir.* He's a very productive writer. *huwwa fadd kaatib kulliš muntij.*
profession - **1.** *mihna* pl. *mihan, zirfa* pl. *ziraf.* My son is preparing himself for the legal profession. *ʔibni da-yhayyiʔ nafsa l-mihnat il-muzaamaat.* **2.** *silk.* He is in the teaching profession. *huwwa b-silk it-taɛliim.*
professional - **1.** *muztarif* pl. *-iin, mumtahin* pl. *-iin.* He's a professional gambler. *huwwa fadd qumarči muztarif.* **2.** *ṣaazib mihna* pl. *ʔaṣzaab mihan.* All of our friends are professional people. *kull ʔaṣdiqaaʔna min ʔaṣzaab il-mihan.*
professor - *ʔustaaδ* pl. *ʔasaatiδa, proofisoor* pl. *-iyya.*
proficiency - When I applied for the job, they gave me a proficiency test in typing. *lamma qaddamit ɛal-waδiifa, ʔinṭooni mtizaan kafaaʔa biṭ-ṭibaaɛa.*
proficient - *baariɛ.* How long did it take you to become proficient in English? *šgadd ʔaxaδak ʔila ʔan ṣirit baariɛ bil-ingiliizi?*
to become proficient - *biraɛ (a baraaɛa).* You can't expect to become proficient in typing and shorthand in a month. *la-tintiδir tibraɛ biṭ-ṭibaaɛa wil-ixtizaal xilaal šahar.*
profit - **1.** *ribiz* pl. *ʔarbaaz.* I sold it at a profit. *biɛitha b-ribiz.* **2.** *faaʔida* pl. *fawaaʔid, maksab* pl. *makaasib.* I don't expect to get any profit out of that. *ma-atwaqqaɛ ʔay faaʔida min waraaha.*
to make a profit - *ribaz (a ribiz).* He makes a profit of at least 10% on every item. *yirbaz ɛala l-ʔaqall ɛašra bil-miyya ɛala kull silɛa.*
to profit - *ntifaɛ (i ntifaaɛ) stafaad (i stifaada).* Did you profit much from the lecture? *stafaadeet ihwaaya mnil-muzaaδara?* **One profits from his mistakes. *l-waazid yitɛallam min ʔaġlaaṭa.*
profitable - *murbiz, mufiid, naafiɛ.* Is it a profitable business? *haš-šaġla murbiza?*
profound - *ɛamiiq.* He had a profound influence on me. *čaan ʔila taʔθiir ɛamiiq ɛalayya.*
profusion - *kuθra.* There is a profusion of roses blooming in the garden. *ʔaku kuθra b-ward ij-juuri mfattaz bil-zadiiqa.*
program - **1.** *manhaj* pl. *manaahij.* The program sells for a dirham. *l-manhaj da-yinbaaɛ ib-dirham.* -- What's on our program tonight? *šinu manhajna hal-leela?* **2.** *barnaamij* pl. *baraamij.* How did you like the program? *šloon ɛijabak il-barnaamij?*
progress - *taqaddum.* The students are making good progress. *t-talaamiiδ da-yṣiir ɛidhum taqaddum mazsuus.* -- Are you making any progress with your book? *da-yṣiir ɛindak ʔay taqaddum b-iktaabak?*
to progress - **1.** *tzassan (a tazassun).* You've progressed a lot in the six weeks I've been away. *ʔinta hwaaya tzassanit xilaal il-ʔasaabiiɛ is-sitta lli ġibit biiha.* **2.** *tqaddam (a taqaddum), traqqa (a triqqi).* Our country has progressed fast during the past few years. *baladna tqaddam sariiɛ xilaal is-sanawaat il-ʔaxiira.* **3.** *tqaddam (a taqaddum).* We progressed slowly toward the enemy. *tqaddamna b-buṭuʔ ɛala l-ʔaɛdaaʔ.*
progressive - *mitjaddid* pl. *-iin, mitqaddim* pl. *-iin, mitdarrij* pl. *-iin.* He's a progressive teacher. *huwwa muɛallim mitjaddid.*
progressively - *bit-tadriij.* The war grew progressively worse. *l-zarub saaʔat bit-tadriij.*
to **prohibit** - **1.** *minaɛ (a maniɛ) n-.* The law prohibits smoking here. *l-qaanuun yimnaɛ it-tadxiin ihnaa.* **2.** *zarram (u tazriim) t-.* The Moslem religion prohibits alcoholic drinks. *l-ʔislaamiyya zarramat šurb il-xamur.*
project - *mašruuɛ* pl. *mašaariiɛ.* We're working on a project together. *da-ništuġuḷ suwa b-fadd mašruuɛ.*
to project - **1.** *ɛiraδ (u ɛaruδ) n-.* The film was projected on the wall. *l-filim inɛiraδ ɛal-zaayiṭ.* **2.** *ṭilaɛ (a ṭuluuɛ), biraz (i bariz, buruuz).* The rear end of our new car projects one foot out of our garage. *muʔaxxar sayyaaratna j-jidiida yiṭlaɛ qadam waazid imnil-garaaj.*
projector - *prujaktar* pl. *-aat.*
to **prolong** - *ṭawwal (i taṭwiil) t-.* You are only prolonging the agony. *ʔinta bass da-ṭṭawwil il-ɛaδaab.*
prominent - *baariz, muɛtabar.* He's a prominent artist. *huwwa fannaan baariz.* -- He has a prominent chin. *ɛinda fadd zinič baariz.*
promise - **1.** *waɛad* pl. *wuɛuud.* You didn't keep your promise. *ma-wuffeet ib-waɛdak.* **2.** *ʔamal, tabaašiir.* There is some promise of change. *ʔaku ʔamal bit-taġyiir.*
to promise - *wuɛad (a waɛad), niṭa (i naṭi) n- kalaam.* We promised him a present. *wuɛadnaa b-hadiyya.* -- Promise me that you won't do it again. *ʔooɛidni ʔan ma-tsawwiiha marra lux.*
promising - *mbaššir bil-xeer.* The horse lost the race after a promising start. *l-izṣaan xiṣar is-sibaaq baɛad bidaaya mbaššra bil-xeer.*
promissory note - *kumpyaala* pl. *-aat.*
to **promote** - **1.** *raffaɛ (u tarfiiɛ) t-.* He was promoted to captain. *traffaɛ ʔila raʔiis.* **2.** *šajjaɛ (i tšijjiɛ) t-.* Most countries promote their foreign trade. *ʔakθar id-duwal itšajjiɛ tijaaratha l-xaarijiyya.*
promotion - *tarfiiɛ.* My promotion is overdue. *tarfiiɛi tʔaxxar.*

prompt - **1.** *sariiε, εaajil.* I expect a prompt reply. *ʔatwaqqaε jawaab sariiε.* **2.** *bil-wakit.* He's prompt in paying his debts. *yidfaε deena bil-wakit.*
to prompt - *zaffaz (i tziffiz) t-.* What prompted you to say that? *šinu lli zaffazak itguul haay?*
promptly - **1.** *biδ-δabuṭ.* We start promptly at five. *nibdi saaεa xamsa biδ-δabuṭ.* **2.** *zaalan, εal-fawr.* The police arrived promptly. *š-šurṭa wuṣlat zaalan.*
pronoun - *δamiir* pl. *δamaaʔir.*
to **pronounce** - **1.** *lufaδ (u lafuδ) n-.* Am I pronouncing the word correctly? *da-alfuδ il-kalima ṣaziiz?* **2.** *ʔiṭaq (u nuṭuq) n- b-.* The judge will pronounce sentence tomorrow. *l-zaakim raz-yinṭuq bil-zukum bil-εuquuba baačir.*
pronounciation - *lafuδ* pl. *ʔalfaaδ.* That's not correct pronunciation. *hal-lafuδ muu ṣaziiz.*
proof - **1.** *burhaan* pl. *baraahiin, daliil* pl. *ʔadilla.* What proof do you have of that? *šinu burhaanak εala haay?* **2.** *ʔiθbaat.* There's definite proof that he killed her. *ʔaku ʔiθbaat ʔakiid ʔannahu huwwa lli qitalha.* **3.** *miswadda* pl. *-aat.* I've just finished reading proof on my new article. *hastawwni xallaṣit iqraayat il-miswadda l-maqaalti j-jidiida.*
propaganda - *diεaaya.*
to **propagate** - **1.** *kaθθar (i takθiir).* There are many ways of propagating this plant. *ʔaku ṭuruq mutaεaddida t-takθiir hal-ʔašjaar.* **2.** *nišar (u našir) n-.* The first four caliphs propagated the Islamic religion. *l-xulafaaʔ ir-raašidiin nišraw il-ʔislaam.*
propeller - *parawaana* pl. *-aat.*
proper - **1.** *ṣaziiz, laayiq.* That isn't the proper way to handle people. *haaδi muu ṭ-ṭariiqa ṣ-ṣaziiza l-muεaamalat in-naas.* **2.** *munaasib, mulaaʔim.* This isn't the proper time to ask questions. *haaδa muu l-wakt il-mulaaʔim il-suʔaal ʔasʔila.* **3.** *ʔaṣli*.* In 1937 the Japanese invaded China proper. *sana ʔalf w-tisiε miyya w-sabεa w-tlaaθiin l-yaabaaniyyiin ġizaw ʔarδ iṣ-ṣiin il-ʔaṣliyya.* **4.** *muxtaṣṣ.* You have to talk to the proper person. *laazim tizči wiyya š-šaxṣ il-muxtaṣṣ.*
properly - **1.** *ka-ma yajib, zasb il-ʔuṣuul.* I'll show you how to do it properly. *raz-araawiik išloon itsawwiiha ka-ma yajib.* **2.** *b-liyaaqa.* Can't you behave properly? *ma-tigdar titṣarraf ib-liyaaqa?*
property - **1.** *muluk* pl. *ʔamlaak.* All the furniture is my property. *kull il-ʔaθaaθ mulki.* -- He has a mortgage on his property. *msawwi rahan εala mulka.* **2.** *xaaṣṣiyya* pl. *xawaaṣṣ, xaṣaaʔiṣ.* One of the properties of copper is its reddish color. *wazda min xawaaṣṣ iṣ-ṣifir loona l-ʔazmar.*
prophecy - *nubuuʔa* pl. *-aat.*
to **prophesy** - *tnabbaʔ (a tanabbuʔ).* He prophesied that the world would come to an end this coming year. *tnabbaʔ il-εaalam raz-yintihi s-sana j-jaaya.*
prophet - *nabi* pl. *ʔanbiyaaʔ.*
proportion - **1.** *tanaasub.* That picture is all out of proportion. *t-tanaasub ib-haṣ-ṣuura kulla ġalaṭ.* **2.** *nisba.* Everybody is paid in proportion to what he does. *kull waazid yaaxuδ bin-nisba š-šuġla.* **3.** *fiʔa* pl. *-aat, qisim* pl. *ʔaqsaam.* A small proportion of the people approved. *fiʔa qaliila mnin-naas waafqaw.*
**His expenses are entirely out of proportion to his income. *maṣruufaata ma-titnaasab wiyya waaridaata ʔabadan.*
proportional - **1.** *nisbi*.* These figures show the proportional distribution of population. *hal-ʔarqaam itbayyin it-tawziiε in-nisbi lis-sukkaan.* **2.** *mitnaasib.* Your wages will be proportional to your education. *ʔujuurak raz-itkuun mitnaasba wiyya diraastak.*
proportioned - *mitnaasiq, mitnaasib.* Her figure is well-proportioned. *jisimha zilu mitnaasiq.*
proposal - **1.** *εariδ* pl. *εuruuδ.* He made me an interesting proposal. *qaddam-li εariδ muġri.* **2.** *qtiraaz* pl. *-aat.* Your proposal met with the approval of all members. *qtiraazak naal muwaafaqat kull il-ʔaεδaaʔ.* **3.** *xuṭba* pl. *-aat.* Our daughter had two proposals at the same time. *binitna jattha xuṭubteen ib-nafs il-wakit.*
to **propose** - *qtiraz (i qtiraaz).* I propose we go to the movies. *ʔaqtiriz inruuz lis-siinama.*
to propose to - *xiṭab (u xuṭba) n-, ṭilab (u ṭalab) n- ʔiid.* He proposed to her. *xiṭabha* or *ṭilab ʔiidha.*
proposition - **1.** *εariδ, εiraδ* pl. *εuruuδ.* He made me an excellent proposition. *εiraδ εalayya εariδ mumtaaz.* **2.** *šaġla* pl. *-aat.* It is a paying proposition. *haay šaġla murbiza.* **3.** *qtiraaz* pl. *-aat.* Your proposition is very sound. *qtiraazak kulliš maεquul.*
proprietor - *maalik* pl. *millaak, ṣaazib* pl. *ʔaṣzaab.*
pros and cons - *mazaasin w-masaawiʔ.*
prose - *naθir.*
rhymed prose - *sajiε.*
to **prosecute** - *qaam, ʔaqaam (i ʔiqaama) n- daεwa εala.* Do you think the government will prosecute him? *tiftikir il-zukuuma raz-itqiim daεwa εalee?*
prosecutor - *mištiki* pl. *-iin, muddaεi* pl. *-iin.*
prospect - **1.** *ʔamal* pl. *ʔaamaal.* What are his prospects of getting a job? *šgadd εinda ʔamal bil-zuṣuul εal-waδiifa?* **2.** *fikra* pl. *fikir.* I don't like the prospect of having to work with him. *fikrat iš-šuġuḷ wiyyaa ma-tiεjibni.*
**This boy has good prospects. *hal-walad εinda mustaqbal zeen.*
prospective - *muntaδar, mutawaqqaε, maʔmuul.* He is my prospective son-in-law. *huwwa nisiibi l-muntaδar.*
prostitute - *gazba* pl. *gzaab, muumis* pl. *-aat, εaahra* pl. *-aat.*
prostitution - *daεaara, baġaaʔ.*
to **protect** - **1.** *zima (i zami) n-.* I wear these glasses to protect my eyes. *ʔaani ʔalbas hal-manaaδir ʔazmi εyuuni.* **2.** *zaafaδ (u muzaafaδa) t- εala.* I will protect your interests. *ʔaani raz-azaafuδ εala maṣlaztak.* **3.** *daafaε (i difaaε) εan.* Everyone must protect his own property. *kull waazid laazim ydaafiε εan mulka.* **4.** *wuqa (i wuqaaya) n-.* This medicine protects the eyes from disease. *had-duwa yooqi l-εeen imnil-ʔamraaδ.*
protection - *zimaaya.* There is no protection against that. *ma-aku zimaaya δidd haay.*
protectorate - *mazmiyya* pl. *-aat.*
to **protest** - **1.** *ztajj (a ztijaaj).* I protest! *ʔaani ʔaztajj!* **2.** *ʔaṣarr (i ʔiṣraar) n- εala.* He protested his innocence throughout the trial. *ʔaṣarr εala baraaʔta ṭuul il-muzaakama.*
Protestant - *prootistaani** pl. *-iyyiin.*
Protestantism - *prootistaaniyya.*
protocol - *prootookool.*
proton - *prootoon* pl. *-aat.*
proud - **1.** *faxuur.* I am proud of you. *ʔaani faxuur biik* or **ʔaani ʔaftixir biik.* **2.** *ʔaanuuf.* She is too proud to ask for someone's help. *haay ʔaʔnaf min ʔan tistanjid ib-ʔazzad.*
to **prove** - *ʔaθbat (i ʔiθbaat), barhan (i tburhin) t-.* I can prove I didn't do it. *ʔagdar aθbit ib-ʔanni ma-sawweetha.*
to prove to be - *ṭilaε (a ṭuluuε).* The rumor proved to be lies. *hal-zači ṭilεat čiδib.*
proverb - *maθal* pl. *ʔamθaal, qawl maʔθuur* pl. *ʔaqwaal maʔθuura.*
to **provide** - **1.** *jahhaz (i tajhiiz, tjihhiz) t-, zawwad (i tazwiid) t-.* The university is going to provide the laboratory with modern equipment. *j-jaamiεa raz-itjahhiz il-muxtabar ib-lawaazim zadiiθa.* **2.** *hayyaʔ (i thiyyiʔ) t-.* We will provide the place for the meeting. *raz-inhayyiʔ il-mukaan lil-ijtimaaε.* **3.** *waffar (u tawfiir) t-.* We provided all means of comfort. *waffarna kull ʔasbaab ir-raaza.*
to provide for - **1.** *εaal (i ʔiεaala).* He has to provide for the whole family. *laazim yεiil il-εaaʔila kullha.* **2.** *zisab (i ʔizsaab) n- ʔizsaab.* The law provides for such special cases. *l-qaanuun yizsib izsaab miθil hal-qaδaaya l-xaaṣṣa.* **3.** *ztaaṭ (a ztiyaaṭ).* We will provide for a long winter. *raz-niztaaṭ ʔila šita ṭawiil.*
provided, providing - *b-šarṭ, εala šarṭ.* I'll go, provided you come with me. *ʔaruuz ib-šarṭ tiji wiyyaaya.*
province - *liwaaʔ* pl. *ʔalwiya.* Iraq is divided into fourteen provinces. *l-εiraaq minqisim ʔila ʔarbaaṭaεaš liwaaʔ.*
provision - *naṣṣ* pl. *nuṣuuṣ.* There is no provision made for this in the law. *ma-aku naṣṣ εala haaδa bil-qaanuun.*
provisions - *tajhiizaat, maʔuuna.* Our provisions are running low. *tajhiizaatna da-tqill.*
to **provoke** - **1.** *ʔaθaar (i ʔiθaara) n-.* His remark provoked a roar of laughter. *mulaazaδta ʔaθaarat εaaṣifa mniδ-δizik.* **2.** *stafazz (i stifzaaz).* Don't provoke him. *la-tistafizza.* -- His behavior is provoking. *taṣarrufa yistafizz il-waazid.*

**He's provoked about it. *huwwa mitgtaaδ Eanha.*
prune - *Einjaaṣa* (pl. *-aat*) *myabbisa* coll. *Einjaaṣ imyabbas.*
to prune - *qallam* (*i taqliim*) *t-*. The rosebushes need to be pruned. *Eruug il-warad yinraad-ilha titqallam.*
psychiatrist - *ṭabiib nafsaani* pl. *ʔaṭibbaaʔ nafsaaniyyiin.*
psychology - *Eilm in-nafs.*
public - 1. *Eumuum, naas.* Is this park open to the public? *hal-ʒadiiqa maftuuʒa lil-Eumuum?* 2. *Eaamm.* Public opinion is against him. *r-raʔi l-Eaamm δidda.* -- Public health requires these measures. *ṣ-ṣiʒʒa l-Eaamma tiṭṭallab hal-ʔijraaʔaat.* 3. *Eumuumi*.* Is there a public telephone here? *ʔaku talafoon Eumuumi hnaa?* 4. *Ealani*, Eumuumi*.* I bought this rug at a public auction. *štireeṭ has-sijjaada b-mazaad Ealani.*
**He embezzled public funds. *xtilas ʔamwaal id-dawla.*
**Such books will always find a public. *hiiči kutub itšuuf-ilha qurraaʔ daaʔiman.*
in public - *giddaam in-naas.* You shouldn't behave like this in public. *ma-laazim titṣarraf hiiči giddaam in-naas.*
publication - 1. *našir.* What is the date of publication? *šwakit taariix in-našir?* 2. *našra* pl. *-aat.* This is a useful publication. *haay našra mufiida.*
publicity - *diEaaya.* That's what I call clever pubblicity. *haaδa lli ʔasammii diEaaya maahra.*
to **publish** - *nišar* (*u našir*) *n-*. He hopes to publish his new book very soon. *yitʔammal yinšur iktaaba j-jidiid qariiban.*
publisher - *naašir* pl. *-iin.*
publishing house - *daar našir.*
puddle - *nugra* pl. *nugar, burka* pl. *burak.* Careful, don't step into the puddle! *diir baalak, la-tixṭi bin-nugra!*
puff - *nafas.* I got sick after only one puff. *nafsi liEbat baEad nafas waaʒid.*
pull - 1. *jarra* pl. *-aat.* One more pull and we'll have it open. *jarra lux baEad raʒ-tinfakk.* 2. *waaṣṭa* pl. *-aat, xaaṭraana, δahar.* You need a lot of pull to get a job here. *tiʒtaaj ihwaaya waaṣṭaat yaḷḷa tigdar itʒaṣṣil šuğuḷ ihnaa.*
to pull - 1. *jarr* (*u jarr*) *n-*. Don't pull so hard! *la-tjurr hal-gadd ʒeel.* 2. *šilaE* (*a šaliE*) *n-*. This tooth must be pulled. *has-sinn laazim yinšiliE.*
**Don't pull any funny stuff! *la-tbiiE šaṭaara b-raasi!*
**Don't try to pull the wool over my eyes! *la-tʒaawil itEabbur Ealayya qiriš qalb!* or *la-tʒaawil itlaflifni!*
**He pulled a fast one on me. *doolabni.* or *δirabni kalak.*
**I pulled a big boner. *sawweet min nafsi maδʒaka.*
**Pull over to the side! *ʔoogaf Eala ṣafʒa!* or *ʔuṭbug!*
to pull apart - 1. *faakak* (*i tfaakuk*) *t-*. It took three men to pull them apart. *tlaθ riyaajiil yaḷḷa gidraw yfaakikuuhum.* 2. *faṣṣax* (*i tafṣiix*) *t-*. I had to pull the radio apart in order to find what was wrong. *δṭarreet ʔafaṣṣix ir-raadyo ʒatta ʔalgi l-Eeeb.*
to pull down - 1. *nazzal* (*i tanziil*) *t-*. Shall I pull down the shades? *ʔanazzil il-pardaat?* 2. *hidam* (*i hadim*) *n-*. They're going to pull down all the old houses. *raʒ-yhidmuun kull il-ibyuut il-Eatiiga.*
to pull in - *ṭabb* (*u ṭabb*), *wuṣal* (*a wuṣuul*). When did your train pull in? *qiṭaarak išwakit ṭabb?*
to pull oneself together - *šadd* (*i šadd*) *n- ʒeel~.* Pull yourself together! *šidd ʒeelak!*
to pull out - 1. *šilaE* (*a šaliE*) *n-*. The children pulled out all the weeds. *l-ʔaṭfaal šilEaw kull il-ʒašiiš.* 2. *ṭilaE* (*a ṭuluuE*). The train will pull out any minute. *l-qiṭaar raʒ-yiṭlaE ib-ʔay laʒδa.*
to pull through - *dabbar* (*u tadbiir*) *t-, Eubar* (*u Eabar*). We were afraid she might not pull through it. *činna xaayfiin ma-raʒ-itdabburha.*
to pull up - 1. *ṭubag* (*u ṭabug*). The car pulled up in front of the house. *s-sayyaara ṭubgat giddaam il-beet.* 2. *jarr* (*u jarr*) *n-*. Pull up a chair! *jurr-lak fadd kursi!*
pulley - *bakra* pl. *-aat.*
pulse - *nabuδ.* The nurse took my pulse. *l-mumarriδa ʔaxδat nabδi.*
pump - 1. *maδaxxa* pl. *-aat.* We have a pump in our country house. *Eidna maδaxxa b-beetna r-riifi.* 2. *pamp* pl. *-aat.* I need a new pump for the bicycle. *ʔaʒtaaj pamp jidiid lil-paaysikil.*
to pump - 1. *δaxx* (*u δaxx*) *n-*. Shall I pump some water? *ʔaδuxx išwayya maay?* 2. *stadraj* (*i stidraaj*). Don't let him pump you. *la-txallii yistadrijak.*
to pump up - 1. *δaxx* (*u δaxx*) *n-*. Our water is pumped up from the spring. *l-maay maalna yinδaxx imnil-Eeen.* 2. *nufax* (*u nafux*) *n-*. Will you please pump up the front tires? *baḷḷa ma-tinfux it-taayaraat il-giddaamiyya?*
pumping station - *maʒaṭṭat* (pl. *-aat*) *δaxx.*
pumpkin - *šijrat* (pl. *-aat* coll. *šijar*) *ʔaskala.*
punch - 1. *δarbat* (pl. *-aat*) *jimiE, lakma* pl. *-aat, books* pl. *-aat.* The punched knocked him down. *δarbat ij-jimiE waggEata.* 2. *quwwa.* His speech lacked punch. *ʒadiiθa čaan yinquṣṣa l-quwwa.* 3. *šarbat* pl. *šaraabit.* Would you like some more punch? *tʒibb tišrab baEad šarbat?*
to punch - 1. *ziraf* (*u zaruf*) *n-, giraδ* (*u garuδ*) *n-*. The conductor punched our tickets. *mufattiš il-paaṣ ziraf tiktaatna.* 2. *δirab* (*u δarub*) *n-*, Shut up, or I will punch you in the nose. *ʔinčabb, tara ʔaδurbak bil-xašma.*
puncture - *zuruf* pl. *zuruuf, nugub* pl. *nguub, pančar* pl. *-aat.* Is there a puncture in the tire? *ʔaku zuruf bit-taayar?*
to puncture - *ziraf* (*u zaruf*) *n-, nigab* (*u nagub*) *n-*. He has a punctured eardrum. *ṭablat ʔiδna mazruufa.*
to **punish** - 1. *Eaaqab* (*i muEaaqaba*) *t- Eala.* Violations will be severely punished. *l-muxaalafaat yitEaaqab Ealeeha b-šidda.* 2. *niṭa* (*i naṭi*) *n- qaṣaaṣ.* I think he's been punished enough. *ʔaEtiqid inniṭa qaṣaaṣ kaafi.*
punishment - *Euquuba* pl. *-aat, qaṣaaṣ* pl. *-aat.* The punishment was too severe. *l-Euquuba čaanat kulliš qaasya.*
**Our car has taken a lot of punishment. *sayyaaratna štiEal diinha.*
punitive - *taʔdiibi*.* We have to send a punitive expedition to the strike area. *laazim indizz ʒamla taʔdiibiyya l-manṭiqt il-iδṭiraab.*
pupil - 1. *tilmiiδ* pl. *talaamiiδ, ṭaalib* pl. *ṭullaab.* She has twenty pupils in her class. *Eidha Eišriin tilmiiδ ib-ṣaffha.* 2. *buʔbuʔ* pl. *baʔaabiʔ.* The pupil of the left eye is dilated. *l-buʔbuʔ maal il-Eeen il-yisra twassaE.*
puppy - *juru* pl. *juriwaat, juraawa; buuji* pl. *bwaaj.*
purchase - *šarwa* pl. *-aat.* This boat was a wonderful purchase. *hal-balam čaan xooš šarwa.*
to purchase - *štira* (*i štiraaʔ*). We're going to purchase a new home this fall. *raʒ-ništri beet jidiid hal-xariif.*
pure - 1. *xaaliṣ.* The necktie is pure silk. *r-ribaaṭ ʒariir xaaliṣ.* 2. *naqi*.* Do you have pure alcohol? *Eindak kuhuul naqiyya?* 3. *ṣirf, baʒt.* That's pure nonsense. *haaδi lağwa ṣirfa.*
purely - *baʒt, ṣirf.* This is a purely political matter. *haaδa mawδuuE siyaasi baʒt.*
purge - *taṭhiir* pl. *-aat.* This government needs a purge of all corruption. *hal-ʒukuuma tiʒtaaj ʔila taṭhiir il-fasaad.*
to purge - *ṭahhar* (*i taṭhiir*) *t-*. The government is planning to purge its police department. *l-ʒukuuma naawiya tṭahhir silk iš-šurṭa.*
to **purify** - *ṣaffa* (*i taṣfiya*) *t-*. This water needs to be purified. *hal-maay laazim yitṣaffa.*
purple - *šaraabi*.*
purpose - *ğaraδ* pl. *ʔağraaδ, muraad, mabğa, qaṣid, ğaaya* pl. *-aat.* What's the purpose of all this? *šinu l-ğaraδ min kull haaδa?* -- He left without achieving his purpose. *tirak bala-ma ynaal ğaraδa.* -- What purpose did he have in doing that? *šinu čaan ğaraδa min iswayyaat haay?* -- You can use this tool for many purposes. *tigdar tistaEmil hal-ʔaala l-Eiddat ğaayaat.*
on purpose - *Ean qaṣid, Eamdan, qaṣdan, qaṣṭani.* I left my coat home on purpose. *ʔaani trakit qappuuṭi bil-beet Ean qaṣid.*
purse - 1. *junṭa* pl. *-aat, junaṭ.* This purse doesn't go well with my new dress. *haj-junṭa ma-tirham ʒeen wiyya badilti j-jidiida.* 2. *jaaʔiza* pl. *jawaaʔiz.* The purse was divided among the winners. *j-jaaʔiza tqassmat been ir-raabʒiin.*

to **pursue** - **1.** *taabaƐ (i mutaabaƐa) t-.* I don't want to pursue the subject any further. *ma-ariid ataabiƐ hal-mawḏuuƐ baƐad ʔazyad.* **2.** *Ɛaqqab (i tƐiqqib) t-, tƐaqqab (a tƐiqqib).* The police are pursuing the smugglers. *š-šurṭa da-tƐaqqib il-muharribiin.* **3.** *tibaƐ (i tabiƐ) n-.* We all pursue the policies of our party. *kullna nitbaƐ siyaasat ḥizibna.*

pursuit plane - *ṭiyyaara* (pl. *-aat*) *muṭaarida.*

pus - *qeeḥ, jaraaḥa.*

push - *dafƐa* pl. *-aat.* He gave me such a push that I nearly fell over. *nṭaani fadd šikil dafƐa xallatni ʔoogaƐ taqriiban.*

to push - **1.** *difaƐ (a dafiƐ) n-.* Push the table over by the window. *ʔidfaƐ il-meez il-yamm is-sibbaač.* -- He was pushed way back. *ndifaƐ lil-ʔaxiir.* **2.** *difaƐ (a dafiƐ) n-, daffaƐ (i tadfiiƐ) t-.* Don't push! *la-tidfaƐ!* **3.** *čifat (i čafit).* The people pushed into the elevator *n-naas čiftaw lil-maṣƐad.* **4.** *daas (u doos) n-.* Did you push the button? *dist iz-zirr?* **5.** *ḏabb (i ḏabb) n-.* He tried to push the blame on me. *ḥaawal yḏibb il-loom Ɛalayya.* **6.** *xalla (i txilli) t-.* What pushed you to do it? *š-xallaak itsawwiiha?*

**I tried to push my way through the crowd. *ḥaawalit ʔašuqq ṭariiqi been ij-jamaahiir.*

to push off - *ṭilaƐ (a ṭuluuƐ, ṭiluuƐ).* Right after we pushed off, the boat capsized. *baƐad-ma ṭilaƐna b-išwayya ngilab il-balam.*

pus - *qeeḥ, jaraaḥa.*

to **put** - **1.** *ḥaṭṭ (u ḥaṭṭ) n-, xalla (i txilli) t-.* Put the table over there. *ḥuṭṭ il-meez ihnaak.* -- Put an ad in the paper. *ḥuṭṭ iƐlaan bij-jariida* or *ʔunšur.* **2.** *wuḏaƐ (a waḏiƐ) n-.* That puts me in an embarrassing position. *haaḏa yooḏaƐni b-waḏiƐ ḥarij.* -- I'll have to put an end to this situation. *raḥ-ʔooḏaƐ ḥadd il-hal-ḥaala.*

**I wouldn't put any faith in that story. *hal-iḥčaaya ma-Ɛaleeha Ɛtimaad.*

**Why don't you put it straight to him? *leeš ma-tgul-la-yaaha b-ṣaraaḥa?*

**Put it this way; we don't like each other. *b-kalima ʔuxra; ʔiḥna waaḥid ma-yḥibb il-laax.*

to put across - **1.** *fahham (i tafhiim).* I don't know how to put it across to him that... *ma-da-ʔadri šloon afahhma ʔinna...* **2.** *ʔanha (i ʔinhaaʔ), xallaṣ (i taxliiṣ).* Did you put the deal across? *ʔanheet iṣ-ṣafqa?*

to put aside - **1.** *xalla (i txilli) t- Ɛala ṣafḥa.* She's been putting aside a little money each month. *da-txalli šwayya fluus Ɛala ṣafḥa kull šahar.* **2.** *ḏabb (i ḏabb) n- Ɛala ṣafḥa.* Put that newspaper aside and let us finish this. *ḏibb ij-jariida Ɛala ṣafḥa w-xalli nxalluṣ haay.*

to put away - *ḏamm (u ḏamm) n-.* Put your jewelry away in a safe place. *ḏumm mujawharaatak ib-makaan ʔamiin.* -- Put your summer clothes away. *ḏumm ihduumak iṣ-ṣeefiyya.*

to put back - *rajjaƐ (i tarjiiƐ) t-, radd (i radd) n-.* Put the book back where you got it. *rajjiƐ il-iktaab imneen-ma ʔaxaḏta.*

to put to bed - *nayyam (i tanyiim), nawwam (u tanwiim).* I have to put the kids to bed. *laazim ʔanayyim il-ʔaṭfaal.*

to put down - **1.** *nazzal (i tnizzil, tanziil) t-, ḥaṭṭ (u ḥaṭṭ) n-.* Put the box down here. *nazzil iṣ-ṣanduug ihnaa.* **2.** *kitab (i kitaaba) n-.* Put down your name and address. *ʔiktib ʔismak w-Ɛinwaanak.* **3.** *qimaƐ (a qamiƐ) n-, ʔaxmad (i ʔixmaad) n-.* The army put down the revolution. *j-jeeš qimaƐ iθ-θawra.*

to put in - **1.** *ṣiraf (u ṣaruf) n-.* They put in a lot of time on that job. *ṣirfaw ihwaaya wakit Ɛala haš-šuġuḷ.* **2.** *rakkab (u tarkiib) t-.* Did they put in a new windowpane? *rakkbaw jaama jidiida liš-šibbaač?*

to put in a word for - *ḥiča (i ḥači) l-, tšaffaƐ (a tšiffiƐ).* I want you to put in a word for me with the director. *ʔariidak tiḥčii-li wiyya l-mudiir.*

to put in order - *rattab (i trittib, tartiib) t-, naḏḏam (u tniḏḏim, tanḏiim) t-.* He's putting his affairs in order. *da-yrattib ʔumuura.*

to put into words - *Ɛabbar (u taƐbiir) t- Ɛan.* This is something hard to put into words. *haaḏa fadd šii ṣaƐub it-taƐbiir Ɛanna.*

to put off - **1.** *nayyam (i tanyiim).* I can't put the matter off any longer. *ma-agdar anayyim il-qaḏiyya baƐad.* **2.** *Ɛaṭṭal (i taƐṭiil, tƐiṭṭil) t-, Ɛawwag (i taƐwiig) t-.* Let's put off the decision until tomorrow. *xalli nƐaṭṭil il-qaraar li-baačir.* **3.** *ʔajjal (i tʔijjil, taʔjiil) t-.* I can't put off the appointment. *ma-agdar aʔajjil il-mawƐid.* **4.** *maaṭal (i mumaaṭala) t-.* Can't you put him off for a while? *ma-tigdar itmaaṭla mudda?*

to put on - **1.** *libas (a libis) n-.* Put your hat on! *ʔilbas šafiqtak!* -- Which dress shall I put on? *ʔay badla ʔalbas?* **2.** *šiƐal (i šaƐil) n-, Ɛilag (i Ɛalig) n-, fitaḥ (a fatiḥ) n-, fakk (u fakk) n-.* Put on the light, please. *baḷḷa ʔišƐil iḏ-ḏuwa.*

**I've put on three pounds. *zaad wazni tlaθ paawnaat.*

**Don't you think her accent is put on? *ma-tiftikir lahjatha mitṣannƐa?*

to put oneself out - *tkallaf (a takalluf), ġaθθ (u ġaθθ) n- nafs~.* Don't put yourself out on my account. *la-titkallaf Ɛala muudi.*

to put out - **1.** *ṭaffa (i ṭṭiffi, taṭfiya) t-.* The fire was put out quickly. *l-ḥariig iṭṭaffa bil-Ɛajal.* -- Put out the light before you leave. *ṭaffi ḏ-ḏuwa gabuḷ-ma truuḥ.* **2.** *ṭallaƐ (i ṭṭilliƐ, taṭliiƐ) t-.* Put him out if he makes too much noise. *ṭallƐa barra ʔiḏa ysawwi laġwa hwaaya.* **3.** *nišar (u našir) n-.* Who's putting out your book? *minu da-yinšur iktaabak?*

to put over on - *Ɛabbar (u taƐbiir) t- Ɛala.* You can't put anything over on him. *ma-tigdar itƐabbur Ɛalee šii.*

to put through - *naffaḏ (i tanfiiḏ) t-.* He put his own plan through. *naffaḏ mašruuƐa l-xaaṣṣ.*

to put to death - *Ɛidam (i ʔiƐdaam) n-.* The criminal was put to death this morning. *l-mujrim inƐidam hal-yoom iṣ-ṣubuḥ.*

to put together - **1.** *ḥaṭṭ (u ḥaṭṭ) n- suwa.* Don't put the dog and the cat together, they will fight. *ma-tḥuṭṭ il-čalib wil-bazzuun suwa tara yitƐaarkuun.* **2.** *rakkab (u tarkiib) t-.* We must put the pieces together. *laazim inrakkub il-wuṣal suwa.*

to put up - **1.** *niṣab (u naṣub) n-.* New telephone poles are being put up. *Ɛawaamiid talafoon jidiida yinnuṣbuun.* **2.** *Ɛiraḏ (u Ɛariḏ) n-, nazzal (i tanziil) t-.* The farm will be put up for sale this week. *l-mazraƐa raḥ-tinƐiriḏ lil-beeƐ hal-isbuuƐ.* **3.** *Ɛammar (u taƐmiir) t-, bina (i binaaʔ, bani) n-.* This building was put up in six months. *hal-binaaya tƐammrat ib-sitt išhur.* **4.** *ḥaṭṭ (u ḥaṭṭ) n-.* We put up a fence around the house. *ḥaṭṭeena siyaaj daayir-ma daayir il-beet.* **5.** *xalla (i txilli) t-, ḥaṭṭ (u ḥaṭṭ) n-.* Each of them put up a thousand dollars. *kull waaḥid minhum xalla ʔalif duulaar.* **6.** *ʔabda (i ʔibdaaʔ) n-.* They didn't put up a fight. *ma-ʔabdaw muqaawama.*

**Who'll put up the bail for him? *minu raḥ-yitkallafa?*

**Can you put us up for the night? *tigdar itbayyitna?*

to put up to - *dalla (i tdilli) t-.* His friends put him up to it. *ʔaṣdiqaaʔa dalloo Ɛaleeha.*

to put up with - *tḥammal (a tḥimmil).* I don't know why you put up with it. *ma da-ʔadri lweeš titḥammalha.*

puzzle - **1.** *ḥazzuura* pl. *-aat, ḥazaaziir.* Can you solve the puzzle? *tigdar itḥill hal-ḥazzuura?* **2.** *laġiz* pl. *ʔalġaaz.* That is a puzzle to me. *haaḏi laġiz bin-nisba ʔili.*

to puzzle - *ḥayyar (i tḥiyyir) t-.* His letter had us puzzled. *maktuuba ḥayyarna.*

to puzzle out - *ḥizar (i ḥazir) n-, ḥall (i ḥall) n-.* I can't puzzle it out. *ma-agdar ʔaḥzirha.*

pyramid - *haram* pl. *ʔahraam.*

Q

quack - *dajjaal* pl. *-iin, mušaƐwiδ* pl. *-iin.* The Ministry of Health has been able to track down a great many quacks and prevent them from practicing medicine. *wizaart iṣ-ṣiħħa twaffqat bil-Ɛuθuur Ɛala d-dajjaaliin ihwaaya w-maniƐhum min mumaarasat iṭ-ṭibb.*
quadrangle - *šikil rubaaƐi* pl. *ʔaškaal rubaaƐiyya.*
quake - *zilzaal* pl. *zalaazil, hazza* (pl. *-aat*) *ʔarḍiyya.*
qualification - **1.** *muʔahhila* pl. *-aat.* Do you think she has the necessary qualifications for the job? *tiƐtiqid Ɛidha l-muʔahhilaat il-laazima lil-waḍiifa.* **2.** *taħaffuδ.* I agree to it with some qualification. *ʔawaafiq Ɛalee maƐa baƐδ it-taħaffuδ.*
qualified - *ʔahil, ṣaaliħ, laayiq.* He is well-qualified for the position. *haaδa ʔahil jiddan lil-waḍiifa.* -- He is not qualified to marry into such a rich and famous family. *haaδa muu ʔahil yitzawwaj min Ɛaaʔila mašhuura ġaniyya miθil haay.*
to **qualify** - **1.** *ħaddad (i taħdiid) t- maƐna.* I want to qualify my previous statement. *ʔariid ʔaħaddid maƐna kalaami s-saabiq.* **2.** *ʔahhal (i taʔhiil) t-.* That does not qualify you for this kind of job. *haaδa ma-yʔahhlak il-han-nooƐ šuġuḷ.* **3.** *ṣilaħ (a ṣalaaħ), laag (i liyaaq).* You don't qualify for the job. *ma-tiṣlaħ lil-waḍiifa.*
quality - **1.** *xiṣla* pl. *xiṣal, ṣifa* pl. *-aat.* He has many good qualities. *Ɛinda hwaaya xiṣal zeena.* **2.** *miiza* pl. *-aat.* This machine has special qualities. *hal-makiina biiha miizaat xaaṣṣa.* **3.** *nawƐiyya* pl. *-aat.* It is a matter of quality, not quantity. *l-masʔala masʔalat nawƐiyya muu kammiyya.*
quandary - *ħiira.*
quantity - *kammiyya* pl. *-aat, miqdaar* pl. *maqaadiir.* We have a sufficient quantity on hand for the present. *Ɛidna kammiyya kaafya mawjuuda bil-wakt il-ħaaḍir.* -- **This item is available in quantity. *hal-maadda mitwaffra b-kammiyyaat čibiira.*
quarantine - *ħajir ṣiħħi, Ɛazil.* You will have to spend three days in quarantine. *laazim tibqa tlaθt iyyaam bil-ħajir iṣ-ṣiħħi.*
to quarantine - *ħijar (u ħajir) n-.* They quarantined all the passengers on the plane. *ħijraw kull rukkaab iṭ-ṭiyyaara.*
quarrel - **1.** *Ɛarka* pl. *-aat.* The policeman broke up the quarrel in the street. *š-šurṭi faḍḍ il-Ɛarka biš-šaariƐ.* **2.** *xiṣaam* pl. *-aat.* The quarrel between the two politicians has become serious. *l-xiṣaam been is-siyaasiyyeen ṣaar jiddi.* **3.** *nizaaƐ* pl. *-aat.* The farmers took their quarrel over water rights to the Bureau of Irrigation. *l-fallaaħiin waṣṣlaw nizaaƐhum Ɛala ħuquuq is-saqi l-daaʔirt ir-rayy.*
to quarrel - **1.** *tƐaarak (a Ɛarka).* This man quarrels with everyone. *haaδa yitƐaarak wiyya l-kull.* **2.** *txaaṣam (a taxaaṣum), tjaadal (a tajaadul).* The committee members quarreled over financial matters. *ʔaƐḍaaʔ il-lujna txaaṣmaw ħawl iš-šuʔuun il-maaliyya.* **3.** *tnaazaƐ (a tanaazuƐ).* The sons of the deceased quarreled over his estate the day after he died. *wild il-marħuum itnaazƐaw Ɛala tarakta ʔawwal yoom baƐad wafaata.*
quarrelsome - **1.** *jadali*.* He is so quarrelsome nobody likes him. *haaδa fadd waaħid jadali maħħad yħibba.* **2.** *qarač.* She is the most quarrelsome women in the whole neighborhood. *haay ʔakθar wiħda qarač bil-maħalla.* **3.** *wakiiħ, wakiħ.* He is a quarrelsome boy, always picking fights with the other children. *haaδa walad wakiħ kull wakit ydawwir Ɛarkaat wiyya l-wulid il-baaqiyyiin.*
quarry - *maqlaƐ* pl. *maqaaliƐ, maħjar* pl. *maħaajir.* All the stone is from a local quarry. *kull iṣ-ṣaxar min maqlaƐ maħalli.*
quarter - **1.** *rubuƐ* pl. *ʔarbaaƐ, čaarak* pl. *čwaariik.* It's a quarter to seven. *saaƐa sabƐa ʔilla rubuƐ.* **2.** *rubuƐ* pl. *ʔarbaaƐ.* Three quarters of the harvest was damaged. *tlatt irbaaƐ il-maħṣuul tilaf.* **3.** *ħayy* pl. *ʔaħyaaʔ.* These are the old quarters of the city. *haay il-ʔaħyaaʔ il-qadiima mnil-madiina.* **4.** *maskan* pl. *masaakin.* The officers' quarters are at the far end of the camp. *masaakin iḍ-ḍubbaaṭ ib-nihaayat il-muƐaskar.* **5.** *waṣaṭ* pl. *ʔawṣaaṭ.* It is maintained in some quarters that the plan will not work. *yguuluun ib-baƐḍ il-ʔawṣaaṭ ʔann il-xiṭṭa ma-raħ-tinjaħ.*
to quarter - *sakkan (i taskiin) t-.* They quartered the troops in the schoolhouse during the emergency. *sakknaw ij-jinuud ib-binaayt il-madrasa ʔaθnaaʔ ħaalt iṭ-ṭawaariʔ.*
quarterly - **1.** *majalla* (pl. *-aat*) *faṣliyya.* This article appeared in the quarterly published by the society. *hal-maqaal innišar bil-majalla l-faṣliyya lli tuṣdurha j-jamƐiyya.* **2.** *kull itlaθt išhur, ʔarbaƐ marraat bis-sana.* We pay the interest on the loan quarterly. *nidfaƐ il-faayiz Ɛala d-deen kull itlaθt išhur.*
quarter-master - *ḍaabuṭ* (pl. *ḍubbaaṭ*) *ʔiƐaaša.*
quarters - *maskan* pl. *masaakin.* Did you find decent quarters? *ligeet-lak fadd maskan muħtaram?*
at close quarters - *mitlaaziim, maxbuuṣ.* They fought at close quarters. *tƐaarkaw mitlaazmiin.*
quartz - *kwaarits.*
quaver - *raƐša* pl. *-aat, rajfa* pl. *-aat.* There was a quaver in her voice as she asked the question. *čaan ʔaku raƐša b-ħissha min siʔlat is-suʔaal.*
to quaver - *riƐaš (i raƐiš), rijaf (i rajif).* The old man is feeble, and his voice quavers when he talks. *š-šaayib ḍaƐiif w-ħissa yirƐiš min yiħči.*
quay - *raṣiif* pl. *ʔarṣifa.*
queasy - **I feel queasy from all the rich food. *nafsi da-tilƐab min kull il-ʔakil id-dasim.*
queen - **1.** *malika* pl. *-aat.* Her majesty, the Queen, has come! *ṣaaħibat ij-jalaala, l-malika, jatti!* **2.** *waziir* pl. *wuzaraaʔ.* I am going to take your queen with the knight. *raħ-aaxuδ waziirak bil-ħṣaan.* **3.** *bnayya* pl. *banaat, qizza* pl. *-aat.* I have two jacks and three queens in my hand. *Ɛindi waladeen w-itlaθ banaat b-iidi.*
queer - **1.** *nimuuna, Ɛantiika.* He is a queer bird. *haaδa fadd waaħid nimuuna.* **2.** *šaaδδ.* What a queer idea! *šloon fikra šaaδδa!*
to **quell** - *qimaƐ (a qamiƐ) n-, ʔaxmad (i ʔixmaad) n-.* Troops were quickly dispatched to quell the uprising. *j-jiyuuš indazzat ib-surƐa ħatta tiqmaƐ iθ-θawra.*
to **quench** - *ruwa (i rawi) n-.* This won't quench my thirst. *haaδa ma-yirwi Ɛaṭaši.*
querulous - *naħis.* She has become a querulous old lady. *ṣaayra fadd Ɛajuuz naħsa.*
query - *stifhaam* pl. *-aat, stiƐlaam* pl. *-aat.* This pamphlet should answer any queries there might be. *hal-kurraasa laazim itjaawab Ɛala kull il-istifhaamaat.*
quest - *baħθ.* The quest for happiness continues all our life. *l-baħθ Ɛan is-saƐaada yistamirr ṭuul Ɛumurna.*
question - **1.** *suʔaal* pl. *ʔasʔila.* Have you any further questions. *Ɛindak ʔasʔila lux?* **2.** *qaḍiyya* pl. *qaḍaaya.* It was a question of saving a human life. *čaanat qaḍiyyat ʔinqaaδ ħayaat bašariyya.* **3.** *masʔala* pl. *masaaʔil.* It's still an open question. *baƐadha masʔala biiha ʔaxiδ w-radd.*
**That's completely out of the question. *haaδa mustaħiil.* or *haay la-tsoolifha.* or *haay ṭalliƐha min l-iħsaab.*
beyond question - *ma-bii suʔaal, foog iš-šubhaat, ma-maškuuk bii.* His honesty is beyond question. *nazaahta ma-biiha suʔaal.*
in question - *maqṣuud, maƐni.* The gentleman in question was not there. *r-rijjaal il-maqṣuud ma-čaan ihnaak.*
to ask a question - *siʔal (a suʔaal) n-.* They asked a lot of questions. *siʔlaw ihwaaya ʔasʔila.*
to question - **1.** *stajwab (i stijwaab).* The police questioned him all night long. *š-šurṭa stajwiboo ṭuul il-leel.* **2.** *šakk (u šakk) n- b-.* I question his sincerity. *ʔašukk ib-ʔixlaaṣa.*
question mark - *Ɛalaamat* (pl. *-aat*) *istifhaam, Ɛalaamat* (pl. *-aat*) *suʔaal.*
questionnaire - *qaaʔimat* (pl. *-aat*) *ʔasʔila.*
queue - *sira* pl. *-aawaat.* The queue in front of the ticket window was so long I didn't want to wait. *s-sira qiddaam šibbaak il-biṭaaqaat čaan hal-gadd ṭuwiil ma-ridt antiḍir.*
to queue up - *liħam (a) n- sira.* People usually queue up for the buses at rush hours. *n-naas Ɛaadatan yilħamuun sira Ɛal-paaṣ wakt il-izdiħaam.*
quick - **1.** *sariiƐ, Ɛaajil.* That was a quick decision. *haaδa čaan qaraar sariiƐ.* -- All his movements are quick. *kull ħarakaata sariiƐa.* **2.** *laħam ħayy.* I

cut my fingernail to the quick. *gaṣṣeet iδifri lil-laʒam il-ʒayy.*
**His remark touched the quick. *ʒičaayta wuṣlat il-laʒam il-ʒayy.* or *ʒičaayta daggat bil-Ɛaδum.*
to be quick - *staƐjal (i stiƐjaal).* Be quick about it. *staƐjil biiha.*
to **quicken** - *Ɛajjal (i tƐijjil) t- b-, sarraƐ (i tasriiƐ) t-.* He quickened his steps. *Ɛajjal ib-xaṭwaata.*
quickly - *b-surƐa, bil-Ɛajal.* He does things quickly. *ysawwi kullši b-surƐa.*
quicksilver - *zeebag, sleemaani.*
quick-tempered - *ʒaadd iṭ-ṭabuƐ.* She is very quick-tempered. *hiyya kulliš ʒaaddat iṭ-ṭabuƐ.* or **raasha ʒaarr.*
quiet - **1.** *haadiʔ.* I live in a quiet neighborhood. *ʔaskun ib-ṭaraf haadiʔ.* **2.** *ṣanṭa, haadiʔ.* It is very quiet here. *kulliš ṣanṭa hnaa.* **3.** *saakit, ṣanṭa.* Why are you so quiet? *leeš saakit?* or *š-biik hal-gadd ṣanṭa?* **4.** *sukuut, ṣanṭa.* Quiet, please! *sukuut, rajaaʔan!* or *ṣanṭa, rajaaʔan!*
to keep quiet - *buqa (a baqaaʔ) saakit, sikat (u sukuut).* Why didn't you keep quiet? *lweeš ma-buqeet saakit?*
to quiet - **1.** *hadda (i tahdiya, thiddi) t-, sakkat (i taskiit) t-.* Samira, go see if you can quiet the baby. *samiira, ruuʒi šuufi ʔiδa tgidriin ithaddiin j-jaahil.* **2.** *hidaʔ (a huduuʔ).* Let's wait until the excitement quiets down a bit. *xal-nintiδir ʔila ʔan yihdaʔ il-ʒamaas.* — She quieted down after a while. *hidʔat baƐad fadd fatra.*
quilt - *lʒaaf* pl. *liʒfaan.*
quince - *sfarjala* pl. *-aat* coll. *sfarjal, ʒeewaaya* pl. *-aat, ʒeewaat* coll. *ʒeewa.*
quinine - *kiniin, kiina, qanaqiina.*
to **quit** - **1.** *baṭṭal (i tbuṭṭul) t- min.* He quit his job yesterday. *baṭṭal min šuġļa l-baarʒa.* — Quit it! *baṭṭil!* or **bass Ɛaad!* or **juuz* — Let's call it quits! *xalli nbaṭṭil!* **2.** *jaaz (u jooz) n-.* I told him a thousand times to quit and he didn't. *gilit-la ʔalif marra yjuuz laakin ma-jaaz.*
**It's time to quit. *ṣaar wakt it-tabṭiila.* or *ṣaar wakt il-ʒalla.* or *þaaydoos.*
quite - **1.** *hwaaya, kulliš.* That's quite possible. *haay kulliš jaaʔiz.* — It turned quite cold during the night. *burdat kulliš ihwaaya bil-leel.* **2.** *ṣudug* That was quite an experience. *haay ṣudug čaanat tajruba.* **3.** *tamaaman, b-δabuṭ, kulliš.* Are you quite sure that you can't go? *ʔinta mitʔakkid tamaaman ma-tigdar itruuʒ?*
quiz - *xtibaar* pl. *-aat.* The teacher gives us a short quiz everyday. *l-muƐallim yinṭiina xtibaar qaṣiir kull yoom.*
quorum - *niṣaab.* We couldn't vote on the bill because we didn't have a quorum. *ma-gidarna nṣawwiṭ Ɛal-laaʔiʒa li-ʔan ma-ʒiṣal in-niṣaab.*
quota - *koota, ʒiṣṣa, taxṣiiṣaat.* There is some talk of increasing the quota for foreign cars next year. *ʔaku ʒači ʒawl ziyaadat il-koota lis-sayyaaraat il-ʔajnabiyya sant ij-jaaya.*
quotation - **1.** *stišhaad* pl. *-aat.* His speech was full of quotations. *ʒadiiθa čaan malyaan bil-istišhaadaat.* **2.** *siƐir* pl. *ʔasƐaar.* This newspaper publishes the stock market quotations. *haj-jariida tinšur ʔasƐaar il-boorṣa.*
quotation mark - *Ɛalaamat* (pl. *-aat*) *ʒaṣir.*
to **quote** - **1.** *staš̌had (i stišhaad) b-.* That's quoted on page ten. *haay mustašhad biiha b-ṣafʒa Ɛašra.* **2.** *Ɛiraδ (i Ɛariδ) n-, niṭa (i) n-.* What price did he quote you? *šinu s-siƐir il-Ɛiraδ-ilk-iyyaa?*
**Don't quote me. *la-tinqulha Ɛann ilsaani.*
quotient - *ʒaaṣil il-qisma.* If you divide fifteen by five the quotient is three. *ʔaδa tqassim ixmuṣṭaƐas Ɛala xamsa ʒaaṣil il-qisma tlaaθa.*

R

rabbit - *ʔarnab* pl. *ʔaraanib.*
race - **1.** *sibaaq* pl. *-aat, reesiz.* When does the race start? *šwakit yibdi s-sibaaq?* **2.** *jinis* pl. *ʔajnaas.* The yellow race is found in eastern Asia. *j-jins il-ʔaṣfar mawjuud ib-šarq ʔaasya.*
to race - *tsaabaq (a musaabaqa), tġaalab (a taġaalub, muġaalaba).* Let's race. *xal-nitsaabaq.*
**Don't race the engine. *la-tijhid il-makiina.*
**The car raced through the streets. *s-sayyaara čaanat ṭaayra biš-šawaariƐ.*
rack - **1.** *raff* pl. *rfuuf.* Put the books back on the rack. *rajjiƐ il-kutub Ɛar-raft.* — Put your baggage up on the rack. *ʒuṭṭ junaṭak Ɛar-raff.* **2.** *tiƐlaaqa* pl. *-aat.* I hung my coat on the rack. *Ɛallaqit sitirti Ɛat-tiƐlaaqa.* **3.** *mišjab* pl. *mašaajib.* The soldiers put the guns on the rack. *j-junuud ʒaṭṭaw il-banaadiq bil-mišjab.*
**Don't rack your brains over it. *la-tdawwux raasak biiha.*
racket - **1.** *hoosa* pl. *-aat.* The children are making an awful racket. *l-ʔaṭfaal da-ysawwuun ġeer hoosa.* **2.** *liƐba* pl. *liƐab.* This whole business is nothing but a racket. *haš-šaġla liƐba mnil-ʔasaas.* **3.** *rakit* pl. *-aat, maδrab* pl. *maδaarib.* Her racket is much too heavy for you. *r-rakit maalha kulliš θigiil Ɛaleek.*
radiator - *raadeeta* pl. *-aat.* Something is wrong with the radiator of my car. *ʔaku šii bir-raadeeta maal sayyaarti.*
radical - **1.** *miṭṭarrif* pl. *-iin.* I consider him a radical. *ʔaani ʔaƐtabra miṭṭarrif.* — He has very radical views. *Ɛinda wajhaat naδar kulliš miṭṭarrfa.* **2.** *ʔasaasi**. He wants to make some radical changes. *yriid ysawwi baƐδ it-taġyiiraat il-ʔasaasiyya.*
radio - *raadyo* pl. *-uwwaat.* Was it announced over the radio? *nδaaƐat bir-raadyo?*
to radio - *δaaƐ (i ʔidaaƐa) n-.* They radioed from the plane that they were in trouble. *δaaƐaw imniṭ-ṭayyaara bi-ʔan Ɛidhum muškila.*
radio station - *maʒaṭṭat* (pl. *-aat*) *ʔiδaaƐa.*
radish - *fijlaaya* pl. *-aat* coll. *fijil.* Shall I slice up the radishes? *ʔagaṣgiṣ il-fijil?*
raft - *čalač* pl. *člaač, kalak* pl. *klaak.*
rag - *xirga* pl. *xirag, wuṣla* pl. *wuṣal.* Do you have a rag to dust the table? *Ɛindič fadd wuṣla l-masʒ il-meez?*
to **rage** - **1.** *haaj (i hiyaaj, hayajaan), ʒtadd (a ʒidda), θaar (u θawra).* He raged like a bull. *haaj miθl iθ-θoor.* **2.** *gabb (u gabb).* The storm raged all night long. *l-Ɛaaṣifa δallat gaabba ṭuul il-leel.*
ragged - *mxaļgan.* They were wearing ragged clothes. *čaanaw laabsiin ihduum imxaļgina.*
rail - *sičča* pl. *sičač, sikka* pl. *sikak.* A loose rail caused the accident. *faad qisim raaxi mnis-sičča sabbab il-ʒaadiθ.*
railing - *mʒajjar* pl. *-aat.* Hold on to the railing. *ʔilzam l-imʒajjar.*
railroad - *qiṭaar* pl. *-aat, sikkat* (pl. *sikak*) *ʒadiid.* I prefer to go by railroad. *ʔafaδδil aruuʒ bil-qiṭaar.* — Our house is near the railroad. *beetna yamm is-sikka.*
railroad station - *maʒaṭṭat* (pl. *-aat*) *qiṭaar.*
rain - *muṭar* pl. *ʔamṭaar.* We stayed home because of the rain. *bqeena bil-beet ib-sabab il-muṭar.*
to rain - *muṭar (u muṭar).* It rained hard all morning. *muṭrat ib-quwwa ṭuul iṣ-ṣubuʒ.*
rainbow - *qooz qazaʒ, gooz gadaʒ.*
raincoat - *mšammaƐ* pl. *-aat.*
rainy - *mumṭir.*
raise - *ziyaada* pl. *-aat, tarfiiƐ* pl. *-aat.* They gave me a raise. *nṭooni ziyaada.*
to raise - **1.** *šaal (i šeel) n-.* Use the jack to raise the car. *staƐmil ij-jagg il-šeel is-sayyaara.* — They didn't even raise their heads from their work as we passed. *wala šaalaw ruushum min šuġuļhum min marreena.* **2.** *rufaƐ (a rafuƐ) n-.* All those in favor, raise your hands. *kull il-muʔayyidiin, ʔirfaƐu ʔiideekum.* — They raised the siege and withdrew. *rifƐaw il-ʒiṣaar w-insiʒbaw.* **3.** *rtifaƐ (i rtifaaƐ)* The bread won't raise without yeast. *l-Ɛajiin ma-yirtifiƐ bala xumra.* **4.** *Ɛalla (i taƐliya) t-.* Raise the picture a little; it's not all on the screen. *Ɛalli ṣ-ṣuura šwayya, muu kullha Ɛal-þarda.* — Raise the volume a little on the radio. *Ɛalli ʒiss ir-raadyo šwayya.* **5.** *ṣaƐƐad (i taṣƐiid) t-.* He showed us how they raise and lower the irrigation gates. *raawaana šloon yṣaƐƐiduun w-ynazziluun ʔabwaab is-saqi.* **6.** *zayyad (i tazyiid, ziyaada) t-.*

The rent will be raised on October first. *l-ʔajaar raz-yitzayyad ib-ʔawwal tišriin ʔawwal.* -- The company has promised to raise our salaries all across the board. *š-šarika wuEdat itzayyid rawaatibna jamiiEan.* **7.** *raqqa (i tarqiya) t-.* They raised him from clerk to supervisor. *raqqoo min kaatib ʔila mulaaziṣ.* **8.** *ziraE (a zariE) n-.* They raise a lot of wheat here. *yzirEuun ihwaaya zunṭa hnaa.* **9.** *rabba (i tarbiya) t-.* She has raised nine children. *rabbat tisiE ʔaṭfaal.* -- Most farmers here raise sheep. *ʔakθar iz-zurraaE ihnaa yrabbuun ǧanam.* **10.** *dabbar (u tadbiir) t-.* I couldn't raise the money. *ma-gdarit adabbur l-ifluus.* **11.** *jimaE (a jamiE) n-.* Our club is raising money to aid the flood victims. *naadiina da-yijmaE ifluus il-ʔiǧaaθat mankuubi l-fayaṣaan.*

**The kids are raising the roof again. *j-jihaal da-yguḷbuun id-dinya marra lux.*

to raise a question - *ʔaθaar (i ʔiθaara) mawṣuuE.* Who raised the question? *minu ʔaθaar il-mawṣuuE?*

range - **1.** *ṭabbaax* pl. *-aat.* We just bought a new range. *hastawwna štireena ṭabbaax jidiid.* **2.** *marEa* pl. *maraaEi.* In the spring the sheep go out on the range. *bir-rabiiE il-ǧanam yruuzuun lil-marEa.* **3.** *saaza* pl. *-aat, maydaan* pl. *mayaadiin.* The new recruits spent their first day on the firing range today. *l-mujannadiin ij-jiddad giṣaw yoomhum il-ʔawwal ib-saazt ir-rami hal-yoom.* **4.** *mada* pl. *-aayaat, marma* pl. *maraami, niṭaaq* pl. *ʔanṭiqa.* The tanks were out of range of our guns. *d-dabbaabaat čaanat xaarij niṭaaq madaafiEna.*

to range - **1.** *traawaz (a taraawuz).* The prices range from one to five dinars. *l-ʔasEaar titraawaz min diinaar ʔila xamis danaaniir.* **3.** *tjawwal (a tajawwul).* The bedouin range the western desert with their flocks. *l-badu yitjawwaluun biṣ-ṣazraaʔ il-ǧarbiyya wiyya qiṭEaanhum.*

rank - **1.** *rutba* pl. *rutab.* What's the officer's rank? *šinu rutbat haṣ-ṣaabuṭ?* **2.** *kaθθ.* His face was covered by a rank growth of beard. *wuččа čaan imǧaṭṭa b-lizya kaθθa.*

rapid - *sariiE.*

rare - **1.** *naadir.* That's a rare flower. *haaδi warda naadra.* **2.** *Ean-nuṣṣ.* I'd like my steak broiled rare. *ʔariid il-lazam maali mašwi Ean-nuṣṣ.*

rarely - *naadiran, mnin-naadir.* That rarely happens. *haaδa naadiran yizduθ.*

rascal - *šiiṭaan, šayṭaan* pl. *šayaaṭiin.*

rash - **1.** *zaṣaf.* There is a rash on his face. *ʔaku zaṣaf ib-wuččа.* **2.** *mooja* pl. *ʔamwaaj.* Last month there was a rash of robberies. *š-šahr il-faat čaan ʔaku moojat boog.* **3.** *mitsarriE, bala tarawwi, bala ʔimEaan.* Don't make any rash promises. *la-tinṭi wuEuud bala tarawwi.*

rat - *jreedi* pl. *-iyya.*

rate - **1.** *siEir* pl. *ʔasEaar, ʔujra* pl. *ʔujur, ʔujuur.* What are the rates for single rooms? *šgadd siEr il-ǧurfa ʔumm sariir waazid?* -- What are the new rates for airmail? *šinu l-ʔujuur ij-jidiida lil-bariid ij-jawwi?* -- The rate of interest is four per cent. *siEr il-faaʔida ʔarbaEa bil-miyya.* **2.** *muEaddal.* At this rate we'll never get done. *Eala hal-muEaddal wala raz-inxalliṣ.*

at any rate - *Eala kull zaal.* At any rate, I'd like to see you. *Eala kull zaal, ʔaani da-ariid ašuufak.*

first-rate - *daraja ʔuula, ṣinif ʔawwal, mumtaaz.* It's definitely a first-rate hotel. *haaδa bila šakk ʔuteel daraja ʔuula.*

rather - **1.** *šwayya, nawEan-ma.* The play was rather long. *r-ruwaaya čaanat nawEan-ma ṭwiila.*

**I would rather wait. *ʔaani ʔafaṣṣil antiṣir.*

**I'd rather die than give in. *ʔaani ʔafaṣṣil il-moot Eat-tasliim.*

ration - *quṣEa* pl. *quṣaE, taEyiin* pl. *-aat.* Our rations consisted of bread and soup. *quṣEatna čaanat xubuz w-šoorba.*

to ration - *wazzaE (i tawziiE) bil-biṭaaqaat, zaddad (i tazdiid) t- tawziiE.* Sugar was rationed. *š-šakar itwazzaE bil-biṭaaqaat.* -- They rationed the meats. *zaddidaw tawziiE il-lazam.*

rattle - *xirxaaša* pl. *xaraaxiiš.* They bought the baby a rattle. *štiraw xirxaaša liṭ-ṭifil.*

to rattle - **1.** *ṭarbag (i ṭarbaga), xašxaš (i xašxaša, txišxiš) t-.* Do you have to rattle the dishes that way? *ʔaku muujib iṭṭarbig hiiči bil-immaaEiin?* -- There is a kind of snake that rattles. *ʔaku nooE imnil-zayyaat itxašxiš.* **2.** *šawwaš (i tašwiiš) t-, xarbaṭ (u xarbaṭa) t-.* Don't rattle me. *la-tšawwišni.*

to rattle on - *θarθar (i θarθara), liǧa (i laǧwa).* She can rattle on like that for hours. *tigdar itθarθir haš-šikil il-muddat saaEaat.*

to rave - *hiδa (i hiδyaan).* He raved like a madman. *hiδa miθl il-majnuun.*

raw - **1.** *niyy.* The meat is almost raw. *l-lazam niyy taqriiban.* **2.** *miltihib.* My throat is raw. *zarduumi miltihib.*

**He got a raw deal. *ṣaaba ǧubun.*

ray - **1.** *šuEaaE* pl. *ʔašiEEa.* Ordinary panes of glass keep out ultraviolet rays. *j-jaam il-Eaadi yimnaE il-ʔašiEEa fooq il-banafsajiyya.* **2.** *baṣiiṣ.* There's still a ray of hope. *li-hassa ʔaku fadd baṣiiṣ imnil-ʔamal.*

rayon - *rayoon.*

razor - *muus* pl. *mwaas.* I have to strop my razor. *laazim ʔazidd il-muus maali.*

safety razor - *makiinat* (pl. *makaayin*) *ziyaan.* I can't find my safety razor. *ma-da-agdar algi makiinat iz-ziyaan maalti.*

razor blade - *muus* pl. *mwaas, mwaasa.* Please buy me a dozen razor blades. *ʔarjuuk ištirii-li darzan imwaasa.*

to **reach** - **1.** *madd (i madd) ʔiid~.* The little fellow reaches for everything he sees. *haz-zaEṭuuṭ ymidd ʔiida Eala kullši yšuufa.* -- He reached into his pocket. *madd ʔiida b-jeeba.* **2.** *mtadd (a mtidaad).* The garden reaches all the way to the river. *l-zadiiqa timtadd liš-šaṭṭ.* **3.** *wuṣal (a wuṣuul) ʔila.* The rumor even reached us. *l-ʔišaaEa wuṣlat zatta ʔilna.* -- The radio reaches millions of people. *r-raadyo yooṣal ʔila malaayiin imnin-naas.* -- We reached the city at daybreak. *wuṣalna l-wlaaya wučč iṣ-ṣubuz.* **4.** *ttiṣal (i ttiṣaal) b-.* There was no way of reaching him. *ma-čaan ʔaku fadd ṭariiqa nittiṣil bii.* **5.** *naaš (u nooš) n-.* Can you reach that shelf? *tigdar itnuuš δaak ir-raff?* **6.** *naawaš (u mnaawaša).* Reach me the hammer. *naawušni č-čaakuuč.*

reaction - **1.** *radd fiEil.* What was his reaction? *š-čaan radd il-fiEil Einda?* **2.** *tafaaEul.* You can speed up the reaction if you beat the mixture. *tigdar itsarriE it-tafaaEul ʔiδa tsaxxin il-maziij.*

reactionary - *rajEi**.*

to **read** - **1.** *qira (a qraaya) n-.* You should read this book. *laazim tiqra hal-iktaab.* -- The text reads differently. *l-matin yiqra ǧeer šikil.* -- Please read it to me. *ʔarjuuk iqraa-li-yyaaha.* **2.** *ʔaššar (i taʔšiir) t- Eala.* The thermometer reads 35 degrees. *l-mizraar yʔaššir xala xamsa w-itlaaθiin daraja.*

reader - **1.** *qaariʔ* pl. *qurraaʔ.* This newspaper has more than a million readers. *haj-jariida ʔilha ʔazyad min milyoon qaariʔ.* **2.** *ktaab* (pl. *kutub*) *muṭaalaEa.* Do you have my English reader? *Eindak iktaab il-muṭaalaEa l-ʔingiliizi maali?*

readily - *bila taraddud, b-surEa, bil-Eajal.* He admitted it readily. *Etiraf biiha bila taraddud.* -- She consented readily. *qiblat ib-surEa.*

reading - *qiraaʔa.* He got excellent in reading. *ʔaxaδ jayyid jiddan bil-qiraaʔa.*

ready - **1.** *zaaṣir* . When will dinner be ready? *šwakit ykuun il-Eaša zaaṣir?* **2.** *mistiEidd, zaaṣir.* I'm ready for anything. *ʔaani mistiEidd il-kullši.* **3.** *jaahiz.* The house is ready for occupancy. *l-beet jaahiz lis-sikna.* **4.** *jawwa l-ʔiid.* I don't have any ready cash just now. *ma-aku fluus jawwa ʔiidi hassa.*

to get ready - **1.** *staEadd (i stiEdaad), tzaṣṣar (a tazaṣṣur).* Get ready, go! *ʔistaEiddu, ʔibdaʔ!* -- My brother is getting ready to go out. *ʔaxuuya da-yitzaṣṣar liṭ-ṭalEa.* **2.** *zaṣṣar (i tazṣiir) t-.* My wife is getting the food ready. *marti da-tzaṣṣir il-ʔakil.*

ready-made - *jaahiz, zaaṣir.* Do you buy your clothes ready-made? *tištiri hduumak jaahza?*

real - **1.** *zaqiiqi**. That's not his real name. *haaδa muu ʔisma l-zaqiiqi.* **2.** *ʔaṣli**. Is this real silk? *haaδa zariir ʔaṣli?* **3.** *min ṣidug.* That's what I call a real friend. *haaδa l-asammii ṣadiiq min ṣidug.* **4.** *waaqiE.* That never happens in real life. *haaδa ʔabad ma-yizduθ bil-waaqiE.*

real estate - *ʔamlaak.*

reality - *zaqiiqa, waaqiE.*

to **realize** - **1.** *zaqqaq (i tazqiiq) t-.* He never realized his ambition to become a doctor. *ʔabadan ma-zaqqaq ṭumuuza bi-ʔan yṣiir ṭabiib.* **2.** *ṭallaE (i taṭliiE) t-.* He realized quite a profit on that deal. *ṭallaE xooš ribiz ib-δiič iš-šagla.* **3.** *tṣawwar (a taṣawwur).* I simply can't realize he's dead. *ma-da-agdar aṭṣawwar ʔanna mayyit.* -- I didn't realize it was so late. *ma-tṣawwarit hal-gadd il-wakit mitʔaxxir.* **4.** *ʔadrak (u ʔidraak).* Does he realize how sick he is? *da-yidruk išgadd mariiṣ huwwa?*

5. *qaddar (i taqdiir) t-*. He doesn't realize how much work is involved. *ma-da-yqaddir išgadd biiha šuğuļ.* -- I never realized the danger. *ma-qaddart il-xaṭar ʔabadan.*

really - 1. *ƶaqiiqatan, ṣ-ṣudug.* Do you really mean it? *ʔinta ƶaqiiqatan tiƐniiha.* -- I really wanted to stay at home. *ṣ-ṣudug ʔaani ridit ʔabqa bil-beet.* 2. *bil-ƶaqiiqa.* He is really younger than he looks. *huwwa bil-ƶaqiiqa ʔaṣğar min-ma ybayyin Ɛalee.* **I really don't know. *waḷḷa ma-adri.*

rear - 1. *δahar* pl. *δuhuur.* The rear of the house is being painted. *δahr il-beet da-yinṣubuğ.* 2. *maqƐad* pl. *maqaaƐid.* She fell on her rear. *wugƐat Ɛala maqƐadha.* 3. *xalfi**. The rear row is empty. *s-sira l-xalfi faariğ.* 4. *warraani**. The rear windows haven't been cleaned yet. *š-šibaabiič il-warraaniyya baƐad ma-tnaδδfat.*

in the rear - *bil-xalf, li-wara.* The emergency exit is in the rear. *baab iṭ-ṭawaari bil-xalf.*

to **rearrange** - *ʔaƐaad (i ʔiƐaada) tartiib, tanδiim.* You ought to rearrange the furniture. *laazim itƐiid tartiib il-ʔaθaaθ.*

reason - 1. *daaƐi* pl. *dawaaƐi.* She really has no reason for acting like that. *ƶaqiiqatan ma-aku daaƐi hiyya titṣarraf haš-šikil.* 2. *baaƐiθ* pl. *bawaaƐiθ.* I see no reason for complaint. *ma-ašuuf baaƐiθ liš-šakwa.* 3. *sabab* pl. *ʔasbaab, Ɛilla* pl. *Ɛilal.* Is that the reason you didn't go? *haaδa sabab Ɛadam rooƶtak?* 4, *Ɛaqil, ṣawaab.* Please use your reason. *rajaaʔan ƶakkum Ɛaqlak.* -- If this keeps up, I'll lose my reason. *ʔiδa haay raƶ-tistimirr ʔaani raƶ-afqud ṣawaabi.*

to reason - *tƶaajaj (a taƶaajuj), tfaaham (a tafaahum).* You can't reason with him. *ma-tigdar titƶaajaj wiyyaa.*

reasonable - 1. *maƐquul.* She's a very reasonable person. *hiyya fadd waƶda kulliš maƐquula.* 2. *mnaasib.* They sell their books at reasonable prices. *ybiiƐuun kutubhum ib-ʔasƐaar imnaasba.*

reasonably - *b-Ɛaqil.* He acted reasonably. *tṣarraf ib-Ɛaqil.*

to **rebel** - *Ɛiṣa (a Ɛiṣyaan).* The troops rebelled against their commander. *j-junuud Ɛiṣaw Ɛala qaaʔidhum.* **My stomach simply rebelled. *nafsi ma-qiblat.*

to **recall** - 1. *tδakkar (a taδakkur).* Do you recall whether he was there or not? *titδakkar ʔiδa huwwa čaan ihnaak loo laa?* 2. *stadƐa (i stidƐaaʔ).* I read in the paper that your government has recalled its ambassador. *qireet bij-jariida ƶukuumatkum istadƐat safiirha.*

receipt - 1. *waṣil* pl. *wuṣuulaat.* Please give me a receipt. *rajaaʔan inṭiini waṣil.* 2. *daxaḷ.* The receipts were low today. *d-daxaḷ čaan qaliil hal-yoom.* 3. *wuṣuul.* Please acknowledge receipt of this letter. *rajaaʔan ʔaƐlimuuna b-wuṣuul hal-maktuub.*

to receipt - **Please receipt this bill. *ʔarjuuk ʔaššir hal-qaaʔima Ɛtiraafan bil-wuṣuul.*

to **receive** - 1. *stilam (i stilaam).* Did you receive my telegram? *stilamit barqiiti?* 2. *qubaδ (u qabuδ) n-.* You'll receive your salary in case on the first of the month. *raƶ-tiqbuδ raatbak ib-ʔawwal iš-šahar.* 3. *staqbal (i stiqbaal).* They received us cordially. *staqbiloona b-tarƶiib.*

receiver - 1. *simmaaƐa* pl. *-aat.* You didn't put the receiver back on the hook. *ma-rajjaƐt is-simmaaƐa b-makaanha.* 2. *mustalim* pl. *-iin.* Write the receiver's name legibly. *ʔiktib ism il-mustalim ib-wuδuuƶ.*

recent - 1. *ƶadiiθ.* Television is a comparatively recent invention. *t-talafizyoon fadd ixtiraaƐ ƶadiiθ nisbiyya.* 2. *jidiid.* Don't you have any recent issues? *ma-Ɛindak ʔay ʔaƐdaad jidiidaʔ.* 3. *ʔaxiir.* Did you hear of the recent revolution in the north? *simaƐit Ɛan iθ-θawra l-ʔaxiira biš-šimaal?*

recently - *ʔaxiiran, ƶadiiθan.* I heard it recently. *smaƐitha ʔaxiiran.*

reception - 1. *stiqbaal.* He gave us a warm reception. *staqbalna stiqbaal ƶaarr.* 2. *ltiqaaṭ.* Reception is poor today on the radio. *l-iltiqaaṭ muu zeen hal-yoom bir-raadyo.* 3. *ƶaflat* (pl. *-aat*) *istiqbaal.* Have you been invited to the reception? *nƐizamit il-ƶaflat l-istiqbaal?*

recess - 1. *furṣa* pl. *furaṣ, fatra* pl. *-aat.* We have a short recess at ten in the morning. *naaxuδ furṣa gṣayyra saaƐa Ɛašra ṣ-ṣubuƶ.* 2. *liiwaan* pl. *lawaawiin.* The recesses of the mosque are cool. *lawaawiin il-masjid baarda.*

recipe - *waṣfa* pl. *-aat.* Do you have a simple recipe for a cake? *Ɛindič fadd waṣfa baṣiiṭa maal keek?*

reckless - *ʔahwaj.* He's reckless driver. *huwwa fadd saayiq ʔahwaj.*

recognition - *taqdiir, Ɛtiraaf.* He didn't get the recognition he deserved. *ma-ƶaṣṣal Ɛala t-taqdiir illi yistiƶiqqa.*

to **recognize** - 1. *Ɛiraf (u maƐrifa) n-.* At first I didn't recognize you. *bil-ʔawwal ma-Ɛraftak.* 3. *Ɛtiraf (i Ɛtiraaf).* The United States does not recognize that country. *l-wilaayaat il-muttaƶida ma-tiƐtirif ib-had-dawla.*

to **recommend** - *waṣṣa (i tawṣiya) b-.* I recommended her highly to him. *waṣṣeeta kulliš biiha.* or *nṭeeta biiha tawṣiya qawwiyya.*

recommendation - *tawṣiya* pl. *-aat.* I did it on your recommendation. *sawweetha ƶasab tawṣiitak.*

record - 1. *qayd* pl. *qiyuud.* I can't find any record of that bill. *ma-da-agdar algi ʔay qayd ib-hal-qaaʔima.* 2. *sijill* pl. *-aat.* He has a criminal record. *Ɛinda sijill sawaabiq.* 3. *taariix.* That was the worst earthquake on record. *haaδa čaan ʔaswaʔ zilzaal bit-taariix.* or *haaδa čaan ʔawsaʔ zilzaal imsajjal.* 4. *ṣṭiwaana* pl. *-aat, qawaana* pl. *-aat.* They have a good selection of classical records. *Ɛidhum xooš majmuuƐa mnil-iṣṭiwaanaat il-iklaasiikiyya.* 5. *raqam qiyaasi* pl. *ʔarqaam qiyaasiyya.* He broke all records in free style swimming. *kisar kull il-ʔarqaam il-qiyaasiyya bis-sibaaƶa l-ƶurra.* -- We had a record crop this year. *ṣaar Ɛidna maƶṣuul qiyaasi has-sana.*

to record - 1. *sajjal (i tasjiil) t-.* Have you recorded everything he said? *sajjalit kullši gaala?* -- Can I use your tape recorder to record something? *ʔagdar astaƐmil il-musajjil maalak ƶatta ʔasajjil šii?* 2. *qayyad (i taqyiid) t-.* Record all payments in this book. *qayyid kull il-madfuuƐaat ib-has-sijill.*

to **recover** - 1. *tšaafa (a tašaafi), tƐaafa (a taƐaafi).* He recovered from his illness quickly. *bil-Ɛajal itšaafa min maraδa.* 2. *starjaƐ (i stirjaaƐ).* Did you finally recover your watch? *taaliiha starjaƐit saaƐtak?* 3. *staradd (i stirdaad), staƐaad (i stiƐaada).* He recovered his balance immediately. *staradd muwaazanta bil-Ɛajal.*

recovery - *šafaaʔ.* He's on the road to recovery. *huwwa b-ṭariiqa liš-šafaaʔ.*

red - 1. (m.) *ʔaƶmar* (f.) *ƶamra,* pl. *ƶumur.* I want to buy a red hat. *ʔard aštiri šafqa ƶamra.* 2. *ʔaƶmar.* Red is not becoming to her. *l-ʔaƶmar ma-yluug-ilha.*
**I'd rather be dead than Red. *ʔafaδδil il-moot Ɛaš-šuyuuƐiyya.*
**I saw red when I heard that. *faar dammi min ismaƐitha.*

Red Crescent - *l-hilaal il-ʔaƶmar.*

Red Cross - *ṣ-ṣaliib il-ʔaƶmar.*

to **reduce** - 1. *xaffaδ (u taxfiiδ) t-, nazzal (i tanziil) t-.* We reduced the prices ten per cent. *xaffaδna l-ʔasƐaar Ɛašra bil-miyya.* 2. *qallal (i taqliil) t-, naggaṣ (i tangiiṣ) t-.* We have to reduce our expenses. *laazim inqallil maṣaariifna.* 3. *δaƐƐaf (i taδƐiif), nazzal (i tanziil).* He can reduce his weight whenever he wants to. *yigdar ynazzil wazna šwakit-ma yriid.*

to **refer** - 1. *ƶawwal (i taƶwiil) t-, ƶaal (i ʔiƶaala) n-.* They referred me to the manager. *ƶawwlooni Ɛal-mudiir.* 2. *šaar (i ʔišaara) n-.* She referred to it in her book. *šaarat ʔilha b-iktaabha.*

reference - 1. *marjiƐ* pl. *maraajiƐ.* You may give my name as a reference. *tigdar tinṭi ʔismi ka-marjiƐ.* 2. *ktaab* (pl. *kutub*) *tawṣiya.* May I see your references? *ʔagdar ašuuf kutub it-tawṣiya maaltak?*

to **reflect** - *Ɛikas (i Ɛakis) n-.* The mirror reflects the light. *l-imraaya tiƐkis iδ-δuwa.* 2. *fakkar (i tafkiir).* I need time to reflect on it. *ʔariid wakt afakkir biiha.*

reflection - 1. *xayaal.* You can see your reflection in the water. *tigdar itšuuf xayaalak bil-maay.* 2. *taƐriiδ.* That's no reflection on you. *haaδa muu taƐriiδ biik.*

reform - *ʔiṣlaaƶ* pl. *-aat.* He introduced many reforms. *ʔadxal ʔiṣlaaƶaat ihwaaya.*

to reform - 1. *ʔaṣlaƶ (i ʔiṣlaaƶ).* He's always trying to reform the world. *daaʔiman yriid yiṣliƶ id-dinya.* 2. *nṣilaƶ (i).* I'm sure he'll reform. *ʔaani mitʔakkid raƶ-yinṣiliƶ.*

refreshing - *munƐiš.* On the banks of the Tigris the breeze is always refreshing. *Ɛala δifaaf dijla l-hawa daaʔiman munƐiš.*

refreshments - *muraṭṭibaat.* Refreshments were served during the intermission. *twazzƐat il-muraṭṭibaat ʔaθnaaʔ il-fatra.*

refrigerator - *θillaaja* pl. *-aat.*

refugee - *laajiʔ* pl. *-iin.*

refund - *ʔirjaaƐ* pl. *-aat, tarjiiƐ* pl. *-aat.* No refunds without a receipt. *ʔirjaaƐ il-mabaaliġ ma-ykuun ʔilla b-waṣil.*
to refund - *rajjaƐ (i tarjiiƐ) t-, ʔaƐaad (i ʔiƐaada) n-.* I'll refund your expenses. *Ɛuud arajjiƐ-lak maṣaariifak.*
refusal - *rafuḍ.* I didn't expect a refusal from him. *ma-twaqqaƐit minna r-rafuḍ.*
refuse - *ʔawsaax.* You'll find a refuse box outside. *tilqi ṣanduug ʔawsaax barra.*
to refuse - *rufaḍ (u rafuḍ) n-.* He doesn't refuse me anything. *ma-yirfuḍ-li ʔay ṭalab.*
regard - **1.** *xuṣuuṣ, šaʔn.* In that regard, I agree with you. *b-hal-xuṣuuṣ attifiq wiyyaak.* **2.** *Ɛtibaar.* He has no regard at all for others. *maa Ɛinda ʔayy iƐtibaar lil-ʔaaxariin.* **3.** *ḥtiraam* pl. *-aat.* Give my regards to your wife. *qaddim iḥtiraamaati l-zawujtak.*
to regard - **1.** *Ɛtibar (u Ɛtibaar).* We regard him as an authority on law. *niƐtabura ḥujja bil-qaanuun.* **2.** *qaddar (i taqdiir).* I regard him highly. *ʔaani ʔaqaddra hwaaya.*
region - *manṭiqa* pl. *manaaṭiq, ʔiqliim* pl. *ʔaqaaliim.*
register - *sijill* pl. *-aat, qayd* pl. *qyuud.* Did you sign the register? *waqqaƐit is-sijill?*
to register - *sajjal (i tasjiil) t-.* He's not registered at this hotel. *huwwa ma-mitsajjil ib-hal-ʔuteel.* -- I couldn't vote because I forgot to register. *ma-gdarit aṣawwut li-ʔan niseet ʔasajjil.* -- Where can I register this letter? *ween ʔagdar ʔasajjil hal-maktuub.*
registered - *musajjal.* I got a registered letter today. *stilamit maktuub musajjal hal-yoom.* --
regret - **1.** *ʔasaf.* I had to decline the invitation with regret. *ḍṭarreet ʔaƐtiḍir Ɛan id-daƐwa maƐa l-ʔasaf.* **2.** *Ɛtiḍaar.* Mr. and Mrs. Doe send their regrets. *s-sayyid wis-sayyida flaan yqaddimuun iƐtiḍaarhum.*
**I'd rather wait than have regrets later. *ʔaani ʔafaḍḍil antiḍir Ɛala ʔan ʔakuun mitnaddim baƐdeen.*
to regret - **1.** *tʔassaf (a taʔassuf), ʔisaf (a ʔasaf).* I've always regretted not having traveled much. *tʔassafit daaʔiman bi-ʔanni ma-saafarit ihwaaya.* **2.** *nidam (a nadam).* He regretted having said it. *nidam Ɛala goolatha.*
regrettable - *muʔsif.* This is a regrettable mistake. *haaḍi ġalṭa muʔsifa.*
regular - **1.** *Ɛtiyaadi*, Ɛaadi*.* The regular price is 5 dinars. *s-siƐr il-iƐtiyaadi xams idnaaniir.* **2.** *muntaḍam.* His pulse is regular. *nabḍa muntaḍam.* **3.** *mnaḍḍam.* He lives a very regular life. *yƐiiš ḥayaat imnaḍḍma kulliš.*
regularly - *b-intiḍaam.* He pays regularly. *huwwa yidfaƐ b-intiḍaam.*
to **regulate** - **1.** *naḍḍam (i tanḍiim) t-.* I can't regulate the temperature. *ma-da-agdar ʔanaḍḍim il-ḥaraara.* **2.** *ḍubaṭ (u ḍabuṭ) n-.* Can you regulate the carburetor? *tigdar tuḍbuṭ il-kaabreeta?*
regulation - *niḍaam* pl. *ʔanḍima.* That's against police regulations. *haaḍi muxaalifa l-ʔanḍimat iš-šurṭa.*
rein - *rašma* pl. *-aat.*
to **reject** - *rufaḍ (u rafuḍ) n-.* My application was rejected. *ƐariiḍṬi nrufḍat.*
related - *mitƐalliq.* I want all the information related to this matter. *ʔariid kull il-maƐluumaat il-mitƐalliqa b-hal-ʔamur.*
**We're related on my mother's side. *Ɛidna qaraaba min jihat ʔummi.*
**That's a related matter. *haaḍa mawḍuuƐ ʔila Ɛalaaqa.*
relation - **1.** *Ɛalaaqa* pl. *-aat.* The relations between the two countries are strained. *l-Ɛalaaqaat been il-baladeen itwattrat.* **2.** *ṣila* pl. *-aat, Ɛalaaqa* pl. *-aat.* Why don't you talk to him, you have better relations with him. *leeš maa ʔinta tiḥči wiyyaa, ṣiltak bii ʔaḥsan.* **3.** *qariib* pl. *qaraayib.* Are they all your relation? *haḍoola kullhum qaraaybak?*
relationship - *Ɛalaaqa.* What's the relationship between those two? *šinu l-Ɛalaaqa been hal-iθneen?*
relative - **1.** *qariib* pl. *ʔaqribaaʔ, garaayib.* He is a relative of mine. *haaḍa qariibi.* or *haaḍa garaaybi.* **2.** *nisbi*.* He said: Everything in life is relative. *gaal: kullši nisbi bil-ḥayaat.*
to **relax** - **1.** *raxxa (i tarxiya) t-.* Relax your muscles. *raxxi ƐaḍalaaṬak.* **2.** *rtaaḥ (a raaḥa).* I can't relax until it's finished. *ma-agdar artaaḥ ʔila ʔan tixlaṣ.* **3.** *hidaʔ (a huduuʔ).* Relax! Nobody's going to hurt you. *ʔihdaʔ, maḥḥad raḥ-yʔaḍḍiik.*
release - *ʔifraaj (pl. -aat) Ɛan-, ʔiṭlaaq siraaḥ.* The lawyer has applied for her release. *l-muḥaami qaddam ṭalab lil-ʔifraaj Ɛanha.*
to release - **1.** *ʔafraj (i ʔifraaj) n- Ɛan, ʔaṭlaq (i ʔiṭlaaq) n- siraaḥ.* The police released him right away. *š-šurṭa ʔafrajaw Ɛanna ḥaalan.* **2.** *fakk (u fakk) n-.* Release the safety catch. *fukk miftaaḥ il-ʔamaan.*
reliable - **1.** *Ɛalee Ɛtimaad.* He is a reliable person. *huwwa fadd šaxiṣ Ɛalee Ɛtimaad.* -- **This is a reliable firm. *haaḍi fadd šarika tiƐtimid Ɛaleeha.* **2.** *mawθuuq b-.* I got it from a reliable source. *ḥaṣṣalitha min maṣdar mawθuuq bii.*
relief - **1.** *faraj.* There is no hope of immediate relief from the heat. *ma-aku ʔamal faraj qariib imnil-ḥarr.* **2.** *ʔiƐaana.* They want to organize a relief committee. *yriiduun yšakkluun lujna lil-ʔiƐaana.*
to give relief - *rayyaḥ (i taryiiḥ) t-.* Did the medicine give you any relief? *d-duwa rayyaḥak išwayya?*
to **relieve** - **1.** *xaffaf (u taxfiif) t-.* This will relieve your headache. *haay raḥ-itxaffuf wujaƐ raasak.* **2.** *raaḥ (i ʔiraaḥa).* Why don't you tell me the story and relieve me of my anxiety. *leeš ma-tiḥčii-li l-qiṣṣa w-itriiḥni min qalaqi.* **3.** *xallaṣ (i taxliiṣ) t-.* We're trying to find a servant to relieve my wife of the cleaning. *da-nḥaawil nilqi xiddaama ḥatta nxalliṣ marti mnit-tanḍiif.*
**We relieve one another. *ʔiḥna nḥill waaḥid maḥall il-laax.*
religion - *diin* pl. *ʔadyaan.*
religious - **1.** *mitdayyin* pl. *-iin, taqi* pl. *-iyyiin.* He's very religious. *huwwa kulliš mitdayyin.* **2.** *diini.** He belongs to a religious order. *huwwa min ʔatbaaƐ ṭariiqa diiniyya.*
to **rely on** - *Ɛtimad (i Ɛtimaad) Ɛala.* You can't rely on him. *ma-tigdar tiƐtimid Ɛalee.*
to **remain** - *ḍall (a), buqa (a baqaaʔ).* He remained silent. *ḍall saakit.* -- There remains nothing else for us to do but wait. *ma-yibqaa-nna šii nsawwii ġeer nintiḍir.*
**That remains to be seen. *haaḍi raḥ-itbayyin baƐdeen.*
remaining - *baaqi.* What did you do with the remaining cards? *š-sawweet bil-biṭaaqaat il-baaqya?*
remains - **1.** *ʔaaθaar.* I'm anxious to see the historical remains. *ʔaani muštaaq ʔašuuf il-ʔaaθaar it-taariixiyya.* **2.** *mayyit* pl. *moota.* The remains were taken to Najaf for burial. *l-mayyit inʔixaḍ lin-najaf lid-dafin.*
remark - *mulaaḥaḍa* pl. *-aat.* That remark wasn't called for. *hal-mulaaḥaḍa maa ʔilha daaƐi.*
remarkable - *fawq il-Ɛaada, xaariq.* What's so remarkable about it. *šinu l-fawq il-Ɛaada biiha?*
remedy - *Ɛilaaj* pl. *-aat, duwa* pl. *ʔadwiya.* That's a good remedy for colds. *haaḍa xooš Ɛilaaj lin-našla.*
to remedy - *Ɛaalaj (i muƐaalaja) t-, daawa (i mudaawaat) t-.* I don't know how that can be remedied. *ma-ʔadri haay išloon titƐaalaj.*
to **remember** - *tḍakkar (a taḍakkur), tfaṭṭan (a tafaṭṭun).* It was in May, as far as I remember. *čaanat ib-maayis, ḥasab-ma ʔatḍakkar.*
**I simply can't remember his name. *ʔisma ʔabad ma-da-yiji Ɛala baali.*
**He always remembers us at Christmas. *daaʔiman nuxtur Ɛala baala b-Ɛiid il-miilaad.*
**Remember to turn out the light. *la-tinsa ṭṭaffi ḍ-ḍuwa.*
**Remember me to your father. *sallim-li Ɛala ʔabuuk.*
to **remind** - **1.** *ḍakkar (i taḍkiir).* He reminded me of my promise. *ḍakkarni bil-waƐad maali.* -- He reminds me of his father. *yḍakkirni b-ʔabuu.* **2.** *jaab (i) b-baal, ḍakkar (i taḍkiir).* Remind me about it later. *jiibha b-baali baƐdeen.*
reminder - *taʔkiid* pl. *-aat.* I'll send him a reminder, if he doesn't pay by tomorrow. *ʔadizz-la taʔkiid ʔiḍa ma-yidfaƐ baačir.*
remnant - *baqiyya* pl. *baqaaya, faḍla* pl. *-aat.* How much do you want for those three remnants? *hal-itlaθ baqaaya maal l-iqmaaš beeš itbiiƐhum?*
remote - *kulliš biƐiid.* There's a remote possibility that it will succeed. *ʔaku ḥtimaal kulliš biƐiid raḥ-yinjaḥ.*
to **remove** - **1.** *nizaƐ (a naziƐ) n-, šaal (i šiyal) n-.* Please remove your hat. *ʔarjuuk ʔinzaƐ šafugtak.* **2.** *zaal (i ʔizaala), šaal (i).* This should remove all doubt. *haay laazim itziil kull šakk.*

3. *rawwaʒ (i tarwiiʒ) t-, zaal (i), šaal (i).* That cleaner will remove all stains. *hal-maadda l-munaδδifa trawwiʒ kull il-lakkaat.* 4. *Ɛizal (i Ɛazil) n-.* He was removed from office. *nƐizal imnil-waδiifa.* 5. *niqal (u naqil) n-.* The phone was removed from here. *t-talafoon inniqal minnaa.*

to **renew** - *jaddad (i tajdiid) t-.* I went to the police to renew my license. *riʒit liš-šurṭa ʔajaddid ʔijaazti.*

rent - *ʔiijaar* pl. *-aat.* How much rent do you pay for your house? *šgadd tidfaƐ ʔiijaar ib-beetak?*

to rent - 1. *ʔajjar (i taʔjiir) t-, staʔjar (i stiijaar).* I rented a room for three months. *ʔajjarit ġurfa l-itlaθt iʃhur.* -- They rented a garage. *staʔjiraw garaaj.* 2. *ʔajjar (i taʔjiir).* He rented me the room for one month. *ʔajjarni l-ġurfa šahar waaʒid.*

repair - 1. *taṣliiʒ* pl. *-aat.* The car needs only minor repairs. *s-sayyaara tiʒtaaj taṣliiʒaat baṣiiṭa bass.* 2. *taƐmiir* pl. *-aat, tarmiim* pl. *-aat, taṣliiʒ* pl. *-aat.* This house needs a lot of repairs. *hal-beet yirraad-la hwaaya taƐmiir.*

to repair - 1. *ṣallaʒ (i taṣliiʒ) t-.* He repaired the radio for me. *ṣallaʒ-li r-raadyo.* 2. *rammam (i tarmiim) t-, Ɛammar (u taƐmiir) t-, ṣallaʒ (i).* When are you going to repair this house? *šwakit raʒ-itrammim hal-beet?*

to **repeat** - *Ɛaad (i ʔiƐaada) n-, karrar (i takriir) t-.* Repeat what I just said. *Ɛiid illi gilta hassa.* -- They repeat everything they hear. *ykarriruun kullši l-ysimƐuu.*

to **replace** - 1. *ʒall (i ʒall) maʒall, ʔaxaδ (u ʔaxiδ) mukaan.* We haven't been able to get anyone to replace her. *ma-da-nigdar nilgi ʔaʒʒad yʒill maʒallha.* 2. *baddal (i tabdiil) t-.* They replaced some tubes and made other repairs in the t.v. set. *baddilaw baƐaδ laampaat w-sawwaw taṣliiʒaat ʔuxra b-jihaaz it-talafizyoon.* 3. *stabdal (i stibdaal).* The prime minister is going to replace two members of his cabinet. *raʔiis il-wuzaraaʔ raʒ-yistabdil Ɛuδween min ʔaƐδaaʔ wizaarta.*

reply - *jawaab* pl. *ʔajwuba, radd* pl. *ruduud.* I never received a reply to my letter. *ʔabad ma-stilamit jawaab il-maktuubi.*

to reply - *jaawab (u ʔijaaba), radd (i radd).* He replied to my letter immediately. *jaawab Ɛala maktuubi ʒaalan.*

report - *taqriir* pl. *taqaariir.* I've already read the report. *ʔaani qreeta lit-taqriir.*

to report - 1. *ruwa (i rawi) n-.* The newspapers reported the accident in detail. *j-jaraayid ruwat il-ʒaadiθ bit-tafṣiil.* 2. *ballaġ (i tabliiġ) t-Ɛan.* Somebody must have reported him to the police. *fadd ʔaʒʒad laazim ballaġ iš-šurta Ɛanna.*

to report to - *raajaƐ (i muraajaƐa).* Tomorrow report to the director for your work. *bukra raajiƐ il-mudiir Ɛan šuġlak.*

**To whom do I report? *minu l-marjaƐ maali?*

report card - *waθiiqat* (pl. *waθaayig*) *darajaat.* She always comes home with good report cards in her hand. *daaʔiman tiji lil-beet w-b-ʔiidha waθaayiq darajaat mumtaaza.*

reporter - *ṣuʒufi* pl. *-iyyiin.*

to **represent** - *maθθal (i tamθiil) t-.* Who is representing the defendant? *minu da-ymaθθil il-muddaƐa Ɛalee?* -- What does this symbol represent? *har-ramiz š-ymaθθil?*

representative - 1. *mumaθθil* pl. *-iin.* He is the European representative of a big concern. *haaδa l-mumaθθil l-ʔooruppi l-šarika čibiira.* 2. *naaʔib* pl. *nuwwaab.* Who's the representative from your district? *minu n-naaʔib min manṭiqtak.*

reproach - *taƐniif, muʔaaxaδa.* I didn't mean that as a reproach. *ma-qṣadit il-muʔaaxaδa.*

to reproach - *waaxaδ (u muwaaxaδa) t-, zijar (u zajir) n-.* My mother is always reproaching me for my extravagance. *ʔummi daaʔiman twaaxiδni Ɛala ʔisraafi.*

reputation - 1. *sumƐa, šuhra, ṣiit.* He has a good reputation. *Ɛinda sumƐa ṭayyba.* 2. *maƐruuf Ɛan.* He has a reputation for being a good worker. *maƐruuf Ɛanna b-ʔanna šaaġuul.*

request - *ṭalab* pl. *-aat, rajaaʔ* pl. *-aat.* They granted the request. *waafqaw Ɛaṭ-ṭalab.* -- I am writing you at the request of a friend. *ʔaani da-ʔaktib-lak binaaʔan Ɛala rajaaʔ ṣadiiq.*

to request - *trajja (a tarajji) min.* I must request you to leave this place. *ʔaani muδṭarr ʔatrajja minnak titruk hal-maʒall.*

to **require** - 1. *stalzam (i stilzaam).* A thing like that requires careful study. *fadd šii miθil haaδa yistalzim diraasa daqiiqa.* 2. *ʒtaaj (a ʒtiyaaj), nraad (a) l-, ṭṭallab (a taṭallub).* That requires no proof. *haaδa ma-yiʒtaaj ʔay ʔiθbaat.* -- How much time will that require? *haay šgadd yinraad-ilha wakit?* -- How much money does that require? *šgadd ifluus haay tiṭṭallab?* 3. *ṭilab (u ṭalab) n-.* Do you require a deposit? *tiṭlubuun taʔmiinaat?* 4. *stadƐa (i stidƐaaʔ), qtiδa (i qtiδaaʔ).* The situation requires firm measures. *l-ʒaala tistadƐi ʔijraaʔaat ṣaarima.*

requirement - 1. *mutaṭallab* pl. *-aat.* The requirements for graduation are numerous. *mutaṭallabaat it-taxarruj kaθiira.* 2. *ʒtiyaaj* pl. *-aat, ʒaaja* pl. *-aat.* He asked us to estimate what our manpower requirements in the crafts will be. *ṭilab min Ɛidna nqaddir išgadd raʒ-itkuun ʒaajatna mnil-Ɛummaal il-maahriin.* 3. *šarṭ maṭluub* pl. *šuruuṭ maṭluuba.* Does he meet our requirements? *titwaffar bii š-šuruuṭ il-maṭluuba?*

to **resemble** - *šibah (a šibih), ṭilaƐ (a ṭuluuƐ) Ɛala.* Don't you think he resembles his mother? *ma-tiƐtiqid yišbah ʔumma?* or *ma-tiƐtiqid ṭaaliƐ Ɛala ʔumma?*

reservation - 1. *ʒajiz* pl. *ʒujuuz.* I want to cancel my reservation. *ʔariid ʔalġi l-ʒajiz maali.* 2. *taʒaffuδ* pl. *-aat.* He said it with some reservation. *qaalha maƐa baƐδ it-taʒuffuδ.*

reserve - 1. *ʒtiyaaṭi.* I'm afraid we'll have to dig into our reserves. *ʔaƐtiqid raʒ-niδṭarr nistaƐmil il-iʒtiyaaṭi maalna.* -- One-fifth of the world's oil reserves are in Kuwait. *xumis iʒtiyaaṭi l-Ɛaalam mnin-nafuṭ bil-kuwayt.* 2. *ʒtiyaaṭ.* He is a reserve officer. *haaδa δaabuṭ iʒtiyaaṭ.*

to reserve - 1. *ʒijaz (i ʒajiz) n-.* Can you reserve a place for me? *tigdar tiʒjiz-li maʒall?* 2. *ʒufaδ (u ʒufuδ) n-.* He reserved the right of using the car for himself. *ʒufaδ ʒaqq istiƐmaal is-sayyaara l-nafsa.*

reserved - 1. *haadiʔ* pl. *-iin.* I found him very reserved. *šifta kulliš haadiʔ.* 2. *maʒjuuz.* All seats are reserved. *kull il-maʒallaat maʒjuuza.*

to **resign** - *staqaal (i stiqaala).* He resigned as chairman of the committee. *staqaal min riʔaasat il-lujna.*

resignation - 1. *stiqaala* pl. *-aat.* He handed in his resignation today. *qaddam istiqaalta l-yoom.* 2. *stislaam, ʔiδƐaan.* He received the news with resignation. *tqabbal il-ʔaxbaar b-istislaam.* 3. *tasliim.* We have nothing left but resignation to the will of God. *ma-Ɛidna ġeer it-tasliim l-ʔiraadat ʔaḷḷa.*

resigned to - *raaδi b-.* She's resigned to her fate of remaining an old maid for the rest of her life. *raaδya b-qismatha tibqa bnayya ṭuul Ɛumurha.*

to **resist** - *qaawam (u muqaawama) t-.* He tried to resist, but the police arrested him. *ʒaawal yqaawum laakin iš-šurṭa ʔalqat il-qabuδ Ɛalee.* -- I couldn't resist the temptation. *ma-gdart aqaawum il-ʔiġraaʔ.*

resistance - *muqaawama.* He didn't put up any resistance. *ma-bayyan ʔay muqaawama.*

to **resole** - *ʒaṭṭ (u ʒaṭṭ) n- naƐal.* I'm having my shoes resoled. *da-aʒuṭṭ naƐal il-qundarti.*

resolution - *qaraar* pl. *-aat.* The resolution was adopted unanimously. *l-qaraar iṭṣaddaq bil-ʔijmaaƐ.*

resort - *maljaʔ* pl. *malaajiʔ.* As a last resort I can turn to him. *ka-ʔaaxir maljaʔ agdar arjaƐ ʔila.*

health resort - *maṣaʒʒ* pl. *-aat.* She's not going to a health resort this year. *ma-raʒ-itruuʒ lil-maṣaʒʒ has-sana.*

summer resort - *maṣiif* pl. *maṣaayif.* Do you know a nice summer resort? *tuƐruf fadd maṣiif laṭiif?*

to resort - *ltijaʔ (i ltijaaʔ).* I don't want to resort to force. *ma-ʔariid altijiʔ lil-quwwa.*

resource - 1. *wasiila* pl. *wasaaʔil.* I have exhausted all resources. *stanfaδit kull il-wasaaʔil.* 2. *mawrid* pl. *mawaarid.* Oil is one of our important resources. *n-nafuṭ ʔaʒad mawaaridna l-muhimma.*

respect - 1. *ʒtiraam.* He has won the respect of everyone. *ktisab iʒtiraam ij-jamiiƐ.* 2. *jiha* pl. *-aat, naaʒya* pl. *nawaaʒi.* We were satisfied in every respect. *činna raaδiin min kull ij-jihaat.*

to respect - *ʒtiram (u ʒtiraam).* I respect your opinion. *ʔaani ʔaʒturum raʔyak.* -- You must respect your elders. *laazim tiʒturum il-ʔakbar minnak.*

respectable - *muʒtaram* pl. *-iin, muƐtabar* pl. *-iin.* Respectable people don't go in a place like that. *n-naas il-muʒtaramiin ma-yṭubbuun hiiči makaan.*

respected - *muztaram* pl. *-iin, muEtabar* pl. *-iin.* He is a respected business man in this city. *huwwa fadd rajul ?aEmaal muztaram ib-hal-wlaaya.*
responsibility - *mas?uuliyya* pl. *-aat.* I'll take the responsibility. *?aani raz-atzammal il-mas?uuliyya.*
responsible - *mas?uul* pl. *-iin.* They held him responsible for the damage. *Etibroo mas?uul Eann iδ-δarar.*
rest - 1. *baaqi, baqiyya.* Eat some now and save the rest. *?ukul qisim hassa w-δumm il-baaqi.* -- You raise the money, and I'll do the rest. *?inta dabbur l-ifluus w-?aani Ealayya l-baaqi.* -- Where are the rest of the boys? *ween baqiyyat il-wulid?* 2. *raaza.* I went to the mountains for a rest. *rizit lij-jibaal il-ṭalab ir-raaza.* 3. *stiraaza* pl. *-aat.* Let's take a short rest. *xal-naaxuδ fadd istiraaza gṣayyra.*
at rest - *raakid, waaguf.* Wait until the pointer is at rest. *?intiδir ?ila ?an ykuun il-mu?aššir raakid.*
**This will put your mind at rest. *haay raz-itrayyiz fikrak.*
to take a rest - *staraaz (i stiraaza), rtaaz (a raaza).* Let's take a little rest. *xal-nirtaaz išwayya.*
to rest - 1. *rtaaz (a raaza), staraaz (a stiraaza).* Rest awhile. *?irtaaz išwayya.* 2. *rayyaz (a taryiiz), ?araaz (i ?iraaza).* Try to rest your eyes. *zaawil itrayyiz Eeenak.* 3. *wugaE (a wuguuE).* The whole responsibility rests on him. *kull il-mas?uuliyya toogaE Ealee.* 4. *taččа (i tatčiya, ttičči) t-.* The ladder was resting against the wall. *d-daraj čaan mittačča Eal-zaayiṭ.*
**The decision rests with you. *l-qaraar b-iidak.*
to rest assured - *ṭma?ann (i ṭmi?naan).* Rest assured that I'll do what you want. *ṭma?inn raz-?asawwi lli triida.*
restaurant - *maṭEam* pl. *maṭaaEum, looqanṭa* pl. *-aat.* Is there a good restaurant around here? *?aku maṭEam zeen ib-hal-manṭiqa?*
restless - *qaliq* pl. *-iin.* I'm very restless today. *?aani kulliš qaliq il-yoom.*
to **restore** - 1. *staEaad (i stiEaada).* The police restored order. *š-šurṭa staEaadaw in-niδaam.* 2. *rajjaE (i tarjiiE) t-.* All the stolen goods were restored. *kull il-masruuqaat trajjEat.* 3. *jaddad (i tajdiid) t-.* The government is going to restore this old mosque. *l-zukuuma raz-itjaddid haj-jaamiE il-Eatiig.*
to **restrain** - 1. *ṣayṭar (i ṣayṭara) Eala.* She couldn't restrain her curiosity. *ma-gidrat itṣayṭir Eala fuδuulha.* 2. *δubaṭ (u δabuṭ) n-.* Can't you restrain your children? *ma-tigdar tuδbuṭ ijhaalak?*
rest room - *mirzaaδ* pl. *maraaziiδ, ?adabxaana* pl. *?adabxaayin, xalwa* pl. *xalaawi, beet* (pl. *byuut*) *maay.*
result - *natiija* pl. *nataa?ij.* The results were very satisfactory. *n-nataa?ij kaanat kulliš murδiya.*
retail - *bil-mufrad.* He sells wholesale and retail. *ybiiE bij-jumla w-bil-mufrad.*
to retail - *baaE (i beeE) n- bil-mufrad.* This coat retails at about thirty dinars. *hal-qappuuṭ yinbaaE bil-mufrad ib-zawaali tlaaθiin diinaar.*
to **retire** - 1. *nsizab (i nsizaab).* He has retired from public life. *nsizab imnil-zayaat il-Eaamma.* 2. *tqaaEad (a taqaaEud).* He'll be able to retire next year. *ykuun b-imkaana yitqaaEad is-sana j-jaaya.*
retreat - *taraajuE* pl. *-aat, taqahqur* pl. *-aat, nsizaab* pl. *-aat.* The retreat was orderly. *t-taraajuE čaan muntaδam.*
to retreat - *traajaE (a taraajuE), tqahqar (a taqahqur), nsizab (i nsizaab).* They were forced to retreat after two day's fighting. *δṭarraw yitraajEuun baEad qitaal yoomeen.*
return - 1. *waarid* pl. *-aat.* How much of a return did you get on your investment? *šgadd waarid ?ijak min tašģiil ifluusak?* 2. *rajEa* pl. *-aat, Eawda* pl. *-aat.* I found many things changed on my return. *b-rajiEti šift ihwaaya ?ašyaa? mitbaddla.* 3. *murajjaE.* I didn't use my return ticket. *ma-staEmalit biṭaaqati l-murajjaE.*
to return - 1. *rijaE (a rujuuE).* When did you return? *šwakit rijaEit?* -- I've returned to my original idea. *rjaEit ?ila ra?yi l-Eatiig.* 2. *rajjaE (i tarjiiE) t-.* She didn't return my visit. *ma-rajjEat-li z-ziyaara.* 3. *Eaad (i ?iEaada), rajjaE (i tarjiiE).* Don't forget to return the book. *la-tinsa tEiid l-iktaab.*

returns - *nataa?ij.* Have the election returns come in yet? *nataa?ij il-intixaabaat wuṣlat loo baEad?*
**Many happy returns! *?aḷḷa yEiida Ealeek bis-suruur.*
revenge - *θaar, ntiqaam.*
to revenge - *θi?ar (a θaar), ntiqam (i ntiqaam).* He revenged the death of his father. *θi?ar qatil ?abuu.* or ***?axaδ θaar ?abuu.*
reverse - 1. *gufa, θaani.* Don't forget to fill in the reverse side of the card. *la-tinsa titrus gufa l-kaart.* or *la-tinsa titrus il-wujj iθ-θaani mnil-kaart.* 2. *bagg.* Put the transmission in reverse. *xalli l-giir Eal-bagg.*
to reverse - 1. *rijaE (a rujuuE) li-wara.* Tell him to reverse. *gul-la yirjaE li-wara.* 2. *Eikas (i Eakis) n-.* In order to put it together, reverse the procedure. *zatta trakkibha, ?iEkis il-Eamaliyya.*
review - *muraajaEa* pl. *-aat.* He publishes book reviews in this magazine. *yinšur muraajaEaat bil-kutub ib-hal-majalla.*
to review - *niqad (u naqid) n-.* Who's going to review the play? *minu raz-yinqud it-tamθiiliyya?*
review lesson - *daris* (pl. *druus*) *muraajaEa.*
to **revolt** - *θaar (u θawra).* Why did they revolt? *leeš θaaraw?*
revolution - 1. *θawra* pl. *-aat.* He was the hero of the revolution and was later killed. *čaan baṭal iθ-θawra w-baEdeen inkital.* 2. *farra* pl. *-aat.* How many revolutions does this motor make per minute? *čam farra tiftarr hal-makiina bid-daqiiqa?*
to **revolve** - 1. *daar (u dawaraan).* The moon revolves around the earth. *l-gumar yduur zawl il-?arδ.* 2. *ftarr (a ftiraar).* The wheel revolves on its axle. *č-čarix yiftarr zawil mazwara.*
reward - *jaa?iza* pl. *jawaa?iz, mukaafa?a* pl. *-aat.* He was promised a substantial reward. *nwiEad ib-jaa?iza θamiina.*
to reward - *jaaza (i mujaazaat) t-, kaafa? (i mukaafa?a) t-.* He was well rewarded for his diligence. *zeen itkaafa? Eala jtihaada.*
rhyme - *qaafiya* pl. *qawaafi.* This word doesn't fit the rhyme. *hač-čilma ma-tiji Eal-qaafiya.*
rhymed prose - *sajiE.*
rib - 1. *δilaE* pl. *δluuE.* He's so thin you can see his ribs. *huwwa δiEiif ?ila daraja tšuuf iδluuEa.* -- Two ribs of my boat were broken. *nkisrat δilEeen min iδluuE il-balam maali.* 2. *siim* pl. *syaam.* The wind broke one of the ribs of my umbrella. *l-hawa kisar siim min isyaam šamsiiti.*
ribbon - 1. *qirdeela* pl. *-aat.* She was wearing a blue ribbon in her hair. *čaanat laabsa qirdeela zarga b-šaEarha.* 2. *šariiṭ* pl. *šaraayiṭ.* I need a new ribbon for my typewriter. *?aztaaj šariiṭ jidiid il-?aalat iṭ-ṭaabiEa maalti.*
rice - 1. *timman.* I'd like a pound of rice. *?ariid paawan timman.* 2. *šilib, timman.* This man is one of the biggest rice merchants in Iraq. *haaδa min ?akbar tujjaar iš-šilib bil-Eiraaq.*
rich - 1. *zangiin* pl. *zanaagiin, ģani* pl. *?aģniyaa?.* He is a rich man. *haaδa waazid zangiin.* 2. *θari* pl. *?aθriyaa?.* He comes from a rich family. *huwwa min Eaa?ila θariyya.* 3. *dasim.* The food is too rich. *l-?akil kulliš dasim.* 4. *xaṣib.* It's rich soil. *hiyya ṭurba xaṣba.*
rickets - *kusaaz.*
riddle - *laģiz* pl. *?alģaaz, zazzuura* pl. *-aat.*
ride - 1. *rukba* pl. *rukab.* It's only a short ride by bus. *hiyya muu ?azyad min rukbat paaṣ qaṣiira.* 2. *farra* pl. *-aat.* Let's take a ride in the car. *xalli nsawwii-nna fadd farra bis-sayyaara.* or *xal-niṭlaE bis-sayyaara.*
**He gave me a ride all the way. *waṣṣalni b-sayyaarta kull iṭ-ṭariiq.*
to ride - 1. *rikab (a rukuub) n-.* Do you know how to ride a motorcycle? *tuEruf tirkub maaṭoorsikil?* -- We rode in a beautiful car. *rikabna b-sayyaara zilwa.* 2. *miša (i maši).* This car rides smoothly. *has-sayyaara timši miθl id-dihin.*
**Stop riding me! *bass Eaad itlizz!* or *ma-tfukk yaaxa Eaad!*
ridiculous - *saxiif, saxaafa.* Don't be ridiculous! *la-ṭṣiir saxiif!* -- That's ridiculous. *haay saxaafa.* or *haaδa šii saxiif.*
rid of - *xalṣaan min.* I'm glad I'm rid of it. *?aani farzaan xalṣaan minna.*
to get rid of - *xilaṣ (a xalaaṣ) min, txallaṣ (a taxalluṣ) min.* I got rid of her at last. *?axiiran*

ixlaṣit minha.

rifle - *bunduqiyya* pl. *banaadiq, tufga* pl. *tufag.*

right - **1.** *ẓaqq* pl. *ẓuquuq.* I insist on my rights. *ʔaani ʔaṣirr Ɛala ẓuquuqi.* -- You have no right to say that. *ma-ʔilak ẓaqq itguul haay.* -- He's right. *l-ẓaqq wiyyaa.* **2.** (m.) *yamiin* (f.) *yimna.* I've lost the glove for my right hand. *ḍayyaƐit ič-čaff maal ʔiidi l-yimna.* **3.** *qaaʔim.* A right angle has ninety degrees. *z-zaawiya l-qaaʔima biiha tisƐiin daraja.* **4.** *munaasib.* He came just at the right time. *ʔija bil-wakt il-munaasib tamaaman.* **5.** *ṣaẓiiẓ.* Are we going the right way? *ʔiẓna da-nimši Ɛaṭ-ṭariiq iṣ-ṣaẓiiẓ?* **6.** *raʔsan, fadd raas, Ɛadil.* I'm coming right home from the office. *raẓ-ʔaji mniš-šuġuḷ lil-beet raʔsan.* **7.** *tamaaman.* The house is right next to the church. *l-beet yamm il-kaniisa tamaaman.* **8.** *zeen.* We'll leave tomorrow if the weather is right. *nitlaƐ baačir ʔiδa j-jaww zeen.*

**You can't be in your right mind. *ʔinta laazim muu b-kaamil Ɛaqlak.*

**It serves him right! *yistaahil!* or *yistaẓiqq!*

**Go right ahead. *fuut ib-faalak.* or *twakkal Ɛal-aḷḷa!*

**He's right here next to me. *hiyyaata hnaa b-ṣaffi.*

right away - *ẓaalan, raʔsan, fawran.* Let's go right away or we'll be late. *xalli nruuẓ ẓaalan w-ʔilla nitʔaxxar.* -- Tell him to come to see me right away. *gul-la yiji ywaajihni fawran.*

right now - *hassa.* I'm busy right now. *ʔaani mašġuul hassa.*

right off - *fawran.* I can't answer that right off. *ma-agdar ajaawub Ɛala haay fawran.*

rightful - *šarƐi*.* He is the rightful owner of the house. *huwwa l-maalik iš-šarƐi lil-beet.*

right-hand - (m.) *yamiin* (f.) *yimna.* The school is on the right-hand side of the street. *l-madrasa Ɛaj-jiha l-yimna mniš-šaariƐ.*

**He's the boss's right-hand man. *huwwa l-ʔiid il-yimna lir-raʔiis.*

rim - *ʔaṭaar* pl. *-aat.* The rim of my glasses is broken. *ʔaṭaar manaaḍri maksuur.*

ring - **1.** *miẓbas* pl. *maẓaabis, xaatam* pl. *xawaatim.* She wears a ring on her right hand. *tilbas miẓbas b-iidha l-yimna.* **2.** *ẓalqa* pl. *-aat.* Tie the rope to the iron ring. *šidd il-ẓabil ib-ẓalaqt il-ẓadiid.* **3.** *dagga, ranna.* That bell has a peculiar ring. *haj-jaras ʔila ranna ġariiba.* **4.** *ring* pl. *-aat.* I had the mechanic put in a new set of rings. *xalleet il-fiitarči yẓuṭṭ-li ṭaxum ringaat jidiida.*

to give a ring - *dagg (u) talafoon.* Give me a ring tomorrow. *dugg-li talafoon baačir.*

to ring - **1.** *rann (i rann).* The noise is still ringing in my ears. *l-laġwa baƐadha da-trinn ib-ʔiδni.* **2.** *dagg (u dagg).* The phone rang. *dagg it-talafoon.* -- Did you ring the bell? *daggeet ij-jaras?*

**Somehow it doesn't ring true. *ʔašu ma-tbayyin ṣudug.*

rinse - *xaḍḍa* pl. *-aat.* Two rinses will be enough. *xaḍḍteen itkaffi.*

to rinse - **1.** *xaḍḍ (u xaḍḍ) n-.* I rinse my wash twice. *ʔaani ʔaxuḍḍ il-ġasiil maali marrteen.* -- Rinse the glasses under the faucet. *xuḍḍ il-iglaaṣaat jawwa il-buuri.* **2.** *maḍmaḍ (u maḍmaḍa) t-.* Rinse out your mouth with water and a little salt. *maḍmuḍ ẓalgak ib-maay w-šwayya miliẓ.*

riot - **1.** *hayaaj, Ɛarbada, šaġab.* Two people were killed in the riot. *šaxṣeen inkitlaw ʔaθnaaʔ il-hayaaj.* -- The riot was caused by several drunkards. *l-Ɛarbada sababha čam sakraan.*

**He's a riot. *haaδa fadd imṣannifči.*

to riot - *šaaġab (i mušaaġaba).* They ignored the presence of the police and kept on rioting all night. *ʔahmilaw wujuud iš-šurṭa w-ḍallaw yšaaġbuun ṭuul il-leel.*

rip - **1.** *šagg* pl. *šguug, mazig* pl. *mzuug.* Do you know you have a rip in your jacket? *tidri ʔaku mazig ib-sitirtak?* **2.** *fatig* pl. *ftuug.* There is a rip in the seam of your shirt under the arm. *ʔaku fatig ib-θoobak jawwa ʔubṭak.*

to rip - **1.** *mizag (i mazig) n-, šagg (u šagg) n-.* I ripped my pants climbing the fence. *šaggeet panṭurooni ʔaθnaaʔ-ma činit ʔatšalbah Ɛas-siyaaj.* **2.** *fitag (i fatig) n-.* I have to rip out the seams. *laazim ʔaftig l-ikwaaka.*

ripe - **1.** *laaẓig, naaḍij.* The apples aren't ripe yet. *t-tiffaaẓ baƐda maa laaẓig.* **2.** *mithayyiʔ.* The situation is ripe for trouble. *l-waḍiƐ mithayyiʔ lil-mašaakil.*

**He lived to a ripe old age. *Ɛammar ihwaaya.*

to **rise** - **1.** *ṭilaƐ (i ṭuluuƐ), ʔašraq (i šuruuq).* The sun rises early. *š-šamis titlaƐ min wakit.* **2.** *ṣiƐad (a ṣuƐuud).* Over there the road rises again. *hnaak iṭ-ṭariiq yiṣƐad marra lux.* **3.** *rtifaƐ (i rtifaaƐ), ṣiƐad (i ṣuƐuud).* The river is rising rapidly. *n-nahar da-yirtifiƐ bil-Ɛajal.* -- Prices are still rising. *l-ʔasƐaar baƐadha da-tirtifiƐ.* **4.** *gaam (u qiyaam).* All rose from their seats. *kullhum gaamaw min makaanaathum.* **5.** *nnufax (u nnifaax).* The cake is rising. *l-keeka da-tinnufux.*

**He rose from the ranks. *haaδa maslaki.*

risk - *muxaaṭara* pl. *-aat, mujaazafa* pl. *-aat.* I can't take such a risk. *ma-agdar asawwi hiiči mujaazafa.*

to risk - *xaaṭar (i muxaaṭara) b-, jaazaf (i mujaazafa) b-.* He risked his life to save her. *xaaṭar ib-ẓayaata ẓatta yungiδha.* -- He's risked his entire fortune. *jaazaf ib-kull θaruuta.*

**He risked his life. *ẓaṭṭ ẓayaata Ɛala čaffa.*

rival - *munaafis* pl. *-iin, muzaaẓim* pl. *-iin.* They were rivals for many years. *čaanaw munaafsiin il-baƐaḍhum il-muddat isniin ihwaaya.* -- He works for a rival company. *yištuġul ib-fadd šarika muzaaẓima.*

river - *nahar* pl. *ʔanhaar, ʔanhur; šaṭṭ* pl. *šṭuuṭ.* What's the name of this river? *han-nahar š-isma?*

road - *ṭariiq* pl. *ṭuruq, darub* pl. *druub.* Where does this road go to? *haṭ-ṭariiq li-ween ywaṣṣil?* -- He's on the road to recovery. *huwwa b-ṭariiq lis-šafaaʔ.*

to go on the road - **1.** *ṭilaƐ (a) yiftarr.* Our salesman is going on the road next week. *d-dawwaar maalna raẓ-yiṭlaƐ yiftarr ʔisbuuƐ ij-jaay.* **2.** *sawwa (i) jawla, qaam (u) b-jawla.* Next month our team is going on the road for two weeks. *š-šahr ij-jaay fariiqna raẓ-ysawwi jawla l-muddat ʔisbuuƐeen.*

roar - **1.** *hadiir.* We can hear the roar of the waterfall from here. *nigdar nismaƐ hadiir iš-šallaal minnaa.* **2.** *zaʔiir.* It sounded like the roar of a lion. *čaan Ɛabaalak zaʔiir maal ʔasad.*

to roar - **1.** *ziʔar (a zaʔiir).* When he's angry he roars like a lion. *Ɛinda-ma yiġḍab yizʔar miθl il-ʔasad.* **2.** *qahqah (i qahqaha).* They roared with laughter. *qahqihaw imniḍ-ḍaẓik.*

to **roast** - *šuwa (i šawi) n-.* You didn't roast the meat long enough. *ma-šuweet il-laẓam mudda kaafya.* There's leg of lamb roasted in the oven for dinner. *ʔaku rijil quuzi mašwi lil-Ɛaša.*

to **rob** - **1.** *baag (u boog) n-.* I've been robbed. *nbaageet.* **2.** *sallab (i tasliib) t-, nihab (a nahib) n-.* They'll rob you of your last cent. *raẓ-ysalliibuun ʔaaxir filis Ɛindak.*

robbery - **1.** *booga* pl. *-aat, sariqa* pl. *-aat.* When was the robbery committed? *šwakit ṣaarat il-booga?* **2.** *tasliib, nahab, boog.* That's highway robbery! *haaδa tasliib!*

robe - **1.** *roob* pl. *-aat.* Please get me my robe and my slippers. *ʔarjuuk jiib-li r-roob win-naƐal maali.* **2.** *zbuun* pl. *-aat, Ɛabaaya* pl. *Ɛibi.* The chiefs who come from their tribes wear inner and outer robes. *š-šiyuux illi yjuun min Ɛašaayiirhum ylibsuun zbuunaat w-Ɛibi.*

rock - **1.** *ṣaxra* pl. *ṣaxar.* They had to blast the rock. *ḍṭarraw ynisfuun iṣ-ṣaxra.* **2.** *ẓjaara* pl. *ẓjaar.* He was throwing rocks. *čaan da-yšammur iẓjaar.*

to rock - **1.** *htazz (a htizaaz).* The floor rocked under our feet. *l-gaaƐ ihtazzat jawwa rijleena.* -- The boat's rocking. *l-balam da-yihtazz.* **2.** *hazz (i hazz) n-.* She rocked the cradle until the baby fell asleep. *hazzat il-kaaruuk ʔila ʔan naam ij-jaahil.* **3.** *xaḍḍ (u xaḍḍ) n-.* She showed us how to rock the churn to make butter. *šawwfatna šloon inxuḍḍ iš-šičwa ẓatta nsawwi zibid.*

rocky - *ṣaxri*.* This soil is too rocky for farming. *hal-ʔarḍ ṣaxriyya, ma-tiṣlaẓ liz-ziraaƐa.*

rod - *šiiš* pl. *šyaaš.* The parts are connected by an iron rod. *l-wuṣal mittaṣla waẓda bil-lux ib-šiiš.*

lightning rod - *maaniƐat* (pl.*-aat*) *ṣawaaƐiq.* Most large buildings have lightning rods. *ʔakθar il-Ɛimaaraat biiha maaniƐaat ṣawaaƐiq.*

role - *door* pl. *ʔadwaar.* He played an important role. *liƐab door muhimm.*

roll - **1.** *laffa* pl. *-aat.* He used up a whole roll of wrapping paper. *staᶓmal laffa kaamla min waraq it-taġliif.* **2.** *ṣammuuna* pl. *-aat,* coll. *ṣammuun.* Shall I get bread or rolls? *š-aaxuδ xubuz loo ṣammuun?*

roll of film - *filim* pl. *ʔaflaam.* I'd like two rolls of 120 film. *ʔariid filmeen zajam miyya w-ᶓišriin.*

to roll - **1.** *daᶓbal (i tdiᶓbil) t-, dazraj (i dazraja, tdizrij) t-.* Don't roll the barrel. *la-tdaᶓbil il-barmiil.* **2.** *tdaᶓbal (a tadaᶓbul), tdazraj (a tadazruj).* The ball rolled under the table. *ṭ-ṭooba tdaᶓbilat jawwa l-meez.* **3.** *tmaayal (a tamaayul).* The ship was rolling heavily. *l-baaxira čaanat da-titmaayal ib-šidda.* **4.** *dačč (a) n- b-roola.* The tennis court must be rolled. *saazt it-tanis laazim tindačč bir-roola.* or *saazt it-tanis yird-ilha doos bir-roola.* **5.** *laff (i laff) n-.* I roll my own cigarettes. *ʔaani ʔaliff jigaayri.*

to roll around - **1.** *tmarġal (a tmurġul).* The buffalo rolled around in the mud. *j-jaamuusa tmarġilat biṭ-ṭiin.* **2.** *tdaᶓbal (a tdiᶓbil).* The marbles rolled around in the box. *d-duᶓbul itdaᶓbal biṣ-ṣanduug.*

to roll out - **1.** *furaš (u fariš) n-.* The servant rolled out the mattress on the bedstead. *l-xaadim furaš id-doošag ᶓas-sariir.* **2.** *fakk (u fakk) n-.* Roll the dough out thin. *fukki l-ᶓajiin xafiif.*

to roll over - **1.** *giḷab (u gaḷub) n-.* The nurse rolled the patient over. *l-mumarriṣa guḷbat il-mariiṣ.* -- The horse rolled over on the grass. *l-izṣaan ngiḷab ᶓala ṣafzat il-lux ᶓal-zašiiš.* **2.** *tgaḷḷab (a tguḷḷub).* I rolled over in bed. *tgaḷḷabit bil-ifraaš.*

to roll up - *laff (i laff) n-.* We rolled up the rug. *laffeena z-zuuliyya.*

rollcall - *tiᶓdaad.* Did the sergeant take a roll call? *l-ᶓariif sawwa tiᶓdaad.*

Roman - *roomaani*.* Use Roman numerals. *ʔistaᶓmil ʔarqaam roomaaniyya.*

Rome - *rooma.*

roof - **1.** *ṣaṭiz* pl. *ṣṭuuz.* In Iraq people sleep on the roof in the summer. *bil-ᶓiraaq in-naas ynaamuun biṣ-ṣaṭiz biṣ-ṣeef.* **2.** *saguf* pl. *sguuf.* I burned the roof of my mouth. *zragit saguf zalgi.*

room - **1.** *ġurfa* pl. *ġuraf, gubba* pl. *gubab.* Where can I get a furnished room? *ween ʔalgi ġurfa mʔaθθiθa?* **2.** *mukaan* pl. *-aat.* Is there any room left for my baggage? *buqa mukaan ij-junaṭi?* **3.** *manaam, sakan.* What do they charge for room and board? *šgadd yaaxδuun ᶓala l-ʔakil wil-manaam?*

roomy - *waasiᶓ, razib.* We have a roomy apartment. *ᶓidna fadd šaqqa waasᶓa.*

rooster - *diič* pl. *dyuuča.*

root - *ᶓirig* pl. *ᶓruug, jaδir* pl. *jδuur.* The roots of this tree are very deep. *ᶓruug haš-šajar kulliš ġamiija.* -- The root of the tooth is decayed. *ᶓirg is-sinn xaayis.*

to take root - **1.** *ṭallaᶓ (i taṭliiᶓ) ᶓuruug.* How can you tell whether the cutting has taken root? *šloon tuᶓruf ʔiδa l-qalam ṭallaᶓ ᶓuruug?* **2.** *diraj (u duruuj).* The custom never really took root. *l-ᶓaada bil-zaqiiqa ʔabad ma-dirjat.*

to root out - *staʔṣal (i stiʔṣaal).* We must root out crime. *laazim nistaʔṣil il-ʔijraam.*

**He stood there as if rooted to the spot. *wugaf ihnaak ᶓabaalak mitbasmur ib-mukaana.*

rope - *zabil* pl. *zbaal.* He was leading the calf by a rope. *čaan gaayid il-ᶓijil ib-zabil.*

**Give him enough rope and he'll hang himself. *raxxii-la l-zabil išwayya w-šuuf išloon yidmur nafsa.*

**I'm at the end of my rope. *ʔaani stanfaδit kull-ma b-ṭaaqti.*

**He knows all the ropes. *yuᶓruf kull il-idruub.*

to rope off - *giṭaᶓ (a gaṭiᶓ) b-zabil.* They roped off the street for the parade. *giṭᶓaw iš-šaariᶓ ib-zabil lil-istiᶓraaṣ.*

rose - *wardat (pl. -aat) juuri,* coll. *warid juuri.* He brings me roses everyday. *yjiib-li warid juuri yoomiyya.*

rosebush - *hiraš (pl. hruuš) warid juuri.*

to **rot** - *xaas (i xayasaan).* The fruit is rotting on the trees. *l-fawaakih da-txiis ᶓal-ʔašjaar.*

rotten - **1.** *xaayis.* The peaches are rotten. *l-xoox xaayis.* **2.** *qaδir.* They played a rotten trick on us. *liᶓbaw ᶓaleena fadd liᶓba qaδra.*

rough - **1.** *xašin.* Why are your hands so rough? *leeš ʔiidak hiiči xašna?* -- He has a rough voice. *ᶓinda ziss xašin.* -- The bench is made of rough planks. *l-maṣṭaba msawwaaya min looz xašin.* -- She isn't used to such rough work. *ma-mitᶓallma ᶓala hiiči šuġuḷ xašin.* **2.** *waᶓir.* This road is very rough. *haṭ-ṭariiq kulliš waᶓir.* **3.** *taqriibi*.* This will give you a rough idea. *haaδa yinṭiik fikra ṭaqriibiyya.*

roughly - **1.** *b-qaswa.* You've got to treat him roughly. *laazim itᶓaamla b-qaswa* or *laazim tiqsi wiyyaa.* **2.** *taqriiban.* Can you tell me roughly how much it will be? *tigdar itgul-li taqriiban išgadd raz-itkuun?*

roughneck - *qaasi* pl. *qusaat.*

round - **1.** *jawla* pl. *-aat.* He was knocked out in the first round. *nṣirab nookaawt ib-ʔawwal jawla.* **2.** *doora* pl. *-aat.* Let's have another round of coffee. *xal-nišrab doora θaanya gahwa.* -- The watchman made his last round and went to bed. *n-naaṭuur daar doorta l-ʔaxiira w-raaz ynaam.* **3.** *mdawwar, daaʔiri*.* I bought a round copper tray. *štireet ṣiiniyya ṣifir imdawwura.*

to round off - **1.** *qarrab (u taqriib) t-.* Round off your answer to the nearest ten. *qarrub jawaabak l-zadd il-ᶓašaraat.* **2.** *kawwar (u takwiir) t-.* I'm not interested in details, round off the result and give me it. *maa ᶓalayya b-tafaaṣiil; kawwur-li n-natiija w-inṭiini-yyaaha.* **3.** *ᶓaddal (i taᶓdiil) t-.* Round off the edges a little. *ᶓaddil il-zawaaši šwayya.*

to round out - *kammal (i ʔikmaal) t-.* I need this to round out my collection. *ʔaani ʔaztaaj haay zatta ʔakammil majmuuᶓti.*

round trip - *rooza w-jayya, rawaaz w-majiiʔ.* How much is the round trip? *šgadd itkallif ir-rooza wij-jayya?*

round-trip ticket - *biṭaaqa (pl. -aat) murajjaᶓ.* He bought a round-trip ticket. *štira biṭaaqa murajjaᶓ.*

rout - *hazima* pl.*-aat, hazaaʔim.* The demonstration ended with the complete rout of the students. *l-muṣaahara ntihat ib-haziima kaamla min qibal iṭ-ṭullaab.*

route - *ṭariiq* pl. *ṭuruq.* Which route did you take? *ʔay ṭariiq ʔaxaδit.*

row - *hoosa* pl. *-aat, laġwa* pl. *-aat, laġaawi.* My neighbors made a terrible row last night. *jiiraani sawwa hoosa faṣiiᶓa il-baarza bil-leel.* -- I had a row with him. *ṣaar ᶓindi laġwa wiyyaa.*

row - *sira* pl. *-aayaat, -aawaat.* We had seats in the first row. *čaan ᶓidna maqaaᶓid bis-sira l-ʔawwal.*

in a row - *marra wara l-lux, marra ᶓala marra.* He won three times in a row. *ribaz itlaθ marraat marra ᶓala marra.*

to row - *jidaf (i jadif) n-.* We rowed across the lake. *jidafna l-ṣafzat il-lux imnil-buzayra.*

rowboat - *balam* pl. *blaam.*

royal - *maliki*.*

rub - *farka* pl. *-aat.* One rub with this material will remove the spot. *farka wizda b-hal-maadda trawwiz il-lakka.*

to rub - **1.** *jallaġ (i tajliiġ) t-.* My shoes rub at the heel. *qundarti da-tjalliġ rijli mnič-čaᶓab.* **2.** *misaz (a masiz) n-.* Keep rubbing it until it shines. *ṣall imsaz biiha ʔila ʔan itguum tilmaᶓ.* **3.** *furak (u farik) n-.* He rubbed his hands together to get warm. *furak ʔiid ib-ʔiid zatta yizma.* -- Rub his back with alcohol. *ʔufruk ṣahra kuzuul.*

to rub against - *zakk (u zakk) n- b-, tnassaz (a tmissiz) b-.* The cat rubbed against my leg. *l-bazzuuna zakkat nafisha b-rijli.*

to rub down - *dallak (i tadliik).* The public baths employ men to rub down their customers. *l-zammaamaat iš-šaᶓbiyya tšaġġul čam rijjaal ydallikuun il-maᶓaamiil.*

to rub in - *furak (u farik) n- b-.* Rub the salve in well. *ʔufruk zaayid id-dihin.*

**I know I'm wrong, but you don't have to rub it in. *ʔadri ʔaani ġalṭaan bass ma-aku zaaja tᶓiid w-tiṣqul.*

to rub out - *misaz (a masiz) n-.* You forgot to rub out the price. *niseet timsaz is-siᶓir.*

rubber - **1.** *maṭṭaaṭ, laastiik.* These tires are made of synthetic rubber. *hat-taayaraat maṣnuuᶓa min maṭṭaaṭ iṣṭinaaᶓi.* **2.** *kaaluuš.* I lost one of my rubbers yesterday. *ṣayyaᶓit farda min kaaluuši l-baarza.*

rubbish - **1.** *zibil.* Don't mix the rubbish in with the garbage. *la-tuxbuṭ iz-zibil wiyya baqaaya* *l-ʔakil.* 2. *xaruṭ.* Don't talk such rubbish! *la-tiḥči hiiči xaruṭ!*

rude - *jilif* pl. *ʔajlaaf.* Don't be so rude! *la-tṣiir hal-gadd jilif.*

rudeness - *jalaafa.* His rudeness is inexcusable. *jalaafta ma-yinṣufuḥ ɛanha.*

rug - *sijjaada* pl. *-aat, zuuliyya* pl. *zwaali.*

ruin - *xaraab, damaar, halaak.* You'll be the ruin of me. *raḥ-itkuun sabab damaari.*

to ruin - 1. *tilaf (i ʔitlaaf), dumar (u damur).* The rain will ruin the crop. *l-muṭar raḥ-yitlif il-maḥṣuul.* 2. *xarrab (u taxriib) t-, dammar (u tadmiir) t-.* The volcano ruined the city. *l-burkaan xarrab il-wlaaya.* 3. *hilak (i halaak).* The war ruined them. *l-ḥarub hilkathum.* 4. *dumar (u damur) n-, dammar (u tadmiir) t-.* His new suit is completely ruined. *badilta j-jidiida ndumrat tamaaman.*

ruins - 1. *xaraayib.* The city is in ruins. *l-madiina ṣaayra xaraayib.* 2. *ʔaṭlaal, ʔaaθaar.* They discovered the ruins of an old temple. *ktišfaw ʔaṭlaal maɛbad qadiim.*

rule - 1. *ḥukum.* In old times Spain was under Arab rule. *b-zamaan il-qadiim ʔispaanya čaanat taḥat ḥukum il-ɛarab.* 2. *niðaam* pl. *ʔanðima.* That's against the rules. *haaða muxaalif lil-ʔanðima.* 3. *ʔuṣuul.* I'm sticking to the rules. *ʔaani mitqayyid bil-ʔuṣuul.* 4. *qaaɛida* pl. *qawaaɛid.* This rule doesn't apply here. *hal-qaaɛida ma-tinṭubuq ihnaa.*

as a rule - *ɛtiyaadiyyan.* As a rule, I don't smoke. *ɛtiyaadiyyan ʔaani ma-adaxxin.*

to rule - *ḥikam (u ḥukum) n-.* They wanted to rule the entire world. *raadaw yḥukmuun id-dinya kullha.*

to rule out - *nifa (i nafi) n-.* This doesn't rule out the other possibility. *haaða ma-yinfi l-iḥtimaal il-laax.*

ruler - 1. *ḥaakim* pl. *ḥukkaam.* He was an absolute ruler. *čaan ḥaakim muṭlaq.* 2. *masṭara* pl. *masaaṭir.* The ruler is too short. *l-masṭara kulliš iqṣayyra.*

to **rumble** - 1. *ṭargaɛ (i ṭargaɛa).* We heard trucks rumbling over the bridge. *smaɛna looriyaat da-ṭṭargiɛ ɛaj-jisir.* 2. *qarqar (i qarqara).* My stomach is rumbling. *baṭni da-tqarqir.*

rumor - *ʔišaaɛa* pl. *-aat.* The rumor spread like wildfire. *l-ʔišaaɛa ntišrat miθl il-barq.*

run - 1. *darub* pl. *druub.* The city bus makes ten runs to Kufa every day. *paaṣ il-ʔamaana yruuḥ ɛašra druub lil-kuufa kull yoom.* 2. *salit.* You've got a run in your stocking. *jwaariibič bii salit.* or ***jwaariibič insilat minna xeeṭ.*

in the long run - *bil-mudda, ɛala muruur iz-zaman, wiyya l-wakit.* In the long run you'll get tired of that. *bil-mudda raḥ-tiɛjaz minha.*

to run - 1. *rikað (u rikið).* Don't run so fast. *la-tirkuð hiiči sariiɛ.* 2. *miša (i maši).* My car runs smoothly. *sayyaarti timši miθl id-dihin.* 3. *štiġal (u šuġuḷ).* Why do you keep the motor running? *leeš da-txalli l-makiina tištuġul?* -- How many weeks has this movie been running? *hal-filim čam isbuuɛ ṣaar-la da-yištuġul?* or *hal-filim išgadd ṣaar-la maɛruuð?* 4. *šaġġal (i tašġiil) t-.* Can you run a washing machine? *tigdar itšaġġil makiina maal ġasl ihduum?* 5. *kišaf (i kašif).* The color runs. *l-loon yikšif.* 6. *faat (u foot).* How often does this bus run? *kull išgadd hal-paaṣ yfuut?* 7. *jira (i jarayaan).* The irrigation ditch has water running through it. *s-saagya da-yijri biiha maay.* -- Does that run in the family? *haaða yijri b-damm il-ɛaaʔila?* 8. *daar (i ʔidaara) n-.* He's been running the business for three years. *ṣaar-la tlaθ isniin da-ydiir iš-šuġuḷ.* 9. *marr (u marr).* The road runs right in front of my house. *š-šaariɛ ymurr giddaam beeti.* 10. *wuṣal (a wuṣuul), bilaġ (i buluuġ).* The casualties ran into thousands. *l-ʔiṣaabaat wuṣlat ʔila ʔaalaaf.* 11. *fawwat (i tafwiit) t-.* Run the rope through this loop. *fawwit il-ḥabil min hal-ḥalqa.* 12. *txallal (a taxallul).* The theme runs through the novel from beginning to end. *l-fikra titxallal il-quṣṣa mnil-bidaaya lin-nihaaya.*

to run across - *ṣaadaf (i muṣaadafa) t-.* Maybe I'll run across him someday. *yimkin ʔaṣaadfa fadd yoom.*

to run aground - *gayyaš (i tagyiiš).* My boat ran aground. *balami gayyaš.*

to run around - 1. *xawwar (u taxwiir), daar (u dawaraan), ftarr (a farr).* Where have you been running around? *ween činit da-txawwur?* 2. *miša (i maši), ṣaaḥab (i muṣaaḥaba).* He's running around with a bad crowd. *mṣaaḥib-la muu xooš jamaaɛa.*

to run away - 1. *hirab (u huruub, harab), farr (u firaar).* His wife has run away. *marta hurbat.* -- The thief ran away before the police arrived. *l-ḥaraami farr gabuḷ-ma tiji š-šurṭa.* 2. *nhizam (i hazиima), ɛallag (i taɛliig).* When he saw us, he ran away. *min šaafna nhizam.* or ***min šaafna šammaɛ il-xeeṭ.*

to run down - 1. *tqaṣṣa (a taqaṣṣi).* We ran down all the clues. *tqaṣṣeena kull il-ʔadilla.* 2. *siḥag (a saḥig) n-.* He was run down by a truck. *nsiḥag ib-sayyaarat loori.* 3. *ḥiča (i ḥači) ɛala.* She's always running her friends down behind their backs. *haay daaʔiman tiḥči ɛala ʔaṣdiqaaʔha waraahum.* 4. *xilaṣ (a xalaaṣ) naṣub-.* The clock has run down. *s-saaɛa xilaṣ naṣubha.*

to run dry - *nišaf (a našif), yibas (a yibis).* The well ran dry last summer. *l-biir nišaf is-sana l-faatat.*

to run errands - *ṭṣaxxar (a taṣaxxur).* I don't have time to run errands for you. *maa ɛindi wakit aṭṣaxxar-lak.*

to run for - *raššaḥ (i taršiiḥ) t- l-.* Who's running for the lower house from this district? *minu mraššiḥ lin-niyaaba min hal-manṭiqa?*

to run into - 1. *diɛam (a daɛim) b-.* He ran the car into a tree. *diɛam is-sayyaara b-šajara.* 2. *ṣaadaf (i muṣaadafa).* We ran into them in Paris last summer. *ṣaadafnaahum ib-paariis iṣ-ṣeef il-maaði.*

**He's running into debt. *da-ywaggiɛ nafsa b-deen.*

to run low - *šaḥḥ (i šaḥḥ).* My money is running low. *fluusi da-tšiḥḥ.*

to run off - 1. *ɛallag (i taɛliig), hirab (a huruub), nhizam (i nhizaam).* He ran off with the club's funds. *ʔaxað ifluus in-naadi w-ɛallag.* 2. *ṭufaḥ (a ṭafuḥ).* The water ran off the fields. *l-maay ṭufaḥ imnil-ḥuquul.*

to run out - 1. *xilaṣ (a xalaaṣ), nifað (a nafaað).* Our supply of sugar has run out. *xilaṣ mawjuudna mniš-šakar.* -- All their supplies ran out. *nifðat kull maʔuunathum.* 2. *hajjaj (i tahjiij) t- min.* They ran him out of town. *hajjijoo mnil-balad.*

to run over - 1. *ṭufaḥ (a ṭafuḥ).* Watch out that the bathtub doesn't run over. *diir baalak la-txalli il-baanyo yiṭfaḥ.* 2. *siḥag (i saḥig) n-.* Watch out you don't run over the children. *diir baalak la-tisḥag ij-jihhaal.* 3. *raajaɛ (i muraajaɛa).* Run over your part before the rehearsal. *raajiɛ doorak gabḷ it-tadriib.*

to run the risk - *tḥammal (a taḥammul) xaṭar, xaaṭar (i muxaaṭara), jaazaf (i mujaazafa).* He ran the risk of losing all his money. *tḥammal xaṭar xaṣaarat kull ifluusa.*

rundown - 1. *puxta, xaraaba.* The house is rundown. *l-beet ṣaayir puxta.* or *l-beet ġaadi xaraaba.* 2. *minhaar, minḥaṭṭ, talfaan.* His health is rundown; he needs a tonic. *ṣiḥḥta minḥaṭṭa, yriid-la muqawwiyyaat.* 3. *minhadd, barbaad.* She looks terribly rundown. *ybayyin ɛaleeha minhadda tamaaman.* or *ybayyin ɛaleeha ṣaayra barbaada.* 4. *mulaxxaṣ* pl. *-aat.* They gave us a rundown on the news. *nṭoona mulaxxaṣ il-ʔaxbaar.*

rung - *darja* pl. *-aat.* The top rung of the ladder is broken. *d-darja l-foogaaniyya maal id-daraj maksuura.*

runner - *raakuuð* pl. *ruwaakiið.* He's a famous runner. *haaða fadd raakuuð mašhuur.*

rupture - *fatiq* pl. *ftuuq.* He has a rupture. *ɛinda fatiq.*

ruse - *ḥiila* pl. *ḥiyal, xudɛa* pl. *xudaɛ.* We had to resort to a ruse. *ðṭarreena niltiji ʔila xudɛa.*

rush - 1. *bardiyya* pl. *-aat* coll. *bardi.* This mat is made of rushes. *hal-ḥaṣiir min bardi.* 2. *ɛajala.* What's the rush for? *ɛala weeš hal-ɛajala?* 3. *zdiḥaam.* Let's wait till the rush is over. *xal-nintiðir ʔila ʔan yixlaṣ il-izdiḥaam.*

to rush - 1. *xubaṣ (u xabṣa) n-.* Don't rush me, I'm going to do it. *la-tuxbuṣni ʔaani raḥ-asawwiiha.* 2. *staɛjal (i stiɛjaal).* Don't rush, we have lots of time. *la-tistaɛjil, ɛidna hwaaya wakit.* -- She rushed through her work and was done by noon. *staɛjilat ib-šuġuḷha w-xallṣat ið-ðuhur.* 3. *maššа (i tamšiya) t- bil-ɛajal.* They rushed the bill through. *maššaw il-laaʔiḥa*

bil-Ɛajal. **4.** *wadda (i tawdiya) bil-Ɛajal.* They rushed him to the hospital. *waddoo lil-mustašfa bil-Ɛajal.* **5.** *hijam (i hujuum).* The blood rushed to his head. *d-damm hijam ʔila raasa.*
Russia - *ruusya.*
Russian - **1.** *ruusi** pl. *ruus.* Those technicians are Russians. *hal-fanniyyiin ruus.* **2.** *ruusi.* They have a class in Russian I want to join. *Ɛidhum daris bir-ruusi ʔariid ʔaštirik bii.*
rust - *zinjaar, ṣadaʔ.* Before you paint the fence, scrape off the rust. *ɣukk iz-zinjaar gabuḷ-ma tiṣbuġ is-siyaaj.*
to rust - *zanjar (i zinjaar) t-, ṣadda (i ṣuduuʔ).* Oil the machine or it will rust. *dahhin il-makiina wa-ʔilla tzanjir.*
to **rustle** - *xašxaš (i xašxaša).* I thought I heard something rustle. *ʔaḍinn ismaƐit šii yxašxiš.*
rusty - *mzanjir, mṣaddi.* He scratched his hand on a rusty nail. *jilaġ ʔiida b-bismaar imzanjir.* -- The knife is rusty. *s-siččiina mṣaddya.*
**I'm afraid my French is a little rusty. *ʔaxša l-ifransi maali yinraad-la ṣaqil.*
rut - *nugra* pl. *nugar.* Keep out of the ruts made by the cars ahead of us. *twaxxar imnil-nugra s-sawwatha s-sayyaaraat il-gabuḷna.*
in rut - *ɣaamya, mithayyja.* Don't let the dog out; she's in rut. *la-txalli č-čalba tiṭlaƐ; tara ɣaamya.*

S

sack - *čiis* pl. *čyaas.* I want a sack of rice. *ʔariid čiis timman.*
sacred - *muqaddas.* The mosque is a sacred place. *j-jaamiƐ makaan muqaddas.*
**Nothing is sacred to him. *ma-yuƐruf il-ɣaraam.*
sacrifice - **1.** *taḍɣiya* pl. *-aat.* They made many sacrifices for their children. *hwaaya qaddimaw taḍɣiyaat il-wilidhum.* **2.** *xaṣaara.* I sold my car at a big sacrifice. *biƐit sayyaarti b-xaṣaara čbiira.*
to sacrifice - *ḍaɣɣa (i taḍɣiya) t-.* She sacrificed her life to him. *ḍaɣɣat ɣayaatha min ʔajla.*
sad - *ɣaziin.* Why is he so sad? *leeš huwwa hal-gadd ɣaziin?*
saddle - *sarij* pl. *sruuj.* Can you ride without a saddle? *tigdar tirkab bila sarij?*
to saddle - *sarrij (i tasriij) t-.* Do you know how to saddle a horse? *tuƐruf išloon itsarrij l-iɣṣaan?*
**He saddled me with all his troubles. *δabb kull maṣaayba b-raasi.* or *δabb kull ihmuuma Ɛalayya.*
safe - **1.** *qaaṣa* pl. *-aat, xzaana* pl. *-aat, xazaayin.* We keep our safe in the office. *ʔiɣna nẓuṭṭ qaaṣatna bid-daaʔira.* **2.** *b-ʔamaan.* You are safe now. *ʔinta hassa b-ʔamaan.* **3.** *ʔamiin, maʔmuun.* This neighborhood isn't quite safe. *hal-manṭiqa muu hal-gadd ʔamiina.* **4.** *saliim.* That's a safe guess. *haaδa taxmiin saliim.*
**Is the bridge safe for cars? *j-jisir yitɣammal sayyaaraat?*
**To be on the safe side, let's ask him again. *ɣatta nkuun mitʔakkidiin, xalli nsiʔla marra lux.*
safe and sound. *ṣaaġ saliim.* He's back safe and sound. *rijaƐ ṣaaġ saliim.*
safely - *b-salaama.* They arrived safely. *wuṣlaw ib-salaama.*
safety - *salaama.* This is for your personal safety. *haaδi l-salaamtak iš-šaxṣiyya.*
**First the children were brought to safety. *ʔaxδaw il-aṭfaal bil-ʔawwal ʔila makaan amiin.*
safety razor - *makiinat* (pl. *makaayin*) *ɣilaaqa, zyaan.*
to **sag** - **1.** *hubaṭ (u habuṭ), rtixa (i rtixaaʔ).* The bookshelf sags in the middle. *raff il-kutub haabuṭ imnin-nuṣṣ.* **2.** *xisaf (u xasuf).* The mattress sags in the middle. *l-ifraaš xaasif imnin-nuṣṣ.*
Sahara Desert - *ṣ-ṣaɣraaʔ il-kubra.*
sail - *šraaƐ* pl. *-aat.* The wind tore the sail. *l-hawa šagg l-išraaƐ.*
to sail - *tirak (u tarik), ṭilaƐ (a ṭluuƐ).* The boat sails at five. *s-safiina titruk saaƐa xamsa.*
**We go sailing every week. *kull isbuuƐ niṭlaƐ bil-balam ʔabu širaaƐ.*
**Do you know how to sail a boat? *tuƐruf išloon itquud balam širaaƐi?*
sailboat - *balam širaaƐi* pl. *blaam širaaƐiyya.*
sailor - *baɣɣaar* pl. *baɣɣaara.* How many sailors are on the boat? *čam baɣɣaar ʔaku Ɛas-safiina?*
sake - *xaaṭir, muud, ʔajil.* I did it for your sake. *sawweetha Ɛala muudak.* -- He gave his life for his country's sake. *ḍaɣɣa b-nafsa min ʔajil bilaada.* -- At least do it for your son's sake! *Ɛal-aqall sawwiiha l-xaaṭir ibnak.*
**For the sake of argument, let's say he did go. *xalli niftiriḍ ʔinna raaɣ.*
salad - *zalaaṭa.*
salary - *raatib* pl. *rawaatib, maƐaaš* pl. *-aat.* How can you manage on that salary? *šloon itdabbur ʔamrak ib-har-raatib?*
sale - **1.** *beeƐ.* The sale of alcoholic drinks to minors is prohibited. *beeƐ il-mašruubaat liṣ-ṣiġaar mamnuuƐ.* -- Our neighbor's house is for sale. *beet jiiraanna lil-beeƐ.* -- Sales of cotton goods have doubled this year. *beeƐ il-mantuujaat il-quṭniyya ḍ̣aaƐaf has-sana.* **2.** *tanziilaat.* I bought this coat at a sale. *štireet hal-qappuuṭ min maɣall Ɛinda tanziilaat.*
salesclerk - *bayyaaƐ* pl. *-a, -iin.* He's a salesclerk in a department store. *huwwa bayyaaƐ ib-maɣall tijaari.*
salesman - *bayyaaƐ* pl. *-a, -iin.* One of our salesmen will call on you tomorrow. *waaɣid min bayyaaƐiinna raɣ-yzuurak baačir.*
salt - **1.** *miliɣ.* Pass me the salt, please. *naawušni l-miliɣ rajaaʔan.* **2.** *mmallaɣ.* Do you have salt cheese? *Ɛindak jibin immallaɣ?*
to salt - *mallaɣ (i tamliiɣ) t-.* Did you salt the soup? *mallaɣti š-šoorba?*
to salt away - *xazzan (i taxziin) t-, ṣammad (u taṣmiid) t-.* He salted away a tidy sum of money. *haada xazzan xooš kammiyya mnil-ifluus.*
salt flat - *ṣabxa* pl. *-aat.*
salt shaker - *mamlaɣa* pl. *mamaaliɣ.*
salt works - *mamlaɣa* pl. *mamaaliɣ.* We visited the salt works near Basra. *zirna l-mamlaɣa qurb il-baṣra.*
salty - *maaliɣ.* The fish is awfully salty. *s-simač kulliš maaliɣ.*
same - **1.** *nafis.* I can be back on the same day. *ʔagdar arjaƐ ib-nafs il-yoom.* -- We're the same age. *ʔiɣna b-nafs il-Ɛumur.* or **ʔiɣna Ɛumurna suwa.* -- Thanks, the same to you! *šukran, ʔatmannaa-lak nafs iš-šii.* or **ʔinta hammeen.* **2.** *suwa.* That's all the same to me. *kullha suwa Ɛindi.* or **haay kullha fadd šii bin-nisba ʔili.*
all the same - *maƐa δaalik.* All the same, I want to see it. *maƐa δaalik, ʔariid ašuufha.*
sample - *namuuδaj* pl. *namaaδij, namuuna* pl. *namaayin.* Do you have a sample of the material with you? *Ɛindak namuuδaj imnil-iqmaaš jaayba wiyyaak?*
sand - *ramuḷ.*
sandal - *naƐal, naƐaal* pl. *niƐil.*
sandwich - *sandwiiča* pl. *-aat.* Take a few sandwiches along. *ʔuynδ wiyyaak čam sandwiiča.*
to sandwich in - *ɣiṣar (i ɣaṣir) n-.* He was sandwiched in between two stout women. *nɣiṣar been niswaan iθneen ismaan.*
sanitary - *ṣiɣɣi**. Your kitchen is not sanitary enough. *maṭbaxak muu ṣiɣɣi kaafi.*
sarcastic - *mithakkim* pl. *-iin.*
sardine - *sardiina* pl. *-aat* coll. *sardiin.*
satisfaction - *rtiyaaɣ, ʔirḍaaʔ.* It gives me great satisfaction to hear that. *ʔašƐur b-irtiyaaɣ čibiir min asmaƐha.*
**Was everything settled to your satisfaction? *ntihat il-masʔala miθil-ma triid?* or *kullši čaan ṣaayir Ɛala keefak?*
satisfactory - *murḍi.* His condition is satisfactory. *ɣaalta murḍiya.*
to be satisfactory - *wufa (i wafooʔ) bil-maraam.* This room is quite satisfactory. *hal-ġurfa toofi bil-maraam tamaaman.*
to **satisfy** - **1.** *ʔarḍa (i ʔirḍaaʔ) n-, raḍḍa (i tarḍiya) t-.* Your answer doesn't satisfy me. *jawaabak ma-yirḍiini.* -- I'm not satisfied with my new apartment. *ʔaani ma-raaḍi Ɛala šuqqti j-jidiida.* -- You can't satisfy everybody. *ma-tigdar itraḍḍi kull waaɣid.* **2.** *qinaƐ (a qanaaƐa) n-.* We'll have to be satisfied with less. *laazim niqnaƐ ib-ʔaqall.*

Saturday - *s-sabit, yoom is-sabit.*
sauce - **1.** *marga* pl. *-aat* coll. *marag.* How do you make the sauce for this dish? *šloon itsawwi l-marga maal hal-ʔakla?* **2.** *ṣooṣ* pl. *-aat, ṣaaṣ* pl. *-aat.* Put some sauce on your kabob. *xalli šwayya ṣooṣ ɛala l-kabaab.*
saucepan - *jidir* pl. *jduur, jduura; gidir* pl. *gduur, gduura.*
saucer - *maaɛuun* pl. *mwaaɛiin, ṣaẓan* pl. *ṣẓuun.*
Saudi - *suɛuudi* pl. *-iyyiin.* I met a Saudi yesterday. *laageet fadd suɛuudi l-baarẓa.*
Saudi Arabia - *l-mamlaka l-ɛarabiyya s-suɛuudiyya.*
savage - **1.** *waẓši* pl. *-iyyiin, wuẓuuš; hamaji* pl. *-iyyiin, hamaj.* You're behaving like a savage. *ʔinta titṣarraf miθl il-wuẓuuš.* **2.** *qaasi.* He started a savage attack on the government. *bida hijuum qaasi ɛal-ẓukuuma.*
to **save** - **1.** *ʔanqaδ (u ʔinqaaδ) n-.* He saved her life. *ʔanqaδ ẓayaatha.* **2.** *ṣ̌amm (u ṣ̌amm) n-, ẓtifaṣ̌ (u ẓtifaaṣ̌) b-.* Could you save this for me until tomorrow? *tigdar itṣ̌umm-li haay ʔila baačir?* -- Why do you save these old papers? *lweeš tiẓtifuṣ̌ ib-hal-ʔawraaq il-ɛatiiga?* **3.** *ẓijaz (i ẓajiz) n-.* Is this seat being saved for anyone? *hal-makaan maẓjuuz il-ʔaẓẓad?* **4.** *jimaɛ (a jamiɛ) n-, jammaɛ (i tajmiiɛ) t-.* He saves stamps. *yijmaɛ ṭawaabiɛ.* **5.** *waffar (i tawfiir) t-, ddixar (a ddixaar).* Have you saved any money? *waffarit ʔay ifluus?* **6.** *xallaṣ (i taxliiṣ) t- min, jannab (i tajniib) t- min.* You could have saved yourself the trouble. *čaan xallaṣit nafsak min-had-dooxa.*
**Save your breath. He's not listening. *la-ttaɛɛib nafsak, huwwa ma-daayir-lak baal.*
savings - *muddaxaraat.* He's used up all his savings. *ṣiraf kull muddaxaraata.*
saw - *minšaar* pl. *manaašiir.* Could I borrow a saw from you? *ʔagdar aṭlub minšaar minnak?*
to saw - *gaṣṣ (u gaṣṣ) n-, širaẓ (a šariẓ) n-.* He's been sawing wood all morning. *ṣaar-la mniṣ-ṣubuẓ yguṣṣ xišab.*
to **say** - **1.** *gaal (u gool) n-.* What did you say? *š-gilit?* -- The paper says rain. *j-jariida tguul raẓ-tumṭur.* -- What does the sign say? *š-itguul haay il-ʔišaara?* -- I'll meet you, say, in an hour. *ʔašuufak, xalli ngul baɛad saaɛa.* -- They say he speaks several languages. *yguuluun huwwa yitkallam ɛiddat luġaat.* **2.** *kitab (i kitaaba) n-, δikar (u δikra) n-, gaal (u gool) n-.* The papers didn't say a thing about it. *j-jaraayid ma-kitbat ʔay šii ɛanha.*
**There's much to be said for his suggestion. *qtiraaẓa yistiẓiqq il-ihtimaam.*
to say good-by - *waddaɛ (i tawdiiɛ) t-.* I said good-by to him yesterday. *waddaɛta l-baarẓa.*
to say nothing of - *min ɛada.* It takes a lot of time, to say nothing of the expense. *taaxuδ ihwaaya wakit haay min ɛada l-maṣaariif.*
saying - *qawl* pl. *ʔaqwaal, maθal* pl. *ʔamθaal.* That's a very common saying. *haaδa qawl kulliš šaayiɛ.*
**That goes without saying. *haaδa ma-bii munaaqaša.*
scaffold - *skalla* pl. *-aat, ʔaskala* pl. *-aat.* He fell from the scaffold. *wugaɛ min ɛal-iskalla.*
scale - *miqyaas* pl. *maqaayiis.* I bought myself a new scale. *štireet-li fadd miqyaas jidiid.* -- The scale is one to one thousand. *miqyaas ir-rasim waaẓid ɛala ʔalif.* **2.** *sullam* pl. *salaalim.* She practices musical scales all day. *titdarrab ɛala s-sullam il-mawsiiqi ṭuul in-nahaar.* **3.** *gišir* pl. *gšuur, filis* pl. *fluus.* The fish has big scales. *s-simča ɛidha gšuur ikbaar.* **4.** *miizaan* pl. *mawaaziin, miyaaziin.* Put the meat on the scales. *xalli l-laẓam bil-miizaan.*
to scale - **1.** *ṣiɛad (a ṣaɛuud) n-ɛala, tsallaq (a tasalluq).* Ten of us scaled the wall. *ɛašra minna ṣiɛdaw ɛal-ẓaayiṭ.* **2.** *gaššar (i tagšiir) t-.* The fish hasn't been scaled yet. *s-simča ma-tgašširat baɛad.*
scandal - *faṣiiẓa* pl. *faṣaayiẓ.*
scar - *ʔaθar* (pl. *ʔaaθaar*) *jiriẓ, ʔuxut.* He has a scar on his right cheek. *ɛinda ʔaθar jiriẓ ɛala xadda l-ʔayman.*
scarce - *naadir.* Gold coins have become scarce. *l-ɛumla δ-δahabiyya ṣaayra naadra jiddan.*
**Eggs are scarce at this time of year. *l-beeṣ̌ yqill ib-hal-wakit imnis-sana.*
scarcely - *bil-kaad.* I scarcely know him. *ʔaani bil-kaad ʔaɛurfa.*
scare - *fazaɛ, fazza.* You gave me an awful scare. *fazzaɛitni fazaɛ faṣiiɛ.* or ***xawwafitni hwaaya.*
to scare - **1.** *xawwaf (i taxwiif) t-.* The dog scared me to death. *č-čalib xawwafni hwaaya.* **2.** *xaaf (a xoof) n-.* I scare easily. *ʔaani ʔaxaaf bil-ɛajal.*
**We were scared stiff. *jimadna mnil-xoof.*
**Where did he scare up the money? *mneen jaab l-ifluus?* or *mneen dabbar l-ifluus?*
scarf - *laččaaf* pl. *-aat.*
scarlet - *qirmizi*.*
to **scatter** - *tfarraq (a tafarruq), ṭaššar (i taṭšiir) t-.* The crowd scattered when the police arrived. *j-jamhuur itfarraq min wuṣlat iš-šurṭa.* -- The books were scattered all over the floor. *l-kutub čaanat imṭaššara b-kull ṣafẓa ɛal-gaaɛ.*
scene - **1.** *mašhad* pl. *mašaahid, manṣ̌ar* pl. *manaaṣ̌ir.* That's in the third scene of the second act. *haaδa bil-mašhad iθ-θaaliθ imnil-faṣl iθ-θaani.* **2.** *furja* pl. *-aat.* Don't make a scene. *la-tsawwiina furja.*
behind the scenes - *jawwa l-ɛabaa, wara s-sitaar.* Nobody knows what's going on behind the scenes. *maẓẓad yidri š-da-yṣiir jawwa l-ɛabaa.*
scenery - **1.** *mašaahid, manaaṣ̌ir.* Who designed the scenery? *minu ṣammam il-mašaahid?* **2.** *manaaṣ̌ir.* We didn't have time to look at the scenery. *ma-ṣaar ɛidna wakit inšuuf il-manaaṣ̌ir.*
scent - **1.** *riiẓa* pl. *-aat.* The dogs have got the scent. *č-čilaab šammaw ir-riiẓa.* **2.** *ẓassat iš-šamm.* Our dog has a keen scent. *čalibna ɛinda ẓassat iš-šamm ẓadda.*
to scent - **1.** *štamm (a štimaam) riiẓat-.* The dogs have scented the fox. *č-čilaabištammaw riiẓat iθ-θaɛlab.* **2.** *ɛaṭṭar (i taɛṭiir) t-.* She scented the clothes. *ɛaṭṭirat il-ihduum.*
schedule - *jadwal* pl. *jadaawil.* We'll have to work out a schedule if we want to finish on time. *laazim insawwi jadwal ʔiδa ridna axalliṣ ɛal-wakit.*
on schedule - *ɛal-wakit.* The train arrived on schedule. *l-qiṭaar wuṣal ɛal-wakit.*
to schedule - *ẓaddad (i taẓdiid) t- wakit, ɛayyan (i taɛyiin) wakit.* The meeting's scheduled for tomorrow. *l-ijtimaaɛ itẓaddad wakta baačir.*
scheme - **1.** *xuṭṭa* pl. *xuṭaṭ, mašruuɛ* pl. *mašaariiɛ, manhaj* pl. *manaahij.* Has he thought up a new scheme? *haaδa fakkar ib-xuṭṭa jidiida?* **2.** *tartiib* pl. *-aat.* We've changed the color scheme. *ġayyarna tartiib il-alwaan.*
to scheme - *dabbar (u tadbiir) t-, muʔaamara.* They're always scheming. *humma ɛala ṭuul ydabbruun muʔaamaraat.*
scholar - *ɛaalim* pl. *ɛulamaaʔ, ṭaalib* (pl. *ṭullaab*) *ɛilim.* He's a great scholar. *huwwa ɛaalim čibiir.*
school - *madrasa* pl. *madaaris.* Do you go to school? *ʔinta truuẓ lil-madrasa?*
science - *ɛilim* pl. *ɛiluum.* He's more interested in science than art. *ɛinda raġba bil-ɛilim ʔakθar imnil-fann.*
scientific - *ɛilmi*.*
scientist - *ɛaalim* pl. *ɛulamaaʔ.*
scissors - *mugaṣ* pl. *mugaṣṣaat, mgaaṣa, mgaṣṣ* pl. *-aat, mgaaṣiiṣ.* The scissors are dull. *l-mugaṣ ʔaɛma.*
to **scold** - *zaff (i zaff) n-, razzal (i tarziil) t-.* My mother scolded me. *ʔummi zaffatni.*
to **scorch** - *ẓirag (i ẓarig) n-.* I nearly scorched my dress. *ẓragit badilti ʔilla šwayya.*
**The sun is scorching hot. *š-šamis da-tilfaẓ.*
scorcher - **It's a scorcher today. *hal-yoom ẓaarr.*
score - **1.** *majmuuɛ.* What's the score? *šgadd il-majmuuɛ?* or ***šgadd ṣaarat in-nuqaaṭ?* **2.** *θaar.* I have a score to settle with him. *ɛindi θaar wiyyaa laazim ʔanhii.*
**Scores of people died in the epidemic. *ɛadad čibiir maat imnil-wabaaʔ*
to score - *sajjal (i tasjiil) t-.* We scored five points in the second half. *sajjalna xamis nuqaaṭ bin-nuṣṣ iθ-θaani.*
scorpion - *ɛagrab* pl. *ɛagaarub.*
scoundrel - *saafil* pl. *safala, minẓaṭṭ* pl. *-iin.*
to **scour** - *jilaf (ijalif) n-.* She scoured the kettle. *jilfat il-quuri.*
scouring pad - *ṣummaaṭa* pl. *-aat, jillaafa* pl. *-aat.*
scrambled eggs - *beeṣ̌ maṭruug.*
scrap - **1.** *wuṣla* pl. *wuṣal.* That's only a scrap of paper. *haaδi mjarrad wuṣlat waraq.* **2.** *ɛarka* pl. *-aat.* They had an awful scrap last night. *čaanat beenaathum ɛarka θixiina l-baarẓa bil-leel.*
to **scrape** - **1.** *gišaṭ (i gašiṭ) n-.* He scraped his hand on the rock. *gišaṭ ʔiida biṣ-ṣaxra.*
to scrape off - *ẓakk (u ẓakk) n-.* Scrape the

paint off before you paint. *zukk iṣ-subuġ gabuḷ-ma tiṣbuġ.*
to scrape together - *lamm (i lamm) n-, jimaƐ (a jamiƐ) n-.* I couldn't scrape the money together. *ma-gdarit alimm il-ifluus.*
scrap metal - *sikraab.* He deals in scrap metal. *yištuġuḷ bis-sikraab.*
scratch - **1.** *xadiš* pl. *xuduuš, txirmuš* pl. *-aat.* What's that scratch on your cheek? *šinu hal-xadiš ib-xaddak?* **2.** *šuxuṭ* pl. *šxuuṭ.* How'd that scratch get on the table? *mneen jaa haš-šuxuṭ Ɛal-meez?*
**We escaped without a scratch. *nhizamna min duun ʔay ʔaδδa.*
**After the fire he had to start from scratch. *baƐd il-zariiq iḍṭarr yibdi mnil-ʔawwal.*
to scratch - **1.** *xaddaš (i taxdiiš) t-, xidaš (i xadiš) n-.* Be careful not to scratch the furniture. *diir baalak la-txaddiš il-ʔaθaaθ.* **2.** *šixaṭ (u šaxuṭ) n-.* This pen scratches. *hal-qalam yišxuṭ.*
to scratch out - *šiṭab (u šaṭub) n-, šixaṭ (u šaxuṭ) n-.* Scratch out the last sentence. *ʔišṭub ij-jumla l-ʔaxiira.*
scream - *ṣarxa* pl. *-aat, ṣeeza* pl. *-aat, ṣyaaz.* I thought what I heard was a scream. *δanneet illi smaƐitha ṣarxa.*
**He's a scream! *huwwa kulliš muḍzik.*
to scream - *ṣirax (u ṣraax).* The child screamed with fright. *ṭ-ṭifil ṣirax imnil-xoof.*
screen - **1.** *sitaar* pl. *sataaʔir, zaajiz* pl. *zawaajiz.* Change behind the screen. *baddil wara s-sitaar.* **2.** *šaaša* pl. *-aat.* He looks older on the screen. *ybayyin ʔakbar min Ɛumra Ɛaš-šaaša.* **3.** *teel.* We need a new screen on that window. *niztaaj teel jidiid Ɛala haaδa š-šibbaak.*
screw - *burġi* pl. *baraaġi.* These screws need tightening. *hal-baraaġi tiztaaj taqwiya.*
to screw - *buram (u barum) n-.* He screwed the nut on the bolt. *buram ij-jooza Ɛal-burġi.*
**Screw the cap on tight. *šidd il-qabaġ zeen.*
**Things are all screwed up at work. *kull il-masaaʔil imxarbuṭa biš-šuġuḷ.*
**If I can screw up enough courage, I'll ask for a raise. *ʔiδa ʔagdar ašidd zeeli, raz-aṭlub ziyaadat raatib.*
screw driver - *darnafiis* pl. *-aat, mfall* pl. *-aat.*
to **scrub** - *furak (u farik) n-.* We've got to scrub the floor. *laazim nifruk il-gaaƐ.*
sculptor - *nazzaat* pl. *-iin, maθθaal* pl. *-iin.*
scythe - *minjal* pl. *manaajil.*
sea - *bazar* pl. *bizaar.* How far are we from the sea? *šgadd nibƐid imnil-bazar?* -- The Nile empties into the Mediterranean Sea. *n-niil yṣubb bil-bazr il-ʔabyaḍ il-mutawaṣṣiṭ.*
seal - **1.** *faqma* pl. *-aat.* We watched them feed the seals. *tfarrajna Ɛaleehum yṭaƐƐmuun il-faqmaat.* **2.** *ṭamġa* pl. *-aat, xatim* pl. *ʔaxtaam.* The papers bore the official seal. *l-ʔawraaq zaamla ṭ-ṭamġa r-rasmiyya.* **3.** *xatim* pl. *ʔaxtaam.* Somebody must have broken the seal. *waazid laazim kaasir il-xatim.*
to seal - *sadd (i sadd) n-, lizag (i lazig) n-.* Have you sealed the letter yet? *saddeet il-maktuub loo baƐad?*
seam - *xyaaṭ* pl. *-aat.* Rip open the seam. *ʔiftig l-ixyaaṭ.*
search - *baziθ* pl. *buzuuθ, taftiiš* pl. *-aat.* The police made a thorough search. *š-šurṭa qaamat ib-baziθ šaamil.*
to search - **1.** *fattaš (i taftiiš) t-.* We'll have to search you. *laazim infattišak.* **2.** *dawwar (i tadwiir) t-.* I've searched the whole house. *dawwarit il-beet kulla.* **3.** *bizaθ (a baziθ) n-, dawwar (i), fattaš (i).* We searched for him everywhere. *bizaθna Ɛalee b-kull makaan.*
seasick - **I was terribly seasick on my last trip. *ṣaabni dawaar bazar kulliš qawi bis-safra l-faatat.*
seasickness - *dawaar bazar.*
season - **1.** *faṣil* pl. *fuṣuul.* Which season do you like best, winter or summer? *yaa faṣil itzibb ʔakθar, š-šita loo ṣ-ṣeef?* **2.** *mawsim* pl. *mawaasim.* This is the best season for swimming. *haaδa ʔazsan mawsim lis-sibiz.*
to season - *zaṭṭ (u) bahaaraat Ɛala.* What did you season the meat with? *š-zaṭṭeet Ɛal-lazam?*
seasoned - *mjarrub.* They were seasoned troops. *čaanaw ijnuud imjarrubiin.*
seat - *maqƐad* pl. *maqaaƐid.* This seat needs fixing. *hal-maqƐad yiztaaj taṣliiz.* -- The pants are tight in the seat. *l-panṭuroon ḍayyig imnil-maqƐad.*
to have a seat - *giƐad (u guƐuud) n-.* Please have a seat. *tfaḍḍal, ʔugƐud.*
to seat - **1.** *gaƐƐad (i tagƐiid) t-.* Seat the children in the front row. *gaƐƐid il-ʔaṭfaal biṣ-ṣaff il-ʔamaami.* **2.** *lizam (i lazim) n-, kaffa (i takfiya) t-.* The theater seats five hundred people. *s-siinama tilzam xamis miit saxiṣ.*
second - **1.** *θaanya* pl. *θawaani.* He ran a hundred yards in ten seconds. *rikaḍ miit yarda b-Ɛašir θawaani.* **2.** *lazḍa* pl. *-aat.* Wait a second. *ʔintiḍir lazḍa.* **3.** *θaani.* Will you please give me the second book from the left? *baḷḷa ma-tinṭiini l-iktaab iθ-θaani lli min Ɛal-yisra?* -- Give me a second class ticket to Basra, please. *rajaaʔan inṭiini taδkara daraja θaanya lil-baṣra.*
in the second place - *θaanyan.* In the first place I have no time, and in the second place I don't want to go anyway. *ʔawwalan ma-Ɛindi wakit, w-θaanyan ʔaani ma-ariid aruuz Ɛala kull zaal.*
to second - *θanna (i taθniya) t-, Ɛala.* I second the motion. *ʔaθanni Ɛal-iqtiraaz.*
second-hand - **1.** *mustaƐmal.* He bought the book second-hand. *štira l-iktaab mustaƐmal.* **2.** *min maṣdar θaanawi.* I only know that story secondhand. *ʔaƐruf hal-quṣṣa min maṣdar θaanawi bass.*
secondly - *θaanyan.* Secondly, I don't want to go anyway. *θaanyan ma-ariid aruuz Ɛala kull zaal.*
second-rate - *daraja θaanya.* It's definitely a second-rate hotel. *bit-taʔkiid haaδa findiq daraja θaanya.*
secret - **1.** *sirr* pl. *ʔasraar.* Let me in on the secret. *xabburni Ɛan is-sirr.* **2.** *sirri*.* They have a secret plan. *Ɛidhum xuṭṭa sirriyya.*
secretary - *sikirteer* pl. *-iyya.* She's my secretary. *hiyya s-sikirteera maalti.* -- I talked to the second secretary at the embassy. *zčeet wiyya s-sikirteer iθ-θaani bis-safaara.*
secretly - *bis-sirr, sirran, bil-xifya.* They met secretly. *jtimƐaw bis-sirr.*
sect - *maδhab* pl. *maδaahib, ṭaaʔifa* pl. *-aat, ṭawaaʔif.*
section - **1.** *juzuʔ* pl. *ʔajzaaʔ.* You'll find it in section three of chapter one. *tšuufa bij-juzʔ iθ-θaaliθ imnil-faṣl il-ʔawwal.* **2.** *qisim* pl. *ʔaqsaam, manṭiqa* pl. *manaaṭiq.* I was brought up in this section of Baghdad. *ʔaani rbeet ib-hal-qism min baġdaad.*
secure - **1.** *mṣoogar, maḍmuun.* It's a secure investment. *hiyya šaġla mṣoogra.* **2.** *bil-amaan.* Nobody feels secure these days. *mazzad yišƐur bil-amaan hal-ʔayyaam.* **3.** *mašduud.* Is the load secure? *l-zimil mašduud zeen?*
to secure - *ḍiman (i ḍamaan) n-.* His future is secured. *mustaqbala maḍmuun.*
security - **1.** *ṭamaʔniina.* We feel a sense of security if we lock our door at night. *nišƐur ib-ṭamaʔniina ʔiδa qfalna baabna bil-leel.* **2.** *ḍamaan.* What security can you give me? *ʔay ḍamaan tigdar tinṭiini?* **3.** *rahin* pl. *ruhuun.* I had to leave my watch as security. *ḍṭarreet azuṭṭ saaƐati ka-rahin.* **4.** *ʔamin.* The meeting of the security council lasted an hour. *jtimaaƐ majlis il-ʔamin ṭawwal saaƐa.*
securities - *ʔashum w-sanadaat.* He's invested most of his money in securities. *šaġġaḷ muƐḍam amwaala bil-ʔashum wis-sanadaat.*
to **see** - **1.** *šaaf (u šoof) n-.* May I see your passport? *ʔagdar ašuuf jawaaz safarak?* **2.** *tṣawwar (a taṣawwur), šaaf (u šoof) n-.* I don't see it that way. *ma-aṭṣawwarha hiiči.* **3.** *ltiga (i ltigaaʔ).* I'd like to see more of you. *ʔazibb altigi wiyyaač ʔakθar.*
**Anybody can see through him. *ʔay waazid yigdar yuƐruf šaku b-gaḷba.*
**I'll see you through this year. *raz-abqa asaaƐdak ʔila nihaayat haay is-sana.*
**Please see to it that this letter is mailed today. *rajaaʔan itʔakkad bi-ʔan hal-maktuub yruuz bil-bariid il-yoom.*
**See to it that you are on time. *tʔakkad min ʔan tiji Ɛal-wakit.*
to see one home - *waṣṣal (i tawṣiil) t- lil-beet.* May I see you home? *tismazii-li awaṣṣlič lil-beet?*
seed - *bazra* pl. *-aat* coll. *bazir, zabba* pl. *-aat, zubuub* coll. *zabb.* Did you buy any seeds? *štireet bazir?* -- Some types of oranges have no seeds. *baƐaḍ ʔanwaaƐ il-purtaqaal ma-biiha zabb.*
to seed - *biδar (i baδir) n-, ṭašš (u ṭašš) n- bazir.* When did you seed this field? *šwakit biδarit hal-zaqil?*
to **seem** - **1.** *bayyan (i tabyiin) t-.* I seem to be in-

terrupting. *ybayyin ʔanni da-aqaaṭiɛ.*
2. *bida (u badu).* It seems to me he wanted to go last week. *yibduu-li čaan yriid yruuz ðaak il-isbuuɛ.* or *ɛala ma-aɛtiqid raad yruuz ðaak il-isbuuɛ.*

to **seize** - **1.** *kumaš (u kamuš) n-, lizam (a lazim) n-.* He seized the rope with both hands. *kumaš il-zabil b-iidteena.* **2.** *milak (i malik) n-, lizam (a) n-.* Fear seized him. *milaka l-xoof.* **3.** *sayṭar (i sayṭara) t- ɛala, lizam (a) n-.* The police seized his papers. *š-šurṭa sayṭarat ɛala ʔawraaqa.* **4.** *ġtinam (i ġtinaam), ntihaz (i ntihaaz).* If I don't seize this opportunity, it may be too late. *muztamal yruuz ɛalayya kullši ʔiða ma-aġtinim hal-furṣa.*

seldom - *naadiran, naadiran-ma.* I seldom see him in the coffee shop. *naadiran-ma ʔašuufa bil-gahwa.*

to **select** - *ntixab (i ntixaab), xtaar (a xtiyaar).* Have you selected anything yet? *ntixabit šii loo baɛad?*

selection - *majmuuɛat il-ʔaškaal.* We have a big selection of shirts. *ɛidna majmuuɛat il-ʔaškaal imniθ-θiyaab.*

selfish - *ʔanaani*.* How can anyone be so selfish? *šloon waazid yigdar ykuun hal-gadd ʔanaani?*

to **sell** - **1.** *baaɛ (i beeɛ) n-.* Did you sell your old car? *biɛit sayyaartak il-qadiima?* — Sorry the tickets are all sold out. *maɛa l-ʔasaf, it-taðaakir inbaaɛat kullha.* **2.** *nbaaɛ (a).* How are the glasses selling? *šloon da-tinbaaɛ l-iglaaṣaat?*
**He sold us out to the enemy. *xaanna wiyya l-ʔaɛdaaʔ.* or *huwwa wiša biina lil-ʔaɛdaaʔ.*

Semite - *saami* pl. *-iyyiin.* The Semites established the first civilization in Iraq. *s-saamiyyiin ʔanšaʔuu ʔawwal zaḍaara bil-ɛiraaq.*

Semitic - *saami*.* Arabic is a Semitic language. *l-luġa l-ɛarabiyya hiyya luġa saamiyya.*

to **send** - *dazz (i dazz) n-, ʔarsal (i ʔirsaal) n-, biɛaθ (a baɛiθ) n-.* Send it by mail. *dizzha bil-bariid.*
to send for - *stadɛa (i stidɛaaʔ).* Have you sent for the doctor? *stadɛeet ṭabiib?*
to send in - *daxxal (i tadxiil) t-.* Send him in. *daxxla.* or ***xallii yidxul.*
to send out for - *dazz (i dazz) n- ɛala.* Shall I send out for ice cream? *triid adizz ɛala doondirma?*

senior - *ʔaqdam, ʔasbaq.* He's the senior man in the office. *huwwa ʔaqdam waazid bil-maktab.*

sensation - **1.** *ḍajja, zamaas.* His speech created a sensation. *zadiiθa ʔaθaar ḍajja čibiira.* **2.** *šuɛuur.* It's a very pleasant sensation. *huwwa fadd šuɛuur laṭiif.*

sense - **1.** *zaassa* pl. *-aat.* My dog has a keen sense of smell. *čalbi ɛinda zaassat šamm qawiyya.* **2.** *ʔidraak, ɛaqil.* I hope he has sense enough to take a taxi. *ʔaamal ʔan ykuun ɛinda ʔidraak kaafi zatta yaaxuð taksi.* **3.** *šuɛuur.* It gives us a sense of security. *tinṭiina šuɛuur bil-iṭmiʔnaan.*
**There's no sense in doing that. *ma-ʔilha maɛna tsawwiiha.*
in a sense - *min naaziya, min jiha.* That's true, in a sense. *min naaziya haaða ṣaziiz.*
to sense - *zass (i ziss) n-, ʔadrak (i ʔidraak) n-.* I sensed right away that something was wrong. *zasseet raʔsan ʔaku fadd šii ġalaṭ.*

senseless - *ma-biiha ɛaqil.* It would be senseless to go out in this rain. *ma-biiha ɛaqil ʔiða tiṭlaɛ barra b-hal-muṭar.*

sensible - *ɛaaqil, mudrik.* Be sensible! *kuun ɛaaqil!*

sensitive - *zassaas.* I'm sensitive to cold. *ʔaani zassaas lil-barid.*

sentence - **1.** *jumla* pl. *jumal.* I didn't understand the last sentence. *ma-ftihamt ij-jumla l-ʔaxiira.* **2.** *zukum* pl. *ʔazkaam.* The judge has just pronounced sentence. *l-zaakim hassa ʔaṣdar il-zukum.*
to sentence - *zikam (u zukum) n-.* He was sentenced to five years. *nzikam xams isniin.*

sentry - *zaaris* pl. *zurraas.* The sentry didn't let me pass. *l-zaaris ma-xallaani ʔafuut.*

separate - *minfiṣil.* Could we have separate rooms? *nigdar naaxuð ġuraf minfaṣla?*
to separate - **1.** *farraq (i tafriiq) t-.* I could hardly separate those two. *b-ṣuɛuuba gdarit atfarriq haθ-θineen.*
2. *qassam (i taqsiim) t-.* Separate the group into five sections. *qassim ij-jamaaɛa ʔila xamis aqsaam.*

separately - *ɛala zida.* Can you buy each volume separately? *tigdar tištiri kull juzuʔ ɛala zida?*

September - *ʔayluul.*

sergeant - *ɛariif* pl. *ɛurafaaʔ*

series - *silsila* pl. *-aat.* He's written a series of articles about it. *kitab silsilat maqaalaat ɛanha.*

serious - **1.** *jiddi* pl. *-iyyiin.* Why are you so serious? *leeš ʔinta hal-gadd jiddi?* **2.** *muhimm.* It isn't serious. *muu šii muhimm.* **3.** *xaṭar, xaṭiir.* That's a serious mistake. *haaða ġalṭa xaṭra.*
**Are you serious? *da-tizči jidd?*

seriously - *jiddiyyaat, ɛan jidd.* Don't take it so seriously. *la-taaxuðha jiddiyyaat.* — I'm seriously considering getting married. *ʔaani jiddiyyaat da-afakkir biz-zawaaj.*

sermon - *xuṭba* pl. *-aat.* The Imam gave a good sermon Friday. *l-ʔimaam xuṭab xuṭba zeena yoom ij-jumɛa.*

servant - *xaadim* pl. *xadam, xiddaam.* I'm not your servant. *ʔaani muu xaadim maalak.*

serve - *sirv, seef.* Whose serve is it? *b-iid man is-sirv?*
to serve - **1.** *qaddam (i taqdiim) t-.* Shall I serve the drinks now? *ʔaqaddim il-mašruubaat hassa?*
2. *xidam (i xadim).* He served in the Navy. *xidam bil-baẓriyya.*
**This will serve as a substitute. *haay raz-itquum maqaamha.*
**Dinner is served! *l-ɛaša zaaḍir.* or *l-ɛaša jaahiz.* **That serves you right! *tistaahilha!*

service - **1.** *xidma.* The service is bad in this restaurant. *l-xidma muu zeena b-hal-maṭɛam.* -- This is a civil service regulation. *haaða qaanuun il-xidma l-madaniyya.* **2.** *jeeš, jayš.* How long have you been in the service? *šgadd ṣaar-lak bij-jayš?*

service station - *mazaṭṭat (pl. -aat) paanziin, paanziinxaana* pl. *-aat.* Let's stop at the next service station. *xal-noogaf ib-muzaṭṭat il-paanziin ij-jaaya.*

set - *ṭaxum* pl. *ṭxuum, majmuuɛa* pl. *-aat.* We have a whole set of these ash trays. *ɛidna ṭaxum kaamil min haṭ-ṭablaat ij-jigaayir.*
all set - *zaaḍir.* Everything all set? *kullši zaaḍir?*
to set - **1.** *zaṭṭ (u zaṭṭ), xalla (i).* Set it on the desk. *zuṭṭha ɛal-meez.* **2.** *niṣab (u naṣub) n-.* I set my watch by the station clock. *niṣabit saaɛati ɛala saaɛat il-muzaṭṭa.* **3.** *ɛayyan (i taɛyiin) t-, zaddad (i tazdiid) t-.* Why don't you set the time? *leeš ma-tɛayyin il-wakit?* **4.** *karrak (i takriik) t-.* Is the hen setting on the eggs? *d-dijaaja mkarrika ɛal-beeḍ?* **5.** *jabbar (u tajbiir) t-.* The doctor will have to set your arm. *ṭ-ṭabiib laazim yjabbur ʔiidak.* **6.** *rakkab (i tarkiib) t-.* He set the stone in a ring for me. *rakkab-li l-zajar ɛal-mizbas.* **7.** *ġurab (u ġarub) n-.* The sun has already set. *š-šamis ġurbat.* **8.** *ṣaffaf (i taṣfiif) t-.* I want my hair washed and set. *ʔariid šaɛri yinġisil w-yiṭṣaffaf.* **9.** *bida (i bidaaya).* He set to work immediately. *bida bil-ɛamal zaalan.*
10. *zaḍḍar (i tazḍiir) t-.* Quick, set the table! *zaḍḍiri l-meez bil-ɛajil.*
**You've got to set a good example. *laazim tijɛal min nafsak maθal il-ġeerak.*
to set ahead - *qaddam (i taqdiim) t-.* I set my watch five minutes ahead. *qaddamit saaɛti xams diqaayiq.*
to set at - *zaddad (i tazdiid) t-.* He set the price at fifty dinars. *zaddad is-siɛir ib-xamsiin diinaar.*
to set down - *nazzal (i tanziil) t-.* Set the box down gently. *nazzil iṣ-ṣanduug ɛala keefak.*
to set free - *ʔaṭlaw (i ʔiṭlaaq) siraaz.* The prisoners were set free. *l-masjuuniin ʔaṭliqaw saraazhum.*
to set off - *fajjar (i tafjiir) t-.* They didn't have time to set off the explosives. *ma-čaan ɛidhum wakit yfajjruun il-mutafajjiraat.*
to set on - *šayyaš (i tašyiiš) t-, ɛala.* He set the dogs on me. *šayyaš ič-čilaab ɛalayya.*
to set out - *twajjah (a tawajjuh), saafar (i safar).* He set out for home on Monday. *twajjah il-beeta yoom iθ-θineen.*
to set straight - *ɛaddal (i taɛdiil) t-.* Can you set me straight on this? *tigdar itɛaddilni b-haay?*
to set up - **1.** *niṣab (u naṣub) n-.* The new machines have just been set up. *l-makaayin ij-jidiida hassa nnuṣbat.* **2.** *ʔassas (i taʔsiis) t-.* Are you going to set up housekeeping? *raz-itʔassis beet?* — His father set him up in business. *ʔabuu ʔassas-la šuġul.*

to **settle** - **1.** *ṣaffa (i taṣfiya) t-.* He settled his bill with his creditors. *ṣaffa zsaaba maɛa d-dayyaana.*

2. *ẓall (i ẓall) n-.* You must settle the misunderstanding between yourselves. *laazim itẓilluun il-xilaaf beenaatkum.* 3. *stawṭan (i stiiṭaan).* The Americans settled their country gradually. *l-amriikaan istawṭinaw baladhum bit-tadriij.* 4. *sakkan (i taskiin) t-.* The government is going to settle farmers on the newly developed land. *l-ẓukuuma raẓ-itsakkin il-fallaaẓiin bil-ʔaraaḍi l-mustaθmara ẓadiiθan.* 5. *staqarr (i stiqraar).* The Bedouin don't want to settle anywhere. *l-badu ma-yriiduun yistiqirruun ib-ʔay mukaan.* 6. *ṭaax (u ṭoox).* The wall has settled a little. *l-ẓaayiṭ ṭaax išwayya.* 7. *trassab (a tarassub).* Wait until the coffee grounds have settled. *ntiḍir ʔila ʔan yitrassab it-tilif maal il-gahwa.* 8. *niha (i nahi) n-.* That settles the matter. *haaδa yinhi l-masʔala.*

settled people - *ẓaḍar.* There is a great difference in the lives of nomad and settled peoples. *ʔaku fariq čibiir ib-ẓayaat il-badu wil-ẓaḍar.*

settlement - 1. *ttifaaq* pl. *-aat.* They couldn't reach a settlement. *ma-gidraw yooṣluun ʔila ttifaaq.* 2. *maʔwa* pl. *maʔaawi, mustaqarr* pl. *-aat.* We uncovered the remains of an ancient settlement. *ktišafna ʔaaθaar maʔwa qadiim.*

seven - 1. *sabiƐ.* He's seven years old. *Ɛumra sabiƐ siniin.* 2. *sabiƐt.* I was there seven days. *buqeet ihnaak sabiƐt iyyaam.* 3. *sabƐa* pl. *-aat.* These numbers are all sevens. *har-raqum kullha sabƐaat.*

seventeen - *ṣbaaṭaƐaš.*

seventeenth - *l-iṣbaaṭaƐaš.*

seventh - *saabiƐ.*

seventieth - *s-sabƐiin.*

seventy - *sabƐiin.*

several - *Ɛidda.* I'd like to stay here for several days. *ʔard abqa hnaa Ɛiddat ʔayyaam.*

severe - 1. *qaasi.* It was a very severe winter. *čaan iš-šita qaasi.* 2. *šadiid, ẓaadd.* She complains of severe pains. *hiyya tiški min ʔaalaam šadiida.*

to **sew** - *xayyaṭ (i taxyiiṭ) t-.* She sews her own clothes. *txayyiṭ ihduumha b-nafisha.* -- Please sew the buttons on for me. *rajaaʔan xayyiṭ-li d-dijam.*

sewer - *burbux* pl. *baraabix.* The sewer is clogged. *l-burbux masduud.*

sex - 1. *jinis.* In your application, state your age and sex. *b-ṭalabak ʔiδkur il-Ɛumur wij-jinis.* 2. *jinsi*.* She's got a lot of sex appeal. *Ɛidha hwaaya jaaδibiyya jinsiyya.*

sexual - *jinsi*.* He has sexual relations with her. *Ɛinda Ɛilaaqa jinsiyya wiyyaaha.*

sexy - *muhayyij.* She's a very sexy girl. *hiyya fadd bint kulliš muhayyija.*

shabby - 1. *mšaggig.* His suit looks shabby. *badilta tbayyin imšaggiga.* 2. *xasiis, danii?.* That was very shabby of him. *haay čannat kulliš xasiis minna.*

shade - 1. *ḍill, fayy.* Let's stay in the shade. *xal-nibqa biḍ-ḍill.* 2. *ṗarda* pl. *-aat.* Pull down the shades. *nazzil il-ṗardaat.* 3. *loon* pl. *ʔalwaan.* This red is too dark a shade. *haaδa l-loon il-ʔaẓmar išwayya ṭoox.*

shadow - *xayaal* pl. *-aat.* The trees cast long shadows. *l-ʔašjaar itsawwi xayaalaat iṭwiila.*
 **There is not a shadow of doubt about it. *ma-biiha šakk ʔabadan.*
 to shadow - *raaqab (i muraaqaba) t-.* They assigned a detective to shadow him. *Ɛayynaw šurṭi sirri ẓatta yraaqba.*

shady - That's a shady business. *haay šağla mašbuuha.*
 **It's shady over here. *biiha fayy ihnaa.*

shaft - *šaft* pl. *-aat.* The shaft on this machine is bent. *šaft hal-makiina maƐwuuj.*

to **shake** - 1. *hazz (i hazz) n-.* He shook his head. *hazz raasa.* 2. *xaḍḍ (u xaḍḍ) n-.* Shake it well before using it. *xuḍḍha zeen gabuḷ-ma tistaƐmilha.* 3. *rajj (u rajj) n-.* The earthquake shook everything in the city. *z-zalzila rajjat kullši bil-madiina.*
 **Come on, shake a leg! *yaḷḷa, staƐjil!*
 to shake hands - *tṣaafaẓ (a taṣaafuẓ).* They shook hands. *tṣaafẓaw.*

shaky - 1. *mirtiƐiš.* I'm still shaky. *ʔaani baƐadni mirtiƐiš.* 2. *mgaḷgaḷ.* The table's shaky. *l-meez imgaḷgaḷ.*

shall - *raẓ-, Ɛuud.* We shall see who's right. *raẓ-inšuuf minu maḍbuuṭ.*
 **I'll never go there. *ʔabad ma-aruuẓ ihnaak.*
 **Shall I wait? *triid antiḍir?*

shallow - 1. *ḍaẓil.* The lake is very shallow in this area. *l-buẓayra kulliš ḍaẓla b-hal-manṭiga.* -- He's a very shallow person. *huwwa fadd waaẓid kulliš ḍaẓil.* 2. *muu ğamiij.* Put it in a shallow bowl. *ẓuṭṭha b-minčaasa muu ğamiija.*

shame - 1. *xajal.* Haven't you any shame? *ma-Ɛindak ʔay xajal?* or ***ma-tistiẓi ʔabad?* 2. *Ɛeeb.* Shame on you! *Ɛeeb Ɛaleek.*
 **What a shame you can't come! *maƐa l-ʔasaf ma-tigdar tiji.*

shape - 1. *šikil* pl. *ʔaškaal.* What shape is the table? *šloon šikla lil-meez.* 2. *ẓaala* pl. *-aat.* What shape is the car in? *šloon ẓaalat is-sayyaara?* 3. *waḍƐiyya* pl. *-aat, ẓaala* pl. *-aat.* I'm in bad shape. *waḍƐiiti muu zeena.*
 in shape - *ẓaaḍir.* Is everything in shape? *kullši ẓaaḍir?*
 out of shape - *muƐaqqač, maƐquuč.* The hat's all out of shape. *š-šafqa kullha mƐaqqača.*
 to shape up - *tẓassan (i taẓassun).* Things are gradually shaping up. *l-ʔašyaaʔ tadriijiyyan da-titẓassan.*

share - 1. *ẓuṣṣa* pl. *ẓuṣaṣ, sahim* pl. *ʔashum.* Everybody has to pay his share. *kull waaẓid laazim yidfaƐ ẓuṣṣta.* 2. *sahim* pl. *ʔashum.* How many shares did you buy? *čam sahim ištireet?*
 to share - *tšaarak (i tašaaruk) b-.* Let's share the cake. *xalli nitšaarak bil-keeka.*
 to share with - *šaarak (i mušaaraka) b-.* Will you share my lunch with me? *tigdar itšaarakni bil-ğada?*

shareholder - *musaahim* pl. *-iin.*

shark - *koosaj* pl. *kwaasij.*
 loan shark - *muraabi* pl. *-iin.*

sharp - 1. *ẓaadd.* Do you have a sharp knife? *Ɛindak siččiina ẓaadda?* 2. *laaδiƐ, saliiṭ.* She has a sharp tongue. *Ɛidha lsaan laaδiƐ.* 3. *biḍ-ḍabuṭ, tamaaman.* We have to be there at five o'clock sharp. *laazim inkuum ihnaak saaƐa xamsa biḍ-ḍabuṭ.*
 **Keep a sharp eye on him. *raaqba zeen.*

to **sharpen** - 1. *ẓadd (i ẓadd) n-.* This knife needs sharpening. *has-siččiina tiẓtaaj ẓadd.* 2. *qaṭṭ (u qaṭṭ) n-, bira (i bari) n-.* Sharpen the pencil for me, please. *quṭṭ-li l-qalam min faḍlak.*

shave - *ẓilaaqa* pl. *-aat, ziyaan* pl. *-aat.* I want a shave and a haircut. *ʔariid ẓilaaqat wujji w-ziyaan šaƐari.*
 to shave - *zayyan (i zyaan) t-, ẓilaq (i ẓalooqa) n-.* Who shaved you? *minu zayyanak?* or *minu ẓilaq wiččak?*

she - *hiyya, haaδi, haay.* She is a capable woman. *hiyya mrayya muqtadra.*
 **She was in town last night. *čaanat bil-balad il-baarẓa bil-leel.*

shed - *Ɛambaar* pl. *Ɛanaabiir, maxzan* pl. *maxaazin.* Put the tools back in the shed. *rajjiƐ il-ʔadawaat lil-Ɛambaar.*
 to shed - 1. *ʔalqa (i ʔilqaaʔ) n-.* That sheds some light on the matter. *haaδa yilqi ḍaww Ɛal-mawḍuuƐ.* 2. *nizaƐ (a naziƐ), δabb (i δabb) n-.* As soon as I got into my room I shed all my clothes. *ʔawwal-ma wuṣalit il-ğurufti nizaƐit kull ihduumi.* 3. *δiraf (i δarif) n-.* She shed bitter tears. *δirfat dumuuƐ ẓaarra.* 4. *δabb (i δabb).* My dog's shedding his hair. *čalbi da-yδibb šaƐra.* 5. *minaƐ (a maniƐ).* This overcoat doesn't shed water at all. *hal-qaṗṗuuṭ ma-yimnaƐ il-muṭar bil-marra.*

sheep - *xaruuf* pl. *xurfaan, ğanma* pl. *ʔağnaam* coll. *ğanam.*

sheer - 1. *ṣirf.* That's sheer nonsense. *haaδi saxaafa ṣirf.* 2. *šaffaaf.* I'd like some sheer material like voile. *ʔariid iqmaaš šaffaaf miθl il-waayil.*

sheet - 1. *čarčaf* pl. *čaraačif.* Shall I change the sheets? *triid ağayyir ič-čaraačif?* 2. *quṭƐa* pl. *-aat.* Please give me a sheet of paper. *rajaaʔan inṭiini fadd quṭƐat waraq.* 3. *ṭabqa* pl. *-aat, looẓa* pl. *-aat.* We bought a sheet of plywood. *štireena ṭabqat xišab muƐaakis.*
 **She turned as white as a sheet. *wujihha ṣaar ʔaṣfar miθl il-kurkum.*

sheik - *šeex* pl. *šyuux.*

shelf - *raff* pl. *rfuuf.* The shelves are empty. *r-rufuuf xaalya.*

shell - 1. *gišir* pl. *gšuur.* The hazelnut shell is hard. *gišr il-findig qawi.* 2. *qumbula* pl. *qanaabil.* A shell exploded near our house. *fadd qumbula nfijrat yamm beetna.* 3. *ṣidfa* pl. *-aat.* coll. *ṣidaf.* What'll I do with the shells of the snails? *š-asawwi b-ṣidaf il-ẓalazuun haay?*
 to shell - 1. *gaššar (i tagšiir) t-.* Do you want to shell the nuts? *triid itgaššir ij-jooz?* 2. *fallas (i tafliis) t-, gaššar (i tagšiir) t-.*

The peas have to be shelled. *l-bazaalya laazim titfallas.* 3. *ḍirab (u ḍarib) n- bil-qanaabil.* The army shelled the town. *j-jayš ḍirbaw il-madiina bil-qanaabil.*

shelter - *maljaʔ* pl. *malaajiʔ*, *maʔwa* pl. *-aat.* We found shelter in a hut during the storm. *ttixaδna l-kuux maljaʔ ʔaθnaaʔ il-εaaṣifa.*

to shelter - *ʔaawa (yiʔwi ʔiiwaaʔ).* They sheltered and fed us. *ʔaawoona w-ṭaεεmoona.*

shepherd - *raaεi* pl. *raεyaan.*

shield - *diriε* pl. *duruuε.* He has a collection of shields and swords. *εinda majmuuεa min id-duruuε wis-siyuuf.*

to shield - **1.** *ḥima (i ḥimaaya) n-, ḥifaḍ (a ḥafiḍ) n-.* You ought to shield your eyes against the sun. *laazim tiḥmi εeenak imniš-šamis.* **2.** *tsattar (a tasattur) εala, ḥima (i ḥimaaya) n-.* He must be shielding someone. *laazim da-yitsattar εala fadd ʔaḥḥad.*

shift - *dafεa* pl. *-aat, wajba* pl. *-aat.* Our workers work in two shifts. *εummaalna yištaġluun εala dafiεteen.*

to shift - **1.** *baddal (i tabdiil) t- geer.* You ought to shift into second. *laazim itbaddil geer εaθ-θineen.* **2.** *ġayyar (i taġyiir) t-, baddal (i tabdiil) t-.* We have to shift the meeting to Tuesday. *laazim inġayyir il-ijtimaaε ʔila θ-θilaaθaa.* **3.** *tġayyar (a taġayyur).* The direction of the wind has shifted. *l-hawa tġayyar ittijaaha.*

**I've always had to shift for myself. *ʔaani činit miḍṭarr daaʔiman ʔadabbur ʔumuuri b-nafsi.*

shin - *saaq.* I got kicked in the shinbone. *ʔakalit ḍarba εala εaḍmat saaqi.*

shine - *lamεa.* See if you can take the shine out of these pants. *šuuf ʔiδa tigdar itwaxxir il-lamεa min hal-panṭaroon.*

to shine - **1.** *šaεε (i šaεε) n-, limaε (a lamiε) n-.* Her eyes were shining with joy. *εyuunha čaanat da-tšiεε imnil-faraḥ.* **2.** *baddaε (i tabdiiε) t-.* He's good in all his subjects, but mathematics is where he shines. *haaδa zeen ib-kull idruusa bass ybaddiε εala l-ʔaxaṣṣ bir-riyaaḍiyyaat.* **3.** *subaġ (u sabuġ) n-.* I have to shine my shoes. *laazim ʔaṣbuġ qundarti.*

**The sun isn't shining today. *š-šamis ma-ṭaalεa l-yoom.*

ship - *baaxira* pl. *bawaaxir.* When does the ship leave? *šwakit itġaadir il-baaxira?*

to ship - *šiḥan (a šaḥin) n-, dazz (i dazz) n-.* Has the case been shipped yet? *ṣ-ṣanduug inšiḥan loo baεad?*

shipment - *šaḥna* pl. *-aat, ʔirsaaliyya* pl. *-aat.* We've just received a new shipment of shoes. *hassa stilamna šaḥna jdiida mnil-ʔaḥδiya.*

shipwreck - *ḥuṭaam safiina.*

shirt - *θoob* pl. *θyaab, qamiiṣ* pl. *qumṣaan.* Are my shirts back from the laundry? *θyaabi rijεat imnil-makwi?*

**He'd give you the shirt off his back. *ʔiida muu ʔila.* or *huwwa kulliš barmaki.*

**Keep your shirt on, I'll be right there. *la-taxbusni, ʔaani jaay.*

shish kebab - *tikka.*

to **shiver** - *rijaδ (i rajiδ) n-, riεaš (i raεiš) n-.* The child shivered with cold. *ṭ-ṭifil rijaf imnil-barid.*

shock - **1.** *ṣadma* pl. *-aat.* His death was a great shock to us all. *mootta čaanat ṣadma εaniifa εaleena kullna.* — He's still suffering from shock. *baεad yqaasi mniṣ-ṣadma.* **2.** *natil.* You can get a bad shock from this machine. *mumkin taakul natil qawi min hal-makiina.* **3.** *koom* pl. *ʔikwaam.* They stacked up the wheat in shocks. *kaddisaw l-ḥunṭa εala šikil ikwaam.*

to get a shock - *nnital (i).* I got a shock from the lamp. *nnitalit inniḍ-ḍaww.*

to shock - *ṣiεaq (a ṣaεiq) n-, ṣidam (i ṣadim) n-.* I was shocked by the death of his father. *nṣiεaqit ib-xabar moot ʔabuu.*

shockproof - *ḍidd il-kasar.* This watch isn't shockproof. *has-saaεa muu ḍidd il-kasar.*

shoe - **1.** *qundara* pl. *qanaadir, ḥiδaaʔ* pl. *ʔaḥδiya.* I'd like a pair of shoes. *ʔariid zooj qanaadir.* **2.** *naεal* pl. *nεaalaat.* The horse lost one shoe. *l-iḥṣaan waggaε naεal min inεaalaata.*

to shoe - *naεεal (i tanεiil).* The horse needs shoeing. *l-iḥṣaan yirraad-la tanεiil.*

shoehorn - *karata* pl. *-aat.*

shoelace - *qiiṭaan* pl. *qyaaṭiin.* I want a pair of shoelaces. *ʔariid zooj iqyaaṭiin.*

shoemaker - *qundarči* pl. *-iyya.* Is there a shoemaker nearby? *ʔaku qundarči qariib minnaa?*

shoe polish - *ṣubuġ qanaadir.*

shoeshine - *ṣubuġ qundara.* I need a shoeshine. *ʔaḥtaaj ṣubuġ qundara.*

to **shoot** - **1.** *rima (i rami), ʔaṭlaq (i ʔiṭlaaq).* He shot the gun four times. *rima l-bunduqiyya ʔarbaε marraat.* **2.** *ḍurab (u ḍarub) b-riṣaaṣ.* He shot him in the back and killed him. *ḍuraba riṣaaṣ ib-ḍahra w-mawwata.* **3.** *xiṭaf (u xaṭuf) n-.* The car shot past us. *s-sayyaara xuṭfat min yammna.* **4.** *maddad (i tamdiid), tallaε (i taṭliiε).* The seed, when it starts growing, shoots out roots. *l-ḥabba min tinbit itmaddid ijduur.* **5.** *ʔaxaδ (u ʔaxiδ) n-.* I shot eight pictures today. *ʔaxaδit θaman ṣuwar il-yoom.*

**You ought to be shot for that. *yinraad-lak taεliig εaleeha.*

to shoot down - *waggaε (i tawgiiε) t-.* They shot down one of our planes. *waggaεaw wiḥda min ṭiyyaaraatna.*

shop - *dukkaan* pl. *dakaakiin, maḥall* pl. *-aat. maxzan* pl. *maxaazin.* There are many shops on this street. *ʔaku hwaaya dakaakiin ib-haš-šaariε.*

to shop - *tsawwag (a tsuwwug).* We shop at the market. *ʔiḥna nitsawwag imnis-suug.*

**I want to shop around before I buy the present. *ʔariid aduur išwayya w-aaxuδ fikra gabuḷ-ma ʔaštiri l-hadiyya.*

shopping - *miswaag.* I still have a lot of shopping to do. *baεad εindi hwaaya miswaag.*

shore - *saaḥil* pl. *sawaaḥil.* How far is it to the shore? *šjadd yibεid is-saaḥil?*

short - **1.** *šooṭ* pl. *-aat.* There was a short in your radio. *saar šooṭ ib-waayaraat ir-raadyo maalak.* **2.** *gṣayyir.* He's rather short. *huwwa gṣayyir.* — She wears short dresses. *tilbas malaabis igṣayyra.* — Cut my hair short. *guṣṣ šaεri gṣayyir.* **3.** *naaqiṣ.* His books are short today. *ḥsaaba naaqiṣ hal-yoom.*

in short - *muxtaṣar il-kilaam, xaṣm il-ḥači.* In short, I can't come. *muxtaṣar il-kilaam, ma-agdar ʔaji.*

to cut short - *ġaṣṣar (i tagṣiir) t-.* They had to cut their trip short. *ḍṭarraw ygaṣṣruun safrathum.*

to run short - *nugaṣ (u naguṣ).* Our ammunition is running short. *δaxiiratna da-tinguṣ.*

shortage - **1.** *naqiṣ, qilla.* The shortage of materials is reducing our production. *naqṣ il-mawaadd il-ʔawwaliyya da-yxaffuḍ intaajna.* **2.** *εajiz, naqiṣ.* The auditors discovered a shortage in his accounts. *l-mudaqqiqiin iktišfaw εajiz b-iḥsaabaata.*

shortcoming - *εeeb* pl. *εiyuub.* The house has many shortcomings. *l-beet bii εiddat εiyuub.*

short cut - *ṭariiq muxtaṣar* pl. *ṭuruq muxtaṣara.* He knows a short cut to the beach. *yuεruf ṭariiq muxtaṣar liš-šaaṭi.*

to **shorten** - *gaṣṣar (tgiṣṣir) t-.* Shorten the pants for me, please. *gaṣṣir-li l-panṭaroon rajaaʔan.*

shorter - *ʔaqṣar, ʔagṣar.* These pants are shorter than mine. *haay il-panṭaroonaat ʔaqṣar min maalti.*

shortly - *baεd išwayya.* He'll be here shortly. *raḥ-ykuun ihnaa baεd išwayya.*

shorts - **1.** *lbaas* pl. *-aat, libsaan.* He ordered six pairs of shorts. *waṣṣa εala sitt libsaan.* **2.** *panṭaroon igṣayyir* pl. *-aat igṣayyra.* The girls all wore shorts and sweaters. *kull il-banaat libsaw panṭaroonaat igṣayyra w-bluuzaat ṣuuf.*

short wave - *mawja qaṣiira.* You can get short wave too, on this radio. *tigdar itḥaṣṣil εala mawja qaṣiira hamm ib-har-raadyo.*

shot - **1.** *ṭalqa* pl. *-aat.* Did you hear a shot? *smaεit ṭalqa?* **2.** *niišaanči* pl. *-iyya, neešinči,* pl. *-iyya.* He's a good shot. *huwwa xooš niišaanči.* **3.** *laqṭa* pl. *-aat, ṣuura* pl. *ṣuwar.* We got good shots of the prime minister. *ʔaxaδna xooš laqṭaat il-raʔiis il-wuzaraaʔ.* **4.** *ʔubra* pl. *ʔubar.* Are you getting shots? *da-taaxuδ ʔubar?* **5.** *mitwattir.* His nerves are all shot. *ʔaεṣaaba mitwattra.* **6.** *mistahlak.* That machine's all shot. *haay il-makiina mistahlika.*

**He thinks he's a big shot. *yitṣawwar nafsa fadd šaxṣiyya.*

to take a shot - *ʔaṭlaq (i ʔiṭlaaq) riṣaaṣ.* Somebody took a shot at him. *fadd waaḥid ʔaṭlaq εalee riṣaaṣ.*

shoulder - *čitif* pl. *čtaaf, čtaafaat.* His shoulders are broad. *čtaafa εariiḍa.*

**I gave it to him straight from the shoulder. *kallamta b-ṣaraaḥa.*

**We'll have to put our shoulders to the wheel.

laazim nibδil ʔaqṣa juhudna.
to give the cold shoulder - *tjaahal (i tajaahul), Eaamal (i muEaamala) ib-buruud.* Why'd you give him the cold shoulder? *leeš itjaahalta?*
to shoulder - 1. *xalla (i txilli) t- Eala čitif-.* He shouldered the sack of wheat and walked home. *xalla čiis il-ḥunṭa Eala čitfa w-miša lil-beet.* **2.** *ʔaxaδ (u) Eala Eaatiq-, tḥammal (a taḥammul).* He shouldered the responsibility. *ʔaxaδ il-masʔuuliyya Eala Eaatqa.* — Why should I shoulder the blame for it? *leeš ʔaani laazim atḥammal il-loom?* **3.** *tnakkab (a tanakkub).* The soldiers shouldered their rifles and marched off. *j-jinuud itnakkbaw banaaduqhum w-mišaw.*
to **shout** - *ṣayyaḥ (i tṣiyyiḥ) t-, ṣaaḥ (i ṣyaaḥ) n-.* You don't have to shout! *ma-aku ḥaaja tṣayyiḥ!* **The speaker was shouted down by the crowd. *ṣyaaḥ ij-jamaahiir xalla l-xaṭiib yiskut.*
shouting - *ṣyaaḥ.* Your shouting is getting on my nerves. *ṣyaaḥkum da-ysawwiini Eaṣabi.*
shove - *dafEa* pl. *-aat.* He gave me a shove that knocked me over. *difaEni dafEa waggaEatni.*
to shove - 1. *daffaE (i tadfiiE) t-, daEEač (i tadEiič) t-.* Don't shove! *la-tdaffiE!* **2.** *difaE (a dafiE) n-.* They shoved him in front of a bus. *difEoo giddaam il-baaṣ.*
to shove around - *jaawaz (a tajaawuz) Eala.* People keep shoving him around. *n-naas yjaawzuun Ealee.*
shovel - *karak* pl. *-aat, mijraf* pl. *-aat.* You'll need a pickax and shovel. *raḥ-tiḥtaaj qazma w-karak.*
to shovel - *kuraf (u karuf).* Shovel this sand into the truck. *ʔukruf ir-ramul w-δibba bil-loori.*
show - 1. *Eariδ* pl. *Euruuδ.* Other than that, how did you like the show? *ma-Eada haaδa, šloon Eijabak il-Eariδ?* **2.** *door* pl. *ʔadwaar, Eariδ* pl. *Euruuδ.* When does the first show start? *s-saaEa beeš yibdi d-door il-ʔawwal?*
to show - 1. *raawa (i muraawaʔa) t-, bayyan (i tabyiin) t-.* Show me how you do it. *raawiini šloon itsawwiiha.* **2.** *bayyan (i tabyiin) t-.* Only his head showed above water. *bass raasa bayyan min foog il-mayy.* **3.** *dalla (i tdilli).* Could you show me the way? *tigdar itdilliini ṭ-ṭariiq?* **4.** *Eiraδ (i Eariδ) n-.* What are they showing at the theater this evening? *š-raḥ-yEirδuun bis-siinama hal-leela?* **5.** *ʔaδhar (i ʔiδhaar) n-.* The investigation didn't show a thing. *t-taḥqiiqaat ma-ʔaδharat šii.* **6.** *δihar (i ʔiδhaar).* I'm going to show you for what you are. *raḥ-aδihrak Eala ḥaqiiqtak.*
**This picture shows a new automobile. *haṣ-ṣuura marsuuma sayyaara jdiida.*
to show around - *farraj (i tafriij) t- Eala.* She's showing her guests around the town. *da-tfarrij iδyuufha Eal-madiina.*
to show off - *tbaaha (i tabaahi), raawa (i muraawaʔa) nafs~.* He's just showing off. *huwwa bass da-yitbaaha.* — He likes to show his children off. *yEijba yitbaaha b-awlaada.*
to show up - 1. *jaa (i majiiʔ), bayyan (i tabyiin) t-.* Nobody showed up. *maḥḥad jaa.* **2.** *δihar (a δuhuur).* Yellow shows up well against a black background. *l-ʔaṣfar yiδhar zeen Eala gaaEiyya sooda.*
showcase - *jaamxaana* pl. *-aat.* Let me see that ring in the showcase. *raawiini l-miḥbas illi bij-jaamxaana.*
shower - 1. *zaxxa* pl. *-aat.* We were caught in a heavy shower. *liḥmatna zaxxa qawiyya.* **2.** *duuš* pl. *-aat.* Does your new apartment have a shower? *š-šiqqa j-jidiida maaltak biiha duuš?*
to shower - *ġarrag (i tġirrig) t-.* Their friends showered them with presents. *ʔaṣdiqaaʔhum ġarrgoohum bil-hadaaya.*
show-off - *mbahaayči* pl. *-iyya.* He's a big show-off. *huwwa mbahaayči.*
shrewd - *miqtidir, ḥaadiq.* He's a shrewd businessman. *huwwa fadd rajul ʔaEmaal miqtidir.*
shrill - *rafiiE.* She has a shrill voice. *Eidha ḥiss rafiiE.*
shrimp - 1. *rubyaan.* We're having shrimp for dinner. *raḥ-ykuun Eidna rubyaan bil-Eaša.* **2.** *qizim* pl. *ʔaqzaam.* He's a little shrimp. *huwwa qizim.* or **haaδa nuṣṣ neeča.
to **shrink - 1.** *xašš (u xašš) n-.* Does this material shrink when washed? *hal-iqmaaš yxušš bil-ġasil?* **2.** *nkumaš (i nkimaaš).* The meat shrank when we cooked it. *l-laḥam inkumaš min ṭubaxnaa.* **3.** *tjabjab (a tajabjub).* He shrinks from responsibility. *haaδa yitjabjab imnil-masʔuuliyya.*
shrub - *šujayra* pl. *-aat.*
to **shrug** - *hazz (i hazz) n-.* He shrugged his shoulders. *hazz ičtaafa.*
to **shuffle - 1.** *xarbaṭ (u txurbuṭ) t-, xilaṭ (i xaliṭ) n-.* Have the cards been shuffled? *l-waraq itxarbaṭ?* **2.** *šaḥḥaṭ (i tašḥiiṭ) b-.* Stop shuffling your feet; you're ruining your shoes! *bass Eaad itšaḥḥiṭ ib-rijlak, muu Eidamit qundartak!*
to **shut - 1.** *sadd (i sadd) n-.* Please shut the door! *sidd il-baab rajaaʔan!* **2.** *ḥibas (i ḥabis) n-.* Who shut the dog in the garage? *minu ḥibas ič-čalib bil-garaaj?*
to shut down - *Eaḍḍal (i tEiḍḍil).* Why'd the factory shut down? *leeš il-maEmal Eaḍḍal.*
to shut off - 1. *giṭaE (a gaṭiE) n-, gaṣṣ (u gaṣṣ) n-.* The workers shut off our water for two days. *l-Eummaal giṭEaw il-mayy Eanna li-muddat yoomeen.* **2.** *sadd (i sadd) n-.* Shut off the water. *sidd il-mayy!*
to shut up - *sikat (u sukuut) n-.* Shut up! *ʔiskut!* or **nčabb!
shutter - 1. *ʔabajoor* pl. *-aat.* Open the shutters, please. *fukk il-ʔabajooraat, min faδlak.* **2.** *ḥaajiz* pl. *ḥawaajiz, ḥaajib* pl. *ḥujjaab.* The lens shutter in my camera is stuck. *ḥaajiz il-Eadasa maal kaamarti mšakkal.* **3.** *kabang* pl. *-aat.* The storekeeper shut the door and rolled down the shutter. *ṣaaḥib il-maḥall sadd il-baab w-nazzal il-kabang.*
shy - *xajuul* pl. *-iin.* Don't be so shy! *la-tkuun hal-gadd xajuul.* or **la-tistiḥi.
to shy - *jifal (i jafil).* The horse shied at the car. *l-iḥṣaan jifal imnis-sayyaara.*
to shy away from - *tjannab (a tajannub).* He shies away from hard work. *yitjannab iš-šuġuḷ iš-šaaq.*
sick - *mariiδ* pl. *marδa.* He's sick in bed. *huwwa mariiδ bil-ifraaš.* — The sick are given the best of care. *l-marδa ydaaruuhum zeen.*
**I get sick when I fly. *nafsi tilEab min aṭiir.*
**I'm getting sick and tired of this job. *malleet min iš-šaġḷa.* or *biδEat nafsi mniš-šaġḷa.*
to be taken sick - *tmarraδ (a tamarruδ).* He was suddenly taken sick. *Eala ġafla tmarraδ.*
sickle - *minjal* pl. *manaajil.*
sickness - *maraδ* pl. *ʔamraaδ.*
side - 1. *jiha* pl. *-aat, ṣoob* pl. *ʔaṣwaab, jaanib* pl. *jawaanib.* On this side of the street there are only a few houses. *min haj-jiha mniš-šaariE ʔaku šwayya ḥwaaš bass.* — I saw him on the other side of the city. *šifta biṣ-ṣoob iθ-θaani mnil-madiina.* **2.** *jaanib* pl. *jawaanib.* He is on our side. *huwwa min jaanibna.* **3.** *jaanibi*.* Please use the side door. *rajaaʔan istaEmil il-baab ij-jaanibiyya.* **4.** *xaaṣra* pl. *xawaaṣir.* She's a thorn in his side. *waagfa siččiina b-xaaṣirta.*
**To be on the safe side, I asked him again. *siʔalta marrt il-lux ḥatta atʔakkad.*
side by side - *ṣuwa.* They walked along silently side by side. *mišaw bil-hiduuʔ ṣuwa.*
to take sides - *nḥaaz (a nḥiyaaz) ʔila jiha, ʔayyad (i taʔyiid) t- jiha.* It's difficult to take sides on this question. *ṣaEub waaḥid yinḥaaz ʔila jiha b-hal-qaδiyya.*
to side with - *nḥaaz (a nḥiyaaz) l-, ʔayyad (i taʔyiid) t- l-.* You always side with him! *ʔinta daaʔiman tinḥaaz-la.*
sidewalk - *raṣiif* pl. *ʔarṣifa.*
siege - *ḥiṣaar* pl. *-aat.*
sieve - *munxuḷ* pl. *manaaxuḷ.*
to **sift** - *nixaḷ (u naxiḷ) n-.* The flour has to be sifted first. *ṭ-ṭaḥiin laazim yinnuxuḷ bil-ʔawwal.*
to **sigh** - *tḥaṣṣar (a taḥaṣṣur), tnahhad (a tanahhud).* What are you sighing about? *leeš da-titḥaṣṣar?*
sight - 1. *naδar, baṣar.* He lost his sight in the accident. *fuqad naδara bil-ḥaadiθ.* **2.** *manδar* pl. *manaaδir.* That's a beautiful sight! *haaδa manδar jamiil waḷḷa!*
**I recognized you at first sight. *ʔawwal ma-šiftak Eiraftak.*
**Don't lose sight of him. *la-txallii yġiib Ean naδarak.*
**They had orders to shoot him on sight. *čaan Eidhum ʔawaamir yitliquun in-naar ʔawwal-ma yšuufuu.*
sights - *maEaalim.* Have you seen the sights of the town? *šifit maEaalim il-madiina?*
by sight - *bil-wujih.* I know him only by sight. *ʔaEurfa bass bil-wujih.*
in sight - *mbayyin, δaahir.* The end is not yet in sight. *n-nihaaya baEadha ma-mbayyna.*
to catch sight of - *limaḥ (a lamiḥ).* As soon as he caught sight of you, he vanished. *ʔawwal-ma limaḥak, ixtifa.*

sign - 1. *quṭεa* pl. *quṭaε, ʔišaara* pl. *-aat, εalaama* pl. *-aat, yaafṭa* pl. *-aat.* What does that sign say? *š-maktuub εal-quṭεa?* **2.** *baadira* pl. *-aat.* Is that a good sign? *haay baadira ṭayyba?* **3.** *ʔišaara* pl. *-aat.* He gave us a sign to follow him. *nṭaana ʔišaara ntibεa.* **4.** *daliil* pl. *dalaaʔil.* All signs point to an early winter. *kull id-dalaaʔil itšiir εala ʔinna š-šita raḥ-yiji mubakkir.*

to sign - *waqqaε (i tawqiiε) t-, muδ̣a (i ʔimδ̣aaʔ, maδ̣i) n-.* He forgot to sign the letter. *nisa ywaqqiε ir-risaala.* -- Don't forget to sign in. *la-tinsa timδ̣i min tiji.*

to sign up - *sajjal (i tasjiil).* I signed up for three courses. *sajjalit ib-iθlaθ mawaaδ̣iiε.*

to sign over - *sallam (i tsillim).* He signed over the business to his son. *sallam šuğla l-ʔibna.*

signal - *ʔišaara* pl. *-aat.* We agreed on a signal. *ttifaqna εala ʔišaara.* -- We're getting a strong signal from him. *da-nitlaqqa ʔišaara qawiyya minna.*

to signal - *ʔaššar (i taʔšiir) t-.* Will you signal the waiter, please? *ma-tʔaššir lil-booy, baḷḷa?*

signalman - *maʔmuur (pl. -iin) seer.* The signalman stopped the train in time. *maʔmuur is-seer waggaf il-qiṭaar bil-wakt il-munaasib.*

signature - *tawqiiε* pl. *tawaaqiiε.* The letter has no signature. *l-maktuub ma-εalee tawqiiε.*

signet ring - *muhur* pl. *mhaar.* He signs documents with his signet ring. *yumhur il-waθaayiq bil-muhur maala.*

silence - 1. *sukuun, sukuut.* There was complete silence in the room. *čaan ʔaku sukuun šaamil bil-ğurfa.* **2.** *hiduuʔ.* They listened in silence. *ntibhaw ib-hiduuʔ.*

to silence - *sakkat (i taskiit) t-.* I couldn't silence him. *ma-gdart asakkta.*

silent - 1. *saakit.* Why are you so silent? *leeš ʔinta hal-gadd saakit?* **2.** *ṣaamit.* She used to play in silent pictures. *čaanat itmaθθil bil-ʔaflaam iṣ-ṣaamita.*

silk - *ḥariir.* How much is this silk? *beeš hal-ḥariir?*

silly - 1. *ʔaḥmaq.* That's a silly thing to do. *haaδa εamal ʔaḥmaq.* **2.** *saxiif, fuṭiir.* That was a silly thing to say. *kalaamak ṣaxiif.* -- Don't be so silly! *la-tṣiir hal-gadd saxiif.* **3.** *ʔablah.* He's not so silly as he looks. *huwwa muu hal-gadd ʔablah miθil-ma da-ybayyin εalee.*

silver - 1. *fuδ̣δ̣a.* I gave her a lighter made of silver. *nṭeetha qiddaaḥa min fuδ̣δ̣a.* **2.** *fuδ̣δ̣i*.* She's wearing a silver ring. *laabsa miḥbas fuδ̣δ̣i.*

similar - *mušaabih, šabiih, mumaaθil.* I know of a similar case. *ʔaεruf qaδ̣iyya mušaabiha.*

simple - 1. *başiiṭ, sahil.* That's quite a simple matter. *haaδa fadd mawδ̣uuε kulliš başiiṭ.* **2.** *saaδij* pl. *suδδaj, başiiṭ* pl. *buşaṭaaʔ.* I may sound simple to you, but I don't understand it. *mumkin tiṭṣawwarni saaδij, laakin ma-da-aftihimha.*

simplicity - 1. *tabṣiiṭ.* For the sake of simplicity let's say that... *min ʔajil tabṣiiṭ il-mawδ̣uuε xalli nguul...* **2.** *baṣaaṭa.* All his designs are characterized by simplicity. *kull taṣaamiima tiğlib εaleeha l-baṣaaṭa.*

simply - 1. *qaṭεan.* That's simply impossible! *haaδi mustaḥiila qaṭεan!* **2.** *b-baṣaaṭa.* He explained it to the children simply. *širaḥha lil-ʔaṭfaal ib-baṣaaṭa.*

sin - *δanib* pl. *δinuub, maεṣiya* pl. *maεaaṣi.* He's committed a lot of sins. *rtikab εiddat δinuub.*

to sin - *ʔaδnab (i ʔiδnaab).* He sins more than he does good. *yiδnib ʔakθar min-ma ysawwi xeer.*

Sinai Peninsula - *šubuh jaziirat siina.*

since - 1. *min.* He hasn't been here since Monday. *ma-caan ihnaa min yoom il-iθneen.* **2.** *min wakit-ma, min.* I haven't seen anyone since I got back. *ma-šifit ʔaḥḥad min wakit-ma rijaεit.* **3.** *li-ʔan.* Since I didn't have the money I couldn't go. *ʔaani ma-gdarit aruuḥ li-ʔan ma-čaan εindi fluus.*

ever since - *min δaak il-wakit.* I haven't spoken with him ever since. *ma-ḥčeet wiyyaa min δaak il-wakit.*

sincere - *muxliṣ.* He's a sincere person. *huwwa fadd waaḥid muxliṣ.*

sincerely - *min kull εaqil-, min ṣudug, min kull galub-.* You sincerely believe it? *min kull εaqlak tiεtiqid biiha?*

to **sing** - *ğanna (i ğina) t-.* I don't sing very well. *ma-ʔağanni zeen.*

to **singe - 1.** *ḥirag (i ḥarig) n-.* I singed my eyebrows when I got too close to the fire. *ḥragit ḥwaajbi min itqarrabit lin-naar.* **2.** *lahhab (i tlihhib).* After you pluck the chicken's feathers, singe it. *baεad-ma tintif riiš id-dijaaja, lahhibha.*

singer - *mğanni* pl. *-iin.* He's a well-known singer. *huwwa mğanni maεruuf.*

single - 1. *ʔaεzab* pl. *εuzzaab.* Are you married or single? *ʔinta mitzawwij loo ʔaεzab?* **2.** *waaḥid.* He made just a single mistake. *sawwa fadd ğalṭa waḥda bass.*

**He didn't make a single mistake. *ma-sawwa wala ğalṭa.*

to single out - *xtaar (a xtiyaar), ntixab (i ntixaab).* Why did they single you out? *leeš bass ʔilak xtaarook?*

singular - *mufrad.* ''Boy'' is the singular of ''boys.'' *walad mufrad ʔawlaad.*

sink - *mağsala, mağsal* pl. *mağaasil.* The dishes are still in the sink. *l-imwaaεiin baεadha bil-mağsala.*

to sink - 1. *ğirag (a ğarag) n-.* The ship sank in 10 minutes. *s-safiina ğirgat ib-εašir daqaayiq.* **2.** *ğarrag (i tğirrig) t-.* They sank three enemy ships. *ğarrigaw itlaθ bawaaxir lil-εadu.* **3.** *ṭumaṣ (u ṭamuṣ).* The car sank into the mud. *s-sayyaara ṭumṣat biṭ-ṭiin.* **4.** *hibaṭ (u hubuuṭ) n-.* The house has sunk ten inches. *l-beet hibaṭ εašir injaat.* **5.** *tdahwar (a tadahwur).* His health is sinking rapidly. *ṣiḥḥta gaaεid titdahwar ib-surεa.*

sip - *šafṭa* pl. *-aat, maṣṣa* pl. *-aat.* I only had a sip of my coffee. *ʔaxaδit šafṭa wiḥda mnil-gahwa.*

to sip - *rišaf (u rašif) n-, šifaṭ (u šafuṭ) n-.* He sipped the hot coffee. *rišaf il-gahwa il-ḥaarra.*

sir - 1. *sayyid* pl. *saada.* Sir, the colonel is here. *sayyidi, l-εaqiid ihnaa.* **2.** *ʔustaaδ* pl. *ʔasaatiδa.* Yes sir, I'll call him now. *naεam ʔustaaδ, raḥ-axaabra hassa.* **3.** *εamm* pl. *ʔaεmaam.* No sir, I didn't break the vase. *laa εammi, ma-ksart il-mazhariyya.* or *laa εammu, ma-ksart il-mazhariyya.*

sister - *ʔuxut* pl. *xawaat.* Do you have any sisters? *εindak xawaat?*

sister-in-law - *ʔuxut (pl. xawaat) mara-, mart ʔaxu-* pl. *mrayyaat ʔuxwa-.* She's my sister-in-law. *hiyya ʔuxut marti.*

to **sit** - *giεad (u gaεid), jilas (i jiluus).* We sat in the front row. *gεadna biṣ-ṣaff il-ʔamaami.*

to sit in on - *ḥiδ̣ar (a ḥuδ̣uur).* I sat in on all the conferences. *ḥiδ̣arit kull il-muʔtamaraat.*

to sit up - *sihar (a suhuur).* We sat up all night waiting for him. *siharna ṭuul il-leel nintaδ̣ra.*

sitting - 1. *gaεda* pl. *-aat.* He finished the food in one sitting. *xallaṣ il-ʔakil ib-gaεda wiḥda.* **2.** *guεuud, gaεid.* Sitting at home alone makes her nervous. *guεuudha waḥḥadha bil-beet ysawwiiha εaṣabiyya.*

situation - *mawqif* pl. *mawaaqif.* She saved the situation. *hiyya ʔanqiδat il-mawqif.*

six - 1. *sitta.* Will six be enough? *sitta tkaffi?* **2.** *sitt.* They were here six days ago. *čaanaw ihnaa gabuḷ sitt iyyaam.*

**It's six of one and half a dozen of another. *xooja εali, mulla εali.*

sixteen - *ṣiṭṭaεaš.*

sixteenth - *ṣ-ṣiṭṭaεaš.*

sixth - *saadis.*

sixtieth - *s-sittiin.*

sixty - *sittiin.*

size - 1. *qiyaas* pl. *-aat.* What size shoe do you wear? *ʔay qiyaas qandara tilbas?* **2.** *ḥajim* pl. *ʔaḥjaam, ḥujuum.* What size refrigerator are you going to buy? *ʔay ḥajim θallaaja raḥ-tištiri?*

to size up - *qaddar (i tqiddir) t-.* How do you size up the situation? *šloon itqaddir il-waδ̣iε?*

skate - *skeet* pl. *-aat.* A wheel came off my skate. *č-čarix wugaε imnil-iskeet maali.*

to skate - *tzallaj (a tazalluj).* We Baghdadis don't skate. *ʔiḥna l-bağdaadiyyiin ma-nitzallaj.*

skeleton - *haykal* pl. *hayaakil.*

skeptical - *šakkaak.* Don't be so skeptical! *la-tkuun hal-gadd šakkaak.*

sketch - *muxaṭṭaṭ* pl. *-aat.*

to **ski** - *tzaḥlag (a tazaḥlug).* I never learned how to ski on snow. *ʔabad ma-tεallamit išloon atzaḥlag εaθ-θalij.*

to **skid** - *tzaḥlag (a tazaḥlug).* The car started to skid. *s-sayyaara gaamat titzaḥlag.*

skill - *mahaara, baraaεa.* That requires a lot of skill. *δiič tiṭṭallab ihwaaya mahaara.*

skilled - *maahir* pl. *-iin.* He is a skilled cabinetmaker. *huwwa najjaar moobilyaat maahir.*

skillfully - *b-mahaara, b-baraaεa.* You got yourself out of that problem very skillfully. *xaḷḷaṣit nafsak imnil-muškila b-mahaara.*

to **skim** - *šaal (i šiyaala) n- il-gišwa.* I skimmed the

milk. *šilt il-gišwa mnil-ᶎaliib.*
to skim through - *ṭṣaffaᶎ (a taṣaffuᶎ).* I just skimmed through the book. *ṭṣaffaᶎit il-iktaab bass.*
skin - **1.** *jilid* pl. *jluud.* She had very sensitive skin. *Ɛidha jilid kulliš ᶎassaas.* **2.** *farwa* pl. *-aat.* How many skins will you need for the coat? *čam farwa tiᶎtaaj lis-sitra?* **3.** *gišir* pl. *gšuur.* These apples have a thick skin. *hat-tiffaaᶎ gišra θixiin.* **4.** *jildi**. He's got a skin disease. *Ɛinda maraḍ jildi.*
I got a passing grade by the skin of my teeth. *ᶎaṣṣalit Ɛala darajt in-najaaᶎ Ɛal-ᶎaaffa.*
to skin - **1.** *ṣilax (a ṣalix).* After you slaughter the calf, skin it. *baƐad-ma tiδbaᶎ il-Ɛijil ʔiṣlaxa.* **2.** *jilax (a jalix), jilaġ (a jaliġ).* When he fell he skinned his knee. *min wugaƐ jilax rukubta.*
to **skip** - **1.** *ṭufar (u ṭafur) n-.* Skip a few lines. *ʔuṭfur čam ṣaṭir.* — Can you skip rope? *tuƐruf tuṭfur Ɛal-ᶎabil?* **2.** *Ɛubar (u Ɛabur, Ɛubuur) n-,* I skipped second grade. *Ɛubarit iṣ-ṣaff iθ-θaani.* **3.** *giḷab (u gaḷub) n-.* Skip a few pages. *ʔugḷub Ɛiddat ṣafᶎaat.* **4.** *tirak (u tarik).* Skip the hard words. *ʔitruk il-kalimaat iṣ-ṣaƐba.* **5.** *nhizam (i nhizaam) min.* He skipped town. *nhizam imnil-madiina.*
skirt - *tannuura* pl. *-aat, tnaaniir.* Her skirt is too long. *tannuuratha ṭwiila.*
skull - *jumjuma* pl. *jamaajim.* He fractured his skull. *nkisrat jumjumta.*
skullcap - *Ɛaraqčiin* pl. *-aat.* They wear skullcaps under their headcloths. *yilbasuun Ɛaraqčiin jawwa l-yeešmaaġ.*
sky - *sima* pl. *samawaat.* How does the sky look today? *šloon is-sima l-yoom?*
**The news came out of a clear blue sky. *l-ʔaxbaar nizlat miθl iṣ-ṣaaƐiqa.*
**He praised her to the skies. *midaᶎha hwaaya.*
slack - **1.** *waaguf, kasaad.* Business is slack. *š-šuġuḷ waaguf.* **2.** *baṭiiʔ.* His work has become very slack. *šuġḷa šaayir kulliš baṭiiʔ.* **3.** *raxi**. Your tentropes are too slack. *ᶎbaal xeemtak raxiyya.*
slacks - *panṭaroon* pl. *-aat.*
to **slap** - *liṭam (u laṭum) n-.* She slapped him when he tried to kiss her. *liṭmata min ᶎaawal ybuusha.*
slaughter - *majzara* pl. *majaazir, maδbaᶎa* pl. *maδaabiᶎ.* The slaughter was terrific. *l-majzara čaanat faḍiiƐa.*
to slaughter - *δibaᶎ (a δabiᶎ) n-.* We usually slaughter sheep on holidays. *Ɛaadatan niδbaᶎ xaruuf ib-ʔayyaam il-Ɛiid.*
slave - *Ɛabid* pl. *Ɛabiid.* He treats them like slaves. *yƐaamilhum Ɛabaalak Ɛabiid.*
**I've really slaved today. *štiġaḷit miθl iᶎmaar il-yoom.*
sleep - *noom.* Sleep is important. *n-noom muhimm.*
to get sleep - *naam (a noom).* I didn't get enough sleep last night. *ma-nimit kaafi l-baarᶎa bil-leel.*
to sleep - *naam (a noom).* Did you sleep well? *nimit zeen?*
**Sleep on it before you decide. *δakkir biiha hal-leela gabuḷ-ma tqarrir.*
sleepy - *naƐsaan, mnaƐƐis.* I'm still sleepy. *baƐadni naƐsaan.*
to make sleepy - *naƐƐas (i tanƐiis) t-.* The heat's making me sleepy. *l-ᶎaraara tnaƐƐisni.*
sleeve - *ridin, rdaan* pl. *ridaanaat.* The sleeves are too short. *r-ridaanaat kulliš igṣaar.*
**He laughed up his sleeve. *ḍiᶎak ib-Ɛibba.*
slender - *rašiig.* She's gotten very slender. *ṣaayra kulliš rašiiga.*
slice - **1.** *quṭƐa* pl. *quṭaƐ, wuṣla* pl. *wuṣal.* How many slices of bread shall I cut? *čam quṭƐat xubuz ʔaguṣṣ?* **2.** *šiif* pl. *šyaaf.* Have another slice of watermelon. *ʔuxuδ šiif laax raggi.*
to slice - **1.** *šarraᶎ (i tširriᶎ) t-.* Do you want to slice the roast? *triid itšarriᶎ il-laᶎam?* **2.** *šayyaf (i tašyiif).* Slice up the cucumbers. *šayyifi l-ixyaara.*
slide - **1.** *slaayda* pl. *-aat.* He gave a lecture with slides. *niṭa muᶎaaḍara b-islaaydaat.* **2.** *ziᶎlaaga* pl. *-aat.* The city put a new slide in the playground. *l-baladiyya ᶎaṭṭat ziᶎlaaga jdiida bil-malƐab.*
to slide - *zaᶎlag (i tziᶎlig).* Pick the desk up; don't slide it on the floor. *šiil il-meez, la-tzaᶎilga (Ɛal-gaaƐ).*
slight - **1.** *baṣiiṭ, ṭafiif, qaliil.* There's a slight difference. *ʔaku xtilaaf baṣiiṭ.* **2.** *xafiif.* He has a slight cold. *Ɛinda našla xafiifa.* **3.** *naᶎiif.* She's very slight. *hiyya kulliš naᶎiifa.*
slightest - *ʔaqall.* I haven't the slightest doubt. *ma-Ɛindi ʔaqall šakka.*
slim - **1.** *naᶎiif, ḍaƐiif.* She's gotten very slim. *ṣaarat kulliš naᶎiifa.* **2.** *ḍiƐiif.* His chances are very slim. *ʔamala kulliš ḍiƐiif.*
sling - **1.** *miƐčaal* pl. *maƐaačiil, miƐčaan* pl. *maƐaačiin.* David killed Goliath with a sling. *daawuud qital jaaluut bil-miƐčaal.* **2.** *Ɛillaaga* pl. *-aat.* They put his broken arm in a sling. *Ɛalligoo ʔiida b-Ɛillaaga.*
slingshot - *muṣyaada* pl. *-aat.* I'm looking for some rubber to make a slingshot. *da-adawwir Ɛala wuṣlat laastiig ᶎatta asawwi muṣyaada.*
slip - **1.** *beet* pl. *byuut.* Our pillows need new slips. *mxaadiidna yinraad-ilha byuut jidiida.* **2.** *ʔatag* pl. *-aat.* Your slip is showing. *ʔatagič da-ybayyin.* **3.** *zalla* pl. *-aat, zalga* pl. *-aat.* It was just a slip of the tongue. *čaanat bass zallat ilsaan.* **4.** *wuṣla* pl. *wuṣal.* He wrote it on a slip of paper. *kitabha Ɛala wuṣlat waraq.*
to give someone the slip - *mulaṣ (a maluṣ) min, filat (i falit) min.* He's given us the slip again. *mulaṣ min Ɛidna marra lux.*
to slip - **1.** *zilaq (a zalaq), tzaᶎlag (a tziᶎlig).* I slipped on the ice. *zlagit Ɛaθ-θalij.* **2.** *ṭilaƐ (a ṭuluuƐ) min.* It slipped my mind completely. *ṭilaƐ min baali tamaaman.*
**He slipped the policeman some money. *Ɛabbar ifluus liš-šurṭi.*
**Wait until I slip into a coat. *ʔintiḍir ʔila ʔan ʔalbas sitra.*
to slip away - *šilaƐ (a šaliƐ), nass (i nass).* Let's slip away, before he sees us. *xalli nišlaƐ gabuḷ-ma yšuufna.*
to slip by - *faat (u foot).* I let the chance slip by me. *xalleet il-furṣa tfuutni.*
to slip out - **1.** *filat (i falit) min.* I really didn't want to tell him, but it just slipped out. *bil-ᶎaqiiqa ma-ridt agul-la, bass filtat min ilsaani.* — The bird slipped out of my hand. *l-Ɛaṣfuur filat min ʔiidi.* **2.** *zubag (u zabug), filat (i falit).* The fish slipped out of my hand. *zubgat is-simča min ʔiidi.*
to slip up - **1.** *xarbaṭ (u txurbuṭ).* I slipped up badly on the next question. *xarbaṭit ihwaaya bis-suʔaal iθ-θaani.* **2.** *twahdan (a twihdin).* I don't know how I could have slipped up on that job. *ma-ʔadri šloon itwahdanit ib-haš-šaġḷa.*
slipper - **1.** *naƐaal* pl. *-aat, niƐil.* I can't find my slippers. *ma-da-ʔagdar algi naƐaali.* **2.** *baabuuj* pl. *bwaabiij.* My wife lost her slippers. *zoojti ḍayyƐat baabuujha.*
slippery - **1.** *zalag.* The streets are very slippery. *š-šawaariƐ kulliš zalag.* **2.** *mitqallib* pl. *-iin.* He's a slippery character. *huwwa waaᶎid mitqallib.*
slit - *fatᶎa* pl. *-aat, šagg* pl. *šguug.* Make the slit a bit longer. *sawwi l-fatᶎa šwayya ʔaṭwal.*
to slit - *gaṣṣ (u gaṣṣ).* The criminals slit his throat. *l-mujrimiin gaṣṣaw joozta.*
slogan - **1.** *šiƐaar* pl. *-aat.* The students wrote slogans on the walls. *ṭ-ṭullaab kitbaw šiƐaaraat Ɛal-ᶎiiṭaan.* **2.** *hitaaf* pl. *-aat.* I didn't hear their slogans. *ma-smaƐit hitaafaathum.*
slope - *munᶎadar* pl. *-aat, nᶎidaar* pl. *-aat, dihidwaana* pl. *-aat.* Is the slope very steep? *l-munᶎadar qawi?*
to slope - *nᶎidar (i nᶎidaar).* The floor slopes. *l-gaaƐ minᶎadra.*
sloppy - **1.** *mbahdal, mbahδal.* Don't be so sloppy! *la-tkuun hal-gadd imbahdal.* **2.** *mxarbaṭ.* They always do sloppy work. *daaʔiman ysawwuun šuġuḷ imxarbaṭ.*
slot - *fatᶎa* pl. *-aat.* Put ten fils in the slot when you want to call from a public phone. *ᶎuṭṭ Ɛašr ifluus bil-fatᶎa min itriid itxaabur min talafoon Ɛumuumi.*
slow - **1.** *baṭiiʔ.* He's very slow in his work. *huwwa kulliš baṭiiʔ ib-šuġḷa.* **2.** *muʔaxxira, mqaṣṣira.* Your watch is slow. *saaƐtak imʔaxxira.* **3.** *haadi, xafiif.* Cook the soup over a slow fire. *ʔuṭbux iš-šoorba Ɛala naar haadiya.*
to slow down - **1.** *xaffaf (u taxfiif) t-, tmahhal (a tamahhul).* Slow down when you come to an intersection. *xaffuf min ṭoosal lit-taqaaṭuƐ.* — Slow down; I can't keep up with you. *xaffuf mašyak; ma-agdar alaᶎᶎig biik.* **2.** *tmaahal (a tamaahul).* He's slowing down in his work. *da-yitmaahal ib-šuġḷa.*
slowly - *yawaaš, b-buṭuʔ.* Drive slowly. *suuq yawaaš.*

or **suuq ʕala keefak.
sly - makkaar, maakir.
small - 1. ṣġayyir pl. ṣġaar. The room is rather small. l-ġurfa šwayya ṣġayyra. 2. baṣiiṭ, qaliil. The difference is very small. l-ixtilaaf kulliš baṣiiṭ. 3. waðiiʕ. That was an awfully small thing to do. haaða ʕamal waðiiʕ.
smaller - ʔaṣġar. I haven't anything smaller. ma-ʕindi šii ʔaṣġar.
smallpox - jidri. We have all been vaccinated against smallpox. kullatna ṭṭaʕʕamna ðidd ij-jidri.
smart - 1. laṭiif, ʔaniiq. That's a smart dress. haaði badla laṭiifa. 2. ðaki pl. ʔaðkiyaaʔ. He's a smart boy. haaða walad ðaki.
to smart - ẓirag (i ẓarig). The wound smarts. j-jiriẓ yiẓrig.
to **smash** - kassar (i tkissir) t-, ẓaṭṭam (a tẓuṭṭum) t-. The boys smashed the window. l-wilid kassiraw iš-šibbaač.
smell - 1. riiẓa pl. -aat. What's that smell? šinu har-riiẓa? 2. šamm. His sense of smell is keen. ẓaassat iš-šamm maalta ẓaadda.
to smell - 1. štamm (a štimaam). Do you smell gasoline? tištamm riiẓt il-baanziin? 2. niṭa (i) riiẓa. It smells like cooked lamb. tinṭi riiẓat laẓam il-ġanam il-mašwi.
smile - btisaama pl. -aat. She has a charming smile. ʕidha fadd ibtisaama jaððaaba.
**She was all smiles. wujihha čaan ðaẓuuk.
to smile - btisam (i btisaam). Did I see you smile? šiftak tibtisim?
smoke - duxxaan. Where's that smoke coming from? mneen da-yiji had-duxxaan?
to smoke - daxxan (i tadxiin, tdixxin) t-. Do you smoke? ʔinta tdaxxin? — The stove is smoking again. ṭ-ṭabbaax da-ydaxxin marra lux.
smoking - tadxiin. Smoking is forbidden here. t-tadxiin mamnuuʕ ihnaa!
smooth - 1. naaʕim, ʔamlas. Her skin is very smooth. jilidha kulliš naaʕiim. 2. haadiʔ. The sea was very smooth. l-baẓar čaan kulliš haadiʔ.
**I can't get a smooth shave with this blade. hal-muus ma-ynaʕʕim zeen.
to smooth down - nawwam (u tanwiim) t-, ṣaffaf (u taṣfiif) t-. Smooth down your hair. nawwum šaʕrak.
to smooth out - ʕaddal (i taʕdiil) t-, rattab (i tartiib) t-. Smooth out the tablecloth. ʕaddil ġaṭa l-meez.
smoothly - b-huduuʔ, b-salaam. Everything went smoothly. kullši miša b-huduuʔ.
to **smother** - 1. xinag (u xanig) n-. He smothered the child with the pillow. xinag iṭ-ṭifil bil-imxadda. 2. xtinag (i xtinaag). We nearly smothered. xtinagna ʔilla šwayya.
to **smuggle** - harrab (i tahriib) t-. They smuggled in arms. harribaw islaaẓ lid-daaxil.
snail - ẓalazuuna pl. -aat coll. ẓalazuun; zalanṭaẓa pl. -aat coll. zalanṭaẓ.
snake - ẓayya pl. -aat, ẓayaaya.
snap - 1. ṭabbaaga pl. -aat. I have to sew snaps on my dress. laazim axayyiṭ ṭabbaagaat ʕala nafnuufi. 2. ẓaraka, ruuẓ. Put some snap in your marching. xallu šwayya ẓaraka b-mašiikum. 3. sariiʕ. Don't make snap judgments. la-tinṭi ʔaẓkaam sariiʕa.
**The exam was a snap. l-intiẓaan čaan baṣiiṭ. or l-imtiẓaan čaan zalaaṭa.
to snap - 1. ṭagg (u ṭagg). If the cucumber's fresh and crisp, just bend it and it snaps. l-ixyaara, ʔiða hašša, bass tiðniiha ṭṭugg. 2. dagg (u dagg). He snaps two fingers when he sings. min yġanni ydugg iṣbiʕteen. 3. nitar (u natir) n-. I don't know why he snapped at me that way. ma-adri leeš nitar biyya hiiči.
**Snap out of it! trukha! or ʔinsaaha!
**The dog snapped at me. č-čalib ẓaawal yʕaððni.
to snap up - fall (i fall). Snap it up! The train leaves in half an hour. fillha! l-qiṭaar raẓ-yitẓarrak baʕad nuṣṣ saaʕa.
snappy - ʔaniiq pl. -iin. He's a snappy dresser. huwwa ʔaniiq bil-libis.
**Come on, make it snappy. yaḷḷa, bil-ʕajal!
snapshot - ṣuura pl. ṣuwar. Where did you take these snapshots? ween ʔaxaðit haṣ-ṣuwar?
to **sneak** - dixal (u duxuul) bil-baskuut. He must have sneaked into the house. laazim dixal il-beet bil-baskuut.
sneaky - saxtači pl. -iyya. He's pretty sneaky. huwwa saxtači.
sneeze - ʕaṭsa pl. -aat. That sure was a loud sneeze. ẓaqiiqatan čaanat ʕaṭsa qawiyya.
to sneeze - 1. ʕiṭaṣ (i ʕaṭiṣ). I sneezed from the dust. ʕiṭaṣit imnil-ʕajaaj. 2. ʕaṭṭaṣ (i tʕiṭṭiṣ) t-. He's been sneezing all morning. ṣaar-la da-yʕaṭṭiṣ imniṣ-ṣubuẓ.
to **sniff** - štamm (a šamm) šamšam (i tšimšim). He sniffed the food. štamm riiẓt il-ʔakil.
to **snore** - šixar (u šaxiir). He snored all night long. čaan yišxur il-leel kulla.
snow - θalij. How deep is the snow? šgadd ġumj iθ-θalij?
to snow - θilaj (i θalij). It snowed all night. buqat tiθlij il-leel kulla.
**We're snowed under with work. ġiragna biš-šuġuḷ.
so - 1. hiiči, ṣudug, ṣaẓiiẓ, tamaam. Isn't that so? muu hiiči? 2. laʕad, ʔiðan, yaʕni. So you think it's a good idea. laʕad tiʕtiqid haay xooš fikra. — So you don't want to go. yaʕni ma-triid itruuẓ. — So what? šinu, yaʕni? 3. hamm, hammeen, hammeena. If I can do it, so can you. ʔiða ʔaani ʔagdar asawwiiha, ʔinta hamm tigdar. 4. hal-gadd. Why are you so lazy? ʔinta leeš hal-gadd kaslaan? 5. ʔila daraja. I'm so tired, I can't work. ʔaani taʕbaan ʔila daraja ma-agdar aštuġuḷ. 6. kulliš. You look so tired! mbayyin ʕaleek kulliš taʕbaan.
**So long! fiimaanillaa! or maʕa s-salaama!
**I need five dinars or so. ʔaẓtaaj ẓawaali xams idnaaniir.
so as to - ẓatta. I did some of the work so as to make things easier for you. sawweet qisim imniš-šuġuḷ ẓatta axaffif ʕaleek.
so far - li-hassa, l-ẓadd il-ʔaan, l-ẓadd hassa. I haven't had any news so far. li-hassa ma-ʕindi ʔay ʔaxbaar. — How are things? So far, so good. šloon il-ʔaẓwaal? li-hassa, kullši zeen.
so far as - ẓasab-ma. So far as I know, he's still in Australia. ẓasab-ma ʔaʕruf huwwa baʕda b-ʔusturaalya.
so much - 1. hal-gadd. Not so much rice please. muu hal-gadd timman, min faðlak. 2. jiddan, hwaaya. Thanks ever so much. ʔaškurak kulliš ihwaaya.
so on - ʔila ʔaaxirihi. He went to the market and bought potatoes, tomatoes, and so on. raaẓ lis-suug w-ištira puteeta, ṭamaaṭa, w-ʔila ʔaaxirihi.
so so - nuṣṣ w-nuṣṣ, yaʕni. How are you? So so. šloonak? nuṣṣ w-nuṣṣ.
so that - ẓatta. I'm telling you so that you'll know. ʔaani da-agul-lak ẓatta tuʕruf.
to **soak** - 1. nigaʕ (a nagiʕ) n-. Leave the beans to soak. xalli l-baagilla bil-maay ẓatta tingaʕ. 2. naggaʕ (i tangiiʕ, tniggiʕ) t-. We soaked the laundry overnight. naggaʕna l-ihduum ṭuul il-leel. 3. šarrab (u tšurrub, tašriib) t-. Soak the bread in the gravy. šarrib il-xubuz bil-marga.
to soak up - mtaṣṣ (a mtiṣaaṣ), maṣṣ (u maṣṣ). The sponge will soak the water. l-isfanja timtaṣṣ il-maay.
soaked - mnaggaʕ pl. -iin, mballal pl. -iin. We came home soaked. wuṣalna lil-beet imnaggaʕiin.
to get soaked - tnaggaʕ (a tanaggaʕ), tballal (a taballul). I got soaked because I didn't have an umbrella. tnaggaʕit li-ʔan ma-čaanat ʕindi šamsiyya.
soap - ṣaabuuna pl. -aat coll. ṣaabuun. I want a cake of soap. ʔariid qaalab ṣaabuun.
to soap - ṣooban (i tṣoobin). Dad is soaping his face. ʔabuuya da-yṣoobin wujja.
**Soap your face well before shaving. xalli ṣ-ṣaabuun zeen gabḷ il-ẓilaaqa.
sob - šahgat (pl. -aat) bači. We heard sobs in the next room. smaʕna šahgaat bači bil-ġurfa l-muqaabila.
to sob - šihag (a šahig) mnil-bači. The child sobbed bitterly. ṭ-ṭifil šihag imnil-bači ẓeel.
sober - ṣaaẓi pl. -iin. You never find him real sober. ʔabad ma-tilgii ṣaaẓi tamaaman.
to sober up - ṣiẓa (a ṣaẓi). He sobered up quickly. ṣiẓa bil-ʕajal.
soccer - kurat il-qadam. Soccer is a very popular sport in Iraq. kurat il-qadam fadd liʕba kulliš mazbuuba bil-ʕiraaq.
social - jtimaaʕi*. Social conditions have changed tremendously. l-ʔaẓwaal il-ijtimaaʕiyya tġayyirat kulliš ihwaaya.
socialism - l-ištiraakiyya.
socialist - štiraaki pl. -iyyiin.
socialistic - štiraaki*.
society - 1. mujtamaʕ. He doesn't feel at ease in society. ma-yaaxuð ẓurriita min huwwa b-mujtamaʕ. 2. jamʕiyya pl. -aat. The society was founded ten

years ago. *j-jamɛiyya tʔassisat gabuḷ ɛašr isniin.*
sociological - *jtimaaɛi*.* I subscribed to a sociological journal. *štirakit ib-majalla jtimaaɛiyya.*
sociologist - *ɛaalim jtimaaɛi* pl. *ɛulamaaʔ ijtimaaɛiyyiin.*
sociology - *ɛilm il-ijtimaaɛ.*
sock - **1.** *lakma* pl. *-aat, books* pl. *-aat.* I'd give him a sock on the jaw if I were you. *loo b-makaanak, ʔanṭii lakma ɛala faččа.* **2.** *takk, fardat ijwaariib* pl. *jwaariib.* I want three pairs of socks. *ʔariid itlaθ izwaaj ijwaariib.*
soda - *ṣooda, sooda.* Bring me a bottle of soda water. *jiib-li buṭil ṣooda.*
soft - **1.** *raxu.* The ground's too soft to drive on. *l-gaaɛ raxwa; ma-tigdar itsuuq ɛaleeha.* **2.** *layyin.* The bread is soft. *l-xubuz layyin.* — He's too soft with the prisoners. *huwwa kulliš layyin wiyya l-masaajiin.* **3.** *ðaɛiif.* He's soft from lack of exercise. *huwwa ðaɛiif ib-sabab ɛadam liɛib riyaaða.* **4.** *raqiiq, ɛaðib, naaɛim.* Her voice is soft. *ṣootha raqiiq.* **5.** *xafiif.* A soft light would be better. *tkuun ʔaẓsan loo ð-ðuwa xafiif.* **6.** *sahil.* He's got a soft job. *šagiḷta sahla.*
soft drinks - *muraṭṭabaat.* Only soft drinks are served here. *hnaa ɛidna bass muraṭṭabaat.*
soil - *turba.* The soil here is very fertile. *t-turba hnaa kulliš xaṣba.*
to soil - *waṣṣax (i tawṣiix, twuṣṣux) t-.* You soiled your suit. *ʔinta waṣṣaxit qaaṭak.*
soiled - *mwaṣṣax, waṣix.* Everything is soiled. *kullši mwaṣṣax.*
soldier - *jundi* pl. *jnuud.*
sole - **1.** *čaff rijil* pl. *čfuuf rijleenaat.* I have a cut on my sole. *ɛindi jiriẓ b-čaff rijli.* **2.** *naɛal.* The soles of the brown shoes are worn. *naɛal il-qundara j-joozi gaayim.* **3.** *waẓiid* pl. *-iin.* He was the sole survivor. *huwwa čaan il-waẓiid illi nija.*
to sole - *ẓaṭṭ (u ẓaṭṭ) naɛal.* I have to have my shoes half-soled. *laazim aẓuṭṭ nuṣṣ naɛal il-qundarti.*
solely - *waẓid-.* I'm solely responsible. *ʔaani waẓdi l-masʔuul.*
solid - **1.** *ṣatib, jaamid.* Is the ice solid? *θ-θalij ṣaar ṣalib?* **2.** *kaamil.* We waited a solid hour for him. *ntiðarnaa l-muddat saaɛa kaamla.* **3.** *qawi*, tukma.* This chair doesn't seem very solid to me. *ma-ašuuf hal-iskamli kulliš qawi.* **4.** *xaaḷiṣ.* This ring is made of solid gold. *hal-miẓbas maɛmuul min ðahab xaaḷiṣ.* **5.** *jaamid* pl. *jawaamid.* All liquids turn into solids by cooling. *jamiiɛ is-sawaaʔil titẓawwal ʔila jawaamid bil-buruuda.*
solution - **1.** *maẓluul* pl. *maẓaaliil.* You need a stronger solution. *tiẓtaaj maẓluul ʔaqwa.* **2.** *ẓall* pl. *ẓuluul.* We'll find some solution for it. *raẓ-inšuuf-ilha ẓall.*
to **solve** - *ẓall (i ẓall) n-.* I can't solve the riddle. *ma-ʔaqdar aẓill il-laġiz.*
some - **1.** *šwayya.* He lent me some money. *daayanni šwayya fluus.* **2.** *baɛað.* Some people can't stand noise. *baɛð in-naas ma-ygidruun yitẓammaluun ið-ðajja.* **3.** *qisim.* Some of us are going by train and some by car. *qisim min ɛidna raẓ-yruuẓuun bil-qiṭaar w-qisim bis-sayyaara.* **4.** *ẓawaali.* We stayed some two or three hours. *buqeena ẓawaali saaɛateen ʔaw itlaaθa.* **5.** *fadd.* You'll regret that some day. *fadd yoom raẓ-tindam ɛaleeha.*
somebody - *fadd šaxiṣ, waaẓid.* Somebody asked for you. *fadd šaxiṣ siʔal ɛannak.*
somehow - **1.** *b-šikil imnil-ʔaškaal.* We'll do it somehow. *ɛuud insawwiiha b-šikil imnil-ʔaškaal.* **2.** *b-ṣuura mniṣ-ṣuwar.* The letter got lost somehow. *l-maktuub ðaaɛ ib-ṣuura mniṣ-ṣuwar.*
someone - *fadd ʔaẓẓad, fadd waaẓid.* Is there someone here who can play the lute? *ʔaku fadd ʔaẓẓad ihnaa yuɛruf ydugg ɛuud?*
something - *šii, fadd šii.* Is something the matter? *ʔaku šii?* — That's something to think about. *haaða fadd šii yiswa t-tafkiir.* — Something or other reminded me of home. *fadd šii ðakkarni b-ʔahli.*
sometime - *fadd yoom, fadd wakit.* Why don't you visit us sometime? *leeš ma-tzuurna fadd yoom.*
sometimes - *ʔaẓyaanan, baɛð il-ʔaẓyaan, dooraat, marraat, noobaat.* Sometimes it gets very hot here. *ʔaẓyaanan iṭṣiir kulliš ẓaarra hnaa.*
somewhat - *šwayya, nooɛan-ma.* I feel somewhat tired. *da-ʔašɛur išwayya taɛbaan.*
somewhere - *b-fadd makaan, b-fadd maẓall.* I saw it somewhere, but I don't remember where. *šifitha b-fadd makaan bass ma-atðakkar ween.*
son - *walad* pl. *wulid, ʔibin* pl. *wulid.* Has he any sons? *ʔaku ɛinda wulid?* — Is this your son? *haaða ʔibnak?*
song - *ġunnuwwa* pl. *-aat, ʔuġniya* pl. *ʔaġaani, ġanniyya* pl. *-aat.* Do you know the song? *tuɛruf il-ġunnuwwa?*
**He always gives me the same song and dance. *daaʔiman yɛiid ɛalayya nafs il-fatlaṗiič.*
**We bought the chair for a song. *štireena l-iskamli b-ʔaxu l-balaas.*
son-in-law - *zooj binit* pl. *ʔazwaaj banaat, rajil bint* pl. *rjuula banaat.* My son-in-law is no good. *zooj binti ma-yiswa filis.*
soon - *qariiban, baɛd išwayya.* He's coming back soon. *raẓ-yirjaɛ qariiban.*
**It's too soon to tell what's the matter with him. *baɛad li-hassa ma-nigdar niɛruf šaku bii.*
**I'd just as soon not go. *ʔafaððil ma-aruuẓ.* or *ʔaẓsan-li ma-aruuẓ.*
as soon as - *ʔawwal-ma.* Let me know as soon as you get here. *gul-li ʔawwal-ma tooṣal l-ihnaa.*
sooner - *ʔasraɛ.* The sooner you come, the better. *šgadd-ma tiji ʔasraɛ, baɛad ʔaẓsan.*
**No sooner said than done. *ʔaxalliṣ-lak-iyyaaha b-laẓðatha.*
sooner or later - *ɛaajilan ʔaw ʔaajilan, ʔawwal w-taali.* Sooner or later we'll have to make up our minds. *ɛaajilan ʔaw ʔaajilan laazim inqarrir.*
to **soothe** - *sakkan (i taskiin) t-, hadda? (i tahdiiʔ) t-.* This salve will soothe the pain. *had-dihin raẓ-ysakkin il-wajaɛ.*
sore - **1.** *jariẓ* pl. *jruuẓ.* The sore is pretty well healed up. *j-jariẓ taqriiban liẓam.* **2.** *ẓabb* pl. *ẓabaabi.* His leg was covered with sores. *rijla čaanat imġaṭṭaaya bil-ẓabaabi.* **3.** *ẓassaas.* That's a sore point with him. *haay masʔala ẓassaasa bin-nisba ʔila.* **4.** *zaɛlaan* pl. *-iin.* Are you sore at me? *ʔinta zaɛlaan ɛalayya?*
**I have a sore toe. *ɛindi ʔiṣbiɛ ib-rijli da-yoojaɛni.*
**Where's the sore spot? *ween manṭiqt il-wajaɛ?*
to get sore - *ziɛal (a zaɛal) n-.* You needn't get sore so quickly. *ma-aku ẓaaja tizɛal bil-ɛajal.*
sorrow - *qahar, ẓizin* pl. *ʔaẓzaan.* She can't get over her sorrow. *ma-da-tigdar tinsa qaharha.*
sorry - **1.** *mitʔassif* pl. *-iin, ʔaasif* pl. *-iin.* I'm really sorry. *ʔaani ẓaqiiqatan mitʔassif.* — I'm sorry to say it can't be done. *ʔaasif ʔan ʔaguul ma-mumkin iṭṣiir.* **2.** *l-ɛafu, ʔaasif, mitʔassif.* Sorry! Did I hurt you? *l-ɛafu, ʔaððeetak?*
**I'm sorry for her. *ʔašɛur ib-ʔasif ittijaahha.*
sort - *nooɛ* pl. *ʔanwaaɛ, šikil* pl. *ʔaškaal, ṣinif* pl. *ʔaṣnaaf.* I can't get along with that sort of person. *ma-agdar attifiq wiyya šaxiṣ min han-nooɛ.*
**What sort of person is he? *huwwa šinu min šii?*
sort of - **1.** *nooɛan-ma, fadd nooɛ.* She's sort of nice. *hiyya laṭiifa nooɛan-ma.* **2.** *taqriiban.* I sort of knew it was going to happen. *taqriiban ɛirafit haaða čaan raẓ-yṣiir.*
to sort - *ṣannaf (i taṣniif) t-, ɛizal (i ɛazil) n-.* Have the stockings been sorted? *j-jwaariib iṭṣannifat?*
soul - **1.** *ruuẓ* pl. *rwaaẓ.* If someone dies, his soul will go to heaven. *ʔiða l-waaẓid ymuut, truuẓ ruuẓa lis-sima.* **2.** *ʔaẓẓad, ʔinsaan, nafis.* There wasn't a soul to be seen. *ma-čaan ʔaẓẓad mawjuud.*
**He's with us heart and soul. *huwwa wiyyaana tamaaman.*
sound - **1.** *ṣawṭ* pl. *ʔaṣwaaṭ.* Light travels faster than sound. *ð-ðuwa yintiqil ʔasraɛ imniṣ-ṣooṭ.* **2.** *ẓiss* pl. *ẓsuus, ṣooṭ* pl. *ʔaṣwaaṭ.* What was that sound? *š-čaan ðaak il-ẓiss?* **3.** *naġma, ranna.* I recognized her by the sound of her voice. *ɛirafitha min naġmat ẓissha.* **4.** *saliim, matiin, qawi*.* He has a sound constitution. *ɛinda bunya saliima.*
**That's a sound bit of advice. *haay xooš naṣiiẓa.*
**He's sound asleep. *huwwa ġaat bin-noom.*
safe and sound - *ṣaaġ saliim.* He's back, safe and sound. *rijaɛ ṣaaġ saliim.*
to sound - *bayyan (i tabyiin) t-.* The report sounds good. *t-taqriir ybayyin zeen.*
to sound out - *jass (i jass) nabað-.* I'll have to sound him out first. *laazim ʔawwal ajiss nabða.*
soup - *šoorba* pl. *-aat.* Bring us the soup. *jiib-ilna š-šoorba.*
sour - *ẓaamuð, mẓammuð.* The milk has turned sour. *l-ẓaliib ṣaar ẓaamuð.*
**Don't make such a sour face. *la-tṣiir hiiči*

mEabbis.
source - **1.** *maṣdar* pl. *maṣaadir.* I have it from a reliable source. *ʒaṣṣalit Ealeeha min fadd maṣdar mawθuuq bii.* **2.** *ʔasaas* pl. *-aat, ʔusus.* Have you found the source of the trouble? *Eirafit ʔasaas il-muškila?* **3.** *manbaE* pl. *manaabiE.* The source of the river is north of here. *manbaE in-nahar imniš-šimaal.*
south - *jinuub.* The wind is coming from the south. *r-riyaaʒ jaaya mnij-jinuub.* — The arrow points south. *s-sahim yʔaššir Eaj-jinuub.*
southern - *jinuubi*.* This plant is found only in southern regions. *han-nabaat yinligi bil-manaaṭiq ij-jinuubiyya bass.*
souvenir - *tiδkaar* pl. *-aat.* I want to buy some souvenirs here. *ʔard aštirii-li čam tiδkaar minnaa.*
sovereign - *δaat siyaada.* Iraq is a soverign state. *l-Eiraaq dawla δaat siyaada.*
Soviet - *soofyaati*.* They're in the Soviet sphere of influence. *humma b-manṭiqat in-nufuuδ is-soofyaati.*
Soviet Russia - *ruusya s-soofyaatiyya.*
sow - *xanziira* pl. *-aat.*
to **sow** - *biδar (i baδir) n-.* He's sowing the field with wheat. *da-yibδir ʒunṭa bil-ʒaqil.*
space - **1.** *faḍaaʔ.* They've just fired another rocket into space. *hassa ʔaṭliqaw ṣaaruux laax lil-faḍaaʔ.* **2.** *makaan.* The desk takes up too much space. *l-meez yaaxuδ makaan kulliš ičbiir.* **3.** *majaal* pl. *-aat.* There's a large space between the houses. *ʔaku majaal waasiE been il-beeteen.* **4.** *faḍwa* pl. *-aat, saaʒa* pl. *-aat.* There's an open space behind the house. *ʔaku faḍwa wara l-beet.* **5.** *xilaal, mudda, fatra.* He did the work in the space of two weeks. *sawwa š-šuğuḷ ib-xilaal ʔusbuuEeen.*
**He was staring out into space. *čaan ṣaafun.* or *čaan ḍaarub daalğa.*
to space - *baaEad (i mubaaEada) t-.* The posts are spaced a foot apart. *l-Eawaamiid mitbaaEida Ean-baEaḍha masaafa qadam.*
spade - *misʒaa* pl. *masaaʒi.* Grab a spade and dig. *ʔuxuδ-lak misʒaa w-ʔuʒfur.*
**Why don't you call a spade a spade? *leeš ma-tiʒči l-ʒaqiiqa?*
spare - **1.** *faraağ.* What do you do in your spare time? *š-itsawwi b-wakit faraağak?* **2.** *ʒtiyaaṭi*.* Can you find spare parts for your radio? *tigdar itʒaṣṣil Eala ʔadawaat iʒtiyaaṭiyya r-raadyuwwak?* **3.** *zaayid.* Is there any spare room in that car? *ʔaku makaan zaayid b-has-sayyaara?* **4.** *ʔiḍaafi*, yadag, speer.* We never travel without a spare tire. *ʔabadan ma-nsaafir bila taayir speer.*
to spare - **1.** *waffar (u tawfiir) t- Ean.* You can spare yourself the trouble. *tigdar itwaffur Ean nafsak il-ʔizEaaj.* **2.** *xalla (i) min.* Spare me the details. *xalliini mnit-tafaaṣiil.* **3.** *staǧna (i stignaaʔ) Ean.* Can you spare the pencil? *tigdar tistağni Ean il-qalam?* **4.** *simaʒ (a samiʒ) b-.* Can you spare me a minute of your time? *tismaʒ-li b-daqiiqa min waqtak?* **5.** *ʔabqa (i ibqaaʔ) Eala.* The commander spared the captives' lives by putting them in a prison outside the city. *l-qaaʔid ʔabqa Eala ʒayaat il-ʔasraaʔ ib-waḍiEhum ib-sijin xaarij il-madiina.*
**He spared no expense. *ma-buxal ib-šii.*
sparingly - *b-iqtiṣaad, b-tadbiir.* Use it sparingly. *staEmilha b-iqtiṣaad.*
spark - *šaraara* pl. *-aat.* The fire was started by a spark. *l-ʒariiq bidat ib-fadd šaraara.*
to **sparkle** - *tlaʔlaʔ (a tliʔliʔ).* The moonlight is sparkling on the water. *ḍuwa il-gumar gaaEid yitlaʔliʔ Eal-maay.*
spark plug - *plakk* pl. *-aat.* I need new spark plugs for my car. *ʔaʒtaaj plakkaat jidiida l-sayyaarti.*
sparrow - *Eaṣfuur* pl. *Eaṣaafiir.*
to **speak** - *ʒiča (i ʒači) n-, tkallam, (a takallum).* Am I speaking clearly enough? *da-ʔaʒči b-wuḍuuʒ?* — May I speak to you? *ʔagdar aʒči wiyyaak?*
**It's nothing to speak of. *muu fadd šii yiswa δikir.* or *ma-biiha šii muhimm.*
to speak to - *kallam (i tkillim).* He spoke to me for half an hour. *kallamni l-muddat nuṣṣ saaEa.*
to speak up for - *daafaE (a difaaE) Ean.* Nobody spoke up for him. *maʒʒad daafaE Eanna.*
speaker - *muʒaddiθ* pl. *-iin, mutkallim* pl. *-iin.* He's an excellent speaker. *huwwa muʒaddiθ mumtaaz.*
speaking - *kalaam, ʒači.* I prefer speaking to writing. *ʔafaḍḍil il-kalaam Eal-kitaaba.*
**We're not on speaking terms. *ʔiʒna ma-nitʒaača.*
spear - *rumuʒ* pl. *rimaaʒ.*
special - *xaaṣṣ, xuṣuuṣi*.* I'm saving it for a special occasion. *ʔaani ḍaamunha l-munaasaba xaaṣṣa.*
specialty - *xtiṣaaṣ* pl. *-aat.* Children's diseases are his specialty. *ʔamraaḍ il-ʔaṭfaal ixtiṣaaṣa.*
specific - *muEayyan.* He proposed specific means to remedy the situation. *qaddam iqtiraaʒaat muEayyana l-muEaalajat il-waḍiE.*
specifications - *muwaaṣafaat.* We can build it to your specifications. *nigdar nibniiha ʒasab muwaaṣafaatkum.*
spectator - *mitfarrij* pl. *-iin.*
speech - **1.** *nuṭaq.* He lost his speech after the accident. *fuqad nuṭqa baEd il-ʒaadiθ.* **2.** *xuṭba* pl. *xuṭab.* That was a very good speech. *haay čaanat kulliš xooš xuṭba.*
speed - *surEa.* Let's put on a little speed. *xalli nʔayyid is-surEa šwayya.*
to speed - *Eadda (i taEdiya) t- s-surEa, faat (u foota) n- s-surEa, ʔasraE (i ʔisraaE).* You're speeding now. *ʔinta mitEaddi s-surEa hassa.*
to speed up - *Eajjal (i taEjiil) t-, staEjal (i stiEjaal).* Can you speed things up a little? *tigdar itEajjil išwayya?*
speed limit - *surEa maʒduuda.* The speed limit is thirty-five miles an hour. *s-surEa l-maʒduuda xamsa w-itlaaθiin miil bis-saaEa.*
spell - **1.** *siʒir.* She's completely under his spell. *maʔxuuδa b-siʒra tamaaman.* or ***hiyya masʒuura bii.* **2.** *nooba* pl. *-aat.* Does she often get spells like that? *hiyya daaʔiman tijiiha hiiči n-noobaat?*
to spell - **1.** *thajja (a thijji).* Please spell your name. *ʔarjuuk ithajja ʔismak.* **2.** *naab (u niyaaba) n- Ean.* Let me spell you awhile. *xalliini anuub Eannak išwayya.*
to **spend** - **1.** *ṣiraf (u ṣaruf) n-.* We spent a lot of money. *ṣrafna hwaaya fluus.* **2.** *giḍa (i gaḍi) n-.* I'd like to spend my vacation here. *yiEjibni ʔagḍi ʔijaazti hnaa.*
sperm - *mani.*
sphere - **1.** *kura* pl. *-aat.* How do you find the capacity of a sphere? *šloon itʒaṣṣil Eala siEat il-kura?* **2.** *manṭiqa* pl. *manaaṭiq.* They're in the Russian sphere of influence. *humma b-manṭiqt in-nufuuδ ir-ruusiyya.*
spice - *bhaar* pl. *-aat.* Do you use spices much in your cooking? *tistaEmiliin ihwaaya bhaaraat bit-ṭabux?*
to spice - *xalla (i) bhaaraat.* She spiced the food too much. *xallat ihwaaya bhaaraat bil-ʔakil.*
**The meat is highly spiced. *l-laʒam bii hwaaya bhaaraat.*
spider - *Eankabuut* pl. *-aat, Eanaakib.*
to **spill** - *čabb (i čabb) n-.* Who spilled the milk? *minu čabb il-ʒaliib?*
spin - *farra* pl. *-aat.* We took a spin in his car. *ʔaxaḍna farra b-sayyaarta.*
to spin - **1.** *farr (u farr) n-.* He spun the top. *farr il-muṣraE.* **2.** *ftarr (a farr).* My head is spinning. *raasi da-yiftarr.* or ***raasi daayix.* **3.** *ğizal (i ğazil) n-, fital (i fatil) n-.* The thread isn't spun evenly. *l-xeeṭ ma-mağzuul bit-tasaawi.*
to spin around - *ltaaf (a ltifaaf), ndaar (a).* He spun around and fired. *ltaaf w-ʔaṭlaq riṣaaṣa.*
spinach - *sbeenaağ.*
spine - **1.** *šawka* pl. *-aat.* I've got a spine from the cactus in my hand. *ʔaku šawkat ṣubbeer b-iidi.* **2.** *Eamuud faqari, Eawaamiid faqariyya.* He broke his spine in the accident. *kisar il-Eamuud il-faqari maala bil-ʒaadiθ.*
spiral - *malwi*, lawlabi* ʒalazuuni*.* The minaret has a spiral staircase. *l-manaara biiha daraj malwiyya.*
spirit - **1.** *ruuʒ* pl. *ʔarwaaʒ, jinni* pl. *jinn.* The natives believe in evil spirits. *s-sukkaan yiEtiqduun bil-ʔarwaaʒ iš-širriira.* **2.** *rooʒ* pl. *ʔarwaaʒ.* I assume his spirit went to heaven when he died. *ʔaftiriḍ rooʒa raaʒat lij-janna min maat.* **3.** *himma.* That's the proper spirit! *haay il-himma ṣ-ṣaʒiiʒa!*
in good spirits - *mirtaaʒ.* I hope you're in good spirits. *ʔinšaaḷḷa tkuun mirtaaʒ.*
in low spirits - *mahmuum.* He seemed to be in low spirits. *ybayyin Ealee mahmuum.*
spiritual - *ruuʒi*.* There's a spiritual bond between them. *ʔaku fadd raabiṭa ruuʒiyya beenaathum.*
spit - **1.** *ṣiix* pl. *ṣiyaax, šiiš* pl. *šiyaaš.* They're roasting a sheep on a spit. *gaaEid yʒammiṣuun il-xaruuf ib-ṣiix.* **2.** *tafla* pl. *-aat, tfaal.* His spit is yellow because he uses snuff. *t-tafla maalta ṣafra li-ʔan yistaEmil barnuuṭi.*
to spit - *tifal (i tfaal), biṣaq (u biṣaaq).* He spat on the ground. *tifal Eal-gaaE.*

spite - *nikaaya.* He did it just for spite. *sawwaaha bass lin-nikaaya.*
in spite of - *b-rağum min, b-rağum εan.* I went in spite of the rain. *riζit ib-rağum min il-muṭar.*
to spite - *ğaaḍ (i ʔigaaḍa) n-.* Are you doing that just to spite me? *ʔinta da-tsawwiha ζatta tğiiḍni bass?*
to **splash** - **1.** *ṭaffar (i taṭfiir) t-.* The car splashed water on me. *s-sayyaara ṭaffirat εalayya ṃaay.* **2.** *ṭṭaffar (a taṭaffur).* The water splashes in all directions. *l-ṃaay da-yiṭṭaffar il-kull jiha.* **3.** *ṭabbaš (u taṭbiiš, ṭṭubbuš) t-.* The boy splashed through the shallow water. *l-walad ṭabbaš bil-geeš.*
splendid - *raaʔiε, faaxir, mumtaaz.* That was a splendid idea! *δiič čaanat fadd fikra raaʔiεa.*
splint - *jabiira* pl. *jabaayir.* His arm has to be put in splints. *ʔiida laazim tinζaṭṭ bij-jabaayir.*
splinter - *sillaaya* pl. *-aat, liiṭa* pl. *-aat.* I've got a splinter under my nail. *ʔaku sillaaya jawwa ʔiḍifri.*
split - **1.** *nšiqaaq* pl. *-aat, xilaaf* pl. *-aat.* There was a split in the party. *čaan ʔaku nšiqaaq bil-ζizib.* **2.** *faṭir* pl. *fṭuur, šagg* pl. *šguug.* There's a split in that board. *ʔaku faṭir ib-hal-looζa.*
to split - **1.** *filaq (u faliq) n-, šagg (u šagg) n-, filaε (a faliε) n-.* The lightning split the tree from top to bottom. *ṣ-ṣaaεiqa filqat iš-šajara min foog li-jawwa.* **2.** *nšaqq (i nšiqaaq).* The party has split into three groups. *l-ζizib inšaqq ʔila tlaθ ʔaqsaam.* **3.** *tgaasam (a tagaasum).* They split the profits with the workers. *tgaasmaw il-ʔarbaaζ wiyya l-εummaal.* **4.** *qassam (i taqsiim) t-.* The directors split the profits between the workers and investors. *l-mudaraaʔ qassmaw il-ʔarbaaζ been il-εummaal wil-mustaθmiriin.* **5.** *fitag (u fatig) n-.* Your pants have split in the seat. *panṭaroonak infitag bil-maqεad.*
**I nearly split my sides laughing. *ridt amuut imniḍ-ḍiζik.* or *ṭaggat baṭni mniḍ-ḍiζik.*
to split hairs - *daqdaq (i tdiqdiq).* Don't split hairs, please. *baḷḷa la-tdaqdiq.*
to **spoil** - **1.** *xaas (i xees), jaaf (i jeef).* The apples are beginning to spoil. *t-tiffaaζ da-yibdi yxiis.* **2.** *jaaf (i jeef).* The meat will spoil in this heat. *l-laζam raζ-yjiif ib-hal-ζaraara.* **3.** *fisad (i fasid), xirab (a xarbaan).* The eggs have spoiled. *l-beeḍ fisad.* **4.** *dallal (i tadliil) t-.* You're spoiling him. *ʔinti da-tdallilii.*
spoke - *siim* pl. *siyaama.* I broke two spokes in the front wheel. *ksarit siimeen bič-čarx il-giddaami.*
sponge - **1.** *sfanja* pl. *-aat* coll. *sfanj.* Where'd you buy that sponge? *mneen ištireet haay il-isfanja?* **2.** *ṭufeeli* pl. *-iyya, -iyyiin.* He's an awful sponge. *huwwa ṭufeeli.*
to sponge off - **1.** *misaζ (a masiζ) bil-isfanja.* She sponged off the water. *misζat il-ṃaay bil-isfanja.* **2.** *ṭṭaffal (a taṭafful) εala.* He's always sponging off his friends. *daaʔiman yiṭṭaffal εala ʔaṣdiqaaʔ.*
spoon - *xaašuuga* pl. *xwaašiig.* A spoon fell off the table. *fadd xaašuuga wugεat imnil-meez.*
sport - *liεba* (pl. *-aat*) *riyaaḍiyya.* Soccer is a good sport. *kurat il-qadam xooš liεba riyaaḍiyya.*
sports - *riyaaḍa.* Do you go in for sports? *tζibb ir-riyaaḍa?*
spot - **1.** *buqεa* pl. *buqaε, latxa* pl. *-aat, lakka* pl. *-aat.* You have a spot on your tie. *ʔaku buqεa εala ribaaṭak.* **2.** *mukaan* pl. *-aat, ʔamaakin.* I stood in the same spot for a whole hour. *buqeet ib-nafs il-mukaan il-muddat saaεa kaamila.* -- A cup of coffee would just hit the spot. *fadd finjaan gahwa hassa ykuun ib-mukaana tamaam.* **3.** *nuqṭa* pl. *nuqaaṭ.* You've touched a sore spot. *ʔinta ṭarraqit ʔila nuqṭa ζassaasa.* **4.** *manṭiqa* pl. *manaaṭiq, mukaan* pl. *-aat, nuqṭa* pl. *nuqaaṭ.* Where is the sore spot? *ween manṭiqat il-ʔalam?*
on the spot - **1.** *b-laζḍatha.* They fired him on the spot. *ṭirdoo b-laζḍatha.* **2.** *b-nafs il-makaan.* I was right on the spot when the accident happened. *min ṣaar il-ζaadiθ, činit ib-nafs il-makaan.* **3.** *b-waḍiε ζarij.* You put me on the spot. *ʔinta xalleetni b-waḍiε ζarij.* or ***ζrajit mawqifi.*
to spot - **1.** *limaζ (a lamiζ) n-.* I spotted him in the crowd. *limaζta bil-xabṣa.* **2.** *mayyaz (i tamyiiz) t-.* I could spot him anywhere. *ʔagdar ʔamayyza ween-ma čaan.*
sprain - *faṣix* pl. *fṣuux.* You've got a bad sprain there. *εindak faṣix qawi.*
to sprain - *fuṣax (u faṣix) n-.* She sprained her ankle. *fuṣxat marfaq rijilha.*
to **spray** - *rašš (i rašš) n-.* We have to spray the peach trees. *laazim inrišš ʔašjaar il-xoox.*
spread - **1.** *ntišaar, tawassuε.* They tried to check the spread of the disease. *ζaawlaw ywaggfuun intišaar il-maraḍ.* **2.** *čarčaf* pl. *čaraačif.* They put new spreads on the beds. *ζaṭṭaw čaraačif ijdiida εač-čarpaayaat.*
to spread - **1.** *nišar (u našir) n-.* The gardener is spreading manure on the lawn. *l-bustanči da-yinšur l-ismaad εaθ-θayyal.* **2.** *mtadd (a mtidaad), ntišar (a ntišaar).* The fire's spreading rapidly. *n-naar da-timtadd ib-surεa.* -- The news spread quickly. *l-ʔaxbaar intišrat bil-εajal.* **3.** *wazzaε (i tawziiε) t-.* The payments were spread over several years. *d-dafεaat itwazzεat εala εiddat isniin.*
to spread out - **1.** *furaš (u fariš) n-, madd (i madd) n-.* Spread the map out. *ʔufruš il-xariiṭa.* **2.** *mtadd (a mtidaad).* We saw the whole valley spread out below us. *šifna l-waadi kulla mimtadd jawwaana.*
spring - **1.** *rabiiε.* We arrived in spring. *wuṣalna bir-rabiiε.* **2.** *εeen* pl. *εyuun; nabiε, yambuuε* pl. *yanaabiiε.* There's a spring behind our house. *ʔaku εeen wara beetna.* **3.** *zumbalag* pl. *-aat.* The spring in my watch is broken. *z-zumbalag maal saaεti maksuur.* **4.** *sipring* pl. *-aat.* We broke a spring on the car on our trip. *ksarna sipring is-sayyaara b-safratna.*
to spring - **1.** *gumaz (u gamuz) n-.* He sprang from his seat. *gumaz min kursiyya.* **2.** *ṭilaε (a ṭuluuε).* All the rumors spring from the same source. *kull il-ʔišaaεaat tiṭlaε min nafs il-maṣdar.* **3.** *nibaε (a nabiε).* The plant sprang up overnight. *z-zariε nibaε εala ğafla.*
to **sprinkle** - *rašš (i rašš) n-, ṭašš (a ṭašš) n-.* Have the streets been sprinkled yet? *š-šawaariε inraššat loo baεad?*
spy - *jaasuus* pl. *jawaasiis.* We're going to send a team of spies to Saudi Arabia. *raζ-indizz jamaaεat jawaasiis lil-mamlaka l-εarabiyya s-saεuudiyya.*
to spy - *tjassas (a tajassus).* They caught him spying on a military installation. *lizmoo da-yitjassas ib-muʔassasa εaskariyya.*
squad - *ζaḍiira* pl. *ζaḍaayir.* An eight man squad was guarding the intersection. *ζaḍiira min iθman irjaal čaanaw yζirsuun it-taqaaṭuε.*
square - **1.** *saaζa* pl. *-aat.* Our windows look out on a large square. *sbaabiična tišrif εala saaζa čbiira.* **2.** *murabbaε* pl. *-aat.* That's not a square, that's a rectangle. *haaδa muu murabbaε, haaδa mustaṭiil.* **3.** *εadil.* He's a pretty square fellow. *huwwa fadd waaζid εadil.*
**I haven't eaten a square meal in days. *ṣaar ihwaaya ma-maakil ʔakla dasma.*
**Our back yard is twenty feet square. *s-saaζa l-warraaniyya maalatna εala šikil murabbaε ṭuula w-ḍilεa εišriin qadam.*
**This squares our account. *haaδa ysaddid iζsaabna.*
squash - *šijra* pl. *-aat* coll. *šijar.* Buy some squash while you're at the market. *štiri šwayya šijar min itkuun bis-suug.*
to squash - **1.** *jiεaṣ (i jaεiṣ) n-, εiqač (i εaqič) n-.* I squashed my hat when I sat down. *jiεaṣit šafuqti min giεadit.* **2.** *ζiṣar (i ζaṣir) n-.* I squashed my finger in the door. *ζṣarit ʔiṣibεi bil-baab.*
to **squeal** - **1.** *ṣirax (u sraax), εaaṭ (i εyaaṭ).* The child squealed with joy. *j-jaahil ṣirax imnil-faraζ.* **2.** *wiša (i wišaaya) n-.* Somebody must have squealed on us to the police. *waaζid laazim ykuun wiša biina liš-šurṭa.*
to **squeeze** - **1.** *εiṣar (i εaṣir) n-.* Don't squeeze my hand so hard. *la-tiεṣir ʔiidi hal-gadd ζeel.* -- I'll squeeze the oranges. *raζ-aεṣir il-purtaqaal.* **2.** *diζas (a daζis) n-.* I can't squeeze another thing into my suitcase. *ma-ʔagdar adζas ʔay šii laax ib-jinuṭṭi.*
squirrel - *sinjaab* pl. *sanaajiib.*
to **squirt** - *rašš (i rašš) n-.* The elephant squirted water on the spectators. *l-fiil rašš il-ṃaay εal-mutafarrijiin.*
to **stab** - *ṭiεan (a ṭaεin) n-.* He was stabbed in the brawl. *nṭiεan bil-εarka.* -- He's just waiting for a chance to stab me in the back. *da-yintihiz furṣa ζatta yiṭεanni mnil-xalf.*
stable - **1.** *ṣṭabil* pl. *-aat.* Where are the stables?

ween l-iṣṭablaat? 2. *mustaqirr.* They haven't had a stable government for years. *ma-ṣaar* *Eidhum ẓukuuma mustaqirra min mudda ṭwiila.* 3. *θaabit.* A stable currency is absolutely necessary. *wujuud Eumla θaabita ṣaruuri jiddan.*

stack - *kudis* pl. *ʔakdaas, koom* pl. *ʔakwaam.* I had to go thru a whole stack of newspapers to find it. *čaan laazim adawwur akdaas imnij-jaraayid ẓatta algaaha.*

to stack - *kaddas (i takdiis) t-, kawwam (u takwiim) t-.* Stack the books in the corner. *kaddis il-kutub biz-zuwiyya.*

staff - *muwaδδafiin.* He dismissed part of his staff. *ṭirad qisim min muwaδδafii.*

general staff - *qiyaadat il-ʔarkaan.* That officer has been attached to the general staff. *haaδa δ-δaabuṭ iltazaq ib-qiyaadat il-ʔarkaan.*

stage - 1. *masraẓ* pl. *masaariẓ.* That hall has a nice stage. *haay il-qaaEa biiha masraẓ ẓilu.* 2. *marẓala* pl. *maraaẓil.* It depends on what stage it's in. *tiEtimid Eala l-marẓala lli hiyya biiha.*

to stage - *qaam (u qiyaam) n- b-.* They staged the robbery in broad daylight. *qaamaw bis-sariqa b-waδaẓ in-nahaar.*

to **stagger** - *ṭṭootaẓ (a taṭooṭuẓ), trannaẓ (a tarannuẓ).* I saw him stagger out of a bar. *šifta ṭaaliE imnil-baar yiṭṭootaẓ.* -- The blow staggered him. *δ-δarba xallata yiṭṭootaẓ.*

staggering - *muδhil, xayaali*, faδiiE.* The prices are staggering. *l-ʔasEaar ṣaayra muδhila.* -- Expenditures have reached staggering proportions. *l-maṣruufaat wuslat ʔila ẓadd faδiiE.* or ***l-maṣruufaat itjaawzat il-maEquul.*

stagnant - *xaayis, jaayif.* The water is stagnant. *l-maay xaayis.*

stain - *buqEa* pl. *buqaE, laṭxa* pl. *-aat.* I can't get the stains out of my shirt. *ma-agdar ašiil il-buqaE min θoobi.*

to stain - *lawwax (w talwiix) t-.* You've stained your shirt. *lawwaxit θoobak.*

stairs - *daraj* pl. *-aat.* Take the stairs to your right. *ʔuxuδ id-daraj illi Eala yamiinak.*

stake - 1. *Eamuud* pl. *ʔaEmida.* You get the stakes for the fence. *ʔinta jiib il-ʔaEmida maal is-siyaaj.* 2. *θbaat* pl. *-aat, watad* pl. *ʔawtaad.* He drove in a stake to tie up the cow to. *dagg iθbaat ẓatta yšidd il-haayša bii.*

**There's too much at stake. *biiha hwaaya muxaaṭara.*

**His life is at stake. *ẓayaata muhaddada bil-xaṭar.* or *da-yraahin Eala ẓayaata.*

**My money's at stake. *jaazafit ib-ʔamwaali.*

stakes - *rihaan, rahin.* They doubled the stakes. *δaaEfaw ir-rihaan.*

to **stall** - 1. *ṭufa (i ṭafi) n-.* The motor's stalled again. *l-muẓarrik inṭufa marra lux.* 2. *maaṭal (i mumaaṭala).* Quit stalling! *la-tmaaṭil, Eaad!* or *yeezi mumaaṭala.*

to **stammer** - *tlaEθam (a tliEθim), watwat (i twitwit).* He stammers when he talks. *huwwa yitlaEθam ib-kalaama.*

stamp - 1. *ṭaabiE* pl. *ṭawaabiE.* Give me five ten-fils stamps, please. *nṭiini xamis ṭawaabiE ʔumm Eašr ifluus rajaaʔan.* 2. *ṭamġa* pl. *-aat, xatim* pl. *ʔaxtaam.* Where's the ''Air Mail'' stamp? *ween ṭamġat il-bariid ij-jawwi?*

to stamp - 1. *ṭumaġ (u ṭamuġ) n-.* I stamped all the papers. *ṭumaġit kull il-ʔawraaq.* 2. *dagg (u dagg).* She stamped her foot. *daggat rijilha.*

to stamp out - 1. *ʔaxmad (i xamid, xumuud) n- b-rijil-.* He stamped out the fire. *ʔaxmad in-naar ib-rijla.* 2. *qiδa (i qaδi) n- Eala.* All opposition was ruthlessly stamped out. *kull il-muEaaraδa nqiδat Ealeeha.*

stand - *mawqif* pl. *mawaaqif.* He's changed his stand on this matter several times. *ġayyar mawqifa bin-nisba l-mawδuuE Eiddat marraat.*

**The witness will take the stand! *š-šaahid yaaxuδ makaana.*

to stand - 1. *wugaf (a wuguuf).* He's standing in the rain. *huwwa waaguf bil-muṭar.* 2. *ṣimad (i ṣumuud), θibat (i θubuut, θabaat).* The soldiers stood their ground. *j-jinuud ṣimdaw ib-maraakizhum.* 3. *buqa (a baqaaʔ) θaabit.* He stood his ground. *buqa θaabit Eala mawqifa.* 4. *qaawam (u muqaawama).* The city's defenders stood for three days. *l-mudaafiEiin Ean il-madiina qaawumaw itlaθt iyyaam.* 5. *waggaf (u tawgiif) t-.* Stand the ladder in the corner. *wagguf id-daraj biz-zuwiyya.* 6. *tẓammal (a taẓammul).* I can't stand it any longer there. *ma-agdar atẓammal ʔakθar ihnaak.* 7. *waajah (i muwaajaha), jaabah (i mujaabaha).* You'll have to stand trial if they catch you. *laazim itwaajih muẓaakama ʔiδa lizmook.*

**You don't stand a chance of getting accepted. *ma-aku ʔamal tinqibil.*

**What I said the other day still stands. *ʔilli gilta l-baarẓa baEda maaδi.* or *ʔilli gilta l-baarẓa baEda ma-tġayyar.*

**You can have it as it stands for 50 dinars. *tigdar taaxuδha miθil-ma hiyya b-xamsiin diinaar.*

to stand by - 1. *ṭubag (u ṭabug).* He always stands by his friends. *daaʔiman yiṭbug wiyya ʔaṣẓaaba.* 2. *biqa (a biqaaʔ) Eala.* I'm standing by my decision. *ʔaani baaqi Eala qaraari.*

**Stand by, I may need you later. *kuun ẓaaδir, yimkin ʔaẓtaajak baEdeen.*

**He stood by, doing nothing. *wugaf miθl il-looẓ.*

to stand for - 1. *ʔayyad (i taʔyiid) t-.* He stands for greater cooperation with neighboring states. *yʔayyid ziyaadat it-taEaawun maEa l-ʔaqṭaar il-mujaawira.* 2. *maθθal (i tamθiil).* The olive branch stands for peace. *ġuṣn iz-zaytuun ymaθθil is-salaam.* 3. *qibal (a qubuul) n-.* I won't stand for that sort of treatment. *ma-ʔaqbal hiiči muEaamala.*

**He stands for equality. *huwwa min duEaat il-musaawaat.*

to stand on - *Etimad (i) Eala.* I'll stand on my record. *ʔaEtimid Eala l-maaδi maali.*

to stand out - *biraz (i buruuz), δihar (u δuhuur).* She stands out in a crowd. *hiyya δaahra been il-majmuuEa.* -- He stands out in physics. *huwwa kulliš baariz bil-fiizya.*

to stand up - 1. *wugaf (a wuguuf).* Don't bother standing up. *la-tzaẓẓim nafsak w-toogaf.* 2. *qaawam (u muqaawama), ṣumax (u ṣamux), kadd (u kadd).* The car has stood up well. *s-sayyaara ṣumxat zeen.*

**She stood me up at the last minute. *Etidrat ib-ʔaaxir laẓδa.*

to stand up for - *saaEad (i musaaEada) daafaE (i difaaE).* If we don't stand up for him, no one else will. *ʔiδa ma-saaEadnaa, maẓẓad raẓ-ysaaEda.*

standard - 1. *miqyaas* pl. *maqaayiis.* You can't judge him by ordinary standards. *ma-tigdar tuẓkum Ealee bil-maqaayiis il-Eaadiyya.* 2. *miEyaar* pl. *maEaayiir, miqyaas* pl. *maqaayiis.* Their standards are high. *maEaayiirhum Eaalya.* 3. *mustawa* pl. *-ayaat.* Their standard of living is lower than ours. *mustawa maEiišathum aqall min Eidna.* 4. *Etiyaadi*.* We carry all the standard sizes. *Eidna kull il-ʔaẓjaam il-iEtiyaadiyya.*

stand-by - *ẓaalat inδaar.* I'm on stand-by this week. *ʔaani b-ẓaalat inδaar hal-isbuuE.*

standing - 1. *maqaam, markaz.* He has a high standing in the community. *maqaama Eaali bil-mujtamaE.* 2. *saakin, raakid.* It's standing water. *haaδa l-maay saakin.* 3. *wuguuf.* There's standing room only. *ʔaku maẓall lil-wuquuf bass.*

**They're friends of long-standing. *humma ʔaṣdiqaaʔ ṣaar-ilhum zamaan.*

star - 1. *najma* pl. *-aat, njuum.* The sky's full of stars. *s-simaaʔ malyaana njuum.* 2. *baṭal* pl. *ʔabṭaal.* Who was the star in that picture? *minu čaanat il-baṭala b-δaak il-filim?*

**He's my star pupil. *haaδa ʔaẓsan ṭaalib Eindi.*

starch - *niša.* Put some starch in the shirts. *xalli šwayya niša liθ-θiyaab.*

to starch - *našša (i tanšiya).* Did you starch the shirts? *naššeet iθ-θiyaab?*

to **stare** - *baẓlaq (i baẓlaqa).* He just stared into space. *baẓlaq bis-sima.*

start - *bidaaya.* It was all wrong from the start. *čaan muxṭiʔ imnil-bidaaya.*

**You gave me quite a start. *fazzazitni.* or *jaffalitni.*

to start - 1. *bida (i bidaaya) n-.* The movie has just started. *l-filim hassa bida.* -- How did the fire start? *šloon bida l-ẓariiq?* 2. *bida (i bidaaya) n- b-.* Who started this rumor? *minu bida b-hal-ʔišaaEa?* 3. *šaġġal (i tašġiil) t-, ẓarrak (i taẓriik).* Start the motor. *šaġġil il-muẓarrik.* 4. *šiEal (i šaEil) n-.* Let's start a fire and get warm. *xalli nišEil naar w-nitdaffa.* 5. *tẓarrak (i taẓarruk).* The train started slowly. *l-qiṭaar itẓarrak ib-buṭuʔ.*

starting - *btidaaʔan.* Starting today the bus will stop here. *btidaaʔan imnil-yoom il-baaṣ raẓ-yoogaf ihnaa.*

to **startle** - *jaffal (i tajfiil) t-, fazzaz (i tafziiz) t-.* The noise startled me. *ṣ-ṣawt jaffalni.*
to be startled - **1.** *jifal (i jafil).* I was startled by the shot. *jifalit imniṭ-ṭalqa.*
to **starve** - **1.** *jaaε (u juuε).* Thousands of people starved. *ʔaalaaf imnin-naas jaaεaw.* **2.** *jawwaε (i tajwiiε) t-.* We can't attack them, we'll have to starve them out first. *ma-nigdar inhaajimhum hassa, xalli njawwiεhum ʔawwal.*
**They almost starved to death. *taqriiban maataw imnij-juuε.*
state - **1.** *wilaaya* pl. *-aat.* What's the largest state in the U.S.? *šinu hiyya ʔakbar wilaaya bil-wilaayaat il-muttaḥida.* **2.** *dawla* pl. *-aat, duwal, ḥukuuma* pl. *-aat.* The railroads are owned by the state. *s-sikak il-ḥadiidiyya timlikha d-dawla.* **3.** *ḥaala* pl. *-aat, waḍεiyya* pl. *-aat, ḥaal* pl. *ʔaḥwaal, waḍiε* pl. *ʔawḍaaε.* His affairs are in a bad state. *ʔumuura b-ḥaala mxarbuṭa.* — Don't speak to her when she's in this state. *la-tkallimha w-hiyya b-hal-waḍεiyya.* **4.** *ḥukuumi*.* It's a state hospital. *haaδa mustašfa ḥukuumi.* **5.** *xaarijiyya.* He works for the state department. *yištuġul ib-wizaart il-xaarijiyya.*
to state - **1.** *gaal (u gool) n-.* You just stated that you were not there. *hassa gilit ma-činit ihnaak.* **2.** *waḍḍaḥ (i tawḍiiḥ) t-, bayyan (i tabyiin) t-.* The terms are stated in the contract. *š-šuruuṭ imwaḍḍaḥa bil-εaqid.* — I thought he stated his case well. *ʔaεtiqid bayyan qaḍiita zeena.*
statement - **1.** *bayaan* pl. *-aat.* The prime minister issued his policy statement to parliament. *raʔiis il-wuzaraaʔ qaddam bayaan siyaasta lil-majlis.*
2. *kašif* (pl. *kšuuf*) *ḥisaab.* My bank sends me a statement each month. *l-bang ydizz-li kašf il-ḥisaab kull šahar.*
static - *wašwaša, xašxaša.* There's so much static I can't get the station. *hwaaya ʔaku wašwaša bir-raadyo; ma-da-agdar aṭalliε il-maḥaṭṭa.*
station - *maḥaṭṭa* pl. *-aat.* Get off at the next station. *ʔinzil bil-maḥaṭṭa j-jaaya.* — We're going to visit a radio station. *raḥ-inzuur maḥaṭṭat il-ʔiδaaεa.*
to station - *xalla (i txilli) t-.* The police stationed a man at the door. *š-šurṭa xallat ḥaaris εal-baab.*
**Where are you stationed? *ween markazak?*
stationery - *qirṭaasiyya.* I need some stationery. *ʔaḥtaaj išwayya qirṭaasiyya.*
statue - *timθaal* pl. *tamaaθiil.*
stay - *baqaaʔ* pl. *-aat.* Our stay in the mountains during the summer was very pleasant. *baqaaʔna bij-jibal biṣ-ṣeef čaan kulliš laṭiif.*
to stay - *buqa (a baqaaʔ).* How long will you stay? *šgadd raḥ-tubqa?* — Are you staying with friends? *baaqi wiyya ʔaṣdiqaaʔak?* — You've stayed away a long time. *buqeet biεiid mudda ṭuwiila.*
to stay up - *siḥar (a sahar).* Our children stay up until nine o'clock. *wilidna yisharuun lis-saaεa tisεa.*
steady - **1.** *θaabit.* This needs a steady hand. *haay tiḥtaaj-ilha ʔiid θaabta.* — We kept a good steady pace. *ḥaafaḍna εala surεa θaabta.* **2.** *mustamirr.* He's made steady progress. *ḥaṣṣal εala taqaddum mustamirr.* **3.** *daaʔimi*, mustamirr.* He's one of our steady customers. *huwwa min maεaamiilna d-daaʔimiyyiin*
to **steal** - *baag (u boog) n-, siraq (u sariq) n-.* He stole all my money. *baag kull ifluusi.*
to steal away - *nass (i nass).* We had to steal away. *ḍṭarreena nniss.*
steam - **1.** *buxaar.* There's steam coming from the teapot. *ʔaku buxaar da-yiṭlaε imnil-quuri.*
2. *buxaari*.* He showed us a model of a steam engine. *raawaana nimuuδaj makiina buxaariyya.*
**You'll have to get up some steam if you want to get done on time. *yinraad-lak himma ʔiδa činit itriid itxaḷḷiṣ bil-wakit.*
to steam - *baxxar (i tabxiir) t-.* The rice is still steaming. *t-timman baεda ybaxxir.*
steamer - *baaxira* pl. *bawaaxir.* The steamer sails at 10 o'clock. *l-baaxira titruk is-saaεa εašra.*
steel - *fuulaaδ.* The bridge is built entirely of steel. *j-jisir mibni kulla min fuulaaδ.*
steep - **1.** *minḥidir ib-šidda, kulliš minḥidir.* Be careful, the stairs are steep. *diir baalak, id-daraj minḥadra b-šidda.* **2.** *εaali.* The price is too steep. *s-siεir kulliš εaali.*
to steep - *xidar (a xadir) n-.* Let the tea steep a little longer. *xalli č-čaay yixdar ʔakθar.*

to **steer** - **1.** *wajjah (i tawjiih) t-.* Steer the launch in to shore. *wajjih il-maaṭoor εaj-juruf.* — Steer the car to the right of that policeman. *wajjih is-sayyaara b-jihat il-yamiin min haš-šurṭi.* **2.** *deewar (u tdeewur).* Okay, you steer and I'll push. *zeen, ʔinta tdeewur w-ʔaani ʔadfaε.* **3.** *dazz (i dazz) n-.* He's steered a lot of customers my way. *dazz-li maεaamiil ihwaaya.*
**Better steer clear of him. *tčaffa šarra.*
to steer away - *waxxar (i twixxir) t-, baεεad (i tabεiid) t-.* Steer away from those kids. *waxxir is-sayyaara min haj-jihaal.*
steering wheel - *sikkaan* pl. *-aat.*
stem - *saag* pl. *siigaan.* Don't cut the stems too short. *la-tguṣṣ is-siigaan igṣaar.*
step - **1.** *daraja* pl. *-aat.* The steps are carpeted. *d-darajaat mafruuša bis-sijjaad.* **2.** *xuṭwa* pl. *-aat, xuṭaw.* He took one step forward. *tqaddam xuṭwa li-giddaam.* — We built up our business step by step. *bineena šuġuḷna xuṭwa xuṭwa.* **3.** *ʔijraaʔ* pl. *-aat.* The government is taking steps to wipe out crime. *l-ḥukuuma gaaεid tittixiδ l-ʔijraaʔaat lil-qaḍaaʔ εala jaraaʔim.*
**Watch your step. *laaziḍ min timši.*
to step - **1.** *wugaf (a wuguuf).* Perhaps if you step on a chair you can reach it. *yimkin itnuušha ʔiδa wugafit εala kursi.* **2.** *daas (u doos).* I stepped into the mud. *disit εaṭ-ṭiin.*
**Step lively! *xuff rijlak!*
to step aside - *tnaḥḥa (a tanaḥḥi), waxxar (i twixxir) t-.* I stepped aside to let him by. *tnaḥḥeet w-xalleeta ymurr.*
to step in - **1.** *dixal (u duxuul).* I saw him step into the store. *šifta yidxul bil-maxzan.*
2. *tdaxxal (a tadaxxul).* The president himself may have to step in. *r-raʔiis nafsa muḥtamal yitdaxxal.*
to step off - *nizal (i nizuul).* He just stepped off the train. *hassa nizal imnil-qiṭaar.*
to step out - *ṭilaε (a ṭuluuε).* He just stepped out for a minute. *ṭilaε daqiiqa w-yirjaε.*
to step up - **1.** *zayyad (i tazyiid) t-.* We'll have to step up the pace. *laazim inzayyid is-surεa.*
2. *šaddad (i tašdiid) t-.* The government stepped up its campaign against VD. *l-ḥukuuma šaddidat ḥamlatha ḍidd il-ʔamraaḍ iz-zuhriyya.* **3.** *jaa (yiji majiiʔ) yamm.* A strange man stepped up to me on the street. *šaxiṣ ġariib jaa yammi εaš-šaariε.*
sterile - **1.** *muεaqqam.* Get me a sterile dressing. *jiib-li gooz muεaqqam.* **2.** *εaqiim, εaaqir.* I think my wife is sterile. *ʔaḍinn zawijti εaqiima.*
to **sterilize** - *εaqqam (i taεqiim) t-.* Sterilize the needle before you use it. *εaqqim il-ʔubra gabuḷ-ma tistaεmilha.*
sterling - *ʔaṣli*.* That's sterling silver. *haay fuḍḍa ʔaṣliyya.*
stern - **1.** *muʔaxxira* pl. *-aat.* Sit in the stern of the boat and I'll row. *ʔugεud ib-muʔaxxirat il-balam w-ʔaani ʔajlif.* **2.** *jaaf, mεabbis.* He's a stern man. *huwwa jaaf.*
stew - *marga* pl. *-aat* coll. *marag.* We had okra stew and rice. *ʔakalna margat baamya w-timman.*
**He's in a stew again. *huwwa mithayyij marra lux.*
to stew - *ṭubax (u ṭabux) n-.* Shall I stew the chicken or roast it? *triidni ʔaṭbux id-dijaaj ʔaw aḥammuṣa?*
stick - *εuuda* pl. *εuwad, εaṣa* pl. *εiṣi.* He hit me with a stick. *ḍirabni bil-εuuda.*
to stick - **1.** *naġġaz (u tanġiiz) n-, čakčak (i tčikčik) t-.* Something is sticking me. *fadd šii da-ynaġġizni.* **2.** *čakk (u čakk) n-.* I stuck my finger. *čakkeet ʔuṣbaεi.* **3.** *lizag (a lazig) n-.* This stamp doesn't stick. *haaδa ṭ-ṭaabiε ma-yilzag.* **4.** *čallab (i tačliib, tčillib).* The door always sticks in damp weather. *l-baab daaʔiman yčallib bir-riṭuuba.* **5.** *biqa (a baqaaʔ) n-.* Nothing sticks in his mind. *ma-yibqa šii b-damaaġa.* **6.** *xalla (i txilli) t-.* Just stick it in your pocket. *bass xalliiha b-jeebak.* **7.** *daxxal (i tadxiil) t-, ḥaṭṭ (u ḥaṭṭ).* He sticks his nose into everything. *ydaxxil nafsa b-kullši.* or **ḥummuṣ bij-jidir yinbuṣ.*
to stick out - *tḥammal (a taḥammul).* Try and stick it out a little longer. *ḥaawil titḥammalha šwayya ʔakθar.*
to stick to - **1.** *tmassak (a tamassuk) b-.* I'm sticking to my opinion. *ʔaani mitmassik ib-raʔyi.* or *ʔaani muṣirr εala raʔyi.* **2.** *lizag (a lazig) n- εala.* That won't stick to a smooth surface. *haaδa ma-yilzag εala saṭiḥ ʔamlas.*

to stick up - *daafaɛ (i difaaɛ) n-*. He stuck up for me. *daafaɛ ɛanni.*
sticky - 1. *mdabbug.* My fingers are all sticky with honey. *ʔaṣaabɛi mdabbga mnil-ɛasal.* 2. *raṭib.* It's awfully sticky today. *kulliš raṭba l-yoom.*
**He's got sticky fingers. *ʔiida ṭwiila.*
stiff - 1. *yaabis.* His collars are always stiff. *yaaxta ɛala ṭuul yaabsa.* 2. *qawi**. The steering is awful stiff! *l-isteerin kulliš qawi.* 3. *mitšannij.* My legs are stiff. *rijlayya mitšannija.* 4. *naašif.* Don't be so stiff! *la-tkuun kulliš naašif!* 5. *ṣaɛub.* Was it a stiff examination? *čaan l-imtiḥaan ṣaɛub?* 6. *čibiir.* He paid a stiff fine. *difaɛ ğaraama čbiira.*
to be stiff - *tṣallab (a taṣallub).* Relax and don't be stiff when you're swimming. *raxxi nafsak; la-titṣallab min tisbaḥ.*
still - 1. *haadi?, saakin.* The night was still. *l-leel čaan haadi?.* 2. *waaguf.* The wheels of industry were still. *ɛajalaat iṣ-ṣinaaɛa čaanat waagfa.* 3. *baɛad-, la-zaal (a).* I'm still of the same opinion. *ʔaani baɛadni b-nafs ir-raʔi.* — This box is big, but that box is still bigger. *has-sanduug kabiir, laakin δaak iṣ-ṣanduug baɛda ʔakbar.* -- It's still raining. *la-tzaal timṭur.* — I'm still eating. *la-azaal ʔaakul.* — They were still playing. *čaanaw la-yzaaluun yilɛabuun.*
to hold still - *wugaf (a wuguuf).* Hold still a minute! *ʔoogaf daqiiqa!* or *la-titḥarrak!*
to keep still - *sikat (u sukuut).* Why don't you keep still? *leeš ma-tiskut?*
to **stimulate** - 1. *nabbah (i tanbiih) t-.* Coffee stimulates the nerves. *l-gahwa tnabbih il-ʔaɛṣaab.* -- We stimulated the muscle with an electric current. *nabbahna l-ɛaδala bit-tayyaar il-kahrabaaʔi.* 2. *šajjaɛ (i tašjiiɛ) t-.* We must stimulate foreign trade. *laazim inšajjiɛ it-tijaara l-xaarijiyya.*
**Running fast stimulates the breathing. *r-rikiδ is-sariiɛ yzayyid surɛat it-tanaffus.*
stingy - *baxiil* pl. *buxalaaʔ.* Don't be stingy! *la-tṣiir baxiil!*
stir - 1. *harja* pl. *-aat.* There was a stir in the crowd when he got up to speak. *ṣaarat harja bin-naas min gaam da-yiḥči.* 2. *ḥarika* pl. *-aat, xarxaša* pl. *-aat.* I heard a stir in the bush. *simaɛit ḥarika bid-dağal.*
to stir - 1. *xaaṭ (u xooṭ).* She forgot to stir the soup. *nisat itxuuṭ iš-šoorba.* 2. *ḥarrak (i taḥriik) t-, hazz (i hazz) n-.* The wind stirred the branches. *l-hawya ḥarrkat il-ğuṣuun.* 3. *tḥarrak (a taḥarruk).* He's stirring. *da-yitḥarrak.*
stirring - *muθiir, muhayyij.* He made a stirring speech. *xiṭab xiṭaab muθiir.*
stitch - *nabδa* pl. *-aat.* The injury needed four stitches. *j-jariḥ inraad-la ʔarbaɛ nabδadt.* — **When is the doctor going to take out the stitches? *yamta ṭ-ṭabiib raḥ-yjurr il-xeeṭ?*
**I haven't done a stitch of work today. *ma-štiğalit wala ḥabbaaya l-yoom.* or *ma-sawweet wala nitfat šuğuḷ hal-yoom.*
**Don't take big stitches. *la-txayyiṭ xašin.*
to stitch - *xayyaṭ (i taxyiiṭ) t-.* Did you stitch the hem yet? *xayyaṭit il-ḥaašya loo baɛad?*
stock - 1. *majmuuɛa* pl. *-aat.* He has a large stock of shirts. *ɛinda majmuuɛa čbiira mnil-qumṣaan.* 2. *saham* pl. *ʔashum.* I advise you not to buy these stocks. *ʔanṣaḥak la-tištiri hal-ʔashum.* 3. *ʔaxmaṣ* pl. *ʔaxaamiṣ.* The stock of a rifle is usually made of wood. *ʔaxmaṣ il-bunduqiyya ɛaadatan maɛmuul min il-xišab.*
**I don't put much stock in what he says. *ma-axalli wazin il-ḥačya.* or *ma-aɛtimid ɛala ḥačya.*
in stock - *maxzuun.* What colors do you have in stock? *ʔay ʔalwaan maxzuuna ɛindak?*
out of stock - *xalṣaan.* Sorry, that color is out of stock. *mitʔassif δaak in-nooɛ xalṣaan.*
to take stock - 1. *jirad (u jarid) n-.* Next week we're going to take stock. *l-isbuuɛ ij-jaay raḥ-nijrud.* 2. *raajaɛ (i muraajaɛa).* Let's take stock of what we've done. *xalli nraajiɛ illi sawweenaa.*
to stock - *xizan (i xazin) n-.* We don't stock that brand. *ma-nixzin hal-maarka* or **ma-ɛidna hal-maarka.*
stocked - 1. *mjahhaz.* Our store is stocked with everything. *maxzanna mjahhaz ib-kullši.* 2. *maxzuun.* Sorry that color isn't stocked by us. *mitʔassif hal-loon muu maxzuun ɛidna.*
stock exchange - *boorṣa* pl. *-aat.*
stockholder - *musaahim* pl. *-iin.* I'm a stockholder in that company. *ʔaani musaahim ib-δiič iš-šarika.*
stocking - *juuraab* pl. *juwaariib.* I'd like three pairs of stockings. *ʔaḥibb itlaθ izwaaj juwaariib.*
stomach - 1. *miɛda* pl. *-aat.* He has an upset stomach. *miɛidta mxarbaṭa.* 2. *baṭin* pl. *bṭuun.* Don't lie on your stomach. *la-tinbuṭiḥ ɛala baṭnak.*
**I'm sick to my stomach. *nafsi da-tilɛab.*
to stomach - *tḥammal (a taḥammul).* I can't stomach that fellow. *ma-agdar atḥammal haš-šaxiṣ.*
stone - 1. *ḥjaara* pl. *-aat.* He killed two birds with one stone. *qital ɛaṣfuureen b-iḥjaara.* 2. *nuwaaya* pl. *-aat,* coll. *nuwa.* Swallowing peach stones is dangerous. *baliɛ nuwa l-xoox xaṭar.* 3. *min iḥjaar, ḥajari**. We sat on a stone bench. *giɛadna ɛala maqɛad min iḥjaar.* — We noticed a stone statue. *laaḥaδna timθaal ḥajari.*
**He left no stone unturned. *ma-xalla zwiyya ma-dawwarha.*
stool - 1. *taxta* pl. *-aat.* When he milks the cow, he sits on a stool. *min yiḥlib il-haayša yigɛud ɛala taxta.* 2. *xuruuj.* We have to make three tests, for the blood, the urine, and the stool. *laazim insawwi θlaθ taḥliilaat lid-damm, lil-bool w-lil-xuruuj.*
stoop - *ḥanya* pl. *-aat.* He has a slight stoop. *ɛinda ḥanya šwayya.*
to stoop - *nḥina (i nḥinaaʔ), naṣṣa (i tnaṣṣi).* He stooped to pick up the newspaper. *naṣṣa ḥatta yitnaawaš ij-jariida.*
to stoop to - *tnaazal (a tanaazul), nizal (i nuzuul).* I don't think she'd stoop to such a thing. *ma-aδinnha titnaazal il-hiiči šii.*
stop - 1. *mawqif* pl. *mawaaqif.* You have to get off at the next stop. *laazim tinzil bil-mawqif ij-jaay.* 2. *waqfa* pl. *-aat.* We have a ten-minute stop in Basra. *ɛidna waqfat ɛašir daqaayiq bil-baṣra.* 3. *ḥadd.* We'll have to put a stop to that practice. *laazim nooδaɛ ḥadd il-hal-ɛaada.* or **laazim inbaṭṭil hal-ɛaada.*
to stop - 1. *wugaf (a wuguuf) n-.* The bus stops on the other side of the street. *l-paaṣ yoogaf ib-ṣafḥat il-lux imniš-šaariɛ.* -- My watch stopped. *saaɛti wugfat.* — I stopped for a drink of water on the way. *wugafit bit-ṭariiq ḥatta ʔašrab maay.* 2. *waggaf (u tawgiif) t-.* Stop the car at the next street. *wagguf is-sayyaara biš-šaariɛ ij-jaay.* 3. *baṭṭal (i tabṭiil) t-.* Please stop that noise. *ʔarjuuk baṭṭil hal-ḥiss.* -- Stop it! *baṭṭil!* or **bass ɛaad!*
to stop over - *wugaf (a wuguuf) b-, biqa (a baqaaʔ) b-.* Why don't you stop over at my house on the way? *leeš ma-toogaf ib-beeti ɛala ṭariiqak?*
to stop overnight - *baat (a beetuuta).* We'll stop in Hilla overnight. *raḥ-inbaat bil-ḥilla.*
to stop short - *sakkat (i taskiit) t-.* I stopped him short before he could say much. *sakkatta b-surɛa gabuḷ-ma gidar yiḥči hwaaya.*
to stop up - *sadd (i sadd) n-.* You're going to stop up the drain. *raḥ-itsidd il-balluuɛa.*
stopper - *saddaad* pl. *-aat.* Put the stopper in the kettle. *xalli s-saddaad bil-buṭil.*
store - 1. *maxzan* pl. *maxaazin, maḥall* pl. *-aat, dukkaan* pl. *dukaakiin.* I know a store where you can buy a good suit. *ʔaɛruf fadd maxzan tigdar tištiri minna badla zeena.* 2. *δaxiira* pl. *δaxaayir, muuna* pl. *muwan.* We have a sufficient store of food in the basement. *ɛidna δaxiira kaafya mnil-ʔakil bis-sirdaab.* -- The army has a large store of rifles in the city. *j-jeeš ɛinda δaxiira čabiira min it-tufag bil-madiina.*
**Who knows what the future has in store for us? *minu yuɛruf iš-δaamm-inna l-mustaqbal?*
to store - *xizan (i xazin) n-, δamm (u δamm) n-, ḥiraz (i ḥariz).* Where shall I store the potatoes? *ween ʔaxzin il-puteeta?*
**I stored up a lot of energy during my vacation. *tnaššaṭit ihwaaya b-ɛuṭulti.*
storm - *ɛaaṣifa* pl. *ɛawaaṣif.* There was a big storm last night. *jatt ɛaaṣifa čibiira l-baarḥa bil-leel.*
to storm - *ṣaarat (i) ɛaaṣifa.* It's going to storm tonight. *raḥ-itṣiir ɛaaṣifa hal-leela.*
stormy - *ɛaaṣif.*
story - 1. *saaluufa* pl. *-aat, suwaaliif, quṣṣa* pl. *quṣaṣ, ḥčaaya* pl. *-aat.* Do you want me to tell you a story? *triidni ʔaḥčii-lak saaluufa?* — It's always the same old story. *daaʔiman nafs il-iḥčaaya* or *daaʔiman nafs il-quṣṣa l-ɛatiiga.* 2. *ṭaabig* pl. *ṭawaabig.* The building has five stories. *l-binaaya biiha xamis ṭawaabiq.*
stout - *simiin* pl. *smaan.* He's a stout man. *huwwa*

rijjaal simiin.

to get stout - *siman (a simin).* He's gotten very stout lately. *siman ihwaaya b-hal-ʔayyaam.*

stove - 1. *ṭabbaax* pl. *-aat, ʔoojaaġ* pl. *-aat.* Put the meat on the stove. *xalli l-laḥam ʕaṭ-ṭabbaax.* 2. *ṣooba* pl. *-aat.* I need a stove in my bedroom. *ʔaḥtaaj ṣooba b-ġurfat noomi.*

straight - 1. *ʕadil.* Draw a straight line. *ʔirsim xaṭṭ ʕadil.* — He gave me a straight answer. *jaawabni jawaab ʕadil.* — She's always straight with me. *hiyya daaʔiman ʕadla wiyyaaya.* — Is my hat on straight? *šafuqti ʕadla?* — She stands very straight. *toogaf kulliš ʕadil.* — He worked for fifteen hours straight. *štiġal xumuṣṭaʕaš saaʕa ʕadil.* 2. *ʕadil, raʔsan.* Go straight home. *ruuḥ ʕadil lil-beet.* 3. *saada.* I take my arrack straight. *ʔaaxuδ il-ʕarag maali saada.* 4. *tamaam, tamaaman.* Try to get the story straight. *ḥaawil tifham il-quṣṣa tamaam.* — You didn't get me straight. *ma-fhamitni tamaam.* — Our house is straight across from the church. *beetna tamaaman guḅaal il-kaniisa.*

**He can't think straight. *fikra mšawwaš.*

**Now let's get this straight! I'm the boss here! *fukk ʕeenak! ʔaani r-raʔiis ihnaa!*

straight ahead - *guḅaḷ.* Walk straight ahead. *ʔimši guḅaḷ.*

to **straighten** - *ʕaddal (i taʕdiil) t-.* Can you straighten the rod? *tigdar itʕaddil iš-šiiš?* — Straighten the tablecloth. *ʕaddil čarčaf il-meez.*

to straighten out - 1. *ʕaddal (i taʕdiil) t-.* Have you straightened out your financial affairs? *ʕaddalit ʔumuurak il-maaliyya?* 2. *ṣaalaḥ (i muṣaalaḥa).* Have you straightened out everything between them? *ṣaalaḥit beenhum* or *ṣaalaḥithum?* 3. *ʕidal (a ʕadil), tʕaddal (a taʕaddul).* Tomorrow everything will straighten out. *bukra kullši yiʕdal.*

to straighten up - *ʕaddal (i taʕdiil) t-, rattab (i tartiib) t-.* Will you please straighten up the room? *ʔarjuuk ʕaddil il-ġurfa.*

strain - 1. *mataaʕib.* He can't stand the strain of modern living. *ma-yigdar yitḥammal mataaʕib il-ḥayaat il-ḥadiiθa.* 2. *šilʕaan gaḷub.* Reading this small print is a strain. *qraayat hal-kitaaba n-naaʕima šilʕaan gaḷub.* 3. *tawattur.* What caused the strain in relations between the two countries? *š-sabbab tawattur il-ʕalaaqaat been id-dawilteen?*

**I don't think the rope will stand the strain. *ma-aδinn il-ḥabil raḥ-yitḥammal.*

to strain - 1. *šilaʕ (a šaliʕ, šilʕaan) n- gaḷub-, taʕʕab (i tatʕiib) t-.* That last effort strained me. *hal-majhuud il-ʔaxiir šilaʕ gaḷbi.* — Reading this small print strained my eyes. *qraayat hal-kitaaba n-naaʕima taʕʕab ʕeeni.* — Don't strain yourself. *la-tišlaʕ gaḷbak* or *la-ttaʕʕib nafsak.* 2. *wattar (i tawtiir) t-.* The blockade strained relations between the two countries. *l-ḥiṣaar wattar il-ʕalaaqaat been id-dawilteen.* 3. *ṣaffa (i taṣfiya) t-.* She strained the rice. *ṣaffat it-timman.*

strained - 1. *mitwattir.* Relations between the two countries are strained. *l-ʕalaaqaat been id-dawilteen mitwattra.* 2. *mṣaffa.* I prefer strained honey. *ʔafaḍḍil ʕasal mṣaffa.*

strainer - *maṣfi* pl. *maṣaafi.*

strait - *maḍiiq* pl. *maḍaayiq.*

Straits of Gibraltar - *maḍiiq jibal ṭaariq.*

strange - *ġariib, ʕajiib.* All this is strange to me. *kull haaδa ġariib ʕalayya.* — What a strange question! *šloon suʔaal ġariib!*

stranger - *ġariib* pl. *ġurabaaʔ.* The stranger gave me a book. *l-ġariib inṭaani ktaab.*

strap - *seer* pl. *-aat, syuur.* The man beat his horse with a leather strap. *r-rijjaal ḍirab iḥṣaana b-seer jilid.*

straw - 1. *tibin.* We feed our horse straw. *ninṭi l-iḥṣaan maalna tibin.* 2. *muṣṣaaṣa* pl. *-aat, guṣba* pl. *-aat* coll. *guṣab.* Please bring me a drinking straw. *ʔarjuuk jiib-li muṣṣaaṣa.*

**That's the last straw! *wuṣlat ḥaddha!*

strawberry - *čilka* pl. *-aat.* coll. *čilak; šilleeka* pl. *-aat.* coll. *šilleek.*

stray - 1. *taayih.* He was hit by a stray bullet. *nḍirab ib-riṣaaṣa taayha.* — Have you found the stray lamb? *ligeet iṭ-ṭili t-taayih?* 2. *saayib.* Stray dogs are becoming a problem. *l-ičlaab is-saayba da-tṣiir muškila.*

to stray - *taah (i teeh).* The lamb strayed from the flock. *ṭ-ṭili taah min il-qaṭiiʕ.*

stream - 1. *šaṭṭ* pl. *šṭuuṭ, nahar* pl. *ʔanhaar, ʔanhur.* Where can we ford the stream? *ween nigdar niʕbur iš-šaṭṭ ixyaaδa?* 2. *saagya* pl. *suwaagi, saajya* pl. *swaaji.* A little stream flows through our farm. *fadd saagya ṣġayyra tijri b-mazraʕatna.* 3. *seel* pl. *syuul.* A stream of refugees left the city. *seel min il-laajiʔiin tirak il-wlaaya.* 4. *majra* pl. *majaari.* You interrupted my stream of thought. *giṭaʕit majra ʔafkaari.*

to stream - 1. *jira (i jarayaan).* Tears streamed down her cheeks. *d-dumuuʕ jirat ʕala xduudha.*

street - *šaariʕ* pl. *šawaariʕ, jaadda* pl. *-aat, darub* pl. *druub.* I met him on the street. *laageeta bi-š-šaariʕ.*

streetcar - *traam* pl. *-aat, traamwaay* pl. *-aat.*

street light - *ḍuwa* (pl. *-aayaat, ʔaḍwiya*) *šaariʕ.* The street lights go on at dark. *ḍuwaayaat iš-šawaariʕ tištiʕil lamma tṣiir ḍalma.*

strength - *quwwa.* I don't have the strength to do my work. *ma-ʕindi quwwa ḥatta ʔasawwi šuġli.* — I've lost all my strength. *fiqadit kull quuti.* — The strength of the enemy surprised us. *quwwat il-ʕadu ʔadhišatna.*

**He doesn't know his own strength. *ma-yiʕruf nafsa šgadd qawi.*

on the strength of - *binaaʔan ʕala.* We hired him on the strength of your recommendation. *šaġġaḷnaa binaaʔan ʕala tawṣiitak.*

strenuous - *mutʕib, mujhid.* That's a strenuous job. *haaδi fadd šaġla mutʕiba.* or **haaδi fadd šaġla tišlaʕ il-gaḷub.*

stress - *tašdiid* pl. *-aat.* The stress is on the second syllable of the word. *t-tašdiid ʕala l-maqṭaʕ iθ-θaani mnil-kalima.*

to stress - 1. *ʔakkad (i taʔkiid) t- ʕala, šaddad (i tašdiid) t- ʕala.* She stressed the importance of honesty. *ʔakkidat ʕala ʔahammiyyat il-ʔamaana.* 2. *šaddad (i).* We stress the second syllable of the word. *nšaddid ʕala l-maqṭaʕ iθ-θaani mnil-kalima.*

stretch - *masaafa* pl. *-aat, qisim* pl. *ʔaqsaam.* We had to run the last stretch. *njibarna nirkuḍ il-masaafa l-ʔaxiira.*

at a stretch - *ʕala fadd jarra, bala wagfa.* He works about ten hours at a stretch. *yištiġuḷ ḥawaali ʕašir saaʕaat ʕala fadd jarra.*

to stretch - 1. *kabbar (u takbiir) t-.* Can you stretch my shoes a little bit. *tigdar itkabbur qundarti šwayya.* 2. *tkabbar (a takabbur).* The gloves will stretch. *l-ičfuuf titkabbar.* 3. *maṭṭa (i tamṭiya) t-.* You stretched the elastic too much. *maṭṭeet il-laastiik ihwaaya.* 4. *tmaṭṭa (a tamaṭṭi) tmaġġaṭ (a tamaġġuṭ).* The lion yawned and stretched. *s-sabiʕ itθaawab w-itmaṭṭa.*

**The wheat fields stretch out for miles. *ḥuquul il-ḥunṭa mimtadda l-ʕiddat ʔamyaal.*

to stretch out - *madd (i madd) n-.* He stretched out his hand. *madd ʔiida.*

stretcher - *naqqaala* pl. *-aat, maḥaffa* pl. *-aat, sadya* pl. *-aat.* They took him to the hospital on a stretcher. *šaaloo lil-mustašfa bin-naqqaala.*

strict - *mitšaddid.* His father is very strict. *ʔabuu kulliš mitšaddid.*

strike - *ʔiḍraab* pl. *-aat.* How long did the strike last? *l-ʔiḍraab išgadd ṭawwal?*

to go on strike - *sawwa (i taswiya) ʔiḍraab, ʔaḍrab (i ʔiḍraab).* We're going on strike tomorrow. *raḥ-insawwi iḍraab baačir.*

to strike - 1. *ḍirab (u ḍarub) n-.* Who struck you? *minu ḍirabak?* 2. *ṭaxx (u ṭaxx) b-.* The ship struck a rock. *s-sifiina ṭaxxat ib-ṣaxra.* 3. *wugaʕ (a wuguuʕ) ʕala, ḍirab (u ḍarub) n-.* Lightning struck the tree. *ṣ-ṣaaʕiqa wugʕat ʕala š-šajara.* 4. *dagg (u dagg).* The clock just struck ten. *s-saaʕa hassa daggat ʕašra.* 5. *šiʕal (i, šaʕil) n-.* Strike a match. *ʔišʕil šixxaaṭa.* 6. *liga (i lagi).* The government struck oil in the north. *l-ḥukuuma ligat nafuṭ biš-šimaal.* 7. *ʕiqad (i ʕaqid) n-.* Did you strike a bargain? *ʕiqadit ṣafqa?* 8. *lifat (i lafit) n-.* That was the first thing that struck my eye. *haaδa čaan awwal šii lifat naḍari.*

**It strikes me he's acting very strangely. *ybayyin ʕalee da-yitṣarraf ib-ṣuura ġeer ṭabiiʕiyya.*

**Does that strike a familiar note? *haaδa yjiib šii b-baalak?* or *haaδa yδakkrak ib-šii?*

to strike off - *šiṭab (u šaṭub) n-.* Strike his name off the list. *ʔišṭub isma mnil-qaaʔima.*

to strike out - 1. *šiṭab (u šaṭub) n-, ḥiδaf (i ḥaδif) n-.* Strike out the first paragraph. *ʔišṭub il-faqara l-ʔuula.* 2. *tḥarrak (a ḥaraka).* The patrol struck out into the desert. *d-dawriyya tḥarrikat biṣ-ṣaḥraaʔ.*

to strike up a friendship - *ṭṣaadaq (a taṣaaduq).* The two of them struck up a friendship very quickly. *θneenhum ṭṣaadqaw ib-surεa.*

striker - *muḍrib* pl. *-iin.* The strikers have agreed to negotiate. *l-muḍribiin waafqaw yitfaawḍuun.*

striking - **1.** *zaahi.* She likes to wear striking colors. *tḥibb tilbas ʔalwaan zaahya.* **2.** *εajiib.* There's a striking resemblance between the two. *ʔaku šabah εajiib beenaathum.*

string - **1.** *xeeṭ* pl. *xyuuṭ.* This string is too short. *hal-xeeṭ kulliš igṣayyir.* **2.** *watar* pl. *ʔawtaar.* I have to buy a new string for my violin. *laazim ʔaštiri watar jidiid lil-kamanja maalti.*

**He's still attached to his mother's apron strings. *baεda taḥat ṣayṭarat ʔumma.* or *baεda laazig ib-ʔumma.*

to string - **1.** *liḍam (u laḍum) n-.* Where can I have my pearls strung? *ween ʔagdar ʔalḍum il-liilu maali?* **2.** *waṣṣal (i tawṣiil) t-.* How are you going to string the wire to the garage? *šloon raḥ-itwaṣṣil il-waayir lil-garaaj?*

string bean - *faaṣuulaaya* pl. *-aat* coll. *faaṣuuliyya, faaṣuulya.*

to **strip** - **1.** *ṣallax (i taṣliix) t-.* They strip the cars of everything valuable before they scrap them. *yṣallixuun is-sayyaaraat min kullši l-yiswa gabuḷ-ma ysakribuuha.* **2.** *šilaε (a šaliε) n-.* The captain stripped the medals from his chest. *r-raʔiis šilaε il-madaalyaat min ṣadra.* **3.** *jarrad (i tajriid) t-.* They stripped the king of all his privileges. *jarridaw il-malik min kull imtiyaazaata.*

to strip off - *nizaε (a naziε).* She stripped off her clothes. *nizεat ihduumha.* or ***ṭṣallxat.*

stripe - **1.** *qalam,* pl. *qlaam.* The tie has red and white stripes. *l-booyinbaağ bii qlaam ḥumur w-biiḍ.* **2.** *xeeṭ* pl. *xyuuṭ.* If you get drunk again, we'll take your stripes away. *ʔiδa skarit marrt il-lux, naaxuδ ixyuuṭak minnak.*

striped - *mqallam.* She's wearing a striped dress. *laabsa nafnuuf imqallam.*

stroke - **1.** *nfijaar* (pl. *-aat*) *bid-damaağ.* He died of a stroke. *maat min ʔaθar infijaar bid-damaağ.* **2.** *ḍarba* pl. *-aat.* With a few strokes of the oars, he was in midstream. *b-čam ḍarbat mijdaaf, wuṣal il-nuṣṣ iš-šaṭṭ.* **3.** *jarra* pl. *-aat.* With a stroke of the pen, he was sentenced to hang. *b-jarrat qalam, inḥikam εalee bil-ʔiεdaam.*

**It was a real stroke of luck to get this apartment. *taḥṣiil haš-šaqqa čaan ḥaḍḍ εadil.*

**At one stroke everything was changed. *kullši tbaddal fadd nooba.*

**He arrived at the stroke of four. *wuṣal is-saaεa ʔarbaεa biḍ-ḍabuṭ.*

to stroke - *massad (i tamsiid) t- l-.* Our cat loves to be stroked. *bazzuunatna tḥibb yitmassad-ilha.*

stroll - *mašya* pl. *-aat.* A short stroll won't tire you much. *mašya ṣğayyra ma-ttaεεbak ihwaaya.*

**I'd like to take a stroll around the square. *ʔariid ʔatmašša ḥawl is-saaḥa.*

to stroll - *tmašša (a tmašši).* Let's stroll through the town, *xalli nitmašša bil-madiina.*

strong - **1.** *qawi*.* He has strong hands. *εinda ʔiideen qawiyya.* **2.** *šadiid, qawi*.* There's a strong wind blowing today. *ʔaku hawa šadiid da-yhibb il-yoom.*

struggle - **1.** *mašaqqa* pl. *-aat.* I only beat him after a hard struggle. *ma-ğiḷabta ʔilla b-mašaqqa.* **2.** *mukaafaḥa.* The struggle against illiteracy in Iraq has made progress. *mukaafaḥat il-ʔummiyya bil-εiraaq itqaddimat.* **3.** *kifaaḥ* pl. *-aat, mukaafaḥa* pl. *-aat.* They got their freedom through a long struggle. *ḥaṣṣlaw εal-istiqlaalhum ib-kifaaḥ ṭuwiil.* **4.** *tbaaṭaḥ (a tabaaṭuḥ).* I've been struggling with this problem for some time. *ṣaar-li mudda da-ʔatbaaṭaḥ wiyya hal-muškila.* **5.** *jaahad (i jihaad).* The government is struggling to improve economic conditions. *l-ḥukuuma da-tjaahid ḥatta tḥassin il-ʔaḥwaal il-iqtiṣaadiyya.*

to struggle against - *kaafaḥ (i mukaafaḥa) t-.* We had to struggle against the current. *ḍṭarreena nkaafiḥ it-tayyaar.*

**We had a hard struggle to get the piano up to the second floor. *mitna gabuḷ-ma nṣaεεid il-ṗiyaano liṭ-ṭaabiq iθ-θaani.*

stubborn - *εnaadi, εnuudi* pl. *-iyyiin.* He's terribly stubborn. *huwwa kulliš iεnaadi.*

to get **stuck** - **1.** *nḥiṣar (i nḥiṣaar).* I got stuck in the chair. *nḥiṣarit bil-kursi.* **2.** *ṭumas (u ṭamus). nḥiṣar (i nḥiṣaar).* My car got stuck in the mud. *sayyaarti ṭumsat biṭ-ṭiin.* **3.** *twarraṭ (a tawarruṭ), txoozaq (a taxoozuq).* I got stuck with this car. *twarraṭit ib-has-sayyaara.*

**I got stuck on this passage. *εiṣat εalayya haay ij-jumla.*

stuck-up - *mitkabbur.* She is stuck-up *hiyya mitkabbra.* or ***šaayla xašimha.*

student - *tilmiiδ* pl. *talaamiiδ, ṭaalib* pl. *ṭullaab.* How many students are there at the medical school? *čam tilmiiδ ʔaku b-kulliyyat iṭ-ṭibb?*

studio - *stoodyo* pl. *-waat.* I've got to see a man at the Iraqi Broadcasting Studios. *laazim ʔašuuf fadd rijjaal b-istoodyowaat il-ʔiδaaεa l-εiraaqiyya.*

study - **1.** *diraasa* pl. *-aat.* Has he finished his studies? *xallaṣ diraasta?* **2.** *baḥiθ* pl. *buḥuuθ, ʔabḥaaθ.* He has published several studies in that field. *nišar εiddat abḥaaθ ib-hal-mawḍuuε.*

to study - **1.** *diras (u diraasa) n-.* We studied the map before we started our trip. *dirasna l-xariiṭa gabuḷ-ma nibdi safratna.* -- He's studying Chinese. *da-yidrus ṣiini.* **2.** *biḥaθ (a baḥiθ) n-, diras (u daris) n-.* The government is studying the problem. *l-ḥukuuma da-tibḥaθ il-muškila.*

stuff - *ğaraaḍ, ʔašyaaʔ.* Throw that old stuff away! *δibb hal-ğaraaḍ il-εatiiga!*

**Now we'll see what sort of stuff he's made of. *hassa nšuuf šinu maεdana.*

to stuff - **1.** *ḥannaṭ (i taḥniiṭ).* He stuffs animals for the museum. *yḥanniṭ ḥaywaanaat lil-matḥaf.* **2.** *ḥašša (l taḥšiya) t-, εabba (i taεbiya) t-.* Stuff cotton in your ears. *ḥašši guṭun b-iδnak.* -- Can you stuff all these things in one suitcase? *tigdar itεabbi kull hal-ğaraaḍ ib-fadd janṭa?* **3.** *tiras (i/u taris) n-, dačč (i dačč) n-.* We stuffed our bellies with food. *daččeena bṭuunna bil-ʔakil.*

stuffed - **1.** *masduud.* My nose is all stuffed up. *xašmi masduud.* **2.** *maḥši, nḥašša.* We had stuffed turkey for lunch. *tğaddeena diič hindi maḥši.*

to **stumble** - *εiθar (a εaθir).* I stumbled over a stone. *εiθarit b-iḥjaara.*

stupid - **1.** *ğabi, baliid.* He isn't at all stupid. *huwwa muu ğabi ʔabadan.* **2.** *saxiif.* That's a stupid idea. *haay fikra saxiifa.*

sty - *ḥadigdiga,* pl. *-aat.* I'm getting a sty on my left eye. *da-tiṭlaε-li ḥadigdiga b-εeeni l-yisra.*

style - **1.** *ʔisluub* pl. *ʔasaaliib.* His style of writing is very poor. *ʔisluuba bil-kitaaba kulliš ḍaεiif.* **2.** *mooda* pl. *-aat.* It's the latest style. *haay ʔaaxir mooda.* — She's always in style. *hiyya εal-mooda daaʔiman.*

subject - **1.** *mawḍuuε* pl. *mawaaḍiiε, qaḍiyya* pl. *qaḍaaya.* I don't know anything about that subject. *ma-aεruf šii εan haaδa l-mawḍuuε.* **2.** *raεiyya* pl. *raεaaya.* He is a British subject. *huwwa min raεaaya ʔingiltara.* **3.** *mubtadaʔ.* The subject of this sentence is the word "Ali". *l-mubtadaʔ ib-haj-jumla huwwa l-kalima "εali".* **4.** *muεarraḍ.* This schedule is subject to change. *haaδa j-jadwal muεarraḍ lit-tağyiir.*

**I'm always subject to colds. *ʔaani ʔanniših ib-surεa.*

to subject - *ʔaxḍaε (i xuḍuuε).* The Mongols subjected all of Asia to their rule. *l-mağuul ʔaxḍiεaw kull ʔaasya l-ḥukumhum.*

to **submit** - **1.** *qaddam (i taqdiim) t-.* I'll submit my report on Monday. *raḥ-ʔaqaddim taqriiri yoom iθ-θineen.* **2.** *riḍax (u riḍuux).* The criminal submitted to search. *l-mujrim riḍax lit-taftiiš.* **3.** *xiḍaε (a xuḍuuε).* The boss forces everyone to submit to his ideas. *r-raʔiis yijbur il-kull yixḍaεuun il-ʔaaraaʔa.* **4.** *staslam (i stislam).* His mother had to submit to an operation. *ʔumma ḍṭarrat tistaslim il-εamaliyya.*

to **subscribe** - **1.** *štirak (i štiraak).* I subscribed to both papers. *štirakit bij-jariidteen.* **2.** *šaarak (i mušaaraka) t-.* I don't subscribe to your opinion. *ma-ʔašaarkak ib-raʔyak.*

substantial - **1.** *čbiir, ḍaxum.* He lost a substantial sum of money. *xiṣar kammiyya čbiira mnil-ifluus.* or *xiṣar mablağ ḍaxum.* **2.** *jawhari*.* I don't see any substantial difference. *ma-ašuuf ʔay faraq jawhari.* **3.** *tukma.* Don't use that ladder; it's not substantial. *la-tistaεmil had-daraj; haaδa muu tukma.*

substantially - *jawhariyyan.* The two are substantially alike. *l-iθneen jawhariyyan yitšaabhuun.*

substitute - **1.** *badal, εuwaḍ.* Vegetable oil is occasionally used as a substitue for animal fat. *d dihin in-nabaati ʔaḥyaanan yustaεmal ka-badal lid-dihin il-ḥaywaani.* **2.** *bdaal.* If you can't be here tomorrow, send a substitute. *ʔiδa ma-tigdar*

itkuun ihnaa baačir, dizz waazid ibdaalak.
to substitute for - 1. *ɛawwaδ (i taɛwiiδ) t-b-makaan-.* I'll substitute red for green. *raz-ʔaɛawwuδ ʔazmar ib-makaan il-ʔaxδar.* **2.** *ʔaxaδ (u) makaan-.* Can you substitute for me today? *tigdar taaxuδ makaani l-yoom?*
to **subtract** - *ṭiraz (a ṭariz) n-.* He subtracted six from ten. *tiraz sitta min ɛašra.*
subtraction - *ṭariz.*
suburb - *δaaziya* pl. *δawaazi.* Their house is in the suburbs of the city. *beethum ib-δawaazi il-madiina.*
to **succeed** - *jaa (i majii?) wara.* Who succeeded him in office? *minu jaa waraa bil-waδiifa.* **2.** *nijaz (a najaaz).* He succeeds in everything he undertakes. *yinjaz ib-kull-ma yaaxuδ ɛala ɛaatqa.*
success - *najaaz* pl. *-aat.* Congratulations on your success! *tahaaniina ɛala najaazak!* -- The play wasn't much of a success. *t-tamθiiliyya ma-zaṣṣlat ɛala najaaz ihwaaya.*
successful - *naajiz* pl. *-iin.* He's a successful businessman. *huwwa rajul ʔaɛmaal naajiz.*
successor - *xalaf* (hereditary). The sheik's oldest son becomes his successor. *ʔakbar awlaad iš-šeex yṣiir xalafa.*
such - 1. *hiiči, miθil haaδa.* Such statements are hard to prove. *hiiči ɛibaaraat yiṣɛab barhanatha.* — I've never heard such nonsense before. *ma-smaɛit miθil hal-laġwa gabuḷ.* — I heard some such thing. *simaɛit hiiči šii.* or *simaɛit šii min haaδa l-qabiil.* **2.** *hal-gadd.* Don't be in such a hurry. *la-tistaɛjil hal-gadd.* — It was such a long movie that we didn't get out till midnight. *hal-gadd-ma čaan filim ṭuwiil, ma-ṭlaɛna ʔilla l-nuṣṣ il-leel.*
as such - *b-zadd δaat-.* The work as such isn't difficult. *š-šuġuḷ ib-zadd δaata muu ṣaɛub.*
such as - *miθil.* We sell things such as hats and shirts. *nbiiɛ ʔašyaaʔ miθil šafqaat w-iθyaab.*
to **suck** - *maṣṣ (u maṣṣ) n-.* Our baby sucks his thumb. *ṭifilna ymuṣṣ ibhaama.*
suction - *maṣṣ, mtiṣaaṣ.*
Sudan - *s-suudaan.*
Sudanese - *suudaani** pl. *-iyyiin.*
sudden - *fujaaʔi**. There's been a sudden change in the weather. *ṣaar tabaddul fujaaʔi bij-jaww.*
all of a sudden - 1. *fujʔatan, ɛala ġafla, baġtatan.* All of a sudden I remembered that I had to mail a letter. *fujʔatan itδakkarit laazim ʔaδibb bil-bariid.*
to **sue - 1.** *štika (i šikaaya).* We sued him for damages. *štikeena ɛalee b-ṭalab it-taɛwiiδ.* **2.** *ṭilab (u ṭalab).* They'll sue for peace. *raz-yṭulbuun iṣ-ṣuluz.*
Suez - *s-suwees.*
to **suffer - 1.** *tɛaδδab (a ɛaδδaab), qaasa (i muqaasaat).* Did she suffer very much? *tɛaδδbat ihwaaya?* **2.** *tkabbad (a takabbud).* They suffered heavy losses. *tkabbdaw xasaayir faadza.*
sufficient - *kaafi.*
to **suffocate** - *xtinag (i xtinaaq).* I nearly suffocated. *taqriiban ixtinagit.*
sugar - *šakar.* Please pass me the sugar. *ʔarjuuk, ɛabbur-li š-šakar.*
to **suggest - 1.** *qtiraz (i qtiraaz).* I suggest that we go to the movies. *ʔaqtiriz inruuz lis-siinama.* **2.** *lammaz (i talmiiz).* Are you suggesting that I'm wrong? *da-tlammiz bi-ʔanni ġalṭaan.* **3.** *δakkar (i taδkiir) b-, jaab (i jeeb) b-baal-.* Does this suggest anything to you? *haaδa yδakkrak ib-šii?* or *haaδa yjiib šii b-baalak?*
suggestion - *qtiraaz* pl. *-aat.* Your suggestion is very reasonable. *qtiraazak kulliš maɛquul.*
suicide - *ntizaar* pl. *-aat.* Suicide cases are rare here. *zawaadiθ il-intizaar naadra hnaa.*
to commit suicide - *ntizar (i ntizaar).* He committed suicide because he owed a lot of money. *ntizar li-ʔan čaan maṭluub ifluus ihwaaya.*
suit - 1. *qaaṭ* pl. *quuṭ, badla* pl. *-aat.* He needs a new suit. *yiztaaj qaaṭ jidiid.* **2.** *daɛwa* pl. *daɛaawi.* If you don't pay today, we shall bring suit. *ʔiδa ma-tidfaɛ il-ifluus il-yoom, nqiim daɛwa ɛaleek.* **3.** *nooɛ* pl. *ʔanwaaɛ, qisim* pl. *ʔaqsaam.* The four suits in cards are: hearts, diamonds, spades and clubs. *ʔanwaaɛ il-waraq il-ʔarbaɛa hiyya kuupa w-dinar w-maača w-sinak.*
**If he takes one, I'll follow suit. *ʔiδa yaaxuδ waazid, ʔaani ʔasawwi miθla.*
to suit - 1. *raδδa (i tarδiya).* It's hard to suit everybody. *ṣaɛub itraδδi kull in-naas.* **2.** *naasab (i munaasaba) t-, waalam (i muwaalama) t-.* These books are suited to the age of the children. *hal-kutub itnaasib ɛumr il-ʔaṭfaal.* **3.** *waafaq (i muwaafaqa), naasab (i), waalam (i).* Does this suit your taste? *haaδa ywaafiq δawqak?* -- Which day would suit you best? *yaa yoom ywaafqak ʔazsan?* **4.** *laag (u loog, liyaaga) l-.* Red doesn't suit you. *l-ʔazmar ma-yluug-lak.*
to be suited - 1. *laag (u).* Is she suited for this kind of work? *hiyya laayga l-hal-waδiifa?* **2.** *ṣilaz (a ṣalaaziyya).* This land isn't suited for growing wheat. *hal-ʔarδ ma-tiṣlaz il-ziraaɛat il-zunṭa.* **3.** *laaʔam (i mulaaʔama).* This climate isn't suited for people with TB. *hal-manaax ma-ylaaʔim il-masluuliin.*
**Suit yourself. *keefak.*
suitable - *mnaasib, ṣaaliz, mlaaʔim.* We can't find a suitable apartment. *ma-nigdar nilgi beet imnaasib.*
suitcase - *junṭa* pl. *junaṭ.* I have three suitcases and one trunk. *ɛindi tlaθ junaṭ w-ṣanduug waazid.*
sullen - *ɛabuus, mɛabbis.*
sultan - *sulṭaan* pl. *salaaṭiin.*
sultanate - *salṭana* pl. *-aat.*
sultry - *šarji**. It's awfully sultry today. *l-yoom il-hawa kulliš šarji.*
sum - 1. *majmuuɛ* pl. *-aat.* Just tell me the full sum. *bass gul-li l-majmuuɛ.* **2.** *mablaġ* pl. *mabaaliġ.* I still owe him a small sum. *baɛadni madyuun-la mablaġ iṣġayyir.*
to sum up - *laxxaṣ (i talxiiṣ) t-.* Let me sum up briefly. *xalli ʔalaxxiṣ b-ixtiṣaar.*
Sumeria - *soomar.*
Sumerian - *soomari** pl. *-iyyiin.* The Sumerians lived in lower Iraq. *s-soomariyyiin siknaw jinuub il-ɛiraaq.*
summary - *xulaaṣa* pl. *-aat, mulaxxaṣ* pl. *-aat.* Read the book and give me a summary. *ʔiqra l-iktaab w-inṭiini l-mulaxxaṣ.*
summer - 1. *ṣeef* pl. *ṣyaaf.* I spent three summers in the mountains. *biqeet itlaθ iṣyaaf bij-jibaal.* -- Does it get hot here in summer? *tṣiir zaarra hnaa biṣ-ṣeef?* **2.** *ṣeefi*, ṣayfi**. I need a new summer suit. *yirraad-li badla ṣeefiyya jdiida.*
summer resort - *maṣiif* pl. *maṣaayif.*
to **summon** - *ṣaaz (i ṣeez) n-.* The boss summoned me to his office. *r-raʔiis ṣaazni l-ġurufta.*
to summon up - *stajmaɛ (stijmaaɛ).* He couldn't summon up the courage to enter the cold water. *ma-gidar yistajmiɛ šajaaɛta zatta yxušš bil-maay il-baarid.*
sun - *šamis* pl. *šmuus.* The sun has just gone down. *š-šamis tawwha ġurbat.*
to sun - *šammas (i tšimmis), tšammas (a tšimmis).* We saw a snake sunning himself on a rock. *šifna fadd zayya da-tšammis nafisha ɛala ṣaxra.*
sunbeam - *šuɛaaɛ* (pl. *ʔašiɛɛat*) *šamis.*
Sunday - *yoom* (pl. *ʔayyaam*) *il-ʔazzad.*
sundown - *miġrib.* He usually comes home around sundown. *ɛaadatan yiji lil-beet wakt il-miġrib.*
sunlight - *δuwa šamis.*
Sunna - *sunna.* The Sunna consists of the deeds and sayings of the Prophet. *s-sunna hiyya ʔafɛaal w-ʔazaadiiθ in-nabi.*
Sunni, Sunnite - *sinni** pl. *-iyyiin, sinna.*
sunny - 1. *mišmis.* The front rooms are sunny. *l-ġuraf il-ʔamaamiyya mišmisa.* **2.** *ṣaazi.* We'll have a sunny day tomorrow. *baačir id-dinya raz-itṣiir ṣaazya.*
sunrise - *šuruuq.*
sunset - *l-ġuruub.*
sunshine - *ʔašiɛɛat šamis, δuwa šamis.* The sunshine is strong today. *ʔašiɛɛat iš-šamis qawiyya l-yoom.*
sunstroke - *δarbat* (pl. *-aat*) *šamis.* He died of sunstroke. *maat min δarbat šamis.*
superior - 1. *raʔiis* pl. *ruʔasaaʔ.* Is he your superior on the job? *huwwa raʔiisak biš-šuġuḷ?* **2.** *mumtaaz.* This is of superior quality. *haaδa min nooɛ mumtaaz.*
superiority - *tafawwuq.* Their superiority in numbers is weakened by their lack of experience. *tafawwuqhum bil-ɛadad qallat ʔahammiita l-ɛadam xibrathum.*
superiority complex - *murakkab iš-šuɛuur bil-ɛaδama.* He has a superiority complex. *ɛinda murakkab iš-šuɛuur bil-ɛaδama.*
superstition - *xuraafa* pl. *-aat.*
superstitious: **He's terribly superstitious. *hwaaya yiɛtiqid bil-xuraafaat.*
supervision - *ʔišraaf.* They are under constant supervision. *humma tazat ʔišraaf mustamirr.*
supper - *ɛaša* pl. *-aayaat.* I've been invited for supper. *ʔaani maɛzuum ɛala ɛaša.*

to have supper - *tεašša (a taεašši).* Would you like to have supper with us tonight? *tḥibb titεašša wiyyaana hal-leela?*
supplement - **1.** *mulḥaq* pl. *malaaḥiq.* The supplement to the phone book is small this year. *mulḥaq daliil it-talafoon has-sana ṣġayyir.* **2.** *ʔiḍaafa* pl. *-aat.* The doctor recommended using vitamins as a supplement to the diet. *ṭ-ṭabiib wuṣaf istiεmaal il-fiitaamiinaat ka-ʔiḍaafa ʔila l-ġiḏaaʔ.*
supply - **1.** *kammiyya* pl. *-aat.* We still have a big supply of bicycles. *baεad εidna kammiyya čibiira mnil-baaysiklaat.* **2.** *ḏaxiira* pl. *ḏaxaayir, maxzuun* pl. *-aat.* Our potato supply is almost gone. *ḏaxiiratna min il-puteeta taqriiban xilṣat.* **3.** *tajhiiz* pl. *-aat.* The hospital needs more medical supplies. *l-mustašfa yiḥtaaj tajhiizaat ṭibbiyya ʔakθar.*
to supply - **1.** *jahhaz (i tajhiiz) t-.* Our bakery supplies all the big hotels. *maxbazna yjahhiz kull il-ʔuteelaat ič-čibiira.* **2.** *zawwad (i tazwiid) t-.* He always supplies us with cigarettes. *huwwa daaʔiman yzawwidna bij-jigaayir.* **3.** *mawwan (i tamwiin) t-.* We have a contract to supply the police with ammunition. *εidna qunṭaraat inmawwin iš-šurṭa bil-εitaad.*
support - **1.** *taʔyiid.* You can count on my support. *tigdar tiεtimid εala taʔyiidi.* **2.** *dinga* pl. *dinag.* We've got to put supports under the bridge. *laazim inxalli dinag jawwa j-jisir.*
in support of - *taʔyiidan l-.* Can you offer any evidence in support of your statement. *tigdar itqaddim ʔay burhaan taʔyiidan il-εibaartak.*
to support - **1.** *ʔayyad (i taʔyiid) t-, sinad (i sanid) n-.* All the parties are supporting him. *kull il-ʔaḥzaab da-tʔayyida.* -- I'll support your election campaign. *raḥ-asnid ḥamiltak il-intixaabiyya.* **2.** *εaal (i ʔiεaala) n-, εayyaš (i taεyiiš) t-.* He has to support his parents. *laazim yεiil ʔumma w-ʔabuu.* **3.** *diεam (a daεim) n-.* Have you got evidence to support your claim? *εindak daliil yidεam iddiεaaʔak?*
to support oneself - *qaam (u qiyaam) ib-nafs^.* I have supported myself ever since I was fifteen. *qumit ib-nafsi min čaan εumri xmuṣṭaεaš sana.*
to **suppose** - *furaḍ (u faraḍ), ftiraḍ (i ftiraaḍ).* Let's suppose that I'm right. *xalli nifruḍ ʔaani ṣaḥiiḥ.* **2.** *ḍann (i ḍann).* I suppose so. *ʔaḍinn hiiči.*
supposed to - **1.** *mafruuḍ bii.* He's supposed to be rich. *l-mafruuḍ bii huwwa ġani.* **2.** *laazim.* I was supposed to go out tonight, but I'm too tired. *čaan laazim ʔaṭlaε hal-leela, laakin ʔaani kulliš taεbaan.*
supposing - *εala fariḍ, faraḍan.* Supposing he doesn't come tonight, what'll we do? *εala fariḍ ma-yiji hal-leela, š-insawwi?*
sure - **1.** *ʔakiid, muʔakkad.* That's a sure thing. *haaḏa šii ʔakiid.* **2.** *ṭabεan, maεluum, ʔakiid, muʔakkad.* Sure, I'd be glad to. *ṭabεan, εala εeeni.* **3.** *waḷḷa.* I'd sure like to see him again. *waḷḷa ʔariid asuufa marrt il-lux.* **4.** *mitʔakkid.* Are you sure of that? *ʔinta mitʔakkid min ḏaak?*
for sure - *bit-taʔkiid.* Be there by five o'clock for sure. *kuun ihnaak saaεa xamsa bit-taʔkiid.*
sure enough - *fiεlan.* You thought it would rain, and sure enough it did. *ʔinta gilit raḥ-tumṭur, w-fiεlan muṭrat.*
to be sure - *tʔakkad (a taʔakkud).* Be sure to come tomorrow. *tʔakkad tiji baačir.*
**He's sure to be back up nine o'clock. *bit-taʔkiid raḥ-yirjaε saaεa tisεa.*
to make sure - *tʔakkad (a taʔakkud), tḥaqqaq (a taḥaqquq).* Make sure that you take everything with you. *tʔakkad taaxuḏ kullši wiyyaak.* -- I just wanted to make sure that nothing was wrong. *bass ridit ʔatḥaqqaq ma-aku šii.*
surely - *bit-taʔkiid, ʔakiid.* Will you be there? Surely. *raḥ-itkuun ihnaak? bit-taʔkiid.* -- He can surely do that. *bit-taʔkiid yigdar ysawwi haaḏa.*
**I surely thought it would be finished. *činit mitʔakkid raḥ-tixḷaṣ.*
surface - *saṭiḥ* pl. *suṭuuḥ, wujih* pl. *wujuuh.*
surgeon - *jarraaḥ* pl. *-iin.*
surgery - *jiraaḥa.*
surplus - **1.** *ziyaada* pl. *-aat.* There is a surplus in the wheat crop this year that they don't know what to do with. *ʔaku ziyaada b-maḥṣuul il-ḥunṭa has-sana ma-yidruun s-ysawwuu biiha.* **2.** *zaayid.* The Labor Office has forbidden the company to discharge its surplus employees. *mudiiriyyat šuʔuun il-εummaal minεat il-istiġnaaʔ εann il-εummaal iz-zaaydiin.*

surprise - **1.** *mufaajaʔa* pl. *-aat.* I've got a surprise for you. *εindi mufaajaʔa ʔilak.* **2.** *dahša* pl. *-aat.* You'll get the surprise of your life. *raḥ-tindihiš dahša ma-ṣaar miθilha.* or *raḥ-tindihiš ʔakbar dahša b-ḥayaatak.*
to catch by surprise - *faajaʔ (i mufaajaʔa) t-, baaġat (i mubaaġata) t-.* The rain caught me by surprise. *l-muṭar faajaʔni.* or *l-muṭar baaġatni.*
to take by surprise - *ʔaxaḏ (u) εala ġafla, baaġat (i mubaaġata) t-.* You took me by surprise. *ʔaxaḏitni εala ġafla.* or *baaġatitni tamaaman.*
to surprise - *ʔadhaš (i dahša) n-, εajjab (i εajab) t-.* I wanted to surprise you. *ridit ʔadihšak.* or *ridit ʔaεajjbak.* -- Nothing surprises me any more. *ma-aku šii yεajjibni baεad.* -- I'm surprised at you. *ʔaani mitεajjib εaleek.* -- I'm not surprised at anything you do. *š-ma tsawwi ma-yidhišni.*
to **surrender** - **1.** *sallam (i tasliim) t-.* He surrendered to the police. *sallam liš-šurṭa.* **2.** *staslam (i stislaam).* The enemy surrendered. *l-εadu staslam.*
to **surround** - **1.** *ḥaaṭ (i ʔiḥaaṭa) n-.* A high fence surrounds the house. *siyaaj εaali yḥiiṭ il-beet.* **2.** *ṭawwaq (u taṭwiiq) t-, ḥaaṣar (i ḥiṣaar, muḥaaṣata) t-.* We're surrounded. *ʔiḥna mṭawwaqiin.*
suspect - *mašbuuh* pl. *-iin.* He's a suspect in that case. *huwwa mašbuuh ib-ðiič il-qaḍiyya.*
to suspect - *šakk (u šakk) b-, rtaab (a rtiyaab) b-, štibah (i štibaah) b-.* Do you suspect anything? *tšukk ib-šii? or tirtaab ib-šii?*
to **suspend** - **1.** *waqqaf (i tawqiif) t-.* The bank has suspended payment due to the robbery. *l-bang waqqaf id-dafiε b-sabab il-booga.* **2.** *fuṣal (u faṣil) n-, ṭirad (u ṭarid) n-.* He was suspended for a year. *nfuṣal il-muddat sana.* -- He was suspended from school for a week. *nṭirad imnil-madrasa l-muddat isbuuε.* **3.** *siḥab (a saḥib) n-, waqqaf (i).* The department of health suspended the restaurant's license for a month. *wizaart iṣ-ṣiḥḥa siḥbat ʔijaazat il-maṭεam il-muddat šahar.* **4.** *sadd (i sadd) n-, εaṭṭal (i taεṭiil).* The government suspended the newspaper. *l-ḥukuuma saddat ij-jariida.* **5.** *εallag (i taεliig) t-.* The worksmen suspended the chandelier from the ceiling by a heavy chain. *l-εummaal εalligaw iθ-θirayya mnis-saguf ib-silsila qawiyya.*
suspense - *ḥiira.* I can't stand the suspense any longer. *ma-ʔatḥammal il-ḥiira baεad.*
suspicion - *šakk* pl. *škuuk.* What aroused your suspicion? *šinu ʔaθaar šakkak?* or ***š-xallaak tirtaab?*
suspicious - **1.** *muriib* pl. *iin.* That place looks suspicious. *hal-maḥall ybayyin muriib.* **2.** *šakkaak* pl. *-iin.* My husband is very suspicious. *rajli kulliš šakkaak.*
**I immediately got suspicious. *ḥaalan šakkeet.* or *ḥaalan irtaabeet.*
swallow - **1.** *jurεa* pl. *-aat, juraε.* I only took one swallow. *širabit bass jurεa waḥda.* **2.** *bint (*pl. *banaat) sinduhind.* The swallows come in the spring and build their nests. *banaat sinduhind yjuun bir-rabiiε w-yibnuun iεšuušhum.*
to swallow - *bilaε (a baliε) n-.* My throat hurts me so much I can't swallow anything. *balεuumi hal-gadd yoojaεni ma-agdar ablaε šii.*
**He swallowed the bait hook, line and sinker. *l-ḥiila εubrat εalee.*
swamp - *hoor* pl. *ʔahwaar, mustanqaε* pl. *-aat.* How far does the swamp go? *l-hoor išgadd yimtadd?*
to swamp - **1.** *ġirag (a ġarig).* I was swamped with work last week. *ġiragit biš-šuġuḷ l-isbuuε il-faat.* **2.** *tiras (i taris) n-.* A large wave swamped our boat. *fadd mooja čibiira tirsat balamna maay.*
swarm - *jamaaεa* pl. *-aat.* They saw a swarm of bees. *šaafaw jamaaεat naḥal.*
to swarm - *εajj (i εajj).* The swamp is swarming with mosquitoes. *l-mustanqaε yεijj bil-baqq.*
to **sway** - **1.** *htazz (a htizaaz).* The trees swayed in the wind. *l-ʔašjaar ihtazzat bil-hawa.* **2.** *ʔaθθar (i taʔθiir) t- εala.* No one can sway him once his mind is made up. *maḥḥad yigdar yʔaθθir εalee baεad-ma ysawwi fikra.*
to **swear** - **1.** *ḥilaf (i ḥalif) n-, ʔaqsam (i qasam) n-.* She swears she's telling the truth. *tiḥlif da-tguul iṣ-ṣudug.* -- Do you swear to that? *tiḥlif εala haaḏa?* or *tiqsim εala haaḏa?* **2.** *šattam (i taštiim) t-, sabb (i sabb) n-.* He swears constantly. *yšattim εala ṭuul.* or *ysibb εala ṭuul.*
to swear in - *ḥallaf (i taḥliif).* They swore the

witness in on the Koran, and later began asking him questions. *ẓallifaw iš-šaahid bil-qur?aan w-baƐdeen gaamaw yis?aluu ?as?ila.*
sweat - *Ɛarag.* He wiped the sweat from his brow. *misaẓ il-Ɛarag min guṣṣṭa.*
to sweat - *Ɛirag (a Ɛarag).* This kind of work makes you sweat. *han-nooƐ imniš-šuġuḷ yxalliik tiƐrag.*
sweaty - *Ɛargaan.* I'm sweaty all over. *?aani Ɛargaan min foog li-jawwa.*
to **sweep** - **1.** *kinas (u kanis) n-.* Did you sweep the bedroom? *kinasti ġurfat in-noom?* **2.** *siẓal (a saẓil) n- b-.* Her dress sweeps the ground. *nafnuufha da-yisẓal bil-gaaƐ.*
to sweep away - *ktisaẓ (i ktisaaẓ).* The flood waters swept away the town. *ṃaay il-fayaḍaan iktisaẓ l-wlaaya.*
sweet - **1.** *ẓilu.* The dates are very sweet. *t-tamur ẓilu kulliš.* **2.** *ẓabbuub.* She is a sweet girl. *hiyya bint ẓabbuuba.*
sweetheart - *ẓabiib* pl. *?aẓibbaa?.* She's his sweetheart. *hiyya ẓabiibta.*
sweets - *ẓalawiyyaat.* I don't care much for sweets. *ma-aẓibb il-ẓalawiyyaat.*
swell - *xooš.* She's a swell person. *hiyya xooš ?aadmiyya.*
to swell - *wuram (a waram).* My finger is all swollen. *?iṣibƐi kulla waarum.*
swelling - *waram.* Has the swelling gone down? *l-waram nizal?*
to **swim** - *sibaẓ (a sibiẓ, sibaaẓa).* Do you know how to swim? *tuƐruf tisbaẓ?*
swimming - *sibaaẓa.* Swimming is the only sport I enjoy. *s-sibaaẓa hiyya r-riyaaḍa l-waẓiida lli ?atwannas biiha.*
swimming pool - *masbaẓ* pl. *masaabiẓ.*
swing - *marjiiẓa, marjuuẓa* pl. *maraajiiẓ.* We have a swing in our garden. *Ɛidna marjuuẓa b-ẓadiiqatna.*
in full swing - *b-?awj.* The party is in full swing. *l-ẓafla b-?awijha.*
to swing - **1.** *marjaẓ (i tmirjiẓ, marjaẓa) t-.* You swing me, and then I'll swing you. *?inta marjiẓni w-baƐdeen ?aani ?amarjiẓak.* **2.** *tmarjaẓ (a tamarjuẓ).* You'll fall off if you swing so hard. *toogaƐ ?iḍa titmarjaẓ hal-gadd ẓeel.* **3.** *hazz (i hazz) n-.* She swings her arms when she walks. *thizz iideeha lamma timši.*
to swing around - *furr (u farr) n-, deewar (u tdeewur).* Swing the car around. *furr is-sayyaara.*
switch - **1.** *swiič* pl. *-aat.* The light switch is next to the door. *swiič iḍ-ḍuwa yamm il-baab.* **2.** *mugaṣṣ* pl. *-aat.* The last car jumped the track at the switch. *?aaxir faargoon ṭilaƐ imnis-sikka yamm il-mugaṣṣ.*
to switch - **1.** *ẓawwal (i taẓwiil) t-.* The train was switched to another track. *l-qiṭaar itẓawwal ?ila ġeer sikka.* **2.** *daar (i deer) n-.* Switch the radio to short wave. *diir ir-raadyo Ɛal-mooja l-qaṣiira.* **3.** *baadal (i mubaadala) t-.* Let's switch places. *xalli nitbaadal ib-mukaanaatna.*
**I don't know how we switched coats. *ma-aƐruf išloon ?axaḍna qappuuṭ waaẓid il-laax bil-ġalaṭ.*
to switch off - *ṭaffa (i taṭfiya) t-.* Switch off the light. *ṭaffi ḍ-ḍuwa.*
to switch on - *šiƐal (i šaƐil) n-.* Switch on the light. *?išƐil iḍ-ḍuwa.*
sword - *seef* pl. *syuuf.*
syllable - *maqṭaƐ* pl. *maqaaṭiƐ.* The accent is on the first syllable. *t-ta?kiid Ɛala l-maqṭaƐ il-?awwal.*
symbol - *ramiz* pl. *rumuuz.*
symbolic - *ramzi*.* That sign has the same symbolic meaning all over the world. *hal-?išaara biiha nafs il-maƐna r-ramzi b-kull il-Ɛaalam.*
to **symbolize** - *rimaz (i ramiz).* The statue over there symbolizes our struggle against imperialism. *hat-timθaal yirmiz ?ila mukaafaẓatna lil-istiƐmaar.*
to **sympathize with** - **1.** *šaarak (i mušaaraka) b-šuƐuur.* I sympathize with you. *?ašaarkak ib-šuƐuurak.* **2.** *Ɛiṭaf (u Ɛaṭuf) Ɛala.* I sympathize with the flood victims. *?aƐṭuf Ɛala l-mutaḍarririin bil-fayaḍaan.*
sympathy - *Ɛaṭuf.* I have no sympathy for her. *ma-Ɛindi ?ay Ɛaṭuf Ɛaleeha.* or ***gaḷbi ma-yinkisir Ɛaleeha.*
Syria - *suurya.*
Syrian - **1.** *suuri* pl. *-iyyiin, šaami* pl. *-iyyiin.* There were a number of Syrians on the boat. *čaan ?aku Ɛiddat suuriyyiin bil-markab.* **2.** *suuri*, šaami*.* He speaks the Syrian dialect very well. *yiẓči l-lahja s-suuriyya kulliš zeen.*
system - **1.** *niḍaam* pl. *?anḍima.* They're hoping to change their system of government. *da-yit?ammaluun ybaddiluun niḍaam ẓukuumathum.* **2.** *jihaaz* pl. *?ajhiza.* We're studying the respiratory system. *da-nidrus jihaaz it-tanaffus.* **3.** *?isluub* pl. *?asaaliib.* I have a better system. *Ɛindi ?isluub ?aẓsan.* **4.** *jisim* pl. *?ajsaam.* My system can't take it. *jismi ma-yitẓammala.*
systematic - *mnaḍḍam.* He's very systematic. *huwwa kulliš imnaḍḍam.*
systematically - *b-ṣuura mnaḍḍama.* You'll have to work more systematically. *laazim tištuġuḷ ib-ṣuura mnaḍḍama ?akθar.*

T

tab - **1.** *Ɛalaama* pl. *-aat.* The tab on this file is worn out. *l-Ɛalaama maal hal-faayil imšaggiga.* **2.** *ẓsaab* pl. *-aat.* How much is the tab? *šgadd il-iẓsaab?*
to keep tabs on - *raaqab (i muraaqaba).* The police are keeping tabs on him. *š-šurṭa da-yraaqbuu.*
table - **1.** *meez* pl. *myuuza.* Put the table in the middle of the room. *ẓuṭṭ il-meez ib-nuṣṣ il-gubba.* **2.** *jadwal* pl. *jadaawil.* The figures are given in the table on page 20. *l-?arqaam mawjuuda bij-jadwal ib-ṣafẓa Ɛišriin.*
**The tables are turned. *nƐiksat il-?aaya.*
to table - *?ajjal (i) in-naḍar b-.* Why has the committee tabled the motion? *lweeš il-lujna ?ajjilat in-naḍar bil-iqtiraa?*
tablecloth - *čarčaf (pl. čaraačif) meez, mšammaƐ* pl. *-aat* (oilcloth).
table of contents - *fihras* pl. *fahaaris, jadwal (pl. jadaawil) muẓtawiyaat.*
tablespoon - *xaašuuga (pl. xwaašiig) maal ?akil, qaašuuga (pl. qwaašiig) maal ?akil.*
tablet - **1.** *daftar (pl. dafaatir) miswadda.* I've used a whole tablet of paper on this case. *xallaṣit daftar miswadda kaamil Ɛala hal-qaḍiyya.* **2.** *ẓabbaaya* pl. *-aat, ẓubuub* coll. *ẓabb.* The doctor told me to take two tablets before each meal. *ṭ-ṭabiib gal-li ?ablaƐ ẓabbaayteen gabḷ il-?akil.*
table tennis - *ṗing ṗoong.*
taboo - *mẓarram.* It's taboo for girls to go out alone at night. *mẓarram Ɛal-banaat yṭilƐuun bil-leel waẓẓadhum.*
tack - **1.** *danbuus* pl. *danaabiis.* Tacks don't hold well on this bulletin board. *d-danaabiis ma-tilzam zeen Ɛala hal-looẓa maal il-?iƐlaanaat.* **2.** *bismaar* pl. *basaamiir.* This tack came out of the sofa. *nšilaƐ ḥal-bismaar imnil-qanafa.*
to tack - *danbas (itdinbis).* The tailor tacked the sleeve on the coat during the last fitting. *l-xayyaaṭ danbas ir-ridaan bis-sitra b-?aaxir iṗraawa.* -- Tack this notice on the bulletin board. *danbis hal-iƐlaan ib-looẓat il-iƐlaanaat.*
tackle - *ġaraaḍ.* I brought my fishing tackle along. *jibit ġaraaḍ ṣeed is-simač wiyyaaya.*
to tackle - *Ɛaalaj (i muƐaalaja).* You've tackled the problem the wrong way. *Ɛaalajit il-muškila b-ṭariiqa muu ṣaẓiiẓa.* or *Ɛaalajt il-muškila ġalaṭ.*
**The policeman tackled the thief outside the house. *š-šurṭi kumaš il-ẓaraami w-waggaƐa barra l-beet.*
tact - *labaaqa.* This situation calls for a certain amount of tact. *hal-ẓaala tiṭṭallab išwayya labaaqa.*
tactic - *taktiik* pl. *-aat, ?isluub* pl. *?asaaliib.* He's still using the same old tactics to get his own way. *baƐda da-yistaƐmil nafs it-taktiikaat ẓatta yẓaṣṣil illi yriida.* -- The commander changed his tactics to deal with guerrilla warfare. *l-qaa?id baddal ?asaaliiba l-ẓarbiyya ẓatta tlaa?im ẓarb il-Ɛiṣaabaat.*
tag - *biṭaaqa* pl. *-aat.* Put a tag on the package.

ħuṭṭ biṭaaqa ʕar-ruzma.
to tag after - *liħag (a laħig).* His son has been tagging after him all day. *ʔibna liħaga ṭuul in-nahaar.*
**Can I tag along? *ʔagdar aruuħ wiyyaak?*
tail - 1. *δeel* pl. *δyuul.* My dog has a short tail. *čalbi ʕinda δeel igṣayyir.* **2.** *δyaal* pl. *-aat.* Put your shirt tail inside your pants. *xaššis iδyaal θoobak bil-ṗanṭiruun.*
**I can't make head or tail of what he says. *ħčaayta ma-biiha laa raas w-laa čaʕab.*
**Heads or tails? *ṭurra loo kitba?* or *šiir loo xaṭṭ?*
at the tail end - *b-ʔaaxir, b-čaʕab.* We arrived at the tail end of the first act. *wuṣalna b-ʔaaxir il-faṣl il-ʔawwal.* -- We were at the tail end of the line. *činna b-čaʕab xaṭṭ il-intiδaar.*
to tail - *tibaʕ (a tabiʕ) n-, liħag (a laħig) n-.* There's a car tailing us! *ʔaku sayyaara da-titbaʕna!*
tail light - *baaklaayt* pl. *-aat, ḍuwa warraani* pl. *ḍuwaayaat warraaniyya.* I'm having the tail light on my car fixed. *da-aṣalliħ il-baaklaayt maal sayyaarti.*
tailor - *xayyaaṭ* pl. *-iin, xyaayiiṭ.* Where is there a good tailor? *ween ʔaku xayyaaṭ zeen?*
to tailor - *xayyaṭ (i xiyaaṭa) t-.* He tailored the suit the way I wanted it. *xayyaṭ il-badla miθil-ma riditha.*
tailoring - *xyaaṭa, xyaaṭ.* Tailoring is a trade which brings in good money. *l-ixyaaṭa mihna tjiib xooš ifluus.* -- The tailoring costs much more than the material. *l-ixyaaṭa tkallif ihwaaya ʔakθar imnil-iqmaaš.*
tailor-made - *tifṣaal.* All his clothes are tailor-made. *kull ihduuma tifṣaal.*
tails - *fraak.* We have to wear tails to the party this evening. *laazim nilbas ifraak bil-ħafla hal-leela.*
taint - 1. *ṣnaan.* The milk has an onion taint to it. *l-ħaliib bii ṣnaan buṣal.* **2.** *laṭxa* pl. *-aat, waṣma* pl. *-aat.* This will be a taint on my reputation. *haaδi raħ-itṣiir laṭxa b-sumuʕti.*
**Cover the butter or the onions will taint it. *ġaṭṭi z-zibid ħatta la-yaaxuδ ṭaʕam buṣal.*
take - *daxal.* The take ran to fifty thousand dollars. *d-daxal waṣṣal ʔila xamsiin ʔalf doolaar.*
to take - 1. *ʔaxaδ (u ʔaxiδ) n-.* Who took my ties? *minu ʔaxaδ booyinbaaġaati?* -- Who took first prize? *minu ʔaxaδ ij-jaaʔiza l-ʔuula?* -- You can take it back; I won't need it any more. *tigdar taaxuδha; baʕad ma-aħtaajha.* -- Who took his place? *minu ʔaxaδ makaana?* -- I'm taking Ahmad to the movies with me. *ʔaani maaxiδ ʔaħmad lis-siinama wiyyaaya.* -- We took many pictures. *ʔaxaδna hwaaya ṣuwar.* -- Take the measurements of this table. *ʔuxuδ qiyaasaat hal-meez.* -- We always take a nap after lunch. *ʔiħna daaʔiman naaxuδ ġafwa baʕd il-ġada.* -- Did the doctor take your temperature this morning? *ṭ-ṭabiib ʔaxaδ ħaraartak hal-yoom iṣ-ṣubuħ?* -- Let's take a quick dip. *xalli naaxuδ-inna fadd ġaṭṭa.* -- We've taken all the necessary precautions. *ʔaxaδna kull il-iħtiyaaṭaat il-laazma.* -- Take my advice. *ʔuxuδ naṣiiħti.* or *ʔiqbil naṣiiħti.* -- Don't take it so seriously! *la-taaxuδha hal-gadd jidd.* -- That takes too much time. *haay taaxuδ ihwaaya wakit.* or ***haay tiħtaaj ihwaaya wakit.* -- He takes too many liberties. *yaaxuδ ħurriita ʔakθar imnil-laazim.* -- We'll take the room with twin beds. *raħ-naaxuδ il-ġurfa ʔumm ifraašeen.* -- My rook will take your pawn. *qaliʕti raħ-taaxuδ ij-jundi maalak.* or ***raħ-ʔagtul ij-jundi maalak bil-qalʕa.* -- Did you take these figures from the latest report? *ʔaxaδit hal-arqaam imnit-taqriir il-ʔaxiir?* **2.** *nraad (a).* It won't take much gas to get there. *ma-yinraad ihwaaya ḅaanziin ħatta nooṣal l-ihnaak.* -- That doesn't take much brains. *haay ma-yinraad-ilha hwaaya muxx.* **3.** *lizam (a lazim).* She took the child by the hand and led him across the street. *lizmat ʔiid ij-jaahil w-ʕabbrata iš-šaariʕ.* **4.** *wadda (i).* What else do you want to take along with you? *baʕad š-itriid itwaddi wiyyaak?* **5.** *šaal (i šeel).* My last smallpox vaccination didn't take. *ʔaaxir marra ḍirabit jidri ma-šaal.* **6.** *sawwa (i taswiya).* The government is going to take a census next year. *l-ħukuuma raħ-itsawwi ʔiħṣaaʔ infuus is-sana j-jaaya.* **7.** *liqa (i ʔilqaaʔ).* Why don't you take a look at the house and tell me what you think? *leeš ma-tilqi naḍra ʕal-beet w-itgul-li raʔyak?*
8. *tħammal (a taħammul).* I'll take the responsibility. *ʔaani raħ-atħammal il-masʔuuliyya.* -- Why should I take the blame for his mistake? *leeš laazim atħammal il-loom ʕan ʔaġlaaṭa?* **9.** *rikab (u rikib) b-, raaħ (u rooħ) b-.* Why don't you take the bus? *leeš ma-tirkab bil-ṗaaṣ?* **10.** *bilaʕ (a baliʕ) n-.* Take one pill before each meal. *ʔiblaʕ ħabbaaya gabuḷ kull wajbat ʔakil.* **11.** *ṭawwal (i taṭwiil).* How long will the trip from here to the market take? *r-rooħa minnaa lis-suug išgadd iṭṭawwil?* **12.** *fiham (a fahim), ʔawwal (i taʔwiil).* He took my remark the wrong way. *fiham qaṣdi bil-ġalaṭ.* or *ʔawwal iħčaayti bil-ġalaṭ.*
**Take it easy! You've got all day. *la-tistaʕjil; ʕindak il-yoom kulla.*
**Take it easy! Don't let that upset you. *la-tdiir baal; la-txalli haaδa yziʕjak.*
**He took me at my word. *sawwa ħčaayti maal.*
**How did he take to your suggestion? *ʕijaba qtiraaħak?* or *giṭaʕ ʕaqla b-iqtiraaħak?* or *š-čaan raʔya b-iqtiraaħak?*
**I take it you're in trouble again. *ybayyin ʔinta mwarriṭ nafsak marra lux.*
**I took him down a peg or two. *xalleeta yuʕruf qadra šinu.* or *kisarit xašma šwayya.*
**She took the stand as witness for the defense. *wugfat ka-šaahda lid-difaaʕ.*
**Take a look! Isn't that a beautiful horse? *baawiʕ! hal-iħṣaan muu ħilu?*
**They took the town by storm. *hijmaw fadd hajma w-iħtallaw il-wlaaya.*
**How much will you take for your car? *šgadd itriid ib-sayyaartak?*
to take after - 1. *ṭilaʕ (a ṭuluuʕ) ʕala.* He takes after his father. *ṭaaliʕ ʕala ʔabuu.* **2.** *rikaḍ (u rikiḍ) wara, ʕala.* She took after the dog with a stick. *šaalat il-ʕuuda w-rikaḍat wara č-čalib.*
to take away - 1. *ʔaxaδ (u ʔaxiδ) n-, wadda (i).* The police took him away. *š-šurṭa ʔaxδoo.* or *š-šurṭa waddoo.* -- She took my books away with her. *waddat kutbi wiyyaaha.* **2.** *waxxar (i tawxiir) t-.* Please take the dog away from the table. *baḷḷa waxxir ič-čalib imnil-meez.* **3.** *ṭiraħ (a ṭariħ) min.* Take three away from five. *ʔiṭraħ itlaaθa min xamsa.* **4.** *šaal (i šeel).* Please take those dirty cups away. *baḷḷa ma-tšiil hal-kuubaat il-waṣxa.* **5.** *ħaṭṭ (u ħaṭṭ).* His eccentric behavior takes away from his prestige among the students. *tṣarrufa š-šaaδδ yħuṭṭ min qadra been it-talaamiiδ.*
to take back - 1. *siħab (a saħib).* I take back what I said. *ʔasħab kalaami.* **2.** *rajjaʕ (i tarjiiʕ) t-.* You can take it back to the tailor. *tigdar itrajjiʕha lil-xayyaaṭ.* -- We already hired someone else, so we can't take him back now. *ʕayyanna waaħid ġeera w-baʕad ma-nigdar inrajjʕa.*
**This music takes me back to my days in Paris. *hal-mawsiiqa tδakkirni b-ʔayyaam ṗaariis.*
to take down - 1. *nazzal (i tanziil) t-.* Take the picture down from the wall. *nazzil iṣ-ṣuura min ʕal-ħaayiṭ.* **2.** *sajjal (i tasjiil) t-.* Take down my address. *sajjil ʕinwaani.* **3.** *ḍubaṭ (u ḍabuṭ) n-.* Who's taking down the minutes? *minu da-yiḍbuṭ ij-jalsa?*
to take for - *tṣawwar (a taṣawwur).* Sorry, I took you for someone else. *l-ʕafu, tṣawwartak ġeer waaħid.* or ***l-ʕafu, ʕabaali ġeer waaħid.* -- What do you take me for? A liar? *š-da-tṣawwarni? čaδδab?* or ***š-ʕabaalak? ʔaani čaδδaab?*
to take in - 1. *sawwa (i taswiya)* We take in about 30 dinars a day. *da-nsawwi ħawaali θlaaθiin diinaar bil-yoom.* **2.** *gaṣṣaf (i tagṣiif).* Will you take this dress in at the waist? *baḷḷa ma-tgaṣṣfiin han-nafnuuf min yamm il-xiṣir?* **3.** *tkallaf (a takalluf) b-.* Our uncle took us in after our parents died. *ʕammna tkallaf biina baʕad-ma maataw ʔabuuna w-ʔummna.* **4.** *tqašmar (a qašmara).* Have you been taken in again? *tqašmarit marra lux?* **5.** *raaqab (i muraaqaba), laaħaδ (i mulaaħaδa).* He sat there, taking it all in. *giʕad ihnaak yraaqib kullši.* **6.** *ʔaxaδ (u ʔaxiδ) n-.* The police took him in for questioning. *š-šurṭa ʔaxδoo lil-markaz lit-taħqiiq.*
to take off - 1. *ʔaxaδ (u) ʔijaaza.* I'm taking off for the rest of the day. *raħ-ʔaaxuδ ʔijaaza baqiit in-nahaar.* **2.** *ṭaar (i ṭayaraan)* When does the plane take off? *šwakit iṭṭiir iṭ-ṭiyyaara?* **3.** *nizaʕ (a naziʕ).* I'm going to take off my coat. *raħ-anzaʕ il-qappuuṭ maali.* **4.** *nazzal (i tanziil), naggaṣ (i tangiiṣ).* He took a few dollars off the

price for me. *nazzal-li čam doolaar imnis-siεir.*
to take on - 1. *lizam (a lazim) n-.* I took on a new job yesterday. *lizamit šağla jdiida l-baarza.* **2.** *šağğal (i tašğiil) t-, εayyan (i taεyiin) t-.* I hear the factory is taking on some new men. *smaεit il-maεmal raz-yšağğil εummaal jiddad.* **3.** *ʔaxaδ (u ʔaxiδ).* The situation has taken on a new aspect since then. *min δaak il-wakit il-hassa l-zaala ʔaxδat maδhar jidiid.* **4.** *δaaf (i ʔiδaafa) n-.* We'll take on two more coaches at the next station. *raz-inδiif fargooneen lux bil-mazatta j-jaaya.*
**I'll take him on any day! *ʔaani ʔanaazla ʔay yoom.* or *ʔaani mistaεidd-la šwakit-ma yriid.*
to take out - 1. *tallaε (i tatliiε) t-.* Did you take the meat out of the refrigerator? *tallaεt il-lazm imniθ-θallaaja?* -- Why do you take it out on me? *leeš da-ttalliεha b-raasi?* or *leeš da-ttalliε zeefak biyya.* **2.** *wadda (i) b-.* When did he take his children out last? *šwakit čaanat ʔaaxir marra wadda jhaala b-fadd mukaan?*
to take over - *stilam (i stilaam).* He took over my job. *stilam šuğli.* -- Who has taken over the management of the factory? *minu stilam ʔidaarat il-maεmal?*
to take up - 1. *ʔaxaδ (u ʔaxiδ).* That takes up a lot of space. *haay taaxuδ ihwaaya makaan.* **2.** *saεεad (i tasεiid).* Please take this book up with you when you go. *balla ma-tsaεεid hal-iktaab wiyyaak min itruuz foog?* **3.** *εaašar (i muεaašara).* I wouldn't take up with those people if I were you. *ʔaani loo b-makaanak ma-ʔaεaašir δoola.* or *ʔaani loo b-makaanak ma-ʔamši wiyya δoola n-naas.* or *ʔaani loo b-makaanak ma-ʔatεaašir wiyya δoola n-naas.* **4.** *bida (i badi).* Can you take up where he left off? *tigdar tibdi mneen-ma battal?* **5.** *tδaakar (i taδaakur) εan.* You'll have to take that matter up with someone else. *laazim titδaakar wiyya ğeeri εan hal-mawδuuε.*
taken - 1. *maʔxuuδ.* All seats on the bus were taken. *kull il-maqaaεid bil-paas maʔxuuδa.* or ***l-paas imqappuṭ.* **2.** *mazjuuz.* All seats are taken for tonight's performance. *kull il-maqaaεid il-zaflat hal-leela mazjuuza.* **3.** *muğram.* She's really taken with that dress. *hiyya zaqiiqatan muğrama b-δaak in-nafnuuf.*
taking - *ʔaxiδ.* Taking pictures is forbidden here. *ʔaxiδ is-suwar mamnuuε ihnaa.*
**She has very taking ways. *tasarrufaatha tiszar l-waazid.*
tale - 1. *saalfa* pl. *swaalif, saaluufa* pl. *-aat, swaaliif.* Children love to listen to fairy tales. *j-jihaal yzibbuun yismaεuun swaalif.* **2.** *qussa* pl. *qusas.* She made up that tale to get even with them. *xtirεat hal-qussa zatta taaxuδ zeefha minhum.*
talebearer - *fattaan* pl. *-iin, -a; waaši* pl. *-iin, wušaat.*
talent - 1. *mawhiba* pl. *mawaahib.* He has a talent for mathematics. *εinda mawhiba bir-riyaaδiyyaat.* -- She discovered her artistic talent late in life. *ktišfat mawhibatha l-fanniyya b-ʔawaaxir εumurha.* **2.** *qaabliyya* pl. *-aat.* He has a talent for getting into trouble. *εinda qaabliyya l-xalq il-mašaakil il-nafsa.* or ***ywaggiε nafsa b-mašaakil.*
**I never saw so much talent on one program. *b-εumri ma-šaayif hal-gadd naas mawhuubiin ib-fadd manhaj.*
talk - 1. *zadiiθ* pl. *ʔazaadiiθ.* His talk was much too long. *zadiiθa čaan ʔatwal imnil-laazim.* -- Her marriage is the talk of the town. *zawaajha saar zadiiθ il-majaalis.* **2.** *zači.* Oh, that's just talk! *haaδa bass zači.* -- What kind of talk is that? *haaδa šloon zači?* or *šinu hal-zači?*
to have a talk with - *ziča (i zači) wiyya, zaača (i).* I had a long talk with him. *začeet wiyyaa zači tuwiil.* or *zaačeeta fadd mudda twiila.*
**I'd like to have a talk with you. *ʔard azči wiyyaak išwayya.* or *ʔard atzaača wiyyaak išwayya.*
to talk - *ziča (i zači).* Don't you think he talks too much? *ma-tiεtiqid huwwa yizči hwaaya?* -- How can he talk with food stuffed in his mouth? *šloon yigdar yizči w-zalga matruus ʔakil?*
to talk into - *qannaε (i taqniiε), sawwa (i) l-wahas.* Do you suppose we can talk them into coming with us? *tiεtiqid nigdar inqanniεhum yjuun wiyyaana?* or *tiεtiqid nigdar insawwii-lhum wahas yjuun wiyyaana?*
to talk nonsense - *liğa (i lağwa, laaği).* Don't talk nonsense! *la-tilği* or *la-tizči zači faariğ.*

to talk over - *bizaθ (a baziθ, daanaš (i mudaanaša), tδaakar (a muδaakara).* Talk the matter over with him. *ʔibzaθ il-mawδuuε wiyyaa.* or *tδaakar wiyyaa bil-mawδuuε.* -- Let's talk it over. *xal-nitdaanaš biiha.*
talkative - *θarθaar* pl. *-iin, lağwi* pl. *-iyya.* I don't like real talkative people. *ma-azibb iθ-θarθaariin.*
**Our son knows how to speak, but he's just not talkative. *ʔibinna yuεruf yizči, bass ma-yizči hwaaya.*
tall - 1. *tuwiil* pl. *twaal.* She's tall and thin. *hiyya twiila w-δiεiifa.* **2.** *εaali.* There aren't many tall buildings in that city. *ma-aku hwaaya bnaayaat εaalya b-δiič l-wlaaya.*
**He's one meter, and sixty centimeters tall. *tuula matir w-sittiin santimatir.*
**How tall are you? *šgadd tuulak?*
tallow - *šazam.*
to **tally -** *εadd (i εadd) n-.* They have a machine to tally the votes. *εidhum makiina l-εadd il-ʔaswaat.*
tamarind - *tamur hind.* Tamarind makes a refreshing drink. *šarbat tamur hind kulliš munεiš.*
tamarisk - *ʔaθil.*
tambourine - *daff* pl. *dfuuf.*
tame - 1. *ʔaliif.* The birds there are so tame they eat out of your hand. *t-tuyuur ihnaak hal-gadd ʔaliifa taakul min ʔiid il-waazid.* **2.** *haadiʔ.* All in all, it was a pretty tame evening. *b-suura εaamma čaanat fadd leela haadʔa.*
to become tame - *ʔilaf (i ʔulfa).* Birds become tame if you feed them every day. *t-tuyuur yiʔlifuun ʔiδa ttaεεumhum yoomiyya.*
to tame - *rawwaδ (i tarwiiδ) t-.* He tames wild animals. *yrawwiδ zaywaanaat wazšiyya.* -- Lions are easily tamed. *s-sibaaε titrawwaδ ib-suhuula.*
to tame down - *εiqal (a εaqil), hidaʔ (a huduuʔ).* He's tamed down a lot since he left school. *εiqal ihwaaya baεad-ma tirak il-madrasa.*
to **tamp -** *dačč (i dačč) n-.* Tamp the earth down well before you lay the tile. *dičč il-gaaε zeen gabul-ma tzutt il-kaaši.*
tamper - *madagga* pl. *-aat.* Do you have a tamper I can borrow? *εindak madagga ʔagdar ʔatdaayanha?*
to tamper - *liεab (a liεib).* We caught him tampering with the mail. *lizamnaa yilεab bil-makaatiib.* -- Don't tamper with the radio. *la-tilεab bir-raadyo.*
tan - 1. *samaar.* Where did you get that nice tan? *mneen jaak has-samaar?* **2.** *gahwaaʔi ʔaačuğ, joozi ʔaačuğ.* I lost my tan gloves. *δayyaεit ičfuufi l-gahwaaʔiyya ʔaačuğ.*
to tan - 1. *dibağ (u dbaağa, dabuğ), dabbağ (u tdubbuğ).* What do you use when you tan hides? *š-tistaεmiluun min itdibğuun ij-jiluud?* **2.** *smarr (a smiraar).* She tans easily. *tismarr ib-suhuula.*
**I'll tan your hide if you don't behave! *tara ʔahri jildak ʔiδa ma-raz-itsiir ʔaadmi.* or *tara ʔadabbuğ jildak ʔiδa ma-raz-itsiir ʔaadmi.*
tangerine - *laalangiyya* pl. *-aat* coll. *laalingi.*
Tangier - *tanja.*
tangle - 1. *šarbaka* pl. *-aat.* This tangle in the strings can't be undone. *haš-šarbaka bil-ixyuuṭ ma-tinfakk.* **2.** *warta* pl. *-aat.* You've certainly got yourself in a tangle this time. *sudug waggaεit nafsak ib-warta hal-marra.*
to tangle - 1. *εaggad (i taεgiid) t-, šarbak (i šarbaka) t-.* The cat tangled the string. *l-bazzuuna εaggidat il-xeet.* **2.** *warrat (i tawriit) t-.* Don't tangle with him! *la-twarrit nafsak wiyyaa!*
tangled - 1. *mεaggad.* The yarn is tangled. *s-suuf imεaggad.* **2.** *makfuuš.* His hair is tangled. *šaεra makfuuš.*
tank - 1. *taanki* pl. *-iyyaat.* He took a few fish out of the tank. *ʔaxaδ čam simča mnit-taanki.* -- Fill up the tank with gas. *ʔimli it-taanki baanziin.* **2.** *dabbaaba* pl. *-aat.* A column of tanks led the attack. *ratil imnid-dabbaabaat itsaddrat il-hijuum.* **3.** *εanbaar* pl. *εanaabiir, taanki* pl. *-iyyaat.* Every house in Baghdaad has a water tank on the roof. *b-kull beet ib-bağdaad ʔaku εanbaar maay biš-satiz.* **4.** *jidir* pl. *jduur, jduura.* The hot-water tank is rusty. *jidir il-zammaam maalna mzanjar.*
tanning - *dibaağa.* Mosul has a tanning factory. *l-moosil biiha maεmal dibaağa.*
**His father gave him a good tanning. *ʔabuu bisata basta zeena.*

tap - 1. *dagga* pl. *-aat.* I heard two taps on the window. *smaƐit daggteen Ɛaš-šibbaač.* 2. *mzambila* pl. *-aat, ẓanafiyya* pl. *-aat.* The tap on the barrel is dripping. *l-imzambila maal il-barmiil da-tnaggiṭ.* 3. *naƐalča* pl. *-aat.* Please put taps on these shoes. *baḷḷa dugg il-hal-qundara naƐalčaat.*
**He always has some story on tap. *Ɛinda daa?iman iẓčaayaat ẓaaḍra.*
to tap - 1. *nigar (u nagir), dagg (u dagg).* He tapped on the window. *nigar Ɛaš-šabbaač.* 2. *ẓaṭṭ (u ẓaṭṭ) n- raqaaba Ɛala.* The police tapped his telephone. *š-šurṭa ẓaṭṭaw raqaaba Ɛala talafoona.* 3. *dagg (u dagg).* She tapped me on the shoulder. *daggat Ɛala čitfi.*
**They tapped the water main for the new house. *jarraw maay imnil-?abbi lil-beet ij-jidiid.*
tape - *šariiṭ* pl. *?ašriṭa, šaraayiṭ.* He has several tapes of Iraqi music. *Ɛinda čam šariiṭ imnil-mawsiiqa l-Ɛiraaqiyya.* -- I'd like five yards of the white tape. *?ariid xamis yardaat imniš-šariiṭ il-?abyaḍ.*
**Getting through this red tape will take a long time. *jtiyaaz har-rasmiyyaat yaaxuδ wakit ihwaaya.*
to tape - 1. *lizag (i lazig).* Please tape an address label on that package. *baḷḷa ?ilzig biṭaaqat Ɛinwaan Ɛala δiič ir-ruzma.* 2. *sajjal (i tasjiil) t-.* Last night we taped the President's speech. *l-baarẓa bil-leel sajjalna ẓadiiθ ir-ra?iis.*
tape measure - *šariiṭ* (pl. *šaraayiṭ*) *qiyaas.*
tape recorder - *musajjil* pl. *-aat.*
tapeworm - *duuda* (pl. *diidaan*) *waẓiida.*
tar - *giir, jiir.*
target - 1. *niišaan* pl. *-aat, hadaf* pl. *?ahdaaf.* Did you set up the target? *niṣabt il-hadaf?* 2. *ġaraḍ* pl. *?aġraaḍ, hadaf* pl. *?ahdaaf.* Our target for this month is to sell 1,000 suits. *ġaraḍna haš-šahar inbiiƐ ?alif badla.*
tariff - *gumruq, rasim* pl. *rsuum, taƐriifa* pl. *-aat.* The tariff on silk is high. *l-gumruq Ɛal-ẓariir Ɛaali.*
tarnish - 1. *sawaad.* Clean the tarnish from those spoons. *naḍḍuf is-sawaad min hal-iqwaašiig.* 2. *zinjaar.* Clean the tarnish off the brass tray. *naḍḍuf iz-zinjaar min iṣ-ṣiiniyya l-iprinj.*
to tarnish - 1. *swadd (a sawaad).* The silverware will tarnish if you don't keep it in its box. *l-fuḍḍiyyaat tiswadd ?iδa ma-tḍummha ib-ṣanduugha.* 2. *zanjar (i zinjaar).* That brass doorknob will tarnish quickly. *hal-yaddt il-baab il-iprinj itzanjir bil-Ɛajal.*
tarpaulin - *čaadir* pl. *čwaadir.* Cover the load with a tarpaulin. *ġaṭṭi l-ẓimil ib-čaadir.*
tart - *ẓaamuḍ.* The apples have a tart taste. *t-tiffaaẓ bii ṭaƐam ẓaamuḍ.*
task - *šaġla* pl. *-aat.* He is equal to his task. *yiṭlaƐ min ẓagg haš-šaġḷa.*
to take to task - *zaff (i zaff) n-.* We'll have to take him to task for his laziness. *laazim inziffa Ɛala kasala.*
taste - 1. *ṭaƐam.* This meat has a peculiar taste. *hal-laẓam bii fadd ṭaƐam ġariib.* -- I have a bad taste in my mouth. *?aku fadd ṭaƐam ma-ṭayyib ib-ẓalgi.* 2. *δawq* pl. *?aδwaaq.* I'd have given you credit for better taste. *tṣawwarit δawqak ?aẓsan min haaδa.*
**Let me have a taste of it. *xalli ?aδuuga.*
to have a taste for - *staδwaq (i stiδwaaq).* He has a taste for classical music. *yistaδwiq il-moosiiqa l-iklaasiikiyya.*
to taste - *δaag (u δoog), δaaq (u δooq).* Just taste this coffee! *bass δuug hal-gahwa!*
The soup taste good. *š-šoorba ṭaƐamha ṭayyib.* --It tastes of vinegar. *ṭaƐamha yinṭi Ɛala xaḷḷ.* or *bii ṭaƐam xaḷḷ.*
tasteless - 1. *ma-bii ṭaƐam.* The food is tasteless. *l-?akil ma-bii ṭaƐam.* 2. *ma-bii δawq.* Her clothes are tasteless. *libisha ma-bii δawq.*
tasty - *laδiiδ, ṭayyib.* This food is very tasty. *hal-?akil kulliš laδiiδ.*
tavern - *mayxaana* pl. *-aat.*
tax - *ḍariiba* pl. *ḍaraayib.* Have you paid your taxes yet? *difaƐt iḍ-ḍaraayib maaltak loo baƐad?*
to tax - *furaḍ (u fariḍ) n- ḍariiba.* Everybody was taxed two dinars. *nfurḍat ḍariiba diinaareen Ɛala kull waaẓid.* -- It is not governmental policy to tax essential commodities. *muu min siyaast il-ẓukuuma tufruḍ ḍariiba Ɛas-silaƐ iḍ-ḍaruuriyya.*
tax collector - *jaabi* (pl. *jubaat*) *ḍariiba.*
taxi - *taksi, taaksi* pl. *-iyyaat.* I took a taxi from the station. *?axaδit taaksi mnil-maẓaṭṭa.*
taxi driver - *saayiq* (pl. *suwwaaq*) *taaksi.*
taxpayer - *daafiƐ* (pl. *-iin*) *ḍariiba.*
tea - *čaay.* In Iraq they serve tea in small glasses. *bil-Ɛiraaq yqaddmuun ič-čaay b-istikaanaat.*
to **teach** - 1. *Ɛallam (i taƐliim) t-, darras (i tadriis) t-.* Will you teach me German! *tƐallimni ?almaani?* -- He teaches in a boys' school. *huwwa ydarris ib-madrasa maal wilid.* 2. *Ɛallam (i).* I'll teach him not to disturb me! *raẓ-aƐallma baƐad ma-yizƐijni.*
teacher - *muƐallim* pl. *-iin, mudarris* pl. *-iin.* He always wanted to be a teacher. *daa?iman raad yṣiir muƐallim.*
teaching - *tadriis, taƐliim.* Teaching Arabic isn't too hard. *tadriis il-Ɛarabi muu kulliš ṣaƐub.*
teachings - *taƐaaliim.* Muslims follow the teachings of the Koran. *l-muslimiin yitbaƐuun taƐaaliim il-qur?aan.*
tea cup - *kuub* (pl. *kwaab*) *čaay.*
tea glass - *stikaan* pl. *-aat.*
tea house - *čaayxaana* pl. *-aat.*
teak - *ṣaaj.* Our dining room table is teak. *meez ?akilna min ṣaaj.*
tea kettle - *kitli* pl. *-iyyaat.*
team - 1. *firqa* pl. *firaq.* Our team has won every football game it entered this year. *firqatna ġulbat kull sibaaq kurat qadam dixlat bii has-sana.* 2. *zooj* pl. *zwaaj, majmuuƐa* pl. *-aat.* That carriage sports a beautiful team of horses. *δiič il-Ɛarabaana biiha xooš zooj xeel badiiƐa.*
to team up - *tjammaƐ (a tajammuƐ).* They teamed up against me. *tjammƐaw Ɛalayya.* -- We teamed up in groups of six to play volley ball. *tjammaƐna kull sitta suwa ẓatta nilƐab kurat iṭ-ṭaa?ira.*
team mate - *Ɛuḍu* (pl. *?aƐḍaa?*) *firqa.* He's one of my team mates. *huwwa waaẓid min ?aƐḍaa? firaqti.*
teamwork - *takaatuf, taḍaamun.* Good teamwork allowed us to finish the job ahead of time. *t-takaatuf xallaana nxaḷḷiṣ iš-šuġuḷ gabḷ il-mawƐid.*
tea pot - *quuri* pl. *-iyyaat, quwaari.*
tear - *šagg* pl. *šguug.* Can this tear be mended? *haš-šagg mumkin yitxayyaṭ.*
to tear - 1. *šagg (u šagg) n-.* Don't tear the paper! *la-tšigg il-warqa!* 2. *nšagg (a).* Careful, the canvas is tearing! *diir baalak, ič-čaadir da-yinšagg.* 3. *nitaš (i natiš) n-.* She tore the letter out of his hand. *nitšat il-maktuub min ?iida.* 4. *gass (u gaṣṣ) n-, giṭaƐ (a gaṭiƐ) n-.* Tear the coupon out of the magazine. *guṣṣ il-koopoon imnil-majalla.* -- The button tore off. *d-dugma ngiṭƐat.* 5. *šilaƐ (a).* Who tore this page out of the book? *minu šilaƐ haṣ-ṣafẓa mnil-iktaab?*
to tear down - *fallaš (i tafliiš, tfalliš) t-.* He tore his house down. *fallaš beeta.*
to tear open - *fakk (u fakk), fitaẓ (a fatiẓ).* Who tore the package open? *minu fakk ir-ruẓma?*
to tear up - 1. *šaggag (i tašgiig).* I hope you tore that letter up. *?at?ammal ?inta šaggagit δaak il-maktuub.* 2. *fakk (u fakk), ẓaffar (u tẓuffur).* The workmen tore up the street in front of the house. *l-Ɛummaal fakkaw iš-šaariƐ igbaaḷ il-beet.*
tear - *damƐa* pl. *-aat,* coll. *dmuuƐ.* Tears ran down her cheeks. *d-dimuuƐ inẓidrat Ɛala xduudha.*
**Tears won't help you. *l-biča ma-yfiidič.*
to tear - *dammaƐ (i tadmiiƐ).* My eyes are tearing. *Ɛyuuni da-tdammiƐ.*
tear gas - *ġaaz musiil lid-dumuuƐ.*
to **tease** - *daahar (i duhur, mudaahara).* Everyone teases him. *l-kull ydaahruu.* -- Don't tease the dog. *la-tdaahir ič-čalib.*
tea shop - *čaayxaana* pl. *-aat.*
teasing - *mdaahara.* I don't like this kind of teasing. *ma-yiƐjibni hiiči mdaahara.*
tea spoon - *xaašuugat* (pl. *xwaašiig*) *čaay.*
technical - *fanni**. The broadcast was called off for technical reasons. *twaqqfat il-?iδaaƐa l-?asbaab fanniyya.* -- There are several technical institutes in Iraq. *?aku Ɛiddat maƐaahid fanniyya bil-Ɛiraaq.*
technicality - *sabab fanni* pl. *?asbaab fanniyya.* We lost the game due to a technicality. *xṣarna s-sibaaq il-sabab fanni.*
technician - *fanni* pl. *-iyyiin.*
technique - *ṭariiqa* pl. *ṭuruq, ?usluub* pl. *?asaaliib.* We'll have to improve our teaching techniques. *laazim inẓassin ṭariiqatna bit-tadriis.*
tedious - *mumill, muḍawwij.*
teen-ager - *muraahiq* pl. *-iin.*
to **telecast** - *Ɛiraḍ (i Ɛariḍ) bit-talafizyoon.*
telegram - *barqiyya* pl. *-aat.* I want to send a telegram. *?ariid adizz barqiyya.*

telegraph - *barq.* Where's the telegraph office? *ween daa?irt il-barq?*
to telegraph - *?abraq (i ?ibraaq) l-.* Did he telegraph you? *?abraq-lak?*
telegraph operator - *ma?muur (pl. -iin) barq.*
telephone - *talafoon* pl. *-aat.* May I use your telephone, please? *tismaz-li ?astaƐmil talafoonak min faδlak?*
to telephone - *xaabar (u muxaabara).* Did anybody telephone? *?azzad xaabar?*
telephone booth - *maqṣuurat (pl. -aat) talafoon.*
telephone call - *muxaabara* pl. *-aat.* I have to pay for every telephone call. *laazim adfaƐ Ɛala kull muxaabara.*
telephone directory - *daliil (pl. ?adillat) talafoon.* His name is in the telephone directory. *?isma b-daliil it-talafoon.*
telephoning - *muxaabara.* Telephoning won't take much time. *l-muxaabara ma-taaxuδ ihwaaya wakit.*
telescope - *taliskooþ* pl. *-aat.*
teletype - *talitaayþ.*
to **televise** - *Ɛiraδ (i Ɛariδ) bit-talafizyoon.*
television - *talafizyoon.*
to **tell** - **1.** *gaal (u gawl) l-.* Tell him your name. *gul-la š-ismak.* -- Tell me, what are you doing tonight? *gul-li š-raz-itsawwi hal-leela.* **2.** *ziča (i zači), gaal (u).* I wish I could tell you the whole story. *yaa reet ?agdar ?azčii-lak il-quṣṣa kullha.* **3.** *Ɛiraf (u).* You can tell by his voice that he has a cold. *tigdar tuƐruf min zissa ?inna manšuul.* **4.** *zizar (i zazir).* Nobody could have told that in advance. *mazzad čaan yigdar yizzir haay li-giddaam.* **5.** *farraq (i tafriiq).* I can't tell one from the other. *ma-?agdar afarriq waazid imnil-laax.* **6.** *sabbaz (i tasbiiz).* That old man is always telling his beads. *š-šeex daa?iman ysabbiz ib-masbazta.*
**Can your little boy tell time yet? *?ibnak yigdar yiqra s-saaƐa loo baƐad?*
**To tell the truth, I don't know. *bil-zaqiiqa, ?aani ma-?adri.* or ***walla, ma-?aƐruf.*
**You can tell by looking at him that he's been working hard. *ybayyin Ɛalee čaan da-yištuġul ib-himma.*
to tell a lie - **1.** *kiδab (i kiδib), čiδab (i čiδib).* I told her a lie to get out of going to the party. *kiδabit Ɛaleeha zatta la-aruuz lil-zafla.* **2.** *čaδδab (i).* He's always telling lies. *Ɛala ṭuul yčaδδib.*
to tell apart - *farraq (i tafriiq) been, mayyaz (i tamyiiz) been.* I can't tell these two materials apart. *ma-agdar afarriq been hal-iqmaašeen.*
teller - *ṣarraaf* pl. *-iin, ṣaraariif.* He has worked ten years as teller in that bank. *štiġaḷ ṣarraaf Ɛašr isniin ib-δaak il-þang.*
temper - **1.** *ṭabuƐ* pl. *?aṭbaaƐ.* He has an even temper. *ṭabƐa haadi.* **2.** *ṣalaaba.* This steel has more temper than iron. *hal-fuulaaδ bii ṣalaaba ?azyad imnil-zadiid.*
to lose one's temper - *ztadd (a ztidaad).* He loses his temper easily. *yiztadd bil-Ɛajal.*
to temper - *siga (i sagi).* In Damascus they have tempered steel for hundreds of years. *biš-šaam yisguun il-fuulaaδ ṣaar-ilhum miyyaat isniin.*
temperamental - *Ɛaṣabi*.* She's very temperamental. *hiyya kulliš Ɛaṣabiyya.* or ***xulugha δayyig.*
temperance - *Ɛtidaal.* He lives by temperance. *yƐiiš b-iƐtidaal.*
temperate - *muƐtadil.* He is very temperate in his habits. *huwwa kulliš muƐtadil ib-Ɛaadaata.* -- Europe is situated in the temperate zone. *?ooruþþa waaqƐa bil-manṭiqa l-muƐtadila.*
temperature - **1.** *ṣxuuna, darajat zaraara.* Her temperature went down today. *ṣxuunatha nizlat il-yoom.* **2.** *darajat zaraara.* What was the highest temperature yesterday? *šgadd čaanat ?aƐla darajat zaraara l-baarza?*
temple - **1.** *maƐbad* pl. *maƐaabid.* This church is built on the ruins of a Roman temple. *hal-kaniisa nbinat Ɛala xaraayib maƐbad roomaani.* **2.** *tooraat.* I love to spend Friday night in the temple. *?azibb agδi masaa? ij-jumƐa bit-tooraat.* **3.** *ṣaabir* pl. *ṣwaabir.* The bullet struck him in the temple. *r-riṣaaṣa δurbata b-ṣaabra.*
temporary - *muwaqqat, waqti.** This is only a temporary solution. *hal-zall muwaqqat bass.*
to **tempt** - *ġira (i ?iġraa?).* That doesn't tempt me. *haaδa ma-yiġriini.* or ***haaδa ma-ysawwii-li waahis.*
**I was tempted to tell him the truth. *ṣaar-li waahis agul-la l-zaqiiqa.*
temptation - *?iġraa?* pl. *-aat.*
tempting - *muġri.* He made me a very tempting offer. *Ɛiraδ Ɛalayya Ɛariδ muġri.*
ten - **1.** *Ɛašra.* It's ten o'clock. *s-saaƐa bil-Ɛasra.* **2.** *Ɛaširt.* We're going on a vacation in ten days. *raayziin ib-?ijaaza baƐad Ɛaširt iyyaam.* **3.** *Ɛašir.* He has ten men working for him. *Ɛinda Ɛašir rayaajiil yištaġluu-la.*
tenacious - *muṣirr, Ɛanuud.*
tenaciously - *b-?iṣraar.* He holds to his opinion tenaciously. *mitmassik ib-ra?ya b-?iṣraar.*
tenant - *mista?jir* pl. *-iin.* He has been our tenant for ten years. *huwwa mista?jir Ɛidna ṣaar-la Ɛašr isniin.*
to **tend** - **1.** *maal (i mayalaan).* He tends to be partial in his judgments. *ymiil lit-tazayyuz ib-qaraaraata.* **2.** *daar (i) baal~.* Tend to your own business! *diir baalak Ɛala šuġlak.* -- Who's going to tend to the furnace? *minu raz-ydiir baala Ɛal-firin?*
tendency - **1.** *mayl* pl. *myuul.* He has a tendency to exaggerate. *Ɛinda mayl lil-mubaalaġa.* **2.** *mayl* pl. *myuul, ttijaah* pl. *-aat.* He has leftist tendencies. *Ɛinda myuul yasaariyya.*
tender - **1.** *fargoon (pl. -aat) wuquud.* Only the locomotive and the tender were derailed. *bass il-makiina w-faargoon il-wuquud ṭilƐaw imnis-sičča.* **2.** *ṭari*.* The meat is so tender you can cut it with a fork. *l-lazam hal-gadd ṭari l-waazid yguṣṣa bič-čaṭal.* **3.** *zassaas.* The bruise is still tender. *r-raδδ baƐda zassaas.*
tendon - *watar* pl. *?awtaar.*
tenement - *beet (pl. byuut) nizil.*
tennis - *tanis.*
tennis court - *saazat (pl. -aat) tanis.*
tennis racquet - *rakit* pl. *-aat.*
tennis shoes - *qundara (pl. qanaadir) laastiig, qundarat (pl. qanaadir) riyaaδa.*
tense - **1.** *mitwattir.* The situation was tense. *l-zaala čaanat mitwattra.* -- **He's very tense these days. *?aƐṣaaba kulliš mitwattra hal-?ayyaam.* **2.** *ṣiiġa* pl. *ṣiyaġ.* That verb is in the past tense. *hal-fiƐil ib-ṣiiġat il-maaδi.*
tension - *tawattur.* The world is in a state of tension these days. *l-Ɛaalam ib-zaalat tawattur hal-?ayyaam.*
**Those are high tension power lines. *hal-waayaraat biiha quwwa kahrabaa?iyya Ɛaalya.*
tent - *xeema* pl. *-aat, xiyam; čaadir* pl. *čwaadir.* The tent is made of canvas. *l-xeema maƐmuula mnil-junfaaṣ.*
tenth - **1.** *Ɛaašir.* This is the tenth year I've been working at the same job. *haay is-sana l-Ɛaašra ?aani ?aštuġuḷ nafs iš-šuġuḷ.* **2.** *Ɛušur* pl. *?aƐšaar.* It's not even one tenth finished. *?aṣlan Ɛušurha ma-xilaṣ.*
**We get paid on the tenth of the month. *niqbuδ rawaatibna yoom Ɛašra biš-šahar.*
term - **1.** *šarṭ* pl. *šuruuṭ.* He gave us very good terms. *nṭaana šuruuṭ mumtaaza.* **2.** *faṣil* pl. *fuṣuul.* When does the fall school term begin? *šwakit yibdi faṣl id-diraasa lil-xariif?* **3.** *mudda* pl. *mudad.* He spent a four-year term in the presidency. *giδa muddat ?arbaƐ isniin bir-ri?aasa.* **4.** *ṣṭilaaz* pl. *-aat.* Do you know the technical term for it? *tuƐruf l-iṣṭilaaz il-fanni maalha?* **5.** *Ɛibaara* pl. *-aat.* I told him in no uncertain terms what I think of him. *git-la ra?yi bii b-Ɛibaaraat ṣariiza.* **6.** *Ɛilaaqa* pl. *-aat.* We're on bad terms. *Ɛilaaqaatna muu zeena.*
**We have been trying to come to terms for months now. *ṣaar-inna ?ašhur da-nriid nitfaaham.* or *ṣaar-inna ?ašhur da-nriid nooṣal ?ila ttifaaq.*
terminal - **1.** *mazaṭṭa* pl. *-aat.* We have to pick up the trunks at the freight terminal. *laazim naaxuδ junaṭna min mazaṭṭat iš-šazin.* **2.** *raas* pl. *ruus.* The terminals of the battery are corroded. *ruus il-þaatri mzanjira.* **3.** *nihaa?i*.* You receive a month's terminal pay when you resign. *taaxuδ raatib šahar nihaa?i Ɛinda-ma tistaqiil.*
to **terminate** - **1.** *?anha (i ?inhaa?), fuṣax (u faṣix).* The company terminated his services. *š-šarika ?anhat xadamaata.* -- The landlord terminated our lease. *ṣaazib il-muluk fuṣax Ɛaqd il-?iijaar maalna.* **2.** *xilaṣ (a), ntiha (i ntihaa?).* My lease terminates in June. *Ɛaqd il-?iijaar maali yixlaṣ ib-zuzeeraan.*
terminology - *ṣṭilaazaat.* Their terminology is not

clear. *ṣṭilaaḥaathum muu waaḍḥa.*

termites - *ʔarḍa.* Our house has termites. *beetna bii ʔarḍa.*

terrace - *ṭarma* pl. *-aat.* Let's all go sit on the terrace. *xall-inruuḥ kullna nigεud biṭ-ṭarma.*

terrain - *ʔaraaḍi.* Around Baghdad the terrain is level. *yamm baġdaad il-ʔaraaḍi minbasṭa.*

terrible - **1.** *faḍiiε.* There was a terrible accident this morning. *čaan ʔaku ṣṭidaam faḍiiε il-yoom iṣ-ṣubuḥ.* **2.** *mxarbaṭ.* The weather is terrible. *j-jaww kulliš imxarbaṭ.* or ***j-jaww kulliš muu zeen.*

terribly - *kulliš.* I'm terribly sorry. *ʔaani kulliš mitʔassif.*

terrific - **1.** *εaḍiim.* His poetry is terrific. *qaṣiidta εaḍiima.* **2.** *haaʔil, šadiid.* Did you hear that terrific explosion today? *simaεt il-infijaar il-haaʔil il-yoom?* -- He's under terrific pressure. *huwwa taḥat ḍaġiṭ šadiid.*

to **terrify** - *riεab (i ʔirεaab).* He brought me news that terrified me. *jaab-li xabar riεabni bii.*

to be terrified - *rtiεab (i).* I was terrified. *rtiεabit* or ***mitit imnil-xoof.*

terrifying - *muxiif, murεib.*

territory - *ʔaraaḍi.* We will defend our territory. *raḥ-indaafiε εan ʔaraaḍiina.*

terror - *xoof, ruεub.* We were speechless with terror. *činna jaamdiin imnil-xoof.*

terrorism - *ʔirhaab.* The dictator ruled through terrorism. *d-diktaatoor ḥikam bil-ʔirhaab.*

terrorist - *ʔirhaabi* pl. *-iyyiin.*

to **terrorize** - *ʔarhab (i ʔirhaab).* The bandits terrorized the countryside. *quṭṭaaε iṭ-ṭuruq ʔarhibaw in-naas bil-ʔaryaaf.*

test - **1.** *mtiḥaan* pl. *-aat.* You have to take a test before you get a driver's license. *laazim taaxuδ imtiḥaan gabuḷ-ma tḥaṣṣil εala ʔijaazat siyaaqa.* -- Did you pass all your tests? *nijaḥit ib-kull imtiḥaanaatak?* **2.** *faḥiṣ* pl. *fuḥuuṣ.* I had an eye test today. *čaan εindi faḥṣ iεyuun il-yoom.* **3.** *xtibaar* pl. *-aat.* He made several tests during his experiment. *sawwa εiddat ixtibaaraat ʔaθnaaʔ tajrubta.*

to test - **1.** *mtiḥan (i mtiḥaan).* I'll test half the class today. *raḥ-amtiḥin nuṣṣ iṣ-ṣaff il-yoom.* -- I was tested in arithmetic today. *mtiḥanit bil-ḥisaab hal-yoom.* **2.** *fuḥaṣ (a faḥiṣ).* Test the brakes. *ʔifḥaṣ l-ibreek.* -- Test this urine for sugar. *ʔifḥaṣ il-bool w-šuuf ʔiδa bii šakar.*

testicle - *xuṣwa* pl. *xaṣaawi.*

to **testify** - **1.** *bayyan (i bayaan).* Have you anything further to testify? *εindak baεad šii tbayyna.* **2.** *šihad (a šahaada).* Can you testify to his honesty? *tigdar tišhad ib-ʔamaanta?*

testimony - *šahaada* pl. *-aat.* Can you add anything further to your testimony? *ʔaku baεad šii tḍiifa l-šahaadtak.*

testing - **1.** *mtiḥaan.* The system of testing in this school is excellent. *ṭariiqat il-imtiḥaan ib-hal-madrasa mumtaaza.* **2.** *tajaarub.* We're about ready to resume atomic testing. *ʔiḥna εala wašak inεiid it-tajaarub iδ-δarriyya.*

test tube - *ʔinbuubat (pl. ʔanaabiib) ixtibaar.*

tetanus - *l-igzaaz, l-kuzaaz, l-gazzaaz, l-kazzaaz.*

text - *naṣṣ* pl. *nuṣuuṣ.* The text of the speech is on page two. *naṣṣ il-xiṭaab mawjuud ib-ṣafḥa θneen.*

textbook - *ktaab madrasi* pl. *kutub madrasiyya, ktaab muqarrar* pl. *kutub muqarrara.*

textile - **1.** *nasiij.* There is a new textile plant in Mosul. *ʔaku maεmal nasiij jidiid bil-muuṣil.* **2.** *qmaaš* pl. *ʔaqmiša, nasiij* pl. *ʔansija.* Egypt is famous for its cotton textiles. *miṣir mašhuura b-ʔaqmišatha l-quṭniyya.*

texture - *malmas* pl. *malaamis.* Silk has a smooth texture. *l-ḥariir malmasa naaεim.*

than - **1.** *min.* He's older than his brother. *huwwa ʔakbar min ʔaxuu.* -- I appreciate him more than ever. *ʔaqaddra ʔazyad min gabuḷ.* **2.** *badal-ma, bidaal-ma.* I'd rather stay home than go to that dull play. *ʔafaḍḍil abqa bil-beet badal-ma ʔaruuḥ ib-har-ruwaaya l-itδawwij.*

to **thank** - *šikar (u šukur).* I haven't even thanked him yet. *baεad li-hassa ma-škarta.*

**Thank goodness! *l-ḥamdu l-illaa.*

thankful - *mamnuun, šaakir.* We are very thankful to you. *ʔiḥna hwaaya mamnuuniin.*

thanks - **1.** *šukur.* I don't expect any thanks or praise. *ma-ʔantiḍir ʔay šukur aw θanaaʔ.* **2.** *faḍil.* It's no thanks to him that I'm here. *l-faḍil muu ʔila b-jayti.*

**Thanks a lot. *šukran jaziilan.*

that - **1.** *(m.) δaak, haaδaak (f.) δiič, haaδiič.* What's that? *δaak šinu?* or *šinu haaδaak?* -- That girl is my sister. *δiič il-bint ʔuxti.* or *δiič l-ibnayya ʔuxti.* -- What does that mean? *šinu maεna δaak?* or *δiič iš-tiεni?* **2.** *lli, l-.* Do you know the story that he told us? *tuεruf l-iḥčaaya l-ḥičaa-lna-yyaaha?* -- Who's the man that just came in? *minu r-rijjaal illi ʔija hassa?* **3.** *ʔann.* They told me that you were ill. *gaaloo-li ʔannak činit wajεaan.* **4.** *hal-.* I don't want that much milk. *ma-ariid hal-gadd ḥaliib.*

at that - **1.** *walaw hiiči.* Even at that I wouldn't pay more. *walaw hiiči ʔaani ma-adfaε ʔazeed.* **2.** *maεa haada.* At that it costs only two dinars. *maεa haaδa, ykallif diinaareen bass.* **3.** *εala hal-ḥaṭṭa, εala haš-šikil.* We'll leave it at that. *xalli nxalliiha εala hal-ḥaṭṭa.*

that is - *yaεni.* I'll come tomorrow, that is, if it doesn't rain. *ʔaji baačir, yaεni, ʔiδa ma-muṭrat.*

thaw - *δawabaan θalij, mooε θalij.* This year the thaw set in rather early. *δawabaan iθ-θalij bida min wakit has-sana.*

to thaw - *δaab (u) iθ-θalij, maaε (u) iθ-θalij.* It's thawing. *θ-θalij da-yδuub.* -- Has the refrigerator thawed out yet? *maaε iθ-θalij il-biθ-θallaaja?*

the - *l-.* The house is big. *l-beet ičbiir.* -- Please pass me the butter. *baḷḷa naawušni z-zibid.*

**The sooner we're paid the better. *kull-ma yinṭuuna fluusna min wakit, ʔaḥsan.*

theater - **1.** *qaaεat (pl. -aat) tamθiil.* Our theater has a modern stage. *qaaεat it-tamθiil maalatna biiha masraḥ εaṣri.* **2.** *siinama* pl. *-aat.* Most movie theaters in Baghdad are in Bab el Sharji. *ʔakθar is-siinamaat ib-baġdaad ib-baab iš-šarji.*

theft - *booga* pl. *-aat, sariqa* pl. *-aat.* The theft was discovered the next morning. *ktišfaw il-booga θaani yoom iṣ-ṣubuḥ.*

their - *-hum.* Do you know their address? *tuεruf εinwaanhum?*

theirs - **1.** *maalhum.* This book is theirs. *hal-iktaab maalhum.* **2.** *maalathum.* We'll go in our car, and they'll take theirs. *nruuḥ ib-sayyaaratna, w-humma yruuḥuun ib-maalathum.*

**Our house isn't as big as theirs. *beetna muu b-gadd beethum.*

**Are you a friend of theirs? *ʔinta ṣadiiqhum?*

them - **1.** *-hum.* I don't want to have anything to do with them. *ma-ariid adaxxil nafsi wiyyaahum.* **2.** *-ha.* The papers are on the floor; will you please pick them up? *l-ʔawraaq bil-gaaε; ma-tšiilha baḷḷa?*

theme - **1.** *mawḍuuε* pl. *mawaaḍiiε.* Why did you pick that theme? *lweeš intixabit hal-mawḍuuε?* **2.** *ʔinšaaʔ* pl. *-aat.* Have you finished your theme for tomorrow? *kitabit il-ʔinšaaʔ maalak maal baačir?*

themselves - *nafishum.* They did it themselves. *humma sawwooha b-nafishum.*

**The pair divided the money between themselves. *θneenhum itqaasmaw l-ifluus beenhum.*

then - **1.** *baεdeen, t-taali.* What did he do then? *w-baεdeen iš-sawwa?* **2.** *laεad.* Then everything is O.K. *laεad kullši zeen.* -- Well, then, let's go. *zeen, laεad xalli nruuḥ.* **3.** *εuud, δaak il-wakit.* Call Tuesday. We'll know by then. *xaabur iθ-θilaaθa, εuud yṣiir εidna maεluum.* **4.** *δaak il-wakit.* He did it right then, rather than waiting. *sawwaaha b-δaak il-wakit, badal-ma yintiḍir.*

**We go to the movies now and then. *nruuḥ lis-siinama been mudda w-mudda.*

then and there - *raʔsan.* Why didn't you take it then and there? *leeš ma-ʔaxaδitha raʔsan?*

theoretical - *naḍari*.* That's a theoretical solution. *haaδa ḥall naḍari.*

theoretically - *naḍariyyan.* Theoretically the experiment should turn out all right. *naḍariyyan it-tajruba laazim tinjaḥ.*

theory - *naḍariyya* pl. *-aat.*

there - *hnaak.* Have you ever been there? *b-εumrak raayiḥ ihnaak?*

**I'm afraid he's not quite all there. *ybayyin maxxuuṭ.*

**There you are! I was looking all over for you. *hiyyaatak, činit da-adawwir εaleek ib-kull makaan.*

there is, are - *ʔaku.* There are a few good hotels in town. *ʔaku čam ʔuteel zeen bil-wlaaya.* -- Are

there such people? *ʔaku hiiči naas?* -- There aren't enough chairs. *ma-aku skamliyyaat kaafya.*
thereabouts - *ðiič il-ʔaṭraaf.* Are there any banks thereabouts? *ʔaku bang ib-ðiič il-ʔaṭraaf?*
therefore - *li-ðaalik, li-haaða.* Therefore I assume it is so. *li-ðaalik ʔaƐtiqid hiyya haš-šikil.*
thermometer - *tarmoomatir* pl. *-aat.*
these - **1.** *ðoola, haaðoola.* I like these better. *ðoola yƐijbuuni ʔazeed.* -- These are good workmen. *haaðoola xooš Ɛummaal.* **2.** *hal-.* These boys are good students. *hal-wulid xooš talaamiið.* -- These cigarettes are Turkish. *haj-jigaayir turkiyya.* -- Everything is very expensive these days. *kullši ġaali hal-ʔayyaam.*
**I'll attend to it one of these days. *raz-asawwiiha yoom imnil-ʔayyaam.*
thesis - **1.** *naðariyya* pl. *-aat, farðiyya* pl. *-aat.* His thesis proved to be right. *naðariita nθibtat ṣizzatha.* **2.** *ʔuṭruuza* pl. *-aat.* He wrote an excellent master's thesis. *kitab ʔuṭruuza mumtaaza l-šihaadat il-maajisteer.*
they - *humma.* They're my friends. *humma ʔaṣdiqaaʔi.* **They're leaving tomorrow. *msaafriin baačir.* **They work for me. *yištiġluu-li.*
thick - *θixiin.* The soup is too thick. *š-šoorba kulliš θixiina.* -- This board isn't that thick. *hal-looza maa hal-gadd θixiina.* -- He's too thick to understand that. *haaða damaaġa θxiin; ma-yifham hiiči ʔašyaaʔ.*
**The crowd was very thick at the scene of the accident. *čaan qalaðaalig ib-mazall il-zaadiθ.*
**I'll go through thick and thin for him. *ʔatzammal il-murr wil-zaamuð Ɛala muuda.*
**Wherever there's a fight, he's in the thick of it. *ween-ma ʔaku Ɛarka, tilgii b-nuṣṣha.*
to **thicken** - **1.** *θixan (a θuxuuna).* The sauce will thicken if you leave it on the fire to boil. *l-marga raz-tiθxan ʔiða txalliiha Ɛan-naar itfawwur.* **2.** *θaxxin (i taθxiin) t-.* Thicken the sauce with tomato paste. *θaxxin il-marga b-maƐjuun ṭamaaṭa.*
thicket - *daġal* (coll.).
thickness - *θuxun.* What is the thickness of that cardboard? *šgadd θuxun hal-imqawwaaya?*
thickset - *mraṣraṣ.* He's quite thickset. *haaða kulliš mraṣraṣ.*
thick-skinned - *safiiz.* She's thick-skinned, so she didn't mind the insult. *haaði safiiza, w-ma-daarat baal lil-ʔihaana.*
thief - *zaraami* pl. *-iyya.* Stop, thief! *ʔilzamuu l-zaraami!*
thievery - *boog.*
thigh - *fuxuð* pl. *fxaað.*
thimble - *kuštubaan* pl. *-aat.*
thin - **1.** *xafiif.* The paper is too thin. *hal-warqa kulliš xafiifa.* -- That soup is rather thin. *š-šoorba xafiifa šwayya.* **2.** *ðƐiif* pl. *ðaƐfaan.* She's gotten thin. *ṣaayra ðƐiifa.* or *ðuƐfat.* -- Her face has gotten very thin. *wujihha ṣaayir kulliš ðiƐiif.* **3.** *rifiiƐ.* That stick's too thin. *hal-Ɛuuda kulliš rifiiƐa.* **4.** *waahi.* That's a pretty thin excuse. *haaða fadd Ɛuður kulliš waahi.*
**I'll go through thick and thin for him. *ʔatzammal il-murr wil-zaamuð Ɛala muuda.*
to get thin - *ðiƐaf (a ðuƐuf).* You've gotten thin. *ðiƐafit.*
to thin - **1.** *xaff (u xaff).* His hair is thinning. *šaƐra da-yxuff.* **2.** *xaffaf (u taxfiif).* Thin this paint. *xaffuf haṣ-ṣubuġ.*
to thin out - *xaff (u xaff).* Let's wait until this crowd thins out. *xal-nintiðir ʔila ʔan yxuff il-izdizaam.*
thing - *šii* pl. *ʔašyaaʔ, zaaja* pl. *-aat.* Some funny things have been going on here. *šwayya ʔašyaaʔ ġariiba da-tṣiir ihnaa.* -- I don't know the first thing about it. *ma-aƐruf ʔay šii Ɛanha.* -- We've heard a lot of nice things about you. *smaƐna hwaaya ʔašyaaʔ zeena Ɛannak.* -- It all adds up to the same thing. *ʔawwal w-taali kullha fadd šii.* -- That's an entirely different thing. *haaða fadd šii yixtilif tamaaman.*
**I didn't have a thing to do with it. *ma-čaan ʔili ʔay Ɛalaaqa b-haaða.*
the real thing - *min ṣudug.* This time it's the real thing. *han-nooba min ṣudug.*
the thing (to do, etc.) - *ʔazsan šii.* The thing to do is to go home. *ʔazsan šii waazid yruuz lil-beet.*
things - **1.** *hduum.* Put on your things and let's go for a walk. *ʔilbas ihduumak w-xalli nitlaƐ nitmašša.* **2.** *l-ʔumuur, l-ʔazwaal.* Things have got to improve. *l-ʔumuur laazim titzassan.* **3.** *ġaraað.* Have you packed your things yet? *lammeet ġaraaðak loo baƐad?*
of all things - *Ɛajiib.* Well of all things, what are you doing here? *Ɛajiib, ʔinta š-da-tsawwi hnaa?*
to see things - *txayyal (a taxayyul).* You're just seeing things. *ʔinta bass da-titxayyal.*
to **think** - **1.** *ftikar (i ftikaar), fakkar (i tafkiir).* Don't you think it's too warm? *ma-tiftikir id-dinya kulliš zaarra?* **2.** *Ɛtiqad (i Ɛtiqaad).* I think he stated it plainly. *ʔaƐtiqid huwwa bayyanha b-wuðuuz.* -- He thinks his son is clever. *yiƐtiqid ʔibna kulliš šaaṭir.* **3.** *ðann (i ðann).* I thought you were from the country. *ðanneet ʔinta min sukkaan il-ʔaryaaf.* -- I don't think I'll go. *ma-aðinn raz-aruuz.* **4.** *šaaf (u šoof).* I don't think it's in your interest to do this. *ma-ašuuf min maṣlaztak itsawwi haay.*
**He's never really learned how to think. *ʔabad ma-tƐallam yistaƐmil fikra.*
**That's what you think, but you're wrong! *haaða raʔyak, laakin ʔinta ġalṭaan!*
**Now he thinks differently. *hassa tbaddal fikra.*
**He thinks nothing of driving all night. *ma-yhimma loo saaq il-leel kulla.*
to think about - *fakkar (i tafkiir) b-.* I've been thinking about it all afternoon. *ṣaar-li n-nahaar kulla da-afakkir biiha.* -- They're thinking about getting married. *da-yfakkruun biz-zawaaj.*
to think out - *tbaṣṣar (a tabaṣṣur) b-.* He doesn't think things out very far. *ma-yitbaṣṣar ihwaaya bil-ʔumuur.*
to think over - *fakkar (i tafkiir) b-, daanaš (i mudaanaša) fikr~.* He's still thinking it over. *baƐda da-ydaaniš fikra.* or *baƐda da-yfakkir biiha.*
thinker - *mufakkir* pl. *-iin.* Plato was a great thinker. *ʔaflaaṭuun čaan mufakkir Ɛaðiim.*
thinking - *tafkiir.* Thinking about it won't help. *t-tafkiir biiha ma-bii faaʔida.*
**That's wishful thinking. *haaði tamanniyaat.*
thinly - **Put the paint on thinly. *la-tkaθθir iṣ-ṣubuġ.* **The valley is thinly forested. *hal-waadi bii šwayya ašjaar.* **This area is thinly settled. *hal-manṭiqa ma-mizdazma bis-sukkaan.*
thinner - **1.** *ʔaðƐaf.* He's thinner than his brother. *huwwa ʔaðƐaf min ʔaxuu.* **2.** *ʔaxfaf.* Can you make it a little thinner? *ma-tsawwii šwayya ʔaxfaf?* **3.** *ʔarfaƐ, ʔaðƐaf.* It'll have to be thinner to fit. *laazim itkuun ʔarfaƐ zatta tirham.*
to get thinner - *ðaƐƐaf (u taðƐiif) nafs~.* She wants to get thinner. *triid itðaƐƐuf nafisha.*
thinness - *ðuƐuf.* Her thinness worries me. *ðuƐufha da-yiqliqni.*
third - **1.** *θuluθ, θiliθ.* A third of that will be enough. *θuluθ haay ykaffi.* **2.** *θaaliθ.* We couldn't stay for the third act. *ma-gdarna nibqa lil-faṣl iθ-θaaliθ.*
third-class - **1.** *daraja θaalθa.* Give me one third-class ticket to Basra. *nṭiini tikit daraja θaalθa lil-baṣra.* **2.** *θaaliθ baab, θaaliθ daraja.* This wool is third class. *haṣ-ṣuuf θaaliθ baab.*
thirdly - *θaaliθan.* First of all it's expensive, secondly it's impractical, and thirdly it's difficult to get. *ʔawwalan ġaalya, θaaniyan muu Ɛamaliyya, w-θaaliθan ṣaƐub tazṣiilha.*
thirst - **1.** *Ɛaṭaš.* I can't quench my thirst. *ma-da-ʔagdar ʔarwi Ɛaṭaši.*
**He still has his thirst for adventure. *baƐda yzibb il-muġaamaraat.*
thirsty - *Ɛaṭšaan* pl. *Ɛaṭaaša, -iin.* I'm very thirsty. *ʔaani kulliš Ɛaṭšaan.* -- We all are very thirsty. *kullna činna Ɛṭaaša.*
thirteen - *tlaṭṭaƐaš.*
thirteenth - *l-itlaṭṭaƐaš.* He came on the thirteenth. *jaa yoom l-itlaṭṭaƐaš.* -- I stopped reading after the thirteenth page. *baṭṭalt il-iqraaya baƐd iṣ-ṣaziifa l-itlaṭṭaƐaš.* -- Who was thirteenth in the class? *minu ṭilaƐ itlaṭṭaƐaš biṣ-ṣaff?*
thirtieth - *l-itlaaθiin.*
thirty - **1.** *tlaaθiin.* This month has thirty days. *haš-šahar bii tlaaθiin yoom.* **2.** *nuṣṣ.* It's three-thirty. *is-saaƐa tlaaθa n-nuṣṣ.*
this - (m.) *haaða, hal-.* (f.) *haaði, haay,*

hal-. Do you know this man? *tuEruf har-rijjaal?* -- Is this the same tie I saw? *haaδa nafs ir-ribaaṭ iš-šifta?* -- This is on me. *haay Eala ẓsaabi* or *haaδa Ealayya.* -- What's this? *šinu haay?* or *haay šinu?* -- This is just what I wanted to avoid. *haay ič-činit da-ariid ʔatfaadaaha.*

**I'm going to see him this afternoon. *raẓ-ašuufa l-yoom il-Eaṣir.*

**They talked about this and that. *ẓičaw Eal-ʔaku wil-maaku.*

thorn - *šooka* pl. *-aat* coll. *šook.* The tree is full of thorns. *š-šajara matruusa šook.*

thorny - 1. *bii šook.* Watch out, that plant is thorny. *diir baa lak, haz-zariE bii šook!* 2. *šaaʔik, muẓrij.* That is a very thorny question. *haaδa fadd mawδuuE šaaʔik.*

thorough - 1. *mutqan.* He's very thorough in everything he does. *huwwa kulliš mutqan ib-kullši l-ysawwii.* 2. *šaamil, kaamil.* He submitted a thorough report. *qaddam taqriir šaamil.*

**He gave him a thorough beating. *bisaṭa basṭa zeena.*

thoroughbred - *ʔaṣiil.* Those horses are thoroughbreds. *hal-xeel ʔaṣiila.*

thoroughfare - *šaariE* pl. *šawaariE.* Rashid St. is the main thoroughfare in Baghdad. *šaariE ir-rašiid huwwa š-šaariE ir-raʔiisi b-baġdaad.*

thoroughly - 1. *b-diqqa.* Read it thoroughly. *ʔiqraa b-diqqa.* 2. *tamaaman.* I'm thoroughly convinced he's wrong. *ʔaani muqtiniE tamaaman ʔanna ġalṭaan.*

those - *δoolaak, δoola.* Who are those people you were talking to? *minu humma δoolaak ič-činit da-tiẓči wiyyaahum?*

though - 1. *maEa ʔann, w-law.* Though he knew it, he didn't tell me anything about it. *maEa ʔanna yuErufha, ma-gal-li Eanha.* -- I bought several shirts, though I didn't need them. *štireet čam θoob w-law ma-aẓtaajhum.* 2. *laakin, bass.* All right, I'll do it! Not now, though. *zeen, Euud asawwiiha! bass muu hassa.* 3. *maEa haaδa, Eal-kull ẓaal.* You've ordered it, though, haven't you? *ʔinta waṣṣeet Ealee, maEa haaδa, muu?*

as though - *Eabaalak.* It looks as though it may rain. *šikilha Eabaalak raẓ-tumṭur.*

thought - 1. *tafkiir.* The very thought of it makes me sick. *mujarrad it-tafkiir bii ylaEEb in-nafis.* 2. *fikra* pl. *-aat, fikar.* The thought occurred to me. *l-fikra xiṭrat-li* or *l-fikra jatti Eala baali.* 3. *muraaEaat.* Can't you show a little thought for others? *ma-tbayyin išwayya muraaEaat lil-ʔaaxariin?*

to be lost in thought - *ṣufan (u ṣafna).* He was lost in thought. *čaan ṣaafun.*

to give thought - *fakkar (u tafkiir) b-.* I'll have to give this matter some thought. *laazim ʔafakkir ib-hal-mawδuuE.*

**Don't give it another thought! *la-tdawwix raasak biiha.* or *la-yibqa baalak yammha.*

thoughtful - *ṣaafun.* Why do you look so thoughtful? *š-biik ṣaafun?*

**It's very thoughtful of you to bring me flowers. *haaδa fadd šuEuur kullis laṭiif minnak itjiib-li warid.*

thoughtless - *ṭaayiš.* That was a thoughtless act. *haaδa fadd taṣarruf ṭaayiš.*

**She's so thoughtless. *ma-traaEi šuEuur il-ʔaaxiriin.*

thousand - *ʔalf* pl. *ʔaalaaf.*

thousandth - 1. *l-ʔalf.* This is our thousandth shipment. *haaδi rsaaliyyatna l-ʔalf.* 2. *waaẓid imnil-ʔalf.* I own a thousandth of the company. *ʔamluk waaẓid imnil-ʔalf min haš-šarika.*

thrashing - *basṭa* pl. *-aat.* Did he ever get a thrashing! *ṣ-ṣudug ʔakal basṭa!*

thread - 1. *xeeṭ* pl. *xyuuṭ.* Have you a needle and thread? *Eindič ʔubra w-xeeṭ?* 2. *sinn* pl. *snuun.* The thread on this screw is worn out. *sinn hal-burġi saayif.*

to thread - 1. *liδam (u laδum).* I'll thread the needle for you. *ʔaani ʔalδum-lič il-ʔubra.* 2. *ṭallaE (i) sinn.* Would you thread this pipe for me? *balla ma-tṭalliE-li sinn il-hal-buuri?*

threat - *tahdiid* pl. *-aat.* Your threats don't scare me. *tahdiidaatak ma-yxawwufni.*

to **threaten** - *haddad (i tahdiid).* He threatened to leave if they didn't increase his salary. *haddad ybaṭṭil ʔiδa ma-yzayyduun maEaaša.* -- The epidemic threatened the whole city. *l-maraδ haddad il-wlaaya kullha.*

three - 1. *tlaaθa.* Three and three equals six. *tlaaθa w-itlaaθa tsaawi sitta.* 2. *tlaθt.* I've been here three days. *činit ihnaa tlaθt iyyaam.* 3. *tlaθ.* He brought three books. *jaab itlaθ kutub.*

to **thresh** - *diras (i draas) n-, daas (u).* In northern Iraq, they still thresh grain by oxen. *b-šimaal il-Eiraaq, baEadhum ydirsuun il-ẓubuub biθ-θiiraan.*

threshing machine - *makiinat* (pl. *makaayin*) *diraas.*

threshold - *Eitba* pl. *Eitab.*

thrift - *qtiṣaad.* Scotsmen are known for their thrift. *l-iskutlandiyyiin mašhuuriin bil-iqtiṣaad.*

thrifty - *muqtiṣid.* She's a thrifty housewife. *hiyya fadd ʔumm beet muqtaṣda.*

to **thrill** - 1. *ṭurab (i ṭarab).* The music thrilled him. *ṭurbata l-mawsiiqa.* 2. *ʔaθaar (i ʔiθaara) mašaaEir.* Seeing the site of Sumer for the first time thrilled me. *šoofat mawqiE soomar il-ʔawwal marra ʔaθaar mašaaEri.*

to be thrilled - *ṭaar (i) Eaqil-.* Jamil was thrilled with his present. *jamiil Eaqla ṭaar bil-hadiyya.*

thrilling - *raayiE.* This is a thrilling view! *haaδi fadd manδar raayiE!*

to **thrive** - 1. *ntiEaš (i ntiEaaš).* The economy is thriving. *l-waδE il-iqtiṣaadi da-yintiEiš.* 2. *nima (u nimu).* Cattle thrive here. *l-baqar yinmu b-hal-manṭiqa.* 3. *traEraE (a taraEruE).* The children are thriving. *j-jihaal da-yitraEraEuun.*

throat - *zarduum* pl. *zraadiim, balEuum* pl. *blaaEiim.* The doctor painted my throat with iodine. *ṭ-ṭabiib dihan zarduumi b-yood.*

**He'd cut your throat for two cents. *yguṣṣ rugubtak Eala filseen.*

**He jumped down my throat. *miharni.* or *zaffni.*

**She wanted to say something, but the words stuck in her throat. *raadat itguul fadd šii bass Eiṣat ič-čilma b-ẓaligha.*

to **throb** - *nubaδ (u nabuδ).* The blood is throbbing in my veins. *d-damm da-yinbuδ ib-damaaraati.*

throne - *Earš* pl. *Euruuš.*

through - 1. *been.* The president's party drove through cheering crowds. *r-raʔiis w-ẓašiita marraw ib-sayyaaraathum been ij-jamaahiir il-haatfa.* 2. *min.* You have to go through the hall to get to the kitchen. *laazim itfuut imnil-hool ẓatta truuẓ lil-maṭbax.* 3. *Ean ṭariiq.* You'll have to go through the sergeant to see the captain. *laazim itruuẓ Ean ṭariiq il-Eariif ẓatta tšuuf ir-raʔiis.* 4. *b-sabab, b-natiijat.* The work was held up two weeks through his negligence. *wugaf iš-šuġuḷ muddat isbuuEeen b-sabab ihmaala.*

**We went through the woods. *xtiragna l-ġaaba.* or *gṭaEna l-ġaaba fadd ṣafẓa lil-lux.*

**The carpenter bored a hole through the wood. *n-najjaar ziraf zuruf bil-xišba.*

**The deal fell through. *ṣ-ṣafqa ma-nijẓat.*

**There's no through train from Kirkuk to Basra. *ma-aku qiṭaar yruuẓ fadd raas min karkuuk lil-baṣra.*

**Is this a through street? *haaδa šaariE yxarrij?*

through and through - 1. *mnil-ʔasaas, mnil-Eirig.* He's bad through and through. *haaδa muu xooš ʔaadmi mnil-ʔasaas.* 2. *min foog li-jawwa.* We were soaked through and through. *tnaggaEna min foog li-jawwa.*

to be through - *xaḷḷaṣ (i).* I'll be through work at five o'clock. *ʔaxaḷḷiṣ imniš-šuġuḷ is-saaEa xamsa.*

**I am through with it. *maa-li laazim bii baEad.*

**If you ever do that again, we're through. *tara ʔiδa tsawwi haay marra lux, wala ʔašuuf wiččak baEad.*

throughout - 1. *ṭuul.* You can get these vegetables throughout the year. *tigdar tilgi hal-xuδra ṭuul is-sana.* 2. *b-kull ʔanẓaaʔ.* This hotel is famous throughout the world. *hal-ʔuteel maEruuf ib-kull ʔanẓaaʔ il-Eaalam.*

throw - *šamra* pl. *-aat, δabba* pl. *-aat.* That was some throw! *haay šloon šamra ẓilwa!*

to throw - 1. *šumar (u šamur), δabb (i δabb).* Let's see how far you can throw the ball. *xalli nšuuf iš-biEid tigdar tišmur it-ṭooba.* -- He throws himself into it heart and soul. *δaabib nafsa Ealeeha min kull galba.* 2. *waggaE (i), šumar (u).* The horse threw him. *l-ẓiṣaan waggaEa.* 3. *buṭaẓ (a baṭiẓ).* He threw his opponent in a few seconds. *buṭaẓ xaṣma b-čam θaaniya.* 4. *wajjah (i).* Throw that light this way, please. *baḷḷa wajjih iṣ-ṣuwa*

l-haṣ-ṣafza.
to throw away - *δabb (i δabb).* Throw the papers away. *δibb hal-ʔawraaq.* -- He's just throwing his money away. *da-yδibb ifluusa biš-šaṭṭ.*
to throw back - *δabb (i δabb) n-.* Throw the fish back in the river. *δibb is-simča biš-šaṭṭ.*
to throw down - *šammar (u), šumar (u šamur).* Don't throw your things down so carelessly. *la-tšammur ġaraaδak haš-šikil bala htimaam.*
to throw in - *čammal (i tčimmil).* The baker threw in a few extra loaves of bread. *l-xabbaaz čammal čam ṣammuuna.*
**Ahmad threw in the towel. *ʔazmad sallam.* or *ʔazmad istaslam.*
to throw off - **1.** *nizaε (naziε).* He threw off his coat and joined the fight. *nizaε sitirta w-ištirak bil-εarka.* **2.** *txallaṣ (a) min.* How did you manage to throw off your cold? *šloon igdarit titxallaṣ imnin-našla?*
to throw out - **1.** *δabb (i δabb) n-.* I threw my old shoes out. *δabbeet qanaadri l-εatiiga.* **2.** *ṭirad (u tarid) n-, čallaq (i tčliiq) t-.* She almost threw me out. *yaεni ʔilla šwayya čaan ṭirdatni.* or *baεad išwayya tčalliqni.*
**The judge threw the case out of court for lack of evidence. *l-zaakim radd id-daεwa l-εadam wujuud ʔadilla.*
to throw up - **1.** *ṭagg (u) b-wijj.* That's the second time you've thrown that up to me. *haay il-marra θ-θaanya ṭṭuggha b-wijji.* **2.** *zaaε (u zooε), zawwaε (i tazwiiε).* I throw up whenever I see blood. *kull-ma ašuuf damm ʔazuuε.* **3.** *baṭṭal (i) min.* He threw up a good job to run for the election. *baṭṭal min saġla zeena zatta yraššiz nafsa lil-intixaab.*
thud - *ṭabba* pl. *-aat.* I heard a thud in the next room. *simaεit ṭabba b-ġuruft il-lux.*
thumb - *ʔibhaam* pl. *-aat.* I burned my thumb. *zragit ibhaami.*
**I'm all thumbs today. *š-ma ʔasawwi b-ʔiidi l-yoom ma-yiṭlaε tamaam.* or *ʔaani mxarbuṭ il-yoom.*
**He's too much under his wife's thumb. *yimši b-zukum marta ʔakθar imnil-laazim.* or *marta raakbata.*
**He sticks out like a sore thumb. *δaakuwa mbayyin.* or *δaakuwa ma-yinδamm.*
to thumb through - *warraq (i).* I thumbed through the telephone book. *warraqit ib-daliil it-talafoon.*
thumb tack - *danbuus* pl. *dnaabiis.* We put up the notice with thumb tacks. *εallaqna l-iεlaan ib-danaabiis.*
thunder - *garguuεa* pl. *garaagiiε, raεad.* Did you hear the thunder last night? *smaεt il-garaagiiε il-baarza bil-leel?*
**A thunder of applause greeted the speaker. *staqbilaw il-xaṭiib ib-fadd εaaṣifa mnit-taṣfiiq.*
to thunder - *gargaε (i gargaεa), riεad (i raεad).* It's beginning to thunder. *bidat itgargiε.* or *bidat id-dinya tirεid.*
**You shouldn't have let him thunder at you like that. *ma-čaan laazim itxallii yirεid w-yizbid εaleek haš-šikil.*
thunderstorm - *εaaṣifa* pl. *εawaaṣif.* We missed the thunderstorm. *l-εaaṣifa ma-jatti εaleena.*
Thursday - *yoom il-xamiis.* That can wait till Thursday. *xalliiha ʔila yoom il-xamiis* or *xalliiha lil-xamiis.*
to **thwart** - *xayyab (u).* His action thwarted our plans. *ṭṣarrufa xayyab xiṭaṭna.*
thyme - *zaεtar, saεtar.*
tick - **1.** *garaada* pl. *-aat* coll. *garaad.* The dog is covered with ticks. *č-čalib malyaan garaad.* **2.** *doošag* pl. *dwaašig.* We had to sleep on straw ticks. *δṭarreena nnaam εala dwaašig maal zalfa.* **3.** *dagga* pl. *-aat.* The room is so quiet you can hear the tick of the clock. *l-gubba hiiči ṣanṭa tigdar tismaε daggaat is-saaεa.*
to tick - *dagg (u dagga).* I can hear the watch tick. *da-ʔagdar asmaε is-saaεa tdugg.*
ticket - **1.** *biṭaaqa* pl. *-aat, biṭaayiq; tikit* pl. *-aat.* Can you get us three tickets for the play? *tigdar itdabburna tlaθ biṭaaqaat lir-ruwaaya?* -- You can buy a ticket on the train. *tigdar tištiri tikit bil-qiṭaar.* **2.** *qaaʔimat muraššaziin.* The National Party has a good ticket. *l-zizb il-waṭani εinda qaaʔimat muraššaziin zeena.*
ticking - **1.** *xaam iš-šaam.* How much is this ticking a yard? *hal-xaam iš-šaam beeš iδ-δiraaε?*
2. *ṭagṭaga.* I just heard a strange ticking in the machine. *hassa smaεit ṭagṭaga ġariiba bil-makiina.*
tickle - *šaxṭa* pl. *-aat.* I've a tickle in my throat. *εindi fadd šaxṭa b-zarduumi.*
to tickle - *daġdaġ (i daġdaġa) t-.* He doesn't laugh even if you tickle him. *ma-yiδzak zatta loo daġdaġta.*
ticklish - *zassaas.* That's a ticklish question. *haaδa fadd mawδuuε zassaas.*
**Are you ticklish? *tġaar ib-suhuula?* or *d-daġdaġa tʔaθθir biik?*
tide: **The tide is coming in. *l-bazar raz-yirtifiε.*
high tide - *madd.* It was high tide when the ship came up the river. *s-sifiina dixlat in-nahar wakt il-madd.*
low tide - *jazir.* You can walk out to the island at low tide. *wakt il-jazir tigdar timši lil-jazra.*
to tide over - *ṭallaε (i taṭliiε), dabbar (u) ʔamur.* Two dinars will tide me over until Monday. *diinaareen iṭṭalliεni l-yoom iθ-θineen.*
tidy - **1.** *mhandam, mnaδδam, mrattab.* He is a very tidy person. *huwwa fadd waazid kulliš imhandam.* **2.** *mrattab, mnaδδam.* Her room is always tidy. *ġurfatha daaʔiman imrattba zeen.* **3.** *čbiir.* He's inherited a tidy fortune. *wiraθ θarwa čbiira.*
tie - **1.** *ṣila* pl. *-aat, raabiṭa* pl. *rawaabiṭ.* The two countries are bound by economic and military ties. *d-dawulteen murtabṭiin ib-ṣilaat iqtiṣaadiyya w-εaskariyya.* **2.** *raabiṭa* pl. *rawaabiṭ.* Family ties are stronger in the Middle East than in the West. *r-rawaabiṭ il-εaaʔiliyya biš-šarq il-ʔawsaṭ ʔaqwa mnil-ġarb.* **3.** *booyinbaaġ* pl. *-aat, ribaaṭ* pl. *ʔarbiṭa.* He wears expensive ties. *yilbas booyinbaaġaat ġaalya.* **4.** *loog* pl. *-aat.* The ties on this line need replacing. *l-loogaat maal has-sičča yinraad-ilha taġyiir.* **5.** *taεaadul.* The game ended in a tie. *s-sibaaq intiha b-taεaadul.*
to tie - **1.** *šadd (i šadd).* I have to tie my shoelaces. *xalli ašidd qiiṭaan qundarti.* **2.** *tεaadal (a taεaadul).* They tied us in the last minute's play. *tεaadlaw wiyyaana b-ʔaaxir lazδa mnil-liεib.* **3.** *εigad (u εagid).* Tie that knot securely. *ʔuεgud hal-εugda zeen.*
**My hands are tied. *ʔaani mčattaf.*
to tie down - *ribaṭ (u rabuṭ).* I don't want to tie myself down. *ʔaani ma-ard arbuṭ nafsi.*
to tie in - *riham (a rahum).* This ties in nicely with what we know. *haaδa yirham zeen wiyya l-nuεurfa.*
to tie on - *šadd (i šadd) b-, rubaṭ (u rabaṭ) b-.* Tie on another piece of string. *šidd biiha wuṣla lux xeeṭ.*
to tie up - **1.** *rubaṭ (u rabaṭ), šadd (i šadd).* Please tie up these papers for me. *ʔarjuuk urbuṭ-li hal-ʔawraaq ib-xeeṭ.* -- Did you tie up the boat? *rbaṭṭa lil-balam?* **2.** *šaġġal (i tašġiil).* He's tied up all his money in real estate. *šaġġal kull ifluusa b-muεaamalaat il-ʔamlaak.* **3.** *εaṭṭal (i taεṭiil).* The accident tied up traffic. *l-zaadiθ εaṭṭal il-muruur.*
tied up - **1.** *mirtibiṭ.* Are you tied up this evening? *ʔinta mirtibiṭ ib-šii hal-leela?* **2.** *mašġuul.* I was tied up all afternoon. *činit mašġuul tamaaman ṭuul wara δ-δuhur.* **3.** *mšaġġal.* I'm sorry, my money's tied up right now. *mitʔassif ifluusi mšaġġila hassa.*
**Rashid St. is generally tied up at noontime. *šaariε ir-rašiid εaadataan ma-yinfaat bii mnil-xabṣa δ-δuhriyya.*
tiger - *namur* pl. *nmuur, nmuura.* We're going to hunt tigers. *raz-inṣiid inmuur.*
tight - **1.** *zeel.* Shut your eyes tight. *sidd iεyuunak zeel.* -- Hold tight to the horse's neck. *čallib ib-rugbat l-izṣaan zeel.* **2.** *δabb, maδbuub.* I tied my shoelaces too tight. *šaddeet qiiṭaan qundarti δabb.* -- Is the jar sealed tight? *qabaġ iš-šiiša maδbuub zeen?* or *qabaġ iš-šiiša masduud δabb?* **3.** *δayyig.* This jacket is too tight for me. *has-sitra kulliš δayyga εalayya.* **4.** *sakraan.* Boy was I tight last night! *ʔamma ʔaani ṣudug činit sakraan il-baarza bil-leel!* **5.** *baxiil.* He's very tight with his money. *huwwa kullis baxiil b-ifluusa.* **6.** *šaazz.* Money is very tight now. *l-ifluus šaazza hassa.*
**I've been in many a tight spot before. *ʔaani yaa-ma waagiε ib-warṭa gabuḷ.* or *ʔaani maarr ib-ʔayyaam εaṣiiba gabuḷ.*
to sit tight - *ṣubar (u ṣabur).* You just sit tight; and we'll be with you in half an hour.

ʔiṣbur ib-makaanak; ʔiẓna raẓ-inkuun yammak baɛad nuṣṣ saaɛa.
to **tighten** - *ṣabb (u ṣabb).* Tighten the rope. *ṣubb il-ẓabil.*
tightlipped - *skuuti* pl. *-iyya, katuum* pl. *-iin.* Nuri is quite tightlipped. *nuuri kulliš iskuuti.*
tightly - *ṣabb, b-ẓeel.* He tied the package tightly. *šadd ir-ruzma ṣabb.*
Tigris River - *nahar dijla.*
tile - *kaašiyya* pl. *-aat* coll. *kaaši.* A tile fell off the bathroom wall. *kaašiyya wugɛat min ẓaayiṭ il-ẓammaam.*
to tile - *ṭabbag (i taṭbiig) t- b-kaaši.* We have to tile the kitchen floor. *laazim inṭabbug gaaɛ il-muṭbax bil-kaaši.*
till - **1.** *daxal.* Is there any money in the till? *ʔaku fluus bid-daxal?* **2.** *ʔila ʔan, ẓatta.* Wait till I come back. *ntiṣir ʔila ʔan ʔarjaɛ.* **3.** *ʔila, ẓatta.* I won't be able to see you till next week. *ma-raẓ-agdar ašuufak ʔila l-isbuuɛ ij-jaay.*
tilt - *meela* pl. *-aat.* The telephone pole has taken on a bad tilt. *ɛamuud it-talafoon maal meela qawiyya.*
at a tilt - *maayil, mnakkas.* The Iraqi cap is worn at a tilt. *s-sidaara l-ɛiraaqiyya tinlibis maayla.*
to tilt - **1.** *mayyal (i tmiyyil), nakkas (i tankiis).* If you tilt the bottle, you may be able to get it out of the refrigerator. *loo tmayyil il-buṭil muẓtamal tigdar iṭṭallɛa mniθ-θillaaja.* -- Tilt your hat forward a bit. *nakkis šafuqtak išwayya.* -- Tilt the flag forward during the parade. *nakkis il-ɛalam ʔaθnaaʔ il-istiɛraaṣ.* **2.** *ẓina (i ẓani), mayyal (i).* I can't tilt my head to either side. *ma-ʔagdar ʔaẓni raasi li-ṣafẓa.*
timber - **1.** *ʔašjaar maal xišab.* Iraq has little timber. *l-ɛiraaq ma-bii hwaaya ʔašjaar maal xišab.* **2.** *dalag* pl. *-aat, jiṣaɛ* pl. *jiṣuuɛ.* The timbers on our roof are rotting. *d-dalagaat ib-sagufna xaaysa.*
time - **1.** *wakit* pl. *ʔawkaat.* It's time to leave. *ṣaar wakt ir-rooẓa.* -- What time are we to go? *š-wakit raẓ-inruuẓ.* -- These are hard times. *haay ʔawkaat ɛaṣiiba.* or ***haaδi muu xooš ʔayyaam.* **2.** *marra* pl. *-aat, nooba* pl. *-aat.* This is my first time here. *haay ʔawwal marra ʔaji hnaa.* -- Four times five equals twenty. *ʔarbaɛ marraat xamsa, ɛišriin.* or *ʔarbaɛa b-xamsa ysaawi ɛišriin.* -- Two times two equals four. *marrteen iθneen ysaawi ʔarbaɛa.* **3.** *l-ʔayyaam, z-zaman.* Time will tell. *l-ʔayyaam tikšifha.* **4.** *mudda.* The time is up tomorrow. *l-mudda tixlaṣ baačir.* -- I worked a long time. *štiġalit mudda ṭwiila.* -- He comes to see us from time to time. *yiji yšuufna been mudda w-mudda.* or *yiji yšuufna been ẓiin w-ʔaaxar.* **5.** *tawqiit.* The news in Arabic is broadcast from London at 6 P.M. Greenwich time or 9 P.M. Baghdad local time. *l-ʔaxbaar bil-ɛarabi tinδaaɛ min landan bil-leel saaɛa sitta ẓasab tawqiit grinič ʔaw saaɛa tisɛa ẓasab tawqiit baġdaad il-maẓalli.* **6.** *tawqiiɛ.* The drum beats the time in music. *d-dumbuk yiḍbuṭ it-tawqiiɛ bil-mawsiiqa.* **7.** *zaman, ʔawaan.* That research is ahead of the times. *hal-buẓuuθ ġaalba z-zaman.* That design was too far ahead of its time. *hat-taṣmiim saabiq ʔawaana.* **8.** *muwaqqat.* The revolutionaries set a time bomb in the plane. *θ-θuwwaar ẓaṭṭaw qumbula mwaqqita biṭ-ṭiyyaara.*
**Would you know what time of day it is? *tuɛruf is-saaɛa b-eeš?*
**They gave him a bad time. *ṣawwjoo or ʔaδδoo hwaaya.*
a long time ago - *min zamaan, gabul mudda ṭwiila.* I met her a long time ago. *tɛarrafit biiha min zamaan.* -- She left a long time ago. *raaẓat min zamaan.* or ***ṣaar-ilha hwaaya min raaẓat.*
all the time - *ɛala ṭuul, daaʔiman.* We had good weather all the time. *čaan ij-jaww mumtaaz ɛala ṭuul.* -- He's here all the time. *huwwa daaʔiman ihnaa.*
at times - *ʔaẓyaanan, dooraat.* At times I work fourteen hours at a stretch. *ʔaẓyaanan ʔaštuġul ʔarbaaṭaɛaš saaɛa ɛala fadd jarra.* -- I see him at times. *ʔašuufa dooraat.*
for the time being - *b-hal-ʔaθnaaʔ, muwaqqatan.* Stay here for the time being. *ʔibqa hnaa b-hal-ʔaθnaaʔ.*
in good time - *b-wakitha.* You'll know it in good time. *ɛuud tuɛrufha b-wakitha.*
in time - **1.** *b-natiija, ʔaxiiran, bil-wakt il-munaasib.* I'm sure we'll come to an agreement in time. *ʔaani mitʔakkid raẓ-noosal il-fadd ittifaaq bin-natiija.* **2.** *bil-wakt il-munaasib.* The doctor arrived in time to save her. *d-diktoor wuṣal bil-wakt il-munaasib ẓatta yinquδha.*
on time - **1.** *ɛal-wakit.* Please be on time. *balla kuun ɛal-wakit.* **2.** *bil-ʔaqṣaaṭ.* He bought the car on time. *štira s-sayyaara bil-ʔaqṣaaṭ.*
time after time - *marra ɛala marra, yaama w-yaama, marraat.* I've asked him time after time not to do it. *yaama w-yaama ridit minna ma-ysawwiiha.*
to have a good time - *twannas (a winsa).* Did you have a good time? *twannasit?*
to time - **1.** *ɛayyan (i taɛyiin) wakit.* We timed the conference to start after the holiday. *ɛayyanna wakt il-muʔtamar ẓatta yibdi wara l-ɛuṭla.* **2.** *lizam (a) wakit, ṣubaṭ (u) wakit.* Who timed the race? *minu lizam wakt is-sibaaq?*
time keeper - *muwaqqit* pl. *-iin.*
timely - *b-wakit-.* That's a timely article. *haaδa fadd maqaal ib-wakta.*
timer - *muwaqqit* pl. *-aat.* Set the timer for 5 minutes. *ʔinṣub il-muwaqqit ʔila xamis daqaayiq.*
timesaver: **Canned foods are great timesavers. *l-muɛallabaat itxalli l-waaẓid yiqtiṣid bil-wakit.*
timetable - *jadwal (pl. jadaawil) ʔawqaat.*
timid - *mitwahwih, xajuul.* Don't be so timid! *la-tṣiir hal-gadd mitwahwih.*
timing - *tawqiit.* The hold-up relied on precise timing. *s-sariqa ɛtimdat ɛala tawqiit daqiiq.*
**The timing of his speech was excellent. *xiṭaaba jaa bil-wakt il-munaasib.*
tin - **1.** *tanak.* The price of tin went up last week. *ʔasɛaar it-tanak ṣiɛdat bil-isbuuɛ il-faat.* **2.** *quuṭiyya* pl. *qwaaṭi.* Give me a tin of tobacco. *nṭiini quuṭiyyat titin.*
tinder - *ɛilga.* Bring a little tinder so I can start the fire. *jiib-li šwayyat ɛilga ẓatta ašɛil in-naar.*
to **tingle** - *nammal (i).* My foot's tingling. *rijli mnammla.*
to **tinkle** - *ṭagṭag (i ṭagṭaga).* The ice cubes tinkle in the glass. *θ-θalij da-yṭagṭig bil-iglaaṣ.*
tinsmith - *tanakči* pl. *-iyya.*
tint - *loon* pl. *ʔalwaan.* Use a lighter tint for the wall. *staɛmil loon ʔaftaẓ il-haaδa l-ẓaayiṭ.*
to tint - **1.** *ṣubaġ (u).* I want my hair tinted blond. *ʔariid ʔaṣbuġ šaɛri ʔašgar.* **2.** *lawwan (i talwiin).* We've tinted one of the photographs. *lawwanna waaẓid imnir-rusuum.*
tiny - *ṣġayyir.* Where'd you get such a tiny radio? *ween ligeet hiiči raadyo ṣġayyir?*
tip - **1.** *raas* pl. *ruus.* They landed on the northern tip of the island. *nizlaw ib-raas ij-jaziira š-šimaali.* -- My shoes are worn at the tips. *qundarti saafat imnir-raas.* **2.** *ṭarf* pl. *ʔaṭraaf.* The word is on the tip of my tongue. *č-čilma ɛala ṭarf ilsaani.* **3.** *zabaana* pl. *-aat.* Do you have cigarettes with tips? *ɛindak jigaayir ʔumm iz-zabaana?* **4.** *naṣiiẓa* pl. *naṣaayiẓ.* Let me give you a tip. *xalli nṭiik fadd naṣiiẓa.* **5.** *ʔixbaariyya* pl. *-aat.* The police found him through a tip. *š-šurṭa ligoo ɛan ṭariiq ixbaariyya.* **6.** *baxšiiš* pl. *-aat.* How much of a tip shall I give the waiter? *šgadd anṭi baxšiiš lil-booy?*
to tip - *niṭa (i) baxšiiš.* Did you tip the porter? *nṭeeta baxšiiš lil-ẓammaal?*
to tip off - *niṭa (i) maɛluumaat, ʔixbaariyya.* Who tipped you off? *minu nṭaak il-maɛluumaat?*
to tip over - **1.** *gulab (u galub) n-.* The maid tipped the chair over. *l-xaadma gulbat l-iskamli.* **2.** *ngilab (u ngilaab).* The boat tipped over. *l-balam ingilab.*
tiptoe - *ʔaṭraaf ʔaṣaabiɛ.* The children came in on tiptoe. *j-jihaal xaššaw ɛala ʔaṭraaf il-ʔaṣaabiɛ.*
tiptop - *mumtaaz.* My car's in tiptop condition. *sayyaarti b-ẓaala mumtaaza.*
tire - *taayar* pl. *-aat.* Did you put air in the tires? *nfaxt it-taayaraat?*
to tire - **1.** *taɛɛab (i tatɛiib).* The long journey tired us thoroughly. *s-safra ṭ-ṭwiila taɛɛbatna kulliš.* **2.** *tiɛab (a taɛab, taɛbaan).* I tire very easily in this hot weather. *ʔaani ʔatɛab bil-ɛajal ib-haj-jaww il-ẓaarr.* **3.** *mall (i malal), ṣaaj (u ṣooj, ṣawajaan).* I'm tired of her

nagging. *malleet min nagnagatha.*
tired - *taɛbaan.* He looks tired. *ybayyin taɛbaan.*
tiresome - 1. *mumill.* What a tiresome person he is! *haaδa ṣudug fadd šaxiṣ mumill.* 2. *mutɛib.* This is very tiresome work. *haš-šuġuḷ kulliš mutɛib.*
tissue - 1. *nasiij* pl. *ʔansija.* Was there much tissue injured? *čaan aku hwaaya ʔansija mitʔaδδaaya?* 2. *čaffiyya* (pl. *čfaafi*) *waraq.* Buy me a box of tissues. *štirii-li quuṭiyya čfaafi waraq.*

tissue paper - *waraq xafiif.* Wrap it in tissue paper. *liffha b-waraq xafiif.*
title - 1. *ʔisim* pl. *ʔasmaaʔ.* Do you know the title of the book? *tuɛruf ʔism il-iktaab?* 2. *laqab* pl. *ʔalqaab.* What's his title? *šinu laqaba?* 3. *ɛinwaan* pl. *ɛanaawiin.* What's the title of your position? *šinu ɛinwaan waḍiiftak?* -- The title page is missing from this book. *ṣafzat il-ɛinwaan ḍaayɛa min hal-iktaab.* 4. *mulkiyya* pl. *-aat.* Whose name is the title of the car in? *b-ism man mulkiit is-sayyaara?*
to - 1. *l-, ʔila.* I have to go to the library. *laazim aruuz lil-maktaba.* -- He went through his fortune to the last cent. *ṣiraf kull θaruuta l-ʔaaxir filis.* 2. *b-.* I told him that to his face. *gilt-ilh-iyyaa b-wučča.* -- What do you say to this? *š-itguul ib-haay.* 3. *wiyya.* Did you talk to him? *zčeet wiyyaa?* 4. *ɛala.* Apply this ointment to the inflamed area. *zuṭṭ hal-marham ɛal-manṭiqa l-miltahba.*
**I'm trying to help you. *ʔaani bass da-ariid aɛaawnak.*
**I must go to bed. *laazim anaam.*
**It doesn't mean much to him. *ma-yhimma.*
**It's ten minutes to four. *s-saaɛa ʔarbaɛa ʔilla ɛašra.*
toad - *ɛugrugga* pl. *-aat, ɛagaariig* coll. *ɛugrugg, ɛagruug.*
toadstool - *raas* (pl. *ruus*) *fṭirr* coll. *fṭirr.*
toast - *naxab* pl. *ʔanxaab.* Let's drink a toast to the newlyweds. *xal-nišrab naxab il-ɛuruus wil-ɛirriis.*
to toast - 1. *zammaṣ (i tazmiiṣ).* Shall I toast the bread? *triidni ʔazammiṣ il-xubuz?* 2. *širab (a) naxab.* Let's toast the host. *xal-nišrab naxab id-daaɛi.*

tobacco - *titin.*
tobacco dealer - *titinči* pl. *-iyya.*
tobacco shop - *maxzan* (pl. *maxaazin*) *jigaayir.*
today - *hal-yoom, l-yoom.* What's on the menu today? *šaku ɛidkum ʔakil hal-yoom?* -- I haven't read today's paper yet. *baɛadni ma-qreet jariidt il-yoom.*
toe - *ʔiṣbiɛ* (pl. *ʔaṣaabiɛ, ʔaṣaabiiɛ*) *rijil.* My toes are frozen. *ʔaṣaabiiɛ rijli mθallja.*
**I didn't mean to stop on anybody's toes. *ma-qṣadit il-ʔisaaʔa l-ʔazzad.* or *ma-qṣadit ʔatɛarraḍ l-azzad.*
**I have to be on my toes all the time. *laazim ʔafukk iɛyuuni ɛala ṭuul.* or *laazim ʔakuun mityaqqiḍ ɛala ṭuul.*
together - *suwa.* We work together. *ništuġuḷ suwa.* -- I saw my friend and his wife walking together. *šifit ṣadiiqi w-marta yitmaššuun suwa.*
to get together - *jtimaɛ (i jtimaaɛ).* Can we get together some evening? *nigdar nijtimiɛ fadd leela?*
to stick together - *tɛaaḍad (a taɛaaḍud).* Let's stick together in this matter. *xalli nitɛaaḍad ib-hal-masʔala.*
toilet - *mirzaaḍ* pl. *maraaziiḍ, xalaaʔ* pl. *-aat.* Where's the toilet? *ween il-mirzaaḍ?*
toilet paper - *waraq maraaziiḍ, waraq xalaaʔ.* Muslims use water instead of toilet paper. *l-misilmiin yistaɛmiluun maay ibdaal waraq il-maraaziiḍ.*
token - 1. *daliil* pl. *dalaaʔil, ɛalaama* pl. *-aat, tiδkaar* pl. *-aat.* He gave it to me as a token of his friendship. *nṭaani-iyyaaha ka-daliil ɛala ṣadaaqta.* 2. *ʔismi*.* We may be able to satisfy them with a token payment. *yimkin nigdar nirḍiihum ib-fadd mablaġ ʔismi.*
tolerance - 1. *tazammul.* This steel has high tolerance for heat. *hal-fulaaḍ ɛinda tazammul qawi lil-zaraara.* 2. *tasaamuz.* Tolerance is difficult in religion and politics. *t-tasaamuz bid-diin w-bis-siyaasa ṣaɛub.*
tolerant - *mitsaamiz.* Our boss is very tolerant. *mudiirna kulliš mitsaamiz.*
to **tolerate** - *tsaamaz (a) b-.* I won't tolerate inefficiency. *ma-raz-ʔatsaamaz ib-zaalat ɛadam il-kafaaʔa.*

toll - 1. *ɛibriyya* pl. *-aat.* You have to pay a toll on this bridge. *laazim tidfaɛ ɛibriyya ɛala haj-jisir.* 2. *ɛadad.* The plane crash took a heavy toll of life. *raaz ɛadad ičbiir imniḍ-ḍazaaya b-zaadiθ iṭ-ṭiyyaara.*
toll bridge: **This is a toll bridge. *haaδa j-jisir yaaxδuun ɛalee ɛibriyya.*
tomato - *ṭamaaṭaaya* pl. *-aat* coll. *ṭamaaṭa.* Make the salad with tomatoes and cucumbers. *sawwi z-zalaaṭa min ṭamaaṭa w-ixyaar.*
tomato juice - *ɛaṣiir ṭamaaṭa.*
tomato sauce - *maɛjuun ṭamaaṭa.*
tomb - 1. *qabur* pl. *qubuur.* He placed a wreath on the tomb of the unknown soldier. *zaṭṭ ʔikliil ɛala qabr ij-jundi il-majhuul.* 2. *ḍariiz* pl. *ḍaraayiz.* They went to visit Husayn's tomb in Karbala. *raazaw yzuuruun ḍariiz il-zusayn ib-karbala.*
tomcat - *hirr* pl. *hruura.*
tomorrow - *baačir.* I'll be back tomorrow. *raz-ʔarjaɛ baačir.* -- It'll be in tomorrow's paper. *tiṭlaɛ ib-jariidat baačir.* -- I won't see him till tomorrow morning. *ma-raz-ašuufa gabuḷ baačir iṣ-ṣubuz.*
ton - *ṭann* pl. *ṭnuun.* We order a ton of coal. *waṣṣeena ɛala ṭann fazam.* -- That's a ten-ton truck. *hal-loori ʔabu ɛašr iṭnuun.*
tone - 1. *lahja* pl. *-aat, ṣooṭ* pl. *ʔaṣwaaṭ.* You shouldn't speak to her in such a rough tone. *ma-laazim tizči wiyyaaha b-hiiči lahja zaadda.* 2. *ṣooṭ* pl. *ʔaṣwaaṭ.* This violin has a beautiful tone. *hal-kamanja ṣooṭha kulliš zilu.* 3. *loon* pl. *ʔalwaan.* His car is two-tone. *sayyaarta looneen.*
to tone down - *hidaʔ (a huduuʔ), ɛiqal (a ɛaqil).* He's toned down a lot since he came here. *hidaʔ ihwaaya min ʔija l-ihnaa.*
tongs - 1. *maaša* pl. *-aat.* Use tongs to stir the coals. *zarrik ij-jamur bil-maaša.* 2. *milgaṭ* pl. *malaagiṭ.* He picked up a lump of sugar with the tongs. *šaal fuṣṣ šakar bil-milgaṭ.*
tongue - *lisaan* pl. *-aat, lisin, ʔalsina.* Let me see your tongue. *xal-ʔašuuf ilsaanak.* -- She has a sharp tongue. *ɛidha lsaan zaadd.* or *lsaanha miθl is-siččiin.* -- The tongue on my shoe is torn off. *ngiṭaɛ ilsaan qundarti.*
tonic - 1. *muqawwi* pl. *-iyaat.* What you need is a good tonic. *yinraad-lak fadd muqawwi zeen.* 2. *toonik.* Do you like gin and tonic? *yɛijbak jin w-toonik?* 3. *dihin.* The barber put some tonic on my hair. *l-imzayyin zaṭṭ dihin ib-šaɛri.*
tonight - *hal-leela, l-leela.* What shall we do tonight? *š-insawwi hal-leela?* -- Have you seen tonight's paper? *šift ij-jariida maalat hal-leela?*
tonnage - *ṭann zumuula.* What's the tonnage of that vessel? *čam ṭann zumuulat δiič il-baaxira?*
tonsil - *looza* pl. *-aat.* My tonsils are swollen. *loozteeni miltahba.*
tonsilitis - *ltihaab il-loozteen.*
too - *hamm, hammeen.* May I come, too? *ʔagdar ʔaani hamm ʔaji?*
**This is too hot. *haay kulliš zaarra.*
**Don't stay away too long. *la-ṭṭawwal barra hwaaya.*
**This board is too long. *hal-looza ʔaṭwal imnil-laazim.*
**The play was none too good. *r-ruwaaya ma-čaanat kulliš zeena.*
tool - 1. *ʔadaat* pl. *ʔadawaat, ʔaala* pl. *-aat.* Be careful with those new tools. *diir baalak ɛala hal-ʔadawaat ij-jidiida.* 2. *ʔaala* pl. *-aat.* The mayor is only a tool in the hands of his party. *raʔiis il-baladiyya muu ʔazyad min ʔaala b-iid il-zizib maala.*
tooled leather - *jilid mašġuul, jilid manquuš.*
to **toot** - *ṭawwaṭ (u ṭṭuwwuṭ), dagg (u).* Toot your horn at this corner. *ṭawwuṭ ib-haaδa l-mafrag.*
tooth - *sinn* pl. *snuun.* This tooth hurts. *has-sinn ywajjiɛ.* -- The saw has a broken tooth. *l-minšaar bii sinn maksuur.*
**She has a sweet tooth. *tzibb il-zalaa hwaaya.*
**We fought against it tooth and nail. *qaawamnaaha b-kull šidda.*
toothache - *wajaɛ sinn.* I have a toothache. *ɛindi wajaɛ sinn.*
toothbrush - *firčat* (pl. *firač*) *isnuun.*
tooth paste - *maɛjuun isnuun.*
top - 1. *raas* pl. *ruus.* The storm broke off the top of our palm tree. *l-ɛaaṣifa kisrat raas in-naxla maalatna.* -- You'll find that passage at the top of page 32. *tšuuf hal-faqara b-raas ṣafza θneen w-iθlaaθiin.* 2. *qumma* pl. *qumam.* How far is it to

the top of the mountain? *šgadd il-masaafa l-qummat haj-jibal?* 3. *Ɛilu, ʔaƐla.* She shouted at the top of her voice. *ṣaaζat ib-Ɛilu ζissha* or ***ṣaaζat ib-kull ζissha.* 4. *foogaani**. There's still one room vacant on the top floor. *li-hassa ʔaku ġurfa faarġa bil-qaaṭ il-foogaani.* — Your handkerchiefs are in the top drawer. *čfaafiyyak bil-imjarr il-foogaani.* 5. *tanta* pl. *-aat.* It's such nice weather, let's put the top down. *j-jaww kulliš laṭiif, xalli nnazzil it-tanta.* 6. *muṣraƐ* pl. *maṣaariƐ.* Do you know how to spin a top? *tuƐruf tilƐab muṣraƐ?* 7. *foog.* The book is lying on top. *l-iktaab maζṭuuṭ li-foog.* — We searched the house from top to bottom. *fattašna l-beet min foog li-jawwa.* 8. *ʔaqṣa.* We drove at top speed all the way down here. *siqna b-ʔaqṣa surƐa ṭuul iṭ-ṭariiq l-ihnaa.*
**I don't know why he blew his top. *ma-ʔadri leeš haaj.*
**I slept like a top last night. *nimit miθl il-iζjaara l-baarζa bil-leel.*
to top off - *ʔanha (i), xallaṣ (i).* Let's top off the evening with a glass of wine. *xalli ninhi l-leela b-fadd iglaaṣ šaraab.*
**To top it all off, he stole my wallet. *w-ičmaala, baag ij-jizdaan maali.* or *foogaaha, baag jizdaani.*
topic - *mawδ̣uuƐ* pl. *mawaaδ̣iiƐ.* This is quite a timely topic. *haaδa fadd mawδ̣uuƐ ib-wakta.*
topsoil - *zimiij.* The rains are washing away the topsoil. *l-ʔamṭaar da-tijruf iz-zimiij.*
topsy-turvy - *raas Ɛala Ɛaqib.* Everything was topsy-turvy. *kullši čaan magluub raas Ɛala Ɛaqib.*
torch - *mašƐal* pl. *mašaaƐil.*
torment - *Ɛaδaab.* I can't stand the torment anymore. *ma-atζammal il-Ɛaδaab baƐad.*
to torment - 1. *ʔaδδa (i).* Stop tormenting that cat! *bass Ɛaad itʔaδδi hal-bazzuuna.* 2. *marmar (u tmurmur) l-, Ɛaδδab (i taƐδiib).* She tormented her father all day. *hiyya marmurat il-abuuha ṭuul in-nahaar.* or *Ɛaδδibat ʔabuuha ṭuul in-nahaar.*
torn - *mašguug.* Which pocket is torn? *yaa jeeb mašguug?*
tornado - *fittaala* pl. *-aat.*
torpedo - *toorbiid* pl. *-aat.*
torrent - *seel* pl. *siyuul.* The heavy rain caused several small torrents. *l-muṭar il-qawi sabbab Ɛiddat siyuul iṣġayyra.*
**The rain came down in torrents. *l-muṭar gaam yinzil miθl il-girab.*
torrid zone - *l-manṭiqa l-istiwaaʔiyya.* Most of Africa lies within the torrid zone. *muƐδ̣am ʔafriiqya waaqƐa bil-manṭiqa l-istiwaaʔiyya.*
tortoise - *sulζafaat* pl. *salaaζif, ragga* pl. *-aat* coll. *ragg.*
torture - 1. *Ɛaδaab, marmara.* Life with her is just torture. *l-ζayaat wiyyaaha Ɛaδaab bass.* 2. *taƐδiib.* Confessions obtained by torture are illegal. *l-iƐtiraafaat il-titζaṣṣal bit-taƐδiib muu qaanuuniyya.*
to torture - *Ɛaδδab (i taƐδiib).* The police tortured him to get a confession. *š-širṭa Ɛaδδiboo ζatta yaaxδuun minna Ɛtiraaf.*
to **toss** - 1. *šimar (u šamur).* Toss me the ball over here. *šmur-li ṭ-ṭooba li-hnaa.* 2. *tgaḷḷab (u tguḷḷub).* Last night I tossed and turned all night long. *l-baarζa bil-leel δ̣alleet atgaḷḷab b-ifraaši.*
tot - *ṣġayyruun* pl. *-iin.* She's just a tiny tot. *baƐadha ṣġayyruuna.*
total - *majmuuƐ* pl. *majaamiiƐ, yakuun* pl. *-aat.* Subtract ten from the total. *ʔiṭraζ Ɛašra mnil-majmuuƐ.* — My total earnings for this month were two hundred dollars. *majmuuƐ il-ζaṣṣalta haš-šahar miiteen doolaar.*
to total - 1. *waṣṣal (i).* His income totals two thousand dollars a year. *daxla ywaṣṣil ʔalfeen doolaar bis-sana.* 2. *ζisab (i ζsaab), jimaƐ (a jamiƐ).* Let's total up our expenses for the month. *xalli niζsib maṣruufaatna maal iš-šahar.*
to **totter** - *tmaayal (a tamaayul).* The old man got up and tottered toward the door. *š-šaayib gaam w-itmaayal lil-baab.*
tottering - *mitdaaƐi.* The bridge is tottering. *j-jisir mitdaaƐi.*
touch - 1. *ṭaxxa* pl. *-aat.* She jumps at the slightest touch. *tugmaz min ʔaqall ṭaxxa.* or ***tugmaz bass waaζid ygiisha.* 2. *malmas.* Silk is soft to the touch. *l-ζariir naaƐim il-malmas.* 3. *nugṭa* pl. *nugaaṭ.* The soup still needs a touch of salt. *š-šoorba baƐadha tiζtaaj fadd nugṭat miliζ.* 4. *ʔaθar* pl. *ʔaaθaar.* The patient has a touch of fever. *l-mariiδ̣ Ɛinda ʔaθar iṣxuuna.*
**The game was touch and go towards the end. *natiijat is-sibaaq čaanat imƐalliga.*
to get in touch with - *ttiṣal (i ttiṣaal) b-.* I have to get in touch with him right away. *laazim attiṣil bii ζaalan.*
to touch - *gaas (i), ṭaxx (u ṭaxx).* Please don't touch that! *baḷḷa la-tgiisha l-haay.* -- He won't touch liquor. *ma-ygiis il-mašruub.*
**I touched him for two dinars. *šilaƐit minna diinaareen.* or *tdaayanit minna diinaareen.*
to touch off - *ʔadda (i taʔdiya) ʔila.* His remarks touched off a violent argument. *mulaaζaδ̣aata ʔaddat ʔila fadd jadal Ɛaniif.*
to touch on - 1. *šaar (i) ʔila, ṭṭarraq (a) ʔila.* The speaker touched on many points during his talk. *l-muζaaδ̣ir šaar ʔila Ɛiddat nuqaaṭ ib-ζadiiθa.* 2. *wuṣal (a wuṣuul) ʔila.* His remarks touch on blasphemy. *ζačya yooṣal ʔila darajt il-kufur.*
to touch up - *sawwa (i) rituuš l-.* They haven't touched up the picture yet. *baƐad li-hassa ma-sawwoo-lha rituuš liṣ-ṣuura.*
touched - *mašxuuṭ.* Don't mind him! He's a little touched. *la-tdiir-la baal, haaδa mašxuuṭ.*
to be touched - *tʔaθθar (i taʔaθθur)* She was deeply touched by the story. *tʔaθθrat kulliš imnil-iζčaaya.*
**I was deeply touched by his kindness. *luṭfa ʔaxjalni.*
touchy - 1. *mitnarfiz.* She's very touchy. *hiyya kulliš mitnarfiza.* 2. *ζassaas.* That's a very touchy subject. *haaδa fadd mawδ̣uuƐ kulliš ζassaas.*
tough - 1. *qawi.* The meat is awfully tough. *l-laζam kulliš qawi.* 2. *zaζim.* That's a tough assignment. *haay fadd šaġḷa zaζma.* 3. *larr.* He's a real tough character. *huwwa fadd waaζid ʔabu jaasim larr.* 4. *suuʔ.* He's had tough luck. *jaabah suuʔ ζaδ̣δ̣.*
**That's a tough nut to crack. *haay fadd muškila ma-tinζall.*
to **toughen** - *Ɛallam (i) Ɛal-xušuuna.* A year in the army will toughen him. *fadd sana bij-jeeš tƐallma Ɛal-xušuuna.*
tour - *jawla* pl. *-aat.* He made a tour through Europe and Asia. *sawwa jawla b-ʔawruppa wib-ʔaasya.*
to tour - *jaal (u jawla).* The troupe is now touring South America. *l-firqa hassa da-tjuul ʔamriika j-jinuubiyya.*
tourist - *saayiζ* pl. *suwwaaζ, siyyaaζ.* Many tourists come here during the summer. *hwaaya suwwaaζ yijuun ihnaa ʔaθnaaʔ iṣ-ṣeef.*
tourist class - *darajat is-siyaaζa, daraja θaanya.*
to **tow** - *jarr (u jarr).* Can you tow my boat over to that side? *baḷḷa tigdar itjurr il-balam maali l-δaak iṣ-ṣoob?*
toward(s) - 1. *b-ittijaah, Ɛala ttijaah.* He drove off toward Karrada. *saaq b-ittijaah il-karraada.* 2. *qariib, wujj.* I'll be there towards evening. *ʔakuun ihnaak qariib il-miġrib.* 3. *wiyya, naζu.* He was very nice toward me. *čaan kulliš laṭiif wiyyaaya.*
towel - *pašxiir* pl. *pašaaxiir, xaawli* pl. *-iyyaat, manšafa* pl. *manaašif.*
tower - *burij* pl. *braaj.* Lightning struck the tower last night. *ṣ-ṣaaƐiqa nizlat Ɛal-burij il-baarζa bil-leel.*
town - 1. *wlaaya* pl. *-aat, madiina* pl. *mudun, balda* pl. *-aat.* What's the name of this town? *hal-wlaaya š-isimha?* 2. *baladi**. He's a member of the town council. *huwwa Ɛaδ̣u majlis baladi.*
tow rope - *ζabil (pl. ζbaal) maal jarr.*
tow truck - *saaζiba* pl. *-aat.* Send me a tow truck *dizz-li s-saaζiba.*
toxic - *saamm.* These fumes are toxic. *hal-ġaazaat saamma.*
toy - *malaaƐiib, laƐƐaaba* pl. *-aat* coll. *laƐƐaab.* I'll bring him some toys. *raζ-ajiib-la malaaƐiib.*
to toy - *ṣufan (u).* I was toying with this idea. *činit da-ʔaṣfun ib-hal-fikra.*
trace - *ʔaθar* pl. *ʔaaθaar.* The police found traces of poison in the food. *š-šurṭa ligaw ʔaθar simm bil-ʔakil.* -- He disappeared without leaving a trace. *xtifa bala ma-yitruk ʔaθar.*
to trace - 1. *ttabbaƐ (a tatabbuƐ), qtifa (i qtifaaʔ).* They traced him by his footsteps. *ttabbiƐoo b-ʔaaθaar ʔaqdaama.* or *qtifaw ʔaaθaar ʔaqdaama.* 2. *nisab (i nisba).* We traced the story

to him. *nisabna l-izčaaya ʔila.* 3. *stansax (i stinsaax).* Did you trace the floor plan? *stansaxit muxaṭṭaṭ il-binaaya?*

tracer - *taʔkiid.* We'll send a tracer after that letter. *raz-indizz taʔkiid ɛala δaak il-kitaab.*

trachoma - *traaxooma.*

tracing paper - *waraq istinsaax.*

track - *ʔaθar* pl. *ʔaaθaar.* There were many animal tracks around the spring. *čaan ʔaku ʔaaθaar zayawaanaat ihwaaya zawl il-ɛeen.* 2. *darub* pl. *druub.* There is an old track in the desert which leads to the well. *ʔaku darub ɛatiig biṣ-ṣazraaʔ yʔaddi lil-biir.* 3. *xaṭṭ* pl. *xuṭuuṭ, sičča* pl. *sičač.* The train will arrive on Track Two. *l-qiṭaar yooṣal ɛal-xaṭṭ iθ-θaani.* -- The tracks between Hilla and Kufa are being repaired. *s-sičča been il-zilla wil-kuufa da-titṣallaz.* 4. *zanjiil* pl. *znaajiil.* The left track on the tractor is broken. *z-zanjiil il-ṣafzat il-yisra maal l-itraaktar magṭuuɛ.* 5. *ttijaah* pl. *-aat.* You're on the right track. *ʔinta mittijih bil-ittijaah iṣ-ṣaziiz* or **ʔ*inta maaši zeen.*
**I'm afraid you're entirely off the track. *ʔaɛtiqid ʔinta maaši ġalaṭ.*

to keep track of - 1. *ṣubaṭ (u ṣabuṭ).* Keep close track of your expenses. *ʔiṣbuṭ maṣruufaatak.* 2. *raaqab (i mu,aaqaba).* The police kept track of him. *š-šurṭa raaqbata.*

to track - *ttabbaɛ (a tatabbuɛ) ʔaθar.* We tracked the fox to his lair. *ttabbiɛna ʔaθar iθ-θaɛlab lil-ġaar maala.*

to track up - *waṣṣax (i).* You're tracking up the kitchen with your feet. *ʔinta da-twaṣṣix gaaɛ il-muṭbax ib-rijlak.*

tract - 1. *qiṭɛa* pl. *qiṭaɛ, muqaaṭaɛa* pl. *-aat.* Several oil companies are prospecting in this tract. *ɛiddat šarikaat nafuṭ da-tnaqqib ib-hal-muqaaṭaɛa.* 2. *kurraasa* pl. *-aat.* The chamber of commerce published a tract on the oil question. *ġurfat it-tijaara nišrat kurraasa ɛan muškilat in-nafuṭ.* 3. *jihaaz* pl. *ʔajhiza.* Her digestive tract is weak. *jihaaz il-haṣum maalha ṣaɛiif.*

traction - *sazib.* Rear-engined cars have better traction than others. *s-sayyaaraat illi makiinatha li-wara sazibha azsan min ġeerha.*

tractor - *traaktar* pl. *-aat.*

trade - 1. *tijaara.* Our trade with the Far East has fallen off. *tijaaratna wiyya š-šarq il-ʔaqṣa qallat.* 2. *ṣanɛa* pl. *ṣanaayiɛ, mihna* pl. *mihan.* The boy has to learn a trade. *l-walad laazim yitɛallam fadd ṣanɛa.* -- I'm a butcher by trade *mihinti gaṣṣaab.* 3. *šuġul, maɛmiil.* He's taking away my trade. *kassad ɛalayya šuġli.* 4. *tijaari**. They published new trade regulations. *ʔaṣdiraw ʔanṣima tijaariyya jdiida.*

to trade - 1. *baddal (i tabdiil).* I've traded my typewriter for a bicycle. *baddalit ʔaalt iṭ-ṭaabiɛa maalti b-paaysikil.* 2. *taajar (i tijaara).* Iraq trades mostly with England. *l-ɛiraaq ytaajir ɛal-ʔakθar wiyya ʔingiltara.*

trader - *taajir* pl. *tujjaar.*

tradesman - *dukkaanči* pl. *-iyya.*

trade wind - *riiz tijaari* pl. *riyaaz tijaariyya.*

tradition - *taqliid* pl. *taqaaliid.* This is a tradition we have been following for centuries. *haaδa fadd taqliid ʔizna taabɛii min ɛuṣuur.*

traditional - *taqliidi**.

traffic - 1. *muruur.* Traffic is heavy on Rashid Street. *l-muruur qawiyya b-šaariɛ ir-rašiid.* 2. *tijaara.* The United Nations is trying to control the traffic in narcotics. *hayʔat il-ʔumam itriid tuṣbuṭ tijaarat il-muxaddiraat.*
**This street is closed to traffic. *haaδa š-šaariɛ masduud.*

traffic jam - *zdizaam* (pl. *-aat*) *sayyaaraat.*

traffic light - *ʔaḍwiyat* (pl. *-aat*) *muruur.*

tragedy - 1. *faajiɛa* pl. *fawaajiɛ.* What a tragedy the accident was! *šloon faajiɛa čaan il-zaadiθ!* 2. *ruwaaya* (pl. *-aat*) *muzzina.* The Baghdad Theatre Group is presenting a tragedy this week. *l-firqa t-tamθiiliyya l-baġdaadiyya raz-itqaddim ruwaaya muzzina hal-isbuuɛ.*

tragic - *muʔlim, mufjiɛ.* That accident was tragic. *δaak il-zaadiθ čaan muʔlim.*

trail - 1. *ṭariiq* pl. *ṭuruq.* The trail leads into the woods. *ṭ-ṭariiq yʔaddi l-daaxil il-ġaaba.* 2. *ʔaθar* pl. *ʔaaθaar.* A trail of blood caught their eye. *ʔaθar imnid-damm lifat naṣarhum.*
**The police are on his trail. *š-šurṭa mɛaqqbata.* or *š-šurṭa waraa.*

to trail - *lizag (a).* Somebody trailed me all the way home. *fadd waazid lizagni ṭuul iṭ-ṭariiq lil-beet.*

train - 1. *qiṭaar* pl. *-aat.* When does the train leave? *šwakit yitzarrak il-qiṭaar?* 2. *dyaal* pl. *-aat.* The bride wore a dress with a long train. *l-ɛaruus libsat badla biiha dyaal ṭuwiil.*

to train - 1. *darrab (u tadriib).* He trains the new employees. *huwwa ydarrub il-muwaṣṣafiin il-jiddad.* 2. *tmarran (a tamriin).* He's been training for the fight for weeks. *ṣaar-la ʔasaabiiɛ da-yitmarran lil-mulaakama.*

trainer - 1. *mudarrib* pl. *-iin.* He's a boxing trainer. *haaδa mudarrib mulaakama.* 2. *ṭiyyaara* (pl. *-aat*) *maal tadriib.* That's a trainer for new pilots. *haay ṭiyyaara maal tadriib liṭ-ṭayyaariin ij-jiddad.*

training - 1. *tamriin, tadriib.* He's still in training. *baɛda tazt il-tamriin.* 2. *tadriib.* The Post Office Department maintains a training school for its employees. *mudiiriyyat il-bariid ɛidha madrasat tadriib il-mustaxdamiiha.*

trait - *ṣifa* pl. *-aat, xiṣla* pl. *xiṣal.* She has many fine traits. *ɛidha hwaaya ṣifaat zeena.*

traitor - *xaaʔin* pl. *-iin, xwaana, xawana.*

tramp - *mhatlaf* pl. *-iin, mitšarrid* pl. *-iin.* He looks like a tramp. *huwwa ɛabaalak fadd waazid imhatlaf.*

to **trample** - *dawwas (i tadwiis) t-.* The horses trampled the children. *l-xeel dawwisat il-ʔaṭfaal.*

transaction - *muɛaamala* pl. *-aat.* We completed the transaction in the lawyer's office. *kammalna l-muɛaamala b-maktab il-muzaami.*

to **transcribe** - *stansax (i stinsaax).* Can you transcribe this into Roman script? *tigdar tistansix haaδa ʔila zruuf laatiiniyya?*

transcript - *waθiiqa* pl. *waθaayiq.* The registrar requires a transcript of my studies in Baghdad. *musajjil ij-jaamiɛa ṭilab waθiiqa b-diraasti b-baġdaad.*

transfer - *naqil.* I have asked for a transfer to Baghdad. *ṭlabit naqil il-baġdaad.*

to transfer - 1. *baddal (i tabdiil).* Where do we transfer buses? *ween inbaddil il-paaṣ?* 2. *niqal (u naqil) n-, zawwal (i tazwiil).* The commander transferred half his forces to the front. *l-qaaʔid niqal nuṣṣ quwwaata lij-jabha.* -- He transferred the property to her name. *zawwal milkiyyat il-muluk ʔilha.* -- He'd like to be transferred. *yriid yinniqil.*

to **transform** - *zawwal (i tazwiil).* This station transforms oil fuel into electric energy. *hal-muzaṭṭa tzawwil iṭ-ṭaaqa l-zaraariyya maal in-nafuṭ ila quwwa kahrabaaʔiyya.*

transformer - *muzawwil* pl. *-aat.* The transformer in my radio is burnt out. *l-muzawwil bir-raadyo maall ztirag.*

transfusion - *naqil.* The patient needs a blood transfusion. *l-mariiṣ yinraad-la naqil damm.*

transient - *maarr* pl. *-iin, ɛaabir* pl. *-iin.* The airport has sleeping and dining facilities for transients. *l-maṭaar imjahhaz ib-mazall noom w-ʔakil lir-rukkaab il-maarriin.*

transit - *traansiit.* These goods are in transit. *hal-biṣaaɛa traansiit.*

transition - *ntiqaal* pl. *-aat.* Our country is in a period of transition. *bilaadna b-fatrat intiqaal.*

to **translate** - *tarjam (u tarjuma).* How do you translate this? *šloon ittarjum haay?*

translation - *tarjuma* pl. *taraajum.*

translator - *mutarjim* pl. *-iin.*

transmission - *geer* pl. *-aat, transmišin* pl. *-aat.* Something seems to be wrong with the transmission of my car. *l-geer maal sayyaarti bii šii.*

transmitter - *mursila* pl. *-aat.* The Baghdad Radio transmitters are at Abu-Ghrayb. *mursilaat mazaṭṭat ʔiδaaɛat baġdaad b-abu ġreeb.*

transparent - 1. *šaffaaf.* The water is quite transparent here. *l-maay šaffaaf ihnaa.* 2. *makšuuf.* His methods are transparent. *ʔasaaliiba makšuufa.*

to **transplant** - *niqal (u naqil).* I'm going to transplant the seedlings today. *raz-ʔanqul il-ištuul il-yoom.*

transport - 1. *tasfiir.* Our primary concern was the transport of troops. *hammna l-ʔawwal čaan tasfiir ij-jiyuuš.* 2. *markab* (pl. *maraakib*) *naqil.* Two transports were sunk by submarines. *l-ġawwaaṣaat ġirgaw markabeen naqil.* 3. *ṭayyaarat* (pl. *-aat*) *naqil.* He's piloting a transport. *da-yquud ṭayyaarat naqil.*

to transport – *niqal (u naqil).* The Navy will transport these troops. *l-baẓriyya raẓ-tunqul haj-jiyuuš.*
transportation – *waasṭat naqil.* I'll need some transportation. *yinraad-li waasṭat naqil.*
trap – **1.** *fuxx* pl. *fxaax, šarak* pl. *ʔašraak.* The police set a trap for him. *š-surṭa nisboo-la fuxx.* **2.** *miṣyaada* pl. *-aat.* We caught three rats in the trap. *ṣidna tlaθ ijreediyya bil-miṣyaada.*
to trap – *ẓiṣar (i ẓaṣir)* The boys trapped the cat in a corner. *l-wulid ẓiṣraw il-bazzuuna biz-zuwiyya.*
trash – *zibil* pl. *zbaalaat.* Burn the trash! *ʔiẓrig iz-zibil.* -- We don't buy such trash. *ʔiẓna ma-ništiri hiiči zbaalaat.*
travel – *safar* pl. *-aat.* Travel in winter is difficult. *s-safar ṣaƐub biš-šita.* -- Let him tell you about his travels. *xal-yiẓčii-lak Ɛala safraata.*
to travel – **1.** *saafar (i safar).* I traveled a lot when I was in the Army. *saafart ihwaaya min činit bij-jeeš.* **2.** *ftarr (a farr), daar (u dawaraan).* He has traveled all over Europe. *ftarr kull ʔawruppa.* **3.** *saaẓ (i siyaaẓa).* She has been traveling for a month. *ṣaar-ilha šahar da-tsiiẓ.*
**He must have been traveling sixty miles an hour. *laazim čaan da-ysuuq sittiin miil bis-saaƐa.*
traveller – *musaafir* pl. *-iin.*
travelling salesman – *bayyaaƐ, baayiƐ mitjawwil* pl. *bayyaaƐa mitjawwiliin.*
tray – *ṣiiniyya* pl. *ṣawaani.* Put the cups on the tray. *ẓuṭṭ il-kuubaat biṣ-ṣiiniyya.*
treason – *xiyaana.*
treasure – *kanz* pl. *knuuz.*
treasurer – *ʔamiin (*pl. *ʔumanaaʔ) ṣanduug.*
treasury – **1.** *xaziina* pl. *xazaayin.* The country's treasury is almost empty. *xaziint id-dawla taqriiban faarġa.* **2.** *maaliyya.* He works in the Treasury Department. *yištuġul ib-wizaart il-maaliyya.*
treat – *laδδa* pl. *-aat.* It's a treat to read his books. *qraayat kutba laδδa.*
**This time the treat's on me. *hal-marra Ɛalayya.* or *hal-marra Ɛala ẓsaabi.*
to treat – **1.** *Ɛaamal (i muƐaamala).* He treats me like a child. *yƐaamilni Ɛabaalak ṭifil.* **2.** *Ɛaalaj (i muƐaalaja).* Dr. Ahmad is treating me. *d-daktoor aẓmad da-yƐaalijni.* **3.** *difaƐ (a dafiƐ) Ɛala.* He treated everybody. *difaƐ Ɛal-kull.*
to treat lightly – *stixaff (i stixfaaf), stahwan (i stihaana).* You shouldn't treat that so lightly. *ma-laazim tistixiff ib-haaδa.*
treatment – *tadaawi, muƐaalaja.* I'm going to the doctor's tomorrow for treatment. *ʔaani raayiẓ liṭ-ṭabiib baačir lit-tadaawi.* **2.** *muƐaamala* pl. *-aat.* I don't like that kind of treatment. *ma-tiƐjibni hiiči muƐaamala.*
treaty – *muƐaahada* pl. *-aat.* The treaty has to be ratified by the Senate. *l-muƐaahada laazim tiṭṣaddaq min majlis il-ʔaƐyaan.*
tree – *šajara* pl. *-aat, ʔašjaar* coll. *šajar.* We have a tree in front of our house. *Ɛidna šajara giddaam il-beet.*
trellis – *qamariyya* pl. *-aat.*
to **tremble** – *rijaf (i rajif).* He trembled with fear. *rijaf imnil-xoof.*
tremendous – **1.** *haaʔil, Ɛaḍiim.* That's a tremendous undertaking. *haaδa mašruuƐ haaʔil.* --There's a tremendous difference between them. *ʔaku xtilaaf Ɛaḍiim beenaathum.* **2.** *Ɛaḍiim.* They've just got out a tremendous new record. *ṭallƐaw iṣṭiwaana jdiida Ɛaḍiima.*
tremendously – *kulliš ihwaaya.* Social conditions have changed tremendously. *l-ʔaẓwaal il-ijtimaaƐiyya tġayyrat kulliš ihwaaya.*
tremor – **1.** *hazza* pl. *-aat.* Several weak earth tremors took place yesterday. *Ɛiddat hazzaat ʔarḍiyya xafiifa ṣaarat il-baarẓa.* **2.** *raƐša* pl. *-aat, rtiƐaaš* pl. *-aat.* He has a tremor in his hand. *Ɛinda raƐša b-ʔiida.*
trench – *xandaq* pl. *xanaadiq.* Civilians were forced to dig trenches. *l-madaniyyiin njubraw yuẓufruun xanaadiq.*
trend – *ttijaah* pl. *-aat.* The trend in Iraq is to wear Western suits. *l-ittijaah bil-Ɛiraaq hassa naẓu libs il-malaabis il-ġarbiyya.*
to **trespass** – *tƐadda (a).* You were trespassing on my property. *ʔinta činit da-titƐadda min gaaƐi.*
trestle – *skalla* pl. *-aat.* The workmen set up a trestle. *l-Ɛummaal nuṣbaw iskalla.*
trial – **1.** *muẓaakama* pl. *-aat.* The case was never brought to trial. *d-daƐwa ʔabadan ma-nƐirḍat lil-muẓaakama.* — He's on trial for murder. *huwwa hassa taẓt il-muẓaakama Ɛan qaḍiyyat qatil.* **2.** *tajruba* pl. *tajaarub.* He's been through a lot of trial and tribulation. *marr b-ihwaaya tajaarub w-šadaaʔid.* -- Children learn through trial and error. *l-ʔaṭfaal yitƐallmuun bit-tajruba.* -- I took the radio on trial. *qbalit ir-raadyo Ɛala šarṭ it-tajruba.*
to give a trial – *jarrab (u).* Why don't you give the car a trial? *leeš ma-tjarrub is-sayyaara fadd mudda?* -- We'll give you a week's trial. *raẓ-injarrbak fadd isbuuƐ.*
triangle – *muθallaθ* pl. *-aat.* A triangle has three sides. *l-muθallaθ bii tlaθ aḍaaƐ.*
triangular – *muθallaθ iš-šikil.* The race was run on a triangular course. *s-sibaaq jira Ɛala saaẓa muθallaθat iš-šikil.*
tribal – *Ɛašaaʔiri*.* The group is studying tribal customs. *j-jamaaƐa da-tidrus il-Ɛaadaat il-Ɛašaaʔiriyya.*
tribe – *Ɛašiira* pl. *Ɛašaayir, qabiila* pl. *qabaaʔil.* He's the head of a tribe from the South. *huwwa šeex Ɛašiira bij-jinuub.*
tribesman – *ʔibin Ɛašaayir.*
tribunal – *hayʔat (*pl. *-aat) taẓkiim.* We'll take the dispute to an international tribunal. *raẓ-naaxuδ han-nizaaƐ il-hayʔat taẓkiim dawliyya.*
tributary – *raafid* pl. *rawaafid.* The Diyala river is a tributary of the Tigris. *nahr idyaala min rawaafid nahar dijla.*
tribute – **1.** *xaawa* pl. *-aat, jizya* pl. *-aat.* The Assyrians exacted tribute from many nations. *l-ʔaašuuriyyiin furḍaw xaawa min ihwaaya duwal.* **2.** *madiẓ.* He paid you a fine tribute. *midaẓak madiẓ zeen.* or ***ʔaθna Ɛaleek.*
trick – **1.** *ẓiila* pl. *ẓiyal.* I'm on to his tricks. *ʔaani ʔaƐruf ẓiyala.* -- Do you know any card tricks? *tuƐruf ẓiila maal waraq?* **2.** *šaṭaara* pl. *-aat.* Don't try your tricks on me! *la-tẓaawil itbiiƐ šaṭaartak ib-raasi.* **3.** *nukta* pl. *nukat.* He played a trick on us. *sawwa biina nukta.* **4.** *waawi.* Watch out, there's a trick to that! *diir baalak haay biiha waawi!* **5.** *darub* pl. *druub.* He knows all the tricks. *yindall kull il-idruub.* **6.** *fann* pl. *fnuun.* There's a trick to fixing this dish. *ṭabix hal-ʔakla yinraad-la fann.* **7.** *siẓri*.* Have you seen Ali's trick box? *šift iṣ-ṣanduug is-siẓri maal Ɛali?*
**I've got a trick knee. *rukubti maƐyuuba.*
**There's no trick to it. *haay ma-yinraad-ilha šii.* or *haay sahla.* or *haay basiiṭa.*
to trick – *qašmar (u qašmara).* He tricked me again. *qašmarni marrt il-lux.* -- They tricked us into signing. *qašmaroona w-xalloona nimḍi.*
to **trickle** – *xarr (u xarr).* The water trickled out of the faucet. *l-maay xarr imnil-buuri.*
trickster – *ġaššaaš* pl. *-iin, ẓayyaal* pl. *-iin.* He has a reputation for being a trickster. *haaδa mašhuur ib-kawna ġaššaaš.*
tricky – *daqiiq.* That's a tricky question. *haaδa fadd mawḍuuƐ daqiiq.*
trifle – **1.** *šaqa, liƐib.* That's no trifle. *haay muu šaqa.* **2.** *šii ṭafiif* pl. *ʔašyaaʔ ṭafiifa, šii taafih* pl. *ʔašyaaʔ taafha.* Don't bother about trifles. *la-tihtamm bil-ʔašyaaʔ iṭ-ṭafiifa.* **3.** *šwayya, ʔismin, šaƐra.* The trousers are a trifle too long. *l-panṭaruun išwayya ṭwiil.* -- The food was good but just a trifle salty. *l-ʔakil čaan zeen bass ʔismin maaliẓ.*
**He was only trifling with her. *čaan da-yilƐab ib-raasha.*
**He's no man to trifle with. *haaδa fadd waaẓid yinẓisib-la ẓsaab.*
trifling – *ṭafiif, taafih.* That's such a trifling matter! *haaδa šii kulliš ṭafiif.*
trigger – *zinaad* pl. *-aat.* The trigger on this pistol has a light pull. *l-iznaad maal hal-musaddas sahil yindaas.*
trigonometry – *Ɛilm il-muθallaθaat, ẓsaab il-muθallaθaat.*
trim – **1.** *ẓaašya* pl. *ẓwaaši.* Most cars now have chrome trim. *ʔakθar is-sayyaaraat biiha ẓwaaši min neekal.* **2.** *taƐdiil* pl. *-aat.* My hair isn't long, but it needs a trim. *šaƐri muu ṭuwiil, laakin yiẓtaaj taƐdiil.* **3.** *mrattab.* She always looks very trim. *hiyya daaʔiman kulliš imrattba.* **4.** *naẓiif.* She has a trim figure. *Ɛidha qiwaan naẓiif.*
to trim – **1.** *Ɛaddal (i).* Just trim my hair a little. *bass Ɛaddil šaƐri šwayya.* **2.** *garṭaf (u*

garṭafa). I'm trimming my mustache. *da-agarṭuf išwaarbi.* **3.** *zawwag (u zwaaga) t-.* She trimmed her hat with feathers. *zawwgat šafqatha bir-riiš.*
trimming - **1.** *naqiš.* The trimming on her dress is red. *n-naqiš ɛala badlatha ʔazmar.* **2.** *zbaaša* pl. *-aat.* We had turkey and all the trimmings. *ʔakalna diič hindi w-izbaašaata.*
**He gave me a trimming. *buṣaṭni baṣṭa zeena.*
**We really got a trimming in our last game. *ṣudug tdammarna b-liɛbatna l-ʔaxiira.*
trip - **1.** *safra* pl. *-aat.* How was your trip? *šloon čaanat safirtak?* -- Have a pleasant trip. *ʔatmannaa-lak safra zeena.* **2.** *rooza* pl. *-aat, rajɛa* pl. *-aat.* The trip there was quicker than the trip back. *r-rooza čaanat ʔashal imnir-rajɛa.*
to trip - **1.** *ɛiθar (a ɛaθir).* Be careful not to trip on the stairs. *diir baalak la-tiɛθar bid-daraj.* **2.** *ðirab (u) band.* He tripped me. *ðirabni band.*
to trip up - **1.** *ligaf (u laguf), ṣaad (i ṣeed).* My professor tripped me up on that question. *l-ʔustaað ligafna b-has-suʔaal.* **2.** *ġilaṭ (a ġalaṭ).* I must have tripped up somewhere. *laazim iġlaṭit ib-fadd makaan.*
tripe - **1.** *karša.* I can't eat tripe. *ma-agdar aakul il-karša.* **2.** *laġwa, zači faasix.* That's just tripe! *haaði laġwa!*
to **triple** - *ðaaɛaf (u) itlaθ marraat.* He tripled his earnings. *ðaaɛaf ʔarbaaza tlaθ marraat.*
triplet - **She had triplets. *jaabat itlaaθa.*
tripod - *seepaaya* pl. *-aat.*
trite - *baayix.* That joke's too trite. *han-nukta ṣaarat baayxa.*
triumph - *ntiṣaar* pl. *-aat.*
triumphant - *muntaṣir.*
trivial - *taafih, ṭafiif.* That's a trivial matter. *haay fadd šii taafih.*
trolley - *traam* pl. *-aat.* In Cairo they still have trolleys. *baɛad ʔaku traamaat bil-qaahira.*
troop - **1.** *firqa* pl. *firaq.* My nephew is in a boy scout troop. *ʔibn axuuya b-firqat il-kaššaafa.* **2.** *jundi* pl. *junuud.* Get the troops out of the sun! *xalli j-junuud la-yoogfuun biš-šamis!*
to troop in - *xašš (u xašš).* The students all trooped in when the bell rang. *t-talaamiið xaššaw kullhum min dagg ij-jaraṣ.*
trophy - *kaʔs* pl. *kuʔuus.* Our school took the trophy this year. *madrasatna ʔaxðat il-kaʔs has-sana.*
Tropic of Cancer - *madaar is-saraṭaan.*
Tropic of Capricorn. *madaar ij-jadi.*
tropical - *stiwaaʔi*.* Central Africa has a tropical climate. *ʔafriiqya l-wuṣṭa jawwha stiwaaʔi.*
tropics - *l-manṭiqa l-istiwaaʔiyya.* Much of Africa lies within the tropics. *ʔakθar ʔafriiqya waaqɛa bil-manṭiqa l-istiwaaʔiyya.*
trot - *xabab.* That horse has a nice trot. *hal-izṣaan xababa zilu.*
to trot - *xabb (u xabb).* The horse trotted around the field. *l-izṣaan xabb zawl is-saaza.*
trouble - **1.** *muškila* pl. *-aat.* What's your trouble? *šinu muškiltak?* or **šbiik? **2.** *ʔizɛaaj* pl. *-aat.* This trouble is quite unnecessary. *haaða fadd ʔizɛaaj ʔabad ma-ʔila muujib.* **3.** *ðṭiraab* pl. *-aat; qalaaqil.* There's been trouble up at Mosul. *ʔaku ðṭiraabaat bil-muuṣil.* **4.** *zazma* pl. *-aat.* Don't put yourself to any trouble. *la-tjurr zazma.* or ***la-titkallaf.* **5.** *warṭa* pl. *-aat.* He's in trouble again. *hamm wugaɛ ib-warṭa.* or ***hammeena twarraṭ.*
**What's the trouble? *š-ṣaar?* or *šaku?*
to trouble - **1.** *ʔazɛaj (i ʔizɛaaj), dawwax (u tduwwux) raas.* I'm sorry, but I'll have to trouble you again. *mitʔassif bass ʔaani miðṭarr ʔaziɛjak marra lux.* **2.** *šawwaš (i tašwiiš) t-.* The news troubled me very much. *l-ʔaxbaar šawwšatni kulliš.* **3.** *qilaq (i qalaq).* What's troubling you? Is it some bad news? *šinu l-qaalqak, ʔaku ʔaxbaar muu zeena?* or *šbiik mitšawwiš, ʔaku ʔaxbaar muu zeena?* **4.** *ʔaððа (i ʔaðiyya).* My arm has been troubling me ever since my accident. *ʔiidi da-tʔaððiini min ṣaar il-zaadiθ li-hassa.*
**What's troubling you? Is it your eyes again? *šbiik, hamm iɛyuunak?* or *šbiik mazɛuuj, hamm iɛyuunak?*
**May I trouble you for a match? *tismaz-li b-šixxaaṭa?*
troubled - **1.** *ɛasiir, ɛaṣiib.* We are living in troubled times. *da-nɛiiš ib-ʔayyaam ɛasiira.* or *da-nɛiiš ib-fadd zaman ɛaṣiib.* **2.** *qaliq.* I've been very troubled about his health lately. *ṣirit kulliš qaliq ɛala ṣizzta bil-mudda l-ʔaxiira.*
troublesome - **1.** *mdawwix.* My tooth has been troublesome. *sinni mdawwixni.* **2.** *muzɛij, qallaaq.* That pupil is troublesome today. *hat-tilmiið muzɛij il-yoom.*
trough - **1.** *zooð (pl. ʔazwaað) saqi.* The watering trough leaks. *zooð is-saqi da-yxurr.* **2.** *miɛlaf* pl. *maɛaalif.* Throw some more food in the trough. *zuṭṭ baɛad ɛalaf bil-miɛlaf.*
trousers - *panṭaruun* pl. *-aat.*
trousseau - *jhaaz* pl. *-aat.*
trowel - *maalaj* pl. *mwaalij, zaffaara* pl. *-aat.*
truce - *hudna* pl. *-aat.* The two countries agreed to a truce. *d-dawilteen ittifqaw ɛala hudna.*
truck - *loori* pl. *-iyyaat.* Where can I park my truck? *ween ʔagdar awagguf il-loori maali?*
to truck - *niqal (u) bil-loori, wadda (i) bil-loori.* He trucks his produce to the warehouse. *da-yinqul l-imxaððar maala lil-ɛalwa bil-loori.*
trucker - *saayiq loori* pl. *suwwaaq looriyyaat.* The truckers went on strike today. *suwwaaq il-looriyyaat sawwaw ʔiðraab il-yoom.*
truck farm - *mazraɛat (pl. -aat) xuðar.*
truck farmer - *zarraaɛ xuðar.*
truck farming - *zariɛ xuðar.*
true - **1.** *ṣudug, ṣaziiz.* Is that story true? *hal-izčaaya ṣuðug?* -- He is a true scholar. *huwwa ṭaalib ɛilim min ṣudug.* **2.** *muxlaṣ, ṣudug.* He's a true friend. *huwwa ṣadiiq muxlaṣ.* -- He stayed true to his principles. *buqa muxliṣ il-mabaadʔa.* **3.** *ṭibq il-ʔaṣil.* I swear this is a true copy. *ʔašhad bi-ʔan haay nusxa ṭibq il-ʔaṣil.*
truffle - *čimaaya* pl. *-aat.* coll. *čima.*
truly - *zaqiiqatan, bil-zaqiiqa.* I am truly sorry. *ʔaani mitʔassif zaqiiqatan.*
trumpet - *buuq* pl. *ʔabwaaq, buuri* pl. *bwaari.*
trunk - **1.** *jiðiɛ* pl. *jðuuɛ.* The trunk of the tree is completely hollow. *jiðɛ iš-šajara kulla faariġ.* -- The human body consists of head, trunk, and limbs. *jisim il-ʔinsaan yitkawwan min raas w-jiðiɛ w-ʔaṭraaf.* **2.** *ṣanduug* pl. *ṣanaadiig.* Are the trunks packed yet? *ṣ-ṣanaadiig kullha matruusa loo baɛad?* **3.** *čiswa* pl. *-aat, čisaw, panṭuroon (pl. -aat) riyaaða.* These trunks are too tight. *hač-čiswa kulliš ðayyga.* **4.** *raʔiisi*.* The Karbala branch joins the trunk line at Hindiyya. *l-xaṭṭ il-farɛi maal karbala yittiṣil bil-xaṭṭ ir-raʔiisi b-saddat il-hindiyya.*
truss - **1.** *zzaam* pl. *zizim.* He has to wear a truss. *laazim yilbas izzaam.* **2.** *rabbaaṭ* pl. *-aat.* The new bridge is built with steel trusses. *j-jisir ij-jidiid mabni ɛala rabbaaṭaat min fuulaað.*
trust - **1.** *θiqa.* I'm putting my trust in you. *ʔaani zaaṭṭ θiqti biik.* **2.** *wiṣaaya* pl. *-aat.* That orphan's money is in a trust. *fluus hal-yatiim mazṭuuṭa tazt il-wiṣaaya.* **3.** *ʔtimaan.* I'm investing my money in a trust company. *da-ašaġġil ifluusi b-šarikat iʔtimaan.*
to trust - **1.** *wiθaq (a θiqa) b-, ʔamman (i taʔmiin) b-.* I don't trust him. *ʔaani ma-ʔaθiq bii.* -- Can you trust me until payday? *tigdar itʔammin biyya l-yoom il-maɛaaš?* **2.** *tʔammal.* I trust you slept well. *ʔatʔammal nimit zeen.*
to trust to - *ɛtimad (i) ɛala.* You shouldn't trust too much to your memory. *ma-laazim hal-gadd tiɛtimid ɛala ðakirtak.*
trustee - *waṣi* pl. *ʔawṣiyaaʔ.* The judge appointed Ahmad as trustee for his nephew's estate. *l-qaaði ɛayyan ʔazmad waṣi ɛala ʔamlaak ibin ʔaxuu.*
trusteeship - *wiṣaaya.* This country was under trusteeship a long time. *had-dawla čaanat tazt il-wiṣaaya mudda ṭuwiila.*
trustful - **He's too trustful. *yʔammin bin-naas ihwaaya.*
trustworthy - *ʔamiin* pl. *ʔumanaaʔ* That man isn't very trustworthy. *haada r-rijaal muu kulliš ʔamiin.*
truth - *ṣudug, zaqiiqa, ṣaziiz, ṣizza.* That's the truth. *haaða iṣ-ṣudug.* -- I told him the plain truth. *gitt-la l-zaqiiqa miθil-ma hiyya.*
truthful - *ṣaadiq.* Ali is very truthful. *ɛali kulliš ṣaadiq.*
truthfulness - **1.** *ṣidiq.* His truthfulness is beyond question. *ṣidqa ma-bii šakk.* **2.** *ṣizza.* I'm not challenging the truthfulness of that statement. *ma-da-ʔanaaqiš ṣizzat it-taṣriiz.*
try - *muzaawala* pl. *-aat.* They reached the mountaintop on the first try. *wuṣlaw il-qummat ij-jibal ib-ʔawwal muzaawala.*
to try - **1.** *jarrab (u tajruba) t-.* I'd like to try it. *yiɛjibni ʔajarrubha.* -- Have you tried this medicine yet? *jarrabit had-duwa loo baɛad?* **2.** *zaawal (i muzaawala).* Try to reach him in his

office. *ʒaawil tittiṣil bii b-daaʔirta.* 3. *δaag (u δoog) n-.* Try some of the peppers. I think you'll like them prepared this way. *δuug išwayya mnil-filfil, ʔaδinn yƐijbak maṭbuux hiiči.* 4. *ʒaakam (u muʒaakama).* Who's going to try the accused? *minu raʒ-yʒaakim il-muttaham?* 5. *šaaf (u šoof), naδar (u).* Which judge is trying the case? *yaa ʒaakim da-yšuuf id-daƐwa?*

to try on - *gaddar (i).* I'd like to try that suit on again. *ʔariid agaddir hal-qaaṭ marra lux.* or *ʔariid ʔašuuf marra lux išloon il-qaaṭ yugƐud Ɛalayya.*

to try out - *jarrab (u tajruba) t-.* I'm going to try out a new car. *raʒ-ʔajarrub fadd sayyaara jidiida.*

trying - *Ɛaṣiib.* Those were trying times. *haay ʔawqaat Ɛaṣiiba.*

tub - 1. *ṭašit* pl. *ṭšuut.* The wash is still in the tub. *l-ihduum baƐadha biṭ-ṭašit.* 2. *baanyo* pl. *-owaat.* Did you wash out the bath tub after you took a bath? *ġisalt il-baanyo baƐad-ma ʔaxaδit ʒammaam?*

tube - 1. *ʔinbuuba* pl. *-aat, buuri* pl. *-iyyaat.* They had to feed him through a tube. *δṭarraw yinṭuu ʔakal b-inbuuba.* 2. *čuub* pl. *-aat, čuup* pl. *-aat.* I need a new tube for my bicycle. *ʔaʒtaaj čuub jidiid lil-paaysikil maali.* 3. *tyuub* pl. *-aat, dabba* pl. *-aat.* I want a large tube of tooth paste. *ʔariid fadd ityuub čibiir maƐjuun maal isnuun.* 4. *lampa* pl. *-aat.* My radio needs a new tube. *r-raadyo maali yinraad-la lampa jidiida.*

tubercular - *masluul.*

tuberculosis - *sill.*

tubing - *buuri* pl. *bwaari.* I need two hundred meters of tubing. *ʔaʒtaaj miiteen matir buuri.*

tubular - *Ɛala šikil ʔinbuub, Ɛala šikil buuri.*

tuck - *kasra* pl. *-aat, ṭawya* pl. *-aat.* The dress needs some tucks at the waist. *n-nafnuuf yinraad-la čam kasra mnil-xiṣir.*

to tuck in - 1. *laflaf (i tliflif).* Mother used to tuck us in at night. *ʔummi čaanat tlaflifna bil-liʒfaan bil-leel.* 2. *xaššaš (i taxšiiš) t-.* Your shirt tail is out; tuck it in your pants. *θoobak ṭaaliƐ; xaššiša bil-panṭuroon.*

to tuck up - *šaal (i šeel) n-.* She tucked up her skirts and ran. *šaalat išyaalha w-rikδat.*

Tuesday - *yoom iθ-θilaaθaa, yoom it-tilaaθaa.* I'll be back on Tuesday. *ʔarjaƐ yoom it-tilaaθaa.*

tuft - 1. *kafša* pl. *-aat.* The squirrel has only one tuft of hair on its tail. *s-sinjaab Ɛinda bass kafšat šaƐar waʒda b-δeela.* 2. *kooma* pl. *kuwam.* There's a rabbit behind that tuft of grass. *ʔaku ʔarnab wara koomt il-ʒašiiš δiič.* 3. *kaƐkuula* pl. *-aat, kaƐaakiil.* This type of pigeon has a tuft on its head. *han-nooƐ ʒamaam Ɛinda kaƐkuula.*

tug - *maatoor* pl. *-aat.* Two tugs are towing the barge. *maatooreen da-yjarruun id-duuba.*

to tug - *saʒsal (i tsiʒsil), jarjar (i tjirjir).* Stop tugging at me! *bass Ɛaad itsaʒsil biyya!*

tug of war - *jarr il-ʒabil.* Who won the tug of war? *minu gilab ib-jarr il-ʒabil?*

tuition - *ʔujuur id-diraasa.* Have you paid your tuition yet? *dfaƐit ʔujuur id-diraasa loo baʒad?*

tumble - *wagƐa* pl. *-aat, čuqlumba* pl. *-aat.* She took quite a tumble yesterday. *tčaqlibat fadd čuqlumba zeena l-baarʒa.*

to tumble down - *tčaqlab (a tčiqlib), tdaƐbal (a tdiƐbil).* He tumbled down the stairs. *tčaqlab imnid-daraj.*

tumbler - *glaaṣ* pl. *-aat, bardaaġ* pl. *baraadiiġ.* He brought me some water in a tumbler. *jaab-li šwayya maay ib-bardaaġ.*

tumor - *waram* pl. *wuruum.*

tune - *naġma* pl. *-aat, laʒin* pl. *ʔalʒaan.* Do you know that tune? *tuƐruf hal-laʒin?*

**He keeps harping on the same tune. *yδill ydugg Ɛala nafs il-watar.*

in tune - *manṣuub.* Is your violin in tune? *l-kamanja maaltak manṣuuba?*

**Their government is in tune with the times. *niδam il-ʒukum maalhum yitlaaʔam wiyya z-zamaan.*

out of tune - 1. *našaaz.* She always sings out of tune. *daaʔiman itġanni našaaz.* 2. *ma-manṣuub.* The lute is out of tune. *l-Ɛuud ma-manṣuub.*

to tune in - *ṭallaƐ (i).* You haven't tuned the station in properly. *ʔinta ma-ṭallaƐt il-muʒaṭṭa zeen.* or ***r-raadyo muu Ɛal-maʒaṭṭa.*

to tune up - 1. *niṣab (u naṣub) ʔaalaat˜.* The orchestra is tuning up. *l-firqa da-tinṣub ʔaalaatha.* 2. *δubaṭ (u δabuṭ) n-, qassam (i taqsiim) t-.* Did you tune up the motor? *δubaṭṭ il-makiina?*

tuning - *naṣub.* The piano needs tuning. *l-ipyaano yinraad-la naṣub.*

Tunis - *tuunis.*

Tunisia - *tuunis.*

Tunisian - *tuunisi** pl. *-iyyiin.*

tunnel - *nafaq* pl. *ʔanfaaq.*

turban - *Ɛmaama* pl. *-aat, Ɛmaayim; laffa* pl. *-aat, čarraawiyya* pl. *-aat.*

turbine - *tarbiin* pl. *-aat.*

turbulence - *δṭiraab.* There's some turbulence ahead so we'll change course. *raʒ-inbaddil ittijaahna li-ʔan ʔaku δṭiraab bij-jaww giddaamna.*

turbulent - *miδṭirib.* It is a very turbulent situation. *l-ʒaala čaanat miδṭarba kulliš.*

Turcoman - *turkumaani* pl. *turkumaan.* Most Turcomans in Iraq live around Kirkuk. *ʔakθar it-turkumaan bil-Ɛiraaq ib-manṭiqat karkuuk.*

turf - *Ɛišib.*

Turk - *turki* pl. *ʔatraak.*

Turkey - *turkiya.*

turkey - *diič hindi* pl. *dyuuča hindiyya, Ɛališiiš* pl. *-aat.*

Turkish - *turki** pl. *ʔatraak.* Is he a Turkish citizen? *huwwa jinsiita turki.* -- How do you say it in Turkish? *šloon itguulha bit-turki?* -- I stopped by the Turkish bath to see Ali. *marreet bil-ʒammaam it-turki ʒatta ašuuf Ɛali.*

Turkish delight - *ʒalquum, luqum.*

Turkish towel - *xaawli* pl. *-iyyaat, paškiir* pl. *pašaakiir.*

turn - 1. *farra* pl. *-aat.* He gave the wheel a half turn. *farr ič-čarix nuṣṣ farra.* -- Give the valve three turns to the right. *furr is-ṣammaam itlaθ farraat lil-yamiin.* 2. *loofa* pl. *-aat.* Take the first turn to the right. *duur ib-ʔawwal loofa Ɛal-yamiin.* 3. *nooba* pl. *-aat, door* pl. *ʔadwaar.* It's my turn now. *hassa noobti.* -- You will be called up in turn. *raʒ-tinṣaaʒ bid-door.*

**We encountered difficulties at every turn. *Ɛtirδatna ṣuƐuubaat min kull naaʒiya.*

**The meat is cooked to a turn. *l-laʒam maṭbuux Ɛal-ʔuṣuul.*

**Last night he took a turn for the worse. *l-baarʒa bil-leel ṣiʒʒta tdahwurat.*

**The political situation has taken a turn for the better. *l-ʒaala s-siyaasiyya ṣaar biiha taʒassun.*

good turn - *maƐruuf, zeeniyya* pl. *-aat.* Ali did me a good turn. *Ɛali sawwaa-li zeeniyya.*

to take turns - *tnaawab (a tanaawub).* We'll take turns driving. *raʒ-nitnaawab bis-siyaaqa.*

to turn - 1. *daar (i deer), farr (u farr).* I can't turn the key. *ma-da-ʔagdar ʔadiir il-miftaaʒ.* -- She turned her back on me. *daarat-li δaharha.* -- Turn your chair to the light. *furr il-kursi maalak Ɛaδ-δuwa.* 2. *čirax (u čarix, čiraaxa) n-.* He turned these chess pieces on a lathe. *čirax quṭaƐ haš-šiṭranj bit-toorna.* 3. *gallab (u tagliib) t-.* She turned the pages slowly. *gallubat iṣ-ṣaʒaayif Ɛala keefha.* -- The police turned the room upside down. *š-šurṭa gallibaw il-ġurfa min foog li-jawwa.* or *š-šurṭa nabbišaw il-ġurfa.* 4. *laƐƐab (i talƐiib).* The sight turned my stomach. *l-manδar laƐƐab nafsi.* 5. *wajjah (i tawjiih) t-, daar (i deer).* Turn the hose on the fire! *wajjih il-buuri Ɛan-naar.* 6. *ṣaar (i).* He's just turned fifty to-day. *ṣaar Ɛumra xamsiin sana l-yoom.* -- They turned traitor. *ṣaaraw xawana.* 7. *gilab (u galub) n-, baddal (i tabdiil) t-.* I want to turn these stocks into cash. *ʔariid ʔaglub has-sandaat ʔila naqid.* 8. *ftarr (a farr).* The wheels turned slowly. *l-ičruux iftarrat yawaaš.* 9. *ltifat (i ltifaat).* She turned to look at him. *ltiftat ʒatta tbaawiƐ Ɛalee.* 10. *ngilab (u).* The tide of battle will turn. *majra l-maƐraka raʒ-yingulub.* or *l-ʔaaya raʒ-tingulub.* 11. *liwa (i lawi) n-.* It's the second time today that I turned my ankle. *haay θaani marra hal-yoom ʔalwi rijli.* 12. *twajjah (i tawajjuh).* I don't know who to turn to. *ma-adri ʔil-man ʔatwajjah.* 13. *tʒawwal (a taʒawwul).* The water turned to steam. *l-maay itʒawwal ʔila buxaar.*

**She turned red. *ʒmarrat.*

**The milk turned sour. *l-ʒaliib iʒmaδδ.*

**They turned pale when they heard the news. *ṣfarraw min simƐaw il-xabar.*

to turn around - 1. *ndaar (a).* Turn around and let me see the back of your jacket. *ndaar w-xalli ʔašuuf δahar sitirtak.* 2. *deewar (u deewara) t-.* Turn around, the street is closed. *deewur, iš-šaariƐ masduud.*

to turn back - *rijaƐ (a rujuuƐ).* Let's turn back. *xal-nirjaƐ.*
to turn down - 1. *rufaḍ (u rafuḍ) n-, radd (i radd) n-.* The management turned down my application. *l-ʔidaara rufḍat ṭalabi.* 2. *ṭawwa (i), Ɛiwaj (i).* Please don't turn down the corners of my book. *la-tiƐwij zawaaši l-waraq b-iktaabi.* 3. *naṣṣa (i tanṣiya), nazzal (i tanziil).* Will you turn down the radio, please? *naṣṣi r-raadyo, min faḍlak.* 4. *faat (u foot) n- b-, deewar (u deewara) t- b-.* Turn down this road. *fuut ib-haṭ-ṭariiq.*
to turn in - 1. *xašš (u xass) min, faat (u foot) min.* Driver, turn in here! *saayiq, xušš minnaa!* 2. *naam (a noom).* We ought to turn in early tonight. *laazim innaam Ɛala wakit hal-leela.* 3. *wiša (i wišaaya) b-.* We turned him in to the police. *wišeena bii biš-šurṭa.* 4. *qaddam (i taqdiim).* He turned in his resignation. *qaddam istiqaalta.* 5. *sallam (i tasliim).* You must turn your gun in to the police. *laazim itsallim bunduqiitak liš-šurṭa.*
to turn into - *ṣaar (i), ngiḷab (i ngiḷaab).* The wine turned into vinegar. *š-šaraab ingiḷab ʔila xaḷḷ.* — He has turned into a poet. *ngiḷab šaaƐir.* or *ṣaar šaaƐir.*
to turn loose - *fakk (u fakk), hadd (i hadd).* He turned his dog loose. *fakk čalba.*
to turn off - 1. *sadd (i sadd) n-, qiṭaƐ (a qaṭiƐ) n-.* Did you turn off the gas? *saddeet il-ġaaz?* 2. *ṭaffa (i taṭfiya).* Turn off the radio. *ṭaffi r-raadyo.*
to turn on - 1. *šiƐal (i šaƐil) n-.* Why don't you turn on the light? *leeš ma-tišƐil iḍ-ḍuwa?* 2. *fakk (u fakk) n-, šiƐal (i šaƐil) n-.* Who turned on the radio? *minu fakk ir-raadyo?*
to turn out - 1. *ṭirad (u ṭarid) n-.* They turned me out of my room in the hotel. *ṭirdooni min ġurufti bil-ʔuteel.* 2. *giḷab (u gaḷub) n-.* Turn the right side of the material out. *ʔugḷub l-iqmaaš Ɛala wučča.* 3. *ṭallaƐ (i taṭliiƐ) t-, ʔantaj (i ʔintaaj).* The factory turns out 500 pairs of shoes a day. *l-maƐmal yṭalliƐ xamis miit zooj qanaadir bil-yoom.* 4. *ṭilaƐ (a ṭuluuƐ) n-.* How did the elections turn out? *šloon ṭilƐat natiijt il-intixaabaat?* — The snapshots didn't turn out right. *ṣ-ṣuwar ma-ṭilƐat zeen.* 5. *ziḍar (a zuḍuur).* A large crowd turned out for the meeting. *jamaaƐa čibiira mnin-naas ziḍrat il-ijtimaaƐ.*
to turn over - 1. *giḷab (u gaḷub) n-.* I nearly turned over the table. *baƐad išwayya ʔagḷub il-meez.* 2. *ngiḷab (u ngiḷaab).* Our boat turned over. *balamna ngiḷab.* 3. *sallam (i tasliim) t-.* Everyone has to turn over his weapons to the police. *l-kull laazim ysallmuun ʔaslizathum liš-šurṭa.* — He turned his business over to his son. *sallam šuġḷa l-ʔibna.* 4. *gaḷḷab (u tagḷiib).* Turn it over in your mind before you give me your answer. *gaḷḷubha b-Ɛaqlak zeen gabuḷ-ma tinṭiini jawaab.*
to turn up - 1. *ḍihar (a ḍuhuur), ṭilaƐ (a ṭuluuƐ).* I guess the file will probably turn up when were not looking for it. *ʔaƐtiqid hal-faayil Ɛala l-ʔakθar raz-yiḍhar min ma-da-ndawwir Ɛalee.* 2. *nubaṣ (u nabuṣ), ḍihar (a ḍuhuur).* The missing man suddenly turned up here in Baghdad. *r-rijjaal iḍ-ḍaayiƐ fujʔatan nubaṣ ihnaa b-baġdaad.*
turning - 1. *tazawwul.* That was the turning point. *haay čaanat nuqṭat it-tazawwul.* 2. *taraajuƐ, nukuuṣ.* There'll be no turning back now. *ma-aku majaal lit-taraajuƐ.*
turnip - *šalġama* pl. *-aat* coll. *šalġam.*
turnkey - *sajjaan* pl. *-iin.*
turnover - 1. *taġyiir* pl. *-aat.* There's a big turnover of employees in this office. *ʔaku hwaaya taġyiir bil-muwaḍḍafiin ib-had-daaʔira.* 2. *beeƐ w-šira.* My uncle's store has a big turnover. *ʔaku hwaaya beeƐ w-šira b-dukkaan Ɛammi.* 3. *kleecaaya* pl. *-aat* coll. *kleeča.* They served date turnovers with tea. *qaddmaw kleeča maal tamur wiyya čaay.*
turpentine - *tarpantiin.*
turquoise - *feeruuz, šaḍir.* My sister has a turquoise stone in her ring. *ʔuxti Ɛidha faṣṣ feeruuz bil-mizbas maalha.*
turret - *burij* pl. *ʔabraaj.* The old castle has turrets on the walls. *l-qalƐa l-Ɛatiiqa biiha ʔabraaj bil-izyaaṭiin.* — The tank returned with its turret damaged. *d-dabbaaba rijƐat ib-burij imzaṭṭam.*
turtle - *ragga* pl. *-aat* coll. *ragg, sulzafaat* pl. *salaazif, rafuš* pl. *rfuuš.*
turtledove - *fuxtaaya* pl. *-aat, faxaati.*
turtleneck sweater - *bluuz (pl. -aat) ʔabu rugba.* He's wearing a turtleneck sweater. *yilbas bluuz ʔabu rugba.*
tusk - *naab* pl. *ʔanyaab.*
tutor - *muƐallim xuṣuuṣi* pl. *muƐallimiin xuṣuuṣiyyiin.* You need a tutor in mathematics. *yinraad-lak muƐallim xuṣuuṣi bir-riyaaḍiyyaat.*
tuxedo - *qaaṭ (pl. quuṭ) smookin.*
twang - *xanna.* He talks with a twang. *Ɛinda xanna b-začya.*
tweezers - *mingaaš* pl. *-aat, minaagiiš.*
twelfth - *l-iθnaƐaš.*
twelve - *θnaƐaš.*
twentieth - *l-Ɛišriin.*
twenty - *Ɛišriin.*
twice - 1. *marrteen, noobteen.* I was invited there twice. *ʔaani marrteen maƐzuum ihnaak.* 2. *ḍiƐf.* That way will take twice as long. *haṭ-ṭariiq yaaxuḍ ḍiƐf il-mudda.* — I paid twice as much. *dfaƐit ḍiƐf hal-miqdaar.*
twig - *ġuṣun iṣġayyir* pl. *ʔaġṣaan iṣġayyra.*
twin - *toom* pl. *twaam.* Those two boys are twins. *hal-waladeen toom.* — She's his twin sister. *hiyya ʔuxta t-toom.*
twine - *suutli.* I need some more twine to tie this package. *ʔariid išwayya laax suutli zatta ʔašidd ir-ruzma.*
to twine - *tsallaq (a tasalluq).* The grapevine twines around the trellis. *Ɛarag il-Ɛinab yitsallaq Ɛala ðiič il-qamariyya.*
twinge - *naġza* pl. *-aat.* I just felt a twinge in my side. *zasseet fadd naġza b-xaaṣirti.*
to **twinkle** - *tlaʔlaʔ (a talaʔluʔ).* The stars were twinkling. *n-nijuum čaanat da-titlaʔlaʔ*
to **twirl** - 1. *farr (u farr).* He twirled his umbrella. *farr šamsiita.* 2. *ftarr (a).* The pencil twirled on the end of the string. *l-qalam l-imƐallag bil-xeeṭ gaam yiftarr.* 3. *fital (i fatil), biram (u barum).* The officer twirled his moustache. *ḍ-ḍaabuṭ fital išwaarba.*
twist - 1. *barma* pl. *-aat.* He gave the donkey's tail a good twist. *buram ðeel iz-zumaaḷ barma qawiyya.* 2. *wuṣla* pl. *-aat.* Add a twist of lemon peel. *zuṭṭ fadd wuṣlat gišir nuumi zaamuḍ.*
to twist - 1. *luwa (i lawi) n-.* He twisted my arm until it hurt. *luwa ʔiidayya ʔila ʔan gaamat toojaƐni.* — I nearly twisted my ankle. *luweet rijli ʔilla šwayya.* — Twist the two ends of the wire together. *ʔilwi nihaayteen il-waayar suwa.* 2. *farr (u farr) n-.* Twist the screw two more turns to the right. *furr il-burġi marrteen lux lil-yimna.* 3. *tlawwa (a talawwi).* The road twists through the mountains. *ṭ-ṭariiq yitlawwa been ij-jibaal.*
**She twisted him around her little finger. *labista b-iṣbaƐha miθl il-mizbas.*
twister - *fitteela* pl. *-aat.* The twister blew off the garage roof. *l-fitteela ṭayyrat sagf il-garaaj.*
to **twitch** - *raff (u raff).* My eye is twitching. *Ɛeeni da-truff.*
to **twitter** - *waṣwaṣ (i waṣwaṣa).* The sparrows are twittering. *l-Ɛaṣaafiir da-twaṣwiṣ.*
two - 1. *θneen, θinteen.* There's no one here but the two of us. *ma-aku ʔazzad ihnaa ġeer ʔizna θ-θineen.* — It is two o'clock. *s-saaƐa θinteen.* — The two of you come here! *θneekum taƐaalu hnaa!* — They came in by twos. *dixlaw iθneen iθneen.* 2. *-een.* He owns two houses and two cars. *yimluk beeteen w-sayyaarteen.* — A two-passenger car is not big enough for our family. *sayyaara maal nafareen maa kaafya l-Ɛaaʔilatna.*
two-faced - *ʔabu wijheen.* He's two-faced and sneaky; don't trust him. *haaða ʔabu wijheen w-zayyaal; la-taθiq bii.*
two hundred - *miiteen.*
type - 1. *nooƐ* pl. *ʔanwaaƐ, šikil* pl. *ʔaškaal.* What type of shoe did you have in mind? *ʔay nooƐ qundara Ɛaqlak qaaṭiƐ bii.* 2. *faṣiila* pl. *faṣaaʔil.* Do you remember your blood type? *titðakkar min ʔay faṣiila dammak?* 3. *zarf* pl. *zruuf.* Which kind of type do you want? *ʔay nooƐ imnil-izruuf itriid?* 4. *ṣinif* pl. *ʔaṣnaaf.* He's not my type. *haaða muu min ṣinfi.*
to type - 1. *ṭubaƐ (a ṭabuƐ) n-.* Can you type? *tigdar tiṭbaƐ?* 2. *ṣannaf (i taṣniif) t-.* Nurse, have you typed that blood yet? *yaa mumarriḍa, ṣannafti had-damm loo baƐad?*
typesetter - *munaḍḍid* pl. *-iin.*
typewriter - *ṭaabiƐa* pl. *-aat.* Bring the typewriter here. *jiib iṭ-ṭaabiƐa hnaa.*
typewriting - *ṭabuƐ, ṭibaaƐa.* Do they teach typewriting at this school? *yƐallimuun ṭabuƐ*

ib-hal-madrasa?
typhoid - *tiifo.*
typhus - *tiifoos.*
typical - **1.** *ʔaṣli*.* This is a typical example of an old Iraqi house. *haaδa namuuδaj ʔaṣli lil-beet il-ɛiraaqi l-qadiim.* **2.** *ṣamiim* pl. *-iin.* He's a typical Iraqi. *huwwa ɛiraaqi ṣamiim.*
  **That's typical of him. *haaδi daggaata.*
typist - *kaatib* (pl. *kuttaab*) *ṭaabiɛa.* He's a good typist. *haaδa xooš kaatib ṭaabiɛa.*
tyranny - *ẓulum, stibdaad.*
tyrant - *ẓaalim* pl. *ẓullaam, mustabidd* pl. *-iin.* He's a tyrant in the office, but he's active in community welfare. *haaδa ẓaalim bid-daaʔira, laakin ysawwi xeer ihwaaya lil-mujtamaɛ.*

U

udder - *dees* pl. *dyuus, ẓariɛ* pl. *ẓruuɛ, θadi* pl. *θidaaya.*
uglier - *ʔabšaɛ, ʔaqbaz.* She's uglier than her sister. *hiyya ʔabšaɛ min ʔuxutha.*
ugly - **1.** *qabiiz, bašiɛ.* She's so ugly! *hiyya kulliš qabiiza.* **2.** *muġriẓ, qabiiz.* They're spreading ugly rumors about him. *da-yšayyɛuun ʔišaaɛaat muġriẓa ɛanna.*
ulcer - *qurza* pl. *-aat, quraz.*
ulterior - *xafi.* I think there is an ulterior motive behind his action. *ʔaɛtiqid ʔaku ġaraẓ xafi b-ɛamala.*
ultimate - *nihaaʔi*, ʔaxiir, ʔaaxar.* Is this your ultimate goal? *haay ġaaytak in-nihaaʔiyya?* or *haaδi ʔaaxar ġaaya triidha?*
ultimatum - *ʔinδaar nihaaʔi* pl. *ʔinδaaraat nihaaʔiyya.* We issued an ultimatum to the enemy. *dazzeena ʔinδaar nihaaʔi lil-ɛadu.*
ultra - **1.** *miṭṭarrif.* He is ultra-Conservative. *huwwa muzaafiẓ miṭṭarrif.* **2.** *fooq.* We studied ultra-violet rays in physics. *dirasna l-ʔašiɛɛa fooq il-banafsajiyya bil-fiizyaa?*
umbilical cord - *zabil* (pl. *zbaal*) *ṣurra.*
umbrella - *šamsiyya* pl. *-aat, šamaasi.*
umpire - *zakam* pl. *muzakkimiin, muzakkim* pl. *-iin.*
un- - **1.** *ma-, muu, ġeer.* This is an unusual situation. *haaδi zaala ma-ɛtiyaadiyya.* -- Last night we had unexpected company. *l-baarza bil-leel joona xuṭṭaar ma-mutwaqqaɛiin.* --That's very unlikely. *haay kulliš ma-muztamala.* -- I am uncomfortable here! *ʔaani muu mirtaaz ihnaa.* -- His trip is still uncertain. *safirta baɛadha muu ʔakiida.* -- I'm still uncertain as to whether I'll go. *ʔaani li-hassa ġeer mitʔakkid ʔiδa raz-aruuz.* -- The climate here is unhealthy. *j-jaww ihnaa ġeer ṣizzi.* **2.** *ma-.* It's quite unlike anything I've seen before. *haaδa ma-yišbah ʔay šii ʔaani šaayfa gabuḷ.* -- This is undesirable. *hiiči šii ma-yinraad.* -- This is unfit to eat. *haaδa ma-yiṣlaz lil-ʔakil.* **3.** *biduun, bila.* This radio has an unconditional guarantee. *har-raadyo bii taɛahhud biduun šarṭ.* -- That's undoubtedly the reason he quit. *haaδa bila šakk sabab ṭaliɛta.* -- The fort was left unmanned. *l-qalɛa ntirkat biduun junuud.* -- He did it unconsciously. *sawwaaha bila šuɛuur.* **4.** *xilaaf.* That's quite unlike him. *haay tamaaman xilaaf ɛaadta.* **5.** *ma-ʔil-.* That remark is uncalled for. *hal-izčaaya ma-ʔilha muujib.* -- Your fears are unfounded. *xoofak ma-ʔila muujib.* -- The statement is unfounded. *hal-izčaaya ma-ʔilha ʔasaas.* -- It was an unparalleled success. *čaan fadd najaaz ma-ʔila maθiil.*
  **She's been so unfortunate. *ɛala ṭuul hiyya ma-čaanat mazẓuuẓa.*
  **He was unfaithful to his wife. *čaan da-yxuun zawujta.* or *ma-čaan muxliṣ iz-zawujta.*
  **He is unusually bright. *δakaaʔa ʔakθar imnil-iɛtiyaadi.*
  to un- - *fakk* (u *fakk*). I can't unlatch the door. *ma-agdar ʔafukk il-lisaan maal il-baab.* -- He unbuttoned his shirt. *fakk id-dugma maal θooba.* or *fakk θooba.* -- They uncoupled the engine at Hindiyya. *fakkaw makiint il-qiṭaar bil-hindiyya.* -- He unbuckled his belt. *fakk izzaama.*
unabridged - *kaamil.* This is the unabridged edition of his book. *haaδi n-nusxa l-kaamila min iktaaba.*
unanimous - *ʔijmaaɛi*.* It needs unanimous approval. *tiztaaj ʔila muwaafaqa ʔijmaaɛiyya.*
unanimously - *bil-ʔijmaaɛ.* They elected him unanimously. *ntixaboo bil-ʔijmaaɛ.*
unarmed - *ʔaɛzal.* The robber was unarmed. *l-zaraami čaan ʔaɛzal.*
unbeliever - *kaafir* pl. *kuffaar.*
uncertainty - *ziira.* Don't leave us in such uncertainty. *la-txalliina b-hiiči ziira.*
uncivil - *xašin, jaaff.* He was very uncivil to us. *čaan kulliš xašin wiyyaana.*
uncle - *ɛamm* pl. *ɛmuum* (paternal), *xaaḷ* pl. *xwaaḷ* (maternal).
unclean - *nagis.* I can't pray now; I'm unclean. *hassa ma-agdar aṣalli li-ʔanni nagis.*
uncomfortable - *mitδaayiq.* I felt uncomfortable when my father was there. *zasseet mitδaayiq min ʔabuuya čaan ihnaak.*
uncompromising - *mitɛannit* pl. *-iin, mɛaanid* pl. *-iin.* The union leaders are very uncompromising. *zuɛamaaʔ in-naqaaba kulliš mitɛannitiin.*
unconscious - *ġaayba ruuz~.* He's still unconscious. *baɛda ġaayba ruuza.*
uncouth - *xašin.*
to **uncover** - **1.** *kaššaf* (i *takšiif, tkiššif*). Don't uncover that pot. *la-tkaššif ij-jidir.* **2.** *ktišaf* (i *ktišaaf*). I uncovered something new in that case. *ktišafit fadd šii jdiid bid-daɛwa.*
uncovered - *makšuuf, mkaššaf.* Their heads are uncovered. *ruushum makšuufa.*
under - **1.** *jawwa, tazat.* The slippers are under the bed. *n-naɛal jawwa č-čarpaaya.* -- Can you swim under water? *tigdar tisbaz jawwa l-maay?* **2.** *tazat.* Are you under medical treatment? *ʔinta tazt it-tadaawi hassa?* -- The police put him under surveillance. *š-šurṭa zaṭṭoo tazt il-muraaqaba.* **3.** *b-.* Under the new system, there will be elections soon. *bin-niδaam ij-jidiid raz-iṣṣiir intixaabaat qariiban.* -- Under these circumstances that could never happen. *b-hiiči ẓuruuf δiič ʔabad ma-tṣiir.* **4.** *ʔaqall min, tazat, jawwa.* This meat weighs under a kilo. *hal-lazam wazna ʔaqall min keelu.* -- They cannot vote since they are under legal age. *ma-ygidruun yṣawwtuun li-ʔan jawwa s-sinn il-qaanuuni.* **5.** *jawwaani*.* Their underclothing is wool. *hduumhum ij-jawwaaniyya min ṣuuf.* **6.** *naaʔib* pl. *nuwwaab.* He's the under-secretary of defense. *huwwa naaʔib waziir id-difaaɛ.*
  **I'm under contract with the government. *ʔaani maaẓi ɛaqid wiyya l-zukuuma.*
  **Don't forget you are under oath. *la-tinsa ʔinta zaalif yamiin.*
  **Is the fire under control? *n-naar mṣayṭar ɛaleeha?*
underarm - *ʔubuṭ* pl. *ʔubaaṭ* This salve will prevent underarm perspiration. *had-dihin yimnaɛ il-ɛarag imnil-ʔubuṭ.*
underdog - *miskiin* pl. *masaakiin.* He always helps the underdog. *huwwa daaʔiman yɛaawun il-masaakiin.*
underground - **1.** *jawwa l-gaaɛ.* The city has underground telephone lines. *ʔaslaak it-talafoon maal hal-wlaaya jawwa l-gaaɛ.* **2.** *muqaawama sirriyya.* He served with the underground during the war. *xidam wiyya l-muqaawama s-sirriyya ʔaθnaaʔ il-zarb.*
underhand - *min jawwa.* Throw the ball underhand. *ʔušmur iṭ-ṭooba min jawwa.*
underlying - *ʔasaasi*.* Do you understand the underlying causes? *tuɛruf il-ʔasbaab il-ʔasaasiyya?*
to **undermine** - *zufar* (u *zafur*) *n- jawwa.* The river undermined the wall and brought it down. *n-nahar zufar jawwa l-zaayiṭ w-waggaɛa.* -- He undermined my position and got me fired. *huwwa l-zufar jawwaaya w-xallaani ʔanṭirid.*
underneath - *jawwa.* I found the ball underneath the bed. *ligeet iṭ-ṭooba jawwa č-čarpaaya.*
undernourishment - *suuʔ taġδiya.*
underpants - *lbaas* pl. *-aat, libsaan.*
underprivileged - *mazruum* pl. *-iin.* He built a hospital for underprivileged children. *bina mustašfa*

lil-ʔaṭfaal il-maɀruumiin.
to **underrate** - *staxaff (i stixfaaf) b-, qallal (i taqliil) min.* We underrated his strength. *staxaffeena b-quuta.*
to **undersell** - *kisar (i).* That store undersold us. *δaak il-maɀall kisarna.*
undershirt - *faaniila* pl. *-aat.*
to **understand** - *ftiham (i ftihaam), fiham (a fahim).* He doesn't understand Russian. *ma-yiftihim ruusi.* -- I understand from his letter that he likes his work. *ʔafham min maktuuba š-šaġḷa Ɛijbata.*
understanding - **1.** *ʔidraak.* He has keen understanding. *Ɛinda xooš ʔidraak.* **2.** *tafaahum.* There's a close understanding between them. *ʔaku beenaathum tafaahum zeen.* **3.** *mudrik.* He's a very understanding man. *huwwa fadd waaɀid mudrik.*
**They've reached an understanding on the Berlin question. *tfaahmaw Ɛala qaḍiyyat barliin.*
understood - *mafhuum.* Of course that's understood! *ṭabƐan haay mafhuum!*
to **undertake** - **1.** *qaam (u qiyaam) b-.* I hope you're not planning to undertake that trip alone. *ʔatʔammal ʔinta ma-raɀ-itquum ib-has-safra waɀdak.* **2.** *tkaffal (a takafful).* He undertook to pay for his nephew's education. *tkaffal ib-maṣaariif taθqiif ʔibn axuu.*
undertaking - **1.** *taɀammul.* His undertaking that responsibility was a big favor. *taɀammula hal-masʔuuliyya čaan fadd luṭuf kabiir.* **2.** *mašruuƐ* pl. *mašaariiƐ.* The government is encouraging industrial undertakings. *l-ɀukuuma da-tšajjiƐ il-mašaariiƐ iṣ-ṣinaaƐiyya.*
undertaker - *mġassil* pl. *-iin.*
underwear - *hduum jawwaaniyya.*
underworld - *muɀiiṭ ʔijraam.* He grew up in the underworld. *nišaʔ ib-muɀiiṭ il-ʔijraam.*
to **underwrite** - *ḍiman (i ḍamaan).* Will the International Bank underwrite this loan? *l-bang id-dawli raɀ-yiḍmin hal-qarḍ?*
to **undo** - **1.** *ɀall (i ɀall), fall (i fall), fakk (u fakk).* Help me undo this knot. *Ɛaawinni nɀill hal-Ɛugda.* **2.** *Ɛaddal (i taƐdiil).* We'll need a week to undo this mess. *yinraad-ilna sbuuƐ ɀatta nƐaddil hal-xarbaṭa.*
**Now it's happened; it can't be undone. *hassa baƐad ṣaarat w-ma-aku majaal lit-taraajuƐ.*
undoing - *xaraab.* Drink was the cause of his undoing. *š-šurub čaan sabab xaraaba.*
to **undress** - **1.** *nazzaƐ (i tnizziƐ, tanziiƐ).* I'll undress the children. *ʔaani raɀ-anazziƐhum lij-jahaal.* **2.** *nizaƐ (a naziƐ) hiduum.* The phone rang just as I was undressing. *dagg it-talifoon ʔawwal-ma bdeet anzaƐ ihduumi.*
undulent fever - *ɀummat maalṭa.*
unduly - *ʔakθar imnil-laazim.* You are unduly severe. *ʔinta qaasi ʔakθar imnil-laazim.*
undying - *ʔila l-ʔabad.* You have my undying gratitude. *raɀ-abqa mamnuun ʔilak ʔila l-ʔabad.*
uneasily - *b-qalaq.* He sat waiting there uneasily. *giƐad da-yintiḍir ib-qalaq.*
uneasy - **1.** *mitqayyid.* I feel uneasy in his company. *ʔaɀiss mitqayyid min ʔakuun wiyyaa* or ***ma-ʔaaxuδ ɀurriiti hal-gadd min ʔakuun wiyyaa.*
2. *ma-mistiqirr.* This is an uneasy situation. *hal-waḍiƐ ma-mistiqirr.* **3.** *mitšawwiš.* He left his wife very uneasy. *xalla marta mitšawwša kulliš.*
unemployed - *Ɛaaṭil* pl. *-iin, baṭṭaal* pl. *-a.* He's unemployed now. *huwwa hassa Ɛaaṭil.*
unemployment - *Ɛaṭaala, baṭaala.* Unemployment this year is less than before. *l-Ɛaṭaala has-sana ʔaqall min gabuḷ.*
UNESCO - *yuuniskoo.*
unexpectedly - *Ɛala ġafḷa.* The accident occurred unexpectedly. *l-ɀaadiθ ṣaar Ɛala ġafla.*
unfinished - *Ɛan-nuṣṣ, ma-xalṣaan, naagiṣ.* The contractor left the work unfinished. *l-qunṭarči tirak iš-šuġuḷ Ɛan-nuṣṣ.*
unfortunate - *muʔsif.* That's an unfortunate mistake! *haaδi ġalṭa muʔsifa.*
unfortunately - *l-suuʔ il-ɀaḍḍ.* Unfortunately, negotiations aren't advancing very well. *l-suuʔ il-ɀaḍḍ, il-mufaawaḍaat ma-da-titqaddam hal-gadd zeen.*
ungrateful - *naakir (pl. -iin) ij-jamiil.* He's an ungrateful boy. *hal-walad naakir ij-jamiil.*
unharmed - *salaamaat.* He escaped unharmed. *ṭilaƐ salaamaat.*
to **unhitch** - *ɀall (i ɀall), fakk (u fakk).* They unhitched the horses from the carriage. *ɀallaw il-xeel imnil-Ɛarabaana.*
to **unhook** - *fakk (u fakk).* Unhook the garden gate, please. *baḷḷa ma-tfukk baab il-ɀadiiqa.*
unification - *tawɀiid.* The foreign ministers are considering unification of the country. *wuzaraaʔ il-xaarijiyya da-ydursuun tawɀiid il-balad.*
uniform - **1.** *badla (pl. -aat) rasmiyya.* They gave us new uniforms. *nṭoona badlaat rasmiyya jdiida.* **2.** *Ɛala namaṭ waaɀid.* Their products aren't of very uniform quality. *muntajaathum muu Ɛala namaṭ waaɀid.*
uniformity - *tanaasuq.* We need more uniformity in our administrative practices. *niɀtaaj ʔila tanaasuq ʔakθar bil-ʔidaara,*
to **unify** - *waɀɀad (i tawɀiid).* Bismarck unified Germany. *bismaark waɀɀad ʔalmaanya.*
unilateral - *min jaanib waaɀid.* We will not accept any unilateral decision. *ma-niqbal qaraar min jaanib waaɀid.*
union - **1.** *ttiɀaad* pl. *-aat.* Racial segregation is still in vogue in the Union of South Africa, unfortunately. *t-tamyiiz il-Ɛunṣuri baƐda mawjuud b-ittiɀaad januubi ʔafriiqya l-suuʔ il-ɀaḍḍ.*
2. *naqaaba* pl. *-aat.* Are you a member of the union? *ʔinta Ɛuḍu bin-naqaaba?*
unique - *waɀiid.* It was a unique experience. *čaanat tajruba waɀiida min nooƐha.*
unison - *ṣoot waaɀid.* Repeat this statement in unison. *Ɛiidu haj-jumla b-ṣoot waaɀid.*
unit - **1.** *qisim* pl. *ʔaqsaam.* This book is divided into twelve units. *l-iktaab imqassam ʔila θnaƐaš qisim.* **2.** *wiɀda* pl. *-aat.* He's been assigned to another unit. *nniqal il-ġeer wiɀda.*
to **unite** - **1.** *ttiɀad (i ttiɀaad).* Egypt and Syria united to form the UAR. *miṣir w-suurya ttiɀdaw w-sawwaw ij-jamhuuriyya l-Ɛarabiyya l-muttaɀida.*
2. *waɀɀad (i tawɀiid).* Saladin united the Muslims against the Crusaders. *ṣalaaɀ id-diin waɀɀad il-muslimiin ḍidd iṣ-ṣaliibiyyiin.*
United Arab Republic - *j-jamhuuriyya l-Ɛarabiyya l-muttaɀida.*
United Nations - *l-ʔumam il-muttaɀida.*
United States - *l-wilaayaat il-muttaɀida.*
unity - **1.** *ttiɀaad.* The Arabs need unity. *l-Ɛarab yinraad-ilhum ittiɀaad.* **2.** *wiɀda.* Arab unity is the goal of many parties. *l-wiɀda l-Ɛarabiyya ġaayat ihwaaya ʔaɀzaab.*
universal - **1.** *Ɛaamm.* There is universal agreement on that. *ʔaku ttifaaq Ɛaamm Ɛal-haay.*
2. *Ɛaalami.** Gandhi had a universal message. *ġaandi risaalta čaanat Ɛaalamiyya.*
universe - *Ɛaalam, koon, dinya.*
university - **1.** *jaamiƐa* pl. *-aat.* How many students are there at this university? *šgadd ʔaku ṭullaab ib-haj-jaamiƐa?* **2.** *jaamiƐi**. University life is loads of fun. *l-ɀayaat ij-jaamiƐiyya kulliš laṭiifa.*
unknown - *majhuul.* We visited the grave of the unknown soldier. *zirna qabr ij-jundi l-majhuul.*
unless - **1.** *ʔilla ʔiδa.* We're coming, unless it rains. *ʔiɀna jaayiin ʔaḷḷaahumma ʔilla ʔiδa tumṭur id-dinya.* **2.** *ʔiδa ma-.* Unless you tell me why, I won't do it. *ʔiδa ma-tgul-li leeš, tara ʔaani ma-asawwiiha.*
to **unload** - *farraġ (i tafriiġ) t-.* They haven't unloaded the ship's cargo yet. *baƐad ma-farrġaw ɀumuulat il-markab.* -- Unload your gun before you go in the car. *farrig it-tufga maaltak gabuḷ-ma txušš bis-sayyaara.*
unlucky - **1.** *mašʔuum.* It was an unlucky coincidence. *čaanat fadd ṣidfa mašʔuuma.* **2.** *ma-maɀḍuuḍ.* I don't know why I'm so unlucky. *ma-adri leeš ʔaani hal-gadd ma-maɀḍuuḍ.*
to **unmask** - *bayyan (i tabyiin), kišaf (i kašif).* They unmasked the traitor. *bayynaw il-xaaʔin.*
unoccupied - *faariġ.* That house is unoccupied. *δaak il-beet faariġ.*
unpleasant - *muzƐij.* I got some unpleasant news today. *jatni šwayya ʔaxbaar muzƐija l-yoom.*
unrest - *qalaaqil.* We heard there's unrest in Najaf. *smaƐna ʔaku qalaaqil bin-najaf.*
unruly - *wakiiɀ, wakiɀ.* He's an unruly child. *huwwa walad wakiiɀ.*
unstable - *qaliq.* This chemical compound is unstable. *hal-murakkab il-kiimyaawi qaliq.*
to **untangle** - **1.** *ɀall (i ɀall), fakk (u fakk).* Can you please untangle this string? *baḷḷa ma-tɀill hal-ixyuuṭ l-imčabbina.* **2.** *faḍḍ (u faḍḍ).* The police untangled the traffic jam. *šurṭat il-muruur*

faṣṣaw izdiζaam is-sayyaaraat.
untidy - *mxarbaṭ.* His wife is very untidy. *marta kulliš mxarbaṭa.*
to **untie** - *fakk (u fakk).* Can you untie this knot for me? *tigdar itfukk-li hal-εuqdaʔ* -- Wait till I untie the package. *ntiṣir ʔila ʔan ʔafukk ir-ruzma.*
until - **1.** *l-, ζatta.* Wait until tomorrow. *ntiṣir il-baačir.* **2.** *ʔila ʔan, ζatta.* Wait until he comes. *ntiṣir ʔila ʔan yiji.*
to **unveil** - *zaaζ (i) sitaar εan.* The president will unveil the monument next week. *raʔiis ij-jamhuriyya raζ-yziiζ is-sitaar εan in-naṣub it-tiδkaari l-isbuuε ij-jaay.*
up - **1.** *foog.* I'm up here. *ʔaani foog ihnaa.* -- Would you please put it up there? *baḷḷa ma-tζuṭṭa foog ihnaakʔ* -- You can find a nice room for a dinar and up. *tigdar tilgi ġurfa zeena hnaa min diinaar w-foog.* **2.** *gaaεid.* Is he up already? *huwwa min hassa gaaεid imnin-noomʔ* **3.** *εaks.* Shall we head up the river? *ma-xal-nittijih εaks il-ṃaayʔ* **4.** *matruuk, εala.* The decision is up to you. *l-qaraar matruuk ʔilak* or *l-qaraar εaleek.*
**Your time is up. *xilaṣ waktak.*
**He was walking up and down the room. *čaan da-yruuζ w-yiji bil-guḅḅa.*
**We all have our ups and downs. *haay id-dinya, yoom ʔilak w-yoom εaleek* or *haay id-dinya, yoom tiṣεad yoom tinzil.*
up to - **1.** *l-ζadd.* Because of the storm, trains were up to two hours late. *b-sabab il-εaaṣifa il-qiṭaaraat čaanat mitʔaxxra l-ζadd saaεteen.* **2.** *gadd.* He isn't up to the job. *huwwa muu gadd haš-šaġla.*
**What's he up to this time? *han-nooba šaku εindaʔ*
up to now - *li-hassa.* Up to now he hasn't answered. *baεad li-hassa ma-jaawab.*
uphill - **This road goes uphill for a mile and then descends. *haṭ-ṭariiq yiṣεad fadd miil w-baεdeen yinzil.*
upkeep - *ṣiyaana.* My car requires a lot of expenses for upkeep. *sayyaarti yinraad-ilha hwaaya maṣaariif liṣ-ṣiyaana.*
upper - *foogaani*.* The fire started on the upper floor. *n-naar bidat imnil-qaat il-foogaani.*
**Write the page number in the upper right-hand corner. *ζuṭṭ ʔarqaam iṣ-ṣafζaat li-foog bij-jiha l-yimna.*
to **uproot** - *šilaε (a šaliε), qilaε (a qaliε).* The storm uprooted several trees. *l-εaaṣifa šilεat čam šajara.*
upset - **1.** *maqluuq, mitšawwiš.* He was all upset. *čaan kulliš maqluuq.* **2.** *mitxarbuṭ.* I have an upset stomach. *miεidti mitxarbuṭa.*
to upset - **1.** *giḷab (u gaḷub), waggaε (i twuggiε).* Be careful or you'll upset the pitcher. *diir baalak, tara raζ-tugḷub id-doolka.* -- You're upsetting the boat! *ʔinta raζ-tugḷub il-balam!* **2.** *xarbaṭ (u).* Nothing ever upsets him. *ma-aku fadd šii yxarbuṭa.*
upside down - *bil-magḷuub.* That picture is upside down. *haṣ-ṣuura maζṭuuṭa bil-magḷuub.*
to turn upside down - *giḷab (u gaḷub).* They turned the whole house upside down. *guḷbaw il-beet kulla.*
upstairs - **1.** *foogaani*.* The upstairs apartment is vacant. *š-šiqqa l-foogaaniyya faarġa.* **2.** *foog.* He's upstairs. *huwwa foog.* **3.** *foog, li-foog.* Bring our bags upstairs. *ṣaεεid jinaṭna li-foog.*
up-to-date - **1.** *εala ʔaaxir ṭarz, εala ʔaaxir ṭiraaz, ζadiiθ.* She has an up-to-date kitchen. *εidha maṭbax εala ʔaaxir ṭarz.* **2.** *l-ζadd il-yoom.* My books are posted up to date. *dafaatri t-tijaariyya mnaṣṣma l-ζadd il-yoom.*
urge - *daafiε* pl. *dawaafiε.* I felt the urge to tell him what I thought of him. *ζasseet ib-fadd daafiε agul-la raʔyi bii.*
to urge - **1.** *ζaθθ (i).* If you urge her a bit, she'll do it. *hiyya tsawwiiha loo šwayya tζiθθha.* **2.** *šajjaε (i tašjiiε).* She urged us to stay longer. *šajjεatna nibqa mudda ʔaṭwal.* **3.** *ζarraṣ (i taζriiṣ).* His mother urged him to commit the crime. *ʔumma ζarriṣata ysawwi haj-jariima.*
urgent - *mustaεjal.* I have an urgent request. *εindi fadd ṭalab mustaεjal.*
use - **1.** *stiεmaal* pl. *-aat.* How long has this method been in use? *šgadd ṣaar-ilha haṭ-ṭariiqa bil-istiεmaal.* **2.** *faaʔida.* Will that be of any use to you? *haay biiha faaʔida ʔilakʔ* or ***haay itfiidakʔ* -- What's the use of arguing? *šinu l-faaʔida mnil-mujaadalaʔ* **3.** *ζaaja.* I have no use for that. *ma-ʔili ζaaja b-haay.* or ***ma-aζtaaj haay.*
**It's no use, we've got to do it. *ma-aku čaara, ʔiζna laazim insawwiiha.*
to make use of - *staġall (i stiġlaal).* He made good use of the opportunity. *staġall il-furṣa zeen.*
to use - *staεmal (i stiεmaal).* I can't use that. *ma-agdar astaεmil haay.* -- What toothpaste do you use? *yaa maεjuun isnuun tistaεmilʔ* -- We'll use this room as a classroom. *raζ-nistaεmil hal-ġurfa ka-ṣaff.*
to use up - *stahlak (i stihlaak), stanfaδ (i stinfaaδ), xallaṣ (i taxliiṣ), ṣiraf (u ṣaruf).* We've used up all our supplies. *stanfaδna kull il-mawjuud il-εidna.* -- His car uses up a lot of gasoline. *sayyaarta tistahlik ihwaaya ḅaanziin.*
used - **1.** *čaan.* I used to live here. *činit askun ihnaa.* -- He used to eat in restaurants before he got married. *čaan da-yaakul bil-maṭaaεim gabuḷ-ma tzawwaj.* **2.** *mitεawwid.* I'm not used to hard work. *ʔaani ma-mitεawwid εala š-šuġuḷ iṣ-ṣaεub.*
to get used to - *taεawwad (a) εala.* She's gotten used to getting up at seven o'clock. *hiyya tεawwdat εal-gaεda s-saaεa sabεa.*
useful - *mufiid, naafiε.* A maid is useful around the house. *l-xaddaama mufiida bil-beet.* -- I've found this book very useful. *šifit hal-iktaab kulliš naafiε.*
useless - *ma-aku faaʔida, ma-bii faaʔida.* It's useless to try to convince him. *ma-aku faaʔida tζaawil itqannεa.* --This map is useless to me. *hal-xariiṭa ma-biiha faaʔida ʔili.*
usher - *tašriifaati* pl. *-iyya, daliil* pl. *-iin, ʔadillaaʔ.* The usher will show you your seats. *t-tašriifaati raζ-yraawiikum maqaaεidkum.*
to usher - *dalla (i tdilli) t-.* We were ushered to our seats. *tdalleena εala maqaaεidna.*
usual - *εtiyaadi*.* Our usual hours are from 8 to 3. *dawaamna l-iεtiyaadi mniθ-θamaanya ʔila θ-θalaaθa.* -- We'll meet at the usual place. *raζ-niltiqi bil-mukaan il-iεtiyaadi.*
as usual - *kal-εaada, εal-εaada.* It's raining, as usual. *da-tumṭur kal-εaada.* -- Everything went along as usual. *kullši miša εal-εaada.*
usually - *εaadatan.* I usually visit them twice a week. *εaadatan ʔazuurhum marrteen bil-isbuuε.*
utensil - *ʔadaat* pl. *ʔadawaat.* We bought some new cooking utensils. *štireena ʔadawaat ṭabux ijdiida.*
utmost - **1.** *kulliš.* The matter is of the utmost importance. *l-qaṣiyya kulliš muhimma.* **2.** *ʔaqṣa.* He expended the utmost energy. *biδal ʔaqṣa juhda.*
utter - *kulliš.* Things are in a state of utter confusion in the office. *l-ʔumuur kulliš imxarbuṭa bid-daaʔira.*
to utter - *gaal (u gool).* I couldn't utter a single word. *ma-gdart aguul wala čilma.*

V

vacant - **1.** *faariġ, xaali.* The house has been vacant for a week. *l-beet ṣaar-la sbuuε faariġ.* -- Next to our house there is still a vacant lot. *yamm beetna ʔaku saaζa faarġa.* **2.** *šaaġir* pl. *šawaaġir.* We have no position vacant at the moment. *ma-εidna waṣiifa šaaġra hassa.*
to **vacate** - *farraġ (i tafriiġ), ṭilaε (a ṭuluuε) min.* When are you going to vacate the house? *šwakit raζ-itfarriġ il-beetʔ*
vacation - *εuṭla* pl. *εuṭal.* The children are looking forward to their vacation. *j-jahaal da-yintaṣruun εuṭlathum ib-faariġ iṣ-ṣabur.*
on vacation - *mujaaz, bil-ʔijaaza.* Ali is on vacation. *εali mujaaz.*

vague - *mubham, muu waaδiz.* He gave me a vague answer. *jaawabni jawaab mubham.*
vaguely - *muu b-wuδuuz.* I remember him vaguely. *ma-atδakkara b-wuδuuz.*
vain - *maġruur, šaayif nafs~.* She's terribly vain. *hiyya kulliš maġruura.*
  in vain - *ɛabaθan.* The doctor tried in vain to save the boy's life. *d-daktoor ɛabaθan zaawal yinquδ zayaat il-walad.*
valid - **1.** *ṣaziiz.* I don't think your argument is valid. *ma-aɛtiqid jadalak ṣaziiz.* **2.** *ṣaaliz, naafiδ, il-mafɛuul.* Is my license still valid? *ʔijaazti baɛadha ṣaalza?*
  **Your passport isn't valid any more. *paaṣportak xilṣat il-mudda maalta.*
valley - *waadi* pl. *widyaan.*
valuable - *θamiin, nafiis.* That's a valuable ring. *haaδa mizbas θamiin.*
valuables - *ʔašyaaʔ θamiina.* You'd better lock your valuables in the safe. *ʔazsan loo tzuṭṭ ʔašyaaʔak iθ-θamiina bil-qaaṣa.*
value - **1.** *qiima* pl. *qiyam.* This coin has no value. *hal-qiṭɛat in-nuquud ma-ʔilha qiima.* -- Even though it's rare, it's of no value to me. *walaw hiyya naadra, bass ma-ʔilha qiima bin-nisba ʔili.*
2. *wazin.* I don't attach any value to his opinions. *ma-anṭi ʔay wazin il-ʔaaraaʔa.*
  to value - **1.** *ɛtazz (a ɛtizaaz) b-, qaddar (i taqdiir).* I value his friendship very highly. *hwaaya ʔaɛtazz ib-ṣadaaqta.* **2.** *θamman (i taθmiin), saam (u soom).* What do you value your house at? *beeš itθammin beetak?* or **š-tiftikir beetak yiswa?*
valve - *ṣammaam* pl. *-aat.* The worker opened a valve to let oil into the pipeline. *l-ɛaamil fakk iṣ-ṣammaam zatta n-nafuṭ yijri bil-buuri.* **2.** *walf* pl. *-aat.* Your valves need adjusting. *l-walfaat yinraad-ilha δabuṭ.*
to **vanish** - *xtifa (i xtifaaʔ).* My pencil has vanished. *qalami xtifa.*
vapor - *buxaar* pl. *ʔabxira.* On sunny days a lot of vapor goes into the atmosphere. *bil-ʔayyaam il-mušmiša hwaaya buxaar yiṣɛad lij-jaww.*
variable - *muu θaabit.* The weather is variable these days. *j-jaww muu θaabit hal-ʔayyaam.*
variety - **1.** *taškiila* pl. *-aat.* We have a wide variety of shirts. *ɛidna taškiila čbiira mniθ-θiyaab.* **2.** *nooɛ* pl. *ʔanwaaɛ.* How many varieties of apples grow in your orchard? *čam nooɛ imnit-tiffaaz ɛindak ib-bistaanak?* **3.** *tanawwuɛ.* There's not much variety in my life. *ma-aku tanawwuɛ ib-zayaati.*
various - *mixtalif.* I have various reasons. *ɛindi ʔasbaab mixtalfa.*
varnish - *waarniiš.* How long does it take the varnish to dry? *šgadd yṭawwil il-waarniiš zatta yeebas?*
  to varnish - *δirab (u δarub) waarniiš.* We just varnished the doors. *tawwna δirabna l-buub waarniiš.*
to **vary** - *xtilaf (i xtilaaf).* The length varies in each case. *ṭ-ṭuul yixtilif ib-kull zaala.*
vase - *mazhariyya* pl. *-aat.*
veal - *lazam ɛijil.*
vegetable - *mxaδδar* pl. *-aat, mxaaδiir.*
vehicle - *ɛajala* pl. *-aat.*
veil - *puuši* pl. *pwaaši, puušiyya* pl. *-aat.* Many Iraqi women still wear veils. *hwaaya niswaan ɛiraaqiyyaat baɛadhum yilibsuun puušiyya.*
vein - *damaar* pl. *-aat, wariid* pl. *ʔawrida.* The medicine has to be injected into the vein. *d-duwa laazim yinδurub bid-damaar.*
velvet - *qadiifa.*
venereal disease - *maraδ zuhri* pl. *ʔamraaδ zuhriyya.* Gonorrhea is a venereal disease. *s-sayalaan maraδ zuhri.*
Venice - *l-bunduqiyya.*
venom - *samm* pl. *sumuum.*
vent - *majra (pl. majaari) hawa, manfaδ (pl. manaafiδ) hawa, baadgiir* pl. *-aat.* Open the vent! *fukk majra l-hawa.*
  to give vent - *naffas (i tanfiis).* She gave vent to her anger. *naffisat ɛan gaḷubha.*
ventilation - *tahwiya* pl. *-aat.* This room need ventilation. *hal-ġurfa yinraad-ilha tahwiya.*
venture - *mujaazafa* pl. *-aat, muxaaṭara* pl. *-aat.* It was a dangerous venture. *čaanat mujaazafa xaṭra.* -- I'm going into a new business venture. *raz-asawwi fadd mujaazafa tijaariyya.*
  to venture - **1.** *xaaṭar (i muxaaṭara), jaazaf (i mujaazafa).* I wouldn't venture to go out in this weather. *ma-ard axaaṭir aṭlaɛ ib-hiici jaww.*
2. *jaazaf (i mujaazafa).* Nothing ventured, nothing gained. *ma-tjaazif, kullši ma-tzaṣṣil.*
verb - *fiɛil* pl. *ʔafɛaal.*
verbal - *šafahi*, šafawi*.* We have a verbal agreement. *beenaatna ɛaqid šafahi.*
verdict - *zukum* pl. *ʔazkaam, qaraar* pl. *-aat.* The court issued the verdict. *l-mazkama ṣaddrat il-zukum.*
verge - **1.** *zaaffa.* She's on the verge of a breakdown. *hiyya ɛala zaaffat l-inhiyaar il-ɛaṣabi.* **2.** *wašak.* I was on the verge of telling him. *činit ɛala wašak agul-la.*
verse - **1.** *šiɛir.* The play is written in verse. *r-ruwaaya ɛala šikil šiɛir.* **2.** *beet* pl. *ʔabyaat.* Let's read the first verse of the poem. *xalli niqra ʔawwal beet imnil-qaṣiida.* **3.** *qisim* pl. *ʔaqsaam.* Let's sing only the first verse. *xalli nġanni ʔawwal qisim bass.*
version - *ruwaaya* pl. *-aat.* I heard another version. *simaɛit ruwaaya lux.*
versus - *δidd.* This is the case of the cotton company versus the ministry of agriculture. *haaδa daɛwat šarikat il-guṭin δidd wizaarat iz-ziraaɛa.*
vertical - *ɛamuudi*.* The Nabi Shiit minaret in Mosul isn't vertical. *manaarat in-nabi šiit il-bil-mooṣil muu ɛamuudiyya.*
very - **1.** *kulliš.* The bank is not very far from here. *l-bang muu kulliš biɛiid minnaa.* -- We're very satisfied with the new cook. *ʔizna kulliš mirtaaziin min iṭ-ṭabbaax ij-jidiid.*
2. *biδ-δabuṭ, nafs, biδ-δaat.* That's the very thing I want. *haaδa iš-šii illi ariida biδ-δabuṭ.*
3. *nafs, biδ-δaat.* She left that very day. *raazat ib-nafs il-yoom.*
  **He came the very next day. *ma-ṭawwal iθ-θaani yoom w-ʔija.*
vessel - *sifiina* pl. *sufun, markab* pl. *maraakub.* Several large vessels were docked in the harbor. *ɛiddat sufun ikbaar waččat bil-miinaaʔ.*
vest - *yalag* pl. *-aat, zaxma* pl. *-aat, zixam.* He usually wears a vest. *ɛaadatan yilbas yalag.*
vestige - *ʔaθar* pl. *ʔaaθaar.*
veteran - **1.** *muzaarib* pl. *-iin.* He's an old veteran. *haaδa muzaarib qadiim.* **2.** *mdarrab* pl. *-iin, muzannak* pl. *-iin.* He's a veteran politician. *huwwa siyaasi mdarrab.*
  **He's a veteran of the North African campaign of World War II. *zaarab ib-šimaal ʔafriiqya bil-zarb iθ-θaanya.*
veterinarian - *bayṭari* pl. *-iyya, beeṭaar* pl. *-iyya.* The veterinarian can tell you what's wrong with your horse. *l-bayṭari yigdar ygul-lak iš-bii l-izṣaan maalak.*
viaduct - *jisir* pl. *jsuura.*
to **vibrate** - *htazz (a htizaaz), rijaf (i rajif).* Pluck the string and watch it vibrate. *ʔuδrub il-watar w-šuufa šloon yihtazz.* -- The steering wheel vibrates at high speed. *l-isteerin yirjif min itsuuq ib-surɛa.*
vice - **1.** *raδiila* pl. *raδaayil.* Gambling is a vice. *liɛb il-iqmaar raδiila.* **2.** *naaʔib* pl. *nuwwaab.* He's the vice-president. *huwwa naaʔib ir-raʔiis.*
vicinity - **1.** *manṭiqa.* Is there a tailor in this vicinity? *ʔaku xayyaaṭ ib-hal-manṭiqa?* or **ʔaku xayyaaṭ qariib minnaa.* **2.** *zawaali.* The weather is bad in the vicinity of Washington. *j-jaww muu zeen zawaali waašinṭan.*
vicious - *šaris, xabiiθ.* The dog is vicious. *č-čalib šaris.*
  **She has a vicious tongue. *lsaanha waṣix* or *lsaanha yguṣṣ.*
victim - *δaziyya* pl. *δazaaya.* He was the victim of an auto accident. *raaz δaziyyat zaadiθ taṣaadum.*
victor - *mintiṣir* pl. *-iin.* We were the victors in that struggle. *ʔizna činna l-mintiṣriin ib-δaak il-kifaaz.*
victorious - *mintiṣir.* The victorious army entered the city. *j-jayš il-mintiṣir dixal l-wlaaya.*
victory - *ntiṣaar* pl. *-aat, naṣir* pl. *ʔanṣaar.* That was a great victory. *čaan fadd intiṣaar ɛaδiim.*
view - **1.** *manδar* pl. *manaaδir.* You have a nice view from here. *ɛindak xooš manδar minnaa.* **2.** *raʔi* pl. *ʔaaraaʔ.* Our views differ. *ʔaaraaʔna tixtilif.*
3. *naδar.* In view of these developments, we'll have to change our plans. *bin-naδar ʔila hat-taṭawwuraat, laazim inġayyir xuṭaṭna.* -- Here's my point of view. *haay wujhat naδari.*

in view - *mbayyin.* Is the ship in view? *s-sifiina mbayyna?*
to come into view - *bayyan (i).* The ship finally came into view. *s-sifiina taaliiha bayynat.*
vile - **1.** *qaδir* pl. *-iin, saafil* pl. *safala.* He's really a vile person. *huwwa fadd waazid kulliš qaδir.* **2.** *muzɛij.* What vile weather we're having! *ġeer jaww muzɛij haaδa!*
village - *qarya* pl. *qura.* He lives in the village. *da-yiskun bil-qarya.*
vinegar - *xall.*
to **violate** - *xaalaf (i muxaalafa).* That's not the first time he's violated the law. *haay muu ʔawwal marra yxaalif biiha l-qaanuun.*
violation - *muxaalafa* pl. *-aat.* He has three violations on his record. *ɛinda tlaθ muxaalafaat.*
violent - **1.** *ɛaniif* pl. *-iin.* He's a violent person. *huwwa fadd waazid kulliš ɛaniif.* **2.** *zaadd.* We had a violent argument. *ṣaarat beenaatna munaaqaša zaadda.* **3.** *faδiiɛ.* He died a violent death. *mootta čaanat faδiiɛa.*
violet - **1.** *wardat* (pl. *-aat,* coll. *warid) banafša.* We have violets in our garden. *ɛidna warid banafša b-zadiiqatna.* **2.** *banafsaji*.* Her dress is violet. *badlatha banafsajiyya.*
violin - *kamanja* pl. *-aat.*
virgin - **1.** *baakir, baakra* pl. *bawaakir, bnayya* pl. *-aat.* She's a virgin. *hiyya baakir.* **2.** *ɛaδraaʔ* pl. *ɛaδaara.* He told the story of the Virgin Mary. *ziča quṣṣat maryam il-ɛaδraaʔ.*
virtue - **1.** *zasana* pl. *-aat.* His virtues are undeniable. *zasanaata ma-tunkar.* **2.** *faδil.* He has risen to this position by virtue of his education. *wuṣal il-hal-manṣab ib-faδil θaqaafta.*
visa - *viiza* pl. *-aat, taʔšiira* pl. *-aat.*
vise - *mangana* pl. *-aat.*
visibility - *mada r-ruʔya.* The visibility is limited today. *mada r-ruʔya mazduuda hal-yoom.*
visible - *mbayyin, waaδiz.* The ship isn't visible yet. *l-baaxira baɛad li-hassa ma-mbayyna.*
vision - *naδar.* His vision is getting poor. *naδara da-yiδɛaf.* — He's a man of great vision. *huwwa fadd waazid ɛinda naδar baɛiid.*
visit - *ziyaara* pl. *-aat.* That was an unexpected visit. *δiič čaanat fadd ziyaara ma-mutawaqqaɛa.*
to pay a visit - *zaar (u ziyaara) n-.* He paid me a visit last week. *zaarni bil-isbuuɛ il-faat.*
to visit - *zaar (u ziyaara).* He wanted to visit you. *raad yzuurak.* — Have you visited our museum yet? *zirt il-matzaf maalna loo baɛad?*
visitor - *xiṭṭaar, zaaʔir* pl. *zuwwaar.* We're having visitors tonight. *ɛidna xiṭṭaar hal-leela.* — No visitors are allowed in this ward. *z-zuwwaar mamnuuɛ yduxluun ib-har-radha.*
vital - **1.** *zayawi*.* It's of vital importance to me. *haaδa fadd šii zayawi bin-nisba ʔila.* **2.** *muhimm.* He's well posted on the vital issues of the day. *huwwa miṭṭiliɛ ɛala kull il-ʔašyaaʔ il-muhimma l-iṭṣiir.*
vitality - *zayawiyya.* He has a lot of vitality. *ɛinda zayawiyya mumtaaza.*
vitamin - *fiitaamiin* pl. *-aat.*
vivid - **1.** *xaṣib.* He has a vivid imagination. *ɛinda xayaal xaṣib.* **2.** *barraaq, zaahi.* He uses vivid colors in his paintings. *yistaɛmil ʔalwaan barraaqa bir-risuum maalta.* **3.** *waaδiz.* He gave us a vivid description of his experience. *nṭaana waṣuf waaδiz ɛan tajaaruba.*
vocal cords - *zbaal ṣawtiyya.*
voice - *ṣoot* pl. *ʔaṣwaat, ziss* pl. *zsuus.* His voice carries well. *zissa yinsimiɛ zeen.*
to voice - *jaahar (i mujaahara).* Don't be afraid to voice your opinions. *la-txaaf itjaahir ib-muɛaaraδṭak.*
void - *malġi, baaṭil.* This check is void. *haṣ-ṣakk mafɛuula baaṭil.* — The contract is null and void. *l-ɛaqid mafɛuula baaṭil.*
to void - *baṭṭal (i tabṭiil).* I'll void the check. *raz-abaṭṭil ič-čakk.*
volcano - *burkaan* pl. *baraakiin.*
volley-ball - *kurat iṭ-ṭaaʔira.*
volt - *voolt* pl. *-aat.*
volume - **1.** *jizuʔ* pl. *ʔajzaaʔ, mujallad* pl. *-aat.* The book was published in two volumes. *l-iktaab innišar ib-juzʔeen.* **2.** *zajim* pl. *zjuum.* What's the volume of this tank? *šinu zajim hal-ɛumbaar?* **3.** *jumla.* The factory's producing clothing in volume. *l-maɛmal da-yintij ihduum bij-jumla.*
voluntarily - *b-ixtiyaar-, min keef-.* He did it voluntarily. *sawwaaha b-ixtiyaara.*
voluntary - *xtiyaari*.* Education is voluntary after 16. *d-diraasa xtiyaariyya baɛad sinn iṣ-ṣiṭṭaɛaš.*
volunteer - *miṭṭawwiɛ* pl. *-iin.* Can you get some volunteers to do it? *tigdar tilgi fadd čam miṭṭawwiɛ ysawwuuha?*
to volunteer - **1.** *ɛiraδ (u ɛariδ), tbarraɛ (a tabarruɛ) b-.* He volunteered his services. *ɛiraδ xadamaata.* **2.** *ṭṭawwaɛ (a taṭawwuɛ).* Who'll volunteer for this job? *minu yiṭṭawwaɛ il-haš-šaġla?*
to **vomit** - *zaaɛ (u zooɛ), zawwaɛ (i tazwiiɛ), δabb (i δabb) min raas~, gilab (u galub).* He got drunk and vomited. *sikar w-zawwaɛ.*
vote - **1.** *ṣawt* pl. *ʔaṣwaat.* They elected him by a majority of 2000 votes. *ntixboo b-akθariyyat ʔalfeen ṣawt.* **2.** *taṣwiit.* Minors have no vote. *l-iṣġaar ma-ɛidhum zaqq it-taṣwiit.* — The motion was put to a vote. *zaṭṭaw l-iqtiraaz bit-taṣwiit.*
to vote - **1.** *ntixab (i ntixaab), ṣawwat (i taṣwiit).* I couldn't vote in the last elections. *ma-gdart antixib bil-intixaabaat il-faatat.* — Who'd you vote for? *ʔilman intixabit?* **2.** *ṣawwat (i taṣwiit).* Shall we vote on it? *nṣawwit biiha?* **3.** *qarrar (i taqriir).* The board voted five hundred dinars for relief. *l-majlis qarrar taxṣiiṣ xamis miit diinaar lil-ʔiɛaanaat.*
to vote down - *rufaδ (u) bit-taṣwiit.* They voted down the proposal. *rufδaw l-iqtiraaz bit-taṣwiit.*
voter - *naaxib* pl. *-iin, muntaxib* pl. *-iin.* We have 200 voters in this section. *ɛidna miiteen naaxib ib-hal-muzalla.*
to **vouch** - *šihad (a šahaada).* I vouch for him. *ʔaani ašhad-la.*
to **vow** - **1.** *tɛahhad (a taɛahhud).* He vowed not to do it again. *tɛahhad ma-ysawwiiha baɛad.* **2.** *zilaf (i zalif).* He vowed to avenge his brother's death. *zilaf yaaxuδ θaar ʔaxuu l-maat.*
voyage - *safra* pl. *-aat.*
vulgar - **1.** *baδiiʔ.* He uses vulgar language. *yistaɛmil zači baδiiʔ.* **2.** *faδδ, xašin.* He's a vulgar person. *haaδa fadd waazid faδδ.*
vulnerable - *ɛurδa.* Our position is vulnerable to attack. *mawqifna ɛurδa lil-hijuum.*
vulture - *zdayya* pl. *-aat.* Vultures eat only carrion. *l-izdayyaat yaakluun fṭaayis bass.*
vulva - *farij* pl. *fruuj.*

W

to **wad** - *kaɛbar (u kaɛbara).* He wadded up the paper and threw it away. *kaɛbar il-waraq w-δabba.*
to **waddle** - *tdaɛbal (a tdiɛbil).* The duck waddled over to the water. *l-baṭṭa tdaɛbilat lil-mayy.*
to **wade** - **1.** *xaaδ (u xooδ) n-.* The soldiers waded ashore. *j-jinuud xaaδaw lis-saahil.* — We waded across the stream. *giṭaɛna š-šaṭṭ xooδ.* **2.** *δabb (i δabb) nafs~.* I waded into my work. *δabbeet nafsi ɛaš-šuġul.*
waders - *ʔazδiyat xooδ.* He bought a pair of waders to go fishing. *štira ʔazδiyat xooδ zatta yṣiid simač.*
to **wag** - *hazz (i hazz) n- b-.* The dog wagged its tail. *č-čalib hazz ib-δeela.*
wage - *ʔujra* pl. *ʔujuur.* They're not paying a decent wage. *ma-ydifɛuun ʔujra zeena.*
to wage - *θaar (i ʔiθaara).* They can't wage a long war. *ma-ygidruun yθiiruun zarb iṭwiila.*
wage rates - *mustawa ʔujuur.* Wage rates are rising. *mustawa l-ʔujuur da-yirtifiɛ.*
wagon - *ɛarabaana* pl. *-aat.* Hitch the horses to the new wagon. *šidd il-xeel bil-ɛarabaana j-jidiida.*
waist - *xiṣir,* pl. *xṣuur, xaaṣra* pl. *xawaaṣir.* I took the pants in at the waist. *gaṣṣafit il-panṭaruun min yamm il-xiṣir.*
wait - *ntiδaar* pl. *-aat.* The hour's wait was aggravating. *saaɛat l-intiδaar čaanat muzɛija.*

to lie in wait - *traṣṣad (a taraṣṣud).* They were lying in wait for us. *čaanaw mitraṣṣdiinna.*
to wait - **1.** *ntiδar (i ntiδaar), ṣṭubar (u ṣṭubaar, ṣabur).* Wait a moment. *ntiδir išwayya.* -- Have you been waiting long? *ṣaar-lak ihwaaya mintiδir?* -- I can hardly wait to see him. *ma-da-agdar aṣṭubur εala šoofta.* **2.** *tʔajjal (a taʔajjul).* Can that business wait till tomorrow? *hal-masʔala mumkin titʔajjal il-baačir?* **3.** *εaṭṭal (i taεṭiil) t-.* We'll wait dinner for him. *εuud inεaṭṭil il-εaša εala muuda.* **4.** *ṣubar (u ṣabur).* I can't wait till that day comes. *ma-da-agdar aṣbur ʔila ʔan yiji δaak il-yoom.*
to wait for - *ntiδar (i ntiδaar).* I'll wait for you until five o'clock. *ʔantiδrak il-saaεa xamsa.* -- Wait for his answer. *ntiδir jawaaba.*
to wait on - *šaaf (u) šuğuḷ.* Will you please wait on me now? *baḷḷa ma-tšuuf šuğḷi εaad?*
waiter - *booy* pl. *-aat.* He's a waiter in a restaurant. *huwwa booy maal maṭεam.*
waiting room - *ğurfat* (pl. *ğuraf*) *intiδaar.* Is there a waiting room at the airport? *ʔaku ğurfat intiδaar bil-maṭaar?*
to **wake** - *gaεεad (i tgiεεid).* Please wake me at seven o'clock. *baḷḷa gaεεidni saaεa sabεa.*
to wake up - **1.** *fazzaz (i) mnin-noom, gaεεad (i) mnin-noom.* The noise woke me up in the middle of the night. *ṣ-ṣoot fazzazni mnin-noom ib-nuṣṣ il-leel.* **2.** *giεad (u).* I didn't wake up until eight this morning. *ma-gεadt imnin-noom ʔilla saaεa θmaanya ṣ-ṣubuḥ.*
**It's high time you wake up to the fact that.... *laazim itfukk εeenak muu θixnat....*
walk - *mašya.* Did you have a nice walk? *ʔaxaδit-lak xooš mašya?* -- You can recognize him by his walk. *tigdar itεurfa min mašiita.*
to go for a walk - *tmašša (a tamašši).* Let's go for a walk. *xalli nitmašša.*
to walk - **1.** *miša (i miši).* Shall we walk or take the bus? *raḥ-nimši loo naaxuδ ḅaaṣ?* -- Can the baby walk yet? *j-jaahil yigdar yimši loo baεad?* **2.** *mašša (i).* Did you walk the dog? *maššeet ič-čalib?*
to walk down - *nizal (i).* We were walking down the stairs. *činna da-ninzil id-daraj.*
to walk out on - *ṭilaε (a), baṭṭal (i).* Our girl walked out on us. *l-xaddaama ṭilεat.*
to walk up - *ṣiεad (a ṣuεuud).* He can't walk up the stairs. *ma-yigdar yiṣεad id-daraj.*
wall - *ḥaayiṭ* pl. *ḥiiṭaan, ḥyaaṭiin.* Hang the picture on this wall. *εallig iṣ-ṣuura εala hal-ḥaayiṭ.* -- Only the walls are still standing. *bass l-iḥyaaṭiin baεadha baaqya.*
to wall up - *bina (i bnaaya).* They're walling up the doorways and windows in that building. *da-ybnuun iš-šabaabiič wil-ibwaab maal hal-ibnaaya.*
wallet - *jazdaan* pl. *-aat, jazaadiin.* I lost my wallet. *δayyaεit jazdaani.*
walnut - **1.** *jooza* pl. *-aat* coll. *jooz.* Let's buy some walnuts. *xal-ništiri jooz.* **2.** *xišab jooz.* This table is made of walnut. *hal-meez imsawwa min xišab jooz.*
walnut tree - *jooza, šajrat* (pl. *-aat, ʔašjaar* coll. *šajar*) *jooz.* We have a walnut tree in our garden. *εidna jooza b-ḥadiiqatna.*
want - *maṭlab* pl. *maṭaaliib.* My wants are very modest. *maṭaaliibi basiiṭa.*
**I'll take it for want of something better. *raḥ-aqbalha li-ʔan ma-aku šii ʔaḥsan.*
to want - *raad (i ʔiraada) n-.* He knows what he wants. *yuεruf š-yriid.* -- I want two sandwiches. *ʔariid sandwiičteen.* -- How much do you want for your furniture? *šgadd itriid anṭiik ib-hal-ʔaθaaθ?* -- I want to go swimming. *ʔariid asbaḥ.*
want ad - *ʔiεlaan* pl. *-aat.*
wanted - *maṭluub.* He is wanted by the police. *huwwa maṭluub imniš-šurṭa.*
war - *ḥarb* pl. *ḥuruub.* Where were you during the last war? *ween činit ʔaθnaaʔ il-ḥarb il-ʔaxiira?*
holy war - *jihaad.*
ward - *qaawuuš* pl. *qwaawiiš, radha* pl. *-aat.* They had to put him in the ward because all the rooms were taken. *δṭarraw yḥuṭṭuu bil-qaawuuš li-ʔan kull il-ğuraf mašğuuḷa.*
warden - *mudiir* (pl. *mudaraaʔ*) *sijin.*
wardrobe - **1.** *qanṭoor* pl. *-aat.* What are your clothes doing in my wardrobe? *εajab ḥaaṭiṭ ihduumak bil-qanṭoor maali?* **2.** *ṭaxum ihduum.* She bought herself a complete wardrobe. *štirat ṭaxum kaamil ihduum.*
warehouse - *maxzan* pl. *maxaazin.*
warm - **1.** *daafi.* It's warm today. *j-jaww daafi l-yoom.* **2.** *dafyaan.* Are you warm enough? *ʔinta dafyaan zeen?*
to warm - **1.** *daffa (i).* Come in and warm yourself by the fire. *taεaal jawwa w-daffi nafsak yamm in-naar.* **2.** *ḥima (i ḥami) n-.* Please warm up the soup for me. *baḷḷa ḥmii-li š-šoorba.*
to warm up - *maal (i).* I can't warm up to him. *ma-agdar amiil ʔila.*
warmth - *ḥamaawa.* The warmth of the fire reached me over here. *jatni ḥamaawat in-naar l-ihnaa.*
to **warn** - **1.** *ḥaδδar (i taḥδiir).* They warned me about him. *ḥaδδrooni minna.* **2.** *niδar, ʔanδar (i ʔinδaar).* The government warned that demonstrators would be jailed. *l-ḥukuuma ʔanδirat ib-ḥabs illi ysawwuun muδaaharaat.*
warning - *taḥδiir* pl. *-aat.* The government broadcast a warning about the flood. *l-ḥukuuma ʔaδaaεat taḥδiir εan il-fayaδaan.*
to **warp** - **1.** *εakkaf (u).* This wood will warp. *han-nooε imnil-xišab yεakkuf.* **2.** *tεawwaj (a).* The records will be warped in the heat. *l-iṣṭiwaanaat titεawwaj bil-ḥaraara.*
wash - *hduum mağsuula.* The maid hung the wash on the line. *l-xaddaama šarrat l-ihduum il-mağsuula εal-ḥabil.*
to wash - **1.** *ğisal (i ğasil) n-.* Wash these shirts, please. *baḷḷa, ğisli hal-ihduum.* -- This floor hasn't been washed yet. *l-gaaε baεadha ma-nğislat.* **2.** *ğassal (i), ğisal (i).* Did you wash your face? *ğassalit wujjak?*
to wash away - *jiraf (u jaruf) n-.* Last year the flood washed away the bridge. *s-sant il-faatat il-fayaδaan jiraf ij-jisir.*
to wash up - *ğassal (i), ğisal (i).* I'd like to wash up before supper. *ʔariid ağassil gabuḷ il-ʔakil.*
**He's washed up. *ntiha ʔamra.*
**Our plans for a trip are all washed up. *mašruuεna maal is-safra fišal.*
waste - **1.** *tabdiid.* That's plain waste. *haaδa tabdiid waaδiḥ.* **2.** *maδyaεa.* It's a waste of time and energy. *haay maδyaεa lil-wakit wij-jahid.*
**Haste makes waste. *l-εajala mniš-šayṭaan.*
to go to waste - **1.** *baar (u boor).* A good cook doesn't let anything go to waste. *ṭ-ṭabbaaxa z-zeena ma-txalli šii ybuur.* **2.** *raaḥ (u) εabaθ, δaaε (i δiyaaε).* His talents are going to waste. *qaabliyyaata raayḥa εabaθ.*
to lay waste - *dumar (u damur) n-.* The storm has laid waste the entire area. *l-εaaṣifa dumrat il-manṭiqa kullha.*
to waste - *δayyaε (i taδyiiε).* He wastes a lot of time talking. *yδayyiε ihwaaya wakit bil-ḥači.*
wastebasket - *sallat* (pl. *slaal*) *muhmalaat.*
watch - *saaεa* pl. *-aat.* By my watch it's five. *bil-xamsa ḥasab saaεati.*
to watch - **1.** *tfarraj (i) εala.* I've been watching this program for about an hour. *ṣaar-li ḥawaali saaεa da-atfarraj εala hal-manhaj.* **2.** *baawaε (i mubaawaεa), šaaf (u).* Watch how I do it. *baawiε išloon da-asawwiiha.* **3.** *daar (i) baal˜.* Who's going to watch the children? *minu raḥ-ydiir baala εaj-jihaal?* **4.** *raaqab (u muraaqaba).* That fellow needs close watching. *haaδa waaḥid laazim yraaqba zeen.* **5.** *fakk (u) εeen˜, daar (i) baal˜.* Watch yourself with him. *fukk εeenak zeen wiyyaa.*
to watch out - *daar (i) baal˜.* Watch out when you cross the street. *diir baalak min tuεbur iš-šaariε.*
to watch out for - *traqqab (a).* I'll be watching out for you to arrive at the station. *raḥ-atraqqab wuṣuulak lil-maḥaṭṭa.*
watchmaker - *saaεači* pl. *-iyya.*
watchman - *ḥaaris* pl. *ḥurraas.*
water - *ṃaay, ṃayy.* Please give me a glass of water. *baḷḷa nṭiini glaaṣ ṃaay.*
to water - **1.** *siga (i sagi) n-.* I water the garden every day. *ʔaani ʔasgi l-ḥadiiqa yoomiyya.* -- Have the horses been watered yet? *sgeet il-xeel loo baεad?* **2.** *dammaε (i tadmiiε).* My eyes are watering. *εyuuni da-tdammiε.* **3.** *saal (i seel).* The cake makes my mouth water. *l-keeka xallat luεaabi ysiil.*
waterfall - *šallaal* pl. *-aat.*
watermelon - *raggiyya* pl. *-aat* coll. *raggi.*
waterproof - **1.** *δidd il-muṭar.* Is this coat waterproof? *hal-miεṭaf δidd il-muṭar?* **2.** *δidd il-ṃayy.* Is this watch waterproof? *has-saaεa δidd il-ṃayy?*
wave - **1.** *mooja* pl. *ʔamwaaj* coll. *mooj.* The waves are very high today. *l-mooj kulliš εaali l-yoom.*

2. *mawja* pl. *-aat.* A wave of enthusiasm swept the country. *fadd mawja mnil-ʒamaas ištaaʒat il-balad.*
to wave - 1. *rafraf (i rafrafa) t-.* The flags were waving in the breeze. *l-iεlaam čaanat da-trafrif bil-hawa.* 2. *ʔaššar (i taʔšiir).* I waved to him with my hand. *ʔaššarit-la b-iidi.*
wax - *šamiε.*
way - 1. *ṭariiq* pl. *ṭuruq.* Is this the way to Baghdad? *haaδa ṭ-ṭariiq il-baġdaad?* — Are you going my way? *raayiʒ εala ṭariiqi?* 2. *ṭariiqa* pl. *ṭuruq.* That's just his way of dealing with employees. *haaδi εaadatan ṭariiqat muεaamalta lil-muwaδδafiin.* — There are different ways of doing things. *ʔaku εiddat ṭuruq.* 3. *šikil.* You shouldn't treat people this way. *ma-laazim itεaamil in-naas ib-haš-šikil.* — That's the way he wants it. *yriidha haš-šikil.* 4. *darub.* Do you know your way around here? *tuεruf darbak ib-hal-manṭiqa?* or ***tindall hal-manṭiqa?* 5. *maṣaariif.* He paid my way. *huwwa difaε l-maṣaariif maalti.* — I paid my own way at college. *dfaεit maṣaariif daraasti min jeebi l-xaaṣṣ.* 6. *ʔamir.* He'll make his way wherever he is. *yigdar ydabbur ʔamra ween-ma tδibba.*
**Everything is going along (in) the same old way. *kullši baεda miθil-ma čaan.*
**Everything turned out the way they wanted. *kullši ṣaar miθil-ma raadaw.*
**Have it your own way! *miθil-ma triid.* or *keefak.*
**I'm afraid he's in a bad way. *ʔaxaaf ʒaalta muu zeen.*
**I don't see my way clear to do it now. *ma-ašuuf imnil-munaasaba ʔasawwiiha hassa.*
**Christmas is still a long way off. *baεad ihwaaya l-krismas.*
a long way - *biεiid.* The school is a long way from our house. *l-madrasa biεiida εan beetna.*
by the way - *bil-munaasaba.* By the way, are you coming with us tonight? *bil-munaasaba ʔinta jaay wiyyaana hal-leela?*
by way of - 1. *εala ṭariiq.* We went by way of Damascus. *riʒna εala ṭariiq iš-šaam.* 2. *εala sabiil.* He said it by way of a joke. *gaalha εala sabiil in-nukta.*
in a way - *min jiha, nooεan-ma.* In a way he's right. *min jiha huwwa ṣaʒiiʒ.*
in no way - *ʔabadan.* This is in no way better than what you had before. *haay ʔabadan muu ʔaʒsan min illi čaanat εindak gabuḷ.*
in the way of - *min.* What have you got in the way of radios? *šaku εidkum imnir-raadyowaat?*
in what way - *šloon.* In what way is that better? *šloon haay aʒsan?*
out of the way - *muu εar-rijil.* This place is somewhat out of the way. *hal-muʒall išwayya muu εar-rijil.*
right of way - *ṭariiq.* You shouldn't have gone through, I had the right of way. *ma-čaan laazim itfuut, ṭ-ṭariiq čaan ʔili.*
to get under way - *tqaddam (a), btida (i).* The project is slowly getting under way. *l-mašruuε da-yitqaddam išwayya šwayya.*
to give way - *ngiṭaε (i).* The rope's giving way. *l-ʒabil da-yingiṭiε.*
to go out of one's way - 1. *tkallaf (a).* I don't want you to go out of your way for my sake. *ma-ariidak titkallaf εala muudi.* 2. *biδal (i baδil) juhuud~.* We went out of our way to make him comfortable. *bδalna juhuudna ʒatta nxallii yirtaaʒ.*
way out - *maxraj* pl. *maxaarij.* I don't see any way out of this mess. *ma-da-ašuuf ʔay maxraj min hal-wurṭa.*
we - *ʔiʒna.* We're not the ones responsible. *ʔiʒna muu l-masʔuuliin.*
**We have a house in Najef. *εidna beet bin-najaf.*
**We haven't seen him. *ma-šifnaa.*
weak - 1. *xafiif.* Would you like your tea weak or strong? *triid čaayak xafiif loo ṭoox?* 2. *δaεiif.* He's still weak from his illness. *baεda δaεiif imnil-maraδ.* — The bridge is weak. *j-jisir δaεiif.*
to **weaken - 1.** *δaεεaf (u).* The flood weakened the bridge. *l-fayaδaan δaεεaf ij-jisir.* 2. *ʔaδεaf (u ʔiδεaaf).* Aspirin weakens you. *l-ʔaspariin yδiεfak.*
weakness - *nuqṭat (pl. nuqaaṭ) δuεuf.* That's his biggest weakness. *haaδi ʔahamm nuqṭat δuεuf εinda.*
wealth - *θarwa.* They wasted the wealth of the nation. *δayyεaw θarwat il-balad.*
wealthy - *zangiin* pl. *znaagiin, ġani* pl. *ʔaġniyaaʔ.* She married a wealthy merchant. *tzawwjat fadd taajir zangiin.*
weapon - *slaaʒ* pl. *ʔasliʒa.* All weapons have to be turned over to the police. *kull il-ʔasliʒa laazim titsallam liš-šurṭa.*
wear - 1. *hduum.* I'm sorry, we carry only men's wear. *mitʔassif, εidna hduum iryaajiil bass.* 2. *libis.* There's still a lot of wear left in this suit. *hal-qaaṭ baεad bii libis ihwaaya.*
**The cuffs are showing signs of wear. *r-ridaanaat mbayyna saayfa.*
to wear - 1. *libas (a libis) n-.* He never wears a hat. *ʔabad ma-yilbas šafqa.* — What did she wear? *š-libsat?* 2. *ṭawwal (i).* This coat didn't wear well. *hal-miεṭaf ma-ṭawwal ihwaaya.*
**She wears her hair short. *hiyya tguṣṣ šaεarha gṣayyir.*
to wear down - *gaam (u).* These heels are all worn down. *hal-iččuuba maal iqnaadir kullha gaamat.*
**We finally wore him down. *taaliiha nazzalnaa εan baġilta.*
to wear off - 1. *burad (a).* Wait till the excitement wears off. *ntiδir ʔila ʔan tibrad il-hoosa.* 2. *raaʒ (u).* The paint has worn off my car in several spots. *ṣ-ṣubuġ maal sayyaarti raaʒ min čam makaan.*
to wear out - 1. *stahlak (a stihlaak).* The tires are all worn out. *t-taayaraat kullha stahilkat.* — Our furniture is worn out. *ʔaθaaθna stahlak.* 2. *šaggag (i) t-.* He wore out his shoes quickly. *šaggag qundarta bil-εajil.* 3. *hilak (i halaak).* Just don't wear yourself out! *la-tihlik nafsak.*
weather - *jaww, ṭaqis, manaax.* How is the weather today? *šloon ij-jaww il-yoom?*
**I'm a little under the weather today. *ma-da-aʒiss hal-gadd zeen hal-yoom.*
to weather - *dabbar (i tadbiir) ʔamr~.* How did you weather the flood? *šloon dabbarit ʔamrak bil-fayaδaan.*
to **weave -** *ʒaak (u ʒook, ʒyaaka) n-.* The children wove this rug at school. *l-ʔaṭfaal ʒaakaw hal-ibṣaaṭ bil-madrasa.*
weaver - *ʒaayič, ʒaayik* pl. *ʒiyyaač.* He's a weaver. *huwwa ʒaayič.*
wedding - *εiris* pl. *ʔaεraas.* I was at the wedding but not at the reception. *činit bil-εiris bass muu bil-ʒafla.*
Wednesday - *l-ʔarbaεaa.*
weeds - *ʒašiiš.* The whole garden is full of weeds. *l-ʒadiiqa matruusa ʒašiiš.*
to weed - *šilaε (a šaliε) ʒašiiš.* I've got to weed the garden. *laazim ʔašlaε il-ʒašiiš imnil-ʒadiiqa.*
week - *sbuuε* pl. *ʔasaabiiε.* I'll be back in three weeks. *raʒ-arjaε ib-xilaal itlaθ asaabiiε.*
by the week - *sbuuεiyya.* They pay by the week. *ydifεuun isbuuεiyya.*
weekend - *εuṭlat isbuuε* pl. *εuṭal ʔasaabiiε.* We decided to spend the weekend at the lake. *qarrarna nigδi εuṭlat il-isbuuε bil-buʒayra.*
weekly - 1. *sbuuεi*.* He publishes a weekly newspaper. *yṭalliε jariida sbuuεiyya.* 2. *marra bil-isbuuε, sbuuεiyyan.* This magazine appears weekly. *hal-majalla tiṭlaε marra bil-isbuuε.*
to **weep -** *biča (i).* She wept bitter tears. *bičat ib-ʒurga.*
to **weigh -** *wuzan (i wazin) n-.* Please weigh this package for me. *baḷḷa ʔoozin-li har-ruzma.* — He always weighs his words carefully. *daaʔiman yoozin iʒčaayaata zeen.*
**This piece of meat weighs four pounds. *hal-wuṣlat il-laʒam wazinha ʔarbaε keeluwwaat.*
**The responsibility weighs heavily on me. *hal-masʔuuliyya kulliš zaʒma.*
weight - 1. *εyaar* pl. *-aat.* The weights are under the scale. *l-iεyaaraat jawwa l-miizaan.* 2. *wazin, θugul.* Did you put down the weight of the package? *sajjalit wazn ir-ruzma?* — Don't attach too much weight to what he says. *la-tinṭi hwaaya wazin il-ʒačya.* 3. *ʒsaab, wazin.* His opinion carries great weight. *raʔya yinʒisib-la ʒsaab.* or *raʔya ʔila wazin.*
weird - *ġariib.* That's a weird story. *haay iʒčaaya ġariiba.*
welcome - 1. *stiqbaal* pl. *-aat.* They gave us a warm welcome. *staqbiloona stiqbaal ʒaarr.* or ***raʒʒibaw biina zeen.* 2. *εal-maraam.* This is a welcome change in government policy. *hat-taġyiir ib-siyaasat il-ʒukuuma čaan εal-maraam.*
**You're always welcome here. *šwakit ma-tiji ʔahlan wa-sahlan.* or *haaδa miθil beetkum.*
**You're welcome. *ʔahlan wa-sahlan.* or *mamnuun.*
to welcome - *staqbal (i), raʒʒab (i) b-.* They

welcomed us warmly. *staqbiloona bit-tirzaab.* or *razzibaw biina.*
to **weld** - *lizam (i lazim).* He's welding the bumper on my car. *da-yilzim id-daεεaamiyya maal sayyaarti.*
welfare - *raxaa?.* The welfare of the country depends on this project. *raxaa? il-bilaad yiεtimid εala haaδa l-mašruuε.*
well - 1. *biir* pl. *byaar.* They're digging a well back of the house. *da-yzaffruun biir wara l-beet.* 2. *zeen.* Do you know him well? *tεurfa zeen?* — I'm not feeling well today. *?aani ma-da-aziss hal-gadd zeen il-yoom.* — The new business is doing very well. *š-šuġuḷ zeen da-yimši.* — Please let me do it. Very well. *baḷḷa xalliini asawwiiha. zeen.* 3. *hwaaya.* There were well over 1000 people. *čaanaw ihwaaya ?azyad min ?alif waazid.* 4. *haa.* Well, where did you come from? *haa, mneen jeet?*
**Leave well enough alone. *?azsan-lak itxalliiha miθil-ma hiyya.*
as well as - *miθil-ma, miθil.* He talks Arabic as well as I do. *yizči εarabi miθil-ma ?azči ?aani.* or *yizči εarabi miθli.*
**He knows Arabic as well as several other languages. *yuεruf εarabi w-yuεruf luġaat ?uxra.*
**He couldn't very well refuse to come. *ma-čaan aku majaal yirfuδ id-daεwa.*
**He could very well change his mind. *?aku ztimaal kabiir ybaddil fikra.*
to get well - *ṭaab (i), ṣaar (i) zeen.* First I must get well again. *xalli ?aṭiib ?awwal.* — I hope you get well soon! *nšaalla tṣiir zeen εan qariib.*
well-behaved - *εaaqil, m?addab.* She's a well-behaved child. *haay fadd ṭifla kullis εaaqla.*
well-done - *maṭbuux zeen, mištiwi zeen.* The meat is well-done. *l-lazam maṭbuux zeen.*
well-to-do - *zangiin.* His family is well-to-do. *εaa?ilta zangiina.*
west - 1. *ġarb.* The wind is from the west. *l-hawa mnil-ġarb.* — The sign points west. *s-sahim y?aššir εal-ġarb.* 2. *ġarbi*.* There's a west wind today. *?aku hawa ġarbi l-yoom.*
western - *ġarbi*.* The Syrian Desert extends into the western part of Iraq. *baadiyat iš-šaam timtadd lil-qism il-ġarbi mnil-εiraaq.*
westward - *lil-ġarb.* They headed westward. *ttijhaw lil-ġarb.*
wet - 1. *mballal, mitnaggiε, mnaggaε.* My socks are wet. *jwaariibi mballila.* — I'm wet through and through. *?aani mitnaggiε min foog li-jawwa.* 2. *raṭib.* We had a wet summer. *marr εaleena ṣeef raṭib.* 3. *jdiid.* The paint is still wet. *ṣ-ṣubuġ baεda jdiid.* or ***ṣ-ṣubuġ baεda ma-yaabis.*
to get wet - *tnaggaε (a tniggiε), tballal (a).* I got wet yesterday in the rain. *tnaggaεit imnil-muṭar il-baarza.*
to wet - *baal (u bool).* The baby wet his pants. *ṭ-ṭifil baal b-ilbaasa.*
whale - *zuuta* pl. *-aat, zuwat* coll. *zuut.*
what - 1. *š-.* What would you like to eat? *š-yεijbak taakul?* 2. *šinu.* What things are missing? *šinu l-?ašyaa? in-naagṣa?* — What's the color of the gloves? *šinu loon ič-čufuuf?* 3. *šloon, šgadd.* What beautiful flowers you have in your garden! *šloon zilu hal-warid il-εindak bil-zadiiqa.* — What nonsense! *šloon laġwa* 4. *beeš.* What time is it? *s-saaεa beeš?* 5. *yaa.* Do you know what train we're supposed to take? *tuεruf yaa qiṭaar laazim naaxuδ?* 6. *lli.* That's just what I wanted to avoid. *haaδa š-šii lli ridt atzaašaa.*
**He certainly knows what's what. *mu?akkad huwwa yuεruf š-aku š-ma-aku.*
**He didn't get there in time, but what of it? *ma-wuṣal l-ihnaak εal-wakit, bass š-yhimm?*
**What about me? *w-?aani?*
what...for - *luweeš, leeš, ?ilweeš.* What did you do that for? *luweeš sawweetha haay?*
what's more - 1. *bil-?iδaafa.* (And) what's more, he is very efficient. *w-bil-?iδaafa l-haaδa, huwwa qadiir.* 2. *hamm.* I'm leaving, and what's more, I'm taking the furniture. *raz-aruuz w-aaxuδ il-?aθaaθ hamm.*
whatever - 1. *š-ma.* Whatever he does is all right with me. *š-ma ysawwi ma-yxaalif.* — Do whatever you want. *sawwi š-ma triid.* — She's lost whatever respect she had for him. *δayyεat iš-ma čaan εidha mnil-iztiraam ?ila.* 2. *š-.* Whatever made you do that? *š-xallaak itsawwi haay?* 3. *?abadan.* I have no money whatever. *ma-εindi fluus ?abadan.*
whatsoever - *?abadan.* I have no money whatsoever. *ma-εindi fluus ?abadan.*
wheat - *zunṭa.* They raise a lot of wheat in Iraq. *yzirεuun ihwaaya zunṭa bil-εiraaq.*
wheel - *čarix* pl. *čruux.* This wheel on that wagon is broken. *č-čarix maal hal-εarabaana maksuur.*
to wheel - *difaε (a dafiε) n-.* Wheel the baby carriage into the garage. *?idfaε εarabaant ij-jaahil lil-garaaj.*
to wheel around - *ftarr (a).* He wheeled around suddenly and fired. *εala ġafla ftarr w-šawwat.*
when - 1. *šwakit, ?eemta.* When can I see you again? *šwakit ašuufak marra lux?* 2. *min, lamma, lamman.* When he calls up tell him I'm not here. *min yxaabur gul-la ?aani ma-hnaa.* — When the work is done you can go. *tigdar itruuz min yixlaṣ iš-šuġuḷ.* — I wasn't home when he called. *ma-činit bil-beet lamma xaabar.*
**There are times when I enjoy being alone. *tiji awqaat yiεjibni ?akuun il-wazdi.*
whenever - 1. *swakit-ma.* Come to see us whenever you have time. *zuurna šwakit-ma yṣiir εindak wakit.* 2. *kull-ma.* Whenever we have a picnic it rains. *kull-ma nsawwi safra, tguum tumṭur.*
**Whenever did you find time to write? *šloon dabbarit wakit zatta tiktib?*
where - 1. *ween.* Where is the nearest hotel? *ween aqrab ?uteel?* — Where does the difference lie? *ween l-ixtilaaf?* 2. *illi.* We found him just where we expected him to be. *lgeenaa bil-makaan illi twaqqaεna nilgii bii.* — They will send them where they're needed most. *εuud ydizzuuhum il-makaan illi yiztaajuuhum bii hwaaya.*
where...from - *mneen.* Where does your friend come from? *ṣadiiqak mneen?*
wherever - *ween-ma.* Wherever you are, don't forget to write me. *la-tinsa tiktib-li ween-ma tkuun.* — Wherever you go in this country you'll find good roads. *ween-ma truuz ib-hal-balad, kull iṭ-ṭuruq zeena.*
whether - *?iδa, loo.* I'd like to know whether he's coming. *?ard aεruf ?iδa raz-yiji loo laa.*
whey - *rooba.*
which - 1. *yaa, ?ay.* Which bag did you pick out? *yaa janṭa ?axaδti?* 2. *yaahu.* Which is yours? *yaahu maalak?* 3. *lli.* Please return the book which you borrowed. *baḷḷa rajjiε l-iktaab illi ṭlabta.*
whichever - *?ay.* Take whichever one you want. *?uxuδ ?ay waazid itriida.*
while - 1. *šwayya, fadd mudda, fadd fatra.* You'll have to wait a while. *laazim tintiδir išwayya.* 2. *min, lamma, b-?aθnaa?-ma.* He came while we were out. *?ija min činna ṭaalεiin.* 3. *bayna-ma.* Some people live in luxury, while others are dying of starvation. *baεaδ in-naas yεiišuun ib-baδax bayna-ma ġeerhum mayytiin imnij-juuε.* 4. *ma-daam.* I want to go in while it's still light. *?ariid aruuz ma-daam baεadha δaawya.*
to while away - *giδa (i giδyaan).* I while away my time reading. *da-agδi wakti ?aqra.*
whip - *qamči* pl. *qamaači, qirbaač* pl. *qaraabiič.* The driver snapped the whip. *l-εarabanči ṭagg il-qamči maala.*
to whip - *δirab (u) bil-qamči.* He whipped the horse mercilessly. *δirab il-xeel maalta bil-qamči bala razam.*
whisky - *wiiski.*
whisper - *hamis.* I heard a whisper in the next room. *smaεit hamis bil-ġurfa l-yammna.*
in a whisper - *mšaawra.* They spoke in a whisper so that no one would hear them. *zičaw imšaawra zatta lazzad yismaεhum.*
to whisper - *himas (i), šaawar (i mušaawara).* She whispered the word in my ear. *himsat ič-čilma b-?iδni* or *šaawratni bič-čilma.*
whistle - 1. *ṣaafira* pl. *-aat.* The policeman lost his whistle. *š-šurṭi δayyaε iṣ-ṣaafira maalta.* 2. *maaṣuula* pl. *-aat.* The boy broke his whistle. *l-walad kisar il-maaṣuula maalta.* 3. *ṣoofra* pl. *-aat.* The signal was one long and two short whistles. *l-?išaara čaanat ṣoofra ṭwiila w-ṣoofirteen igṣaar.*
to whistle - *ṣoofar (i ṣoofra).* He whistled as he walked along. *čaan da-yimši w-yṣoofir.* — He whistled to the cab. *ṣoofar-la lit-taksi.*
white - 1. *?abyaδ.* She wore a white dress at the party. *libsat nafnuuf abyaδ bil-zafla.* 2. *bayaaδ.* I put the whites of four eggs in the cake. *zaṭṭeet bayaaδ arbaε beeδaat bil-keeka.*
whitewash - *byaaδ.* The whitewash is peeling off the walls. *l-ibyaaδ maal il-zaayiṭ da-yoogaε.*

to whitewash - *bayyaδ (i tabyiiδ) t-.* How long will it take you to whitewash the garage? *šgadd mudda yinraad-lak ʒatta tbayyiδ il-garaaj?*
who - 1. *minu.* Who used this book last? *minu ʔaaxir waaʒid istaƐmal hal-iktaab?* **2.** *lli.* Did you notice the man who just passed by? *laaʒaδţ ir-rijjaal il-marr minnaa hassa?* **3.** *man.* Who did you give it to? *ʔil-man inţeetha?*
who...for - *Ɛala man.* Who are you looking for? *Ɛala man da-tdawwur?*
whoever - *minu-ma.* Whoever wants it may have it. *minu-ma yriidha xal-yaaxuδha.*
whole - *kaamil, kull.* I intend to stay a whole week. *b-niiti ʔabqa sbuuƐ kaamil.* -- He ate the whole thing himself. *ʔakal kullši waʒda.*
on the whole - *b-şuura Ɛaamma, šii Ɛala šii.* On the whole, I agree with you. *b-şuura Ɛaamma ʔaani attifiq wiyyaak.*
wholesale - *bij-jumla.* They sell only wholesale. *ma-ybiiƐuun ğeer bij-jumla.* -- The president gave out wholesale pardons. *raʔiis ij-jamhuuriyya ţallaƐ Ɛafu bij-jumla.*
wholesale price - *siƐir ij-jumla.* What's the wholesale price? *šinu siƐr ij-jumla?*
whooping cough - *suƐaal diiki.* My kids all have whooping cough. *wuldi kullhum Ɛidhum suƐaal diiki.*
whore - *gaʒba* pl. *-aat, gʒaab.*
whose - 1. *maal man.* Whose watch is this? *maal man has-saaƐa?* **2.** *lli.* There's the lady whose bag you found yesterday. *haaδi l-imrayya lli lgeet janţatha l-baarʒa.*
why - *luweeš, leeš, ʔilweeš.* Why is the train so crowded this morning? *luweeš il-qiţaar hal-gadd xabşa ļ-yoom?*
**Why, what do you mean? *haa! š-tuqşud?*
**Why there he is! *haa, hiyyaata.*
that's why - *li-haaδa, l-has-sabab.* That's why I didn't call you. *li-haaδa ma-xaabartak.*
wick - *ftiila* pl. *ftaayil.*
wide - 1. *Ɛariiδ.* The garage doorway isn't wide enough. *l-baab maal il-garaaj muu hal-gadd Ɛariiδa.* — The window is very wide. *š-šibbaač Ɛariiδ ihwaaya.* **2.** *čbiir, waasiƐ.* We have a wide selection of shoes. *Ɛidna majmuuƐa čbiira mnil-ʔaʒδiya.* **3.** *waasiƐ.* Our firm has wide commercial connections. *šarikatna Ɛidha Ɛalaaqaat tijaariyya waasƐa.*
**The window is two feet wide. *š-šibbaač Ɛurδa fuuteen.*
wide-awake - *şaaʒi.* I'm wide awake. *ʔaani şaaʒi tamaaman.*
**He's a wide-awake fellow. *Ɛeena mafkuuka zeen.*
wide-eyed - **He looked at me wide-eyed. *fakk iƐyuuna mitƐajjib.*
to **widen** - *Ɛarraδ (i taƐriiδ) t-.* They're going to widen our street. *raʒ-yƐarrδuun šaariƐna.*
wide open - *Ɛala gfaaha.* He left the door wide open. *xalla l-baab mafkuuka Ɛala gfaaha.*
widespread - 1. *mintišir.* How widespread is this opinion? *šgadd mintašra hal-fikra?* **2.** *šaayiƐ.* This custom is widespread here. *hal-Ɛaada šaayƐa hnaa.* **3.** *waasiƐ, šaamil.* The hailstorm caused widespread damage. *l-ʒaaluub sabbab δarar waasiƐ.*
widow - *ʔarmaļa* pl. *ʔaraamiļ.*
widower - **That man is a widower. *har-rijjaal marta mayyta.*
width - *Ɛuruδ.* What's the width of this window? *šgadd Ɛuruδ haš-šibbaač?* -- The room is nine feet in width. *l-ğurfa Ɛuruδha tisiƐ fuutaat.* — We need double-width material for the drapes. *niʒtaaj iqmaaš ʔabu Ɛurδeen lil-pardaat.*
wife - *zawja* pl. *-aat.* She's the wife of the prime minister. *haay zawjat raʔiis il-wuzaraaʔ.*
wild - 1. *waʒši*.* There are no wild animals in this area. *ma-aku ʒaywaanaat waʒšiyya b-hal-manţiqa.* **2.** *wakiiʒ, wakiʒ.* The children are too wild. *l-wulid kulliš wukkaʒ.* **3.** *mitʒammis.* I'm not wild about it. *ʔaani muu kulliš mitʒammis Ɛaleeha.*
**He lead a wild life when he was young. *čaan ţaayiš min čaan işğayyir.*
**My boy is wild about ice cream. *ʔibni ymuut Ɛad-doondirma.*
to go wild - 1. *tʒammas.* The crowd went wild when they heard the news. *n-naas itʒammsaw min simƐaw il-axbaar.* **2.** *haaj (i).* The crowd went wild and attacked the embassy. *n-naas haajaw w-hijmaw is-safaara.*
to run wild - *nhadd (a).* The dog has run wild since his master died. *č-čalib inhadd min maat şaaʒba.*
wilderness - *čool* pl. *čwaal.* They wandered in the wilderness. *taahaw bič-čuwaal.*
wilds - **Their house is way out in the wilds. *beethum ib-ʔaaxir id-dinya.*
will - 1. *ʔiraada.* He has a strong will. *Ɛinda ʔiraada qawiyya.* **2.** *waşiyya* pl. *waşaaya.* He died without making a will. *maat bala-ma yiktib waşiyya.*
at will - *b-keef-.* They come and go at will. *yruuʒuun w-yijuun ib-keefhum.*
to will - *waşşa (i tawşiya).* He willed all his property to the hospital. *waşşa kull ʔamlaaka lil-mustašfa.*
will - 1. *Ɛuud.* I'll meet you at three o'clock. *Ɛuud ašuufak saaƐa tlaaθa.* -- We'll see what can be done. *Ɛuud inšuuf iš-nigdar insawwi.* **2.** *raʒ-.* They'll be surprised to see you here. *raʒ-yitƐajjbuun min yšuufuuk ihnaa.* — I thought that would happen. *tşawwarit hiiči šii raʒ-yşiir.* -- I won't be able to do that. *ma-raʒ-agdar asawwi haay.* — He won't get anywhere that way. *ma-raʒ-yooşal in-natiija b-haţ-ţariiqa.*
**Won't you come in for a minute? *baļļa ma-txušš išwayya?*
**Will you please reserve a room for me. *baļļa-ma tiʒjiz-li ğurfa?*
**This hall will hold a thousand people. *hal-qaaƐa tilzam ʔalif waaʒid.*
**What would you like to drink? *š-yƐijbak tišrab?*
**We would rather live outside of town. *ʔiʒna nfaδδil niskun xaarij l-wlaaya.*
**Would you rather go to the theater? *tfaδδil itruuʒ lis-siinama?*
**He would never take the job. *ʔabad ma-yiqbal haš-šuğuļ.*
**He'll go for days without smoking. *ʔaʒyaanan yibqa Ɛiddat ʔayyaam bala ma-ydaxxin.*
willing - **I'm willing to try anything. *ma-Ɛindi maaniƐ š-ma-ykuun.* or *ʔaqbal asawwi kullši.*
will power - *quwwat ʔiraada.* He has amazing will power. *Ɛinda quwwat ʔiraada Ɛajiiba.*
to **wilt** - *δibal (a δabil).* The flowers have wilted. *l-warid δibal.*
to **win - 1.** *ğilab (u ğuļub).* I'm going to win this time. *raʒ-ağļub hal-marra.* — Which team do you think will win? *yaa firqa titşawwar raʒ-tuğļub?* **2.** *ribaʒ (a rabiʒ).* I won five hundred fils. *rbaʒit xamis miit filis.*
to win over - *stimaal (i).* Can you win him over to our side? *tiğdar tistimiila j-jaanibna?* or *tigdar itqannƐa yşiir wiyyaana?*
winch - *bakra* pl. *-aat.*
wind - *hawa.* There was a violent wind last night. *čaan ʔaku hawa kulliš Ɛaali l-baarʒa bil-leel.*
**There's something in the wind. *ybayyin aku šii bij-jaww.*
**I took the wind out of his sails. *faššeet ijraaba.*
to get wind of - *ʒass (i), Ɛiraf (u) b-.* I got wind of the story yesterday. *ʒasseet bil-quşşa l-baarʒa.*
to **wind - 1.** *tƐarraj (a taƐarruj).* The road winds through the mountains. *ţ-ţariiq yitƐarraj been ij-jibaal.* **2.** *laff (i laff) n-.* Wind it around my finger. *liffha daayir-ma daayir ib-şibƐi.* **3.** *kawwak (u takwiik) t-.* I forgot to wind my watch. *nseet akawwuk saaƐti.*
to wind up - 1. *laff (i laff) n-.* Will you help me wind up this yarn? *ma-tƐaawunni ʔaliff haş-şuuf?* **2.** *rattab (i tartiib).* They gave him two weeks' time in which to wind up his affairs. *nţoo sbuuƐeen ʒatta yrattib ʔumuura.*
to get **winded** - *nihat (a).* I get winded easily when I run. *ʔanhat bil-Ɛajil min arkuδ.*
winding sheet - *čifan* pl. *čfaana.*
windmill - *ţaaʒuunat* (pl. *ţwaaʒiin*) *hawa, makiina* (pl. *makaayin*) *hawaaʔiyya.*
window - 1. *šibbaač* pl. *šbaabiič.* Please open the windows. *baļļa fukk iš-šibaabiič.* **2.** *jaamxaana* pl. *-aat.* Put these on display in the window. *ʔiƐriδ hal-ʔašyaaʔ bij-jaamxaana.*
windowpane - *jaama* pl. *-aat.* The stone broke the windowpane. *l-iʒjaara kisrat ij-jaama.*
windpipe - *qaşaba* (pl. *-aat*) *hawaaʔiyya.*
windshield - *jaama* (pl. *-aat*) *giddaamiyya.*
windy - **It's windy today. *ʔaku hawa hwaaya l-yoom.*
wine - *šaraab.* Do you have aged wine? *Ɛindak šaraab muƐattaq?*
wing - 1. *jnaaʒ* pl. *-aat.* The pigeon broke its wing. *ţ-ţeer inkisar ijnaaʒa.* — The office is in the left wing of the building. *d-daaʔira bij-jinaaʒ il-Ɛal-yisra mnil-binaaya.* **2.** *ʒimaaya.* She took him under her wing. *šimlata b-ʒimaayata.*

**I watched the play from the wings. *tfarrajit Ear-ruwaaya min şafzat il-masraz wara l-parda.*

wink - 1. *ġamza* pl. *-aat.* She gave me a knowing wink. *ġumzat-li ġamzat waazid yidri.* 2. *lazδa.* I didn't sleep a wink. *ma-ġumδat Eeeni wala lazδa.*

**He was gone in a wink. *ġaab miθil lamz il-başar.*

to wink - *ġumaz (u ġamuz).* Did she wink at you? *ġumzat-lak?*

winter - *šita* pl. *-aayaat.* We don't travel in winter. *ma-nsaafir biš-šita.*

to wipe - *naššaf (i tanšiif) t-.* I'll wash the dishes if you wipe them. *ʔaġsil l-imwaaEiin ʔiδa ʔinta tnaššifhum.*

to wipe off - *misaz (a masiz) n-.* First let me wipe off the dust. *xalli ʔamsaz it-tiraab ʔawwal.*

to wipe out - *qiδa (i qaδaaʔ) n- Eala.* The earthquake wiped out the whole town. *z-zilzaal qiδa Eal-wlaaya kullha.*

wire - 1. *silk* pl. *ʔaslaak, siim* pl. *syuuma, waayir* pl. *-aat.* The wire isn't strong enough. *s-silk muu hal-gadd qawi.* 2. *barqiyya* pl. *-aat.* Send him a wire. *dizz-la barqiyya.*

by wire - *barqiyyan.* I'll let you know by wire. *Euud axabbrak barqiyyan.*

to wire - *dazz (i dazz) barqiyya l-.* He wired me to meet him at the station. *dazz-li barqiyya alaagii bil-muzaṭṭa.*

wisdom - *Eaqil.* That needs courage and wisdom. *haay yinraad-ilha šajaaEa w-Eaqil.*

wise - *Eaaqil.* He's a very wise man. *huwwa fadd waazid kulliš Eaaqil.*

**When are you going to get wise to yourself? *šwakit raz-yiji Eaqlak ib-raasak?*

**Don't be such a wise guy. *ʔiθgal išwayya.*

to put one wise - *fahham (i tafhiim) t-.* Don't you think we ought to put him wise? *ma-tiEtiqid ʔazsan infahhma š-aku š-ma-aku?*

wish - 1. *raġba* pl. *-aat.* My wishes are easily satisfied. *raġbaati sahil tazqiiqha.* 2. *tamanniya* pl. *-aat.* Best wishes for the New Year! *ʔaṭyab it-tamanniyaat ib-munaasabat raas is-sana.*

to wish - *tmanna (a tamanni).* We wished him luck on his trip. *tmanneenaa-la safra mwaffqa.* -- I wish I could stay here longer. *ʔatmanna loo ʔagdar abqa mudda aṭwal.* -- I wouldn't wish it on my worse enemy. *ma-atmannaaha l-Eaduwwi.*

**I wish I'd done that. *yaareet sawweetha.*

to wish for - *tmanna (a tamanni).* What do you wish for most? *š-titmanna hassa ʔazyad šii?*

witch - *sazzaara* pl. *-aat, saazira* pl. *-aat.*

with - 1. *wiyya, maEa.* I'll have lunch with him today. *raz-atġadda wiyyaa l-yoom.* -- Do you want something to drink with your meal? *yEijbak tišrab šii wiyya l-ʔakil?* -- He took the book with him. *ʔaxaδ l-iktaab wiyyaa.* 2. *maEa, b-.* With pleasure! *maEa l-mamnuuniyya.* 3. *b-.* With all the money he's spent he should have a better house than that. *b-hal-ifluus l-işrafha čaan laazim ykuun Einda beet ʔazsan min haaδa.* -- The house was crawling with ants. *l-beet čaan yruuš bin-namil.* 4. *bin-nisba ʔil-.* With him it's all a matter of money. *bin-nisba ʔila hiyya mawδuuE ifluus bass.* 5. *raġum.* With all the work he's done he still isn't finished. *raġum kull iš-šuġuḷ is-sawwaa huwwa li-hassa baEad ma-mxalliş.* 6. *Eind.* He's staying with us. *huwwa naazil Eidna.* 7. *min.* She was beaming with happiness. *wujihha čaan da-yiδzak imnil-faraz.*

to withdraw - 1. *sizab (a sazib) n-.* I withdraw the motion. *ʔaszab il-iqtiraaz.* 2. *nsizab (i nsizaab).* Because of health reasons I will withdraw from the elections. *ʔaani raz-ansizib imnil-intixaabaat il-ʔasbaab şizziyya.*

to wither - *δibal (a).* Her face is withered. *wujihha δablaan.*

within - 1. *xilaal.* I expect an answer within three days. *ʔatwaqqaE jawaab xilaal itlaθt iyyaam.* 2. *δimin.* Speeding is forbidden within the city limits. *s-surEa mamnuuEa δimin zuduud l-wlaaya.* -- This is within my authority. *haay δimin şulṭaati.* 3. *ib-xilaal.* The letters came within a short period. *l-makaatiib wuşlat ib-xilaal fatra qaşiira.*

**We're within 3 miles of the city. *ʔizna b-biEid itlaθ amyaal imnil-wlaaya.*

without - *blayya, bala, biduun, min ġeer.* Can I get in without a ticket? *ʔagdar axušš iblayya tikit?* -- He left without permission. *ṭilaE biduun ʔijaaza.* -- She left the room without saying a word. *tirkat il-ġurfa blayya-ma tguul wala čilma.*

witness - *šaahid* pl. *šhuud.* The witnesses haven't been examined yet. *š-šuhuud baEad ma-nsiʔlaw li-hassa.*

to witness - 1. *šihad (a) Eala.* We witnessed his signature. *šhadna Eala tawqiiEa.* 2. *šaaf (u šoof).* Did you witness the accident? *šift il-zaadiθ min şaar?* 3. *tfarraj (a tafarruj) Eala.* A huge crowd witnessed the game. *hwaaya naas itfarrjaw Eas-sibaaq.*

witty - *mnakkit laaδiE.* He's very witty. *huwwa mnakkit laaδiE.*

wolf - *δiib* pl. *δiyaab.* The wolves have been killing our sheep. *δ-δiyaab da-yaakluun xurfaanna.*

**He's a wolf in sheep's clothing. *bil-wujih imrayya w-bil-gufa sillaaya.* or *jawwa Eanaamta ʔaku miit ibliis.*

woman - *mara* pl. *niswaan, mrayya* pl. *-aat.* That woman is selling yoghurt. *δiič il-mara da-tbiiE liban.*

womb - *razam* pl. *ʔarzaam.*

wonder - *muEjiza* pl. *-aat.* The medicine works wonders. *had-duwa ysawwi muEjizaat.* -- It's a wonder that you got here at all. *wuşuulak ihnaa b-zadd δaata čaan muEjiza.*

**No wonder it's cold with the window open. *ṭabEan itşiir barda ʔiδa iš-šibbaač mafkuuk.*

to wonder - *staġrab (u stiġraab).* I shouldn't wonder if it were true. *ma-astaġrub ʔiδa čaanat şudug.*

**I was wondering where you were. *ridt aEruf Eajaban inta ween.*

**I wonder what he'll do now. *Eajaban iš-raz-ysawwi hassa.*

wonderful - *mumtaaz.* That's a wonderful book. *haaδa ktaab mumtaaz.*

wood - 1. *xišab.* What kind of wood is this? *šinu nooE hal-xišab?* 2. *zaṭab.* Those people are collecting wood for the fire. *δoola da-ylimmuun zaṭab lin-naar.*

wooden - *min xišab.* The pan has a wooden handle. *ṭ-ṭaawa biiha yadda min xišab.* -- The room is divided by a wooden partition. *l-ġurfa maqsuuma b-zaajiz min xišab.*

woods - *ġaaba* pl. *-aat.* Is there a path through the woods? *ʔaku ṭariiq imnil-ġaaba?*

**We're not out of the woods yet. *baEadha zaalatna ma-mistaqirra.*

wool - *şuuf.* The blanket is made of pure wool. *hal-baṭṭaaniyya şuuf xaaliş.*

woolen - *min şuuf.* I bought a woolen sweater. *štireet ibluuz min şuuf.*

woolens - *şuufiyyaat.* Did you put moth balls in your woolens? *zaṭṭeet naftaaliin wiyya ş-şuufiyyaat maaltak?*

word - 1. *čilma, kalima* pl. *-aat.* We have to learn fifty new words between now and tomorrow. *laazim nizfaδ xamsiin čilma minnaa l-baačir.* -- How do you spell that word? *šloon tithajja hač-čilma?* -- I don't want to hear another word about this. *ma-ariid asmaE wala čilma baEad Ean hal-mawδuuE.* -- I remember the tune, but I forget the words. *ʔatδakkar l-lazan bass naasi l-kalimaat.* 2. *waEad.* He gave his word that he would finish the job in time. *niṭa waEad yxalliş iš-šuġuḷ ib-wakta.* 3. *xabar.* Try to send them word we need reinforcements. *zaawil itdizz-ilhum xabar Ean zaajatna lil-musaaEada.*

**You can take his word for it. *Etimid Eala zčaayta.*

**He doesn't let you get a word in edgewise. *ma-yxalli ʔazzad yizči.*

**In a word, no. *muxtaşar mufiid, laa.*

to word - *rattab (i tartiib) kalimaat.* How do you want to word the telegram? *šloon itriid itrattib kalimaat il-barqiyya?*

wording - **The wording of this sentence is bad. *Eibaaraat haj-jumla ma-mrattba.*

work - 1. *šuġuḷ* pl. *ʔašġaaḷ.* The Department of Public Works is being reorganized. *ʔaEaadaw tanδiim mudiiriyyat il-ʔašġaaḷ il-Eaamma.* -- The work is boring. *š-šuġuḷ yδawwij.* -- He's been out of work since the factory closed. *huwwa gaaEid bila šuġuḷ min saddaw il-maEmal.* 2. *muʔallafa* pl. *-aat.* All of that author's works are very popular. *kull muʔallafaat hal-kaatib naajza.* 3. *Eamal* pl. *ʔaEmaal.* All that painter's works are very popular. *kull ʔaEmaal haaδa r-rassaam naajza.* 4. *qiṭEa* pl. *qiṭaE.* That work of art is in the Egyptian museum. *hal-qiṭEa l-fanniyya bil-matzaf il-mişri.*

**It took a lot of work to convince him we were right. *tEabna yaḷḷa qanna'naa.*

to work - 1. *štiġaḷ (u štiġaal).* I work from eight to five. *ʔaštuġuḷ imniθ-θimaanya lil-xamsa.* -- The elevator doesn't work. *l-maşEad ma-yištuġuḷ.*

2. *šaġġaḷ.* He works his employees very hard. *yšaġġiḷ εummaala kulliš ihwaaya.* — Do you know how to work an adding machine? *tuεruf išloon itšaġġiḷ makiinat iḥsaabaat?* 3. *nijaḥ (a najaaḥ).* This trick doesn't always work. *hal-liεba muu daaʔiman tinjaḥ.* 4. *fakk (u).* I had to work my way through the crowd. *δ̣ṭarreet afukk-li ṭariiq been in-naas bil-itdiffiε.*

to work loose – *rixa (a).* Several screws have worked loose on the machine. *čam burġi rixat bil-makiina.*

to work on – 1. *qannaε (i).* We're working on him to give us the day off. *da-nqannεa ḥatta yinṭiina yoom εuṭla.* 2. *štiġaḷ (u) b-.* The mechanic is just working on your car now. *l-miikaaniiki da-yištuġuḷ ib-sayyaartak hassa.*

to work out – 1. *rattab (i tartiib) t-, hayyaʔ (i tahyiiʔ) t-.* The plan is well worked out. *l-mašruuε mitrattib zeen.* 2. *nijaḥ (a najaaḥ).* How do you think this idea would work out? *šgadd tiṭṣawwar hal-fikra raḥ-tinjaḥ?* 3. *miša (i miši).* How did things work out? *šloon mišat il-ʔumuur?*

worker – *εaamil* pl. *εummaal.* He's the best worker in my factory. *haaδa ʔaḥsan εaamil bil-maεmal maali.*

**He's a hard worker. *haaδa kulliš šaaġuuḷ.*

working hours – *dawaam.* May I call you during working hours? *ʔagdar axaabrak ʔaθnaaʔ id-dawaam?*

workman – *εaamil* pl. *εummaal.*

works – *makiina* pl. *makaayin.* The works of that clock need repairing. *l-makiina maal has-saaεa yinraad-ilha taṣliiḥ.*

water works – *ʔisaalat maaʔ.* The water works are outside the city. *ʔisaalat il-maaʔ barra l-wlaaya.*

world – 1. *dinya.* He's traveled all over the world. *daar id-dinya kullha.* — I wouldn't hurt him for anything in the world. *ma-ʔaδδii loo yinṭuuni mulk id-dinya.* 2. *εaalam.* The Red Cross is a world-wide organization. *muʔassasat iṣ-ṣaliib il-ʔaḥmar mintašra b-kull il-εaalam.*

**Where in the world have you been? *b-yaa ẓwiyya činit δ̣aamum nafsak?*

**It will do him a world of good to go somewhere else. *hwaaya l-maṣlaḥta loo yruuḥ il-ġeer makaan.*

**My father thinks the world of you. *ʔabuuya yqaddrak kulliš ihwaaya.*

worm – *duuda* pl. *-aat* coll. *duud.* Do you use worms for bait? *ʔinta tistaεmil duud liṭ-ṭuεum?*

wormy – *mdawwid.* These dates are wormy. *hat-tamur kulla mdawwid.*

worn – *mistahlik, gaayim.* My coat is pretty worn. *sitirti mistahlika.*

worn-out – *taεbaan kullis.* He looks worn-out. *ybayyin εalee taεbaan kulliš.*

worry – *dooxat raas, qalaq.* Her son gave her a great deal of worry. *ʔibinha sabbab-ilha hwaaya dooxat raas.*

to worry – 1. *šawwaš (u), qilaq (i qalaq) n-.* His silence worries me. *sukuuta da-yšawwušni.* 2. *tšawwaš (a).* I'm worried about him. *fikri mitšawwiš εalee.*

**I won't let that worry me. *ma-adawwux raasi b-haay.*

**The future doesn't worry him. *ma-yxaaf imnil-mustaqbal.*

**I don't have time to worry about that. *ṣ-ṣidug ma-εindi wakt il-haay.*

worse – 1. *ʔamarr, ʔangas.* He's feeling worse this morning. *hal-yoom ṣiḥḥta baεad amarr.* — The weather is worse now than it was in the morning. *j-jaww hassa ʔangas imniṣ-ṣubuḥ.* 2. *ʔaswaʔ.* His business is going from bad to worse. *šuġḷa da-yiṭṭawwar min sayyiʔ ʔila ʔaswaʔ.* 3. *ʔatεas.* He's even worse off now. *ḥaalta hassa baεad ʔatεas.*

**He's none the worse for it. *ma-ṣaaba ʔay δ̣arar min waraaha.*

**Her condition is getting worse and worse. *ḥaalatha da-titdahwar.*

worship – *εibaada.* The worship of idols was prevalent before Islam. *εibaadat il-ʔaṣnaam čaanat mawjuuda gabḷ il-ʔislaam.*

to worship – *εibad (i εbaada) n-.* He worships his wife. *yiεbidha l-marta.*

worst – 1. *ʔaswaʔ.* But wait, I haven't told you the worst. *yawaaš, baεad ma-git-lak ʔaswaʔ šii.* 2. *ʔangas.* I got the worst piece. *jatni ʔangas wuṣla.* 3. *ʔatεas.* That's the worst accident I've seen in my life. *δaak ʔatεas ḥaadiθ taṣaadum šaayfa b-εumri.*

**I get the worst of it when I argue with him. *kull-ma atnaaqaš wiyyaa, ʔaani ʔaakulha.*

**We're over the worst of it. *šarrha faat.*

at worst – *b-ʔatεas il-ḥaalaat.* At worst, the storm won't last longer than a week. *b-ʔatεas il-ḥaalaat, il-εaaṣifa ma-ṭṭawwil ʔaẓyad min isbuuε.*

worth – 1. *qiima* pl. *qiyam.* He didn't appreciate her true worth. *ma-qaddar qiimatha l-ḥaqiiqiyya.* 2. *ḥagg.* Give me 10 fils worth of peanuts. *ʔinṭiini ḥagg εašr ifluus fistiq εabiid.*

**Give me fifty fils worth of almonds. *nṭiini b-xamsiin filis looẓ.*

**Did you get your money's worth in the night club last night? *εaad ṭallaεt ifluusak il-ḥaṭṭeetha bil-malha l-baarḥa bil-leel?*

to be worth – 1. *siwa (a).* It's worth the trouble. *tiswa dooxt ir-raas.* — That horse is worth five hundred dinars. *hal-iḥṣaan yiswa xamis miit diinaar.* 2. *stiḥaqq (i stiḥqaaq).* His idea is worth trying. *fikirta tistiḥiqq it-tajruba.*

**Pay him what he's worth. *ʔinṭii εala gadd taεaba.*

**He's worth about two million dinars. *yimlik-la fadd milyooneen diinaar.*

**I'll make it worth your while. *ʔaraδ̣δ̣iik.* or *ma-titnaddam.*

worthless – *ma-il- qiima.* That money is worthless now. *hal-ifluus baεad ma-ilha qiima.*

**The painting is practically worthless. *haṣ-ṣuura ma-tiswa šii.*

worthy – *nabiil.* They did it for a worthy cause. *sawwooha l-ġaaya nabiila.*

wound – *jariḥ* pl. *jruuḥ.* It will be a couple of months before the wound in his leg is healed. *yinraad-la šahreen ḥatta j-jariḥ illi b-rijla yṭiib.*

to wound – *jiraḥ (a jariḥ) n-, jarraḥ (i tajriiḥ).* Several men were wounded in the action. *čam waaḥid injirḥaw ib-δaak il-hijuum.* — The explosion wounded three soldiers. *l-infijaar jiraḥ itlaθ jinuud.*

to wrap – *laff (i laff) n-, ġallaf (i).* Shall I wrap it up for you? *triid aliff-ilk-iyyaaha?*

**He's all wrapped up in his work. *δaabib nafsa εaš-šuġuḷ.* or *minhimik biš-šuġuḷ.* or *ṭaamuṣ biš-šuġuḷ.*

wrapping paper – *waraq taġliif.*

wreath – *ʔikliil* pl. *ʔakaaliil.*

wreck – 1. *ʔanqaaδ̣.* The bodies are still buried in the wreck. *j-jiθaθ baεadha madfuuna bil-ʔanqaaδ̣.* 2. *ḥaadiθ* pl. *ḥawaadiθ.* Was anybody killed in the wreck? *ʔaḥḥad maat bil-ḥaadiθ?*

**He's a complete wreck. *ʔaεṣaaba minhaara.*

to wreck – 1. *ḥaṭṭam (u taḥṭiim).* The collision wrecked the car. *t-taṣaadum ḥaṭṭamha lis-sayyaara.* 2. *dammar (u tadmiir).* The explosion wrecked the whole plant. *l-infijaar dammar il-maεmal.* 3. *dumar (u damur) n-.* The strike wrecked his business. *l-ʔiδ̣raab dumar šuġḷa.*

wrench – *ṣpaana* pl. *-aat, ṣpaayin.*

to wrestle – 1. *tṣaaraε (a taṣaaruε).* He likes to wrestle better than box. *yεijba yiṭṣaaraε ʔaẓyad min-ma yitlaakam.* 2. *εaalaj (i muεaalaja) t-.* I've been wrestling with this problem for hours. *ṣaar-li tlaθ saaεaat da-aεaalij hal-qaδ̣iyya.*

wretched – *δ̣aayij.* I still feel wretched. *baεadni δ̣aayij.*

to wring – 1. *εiṣar (u εaṣir).* Wring out the clothes. *ʔiεṣur il-ihduum.* 2. *luwa (i lawi).* She wrung the chicken's neck. *luwat rugbat id-dijaaja.*

wringer – *εaṣṣaara* pl. *-aat.* The wringer on my washing machine is broken. *εaṣṣaart il-ġassaala maalti maksuura.*

wrinkle – *tajεiid* pl. *tajaaεiid.* Her face is full of wrinkles. *wujihha matruus tajaaεiid.*

to wrinkle – 1. *εaknaš (i tεikniš) t-.* He wrinkled his forehead. *εaknaš wujja.* 2. *tεaqqač (a taεaqqič).* This silk wrinkles easily. *hal-ḥariir yitεaqqač bil-εajil.*

wrist – *rusuġ* pl. *ʔarsaaġ.* You've got a sprained wrist. *ʔaku εindak rusuġ mafṣuux.*

wrist watch – *saaεat* (pl. *-aat*) *iid.*

to write – *kitab (i kitba, kitaaba) n-.* Write your name on the first line. *ʔiktib ismak εala ʔawwal saṭir.*

to write down – *sajjal (i tasjiil).* Write down that telephone number before you forget it. *sajjil har-raqam maal it-talafoon gabuḷ-ma tinsaa.*

to write off – *ḥisab (i ḥsaab) n-.* You'd better write that off as a bad debt. *ʔaḥsan-lak iḥsib had-deen mayyit.*

writer – *kaatib* pl. *kuttaab.* My son wants to become a story writer. *ʔibni yriid iyṣiir kaatib quṣaṣi.*

writing – *kitba, kitaaba* pl. *-aat.* I can't read his

writing. *ma-agdar aqra kitibta.*
**I don't get around to writing. *ma da-yṣiir Ɛindi wakit ʔaktib.*
in writing - *maktuub.* I'd like to have that in writing. *ʔariid haay maktuuba.*
writings - *kitaabaat.* I don't understand his writings. *ma-agdar aftihim kitaabaata.*
wrong - **1.** *ġalaṭ.* He admitted that he was in the wrong. *Ɛtiraf ib-ġalaṭa.* — I must have added the figures up wrong again. *laazim hamm ijmaƐit l-ʔarqaam ġalaṭ.* — You're heading in the wrong direction. *ttijaahak muu ṣaziiz.* or *ttijaahak ġalaṭ.* **2.** *ġalṭaan.* I'm afraid you're wrong. *ʔaƐtiqid inta ġalṭaan.* -- I'll admit that I was completely wrong about him. *ʔaƐtirif ʔaani činit ġalṭaan ib-raʔyi bii.* **3.** *muu tamaam.* Something is wrong with the telephone. *ʔaku šii muu tamaam ib-hat-talafoon.*
**He got out on the wrong side of the bed. *hal-yoom wujja magluub.*
**Is anything wrong with you? *yoojƐak šii?*
**What's wrong with you? *š-biik?*
to do wrong - *ġilaṭ (a ġalaṭ).* He thinks he can do no wrong. *yiƐtiqid huwwa ʔabad ma-yiġlaṭ.*
to wrong - *ẓilam (u ẓulum) n-, ġidar (i ġadir) n-.* He thinks he's been wronged. *yiƐtiqid inna huwwa maẓluum.*
wrongfully - *ẓulman w-Ɛidwaanan, bil-taƐaddi.* He was wrongfully accused of incompetence. *ttihmoo b-Ɛadam il-qaabliyya ẓulman w-Ɛidwaanan.*

X

X-ray - **1.** *ʔašiƐƐat* (pl. *-aat*) *ʔeeks.* Who discovered the X-ray? *minu ktišaf ʔašiƐƐat ʔeeks?* **2.** *ʔašiƐƐa* pl. *-aat.* May I see the X-ray? *ʔagdar ašuuf il-ʔašiƐƐa?*
to X-ray - *ʔaxaδ (u ʔaxiδ) ʔašiƐƐa l-.* The dentist X-rayed my teeth. *ṭabiib il-ʔasnaan ʔaxaδ ʔašiƐƐa l-isnuuni.*

Y

yard - **1.** *yaarda* pl. *-aat.* I'd like to have five yards of this material. *ʔariid xamis yaardaat min hal-iqmaaš.* **2.** *saaza* pl. *-aat.* The house has a yard for the children to play in. *l-beet bii saaza yliƐbuun biiha j-jihaal.* **3.** *skalla* pl. *-aat.* You may be able to get that at the lumber yard. *balki tigdar tilgiiha bil-iskalla maal xišab.*
yarn - *ġazil.* I'll take six balls of that green yarn. *ʔariid xamis laffaat min δaak il-ġazil il-ʔaxẓar.*
to **yawn** - *tθaawab (a taθaawub).* He began to yawn from drowsiness. *bida yitθaawub imnin-naƐas.*
year - *sana* pl. *-awaat, sniin.* He's thirty years old. *Ɛumra tlaaθiin sana.* -- I haven't seen him for years. *ṣaar-li sniin ma-šaayfa.*
**Year in, year out, the same routine. *sana txušš, sana tiṭlaƐ, ma-aku taġyiir.*
yearly - *sanawi*.* How much is the yearly rent? *šgadd il-ʔajaar is-sanawi?*
**My uncle pays us a yearly visit. *Ɛammi yzuurna marra bis-sana.*
yeast - *xumra* pl. *-aat, xamiira* pl. *-aat.*
yell - *Ɛeeṭa* pl. *-aat.* He let out a yell and died. *Ɛaaṭ fadd Ɛeeṭa w-maat.*
to yell - *Ɛayyaṭ (i taƐyiiṭ).* Don't yell; you'll wake the neighbors. *la-tƐayyiṭ, raz-itgaƐƐid ij-juwaariin.*
yellow - *ʔaṣfar.* She's wearing a yellow dress. *laabsa nafnuuf aṣfar.*
**He's yellow. *haaδa jabaan.*
yes - *ʔii, naƐam, bali.* Yes, I'll be glad to go. *ʔii, aruuz maƐa l-mamnuuniyya.*
yes man - *ʔabu bali.* He's a yes man. *haaδa ʔabu bali.*
yesterday - *l-baarza.* I saw him yesterday. *šifta l-baarza.*
yet - **1.** *baƐad* (with negative). Haven't you read the book yet? *ma-qreet l-iktaab baƐad?* -- He hasn't come yet. *ma-jaa baƐad.* **2.** *loo baƐad.* Did you see the new play yet? *šift it-tamθiiliyya j-jidiida loo baƐad?* -- Have you selected anything yet? *stangeet šii loo baƐad?* **3.** *laakin, bass.* He didn't want to go, yet he had to. *ma-raad yruuz laakin iẓṭarr.* **4.** *maƐa haaδa.* And yet you can't help liking him. *maƐa haaδa ma-tigdar ʔilla tzibba.*
to **yield** - **1.** *ṭallaƐ (i taṭliiƐ) t-, jaab (i jeeb).* His business doesn't yield much profit. *maṣlazta ma-ṭṭilliƐ ihwaaya ribiz.* **2.** *nitaj (i ʔintaaj) n-.* This farm yields a pretty good income. *hal-mazraƐa tintij xooš waarid.* **3.** *xiẓaƐ (a xuẓuuƐ), ʔaδƐan (i ʔiδƐaan), riẓax (a ruẓuux).* We'll never yield to force. *ʔabadan ma-nixẓaƐ lil-quwwa.*
yoghurt - *laban.*
yolk - *ṣafaar.*
you - **1.** (m.) *ʔinta* (f.) *ʔinti* (pl.) *ʔintum.* Are you the new clerk? *ʔinta l-kaatib ij-jidiid?* **2.** (m.) *-ak,* (f.) *-ič,* (pl.) *-kum.* I haven't seen you in a long time. *ma-šiftak min zamaan.*
young - *jaahil.* Who's that young man? *minu δaak ir-rijjaal ij-jaahil?* -- She's very young for her age. *tbayyin jaahla bin-nisba l-Ɛumurha.*
**The night is still young. *l-leel baƐda b-ʔawwala.*
young people - *šabaab.* The young people had a lot of fun. *š-šabaab itwannsaw ihwaaya.*
yours - *maal-.* This hat is yours, sir. *haš-šafqa maalak, yaa ʔustaaδ.* This doll is yours. *hal-laƐƐaaba maaltič.* -- My bag is bigger than yours. *jinuṭṭi ʔakbar min maaltak.*
**Is he a friend of yours, Mr. Smith? *haaδa min ʔaṣdiqaaʔak, yaa mistir smiθ?*
yourself - *nafs-.* Did you hurt yourself? *ʔaδδeet nafsak?*
youth - *šabaab.* He had to work hard in his youth. *ẓṭarr yištuġuḷ ihwaaya b-šabaaba.*
yo-yo - *yooyo* pl. *-owaat.*

Z

zebra - *zibra* pl. *-aat.*
zero - *ṣifir* pl. *ṣfaara.* Add another zero. *zuṭṭ ṣifir laax.* -- The temperature is zero. *darajat il-zaraara ṣifir.*
zinc - *qaṣdiir, tuutya.*
Zion - *ṣahyuun.*
Zionism - *ṣ-ṣahyuuniyya.*
Zionist - *ṣahyuuni** pl. *-iyyiin, ṣahaayna.*
zipper - *zanjiil* pl. *zanaajiil.* I broke the zipper on my sweater. *ksarit iz-zanjiil maal ibluuzi.*
zither - *qaanuun* pl. *qawaaniin.*
zone - *manṭiqa* pl. *-aat, manaaṭiq.* Iraq is located in the temperate zone. *l-Ɛiraaq waaqiƐ bil-manṭiqa l-muƐtadila.*
zoo - *zadiiqat* (pl. *zadaayiq*) *zaywaanaat.*
zoology - *Ɛilim il-zaywaanaat.*

Arabic – English

Foreword

The time for reissuing these classic Iraqi Arabic/English dictionaries could not be more appropriate. Political interest in Iraq, combined with generally heightened interest in the Middle East, indicate that the study of the Iraqi dialect will take on increased importance in the near future. The need for reference materials such as this has dramatically increased. We are fortunate that so much Iraqi material was described in the 1960s because it is needed now more than ever.

The project to describe the Arabic colloquial dialects was conceived and headed by Richard S. Harrell, for whom Georgetown's original Arabic series was named. His foresight resulted in grants to write reference grammars, classroom courses, and bilingual dictionaries in four Arabic dialects: Iraqi, Moroccan, Egyptian, and Syrian. (Some of these books never appeared, due to Harrell's untimely death in 1964.) The Iraqi texts are complete—we have the Arabic–English and English–Arabic dictionaries, as well as a comprehensive reference grammar and an introductory speaking course.

Designing dictionaries of spoken Arabic when Arabic-to-English always poses theoretical problems: Should words be listed by root, with use restricted to those who know Arabic structure? Should words be in straight alphabetical order, which omits information about related words from the same root? Which alphabetical order? Should transcription be in the Latin alphabet, the Arabic alphabet, or both? Which nonstandard Arabic features should be transcribed and how? How should the semantic fields of words be determned and illustrated? What about classicisms?

In this Arabic-to-English dictionary, only Latin-alphabet transcription is used. Words are arranged by root (for example, q-w-m) and letters are listed in the order of the Arabic alphabet. Idioms are marked but not stylistic register. This dictionary, then, is both logical and accessible to the user who has at least a beginning knowledge of the Arabic language but may not be fully comfortable with the Arabic alphabet.

Under Harrell's brilliant leadership, a team of scholars produced these dialect materials by conducting original field research, eliciting data, and combining it with grammatical analysis. This was truly a pioneering effort in the field of Arabic dialectology, one that has not been equalled in all the years since.

Margaret Nydell
Georgetown University
March 2003

The Arabic Research Program
Institute of Languages and Linguistics
Georgetown University

The Arabic Research Program was established in June of 1960 as a contract between Georgetown University and the United States Office of Education under the provisions of the Language Development Program of the National Defense Education Act.

The first two years of the research program, 1960–62 (contract number SAE-8706), were devoted to the production of six books, a reference grammar, and a conversational English–Arabic dictionary in the cultivated spoken forms of Moroccan, Syrian, and Iraqi Arabic. The second two years of the research program, 1962–64 (contract number OE-2-14-029), have been devoted to the further production of Arabic–English dictionaries in each of the three varieties of Arabic mentioned above, as well as comprehensive basic courses in the Moroccan and Iraqi varieties.

The eleven books of this series, of which the present volume is one, are designed to serve as practical tools for the increasing number of Americans whose lives bring them into contact with the Arab world. The dictionaries, the reference grammars, and the basic courses are oriented toward the educated American who is a layman in linguistic matters. Although it is hoped that the scientific linguist and the specialist in Arabic dialectology will find these books both of interest and of use, matters of purely scientific and theoretical importance have not been directly treated as such, and specialized scientific terminology has been avoided as much as possible.

As is usual, the authors or editors of the individual books bear final scholarly responsibility for the contents, but there has been a large amount of informal cooperation in our work. Criticism, consultation, and discussion have gone on constantly among the senior professional members of the staff. The contribution of more junior research assistants, both Arab and American, is also not to be underestimated. Their painstaking assembling and ordering of raw data, often in manners requiring considerable creative intelligence, has been the necessary prerequisite for further progress.

In most cases the books prepared by the Arabic Research Program are the first of their kind in English, and, in some cases, the first in any language. The preparation of them has been a rewarding experience. It is hoped that the public use of them will be equally so. The undersigned, on behalf of the entire staff, would like to ask the same indulgence of the reader as Samuel Johnson requested in his first English dictionary: To remember that although much has been left out, much has been included.

Richard S. Harrell
Professor of Linguistics
Georgetown University

Director
Arabic Research Program

Before his death in late 1964, Dr. Harrell had done the major part of the work of general editor for the last five books of the Arabic series, and to him is due the credit for all that may be found of value in that work. It remained for me only to make some minor editing decisions and to see these books through the process of proofreading and printing; for any errors of inadequacies in the final editing, the responsibility is mine alone.

Wallace M. Erwin
Associate Professor of
Linguistics and Arabic
Georgetown University

Editors' Introduction

This book is a dictionary of the colloquial Arabic spoken in Baghdad. Expressions peculiar to the area immediately south of Baghdad have been included, but because of practical limitations the quite distinct Iraqi dialects spoken in the other two major cities, Mosul and Basra, have not been considered. The Arabic dealt with is that used by an educated Iraqi in everyday speech.

This volume is intended as a comprehension dictionary for native speakers of American English; that is, one designed to allow Americans to understand Iraqi Arabic. Like a monolingual English dictionary, it presumes a thorough knowledge of English. It is therefore not intended to help Iraqis reproduce English.

The use of this dictionary requires a basic knowledge of the structure and phonology of Arabic, and of the standard arrangement of an Arabic dictionary. For a treatment of the grammar of spoken Iraqi Arabic, the reader is referred to several available books, among them Wallace Erwin's *Reference Grammar of Iraqi Arabic,*[1] and McCarthy & Raffouli's *Spoken Arabic of Baghdad.*[2] The entries are ordered according to the traditional Arabic root system, with the roots arranged in accordance with the Arabic alphabet, including the purely colloquial Iraqi phonemes *p*, *č*, and *g* at positions dictated by phonology. Thus *p* follows *b*, *č* follows *j* (rather than *k*), and *g* follows *q*.

Foreign borrowings and Arabic words no longer identified with their original roots (such as *šarbat*) are listed alphabetically. In the case of some Persian and Turkish words which form compounds with Arabic words, the affix is listed separately, and also under the roots of the Arabic words it combines with (cf. *-xaana* and *-sizz*).

Under the root, which is alphabetized by its main two, three, or four root consonants, are listed first the ten measures, or forms, of the verb. They are: *faɛal*, *faɛɛal*, *faaɛal*, *ʔafɛal*, *tfaɛɛal*, *tfaaɛal*, *nfiɛal*, *ftiɛal*, *fɛall*, and *stafɛal*. Many historically fourth-measure verbs in Iraqi Arabic have acquired perfect forms corresponding to those of first-measure verbs. Such originally fourth-measure verbs have been listed immediately after the first true measure.

In accordance with traditional Arabic practice, verbs are listed in the third person singular of the perfect. The perfect is followed in parentheses by the stem vowel and the verbal noun or nouns. After the verbs come the nominal forms, arranged generally by length and complexity. Forms ending in *i* are followed by an asterisk when they follow the pattern: feminine *-iyya*, masculine plural *-iyyiin*, feminine plural *-iyyaat*. Additional irregular plural forms follow the asterisk (e.g., *baɛθi** pl. *baɛθiyya*).

The instance noun of a verbal noun, that is, a single instance of the action, or the product of it, is commonly indicated by the abbreviation "i.n.", with no translation (e.g., *ḥamis* frying. *ḥamsa* pl. *-aat* i.n. of *ḥamis*—i.e., a single act of frying.) Similarly, the unit noun of a collective is simply defined by the abbreviation "un.n.", with no translation, for the sake of economy—e.g., *čaraz* (coll.) nut(s). *čaraza* pl. *-aat* un.n. of *čaraz*.

After the nominal forms come the elative and the active and passive participles. In glossing participles, we have not listed the verbal usages, as they are readily inferred from the preceding verb. Only the nominal and adjectival meanings are given. Where the participle functions only as such as Iraqi Arabic, it is not normally listed at all.

Plurals of participles are not usually shown when the predominant usage is adjectival and inflection follows the usual adjectival pattern. When the participle is used primarily as a noun, the masculine plural is usually given (e.g., *kaatib* pl. *-iin*). Plurals that differ from the plural of the first nominal form or participle glossed (and in the case of verbs, the stem vowel and verbal nouns that differ from those of the first verb glossed) are placed in parentheses before the new definition (*cf.* *ɛidal* under *ɛ-d-l*).

In all entries, idiomatic usages within a given semantic range follow the rest of the examples and are set off by a double virgule. In those few instances where idiomatic expressions do not fit into any one meaning of the word, they are set in a separate paragraph at the end of the entry and marked with a paragraph sign.

To delimit the semantic range and to show the syntactic aspects of the entries, numerous illustrative examples have been provided, particularly of verbs, adjectives, prepositions, and particles. Nouns have not usually been illustrated, except when they show unusual or idiomatic usages.

In translating common Iraqi phrases and sentences used as illustrations, it was not always possible to keep the style equivalent in the two languages. An example is the commonly used noun *jaahil*. In many cases, it means "baby," occasionally it can be translated as "boy" or "child," but, in most cases, the only word that sounded right in the same context was "kid"—definitely not on the same stylistic level as *jaahil*. The level of the English translation then is not to be relied on as an indication of the stylistic level of the Arabic original.

The transcription used for the consonants of Iraqi Arabic is as follows in the alphabetical order used for the entries:

ʔ —glottal stop; like the catch between the vowels in oh-oh.
b— voiced bilabial stop; similar to English *b* as in *bake*.
p— voiceless bilabial stop; similar to English *p* as in *pole*.
t— voiceless dental stop; similar to English *t* as in *take*.
θ— voiceless interdental spirant; similar to English *th* as in *thank*.
j— voiced palatal affricate; similar to English *j* as in *jail*.
č— voiceless palatal affricate; similar to English *ch* as in *cheese*.
ɂ— voiceless pharyngeal spirant; no English equivalent.
x— voiceless velar spirant; no English translation but similar to German *ch* as in *Bach*.
d— voiced dental stop; similar to English *d* as in *desk*.
δ— voiced interdental spirant; similar to English *th* as in *than*.
r— alveolar flap, generally voiced; unlike American English *r* but somewhat similar to the *t* or *d* flap of American English *Betty* or *body*.
z— voiced dental spirant; similar to English *z* as in *zeal*.
s— voiceless dental spirant; similar to English *s* as in *seen*.
š— voiceless palatal spirant; similar to English *sh* as in *sheep*.
ṣ— voiceless dental spirant, velarized; no equivalent in English.
δ̣— voiceless interdental spirant, velarized; no equivalent in English.
ṭ— voiceless dental stop, velarized; no equivalent in English.
ɛ— voiced pharyngeal spirant; no equivalent in English.
ġ— voiced velar spirant; no equivalent in English, but similar to some occurrences of French *r*.
f— voiceless labio-dental spirant; similar to English *f* as in *fan*.
q— voiceless post-velar stop; no equivalent in English.

g—voiced velar stop; similar to English *g* as in *get*.

k—voiceless velar stop; similar to English *k* as in *kick*.

l—voiced alveo-dental lateral; unlike most English *l*'s but similar to *l* in *million* as pronounced by some speakers.

ḷ—voiced alveo-dental lateral, velarized; similar to English *l* in *mill* (treated as *l* in ordering of entries).

m—voiced bilabial nasal; similar to English *m* as in *meat*.

n—voiced dental nasal; similar to English *n* as in *neat*.

h—voiceless glottal spirant; similar to English *h* as in *home*.

The semivowels are as follows:

w— voiced high back rounded semivowel; similar to English *w* as in *way*.

y— voiced high front unrounded semivowel; similar to English *y* as in *yell*.

The above constitute the alphabet in this book. In addition, Iraqi Arabic contains a number of long and short vowels which are not included in the alphabet. The short vowels are as follows:

a—short low central vowel; the quality of this vowel varies with its environment and is similar to the English *a* as in *father*, or a sound between the vowels of *father* and *fought*, or *bet* and *bat*.

i—short high front unrounded vowel; the quality of this vowel varies with its environment and is similar to the English *i* as in *machine*, or in *bit*, or in *sister*.

o—short mid back rounded vowel; similar to the first part of the diphthong in English *boat*.

u—short high back rounded vowel; the quality of this vowel varies with its environment, and is similar to the vowel of English *boot*, or to a sound between the vowels of *bull* and *ball*, or to the vowel sound of English *book*.

The long vowels are as follows:

aa—long low central vowel; this vowel, when not next to a velarized consonant, is between the vowels of English *had* and *hod*, but longer. Next to a velarized consonant, it ranges between the vowel of English *hod* and *haul*.

ee—long mid front unrounded vowel; this vowel is between the vowel sounds of English *fez* and *phase*, or else has diphthong quality, the first part being like the sound of *eat*, the second like the sound of *let*.

ii—long high front unrounded vowel similar to the *i* of English as in *machine*.

oo—long mid back rounded vowel; this vowel, when not next to a velarized consonant, has the quality of the first element in the diphthong of English *chose*, of if next to a velarized consonant, it is similar to the vowel of English *ball*.

uu—long high back rounded vowel; if next to a velarized consonant, it is between the vowel of *choose* and the first element of the diphthong of *chose* in English; otherwise it is similar to the vowel of English *choose*.

In order to preserve the root, we have not shown the assimilation of root consonants to adjacent consonants. In addition, the assimilation of structural elements indicating the measure of a verb has not been shown in the entry, in order to preserve the structure intact. In the illustrative examples, however, assimilation has been allowed to vary freely. Therefore, under the root *ṣ-d-*

m, the eighth measure is shown as *ṣtidam*, but in any examples, it will generally appear as *ṣṭidam*, and while the fifth-form verb of the root *z-w-j* will be shown as *tzawwaj*, examples will vary from that to the more common *dzawwaj* or *zzawwaj*.

The material used in this dictionary is all original and was provided by the Iraqi native speakers on the staff, using a small number of radio scripts in colloquial Iraqi Arabic as a starting point from which to build a corpus. The standard works consulted for certain etymological questions were Hans Wehr's *Dictionary of Modern Written Arabic*,[3] Steingass's *Persian-English Dictionary*,[4] and Hony's *English-Turkish Dictionary*.[5]

Arabic entries and illustrative examples were provided by Faisal Al-Khalaf, Husain Mustafa, and, in the later stages, also by Majid Damah. Compilation was done by Darrel Smith, Ronald G. Wolfe, and the editors. The editing procedure was set up and supervised by Karl Stowasser, who was the lexicographic consultant for the entire Arabic Research Program. Valuable assistance in handling grammatical points was provided by Wallace M. Erwin. Final editing and proofreading were the responsibility of Daniel R. Woodhead.

The editors wish to express their appreciation to Georgetown University for providing an academic home during the compiling of this dictionary, and, above all, to the authors of the National Defense Education Act and its administrators in the Department of Health, Education, and Welfare, who made possible for us its undertaking.

Notes

1. Wallace M. Erwin, *A Short Reference Grammar of Iraqi Arabic*, Washington: Georgetown University Press, 1963.

2. R. J. McCarthy, S.J., and Farraj Raffouli. *Spoken Arabic of Baghdad: Part One.* Beirut: Librairie Orientale, 1964.

3. Hans Wehr, *A Dictionary of Modern Written Arabic*, edited by J Milton Cowan. Ithaca, N.Y.: Cornell University Press, 1961.

4. F. Steingass, *Persian-English Dictionary.* London: Routledge & Kegan Paul, Ltd., 1892.

5. H. C. Hony, *A Turkish-English Dictionary.* London: Oxford, at Clarendon Press, 1957.

Abbreviations and Symbols

anat.	anatomy
archeol.	archeology
arith.	arithmetic
athlet.	athletics
auto.	automotive
biol.	biology
bot.	botany
chem.	chemistry
coll.	collective
com.	commerce
conj.	conjunction
econ.	economy
e.g.	for example
el.	electricity
equiv.	equivalent
esp.	especially
fem.	feminine
fig.	figuratively
geom.	geometry
gram.	grammar
i.e.	that is
i.n.	instance noun
intens.	intensive
invar.	invariable
jur.	jurisprudence
masc.	masculine
math.	mathematics
med.	medicine
mil.	military
mus.	music
pass.	passive
phot.	photography
phys.	physics
pl.	plural
pol.	politics
psych.	psychology
recip.	reciprocal
refl.	reflexive
s(ing).	singular
specif.	specifically
techn.	technology
trans.	transitive
un.n.	unit noun
var.	variant
W.	west, western
zool.	zoology

=	equals, equivalent to
*	indicates that inflection follows the pattern: fem. -*iyya*, masc. pl. -*iyyiin*, fem. pl. -*iyyaat*
||	indicates an idiomatic expression
¶	indicates an idiomatic expression not directly related to any semantic range of the entry
/ /	enclose prescriptive syntactic information
<	indicates probable derivation of the word or expression

ʔ

ʔ-a-b
ʔaab August.
ʔ-a-b-r-u
ʔaabru: waraq ʔaabru construction paper, glossy and colored on the face, plain white on the back.
ʔ-a-b-r-y
ʔaabri = *ʔaabru.*
ʔ-a-θ-w-r
*ʔaaθuuri** **1.** Assyrian, referring to a Christian people living NE of Mosul in Iraq. **2.** an Assyrian. **3.** Assyrian (language).
ʔ-a-č-ġ
ʔaačuġ (invar.) **1.** light, light colored. *maawi ʔaačuġ* light blue. **2.** uncovered, unguarded (chiefly in backgammon). *puul ʔaačuġ* an unguarded piece. **3.** unemployed, idle. *kull ʔaṣdiqaaʔi štiġlaw w-aani bqeet ʔaačuġ.* All my friends went to work and I remained idle.
ʔ-a-x
ʔaax an exclamation, approx.: ow! ouch!, and a cry of distress, approx.: oh! *ʔaax, raasi yoojaƐni!* Oh, my head hurts!
ʔ-a-d-m
ʔaadam Adam. || *bani ʔaadam* (invar.) human being, man.
ʔaadmi pl. *ʔawaadim* **1.** human being, person. *ma-yṣiir tƐaamilni hiiči. ʔaani ʔaadmi, muu čalib.* You can't treat me that way. I'm a human being, not a dog. *jiiraanna xooš awaadim.* Our neighbors are nice people. **2.** valet, man servant. **3.** a good man, nice guy. || *ʔibin ʔawaadim* man from a good family, well-bred man.
ʔaadmiyya pl. *-aat* **1.** person (fem.), woman, girl. **2.** a good girl. *ṣiiri ʔaadmiyya; la-tsawwiin hiiči baƐad.* Be a good girl; don't do that again.
ʔ-a-δ-a-r
ʔaaδaar March.
ʔ-a-z-n-y-f
ʔaazniif variant form of the game of dominoes.
ʔ-a-s
ʔaas pl. *-aat* ace (playing cards).
ʔ-a-s-q-y
ʔaasqi pl. *-iyyaat* **1.** elastic, elastic fabric. **2.** suspenders. **3.** garters. **4.** coatrack, usually a board with hooks, attached to the wall of an entryway. Also occasionally a stand, with a mirror, for the same purpose.
ʔ-a-s-y-a
ʔaasya Asia.
*ʔaasyawi** **1.** Asian. **2.** Asiatic.
ʔ-a-š
ʔaaš a thick type of soup made from several kinds of grains and vegetables.
ʔaašči pl. *-iyya* cook.
ʔa-š-w-r
ʔaašuur Assyria.
*ʔaašuuri** **1.** Assyrian **2.** an Assyrian.
ʔ-a-f
ʔaafa see under *ʔ-w-f.*
ʔ-a-l
ʔaal, ʔaala see under *ʔ-w-l.*
ʔ-a-l-w-b-a-l-w
ʔaalubaalu (coll.) variety of large cherries resembling plums.
ʔaalubaaluwwa pl. *-aat* un. n. of *ʔaalubaalu.*
ʔ-a-l-w-č-a
ʔaaluuča (coll.) a variety of dried plums.
ʔaaluučaaya pl. *-aat* un. n. of *ʔaaluuča.*
ʔ-a-n-a
ʔaana: ʔabu l-ʔaana the one responsible, the one in charge.
ʔ-a-n-y
ʔaani I.
ʔ-a-h
ʔaah see under *ʔ-w-h.*
ʔ-a-h-y-n
ʔaahiin cast iron.
ʔ-b
ʔab pl. *ʔaabaaʔ* (for construct state, see *ʔ-b-w*) **1.** father. **2.** Father (title of a Christian priest). *l-ʔab sarkiis muu bil-kaniisa hassa.* Father Sarkis isn't in the church now.
ʔaban: ʔaban Ɛan jidd for generations. *hal-beet mulukna ʔaban Ɛan jidd.* This house has been our property for generations.
ʔ-b-b-y
ʔabbi pl. *-iyyaat* **1.** main. *ʔabbi l-maay* water main. **2.** main line (elec.). **3.** main switch, master switch (elec.).
ʔ-b-d
ʔabbad to be eternal, perpetual, to last forever. *xoo muu raƐ-itʔabbid; laazim itmuut fadd yoom.* Well you're not going to last forever; you've got to die some day.
ʔabad (limited to a few phrases) *ʔabad ma-* never. *ʔabad ma-agul-la.* I'll never tell him. *ʔila l-ʔabad* forever, to the end. *haaδa*

muxliṣ ʔila l-ʔabad. He's faithful to the end. *ma-ʔansa faḍlak* ʕ*alayya ʔila l-ʔabad.* I won't ever forget the favor you did me.

*ʔabadi** eternal, everlasting. || *n*ʕ*ikam ʔabadi* He was sentenced to life imprisonment.

ʔabadan **1.** /with neg./ never. *ʔabadan ma-yiji hnaa.* He never comes here. **2.** at all. *ma-*ʕ*indi fluus ʔabadan.* I don't have any money at all. **3.** /alone/ never, not at all. *ʔabadan! ma-aqbal itruu*ʕ *wiyyaa.* Never! I won't have you go with him. *ʔabadan! wala fakk* ʕ*alga.* Not at all! He didn't even open his mouth.

muʔabbad (limited to a few phrases) || *ma*ʕ*kuum muʔabbad* sentenced to life imprisonment. ʕ*ukum muʔabbad* a life sentence. *sijin muʔabbad* life imprisonment.

ʔ-b-d-s-x-a-n

ʔabdasxaana toilet, especially that of a mosque.

ʔ-b-δ

ʔabuδiyya type of poetry in which homonymous endings are used for three lines and *-iyya* for the fourth. Usually used in song prologue, and popular in rural areas.

ʔ-b-r

ʔubra pl. *ʔubar* **1.** needle. **2.** by extension, hypodermic syringe, and loosely, a shot, an injection. || *δa*ʕ*faan. ṣaayir ʔubra w-xeeṭ.* You're skinny. You've gotten thin as a rail (lit. needle and thread).

ʔ-b-r-g

ʔibriig pl. *ʔabaariig* pitcher (for water).

ʔ-b-ṭ

ʔubuṭ, ʔubaaṭ pl. *ʔubaaṭaat* armpit(s). *jawwa l-ʔubuṭ* **1.** underarm, armpit. **2.** under the arm. *šaayil jariidta jawwa ʔubṭa.* He's carrying his newspaper under his arm. *haaδa ʔaṭwal minna hwaaya; yxallii jawwa ʔubṭa.* That guy's a lot taller than he; he can put him under his arm. || *l-mu*ʕ*aawin xaall il-mudiir jawwa ʔubṭa.* The assistant's gotten the director under his control. *haaδa s-im*ʕ*arrfa yil*ʕ*ab šiṭranj? ʔagdar axallii jawwa ʔubṭi.* What does *he* know about playing chess? I can put him in my pocket. *ʔaṣdiqaaʔa xaššaw jawwa ʔubṭa w-xalloo ybii*ʕ *kull ʔamlaaka.* His friends got hold of him and had him sell all his property. *xašš jawwa ʔubṭa w-xallaa yiṣruf kull ifluusa* ʕ*ar-raaqiṣaat.* He got hold of him and had him spend all his money on dancers.

ʔ-b-l-y-s

ʔibliis /never with definite article/ **1.** the Devil. *ʔibliis stawla* ʕ*ala* ʕ*aqla.* The Devil has gotten control of him. **2.** (pl. *ʔabaaliis, ʔabaalisa*) devil. *haaδa ʔibliis; ma-yinġulub.* He's a devil; he can't be beaten.

¹ʔ-b-n

ʔabban to eulogize a deceased person, deliver a funeral sermon. *ʔabbana b-qaṣiida mumtaaza.* He eulogized him with an excellent poem.

taʔbiin commemoration, eulogizing. ʕ*aflat taʔbiin* commemorative celebration (in memory of a dead person).

*taʔbiini** commemorative. ʕ*afla taʔbiiniyya* commemorative ceremony.

²ʔ-b-n

ʔibin pl. *wilid* **1.** son. *ʔibni* my son, and by extension, kid, sonny. *ʔibn il-*ʕ*amm* (uncle's son) = cousin on the father's side. *ʔibn il-xaal* (uncle's son) = cousin on mother's side. *ʔibn il-ʔax* (brother's son) = nephew. *ʔibin* ʕ*araam* illegitimate son, bastard, son of a bitch, stinker. *ʔibin ga*ʕ*ba* son of a whore, son of a bitch, stinker. *ʔibin ʔabuu* (his father's son) brave, clever man. **2.** one of, one from, member of. *ʔibin ṣaffi* a member of my class. *ʔibin ṭaraf* and *ʔibn il-ma*ʕ*alla* man from the neighborhood. *ʔibin wlaayti* man from my home town. *ʔibin iθlaaθiin* a man of thirty. *ʔibn is-sabit* Jew. *ʔibin* ʕ*arab* an Arab. *ʔibin ʔawaadim* and *ʔibin* ʕ*amuula* honorable, respected, dignified man. *ʔibin nuṣṣ id-dinya* man of great influence from an important family.

³ʔ-b-n

ʔaban see under *ʔ-b.*

ʔ-b-n-w-s

ʔabanoos ebony.

ʔ-b-h

ʔubbaha splendor, luxury, ostentation.

ʔ-b-w

ʔabu **1.** (construct state of *ʔab*) father. *ʔabuu* his father. *ʔabuuk* your father. *ʔabuuya* my father. *ʔabu* followed by name of oldest son: a friendly way of addressing or speaking of a man. By extension, *ʔabu* followed by a conventional male name: a form of address among friends to a man who is not married and has no children. *ʔabuuna* (our father) respectful title for a Christian priest. **2.** owner of, possessor of, one distinguished by *ʔabu l-jaraayid* the newspaper boy, newspaper vendor. *kursi ʔabu yaddteen* arm chair. *ʔabu beet* household manager. *huwwa ʔabu beet mumtaaz. yuʕruf iš-yištiri.* He's a fine manager of household affairs. He knows what to buy. || *ʔabu j-jaʕal* dung beetle. *ʔabu j-jinneeb* crab. *ʔabu breeṣ* a type of small lizard. *ʔabu flees* miser, penny-pincher.

l-ʔabaween the parents. *ʕtiraam il-ʔabaween waajib.* Respecting the parents is a duty.

*ʔabawi** paternal, fatherly. *waajib ʔabawi* paternal duty. *ʕanaan ʔabawi* fatherly affection.

ʔubuwwa fatherhood, paternity.

ʔ-b-y

tʔabba to be careful, cautious, to proceed with caution. *laazim titʔabba min tiʕči wiyyaa tara yitʔaδδa.* You should be careful when you talk to him or he'll take offense. *laazim titʔabba fadd čam yoom w-baʕdeen ʔukul iš-ma triid.* You should watch yourself for a few days and then eat whatever you want. *laazim titʔabba mnil-barid li-ʔannak mariiδ.* You should stay out of the cold because you are sick. *ʔinta ma-titʔabba ʔilla waaʕid ykassir raasak ṣudug.* You won't learn prudence until someone really breaks your head.

*ʔabi** proud, prideful. *haaδa ma-yiqbal inhaana. nafsa ʔabiyya.* He won't take insults. He has a proud nature. *walad ʔabi* a proud boy.

ʔ-t-g

ʔatag pl. *-aat* **1.** slip. **2.** petticoat, half-slip.

ʔ-t-m

maʔtam pl. *maʔaatim* **1.** funeral procession. **2.** wake, mourning ceremony.

ʔ-θ-θ

ʔaθθaθ to furnish (a house, etc.) *da-aʔaθθiθ il-beet ij-jidiid.* I'm furnishing the new house.

tʔaθaθθ pass. of *ʔaθθaθ.*

ʔaθaaθ furniture, furnishings.

ʔ-θ-r

ʔaθθar /with *b-, ʕala*/ **1.** to affect, influence, have an effect upon. *δ-δarub ma-da-yʔaθθir bii.* Beating doesn't have any effect on him. *had-duwa ma-da-yʔaθθir biik baʕad.* That medicine doesn't have any effect on you any more. *kuθrat iš-šurub imʔaθθira ʕala naδara.* Too much drinking has affected his vision. *l-muʕallim ʔaθθar ʕala tafkiir talaamiiδa.* The teacher influenced the thinking of his students. **2.** to move, touch emotionally. *ʕčaayta ʔaθθirat biyya.* His story moved me. **3.** to anger, make mad. *δirab ʔaxuu l-iṣġayyir ʕijil w-ʔaθθarni hwaaya.* He slapped his little brother on the back of the neck and angered me very much.

tʔaθθar pass. of *ʔaθθar. l-lakka b-haθ-θoob wala tʔaθθrat bil-ġasil.* The stain in this shirt wasn't affected at all by the washing. *ʕeeni titʔaθθar biš-šamis. laazim ʔalbas manaaδir šamis.* My eyes are affected by the sun. I have to wear sunglasses. *čaan il-filim muʔlim, w-itʔaθθar bii hwaaya.* The film was sad, and he was touched very much by it. *tʔaθθar min iʕčaaytak ihwaaya.* He got very mad at your remark.

ʔaθar pl. *ʔaaθaar* **1.** track, print. *ʔaaθaar aqdaam* footprints. *ʔaaθaar aṣaabiʕ* fingerprints. **2.** trace, vestige. *nhizmaw w-ma-tirkaw waraahum ʔaθar.* They escaped without leaving a trace. *ligaw ʔaθar zarniix ib-miʕidta.* They found a trace of arsenic in his stomach. **3.** (mostly pl.) ruin, historical monument, antiquity. || *ʕilm il ʔaaθaar* archaeology. **4.** effect. *ʔaθar l-maraδ baʕda mbayyin ʕaleek.* The effect of the disease is still showing on you. *ʔila ʔaθar rajʕi.* It has retroactive effect. **5.** impression. *xiṭaaba tirak ʔaθar ʕamiiq ib-nufuusna.* His speech left a deep impression on us.

*ʔaθari** ancient, antique. *qiṭaʕ nuquud ʔaθariyya.* antique coins.

ʔaθaari (invar.) it seems, it turns out. *ʔaθaari yriiduuni ʔaskun wiyyaahum ʕatta ʔaṣruf ʕaleehum.* It seems they want me to live with them so I can spend my money on them. *ʕabaali jiiraanna muʕallim; ʔaθaari δaabuṭ.* I thought my neighbor was a teacher; it turns out he's an officer. *ʔaθaariihum min wlaayatna.* It seems they're from our city.

taʔθiir effect. *had-duwa ma-ʔila ʔay taʔθiir ʕala maraδak.* This medicine has no effect on your illness. *ziyaart ir-raʔiis raʕ-ykuun ʔilha taʔθiir qawi ʕala ʕalaaqaatna.* The president's visit will have a pronounced effect on our relations.

taʔaθθur emotion, agitation. *t-taʔaθθur da-ybayyin ʕala wučča.* Emotion is showing on his face.

maʔθuur handed down, traditional. *qawl maʔθuur* a traditional saying.

muʔaθθir **1.** touching, moving. *quṣṣat il-filim muʔaθθira.* The story of the movie is touching. **2.** effective. *hal-bunduqiyya muʔaθθira min masaafat xamis miit matir.* This rifle is effective at a distance of five hundred meters.

ʔ-θ-l
ʔaθal tamarisk.
ʔ-θ-m
ʔiθam (*i ʔiθim*) to sin. *ʔiθamit ʕind aḷḷa*. You sinned in the eyes of God.
ʔiθim pl. *ʔaaθaam* sin.
ʔ-θ-y-r
ʔaθiir ether.
ʔ-j-r
ʔajjar 1. to rent, let, lease. *ʔajjarni d-dukkaan maala*. He rented me his shop. *ʔajjar-li beeti b-xooš siʕir*. He leased my house for me at a good price. 2. to rent, hire, lease. *ʔajjarna balam muddat saaʕteen*. We rented a boat for two hours.
tʔajjar pass. of *ʔajjar*. *maʕa l-ʔasaf, il-beet itʔajjar il-baarḥa*. I'm sorry, the house was rented yesterday.
staʔjar to hire, rent, charter. *minu staʔjar beetak?* Who rented your house?
ʔajir reward, recompense. *ʔajrak ʕaḏiim ʕind ʔaḷḷa*. Your reward will be great in Heaven.
ʔujra pl. *ʔujuur* 1. rent, rental, hire. 2. pay (rate), wage (rate). *šgadd ʔujurtak bil-yoom?* How much is your pay per day? *š-šarika qarrirat idzayyid ʔujuur il-ʕummaal*. The company decided to increase the wages of the workers. 3. fee, rate, fare. *ʔujrat il-p̣aaṣ* bus fare. *šgadḍ il-ʔujra ʕala hal-maktuub biṭ-ṭiyyaara?* How much is the airmail rate on this letter? *ʔujuur id-diraasa* tuition.
ʔiijaar rent, rental. *ʔaku yammkum beet lil-ʔiijaar?* Is there a house for rent near you?
maʔjuur hired, bribed, bought. *ʕamiil maʔjuur lil-istiʕmaar*. a hired agent of imperialism. *haaδa waaḥid maʔjuur*. He's in the pay of someone.
muʔajjir pl. *-iin* landlord, lessor.
mistaʔjir pl. *-iin* tenant, renter, lessee.
ʔ-j-r-r
ʔaajirr (coll.) hard, overfired brick(s).
ʔaajirra pl. *-aat* a hard, overfired brick.
ʔ-j-l
ʔajjal 1. to postpone, delay, defer, put off. *ʔajjalt is-safra maalti l-isbuuʕ ij-jaay*. I postponed my trip till next week. *ma-ʕindi fluus. tigdar itʔajjil-li hal-qiṣiṭ?* I haven't got any money. Can you defer this payment for me? *ʔajjilaw ij-jundiyya maalti ʔila s-sana j-jaaya*. They deferred my military service till next year.
tʔajjal pass. of *ʔajjal*. *l-ijtimaaʕ itʔajjal ʔila yoom il-xamiis*. The meeting's been postponed to Thursday.
li-ʔajil, min ʔajil for the sake of, because of. *δaḥḥeet ib-waδiifti l-ʔajlak*. I sacrificed my job for your sake. *min ʔajil haaδa, ma-nigdar inšaġġlak*. Because of this, we can't employ you.
ʔajal pl. *ʔaajaal* (appointed) time, instant of death. *ʔajala jaay*. His time is coming. *l-ʔaajaal b-iid ʔaḷḷa*. Men's lives are in God's hands.
taʔjiil pl. *-aat* delay, postponement.
muʔajjal 1. postponed, delayed, deferred. 2. sum of money arranged before marriage to be paid to the wife in the event of divorce.
ʔ-j-n
ʔujun: ʔujun ʔujun bit by bit, slowly, carefully, gently.
ʔ-j-y
ʔija (*yiji*) var. of *jaa*, which see under *j-y*.
ʔ-ḥ-d
l-ʔaaḥaad (pl.) the units (math.).
l-ʔaḥḥad, yoom il-ʔaḥḥad Sunday.
ʔaḥḥad someone, anyone. *ma-aku ʔaḥḥad ihnaa*. There isn't anyone here. *maḥḥad, laḥḥad* no one, nobody. *maḥḥad xaabarak*. No one called you. *laḥḥad yiḥči*. Don't anyone say anything.
see also *w-ḥ-d*.
ʔ-ḥ-n-a
ʔiḥna we.
ʔ-x
ʔax pl. *ʔuxwa* (in construct *ʔuxwat-, ʔuxuut-*), *ʔixwaan, xuwwaan* (for construct state, see *ʔ-x-w*) 1. brother ‖ *l-ʔax* polite term for a stranger. *minu l-ʔax w-mineen?* Who is the gentleman and where is he from? 2. brother (in a religious or ideological sense). *l-ʔixwaan il-muslimiin* The Moslem Brotherhood. *ʔaxi* (familiar form of address) friend, buddy, pal.
ʔ-x-t
ʔuxut pl. *xawaat* 1. sister. ‖ *l-ʔuxt* (polite form of address or way of referring to a woman of approximately the same age as the speaker; approx.:) the lady. 2. /with feminine nouns/ mate, twin, the same as. *haay ʔuxut sayyaarti*. This one is exactly like my car. ‖ *štireetha ʔuxt il-balaaš*. I bought it for next to nothing. 3. Baghdad boil, a long-term skin eruption which leaves a large, round, flat depression on healing.
ʔ-x-δ
ʔaxaδ (*yaaxuδ ʔaxiδ*) 1. a. to take (something). *ʔuxuδ išgadd-ma triid*. Take as

much as you want. || *l-xayyaaṭ ʔaxað-li ʔoolči.* The tailor took my measurements. *ʕind yaa rassaam ʔaxaðit har-rasim?* Which photographer's did you have this picture taken at? *xal-naaxuð haṭ-ṭariiq. haaða ʔaqṣar.* Let's take this road. It's shorter. *raḥ-aaxuð hal-šuġuḷ ʕala ʕaatqi.* I will take this job on myself. *ʔaxað-la faal.* He told his fortune. *nṭii ʕašir ifluus ḥatta yaaxuð-lak faal.* Give him ten fils so he will tell your fortune. *ʔuxuð girfa. ṣaar loo laa?* Face the facts. Did it happen or not? *ʔuxuð girfa. ʔawwal-ma xallaṣ il-kulliyya, ṣaar ʔustaað.* Face it. As soon as he finished college, he became a professor. **b.** to take, take away. *minu ʔaxað qalami?* Who took my pencil? *ʔilḥag-la. l-ṃaay ʔaxaða.* Go get him. The current's taken him. *ʔaḷḷa yaaxuð ruuḥak!* May God take your life! *ʔaxað waḥda min banaathum.* He married one of their daughters. *ʔaxðoo jundi.* They took him into the army. *ʔaxað wujihha,* or *ʔaxað bakaaratha.* He took her virginity. || *xalli nruuḥ naaxuð min xaaṭra.* Let's go ease his mind (of grief, anger, etc.). **2.** to take along. *raḥ-aaxðak wiyyaaya.* I'll take you with me. **3.** to get, receive, obtain. *ʔaxaðit jawaab loo baʕad?* Did you get an answer yet? *ʔaxaðit xabar raḥ-yiji.* I got word he's coming. *šgadd taaxuð bil-isbuuʕ?* How much do you get per week? *l-yoom naaxuð maʕaašna.* We get our pay today. *šgadd ʔaxaðit bil-ḥisaab?* How much did you get in arithmetic? *r-raadyo maali ma-da-yaaxuð miṣir.* My radio won't get Egypt. *ʔaxaðit ḥeefak minna?* Did you take your revenge on him? *laazim itruuḥ il-daaʔirt il-bariid w-taaxð ir-ruzma b-nafsak.* You have to go to the Post Office and pick up the package yourself. **4.** to accept, take. *ʔuxða ʕala gadd ʕaqla.* Accept him for what he is. *la-taaxuð kalaama raas.* Don't take what he says seriously. *min gilit iš-šuġuḷ ma-da-yimši, ʔaxað ʕala nafsa w-ziʕal.* When I said the work's not moving, he took it personally and got mad. *ma-agdar atfaaham wiyyaa. ma-yaaxuð w-ma-yinṭi.* I can't reach an understanding with him. He won't give and take. **5. a.** to take, require. *ʕabaali ʔaxaḷḷiṣ haš-šaġḷa b-saaʕa laakin ʔaxðat nahaar kaamil.* I thought I'd finish this job in an hour but it took a full day. **b.** to take up, occupy, take. *hal-meez yaaxuð makaan ihwaaya.* This desk takes up a lot of room. *raḥ-ʔaaxuð iṣ-ṣadir waḥdi w-artaaḥ.* I'm going to take the front seat to myself and be comfortable. **6. a.** /with *b-*/ (to begin) to take on, acquire. *ðall naaʕim ʔila ʔan ṣaar ʕumra ʔarbaaṭaʕaš w-axað biṭ-ṭuul.* He remained small until he was fourteen years old and then he took on some height. *da-yaaxuð bil-ʕuruð li-ʔan marta tʔakkla zeen.* He's getting fat because his wife feeds him well. **b.** to adopt, follow. *ʔuxuð ib-raʔya li-ʔan yiftihim.* Follow his opinion because he knows what he is talking about. **c.** to take up, take on, acquire, absorb. *l-ḥaayiṭ maaxið ruṭuuba.* The wall's taken up moisture. *l-ʔakil bil-quuṭiyya jaayif li-ʔan ʔaxað hawa.* The food in the can is rotten because it got some air in it. **7. a.** to catch, contract, get. *ʔaxaðit barid li-ʔan rijaʕit il-baarḥa bil-leel bil-muṭar.* I caught cold because I came back last night in the rain. *ma-ʔaʕtiqid ʔaxðat; laazim inwaddiiha lil-faḥal marrt il-lux.* I don't think she took; we'll have to take her to the stud again. **b.** to take hold, catch hold, catch on. *j-jidri maali ma-ʔaxað.* My smallpox vaccination didn't take. *ʕuudt iš-šixxaaṭ ma-da-taaxuð. yimkin imballila.* The match won't strike. Maybe it's wet. **8.** to engage in, accomplish, make, take. *ʔuxuð-lak farra bis-suug ʔila ʔan axaḷḷiṣ šuġḷi.* Take a turn in the market till I finish my business. *baʕad-ma yugʕud imnin-noom, yaaxuð išnaaw.* After he gets out of bed, he does push-ups. **9.** to take up, assume, strike (a pose, position, etc.) *ʔuxuð waðiʕ istiʕdaad min tiḥči wiyya ð-ḍubbaaṭ.* Assume a position of attention when you speak to officers. *ʔuxuð ḥaðarak minna.* Be on your guard against him. || *min ymurr ið-ðaabuṭ, ʔuxuð-la salaam.* When the officer passes by, give him a salute. **10.** to take, catch, get the better of. *ʔaxaðni flaaḥa mlaača. ðall yiḥči nuṣṣ saaʕa wala xallaani ajaawba.* He took me by storm. He kept talking a half hour and didn't give me a chance to answer him. *ʔaxaðni kraaxa; ma-nṭaani majaal ʔaḥči wala čilma.* He took me by storm; didn't give me a chance to say a word. *ʔaxaðni ʕala ġafla* or *ʔaxaðni ġafuḷ.* He took me by surprise. *ʔaxaðni n-noom min činit da-ʔaqra j-jariida.* Sleep overcame me while I was reading the newspaper. *ʔaxðatha l-ʕabra.* She was overcome by sobbing.

ʔaaxaδ to blame, censure. *la-tʔaaxδa. baʕda jidiid.* Don't blame him. He's still inexperienced.

nʔixaδ pass. of *ʔaxaδ.*

ttixaδ **1.** to take. *ttixaδna kull it-tadaabiir iδ-δuruuriyya.* We took all the necessary measures. **2.** to take on, assume, adopt. *ttixaδ mawqif muʕaadi lil-ḥukuuma.* He took a position unfriendly to the government. *l-ḥukuuma ttixδat qaraar xaṭiir.* The government adopted an important decision. **3.** to take as, employ as, use as. *ttixaδ maraδa ḥijja ḥatta ma-yruuḥ liš-šuġul.* He used his sickness as an excuse not to go to work. *ttixaδni ʔaala l-taḥqiiq ʔaġraaδa.* He used me as a tool to achieve his ends.

ʔaxiδ **1.** taking, receiving, acceptance. **2.** taking away, removal. || *ʔaxiδ w-radd* dispute, controversy, debate. *haaδa ma-bii ʔaxiδ w-radd.* There's no argument about that. *l-qaδiyya been ʔaxiδ w-radd.* The matter is in dispute.

muʔaaxaδa censure, blame. *bala mu-ʔaaxaδa, raḥ-aδṭarr aturkak.* No offense, but I'm going to have to leave you.

ʔ-x-r

ʔaxxar **1.** to delay, make late, hold up. *δall yiḥči w-ʔaxxarni nuṣṣ saaʕa.* He kept talking and delayed me a half hour. *l-muṭar ʔaxxar taqaddumna.* The rain slowed our advance. *ʔariid il-ʔiijaar waaḥid biš-šahar. la-ykuun itʔaxxra.* I want the rent the first of the month. You're not to hold it up. **2.** to postpone, put off. *ʔaxxraw il-ijtimaaʕ ʕala muudi.* They postponed the meeting on my account. *dizz il-maktuub il-yoom; la-tʔaxxra ʔila baačir.* Send the letter today; don't put it off till tomorrow.

tʔaxxar **1.** to be delayed. *wuṣuul iṭ-ṭiyyaara tʔaxxar nuṣṣ saaʕa.* The plane's arrival was delayed a half hour. **2.** to become late, get late, be late. *l-wakt itʔaxxar. xalli nruuḥ.* It's gotten late. Let's go. *l-muṭar itʔaxxar has-sana.* The rain is late this year. *leeš itʔaxxarit halgadd? l-filim bida hassa.* Why'd you take so long? The movie's begun now. **3.** /with *ʕan*/ to fall behind. *tʔaxxar ʕan jamaaʕta li-ʔan itmarraδ is-sana l-faatat.* He fell behind his group because he got sick last year.

ʔaaxir **1.** pl. *ʔawaaxir* last, end, last portion. *ʔaaxir iš-šahar* the last (part) of the month. *hal-ḥači ma-ʔila ʔaaxir.* There's no end to this talk. **2.** last, final. *haay ʔaaxir marra raḥ-agul-lak.* This is the last time I'm going to tell you. *ʔaaxir kalaam, diinaareen.* The final price is two dinars. **3.** latest. *sayyaartak ʔaaxir moodeel.* Your car's the latest model. || *ʔaaxir šii, gal-li ma-yriid hal-waδiifa.* Finally, he told me he didn't want the job. *ʔila ʔaaxirihi* etc., and so on. *l-baarḥa bil-leel sikarna, w-liʕabna qmaar, riḥna lil-kallačiyya, ʔila ʔaaxirihi.* Last night we got drunk, played cards, went to the red light district, and so on.

ʔaaxar fem. *ʔuxra* another. *haaδa mawδuuʕ ʔaaxar.* That's another matter. *r-rijjaal il-ʔaaxar ma-gaal šii.* The other man didn't say anything. || *min wakt il-ʔaaxar, inruuḥ lil-masbaḥ.* From time to time, we go swimming.

laax (contr. of *l-ʔaaxar*) other. *ʔarjuuk, inṭiini čaay laax.* Please give me another tea.

lux (contr. of *l-ʔuxra*) other. *raawiini ʔiidak il-lux.* Show me your other hand. *šifta marra lux.* I saw him another time.

l-ʔaaxra the hereafter, the world to come.

ʔaxiir **1.** last. *ʔinta daaʔiman ʔaxiir waaḥid yooṣal.* You're always the last one to arrive. **2.** latest. **3.** rearmost. **4.** rear, back, rear section. *ma-aku mukaan ihnaa. ʔugʕud bil-ʔaxiir.* There's no room here. Sit in the rear.

ʔaxiiran **1.** finally, eventually. *ʔaxiiran, štira s-sayyaara t-tanta.* Finally, he bought the convertible. **2.** lately. *š-šahr il-faat, iš-šuġuḷ ma-čaan zeen, laakin ʔaxiiran itḥassan.* Last month, business wasn't good, but lately it's picked up.

taʔxiir pl. *-aat* delay, postponement.

muʔaxxar **1.** delayed, postponed. **2.** sum of money agreed upon before marriage to be paid to the wife in the event of divorce.

mitʔaxxir **1.** late, delayed. *leeš hiiči mitʔaxxir?* Why are you so late? **2.** backward, underdeveloped. *ʔahil hal-manṭiqa kulliš mitʔaxxriin.* The people of this area are very backward.

ʔ-x-ṭ-b-w-ṭ

ʔuxṭubuuṭ pl. *-aat* octopus.

ʔ-x-w

ʔaxu /construct state of *ʔax*/. **1.** brother. *ʔaxuu* his brother. *ʔaxuuk* your brother. *ʔaxuuya* my brother. **2.** (by extension) pal, buddy, friend. **3.** /with masculine nouns/ mate, equal, like. *šifit beet ʔaxu beeti tamaaman!* I saw a house exactly like my house! *haaδa fadd xooš walad. ma-*

yinligi ʔaxuu. He's a real nice guy. One like him can't be found. || *štireena hal-beet ʔaxu l-balaaš.* We bought this house dirt cheap.

xuuya (familiar form of address) pal, buddy, friend.

*ʔaxawi** brotherly, fraternal. *ɛubb ʔaxawi* **1.** brotherly love, deep friendship between two men. **2.** platonic friendship with a girl.

ʔixaaʔ brotherhood, fraternity. *jam-ɛiyyat il-ʔixaaʔ il-waṭani* Society of National Brotherhood.

ʔuxuwwa friendship, brotherhood. *la-tsawwi hiiči ʔašyaaʔ ʔiδa triid ʔuxuw-watna tistamirr.* Don't do that sort of thing if you want our friendship to last.

taʔaaxi friendship. *t-taʔaaxi beenkum yɛajjib.* The friendship between you is amazing.

ʔ-d-a-t

ʔadaat, see *ʔ-d-w.*

ʔ-d-b

ʔaddab **1.** to rear properly, bring up right, teach manners. *yiδ̣har ʔahlak ma-ʔaddibook.* Apparently your family didn't bring you up right. **2.** (by extension) to teach a lesson. *ʔiδ̣a ma-tiskut, tara aji ʔaʔaddbak.* If you don't shut up, I'll come and teach you a lesson. **3.** to punish, discipline. *min yiji ʔabuuk ʔagul-la yʔaddbak.* When your father comes I'll tell him to punish you.

tʔaddab to be or become polite. *tʔaddab, lak! la-tiɛči hiiči giddaam in-niswaan.* Watch your manners, you! Don't talk like that in front of women.

ʔadab pl. *ʔaadaab* **1.** literature. *kulliyyt il-ʔaadaab* College of Arts. **2.** manners, breeding, upbringing. *qaliil il-ʔadab* lacking in manners. **3.** (pl. *-aat*) toilet.

ʔadabsizz pl. *-iyya* mannerless, crude, boorish, impolite.

*ʔadabi** literary. *majalla ʔadabiyya* literary magazine.

ʔadabiyyan morally, socially. *ʔinta ʔadabiyyan masʔuul ɛan ʔibnak.* You're morally responsible for your son. *ʔiδa ma-tsallim ɛaleeha, ʔadabiyyan ma-ṣaɛiiɛ.* If you don't say hello to her, it's not socially correct.

ʔadiib pl. *ʔudabaaʔ* writer, author, literateur.

taʔdiib discipline. *majlis taʔdiib* disciplinary board.

muʔaddab well-mannered, well brought up. *walad kulliš muʔaddab* a very well brought up boy.

ʔ-d-b-x-a-n

ʔadabxaana pl. *-aat* toilet, rest room, w.c.

ʔ-d-m

ʔaadmi see under *ʔ-a-d-m.*

ʔ-d-w

ʔadaat pl. *ʔadawaat* **1.** tool, piece of equipment, and by extension, a person being used as a tool. || *ʔadaat it-taɛriif* the definite article (gram.). **2.** piece, part (of a machine, etc.). *ʔadawaat iɛtiy-aaṭiyya* spare parts.

ʔ-d-y

ʔadda **1.** to lead. (see also *wadda* under *w-d-y.*) *haṭ-ṭariiq ween yʔaddi?* Where's this road lead? *ɛamalak haaδa yʔaddi ʔila nataaʔij xaṭiira.* This action of yours will lead to serious consequences. **2.** to carry out, discharge, do, fulfill. *š-šurṭi ʔadda waajba.* The policeman did his duty. *has-sayyaara tʔaddi l-maṭluub.* This car will do what you require. **3.** to perform, execute, render. *l-ɛaras ʔadda t-taɛiyya l-ʔamiir il-liwaaʔ.* The guard rendered a salute to the major general. || *ʔadda l-yamiin il-qaanuuniyya.* He took the oath of office. **4.** to pay, hand over. *ʔiδa ma-tʔaddi l-ifluus, ma-axalliik tiṭlaɛ.* If you don't pay the money, I won't let you leave.

ʔ-δ-a

ʔiδa **1.** if. *ʔiδa siʔal ɛanni, gul-la raaɛ lis-siinama.* If he asks about me, tell him I went to the movie. **2.** whether, if. *ʔiδa yištiriiha ʔaw ma-yištiriiha, tinbaaɛ θaani yoom.* Whether he buys it or doesn't buy it, it'll be sold some other day.

ʔilla ʔiδa except that, unless. *raɛ-aštiki ɛaleek ʔilla ʔiδa nṭeetni fluusi l-yoom.* I'll take you to court unless you give me my money today.

ʔ-δ-r

ʔiδra see under *δ-r-y.*

¹ʔ-δ-n

ʔiδan (*i*) to give permission. *minu ʔiδan-lak itxušš ib-hal-ġurfa* ? Who gave you permission to enter this room?

ʔaδδan to give the call to prayer. (see also *w-δ-n*). *ʔaδδan iδ̣-δ̣uhur loo baɛad?* Has he called the noon prayer yet?

staʔδan to ask permission. *laazim tistaʔδin gabuḷ-ma tiṭlaɛ.* You should ask permission before you leave.

ʔiδin permission, authorization. *b-ʔiδn illaah* God willing, with God's permission.

ʔiδin (f.) pl. *ʔiδaanaat* ear. /the

sing. can be used for plural also, eg./ *zirfaw ʔiδinha.* They pierced her ears. || *nṭii ʔiδn iṭ-ṭarša.* Pay no attention to him (lit., give him the deaf ear).

ʔiδaan pl. *-aat* ear /the sing. can be used for sing. and pl./

ʔaδaan pl. *-aat* a call to prayer (see also *w-δ-n*).

maʔδuuniyya pl. *-aat* permission, authorization.

²ʔ-δ-n

ʔiδan (formal equivalent of *laɛad*) therefore, then. *ʔiδan ma-raḥ-tiji?* Then you're not going to come? *ʔiδan, ɛala hal-ḥači, ma-raḥ-tigdar tištuġuḷ.* Therefore, from what's been said, you won't be able to work.

ʔ-δ-y

ʔaδδa **1.** to hurt. *hiddni; da-tʔaδδiini.* Let me go; you're hurting me. **2.** to harm, do harm. *ʔiδa ma-tismaɛ kalaama, yʔaδδiik.* If you don't listen to what he says, he can do you harm. **3.** to damage, do damage. *l-muṭar ʔaδδa z-zariɛ has-sana.* Rain damaged the crops this year. **4.** to molest, annoy, irritate, trouble, pester. *ʔiδa tḍall itʔaδδiiha, yjuuz itɛawwirha.* If you keep on pestering her, you might injure her.

ʔaaδa = *ʔaδδa. diir baalak la-tʔaaδi j-jaahil.* Careful you don't hurt the kid. *jiiraani da-yʔaaδiini hwaaya.* My neighbor's annoying me a lot.

tʔaδδa **1.** to get hurt, hurt oneself. *tʔaδδeet ihwaaya min haš-šaraaka.* I've hurt myself a lot in this partnership. **2.** to feel hurt, feel sorry. *tʔaδδeet ihwaaya min simaɛit xabar faṣlak.* I was very sorry to hear about your getting fired. **3.** to be hurt, suffer. *tʔaδδa hwaaya b-šabaaba.* He suffered a lot in his youth. *šuġḷi tʔaδδa hwaaya ṭuul ramaḍaan.* My business has suffered a lot all Ramadan.

ʔaδa **1.** harm, damage, injury. **2.** trouble, grief, misfortune. **3.** annoyance, trouble, irritation.

ʔaδiyya pl. *-aat* trouble, annoyance.

muuδi, muʔδi **1.** harmful, damaging, injurious, noxious. **2.** hateful, spiteful, mean, offensive. **3.** annoying, irksome, irritating, troublesome.

ʔ-r-t-w-a-z

*ʔirtiwaazi** artesian. *biir ʔirtiwaazi* artesian well.

ʔ-r-θ

ʔiriθ = *wiriθ,* which see under *w-r-θ.*

ʔ-r-x

ʔarrax to date, affix the date to. *la-tinsa tʔarrix il-maktuub gabuḷ-ma ddizza.* Don't forget to date the letter before you send it.

taariix pl. *tawaariix* **1.** date. *taariix il-yoom* today's date. *ʔila hat-taariix* to date, to this date. **2.** history. *taariix ḥayaat* life story, biography.

*taariixi** historical. *mawqiɛ taariixi* historical site.

muʔarrix pl. *-iin* historian, chronicler.

ʔ-r-d-n

l-ʔardun Jordan. *nahr il-ʔardun* the Jordan River. *šarq il-ʔardun* Trans-Jordan.

*ʔarduni** **1.** Jordanian. **2.** a Jordanian.

ʔ-r-z

ʔarz cedar, cedar tree.

ʔ-r-ḍ

ʔarḍ **1.** earth, ground. *l-ʔarḍ* the earth. **2.** (pl. *ʔaraaḍi*) land, piece of land.

*ʔarḍi** **1.** ground. *ṭaabiq ʔarḍi* ground floor. **2.** (pl. *-iyya*) electrical ground, ground wire.

ʔarḍiyya pl. *-aat* **1.** floor. **2.** ground, background (of a fabric, painting, etc.). **3.** charge for use of floor space, storage charge.

ʔarḍa (pl. only) termites.

ʔ-r-q

ʔiraq (*i ʔaraq*) to have or get insomnia. *ʔiraqit il-baarḥa bil-leel w-ma-gdarit anaam.* I got insomnia last night and couldn't sleep.

ʔaraq insomnia.

ʔ-r-m-n

*ʔarmani** pl. *ʔarman* **1.** Armenian, **2.** an Armenian.

ʔ-r-n-b

ʔarnab pl. *ʔaraanib* rabbit.

ʔ-r-w-l

ʔarwal pl. *ʔaraawil* monitor lizard, uran.

ʔ-r-y-l

ʔaryal pl. *-aat* aerial, antenna.

ʔ-z-z-a

ʔazzaači pl. *-iyya* pharmacist, druggist.

ʔazzaxaana pl. *-aat* pharmacy, drug store.

ʔ-z-m

tʔazzam to become critical. *l-ḥaala tʔazzmat baɛad ṣuquuṭ il-wizaara.* The situation got critical after the fall of the cabinet.

ʔazma pl. *-aat* crisis.

ʔ-s-t-a-δ

ʔustaaδ pl. *ʔasaatiδa* **1.** professor. **2.** master. *ʔustaaδ biš-šiṭranj* a master at chess. *ʔustaað bil-maqaam* a master in singing the *maqaam*. **3.** sir (a polite form of address to an educated man). || *daftar il-ʔustaað* ledger.

ʔ-s-t-r-a-l

ʔusturaalya Australia.

*ʔusturaali** **1.** Australian. **2.** an Australian. **3.** draft horse. **4.** (as a contemptuous form of address) dumb ox.

ʔ-s-t-f-n-y-k

ʔastafaniik creosote.

ʔ-s-t-w-a-n

ʔustuwaana pl. *-aat* **1.** cylinder. **2.** phonograph record.

ʔ-s-d

staʔsad **1.** to become strong, rugged, tough. *hal-walad ič-čibiir istaʔsad bil-imɛalla.* This big kid has become the toughest in the neighborhood. **2.** to achieve power, influence. *haaða staʔsad min izzawwaj bitt il-mudiir.* That guy's sitting pretty since he married the director's daughter.

ʔasad pl. *ʔusuud* **1.** lion. **2.** (by extension) a brave man.

ʔ-s-l

ʔasal rush, a variety of marsh grass used in weaving.

ʔ-s-m

ʔisim, see *s-m-y.*

ʔ-s-r

ʔisar (*i ʔasir*) **1.** to capture. *l-ɛadu ʔisar miyya min jinuudna.* The enemy captured one hundred of our soldiers. **2.** (by extension) to captivate. *ʔisrata b-jamaalha.* She captivated him by her beauty.

ʔassar to capture. *ʔassarna faṣiil min jinuud il-ɛadu.* We captured a platoon of the enemy's soldiers.

tʔassar to be captured. *waaɛid min ḍubbaaṭna tʔassar.* One of our officers was captured.

ʔasir captivity.

ʔasiir pl. *-iin, ʔasra* captive, prisoner. *ʔasiir ɛarub* prisoner of war.

ʔusra pl. *ʔusar* clan, dynasty, family.

ʔ-s-s

ʔassas **1.** to lay a foundation. *šwakit raɛ-itʔassis w-tibni?* When are you going to lay the foundation and start building? **2.** to found, establish, set up. *ʔassas jamɛiyya lil-ʔasaatiða.* He founded a society for professors.

tʔassas to be founded. *n-naadi tʔassas is-sana l-faatat.* The club was founded last year.

ʔuss exponent of a power (math.). *ɛašra ʔuss ixmuṣṭaɛaš* ten to the fifteenth power.

ʔasaas **1.** foundation, basis. *ɛala l-ʔasaas* on the basis of. *min ʔasaas* from the beginning, thoroughly. **2.** (pl. *-aat*) foundation (of a building, etc.).

*ʔasaasi** basic, fundamental. *s-sabab il-ʔasaasi* the basic reason. || *ɛajar ʔasaasi* cornerstone.

taʔsiisaat facilities, utilities (plumbing and wiring, etc.).

ʔ-s-f

ʔisaf (*a ʔasaf*) to feel sorry, be sad *ʔisafit ihwaaya min simaɛit ib-maraḍak.* I was very sorry to hear of your sickness. *ṭiradta w-baɛdeen ʔisafit ɛala ɛamali.* I fired him and then regretted my act.

tʔassaf = *ʔisaf. tʔassafit min simaɛit ib-naqlak.* I was sorry to hear of your transfer.

ʔasaf regret. || *maɛa l-ʔasaf, b-kull ʔasaf* unfortunately.

ʔaasif sorry, regretful. *ʔaani ʔaasif laakin ma-agdar asawwi šii.* I'm sorry but I can't do anything.

muʔsif regrettable. *haaða ɛaadiθ muʔsif.* That's a regrettable accident.

mitʔassif sorry, regretful. *mitʔassif, ma-ɛindi xurda.* Sorry, I don't have any change.

ʔ-s-f-n-j

ʔisfanj sponge.

ʔ-s-f-n-y-k

ʔasfaniik creosote.

ʔ-s-q-f

ʔasqaf pl. *ʔasaaqifa* bishop.

ʔ-s-k-l

ʔaskala pl. *-aat* **1.** scaffold, scaffolding. **2.** pier, wharf. **3.** pumpkin. *šijar ʔaskala* pumpkin.

ʔ-s-y

maʔsa pl. *maʔaasi* tragedy. (see also *w-s-y*).

ʔ-š-a-r-p

ʔišaarp pl. *-aat* kerchief, woman's scarf.

ʔ-š-r

ʔaššar **1.** to check, indicate, mark. *ʔaššir ɛal-mawaadd illi tistilimha.* Check the items you receive. *qiis ib-hal-masṭara w-ʔaššir ib-qalam basma.* Measure with this ruler and make a mark with a lead pencil. *jibit-lak miswaddat il-maktuub ɛatta tʔašširha gabuḷ-ma niṭbaɛa.* I brought you the draft of the letter to O.K. before we type it. **2.** to indicate, point to, point out. *ʔaššir-li ɛar-rijjaal ʔilli šifta* *da-yxušš bil-beet il-baarḥa.* Point out the man you saw entering the house yesterday. *ʔubrat il-booṣla da-tʔaššir ʕaš-šimaal.* The compass needle is pointing toward the north. **3.** to signal, gesture. *lamma ʔaššir-lak, ʔibdi tsajjl il-ḥači.* When I signal you, start to record the talk. *ma-yigdar yiḥči bila-ma yʔaššir.* He can't talk without making gestures. **4.** to note, make note of. *ʔaššir il-mulaaḥaðaat il-ʔagul-ilk-iyyaaha w-qaddim-li biiha taqriir.* Make a note of the comments I give you and submit a report about them to me.

ʔišaara pl. *-aat* signal, sign. *ʔišaarat ðarub* multiplication sign. *ʔintiini ʔišaara min itkuun ḥaaðir.* Give me a signal when you are ready.

muʔaššir pl. *-iin* pointer, indicator.

ʔ-š-w

ʔašu, ʔašuu **1.** it seems, it looks as if, it appears. *l-kutub weenha? ʔašu ma-aku.* Where are the books? Looks like there aren't any. *ʔašu ma-da-tbayyin hal-ayyaam.* It seems you're not coming around these days. *ʔašu miθil ḥissha.* It seems just like her voice. **2.** (interjection, approx.:) well then, okay then, well now. *haaða ġalaṭ? ʔašu ʔinta jaawub.* That's wrong? Okay then, you answer it. *ʔašu taʕaal w-xalli ʔafḥaṣa.* Now come here and let me examine it. *ʔašu ʔugʕud ihnaa ḥatta ʔalabbsak qundara.* Well sit down here so I can put shoes on you.

ʔ-ṣ-ṭ-a

ʔusṭa pl. *-awaat* master of a trade, also, form of address for such a man. *ʔusṭa bin-nijaara* master carpenter. || *ʔusṭa ʕumraan* a variety of dates.

ʔ-ṣ-ṭ-w-a-n

ʔisṭiwaana pl. *-aat* **1.** cylinder. **2.** phonograph record.

ʔ-ṣ-ṭ-w-r

ʔusṭuura see under *ṣ-ṭ-r*.

ʔ-ṣ-ṭ-w-l

ʔusṭuul pl. *ʔaṣaaṭiil* (naval) fleet.

ʔ-ṣ-l

tʔaṣṣal to become firmly rooted, deep-rooted, ingrained. *l-ʕaada tʔaṣṣilat bii min čaan iṣġayyir.* The habit became ingrained in him when he was young.

ʔaṣil pl. *ʔuṣuul* **1.** origin, source, original form or state. *ʔaṣl il-iḥčaaya* the story in its original form. || *bil-ʔaṣil* originally, in the beginning. *has-sayyaara bil-ʔaṣil čaanat maalti.* This car was originally mine. *mnil-ʔaṣil* to begin with, from the beginning. *l-paaysikil čaan maksuur imnil-ʔaṣil. muu ʔaani kisarta.* The bicycle was broken from the beginning. I wasn't the one who broke it. **2.** foundation, basis. **3.** one who counts, important one. *la-tġaar minhum. ʔinta l-ʔaṣil.* Don't be jealous of them. You're the important one. **4.** lineage, stock, descent, pedigree. **5.** (pl. only) customs, traditions, proprieties. *ḥasb il-ʔuṣuul* properly, according to the rules. **6.** (pl. *ʔaaṣaal*) plant, seedling, set.

ʔaṣlan actually, as a matter of fact. *ʔaṣlan ma-činit ib-baġdaad il-baarḥa.* Actually I wasn't in Baghdad yesterday. *ma-raḥ-adfaʕ šii. ʔaṣlan kull it-talaamiið gaalaw nafs iš-šii.* I'm not going to pay anything. Actually, all the students said the same thing.

*ʔaṣli** **1.** original. *n-nusxa l-ʔaṣliyya* the original copy. *t-taayaraat il-ʔaṣliyya maal sayyaara* the original tires on a car. **2.** genuine, authentic. *ġaraað ʔaṣliyya* genuine parts. **3.** real. *čaððaab ʔaṣli* a real liar. *ʔakil ʕiraaqi ʔaṣli* real Iraqi food. **4.** primary, initial. *waaḥid ʔaṣli* low low, the lowest gear on a 4-speed truck transmission, and, by extension, 1st gear on a 4-speed auto transmission.

ʔuṣuuli in accordance with traditions, rules, established practice. *la-tiqlaq abadan. ʕamalak ʔuṣuuli kulliš.* Don't worry at all. Your action is quite proper.

ʔaṣiil of pure or noble origin. *ḥṣaan ʔaṣiil* a purebred horse.

mitʔaṣṣil deep-rooted, deep-seated. *l-ʕaada mitʔaṣṣla bii.* The habit is deep-rooted in him.

ʔ-ṭ-r

ʔiṭaar pl. *-aat* (picture) frame.

ʔ-ṭ-r-q

ʔaṭraqči pl. *-iyya.* rug merchant.

ʔ-ṭ-l-ṣ

ʔaṭlaṣ pl. *ʔaṭaaliṣ* atlas, collection of maps.

*ʔaṭlaṣi** Atlantic. *l-muḥiiṭ il-ʔaṭlaṣi* the Atlantic Ocean.

ʔ-ṭ-l-n-ṭ

*ʔaṭlanṭi** Atlantic. *l-muḥiiṭ il ʔaṭlanṭi* the Atlantic Ocean.

ʔ-ġ-a

ʔaġa pl. *-awaat* **1.** rich landowner. **2.** lord, master (as form of address). *ʔaġaati* My lord. **3.** better, superior. *huwwa ʔaġaatak biš-šiṭranj.* He's your superior at chess. *la-tiḥči ʕalayya hiiči. ʔaani ʔaġaatak.*

Don't talk about me like that. I'm a better man than you.

ʔ-ġ-š-m

ʔaġšamči pl. *-iyya* night watchman who guards until midnight, when he is relieved by the *ṣabbaḥči*.

ʔ-f-f

tʔaffaf to moan, groan, complain. *kull-ma ʔanṭii šwayya šuġul, yitʔaffaf.* Whenever I give him a little work, he moans and groans.

ʔuff, ʔooff (an exclamation of dismay or pain, approx.:) oh. *ʔuff, yaa rabbi! šloon wiyya hal-walad?* Oh, my God! What are we going to do with this boy? *ʔooff, ʔooff, raasi da-ymawwitni!* Oh, oh, my head is killing me! || *ʔooff minnak! raḥ-ahijj.* You're a pain in the neck! I'm leaving.

ʔ-f-r-y-q

ʔafriiqya Africa.

*ʔafriiqi** **1.** African. **2.** an African.

ʔ-f-ġ-a-n

l-afġaan **1.** the Afghans. (coll.). **2.** Afghanistan.

*ʔafġaani** **1.** Afghanistani, Afghan. **2.** an Afghanistani, an Afghan.

ʔ-f-ġ-a-n-s-t-a-n

ʔafġaanistaan Afghanistan.

ʔ-f-q

ʔufuq horizon. || *ʔufqa waasiʕ.* His horizon is wide, i.e.; He has imagination.

*ʔufqi** horizontal.

ʔ-f-l

*ʔafli** late, planted at the end of the season.

ʔ-f-n-d-y

ʔafandi pl. *-iyya* **1.** gentleman, a non-Westerner wearing Western clothes. **2.** a jocular or ironic form of address. *ʔafandi, ma-tištuġuḷ ʕaad!* Get to work, Mac!

ʔ-f-y-w-n

ʔafyuun opium.

ʔ-q-l-m

ʔiqliim pl. *ʔaqaaliim* **1.** territory, region. **2.** province, district, administrative subdivision.

ʔ-g-r

ʔagar: ʔagar . . . ʔagar whether . . . or, either . . . or. *ʔagar minna ʔagar minnak, ʔaani ʔariid ifluusi.* Whether it's from him or from you, I want my money.

ʔ-k-d

ʔakkad **1.** to confirm, make sure about, check on. *ʔakkid ʕalee yiktib il-maktuub.* Make sure that he writes the letter. **2.** to confirm. *ʕali ʔakkad-li l-xabar.* Ali confirmed the story for me. **3.** to give assurance. *ʔakkad-li ʔanna ma-yʕurfa.* He assured me that he doesn't know him.

tʔakkad **1.** to be assured. *tʔakkad, ʔaani ma-ʔili ʕalaaqa bil-mawḏuuʕ.* Rest assured, I have no connection with the matter. **2.** to be confirmed. *hassa l-xabar itʔakkad.* The news has been confirmed now. **3.** to be or become sure, certain, convinced, to reassure oneself, convince oneself. *tʔakkad gabuḷ-ma tiḥči.* Be sure of yourself before you speak out.

taʔkiid pl. *-aat* **1.** assurance, confirmation. *kull hat-taʔkiidaat w-ma-tṣaddig?* All these assurances and you don't believe it? **2.** follow-up, check (on a previous letter). || *bit-taʔkiid* certainly, assuredly, surely. *raḥ-aji saaʕa xamsa bit-taʔkiid.* I'll come at five o'clock without fail. *b-kull taʔkiid! maḥḥad yistiḥiqq tarfiiʕ ʔakθar minna.* Certainly! No one deserves promotion more than he does.

ʔakiid certainly, surely. *ʔakiid; haaḏa ma-yinraad-la ḥači.* Certainly; this needs no discussion. *haaḏa ʔakiid raḥ-yuġlub.* That one's certainly going to win.

muʔakkad certain, sure, confirmed. *haaḏa šii muʔakkad.* That's a sure thing.

mitʔakkid positive, certain, sure. *ʔinta mitʔakkid huwwa lli ḏirabak jeeb?* Are you sure he's the one who picked your pocket?

ʔ-k-d-n-y

ʔikkidinya loquat.

ʔ-k-l

ʔakal (*yaakul ʔakil*) (active participle *ʔaakil* or *maakil*) **1.** to eat. *ma-akalit šii ṭuul in-nahaar.* I haven't eaten a thing all day long. *maʔkuul il-ʕaafya.* May it be eaten in health. || *saaʕtak taakul išʕiir.* Your watch is running slow (lit. eating barley). **2.** to eat up, consume, take. *l-qaaṭ yaakul iθlaθ yaardaat.* The suit will take three yards. *laazim tidfaʕ id-deen li-ʔan il-faayiz raḥ-yaakul il-beet.* You should pay the debt because the interest will take the house. || *bij-jahannam; ʕasa naarhum taakul ḥaṭab-hum.* To hell (with them); let them kill each other off (let their fire consume their firewood). **3.** to gnaw, eat away, corrode, erode. *z-zinjaar maakil il-buuri.* Rust has eaten away the pipe. *l-ṃaay maakil ij-juruf ihwaaya minnaa.* The water's eaten away the bank extensively here. *l-ʔuxut maakla kull wučča.* The Baghdad boil has covered his whole face.

|| *ḥčaaytak da-taakul ib-galbi.* Your remark is gnawing at my heart. *laazim ʔanṭii fluusa; haaδa ʔakal raasi.* I've got to give him his money; he's insistent as hell (lit.: ate my head.) **4.** to take, get (something unpleasant). *ʔakal il-ʔihaana w-sikat.* He took the insult and kept quiet. *ʔaxuuya lḥag-li, tara ʔakalitha.* Help me out, friend, or I've had it. *raḥ-taakulha ġeer ʔakla.* You're going to get a real comeuppance. **5.** to capture, take. *l-billi yaakul il-ʔikilli.* The ace beats the deuce. *j-jundi maali raḥ-yaakul il-iḥṣaan maalak.* My pawn will capture your knight. || *muu ʕeeb taakul ḥaraam?* Don't you think it's wrong to be so dishonest? *ʔakal ḥaqqi. ma-nṭaani kull ill-aṭlubh-iyyaa.* He cheated me out of what was mine. He didn't give me all that he owes me.

ʔakkal to feed. *la-tinsiin itʔakkliin ij-jaahil.* Don't forget to feed the baby.

tʔakkal to be corroded, eaten away. *č-čaamulluġ tʔakkal mniz-zinjaar.* The fender was eaten away by rust.

nʔikal pass. of *ʔakal. l-ʔakil kulla nʔikal.* The food's all been eaten.

ʔakil **1.** eating, dining. *ġurfat ʔakil* dining room. *xaašuugat ʔakil* tablespoon. **2.** food.

ʔakla pl. *-aat* **1.** meal, repast. **2.** dish, bit of food.

ʔakkaal pl. *-iin, -a* big eater, glutton.

ʔakuul pl. *-iin* hearty eater, gourmand.

maʔkuulaat (pl. only) foodstuffs, food. *maʔkuulaat muʕallaba* canned foods.

ʔ-k-l-l-y

ʔikilli deuce (in native Iraqi card games).

ʔ-k-w

ʔaku there is, there are. *ʔaku xamsiin diinaar ib-jeebi.* There's fifty dinars in my pocket. *ʔaku ʔaḥḥad bil-beet?* Is there anyone at home? || *ʔaku ʕinda* he has. *ʔaku ʕindak qalam?* Do you have a pencil?

ma-aku there isn't, there is no, there is nothing. *staʕjil, ma-aku wakit.* Hurry, there's no time. *ma-aku ġeer baačir aruuḥ ʕaš-šurṭa.* There's nothing else to do but to go to the police tomorrow. *da-ykattiluun ib-han-naas w-ma-aku.* They're slaughtering those people and there's no end to it.

š-aku what is there? what? || *š-aku b-? š-aku ʕind-?* what about? what is there about? what is wrong with? *ṭ-ṭabiib raad yuʕruf š-aku bii.* The doctor wanted to know what was ailing him. *š-aku ʕindak mistaʕjil?* Why are you hurrying? *š-aku ma-aku?* What's been going on lately? How have you been?

ʔ-l-a

ʔila **1.** to, toward. *waṣṣalni ʔila hnaa.* He brought me here. **2.** up to, as far as. *liḥagni ʔila d-daaʔira.* He followed me as far as the office. **3.** till, until, up to. *ʔila hassa, ma-jaa.* Up to now, he hasn't come. *ʔajjalna l-ijtimaaʕ ʔila baačir.* We postponed the meeting till tomorrow. || *ʔila ʔaaxirihi* and so on, et cetera. *ʔila ʔan* until. *ntaδra ʔila ʔan yirjaʕ.* Wait for him until he comes back.

ʔ-l-b

ʔilba milk from a fresh cow or goat, boiled to a thick consistency.

ʔ-l-j

ʔalij, ʔalič base down (of the animal knuckles used in boys' games.). *č-čaʕab maali wugaf ʔalij.* My bone landed base down. || *huwwa fadd waaḥid balaaʔ. kull-ma δδibba, yoogaf ʔalič.* He's a real hot shot. Every time you throw him, he lands on his feet.

ʔ-l-č-ġ

ʔalčaġ pl. *ʔalaačiġ* rotten, low-down, no-good.

[1]*ʔ-l-f*

ʔalif pl. *ʔaalaaf, ʔuluuf.* thousand.

[2]*ʔ-l-f*

ʔalif name of the first letter in the alphabet. *l-ʔalifbaaʔ* the alphabet.

[3]*ʔ-l-f*

ʔilaf (a *ʔalif*) **1.** to be or become tame. *baʕad xams isniin, il-ʔasad ʔilaf.* After five years, the lion grew tame. **2.** to be or become accustomed to, habituated to, used to. *min ʔawwal nahaar, ʔilafit ḥayaat ij-jibaal.* From the first day, I got used to the life in the mountains. *yoom, yoomeen, w-yiʔlaf ʕaleekum.* A day or so and he'll get used to you.

ʔallaf **1.** to form, make up, put together. *xalli nʔallif lujna tidrus il-muškila.* Let's form a committee to study the problem. **2.** to compose, compile, write. *ʔallafit iktaab ʕan il-ʕiraaq.* I wrote a book about Iraq.

tʔallaf to be formed, made up, compiled, to consist. *l-lujna mitʔallfa mnil-mudiir w-muʕaawna.* The committee consists of the director and his assistant.

ʔtilaf to harmonize, agree, go well, get along well. *ma-raḥ-asaafir li-ʔan ma-aʔtilif wiyyaahum.* I'm not going to go because I don't get along with them.

ʔulfa close association, intimate relationship.

ʔaliif **1.** tame. *ʔasad ʔaliif* a tame lion. **2.** domestic, domesticated. *ʕaywaanaat ʔaliifa* domestic animals. **3.** friendly. *jaahil ʔaliif* a friendly baby.

ʔtilaaf **1.** harmony, concord, agreement. **2.** (pl. *-aat*) political coalition.

*ttilaafi** coalition. *wizaara ttilaafiyya* coalition government.

maʔluuf **1.** familiar, accustomed, habituated. **2.** usual, customary, familiar (thing or action). *wujuud ij-jinuud wid-dabbaabaat biš-šawaariʕ ṣaar šii maʔluuf.* The presence of soldiers and tanks in the streets has become a usual thing.

muʔallif pl. *-iin* author, writer.

[1]*ʔ-l-l-a*

ʔilla **1.** except. *dazzeethum kullhum ʔilla ʔaani.* You sent them all except me. *ma-ašuufa ʔilla marra bil-isbuuʕ.* I don't see him except once a week. **2.** just, only. *ʔilla ʔariid il-p̣aaysikil maali. b-eeš ʔalʕab?* I just want my bicycle. What'll I play with? *ma-aqbal. ʔilla ʔariid qalami nafsa.* I don't want (this). I only want my own pen. *ʔilla ʔaštiri han-nooʕ. ma-aštiri ġeera.* I'll only buy this type. I won't buy other than it. *laa. ʔilla ʔalif diinaar.* No. It's nothing but a thousand dinars. *yaʕni ʔilla hal-qaaṭ loo ma-yṣiir?* In other words either this suit or nothing doing? **3.** (denoting inevitability or necessity, approx.:) must. *waḷḷa ma-yṣiir. ʔilla tiji.* No, that can't be. You've got to come. *šifta bij-jaadda w-ma-ʕaačaani. haaδa ʔilla zaʕlaan.* I saw him on the way and he didn't speak to me. He must be mad. *yaʕni ʔilla twaṣṣix il-gubḅa min tilʕab?* Do you have to dirty the room when you play? *xalli ašuufa, ʔilla amawwta mnil-baṣiṭ.* Let me see him, and I'll beat him to death! *bass ašuufa ʔilla ʔabuṣṭa!* As soon as I see him I'll sure beat him up good.

ʔilla ʔiδa unless. *raʕ-aštiki ʕalee ʔilla ʔiδa nṭaani l-ifluus il-yoom.* I'm going to sue him unless he gives me the money today.

w-ʔilla, willa or, or else, otherwise. *tiskut willa ʔaji amawwtak.* You be quiet or I'll come kill you. *triid haaδa willa δaak?* Do you want this one or that? *ma-ʕindi fluus, willa čaan jeet wiyyaa-kum.* I've got no money, or else I would've come with you. *ma-staʕmal id-duwa maala, willa čaan ṭaab.* He didn't take his medicine, or otherwise he'd've gotten well. *ġeer ʔaxuu l-mudiir? willa haaδa š-yraffʕa?* Isn't it that his brother is the director? How else would he get promoted?

[2]*ʔ-l-l-a*

ʔaḷḷa God, Allah. *yaa ʔaḷḷa! šloon wiyyaak?* My God! what'm I going to do with you? *la-ddiir baal. xalliiha yamm aḷḷa.* Don't worry. Leave it in God's hands. *ʔaḷḷa ʕaleek la-tgul-la.* By God, don't you tell him. *ʔaḷḷa šaahid, ma-qibal yaaxuδ ifluus.* As God is my witness, he wouldn't take any money. || *ʕala ʔaḷḷa, ʕal-aḷḷa.* Can't complain. (an answer to *šloonak?*, *šloon siʕʕtak?*, etc.) *beet ʔaḷḷa* 1. the Kaaba. 2. (by extension) Mecca.

baḷḷa (< *bi-ʔaḷḷa* by God) **1.** please. *baḷḷa ma-jjuuz minni? ʔaani taʕbaan.* Won't you please leave me alone? I'm tired. *baḷḷa ma-tnaawušni l-miliʕ?* Would you please pass me the salt? **2.** (an expression of surprise) really? my gosh! *baḷḷa? w-išloon laʕad ma-ygul-li?* Really? Then how come he didn't tell me? || *baḷḷa ʕaleek* my gosh, my word. *baḷḷa ʕaleek! šifta š-sawwa biyya baʕad taʕabi wiyyaa?* My gosh! Did you see what he did to me after all I did for him? *baḷḷa ʕaleek! š-gal-lak?* Oh come on! What did he tell you?

maašaaḷḷa (< *maa šaaʔa ḷḷaah* whatever God willed) **1.** good, thank goodness. *maašaaḷḷa, ṣiʕʕtak itʕassinat.* Good, your health has improved. **2.** (an exclamation of surprise) amazing! *maašaaḷḷa! yaahu l-yiji yṣiir waziir.* Amazing! Anyone who comes along can become a minister.

smaḷḷa (< *ʔisim ʔaḷḷaah* the name of God, a phrase to ward off potential evil, to express solicitousness and occasionally, admiration.) *smaḷḷa! xoo ma-tʕawwarit?* God save you! You didn't get hurt, did you? *smaḷḷa! biʕiid iš-šarr ʕanna.* Heaven forbid. I hope he'll be all right. *smaḷḷa ʕalee, ṣaxxan išwayya!* Poor thing, he's gotten a slight fever! *smaḷḷa yaaḅa, sloon ibnayya ʕilwa!* God, man, what a pretty girl!

nšaaḷḷa (< *ʔin šaaʔa ḷḷaah* if God wills) God willing, if possible, it's to be hoped. *nšaaḷḷa tṣiir waziir.* You'll become a minister, I hope. (Often a mere mechanical phrase when speaking of a plan or happening in the near or distant future.)

nšaaḷḷa raḥ-aštiri sayyaara l-yoom. I'm planning to buy a car today. (Sometimes indicating an intentional vagueness of one's own plans.) *tiji baačir? nšaaḷḷa.* Are you coming tomorrow? I might.

waḷḷa (< *w-ʔaḷḷaah* by God) **1.** definitely, really. *waḷḷa ma-aqbal ʔaqall min miit diinaar.* I really won't accept less than one hundred dinars. *waḷḷa, ma-aððakkar.* Gosh, I don't remember. **2.** (as a mere expletive) well, uh, umm. *waḷḷa, ʔabuuya baʕda mariið.* My father's still sick. **3.** (an expression of surprise) really? my gosh! *waḷḷa? ṣudug inqibal bij-jaamiʕa?* Really? Did he actually get accepted in the university?

yaḷḷa (< *yaa ʔaḷḷa*) **1.** (exclamation) oh God! *yaḷḷa, yaḷḷa! ḥaṣṣalit waðiifa zeena w-ʔahli yirduuni ʔatrukha.* Oh my God! I got a good job and my family wants me to leave it. **2.** come on, go on, hurry up. *yaḷḷa, ʕali, xalli nruuḥ!* Come on, Ali, let's go! *di-yaḷḷa, xal-naakul.* Oh come on, let's eat. *di-yaḷḷa haaða muu kattaal!* Oh come now, he's not a killer! **3.** then. *nriidha tkammil il-kulliyya yaḷḷa tidzawwaj.* We want her to finish college then get married. *min ʕiraf ʔaani ʔaxuuk yaḷḷa ḥiča wiyyaaya.* When he learned I'm your brother, then he talked to me. *nṭeeta diinaar yaḷḷa qibal.* I gave him a dinar, then he accepted. **4.** just, just barely. *l-ifluus il-ʕindi yaḷḷa tkaffi.* The money I've got will just do. *baʕadni yaḷḷa bideet. la-tistaʕjil.* I just started. Don't be in a hurry.

ḥayyaḷḷa (< *ḥayya ʔaḷḷa* God present, grant.) anything at all, anyone at all. *da-ywaððifuun ḥayyaḷḷa; l-ʕinda ša-haada wil-ma-ʕinda.* They're hiring just anyone; those who have a degree and those who don't. *nṭiini ḥayyaḷḷa hal-mawjuud. l-ḥajim muu muhimm.* Give me whatever's available. The size isn't important. *l-loon ma-yifruq. ḥayyaḷḷa.* The color doesn't make any difference. Anything. *triid iqmaaš min nooʕ muʕay-yin loo ḥayyaḷḷa?* Do you want a particular kind of cloth or just anything?

ʔ-l-l-w-l

ʔaḷḷuuḷ (a derogatory term for God) *š-itgul-la l-ʔaḷḷuuḷ illi yinṭi fluus il-hiiči naas?* What would you say to a God that enriches such people?

ʔ-l-l-y

ʔilli (relative pronoun) **1.** who, which, that. *minu lli gal-lak?* Who's the one who told you? *ʔuxð il-qalam ʔilli triida.* Take the pencil that you want. **2.** whoever, whichever, whatever. *ʔilli ywaafuq, yirfaʕ ʔiida.* Whoever agrees, raise his hand.

ʔ-l-m

ʔallam to cause pain to (someone), to pain, hurt, grieve. *manðar il-majruuḥiin ʔallamni kulliš.* The sight of the wounded caused me great pain. *ḥčaayta ʔallimatni hwaaya.* His remark hurt me a lot. *j-jariḥ da-yʔallimni.* The wound is hurting me.

tʔallam to suffer pain. *tʔallamit min simaʕta yiḥči hiiči ʕan il-laajiʔiin.* I was grieved to hear him talk like that about the refugees. *tʔallamit kulliš min simaʕit ib-xabar wafaata.* I was deeply pained when I heard the news of his demise.

ʔalam pl. *ʔaalaam* pain, suffering, agony.

ʔaliim painful, grievous, sad.

muʔlim painful, sore, grievous, sad.

mitʔallim in pain, suffering, grieved, saddened, hurt.

ʔ-l-m-a-ẓ

ʔaḷmaaẓ (coll.) diamonds(s).

ʔaḷmaaẓa pl. *-aat* diamond.

ʔaḷmaaẓa the root of a variety of the taro plant, resembling ginger root in appearance.

ʔ-l-m-a-n

l-ʔaḷmaan the German people, the Germans.

*ʔaḷmaani** pl. *ʔaḷmaan* **1.** German. **2.** a German.

ʔaḷmaaniya Germany.

ʔ-l-m-n-y-w-m

ʔalaminyoom aluminum.

ʔ-l-h

ʔilaah pl. *ʔaaliha* god, deity. *yaa ʔilaahi!* My God! *ʔilaah il-ḥarb* the god of war.

ʔilaaha pl. *-aat* goddess.

*ʔilaahi** divine, of God. *ġaðab ilaahi.* divine wrath.

ʔaḷḷaah. God, Allah. *ʔaḷḷaah yinṭiik il-ʕaafya.* God give you strength. (Said to someone carrying a heavy load, or engaged in strenuous or difficult work.) *ʔaʕuuðu bi-llaah.* God forbid (lit. I take shelter with God). *qasaman bi-llaah, ma-aʕruf.* I swear by God I don't know. *li-llaah darra, šloon šaaʕir!* My God what a poet! (lit. his achievement is due to God). *l-ḥamdu li-llaah* thank God, praise God. *l-ḥamdu li-llaah, ṣiḥḥti zeena.* I'm in good health, thank you. *subħaan aḷḷaah* (lit., praise the Lord, an expression of surprise) my God, my goodness. *subħaan aḷḷaah, l-ʕaam caan miflis w-hassa zangiin.* My God, last year he was broke, and now he's rich. *subħaan aḷḷaah ʕala haj-jamaal.* My goodness what beauty! *subħaan aḷḷaah ʕala hač-čiδib!* My God what a lie! *subħaan aḷḷaah, l-ma-ʕinda waaṣṭa, ma-yimši šuġḷa.* My God, anyone without pull won't get anywhere.

maašaaḷḷa (lit. whatever God intend, an expression of surprise) good, amazing. *maašaaḷḷa ʔibni nijaħ ib-kull id-duruus.* Great! My son passed in all subjects. *maašaaḷḷa! haaδa šloon yṣiir waziir?* Amazing! How can that guy become a minister?

nšaaḷḷa If God wills, God willing. *nšaaḷḷa, raħ-aruuħ lee baačir.* God willing, I'm going to go see him tomorrow. *nšaaḷḷa tinjaħ.* I hope you pass.

b-ismillaah in the name of God. *gabuḷ-ma taakul, guul b-ismillaah.* Before you eat, say "In the name of God."

waḷḷaahi (< *wa-ʔaḷḷaahi* by God) = *waḷḷa,* which see under ²*ʔ-l-l-a.*

ʔaḷḷaahumma Oh God. *ʔaḷḷaahumma ʔuxuδ ruuħa.* Oh God kill him! || *ʔaḷḷaahumma ʔilla ʔiδa* that is, unless. *raħ-agδ̣i ṣ-ṣeef kulla hnaa; ʔaḷḷaahumma ʔilla ʔiδa xilṣat ifluusi.* I'm going to spend the whole summer here; that is unless my money runs out.

ʔ-l-w-y-š

ʔilweeš = *leeš,* which see under *l-y-š.*

ʔ-m-b-r-a-ṭ-w-r

ʔimbraaṭoor pl. *-iyya* emperor.

*ʔimbraaṭoori** imperial.

ʔimbraaṭooriyya pl. *-aat* empire.

ʔ-m-p-y-r

ʔampeer pl. *-aat* ampere.

ʔ-m-r

ʔumar (*u ʔamur*) to order, command, bid, direct. *l-mudiir ʔumarni ʔaṭbaʕ hal-maktuub.* The director ordered me to type this letter. *l-lujna ʔumrat ib-ṭarda.* The committee ordered his discharge. || *tuʔmur* (lit., you command) a polite acknowledgement of an order, approx.: yes sir. *tuʔmur. hassa ʔaṭbaʕa.* Yes sir. I'll type it now.

ʔammar to give authority. *minu ʔammarak ʕaleena?* Who set you over us?

tʔammar to behave imperiously, be domineering, throw one's weight around. *bass itraffaʕ, gaam yitʔammar ʕaleena.* As soon as he got promoted, he began to lord it over us.

tʔaamar to plot, conspire. *tʔaamraw ʕala ħayaat il-waziir.* They plotted against the life of the minister.

ʔtumar ib-ʔamur to obey, take orders. *ma-yiʔtumur ib-ʔamur ʔaħħad.* He won't take orders from anyone.

ʔamur pl. *ʔawaamir* **1.** order, command, directive, instruction. *sawweetha ħasab ʔamrak.* I did it according to your order. || *b-ʔamrak* (polite reply to an order, approx.:) Yes, sir! Just as you say! *jawwa ʔamri* at my disposal. *ṣiiġt il-ʔamur* (gram.) imperative mood. **2.** (pl. *ʔumuur*) matter, affair, concern, business. || *b-ʔawwal il-ʔamur* in the beginning, at first. || *ybayyin giδa ʔamra.* Looks like it's all over for him. *š-agdar asawwi? ʔamri l-aḷḷa.* What can I do? My fate is up to God.

ʔimaara pl. *-aat* principality, emirate.

ʔamiir pl. *ʔumaraaʔ* **1.** prince, emir. **2.** commander, one who gives orders, leader. || *ʔamiir liwaaʔ* military rank corresponding to American major general.

ʔamiira pl. *-aat* princess.

*ʔamiiri** state, government. *ʔarδ̣ ʔamiiriyya* state land.

muʔaamara pl. *-aat* plot, conspiracy.

maʔmuur pl. *-iin* **1.** subordinate, one who takes orders. *ʔinta l-ʔaamir w-aani l-maʔmuur ib-had-daaʔira.* You're the boss and I'm the one who takes orders in this office. **2.** one delegated authority, official. *maʔmuur il gumrug* customs official. *maʔmuur il-markaz* the chief of a police station. *maʔmuur bariid* postmaster.

maʔmuuriyya pl. *-aat* assignment, mission.

mitʔaamir pl. *-iin* conspirator.

muʔtamar pl. *-aat* conference, convention, congress.

stimaara pl. *-aat* form, blank.

ʔ-m-r-k

tʔamrak to become Americanized. *min rooħta l-ʔamriika, tʔamrak.* Since his trip to America, he's become Americanized.

ʔamriika, ʔameerka America.

*ʔamriiki** pl. *ʔamriikaan* American.

*ʔameerki** pl. *ʔameerkaan* American.

*ʔamriikaani** pl. *ʔamriikaan* American.

*ʔameerkaani** pl. *ʔameerkaan* American.

ʔ-m-z-g

ʔumzug pl. *-aat* cigarette holder.

ʔ-m-s

ʔamis yesterday. *ʔawwal ʔamis* day before yesterday.

ʔ-m-l

ʔammal **1.** to raise hopes, give reason to hope. *ʔammalni tooṣal is-sayyaara raas iš-šahar.* He gave me hope the car would come at the beginning of the month. **2.** to put off, keep waiting, ask to wait. *min ṭaalabta bil-ifluus, ʔammalni ʔila ʔan yaaxuð maʕaaša.* When I dunned him for the money, he asked me to wait until he gets his salary. *riḥit ʕalee ʕala šuġuḷ w-ʔammalni l-baačir.* I went to him for work and he put me off until tomorrow. **3.** to hope, expect. *walaw ma-qaari zeen, yʔammil yinjaḥ.* Although he hasn't studied well, he expects to pass.

tʔammal **1.** to hope. *ʔatʔammal il-beet yʕijbak.* I hope you'll like the house. **2.** to expect. *ʔatʔammal ṣadiiqi yooṣal baačir.* I expect my friend to arrive tomorrow. **3.** to wait, be patient. *tʔammal išwayya. la-tistaʕjil.* Wait a while. Don't be in a hurry.

ʔamal pl. *ʔaamaal* hope, expectation.

ʔ-m-m

ʔamm (*i ʔamm*) to lead in prayer. *minu raḥ-yʔimm ij-jamaaʕa l-yoom?* Who's going to lead the congregation in prayer today?

ʔammam to nationalize. *l-ḥukuuma ʔammimat ṣinaaʕat is-simant.* The government nationalized the cement industry.

tʔammam to be nationalized. *kull il-bunuug itʔammimat ib-hal-balad.* All the banks in this country were nationalized.

ʔumm pl. *ʔummahaat* **1.** mother. || *l-ḥaaja ʔumm il-ixtiraaʕ.* Necessity is the mother of invention. **2.** the woman with, the one with. *ʔumm il-xubuz* the baker woman. *ʔumm θoob il-ʔaxḍar* the one in the green dress. *siččiina ʔumm il-yaay.* switchblade knife. *jaamxaana ʔumm baabeen* china closet with two doors.

ʔumma pl. *ʔumam* people, nation. *l-ʔumam il-muttaḥida.* The United Nations.

ʔummaaya pl. *-aat* **1.** diminutive of *ʔumm* mother. **2.** matriarch, woman in charge.

ʔummiyya illiteracy, analphabetism.

*ʔummi** **1.** illiterate. **2.** an illiterate.

*ʔumami** international.

ʔumuuma **1.** motherhood. **2.** maternity.

ʔamaam **1.** in front of, ahead of. *l-firqa l-moosiiqiyya da-timši ʔamaam ij-jeeš.* The band's marching ahead of the army. *l-mulaazim yimši ʔamaam jinuuda.* The lieutenant walks at the head of his troops. **2.** in front of, in the presence of. *ma-ariidak tiḥči hiiči ḥači ʔamaam ij-jihaal.* I don't want you to talk that way in front of the children. *l-ḥaadiθa ṣaarat ʔamaam iʕyuuni.* The accident occurred right before my eyes. **3.** front. *baawiʕ lil-ʔamaam.* Look to the front. Face forward. *xal-nigʕud bil-ʔamaam.* Let's sit down front. || *ʔila l-ʔamaam — sir!* Forward — march!

*ʔamaami** front, forward. *l-xuṭuuṭ il-ʔamaamiyya* the front lines. *ġurfa ʔamaamiyya* front room.

ʔimaam pl. *ʔaʔimma,* and *ʔimaami* pl. *-iyya* **1.** imam, religious official. **2.** prayer leader.

[1]*ʔ-m-m-a*

ʔamma **1.** as for, as to, as far as . . . is concerned. *ʔamma ʔaani, raḥ-akuun mašġuuḷ baačir.* As for me, I'll be busy tomorrow. **2.** but. *ʔamma hal-muxtabar bass l-istiʕmaal il-muʕallimiin.* But this lab is just for the teachers' use. **3.** (an exclamation of surprise or astonishment, approx.:) my! well now! *ʔamma tamaam ṭilaʕ miθil-ma gilit.* My! He sure did turn out like you said. *ʔamma haay ṣudug xooš nukta.* Well now that's really a good joke! *ʔamma tamaam! šloon ma-jatti ʕala baali?* Well of course! How come I didn't think of it? **4.** what, what a. *ʔamma jamaal!* What beauty! *ʔamma ʕyuun!* What eyes!

[2]*ʔ-m-m-a*

ʔimma either. *ʔariid ʔimma haaða loo ðaak.* I want either this or that.

[1]*ʔ-m-n*

ʔiman (*a ʔamin, ʔamaan*) to be safe from, be secure from. *š-šurṭa lizmat hal-ʔašqiyaaʔ win-naas ʔimnaw šarra.* The police caught that thug and people are safe from his wickedness.

ʔamman **1.** to assure, ensure, guarantee, safeguard. *ḥaṣṣal ʕala šahaada w-ʔamman mustaqbala.* He got a degree and ensured his future. **2.** to place in safekeeping, to leave in trust. *ʔamman garaaḍa ʕindi.* He left his things in my keeping. *xalli nʔammin jinaṭna bil-maḥaṭṭa.* Let's check our bags in the station. **3.** to assure, reassure, to set (someone's) mind at ease. *ʔammanni min ṭaraf il-ʔwaḍiifa.* He reassured me about the position. *ʔammanni kullši yixlaṣ baačir.* He assured me everything would be done tomorrow. **4.** /with *ɛala/* to confirm, corroborate, bear out. *kull il-mawjuudiin ʔammnaw ɛala ɛčaayta.* All those present confirmed his statement. **5.** to get insurance, take out insurance. *ʔamman ɛala maxzana δidd il-ɛariiq.* He insured his warehouse against fire. **6.** to believe, be assured, trust, have faith. *min šaafni, yaḷḷa ʔamman ʔaani b-baġdaad.* When he saw me, then he believed I was in Baghdad. *yiδhar ma-tʔammin b-iɛčaayti.* It seems you don't believe my story. *ma-yʔammin ib-aɛɛad.* He doesn't trust anyone. *ma-da-yʔammin min ɛummaala. ma-yxalli fluus ɛal-meez ʔabadan.* He doesn't trust his workers. He doesn't ever leave money on the table. *ʔammin, ma-raɛ-ʔaɛči l-ʔaɛɛad.* Rest assured, I'm not going to talk to anyone. **7.** to feel safe. *ma-da-yʔammin yruuɛ waɛda bil-leel.* He doesn't feel safe going out alone at night.

ʔaaman to believe. *haaδa ma-yʔaamin ib-ʔaḷḷa.* He doesn't believe in God. *hassa ʔaamanit illi git-lak iyyaa ṣudug?* Now do you believe that what I told you is true?

tʔamman **1.** to be placed in safekeeping. *jinaṭi ma-yimkin titʔamman bil-maṭaar ʔakθar min yoom waaɛid.* My suitcases can't be left in safekeeping at the airport more than one day. **2.** to rest assured, have peace of mind. *tʔamman ma-aġuššak.* Rest assured that I won't cheat you. **3.** to be trustworthy, reliable, honest. *ʔard ʔagul-la fadd sirr. tiɛtiqid yitʔamman?* I want to tell him a secret. Do you think he is trustworthy? *la-tiššaarak wiyyaa. haaδa ma-yitʔamman.* Don't go in partnership with him. He can't be trusted.

ʔamin **1.** safety. **2.** security, peace. *l-ʔamm il-ɛaamm* public safety. *majlis il-ʔamin* the Security Council (of the United Nations). || *šurṭat il-ʔamin* security forces, investigative branch of the Iraqi police system.

ʔamaan security, safety. || *fiimaanillaa.* Good-bye (lit., in God's protection). **2.** secure, safe. *maaku ɛaaja tuqful il-baab; id-dinya ʔamaan.* No need to lock the door; the area's safe. *d-dinya ʔamaan.* All is well.

ʔamiin **1.** trustworthy, reliable, honest. **2.** (pl. *ʔumanaaʔ*) one entrusted with something, trustee, custodian, guardian, keeper. *ʔamiin iṣ-ṣanduuq* **1.** treasurer. **2.** cashier. *ʔamiin il-maktaba* custodian of the library. *ʔamiin il-matɛaf* curator of the museum. *ʔamiin ɛaamm* secretary general. *ʔamiin il-ɛaaṣima* an appointed officer in the Baghdad city government with limited administrative responsibility.

ʔamaana **1.** trustworthiness, reliability. **2.** honesty. **3.** confidence, trust, good faith. **4.** (pl. *-aat*) something deposited in trust, trust, charge. **5.** office or position of trust, trusteeship. *ʔamaant iṣ-ṣanduuq* office or position of treasurer or cashier.

taʔmiin **1.** assurance. **2.** safeguarding. **3.** assurance, reassurance. **4.** insurance. **5.** (usually pl.) *taʔmiinaat* security, deposit, surety bond.

ʔiimaan faith, belief. || *b-iimaanak* by your faith, on your honor. *b-iimaanak š-gal-lak?* By your faith, what did he tell you?

maʔmuun **1.** trustworthy, reliable. *ma-nigdar nitruk ij-jihaal wiyyaa. haaδa waaɛid ma-maʔmuun.* We can't leave the children with him. He's not trustworthy. **2.** safe, secure. *nigdar inxayyim ihnaa; hal-manṭaqa maʔmuuna.* We can camp here; this area is safe.

²ʔ-m-n

ʔaṃaan (an expression of enthusiastic approval of a singer) great, wonderful. *ʔaṃaan, ʔaṃaan, yaa ɛeeni!* Great, great!

ʔ-m-w

*ʔamawi** **1.** Ummayyad. **2.** an Ummayyad.

ʔ-m-y-b-a

ʔamiiba pl. *-aat* amoeba.

ʔ-m-y-r-a-l

ʔamiiraal pl. *-iyya* admiral.

ʔ-n

ʔan (with pronominal suffix, generally *ʔin-*, masc.s. *ʔinn-*) that. *ma-daam ʔiɛna bil-ḅang, mnil-aɛsan ʔan niṣruf ič-čikuuk.* As long as we're in the bank, it's best that we cash the checks. *ttifqaw ʔan yirɛuun lis-siinama suwa.* They agreed to go to the movies together. *gaal ʔinhum ma-yɛibbuun ydirsuun.* He said that they don't like to study. *gaal ʔinna raajiɛ baɛad nuṣṣ saaɛa.* He said that he's coming back after a half hour. *gal-li ʔinna l-qaδiyya raɛ-tintihi baačir.* He told me that the matter would be settled tomorrow. *ʔila ʔan* until. *ntiδirni hnaa ʔila ʔan axaḷḷiṣ.* Wait for me here till I finish. *bi-ʔan* to the effect that. *ṭayyar ʔišaaɛa bi-ʔan il-waziir raɛ-yistaqiil.* He spread a rumor to the effect that the minister was going to resign. *raad yiqniɛhum bi-ʔan ʔaani l-muṣwič.* He wanted to convince him that I was to blame. *ɛala ʔan* provided that, providing. *waafaq yištiriiha ɛala ʔan yinṭuu taxfiiḏ xamsa bil-miyya.* He agreed to buy it providing they gave him a five per cent discount. *štirṭaw ɛalee ɛala ʔan yidfaɛ nuṣṣ il-mablaġ.* They set a condition that he pay half the amount. *li-ʔan* because, since. *ma-štireeta li-ʔan ġaali.* I didn't buy it because it's expensive. *l-muɛallim ma-raɛ-yiji li-ʔanna mariiḏ.* The teacher isn't going to come because he's sick. *walaw ʔan* even though. *ʔaxaδitha minna walaw ʔan čaan ymaaniɛ.* I took it from him even though he objected. *laazim yištuġul walaw ʔan ma-yriid.* He has to work even though he doesn't want to.

ʔ-n-a-n

*ʔanaani** selfish. *xalli-ʔastaɛmil il-qaamuus. la-tṣiir ʔanaani.* Let me use the dictionary. Don't be selfish.

ʔanaaniyya selfishness.

ʔ-n-b

ʔannab to rebuke, censure, upbraid, scold (someone). *ʔannabta miit marra laakin ma-yjuuz.* I rebuked him a hundred times but he won't stop. *ḏamiiri da-yʔannibni li-ʔan ma-nṭeeta l-ifluus.* My conscience is bothering me because I didn't give him the money.

ʔ-n-b-b

ʔunbuub, ʔunbuuba pl. *ʔanaabiib* tube, pipe. *ʔunbuub ixtibaar* test tube. *xaṭṭ ʔanaabiib nafuṭ* oil pipeline.

ʔ-n-b-y-q

ʔinbiiq pl. *ʔanaabiiq* retort (chem.).

ʔ-n-t

ʔinta fem. *ʔinti* pl. *ʔintum* you. *ʔinta š-aɛleek?* What's it to you?

ʔ-n-θ

ʔannaθ to make feminine (gram.). *šloon itʔanniθ hač-čilma?* How do you make this word feminine?

tʔannaθ pass. of *ʔannaθ. hal-ʔisim ma-yitʔannaθ.* This noun doesn't become feminine.

ʔunθa pl. *ʔinaaθ* 1. female. 2. a female. *l-ʔunθa taaxuδ nuṣṣ iδ-δakar bil-miiraaθ.* The female gets half of what the male gets in the inheritance. *ʔunθa l-ɛankabuut tuktul il-faɛal.* The female spider kills the male.

ʔunuuθa femininity.

muʔannaθ feminine. *čilma muʔannaθa* feminine word.

see also *n-θ-y.*

ʔ-n-j-y-l

ʔinjiil pl. *ʔanaajiil* 1. gospel. 2. Bible.

ʔ-n-č

ʔinč pl. *-aat* inch.

ʔ-n-s

staʔnas, staanas to enjoy oneself, have a good time. *staʔnasit wiyyaak ihwaaya.* I enjoyed myself a lot with you. *xal-nibqa baɛad; ʔaani mistaʔnis.* Let's stay a little longer; I'm having a good time. *mistaʔnis bil-paaysikil kulliš.* He's having a good time with the bicycle.

ʔins (coll.) man, mankind, humanity. *laa ʔins wala jinn* neither man nor beast.

*ʔinsi** 1. human. 2. human being.

naas (masc. or fem.) people.

ʔinsaan 1. man, mankind, humankind, the human race. 2. human being, man.

*ʔinsaani** 1. human. 2. humane, humanitarian.

ʔinsaaniyya 1. humanity, humaneness, kindness. 2. humanity, mankind. 3. (pl. *-aat*) humane act, humane deed, a kindness.

ʔaanisa pl. *-aat, ʔawaanis* young lady, miss (also as a polite form of address).

ʔ-n-f

ʔinaf (a *ʔanafa*) to disdain, scorn. *ʔaani ʔaʔnaf ʔaštuġuḷ wiyya hiiči naas.* I am too proud to work with such people.

staʔnaf to appeal (a legal case). *raɛ-astaʔnif id-daɛwa.* I'm going to appeal the case.

ʔanif pl. *ʔunuuf* nose. || *raġum ʔanf* in spite of, in defiance of. *sawweetha raġum ʔanfak.* I did it in spite of you.

*ʔanfi** nasal. *j-jiyuub il-ʔanfiyya* the nasal sinuses.

ʔanafa 1. pride. 2. haughtiness. 3. scorn, disdain.

stiʔnaaf appeal (to the lower courts). || *qaddam istiʔnaaf.* He made an appeal. *maɛkamt il-istiʔnaaf* appeals court.

ʔ-n-f-l-w-n-z-a

ʔinflawanza influenza.

ʔ-n-q

tʔannaq to be chic, elegant. *yitʔannaq ib-libsa hwaaya.* He's very elegant in his dress.

ʔanaaqa elegance.

ʔaniiq neat, chic, elegant.

ʔ-n-g-l-ṭ-r-a

ʔingilṭara England.

ʔ-n-g-l-y-z

*ʔingiliizi** 1. English. 2. (pl. *ʔingiliiz*)

Englishman. *l-ʔingiliiz* the English, the British.

ʔ-n-n

ʔann (*i ʔaniin*) to moan, groan. *buqa yʔinn liṣ-ṣubuḥ.* He kept moaning until morning.

ʔanna pl. *-aat* moan.

ʔaniin moaning.

see also *w-n-n.*

ʔ-n-n-a-s

ʔananaas pineapple.

ʔ-n-y

tʔanna to act slowly, proceed deliberately and unhurriedly, take one's time. *loo titʔanna, ma-tiġlaṭ.* If you take your time, you won't make a mistake. *tʔanna. ʔudrus il-mawḍuuʕ gabuḷ-ma tiḥtajj.* Take your time. Study the matter before you protest.

taʔanni deliberateness, unhurriedness.

ʔ-n-y-m-y-a

ʔaniimiya anemia.

ʔ-h-b

tʔahhab to be ready, get ready, to prepare oneself. *tʔahhabtu lis-safra loo baʕad?* Are you ready for the trip yet?

ʔ-h-r

ʔaahra pl. *-aat* whore, prostitute.

ʔ-h-l

ʔahhal to qualify, fit, make suitable. *naḍara ma-yʔahhla yṣiir ṭayyaar.* His eyesight doesn't qualify him to be a pilot. *θaqaafta ma-tʔahhla l-hal-waḍiifa.* His education doesn't qualify him for this position.

tʔahhal to get married. *simaʕit ʔaxuuk raḥ-yitʔahhal.* I heard your brother's going to get married.

staahal to deserve, merit, be worthy of. *staahal it-tarfiiʕ.* He deserved the promotion. *tistaahil. ma-git-lak ʔugʕud raaḥa?* You deserve it. Didn't I tell you to be good? *mistaahil, ḥeel bii. laazim čaan yinṭirid min zamaan.* He deserved it, and more. He should have been fired long ago. *leeš ma-yistaahilha? qaabil ʕaaʔilatha ʔaḥsan min ʕaaʔilta?* Why isn't he worthy of her? Is her family better than his? *mistaahilha w-šaayif il-xeer, inšaaḷḷa.* You deserve it. Good luck. (congratulatory phrase for use on occasions of new acquisitions).

ʔahal pl. *ʔahaali* **1.** family, relatives. **2.** wife. **3.** people. *ʔahal baġdaad* the people of Baghdad. *ʔahl is-sayyaaraat* the people owning cars.

ʔahaali **1.** people, populace. *ʔahaali l-manṭaqa* the population of the area. **2.** civilian populace (as distinct from government employees). **3.** natives, native population.

ʔahlan welcome. *ʔahlan wa-sahlan, ʔahlan biik* welcome!

*ʔahli** **1.** civil, civilian. *malaabis ʔahliyya* civilian clothes. **2.** civil, national. *ḥarb ʔahliyya.* civil war. **3.** private. *bang ʔahli.* private bank. *madrasa ʔahliyya* private school. **4.** family, domestic. *waquf ʔahli* family wakf.

ʔahliyya **1.** aptitude, suitability, fitness, competence. **2.** relatives, family.

maʔhuul inhabited, populated. *manṭiqa ma-maʔhuula* an uninhabited area.

muʔahhilaat (pl. only) qualifications, aptitudes.

mitʔahhil married.

ʔ-w

ʔaw or. *loo ddaayinni l-ifluus ʔaw idgul-li mneen addaayanha.* Either lend me the money or tell me where I can borrow it. *ʔimma tiji wiyyaaya ʔaw tibqa bil-beet.* Either come with me or stay at home. || *ʔaw haaḏa ʔaw ḏaak.* Either this or that.

ʔ-w-t-y

ʔuuti pl. *-iyyaat* iron, flatiron. || *ḍirab ʔuuti* to iron, press. *ḍrabti θ-θoob maali ʔuuti?* Did you iron my shirt?

ʔ-w-t-č-y

ʔuutači pl. *-iyya* **1.** presser, ironer. **2.** presser's shop, cleaner's.

ʔ-w-t-y-l

ʔuuteel, ʔuteel pl. *-aat* hotel.

ʔ-w-j

ʔawj peak, top (e.g., of power or fame).

ʔ-w-j-a-ġ

ʔoojaaġ pl. *-aat* fireplace, hearth.

ʔ-w-d

ʔooda pl. *-aat, ʔuwad* room.

ʔ-w-r-p-p-a

ʔawruppa Europe.

*ʔawruppi** European (adj. and n.).

ʔ-w-r-t-y

ʔoorti pl. *-iyyaat* sheet, bedsheet.

ʔ-w-r-ṭ

ʔoorṭa pl. *-aat* a kind of very large Persian rug.

ʔ-w-f

ʔaafa pl. *-aat, ʔafawaat, ʔawaafi* (m. and f.) **1.** tough person, tough, tough guy, terror. **2.** rascal, sly guy. **3.** efficient person, one who gets things done, whiz.

ʔ-w-f-f

ʔooff see under *ʔ-f-f.*

ʔ-w-g-y
ʔuugiyya var. of *wgiyya,* which see under *w-g-y.*
ʔ-w-k-s-j-y-n
ʔooksijiin oxygen.
ʔ-w-l
ʔawwal to interpret. *ʔawwil iḥčaayti miθil-ma triid. ma-yhimm-li.* Interpret my remark any way you want. I don't care.

ʔaal family, clan. *ʔaal il-ʕabdi* the 'Abdi family.

ʔaala pl. *-aat* 1. instrument. *ʔaala muusiiqiyya* musical instrument. *ʔaala jiraaḥiyya* surgical instrument. 2. mechanical device, gadget. 3. small part (of a device). *ʔaalaat saaʕa* works of a watch, watch movement. *ʔaalaat talafizyoon* parts of a television set. 4. spices (mainly dill, parsley, and fenugreek) used to season spinach.

*ʔaali** 1. mechanical. 2. mechanized, motorized. *quwwa ʔaaliyya* mechanized force.

ʔaalaati pl. *-iyya* musician.

ʔawwal fem. *ʔuula* pl. *ʔawaaʔil* 1. first. *ʔawwal marra* the first time. *j-jaaʔiza l-ʔuula* the first prize. 2. beginning. *ʔawwal iš-šaariʕ* the beginning of the street. *ʔawwal l-isbuuʕ* the beginning of the week. *mnil-ʔawwal* from the beginning. *čaan imnil-ʔawwal gut-li ḥatta ma-atʕab nafsi.* You should have told me in the first place so I wouldn't go to such effort. 3. earlier, previous. *ʔaḥsan imnil-ʔawwal.* better than before. || *ʔawwal il-baarḥa, ʔawwalt il-baarḥa* the day before yesterday. 4. (pl. only) *ʔawwaliin* forerunners, forebears. *kutub il-ʔawwaliin wil-ʔaaxiriin.* the books of early and contemporary (Islamic) writers.

¶ *bil-ʔawwal* in the beginning, at first, to begin with. *bil-ʔawwal ma-qibal laakin qannaʕta.* At first he wouldn't agree but I convinced him. *bil-ʔawwal xalli agul-lak š-ṣaar.* First of all let me tell you what happened. *ʔawwal-ma* as soon as, the moment that. *ʔawwal-ma šifta, ʕirafit ʔinna mujrim.* As soon as I saw him, I knew he was a criminal.

ʔawwalan first, firstly, first of all. *ʔawwalan xalli nḥaḍḍir il-ġaraaḍ.* First let's get the things ready.

*ʔawwali** first, initial. *miswadda ʔawwaliyya* first draft. *jtimaaʕ ʔawwali* preliminary meeting. *ntixaabaat ʔawwaliyya* primary elections (the popular choosing of electors). || *mawaadd ʔawwaliyya* raw materials.

ʔawwaliyya pl. *-aat* 1. precedence, priority. 2. first place. 3. (pl. only) *ʔawwaliyyaat* file, records.

taʔwiil pl. *-aat* interpretation, explanation.

ʔ-w-l-č-y
ʔoolči pl. *-iyya* tape, tapeline, tape measure. || *ʔaxað ʔoolči* to take measurements. *l-xayyaaṭ ʔaxað-li ʔoolči.* The tailor took my measurements.

ʔ-w-n
l-ʔaan now. *sawwi hal-muʕaamala l-ʔaan, rajaaʔan.* Do this job now, please. *ḥatta l-ʔaan ma-ṣaar šii.* Until now, nothing's happened. *baʕd il-ʔaan, ma-ariidak itsawwi hiiči šii.* From now on, I don't want you to do such a thing. *mnil-ʔaan fa-ṣaaʕidan* and *mnil-ʔaan w-ṣaaʕid* from now on. *mnil-ʔaan fa-ṣaaʕidan, waqt id-dawaam raḥ-yid-ġayyar.* From now on, working hours will be changed.

ʔawaan pl. *ʔaawina* time. *gabuḷ ʔawaana* prematurely. *ʔilla baʕad fawaat il-ʔawaan* until the time was past.

ʔ-w-h
tʔawwah to moan, groan. *baʕdak titʔawwah li-hassa?* Are you still moaning?

ʔaaha pl. *-aat* moan, groan.

ʔ-w-y
ʔaawa (i *muʔaawaat*) to shelter, take in, put up. *ʔaawaahum ʔila ʔan ligaw beet jidiid.* He put them up until they found a new house. *haš-šeex ʔaawa kull il-inhizmaw mniš-šimaal.* That ruler sheltered all who fled from the north.

ʔaawa: ʔibin ʔaawa (formal term for *waawi*) jackal.

maʔwa pl. *maʔaawi* shelter, refuge.

[1]*ʔ-y*
ʔii 1. yes. 2. look, okay. *ʔii, ma-truuḥ ʕaad!* Look, why don't you get lost!

[2]*ʔ-y*
ʔay /before cons./, *ʔayy* /before vowel/ 1. what? which? *ʔay nooʕ?* What kind? Which type? || *ʔay mudiir w-ʔay baṭṭiix?* What sort of a director is that (lit., what director and what melon)? 2. any. *ʔay waaḥid* anyone, whoever. *ʔay šii* anything, whatever.

ʔayyu 1. which? which one? 2. whichever, whatever

[1]*ʔ-y-a*
ʔaaya pl. *-aat* 1. wonder, marvel. *hiyya*

ʔaaya bij-jamaal. She's a marvel of beauty. **2.** a verse of the Koran.

[2]*ʔ-y-a*

ʔayaa see under *y-a.*

ʔ-y-a-r

ʔayyaar May.

ʔ-y-a-ġ

ʔayaaġ pl. *-aat* **1.** pay, salary. **2.** funds, money. **3.** price, amount.

ʔ-y-j-a-b

ʔiijaab see under *w-j-b.*

[1]*ʔ y-d*

ʔayyad **1.** to support, back. *kull il-muwaδδafiin ʔayydaw il-mudiir ib-mawqifa.* All the employees supported the director's stand. **2.** to confirm, corroborate. *ʕali ʔayyad il-xabar.* Ali confirmed the news.

taʔyiid **1.** support, backing. **2.** confirmation, corroboration.

[2]*ʔ-y-d*

ʔiid pl. *-een* **1.** hand. *šifithum ʔiid ib-ʔiid.* I saw them hand in hand. *maa-la ʔiid bil-qaδiyya.* He has no hand in the matter. *ʔiδa wugaʕ b-iideehum ymawwtuu.* If he falls into their hands they'll kill him. *ṭ-ṭamaaṭa ma-toogaʕ bil-ʔiid biš-šita.* Tomatoes aren't available in winter. *hiiči raadyo b-has-siʕir ma-yoogaʕ bil-ʔiid ʕala ṭuul.* Such a radio for this price can't be gotten all the time. *saaʕat ʔiid* wrist watch. || *ʔiid min wara w-ʔiid min giddaam.* empty-handed. *laʕʕib ʔiidak!* Pay up! *ʔiida xafiifa.* He's a fast worker. *ʔaax min ʔiidak, mawwatitni!* Darn you, you'll be the death of me! *haaδa kulla min ʔiidak.* This is all your doing. This is all your fault. *kullhum yištuġluun jawwa ʔiidi.* They all work under my supervision. *ʔaku jawwa ʔiidak miit diinaar?* Do you have one hundred dinars at hand? *has-sayyaara šuġuḷ ʔiid.* This car is hand made. **2.** arm. *ʔiida magṭuuʕa mnič-čitif.* His arm's cut off at the shoulder. || *ʔiideehum ṭuwiila.* They're light-fingered. **3.** handle (see also *yadda* under *y-d-d*).

ʔ-y-r-a-n

ʔiiraan Iran.

*ʔiiraani** **1.** Iranian. **2.** an Iranian.

ʔ-y-r-y-l

ʔeeryal pl. *-aat* aerial, antenna.

ʔ-y-s

ʔayyas to give up hope, to despair. *ʔayyas imnit-tarfiiʕ.* He gave up hope of promotion. *ʔayyis! ma-raʕ-yiji il-yoom.* Forget it! He won't come today.

ʔ-y-š

ʔeeš what? /used only following prepositions/ *ʕal-eeš* and *ʕala-weeš* why? what for? (see also *l-eeš*). *ʕal-eeš zaʕlaan?* What are you mad about? *ʕala-weeš hal-iṣyaaʕ?* What's all the shouting about?

minn-eeš **1.** from what? *minn-eeš maʕmuula?* What is it made of? **2.** why? for what reason?

l-eeš, lu-weeš, ʔil-weeš what for? why? *l-eeš ma-tiji wiyyaana?* Why don't you come with us?

b-eeš **1.** with what? how? *beeš jaa, bil-qiṭaar?* How'd he come, on the train? **2.** at what, how much. *beeš kallifatak?* How much did it cost you? *s-saaʕa beeš?* What time is it?

ʔ-y-š-a-r-p

ʔiišaarp̣ pl. *-aat* kerchief, (woman's) scarf.

ʔ-y-δ

ʔayδan also, too. *l-muʕallim ʔayδan gal-li.* The teacher also told me.

ʔ-y-l-w-l

ʔayluul, ʔeeluul September.

ʔ-y-y

ʔayy, ʔayyu see under *ʔ-y.*

B

b-

b- **1. a.** in, at, into. *huwwa muu bil-ġurfa hassa.* He's not in the room now. *ʔabuuya baʕda bid-daaʔira.* My father's still at the office. *sibaʕit biš-šaṭṭ il-yoom.* I swam in the river today. *ma-aku miθla bid-dinya.* There's no one like him in the world. *qireeta bij-jariida.* I read it in the paper. *dawwir ib-been hal-iqlaam, balki tšuuf illi triida.* Look through these pencils; maybe you'll find the one you want. *xašš bil-gubba.* He went into the room. *ʕaṭṭeet šakar bič-čaay loo baʕad?* Did you put sugar in the tea yet? *ʕuṭṭ dihin ib-šaʕrak ʕatta yugʕud.* Put some oil on your hair so it'll stay down. *xašš ib-beenaathum w-faakak-hum.* He stepped in between them and separated them. || *has-salla ʔaʕtiqid biiha keeluween ʕala l-aqall.* I figure this basket weighs two kilos at least. *š-biiha s-sayyaara? ma-timši baᶜad?* What's wrong with the car? Won't it run anymore? *š-bii? ma-da-yištuġul ˀabadan.* What's ailing him? He never works. *biihum tiifoo. ma-laazim itxušš bil-gubba.* They've got typhoid. You mustn't go in the room. *hassa biik. ˀinta ˀurkuδ.* Now you're "it". You run. **b.** in, at (time). *bil-leel* at night. *bin-nahaar* in the day. *biš-šita* in the winter. *biṣ-ṣeef* in the summer. *b-ˀawwal iš-šahar* the first of the month. *bil-wakt il-muᶜayyan* at the appointed time. *sawwaaha b-nuṣṣ saaᶜa.* He did it in a half hour. *ṣrafit ihwaaya fluus ib-haš-šahar.* I spent a lot of money this month. *b-ᶜayaati ma-šaayif hiiči.* I've never seen such a thing in my life. *s-saaᶜa bil-xamsa.* It's five o'clock. *s-saaᶜa beeš, yaa šabaab?* What time is it, fellows? *beeš saaᶜtak?* What time have you got? *s-saaᶜa beeš tiji?* At what time will you come? **c.** in, at (signifying the pursuit of an action). *ġilabta biš-šiṭranj.* I beat him at chess. *xiṣar ifluusa bil-iqmaar.* He lost his money in gambling. *ġilab diinaar bir-reesiz.* He won a dinar at the races. *nijaᶜit bil-imtiᶜaan.* I passed the exam. *yδayyiᶜ wakta bil-liᶜib.* He wastes his time in play. *maxbuuṣ biš-šuġuḷ.* He's all wrapped up in the work. *tᶜaarkaw bil-ᶜači.* They had an argument. **2.** with, by means of. *ġisla b-ṃaay w-ṣaabuun.* Wash it with water and soap. *yiktib ib-qalam baṣma.* He writes with a pencil. *raᶜ-itruuᶜ bil-qiṭaar?* Are you going to go by train? *zaᶜᶜalni b-ᶜačya.* He angered me with his talk. *xaabra bit-talafoon.* Call him on the phone. *nišraw il-xabar bil-iδaaᶜa.* They broadcast the news on the radio. *tzaᶜlag ib-gišir mooz.* He slipped on a banana peel. *xtinag ib-ᶜaδum simač.* He choked on a fish bone. *beeš jaa? bil-qiṭaar?* How'd he come? On the train? *ruuᶜ beeš-ma yᶜijbak.* Go any way you want. (by redundant use of *b*) *b-beeš* = *b-eeš*. *b-beeš ˀaakul? ma-ᶜindi fluus.* How'll I eat? I don't have any money. **3.** for (price). *štireet il-qaaṭ ib-ᶜišriin diinaar.* I bought the suit for twenty dinars. *ˀabiiᶜhum id-darzan ib-ᶜašriin filis.* I sell them for twenty fils a dozen. *šgadd difaᶜit-la bis-sayyaara?* How much did you pay him for the car? *ˀaxaδitha b-balaaš.* I got it for free. *haθ-θoob beeš?* How much is this shirt? *raᶜ-aštriiha beeš-ma yguul.* I'll buy it for whatever he says. **4.** by. *firqatna ġilbathum ib-xamis nuqaaṭ ˀazyad.* Our team beat them by five points. *ˀaani ˀakbar min ˀaxuuya b-xams isniin.* I'm five years older than my brother. *ˀuδrub xamsa b-sitta.* Multiply five by six. *masaaᶜat hal-ġurfa sitt amtaar ib-xamsa.* The area of this room is six meters by five. **5.** per. *šgadd taaxuδ bil-yoom?* How much do you get a day? *ˀaṣruf miit diinaar biš-šahar.* I spend a hundred dinars a month. *ˀašuufhum marra bis-sana.* I see them once a year. *ˀiblaᶜ itlaθ ᶜabbaat bil-yoom.* Take three pills a day. **6.** in the condition or state of (frequently paraphrases an English adverb). *yaḷḷa bil-ᶜajal!* Come on, make it snappy! *jaa b-surᶜa.* He came in a hurry. *ˀilibsa bil-ᶜaafya.* Wear it in health. *bil-xeer, inšaaḷḷaah!* Hope you have good luck. *šifta biṣ-ṣidfa.* I saw him by accident. *ma-aku ˀaᶜᶜad ib-quuta.* There's no one with his strength. **7.** (as a particle of oath, approx.:) by. *b-diinak, ˀaani git-lak hiiči?* By your religion, did I tell you that? *b-šarafi, ˀaani ma-aᶜurfa.* On my honor, I don't know him.

b-a-ˀ

baaˀ name of the letter *b*.

b-a-b-a

ḅaaḅa pl. *-awaat* **1.** pope. **2.** (a familiar form of address by a child to his father) daddy, papa. **3.** = *yaaḅa* man, friend, pal, buddy (form of address).

*ḅaaḅawi** papal. *ˀamur baabawi* a papal edict.

l-ḅaaḅawiyya Papacy.

b-a-b-l

baabil Babylon.

*baabili** **1.** Babylonian. **2.** a Babylonian.

b-a-b-n-g

baabunnag camomile (bot.).

b-a-p-w-r

ḅaapuur pl. *-aat, ḅwaapiir* **1.** a long cigarette holder, consisting of two types; one in which the cigarette fits upright, and one in which it fits lengthwise. Often decorated with engraving, it is peculiar to the rural North. **2.** opium pipe. *ˀabu ḅaapuur* and *šarraab ḅaapuur* dope addict.

b-a-b-w-j

baabuuj pl. *bwaabiij* slipper, a sandal-like slipper worn mostly by women.

b-a-t-r-y

baatri pl. *-iyyaat* battery.

b-a-j-y

baaji pl. *-iyyaat* /fem./ close friend

(among women), also a polite term of address among women not related by blood.

b-a-d-k-y-š

ḅaadkeeš cupping, the application of suction to draw blood into an area of the body.

b-a-d-g-y-r

baadgiir pl. *-aat* **1.** air vent, air duct. **2.** chimney.

b-a-d-m

ḅaadam (coll.) a variety of hard glazed cookie.

baadma pl. *-aat* un.n. of *ḅaadam.*

b-ʔ-r

buʔra pl. *buʔar* focus, focal point.

*buʔri** focal. *ṭuul buʔri* focal length.

b-a-r

baar pl. *-aat* **1.** bar, counter. **2.** bar, tavern.

b-a-r-w-d

baaruud gunpowder. || *ṣaar miθl il-baaruud.* He became apoplectic.

b-a-r-y

baarya pl. *bwaari* large, heavy, woven bamboo mat.

[1]*b-a-z*

baaza cotton flannel.

[2]*b-a-z*

baaz pl. *-aat* falcon.

b-a-z-b-n-d

ḅaazḅand pl. *-aat* a talisman in the form of a leather bracelet worn on the upper arm.

b-ʔ-s

baʔs: laa baʔs **1.** no objection. *laa baʔs. xuδha.* No objections. Take it. **2.** not bad. *ṣiƐƐta laa baʔs biiha.* His health is pretty good. *laa baʔs bii, laakin ma-yiswa rubuƐ diinaar.* It's all right, but it's not worth a quarter dinar.

buʔs misery, wretchedness.

baaʔis wretched, miserable.

b-a-s-w-r-g

baasoorag, baasuurag (coll.) an edible nut, similar to the almond but smaller, with a smooth, dark shell.

baasoorga pl. *-aat* un. n. of *baasoorag.*

b-a-š

baaš /in compounds/ head, chief. *baaš Ɛammaal* head porter. *baaš kaatib* chief clerk.

b-a-š-b-z-ġ

baašbuzuġ, baašbuzuq native or eastern dress. *ma-yṣiir tiji lid-daaʔira laabis baašbuzuġ.* You can't come to the office in native clothes. *haaδa l-baašbuzuġ, š-imƐarrfa?* That guy in native dress, what does he know?

b-a-š-k

baašak pl. *bwaašik* sparrow hawk.

b-ṣ-ṭ-r-m-a

baaṣṭirma (coll.) a type of large flat sausage stuffed with highly seasoned meat.

baaṣṭirmaaya pl. *-aat* un. n. of *baaṣṭirma.*

b-a-ġ-a

baaġa **1.** plastic. **2.** celluloid.

b-a-g

baaga pl. *-aat* bunch, bouquet.

b-a-l

baala pl. *-aat* bale.

b-a-l-d-y

baaldi pl. *-iyyaat* drum, metal barrel.

b-a-l-w

baaḷo, Ɛaflat baaḷo ball, formal dance.

b-a-l-w-n

ḅaaloon pl. *-aat* **1.** balloon. **2.** dirigible, blimp.

b-a-l-y

baalee ballet.

b-a-m-y-a

ḅaamya (coll.) okra.

ḅaamyaaya pl. *-aat* or *baamyaat* pod of okra.

b-a-n-z-y-n

ḅaanziin gasoline.

ḅaanziinxaana pl. *-aat* gas station.

b-a-n-y-a

ḅaanya var. of *ḅaamya,* which see under *b-a-m-y-a*

b-a-n-y-w

baanyo pl. *-waat* bathtub.

b-a-n-y-a-n

*ḅaanyaani** pl. *ḅaanyaan* **1.** Hindu, or any non-Moslem Indian. **2.** an ignorant person.

b-b-t-w-t-y

bibituuti pl. *-iyyaat* parrot.

b-b-ġ-a-ʔ

babaġaaʔ pl. *-aat* parrot.

b-b-m-t-w

bibimattu pl. *-waat* parrot.

b-t-a-t-a

bataata (coll.) potato(es)

bataataaya pl. *-aat* potato.

[1]*b-t-t*

batt (*i batt*) to decide. *l-mudiir baƐad ma-batt ib-qaδiitak.* The director hasn't yet decided on your case. *l-mawδuuƐ baƐad ma-mabtuut bii.* The matter still hasn't been decided upon.

bataatan positively, absolutely, definitely, decidedly, categorically. *t-tadxiin mamnuuƐ bataatan.* Smoking is absolutely forbidden.

baatt definite, decided, absolute. *jawaab*

baatt definite answer. *maniɛ baatt* categorical prohibition.

²b-t-t

batt luck, break. *jaab xooš batt w-ġilabhum kullhum.* He had good luck and beat them all.

³b-t-t

batt pl. *btuut* thin bracelet, usually worn several at a time.

⁴b-t-t

bitt var. of *bint,* which see under *b-n-t.*

b-t-r

bitar (*i batir*) 1. to cut off, sever. *bitar gumɛ il-ixyaara bis-siččiina.* He chopped off the cucumber stem with the knife. *čruux il-qiṭaar bitrat rijlee.* The train wheels severed his legs. *la-tibtir il-iɛčaaya; gull-inna š-ṣaar.* Don't cut the story short; tell us what happened. 2. to amputate. *ṭ-ṭabiib bitar ʔiida.* The doctor amputated his arm.

battar 1. to chop off. *battar iδyuul xeelhum ɛatta yintiqim minhum.* He cut off their horses' tails to get revenge on them. 2. to flow steadily. *njirɛat ʔiida bis-siččiin wid-damm ḍall ybattir.* His hand got cut on the knife and the blood kept flowing.

nbitar to be cut off, be severed. *ʔiida nbitrat bil-ɛaadiθ.* His arm was severed in the accident.

ʔabtar having a bobbed, docked, or clipped tail. *čalib ʔabtar* dog with a bobbed tail.

battaar sharp. *has-seef ṣaar-la b-ɛaaʔilti miit sana w-baɛda li-hassa battaar.* This sword has been in my family a hundred years and it's still sharp as a razor. *lsaana battaar.* His tongue is sharp.

b-θ-θ

baθθ (*i baθθ*) 1. to spread, tell (a secret, etc.). *la-tiɛčii-la l-quṣṣa, tara ybiθθha been in-naas.* Don't tell him the story or he'll spread it around. 2. to broadcast, transmit. *maɛaṭṭat baġdaad itbiθθ ɛala mawijteen.* The Baghdad station transmits on two wave lengths.

b-θ-l

biθil 1. (tea) leaves. 2. (coffee) grounds.

b-j-a-m

bijaama pl. *-aat* pajamas.

b-j-j

bajj (*i bajj*) to spray or squirt (a liquid) from the mouth. *j-jaahil bajj ṃayy ɛal-bazzuuna.* The kid spat water on the cat.

b-j-ɛ

tbajjaɛ to boast, brag. *bass itwaḍδaf, gaam yitbajjaɛ ib-maqdirta.* As soon as he was hired, he began to brag about his ability.

tabajjuɛ bragging.

mitbajjiɛ bragger, braggart.

b-j-ġ

bajaġ pl. *-aat* 1. good-looking young man, pretty boy. 2. jack, knave (in cards).

b-j-l

bajal a mild form of syphilis causing sores on the belly.

b-č-b-č

tbačbač to whine, wheedle, pout tearfully. *ḍallat titbačbač ɛatta štiraa-lha l-badla.* She kept whining around until he brought the suit for her.

see also *b-č-y.*

b-č-r

bičir /masc. and fem./ first child, first-born.

baačir tomorrow. || *ɛugub baačir* the day after tomorrow. *ʔabu baačir* (lit. the father of tomorrow, i.e.:) the master of his own fate. *minu ʔabu baačir?* Who knows what the future will bring?

see also *b-k-r.*

b-č-y

biča (*i bači, biča*) to cry, weep. *ruuɛ šuuf leeš ij-jaahil da-yibči.* Go see why the baby's crying. *min maat abuuha, bičat ihwaaya.* When her father died, she cried very much. *tibči min* (or *ɛala*) *ʔagall šii.* She cries at the slightest thing. *yibčuun min* (or *ɛala*) *mootat abuuhum.* They're crying over their father's death.

bačča to make cry. *ʔaxaδ iṭ-ṭooba mnij-jaahil w-baččaa.* He took the ball away from the child and made him cry.

tbačča to be made to cry. *yitbačča b-ʔaqall šii.* He bawls at any little thing.

tbaača to implore tearfully, plead. *raaɛ lil-mudiir w-itbaačaa-la ɛatta ma-ynuqla.* He went to the director and cried on his shoulder so that he wouldn't transfer him.

nbiča pass. of *biča. l-maaḍi ma-yinbiči ɛalee.* The past isn't worth crying over.

bači crying, weeping.

b-ɛ-b-ɛ

baɛbaɛ 1. to prosper, be prosperous. *haaδa baɛbaɛ ʔaθnaaʔ il-ɛarb.* He prospered during the war. *mbaɛbiɛ li-ʔan yištuguḷ wiyya ɛašir banaat.* He's in clover since he's working with ten girls. 2. to enjoy oneself, have a good time. *baɛbiɛ, ʔaḷḷa rabbak.* Enjoy yourself, God's taking care of you.

tbaħbaħ = *baħbaħ. tbaħbaħ min idzawwaj bint it-taajir.* He became prosperous when he married the merchant's daughter. *tbaħbaħ ib-haš-šuġuḷ is-sahil.* He enjoyed himself with that easy job.

baħbuuħ merry.

mbaħbiħ prosperous, well-to-do. *malʕuun imbaħbiħ, da-yħaṣṣil ʕašr idnaaniir bil-yoom.* The prosperous son of a gun, he's making ten dinars a day.

b-ħ-t

baħt pure, unadulterated, sheer. *haaδa čiδib baħt.* That's pure lies. *haay li-manfaʕtak iš-šaxsiyya l-baħta.* That's for your own personal benefit. *l-ħaqiiqa l-baħta* the unadulterated truth.

b-ħ-θ

biħaθ (*a baħiθ*) **1.** to look, search. *š-šurṭa da-tibħaθ ʕannak.* The police are looking for you. *biħaθ bil-ġurfa w-ma-liga šii.* He searched the room and didn't find anything. **2.** to study, examine, investigate. *l-wizaara da-tibħaθ mawqifna b-hal-muškila.* The cabinet's studying our stand on this problem. **3.** to discuss. *biħaθnaaha wiyya l-mudiir.* We discussed it with the director. **4.** to scratch, dig. *d-dijaaj da-yibħaθ bil-ħadiiqa.* The chickens are scratching in the garden.

baaħaθ to talk to, consult with, confer with. *mumaθθilna baaħaθ mumaθθil iš-šarika ħawil ziyaadt il-ʔujuur.* Our representative talked to the company representative about the pay raise.

tbaaħaθ to confer, discuss together. *raħ-nitbaaħaθ bil-qaδ̣iyya.* We're going to confer on the matter.

baħiθ pl. *buħuuθ, ʔabħaaθ* **1.** research. *baħiθ ʕilmi* scientific research. **2.** report, paper. *qaddam baħiθ bil-muʔtamar.* He presented a paper at the conference.

mubaaħaθa pl. *-aat* talk, conference, negotiation.

b-ħ-ħ

baħħ (*i baħħ, baħħa*) to be or become hoarse, husky, harsh. *ħissi baħħ imnil-iʕaaṭ.* My voice got hoarse from shouting.

baħħa hoarseness.

mabħuuħ hoarse. *š-biik? ħissak mabħuuħ!* What's the matter? your voice's hoarse!

b-ħ-r

ʔabħar to sail, put to sea. *l-baaxira tibħir yoom il-iθneen iṣ-ṣubuħ.* The ship sails Monday morning.

baħħar to look closely, look carefully. *baħħir ib-har-rasim w-gul-li minu hal-mara.* Examine this picture closely and tell me who this woman is.

tbaħħar = *baħħar. ma-aku ħaaja titbaħħar bii halgadd. ʔaʔakkid-lak ʔaṣli.* No need to examine it so closely. I assure you it's genuine.

baħar pl. *ʔabħur, bħaar, bħuur* sea. || *l-kiimiya baħar; maħħad yigdar yixtimha.* Chemistry is like a sea; no one can know it all.

l-baħreen Bahrain.

*baħraani** pl. *bħaarna* **1.** Bahraini, from Bahrain. **2.** a Bahraini.

*baħri** **1.** sea, marine. *ħaywaan baħri* marine animal. **2.** naval. *δaabuṭ baħri* naval officer.

baħriyya pl. *-aat* navy.

baħħaar pl. *-a* sailor.

buħayra pl. *-aat* lake.

mitbaħħir experienced, familiar. *mitbaħħir ib-farʕa.* He's thoroughly familiar with his specialty.

b-ħ-l-q

baħlaq to stare. *leeš da-tbaħliq ib-wičči?* Why are you staring at me? *min šaaf il-ʔabu l-miyya, ʕeena baħliqat.* When he saw the hundred dinar bill, his eyes opened wide.

b-x-t

baxat luck. *šloon baxat ʕinda! kull-ma yilʕab, yirbaħ.* What luck he has! Every time he plays, he wins. || *ʔaani b-baxtak; la-tuδ̣rubni!* I'm at your mercy; don't hit me! *b-baxtak! twannas!* You lucky guy! Have a good time! *b-baxtak! ʔaani gilit fadd šii ma-zeen?* Now I ask you! Did I say anything wrong? *b-baxt ʔalla, fukkni. ʕindi ʕašr ijhaal.* For the love of God, let me go! I have ten kids. *ʕala baxtak; ʔaani ʔaguul hiiči šii?* By your conscience; would I say such a thing? *ʕala baxtak, n-nahaar kulla ma-akalit.* Have a heart, I haven't eaten all day. *ʕala baxtak! šloon raħ-aṭaʕʕum ij-jihaal?* My God! How'm I going to feed the kids? *ʕala baxtak! l-maskiin! šwakit maat?* For God's sake! The poor guy! When'd he die? *ʕala baxtak; l-ḅaanziin xilaṣ.* Now what do we do? We're out of gas.

mabxuut **1.** fortunate, lucky. **2.** lucky person.

b-x-t-r

tbaxtar to strut. *yitbaxtar ib-mašiita.* He struts when he walks.

baxtara strutting.

b-x-x

ḅaxx (*u ḅaxx*) to spray, sprinkle. *ḅuxx*

išwayya ṃaay ɛaθ-θoob gabuḷ-ma ðður-ba ˀuuti. Sprinkle a little water on the shirt before you iron it. *ḅuxx it-timman b-išwayyat ṃayy.* Sprinkle the rice with a little water.

b-x-r

ḅaxxar 1. to vaporize, evaporate. *š-šamis biṣ-ṣeef itḅaxxir ihwaaya ṃaay imnil-buɛayra.* The sun evaporates a lot of water from the lake in the summer. 2. to disinfect, fumigate. *ḅaxxiraw it-tamur ɛatta yṣaddruu.* They fumigated the dates in order to export them. 3. to expose to burning incense. *ḅaxxiraw il-ġurfa li-ˀan iš-šeex ɛinda xuṭṭaar.* They burned incense in the room because the chief is having guests. *ḅaxxiraw lil-mariið ɛatta yṭurduun iš-šiiṭaan.* They burned incense for the sick man in order to chase away the Evil One.

tḅaxxar 1. to evaporate. *l-ṃayy yitḅaxxar bil-ɛaraara.* Water evaporates with the heat. 2. to disappear, evaporate. *gabuḷ-ma axušš lil-imtiɛaan, maɛluumaati kullha tḅaxxrat.* Before I went in for the exam, my knowledge all disappeared. *hassa čaan ihnaa; ɛabaalak itḅaxxar.* He was just here; looks as if he vanished into thin air.

buxaar 1. steam. 2. fumes, vapor.

bxaara a variety of small preserved plum, mostly imported from Afghanistan or Iran.

*buxaari** 1. steam, steam-driven. *makiina buxaariyya* steam engine. 2. (pl. *-iyyat*) chimney.

buxuur incense.

mabxara pl. *maḅaaxir* censer.

baaxira pl. *bawaaxir* steamer, steamship. *raaɛ bil-baaxira.* He went by steamer.

taḅaxxur evaporation.

b-x-š-y-š

baxšiiš tip, gratuity.

b-x-l

bixal (*a buxul*) to be stingy, niggardly, miserly. *ˀinta šloon ṣadiiq! tibxal ɛalayya b-hal-kaamira l-ma-tiswa.* Some friend you are! You're being stingy with me about this worthless camera. *la-tibxal ɛala nafsak bil-ˀašyaaˀ ð-ðaruuriyya.* Don't stint yourself on the necessities. *la-tibxal ɛaleena b-ziyaartak.* Don't be stingy with your visits to us.

buxul stinginess.

baxiil pl. *buxalaaˀ* 1. stingy, miserly, niggardly. 2. stingy person.

ˀabxal more or most stingy, miserly.

b-d-ˀ

bida (*i badi, badwa, bidaaya*) to begin, start. *l-filim bida gabuḷ xamis daqaayiq.* The film started five minutes ago.

badda to give precedence or priority to. *ybaddi l-xuṭṭaar ɛala nafsa.* He puts the guests before himself. *ybaddi ṣadiiqa ɛala ˀaxuu.* He prefers his friend over his brother.

btida to begin, start. *šwakit raɛ-nibtidi ništuġuḷ?* When are we going to start working?

bidaaya pl. *-aat* beginning, start. *bil-bidaaya* at first, in the beginning. *maɛkamt il-bidaaya* court of first instance, ranking above *maɛkamt iṣ-ṣuluɛ,* and handling suits and crimes involving money.

badaaˀa formal variant of *bidaaya.*

badwa pl. *-aat* beginning, start.

mabdaˀ pl. *mabaadiˀ.* 1. principle. 2. doctrine, ideology. *mabaadiˀ* 1. fundamentals, guiding principles. *mabaadiˀ il-qiraaˀa* fundamentals of reading. 2. ideology. *l-mabaadiˀ l-haddaama* the subversive ideology, i.e. communism.

*mabdaˀi** initial, preliminary. *ɛall mabdaˀi* initial solution, temporary solution. *diraasa mabdaˀiyya* preliminary study. || *b-ṣuura mabdaˀiyya* provisionally, tentatively. *waafaq ib-ṣuura mabdaˀiyya, laakin baɛdeen ġayyar raˀya.* He agreed tentatively, but then he changed his mind. *b-ṣuura mabdaˀiyya, ma-ɛindi maaniɛ, laakin yumkin tiṭlaɛ mašaakil.* Offhand, I have no objections, but problems may arise.

mabdaˀiyyan 1. initially, originally, as a beginning, to start with. *ṣirafna miit ˀalf diinaar mabdaˀiyyan ɛala binaaˀ ˀuteelaat biš-šimaal.* We spent one hundred thousand dinars initially for building hotels in the North. 2. provisionally, tentatively. *waafaq mabdaˀiyyan laakin baɛdeen ġayyar raˀya.* He agreed provisionally but then changed his mind. *l-ɛukuuma xaṣṣiṣat milyoon diinaar mabdaˀiyyan, ˀila ˀan yijtimiɛ il-majlis.* The government appropriated a million dinars provisionally till parliament convenes.

*bidaaˀi** primitive. *ɛiiša bidaaˀiyya* a primitive way of life.

btidaaˀan min starting with, beginning from, as of. *btidaaˀan min baačir, d-dawaam raɛ-yibdi saaɛa θmaanya.* As of tomorrow, office hours will commence at eight o'clock.

*btidaaʔi** primary, elementary. *madrasa btidaaʔiyya* elementary school.

baadiʔ beginning. *b-baadiʔ il-ʔamur, ma-qibal.* At first, he wouldn't agree.

mubtadiʔ pl. *-iin* **1.** beginner, novice. **2.** subject of an equational sentence. (gram.)

[1]*b-d-d*

baddad to waste, squander. *baddidaw kull juhuudhum.* They wasted all their efforts. *baddad ifluusa.* He squandered his money.

stabadd **1.** to act arbitrarily, high-handedly. *l-mudiir istibadd bil-muwaδδafiin.* The director acted arbitrarily with the employees. *stibadd ib-raʔya w-ma-twaṣṣalna ʔila natiija.* He was obstinate and we didn't reach any conclusion. **2.** to act despotically, tyrannically. *d-diktaatoor istibadd ib-ḥukma.* The dictator was a tyrant in his rule.

stibdaad **1.** arbitrariness. **2.** despotism.

*stibdaadi** despotic. *ḥukum istibdaadi* despotic rule.

mistibidd **1.** arbitrary, high-handed, tyrannical, despotic. *l-mudiir is-saabiq čaan mistibidd.* The former director was high-handed. *malik mistibidd* a tyrannical king. || *huwwa mistibidd ib-raʔya.* He's opinionated. **2.** despot, tyrant.

budd way out, escape (usually in set phrases as:) *laa budd min . . .* there is no escape from . . . it is inevitable that . . . . *laa budd ingul-la.* We have no choice but to tell him. *laazim tijuun min kull w-laa budd.* You absolutely must come without fail. *min kull budd* in any case, under any circumstances, without fail. *ʔariidak tiḥči wiyya l-mudiir il-yoom min kull budd.* I want you to talk to the director today definitely.

[2]*b-d-d*

bidd (in the phrase:) *εala bidd* on one's own. *baṭṭal imniš-šarika w-da-yištuġul εala bidda.* He quit the company and is working on his own.

b-d-δ-a-t

badδaat see under *δ-w-t.*

b-d-r

badir full moon. *l-gumar badir il-leela.* The moon is full tonight. *dzawwaj wiḥda miθl il-badir.* He married a girl pretty as the full moon.

baadira pl. *bawaadir* sign, omen. *haay baadrat xeer.* That's a good sign. *muu xooš baadra; ma-da-yṭiiεuun il-ʔawaamir.* That's a bad sign; they're not obeying orders.

b-d-ε

baddaε to achieve excellence, to excel, be outstanding. *baddaεit bil-imtiḥaan.* I did very well in the examination. *l-gooḷči baddaε.* The goalkeeper did an excellent job. *haaδa ṣudug baddaε ʔibdaaε ib-haṣ-ṣuura.* He really came up with something fine in this picture.

bidεa pl. *bidaε* (heretical) innovation.

badiiε excellent, outstanding, wonderful, marvelous. *sloon manδar badiiε!* What a marvelous view!

badaaεa (invar.) an outstanding, amazing thing, a marvel, a wonder. *čaanat ṭaalεa badaaεa.* She looked wonderful. *badaaεa! waḷḷa, yistaahil yṣiir wazir!* Wonderful! He really deserves to be a minister. *haaδa xabar badaaεa.* That's great news.

ʔabdaε more or most outstanding, excellent, wonderful, amazing.

ʔibdaaε unique, wonderful achievement. *ʔilqaaʔa čaan ʔibdaaε.* His recitation was an excellent thing. *tamθiila ma-bii ʔibdaaε.* There's no excellence in his acting. *nṭoo madaalya εala ʔibdaaεa b-hat-timθaal.* They gave him a medal for his achievement with this statue.

mubdiε **1.** outstanding, exceptional, unique. **2.** outstanding person.

b-d-g

bidag (*i badig*) **1.** to be aware, to note. *ʔinta da-tibdig εal-qaṣid maala?* Are you aware of his intention? *baadig εala hač-čiδib?* Did you catch those lies? **2.** to pay attention. *ʔibdig εalee w-šuuf iš-da-yiḥči.* Pay attention to him and see what he is saying. *ʔiδa ma-tibdig-li, šloon tiftihim?* If you don't pay attention to me, how will you comprehend?

b-d-l

baddal **1.** to exchange, replace. *ʔagdar abaddil haθ-θoob? ṭilaε iṣġayyir εalayya.* Can I exchange this shirt? It's too small for me. *ʔagdar abaddil hal-qalam ib-haaδaʔ* Can I exchange this pen for that one? *l-fiitarči baddal plakkeen ib-sayyaarti.* The mechanic changed two spark plugs in my car. *minu baddal il-qappuuṭ maali?* Who switched overcoats with me? *laazim inbaddil hal-faṣiil li-ʔan ṣaar-la bij-jabha mudda ṭuwiila.* We've got to replace that platoon because they've been in the front lines a long time. **2.** to change, alter. *baddilaw mawqiε ij-jisir.* They changed the site of the bridge. *baddal siyaasta min rijaε imnil-*

*mu*ʔ*tamar.* He changed his policy when he returned from the conference. *hal-kalima tbaddil kull maʕna j-jumla.* That word alters the whole meaning of the sentence. *ma-adri š-baddala.* I don't know what changed him. **3.** to change, change clothes, to get dressed. *ʔida ma-ṭaaliʕ baʕad, leeš ma-tbaddil?* If you're not going out again, why don't you change clothes? *ntiðirni ʕatta ʔabaddil.* Wait for me while I change. *guum, baddil. ṣaar wakt il-madrasa.* Get up; get dressed. It's time for school. *yaḷḷa, baddil ihduumak.* Come on, get dressed. *ʔabuuya baʕda ma-mbaddil. yguul "xall yintaðruuni."* My father's not dressed yet. He says, "Have them wait for me." *šuuf ʕali šloon imbaddil! ṭaaliʕ falla.* Look at Ali, all dressed up! He looks sharp. *šloon ʕilu mbaddil!* How nicely dressed he is! **4.** to shift, switch, change. *ma-tigdar tiṣʕad ij-jibal iða ma-tbaddil ʕaθ-θineen.* You won't be able to get up the mountain unless you shift into second. *ma-ftihamit wala čilma li-ʔan kull saaʕ ybaddil imnil-ʕarabi lil-ʔingiliizi.* I didn't understand a word because every moment he switches from Arabic to English.

baadal **1.** to exchange, trade. *leeš abaadil iʕṣaani b-iʕṣaanak illi ma-ġilab ʔabadan?* Why should I trade my horse for your horse which has never won? **2.** to reciprocate. *baadalha l-ʕubb.* He returned her love.

tbaddal **1.** *to change. min ṣaar muwaððaf, itbaddal ihwaaya.* When he became an official, he changed a lot. **2.** to be changed. *raqam talafooni tbaddal.* My telephone number was changed.

tbaadal to exchange. *l-waziireen tbaadlaw il-ʔaaraaʔ ʕawl il-mawðuuʕ.* The two ministers exchanged opinions on the case. *tbaadlaw ib-saaʕaathum.* They exchanged watches.

badal (no pl.) **1.** substitute, alternate, replacement. *ðayyaʕ il-qalam maali w-inṭaani haaða b-badala.* He lost my pencil and gave me this in place of it. *ʔanṭiik badal il-qalam illi ðayyaʕit-lak-iyyaa.* I'll give you a replacement for the pencil I lost. **2.** compensation, reimbursement, recompense, allowance. *badal layaali* overnight travel allowance. **3.** fee, rate, price. *badal il-ištiraak* subscription rate. **4.** (pl. *-aat*) an exemption fee, paid to reduce the length of one's military service. **5.** in place of, instead of. *haak diinaareen badal iktaabak li-ʔan ðayyaʕta.* Here's two dinars in place of your book since I lost it.

badal-ma instead of. *badal-ma ysaaʕidni, ʕaafni w-raaʕ.* Instead of helping me, he left me and went off.

badalan min, badalan ʕan instead of. *staʕmil had-duwa badalan min id-duwa l-ʕatiig.* Use this medicine instead of the old kind. *huwwa raaʕ badalan ʕanni.* He went instead of me.

badalči pl. *-iyya* man who has paid the fee to shorten his military service.

badla pl. *-aat* suit (of clothing). *badla rasmiyya* uniform. *badla ʕaskariyya* military uniform.

bdaal, b-bidaal in lieu of, in place of, in exchange for. *ʔariid diinaar ibdaal il-qalam illi ksarit-li-yyaa.* I want a dinar in exchange for the pen you broke. *ma-aku ṭamaaṭa bis-suug. š-itriid ib-bidaalha?* There aren't any tomatoes in the market. What do you want in place of them? *maa-li xulug. ruuʕ ib-bidaali.* I don't feel well. Go in my place. *triid qalami? zeen, iš-tinṭiini bdaala?* You want my pen? Okay, what'll you give me in exchange for it? || *ʔaḷḷa bdaalak.* I wouldn't cheat you (lit., God is in your place).

bdaal-ma **1.** in exchange for (the fact that). *bdaal-ma saaʕaditni raʕ-aštuġuḷ ib-mukaanak.* In exchange for your helping me, I'm going to work in your place. **2.** instead of. *bdaal-ma tilʕab, taʕaal idrus.* Instead of playing, come and study.

baddaala pl. *-aat* **1.** telephone exchange. **2.** switchboard.

tabaadul exchange. *tabaadul il-ʔaaraaʔ* exchange of opinions. *tabaadul ʔiṭlaaq in-naar* exchange of gunfire.

b-d-n

badan pl. *ʔabdaan* **1.** body, trunk, torso. **2.** physique. *faʕiṣ badan* physical examination. *ṭabiib ʔabdaan* general practitioner (commonly excluding eye, ear, nose, and throat).

*badani** physical. *riyaaða badaniyya* physical exercise.

b-d-h

badiihi **1.** self-evident, obvious. *masʔala badiihiyya* a self-evident matter. **2.** naturally, obviously. *badiihi yʕurfa li-ʔan haay šaġiḷta.* Of course he knows it because that's his business.

badiihiyya pl. *-aat* **1.** axiom, self-evident fact. **2.** truism, platitude.

[1]*b-d-w*
ʔabda to express, utter, voice. *tḥibb tibdi raʔyak bil-mawḍuuḥ?* Do you want to express your opinion on the subject? *ʔabda raġubta b-širaaʔ il-beet.* He expressed his desire to buy the house. **2.** to offer. *ṣ-ṣulṭaat ʔabdat-ilhum kull il-musaaḥadaat il-mumkina.* The authorities offered them all possible assistance.
bidwi, bdiwi, badawi** pl. *badu* **1.** Bedouin, nomad, nomadic. *xeel bidwi* Bedouin horses. *ḥayaat ibdiwi* nomadic life. *ʔaġaani badawiyya* Bedouin songs. **2.** a nomad, a Bedouin.
badawiyya pl. *-aat* Bedouin woman or girl.
badaawa Bedouinism, nomadism. *ḥayaat il-badaawa tqawwi l-ajsaam.* The Bedouin life strengthens the body.
baadi evident, apparent. *l-faraḥ baadi ḥala wičča.* Joy is evident on his face.
baadya pl. *bawaadi* desert.

[2]*b-d-w*
badwa see under *b-d-ʔ.*

b-d-w-n
biduun = bi-duun which see under *d-w-n.*

[1]*b-d-y*
badda to spill. *badda l-mayy ḥaz-zuuliyya.* He spilled the water on the carpet.
tbadda to be spilled. *šloon itbadda š-šakar?* How'd the sugar get spilled?

[2]*b-d-y*
bida, badwa, bidaaya see under *b-d-ʔ.*

[3]*b-d-y*
baadya see under *b-d-w.*

b-δ-ʔ
baδiiʔ foul, obscene, dirty. *ḥači baδiiʔ* dirty talk. *baδiiʔ il-lisaan* foul-mouthed.

b-δ-x
biδax (i baδix) to spend lavishly. *yibδix ḥala wilda hwaaya.* He spends a lot on his sons. *biδax ihwaaya bil-ḥafla s-sawwaaha lil-waziir.* He really put on the dog in the party he gave for the minister.
baδix **1.** extravagance. **2.** splendor, high style.
baδδaax pl. *-iin* spendthrift, wastrel.

b-δ-δ-a-t
baδδaat see *baδ-δaat* under *δ-w-t.*

b-δ-r
baδδar **1.** to waste, squander. *baδδar kull ifluusa ḥal-winsa.* He squandered all his money on pleasure. **2.** to go to seed. *laazim axalli ṭamaaṭa waḥda tbaδδir lis-sana j-jaaya.* I have to let one tomato go to seed for next year.
tbaδδar to be wasted. *kull juhuudi tbaδδirat.* All my efforts were wasted.
baδir (coll.) pl. *biδuur, bδuuraat* seed(s)
baδra pl. *-aat, biδuur* seed.
mubaδδir pl. *-iin* spendthrift.

b-δ-l
biδal (i baδil) to give or spend freely. *ḥinda stiḥdaad yibdil ḥala ʔaṣdiqaaʔa.* He's ready to spend freely on his friends. *biδalit kull juhdi ḥatta asaaḥda.* I made every effort to help him. *biδalt il-ġaali wir-rixiiṣ ib-sabiilak.* I sacrificed everything for your sake.
tbaδδal to debase, cheapen oneself, to display crude, vulgar traits. *tbaδδal ib-ʔawaaxir ʔayyaama.* He got vulgar in his old age. *l-mudiir mitbaδδil. tšuufa bil-mayxaanaat wiyya l-igḥaab.* The director's degraded himself. You see him in the bars with prostitutes.
mitbaδδil vulgar, crude, cheap, debased.
mabδuul **1.** spent, given, sacrificed freely. **2.** plentiful, abundant, rife. *han-nooḥ imnil-uqmaaš mabδuul bis-suug.* This type of cloth is very plentiful in the market.

[1]*b-r-ʔ*
l-baari the Creator.

[2]*b-r-ʔ*
barra to clear, acquit, absolve. *barrata l-maḥkama mnid-daḥuuteen.* The court cleared him of the two charges.
tbarra **1.** to disassociate oneself. *tbarra min ʔibna bil-maḥkama.* He disowned his son in court. **2.** to be acquitted, be cleared. *ḥali tbarra laakin šariika nḥikam santeen.* Ali was acquitted but his partner got two years.
bari, bariiʔ pl. *-iin, ʔabriyaaʔ* **1.** free, rid. *ʔaani bari minnak w-min ḥašiirtak.* I'm having nothing to do with you and your relatives. **2.** guiltless, innocent. *ṭilaḥ bari.* He turned out to be innocent. **3.** guileless, harmless. *ḥčaaya bariiʔa* an innocent remark.
baraaʔa **1.** innocence, guiltlessness. *ḥukm il-baraaʔa* acquittal decision. **2.** guilelessness, naiveté. **3.** (pl. *-aat*) patent (on an invention).
tabriya, tabriʔa acquittal. || *ḥiḍar il-maḥkama w-ṭilaḥ tabriya.* He went to court and came out a free man.

b-r-b-x
burbux pl. *baraabix* **1.** drain, drainpipe. **2.** section of drainpipe.

b-r-b-a-d
burbaad (invar.) worn out. *ma-δδibb*

qaaṭak? muu ṣaar burbaad! Why don't you throw away your suit? It's become worn out. *ma-yigdar yištuġul; ṣaayir burbaad.* He can't work; he's all worn out.

b-r-b-r

barbar to jabber, prattle, chatter. *ṣaar-la saaʕa ybarbir.* He's been jabbering away for an hour.

l-barbar the Berbers.

*barbari** 1. Berber. 2. barbarian. *juyuuš barbariyya.* barbarian armies.

barbari pl. *baraabira* 1. a Berber. 2. a barbarian.

barbariyya barbarianism, barbarism.

b-r-b-ʕ

barbaʕ 1. to thrive, prosper. *l-ġanam raħ-itbarbiʕ ib-hal-xaðaar.* The sheep will thrive in this pasturage. *barbaʕ ib-haš-šuġul.* He prospered in that business. *barbiʕ! ʔalla rabbak.* Enjoy yourself! God's taking care of you. 2. to soak, sop, dip, dunk. *barbiʕ il-xubza bil-ħaliib w-inṭiiha liṭ-ṭifil.* Soak the piece of bread in milk and give it to the baby.

tbarbaʕ to be soaked, sopped, dipped, dunked. *l-xubza tbarbiʕat biš-šoorba.* The bread was soaked in the soup.

b-r-b-y-n

barbiin an edible wild green plant.

b-r-j

burij pl. *buruuj, ʔabraaj* 1. tower. *burj il-muraaqaba* watch tower, control tower. 2. dovecote, pigeon house. 3. sign of the zodiac.

baarija pl. *bawaarij* battleship.

b-r-j-z

birjiz pl. *baraajiz* riding breeches, jodhpurs.

b-r-ħ

l-baarħa yesterday. || *ʔawwal il-baarħa* and *ʔawwalt il-baarħa* day before yesterday.

[1]*b-r-d*

burad (*a barid*) to cool, cool off (also figuratively). *l-mayy burad hassa; tigdar tišrab minna.* The water's cooled off now; you can drink some of it. *burdat id-dinya hwaaya.* The weather got very cold. *raħ-ysaafir ʔaxuuk? laa, yiðhar burad ʕan il-qaðiyya.* Is your brother going to go? No, it looks like he's cooled toward the idea. *tigdar itħaačii. burad hassa.* You can talk to him now. He's cooled off.

barrad to cool, chill. *barrad il-mayy biθ-θallaaja.* He cooled the water in the refrigerator. *l-muṭar barrad ij-jaww.* The rain cooled the air. *barradha l-marta b-ħačya l-laṭiif.* He cooled his wife's anger with his gentle words. *lamma ħičaa-li ʕan ħarr uwlaayta barradni ʕan ir-rawaaħ leeha.* When he told me about his city's hot weather, he dampened my enthusiasm for going there.

tbarrad 1. to be cooled. *l-maay ma-yitbarrad ʔakθar min haaða; yijmad.* The water can't be cooled any more than that; it'll freeze. 2. to cool off, cool oneself. *fakkeet yaaxti ħatta atbarrad išwayya.* I opened my collar so I could cool off a bit.

stabrad to catch a cold. *laazim istabrad il-baarħa bil-leel.* He must have caught a cold last night.

barid 1. cold, coldness, coolness, chill. *garṣat barid* a touch of cold. 2. cold, catarrh. *ʔaxað barid.* He caught cold.

barda pl. *-aat* cold spell, cold snap, frost.

buruud 1. coldness, coolness. *ṣaar beenaathum buruud.* They've gotten cool to each other. *qaabalni b-buruud.* He received me halfheartedly. 2. emotional coldness. *buruud ṭabʕa yʕajjib.* His coolness of disposition is amazing.

buruuda coldness, coolness, (also of emotions).

barraada pl. *-aat* water cooler.

bardaan cold. *lbasit qappuuṭ w-baʕadni bardaan.* I put on an overcoat and I'm still cold.

ʔabrad colder, coldest.

baarid cold, cool, chilly. || *fadd waaħid baarid kulliš* a real slowpoke. *titin baarid* mild tobacco. *nukta baarda* a dull joke. *ṭabuʕ baarid* a phlegmatic disposition. *damma baarid.* He's cool headed. *raasa baarid.* He has no problems. He is carefree.

mubarrida pl. *-aat* 1. cooling device. 2. air conditioner.

[2]*b-r-d*

burad (*u biraada*) to file. *burad il-miħbas ħatta gidar ylibsa.* He filed out the ring until he could slip it on.

barraad fitter, mechanic (esp. in the military).

biraada fitter's trade or work.

braada iron filings.

mubrad, mabrad pl. *mabaarid* file, rasp.

[3]*b-r-d*

bariid post, mail.

*bariidi** postal. *ħawaala bariidiyya* postal money order.

b-r-d-ġ

bardaaġ pl. *baraadiiġ* drinking glass.

b-r-d-y
bardi (coll.) papyrus.
bardiyya pl. *-aat* papyrus branch.
|| *yṭuuf ʕala bardiyya.* He's happy-go-lucky (lit., he'd float on a papyrus twig).

[1]*b-r-r*
barr (*u barr*) /with *b-*/ to fulfill, keep. *baʕad santeen, barr ib-waʕda.* After two years, he kept his promise.
barrar to warrant, justify, vindicate. *šloon itbarrir mawqifak?* How do you justify your stand?
baarr dutiful, devoted. *walad baarr* a dutiful son. *zawj baarr* devoted husband.
mabruur blessed. *ʕamal mabruur* a blessed act.
mubarrir pl. *-aat* justification, excuse.

[2]*b-r-r*
barr **1.** dry land, terra firma. *bil-barr wil-baḥar* on land and sea. **2.** desert wilderness.
*barri** **1.** land, terrestrial. *quwwaat barriyya* land forces. **2.** wild. *ḥaywaanaat barriyya* wild animals.
barra **1.** (prep.) outside. *xalli č-čalib barra l-beet.* Leave the dog outside the house. **2.** (adv.) out, outside. *j-jihaal da-yilʕabuun barra.* The children are playing outside. *laa, baʕda barra. raḥ-yirjaʕ il-baġdaad baačir.* No he's still away. He'll return to Baghdad tomorrow. *ṭilaʕ barra.* He went out.
*barraani** **1.** outside, outer, exterior. *ṣ-ṣafḥa l-barraaniyya* the outer side. *ṭ-ṭabaqa l-barraaniyya* the exterior layer. **2.** external, extrinsic. *haaḏa šii barraani maa-la ʕilaaqa bil-masʔala.* That's an external thing that has no connection with the problem. *huwwa rajul barraani maa-la daxal bil-mawḏuuʕ.* He's an outsider who has no concern with the matter. *nsawwi rahan barraani beeni w-beenak.* Let's make a side bet between us.

b-r-z
buraz (*u buruuz*) **1.** to appear, show up, emerge. *buraz ḏakaaʔa min xallaṣ id-diraasa il-ibtidaaʔiyya.* His intelligence showed up when he finished elementary education. **2.** to stand out, attain prominence. *biraz been il-muwaḏḏafiin ib-mudda qaṣiira.* He stood out among the employees in a short time. *biraz bil-ḥizib.* He became prominent in the party. **3.** to display, show. *ʔubruz hawiitak lil-imwaḏḏaf gabuḷ-ma-txušš.* Show your identification to the official before you go in.
baaraz **1.** to duel, engage in a sword fight with. *l-baṭal hijam ʕalee w-baaraza.* The hero charged him and engaged him in swordplay. **2.** to compete in a contest. *ʔaani ḥaaḏir abaarzak biš-šiṭranj.* I'm ready to take you on in chess.
ʔabraz to present, show, display. *ʔabraz kull-ma ʕinda min waθaayiq ḥatta yiksib id-daʕwa.* He presented all he had in the way of documents to win the case. *ʔabraz hawiita bil-baab gabuḷ-ma yxušš.* He showed his identification at the gate before entering.
tbaaraz reciprocal of *baaraz.* *ṣaar-ilhum nuṣṣ saaʕa da-yitbaarzuun.* They've been dueling for a half hour. *hal-iθneen da-yitbaarzuun ʕal-ʔawwaliyya.* Those two are competing for first place.
buruuz prominence, eminence.
ʔabraz more or most prominent, outstanding, etc.
mubaaraza pl. *-aat* **1.** swordfight, duel. **2.** competition, contest.
ʔibraaz presentation, showing.
baariz **1.** prominent. *ʕuḏu baariz bil-ḥizib* a prominent member of the party. **2.** raised, embossed, in relief. *ḥuruuf baariza* embossed letters.

b-r-z-n
barazaan pl. *-aat* horn, trumpet, bugle.

[1]*b-r-ṣ*
baraṣ **1.** a birth defect resulting in unpigmented patches of skin. **2.** (by extension) albinism.
breeṣ: ʔabu breeṣ pl. *ʔabu breeṣaat* lizard, wall gecko.
ʔabraṣ fem. *barṣa* pl. *buruṣ, barṣiin* **1.** having light patches of skin. **2.** person with light patches of skin. **3.** albino. **4.** an albino.

[2]*b-r-ṣ*
burṣa, boorṣa pl. *-aat* bourse, stock exchange.

b-r-ṭ-l
barṭal to bribe. *barṭala b-xamsiin diinaar.* He bribed him with fifty dinars.
tbarṭal to be bribed. *haaḏa yitbarṭal bil-ʕajal.* He's easily bribed.
barṭiil, burṭiil pl. *baraaṭiil* bribe.

b-r-ṭ-m
barṭam to pout. *lamma ma-nṭeeta l-paaysikil, barṭam w-baʕd išwayya yibči.* When I didn't give him the bicycle, he pouted and was about to cry.

baraaṭim (pl. only) 1. pout, pouting. 2. thick lips.

b-r-ع

biraع (*a baraaعa*) to be skillful, proficient. *biraع ib-taqliid il-mumaθθiliin.* He was skillful at impersonating actors.

tbarraع 1. to donate, contribute, give freely. *yitbarraع ihwaaya lij-jamعiyyaat il-xayriyya.* He contributes a lot to charitable organizations. *tbarraع ib-ʔalif diinaar.* He donated a thousand dinars. 2. to volunteer. *tbarraع yibni ġurfa jidiida lij-jaamiع.* He volunteered to build a new room on the mosque.

baraaعa skill, proficiency.

ʔabraع more or most skillful, proficient.

tabarruع pl. *-aat* donation, contribution.

baariع skilled, skillful, proficient. *baariع bir-rasim* skillful at drawing. *xaṭiib baariع* a skillful speaker.

b-r-ع-m

burعum pl. *baraaعim* bud (bot.).

b-r-ġ-θ

barġuuθ (coll.) flea(s).

barġuuθa pl. *baraaġiiθ* flea.

b-r-ġ-š

barġaš (coll.) small, nonbiting, swarming insect(s), midge(s).

barġaša pl. *-aat, baraaġiiš* un.n. of *barġaš.*

b-r-ġ-l

burġul bulgur, boiled, dried and crushed wheat.

b-r-ġ-y

burġi pl. *baraaġi* 1. screw, bolt. 2. winding stem (of a watch).

b-r-q

biraq (*u*) 1. to flash (of lightning). *s-sima birqat w-riعdat.* There was thunder and lightning. 2. to wire, telegraph, cable. *biraq-li barqiyya yṭaalibni bil-ifluus.* He wired me asking for the money.

barq pl. *buruuq* 1. lightning, flash of lightning. 2. telegraph. *daaʔirt il-barq* telegraph office.

*barqi** 1. telegraph, telegraphic. *l-muwaaṣalaat il-barqiyya* telegraph connections. *xaṭṭ barqi* telegraph line. 2. (pl. *-iyyaat, baraaqi*) light, lamp, specif., light bulb, flashlight. || *barqi ʔabu ftiila* and *barqi looks* gas mantle lantern.

barqiyya pl. *-aat* telegram, wire, cable.

b-r-g

briig pl. *burgaan* pitcher.

b-r-k

burak (*a buruuk*) to kneel. *burak عala rukubta w-neešan عal-hadaf.* He knelt on one knee and aimed at the target.

baarak 1. to bestow a blessing (said of God). || *ʔaḷḷaahumma zid wa-baarik.* God increase and bless. *ʔaḷḷa ybaarik. yoom عala yoom da-yṣiir ʔazgan.* Bless his heart. Day by day he gets richer. 2. to offer congratulations, felicitations. *baarak-la عan-najaaح.* He congratulated him on his success. *smaعit jaa-la walad. xalli nruuح inbaarik-la.* I heard he has a son. Let's go congratulate him. *ʔaškurak, ʔaḷḷa ybaarik-lak.* Thank you, the same to you (an answer to *mbaarak*).

tbarrak to be blessed, get a blessing. *xalli ʔatbarrak bil-ح aayiṭ maal ij-jaamiع.* Let me get a blessing from touching the wall of the mosque.

burka, birka pl. *birak* puddle, pool, pond.

baraka blessing, boon. *has-sana baraka. l-maحṣuul kulliš zeen.* This year is a lucky one. The harvest is very good. *hal-ifluus ma-biiha baraka.* This money doesn't do any good. *maašaḷḷa baraka; yoom عala yoom yziid.* God's been bounteous; there's more every day. *عal-baraka najaaحak.* Congratulations on your success. *min barakt ʔaḷḷa, šuġḷi zeen.* Thank God, my business is good.

mbaarak (lit. blessed, fortunate, approx.:) congratulations. *mbaarak, simaعit nijaحit.* Congratulations, I heard you passed. *mbaarak عala qaaṭak ij-jidiid.* Congratulations on your new suit. *mbaarak عiidak.* Blessings on your feast day.

mabruuk. a less common equivalent of *mbaarak.*

b-r-k-a-n

burkaan pl. *baraakiin* volcano.

*burkaani** volcanic. *حajar burkaani* volcanic rock. *manṭiqa burkaaniyya* a volcanic region.

b-r-l-m-a-n

barlamaan pl. *-aat* parliament.

*barlamaani** parliamentary.

b-r-m

buram (*u barum*) 1. to twist. *ʔubrum il-xeeṭ w-šammiعa حatta yuqwa.* Twist the string and wax it so it'll be strong. *buram ʔiidi w-ʔaδδaani.* He twisted my arm and hurt me. 2. to brag, talk big, show off. *š-daعwa tubrum halgadd?* Why do you brag so much?

baaram to brag, talk big. *haaδa ybaarum ihwaaya.* He brags a lot.

tbaaram 1. = *baaram. kull-ma yšuuf*

banaat, yguum yitbaaram. Wherever he sees girls, he starts talking big. **2.** to brag to each other. *ˀibni w-ˀibnak čaanaw yitbaarmuun.* My son and your son were bragging to each other.

barum **1.** twisting. **2.** bragging, showing off.

braam bragging, showing off.

barraam pl. *-a* braggart, bragger.

mubram real, veritable. *haṭ-ṭifil ġaδab mubram.* That kid's a real pest. *balaaˀ mubram* a real terror, one hell of a thing. *hal-mulaakim balaaˀ mubram; yiδrub neekawt.* That boxer's a real terror; he's got a knockout punch. *l-mudiir ij-jidiid balaaˀ mubram.* The new director is a real ball of fire.

b-r-m-a

burma (coll.) bourma, a Mid-Eastern pastry.

burmaaya pl. *-aat.* un.n. of *burma.*

b-r-m-a-ˀ

*barmaaˀi** amphibious. *l-ḥaywaanaat il-barmaaˀiyya* the amphibious animals.

b-r-m-j

baraamij pl. of *barnaamij* which see under *b-r-n-a-m-j.*

b-r-m-k

barmaki pl. *-iyya* generous. || *xal̤l̤ barmaki* sweetened, dark-colored vinegar.

b-r-m-l

barmiil pl. *baraamiil* barrel, drum.

b-r-n-a-m-j

barnaamij pl. *-aat, baraamij* program, schedule, list. *barnaamij ˀiδaaʕa* broadcasting schedule, list of programs.

b-r-n-z

brunz bronze.

*brunzi** **1.** bronze. *timθaal ibrunzi* a bronze statue. **2.** bronze-like, bronze-colored.

b-r-n-ṣ

burnuṣ pl. *baraaniṣ* burnoose, hooded robe.

b-r-n-w-ṭ

barnuuṭi snuff.

b-r-n-y-ṭ

burneeṭa pl. *-aat, baraaniiṭ* hat.

b-r-h-n

barhan to prove, demonstrate. *barhan ˀanna waaḥid minna.* He proved that he's one of us. *tigdar itbarhin ʕala ḥaqiiqat qawlak?* Can you prove the truth of what you say?

burhaan pl. *baraahiin* proof.

¹b-r-y

bira (*i bari*) to sharpen (a pencil). *hal-muqṭaaṭa tibri l-qalam mumtaaz.* This sharpener sharpens the pencil very well.

baara to vie with, compete with. *baʕad-ma ġilab kull il-mitnaafsiin, raḥ-ybaari l-baṭal nafsa.* Now that he's beat all contenders, he's going to compete with the champion himself.

tbaara to vie, compete with each other. *wiyya ˀay firqa raḥ-titbaaruun l-isbuuʕ ij-jaay?* Which team are you going to compete with next week?

mubaaraa pl. *mubaarayaat* match, tournament, contest. *mubaaraat kurat il-qadam* football game.

²b-r-y

baarya pl. *bwaari* large woven bamboo mat.

b-r-y-a-n

bariyaani a dish made of rice, meat, and hot spices, originally from India.

b-r-y-s-m

briisam silk.

b-r-y-n

bariina pl. *baraayin* drill.

b-z-a-l-y

bazaalya green peas.

b-z-b-z

bazbaz to dart, shift (of the eyes). *ʕyuuna tbazbiz ʕala ṭuul.* His eyes dart about all the time.

bizbiz, and *bizbiz l-igbuur* pl. *bizaabiz* grave rat, a nocturnal animal resembling the mink.

¹b-z-r

bizar (*i bazir*) to beget. || *yisˀal ʕan-naġal w-minu l-ibzara.* He's a nosy old busybody (lit., he asks about the bastard and who begat him).

bazzar to go to seed. *l-warid bazzar.* The flower's gone to seed. *l-beetinjaan bazzar.* The eggplant has gotten old and seedy.

bazir (coll.) pl. *bzuuraat* **1.** seed(s). **2.** semen. **3.** offspring, kid(s), brat(s).

bazra pl. *-aat, bzuur* **1.** seed. **2.** offspring, kids, brats.

bzaar: || *δaaʕ ʕalee l-ibzaar.* He lost track of the total. *txarbaṭ ʕalee l-ibzaar.* He got confused.

bzaara pl. *-aat* date molasses factory.

²b-z-r

bzaar pl. *-aat* scaffold.

¹b-z-z

bazz (*i bazz*) **1.** to defeat, beat, outstrip, excel. *bazz kull it-talaamiiδ bir-riyaaδiyyaat.* He outdid all the students in sports. **2.** to spit or spray. *j-jaahil bazz* *il-mayy ʕal-bazzuuna.* The child spat the water on the cat.

btazz to take away (unlawfully). *btazz ʔamwaal il-ʔaġniyaaʔ b-imʕallta bit-tahdiid.* He extracted money from the rich in his neighborhood by threats. *btazz amwaalhum biduun ʔan yšiʕruun.* He got their money without them catching on.

btizaaz extortion, robbery, fleecing.

²b-z-z

bazzaaz pl. *-a, -iin* cloth merchant, yard goods dealer.

bzaaza cloth trade.

bizz a large Iraqi food fish.

b-z-z-w-n

bazzuun pl. *bzaaziin* cat, tom cat.

bazzuuna pl. *-aat, bzaaziin* 1. cat, female cat. 2. hoist, chain hoist, chain falls, and by extension, derrick, crane.

b-z-ʕ

bizaʕ (*a baziʕ*) to be or become exasperated, disgusted, fed up. *bzaʕit min ʔaʕmaalak.* I've gotten fed up with your actions.

bazzaʕ to exasperate, irritate. *bazzaʕitni. bass ʕaad!* You've exasperated me. That's enough, now!

b-z-q

buzuq pl. *-aat* a mandolin-like musical instrument.

b-z-l

bizal (*i bazil*) to drain. *wizaarat iz-ziraaʕa qarrirat tibzil hal-manṭiqa.* The Ministry of Agriculture has decided to drain this area. *ʔibizli t-timman zeen ʕatta la-yinlakk.* Drain the rice well so it won't stick together.

mabzal pl. *mabaazil* drainage ditch.

b-z-m

buzma pl. *-aat, buzam* cuff (of a shirt sleeve).

b-z-y-m

bziim pl. *-aat, bzaayim* buckle.

b-s-t-j

bastaj frankincense, used primarily for chewing gum. *ʕilič bastaj* frankincense gum.

b-s-t-n

bistaan pl. *bsaatiin* orchard, grove.

bastana horticulture.

b-s-t-w-g

bastuuga pl. *-aat* glazed pottery jar.

b-s-r

baasuur pl. *bwaasiir* hemorrhoid.

b-s-s

bass 1. enough. *bass; la-txalli baʕad.* That's enough; don't put in any more. *buṣaṭṭa ʕatta gaal bass.* I beat him till he said uncle. *bassak ʕaad! šgadd tiʕči!* That's enough out of you now! You talk too much! 2. only, just. *bass ṣaar ʕumra ʕašr isniin, gaam yriid paaysikil.* He just turned ten, and here he wants a bicycle. *bass jarr nafas waaʕid min ij-jigaara w-δabbha.* He just took one puff of the cigarette, and threw it away. *ʕindi bass itlatt iyyaam ʕuṭla.* I've only got three days' vacation. *bass yguʕʕ il-leel kulla.* He simply coughs all night. *bass loo ʕindi xams idnaaniir!* If I only had five dinars! 3. but, however, on the other hand. *haaδa ṭibiix mumtaaz, bass ʔaʕtiqid yṣiir ʔaʕṣan ʔiδa tʕuṭṭ bii šwayya filfil.* This is excellent food, but I think it'll be better if you put in some pepper. *bass il-muṣiiba wiyya ʔibin xaalič.* But the problem is with your cousin. || *w-bass* and that's it, and no back talk. *tkuun ihnaa saaʕa xamsa w-bass.* Be here at five and no arguments.

b-s-f-w-r

l-busfoor The Bosporus.

b-s-k-t

biskit (coll.) cookie(s), biscuit(s).

biskita, biskitaaya pl. *-aat* cookie, biscuit.

b-s-k-w-y-t

biskwiit (coll.) cookie(s), biscuit(s).

biskwiita pl. *-aat* cookie, biscuit.

b-s-k-w-t

baskuut = *b-sukuut,* which see under *s-k-t.*

¹b-s-l

stabsal to be fearless, defy death. *haj-jundi stabsal bil-maʕraka.* This soldier defied death in battle. *j-jeeš il-ʕiraaqi stabsal bid-difaaʕ ʕan il-ʕiraaq.* The Iraqi Army was intrepid in its defense of Iraq.

basaala courage, bravery.

stibsaal heroism.

baasil brave, feerless, intrepid. *j-jeeš il-baasil* the fearless army.

²b-s-l

bisal (*i basil*) to cull. *ma-agdar ʔabiiʕ-lak ṭamaaṭa gabuḷ-ma ʔabsilha.* I can't sell you any tomatoes before I cull them.

basil 1. culling, sorting the bad from the good. 2. culls, throw-aways, things culled out. *l-ixyaar iz-zeen inbaaʕ w-ma-buqa ġeer il-basil.* The good cucumbers are sold out and nothing is left but the culls.

b-s-m

bassam to smile. *ma-δiʕak, laakin bassam.* He didn't laugh, but he smiled.

tbassam = *bassam. min yiʕči, yitbassam.* He smiles when he talks.

btisam = *bassam*. *min yibtisim, tigdar itšuuf sinna δ-δahab.* When he smiles, you can see his gold tooth. *ɛala ṭuul itšuufa mibtisim.* You always see him smiling.

basma pl. *-aat* smile.

btisaam smiling, smile.

btisaama pl. *-aat* smile.

b-s-m-r

basmar to nail, fasten with nails. *basmir hal-qiṭɛa ɛal-baab.* Nail this sign on the door.

tbasmar to be nailed. *hal-looɛa matitbasmar b-suhuula.* That board can't be nailed easily. || *min šaafni, tbasmar ib-mukaana.* When he saw me, he was riveted to the spot.

bismaar pl. *bsaamiir* **1.** nail. **2.** corn (on the foot).

b-š-t

bišit pl. *bšuut, bšaati* a thin aba worn in summer.

b-š-t-a-w

bištaawa pl. *-aat* flintlock pistol, old-fashioned handgun.

[1]*b-š-r*

bišar (*i bašir*) **1.** to rejoice. *ʔibšir! ɛammak ṣaar mudiirna.* Rejoice! Your uncle has been made our director. || *naδδuf il-ġurfa zeen . . . ʔibšir!* Clean the room well . . . Yes sir! **2.** to be cordial. *l-mudiir bišar bii hwaaya.* The manager was very cordial to him.

baššar **1.** to bear glad tidings, to tell (someone) good news. *ɛammak, marta jaabat walad. ruuɛ baššira.* Your uncle's wife had a boy. Go give him the good news. *baššarak ʔaḷḷaa bil-xeer.* (polite reply to someone bringing good news, approx.:) May God gladden you also with good tidings. **2.** /with *b-*/ to spread, propagate, preach. *da-ybaššruun bil-islaam b-afriiqiya.* They're spreading Islam in Africa.

stabšar to rejoice, be delighted, be happy. *stabšar ihwaaya b-hal-xabar.* He became very happy with this news.

bšaara pl. *bšaayir* good news, glad tidings.

bašiir pl. *-iin* bearer of good news.

tabšiir missionary activity.

mubaššir pl. *-iin* **1.** bearer of glad tidings. **2.** missionary, evangelist.

[2]*b-š-r*

baašar **1.** /with *b-*/ to begin, start in, commence. *raɛ-abaašir bil-binaaʔ baačir.* I'm going to start building tomorrow. *baašarit ib-šuġḷi j-jidiid il-baarɛa.* I began work in my new job yesterday. **2.** to treat, attend, give medical treatment to. *ṭabiibna baašara.* Our doctor treated him.

bašar pl. *-iin* **1.** human being, man. **2.** mankind, men. || *ma-tilgi miθla bil-bašar.* You won't find anyone like him in the world.

*bašari** human. *j-jins il-bašari* the human race.

bašara complexion. *bašara ṣamra* dark complexion.

bašariyya mankind, human race.

mubaašara **1.** start, commencement, beginning. **2.** medical treatment.

mubaašaratan immediately, directly. *raɛ-aruuɛ ɛalee mubaašaratan w-agul-la.* I'm going to go straight to him and tell him.

mubaašir **1.** direct, immediate. *s-sabab il-mubaašir il-maraδa* the direct reason for his illness. **2.** (pl. *-iin*) bailiff, usher in a courtroom.

[1]*b-š-š*

bašš (*i bašš*) **1.** to smile. *bašš ib-wuččna w-raɛɛab biina.* He smiled at us and welcomed us. **2.** to be friendly, cheerful. *min zirta, bašš biyya.* When I visited him, he was very friendly to me.

bašuuš smiling, cheerful, friendly. *wijih bašuuš* cheerful face.

bašaaša pl. *-aat* smile, happy face. *b-bašaaša* cheerfully. *staqbalni b-bašaaša.* He received me with a big smile.

[2]*b-š-š*

bašš (*i bašš*) to run, blot. *hal-waraq, ybišš bii l-ɛibir.* Ink runs on this paper.

[3]*b-š-š*

bašš (coll.) a variety of large, light-colored domesticated duck.

bašša pl. *-aat, bšuuš* un. n. of *bašš*.

b-š-ɛ

bašiɛ **1.** ugly. *wujih bašiɛ* ugly face. **2.** disgusting, repulsive. *jariima bašɛa* a disgusting crime. **3.** (pl. *bašɛiin*) ugly person.

bašaaɛa ugliness.

ʔabšaɛ **1.** uglier, ugliest. **2.** more or most disgusting, revolting, loathsome.

b-š-q

bašqa (invar.) different. *laa, haaδa mawδuuɛ bašqa.* No, that's another matter.

b-ṣ-b-ṣ

baṣbaṣ /with *b-*/ **1.** to wag. *č-čalib baṣbaṣ-li b-δeela.* The dog wagged his tail at me. **2.** to cast sly, stealthy glances. *min yšuuf ibnayya, ṣall ybaṣbuṣ ʕaleeha.* When he sees a girl, he keeps making eyes at her. *la-tiktib giddaama tara ybaṣbuṣ.* Don't write in front of him or he'll look on.

tbaṣbaṣ to fawn, apple-polish, curry favor. *daaʔiman yitbaṣbaṣ lil-mudiir.* He's always fawning on the director.

[1]*b-ṣ-r*

tbaṣṣar to reflect, ponder. *laazim titbaṣṣar bil-ʔumuur.* You have to think things through.

tbaaṣar to confer. *xal-nitbaaṣar bil-qaṣiyya w-inšuuf fadd ḥall.* Let's confer on the matter and find a solution.

baṣar vision, eyesight. *baṣara ṣaʕiif.* His eyesight is weak. *qaṣiir il-baṣar* near-sighted. || *xtifa b-lamḥ il-baṣar.* He disappeared in the blink of an eye. *biṣ-ṣaḥraaʔ itšuuf ramuḷ ʕala madd il baṣar.* In the desert the sand stretches as far as the eye can see.

baṣiir **1.** seeing, endowed with vision. || *l-ʕeen baṣiira wil-yad qaṣiira.* I see your problem but I can't help (lit., the eye sees but the arm is short). **2.** (as a euphemism) blind. *l-miskiin baṣiir bil-ʕeenteen.* The poor man's blind in both eyes.

[2]*b-ṣ-r*

l-baṣra Basra (port in South Iraq). *nuumi baṣra* a condiment made of dried lemons imported through Basra.

*baṣri** **1.** Basra-, of, from, or pertaining to Basra. **2.** native of Basra.

*baṣraawi** **1.** from, of, or pertaining to Basra. **2.** (pl. *-iyyiin, bṣaarwa*) native of Basra.

b-ṣ-ṭ

buṣaṭ (*u baṣuṭ*) to beat, thrash. *š-šurṭa ʔijaw w-bidaw ybuṣṭuun iṭ-ṭullaab.* The police arrived and began to beat the students. *ʔibn ij-jiiraan buṣaṭni.* The neighbor's son beat me up.

baṣṣaṭ **1.** to spread out, display (i.e. wares, merchahdise. *raḥ-abaṣṣiṭ giddaam hal-ibnaaya. ybayyin ʔaku hwaaya naas ihnaa.* I'm going to spread out my wares in front of this building. It seems there's a lot of people here. **2.** (by extension) to open, open up, open for business. *ma-laazim itbaṣṣiṭ yoom ij-jimʕa.* You shouldn't open for business on Friday. **3.** to simplify. *tigdar itbaṣṣiṭ-li hal-qaṣiyya? ma-da-afhamha.* Can you simplify this thing for me? I don't understand it. *baṣṣaṭitha lil-qaṣiyya hwaaya.* You've over-simplified the matter.

tbaaṣaṭ to fight, beat each other. *tbaaṣaṭ wiyya ṣaaḥib il-maḥall.* He got in a fight with the owner of the shop.

baṣṭa pl. *-aat* **1.** display of wares, merchandise. **2.** a beating, thrashing, flogging.

bṣaaṭ pl. *buṣuṭ* a kind of floor mat or rug, thin and simple in pattern.

baṣiiṭ **1.** simple, uncomplicated. *muškila baṣiiṭa* a simple problem. *ʕaqliita baṣiiṭa.* He has a simple mind. || *baṣiiṭa. xalliiha ʕalayya. ʔinta ʔidfaʕ marrt il-luxx.* It's nothing. Leave it to me. You pay next time. *baṣiiṭa. darbi minna.* No trouble. It's on my way. *baṣiiṭa. ma-aku ḥaaja tiškurni.* Don't mention it. There's no need to thank me. *baṣiiṭa. ʔaani adabbur-lak-iyyaa baačir.* No problem. I'll arrange it for you tomorrow. *maḥḥad tʕawwar; la-txaabur iš-šurṭa. baṣiiṭa, baṣiiṭa.* No one's injured; don't call the police. It's nothing. **2.** small, modest, trivial, trifling. *mablaġ baṣiiṭ* a small sum. *šii baṣiiṭ* a trivial thing, nothing. *našla baṣiiṭa* an ordinary cold, a little cold. **3.** (pl. *-iin, buṣaṭaaʔ*) naive, simple. *ʔahal il-quraʔ hwaaya buṣaṭaaʔ.* The villagers are very ingenuous.

l-baṣiiṭa the earth, the world. *ʕala wajh il-baṣiiṭa* on the face of the earth.

baṣaaṭa **1.** simplicity, uncomplicatedness, plainness. **2.** naivete, ingenuousness.

ʔabṣaṭ **1.** more or most uncomplicated, etc. **2.** more or most insignificant, etc. **3.** more or most naive, ingenuous, etc.

b-ṣ-l

buṣal (coll.) pl. *ʔabṣaal* **1.** onion(s). **2.** bulb(s). || *raḥ-yizraʕ buṣal.* He's pushing up daisies.

buṣla pl. *-aat* un. n. of *buṣal.*

b-ṣ-m

buṣam (*u baṣum*) **1.** to stamp, print. *bin-najaf aku maḥallaat tubṣum pardaat, čaraačif, w-buqač.* In Nejef there are places that hand print curtains, handkerchiefs and cloths for bundling up articles. **2.** to trace. *buṣam nusxa ʕala hal-xariiṭa.* He made a tracing of this map.

baṣma pl. *-aat* imprint, impression. *basmat ʔaṣaabiʕ* fingerprint. || *qalam baṣma* pencil.

baṣmači pl. *-iyya* an artisan who hand prints material.

baṣṣaam pl. *-a* = *baṣmači.*

b-δ-ε

biδaaεa pl. *baδaayiε* goods, merchandise, wares, commodities.

b-ṭ-ʔ

buṭa (*i buṭuʔ*) **1.** to be slow, take a long time. *leeš tubṭi halgadd bil-libis?* Why are you so slow getting dressed? **2.** to tarry, linger. *ruuħ, bass la-tubṭi.* Go, but don't be long. *buṭa hwaaya bis-suug; ma-adri š-ṣaar bii.* He's stayed a long time at the market; I don't know what happened to him.

baṭṭa to slow up, delay, make late. *la-tbaṭṭi š-šuġul εindak.* Don't hold the work up at your end. *ʔuxδa wyaak bass la-tbaṭṭii.* Take him with you but don't make him late.

stabṭa to consider (someone or something) late, slow, to get impatient about, wait anxiously for. *stabṭeet in-najjaar w-gumit aštuġuḷ bil-maktaba b-nafsi.* I got tired of waiting for the carpenter and started to work on the bookcase myself. *stabṭeenaak w-xaabarna š-šurṭa.* We got worried about you and called the police. *la-tistabṭuuni. yjuuz ʔatʔaxxar.* Don't be expecting me. I might be late.

buṭuʔ slowness, tardiness. *b-buṭuʔ* slowly.

baṭiiʔ slow. *muwaδδaf baṭiiʔ* a slow worker. *yištuġuḷ baṭiiʔ.* He works slowly.

*buṭi** **1.** slow. *buṭi bit-tafkiir* slow thinking. **2.** late. *d-dinya buṭiyya, l-wakit buṭi* It's late. *ṣaar buṭi.* It's gotten late.

ʔabṭaʔ, ʔabṭa **1.** slower, slowest. **2.** later, latest.

b-ṭ-b-ṭ

baṭbaṭ to blister, become blistered. *ʔiidi baṭbuṭat min šilt ij-jidr il-ħaarr.* My hand got blistered when I lifted the hot pot.

buṭbaaṭa pl. *-aat* blister.

b-ṭ-ħ

buṭaħ (*a baṭuħ*) to throw down, fell, prostrate. *triidni abuṭħak baṭiħt il-lux?* Do you want me to throw you again? *ʔaani baaṭħa gabuḷ miit marra.* I've thrown him a hundred times before. *minu yibṭaħ, ʔinta loo ʔaxuuk?* Who throws the other, you or your brother? *min itṣaaraεna l-baarħa, buṭaħta marrteen.* When we wrestled yesterday, I pinned him twice.

baaṭaħ to wrestle with (someone). *raħ-abaaṭħa l-εali baačir.* I'm wrestling with Ali tomorrow.

tbaaṭaħ to wrestle each other, wrestle with each other. *wiyyaa man raħ-titbaaṭaħ baačir?* Who are you wrestling with tomorrow?

nbuṭaħ **1.** pass. of *buṭaħ.* **2.** to prostrate oneself, lie down, sprawl flat. *bass difaεta, nbuṭaħ.* I just pushed him and he fell down.

baṭħa pl. *-aat* fall, pin (wrestling).

mabṭuuħ **1.** stretched out, prone. *šifta mabṭuuħ εala baṭna, jawwa l-qanapa.* I found him lying on his stomach, under the couch. **2.** the loser, one who got pinned (wrestling).

b-ṭ-x

baṭṭiix (coll.) melon(s), canteloupe(s).

baṭṭiixa pl. *-aat* un. n. of *baṭṭiix.*

b-ṭ-r

baṭṭar to make reckless, dissatisfied. *l-waδiifa baṭṭrata.* The job went to his head.

tbaṭṭar to have big ideas, to be dissatisfied with one's lot. *gaam yitbaṭṭar min ṣaar mudiir.* He got delusions of grandeur when he became a director. *la-titbaṭṭar. muu εindak sayyaara!* Don't be malcontent. You already have a car! *la-titbaṭṭar, tara haay xooš waδiifa.* Don't hold out, 'cause that's a good position. *da-yitbaṭṭar εaleena. ʔay waδiifa ninṭii, ma-yirδa.* He's being high hat with us. Any position we give him, he's not satisfied.

buṭar desire for something better, dissatisfaction.

baṭraan **1.** discontent, dissatisfied with one's lot. **2.** malcontent, person who is dissatisfied with his lot.

mitbaṭṭir = *baṭraan.*

b-ṭ-r-ṣ

buṭruṣ Peter.

b-ṭ-r-y

baṭariyya pl. *-aat* battery (mil.).

b-ṭ-r-y-q

baṭriiq Patriarch.

baṭriiqiyya Patriarchate.

¹b-ṭ-š

buṭaš (*u baṭiš*) to throw down, knock down. *šaala w-buṭaša bil-gaaε.* He lifted him and threw him on the ground.

nbuṭaš to throw oneself down. *bass jaa lil-beet, xašš lil-gubba w-inbuṭaš εal-gaaε.* As soon as he reached the house, he went in the room, and threw himself on the floor.

²b-ṭ-š

baṭṭuuš a variety of small melon.

¹b-ṭ-ṭ

baṭṭ (coll.) ducks.

baṭṭa pl. *-aat, bṭuuṭ* duck. || *timši miθl il-baṭṭa.* She wiggles her hips nicely when she walks.

[2]*b-ṭ-ṭ*

baṭṭ (*u*) to poke, prick (the eye). *ˀaxuuya baṭṭ εeeni b-iṣibεa.* My brother poked me in the eye with his finger.

nbaṭṭ pass. of *baṭṭ. diir baalak; la-tinbaṭṭ εeenak.* Watch out; don't get poked in the eye. *εeeni nbaṭṭat bil-εarka.* My eye was poked during the fight.

b-ṭ-q

biṭaaqa pl. *-aat, biṭaayiq* **1.** ticket. **2.** card. *biṭaaqat taεziya.* card of condolence. *biṭaaqat muεaayada* greeting card.

[1]*b-ṭ-l*

buṭal (*a, u*) to be or become null, void, invalid, to expire, become obsolete. *l-paaspoort maalak buṭal; laazim taaxuδ ġeera.* Your passport has expired; you'll have to get another one. || *n-nafnuuf il-qaṣiir buṭlat l-mooda maalta.* The short dress has gone out of style.

baṭṭal **1.** to stop, cease, leave off, quit. *l-muṭar baṭṭal.* The rain stopped. *ma-tbaṭṭil, haaδa wala yuġḷub.* Aw quit it! He'll never win. *ṣaar-la sbuuε imbaṭṭil it-tadxiin.* He's been off smoking for a week. *leeš baṭṭalit min šuġḷak?* Why'd you quit your job? **2.** to make (someone) stop, cease, quit. *δall yliεε εalayya ˀila ˀan baṭṭalni mnil-εaada.* He kept after me until he made me quit the habit. **3.** to fire, lay off. *baṭṭilooni mniš-šuġuḷ.* They laid me off the job.

buṭul falseness, untruth. *šihaadta buṭul.* His testimony is false. *hal-εači kulla buṭul.* That talk is all false.

baṭaala **1.** idleness, inactivity. **2.** unemployment.

baṭṭaal unemployed, out of work. *ṣaar-li šahreen baṭṭaal.* I've been unemployed for two months.

baaṭil **1.** groundless, baseless, unfounded, false. || *bil-baaṭil* idly, groundlessly. *la-tithim il-εaalam bil-baaṭil.* Don't accuse people without evidence. **2.** null, void, invalid. *kumpyaala baaṭla* a voided promissory note.

[2]*b-ṭ-l*

baṭal pl. *ˀabṭaal* **1.** hero. *dawr il-baṭal* the role of the hero. **2.** champion. *baṭal il-mulaakama bil-wazn iθ-θaqiil* heavyweight boxing champion.

buṭuula **1.** heroism, bravery, valor. **2.** lead, leading role. *dawr il-buṭuula.* the leading role, the starring role. **3.** championship.

[3]*b-ṭ-l*

buṭil pl. *bṭuula* bottle.

b-ṭ-m

buṭum (coll.) terebinth nut(s).

buṭma pl. *-aat* terebinth nut.

buṭmaaya pl. *-aat.* variant of *buṭma.*

b-ṭ-n

baṭṭan to line (a garment). *l-xayyaaṭ baṭṭan sitirti b-εariir.* The tailor lined my jacket with silk. *l-iqmaaš maal il-qanapa mbaṭṭan ib-guuniyya.* The cloth on the sofa is lined with burlap.

baṭin pl. *bṭuun* **1.** belly, stomach, abdomen. **2.** pregnancy, delivery. *ˀawwal baṭin jaabat walad.* On her first pregnancy she had a boy. *jaabat tlaθ ibṭuun.* She's had three babies. **3.** interior, inside. *šaku b-baṭn iṣ-ṣanduug?* What's inside the trunk? *εaṭṭ diinaar ib-baṭn il-iktaab.* He put a dinar in the book. *l-walad maat ib-baṭinha.* The child died inside her. *šaggaw baṭinha w-ṭaḷḷεaw ij-jaahil.* They opened her womb to remove the baby.

bṭaana pl. *-aat* lining (of a garment).

*baaṭini** internal. *maraδ baaṭini.* internal disease.

baṭṭaaniyya pl. *-aat* blanket.

b-ṭ-n-a-š

baṭanaaš: δirab baṭanaaš to spin, slip, lose traction (esp. of a wheel). *la-tduus εal-baanziin ihwaaya tara tuδrub baṭanaaš.* Don't give it too much gas or you'll spin the wheels. *l-wiil da-yiδrub baṭanaaš.* The wheel's spinning.

b-ε-b-ṣ

baεbaṣ (vulgar) **1.** to poke, or pretend to poke, lewdly with a finger. *min čaanat timši giddaama, baεbaṣha w-širad.* As she was walking in front of him, he poked her and ran away. **2.** to make a lewd gesture with the middle finger, suggesting poking.

baεbuus, baεbuuṣa pl. *baεaabiiṣ* **1.** act of lewd poking. **2.** (by extension) the middle finger. || *huwwa b-gadd il-baεbuuṣ w-yiεči kbaar.* He's a runty little shrimp and still he talks big.

b-ε-θ

biεaθ (*a baεiθ*) to send, send out, dispatch. *leeš ma-tibεaθ-la maktuub?* Why don't you send him a letter?

l-baعθ, ḥizb il-baعθ the Ba'ath Party, Renaissance Party.

*baعθi** 1. of or pertaining to the Ba'ath Party. 2. member of the Ba'ath Party.

biعθa pl. *-aat* 1. delegation, mission. *biعθa عaskariyya* military mission. 2. student exchange (for studying abroad at Government expense). *ṭaalib biعθa* bursary student.

baaعiθ reason, cause, motive. *l-baaعiθ عaj-jariima* the motive for the crime.

mabعuuθ 1. dispatched, delegated. 2. (pl. *-iin*) envoy, delegate.

b-ع-θ-r

baعθar 1. to scatter, strew. *la-tbaعθir ġaraaḍak ihnaa w-ihnaak.* Don't scatter your things all around. 2. to squander. *baعθar kull ifluusa عal-igḥaab.* He squandered all his money on whores.

tbaعθar to become scattered. *ġaraaḍi tbaعθar min wugعat ij-junṭa.* My things got scattered when the suitcase fell.

b-ع-d

biعad to go far away, become distant. *l-mawkib biعad minna hwaaya.* The parade has gotten a long way from us. *ṭ-ṭiyyaara biعdat ihwaaya. ma-agdar ašuufha baعad.* The plane has gotten very distant. I can't see it anymore. *biعadna عan il-wlaaya; tara il-baanziin yixlaṣ.* We've gotten far from the city; the gas may run out.

baععad 1. = *biعad. baععadna عan ij-juruf. xal-nirjaع.* We've gotten far from the shore. Let's go back. *min yšawwit, ybaععid ihwaaya.* When he shoots for a goal, he overshoots it by quite a lot. 2. to remove, move away. *baععid il-manqal min yammi.* Move the brazier away from me. 3. to deport. *l-ḥukuuma baععdata ʔila ʔiiraan li-ʔan dixal il-عiraaq bala paaspoort.* The government deported him to Iran because he entered Iraq without a passport.

ʔabعad 1. to banish, exile. *majlis il-wuzaraaʔ ʔabعada.* The council of ministers exiled him. 2. to remove, send away, deport. *š-šurṭa ʔabعidoo عan il-عiraaq.* The police threw him out of Iraq.

tbaععad reflex. of *baععad. tbaععad minna, tara yعaḍḍak.* Get away from him, or he'll bite you.

btiعad 1. to move or go far away, to get distant. *btiعad عan ij-juruf w-ġirag.* He got far away from the shore and sank. *l-maaṭoor ibtiعad ihwaaya; ma-dagdar inšuufa baعad.* The launch has gotten very far away; we can't see it any more. 2. to withdraw, pull away, avoid. *btiعad عan jamaaعta li-ʔan gaamaw ysikruun w-yilعabuun iqmaar.* He's moved away from his group because they began to drink and gamble. *min itšuufa, btiعid عanna; daaʔiman yšiil musaddas.* When you see him, keep away from him; he always carries a pistol. *ḥaawil tibtiعid عan hiiči mašaakil.* Try to avoid problems like this.

stabعad to consider unlikely, to doubt. *ʔastabعid yiji baačir.* I doubt he'll come tomorrow. *ʔastabعid quṣṣṭa عan il-ḥaadiθ.* I doubt his account of the accident. *ʔastabعid hal-عamal minnak.* I wouldn't have expected that of you. *ma-astabعid haaḏa minna ʔabadan.* I wouldn't ever put that past him.

buعud, biعid 1. remoteness. 2. (pl. *ʔabعaad*) distance. *عala buعud miit matir* at a distance of one hundred meters. *min biعid* from a distance. *buعud naḏar* 1. farsightedness, hyperopia. 2. foresightedness, foresight.

baعad 1. still, yet. *baعda da-yaakul.* He's still eating. *baعadha mariiḍa.* She's still sick. *waṣṣa s-sayyaara gabuḷ šahar laakin baعad ma-stilamha.* He ordered the car a month ago but he still hasn't received it. *xaḷḷaṣit loo baعad?* Have you finished yet? *laakin baعad ma-šaafa liṭ-ṭabiib.* But he hasn't seen the doctor yet. 2. after. *raḥ-ʔarjaع baعd išwayya.* I'll return after a while. *raḥ-yooṣal l-ihnaa baعad šahar.* He'll arrive here a month from now. *sbaḥna šwayya baعd iḏ-ḏuhur.* We swam a bit in the afternoon. 3. more. *triid baعad ifluus?* Do you want more money? *baعad š-itriid?* What else do you want? *xilaṣ! ʔaani š-عalayya baعad?* That settles it! What does it matter to me anymore? *baعad-li θlaθ idnaaniir w-yṣiir عindi ʔalif.* Just three more dinars and I'll have a thousand. *šgadd baعad-lak w-itxalliṣ?* How much longer until you finish?

baعad-ma (conj.) after. *baعad-ma tعaššeena, riḥna lis-siinama.* After we had supper, we went to the movies.

biعiid, baعiid 1. far, distant. *beetna biعiid.* Our house is far away. *baعiid in-naḏar.* farsighted, foresighted. *baعiid il-iḥtimaal* unlikely, improbable. *muu baعiid yiji b-nafs il-waqit illi nitlaع bii.* It isn't unlikely that he'll come at the same time we're leaving. *biʕiid ʕannak* (a polite expression used when speaking of an unpleasant occurrence, approx.:) May it never happen to you. *biʕiid ʕannak, nṭaak ʕumra l-baarḥa.* God forbid. He died yesterday. *min biʕiid* distantly. *yigrab-li min biʕiid.* He's distantly related to me. *maa-li bii ʕalaaqa, laa min giriib wala min biʕiid.* I've no connection with him, neither close nor distant. *l-baʕiid* a way of referring to someone not present, whom the speaker is condemning.

baʕdeen 1. then, after that. *w-baʕdeen iš-ṣaar?* And then what happened? 2. afterwards, later. *ʔaḥči wiyyaak baʕdeen.* I'll talk to you later. || *w-baʕdeen min ʔiidak? š-raḥ insawwi?* What's next from you? What are we going to do? *w-baʕdeen wiyyaak? ma-tiskut ʕaad!* What's next? Why don't you shut up!

ʔibʕaad banishment, deportation, expulsion.

mubʕad deportee, exile.

mustabʕad unlikely, improbable. *quṣṣa mustabʕada* an unlikely story.

b-ʕ-r

biʕiir pl. *biʕraan, ʔabaaʕir* camel.

b-ʕ-r-r

baʕrar to defecate (of sheep, goats, and camels). *l-xaruuf da-yimši w-ybaʕrir.* The sheep's walking along and dropping dung. || *haaδa ybaʕrir ib-ḥačya. la-tdiir-la baal.* He's talking nonsense. Don't pay any attention to him.

baʕruur (coll.) dung, manure (sheep, goat, or camel).

baʕruura pl. *-aat* un. n. of *baʕruur.*

b-ʕ-ṣ

buʕaṣ (*a baʕuṣ*) (vulgar) 1. to poke lewdly with the finger. *biʕaṣṭa min šifta laabis qaaṭ jidiid.* I poked him when I saw him wearing a new suit. 2. to nonplus, confound, deflate. *buʕaṣa b-hal-iḥčaaya.* He took the wind out of his sails with that remark. 3. to mess up, foul up, ruin, wreck. *buʕaṣha l-qaδiyyat is-safra. ma-raḥ-yjiib sayyaarta.* He messed up the business of the trip. He's not going to bring his car. *buʕaṣa b-hal-muʕaamala.* He messed him up on that deal.

b-ʕ-δ̣

baʕaδ̣ some, a few. *baʕδ̣ it-talaamiiδ* some of the students. || *baʕδ̣ iš-šii* something, a little bit. *ʔisʔal ʕali; yiftihim baʕδ iš-šii b-hal-mawδuuʕ.* Ask Ali; he knows a little about this subject. *ʕala baʕδ̣* /plus pronominal ending/ up to sorts, one's usual self. *š-biik il-yoom? muu ʕala baʕδ̣ak.* What's ailing you today? You aren't your usual self. *baʕaδ maʕa baʕaδ̣* each other, among themselves. *xalliihum yitbaaṣṭuun baʕaδ̣hum maʕa baʕaδ̣.* Let them fight it out among themselves.

baʕδ̣an sometimes, at times, occasionally. *baʕδ̣an wala yiʕjibni ʔaštuġul.* Sometimes I don't like to work at all.

b-ġ-t

baaġat to surprise, come unexpectedly upon. *š-šurṭa baaġtoo min čaan da-yiksir il-qaaṣa.* The police surprised him while he was cracking the safe.

ʕala baġta, baġtatan all of a sudden, suddenly. *ʕala baġta smaʕna ʕyaaṭ.* All of a sudden we heard shouting. *baġtatan ič-čalib gumaz ʕalayya.* Suddenly the dog jumped at me.

b-ġ-d-a-d

baġdaad Baghdad.

*baġdaadi** pl. *bġaadda* 1. from Baghdad, Baghdadi. 2. native of Baghdad, Baghdadi.

b-ġ-δ̣

buġaδ̣ (*u baġuδ̣*) to loathe, detest, hate. *leeš tubġuδ̣ni?* Why do you hate me?

nbuġaδ̣ pass. of *buġaδ̣. nbuġaδ̣ min kull it-talaamiiδ.* He's hated by all the students.

buġuδ̣ hatred, hate.

ʔabġaδ̣ more or most hated, loathed, detested.

mabġuuδ̣ hated, loathed, detested.

b-ġ-l

baġal pl. *bġaal* mule.

baġla pl. *-aat* female mule.

b-ġ-y

nbiġa /in pres. tense/ to be necessary, desirable. *čaan yinbiġi tgul-la.* You should have told him. *ma-tδ̣inn yinbiġi tiftaḥ daftar ijdiid?* Don't you think you ought to start a new ledger?

baġaaʔ prostitution.

mabġa pl. *mabaaġi* brothel. *l-mabġa l-ʕaamm* the red light district.

buġya pl. *-aat* desired object, goal. *tirakha baʕad-ma naal buġiita.* He left her after he got what he wanted.

b-q-b-q

baqbaq 1. to bubble, gurgle. *t-timman da-ybaqbuq. xalli ʕalee šwayya maay.* The rise is bubbling. Put some water in it.

2. to cluck. *d-dijaaja da-tbaqbuq.* The hen is clucking.

baqbaqa bubbling.

buqbaaqa pl. *-aat, buqaabiiq* bubble.

b-q-č

baqqač to bundle, gather up in a bundle. *baqqač il-ihduum w-axaðha lil-makwi.* He bundled up the clothes and took them to the cleaner's.

buqča pl. *buqač* a large, cotton cloth used to tie up things in a bundle.

baqča pl. *-aat* small flower garden.

b-q-r

baqar (coll.) cow(s), cattle. *laħm il-baqar* beef.

baqara pl. *-aat* cow.

b-q-ṣ-m

baqṣam (coll.) rusk(s), zwieback.

baqṣama pl. *-aat* rusk, zwieback.

b-q-l-a-w

baqlaawa (coll.) baklava, a Near Eastern confection.

baqlaawaaya pl. *-aat* a piece of baklava.

b-q-y

buqa (*a baqaaʔ*) **1.** to remain, stay. *buqeet ib-baġdaad isbuuʕ.* I stayed in Baghdad a week. *ʔinta jaay wiyyaana loo baaqi?* Are you coming with us or staying? *ma-adri ween buqa; huwwa s-suug hiyyaata!* I don't know where he's keeping himself; the market is close-by here. *buqa ʕindi bass diinaareen.* I've only got two dinars left. *ʔiða jooʕaan, ʔaku ʔakil baaqi.* If you're hungry, there's some food left. *baaqii-la santeen ʕat-taxarruj.* He's got two years left to graduation. *šgadd baaqi ʕal-ʕiid?* How much longer till the holiday? *l-laħam yubqa biθ-θallaaja sbuuʕ w-ma-yitlaf.* Meat will last in the refrigerator a week and not spoil. **2.** to continue, go on, keep on. *buqeena nilʕab saaʕa.* We kept on playing for an hour. || *ma-buqa ġeer tið̣rubni.* There's nothing left now except for you to hit me.

baqqa to cause or allow (something or someone) to remain, stay, or be left. *baqqeet šii mnil-ʔakil, loo ʔakalta kulla?* Did you leave any of the food, or did you eat it all? *baqqii ʕan-naar išwayyt il-lux.* Leave it on the fire a little longer. *l-mudiir baqqaani ʔaštuġuḷ ʔila hassa.* The director kept me working till now.

tbaqqa pass. of *baqqa. šgadd raħ-yitbaqqa mnid-deen?* How much of the debt will be left?

nbuqa pass. of *buqa. hal-maħall ma-yinbuqi bii ʔakθar min saaʕa liʔan ħaarr.* You can't stay in this place more than an hour, it's so hot.

baqaaʔ remaining, staying.

baqiyya **1.** remainder, rest. *baqiyyt il-fluus* the rest of the money. *l-baqiyya* the rest, the others. || *l-baqiyya b-ħayaatak.* polite formula for expressing condolences to the bereaved. **2.** well, so. *baqiyya—la-tfaatiħni b-hal-mawð̣uuʕ baʕad.* So—don't bring up the matter with me again.

baaqi **1.** rest, remainder. **2.** remainder (arith.). **3.** everlasting, eternal. *l-ħayy il-baaqi* the Eternal Being.

b-g-ʕ

baggaʕ to get stained, spotted. *šuuf θoobi baggaʕ mnil-ʕarag.* Look how my shirt got stained from the sweat.

ʔabgaʕ fem. *bagʕa* pl. *buguʕ, bagʕiin* spotted, speckled (of animals). *ħṣaan ʔabgaʕ* piebald horse.

b-g-g

ḅagg (coll.) **1.** mosquito(es) **2.** gnat(s).

ḅagga pl. *-aat* un. n. of *ḅagg.*

b-g-l

baggaaḷ pl. *-iin, bgaagiiḷ* grocer.

bgaaḷa grocery business.

b-k-t-y-r-y-a

baktiirya bacteria.

b-k-r

btikar **1.** to invent. *btikar makiina jdiida.* He invented a new machine. **2.** to originate, create, start. *paariis tibtikir ʔaħdaθ ʔazyaaʔ in-niswaan.* Paris creates the latest women's fashions.

bakra pl. *-aat, bakar.* **1.** spool, reel. **2.** pulley. **3.** winch.

bukra = *baačir,* which see under *b-č-r.*

bakaara virginity.

baakir, baakra pl. *bawaakir* virgin.

btikaar pl. *-aat* **1.** creation, fashion design. **2.** creative idea.

b-k-l

bukla pl. *-aat* forelock, lock of hair on the fore part of the head.

b-k-l-w-r-y-a

bakaloorya baccalaureate. *mtiħaan bakaloorya* baccalaureate examination. *šahaada bakaloorya* high school degree, baccalaureate.

b-k-l-w-r-y-s

bakalóoryus and *bakalóoryoos* (invar.) bachelor's degree. *šahaada bakalooryus* bachelor's degree. *bakalooryus bil-ʕuluum* bachelor of science degree.

b-l-a

bila (prep.) without. *dixal is-siinama bila biṭaaqa.* He went in the movie without a ticket. || *bila laġwa. ma-yčijbak, la-tiji.* No nonsense. If you don't want to, don't come. *bila začal. ma-aku mukaan bis-sayyaara.* Don't get mad. There isn't any room in the car.

bila-ma (conj.) without, unless. *raḥ-aġul-lak bila-ma tis'al.* I'll tell you without your asking. *marrat 'ayyaam bila-ma nismač minna.* Days passed without our hearing from him. *ma-tigdar itsuuq bila-ma titčallam siyaaqa.* You can't drive unless you take driving lessons.

b-l-a-š

balaaš see under *b-l-š*.

[1]*b-l-b-l*

bilbil pl. *balaabil* nightingale.

[2]*b-l-b-l*

balbuula pl. *-aat* spout (of a pitcher, teapot, etc.)

b-l-d

balda pl. *-aat* city, town, community.

balad, blaad pl. *buldaan* country. || *šuġul iblaad* foreign manufacture, foreign workmanship.

*blaadi** foreign. *biðaača blaadiyya* foreign goods.

*baladi** municipal. *l-majlis il-baladi* the municipal council.

baladiyya municipal administration, city government.

baliid pl. *-iin, buladaa'* stupid. *tilmiið baliid* a stupid student.

balaada stupidity.

'ablad more or most stupid.

b-l-s-m

balsam balsam, balm.

b-l-š

bilaš (*a bilša*) **1.** to become involved, get entangled, get mixed up. *ma-ard 'ablaš wiyya hiiči naas.* I don't want to get mixed up with that kind of people. *šloon tiblaš ib-hiiči šaġla?* How did you ever get messed up in such a deal? **2.** to get stuck, get a bad deal, get the dirty end of the stick. *walla bilašit ib-has-sayyaara l-palašqa.* I really got stuck with this junky car. *dzawwajha w-bilaš biiha.* He married her and got stuck with her.

ballaš **1.** to stick, give (someone) the dirty end of the stick. *š-ballašak ib-has-sayyaara?* How'd you get stuck with this car? *walla, ballašni b-haš-šarwa.* Gosh, he stuck me on that deal. *wallaahi, ma-ridit 'aštiriiha bass huwwa ballašni.* By golly, I didn't want to buy it but he stuck me with it. **2.** to commence, start, go ahead. *šwakit raḥ-itballiš bil-binaa'?* When are you going to start building?

tbaalaš to pick fights, get into fights. *la-titbaalaš wiyya l-čaalam.* Don't fight with people.

bilša pl. *-aat* **1.** mess, muddle. **2.** bother, pain in the neck.

balaaš (invar.) free, gratis. *nṭaani qalam basma balaaš.* He gave me a pencil free. *b-balaaš* for free, for nothing. *stireetha balaaš.* I bought it cheap. *yaa balaaš! walla balaaš!* My, that's cheap, that's a steal! *l-balaaš ma-yinḥaaš.* You don't get something for nothing.

[1]*b-l-ṭ*

ballaṭ to pave. *raḥ-yballṭuun iš-šaarič w-nixlaṣ imnit-tiraab.* They're going to pave the street and we'll be rid of the dust. *xalli sayyaartak ihnaa. šaaričhum ma-mballaṭ.* Leave your car here. Their street isn't paved.

tabliiṭ paving, pavement, surface (of a road or sidewalk).

mballaṭ paved. *šawaarič mballaṭa* paved streets.

[2]*b-l-ṭ*

balluuṭ (coll.) **1.** oak(s) **2.** acorn(s).

balluuṭa pl. *-aat* **1.** oak. **2.** acorn.

[3]*b-l-ṭ*

balṭa pl. *-aat* axe, hatchet.

b-l-č

bilač (*a balič*) to swallow. *lsaani miltihib; ma-agdar 'ablač riigi.* My tongue's swollen; I can't swallow. *ma-yigdar yiblač il-ḥabbaaya bila mayy.* He can't swallow the pill without water. **2.** to swallow, put up with, stomach. *ma-agdar ablač hal-'ihaanaat.* I can't put up with these insults.

ballač to make swallow. *l-'umm balličat ibinha l-ḥabbaaya.* The mother forced her son to swallow the pill.

balluuč, balluuča pl. *-aat, blaaliič* drain, cesspool.

b-l-č-m

balčam to astound, dumbfound. *ḥčaayta balčimatni.* His remark floored me.

tbalčam **1.** to be unable to speak, to stammer. *kull-ma l-mučallim yis'ala su'aal, yitbalčam.* Whenever the teacher asks him a question, he gets tongue-tied. **2.** to be hesitant to speak, to hem and haw, beat around the bush. *lamma ṭlabit minna yinṭiini n-natiija, gaam yitbalčam.* When I asked him to give me the result, he started hemming and hawing.

balčuum pl. *blaačiim* **1.** throat. **2.** (pl.

only) *blaaεiim* tonsils. || *ʔidhan balεuuma εatta ymašši qaδiitak.* Bribe him so he'll put your case through.

b-l-ġ

bilaġ (*a buluuġ*) **1.** to reach, get to, arrive at, come to. *t-taεaddi bilaġ εadda; baεad ma-atεammal.* The aggression has reached its limit; I can't take anymore. *yxalluu yitṣarraf b-ifluusa min yibluġ sinn ir-rušid.* They'll let him manage his money when he comes of age. **2.** to reach puberty, become sexually mature. *raε-yzawwjuu bass yiblaġ.* They're going to get him married as soon as he reaches puberty.

ballaġ **1.** to convey, transmit, impart, communicate, report. *ballaġ taεiyyatna lil-ʔahal wil-ʔaṣdiqaaʔ.* He conveyed our greetings to the family and friends. **2.** to notify officially. *ballaġta bid-daεwa l-baarεa.* I served him with a summons yesterday. *ballġata š-šurṭa b-luzuum εuδuura lil-maεkama.* The police notified him he had to appear in court.

baalaġ to exaggerate. *ybaaliġ ihwaaya b-waṣfa l-ʔay šii.* He exaggerates a lot in describing anything.

tballaġ pass. of *ballaġ*. *tballaġ w-raε-yiεδar il-muεaakama.* He was officially notified and he's going to attend the trial.

balaaġ pl. *-aat* communication, report, communiqué, bulletin.

buluuġ, biluuġ **1.** attainment, reaching, arrival at. **2.** puberty, sexual maturity. *sinn il-biluuġ* the age of puberty.

mablaġ pl. *mabaaliġ* **1.** amount, sum of money. **2.** (by extension) price, cost.

tabliiġ pl. *-aat* subpoena, summons.

mubaalaġa pl. *-aat* exaggeration.

baaliġ **1.** adolescent, having reached puberty. **2.** an adolescent. **3.** adult, mature. **4.** an adult.

muballiġ pl. *-iin* process server (of a court).

b-l-ġ-m

balġam phlegm.

b-l-f

bilaf (*i balif*) to bluff, deceive, trick. *bilafha w-ʔaxaδ ifluusha minha.* He tricked her and took her money. *bilafa w-xallaa ydaayna fluus.* He bluffed him and made him loan him money.

balfa pl. *-aat* bluff, trick.

ballaaf pl. *-a, -iin* trickster, deceiver, bluffer.

b-l-q-w-n

balqoon, baalqoon pl. *-aat* balcony.

b-l-k

balki, balkat, balkan perhaps, maybe. *balki maat baačir; xalli nisʔala hassa.* Maybe he'll die tomorrow; let's ask him now. *ntiδir fadd εašir daqaayiq; balkat yiji.* Wait about ten minutes; perhaps he'll come. *smaεit ṣaar janaraal . . . balkat.* I heard he became a general . . . It could be.

b-l-k-w-n

balkoon, baalkoon pl. *-aat* balcony.

b-l-l

ballal to wet, soak, moisten. *ballil ʔiidak gabul-ma tiεjin il-εajiin.* Wet your hands before you knead the dough. *l-muṭar ballal ihduumi.* The rain soaked my clothes. *ballal iṭ-ṭaabiε b-ilsaana w-lizaga.* He moistened the stamp with his tongue and stuck it on. || *l-imballal ma-yxaaf imnil-muṭar.* What more is there to lose? (lit., whoever's gotten soaked isn't afraid of the rain).

tballal to get wet, be soaked. *tballalit bil-muṭar.* I got wet in the rain.

balla: haaδa zaad iṭ-ṭiin balla. That made things worse.

b-l-l-y

billi pl. *-iyyaat* ace (in cards).

b-l-m

balam pl. *blaam* **1.** small rowboat, skiff. **2.** lateen rigged sailing barge, dhow. **3.** large porcelain serving platter.

ballaam pl. *-a* man who operates a rowboat.

b-l-h

balaaha **1.** stupidity. **2.** idiocy.

ʔablah idiot, stupid person.

b-l-h-r-s

bilhaarisya, bilhaariizya bilharziasis, schistosomiasis.

b-l-w

balwa see under *b-l-y*.

b-l-w-r

balluur (coll.) **1.** crystal. **2.** crystal glass.

balluura pl. *-aat* piece of crystal.

*balluuri** crystal, crystalline.

b-l-w-z

bluuz pl. *-aat* **1.** blouse. **2.** sweater, pullover.

¹*b-l-y*

bila (*i bali*) **1.** to accuse. *j-jiiraan biloo bil-booga.* The neighbors accused him of the theft. **2.** to afflict, try, torment. *l-muεallim bilaana bil-imtiεaanaat.* The teacher bothered us continually with examinations. *bilaani b-ibna.* He pestered me continually about his son.

baala to care, be concerned. *min git-la marta maatat, wala baala.* When I told him his wife died, he wasn't concerned at all. *yiḉči š-ma-yriid w-ma-ybaali.* He says what he wants and doesn't worry about the consequences. *ma-smaḉit il-ˀaxbaar? ˀašu wala mbaali.* Didn't you hear the news? It seems you're not concerned at all.

nbila pass. of *bila. xaṭiyya, nbila bil-booga.* Poor guy, he was accused of the theft.

btila **1.** to be afflicted, get stuck. *ˀaxuuya maat w-xallaani ˀabtili b-wilda.* My brother died and left me saddled with his kids. *yaḉni btileet biik? ma-tištuġuḷ!* How'd I get stuck with you? Get to work! *btileet ib-sayyaarti; kull yoom yiṭlaḉ biiha ḉeeb jidiid.* I got stuck on my car; every day a new defect turns up in it. *xaṭiyya, mibtili b-ibna.* Poor guy, he's got his hands full with his son. **2.** to get involved, get in trouble. *la-timši wiyyaa, tara tibtili.* Don't associate with him, or you'll find yourself in trouble. *xalli nruuḉ gabuḷ-ma tiji š-šurṭa tara nibtili.* Let's go before the police come or we may get ourselves in trouble. *waḷḷa btileet! ma-adri ˀil-man axdim.* God, I'm in a mess! I don't know who to take orders from. *bii-man ibtileet! haaδa yuḉruf nuṣṣ id-dinya.* Look who you've tangled with! He knows everybody. || *fuut min giddaami gabuḷ-ma ˀabtili biik.* Get out of my sight before I get your blood on my hands.

balaaˀ, bala affliction, visitation. *haaδa balaaˀ min ˀaḷḷa.* This is an affliction from God. || *haaδa balaaˀ maal ˀaḷḷa. yoomiyya ysawwii-la ḉarka.* He's a holy terror. Every day he starts a fight. *haaδa čalib loo bala ˀaswad?* Is that a dog or a black terror?

balwa pl. *balaawi* tribulation, affliction, misfortune, distress, calamity. *haaδa ġeer balwa; yoomiyya jaayib is-sayyaara lil-garaaj.* He's a real affliction; he brings the car to the garage every day. *haaδa ġeer balwa; kull in-naas yxaafuun minna.* He's a real terror; everyone's scared of him. *la-tiddaaxal tara waraaha balwa.* Don't interfere because there's only misfortune to come of it.

mubaalaa attention, heed. *bala mubaalaa* without paying attention, unconcernedly.

btilaaˀ affliction, tribulation. *btilaaˀa bil-iqmaar ḉaṭṭama.* His affliction with gambling destroyed him. *haaδa šloon ibtilaaˀ min ˀaḷḷa! walaa yištuġuḷ; yδibb kull iš-šuġuḷ ḉalayya.* What an affliction he is! He won't work; he lets me do it all.

*laa-ˀubaali** **1.** indifferent, unconcerned, careless, heedless, inattentive. **2.** indifferent, unconcerned person.

²*b-l-y*

bali **1.** yes, of course, certainly. *bali, tamaam.* Yes, that's right. *bali, ˀatṣawwar yigdar yinjaḉ.* Yes, I think he can succeed. *bali, ˀaġaati! leeš laa?* Sure, man! Why not? *bali, ˀaġaati! leeš ma-yirkab káadi-laak ˀiδa zzawwaj waḉda zangiina?* Sure, man! Why shoudn't he ride in a Cadillac if he's married a rich girl? || *ˀabu bali* yes man, sycophant. **2.** (as a question) pardon? eh? *bali? š-gilit? ma-smaḉit.* Pardon? What'd you say? I didn't hear.

b-l-y-a-r-d

bilyaard billiards.

b-l-y-w-n

bilyoon pl. *balaayiin* billion.

b-m-b-a-r

bumbaar variant of *mumbaar* which see under *m-m-b-a-r*.

b-n-t

bint, bitt pl. *banaat* **1.** daughter. *binti* my daughter, and by extension, approx., kid, little girl. || *bint il-ḉamm* (uncle's daughter) = cousin on father's side. *bint il-xaaḷ* (uncle's daughter) = cousin on mother's side. *bint il-ˀax* (brother's daughter) = niece. *bint ˀabuuha* (her father's daughter) a girl displaying commendable traits. *bint ḉaraam* illegitimate daughter, and by extension, bitch, brat. *bint gaḉba* daughter of a whore, and by extension, bitch. **2.** one of, one from, a member of. *bint il-imḉalla* a woman from the neighborhood. *bint iθ-θilaaθiin* a woman of thirty. *bint ḉarab* an Arab woman. || *bint wurdaan, bitt murdaan* cockroach. *bint iš-šaqqa* ladybug, ladybird beetle. **3.** queen (in cards).

see also *bnayya* under *b-n-y*.

b-n-j

bannaj to anesthetize. *d-duktoor ma-bannajni gabḷ il-ḉamaliyya.* The doctor didn't anesthetize me before the operation.

banj anesthetic.

¹*b-n-d*

bannad **1.** to stop working, be idle (with a commercial vehicle). *raḉ-ˀabannid is-sayyaara s-saaḉa xamsa.* I'm going to put the car away at five. *raḉ-inbannid baačir.*

We're not going to drive tomorrow. *šuġl it-taksiyyaat muu zeen. ṣaar-li sbuuƐ imbannid.* The taxi business is bad. I haven't been driving for a week. **2.** to suspend. *bannidaw haj-jaaki sbuuƐeen.* They suspended that jockey for two weeks.

²*b-n-d*

band pl. *bunuud* **1.** a bundle of 100 large sheets of paper. **2.** clause, article, paragraph (of a contract).

¶ *ðirab band* to trip, cause to stumble. *ðirabni band w-waggaƐni.* He tripped me and made me fall.

banid var. of *band.* || *xeeṭ banid* wrapping string, parcel string.

³*b-n-d*

ḅanid pl. *ḅnuud* bonnet, hood (of a car).

b-n-d-q

bunduq (coll.) **1.** hazelnut(s), filbert(s). **2.** hazel, hazel tree(s).

bunduqa pl. *-aat, banaadiq* un. n. of *bunduq.*

bunduqi pl. *bunduqiyya* (military) gunsmith, armorer.

bunduqiyya pl. *banaadiq* **1.** rifle, gun. **2.** shotgun.

l-bunduqiyya Venice.

b-n-ṭ-r-w-n

ḅanṭaruun pl. *-aat, ḅanaaṭiir* pants, trousers.

b-n-f-s-j

*banafsaji** violet (adj). || *ˀašiƐƐa fooq il-banafsajiyya* ultra-violet rays.

b-n-f-š

banafša a purplish carbonated drink.

b-n-g

ḅang pl. *ḅinuug* bank, banking house.

b-n-n

*bunni** brown, coffee colored. *qaaṭ bunni* a brown suit.

b-n-n-y

bunni (coll.) a common variety of edible fish similar to the carp.

bunniyya pl. *-aat* un. n. of *bunni.*

¹*b-n-y*

bina (*i binaaˀ*) to build, construct, erect. *binaa-la beet jidiid.* He built himself a new house. *štireet qiṭƐa rukun. raƐ-abniiha beet.* I bought a corner lot. I'm going to build a house on it.

binaaˀ building, construction.

binaaˀan Ɛala based on, due to, on the basis of. *binaaˀan Ɛala maraða, nṭoo ˀijaaza šahar.* Due to his illness, they gave him a month's leave. *binaaˀan Ɛala haaða, kull it-tarfiiƐaat itwaqqfat.* Because of this, all promotions have been stopped.

bunya build, frame, physique, constitution.

banna pl. *-aaya* mason, master bricklayer.

binaaya **1.** building, construction. **2.** (pl. *-aat*) building, structure, edifice.

mabni built, made, constructed. *mabni min ṣaxar* built of stone.

²*b-n-y*

tbanna **1.** to adopt. *tbanneena yatiim imnil-maytam il-ˀislaami.* We adopted an orphan from the Islamic Orphanage. **2.** to adopt, take an interest in, take up the cause of. *waziir id-daaxiliyya nafsa tbanna hal-mašruuƐ.* The Minister of the Interior himself has embraced this project.

bani ˀaadam, banyaadam human being, man. *banyaadam! ma-yitˀamman.* He's only human. You can't trust him. *l-banyaadam ṭammaaƐ.* Man is greedy. (see also *ˀ-b-n*)

bnayya pl. *-aat* **1.** daughter. **2.** girl. **3.** virgin, maiden. (see also *bint* under *b-n-t.*)

b-h-t

bihat (*a bahit*) **1.** to be or become astonished, amazed, surprised, flabbergasted. *bihatit min xašš Ɛalayya w-raawaani ˀalif diinaar.* I was amazed when he came up and showed me a thousand dinars. **2.** to astonish, amaze, surprise. *xabar naqla bihatni. wala čint aṭṣawwar yinniqil.* The news of his transfer amazed me. I'd never have imagined he'd be transferred.

nbihat to be amazed, astonished. *nbihatit min simaƐit ṭṭalligat.* I was amazed when I heard she was divorced.

buhtaan slander, lies.

baahit pale, faded. *loon baahit* a pale color.

mabhuut amazed, astonished, surprised, startled. *š-biik mabhuut? ma-tiƐči!* What're you, flabbergasted? Talk, why don't you!

b-h-j

btihaj to be glad, happy, delighted. *btihaj ihwaaya b-xabar najaaƐ ˀibna.* He was very joyful at the news of his son's success.

bahja pl. *-aat* joy, delight.

b-h-d-l

bahdal **1.** to ridicule, embarrass. *Ɛala diinaareen, bahdalni giddaam in-naas.* For two dinars, he ridiculed me in front of people. **2.** to make a mess of, disrupt, ruin.

l-muṭar bahdalna w-δṭarreena nbaddil. The rain made a mess of us and we had to change clothes. *leeš imbahdil nafsak hiiči? ma-tilbas ihduum zeena!* Why're you letting yourself go? Wear some good clothes! *ʔiδa ašuufa, abahdil aḥwaala.* If I see him, I'll mess him up. **3.** to waste, squander. *ʔabuu xallaf-la θarwa, laakin bahdalha bil-ʕajal.* His father left him a fortune, but he squandered it right away.

tbahdal to be or become mixed up, get in bad shape, go to ruin. *min idzawwajit, tbahdalit; ʕala ṭuul miflis.* When I got married, I got all messed up; I'm always broke.

bahdala pl. *-aat* **1.** abuse, insult. *l-bahdala ma-tinfaʕ wiyyaa.* Abuse won't do any good with him. **2.** humiliation, degradation. *š-šuġuḷ ib-had-daaʔira bahdala. maḥḥad yiḥturum il-waaḥid.* Working in this office is a trauma. No one respects you. **3.** mess, disorder, sloppiness. *šinu hal-bahdala? ma-tṣaffuṭ ġaraaδak!* What's this mess? Arrange your things, will you!

mbahdal sloppy, unkempt. *šuufa šloon imbahdal, laa mmaššiṭ wala mzayyin.* Look how sloppy he is, uncombed and unshaven.

b-h-δ-l

bahδal variant of *bahdal.*

[1]*b-h-r*

buhar (*u bahar*) to dazzle, overwhelm. *δuwa š-šamis buhar ʕeeni.* The sunlight dazzled me. *jamaalha yibhur.* Her beauty is dazzling.

nbuhar pass. of *buhar. nbuhar ib-jamaalha.* He was dazzled by her beauty.

buhra a Moslem sect concentrated in India and Pakistan.

bahaar pl. *-aat* spice, seasoning.

baahir splendid, brilliant, dazzling. *najaaḥ baahir* a brilliant success.

[2]*b-h-r*

bahaar the beginning of Spring.

*bahaari** spring, vernal. *qaaṭ bahaari* spring suit.

b-h-δ

baahiδ excessive, exorbitant, enormous. *mablaġ baahiδ* an enormous sum of money.

b-h-l

buhul (invar.) stupid, backward. *niswaan buhul* stupid women.

bahluul pl. *bahaaliil* **1.** clown, buffoon, jester. **2.** dunce, simpleton, fool.

b-h-m

bahiima pl. bahaayim **1.** beast of burden. **2.** a stupid animal.

ʔibhaam, bhaam pl. *-aat* **1.** thumb. **2.** big toe.

mubham vague, ambiguous. *ḥači mubham* vague talk.

b-h-w

bahu large hall, auditorium, recreation hall.

b-h-y

baaha to pride oneself, be proud, boast. *ʕala ṭuul ybaahi b-sayyaarta.* He's always bragging about his car.

tbaaha = *baaha. š-daʕwa titbaaha b-nafsak!* You sure are proud of yourself!

*bahaaʔi** pl. *-iyya* **1.** Bahai. **2.** a Bahai, adherent of the Bahai sect.

l-bahaaʔiyya Bahai, the Bahai religion.

b-w-b

bawwab **1.** to divide into parts or sections. *l-iktaab imbawwab ʔila tlaθ abwaab.* The book's divided into three parts. **2.** to classify, arrange in groups. *ʔariidak itbawwub-li hal-maʕluumaat.* I want you to classify this information for me.

baab pl. *ʔabwaab, biibaan* (masc. and fem.) **1.** door, doorway. **2.** gate, gateway. || *baab aš-šarji* (the South Gate) a quarter of Baghdad. **3.** sluice gate. **4.** part, section (of a book). **5.** class, type, category. *qmaaš min ʔawwal baab* top quality cloth.

¶ *la-tfukk hiiči baab.* Don't get started on that. *ʔabiiʕ purṭuqaal ʕala baab ʔaḷḷa.* I sell oranges for a living. *haaδa ʕala baab ʔaḷḷa. š-ma-dgul-la yṣaddig.* He's dim-witted. Whatever you tell him, he'll believe.

bawwaab pl. *-iin* doorman.

bawwaaba pl. *-aat* gate, sluice gate.

tabwiib arrangement, grouping.

b-w-ḥ

baaḥ (*u, i booḥ, beeḥ*) /with *b-*/ to disclose, divulge, reveal. *loo itkutla ma-ybuuḥ bis-sirr.* Even if you kill him he won't reveal the secret.

baaḥ (*i ʔibaaḥa*) to permit, allow, sanction. *l-qaaʔid baaḥ lij-jinuud yḥirguun iz-zariʕ.* The commander allowed the soldiers to burn the crops.

ʔibaaḥi **1.** licentious, amoral. *fikra ʔibaaḥiyya* an amoral idea. *ḥukuuma ʔibaaḥiyya* an amoral government. **2.** libertine, freethinker.

ʔibaaḥiyya freethinking, libertinism.

b-w-x

bawwax to steam, give off steam.

l-ħammaam da-ybawwix. ruuħ ʔiġsil. The Turkish bath is steaming. Go take a bath. *bawwax it-timman. nazzil naara šwayya.* The rice has boiled. Turn down the fire under it a little.

booxa, bwaax steam.

b-w-r

baar (u boor, bawaar) **1.** to go to waste, to be left over. *da-yaakluun kullši; ma-aku šii raħ-ybuur.* They're eating everything; nothing's going to be left over. **2.** to be unsaleable, stay on the shelf. *hal-biðaaʕa baarat, maħħad yištiriiha.* These goods didn't move; no one will buy them. **3.** to fail to get a husband, become an old maid. *binti ma-raħ-itbuur li-ʔan zangiina.* My daughter won't be left on the shelf because she's rich.

boor: ʔaraaði boor wasteland.

baayir **1.** waste, uncultivated, unused, unwanted. *ʔaraaði baayra* wasteland. **2.** unsold, left over, unwanted. *baðaayiʕ baayra* goods left on the shelves.

baayra pl. *-aat* **1.** an old maid. **2.** a woman whose husband has married a second wife.

b-w-r-a-n

booraani fried slices of eggplant, usually mixed with yoghurt and garlic.

b-w-r-g

buurag **1.** borax. **2.** a type of stuffed pastry.

b-w-r-y

buuri pl. *-iyyaat, bwaari* **1.** bugle. **2.** pipe, tube.

[1]b-w-z

bawwaz to pout, look glum. *min axaδt il-laʕʕaaba minha, bawwzat.* When I took the doll from her, she pouted. *š-biik imbawwiz? ʔaku šii?* Why are you so glum? Is something wrong?

buuz pl. *-aat* snout, muzzle (of an animal), and by extension, a derogatory term for chin. *šifta šloon buuz ʕalee?* Did you see what a chin he's got? || *mišš buuzak! ma-raħ-itħaṣṣil šii.* Wipe your chin! You won't get anything.

[2]b-w-z

bawwaẓ to shuffle. *bawwiẓ il-waraq zeen.* Shuffle the cards well.

b-w-s

baas (u boos) to kiss. *baas ibna b-guṣṣṭa.* He kissed his son on the forehead.

bawwas /with *b-*/ to kiss repeatedly, cover with kisses. *ðall ybawwis biiha nuṣṣ saaʕa.* He kept on kissing her for a half hour.

tbaawas to kiss one another. *baʕad-ma tlaagaw, tbaawasaw.* After they met, they kissed each other.

boosa pl. *-aat* kiss.

[1]b-w-š

bawwaš to put in neutral. *bawwiš il-geer.* Put the gears in neutral.

booš (invar.) **1.** empty. *l-ikwaaba l-booš* the empty cups. **2.** vain, useless. *taʕabi kulla raaħ booš.* All my efforts went to waste. **3.** neutral (automotive). *l-makiina gaaʕid tištuġuḷ bil-booš.* The motor's running in neutral. *δibb il-geer ʕal-booš.* Put the gearshift in neutral. **4.** looseness, play. *booš il-isteerin da-yziid yoom ʕala yoom.* The play in the steering is increasing all the time. **5.** (pl. *-aat*) an empty, a "dead soldier" (bottle or can), an empty cup, empty glass, etc. **6.** (pl. *-aat, bwaaš*) a worthless card. *ʔiidi čaanat kullha bwaaš.* My hand was all worthless cards.

[2]b-w-š

bawwaš, tbawwaš, buuši, buušiyya = *pawwaš*, etc. which see under *p-w-š*.

b-w-ṣ-l

booṣla, buuṣala pl. *-aat* compass.

b-w-ʕ

baawaʕ **1.** to observe, watch. *baawuʕ iš-da-asawwi ħatta tsawwi miθli.* Observe what I do so you can do it the same way. **2.** to look. *baawiʕ imniš-šibbaač w-šuuf iš-ṣaar jawwa.* Look out the window and see what happened down below. *baawiʕ jawwa l-qanapa.* Look under the couch. || *baawiʕ da-agul-lak! ʔaani ma-axaaf min it-tahdiid.* Now you look here! I'm not afraid of threats.

b-w-f-y

buufee pl. *-eyaat* buffet, sideboard.

b-w-q

buuq pl. *bwaaq* **1.** bugle. || *buuq in-noom* taps. **2.** spokesman, mouthpiece. *buuq lil-mustaʕmiriin* a mouthpiece for the imperialists.

buuqi pl. *-iyya* (mil.) bugler.

[1]b-w-g

baag (u boog) **1.** to rob, burglarize. *l-ħaraamiyya baagaw il-beet.* The thieves robbed the house. **2.** to steal. *baag nuṣṣ diinaar minni.* He stole half a dinar from me. || *baag ʔalif diinaar bil-iħsaab.* He embezzled a thousand dinars. *ʔabuug nafsi mniš-šuġuḷ nuṣṣ saaʕa.* I'll drag myself away from work for a half hour. *lahhi ʔibni ħatta ʔabuug nafsi.* Keep my son busy so I can sneak away.

bawwag to steal (habitually). *b-ʔay šuġuḷ itxallii, yguum ybawwug.* Any job you put him in, he starts to steal. *da-ybawwug ifluus iš-šarika.* He's stealing the company's money.

boog thievery, robbery, larceny, stealing. || *boog bil-iḥsaab* embezzlement.

booga pl. *-aat* **1.** a theft, a robbery. **2.** loot, swag, take, stolen goods.

¶ *bil-booga* stealthily, secretly, on the sly. *j-jaahil xašš lil-gubba bil-booga w-jarr šaعri.* The kid came into the room stealthily and pulled my hair. *da-yiji lil-mabġa bil-booga.* He goes secretly to the red-light district.

[2]*b-w-g*

baaga pl. *-aat* bunch, bouquet.

[1]*b-w-l*

baal (*u bool*) to urinate, make water. *la-tbuul bid-darub.* Don't urinate in the street.

bawwal to make (someone) urinate. *bawwli j-jaahil.* Take the kid to the potty.

bool urine. || *maraδ̣ il-bool is-sukkari.* sugar diabetes.

boola pl. *-aat* an act of urination.

mibwala, mabwala pl. *-aat, mabaawil* **1.** urinal. **2.** public urinal.

[2]*b-w-l*

baal **1.** mind. *baala mašġuul ihwaaya.* He's very preoccupied. *xalli baalak yamm it-talafoon.* Keep your mind on the telephone. *ʔisma raaḥ min baali.* His name slipped my mind. *xalliiha عala baalak. muu tinsa.* Keep it in mind. Don't you forget. *ʔisma muu عala baali.* His name doesn't come to mind. *ʔisma hassa jaa عala baali.* His name just came to me. *b-baalak min nizal iθ-θalij ihnaa qabl isbuuع?* Do you recall when the snow fell here a week ago? || *hiiči muškila ma-čaanat laa bil-baal wala bil-xaaṭir.* Such a problem could never have been expected. *baalak wiyyaak . . .!* Take care not to . . .! Mind that you don't . . .! *baalak wiyyaak itruuḥ min ʔaṭlaع.* Make sure you don't leave while I'm out. *baalak wiyyaak timši wiyya hiiči naas.* Watch yourself that you don't associate with such people. **2.** attention. *baalak عanni! hassa ʔaftaḥ il-baab ib-fadd dafعa.* Watch me! I'm going to open the door with one push. || *daar baal* to pay attention, give heed. *xawwufoo bass ma-daar baal w-xašš bil-maqbara.* They tried to frighten him but he paid no attention and went into the graveyard. *la-ddiir-la baal iš-ma yiḥči.* Don't pay any attention to him whatever he says. *diir baalak عala šuġlak.* Pay attention to your work. *diir baalak عala ġaraaδ̣i.* Watch my things. *diir baalak imnis-sayyaara!* Watch out for that car! *δ̣all baala.* He was worried, apprehensive. *la-yδ̣all baalkum. raḥ-atʔaxxar il-leela.* Don't worry. I'm going to be late tonight. *w-baalak w-baalak* a derisive expression of exaggerated emphasis. *ʔašu dguul raḥ-asaaعdak w-baalak w-baalak w-ma-bayyan šii minnak.* It seems you say "I'll help you" and this and that and nothing has appeared from you. *baalak w-baalak; wuعad yintiina fluus w-ma-qbaδ̣na šii.* He made a big fuss; he promised to give us some money and we didn't get a thing.

عabaal- (contraction of *عala baal*) /with pronominal suffix, approx.:/ it seemed, it would have seemed. *min dagg it-talafoon, عabaali ʔinta.* When the phone rang, I thought it was you. *twahhamit. عabaali ʔaxuuya.* I got confused. I thought it was my brother. *عabaalkum ajuuz imniṭ-ṭalab? raḥ-aštiki عaleekum.* Did you think I would abandon the debt? I'll sue you. *laعad š-aعbaalak? bass inta tuعruf?* So what did you think? You're the only one who knows? *gaam yṣayyiḥ عalayya عabaala yxawwufni.* He began to shout at me like he thought he'd scare me. *wugaع bil-ʔakil dagg عabaalak ma-maakil muddat šahar.* He dug into the food as though he hadn't eaten for a month.

b-w-m

buum (coll.) owl(s).

buuma pl. *-aat, buwam* un. n. of *buum.* || *ʔayaa buuma! hamm ma-dabbarha.* What a dunce! He failed again. *la-tṣiir buuma. ʔiδa yδ̣urbak, ʔinta hamm ʔuδ̣urba.* Don't be a chicken. If he hits you, hit him back. *haaδa buuma. l-kull ykarribuun عalee.* He's a sheep. Everyone loads him with work.

b-w-y

booya pl. *-aat* paint.

b-w-y-n-b-a-ġ

booyinbaaġ pl. *-aat* necktie.

b-y

bee name of the letter *b.*

b-y-b-m-t-t-w

biibimattu pl. *-uwwaat* parrot.

b-y-b-y

biibi pl. *-iyyaat* grandmother, granny.

biibiyya pl. *-aat* var. of *biibi.*

b-y-t

baat (*a mabiit, beeta*) **1.** to spend the night, stay overnight. *l-xuṭṭaar raḥ-ybaat ʕidna l-yoom.* The guest is going to stay overnight with us tonight. **2.** to sit overnight. *ʔiδa l-ʔakil ybaat, ma-yṣiir ṭayyib.* If the food sits overnight, it won't be tasty.

bayyat **1.** to put up for the night. *bayyiti binti w-baačir ʔaji ʔaaxuδha.* Keep my daughter overnight and tomorrow I'll come and get her. **2.** to keep overnight, let stand overnight. *triidni aδibb il-ʔakil il-baaqi, loo abayyita li-baačir.* Do you want me to throw out the remaining food, or keep it till tomorrow. *bayyit il-ṃaay ʕat-tiiġa, yibrad lis-subuḥ.* Let the water stand overnight on the wall of the roof to get cold for the morning. **3.** to put, place. *bayyit il-geer ʕal-waaḥid.* Put the gearshift in first. *bayyit ir-rahan ʕind axuuk.* Put the money for the bet in your brother's care. *tiskut loo ʔaji ʔabayyit irṣaaṣa b-raasak.* Shut up or I'll put a bullet in your head.

beet pl. *byuut* **1.** house, home. *bil-beet* at home. *ʔaani raayiḥ lil-beet.* I'm going home. || *maal beet* home-made, home. *xubuz maal beet* home-made bread. *ṭabux maal beet* home cooking. **2.** family. *beet ič-čalabi* the Chalabi family. *beet ʕammi* my uncle's family. **3.** case, covering, sheath, box. || *beet musaddas* pistol holster. **4.** (pl. *byuut, byaat*) verse, line (of a poem or song). || *beet il-qaṣiid* main point, gist, essence (of a story, etc.).

*beeti** home-, domestic, house-. *ʔašġaal beetiyya* household chores.

beeta, beetuuta pl. *-aat* overnight stop, stay.

mabiit pl. *-aat* **1.** overnight stop, stay. **2.** shelter for the night.

baayit left overnight, stale, old.

b-y-t-n-j-a-n

beetinjaan (coll.) eggplant(s).

beetinjaana pl. *-aat* eggplant.

beetinjaanaaya pl. *-aat* eggplant.

b-y-j-a-m

beejaama pl. *-aat* pyjamas.

b-y-ḥ

baaḥ, beeḥ see under *b-w-ḥ.*

b-y-x

baayix stale, insipid, flat. *nukta baayxa* a bad joke. *ḥčaaya baayxa* an insipid remark.

b-y-d

baad (*i ʔibaada*) to destroy, exterminate. *l-iflitt baad kull il-ḥašaraat.* The flyspray killed all the insects.

baayid, baaʔid past, bygone. *l-ʕahd il-baayid* the bygone era, the former regime.

b-y-d-r

beedar pl. *-aat, bayaadir* **1.** threshing floor, threshing area. **2.** pile, heap. *beedar tibin* pile of straw. *beedar duxun* pile of millet.

b-y-d-q

baydaq pl. *bayaadiq* pawn (in chess).

[1]*b-y-r*

biir pl. *byaar, ʔaabaar.* well. *ʔaabaar in-nafuṭ* oil wells.

[2]*b-y-r*

biira pl. *-aat* **1.** beer. **2.** a beer, a bottle of beer.

b-y-r-ġ

beeraġ pl. *byaariġ* banner, flag.

b-y-r-q

beeraq pl. *bayaariq* flag, banner, standard.

b-y-r-l-y

biirli pl. *-iyyaat* ace (playing card).

b-y-r-w-t

bayruut, beeruut Beirut.

bayruuti, beeruuti, pl. *-iyya, bayaarita* **1.** Beiruti, from Beirut. **2.** a Beiruti, a native of Beirut.

b-y-z-n-ṭ

biizanṭi beezanṭi** **1.** Byzantine. *l-ḥaδ̣aara l-biizanṭiyya* Byzantine civilization. **2.** a Byzantine.

b-y-š

beeš = *b-eeš* which see under *ʔ-y-š.*

b-y-δ̣

baaδ̣ (*i beeδ̣*) to lay (an egg). *d-dijaaja baaδ̣at il-yoom.* The hen laid today. *baaδ̣at id-dijaaja xamis beeδ̣aat ib-hal-isbuuʕ.* The hen laid five eggs this week. || *ma-tbiiδ̣ha lil-iḥčaaya ʕaad!* Come on, out with it!

bayyaδ̣ **1.** to make white, whiten. *l-ḥarub bayyiδ̣at šaʕri.* The war turned my hair white. || *bayyaδ̣ ʔaḷḷaa wiččak.* A phrase said to the bearer of good news, lit., May God lighten your face. **2.** to whitewash. *l-yoom raḥ-inbayyiδ̣ il-ḥiiṭaan.* Today we're going to whitewash the walls. **3.** to make a fair copy, to copy neatly. *da-aktib id-daris ib-hal-ʔawraaq w-baʕdeen ʔabayyiδ̣a bid-daftar.* I'm writing the lesson on these slips of paper and later I'll enter them neatly in the notebook. **4.** to lay eggs. *had-dijaaja ma-tbayyiδ̣ ʔabadan.* This chicken doesn't ever lay. **5.** to tinplate, cover with tin. *laazim itbayyiδ̣ il-ijduura gabuḷ-ma* *tuṭbux biiha.* You should coat the inside of the pots with tin before you cook with them.

byaḏḏ to turn white. *šaʕra kulla byaḏḏ.* His hair all turned white.

beeḏ (coll.) egg(s). || *beeḏ il-laglag* a frothy, colored confection.

beeḏa pl. *-aat* egg.

*bayḏawi** egg-shaped, oval.

bayaaḏ 1. white, whiteness. *ʕaleeha geer bayaaḏ.* She has a very light complexion. || *ṭilaʕ ib-bayaaḏ il-wujih. ma-θibat ḏidda šii.* He came out smelling like a rose. Nothing was proven against him. 2. white, white part. *bayaaḏ il-beeḏ* egg white, albumen. *bayaaḏ il-ʕeen* white of the eye. 3. whitewash.

bayyaaḏ pl. *-a, byaayiiḏ* tinner, man who plates copper pots.

bayyaaḏa pl. *-aat* layer, good layer, productive hen.

ˀabyaḏ fem. *beeḏa* pl. *biiḏ* white. *θoob ˀabyaḏ* white shirt. || *haaḏa ṣaḥiifta beeḏa.* His record's clean. *silaaḥ ˀabyaḏ* bayonet, sword, cold steel.

mabiiḏ pl. *mabaayiḏ* ovary.

mbayyiḏ tinner, tinplater.

mibyaḏḏa pl. *-aat* fair copy, final copy.

b-y-ṭ-r

beeṭar, bayṭar to beat severely. *beeṭroo l-baarḥa.* They beat the devil out of him yesterday.

*beeṭari** veterinary. *ṭ-ṭibb il-beeṭari* veterinary medicine.

beeṭari pl. *-iyya* veterinarian.

beeṭaar pl. *bayaaṭara* veterinarian.

beeṭara veterinary science.

b-y-ʕ

baaʕ (*i beeʕ*) to sell. *simaʕit biʕt il-beet maalak.* I heard you sold your house. *baaʕni sayyaarta.* He sold me his car. || *da-ybiiʕ razaana b-raasi.* He's trying to show off his dignity to me. *la-tbiiʕ šaqaawa b-raasi.* Don't get tough with me.

bayyaʕ to make sell, cause to sell. *wild ij-jiiraan raḥ-ybayyiʕuuna l-beet.* The neighbors' kids are going to force us to sell the house.

beeʕ pl. *buyuuʕ* sale. || *lil-beeʕ* for sale.

beeʕa pl. *-aat* sale.

bayyaaʕ pl. *-a, -iin* salesman, sales clerk.

bayyaaʕa pl. *-aat* salesgirl.

baayiʕ seller.

b-y-ʕ-a-r

bee-ʕaar see under *ʕ-w-r.*

b-y-g

beeg (formerly a title of respect, now used sarcastically:) *haaḏa beeg; ma-yištuġul.* He's a privileged character; he doesn't work. *šinu, yaa beeg, qaabil niseetni?* Hey, stuck up, have you forgotten me?

b-y-n

bayyan 1. to explain, expound. *bayyan-li l-qaḏiyya bit-tafṣiil.* He explained the matter to me in detail. 2. to appear, show up, become evident. *l-tayyaara bayynat min biʕiid.* The plane appeared in the distance. *bayyan šii min qaḏiyyat taʕyiinak?* Has anything come up on the business of your appointment? *ʕali baʕda da-ybayyin bil-gahwa kull leela?* Does Ali still show up in the coffee shop every evening? *hassa mawqifa bil-qaḏiyya bayyan.* Now his stand on the matter has come out. *l-maraḏ bayyan ʕaleek. ˀaḥsan-lak itruuḥ lil-beet.* The illness has begun to show on you. You'd better go home. 3. to be visible, to show. *ṭ-ṭayyaara baʕadha tbayyin.* The plane is still visible. *bin yiḏḥak, snuuna kullha tbayyin.* When he grins, his teeth all show. *ˀiktib ib-hal-qalam ḥatta l-kitaaba tbayyin.* Write with this pen so the writing will show up. 4. to seem, appear to be. *ybayyin ḏijit. tḥibb nirjaʕ?* It looks like you're bored. Would you rather we go back? *ybayyin ʕaleek taʕbaan.* It seems that you're tired, you look tired.

tbayyan to turn out, prove to be, appear. *tbayyan-li ˀinna muu ṣadiiq.* It became evident to me that he's not a friend. *tbayyan bil-ˀaxiir il-ḥukuuma ma-raḥ-itsawwiiha.* It turned out finally that the government isn't going to do it. *yitbayyan-li ma-ˀilhum θiqa b-ˀay waaḥid.* It looks to me like they have no confidence in anyone.

been 1. between. *been id-dinagteen* between the two columns. *beenhum, beenaathum* between them. *dixal ib-beenaathum w-faakakhum.* He stepped in between them and separated them. *haaḏa qaḏiyya beeni w-beenak bass.* This is a matter just between me and you. || *been yoom w-yoom* from day to day, occasionally. *been mudda w-mudda* from time to time, now and then. 2. among, amidst. *been il-kutub* among the books. *b-been hal-iqlaam* among these pencils. *been ij-jamaaʕa* in the midst of the group. 3. bad luck, misfortune. *ween-ma yruuḥ laaʕga l-been.* Wherever he goes bad luck is after him. **4.** death. *ʔinšaaḷḷa yaaxδak il-been.* Plague take you! (lit. God grant that death take you). *šaala l-been.* Death claimed him, he died.

bayaan pl. *-aat* **1.** statement, official report. **2.** announcement, proclamation. *baayin ʕala* /plus pronominal endings/ it seems that, it appears that. *baayin ʕalee yriid yištirii-lha hadiyya.* He seems to want to buy her a gift. *baayin ʕaleek taʕbaan.* You seem to be tired.

P

p-a-p-a

p̣aap̣a pl. *-awaat* pope

p̣aap̣awiyya Papacy.

p-a-t-r-y

paatri variant of *baatri,* battery.

p-a-č-a

paača pl. *-aat* **1.** leg, calf of the leg. **2.** a stew made of meat from the head, feet, stomach, and neck of an animal.

paačači pl. *-iyya* man who cooks and serves *paača.*

p-a-r-a

p̣aara pl. *-aat* the smallest unit of Turkish money, hence, an insignificant, almost worthless thing. *ma-yiswa wala p̣aara.* It's not worth a red cent.

p-a-š

paaša pl. *-awaat* **1.** pasha. **2.** a well-liked, popular fellow. *haaδa xooš walad — paaša.* He's a good guy — a prince.

p-a-ṣ

paaṣ pl. *-aat* **1.** pass, authorization paper. **2.** (or *baaṣ*) bus.

p-a-ṣ-ṭ-w-n

paaṣṭoon pl. *-aat* walking stick, cane.

p-a-ṭ

paaṭa even. *liʕabit waraq saaʕa w-iṭlaʕit paaṭa.* I played cards an hour and broke even.

p-a-l-ṭ-w

paalṭo pl. *-owaat* coat, overcoat.

p-a-n-d-a-n

paandaan pl. *-aat* fountain pen, ink pen. *qalam paandaan* fountain pen.

p-a-n-s-y-w-n

paansyoon pl. *-aat* **1.** boarding house. **2.** apartment house.

p-a-y

paaya pl. *-aat* **1.** leg. *paayaat il-qanafa mṭaʕṭiʕa.* The sofa legs are wobbly. **2.** step, stair. *s-sirdaab yinzil ʕišriin paaya.* The cellar is twenty steps deep. **3.** step, notch, degree. *ṣaʕʕdoo paaya lux; sawwoo mulaaḥiδ.* They raised him another step; made him a supervisor. *nazzalit xašma paaya.* I took him down a peg.

p-a-y-d-a-r

paaydaar pl. *-aat* pedal (bicycle). *ʔuδṛub paaydaar ḥeel.* Pedal hard.

p-a-y-d-w-s

paaydoos quitting time, closing time, time to stop work. *ma-tigdar tištiri ṭaabiʕ. hassa paaydoos.* You can't buy any stamps. It's closing time.

p-a-y-s-k-l

paaysikil pl. *-aat* bicycle.

p-t-t

putta an expensive sort of iridescent, silk fabric.

p-t-w

patu pl. *-uwaat* blanket.

p-t-y-t-a

puteeta (coll.) potato(es).

puteetaaya pl. *-aat* potato.

p-x-t-a

puxta (invar.) mush. *š-daʕwa ṭubaxti l-ʔakil halgadd? ṣaayir puxta.* Why'd you cook the food so much? It's gotten mushy. || *ṣaar puxta mnit-taʕab.* He got dead tired.

p-r-a-w

praawa pl. *-aat* tailor's fitting. *l-xayyaaṭ sawwaa-li praawteen.* The tailor gave me two fittings.

p-r-t-q-a-l

purtiqaal, puritqaal (coll.) orange(s).

purtiqaala pl. *-aat* orange.

*purtiqaali** orange, orange colored.

p-r-č

pirča, etc. = *firča,* etc., which see under *f-r-č.*

p-r-č-m

parčam to rivet. *parčimaw šeelmaan il-ibnaaya.* They riveted the girders of the building. || *parčamha lil-qaδiyya.* He took care of the matter once and for all. He settled the matter finally.

tparčam to be riveted. *hal-ḥadiida laazim titparčam wiyya lli yammha.* This piece of metal has to be riveted to the one next to it.

parčam pl. *paraačim* rivet. || *gaaṣṣa*

šaʕarha parčam. She has her hair cut into bangs.

p-r-d

parda pl. *-aat* curtain, drapery.

p-r-d-s-w-n

pardasuun pl. *-aat* overcoat, topcoat.

p-r-d-ġ

pardaġ (*i*) to shave close. *l-ʕallaaq pardaġ wičči kulliš zeen.* The barber gave me a very close, smooth shave.

pirdaaġ pl. *paraadiiġ* drinking glass, tumbler.

p-r-ṭ

puraṭ (*u paruṭ*) to disclose inadvertently (a secret). *diir baalak la-tupruṭ is-sirr.* Watch out you don't give away the secret. *puraṭha lil-iʕčaaya.* He let the cat out of the bag.

p-r-g-a-l

purgaal pl. *paraagiil* compass (drawing), dividers.

p-r-k-n-d-a

parakanda pl. *-iyya* **1.** disorderly, untidy, disorganized. *la-tṣiir parakanda. rattib ġaraaðak.* Don't be disorderly. Straighten up your things. **2.** untidy person.

p-r-n-j

prinj **1.** brass. **2.** bronze.

p-r-w-a-n

parawaana pl. *-aat* propeller, fan.

p-r-y-m-z

preemiz pl. *-aat* Primus stove.

p-s-t

pasta pl. *-aat* **1.** a kind of Iraqi folk song or verse. **2.** tale, story. *ṭallaʕ-li ġeer pasta ʕatta ybarrir ġiyaaba.* He told me quite a tale to justify his absence. *la-tfukkii-li pastat iz-zawaaj min jidiid.* Don't go bringing up that marriage business again.

p-s-t-r

pastar (*i*) to pasteurize. *l-maʕmal ypastir il-ʕaliib gabuḷ-ma yʕabbii bil-ubṭaala.* The plant pasteurizes the milk before they fill the bottles with it.

mpastar pasteurized. *ʕaliib impastar* pasteurized milk.

p-s-k-w-l

paskuula pl. *-aat* tassel (on a fez).

p-š-t

pušt pl. *-iyya* a bad character, degenerate.

p-š-ṭ-m-a-l

pašṭamaal pl. *-aat* sarong-like, tight-fitting garment, usually worn in public baths, etc.

p-š-k-y-r

paškiir pl. *pašaakiir* hand towel.

p-ṣ-w-a-n

paṣwaan, paṣwanči pl. *-iyya* night watchman.

p-l-a-t-y-n

plaatiin **1.** platinum. **2.** pl. *-aat* breaker points (automotive).

p-l-a-y-s

plaayis pl. *-aat* pliers, pincers.

p-l-s-y

plisee pl. *plisaat* pleat (in clothing).

p-l-š-q-a

palašqa pl. *-aat* **1.** crude, simple wagon or cart. **2.** dilapidated car, jalopy. *ma-tbiiʕ has-sayyaara? ṣaarat palašqa.* Why don't you sell that car? It's gotten to be a jalopy.

p-l-k

pulka pl. *-aat, pulak* **1.** spangle. **2.** fringe.

p-l-k-k

plakk pl. *-aat* **1.** (electrical) plug. **2.** spark plug. **3.** electrical outlet.

p-l-m-n

puḷman: sayyaara puḷman "Pullman" bus, an air conditioned passenger trailer and tractor.

p-l-y-s

puliis pl. *-iyya* police, policeman.

p-n-t-r

pantar: qandara šikil pantar shoes with decorative stitched welts on the toes and sides.

p-n-č-r

pančar to break down, fail mechanically. *pančirat is-sayyaara b-nuṣṣ id-darub.* The car broke down halfway down the road. || *wuṣal iṣ-ṣaff ir-raabiʕ w-pančar.* He got to the fourth grade and couldn't get any further. *da-agul-lak ṣiʕʕti mpančira. kallif ġeeri ysawwiiha.* I tell you my health is run down. Have someone else do it.

pančar pl. *-aat, panaačir* **1.** puncture, leak, hole. **2.** flat.

pančarči pl. *-iyya* tire repairman.

p-n-d-w-l

panduul pl. *-aat* pendulum.

p-n-ṭ-r-w-n

panṭaruun, panṭaroon pl. *-aat, panaaṭiir* pants, slacks, trousers.

p-n-k

panka pl. *-aat* electric fan.

p-h-r-y-z

pahriiz diet, prescribed regimen.

p-h-l-w-a-n

pahlawaan pl. *-iyya* **1.** circus performer. **2.** acrobat. **3.** strongman.

p-w-t-a-z
puutaaza var. of *puutaasa.*
p-w-t-a-s
puutaasa pl. *-aat* torpedo, a home-made, impact-detonating firecracker.
p-w-t-y-n
pootiin pl. *-aat* (pair of) leather boots.
p-w-d-r
poodra powder.
p-w-š
pawwaš to cause to wear the veil, to veil. *tpawwiš* ح*atta banaatha l-iṣġaar.* She makes even her little girls wear the veil.
tpawwaš 1. to put on the veil, to veil oneself. *laazim titpawwšiin gabuḷ-ma ṭṭil*ع*iin.* You should put on your veil before you go out. 2. to wear a veil, go veiled. *hiyya titpawwaš* ح*atta ma*ححad *yu*ع*rufha.* She wears a veil so no one will know her.
puuši pl. *-iyyaat, pwaaši* veil.
puušiyya pl. *-aat* var. of *puuši.*
p-w-ṣ-ṭ
pooṣṭa pl. *-aat* 1. mail, post. *dizz-li l-*ʔ*awraaq bil-pooṣṭa.* Send me the papers by mail. 2. post office. *raa*ح *lil-pooṣṭa* ح*atta yištiri ṭawaabi*ع. He went to the post office to buy some stamps. 3. group of travelers. *ra*ح*-itruu*ح *wiyya hal-pooṣṭa li-*ʔ*an kullhum tu*ع*rufhum.* You will go with this group because you know all of them.
pooṣṭači pl. *-iyya* postman.
p-w-ṭ
pawwaṭ to wrinkle and lose its shape. *min tiġsil is-sitra, tpawwuṭ.* As soon as you wash the jacket, it will wrinkle out of shape.
pooṭ pl. *-aat* faux pas, social error, slip. *ṣaa*ح*ibna kisar ġeer pooṭ il-baar*ح*a* ع*ind il-waziir.* Our friend pulled a big faux pas yesterday with the minister.
p-w-ṭ-r
pooṭar to powder, apply powder. *pooṭrat il-mukaanaat il-miltahba b-jism ij-jaahil.* She powdered the inflamed areas on the baby's body.
tpooṭar to powder oneself. *da-titpooṭar giddaam il-umraaya.* She's powdering herself in front of the mirror.
pooṭra 1. powder, face powder. 2. talcum powder, baby powder.
p-w-k
paawak to pay back, pay off, settle (a debt). *paawakit kull idyuunak.* You paid back all your debts.
tpaawak to settle with each other, settle up. *nṭaani l-ifluus w-itpaawakna.* He gave me the money and we were even.
paak even. *laa, ma-xṣarit; ṭla*ع*it paak.* No, I didn't lose; I broke even.
p-w-l
puul pl. *pwaala* 1. piece, man (backgammon, dominoes, etc.). 2. (archaic) postage stamp. 3. small Persian coin.
p-w-l-a-d
puulaad fine quality steel, spring steel.
p-y-a-d-a
pyaada on foot, walking. *sayyaarti xarbaana; jeena pyaada.* My car's out of commission; we came on foot.
p-y-p
piip pl. *pyaap(a)* barrel, keg, drum.
p-y-ṣ-w-a-n
peeṣwaan pl. *-iyya* night watchman.
p-y-k
peek pl. *-aat* 1. shot, dram (of liquor). 2. shot glass, jigger.

T

*t-a-*ʔ
*taa*ʔ name of the letter *t.*
t-a-b-w-t
taabuut pl. *twaabiit* coffin, casket.
t-a-r-y-x
taariix see ʔ*-r-x.*
t-a-z-a
taaza (invar.) 1. fresh. *fawaakih taaza* fresh fruit. 2. recent, new. *xabar taaza* recent news.
t-a-l
taal (coll.) palm seedling(s), palm shoot(s), slip(s).
taala pl. *-aat* un. n. of *taal.*
t-a-n-k-y
taanki pl. *-iyaat* tank, metal container.
t-b-d-w-r
tabbaduur (coll.) cork.
tabbaduura pl. *-aat* piece of cork, cork.
t-b-s-y
tabsi pl. *-iyaat* 1. tray. 2. large, flat pan.
*t-b-*ع
*tiba*ع *(a tabi*ع*)* 1. to follow, pursue, to trail, track. ʔ*itba*ع*a w-šuufa ween yruu*ح. Follow him and see where he goes. 2. to come after, succeed, follow. *hal-barid*

wil-muṭar raḥ-yitbaɛhum ṣaḥu. Clear weather will follow this rain and cold. **3.** to use as a guide, adhere to, follow. *loo titbaɛ hat-taɛliimaat, tilgi l-mukaan ib-suhuula.* If you adhere to these directions, you'll find the place easily. *l-mudiir ij-jidiid da-yitbaɛ siyaasat taqliil il-maṣruufaat.* The new director is following a policy of cutting expenditures. **4.** to be attached to, be fastened to. *ɛinda beet yitbaɛa muštamal w-garaaj.* He has a house with a cottage and a garage attached to it. **5.** to be attached to, under the authority of. *hal-fariɛ yitbaɛ il-fariɛ ir-raʔiisi lli b-baġdaad.* This branch office is subsidiary to the main branch which is in Baghdad.

tabbaɛ to follow, follow along. *ʔaani ʔaqra w-inta tabbiɛ w-gul-li ʔiδa ʔaġlaṭ.* I'll read and you follow along and tell me if I make a mistake. *ma-yigdar yiqra ʔiδa ma-ytabbiɛ.* He can't read if he doesn't follow the line with his finger.

taabaɛ **1.** to keep under surveillance, watch, keep an eye on, follow the progress of. *ẓall ytaabiɛ il-qaẓiyya ib-nafsa.* He kept an eye on the case personally. **2.** to continue, go on with, pursue. *taabaɛ il-xiṭaab maala baɛad-ma ṣallḥaw il-makrafoon.* He continued his speech after they fixed the microphone.

ttabbaɛ to track down, trail, follow, pursue. *š-šurṭa ttabbiɛata ʔila baṣra.* The police traced him to Basra. *č-čilaab ittabbiɛat ʔaθar il-ḥaraamiyya.* The dogs followed the criminals' tracks.

ttibaɛ to adhere to, follow, go along with, pursue. *loo mittibiɛ taɛliimaati, hal-ġalṭaat ma-čaan ṣaarat.* If you'd followed my instructions, these mistakes wouldn't have happened. *l-wizaara j-jidiida da-tittibiɛ siyaast il-ḥiyaad.* The new cabinet is pursuing a policy of neutrality.

tibbaaɛa pl. *-aat* pointer (used to follow the line in reading).

taabiɛ **1.** following, succeeding. *hal-maqaal taabiɛ il-maqaali maal l-isbuuɛ il-faat.* This article is a continuation of my article of last week. **2.** subordinate. *haš-šarika taabɛa š-šarikatna.* That company is subordinate to our company. *had-duwal čaanat taabɛa lil-ḥukm il-ingiliizi.* Those countries were under British rule. **4.** (pl. *ʔatbaaɛ*) follower, disciple. *ʔatbaaɛa kullhum tirkoo.* His followers all left him.

matbuuɛ **1.** followed, succeeded. **2.** (pl. *-iin*) leader.

t-b-ġ

tabuġ, tibiġ tobacco.

t-b-l

tibal, tabal pl. *-aat* **1.** burden, hardship. **2.** burdensome or troublesome person.

tabbuula a type of salad made with bulgur.

t-b-l-y

tibilya pl. *-aat* thick strap used for climbing palm trees, safety strap.

t-b-n

tiban (*i tabin*) to founder. *la-tʔakkil il-iḥṣaan ihwaaya, tara ttibna.* Don't feed the horse too much or you'll founder him. || *l-baarḥa tbanitha zeen bil-ɛaziima.* Yesterday I really stuffed myself at the dinner party.

ntiban to be or become foundered. *la-tinṭii lil-iḥṣaan šiɛiir ihwaaya tara yintibin.* Don't give the horse too much barley or he'll get foundered.

tibin straw.

*tibni** straw colored.

t-p-p

tappa pl. *-aat* hilltop.

t-t-n

titin tobacco. || *titna xalṣaan.* 1. He's on his last legs. He's about gone. 2. He's lost his virility. He's impotent.

titinči, tatanči pl. *-iyya* tobacconist, tobacco vendor, cigarette maker.

t-j-r

taajar to do business, deal, buy and sell, trade. *ytaajir bil-ḥariir.* He deals in silk. *huwwa ytaajir ib-ʔaɛraaẓ in-naas.* He buys and sells people's honor.

taajir pl. *tujjaar* merchant, dealer, trader. *taajir jumla* wholesaler. *taajir mufrad* retailer.

tijaara commerce, trade, business. *wizaarat it-tijaara* Ministry of Commerce.

*tijaari** commercial, trading, business. *šarika tijaariyya* trading company.

t-j-h

ttijah see under *w-j-h.*

t-č-č

tičča pl. *tičač* drawstring (in the waistband).

t-č-l

ntičal variant of *ttikal,* which see under *w-k-l.*

t-č-w

tačča **1.** to lean, prop up. *tačči kiis it-timman ɛala fadd šii ḥatta ma-yoogaɛ.* Lean the sack of rice against something so it won't fall over. *taččii-la lil-mariið ḉatta yufḉaṣa ṭ-ṭabiib.* Support the sick man so the doctor can examine him.

ntiča to lean, rest one's weight. *ma-yigdar yoogaf; laazim yintiči ḉal-ḉaayiṭ.* He can't stand up; he'll have to lean against the wall. *xalli l-umxadda waraak w-intiči ḉaleeha.* Put the pillow behind you and lean back against it.

tačwa pl. *-aat* **1.** prop, support, stay. **2.** back (of a seat).

see also *w-č-y*.

t-ḉ-t

taḉat **1.** (prep.) under. *š-šurṭa ḉaṭṭat hal-beet taḉt il-muraaqaba.* The police put that house under surveillance. *xalla sayyaarta taḉat taṣarrufi.* He put his car at my disposal. **2.** (adv.) down below, downstairs. *nazzil hal-ˀaġraað taḉat.* Take these things downstairs. *ˀintiðirni taḉat.* Wait for me downstairs. *dawwarna l-binaaya min foog ˀila taḉat.* We searched the building from top to bottom.

*taḉtaani** lower, underneath. *l-qaaṭ it-taḉtaani* the lower floor. *malaabis taḉtaaniyya* underclothes.

t-ḉ-d

ttiḉad see under *w-ḉ-d*.

t-ḉ-f

tiḉaf (*i*) to present. *tiḉafni b-hadiyya faaxra.* He presented me with an exquisite present. *ˀitḉifna b-čam nukta.* Favor us with some jokes.

tuḉfa pl. *tuḉaf* **1.** unique object, curiosity, rarity. *hat-timθaal tuḉfa; ma-aku miθla.* This statute is a rarity; there's no other like it. **2.** work of art. *l-matḉaf malyaan tuḉaf fanniyya.* The museum's full of unique works of art. **3.** something exceptionally good, something special, really something. *han-nooḉ imnit-tiffaaḉ tuḉfa.* This kind of apple is something special. *hal-maqaal tuḉfa; laazim tiqraa.* This article is a great one; you must read it. *baanii-la beet tuḉfa.* He's built himself a marvelous house.

matḉaf pl. *mataaḉif* **1.** museum. **2.** (art) gallery.

t-x-t

taxat pl. *txuut* unupholstered couch, bench with back and arms. || *yuðrub bit-taxat.* He tells fortunes. He predicts the future. *huwwa taxta naaguṣ.* He's slightly crazy. His mind has slipped a notch.

taxta pl. *-aat* **1.** small box-like stool. **2.** chopping board, bread board. **3.** card for winding yarn on.

t-x-t-x

taxtax **1.** to be stunned, stupefied, overwhelmed. *min šaaf jamaalha, taxtax.* When he saw her beauty, he was stupefied. **2.** to seduce, overcome the resistance of. *ˀiða triid ittaxtixha, ˀinṭiiha mašruub.* If you want to weaken her resistance, give her a drink.

t-x-t-r-w-a-n

taxtaruwaan pl. *-aat* **1.** sedan chair **2.** litter for carrying a coffin.

t-x-m

tixam (*i taxim*) **1.** to satiate, fill up. *ma-agdar ˀaakul wala šii, li-ˀan il-ˀakla tixmatni.* I can't eat a thing — the meal filled me up. **2.** to give indigestion, make sick. *hal-akla d-dihiina tixmatni.* That greasy food gave me indigestion.

taxxam to loaf, hang around, dawdle, kill time. *ma-ḉinda šuġuḷ. bass ytaxxim bid-daraabiin.* He has no job. He just loafs around in the streets.

ntixam **1.** to be satiated, filled up. *min yšuuf ˀakil, yoogaḉ bii dagg, ˀila ˀan yintixum.* When he sees food, he digs in until he's stuffed. **2.** to get indigestion, get sick. *ntixamit. laazim ˀaaxuð fadd šii yṣarruf il-ˀakil.* I've got indigestion. I should take something to digest the food.

tuxma indigestion, dyspepsia.

tuxum pl. *txaama* cigarette holder.

t-r-a

tara (particle) **1.** or, or else, otherwise. *ˀoogaf, tara ˀarmiik!* Stop or I'll shoot! *la-titgarrab yamm ič-čalib, tara yḉaððak.* Don't go near the dog or else he'll bite you. *la-tištiri has-sayyaara, tara titwarraṭ biiha.* Don't buy this car, or you'll have trouble with it. **2.** since, because. *la-tšuuf hal-filim, tara ma-yiswa.* Don't see that film, 'cause it's not worth it. **3.** I tell you, I warn you, mind you. *ˀiða ma-tinṭiini l-ifluus tara ˀaštiki ḉaleek.* If you don't give me the money, I warn you I'm going to sue. *tara ma-ariidak tiḉči wiyyaa.* Mind you, I don't want you to talk with him. **4.** well, well then, well now, so. *tara l-yoom jumḉa. nṭiini l-ifluus miθil-ma wuḉadit.* Well, today's Friday. Give me the money like you promised. **5.** actually, after all. *tara ṣudug haaða xooš walad.* You know, he really is a good fellow.

t-r-a-m

traam pl. *-aat* streetcar, tram.

t-r-a-m-w-a-y

traamwaay pl. *-yaat* streetcar, tram.

t-r-b

tarrab to make dusty, get dirty, cover with dust. *wugaɛ w-tarrab ihduuma.* He fell and got his clothes dusty.

ttarrab to become dusty or dirty. *la-txušš ib-maɛmal il-ičbintu tara tittarrab.* Don't go in the cement factory or you'll get dusty.

turba pl. *turab* **1.** soil, earth. **2.** ground. **3.** clean piece of clay, usually taken from the river at the holy city of Karbala, used by the Shiah sect of Islam in their prayer rites.

traab pl. *turbaan* dirt, dust, soil, earth.

*traabi** **1.** dusty. **2.** powdery, dust-like.

t-r-b-s

tirbaas pl. *taraabiis* bolt, latch. *bunduqiyya ʔumm it-tirbaas* bolt-action rifle.

t-r-j-m

tarjam to translate, interpret. *tarjum-li hal-maqaala lil-ɛarabi.* Translate this article into Arabic for me. *ʔaani ma-ʔaɛruf ɛarabi, laakin raḥ-ajiib waaḥid wiyyaaya ytarjum-li.* I don't know Arabic, but I'll bring someone along to interpret for me.

tarjuma, tarjama pl. *taraajim* translation, interpretation.

mutarjim pl. *-iin* translator, interpreter.

turjumaan pl. *-iyya* translator, interpreter.

t-r-č-y

tirčiyya pl. *taraači* earring.

t-r-s

tiras (*u taris*) to fill, fill up. *j-jaahil tiras jeeba bič-čukleet.* The child filled his pocket with candy.

tarras to fill, fill up. *ʔaani ʔanaawšak il-piip w-inta tarris il-ubṭaaḷa.* I'll hand you the barrel and you fill the bottles.

ntiras to be or become filled, get full. *ntiras is-sirdaab ṃayy.* The cellar got filled with water.

taras pl. *-iyya* **1.** person of low morals, person with bad character. **2.** clever person, sly fox, sneak.

t-r-f

taraf luxury, opulence, affluence.

tarif neat, clean, tidy. *beet tarif* a tidy house. *hduum tarfa* neat clothes.

taraafa neatness, cleanness, tidiness.

t-r-q-w

tarquwa, ɛaḍum it-tarquwa clavicle, collarbone.

t-r-k

tirak (*u tarik*) **1.** to give up, forswear, swear off. *laazim titruk hal-ɛaada.* You've got to stop this habit. *čaan yilɛab uqmaar bass baɛdeen tirak.* He used to gamble but later gave it up. *ṣaar-la mudda taarik it-tadxiin.* He's been off smoking for some time. **2.** to leave. *ʔiδa ma-ligeeta, truk-la xabar.* If you don't find him, leave him a message. *ma-tirak-li majaal lit-tafaahum.* He didn't give me a chance to explain. **3.** to leave, abandon, forsake, give up, leave behind. *ma-yṣiir titruk sayyaartak ib-nuṣṣ iš-šaariɛ.* You can't just leave your car in the middle of the street. **4.** to leave alone, stay away from. *turka! l-ʔilḥaaḥ ma-yfiid.* Leave him alone! Insisting won't help. *turka l-hal-mawḍuuɛ.* Drop the subject.

tarrak to cause to give up. *laazim atar-rikak il-ɛaada.* I've got to cure you of the habit.

tarka pl. *-aat* small amount, dash, pinch. *tarkat miliḥ* pinch of salt.

tarika pl. *-aat* heritage, legacy, bequest.

t-r-k-m-a-n

turkmaani pl. *turkmaan* Turkoman (a Turkic people in North Iraq, who speak a dialect of Turkish).

*turkmaani** Turkoman, Turkomanic.

t-r-k-y

turkya Turkey.

turki pl. *turuk, ʔatraak* Turk, person from Turkey.

*turki** Turkish.

t-r-w-a-k

tirwaaka pl. *-aat* three-quarter length jacket, worn by women.

t-r-y-a-k

tiryaak opium.

tiryaaki pl. *-iyya* **1.** person addicted to opium, dope addict. **2.** person fond of strong tea.

tiryakči pl. *-iyya* = *tiryaaki.*

t-r-y-š

tiriiša pl. *traayiš* slat, lath, long, thin piece (of wood, metal, etc.).

t-r-y-ɛ

ttaryaɛ to belch, burp. *min yaakul fijil yittaryaɛ ihwaaya.* When he eats radishes he belches a lot.

taryuuɛa pl. *-aat* belch, burp.

t-s-ɛ

tisɛa pl. *-aat* nine.

tsaaṭaɛaš nineteen.

tusuɛ pl. *ʔatsaaɛ* a ninth part, one-ninth.

tisɛiin ninety.
taasiɛ ninth (ordinal).

t-s-g-a
tisgaa pl. *-ayaat* carpenter's workbench.

t-s-k-r
taskara pl. *tasaakir* **1.** note of authorization or recommendation. **2.** permit, pass, authorization card.

t-š-r-n
tašran to become inflamed. *j-jariɛ maal ʔiidak imtašrin.* The wound on your hand is blue and swollen.

t-š-r-y-n
tašriin: tašriin ʔawwal, tašriin il-ʔawwal October. *tašriin θaani, tašriin iθ-θaani.* November.

t-š-q-l
tašqal /with *ɛala*/ to cheat, swindle, dupe. *diir baalak minna; haaδa ytašqil ɛan-naas.* Watch out for him; he cheats people. *ma-yigdar ybiiɛ-lak il-paaṣ. tašqal ɛaleek.* He can't sell you the bus. He swindled you.

t-ṣ-f
ttiṣaf see *w-ṣ-f*.

t-ṣ-l
ttiṣal see *w-ṣ-l*.

t-ɛ-b
tiɛab (*a taɛab*) **1.** to work hard, toil, slave. *tiɛabit ɛala hal-beet ihwaaya.* I put a lot of effort into this house. *niseet išgaad tiɛabit ɛaleek min čint iṣġayyir?* Have you forgotten how much trouble I went to for you when you were young? **2.** to be or become tired, weary. *tiɛabit; xalli ʔastiriiɛ išwayya.* I've gotten tired; let me sit down a bit.
taɛɛab **1.** to make tired, to tire, to weary. *r-rikiδ taɛɛabni hwaaya.* The running tired me a lot. **2.** to trouble, inconvenience, bother. *taɛɛabtak ihwaaya b-hal-qaδiyya.* I've caused you a lot of trouble with this matter.
taɛab **1.** fatigue, weariness, tiredness. **2.** (pl. *ʔatɛaab*) trouble, effort, exertion, inconvenience.
taɛbaan tired, weary, exhausted.
ʔatɛab **1.** more or most tired. **2.** more or most tiring.
mutɛib **1.** tiring, difficult, wearisome. **2.** dull, boring, tedious.

t-ɛ-s
taɛis, taɛiis pl. *-iin, tuɛsaaʔ* **1.** miserable, wretched, unfortunate, poor. **2.** miserable person, wretch.
taɛaasa misery, wretchedness.
ʔatɛas more or most miserable.

t-ɛ-δ̣
ttiɛaδ̣ see *w-ɛ-δ̣*.

t-ɛ-l
taɛaal (imperative direct address) **1.** come, come here. *taɛaal yammi. daaɛčii-lak šii.* Come here. I'll tell you something. *ruuɛ w-taɛaal bil-ɛajal.* Go and come back quickly. *taɛaal, itšuuf bii-man ibtileet.* Come here and look who I got stuck with! **2.** come on, let's go. *taɛaal fahhma lil-ʔustaaδ.* Come on, explain to the gentleman. *di-taɛaal ɛaad! muu ṣaar-li saaɛa antaδ̣rak?* Come on there! Haven't I been waiting for you an hour already? *taɛaal da-agul-lak, haššaġḷa ma-tinraad.* Let me tell you, that work isn't desirable.

t-ɛ-l-g
tiɛlaaga, see *ɛ-l-g*

t-f-ɛ
taffaɛ to glow with good health, to have rosy cheeks. *taffaɛ wijh ij-jaahil ɛala hal-hawa wil-ʔakil.* The child's face glowed with good health from this climate and food. *šuuf wičča šloon imtaffiɛ!* Look how pink-cheeked and healthy he is!
tiffaaɛ (coll.) **1.** apple(s). **2.** apple tree(s).
tiffaaɛa pl. *-aat* un. n. of *tiffaaɛ*.

t-f-x
tufax, tuffaaxa, etc. var. of *nufax,* etc., which see under *n-f-x*.

t-f-r
tafar pl. *-aat* crupper, breeching strap (of donkey's harness).

t-f-q
ttifaq see *w-f-q*.

t-f-g
ttaffag to arm oneself with a rifle, to take up arms. *ttaffugaw gabuḷ-ma yhijmuun.* They armed themselves with rifles before they attacked.
tufga pl. *tufag* rifle, gun. *tufgat ṣeed* shotgun. *tufgat ṣačim* BB gun, air rifle.
taffaag pl. *-a* rifleman.
mtaffag carrying a rifle, armed.

¹t-f-l
tifal (*i tafil*) to spit, expectorate. *tiflat ib-wičča li-ʔan faššar ɛaleeha.* She spit in his face because he talked dirty to her. || *waaɛidhum taafil ib-ɛalg iθ-θaani.* They both say exactly the same thing.
taffal to spit, expectorate. *la-ttaffil bil-gaaɛ. staɛmil čaffiyya.* Don't spit on the floor. Use a handkerchief.
tfaal spit, spittle, saliva.

matfala pl. *-aat, mataafil* cuspidor, spittoon.

²*t-f-l*

tifil var. of *tilif,* which see under *t-l-f.*

t-f-h

tafaaha triviality, paltriness, insignificance.

ˀatfah more trivial, unimportant, most trivial, unimportant.

taafih trivial, paltry, unimportant, trifling, insignificant.

t-q-n

tiqan (*i ˀitqaan*) to master, know thoroughly. *biqa b-amriika santeen w-tiqan il-ˀingiliizi.* He stayed in America two years and mastered English.

ˀitqaan, ttiqaan 1. perfection. 2. proficiency, skill. 3. mastery, command.

t-q-y

ttiqa see *w-q-y.*

*taqi** devout, pious, God-fearing.

ˀatqa more or most devout, pious.

taqwa piety, devoutness, godliness.

t-k-t

tikit pl. *-aat* ticket.

t-k-s-y

taksi pl. *-iyyaat* taxi, taxicab.

t-k-k

takk 1. one of a pair, mate, match. *ween takk haj-jooraab?* Where's the mate to this sock? *ḏaaع takk min qundarti.* One of my shoes got lost. *ween takkak? muu ˀintu kull yoom suwa?* Where's your bosom buddy? Aren't you always together? 2. one, a single. *ˀagdar amawwtak ib-takk ع ijil.* I could kill you with a single slap. 3. alone, only. *laa, ˀaani b-takk nafsi.* No, I'm all by myself. *sawwaaha b-takk nafsa.* He did it all by himself.

tikka 1. cabob, shish kebab, meat cooked on a skewer. 2. drawstring (in the waistband).

t-k-l

ttikal see under *w-k-l.*

t-k-m

tikma pl. *tikam* 1. pillar, column. 2. brace, support. 3. (invar.) well-built, solid, stout. *beet tikma* a sturdy house.

t-k-k-y

tukki (coll.) 1. mulberry(s). 2. mulberry tree(s).

tukkiyya pl. *-aat* un. n. of *tukki.*

t-k-y

takya pl. *-aat* 1. monastery of a Moslem order. 2. school for the study of a branch of Moslem theology.

t-l-θ

tlaaθa, tlaaθiin see under *θ-l-θ.*

t-l-ṭ-ع-š

tlaṭṭaعaš see *θ-l-θ.*

t-l-ġ-r-a-f

talaġraaf pl. *-aat* 1. telegraph. 2. telegram, wire, cable.

*talaġraafi** telegraphic. *muwaaṣalaat talaġraafiyya* telegraph communications.

t-l-f

tilaf (*a talaf*) 1. to be or become damaged, spoiled, ruined. *xalli l-laعam biθ-θallaaja gabuḷ-ma yitlaf.* Put the meat in the refrigerator before it spoils. || *tlafit imniddiraasa.* I got worn out from studying. *tlafit عaleeha, laakin ma-daarat-li baal.* I went to pieces over her, but she didn't pay me any attention. 2. to destroy. *ˀitlif kull il-ˀawraaq illi عindak gabuḷ-ma ykibsuun il-beet.* Destroy all the papers you have before they raid the house. 3. to ruin, spoil. *tilaf ṣiععta b-širb il-عarag.* He ruined his health drinking liquor. 4. to waste, squander. *tilaf ifluusa bil-iqmaar.* He frittered away his money gambling.

talaf 1. damage, destruction. 2. waste, spoilage.

tilif, tifil 1. pulp (of fruit, etc.). 2. grounds (of coffee). 3. leaves (of tea).

talafiyya pl. *-aat* casualty, loss, damage.

tallaaf pl. *-iin* wastrel, spendthrift, squanderer.

talfaan 1. damaged, ruined, destroyed. *madiina talfaana* a ruined city. 2. spoiled, rotten. *laعam tilfaan* spoiled meat. *fawaakih talfaana* rotten fruit. 3. worn-out. *sayyaara talfaana* a worn-out car.

ˀitlaaf destruction, annihilation.

t-l-l

tall pl. *tlaal, tluul* hill, mound, elevation, rise.

tallači pl. *-iyya* gambler, gambling house owner.

tallaxaana pl. *-aat, tallaxaayin.* gambling den, casino.

t-l-m-δ

ttalmaδ to be or become a student or apprentice. *huwwa ttalmaδ عala ˀiid halustaaδ.* He became a student under that professor.

talmaδa student status, student life. *ˀayyaam it-talmaδa* student days.

tilmiiδ pl. *talaamiiδ* pupil, student.

t-l-w

tila (*u, i tilaawa*) 1. to read aloud, recite. *tila عaleena t-taعliimaat.* He read the instructions aloud to us. 2. to follow after, succeed, come behind. *hal-hadiyya raḥ-titliiha hadaaya.* Gifts will follow this gift.

tilaawa oral reading, recitation, recital.

taali pl. *tuwaali* 1. final portion, last part, end. *b-taali ʕumra, ṣaar middayyin.* Toward the end of his life, he became religious. *taaliiha ṭilaʕ ma-yuʕruf šii.* In the end he turned out not to know a thing. *l-ʕinab iz-zeen yinzil ib-tuwaali l-moosim.* The good grapes appear toward the last days of the season. *haay it-tuwaali. ˀusbuuʕ ij-jaay ma-tilgi ṭamaaṭa bis-suug.* These are the last ones. Next week you won't find tomatoes in the market. *ˀinta ruuḥ. ˀaani ˀaji taali.* You go ahead. I'll come later. *ˀuxδu kifaayatkum. ˀaani ˀabqa bit-taali.* Take what you need. I'll wait until last. || *ʕidna xooš qumṣaan. ˀilḥagu ʕala taaliiha.* We have fine quality shirts. Get them while they last. *haaδa maa-la taali. ma-šifta š-sawwa biyya?* You just can't tell about him. Did you see what he did to me? 2. outcome, result, conclusion, final issue. *haay taaliiha? muu ˀaani ṣadiiqak?* Is that the end result? Aren't I your friend? *t-taali raḥ-tištiki bil-ifluus ʕala jiiraanha.* The upshot is that she's going to sue her neighbor for the money. *ˀiδa ma-tidrus, ma-dgul-li šinu taaliyyak?* If you don't study, would you tell me just what'll become of you? *ṣaar-li miit marra ˀadaaʕiik bil-ifluus w-ma-tinṭiini. taaliiha wiyyaak?* I've asked you a hundred times for the money and you don't give it to me. What am I going to do with you? *taaliiha wiyya ˀibnak? baʕda da-yišlaʕ wardi.* What's going to become of your son? He's still pulling up my flowers. *t-taali š-ṣaar?* Then what happened? || *taali-ma taali* finally, after all that, in the end. *taali-ma taali, ma-yriid ysaaʕidni.* After all that, he doesn't want to help me.

*taalaani** toward the end, at the last, end, final, concluding, terminal. *naawišni l-iktaab it-taalaani.* Hand me the book on the end.

t-m-b-a-k

timbaak a kind of tobacco, used mostly in the narghile.

t-m-t-m

tamtam to mutter, mumble. *da-ttamtim w-ma-da-ˀafham.* You're muttering and I can't understand.

t-m-r

tamur (coll.) date(s) (particularly dried dates). || *tamur hindi* tamarind.

tamra pl. *-aat* 1. a date. 2. clump, chunk, piece of packed dates.

tamraaya pl. *-aat* date.

t-m-s-a-ḥ

timsaaḥ pl. *tamaasiiḥ* 1. crocodile. 2. alligator.

t-m-m

tamm 1. to stay, remain, abide. *leeš ma-ttimm ʕidna hal-leela?* Why don't you stay with us tonight? *ween tammeet li-hassa?* Where've you been till now? *ma-tamm ˀaḥḥad ma-simaʕ.* No one remained who hadn't heard. 2. to continue to completion, to be complete. *farḥatna ma-ttimm ˀiδa ma-tiji.* Our joy won't be complete if you don't come.

tammam to complete, finish, wind up, conclude. *tammim šuġļak w-taʕaal.* Finish your work and come on.

tamaam 1. completeness, entirety, wholeness. *stilamt ifluusi bit-tamaam.* I received my money in full. 2. exact, real, true, complete. *huwwa ṣadiiq tamaam.* He's a real friend. 3. true, correct, right. *haaδa tamaam, laakin . . .* That's true, but. . . . *waļļa, tamaam! haaδa xooš walad.* You can say that again! He's a nice guy. *tamaam, bass haaδa muu ʕuδur.* All right, but that's not an excuse. *haaδa tamaam! haaδa biδ-δabuṭ il-loon il-ˀariida.* That's it! That's the color I want exactly. *ˀamma tamaam ṭilaʕ miθil-ma gilit.* He sure did turn out like you said.

tamaaman 1. precisely, exactly. 2. completely, entirely.

taamm 1. complete, perfect. 2. genuine, real.

tatimma pl. *-aat* 1. supplement. 2. completion.

t-m-m-n

timman rice.

t-m-m-w-z

tammuuz July.

t-n-b-l

tanbal pl. *-iyya, tanaabil* 1. lazy, slothful, indolent. 2. lazy person. || *tanbal bin-noom* heavy sleeper, deep sleeper.

tanbalxaana pl. *-aat* a place to relax, and take one's ease. *min tiji liš-šuġuļ laazim tištuġuļ; haaδi muu tanbalxaana!* When you come to work, you better work; this isn't any place to goof off!

t-n-t

tanta pl. *-aat* convertible top (of an automobile). *sayyaara tanta* convertible car.

t-n-t-r-y-w-k

tantaryook tincture of iodine.

t-n-ع

tannaع (vulgar) to bend over.

t-n-g

tannag to draw tight, make taut, stretch, strain. *tannig il-ḥabil gabuḷ-ma txalli l-ihduum ع alee.* Stretch the rope tight before you put the clothes on it. *l-xayyaaṭ tannag sitirti kulliš.* The tailor made my coat very tight. *ع abbi l-guuniyya timman bass la-ttannigha.* Fill the gunny sack with rice but don't strain it. *l-waḏع is-siyaasi mtannig.* The political situation is tense. *l-ع alaaqaat beenaathum imtanniga.* Relations between them are strained.

ttannag to be made taut or tight, to be strained. *l-ḥabil ittannag.* The rope was tightened. || *ma-agdar ʔaakul. ttannagit.* I can't eat. I'm already full.

tang **1.** tight, strained. *hduum tanga* tight clothes. **2.** tense, nervous. *rijjaal tang* a nervous man.

tunga pl. *tinag* clay water jug.

t-n-g-n-f-s

tanganafas asthma.

t-n-k

tanak tin.

tanaka pl. *-aat* **1.** piece of tin. **2.** jerry can, five-gallon can.

tanakči pl. *-iyya* **1.** tinsmith **2.** automobile body and fender repairman.

t-n-n

tinniin pl. *tananiin* dragon.

t-n-w-r

tannuur pl. *tnaaniir* large, mud outdoor oven for baking bread.

tannuura pl. *-aat* woman's skirt.

t-n-y

tina (*i, a tani*) to wait, to await, wait for. *tnaa fadd išwayya. hassa yiji.* Wait for him a little while. He's coming now. *raḥ-nitniik w-ma-naakul ʔila ʔan tiji.* We will wait for you and not eat until you come. *ʔinta ʔil-man taani?* Who are you waiting for?

t-h-m

tiham (*i*) to accuse, charge. *leeš da-tithim ṣadiiqak?* Why are you accusing your friend? *š-šurṭa tihmata bil-booga.* The police charged him with the theft. *raad yšuuf illi taahma.* He wanted to see whoever accused him.

ntiham to be accused, charged. *ntiham bil-qatil.* He was accused of murder.

tuhma pl. *tuham* accusation, charge. see also *w-h-m.*

t-w-a-l-y

tuwaali see under *t-l-w.*

t-w-a-l-y-t

twaaleet coiffure, hairdo (also, long hair style for men).

t-w-b

taab **1.** to forswear, renounce, turn from. *l-qumarči taab min liع b il-uqmaar.* The gambler swore off gambling. *raaḥ il-beet aḷḷa w-taab min ʔakl il-ḥaraam.* He went to Mecca and swore off cheating. **2.** to learn one's lesson, to go straight, reform. *min ðiič il-basṭa, taab. baع ad ma-yðibb iḥjaar ع an-naas.* Since that beating, he's reformed. He doesn't throw rocks at people any more. *raḥ-abusṭak ʔila ʔan itguul "tibit."* I'm going to beat you till you say "I've learned my lesson!".

tawwab to cause to go straight, reform, teach a lesson to. *l-xaṣaara tawwubata min haš-šaġḷa.* The losses made him give up this business. *tawwabta. baع ad wala ybuug.* I straightened him out. He won't steal again.

tooba repentance, contrition. || *t-tooba. . . !* May I never. . . ! I've learned my lesson about. . . ! *l-ʔumm busṭat ibinha ḥatta gaal "it-tooba!".* The mother beat her son until he said "I'll never do it again!". *t-tooba ʔiða ʔakfal waaḥid min hiiči naas!* That's the last time I'll ever co-sign with one of those people!

t-w-t-y

tuutya zinc.

t-w-θ

tuuθ (coll.) mulberry wood, mulberry trees.

tuuθa pl. *-aat* mulberry tree.

tuuθiyya pl. *twaaθi* billy club, nightstick.

t-w-j

tawwaj to crown. *tawwijoo malik ع al-ع iraaq.* They crowned him king of Iraq.

taaj pl. *tiijaan* crown, miter.

t-w-r-a

toora pl. *-aat* **1.** Torah. **2.** synagogue.

t-w-r-n

toorna pl. *-aat* lathe.

toornači pl. *-iyya* machinist, lathe operator.

t-w-ṣ-y

tawṣiya, tuuṣaa see under *w-ṣ-y.*

t-w-k-y

tuuki a children's game similar to hopscotch.

t-w-m

toom pl. *twaama* **1.** twin. *marta jaabat*

toom. His wife had twins. *ˀaxuu t-toom* his twin brother. **2.** one of any multiple birth. *marta jaabat iθlaθ itwaama.* His wife had triplets.

t-w-w

taww- /with pronominal suffix/ just now, just this minute, just a second ago. *tawwni wuṣalit. xalli ˀartaaḥ.* I just arrived. Let me rest. *tawwa čaan ihnaa.* He was just here. || *hassa tawwak!* Now you're on the right track! You've hit the nail on the head!

t-y-t-y

tiiti pl. *-iyya* ticket taker, conductor.

t-y-x

taax (*i*) to wear out, to become dilapidated, old, run-down. *sikanna bil-beet ˀila ˀan taax.* We lived in the house till it wore out. *la-timši ʕaṣ-ṣaṭiḥ tara taayix.* Don't walk on the roof because it's dilapidated.

t-y-r

tayyaar pl. *-aat* **1.** current, flow, stream, movement. *tayyaar kahrabaaˀi* electric current. **2.** draft (of air).

t-y-z-a-b

tiizaab aqua regia (chem.).

t-y-s

tees pl. *tyuus* billy goat.

t-y-ġ

tiiġa pl. *tiyaġ* wall around the roof of a house.

t-y-f-w

tiifu typhoid.

t-y-f-w-s

tiifoos typhus.

t-y-l

teel pl. *tyuul* **1.** wire. **2.** metallic thread. **3.** wire screen, window screen. **4.** power line, high-tension line. || *la-tindagg ibteela.* Don't get mixed up with him.

t-y-n

tiin (coll.) **1.** fig(s). **2.** fig tree(s).

tiina pl. *-aat* un. n. of *tiin.*

t-y-h

taah (*i*) to get lost, go astray, lose one's way, wander, stray. *ṭilaʕ liṣ-ṣeed w-taah bič-čool.* He went out hunting and got lost in the wilderness. *fikri taayih; ma-daagdar aštuġuḷ.* My mind is wandering; I can't work.

tayyah to lose, mislead, lead astray, confuse, confound. *š-šurṭi ṛaad yilzamni laakin rikaḍit w-tayyahta.* The policeman tried to catch me but I ran and lost him. *min wuṣalit yamm is-siinama, tayyaht iṭ-ṭariiq.* When I got near the movie, I lost the way. *la-ttayyih ʕalayya l-iḥsaab.* Don't make me lose count. *haš-šawaariʕ ittayyih.* These streets are confusing.

tyaah anarchy, confusion.

taayih **1.** lost, stray, errant, wandering. *ṛṣaaṣa taayha* a stray bullet. **2.** confused, perplexed.

θ

θ-a

θaa name of the letter *θ.*

θ-ˀ-r

θiˀar (*a θarr*) to take blood revenge. *raḥ-niθˀar min kull ˀaʕdaaˀna.* We're going to take revenge on all our enemies. *ʕaaˀilta θiˀarat-la.* His family avenged him.

θaar pl. *-aat* revenge, vengeance, blood revenge.

θ-b-t

θibat (*i θabiṭ*) **1.** to be steady, firm, unshakable, stable. *halgadd-ma šaarub, ma-da-yigdar yiθbit ʕala rijlee.* He's so drunk, he can't stay on his feet. **2.** to hold on, to abide, stick. *θibat ʕala raˀya.* He held to his opinion. *haaḍa ma-yiθbit ʕala kalaama.* He doesn't stick to his word. **3.** to withstand, resist, hold out. *jeešna θibat bil-maʕraka ˀila n-nihaaya.* Our army held out in the battle till the end. **4.** to be or become established, proven, definite. *j-jariima θibtat ʕalee.* The crime was proven against him. *θibat ˀinna huwwa l-baayig.* It was established that he's the thief. *θibat-li maa-la ʕalaaqa bil-mawḍuuʕ.* It's clear to me that he has no connection with the matter.

θabbat **1.** to set firmly, stabilize. *θabbitha b-mukaanha zeen, la-toogaʕ.* Set it in place well, so it doesn't fall. **2.** to appoint permanently, confirm. *θabbitoo b-waḍiifta baʕad intihaaˀ muddat it-tajruba.* They appointed him to his position permanently at the end of the probationary period.

ˀaθbat to prove, establish, validate. *xalli -aθbit-lak l-iḥčaaya.* Let me prove the story to you. *ˀaθbat šajaaʕta giddaam in-naas.* He established his bravery before the people.

tθabbat to make sure of, become certain of, verify, establish. *la-tinṭii l-ifluus gabuḷ-*

ma titθabbat min hawiita. Don't give him the money before you establish his identity.

θubuut **1.** permanence, stability. **2.** certainty, sureness. || *θubuut ramaḏaan* official determination of the beginning of Ramadan (by two witnesses who have seen the moon).

θbaat pl. *-aat* **1.** proof, corroboration. **2.** stake, peg, pin.

ˀaθbat more or most stable, certain, reliable, etc.

θaabit **1.** steady, invariable, constant, stable. || *n-nisba θ-θaabita* pi (math.). **2.** permanent, lasting, durable, enduring. *ṣubuġ θaabit* color-fast dye. *ḥibir θaabit* indelible ink. **3.** confirmed, proven, established.

θ-b-r

θubar (*u θabur*) **1.** to pester, keep after, bother continually. *l-baarḥa ḏall yiḥčiinna ʕala muġaamaraata w-θubarna ˀarbaʕ saaʕaat.* Yesterdy he kept talking to us about his adventures and pestered us for four hours. *θubarni ʕal-ifluus.* He pestered me for the money. *j-jaahil θubarni, n-nahaar kulla yibči.* The baby gave me a pain—he's been crying all day. **2.** to puzzle, perplex, stump, stymie. *l-ˀustaaḏ θubarna bil-imtiḥaan ib-suˀaal ṣaʕub.* The professor stymied us on the exam with a hard question.

nθubar **1.** to be or become puzzled, perplexed, stumped, stymied. *nθubarit bil-imtiḥaan w-majaawabit zeen.* I got muddled on the exam and didn't answer well. **2.** to be or become caught, stuck. *nθubarit bii w-ma-txallaṣit minna ˀilla b-ṣuʕuuba.* I got stuck with him and only got away from him with difficulty.

θ-x-n

θixan (*a*) **1.** to thicken, to be or become thick. *baqqi l-imrabba ʕan-naar ḥatta tiθxan.* Leave the jam on the fire so that it'll thicken. *min istaʕmal had-duwa, bida šaʕra yiθxan.* When he used that medicine his hair began to get thicker. **2.** to be or become thick, fat, heavy. *haaḏa l-faayil θixan ihwaaya; ˀiftaḥ-la mulḥaq.* That file's gotten awfully fat; start an appendix to it. *raḥ-yiθxan ʕala hal-ˀakil.* He's going to get fat on this food. **3.** to become serious, complicated, more involved, more serious. *θixnat il-qaḏiyya beenaathum w-wuṣlat lil-imbaaṣaṭ.* The matter got serious between them and it came to blows.

θaxxan **1.** to make thick, thicken. *n-naar raḥ-iθθaxxin il-imrabba ˀiḏa ma-ṭṭaffiiha.* The fire will make the jam thick if you don't turn it off. **2.** to exaggerate. **3.** to overdo, go too far. *muu θaxxanitha? ma-ˀaʕtiqid halgadd baxiil.* Aren't you exaggerating? I don't think he's that stingy. *ṭlaʕit imnid-daaˀira ʕišriin marra hal-yoom. muu θaxxanitha?* You've left the office twenty times today. Aren't you overdoing it? *yeezi ʕaad; muu θaxxanitha!* Hold on now; you've gone too far!

θuxun, θxuuna **1.** thickness, density. **2.** seriousness, severity, complexity.

θixiin pl. *θxaan* **1.** thick, dense. **2.** thick, fat, heavy. **3.** serious, complicated, deep, weighty.

ˀaθxan **1.** thicker, thickest. **2.** more or most serious, complicated.

θ-d-y

θida, θadi pl. *θidaaya* breast, udder.

θ-r-b

θirib (coll.) pl. *θuruub* fish eggs, roe.

θirba pl. *-aat* un. n. of *θirib.*

θ-r-θ-r

θarθar to chatter, prattle. *ṣaar-lak saaʕa tθarθir. ma-tiskut ʕaad!* You've been chattering an hour. Why don't you shut up!

θarθara chatter, idle talk.

θarθaar pl. *-iin* chatterbox, prattler.

θ-r-d

θirad to crumble, break (bread). *ˀiθrid il-xubuz bil-maaʕuun.* Crumble the bread in the plate.

θiriid crumbled bread with stew or broth poured over it.

maθruuda a dish made of pieces of dried bread and spices boiled in water.

θ-r-m

θiram (*u θarum*) to chop, cut up. *ˀiθrum il-laḥam naaʕim.* Chop the meat fine.

θarram to chop up, cut up. *θarram il-buṣal w-xallaa ʕaẓ-ẓalaaṭa.* He chopped up the onions and put them on the salad.

tθarram to be chopped, to get cut up. *l-laḥam ma-yitθarram ib-has-siččiina.* The meat can't be chopped with this knife.

nθiram to be chopped, to get cut up. *l-laḥam laazim yinθirim ˀawwal.* The meat has to be cut up first.

θurma pl. *θuram* shred, small piece.

θ-r-y

θira (*i*) to become wealthy, rich, to prosper. *ˀiḏa tudxul ib-haš-šaġla, tiθri.* If you get into this business, you'll get rich.

*θari** pl. *ˀaθriyaaˀ* **1.** wealthy, rich. **2.** rich person.

θarwa pl. *-aat* wealth, riches, fortune.

θrayya pl. *-aat* chandelier.

muθri pl. *-iyyiin* **1.** wealthy, rich. **2.** rich person.

θ-ع-l-b

θaعlab pl. *θaعaalib* fox.

θaعlabiyya tapioca.

θ-ġ-r

θaġra pl. *-aat* breach, crack, rift, opening.

θ-q-f

θaqqaf to impart education or culture, to educate. *hal-kutub raح-itθaqqifak.* These books will give you an education.

tθaqqaf to acquire education or culture, to become educated. *ʔiδa triid tiθθaqqaf, ʔudxul kulliyya.* If you want to get educated, enter a college.

θaqaafa education, culture.

*θaqaafi** educational, cultural, intellectual. *mulحaq θaqaafi* cultural attaché.

ʔaθqaf more or most cultured, refined, educated.

mθaqqaf educated, cultured, refined.

θ-q-l

tθaaqal to feel imposed upon, to be recalcitrant, reluctant. *min simaع ʔariid ʔaruuح wiyyaa, tθaaqal.* When he heard that I want to go with him, he felt imposed upon. *la-titθaaqal. haaδa ṣadiiqak; laazim itsaaعda.* Don't feel burdened. He's your friend; you must help him. *min itkallfa b-šii, yitθaaqal.* When you ask him to do something, he moans and groans.

staθqal to consider burdensome, to find onerous. *yistaθqil ʔay šuġuḷ tinṭii.* He considers any work you give him as an imposition. **2.** to find annoying or unpleasant, to dislike. *ʔastaθqila l-haaδa. ma-agdar ʔagعud wiyyaa.* I find him boring. I can't sit with him. *ʔastaθqil ihwaaya r-rooحa lil-maṭaar.* I dislike going to the airport very much.

θuqul pl. *ʔaθqaal* weight, burden, load. *rami θ-θuqul* the shot put (athlet.). *rafiع il-ʔaθqaal* weight-lifting (athlet.).

θaqiil **1.** heavy. **2.** burdensome, oppressive, unpleasant.

ʔaθqal **1.** heavier, heaviest. **2.** more or most burdensome, oppressive, unpleasant, etc.

miθqaal pl. *mθaaqiil* a unit of jeweler's weight. || *yiحči bil-imθaaqiil.* He's a man of few words.

see also *θ-g-l.*

θ-q-y

θiqa see *w-θ-q.*

θ-g-l

θigal (*a*) **1.** to be or become heavy, burdensome. *ṣ-ṣanduug θigal. ma-agdar ašiila baعad.* The trunk's gotten heavy. I can't lift it anymore. *ʔiδa yiθgal حiml iz-zumaaḷ, ma-yimši sariiع.* If the donkey's load is heavy, he won't go fast. **2.** to be or become serious, somber. *min izzawwaj, θigal ihwaaya.* Since he got married, he's gotten awfully serious.

θaggal **1.** to make heavy, weight, weight down. *θaggil il-ʔawraaq ib-šii حatta la-yṭayyirha l-hawa.* Weight the papers with something so the wind won't blow them around. **2.** to make too heavy. *la-tحuṭṭ baعad tara θθaggil il-حimil عal-iحṣaan.* Don't put any more or you'll make the load too heavy for the horse. **3.** to make difficult, troublesome, or onerous. *l-ʔustaaδ θaggal il-ʔasʔila b-hal-imtiحaan.* The teacher made the questions on this exam difficult. **4.** to overload. *sayyaart il-حimil maaltak ma-raح-timši, li-ʔan θaggalitha.* Your truck won't go because you overloaded it. **5.** /with *عala*/ to be a burden to, to inconvenience. *xalli nruuح, عaad. θaggaḷna عaj-jamaaعa hwaaya.* Let's go, then. We've inconvenienced them too much. **6.** to make indifferent, make cool. *šinu l-imθagglak عalayya?* What's made you so cool to me?

θuguḷ pl. *θgaaḷ* **1.** weight, burden, load. **2.** seriousness, gravity, importance. || *daybiiع θugul ib-raasi.* He's being pompous toward me. **3.** inconvenience, bother, trouble.

θigiil **1.** heavy. **2.** burdensome, weighty, cumbersome, opressive, unpleasant, onerous. **3.** serious, grave, somber. || *damma θgiil.* He's a dull bore. He's too serious. *samعa θigiil.* He's hard of hearing.

θiggaala pl. *-aat* paperweight.

ʔaθgaḷ **1.** heavier, heaviest. **2.** more or most burdensome, unpleasant, serious, etc.

θ-k-l

θikal (*i*) to lose (in death), to be bereaved of a loved one. *θiklatak ʔummak, ʔinšaaḷḷaa! ma-truuح minaa!* May your mother lose you, God willing! Get out of here! *ʔaθkil ibni ʔiδa ʔaعruf šii عan haaδa.* May I lose my son if I know anything about that.

θ-k-n

θakana pl. *-aat* barracks (mil.).

θ-l-θ

tlaaθa three.

tlaṭṭaعaš thirteen.

tlaaθiin thirty.

θ-θilaaθaa, yoom iθ-θilaaθaa. Tuesday.

θiliθ, θuluθ pl. *ʔaθlaaθ* third, one third, a third part.

θaaliθ third (ordinal).

*θulaaθi** tri-partite, tri-, triliteral. *fiʕil θulaaθi* triliteral verb, verb with three radicals.

θaaluuθ Trinity. *θ-θaaluuθ il-muqaddas* the Holy Trinity.

muθallaθ **1.** tripled, triple, triangular. **2.** (pl. *-aat*) triangle. **3.** (pl. only) trigonometry.

θ-l-j

θilaj (*i θalij*) to snow, sleet. *šuuf! id-dinya da-tiθlij!* Look! It's snowing! *b-manṭiqt ij-jibaal, θiljat ihwaaya hal-isbuuʕ.* In the mountain area, it snowed a lot this week.

θallaj to be or become frozen (fig.), to get cold. *θallajit. nṭiini baṭṭaaniyya lux.* I'm half frozen. Give me another blanket. *θallijat rijlayya mnil-barid.* My legs froze from the cold. *d-dinya θalljat. xalli nsawwi manqala.* The weather's gotten cold. Let's start the brazier.

θalij pl. *θuluuj* **1.** snow. **2.** sleet. **3.** ice.

*θalji** **1.** snowy. **2.** icy, ice-, glacial. *l-ʕaṣr iθ-θalji* the Ice Age. *manaaṭiq θaljiyya* arctic regions.

θallaaja pl. *-aat* **1.** refrigerator, icebox. **2.** iceberg.

muθallaj iced, icy, ice-cold. *čaay muθallaj* iced tea.

θ-l-ṭ-ṭ-ʕ-š

θlaṭṭaʕaš = *tlaṭṭaʕaš* which see under *θ-l-θ.*

θ-l-m

θilam (*i θalim*) to chip, nick, break the edge of, make jagged. *θilam il-maaʕuun min čaan yġisla.* He chipped the edge of the dish when he was washing it. *minu θilam has-siččiina?* Who nicked this knife?

θallam to chip, nick. *θallam il-kaasa b-ʕiddat mukaanaat.* He chipped the edge of the bowl in several places. *has-siččiina kullha mθallma.* This knife is all nicked.

θilma pl. *-aat, θilam* chip, nick, notch.

θ-m-r

θumar (*u θamur*) **1.** to bear, bear fruit. *haš-šajara ma-tiθmur.* This tree doesn't bear. **2.** to bear fruit, to show results. *taʕabna bida yuθmur ʔaxiiran.* Our work has finally begun to show results.

ʔaθmar = *θumar. juhuudi ma-ʔaθmurat.* My efforts didn't bear fruit.

staθmar to invest profitably, to exploit, utilize, derive benefit from. *staθmar ifluusa b-šarikat is-simant.* He invested his money in the cement company.

θamar (coll.) pl. *ʔaθmaar* fruit(s). || *milʕ il-ʔaθmaar* an alkaline powder taken for the relief of indigestion.

θamara pl. *-aat, ʔaθmaar* **1.** fruit. **2.** benefit, gain, profit. *taʕabak ma-bii θamara.* You're wasting your effort.

stiθmaar **1.** investment, utilization, exploitation. **2.** exploitation, selfish or unfair utilization.

mustaθmir pl. *-iin* **1.** investor. **2.** exploiter.

[1]*θ-m-n*

θamman to appraise, assess, to set a value on. *l-lujna raʕ-tiji baačir itθammin il-beet.* The committee will come tomorrow to appraise the house.

tθamman to be appraised, assessed. *saaʕti tθammanat b-qiimat ʕašr idnaaniir.* My watch was appraised at ten dinars. || *haaδa fadd šii ma-yitθamman.* That's a priceless thing.

θaman pl. *ʔaθmaan* **1.** price, cost. **2.** value.

θamiin costly, precious, valuable.

ʔaθman more or most valuable, precious, costly.

[2]*θ-m-n*

θmaanya eight.

θmunṭaʕaš eighteen.

θmaaniin eighty.

θumun pl. *ʔaθmaan* eight, one eighth, an eighth part.

θaamin eighth (ordinal).

muθamman **1.** eight-fold. **2.** eight-sided, octagonal. **3.** (pl. *-aat*) octagon.

θ-n-ʕ-š

θnaʕaš twelve.

θ-n-y

θina (*i θani*) **1.** to double, double up, fold. *l-pahlawaan θina š-šiiš.* The strongman bent the bar. *ʔiθni ʕaašyat ič-čarčaf w-xayyiṭha.* Fold the edge of the sheet and sew it up. **2.** to bend, bend over. *ʔiθni nafsak ʕal-yamiin.* Bend over to the right.

θanna to do twice, repeat. *sawweetha marra wiʕda — ma-yxaalif. ʔiδa tθanni, ʔabuṣṭak.* You did it once — that's O.K. If you do it again, I'll beat you up.

ʔaθna /with *ʕala*/ to praise, laud, commend. *l-waziir ʔaθna ʕala xiṭaaba.* The minister praised his speech.

tθanna to walk with a graceful gait.

šuufha šloon titθanna b-mašiiha! Look how she undulates when she walks!

nθina 1. to be or become doubled, folded. *haz-zuuliyya ma-tinθini.* This carpet won't fold up. 2. to bend, bend over, lean, incline. *la-tčuṭṭ halgadd θugul ʕat-teel tara yinθini.* Don't put so much weight on the wire or it'll get bent. *ʔinθini l-jihat il-yisaar.* Lean to the left side.

staθna to exclude, except, exempt. *ʕaaqibhum kullhum w-la-tistaθni ʔaččad.* Punish them all and don't make an exception for anyone. *l-qaanuun yistaθni l-wuzaraaʔ imnil-xidma l-ʕaskariyya.* The law exempts cabinet ministers from military service.

ʔaθnaaʔ 1. during, in the course of. *la-txalli ʔaččad yxušš lil-ġurfa ʔaθnaaʔ il-ijtimaaʕ.* Don't let anybody come in the room during the meeting. 2. time, moment, instant. *b-hal-ʔaθnaaʔ, bayyan rajilha.* At that moment, her husband appeared. *baʕaḏ ʔaθnaaʔ išgadd xooš walad!* Sometimes he's such a nice guy!

ʔaθnaaʔ-ma while, when. *la-tizʕijni ʔaθnaaʔ-ma da-aštuġuḷ.* Don't bother me while I'm working.

θanya pl. *-aat* 1. fold. 2. cuff.

θneen pl. *-aat* 1. two. 2. pair. 3. deuce, two (cards). 4. /plus pronominal suffix/ both, both of, the two of. *ʕali w-axuu θneenhum ijaw.* Ali and his brother both came.

l-iθneen, yoom il-iθneen Monday.

θneenaat- /plus pronominal suffix/ = *θneen* 4. *θneenaathum zaʕlaaniin ʕalayya.* They're both mad at me.

θaani 1. second (ordinal). 2. next, following.

θaaniyan secondly, in the second place, furthermore. *ʔawwalan ma-šifta. w-θaaniyan š-aʕlayya?* First of all I didn't see him. And secondly, what's it to me?

θaaniya pl. *θawaani* second (unit of time).

*θaanawi** 1. secondary. *madrasa θaanawiyya* secondary school, high school. 2. minor. *masʔala θaanawiyya* a minor matter.

θaanawiyya secondary school, high school. *xirriij θaanawiyya* high school graduate.

stiθnaaʔ pl. *-aat* exception, exclusion. || *b-istiθnaaʔ* with the exception of, except, excluding.

*stiθnaaʔi** exceptional, special. *jalsa stiθnaaʔiyya* emergency session.

θ-n-y-n

θneen see under *θ-n-y.*

θ-w-b

tθaawab to yawn. *ʔašu da-titθaawab. ʔinta naʕsaan?* I see you're yawning. Are you sleepy?

θoob pl. *θyaab* 1. shirt. 2. blouse.

θawaab pl. *-aat* 1. reward from God for good deeds. 2. merit, credit (in the eyes of God).

ʔaθwab more or most meritorious, deserving reward (in the eyes of God).

θ-w-r

θaar (*u*) 1. to revolt, rebel, make a revolution. *baʕḏ il-qabaaʔil θaarat ʕal-čukuuma.* Some of the tribes revolted against the government. 2. to erupt, explode, flare up. *hal-burkaan θaar marrteen has-sana.* This volcano erupted twice this year. || *yθuur bil-ʕajal, min aqall čilma.* He flares up easily, at the slightest thing. *θaar il-ʕajaaj min faatat il-xeel.* The dust swirled up when the horses passed. 3. to fire, go off. *θaar il-musaddas b-iid il-walad.* The revolver went off in the boy's hand. *haṭ-ṭalqa faasda. ma-tθuur.* This bullet is defective. It won't go off.

θawwar 1. to incite to revolution, to stir up, arouse. *θawwar kull il-qabaaʔil ʕal-čukuuma.* He stirred up all the tribes against the government. 2. to have an erection.

ʔaθaar 1. to stir up, arouse, kindle, provoke. *la-tθiir-inna muškila.* Don't stir up trouble for us. 2. to raise, pose, bring up, interject. *bukra rač-ʔaθiir il-mawḏuuʕ w-ašuuf š-yguuluun.* Tomorrow I'll bring up the subject and see what they say.

staθaar to provoke, inflame, arouse, infuriate. *ʔinta rač-tistiθiira b-hal-iččaaya.* You'll infuriate him with that remark.

θoor pl. *θiiraan* 1. bull, steer. 2. ox. 3. (by extension) a stubborn, bull-headed person.

θawra pl. *-aat* 1. revolution, rebellion, revolt. 2. commotion, turmoil.

*θawri** revolutionary.

*θawrawi** revolutionary.

θaayir, θaaʔir 1. rebellious, agitated, stirred up. 2. (pl. *θuwwaar*) rebel, insurgent, revolutionary.

muθiir **1.** exciting. **2.** provocative, stimulating.

see also *θ-ʔ-r*

θ-w-l

θuwal (*i θawil*) to confuse, muddle, mix up. *giʕad yammi w-ḏall yiḏʕak ʔila ʔan θuwalni.* He sat near me and kept laughing until he mixed me up. *š-θuwalak? muu tuʕruf il-mawḏuuʕ zeen!* What came over you? You know the subject well!

θawwal to confuse, unnerve, upset. *θawwalitni b-ṭalabaatak!* You've driven me crazy with your demands!

nθuwal to become confused, mixed up. *nθiwalit; ma-gdarit ajaawub ʔasʔilat il-mudiir.* I got confused; I couldn't answer the director's questions.

θwall to be or become confused, disturbed, mixed-up. *min waaʕid yraaqba biš-šuġuḷ, yiθwall.* When someone watches him at work, he gets all confused.

ʔaθwal fem. *θoola* pl. *θuul, θooliin.* **1.** confused, scatter-brained, absent-minded. **2.** scatter-brained person.

θ-w-m

θuum garlic. *raas θuum* a clove of garlic.

θ-y

θee (variant of *θaa*) name of the letter *θ*.

θ-y-r

θaayir, muθiir, etc. see *θ-w-r*.

θ-y-l

θayyil **1.** grass. **2.** lawn.

J

j-a

jaa see under *j-y-a*.

j-a-j

jaaj (coll.) chicken(s) (var. of *dijaaj*, which see under *d-j-j*).

jaaja pl. *-aat* chicken.

j-a-r

jaara pl. *-aat* afterbirth, placenta.

j-a-m

jaam (coll.) glass, plate glass, sheet glass.

jaama pl. *-aat* **1.** pane of glass. **2.** photographic plate or negative.

jaamxaana pl. *-aat* **1.** glassed cabinet. **2.** showcase. **3.** store show window.

j-a-m-w-s

jaamuus pl. *jwaamiis* buffalo, water buffalo.

jaamuusa pl. *-aat, jwaamiis* buffalo cow.

j-a-h

jaah standing, dignity, position.

j-a-w

jaawa Java.

*jaawi** **1.** Javanese. **2.** *jaawi, xišab jaawi* a type of hardwood.

j-a-w-n

jaawan pl. *-aat, jwaawiin* **1.** large mortar, large bowl. **2.** hollowed log used as a mortar. **3.** whirlpool.

j-ʔ-z

jaaʔiza see *j-w-z*.

j-b-b

jubba pl. *jubab* a long, plain outer garment, collarless, with wide sleeves, usually worn by religious men.

j-b-j-b

tjabjab to be unsure, hesitant, timid, shy. *di-fuut gul-la! la-tidjabjab!* Go on in and tell him! Don't be hesitant! *huwwa da-yidjabjab min-hal-waḏiifa.* He's not too sure about this position. *ʔaani da-adjabjab minna hwaaya.* I am very unsure about him.

j-b-r

jubar (*u jabur*) to force, compel, coerce. *jubrooni ʔazzawwajha.* They forced me to marry her.

jabbar to set (a broken bone). *l-imjabbur jabbar ʔiidi l-maksuura.* The bonesetter set my broken arm.

njubar **1.** to be forced, compelled. *njubarit atruk šuġḷi w-aruuʕ wiyyaahum.* I had to leave my work and go with them. **2.** to fall in love. *njubar biiha w-idzawwajha.* He fell in love with her and married her.

jabir **1.** strong. **2.** thick, large (in circumference). **3.** algebra.

jabur force, coercion, compulsion, duress.

jabran forcibly, by force. *ma-qibal yruuʕ laakin iš-šurṭa waddoo jabran.* He wouldn't go but the police took him forcibly. *ʔibni ma-yidrus ʔilla jabran.* My son won't study unless forced to. *š-b-iidi? sawweetha jabran.* What could I do? I did it because I had to. || *jabran ʕan* in spite of, despite. *ḏṭarreet ʔaqbal iš-šaġḷa jabran ʕanni.* I had to accept the job in spite of myself. *ʕayynaw hal-muwaḏḏaf jabran ʕan raʔiisa.* They appointed that employee against the wishes of his boss.

*jabri** compulsory, obligatory, forced.

jabbaar **1.** thick, large (in circumference). **2.** almighty, omnipotent (God). **3.** (pl. *jabaabira*) mighty, powerful, strong. **4.** strong person.

ʔajbar **1.** stronger, strongest. **2.** thicker, thickest.

*ʔijbaari** compulsory, obligatory, forced. *jundi ʔijbaari* draftee. || *ʔaxδoo ʔijbaari.* They drafted him.

majbuur **1.** forced, compelled. **2.** in love, enamored. *huwwa majbuur biiha.* He's in love with her.

mjabbir pl. *-iin* bonesetter.

mjabbirči pl. *-iyya* bonesetter.

j-b-l

jibal pl. *jbaal* mountain.

*jabali** **1.** mountainous, hilly, mountain-. **2.** mountain dweller, mountaineer.

j-b-n

jiban (*i jubun*) **1.** to be cowardly, fearful, scared, afraid. *min šaaf il-ʔasad giddaama, jiban.* When he saw the lion before him, he was scared. **2.** to mix (mortar, cement). *ʔijbin haj-juṣṣ ḥatta nibni bii ṭ-ṭaabuug.* Mix this mortar so that we can use it to lay the bricks.

jabban to curdle, become curdled. *l-ḥaliib jabban. ṣaar miθl il-qaalab.* The milk's curdled. It's gotten solid.

jabna pl. *-aat* mixing, batch (of mortar, cement).

jibin cheese.

jabaan pl. *jubanaaʔ* coward.

majibna part of the stomach of the baby lamb, used as a fermenting agent in making cheese.

j-b-h

jaabah to confront, face, encounter. *laazim injaabha bil-ḥaqiiqa.* We'll have to face him with the truth. *raḥ-itjaabih ṣuʕuubaat ihwaaya b-has-safra.* You will encounter many hardships on this journey.

jabha pl. *jabahaat* **1.** front, front part, facade. **2.** forehead, brow. **3.** front lines, front (mil.).

j-b-y

jiba (*i jibaaya*) to collect, levy (taxes). *l-ḥukuuma tijbi iδ-δaraayib imnil-fuqaraaʔ w-ijjuuz imniz-zanaagiin.* The government collects taxes from the poor and leaves the rich alone.

jabba (taboo) to sit or lie down, with the buttocks prominently displayed. *šaayfa min yugʕud išloon yjabbi?* Have you seen how he sticks his butt out when he sits down? *leeš imjabbi ʕal-gaaʕ? ma-dguum!* Why are you prostrated on the ground? Get up!

jaabi pl. *jubaat* **1.** collector, collection agent. **2.** bus conductor.

j-p-s

jips **1.** gypsum. **2.** plaster of paris.

j-t-t

jatt **1.** clover **2.** hay.

j-θ-θ

jiθθa pl. *jiθaθ* corpse, cadaver, body.

jiθiiθ pl. *-iin, jθaaθ.* **1.** fat, obese, corpulent. **2.** obese person.

j-θ-m

jiθmaan pl. *-aat* body, remains, corpse.

jeeθuum pl. *-aat* **1.** incubus. **2.** nightmare.

j-ḥ-d

jiḥad (*a juḥuud*) to disclaim, disavow, deny. *haaδa jiḥad in-niʕma.* He proved ungrateful.

jaaḥid pl. *-iin* denier. *ʔaḷḷa yjaaziik, yaa jaaḥid in-niʕma!* God damn you, you ungrateful wretch!

j-ḥ-r

juḥur pl. *jḥaar, jḥuur* (vulgar) **1.** anus. **2.** buttocks.

j-ḥ-š

jaḥḥaš to marry a woman, consummate the marriage, and then divorce her (in order to make her eligible to re-marry her former husband). *jaḥḥašha ḥatta yigdar yidzawwajha rajilha s-saabiq.* He married her, slept with her, and divorced her so that her former husband could marry her.

jaḥaš pl. *jḥaaš, jḥuuš* young donkey.

j-ḥ-f-l

jaḥfal pl. *jaḥaafil* group, battle group (mil.). *ʔaamir ij-jaḥfal* battle group commander.

j-ḥ-y-m

jaḥiim hell, hellfire.

j-d-ḥ

jidaḥ (*a jadiḥ*) to spark, make sparks. *han-nooʕ imnil-ḥajar ma-yijdaḥ zeen.* This kind of flint doesn't spark well.

jiddaaḥa pl. *-aat* cigarette lighter.

¹*j-d-d*

jidd pl. *jduud, ʔajdaad* grandfather.

jidda pl. *-aat* **1.** grandmother. **2.** midwife.

²*j-d-d*

jaddad **1.** to renew, revive. *xalli njaddid ʕalaaqatna.* Let's renew our relationship. *ma-tigdar itsaafir ʔiδa ma-djaddid il-paaspoort.* You can't travel if you don't renew your passport. **2.** to remodel, restore, renovate, modernize. *laazim injaddid il-beet gabuḷ-ma nʔajjra.* We've got to renovate the house before we rent it. **3.** to begin anew, start, try again. *fluusak xilṣat. raḉ-itbaṭṭil loo jjaddid?* Your money's gone. Are you going to quit or play again? *ma-maḉquula šbaḉit. jaddid!* You can't possibly be full. Have some more!

tjaddad **1.** to be started anew, be revived. *l-mašaakil idjaddidat biš-šimaal.* The troubles have cropped up again in the North. **2.** to be modern, keep up to date. *yidjaddad ib-kull aḉmaala.* He keeps up to date in everything he does.

jidd seriousness, earnestness. *da-agul-lak-iyyaa b-kull jidd.* I'm telling you this in all seriousness. || *da-tiššaaqa loo jidd?* Are you kidding or serious?

jiddan very much. *ʔaḉturum ʔabuuya jiddan.* I respect my father very much.

*jiddi** serious, earnest, sincere.

jiddiyya pl. *-aat* earnestness, seriousness, gravity. || *jiddiyyaat. ma-da-ʔaššaaqa.* Seriously. I'm not joking.

jiddiyyan seriously, earnestly, in earnest.

jidiid new, recent. || *min jidiid* anew, again, from the start.

ʔajdad newer, newest, more or most recent.

jaadd serious, in earnest. *čaan jaadd min ḉičaaha.* He was serious when he said it.

jaadda pl. *-aat* boulevard, main street, large street.

mitjaddid modern, progressive, up-to-date.

mistajidd new, recent. *jundi mistajidd* (military) recruit.

¹*j-d-r*

jaddar to be or become infected with smallpox. *jaddar min čaan ḉumra xams isniin.* He had smallpox when he was five years old. *ʔaani mjaddir gabuḷ.* I've had smallpox before.

jidri **1.** smallpox. **2.** smallpox vaccination. *ḍarub jidri* smallpox vaccination.

²*j-d-r*

jadiir **1.** worthy, deserving. **2.** proper, suited, suitable, fit, appropriate. *haaδa muu jadiir ib-hal-waḍiifa.* That man's not qualified for this position.

ʔajdar more or most worthy, deserving, etc.

jadaara **1.** worthiness. **2.** fitness, suitability, aptitude, qualification. **3.** appropriateness.

³*j-d-r*

jidir pl. *jduur, jduura* pot, cooking vessel.

jidriyya pl. *-aat* small pot.

j-d-f

jidaf, mijdaaf = *jiδaf, mijδaaf,* which see under *j-δ-f.*

j-d-l

jaadal to debate, argue with, bicker with. *jaadalni b-mawḍuuḉ ma-yuḉruf ḉanna šii.* He argued with me on a subject he knew nothing about.

tjaadal to engage in argument, to argue with each other. *jjaadlaw saaḉa w-ma-tfaahmaw.* They argued an hour and didn't reach an understanding. *jjaadal wiyyaana ḉala šii taafih.* He argued with us about a trivial thing.

jadal debate, dispute, argument, controversy.

*jadali** pl. *-iyyiin* **1.** disputant. **2.** an argumentative person.

jidaal pl. *-aat* quarrel, argument, debate.

mujaadala pl. *-aat* argument, discussion, debate, quarrel.

j-d-w

jadwa, jidwa benefit, advantage, gain, avail. *bala jadwa* or *min ġeer jadwa* to no avail, with no benefit. *min jadwa* concerning, about. *min jadwa l-ifluus il-aṭulbak-iyyaaha; tara ariidha.* About the money you owe me; well, I want it.

j-d-w-l

jadwal pl. *jadaawil* **1.** canal. **2.** small stream, brook. **3.** table, schedule, chart. *jadwal mawaaḉiid il-qiṭaar* train schedule. *jadwal iḍ-δarub* multiplication table.

j-d-y

jadda = *gadda,* which see under *g-d-y.*

jidya begging.

mjaddi pl. *mjaadi* = *mgaddi* which see under *g-d-y.*

j-δ-b

jiδab (*i jaδib*) to attract, draw in, pull in. *l-miġnaṭiiz yijδib il-ḉadiid.* A magnet attracts iron. *b-hal-manhaj, nigdar nijδib kull iš-šabaab.* With this program, we can attract all the young people. *b-xiṭaaba, jiδabhum kullhum lil-ḉizib.* With his speech, he drew them all into the political party.

jaδδaab attractive, appealing, enticing. *manδar jaδδaab* an attractive sight.

jaaδibiyya **1.** attraction, lure, enticement. **2.** attractiveness, charm. **3.** magnetic force. **4.** gravitational force, gravity.

jaδaba pl. *-aat* nut, lunatic, oddball.

j-δ-r

jaδir pl. *jδuur* root. *jaδir tarbiiɛi* square root (math.).

j-δ-ɛ

jiδiɛ pl. *jδuuɛ* **1.** tree trunk. **2.** stump.

j-δ-f

jiδaf (*i jaδif*) to row, paddle. *l-balam čaan bii fadd waaɛid yijδif.* There was one person in the boat rowing.

mijδaaf pl. *majaaδiif* oar, paddle.

j-r-ˀ

jiraˀ (*a jurˀa*) to dare, have the courage. *ma-yijraˀ yiɛči wiyyaa.* He doesn't dare talk with him.

tjarraˀ **1.** to dare, to have the nerve. *šloon tidjarraˀ tiɛči wiyya l-mudiir hiiči?* How do you dare talk with the director like that? **2.** to be insolent, disrespectful, to take liberties. *ˀariid hal-muwaδδaf yinfuṣil li-ˀan idjarraˀ ɛalayya.* I want that employee to be fired because he was insolent toward me.

jariˀ, jariiˀ **1.** courageous, bold, daring. **2.** insolent, immodest, forward.

jurˀa courage, daring, nerve.

ˀajraˀ **1.** more or most bold, courageous, daring. **2.** more or most insolent, forward.

[1]*j-r-b*

jarrab to test, try out. *jarrub hal-miftaaɛ. balki tigdar itfukk il-baab.* Try this key. Maybe you can open the door.

jrabb **1.** to get the mange. *čalbi jrabb.* My dog got mange. **2.** to fade, lose color. *qaaṭi jrabb imniš-šamis.* My suit faded from the sun.

jarab **1.** mange. **2.** scabies, itch.

ˀajrab pl. *jirbiin* mangy.

jarba pl. *-aat* (fem.) mangy.

jraab pl. *jurbaan* fraud, blowhard, incompetent.

tajruba pl. *tajaarub* **1.** experiment, test. *t-tajruba ma-nijɛat.* The experiment didn't succeed. **2.** trial, test. *baɛda taɛt it-tajruba, w-ma-yistiɛiqq ˀijaaza b-raatib.* He's still on probation and isn't entitled to vacation with pay. **3.** experience, practice. *titɛallam bit-tajruba.* You learn by experience. *haaδa šaayif tajaarub ihwaaya; štiġal wiyya ˀanwaaɛ in-naas.* He's had a lot of experiences; he's worked with different types of people.

mjarrib **1.** experienced, seasoned. *ɛaamil imjarrib* an experienced workman. **2.** experimenter, tester, examiner.

[2]*j-r-b*

jiriib = *giriib,* which see under *g-r-b.*

jraab = *graab,* which see under *g-r-b.*

j-r-b-z

jarbaza pl. *-aat* irascible person, crank, crab, grouch.

j-r-b-w-ɛ

jarbuuɛ pl. *jaraabiiɛ* **1.** jerboa, kangaroo rat. **2.** a kind of desert lizard.

j-r-θ-m

jarθuum pl. *jaraaθiim* microbe, germ.

j-r-j-r

jarjar **1.** to jerk, tug, pull. *ma-yriid yruuɛ. la-djarjir bii.* He doesn't want to go. Don't tug at him. **2.** to stall, procrastinate, hedge, delay. *δall yjarjir sana w-baɛdeen difaɛ il-ifluus.* He kept stalling for a year and then paid the money.

jirjiir pl. *-iin* procrastinator, staller.

j-r-j-y-t

jirjeet a kind of thin, translucent cloth.

j-r-ɛ

jiraɛ (*a jariɛ*) to wound, injure, cut. *jiraɛa b-ṣadra, w-waddoo lil-mustašfa.* He wounded him in the chest, and they took him to the hospital. *la-tilɛab bil-muus, tara tijraɛ nafsak.* Don't play with the razor blade, or you'll cut yourself. *la-tijraɛ ɛawaaṭfa b-hiiči kalimaat.* Don't hurt his feelings with such remarks.

jarraɛ to wound, cut to pieces, cut up. *šloon imzayyin! jarraɛni.* What a barber! He cut me all up.

tjarraɛ pass. of *jarraɛ.*

njiraɛ pass. of *jiraɛ.*

jariɛ pl. *jruuɛ* wound, cut, injury.

jiraaɛa surgery.

*jiraaɛi** surgical.

jarraaɛ pl. *-iin* surgeon.

jaariɛ **1.** dangerous, injurious. *ˀaalaat jaariɛa* dangerous instruments. **2.** rapacious, predatory. *ṭyuur jaariɛa* predatory birds.

j-r-d

jirad (*i jarid*) to take stock, make an inventory. *raɛ-tiji lujna tijrid il-maxzan baačir.* A committee's coming to inventory the stores tomorrow.

jarrad to divest, strip, dispossess, deprive. *jarridoo min rutubta w-madaalyaata.* They stripped him of his rank and medals.

njirad pass. of *jirad. l-maxzan laazim yinjirid marra bis-sana.* The store should be inventoried once a year.

jaraad (coll.) locust(s).

jaraada pl. *-aat* locust.

jariida pl. *jaraayid* newspaper.

jirriid (coll.) palm branch(es) stripped of leaves, palm-leaf stalk(s).

jirriida pl. *-aat* un. n. of *jirriid.*

jweerid: ʔabu jweeriid the first cold wind of fall, the harbinger of autumn.

mujarrad **1.** stripped, divested, bare. *ʔakθar in-nujuum ma-tinšaaf bil-ʕeen il-mujarrada.* Most of the stars can't be seen with the naked eye. **2.** pure, mere, nothing more than. *haaδa mujarrad suʔaal, laa ġeer.* This is merely a question, nothing else. *b-mujarrad-ma* as soon as, the moment that .... *b-mujarrad-ma tiḍḥak, yizʕal.* If you barely laugh, he gets mad.

j-r-d-m

jardam to infect with leprosy, or loosely, any skin blemish. *la-truuḥ yamma tara yjardimak.* Don't go near him or he'll infect you with leprosy.

tjardam to be or become infected with leprosy or, loosely, any skin blemish. *wičča djardam imnilbagg.* His face was blotched by mosquito bites.

jirdaam leprosy.

mjardam **1.** leprous. **2.** leper.

j-r-r

jarr (*u jarr*) **1.** to pull, tug, jerk. *l-muʕallim jarr iδn it-tilmiiδ lamma ḍurab il-yamma.* The teacher pulled the student's ear when he hit the one beside him. || *jarr ḥaṣra wara ḥaṣra.* He heaved sigh after sigh. *jarr-la nafas min jigaarti.* He took a puff from my cigarette. **2.** to tow, pull, drag along, draw. *čaan ij-jaahil yjurr ʕarabaanta b-ḥabil.* The child was pulling his wagon with a rope. *jarr sayyaarti b-sayyaarta lil-garaaj.* He towed my car with his car to the garage. **3.** to extract, draw out, pull out. *jarr ʕalayya xanjar.* He pulled a knife on me. *jarrat ir-raqum maali bil-yaanaṣiib.* She drew my number in the lottery. || *jurr iidak tara amawwtak.* Take your hand off or I'll kill you. *jurr nafsak min hal-qaḍiyya.* Get out of that affair. *triid naaxuδ raaḥa šwayya mniš-šuġul loo njurrha fadd jarra?* Shall we take a short rest from working or get right on with it? *jarreenaaha fadd jarra l-baġdaad.* We hurried straight through to Baghdad.

njarr **1.** pass. of *jarr.* **2.** /with *min*/ to shun, avoid, stay away from. *kull il-muwaḍḍafiin yinjarruun minna.* All the employees shy away from him. *ʔiδa tinjarr min ʕidhum, ʔaḥsan-lak.* If you avoid them, it'll be better for you.

jtarr to ruminate. *baawiʕ! il-haayša da-tijtarr.* Look! The cow is chewing its cud.

jarr pulling, towing, tugging, drawing, dragging. *sibaaq jarr il-ḥabil* tug-of-war contest. *ḥaruf jarr* preposition (gram.).

jarra pl. *-aat* a pull, a tug, a jerk. || *yigdar ybaddil il-waḍiʕ ib-jarrat qalam.* He can alter the situation with a stroke of the pen.

jarra pl. *-aat* large earthenware jug.

mujtarr **1.** ruminant. **2.** a ruminant.

jarraar pl. *-aat drawer* (of desk, etc.).

mjarr pl. *-aat* drawer (of a desk, etc.).

jarraara pl. *-aat* trailer.

j-r-r-y

jirri (coll.) a type of catfish.

jirriyya pl. *-aat* un.n. of *jirri.*

j-r-š

jiraš (*u jariš*) to grind, crush, crack (grain, etc.). *ʔijruš išwayyat ʕadas lis-šoorba.* Grind up a few lentils for the soup.

jiriiš ground grain.

jaaruuša pl. *-aat* grinder, cracking machine.

majraša pl. *majaariš* grinder, cracking machine.

j-r-ṣ

jaraṣ pl. *jraaṣ* bell.

j-r-ʕ

jiraʕ (*a jariʕ*) **1.** to gulp, swallow, drink down hurriedly. *jiraʕ nuṣṣ iglaaṣ ʕarag ib-šurba waḥda.* He downed half a glass of arrack in one draught. **2.** to endure, bear, stand, take. *ḍall ʕidna yoomeen bass ma-gdart ajirʕa.* He was with us for two days but I couldn't stand him. *jiraʕt il-murr min ʔiid hal-walad.* I've had nothing but trouble from this boy.

jarraʕ = *jiraʕ.*

njiraʕ to be bearable, sufferable. *dihn il-xirwiʕ ma-yinjiriʕ.* Castor oil is unbearable.

jurʕa pl. *-aat, juraʕ* **1.** mouthful, gulp, swallow. **2.** dose (of medicine).

see also *č-r-ʕ.*

j-r-f

jiraf (*u jaruf*) **1.** to sweep away, carry downstream. *l-ṃaay jiraf il-balam min ḍayyaʕit il-mijdaaf.* The water took the boat when I lost the oar. **2.** to wash away. *l-ṃaay jiraf kull il-ġaraaḍ il-xalleenaaha ʕaš-šaaṭi.* The water washed away all the things we left on the bank.

njiraf pass. of *jiraf.*

juruf pl. *jruuf* bank, edge, brink (of a body of water).

mijrafa pl. *majaarif* a kind of shovel shaped like a hoe with a curved blade.

j-r-m

jiram (*i ˀijraam*) to commit a crime or offense, to do wrong. *ˀiδa yijrim marra θaanya, ma-yiɛfi ɛanna l-ḥaakim.* If he commits another crime, the judge won't pardon him. *jiram ɛala wilda; ma-daxxalhum madaaris.* He wronged his children; he didn't put them in school.

njiram to be wronged, mistreated, cheated. *njiramit ib-haš-šarwa.* I got cheated on that deal.

jurum pl. *ˀajraam* crime, offense.

ˀijraam crime. *mukaafaḥat il-ˀijraam* crime prevention. *ɛilm il-ˀijraam* criminology.

jariima pl. *jaraayim* crime.

mujrim pl. *-iin* criminal.

j-r-w

jiru pl. *jraawa* puppy, whelp, cub.

¹*j-r-y*

jira (*i jari*) **1.** to flow, stream, run. *l-ṃayy da-yijri bis-saagya ṣaar-la saaɛteen.* The water has been running in the ditch for two hours. **2.** to take place, come to pass, happen, occur. *ḥawaadiθ ir-ruwaaya tijri bij-jibaal.* The action of the story takes place in the mountains. *loo tidri š-jira biyya!* If you only knew what happened to me! *kullši jira b-laḥδa waḥda.* Everything happened at once. || *š-jaarii-lak tištiri sayyaara mustaɛmala w-titwarraṭ biiha?* What ever impelled you to buy a used car and get stuck with it?

jaara to co-operate with, go along with, to adapt to, adjust to. *jaarii. baɛad-la sbuuɛeen yinniqil.* Go along with him. He's got two more weeks before he's transferred.

ˀajra to carry out, perform. *ˀajra tajaarub ihwaaya ɛala had-duwa.* He conducted many experiments on that medicine.

jarayaan **1.** flow, movement. **2.** current.

ˀijraaˀ pl. *-aat* **1.** performance, execution, act of carrying out. **2.** measure, step, proceeding. *l-ḥukuuma raḥ-taaxuδ ˀijraaˀaat šadiida δidd il-miṭδaahiriin.* The government's going to take stern measures against the demonstrators. *raḥ-aaxuδ ˀijraaˀaat qaanuuniyya b-ḥaqqak.* I'm going to take legal steps against you.

jaari flowing, running, circulating. *l-ṃaay ij-jaari naδiif.* Flowing water is clean.

majra pl. *majaari* **1.** watercourse, stream. **2.** channel, streambed. **3.** flow, stream. *laazim ˀaku šii saadd majra l-ṃaay. n-nahar da-yiṣɛad.* There must be something blocking the flow of water. The river's rising. *gitɛaw ɛan iθ-θuwwaar majra l-ṃaay.* They cut off the supply of water to the rebels. **4.** course, progress, passage (of events). *ṣaar-li mudda ma-da-attibiɛ majra l-ḥawaadiθ b-amriika.* For some time I haven't been following the course of events in America.

mujaaraatan li- out of regard for. *biqeet saakit mujaaraatan iš-šuɛuura.* I kept still out of regard for his feelings.

²*j-r-y*

jirri see under *j-r-r-y*.

j-r-y-d

jreedi pl. *-iyya* rat. *jreedi naxal̩* a large tree-climbing rodent.

j-z-ˀ

jazzaˀ to divide, break up, separate, partition, cut up. *ˀiδa djazziˀ is-suˀaal, yinfihim ib-suhuula.* If you break up the question, it will be easily understood.

juzuˀ pl. *ˀajzaaˀ* **1.** part, portion. *qreet juzuˀ imnil-iktaab w-ma-ɛijabni.* I read a part of the book and I didn't like it. **2.** fraction. *l-beet ma-kallafa ˀilla juzuˀ baṣiiṭ min θaruuta.* The house didn't cost him more than a small fraction of his fortune. **3.** one of the thirty sections of the Koran. **4.** volume, section, part. *štireet ij-juzˀ il-ˀawwal imnil-iktaab.* I bought the first volume of the book.

*juzˀi** **1.** partial. **2.** minor, trivial, insignificant, petty.

j-z-j-z

jaẓjaẓ to squeak. *hal-yamani yjaẓjuẓ. laazim xooš šuġul̩.* These slippers squeak. They must be well made.

j-z-d-a-n

jizdaan pl. *-aat, jazaadiin* **1.** wallet. **2.** change purse.

j-z-r

jazzar to be or become dried out. *la-tfukk ij-jidir, ḥatta la-yjazzir iš-šuwanδar.* Don't open up the pot, so the beets won't dry out.

jizar (coll.) carrot(s). *raas jizar* a carrot, one carrot.

jizra pl. *-aat* carrot.

jazir **1.** ebb (of the tide). **2.** low tide. **3.** shortage, deficiency. *ˀaku jazir bil-iḥsaab.* There is a shortage in the accounts.

jazra pl. *-aat* **1.** island. **2.** sandbar.

jaziira pl. *jazaayir, juzur* island. *šibih jaziira* peninsula. || *j-jaziira* the desert between the Tigris and the Euphrates.
l-jazaaʔir Algeria.
*jazaaʔiri** 1. Algerian, from Algeria. 2. an Algerian.
majzara pl. *majaazir* 1. slaughterhouse. 2. massacre, slaughter, carnage.

j-z-z
jazz (*u jazz*) 1. to shear, clip off. *da-yjuzzuun ṣuuf il-xaruuf.* They're shearing the sheep. 2. to squeak. *qundarti j-jidiida da-djuẓẓ.* My new shoes are squeaking.
jizza pl. *jizaz* fleece. *jizzat ṣuuf* the wool from one sheep, a clip of wool.

j-z-ʕ
jizaʕ (*a jazaʕ, juzuuʕ*) 1. to be or become bored, to tire. *j-jaahil ma-yijzaʕ imnil-liʕib.* The child doesn't get tired of playing. 2. to be or become disgusted, fed up, impatient, dissatisfied. *ṭaalabta bil-ifluus mudda w-baʕdeen jizaʕit.* I asked him for the money a few times and then got disgusted.
jazzaʕ to make restless, impatient, disgusted, to upset, make nervous. *ʔaḍall adugg ib-raasa ḥatta ʔajazziʕa.* I keep pestering him until I get his goat.

j-z-f
jaazaf 1. to act recklessly, heedlessly, to take chances. *la-jjaazif halgadd; suuq ʕala keefak.* Don't take chances so much; drive slowly. 2. /with *b-*/ to risk, hazard, stake. *jaazaf ib-ḥayaata ḥatta yinquð il-mara.* He risked his life to save the woman.
mujaazafa pl. *-aat* 1. risk, hazard. 2. recklessness. 3. dangerous adventure.
mujaazif 1. reckless, foolhardy. 2. adventurous.

[1]*j-z-m*
jizam (*i jazim*) to be certain, positive, sure. *ma-tigdar tijzim bi-ʔan iṣ-ṣuuč minna.* You can't be positive that the blame is his.
jaazim 1. decisive. 2. final, definite. 3. absolutely certain, firmly convinced.

[2]*j-z-m*
juzma pl. *juzam* (pair of) rubber boots.

j-z-w
jazwa pl. *-aat* coffee pot (for Turkish coffee).

j-z-y
jazza 1. to fine. *l-ḥaakim jazzaani diinaareen.* The judge fined me two dinars. 2. to reward. *jazzaak ʔaḷḷaa xeer.* May God reward you.
jaaza 1. to repay, recompense. *yiji yoom ʔajaaziik ʕala faḍlak.* The day will come when I'll repay you for your favor. 2. to reward. *ʔaḷḷa yjaaziik ʕala ʕamalak.* May God reward you for your act. 3. to punish. *ʔiða ma-tḥaððir waḍiiftak, l-muʕallim yjaaziik.* If you don't prepare your lessons, the teacher will punish you.
tjaaza pass. of *jaaza.*
jazaaʔ pl. *-aat* 1. reward. *ʔilli yitṣaddaq ʕal-fuqaraaʔ, jazaaʔa ʕind ʔaḷḷa ʕaḍiim.* The man who gives to the poor will have a great reward in heaven. 2. punishment, penalty. *marrt il-lux jazaaʔak ykuun ḥabis.* Next time your punishment will be jail. || *maḥkamt ij-jazaaʔ* Penal Court (the second from the bottom of criminal court hierarchy, above *ṣulḥ* and below *kubra*). 3. fine, judgment. *ʔiða ma-tidfaʕ ij-jazaaʔ, yḥibsuuk ʔusbuuʕeen.* If you don't pay the fine, they'll jail you for two weeks.

j-s-b
jasib (coll.) dried date(s).
jasba pl. *-aat* un. n. of *jasib.*

j-s-r
jisar (*u jasaara*) 1. to venture, dare. *šloon jisarit w-git-la lil-muʕallim hiiči?* How could you be so bold as to tell the teacher such a thing? *ʔiða tijsur ib-čilma wiḥda, ašugga l-ḥalgak.* If you dare say one word, I'll smack you. 2. to have the courage, have the nerve. *ma-yijsur yuṭlub minna l-ifluus.* He doesn't have the nerve to ask him for the money. 3. to be disrespectful, impudent, insolent. *hal-walad yijsur ʕala ʔabuu.* This boy is disrespectful toward his father.
jassar to embolden, encourage, to make disrespectful, impudent. *šinu lli jassarak hiiči?* What was it made you so impudent?
tjaasar to be bold, forward, insolent, impudent. *ʕeeb tijjaasar ʕal-ʔabuuk!* Shame on you, being insolent to your father! *ṭ-ṭaalib idjaasar ʕal-mudarris.* The student was impudent toward the instructor.
jisir pl. *jsuur, jsuura* 1. bridge, span, overpass, viaduct. 2. dental bridge. 3. beam, girder, rafter.
jasir 1. bold, courageous. 2. impudent, insolent, forward.
jasuur = *jasir.*
jasaara 1. boldness, courage. 2. insolence, impudence, forwardness, nerve.
ʔajsar more or most insolent, impudent, etc.

j-s-s

jass (*i, u jass*) **1.** to feel, probe, examine by touch. *ṭ-ṭabiib jass in-nabuð maala.* The doctor felt his pulse. || *xalli njuss nabða gabul-ma nisʔala.* Let's feel him out before we ask him. **2.** to try to find out, try to gain information. *jiss-li l-xabar ɛatta ʔaɛruf š-asawwi.* Find out for me what's happening so I'll know what to do.

tjassas to spy, engage in espionage. *dazzoo yidjassas-ilhum.* They sent him to spy for them.

jaasuus pl. *jwaasiis* spy.

jaasuusiyya spying, espionage.

j-s-m

jassam to play up, magnify, enlarge, exaggerate. *ma-aku šii. haaða ṣaaɛbak yjassim il-ʔumuur.* It's nothing. Your friend here just builds things up out of proportion.

tjassam to become corporeal, materialize, assume form, take shape. *djassimat ʔamaama ɛaadiθat mootat ɛamma w-biča.* A vision of the death of his uncle materialized before him and he cried.

jisim pl. *ʔajsaam* **1.** body, **2.** figure, form, shape. **3.** bulk, mass.

jasiim huge, immense.

jasaama **1.** size, volume. **2.** immensity.

mujaasam **1.** bodily, corporeal. **2.** material, tangible. **3.** three-dimensional. *xariiṭa mujassama* three-dimensional relief map. *handasa mujassama.* Solid geometry.

j-š-ɛ

jašaɛ greediness, covetousness.

jašiɛ greedy, covetous.

ʔajšaɛ more or most covetous.

j-ṣ-ṣ

juṣṣ **1.** lime. **2.** mortar, plaster.

j-ṭ-l

jiṭal (*u*) to lay, place horizontal. *ʔijṭul ij-jaahil ɛal-meez w-laflifa.* Lay the child on the table and wrap him up.

jaṭṭal to lay out, flatten. *ðurabhum booksaat w-jaṭṭalhum ɛal-gaaɛ.* He hit them several times and laid them on the ground.

njiṭal to lie down, recline. *taɛbaan; raɛ-anjiṭil ɛal-ifraaš.* I'm tired; I'm going to lie down on the bed.

j-ɛ-b

jiɛib pl. *jɛuuba* (vulgar) hips, buttocks.

jaɛaba pl. *-aat* clump of flesh on a bird's tail, pope's nose.

see also *č-ɛ-b.*

j-ɛ-d

jaɛɛad **1.** to curl, make curly. *šaɛrič ɛilu. ma-aku ɛaaja itjaɛɛdii.* Your hair's nice. There's no need to curl it. **2.** to wave. *ween jaɛɛadti šaɛrič?* Where'd you get your hair waved?

tjaɛɛad **1.** pass. of *jaɛɛad.* **2.** to become wrinkled. *mnil-wajɛa ðiɛaf w-jilid wučča djaɛɛad.* He got thin from the illness and the skin of his face became wrinkled.

mjaɛɛad **1.** curly, kinky. *šaɛarha mjaɛɛad min ṭabiiɛta.* Her hair is naturally curly. **2.** wrinkled, creased, furrowed. *baɛda jaahil laakin wičča mjaɛɛad.* He's still young but his face is wrinkled.

tajaaɛiid (pl. only) wrinkles, lines (in the face).

j-ɛ-r

jiɛar (*a*) to bray. *šuufa šloon da-yijɛar miθl iz-zumaaḷ. ma-yigdar yiɛči yawaaš.* Look at him braying like a donkey. He can't talk softly.

j-ɛ-ṣ

jiɛaṣ (*a jaɛiṣ*) to crush, mash, squash. *ɛala keefak! la-tijɛaṣ iṭ-ṭamaaṭa.* Watch it! Don't mash the tomatoes. *la-tugɛud yamm haaða s-simiin tara yijɛaṣak.* Don't sit next to that fat guy or he'll squeeze you. *raɛ-tiṭṣaaraɛ wiyya has-simiin? haaða yigdar yijɛaṣha.* Are you going to wrestle with that fat guy? He could squash you.

j-ɛ-l

jiɛal (*a*) to consider, regard, assume. *nṭiiha čam filis w-ijɛalha ṣadaqa.* Give her a little money and consider it charity. *ʔijɛal nafsak ma-tidri w-ʔisʔala.* Pretend you don't know and ask him.

jaɛal: ʔabu jaɛal dung roller, dung beetle.

j-ɛ-m-r

mjaɛmar lop-sided, misshapen.

j-ɛ-m-ṣ

jaɛmaṣ (vulgar) to talk nonsense. *la-tintibih-la. da-yjaɛmuṣ.* Don't pay any attention to him. He's just talking nonsense.

jaɛmuuṣ pl. *jaɛaamiiṣ* (vulgar) the product of an act of defecating, a piece of feces.

j-f-t

jaffat to overhaul, rebuild (a motor). *šwakit raɛ-itjaffit makiint is-sayyaara?* When are you going to overhaul the car motor?

jift **1.** an even number, multiple of two.

ʔiδa djiib jift, tuġlub. If you get an even number, you win. **2.** double. *bunduqiyya jift* double-barreled shotgun.

jufta pl. *jufat* in dominoes, a piece with the same number on both ends.

j-f-r

jufra pl. *jufar* **1.** pit, hole in the ground. **2.** dug-out arena or ring for wrestling and athletic contests.

j-f-f

jaff (*i jafaaf*) to dry, become dry. *xallaaha biš-šamis ʕatta djiff.* He put it in the sun to dry.

jaffaf to dry out, make dry. *yjaffifuun il-fawaakih ʕatta yaakluuha biš-šita.* They dry fruits in order to eat them in the winter.

jaaff **1.** dry. *baġdaad jawwha jaaff biṣ-ṣeef.* Baghdad's climate is dry in the summer. *qalam ʕibir jaaff* ball-point pen. **2.** stale, uninteresting, dry. *yisʔal ʔasʔila jaaffa.* He asks uninteresting questions.

j-f-l

jifal (*i jafil*) **1.** to start, jump with fright. *jifalit min ṭilaʕ-li min wara l-baab.* I got a start when he came out from behind the door. **2.** to shy. *l-iʕṣaan jifal min simaʕ iṭ-ṭalqa.* The horse shyed when he heard the shot.

jaffal to startle, frighten. *xal-nixtil wara l-baab w-injaffla.* Let's hide behind the door and startle him.

j-f-n

jifin pl. *jfuun* eyelid.

j-l-b

jilab (*i jalib*) **1.** to attract, draw. *hduum har-rijjaal tijlib in-naδar.* This man's clothes attract attention. **2.** to bring, bring about, cause. *ʔinta raʕ-tijlib-inna mašaakil.* You will bring us problems.

jalab **1.** of poor quality, shoddy, cheap. **2.** imitation, copied.

jallaab cold and refreshing, invigorating.

j-l-x

jilax (*i jalix*) to scratch, scrape open, wound. *l-bazzuuna xarmušatni w-jilxat ʔiidi.* The cat clawed me and scratched my hand.

jallax to scratch up. *j-jihaal itʕaarkaw w-waaʕid jallax wučč il-laax.* The children had a fight and one scratched the other's face all up.

tjallax to get all scratched. *leeš ijjallxat ʔiidak hiiči?* How'd your hand get all scratched up like that?

njilax to be scratched, scraped. *njilxat rukubta min čaan yiʕbi.* His knee got scraped when he was crawling.

jalix pl. *jluux* scratch, scrape.

j-l-d

jilad (*i jalid*) to whip, flog, lash. *gabulma yjilduu, ṭ-ṭabiib fuʕaṣa.* Before they flogged him, the doctor examined him.

jallad to bind (a book). *beeš jalladit l-iktaab?* How much did it cost you to bind the book?

tjallad to take heart, buck up, compose oneself. *jjallad; la-tbayyin δuʕfak giddaam in-naas.* Pull yourself together; don't show your weakness in front of people.

jilid pl. *jluud* **1.** skin, hide, pelt. **2.** leather.

*jildi** dermal, pertaining to the skin. *ʔamraaδ jildiyya* skin diseases.

jalid: ṭeer jalid tame pigeon, homing pigeon.

jalda pl. *-aat* lash, stroke with a whip.

jallaad pl. *-iin* executioner, hangman.

mujallid pl. *-iin* book-binder.

mujallad **1.** bound (book). **2.** (pl. *-aat*) volume (of a book).

j-l-s

jalsa pl. *-aat* session, meeting, gathering.

majlis pl. *majaalis* conference, council, congress. *majlis il-ʔumma* parliament. *majlis il-ʔaʕyaan* the senate. *majlis in-nuwwaab* the lower house, chamber of deputies. *majlis il-ʔamin* the Security Council. *majlis il-ʔidaara* board of directors.

j-l-ṭ

jilaṭ (*u jaliṭ*) **1.** to make a mistake, foul up, goof. *tidri, jilaṭit ġeer jalta! dazzeet-ilhum ʔasʕaar ʔaqall min it-takliif.* You know, I made a bad mistake! I sent them prices that are below cost. *jilaṭit bis-suʔaal iθ-θaani maal il-imtiʕaan.* I made a mistake on the second question of the exam. *ween-ma truuʕ, tijluṭha.* You foul up everywhere you go. *jilaṭit jalṭa fišalit minha hwaaya.* I goofed and was very embarassed about it. **2.** to tell inadvertently, give away. *diir baalak la-tijluṭha lil-iʕčaaya.* Watch out you don't spill the story.

j-l-ġ

jilaġ, etc. variant of *jilax,* etc. which see under *j-l-x.*

j-l-f

jilaf (*i jalif*) to scrub, scour. *jilfi rijlič zeen; baʕadha waṣxa.* Scrub your feet well; they're still dirty. *da-tijlif gufa j-jidir b-masɛuuq xaaṣṣ.* She's scouring the outside of the pot with a special powder.

jilf pl. *ʔajlaaf* **1.** boorish, rude, ill-mannered. **2.** rude person.

*jilfi** **1.** uncivilized, crude, common. **2.** colloquial, informal. *ɛiraaqi jilfi* colloquial Iraqi. *ma-yṣiir tiɛči jilfi biṣ-ṣaff.* You shouldn't use colloquial speech in class.

jallaafa pl. *-aat* scouring pad.

j-l-f-ṭ

jalfuuṭa pl. *jlaafiiṭ* gristle, fat, waste (of meat).

j-l-q

juluq: δarb ij-juluq masturbation.

j-l-g

jlagg to sag, droop (of the eyelid). *ɛeena jlaggat min čaan jaahil.* His eyelid drooped when he was a child.

ʔajlag fem. *jalga* pl. *julug, jalgiin* having a drooping eyelid.

j-l-l

jall (i jalaal) **1.** to be great, exalted, sublime. *ʔaḷḷa ɛazza w-jall.* God is powerful and exalted. **2.** /with *ɛan*/ to be above, too good for. *haaδa yjill ɛan hiiči ɛamal.* He's above such an act.

ʔajall to revere, venerate, esteem highly, exalt. *hal-ɛaalim id-diini kullhum yijilluu.* They all revere this religious advisor. || *ʔajallak ʔaḷḷaa* (an expression of apology for mentioning a distasteful topic, approx.:) Pardon the expression, but. . ., excuse me for saying so, but. . . . *ʔajallak ʔaḷḷaa, haaδa čaδδaab ɛaqiir.* You should pardon the expression, he's a low-down liar.

jalla (coll.) animal droppings, dung (specifically, of a donkey, horse, or camel).

jillaaya pl. *-aat* un. n. of *jalla.*

jilla pl. *jilal* basket made of palm leaves.

jaliil **1.** revered, respected. **2.** exalted, lofty, sublime.

jlaal pl. *-aat* canvas packsaddle (for a donkey).

jalaala majesty. *ṣaaɛib ij-jalaala l-malik.* His Majesty the King.

majalla pl. *-aat* **1.** periodical. **2.** magazine. **3.** bulletin, journal.

[1]*j-l-y*

jila (i jali) **1.** to polish, shine, clean. *ʔagdar ʔajli ṣ-ṣiiniyya w-axalliiha tilmaɛ.* I can polish the tray and make it shine. **2.** *(i jalaaʔ)* to evacuate, pull out, depart. *j-jeeš il-ʔajnabi jila ɛan ij-jaziira.* The foreign army pulled out of the island.

jaali heartburn, indigestion. *ʔakalt ihwaaya w-ṣaar ɛindi jaali.* I ate a lot and got indigestion.

jaaliya pl. *-aat* colony (of foreigners).

[2]*j-l-y*

jillaaya, see under *j-l-l.*

j-m-b

jamb = janb, which see under *j-n-b.*

j-m-b-a-z

jumbaaz gymnastics.

*jumbaazi** pl. *-iyya* **1.** gymnast. **2.** dishonest shopkeeper.

j-m-j-m

jimjima pl. *jmaajim* skull.

[1]*j-m-d*

jimad (a) **1.** to freeze. *l-ṃayy jimad ib-surɛa.* The water froze quickly. **2.** to congeal, harden, set, become solid. *š-šoorba jimdat bil-hawa l-baarid.* The soup congealed in the cool air. *l-kankari yriid-la saaɛa ɛatta yijmad.* The concrete needs an hour to set. **3.** to stop dead, stand stock still, freeze. *ṣ-ṣayyaad, min šaaf is-sabiɛ, jimad.* The hunter froze when he saw the lion.

jammad **1.** to freeze. *θallaajatna tjammid il-ṃayy bil-ɛajal.* Our refrigerator freezes water quickly. *ṣaaɛ bii ṣeeɛa jammada b-mukaana biiha.* He gave him a shout that froze him in his place. **2.** to freeze (assets). *l-ɛukuuma jammidat ʔamwaal haš-šarikteen.* The government froze the assets of these two companies.

tjammad to be or become frozen. *b-haj-jaww, il-ṃayy yidjammad ib-surɛa.* In this weather, water becomes frozen quickly.

jamaad pl. *-aat* **1.** a solid. **2.** inorganic body. **3.** inanimate body, inanimate being.

jumuud **1.** inactivity, inaction. **2.** lethargy, apathy.

jaamid **1.** frozen. **2.** hard, solid. **3.** stiff. **4.** inanimate. **5.** dry, dull, boring. **6.** impervious to progress or innovation, ultraconservative.

[2]*j-m-d*

jamaadi: jamaadi l-ʔawwal Jumada I, the fifth month of the Moslem year. *jamaadi θ-θaani* Jumada II, the sixth month of the Moslem year.

j-m-r

jammar **1.** to cut the core from a young palm tree. *jammar it-taala bil-faas.* He cored the young palm tree with the adze. **2.** to place fresh coals upon. *baḷḷa jammur-li n-nargiila.* Put fresh coals on the narghile for me, please.

jamur (coll.) ember(s), live coal(s).

jamra pl. *-aat* ember, live coal. || *j-jamra l-xabiiθa* anthrax.

jummaar edible heart of the young palm tree.

j-m-s

jimas (coll.) buffalo(es), water buffalo(es).

j-m-ε

jimaε (*a jamiε*) **1.** to collect. *ṭ-ṭullaab da-yijmaεuun fluus lil-hilaal il-ʔaḥmar.* The students are collecting money for the Red Crescent. **2.** to gather, collect (specimens). *ʔaxuuya yijmaε ṭawaabiε.* My brother collects stamps. **3.** to assemble. *l-mudiir jimaε kull it-talaamiiδ.* The principal called all the students together. *subḥaan ij-jimaεhum.* Only the Sublime could have brought them together. **4.** to add, add up, total. *ʔijmaε hal-ʔaεdaad.* Add up these figures. **5.** to make plural, pluralize. *šloon tijmaε hal-ʔisim?* How do you make this noun plural?

jammaε to save, pile up, amass, accumulate. *ṣaar-li santeen ajammiε fluus ḥatta aštiri raadyo.* I've been saving money for two years to buy a radio.

jaamaε to have sexual intercourse. *ma-laazim idjaamiε ihwaaya w-inta mariiδ.* You shouldn't have intercourse often when you're sick.

tjammaε **1.** to assemble, congregate, gather. *ṭ-ṭullaab jjammiεaw b-saaḥt il-madrasa.* The students gathered in the school yard. *quwwaat il-εadu jjammiεat xaarij il-madiina.* The enemy forces assembled outside the city. **2.** to accumulate, collect. *l-maay jjammaε bis-sirdaab.* The water collected in the basement.

tjaamaε reciprocal of *jaamaε*.

njimaε pass. of *jimaε*.

jtimaε **1.** to assemble, meet, convene. *l-lujna raḥ-tijtimiε baačir.* The committee will meet tomorrow. **2.** to meet, confer, get together. *l-mudiir jtimaε wiyya l-waziir marrteen hal-isbuuε.* The director has conferred with the minister twice this week.

jamiε **1.** gathering. **2.** collection. **3.** accumulation. **4.** addition. **5.** (pl. *jumuuε*) plural.

jimiε pl. *jmuuε* **1.** fist, clenched hand. **2.** a blow with the fist.

jumεa: *j-jumεa, yoom ij-jumεa* Friday.

jamεiyya pl. *-aat* organization, association, club, society. *jamεiyyt ir-rifq bil-ḥaywaan.* The Humane Society.

jamiiε all, entirety. *xabbarit jamiiε it-talaamiiδ.* I told all the students. || *j-jamiiε* everyone, everybody. *j-jamiiε waafqaw.* Everyone agreed.

ʔajmaε: *ʔajmaεiin* (reply to a wish for good health, fortune, etc., approx.:) May it be the same for all.

jamaaεa pl. *-aat* group, gang, bunch. *šifta yiḥči wiyya jamaaεa mnil-fallaaḥiin.* I saw him talking with a group of peasants. *haay jamaaεti. kull yoom nigεud bil-gahwa suwa.* This is my gang. We sit in the coffee shop together every day. || *jamaaεaat jamaaεaat* by groups, in groups. *l-muṣalliin da-yṭilεuun mnij-jaamiε jamaaεaat jamaaεaat.* The worshippers are coming out of the mosque in groups.

majmaε pl. *majaamiε* **1.** meeting place, assembly point. **2.** convention, assembly, gathering. **3.** academy. *majmaε εilmi* academy of sciences.

jimaaε sexual intercourse.

ʔijmaaε unanimity. *waafqaw εal-iqtiraaḥ bil-ʔijmaaε.* They agreed on the proposal unanimously.

jtimaaε pl. *-aat* **1.** meeting. **2.** get-together, gathering, assembly. **3.** community life, social life. *εilm il-ijtimaaε* sociology.

*jtimaaεi** **1.** social. *l-ḥaala l-ijtimaaεiyya bil-εiraaq zeena.* Social conditions are good in Iraq. *wizaart iš-šuʔuun il-ijtimaaεiyya* ministry of social affairs. **2.** sociological. *εaalim ijtimaaεi* sociologist. **3.** sociable, friendly. *leeš ma-tṣiir ijtimaaεi w-itruuḥ tiḥči wiyya l-xuṭṭaar?* Why don't you be sociable and go talk with the guests?

jaamiε **1.** comprehensive, extensive, broad, general. **2.** (pl. *-iin*) collector. **3.** compiler (of a book). **4.** (pl. *jawaamiε*) mosque.

jaamiεa pl. *-aat* **1.** league, union, association *j-jaamiεa l-εarabiyya* the Arab League. **2.** university.

majmuuε **1.** collected, gathered. **2.** (pl. *majaamiiε*) sum, total. **3.** totality, whole.

majmuuεa pl. *-aat* **1.** collection (of objects). **2.** group. **3.** aggregate. **4.** complex.

mujtamaε pl. *-aat* society, community, human society.

[1]*j-m-l*

jammal to beautify, make beautiful. *da-yjammiluun iš-šawaariε ib-saεaf w-δuwaayaat.* They're beautifying the streets with palm branches and lights. *l-ɛadiiqa djammil il-beet.* The garden makes the house beautiful.

jaamal to be polite, courteous. *jaamalni b-šurb il-gahwa, walaw iṭ-ṭabiib maanɛa.* He was polite to me, drinking the coffee even though the doctor had told him not to. *l-ˀustaað yjaamil ṭullaaba hwaaya.* The professor treats his students very politely. *ma-aku ɛaaja jjaamilni. ˀaani muu ġariib.* No need to treat me special. I'm not a stranger.

tjammal to beautify oneself, make oneself pretty. *ɛumurha sittiin sana w-yiɛjibha tidjammal.* She's sixty years old and still likes to make herself pretty.

tjaamal to be polite with one another, treat each other with courtesy. *b-beenhum ɛadaawa bass da-yidjaamluun giddaamna.* There is animosity between them but they're being polite to each other in our presence.

jumla pl. *jumal* **1.** totality, sum, total. *min jumlat il-ˀašyaaˀ illi gaalha ɛannak, ˀannak kaððab.* Among the things he said about you was that you're a liar. **2.** group, body. *l-ɛukuuma da-tufṣul muwaððafiin bij-jumla.* The government is firing employees in whole groups. **3.** wholesale. *bayyaaɛ jumla* wholesale dealer. *hal-maxzan ybiiɛ bij-jumla.* This store sells wholesale. **4.** (gram.) sentence, clause. *ˀinṭiini jumla biiha hač-čilma.* Give me a sentence with this word in it.

jamaal beauty.

jamiil **1.** beautiful, pretty, comely, handsome. **2.** (pl. *-aat*) favor, good turn, service. *naakir ij-jamiil* ungrateful.

ˀajmal more or most beautiful, handsome, etc.

mujaamala pl. *-aat* **1.** courtesy. **2.** amiability, civility. **3.** flattery.

[2]*j-m-l*

jimal pl. *jimaal* camel, male camel.

jammaal pl. *-a* **1.** camel driver. **2.** camel herder.

[3]*j-m-l*

jammaali: saguf jammaali pitched roof.

j-m-l-w-n

jamaloon: saguf jamaloon pitched roof.

j-m-h-r

tjamhar to gather, flock together. *leeš han-naas mijjamhiriin ihnaa?* Why are these people gathered here?

jamhuur pl. *jamaahiir* **1.** crowd, throng, group, mass (of people). *š-šurṭa farriqat ij-jamaahiir.* The police broke up the crowds. **2.** the public, the people, the masses. *j-jamhuur ma-yˀayyid il-ɛukuuma b-siyaasatha.* The public doesn't support the government in its policy.

*jamhuuri** republican. *niðaam jamhuuri* republican system (of government).

jamhuuriyya pl. *-aat* republic.

[1]*j-n-b*

jannab to avert from, ward away from. *haaða yjannibak ihwaaya mašaakil.* That'll spare you a lot of problems.

tjannab to avoid, keep away from. *laazim tijjannab hal-walad.* You've got to avoid that boy.

jtinab = *tjannab. ɛaawil tijtinib tug-ɛud yamma.* Try to avoid sitting near him.

janb **1.** side. *maraḍ ðaat ij-janb* pleurisy. **2.** = *yamm* which see under *y-m-m.*

janaab a title of respect (also used facetiously). *yaa janaab il-ɛaakim . . .* Your Honor . . . . *janaabak, leeš ziɛalit?* Why did Your Lordship get angry?

janabaat (invar.) in a state of ritual impurity from sexual intercourse (of men only). *ma-agdar axušš bij-jaamiɛ; ˀaani janabaat.* I can't go in the mosque; I'm unclean.

jinuub, januub south.

*jinuubi** southern. *lahja jinuubiyya* southern accent.

jinneeb: ˀabu jinneeb crab.

jaanib pl. *jawaanib* side, faction. *j-jaanbeen ma-ttifqaw ɛala šii.* The two sides didn't agree on anything. *ˀaani min jaanbak.* I'm on your side.

*jaanibi** lateral, side. *ˀaxaðna manḍar jaanibi lil-binaaya.* We took a side view of the building.

*ˀajnabi** **1.** foreign, alien. **2.** (pl. *ˀajaanib*) foreigner, alien.

mujnib, mijnib in a state of religious impurity from sexual intercourse (of men only). *ma-agdar aṣalli; ˀaani mijnib.* I can't pray; I'm unclean.

[2]*j-n-b*

jinnab hemp.

j-n-j-l

jinjil pl. *-aat* sty, growth on the eye.

janaajiil or *jnaajil* (pl. only) gold or silver anklets with bells attached, worn by small children learning to walk.

j-n-ɛ

jannaɛ **1.** to fledge. *fruux iṭ-ṭeer janniɛat w-raɛ-iṭṭiir.* The squabs have fledged and are about to fly. **2.** to strut, walk with the chest stuck out. *šuufa šloon* *imjanniɛ. ɛabaa-lak huwwa baṭal.* Look at him all puffed up. You'd think he's a champion.

junɛa pl. *junaɛ* misdemeanor (jur.).

jnaaɛ pl. *-aat, ʔajniɛa* wing (of a bird, airplane, building, or air force).

[1]*j-n-d*

jannad to draft, conscript, induct, recruit. *l-ɛukuuma raɛ-ijjannid kull šaabb illi yigdar yšiil islaaɛ.* The government's going to induct every young man who can bear arms.

tjannad to be drafted, recruited. *kull wuldi jjannidaw.* All my sons were drafted.

jundi pl. *jinuud* **1.** soldier. *jundi nafar* private. *jundi ʔawwal* private first class. **2.** pawn (in chess).

jundiyya **1.** the army, the military. **2.** military service.

[2]*j-n-d*

jinda pl. *-aat, jinad* porter's back pad.

j-n-d-r-m

jandirma pl. *-aat* dullard, dim-wit, lout.

j-n-d-l

jandala pl. *-aat* or *janaadil* **1.** giant. **2.** big person.

j-n-z

jannaz to kill, murder. *jannaza mnil-baṣuṭ.* He beat him within an inch of his life.

tjannaz to act dead, be lazy. *la-tijjannaz. xuff ʔiidak.* Don't goof off. Get a move on.

janaaza pl. *-aat, janaayiz* coffin (with corpse), bier. || *ʔaani ṣaayir janaaza.* I'm dead tired.

jannaaz pl. *-a* person who accompanies the deceased from where he died to the city where he is to be buried.

j-n-s

tjannas to become a naturalized citizen. *raɛ-ajjannas bij-jinsiyya l-ɛiraaqiyya.* I'm going to get naturalized with Iraqi citizenship.

jinis pl. *ʔajnaas* **1.** kind, sort, variety. *ɛindi ṭyuur min kull jinis.* I have all varieties of pigeons. *ɛinda ɛašir quuṭ; kull waaɛid jinis.* He has ten suits, each one a different kind. *la-timši wiyyaa. haaδa muu min jinsak.* Don't hang around with him. He's not your sort of person. **2.** sex, gender. *j-jins il-laṭiif* the fair sex. **3.** race. *j-jins il-bašari* the human race. *j-jins iz-zinji* the Negro race.

*jinsi** **1.** generic. **2.** sexual. **3.** racial.

jinsiyya pl. *-aat* nationality, citizenship.

j-n-ṭ

junṭa pl. *junaṭ* **1.** suitcase, valise, satchel. **2.** briefcase. **3.** (woman's) purse, handbag.

j-n-f-ṣ

jinfaaṣ **1.** canvas. **2.** sackcloth.

j-n-n

jann (*i junuun*) to be or become insane. *ṣaar ɛinda maraḍ ɛaṣabi w-baɛdeen jann.* He got a nervous disease and later went insane. *min šaaf jamaalha, jann.* When he saw her beauty, he went out of his mind.

jannan to make insane, to craze, madden. *ʔibnak jannanni l-yoom.* Your son drove me nuts today. *jamaalha yjannin.* Her beauty is maddening.

njann to become insane. *ʔiδa yšuuf ʔibna mariiḍ, yinjann.* If he finds out his son is sick, he'll go out of his mind.

jinn (coll.) genie(s), jinn.

jinni pl. *jnuun* genie, jinni.

janna heaven, paradise.

janiin pl. *ʔajinna* embryo, fetus.

junuun **1.** insanity, madness, mania. **2.** delusion. *junuun il-ɛaḍama* delusions of grandeur, superiority complex.

*junuuni** crazy, insane, mad.

majnuun **1.** crazed, crazy, insane, mad. **2.** (pl. *majaaniin*) **1.** madman, maniac, lunatic. **2.** fool.

j-n-y

jina (*i jani*) /with *ɛala*/ to wrong, injure, harm. *jina ɛala wilda. ma-daxxalhum madrasa.* He wronged his children. He didn't enter them in school. *jinaw ɛalee. haaδa ma-yistaɛiqq il-faṣil.* They wronged him. He doesn't deserve firing.

jinaaya pl. *-aat* felony, crime.

*jinaaʔi** criminal. *ɛamal jinaaʔi* a criminal act.

jaani pl. *junaat* **1.** perpetrator (of a crime). **2.** culprit, criminal.

j-h-d

jaahad **1.** to strive, endeavor, to put forth one's best effort. *jaahid tqannɛa yiji wiyyaana.* Do your best to persuade him to come with us. *šgadd-ma jaahadit ʔabaddil fikra, ma-faad.* As much as I tried to change his mind, it still didn't work. **2.** to fight, to do battle. *kullna mustaɛiddiin injaahid fii sabiil il-waṭan.* We're all ready to fight in our country's behalf.

ʔajhad to strain, overtax, overwork. *la-tijhid nafsak biš-šuġuḷ. muu zeen.* Don't strain yourself with work. It's not good.

jtihad to work hard, put forth one's best

effort. *ʔiδa tijtihid, tinjaς.* If you work hard, you'll succeed. *jtihadit-lak ihwaaya laakin inṭaw il-waδiifa l-ġeerak.* I did all I could for you but they gave the job to someone else.

juhud effort, attempt, endeavor. *kull juhud* every possible effort. *biδalit kull juhdi ςatta aṣaaliςhum.* I did all I could to reconcile them. || *juhud imkaan* as far as possible, as much as possible. *ςaawalit juhd imkaani, laakin ma-raad.* I tried as hard as I could, but he wasn't willing.

jihaad jihad, holy war.

ʔijhaad overwork, overexertion, strain. *ʔijhaad ζaṣabi* nervous strain.

jtihaad **1.** effort, exertion, pains, trouble. **2.** (pl. *-aat*) an individual interpretation of a religious matter, based on Koran, *ςadiiθ,* or other *jtihaad.* **3.** interpretation, individual opinion.

majhuud pl. *-aat* effort, endeavor, exertion, work, trouble.

mujaahid pl. *-iin* **1.** warrior, religious warrior. **2.** fanatic crusader.

mujtahid **1.** diligent, industrious. **2.** (pl. *-iin*) an interpreter of the Koranic law, through precedents.

j-h-r

jaahar to declare openly, publicly. *yjaahir ib-aaraaʔa. ma-yxaaf min ʔaςςad.* He expresses his opinions openly. He's not afraid of anyone.

jahran publicly, openly, in public. *ma-xaaf. gaalha jahran.* He wasn't afraid. He said it openly.

mijhar pl. *-aat, majaahir* microscope.

*mijhari** microscopic.

j-h-z

jahhaz to supply, provide, furnish, equip. *jahhazna j-jayš ib-ʔaςdaθ il-ʔasliςa.* We supplied the army with the most modern arms.

tjahhaz pass. of *jahhaz. humma daaʔiman yidjahhazuun ib-dafaatir w-ʔaqlaam.* They are always provided with notebooks and pencils.

jihaaz pl. *ʔajhiza* **1.** apparatus, instrument, appliance, gadget, utensil. **2.** things bought with the *muqaddam* for a bride to start housekeeping, trousseau. **3.** system. *j-jihaaz il-ζaṣabi* the nervous system.

tajhiiz **1.** equipping, equipment. **2.** (pl. *-aat*) equipment, gear, materiel.

jaahiz ready-made. *malaabis jaahza* ready-made clothes.

j-h-ḍ

jhaaḍ miscarriage, abortion. *ṣaar ζindha jhaaḍ baζad-ma wugζat imnid-daraj.* She had a miscarriage after she fell down the stairs.

j-h-l

tjaahal **1.** to ignore, disregard. *jjaahala. sawwi nafsak ma-šifta.* Ignore him. Make as if you didn't see him. **2.** to pretend ignorance, feign a lack of knowledge. *la-tijjaahal. tidri ζalee-man da-niςči.* Don't pretend ignorance. You know who we're talking about.

jahl **1.** ignorance. **2.** illiteracy.

jaahil pl. *jahala* **1.** ignorant, uneducated, illiterate. **2.** uneducated person. **3.** (pl. *jhaal, jahhaal*) baby, child, youngster, kid.

ʔajhal **1.** more or most ignorant, uneducated. **2.** more or most youthful.

majhuul unknown.

j-h-m

jhaama pl. *-aat, jhaayim* (an insulting term for face, approx.:) mug, puss, ugly face.

j-h-n-m

jihannam hell, hellfire. *bij-jihannam! yistaahil.* To hell with him! He deserves it.

j-h-y

jiha see *w-j-h.*

j-w-b

jaawab **1.** to answer, reply to, respond to. *ςatta loo ysibbak, la-djaawba.* Even if he insults you, don't answer him. *jaawab ζala suʔaaleen bass.* He answered two questions only.

stajwab to interrogate, examine, question. *š-šurṭa stajwubata saaζa.* The police questioned him an hour.

jawaab pl. *ʔajwiba* answer, reply.

j-w-t

juut jute.

j-w-d

jaad (*u juud*) /with *b-*/ to grant or bestow generously. *jaad ζaleena b-ʔalif diinaar.* He generously granted us a thousand dinars. *leeš ma-jjuud ζaleena b-sukuutak!* Why don't you favor us with your silence!

jawwad to recite the Koran. *fitaς il-qurʔaan w-gaam yjawwid.* He opened the Koran and began to recite.

ʔajaad to excel at, be a master of, to do (something) well, know (something) well. *huwwa yjiid il-ζazif ζal-kamanja.* He excels at playing the violin. *yijiid it-tlaθ lugaat.* He knows three languages well.

juud **1.** generosity, liberality, openhandedness. **2.** (pl. *jwaad*) small bag made from an animal skin.

jawda goodness, excellence.
jayyid 1. good, perfect. 2. excellent, outstanding.
ˀajwad better, best.
ˀajaawiid (pl. only) generous people.

[1]*j-w-r*

jaar (*u joor*) /with *ʕala*/ to wrong, persecute, oppress, commit an outrage against. *jjuur ʕal-walad ˀiδa tdizza lis-suug ib-hal-muṭar.* You're being unfair to the boy if you send him to the market in this rain.
jaawar 1. to be the neighbor of, to live next door to. *jaawarna santeen w-baʕdeen itḥawwal.* He was our neighbor for two years and then he moved. 2. to border, border on. *ˀiiraan itjaawir il-ʕiraaq.* Iran borders on Iraq.
tjaawar pass. of *jaawar.*
stajaar to seek refuge, protection, help, aid. *raḥ-nistajiir ib-ˀay waaḥid yigdar yinquδna.* We will appeal for aid from anyone who can save us.
joor 1. injustice. 2. oppression, tyranny.
jaar pl. *jiiraan* neighbor.
jiiraan pl. *jiyaariin* or *jwaariin* neighbor.

[2]*j-w-r*

juuri: *warid juuri* damask rose.

j-w-r-a-b

jooraab pl. *jwaariib* (pair of) socks, stockings. *takk jooraab* one sock, a stocking.

[1]*j-w-z*

jaaz (*u jooz, jawaaz*) 1. to be possible, conceivable. *kull šii yjuuz.* Anything's possible. *yjuuz. laakin ma-aṭṣawwar hiiči.* It's possible. But I don't think so. *xaabra hassa. yjuuz bil-beet.* Call him now. He may be home. *šloon iyjuuz-lak iṭṭallʕa mniš-šuġul?* What gives you the right to fire him? 2. /with *min*/ to stop, quit, give up. *juuz min ˀakil il-ixyaar; ma-zeen ˀilak.* Stop eating cucumbers; it's not good for you. *qaabil ˀaani jaayiz min ḥayaati, ˀarkab ṭiyyaara wiyyaa?* You think I've given up my life, to ride an airplane with him? 3. to let go of, let alone. *juuz min haj-jaahil!* Leave that child alone! *š-šurṭi jaaz minni baʕad-ma raaweeta hawiiti.* The cop let me go after I showed him my identification.
jaawaz 1. to overstep, go beyond. *jaawaz kull il-ḥuduud bil-ḥači maala.* He overstepped all the bounds with his talk. 2. to exceed, surpass. *miizaaniyyatna jaawazat il-malyoon diinaar has-sana.* Our budget exceeded a million dinars this year.
tjaawaz to overstep, exceed, go beyond. *djaawaz il-ḥuduud ib-ḥačya.* He stepped out of bounds in what he said.
jtaaz 1. to pass through, go through, traverse. *jtaaz il-ġaaba waḥda.* He passed through the woods by himself. 2. to cross, go across. *jeeš il-ʕadu jtaaz ḥduudna l-baarḥa.* The enemy army crossed our borders yesterday. *xan-nijtaaz iš-šaariʕ min-naa.* Let's cut across the street here. 3. to get through, come through. *jtaaz il-imtiḥaan ib-tafawwuq.* He passed the exam with flying colors.
jawaaz 1. possibility, conceivability. 2. quitting, giving up. 3. relinquishing. 4. (pl. *-aat*) passport.
ˀijaaza pl. *-aat* 1. authorization. 2. license, permit. 3. leave, vacation. *ˀijaaza diraasiyya* leave of absence for study.
tajaawuz pl. *-aat* 1. encroachment, unwarranted act. 2. overdraft, overdrawing (of an account).
jaaˀiz possible, conceivable.
jaaˀiza pl. *jawaaˀiz* 1. prize, award, premium. 2. reward.
mujaaz 1. on vacation, on leave. 2. licensed, authorized.

[2]*j-w-z*

jooz (coll.) walnut(s). *jooz hind, jooz hindi* coconut(s).
jooza pl. *-aat* 1. un. n. of *jooz.* 2. Adam's apple.
*joozi** walnut-colored, nut brown.
joozbawwa nutmeg.

j-w-ʕ

jaaʕ (*u jooʕ*) to be or become hungry. *š-ib-saaʕ jiʕit! hassa ˀakalna.* You sure got hungry fast! We just ate.
jawwaʕ 1. to starve, cause to starve. *leeš da-jjawwiʕ il-iḥṣaan maalak?* Why are you starving your horse? 2. to make hungry. *hawa j-jibaal yjawwiʕ.* Mountain air makes one hungry.
juuʕ hunger, starvation.
juuʕi pl. *-iyyiin* cadger, freeloader, sponger, cheapskate.
juuʕiyyaat sponging, freeloading. *ma-djuuz mnij-juuʕiyyaat!* Why don't you quit sponging!
juuʕaan pl. *-iin, jwaaʕa* hungry, starved, famished.
majaaʕa pl. *-aat* famine.

j-w-ʕ-r

jooʕar to bray. *waxxir haz-zumaaḷ minnaa. da-yjooʕir ʕala ṭuul.* Get this donkey away from here. He brays continuously.

j-w-q

jooq pl. *ˀajwaaq* band, orchestra.

j-w-l

tjawwal to wander around, roam, rove about. *yiċjibni ˀadjawwal ib-paariis.* I like to go wandering around in Paris. **2.** to patrol, make the rounds. *š-šurṭa tidjawwal bil-manaaṭiq il-ċassaasa bil-balda.* The police patrol the sensitive areas in the city.

jawla pl. *-aat* **1.** tour, excursion, outing. **2.** circuit, round, patrol. **3.** round (in sports).

jawwaal pl. *-a* senior Boy Scout, older than a *kaššaaf.*

majaal pl. *-aat* **1.** room, space. *ˀaku majaal kaafi lis-sayyaara tfuut jawwa ṭ-ṭaag.* There's clearance enough for the car to go under the arch. **2.** place, opening. *maaku majaal bil-milaak inċayyna.* There's no opening we can appoint him to in the organization. **3.** field, domain, sphere. *huwwa maċruuf bil-majaal is-siyaasi.* He is well-known in the political field. **4.** free scope, freedom, opportunity, chance. *b-hal-waδiifa, ċindi majaal waasiċ ˀastaċmil δakaaˀi.* In this job, I have great opportunity for using my intelligence. *raċ-axaabrak ˀiδa ṣaar-li majaal.* I'll call you if I get a chance.

tajawwul going about, moving around. *maniċ tajawwul* curfew.

mutajawwil moving, wandering, itinerant, travelling, roving.

j-w-m

juuma pl. *juwam* **1.** hole in the ground or floor for mounting a loom. **2.** a loom.

j-w-n

jaawan see *j-a-w-n.*

j-w-h-r

jawhar pl. *jawaahir* essence, quintessence, essential nature. *jawhar il-ċaqiiqa* the real truth. *jawhar il-insaan* man's essential nature.

joohar tint, dye, coloring.

jawhara pl. *jawaahir* gem, jewel, precious stone.

jooharči pl. *-iyya* **1.** jeweler. **2.** merchant who charges high prices, profiteer.

mujawharaat (pl. only) **1.** jewelry. **2.** jewels, gems.

j-w-w

jaww pl. *ˀajwaaˀ* **1.** air. *j-jaww baarid ihnaa bil-leel.* The air's cold here at night. **2.** atmosphere. *j-jaww ib-had-daaˀira muu muriiċ.* The atmosphere in this office is not relaxed. **3.** weather, climate. *jaww mumṭir* rainy weather.

*jawwi** air, aerial, aero-. *bariid jawwi* air mail.

jawwa **1.** in, inside. *xašš jawwa.* He went inside. *fuut bil-paaṣ w-ugċud jawwa kulliš.* Get on the bus and sit all the way in the back. || *jawwa l-ċabaa* behind the scenes, unseen, covert. **2.** down, downstairs. *xall ninzil jawwa.* Let's go downstairs. **3.** under, beneath, underneath. *č-čalib naayim jawwa s-sayyaara.* The dog is sleeping under the car. || *jawwa l-ˀiid* at hand, handy, available.

*jawwaani** **1.** inner, inside, interior. **2.** lower, bottommost. **3.** under-.

juwwa pl. *-aat, juwaw* patch, plot, bed (in a garden). *juwwat ṭamaaṭa* bed of tomatoes.

j-y

jaa or *ˀija* (*i jayya*) **1. a.** to come, come to. *jaa lid-daaˀira mitˀaxxir.* He came to the office late. *ˀijoona xuṭṭaar il-baarċa.* We had guests yesterday. *ṣadiiqak jaa ċaleek il-baarċa.* Your friend came to see you yesterday. *jaani min wara w-δirabni.* He approached me from behind and hit me. || *l-ma-yiji wiyyaak, taċaal wiyyaa.* If he doesn't go along with you, compromise (lit. whoever won't come with you, go with him). *ˀiδa tiji wiyyaa bil-liin, yiqbal.* If you approach him gently, he will agree. *ˀiδa tijii b-ilsaan ṭayyib, ywaafuq.* If you approach him in a nice manner, he'll agree. *ˀisma ma-da-yiji ċala baali.* His name doesn't occur to me. *δall yruuċ w-yiji bil-gubba.* He kept pacing back and forth in the room. *jatni xooš fikra.* A good idea occurred to me. *jaak xabar min axuuk?* Have you gotten any news from your brother? *jatti b-raasi w-δirabta.* I got mad and hit him. **b.** to arrive. *šwakit tiji ṭ-ṭiyyaara?* What time does the plane arrive? *ˀajala jaa w-maat.* His time came and he died. *jaa l-muṭar w-dumar kull il-warid.* The rain came and damaged all the flowers. *min yiji l-xeer, yiji fadd marra.* When properity comes, it comes all at one time. *min tiji l-ċuṭla, raċ-atċallam sibiċ.* When vacation comes around, I'll learn swimming. *hamm jaa ṣ-ṣeef.* Summer has come again. *jaa wakt ir-raggi.* Watermelons are in season. || *ˀija δahra.* He had an orgasm. *hal-iqmaaš yiji b-xams alwaan.* This cloth comes in five colors. **c.** to reach, get to. *l-maay jaani ṣ-ṣadri.*

The water came to my chest. *ṃayy ij-jadwal yiji lil-iƹzaam.* The water in the channel comes up to the waist. **2.** to come to, accrue to, come one's way. *da-yijii xooš mawrid imnil-bistaan.* He's getting a good income from the orchard. *min maat ˀabuu, jatta fluus ihwaaya.* When his father died, he came into a lot of money. *jattak ziyaada wiyya baqiit il-ƹummaal?* Did you get a raise with the rest of the workers? *jaani l-ˀaas.* I got the ace. *jaa walad.* He had a son. *š-da-yjiik min wara ˀaδiit in-naas?* What are you gaining from hurting people? *tgarrab ƹal-panka. ma-da-yjiik hawa.* Move closer to the fan. You aren't getting any air. **3.** to descend upon, befall. *š-jaak? muu tuƹruf il-ˀajwiba!* What came over you? You know the answers! *ˀiδa dġammuδ ƹeenak, yijiik in-noom.* If you close your eyes, sleep will come to you. *jaani n-noom. xall-nirjaƹ lil-beet.* I've gotten sleepy. Let's go home. *jatni d-dooxa w-aani da-aktib.* I was overcome by dizziness as I was writing. *ˀahli ma-jatha l-ƹaada šahreen.* My wife hasn't gotten her period for two months. *jaak il-moot ˀinšaaḷḷah.* I hope death takes you. **4.** (as a set phrase) approximately. || *ƹindi yiji xams idnaaniir.* I have almost five dinars. **5.** /with *ƹala*/ to fit, be big enough. *haš-šafqa ma-tiji ƹaleek.* This hat is too small for you.

jayya pl. *-aat* **1.** coming, arrival. *jayyta čaanat ib-maƹallha.* His arrival was timely. *jayytak imneen?* Where did you arrive from? *ˀija l-barid fadd jayya.* The cold weather came all at once. **2.** visit, call. *bqeet daqiiqteen. haaδi muu jayya!* You stayed two minutes. That's no visit!

¹*j-y-b*

jaab (*i jeeb*) **1.** to bring, fetch. *jaab-li saaƹa min iswiisra.* He brought me a watch from Switzerland. *ˀiδa tbiiƹha hassa, djiib-lak xooš ifluus.* If you sell it now, it will bring you a good price. **2.** to come up with, get hold of. *ma-jjiib il-ifluus ƹaad! muu ṣaar šahreen aṭaalbak?* Why don't you come up with the money, then! Haven't I been after you for two months? **3.** to bring out, come out with, pull off. *jaab l-iƹčaaya b-mukaanha.* He made a pertinent remark. *jaab xooš naqiš w-gidar yaaxuδha minha.* He pulled a slick trick and was able to get it from her. **4.** to receive, get, have. *jaab xooš čaanṣ. ġilab miit diinaar.* He had good luck. He won a hundred dinars. *jibit duušeeš.* I drew a double six. **5.** to give birth to, have (a child). *zawijti jaabat walad.* My wife had a boy.

jayyab to attend (a woman) in childbirth. *ˀayy ṭabiib jayyab martak?* Which doctor attended your wife in childbirth? *jiiraanatna da-tiṭlag w-ma-aku wiƹda djayyibha.* Our neighbor is in labor and there's no one to act as midwife for her.

jeebuuba pl. *-aat* delivery, birth (of a baby).

²*j-y-b*

jeeb pocket. || *diir baalak minna, tara yuδrub jeeb.* Be careful of him, because he picks pockets.

j-y-d

jayyid, see *j-w-d.*

j-y-r

jayyar **1.** to cover with asphalt, to pave with asphalt. *jayyiraw il-ṭariiq kulla.* They paved the entire road with asphalt. **2.** to endorse (a check). *jayyarta lič-čakk?* Did you endorse the check?

jiir asphalt. || *bij-jiir!* Good riddance! He deserves what he gets! *w-iδa ṣiqaṭ, bij-jiir!* And if he fails, the hell with him! *xisar ihwaaya bil-uqmaar . . . bij-jiir!* He lost a lot gambling . . . That's good enough for him!

j-y-r-a-n

jiiraan see under *j-w-r.*

j-y-š

jeeš pl. *jiyuuš* army, armed forces.

j-y-f

jaaf (*i jeef*) to be or become putrid, to stink. *j-jiθθa buqat maδbuuba hnaa ˀila ˀan jaafat.* The body was left here till it began to stink. *l-laƹam jaaf. laazim tδibba.* The meat's spoiled. You'd better throw it out. *l-mayy ˀiδa yibqa b-mukaan waaƹid, yjiif.* If water stays in one place, it becomes foul.

jayyaf to go too far, carry something too far. *haaδa jayyafha. kull yoom yiṭlaƹ gabḷ id-dawaam.* He's carried it too far. Every day he leaves early.

jiifa pl. *jiyaf* **1.** rotting carcass, carrion. **2.** bad odor, stink, putrid smell.

jaayif **1.** stinking, putrid. **2.** rotten, spoiled.

j-y-l

jiil pl. *ˀajyaal* generation.

j-y-m

jiim name of the letter *j.*

j-y-y

jayya see under *j-y.*

Č

č-a

čaa = *laɛad,* which see under *l-ɛ-d.*

č-a-d-r

čaadir pl. *čwaadir* see under *č-w-d-r.*

č-a-r

čaara pl. *-aat* **1.** cure, remedy. *hal-maraδ ma ˀila čaara.* There's no cure for this disease. *ma-yṣiir-la čaara. raɛ-ymuut.* There's no curing him. He's going to die. || *šinu čaarta l-haaδa? kull sana yiṣquṭ bil-madrasa.* What's to be done with him? He fails in school every year. **2.** escape, way out. *ma-aku čaara. laazim iysawwi ɛamaliyya.* There's no way out. He has to have an operation. *haay ma-ˀilha-ġeer čaara.* There's no other solution for it. || *tigdar itsawwi fadd čaara w-itšuuf-la šuġuḷ?* Could you manage somehow to find work for him?

č-a-r-k

čaarak pl. *čwaariik* **1.** one-fourth, a quarter. *čaarak saaɛa* a quarter hour. **2.** one-fourth of a *mann,* six kilograms. *štiri čaarak išɛiir lid-dijaaj.* Buy six kilograms of barley for the chickens.

č-a-q-w-č

čaaquuča pl. *-aat* pocket knife.

č-a-k

čaak (invar.) base down, the winning position. (said of the *čaɛab,* the bone used to play a popular children's game). *č-čaɛab maali wugaf čaak.* My bone landed base down. || *šloon ma-tδibba, yooguf čaak.* No matter what happens, he comes out all right.

č-a-k-w-č

čaakuuč pl. *čwaakiič* hammer.

č-a-m

čaam, xišab čaam an inexpensive, light-colored, lightweight wood used for boxes, shelves, cheap furniture, etc.

č-a-m-l-ġ

čaamulluġ, čaamurluġ pl. *-aat* fender (of a car, etc.).

č-a-w-w-š

čaawuuš pl. *čwaawiiš* crew boss, foreman.

č-a-y

čaay pl. *-aat* **1.** tea. || *čaay daarsiin* cinnamon and hot water. *čaay ɛaamuδ* beverage made with dried lemons and hot water. **2.** cup of tea.

čaayači, čaayči pl. *-iyya* tea vendor.

čaayxaana pl. *-aat* tea house, café.

čaayxaanči pl. *-iyya* tea shop owner.

č-b-b

čabb (*i čabb*) **1.** to pour out. *čibb hal-mayy il-waṣix barra.* Pour this dirty water outside. **2.** to spill. *diir baalak la-tčibb ič-čaay maali.* Careful, don't spill my tea. **3.** to ejaculate (semen).

nčabb **1.** to be spilled, to get poured out. *nčabb il-ɛaliib kulla.* All the milk was spilled. **2.** (impolite) to shut up, be quiet, quit talking. *nčabb! la-tiɛči šii baɛad.* Shut up! Don't say anything else.

č-b-č-b

čabčab to splash, slop. *j-jaahil da-yčabčib mayy ɛala hduuma.* The baby's splashing water on his clothes. *tiras il-gidir mayy w-δall yitčabčab.* He overfilled the pot with water and it kept spilling out.

tčabčab to slosh out, spill over.

č-b-r

čibiir see under *k-b-r.*

č-b-s

čibas (*i čabis*) **1.** to pack, place in containers (esp. dates). *čibasna ɛallaanteen tamur.* We packed two baskets of dates. **2.** to pickle, marinate, preserve. *raɛ-itčibsuun has-sana ṭurši willa laa?* Are you going to put up pickles this year or not?

čibbaasa pl. *-aat* weight put on top of food while frying it.

č-b-n

čabban to be or become matted, thick. *šaɛri mčabbin. yriid-la ġasil.* My hair is snarled. It needs washing. || *damaaġa mčabbin* or *raasa mčabbin.* He's got a thick head. He's terribly slow-witted.

čiban a felt material used for saddle blankets.

čibna pl. *-aat* saddle blanket, felt pad.

č-b-n-t-w

čbintu **1.** cement. **2.** plaster, mortar.

č-t-a

čata **1.** (invar.) undisciplined, helter-skelter, disorganized, a mess. *d-dawaam ib-had-daaˀira čata. kull-man yruuɛ w-yiji b-keefa.* Working hours in this office are loose and informal. Everyone goes and comes as he pleases. **2.** (pl. *čatawaat*) an undisciplined person, a slacker, an idler, a goof-off. *ma-ydiir baal* *liš-šuġuḷ. haaδa čata.* He doesn't pay attention to work. He's a goof-off. *ᶜatta loo tkuun čata biṣ-ṣaff, ynajjiᶜak.* Even if you're a lazy slacker in class, he'll promote you.

č-t-f

čattaf to bind, tie up. *čattifaw il-mujrim w-ᶜaṭṭoo bis-sayyaara.* They bound up the criminal and put him in the car. || *l-mudiir ij-jidiid čattafni. ma-yxalliini ˀamḍi wala maktuub.* The new director's tied my hands. He won't let me sign even a single letter.

tčattaf to fold one's arms. *tčattaf w-wugaf giddaami.* He folded his arms and stood in front of me.

čitif pl. *čtaaf, čtaafaat* shoulder. || *nṭaa čitif.* He helped him. He gave him a hand.

čattaafiyya pl. *-aat* shoulder pad (in clothing).

č-d-m

čidam (coll.) sandstone.

čidmaaya pl. *-aat* piece of sandstone.

č-δ-b

čiδab (*i čiδib*) to lie, tell a lie. *la-tṣaddig bii. yičδib ihwaaya.* Don't believe him. He lies a lot.

čaδδab **1.** to tell lies, prevaricate, speak untruthfully. *ˀiᶜči ṣ-ṣudug. la-tčaδδib.* Tell the truth. Don't tell lies. **2.** to deny, refute, disprove. *čaδδibaw xabar zawaaja.* They denied the news of his marriage. || *ma-čaδδab xabar.* He didn't hesitate. He wasted no time. *gut-la lil-mujaamala "ˀiδa tiᶜtaaj ifluus, ˀaani ᶜindak." ma-čaδδab xabar w-ṭilab diinaareen.* I told him out of politeness "If you need money, I'm at your service." He took me at my word and asked for two dinars.

čiδba pl. *-aat* lie, untruth, falsehood.

čaδδaab pl. *-iin* liar, prevaricator.

ˀačδab more or most untruthful. *haaδa ˀačδab il-kull.* He's the biggest liar of all.

č-r-p-a-y

čarpaaya pl. *-aat, čaraapi* bed, bedstead. *čarpaaya ˀumm nafareen* double bed.

č-r-č-b

čarčab to put into a frame, to frame. *čarčab iṣ-ṣuura w-xallaaha ᶜal-meez.* He framed the picture and put it on the table.

čarčuuba pl. *-aat, čaraačiib* picture frame.

č-r-č-f

čarčaf pl. *čaraačif* **1.** large cloth. **2.** tablecloth. **3.** bedsheet. || *čarčaf imxadda* pillowcase.

č-r-x

čirax (*a čarix*) to turn on a lathe. *yičrax il-xišba w-ysawwi minha muṣraᶜ.* He turns the wood and makes a top out of it.

čarix pl. *čruux* wheel. *kursi ˀabu čruux* wheelchair.

čarraax pl. *-a, -iin* **1.** lathe operator. **2.** man who sharpens knives, scissors, etc., on a grinding wheel, scissors grinder.

čarxači pl. *-iyya* night watchman, patrolman.

č-r-x-l

čarxala pl. *-aat* spin, turn, revolution. *ˀinṭi l-ˀarqaam čarxala zeena gabuḷ-ma djurr.* Give the numbers a good spin before you draw. || *xan-naaxδ-inna fadd čarxala bis-suug balki nilgii.* Let's take ourselves a spin around the marketplace and perhaps we'll find him.

č-r-d

čarid pl. *čruud* cigar.

č-r-d-a-ġ

čirdaaġ pl. *čaraadiiġ* summer cabin, a hut built on the river.

č-r-z

čarraz to eat seeds or small nuts by cracking them and separating the hulls in the mouth. *ᶜeeb itčarriz ᶜabb bis-siinama.* Shame on you eating seeds in the movie.

čaraz pl. *-aat* mixed nuts, seeds. *maᶜall čarazaat* nut store.

č-r-s

čarras to daydream, be distracted, let one's attention wander. *ṭabᶜan ma-tuᶜruf ˀiδa tčarris biṣ-ṣaff.* Of course you won't know if you daydream in class.

čarsi pl. *-iyya* **1.** daydreamer. **2.** absent-minded person.

č-r-ᶜ

čarraᶜ to drink like an animal, to drink sloppily, gulp down, guzzle. *la-tčarriᶜ bil-ᶜaliib; muu xallaṣta!* Don't gulp the milk down; you've almost finished it! *la-tčarriᶜ min tišrab! ᶜuṭṭ bil-iglaaṣ w-išrab.* Don't put your nose in it when you drink! Put it in the glass and drink properly.

č-r-ġ-d

čarġad pl. *čaraaġid* woman's headcloth.

č-r-q-ᶜ

tčarqaᶜ to be or become worn out, run down. *buqat is-sayyaara ᶜinda santeen w-baᶜdeen itčarqiᶜat.* He had the car for two years and then it went to pieces.

mčarqaᶜ worn out, run down, dilapidated.

č-r-k

čuruk (invar.) bad, no good, undesirable. *har-raaδyo ṭilaɛ čuruk.* This radio has turned out to be a bad one. *hal-ibnayya čuruk; ɛaleeha ɛači hwaaya.* That girl's no good; there's a lot of talk about her.

čurak (coll.) a kind of bread, shaped like a pretzel.

čurka or *čurkaaya* pl. *-aat* un. n. of *čurak.*

čaarak see *č-a-r-k.*

č-r-n-q

črunqa pl. *-aat* syringe, hypodermic syringe.

č-r-w-y

čarraawiyya pl. *-aat* **1.** cloth wound around the head. **2.** small, simple turban.

č-r-y

mčaari pl. *-iyya* muleteer, donkey driver.

č-z-z

čazz (*i u čazz*) **1.** to mark over, cross out. *ma-ɛindi missaaɛa. tigdar itčizz ič-čilma bil-qalam.* I don't have an eraser. You can cross out the word with the pencil. **2.** to squeak. *qundarti ij-jidiida tčuzz.* My new shoes squeak.

č-z-m

čazma pl. *čizam* (pair of) rubber boots, waders.

č-s-w

čiswa pl. *-aat, čisaw* bathing suit, swimming trunks.

č-s-y

čassa **1.** to lose one's nerve, become frightened, back down, turn tail. *hijam ɛalayya bil-xanjar, w-min šaaf b-iidi musaddas, čassa.* He attacked me with a dagger, but when he saw the pistol in my hand, he lost his enthusiasm. *č-čalib rikaδ ɛalayya laakin min šilt il-ɛuuda, čassa.* The dog ran at me, but when I picked up the stick, he cringed away. **2.** to quiet down, shut up, be quiet, be still. *ma-tčassi ɛaad ? muu δawwajitna?* Why don't you shut up? Haven't you annoyed us enough? **3.** to become tired, worn out, run down. *miša miileen w-čassa.* He walked two miles and got pooped out. *l-paatri da-yčassi ɛindi.* The battery is going dead on me.

č-ṭ-l

čaṭal, čaṭla pl. *-aat* **1.** fork (utensil). **2.** shuttle, shuttle train. **3.** jumper cable (elec.). *jiib sayyaartak yamm sayyaarti w-insawwi čaṭal ɛal-paatri maalak.* Bring your car up to mine and we'll run a jumper to your battery.

č-ɛ-b

čaɛɛab to speak boldy, speak roughly. *kullna nxaaf niɛči wiyyaa. bass ɛali yčaɛɛib-la.* All of us are afraid to talk to him. Only Ali tells him off. *šifta šloon čaɛɛab-la? ma-nṭaa furṣa yjaawub.* Did you see how he raked him over the coals? He didn't give him a chance to answer.

čaɛab pl. *čɛuub* **1.** bottom, lower part. *ʔaku šakar baaqi b-čaɛb il-kuub.* There's still some sugar in the bottom of the cup. **2.** sole, or heel (of a shoe). **3.** end, last part. *čaɛab šahar w-ma-ɛindi fluus.* It's the end of the month and I don't have any money. **4.** back, rear part. *biṣ-ṣaff ma-yigɛud ʔilla bič-čaɛab.* In class he doesn't sit anywhere except in the back. **5.** a bone from the lower leg of the sheep, in the form of a truncated cone, cleaned, often dyed, and used in boys' games.

čaɛbiyya pl. *-aat* the portion in the bottom, in the rear, at the end, the tailings, the last portion. *čaɛbiyyat id-doondirma tkuun jaamda ʔakθar.* The ice cream in the bottom is more solid.

č-ɛ-č-l

čaɛčuula variant of *kaɛkuula,* which see under *k-ɛ-k-l.*

č-f-t

čifat (*i čafit*) **1.** to crowd, cram, jam, stuff, force. *ʔaxaδ il-fluus w-čifatha b-jeeba.* He took the money and stuffed it down into his pocket. *ʔičfit l-iktaab been baqiyyt il-kutub.* Jam the book in among the rest of the books. *ʔičfit kull ij-jihaal bil-ɛooδ il-waraani.* Stick all the kids in the back seat. || *čiftoo bis-sijin.* They stuck him in jail. **2.** to intrude, burst in, to enter suddenly. *dugg il-baab bil-ʔawwal. la-tičfit.* Knock on the door first. Don't burst in. *čiftaw fadd čafta.* They burst right in. **3.** to spring, pounce, jump suddenly. *čifat ɛalee č-čalib w-mallaxa.* The dog pounced on him and ripped him up. **4.** to hit. *čifata b-lakma w-waggaɛa.* He hit him a blow and knocked him down. || *l-ɛaakim čifata b-santeen ɛabis.* The judge hit him with a two-year sentence. *l-mudiir čifata b-ġaraama yoomeen.* The director docked him two days pay.

tčaafat to clash, exchange blows. *tšaatmaw bil-ʔawwal w-baɛdeen itčaaftaw.* First they exchanged insults and then they got into a fist fight.

čafta: fadd čafta all at once. *ʔaxaδ rawaatba kullha fadd čafta.* He took all his earnings in one lump sum.

čaffaat pl. *-a* **1.** intruder, interloper. **2.** brash person, brazen person.

č-f-č-r

čafčiir pl. *čafaačiir* a slightly concave metal spatula with holes in it.

č-f-f

čaff pl. *čfuuf* **1.** inside part of the hand, palm. **2.** handful. **3.** glove. || *ḍirab čaff* 1. to swim with an overhand stroke. *l-yoom raɛ-aɛallmak tuḍrub čaff.* Today I'm going to teach you to swim with an overhand stroke. 2. to work hard. *ṣaar-li saaɛa da-aḍrub čaff ib-haš-šuġuḷ w-ma-xallaṣit.* I've been battling this work for an hour and haven't finished.

čaffiyya pl. *čfaafi* handerchief.

č-f-n

čaffan to wrap in a winding sheet. *čaffinaw il-mayyit ib-xaam ʔabyaḍ.* They wrapped the corpse in a white cloth.

čifan pl. *čfaana* winding sheet.

[1]*č-f-y*

čifa (*i čafi*) **1.** to save, spare from. *čfiini šarrak tara amawwtak.* Spare me your unpleasantness or I'll murder you. *ʔaḷḷa yičfiik šarra.* God protect you from him. **2.** to turn over, invert, turn upside down. *min čifoo ɛala wičča, šaafaw is-siččiina b-ḍahra.* When they turned him over on his stomach, they saw the knife in his back. *ʔičfi l-maaɛuun ɛala wičča.* Turn the dish upside down. **3.** to spread out, stretch out, flatten. *ḍirabta band w-čifeeta ɛala wičča.* I tripped him and sent him sprawling. *ṭ-ṭabiib čifaa ɛala wičča.* The doctor laid him face down.

tčaffa to avoid, keep away from. *xall nitčaffa š-šarr w-infuut minnaa.* Let's avoid trouble and go this way.

nčifa **1.** to be inverted, get turned over. *nčifa j-jidir w-raaɛ kull il-ʔakil.* The pot got turned over and all the food spilled. **2.** to fall flat, to sprawl. *j-jaahil kull saaɛ yinčifi ɛala wičča.* The baby falls on his face all the time. *ma-qibal yinčifi ɛala wičča, w-xalla l-ɛariif yizɛal.* He refused to stretch out on his belly, and made the sergeant mad.

[2]*č-f-y*

čaffiyya see under *č-f-f.*

č-q-l

ʔačqal fem. *čaqla* pl. *čuqul, čaqliin* **1.** cross-eyed or walleyed. *ɛyuuna čuqul* His eyes are crossed. **2.** cross-eyed or walleyed person.

č-q-l-b

čaqlab to send tumbling. *difaɛni w-čaqlabni min foog id-daraj.* He pushed me and sent me tumbling from the top of the stairs.

tčaqlab to tumble, fall head over heels. *ɛiθar b-iɛjaara w-itčaqlab.* He tripped on a rock and took a tumble.

č-q-l-m-b

čuqlumba pl. *-aat* somersault, tumble.

č-k-k

čakk (*u čakk*) to prick, stick. *čakkni b-dambuus.* He pricked me with a pin.

čakk pl. *-aat, čkuuk* check.

čikk: čikk maal naddaaf a short, heavy, wooden mallet used by the cotton teaser to strike his bow.

č-k-l-y-t

čukleet **1.** chocolate. **2.** various types of wrapped candies, such as caramels, toffee, etc. || *bazir čukleet* person who has lived a wealthy, soft life.

č-k-m-č

čakmača pl. *-aat* **1.** drawer. **2.** glove compartment (of a car).

č-k-n-m

mčaknam cozy, comfortable, snug. *ġurfa mčaknama* a cozy room.

č-l-b

čilab (*i*) **1.** to ruin, spoil. *hiyya lli čilbat ibinha, halgadd-ma dallilata.* She's the one who ruined her son, she's spoiled him so much. *l-ifluus čilbata. štiraa-la tlaθ sayyaaraat.* The money's spoiled him. He's bought three cars. **2.** to make a swine of. *l-waḍiifa j-jidiida čilbata. ma-gaam yinjiriɛ baɛad.* The new position's made a swine of him. He's no longer bearable.

čallab **1.** to stick, cling, hold on. *ṭayyaart ij-jaahil xarrat w-čallibat biš-šijra.* The kid's kite nose dived and hung up in the tree. *ʔaku xeet imčallib ib-sitirtak.* There's a thread hanging on your coat. *šuuf ij-jaahil imčallib bil-ɛarabaana.* Look at the kid hanging onto the carriage! *hiddni! š-aku ɛindak imčallib biyya.* Turn me loose! Why are you holding onto me? *š-čallabit biyya miθil il-garaada? muu gitlak ma-ɛindi fluus ʔanṭiik!* Why are you hanging on like a leech? I told you I've got no money to give you. || *š-yxallṣak minna? ġargaan w-imčallib ib-sibbaaɛa.* How can you get away from him? He's a drowning man grasping at a float. **2.** to insist. *čallab biyya ʔilla ʔatġadda wiyyaa.* He insisted that I have lunch with him. *mčallib ʔilla yruuɛ wiyyaahum.* He's insisting on going with them. *čallab biyya* *ˀaruuḥ wiyyaa.* He insisted I go with him.

tčaalab to assail one another, to grapple with, fight each other. *tšaatmaw w-itčaalbaw w-baʕdeen faakaknaahum.* They exchanged insults and grappled with each other and then we separated them.

nčilab **1.** to become swell-headed, get too big for one's breeches. *nčilab min ṣaarat ʕinda fluus. yriid yizzawwaj bint il-malik.* He got big ideas when he became rich. He wants to marry the king's daughter. **2.** to become a swine. *ˀašuu min idzangan, nčilab.* It seems since he became rich, he's lost his manners. **3.** to be seized by hydrophobia. *čalibna nčilab.* Our dog got rabies.

čalib pl. *člaab* dog. || *ftirr ičlaab* poisonous mushroom, toadstool.

čalba pl. *-aat* female dog, bitch.

čalabi pl. *-iyya* **1.** man from a wealthy class of merchants and landlords. **2.** dignitary.

čalabiyya pl. *-aat* tall, slender, and attractive girl.

čillaab pl. *člaaliib* **1.** hook. **2.** safety pin.

čillaabteen pl. *-aat* pliers.

čilleeb persistent person.

ˀačlab more or most uncivilized.

mačluub **1.** infected with hydrophobia, rabid, mad. **2.** rabid dog. **3.** madman, lunatic.

č-l-č

čalač = *kalak* which see under *k-l-k.*

č-l-k

čilak (coll.) strawberry(s).

čilka pl. *-aat* un. n. of *čilak.*

č-l-m

čilma pl. *-aat, čilam* **1.** word. **2.** remark. (see also *k-l-m*).

č-l-w

čilwa pl. *-aat, čalaawi* kidney.

č-m

čam **1.** how many? how much? *čam walad ʕindak?* How many boys do you have? **2.** so many! so much! *čam marra gut-la w-ma-faad!* I told him so many times and it did no good! **3.** some, a few. *ˀaʕtiqid il-qiṭaar raḥ-yooṣal baʕad čam daqiiqa.* I think the train will arrive in a few minutes. *ˀinṭiini fadd čam diinaar; ˀariid atsawwag.* Give me a few dinars; I want to go shopping.

č-m-p-a-r

čumpaara pl. *-aat* **1.** finger cymbal. **2.** castanet.

č-m-č

čamča pl. *-aat* ladle, dipper.

č-m-r

čimri dates, picked green and ripened artificially.

č-m-l

čammal to add a bit extra, to put some more in. *haš-šoorba θixiina. čammilha šwayyat mayy.* This soup is thick. Add a little more water to it. *l-xabbaaz čammal-li čam ṣammuuna.* The baker threw in a few extra loaves for me.

čmaala pl. *-aat* or *čmaayil* an extra portion, a bit more. *ˀabuu buṣaṭa w-inta buṣaṭa čmaala.* His father beat him and you beat him more yet. *ˀiδa tištiri xamis keeluwaat ixyaar, yinṭiik ixyaarteen ičmaala.* If you buy five kilograms of cucumbers, he'll give you two extra cucumbers.

č-m-y

čima (coll.) truffle(s).

čimaaya pl. *-aat* truffle.

č-n-t-y-a-n

čintiyaana pl. *-aat* short, double-edged sword.

č-n-g-l

čangaḷ to fasten together, hook together. *čangiḷ il-yaaxa ˀila ˀan yṣiir ʕindi wakit axayyiṭ id-dugma.* Pin the collar together until I have time to sew on the button. *čangiḷ hal-faargooneen b-makiint il-qiṭaar.* Couple these two boxcars to the train engine.

čingaaḷ pl. *čnaagiiḷ* **1.** fastener, catch, hook. **2.** safety pin. **3.** stevedore's hook, bale hook. **4.** fork (for eating).

č-n-n

stačann to settle down, make a home. *raḥ-aštiri hal-beet w-astačinn bii.* I'm going to buy this house and settle down in it.

čanna pl. *čnaayin* **1.** daughter-in-law. **2.** loosely, woman married to any junior member of a household.

čann- /followed by pronominal suffix/ **1.** as though, as if. *yṣayyiḥ čanna zumaal.* He shouts as though he were a donkey. *yimši čanna ṭaawuus.* He walks like a peacock. *gaaʕidiin čannhum muluuk.* They're sitting as though they were kings. **2.** like. *ḥissa čanna ḥiss ˀabuuk.* His voice is like your father's voice. *qaṣiir w-imdaḥdaḥ čanna čikk maal naddaaf.* He's short and pudgy like a cotton-teaser's mallet. **3.** it seems as though, it looks as if, it appears that. *čannḥa taahat biṭ-ṭariiq.*

It looks as though she got lost on the way. *čannak ma-triid itruuɛ.* It looks as though you don't want to go. *čanna ɛali bil-baab.* It seems to be Ali at the door.

č-h-r

čihra pl. *-aat, čihar* (insulting term for face, approx.:) mug, puss, ugly face. *la-traawiini čihirtak baɛad.* Don't let me see your ugly mug again. *ɛaleeha čihra ma-titbaawaɛ.* She has an unsightly face.

čihrasizz (invar.) ugly, homely. *hiyya cihrasizz.* She's ugly.

č-w-b

čuub pl. *-aat, čwaab, čwaaba* **1.** tube, inner tube. **2.** bladder (of a ball).

č-w-p

čuup pl. *-aat, čwaap, čwaapa* variant of *čuub.*

č-w-t

čawwat to add bluing (to laundry), to whiten. *raɛ-tiġsil il-qamiiṣ w-itčawwita.* She will wash the shirt and blue it.

čwiit a blueing agent used in washing clothes.

č-w-x

čoox **1.** heavy broadcloth. **2.** felt.

č-w-d-r

čoodar to pitch a tent, to make camp. *xall-inčoodir ihnaa hal-leela.* Let's camp here tonight. || *ˀašuu ṣaar-lak imčoodir ihnaa saaɛteen. šaku ɛindak?* You've been hanging around here two hours. What are you after?

čaadir pl. *čwaadir* tent.

č-w-l

čool **1.** wilderness, wasteland, desert. || *ˀiδa truuɛ lil-madrasa bil-leel, tilgiiha čool.* If you go to the school at night you'll find it deserted.

č-w-n

čaan see under *k-w-n.*

č-w-y

čuwa (*i čawi*) **1.** to burn, sear, scald. *l-ṃayy il-ɛaarr čuwa ˀiida.* The hot water scalded his hand. **2.** to cauterize. *ˀiδa tičwi j-jariɛ, yṭiib ib-saaɛ.* If you cauterize the wound, it will heal quickly. *čuwa l-ɛabbaaya lli b-wičča b-jigaara.* He burned the pimple on his face with a cigarette. **3.** to brand. *b-ˀamriika, yičwuun il-hooš ib-ɛalaamaat xaaṣṣa ɛatta ma-tinbaag.* In America, they brand cattle with personal markings so they won't get stolen.

čawwa = *čuwa.*

nčuwa to be burned, be seared, be scalded. *j-jaahil inčuwa bis-samaawar.* The child got burned on the samovar.

čawya pl. *-aat* **1.** burn. **2.** burn scar. **3.** brand.

čaawya pl. *-aat* soldering iron.

č-y-t

čayyat **1.** to plunge, dive, jump. *la-tčayyit bil-ṃayy tara muu ġamiij.* Don't plunge into the water in case it isn't deep. **2.** to burst in. *dugg il-baab ɛalee. muu tčayyit.* Knock at the door for him. Don't just burst in.

čiit an inexpensive, lightweight cotton cloth.

č-y-s

čayyas **1.** to scrub with a coarse cloth mitten. *l-ˀumm čayyisat rijleen ˀibinha.* The mother scrubbed her son's legs. **2.** to bog down, get stuck. *čayyasit biṭ-ṭiin ˀila rukubti.* I bogged down in the mud to my knees. *sayyaarti čayyisat biṭ-ṭiin.* My car got stuck in the mud. || *simaɛit ɛali čayyas bil-imtiɛaan.* I heard Ali failed on the exam.

čiis pl. *čiyaas* **1.** bag, sack, pouch, purse, pocket. **1.** a mitten made of coarse, heavy cloth, used to scrub the skin.

č-y-f

čeef because, since. *ma-agdar aruuɛ lis-siinama čeef ma-ɛindi fluus.* I can't go to the movies because I haven't got any money.

č-y-l

čaal (*i*) to measure out. *čiil-li čeelteen ˀiδra.* Measure out two ladles of corn for me.

čayyal to stockpile, store up. *kull ribiiɛ yčayyluun ɛunṭa tkaffiihum is-sana kullha.* Every spring they buy up enough wheat to last them the whole year.

čeela pl. *-aat* **1.** a container of no standard size used by merchants to measure out grain, etc. **2.** bullet. **3.** gunshot.

čayyaal pl. *-a* measurer, person who measures out grain, etc.

č-y-n-k-w

čiinku (coll.) galvanized sheet metal.

čiinkuwwa pl. *-aat* piece of galvanized sheet metal.

ε

ε-a

εaa name of the letter ε.

ε-a-x-a-m

εaaxaam pl. *-iyya* rabbi.

ε-a-n-w-t

εaanuut pl. *εawaaniit* canteen, snack bar.

εaanuuti pl. *-iyya* canteen operator.

[1]ε-b-b

εabb (*i εubb*) **1.** to love, like. *ˀaεibb marti hwaaya.* I love my wife a lot. *ma-aεibb hal-loon.* I don't like this color. *tεibb tiji wiyyaana?* Would you like to come with us? **2.** to kiss. *εabbha b-išfaafha.* He kissed her on her lips.

εabbab to endear, to cause to be loved or liked. *yuεruf išloon yεabbib nafsa lin-naas.* He knows how to endear himself to people.

tεabbab to show love, reveal affection. *daaˀiman yitεabbab-ilha w-hiyya ma-tdiir-la baal.* He's always demonstrating his affection for her and she doesn't pay him any attention.

tεaabab to love each other. *tεaabibaw min humma ṣġaar.* They've loved each other since they were kids.

εubb love, affection. || *εubb il-istiṭlaaε* curiosity. *εubb iδ-δuhuur* love of display, love of being known. *εubb iδ-δaat* love of self, egotism. *wugaε bil-εubb.* He fell in love. *waagiε ib-εubb ibnayya ma-εilwa.* He's in love with an unattractive girl.

εabiib pl. *ˀaεibba, ˀaεbaab* **1.** beloved, lover, sweetheart. *εabiib aḷḷa(ah)* (beloved by God) Mohammed. **2.** dear friend. *ˀaṣdiqaaˀi w-aεbaabi* my closest friends.

εabiiba pl. *εabaayib* beloved (fem.), sweetheart, darling.

maεabba affection, love.

maεabbatan through love, from affection. *sawweeta maεabbatan ˀilak.* I did it out of affection for you.

maεbuub **1.** beloved, dear. **2.** lovable, likeable. **3.** popular.

εabbuub likeable, loveable, friendly, pleasant. *muwaδδafna j-jidiid kulliš εabbuub.* Our new employee is very likeable.

mustaεabb recommended, desirable (said of acts which are not required by religion but which are commendable).

[2]ε-b-b

εabb (coll.) pl. *εubuub* **1.** seed(s), grain(s), kernel(s). **2.** pimple(s), pustule(s), acne. **3.** pill(s), capsule(s), tablet(s), pellet(s).

εabba pl. *-aat* un. n. of *εabb.*

εabbaaya pl. *-aat* var. of *εabba.* || *ma-baaqi wala εabbaaya.* There isn't a single bit left.

[3]ε-b-b

εibb pl. *εbaab, εbuub* large, porous, pottery vessel for storing drinking water.

ε-b-δ

εabbaδ to approve of, think well of. *ˀaani aεabbiδ hal-fikra.* I approve of this idea.

ε-b-r

εibir ink.

maεbara pl. *maεaabir* inkpot, inkwell.

εabaari: ṭeer εabaari bustard.

ε-b-s

εibas (*i εabis*) **1.** to confine, restrict, block. *baḷḷa taεaal bil-εajal; la-tiεbisni.* Please come quickly; don't leave me stranded. *ˀaani maεbuus w-ma-agdar ˀaṭlaε li-ˀan ˀaxuuya raε-yiji.* I'm tied down, and can't go out because my brother's coming. *εibasit il-puul maalak; ma-tigdar itεarrika.* I've blocked your piece; you can't move it. **2.** to jail, imprison. *εibsoo sana w-ṭalliεoo.* They locked him up for a year and turned him loose. **3.** to pen up. *ˀiεbis id-dijaaj gabuḷ-ma δδallum.* Pen the chickens up before it gets dark.

εabbas to jail, lock up. *l-εukuuma εabbisathum kullhum.* The government jailed them all.

nεibas pass. of *εibas.* || *yinεibis ṭabεa b-hal-wlaaya.* He feels depressed in this city.

εabis **1.** imprisonment, confinement, detention, jailing. **2.** (pl. *εubuus*) prison, jail.

maεbuus **1.** blocked, restricted. || *ṭaawli maεbuus* a variant of backgammon in which the opponent's pieces are blocked by landing one's pieces on the same file after them. **2.** (pl. *mεaabiis*) prisoner, convict.

miεbas pl. *mεaabis* ring (jewelry).

mεeebis a game, usually played during the nights of Ramadan, in which one team hides an object in a member's closed fist and the other team must find it.

ح-b-š

l-ḥabaša Abyssinia, Ethiopia.

*ḥabaši** 1. Abyssinian, Ethiopian. 2. (pl. *-iyyiin, ʔaḥbaaš*) an Abyssinian, an Ethiopian.

[1]ح-b-l

ḥabil rope, line, cord. *sibaaq jarr il-ḥabil* tug-o-war. || *šarra ʕal-ḥabil.* He hung him up for all to see (lit., he hung him on the line). *j-jariida šarrat il-waziir ʕal-ḥabil. tguul yaaxuδ rašaawi.* The newspaper exposed the minister. They say he takes bribes. *yilʕab ʕal-ḥableen.* He plays both ends against the middle. *ḥabl is-surra* umbilical cord.

[2]ح-b-l

ḥibal (*a ḥabal*) to be or become pregnant. *ḥiblat baʕad šahreen imniz-zawaaj.* She got pregnant after two months of marriage. *ṭallag marta li-ʔan ma-tiḥbal.* He divorced his wife because she can't have kids.

ḥabbal to make pregnant. *baʕad-ma ḥabbalha, δṭarr yidzawwajha.* Once he'd made her pregnant, he had to marry her.

ḥibla pl. *-aat, ḥbaala.* pregnant. *niswaan ḥiblaat.* pregnant women.

ḥbaala pregnancy.

ḥablaana pl. *-aat* 1. pregnant. 2. pregnant woman.

ح-b-n

ḥubbaana pl. *-aat* pottery drinking cup.

ح-b-y

ḥiba (*i ḥabi*) to crawl, creep. *j-jaahil gaam yiḥbi.* The baby's started to crawl.

ḥaaba to show favoritism, take sides. *l-mulaaḥiδ yḥaabi l-ʔahl wlaayta.* The supervisor favors the people from his home town. *yḥaabi been ij-jihaal.* He plays favorites among the children.

muḥaabaat favoritism.

ح-t-t

ḥatta see ح-t-y.

ح-t-m

ḥattam 1. to make necessary, make a duty. *minu ḥattam ʕaleek ir-rooḥa?* Who made it your duty to go? 2. to impose. *ḥattam ʕala ʔabuu yištirii-la saaʕa.* He insisted that his father buy him a watch.

ḥatman decidedly, definitely, certainly, inevitably. *ḥatman raḥ-aruuḥ.* I'm definitely going to go. *raḥ-tumṭur id-dinya ḥatman.* It will certainly rain.

*ḥatmi** inevitable, irrevocable, unalterable, definite, final, conclusive. *l-ʔimtiḥaan in-nihaaʔi fadd šii ḥatmi.* The final exam is something unavoidable.

ح-t-y

ḥatta (prep.) 1. until, till, up to, as far as. *bqeena nisbaḥ ḥatta s-saaʕa xamsa.* We kept swimming until five o'clock. *buqa bil-paaṣ ḥatta ʔaaxir mawqif.* He stayed on the bus until the last stop. *ma-ṭilaʕ ḥatta šaafhum kullhum.* He didn't leave until he saw them all. 2. (conj.) in order to, so that. *laazim inruuḥ ʕal-wakit ḥatta nlaḥḥig bil-qiṭaar.* We've got to go early in order to catch the train. *ʔiḥčii-la kull il-quṣṣa ḥatta yifham iš-da-yṣiir bid-daaʔira.* Tell him the whole story so that he'll know what's going on in the office. *baʕad ma-šifta liṭ-ṭabiib ḥatta ʔagul-la ʕaleeha.* I still haven't seen the doctor to tell him about it. *laazim tiṭṭiini fluus kaafya ḥatta ʔagdar asaafir.* You'll have to give me enough money so I'll be able to travel. 3. even. *bil-beet ʕidna kullši, ḥatta talafizyoon.* We've got everything in the house, even a television. *ma-yifši b-ʔay sirr ḥatta loo tbuṣṭa.* He won't reveal any secret even if you beat him. || *ḥatta wala* not even, never even. *ḥatta wala ḥiča wiyyaaya.* He didn't even talk to me. *ḥatta wala yisʔal suʔaal.* He never even asks a single question.

ح-θ-θ

ḥaθθ (*i ḥaθθ*) to urge, encourage, prod. *ḥiθθ axuuk ʕad-diraasa tara yisqut.* Urge your brother on to study or he's going to fail.

ح-j-b

ḥijab (*i ḥajib*) 1. to veil, cover, screen, shelter, seclude. *laazim inʕalli l-ḥaayiṭ ḥatta yiḥjib il-ḥadiiqa ʕan iš-šaariʕ.* We've got to raise the wall so it'll screen the garden from the street. 2. to hide, obscure, conceal, block off. *haš-šijra datiḥjib ʕanna l-manδar.* This tree is obscuring the view for us. *la-tibni l-ḥaayiṭ ʕaali tara yiḥjib iš-šamis ʕan il-ḥadiiqa.* Don't build the wall too high or it'll block the sun from the garden.

tḥajjab to put on a veil, to wear a veil. *binta saafira bass marta titḥajjab.* His daughter is unveiled but his wife wears a veil.

ḥijaab 1. (woman's) veil. 2. diaphragm. *l-ḥijaab il-ḥaajiz* the diaphragm (anat.).

ḥaajib pl. *ḥwaajib* eyebrow.

muḥajjab veiled, obscured, screened. *mara muḥajjaba* a woman who goes veiled.

ح-j-j
ḥajj (i ḥajj) to make the pilgrimage (to Mecca). *ḥajj beet ʔaḷḷa.* He made a pilgrimage to Mecca.

ḥaajaj to dispute with, argue with. *sawwiiha miθil-ma git-lak; la-tḥaajijni.* Do it the way I told you; don't give me an argument.

tḥajjaj to make excuses, to find an excuse. *bass tiṭlub minna šii, yguum yitḥajjaj.* Just ask him for something, and he begins to make excuses. *la-titḥajjaj ib-taʕbak.* Don't use your tiredness as an excuse.

tḥaajaj to debate, carry on an argument. *yitḥaajaj wiyya l-muʕallim.* He argues with the teacher.

ḥtajj to protest, object. *š-kull-ma nsawwi, yiḥtajj.* Whatever we do, he objects. *raḥ-aruuḥ is-safaaratna aḥtajj.* I'm going to our embassy to protest. *ḥtajj ʕind il-mudiir.* He protested to the director. *ḥtajj ʕala muʕaamalt iš-šurṭa ʔila.* He protested about the treatment he got from the police.

ḥijja: ðu l-ḥijja Zu'lhijjah, the twelfth month of the Moslem calendar.

ḥijja pl. *-aat, ḥijaj* **1.** excuse, pretext. *b-ḥijjat mariið ma-jaa liš-šuġuḷ tlat-iyyaam.* On the pretense of being sick, he didn't come to work for three days. *ṭallaʕ ḥijja ḥatta ma-yiruuḥ.* He made up an excuse not to go. **2.** a pilgrimage to Mecca. **3.** deed, title (to real property).

ḥujja pl. *ḥujaj* authoritative source, competent authority.

ḥajji pl. *ḥijjaaj* person who has made the pilgrimage, pilgrim.

ḥtijaaj protest, objection, exception.

[1]ح-j-r
ḥajir: ḥajir iṣ-ṣiḥḥi quarantine.

ḥujra pl. *ḥujar* **1.** room. **2.** an office stall in an old building. **3.** stall in an automobile repair shop rented by a specialist such as a body and fender man.

maḥjar ṣiḥḥi pl. *maḥaajir ṣiḥḥiyya* **1.** quarantine station. **2.** sanatorium for communicable diseases.

mḥajjar pl. *-aat* balustrade, banister.

[2]ح-j-r
ḥajjar **1.** to turn to stone, petrify, harden (fig.). *š-biik? ʔašu damaaġak ḥajjar il-yoom.* What's the matter with you? It seems like you've got rocks in your head today. *gaḷba ḥajjar min kuθrat-ma šaaf qatil bil-ḥarb.* He became hard-hearted from seeing so much killing in the war. **2.** to scrub with pumice. *ḥajjir rijlak gabuḷ-ma tiġsilha biṣ-ṣaabuun.* Scrub your feet with pumice before you wash them with soap.

tḥajjar pass. of *ḥajjar.*

ḥajar pl. *ḥjaar* **1.** stone, rock. *l-ḥajar il-ʔasaasi* the cornerstone. **2.** (pl. *-aat*) pumice stone. **3.** jewel (watchmaking). **4.** flint (in a lighter).

*ḥajari** stony, stone. *l-ʕaṣr il-ḥajari* the Stone Age.

ḥjaar (coll.) rock(s), stone(s).

ḥjaara pl. *-aat* rock, stone.

maḥjar pl. *maḥaajir* (stone) quarry.

mitḥajjar petrified, hardened (fig.). *gaḷba mitḥajjir. manðar il-qatil ma-yʔaθθir ʕalee.* He's hard-hearted. The sight of killing doesn't affect him. *haaða damaaġa mitḥajjir.* That guy's thick-headed.

ح-j-z
ḥijaz (i ḥajiz) **1.** to separate. *ma-aku šii yiḥjiz ḥadiiqatna min ḥadiiqathum.* There's nothing separating our garden from their garden. **2.** to sieze, confiscate. *l-ḥukuuma ḥijzat ʕala kull ʔamwaala.* The government seized all his property. *l-ḥukuuma ḥijzat il-beet maala.* The government seized his house. **3.** to reserve. *ʔiḥjiz-li ġurfa b-nafis ʔuteelak.* Reserve me a room in the same hotel you're in. **4.** to make a reservation. *ḥijazit il-yoom biṭ-ṭiyyaara.* I made a reservation today on the plane.

ḥaajaz to separate, come between. *šuuf waaḥid da-ymawwit il-laax! ḥaajizhum.* Look, one of them's killing the other! Separate them. *xalliihum yitʕaarkuun. la-tḥaajiz beenhum.* Let them fight. Don't separate them.

ḥajiz **1.** separation. **2.** seizure, confiscation. **3.** reservation.

ḥijaaz Hijaz, or, by extension, Saudi Arabia.

*ḥijaazi** **1.** from Hijaz, or, by extension, from Saudi Arabia. **2.** person from Hijaz or from Saudi Arabia.

ḥaajiz pl. *ḥawaajiz* **1.** divider. **2.** partition, dividing wall, screen. || *l-ḥijaab il-ḥaajiz* the diaphragm.

ح-j-l
ḥijil pl. *ḥjuul* (pair of) anklets.

ḥajla pl. *-aat* a small stand with wheels for teaching children to walk.

mḥajjal **1.** wearing anklets. *mara mḥajjala* ankleted woman. || *ṭeer imḥajjal* pigeon with feathers covering its feet. **2.** white-footed, white-ankled. *ḥṣaan imḥajjal* white-ankled horse.

ḥ-j-m

ḥijam (*i ḥijaama*) to cup, subject to blood-letting. *l-yoom ḥijmoo w-axδaw damm ihwaaya minna.* Today they cupped him and took a lot of blood. *huwwa ḥijam marrteen haš-šahar.* He was bled twice this month.

ḥajim pl. *ḥujuum, ʔaḥjaam* bulk, size, volume. *ḥajim ir-raadyo čibiir.* The radio's too large a size. *ḥajim tanki* volume of a tank.

ḥajjaam pl. *-a* blood-letter, cupper.

ḥijaama cupping, bloodletting.

ḥ-č-y

ḥiča (*i ḥači*) **1.** to tell, relate, report. *ʔiḥčii-li, š-ṣaar?* Tell me, what happened? *ḥčaa-li ḥčaaya ṭuwiila.* He told me a long story. **2.** to say, utter. *ḥiča hwaaya ʔašyaaʔ ma-ʕijbatni.* He said many things I didn't like. *ma-ḥiča wala čilma.* He never said a word. *ma-smaʕit š-iḥčeet.* I didn't hear what you said. **3.** to speak, talk. *ḥičeet wiyyaa bit-talafoon.* I talked with him on the telephone. *ḥiča hwaaya bil-ḥafla.* He talked a lot at the party. *ʔiδa ma-dzuurni ma-aḥči wiyyaak baʕad.* If you don't visit me, I won't talk to you any more. *ṣaar mudda ma-yiḥči wiyya ʔabuu.* He hasn't been speaking to his father for some time. *yiḥči ʕan-naas.* He runs people down. *ḥiča min yammak min ntiqdook.* He spoke in your behalf when they criticized you. *ʔariidak tiḥčii-li wiyya l-mudiir.* I want you to put in a word for me with the director. *l-mudiir ṣaaḥa l-ġurufta w-ḥiča ʕalee.* The director called him into his office and dressed him down.

ḥačča to force to speak, make talk. *raḥ-aḥaččii bil-guwwa.* I'm going to make him talk by force. *la-tḥaččiini. xalli l-qaδiyya msattira.* Don't make me talk. Let the matter rest.

ḥaača to talk to, speak to, converse with. *ʔariidak itḥaačii-li-yyaa lil-mudiir.* I'd like you to speak to the director for me. *šifta l-yoom laakin ma-ḥaačeeta.* I saw him today but I didn't speak to him. *ḥaačeet il-mudiir ʕala tarfiiʕi?* Did you talk to the director about my promotion? *ṣaar-li mudda ma-aḥaačii.* I haven't been speaking to him for some time.

tḥačča to be willing to talk. *hal-muwaδδaf ma-yitḥačča. la-traajiʕa b-qaδiitak.* That official won't talk. Don't go to him with your case. *loo bass itḥačča, čaan ʔatfaaham wiyyaa.* If he had only been willing to talk, I would have reached an understanding with him. *min ṣaar mudiir, ma-gaam yitḥačča.* Since he's become a director, he doesn't speak. *haaδa ma-yitḥačča. ʕabaala bass huwwa ʕinda sayyaara.* He won't even talk terms. He thinks he's the only one with a car for sale.

tḥaača to talk to one another, to converse. *ṣaar-ilhum saaʕa da-yitḥaačuun.* They've been talking together for an hour. *ṣaar-ilhum sana ma-yitḥaačuun.* They haven't been speaking to each other for a year.

nḥiča to be said, uttered. *hiiči šii ma-yinḥiči giddaam in-niswaan.* This sort of thing isn't said in front of women.

ḥači **1.** talking, speaking. **2.** speech, talk. || *xooš ḥači!* Good idea! That's the spirit! Now you're talking!

ḥčaaya pl. *-aat* **1.** story, narrative, tale. **2.** remark, utterance.

ḥaččaay pl. *-a* **1.** orator, convincing or persuasive speaker. **2.** glib person, fast-talker. **3.** talkative person, articulate person.

ḥ-d-b

ḥaddab to stoop, hunch the back. *haš-šaayib yḥaddib min yimši.* That old man hunches his back when he walks.

tḥaddab to become hunched. *δahra tḥaddab min ṣaar ʕumra sittiin.* His back became hunched by the time he was sixty.

ḥidba pl. *-aat, ḥidab* hump on the back.

ʔaḥdab fem. *ḥadba* pl. *ḥidib, ḥadbiin* **1.** hunchbacked. **2.** a hunchback.

ḥ-d-θ

ḥidaθ (*i ḥuduuθ*) to happen, occur, take place. *l-ḥaadiθa ween ḥidθat?* Where'd the accident occur?

ʔaḥdaθ to found, establish. *ʔaḥdiθaw šuʕba jidiida bid-daaʔira.* They set up a new section in the office.

tḥaddaθ to speak, talk. *raḥ-yitḥaddaθ ʕan il-ʔumam il-muttaḥida.* He'll speak about the U.N.

ḥadiiθ **1.** modern, up to date. *ʔajhiza ḥadiiθa* modern equipment. *makaayin ḥadiiθa* modern machinery. **2.** (pl. *ʔaḥaadiiθ*) talk, address, speech. **3.** Prophetic tradition, Hadith, the deeds and sayings of the Prophet.

ʔaḥdaθ more or most modern, up-to-date.

muḥaadaθa pl. *-aat* conversation, discussion, talk, parley. || *daris muḥaadaθa* speech class.

ḥaadiθ, ḥaadiθa pl. *ḥawaadiθ* **1.** occurrence, event, incident, happening. *ḥaadiθ wafaat* a death. *ḥaadiθ qatil* a killing. *ḥaadiθ daᶜis* pedestrian accident. **2.** accident, mishap.

ḥ-d-j

ḥadiija pl. *ḥadaayij* camel saddle.

ḥ-d-d

ḥadd (*i ḥadd*) **1.** to sharpen, hone. *s-siččina ᶜamya. laazim itḥiddha.* The knife's dull. You'd better sharpen it. || *l-bazzuuna naayma jawwa l-qafaṣ. ybayyin ḥaadda isnuunha ᶜaṭ-ṭeer.* The cat's lying under the cage. Looks like she's after the bird. *ḥišdaw jiyuushum ᶜal-ḥuduud. ybayyin ḥaaddiin isnuun ᶜaleena.* They've massed their troops on the border. They seem to be ready to pounce on us. *l-mudiir ḥaadd isnuuna ᶜaleek.* The director's got it in for you. *yiðhar ṣadiiqak ḥadd isnuuna ᶜala hal-waðiifa.* It looks like your friend has really worked up an appetite for this job. *ḥidd isnuunak; tara hal-furṣa ma-tiḥṣal baᶜad.* Get ready; maybe the chance won't come again. **2.** to impede, hinder, check, curb. *l-muṭar raḥ-yḥidd min šiddat il-ḥarr.* The rain will reduce the intensity of the heat. **3.** to border upon, be adjoining. *ʔiiraan itḥidd il-ᶜiraaq imniš-šarq.* Iran borders Iraq on the east.

ḥaddad **1.** to delimit, demarcate. *lujna raḥ-itḥaddid il-ḥuduud been il-ᶜiraaq w-iiraan.* A committee's going to demarcate the border between Iraq and Iran. *raḥ-yiji muhandis yḥaddid il-gaaᶜ maalti.* A surveyor's coming to set the boundaries of my land. **2.** to limit, restrict, confine. *l-ḥukuuma ḥaddidat masaaḥt il-gaaᶜ illi laazim tinziriᶜ titin.* The government limited the amount of land which can be planted in tobacco. *š-maʔasawwi b-keefi. qaabil itriid itḥaddidni?* Whatever I do is my business. Do you mean you want to restrict me? **3.** to hobble, chain. *ḥaddidaw il-masjuun b-iznaajiil iġlaað.* They hobbled the prisoner with thick chains. **4.** to set a limit, fix a deadline. *ḥaddad-li ʔila yoom ij-jumᶜa ʔarajjiᶜ-la l-ifluus.* He gave me until Friday to return the money. *ḥaddad-li l-waqit l-ʔaxalluṣ iš-šuġuḷ bii.* He set a deadline for me to finish the work. **5.** to determine, appoint, assign, schedule, establish, set down. *ḥaddad-li s-saaᶜa lli ʔašuufa biiha.* He set the time for me to see him. **6.** to fix. *raaṭib il-muwaððaf mḥaddad bil-qaanuun.* The employee's salary is fixed by law.

ḥaadad to border, adjoin. *l-ᶜiraaq yḥaadid turkiya mniš-šimaal.* Iraq borders Turkey in the north.

ḥtadd to be or become angry. *š-daᶜwa tiḥtadd bil-ᶜajal?* Why do you get mad so fast? *ḥtadd ᶜalayya ᶜala šii mayiswa.* He got mad at me over a trifle.

ḥadd pl. *ḥuduud* **1.** border, boundary, borderline. *ḥuduud il-balad ṭuulha miiteen miil.* The borders of the country are two hundred miles long. **2.** limit, end. *ṭamaᶜa ma-ʔila ḥadd.* His greed has no limit. *haaδa ḥaddak. ʔiδa tguul čilma lux, ʔadumrak.* That's enough from you. If you say one more word, I'll beat you up. *waggafta ᶜind ḥadda, li-ʔan θaxxanha.* I stopped him right there, because he went too far. || *š-ḥadda!* He wouldn't dare! *š-ḥaddi ʔaᶜtirið! yufṣulni bil-ᶜajal.* I don't dare object! He would fire me right away. *š-ḥadda yṭubb! č-čalib yᶜaððа.* He wouldn't dare go in! The dog would bite him. **3.** extent, degree, point. *huwwa baxiil ʔila ḥadd ᶜajiib.* He's stingy to an extraordinary degree. *čaan yiᶜtimid ᶜalayya ʔila ḥadd kabiir.* He used to depend on me to a large extent. *ʔila ḥadd* until, till, up to, to the extent of, to the point of. *rikað ʔila ḥadd ij-jisir, w-ṭaᶜab.* He ran as far as the bridge and got tired. *ᶜraakhum wuṣal il-ḥadd ið-ðarub.* Their fight reached the point of blows. *wuṣlat ʔila ḥadd ma-yinḥimil baᶜad.* It's reached the point where it's not bearable any more. *biδal juhda ʔila ʔaqṣa ḥadd il-musaaᶜadti.* He exerted his efforts to the utmost extent in helping me. *ʔila ḥadd il-ʔaan* till now, up to now. *l-ḥadd il-ʔaan, ma-jaa.* Up to now, he hasn't come. *ʔila ḥadd-ma* to the point that. *laḥḥ ᶜalayya ʔila ḥadd-ma ðawwajni.* He kept insisting, to the point where he irritated me. || *b-ḥadd δaata* by itself, in itself, as such. *r-raggi b-ḥadd δaata mudarrir.* Watermelon by itself is a diuretic.

ḥidda **1.** sharpness, intensity, severity. **2.** rage, fury, anger.

ḥidaad mourning. *ᶜilnaw ḥidaad ᶜala raʔiis il-wuzaraaʔ.* They declared (a period of) mourning for the prime minister.

ḥidaadan in mourning, as mourning. *laabis ʔaswad ḥidaadan ɛala marta.* He's wearing black in mourning for his wife.

ḥadiid 1. iron. *ḥadiid il-xaam* crude iron, pig iron. 2. (loosely) steel, or any metal. || *ʔaɛṣaab min ḥadiid* nerves of steel. *sikkat ḥadiid* railroad, railroad tracks.

ḥadiida pl. *ḥadaayid.* piece of iron.

*ḥadiidi** iron, made of iron or, loosely, of any metal. || *ɛaδalaat ḥadiidiyya.* iron muscles.

ḥaddaad pl. *-iin* blacksmith.

ḥdaada blacksmithing, trade of smithing.

taḥdiid 1. demarcation. *taḥdiid il-ḥuduud* demarcation of the border. 2. restriction. *taḥdiid il-ʔasɛaar* price restriction. || *bit-taḥdiid* specifically. *l-mudiir ɛayyan ʔismak bit-taḥdiid.* The director selected your name specifically. *ma-ʔaɛruf minu humma bit-taḥdiid.* I don't know who they are specifically.

ʔaḥadd 1. sharper, sharpest. 2. more or most intense, severe, etc. 3. more or most vehement, impetuous, etc.

ḥaadd 1. sharpened, sharp, keen. *siččiina ḥaadda* a sharp knife. *zaawiya ḥaadda* acute angle. 2. acute, severe, intense. *ltihaab ḥaadd.* acute inflammation. 3. fiery, vehement, impetuous. *ṭabɛa ḥaadd. yizɛal bil-ɛajal.* He has a fiery nature. He gets mad easily.

maḥduud limited, delimited, restricted, fixed. *kammiyya maḥduuda* a limited number, a small number. *laazim itšuuf il-mudiir. ʔaani ṣuluṭṭi maḥduuda.* You'll have to see the director. My powers are limited. *šarika maḥduuda* a limited company, a corporation.

mistaḥadd pl. *-aat* whetstone, sharpening stone.

ḥ-d-r

ḥidar (*i ḥadir*) to wash away, sweep away, carry downstream. *l-mayy ḥidar il-balam.* The current carried the boat downstream.

nḥidar pass. of *ḥidar. l-balam ingiṭaɛ w-inḥidar wiyya l-mayy.* The boat got free and was washed away with the current.

ḥidriyya pl. *ḥadaari* skull cap.

ḥaddaar fast, swirling. *la-tisbaḥ ihnaa; l-mayy ḥaddaar.* Don't swim here; the current's fast.

nḥidaar 1. slant, dip, pitch, descent, slope. *nḥidaar qawi* steep slope, steep incline, steep pitch. 2. fall. *nhidaar in-nahar* the fall of the river.

minḥadir, minḥidir. slanting, sloping. *gaaɛ minḥadra* sloping land.

ḥʔd-q

ḥadaqa pl. *-aat* pupil (of the eye).

ḥadiiqa pl. *ḥadaayiq* 1. garden. 2. public park. *ḥadiiqat ḥaywaanaat* zoo.

ḥ-d-g-d-g

ḥidigdiga pl. *-aat* sty (med.).

[1]ḥ-d-y

ḥida (*i ḥadi*) to sing or chant to camels, to urge them on. *ḥida lij-jimaal min bidat titɛab.* He sang at the camels when they began to tire.

tḥadda 1. to challenge. *ʔatḥaddaak ʔan tilɛab šiṭranj.* I challenge you to play chess with me. 2. to defy, oppose, resist. *la-titḥadda ṣulṭat il-mudiir.* Don't defy the director's authority.

ḥida, ḥadi singing (to urge on camels).

[2]ḥ-d-y

ḥdayya pl. *-aat* kite (zool.).

[3]ḥ-d-y

ḥida, see under *w-ḥ-d.*

ḥ-δ-r

ḥiδar (*a ḥaδar*) to be cautious, beware, be on guard. *ʔiḥδar min haš-šaxiṣ.* Watch out for that guy.

ḥaδδar to warn, caution, put on guard. *ma-ḥaδδartič min iṭ-ṭalɛa bil-leel?* Didn't I warn you about going out at night?

tḥaδδar to take care, be careful, be wary. *tḥaδδar imnis-sayyaaraat.* Watch out for the cars.

ḥtiδar to be on guard, take care, be cautious. *ḥtiδar imnil-mudiir li-ʔan simaɛ ɛanna ḥači gabuḷ.* He was on his guard against the director, since he'd heard talk about him before.

ḥaδar caution, wariness, watchfulness. *b-ḥaδar* cautiously, with caution. *j-junuud xaššaw lil-beet ib-ḥaδar.* The soldiers entered the house cautiously. *ɛala ḥaδar* on guard, alert, watchful. *kuunuu ɛala ḥaδar. mumkin yhijmuun ɛaleena hal-leela.* Be on your guard. They may attack us tonight. || *ʔuxuδ ḥaδarak minna.* Be on your guard with him.

ḥaδir cautious, wary, careful.

taḥδiir warning, cautioning.

maḥδuur pl. *maḥaaδiir* 1. something to beware, something to be careful about. *ʔuṣruf l-ifluus; ma-aku ʔay maḥδuur, li-ʔan il-imwaafaqa raḥ-tiji baačir.* Spend the money; there's nothing to worry about since the authorization's coming tomorrow. **2.** danger, peril. *ˀaḷḷa yidfaʕ ʕannak kull maζδuur.* God protect you from any peril.

ζ-δ-f

ζiδaf (*i ζaδif*) to delete, cancel, drop, omit, leave out, take away. *ζiδfaw ˀisma mnil-qaaˀima.* They removed his name from the list. *ζiδfaw ˀalif diinaar min miizaaniyyat šuʕubti.* They cut out a thousand dinars from my section's budget.

ζaδif removal, dropping.

ζiδδaaf a variety of wild bird.

ζ-δ-f-r

ζaδaafiir: b-ζaδaafiira in its entirety. *ζčaa-li l-ζaqiiqa b-ζaδaafiirha.* He told me the truth in its entirety.

ζ-δ-y

ζaaδa to parallel, run parallel to. *ṭ-ṭariiq yζaaδi n-nahar il-masaafat miil.* The road parallels the river for a mile.

ζiδaaˀ pl. *ˀaζδiya* shoe. *ˀibin ζiδaaˀ* (insulting epithet, approx.:) son of a bitch, jerk. *maʕmal ˀaζδiya.* shoe factory.

b-muζaaδaa along, alongside of, parallel to. *xan-nimši b-muζaaδaat iš-šaṭṭ.* Let's walk along the river.

muζaaδi next to, along. *n-nahar muζaaδi lis-sičča.* The river's next to the tracks.

ζ-r-b

ζaarab to fight, combat, battle. *jeešna da-yζaarub ib-jabihteen.* Our army's fighting on two fronts. *raζ-inζaarub il-ˀaʕdaaˀ lil-moot.* We'll battle the enemy to the death. *jamʕiyyatna tζaarub il-uqmaar.* Our association is combatting gambling. *kull il-mwaδδafiin da-yζaar-buuni liˀan ˀaani l-waζiid ʕindi šahaada ʕaalya.* All the other employees are giving me a hard time because I'm the only one with an advanced degree.

tζaarab to fight (each other), be engaged in war. *tζaarabna wiyya had-dawla l-muddat sitt išhur.* We fought with that nation for a period of six months.

ζarub pl. *ζuruub* (fem.) **1.** war, warfare. **2.** fight, battle, combat.

*ζarbi** war, military, martial. *l-kulliyya l-ζarbiyya* the military academy.

ζarba pl. *ζiraab* bayonet.

ζraab pl. *-aat* rock fight, a fight with slings.

ζarbaaˀ pl. *ζaraabi* chameleon.

miζraab pl. *maζaariib* recess in a mosque indicating the direction of prayer, mihrab, prayer niche.

ζ-r-θ

ζiraθ (*i ζariθ, ζiraaθa*) to plow, plow up. *raζ-yζirθuun il-gaaʕ w-yizraʕuuha ζunṭa.* They'll plow up the land and plant it in wheat.

miζraaθ pl. *maζaariiθ* plow.

ζ-r-j

ζiraj (*i ζarij, ˀiζraaj*) to embarrass, to put (someone) on the spot, to put in a tight spot. *leeš ζirajitni giddaam marti?* Why'd you put me on the spot in front of my wife?

ζarraj to be persistent. *ζarraj ʕala ˀabuu yištirii-la paaysikil.* He insisted that his father buy him a bicycle.

ˀaζraj = *ζiraj. ˀaζrajitni b-has-suˀaal.* You've embarrassed me with this question.

nζiraj pass. of *ζiraj. min siˀalni s-suˀaal, inζirajit w-ma-ʕirafit š-ajaa-wub.* When he asked me the question, I was embarrassed and didn't know what to answer. *nζiraj w-iδṭarr yidfaʕ il-mablaġ.* He got put on the spot and was forced to pay the sum.

ζaraj: suug il-ζaraj auction place, auction marketplace.

ζarij **1.** difficult, embarrassing. *xallaani b-waδiʕ ζarij.* He put me in a bind. **2.** critical. *l-ζaala bil-balda ζarja.* The situation in the city is critical.

ζ-r-ζ-r

ζirζaara pl. *-aat* palm of the hand.

ζ-r-r

ζarrar **1.** to liberate, free. *raζ-aζarrir il-waṭan.* I'm going to free the country. **2.** to edit, redact. *minu yζarrir haj-jariida?* Who edits this newspaper?

tζarrar to be freed. *l-ʕabiid itζar-riraw min zamaan.* The slaves were freed long ago.

ζtarr to be or become heated, hot. *ζtarreet. baḷḷa ma-tfukk iš-šibbaač?* I'm hot. Would you please open the window?

ζurr pl. *ˀaζraar* **1.** pure, unadulterated. || *dihin ζurr* clarified butter. **2.** free. *ṣaζaafa ζurra* free press. **3.** liberal (pol.). *tafkiir ζurr* liberal thinking. **4.** a liberal. *ζizb il-ˀaζraar* the Liberal Party.

ζurri: ṭiin ζurri a type of red alluvial clay.

ζurriyya pl. *-aat* **1.** freedom, liberty. **2.** independence.

ζariir silk.

ζariira a pudding of starch and sugar, served hot.

ζaraara **1.** heat. **2.** warmth (also of

emotions). **3.** temperature. *darajt il-ḥaraara* the temperature. **4.** fever blister, cold sore.

miḥraar pl. *maḥaariir* thermometer.

ʔaḥarr hotter, hottest.

taḥriir **1.** liberation, emancipation. **2.** editing. *mudiir it-taḥriir* editor-in-chief.

*taḥriiri** recorded in writing, written, in writing. *mtiḥaan taḥriiri* written examination. *b-ṣuura taḥriiriyya* in written form.

ḥaarr **1.** hot. *nahaar ḥaarr* a hot day. || *raasa ḥaarr* He's hot-tempered. **2.** strong, hot, biting. *titin ḥaarr* strong tobacco.

muḥarrir pl. *-iin* **1.** liberator, emancipator. **2.** editor.

mitḥarrir **1.** emancipated. *haaḏi mitḥarrira b-ʔaaraaʔha.* She's emancipated in her opinions. **2.** liberal-minded, liberal. *l-malik ij-jidiid mitḥarrir.* The new king is liberal-minded.

ḥ-r-z

ḥiraz (*i ḥariz*) to stockpile, store up. *l-buṣal ihwaaya bis-suug. xan-niḥriz čam keelu minna.* Onions are plentiful at the market. Let's stock up with a few kilos of them.

ʔaḥraz /with *ʕala*/ to achieve, obtain, attain. *ʔaḥraz ʕala darajaat qawiyya.* He achieved good grades.

ḥiriz **1.** custody, protection. *b-ḥirz ir-raḥmaan* (under the protection of the Merciful) God be with you. (Said to anyone starting on a journey.) **2.** (pl. *ḥuruuz*) amulet.

ḥ-r-s

ḥiras (*i ḥaris, ḥiraasa*) **1.** to guard, watch. *xams ijnuud yḥirsuun il-muxayyam kull leela.* Five soldiers guard the camp each night. *l-maʕmal ma-čaan maḥruus min iḥtirag.* The factory wasn't guarded when it caught fire. **2.** to secure, protect, safeguard, preserve, keep. *ʔaḷḷa yḥirsak.* God preserve you. *dizz wiyyaahum sayyaara mṣaffaḥa tiḥrishum.* Send an armored car along to protect them.

tḥarras to beware, be wary, be on guard. *tḥarras minna. tara haaḏa fattaan.* Be wary of him. He's a talebearer.

ḥtiras = *tḥarras. haš-šaxuṣ ʔaḥtiris minna hwaaya.* I am very much on my guard with this fellow. *ʔiḥtiris ihwaaya tara taaxuḏ barid.* Be very careful or you'll catch cold.

ḥaras **1.** watch, guard. *waaguf ḥaras* standing guard. *ʕali waaguf ḥaras il-leela.* Ali's standing guard tonight. **2.** guard detachment, guard, escort. **3.** sentry, guard.

ḥiraasa **1.** guarding, watching. **2.** watch, guard duty. *ḍariibat il-ḥiraasa* night watch tax.

ḥtiraas **1.** caution, wariness. **2.** precaution, taking precautions.

ḥaaris pl. *ḥurraas* **1.** watchman. **2.** guard, sentry.

maḥruus **1.** guarded, safeguarded. *l-muʕaskar maḥruus zeen.* The post is well guarded. **2.** protected (by God). *ruuḥ, maḥruus ib-aḷḷa.* God go with you. **3.** (pl. *-iin*) a polite term for a man's son. *ṭaab il-maḥruus min mariḍta willa baʕad?* Has your boy recovered from his sickness yet?

ḥ-r-š

ḥaaraš to provoke, incite, stir up trouble with. *leeš ḥaarašta? ma-git-lak ijjuuz minna?* Why'd you provoke him? Didn't I tell you to leave him alone?

tḥarraš **1.** to start trouble, pick a fight. *daaʔiman yitḥarraš ib-wild ij-jiiraan.* He's always provoking the neighbor's kids. **2.** to be forward, be rude, be fresh. *la-titḥarraš bil-baanaat.* Don't get fresh with the girls.

tḥaaraš **1.** to pick a quarrel, to provoke or start trouble. *ʔiḏa ma-titḥaaraš bii, ma-yʔaḏḏiik.* If you don't provoke him, he won't hurt you. *leeš titḥaaraš biṣ-ṣiġaar? ruuḥ ʕal-ib-gaddak.* Why pick on the little kids? Go find someone your own size. **2.** to be forward, be rude, be fresh. *la-titḥaaraš biiha. haaḏi binit mastuura.* Don't get fresh with her. She's a chaste girl.

ḥariš (coll.) a variety of small fish.

ḥarša pl. *-aat* un. n. of *ḥariš.*

ḥirša pl. *-aat* provocation, act of provocation.

ḥ-r-ṣ

ḥiraṣ (*i, a ḥiriṣ*) /with *ʕala*/ to be concerned with, be intent upon. *yiḥriṣ ʕala maṣlaḥat balada.* He is very concerned with the welfare of his country. *yiḥraṣ ʕala kull daqiiqa min wakta.* He husbands every minute of his time.

ḥiriṣ dedication, intentness, concern. *ḥiriṣ ʕad-diraasa* dedication to studying.

ḥariiṣ concerned, dedicated, intent. *ḥariiṣ ʕala sumuʕta* concerned about his reputation. *š-daʕwa halgadd ḥariiṣ?*

ʔuxuδ raaḥa. Why so eager? Take a rest.

ʔaḥraṣ more or most dedicated, concerned, intent.

ḥ-r-ḍ

ḥarraḍ to incite, provoke, rouse, stir up. *ḥarraḍ it-talaamiiδ ʕal-iḍraab.* He incited the students to strike.

muḥarriḍ pl. *-iin* 1. instigator, inciter, provoker. 2. rabble-rouser, demagogue.

ḥ-r-f

ḥiraf (u) 1. to tilt to one side. *ʔiḥruf il-bismaar lil-yamiin, tara muu ʕadil.* Tilt the nail to the right; it's not straight. *loo-ma ʔaḥruf raasi, čaan l-iḥjaara ṣaabatni.* If I hadn't ducked my head, the stone would have struck me. 2. to turn (someone) aside. *huwwa lli ḥirafha ʕan iṭ-ṭariiq il-ʕadil.* He's the one who turned her aside from the straight and narrow.

ḥarraf to distort, twist, pervert, corrupt, misconstrue. *ʔinta leeš itḥarruf il-ḥači? ʔaani ma-gilit hiiči.* Why do you twist what's said? I didn't say that.

nḥiraf to deviate, digress, turn away, depart. *nḥiraf ʕan il-mabdaʔ illi čaan mitmassik bii.* He deviated from the principle that he had adhered to.

ḥtiraf to take as a profession, to do professionally. *ḥtiraf il-mulaakama.* He made boxing his profession.

ḥaruf pl. *ḥuruuf* 1. letter (of the alphabet). || *ḥaruf ib-ḥaruf* word by word, exactly. *ḥčaa-li l-quṣṣa ḥaruf ib-ḥaruf.* He told me the story word for word. 2. consonant. 3. particle. || *ḥaruf jarr* preposition (gram.).

*ḥarfi** literal, word-for-word, direct. *tarjuma ḥarfiyya* a literal translation. *naqil ḥarfi* a word-for-word copy. *b-ṣuura ḥarfiyya* literally, word for word. *ʔariidak ittarjum-li hal-maktuub ib-ṣuura ḥarfiyya.* I want you to translate this letter for me literally.

ḥarfiyyan 1. literally, directly. *tarjum-li hal-maktuub ḥarfiyyan.* Translate this letter for me literally. 2. word for word, word by word. *ʕaad kalaami ḥarfiyyan.* He repeated my remark word for word. *gal-li kull šii ḥarfiyyan.* He told me the whole thing word by word.

ḥtiraaf professionalism (as opposed to amateurism).

muḥtarif professional. *laaʕib kurat il-qadam muḥtarif* a professional soccer player.

ḥ-r-q

ḥurqa stinging, burning sensation (of heartburn, etc.).

ḥariiq pl. *ḥaraayiq* fire, conflagration.

miḥraqa pl. *maḥaariq* incinerator.

see also *ḥ-r-g.*

ḥ-r-g

ḥirag (i ḥarig) 1. to burn. *jigaartak ḥirgat ʔiidi.* Your cigarette burned my hand. *l-mutaḍaahiriin ḥirgaw is-safaara.* The demonstrators set fire to the embassy. *l-baanyaan yḥirguun il-mayyit.* The Hindus cremate the dead. || *ḥiraga l-galbi. ḍall saaʕa yiḥči ʕala šii ma-yifham bii.* He exasperated me. Kept talking for an hour about something he doesn't understand. *zaʕʕal xaṭiibti ʕalayya w-ḥirag galbi.* He got my fiancee mad at me and burned me up. 2. to burn, sting, smart. *ṣ-ṣaabuun xašš ib-ʕeeni w-gaam yiḥrigha.* The soap got in my eyes and started to sting. *ʕeeni gaamat tiḥrigni mniṣ-ṣaabuun.* My eyes began to sting from the soap.

tḥarrag to be consumed (by an emotion), be pained, eat one's heart out. *baʕdak titḥarrag ʕal-waḍiifa?* Are you still eating your heart out over the position?

ḥtirag 1. to catch fire, burn, burn up. *ḥtirgat sayyaarti w-ma-čaanat ʕindi mitfaʔat ḥariiq.* My car caught fire and I had no fire extinguisher. *l-ʔakil iḥtirag.* The food got burned. || *ḥtirag galbi ʕala hal-faqiir ij-jooʕaan.* My heart bled for that poor, hungry man. *ḥtirag il-ʔaxḍar b-siʕir il-yaabis.* The innocent got hung with the guilty (lit., the green things got burned up with the dry). 2. to burn out. *l-igloob iḥtirag.* The light bulb burned out. 3. to be consumed (with emotion). *ḥtirag min simaʕ itraffaʕit.* He was consumed with jealousy when he heard I got promoted.

ḥarig 1. burning. 2. (pl. *ḥuruug*) burn, burn mark.

maḥruug 1. burned, scorched, charred, burned up. || *maḥruug iṣibʕa* a dish made of dried bread and spices boiled in water. *š-daʕwa galbak maḥruug ʕalee! yistaahil.* My you're awfully agitated about him! He deserves it. 2. irritated, burned up. *ʔinta š-biik maḥruug? ʔaani lli xṣarit ʔalif diinaar.* What are you burned up about? I'm the one who lost the thousand dinars. 3. burned out. *gloob*

maḥruug a burned out light bulb.
see also *ḥ-r-q.*

ḥ-r-k

ḥarrak **1.** to move, to set in motion, make move, propel. *ḥarrik il-meez išwayya. xalli ašuuf š-aku jawwaa.* Move the desk a little. Let me see what's under it. *ʔiδa tḥarrik il-meez, ma-agdar aktib.* If you jiggle the table, I can't write. *ma-yuʕruf yḥarrik hal-makiina.* He doesn't know how to make this machine operate. || *la-tḥarrik saakin!* Let sleeping dogs lie! Don't stir things up! *δall gaaʕid yitfarraj wala ḥarrak saakin.* He just sat watching and never lifted a finger. **2.** to start, get started, get under way. *xalli nḥarrik iṣ-ṣubuḥ saaʕa xamsa.* Let's get started at five in the morning. *ṣiʕdu. raḥ-yḥarrik il-paaṣ.* Get on. The bus is about to leave. **3.** to incite, instigate, provoke, stir up. *ḥarrak il-ʕašaayir ḥatta yθuuruun.* He incited the tribes to revolt. *ḥarrak il-ʕummaal ʕaš-šarika w-xallaahum yδir-buun.* He stirred up the workers against the company and got them to go on strike. *ḥarrakit marta ʕalee.* I stirred up his wife against him. **4.** to vowel, put in vowel markings (gram.). *ʔiktib ič-čilam w-ḥarrikha.* Write the words and put the vowel markings on them.

tḥarrak **1.** to move, stir, budge. *la-titḥarrak. aruuḥ ajirḥak bil-muus.* Don't move. I might cut you with the razor. *bass yugʕud, baʕad ma-yitḥarrak min mukaana.* Once he sits down, then he won't move out of his place. **2.** to start moving, get moving. *tḥarrak ʕaad! ma-buqa wakit.* Get a move on! There's no time left. **3.** to start out, get under way. *šwakit itḥarraktu min il-baṣra?* When'd you start out from Basra? *j-jeeš itḥarrak lil-ḥuduud.* The army moved out toward the border. **4.** to leave, depart. *l-p̣aaṣ itḥarrak gabuḷ xamis daqiiqa.* The bus left five minutes ago. **5.** to be agitated, be excited, to act up. *tḥarrak ʕalee sinna w-ma-gidar ynaam.* His tooth acted up on him and he couldn't sleep.

ḥarik **1.** lively, brisk, agile, nimble. **2.** mischievous.

ḥaraka **1.** movement, motion. **2.** activity. *suug it-timman ma-bii ḥaraka l-yoom.* There's no activity in the rice market today. **3.** traffic. *ḥarakat il-muruur* traffic. **4.** disturbance, trouble. **5.** social movement, cause. **6.** vowel, vowel marking (gram.). **7.** (taboo) erection.

muḥarrik pl. *-iin* trouble-maker, instigator. **2.** (pl. *-aat*) motor, engine.

mitḥarrik **1.** active, lively. **2.** mischievous.

ḥ-r-m

ḥiram **1.** to deprive, dispossess, withhold, deny, refuse. *la-tiḥrumna min šooftak.* Don't deprive us of the pleasure of seeing you. *manʕ it-tajawwul ḥiramni min šoofat ʔaṣdiqaaʔi.* The curfew prevented me from seeing my friends. *la-tiḥrum il-walad imnil-liʕib wiyya ʔaṣdiqaaʔa.* Don't keep the boy from playing with his friends. *ḥaṭṭ ʔiida l-waṣxa bil-ʔakil w-ḥiramna minna.* He put his dirty hand in the food and spoiled it for us. *xaṭiyya, maḥruuma min kull šii.* Poor thing, she's been deprived of everything. **2.** to exclude, cut off. *ḥiram ʔibna č-cibiir min il-miiraaθ.* He excluded his oldest son from the inheritance. *l-kull itraffʕaw. bass ʔaani l-maḥruum.* Everyone got promoted. I'm the only one who was excluded.

ḥarram **1.** to declare unlawful, forbidden, to forbid. *d-diin yḥarrum šurb il-ʕarag.* Religion forbids drinking arrack. *ʔabuuya ḥarram ʕalayya ṭ-ṭalʕa bil-leel.* My father told me not to go out at night. *ḥarram ʕala nafsa ʔay winsa.* He denies himself all pleasure. **2.** to waste, squander sinfully. *la-tḥarrum il-waraq. ʔiδa triid itšaxbuṭ, staʕmil waraq rixiiṣ.* Don't waste the paper. If you want to scribble, use cheap paper.

tḥarram to be wasted, go to waste. *l-gaṣṣaab baaʕ nuṣṣ il-laḥam win-nuṣṣ il-laax itḥarram ʕalee.* The butcher sold half the meat and the other half went to waste. *mawaahba tḥarrmat bij-jeeš.* His talents were wasted in the army.

nḥiram to be deprived. *j-jaahil inḥiram min kullši.* The kid was deprived of everything. *min ṣirit ib-hal-waδiifa, nḥiramit min šoofat wildi.* Since I got this position, I've been prevented from seeing my kids.

ḥtiram to respect, esteem, revere. *laazim tiḥtirum abuuk.* You have to respect your father. *yiḥturum nafsa hwaaya. ma-yiddaaxal ib-qaδaaya j-jihaal.* He's very self-respecting. He doesn't meddle in the children's affairs.

staḥram to consider sinful, unlawful, forbidden. *yistaḥrum min šurb il-mašruubaat ir-ruuḥiyya.* He considers drinking alcoholic beverages sinful. *ma-*

yaaxuδ faaʔida ʕala fluusa li-ʔanna yistaḥrim. He doesn't take interest on his money because he considers it a sin.

ḥaram pl. *ʔaḥraam* **1.** forbidden, prohibited. **2.** holy, sacred, sacrosanct. **3.** forbidden place, esp. the family quarters of a house, where guests are not allowed. **4.** sacred place, consecrated part (of a mosque or shrine). *l-ḥaram iš-šariif* the Kaaba and Mecca.

ḥurma **1.** sanctity, sacredness, inviolability. *kull beet ʔila ḥurma.* Every house is private. **2.** (pl. *-aat*) that which is sacred, sacrosanct, inviolable. **3.** woman, lady. **4.** wife.

ḥaraam forbidden, interdicted, prohibited. *šurb il-ʕarag ḥaraam.* Drinking arrack is forbidden. || *ʔibin ḥaraam* illegitimate son, bastard. *ḥaraam ʕaleek!* Shame on you! You shouldn't do that! *haaδa yaakul maal ḥaraam.* He's dishonest. He cheats. *ḥaraam, bil-ḥaraam* I swear. *bil-ḥaraam, ma-tinṭi.* By God, I won't let you pay. *ḥaraam, ma-aʕruf.* Cross my heart, I don't know.

ḥaraamaat regrettable waste. *taʕabi kulla raaḥ ḥaraamaat.* My effort all went to waste.

ʔiḥraam state of ritual consecration of a Mecca pilgrim.

ḥraam pl. *-aat* **1.** white sheet worn by pilgrims in Mecca. **2.** thin, coarse-textured blanket.

ḥariim **1.** harem. **2.** women of a family. **3.** family.

ḥaraami pl. *-iyya* thief, bandit.

ḥtiraam pl. *-aat* deference, respect, regard, esteem. *qaddim iḥtiraamaati lil-ʔahil.* Give my regards to the family. *b-iḥtiraam* with respect, respectfully. *ʕaamalni b-iḥtiraam.* He treated me with respect.

ḥtiraaman out of respect. *wugfaw iḥtiraaman lil-ḥaakim.* They stood out of respect for the judge.

muḥarram **1.** forbidden, interdicted. *šurb il-ʕarag fadd šii mḥarram.* Drinking arrack is a forbidden thing. **2.** forbidden act. **3.** Muharram, first month of the Moslem calendar.

muḥrim pl. *-iin.* Mecca pilgrim in a state of ritual consecration.

muḥtaram honored, esteemed, respected. *haaδa kulliš muḥtaram been in-naas.* He's very much respected among the people.

ح-r-m-s

ḥirmis very small biting insects.

ح-r-m-l

ḥarmal African rue.

ح-r-n

ḥiran (*i ḥarin*) to be or become obstinate, stubborn, headstrong. *min itkallfa b-šii, yiḥrin.* When you ask him for anything, he gets stubborn. *l-iḥṣaan ḥiran w-ma-yiqbal yimši baʕad.* The horse balked and refused to go on.

ح-r-y

tḥarra **1.** to investigate. *ma-nigdar inʕayynak gabul-ma š-šurṭa titḥarra ʕannak.* We can't appoint you before the police investigate you. **2.** to inquire, make inquiries. *š-šurṭa da-titḥarra ʕannak.* The police are looking for you.

taḥarri pl. *-iyyaat* **1.** investigation. *šurṭat it-taḥarri* detective force. *šurṭi taḥarri* detective. **2.** inquiry, check.

ح-z-b

tḥazzab **1.** to band together, stick together, join forces. *tḥazzbaw δidda li-ʔan yxaafuun minna.* They banded together against him because they're afraid of him. *ʔahil hal-wlaaya yitḥazzibuun. l-ġariib ma-yigdar yʕiiš wiyyaahum.* The people of that town stick together. A stranger can't live with them. **2.** to show favoritism, bias, to take sides. *yitḥazzab il-garaayba.* He shows favoritism toward his relatives. *l-mudiir yitḥazzab ihwaaya. ma-yʕayyin ʔaḥḥad ʔilla min uwlaayta.* The director plays favorites. He only appoints people from his home town.

ḥizib pl. ʔaḥzaab **1.** political party. **2.** faction, clique, group, band.

*ḥizbi** party, factional. *jariida ḥizbiyya* party newspaper. *ġaraδ ḥizbi* party goals.

ḥizbiyya pl. *-aat* **1.** party activity, political campaigning. **2.** partisanship, partiality. **3.** factionalism. **4.** patronage, favoritism.

taḥazzub **1.** group loyalty. **2.** favoritism, bias. **3.** factionalism.

mitḥazzib **1.** partial, biased. **2.** partisan.

ح-z-b-a-l

ḥazbaal— (< *ḥasab baal*) /with pronominal suffix/ in the opinion of . . . *nṭeeta fluus. ḥazbaali ʔaadmi.* I gave him money. I thought he was an honorable man.

ح-z-r

ḥizar (*i ḥazir*) to guess, make a guess. *tigdar tiḥzir š-aku b-iidi?* Can you guess what's in my hand?

ḥazzar to quiz, make guess. *ḥazzarta šgadd kallfatni s-sayyaara.* I made him guess how much the car cost me. *xalli ʔaḥazzrak šii. š-jibit-lak?* Let me quiz you on something. What'd I bring you? *čaan yḥazzirna b-ʔašyaaʔ ma-tiji ʕal-baal.* He was giving us riddles about things you'd never think of.

ḥazzuura pl. *-aat* riddle, puzzle.

ḥ-z-r-a-n

ḥzeeraan June.

ḥ-z-z

ḥazz (*i ḥazz*) **1.** to notch, nick. *ḥazz il-xišba bis-siččiina.* He notched the piece of wood with the knife. **2.** to split. *ðiraba bil-faas w-ḥazza r-raasa.* He hit him with an ax and split his head.

nḥazz **1.** to be or become notched, nicked. *l-aθaaθ kulla nḥazz bin-naqil.* The furniture all got nicked in moving. **2.** to be split. *raasa nḥazz mnið-ðarḅa.* His head was split by the blow.

ḥazz pl. *ḥzuuz* nick, notch.

ḥazaaza pl. *-aat* enmity, hostility, rancor, hatred, hate.

ḥ-z-m

ḥizam (*i ḥazim*) to tie up, bundle, wrap up, pack. *ʔiḥzim hal-faaylaat suwa, w-dizzhum lil-wizaara.* Tie up these files and send them to the ministry.

ḥazzam to strap, strap up. *haṣ-ṣanduug muu qawi. ḥazzma b-qeed.* This trunk isn't very strong. Strap it up with steel bands. || *ḥazzamta b-ziig.* I gave him a Bronx cheer. *min gaal raḥ-yṣiir il-mudiir, ḥazzamta b-ziig.* When he said he's going to be director, I gave him a Bronx cheer.

tḥazzam **1.** to put on a belt. *libas il-panṭaroon bass ma-tḥazzam.* He put on the pants but didn't put on a belt. **2.** to gird oneself, get ready, prepare oneself. *tḥazzamit-la lil-imtiḥaan.* I got ready for the exam. **3.** to pitch in, throw oneself wholeheartedly into. *ma-čaan xaḷḷaṣna š-šuġuḷ kulla loo ma-nitḥazzam-la.* We wouldn't have finished all the work if we hadn't pitched right into it. *tḥazzam-li b-qaðiyyat tarfiiʕi.* He got right down to work on the matter of my promotion. *guum itḥazzam w-naððuf il-beet.* Get to work and clean the house.

ḥazim **1.** packaging, wrapping. **2.** resoluteness, firmness, determination. *b-ḥazim* with firmness, firmly. *la-tṣiir ðaʕiif. ʕaamil il-mwaððafiin ib-ḥazim.* Don't be weak. Handle the employees with firmness.

ḥzaam pl. *ḥizim* **1.** belt. **2.** girdle. **3.** truss, supporter.

maḥzam pl. *maḥaazim* waist.

ḥaazim resolute, decisive, energetic, forceful. *hal-waðiifa yird-ilha fadd rajul ḥaazim; yqarrir šii w-ynaffða.* This position needs a decisive man; one who'll decide a thing and carry it out.

ḥ-z-n

ḥizan (*a ḥizin*) to mourn, be in mourning *ḥiznat ʕala rajilha sniin.* She mourned her husband for years. *ḥiznat sana ʕala ʔibinha l-mayyit.* She mourned her dead son for a year.

ʔaḥzan to grieve, sadden, make sad. *wafaata ʔaḥzinatni hwaaya.* His demise grieved me greatly.

ḥizin **1.** grief, sorrow, sadness. **2.** mourning. *baʕadhum ma-fakkaw il-ḥizin maalhum.* They still haven't come out of mourning.

ḥaziin sorrowing, mournful, grieved. || *maalik il-ḥaziin* heron.

ḥaznaan in mourning. *ma-yiḥliq wičča li-ʔan baʕda ḥaznaan.* He doesn't shave his face because he's still in mourning.

ḥazaayni (invar.) funereal, mourning. *muusiiqa ḥazaayni* mourning music.

muḥzin sad. *hal-filim kulliš muḥzin.* This movie's very sad.

ḥ-s-b

ḥisab (*i ḥsaab*) **1.** to compute, reckon, calculate. *xal-niḥsib maṣrafna haš-šahar.* Let's figure out our expenses for this month. **2.** to count. *ḥisab l-ifluus w-šaaf ʔaku ziyaada.* He counted the money and saw that there was a surplus. **3.** to enumerate. *tigdar tiḥsib-li čam ibin ʕamm ʕindak?* Can you tell me how many cousins you have? *ʔiḥsib-li l-qaarraat il-xamsa.* Enumerate the five continents for me. **4.** to consider, deem, think. *da-yiḥsib nafsa rajjaal.* He considers himself a man. *raffʕoo li-ʔan ḥisboo ʕal-waziir.* They promoted him because they figured he was a protégé of the minister. **5.** to consider, regard, count. *ʔiḥsiba wiyya j-jaayiin.* Count him with those that are coming. *min itkallfa b-šii, ʔiḥisba ṣaar.* When you ask him for something, you can consider it done. *ḥisabni waaḥid min ʔixwaana.* He considered me one of his brothers. || *ʔiḥsibha ʕalayya; haaða jaahil.* Do it for my sake; he's just a kid. **6.** to price. *ʔiða tištiri l-iktaab, ʔaḥsib-lak il-qalam ib-xamsiin filis.* If you buy the book, I'll sell you the pencil for fifty fils. *beeš ḥisboo-lak haθ-θoob?* How much did they charge you for this shirt? || *ḥisab iḥsaab.* He took account of everything. He took everything into consideration. *laazim tiحsib حisaabak gabul-ma tištiriiha.* You must take all things into account before you buy it. *laazim tiحsib-la ʔalf iحsaab.* You should take every little thing about him into consideration. *ʔiحsib iحsaab il-mustaqbal.* Consider the future.

حassab 1. to consider, think. *ma-حassabit yitrukni.* I never thought he would leave me. 2. to ponder, meditate. *š-biik itحassib? عindak muškila?* Why are you pondering? Have you got a problem? 3. to be or become apprehensive, anxious, concerned. *lamma tʔaxxar ibinha, δallat itحassib ihwaaya.* When her son was late, she became very apprehensive.

حaasab 1. to call to account, ask for an accounting. *ysawwuun iš-ma yirduun liʔan ma-aku waaحid yحaasibhum.* They do whatever they want because there's no one to call them to account. 2. to hold responsible, make answerable. *yحaasibni عala kull filis.* He holds me responsible for every penny.

tحaasab to settle a mutual account. *xal-nugعud nitحaasab.* Let's sit down and settle accounts. *ṣudug حiča عalayya? bass ašuufa ʔatحaasab wiyyaa.* Did he really talk about me? Just let me see him and I'll settle with him.

حasab pl. **ʔaحsaab** 1. esteem, high regard. 2. noble descent. *ʔibin حasab w-nasab* man from an esteemed, noble family.

حasab (prep.) according to, in accordance with, commensurate with, depending on. *ʔuṣbuġ il-beet حasab δawqak.* Paint the house according to your own taste. *sawweetha حasab ṭalab il-mudiir.* I did it in accordance with the director's request. *l-qundarči ysawwi qanaadir حasab iṭ-ṭalab.* The shoemaker makes shoes according to demand. || *حasab ʔamrak; hassa raح-ajiib-lak-iyyaa.* At your orders; I'll bring it to you now.

حasab-ma (conj.) according to what, as, as far as. *sawweet-ilh-iyyaa حasab-ma yriid.* I made it for him just the way he wanted. *حasab-ma ʔaعruf, maa-la عilaaqa bil-qaδiyya.* As far as I know, he's got nothing to do with the affair.

حasba pl. **-aat** 1. arithmetical problem. 2. matter, business, question, affair, problem. *حasbat il-beet, iš-ṣaar minha? štireeta loo baعad?* What happened about the matter of the house? Have you bought it yet? *ʔaعtiqid hiyya حasbat عišriin diinaar, muu ʔakθar.* I think it's a matter of twenty dinars, no more.

حsaab 1. arithmetic, calculus. *bintič δaعiifa bil-iحsaab.* Your daughter is weak in arithmetic. 2. count, score. *ʔaani ʔasaffuṭ l-ičyaas w-inta ʔilzam iحsaab.* I'll stack the bags and you keep count. *حisabit miit waaحid w-taah il-iحsaab عalayya.* I counted one hundred people and then lost count. *xal-nilعab ṭaawli w-عali yilzam l-iحsaab.* Let's play backgammon and Ali'll keep score. *ma-ʔila حsaab* countless, innumerable. *حaaṭṭiin karaasi ma-ʔilha حsaab bil-حadiiqa.* They've put innumerable chairs in the garden. *bila حsaab, blayya حsaab* without limits, recklessly, heedlessly. *da-yiṣruf ifluusa blayya حsaab.* He's spending his money heedlessly. 3. bill, check. 4. account, reckoning. *حsaab bil-bang* bank account. *nṭii حsaaba w-xallii ywalli.* Give him what you owe him and make him scram. || *عala حsaab* 1. at the expense of. *čaayak عala حsaabi.* Your tea's on me. *ma-qibal yaaxuδ ifluus. ṣallaحha عala حsaaba.* He wouldn't take any money. He fixed it at his own expense. 2. on the account of, by oneself. *ʔaxaδt is-sayyaara عala حsaabi liʔan mistaعjil.* I took the taxi all to myself because I was in a hurry. *ʔaxaδit sayyaara عala حsaabak loo riحit عibri?* Did you hire a car by yourself or come by jitney? 3. on the account of, for the sake of. *عala حsaabak, raح-aṭurda.* I'll fire him for your sake. *عala ʔayy iحsaab fuṣloo?* On what grounds did they fire him? *sawwa daعwa عala حsaab zawaaj axuu.* He gave a party on the occasion of his brother's marriage. 5. (pl. only) **حsaabaat** accounting. *šuعbat il-iحsaabaat* finance section, accounting section.

حisaabi* arithmetical, mathematical. *عamaliyya حisaabiyya* a mathemtical calculation.

muحaasaba pl. **-aat** 1. accounting. 2. bookkeeping. *daaʔirat il-muحaasabaat* accounting office.

حaasiba pl. **-aat** adding machine, calculator. *ʔaala حaasiba* adding machine.

maحsuub 1. reckoned, figured, calculated, counted. *δariiba maحsuuba wiyya l-kulfa* tax included in the cost. 2. considered, deemed. *ʔinta maحsuub waaحid minna.* You're considered one of us. 3. (pl. **-iin**) protégé, pet, favorite. *huwwa* *maḥsuub ʕal-waziir.* He is a protégé of the minister.

maḥsuubiyya favoritism, patronage.

muḥaasib pl. *-iin* 1. accountant, bookkeeper. 2. paymaster.

ḥ-s-b-a-l

ḥasbaal- = *ḥazbaal-,* which see under *ḥ-z-b-a-l.*

ḥ-s-d

ḥisad (*i ḥasad*) to be envious, to envy. *ḥisadni ʕala waḏiifti j-jidiida.* He envied me my new job.

nḥisad to be envied. *nḥisadit min ištireet sayyaara jidiida.* I've been envied since I bought a new car.

ḥasad envy.

ḥasuud envious.

ḥ-s-r

tḥassar, etc. = *tḥaṣṣar,* etc., which see under [2]*ḥ-ṣ-r.*

ḥ-s-s

ḥass (*i ḥass*) 1. to feel, sense. *xašš lil-gubba, w-wugaf yammi w-ma-ḥasseet bii ʔila ʔan ḥiča wiyyaaya.* He came in the room and stood beside me and I didn't sense it till he spoke to me. *ma-triid tiḥči wiyyaak. ma-da-tḥiss?* She doesn't want to talk to you. Can't you sense it? 2. to notice. *šloon ma-ḥasseet? ṣaarat laġwa čibiira.* How come you didn't notice? There was a big commotion. 3. to discover, find out. *š-šurṭa ḥassat bii da-ybuug w-waqqfoo.* The police found out that he was stealing and arrested him. 4. to wake, wake up. *ma-ḥasseet imnin-noom ʔila ḏ-ḏuhur.* I didn't wake up till noon.

ḥassas 1. to make aware, make conscious. *ḥassasta b-taṣarrufaat il-muwaḏḏafiin ḏidda.* I made him aware of the employees' actions against him. 2. to wake, wake up, cause to wake. *ruuḥ, ḥassis abuuk imnin-noom.* Go wake your father up.

tḥassas to feel around, grope, probe. *nṭifa ḏ-ḏuwa, w-itḥassasit ṭariiqi li-barra.* The light went out and I groped my way outside.

ḥiss (pl. *ḥsuus*) 1. feeling, sensation, sensory perception. 2. voice. 3. sound. 4. noise.

ḥassaas 1. sensitive, readily affected. *fadd šaxiṣ kulliš ḥassaas* a very sensitive person. 2. delicate, sensitive. *ʔaala ḥassaasa* a delicate instrument. 3. delicate, touchy. *masʔala ḥassaasa* a delicate matter.

ḥassaasiyya sensitivity, allergy.

ʔiḥsaas sensitivity, perception. *qillat iḥsaas* insensitivity, obtuseness.

ḥaassa pl. *ḥawaass* 1. sensation. 2. sense. *l-ḥawaass il-xamsa* the five senses. *ḥaassat iš-šamm* the sense of smell.

maḥsuus perceptible, noticeable, tangible. *taḥassun maḥsuus* a noticeable improvement.

ḥ-s-m

ḥisam (*i ḥasim*) 1. to finish, complete, terminate, conclude. *ṣaar-lak titʕaamal saaʕa. ma-tiḥsim il-qaḏiyya, ʕaad!* You've been bargaining for an hour. For goodness' sake, conclude the matter! 2. to decide. *l-mudiir huwwa l-waḥiid illi yigdar yiḥsim hal-masʔala.* The director's the only one who can decide this question. 3. to settle. *leeš ma-tiḥsim qaḏiyyt il-gaaʕ wiyyaahum?* Why don't you settle the matter of the land with them?

ḥaasim 1. decisive. *maʕraka ḥaasma* a decisive battle. 2. final, definite. *jawaab ḥaasim* a definite answer.

ḥ-s-n

ḥassan to improve, make better. *hal-maṭʕam ḥassan il-ʔakil.* This restaurant has improved its food.

ʔaḥsan 1. to master, have command of, be proficient in. *huwwa yiḥsin il-luġa l-ingiliiziyya.* He has a good knowledge of English. 2. to give alms. *yiḥsin ʕal-fuqaraaʔ.* He gives alms to the poor.

tḥassan to be or become improved, get better. *ṣiḥḥta tḥassnat.* His health has improved.

staḥsan to regard as best, appropriate, or advisable. *ʔastaḥsin inruuḥ hassa.* I think we'd better go now. *ʔastaḥsin naqla min haš-šuʕba li-ʔan huwwa wil-mulaaḥiḏ ma-yitfaahmuun.* I approve of his transfer from this section since he and the supervisor don't get along.

ḥisin beauty, loveliness, comeliness.

ḥusin goodness, excellence (in certain expressions:) *ḥusn is-suluuk* good conduct, good behavior. *ḥusn it-taṣarruf* good judgment, discretion. *ḥusin in-niyya* good faith, good intentions. *sawwaaha b-ḥusin niyya.* He did it in good faith. *ḥusn iḏ-ḏann* good opinion. *haaḏa ḥusin ḏannak biyya.* You have a good opinion of me. *ʔaškurak ʕala ḥusin ḏannak.* I thank you for your good opinion. *min ḥusn il-ḥaḏḏ* or *l-ḥusn il-ḥaḏḏ* as good luck would have it, fortunately. *l-ḥusn il-ḥaḍḍ, wuṣanna ʕal-wakit.* Fortunately, we arrived on time.

ḥasin beautiful, handsome, good-looking, comely, lovely. *binithum ḥasna.* Their daughter is pretty. *waaḥid ḥasin* a good-looking man. *ḥasin iṣ-ṣuura* good-looking, having good features. *ʔibnak ḥasn iṣ-ṣuura.* Your son has nice features.

ḥasiin pretty, good-looking. *bnayya ḥasiina* a pretty girl.

ʔaḥsan better, best. *sayyaarti ʔaḥsan min haay.* My car's better than this one. *loo tisʔala ʔawwal ʔaḥsan.* If you ask him first, it would be better. *ʔaḥsan-lak itruuḥ gabul-ma yizʕal.* You'd better go before he gets mad. *haaḏa ʔaḥsan ṭabiib ib-baġdaad.* He's the best doctor in Baghdad. *ʔaani ʔaḥsanhum biš-šiṭranj.* I'm the best of them in chess. *l-ʔaḥsan idgul-la gabul-ma tsawwi šii.* The best thing would be to tell him before you do anything.

ʔaḥsan-ma in preference to, rather than. *ʔaḥsan-ma nxaabra, xalli nruuḥ-la lil-beet.* Better than calling him, let's go see him at home. *baṭṭil ʔaḥsan-ma tixṣar kull ifluusak.* Quit rather than lose all your money.

ḥusnaa, ḥusna: bil-ḥusnaa amicably, in a friendly way. *ʕaamla bil-ḥusna.* Treat him nicely.

ḥasana pl. *-aat* **1.** good deed, charitable deed, benefaction. *sawwiiha ḥasana l-ʔaḷḷa.* Do it as a good deed for God's sake. **2.** merit, advantage, attraction. *haṭ-ṭariiqa ʔilha ḥasanaatha.* This way has its advantages.

taḥsiin pl. *-aat* improvement, improving, betterment.

ʔiḥsaan **1.** performance of good deeds, charity, alms-giving. **2.** (pl. *-aat*) good deed, good turn, favor.

taḥassun pl. *-aat* improvement.

muḥsin **1.** charitable, beneficent, philanthropic. *ʔaʕmaal muḥsina* charitable works. **2.** (pl. *-iin*) philanthropist, charitable person.

ḥ-s-w

ḥasaawi pl. *-iyya* a kind of large, white donkey.

ḥ-š-d

ḥišad (i ḥašid) to gather, mass, concentrate. *ḥišdaw juyuušhum ʕal-ḥuduud.* They massed their troops on the border.

ḥaššad to mass, build up, concentrate. *da-yḥaššduun quwwaathum qurb il-ʕaaṣima.* They're concentrating their forces around the capital.

tḥaššad to be massed, concentrate. *j-juyuuš mitḥaššda b-hal-manṭaqa.* The troops are concentrated in this area.

ḥtišad to come together, assemble, congregate. *ʕaširt aalaaf jundi ḥtišdaw ʕala l-ḥuduud.* Ten thousand troops have assembled on the border.

ḥ-š-r

ḥišar (i ḥašir) **1.** to stuff, pack, jam, squeeze, force. *ʔiḥšir hal-kitaab been baqiyyt il-kutub.* Stick this book in among the rest. *ʔiḥšir qamiiṣi wiyya qumṣaanak bij-janṭa.* Stick my shirt in with your shirts in the bag. *haaḏa walad iṣġayyir. ʔiḥišra biṣ-ṣadir.* He's a small boy. Squeeze him into the front seat. *s-saayiq ḥišar in-naas bil-paaṣ bala ḥsaab.* The driver jammed a whole crowd of people into the bus. *šloon ḥišraw ʔalif šaxiṣ ib-hal-qaaʕa ṣ-ṣiġayyra?* How'd they crowd a thousand people into that small hall? || *ʕala ṭuul yiḥšur nafsa wiyyaana bil-munaaqaša.* He always intrudes himself into our discussion. *la-tiḥšir ismi b-hal-mawḏuuʕ.* Don't bring my name into this affair. *l-mudiir ḥišarni b-hal-lujna.* The director stuck me on this committee. **2.** to jam, stick, get stuck. *l-geer ḥišar. xaabur il-fiitarči.* The gearshift jammed. Call the mechanic.

nḥišar to crowd oneself, push oneself. *kull-ma nigʕud bil-gahwa, yinḥišir beenaatna.* Whenever we sit in the coffee-shop, he crowds in among us.

ḥašir: yoom il-ḥašir Resurrection Day.

ḥašara pl. *-aat* insect, bug. *ʕilm il-ḥašaraat* entomology.

*ḥašari** **1.** lustful, over-sexed. **2.** (fem. and pl. *-iyya*) person with a large, and generally indiscriminate sexuai appetite.

ḥ-š-š

ḥaššaš **1.** to smoke hashish. *ʔahal hal-manṭiqa kullhum yḥaššišuun.* The people of this area all smoke hashish. **2.** to daydream, let one's mind wander. *š-biik imḥaššiš? ma-tdiir baalak ʕaš-šuġuḷ!* What's the matter with you, daydreaming? Pay attention to your work!

ḥašiiš **1.** wild grass, hay. **2.** hemp, hashish, cannabis, or loosely, any narcotic.

ḥašiiša hemp, hashish, cannabis, or loosely, any narcotic.

ḥaššaaš pl. *-iin, -a.* **1.** narcotics addict. **2.** idiot, dope, dunce, ninny.

mḥaššiš **1.** under the influence of

hashish, or other narcotic. *ligoo mḥaššiš w-waqqufoo.* They found him hopped up, and arrested him. **2.** absent-minded. *haaδa mḥaššiš. ma-yiδδakkar ween xalla l-ġaraaḍ.* He's absent-minded. He doesn't remember where he put the things. **3.** (loosely) crazy, out of one's mind. *haaδa mḥaššiš. maaku jtimaaع il-yoom.* He's out of his mind! There's no meeting today.

ح-š-f

ḥašaf (coll.) under-developed, dried up, poor quality dates.

ḥašafa pl. *-aat* **1.** un. n. of *ḥašaf.* **2.** (vulgar) glans penis.

ح-š-g

ḥišag (*i ḥašig*) to crowd, cram, stuff, jam, squeeze. *ʔiḥšig hal-iktaab been baqiyyat il-kutub.* Squeeze this book in with the rest of them.

tḥaššag **1.** to crowd, jostle, brush. *ʕeeb titḥaššag bil-banaat.* It's wrong to go brushing against the girls. **2.** to interfere, meddle. *haaδa yitḥaššag bir-raayiḥ wij-jaay.* He interferes in everyone's affairs.

tḥaašag to crowd, jostle, push each other. *la-titḥaašguun. ʔaku mukaan waasiʕ.* Don't jostle. There's a wide-enough space.

nḥišag to crowd, force oneself. *giʕad bil-paaṣ yammi w-ḍall yinḥišig biyya.* He sat next to me on the bus, and kept crowding me. *ʔibni daaʔiman yinḥišig beeni w-been marti ʕal-qanafa.* My son always squeezes in between me and my wife on the sofa.

ḥašga pl. *-aat* crowd, mob, jam.

ح-š-m

ḥtišam to be modest, proper, conservative, timid. *tiḥtišim ihwaaya b-libisha.* She is very conservative in her dress.

ḥašam compensation for an insult to one's reputation. *hal-iḥčaaya ʕaleeha ḥašam.* That remark calls for recompense.

ḥišma **1.** modesty. **2.** decorum, decency.

maḥšuum blameless, undeserving of shame or guilt, proper, decorous. *ʔinta maḥšuum imnič-čiδib.* You're above lying. *maḥšuum! ʔinta ma-ʔilak ʕilaaqa bil-uqmaar.* You have nothing to be ashamed of! You have no connection with gambling. *maḥšuum; muu bil-ḥeef! ʔinta š-jaabak ʕač-čiδib?* You're not to blame; far from it! What could you have to do with lying?

ح-š-w

ḥiša = *ḥašša.*

ḥašša **1.** to stuff, fill. *ḥašša d-dijaaja b-looz w-kišmiš.* He stuffed the chicken with almonds and raisins. **2.** to fill (teeth). *ṭabiib il-asnaan ḥašša čam sinn.* The dentist filled some teeth. **3.** to stick, stuff, pack. *š-daʕwa mḥašši halgadd guṭin b-iδnak?* Why have you stuffed so much cotton in your ear? **4.** to insert, stick in. *š-imḥašši been il-ʔawraaq?* What's stuck in among the papers? *ḥašša l-iθmaanya wiyya l-ʔaas ḥatta yiblifni.* He stuck the eight with the ace so as to bluff me.

tḥašša to be filled. *has-sinn ma-yitḥašša. laazim nišlaʕa.* This tooth can't be filled. We'll have to pull it.

tḥaaša **1.** to avoid, shun. *ʔaani daaʔiman atḥaašaa li-ʔanna muu xooš rijjaal.* I'm always avoiding him because he's a nasty old man. *tḥaaša tiδkur-la ʔay šii ʕan il-mawḍuuʕ.* Avoid mentioning anything about the subject to him. **2.** to ignore. *da-aḥaawil atḥaašaa. š-ma-yiḥči, ma-adiir-la baal.* I'm trying to ignore him. Whatever he says, I don't pay him any attention.

ḥašu **1.** stuffing, filling, that with which something is filled. *ḥašu maal qanafa* stuffing, or padding of a sofa. *l-ḥašu maal il-filfil* the stuffing in the pepper. **2.** filling (of teeth). *ḥašu maal sinn* filling of a tooth. **3.** verbiage. *l-qaṣiida maalta kullha ḥašu.* His poem is nothing but verbiage.

ḥašwa pl. *-aat* (dent.) a filling.

ḥaša except, with the exception of, excluding. *kull il-banaat imlaʕʕibaat, ḥaša banaatak.* All girls are fast, excepting your girls. *ʕasaahum bil-ʕama min ḥaša ʔibni!* I hope they all go blind, except for my son! *hal-ʔakil ṭurrahaat, ḥaša n-niʕma.* This food is lousy, save what is God's bounty. || *ḥašaak, ʔustaaδ, haaδa zmaal̩.* Saving your presence, sir, that guy's an ass. *ʔinta ḥašaak imnič-čiδib.* You're above lying.

ḥaašya pl. *ḥawaaši* **1.** edge. *ḥaašyat il-pirdaaġ* the edge of the glass. *ḥaasyat iz-zuuliyya* the edge of the carpet. || *hal-qaḍiyya ʔilha ḥawaaši hwaaya baʕad.* There are many more facets to this affair. **2.** retinue, entourage, followers.

*maḥši** stuffed, filled. *ṭamaṭa maḥšiyya* stuffed tomatoes. *hal-baqlaawa maḥšiyya b-looz loo jooz?* Is this baklava filled with almonds or walnuts?

mḥašša stuffed, filled. *dijaaja mḥaššaaya timman w-kišmiš w-looz* chicken stuffed with rice, raisins, and almonds.

ḥ-ṣ-b

ḥaṣṣab to catch or have the measles. *ḥaṣṣab ʔibinha w-ma-raaḥ lil-madrasa.* Her son had measles and didn't go to school.

ḥaṣba, ḥuṣba measles.

ḥ-ṣ-d

ḥiṣad (i ḥaṣid, ḥaṣaad) to reap, harvest. *l-fallaaḥiin da-yḥiṣduun il-ḥunṭa.* The peasants are harvesting the wheat.

nḥiṣad to be harvested. *š-šiʕiir baʕad ma-nḥiṣad.* The barley still hasn't been harvested.

ḥaṣaad pl. *-aat* **1.** harvesting, harvest. **2.** harvest time.

¹*ḥ-ṣ-r*

ḥiṣar (i ḥaṣir) **1.** to enclose. *ʔiḥṣir hač-čilma been qawseen.* Enclose this word between parentheses. **2.** to trap, corner, hem in, encircle. *ḥiṣraw ič-čalib biz-zuwiyya w-kumšoo.* They trapped the dog in the corner and caught him. *ḥiṣar il-malik maali b-hal-xaana w-ma-agdar aḥarrka baʕad.* He trapped my king on that square and I can't move it. *leeš tiḥṣir il-waziir maalak hiiči? muu tiḥtaaja barra.* Why do you hem in your queen like that? You need it outside. *ma-yiʕjibni hal-beet li-ʔan maḥṣuur been binaayaat ʕaalya.* I don't like this house because it's sandwiched in between tall buildings. || *ʔijaani lid-daaʔira w-ḥiṣarni w-ma-ṭilaʕ ʔilla baʕad-ma ʔaxað ifluusa.* He came to me at the office, cornered me and wouldn't leave till he got his money. *ḥiṣarni ʕaṭ-ṭalab maala b-waqit ma-čaan ʕindi fluus.* He pressed me for what I owed him when I didn't have any money. **3.** to narrow down, confine. *ḥiṣraw iš-šubha bil-xaddaama.* They narrowed down the suspicion to the maid. *ʔiḥṣir fikrak ib-šuġlak.* Keep your mind on your work. *ʔiḥṣir fikrak w-ḥaawil tiððakkar.* Put your mind to it and try to remember. || *hal-wlaaya tiḥṣir ir-ruuḥ.* This city's depressing (lit., restricts the spirit).

ḥaaṣar **1.** to surround, encircle. *š-šurṭa ḥaaṣrat il-kulliyya min bidat il-muðaa-haraat.* The police surrounded the college when the demonstrations started. **2.** to besiege. *l-ʕadu ḥaaṣar il-madiina sabiʕt iyyaam gabuḷ-ma tsallim.* The enemy besieged the city for seven days before it surrendered.

nḥiṣar **1.** to get caught, get trapped. *nḥiṣarna b-baab id-daaʔira ʔila ʔan wugaf il-muṭar.* We got caught in the doorway of the office until the rain stopped. *ʔiidi nḥiṣrat bil-baab w-iṣibʕi tʕawwar.* My hand got caught in the door and my finger got hurt. **2.** to be crowded, be jammed. *nḥiṣraw bil-paaṣ w-ma-gidar il-waaḥid yitḥarrak.* They were crowded in the bus so that no one could move. || *ʔiða nḥiṣarit w-ma-ʕindak wala filis, ʔiktib-li.* If you get in a tight spot and don't have a bit of money, write me. **3.** to have a full bladder, to have to go. *j-jaahil inḥiṣar boola. ʔaku mirḥaað ihnaa?* The child has to go to the bathroom. Is there a toilet here? *ʔiða nḥiṣarit, il-maraaḥiið foog.* If you feel the need, the toilet is upstairs.

ḥtiṣar to be or become depressed, feel confined, restless, closed in. *ʔiða yibqa waḥda bil-beet, yiḥtiṣir.* If he stays alone in the house, he will get depressed. *ḥtiṣarit ib-baʕguuba, liʔan maaku šii waaḥid yiltihi bii.* I got depressed in Ba'kuba, because there's nothing to occupy oneself with.

ḥaṣiir (coll.) pl. *ḥiṣraan* woven matting, woven mat(s).

ḥaṣiira pl. *-aat* a woven mat.

ḥiṣaar pl. *-aat* **1.** siege. **2.** blockade. *ḥiṣaar iqtiṣaadi* economic blockade.

muḥaaṣara pl. *-aat* **1.** blockade. **2.** siege.

nḥiṣaar **1.** restrictedness, limitation, confinement. **2.** (tobacco) monopoly. *mudiiriy-yat inḥiṣaar it-tabuġ il-ʕaamma.* Directorate General of the Tobacco Monopoly.

maḥṣuur **1.** limited, restricted, confined. *tijaart ič-čaay maḥṣuura been xamis tujjaar.* The tea trade's restricted to five merchants. **2.** depressed, bored. *činit maḥṣuur ib-hal-uwlaaya l-izġayyra.* I was bored in that small town. **3.** feeling the need to urinate. *ʔaani maḥṣuur. ʔaku xalaaʔ ihnaa?* I've got to go. Is there a toilet here?

²*ḥ-ṣ-r*

tḥaṣṣar **1.** to sigh. *min yismaʕ isimha, yitḥaṣṣar.* When he hears her name, he sighs. **2.** to long. *da-yitḥaṣṣar ʕala šoofat xaṭiibta.* He's longing for the sight of his fiancée. *gaam yitḥaṣṣar ʕala ʔayyaam šabaaba.* He became nostalgic over the days of his youth. **3.** to grieve, be grieved, be upset. *ṣuraf ifluusa kullha w-baʕdeen gaam yitḥaṣṣar ʕal-filis.* He spent all his money and then began to grieve for one fils.

ḥaṣra pl. *-aat* **1.** sigh. *giʕad igbaali*

w-gaam yjurr ḥaṣra wara ḥaṣra. He sat down across from me and began heaving sigh after sigh. **2.** longing, nostalgia. *maat ib-ḥaṣratha.* He almost died of longing for her. || *ḥaṣra ʕala l-ʔayyaam il-faatat.* Ah, what days those were!

ḥ-ṣ-r-m

ḥiṣrim, ḥuṣrum sour, unripe grapes.

ḥ-ṣ-f

ḥaṣaf skin rash.

ḥ-ṣ-l

ḥiṣal (*a ḥuṣuul*) **1.** to happen, occur, take place, come to pass. *ḥiṣal šii b-iġyaabi?* Did anything happen during my absence? *haaδa šii yiḥṣal marra bis-sana.* This is a thing that happens only once a year. *laazim ḥiṣal ʕinda maaniʕ ʔaxxara.* Something must have come up to delay him. *ḥiṣlat il-muwaafaqa ʕala naqlak il-yoom.* The approval of your transfer went through today. **2.** to be extant, available, obtainable. *dawwarit-lak ʕal-iqmaaš laakin ma-ḥiṣal.* I looked for the cloth for you but it wasn't available. *haθ-θoob ma-yiḥṣal minna bis-suug.* A shirt like this isn't to be found in the market. **3.** /with *ʕala*/ to obtain, get, receive, achieve. *šwakit ḥiṣalit ʕala šahaadtak?* When did you get your diploma?

ḥaṣṣal **1.** to obtain, attain, get, receive. *ḥaṣṣal il-waδiifa illi yriidha.* He got the job he wanted. *ḥaṣṣalit-lak il-maʕluumaat ʔilli triidha.* I got you the information that you want. *tigdar itḥaṣṣil-li hal-iktaab imnil-maktaba?* Can you get this book for me from the library? *ḥaṣṣil-li mulaaḥiδ iδ-δaatiyya.* Get me the personnel supervisor (on the phone). *da-yḥaṣṣil ʕašr idnaaniir bil-yoom.* He makes ten dinars a day. || *š-itḥaṣṣil min ʔaδiyyt in-naas?* What do you get from hurting people? **2.** to collect, recover (a debt). *ʔaṭlub ʕali xams idnaaniir w-ma-da-agdar aḥaṣṣilha minna.* Ali owes me five dinars and I can't collect it from him. **3.** to profit, make a profit. *biʕit sayyaarti b-ʔalif diinaar w-ḥaṣṣalit biiha miit diinaar.* I sold my car for a thousand dinars and made a hundred dinars profit on it. *ʔiδa tbiiʕ sayyaartak hassa, ma-raḥ-itḥaṣṣil.* If you sell your car now, you won't make any profit. **4.** to yield a profit, be profitable. *ʔiδa ʔabiiʕha b-hiiči qiima, ma-tḥaṣṣil.* If I sell it for this price it won't yield any profit.

tḥaṣṣal **1.** to be obtained. *hiiči sayyaara ma-titḥaṣṣal ib-ʔaqall min ʔalif diinaar.* That sort of car can't be obtained for less than a thousand dinars. **2.** to be collected. *had-deen ma-yitḥaṣṣal.* This debt can't be collected.

ḥuṣuul obtainment, attainment. *ḥuṣuul ʕaš-šahaada* attainment of a degree.

taḥṣiil pl. *-aat* attainment, obtainment. *taḥṣiil ʕilmi* educational level.

ḥaaṣil pl. *-aat* **1.** product. *ʔahamm ḥaaṣilaat il-ʕiraaq in-nafuṭ wit-tamur.* The most important of the products of Iraq are oil and dates. **2.** crop, harvest. *l-muṭar dammar ḥaaṣilaatna mnit-tamur has-sana.* The rain damaged our date production this year. **3.** gist, essence, main content. || *l-ḥaaṣil* briefly, in brief. *l-ḥaaṣil, kull taʕabna raaḥ ḥaramaat.* To make a long story short, all our effort went for nothing. *l-ḥaaṣil, štireet sayyaara loo laa?* In point of fact, did you buy a car or not? *l-ḥaaṣil, ma-ligeena sayyaara tiʕjibna.* In the end, we didn't find a car we liked.

maḥṣuul pl. *maḥaaṣiil* **1.** produce, product. **2.** crop, harvest. **3.** yield, gain, profit.

ḥ-ṣ-n

ḥaṣṣan to fortify, entrench. *j-jeeš ḥaṣṣan hal-manṭiqa bil-ḥarb il-ʔuula.* The army fortified this area in the first World War.

tḥaṣṣan to take shelter, seek shelter. *loo-ma titḥaṣṣan il-ʕašaayir bij-jibaal, čaan ij-jeeš dammarhum.* If the tribes hadn't taken shelter in the mountains, the army'd have destroyed them. *j-jinuud itḥaṣṣnaw bis-suupeeraat min ṣaar il-hujuum.* The soldiers took cover in the trenches when the attack occurred.

ḥuṣin pl. *ḥuṣuun* fort.

ḥṣaan pl. *ḥuṣun* **1.** horse, specifically, a stallion. *ḥṣaan ibliis* mantis, praying mantis. *ḥṣaan il-baḥar* **1.** sea horse. 2. hippopotamus. **2.** horsepower. *hal-makiina quwwatha miit iḥṣaan.* This motor is one hundred horsepower. **3.** knight (chess).

ḥṣeeni pl. *-iyya* **1.** fox. **2.** jackal.

ḥaṣaana immunity. *ḥaṣaana diplomaasiyya* diplomatic immunity. *ḥaṣaana barlamaaniyya* parliamentary immunity.

taḥṣiin pl. *-aat* fortification, entrenchment.

ḥ-ṣ-w

ḥiṣa (*i ʔiḥṣaaʔ*) to count, enumerate. *han-naas il-bis-siinama š-yiḥṣiihum?* How could you ever count all these people in the movie? *ʕinda fluus š-yiḥṣiiha!* He has more money than he could count!

ḥaṣu (coll.) pebble(s), gravel.

ḥaṣwa pl. *-aat* **1.** pebble, small stone. **2.** stone, calculus (med.).

ʔiḥṣaaʔ **1.** count, counting. *ʔiḥṣaaʔ in-nufuus* census. **2.** statistics. **3.** (pl. *-aat*) statistic, statistical datum.

ʔiḥṣaaʔiyya pl. *-aat* **1.** count. **2.** statistic.

ḥ-ḍ-r

ḥiḍar (a ḥuḍuur) **1.** to attend. *miit šaxiṣ ḥiḍraw il-ijtimaaʕ.* A hundred people attended the meeting. *ma-ḥiḍar il-ḥafla l-baarḥa.* He didn't attend the party yesterday. **2.** to arrive. *ṭ-ṭarafeen ḥiḍraw. triid itšuufhum hassa?* The two parties have arrived. Do you want to see them now? **3.** to appear at, show up at. *ʔiḏa ma-tiḥḍar il-muḥaakama, tixṣar id-daʕwa.* If you don't appear at the trial, you'll lose the case. **4.** to be or become ready. *šuuf il-ʔakil ḥiḍar loo baʕad.* See if the food's ready yet.

ḥaḍḍar **1.** to prepare, make ready, ready. *ḥaḍḍir kull ġaraaḍak lis-safra.* Get all your things ready for the trip. *ʔiḏa tintiḍir xamis daqaayiq, raḥ-aḥaḍḍir-lak id-duwa.* If you wait five minutes, I'll prepare the medicine for you. **2.** to produce, make, manufacture. *šloon itḥaḍḍir ġaaz il-heedrojin?* How do you produce hydrogen gas? **3.** to fetch, get, bring. *tigdar itḥaḍḍir-li miit diinaar il-yoom il-ʕaṣir?* Can you get me a hundred dinars by this afternoon? **4.** to summon forth, make appear. *has-saaḥir yigdar yḥaḍḍir ʔarwaaḥ.* This magician is able to summon spirits.

ḥaaḍar to lecture, give lectures. *ḥaaḍar ib-hal-kulliyya santeen.* He lectured in this college two years.

tḥaḍḍar **1.** to prepare oneself, get ready. *tḥaḍḍarit lil-imtiḥaan zeen.* I prepared well for the exam. *tḥaḍḍarna min zamaan.* We got ready some time ago. **2.** to become civilized, settle down. *ṭuul ʕumrak ma-raḥ-titḥaḍḍar.* You'll never in your life become civilized.

ḥtiḍar to die. *da-yiḥtiḍir w-maḥḥad yamma.* He is dying and there's no one by his side.

ḥaḍar settled population, town dwellers (as opposed to nomads).

*ḥaḍari** **1.** settled, sedentary, non-nomadic. **2.** settled person, town dweller.

ḥaḍra **1.** presence. *ma-laazim itguul hiiči ʔašyaaʔ b-ḥaḍrat naas ʔakbar minnak.* You shouldn't say such things in the presence of older people. **2.** /in construct/ a polite form of address, sometimes used sarcastically. *ḥaḍrat il-ustaad* approx., the good professor, the worthy professor. *ḥaḍrat il-ustaaḏ, loo qaari jariidt il-yoom, čaan šifit maʕluumaatak ġalaṭ.* My dear sir, if you'd read today's paper you'd have seen your information is wrong. *ḥaḍratkum leeš ziʕaltu?* Why did your Grace get mad? **3.** (pl. *-aat*) the main part of the mosque, where people pray. **4.** most sacred chamber of a religious shrine, where the deceased is entombed.

ḥuḍuur **1.** presence. *ḥuḍuurak bil-maḥkama muu ḍaruuri.* Your presence in court isn't necessary. *nṭaa l-ifluus b-iḥḍuuri.* He gave him the money in my presence. **2.** attendance. *l-ḥuḍuur bil-ijtimaaʕ jabri.* Attendance at the meeting is compulsory. **3.** those present, the ones attending. *maḥḥad imnil-ḥuḍuur waafaq.* None of those present would agree.

ḥaḍaara pl. *-aat* **1.** civilization. **2.** culture.

ḥaḍiira pl. *ḥaḍaayir* **1.** patrol (boy scouts). **2.** squad (mil.).

maḥḍar pl. *maḥaaḍir* minutes (of a meeting, etc.).

muḥaaḍara pl. *-aat* lecture.

ḥaaḍir **1.** present. *ʔabuuk hamm čaan ḥaaḍir biz-zawwaaj.* Your father was also present at the marriage. **2.** ready. *l-ʔakil ḥaaḍir.* The food's ready. **3.** dower paid by a man to his bride before their final marriage vows. **4.** *l-ḥaaḍir* the present, the present time. || *bil-ḥaaḍir, bil-wakt il-ḥaḍir* at present, now, at the present time. *bil-wakt il-ḥaadir ma-ʕiddna waḍiifa šaaġra.* At the present time, we don't have a position vacant.

muḥaaḍir pl. *-iin* lecturer, speaker.

mitḥaḍḍir civilized. *dawla mitḥaḍḍra* a civilized country.

ḥ-ḍ-r-m-w-t

ḥaḍramawt Hadhramaut.

*ḥaḍramawti** (pl. *-iyya*) **1.** Hadhramautian, from Hadhramaut. **2.** Hadhramauti, man from Hadhramaut.

ḥ-ḍ-ḍ

ḥaḍḍ pl. *ḥḍuuḍ* **1.** lot, fate, destiny. **2.** luck, fortune. *suuʔ il-ḥaḍḍ* bad luck, misfortune. *min suuʔ il-ḥaḍḍ* or *l-suuʔ il-ḥaḍḍ* unfortunately. *ḥusn il-ḥaḍḍ* good luck. *min ḥusn il-ḥaḍḍ* or *l-ḥusn il-ḥaḍḍ* luckily, fortunately. *l-ḥusn il-ḥaḍḍ, ma-yʕaḍḍ.* Fortunately it doesn't bite. *l-ḥusn ḥaḍḍa, ligaw il-ʔawraaq ḏ-ḍaayʕa.*

Fortunately for him, they found the lost papers.

ḥaḍiiḍ fortunate, lucky. *haaða ḥaḍiiḍ. kull-ma yilʕab waraq yiġlub.* He's lucky. Whenever he plays cards he wins.

ḥ-ḍ-n

ḥiḍan (u ḥaḍin) to embrace, hug. *ḥiḍan ṣadiiqa w-baasa.* He embraced his friend and kissed him.

tḥaaḍan to embrace one another. *min itlaagaw, itḥaaḍnaw.* When they met, they embraced.

ḥuḍun pl. *ʔaḥḍaan* **1.** lap. **2.** bosom. || *ḥuḍnat ḥaṭab* an armload or apronload of firewood.

ḥaḍna pl. *-aat* embrace, hug.

ḥaḍaana: daar ḥaḍaana day nursery, children's home.

ḥaḍiina pl. *ḥaḍaayin* (baby's) diaper.

ḥ-ṭ-b

ḥaṭṭab to gather firewood. *mart il-fallaaḥ itḥaṭṭub w-rajilha ybiiʕ il-ḥaṭab.* The peasant's wife gathers firewood and her husband sells it.

ḥaṭab (coll.) firewood.

ḥaṭba pl. *-aat* stick, piece of firewood.

ḥaṭṭaab pl. *-a* man who gathers and sells firewood.

ḥ-ṭ-ṭ

ḥaṭṭ (u ḥaṭṭ) **1.** to put, place, put down, set down. *ḥuṭṭ booyinbaaġi b-jinuṭṭak, rajaaʔan.* Put my necktie in your suitcase, please. *la-tḥuṭṭ nafsak ib-hal-qaḍiyya.* Don't get yourself into that affair. || *činit ḥaaṭṭ ʕeeni ʕala ʔuxutha, laakin izzawwjat.* I had my eye on her sister, but she got married. **2.** to alight, settle, land. *ḍall iṭ-ṭeer yḥuum nuṣṣ saaʕa gabuḷ-ma yḥuṭṭ.* The bird kept hovering for a half hour before he lit. **3.** /with *min*/ to lower, diminish, reduce, decrease, detract from. *hal-ʕamal ḥaṭṭ min qiimta.* That deed lowered his prestige.

nḥaṭṭ **1.** to be put, placed, put down. || *har-rijjaal ma-yinḥaṭṭ bij-jeeb.* That man can't be pushed around (lit., can't be put in one's pocket). **2.** to deteriorate, decline, go down, decay. *nḥaṭṭat ṣiḥḥta hwaaya bil-ʔašhur il-ʔaxiira.* His health has deteriorated a lot the last few months. *l-waḍiʕ inḥaṭṭ min jatti hal-wizaara lil-ḥukum.* The situation's deteriorated since this government came to power. *nḥaṭṭat ʔaxlaaqa hwaaya min gaam yimši wiyya haj-jamaaʕa.* His morals have declined a lot since he started to go with that crowd. *nḥaṭṭ ihwaaya. gaam ybuug w-yġišš.* He's become awfully debased. He's started to steal and cheat.

maḥaṭṭa **1.** stop, stopping place. *maḥaṭṭat il-paaṣ* bus stop. **2.** station. *maḥaṭṭat il-qiṭaar* railroad station. *maḥaṭṭat il-iðaaʕa* broadcasting station, radio station.

ʔaḥaṭṭ **1.** more or most deteriorated, etc. **2.** more or most debased, etc.

ntiḥaaṭ decline. *nḥiṭaaṭ bil-axlaaq* a decline in morals.

munḥaṭṭ degraded, low, base, vile. *haaða munḥaṭṭ. ma-ʕinda laa ḍamiir wala axlaaq.* He's degraded. He has neither conscience nor morals. *mara munḥaṭṭa* a fallen woman.

ḥ-ṭ-m

ḥaṭṭam to wreck, destroy, ruin. *l-loori diʕam is-sayyaara w-ḥaṭṭamha.* The truck hit the car and demolished it. *l-ʕarag ḥaṭṭam ṣiḥḥta.* Arrack destroyed his health. *ʔiða ašuufa, ʔaḥaṭṭma!* If I see him, I'll bust him up! *šariiki ḥaṭṭamni. ma-yuʕruf yistuġuḷ.* My partner ruined me. He doesn't know how to do business.

tḥaṭṭam pass. of *ḥaṭṭam. ṭ-ṭayyaara wugʕat w-tḥaṭṭmat.* The plane crashed and was wrecked. *tḥaṭṭam min šurb il-ʕarag wil-iqmaar.* He was destroyed by drinking arrack and gambling. *l-miskiin itḥaṭṭam. l-maxzan maala ḥtirag w-xiṣar kull amwaala.* The poor guy was ruined. His store burned and he lost all his money.

ḥiṭaam wreckage, wreck.

ḥ-f-d

ḥafiid pl. *ʔaḥfaad* **1.** grandson. **2.** descendant.

ḥ-f-r

ḥufar (u ḥafur) **1.** to dig. *ḥufar nugra ġamiija bil-ḥadiiqa.* He dug a deep hole in the garden. *j-jinuud da-yḥufruun xanaadiq.* The soldiers are digging trenches. **2.** to drill. *š-šarika da-tuḥfur ʔaabaar nafuṭ jidiida.* The company's drilling new oil wells. *ṭabiib il-asnaan ḥufar sinni w-ḥaššaa.* The dentist drilled out my tooth and filled it. **3.** to carve. *ḥufar ʔisma w-ʔisimha biš-šijra.* He carved his name and her name on the tree.

ḥaffar to dig up, tear up. *l-ʕummaal ḥaffuraw iš-šaariʕ kulla w-ma-ligaw il-buuri l-maksuur.* The laborers dug up the whole street and didn't find the broken pipe. *l-looriyyaat ḥaffrat iš-šaariʕ maalna.* The trucks have torn our street all up.

tḥaffar to be or become dug up. *š-šaariʕ tḥaffar mnil-looriyyaat.* The street got all dug up by the trucks.

nḥufar pass. of *ḥufar.*

ḥufra pl. *ḥufar* hole.

(pl. only) *ḥafriyyaat* excavations (archeol.).

ḥaffaar pl. *-a, -iin* **1.** digger. *ḥaffaar il-igbuur* gravedigger. **2.** driller.

ḥaafir pl. *ḥawaafir* hoof.

maḥfuur inscribed, engraved. *maḥfuur ʕal-marmara maal il-gabur.* Inscribed on the tombstone.

ح-f-ḏ̣

ḥifaḏ̣ (*u ḥufuḏ̣*) **1.** to preserve. *θ-θalij ḥifaḏ̣ ij-jiθθa mudda ṭwiila.* The snow preserved the corpse a long time. **2.** to protect, guard, watch over. *ʔaḷḷa yḥufḏ̣ak.* God protect you. **3.** to put away, store, file. *xallaṣna šuġulna b-hal-iḏbaaraat. ʔariidak tuḥfuḏ̣ha kullha.* We've finished with these files. I want you to put them all away. *laazim tiḥfuḏ̣ kull il-ʔawraaq.* You've got to file all the papers. *l-maktuub maḥfuuḏ̣ ʔili b-šibbaak il-bariid.* The letter's being held for me in care of general delivery. **4.** to set aside, pigeon-hole. *l-mudiir ḥifaḏ̣ ʕariiḏ̣ti. laazim ʔaqaddim ṭalab laax.* The director pigeon-holed my application. I'll have to submit another request. **5.** to memorize, commit to memory. *ḥifaḏ̣it il-qaṣiida kullha?* Did you memorize the whole poem? **6.** to know by heart. *xamsa min ḏoola t-talaamiiḏ yḥufḏ̣uun il-qurʔaan.* Five of those students know the Koran by heart.

ḥaffaḏ̣ to cause to memorize. *ma-aku ḥaaja tḥaffuḏ̣ iṭ-ṭullaab halgadd qaṣaayid.* There's no need to make the students learn so many poems. *ʔabuuya ḥaffaḏ̣ni š-šiʕir.* My father helped me memorize the poetry.

ḥaafaḏ̣ /with *ʕala*/ **1.** to maintain, sustain, keep up, preserve, uphold. *l-ṃaay ḥaafaḏ̣ ʕala mustawaa.* The water maintained its level. *baʕda mḥaafuḏ̣ ʕala siḥḥta.* He's still keeping up his health. *š-šurṭa tḥaafuḏ̣ ʕal-ʔamin.* The police maintain the peace. *ḥaafaḏ̣ ʕala waʕda w-inṭaani l-ifluus miθil-ma gaal.* He kept his promise and gave me the money like he said. **2.** to guard, protect, defend. *j-jayš da-yḥaafuḏ̣ ʕala baġdaad min iθ-θuwwaar.* The army is guarding Baghdad from the rebels. *š-šurṭa ḥaafḏ̣atna ṭuul iṭ-ṭariiq.* The police protected us all the way.

tḥaffaḏ̣ **1.** to protect oneself. *tḥaffaḏ̣ imnil-barid. ʔilbas qappuuṭak.* Protect yourself from the cold. Put on your overcoat. **2.** to be cautious, careful, wary, be on guard. *tḥaffaḏ̣ ib-ḥačyak. la-ykuun idguul šii ġaḷaṭ.* Be careful with what you say. Don't say anything wrong. *haaḏa mujrim xaṭir; tḥaffaḏ̣ minna.* He's a dangerous criminal; be careful of him.

nḥifaḏ̣ pass. of *ḥifaḏ̣.*

ḥtifaḏ̣ /with *b-*/ **1.** to maintain, uphold, reserve. *ʔaḥtifiḏ̣ ib-ḥaqqi ʔalġi l-ʕaqid išwakit-ma ariid.* I reserve the right to break the contract whenever I want. **2.** to keep up, maintain, retain. *ḥtifaḏ̣ ib-siḥḥta ʔila ʔaaxir ʔayyaama.* He kept his health up to the end of his life. **3.** to hold, possess. *ḥtifaḏ̣ bil-ʔawwaliyya min ʔawwal is-sibaaq il-ʔaaxira.* He held first place from the beginning of the race to the end. *ḥtifaḏ̣ bil-ʔawwaliyya tlaθ isniin.* He retained first place for three years. **4.** to keep, retain. *ḥtifaḏ̣ bil-baaqi n-nafsa.* He kept the rest for himself. *raʔiis il-wuzaraaʔ ḥtifaḏ̣ ib-wizaart id-difaaʕ in-nafsa.* The prime minister retained the ministry of defense for himself.

maḥfaḏ̣a pl. *-aat, maḥaafiḏ̣* **1.** folder, (and by extension) file, dossier. **2.** dispatch case, attaché case, brief case, portfolio.

muḥaafaḏ̣a **1.** safeguarding. **2.** protection, defense. **3.** preservation, maintenance. *l-muḥaafaḏ̣a ʕal-ʔamin* preservation of the peace. *muḥaafaḏa ʕal-hiduuʔ* maintenance of order.

ḥtifaaḏ̣ maintenance, preservation. *loo-ma ḥtifaaḏ̣a b-hiduuʔa, čaan itṣiir ʕarka.* But for his maintenance of his calm, there'd've been a fight.

ḥaafiḏ̣ pl. *ḥuffaaḏ̣* man who knows the Koran by heart (used also as a title).

maḥfuuḏ̣a pl. *-aat* memory selection, thing to be memorized. *dars il-maḥfuuḏ̣aat* poetry memorization class.

muḥaafiḏ̣ **1.** conservative. *naaʔib muḥaafiḏ̣* a conservative deputy. **2.** (pl. *-iin*) a conservative. *ḥizb il-muḥaafiḏ̣iin* the conservative party. **3.** director, director general. *muḥaafiḏ̣ il-ḅang il-markazi.* Director of the Central Bank.

ح-f-f

ḥaff (*i ḥfaaf*) to depilate, remove hair, to pluck. *l-yoom raḥ-yḥiffuun lil-ʕaruus.* Today they're going to depilate the bride. *hiyya tḥiff loo dzayyin šaʕar rijleeha?* Does she pluck or shave the hair on her legs?

ɛaaffa pl. *-aat* 1. rim, edge, brim. 2. border. *ɛaṣṣal daraja ɛal-ɛaaffa bil-imtiɛaan.* He got a marginal grade on the exam.

ɛ-f-l

ɛtifal /with *b-*/ to celebrate, have a celebration. *ɛtiflaw ib-foozhum bis-sibaaq.* They celebrated their victory in the game.

ɛafla pl. *-aat* 1. party. 2. ceremony. *ɛaflat taʔbiin* commemorative ceremony for a deceased person. 3. show, presentation, performance. *ɛafla tamθiiliyya* dramatic presentation, play. *šwakit tibtidi l-ɛafla l-hal-filim?* What time does the showing of that movie start? 4. concert. *ɛafla moosiiqiyya* concert. *ɛafla ġinaaʔiyya* a concert of vocal music.

ɛtifaal pl. *-aat* celebration, festival.

ɛtifaalan in celebration. *sawwa ɛafla ɛtifaalan ib-najaaɛ ibinhum.* He gave a party in celebration of their son's graduation.

ɛ-f-n

ɛafna pl. *-aat* a double handful.

ɛ-f-w

ɛtifa to behave with affection, be affectionate. *min riɛna nzuurhum, iɛtifaw biina hwaaya.* When we went to visit them, they were very nice to us.

ɛafaawa friendly reception, welcome, hospitality. *qaabloona b-ɛafaawa.* They received us with open arms.

ɛ-f-y

tɛaffa to be or become barefooted. *laazim titɛaffa gabuḷ-ma ṭṭubb bij-jaamiɛ.* You must be barefooted before you enter the mosque. *tɛaffa. xalli ʔafɛaṣ rijlak.* Take off your shoes and socks. Let me examine your feet.

ɛaafi pl. *ɛiffaay* 1. barefooted. || *teer ɛaafi* a bare-shanked pigeon. 2. barefoot person. 3. ignorant, uneducated. *ɛaafi bil-kiimya* ignorant of chemistry. 4. ignorant person, ignoramus.

ɛ-q-r

ɛaqqar 1. to disparage, decry, deprecate. *riɛit ɛalee l-ġurufta w-ɛaqqarta ɛala š-šii s-sawwaa biyya.* I went to him in his office and told him what I thought of him for what he did to me. *ɛaqqarta ɛala ɛamala d-daniiʔ.* I gave him hell for his filthy trick. 2. to humiliate, humble, debase, degrade. *šloon ɛaqqiroo! la-nṭoo mukaan yigɛud wala aɛɛad ɛiča wiyyaa.* They really humiliated him! They didn't give him a place to sit and no one talked to him. *leeš itɛaqqir nafsak w-truuɛ lil-ɛazaayim bala daɛwa?* Why do you degrade yourself and go to parties without invitation? *ɛaqqar nafsa b-naδ̣ar il-mwaδ̣δ̣afiin.* He's lowered himself in the eyes of the employees. *la-tɛaqqir nafsak w-truuɛ-la. xalli huwwa yijiik.* Don't lower yourself and go to him. Let him come to you.

ɛtiqar to despise, scorn, disdain, look down on. *ʔaani ʔaɛtiqir il-yaaxuδ rašwa.* I despise anyone who take a bribe.

ɛaqiir pl. *-iin, ɛuqaraaʔ* 1. low, base, vulgar. *min ɛaaʔila ɛaqiira* from a low family. 2. mean, cheap, petty. *ɛamal ɛaqiir* a mean action. 3. despicable, contemptible. *šaxiṣ ɛaqiir* a contemptible person.

ɛaqaara 1. meanness, baseness. 2. pettiness. 3. contemptibility.

ʔaɛqar more or most vulgar, despicable.

taɛqiir contempt, disdain, scorn. *ma-aku ɛaaja lit-taɛqiir. ʔiδa ma-triidni ʔaštuġuḷ ihnaa, gul-li.* There's no need for contempt. If you don't want me to work here, tell me.

ɛtiqaar contempt, disdain, scorn. *ɛaamalni b-iɛtiqaar.* He treated me with contempt.

ɛ-q-q

ɛaqq (*i, u ɛaqq*) 1. to be true, turn out to be true, be confirmed. *hassa ɛaqqat il-ɛaqiiqa.* Now the truth has come out. 2. to be right, correct, proper, fitting. *ma-yɛiqq-lak itɛaamilni hiiči.* You have no right to treat me that way. 3. to have a claim, be entitled. *la-yazaal yɛuqqak ib-diinaareen.* He is still entitled to two dinars from you.

ɛaqqaq 1. to realize *ɛaqqaqit kull ʔaamaali.* I've realized all my hopes. 2. to inquire, check. *l-lujna da-tɛaqqiq ɛan maṣiir il-ʔawraaq iδ̣-δ̣aayɛa.* The committee's inquiring into the whereabouts of the lost papers. *leeš ma-tɛaqqiq ɛan maṣdar il-iɛčaaya?* Why don't you check on the source of the story? *ruuɛ ɛaqqiq-li šuuf ṣudug raɛ-yitɛawwluun.* Go find out for me if it's true they're going to move. 3. /with *b-*/ to investigate. *š-šurṭa ɛaqqiqat ib-ɛaadiθ il-qatil, laakin ma-ligat ʔay daliil.* The police investigated the killing, but didn't find any clues. 4. /with *wiyya*/ to interrogate. *š-šurṭa ɛaqqiqat wiyyaa ʔakθar min saaɛa.* The police interrogated him for more than an hour.

tɛaqqaq 1. to prove true, turn out to be true, be confirmed. *l-xabar itɛaqqaq miθil-ma gitlak.* The news turned out to be true, just like I told you. *ʔišaaʕat naqla tḥaqqiqat.* The rumor of his transfer has been confirmed. **2.** to be realized, be effected, come into effect, come to pass. *ʔamala bil-ḥayaat itḥaqqaq.* His goal in life has been realized. **3.** to make sure, reassure oneself. *tḥaqqaq ʔaku ʔaḥḥad ihnaak gabuḷ-ma truuḥ.* Make sure there's someone there before you go. *tḥaqqaq imnil-wakit illi yirduuna bii.* Make sure of the time they want us. **4.** /with *min*/ to check, verify. *ʔariidak itruuḥ titḥaqqaq mnil-xabar.* I want you to go check out the news. *tḥaqqaq min hawiita gabuḷ-ma tinṭii l-ifluus.* Check his identity before you give him the money.

staḥaqq **1.** to be entitled, have a claim. *maḥḥad yistiḥiqqha lil-ifluus ġeer ibna.* No one is entitled to the money but his son. *ma-daam kisarit il-paaysikil maala, sta-ḥaqqak ib-ʕašr idnaaniir.* Inasmuch as you broke his bicycle, he has a claim on you for ten dinars. || *ʔiδa štika ʕaleek, yistaḥiqqak bil-mablag kulla.* If he sues you, he'll get you for the whole amount. **2.** to deserve, merit. *leeš itʕaamla hiiči? ma-yistiḥiqq.* Why do you treat him like that? He doesn't deserve it. *haaδa ma-yistiḥiqq il-waaḥid ysaaʕda.* He doesn't deserve to have anyone help him. **3.** to become payable, fall due. *l-kumpiyaala staḥaqqat il-yoom.* The note became due today. *ʔida ma-tšiil ġaraaḍak, tistiḥiqq ʕaleeha ʔarḍiyya yoomiyya diinaar.* If you don't move your things, a daily charge of a dinar will be due on them. *ʔiδa ma-txaḷḷiṣ iš-šuġuḷ xilaal šahar, tistiḥiqq ġaraama.* If ou don't finish the job within a month, there'll be a penalty due against you.

ḥaqq pl. *ḥuquuq* **1.** truth. *hassa ṭilaʕ il-ḥaqq, w-θibtat baraaʔti.* Now the truth has come out, and my innocence is established. *l-ḥaqq wiyyaak.* You're right. *w-ḥaqq ʔaḷḷa, ma-aʕruf.* It's God's truth, I don't know. **2.** one's due. *ʕaqqak. minu yitḥammal haaδa?* You're entirely justified. Who'd stand for that? *ḥaqqak. ma-čaan laazim ysibbak.* You're right. He shouldn't have insulted you. *ʔaani ma-da-aṭaalib ġeer ib-ḥaqqi.* I'm not asking for anything but what's due me. *ṣudug ḥiča ʕalayya? bass ašuufa, ʔaaxuδ ḥaqqi minna.* Did he really talk about me? Just let me see him and I'll get my revenge on him. *ʔuxuδ ḥaqqak w-xalli ḥaqqi.* Take what's yours and leave what's mine. *kammalit šuġḷi. nṭiini ḥaqqi w-xalli aruuḥ.* I've finished my work. Give me what's due me and let me go. || *ḥaqq hal-ʕaamil rubuʕ diinaar bil-yoom.* This worker's wage is a quarter of a dinar a day. *xalli nqassimha qismat ḥaqq.* Let's make a fair division of it. *l-ḥaqq ḍaayiʕ ib-had-dinya.* There's no justice in this world. *b-ḥaqq* with respect to, concerning, regarding. *hal-iḥčaaya muu zeena b-ḥaqqa.* That story's not so good as regards him. *gaal ihwaaya ʔašyaaʔ zeena b-ḥaqqak.* He said many nice things about you. *bil-ḥaqq* properly, justly, in an appropriate manner. *qassam l-ifluus ʕala wilda bil-ḥaqq.* He divided the money justly among his sons. *yiṭlaʕ min ḥaqqha.* He can handle it. He's capable of it. *ʔinta ʔiḥči wiyyaa. maḥḥad yiṭlaʕ min ḥaqqa ġeerak.* You speak to him. Nobody can handle him except you. **3.** right, title, claim, legal claim. *ḥaqq it-taṣwiiṭ* the right to vote. *ma-ʔilak kull ḥaqq biiha.* You have no right at all to it. *ḥaqqha ddaaʕi bil-ifluus.* She has the right to ask for the money. *min ḥaqqak tuṭlub taʕwiiḍ.* You have the right to ask for damages. *ma-ʔilak ḥaqq ʕalee. ma-ddaayan minnak.* You have no claim against him. He didn't borrow from you. **4.** (pl. only) law, jurisprudence, legal science. *kulliyyat il-ḥuquuq* law school.

ʔaḥaqq more or most worthy, entitled, deserving.

ḥaqiiqa pl. *ḥaqaayiq* **1.** truth, reality. *bil-ḥaqiiqa* really, actually, in fact. *bil-ḥaqiiqa, ġuruftak ʔalṭaf.* Actually, your room is nicer. **2.** fact. **3.** true nature, essence. *hassa ʕirafitha ʕala ḥaqiiqatha.* Now I know her true colors.

ḥaqiiqatan really, actually, truly, in fact, indeed.

*ḥaqiiqi** **1.** real, true, actual. *quṣṣa ḥaqiiqiyya* a true story. *s-sabab il-ḥaqiiqi* the real reason. *ġaayta l-ḥaqiiqiyya* his real goal. **2.** intrinsic, essential. *l-farq il-ḥaqiiqi been iθ-θneen* the essential difference between the two.

*ḥuquuqi** **1.** juristic, law, legal. *daʕwa ḥuquuqiyya* law suit, court case. *maʕluu-maat ḥuquuqiyya* legal knowledge. **2.** (pl. *-iyyiin*) graduate of a law school, lawyer, jurist.

ʔaḥaqqiyya pl. *-aat* legal claim, title, right.

ḥaqqaani pl. *-iyya, -iyyiin* **1.** just, honest, fair. **2.** an honest person.

taḥqiiq 1. realization, actualization, implementation. *taḥqiiq ʔahdaaf il-ḥizib* realization of the goals of the party. 2. (pl. *-aat*) verification, investigation, check. *taḥqiiq il-hawiyya* identity check. *ḥaakim taḥqiiq* a judge who issues warrants for search, seizure, arrest.

muḥaqqiq pl. *-iin* 1. investigator. 2. interrogator.

muḥaqqaq 1. sure, certain, indubitable, unquestionable. *muḥaqqaq raḥ-yiji.* It's certain he'll come. *muḥaqqaq, šloon ma-yifzaʕ-li? haaδa axuuya.* Sure, why shouldn't he back me up? He's my brother. 2. confirmed, established. *jaayta ṣaarat muḥaqqaqa.* His arrival has been confirmed.

muḥiqq correct, right. *ṭlaʕit muḥiqq ib-raʔyak ʕanha, liʔan hassa nkišfat ḥaqiiqatha.* You turned out to be right in your opinion of her, because now her true nature has come out.

mustaḥiqq, mistaḥiqq 1. entitled to. *ṣaar-li šahar mustaḥiqq tarfiiʕ.* I've been entitled to promotion for a month. 2. deserving, worthy. *mustaḥiqq kull musaaʕada* deserving of help. 3. due, payable. *l-kumpiyaala mustaḥiqqa.* The note is due. *d-deen maalak mustaḥiqq ʕalee faayiz.* Your debt has interest due on it. 4. (pl. *-iin*) beneficiary (of a wakf or inheritance).

mustaḥaqq deserved. *mustaḥaqq! loo daaris, ma-čaan ṣiqaṭit.* It was deserved! If you'd studied you wouldn't have failed. *mustaḥaqq biik! ma-git-lak la-tilʕab wiyyaa, tara yδurbak?* You deserved it! Didn't I tell you not to play with him or he'd beat you up?

ح-q-l

ḥaqil pl. *ḥaquul* 1. field. 2. (fig.) realm, domain, field.

ح-q-n

ḥiqan (*u ḥaqin*) to give an enema. *ḥiqan il-mariiδ mayy w-miliḥ ḥatta timši baṭna.* He gave the sick man an enema of salt water so he'd have a bowel movement.

ḥtiqan to become congested. *ḥtiqnat iʕyuuna b-sabab il-ḥassaasiyya.* His eyes became congested because of the allergy.

ḥuqna pl. *-aat, ḥuqan* 1. enema. 2. apparatus for giving an enema, syringe. 3. pain in the neck, dull person, dolt, clod, stick in the mud.

ḥtiqaan congestion. *ḥtiqaan ir-riʔa* lung congestion.

ح-g-g

ḥagg 1. variant of *ḥaqq,* which see under *ḥ-q-q.* 2. (pl. *ḥuguug*) dowry paid for a bride.

ḥugga pl. *ḥugag* oka, a unit of weight equal to four kilograms. *ḥugga ṣṭanbuul* the small Iraqi oka, 1.28 kilos.

ح-g-n

miḥgaan pl. *maḥaagin* funnel.

ح-k-k

ḥakk (*u ḥakk*) 1. to scratch. *la-tḥukk il-ḥabbaaya tara tiltihib.* Don't scratch the pimple or it'll get infected. *δahri yḥukkni w-ma-agdar aḥukka.* My back itches and I can't scratch it. 2. to itch. *raasi yḥukkni. ʔaʕtiqid wasix.* My head itches. I think it's dirty. *ʔašu ʔiidi da-tḥukkni l-yoom. laazim raḥ-aḥaṣṣil šii.* My hand is itching me today. I must be going to get something. || *jilda da-yḥukka.* He's itching for something (lit. his skin is itching him). *ma-git-lak ʔugʕud raaḥa? ybayyin jildak da-yḥukkak.* Didn't I tell you to quit? Looks like you're itching for it. *jilda yḥukka. yriid-la basṭa zeena.* He's itching for a good beating.

tḥakkak to rub, brush. *giʕad yammi bil-paaṣ w-gaam yitḥakkak biyya.* He sat next to me in the bus and began to brush against me.

tḥaakak to engage in tribadism, and hence, to be a lesbian. *ma-triid tizzawwaj liʔan titḥaakak.* She doesn't want to get married because she's a lesbian.

nḥakk to become frayed, worn. *yaaxt iθ-θoob nḥakkat imnil-ġasil.* The shirt collar got worn from washing. *nḥakk il-pantaroon min gadd-ma yizḥaf.* The pants got worn from his crawling so much.

ḥtakk 1. to come in contact, be in contact, be in touch. *la-tiḥtakk bii. tara haaδa ʕaṣabi.* Don't get near him. He's irritable. *ʔaani ma-ridit aḥaačii, bass huwwa ḥtakk biyya.* I didn't want to talk with him but he buttonholed me. 2. to bother, pick at, pick on, cause trouble. *kull-ma nfuut minnaa, yiḥtakk biina.* Whenever we come by here, he starts trouble with us.

ḥakka pl. *-aat* 1. scratching. 2. itching, itch. 3. itch, scabies. 4. rash.

ḥakkaak pl. *-a* lapidary.

ḥakkaaka pl. *-aat* lesbian.

ḥikkaaka the browned rice burned onto the bottom of the pan.

ḥakkaakiyya pl. *-aat* lesbian.

ḥtikaak **1.** friction. **2.** close contact or touch. **3.** friction, dissention, dischord.

maḥkuuk frayed, worn. *leeš ma-txayyiṭ irdaanak il-maḥkuuka?* Why don't you have your frayed cuff repaired?

ḥ-k-m

ḥikam, ḥukam (*u ḥukum*) **1.** to pass judgment, express an opinion, judge. *l-ḥaakim laazim yuḥkum bil-ʕadil.* The judge must judge fairly. **2.** to sentence. *ḥikmoo lij-jaasuus bir-rami bir-riṣaaṣ.* They sentenced the spy to death by firing squad. *ḥukmoo bil-iʕdaam.* They sentenced him to death by hanging. *ḥikama l-ḥaakim ʕašar isniin.* The judge sentenced him to ten years. **3.** to deliver a judgment, rule. *l-ḥakam ḥikam iδ-δarba čaanat ʔaawt.* The referee ruled the ball was out-of-bounds. *l-ḥakam ma-da-yiḥkum zeen. ma-yuʕruf il-qawaaniin.* The referee isn't doing a good job. He doesn't know the rules. **4.** to govern, rule, control, dominate. *ḥikam il-balad ʕišriin sana.* He ruled the country for twenty years. *ḥikamitni b-hal-liʕba. laazim aḥarrik il-malik.* You got the upper hand with that move. I'll have to move the king. **5.**/with *ʕala*/ to insist, demand, order. *minu ḥikam ʕaleek itruuḥ? ʔinta l-čaan ʕaajbak.* Who forced you to go? You're the one who was anxious. *ḥikam ʕalayya laazim aštirii-la paaysikil.* He insisted that I should buy him a bicycle. **6.** to come due, be due, arrive (of prayer time). *šwakit tuḥkum ṣalaat iδ-δuhur?* How soon is the noon prayer due? *ḥukmat ʕaleena ṣ-ṣalaa ʔaθnaa s-safra.* Prayer time came on us during the trip.

ḥakkam **1.** to choose as judge or arbitrator, make the judge. *ḥakkim ʕaqlak b-hal-qaδiyya w-šuuf suuč man.* Let your reason be the judge of this matter and see who's at fault. **2.** to adjust, regulate. *ḥakkim il-ḥanafiyya ʕal-ḥooδ.* Adjust the faucet so it's over the basin. *ḥakkam waqit wuṣuula b-waqit wuṣuuli.* He adjusted his time of arrival to coincide with my time of arrival.

ḥaakam to arraign, bring to trial, try. *ma-yṣiir inḥaakim il-waaḥid marrteen ib-nafs ij-jariima.* We can't try a person twice for the same crime. *ḥaakmoo baʕad-ma θibtat ʕalee ṭ-ṭuhma.* They tried him once his guilt was established.

tḥakkam to have one's own way, deal arbitrarily. *maḥḥad yriid yištuġuḷ ib-haš-šuʕba li-ʔan il-mulaaḥiδ yitḥakkam bil-muwaδδafiin.* No one wants to work in this section because the supervisor handles the employees arbitrarily. *yitḥakkam biihum miθil-ma yriid.* He can do anything he wants with them.

nḥikam to be sentenced. *nḥikam muʔabbad.* He was sentenced to life imprisonment.

ḥtikam to seek judgment, appeal for a decision. *ḥtikmaw ʕind raʔiis il-qabiila.* They sought judgment from the head of the tribe.

ḥukum pl. *ʔaḥkaam* **1.** judgment, verdict, sentence. *ḥukum xafiif* a light sentence. *ḥukum ġiyaabi* sentence in absentia. *ḥukum bil-iʕdaam* death sentence. *ḥukm il-baraaʔa* acqittal. **2.** decision, ruling. *ḥukm il-ḥakam* the decision of the referee. **3.** rule, regulation, provision, ordinance, decree. *ʔaḥkaam il-qaanuun* provisions of the law. || *ʔaḥkaam ʕurfiyya* martial law. *δ-δaruura ʔilha ʔaḥkaam.* Necessity knows no law (lit. necessity has its own rules). *b-ḥukum* 1. by force of. *saw-waaha b-ḥukm il-ʕaada.* He did it from force of habit. 2. almost, as good as, virtually. *b-ḥukm il-mustaḥiil* virtually impossible. **4.** government, regime, rule. *l-ḥukm ij-jamhuuri* the republican form of government. *l-ḥukm it-turki* The Turkish rule. *l-ḥukm iδ-δaati* self-rule, autonomy. **5.** (invar.) inescapable, inevitable, certain, sure. *raas šahar w-maaxiδ maʕaaša. haaδa ḥukum raḥ-yiskar hal-leela.* The first of the month and he's got his pay. He's certainly going to go out drinking tonight. *ḥukum. laazim yijuun minnaa.* It's inevitable. They've got to come by here. *haaδa ḥukum. laazim tḥarrik il-malik maalak.* It's obligatory. You've got to move your king.

ḥakam pl. *-iyya, ḥukkaam* umpire, referee.

ḥikma pl. *ḥikam* **1.** wisdom. **2.** maxim. **3.** rationale, underlying reason.

ḥakiim pl. *ḥukumaaʔ* **1.** wise, judicious. **2.** wise man, sage. **3.** herb doctor.

ḥukuuma pl. *-aat* **1.** government. **2.** administration, cabinet, government.

*ḥukuumi** **1.** government, official. *sayyaara ḥukuumiyya* an official car. **2.** public, state, state-owned. *gaaʕ ḥukuumiyya* public land. **3.** administration, government. *l-manhaj il-ḥukuumi* the administration's program. **4.** pro-administration, pro-government. *n-nuwwaab il-ħukuumiyyiin* the pro-government deputies.

maħkama pl. *maħaakim* court, tribunal.

muħaakama pl. *-aat* trial, court hearing.

ħaakim pl. *ħukkaam* **1.** governor. *ħaakim ʕaskari* military governor. **2.** judge.

ħaakimiyya judgeship, position as judge.

maħkuum ʕalee **1.** sentenced. *huwwa maħkuum ʕalee bil-ʔiʕdaam.* He's been condemned to death. **2.** person who has been sentenced. *rajjʕaw il-maħkuum ʕalee lis-sijin.* They returned the sentenced man to prison.

ħ-l-b

ħilab (*i ħalib*) to milk. *tiħlib il-haayša s-saaʕa ʔarbaʕa ṣ-ṣubuħ kull yoom.* She milks the cow at four a.m. every day. || *r-raaqiṣa ħilbata kull ifluusa.* The dancer milked him of all his money.

nħilab to be milked. *ṣ-ṣaxla nħilbat ħalibteen.* The goat was milked twice.

ħalib milking.

ħalba pl. *-aat* a milking.

ħilba fenugreek.

ħaliib **1.** milk. *δallat tiʕtini bii ħatta ṭilaʕ ħaliib ʔummha min xašimha.* She kept worrying with him until she couldn't take any more. *ħaliib isbaaʕ* arrack (lit., lions' milk). **2.** (by extension) breeding, honor. *ħaliiba ma-yxallii ysawwi hiiči šii.* His breeding won't let him do such a thing. *ħaliiba muu zeen.* He's not honorable (i.e. his womenfolks' milk isn't good). *ħaliiba naδiif w-ma-yxuun ʔay waaħid.* He's an honorable fellow and wouldn't betray anyone. || *ʔinta w-ħaliibak. ʔiδa ʔastaahil ifluus, ʔinṭiini.* I leave it to your honor. If I deserve money, give it to me. *raħ-tuqbuδ min dabaš. huwwa w-ħaliiba.* You'll wind up holding the short end. That's how honorable he is. *ʔinta w-ħaliibak yaa liban.* (an insult implying that one's mother's milk was soured because her character was questionable, approx.:) Your family honor's in question.

*ħaliibi** milky, milk-like. *gloob ħaliibi* frosted light bulb.

ħallaaba pl. *-aat* **1.** milkmaid, dairymaid. **2.** good milker, cow which gives a lot of milk.

ħaaluub (coll.) hail, hailstones.

ħaaluuba pl. *-aat* hailstone.

ħaalib pl. *ħawaalib* ureter.

mħallabi a pudding made from milk, sugar, and rice flour or starch.

ħ-l-j

ħilaj (*i ħalij*) to gin (cotton). *yiħlijuun il-guṭin w-yṣaddiruu.* They gin the cotton and export it.

maħlaj pl. *maħaalij* cotton ginning plant.

ħ-l-ħ-l

ħalħal **1.** to wiggle, jiggle, work back and forth. *ħalħil sinnak ħatta yinšiliʕ.* Work your tooth back and forth so it can be pulled. *tigdar itħalħil ʕamuud il-kahrabaaʔ?* Can you jiggle the power pole? **2.** to move, budge. *haaδa θigiil; ma-agdar aħalħila.* That's heavy; I can't move it. **3.** to loosen (one's) clothes, make (oneself) comfortable. *leeš imħalħil nafsak? muu ʕidna xuṭṭaar!* Why've you loosened your clothes? We have guests!

tħalħal **1.** to wiggle, wobble, shake, move. *sinni da-yitħalħal. raħ-ašlaʕa.* My tooth is loose. I'm going to pull it. **2.** to move oneself, move over. *tħalħal išwayya xaaṭir ʔagʕud yammak.* Move a little so I can sit down next to you. **3.** to loosen one's clothes, make oneself comfortable. *ʔaani taʕbaan w-miħtarr. raħ-atħalħal w-aaxuδ raaħa.* I'm tired and hot. I'm going to loosen up my clothes and take a rest.

ħ-l-z-w-n

ħalazuun pl. *-aat* snail.

*ħalazuuni** spiral. *daraj ħalazuuni* a spiral staircase.

ħ-l-f

ħilaf (*i ħilif*) to swear, vow. *ħilaf baʕad ma-yilʕab iqmaar ʔabadan.* He swore that he'd never gamble again. *ħilaf ib-aḷḷa ma-sawwaa.* He swore by God he didn't do it. *ħilaf yamiin maa-la ʕilaaqa biihum.* He took an oath that he has no connection with them.

ħallaf **1.** to make swear, force to swear. *ħallfa ma-yruuħ.* Make him take an oath that he won't go. *ħallafni ʔiδa ʔili ʕilaaqa bil-booga.* He made me swear as to whether I had any connection with the theft. **2.** to put under oath, swear in. *ħallifoo gabuḷ-ma yinṭi šahaadta.* They swore him in before he gave his testimony.

ħaalaf to form an alliance with, become an ally of. *ħaalafnaahum ħatta nigdar nintiṣir ʕala ʔaʕdaaʔna.* We formed an alliance with them so we could conquer our enemies.

tɛallaf to swear revenge. *baɛad-ma nikat biyya, tɛallafit-la.* After he made a fool of me, I swore I'd even the score with him. *tara l-mudiir mitɛallif-lak. ʔaqall ġalṭa yfuṣlak.* I'm telling you the director's got it in for you. The least mistake and he'll fire you. *la-truuɛ lil-beet, tara abuuk mitɛallif-lak.* Don't go home, because your father's laying for you.

tɛaalaf to join together in an alliance, to ally oneself. *d-dawilteen itɛaalfaw ʔaθnaaʔ il-ɛarb.* The two countries allied themselves during the war. *tɛaalafna wiyyahum.* We allied ourselves with them.

ɛilif pl. *ʔaɛlaaf* 1. swearing, oath-taking, oath. 2. pact, alliance.

ɛaliif 1. allied. *d-duwal il-ɛaliifa* the allied nations. 2. (pl. *ɛulafaaʔ*) ally.

ɛalfa alfa, esparto, a long marsh grass commonly dried and used for packing material.

ɛallaaf pl. *-iin, -a* (chronic) oath-taker, vow-maker.

ɛ-l-q

ɛilaq (i *ɛaliq, ɛilaaqa*) 1. to shave. *yiɛliq wičča marrteen yoomiyya.* He shaves his face twice a day. *haaδa yiɛliq raasa bil-muus.* He shaves his head. 2. to shave off. *rabbaa-la liɛya šahreen w-baɛdeen ɛilaqha.* He grew a beard for two months and then shaved it off. 3. to barber, cut hair. *l-ɛallaaq ġiṣal w-ɛilaq raasi.* The barber washed and cut my hair.

ɛalqa, ɛalaqa pl. *-aat* 1. ring (also nosering, earring). 2. wedding band. 3. link (of a chain). 4. circle (also of people). 5. (vulgar) anus.

ɛallaaq pl. *-iin* barber.

ɛilaaqa pl. *-aat* 1. shaving, shave. *makiinat ɛilaaqa* safety razor. 2. barber's trade, barbering.

ɛ-l-q-w-m

ɛalquum Turkish delight.

ɛalquuma pl. *-aat* piece of Turkish delight.

ɛ-l-g

ɛalig pl. *ɛluug* mouth (also of a bottle, etc.). || *ʔiδa triid kull in-naas yismaɛuun hal-iɛčaaya ɛuṭṭha b-ɛalig ɛali.* If you want everyone to hear that story, let Ali know. *laazim ʔaštuġuḷ kull yoom ɛašir saaɛaat liʔan aṭaɛɛim ɛašr iɛluug.* I have to work ten hours every day since I have ten mouths to feed. *ɛalga waṣix.* He's foul mouthed.

ɛ-l-l

ɛall (i *ɛall*) 1. to untie, unfasten, unravel, undo. *ʔiδaafiirak iṭwaal. tigdar itɛill il-ɛugda.* Your fingernails are long. You can untie the knot. || *la-tṭδayyiɛ waktak. haaδa la-yɛill wala-yirbuṭ.* Don't waste your time. He has no power (lit., he neither unties nor knots). 2. to solve, figure out. *tigdar itɛill hal-laġiz?* Can you solve this riddle? *l-xabiir ma-yigdar yɛill rumuuz iš-šafra.* The expert can't solve the key to the code. 3. to dissolve. *hal-lakka ɛala sitirtak ma-yɛillha ʔilla l-kuɛuul.* That spot on your suit can only be dissolved by alcohol. 4. to disband, break up, dissolve. *l-ɛukuuma ɛallat il-majlis.* The government dissolved parliament. 5. to release, set free, let go. *ɛall nafsa w-inhizam.* He freed himself and escaped. *ɛillni! ma-raɛ-anhizim.* Turn me loose! I'm not going to run away. || *ɛill ɛanni! ma-da-tšuufni mašġuul?* Leave me alone! Don't you see I'm busy? 6. to be let off, be let go. *l-ɛummaal raɛ-yɛilluun s-saaɛa ʔarbaɛa.* The workers will get off at four o'clock. *la-tfattiɛ gabuḷ-ma aṣiiɛ ɛallat.* Don't open your eyes before I call okay. 7. to befall, occur, happen. *šuufa š-ɛall bii! git-la la-yištuġuḷ wiyya haj-jamaaɛa.* Look what happened to him! I told him not to go into business with that crowd. 8. (*ɛalaal*) to be allowed, permitted, lawful, legitimate. *ʔuxtak ma-tɛill ɛaleek.* You're not allowed (to marry) your sister. *ma-yɛill lil-misilma tizzawwaj ġeer il-mislim.* It's not permitted for a Moslem girl to marry anyone but a Moslem. 9. to be or become due, payable. *ɛallat il-waɛdа. ma-git-li twaddiini lis-siinama yoom ij-jumɛa?* The promise has come due. Didn't you tell me you'd take me to the movies Friday? 10. to be or become worthwhile, appropriate, timely. *hassa ɛallat ir-rooɛa l-baġdaad. kull garaaybi hnaak.* Now it's worthwhile going to Baghdad. All my relatives are there.

¶ *ɛall ib-maɛall* to serve in the place of, to take the place of, substitute for. *r-ramuḷ yɛill ib-maɛall il-maay bil-wuδu ɛind iδ-δaruura.* Sand takes the place of water in ritual ablutions when necessary. *ʔinta ɛill ib-maɛalla.* You substitute for him.

ɛallal 1. to analyze. *ɛallal il-mawqif ib-maqaal ṭilaɛ bij-jariida l-yoom.* He analyzed the situation in an article which came out in the paper today. **2.** to make a chemical analysis. *ḥallil hal-maḥluul.* Analyze this solution. **3.** to make permissible or lawful, sanction, justify, warrant. *ʔaḷḷa ḥallal iz-zawaaj ib-ʔarbaʕ niswaan.* God sanctioned marriage to four women. *guum ištuġuḷ, ḥallil maʕaašak.* Get to work and justify your salary. **4.** to declare permissible, permit, allow. *d-diin yḥallil ʔakil ʔanwaaʕ il-luḥuum ʕada l-xanziir.* The religion permits the eating of meats other than pork.

nḥall **1.** to be untied. *l-ʕugda nḥallat.* The knot came loose. **2.** to be solved. *l-muškila nḥallat.* The problem was solved.

ḥtall to occupy, take over. *j-jeeš iḥtall il-madiina.* The army occupied the city. *ʔibni ḥtall is-sirdaab kulla l-nafsa.* My son has taken over the whole basement for himself.

ḥall pl. *ḥuluul* **1.** untying, unfastening, undoing. || *l-muʕaawin huwwa lli b-iida l-ḥall wir-rabuṭ ib-had-daaʔira.* The assistant is the one who has the power in this office (lit., in whose hands is the untying and the knotting). **2.** solution. **3.** chemical solution. **4.** dissolution, disbandment, breaking up. **5.** release, liberation, freeing.

ḥalla pl. *-aat, ḥlaal* large, basket-like nest for pigeons.

ḥalaal **1.** allowed, permitted, permissible, allowable, lawful, legal. *haaδa ḥalaal bil-islaam.* That's permissible in Islam. || *ʔibin ḥalaal* 1. nice guy, good fellow, good man. 2. (as a euphemism for *ʔibin ḥaraam,* approx.:) son of a gun. **2.** due, owed, coming. *ḥalaal ʕaleek. ʔuxδa. min kull gaḷbi.* It's rightfully yours. Take it. I really mean it. *ḥalaal ʕalee l-waḍiifa. yistaahil.* The position is rightly his. He deserves it. *l-ijaaza ḥalaal ʕalee liʔan ṣaar-la santeen ma-maaxiδ ʔijaaza.* The leave is due him since he's gone two years without one. **3.** lawful possession. *haaδa mulki w-ḥalaali. ʔagdar asawwi bii š-ma-ariid.* This is my legal property. I can do what I want with it.

maḥall pl. *-aat* **1.** place, location, site, spot. || *loo b-maḥallak, ma-činit aqbal ib-aqall min miit diinaar.* If I'd been in your place, I wouldn't have accepted for less than one hundred dinars. *min astaqiil, minu raḥ-yaaxuδ maḥalli?* When I resign, who's going to take my place? *b-maḥallha* 1. appropriate. *jaab iḥčaaya kulliš ib-maḥallha.* He came out with a very appropriate remark. 2. justified, warranted. *ḥčaaytak muu b-maḥallha.* Your remark was out of place. **2.** room, space. **3.** seat. **4.** desk, work area. **5.** shop, place. **6.** place, opening. || *maḥall imnil-iʕraab* **1.** grammatical function. *hač-čilma ma-ʔilha maḥall imnil-iʕraab ib-haj-jumla.* This word has no function grammatically in this sentence. 2. (hence, by extension) bearing, relevance. *ḥčaaytak ma-ʔilha maḥall imnil-iʕraab.* Your remark has no relevance.

maḥalli **1.** local. *l-ʔidaara l-maḥalliyya* the local administration. **2.** native, indigenous, local. *sinaaʕaat maḥalliyya* local industries. **3.** (pl. only) *maḥalliyyaat* local news. *tigdar tilgi l-maḥalliyyaat biṣ-ṣaḥiifa θ-θaanya.* You can find the local news on the second page. *qreet xabar iz-zilzaal bil-maḥalliyyaat?* Did you read the earthquake story in the local news?

maḥalla pl. *-aat, mḥaaliil* section, part, quarter (of a city), neighborhood.

ḥallaan, ḥillaan (coll.) **1.** bale(s) of pressed dates. *tamr il-ḥillaan* dates in the bale. **2.** the basket-like wrapping of the bale, woven of palm leaves.

ḥallaana, ḥillaana pl. *-aat* **1.** unit noun of *ḥallaan.* **2.** (by extension, jokingly) derrière (vulgar).

taḥliil pl. *-aat, taḥaaliil* analysis. *taḥliil nafsi* psychoanalysis. *sawwoo-la taḥliil nafsi.* They psychoanalyzed him. *taḥliil damm* blood test. *taḥliil maraḍi* a medical analysis. *muxtabar it-taḥliilaat il-maraḍiyya* medical analysis laboratory.

nḥilaal slackening, loosening, relaxing. *nḥilaal il-ʔaxlaaq* the decline in morals.

ḥtilaal occupation (mil.).

maḥluul **1.** loose, loosened. *burġi maḥluul* a loose screw. **2.** untied, unfastened, free, at large, loose. *qiiṭaan qundartak maḥluul.* Your shoelace is untied. *la-txušš bil-ḥadiiqa, tara č-čalib maḥluul.* Don't go in the garden, because the dog's loose. **3.** weakened, exhausted, languid. *ʔaani maḥluul il-yoom; ma-biyya ḥeel aštuġuḷ.* I'm tired today; I've got no energy to work. **4.** (pl. *maḥaaliil*) solution (chem.). *maḥluul ḥaamḍi* an acidic solution.

muḥallil pl. *-iin* analyzer, analyst.

minḥall loosened, relaxed. *l-axlaaq minḥalla b-hal-balad.* Morals are loose in this country.

ḥ-l-m

ḥilam (*a ḥilim*) **1.** to dream. *ḥilamit il-baarḥa raḥ-aṣiir malik.* I dreamed yesterday that I was going to become a king. *ḥilamit biik il-baarḥa.* I dreamed about you yesterday. **2.** to daydream. *ma-štiġaḷ kullši hal-yoom; da-yiḥlam ib-zawaaja.* He didn't do a thing today; he's dreaming about his marriage. || *da-tiḥlam. baʕad ʕišriin sana ma-tṣiir ṭabiib.* You're dreaming. In twenty years you won't become a doctor.

tḥallam to muse, reflect, daydream. *da-yitḥallam ib-safirta l-paariis.* He's daydreaming about his trip to Paris.

staḥlam to have a nocturnal emission.

ḥilim pl. *ʔaḥlaam* dream. *yʕiiš ib-dinya l-ʔaḥlaam.* He lives in a dream world.

ḥilma pl. *-aat, ḥilam* nipple, teat, mammilla (of a female).

ḥalmaan dreaming, in a state of dreaming. *ʔinta ḥalmaan. ma-aku hiiči šii.* You're dreaming. There's no such thing.

ḥ-l-n

ḥallaan, ḥillaan, etc., see under *ḥ-l-l.*

ḥ-l-w

ḥila (*a ḥalaa, ḥala*) **1.** to become sweet. *kull-ma txalli r-raggi yibqa b-hirša ʔazyad, yiḥla.* The longer you leave the watermelon on the vine, the sweeter it gets. **2.** to become pleasant, nice, enjoyable. *min jaa majiid, ḥilat il-gaʕda.* When Majid came, the session became pleasant. *l-gaʕda ʕaš-šaṭṭ tiḥla wakt il-miġrib.* Sitting by the river gets pleasant at sunset. *baġdaad tiḥla bir-rabiiʕ.* Baghdad gets pleasant in the spring. **3.** to become pretty. *da-tiḥla yoom ʕala yoom.* She's getting prettier day by day.

ḥalla **1.** to make sweet, sweeten. *la-tḥalli č-čaay maali zaayid.* Don't sweeten my tea too much. **2.** to make pleasant, nice, enjoyable. *l-ġina yḥalli l-ḥayaat.* Wealth makes life more enjoyable. **3.** to make pretty, beautify. *nafnuufič il-ʔaswad yḥalliič ʔazyad imnil-laax.* Your black dress becomes you more than the other. *l-laaytaat ʕas-sayyaara mḥallyatha.* The lights on the car have improved its appearance.

ḥalaa, ḥala **1.** sweetness. **2.** pleasantness, niceness. **3.** beauty, prettiness.

ḥilu **1.** sweet, sweetened. *čaay ḥilu* sweetened tea. || *ṃaay ḥilu* fresh water, free of brackish qualities. **2.** pleasant, nice, enjoyable. *ḥači ḥilu* pleasant talk. *da-yiṣruf ib-hal-ifluus il-ḥilwa.* He's spending all that nice money. **3.** handsome, good-looking, pretty. *bnayya ḥilwa* a pretty girl. **4.** (an exclamation of approval, also used sarcastically, approx.:) great! wonderful! *ḥilu! laʕad raḥ-atwannas haṣ-ṣeef.* Wonderful! Then I'm going to have a good time this summer. *ḥilu! ḥilu! leeš ḥarrakt il-malik? muu raḥ-tixṣar!* Great, great! Why'd you move the king? You're going to lose now! **5.** nicely. *šuufha šloon timši ḥilu.* Look how nicely she walks. *čaan da-yidrus ḥilu ḥilu ʔila ʔan jaa ṣadiiqa.* He was studying quite nicely till his friend came. **6.** (pl. *ḥilwiin*) buddy, pal. *ʔahlan bil-ḥilu! šloonak yaaba?* Welcome, old buddy! How are you, man?

ḥilwa pl. *-aat* pretty girl. *taʕaali yaa ḥilwa; nṭii boosa l-abuuč.* Come on, pretty girl; give your father a kiss! *ḥilwat il-maḥalla* the belle of the neighborhood.

ḥalawiyyaat (pl. only) sweet pastries.

ḥalaawa **1.** halvah, a flaky confection of crushed sesame seeds in a base of honey or other syrup. || *ḥalaawat ṣuluḥ* **1.** peace offering. *ma-daam itṣaalaḥna, xalli ʔaġaddiik ḥalaawat ṣuluḥ.* Since we've made up, let me take you to lunch as a peace offering. 2. present to a mediator. *ʕaliyya nṭatha hadiyya l-ʔummha ḥalaawat ṣuluḥ li-ʔan saalḥatha wiyya rajilha.* Aliya gave her mother a present as a token for mediation because she reconciled her and her husband. **2.** an easy thing, a snap. *š-šuġuḷ ib-ʔawwal hal-isbuuʕ čaan ḥalaawa, laakin ṣaar ṣaʕub baʕdeen.* The work at the beginning of this week was a piece of cake, but it got hard later.

ʔaḥla **1.** sweeter, sweetest. **2.** more or most pleasant, etc. **3.** more or most handsome, etc.

ḥ-m-d

ḥimad (*i ḥamid*) to praise, laud, extol. *mudiirak yḥibbak w-yḥimdak.* Your boss likes you and praises you. *l-muʕallim yiḥmid biik ihwaaya.* The teacher praises you a lot. *ʔiḥmid ʔaḷḷa w-šukra! š-itriid baʕad?* Praise God and thank Him! What else do you want?

ḥamid praise, commendation. *l-ḥamdu lil-laah, l-ḥamdilla.* Praise be to God!

Thank God! *l-ḥamdu lil-laah, rijaʕ saalim!* Thank God, he returned safely!

ḥamiid praiseworthy, laudable, commendable. *ṣifa ḥamiida* a laudable quality, a virtue. || *rabbak ḥamiid, ma-sawwaanna šii.* Thank goodness, he didn't do anything to us. *w-ʔalla l-ḥamiid, maa-li ʕilaaqa bii!* My goodness, I had nothing to do with it!

ḥamaad desert.

mḥammadi pl. *-iyyiin* a follower of Mohammed, a Moslem.

ḥ-m-r

ḥammar **1.** to make red, redden, color red. *l-ʕaruus ḥammurat ixduudha zaayid.* The bride put too much rouge on her cheeks. **2.** to roast. *bdaal-ma tfawwirha lid-dijaaja, ḥammurha ʕan-naar.* Instead of boiling the chicken, roast it on the fire. **3.** to brown. *d-dijaaja mistawiya laakin rajjiʕha ʕan-naar w-ḥammurha.* The chicken's done, but put it back on the fire and brown it.

ḥmarr to turn red, become red, redden. *ḥmarrat ʕeena min gadd-ma yifrukha.* His eyes turned red from his rubbing them so much. *ḥmarr wičča mnil-xajal.* He blushed from embarrassment.

ḥimri a kind of reddish-colored fish.

ḥimriin: jibaal ḥimriin a group of mountains in northern Iraq.

ḥumra **1.** redness, red color, red coloration. **2.** rouge, lipstick. *ḥumrat išfaaf* lipstick.

ḥamaar **1.** reddening, blushing. **2.** redness, red coloration.

ḥmaar pl. *ḥamiir* donkey, ass (also as a derogatory term for a human being). *haaδa šinu, hal-iḥmaar?* What does he matter, that jackass?

ʔaḥmar fem. *ḥumra* pl. *ḥumur* red. || *moot ʔaḥmar* violent death. *haay šloon waδiifa! moot ʔaḥmar!* What a job! It's killing!

mḥammar roasted. *dijaaja mḥammara* a roasted chicken.

[1]ḥ-m-s

ḥimas (*i ḥamis*) to excite, stir up. *ḥimasta min gumit ʔaḥči wiyya ṣadiiqta.* I got him all worked up when I started talking with his girl friend.

ḥammas to excite, arouse, stir, make enthusiastic, work up. *l-moosiiqa l-ʕaskariyya ḥammsatni.* The military music stirred me. *ḥammasni ʕala d-duxuul bis-sibaaq.* He made me enthusiastic about entering the race. *xiṭaaba ḥammas ij-jamaahiir, w-gaamaw yhawwsuun.* His speech stirred up the crowd, and they began to go wild.

tḥammas **1.** to be excited, aroused, stirred. *tḥammasit min simaʕt il-xiṭaab.* I was stirred when I heard the speech. **2.** to become enthusiastic, eager, zealous. *tḥammas ihwaaya lil-mašruuʕ w-čaan ʕinda stiʕdaad yuṣruf ifluus.* He grew very enthusiastic toward the project and was ready to spend money.

ḥamaas, ḥamaasa enthusiasm, ardor, fervor, zeal, fanaticism. *b-ḥamaas* with enthusiasm, enthusiastically.

*ḥamaasi** stirring, rousing, thrilling. *ʔanaašiid madrasiyya ḥamaasiyya* stirring school songs.

taḥammus enthusiasm. *b-taḥammus* with enthusiasm, enthusiastically.

mitḥammis enthusiastic, ardent, fiery, zealous. *qawmi mitḥammis* an ardent nationalist.

[2]ḥ-m-s

ḥimas (*i ḥamis*) to fry (meat) in its own juices (without oil or grease). *ḥimsat il-laḥam w-baʕdeen xallat ʕalee mayy.* She fried the meat and then put water in it. || *raḥ-anzaʕ il-yalag. š-šamis ḥimsatni.* I'm going to take off the vest. The sun has broiled me.

ḥamis frying.

ḥamsa pl. *-aat* i. n. of *ḥamis.*

ḥamiis **1.** chunks of meat fried in their own juice with onion. **2.** pieces of liver broiled on a skewer.

maḥmuus **1.** = *ḥamiis.* **2.** boiled heart, lungs, and liver.

ḥ-m-ṣ

ḥammaṣ to roast. *ḥammuṣ il-gahwa zeen gabul-ma tiṭḥanha.* Roast the coffee well before you grind it.

tḥammaṣ to be roasted. *xalli d-dijaaja titḥammaṣ zeen bil-firin.* Let the chicken get well roasted in the oven.

ḥummuṣ chick-peas. || *ḥummuṣ b-iṭḥiina* a dish made of ground chickpeas and sesame oil.

ḥ-m-δ̣

ḥumaδ̣ (*u ḥamuδ̣*) to sour, become sour or unpleasant. *min ṣaar waziir ʔaxlaaqa ḥumδ̣at.* When he became a minister his manners went bad. *djaadlaw išwayya w-baʕdeen ḥumδ̣ad il-qaδ̣iyya.* They argued a little and then the matter really turned sour. *ḥumδ̣at ʕaad! ṣaar-lak isbuuʕ itwaaʕidni bil-ifluus.* It's gone too far! You've been promising me the money for a week.

ħammað̣ **1.** to sour, become sour. *xalli l-ħaliib biθ-θallaja gabuḷ-ma yħammuð̣.* Put the milk in the refrigerator before it sours. **2.** to make (matters) unpleasant. *yeezi ʕaad! muu ħammað̣itha!* Enough now! You've gone too far!

ħumuuð̣a **1.** sourness. **2.** acidity.

ħaamuð̣ **1.** sour, acid. *l-ħiṣrim ħaamuð̣ kulliš.* Green grapes are very sour. *nuumi ħaamuð̣* lemon. || *čaay ħaamuð̣* lemon tea, a hot drink made by boiling crushed dried lemons. **2.** sour, crabby. *nafsa ħaamð̣a; la-tiṭlub minna šii.* He's crabby; don't ask him for anything. *ma-tigdar tiħči wiyyaa; ʔaxlaaqa ħaamð̣a.* You can't talk to him; he's a sourpuss. **3.** (pl. *ħawaamið̣*) acid. **4.** = *čaay ħaamuð̣.*

ħ-m-q

ħumaq (*u ħamuq*) **1.** to be or become angry, mad, furious. *ħumaq bil-ʕajal w-ṭilaʕ imnil-ġurfa.* He got mad right away and left the room. **2.** to anger, make mad, furious. *ħumaqni bil-ħači maala.* He angered me with his talk.

nħumaq to get angry, mad, furious. *nħumaq ʕalayya li-ʔan ma-kammalt iš-šuġuḷ maali.* He got mad at me because I hadn't finished my work.

*ħamaqi** pl. *-iyya* **1.** hot-tempered, easily angered, excitable. **2.** hot-tempered person.

ħamaaqa **1.** stupidity, foolishness. **2.** (pl. *-aat*) stupid, foolish act or deed.

ħamqaan angry, upset, mad. *ʔismaʕ ħissa; da-yṣayyiħ. ybayyin hamm ħamqaan.* Listen to his voice; he's shouting. Looks like he's mad again.

ʔaħmaq fem. *ħamqa* pl. *ħumuq, ħumaqaaʔ, ħamqiin.* **1.** dumb, stupid, foolish, silly. **2.** fool, simpleton, idiot, jerk.

ʔaħmaq more or most foolish.

maħmuuq angry, mad, furious. *leeš maħmuuq? ma-qiṣadha.* Why are you angry? He didn't mean it.

ħ-m-l

ħimal (*i ħamil*) **1.** to bear, hold, support. *hal-kursi ma-yħimlak.* This chair won't bear your weight. **2.** to bear, stand, endure, tolerate. *duktoor, ma-agdar aħmil baʕad. bannijni.* Doctor, I can't take any more. Anesthetize me. *ma-agdar aħimla l-haað̣a. yilġi ʕala ṭuul.* I can't take him. He chatters constantly. *la-tšaaqii tara ma-yiħmil.* Don't tease him because he can't take it. *ħimalha lil-iħčaaya li-ʔan ma-raad ysawwi laġwa.* He took the remark because he didn't want to make a commotion. **3.** to accept, entertain, harbor. *yiħmil ʔafkaar šiyuuʕiyya.* He harbors communist ideas. *ʕaqli ma-yiħmilha. mustaħiil.* My mind won't accept it. It's unbelievable. **4.** to become pregnant. *ħimlat minna.* She got pregnant by him. **5.** to bear, bear fruit. *šijrat il-purtuqaal ħimlat has-sana.* The orange tree bore fruit this year. **6.** /with *ʕala*/ to attack, launch or make an attack against. *min simaʕ raħ-anaafsa ʕal-wað̣iifa, ħimal ʕalayya giddaam in-naas.* When he heard I'm going to compete with him for the position, he attacked me in front of everyone. **7.** to take, take hold. *j-jidri maalak ma-ħimal. laazim tið̣rub marrt il-luxx.* Your vaccination didn't take. You'll have to be vaccinated again.

ħammal **1.** to load. *ħammilaw il-loori raġġi.* They loaded the truck with watermelons. **2.** to load, burden, impose on. *l-mudiir ħammal il-muʕaawin maala masʔuuliyyat kull il-aġlaaṭ bil-iħsaabaat.* The director saddled his assistant with responsibility for all the mistakes in the accounts. *ʕaawanni biš-šuġuḷ w-ħammalni minniyya. hassa yoomiyya yriidni aʕaawna.* He helped me with the job and imposed an obligation. Now he wants me to help him everyday. *ħammal l-ifluus diinaar faayiz.* He added a dinar interest to the money. **3.** to ship, transport. *ħammal ʕišriin maaṭoor ħunṭa lil-baṣra.* He shipped twenty motor barges of wheat to Basra. *raħ-adizz-lak ħammaaleen ħatta tħammil kull il-ġaraað̣.* I will send you two porters so you can transport all the things. **4.** to become infected. *l-ħabbaaya raħ-itħammil ʔiða ma-ddaawiiha b-surʕa.* The pimple will get infected if you don't treat it quickly. **5.** to take hold, take. *j-jidri maalak ma-ħammal.* Your smallpox vaccination didn't take.

tħammal **1.** to be loaded. *ʔariid il-loori yitħammal gabḷ il-muġrub.* I want the truck to be loaded before sundown. **2.** to bear, hold, support, take. *haj-jisir ma-yitħammal looriyyaat.* This bridge won't take trucks. **3.** to bear, stand, sustain, endure, tolerate, stomach. *ma-yitħammal ʔalam.* He can't stand pain. *minu yitħammal hiiči mara?* Who can stand such a woman? *tħammal ir-razaala w-sikat.* He took the insult and kept quiet. *l-waðiʕ ma-yitħammal hiiči ʔijraaʔaat.*

The situation won't allow such measures. **4.** to undergo, suffer. *tḥammilat ihwaaya b-maraḏ ibinha.* She suffered a lot during her son's illness. **5.** to accept, receive, admit, entertain. *ʕaqli ma-yitḥammal raḥ-ybaṭṭil.* My mind won't accept that he's going to quit. *ʕaqli ma-yitḥammal ir-riyaaḏiyyaat.* My mind has no capacity for mathematics.

tḥaamal /with *ʕala*/ to attack, criticize unjustly, pick on. *ma-aku ḥaaja titḥaamal ʕalee b-ġiyaaba.* There's no need for you to attack him in his absence. *l-mudiir ʕala ṭuul yitḥaamal ʕalayya.* The principal always picks on me.

nḥimal to be borne, stood, endured, tolerated, stomached. *l-wujaʕ ma-yinḥimil.* The pain is unbearable. *ḥčaaytak ma-tinḥimil. ʔida tguulha marrt il-lux, keefak.* Your remark was unbearable. If you say it again, you're asking for it. *damma θigiil; ma-yinḥimil.* He's a stick in the mud; he's unbearable.

ḥtimal **1.** to bear, stand, endure, take. *minu yiḥtimil hal-ʕaḏaab?* Who could stand this suffering? *šloon iḥtimalit kull hal-mudda bila mara?* How'd you stand it all this time without a wife? *ma-agdar aḥtimla. ḥačya ysawwiini ʕaṣabi.* I can't stand him. His talk makes me mad. *leeš iḥtimalt il-ihaana? čaan laazin iḏḏurba.* Why'd you take the insult? You should have hit him. **2.** to accept, receive, encompass. *l-ʕaqil ma-yiḥtimil quṣṣta.* The mind boggles at his story. **3.** to feel that something is possible, conceivable, or likely. *ʔaḥtimil yiji l-yoom.* I suppose he'll come today. || *yuḥtamal* it's possible, it's conceivable. *yuḥtamal yiji baačir.* It's possible he'll come tomorrow.

ḥamil pregnancy.

ḥimil pl. *ḥmuul* cargo, load, burden.

ḥamla pl. *-aat* **1.** attack, criticism. **2.** campaign. *ḥamla ntixaabiyya* election campaign. *ḥamla ʕaskariyya* military campaign. **3.** the ceremony of carrying the bride's belongings from her parents' house to the groom's house.

ḥammaal pl. *-iin, ḥmaamiil* porter, carrier.

ḥmaala **1.** porter's trade, occupation of being a porter. **2.** (pl. *-aat*) porterage, fee for carrying.

ḥumuula pl. *-aat* **1.** load capacity, load limit, capacity. **2.** tonnage (of a vessel).

ḥamuula pl. *ḥamaaʔil* stock, family. *ʔibin ḥamuula* a man from good stock.

taḥammul **1.** endurance, tolerance, resistance. *taḥammul liṭ-ṭaʕab* physical endurance, staying power. *taḥammul lil-barid* resistance to cold. **2.** capacity, carrying capacity, strength. *taḥammul il-ifyuuz* the load capacity of the fuse. *taḥammul il-ʔasaasaat ʔakθar šii ʔarbaʕ quuṭ.* The bearing capacity of the foundations is at the most four floors.

ḥtimaal **1.** tolerance, toleration, endurance, resistance. *ḥtimaal lil-ḥarr.* tolerance for heat. **2.** probability, likelihood, potentiality. *ʔaku ḥtimaal tumṭur baačir.* There's a good chance it will rain tomorrow.

muḥtamal **1.** probable, likely. *laazim čaan yooṣal gabuḷ saaʕteen. sayyaarathum ʕatiiga; muḥtamal xurbat.* They should've arrived two hours ago. Their car's old; it's likely it broke down. *muḥtamal yruuḥ biṭ-ṭayyaara l-baġdaad.* He'll likely take the plane to Baghdad. **2.** possible, conceivable. *muḥtamal tumṭur baačir.* It's possible it'll rain tomorrow. *muḥtamal, laakin haaḏa ma-yirkab ṭiyyaara ʔabadan.* It's possible, but he never goes by plane.

ḥaamil pl. *ḥawaamil* **1.** pregnant. *zawijta ḥaamil* (or *ḥaamla*). His wife's pregnant. **2.** (pl. *ḥamala*) holder. *ḥaamil šahaada ʕaalya* a holder of a college degree (or better). **3.** holder, stand, support. *ḥaamil ʔanaabiib ixtibaar* test tube stand.

ḥaamila pl. *-aat* **1.** pregnant woman. **2.** device for carrying or holding. || *ḥaamilat ṭaaʔiraat* aircraft carrier.

mḥammal loaded. *l-loori mḥammal ʔakθar imnil-laazim.* The truck's overloaded.

ḥ-m-m

ḥumma pl. *-ayaat* fever.

ḥamaam (coll.) pigeon(s), dove(s).

ḥamaama pl. *-aat* pigeon, dove.

ḥammaam pl. *-aat* **1.** bath, Turkish bath. *ḥammaam ʕaamm* public bath. **2.** bathroom, room for bathing.

maḥmuum feverish. *l-walad ṣaar-la yoomeen maḥmuum.* The boy's been feverish for two days.

ḥ-m-n

ḥimminiin chicken lice, small parasites found on chickens.

[1]ḥ-m-y

ḥima (*a ḥami*) to become hot, warm. *šuuf il-mayy ḥima loo baʕad.* See if the water has gotten hot yet. || *ʔinti leeš* ḥima ḥammaamič? maḥḥad jaab ʔismič. Don't get your water hot! No one mentioned your name. **2.** (by extension) to become heated. *l-munaaqaša ḥimat w-gaamaw yṣayyḥuun.* The discussion became heated and they began to shout. **3.** to heat, heat up, make warm. *ruuḥi ḥmii-li l-ḥammaam!* Go heat the bath for me!

ḥamma to heat, make warm. *ḥammii-li šwayya ṃaay.* Heat me some water.

tḥamma to warm oneself. *taʕaal itḥamma yamm in-naar.* Come get warm by the fire.

ḥumma pl. *-ayaat* see under *ḥ-m-m.*

ḥamaawa heat, warmth.

ḥamiyya **1.** zeal, ardor, fervor. *ḥamiyya qawmiyya* nationalistic zeal. **2.** enthusiasm. *ṣaaḥib ḥamiyya* a man with enthusiasm, dedicated man. **3.** passion, rage, fury.

ḥaami warm, heated, violent, fierce. *munaaqaša ḥaamya* a heated argument. *liʕib ḥaami* a fierce game.

²*ḥ-m-y*

ḥima (*i ḥami, ḥimaaya*) **1.** to protect, defend, shelter, shield. *l-labwa tiḥmi ʔašbaalha.* The lioness protects her cubs. *j-jeeš yiḥmi l-waṭan mnil-ʔaʕdaaʔ.* The army defends the country from her enemies.

ḥaama **1.** to defend, protect. *la-txaaf; ʔaxuuk ič-čibiir yḥaamiik.* Don't worry; your older brother will protect you. **2.** /with *l-*/ to stand up for. *leeš da-tḥaamii-la? muu haaḏa muu xooš imwaḏ̣-ḏ̣af.* Why do you stick up for him? He's really not a good employee.

ḥtima to seek protection, take shelter or refuge. *j-jaahil iḥtima biyya mnič-čalib.* The child took shelter behind me from the dog. *xall niḥtimi bil-ḥaayiṭ imnil-hawa.* Let's take shelter from the wind behind the wall.

ḥimaaya **1.** protecting, protection. **2.** (pl. *-aat*) protectorate (pol.).

ḥaami pl. *-iin, ḥumaat* protector, defender, guardian. || *ḥaamiiha ḥaraamiiha.* The protector turned out a thief.

ḥaamiya pl. *-aat* **1.** protectress. **2.** garrison (mil.).

*maḥmi** protected. *l-malif maali maḥmi zeen bil-fiil.* My king is well protected by the bishop.

maḥmiyya pl. *-aat* protectorate (pol.).

muḥaamaat legal profession, practice of law.

muḥaami pl. *-iin* lawyer, attorney.

muḥaamiya pl. *-aat* woman lawyer.

³*ḥ-m-y*

ḥama pl. *ḥimyaan* father-in-law. *ḥamaaya* my father-in-law. *ḥamaa* his father-in-law.

ḥama pl. *ḥamawaat* mother-in-law. *ḥamaati* my mother-in-law. *ḥamaata* his mother-in-law.

ḥ-n-j-r

ḥinjara pl. *ḥanaajir* larynx, throat.

ḥ-n-č

ḥinič pl. *ḥnuuč* chin.

ḥ-n-ṭ

ḥannaṭ **1.** to mummify, embalm. *l-maṣriyyiin il-qudamaaʔ čaanaw yḥanniṭuun mootaahum.* The ancient Egyptians used to mummify their dead. **2.** to stuff, preserve. *min ymuut haṭ-ṭeer raḥ-aḥanniṭa w-aḥuṭṭa b-ġurfat il-xuṭṭaar.* When this bird dies I'm going to have him stuffed and put him in the parlor. *bil-muxtabar, yḥanniṭuun il-ḥiyaaya b-saaʔil kiimyaawi.* In the lab, they preserve snakes in a chemical solution.

ḥunṭa wheat.

ḥunṭaaya pl. *-aat* grain of wheat.

ḥ-n-ḏ̣-l

ḥanḏ̣al colocynth, a kind of very bitter wild gourd. || *murr ḥanḏ̣al* as bitter as colocynth.

ḥ-n-f

*ḥanafi** **1.** Hanafitic, pertaining to the theological school founded by Abu Hanifah. **2.** (pl. *-iyya, -iyyiin*) Hanafi, member of the Hanafite school.

ḥanafiyya pl. *-aat* faucet, spigot.

ḥ-n-q-b-a-z

ḥanqabaaz pl. *-iyya* juggler.

ḥ-n-g-r-y-ṣ

ḥingareeṣa pl. *-aat* orgasm, climax.

ḥ-n-n

ḥann (*i ḥaniin*) **1.** to long, yearn, be anxious. *da-aḥinn il-ayyaam it-talmaḏa.* I'm longing for my student days. *da-aḥinn il-šoofatha marrt il-lux.* I'm anxious to see her again. **2.** (*ḥanaan*) to feel compassion, sympathy, to have mercy, take pity. *l-muʕallim ḥann ʕalayya w-najjaḥni.* The teacher took pity on me and passed me. *galba ḥann ʕalayya w-inṭaani l-qappuuṭ albisa.* His heart went out to me and he gave me the overcoat to wear.

ḥannan to fill with compassion, sympathy, or tenderness, to soften. *ʔaḷḷa yḥannin galb il-muʕallim ʕaleek.* May God soften the teacher's heart toward you.

ḥanaan **1.** sympathy, love, affection, tenderness. **2.** compassion, pity.

ḥaniin 1. softhearted, tenderhearted, compassionate. *šuufa šloon ḥaniin! min šaaf ʔaxuu yiḥtaaj ifluus, nṭaa kull ifluusa.* Look how compassionate he is! When he saw his brother needed money, he gave him all his money. 2. moving, touching, tender. *hal-qaari l-qurʔaan ḥissa ḥaniin.* That Koran reader's voice is moving.

ḥannuuna pl. *-aat* small loaf of bread, usually made from the last bit of dough.

maḥanna 1. sympathy, tenderness. 2. compassion, pity.

ʔaḥann 1. more or most compassionate, etc. 2. more or most moving, touching, etc.

[1]ḥ-n-y

ḥina (*i ḥani*) 1. to bow, bend forward, tilt forward. *ʔiḥni raasak ḥatta azayyin rugubtak.* Bend your head forward so I can shave your neck. 2. to bend, bow, curve. *l-kubur ḥina ḍahra.* Age bent his back.

nḥina 1. to bend, curve, twist, turn. *ṭ-ṭariiq yinḥini lil-yisaar minnaa.* The road curves to the left here. 2. to bow. *l-yaabaaniyyiin, min ysallimuun ʕala waaḥid, yinḥinuu-la.* The Japanese bow to a person when they greet him. 3. to bend forward. *nḥina w-šaal il-qalam imnil-gaaʕ.* He bent forward and picked up the pencil from the ground. *raasa nḥina mnin-naʕaas.* His head bent forward from fatigue.

ḥunuw sympathy, compassion, tenderness, affection. *ḥunuwwa ʕala wilda* his affection for his children.

minḥini 1. bent, bowed. *ḍahra minḥini mnil-kubur.* His back is bent with age. 2. leaning, inclined. *haš-šajara minḥanya w-raḥ-toogaʕ. laazim il-hawa čaan kulliš qawi l-baarḥa.* That tree is leaning over and it's about to fall. The wind must have been real strong yesterday.

[2]ḥ-n-y

ḥanna to dye red (with henna), to apply henna to. *ḥannaw ʔiideen il-ʕaruus w-rijleeha.* They dyed the bride's hands and feet with henna.

tḥanna to apply henna to oneself, to use henna as a cosmetic. *banaat il-madaaris ma-yitḥannuun gabuḷ zawaajhum.* Educated girls don't put on henna before their marriage.

ḥinna henna.

ḥ-w-b

ḥooba pl. *-aat* 1. divine retribution, punishment by God. *hal-ʕaalim id-diini ʔila ḥoobta.* That religious man can summon the wrath of God. *qatl ič-čalib ʔila ḥooba. titlaggaaha b-ʔahlak.* Killing the dog will bring retribution. You'll catch it through your family. *šuufa šloon ʕimat ʕeena? haay ḥoobt il-ʔaytaam il-ʔakal ifluushum.* See how he went blind? That's retribution for the orphans whose money he took. 2. revenge, satisfaction. *ʔaxaδit ḥoobti minna. buṣaṭṭa baṣṭa zeena li-ʔan fitan ʕalayya ʕind il-mudiir.* I got my revenge on him. I beat him up because he told the principal on me.

ḥ-w-t

ḥuut pl. *ḥiitaan* whale.

ḥ-w-j

ḥuwaj (*i ḥaaja*) to be necessary. *ma-yiḥwij itwaṣṣilni lil-maṭaar, li-ʔan iš-šarika raḥ-itdizz-li sayyaara.* It isn't necessary for you to take me to the airport, because the company's going to send a car for me. *ma-yiḥtaaj idgul-la l-abuuk; ʔagdar anṭiik l-ifluus.* There's no need to tell your father; I can give you the money.

ḥtaaj 1. to need, want, require, be in want of. *ʔiδa tiḥtaaj šii, gul-li.* If you need anything, tell me. *ʔaani ma-miḥtaaj ʔila ʔayy šii hassa.* I don't need anything right now. *qaδiyyat taʕyiinak yiḥtaaj-ilha dafʕa.* The matter of your appointment requires a push.

ḥaaja pl. *-aat* 1. need, necessity. *ʔaku ḥaaja tsawwi hiiči?* Is there any need to do this? *la-taaxδ il-bariina; ʔili ḥaaja biiha.* Don't take the drill; I need it. *maaku ḥaaja tizʕal. siʔaltak suʔaal basiiṭ.* There's no need to get mad. I asked you a simple question. *ʕind il-ḥaaja* in time of need, when necessary. *ma-aku maaniʕ tistaʕmil sayyaarti ʕind il-ḥaaja.* There's no objection to your using my car if necessary. *b-ḥaaja ʔila* in need of, lacking. *l-muxtabar ib-ḥaaja ʔila ʔadawaat jidiida.* The laboratory's in need of new equipment. 2. pressing need, neediness, poverty, destitution. *loo maa l-ḥaaja, ma-aqbal hiiči šuġuḷ.* Were it not for pressing need, I wouldn't accept such a job. 3. need, necessary article, requisite. *ʔuxuδ ḥaajtak w-xalli l-baaqi.* Take what you need and leave the rest. 4. matter, concern, business, job. *riḥit ʕaš-šaxiṣ illi dazzeetni ʕalee w-giδa ḥaajti.* I went to the person you sent me to and he took care of my business. 5. concern, interest, responsibility. *ʔaani maa-li ḥaaja bil-ġeer. ʔiδa yirduun yitbaaraḥuun, keefhum.* I've got no concern with the others. If they want to donate, let them. *š-ma triid sawwi. ˀaani maa-li ḥaaja.* Do whatever you want. I'm not responsible. *la-txaaf itfuut min yamm iš-šurṭi. maa-la ḥaaja biik.* Don't be afraid of going by the policeman. He has no concern with you. **6.** (pl. only) wares, merchandise. *ybiiʕ ḥaajaat ˀajnabiyya.* He sells foreign goods.

ḥaajiyyaat (pl. only) goods, wares, merchandise.

miḥtaaj pl. *-iin* **1.** in need, needy, poor, destitute. **2.** needy person, poor person.

ḥ-w-č

ḥaač (*u ḥyaača*) = *ḥaak*, etc., which see under *ḥ-w-k*.

ḥ-w-d

ḥaad (*u ḥood*) to drive, herd, urge on. *ḥuuda lil-iḥṣaan liṭ-ṭoola ḥatta nsarrja.* Drive the horse to the stable so we can saddle him. *ḥuud il-ihwaayiš il-baab il-bistaan.* Drive the cows to the orchard gate. *š-šurṭa ḥaadat iṭ-ṭullaab min is-saaḥa ˀila l-markaz.* The police herded the students from the square to the station. || *kull-man yḥuud in-naar il-guruṣṭa.* Everyone looks out for his own interests (lit., everyone pushes the fire toward his own loaf). **2.** to turn aside, drive away, drive off. *ḥuud izmaaylak. da-yaakluun il-warid.* Drive your donkeys away. They're eating the flowers.

ḥ-w-r

ḥawwar to change, alter, amend, modify, remodel, transform, reorganize. *ruuḥ gul-la lli git-lak-iyyaa biḏ-ḏabuṭ. la-tḥawwir šii.* Go tell him what I told you exactly. Don't change anything. *ˀiḥči ʕadil. la-tḥawwir il-kalaam.* Talk straight. Don't alter the words.

tḥawwar pass. of *ḥawwar*.

ḥaara pl. *-aat* neighborhood, area, section (of a city).

*ḥawaari** disciple, follower.

ḥuuriyya pl. *-aat* **1.** houri. *ḥilwa miθl il-ḥuuriyya* very pretty. **2.** nymph. *ḥuuriyyat il-baḥar* mermaid, sea nymph.

miḥwar pl. *maḥaawir* pivot, core, heart, center. *huwwa čaan miḥwar il-ḥadiiθ.* He was the central figure of the discussion.

muḥaawara pl. *-aat* dialogue, conversation, talk.

ḥ-w-z

ḥaaz (*u ḥiyaaza*) see under *ḥ-y-z*.

ḥ-w-š

ḥaaš (*u ḥooš*) to gather, collect, amass, accumulate. *ruuḥ ḥuuš išwayya ḥašiiš lil-xaruuf.* Go gather some grass for the sheep.

ḥooš pl. *ḥwaaš* **1.** court, courtyard, patio. **2.** house.

ḥ-w-ṣ

ḥaaṣ (*u ḥooṣ*) to fidget, be restless, nervous. *š-biik da-tḥuuṣ? ˀašu kull daqiiqa raakiḏ lid-darub.* Why are you fidgeting? Every minute you run to the street. *š-aku ʕindak da-tḥuuṣ? hassa nruuḥ.* Why are you so restless? We're going right away. || *da-yḥuuṣ ʕala hal-waḏiifa.* He's really itching for that job.

ḥ-w-ṣ-l

ḥooṣla pl. *-aat, ḥawaaṣil* **1.** craw, crop, gizzard (of a bird). **2.** patience, endurance. *haaḏa ma-ʕinda ḥooṣla. yizhag bil-ʕajal.* He doesn't have any patience. He gets disgusted quickly.

ḥ-w-ḏ

ḥooḏ pl. *ḥwaaḏ* **1.** basin, trough, tank. **2.** pool, pond. **3.** seat of a car. *l-ḥooḏ il-warraani* the back seat. || *ˀaxaḏni ḥooḏ. ma-nṭaani majaal ˀaḥči.* He talked incessantly. He didn't give me a chance to speak.

ḥ-w-ṭ

ḥaaṭ (*u ḥooṭ*) to surround, encircle, encompass. *ḥaaṭoo ġeer ḥooṭa w-ma-gdart ašuufa.* They clustered around him and I couldn't see him.

ḥawwaṭ to wall in, build a wall around, to encircle, surround. *leeš ma-tḥawwuṭ beetak ib-siyaaj ḥadiidi?* Why don't you surround your house with an iron fence?

ḥtaaṭ to take precautions, to prepare oneself, make provision. *ˀiḏa ma-tiḥtaaṭ lil-muškila, tiddammar.* If you aren't prepared for the problem, you'll be ruined. *laazim tiḥtaaṭ lil-mawḏuuʕ gabul-ma tšuufa.* You should bone up on the subject before you see him.

ḥooṭa pl. *-aat* circle, cluster.

ḥtiyaaṭ **1.** caution, cautiousness, prudence, carefulness. **2.** provision, precaution, care, prevention. *lil-iḥtiyaaṭ* as a precaution, just in case. *ˀuxuḏ wiyyaak qappuuṭ lil-iḥtiyaaṭ.* Take an overcoat with you just in case. **3.** (pl. *-aat*) precaution, precautionary measure, step. *š-šurṭa wij-jeeš ˀaxḏaw kull il-iḥtiyaaṭaat il-laazma l-manʕ il-muḏaaharaat.* The police and army took all precautions necessary to prevent demonstrations. **4.** reserve. *ʕidna firiqteen iḥtiyaaṭ.* We have two divisions in reserve. **5.** (pl. *-iyya*) substitute (sports).

*ħtiyaaṭi** 1. spare, replacement. *ʔadawaat iħtiyaaṭiyya* spare parts. 2. reserve. *quwwaat iħtiyaaṭiyya* reserve forces.

ħaayiṭ pl. *ħiiṭaan, ħyaaṭiin* wall. || *ʔaani muu ħaayiṭ inṣayyiṣ.* I'm nobody to fool around with (lit., I'm not a low wall).

muħiiṭ pl. *-aat* 1. circumference, periphery. 2. ocean. 3. milieu, environment, surroundings.

ħ-w-k

ħaak (*u ħiyaaka*) 1. to weave. *ħaak-li ʕabaaya ṣuuf.* He wove a woolen robe for me. 2. to knit. *bitt ʕammi ħaakat-li bluuz.* My uncle's daughter knitted me a sweater. 3. (*ħook*) to hit, strike. *ħaaka b-boox w-waggaʕa.* He hit him with his fist and knocked him down.

ħyaaka 1. weaving. 2. knitting.

ħook striking, hitting. || *ʔaxaðna ħook bil-ħači maala.* He wouldn't let us get a word in edgewise.

ħaayik pl. *ħiyyaak* weaver.

ħ-w-l

ħaal (*u ħool*) 1. to be perennial (of plants). *han-nooʕ imnil-warid yħuul.* This type of flower comes up each year. 2. to intervene, interfere, interpose. *ma-aku šii yħuul beena w-been is-safra.* Nothing's going to come between him and his trip.

ħaal (*i ʔiħaala*) 1. to transfer. *ħaal deena ʕalayya.* He transferred his debt to me. *ħaal nafsa ʕat-taqaaʕud.* He got himself on pension. 2. to refer. *la-tħiilni ʕala daaʔira ʔuxra. ʔinta xaḷḷiṣ šuġḷi.* Don't refer me to another office. You take care of my business.

ħawwal 1. to change. *ħawwalit miit diinaar ʔila duulaaraat.* I changed a hundred dinars into dollars. 2. to convert (mathematically). *ħawwil hal-kusuur il-iʕtiyaadiyya ʔila kusuur ʕušriyya.* Convert these common fractions to decimal fractions. 3. to transfer. *l-mudiir ħawwala ʔila ġeer waðiifa.* The director transferred him to another job. 4. to remit, send, transmit. *ħawwil-li miit diinaar bil-bariid il-yoom.* Send me a hundred dinars through the post office today. 5. to refer, pass on, hand on. *raħ-aħawwil muʕaamaltak lil-mudiir w-ašuuf š-yguul.* I'm going to refer your affair to the director and find out what he says. *raħ-aħawwila ʕaleek. ʔinta nṭiih-iyyaa.* I'll unload him onto you. You give it to him. 6. to endorse, sign over. *ħawwal ič-čakk ʕalayya w-aani nṭeeta l-ifluus.* He signed the check over to me and I gave him the money. 7. to direct, turn, divert. *ħawwil il-ṃayy ʕala hal-looħ.* Divert the water into this plot. 8. to turn aside, avert. *ma-ħawwal ʕeena ʕan wujhi.* He didn't move his eyes from my face.

ħaawal to try, attempt, endeavor, make an attempt. *ħaawal yinhizim imnis-sijin.* He tried to escape from prison.

tħawwal 1. to be changed, be converted. *kull il-ṃaay itħawwal ʔila buxaar.* All the water turned to steam. 2. to be transferred, reassigned. *ʔiða ma-atħawwal min hal-waðiifa, ʔabaṭṭil.* If I don't get transferred from this position, I'll quit. 3. to move. *tħawwalna min beetna.* We moved out of our house.

ħtaal /with *ʕala*/ to cheat, dupe, deceive, beguile. *ħtaal ʕalee w-ʔaxað minna nuṣṣ diinaar.* He cheated him and took a half dinar from him.

ħwall to be cross-eyed. *ħwall min ṭifuulta.* He's been cross-eyed since childhood.

ħaal pl. *ʔaħwaal* 1. condition, state. *šloon ħaalak?* How're you doing? 2. situation. 3. circumstance. *ʕala kull ħaal* at any rate, in any case, anyhow. *ʕala kull ħaal, la-ddiir-la baal.* At any rate, don't pay attention to him. || *ma-baqqa ʕala ħaali ħaal.* He didn't leave me a thing. 4. (pl. only) *ʔaħwaal* matters, affairs, concerns. *šloon il-ʔaħwaal?* How are things?

ħaal-ma as soon as, the moment that. *gul-li ħaal-ma tšuufa.* Tell me as soon as you see him.

ħaalan immediately, at once, right away. *xaabra ħaalan.* Call him immediately.

ħaala pl. *-aat* 1. condition, state. *ħaalt iṭ-ṭawaariʔ* state of emergency. 2. situation. 3. case. *b-hal-ħaala, ʔinta kuun il-masʔuul.* In this case, you be in charge.

*ħaali** present, current, existing. *l-waðiʕ il-ħaali* the present situation.

ħawl 1. power, might. *la-ħawla wala quwwata ʔilla bil-laah.* There's no power and no strength save in God. 2. (prep.) around, about, in the area of. *ʔaku dakaakiin ihwaaya ħawl il-binaaya.* There are many shops around the building. 3. about, concerning, re. *ħiča wiyyaak ħawl il-mawðuuʕ loo laaʔ?* Did he speak with you about the situation or not?

ħooli pl. *-iyya* 1. a male calf. 2. a

hanger-on, one who fawns on another for ulterior motives.

ḥooliyya pl. *-aat* calf, heifer.

ḥeel **1.** strength, force, power, vigor. || *smaʕit ʕali nṭirad min šuġla? ḥeel bii, yistaahil.* Did you hear that Ali was fired? Good, he deserves it. **2.** (adv.) with force, with vigor. *ʔidfaʕ ḥeel.* Push hard. *ʔilzam il-ḥabil ḥeel.* Hold the rope tight. *la-timši ḥeel.* Don't walk fast. *ʔiḥči ḥeel!* speak up loudly!

ḥiila pl. *ḥiyal* trick, ruse, strategem, subterfuge. *sawwa biyya ḥiila w-ʔaxaδ ifluusi.* He played a trick on me and took my money.

ḥawaala pl. *-aat* (postal) money order.

ḥawaali **1.** around, about, in the area of. *buqeena ṭaayriin ḥawaali baġdaad.* We kept flying around in the area of Baghdad. **2.** approximately, about, roughly. *ʕindi ḥawaali miiteen iktaab.* I have about two hundred books.

ḥayyaal pl. *-iin* cunning, crafty, wily, or sly person. *ʔayaa ḥayyaal! šloon dabbaritha?* You sly fox! How'd you manage it?

ḥawal crossing (of the eyes). || *ḥawal ḥisin* a slight crossing of the eyes, regarded as a mark of beauty. *ʕeenha ḥoola ḥawal ḥisin.* Her eyes are crossed in a charming way.

ʔaḥwal fem. *ḥoola* pl. *ḥuul, ḥooliin* **1.** cross-eyed. **2.** crossed-eyed person.

muḥawwila pl. *-aat* transformer (el.).

muḥaawala pl. *-aat* attempt, endeavor, try.

muḥtaal pl. *-iin* **1.** swindler, cheat, impostor, fraud. **2.** crook, scoundrel.

mustaḥiil **1.** impossible, absurd, preposterous. **2.** (pl. *-aat*) impossible thing, impossibility.

ḥ-w-m

ḥaam (*u ḥoom*) to circle, hover, fly around. *δall iṭ-ṭeer yḥuum nuṣṣ saaʕa gabuḷ-ma yḥuṭṭ.* The bird kept circling for half an hour before he lit. || *ḥaamat iš-šubha ʕalee.* The suspicion centered on him. *ṣaar-la mudda yḥuum ʕala haš-šuġuḷ.* He's been after this job for quite a while.

ḥ-w-w

ḥawwa Eve. *ʔaadam w-ḥawwa.* Adam and Eve.

ḥ-w-y

ḥuwa (*i ḥawi*) **1.** to gather, collect, amass. *yiḥwi b-beeta ʔanwaaʕ il-iṭyuur.* He collects different types of birds at his house. *šwakit raḥ-tiḥwi l-ʕinjaaṣ?* When are you going to pick the plums? **2.** to contain, hold, comprise, include. *bistaana yiḥwi ʔanwaaʕ il-fawaakih.* His garden contains all kinds of fruits. *l-maḥall yiḥwi ʔašyaaʔ mumtaaza.* The store has fine things.

ḥtiwa /with *ʕala*/ to contain, hold comprise, include. *taqriiri yiḥtiwi ʕala kull it-tafaaṣiil.* My report contains all the details. *l-beet yiḥtiwi ʕala θlaθ ġuraf w-maṭbax w-ḥammaam.* The house consists of three rooms and kitchen and bath.

muḥtawayaat (pl. only) contents, ingredients.

ḥ-y

ḥee name of the letter ḥ.

ḥ-y-b-s

mḥeebis see *ḥ-b-s*.

ḥ-y-θ

ḥayθ, ḥeeθ (in certain phases:) *ʔila ḥeeθ* the hell with him, he deserves it, good riddance. *ṣudug ʕali nniqal? ʔila ḥayθ!* Was Ali really transferred? Good riddance. *jiiraanak ma-raaδi ʕannak. — ʔila ḥeeθ.* Your neighbor is not pleased with you. — The hell with him. *b-ḥeeθ* in such a manner that, so that, in order that. *dixalit lil-beet ṣanṭa b-ḥeeθ maḥ-ḥad ḥass biyya.* I entered the house quietly so that no one would hear me.

ḥayθiyya pl. *-aat* dignity, social distinction, high social standing. || *xireet ib-ḥayθiita.* I really told him off.

ḥ-y-č

ḥaayič = *ḥaayik* which see under *ḥ-w-k*.

ḥ-y-d

ḥaad (*i ḥeed*) to deviate, stray, swerve. *ma-yḥiid ʕan ṭariiq il-ḥaqq walaw δidd maṣlaḥta.* He doesn't deviate from the way of truth even though it's against his own good.

ḥiyaad neutrality. *ʕal-ḥiyaad* neutral. *ʔaani ʕala l-ḥiyaad, w-ma-ʔaddaxxal.* I'm neutral, and I won't interfere.

ḥ-y-r

ḥaar (*i ḥiira*) to become confused. *leeš ḥirit? yaa ktaab itriida, ʔuxδa.* Why are you confused? Whichever book you want, take it. *min kuθrat iṣ-ṣuwar, l-waaḥid yḥiir ʕala yaa ṣuura ybaawiʕ.* Because there are so many pictures, one is perplexed as to which picture to look at. *min itxušš il-ġurfatha tḥiir min kuθrat iδ-δahab wil-mujawharaat.* When you enter her room, you'll be astonished at the amount of gold and jewelry. *štireetha w-ḥirit biiha.* I bought it and then didn't know what to do with it.

ḥayyar to perplex, confuse, baffle, puzzle. *gul-li š-itriid. muu ḥayyaritni!* Tell me what you want. You've played games with me enough! *ʔariid ʔaruuḥ. la-tḥayyirni.* I want to go. Don't waste my time. *la-tḥayyirni. triidha loo laa?* Make up your mind. Do you want it or not? *hal-walad ḥayyarni. marra yriid sayyaara w-marra yriid maaṭoor.* This boy's given me a hard time. One time he wants a car and next he wants a motorboat. *jamaalha yḥayyir il-ʕaqil.* Her beauty makes the mind reel.

tḥayyar to become puzzled, perplexed, confused. *tḥayyarit w-ma-adri š-asawwi.* I'm perplexed and don't know what to do. *tḥayyarit, ma-adri ʔaaxuð has-sayyaara loo ðiič.* I am undecided whether to take this car or that.

ḥtaar = *tḥayyar. xaaf ʔaštiriiha w-aḥtaar biiha.* I might buy it and not know what to do with it.

ḥiira confusion, perplexity, puzzlement, bewilderment. || *saafar zawijha w-xal-laaha b-ḥiira.* Her husband went away and left her helpless.

ح-y-z

ḥaaz (*u ḥiyaaza*) /with *ʕala*/. to achieve, attain, obtain, get, receive. *qtiraaḥa ḥaaz ʕala taʔyiid il-kull.* His suggestion received the support of everyone. *ḥaaz ʕala darajat šaraf.* He got honors. He passed with honors.

tḥayyaz to side, take sides, to be biased, be partial. *hal-ḥakam yitḥayyaz il-firqatkum.* This referee is partial to your team.

nḥaaz = *tḥayyaz. nḥaaz il-jaanibhum bil-munaaqaša.* He took sides with them in the discussion.

ḥiiz pl. *-iyya, ḥyuuza* epithet for a man who submits to sodomy for profit or advancement, and by extension, a loose term of contempt.

ḥiyaaza 1. acquisition, obtainment, attainment. 2. possession, holding. *ligaw ib-ḥiyaazta banaadiq w-musaddasaat.* They found rifles and pistols in his possession.

taḥayyuz prejudice, bias.

ح-y-ṣ

ḥiyaaṣa pl. *-aat* 1. cummerbund. 2. wide woven belt.

ح-y-ð̣

ḥaað (*i ḥeeð̣*) to menstruate. *b-ʔay sinn tibtidi l-ibnayya tḥiið̣?* At what age does a girl begin to menstruate?

ح-y-ṭ

ḥaayiṭ, ḥtiyaaṭ, muḥiiṭ, etc., see under ح-w-ṭ.

ح-y-f

staḥyaf 1. to consider (something) wrong, shameful. *da-astaḥyif ʔaðibb haθ-θoob li-ʔan baʕda yinlibis.* I feel it's a shame to throw this shirt out because it still can be worn. 2. to regret. *staḥyafit ma-stireet hal-badla l-mumtaaza.* I was sorry I didn't buy that fine suit of clothes.

ḥeef 1. wrong, injustice. 2. pity, shame, waste. || *ḥeef ʕalee!* What a pity! Too bad! *ḥeef ʕalee, id-daaʔira xiṣrata!* It's a shame the office lost him! *muu bil-ḥeef!* Not a chance! It'll never happen! Not on your life! *haaða yuġḷubni? muu bil-ḥeef!* Him beat me? Not on your life! *muu bil-ḥeef! loo kull ʔaṣdiqaaʔak yiturkuuk ʔaani ma-aturkak.* Not a chance! Even if all of your friends leave you, I won't. 3. revenge. *ruuḥ ʔuxuð ḥeefak imnil-buṣaṭak.* Go get your revenge on the one who beat you up.

ح-y-k

ḥaayik, ḥyaaka, etc., see under ح-w-k.

ح-y-l

ḥaal, ḥeel, ḥiila, ḥayyaal, etc., see under ح-w-l.

ح-y-n

ʔaḥyaan: baʕð̣ il-ʔaḥyaan sometimes, occasionally, once in a while, at times. *baʕð̣ il-ʔaḥyaan ma-yinḥimil.* Sometimes he's insufferable.

ʔaḥyaanan sometimes, occasionally, from time to time. *ʔaḥyaanan ma-afham ʕalee.* Sometimes I don't understand him.

ح-y-w

ḥeewa (coll.) quince(s).

ḥeewaaya pl. *-aat* quince.

ح-y-w-a-n

ḥaywaan see under ح-y-y.

ح-y-y

ḥiya (*i ḥayaat*) 1. to live. *yaḥya l-malik!* Long live the king! 2. to revive, give new life, rejuvenate. *l-muṭar yiḥyiiha lil-gaaʕ.* The rain adds new life to the land. *b-hat-taṣliiḥ, ḥiyeetha lis-sayyaara.* By repairing it like that, you gave the car a new lease on life. 3. to stay awake. *ḥiya liṣ-ṣubuḥ, ʔabad ma-naam.* He stayed up until morning and never slept.

ḥayya 1. to hail, to greet (formally). *j-jamaahiir da-yḥayyuun il-malik.* The crowds are cheering the king. *dixlaw ʕal-*

waziir yḉayyuu. They went in to the minister to wish him well. **2.** to salute. *j-junuud da-yḉayyuun il-ḉalam.* The soldiers are saluting the flag. || *ḉayyaak ˀallaah!* Bravo! Good for you!

ˀaḉya **1.** to celebrate. *ˀaḉyaw δikir il-marḉuum ib-qaṣaaˀid rannaana.* They commemorated the memory of the deceased wtih fine poems. **2.** = *ḉiya* **2.**

ḉtiya to revive, come back to life. *maat baḉd il-ḉamaliyya, bass min sawwoo-la tanaffus iṣṭinaaḉi, ḉtiya.* He died after the operation, but when they gave him artificial respiration, he revived.

stiḉa **1.** to feel ashamed, be ashamed. *ma-tistiḉi? la-tṣayyiḉ ḉala ˀabuuk!* Aren't you ashamed? Don't shout at your father! *huwwa fadd waaḉid ma-yistiḉi. yičδib ḉala ˀay šaxiṣ.* He's a guy who doesn't know shame. He lies about anybody. **2.** to be or become embarrassed, feel embarrassed. *ˀastiḉi ˀaṭlub minna fluus baḉad.* I'm embarrased to ask him for more money. *ma-agdar ˀakallifa biiha. ˀastiḉi.* I can't bother him with it. I'd be embarrassed. **3.** to be bashful, shy, diffident. *ma-qibal yḉaačiiha. yistiḉi hwaaya.* He wouldn't talk to her. He's very bashful.

ḉayy **1.** living, live, alive. *ma-adri ḉayy loo mayyit.* I don't know if he's alive or dead. *yeezi ḉaad! muu wuṣlat il-laḉm il-ḉayy!* Enough now! You've gotten to the quick! **2.** (pl. *ˀaḉyaaˀ*) living being, living thing, organism. *ḉilm il-ˀaḉyaaˀ* biology.

ḉayya: ḉayya ḉala ṣ-ṣalaa! Come to prayer! || *ma-aku ḉaaja tisˀal; l-masˀala mbayyna ḉayya ḉala ṣ-ṣalaa.* There is no need to ask; the matter's as clear as daylight.

ḉayya pl. *-aat, ḉyaaya* snake, serpent, viper. || *ḉayya ṣafra* snake in the grass, dirty rat.

ḉaya, ḉayaaˀ shame, diffidence, timidity, bashfulness.

ḉayaasizz pl. *ḉayaasizziyya* **1.** shameless, bold, brazen. **2.** brazen person.

ḉayaat life. *b-ḉayaati ma-šifit hiiči šii.* I never saw such a thing in my life.

*ḉayawi** vital, essential to life. *masˀala ḉayawiyya* a vital matter.

ḉaywaan pl. *-aat* animal, beast. *la-tṣiir ḉaywaan!* Don't be an animal!

taḉiyya pl. *-aat* **1.** greeting. **2.** salute.

ḉ-y-y-l-l-a

ḉayyaḷḷa see under [2]*ˀ-l-l-a.*

X

x-a

xaa name of the letter *x.*

x-a-x-a-m

xaaxaam pl. *-iyya* rabbi.

x-a-t-w-n

xaatuun, xaatuuna pl. *xwaatiin* **1.** lady. **2.** polite form of address to a lady. **3.** good girl, little lady.

x-a-r-ṣ-y-n

xaarṣiin zinc.

x-a-z-w-q

xaazuuq, see *x-w-z-q.*

x-a-š-w-g

xaašuuga see *x-w-š-g.*

[1]*x-a-k*

xaak the kneeling position (in Greco-Roman wrestling).

[2]*x-a-k*

xaaka dust. *xaakat faḉam* charcoal dust. *xaakat qand* the particles left from breaking up a block of sugar.

x-a-k-y

xaaki khaki.

x-a-m

xaam (invar.) **1.** raw, unworked, unprocessed. *mawaadd xaam* raw materials. *nafuṭ xaam* crude oil. *ḉadiid xaam* crude iron, pig iron, iron ore. *jilid xaam* untanned hide, raw leather. **2.** inexperienced, green, wet behind the ears, naive, artless. *hal-ḉaamil ij-jidiid xaam; ma-yuḉruf kull šii.* That new worker's green; he doesn't know anything. *damaaġa baḉda xaam.* His mind is still undeveloped. **3.** a type of cheap cotton cloth. *xaam ˀasmar* and *xaam sawaaḉil* unbleached cotton cloth. *xaam ˀabyaḏ* bleached cotton cloth.

x-a-n

xaan pl. *-aat* **1.** old fashioned inn, hostelry. **2.** stable (usually boarding beasts of burden). **3.** warehouse, storehouse.

xaana pl. *-aat* **1.** space, row (chess, backgammon, etc.) **2.** space, shelf, cubbyhole.

-xaana the second constituent in a num-

ber of compounds of Turkish and Persian origin, indicating place for—, house for—, and the like, as: *xastaxaana,* lit., a sick house, i.e. hospital; *ˀazzaxaana,* lit., drug house, i.e. pharmacy; *musaafirxaana* lit., traveler's house, i.e. inn. Look up alphabetically, or under Arabic root of first constituent.

xaanči pl. *-iyya* warehouseman.

x-a-w-l-y

xaawli pl. *-iyyaat* towel, hand towel.

x-b-ˀ

xabba see under *x-b-y.*

x-b-θ

xabbaθ to work malicious mischief. *maštiġal ib-mukaan ˀiδa ma-xabbaθ bii.* He's never worked anywhere that he didn't stir up trouble.

xubuθ troublemaking, viciousness.

xabiiθ pl. *xubaθaaˀ* **1.** troublesome, vicious, malicious. *waaʕid xabiiθ* an instigator, troublemaker. **2.** dangerous, serious, deadly, pernicious. *maraḍ xabiiθ* a serious disease.

ˀaxbaθ more or most troublesome, vicious, etc.

x-b-r

xabbar to tell, inform, advise. *xabbarta baačir ma-raʕ-ništuġuḷ.* I told him we're not going to work tomorrow.

xaabar to telephone, phone. *xaabratni marrteen il-baarʕa.* She phoned me twice yesterday.

txaabar to telephone, get in touch. *txaabarit wiyyaa.* I got in touch with him.

xtibar to test, examine, give an examination. *xtibarta w-ṭilaʕ ṣaadiq.* I tested him and he was telling the truth. *l-baarʕa l-mudarris ixtibarna.* Yesterday the teacher gave us an examination.

staxbar **1.** to ask, inquire. *laazim nistaxbur ʕanna.* We have to inquire about it. **2.** to learn, discover, find out. *staxbarna ˀinna haaδa l-mujrim baʕda bil-wlaaya.* We've learned that the criminal's still in town.

xabar pl. *ˀaxbaar* **1.** news item. *ˀaxbaar* news. **2.** news, word, information, report.

ˀixbaar pl. *-aat* summons, subpoena. *jaani ˀixbaar imnil-maʕkama.* I got a summons from the court.

xibra pl. *-aat, xibar* experience.

xabiir pl. *xubaraaˀ* expert.

l-xaabuur a tributary of the Upper Euphrates.

muxaabara pl. *-aat* **1.** correspondence. **2.** communication, contact. **3.** telephone call.

ˀixbaariyya pl. *-aat* tip, information.

muxbir reporter.

muxtabar pl. *-aat* laboratory.

x-b-z

xubaz (*u xabuz*) to bake bread. *ˀumma xubzat ʕišriin gurṣa xubuz.* His mother baked twenty flat, round loaves of bread. || *ṣaar-li xams isniin ˀaštuġuḷ wiyyaa. ʕijanta w-xubazta.* I have worked with him for five years. I know him thoroughly (lit., kneaded and baked him.) *ˀaani ʕaajna w-xaabza.* I know all about it.

xubuz (coll.) bread.

xubza pl. *-aat* piece of bread.

xabza pl. *-aat* batch, mixture (of bread dough).

xabbaaz pl. *-iin, xbaabiiz* baker, bread maker.

xubbaaz, xubbeez mallow.

maxbaz pl. *maxaabiz* bakery, bread shop.

x-b-ṣ

xubaṣ (*u xabuṣ*) to mix up, distract, confuse, bother, rush. *la-tuxbuṣni. xalliini ˀašuuf darbi.* Don't bother me. Let me concentrate on what I'm doing. *š-aku xaabuṣ nafsak? ʕala keefak.* Why are you so worked up? Take it easy.

nxubaṣ to be or become rushed, busy, preoccupied. *čaan ʕidna ʕiris w-inxubaṣna.* We had a wedding and we got all tied up with it. *min yjuu xuṭṭaar yinxubuṣ biihum.* When he has guests he gets completely occupied with them.

xabṣa pl. *-aat* **1.** commotion, hustle and bustle, melee, madhouse. **2.** mess, hodgepodge, rat's nest.

xibiiṣa pl. *-aat* = *xabṣa.*

maxbuuṣ busy, occupied, tied up. *maxbuuṣ ib-šuġḷa* busy with his work.

x-b-ṭ

xubaṭ (*u xabuṭ*) **1.** to mix. *yuxbuṭ jatt w-tibin w-yinṭii lil-iʕṣaan.* He mixes alfalfa and straw and gives it to the horse. **2.** to roil, stir up, muddy. *faatat is-sayyaara bij-jadwal w-xubṭat il-mayy.* The car went through the creek and muddied the water. **3.** to become murky, muddy, roiled. *min iḍḍiif hal-masʕuuq, loon is-saaˀil yuxbuṭ.* When you add this powder, the color of the liquid becomes murky. *n-nahar xaabuṭ min kuθrat il-muṭar.* The river's muddy from all the rain.

xabbaṭ to grope, stumble around. *ḍall yxabbuṭ mudda biḍ-ḍulma ʕatta liga s-suwwiič.* He kept groping around for a while in the dark until he found the switch.

xabṭa pl. *-aat* **1.** a mixing, an instance of mixing. **2.** mixture, batch.

xabaaṭa (invar.) mentally unbalanced, touched in the head, odd, off. *kullhum xabaaṭa.* They're all a little touched.

xabbaaṭa pl. *-aat* mixer, cement mixer.

xaabuṭ muddy, murky, roiled. *maay xaabuṭ* muddy water.

x-b-ḷ

xaḅḅaḷ to drive insane, rob of his senses. *ma-taaxδa l-ʔibnak! muu xaḅḅaḷni!* Look, take your son! He's driven me out of my mind! *jamaalha yxaḅḅuḷ.* Her beauty stuns you.

txaḅḅaḷ to go crazy, go wild. *txaḅḅḷat min maat ʔibinha.* She went crazy when her son died. *min šaaf is-sayyaara, txaḅḅaḷ ɛaleeha.* When he saw the car, he was crazy about it.

xḅaaḷ madness, insanity.

mxaḅḅaḷ pl. *mxaaḅiiḷ* insane person, madman.

mitxaḅḅaḷ angry, infuriated, furious. *l-mudiir mitxaḅḅaḷ li-ʔan nuṣṣ il-muwaδ-δafiin ma-ʔijaw liš-šuġuḷ.* The director's furious because half of the employees didn't show up for work.

x-b-y

xabba to hide, conceal. *gul-li. la-txabbi ɛalayya šii.* Tell me. Don't hide anything from me.

txabba to hide oneself. *ʔija š-šurṭi. txabba.* The policeman's coming. Hide yourself!

xtiba to hide, conceal oneself. *šuuf-lak fadd mukaan tixitibi bii.* Look for some place to hide.

x-t-b

xitteeba hide and seek.

x-t-l

xital (*i xatil*) to hide, conceal oneself. *l-ɛaraami xital bis-sirdaab.* The thief hid in the cellar.

txattal intens. of *xital. luweeš da-titxattal? haaδa ɛammak, muu ġariib.* Why do you keep hiding? This is your uncle, not a stranger.

xatla pl. *-aat* an isolated or concealed spot, a hiding place. *makaan xatla* an isolated spot. || *ween hal-xatla? ma-nšuufak.* Where've you been hiding? We don't see you anymore.

xitteela the game of hide and seek.

x-t-m

xitam (*i xatim*) **1.** to seal. *xitam iδ-δaruf baɛad-ma xalla l-maktuub bii.* He sealed the envelope after he placed the letter in it. **2.** to stamp. *ʔixtim il-ɛariiδa w-waddiiha lil-mudiir.* Stamp the application and take it to the director. *ʔixtim iṭ-ṭawaabiɛ ib-xatam il-yoom.* Cancel the postage stamps with the date stamp. **3.** to conclude, terminate. *xitam il-kalima maalta bit-tarɛiib biδ-δuyuuf.* He concluded his speech by welcoming the guests. **4.** to finish, complete, wind up. *xitam il-maṣlaɛa.* He has finished his apprenticeship. **5.** to read through, read from cover to cover (of the Koran). *ʔibinha xitam il-qurʔaan.* Her son has read the Koran from cover to cover.

xattam to have someone read through. *xattimoo l-qurʔaan gabuḷ-ma ydaxxiluu l-madrasa.* They made him read the Koran before they entered him in school.

xtitam to conclude, finish, terminate. *xtitmaw il-ɛafla bis-salaam ij-jumhuuri.* They concluded the ceremony with the national anthem.

xatim, xatam pl. *ʔaxtaam* seal, stamp.

xaatam pl. *xawaatim* **1.** ring. **2.** anus.

xatma: ward il-xatma hollyhock.

x-θ-r

xiθar (*i xaθir*) to curdle. *xiθar il-ɛaliib willa baɛad?* Has the milk curdled yet?

xaθθar **1.** to curdle. *šarrub ij-jaahil ɛaliib wil-baaqi, xaθθira.* Give the baby a drink of milk and curdle the rest. **2.** to clot, make clot. *had-duwa yxaθθir id-damm.* This medicine makes blood clot.

txaθθar reflex. of *xaθθar. damma yitxaθθar ib-surɛa.* His blood clots quickly. *xalli l-ɛaliib biš-šamis yitxaθθar bil-ɛajal.* Leave the milk in the sun so it'll curdle quickly.

xuθra pl. *-aat* curdling agent.

xaaθir A variety of yoghurt, thinner than *liban.*

x-j-l

xijal (*a xajil*) **1.** to be or become embarrassed. *xijal li-ʔan jawaaba ṭilaɛ ġaḷaṭ.* He got embarrassed because his answer turned out to be wrong. *huwwa yixjal min ʔabuu.* He's embarrassed in front of his father. *xijal min ma-ɛiraf yjaawub.* He was embarrassed when he couldn't answer. **2.** to be ashamed, feel shame. *huwwa fadd šaxuṣ ma-yixjal.* He's a person who feels no shame. *xijal min ʔaɛmaala.* He was ashamed of his action.

xajjal to embarrass, put to shame. *la-ddizza l-haaδa, tara yxajjilna li-ʔan ma-yuɛruf ʔingiliizi.* Don't send him—he'll embarrass us because he doesn't know English. *xajjalna b-kalaama l-xašin.* He embarrassed us with his rough talk. *xajjalitni. maaƐruf išloon ajaaziik.* You've embarrassed me (with favors). I don't know how to repay you.

xajal embarrassment.

xajuul shy, bashful, timid. *walad xajuul ihwaaya* a very timid boy.

xajlaan embarrassed. *tirak il-qaaƐa xajlaan.* He left the hall in embarrassment.

ˀaxjal more or most shy, etc.

muxjil shameful, shocking. *Ɛamal muxjil* a shameful act.

x-d-d

xadd pl. *xduud* cheek. || *tiffaaƐ ˀabu xadd w-xadd* apples that are not all red.

mxadda pl. *mxaadiid* pillow, cushion.

[1]*x-d-r*

xidar (*a xadir*) to become numb, tingle. *giƐadit Ɛala rijli, w-xidrat.* I sat on my leg, and it went to sleep.

xaddar 1. to numb, deaden. *ðuraba ˀubra jawwa s-sinn Ɛatta yxaddir il-mukaan.* He gave him a shot next to the tooth to deaden the area. 2. to anesthetize. *xaddir il-ˀarnab Ɛatta nšarrƐa.* Anesthetize the rabbit so we can dissect it.

xadraan numb, asleep. *ˀiidi xadraana li-ˀan nimit Ɛaleeha.* My arm's asleep because I slept on it.

muxaddir anesthetic, painkilling, tranquilizing. *maadda muxaddira* painkilling agent, material. (pl. *-aat*) narcotics, drugs, dope.

muxaddara pl. *-aat* veiled, secluded from men outside the family. *niswaan muxaddaraat* veiled women.

[2]*x-d-r*

xidar (*a xadir*) to brew, steep. *xidar ič-čaay. subb-inna.* The tea has brewed. Pour for us.

xaddar to brew. *xaddir išwayya čaay lil-xuṭṭaar.* Brew a little tea for the guests.

x-d-Ɛ

xidaƐ (*a xadiƐ*) to deceive, mislead, dupe, gull. *la-txalli maðhara yixdaƐak.* Don't let his appearance fool you. *baƐdak li-hassa maxduuƐ bii?* Are you still taken in by him?

nxidaƐ pass. of *xidaƐ*. *haaða yinxidiƐ bil-Ɛajal.* He's easily taken in.

xaddaaƐ deceptive, deceiving. *maðhara xaddaaƐ.* His appearance is deceiving.

x-d-g

xudug: yiji l-xudug min ðahra. He is ticklish on his back.

x-d-m

xidam (*i xadim*) 1. to serve, be of service, work for. *r-raˀiis xidam il-waṭan mudda ṭuwiila.* The president served his country a long time. *xidam maṣaaliƐ Ɛamma.* He served the interests of his uncle. 2. to serve, be a servant. *xidam ib-beethum šahreen.* He served in their household for two months.

staxdam 1. to employ, hire. *staxdimata l-Ɛukuuma šahreen w-nuṣṣ.* The government employed him for two and a half months. 2. to employ, use, make use of. *nistaxdim ˀaƐdaθ il-ˀajhiza b-hal-muxtabar.* We use the most modern equipment in this lab.

xidma pl. *-aat, xidam, xadamaat* 1. a service. 2. hospitality, duties of a host 3. service, attendance. *l-xidma l-Ɛaskariyya* military service. || *ˀaani b-xidmatkum.* I'm at your service. *bil-xidma.* At your service.

xaduum obliging. *haaða kulliš xaduum. ˀay šii tkallfa bii, ysawwii.* He's very obliging. Anything you ask, he'll do.

xaadim pl. *xadam, xiddaam* servant, manservant.

xaddaama pl. *-aat* maid.

xaadma pl. *-aat* maid.

mustaxdam an employee of the Iraqi civil service having less rights and privileges than the regular employee, or *muwaððaf.*

x-r-b

xirab (*a xaraab*) 1. to be ruined, destroyed, spoiled. *xirbat il-madiina min marr ij-jeeš.* The city was destroyed when the army came through. *l-balad xirab min aƐmaal id-diktaatooriyya.* The country was ruined by the dictatorship's actions. 2. to go bad, spoil (of food). *xirab il-ˀakil.* The food got spoiled. 3. to break down, get out of order, broken. *l-makiina xirbat.* The machine broke down. *has-saaƐa kulliš daqiiqa; tixrab bil-Ɛajal.* This watch is very delicate; it'll get out of order easily. 4. to go bad, be spoiled, change for the worse. *čaan xooš walad laakin xirab min gaam yimši wiyya haj-jamaaƐa.* He used to be a good boy, but he was ruined by going with this group. || *ṣadiiqti xirbat Ɛalayya. laazim ˀaƐƐad gaalha šii Ɛanni.* My girl turned against me. Someone must have told her something about me. 5. to collapse, to pass out. *xirab iš-šaayib min šiddat il-Ɛarr.* The old man collapsed from the intense heat. *j-jaahil wugaɛ ɛala wučča w-xirab.* The child fell on his face and passed out. *j-jaahil xirab imniđ-điɛik.* The kid fell over from laughter.

xarrab **1.** to destroy, ruin, spoil. *ʔalla yxarrub beetak.* I hope God will destroy your house. *l-muṭar ġarrag il-wlaaya w-xarrab kullši.* The rain flooded the city and destroyed everything. **2.** to put out of order, damage. *luweeš xarrabt is-saaɛa?* Why did you mess up the watch? **3.** to lead astray, influence for the worse. *la-timši wiyyaa tara yxarrubak.* Don't run around with him or he'll ruin you. || *la-tgul-lha hal-iɛcaaya, tara txarrubha ɛalayya.* Don't tell her that story or you'll turn her against me. *xarrab beeni w-been marti.* He caused trouble between me and my wife.

xaarab to make mad at each other, stir up trouble between. *raaɛ iddaxxal w-xaarabhum.* He went and interfered and made them mad at each other.

txaarab to get mad at each other, to quarrel, fall out. *kull yoom yitxaarbuun w-yitṣaalɛuun.* Every day they quarrel and make up. *l-ʔibn w-ʔabuu txaarbaw.* The son and his father had a falling out. *txaarabit wiyya ṣadiiqi w-ma-da-nitɛaača.* I quarreled with my friend and we're not speaking.

xaraab **1.** ruin, ruins. **2.** quarrel, split, falling out.

xaraaba pl. *-aat, xaraayib* ruin, ruins, dilapidated building.

xarbaan **1.** broken, out of order. *sayyaarti xarbaana.* My car is broken down. **2.** knocked out, out cold. *buqa xarbaan saaɛteen.* He was out cold for two hours.

x-r-b-ṭ

xarbaṭ **1.** to throw into disorder, mess up, confuse. *l-hawa xarbaṭ šaɛri.* The wind messed up my hair. *xarbaṭ il-ġaraađ w-laazim ʔaɛaddilha.* He mixed up the things and I have to straighten them out. *xarbaṭni b-ɛačya w-ma-gdart ajaawub.* He confused me with what he said and I couldn't answer. *raɛ-aruuɛ ɛalee w-axarbuṭ ʔaɛwaala.* I'll go see him and tell him off. **2.** to get mixed up, to foul up, malfunction. *kull ij-jinuud da-yimšuun ɛadil, bass huwwa yxarbuṭ.* All the soldiers are marching properly; he's the only one who's messing it up. *makiinat sayyaarti da-txarbuṭ. laazim ʔađbuṭha.* The motor in my car is running badly. I've got to tune it. *miɛidti da-txarbuṭ ɛalayya.* My stomach's bothering me. *širab peek w-xarbaṭ, ṣiɛad ɛal-meez, w-gaam yirguṣ.* He had a shot and went wild; got up on the table and started to dance. *da-yxarbuṭ ib-ɛačya.* He gets mixed up in talking. *da-yxarbuṭ w-ma-da-yuɛruf iš-yiɛči.* He talks disjointedly and doesn't know what he is saying. *rijaɛ ɛalee il-wujaɛ li-ʔan xarbaṭ bil-ʔakil.* The pain returned to him because he didn't eat right.

txarbaṭ pass. of *xarbaṭ*. *ʔaɛwaala txarbuṭat min idzawwaj.* Since he got married he's gone to pot. *la-tiɛči min ʔaktib tara ʔatxarbaṭ.* Don't talk when I'm writing or I'll get mixed up. *ʔabuu txarbaṭ bil-leel w-jaaboo-la ṭ-ṭabiib.* His father got sick at night and they brought the doctor for him. *min bilaɛ il-ɛabbaaya txarbaṭ.* When he took the pill, he got worse.

xarbaṭa pl. *xaraabiiṭ* mess, disorder, muddle, confusion.

mxarbaṭ **1.** mixed up, confused. *wađiɛ imxarbaṭ* an unsettled situation. **2.** disorderly, disarranged, messed up. *libis imxarbaṭ* disorderly clothes.

x-r-b-n-d-a

xar(a)banda pl. *xar(a)bandiyya* **1.** an incompetent, incapacitated, or senile person. **2.** something useless or worn out, junk.

x-r-j

xiraj (i xarij) to spend. *xiraj kull ifluusa b-saaɛa wiɛda.* He spent all his money in one hour.

xarraj **1.** to graduate. *j-jaamiɛa xarrijat ʔalfeen ṭaalib has-sana.* The university graduated two thousand students this year. **2.** to deduct, subtract. *xarrij diinaareen imnil-iɛsaab.* Deduct two dinars from the account.

ʔaxraj **1.** to throw out, eject, bounce. *ʔaxrijoo mnil-ɛafla min gaam yṣayyiɛ.* They ejected him from the ceremony when he began to shout. **2.** to direct. *minu ʔaxraj hal-filim?* Who directed this movie?

txarraj **1.** to graduate, be graduated. *txarraj has-sana min ij-jaamiɛa.* He graduated this year from the university. **2.** to manage, to take care of oneself. *la-tdizza waɛda. ma-yuɛruf yitxarraj.* Don't send him alone. He doesn't know how to get around.

staxraj to extract, mine, recover. *yistaxrijuu l-ɛuṭuur imnil-ʔawraad.* They extract scents from flowers. *hal-faɛam ma-yistaxrij ib-suhuula.* This coal can't be mined easily. *l-ˀalmaaz yistaxrijuu mnil-faɛam.* Diamonds are obtained from coal. *l-baaziin yistaxrijuu mnin-nafuṭ.* Gasoline is extracted from petroleum.

xarjiyya spending money.

xuruj, xurij pl. *xuruuj* saddlebags.

xuruuj stool, feces.

xaarij (n.) **1**. outside, exterior. **2**. foreign countries, the outside. *mnil-xaarij.* From outside, from abroad. *bil-xaarij* abroad, in foreign countries. **3**. (prep.) outside, out of. *xaarij il-madiina* outside the city.

*xaariji** **1**. outer, outside, external. *l-istiɛmaal il-xaariji* external use. **2**. non-resident. *ṭullaab xaarijiyyiin* day students. *ɛiyaada xaarijiyya* outpatient clinic.

xaarijiyya foreign office, foreign ministry. *šuˀuun il-xaarijiyya* foreign affairs. *wizaart il-xaarijiyya* ministry of foreign affairs.

maxraj pl. *maxaarij* exit, way out.

muxrij (stage or screen) director.

x-r-x-r

xarxar to drip, to leak. *l-girba maaltak manguuba w-da-txarxir.* Your water bag has a hole in it and is dripping.

x-r-x-š

xarxaš to rattle. *j-jaahil da-yxarxiš ib-quuṭiyya biiha ɛaṣu.* The kid is rattling a tin can with gravel in it.

xirxaaša pl. *-aat* rattle, baby's rattle.

x-r-d-a

xurda change, small change.

xurdawaat (pl.) notions, miscellaneous small articles.

x-r-d-f-r-w-š

xurdafuruuš pl. *-iyya* dealer in notions, or miscellaneous small articles.

x-r-d-l

xardal mustard.

x-r-r

xarr (*u xarr*) **1**. to drip, leak. *min maṭrat id-dinya, xtalit jawwa š-šijra, bass il-mayy buqa yxurr ɛala raasi.* When it rained, I sought shelter under the tree, but the rain kept dripping on my head. *min tumṭur id-dinya sagf il-ġurfa yxurr.* When it rains, the ceiling of the room drips. *ma-buqa bil-kitli mayy. ˀaɛtiqid yxurr minna.* There's no water left in the kettle. I think it leaks out of it. **2**. to fall, fall down, drop, dive, swoop down. *šuuf, šuuf, najma xarrat!* Look, look, a star fell! *ṭayyaart ij-jaahil xarrat w-čallibat bis-šijra.* The kid's kite nose-dived and got hung up in the tree. *ṭ-ṭayyaara xarrat ɛala saaɛt il-ˀalɛaab.* The airplane buzzed the playing field.

x-r-z

xirza pl. *-aat, xiraz* bead.

xreeza a small bead. *ṭamm ixreeza* a children's game in which a small bead is hidden in one of two piles of earth. *ˀabu xreeza.* a type of small, round-shaped river fish.

x-r-s

xarras to silence, make dumb. *ṣaaɛ bii ṣeeɛa xarrasa biiha.* He shut him up with a mighty shout.

xrass to become mute, dumb. *xrass w-iṭrašš min ɛaadiθ is-sayyaara.* He became mute and deaf from the car accident. *š-biik ma-tiɛči? xrasseet?* Why don't you talk? Have you lost your tongue?

ˀaxras fem. *xarsa* pl. *xurus, xirsaan, xaarsiin.* **1**. mute, dumb. **2**. mute, dumb person.

x-r-š

xiraš (*i xariš*) **1**. to startle. *xirašhum ib-ṣeeɛta.* He startled them with his shout. **2**. to astound, amaze. *l-muɛallim xirašna b-ɛačya ɛan il-qumbula δ-δarriyya.* The teacher astounded us with his talk on the atomic bomb. **3**. to annoy, irritate, disturb, bother. *ɛiss ir-raadyo ɛaali yixriš il-ˀiδin.* The volume of the radio is so high it is irritating. *l-maziiqa halgadd ɛaalya xiršatha lil-imɛalla.* The music was so loud that it shook the neighborhood.

xarraš to startle, dumbfound. *ṣeeɛt iz-zumaaḷ itxarriš.* The donkey's screech startles.

xiriiš eccentric, odd, touched in the head.

x-r-ṭ

xiraṭ (*u xariṭ, xaruṭ*) **1**. to talk nonsense, talk through one's hat. *n-nahaar kulla yuxruṭ ib-raasi ɛan il-ˀašyaaˀ is-sawwaaha b-ˀamriika.* All day long he gave me all this talk about the things he did in America. *δall saaɛa yuxruṭ w-sikat baɛdeen.* He spent an hour talking nonsense and finally shut up. **2**. to wipe out. *ˀuxruṭ il-liban il-baaqi b-ṣibɛak.* Wipe out the rest of the yoghurt with your finger.

xariṭ, xaruṭ **1**. rubbish, trash, baloney, nonsense. *ɛačya kulla xariṭ.* Everything he says is nonsense. **2**. worthless thing, junk. *la-tištiri has-sayyaara, tara hiyya xariṭ.* Don't buy that car—it's a piece of junk. **3**. worthless person, incompetent, jerk. *šloona muɛallimkum ij-*

jidiid? xaruṭ. How's your new teacher? Not worth a damn.

xarraaṭ pl. *-a,-iin* braggart, storyteller.

xriiṭ 1. rubbish, junk, worthless thing. 2. worthless person, incompetent.

xariiṭa pl. *xaraayiṭ* map, chart.

ˀaxraṭ more or most useless, etc.

maxruuṭ pl. *maxaariiṭ* cone (geom.). *maxruuṭi** cone-shaped. *jibal maxruuṭi* cone-shaped mountain.

x-r-ṭ-w-m

xarṭuum pl. *xaraaṭiim* trunk (of the elephant). *l-xarṭuum* Khartoum (capital of the Sudan).

x-r-ɛ

xarraɛ to scare, frighten. *jaani min wara w-xarraɛni.* He came from behind and scared me.

txarraɛ to be scared, alarmed. *haaδa ma-yitxarraɛ bil-ɛajal.* He doesn't get scared easily.

xtiraɛ 1. to become scared, alarmed. *xtiraɛ biδ-δalma.* He got scared in the dark. 2. to invent, devise. *minu xtiraɛ ir-raadyo?* Who invented the radio?

xarɛa pl. *-aat* a scare, a fright.

xarraaɛ, xurraaɛa, xarruuɛa pl. *-aat* something frightening, something to frighten people. *hač-čalib ma-yɛaδδ. xaallii xarruuɛa.* That dog doesn't bite. He's just put there to scare people. *xarraaɛ xuδra* scarecrow. *ˀinta šinu hnaa, xarraaɛ xuδra?* What are you here for, a scare crow?

xtiraaɛ pl. *-aat* invention.

muxtariɛ pl. *-iin* inventor.

mixtiriɛ scared. *š-biik mixtiriɛ? ma-aku šii.* Why are you scared? There's nothing wrong.

x-r-f

xraff to become senile, feeble minded. *da-yixraff yoom ɛan yoom.* He's getting more senile every day.

xariif autumn, fall. *faṣl il-xariif* the autumn season.

xaruuf pl. *xirfaan* sheep, and by extention, a stupid person.

xuraafa pl. *-aat* fable, fairy tale.

*xuraafi** fictitious, legendary. *šaxiṣ xuraafi* legendary character. *quṣṣa xuraafiyya* fable.

muxraff senile, feeble minded, and by extension, crazy.

xarfaan 1. senile, feeble minded 2. crazy.

x-r-q

xiraq (*i xariq*) to violate, break (the law). *xiraq il-qaanuun.* He violated the law.

xtiraq 1. to pierce. *r-raṣaaṣa xtirqat il-baab.* The bullet went through the door. 2. to penetrate, pass through. *dabbaabaatna xtirqat xuṭuuṭ il-ɛadu.* Our tanks penetrated the enemy lines.

xaariq, xaariq lil-ɛaada unusual, extraordinary.

x-r-g

xirga pl. *xirag* rag, scrap of cloth.

x-r-k

xurraki pl. *-iyya* coward, pantywaist, creampuff.

x-r-m

xarram 1. to pierce, make holes in, perforate. *ˀariidak itxarrum-li hal-looɛa.* I want you to make holes in this piece of wood for me. 2. to embroider. *ṣadr il-ibluuz maalha mxarram.* The front of her blouse is embroidered.

xurum pl. *xruum* hole. *xurm il-ˀubra* needle's eye.

mxarram 1. perforated. 2. embroidered.

x-r-m-š

xarmaš to scratch. *diir baalak, la-txarmušak il-bazzuuna.* Be careful that the cat doesn't scratch you.

xarmuuš pl. *xraamiiš* stalk or bunch of dates.

x-r-w-ɛ

xirwiɛ castor oil plant. *dihin xirwiɛ* castor oil.

x-r-y

xira (*a xari*) to excrete, defecate, go to the toilet. *j-jaahil xira ɛaz-zuuliyya.* The baby messed on the carpet. *la-txalli ˀibnak yixra biš-šaariɛ.* Don't let your son go in the street. *č-čalib xira giddaam il-baab.* The dog made a mess in front of the door. || *la-tijjaadal wiyyaa, yixra min ɛalga.* Don't argue with him; he talks dirty. *ˀija w-xira bil-waṣṭa.* He came and messed up the works. *ma-aku zambuur yixra ɛasal.* It sounds like baloney to me (lit., there's no wasp which excretes honey).

xarra 1. = *xira. l-bazzuuna da-txarri bil-ɛadiiqa.* The cat is messing in the garden. 2. to allow or cause to defecate. *bawwlii w-xarrii lij-jaahil gabuḷ ma-niṭlaɛ.* Make the child urinate and defecate before we go out.

xara (coll.) pl. *xiryaan, xaryaan.* feces, excrement. || *haaδa ˀaθgal min xara l-ɛaddaad.* He's a real bore (lit., he's heavier than the blacksmith's rubbish).

xarya pl. *-aat* un. n. of *xara.*

ˀaxra worse or worst.

x-z-r

xizar (*i xazir*) **1.** to stare at. *been mudda w-mudda yixzir il-ibnayyaat.* From time to time he stares at the girls. **2.** to glare at. *l-ˀabu xizar ibna min madd iida ḉal-ˀakil.* The father glared at his son when he stretched out his hand toward the food.

xazra pl. *-aat* **1.** stare. **2.** scathing look.

xazar: baḉr il-xazar. The Caspian Sea.

x-z-f

xazaf (ancient) glazed pottery, earthenware.

*xazafi** pottery, earthenware. *ˀawaani xazafiyya* earthenware dishes.

x-z-l

xtizaal shorthand, stenography.

x-z-m

xizzaama pl. *-aat* nose ring (in bulls, male camels, or women). *ṭoob ˀabu xazzaama* an old-fashioned type of cannon (with a ring on it for hitching to a horse).

x-z-n

xizan (*i xazin*) to store. *l-ḉukuuma xiznat it-titin biš-šimaal.* The government stored the tobacco in the north.

xazzan to become infected. *j-jariḉ xazzan.* The wound became infected.

xazna pl. *-aat* treasure.

xzaana pl. *xzaayin.* The hot water reservoir in a public bath house.

xaziina pl. *-aat* treasury, public treasury.

xazzaan pl. *-aat* reservoir.

maxzan pl. *maxaazin* **1.** storeroom, storehouse. **2.** stockroom, supply room. **3.** store, shop.

x-z-y

xazza to disgrace, put to shame. *xazzeetna b-buxlak.* You've shamed us with your stinginess. *raḉ-aruuḉ lee w-axazzii ḉaṭ-ṭalab maali.* I'm going to him and take him to task about my money.

txazza pass. of *xazza.* *ˀiδa ma-nidfaḉ iṭ-ṭalab, tara nitxazza.* If we don't pay the debt, we'll be disgraced.

xtiza to be ashamed. *ma-tixtizi ḉaad! muu ḉeeb?* Aren't you ashamed of yourself? Isn't that something to be ashamed of?

xizi shame, disgrace.

ˀaxza more or most disgraceful, etc.

muxzi pl. *-iya* shameful, disgraceful. *ˀaḉmaal muxziya* disgraceful conduct.

x-s-ˀ

xasa: txasa (invar.) approx., aw, go on! come off it. *txasa! ḉaad walḷa l-yuδrubni ˀamawwta.* Baloney! Boy, anyone hits me, I'll kill him. *txasa, ˀaani ma-axaaf min ˀaḉḉad.* Not me. I'm not afraid of anyone. *firqatna raḉ-tuġlub firqatkum. txasa!* Our team is going to beat your team. How could that be?

x-s-t-x-a-n

xastaxaana pl. *xastaxaayin* hospital.

x-s-s

xass lettuce. *raas xass* a head of lettuce.

xissa meanness, baseness.

xasiis stingy, cheap, mean. *rijjaal xasiis* a stingy man.

x-s-r

xisar = *xiṣar* which see under ²*x-ṣ-r.*

x-s-f

xisaf (*i xasif*) **1.** to give way, cave in. *s-saguf xisaf biihum w-maataw.* The roof caved in under them and they died. *čaanaw gaaḉdiin bil-gahwa w-ˀašu fadd marra xisfat il-gaaḉ biihum.* They were sitting in the coffee shop and all of a sudden the floor sank under them. **2.** to be eclipsed (moon only). *raḉ-yixsif il-gumar baačir.* The moon will be eclipsed tomorrow.

xassaf to dent, make dents in. *j-jaahil dagdag ib-maaḉuun il-faafoon w-xassafa.* The child beat on the aluminum dish and made dents in it.

xasfa pl. *-aat* **1.** dent. **2.** dimple.

xusuuf lunar eclipse.

x-s-l

xasil = *ġasil* which see under *g-s-l.*

x-š-b

xaššab **1.** to become like wood, to stiffen, to become rigid. *wugaḉ ḉala wučča w-xaššab miθl il-mayyit.* He fell on his face and became rigid like a dead person. || *ṣadra xaššab min han-našla l-qawiyya.* His chest dried out and became painful from this strong cold.

xišab wood, lumber, timber. *ṣanduug xišab* a wooden box. *xišab imḉaakas* plywood. *xišab čaam* crate wood. *xišab jaawi* ironwood (lit. Java wood). *xišab jooz* walnut.

xišba pl. *-aat* piece of wood.

*xašabi** wooden. *ṣanduug xašabi* a wooden box.

xaššaab pl. *-a* the man that plays the *xšiba* at Iraqi parties.

xšiba pl. *-aat, xšaab* = *dumbuk,* which see under *d-m-b-k.*

x-š-x-š

xašxaš to rattle, to jingle. *laazim ˀaku šii bii; min itxuδδa yxašxiš.* There must be something in it; when you shake it, it rattles. *da-yxašxiš il-ifluus ib-jeeba.* He's jingling the money in his pocket.

txašxaš to get around, socialize. *yuʕruf kull il-wuzaraaˀ li-ˀanna yitxašxaš ihwaaya.* He knows all the ministers because he gets around a lot.

xašxaša pl. *-aat* rattle, jingle. *xišxaaš* (coll.) poppy, poppies.

xišxaaša pl. *-aat* 1. un. n. of *xišxaaš.* 2. rattle (toy).

x-š-š

xašš (*u xašš*) 1. to enter. *ˀaani ma-xašš ib-beethum ˀabadan.* I have never entered their house. *hal-iktaab čibiir; ma-yxušš ib-jeebi.* This book is too big; it won't go into my pocket. *šooka xaššat ib-ˀiidi.* A thorn pricked my hand. *xušš ʕal-mudiir w-gul-la.* Go on in to the director and tell him. *min xašš lil-beet nizaʕ sitirta.* When he entered the house he took off his jacket. || *haay ma-da-txušš ib-ʕagli.* I can't believe that (lit., this cannot enter my mind). *xašš bil-xamsiin.* He just turned fifty. *xašš wiyyaaha marrteen.* He slept with her twice. 2. to shrink. *hal-uqmaaš yxušš bil-ġasil.* This material shrinks with washing.

xaššaš 1. to put in, insert. *xaššiš il-ġaraaδ jawwa.* Take the things inside. *tigdar itxaššiš ˀiidak bit-tunga?* Can you stick your hand in the jar? 2. to let in, get in. *xaššašni bil-ʕafla bila biṭaaqa.* He got me into the party without a ticket. *kull-ma ˀaruuʕ il-has-siinama yxaššišni balaaš.* Everytime I go to this movie he lets me in for nothing.

xašša pl. *-aat* 1. entry, entrance. 2. (taboo) instance of fornication.

xušša pl. *-aat* fat, pug nose.

x-š-ʕ

xišaʕ (*a xušuuʕ*) 1. to humble oneself. *yṣalli w-yixšaʕ ir-rabba.* He prays and humbles himself to God. 2. to make someone feel humble. *ṣoota yixšaʕ min yiqra l-qurˀaan.* His voice makes one feel humble when he reads the Koran.

xušuuʕ humbleness, humility. *b-xušuuʕ* humbly.

¹*x-š-f*

xišif pl. *xšuuf* fawn (of a gazelle).

²*x-š-f*

xiššaaf (coll.) pl. *xašaašiif* bats (zool.).

xiššaafa pl. *-aat* un. n. of *xiššaaf.*

x-š-l

xašil jewelry.

muxaššalaat (pl.) jewelry, valuables.

x-š-m

xašim pl. *xšuum* 1. nose. || *šaayil xašma ʕaleena.* He stuck up his nose at us. *l-mudiir ij-jidiid kisar xašma, rajjaʕa kaatib.* The new director put him in his place, and demoted him back to clerk. *ṭilʕat is-safra min xašma.* The trip turned out to be a pain. *ˀaksir xašma w-aaxuδ ifluusi minna.* I'll force him to give me my money. 2. breast (of lamb, etc., a cut of meat).

xšuum = *ˀabu xšeem* 1.

xšeem: ˀabu xšeem 1. variety of pigeons with a large protuberance above the beak. 2. man with a large nose.

x-š-n

xašin 1. coarse, rough. *qmaaš xašin* coarse cloth. *jilid xašin* rough skin. 2. rough, crude, uncouth, rude. *walad xašin* an uncouth boy. *ˀaxlaaq xašna* crude manners. 3. rough, hoarse, low-pitched. *ṣoot xašin* low voice, low note. 4. large, coarse. *mišmiš xašin* large apricots. *j-jins il-xašin* men, the stronger sex.

xušuuna 1. coarseness, crudeness. 2. rudeness. *b-xušuuna* 1. coarsely. 2. rudely.

ˀaxšan 1. coarser, rougher. 2. cruder, more uncouth. 3. rougher, deeper, hoarser. 4. larger, coarser.

x-š-y

xiša (*i xaši*) to fear, dread. *ˀiδa tixša rabbak, ma-tbuug.* If you fear your God, you won't steal.

xtiša to feel shame, be ashamed. *la-yistiʕi w-la-yixtiši.* He feels no shame at all. *xtiši! šloon tiʕči hiiči ġiddaam ˀabuuk?* For shame! How can you talk like that in front of your father?

x-ṣ-b

xaṣib fertile. *ˀaraaδi xaṣba* fertile land.

xaṣiib fertile. *l-hilaal il-xaṣiib.* The Fertile Crescent.

xuṣuub fertility.

¹*x-ṣ-r*

txaṣṣar to put one's hands on hips. *txaṣṣar w-wugaf giddaami.* He put his hands on his hips and stood in front of me.

xtiṣar 1. to condense, shorten. *ˀida matixtiṣir il-maqaal maalak, ma-nigdar nnišra.* If you don't condense your article, we can't publish it. 2. to summarize. *ˀixtiṣir maqaal il-waziir ib-ṣafʕa wiʕda.* Summarize the minister's article in one page.

xiṣir pl. *xuṣuur* waist.

xtiṣaar shortening, condensation, summarization. *b-ixtiṣaar* briefly, in a few words.

muxtaṣar 1. brief, short. *maktuub muxtaṣar* a short letter. *ziyaara muxtaṣara* a brief visit. || *ḉafla muxtaṣara* small, informal party or get-together. *muxtaṣar mufiid* in short, in brief, to make a long story short. 2. (pl. *-aat*) summary, synopsis, abstract.

xaaṣra pl. *xawaaṣir* 1. side (between the hip bone and false rib). 2. loin. *laḉam xaaṣra* loin meat.

²x-ṣ-r

xiṣar (*a xaṣir*) to lose. *xiṣarit diinaar bil-iqmaar.* I lost a dinar gambling. *xiṣar id-daḉwa laakin raḉ-yista*ʔ*nif.* He lost the case but he is going to appeal. *daa*ʔ*irta xiṣrata. ma-yilguun* ʔ*aḉsan minna.* His office lost him. They can't find anyone better than he was. *firqatna xiṣrat il-yoom.* Our team lost today.

xaṣṣar to make lose. *la-tṣiir šariika, tara yxaṣṣrak kull ifluusak.* Don't become his partner, or he'll make you lose all your money. *ḉali ma-liḉab zeen, huwwa l-xaṣṣarna.* Ali didn't play well. He caused us to lose.

xaṣaara pl. *-aat xaṣaayir* 1. loss, losses. 2. waste, loss. *yruuḉ ḉumrak xaṣaara.* Your life will go to waste. || *xaṣaara!* or *yaa xaṣaara!* pity! what a shame! what a loss! 3. defeat, loss.

xaṣraan loser.

x-ṣ-ṣ

xaṣṣ (*u xaṣṣ*) 1. to concern, pertain to. *haš-šii ma-yxuṣṣni.* That doesn't concern me. ʔ*aani ma-yxuṣṣni.* ʔ*is*ʔ*al ġeeri.* That's not my business. Ask someone else. 2. to be related to. *ḉali yxuṣṣni.* Ali's related to me. *š-yxuṣṣak haaδa?* How's he related to you? 3. to single out, bestow upon. *ṣadiiqak ḉali yxuṣṣak bis-salaam.* Your friend Ali sends his greetings to you.

xaṣṣaṣ 1. to designate, set aside. *xaṣṣaṣit saaḉa min wakti kull yoom lil-ifransi.* I have set aside one hour of my time every day to study French. 2. to assign, reserve. *xaṣṣaṣna haay il-ġurfa lin-niswaan.* We've reserved this room for women. *hal-ġurfa muxaṣṣaṣa lil-ijtimaaḉaat.* This room is reserved for meetings. 3. to allocate, allot, appropriate. *l-ḉukuuma xaṣṣiṣat milyoon diinaar lij-jisir ij-jidiid.* The government appropriated a million dinars for the new bridge.

txaṣṣaṣ to specialize, become a specialist. *txaṣṣaṣ bil-*ʔ*amraaδ ij-jildiyya.* He specialized in skin diseases.

xtaṣṣ = *txaṣṣaṣ. had-duktoor, beeš muxtaṣṣ?* What does that doctor specialize in? *xtaṣṣ bil-qaanuun ij-jinaa*ʔ*i.* He specialized in criminal law.

xuṣuuṣ /in certain pharses:/ *min xuṣuuṣ* and *b-xuṣuuṣ* in regard to, concerning. *b-hal-xuṣuuṣ* in this respect. *ḉal-xuṣuuṣ* especially.

xuṣuuṣan especially. ʔ*aḉibb il-faakiha, xuṣuuṣan il-ḉinab.* I like fruit, especially grapes.

*xuṣuuṣi** 1. special. *paaṣpoort xuṣuuṣi* special passport. 2. personal, private. *makaatiib xuṣuuṣiyya* personal letters. *sayyaara xuṣuuṣiya* private car.

ʔ*axaṣṣ* /in the phrases:/ *ḉal-axaṣṣ* and *bil-axaṣṣ.* especially. *kullhum xooš wilid, w-ḉal-*ʔ*axaṣṣ haaδa.* They're all good boys, especially that one.

taxaṣṣuṣ specialization.

xtiṣaaṣ 1. jurisdiction, bailiwick. 2. specialty, field, area of competence.

*xtiṣaaṣi** specialist.

xaaṣṣ 1. special. *ḉisab-li-yyaaha b-siḉir xaaṣṣ.* He gave it to me at a special price. *δuruuf xaaṣṣa* special circumstances. || *b-ṣuura xaaṣṣa* especially, particularly. 2. reserved, limited, restricted. *hal-qaaḉa xaaṣṣa lil-*ʔ*aḉδaa*ʔ*.* This hall is reserved for members. *paaṣ xaaṣṣ liṭ-ṭullaab* a bus reserved for students. 3. personal. *ḉaras xaaṣṣ* personal guard. *ṭabiib xaaṣṣ* personal physician. 4. set aside, designated. *duktoor xaaṣṣ lil-imwaδδafiin* a doctor especially for the employees. *mablaġ xaaṣṣ lil-fuqaraa*ʔ*.* an amount earmarked for the poor. 5. private. *qaδiyya xaaṣṣa* a private matter.

xaaṣṣa pl. *xawaaṣṣ, xaaṣṣiyya* property, characteristic, attribute.

xaaṣṣa (invar.) relatives.

xaaṣṣatan especially, particularly.

ʔ*axiṣṣaa*ʔ*i** specialist.

maxṣuuṣ especially, particularly, specifically. *riḉit lee maxṣuuṣ il-hal-qaδiyya.* I went to see him specifically about that matter.

muxaṣṣaṣaat (pl.) 1. allocation, appropriation. 2. allowances, *raatib w-muxaṣṣaṣaat* pay and allowances.

x-ṣ-f

xiṣṣaaf (coll.) a basket-like container for dates, woven of palm leaves.

xiṣṣaafa pl. *-aat* un. n. of *xiṣṣaaf.*

x-ṣ-l

xiṣla pl. *-aat, xiṣaal* **1.** good quality, good characteristic. **2.** character, good character.

x-ṣ-m

xiṣam (u xaṣum) **1.** to deduct, subtract. *ˀiδa ˀaštiri miit wiꞓda, yuxṣum-li čam filis imnis-siɛir.* If I buy a hundred, he deducts a few fils from the price. **2.** to finish, be complete. *qaδ̣iyyat naqli xuṣmat.* The matter of my transfer is completed. *ṣaar-li saaɛa waaguf. ma-tuxṣumha ɛaad.* I've been standing here for an hour. Come on and finish with it. *nṭii ɛašr idnaaniir w-uxṣumha wiyyaa.* Give him ten dinars and be done with him. *ˀagdar axṣumha wiyyaa b-xamsa w-iθlaaθiin diinaar.* I can settle it with him for thirty-five dinars. *ˀiδa δoola tɛayynaw wuzaraaˀ, laɛad xuṣmat il-qaδ̣iyya.* If those guys have been appointed ministers, then it's all over. *laa xuṣmat* how could that be? it's not possible! *šloon xallaṣit šuġul maal šahar ib-nuss saaɛa? laa xuṣmat! laɛad guul "sawweeta šallaali."* How'd you finish a month's work in a half hour? It's impossible! Then say "I did a sloppy job"! *laa xuṣmat, haaδa yṣiir mulaaꞓiδ.* I don't see how he can be a supervisor.

xaṣum **1.** discount. *siɛir il-xaṣum* discount price. **2.** (pl. *xuṣuum*) opponent, opposing team.

x-ṣ-y

xiṣa (i xaṣi) to castrate, emasculate. *ˀiδa tixṣi d-diič, yisman.* If you castrate a rooster, it becomes fat. *ˀiδa yiji l-mudiir ij-jidiid, yixṣiihum kullhum.* If the new director comes, they'll be done for.

xaṣṣa = *xiṣa. šinu šuġla ɛammak? yxaṣṣi dibbaan?* What kind of work does your uncle do? Castrate flies?

xiṣi pl. *xiṣyaan, xaṣaaya.* eunuch, castrate.

xuṣwa pl. *xaṣaawi, xiṣyaan.* testicle, testis.

maxṣi pl. *mxaaṣi* castrated male, eunuch, gelding, capon.

x-δ̣-x-δ̣

xaδ̣xaδ̣ to shake. *la-txaδ̣xiδ l-ibṭoola.* Don't shake the bottles.

x-δ̣-r

xaδ̣δ̣ar **1.** to turn green. *halgadd-ma muṭrat, il-gaaɛ kullha xaδ̣δ̣rat.* Because it rained so much, the whole land became green. **2.** to sprout, send up shoots. *l-bazr iz-ziraɛta kulla ma-xaδ̣δ̣ar.* None of the seeds I planted came up. **3.** to bud, leaf. *š-šajara illi b-ꞓadiiqti xaδ̣δ̣irat.* The tree in my garden leafed. **4.** to become infected. *l-ꞓabbaaya lli b-iidi xaδ̣δ̣irat.* The sore on my hand got infected.

xδ̣arr to turn green. *l-ṃaay bil-ꞓooδ̣ ixδ̣arr.* The water in the pool turned green. *l-giiɛaan raꞓ-tixδ̣arr min hal-muṭar.* The landscape will turn green from this rain.

l-xiδ̣ir a legendary invisible religious man.

xuδ̣ra **1.** greens, salad greens. **2.** (pl. *xuδ̣ar*) vegetable garden. **3.** *xuδ̣rawaat* (pl.) vegetables.

xaδ̣aar **1.** green, green color. **2.** vegetation, herbage, greenery.

ˀaxδ̣ar fem. *xaδ̣ra* pl. *xuδ̣ur* green. *ɛyuunha xuδ̣ur.* Her eyes are green.

xδ̣eeri (coll.) a kind of wild duck, resembling the mallard.

xδ̣eeriyya pl. *-aat* un. n. of *xδ̣eeri.*

xδ̣eeri pl. *-iyya* = *xδ̣eeriyya.*

xiδ̣δ̣eer: ˀabu l-xiδ̣δ̣eer a kind of wild green bird.

xaδ̣raawi A common variety of dates.

mxaδ̣δ̣ar pl. *-aat, mxaδ̣iir* vegetable(s).

mxaδ̣δ̣arči pl. *-iyya* vegetable merchant, greengrocer.

x-δ̣-δ̣

xaδ̣δ̣ (u xaδ̣δ̣) **1.** to shake. *xuδ̣δ̣ il-buṭil gabuḷ-ma tišrab id-duwa.* Shake the bottle before you take the medicine. *xuδ̣δ̣ il-maaɛuun b-išwayyat ṃayy.* Rinse the plate in some water. **2.** to threaten, shake up. *raꞓ-axuδ̣δ̣-ilk-iyyaa xaδ̣δ̣a zeena w-axawwfa biiha.* I will shake him up good for you and make him worry about it.

xδ̣aaδ̣a **1.** rinse water. **2.** (by extension) a worthless person. **3.** buttermilk.

x-δ̣-ɛ

xiδ̣aɛ (a xuδ̣uuɛ) to bow, defer, yield, submit. *l-ɛašaayir kullha xiδ̣ɛat lil-ꞓukuuma.* All the tribes yielded to the government. *hiyya ma-tixδ̣aɛ ir-rajilha.* She doesn't obey her husband.

xaδ̣δ̣aɛ to subdue, subjugate. *l-ꞓukuuma xaδ̣δ̣iɛat il-qabaaˀil bil-quwwa.* The government subdued the tribes by force.

ˀaxδ̣aɛ = *xaδ̣δ̣aɛ. j-jeeš ˀaxδ̣aɛ iθ-θuwwaar.* The army subdued the rebels.

txaδ̣δ̣aɛ to abase oneself, grovel. *min fuṣloo, raaꞓ yitxaδ̣δ̣aꞓ lil-waziir.* When they fired him, he went to grovel at the minister's feet.

x-ṭ-ʔ

xiṭaʔ (*a xaṭaʔ*) to make a mistake. *xiṭaʔ bil-iḥsaab.* He made a mistake in arithmetic.

xiṭa (*i xaṭi*) to miss. *ðirabit itlaθ irṣaaṣaat w-xiṭeeta.* I fired three shots, but I missed him.

xaṭṭaʔ to cause to make a mistake. *bass tiḥči, txaṭṭiʔni.* The minute you speak, you cause me to make a mistake.

staxṭi to deem sinful, consider sinful. *ʔastaxṭi ʔaṣruf ifluus il-yatiim.* I feel it's a sin to spend the orphan's money.

xaṭaʔ pl. *ʔaxṭaaʔ* mistake.

xaṭʔa pl. *-aat* mistake.

xaṭiyya 1. (in certain expressions:) || *la-tšiil xaṭiyyatha. ʔinta ma-mitʔakkid.* Don't accuse her wrongly. You're not really sure. *la-tšiil xaṭiita lir-rajjaal. yjuuz muu suuča.* Don't accuse the man. Maybe it wasn't his fault. 2. (invar.) poor unfortunate, poor wretch. *juuz minna, xaṭiyya.* Let the poor guy alone.

muxṭiʔ mistaken, wrong, at fault.

x-ṭ-b

xiṭab (*u xaṭab*) 1. to speak, give an address. *l-waziir xiṭab bit-talaamiið.* The minister addressed the students. 2. to propose to, get engaged to. *xiṭab-la binayya ḥilwa.* He got engaged to a pretty girl. *xiṭabit binit jiiraanna w-raḥ-nidzawwaj šahr il-laax.* I became engaged to the neighbor's daughter and we will be married next month. 3. to betroth, engage. *dazz ʔumma tuxṭub-la bnayya minhum.* He sent his mother to propose to one of their girls for him.

xaaṭab to speak to, talk to, address. *ʔaani da-axaaṭbak ʔilak.* I'm talking to you.

nxiṭab to be betrothed, become engaged. *nxiṭbat iš-šahr il-faat.* She got engaged last month.

xuṭba pl. *xuṭab* 1. speech, address. 2. sermon. 3. (pl. *-aat*) engagement ceremony, betrothal.

xiṭaab pl. *-aat* speech, address.

xaṭiib pl. *xuṭabaat* 1. preacher, speaker in a mosque. 2. good speaker, orator. 3. (pl. *xuṭbaan*) fiancé, betrothed.

xaṭiiba pl. *-aat* fiancée, betrothed.

xaṭṭaaba betrothal delegation, matchmaking delegation.

x-ṭ-r

xiṭar (*u xaṭir*) 1. to pass, go by. *hassa xiṭar minna.* He just passed by here. 2. (*xuṭuur*) to occur. *ʔisma ma-da-yixṭur ʕala baali.* His name doesn't come to mind. *šinu? ṣaar waziir? haaða šii ma-yixṭur ʕal-baal.* What? He became a minister? I can't imagine that.

xaaṭar to endanger, risk. *ma-aku ḥaaja txaaṭir ib-ḥayaatak.* There's no need for you to risk your life.

ʔaxṭar to notify, serve notice. *ʔaxṭirata l-maḥkama yiṭlaʕ imnil-beet.* The court notified him to vacate the house.

txaṭṭar to recall, recollect, remember. *ma-da-atxaṭṭar ween šaayfa.* I don't remember where I saw him.

nxiṭar to be endangered. *baġdaad inxiṭrat bil-fayaðaan.* Baghdad was endangered by the flood.

xaṭar pl. *ʔaxṭaar* 1. danger, risk. 2. menace, danger. *xaṭar ʕal-mujtamaʕ* a menace to society.

xaṭir dangerous, hazardous, risky, serious. *mujrim xaṭir* a dangerous criminal. *saabiqa xaṭra* a dangerous precedent. *ʕamaliyya xaṭra* a serious operation.

xaṭiir 1. serious, grave. *waðiʕ xaṭiir* a serious situation. *xabar xaṭiir* grave news. 2. important, weighty. *nabaʔ xaṭiir* an important announcement.

xaaṭir 1. (in certain expressions:) *l-xaaṭrak, ib-diinaareen.* For your sake, two dinars. (*l-*)*xaaṭir ʔaḷḷa, ʕindi mara w-aṭfaal. juuz minni.* For God's sake, I've got a wife and kids. Let me go. *l-xaaṭir ʔaḷḷa, bass ʕaad!* For God's sake, quit it! *l-xaaṭir ʔaḷḷa, juuʕaan.* For the sake of Allah. I'm hungry. *ma-ʕindi xaaṭir ʕindak?* Don't I have any influence with you? *xalli nruuḥ naaxuð min xaaṭra. ʔabuu maat il-baarḥa.* Let's go offer our condolences. His father died yesterday. *ruuḥ ʔuxuð min xaaṭir abuuk w-la-txallii zaʕlaan ʕaleek.* Go make up with your father and don't leave him mad at you. *la-yibqa b-xaaṭrak; ma-qṣadit šii.* Don't be offended; I didn't mean anything. 2. so, so as to, so that. *xalli nfuut minnaa xaaṭir ma-yšuufna.* Let's go this way so's he won't see us.

xaaṭraana 1. pull, influence. 2. favoritism. 3. (pl. *-aat*) patron, sponsor.

ʔaxṭar more or most dangerous.

xuṭṭaar pl. *xṭaaṭiir* guest(s), company. || *raaḥ xuṭṭaar.* He went visiting.

maxṭuur endangered, threatened. *ṣiḥḥta maxṭuura.* His health is endangered.

x-ṭ-ṭ

xaṭṭ (*u xaṭṭ*) **1.** to draw (a line). *xuṭṭ xaṭṭ jawwa hač-čilma.* Draw a line under this word. **2.** to print, write, paint (calligraphy). *l-xaṭṭaṭ xaṭṭha lil-quṭƹa b-diinaareen.* The calligrapher printed the sign for two dinars.

xaṭṭaṭ **1.** to draw lines, rule. *xaṭṭiṭ haṣ-ṣafƹa bil-maṣṭara.* Draw lines on this page with the ruler. **2.** mark off, line. *xalli nxaṭṭiṭ saaƹt it-tanis.* Let's mark off the tennis court.

txaṭṭaṭ to apply eyebrow make-up. *l-ƹaruus da-titxaṭṭaṭ giddaam il-umraaya.* The bride is putting on eyebrow make-up in front of the mirror.

xaṭṭ pl. *xuṭuuṭ* **1.** line. **2.** line of communication, route. *xaṭṭ ƹadiidi* railroad line. *l-xuṭuuṭ il-ƹiraaqiyya j-jawwiyya* Iraqi Airlines. *xaṭṭ il-ṗaaṣ* the bus line. **3.** telephone line. *l-xaṭṭ mašğuul.* The line's busy. **4.** line (mil.). *l-xuṭuuṭ il-ʔamaamiyya* the front lines. **5.** handwriting. *xaṭṭ ʔiid* handwriting, penmanship. **6.** calligraphy. *xaṭṭ ir-ruqƹa.* Ruq'a style calligraphy. **7.** letter, note. *xaṭṭ il-ʔistiwaaʔ* the equator. *xaṭṭ il-ƹarḍ* parallel (of latitude). *xaṭṭ iṭ-ṭuul* meridian, circle of longitude.

¶ *ʔaani wyaak ƹala ṭuul il-xaṭṭ.* I'm with you all the way down the line.

*xaṭṭi** written, handwritten. *jawaab xaṭṭi* a written answer.

xuṭṭa pl. *-aat* a diagram drawn on pavement for children's games.

xiṭṭa pl. *xiṭaṭ* **1.** plan, project, design. **2.** policy, line of action, aim, purpose, principle.

xaṭṭaaṭ **1.** calligrapher. **2.** sign painter.

xṭaaṭ eyebrow make-up, eyebrow pencil.

maxṭuuṭ pl. *-aat* (old) manuscript.

x-ṭ-f

xiṭaf (*u xaṭuf*) **1.** to pass, go by. *xiṭaf minnaa miθl il-barq.* He went by here like lightning. *s-sayyaara xiṭfat ib-surƹa.* The car went by fast. *la-tuxṭuf minnaa. l-gaaƹ imballila.* Don't step across here. The ground is wet. **2.** to duck. *ʔuxṭuf raasak. l-baab muu ƹaali.* Duck your head. The doorway's not very high. *loo-ma xiṭafit, čaan ḍirabni ƹajara.* If I hadn't ducked, he'd have hit me with a rock.

nxiṭaf **1.** to be drained away (of color). *nxiṭaf loonha min git-ilha il-xabar.* She turned pale when I told her the news. **2.** to be dumbfounded, petrified. *nxiṭafit min šifit ič-čalib jaay ƹalayya.* I was petrified when I saw the dog coming at me.

xtiṭaf to kidnap, abduct. *xtiṭfaw ʔibn il-waziir.* They kidnapped the minister's son.

xaṭfa pl. *-aat* a short distance, a dash, a hop, skip, and a jump.

maxṭuuf kidnap victim.

x-ṭ-w

xiṭa (*i xaṭi*) to step. *l-yixṭi minnaa, ʔamawwta.* I'll kill anyone who moves from there. *ʔixṭi xaṭwa li-giddaam.* Step forward one pace.

xaṭṭa to pace, walk around. *ṣaar saaƹa da-yxaṭṭi bil-gubba.* He has been pacing the room for one hour.

txaṭṭa **1.** to overstep, transgress. *la-titxaṭṭa l-ƹuduud ib-ƹačyak wiyyaaha.* Don't overstep the bounds in talking with her. *txaṭṭa l-ʔuṣuul ib-taṣarrufaata.* He violated the customs with his behavior. **2.** to cross, go beyond. *la-titxaṭṭa hal-ƹadd. gaaƹna tintihi hnaa.* Don't cross this boundary. Our land ends here. **3.** to disregard, by-pass, go around *la-titxaṭṭa marjaƹak.* Don't by-pass your superior. **4.** to take a stroll. *xan-niṭlaƹ nitxaṭṭa bil-ƹadiiqa.* Let's go out and take a stroll in the garden.

xaṭwa pl. *-aat* step, pace, stride. *xaṭwa ƹaasma* a decisive step.

x-ṭ-y

xiṭa, nxiṭa, staxṭa, xaṭiyya see under *x-ṭ-ʔ*.

x-f-t

xifat (*i xafit*) **1.** to die away, fade. *kull-ma yibtiƹid, yixfit ṣoota.* As he goes farther away, his voice fades. **2.** to become silent, quiet down. *biča mudda w-baƹdeen xifat.* He cried a while and then quieted down. **3.** to die down, subside. *n-naar raƹ-tixfit.* The fire will die down.

xaafit dim, soft, subdued. *ḍuwa xaafit* dim light.

ʔaxfat weaker, softer.

x-f-r

xafar (invar.) **1.** watching, watch, guard. *ṭ-ṭabiib il-xafar* the duty doctor. *mumarriḍa xafar* duty nurse. *jundi xafar* soldier on guard duty. *ṣaydaliyya xafar* pharmacy designated to stay open all night. *r-raʔiis ʔaƹmad xafar baačir.* Captain Ahmed will be on guard duty tomorrow. **2.** guard, guard detachment. *ḍaabuṭ il-xafar* officer of the guard.

xafaara pl. *-aat* duty, watch, guard. || *lizam xafaara.* He was on guard duty.

maxfar pl. *maxaafir* guard post, control post. *maxfar šurṭa* police substation, precinct station. *maxfar ƹuduud* border post, guard station.

maxfuur under escort, under guard. *jaaboo lil-markaz maxfuur.* They brought him to the police station under guard.

x-f-ḏ̣

xaffaḏ̣ to lower, decrease, reduce, drop. *ʔiḏa txaffuḏ̣ is-siƹir, ʔaštiriiha.* If you lower the price, I'll buy it. *xaffuḏ̣ ṣootak. ʔaku jamaaƹa yitṣannaṭuun.* Lower your voice. There are people listening.

nxufaḏ̣ to sink, drop, decrease. *ʔasƹaar iš-šakar inxufḏ̣at hal-ayyaam.* The price of sugar has dropped these days. *l-yoom nxufḏ̣at darajt il-ƹaraara hwaaya.* The temperature went down a lot today.

ʔaxfaḏ̣ more or most subdued, etc.

nxifaaḏ̣ 1. reduction, decrease. 2. dropping, low level (of water).

munxafiḏ̣ low. *rtifaaƹ munxafiḏ̣* low altitude. *ʔasƹaar munxafḏ̣a* low prices.

x-f-f

xaff (*u xiffa*) 1. to become lighter, lose weight, decrease in weight. *min tinzil bil-ṃayy, waznak yxuff.* When you get in the water, your weight decreases. *l-ƹimil xaff ƹalee min ʔaxaḏit qisim minna.* The load was lighter for him after I took some of it. || *taah bil-ġaaba muddat šahar w-ƹaqla xaff.* He was lost in the jungle for a month and he went half crazy. 2. to decrease. *l-wujaƹ xaff.* The pain has let up. *s-surƹa maalta ma-xaffat, tara ma-raƹ-yoogaf.* His speed hasn't decreased; looks like he's not going to stop. 3. to become lighter in color. *la-tƹuṭṭ bii ṃayy baƹad tara loona yxuff.* Don't add anymore water or its color will become lighter. 4. to become easier, lighter. *loo ʔaƹruf ʔingiliizi čaan il-imtiƹaan yxuff ƹalayya.* If I knew English, the exam would be easier for me. *min ʔija l-muwaḏḏaf iθ-θaani, š-šuġuḷ maali xaff.* When the new employee came, my work got lighter. 5. to thin, become thin, sparse. *xal-nibqa bil-beet ʔila ʔan yxuff il-izdiƹaam.* Let's stay at home until the crowd thins out. *šaƹri da-yxuff.* My hair is getting thinner. 6. to speed up, hurry, quicken. *xuff rijlak, tʔaxxarna ƹal-ƹafla.* Speed up. We are late for the party. *xuff ʔiidak, l-mudiir da-yriid il-maktuub.* Hurry up. The director wants the letter.

xaffaf 1. to lighten, make lighter. *laazim inxaffif il-ƹimil ƹatta inṣalliƹ il-pančar.* We've got to lighten the load in order to fix the flat. 2. to decrease, lessen. *min tooṣal qariib imnij-jisir xaffif is-surƹa.* When you get near the bridge, let up on the speed. 3. to ease, lighten, relieve. *raƹ-ʔaḏ̣urbak ʔubra txaffuf il-wujaƹ ƹannak.* I am going to give you a shot to ease your pain. *xallaw wiyyaa waaƹid ƹatta yxaffuf ƹalee š-šuġuḷ.* They put a man with him to make the work lighter on him. *l-maktuub illi dazz-ilha-yyaa xaffaf ƹanha šwayya.* The letter which he sent her lifted her spirits a little. *l-muƹallim raƹ-yxaffif il-ʔasʔila hal-marra.* The teacher is going to simplify the questions this time. 4. to dilute, thin, lighten. *xaffif il-booya, li-ʔanha θxiina kulliš.* Thin the paint; it's too thick. *xaffif il-ƹaamuḏ̣ ƹatta ma-yiƹrig il-malaabis.* Dilute the acid so it won't burn the clothes. *č-čaay ṭoox, xaffif-li-yyaa.* The tea is dark. Lighten it for me. *l-ƹallaaq xaffaf šaƹri bil-mugaṣṣ wil-mišiṭ.* The barber thinned my hair with the scissors and comb.

staxaff 1. to ridicule, despise, disdain, scorn. *staxaff ib-fikirti.* He ridiculed my idea. 2. to value lightly, take lightly. *la-tistixiff ib-haš-šuġuḷ. ʔuṣbur w-šuufa šloon ṣaƹub.* Don't take this work too lightly. Wait and see how hard it gets.

xuff pl. *ʔaxfaaf* hoof (especially of a camel).

xiffa 1. agility, nimbleness. || *xiffat id-damm* amiability, charm, wittiness. 2. looseness, availability (of women).

xafaayfi (invar.) light, digestible. *ʔakla xafaayfi* a little light food, a light meal, a snack.

ʔaxaff 1. more or most lightweight. 2. more or most trivial. 3. more or most sparse. 4. more or most diluted. 5. more or most agile, etc.

xafiif pl. *xfaaf* 1. light, lightweight. *junṭa xafiifa* a light suitcase. *qmaaš xafiif* lightweight cloth. *waraq xafiif* thin paper, onionskin. *ṭabaqa xafiifa* light, thin layer. || *ʔakil xafiif* and *ʔakil xafiif ƹal-miƹda* light, easily digestible food. *maṭra xafiifa* a light shower. *muṭar xafiif* light rain. *ƹukum xafiif* a light sentence. 2. slight, little, trivial, inconsequential. *wujaƹ xafiif* a slight pain. *ƹmuuḏ̣a xafiifa* a little sourness. *ƹumra xafiifa* a little lipstick. || *suʔaal xafiif* an easy question. *šuġuḷ xafiif* easy work. *pookar xafiif* low-stake poker. *qmaar xafiif* gambling for low stakes. **3.** thin, sparse, scanty. *šaʕra xafiif.* His hair is thin. **4.** thin, diluted. *liban xafiif* thin yoghurt. *subuġ xafiif, booya xafiifa* thin paint. || *čaay xafiif* weak tea. **5.** agile, nimble, quick. *ṣiir xafiif, tʕarrak.* Be quick about it; get a move on. *xaadma xafiifa biš-šuġuḷ* a maid who is quick and efficient at her work || *ʔiida xafiifa.* He's a fast worker.

¶ *xafiif id-damm* charming, amiable, witty. *walad xafiif ʕal-miʕda* a sociable, pleasant man. *xafiif il-ʕaqil* simple-minded, feeble-minded. *bnayya xafiifa* a loose, easily available girl.

x-f-g

xufag (*u xafug*) **1.** to palpitate, beat, throb. *gaḷbi da-yuxfug.* My heart is palpitating. **2.** to flap, beat, flutter. *ṭ-ṭeer xufag ijnaaʕa marra w-maat.* The pigeon flapped its wings once and died. **3.** to beat, whip. *ʔuxfug-li beeðṭeen lil-keeka.* Beat me two eggs for the cake. || *xušš jawwa la-yxufgak il-hawa l-baarid.* Go inside so the cold wind won't hit you. **4.** to stucco. *l-banna da-yuxfug il-ʕaayiṭ b-ičbintu xafiif.* The mason's stuccoing the wall with grout.

xaffag to flap, flutter, beat. *šuuf iṭ-ṭeer da-yxaffug ib-jinʕaana.* Look at the bird flapping his wings.

x-f-y

xifa (*i xafi*) **1.** to hide, conceal. *ʔixfiiha b-fadd mukaan gabuḷ-ma yšuufha.* Hide it somewhere before he sees it. **2.** to conceal, keep secret. *ʔagul-lak loo ʔadri. ma-axfi ʕaleek šii.* I'd tell you if I knew. I don't hide anything from you.

txaffa **1.** to hide, keep out of sight. *da-yitxaffa w-maʕʕad yidri ween.* He is in hiding and nobody knows where. **2.** to disguise oneself. *čaan mitxaffi b-ihduum niswaan.* He was disguised in women's clothing.

xtifa **1.** to hide, conceal oneself, keep out of sight. *ṣ-ṣayyaad xtifa ʕatta ma-yšuufa ṭ-ṭeer.* The hunter concealed himself so the bird wouldn't see him. **2.** to disappear, vanish. *šloon ixtifa! hassa čaan mawjuud.* He simply disappeared! He was just here. *š-šakar xtifa mnis-suug.* Sugar's vanished from the market.

xifya secretly, covertly. *sawwaaha xifya bala ʕiss ʔaʕʕad.* He did it secretly without anyone's knowing it.

x-l-b

mixlab pl. *maxaalib* claw, talon.

x-l-j

xaliij pl. *xiljaan* gulf, bay.

x-ḷ-x-ḷ

xaḷxaḷ to shake, jiggle. *min da-yišlaʕ il-bismaar, xaḷxaḷa lil-meez kulla.* When he was pulling the nail, he shook the whole table.

xiḷxaaḷ pl. *xaḷaaxiiḷ* anklet, ankle bracelet (usually heavy and tinkling).

x-l-d

xallad to perpetuate, immortalize. *saw-woo-la tamaaθiil ʕatta yxalliduun ðikraa.* They built statues of him to perpetuate his memory.

txallad to be perpetuated, immortalized. *b-hat-taðʕiya raʕ-yitxallad ðikra.* By that sacrifice his memory will be immortalized.

x-l-s

xtilas to embezzle, misappropriate. *xtilas ʔalif diinaar min ifluus iš-šarika.* He embezzled a thousand dinars from company funds.

xilsa secretly. *ṭilaʕ imnil-beet xilsa w-maʕʕad dira bii.* He left the house secretly and no one knew about it.

xtilaas embezzlement.

muxtalis embezzler.

x-l-ṣ

xiḷaṣ (*a xaḷaaṣ*) **1.** to be freed, get rid of. *baacir raʕ-ʔanniqil w-axlaṣ min haš-šuġuḷ.* Tomorrow I am being transferred and will be relieved of this work. *raʕ-aštiri beet w-ʔaxḷaṣ.* I'm going to buy a house and be done with it. || *ʔixḷaṣ rastak.* Shoot the works! (Play the rest of your money). **2.** to be saved, rescued, to escape. *xiḷaṣ imnil-ʕabis b-iʕjuuba.* He avoided being imprisoned by a miracle. *xiḷaṣ imnil-moot ib-ʔiʕjuuba.* He escaped from death by a miracle. *giðeena ṣ-ṣeef ib-labnaan w-ixḷaṣna min ʕarr* bağdaad. We spent the summer in Lebanon to escape Baghdad's heat. **3.** to be finished, done, all through, over. *sayyaartak xiḷṣat. taʕaal ʔuxuðha.* Your car is ready. Come and get it. *l-qaaṭ maalak xiḷaṣ.* Your suit is finished. *qaðiyyat taʕyiinak xiḷṣat.* The matter of your appointment is all done. **4.** to become finished, used up. *mitʔassif. ma-aku ʔakil; kulla xiḷaṣ.* I'm sorry. There's no food; it's all gone. *l-wakit xiḷaṣ.* The time is up. || *xiḷṣat ruuʕi!* I'm plumb fed up! *xiḷaṣ! ʔaani š-aʕlayya baʕad?* That does it! (That settles it! that's it!) What concern of mine is it then?

xaḷḷaṣ **1.** to save, rescue, free, rid.

l-muʕaami xaḷḷaṣa mnis-sijin. The lawyer saved him from prison. *raʕ-yxaḷḷiṣ il-beet imnid-dibiib.* He's going to rid the house of crawling insects. *maʕʕad yigdar yxaḷḷṣak minni.* No one can save you from me. **2.** to finish, complete, get through. *l-xayyaaṭ ma-xaḷḷaṣ il-qaaṭ maali.* The tailor hasn't finished my suit. *xaḷḷaṣ santeen w-baʕad-la sana.* He completed two years and still has a year to go. *ʔariidak tiʕči wiyyaa w-itxaḷḷiṣ-li l-qaδiyya.* I want you to talk with him and bring this matter to a close. *šwakt itxaḷḷiṣ imniš-šuġuḷ?* What time do you get off work? || *ʔagdar axaḷḷiṣ-lak is-sayyaara b-ʔalif diinaar.* I can get you the car for a thousand dinars. *buṣaṭṭa baṣṭa xaḷḷaṣṭa biiha.* I beat the tar out of him, I gave him a beating he'll never forget. **3.** to use up, finish. *la-txaḷḷiṣ kull il-waraq.* Don't use up all the paper. *la-txaḷḷiṣ kull il-ʔakil; baʕad ʔuxuutak ma-aklaw.* Don't eat up all the food; your brothers haven't eaten yet. *xaḷḷaṣ il-buṭil waʕda.* He finished the bottle alone. **4.** to clear, make it. *min haṣ-ṣafʕa txaḷḷiṣ, laakin yimkin iṭṭuxx bil-ʕaayiṭ min ṣafuʕt il-luxx.* You're clear on this side, but you might hit the wall on the other side. *suuq ʕala keefak. tigdar itxaḷḷiṣ.* Drive slowly —you can make it. *bil-kaad iṭ-ṭiyyaara xaḷḷaṣat imnil-ašjaar.* The airplane just barely cleared the trees.

ʔaxḷaṣ to be devoted, faithful. *ʔaxḷaṣ-ilha ʔila ʔaaxir yoom min ʕayaaṭa.* He was faithful to her till his death.

txaḷḷaṣ to rid oneself. *bil-guwwa yaḷḷa txaḷḷaṣit minna.* I got rid of him only after a lot of trouble. *txaḷḷaṣit imnid-daʕwa lil-ʕafla.* I got out of going to the party. *txaḷḷaṣ min is-suʔaal maali.* He avoided my question.

staxḷaṣ to extract. *nistaxḷiṣ ʕiddat mawaadd imnin-nafṭ il-xaam.* We extract several products from crude oil.

xaḷaaṣ way out, way around. *haay maa minha xaḷaaṣ.* There's no way out of it.

xuḷaaṣa pl. *-aat* **1.** essence, extract. **2.** substance, gist. **3.** summary, resumé. || *xuḷaaṣa* and *l-xuḷaaṣa* in short, in a word, briefly. *l-xuḷaaṣa, haaδa muu ṣadiiq.* In short, he's no friend.

xaḷṣaan **1.** free, rid. *ʔiʕna xaḷṣaaniin min šarra l-ʕamdillaah.* We're rid of his annoying, thank God. *ʔaani xaḷṣaan min hal-mašaakil; baʕadni ma-mitzawwij.* I'm free of those problems; I'm not married yet. **2.** safe, saved, out of danger. *l-madiina xaḷṣaana mnil-ġarig hassa.* The city's safe from the flood now. **3.** finished, done, over. *qaaṭak xaḷṣaan. taʕaal ʔuxδa.* Your suit's ready. Come get it. *l-ʕafla xaṣḷaana.* The party's over. *kullši xaḷṣaan. raʕ-yizzawwaj baačir.* Everything's done. He's going to get married tomorrow. **4.** gone, finished, used up, worn out. *ma-aku xubuz. kulla xaḷṣaan.* There's no bread. It's all gone. *has-sayyaara xaḷṣaana. ma-tiswa* This car's done for. It's not worth anything. *l-mudda xaḷṣaana. laazim tidfaʕ il-yoom.* The time's up. You've got to pay today. || *gaḷbi xaḷṣaan imnil-qahar.* I'm sick from this misery.

maxḷaṣ final offer, firm price. *has-sitra maxḷaṣha b-diinaareen.* The bottom price on this jacket is two dinars. *ma-aku ʕaaja lil-muʕaamala. maxḷaṣ ib-diinaareen.* There's no use in bargaining. The final price is two dinars.

ʔaxḷaṣ more or most faithful, loyal, etc.

ʔixḷaaṣ loyalty.

xaaḷiṣ pure, unadulterated. *δahab xaaḷiṣ* pure gold.

muxḷiṣ loyal, faithful. *ṣadiiq muxḷiṣ* a loyal friend.

x-l-ṭ

xiḷaṭ (*u xaḷuṭ*) **1.** to mix, mingle, blend. *hal-ʕaṣiir qawi. laazim tuxulṭa b-ṃayy.* This juice is too thick. You better mix it with water. *la-tuxḷuṭ hal-ʔawraaq, xaliiha maʕzuula.* Don't mix these papers. Leave them separated. **2.** to be or become confused, mixed up. *daaʔiman axḷuṭ beena w-been axuu.* I always confuse him with his brother. *da-tuxḷuṭ been ič-čilimteen.* You're confusing the two words. *haaδa yuxḷuṭ ib-ʕačya.* He gets all mixed up in his speech.

xaaḷaṭ to mix, associate with. *ʔibnak da-yxaaliṭ jamaaʕa muu zeena.* Your son is mixing with a bad group

xtiḷaṭ **1.** to associate, mix. *ṣadiiqi ma-yʕijba yixtiḷiṭ wiyya l-ġeer.* My friend doesn't like to associate with others. **2.** to get all mixed up. *xtiḷaṭ il-ʕaabil bin-naabil.* Everything got all mixed up.

xaḷṭa pl. *-aat* mixture, blend, mix.

xtiḷaaṭ pl. *-aat* complication (med.).

mxaḷḷaṭ a mixture of candies, nuts, cookies, or fruits. || *mxaḷḷaṭ yaa looz.* the cry of the nut vendor. *mwaδδafiin had-daaʔira mxaḷḷaṭ yaa looz.* The employees in this office are a motley crew.

x-l-ع

xilaع (*a xaliع*) **1.** to dislocate, wrench. *jarrni min ʔiidi w-xilaع čitfi.* He pulled me by my hand and dislocated my shoulder. **2.** to depose, remove, dismiss. *xilعaw il-malik w-xallaw ʔibna b-mukaana.* They dethroned the King and put his son in his place.

xtilaع to tear out, pull out. *xtilaع iš-šijra min juδuurha.* He pulled up the tree by its roots.

xaliع dislocation.

xaliiع wanton, dissolute, dissipated, depraved. *huwwa fadd waaحid xaliiع ma-yistiحi.* He's a depraved fellow who knows no shame.

*xalaaعi** lewd, bawdy. *ṣuwar xalaaعiyya* lewd pictures, pornography.

x-l-f

xilaf (*i xalif*) to break, fail to keep. *xilaf il-mawعid maali.* He broke the date with me. *muu ṣaحiiح tixlif il-waعad.* It isn't right to break the promise.

xaḷḷaf **1.** to have offspring. *xaḷḷaf ʔarbaع aṭfaal.* He had four children. || *ʔanعal ʔabuuk la-abuu l-xaḷḷafak!* Damn your father and your father's father! **2.** to leave behind, leave. *min maat xaḷḷaf θarwa l-wilda.* When he died he left a fortune to his kids.

xaalaf **1.** to contradict. *ʔawwal marra gaalha hiiči w-baعdeen xaalaf nafsa.* The first time he said it this way, and later contradicted himself. **2.** to be different, to differ, to diverge, to be inconsistent, incompatible, not in keeping. *raʔyak yxaalif raʔyi.* Your opinion differs from my opinion. *ʔaani ʔaxaalfak ib-hal-mawḍuuع.* I differ with you on this subject. *yimši daayman عala qaaعidat xaalif tuعraf.* He always follows the principle: Be different and you'll be known. *taṣarrufaata txaalif il-ʔuṣuul.* His conduct is at variance with good manners.. *šurb il-عarag yxaalif id-diin.* Drinking arrack is not in keeping with religion. **3.** break, violate, disobey. *s-saayiq xaalaf il-qaanuun.* The driver violated the law. *ma-yṣiir itxaalif raġbat abuuk.* You mustn't go against your father's wishes. **4.** to matter, to make a difference. *yxaalif šii ʔiδa aruuح?* Would there be any objection to my leaving? *š-yxaalif iδa gilit hiiči?* What difference does it make if I said that? *ma-yxaalif. ma-عindi maaniع.* It doesn't make any difference. I've got no objections.

txallaf to fall behind, lag behind. *ṣiqaṭ biṣ-ṣaff il-xaamis w-itxallaf عan jamaaعta.* He failed in the fifth class and fell behind his group. **2.** to fail to appear, to stay away. *txallaf عan il-xidma l-عaskariyya w-حibsoo.* He failed to appear for his military service and they jailed him.

xtilaf **1.** to differ, be different, vary. *hal-iqmaaš yixtilif, muu miθl illi ʔariida.* This cloth is different, not like the one I want. *ʔaaraaʔ il-xubaraaʔ ixtilfat ib-hal-mawḍuuع.* The opinions of the experts varied on this matter. **2.** to disagree, argue, quarrel. *wilda xtilfaw عala taqsiim il-gaaع.* His sons quarrelled over division of the land. *š-šuhuud ixtilfaw. kull waaحid حiča šikil.* The witnesses disagreed. Each one said something different.

xalfa pl. *-aat* apprentice, assistant.

xuḷfa pl. *xuḷaf* **1.** offspring, issue. **2.** ugly face, mug, puss.

xaliifa pl. *xulafaaʔ* caliph.

xalaafa pl. *-aat* caliphate.

xilaaf pl. *-aat* **1.** difference, disparity, dissimilarity. *xilaaf bir-raʔi* a difference of opinion. **2.** disagreement, difference of opinion. **3.** dispute, controversy.

mixlif pl. *maxaalif* (adj. and n.) young male, immature male (bird).

muxaalafa pl. *-aat.* **1.** violation, infringement. **2.** misdemeanor.

xtilaaf pl. *-aat* difference, disparity.

muxaalif dissenter.

x-l-q

xilaq (*i xaliq*) to create. *ʔaḷḷa xilaq il-ʔarḍ w-is-samaawaat.* God created the earth and the skies. *ʔaḷḷa yixliq w-muحammad yibtili.* Man proposes and God disposes (lit., God creates and Mohammed suffers). Used to express exasperation at a nuisance that must be endured. *la-tgul-li "ma-adri weena"! ʔixilqa!* Don't tell me "I don't know where he is." Pull him out of thin air!

xtilaq to think up, concoct, fabricate. *xtilaq quṣṣa xayaaliyya, win-naas saddgaw bii.* He made up a fanciful story, and people believed him. *l-حaadiθa muu حaqiiqiyya. huwwa xtilaqha.* The incident is not true. He made it up.

xuluq pl. *ʔaxlaaq* **1.** character, behavior. **2.** (pl.) *ʔaxlaaq* manners. **3.** morals.

xilqa pl. *xilaq* face, countenance, looks. *xilqa حilwa* an attractive face. || *xilqata ngiḷbat min simaع bil-xabar.* His face fell when he heard the news. *xilqatha magluuba li-ˀan baɛad ma-mxallya masaaɛiiq.* Her face is a mess because she hasn't put on her make-up yet.

*ˀaxlaaqi** moral. *fuṣloo l-ˀasbaab ˀaxlaaqiyya.* They fired him for moral reasons.

xaluuq polite, well-mannered. *ˀibin jiiraanna šloon xaluuq!* Our neighbors' son is awfully polite.

l-xallaaq The Creator.

maxluuq pl. *-aat* creature.

x-l-g

xuḷug 1. mood, temper, disposition. *xuḷga ḏayyig.* He's short-tempered. *ḏaag xuḷgi bil-beet; xal-niṭlaɛ nitmašša.* I feel confined in the house; let's go for a walk. || *ˀummi ma-ˀilha xuḷug il-yoom.* My mother isn't feeling well today. *la-tiɛči wiyyaa. ma-ˀila xuḷug.* Don't talk to him. He's in a bad mood. *ˀuxuð ˀibnak. ˀaani ma-ˀili xuḷga.* Take your son. I'm not in the mood to put up with him. *maa-li xuḷg id-diraasa wil-imtiɛaanaat.* I don't have the get-up-and-go for study and examinations 2. patience, even temper. *xuḷga ṭuwiil.* His patience is great. *tarbiit il-ˀaṭfaal yriid-ilha xuḷug.* Raising children requires patience.

xaḷag 1. worn out, useless. *xaḷag sayyaara* a beat-up old car. 2. lowly, mere. *xaḷag kaatib* a mere clerk.

mxaḷgan run-down, worn-out, shabby. *mwaððaf imxaḷgan* a seedy official. *sayyaara mxaḷgana* a run-down car.

x-l-l

txallal to come between, be located between. *t-tamθiiliyyaat čaan titxallalha qiṭaɛ muuṣiiqiyya.* Musical selections were interspersed between the dramas.

xtall 1. to become disrupted, disturbed. *čaan da-yimši ɛal-ɛabil laakin xtall tawaazna w-wugaɛ.* He was walking on the rope, but he lost his balance and fell. *xtallat il-muwaaṣalaat been iθ-θawra.* Communications were disrupted during the revolution. *ˀiða txalli ˀiidak hnaa, yixtall it-tawaazun.* If you put your hand here, the balance will be disturbed. *xtall ɛaqla w-waddoo l-mustašfa l-majaaniin.* His mind became disturbed and they took him to the mental hospital.

xaḷḷ vinegar.

xalal pl. *xilaal* defect, deficiency. *xalal miikaaniiki* a mechanical defect.

xilla pl. *-aat* defect, deficiency, flaw, fault, shortcoming.

xilaal 1. interval, space, period. *b-xilaal itlaθ isniin* in the period of three years. 2. (prep.) during. *xilaal hal-mudda* during this time.

ˀixlaal pl. *-aat* 1. breach, infraction, violation. 2. disturbance. *ˀixlaal bil-ˀamin* disturbance of the peace.

xḷaaḷ (coll.) dates, crisp and not yet ripe.

xḷaaḷa pl. *-aat* 1. un. n. of *xḷaaḷ* 2. (vulgar) glans penis.

muxill: || *muxill bil-ˀaadaab* immoral, indecent, improper.

x-l-y

xalla 1. to leave, allow or cause to remain. *tɛaššu w-xalluu-li šwayya.* Eat your supper and leave me a little bit. *xalleeta bis-siinama; raad yšuuf il-filim marrt il-luxx.* I left him behind at the movie; he wanted to see the film another time. *min titlaɛ, la-txalli l-baab mafkuuka.* When you go out, don't leave the door open. *ɛičaw ɛaleeha ɛači w-ma-xallaw šii ma-gaaloo.* They talked about her and didn't leave anything unsaid. *ma-xalla ˀaɛɛad ma-gal-la.* There was no one he didn't tell. || *ɛali gaal hiiči? di-xalliina min haaða; kaððaab.* Ali said that? Spare us from him; he's a liar. 2. to keep, retain, hold. *xalli l-ifluus ɛindak ˀila ˀan ˀaɛtaajha.* Keep the money with you until I need it. *xalli ɛeenak ɛaj-jaahil.* Keep your eye on the child. *baḷḷa xalli hal-qaðiyya ɛala baalak.* Please keep this matter in mind. *xalluu-li mukaan yamm-kum.* Save me a place near you. 3. to put, place. *xalli xamis gaḷnaat baanziin bis-sayyaara.* Put five gallons of gas in the car. *xalli l-iglaaṣ ɛal-meez.* Put the glass on the table. *xalla wahsa bil-iqmaar. laa da-yištuġuḷ wala da-yidrus.* He's put all his energy into gambling. He's neither working nor studying. *leeš xaall haṭ-ṭweerni wiyya ṭyuurak?* Why do you keep that wild pigeon with your domesticated pigeons? *ween xaall il-miftaaɛ?* Where do you keep the key? *bintič xaalla ɛumrat išfaaf.* Your daughter is wearing lipstick. *xaall ɛeena ɛala has-sayyaara; yriid yištiriiha.* He's set on this car; he wants to buy it. || *haaða š-imgaddra yuġḷubni? ˀaxallii b-jeebi.* How can he beat me? He's no problem (lit., I'll put him in my pocket). *leeš xalleet nafsak?* Why did you interfere? 4. to let, allow. *hal-masjuun ma-yxalluun waaɛid yšuufa.* They don't allow anyone to see this prisoner. *xallii yilbas ihduuma.* Let him get dressed.

xalliini ˀafakkir. Let me think. **5.** to cause, make, have. *xalli yruuḥ lil-bang.* Have him go to the bank. *xalla kull in-naas yḍiḥkuun.* He made all the people laugh. *hal-ˀeeryal yxalli r-raadyo yištuğuḷ ˀaḥsan.* This aerial makes the radio operate better. **6.** /in imperative/ (showing inclination, desire, command) let. *xalli ilʕab waraq.* Let's play cards. *yaḷḷa, ʕaad, xalli nruuḥ!* C'mon man, let's go! *ˀiδa ma-ddaawum, yfuṣluuk. xalli.* If you don't show up, they'll fire you. Let them.

ˀaxla **1.** to vacate. *l-ḥukuuma gaalat laazim nixli l-beet maalna.* The government announced we have to vacate our house. **2.** to evacuate. *l-faṣiil iθ-θaani ˀaxla markaza.* The second platoon evacuated its position. *j-jeeš ˀaxla l-madiina mnis-sukkaan.* The army evacuated the populace from the city.

txalla /with *ʕan*/ **1.** to give up, relinquish, abandon. *ma-xalloo yidzawwajha ˀilla lamma txalla ʕan nuṣṣ ˀamlaaka.* They wouldn't let him marry her until he gave up half of his property. *ma-yitxalla ʕan iṣ-ṣadiiq ʕind iš-šidda.* He doesn't abandon a friend during a crisis. **2.** to be left. *l-ifluus ma-yitxalla b-hiiči mukaan.* Money mustn't be left in that sort of place. || *haaδa ma-yitxalla bil-ʕibb.* He's a tough nut to crack (lit. he can't be put in the pocket).

txaḷḷa to visit the toilet. *raaḥ yitxaḷḷa w-hassa yiji.* He went to visit the rest room and he'll be right back.

xtila to go off, retire, be alone, withdraw. *xtila bii w-ğal-la bis-sirr.* He stepped aside with him and told him about the secret.

xalaaˀ, beet il-xalaaˀ toilet, water closet.

xalwa pl. *-aat* secluded, isolated place.

xaḷwa pl. *xaḷaawi* toilet, water closet.

xaliyya, pl. *xalaaya* **1.** cell (biol.). **2.** beehive. *xaliyyat ʕasal.* beehive.

xaali **1.** empty, void. *ṣanduug xaali* an empty chest. **2.** vacant. *beet xaali* a vacant house. **3.** free, clear, devoid. *meezi xaali min ˀawraaq.* My desk is free of papers. *baala xaali.* His mind is clear. || *xubuz xaali* plain bread.

x-m-x-m

xamxam **1.** to become spoiled, tainted. *l-ˀakil xamxam w-δabbeenaa.* The food got a taint to it and we threw it out. **2.** to loaf, lounge. *ma-ʕinda šuğuḷ ğeer yxamxum biš-šawaariʕ.* He has nothing to do but loaf around the streets. **3.** to rummage, fumble about. *leeš da-txamxum bil-ğaraaḍ?* Why are you rummaging in the things?

x-m-d

ximad (*u xumuud*) **1.** to go out, die. *la-titruk in-naar gabuḷ-ma tuxmud.* Don't leave the fire until it goes out. **2.** to calm down, die down, abate. *l-burkaan xumad.* The volcano became quiet. **3.** to quiet down, shut up, be still. *š-gadd tibči! ma-raḥ-tuxmud?* You cry so much! Aren't you going to shut up?

xammad to quench, put out. *δabb ṃayy ʕan-naar w-xammadha.* He threw water on the fire and extinguished it.

ˀaxmad to quell, put down. *j-jeeš ˀaxmad iθ-θawra b-surʕa.* The army quelled the revolt quickly.

xaamid **1.** inactive. *burkaan xaamid* an inactive volcano. **2.** quiet, still, silent. *j-jaahil xaamid hassa.* The kid's quiet now.

x-m-r

xammar **1.** to leaven, raise, let rise. *ma-yṣiir tuxkuz il-ʕajiin bala-ma txammura.* You shouldn't bake the dough without letting it rise. *l-xumra haay ma-txammur l-ʕajiin kulla.* That leaven won't raise all the dough. **2.** to rise. *xalli l-ʕajiin yxammur zeen.* Let the dough rise well. **3.** to let ferment, cause to ferment. *biš-šimaal, yxammuruun ʕaṣiir il-ʕinab, w-ysawwuu šaraab.* In the North, they ferment grape juice and make it into wine. **4.** to ferment. *ʕaṣiir il-ʕinab xammar; baʕad ma-yinšurub.* The grape juice fermented; it's not drinkable any more.

txammar **1.** to veil oneself, wear a veil. *l-badu biṣ-ṣaḥraaˀ yitxammuruun, laakin tigdar itšuuf iʕyuunhum.* The Bedouins in the desert veil themselves but you can see their eyes. *ˀumma ma-tiṭlaʕ ˀiδa ma-titxammar.* His mother doesn't go out without putting on a veil. **2.** to rise. *xalli l-ʕajiin yitxammar zeen gabuḷ-ma txubza.* Let the dough rise well before you bake it. **3.** to ferment. *ʕaṣiir il-ʕinab txammar.* The grape juice has fermented.

xtimar to rise. *xtimar il-ʕajiin. xubzii.* The dough has risen. Bake it.

xamur pl. *xumuur* **1.** wine. **2.** liquor, alcoholic beverage.

*xamri** reddish brown, rosy *loon xamri* wine color. *xduud xamriyya* rosy cheeks.

xumra pl. *-aat* fermenting agent, starter (in making yoghurt, bread), yeast.

xmaar pl. *-aat* veil covering the head and face, worn by women.

xmaariyya pl. *-aat* hangover.

xammaar pl. *-a* **1.** Alcoholic, drunkard. **2.** experienced drinker.

x-m-s

xammas to divide (property) into fifths. *xammisaw ifluusa min maat.* They divided his money into fifths when he died.

xumus pl. *ˀaxmaas* one fifth.

xamsa pl. *-aat* five. *xamis keeluwaat* five kilos. ¦| *l-baarḥa bil-ʕaziima δirabna bil-xamsa.* Yesterday at the dinner party we really dug in (lit. used all five fingers).

xumustaʕaš fifteen.

xamsiin pl. *-aat* fifty.

l-xamiis, yoom il-xamiis Thursday.

xmayyis: ˀabu xmayyis a figurative term for a lion.

l-xaamis the fifth.

muxammas pentagon.

x-m-š

xumaš (*u xamuš*) to snatch, to grab. *lamma ma-nṭaah-iyyaa, xumašha min ˀiida w-širad.* When he wouldn't give it to him, he snatched it from his hand and ran away.

xammaš (intens. of *xumaš*). *luweeš da-txammuš? raḥ-ninṭiik-iyyaahum.* Why are you grabbing so much? We will give them to you.

xamša pl. *-aat* a grab, a snatch.

x-m-ṣ

ˀaxmuṣ butt (of a rifle).

[1]*x-m-l*

xamḷa nap, pile, hairy surface (of a fabric).

xaamil lazy, sluggish. *fadd waaḥid xaamil* a lazy guy.

maxmal velvet.

[2]*x-m-l*

xammaḷ to estimate, appraise, assess. *šgadd itxammuḷ ˀiijaar hal-beet?* How much would you guess the rent of this house to be?

xamaḷ estimate, appraisal, assessment. *b-xamaḷak* in your estimation, in your estimate.

x-m-m

xamm (*u xamm*) **1.** to check, try. *xumm il-ˀakil, šuufa stiwa.* Check the food and see if it's done. *xumm ijyuuba; šuufa šaayil siččiina.* Check his pockets; see if he's carrying a knife. *xumm ij-jaahil, šuufa naayim loo laa.* Check the baby and see if he's sleeping or not. *xumm-li fikra. raḥ-ybiiʕ il-ḥooš loo laa?* Check out this idea for me. Is he going to sell his house or not? *xammeet ib-kull il-maxaazin w-ma-ligeet hiiči qalam.* I've tried in all the stores and couldn't find that sort of pencil. **2.** to test, try. *raad yxummak ˀawwal, yšuufak tiṣlaḥ il-hal-waδiifa.* He wanted to test you first, to see if you're suitable for that job. *čaan da-yxummni. raad yšuuf ˀabuug šii.* He was testing me. He wanted to see if I'd steal something. **3.** to search, explore, rummage. *š-aku ʕindak da-txumm bil-ġaraaδ?* How come you're rummaging through the things? *xumm ij-jaahil w-šuuf ˀiδa ˀaku šii b-jeeba.* Search the child and see if there's anything in his pocket. *xammeet is-suug kulla w-ma-šifit miθil hal-iglaaṣ.* I searched all through the market and didn't see a glass like this. *ˀaani xaamm ˀooruppa kullha.* I've travelled all over Europe.

x-m-n

xamman to assess, appraise, estimate. *raḥ-yiji muwaδδaf yxammin il-beet il-yoom.* An official is coming to appraise the house today. *tigdar itxammin siʕir hal-beet?* Can you estimate the price of this house?

muxammin assessor, appraiser.

x-n-θ

xannaθ **1.** to scare, terrify, cow. *xannaθ-ilk-iyyaa b-ṣeeḥa wiḥda.* He really terrified him with one roar. *xannaθta bis-šiṭranj il-baarḥa. ġilabta xamis marraat w-baʕad ma-yilʕab wiyyaaya.* I cowed him in chess yesterday. I beat him five times and now he won't play with me. **2.** to get scared. *min yšiil ʕalee s-siččiina, yxanniθ.* When he pulls a knife on him, he turns chicken.

txannaθ **1.** to be effeminate. *la-titxannaθ ib-libsak.* Don't be effeminate in your dress. **2.** to turn coward, chicken out. *min šaafni jaay, txannaθ w-sikat.* When he saw me coming, he chickened out and shut up. *fuut ʕalee! la-titxannaθ!* Go get him! Don't be chicken!

xunθaa (no pl.) hermaphrodite.

xaniiθ coward, timid person, chicken. *xaniiθ xabiiθ* trouble-making coward.

xnaaθ, xanaaθ pl. *-aat* (vulgar) vulva.

ˀaxnaθ more or most cowardly. *ˀaxnaθ imniddijaaja.* More cowardly than the chicken.

mxannaθ pl. *maxaaniiθ, mxaanθa.* **1.** effeminate man. **2.** coward, sissy. **3.** powerless, weak, ineffectual person.

x-n-j-r

xanjar pl. *xanaajir* dagger, usually with a curved blade.

xanjarliyya pl. *-aat* small dagger.

x-n-x-n

xanxan to talk nasally, talk through one's nose. *yxanxin ib-ḉačya hwaaya.* He nasalizes his speech a lot. *min yiḉči, yxanxin (ib-xašma).* When he talks, he talks through his nose.

xanxana nasalization, nasal twang.

x-n-d-q

xandaq pl. *xanaadiq* var. of *xandag,* which see.

x-n-d-g

xandag pl. *xanaadig* **1.** moat. **2.** trench.

x-n-z-r

xanzar to glare, stare angrily. *luweeš da-txanzir ḉalayya? š-sawweet?* Why are you glaring at me? What did I do?

txanzar to be or become a swine, a bastard. *min itwaḏḏaf, itxanzar.* When he got the job, he became a swine.

xanziir, xinziir pl. *xanaaziir* pig, hog, swine.

xanziira, xinziira pl. *-aat* **1.** female pig, sow. **2.** water pump, hand pump.

x-n-s

xinas (i, a xanis) **1.** to cower, withdraw, shrink back. *xinas jawwa l-meez.* He cowered under the table. *ṣiiḉ bii, hassa yixnis.* Shout at him and he'll shrink back. **2.** to subside, quiet down, shut up. *min ṣaaḉ ib-ʔibna, xinas.* When he shouted at his son, he shut up. *huwwa xaanis w-gaaḉid.* He's sitting subdued.

xannas to cow, make cower. *xannasa ib-ṣeeḉa waḉda.* He made him cower with one shout.

l-xannaas name for the Devil: || *laabis iklaaw il-xannaas.* He's invisible (lit., he's wearing the Devil's cap).

x-n-ṣ-r

xunṣur pl. *xanaaṣir* little finger.

x-n-f-s

xanfas **1.** to die down, go down, subside, dim. *n-naar xanfisat. ḉuṭṭ-ilha baḉad faḉam.* The fire's died down. Put some more coal on it. *l-faanuus xanfas. yimkin xilaṣ in-nafuṭ.* The lantern has dimmed. Maybe the oil is all gone. *min šiḉalt iṭ-ṭabbaax, il-igloob xanfas.* When I turned on the oven, the light dimmed. *ʔašu l-ṃaay xanfas. ybayyin jiiraanna hamm gaam yizguun ḉadiiqathum.* I notice the water pressure's gone down. Looks like the neighbors have started to water their garden again. **2.** to quiet down, calm down. *xanfas min šaaf ir-rijjaal išloon qawi.* He quieted down when he saw how strong the man was.

x-n-f-s-a-n

xunfisaan (coll.) beetle(s).

xunfisaana pl. *-aat* beetle.

x-n-g

xinag (i xanig) **1.** to choke. *ḉaḏum simač xinagni.* A fishbone choked me. *d-duxxaan ib-hal-maḉall yixnig.* The smoke in this place is choking. **2.** to choke (a motor, usually by putting one's hand over the carburetor mouth). *ʔixnig il-kaabreeta.* Choke the carburetor. **3.** to choke to death, strangle, suffocate, smother. *j-jaahil xinag il-bazzuuna.* The kid strangled the cat. *ligoo bis-sayyaara bil-garaaj mayyit. duxxaan is-sayyaara xinaga.* They found him in the car in the garage. The smoke from the car overcame him. *wugaḉ biš-šaṭṭ wil-ṃaay xinaga.* He fell in the river and drowned.

xannag intens. of *xinag. j-jahhaal da-yxanniguun il-ḉaṣaafiir.* The kids are choking the sparrows.

txaanag **1.** to choke one another. *faakik ij-jahhaal. da-yitxaanguun.* Separate the kids. They're choking each other. **2.** to quarrel, dispute, pick a fight. *ma-aku ḉaaja titxaanag wiyya n-naas.* There is no reason for you to jump down people's throats.

xtinag **1.** to choke. *ma-aku šii. xtinaġit bil-ʔakil.* It's nothing. I choked on the food. *xtinagit imnid-duxxaan.* I choked from the smoke. **2.** to choke to death, suffocate. *wugaf il-ʔakil ib-zarduuma w-ixtinag.* The food caught in his throat and he choked to death. *ṣaar ḉariig bil-ġurfa maala w-ixtinag.* There was a fire in his room and he suffocated. *xtinag jawwa t-tiraab.* He suffocated under the dirt. *wugaḉ bil-ṃaay w-ixtinag.* He fell into the water and drowned.

xanig strangulation, suffocation.

xanga pl. *-aat* **1.** congestion, crowding, jam. **2.** madhouse, mess, crowded place. *s-suug čaan xanga l-yoom.* The market was a madhouse today.

xinnaag id-dijaaj a type of plant poisonous to chickens.

x-n-m

xaanim, xaanum pl. *xawaanim* **1.** (a term of respectful address to a lady, approx.:) madam, ma'am. **2.** (a casual way of referring to a man's wife, approx.:) the little woman, the missus. *ˀija huwwa wil-xaanum maalta.* He and his wife came. *l-xaanim maalta raakubta.* His missus wears the pants in the family.

x-n-n

xann (i xann) to speak nasally, nasalize. *min yiCči yxinn* or *yxinn ib-Cačya.* He speaks nasally. *yxinn ib-xašma.* He talks through his nose.

xanna nasal twang. *ˀabu xanna* man with a nasal twang.

x-n-a-w-a

xanaawa (invar.) sissified, unmanly. *la-tṣiir xanaawa.* Don't be a sissy.

x-w

xoo **1.** an interjection implying apprehension or hope. *xoo ma-simaC?* He hasn't heard, has he? *xoo ma-ziCal?* He didn't get mad, did he? *xoo maa l-ṃaay burad?* The water hasn't cooled off, has it? *xoo ma-triid itruuC hassa.* You don't want to go now, I hope. **2.** thus, therefore, so. *xoo ma-biqa Calayya deen.* So I don't owe anything anymore. *xoo ma-Cindak Cijja baCad.* So you've got no more excuse. **3.** (as an intensifier, approx.:) oh, why, heck. *xoo l-kull yiCrifuun išgadd aCibbak. ma-maCquul asawwi biik hiiči.* Oh everyone knows how much I like you. I couldn't do anything like that to you. *xoo ˀay waaCid yigdar ysawwi haaδa.* Heck, anyone can do that!

x-w-b

xoob = xoo.

x-w-b-y-a-r

xuubyaar milt.

x-w-x

xoox (coll.) peach(es)

xooxa pl. *-aat* peach.

x-w-δ

xuuδa pl. *xuwaδ* helmet.

x-w-r

xaar (u xoor) to tour, wander around. *xirit ˀooruṗṗa kullha.* I went all over Europe.

xawwar to run around, wander, roam. *ˀibinha ma-Cinda šuġuḷ; bass yxawwur bid-daraabiin.* Her son has no job and just bums around the streets.

xoora pl. *-aat* **1.** tour, trip, spin, turn, round. **2.** whirlpool.

xawwaar pl. *-a* well traveled, having gotten around a lot. *yuCruf kull mukaan bil-wlaaya li-ˀanna xawwaar ihwaaya.* He knows every corner of the city because he's gotten around a lot.

x-w-r-d

txoorad to treat. *raC-ˀatxoorad Caleek ib-doondirma.* I'll treat you to an ice cream. *da-yitxoorad Cal-ibnayya b-ifluus ġeera.* He's treating the girl with money that isn't his. *yitxoorad Car-raayiC wij-jaay.* He pays for everyone whether he knows them or not.

xwaarda (invar.) generous. *walad ixwaarda* a generous fellow.

x-w-z-q

xoozaq to stick, cheat, take in. *la-tištiri minna tara yxooziqak.* Don't buy from him or he'll stick you.

txoozaq to get stuck, to be taken in. *ˀaani txoozaqit ib-haš-šarwa.* I got stuck on this deal.

xaazuuq pl. *xawaaziiq* (originally, post or stake, now in expressions, approx.:) shaft. || *ˀakal il-xaazuuq.* He got the shaft, he got taken.

x-w-š

xooš **1.** good, fine, excellent. *xooš sayyaara* a good car. *xooš walad* a nice guy. *xooš. ašuufak is-saaCa sitta.* Good. I'll see you at six. || *xooš Cači!* Good idea! Now you're talking! **2.** = *xoo* which see under *x-w.*

*xooši** tart, bittersweet. *rummaana xoošiyya* a tart pomegranate.

x-w-š-g

xoošag **1.** to eat with a spoon. *šifithum yxoošguun biš-šoorba.* I saw them eating soup with spoons. **2.** to stir with a spoon. *xoošagt ič-čaay zeen?* Did you stir up the tea well enough? **3.** (by extension) to drink tea. *ṭabbeet Caleehum w-ilgeethum yxoošguun.* I dropped in on them and found them drinking tea.

xaašuuga pl. *xawaašiig* spoon, (and by extension,) spoonful. *xaašuugat ˀakil* table spoon. *xaašuugat čaay* demi-tasse spoon. *xaašuugat kuub* teaspoon.

x-w-ṣ

xuuṣ (coll.) palm leaf, palm leaves.

xuuṣa pl. *-aat, xuwaṣ* **1.** palm leaf **2.** a type of bracelet in the form of a coil.

x-w-δ̣

xaaδ̣ (u xooδ̣) to wade. *šaal dišdaašta w-ṭabb yxuuδ̣ bil-ṃayy.* He lifted his robe and went wading in the water.

x-w-f

xaaf (a xoof) to be scared, afraid, worried, concerned, apprehensive. *xifit bil-Carka; wala ṭallaCit raasi.* I was scared during the fight; I never even stuck my head out. *la-txaaf; ič-čalib may-yCaδ̣δ̣.*

Don't be afraid; the dog doesn't bite. *ʔaxaaf ʔaḉči wiyyaa hassa li-ʔan mašġuul.* I'm afraid to talk to him now, because he's busy. *yxaaf min marta.* He's afraid of his wife. *xaaf ʔaḷḷa w-la-tiḉči ḉan-naas.* Fear God and don't talk about people. *ʔaxuuk xaaf ḉaleek huwaaya.* Your brother was worried about you a lot. *la-txaaf ḉalee. huwwa kulliš šaaṭir.* Don't worry about him. He's very clever. || (invar.) *xaaf* or *ʔaxaaf* it's conceivable, perhaps, possibly, maybe. *xaaf yiji lil-beet w-ma-yilgaani.* It's possible he'll come to the house and not find me. *ʔaxaaf ma-ḉinda fluus wil-has-sabab ma-jaa.* I'm afraid he didn't have money and that's the reason he didn't come. *ʔaxaaf min ṭaraf l-ifluus.* Maybe it's about money. *ʔaxaaf ḉan it-tarfiiḉ maali.* Hey, maybe it's about my promotion! *xaaf yisʔal ḉanni gul-la hassa yiji.* Just in case he asks about me, tell him I'm coming right away. *ʔuxuδ wiyyaak ʔakil xaaf idjuuḉ.* Take some food with you in case you get hungry.

xawwaf to scare, frighten, alarm, worry. *ṭilaḉ-li min wara l-baab w-xawwafni.* He jumped at me from behind the door and scared me. *xawwafni kulliš min wugaḉ imnid-daraj.* He scared me to death when he fell down the stairs. *l-ḉaala da-txawwuf.* The situation is alarming. *hač-čalib yxawwuf.* This dog is frightening.

txawwaf pass. of *xawwaf. da-atxawwaf imnil-waδ̣iḉ.* I am alarmed at the situation. *la-tuṭlub minna ysawwiiha. yitxawwaf ihwaaya.* Don't ask him to do it. He's very fearful.

xoof fear, fright.

xawwaaf 1. fearful, timid, fainthearted. *ʔibnak xawwaaf ihwaaya.* Your son's very timid. 2. coward.

ʔaxwaf more or most cowardly. *ʔaxwaf imniddijaaja* more cowardly than the chicken.

x-w-l

xawwal to authorize. *xawwalni ʔawaqqiḉ iṣ-ṣukuuk maalta.* He authorized me to sign his checks.

xaaḷ pl. *xwaaḷ* maternal uncle.

xaaḷa pl. *-aat* 1. maternal aunt. 2. (form of address to a much older woman approx.:) madam. *xaaḷa, tidriin ween daaʔirt il-bariid?* Ma'am, do you know where the post office is?

xaaḷu (as a form of address) = *xaaḷi* my uncle. || *ruuḉ, yaa ẓġayyir; jiib xaaḷu.* Go on, Junior; get Uncle.

taxwiil authorization.

[1]*x-w-n*

xaan (*u xiyaana*) 1. to betray. *rimoo bir-riṣaaṣ li-ʔan xaan waṭana.* They shot him because he betrayed his country. *la-dgul-la bis-sirr tara yxuunak.* Don't tell him the secret or he will give you away. 2. to cheat, deceive. *zawijta txuuna ḉala ṭuul.* His wife's cheating on him all the time.

xawwan to consider or call treacherous, unfaithful, disloyal, or dishonest. *ʔinta da-txawwinni b-šii ma-tuḉruf ḉanna.* You're making me out to be dishonest in something you don't know about. 2. to distrust, be suspicious of. *ma-aku ḉaaja tṣiir šakkaak w-itxawwin in-naas il-yištaġḷuun ḉindak.* There is no need to be suspicious and to mistrust the people who work for you.

xaaʔin pl. *xawana* traitor.

[2]*x-w-n*

xaan, xaana see under *x-a-n.*

[1]*x-w-y*

xuwa (*i xawi*) 1. to extort money from. *l-ʔašqiyaaʔ xuwa l-muumisaat.* The thug extracted protection money from the prostitutes. || *kull-ma ašuufa yixwiini jigaara.* Whenever I see him he bums a cigarette.

xaawa protection, protection money. || *tiin xaawa* a white clay used by women as a beauty cream.

[2]*x-w-y*

xuuya see under *ʔ-x-w.*

x-y

xee name of the letter *x.*

x-y-b

xaab (*i xeeb*) to be dashed, let down, disappointed. *xaab δ̣anni biik.* My opinion of you has been lowered. *xaab ʔamali bil-mudiir ij-jidiid.* My hopes in the new director were dashed.

xayyab to dash, disappoint, let down. *la-txayyib ʔamali biik.* Don't disappoint my hopes for you.

xaayib: || *ʔibn il-xaayba* a failure in life (lit., son of a disappointed woman).

x-y-a-r

xyaar (coll.) cucumber(s).

xyaara pl. *-aat* cucumber.

x-y-r

xayyar to let choose, to give a choice. *xayyarta been iθ-θoob wil-ibluuz.* I gave him the choice between the shirt and the sweater.

txayyar to choose, take one's choice. *loo truuḉ idjiibha, loo ddizz waaḉid yjiibha;*

txayyar. Either you go get it or you send someone to get it; you take your choice.

xtaar to choose, select, pick. *minu xtaar hal-loon?* Who chose this color?

staxaar to ask (God) for guidance. *stixiir ʔaḷḷa gabuḷ-ma tsaafir.* Ask God for proper guidance before you go travelling.

staxyar to choose, pick. *kulla giddaamak. staxyir iš-ma triid.* They're all in front of you. Choose whatever you want.

xeer **1.** good, excellent, outstanding, superior. *has-sana xeer. muṭrat ihwaaya wil-ʕunṭa kulliš zeena.* This year is prosperous. It rained a lot and the wheat is very good. **2.** best. *l-xeer fii-ma xtaarahu ḷḷaa.* Whatever God willed is best. *simaʕit izzawwajit. biiha l-xeer, inšaḷḷa.* I heard you got married. I wish you the best. **3.** good thing, blessing. **4.** good, benefit, advantage. *haaδa ma-bii xeer.* He's not worth anything. || *ʔiδa biik xeer, iṭṣaaraʕ wiyya waaʕid ib-gaddak.* If you're the man you think you are, fight with someone your own size. **5.** charity. *ʕamal il-xeer* charitable work.

¶ *xeer inšaḷḷa. š-aku?* I hope everything's all right. What's wrong? *ʔaškurak, ʔaani b-xeer.* thank you. I'm in good shape. *ʔaḷḷaa bil-xeer!* a polite formula used after someone arrives and sits down. Also the answer to *ʔaḷḷaa bil-xeer. ʕal-xeer, ʕal-xeer! smaʕit nijaʕit.* congratulations! I heard you passed. *ṣabaaʕ il-xeer. šloonak il-yoom?* Good morning. How are you today?

*xayri** charitable. *jamʕiyya xayriyya* a charitable organization.

xayyir **1.** generous man. **2.** charitable, benevolent man.

xiira pl. *-aat* **1.** best, choice, pick, elite, cream. **2.** fortune, lot. || *xalli aaxuδ-lak xiira.* Let me tell your fortune.

ʔaxyar more or most honorable, upstanding, etc.

xtiyaar pl. *-aat* choice, selection, option. || *dzawwajha b-ixtiyaara.* He married her of his own accord. **2.** (pl. *-iyya*) elder, old man.

*xtiyaari** **1.** voluntary. *qaraar ixtiyaari* a voluntary decision. *jundi xtiyaari* an enlistee. **2.** optional. *l-ʕuδuur ixtiyaari.* Attendance is optional. *mawqif ixtiyaari* optional (bus) stop, where the bus need not stop if there are no passengers. **3.** elective. *duruus ixtiyaariyya* elective courses.

muxtaar pl. *mxaatiir* mukhtar, the elected village or neighborhood leader.

x-y-z-r-a-n

xeezaraan (coll.) **1.** cane, rattan. **2.** cane plant.

xeezaraana pl. *-aat* un. n. of *xeezaraana.*

x-y-s

xaas (*i xees*) to spoil, rot, go bad. *ṭ-ṭamaaṭa xaasat.* The tomatoes spoiled. *l-ṃaay bil-ʕooδ xaas.* The water in the pond got stagnant.

xayyas to cause to rot, spoil. *l-ʕarr yxayyis is-simač.* Heat rots fish.

xiisa dirt, filth. || *ʔiδa ʔijaw mufattišiin tiṭlaʕ il-xiisa.* If any inspectors came the dirt would come out.

xaayis rotten, spoiled. *buṣal xaayis* rotten onions. || *haaδa damaaġa xaayis! ʔaku waaʕid yiqbal ib-hiiči mašruuʕ?* He's out of his mind! Is there anyone who'd accept such a plan?

x-y-ṭ

xayyaṭ **1.** to sew. *binta txayyiṭ kulliš zeen.* His daughter sews very well. || *ma-tiʕči. šbiik, ʕalgak mxayyaṭ?* You aren't talking. What's wrong, is your mouth sewed up? *δiraba sitt irṣaaṣaat, xayyaṭa b-mukaana.* He hit him with six bullets and stitched him to the spot. **2.** to tailor. *minu xayyaṭ-lak hal-qaaṭ?* Who made this suit for you?

xeeṭ pl. *xyuuṭ* **1.** thread. || *xeeṭ ʔamal* a thread of hope. **2.** string, twine, cord. **3.** chevron, stripe. **4.** trace, touch, bit.

¶ *qaabil ʔaani xeeṭ in-naayuum? ʔašu yaahu l-yiji yuδrubni.* Am I a weakling? Everybody picks on me.

xyaaṭ seam, seams, sewing.

xyaaṭa sewing. *makiinat ixyaaṭa* sewing machine.

xayyaaṭ tailor. || *xayyaaṭ farfuuri* porcelain mender.

xayyaaṭa pl. *-aat* seamstress.

muxyaṭ pl. *muxaayiṭ* a large needle.

[1]*x-y-l*

xayyal **1.** to be or become entranced. *xayyal ʕala jamaalha.* He was entranced by her beauty. *kull-ma yšuuf ibnaaya ʕilwa yxayyil.* Every time he sees a pretty girl, he becomes entranced. **2.** to become tipsy, intoxicated. *širab-la peek waaʕid w-xayyal.* He had one drink and became tipsy. **3.** to daydream, woolgather. *šuuf, da-yxayyil ʕaleeha!* Look, he's dreaming about her.

txayyal to imagine. *txayyal nafsak malik!* Imagine being a king!

xayaal **1.** imagination. **2.** (pl. *-aat*) fantasy, vision. **3.** shadow.

xyaal pl. *-aat shadow. yxaaf imn ixyaala.* He's afraid of his own shadow.

²*x-y-l*

xeel **1.** horse(s) **2.** knights (chess).

xayyaal pl. *-a* rider, horseman.

xayyaala cavalry. || *šurṭa xayyaala* mounted police.

x-y-m

xayyam **1.** to set up camp, pitch a tent. *xayyamna l-muġrub.* We set up camp at sunset. **2.** to settle (of the night). *l-leel xayyam ʕal-balda w-kull in-naas naamaw.* Night settled over the city and everybody slept.

xeema pl. *xiyam, xyaam* tent. || *ʔabu xeemt iz-zarga* Allah, God.

muxayyam camp ground, camp, encampment.

D

d-a

da- progressive prefix, indicating continued, repeated, or habitual action: *da-yibnuun jisr ijdiid ihnaa.* They're building a new bridge here. *da-ysawwiiha hassa.* He's doing it now. *ma-da-adri ween raaḥ.* I don't know where he went. *ma-da-tiftihim illi git-lak?* Don't you understand what I told you? *ʔii, da-ašuufha hassa.* Yes, I see her now.

d-ʔ-b

daʔib (invar.) habit. *daʔba yiḥči ʕan-naas.* He has a habit of talking about people.

¹*d-a-d*

daad brother (form of address used mostly in supplication). *daad, ma-tsaaʕidni?* Say, old buddy, won't you give me a hand?

daada brother, (form of address; infrequently, by a girl =) sister.

²*d-a-d*

daad **1.** (in certain expressions:) *bass ʕaad. muu raḥ-aṣiiḥ id-daad!* Quit it! I'm about to holler uncle, dammit! *wuld il-imḥalla ṣaaḥaw id-daad minna.* The neighborhood kids have gotten sick of him. *hamm sakraan w-jaay milʔaxxir, d-daad minnak!* Drunk again and coming in late, to hell with you!

d-a-r-s-y-n

daarsiin cinnamon.

d-a-ṭ-l-y

daaṭli (coll.) a type of pastry similar to doughnuts.

daaṭliyya pl. *-aat* a piece of *daaṭli.*

d-a-ġ-l-y

daaġḷi pl. *-iyyaat* king (in non-western card games).

d-a-g-w-r

daaguur pl. *dwaagiir* a removable center door post used to hold shop doors together when the shop is closed.

d-a-l

daal name of the letter *d.*

d-a-l-y-a

daalya dahlia(s) (bot.).

d-a-m

daama **1.** checkers. **2.** a game played by moving counters through a series of depressions around a board.

d-a-n

daan (coll.) **1.** cannonball(s) **2.** bomb(s).

daana pl. *-aat* un. n. of *daan.*

d-a-n-t-y-l

daanteel pl. *-aat* lace.

d-a-y

daaya pl. *-aat* **1.** wet nurse. **2.** seedling.

d-b-b

dabbab to sharpen, point, taper. *dabbib raas il-qalam ib-hal-muus.* Sharpen the pencil point with this razor blade.

dibb pl. *dibaba, dbaab* bear. || *d-dibb il-ʔaṣġar* the Little Bear, Ursa Minor. *d-dibb il-ʔakbar* the Big Bear, Ursa Major.

dabba pl. *-aat* **1.** heavy jug or jar, made of porcelain or sheet metal, used for clarified butter. **2.** tube (toothpaste, medicine, etc.).

dabba (invar.) /with *ðirab*/ **1.** to balk, be obstinate. *ðirab dabba; baʕad ma-yimši.* He balked and won't go any further. *ðirab dabba ʔilla yruuḥ lis-siinama.* He's dead set on going to the movie. **2.** to change one's mind, go back on one's word, back down. *ðirab dabba w-ma-qibal ybiiʕha b-diinaareen.* He went back on his word and refused to sell it for two dinars. **3.** to trick, fool. *ðirabni dabba w-axað ifluusi.* He tricked me and took my money.

dubba (invar.) fat, obese. *mara dubba* a fat woman.

dbiib (coll.) crawling insect(s).

dbiiba pl. *-aat* un. n. of *dbiib.*

ḍabbaaba pl. *-aaṭ* ṭaṇk (mil.).

daabba pl. *dwaabb* **1.** a riding animal, or beast of burden, especially a donkey. **2.** (pl. *dawaabb*) water buffalo.

d-b-r

dubar to be arranged, managed. *dubrat il-qaṣiyya b-suhuula.* The matter was taken care of easily. *l-ifluus dubrat; ʕaṣṣir nafsak lis-safar baačir.* The money is arranged for; get yourself ready for travelling tomorrow.

dabbar **1.** to arrange, manage, handle. *tigdar iddabbur-li ʕašr idnaaniir?* Can you manage to get ten dinars for me? *ma-aʕtiqid ydabburha.* I don't think he can handle it. *huwwa dabbar-li šuġul ib-haš-šarika.* He arranged a job for me with this company. **2.** to contrive, devise, work out. *l-ʕaraamiyya dabbiraw xiṭṭa ybuuguun biiha l-beet.* The thieves worked out a plan for robbing the house.

tdabbar = *dubar.* *ma-aʕtiqid il-ifluus raʕ-tiddabbar.* I don't think the money will come through.

dibir, dubur pl. *ʔadbaar* anus.

tadbiir pl. *tadaabiir* **1.** organization, planning, preparation. *tadbiir manzili.* home economics. **2.** (pl. *tadaabiir*) measure, step move. || *sawwii-li tadbiir; il-quṣuṭ istaʕaqq w-ma-ʕindi fluus.* Show me a way out; the payment is due and I don't have any money.

mdabbar well-organized. *marta mdabbara.* His wife is a good manager.

d-b-č

dabbač to stamp one's feet. *la-ddabbičuun. ṭ-ṭifil naayim.* Don't stamp your feet. The baby's sleeping.

dabča **1.** stamping of feet. **2.** a folk dance in which a group of dancers lined up with locked arms, stamps out the rhythm and sings.

d-b-s

dibis date molasses.

dabbaas pl. *-a* a maker of date molasses.

d-b-š

dabaš (only in the expression:) *qubaṣ min dabaš* he never got it back. *nṭeeta ʕašr idnaaniir w-raʕ-ʔaqbuṣ min dabaš.* I gave him ten dinars and don't expect to get it back.

d-b-ġ

dubaġ (*u dabuġ*) to tan. *ništiri jluud w-nidbuġha.* We buy hides and tan them.

dabbaġ intens. of *dubaġ.* *raʕ-ydabbuġuun ij-jiluud ib-madbaġatna.* They'll have the hides tanned at our tannery. || *jilda mdabbaġ imnil-baṣiṭ; baʕad ma-ymuṣṣ bii.* His hide is tanned from beating, so that it doesn't hurt him anymore. *kull-ma ṭṣurba ma-yʕiss. ʕabaalak jilda mdabbaġ.* No matter how much you hit him he doesn't feel it. He must be tough as leather.

tdabbaġ to be tanned. *j-juluud yird-ilha tanṣiif gabul-ma tiddabbaġ.* The skins need cleaning before they are tanned.

ndubaġ to be tanned. *j-jiluud tindubuġ ihnaa w-baʕdeen yṣaddiruuha.* The hides are tanned here and then they export them.

dbaaġ pomegranate peels used for tanning.

dibaaga, dbaaġa tanning, tanner's trade.

dabbaaġ pl. *-a* *tanner.* || *baačir ywadduun jilda lid-dabbaaġ.* Tomorrow they're going to tan his hide.

madbaġa pl. *madaabiġ* tannery.

madbuuġ tanned. *jluud madbuuġ* tanned hides.

d-b-g

dabbag to make sticky. *staʕmil xaašuuga ʕatta la ddabbug ʔiidak.* Use a spoon so you won't get your hands sticky.

tdabbag to get sticky. *ʔiidi ddabbgat imnit-tamur.* My hand got sticky from the dates.

dubag sticky place, stickiness. *sitirtak biiha dubag.* Your jacket has a sticky-looking spot on it. || *kull il-imwaṣṣafiin da-yirduun haš-šuʕba, laazim biiha dubag.* All the employees want to work in this section. There must be something attractive there.

dabug, dabig sticky. *ʔiida dabig imnič-čukleet.* His hand's sticky from the candy.

d-b-k

dabka = *dabča,* which see under *d-b-č.*

d-b-l

dabla pl. *-aat* a plain ring.

d-b-l-w-m

dibloom pl. *-aat* diploma or associate degree awarded on successful completion of first two years of college.

d-b-l-w-m-a-s

*dibloomaasi** **1.** diplomatic. **2.** diplomat.

dibloomaasiyya diplomacy.

d-b-n-g

dabang pl. *-iyya* stupid, addlebrained, witless.

d-θ-r

daθθar to cover, cover up. *daθθir ij-jaahil ʕatta la-yibrad.* Cover up the kid so he won't get cold.

ndiθar **1.** to be wiped out, be obliterated.

ɛaδaarathum indiθrat min haajmoohum il-maġuul. Their civilization was wiped out when the Mongols attacked them. *l-madiina ndiθrat biz-zilzaal.* The city was obliterated by the earthquake **2.** to die out, disappear. *ˀahla ndiθraw, ma-biqaa-lhum ˀaθar.* His family died out, and no trace of them remains.

tdaθθar **1.** to wrap oneself up. *ddaθθar zeen; d-dinya baarda.* Cover up well; the weather's cold. *daθθar bil-baṭṭaaniyya w-naam.* He wrapped himself in the blanket and went to sleep. **2.** to be covered. *ˀiδa ddaθθar ij-jidir zeen, yinṭubux il-ˀakil bil-ɛajal.* If the pot's well covered, the food will cook quickly.

dθaar pl. *-aat* covers.

d-θ-w

diθu pl. *diθaawa* (a contemptuous term) sloth, sluggard, slob, clod, idiot.

d-j-j

dijaaj (coll.) chicken(s).

dijaaja pl. *-aat* chicken.

¹*d-j-l*

dajjal to swindle, cheat. *la-tištiri min hat-taajir. ydajjil ɛala kull waaḥid.* Don't buy from that merchant. He cheats everyone.

dajal trickery, humbug, deceit.

dajjaal imposter.

²*d-j-l*

(*nahar*) *dijla* the Tigris River.

d-j-n

daajin tamed, domesticated. *ḥaywaanaat daajina* domesticated animals.

daajin pl. *dawaajin* domestic animal (usually chickens, ducks, and rabbits).

d-č-č

dačč **1.** to tamp, pack. *da-ydiččuun iš-šaariɛ bir-roola.* They're packing the street down with the roller. *ˀiδa ma-ddičč il-gaaɛ zeen, ygubb il-kaaši.* If you don't tamp the ground well, the tile will come up. **2.** to stuff, pack, jam. *dičč hal-wuṣla biz-zuruf ḥatta la-yiji hawa baarid.* Stuff this piece of cloth in the hole so cold air won't come in. || *diččha zeen, tara ma-raḥ naakul baɛad lil-miġrib.* Eat your fill—we aren't going to eat again until evening.

dačč tamping, packing.

dačča pl. *-aat, dičač* **1.** a low ledge or platform built against a wall and used as a seat, esp. in Turkish baths. **2.** door step, front step. **3.** brick grave cover. **4.** dunce, blockhead.

d-ḥ-j

daḥḥaj = *daḥḥag* which see under *d-ḥ-g.*

d-ḥ-d-ḥ

tdaḥdaḥ to waddle. *šuufa šloon yiddaḥdaḥ ib-mašya.* Look at how he waddles when he walks.

mdaḥdaḥ dumpy, squat, stocky.

d-ḥ-r

diḥar (*a daḥir*) to defeat, vanquish. *diḥarna jeeš il-ɛadu b-suhuula.* We defeated the enemy army easily.

d-ḥ-s

diḥas (*a daḥis*) to stuff in, stick in, push in, shove in, crowd in. *diḥas saaɛta been il-baṭṭaaniyyaat.* He shoved his watch in between the blankets. *ˀidḥas hal-iktaab been kutbak.* Stick this book in among your books. *kull-ma nugɛud niḥči yidḥas nafsa beenaatna.* Every time we sit down to talk, he butts in among us.

daḥḥas = *diḥas. la-ddaḥḥis ˀay šii baɛad bij-janṭa.* Don't cram anything else into the suitcase.

ndiḥas to crowd oneself in. *j-jaahil indiḥas been ˀabuu w-ˀumma.* The child crowded in between his father and mother.

d-ḥ-g

daḥḥag to look. *ˀiδa ddaḥḥig zeen, tigdar tiqraaha.* If you look carefully, you can read it. *daḥḥig biṣ-ṣanduug.* Look in the trunk. *daḥḥig zeen w-ˀiḥzir haaδa taṣwiir man.* Look very closely and guess whose picture this is.

d-x-t-w-r

daxtoor pl. *-iyya* = *daktoor* which see under *d-k-t-w-r.*

d-x-r

ddixar to save, lay away, be thrifty. *ˀiδa tisrif w-ma-tiddixir, tara taakulha.* If you spend everything and don't save, you'll be sorry. *yiddixir ifluusa b-ṣunduug il-bariid.* He saves his money in the postal savings bank.

d-x-l

dixal (*u duxuul*) to enter, go in. *šuuf it-talaamiiδ dixlaw iṣ-ṣaff loo baɛad.* See if the students have gone into the classroom yet. *ˀidxul, l-baab maftuuḥa.* Come in, the door is open. *quwwaatna dixlat ˀaraaδi l-ɛadu.* Our troops entered enemy territory. *dixal bil-ġurfa laakin ma-šaafni.* He entered the room but he didn't see me. *la-txalli ˀaḥḥad yidxul ɛal-mudiir.* Don't let anyone go in to the director. *l-yikδib yidxul jahannam.* He who lies goes to hell. *ˀibni raḥ-yidxul kulliit it-ṭibb.* My son's going to enter the medical school. *raħ-ʔadxul sibaaq il-miit matir.* I am going to enter the 100-meter dash. *ʔismak dixal ib-qaaʔimt it-tarfiiεaat.* Your name has been put on the promotion list. *xal-nidxul bil-mawδ̣uuε. š-itriid?* Let's get to the subject. What do you want? *has-sana d-dinya raħ-tidxul εala jreedi.* The world is entering the year of the rat. **2.** to consummate the marriage, cohabit, sleep with one's wife. *dixal εal-εaruus usbuuεeen baεad il-εaqid.* He slept with his bride two weeks after the signing of the contract. *smaεit εali dixal il-baarħa?* Did you hear Ali consummated his marriage yesterday? **3.** to be included. *l-εumuula ma-tidxul bis-siεir.* The commission is not included in the price. *δ̣-δ̣ariiba daaxla b-δ̣imn is-siεir.* The tax is included in the price.

daxxal to put in, stick in, place in, enter. *daxxil il-waayar ib-haz-zuruf.* Insert the wire in this hole. *daxxil ič-čalib bil-beet.* Bring the dog in the house. *daxxal ʔiṣibεa b-εeeni.* He stuck his finger in my eye. *l-baarħa ṣiħħta txarbiṭat w-daxxloo l-mustašfa.* Yesterday his condition worsened and they placed him in the hospital. *ma-yiqbal ydaxxil ʔaħħad εal-waziir.* He refuses to let anyone go in to see the minister. *ydaxxil nafsa b-kullši.* He meddles in everything. *la-tdaxxilni b-hal-muškila.* Don't drag me into the problem. *daxxil hal-kalima b-jumla.* Put this word in a sentence. *ma-daxxlaw ʔismak bil-qaaʔima.* They didn't enter your name on the list. *daxxil had-diinaar b-iħsaabi.* Put this dinar on my account.

ʔadxal formal equivalent of *daxxal. l-majlis ʔadxal baεδ̣ it-taεdiilaat ib-hal-qaanuun.* The parliament inserted some amendments in this law.

tdaxxal **1.** to be put in, entered. *hal-waayar laazim yiddaxxal minnaa.* This wire has to go through here. **2.** to involve oneself, take part, interfere. *la-tiddaxxal bis-sayaasa.* Don't involve yourself in politics. *leeš tiddaxxal ib-kull munaaqaša?* Why do you always take part in arguments? *ma-aqbal tiddaxxal ib-šuġḷi.* I won't have you interfering in my affairs. *š-šurṭa ddaxxalaṭ bil-intixaabaat.* The police meddled in the elections.

tdaaxal **1.** = *tdaxxal. gitt-lak miit marra, la-tiddaaxal ib-šuġḷi.* I've told you a hundred times, don't interfere in my business. **2.** to get acquainted, make friends. *š-bil-εajal yiddaaxal! ma-aku ʔaħħad ma-yεurfa.* How fast he makes friends! There's no one that doesn't know him.

daxaḷ pl. *dxuuḷ* **1.** income. *δ̣ariibt id-daxaḷ* the income tax. **2.** receipts, revenues, returns, take. **3.** till, cash drawer. **4.** bank for saving coins.

¶ *b-daxḷ aḷḷa w-b-daxḷak, xaḷḷiṣni minna.* For God's sake and for your own, save me from him.

daxal (in certain expressions:) *maa-la daxal.* he has no business, he has nothing to do with, it's none of his business. *ʔaani maa-li daxal ib-hal-mawδ̣uuε.* I've got nothing to do with that affair. *ʔinta šinu daxalak? haay beeni w-been axuuya.* What's this got to do with you? This is between me and my brother.

daxḷa pl. *-aat* consummation. *yoom id-daxḷa, leelt id-daxḷa* the wedding night.

daxiil (in certain expressions:) *daxiil ʔaḷḷa, ma-dgul-li mneen jibt il-ifluus?* For the love of God, won't you tell me where you got the money? *daxiilak, la-tuδ̣rubni.* Please don't hit me. *δabb nafsa daxiil εalayya.* He threw himself on my mercy.

duxuul entry, entrance, admittance, admission. *siεir id-duxuul* the price of admission. *εiid id-duxuul* Celebration of the Persian New Year, held in springtime, when the world comes under the sign of a different animal.

duxuuliyya admission, admission price.

madxal pl. *madaaxil* entrance.

daaxil interior, inside.

*daaxili** internal, interior, inside. *δ̣ṭiraabaat daaxiliyya* internal disorders. *ʔamraaδ̣ daaxiliyya* internal diseases. *qisim daaxili* (of a school) boarding department, boarding section. *malaabis daaxiliyya* underwear, underclothes.

daaxiliyya interior. *wizaart id-daaxiliyya* ministry of the interior.

d-x-n

daxxan **1.** to fumigate. *daxxin il-ġurfa ħatta yruuħ il-bagg.* Fumigate the room so that the mosquitoes will go away. **2.** to smoke (cigarette, pipe, etc.). *ʔay nooε jigaayir itdaxxin?* What kind of cigarettes do you smoke? **3.** to smoke, give off smoke. *l-xišab da-ydaxxin; yumkin raħ-yištiεil.* The wood's smoking; maybe it'll catch fire. *l-fitiila muu zeena; tdaxxin ihwaaya.* The lantern's no good; it smokes a lot.

duxun millet.

duxxaan **1.** smoke, fumes. **2.** tobacco.

midxana pl. *mdaaxin* chimney, smokestack, funnel.

tadxiin (tobacco) smoking.

mdaxxin irritated, upset. *ṭabb ʕaleena mdaxxin; maḥḥad yidri š-bii.* He came in all upset; no one knows what was ailing him.

d-r-b

darrab **1.** to train, coach, drill. *darrab il-firqa hwaaya gabuḷ is-sibaaq.* He coached the team a lot before the game. *l-muṣaariʕ yiji lil-madrasa kull yoom ydarrub it-talaamiiδ ʕal-muṣaaraʕa.* The wrestler comes to school every day to train the students in wrestling. *δ-δaabuṭ darrab ijnuuda ʕala stiʕmaal is-sungi.* The officer drilled his soldiers on using the bayonet. *darrab ič-čalib maala ʕal-qafuz.* He trained his dog to jump. **2.** to send (someone) on his way, send packing. *nṭii filis w-darrba.* Give him a fils and send him packing.

tdarrab **1.** to get accustomed to, get used to. *ddarrabit ʕala hiiči ḥayaat min činit jundi.* I got used to such a life when I was in the army. **2.** to train, drill, practice. *sawwa nafsa mariiδ ḥatta ma-yiddarrab wiyya j-jinuud.* He pretended to be sick so as not to drill with the soldiers. *ruuḥ iddarrab čam šahar w-baʕdeen taʕaal ʔilʕab šitranj wiyyaaya.* Go practice for a few months and then come play chess with me. **3.** to train (athletics). *da-addarrab lis-sibaaq.* I'm training for the race. *da-ʔaddarrab ʕala rafʕ il-ʔaθqaal kull yoom.* I'm training in weight lifting every day.

darub pl. *druub* **1.** street, road. **2.** way, route. *ʔiδa darbak ʕas-suug matištirii-li keelu šakar.* If you happen to go by the market would you buy me a kilo of sugar. *tigdar idjiib-li ṭawaabiʕ ib-darbak?* Could you bring me some stamps on your way? || *ma-ʕlee b-kull ʔaḥḥad. yruuḥ ib-darba w-yiji b-darba.* He doesn't bother anyone. He goes his own way. *darb ič-čalib ʕal-gaṣṣaab.* He'll be around one of these days (lit., the dog's route goes to the butcher's). *la-tliḥḥ ʕalayya. xalliini ʔašuuf darbi.* Don't pester me. Let me concentrate on what I'm doing. *nṭiini darub ḥatta ʔasawwiiha.* Give me a chance to do it. *ma-nṭeeta darub yiḥči.* You didn't give him a chance to speak. *šift-ilha xooš darub. ʔagdar ʔaxaabir il-mudiir w-huwwa ydabburha.* I've found a good way out. I can call the director and he'll take care of it. **3.** trip, run. *haaδa ʔaaxir darub lil-paaṣ il-hal-leela.* This is the last bus run tonight. *šilt kull il-garaaδ ib-darbeen?* Did you bring all the things in two trips? || *raaḥ wiyyaaha darbeen.* He went with her twice (euphemism for the act of sexual intercourse). *jiib-li darub ramuḷ.* Bring me a load of sand.

tadriib practice, drill, training.

*tadriibi** training. *dawra tadriibiyya* a training course.

mudarrib trainer, coach.

d-r-b-w-n

darbuuna pl. *draabiin* alley, narrow street.

d-r-b-y

darba to roll, cause to roll. *darbii-li l-piip min yammak.* Roll the barrel to me from where you are. || *nṭii ʕašr ifluus w-darbii.* Give him ten fils and be done with him.

tdarba to roll oneself, roll. *j-jahhaal yiʕjibhum yiddarbuun min raas it-tall.* The kids like to roll down from the top of the hill. || *lamma ma-ḥaṣṣal ifluus min ʔabuu, ddarba ʕalayya.* When he didn't get any money from his father, he drifted over to me.

d-r-b-y-n

darbiin pl. *-aat* binoculars.

d-r-j

tdarraj to advance gradually. *ddarraj bil-waδaayif ʔila ʔan ṣaar mudiir.* He rose in grade till he became a director.

stadraj to lure, coax, lead gradually. *stadrijoo ʔila ʔan iʕtiraf bij-jariima.* They coaxed him until he confessed to the crime.

daraj pl. *-aat* **1.** stairs, steps, flight of stairs, staircase. **2.** ladder.

darja pl. *-aat* step, stair.

daraja pl. *-aat* **1.** degree. *darajat ġalayaaan il-maay* the boiling point of water. *darajt il-ḥaraara* the temperature. **2.** thermometer. **3.** degree, extent. *baxiil ʔila daraja faδiiʕa* stingy to an extreme degree. *sawwaani ʕaṣabi ʔila daraja baʕd išwayya aδurba.* He made me so mad I was about to hit him. **4.** class. *daraja ʔuula* first class. *čaδδaab imnid-daraja l-ʔuula* a first-class liar. **5.** grade, mark (in school).

daraaj = *daraj,* which see.

darraaj (coll.) a game bird resembling the pheasant.

darraaja pl. *-aat* un. n. of *darraaj.*

bit-tadriij gradually, by degrees, step

by step. *l-ˀumuur da-titɛassan bit-tadriij.* Things are getting better gradually.

bit-tidaariij var. of *bit-tadriij. l-ɛaafya bit-tidaariij.* Good health comes gradually (Everything takes time).

tadriijiyyan = *bit-tadriij,* which see.

daarij current, prevalent, common, popular. *maθal daarij* a wide-spread saying.

mudarraj pl. *-aat* stand, grandstand, bleachers.

¹*d-r-d*

ˀadrad **1.** toothless. **2.** toothless person.

²*d-r-d*

darid suffering, torment, affliction, misfortune, trouble, bad luck, problem. *kull man mibtili ib-darda.* Everyone's got his own problems. *ma-da-aɛruf šinu darda.* I can't figure out what's eating him. *haaδa dardi. ˀibni seebandi.* That's my luck. My son is a rotter. *leeš in-nahaar kulla ma-yiɛči? bass loo ˀaɛruf šinu darda.* Why hasn't he said anything all day? If only I knew what his trouble was.

d-r-d-m

dardam to mumble, muttter. *ṭilaɛ zaɛlaan w-gaam ydardim.* He went out mad and began to mutter to himself.

d-r-r

darr (*u*) **1.** to shower, heap. *min ṣaar abuuhum waziir, δall ydurr ɛaleehum bil-ifluus.* When their father became minister, he kept them in money. *haš-šaġla darrat ɛaleehum ifluus ihwaaya.* That job showered a lot of money on them. **2.** to be productive, give milk abundantly. *gabuḷ-ma yiɛlibuun il-haayša yxalluun ˀibinha yirδaɛ minha ɛatta tdurr.* Before they milk the cow they let her calf suck so that she will give plenty of milk.

darrar to act as a diuretic, stimulate the kidneys. *l-biira tdarrir.* Beer makes you urinate.

durr (coll.) **1.** pearl(s). **2.** gem(s). **3.** gemstone(s). *durr najaf* crystalline quartz. *ɛačya durr.* His words are precious gems. *yṭaḷḷiɛ durr min ṭiiz il-kurr.* He's talking through his hat (lit., he gets gems from the young donkey's anus).

durra pl. *-aat, durar* un. n. of *durr.*

mudarrir pl. *-a, -aat* (adj. and n.) diuretic.

ˀidraar urine (as medical specimen).

d-r-z-n

darzan pl. *daraazin* dozen.

d-r-s

diras (*u daris*) to study. *min ˀakbar raɛ-adrus handasa.* When I grow up I'm going to study engineering. *ˀidrusha l-hal-qaδiyya zeen w-qaddim-li taqriir.* Study this case well and forward me a report. *ma-dirasit ib-hal-madrasa.* I didn't study at that school. *diras ihwaaya lil-imtiɛaan.* He studied a lot for the exam.

darras to teach. *ydarris il-iqtiṣaad.* He teaches economics.

daris pl. *druus* **1.** class, class period. **2.** course, course of study. **3.** lesson, chapter (of a textbook). **4.** lesson (from experience).

diraasa **1.** study, studying. *diraasa ɛaaliya* graduate study. *ˀujuur id-diraasa* tuition. **2.** (pl. *-aat*) a study, an investigation.

*diraasi** academic, scholastic. *sana diraasiyya* an academic year.

madrasa pl. *madaaris* school.

*madrasi** scholastic, school. *ktaab madrasi* school book, text book.

tadriis teaching.

mudarris teacher, instructor.

d-r-ɛ

diriɛ pl. *druuɛ* **1.** shield. **2.** armor, suit of armor. **3.** mail, suit of mail.

driiɛ dull person, clod, jerk.

mudarraɛ armored. *sayyaara mudarraɛa* armored car. *quwwaat mudarraɛa* armored forces. *firqa mudarraɛa* armored division.

d-r-f-ɛ

darfaɛ to push, shove. *darfaɛni w-waggaɛni.* He pushed me and knocked me down. *ɛala keefak. la-ddarfuɛ.* Take it easy. Don't push. || *ˀiδa ˀija ɛaleek, darfuɛa.* If he comes to you, send him away.

d-r-q

*daraqi** thyroid. *l-ġudda l-daraqiyya* the thyroid gland.

d-r-g

dirga pl. *-aat,* dirag **1.** shield. **2.** disc. **3.** steering wheel.

durga pl. *-aat, durag,* and *darga,* pl. *-aat, darag* var. of *dirga.*

d-r-k

dirak (*i ˀidraak*) **1.** to attain puberty. *zawwjoo gabuḷ-ma yidrik.* They married him off before he became sexually mature. **2.** to understand, grasp, comprehend, realize. *huwwa ma-yidrik hiiči ɛaqaayiq.* He doesn't understand such facts. *ma-dirak qasidhum, w-ˀakalha.* He didn't realize what they were up to, and he got taken.

tdaarak to face, meet, check, take care of, take charge of. *ddaarak il-qaδiyya gabuḷ-ma tiθxan.* Take charge of the matter before it gets any worse. *ˀiδa ṭ-ṭabiib ma-yiddaarak l-majruuḥ b-surʕa, tara ymuut.* If the doctor doesn't see to the patient quickly, he's going to die.

darakiyya danger.

ˀidraak understanding, comprehension, grasp.

madruuk endangered. *ṣiḥḥta madruuka.* His health is endangered.

d-r-m

durraama, dirraama pl. *-aat* (vulgar) glans penis.

d-r-m-k

darmak to stain, spot. *l-ḥibir inčabb ʕalayya w-darmak θoobi.* The ink got spilled on me and stained my shirt.

tdarmak to become spotted, stained. *ṣubaġ iθ-θoob maala w-iddarmak.* He dyed his shirt and it became spotty.

d-r-n-f-y-s

darnafiis pl. *-aat* screwdriver.

d-r-n-g-a

dringa pl. *-aat* = *dumbuk,* which see under *d-m-b-k.* || *sakraan ṣaayir dringa* drunk as a skunk, dead drunk.

d-r-h-m

dirhim pl. *daraahim* **1.** coin of fifty fils. **2.** a weight equalling 1/100 *wgiyya* (10 grams) in the reformed weight system, and 1/96 *wgiyya* in the old.

d-r-w-y-š

darwiiš pl. *daraawiiš* dervish, a member of any of the various Moslem sects which take vows of poverty and self-denial.

d-r-y

dira (*i diraaya*) **1.** to know. *tidri? hal-waδiifa ma-tiʕjibni.* You know what? I don't like this job. *ma-da-nidri š-raḥ-yṣiir baačir.* We don't know what's going to happen tomorrow. *bass ˀadri weena, ˀaruuḥ ʕalee.* If I only knew where he was, I'd go to him. *ma-ˀadri aruuḥ bis-sayyaara loo biṭ-ṭayyaara.* I don't know if I'll go by car or by plane. || *ma-ˀadri minu gal-la.* I wonder who told him. *haaδa š-ma-drii? baʕda jidiid ihnaa.* What does he know? He's still new here. *š-šabʕaan š-ma-drii bij-jooʕaan?* What does the well-fed man know about the hungry? *ˀaani š-ma-driini? ˀisˀal ġeeri.* What do I know? Ask someone else. **2.** to find out. *dira b-naqla, loo baʕad?* Has he learned of his transfer yet?

daara to take care of, care for. *ʕammti daaratni kulliš zeen.* My aunt took good care of me. *leeš gaaʕid? guum daari l-mištiriyya.* Why are you sitting? Get up and wait on the customers. *loo tdaari hruuš il-warid bil-mayy wis-samaad, ma-ymuutuun.* If you'd provide the rose bushes with water and manure, they won't die. *ma-adri leeš baṭṭal. kull il-muwaδδafiin yḥibbuu w-ydaaruu.* I don't know why he quit. All of the employees like him and do things for him.

ndira to be known. *ma-yindiri raḥ-yistiqiil loo yibqa.* It's not known if he's going to resign or stay.

mdaaraa service, care, attention.

ˀadra more or most informed, knowledgeable, etc.

d-r-y-ʕ

tdaryaʕ = *ttaryaʕ,* which see under *t-r-y-ʕ.*

d-r-y-w-l

dreewil pl. *-iyya* driver (of a taxi or car), chauffeur.

d-z-z

dazz (*i dazz*) to send. *dazzeet il-maktuub loo baʕad?* Did you send the letter yet? *dazzeet ˀibni b-šuġuḷ.* I sent my son on an errand. *dazzeet-la xabar w-raḥ-yiji.* I sent him word and he will come.

dazza pl. *-aat* trip, errand.

duzz children's game similar to tic-tac-toe, played with stones or pieces of wood.

d-s-t

dasta pl. *-aat* **1.** deck (of cards). *dastat warag* a deck of cards. **2.** dozen, set of twelve. **3.** mourning or funeral procession for a dignitary by the Shiites.

d-s-t-w-r

dastuur pl. *dasaatiir* constitution.

*dastuuri** constitutional. *l-ḥukum id-dastuuri* constitutional rule.

d-s-s

dass (*i dass*) **1.** to administer surreptitiously. *dassat-la s-samm biš-šoorba ḥatta tmawwta.* She slipped him the poison in the soup to kill him. **2.** to inject double meanings, insinuate. *diir baalak minna tara ydiss bil-ḥači maala.* Watch your step with him; he's insincere in his speech.

dassaas pl. *-iin* plotter, schemer.

dasiisa pl. *dasaaˀis* scheme, plot.

d-s-k-r

daskara pl. *dasaakir* small piece of notepaper (= *taskara*).

d-s-m

tdassam to become greasy, oily (from food). *ma-agdar ˀaakul b-iidi li-ˀan tiddassam.* I can't eat with my hand because it'll get greasy.

dasam pl. *dusuumaat* fat, grease, oil.

dasim **1.** fatty, greasy, oily. *ˀakil dasim* greasy food. *laḥam dasim* fatty meat. **2.** rich. *ḥaliib dasim* rich milk. || *raatib dasim* a fat salary.

ˀadsam **1.** more or most fatty, etc. **2.** richer or richest.

d-š-b-w-l

dašbuul pl. *-aat* dashboard (of a car).

d-š-d-š

dišdaaša pl. *dišaadiiš* an ankle-length robe, with a buttoned opening halfway down the front, the standard dress for children, and adults not wearing western clothing.

[1]*d-š-š*

dašš (*i dašš*) to jingle, make a jingling noise. *min timši ddiśš ib-ḥijilha.* When she walks, she makes a noise with her anklets.

[2]*d-š-š*

dašš = *xašš* which see under *x-š-š*.

d-š-l-m-a

dašlama, dišlama: čaay dašlama tea strained through a lump of sugar held in the mouth.

d-š-l-y

dišli pl. *-iyyaat* gear, cog wheel.

d-š-n

daššan to dedicate, inaugurate. *l-waziir daššan is-siinama j-jidiida.* The minister dedicated the new movie house. **2.** (by extension) to use for the first time. *bukra raḥ-adaššin qaaṭi.* Tomorrow I'm going to wear my suit for the first time. *jidiida; baʕda ma-mdaššina.* It's brand new; never been used.

d-ʕ-b-l

daʕbal **1.** to roll into a ball, to round. *haṭ-ṭiina tigdar iddaʕbilha b-suhuula.* You can round this piece of clay easily. **2.** to roll. *daʕbil-li iṭ-ṭooba.* Roll me the ball. || *daʕbalit-la ḥčaayaat ikbaar laakin wala ziʕal.* I threw some rough phrases his way, but he didn't get mad. *ḥčeet wiyyaa šwayya w-daʕbalta.* I talked to him a bit and sent him on his way.

tdaʕbal to roll. *ṣ-ṣaxra ddaʕbilat min foog ij-jibal.* The rock rolled from the top of the mountain. *min yimši yiddaʕbal, hal-gadd-ma simiin.* When he walks he rolls, because he's so fat.

duʕbul (coll.) marble(s).

duʕbulla pl. *-aat* a marble.

mdaʕbal rounded, round, spherical. *d-duʕbulla muu mdaʕbala.* The marble's out of round. || *lamma čaan ṭifil čaan imdaʕbal.* When he was a child, he was roly-poly. *muu kull imdaʕbal jooz.* All that glitters is not gold. You can't judge a book by its cover (lit. not everything round is a walnut).

d-ʕ-č

diʕač (*a daʕič*) **1.** to jostle, bump, shove, push, squeeze. *la-tidʕačni. b-iidi čaay.* Don't jostle me. I'm holding some tea. *č-čalib diʕač nafsa beenaatna.* The dog pushed himself between us. **2.** to hurt (feelings), make someone feel bad. *diʕačni b-iḥčaayta.* He hurt my feelings with his remark.

daʕʕač **1.** = *diʕač* **1.** *š-biik daddaʕʕič? mistaʕjil?* What's with you pushing? Are you in a hurry? **2.** to wrinkle. *nṭeeta diinaar jidiid w-daʕʕača b-iida.* I gave him a new dinar and he wrinkled it up in his hand.

daaʕač = *diʕač* **1.** *ʕala keefak. la-ddaaʕič.* Take it easy. Don't shove.

tdaʕʕač to become wrinkled. *hduumak iddaʕʕčat. baddilha.* Your clothes are wrinkled. Better change them.

ndiʕač **1.** pass. of *diʕač*. *ndiʕačit bil-izdiḥaam w-čitfi tʕawwar.* I got shoved in the crowd and my shoulder was hurt. *min gal-li ˀiṭlaʕ barra, ndiʕačit min iḥčaayta.* When he told me to get out, I was hurt by his remark. *la-tgul-la siqaṭ bil-imtiḥaan; yindiʕič.* Don't tell him he failed the exam; he'll feel bad. **2.** reflex of *diʕač*. *j-jaahil indiʕač been abuu w-ˀumma.* The child pushed himself in between his father and mother. *ˀagdar andiʕič bil-ḥooδ il-warraani.* I can squeeze in the back seat.

d-ʕ-s

diʕas (*a daʕis*) to run over, knock down. *diʕsata s-sayyaara w-maat.* The car ran over him and he died.

ndiʕas to be run over. *ndiʕas ib-loori w-rijla nfusxat.* He was run over by a truck and his leg was broken.

daʕis running over pedestrians. *ḥawaadiθ id-daʕis* pedestrian accidents.

d-ʕ-m

diʕam (*a daʕim*) **1.** to run into, collide. *čint abaawiʕ li-wara w-diʕamt il-*

ɛamuud. I was looking back, and ran into the pole. *diɛamit il-loori b-sayyaarti.* I ran into the truck with my car. *s-saayiq maali diɛam is-sayyaara w-tilafha.* My chauffeur had an accident with the car and ruined it *sayyaarti diɛmat bil-ɛaayiṭ.* My car collided with the wall. **2.** to support, hold up. *had-dalag yidɛim il-binaaya.* This column holds up the building. **3.** to support, back up. *ʔaani raɛ-adɛim kull illi dgul-la.* I will back up everything you tell him.

tdaaɛam to collide, run into each other. *s-saayiq maali w-saayiqak iddaaɛmaw.* My chauffeur and yours collided.

ndiɛam to be run into, to be hit. *has-sayyaara ndiɛmat ʔarbaɛ marraat.* This car has been in four collisions.

daɛma pl. *-aat* accident, collision.

daɛɛaamiyya pl. *-aat* bumper (auto.).

d-ɛ-y

diɛa (*i, u daɛwa*) **1.** to summon, call for someone, send for someone. *wizaart id-difaaɛ diɛat mawaaliid santi lil-xidma.* The defense ministry called my year group to service. **2.** to invite. *diɛa kull ʔaṣdiqaaʔa lil-ɛaša.* He invited all his friends to supper. **3.** (*i duɛa*) to pray. *diɛa min ʔaḷḷa yinṭii walad.* He prayed to God to give him a boy. *diɛaa-lak bin-najaaɛ.* He prayed for your success. *min buṣaṭ ʔibinha, diɛat ɛalee bil-moot.* When he beat her son, she prayed for his death. **4.** to curse. *leeš da-tidɛi ɛalayya?* Why are you cursing me?

daaɛa (*i mdaaɛaa*) to dun, ask for repayment. *daaɛeeta b-ifluusi ɛiddat marraat.* I dunned him for my money several times.

tdaaɛa **1.** to argue, bicker, fight. *ma-aku ɛaaja tiddaaɛa wiyyaa.* There's no need to argue with him. *ɛali w-marta daaʔiman yiddaɛuun.* Ali and his wife are always fighting. *ʔinta šgadd tiddaaɛa w-tiṭṭaalab wiyya j-jiiraan.* My, how you argue with and make demands of the neighbors.

ddiɛa to claim, allege, maintain. *ddiɛa ʔanna yuɛruf is-sirr.* He claimed he knows the secret.

stadɛa **1.** to summon, call in. *waziir il-xaarijiyya stadɛa safiirna d-daaʔirta.* The foreign minister summoned our ambassador to his office. **2.** to recall. *stadɛeena wafidna gabul nihaayt il-ijtimaaɛ.* We recalled our delegation before the end of the conference. **3.** to call for, require, demand. *l-waḍiɛ stadɛa hal-ʔijraaɛaat.* The situation called for these measures. **4.** to apply, submit an application. *leeš ma-truuɛ tistadɛi? yimkin itɛaṣṣil šii.* Why don't you go apply? Maybe you'll get something. *stadɛeet ɛala waḍiifa b-daaʔirt il-bariid.* I applied for a position in the post office. *stadɛat bil-maɛkama ɛala ɛaqqha mnil-ifluus.* She applied to the court for her share of the money.

daɛwa pl. *-aat* **1.** invitation. **2.** reception, party, fete. **3.** matter, case, affair. *daɛwat šaraf* a matter of honor. *daɛwat diinaareen* a matter of two dinars. || *maa-li daɛwa bii; laazim yidrus ib-nafsa.* He's no concern of mine; he'll have to do his own studying. *haay daɛwat il-imjaddi; tinṭii filis, yriid ɛašra.* That's the story with the beggar; give him a fils and he wants ten. *š-daɛwa halgadd? ma-yiswa ʔazyad min diinaar.* How come so much? It's not worth more than a dinar. *š-daɛwa da-turkuḍ? ʔaku šii?* Why're you running? Anything wrong? *š-daɛwa hal-biča?* Why all this crying? *š-daɛwa šaayil xašmak ɛaleena?* Why are you looking down on us? *š-daɛwa, yaaba? maɛɛad yšuufak.* What's up, pal? We don't see you any more. **4.** (pl. *daɛaawi*) law suit, case, legal proceedings. || *haaḍa daɛaawiyya ma-tixlaṣ.* That guy's always in trouble.

duɛa pl. *ʔadɛiya* **1.** prayer, supplication. **2.** curse, imprecation. **3.** a small scroll or paper carried as an amulet on which is written a religious phrase.

diɛaaya **1.** propaganda. **2.** advertising, promotion.

daaɛa: in *w-daaɛt ʔabuuya, raɛ-asawwiiha.* By my father's honor, I'll do it. *w-daaɛt aḷḷa ma-šaayfa.* By God, I haven't seen him. *w-daaɛtak ma-tinṭi; xalliiha ɛala ɛsaabi.* Not on your life; this is on me.

daaɛi pl. *duɛaat* **1.** proponent, propagandist. **2.** host, person who has invited someone. || *daaɛiik* yours truly, myself. *ʔaani l-sawweeta, daaɛiik.* I am the one who did it, yours truly. **3.** (pl. *dawaaɛi*) reason, cause, motive.

d-ġ-d-ġ

daġdaġ to tickle. *daġdiġ ij-jaahil ɛatta yiḍɛak.* Tickle the kid so he'll laugh.

d-ġ-š

diġaš (*u daġiš*) **1.** to cheat. *diġašni. gal-li hal-iqmaaš ʔingiliizi, ṭilaɛ waṭani.* He cheated me. He said this material was English and it turned out to be a local product. *hal-baggaaḷ yidġuš ib-kullši ybiiʕa.* This grocer cheats on everything he sells. *yidġuš bil-iqmaar.* He cheats at gambling. **2.** to insinuate, imply. *walaw kalimaata barii?a, laakin yidġuš ib-ɛačya.* Even though his words are innocuous, he makes insinuations.

daġaš insinuation, innuendo.

d-ġ-l

daġġaḷ to poke. *la-ddaġġaḷ tara ?abuṣṭak.* Don't poke or I'll sock you one.

daġaḷ (coll.) pl. *?adġaaḷ* **1.** clump(s) of grass or brush. **2.** thorn bush(es).

daġḷa pl. *-aat* **1.** un. n. of *daġaḷ*. **2.** poke, jab.

duġḷa pl. *-aat* = *daġḷa* **2.**

d-ġ-m

?adġam fem. *daġma* pl. *duġum, daġmiin* dark, dull, gloomy. *?alwaan daġma* dark colors. *d-dinya daġma l-yoom.* It's dark today. *loon raṣaaṣi ?adġam* dull grey color. *loon sitirti raṣaaṣi ?adġam.* The color of my jacket is dull gray. **2.** gloomy-looking, sad-looking. **3.** gloomy-looking person.

d-f-t-r

daftar pl. *dafaatir* note book. *daftar xidma* service certificate—a small booklet showing record of military service. *mask id-dafaatir* bookkeeping. || *yilzam daftar ib-maṣruufaata.* He keeps a record of his expenses.

d-f-t-y-r-y-a

daftiirya diphtheria.

d-f-r

dufar (*u dafur*) to kick. *l-iɛṣaan dufara b-rijla w-waggaʕa.* The horse kicked him and knocked him down.

daffar to kick repeatedly. *la-ddaffura; tigdar idgulla ?iṭlaʕ.* Don't keep kicking him; you can tell him to get out.

tdaafar to kick one another. *šuuf il-wilid da-yiddaafruun.* Look at the boys kicking each other.

dafra pl. *-aat* kick (like that of a horse).

d-f-ʕ

difaʕ (*a dafiʕ*) **1.** to push. *l-baab ma-tinfakk ?iδa ma-tidfaʕha ɛeel.* The door won't open if you don't push it hard. *difʕaw sayyaarti lil-baanziinxaana.* They pushed my car to the gas station. *jaani min wara w-difaʕni bil-mayy.* He ran up behind me and shoved me into the water. *wugafit bil-baab ɛatta ma-yxušš laakin difaʕni w-xašš.* I stood in the door so he wouldn't come in, but he pushed me aside and entered. **2.** to get rid of, send away. *?inṭii diinaar w-idifʕa.* Give him a dinar and get rid of him. *?aḷḷa yidfaʕ ʕannak kull bala.* God save you from all misfortune. *dafaʕ aḷḷaah maa kaan ?aʕδam loo mayyit.* God spared him the worst or he'd have died. **3.** to pay. *ma-da-agdar ?abiiʕha; maɛɛad da-yidfaʕ biiha šii.* I can't sell it; nobody will pay anything for it. *šgadd tidfaʕ ib-hat-talafizyoon?* How much would you pay for this TV? *difaʕ idyuuna gabuḷ-ma saafar.* He paid his debts before he left. **4.** to offer. *ma-biʕt is-sayyaara li-?an difʕoo-li biiha miit diinaar.* I didn't sell the car because they offered me (only) a hundred dinars for it.

daffaʕ intens. of *difaʕ* **1.** *la-ddaffiʕ, ʕaad! kullna nxušš.* Don't shove, Mac! We'll all get in. *la-ddaffi biyya. xalliini ?amši ʕala keefi.* Don't push me. Let me walk slowly.

daafaʕ to defend. *daafʕaw ʕan il-muʕaskar ɛatta xilṣat ma?uunathum.* They held the barracks until their ammunition ran out. *daafʕaw ʕan baldathum ɛatta n-nafas il-?axiir.* They defended their city unto the last breath.

tdaafaʕ to push each other. *n-naas iddaafʕaw min fattaɛ il-maxzan.* The people pushed each other when the store opened. *maaku ɛaaja tiddaafaʕ wiyyaa. xaabir iššurta.* There's no reason for you to struggle with him. Call the police.

ndifaʕ **1.** to be pushed. *has-sayyaara ma-tindifiʕ; θigiila.* This car can't be pushed; it's too heavy. **2.** to be gotten rid of, be sent away. *ma-ndifaʕ gabuḷ-ma yaaxuδ diinaar minni.* He wouldn't go away until he got a dinar from me. *ndifiʕ, lak. bass tilġi.* Beat it, bud! You're talking nonsense. **3.** to be carried away, to get worked up. *min yiɛči ʕan id-diin yindifiʕ ihwaaya.* When he talks about religion, he gets all worked up.

dafʕa pl. *-aat* **1.** push, shove, thrust. || *xalli yruuɛ, dafʕat mardi w-?aṣaat kurdi.* Let him go, to hell with him. *haay itbayyin dafʕa; loo yriid yšaġġlak čaan dazzak lil-faɛiṣ.* It looks like he wanted to get rid of you; if he wanted to give you a job, he would have given you a physical exam. **2.** that which comes at any one time, a burst, a spurt, a gush, a rush. **3.** group, bunch. *dafʕat jinuud* a shipment of troops. *dafʕat ifluus* a payment of money.

|| *dafʕa waħda* all at once, at one time. *labbsoona junuud kullna dafʕa waħda.* They took all of us into the army at one time.

madfaʕ pl. *madaafiʕ* gun, cannon.

*madfaʕi** artillery, gun, cannon. *ðaabuṭ madfaʕi* artillery officer. *baṭaariyya madfaʕiyya* artillery battery. *wukur madfaʕi* gun emplacement.

madfaʕiyya artillery.

difaaʕ **1.** defense (also jur. and sports). *wizaarat id-difaaʕ* Ministry of Defense. *muħaami d-difaaʕ* the lawyer for the defense. **2.** (pl. *-iyya*) back (soccer).

*difaaʕi** defensive. *xiṭṭa difaaʕiyya* a defensive strategy.

mudaafiʕ back (in soccer).

d-f-f

daff pl. *dfuuf* tambourine.

daffa pl. *-aat* **1.** rudder (of a boat or plane). || *daffat il-ħukum* the helm of government. **2.** a shallow, conical clay brazier set by one's feet for warmth.

d-f-q

tdaffaq to pour out, gush out. *ṣaarat kasra bis-sadd w-gaam yiddaffaq il-ṃayy minha.* There was a break in the dam and the water began rushing out of it.

d-f-l

difla oleander.

d-f-n

difan (*i dafin*) **1.** to bury, inter. *difnaw il-mayyit bil-maqbara.* They buried the dead man in the cemetery. *z-zilzaal difanha lil-wlaaya.* The earthquake buried the city. *č-čalib difan il-ʕaðum bil-ħadiiqa.* The dog buried the bone in the yard. **2.** to conceal, keep secret. *ʔidfin hal-faayil been il-faaylaat ħatta laħħad yilgii.* Conceal the file among the others so no one will find it. *difnaw il-ħičaaya w-ma-xallooha tiṭlaʕ.* They kept the story secret and didn't let it leak out.

ndifan to be buried. *l-marħuum indifan ib-magbart il-ʕaaʔila.* The deceased was buried in the family cemetery.

dafin **1.** burying, burial. *fluus id-dafin* burial money. *ʔijaazt id-dafin* burial permit. **2.** innuendo, insinuation, implication.

¶ *jeeb dafin* slash pocket (tailoring). *qundara dafin* shoe(s) with thin, inconspicuous soles.

madfuuna stuffed foods.

d-f-w

difa (*a difu*) to get warm, warm up. *laffeet nafsi bil-baṭṭaaniyya w-difeet.* I wrapped myself in the blanket and got warm. *l-ṃayy difa. tigdar tiġsil ʔiða triid.* The water has gotten warm. You can take a bath if you want. *ʔaku ħtimaal id-dinya tidfa l-yoom.* There's a possibility it will warm up today.

daffa to warm. *xalla j-jaahil taħat qappuuṭa ħatta ydaffii.* He put the kid under his overcoat to warm him up. *haṣ-ṣoopa ddaffi l-ġurfa b-nuṣṣ saaʕa.* This heater heats the room in a half hour.

tdaffa to warm oneself, get warm. *taʕaal ʔugʕud yamm in-naar, iddaffa.* Come sit near the fire, and get warm.

dafu, difu warmth.

ʔadfa warmer.

daafi warm. *ṃayy daafi* warm water. *d-dinya daafya.* The weather's warm.

d-q-d-q

daqdaq to be fussy, particular. *ʔiktib il-ʕariiða kulliš zeen, tara hal-imwaððaf ydaqdiq ihwaaya.* Write the petition very well, because that official's awfully fussy.

*diqdaaqi** pl. *-iyya* **1.** particular, fussy. **2.** fussy person.

d-q-q

daqq (*u daqq*) to sicken, make ill (with anxiety, impatience, irritation, etc.). *ħacya yduqq il-muṭi.* His talk would make even a donkey sick. *daqqni; qira l-maktuub ʕašir marraat gabuḷ-ma yifham il-masʔala.* He made me sick; he read the letter ten times before he understood the problem. *raħ-ʔašawwfa l-paaysikil maali w-aduqqa.* I am going to show him my bicycle and make him green with envy.

daqqaq to scrutinize, look closely. *raħ-yiji mufattiš, ydaqqiq iħsaabaatna.* An inspector's coming to check our accounts. *leeš ma-daqqaqt in-naðar, gabuḷ-ma tištirii?* Why didn't you look close before you bought it?

ndaqq pass. of *daqq*. *ndaqq min šaafni raakub il-paaysikil ij-jidiid.* He became green with envy when he saw me riding the new bicycle. *marta ndaqqat min idzawwaj ʕaleeha mara.* His wife was crushed when he married a second wife.

diqqa accuracy, exactness, precision. *b-diqqa* precisely, accurately.

daqiiq **1.** small, minute, tiny. *tafaaṣiil daqiiqa* minute details. *l-ʔamʕaaʔ id-daqiiqa* the small intestine. **2.** precise, exact, accurate. *saaʕa daqiiqa* an accurate watch. *ħsaab daqiiq* a precise account. **3.** delicate, precarious, serious.

qaḍiyya daqiiqa a delicate matter. *waḍiɛ daqiiq* a precarious situation.

daqiiqa pl. *daqaayiq* minute.

ʔadaqq more or most exact, precise.

mudaqqiq a civil servant ranking between the *kaatib* (clerk) and the *mulaaɛiḍ* (supervisor).

d-g-d-g

dagdag **1.** to bang, pound. *š-da-ddagdig? ʔard anaam.* What are you banging? I want to sleep. **2.** to tattoo. *d-daggaaga ddagdig il-ɛaruus w-itɛafɛifha gabuḷ-ma tizzawwaj.* The tattooing woman will tattoo the bride and depilate her before she gets married.

digdiga pl. *-aat* sty (med.).

mdagdag tattoed. *ʔiid imdagdiga* a tattoed hand.

d-g-r

digar (*u dagur*) **1.** to bump, jostle, jiggle. *diir baalak. la-tidgur il-iglaaṣ.* Careful! Don't bump the glass. **2.** to disturb, upset, bother, irritate. *digarni hwaaya b-hač-čilma.* He upset me terribly with that remark.

ndigar pass. of *digar. l-iglaaṣ indigar ib-iidi w-čabb il-ṃayy.* The glass got bumped by my hand and spilled the water. *ʔašu ndigarit ib-hač-čilma.* Seems you were upset by that remark.

d-g-g

dagg (*u dagg*) **1.** to grind, crush, pulverize. *laazim indugg il-gahwa.* We've got to grind the coffee. **2.** to strike. *saaɛt iṣ-ṣaraay hassa daggat bil-xamsa.* The clock on the Serai just struck five. **3.** to beat, throb. *rikaḍit išwayya w-galbi gaam ydugg ɛeel.* I ran a little, and my heart began to beat heavily. **4.** to knock, rap, bang, pound, hammer. *dugg il-baab gabuḷ-ma txušš.* Knock on the door before you go in. *dagg rijla bil-gaaɛ w-gaal ʔilla yištiri sayyaara.* He stamped his foot on the ground and said he's bound he'll buy a car. || *ruuɛ dugg raasak bil-ɛaayiṭ.* Go jump in the lake (lit., go bang your head against the wall). *ʔibnak daggoo ɛeel.* They beat up your son badly. *raɛ-adugg-la barqiyya baačir.* I will send him a telegram tomorrow. *ʔaani mwaafuq; duggha!* I'm agreed; put 'er there! *yiɛjibha ddugg ʔiṣbiɛteen min turguṣ.* She likes to snap her fingers when she dances. *činna saaktiin ʔasu fujʔatan daggha.* We were all quiet and suddenly he broke wind. **5.** to pound in, drive. *dugg hal-bismaar bil-ɛaayiṭ.* Hammer this nail into the wall. *dugg haṣ-ṣuura bil-ɛaayiṭ.* Nail up this picture on the wall. **6.** to bump, touch. *halgadd-ma ṭuwiil, raasa ydugg bis-saguf.* He's so tall, his head bumps the ceiling. *ɛaašyat čarčaf id-doošaq mdandila w-qariib iddugg bil-gaaɛ.* The edge of the bed sheet is dangling down and almost touching the floor. **7.** to beat, strum, play. *ydugg ɛuud zeen.* He plays the lute well. || *dagg-li ṭabul; ma-ḍall aɛɛad ma-simaɛ.* He noised it all over town. There isn't anyone left who hasn't heard. **8.** to ring. *j-jihaal daggaw ij-jaras w-inhizmaw.* The children rang the bell and ran away. || *daggeet-la talafoon, laakin ma-čaan ib-beeta.* I gave him a ring, but he wasn't home. **9.** to ring, resound. *t-talafoon da-ydugg.* The phone is ringing. *leeš ij-jaras da-ydugg?* Why's the bell ringing? **10.** to tattoo. *l-ɛaruus da-ydugguu-lha dagga b-ɛiničha.* They are putting a tattoo on the bride's chin.

¶ *dagg biyya muu xooš dagga.* He pulled a dirty trick on me.

ndagg to get involved. *la-tindagg bii, tara muu xooš ʔaadmi.* Don't get involved with him because he's no good.

dagg (in certain expressions:) || *lizam ʔibna w-wugaɛ bii dagg.* He grabbed his son and beat the tar out of him. *wugaɛ biš-šuġuḷ dagg; wala tġadda.* He really tore into the work; didn't even have lunch. *min yaakul simač, yoogaɛ bii dagg.* When he eats fish, he really digs into it.

dagga pl. *-aat* **1.** knock, bang, rap. **2.** beat, throb. **3.** stroke, striking. **4.** ring, ringing. **5.** tattoo, tattooed mark. **6.** dirty trick.

dugga cracked rice.

daggaag: in *daggaag jidri* a man who gives smallpox vaccinations.

daggaaga pl. *-aat* **1.** door knocker. **2.** a woman who does tattooing.

madguuga a confection made of crushed dates and sesame seeds.

d-g-l

digaḷ **1.** (coll.) a variety of dates. **2.** mast (naut.).

digḷa pl. *-aat* un. n. of *digaḷ* **1.**

d-g-m

digam (*u dagum*) to dull, blunt, to bend or break the tip of. *diġam il-ʔubra w-baɛad ma-txayyiṭ.* He dulled the needle and it won't sew any more.

daggam to button. *daggum qappuuṭak. d-dinya baarda.* Button up your overcoat. It's cold outside.

tdaggam to button oneself up. *ddaggam gabuḷ-ma txušš ʕal-mudiir.* Button up before you go in to see the director.

dugma pl. *dugam, digam.* **1.** button **2.** button, pushbutton. || *dugmat iδ-δuwa* the light switch. *dugmat-il-kameera* camera's shutter release.

d-g-n

daggan to secrete rheum. *min tiltihib il-ʕeen ʕal-ʔaġlab iddaggin.* When the eye gets inflamed, it usually secretes rheum.

digan rheum, sleep, the mucous substance in the eyes.

d-k-t-w-r

daktoor, duktoor pl. *dakaatir* doctor (physician and Ph.D.).

diktooraa Ph.D. *šihaadat id-diktoora* Ph.D. degree.

d-k-k-n

dukkaan pl. *dkaakiin.* shop, small store.

dukkanči pl. *-iyya* shopkeeper.

d-l-ġ

dilaġ (*u daluġ*) to daydream, dream, woolgather. *baawaʕ ʕala rasimha w-dilaġ.* He looked at her picture and daydreamed.

dallaġ = *dilaġ. jaawubni! la-ddalliġ!* Answer me! Don't just sit there staring at nothing!

daalġa pl. *-aat* **1.** an unexpected thing, something sprung at the last minute, a surprise. **2.** question, problem, matter, affair. **3.** a strange or inconceivable thing, an unbelievable event or exploit, a wild tale. **4.** opium dream, pipe dream, daydream. **5.** an odd statement or action, an eccentricity. **6.** a strange person, eccentric, nut.

¶ *yiδrub daalġa* he woolgathers, daydreams, contemplates, meditates.

daalġači pl. *-iyya* woolgatherer, daydreamer, contemplative person, absent-minded person.

d-l-ġ-m

dalġam to look unhappy, glum. *min git-la ma-yṣiir yruuḥ, dalġam.* When I told him he couldn't go, he looked glum.

d-l-g

dalag pl. *-aat, dalgaat.* column, vertical beam, support.

d-l-k

dilak (*u dalik*) to rub. *dilak ṣadra w-xalla ʕalee dihin.* He rubbed his chest and put oil on it.

dallak to massage. *min dallikat δahri raaḥ il-ʔalam minna.* When she massaged my back, the pain left it.

dallaak masseur (in a Turkish bath, massages and washes the body).

mdallikči pl. *-iyya* = *dallaak.*

d-l-l

dall (*u dalaala*) **1.** to show, indicate, demonstrate. *xtiyaarak il-hal-qaaṭ ydull ʕala ḥusun δawqak.* Your choosing this suit shows your good taste. *jawaabak ma-ydull ʕala ʔay šii.* Your answer doesn't show anything. *ʕamalak ydull ʕala ḥusun niitak.* Your action demonstrates your good will. **2.** to prove. *ḥačyak haaδa ma-ydull ʕala ʔanna kaδδaab.* This remark of yours doesn't prove that he's a liar.

dallal **1.** to auction off. *min wuṣalit lil-mazaad, id-dallaal čaan da-ydallil bil-kamanja.* When I got to the auction, the auctioneer was auctioning off the violin. **2.** to peddle, hawk, sell. *jiib dallaal, xalli ydallil bil-qappuuṭ maalak bis-suug.* Get a peddler, let him sell your overcoat. *yaḷḷa, ʔiṭlaʕ, dallil bil-liban, ʕaad!* Go on, get out and peddle the yoghurt, why don't you! || *da-ydallil ib-banaata w-maḥḥad da-yizzawwajhum.* He's trying to get rid of his daughters and no one wants to marry them. **3.** to pamper, spoil. *da-ddallil ibnak ihwaaya.* You're pampering your son too much.

tdallal to be coy, to play hard to get. *kassiḥha l-haay. bass yiʕjibha da-tid-dallal ʕala kull in-naas.* Forget about her. She just likes to be playing hard to get with everyone. *haay qaabla tidzaw-waja laakin da-tiddallala.* She's willing to marry him but she's acting coy. *la-tiddallal; difʕoo-lak xooš ifluus.* Don't play hard to get; they offered you a good salary. *raḥ-addallal ʕaleehum li-ʔan yiḥtaajuuni.* I'm going to hold them up for more because they need me. **2.** to makes demands, ask for favors, take advantage. *l-mara tiddallal ʕala rajilha li-ʔan yḥibbha.* The woman makes demands of her husband because he loves her. *da-yiddallal ʕalayya ʕabaalak ʔaani ʔabuu.* He's asking favors of me as if I were his father. || *ddallal* Gladly! At your service! (answer to a request).

ndall **1.** to find. *ndalleet il-beet loo laa?* Did you find the house or not? *j-jaahil δamm il-qalam maala b-mukaan ma-nin-dalla.* The child hid his pencil in a place where we wouldn't find it. **2.** to know, know where. *tindall beetna?* Do you know where our house is? *maḥḥad* *yindall beethum ween ṣaayir.* Nobody knows where they're living now. *ˀandall, bass li-hassa ma-gal-li š-yriid.* I know, but he still hasn't told me what he wants.

stadall to gather, infer, conclude, draw conclusions. *š-tistidill min hal-kalaam maala?* What do you conclude from what he said?

dalla pl. *dlaal* coffee pot.

dalaal **1.** coyness, coquettishness. **2.** spoiling, coddling, pampering. || *wilid niʕma w-dalaal* and *bazir dalaal* the pampered rich.

daliil pl. *ˀadilla* **1.** proof, evidence, clue. **2.** guide. **3.** guidebook, handbook. *daliil ij-jaamiʕa* the college catalog. **4.** directory, telephone book.

dallaal **1.** auctioneer. **2.** hawker, peddler. **3.** agent, broker. *dallaal sayyaaraat* car dealer.

dlaala pl. *-aat* commission taken by a *dallaal.*

d-l-h-m

dalham **1.** to become dark, cloudy. *d-dinya dalhimat w-yimkin tumṭur.* The sky has turned dark and it might rain. || *ʕala-weeš mdalhim? ˀaʕʕad ˀaδδaak?* Why are you so gloomy? Did somebody treat you bad?

d-l-w

dalu pl. *dlaawa* bucket, pail.

dilu pl. *dlaawa.* simpleton, dope, idiot.

d-l-y

dalla **1.** to direct, give directions. *tigdar iddalliini ʕala maʕaṭṭat il-qiṭaar?* Could you direct me to the train station? || *dalla ˀibni ʕala kull id-diruub il-muu zeena.* He steered my son on all the wrong paths. **2.** to show the way, point out. *ˀiδa taaxuδni bis-sayyaara, ˀagdar adalliik.* If you take me in the car, I can show you the way. *baawiʕ minnaa ʕatta adalliik weena.* Look out from here and I'll show you where it is.

d-m-b-s

dambas **1.** to pin. *dambus il-ibṭaana kullha.* Pin the whole lining in. **2.** to clip. *dambus hal-waraqteen bil-iklips.* Clip these two papers together with the paper clip.

dambuus pl. *danaabiis* **1.** pin, straight pin. **2.** pin, brooch. **3.** mace (weapon).

d-m-b-k

dumbuk pl. *danaabuk* a tapering clay or brass drum with skin head.

d-m-b-l

dimbila pl. *danaabil* boil.

d-m-j

dimaj (*i damij*) to merge, combine, join. *dimjaw šarikathum wiyya šarika θaanya.* They merged their company with another one. *l-qaaˀideen dimjaw quwwaathum w-hijmaw suwa.* The two commanders merged their forces and attacked together. *l-muʕallim dimaj iṣ-ṣaffeen w-darrashum.* The teacher combined the two classes and taught them that way.

d-m-r

dumar (*u damur*) to ruin, damage, wreck. *l-muṭar dumarha l-ʕadiiqti.* The rain ruined my garden. *l-ˀuutači dumar qaaṭi.* The presser made a mess of my suit. *ˀibni muu dmaritni; ma-yṣiir tuṣruf halgadd ifluus.* You've ruined me, son; you can't go around spending so much money. *buṣaṭa xooš baṣṭa; dumara.* He gave him a good beating; messed him up good. *šaǧǧalna lil-miǧrib. dumarni.* He worked us till evening. Knocked me out.

dammar to destroy, ruin, wreck, demolish. *l-qanaabul dammurat il-balda.* The bombs destroyed the city. *l-ʕadu dammar jeešna.* The enemy wiped out our army. *dammarha lis-sayyaara li-ˀan ʕallam kull ˀaṣdiqaaˀa s-siyaaqa biiha.* He ruined the car by teaching all of his friends to drive in it. *l-xaḷḷ ydammur il-marag.* Vinegar ruins stew. *kull-ma ˀalʕab šitranj wiyyaa ydammurni.* Everytime I play chess with him he slaughters me. *l-ˀustaaδ dammarna bil-imtiʕaan.* The professor ruined us with the test.

tdammar to be destroyed, ruined, demolished. *huwwa ma-ṣaar bii šii laakin sayyaarta ddammraṭ.* Nothing happened to him, but his car was wrecked. *l-miskiin iddammar; ṭirdoo mnil-waδiifa w-maʕ-ʕad da-yšaǧǧla.* The poor guy is ruined; they fired him from his job and no one will hire him. || *ddammarit ihwaaya b-has-safra.* I had a lot of troubles on that trip.

ndumar to be destroyed, ruined, demolished. *s-sayyaara ndumrat ib-had-daʕma.* The car was wrecked in this accident. *ʕadiiqta ndumrat imnil-ibzaaziin.* His garden was ruined by the cats. *l-qaaṭ maalak indumar; ṣaar-lak šahar laabsa.* Your suit is a mess; you've been wearing it a month.

dumaar ruin, destruction.

madmuur in bad shape, messed up, ruined.

mudammira pl. *-aat* destroyer (nav.).

d-m-a-r

damaar pl. *-aat* vein (anat.). || *lizama damaar w-ma-gidar yisbaḥ baʕad.* He got a cramp and couldn't swim any farther. *ʔaani ʔaʕruf kull damaaraata.* I can read him like a book. I know what makes him tick.

d-m-ʕ

dimaʕ (*a damiʕ*) to tear, shed tears, water (of the eyes). *lamma yibči ma-tidmaʕ ʕeena ʔabadan.* When he cries his eyes never shed tears. *min itgaššir buṣal iʕyuunha tidmaʕ.* When she peels onions her eyes water.

dammaʕ intens. of *dimaʕ*. *min ybaawiʕ biš-šamis iʕyuuna tguum iddammiʕ.* When he looks at the sun his eyes begin to water.

damiʕ (coll.) pl. *dmuuʕ* tear(s).

damʕa pl. *-aat* un. n. of *damiʕ*.

d-m-ġ

dumaġ (*a dumuġ*) to hit someone on the head, to crown, to brain. *dumaġa ḥeel w-waggaʕa ʕal-gaaʕ.* He brained him and knocked him down.

dammaġ intens. of *dumag*. *ʔibnak daydammġuun bii j-jahhaal.* The kids are beating your son on the head.

damġa pl. *-aat* **1.** blow on the top of the head (with the flat of the hand). **2.** a light blow with the knuckles, generally to the ribs.

damaaġ pl. *ʔadmiġa* **1.** brain. **2.** mind, brains, intelligence.

damaaġsizz pl. *-iyya* brainless.

madmaġa (invar.) person who is easily abused or pushed around.

daamuġ (only in the expression:) || *č-čalib yḥibb daamġa.* A dog loves his tormentor (said of anyone who submits to abuse).

d-m-q-r-a-ṭ

*dimuqraaṭi** 1. democratic **2.** democrat.

dimuqraaṭiyya democracy.

[1]*d-m-m*

damm **1.** blood. || *ʔaḥmar damm* blood red. *wučča ʔaḥmar damm.* His face is blood red. *damma b-raḥaat ʔiida.* He doesn't fear danger (lit., his blood is on the palm of his hand). **2.** (pl. *-aat, dmuum*) a killing, a death, a life. *niṭlubhum dammeen; kitlaw ʕammi w-ibna.* They owe us two lives; they killed my uncle and cousin. *damma ma-raḥ-yruuḥ balaaš. ʔuxuuta raḥ-yintaqmuu-la.* His death won't go for nothing. His brothers will avenge him. || *ʕala xams idnaaniir haaδa yruuḥ lid-damm.* For five dinars he is willing to kill or be killed.

*damawi** **1.** blood. *ʔawʕiya damawiyya* blood vessels. **2.** bloody, sanguinary. *ḥarub damawiyya* a bloody war. **3.** blood-red, bright red. *nafnuuf damawi* a bright red dress.

dammaam pl. *-aat* a flat, circular drum used to wake people in Ramadan, and in religious processions.

d-m-y

damma to bloody, cover with blood. *dammaa bil-basuṭ.* He bloodied him with the beating. *δall yδurba ʔila ʔan dammaa.* He kept hitting him until he'd covered him with blood.

tdamma to be bloodied, be covered with blood. *δallaw yitbaasṭuun ḥatta ddammaw iθneenhum.* They continued to fight until they were covered with blood.

(see also *d-m-m*).

d-m-n

daaman **1.** to become accustomed, get used. *l-bazzuuna daamnat ʕal-beet, w-tiji waḥḥadha.* The cat's gotten used to the house, and comes by herself. **2.** to make a habit, to do regularly. *ʔiδa ddaamin ʕala had-duwa, ṣiḥḥtak titḥassan.* If you take this medicine regularly, your health will improve. *daaman ʕal-čiδib w-ma-yigdar ybaṭṭil baʕad.* He made a habit of lying and he can't stop now. **3.** to get a habit, become addicted. *daaman ʕala širb ij-jigaayir min čaan iṣġayyir.* He became addicted to smoking cigarettes when he was small.

ʔadman to become addicted. *ʔadman ʕala l-ḥašiiš.* He became addicted to hasheesh. *ʔiδa tidmin ʕala širb il-ʕarag, tiddahwar ṣiḥḥtak.* If you addict yourself to drinking arrack, your health will be ruined.

dimin manure.

mudmin **1.** addict. **2.** habitual drunkard. **3.** person who has the habit of smoking.

d-m-y-r

damiiri a kind of brocaded cloth.

d-n-ʔ

daniiʔ pl. *ʔadniyaaʔ* low, base, vile, mean. *ʕamal daniiʔ* a foul deed, a dirty trick.

danaaʔa lowness, vileness, meanness, depravity.

d-n-b-s

danbas, danbuus = *dambas, dambuus,* which see under *d-m-b-s*.

d-n-b-k
dunbuk pl. *danaabuk* = *dumbuk* which see under *d-m-b-k*.
d-n-b-l
dinbila pl. *danaabil* = *dimbila,* which see under *d-m-b-l*.
d-n-j
dannaj = *dannag* which see under *d-n-g*.
d-n-d-l
dandal to lower, let down, dangle. *dandil il-ɛabil bil-biir ɛatta nšuuf iš-ġumja.* Lower the rope into the well so we can see how deep it is. *raɛ-anzil jawwa w-inta dandil-li l-meez.* I'll get down below and you let the table down to me. *ɛaašyat čarčaf id-doošag imdandila w-gariib iddugg bil-gaaɛ.* The edge of the bed sheet is hanging down and almost touching the floor.

ddandal to hang down, hang, dangle. *l-pahlawaan da-yiddandal imnil-ɛabil.* The acrobat's hanging on the rope. *xalli j-jaras yiddandal minnaa.* Hang the bell from here.

danduula pl. *-aat* something dangling, pendant.
d-n-r
dinar diamonds (suit in cards).
d-n-s
dannas to dirty, soil, sully (fig.). *dannas sumɛat il-ɛaaʔila min idzawwajha l-haay.* He dirtied the family's reputation when he married that woman. *la-timši wiyyaa; tara ydannisak ib-ʔaxlaaqa.* Don't hang around with him; he'll contaminate you with his behavior.
d-n-š
daanaš to consult, seek advice from. *ruuɛ daaniš ʔabuuk gabuḷ-ma tištiri s-sayyaara.* Go consult your father before you buy the car.

ddaanaš to confer, talk over something. *ddaanaš wiyya ʔabuuk gabuḷ-ma tqarrir.* Talk it over with your father before you decide.
d-n-g
dannag to bend, bow, lean. *dannag ɛaṭ-ṭifil w-šaala.* He bent over the baby and picked it up. *dannag raasa ɛatta ʔašuuf iš-biiha ɛilbaata.* He bowed his head so I could see what was on the back of his neck. *la-ddannig ihwaaya mniš-šibbaač, tara toogaɛ.* Don't lean too far out the window or you'll fall.

dinga pl. *-aat, dinag* column, pillar, support (especially from the sidewalk to a balcony). || *ʔabu d-dinag* (epithet for a homosexual) queer.
d-n-n
dnaan (coll.) seeds of a variety of grass or weeds sometimes found in rice.

dnaana pl. *-aat* un. n. of *dnaan*.
d-n-y
dina (i): *dinat nafsa ɛala* to stoop to, lower oneself for. *tidni nafsa ɛal-filis.* He'd do anything for a buck. *nafsa dinat ɛal-xaddaama, laakin xaaf min marta.* He felt lust for the maid, but he was afraid of his wife.

danna 1. to bring close, move near. *danni l-iktaab; ma-da-agdar ʔašuuf minnaa.* Move the book closer; I can't see from here. *danni l-maaɛuun yammi ɛatta ʔaakul.* Move the dish near me so I can eat. 2. (*danna nafsa*) to humble, abase, lower oneself. *danna nafsa w-raaɛ yitwassal bii.* He lowered himself and went to beg of him.

tdanna 1. to move close, go near. *ddanna! leeš waaguf biɛiid?* Move closer. Why are you standing so far off? *la-tiddanna yamm ič-čalib, tara yɛaḍḍak.* Don't go near the dog or he'll bite you. 2. to move over, shift one's position. *ddanna swayya w-sawwii-li mukaan.* Move over a little and make a place for me.

dini:* in *nafsa diniyya* greedy, self-indulgent, lacking self control. *nafsa diniyya. kull-ma ysuufa, yriid.* He's greedy. He wants everything he sees.

ʔadna 1. more or most vile. *ʔadna mnil-ʔaaxar* more vile than the other. 2. more or most slight, small, etc. *l-ɛadd il-ʔadna* the lower limit. *s-siɛir il-ʔadna* the lowest price. *ʔiḏa tiɛči ʔadna čilma ʔazɛal.* If you say a single word, I'll get mad. *yizɛal ɛala ʔadna šii.* He gets mad over the least thing. *š-šarq il-ʔadna.* The Near East.

dinya 1. world. || *jaa lid-dinya ʔawwal ramaḍaan.* He was born the first of Ramadan. 2. this world, this life (as opposed to *l-ʔaaxira*). 3. life, existence. *haay id-dinya* and *haay dinya.* That's life. *d-dinya jatti wiyyaa fadd jayya. ṣaar ṣaaɛib ʔaraaḍi w-mazaariɛ.* Things are going his way. He's become the owner of land and farms. || *giḷabha lid-dinya min ʔaxaḏt il-paaysikil minna.* He threw a fit when I took the bicycle from him. 4. weather. *d-dinya ṭayyba l-yoom.* The weather's nice today. *d-dinya da-tumṭur.* It's raining. 5. people, humanity. *s-suug matruus dinya.* The market is full of people.

d-h-d-r

dahdar to roll, cause to roll, let roll. *dahdir il-piip min yammak.* Roll the barrel away from you. *dahdar il-qalam ʕal-meez, w-wugaʕ.* He started the pencil rolling on the table, and it fell off. **2.** to send. *dahdira l-ʕali ʕalee, tara ṣadiiqa.* Send Ali to him, since he's his friend. **3.** to let out (a remark). *dahdarha lil-iʕčaaya giddaam in-naas.* He let the remark slip in front of the people.

tdahdar to roll. *waxxir! ṣ-ṣaxra da-tiddahdar.* Get out of the way! The rock's rolling. *lamma ddahdirat il-loori bila ṣtaap, gumaz is-saayiq minha.* When the truck rolled forward without any brakes, the driver jumped out. *ddahdar imnij-jibal ib-surʕa.* He coasted down the mountain at high speed. *ʔaku sadd ʕaj-jibal ṭagg w-iddahdar il-mayy kulla.* There's a dam on the mountain which broke and all the water ran down.

d-h-d-w

dahda, ydahdi var. of *dahdar,* which see.

dihidwaana pl. *-aat* downgrade, slope, incline.

dihideewa pl. *-aat* = *dihidwaana.*

d-ħ-r

daahar to tease. *la-tizʕal; da-ydaahrak.* Don't get mad; he's teasing you. *la-ddaahirni; tuʕruf ween iktaabi loo laa?* Don't stall me; do you know where my book is or don't you?

tdaahar **1.** to tease one another. *haaδoola ma-da-yitʕaarkun; da-yiddaahruun bass.* They're not fighting; they're just stirring each other up. *haaδa da-yiddaahar wiyyaak, l-iktaab ʕinda.* He's teasing you; he has the book. **2.** to drag things out, to hold up matters. *rubuʕ diinaar. ma-addaahar wiyyaak.* A quarter dinar. I won't haggle with you. *la-tiddaahar. ruuʕ ʕaad. sawwi lli git-lak-iyyaaha.* Don't keep arguing. Go on now. Do what I told you to. *ʔinta šgadd tiddaahar! fuδδni.* You sure do prolong things! Let me be on my way.

dahar pl. *duhuur* **1.** long time, age. **2.** fate, destiny.

*dahri** slowpoke.

duhur **1.** teasing. **2.** delaying, arguing, haggling.

d-h-s

dihas, dahis, etc. var. of *diʕas, daʕis,* which see under *d-ʕ-s.*

d-h-š

dihaš (*i dahiš*) to astonish, surprise, amaze, impress. *ʕamala dihašni.* His action astonished me. *šikla dihašni. ʕabaali waziir.* His appearance impressed me. I thought he was a cabinet member.

ndihaš to be astonished, amazed, surprised. *ndihašit min jawaaba l-xašin.* I was taken aback by his rude answer. *ndihašit min jamaalha.* I was overwhelmed by her beauty. *ndihašit min hal-manδar il-faδiiʕ.* I was stunned by the gruesome sight.

dahša **1.** astonishment, amazement, wonder, surprise. **2.** a magnificent, wondrous thing. || *ʔinta ṭaaliʕ dahša b-hal-qaaṭ ij-jidiid.* You look great in that new suit.

ʔadhaš more or most surprising, astonishing, amazing.

mudhiš amazing, astonishing, surprising.

madhuuš amazed, astonished. *š-biik madhuuš? ma-šaayif ibnayya?* Why are you astonished? Haven't you ever seen a girl?

d-h-l

dihla (invar.) **1.** dense, stupid. **2.** dunce. **3.** roiled, turbid. *mayy dihla* muddy water.

d-h-l-y-z

dihliiz pl. *dahaaliiz* **1.** a narrow passage or corridor. **2.** a tunnel between buildings.

d-h-n

dihan (*i dahin*) **1.** to oil, grease. *dihan ʔiida ʕatta txušš ib-ṣuhuula bil-bastuuga.* He greased his hand so it would go into the jar. *l-makiina biiha ṣooṭ; laazin tidhanha.* The machine's noisy; better oil it. || *dihan is-seer ʕaṭṭa yinṭuu ʔijaaza.* He greased some palms so they'd give him a license. *laazim dihnaw fadd čam ʔiid yalla gidraw yʕaṣṣluun biṭaaqaat.* They must have greased some palms to be able to get tickets. **2.** to rub, massage. *dihan rijla b-zeet iz-zeetuun.* He massaged his leg with olive oil. *dihnat δahra bil-kuʕuul.* She rubbed his back with alcohol. **3.** to salve, apply, smear on, paint on. (medicine, ointment). *dihanit xašmak bid-duwa?* Did you apply the ointment to your nose? *ṭ-ṭabiib dihan balʕuumi b-duwa murr.* The doctor painted my throat with a bitter medicine.

dahhan **1.** to oil. *baʕad-ma tixsil iṭ-ṭaawa, dahhinha ʕatta ma-dzanjir.* After you wash the frying pan, oil it so it won't rust. **2.** to cover with grease, get greasy. *ma-štiġaḷ bil-makiina ʔilla-ma dahhan iida.*

He's never worked on an engine without getting his hands greasy.

dihin **1.** oil (lubricating, edible, or for the skin). **2.** fat, butterfat. || *dihin ʕurr* clarified butter, ghee. **3.** ointment. || *ʕali w-ʔaʕmad ṣaayriin dihin w-dibis.* Ali and Ahmed have become very good friends. *has-sayyaara timši miθl id-dihin.* This car runs like a top. *ʔiida bid-dihin.* He's fat-catting it. He's got it made. He's really living.

*dihni** fatty. *maadda dihniyya* a fatty substance.

dihiin **1.** oily, greasy. *t-timman dihiin.* The rice is too oily. *ʔakil dihiin* greasy food. **2.** rich (in butterfat). *ʕaliib dihiin* rich milk. || *yaaxuδ raatib dihiin.* He gets a fat salary.

dahiin a type of very rich, greasy pastry.

d-h-w-r

dahwar to damage, ruin, destroy. *l-ʕarag dahwar ṣiʕʕta.* Arrack destroyed his health.

tdahwar to deteriorate. *l-waδiʕ iddahwar ib-hal-balad.* The situation has deteriorated in this country. *l-beet iddahwar imnil-muṭar.* The house deteriorated from the rain.

d-h-y

dahha to close (a door). *la-tinsa ddahhi l-baab min tiṭlaʕ.* Don't forget to close the door when you go out.

daahiya pl. *duhaat.* genius, clever, resourceful person.

daahiya pl. *dawaahi* disaster, catastrophe, calamity. *wugaʕ ib-daahiya.* A disaster befell him.

d-w-b

duub barely, hardly, scarcely. *duub wuṣalna ʕal-wakit.* We just barely got there in time. *duubha l-fluus itkaffi.* The money is barely sufficient. || *bid-duub, yaa duub* = *duub. bid-duub laʕʕagna bii.* We just barely caught him. *yaa duub laʕʕagna min ṭilaʕ il-qiṭaar.* We had only just arrived when the train left.

duuba **1.** barge. **2.** flatcar or gondola (R.R.). **3.** sidecar (of a motorcycle).

d-w-b-a-r

duubaara two deuces (in rolling dice).

d-w-b-l-a-j

dooblaaj dubbing (in motion pictures).

d-w-ʕ-s

dooʕas (*i dooʕaas*) to become seriously infected. *njiraʕ iṣibʕa w-dooʕas.* His finger was injured and became badly infected.

d-w-x

daax (*u doox*) **1.** to get dizzy, feel dizzy. *ʔaani ʔaduux ʔiδa ʔaftarr čam marra.* I get dizzy if I spin around a few times. *raasi yduux min ʔawwal peek.* My head starts spinning on the first drink. **2.** to get a headache, be bothered. *dixit min iʕyaaṭ ij-jihaal.* The kids' shouting gave me a headache. *daax raasi min ʕiss il-makaayin.* I got a headache from the noise of the machines. *dixit. ma-tsiktuun, ʕaad.* I'm fed up. Why don't you keep quiet now. **3.** to be put to a lot of bother, have a lot of trouble. *dixit ib-qaδiyytak. ṣaar-li sbuuʕ ma-da-asawwi šii; bass arkuδ-lak.* I've had a lot of trouble with your case. For a week I've been doing nothing but running around for you. *ʕali w-marta čaanaw ib-baġdaad w-dixna biihum.* Ali and his wife were in Baghdad and we ran ourselves ragged for them. *ʔiδa tištiri has-sayyaara l-imčarqiʕa raʕ-idduux biiha.* If you buy this broken down old car you will be constantly having trouble with it. **3.** to get sick, feel nauseous. *ma-ysaafir biṭ-ṭiyyaara li-ʔan yduux biiha.* He doesn't travel by plane because he gets sick on them.

dawwax **1.** to make dizzy. *l-iqraaya bis-sayyaara ddawwixni.* Reading in a car makes me dizzy. **2.** to give someone a headache, bother. *dawwaxitni. ma-tiskut!* You give me a headache. Why don't you shut up! *dawwxni b-ṭalabaata.* He bothered me with his requests. *raʕ-ʔaδall ʔaṭaalba bil-ifluus ʕatta ʔadawwxa w-yinṭiini-yyaaha.* I will keep asking him for the money until I drive him to distraction and he gives it to me.

dooxa **1.** dizziness, vertigo. **2.** headache, trouble, bother, nuisance. **3.** nausea, motion sickness.

d-w-d

dawwad to become wormy, worm-eaten. *t-tamur dawwad, w-ma-yinnikil.* The dates have gotten wormy and can't be eaten.

duud (coll.) **1.** worm(s). **2.** worm-like larva(e), e.g. maggot(s), grub(s). *miθl id-duud, ma-yinʕadduun.* There are so many of them, they can't be counted.

duuda pl. *-aat* un. n. of *duud. duudt il-ʔarδ* earthworm. *duudt il-qazz* silkworm. *d-duuda l-waʕiida* tapeworm.

duudaki pl. *-iyya* (vulgar) homosexual who takes the female role.

d-w-r

daar (*u door*) **1.** to turn, revolve, rotate, circle. *min simaʕni waraa, daar.* When he heard me behind him, he turned. *marra bil-yoom, il-ʔarð idduur ʕala nafisha.* Once a day, the earth revolves on its axis. *ruuḥ il-raas iš-šaariʕ w-duur lil-yisra.* Go to the end of the street and turn left. *l-arð idduur ḥawl iš-šamis.* The earth revolves around the sun. || *s-sana daarat ʕala θoor.* The year has come under the sign of the bull. *z-zaman daar ġeer doora; l-ʕawaaʔil il-ʕatiiga nqirðat.* Times have changed; all the old families have died out. *raasi daar w-ma-da-ʔandall.* I'm all turned around and can't find my way. **2.** /with *ʕala*/ to turn against. *daar ʕalayya w-sabbni.* He turned on me and cursed me. *daaraw ʕalee kullhum w-busṭoo.* They all turned against him and beat him up. **3.** to turn something, turn something around. *min giʕadit yamma, daar-li ðahra.* When I sat near him, he turned his back on me. *duur is-sayyaara; xal-nirjaʕ.* Turn the car around; let's go back. *yaaxat qamiiṣak gaayma. duurha.* Your shirt collar's frayed. Have it turned. *haj-jiha mnil-meez waṣxa. raḥ-aduurha.* This side of the table is dirty. I'm going to turn it around. **4.** to move, transfer, change. *raḥ-induur ʔila geer maxzan.* We're going to move to a new store. *beet ʕammi daaraw ib-beethum ij-jidiid.* My uncle's family moved into their new house. **5.** to tour, travel, go around, wander around. *kull sana yduur ʔawruppa kullha.* Every year he travels all over Europe. *dirna baġdaad kullha b-itlatt iyyaam.* We toured the whole of Baghdad in three days. *da-yduur ʕal-imwaððafiin yijmaʕ minhum ifluus.* He's going around to the employees collecting money from them. *š-aku ʕindak itduur ihnaa bil-leel?* What reason do you have for walking around here at night? || *haaða daayir ʕakka w-makka.* He's been all over. He's widely traveled (lit. he's toured Acre and Mecca.). **6.** to circulate, spread, be current, go around. *l-ʔišaaʕa daarat ib-baġdaad.* The rumor has gone around Baghdad. *hal-mooda daayra has-sana.* This style is in fashion this year.

dawwar **1.** to show around, take on a tour. *dawwarna kull baġdaad ib-sayyaarta.* He showed us around Baghdad in his car. **2.** to look, search. *dawwarit kull ijyuuba w-ma-lgeet šii.* I searched all his pockets and didn't find anything. *ʔiða ddawwur zeen tilgaaha.* If you search carefully you'll find it. *dawwarit bis-suug laakin ma-lgeet miθil hal-qalam.* I looked all over the market and didn't find another pen like this. *haaða da-ydawwir iṭlaayib. yriid yitʕaarak wiyya r-raayiḥ wij-jaay.* He is looking for trouble. He wants to fight with everybody. *yikrahuu li-ʔan yiskar w-ydawwir igḥaab.* They despise him because he drinks and chases after whores. *ʔabuuk da-ydawwur ʕaleek.* Your father is looking for you. || *la-ddawwir dafaatir ʕittag.* Don't bring up old matters.

daawar to alternate, vary, change, exchange. *leeš tilbas hal-qaaṭ kull yoom w-taark il-laax? daawirhum.* Why do you wear this suit every day and leave the other one? Alternate them. *daawir il-ispeer wit-taayaraat.* Rotate the spare and the tires. *daawir il-xall ib-hal-ibṭaala.* Transfer the vinegar into these bottles.

ndaar **1.** to turn. *min simaʕ ḥissi ndaar ḥatta yšuufni.* When he heard my voice he turned so he could see me. **2.** /with *ʕala*/ to turn against, on. *l-ḥači čaan ʕalayya, laakin hassa ndaar ʕaleek.* The talk was against me, but now it's turned against you. *waaḥid minhum indaar ʕalayya; ðirabni miit čillaaq.* One of them turned on me; he kept kicking me. **3.** to sneak in, slip in. *ndaar ʕaleena ḥaraami l-baarḥa bil-leel.* A thief broke into our place last night. *ðayyaʕna l-miftaaḥ w-indaareena min beet ij-jiiraan.* We lost the key and slipped in from the neighbor's house.

daar pl. *duur* house. *daar il-ʔaytaam* orphanage. *daar il-ʕajaza* old folks' home. *daar il-muʕallimiin il-ʕaaliya* teachers college. *daar il-ḥaðaana* nursery (in hospital, etc.).

daara pl. *-aat* **1.** circle. **2.** hand, round (cards).

daara: filfil daara hot pepper(s).

door pl. *ʔadwaar* **1.** round (in sports). **2.** role, part (also of stage and screen). *liʕab door muhimm bit-taḥqiiq.* He played an important role in the investigation. **3.** stage, phase, step. **4.** turn. *d-door ʕaleek.* It's your turn. *raḥ-yooṣlak id-door.* Your turn will come. *bid-door* in turn, by turns.

doora pl. *-aat* **1.** once, one time, time. *doora yiðhak w-doora yibči.* Sometimes he laughs and sometimes he crys. *ftarr daayir* *il-beet doorteen.* He went around the house twice. *ˀaani taɛbaan. ˀinta ruuḥ had-doora.* I'm tired. You go this time. || *fadd doora guul "ˀaani ma-aštirik."* You might as well say "I don't participate." *ˀaani taɛbaan fadd doora; ma-agdar ˀarkuḍ.* I'm completely exhausted; I can't run. *z-zaman daar ġeer doora; l-ɛawaaˀil il-ɛatiiga nqiḍrat.* Times have changed; all the old families have died out.

dawra pl. *-aat* **1.** rotation, turn. **2.** orbit, circuit, lap. **3.** course, training course. **4.** session (of Parliament). || *d-dawra d-damawiyya* blood circulation.

*dawri** round robin, rotating. *sibaaq dawri* round robin tournament.

dawriyya pl. *-aat* patrol.

dwaara (alternate verbal noun of *dawwar:*) *ˀinta da-ddawwir ɛal-ɛarka dwaara. leeš iṭṣayyiḥ ɛalee?* You are really looking for a fight. Why are you hollering at him? *ˀadawwur ɛaleeha dwaara.* I would go to the end of the earth to find it. I'd really look hard for it.

dawwaar pl. *-iin, -a* peddler, hawker, roving vendor.

dawaraan **1.** rotation, revolving. **2.** revolution, circuiting, orbiting.

daaˀira pl. *dawaaˀir* **1.** circle. **2.** agency, bureau, department. **3.** office, office building. ¶ *daaˀirat il-maɛaarif* encyclopedia.

daayir around, surrounding. *daayir il-waṣiṭ* around the center. || *daayir-ma daayir* = *daayir. giɛdaw daayir-ma daayiri.* They sat all around me.

mdawwar round, circular. *wujih imdawwar* a round face.

(see also *d-y-r.*)

d-w-r-b-y-n

doorbiin pl. *-aat* binoculars.

d-w-z-y

duuzi: leemuun duuzi crystalline citric acid, sour salt.

d-w-s

daas (*u doos*) **1.** to step, tread. *la-dduus ib-qundartak ɛaz-zuuliyya.* Don't step on the carpet with your shoes. *rijli l-yisra toojaɛni. ma-agdar ˀaduus ɛaleeha.* My left foot is hurting me. I can't stand on it. || *sabbata li-ˀan daas wiyyaaha zaayid.* She cussed him out because he went too far with her. *duus baanziin! ma-ḍall wakit.* Step on the gas! There's no time left. *xalli nsawwi nafisna ma-nšuufa. duus!* Let's pretend we don't see him. Step on it! **2.** to press, push. *la-dduus ɛaj-jariḥ; yoojaɛni.* Don't press on the wound; it hurts me. *daas iz-zirr w-inhizam.* He pushed the doorbell and ran. *duus il-ɛuuda ḥeel ḥatta txušš biz-zuruf.* Push the stick hard so it'll go into the hole. || *kull-ma yiḥči yduus ɛala galbi.* Everything he says burns me up. *disit b-iida diinaar yalḷa xallaani ˀaxušš.* I slipped him a dinar and only then he let me enter. *šgadd xooš ˀaadmi! loo dduus ɛala raasa ma-yiḥči.* What a nice guy! Even if you hurt him he won't say anything. **3.** to roll over, flatten. *r-roola daasat il-gaaɛ.* The steam roller packed the ground. *s-sayyaara daasat walad.* The car ran over a boy. **4.** to raid. *š-šurṭa daasaw beetna.* The police raided our house.

dawwas to trample. *xalloo jawwa rijleehum w-gaamaw ydawwisunn ɛalee.* They put it under their feet and started stamping on it.

ndaas pass. of *daas. l-kaaši muu yaabis; ma-yindaas ɛalee.* The tile's not dry; it can't be walked on. *l-gaaɛ ma-tindaas baɛad.* The ground can't be packed down anymore. *loo ma-yirkuḍ, čaan indaas.* If he hadn't run, he'd have been run over. *had-dugma ndaasat bil-ġaḷaṭ.* This button was pushed by accident. *ˀinhazmu tara ndaaseena!* Run—we've been raided!

daas pl. *duus* round, game, hand.

doosa pl. *-aat* **1.** plank, walkway, gang plank. **2.** running board.

mdaas pl. *-aat, midis* **1.** slipper with the quarter folded in. **2.** slipper with a low heel and no quarter, mule. || *wičča miθil imdaas.* His face is wrinkled up like the top of a soft shoe.

[1]*d-w-š*

dooš and *laḥam dooš* breast of lamb.

dooša noise, racket, uproar.

[2]*d-w-š*

duuš shower, shower bath.

d-w-š-g

doošag pl. *dwaašig* mattress.

d-w-š-m

doošama **1.** upholstering, upholstery. **2.** upholstering, the upholsterer's trade.

doošamči pl. *-iyya* upholsterer.

[1]*d-w-ġ*

duuġ: liban duuġ thin, diluted yoghurt.

[2]*d-w-ġ*

dwaaġ pl. *-aat* bridal veil, often including the train.

d-w-ġ-r-y

dooġri **1.** straight, direct. *ḥači dooġri* straight talk. *rajuḷ dooġri* an honest man, an upright man. **2.** truth, straight story.

ɛiča d-doogri. l-gaala kulla ṣudug. He told the truth. Everything he said is right.

d-w-q

dooq duck, white duck, duck cloth.

d-w-l

tdaawal to discuss. *da-yiddaawaluun bil-muškila.* They're discussing the problem. *ddaawalit wiyya ˀabuuk ɛan qaðiyyat diraastak?* Did you discuss the matter of your studies with your father?

dawla pl. *duwal* 1. country, state. || *haaða š-kubra! dawla min ġeer ɛasaakir.* What a great man! He's a state by himself (lit. a state without soldiers). 2. dynasty.

*dawli** international. *l-qaanuun d-dawli* international law.

mudaawala pl. *-aat* 1. negotiation. 2. discussion.

tadaawul 1. circulation (of money). 2. negotiation.

d-w-l-a-b

duulaab = *diilaab* which see under *d-y-l-a-b.*

d-w-l-č

doolča pl. *-aat, dwaalič* var. of *doolka.*

d-w-l-k

doolka pl. *-aat, dwaalik* 1. pitcher. 2. dipper resembling a pitcher.

d-w-l-m-a

doolma an all inclusive term for stuffed vegetables.

d-w-m

daam (*u doom*) to last, continue. *l-ɛarub daamat sitt isniin.* The war lasted six years. *l-farɛa ma-daamat-la hwaaya.* The enjoyment didn't last long for him. || *d-dinya ma-dduum l-aɛɛad.* The world doesn't stand still for anyone.

daam (*i ˀidaama*) to perpetuate, make permanent, cause to last. *ˀaḷḷa ydiim hal-niɛma ɛaleek.* God perpetuate this prosperity for you. *ˀaškurak, ˀaḷḷa ydiimak.* Thank you. God keep you.

daawam to commence, begin (to do something on a steady basis). *raɛ-adaawum bil-waðiifa min baačir.* I'm going to start going to work tomorrow. *raɛ-ydaawum bil-madrasa has-sana.* He's going to start attending school this year. 2. to continue. *baɛda da-ydaawum bil-madrasa.* He is still going to school. *raɛ-adaawum ɛala had-duwa.* I'm going to stay on this medicine.

ˀadaam to perpetuate, cause to last. *yaa rabbi, diimha l-hal-niɛma.* Oh, God, let this blessing continue.

ma-daam 1. as long as, while. *tmattaɛ ib-ɛayaatak ma-daamak šabaab.* Enjoy your life while you're still young. 2. as long as, inasmuch as, since, because. *ma-daam ma-ɛindak ifluus, ma-nigdar inwaddiik wiyyaana.* As long as you don't have money, we can't take you with us. *ma-daam ma-jaa, la-tidfaɛ-la fluus.* Since he didn't come, don't pay him any money.

dawaam working day. *saaɛaat id-dawaam* working hours, hours of business. *d-dawaam bil-madrasa* school hours. *ɛidna nuṣṣ dawaam.* We have a half day. || *dawaama muntaðam.* His attendance is regular. *l-ˀaɛwaal maa-lha dawaam; kullši yitbaddal.* Things don't remain the same; everything changes. *ɛala d-dawaam* perpetually, at all times, always. *yitšakka ɛala d-dawaam.* He complains all the time.

daaˀim continuous, continual, unceasing, constant. *b-xaṭar daaˀim* in constant danger.

daaˀiman always. *yzuurna daaˀiman min huwwa b-baġdaad.* He always visits us when he's in Baghdad. *daaˀiman yitšakka.* He always complains.

*daaˀimi** permanent. *waðiɛ daaˀimi* a permanent arrangement. || *b-ṣuura daaˀimiyya* permanently.

doom always, perpetually, continually. *doom yiji mitˀaxxir.* He always arrives late. *doom yiɛčuun ɛan-naas.* They're always talking people down. *dooma yiji mitˀaxxir.* He always comes late. *doomi miflis.* I'm always broke. || *biqa wiyyaaya doom il-wakit.* He stayed with me all the time.

ˀadwam more or most lasting, enduring. *ṣ-ṣuuf ˀadwam imnil-guṭin.* Wool is longer wearing than cotton.

d-w-m-n

doomna pl. *-aat* dominoes.

d-w-n

duun less than, under, below. *ˀilli duun il-iθmunṭaɛaš ma-yṣiir yṣiir muwaððaf.* Anyone under eighteen cannot become a government employee.

b-duun and *bi-duun* (prep.) without. *ṭilaɛ bi-duun šamsiyya b-hal-muṭar.* He went out without an umbrella in this rain. *b-duuna l-gaɛda ma-tiswa.* Without him a gathering isn't worthwhile.

b-duun-ma, bi-duun-ma (conj.) without. *la-truuɛ ib-duun-ma dgulli.* Don't go without telling me.

*duuni** 1. inferior, poor, bad. *qmaaš*

duuni poor quality cloth. **2.** bad, spoiled, rotten. *ṭamaaṭa duuniyya* spoiled tomatoes. **3.** low, lowly, mean, base, despicable, depraved, degenerate. *riyaajiil duuniyyiin* contemptible men. *mara duuniyya* a bad woman, a slut. **4.** (pl. *-iyyiin, -iyya*) bum, degenerate, debased or unscrupulous man.

diiwaan pl. *dawaawiin* **1.** guest house of a village. **2.** collection of poems by one author. **3.** central office, central building (of a ministry).

ˀadwan **1.** worse or worst. **2.** more or most spoiled. **3.** more or most despicable, debased.

d-w-n-d-r-m

doondirma pl. *-aat* ice cream, serving of ice cream. *glaaṣ biskit doondirma* an ice cream cone.

d-w-n-k-y

doonki pl. *-iyyaat* billy club, nightstick.

d-w-n-m

doonam pl. *-aat, dwaanim* a land measure of about 2500 square meters.

d-w-w

dawwa pl. *-aat* a shallow, conical clay brazier set by one's feet for warmth.

d-w-y

duwa (*i dawi*) **1.** to resound, boom, make a dull, booming sound. *simaʕit ʕiss il-madfaʕ yidwi?* Did you hear the cannon boom? *l-makiina ḍallat tidwi l-leel kulla.* The machine kept thudding all night. **2.** to drone. *ṭ-ṭayyaara ṣaar-ilha saaʕa tidwi foog ruusna.* The plane kept droning over our heads.

daawa to treat. *ḍall iṭ-ṭabiib ydaawii šahar.* The doctor continued to treat him for a month. *daaweet is-siflis maalak loo laa?* Have you had your syphilis treated or not?

tdaawa to get treated, be treated. *ʕind yaa ṭabiib da-tiddaawa?* What doctor are you being treated by?

duwa pl. *duwyaat, ˀadwiya* medicine, medication, remedy. *ˀibnak duwaa l-ʕaṣa.* The best medicine for your son is a stick. *l-ʕagrab duwaa in-naʕaal.* The only way you'd be any good is dead (lit., the remedy for a scorpion is a sandal). || *duwa ʕammaam* a depilatory made from quicklime and arsenic, used to remove pubic hairs. *da-yuḍrub duwa ʕammaam.* He's putting on a depilatory.

dawya pl. *-aat* boom, rumbling. *dawyat il-madfaʕ* the cannon's roar.

dwaaya pl. *-aat* inkwell.

d-y

di-, d- /emphatic particle used with imperative:/ *di-taʕaal nitšaarak!* Come on; let's become partners! *di-yaḷḷa! faat il-wakit.* Come on! It's late. *di-guum! xalli nruuʕ lis-siinama.* Get up! Let's go to the movies. *lak di-guum! š-imgaddrak tilʕab wiyyaaya?* Oh go on! How could you play against me? *di-ruuʕ! haaδa š-imfahhma?* Oh go on! What does he understand? *d-ukul xaatir inguum inruuʕ!* Eat up so we can get going. *d-iʕči! muu git-li ʕindak ˀaxbaar?* Speak up! Didn't you tell me you had some news?

dii **1.** come on, let's go. *dii! ˀidfaʕ ʕeel!* Come on! Push hard! *dii! ma-tinzil ʕaad! faat il-wakit.* Let's go! Get down here! It's late. **2.** (an emphatic expression of disagreement, approx.:) aw, come on, good God. *dii! haaδa šloon šuġuḷ yδawwij!* My God! This is such irritating work! *dii! haay hamm gahwa?* Come on! Do you call this coffee?

d-y-θ

dayyuuθ pl. *-iin* **1.** cuckold. **2.** procurer, pimp.

d-y-č

diič pl. *dyuuča* rooster, cock.

diič hindi turkey.

d-y-x

diixa pl. *diyax* date stalk (after the dates are removed).

d-y-r

daar (*i deer*) **1.** to turn, direct. *diir wiččak ʕalayya.* Turn your face to me. *diir it-talafizyoon ʕaleena, ma-da-nšuuf.* Turn the television towards us; we can't see. || *daar baala* to pay attention, look out, be careful. *la-ddiir-la baal; haaδa jaahil.* Don't pay any attention to him; he's a child. *diir baalak ʕaj-jaahil ˀila ˀan ˀarjaʕ imnis-suug.* Look after the kid until I get back from the market. *la-ddiir baal. minu ˀabu baačir?* Don't worry about it. Who knows about tomorrow? *diir baalak minna, tara yčaδδib.* Be careful with him, or he'll lie to you. *diir baalak! la-titʕawwar.* Watch out! Don't get hurt. **2.** to pour. *ˀarjuuk, diir-li finjaan gahwa.* Please pour me a cup of coffee. *diir il-mayy il-baaqi bil-iglaaṣ.* Pour the rest of the water in the glass. **3.** to manage, run, direct. *ma-aʕtiqid yidgar ydiir had-daaˀira.* I don't think he can manage this office. *nigdar indiir baladna blayya nufuuδ ˀajnabi.* We can run our country without foreign influence.

deer pl. *ˀadyira* monastery.
deeri (coll.) variety of dried red dates, common in southern Iraq.
deeriyya pl. *-aat* un. n. of *deeri*.
diira pl. *-aat* district, area, region.
ˀidaara **1.** administration, management, managing. **2.** (pl. *-aat*) administration, management, directorate. **3.** administrative section, administrative office. **4.** managerial ability, administrative ability. || *sawwa ˀidaara* to manage, make do. *marti ma-tigdar itsawwi ˀidaara ʕala miit diinaar biš-šahar.* My wife can't manage on a hundred dinars a month.
*ˀidaari** **1.** administrative. *ˀamur ˀidaari* an administrative order. **2.** administrator.
mudiir pl. *mudaraaˀ* **1.** director, head, chief, manager. **2.** principal (of a school).
mudiiriyya pl. *-aat* bureau, directorate, department, office.
(see also *d-w-r*)

d-y-z
diizi pl. *-iyyaat* small round cooking pot, usually with handles at the side.

[1]*d-y-s*
dees pl. *dyuus* **1.** breast. **2.** udder.
dees il-ʕanz variety of large "white" grape.

[2]*d-y-s*
dayyuus pl. *-iin* **1.** cuckold. **2.** procurer, pimp.

d-y-k
diik, var. of *diič,* which see under *d-y-č*.

d-y-l-a-b
diilaab pl. *duwaaliib, dwaaliib.* wardrobe, cupboard, bureau.
¶ *diilaab hawa* a Ferris wheel.

d-y-l-k-w
diilko pl. *diilkuwwaat* distributor (automotive).

[1]*d-y-n*
daayan to lend, loan. *daayinni xamsiin filis rajaaˀan.* Please lend me fifty fils. *ma-ddaayinni sayyaartak?* Would you lend me your car? *ma-ydaayin ˀaḥḥad.* He doesn't lend to anyone.
ˀadaan to find guilty, convict. *l-maḥkama ˀadaanata.* The court found him guilty.
tdaayan to borrow. *ddaayan minni xams idnaaniir.* He borrowed five dinars from me. *čaan muḏṭarr yiddaayan il-mablaġ.* He was obliged to borrow the amount.
stadaan = *tdaayan*. *stadaan minna fluus ihwaaya.* He borrowed a lot of money from him.
deen pl. *dyuun* **1.** debt. **2.** a loan outstanding, money owed one. **3.** an obligation, a favor (owed, or due one).
¶ *bid-deen* on credit.
dayyaan pl. *-a.* creditor.
madyuun **1.** indebted, in debt. **2.** obligated, under obligation.

[2]*d-y-n*
diin pl. *ˀadyaan* religion. || *d-diin* the religion, i.e., Islam.
diinsizz pl. *-iyya* **1.** faithless, lacking religion, person who violates religious laws. **2.** cruel, heartless, savage, barbarous. **3.** a mild term of jocular condemnation.
*diini** religious, spiritual. *jtimaaʕ diini* religious gathering. *rajul diini* religious functionary.
dayyin religious, pious, godly, devout.
dyaana pl. *-aat* **1.** religious. **2.** confession, denomination, sect.
middayyin religious, pious, devout, godly.

d-y-n-a-r
diinaar pl. *dnaaniir* dinar (the basic unit of Iraqi money, equal to the pound sterling.

d-y-n-a-m-y-t
diinaamiit dynamite. || *ˀiṣbiʕ diinaamiit* a stick of dynamite.

d-y-n-m-w
diinamo pl. *-owaat.* generator, dynamo.

d-y-w-x-a-n
diiwaxaana pl. *-aat* parlor, sitting room (where guests are entertained in traditional households).

d-y-w-r
deewar to turn, turn around. *yalla, deewir; xalli nirjaʕ.* Come on, turn around; let's go back. *xaffif is-surʕa gabuḷ-ma ddeewar.* Slow up before you turn.
tdeewar pass. of *deewar*. *s-sayyaara ma-tiddeewar ib-had-darbuuna.* The car can't be turned around in this alley.
(see also *d-w-r*.)

δ

δ-a-t
δaat see under *δ-w-t*.

δ-a-k
δaak f. *δiič* pl. *δook, δoolaak.* **1.** that, those. **2.** that one, that person, that guy. || *kullši ma-tbaddal; δaak iṭ-ṭaaṣ w-δaak il-ḥammaam.* Everything is unchanged; it's the same old song and dance.

δaak il-yoom the other day.

δaakuwwa (< *δaak huwwa*) **1.** That's him. **2.** There he is.

δaaka f. *δiiča* pl. *δooka, δoolaka* = *δaak.*

δ-a-l

δaal name of the letter *δ*.

δ-b-b

δabb (*i δabb*) **1.** to toss, throw. *δabb-li ṭ-ṭooba.* He threw me the ball. *δabb išwayya šʕiir lid-dijaaj.* He threw a little barley to the chickens. || *δabbha lil-iḥčaaya b-wučča.* He threw the remark in his face. *δabbeet-la ḥači, laakin ma-ftiham.* I threw out a hint to him, but he didn't understand. *j-jaahil δabb nafsa ʕala ʔumma w-ḥiḍanha.* The child threw himself on his mother and hugged her. *δabb nafsa mniṣ-ṣaṭiḥ.* He jumped from the roof. *loo tδibb nafsak ʕaš-šuġuḷ txaḷḷṣa b-saaʕa.* If you throw yourself into the work, you'll finish in an hour. *δabb nafsa tibal ʕalayya ʔila ʔan inṭeeta l-ifluus.* He pressured me until I gave him the money. *δabb nafsa ʕal-moot, w-anqad ḥayaat ʔibna.* He endangered himself and saved his son's life. *b-yaa faṣiil δabbook?* In which platoon did they put you? *δabbooni b-fadd wlaaya ṣġayyra.* They sent me to a small town. *baḷḷa δibbni yamm mawqif il-paaṣ.* Please drop me off near the bus stop. *δabb kull šuġḷa ʕalayya.* He pushed all of his work off on me. *δibb-la ṭuʕum. gul-la ʔiδa yiji ninṭii miit diinaar.* Put out some bait for him. Tell him if he comes we'll give him a hundred dinars. *δabb-la nukta ma-ṭḍaḥḥik.* He cracked a joke that wasn't funny. *miθl il-mayyit. ma-da-yδibb laa ʔiid wala rijil.* He's like a dead man. He isn't moving a hand or a leg. *ʔoogaf ib-mukaanak; la-tδibb wala xaṭwa.* Stop where you are; don't take another step. *t-taksi maali δabb-li diinaareen il-yoom.* My taxi brought in two dinars today. *raḥ-ʔaδibb il-ʔaas.* I am going to play the ace. *δabbeet diinaareen ʕala hal-iḥṣaan w-xisarit.* I put two dinars on this horse and he lost. *δibb il-geer ʕal-waaḥid.* Put the gear into first. *δabbeet ihwaaya ʕaraayiḍ.* I put in many applications. **2.** to throw away, discard. *rajaaʔan δibb iz-zibil barra.* Please throw the garbage outside. *raḥ-albas iθ-θoob fadd marra w-aδibba.* I'm going to wear the shirt one time and throw it away. *j-jaahil δabb iθ-θalij min ʔiida.* The child threw the ice away. || *ʔiδa tištiri has-sayyaara tδibb ifluusak biš-šaṭṭ.* If you buy this car, you'll be throwing your money away. *δabbat il-ḥijaab min dixlat il-kulliya.* She discarded the veil when she entered college. *δibb kullši w-iṭbaʕ hal-maktuub.* Drop everything and type the letter. *δabb marta w-ijhaala w-miltihi bil-winsa.* He dropped his wife and children and is busy having a good time. *ṭ-ṭiyyaara da-tδibb manaašiir.* The plane is dropping pamphlets. *da-yδibb min raasa.* He is throwing up. *ṣallḥaw il-buuri, loo baʕda yδibb mayy?* Did they fix the pipe, or is it still leaking water?

δabba pl. *-aat* habit, custom, quirk.

δ-b-ḥ

δibaḥ (*a δabiḥ*) **1.** to slaughter, butcher. *l-gaṣṣaab δibaḥ iθlaθ ihwaayiš.* The butcher slaughtered three cows. **2.** to cut someone's throat. *l-ḥaraami šaafa naayim bil-ifraaš w-δibaḥa.* The thief found him lying in bed and cut his throat. || *ʔaδbaḥak ʔiδa truuḥ.* I'll kill you if you go. *hal-ḥarr yiδbaḥ.* This heat is murder. *δibaḥitni, laa tištuġuḷ wala txalli ġeerak yištuġuḷ.* You kill me. You don't work and you don't let anyone else work. *δibḥoo mnil-basiṭ.* They just about beat him to death. *δibaḥ nafsa ḥatta ḥaṣṣal ʕal-waḍiifa.* He almost killed himself until he got the job. **3.** to massacre. *j-jeeš δibaḥ ʔahl il-wlaaya.* The army massacred the people of the city.

δabbaḥ **1.** to slaughter (large numbers). *ṣaar-la saaʕa yδabbiḥ ṣuxuul.* He's been slaughtering goats for an hour. **2.** to massacre. *l-ʔašqiyaaʔiyya δabbḥaw rukkaab il-paaṣ.* The gangsters massacred the bus passengers.

nδibaḥ pass. of *δibaḥ*. *nδibaḥit min haš-šuġuḷ.* I'm dead tired from this work.

δbiiḥa pl. *δibaayiḥ* **1.** animal for slaughter, slaughtered animal. **2.** sacrificial animal (given away, to the poor, after sacrifice).

maδbaḥa pl. *maδaabiḥ* massacre, carnage, slaughter.

δ-b-δ-b

δabδab to strew, throw around. *luweeš da-δδabδib kutbak ihnaa w-ihnaa?* Why do you throw your books here and there?

tδabδab **1.** pass. of *δabδab*. *ma-yṣiir ʔaġraaḍak tiδδabδab ihnaa.* Your things shouldn't be strewn around here. **2.** to fluctuate. *š-ṣaar bil-makiina? l-ʔubra da-tiδδabδab.* What happened to the machine? The needle is fluctuating. **3.** to tailor one's opinions or statements to what is expected. *hal-muwaδδaf yiδδabδab lil-mudiir ʔakθar imnil-laazim.* That employee defers to the director unnecessarily. *ʔaɛtaqra li-ʔan miδδabδib.* I despise him because he goes with the prevailing wind.

δ-b-l

δibal (*a δabil*) **1.** to wilt, wither, shrivel. *l-ixyaar δibal bil-ɛarr.* The cucumbers wilted in the heat. **2.** to waste away, get run down. *δiblat imnil-maraδ.* She wasted away with the illness.

δablaan **1.** wilted, withered, dried up. *warid δablaan* a wilted flower. **2.** wasted away, run down. *ʔibnak ybayyin δablaan.* Your son seems run down.

δ-b-n

δabban to become fly-infested. *ʔaɛtiqid il-baagilla raɛ-iδδabbin.* I think the horse beans are going to get flies in them.

δibbaan (coll.) fly, flies.

dibbaana pl. *-aat* fly.

δ-x-r

δuxur mainstay (person). *ʔinta δuxur ʔilna.* You're our mainstay.

δaxiira pl. *δaxaayir* **1.** supplies, stores. **2.** ammunition (mil.).

maδxar pl. *maδaaxir* warehouse, storehouse, especially for pharmaceuticals and drugs.

δ-r-r

δarra pl. *-aat* **1.** atom. **2.** tiny particle. **3.** speck, mote. || *ma-ɛinda wala δarrat ɛaqil.* He doesn't have a bit of sense.

*δarri** atomic. *qumbula δarriyya* atomic bomb.

δurriyya pl. *-aat* offspring, descendants, children.

δ-r-ɛ

δiraɛ (*a δariɛ*) to measure. *ʔiδraɛ il-ġurfa w-gul-li šgadd ṭuulha w-ɛuruδha.* Measure the room and tell me its length and width.

tδarraɛ to resort, have recourse. *yiδδarraɛ ib-ʔaɛδaar ṣaxiifa.* He resorts to stupid excuses.

δraaɛ pl. *-aat, δirɛaan* **1.** arm, forearm. || *ɛaṣṣal il-waδiifa b-iδraaɛa.* He got the job by his own effort. **2.** (pl. *-aat, ʔuδruɛ*) unit of measure, from finger tips to shoulder. *δraaɛ ɛalab* = approx. .68 meter. *δraaɛ baġdaad* = approx. .8 meter. *δraaɛ šaah* = approx. 1 meter.

δ-r-y

δarra to winnow. *da-yδarruun il-ɛunṭa bil-hawa.* They are winnowing the wheat in the wind.

ʔiδra corn. *ʔiδra ṣafra* corn, maize. *ʔiδra beeδa* durra, grain sorghum.

δarwa peak, apex, top (of power or success).

δ-ɛ-n

ʔaδɛan to yield, submit, give in, obey. *ʔiδa ma-yiδɛin, nistaɛmil quwwa wiyyaa.* If he doesn't obey, we'll use force on him. *ʔiδa thaddida yiδɛin-lak.* If you threaten him, he'll give in to you.

δ-q-n

δiqin pl. *δiquun* beard, whiskers (on the chin).

δ-k-r

δikar (*u δikir*) **1.** to recall, remember. *ma-tiδkur iz-zeeniyyaat il-sawweet-lak-iyyaaha?* Don't you recall all the favors I did for you? *hassa δkarit. ʔaxuuk ʔaxaδ qalami.* Now I remember. Your brother took my pen. *ʔiδa taakul ʔakla ṭayyba, ʔuδkurni.* If you eat a good meal, think of me. **2.** to speak of, talk about. *ʔiɛna daaʔiman niδukrak bil-xeer.* We always speak well of you. **3.** to mention. *ʔašu ma-da-yiδkur šii b-hal-maktuub ɛan majiiʔa.* I notice he mentions nothing about his coming in this letter.

δakkar **1.** to remind, call to mind. *balla δakkirni l-yoom ʔaštiri šamsiyya.* Please remind me today to buy an umbrella. *šuuf hal-walad. wučča ma-yδakkrak ib-ɛali?* Look at that boy. Doesn't his face remind you of Ali? **2.** to make a word masculine. *hal-ʔasmaaʔ muʔannaθa. δakkirha.* These nouns are feminine. Make them masculine.

tδakkar to remember, recollect. *ma-da-aδδakkar išwakit gal-li ʔašuufa.* I don't remember what time he told me to see him.

tδaakar to confer, have a talk. *marr ɛalayya lil-beet ɛatta niδδaakar bil-qaδiyya.* He dropped by my house so we could confer about the matter.

δikir **1.** mentioning, mention. || *jaab δikir il-qaδiyya.* He brought up the matter. *hassa činna b-δikrak.* We were just talking about you. *ɛala δikir ʔaxuuk, gul-li hassa š-da-ysawwi.* Speaking of your brother, tell me what he's doing now. **2.** a religious ceremony in which the attributes of God are recited.

δakar pl. *δukuur,* **1.** male. **2.** (pl. *δukuur, δkuura*) penis.

δikra pl. *-ayaat* memory, remembrance, recollection. || *yoom δikra* anniversary.

tiδkaar pl. *-aat* souvenir, memento.

*tiδkaari** memorial, commemorative. *naṣub tiδkaari* monument.

muδaakara pl .*-aat* conference, consultation.

δaakira memory. *quwwat iδ-δaakira* power of recollection.

muδakkar masculine (gram.). *ʔisim muδakkar* a masculine noun.

muδakkara pl. *-aat* **1.** memorandum. **2.** appointment book.

δ-k-y

δakaaʔ intelligence, mental acuteness, brightness.

*δaki** pl. *ʔaδkiyaaʔ* intelligent, clever, bright, smart, sharp-witted.

δ-l-l

δall (*i δall*) **1.** to go down. *siʕr iš-šiʕiir idδall ib-waasṭat il-istiiraad.* The price of barley went down as a result of imports. **2.** to humble, humiliate. *ma-aku ḥaaja dδill nafsak ʕala diinaar.* There's no need to humiliate yourself for a dinar.

δallal **1.** to humble, humiliate. *la-δδallil nafsak giddaama. qaabil huwwa rabbak?* Don't humble yourself in front of him. Do you think he's your God? **2.** to conquer, overcome. *musaaʕadtak raḥ-iδδallil kull iṣ-ṣuʕuubaat.* Your help will overcome all the difficulties.

tδallal **1.** to lower, humble oneself, be humble, cringe. *šuufa šloon yiδδallal min yiḥtaajak.* Look at how he humbles himself when he needs you. **2.** to be overcome, be conquered. *raḥ-tidδallal kull iṣ-ṣuʕuubaat ʔamaami.* All the difficulties facing me will be overcome.

δill, δull subjugation, subjection, submission, humiliation. *ʕiišt iδ-δill ma-tinraad.* A life of subjugation is unacceptable.

δilla = *δill. ʕadam il-istiqlaal δilla.* Lack of freedom is a humiliation.

δaliil **1.** low, down, depressed. *suug iš-šiʕiir δaliil.* The barley market's depressed. **2.** humble, submissive, servile, abject. *šaʕab δaliil* a subservient people.

maδalla = *δill.*

δ-m-r

tδammar to complain, grumble. *da-yiδδammar ihwaaya min haš-šuġuḷ.* He's grumbling a lot about this work.

taδammur complaining, grumbling, griping.

δ-m-m

δamm (*i δamm*) to criticize, find fault with, damn. *yaakul ʕidhum w-yδimmhum.* He eats at their house and then finds fault with them. *yδimm il-ʔakil il-ʔawruppi.* He's always talking down European food. *midaḥ ʕali hwaaya laakin δamm ʔaḥmad.* He praised Ali a lot but he criticized Ahmed.

δamman = *δamm. δammam-la s-safra lij-jinuub.* He discouraged him from making the trip to the south.

δimma pl. *δimam* conscience. || *biδ-δimma?* really? honestly? *b-δimmti* on my honor, honestly. *ʔaxalliiha yamm δimmtak.* I'll leave it to your discretion.

maδamma censure, blame.

maδmuum objectionable, reprehensible. || *ʔaani miθl is-simač, maakuul w-maδmuum.* I'm like the fish, eaten and then despised.

δ-n-b

ʔaδnab to sin. *ʔiδa tiδnib bid-dinya titʕaδδab bil-ʔaaxira.* If you sin in this life you will be tortured in the next life.

δanib pl. *δnuub* **1.** offense, sin, crime, misdeed. **2.** fault, error, mistake.

δinba pl. *-aat* stinger (of an insect).

δinbaaya = *δinba.*

muδnib **1.** guilty. **2.** sinner.

δ-h-b

δahhab to gild. *nṭeeta ṣiiniyyat ič-čaay ḥatta yδahhibha.* I gave him the tea tray to gild.

δahab gold. || *š-daʕwa l-keelo b-diinaar! qaabil δahab.* Imagine, a dinar a kilo! You'd think it was gold. *šloon xooš walad! δahab.* What a good boy! He's a gem.

maδhab pl. *maδaahib* **1.** faith, denomination, religious creed. **2.** school of canonical law. || *b-maδhabak, ʔaani gilit šii?* Honestly, did I say anything?

*maδhabi** sectarian. *taʕaṣṣub maδhabi* sectarian bigotry.

mδahhab, mδahhib gilded. *parda mδahhiba* a gilded curtain.

δ-h-l

δihal (*i δahil, δuhuul*) **1.** to amaze, astonish, astound, dumbfound. *haṣ-ṣuura tiδhil illi yšuufha.* This picture will astonish anyone who sees it. *l-filim bii ḥawaadiθ tiδhil il-ʕaqil.* The film has events in it which stagger the imagination. **2.** to frighten, scare. *šikil hal-ḥaywaan yiδhil.* This animal's looks are frightening.

ʔaδhal = *δihal. ʔaδhalni b-has-suʔaal.* He astonished me with that question. *ʔaδhal il-maḥalla kulla b-jaraaʔima.* He terrorized the whole neighborhood with his crimes.

nδihal pass. of *δihal. nδihalit minna min ṭabb fujʔa.* I was frightened when he burst in. *min simaɛ il-xabar inδihal.* When he heard the news he was astonished.

δ-h-n

δihin pl. *ˀaδhaan* mind.

*δihni** mental, intellectual. *masˀala riyaaδ̣iyya δihniyya* a perplexing mathematical problem. *ˀasˀila δihniyya* questions requiring thought.

δ-w-b

δaab (u δawabaan) **1.** to dissolve. *kull iš-šakar δaab bič-čaay.* All the sugar dissolved in the tea. **2.** to melt. *θ-θalij kulla δaab.* All the ice melted. || *δaabat ruuɛi mniš-šamis.* I wilted from the sun. *δaabat ruuɛi mnij-juuɛ.* I became weak from hunger.

δawwab **1.** to dissolve. *δawwub il-miliɛ ib-hal-kuub.* Dissolve the salt in this cup. **2.** to melt. *δawwub ir-raṣaaṣ ib-hal-xaašuuga.* Melt the lead in this spoon. || *yδawwub il-gaḷub haj-jaahil.* That kid's a pain in the neck.

δ-w-t

δaat **1.** self, ego. *ɛubb iδ-δaat* egoism, self-love, selfishness. *nukraan iδ-δaat* self-denial. **2.** -self. *humma ˀijaw b-δaathum.* They came themselves. *huwwa b-δaata. ma-aku ˀaɛɛad yišbaha.* It was he himself. There is no one that looks like him. || *b-ɛadd δaat* by itself, in itself. *s-safar ib-ɛadd δaata mufiid bass mutɛib.* Travelling in itself is beneficial but tiring. **3.** conscience.

¶ *biδ-δaat* by itself, in itself. *l-has-sabab biδ-δaat ma-raad yruuɛ wiyyaana.* For that very reason he didn't want to go with us. *ˀaani biδ-δaat ma-aɛibba.* I in particular don't like him. *δ̣aat ir-riˀa* pneumonia. *δaat ij-janb* pleurisy.

δawaat: ˀibin δawaat person from a prominent family.

bad-δaat, baδ-δaat inconsiderate.

*δaati**: || *ɛukum δaati* autonomy, self-rule.

δaatiyya personnel. *qism iδ-δaatiyya* personnel section.

δ-w-q

staδwaq to like, appreciate. *ma-yistaδwiq il-ˀakil bil-maṭaaɛim.* He doesn't like the food in restaurants. *ma-tistaδwiq il-faṣaal il-ˀamriikiyya.* She doesn't like American styles. *staδwaqit iṭ-ṭabux maalha.* I appreciated her cooking.

δooq **1.** taste (in food, clothing, etc.). **2.** taste, manners, sense of propriety. **3.** taste, flavor.

see also *δ̣-w-g.*

δ-w-l

δool, δoola see under *h-a-δ-a.*

δ-y-b

δiib pl. *δiyaab* wolf.

δ-y-ɛ

δaaɛ (i ˀiδaaɛa) **1.** to spread, circulate. *l-xabar š-ib-saaɛ δaaɛ! ma-δ̣all ˀaɛɛad ma-simɛa.* How fast the news spread! There's no one who hasn't heard it. **2.** to broadcast, transmit. *raɛ-yδiiɛuun il-ˀaxbaar saaɛa sitta.* They're going to broadcast the news at six o'clock.

nδaaɛ to be broadcast, transmitted. *l-ˀaxbaar inδaaɛat gabuḷ saaɛa.* The news was broadcast an hour ago.

ˀiδaaɛa **1.** announcement, disclosure. **2.** broadcasting, radio. *maɛaṭṭat il-ˀiδaaɛa* broadcasting station, transmitter station (radio and television). **3.** (pl. *-aat*) broadcasting station.

muδiiɛ radio or television announcer.

δ-y-l

δayyal **1.** to add on the end, add an appendage. *daaˀiratna δayyilat il-iktaab ib-ṭalab musaaɛada.* Our office attached an appendage to the letter with a request for assistance. *δayyal il-maktuub ib-ɛibaara ġayyirat kull il-maɛna.* He tacked on the end of the letter a clause changing the whole meaning. **2.** (jocular) to fire, throw out of a job. *ṣadiiqi δayyiloo l-baarɛa.* They fired my friend yesterday.

δeel pl. *δyuul, δyuula* **1.** tail (of an animal or bird, also of an airplane or kite). **2.** hem, border (of a dress, skirt, or robe). **3.** appendix (of a book). **4.** (pl. only) *δyuul* consequences, results. *δyuul iθ-θawra* the consequences of the revolution. || *ˀašu ween-ma ˀaruuɛ tilɛagni. šinu ˀinta, qaabil δeeli?* It seems wherever I go you follow me. What are you, my shadow?

δyaal pl. *-aat* hem, border (of a dress, skirt, or robe). *šaayla iṭ-ṭamaaṭa b-iδyaal ɛabaayatha.* She is carrying the tomatoes in the hem of her aba. *l-ijhaal imčallibiin b-iδyaalaat ˀummahaathum ɛatta la-yδ̣iiɛuun.* The children are holding onto their mothers' coattails so they won't get lost.

δweel (diminutive of *δeel*): *najma ˀumm iδweel* a comet.

R

r-ʔ-a

riʔa, riyya pl. *-aat* lung. || *maraḍ ḍaat ir-riʔa* pneumonia.

*riʔawi** of the lung, pulmonary.

r-a-č-y-t-a

raačeeta pl. *-aat* prescription (med.).

r-a-d-y-t-a

raadeeta pl. *-aat* radiator. || *šaku ʕinda yṣayyiʕ? laazim ir-raadeeta ʕinda ʕaamya.* What's he doing all that shouting for? He must be boiling mad about something.

r-a-d-y-w

raadyo pl. *raadyowwaat* radio.

r-ʔ-s

riʔas (*a riʔaasa*) to lead, head, be in charge of. *minu raʕ-yirʔas ij-jamʕiyya?* Who's going to head the association?

raʔʔas to appoint as leader, place in charge. *ma-dgul-li minu raʔʔasak ihnaa?* Would you just tell me, who made you the boss around here?

traʔʔas to lead, head, be in charge of. *minu traʔʔas il-wafid?* Who headed the delegation?

raas pl. *ruus* **1. a.** head. || *yaʕni qaabil yriid yilʕab ib-raasi?* You mean he thinks he's going to make a fool out of me? *hal-qaḍiyya mxarbuṭa; ma-aʕruf raasha min čaʕabha.* This matter is confusing; I can't make heads or tails of it. *binta ʔijat ʕala raas ʔibna.* His daughter was born immediately after his son. *ʕala ʕeeni w-raasi!* Very gladly, sir! At your service! Just as you say! *ʕala ʕeeni w-raasi. raʕ-asawwi miθil-ma triid.* Certainly! I'll do as you wish. *w-raasak il-ʕaziiz!* Honest! You can be sure! *w-raasak il-ʕaziiz, ma-aʕruf.* Honestly, I don't know. *la-taaxuḍ kalaama raas.* Don't take what he says seriously. **b.** head (as a numerative of livestock). *čam raas ġanam ʕindak?* How many head of sheep do you have? **c.** one, a single. *raas xass* a head of lettuce. *raas šalġam* one turnip. *raas jizar* one carrot. *raas paača* head, feet, and tripe from one animal. || *ma-ʕindi jhaal; raasi w-raas marti.* I have no children; there's only me and my wife. **2.** tip, end. *raas il-xašim* the tip of the nose. *raas is-sillaaya* the tip of the pen point. *raas qalam* point of a pencil. || *ruʔuus ʔaqlaam* notes. *ʔaxaḍit ruʔuus ʔaqlaam bil-muʕaaḍara.* I took notes in the lecture. *ruus il-iṣaabiʕ* tiptoes. *leeš da-timši ʕala ruus ʔiṣaabʕak?* Why are you walking on tiptoe? **3.** top, summit, peak. *raas in-naxla* the top of the palm tree. *raas il-qaaʔima* the top of the list. *ʔitris il-buṭul lir-raas.* Fill the bottle to the brim. *nṭiini keelu tamaaṭa min raas is-salla.* Give me a kilo of tomatoes from the top of the basket. **4.** end, extremity. *raas il-ʔoolči* the end of the tape measure. *raas il-xeet* the end of the string. *raas il-ʕagid* the end of the alley, end of the lane. *raas iš-šaariʕ* end of the block, i.e., corner, intersection. **5.** beginning. *raas iš-šahar* the first of the month. *raas is-sana* the beginning of the year. *ʔiʕčii-li kullši mnir-raas.* Tell me everything from the beginning.

¶ *nṭeeta šaġla baṣiiṭa w-ma-ṭallaʕ minha raas.* I gave him a simple job and he couldn't grasp it. *fadd raas* directly, without delay, straightaway. *ruuʕ lil-beet fadd raas.* Go straight home. *raas gala* by chance, by accident. *jat-ti raas gala.* I got it purely by chance. *b-raasa* pure, unadulterated. *ʕaliib ib-raasa* unadulterated, undiluted milk.

raʔs pl. *ruʔuus* cape, promontory, headland.

raʔsan directly, straight, straightaway. *haṭ-ṭayyaara truuʕ raʔsan il-baġdaad.* This plane goes directly to Baghdad. *raʕ-awaddi s-sayyaara lil-garaaj raʔsan.* I'm going to take the car straight to the garage.

raʔsmaal, raasmaal capital, financial assets.

*raʔsmaali** **1.** capitalistic, capitalist. **2.** a capitalist.

raʔsmaaliyya capitalism.

raʔiis pl. *ruʔasaaʔ* **1.** head, leader, chief, boss. *raʔiis il-ʕiṣaaba* the leader of the gang. *raʔiis ʕurafaaʔ* master sergeant. *raʔiis taʕriir ij-jariida* the editor in chief of the newspaper. **2.** captain (mil.). *raʔiis ʔawwal* major. *raʔiis firqat kurat il-qadam* captain of the football team. **3.** president. *raʔiis ij-jamhuuriyya* president of the republic. *raʔiis il-wuzaraaʔ, raʔiis il-wizaara* prime minister. *raʔiis il-baladiyya* chief of a municipality, mayor. *raʔiis ʔarkaan ij-jayš.* army chief of staff.

*raʔiisi** leading, main, chief, principal. *šaariʕ raʔiisi* a main street. *door raʔiisi* a leading role.

riʔaasa, riyaasa pl. *-aat* presidency.

riˀaast il-wizaara premiership, prime ministry.

marˀuus pl. *-iin* subordinate, underling.

r-ˀ-f

riˀaf (*a raˀif, raˀfa*) to show pity, have mercy, be mericful. *riˀaf bii w-ma-ƹaaqaba ƹal-muxaalafa.* He took pity on him and didn't punish him for the violation.

raˀuuf merciful, compassionate.

ˀarˀaf more or most merciful, compassionate.

r-a-m-y

raami rummy (cards).

r-ˀ-y

raˀi pl. *ˀaaraaˀ* opinion, view.

raaya pl. *-aat* banner, flag.

mraaya pl. *-aat, muri* mirror. || *huwwa bil-wijih imraaya w-bil-gufa sillaaya.* He's nice to your face, but talks behind your back. *mraayat iδ-δahar* the behind.

muraaˀi pl. *-iin* hypocrite.

r-b-b

rabb pl. *ˀarbaab, rbuub* lord, master. *rabb il-ƹaaˀila* the head of the family. *r-rabb* the Lord, God. *yaa rabbi, haay šloon balwa!* My God, what a calamity! || *ˀalla rabbak; l-mudiir axuuk.* God looks after you; the director's your brother. *walad ˀarbaab* refined gentleman, well-liked, respected man.

rubbama perhaps, maybe, possibly. *rubbama tˀaxxraw bit-ṭariiq.* Perhaps they got delayed on the way.

rbaaba pl. *-aat* 1. rebec, a one stringed musical instrument resembling the fiddle. 2. (pl. *rbaayib*) long, drawn-out affair. *sawwaaha rbaaba. ṣaar-la saaƹa yitƹaamal wiyya d-dukkanči.* He made a big production of it. He spent an hour haggling with the proprietor. *ma-txalliṣ ƹaad? sawweetha rbaaba!* Why don't you finish? You've already taken too long! 3. headache, bother. *haay šloon irbaaba! ma-ariid ˀaruuƈ lis-siinama.* What a pain in the neck! I don't want to go to the movies. *laazim ˀaruuƈ lil-maktaba, w-adawwur ƹal-iktaab. haay irbaaba; ˀashal-li ˀaštirii.* I'll have to go to the library and look for the book. That's a bother; it's easier for me to buy it.

rubbaaba pl. *-aat* = *rbaaba* 1.

*rabbaani** divine. *ƹamal rabbaani* act of God.

mrabba pl. *-aat, -aayaat* jam, preserves, jelly.

r-b-ƈ

rubaƈ (*a ribiƈ*) 1. to gain, profit. *ˀufruδ ymuut. ˀinta š-tirbaƈ?* Assume he dies. What would you gain? *rubaƈ ib-haṣ-ṣafqa ƹišriin diinaar.* He made twenty dinars on that deal. 2. to win. *l-biṭaaqa raqam ƹišriin rubƈat diinaar waaƈid.* Ticket number twenty won one dinar. *rubaƈ ˀalif diinaar bil-uqmaar l-baarƈa.* He won a thousand dinars gambling yesterday.

rabbaƈ to grant a profit, to allow to profit. *ˀalla yrabbƈak ib-hal-beeƹa.* God grant that you profit from this sale.

ribiƈ pl. *ˀarbaaƈ* 1. profit, gain. 2. interest (on money). 3. winnings.

rabƈaan pl. *-iin* gainer, winner, profiter.

ˀarbaƈ more or most profitable, lucrative, etc.

raabiƈ 1. profitable, lucrative, gainful. 2. (pl. *-iin*) gainer, winner, profiter.

r-b-d

rabud pl. *rbuud* pointed stick, stake.

rabda: ƈiss rabda clattering, banging, rattling noise.

r-b-r-b

rabrab to complain vociferously, make a fuss. *min ma-liga ƹaša, gaam yrabrub.* When he didn't find any supper, he started raising hell.

r-b-ṭ

rubaṭ (*u rabuṭ*) 1. to bind, tie up. *ˀurbuṭ il-kutub il-hal-xeeṭ.* Tie up the books with this string. 2. to tie, fasten, attach, hitch. *ween triidni ˀarbuṭ l-iƈṣaan?* Where do you want me to hitch the horse? *ˀurbuṭ il-xaruuf biš-šijra.* Tie the sheep to the tree. 3. to connect. *binaw jisir ib-baġdaad yirbuṭ qiṭaar karkuuk ib-qiṭaar il-baṣra.* They built a bridge in Baghdad to connect the Kirkuk railroad with the Basra railroad. 4. to attach, annex. *raƈ-yifuṣluun daaˀiratna min wizaart iz-ziraaƹa w-yirubṭuuha b-wizaart it-tijaara.* They're going to detach our office from the Ministry of Agriculture and attach it to the Ministry of Commerce.

rtubaṭ to bind oneself, commit oneself. *rtubaṭ ib-mawƹid gabul-ma ygul-li.* He got tied up with an appointment before he spoke to me.

rabuṭ 1. binding, tying. || *b-iida l-ƈall wir-rabuṭ.* He has absolute power (lit., in his hands is the untying and the tying). *ma-yfiid tiƈči wiyyaa; l-ƈall wir-rabuṭ b-iid marta.* It won't do you any good to talk to him. She's the one who makes the decisions. 2. connecting, connection. || *ƈačya ma-bii rabuṭ.* His words don't make sense. *taعliiqak ma-čaan ʔila rabuṭ.* Your comment was irrelevant.

rabṭa pl. *-aat* 1. bunch, bale, bundle. 2. necktie.

rbeeṭi pl. *-iyya* an animal penned up for fattening.

ribaaṭ pl. *ʔarbiṭa* necktie.

raabiṭa pl. *rawaabiṭ* 1. bond, tie. *rawaabiṭ ṣadaaqa* bonds of friendship. 2. league, union, association. *raabiṭat iṭ-ṭullaab il-عarab.* Arab Students League.

naamarbuuṭiyyaat sinful, disgraceful actions or deeds.

mirtibuṭ committed, tied up, tied down. *mirtibuṭ ib-mawعid* tied up with an appointment.

r-b-ع

rabbaع to square. *rabbuع hal-عadad.* Square this number.

trabbaع to sit cross-legged. *min yug-عud عaz-zuuliyya, yitrabbaع.* When he sits on the rug, he crosses his legs.

rabuع (group of) friends. *عinda rabuع ihwaaya.* He has a lot of friends. *tṣaa-laحna w-ṣirna rabuع.* We made up and became buddies. *jiib rabعak w-aani ʔajiib rabعi w-xan-nilعab.* You bring your gang and I'll bring my gang and let's play.

rubuع pl. *ʔarbaaع* 1. quarter, one-fourth, fourth part. *tlatt urbaaع is-saaعa* three quarters of an hour. *rubuع fistiq* a quarter kilo of pistachios. *rubuع عarag* a quarter liter bottle of arrack.

rabiiع spring, springtime. || *rabiiع il-ʔawwal* Rabia I, third month of the Moslem calendar. *rabiiع iθ-θaani* Rabia II, fourth month of the Moslem calendar.

ribiiع plenitude, abundance, sufficiency. *waagiع ib-ribiiع.* He's got it made. He's in high cotton.

*rabiiعi** spring. *l-عuṭla r-rabiiعiyya* spring vacation.

ʔarbaعa pl. *-aat* four.

ʔarbaaṭaعaš fourteen.

ʔarbaعiin forty.

*rubaaعi** 1. quadri-partite, consisting of four. 2. (gram.) consisting of four radical letters, quadriliteral.

ʔarbaعaa, yoom il-ʔarbaعaa. Wednesday.

tarbiiع 1. squaring (a number). 2. floor tiling, flooring.

*tarbiiعi** square, quadratic. *jaδir tarbiiعi* square root (math.).

raabiع fourth (ordinal).

marbuuع pl. *-iin* medium sized with broad shoulders.

murabbaع 1. squared, square. *عišriin matir murabbaع* twenty square meters. 2. (pl. *-aat*) square (geom.). 3. square (math.).

r-b-k

ribak (*i rabik*) to confuse. *la-tirbikni; xalliini ʔaحsib.* Don't confuse me; let me count.

ʔarbak = *ribak.*

rtibak to become confused. *rtibakit bil-imtiحaan w-ma-gdart ajaawub zeen.* I got confused on the examination and couldn't answer properly.

r-b-w

rabu asthma.

r-b-y

ruba (*a riba*) to grow, grow up. *ruba wiyya l-عurbaan w-itعallam عaadaathum.* He grew up with the tribes and learned their customs.

rabba 1. to cause to grow, let grow. *da-yrabbii-la šwaarub حatta ykawwin-la šaxṣiyya.* He's growing himself a mustache to give himself a personality. 2. to raise, rear, bring up. *rabba jhaala zeen.* He raised his children well. 3. to raise, breed. *had-dijaaj imrabba عala حunṭa w-išعiir.* These chickens have been raised on wheat and barley. 4. to strengthen, give added vigor. *had-duwa yrabbi il-galub.* This medicine will strengthen the heart.

trabba to be raised, reared, brought up. *عali trabba wiyyaana.* Ali was raised with us.

riba up-bringing, raising, breeding.

tarbiya 1. raising, rearing, bringing up. 2. manners, breeding, civility. 3. education, teaching, pedagogy. 4. breeding, raising (of animals).

mrabba 1. raised, brought up. 2. (pl. *-aat, -ayaat*) preserves, jam, jelly.

murabbiya pl. *-aat* 1. nursemaid. 2. governess.

r-t-b

rattab 1. to arrange, put in order, organize. *rattib hal-biṭaaqaat حasb il-حuruuf il-hajaaʔiyya.* Arrange these cards alphabetically. *rattib ġurfat il-xuṭṭaar.* Straighten up the guest room. *tilbas ihduum rixiiṣa laakin tuعruf itrattib nafisha w-tiṭlaع حilwa.* She wears cheap clothes but she knows how to fix herself up and look nice. 2. to arrange, prepare. *rattabit kullši. ʔiحna nibqa hnaa w-humma yijuun saaعa xamsa.* I arranged everything. We stay here and they will come at five o'clock. *rattib-lak ʕuδur zeen tara zaʕlaan.* Make up a good excuse for yourself because he's mad.

trattab **1.** to be arranged, put in order. *hal-awraaq ʔabad ma-titrattab.* These papers can't be arranged at all. **2.** to be the result or consequence. *tuʕruf š-raḥ-yitrattab ʕala ʕamalak haaδa?* Do you know what's going to result from this action of yours?

rutba pl. *rutab* rank (mil.).

tartiib **1.** order, arrangement. *b-tartiib* in order. *ḥill hal-masaaʔil bit-tartiib* Solve the problems in order. **2.** (pl. *-aat*) layout. *tartiib il-ġuraf* the layout of the rooms.

raatib pl. *rawaatib* salary, pay.

mrattab orderly, neat. *šuuf hal-walad šloon imrattab.* Look how neat that boy is.

r-t-l

ratil pl. *ʔartaal* column (of soldiers, etc.), convoy. *r-ratl il-xaamis* the fifth column.

rteela pl. *-aat* harvestman, daddy long-legs.

r-t-w-š

rituuš retouching (phot.).

r-θ-y

riθa (*i riθaaʔ*) **1.** to elegize, lament, bewail. *riθa l-waziir il-marḥuum ib-qaṣiida faxma.* He elegized the deceased minister wtih a magnificent poem. **2.** to pity, feel sorry. *ʔaani ʔarθi l-ḥaal hal-faqiir.* I'm sorry about this poor man's situation.

riθiyya a dish made of yoghurt and fresh goat's milk.

r-j-ʔ

rajaaʔ, rijiʔ, see *r-j-w.*

r-j-b

rajab Rajab, seventh month of the Moslem calendar.

r-j-j

rajj (*u rajj*) to convulse, shake, rock. *ṭ-ṭullaab rajjaw il-wlaaya bil-muδaaharaat.* The students shook the city with their demonstrations.

rtajj to be convulsed, shake, tremble, quake. *rtajjat il-wlaaya min ʔaṣwaaṭ il-madaafiʕ.* The city shook from the noise of the cannons.

r-j-ḥ

rajjaḥ to prefer, favor, consider preferable. *ʔaani ʔarajjiḥ itxalliṣ šuġulak gabuḷ-ma tiṭlaʕ.* I prefer that you finish your work before you leave.

ʔarjaḥ more or most probable, etc. *ʕal-ʔarjaḥ* most probably, most likely. *ʕal-ʔarjaḥ, yooṣal il-yoom bil-leel.* Most probably, he will arrive tonight.

raajiḥ **1.** preferable. **2.** probable, likely. **3.** heavy, generous, more than fair (of a merchant's weight). *nṭaak wazin raajiḥ.* He gave you more than a fair amount.

marjiiḥa pl. *maraajiiḥ* swing.

r-j-ʕ

rijaʕ (*a rujuuʕ*) **1.** to return, come back, come again. *raḥ-ʔarjaʕ baʕd išwayya.* I'll return after a while. *la-tiji wyaana. ʔirjaʕ!* Don't come with us. Go back! *ʔirjaʕ li-wara!* Move back! || *rijaʕ il-ʕaqla w-jaaz imnil-iqmaar.* He came to his senses and quit gambling. *wugaʕ b-ʔawwal δarba, laakin gaam w-rijaʕ-la b-books.* He fell from the first blow but then he got up and retaliated with a punch. **2.** to recur, come back, return. *l-maraδ rijaʕ ʕalayya.* My sickness recurred. *hamm rijaʕ il-barid.* Cold weather is back again. *biṣ-ṣeef yitlaf, laakin biš-šita tirjaʕ ṣiḥḥta.* In the summer he gets run down but in the winter his health returns. *rijaʕ waahsa biš-šiṭranj.* His interest in chess returned. **3.** to begin again, resume, recommence. *rijaʕ ʕala swaalfa l-ʕatiiga.* He resumed his old stories. **4.** to return to, revert to, go back to, become again. *min idzawwaj, rijaʕ šabaab.* When he got married, he became young again. *ʔiδa tġisla b-haṣ-ṣaabuun, yirjaʕ ʔabyaδ.* If you wash it with this soap, it'll turn white again. || *kull-ma yikbar, yirjaʕ li-wara.* The older he gets, the more he regresses. **5.** to be traceable, go back. *ʔaṣla yirjaʕ il-haaruun ir-rašiid.* His ancestry goes back to Harun al Rashid. **6.** /with *ʕan*/ to go back on, revoke, countermand. *ʔaani waafaqit w-ma-raḥ-arjaʕ ʕan raʔyi.* I agreed and I'm not going to change my opinion. *rijaʕ ʕan kalaama.* He went back on his word. **7.** to derive power from, rely on, depend on. *š-ma-yriid, sawwi! haaδa yirjaʕ lil-waziir.* Whatever he wants, do! He's backed up by the minister.

rajjaʕ **1.** to return, give back. *ʔarjuuk rajjiʕ-li ktaabi.* Please return my book to me. *hal-qaaṭ ma-da-yiʕjibni; raḥ-ʔarajjʕa.* I don't like this suit; I'm going to take it back. *rajjʕoo-lna it-talafoon baʕad-ma difaʕna l-fluus.* They reinstalled the telephone after we paid the money. *l-ʔakil iz-zeen rajjaʕ-li quuti.* The good food gave me back my strength. || *rajjaʕ-la δarba b-δarba* He returned him punch for punch. **2.** to bring back, take back, return. *ʔiδa ʔaruuح wiyyaak, laazim itrajjiعni b-sayyaartak.* If I go with you, you'll have to bring me back in your car. || *ṣaaح عalee w-rajjaع عaqla b-raasa.* He shouted at him and brought him to his senses. *staعmil had-duwa; yrajjعak jaahil.* Take this medicine; it will make a young man of you. **3.** to put back, return. *rajjعooni l-waδiifti is-saabqa.* They returned me to my previous position. *rajjعoo ʔila rutbat raʔiis.* They reinstated him in the rank of captain. || *min yilعab šiṭranj yrajjiع.* When he plays chess, he takes his moves back. **4.** to take back. *min inbiiع šii, baعad ma-nrajjعa.* Once we sell something, we don't take it back. **5.** to move back, set back. *rajjiع il-kursi maalak li-wara šwayya.* Move your chair back a little. *rajjaع is-saaعa maalta عašir daqaayiq.* He set his watch back ten minutes.

raajaع **1.** to consult, ask, check with. *ma-ariidak ṭinṭi ʔay jawaab il-ʔaححad gabuḷ-ma traajiعni.* I don't want you to give an answer to anybody without consulting me. *raajaعit عiddat ʔaṭibbaaʔ laakin maححad عiraf šinu maraδi.* I consulted several doctors but no one found out what my disease was. *raajiع šuعbat iδ-δaatiyya.* Check with the personnel section. *raajiعni baačir bid-daaʔira.* Check with me tomorrow in the office. || *raajiع عaqlak gabuḷ-ma tqarrir.* Think it over before you decide. *raajaعit l-iktaab marrteen gabḷ il-imtiحaan.* I went over the book twice before the exam. **2.** to check, verify, examine critically. *l-muʔallif ma-ṭubaع il-iktaab ʔilla baعad-ma raajaعa muʔallif ʔaaxar.* The author didn't print the book until after another author had reviewed it. *raajaعt il-iحsaab w-maligeet ʔay ġalaṭ.* I checked the accounts and didn't find any error.

trajjaع pass. of *rajjaع.*

traajaع **1.** to consult, confer. *yitraajaع wiyya l-mudiir ib-kull qaδiyya muhimma.* He confers with the director on every important matter. **2.** to withdraw, retreat, fall back, back off. *jeeš il-عadu traajaع miit miil.* The enemy army retreated a hundred miles. **3.** /with *عan*/ to go back on, rescind, countermand, revoke. *ma-da-yiqbal yitraajaع عan qaraara.* He won't agree to go back on his decision.

starjaع to get back, recover, regain. *starjiعaw minna jamiiع il-mabaaliġ.* They recovered all the money from him.

*rajعi** reactionary.

rajعiyya reactionism, reaction.

rajعa pl. *-aat* return, return trip.

marjiع pl. *maraajiع* **1.** source, source material, authoritative reference work. **2.** immediate superior in a chain of command, authority one turns to.

muraajaعa pl. *-aat* review, reiteration, going over.

murajjaع (adj.) round-trip. *tikit murajjaع* a round-trip ticket.

muraajiع pl. *-iin* **1.** petitioner, consulter, person who has business with an official. **2.** (doctor's) patient.

r-j-f

rijaf (*i rajif, rajfa*) to tremble, shiver, shudder, shake. *j-jaahil da-yirjif imnil-barid.* The child is shivering from the cold. *min yṣiir عaṣabi yirjif.* When he becomes angry he trembles.

rijjeefa trembling, shaking, shivering. *lizmata r-rijjeefa.* He was seized with shivering.

r-j-l

trajjal to dismount. *trajjal il-faaris min iحṣaana.* The horseman got down off his horse.

rtijal to improvise, extemporize, deliver off-hand. *š-šaaعir irtijal qaṣiida mumtaaza.* The poet made up a wonderful poem on the spot.

starjal **1.** to act like a man, display masculine manners or qualities. *starjilat w-libsat ihduum riyaajiil.* She looked like a man and wore men's clothing. **2.** to be self-important, overbearing. *min ṣaar عamma waziir starjal ib-raasna.* When his uncle became miinster, he lorded it over us.

rijil (m. or f.) dual *rijilteen* or *rijleen* *pl. rijleen, rijleenaat* **1.** foot. **2.** leg (also of a table, etc.). || *makiina ʔumm rijil* treadle-operated machine, foot-powered machine. *xuff rijlak; tʔaxxarna.* Get a move on; we're late.

rajil pl. *rjuula, riyaajiil* husband.

rijjaal pl. *riyaajiil* man.

*rijaali** men's, for men, male, masculine. *ʔalbisa rijaaliyya* men's clothing.

rujuula manhood, masculinity, virility.

mirjal pl. *maraajil* boiler (of a steam engine).

maraajil (pl. only) feats, deeds, exploits. || *da-ybiiع maraajil ib-raasi.* He's trying to impress me with his exploits. *leeš itbiiع*

maraajil ib-raas il-banaat? ʔiδa biik xeer ruuħ ʕal-wulid. Why do you bully the girls? If you think you're somebody, go pick on the boys.

rtijaal pl. *-aat* improvisation, extemporaneous creation.

*rtijaali** improvised, impromptu, offhand, extemporary, unprepared. *xiṭaab irtijaali* an extemporaneous speech. *ʔaʕmaala kullha rtijaaliyya.* Everything he does is on the spur of the moment.

r-j-w

rija (*i rija, rajaaʔ*) to request, ask. *rijaani atarjum-la l-maktuub.* He asked me to translate the letter for him. || *ʔarjuuk* please. *ʔarjuuk ma-tṣarruf-li d-diinaar?* Would you please change the dinar for me? *ʔarjuuk la-tjiib ʔismi.* Please don't mention my name. || *ʔarjuuk! ʔaani š-aʕlayya?* Now I ask you! What do I have to do with it?

rajja to hear a request, listen to. *ma-yfiid, haaδa ma-yrajji ʔaħħad.* It's no good. He won't listen to anyone.

trajja to request, ask, beg. *jeet atrajja minnak itsawwii-li zeeniyya.* I came to ask you to do me a favor. *ʔatrajjaak itsaaʕid ʔibni.* I beg of you to help my son. *ʔatrajjaak, ma-dgul-li ween il-maktaba?* Would you please tell me where the library is?

rtija to hope for, expect, anticipate. *š-tirtiji minna?* What can you expect from him?

rija pl. *-aayaat* request, plea. *r-rija ma-yinfaʕ wiyyaa.* Begging won't help with him.

rajaaʔ pl. *-aat* 1. hope. *raʔs ir-rajaaʔ iṣ-ṣaaliħ.* Cape of Good Hope. 2. request, plea.

rajaaʔan please. *rajaaʔan, la-tsawwi halgadd ħiss.* Please don't make so much noise.

marju hoped for, anticipated, expected. *haaδa marju minna.* That's expected of him.

r-j-y-m

rajiim pl. *-aat* diet. *sawwa rajiim.* He went on a diet.

r-č-č

račč (*i račč*) to become weak, be weakened. *la-tiġsil θoobak ihwaaya tara yričč bil-ġasil.* Don't wash your shirt too much or it'll be weakened by the washing. *raččeet w-baʕad ma-agdar ʔaštuġuḷ.* I've gotten weak and can't work any more.

ričiič 1. weak, feeble. *qmaaš ričiič* weak cloth, shoddy cloth. *ʕibaara ričiiča* a weak phrase. *ṣiħħta ričiiča.* His health is poor. 2. loose, slack. *l-ħabil ma-mašduud zeen ʕaj-junṭa. ričiič.* The rope isn't tied on the suitcase well. It's loose.

r-ħ

raħ-, raaħ- /followed by imperfect verb/ prefix indicating future tense. *muʔakkad raħ-tumṭur il-yoom.* It's definitely going to rain today. *raħ-tiji lil-ħafla loo laa?* Are you going to come to the party or not? *ma-raħ-ašrab jigaayir ʔiδa yirfaʕuun il-asʕaar.* I'm not going to smoke cigarettes if they raise the prices. *yaʕni šloon wiy-yaak? ma-raħ-itbaṭṭil imniš-šaqa?* Just what's to be done with you? Aren't you ever going to stop teasing?

r-ħ-b

raħħab /with *b-*/ to welcome, make welcome. *min šaafni, raħħab biyya hwaaya.* When he saw me, he welcomed me heartily.

raħaaba: raħaabat ṣadir magnanimity, generosity.

marħaba pl. *maraaħub* welcome! greetings! hello! *marħaba biik* an answer to *marħaba. ʔahlan w-marħaban!* Hello! || *maaku beenaatna ġeer il-marħaba.* We don't do anything more than say hello to each other.

tirħaab pl. *-aat* welcome, greeting. *qaabalni bit-tirħaab.* He received me with open arms.

tarħiib welcoming, welcome, greeting. *ħaflat tarħiib* a welcoming party, reception.

*tarħiibi** welcoming. *ħafla tarħiibiyya* reception, welcoming ceremony.

r-ħ-t

rħaati, raħħaati pl. *-iyaat* funnel.

r-ħ-δ̣

mirħaaδ̣ pl. *maraaħiiδ̣* toilet, lavatory, rest room, latrine.

r-ħ-l

riħal (*a raħiil*) to migrate, move away. *hal-qabiila raħ-tirħal min hal-manṭiqa li-ʔan ma-aku ʕišib kaafi.* This tribe's going to move away from this area because there isn't enough grazing.

raħħal to cause to migrate, to relocate, resettle. *l-ħukuuma raħħilat kull il-qabaaʔil ib-hal-manṭiqa.* The government relocated all the tribes in this area.

raħla pl. *-aat* desk, seat (in school).

riħla pl. *-aat* trip, tour, outing.

raħħaal pl. *-a, ruħħal* migratory,

wandering, nomadic. *qabaaʔil ruɛɛaal* nomadic tribes.

raɛɛaala (no pl.) great traveler, explorer.

marɛala pl. *maraaɛil* phase, stage.

r-ɛ-m

riɛam (*a raɛam, raɛma, marɛama*) to have mercy upon, have comparison for. *ʔaḷḷa yirɛama. čaan xooš ʔaadmi.* God have mercy on him. He was a good man. *tuɛruf il-ɛaakim riɛamak ib-hal-ɛukum?* Do you realize that the judge was merciful to you in that verdict? || *yirɛam ʔabuuk, ma-tɛaawinni!* For goodness sake, will you please give me a hand!

raɛɛam to seek the mercy of God, to ask God to have mercy. *raɛɛam il-ʔabuu.* He asked God to have mercy upon his dead father.

traɛɛam to be merciful, be kind, show mercy. *traɛɛam ɛalee b-badla ɛatiiga.* He showed mercy to him by giving him an old suit.

starɛam to plead for mercy. *l-masjuun qaddam ɛariiδa l-raʔiis ij-jumhuuriyya yistarɛim biiha.* The prisoner presented a petition to the president in which he pleaded for mercy. *starɛam imnil-ɛukuuma yfukkuun ʔibna mnil-ɛabis liʔan ṣiɛɛta muu zeena.* He pleaded with the government to release his son from prison because his health was bad.

raɛam pl. *ʔarɛaam* **1.** womb, uterus. **2.** kinship, family tie, relationship. || *huwwa min ʔarɛaamna.* He's one of our kinfolk. **3.** pity, compassion. *ween ʔahl ir-raɛam? fluus ɛaša ma-ɛindi.* Where are the compassionate people? I don't have money for dinner.

raɛma **1.** compassion, pity. **2.** mercy. *raɛma ɛal-maat-lak* a polite formula for requesting aid. *raɛma ɛal-maat-lak ma-tfukk-li hal-baab.* Would you please open that door for me. **3.** (pl. *-aat*) an act of mercy from God, a blessing. *l-muṭar raɛma.* Rain is a blessing.

raɛiim merciful, compassionate. *gaḷba raɛiim.* He's kind-hearted.

r-raɛmaan the Merciful (i.e. God). *b-ism illaah ir-raɛmaan ir-raɛiim.* In the name of God, the Merciful, the Compassionate. *wir-raɛmaan, ma-adri.* I swear I don't know.

ʔarɛam more or most merciful, compassionate.

marɛama pl. *maraaɛim* merciful deed, act of mercy. *bil-ɛiid il-masaajiin iyɛaṣṣ-luun ɛala maraaɛim.* During the feast the prisoners receive a lightening of their sentences.

stirɛaam pl. *-aat* petition, plea for clemency.

marɛuum **1.** deceased, departed, late. **2.** deceased person.

r-ɛ-y

raɛɛa pl. *-aat, -ayyaat* quern, hand mill.

raɛɛaaya, rɛayya pl. *-aat, riɛi* grinder, molar tooth.

r-x-x

ruxx rook, castle (chess).

r-x-ṣ

rixaṣ (*a ruxuṣ*) to become inexpensive, cheap. *l-ixyaar rixaṣ ihwaaya.* The cucumbers got very cheap. *siɛr iš-šakar yirxaṣ biṣ-ṣeef.* The price of sugar decreases in the summer.

raxxaṣ **1.** to make cheap, inexpensive. *ʔiδa traxxiṣha šwayya, tbiiɛ minha hwaaya.* If you lower the price a little, you'll sell a lot of it. **2.** to permit, allow, give permission. *baɛad-ma raxxaṣni, saafarit.* Once he'd given me permission, I took the trip. **3.** to authorize, license. *minu raxxaṣ-lak itbiiɛ jigaayir hnaa?* Who authorized you to sell cigarettes here?

starxaṣ **1.** to find cheap, regard as inexpensive. *starxaṣa lil-uqmaaš w-ištira minna hwaaya.* He decided the cloth was cheap and bought a lot of it. **2.** to ask permission. *starxaṣ min abuu gabuḷ-ma raaɛ lis-siinama.* He asked permission from his father before he went to the movie. || *ʔaani ʔastarxiṣ.* Excuse me (said when leaving a room or group).

ruxuṣ cheapness, inexpensiveness. *r-ruxuṣ ɛajiib ib-hal-uwlaaya.* Life is amazingly cheap in this city.

ruxṣa permission, authorization. *min ruxuṣtak* if you please, with your permission. *min ruxuṣtak, agdar ʔamurr minnaa?* May I please get through here? *min ruxuṣtak, naawišni s-salla.* Please hand me the basket.

rixiiṣ inexpensive, cheap. *ma-tilgi šii rxiiṣ ihnaa.* You won't find anything cheap here.

ʔarxaṣ more or most inexpensive, etc.

tarxiiṣ pl. *-aat* **1.** permission. **2.** authorization. **3.** price cut, price reduction.

marxuuṣ authorized, permitted. *ʔinta ma-marxuuṣ taaxuδ il-ifluus.* You are not permitted to take the money.

r-x-m

ruxaam marble.

r-x-y

rixa (i raxaawa) **1.** to become loose, slack. *leeš ma-šaddeet il-ʕabil zeen? bass ʕal-lagit l-ihduum bii, rixa.* Why didn't you tighten the rope well? The minute I hung the clothes on it, it sagged. || *min tiʕči wyaa bnayya ʕilwa, yirxa.* Whenever a pretty girl talks with him, he's helpless. **2.** to accede, give in, be persuaded. *ʕaačaaha b-luṭuf ʕatta rixat.* He talked to her gently until she gave in.

raxxa **1.** to slacken, loosen. *raxxi l-ʕabil ʕatta ašidda bil-ʕamuud.* Slacken the rope so I can tie it to the pole. **2.** to persuade, win over, cause to give in. *δall yiʕči wyaaha ʕaz-zawaaj ʔila ʔan raxxaaha.* He kept on talking to her about marriage until he won her over.

traxxa to be loosened, slackened. *hal-burği mzanjir. ma-yitraxxa.* This screw is rusted. It can't be loosened.

rtixa to relax. *rtixi šwayya ʕatta yδ̣urbak ʔubra.* Relax a little so he can give you a shot. *diir baalak. la-tirtixi min yiʕčuun wiyyaak.* Be careful. Don't let down your guard when they're talking to you.

raxu soft. *gaaʕ raxwa* soft ground.

raxaawa **1.** looseness, slackness. **2.** softness.

rixi loose, slack. *šidd il-iʕzaam rixi ʕatta taakul ʔakθar.* Fasten your belt loosely so you can eat more.

taraaxi limpness. || *taraaxi ʔaʕṣaab* semiparalysis.

raaxi loose, slack. *l-qaayis maal il-makiina raaxi.* The fan belt is loose. *l-watar maal il-kamanja raaxi. δ̣uuba.* The violin string is loose. Tighten it. *l-burği raaxi; δ̣ubba.* The screw is loose; tighten it.

r-d-ʔ

tradda to become bad. *ṣiʕʕta traddat ihwaaya.* His health got very poor.

radiiʔ **1.** bad. *huwwa sumuʕta radiiʔa.* His reputation is bad. **2.** of poor quality. *hal-uqmaaš imnin-nooʕ ir-radiiʔ.* This is a shoddy sort of cloth. **3.** in poor condition. *siʕʕta radiiʔa.* His health is poor.

radaaʔa badness, bad condition or state. *radaaʔat ij-jaww* the inclemency of the weather.

ʔardaʔ worse, worst.

r-d-d

radd (u, i radd) **1.** to bring back, take back. *ʔiδa tištiri has-saaʕa baʕad ma-tigdar itruddha.* If you buy this watch you won't be able to return it later. **2.** to return, put back. *ʔuxuδ l-iktaab w-baʕad-ma tiqraa, ridda b-mukaana.* Take the book and after you read it, put it back where it belongs. || *baḷḷa, min tiṭlaʕ, rudd il-baab.* When you go out, please close the door. **3.** to throw back, repel, drive back, drive away. *l-mutaδ̣aahiriin raadaw yhijmuun ʕal-binaaya laakin iš-šurṭa rad-dathum.* The demonstrators were going to attack the building but the police drove them off. **4.** to refuse, reject, turn down, decline. *ma-radd-li ṭalab li-hassa.* He hasn't refused me a request yet. *ma-yridd ʔaʕʕad; baaba ʕala ṭuul maftuuʕ.* He doesn't turn anyone away; his door is always open. **5.** to hand back, give back, return, restore. *min tinṭii diinaar, raʕ-yridd-lak il-baaqi.* When you give him a dinar, he'll give you back the change. **6.** to return. *sallamit ʕalee w-ma-radd is-salaam.* I greeted him and he didn't return the greeting. *zaarna w-laazim inrudd iz-ziyaara.* He visited us and we must return the visit. **7.** /with *ʕala*/ to reply to, answer. *leeš ma-tridd ʕat-talafoon?* Why didn't you answer the telephone? *raʕ-ʔaridd ʕala maqaala bij-jariida.* I'll reply to his article in the newspaper. **8.** to echo, sing a refrain. *l-muğanniya dğanni wij-jooq yridd-ilha.* The singer sings and the band sings the refrain. *min inxaḷḷiṣ raddatna, ʔintu riddu.* When we finish our chorus, you repeat it. **9.** to dictate. *ʔinta ridd-li w-ʔaani ʔaktib.* You dictate to me and I'll write. *l-mudiir radd il-maktuub il-sikirteerta w-kitbata.* The director dictated the letter to his secretary and she wrote it down. || *giʕad yammi bil-imtiʕaan w-radd-li.* He sat next to me in the examination and gave me the answers. **10.** to return, come back, go back. *du-ruuʕ hassa; ʕuud min itrudd anṭiik-iyyaaha.* Go ahead now and then when you come back I'll give it to you. *š-aku ʕinda haaδa? ʔašu da-yruuʕ w-yridd.* What's the matter with that guy? I notice he's pacing back and forth. *raddat ṣiʕʕta min idzawwaj.* His health returned when he got married. *hamm raddeena ʕal-iʕraak wil-mašaakil.* We're back to fights and problems again.

raddad to repeat. *yraddid iš-ma ʔaguul.* He repeats whatever I say.

traddad **1.** to come and go, appear frequently. *da-yitraddad ʕad-daaʔira. š-aku ʕinda?* He's always coming into the office.

What's he up to? **2.** to return, recur. *ˀisma da-yitraddad ʕal-ˀalsina.* His name is frequently mentioned. **3.** to hesitate, waver, be uncertain, doubtful, reluctant. *la-titraddad. ruuḥ ištiriiha.* Don't hesitate. Go and buy it.

staradd to get back. *staradd minna kull il-mablaġ.* He got the whole amount back from him.

radd pl. *ruduud* response, reply, answer. || *radd il-fiʕil* 1. reaction. 2. reversal, turnabout, change of heart. *ṣaar ʕinda radd fiʕil w-fuṣax il-xuṭba.* He had a change of heart and broke the engagement. *been ˀaxiδ w-radd* under discussion, under debate, in dispute. *l-qaḍiyya been ˀaxiδ w-radd.* The matter is in dispute.

radda pl. *-aat* **1.** return, returning. **2.** chorus, refrain (of a song or chant).

raaduud pl. *rwaadiid* leader of a chorus or chant.

raddaad pl. *-a* member of a chorus which repeats a refrain after a singer.

r-d-f

muraadif pl. *-aat* synonym (gram.).

r-d-m

ridam (*i radim*) **1.** to fill in with dirt. *l-ḥukuuma da-tirdim il-mustanqaʕaat.* The government's filling in the swamps. **2.** to hit, crash into. *s-sayyaara ridmat il-ʕamuud.* The car crashed into the pole.

traadam to collide, crash together, crash into each other. *traadmat sayyaara wiyya paaṣ.* A car collided with a bus.

r-d-n

ridin pl. *rdaanaat* sleeve.

rdaan (masc. and fem.) pl. *-aat* sleeve.

r-d-h

radha pl. *-aat* **1.** large room. **2.** ward (in a hospital, etc.).

r-δ-l

raδδal, raδiil, etc. = *razzal, raziil,* etc., which see under *r-z-l.*

r-r-y

raara **1.** to be transparent, sheer. *laabsa ˀatag li-ˀan nafnuufha yraari.* She's wearing a slip because her dress is transparent. **2.** to show through, be visible behind sheer cloth. *wujihha da-yraari min wara l-puušiyya.* Her face shows through from behind the veil.

r-z-b

mirzaab pl. *maraaziib* drainspout (see also *z-r-b*).

r-z-z

razza pl. *-aat* **1.** hasp. **2.** hook latch.

r-z-q

rizaq (*i*) **1.** to provide (with a means of subsistence). *ˀalla yrizqak.* May God provide you with a livelihood. *šuuf išgadd ˀaku bayyaaʕa hnaa, laakin ˀaḷḷa yirziqhum kullhum.* Look how many vendors there are here, but God enables them all to make a living. **2.** to bless with (esp. a child). *ˀaḷḷa rizaqa walad.* God blessed him with a son.

rtizaq to make a living, seek one's livelihood. *da-yirtiziq min beeʕ l-ixyaar.* He's making a living selling cucumbers.

riziq pl. *ˀarzaaq* **1.** livelihood, subsistence, means of living. **2.** provision, ration.

r-z-l

razzal **1.** to give trouble, cause trouble, mess up, ruin. *z-zawaaj razzala w-maxalla ʕinda filis.* Marriage ruined him and left him penniless. **2.** to rebuke, upbraid, scold, berate. *ˀiδa ˀaδδaak, ˀarazzila.* If he hurt you, I'll tell him off.

trazzal to have trouble, get in trouble. *šuufa šloon itrazzal. xisar kull ifluusa bil-uqmaar w-ṭirdoo min šuġḷa.* Look what a mess he's in. He lost all his money gambling and they fired him from his job. *bass yġišš, yitrazzal.* As soon as he cheats, he'll be in trouble. *ˀiδa tuṣquṭ ib-hal-imtiḥaan, titrazzal, li-ˀan yfuṣluuk imnil-madrasa.* If you fail this exam, you've had it, because they will kick you out of school. *ma-čaanat ʕindi šamsiyya w-itrazzalit bil-muṭar.* I had no umbrella, and I really caught it in the rain.

raziil **1.** base, mean, vile, contemptible, despicable. **2.** miserly, cheap, tight, penny-pinching. **3.** a despicable character. **4.** tightwad, miser, skinflint.

razaala pl. *-aat* **1.** trouble, mess, pain, pain in the neck. *ma-aku ġeer ir-razaala min wara z-zawaaj; maṣrafak yiziid w-martak titʕaarak.* There's nothing but trouble to be had from marriage; your expenses increase and your wife nags. *taṣliiḥ is-sayyaaraat razaala. kull yoom ihduumi tiddahan.* Repairing cars is for the birds. Every day my clothes get oil all over them. **2.** rebuke, upbraiding, scolding, berating. **3.** humiliation.

r-z-m

ruzma pl. *ruzam* parcel, package.

razzaam pl. *-iin* **1.** junior clerical worker. **2.** file clerk.

r-z-n

raziin grave, serious, sedate, staid, dignified. *la-tiššaaqa wiyyaa. huwwa fadd waaċid raziin.* Don't joke with him. He's a serious person.

razaana gravity, sedateness, staidness, dignity. *da-ybiiʕ razaana b-raasi.* He's trying to stand on his dignity with me.

raazuuna pl. *rwaaziin* **1.** shelf. **2.** ledge. **3.** mantle. **4.** pigeonhole, niche.

ˀarzan more or most serious, staid, etc.

r-s-b

risab (i rusuub) **1.** to sink to the bottom, settle. *l-masċuuq kulla risab bil-qaʕar.* All the powder settled to the bottom. **2.** to fail, flunk. *risab ib-darseen bil-imtiċaan in-nihaaˀi.* He failed two courses on the final exam.

rassab **1.** to cause to settle. *š-šabb yrassib iṭ-ṭiin.* Alum causes mud to settle. **2.** to cause to fail, fail, give a failing grade. *rassaba l-muʕallim li-ˀan ġašš.* The teacher flunked him because he cheated.

trassab to settle to the bottom. *ˀiδa trakkid il-iglaaṣ, il-ˀamlaaċ raċ-titrassab bič-čaʕab.* If you let the glass sit still, the grains of salt will settle to the bottom.

rusuub **1.** sediment, deposit. **2.** failure (in an examination).

r-s-ċ

marsaċ var. of *masraċ,* which see under *s-r-ċ.*

r-s-x

risax (a rusuux) to be or become firmly established, deeply rooted, to sink in, stick (in the mind). *qreet il-mawδuuʕ ʕiddat marraat ċatta yirsax ib-δihni.* I read up on the subject several times so it would stick in my mind.

rassax to establish, impress, make take root. *l-muʕallim yriid yrassix hal-maʕluumaat ib-ˀaδhaanna.* The teacher wants to impress these instructions on our minds.

r-s-s

riss family background, breeding.

r-s-ġ

rusuġ pl. *ˀarsaaġ* wrist.

r-s-l

raasal to correspond with, carry on a correspondence with. *δalleet araasla muddat sana.* I kept corresponding with him for a year.

ˀarsal to send, forward, ship. *raċ-arsil-lak il-qumṣaan wiyya ˀaxuuk.* I'll send you the shirts through your brother.

traasal to exchange correspondence, correspond with each other. *da-titraasluun loo baṭṭaltu?* Are you all corresponding with each other or did you stop?

rasil: ʕala rasla according to his own desire, however he wishes. *min nooṣal ir-raas iš-šaariʕ, kull waaċid raċ-yruuċ ʕala rasla.* When we get to the corner, everyone will go his own way. *činit maaši ʕala rasli ˀašu fadd marra waaċid hijam ʕalayya.* I was walking along minding my business when suddenly someone attacked me. *ˀinta ruuċ ʕala raslak.* Go ahead with what you were doing.

r-rasuul the Messenger of God, Mohammed.

risaala pl. *rasaaˀil* letter, note.

muraasala pl. *-aat* correspondence, exchange of letters.

ˀirsaaliyya pl. *-aat* **1.** consignment. **2.** shipment.

muraasil pl. *-iin* **1.** correspondent, reporter. **2.** orderly, houseboy (military).

mursila pl. *-aat* (radio) transmitter.

r-s-m

risam (i rasim) **1.** to draw, sketch. *tigdar tirsim fiil?* Can you draw an elephant? **2.** to paint. *l-fannaan risam-li xooš lawċa.* The artist painted a good picture for me. **3.** to sketch, outline (fig.). *risam-li xiṭṭa w-raċ-ˀamši ʕaleeha.* He outlined a plan for me and I'm going to follow it.

raasam to set, fix, or establish a tax or duty on. *ma-tiṭlaʕ imnil-gumrug gabul-ma yrassimuuha.* It won't come out of the customs office until they fix a tax on it.

trassam pass. of *rassam. biδaaʕtak xattitrassam w-baʕdeen ˀuxuδha.* Let your goods have a tax set on them and then take them.

nrisam pass. of *risam.*

rasim **1.** drawing, sketching, art (as a subject in school). **2.** (pl. *rusuum*) picture, sketch, drawing. **3.** (rarely) photograph. **4.** duty, tax, tariff.

*rasmi** official, formal. *libaas rasmi.* formal dress. *malaabis rasmiyya* official dress, uniforms. *b-ṣuura rasmiyya* officially. *raċ-awaajha b-ṣuura rasmiyya.* I'll see him officially.

rasmiyyan officially, formally.

rassaam pl. *-iin* **1.** draftsman. **2.** painter, artist. **3.** (rarely) photographer.

marsuum **1.** drawn, sketched, traced. **2.** painted. **3.** (pl. *maraasiim*) decree, edict. **4.** regulation, ordinance. *maraasiim il-ċafla* rules of the ceremony, protocol, ceremonial procedures, rituals.

r-s-n

risan pl. *ˀarsaan* halter.

r-š-ح
raššaح to nominate, put up as a candidate. *raššiحoo r-riʔaast il-wafid.* They nominated him for the chairmanship of the delegation. **2.** to filter. *n-niššaaf yraššiح kulliš zeen.* Blotter paper filters very well.
traššaح to be nominated. *minu traššaح عan hal-manṭaqa?* Who was nominated from this district?
muraššaح pl. *-iin* candidate, nominee.
r-š-d
ʔaršad to lead, guide, direct, show the way. *ma-aku waaحid yrišda عaṭ-ṭariiq iṣ-ṣaحiiح.* There is no one who can show him the right way.
staršad to be guided. *ʔaani daaʔiman astaršid b-ʔaaraaʔ ʔasaatiδti.* I'm always guided by the opinions of my professors.
rušd: sinn ir-rušd full legal age, majority (18 years or older).
ʔiršaad pl. *-aat* **1.** guidance. **2.** (pl. only) *ʔiršaadaat* instructions, directions, directives.
ršaad pepper grass (eaten as a condiment with food).
raašdi pl. *-iyyaat* a slap on the cheek.
muršid pl. *-iin* adviser.
r-š-r-š
rašraš to sprinkle, spray. *j-jaahil laazim iṣ-ṣoonda w-yrašriš biiha.* The kid's holding the hose and spraying water around with it.
r-š-š
rašš (i rašš) **1.** to sprinkle. *l-ʔakil faahi. rišš عalee šwayya miliح.* The food is flat. Sprinkle a little salt on it. *rušš il-gaaع b-išwayyat mayy حatta yiji hawa baarid.* Sprinkle the ground with a little water so we'll get some cool air. **2.** to water. *raššeet iθ-θayyil willa baعad?* Have you watered the lawn yet?
rašš sprinkling. *sayyaart ir-rašš* sprinkling truck.
rašša i.n. of *rašš.*
raššaaš, raššaaša pl. *-aat* **1.** sprinkling can, watering can. **2.** machine gun.
r-š-q
rašiiq svelte, slender, slim. *har-raaqiṣa rašiiqa.* This dancer's shapely.
rašaaqa shapeliness, slenderness, graceful, slender build.
r-š-m
rašma pl. *-aat* halter.
r-š-w
riša (i rašu) to bribe. *حaawal yirši š-šurṭi bass ma-gidar.* He attempted to bribe the policeman but he couldn't.
rtiša to accept bribery, to be corrupt. *hal-muwaδδaf ma-yirtiši ʔabadan.* This employee won't ever take a bribe.
rašwa pl. *-aat, rašaawi* bribe.
r-š-y
raaši sesame oil.
r-ṣ-d
riṣad (i raṣid) **1.** to observe, watch. *dayirṣid nijuum min foog ij-jibal.* He is observing stars from the top of the hill. **2.** to appropriate, set aside, earmark. *l-حukuuma riṣdat malyoon diinaar il-halmašruuع.* The government appropriated a million dinars for this project.
traṣṣad to observe, watch. *š-šurṭa datitraṣṣad-la. bass ysawwi šii, yčiftuu bissijin.* The cops are keeping their eyes on him. As soon as he does anything, they'll lock him up.
raṣiid pl. *ʔarṣida* **1.** assets, capital. **2.** reserves. **3.** available funds. *čakk bila raṣiid* rubber check, check without funds to cover it. **4.** backing, support. *ma-ʔila raṣiid ibdaaʔirta.* He gets no backing in his office.
marṣad pl. *maraaṣid* observatory.
mirṣaad ambush. || *waaguf bil-mirṣaad.* He's lying in wait. *waaguf-li bil-mirṣaad. š-ma ʔasawwi, yiحtajj.* He's keeping a sharp eye on me. Whatever I do, he protests. *š-šurṭa waagfat-la bil-mirṣaad.* The police are watching him closely.
r-ṣ-r-ṣ
raṣraṣ to fill with melted lead, to weight. *mawwiع išwayya rṣaaṣ w-raṣriṣ ič-čaعab.* Melt a little lead and weight the bone.
r-ṣ-ṣ
raṣṣ (u raṣṣ) to fit tightly together, press together, compress, pack, tamp. *عabbi hal-quuṭiyya b-tamur bass ruṣṣha zeen.* Fill this container with dates and pack them down well.
rṣaaṣ **1.** lead. || *qalam irṣaaṣ* pencil. **2.** (coll.) bullets.
rṣaaṣa pl. *-aat* bullet.
*rṣaaṣi** leaden, lead-colored, dull gray.
r-ṣ-ع
raṣṣaع to set, stud, inlay. *taaj il-malika mraṣṣaع b-yaaquut w-ʔalmaaz.* The queen's crown is set with rubies and diamonds.
raṣعa pl. *-aat* **1.** dent. **2.** dimple.
r-ṣ-f
riṣaf (u raṣif) to pave. *raح-iyruṣfuun iššaariع b-ṭaabuug.* They're going to pave the street with bricks.
traaṣaf to move together, draw closer

to each other, close ranks. *l-ʕariif gaal lij-junuud yitraaṣfuun.* The sergeant told the soldiers to close ranks.

raṣiif pl. *ʔarṣifa* **1.** pavement. **2.** sidewalk. **3.** wharf, dock, pier. **4.** wharfage, fee for using a wharf. **5.** platform (of a railway station).

r-riṣaafa, jaanib ir-riṣaafa name of the section of Baghdad on the east side of the Tigris.

r-ḍ-r-ḍ

raḍraḍ to break, smash, crush. *ʔiḍa ma-tiskut, ʔaraḍriḍ iʕḍaamak.* If you don't shut up, I'll break your bones into pieces. *ʔaani ʔaraḍriḍ ij-jooz w-inta ṭalliʕ il-libb.* I'll crack the walnuts and you take out the meat.

r-ḍ-ḍ

raḍḍ (*u raḍḍ*) to bruise. *wugʕat il-ḥadiida ʕala zandi w-raḍḍata.* The piece of iron fell on my arm and bruised it.

nraḍḍ to become bruised. *fuxḍa nraḍḍ min wugaʕ ʕalee l-kursi.* His thigh got bruised when the chair fell on him.

raḍḍ pl. *rḍuuḍ* bruise, bruising.

raḍḍa pl. *-aat* i.n. of *raḍḍ*.

r-ḍ-ʕ

riḍaʕ (*a riḍaaʕa, raḍiʕ*) **1.** to nurse, suck at the breast. *j-jaahil riḍaʕ ʔila ʔan ṣaar ʕumra santeen.* The baby nursed until he was two years old. *l-ibzaaziin riḍʕaw kull ḥaliib ʔummhum.* The kittens sucked out all their mother's milk. **2.** to nurse, suckle, feed at the breast. *jaabaw daaya ḥatta tirḍaʕ ṭifilhum.* They brought a wet nurse to nurse their baby.

raḍḍaʕ to nurse, suckle, feed at the breast. *guumi raḍḍiʕi j-jaahil!* Go nurse the baby!

raḍiiʕ pl. *ruḍaʕaaʔ, ruḍḍaʕ* suckling, infant, baby.

murḍiʕ nursing, having a nursing child. *hal-mara murḍiʕa.* That woman's nursing a baby.

murḍiʕa pl. *-aat* wet nurse.

r-ḍ-y

riḍa (*a riḍa*) **1.** to be satisfied, be content. *š-ma tinṭii, ma-yirḍa.* Whatever you give him, he isn't satisfied. **2.** to agree, consent. *ma-da-yirḍa yištirik bil-wizaara.* He won't consent to take a position in the cabinet. *ma-yirḍa ybiiʕ ib-has-siʕir.* He won't agree to sell at that price. *ma-da-yirḍa yruuḥ wiyyaana.* He isn't willing to go with us. **3.** to be pleased. *maḥḥad yirḍa ʕala hiiči waḍiʕ.* No one is pleased with these conditions. *ʔaḷḷa yirḍa ʕannak.* May God be pleased with you.

raḍḍa **1.** to satisfy, please, gratify. *haaḍa š-yraḍḍii? kull-ma tinṭii, yriid baʕad.* What can satisfy him? The more you give him, the more he wants. *ma-mraḍḍi ʔaḥḥad imnil-mwaḍḍafiin.* He hasn't made any of the employees happy. *raḍḍa j-jaahil bič-čukleet.* He placated the child with the candy. **2.** to mollify, appease, placate, conciliate. *ʔabuuk zaʕlaan ʕaleek. ruuḥ raḍḍii.* Your father is mad at you. Go make up with him.

raaḍa **1.** to conciliate, propitiate, make up with. *ziʕal ʕaleek. ruuḥ raaḍii.* He's mad at you. Go make up with him. **2.** to reconcile. *ṣaar-ilhum šahar zʕaala. xalli nruuḥ inraaḍiihum.* They've been mad at each other for a month. Let's go reconcile them.

traaḍa to come to terms, settle differences with each other. *ʔitrukhum humma yitraaḍuun waḥḥadhum.* Leave them to settle their differences by themselves.

riḍa agreement, consent, assent, acceptance, approval.

bil-imraaḍaa amicably, with mutual satisfaction. *nḥallat il-muškila bil-imraaḍaa.* The problem was solved amicably.

raaḍi **1.** satisfied, content. *l-muʕallim raaḍi ʕannak.* The teacher's satisfied with you. **2.** willing, ready. *huwwa raaḍi ysawwiiha.* He's willing to do it.

r-ṭ-b

raṭṭab **1.** to moisten, dampen. *l-mubarrida traṭṭub il-hawa ḥatta yubrad.* The air cooler moistens the air so it gets cool. **2.** to become succulent, mellow, ripen. *l-ixlaal baʕda ma-raṭṭab.* The dates still haven't gotten ripe.

starṭab to become excited, become sexually aroused. *yistarṭub min yšuuf banaat.* He gets excited when he sees girls. *starṭab min šaaf iṣ-ṣuwar il-xalaaʕiyya.* He became aroused when he saw the lewd pictures.

raṭib moist, damp, humid. *l-hawa raṭib il-yoom.* The air's humid today. *l-gaaʕ raṭba. la-tuqʕud ʕaleeha.* The ground's damp. Don't sit on it.

ruṭab (coll.) ripe, fresh, succulent date(s).

ruṭba pl. *-aat* un. n. of *ruṭab*.

ruṭuuba moistness, dampness, humidity.

marṭuub damp, moist, wet. *la-timši*

ɛaafi; l-gaaɛ marṭuuba. Don't walk barefooted; the ground's damp.

murattibaat (pl. only) refreshments, soft drinks.

r-ɛ-d

riɛad (*i raɛad*) to thunder. *ʔašu datirɛid w-ma-da-tumṭur.* It seems to be thundering but it isn't raining.

raɛad pl. *ruɛuud* thunder, clap of thunder.

r-ɛ-š

riɛaš (*i raɛiš*) to shake, tremble. *ʔabuuha yirɛiš imnil-kubur.* Her father trembles from old age.

rtiɛaš to shake, tremble. *rtiɛaš badana mnil-xoof.* His body trembled from fear.

raɛša pl. *-aat* tremor, trembling, shaking.

r-ɛ-y

riɛa (*a raɛi*) to graze. *l-ganam da-tirɛa b-hal-manṭiqa.* The sheep are grazing in this area.

raaɛa 1. to observe, heed, respect, comply with. *laazim itraaɛuun il-qaanuun.* You must observe the law. 2. to make allowance for, be lenient with. *l-muɛallim raaɛaana bil-imtiɛaan.* The teacher was lenient with us on the exam. 3. to treat well. *ʔiδa traaɛiini, ʔaštiri minnak ɛala ṭuul.* If you treat me well, I'll always buy from you. *raaɛaani bis-siɛir w-inṭaani θ-θoob ib-diinaar.* He did well by me on the price and gave me the shirt for a dinar.

marɛa pl. *maraaɛi* meadow, grazing land, pasture.

riɛaaya 1. care, attention, consideration, regard. 2. sponsorship, patronage, auspices. *s-sibaaq taɛt riɛaayat il-waziir.* The game is sponsored by the minister.

raaɛi pl. *riɛyaan, ruɛaat* shepherd, herdsman. || *ruɛaat il-baqar il-amriikiyyiin* American cowboys.

r-ġ-a-n

ruġaan patent leather.

r-ġ-b

riġab (*a raġba*) to desire, wish, want. *tirġab tiji wyaaya lis-siinama?* Would you like to come to the movie with me? *has-sayyaara, ṣaar-ilha šahreen maɛruuδa lil-beeɛ w-maɛɛad da-yirġab biiha.* This car has been up for sale for two months and nobody wants it.

raġġab to interest, excite interest. *raġġabta b-beetak yalla štiraa.* I got him interested in your house and he bought it. *ma-čaanat ɛindi niyya ʔaštiriiha, bass ʔinta raġġabitni ɛaleeha.* I had no intention of buying it, but you got me enthusiastic about it.

raġba pl. *-aat* wish, desire, craving. *raġba bid-diraasa* desire to study. *raġba bis-safar* desire to travel.

marguub coveted, sought after, in demand. *has-sayyaaraat marġuuba b-baġdaad.* These cars are in demand in Baghdad.

r-ġ-m

riġam (*u raġum*) to force, compel, coerce. *riġmoo yistiqiil.* They forced him to resign.

ʔarġam to force, compel, coerce. *ʔarġumoo yidfaɛ kull il-mablaġ.* They forced him to pay the whole amount.

raġum, bir-raġum min in spite of, despite. *nijaɛ raġm iṣ-ṣuɛuubaat illi šaafha.* He succeeded despite the hardships that he experienced. *saafar bir-raġum min muɛaaraδat abuu.* He went on a trip in spite of the objection of his father. || *raɛ-ʔaruuɛ raġum ʔanfak.* I will go no matter what you do.

raġman ɛan in spite of, despite. *raɛ-adxul raġman ɛannak.* I'm going in in spite of you.

raaġum 1. reluctant, unwilling. 2. reluctantly, unwillingly. *sawwaaha raaġum.* He did it unwillingly.

r-f-t

raffat to dismiss, discharge. *buqa šahar bil-waδiifa w-baɛdeen raffitoo.* He stayed a month in the position and then they dismissed him.

raftiyya pl. *-aat* clearance paper showing that commodity tax has been collected on a shipment of goods, also used as an invoice.

r-f-j

raafaj 1. to become on intimate terms with, become friends with, associate closely with. *ʔiδa traafja, titɛallam minna hwaaya.* If you become his close friend, you'll learn a lot from him. 2. to go with, be the lover of, keep as a mistress. *raafajha muddat santeen.* He was her lover for two years.

traafaj to become friendly, be intimate with one another. *traafaj wiyya ʔaxuuha ɛatta yidzawwajha.* He became friendly with her brother, so that he could marry her.

rifja pl. *-aat* close friendship, comradeship.

rifiij pl. *rifjaan* friend, buddy, pal.

rifiija pl. *-aat* 1. girl friend. 2. mistress, paramour.

r-f-r-f

rafraf to flap the wings. *l-ḥamaama* *ðallat itrafrif gabul-ma tḥuṭṭ.* The pigeon flapped its wings before it lit. **2.** to flutter, flap. *l-ʕalam da-yrafrif ʕala ṣaṭḥ il-madrasa.* The flag is fluttering on the roof of the school.

r-f-s

rufas (*u rafus*) to kick. *la-truuḥ yamm il-iḥṣaan, tara yurfus.* Don't go near the horse, because he kicks. *rufasa b-baṭna w-xallaa yibči.* He kicked him in his stomach and made him cry.

raffas to keep kicking. *č-čalib il-maðruub ðall yraffus mudda gabuḷ-ma ymuut.* The dog that got hit kicked for a while before he died.

rafsa pl. *-aat* kick.

r-f-š

rafiš pl. *rufuuš* variety of large turtle.

r-f-ð

rufað (*u rafuð*) to reject, turn down, decline, refuse to accept. *baʕad-ma šaaf in-namuuna, rufað kull il-ʔirsaaliyya.* After he saw the sample, he rejected the whole shipment. *ttifqaw yrufðuun ʔayy iqtiraaḥ yqaddima.* They agreed to turn down any suggestion he submitted. *ʔayy madrasa yruuḥ-ilha trufða.* Any school he goes to rejects him. *l-ḥaakim rufað šakwaa.* The judge dismissed his complaint.

rafuð refusal, rejection. *čaan jawaaba bir-rafuð.* His answer was a refusal.

r-f-ʕ

rufaʕ (*a rafuʕ*) **1.** to lift, lift up, raise a loft, heave up, hoist up. *rufaʕ miit keelu b-fadd ʔiid.* He lifted one hundred kilos with one hand. **2. a.** to raise. *rufaʕ il-ʕalam.* He raised the flag. **b.** to raise, increase, make higher. *š-šarika rufʕat is-siʕir lamma zdaad iṭ-ṭalab.* The company raised the price when the demand increased. *rufaʕ ṣooṭa.* He raised his voice. **3.** to remove, take away. *rufaʕ jamiiʕ il-ʕaraaqiil ib-ṭariiq diraasta.* He removed the obstacles in the way of his studies. *rufʕaw ʕanna t-tawbiix.* They removed the reprimand from his record. || *rufaʕ zaḥma* to remove an inconvenience, get out of someone's way. *ʔiḥna raḥ-nirfaʕ iz-zaḥma. ṣaar-inna mudda gaaʕdiin.* We'll get out of your way. We've been sitting around for some time. **4.** to abolish, eliminate, lift, put an end to. *šwakit raḥ-yirfaʕuun manʕ it-tajawwul?* When are they going to lift the curfew? **5.** to submit, present, forward. *rufaʕ taqriir bil-qaðiyya.* He submitted a report on the matter. *l-mulaaḥið širaḥ ʕal-ʕariiða w-rufaʕha r-raʔiis il-mulaaḥiðiin.* The superintendent endorsed the request and forwarded it to the chief superintendent. *rufaʕ qaðiita l-majlis il-wuzaraaʔ.* He took his case to the Cabinet. || *rufaʕ daʕwa ʕala* to instigate legal action against, to sue. *rufaʕ daʕwa ʕaš-šarika.* He sued the company.

raffaʕ **1.** to promote, raise in salary or rank. *bass yraffʕuuni, ʔaʕzimkum ʕala ʕaša b-ʔafxar maṭʕam.* As soon as they promote me, I'll treat you to dinner at the best restaurant. **2.** to thin, make thinner (in diameter). *tigdar itraffuʕ il-ʕuuda bil-mubrad.* You can make the stick thinner with the file.

traffaʕ **1.** to be promoted. *ṣaar-la ʕašr isniin ib-hal-waðiifa w-ma-traffaʕ illa marra wiḥda.* He's been in this position for ten years and only been promoted once. **2.** to become thinner, be made thinner (in diameter). *min tubrud iš-šiiš, yitraffaʕ.* When you file the rod, it becomes thinner. **3.** to be or deem oneself above, to be too good, look down. *ʔatraffaʕ ʔatzawwaj bnayya minhum.* I'm above marrying one of their girls. *ma-aʕtiqid yiqbal haš-šuğuḷ. huwwa yitraffaʕ ʕan hiiči ʔašğaal.* I don't think he'll accept this job. He looks down on such tasks.

traafaʕ /with *b-*/ to plead, present (a case in court). *l-muḥaami traafaʕ ib-daʕuuteen hal-yoom.* The lawyer pleaded two cases today.

rtifaʕ to rise, ascend, go up, become higher. *mustawa l-maay irtifaʕ baʕad il-muṭar.* The water level increased after the rain. *bida yiḥči yawaaš ʔila ʔan ṣaar ʕaṣabi w-ḥissa rtifaʕ.* He started talking softly until he got mad and his voice rose. *biš-šahar ij-jaay, raḥ-yirtifiʕ siʕir il-laḥam.* In the next month, the price of meat will go up.

rafiʕ lifting, hoisting. *rafʕ il-ʔaθqaal* weight lifting.

rufuʕ thinness, slenderness. *jiib-li ʕuuda b-har-rufuʕ.* Bring me a stick this thin.

rifiiʕ **1.** thin in diameter, slender, fine, of small gauge. *xeeṭ rifiiʕ* thin string. **2.** thin, high-pitched. *sooṭ rifiiʕ* a high-pitched voice.

ʔarfaʕ **1.** thinner, thinnest. **2.** more or most high-pitched. **3.** above, too good for.

ˀaani ˀarfaɛ min ˀan ˀasawwi hiiči šii. I'm above doing such a thing.

marfaɛ pl. *maraafiɛ* stand supporting a clay water urn.

tarfiiɛ pl. *-aat* 1. promotion. 2. raise in salary.

muraafaɛa pl. *-aat* court proceeding, hearing, trial.

rtifaaɛ pl. *-aat* 1. rise. 2. increase. 3. altitude, elevation, height.

r-f-f

raff (*u*) to twitch, quiver. *ɛeeni da-truff.* My eye is twitching. *ˀaɛyaanan yruff matni bila sabab.* Sometimes my shoulder twitches without any reason.

raff pl. *rfuuf* 1. shelf. 2. ledge. 3. flight, covey (of birds).

r-f-q

rufaq (*u rifiq*) to be kind, friendly, nice, to show kindness. *rufaq bii l-ɛaakim w-ɛifa ɛanna.* The judge took pity on him and let him go.

raafaq to accompany, escort. *tlaθ ṣuɛu-fiyyiin raafqaw il-wafid.* Three newspapermen accompanied the delegation.

ˀarfaq to enclose, attach, append, add. *laazim tirfuq ṣuurtak wiyya l-istimaara w-iddizzha.* You must enclose your picture with the application and send it in.

rafiiq 1. kind, gentle, tender. 2. (pl. *rifaaq*) friend, buddy, pal. 3. comrade (in Marxist terminology).

muraafaqa association, company, friendly relationship.

muraafiq pl. *-iin* 1. companion, attendant. 2. escort. 3. aide, aide-de-camp, adjutant.

murfaq 1. attached, enclosed. 2. (pl. *-aat*) enclosure.

r-f-h

raffah to make life pleasant and comfortable. *hal-wizaara da-traffih ɛan il-muwaδδafiin ihwaaya.* This administration is making conditions a lot better for the employees. *l-muġanniya tbarraɛat itruuɛ itraffih ɛan ij-jinuud.* The singer volunteered to go bring comfort to the soldiers.

traffah to live in comfort and ease. *ˀiδa yṣiir raatbak miiteen diinaar biš-šahar, titraffah.* If your salary gets to two hundred dinars per month, you'll live well.

rafaahiyya 1. luxury. 2. easy living. 3. personal comfort.

r-q-b

raaqab to watch, observe, regard closely, keep an eye on. *minu raaqab iṣ-ṣaff il-yoom?* Who watched over the class today? *š-šurṭa da-traaqba.* The police have him under surveillance.

traqqab to expect, anticipate, await. *činna nitraqqab wuṣuula b-ˀay laɛδa.* We were expecting his arrival at any moment.

raqiib pl. *ruqabaaˀ* censor.

raqaaba censorship.

muraaqaba 1. observation, surveillance. 2. monitoring, overseeing.

muraaqib pl. *-iin* prefect, monitor.

r-q-d

marqad pl. *maraaqid* mausoleum, tomb.

r-q-ṣ

raqqaaṣ pl. *-a* 1. dancer. 2. (pl. *-aat*) pendulum.

marqaṣ pl. *maraaqiṣ* dance hall, ballroom.

raaqiṣ 1. dancing. *ɛafla raaqiṣa* dancing party. 2. (pl. *-iin*) dancer.

raaqiṣa pl. *-aat* woman dancer.

see also *r-g-ṣ*.

r-q-q

raqq (*i riqqa*) to soften, relent, have pity. *raqq galbi ɛalee w-inṭeeta ˀakil.* I took pity on him and gave him food.

riqqa gentleness, mildness.

raqiiq soft, tender, gentle. *galba raqiiq.* He has a kind heart. He's soft-hearted. *raqiiq il-galub* soft-hearted, tender-hearted, compassionate, tender, gentle.

ˀaraqq more or most compassionate, tender-hearted, etc.

r-q-m

raqqam to affix numbers to, to number. *raqqum ṣafɛaat it-taqriir.* Number the pages of the report.

raqam pl. *ˀarqaam* number, numeral. || *raqam qiyaasi* record, official record (athlet.).

r-q-y

raqqa 1. to promote. *ˀaxuuk, raqqoo willa baɛad?* Did they promote your brother yet? 2. to raise, further, promote, advance. *ybayyin waδiifta raqqata ɛaleena.* It seems his job has set him above us. *š-raqqaak ɛala ˀaṣdiqaaˀak?* What made you feel you are better than your friends?

traqqa 1. to rise, ascend, go up. *l-ˀasɛaar kullha traqqat.* All the prices went up. 2. to advance, progress. *ṭ-ṭibb itraqqa hwaaya bis-siniin il-ˀaxiira.* Medicine has advanced a lot in the last few years.

raaqi 1. advanced, modern. 2. superior, high-grade. 3. educated, refined.

r-g-b

rugba pl. *rugab, rgaab* neck. || *rugbat*

ij-jisir end of the bridge. *b-rugubta xamis jahhaal bil-ʔiδaafa ʔila marta.* He's got the responsibility for five children in addition to his wife on his shoulders.

rgeeba: šijar ʔabu rgeeba long-necked squash.

r-g-š

ragiš pl. *rgaaš* pockmark.

ʔargaš fem. *ragša* pl. *ruguš, ragšiin.* **1.** pockmarked. **2.** person with a pockmarked face.

r-g-ṣ

rigaṣ (*u raguṣ, rigiṣ*) to dance. *hiyya matuζruf turguṣ zeen.* She doesn't know how to dance well. *gaam yurguṣ imnil-faraζ.* He jumped for joy.

raggaṣ to make dance. *jiib iš-šaadi maalak w-raggiṣa.* Bring your monkey and make him dance. || *raggaṣni. marra yriid haaδa w-marra yriid δaak.* He kept me jumping. One time he wants this and next he wants that.

traggaṣ to prance. *yitraggaṣ ib-mašya.* He prances when he walks.

rigṣa pl. *-aat* a dance.

raaguuṣ pl. *rwaagiiṣ* dancer.

see also *r-q-ṣ*.

r-g-ṭ

raggaṭ to speckle, spot. *raggaṭ wuṣlat il-uqmaaš ib-ʔaxδar w-ʔaζmar.* He speckled the piece of cloth with green and red.

ʔargaṭ speckled, spotted. *diič ʔargaṭ* a speckled rooster.

r-g-ζ

rigaζ (*a ragiζ*) **1.** to patch. *rigaζ id-dišdaaša b-wuṣla min ġeer loon.* He patched the robe with a piece of another color. **2.** to slam, slap. *min tiṭlaζ, la-tirgaζ il-baab ζeel.* When you go out, don't slam the door hard. *šaal ič-čalib w-rigaζa bil-gaaζ.* He picked up the dog and slammed him down on the ground. *rigaζa ζijil dawwaxa.* He slapped him and made him dizzy. || *ma-adri šaku. ṣaar saaζa r-riṣaaṣ yirgaζ.* I don't know what's happening. For an hour bullets have been flying around.

raggaζ to patch, mend. *ṣaar xamis marraat raggaζit hal-qundara.* I've mended this shoe for the fifth time now. *da-traggiζ il-panṭaroon.* She's patching the pants. || *hiyya tšugg w-ʔummha traggiζ-ilha.* She misbehaves and her mother patches things up for her.

rugζa pl. *rugaζ* patch. || *har-rugζa l-hal-baabuuj.* They're birds of a feather (lit., this patch for this slipper).

raggaaζ pl. *rgaagiiζ* shoe repairman, cobbler.

r-g-g

ragg (coll.) turtle(s).

ragga pl. *-aat* turtle.

raggi (coll.) watermelon(s).

raggiyya pl. *-aat* watermelon.

rgaag: xubuz irgaag bread baked in thin loaves.

r-g-l

rigaḷ (*u*) to wobble. *č-čarix il-giddaami da-yurguḷ.* The front wheel is wobbling.

ragla rough, bumpy, uneven ground.

r-g-m

rigam (*u ragum*) to cover over, close off, seal off. *rigam iṣ-ṣanduug ib-xišab imζaakas.* He sealed up the box with plywood. *rigam ζalg il-biir ib-čiinku.* He closed up the mouth of the well with sheet metal.

raggam to close up, seal up. *ʔaxaδ il-ibsaamiir wil-xišab w-raggam iṣ-ṣinaadiig.* He took the nails and wood and sealed up the boxes.

r-k-b

rikab (*a rukub, rukuub*) **1.** to ride. *mayigdar yirkab iζṣaan.* He can't ride a horse. **2.** to ride in, ride on, go in, on, or on board, travel in, on, or on board. *j-jaahil raakub ζala matin ʔumma.* The child is riding on his mother's shoulder. *rikab yammi bil-qiṭaar.* He rode beside me on the train. *ʔabadan ma-raakub ṭiyyaara* I've never ridden in an airplane. **3.** to get in, get on, board, climb aboard. *rikab sayyaarta w-raaζ ζalee.* He got in his car and went to see him. **4.** to mount, breed with, mate with. *xaruufna rikab naζjathum.* Our ram mated with their ewe. **5.** to bully, browbeat, intimidate, dominate. *lli yṣiir δaζiif, in-naas yirkabuu.* People bully anyone who is weak. *marta šaafata δaζiif w-rikbata.* His wife saw that he was weak and dominated him.

¶ *rikab raasa* to be stubborn, recalcitrant, untractable. *la-tirkab raasak. ʔiqbal ib-has-siζir.* Don't be stubborn. Agree on this price. *ʔibnak raakub raasa w-mayiqbal yiji.* Your son's gotten stubborn and he doesn't want to come.

rakkab **1.** to cause to ride, give a ride to. *tigdar itrakkubni wiyyaak?* Can you give me a ride with you? **2.** to put on, put aboard. *ʔuxuδ ij-jaahil w-rakkuba bil-paaṣ.* Take the child and put him on the bus. **3.** to mount, fasten, insert, set, place, install. *rakkab ij-jaama biš-šibbaač.* He installed the pane of glass in the window. **4.** to put together, assemble, fit together. *rakkab il-makiina b-saaƐa.* He assembled the machine in one hour. **5.** to cook, fix, or put together a meal. *raƐ-itrakkub baƐad-ma tiji mnis-suug.* She's going to fix a meal as soon as she comes from the market. **6.** to graft. *rakkabit purtaqaal Ɛala sindi.* He grafted an orange onto a grapefruit.

trakkab **1.** to be set in, inserted, mounted, fitted. *baab is-sayyaara ma-titrakkab li-ˀan maƐwuuja.* The car door won't fit because it's bent. **2.** to be composed, made up, consist. *hal-maadda titrakkab min iθlaθ Ɛanaaṣir.* This substance is composed of three elements. **3.** to be grafted. *l-purtaqaal ma-yitrakkab Ɛala rummaan.* An orange can't be grafted onto a pomegranate.

rtikab to commit, perpetrate. *rtikab jaraaˀim ihwaaya.* He committed many crimes.

rukba pl. *rukab* knee.

rikba pl. *-aat* ride.

rkaab, rčaab pl. *-aat* stirrup.

markab pl. *maraakib* ship, vessel, boat.

raakib pl. *rukkaab* passenger, rider.

markuub **1.** ridden. **2.** boarded. **3.** mounted, mated, bred. **4.** (pl. *mraakiib*) (pair of) sandals.

murakkib pl. *-iin* **1.** installer, fitter. *murakkib il-ˀasnaan* prosthodontist. **2.** assembler.

murakkab **1.** mounted, fastened, fixed, fitted, inserted, installed. **2.** assembled, composed, put together, made up. **3.** compound, composite, complex. *ribiƐ murakkab* compound interest. **4.** grafted. *tukki mrakkab* grafted mulberries. **5.** (pl. *-aat*) composite, composition, compound. *murakkab kiimyaawi* chemical compound. **6.** complex (psych.). *murakkab naqiṣ* inferiority complex.

r-k-d

rikad (*u rukuud*) **1.** to be still, motionless. *bass yirkud il-ṃayy, kull iṭ-ṭiin yinzil liččaƐab.* As soon as the water becomes still, all the mud settles to the bottom. *šloon aδurbak ˀubra ˀiδa ma-tirkud?* How can I give you a shot if you don't be still? **2.** to abate, subside. *rikad il-wajaƐ willa baƐad?* Has the pain eased yet?

rakkad **1.** to still, make quiet, motionless. *rakkdii lij-jaahil. dawwaxni b-iṣyaaƐa.* Calm that kid down. He's driving me nuts with his yelling. **2.** to set firmly in place, to place solidly. *rakkid il-kaasa Ɛatta la-toogaƐ.* Set the bowl firmly in place so it won't fall.

rakda pl. *-aat* base, foundation, good, level place.

raakid **1.** still, motionless, stagnant. *ṃaay raakid* stagnant water. **2.** sluggish. *suug il-Ɛunṭa raakid il-yoom.* The wheat market is sluggish today.

r-k-z

rakkaz **1.** to plant in the ground, set up. *rakkiz il-Ɛamuud ib-han-nugra.* Set up the pole in this hole. **2.** to fix, implant. *ˀiqraaha Ɛiddat marraat Ɛatta trakkiz il-maƐluumaat ib-δihnak.* Read it several times so as to fix the information in your mind. **3.** to concentrate. *rakkaz kull ijhuuda Ɛala hal-qaδiyya.* He concentrated all his efforts on this matter. *ma-da-agdar arakkiz min haṣ-ṣoot il-Ɛaali.* I can't concentrate because of this loud noise. **4.** to focus. *rakkiz il-kaamira Ɛala buƐud Ɛašr aqdaam.* Focus the camera at ten feet.

trakkaz pass. of *rakkaz.*

rtikaz **1.** to lean, support one's weight. *rijl il-meez maksuura. yinraad-la šii yirtikiz Ɛalee.* The table leg is broken. It needs something to support its weight on. **2.** to rest, be based. *xalli Ɛjaara min hajjiha Ɛatta yirtikiz Ɛaleeha l-piip.* Put a stone under this side so the barrel will rest on it.

markaz pl. *maraakiz* **1.** station, police station. **2.** position (mil.). **3.** center (of a circle and fig.). **4.** position, situation, office, post. **5.** status, standing, position.

*markazi** central. *l-Ɛukuuma l-markaziyya* the central government.

murakkaz **1.** centralized, concentrated. **2.** condensed, concentrated. *Ɛaamuδ murakkaz* concentrated acid.

r-k-s

rikas (*u rakis*) **1.** to sink, go down, become submerged. *l-Ɛadiid yirkus bil-ṃayy.* Iron sinks in water. **2.** to plunge, fall, drop. *rikas bin-nugra w-itƐawwar.* He fell in the hole and got hurt.

rakkas to push down, submerge, immerse, dunk. *rakkis iθ-θoob zeen biṣ-ṣubuġ.* Immerse the shirt well in the dye.

r-k-δ

rikaδ (*u rakuδ, rikiδ*) to race, rush, run. *Ɛṣaani raƐ-yirkuδ ib-θaani hadda.* My horse will run in the second race. *ˀurkuδ Ɛatta tlaƐƐig bii.* Run so you can catch up to him. *kull-ma yiƐtaaj ifluus, yurkuδ ƹala ˀabuu.* Whenever he needs money, he runs to his father. *rikaḍ-li b-qaḍiyyat il-paaspoort maali.* He did the running around for me on the matter of my passport. || *saaƹti da-turkuḍ.* My watch is too fast. *l-makiina da-turkuḍ; naqqiṣha.* The engine is racing; slow it down. *yirkuḍ wil-ƹaša xubbaaz.* He works hard and gets nowhere (lit., he runs and gets only greens for dinner).

rakkaḍ to make race, rush, run. *laazim itrakkiḍ il-iḥṣaan išwayya gabul-ma tdaxxla s-sibaaq.* You should make the horse run a little before you enter him in the race.

rikiḍ **1.** running. **2.** run, dash. *sibaaq rikḍ iḍ-ḍaaḥiya* cross-country race.

rikḍa pl. *-aat* i. n. of *rikiḍ.*

raakuuḍ **1.** swift, fleet-footed. **2.** (pl. *-iin*) racer, runner.

raakiḍ **1.** running, galloping. **2.** (pl. *-iin*) runner, racer.

r-k-ƹ

rikaƹ to bend the body (in prayer). *min yirkaƹ biṣ-ṣalaa, ḍahara yguum yoojƹa.* When he bends over in prayer, his back begins to hurt.

rukƹa pl. *rukaƹ* in prayer, a bending of the torso from a standing position, followed by putting the forehead to the floor twice.

r-k-k

rakiik = *ričiič* which see under *r-č-č.*

r-k-n

rukun pl. *ˀarkaan* **1.** corner. *kull waaḥid gaaƹid ib-rukun. ybayyin izƹaala.* Everyone is sitting in a corner. It seems they're mad. *štireet qiṭƹa rukun. raḥ-abniiha beet.* I bought a corner lot. I'm going to build a house on it. **2.** (military) staff. *ḍaabuṭ rukun* staff officer. *raˀiis ˀarkaan ij-jeeš* military chief of staff.

r-m-ḥ

rumuḥ pl. *rmaaḥ* lance, spear, javelin.

r-m-d

rumad (*a ramad*) to become inflamed (eye). *rumdat ƹeen ij-jaahil min gadd-ma yilƹab biiha.* The child's eye became inflamed from his playing with it so much.

rammad to inflame, make inflamed. *ṭ-ṭooz yrammid il-ƹeen.* Dust inflames the eyes.

ramad inflammation of the eyes, ophthalmia.

ˀarmad fem. *ramda* pl. *rumud, ramdiin* **1.** sore-eyed, having inflamed, sore eyes. **2.** person with inflamed eyes.

rṃaad ashes.

*rṃaadi** ashen, ash-colored, ash-gray. *qaaṭ irmaadi* a light gray suit.

r-m-z

rimaz (*i ramiz*) /with *ˀila*/ **1.** to symbolize, represent, stand for. *hal-ḥaruf yirmiz ˀila l-hadroojiin.* This letter stands for hydrogen. *l-loon il-maawi bil-xariiṭa yirmiz ˀila l-ṃayy.* The light blue color on the map stands for water. **2.** to use a symbol for, represent with a symbol. *bil-kiimya yirmizuun il-kull maƹdan ib-ramiz.* In chemistry they represent each metal with a symbol. *xan-nirmiz ˀilha ḥaruf laatiini.* Let's use a Latin character to symbolize it.

ramiz pl. *rumuuz* **1.** symbol, symbolic figure, emblem, character. **2.** secret sign, code sign.

*ramzi** symbolic. *hadiyya ramziyya* a symbolic gift.

r-m-š

rimaš (*i ramiš*) to twitch, flutter, to blink. *jifin ƹeeni da-yirmiš ihwaaya.* My eyelid is twitching a lot.

r-m-ḍ

ramaḍaan Ramadan, the ninth month of the Moslem calendar.

r-m-l

trammal to become a widow. *ˀiḍa trammulat, išloon raḥ-itƹayyiš wulidha?* If she became a widow, how would she provide for her children?

ramuḷ sand. || *yuḍrub bit-taxat ramuḷ.* He tells fortunes in sand.

*ramḷi** sandy.

ˀarmaḷa pl. *ˀaraamil* widow.

r-m-n

rummaan (coll.) pomegranate(s).

rummaana pl. *-aat* **1.** pomegranate. **2.** knob, ball.

*rummaani** dark red, maroon.

r-m-y

rima (*i rami*) **1.** to throw, hurl, cast. *rima r-rumuḥ ˀila masaafat miit matir.* He threw the javelin one-hundred meters. **2.** to fire (a gun). *ḍallat il-madaafiƹ tirmi liṣ-ṣubuḥ.* The artillery continued firing till morning. *ˀuxuḍ niišaan zeen gabuḷ-ma tirmi.* Take good aim before you fire. **3.** to shoot (someone). *rimoo b-ṭaliqteen ib-ṣadra.* They shot him twice in the chest. || *ƹyuuna tirmi naar mnil ġaḍab.* His eyes are flashing with anger.

rami **1.** throwing, hurling. *rami l-quruṣ* discus throwing. **2.** firing, shooting. *rami ḥaqiiqi* live firing, firing with live ammunition. *rami bir-riṣaaṣ* death by firing squad.

r-n-ɛ

trannaɛ to stagger, reel, totter, sway. *yitrannaɛ ib-mašya mnis-sukur.* He's staggering from drunkenness.

r-n-d

randa pl. *-aat* **1.** (carpenter's) plane. || *ˀuḏurba randa ˀila ˀan yitsaawa.* Use a plane on it till it's smooth. **2.** food grater.

r-n-d-j

randaj to plane. *n-najjaar randaj il-looḥa w-ṣaarat naaɛma.* The carpenter planed the board and it became smooth.

randaj pl. *ranaadij* (carpenter's) plane.

r-n-g

ring pl. *-aat* **1.** ring (esp. piston ring). *ring mulaakama* boxing ring. **2.** rim (of an automobile wheel). || *ˀaani gaaɛid ɛar-ringaat.* I'm flat broke.

r-n-n

rann (*i rann, ranna*) to ring, resound. *d-dirhim, ˀiḏa ma-yrinn, qabil.* If the dirham doesn't ring, it's counterfeit.

rannaan ringing, resounding. *xiṭaab rannaan* a resounding speech. *šawka rannaana* tuning fork.

r-h-b

rtihab to become afraid, be frightened. *rtihabit imniḏ-ḏalma.* I got scared of the dark.

rahba fear, fright, terror.

ˀirhaab terror, terrorism.

*ˀirhaabi** **1.** terroristic. **2.** (pl. *-iyyiin*) terrorist.

raahib pl. *ruhbaan* (Christian) monk.

raahiba pl. *-aat* nun.

r-h-d-n

rahdan **1.** to set or put in place, place. *t-tunga wugɛat li-ˀan ma-rahdanitha zeen.* The jug fell because you didn't place it carefully. **2.** to situate, get settled, settle. *rahdin martak w-wildak bil-awwal, w-baɛdeen saafir.* Get your wife and children settled first, and then take the trip.

trahdan to become settled, situated. *baɛad-ma ˀatrahdan ib-baġdaad, ˀadawwir ɛala šuġuḷ.* After I get settled in Baghdad, I'll look for work.

r-h-m

riham (*a rahum*) /with *ɛala*/ **1.** to fit. *hal-miftaaḥ ma-yirham ɛal-quful.* This key doesn't fit the lock. *sitirtak tirham ɛalayya tamaam.* Your coat fits me fine. || *min ˀawwal yoom, ˀiida ruhmat ɛaš-šuġuḷ.* From the first day, he took to the work. *šloon rihmat jayytak il-yoom!* Your arrival today was very appropriate! **2.** to harmonize. *hal-booyinbaaġ ma-yirham wiyya hal-qaaṭ.* This tie doesn't go with this suit. **3.** to come to agreement. *ˀinṭii fadd siɛir zeen w-balki tirham wiyyaa.* Give him a good price and maybe you'll come to an agreement with him.

rahham to make fit, to fit. *rahham miftaaḥ ɛala qufl iṣ-ṣanduuq w-fitaḥa.* He fitted a key into the trunk's lock and opened it. *l-xayyaaṭ rahham qaaṭ ˀabuuya ɛalayya.* The tailor fitted my father's suit to me.

traaham to fit with each other, be harmonious with each other. *haθ-θoob w-hal-qaaṭ ma-yitraahmuun.* This shirt and this suit don't go together. *ma-ridit asaafir wiyyaa li-ˀan ma-nitraaham.* I didn't want to travel with him because we don't get along together.

raahim fitting, proper. *hal-iḥčaaya ma-raahma minnak.* That statement isn't proper from you.

marham pl. *maraahim* ointment, salve.

r-h-n

rihan (*a rahin*) to pawn, deposit as security. *rihnat kull ḏahabha.* She pawned all of her jewelry. *ma-daayana fluus illa lamma rihan saaɛta.* He wouldn't lend him any money until he left his watch as security. **2.** to mortgage. *rihanit beeti b-ˀalif diinaar.* I mortgaged my house for a thousand dinars.

raahan to make a bet with (someone), to bet, wager. *raahana ɛala fadd masˀala ɛawiiṣa.* He made a bet with him on a complex issue. *ˀaraahnak raḥ-yidzawwaj.* I'll bet you he is going to get married. *raahan ib-miit diinaar ɛala hal-iḥṣaan.* He wagered a hundred dinars on that horse.

traahan to bet with each other. *traahnaw ɛala miit diinaar.* They bet each other a hundred dinars.

rahan pl. *ruhuun* **1.** pawn, pledge, security. *maṣraf ir-ruhuun* pledge bank, government bank which lends money upon deposit of collateral. **2.** mortgage. **3.** bet, wager. **4.** money deposited on a bet.

rahiina pl. *rahaayin* hostage.

r-h-y

trahha **1.** to be or become skilled, proficient, thoroughly competent. *huwwa raḥ-yitrahha ɛaš-šuġuḷ baɛad fadd sana.* He will become proficient at the job after one year. *nṭoo šaġḷa basiiṭa trahha ɛalee.* They gave him a simple job he could do easily. || *laazim mitrahhi ɛalee. da-yḏurba šloon-ma yriid.* He knows he's got him. He's hitting him any way he wants. **2.** to be in control of the situation, be in good shape, to have an easy time of it. *ˀagdar ˀaxalliṣ šuġḷi gabḷ iδ̣-δ̣uhur w-aani mitrahhi.* I can finish my work before noon and have time to spare. *haaδa ḥači waaḥid mitrahhi.* This is the talk of a man who's comfortably well off.

rahaawa **1.** surplus, extra amount. *ˀariid itxayyiṭ-li qamiiṣ bii rahaawa.* I want you to sew me a shirt that will be a bit large. *hal-panṭaroon bii rahaawa zaayda.* These pants are a little too big. **2.** confidence, assurance, authority. *yiḥči b-rahaawa li-ˀan yuɛruf kullši ɛan il-mawδ̣uuɛ.* He speaks with confidence because he knows all about the subject.

raahi ample, more than enough. *tlaθ yaardaat uqmaaš raahya ɛalayya. yṣiir minha qaaṭ w-yziid išwayya.* Three yards of cloth is ample for me. It will make a suit with a little left over. *has-sitra raahya ɛalayya.* This jacket is too big for me.

mitrahhi **1.** skilled, proficient. **2.** relaxed, at ease, completely in control.

[1]*r-w-b*

raab (u roob) to curdle. *l-ḥaliib raab.* The milk curdled.

rawwab to curdle, make curdle. *rawwub il-ḥaliib ib-hal-kaasa.* Curdle the milk in this bowl.

rooba **1.** curdled milk, curds. **2.** thick yoghurt.

[2]*r-w-b*

roob pl. *ˀarwaab* robe, dressing gown, bathrobe.

r-w-b-y-a-n

ruubyaan a kind of shrimp.

r-w-θ

rawwaθ to defecate, drop dung (of an animal). *waxxir il-iḥṣaan minna gabuḷ-ma yrawwiθ.* Get the horse away from us before he drops his dung.

rooθ dung, manure (horse, donkey, or cow).

r-w-ḥ

raaḥ (u rawaaḥ) **1.** to go, go away, leave, depart. *la-truuḥ. ˀubqa hnaa.* Don't go. Stay here. *hal-lakka ma-truuḥ.* This spot won't go away. *δ̣all yruuḥ w-yiji bil-gubḅa.* He kept pacing back and forth in the room. *taɛabi raaḥ balaaš.* My efforts went for nought. *hal-qaaṭ raaḥ; baɛad ma-yinlibis.* This suit's gone; it can't be worn anymore. *l-qaaṭ raaḥ-la ˀarbaɛ yaardaat uqmaaš.* Four yards of material went into the suit. *hal-beet šgadd raaḥ-la fluus?* How much money did this house cost? **2.** a pre-verb denoting likelihood of some alternate or future action. *la-tsawwi hiiči ˀašyaaˀ giddaam ij-jaahil. yruuḥ yitɛallam minnak.* Don't do such things in front of the child. He might learn from you. *ˀiδa tinṭii lij-jaahil fadd šii yaakla, yruuḥ yiskut.* If you give the kid something to eat, he'll be quiet. *la-tbayyin-la šii. yruuḥ yišnaɛna.* Don't let him in on anything. He's likely to give us away. *ˀuxuδ šamsiyya wyaak la-truuḥ titballal.* Take an umbrella with you or you'll get wet. *la-tilɛab iqmaar la-truuḥ tixṣar.* Don't gamble or you might lose. *jaawba ɛala maktuuba la-yruuḥ yizɛal.* Answer his letter or he might get mad. *ˀunṣub is-saaɛa la-truuḥ toogaf.* Wind the watch or it'll stop.

rawwaḥ **1.** to cause or allow to go away, *l-ḅaanziin yrawwiḥ il-lakkaat.* Gasoline removes spots. *la-trawwiḥ has-sayyaara min ˀiidak.* Don't let this car get through your hands. *čaanat xooš ṣafqa bass inta rawwaḥitha min ˀiidi b-ḥačyak.* It was a good deal but you made it slip through my hands with your remark. **2.** = *rayyaḥ* which see under *r-y-ḥ*.

raawaḥ to mark time, walk in place. *j-jinuud da-yraawḥuun.* The soldiers are marking time. *ṣaar-la tlaθ isniin da-yraawiḥ biṣ-ṣaff ir-raabiɛ.* He's been marking time for three years in the fourth grade.

traawaḥ **1.** to fluctuate, alternate, vary, vacillate. *ˀasɛaar il-badlaat titraawaḥ been ɛašra w-ɛišriin diinaar.* The prices of the suits range between ten and twenty dinars. **2.** to take turns, alternate. *ˀiδa nitraawaḥ biš-šuġuḷ, ma-nitɛab.* If we alternate doing the work, we won't get tired.

raaḥ- see *raḥ-* under *r-ḥ*.

ruuḥ pl. *ˀarwaaḥ* **1.** soul, breath of life. *r-ruuḥ b-iid ˀaḷḷa.* A person's life is in God's hands. *laa, muu mayyit. baɛad bii ruuḥ.* No, he's not dead. There's still life in him. *l-bazzuuna biiha tisɛ arwaaḥ.* The cat has nine lives. *ma-gdarit ˀasaaɛid ˀaḥḥad. yaḷḷa xaḷḷaṣit ruuḥi.* I couldn't help anyone. I barely saved myself. *la-ddaxxil ruuḥak ib-hal-ɛarka.* Don't get yourself involved in this fight. *δ̣all yuδ̣rub ič-čalib ˀila ˀan ṭilɛat ruuḥa.* He continued beating the dog until it died. *ˀiδa tubṣuṭ ibni, ˀaṭalliɛ ruuḥak.* If you whip my son, I'll kill you. || *luwweeš ma-*

saaƐadtuu? kull-man yguul yaa-ruuƐi. Why didn't you all help him? Everyone's looking out for himself. *ruuƐi* an endearing term of address. *š-biik da-tibči, yaa ruuƐi.* Why are you crying, dear? *ma-Ɛinda ʔaƐƐad. haaδa b-ṭarig ruuƐa.* He doesn't have anyone. He's all by himself. **2.** spirit. *wlaayatkum tuqbuδ ir-ruuƐ.* Your town is depressing (lit., constricts the spirit). *ruuƐa ṭwiila.* He has great patience. *min šaaf id-damm, maaƐat ruuƐa.* When he saw the blood, he passed out. **3.** essence, spirit. *ruuƐ iš-šakar* saccharine. || *ruuƐ il-Ɛayaat* a type of cloth, similar to rayon.

*ruuƐi** **1.** spiritual. *zaƐiim ruuƐi mašhuur.* a famous spiritual leader. **2.** spiritous, alcoholic. *mašruubaat ruuƐiyya* alcoholic beverages, spirits.

rooƐa pl. *-aat* an act of going, departing, leaving, or going away. || *raaƐ wir-rooƐa rooƐa.* He went away and was never seen again.

see also *r-y-Ɛ*.

r-w-z

raaz (*u rooz*) to weigh, size up, examine. *ʔagdar aruuz sallat il-xoox w-agul-lak išgadd biiha.* I can examine the basket of peaches and tell you how many are in it. *rizta w-šifta ma-yriid yinṭi.* I sized him up and saw he didn't want to give.

r-w-z-n-a-m

ruuznaama pl. *-aat* calendar.

[1]*r-w-s*

raawas **1.** to apportion equally, evenly, or fairly. *la-tinṭiini mišmiš iṣgaar bass. laazim itraawis.* Don't give me only small apricots. You should be fair. *qassim it-tiffaaƐ Ɛaleena bass raawsa.* Divide the apples among us but be sure to divide them equally. **2.** to settle, resolve, decide. *l-qaδiyya čaanat muƐallaqa w-huwwa l-raawas-li-yyaaha.* The matter was undecided and he is the one who settled it for me. *ma-da-yigdar yraawis il-mawδuuƐ liʔan kull-man da-yriid geer šii.* He isn't able to settle the matter because everybody wants something different.

traawas to be crowded in. *bass Ɛiddna čurpaaya wiƐda. laazim ij-jihaal yitraawsuun.* We only have one bed. The children will have to crowd in together.

[2]*r-w-s*

*ruusi** **1.** Russian. **2.** (pl. *-iyyiin, ruus*) a Russian.

ruusya Russia.

[3]*r-w-s*

raas pl. *ruus* see under *r-ʔ-s*.

r-w-ḍ

rawḍa pl. *-aat: rawḍat il-ʔaṭfaal* kindergarten, nursery school.

r-w-Ɛ

rawwaƐ to frighten, scare, alarm. *hal-xabar rawwaƐ kull il-wlaaya.* This news alarmed the whole city.

rtaaƐ to be or become frightened, scared, alarmed. *j-jahhaal irtaaƐaw min šabbat in-naar.* The children were terrified when the fire broke out.

rawƐa **1.** beauty, splendor, magnificence. **2.** (pl. *rawaaʔiƐ*) a beautiful, splendid, or magnificent thing.

ʔarwaƐ more or most splendid, marvelous, etc.

raaʔiƐ splendid, wonderful, marvelous, glorious, magnificent. *ṣuura raaʔiƐa* a splendid picture.

muriiƐ dreadful, terrible, horrible. *ʔaxbaar muriiƐa* dreadful news.

r-w-f

raaf (*u roof, riyaafa*) to reweave, darn, mend. *raaf mukaan il-Ɛarig bis-sitra kulliš zeen.* He rewove the burned place in the jacket very well. *ruuf il-mukaanaat il-gaayma bij-juwaariib.* Darn the worn places in the socks.

riyaafa reweaving, darning, mending.

rawwaaf pl. *-a* reweaver, mender (of woven material).

r-w-l-a

roola pl. *-aat* **1.** roller. **2.** road roller, steam roller. **3.** hair roller, hair curler.

r-w-m

maraam pl. *-aat* **1.** wish, desire. **2.** aspiration.

r-w-n-q

rawnaq splendor, beauty, glamor, elegance.

r-w-y

ruwa (*i rayy, riwa*) **1.** to quench the thrist. *ma-aku šii yirwi miθl il-mayy il-baarid.* Nothing quenches thirst like cold water. **2.** to water, irrigate. *haj-jadwal yirwi giiƐaan waasƐa.* This creek provides water for a vast area of land.

raawa to show, demonstrate, display. *baƐad-ma raawaani n-namuuna, štireet.* After he showed me the sample, I made a purchase. *raawaani kull kutba.* He showed me all his books. *ʔinta hassa ʔiƐči Ɛalayya. ʔaani baƐdeen ʔaraawiik.* Go ahead and talk about me now. I'll show you later.

trawwa to ponder, reflect, think over.

trawwa w-la-tistaʿjil ib-ḥukmak ʿalee. Think it over and don't be hasty in your judgment of him.

traawa to appear (in a vision or dream), materialize. *jidda traawaa-la.* His grandfather appeared to him. *l-mayyit li-hassa baʿda da-yitraawaa-li.* The vision of the corpse is still real to me now. *bass da-traawaa-lak ʾašbaaḥ.* You're just seeing things.

rtiwa 1. to quench one's thirst. *ðall yišrab mayy ḥatta rtiwa tamaam.* He kept drinking water until he'd quenched his thirst completely. 2. to be watered, irrigated. *xalli l-gaaʿ tirtiwi zeen.* Let the ground get plenty of water.

rayy watering, irrigation, supplying of water. *mudiiriyyat ir-rayy il-ʿaamma* general directorate of irrigation.

rayyaan 1. provided with a good supply of water. 2. juicy, succulent, fresh. *purtaqaala rayyaana* a juicy orange. *bnayya rayyaana* healthy, well-formed girl.

ruwaaya pl. *-aat* 1. tale, story. 2. novel. 3. play, drama. *ruwaaya hazaliyya* a comedy. *kaatib ruwaayaat* 1. novelist. 2. playwright, dramatist.

mraawaa viewing, examination, being shown. *ʾaštiriiha ʿal-imraawaa.* I'll buy it once I see it.

r-y-a-l

ryaal pl. *-aat* rial, two hundred fils coin.

r-y-b

rtaab to feel doubt, suspicion, or misgivings, to be suspicious. *ʾaani ʾartaab minna.* I'm suspicious of him.

riiba pl. *riyab* suspicion, doubt, misgiving.

[1]*r-y-t*

reet . . . ! , yaa reet . . . ! I wish . . . ! How nice it would be if . . . ! Would that . . . ! *reet ðiič il-ʾayyaam tirjaʿ.* I wish those days would return. *reetak ihnaa.* I wish you were here.

[2]*r-y-t*

riita the seeds of a certain plant, ground and used as soap in washing wool and delicate fabrics.

r-y-θ

trayyaθ 1. to stay, linger, tarry. *ma-agdar ʾatrayyaθ li-ʾan ma-aku ṭayyaara baʿd isbuuʿ.* I can't stay because there isn't another plane for a week. 2. to be patient, bide one's time, wait. *la-tsaafir hassa. trayyaθ išwayya.* Don't go on a trip now. Wait a while.

r-y-j-y-m

reejiim diet, regimen. *raḥ-asawwi reejiim.* I'm going to go on a diet.

r-y-ḥ

raaḥ (*i raaḥa*) 1. to give a rest to, rest, let rest. *ṣaar-lak saaʿa tiqra. leeš ma-triiḥ ʿeenak?* You've been reading for an hour. Why don't you rest your eyes? *raḥ-astiqiil w-ariiḥ muxxi.* I'm going to resign and get some peace of mind. *hannooma raaḥatni.* That nap refreshed me. 2. to relieve, free, ease. *l-muwaððaf ij-jidiid raaḥni hwaaya. yuʿruf kullši.* The new employee took a lot off of me. He's very capable. *ʾiða taaxuð haš-šaġla waḥdak, itriiḥni hwaaya.* If you take over this job by yourself, you'll relieve me a lot. *l-muwaððaf ij-jidiid ṭilaʿ šaaġuul. raaḥni min kuθrat iš-šuġuḷ.* The new employee turned out to be a hard worker. He relieved me of a large part of the work.

rayyaḥ, rawwaḥ 1. to rest, give a rest to, let rest. *rayyiḥ il-iḥṣaan maalak.* Rest your horse.

ʾaraaḥ-raaḥ, which see above.

rtaaḥ 1. to rest, relax. *xalli nirtaaḥ išwayya.* Let's rest awhile. *ʾiða taʿbaan, irtaaḥ.* If you're tired, take a break. *ʾugʿud išwayya w-irtaaḥ.* Sit down for a while and relax. *wuṣlaw bis-salaama. hassa agdar artaaḥ.* They arrived safely. Now I can relax. 2. to be relieved, be at ease. *raḥ-arajjiʿ-ilh-iyyaa ḥatta ðamiiri yirtaaḥ.* I'm going to return it to him so my mind will be at ease. *min bilaʿt il-ḥabbaaya, rtaaḥeet.* When I took the pill, I felt relieved. 3. to be satisfied, be pleased. *ʾaani mirtaaḥ min sayyaarti.* I'm well-satisfied with my car.

staraaḥ (*yistaraaḥ* or *yistiriiḥ*) 1. to rest, take a break. *kull nuṣṣ saaʿa yistiriiḥ ʿašir daqaayiq.* Every half hour he rests ten minutes. *tʿabna. xan-nistaraaḥ išwayya.* We got tired. Let's rest a little. 2. to relax, make oneself comfortable. *tfaððal ʾistiriiḥ. hassa yiji l-mudiir.* Please make yourself comfortable. The director will be with you in a moment. || *stariḥ!* At ease! (military command). 3. to be saved, delivered, relieved. *zawwija ḥatta nistaraaḥ minna.* Marry him off so we'll be rid of him.

riiḥ gas (on the stomach). *ṣ-ṣooda zeena lir-riiḥ.* Soda is good for gas on the stomach. || *fatig riiḥ* hernia.

riiḥa pl. *riyaḥ, ʾaryaaḥ, rawaaʾiḥ*

1. scent, odor, fragrance, smell. 2. perfume, cologne.

raaƈa 1. rest, repose. *l-mariiδ̣ yiƈtaaj ʔila raaƈa.* The patient needs rest. *xannaaxuδ̣ raaƈa.* Let's take a rest. *ʔuxuδ raaƈtak. ʔaani ʔagƐud ihnaa.* You take it easy. I'll sit over here. 2. ease, leisure. *b-raaƈtak. šwakit-ma Ɛindak majaal, sawwiiha.* At your convenience. Whenever you get a chance, do it. 3. comfort. *wasaaʔil ir-raaƈa* conveniences. *kursi raaƈa* deck chair, cloth garden chair.

ʔarwaƈ, ʔaryaƈ more or most relaxed.

*ʔaryaƈi** pl. *-iyya* 1. generous, liberal, open-handed. 2. having a relaxed, congenial personality.

ʔaryaƈiyya generosity, open-handedness.

riiƈaan sweet basil.

ṣalaat it-taraawiiƈ a prayer performed during the evening in Ramadan.

muriiƈ 1. restful, reposeful. 2. comfortable. *kursi kulliš muriiƈ* a very comfortable chair.

see also *r-w-ƈ.*

r-y-d

raad (*i reed, reeda*) 1. to want, wish, desire. *š-raad minnak?* What did he want from you? *triid tiji wiyyaaya?* Do you want to come with me? *xaaḷa, ʔibni yriid bintič.* Ma'am, my son would like the hand of your daughter in marriage. *ʔariid min aḷḷa yinṭiini walad.* I'd like God to give me a son. *ma-raad-lak ʔilla l-xeer.* He wished you nothing but the best. *ʔariidak bil-Ɛama.* I wish you were blind. 2. to be desirable, important, necessary. *l-beet yriid-la ṣubuġ.* The house needs paint. *raad-li ʔalbas qaaṭ šitwi l-yoom.* I should have worn a winter suit today.

nraad to be wanted, desired, needed, necessary. *yinraad-li qalam paandaan.* I need a fountain pen.

ʔiraada 1. will, volition. 2. wish, desire. *haaδa δ̣idd ʔiraadti.* That's against my wishes. *kullši ṣaar ƈasb il-ʔiraada.* Everything went as was desired. 3. (pl. *-aat*) decree. *ʔiraada malakiyya* royal decree. 4. will power. *haaδa ʔiraadta δ̣aƐiifa.* His will is weak.

muraad 1. wanted, desired. 2. design, purpose, intention. *tirakha baƐad-ma naal muraada minha.* He left her after he got what he wanted from her.

r-y-z

riiza a kind of thin cotton cloth.

r-y-š

rayyaš to become wealthy, feather one's nest. *maƐluum yrayyiš ʔiδa raatba ṣaar miit diinaar biš-šahar.* Of course he's getting rich if his salary is a hundred dinars a month. *ʔaani raƈ-arayyiš ib-har-raatib.* I'll live in luxury on this salary. || *min yiƈčuun Ɛan il-banaat, yrayyiš ihwaaya.* When they talk about girls, he gets a big charge out of it.

riiš (coll.) feather(s).

riiša pl. *-aat, riyaš* 1. feather. 2. blade of a fan or propeller. 3. windshield wiper blade. 4. nib of a pen.

r-y-δ̣

riyaaδ̣a 1. physical exercise. 2. athletics, sports.

*riyaaδ̣i** 1. athletic, sporting. *ʔalƐaab riyaaδ̣iyya* sports, sporting events. 2. mathematic, mathematical. *masʔala riyaaδ̣iyya* a mathematical problem. 3. (pl. *-iyyiin*) athlete, sportsman.

riyaaδ̣iyyaat mathematics.

r-y-Ɛ

rayyaƐ to thrive, flourish, grow. *l-ġanam itrayyiƐ ib-hal-Ɛišib.* The sheep are thriving in this good pasture. || *ʔakalit raggiyya w-rayyaƐit biiha.* I ate my fill of watermelon.

[1]*r-y-f*

riif pl. *ʔaryaaf* countryside, country (as opposed to city), rural area.

*riifi** rural, rustic, country. *l-ƈayaat ir-riifiyya* the rural life.

[2]*r-y-f*

riyaafa see under *r-w-f.*

r-y-g

rayyag to feed breakfast to, to provide with breakfast. *rayygii lil-walad gabuḷ-ma ddizzii lil-madrasa.* Give the boy some breakfast before you send him to school. *raƈ-arayygak ib-hal-maṭƐam.* I'll treat you to breakfast in this restaurant.

trayyag to eat breakfast. *š-itrayyagit il-yoom?* What did you have for breakfast today?

riig saliva, spittle. *riigi naašif.* My mouth is dry. *min ʔablaƐ riigi, balƐuumi yoojaƐni.* When I swallow, my throat hurts me. || *Ɛala r-riig* before breakfast, on an empty stomach. *li-hassa, baƐadni Ɛala riigi.* I haven't eaten a thing all day. *fukk riigak ib-fadd šii gabuḷ-ma tišrab jigaara.* Get something in your stomach

before you smoke a cigarette.
rayuug, ryuug pl. *-aat* breakfast.

r-y-n
rayyaan see under *r-w-y*.

¹r-y-y
riyya see under *r-ˀ-a*.

²r-y-y
rayy see under *r-w-y*

Z

z-a-t
zaatan anyway, anyhow. *ˀaani zaatan raƹ-ˀabaṭṭil; xalli yṭurduuni.* I'm going to quit anyway; let them fire me.

z-a-r
zaar pl. *-aat* **1.** die. **2.** (pair of) dice. **3.** a large skin-covered earthen drum played at traditional oriental athletic events.

z-a-ġ
zaaġ pl. *-aat, ziiġaan* crow.

z-a-n
zaana pl. *-aat* pole. *ṭafr iz-zaana* pole vaulting.

z-b-b
zibb pl. *zbuuba, zbaab* penis.
zibiib (coll.) large, dried grape(s), raisin(s).
zibiiba pl. *-aat* un. n. of *zibiib*.

z-b-d
zibid butter.
zubda pl. *-aat, zubad* essence, substance, gist, main point. *šinu zubdat il-mawδuuƹ?* What's the essence of the matter?

z-b-r-j-d
zabarjad chrysolite, a dark green semi-precious gem.

z-b-g
zubag (*u zabug*) to slip out, slip away. *zubgat is-simča min iidi.* The fish slipped out of my hand. *j-jaahil čaan wiyyaana w-baƹdeen zubag.* The kid was with us and then slipped away. *ˀuzbug gabuḷ-ma yšuufak.* Slip away before he sees you.
tzabbag to slip, dart, jump. *šuuf haj-jaahil da-yidzabbag been is-sayyaaraat.* Look at that kid zigzagging through the cars.
zeebag quicksilver, mercury.

¹z-b-l
zabbal to throw trash around, cause untidiness. *la-dzabbil. hassa knasna l-beet.* Now don't make a mess. We just swept the house.
zibil garbage, trash, rubbish, refuse.
zbaala trash, garbage, rubbish, refuse.
zabbaal pl. *-a, -iin, zbaabiil* garbage collector, trash man.
mazbala pl. *mazaabil* dump, trash heap. || *d-dijaaja tmuut w-ƹeenha ƹal-mazbala.* He doesn't know when he's well off (lit., the chicken dies with its eye on the trash pile).

²z-b-l
zbiil pl. *ziblaan* flexible basket or satchel made of palm leaves.

z-b-n
zabaana pl. *zabaayin* **1.** casing of heavy paper for custom-made cigarettes. **2.** brass casing of a cartridge.
mzabbun: jigaayir mzabbuna custom-made cigarettes in which the tobacco is packed in a pre-formed casing of heavy paper with one end closed.
zibuun pl. *zibnaat* long, belted robe made of heavy material.

z-t-t
zatt (*i zatt*) to move quickly, rush (trans.). *zitta bis-sayyaara l-beeta w-taƹaal.* Rush him home in the car and come back. *la-txaaf. min tixlaṣ il-ƹafla, ˀaani raƹ-azittha l-beetha.* Don't worry. When the party is over, I'll get her home quickly. *ˀuxuδ minna l-maktuub w-zitta.* Take the letter from him and send him back. *baḷḷa zitt maaƹuun iz-zibid min yammak.* Please slide the butter dish over here from where you are.

z-j-j
zujaaj glass (as substance).
*zujaaji** glass, of glass. *ƹeen zujaajiyya* a glass eye.

z-ƹ-r
zaƹiir, zuƹaar dysentery.

z-ƹ-z-ƹ
zaƹzaƹ to move, shift, displace. *zaƹziƹ il-meez išwayya ƹatta yṣiir mukaan.* Move the table a little so there will be room. *ybayyin masnuud ib-waδiifta. maƹƹad yiqdar yzaƹziƹa.* It seems that he's protected in his job. No one can move him out.
tzaƹzaƹ to move, budge. *hal-piip θigiil ihwaaya w-ma-yidzaƹzaƹ.* This barrel is very heavy and won't budge. *dzaƹzaƹ išwayya ƹatta yṣiir-li mukaan ˀagƹud.* Move over a little so there'll be room for me to sit down.

z-ʕ-f

ziʕaf (*a zaʕif*) 1. to crawl, creep. *šuuf ič-čalib; rijlee maksuura w-da-yizʕaf ʕala baṭna.* Look at the dog; his legs are broken and he's crawling on his stomach. *haj-jaahil ʕumra sana w-nuṣṣ w-baʕda yizʕaf.* This baby's one and a half years old and still crawling. 2. to march. *j-jeeš raʕ-yizʕaf ʕal-ʕuduud il-fajir.* The army will march toward the border at dawn.

zaʕif 1. crawling, creeping. 2. marching, march, advance. 3. a blanket wage increase for all civil servants, decreed periodically to cover cost-of-living increases.

zaaʕif 1. creeping, crawling. 2. marching. 3. (pl. *zawaaʕif*) reptile.

z-ʕ-l-g

zaʕlag 1. to cause to slide, slip. *difaʕa w-zaʕlaga ʕaṭ-ṭiin.* He pushed him and made him slide into the mud. 2. to be slippery. *θ-θalij yzaʕlig.* The ice is slippery.

tzaʕlag 1. to glide, slide, slip, skid. *dzaʕlag ib-gišir mooz w-wugaʕ.* He slipped on a banana peel and fell. *ʔimši ʕala keefak ʕatta la-tidzaʕlag.* Walk slowly so you won't slip. 2. to ski. *raʕ-nitzaʕlag haš-šitwiyya b-jibaal libnaan.* We're going to ski this winter in the mountains of Lebanon.

ziʕlaaga pl. *-aat* 1. slide, place to slide. 2. slippery spot.

z-ʕ-m

zaʕʕam to inconvenience, trouble, bother. *zaʕʕamnaak ihwaaya b-muškilatna.* We've bothered you too much with our problem.

zaaʕam to compete with, vie with. *ybiiʕ rixiiṣ w-maʕʕad yigdar yzaaʕma.* He sells cheaply and nobody can compete with him.

zdiʕam to be crowded, jammed, to teem, swarm. *zdiʕam iš-šaariʕ bin-naas.* The street was crowded with people.

stazʕam to regard as an inconvenience. *stazʕam tawṣiilat ʔaxuuya bis-sayyaara.* He thought it was too much trouble delivering my brother in the car.

zaʕim inconvenient, bothersome, difficult. *ʕubuur iš-šaariʕ ib-had-daqiiqa zaʕim kulliš.* Crossing the street right now is very difficult. *haš-šuġuḷ kulliš zaʕim.* This work is a lot of trouble.

zaʕma pl. *-aat* inconvenience, bother, trouble. || *bala zaʕma, ma-tfukk il-baab?* If it's not too much trouble, would you open the door?

muzaaʕama pl. *-aat* 1. competition. 2. rivalry.

zdiʕaam pl. *-aat* 1. crowd, crush, jam. 2. congestion.

z-x-x

zaxx (*u zaxx*) to rain heavily, pour down rain, pour. *l-muṭar ðall yzuxx ṭuul il-leel.* The rain kept pouring down all night long.

zaxxa pl. *-aat* shower, heavy shower, downpour, cloudburst. *zaxxa xafiifa* a light shower.

z-x-r-f

zaxraf to engrave, carve. *ʔuxuð hal-looʕa w-zaxruf ʕaleeha fadd šii laṭiif.* Take this board and carve some nice design on it.

zuxruf pl. *zaxaarif* engraved decoration, embellishment.

z-x-m

zaxam momentum, impetus (phys.).

zixma pl. *-aat, zixam* brassiere.

z-r-b

zirab (*u zarub*) to have a bowel movement, defecate. *j-jaahil zirab b-ilbaasa.* The baby messed in his pants.

zarrab = *zirab.* *j-jaahil da-yzarrib bišaariʕ.* The child is defecating in the street.

zarba pl. *-aat* feces, stool.

ziriiba pl. *zaraayib* pen, corral, stockade, fold.

mazriib, mizriib pl. *mazaariib* drainspout.

z-r-d

zarad chain mail.

zarda a thick pudding made of rice, milk, and sugar.

z-r-d-w-m

zarduum pl. *zaraadiim* 1. pharynx, throat. 2. larynx, Adam's apple.

z-r-r

zirr pl. *zraar* 1. button, push button. 2. (pl. *zruur*) thigh, leg.

z-r-z-r

zarzuur pl. *zaraaziir* starling.

z-r-š-k

zrišk (coll.) currant(s).

zriška pl. *-aat* currant.

z-r-ʕ

ziraʕ (*a zariʕ*) to plant, grow, raise. *ʔizraʕ haš-šijra b-hal-mukaan.* Plant that tree right here. *raʕ-yʕirθuun il-gaaʕ w-yizraʕuuha ʕunṭa.* They'll plow the land and plant wheat on it. *raʕ-nizraʕ ʕunṭa w-šiʕiir has-sana.* We're going to grow wheat and barley this year. || *balla taعaal ib-surعa. la-tizraعni.* Please come quickly. Don't leave me waiting.

zariع 1. planting, growing, cultivation (of crops). 2. (pl. *zuruuع*) crop, growing crop.

ziraaعa agriculture, farming. *wizaart iz-ziraaعa* ministry of agriculture.

*ziraaعi** agricultural, agrarian, farm-. *wizaart il-iṣlaaح iz-ziraaعi* ministry of agrarian reform. *makaayin ziraaعiyya* farm machinery. *ʔaraaḏi ziraaعiyya* arable lands.

zarraaع pl. *-a* farm-owner, farmer.

mazraعa pl. *mazaariع* farm, plantation.

muzaariع pl. *-iin* farm-owner, farmer.

z-r-f

ziraf (*u zaruf*) to pierce, puncture, make a hole in. *l-qalam zirafa j-jeebi.* The pencil punched a hole in my pocket. *raح-nizruf ʔiδaan l-ibnayya.* We're going to pierce the girl's ears.

zarraf to punch full of holes. *b-iida l-muxyaṭ w-yzarruf bil-umqawwaaya.* He has the big needle in his hand and he's punching holes in the cardboard.

nziraf pass. of *ziraf*. *č-čiis inziraf.* The bag got a hole in it.

zuruf pl. *zruuf* hole. *zurf il-ubra* eye of the needle.

zuraafa pl. *-aat* giraffe.

mizraf pl. *mazaarif* 1. awl. 2. drill.

z-r-q

zaraq: zaraq waraq colored or decorated paper for gift wrapping, etc. || *laabis booyinbaaġ zaraq waraq.* He's wearing a loud, multicolored tie.

z-r-g

zirag (*u*) to dash, hurry, go quickly. *hassa ʔazrug lis-suug w-ʔaštirii-lk-iyyaaha.* I'll dash to the market right now and buy it for you. *kull-ma ʔalzam is-simča, tizrug min ʔiidi.* Every time I try to catch the fish, it slips from my hand.

zragg to become blue, turn blue. *zragg jilda mnil-barid.* His skin turned blue from the cold.

zaraag blueness, blue coloration.

ʔazrag fem. *zarga* pl. *zarag, zargiin* blue.

z-r-k-š

zarkaš to embroider, decorate with brocade embroidery. *zarkišat čarčaf il-meez.* She embroidered the tablecloth.

z-r-n

zarna pl. *-aat* 1. protruding corner, point where three converging lines meet. *tعawwar raasa b-zarnat il-meez.* He hurt his head on the corner of the table. 2. promontory, peak.

z-r-n-y-x

zarniix arsenic.

z-r-w-q

zarwaq to decorate, adorn, embellish. *zarwiq il-hadiyya gabuḷ-ma ddizz-ilh-iyyaa.* Decorate the present before you send it to him. *zarwuqat is-simča b-nuumi ح aamuḏ w-buṣal.* She garnished the fish with lemon and onions.

z-r-y

zari: qmaaš zari a type of cloth brocaded with gold or silver, imported from India.

z-ع-t-r

zaعtar wild thyme.

z-ع-j

ziعaj (*i*) 1. to annoy, bother, upset. *ziعajni b-ʔilحaaحa.* He annoyed me with his insistence. *ziعajni hwaaya min radd ṭalabi.* He upset me a lot when he turned down my request. 2. to disturb, alarm, make uneasy. *jawaaba ziعajni.* His answer bothered me. *la-tizعij nafsak w-itδall itfakkir, raح-yidrus w-yinjaح.* Don't upset yourself and keep thinking about it. He's going to study and pass.

ʔazعaj = *ziعaj*. *ʔazعajni b-taعliiqa s-saxiif.* He annoyed me with his stupid comment.

nziعaj pass. of *ziعaj*. *yinziعij min ʔay čilma tguulha.* He gets upset at anything you say.

z-ع-z-ع

zaعzaع 1. to shake violently, rock. *l-hawa zaعzaع kull il-ʔašjaar.* The wind shook all the trees. 2. to disturb, unsettle, disrupt. *la-tzaعziع ij-jaahil. xallii naayim.* Don't disturb the baby. Let him sleep. *ʔinta zaعzaعitni hwaaya. kull marra tgaععidni b-mukaan.* You've upset me very much. You're always seating me in a different place. 3. to move, displace, dislodge. *haaδa š-iyzaعziعa min manṣaba? j-jees wiyyaa.* What could dislodge him from his position? The army is behind him.

tzaعzaع pass. of *zaعzaع*.

z-ع-ṭ

zaعṭuuṭ pl. *zعaaṭiiṭ* child, young person.

mazعaṭa something for children (used in derisive phrases). *wizaaraathum mazعaṭa.* Their ministry is full of young punks. *haaδa šuġuḷ حukuuma loo mazعaṭa?* Is this government work or child's play?

z-ع-f-r-a-n

zaعfaraan, zuعufraan saffron.

z-ʕ-l
ziʕal (*a zaʕal*) to become annoyed, angry. *yizʕal bil-ʕajal.* He gets mad quickly. *ziʕalit ʕalee min ma-daayanni l-ifluus.* I got mad at him when he didn't lend me the money.
zaʕʕal to vex, annoy, anger. *zaʕʕalni b-hač-čilma.* He made me mad with this remark.
tzaaʕal to be angry at each other. *dzaaʕlaw ʕala šii saxiif.* They stopped speaking to each other over a silly thing.
nziʕal to be angered, made angry. *haaδa ma-yinziʕil minna; baʕda jaahil.* One can't get mad at him; he's still a child.
zaʕal irritation, annoyance, vexation, anger. *tara maaku zaʕal!* Now don't get mad! *maaku ḥaaja liz-zaʕal, siʔalatak suʔaal basiiṭ.* There's no need to get mad. I asked you a simple question. *zaʕalhum daawam šahreen.* They didn't talk to each other for two months. *b-zaʕal* in anger, angrily. *ḥičaaha b-zaʕal.* He said it angrily.
zaʕla pl. *-aat* i. n. of *zaʕal.*
zaʕlaan pl. *-iin, zʕaala* peeved, vexed, annoyed, angry. *marta baʕadha zaʕlaana.* His wife is still mad at him.

z-ʕ-m
zaʕʕam to make leader, appoint as leader. *minu lli zaʕʕamak ʕaleena?* Who put you in charge of us?
tzaʕʕam to be the leader, to command, lead. *minu dzaʕʕam hal-ḥaraka?* Who was leader of this movement?
zaʕam supposing . . . , let's suppose . . . , just suppose . . . , let's assume . . . , let's pretend. . . . *zaʕam ʔaani ʔabuu w-laazim ʔarišda.* Suppose I were his father and had to advise him. *zaʕam ʔaani l-ʕiṣaabači w-inta š-šurṭi.* Pretend I'm the gangster and you're the policeman.
zaʕiim pl. *zuʕamaaʔ* 1. leader. 2. brigadier general.
zaʕaama leadership, controlling position.

z-ġ-r
ẓiġar, ẓuġur, ẓġayyir, etc., = *ṣiġar, ṣuġur, ṣġayyir,* etc., which see under *ṣ-ġ-r.*

z-ġ-l
zaaġal to cheat, break the rules, play unfairly. *ma-alʕab wiyyaa baʕad li-ʔan yzaaġul ihwaaya.* I won't play with him any more because he cheats too much. *zaaġal ʕalayya bil-iḥsaab.* He cheated me on the bill. *haaδa midzawwaj w-yzaaġil. ʕala ṭuul ʔašuufa wiyya banaat.* He's married and he cheats. I see him all the time with girls. || *ʔiḥči ʕadil. la-dzaaġul.* Talk straight. Don't try to beat around the bush.
zuġul cheating, deception, duplicity. *kisab biz-zuġul.* He won by cheating.

z-ġ-l-ṭ
zaġlaṭ to cheat, break the rules. *zaġlaṭ ʕalayya bil-iḥsaab.* He cheated me on the account. *hiyya da-dzaġluṭ w-maḥḥad yidri biiha.* She is slipping around and nobody knows about her.

z-f-t
zaffat to coat with tar or asphalt. *zaffitaw iš-šeelmaan ḥatta ma-yzanjir.* They coated the girders with tar so they wouldn't rust.
zifit tar, asphalt.

z-f-r
zaffar to make stink, to impart a stench to, to soil, dirty. *ʔinta naδδuf is-simča. ʔaani ma-ariid azaffur iidi.* You clean the fish. I don't want to stink up my hands.
tzaffar pass. of *zaffar. dzaffarit min šilit is-simač.* I got smelly when I carried the fish.
zufar 1. the slippery secretion of fish. 2. fishy smell. 3. grease, animal fat.
zafir 1. rancid, rank, stinking. 2. dirty, filthy, unclean. *ḥalga zafir. yfaššir ihwaaya.* He's got a dirty mouth. He's always using bad language.
zufra smell, stench, stink.

z-f-f
zaff (*i zafaaf*) 1. to escort the bride or bridegroom to the new home. *raḥ-yziffuun il-ʕaruus il-yoom bil-leel.* They're going to escort the bride to her new home tonight. 2. to scold, upbraid. *ʔiδa ʕθarit bii, ʔaziffa!* If I run into him, I'll really read him the riot act!
zaffa pl. *-aat* 1. procession which ceremonially escorts the bride or bridegroom on the wedding night. 2. scolding, tirade.

z-q-z-q
zaqzaq to chirp, peep, cheep. *l-ʕaṣfuur da-yzaqziq.* The bird is cheeping.

z-q-q
zaqq (*u zaqq*) to feed (of a bird). *l-ʕaṣfuur da-yzuqq ifraaxa.* The sparrow is feeding its young. || *yeezi tzuqq iz-zaʕṭuuṭ mayy!* You've fed the baby enough water now!

z-q-m
zaqquum an infernal tree mentioned in the Koran, and also its fruit, used figuratively to mean poison. *ʕasa tkuun hal-ʔakla zaqquum.* I hope this meal is poison. *ṣaar*

ɛalayya zaqquum. It was like poison to me.

z-q-n-b

zaqnab to feed (someone) something unpleasant, to cram down the throat, stuff into the mouth. *zaqnibi j-jaahil ɛatta yiskut.* Feed the kid so he'll shut up.

tzaqnab to eat something unpleasant, to stuff in, shovel in. *ṣaar-lak saaɛa tizzaqnab; ma-txaḷḷiṣ ɛaad!* You've been stuffing yourself for an hour; why don't you finish! *leeš ma-tizzaqnab gabuḷ-ma tiji?* Why don't you feed your face before you come?

z-q-n-b-w-t

zaqnabuut an unpleasant meal, (figuratively) poison. *ma-ltaδδeet bil-ɛaša min xabṣatkum. ṣaar ɛalayya zaqnabuuṭ.* I didn't enjoy dinner because of your commotion. It was like poison to me. *zaqnabuut!* May you choke to death! Go eat worms!

z-g-ṭ

zigaṭ (*u zaguṭ*) to kick (of an animal). *z-zumaaḷ zigaṭa.* The donkey kicked him.

zaggaṭ to have a tendency to kick.

zaagaṭ to have a tendency to kick, to be in the habit of kicking. *haz-zumaaḷ yzaaguṭ. diir baalak minna.* This donkey kicks. Be careful of him.

zagṭa pl. *-aat* a kick (of an animal).

z-k-m

zukaam common cold, head cold.

z-k-y

zakka **1.** to vouch for, support, testify in favor of. *ˀaani ˀazakkiik ˀiδa triid tištirik bin-naadi.* I'll vouch for you if you want to join the club. *kullhum zakkoo ɛind il-mudiir.* They all vouched for his integrity to the director. **2.** to recommend. *kullhum zakkoo lir-riyaasa.* They all recommended him for the presidency.

zakaa **1.** alms-giving, alms, charity. **2.** alms tax (Islamic law).

tazkiya pronouncement of support, favorable testimony. || *bit-tazkiya* by acclamation. *ṭilaɛ bit-tazkiya bil-intixaab.* He won the election by acclamation.

z-l-a-b-y

zlaabya a coil-shaped donut-like pastry, fried in oil or butter and covered with syrup.

z-l-a-ṭ

zalaaṭa pl. *-aat* **1.** salad. **2.** a sure or easy thing, a snap, a cinch. *hal-mawδuuɛ zalaaṭa. ma-yinraad-la qraaya.* This course is a cinch. There's no reading required for it.

z-l-j

mizlaaj pl. *mazaalij* (sliding) bolt (on a door).

z-l-z-l

zilzaal pl. *zalaazil* earthquake.

z-l-ṭ

zilaṭ to swallow whole, to gulp down, bolt. *ˀiɛlis il-xubuz zeen. la-tzulṭa.* Chew the bread well. Don't swallow it whole.

nzilaṭ pass. of *zilaṭ. l-mooz yinziluṭ ib-suhuula.* Bananas go down easily.

zalaaṭa see under *z-l-a-ṭ.*

z-l-f

tzallaf to fawn, curry favor, behave in a fawning, obsequious manner, fawn on. *yidzallaf ihwaaya. ma-ɛinda maaniɛ yčaδδib.* He curries favor all the time. He has no compunction about telling lies. *yizzallaf ir-raˀiis id-daaˀira.* He fawns on the chief of the office.

zilif pl. *zluuf* sideburns.

mzallaf pl. *-iin* **1.** greedy. **2.** miserly, stingy.

z-l-g

zilag (*a zalig*) **1.** to slip, slide. *zilag bit-ṭiin w-itwaṣṣaxat ihduuma.* He slipped in the mud and his clothes got dirty. **2.** to make a mistake, commit an error, make a slip. *ˀiɛči ɛala keefak w-la-tizlag.* Talk slowly and don't make a slip.

zallag to cause to make a mistake, to trip up. *yisˀalni hiiči ˀasˀila ɛatta yzalligni.* He asks me these questions to trip me up.

z-l-g-ṭ

zalgaṭ to bolt. *ˀuqful il-baab w-zalgiṭha.* Lock the door and bolt it.

zilgaaṭa pl. *-aat* (door)bolt, lock.

z-l-l

zall to slip, slip up, make a mistake. *mitˀassif. zall ilsaani.* I'm sorry. My tongue slipped.

zalla pl. *-aat* **1.** mistake, error. **2.** slip (of the tongue).

z-l-m

zilma, zlima pl. *zilim* man.

z-l-n-ṭ-ɛ

zalanṭaɛ pl. *-aat* snail. *zaḷanṭaɛ, zaḷanṭaɛ, ṭalliɛ igruunak w-inṭaɛ.* Snail, snail, put out your horns and butt.

z-m-b-l

mzambila pl. *-aat* faucet, spigot.

z-m-b-l-k

zumbalak pl. *-aat* mainspring of a watch. || *mara zumbalak* harridan, shrewish woman.

z-m-b-y-l

zambiil, var. of *zanbiil,* which see under z-n-b-l.

z-m-r

zammar to play the zummara. *ðall yzammur ʔilla ʔan dawwaxna.* He kept on playing the zummara until he made us dizzy.

zummaara pl. *-aat* zummara, a small flute-like wind instrument with a bell-shaped end.

zumra pl. *zumar* gang, group (of people).

z-m-r-d

zumarrad, zumrud (coll.) emerald(s).

zumarrada pl. *-aat* emerald.

z-m-z-m

zamzamiyya pl. *-aat* canteen, flask.

z-m-ṭ

zumaṭ (*u zamuṭ*) to boast, brag, talk big. *ʔašu tizmuṭ w-ma-aku qabuð.* It seems you're always bragging but there's no results.

z-m-l

zaamal to be a friend, colleague, associate of, to maintain a friendship with. *zaamalhum muddat sana w-baʕdeen tirakhum.* He ran around with them for a year and then abandoned them.

tzammal to behave like an ass. *latizzammal ʕaad!* Stop acting like a jackass!

zamiil pl. *zumalaaʔ* **1.** friend, companion, associate, comrade. **2.** colleague.

zamaala pl. *-aat* **1.** comradeship. **2.** colleagueship. **3.** fellowship, friendship. **4.** fellowship, grant, stipend.

zmaaḷ pl. *zmaayiḷ* jackass, donkey.

mzammila pl. *-aat* faucet, spigot.

z-m-n

ʔazman to be or become chronic. *l-gaʕʕa maalta ʔazminat.* His cough has become chronic.

zaman pl. *ʔazmina* time, period, era. *b-zaman il-ʔatraak, kull il-imwaððafiin itʕallmaw turki.* During the Turkish period, all officials learned Turkish.

zamaan, zimaan pl. *ʔazmina* time, age, era, epoch. *b-zamaani hiiči šii ma-čaan yṣiir.* In my day this sort of thing wouldn't have happened. *haaða šloon zamaan illi haaða yṣiir naaʔib?* What sort of times are these when that guy becomes a representative? *haz-zamaan, ma-bii ṣadiiq min ṣudug.* These days there are no real friends. || *ṣaar zimaan ma-šiftak.* I haven't seen you in quite a while. *min zamaan* for quite a long while, for some time, for ages. *ʔaʕurfa min zimaan.* I've known him a long time. *ṣaaʕib iz-zamaan* (Shiah) the Mahdi, the last imam who will come to purify Islam.

muzmin chronic. *dizaantari muzmin* chronic dysentery.

z-m-h-r

zamhariir severe frost, bitter cold.

z-m-y-j

zimiij alluvial mud (used as fertilizer).

z-n-a-n

zanaana, maal zanaana **1.** having to do with women, for women, feminine. *hal-xurdafaruuš ybiiʕ ġaraað maal zanaana.* This variety store sells women's articles. *šloon tilbas hiiči qanaadir? haaði maal zanaana!* How can you wear such shoes? These are for women! *šloon itsawwi hiiči biyya? haaða ʕamal zanaana.* How could you do that to me? That's something a woman would do. **2.** effeminate. *haaða zanaana. ma-yugʕud wiyya r-riyaajiil, yʕibb ʕači n-niswaan.* He's effeminate. He doesn't sit with the men; he likes women's talk. *waaʕid min wilda rijjaal tamaam, wil-laax zanaana.* One of his boys is a real man, but the other is effeminate.

z-n-b-r

zanbuur pl. *znaabiir* wasp, hornet.

z-n-b-r-k

zunburuk var. of *zumbalak* which see under z-m-b-l-k.

z-n-b-q

zanbaq pl. *zanaabiq* **1.** lily. **2.** iris.

z-n-b-l

zanbiil pl. *zanaabiil* large basket woven from palm leaves.

z-n-j

*zanji** pl. *zunuuj* **1.** Negro, black. **2.** a Negro.

z-n-j-r

zanjar to rust, be or become rusted. *l-quful zanjar w-ma-yinfitiʕ.* The lock has rusted and won't open.

zinjaar **1.** rust. **2.** verdigris.

zinjaari: daff zinjaari tambourine.

z-n-j-l

zanjiil pl. *znaajiil* **1.** chain, chain bracelet. **2.** zipper.

z-n-d

zanid pl. *znuud* upper arm, between the shoulder and the elbow.

znaad pl. *-aat* **1.** trigger (of a gun). **2.** cigarette lighter.

z-n-d-q

zandiiq pl. *zanaadiq, zanaadiiqa* atheist, unbeliever, free-thinker.

z-n-z-n
zinzaana pl. *-aat* prison cell.
z-n-g-ṭ
zunguṭa, zunugṭa pl. *-aat, znaagiṭ* pimple, skin blemish.
z-n-g-n
zangan to bestow wealth, make wealthy. *l-waḍiifa ma-tzangin ʔaḥḥad.* Government work won't make anyone wealthy. *ʔiḏa ddabbur il-qaḍiyya, ʔazanginak ib-miit diinaar.* If you take care of the matter, I'll give you a hundred dinars.
tzangan to be or become wealthy, to get rich. *b-wakt il-ḥarub, idzanganaw naas ihwaaya.* During the war, many people got rich.
zangiin pl. *zanaagiin* **1.** wealthy, rich. **2.** a rich man.
zangana wealth, riches.
z-n-m
zaniim **1.** low, despicable, mean, ignoble. **2.** (pl. *-iin*) despicable person.
z-n-y
zina (*i zina*) **1.** to fornicate. **2.** to commit adultery. *ʔiḏa tizni, ʔaḷḷa yʕaaqbak.* If you commit adultery, God will punish you.
zina **1.** fornication. **2.** adultery. || *ʔibin zina* bastard.
zaani, pl. *-iyyiin* fornicator, adulterer.
z-h-d
zahdi a cheap variety of dates.
z-h-r
zdihar to flourish, thrive, prosper. *baġdaad izdiharat ib-zaman il-ʕabbaasiyyiin.* Baghdad flourished during the Abbasid period.
zahar a kind of poison primarily used in poisoning fish.
zuhri: maraḍ zuhri venereal disease.
z-zuhara the planet Venus.
mizhariyya pl. *-aat* flower vase.
z-h-f
zihaf (*i zahif*) to make a mistake, err. *diir baalak la-tizhif tara ma-ysaamḥak.* Be careful not to make a mistake or he won't forgive you.
zahhaf to cause to make a mistake, to cause to err. *la-tiḥči. tara tzahhifni.* Don't talk. You'll make me make a mistake.
zahfa pl. *-aat* mistake, error.
z-h-g
zihag (*a zahig*) to be or become disgusted, fed up, tired. *r-rijjaal zihag min marta.* The man got fed up with his wife.
zahhag to make disgusted, fed up, tired, to antagonize, irritate, exasperate. *yzahhigni. saaʕa yriid is-sayyaara w-saaʕa ma-yriidha.* He disgusts me. One time he wants the car and one time he doesn't. *la-dzahhiga lil-walad tara ybaṭṭil.* Don't antagonize the boy or he will quit.
zahgaan disgusted, fed up, tired, annoyed. *ʔaani zahgaan min hal-ʕiiša.* I'm disgusted with this life.
z-h-w
ziha (*i zahu*) to be radiant, glow, gleam, shine brightly. *š-šaariʕ il-yoom yizhi b-haḏ-ḏuwaayaat.* The street's radiant today with these lights.
z-w-a-n
zwaan (coll.) freckle(s).
zwaana pl. *-aat* freckle.
z-w-j
zawwaj to marry off, to give in marriage. *ʔiḏa tištirik wiyyaaya, ʔazawwijak binti.* If you'll go into partnership with me, I'll marry my daughter to you. *min yitxarraj ʔibni mnil-kulliyya, ʔazawwija.* When my son graduates from college, I'll get him married.
zaawaj to mate. *zaawaj dijaaj ʔameerki wiyya dijaaj ʕiraaqi.* He mated an American chicken with an Iraqi chicken.
tzawwaj to get married. *dzawwijaw gabuḷ sana w-hassa ʕidhum bint.* They got married a year ago and now they have a daughter.
zooj, zawj pl. *ʔazwaaj* **1.** husband. **2.** couple, pair. *zooj qanaadir* a pair of shoes. || *z-zumaaḷ ḏuraba zooj.* The donkey kicked him with his two hind feet. *sawwoo zooj w-ʔaxḏaw fluusa.* They fooled him and took his money.
zawja pl. *-aat* wife.
*zawji** **1.** matrimonial, marital, conjugal. **2.** paired, in pairs. **3.** even. *raqam zawji* an even number.
zawaaj **1.** marriage. *dzangan ib-zawaaja minha.* He got rich from his marriage with her. **2.** wedding. **3.** matrimony.
z-w-d
zaad (*u*) see under *z-y-d*.
zawwad to provide, supply, furnish. *haddaaʔira raḥ-idzawwdak ib-kull il-maʕluumaat.* That office will furnish you with all the information.
zaad **1.** provisions, supplies, stores. **2.** food.
z-w-r
zaar (*u ziyaara*) to visit, call on, pay a visit to. *zirna lubnaan ziyaara gṣayyra iṣ-ṣeef il-faat.* We paid a short visit to Lebanon last summer. *raḥ-azuur il-mudiir ib-beeta.* I will call on the director at his home. *zirna l-ʕatabaat il-muqaddasa.* We

visited the holy places. *raح-idzuur hassana?* Are you going to the holy places this year?

zawwar 1. to guide, show around, conduct on a tour (particularly of a shrine). *šuuf-lak fadd waaحid yzawwrak il-maqaam.* Find yourself someone to guide you around the shrine. 2. to forge, falsify. *yigdar yzawwir ʔay tawqiiع.* He can forge any signature. *ʔalġaw il-intixaabaat li-ʔan čaanat muzawwara.* They voided the elections because they were rigged.

tzaawar to exchange visits, visit each other. *ʔiδa δ̣δ̣alluun tizzaawruun عala ṭuul, yimkin tizzawwajha.* If you keep on visiting with each other a long time, perhaps you will marry her.

zuur: sahaadat zuur false testimony, perjury.

zoor 1. force. *ma-ysawwi šii ʔilla biz-zoor.* He doesn't do anything unless he's forced to. *xoo muu biz-zoor; ma-yiعjibni ʔaruuح lis-siinama hal-leela.* Even force won't help; I don't want to go to the movies tonight. 2. undergrowth, thicket in a marshy area. || *ʔaku xanziir biz-zoor.* There's something that doesn't meet the eye (lit., there's a boar in the marsh growth).

zoorxaana pl. *-aat* a kind of oriental gymnasium, devoted to body-building and physical culture.

zoorxanči an athlete who exercizes in a *zoorxaana.*

ziyaara 1. visiting. 2. (pl. *-aat*) visit. 3. call (social, business, etc.).

zaayir pl. *zuwwaar* 1. visitor, caller, guest. 2 visitor, pilgrim (to a shrine or holy place other than Mecca).

mzawwirči pl. *-iyya* guide at a shrine who leads people in prayers appropriate to the place.

z-w-ع

zaaع (*u zooع*) to vomit, retch, throw up. *s-sakraan zaaع bil-paaṣ.* The drunk vomited in the bus. || *min haddadta, zaaع kull il-ifluus.* When I threatened him, he coughed up all the money.

zawwaع 1. to vomit, retch, throw up. *daax w-zawwaع.* He got dizzy and vomited. 2. to cause to vomit. *ʔumma nṭata duwa حatta dzawwiعa.* His mother gave him some medicine to make him vomit. || *zawwaعta kull il-ifluus.* I squeezed all the money out of him.

zwaaع vomit.

zooعa: maraδ̣ ʔabu zooعa cholera.

z-w-l

zaal 1. (*u zawaal*) to go away, leave, withdraw. *l-xaṭar zaal عanna.* He's out of danger (lit., the danger went away from him). 2. (*i ʔizaala*) to remove, eliminate, to make disappear or vanish. *hal-maحluul yziil il-lakka.* This solution will remove the spot. 3. (*a*) /with negative only/ to cease (often equivalent to English "still, yet"). *humma la-yazaaluun yirكuun maši lil-madrasa.* They haven't stopped walking to school. They still go to school on foot. *huwwa la-yazaal mawjuud ib-baġdaad.* He's still in Baghdad.

zuuliyya pl. *-aat, zwaali* carpet, rug.

mizwala pl. *mazaawil* sundial.

z-w-n

zwaan, zwaana see under *z-w-a-n.*

z-w-y

nzuwa to hide oneself, go into seclusion. *l-bazzuuna tinzuwi min itšuuf ič-čalib.* The cat hides itself when it sees the dog. *min fišal bil-intixaabaat, inzuwa.* When he lost in the election, he went into seclusion.

zaawiya pl. *zawaaya* angle (math.).

zuwiyya pl. *zwaaya* corner, nook.

z-y-b-g

zeebag quicksilver, mercury.

z-y-t

zeet pl. *zyuut* oil (edible, fuel, etc.). || *dihin iz-zeet* olive oil.

zeeti, zayti** oily, oil. *ʔaṣbaaġ zeetiyya* (artist's) oil paints.

z-y-t-w-n

zeetuun (coll.) 1. olive(s). 2. olive tree(s).

zeetuuna pl. *-aat* 1. olive. 2. olive tree.

*zeetuuni** olivaceous, olive-colored, olive-green. *nafnuuf zeetuni* an olive-colored dress.

z-y-ح

zaaح (*i zeeح*) to take away, drive away, remove, banish. *ma-tziiح hal-kutub min yammi حatta ʔagdar aktib?* Would you move these books away from me so I can write? *l-waziir ij-jidiid zaaح il-mudiir min δaak il-manṣab.* The new minister ousted the director from that position. *ʔuxuδ hač-čam daris il-maṭluuba حatta tziiحha عannak.* Take these few required courses so you can get them out of your way.

z-y-d

zaad (*i ziyaada*) 1. to become greater, become more, grow, increase, multiply. *عadad iṭ-ṭullaab zaad.* The number of students increased. *wijaع raasi da-yziid.* My headache is getting more severe. *š-šaṭṭ yziid bir-ribiiع.* The river rises in the spring. **2.** to augment, increase, compound. add to, enlarge. *ziid ič-čaay maali ṃaay.* Add some water to my tea. **3.** (*yzuud*) to be in excess, be left over. *kull ṭaalib ʔaxaδ ktaab w-zaadat xamis kutub.* Every student took a book and five books were left over. *ʔiδa yzuud šii mnil-uqmaaš, anṭiik-iyyaa.* If there's anything left of the cloth, I'll give it to you. **4.** /with *عala* or *عan*/ to exceed, be greater than, be more than. *l-maṣraf zaad عala d-daxal.* The expense exceeded the income.

zayyad **1.** to augment, increase, make greater or more. *l-baggaaḷ raح-yzayyid siعir ij-jizar.* The grocer is going to increase the price of carrots. *zayydaw yoomiiti.* They raised my daily allowance. **2.** /with *عala*/ to outbid, to make a higher bid than. *zayyad عalayya b-diinaareen w-baaعoo-lh-iyyaa.* He raised me two dinars and they sold it to him.

zaayad to bid, offer a bid (at an auction). *d-dallaal عiraḍ ir-raadyo bass maححad zaayad.* The auctioneer showed the radio but no one bid.

zdaad to grow, increase, become more or greater. *la-tidjaadal wiyyaa tara yizdaad ġaḍaba.* Don't argue with him or he'll get madder (lit., his anger will increase).

ziyaada **1.** increase, growth. *ṣaarat ziyaada čibiira biš-šaṭṭ has-sana.* There was a big rise in the river this year. **2.** excess, surplus, overage, overplus. *ṭilعat عidna ziyaada bil-iحsaab.* We had an excess in our accounts. *has-sana raح-iṭṣiir ziyaada bil-miizaaniyya.* This year there is going to be a surplus in the budget. *ġilaṭ bil-iحsaab w-inṭaani xamsiin filis izyaada.* He made a mistake in figuring and gave me 50 fils too much. *عindi fluus it-tikit w-laa filis ziyaada.* I have money for the ticket, but not one fils more. *haay kullha zyaada maa-lha حaaja.* All of these things are unnecessary additions. *z-ziyaada b-kullši muu zeena.* Excess in everything isn't good. **3.** increase, augmentation, raising, stepping up. *ʔinṭooni ziyaada nuṣṣ diinaar bil-yoom.* They gave me a half dinar a day raise. *baaع-li l-ʔaθaaθ ib-siعr it-takliif bala ziyaada.* He sold me the furniture at cost without a mark-up. || *w-ziyaada عala δaalik . . .* and in addition to that . . . *niqala w-ziyaada عala δaalik ġarrama raatib yoomeen.* He transferred him and, in addition to that, docked him two days pay.

ʔazyad more or most excessive, high, great, etc.

mazaad pl. *-aat* auction, public sale.

muzaayada bidding, offering of bids (at an auction).

zaayid **1.** increasing, growing, becoming more or greater. **2.** excessive, immoderate. *haaδi čaanat zaayda minnak. ma-čaan laazim idguul hiiči šii.* That was uncalled for. You shouldn't have said such a thing. **3.** additional, extra. *عindak qalam zaayid?* Do you have an extra pencil? **4.** excess, more than necessary. *č-čaay maali, šakara zaayid.* My tea has too much sugar. *l-عašr idnaaniir zaayda عalayya.* The ten dinars is more than enough for me.

zaaʔida: z-zaaʔida d-duudiyya vermiform appendix (anat.).

z-y-r

ziyaara, zaayir see *z-w-r.*

z-y-ṭ

ziiṭa pl. *-aat* wagtail, water thrush.

z-y-f

zayyaf to counterfeit (money). *ʔaku čam waaحid da-yzayyifuun idnaaniir.* There are several people counterfeiting dinars.

muzayyaf counterfeit, false, spurious. *حubba ʔilha čaan muzayyaf.* His love for her was phony.

[1]*z-y-g*

zayyag to give a Bronx cheer, raspberry. *kull-ma ʔaحči, yzayyig.* Everytime I say something, he gives a Bronx cheer.

ziig pl. *zyaaga* a loud, derisive noise made by putting the tongue between the lips and blowing, Bronx cheer, raspberry. *lamma haddadni jibta b-ziig.* When he threatened me, I gave him the raspberry.

[2]*z-y-g*

ziig pl. *zyaag* shirt-front opening.

z-y-l

zaal (*i*) see *z-w-l.*

z-y-n

zayyan **1.** to adorn, decorate, embellish, ornament, beautify. *zayyinaw il-ġurfa b-wruud.* They decorated the room with flowers. **2.** to shave, give a shave to. *minu zayyanak iṣ-ṣubuح, ʔabu saami?* Who shaved you this morning, Abu Sami? **3.** to shave, get a shave. *liحiitak ṭuwiila. leeš ma-dzayyin?* Your whiskers're pretty long. Why don't you shave? **4.** to cut hair, give a haircut to. *huwwa yzayyin ʔibna b-iida.* He gives his son haircuts himself. **5.** to cut one's hair, get a haircut. *laazim idzayyin raasak.* You have to have a haircut.

tzayyan **1.** to be decorated, be adorned,

be beautified. *š-šawaariع idzayyinat ib-hal-ʔašjaar.* The streets have been improved by these trees. **2.** to shave, get a shave. *ʔaani ʔadzayyan is-saaعa sabعa ṣ-ṣubuح kull yoom.* I shave at seven o'clock every morning. **3.** to get a haircut. *ʔaani raayiح lil-ḥallaaq ʔadzayyan.* I'm going to the barber to get a haircut.

zeen **1.** fine, good, nice. *عinda šuġuḷ zeen.* He has a good job. *hamm zeen ma-git-la.* It's a good thing you didn't tell him. *yaعni, muu zeen minna nṭaak sayyaarta tistaعmilha?* Now, wasn't that nice of him to give you his car to use? *ṣirit zeen loo baعdak mariið?* Did you get well or are you still sick? **2.** (adv.) well, excellently. *marti tuṭbux zeen.* My wife cooks well. **3.** (interjection of compliance or approbation) fine, good, all right, O.K. *zeen, ʔasawwiiha b-ʔaqrab furṣa.* All right, I'll do it the first chance I get. *zeen, ʔaani ʔaعallamak.* O.K., I'll teach you.

zeeniyya pl. *-aat* favor, kindness, good deed.

ziina pl. *-aat* decoration, embellishment, ornament.

zyaan pl. *-aat* **1.** shave. **2.** haircut.

mzayyin pl. *mzaayna* barber.

z-y-y

zayy pl. *ʔazyaaʔ* **1.** costume. **2.** style of dress. *maعrað ʔazyaa* fashion show.

S

s-a-j

saaj teak, teakwood.

s-a-d-a

saada (invar.) **1.** plain, unicolored, uniform. *loon saada* a solid color. *ʔaḥmar saada* solid red. **2.** plain, unadulterated, straight. *ġahwa saada* unsweetened coffee. *čaay saada* unsweetened tea. *عarag saada* straight arrack.

s-a-s

saas a fencing game played with sticks and shields, often to the accompaniment of drum and pipe.

s-a-ع

saaع: b-saaع quickly, speedily, fast, in a hurry, right away. *ʔiða tsidd ij-jidir, yfuur il-mayy ib-saaع.* If you cover the pot, the water will boil quickly. *š-ib-saaع irjaعit!* You sure got back fast! *waddi ʔibni lil-madrasa w-taعaal ib-saaع.* Take my son to school and hurry back.

saaعa pl. *-aat* **1.** time, moment. *beeš is-saaعa rajaaʔan?* What time is it, please? *saaعt il-yooṣal, ʔagul-la.* The minute he comes, I'll tell him. **2.** hour. *d-daris ṭawwal saaعa w-nuṣṣ.* The lesson lasted an hour and a half. **3.** (pl. *-aat, suuع*) watch, clock, timepiece. *saaعa munabbiha* alarm clock. *saaعat ʔiid* wrist watch.

saaعči pl. *-iyya* watchmaker, watch and clock repairman or dealer.

saaعaati pl. *-iyya* var. of *saaعči.*

s-a-q-w

saaqu pl. *saaquwwaat* coat, jacket.

s-ʔ-l

siʔal (a suʔaal) to ask, inquire. *ma-nidri š-raح-yisʔalna bil-imtiḥaan.* We have no idea what he will ask us on the exam. *ʔisʔal minna. balki yuعruf.* Ask him. Perhaps he knows. *š-šurṭa da-tisʔal عannak.* The police are inquiring about you.

tsaʔʔal to be inquisitive, ask questions. *ʔiða titsaʔʔal ihwaaya, yعurfuuk ġariib.* If you ask a lot of questions, they will know you're a stranger.

suʔaal pl. *ʔasʔila* question, query, inquiry.

saʔʔaal inquisitive, curious, given to asking questions.

masʔala pl. *masaaʔil* **1.** problem, question. **2.** controversy, issue, thing in dispute. **3.** matter, affair, case. *š-ṣaar min masʔalt iz-zawaaj?* What came of the wedding matter? *šloon masaaʔil da-tṣiir bid-daaʔira! l-muwaððafiin yitعaarkuun, wil-ġaraað da-tinbaag.* What goings-on are taking place in the office! The employees are fighting with each other and things are being stolen. *ma-djuuz min hal-masaaʔil! muu عeeb tiḥči عan-naas!* Why don't you quit this business! It's wrong to talk against people! || *عinda ġeer masaaʔil!* or *šloon masaaʔil عinda!* He's a real nut! What a character he is!

saaʔil pl. *-iin* **1.** questioner, asker. **2.** beggar.

masʔuul accountable, responsible, in charge. *minu l-masʔuul عann illi ṣaar?* Who's responsible for what happened? *minu l-masʔuul ib-had-daaʔira?* Who's in charge of this office?

masʔuuliyya pl. *-aat* responsibility.

s-a-m

*saami** **1.** Semitic. *l-عunṣur is-saami* the Semitic race, Semitic stock. **2.** a Semite.

s-a-h-w-n

saahuun peanut brittle.

s-b-b

sabb (i sabb, masabba) to insult, abuse, call names, revile, curse. *sabb il-bazzaaz illi ġašša bil-uqmaaš.* He reviled the cloth dealer who cheated him on the material. *ma-yxaaf minna. čam marra sabba b-wičča.* He's not scared of him. Several times he insulted him to his face.

sabbab to cause, bring about, provoke, produce. *ma-da-nuعruf šinu lli da-ysabbib hal-maraḍ.* We don't know what's causing this disease.

tsabbab **1.** /with *min* or *عan*/ to be caused by, be the result or consequence of, to result from, spring from. *har-ruṭuuba da-titsabbab imnil-balluuعa.* This dampness comes from the drain. **2.** /with *b-*/ to be the cause of, be to blame for. *xalla ʔibna yṣiir ṭayyaar w-itsabbab ib-moota.* He let his son become a pilot and caused his death. **3.** to make a living, carry on a business. *xalli r-rijjaal yitsabbab w-ruuح عanna!* Let the man carry on his business; get away from him!

tsaabab to exchange insults, insult each other. *tsaabbaw marra θaanya b-markaz iš-šurṭa.* They exchanged insults again in the police station.

sabab pl. *ʔasbaab* reason, cause. *šinu sabab ʔistiqaalta?* What's the reason for his resignation? *ʔinta činit sabab kull hal-mašaakil.* You were the cause of all these difficulties. || *b-sabab* because of, on account of, due to. *ma-gidar yiji b-sabab il-muṭar.* He couldn't come because of the rain.

masabba pl. *-aat* abuse, insult, vilification. *ʔaani ma-mistiعidd ʔaakul masabba.* I'm not about to take insults.

s-b-t

sabit: yoom is-sabit Saturday.

s-b-č

sibač (i sabič) to thicken, become thick. *fawwurha nuṣṣ saaعa ḥatta tisbič.* Boil it for half an hour so that it'll thicken.

sibbaač pl. *sibbaača* a maker of date molasses.

masbač pl. *masaabič* a place where date molasses is made.

ʔasbač more or most syrupy, viscous, thick, etc.

saabič viscous, syrupy, thick. *šoorba saabča* thick soup.

s-b-ح

sibaح (a sibiح) **1.** to swim, go swimming. *yiعijbak inruuح nisbaح il-yoom?* Would you like to go swimming today? **2.** to bathe, take a bath. *ʔaani mujnib; laazim asbaح gabuḷ-ma aṣaḷḷi.* I'm ritually unclean; I've got to take a bath before I pray.

sabbaح **1.** to cause to swim, let swim. *waddi ʔaxuuk l-iṣġayyir w-sabbحa biš-šaṭṭ.* Take your little brother and let him swim in the river. **2.** to finger one's beads, toy with a string of prayer beads. *ṣaar-lak saaعa da-tsabbiح. ʔiidak ma-tiعbat?* You've been playing with your worry beads for an hour. Hasn't your hand gotten tired?

nsibaح pass. of *sibaح* **1.** *hal-ṃaay baarid. ma-yinsibiح bii.* That water's cold. It can't be swum in.

sibحa pl. *sibaح* prayer beads, a string of beads resembling a rosary.

sabbaaح pl. *-iin* swimmer.

sibbaaحa pl. *-aat* float.

saabuuح pl. *-iin, swaabiiح* expert swimmer, good swimmer.

masbaح pl. *masaabiح* swimming place, swimming pool.

s-b-d-j

sabdaj to scrub with ceruse, apply ceruse. *da-tsabdij wujihha.* She's scrubbing her face with ceruse.

sibdaaj white lead, ceruse, a cosmetic containing white lead.

s-b-r

sabbuura pl. *-aat* **1.** blackboard. **2.** slate.

s-b-z

sabzi spinach.

s-b-s

sbuus (coll.) rice hulls, rice husks.

sbuusa pl. *-aat* un. n. of *sbuus.*

s-b-ع

sabbaع to make brave, courageous. *haaḏa mxannaθ! š-sabbaعa?* He's a coward! What made him brave?

tsabbaع to be made brave, to get up one's courage. *tsabbaع w-raaح ḥiča wiyyaa.* He got up his courage and went to talk with him.

stasbaع **1.** to become brave, work up courage, find courage. *min ʔija ʔabuu, stasbaع w-gaam ysibbni.* When his father came, he got brave and began to insult me. *čaan yxaaf min xayaala. ʔašu hassa stasbaع.* He was afraid of his shadow. Now it seems he's gotten some courage. **2.** /with *عala*/ to overpower, overcome. *šaafa waḥda w-istasbaع عalee.* He saw him alone and overpowered him.

sabiɛ 1. brave. 2. cunning, clever. 3. (pl. *sbaaɛ*) lion.

sabɛa pl. *-aat, sibaɛ* seven. *sabiɛ miyya* seven hundred. *sabiɛ ʔaqlaam* seven pencils. *s-sabɛa b-iidi.* I've the seven in my hand. || *ʔabu sabɛa w-sabɛiin* centipede, millipede.

sbaaṭaɛaš seventeen.

subuɛ pl. *ʔasbaaɛ* one-seventh, seventh part.

sabɛiin seventy.

ʔusbuuɛ, sbuuɛ pl. *ʔasaabiiɛ* week.

ʔusbuuɛi, sbuuɛi** weekly. *maɛaaš isbuuɛi* a weekly salary.

ʔusbuuɛiyyan weekly, by the week.

saabiɛ seventh (ordinal).

s-b-q

sibaq (*i sabiq, sibiq*) 1. to be, come, go, get, act, or happen before or ahead of, to precede, antecede. *l-faḥṣ iṭ-ṭibbi yisbiq it-taɛyiin.* The medical examination precedes the appointment. *ʔaxuuk yisbiqni bit-tarfiiɛ.* Your brother is ahead of me in line for promotion. *huwwa saabiqni b-ṣaffeen biθ-θaanawiyya.* He is two grades ahead of me in high school. || *sibaq w-git-la ɛannak.* I already told him about you. *ma-sibaq w-šifta yṣiir hiiči ɛaṣabi.* I haven't ever seen him so mad before. 2. to surpass, beat, do better than. *madrasathum sibqatna b-kurat is-salla.* Their school beat us in basketball.

tsaabaq to race, compete. *la-titsaabaq wiyyaa. sayyaarta čibiira.* Don't race him. His car is big. *triid titsaabaq wiyyaaya bir-rikiḍ?* Do you want to see if you can outrun me?

sabiq, sibiq 1. antecedence. 2. precedence, priority. || *sabiq lisaan* a slip of the tongue, impulsive utterance.

sibaaq pl. *-aat* 1. race. 2. game, meet, match, contest.

ʔasbaq earlier, or earliest, antecedent. *ʔinta l-ʔasbaq bit-tarfiiɛ.* You are the first in line for promotion.

ʔasbaqiyya 1. precedence, priority. 2. seniority. *ʔintu ʔilkum il-ʔasbaqiyya bit-tarfiiɛ.* You have the seniority for promotion.

musaabaqa pl. *-aat* 1. race. 2. contest. *musaabaqat ʔajmal ṭifil* most-beautiful child contest.

saabiq 1. prior, previous, preceding. *r-rooḥa s-saabqa* the previous trip. 2. former, ex-. *l-waziir is-saabiq* the ex-minister. || *bis-saabiq* in the past, formerly, at one time. *bis-saabiq, čaanaw ysaafruun ib-ɛarabaayin.* In the past, they travelled by carriage. *kas-saabiq* as formerly, as it was before. *rijɛat il-ʔumuur kas-saabiq.* Everything returned to the way it was before.

saabiqa pl. *sawaabiq* precedent, previous case. || *min ʔaṣḥaab is-sawaabiq* previously convicted, having a criminal record. *maɛruuf ɛanna min ʔaṣḥaab is-sawaabiq.* He is known to have been previously convicted.

s-b-k

sabiika pl. *sabaaʔik* ingot. *sabaaʔik δahabiyya* gold bullion.

s-b-l

sabbal to donate for charitable use. *raḥ-asabbil ṭungat ṃayy l-iθwaab ʔabuuya.* I will donate a jar of water (to people passing by) for the sake of my deceased father.

sabiil donated for public use (especially water at a religious shrine). *hal-ṃayy sabiil; muu bi-fluus.* This water has been donated; it isn't to be paid for. || *ʔibn is-sabiil* 1. vagabond, tramp, hobo. 2. wayfarer, traveler. *fii sabiil* for the sake of, in behalf of. *sawweetha fii sabiil aḷḷaah.* I did it for the sake of God. *ɛala sabiil* for the purpose of, by way of, as. *ɛala sabiil it-tajruba* for the purpose of trial, on a trial basis. *ɛala sabiil il-miiθaal* as an example, for the purpose of an example.

sbiil pl. *-aat, sbaayil* clay pipe.

s-b-y

siba (*i sabi*) 1. to capture, take prisoner. *kitlaw zilimhum w-sibaw niswaanhum.* They killed their men and captured their women. 2. to exasperate, vex, bother greatly. *sibaani. kull ɛašir daqaayiq yxaaburni yisʔal ɛala natiijt imtiḥaana.* He has thoroughly exasperated me. Every ten minutes he calls me to ask about the results of his exam. *ʔiṣbir išwayya. muu sibeetni.* Be patient a minute. You've bothered the hell out of me.

sibaaya pl. *-aat* Shiite mourning ceremony.

s-b-y-n-a-ġ

sbeenaaġ spinach.

s-p-r-n-g

sipring pl. *-aat* spring (as an elastic body, e.g.:) *sipringaat lawi* coil springs.

s-p-w-r-t-r

sapoortar athletic supporter.

s-p-y-r

speer pl. *-aat* spare, e.g. spare tire, spare part.

s-p-y-l

spiil pl. *-aat* = *sbiil,* which see under *s-b-l.*

s-t-a-d

staad, staadi pl. *-iyya* supervisor, superintendent, boss. *ɛali, staadi yriidak.* Ali, the boss wants you.

[1]*s-t-t*

sitt a polite term of address used by students when speaking or referring to a female teacher, approx.: Lady, Madame, Miss. *muɛallimt il-ɕisaab sitt hindi.* The mathematics teacher is Miss Hindi.

[2]*s-t-t*

sitta six.

sittaɛaš sixteen.

sittiin sixty.

see also *s-d-s.*

s-t-r

sitar (*u sitir*) **1.** to watch over, protect, guard. *ʔalla yistur ɛaleeha. xooš mara.* God watch over her. She's a fine woman. *ʔalla yistur min hal-ɕarb. yjuuz iddammur il-ɛaalam.* God protect us from this war. It might destroy the world. *jaa yoogaɛ biš-šatt, laakin ʔalla sitar.* He was about to fall into the river, but God prevented it. *laa, ma-tuṣqut. ʔalla yistur!* No, you won't fail. God forbid! **2.** to hide, conceal, cover up. *ma-tmakkan yistur ġaḍaba.* He wasn't able to conceal his anger.

sattar = *sitar. daaʔiman itsattir ɛala bintha.* She always covers up for her daughter.

tsattar to cover, hide, conceal oneself. *da-titsattar w-tiɛtiqid in-naas ma-yɛurfuun ɛanha.* She's covering up and she thinks people don't know about her.

sitra pl. *sitar* **1.** jacket, light coat. **2.** sport coat, suit jacket.

sitaar pl. *sataaʔir* curtain (of a theater). *s-sitaar il-ɕadiidi* the Iron Curtain.

ʔastar more or most proper, honorable, respectable. *ʔaɕsan šii w-ʔastar šii l-waaɕid yuṣruf ɛala-gadd ifluusa.* The best and most proper thing is for one to spend according to how much money he has.

mastuur **1.** hidden, concealed, covered up. **2.** chaste, proper, honorable. *bint mastuura* a nice girl.

s-t-k-a-n

stikaan pl. *-aat* a small glass used for drinking tea.

s-t-m

satami pl. *-iyyaat* bill of lading (com.).

s-t-w

sattaw to cook well, make well-done. *sattuw il-laɕam zeen gabul-ma djiiba.* Cook the meat well-done before you bring it in. *sattawt il-laɕam.* I cooked the meat well-done.

see also *stuwa* under *s-w-y.*

s-t-w-w

staww variant of *hastaww,* which see under *h-s-t-w.*

s-t-y-r-n

steerin pl. *-aat* **1.** steering wheel. **2.** steering mechanism, steering gear, steering.

s-j-d

sijad (*i sujuud*) to bow down, prostrate oneself (in prayer). *maa daam ḍahrak yoojɛak, la-tisjid min itṣalli.* Since your back hurts you, don't bow down when you pray. *ma-yisjid ġeer il-ʔalla.* He doesn't bow down to anyone except God.

sajda pl. *-aat* prostration in prayer.

sijjaad (coll.) **1.** prayer rug(s). **2.** rug(s), carpet(s).

sijjaada pl. *-aat, sjaajiid* un. n. of *sijjaad.*

masjid pl. *msaajid* mosque.

s-j-ɛ

sajiɛ rhymed prose.

s-j-q

sujuq link sausage.

s-j-l

sajjal **1.** to register, record, put on record, enter in a register. *sajjil ʔismak w-ɛinwaanak ihnaa.* Enter your name and address here. *sajjilni; ʔariid ʔaruuɕ lis-safra.* Put me down; I want to go on the trip. *sajjil diinaar b-iɕsaaba.* Enter a dinar on his account. || *la-toogaf ihnaa tara š-šurṭi ysajjil ɛaleek muxaalafa.* Don't stop here or the cop will give you a ticket. **2.** to enter, enroll (in a school, etc.). *ʔariid ʔasajjil ʔibni bil-madrasa.* I want to enroll my boy in the school. **3.** to record, make a recording of, cut a record of. *ʔariid asajjil ʔaġaaniiha j-jidiida.* I want to record her new songs.

sijil pl. *sijillaat* register, list, record. *sijillaat iš-šarika* the company's records. *sijil iz-ziyaaraat* guest register, visitors' book. *sijil il-ġiyaabaat* attendance record.

musajjil pl. *-iin* **1.** recorder, registrar. **2.** (pl. *-aat*) recording device, recorder, tape recorder.

musajjal registered, recorded, listed. *bariid musajjal* registered mail. *ɛalaama musajjala, maarka musajjala* registered trade mark.

s-j-m

nsijam to harmonize, blend in, be in

harmony. *l-loon il-ˀaḥmar ma-yinsijim wiyya hiiči ˀalwaan.* Red doesn't go with such colors. *ma-da-yinsijim wiyya talamiiδ ṣaffa.* He's not getting along with the students in his class. *huwwa ma-minsijim wiyya ˀaṣdiqaaˀa.* He doesn't get along with his friends.

nsijaam harmony.

s-j-n

sijan (i sijin) to jail, imprison, confine. *sijnoo baʕad-ma ṣidar il-ḥukum δidda.* They put him in prison after the sentence was pronounced against him. *l-baarḥa sjanitni bil-ḥarr saaʕteen.* Yesterday you stranded me in the heat for two hours.

nsijan to be jailed, imprisoned. *kitala w-insijan ʕišriin sana.* He killed him and was imprisoned for twenty years.

sijin pl. *sijuun* **1.** prison, jail, penitentiary. **2.** imprisonment, confinement. *sijin ˀinfiraadi* solitary confinement. *sijin šadiid* confinement at hard labor.

masjuun **1.** imprisoned, jailed, confined. *ġirgat il-baaxira w-buqaw masjuuniin bij-jaziira santeen.* The ship sank and they stayed stranded on the island for two years. **2.** (pl. *masaajiin*) prisoner, prison inmate, convict.

s-j-y

saajya pl. *swaaji* irrigation channel, irrigation ditch.

s-č-č

sičča variant of *sikka* which see under *s-k-k.*

s-č-n

siččiin, siččiina pl. *sčaačiin* knife.

s-ḥ-b

siḥab (a saḥib) **1.** to pull, draw, drag. *sayyaarti ma-da-tištuġuḷ. dizz-li loori yisḥabha.* My car isn't running. Send me a truck to tow it. *sayyaart ij-jiip tisḥab kulliš zeen.* A jeep pulls very well. *xallaw panka b-šibbaač il-maṭbax ḥatta tisḥab il-hawa.* They put a fan in the kitchen window to draw the air out. **2.** to withdraw, call back, pull back, pull out. *siḥbaw safiirhum.* They recalled their ambassador. *raḥ-nisḥab jeešna imnil-ḥiduud.* We are going to pull our army back from the borders. **3.** to take back, withdraw. *ˀisḥab kalaamak tara ˀamawwtak.* Take back what you said or I'll kill you. *ˀiδa tsawwi muxaalafa, yisḥabuun ˀijaaztak.* If you break the law, they'll take away your license. || *siḥbaw ˀiida mnil-waδiifa ˀila ˀan ydaqqiquun iḥsaabaata.* They suspended him from the position until they check his books. **4.** to take out, withdraw. *siḥabit miit diinaar imnil-ḅang.* I withdrew a hundred dinars from the bank. *jaabaw ibnayya zġayyra tisḥab ˀarqaam il-faaˀiziin.* They brought a little girl to draw the winners' numbers. **5.** to draw (a check, bill of exchange, etc.). *dizz-li čakk masḥuub ʕala bang ir-raafideen.* Send me a check drawn on the Rafidayn Bank. *siḥab ʕalayya kumpiyaala b-miit diinaar.* He made out a promissory note to me for a hundred dinars. **6.** to pull, draw (a weapon). *siḥab ʕalee l-musaddas w-raad ykutla.* He drew the gun on him and wanted to kill him.

nsiḥab to withdraw, retreat, pull back. *jeešna nsiḥab min hal-manṭiqa.* Our army retreated from the area. *ˀiδa ma-tigdar tidjaadal wiyyaahum, ˀinsiḥib.* If you can't argue with them, back off. *ma-aʕtiqid yintaxbuuni. raḥ-ansiḥib.* I don't think they will elect me. I'm going to withdraw.

saḥib drawing (in a lottery).

saḥba pl. *-aat* **1.** a withdrawal. **2.** a drawing (in a lottery).

saaḥiba pl. *-aat* **1.** tow truck, wrecker. **2.** tractor (for hauling a semitrailer).

s-ḥ-r

siḥar (a siḥir) to enchant, bewitch, charm, infatuate, fascinate. *marta triid tisḥara ḥatta balki yḥibbha.* His wife wants to cast a spell on him so he'll love her. *ˀiʕyuunič siḥratni!* Your eyes have bewitched me!

saḥḥar to serve the Suhuur. *bitna ʕidhum w-čallab ˀilla ysaḥḥirna.* We spent the night with them and he insisted on serving us the Suhuur.

tsaḥḥar to eat the Suhuur. *ma-raḥ-atsaḥḥar hal-leela.* I'm not going to eat the Suhuur tonight.

siḥir **1.** bewitchment, enchantment, beguilement. **2.** magic, sorcery, witchcraft.

*siḥri** magic, magical. *ˀalʕaab siḥriyya* magic tricks. *faanuus siḥri* magic lantern, slide projector.

suḥuur pl. *-aat* Suhuur, the meal before dawn during Ramadan.

saḥḥaar pl. *-a, -iin* sorcerer, magician, wizard.

saḥḥaara pl. *-aat* sorceress, witch.

saaḥir pl. *-iin* magician.

s-ḥ-s-l

saḥsal **1.** to drag or scrape on the ground, to brush the ground. *ʕabaata da-tsaḥsil biṭ-ṭiin.* His robe is dragging in the mud.

da-yimši w-ysaɛsil ib-qundarta. He's walking along and scuffling his shoes. **2.** to slide, drag, pull. *ʔiδa ma-tigdar itšiil ič-čiis, saɛsila.* If you can't carry the bag, drag it.

msaɛsal **1.** dragged. **2.** minimal, barely sufficient. *ġulba msaɛsala* a close victory. *nijaɛ najaaɛ imsaɛsal.* He barely succeeded. *yiɛči ngiliizi msaɛsal.* He barely speaks English. *huwwa fadd waaɛid imsaɛsal.* He's a good-for-nothing loafer.

s-ɛ-q

siɛaaq Lesbianism, tribady.

saɛɛaqiyya pl. *-aat* Lesbian.

saaɛiq overwhelming, crushing. *faaz fooz saaɛiq bil-intixaabaat.* He won an overwhelming victory in the election.

masɛuuq pl. *masaaɛiiq* **1.** powder. **2.** (pl.) make-up, cosmetics.

s-ɛ-g

siɛag (a saɛig) **1.** to crush, mash, flatten. *ʔisɛag ɛaj-jigaara ɛatta tinṭifi zeen.* Crush the cigarette so it'll be really out. *yinraadinna rooḷa tisɛag il-gaaɛ.* We need a steam-roller to pack down the ground. **2.** to run over, run down, trample. *čaan yimši b-nuṣṣ iš-šaariɛ w-siɛgata sayyaara.* He was walking in the middle of the street and a car ran over him. *waxxir, la-ysiɛgak iz-zumaaḷ.* Move out of the way so the donkey won't trample you. *l-yoogaf ib-ṭariiqak, ʔisiɛga.* Whoever stands in your way, run over him. *bass-ma ṣaar mudiir, siɛag il-muwaδδaf illi čaan ynaafsa.* As soon as he became director, he rode roughshod over the employee who was competing with him. **3.** to annihilate, wipe out, destroy. *jeešna siɛag jeeš il-ɛadu.* Our army crushed the enemy army. **4.** to wear in, break in. *l-qundara ʔiδa tisɛagha muddat yoomeen, baɛad ma-toojɛak.* If you break in the shoes for a couple of days, they won't hurt you anymore. *laazim tisɛag makiint is-sayyaara gabuḷ-ma timši b-surɛa zaayda.* You should break in the car's motor before you go at high speed.

saɛɛag intensive of *siɛag. xallaa jawwa rijla w-gaam ysaɛɛig bii.* He put it underneath his foot and started stomping on it.

siɛig worthless, no good. *has-siinama djiib ʔaflaam siɛig.* That theatre brings in no-good movies. *huwwa zeen bil-luġaat bass siɛig bir-riyaaδiyyaat.* He's good in languages but not worth a damn at mathematics.

saɛga humiliation.

msaɛɛag crushed, mashed, flattened, trampled. || *giɛadit iṣ-ṣubuɛ imsaɛɛag.* I got up this morning feeling like I'd taken a beating.

s-ɛ-l

siɛal (a saɛil) to draw, drag, trail. *šuuf ij-jahhaal da-ysiɛluun il-bazzuuna l-mayyta.* Look at the kids dragging the dead cat around.

saɛil dragging.

saɛla i.n. of *saɛil.*

sɛaala fine rice dust left over after polishing. || *šinu hal-isɛaalaat timši wyaahum?* What's this scum you're running around with?

misɛaal: misɛaal il-kabiš the Milky Way.

saaɛil pl. *sawaaɛil* seashore, coastline. || *xaam sawaaɛil* rough, unbleached cotton cloth.

s-ɛ-n

siɛan (a saɛin) to pulverize, grind, crush. *duggi l-miliɛ w-siɛnii zeen.* Pound the salt and pulverize it well.

[1]*s-ɛ-y*

saɛaaya: maraδ is-saɛaaya meningitis.

misɛaa pl. *masaaɛi* spade, shovel.

[2]*s-ɛ-y*

stiɛa, yistiɛi see *ɛ-y-y.*

s-x-t

saxta pl. *-aat* swindle, fraud. *sawwa biyya saxta. gal-li l-uqmaaš ʔingiliizi w-ṭilaɛ waṭani.* He pulled a fast one on me. He told me the cloth was British and it turned out to be locally made. *la-dṣaddig bii. haaδi saxta min ɛinda.* Don't believe him. That's a lot of baloney.

saxtači pl. *-iyya* swindler, fraud, con artist, smooth talker.

s-x-t-y-a-n

suxtiyaan a kind of fine, thin leather.

s-x-r

sixar (a saxir, suxur) /with *min* or *b-*/ to laugh at, ridicule, mock, make fun of. *la-tisxar imnil-ʔaqdaar.* Don't laugh at fate.

saxxar to employ, utilize, make use of. *msaxxir jariidt il-ɛizib il-maṣaalɛa š-šaxṣiyya.* He's using the party newspaper for his personal interest.

masxara pl. *masaaxir* object of ridicule, butt of jokes, laughingstock. || *haaδi muu ʔintixaabaat. haaδi masxara.* This is no election. This is a joke.

s-x-f

saxiif **1.** foolish, stupid, simple-minded.

2. silly, ridiculous, absurd. 3. (pl. *suxafaaʔ*) fool, idiot.
saxaafa pl. *-aat* foolishness, folly, a foolish thing to do.
ʔasxaf more or most foolish.

s-x-l

s-x-l see *ṣ-x-l*.

s-x-y

saxi see under *ṣ-x-y*.

s-d-d

sadd (*i sadd*) 1. to plug, close up, stop up. *biθl il-gahwa sadd il-mağsal.* The coffee grounds stopped up the sink. *saddaw majra l-ṃayy li-ʔan iz-zariʕ kulla ġirag.* They dammed the water channel because all the crops had flooded. *sidd izruuf il-ʕaayiṭ b-ičbintu.* Fill in the cracks in the wall with cement. 2. to block, obstruct, close off. *l-baladiyya saddat iš-šaariʕ li-ʔan da-yballṭuu.* The city closed off the street because they're paving it. *sadd ʕalayya ṭ-ṭariiq.* He blocked my way. *l-beet ij-jidiid gbaalna sadd manðar il-ʕadiiqa ʕaleena.* The new house across from us obstructed our view of the park. 3. to cover, close up, stopper. *ʔiða tsidd ij-jidir, iyfuur il-ṃayy ib-saaʕ.* If you cover the pot, the water will boil quickly. 4. to close, shut. *sidd il-imjarr.* Close the drawer. *sidd il-baab min tiṭlaʕ.* Close the door when you go out. *saddeet iʕsaabi bil-bang.* I closed out my account at the bank. *sidd il-mawðuuʕ! ʕali jaa.* Drop the subject! Ali is coming. *siddha ʕaad!* All right, knock it off! 5. to turn off, shut off, cut off. *saddeet il-ṃaay min ṭilaʕit?* Did you turn off the water when you left? *sidd ið-ðuwa.* Turn off the light. *sadd it-talafoon ib-wučči.* He hung up the telephone on me. 6. to cover, satisfy, meet. *l-ʕukuuma qtirðat milyoon diinaar ʕatta tsidd il-ʕajaz bil-miizaaniyya.* The government borrowed a million dinars to meet the deficit in the budget. *hal-ifluus il-ʕidna tsidd ʕaajaatna.* The money we've got satisfies our needs. 7. to fill, close. *saddeena kull iš-šawaağir.* We filled all the vacancies. *maʕʕad ysidd il-faraağ illi ʕiṣal baʕad wafaata.* No one can fill the gap that was created by his death.
saddad to settle, pay up, cover. *saddad kull idyuuna.* He paid up all his debts.
sadd pl. *suduud* 1. obstacle, obstruction. 2. block. 3. dike. 4. dam.
sadda pl. -*aat* dam.
ṣaddaada pl. *-aat* plug, stopper, cork.

s-d-r

sidir 1. a type of thorny bush or tree. 2. the leaves of this tree, crushed and used as soap in rural areas.
sidaara pl. *sidaayir* 1. a common Iraqi headgear, usually of black velvet. 2. overseas cap (mil.).

s-d-s

sudus pl. *ʔasdaas* a sixth part, one-sixth.
saadis sixth (ordinal).
musaddas pl. *-aat* 1. hexagon. 2. pistol, revolver.
see also under *s-t-t*.

s-d-n

sidaana pl. *sidaayin* a clay container used for storing grain, and the like.

s-d-y

sadda to weave, make a web. *l-ʕankabuut da-ysaddi biz-zuwiyya.* The spider is making a web in the corner. *hirš il-ʕinab sadda ʕaš-šibbaač.* The grape vine has covered the window.
sida pl. *sdaaya* warp (of a fabric).
sadya pl. *-aat* stretcher, litter.

s-ð-j

saaðij pl. *suððaj* 1. simple, naive, innocent, guileless. 2. naive person.

s-r-a-y

saraay see under *ṣ-r-a-y*.

s-r-b

tsarrab 1. to leak, seep out. *l-ṃayy da-yitsarrab min jawwa l-baab.* Water is leaking out from under the door. 2. to leak out, get out, spread. *ma-da-nuʕruf išloon itsarrubat hal-maʕluumaat.* We don't know how this information leaked out.
sirib pl. *ʔasraab* 1. flock, covey, flight (of birds). 2. squadron, group, formation, flight (of aircraft). 3. swarm (of bees).
saraab mirage.

s-r-b-t

sarbat to let go free, to turn loose. *sarbat ičlaaba biš-šawaariʕ.* He let his dogs run loose in the streets. *nṭii xamsiin filis w-saribta.* Give him fifty fils and let him go.
tsarbat to wander away. *liğa nuṣṣ saaʕa w-baʕdeen itsarbat.* He prattled on for a half hour and then wandered away.
sarbuut loafer, lazy bum.

s-r-b-s

sarbas pl. *saraabis* reel.

[1]*s-r-j*

siraj (*i sarij*) to saddle. *ʔisirja lil-iʕṣaan.* Saddle the horse.
sarij pl. *sruuj* saddle.

siraaj light, lamp, lantern. || *loo biδ-δulma loo bis-siraajeen.* It's either a feast or a famine (lit., either in the dark or with two lamps).

siraaja saddlery, saddler's trade.

sarraaj pl. *-iin, -a* **1.** saddler. **2.** leather craftsman.

siruujiyya saddlery, saddler's trade.

²*s-r-j*

sarij serge. *pantaroon sarij* serge pants.

s-r-j-y-n

sirjiin dung, manure (especially of cattle).

s-r-ζ

siraζ (*a sariζ*) **1.** to roam freely, graze freely. *ṣaxlatna da-tisraζ wiyya l-ġanam.* Our goat is grazing with the sheep. **2.** to be distracted, let one's mind wander. *yintibih išwayya lil-muζaaδara w-baζdeen yisraζ.* He pays attention to the lecture for a while and then his mind wanders. **3.** to forget. *ʔiδa ma-tʔakkid ζalee, tara yisraζha lil-qaδiyya.* If you don't remind him, he's going to forget about the matter.

sarraζ **1.** to dismiss, discharge, release, set free. *wizaart id-difaaζ raζ-itsarriζ ʔalif jundi haš-šahar.* The Ministry of Defense is going to dismiss a thousand soldiers this month. **2.** to arrange, do up, fix (the hair). *ṣaar-ilha saaζa tsarriζ šaζarha.* She took an hour doing her hair.

siraaζ release. || *ʔaṭliqaw siraaζa baζad-ma ζurfaw muu huwwa l-muδnib.* They set him free after they learned he wasn't the guilty one.

*sarζi** **1.** forgetful, absent-minded. **2.** (pl. *-iyya*) absent-minded person.

masraζ pl. *masaariζ* stage (of a theater).

tasriiζa pl. *-aat* hairdo, coiffure. *tasriiζt iš-šaζar* hairdo.

s-r-d

sirad (*u sarid*) to tell, present in detail, give a detailed account. *ʔijaani ġaδbaan w-sirad kull illi ζinda.* He came to me angrily and told me everything that was bothering him.

s-r-d-a-b

sirdaab pl. *sraadiib* **1.** cellar. **2.** basement.

s-r-r

sarr (*u*) **1.** to make happy, gladden, delight. *ysurrni hwaaya ʔan titqaddam ib-ζayaatak.* It makes me very happy that you're getting ahead in life. **2.** to tell a secret, to confide in. *ʔagdar ʔasurrak ib-šii w-ma-dguul?* Can I let you in on a secret without your telling?

starr to become happy, be delighted. *min simaζ bil-xabar, starr ihwaaya.* When he heard the news, he became very happy.

sirr pl. *ʔasraar* secret. *kalimat is-sirr* password. *ma-yiktim sirr.* He can't keep a secret.

*sirri** **1.** secret. *jtimaaζ sirri* a secret meeting. *l-ζaada s-sirriyya* masturbation. **2.** confidential, classified. *δbaarta maζfuuδa bil-qalam is-sirri.* His file is kept in the classified section. **3.** secret agent, undercover agent.

suruur joy, happiness, delight, pleasure. || *b-kull suruur* gladly! with pleasure! *b-kull suruur! ma-aku zaζma.* Gladly! It's no trouble.

siriir pl. *sraayir* **1.** bed. **2.** a mat of woven palm stalks.

masruur glad, happy, delighted, pleased. *ʔaani masruur ib-najaaζak.* I am happy about your success.

s-r-s-r

sarsari pl. *-iyya* tramp, vagabond, bum.

s-r-ζ

sarraζ to speed up, expedite. *balki tigdar itsarriζ-li l-masʔala.* Perhaps you can expedite this matter for me.

ʔasraζ (*i ʔisraaζ*) to hurry, hasten, rush, run, dash. *ʔiδa tisriζ, itlaζζag bii.* If you hurry, you'll catch up with him.

tsarraζ to be rash, hasty, be in too much of a hurry. *la-titsarraζ w-tistiqiil. yimkin baačir ybaddil raʔya.* Don't be rash and resign. Maybe tomorrow he'll change his mind. *ʔašuuf loo ma-titsarraζ ʔaζsan.* I think it would be better not to be in a rush.

surζa **1.** speed, velocity. *ysuuq ib-surζa.* He drives fast. **2.** rapidity, quickness, promptness. *š-ma dgulla yṣaddig ib-surζa.* Whatever you tell him, he believes right away.

sariiζ fast, quick, rapid, speedy, swift. *ζṣaan sariiζ kulliš* a very fast horse. || *qiṭaar sariiζ* express train. *sariiζ il-iltihaab* highly inflammable. *sariiζ it-taʔaθθur* easily affected, highly sensitive.

ʔasraζ **1.** faster or fastest. **2.** quicker or quickest.

s-r-f

ʔasraf (*i ʔisraaf*) to waste, squander, spend lavishly, to be extravagant. *ʔiδa tisrif w-ma-tiddixir, tara taakulha.* If you waste and don't save, you'll be in trouble.

musrif **1.** extravagant, wasteful. **2.** spendthrift.

s-r-q
sariqa pl. *-aat* robbery, theft, larceny.
masruuqaat (invar. pl.) stolen goods, loot.

s-r-g-y
surgi pl. *-iyyaat, saraagi* bolt, lock.

[1]*s-r-w*
saru (evergreen) cypress.

[2]*s-r-w*
sira see under *s-r-y*.

s-r-w-a-l
sirwaal̩ pl. *-aat* a sort of loose trousers.

s-r-y
sira (*i sarayaan*) **1.** to spread. *ṣ-ṣaraṭaan da-yisri b-jisma.* Cancer's spreading through his body. **2.** to take effect, be effective. *d-duwa raḥ-yisri mafƐuula b-ðaruf xamis daqaayiq.* The medicine will take effect within five minutes. **3.** to apply, be applicable. *l-qaanuun yisri Ɛal-kull.* The law applies to everyone.

sira pl. *-aayaat, -aawaat* **1.** line, row, column. *xall nugƐud bis-sira l-warraani.* Let's sit in the last row. *ṣuff is-sayyaaraat siraayeen.* Line up the cars in two columns. **2.** row of buttons (on a jacket) *sitra sira waaḥid* single-breasted jacket. *quuṭ siraween.* double-breasted suit. **3.** place in line, turn. *ma-tigdar itguṣṣ biṭaaqa ʔiða ma-taaxuð sira.* You can't buy a ticket if you don't take a place in line. *hassa siraak.* Now it's your turn.

sariyya pl. *saraaya* company (mil.).

saari contagious. *ʔamraaḍ saarya* contagious diseases.

saariya pl. *-aat* **1.** column, pole. *saariyat Ɛalam* flagpole. **2.** mast.

s-z-z
-sizz fem. and pl. *-iyya* a suffix of negation roughly comparable to English -less. *ʔadabsizz* ill-mannered, mannerless. *muxxsizz* stupid, brainless.

s-s-y
sissi (coll.) a kind of edible nut with a fibrous, grayish-white shell, grown in northern Iraq.

sissiyya pl. *-aat* un. n. of *sissi*.

s-ṭ-ḥ
see *ṣ-ṭ-ḥ*.

s-ṭ-r
see *ṣ-ṭ-r*.

s-ṭ-Ɛ
see *ṣ-ṭ-Ɛ*.

s-ṭ-l
see *ṣ-ṭ-l*.

s-Ɛ-d
siƐad (*i*) to please, make happy. *ʔaḷḷa ysiƐdak ib-zawaajak.* God make you happy in your marriage. *marta siƐdata.* His wife made him happy. *yisƐidni Ɛan titwaffaq ib-ḥayaatak.* It pleases me that you're getting ahead in your life.

saaƐad to help, aid, assist. *saaƐadni b-šuġḷi.* He helped me in my work. *kawna mislim saaƐada bil-ʔintixaabaat.* His being a Moslem helped him in the elections. *l-ḥaraara tsaaƐid Ɛala ðawaaban il-ʔamlaaḥ.* Heat is helpful in dissolving salts.

ʔasƐad = *siƐad.*

tsaaƐad to help each other. *ʔiða ma-nitsaaƐad, ma-yiṭlaƐ šuġuḷ.* If we don't help each other, no work will get done.

saƐiid pl. *-iin, suƐadaaʔ* **1.** happy. *ʔaƐtiqid raḥ-iykuun saƐiid ib-zawaaja minha.* I think he'll be happy in his marriage with her. *ʔayyaamkum saƐiida!* Happy holiday! (a greeting used during the two Moslem feast days). **2.** fortunate, lucky. *s-saƐiid illi ma-yiḥtaaj waðiifa.* The lucky one is the guy who doesn't need a government job.

saƐaada **1.** happiness. **2.** good fortune. **3.** a formal title roughly equiv. to His Excellency, His Grace. *saƐaadat il-mudiir* His Excellency the Director.

*suƐuudi** **1.** Saudi. *l-mamlaka is-suƐuudiyya l-Ɛarabiyya.* The Kingdom of Saudi Arabia. **2.** a Saudi Arab.

ʔasƐad **1.** happier or happiest. **2.** more or most fortunate.

musaaƐada pl. *-aat* aid, assistance, help, support, backing. *musaaƐada maaliyya* financial assistance. *musaaƐadaat ʔiqtiṣaadiyya* economic aid. *ʔaani ḥaaðir il-ʔayy musaaƐada tirduuha.* I'm ready to help in any way you want.

saaƐid pl. *sawaaƐid* forearm. || *huwwa s-saaƐid il-ʔayman lil-waziir.* He's the minister's right-hand man.

musaaƐid pl. *-iin* helper, aide, assistant. *Ɛaamil musaaƐid* (chem.) catalyst.

s-Ɛ-r
saƐƐar to price, set a price on, fix the price of. *l-ḥukuuma saƐƐirat ʔakθar il-biðaaʔiƐ il-mustawrada.* The government has fixed the price on most imported goods.

siƐir pl. *ʔasƐaar* price.

siƐra, suƐra pl. *-aat* calorie.

tasƐiira pricing, price-fixing.

s-Ɛ-f
ʔasƐaf **1.** to help, aid, assist. *šloon činit miflis laakin Ɛali ʔasƐafni b-Ɛašr idnaa-*

niir. I was really broke but Ali came to my aid with ten dinars. **2.** to render medical assistance. *ʔasʕifoo bil-ʔooksijiin ʕatta ṣiʕa.* They treated him with oxygen until he regained consciousness.

ʔisʕaaf pl. *-aat* **1.** aid, relief, help. **2.** medical assistance. *ʔisʕaafaat ʔawwaliyya* first aid. *sayyaart il-ʔisʕaaf* ambulance.

saʕaf (coll.) palm frond(s).

saʕfa pl. *-aat* palm frond.

s-ʕ-l

saʕʕal to catch whooping cough. *ʔibni saʕʕal min čaan ʕumra sabʕ isniin.* My son caught whooping cough when he was seven years old.

suʕaal, suʕaal diiki whooping cough.

s-ʕ-l-b

saʕlabiyya variant of *θaʕlabiyya,* which see, under *θ-ʕ-l-b.*

s-ʕ-l-w

siʕluwwa pl. *-aat* large (female) monster, witch, goblin.

s-ʕ-y

siʕa (*i saʕi*) to work, endeavor, try. *siʕaa-li hwaaya laakin ma-ʕaṣṣalt il-waδiifa.* He did his best for me but I didn't get the position. *ʔiδa tisʕi zeen, tinjaʕ.* If you work real hard, you'll succeed. *ma-siʕa w-ṣiqaṭ bil-imtiʕaan.* He didn't study and he failed the exam. *da-yisʕii-lak ib-kisraan ir-rugba. da-yšayyiʕ ʕannak ʔinta šiyuuʕi.* He's trying to hurt you. He's spreading it around that you're a communist.

saʕi money-changer's fee or commission.

saaʕi pl. *suʕaat* messenger, delivery boy. *saaʕi l-bariid* rural mail carrier.

see also *w-s-ʕ.*

s-f-ʕ

sifaaʕ fornication.

s-f-r

sifar (*i sufuur*) to unveil the face. *min maat, banaata sifraw.* When he died, his daughters took off their veils. *banaat baġdaad kullhum sifraw.* Baghdad girls have all removed the veil.

saffar **1.** to send on a journey, send off. *saffarna ʔalif ʕajji hal-isbuuʕ.* We got a thousand pilgrims on their way this week. **2.** to compel to leave, expel, deport. *š-šurṭa saffirat tlaθ ʔajaanib dixlaw bala paaspoort.* The police deported three foreigners who entered without passports.

saafar **1.** to travel, take a trip. *raʕ-asaafir il-ʔawruppa haṣ-ṣeef.* I'm going to travel to Europe this summer. **2.** to leave, depart. *l-wafid raʕ-iysaafir baačir.* The delegation will leave tomorrow. *ʔariid ʔašuufak gabul-ma tsaafir.* I want to see you before you leave town.

safar traveling, travel.

*safari** portable, movable, mobile.

safra pl. *-aat* **1.** trip, journey. **2.** tour, outing.

sufra pl. *sufar* a woven mat placed on the floor to place food on at meal time. || *ʕaδδri s-sufra. raʕ-naakul.* Set the table. We're going to eat.

safiir pl. *sufaraaʔ* ambassador.

sufuur **1.** unveiling, uncovering the face. **2.** without a veil, with the face uncovered. *baġdaad biiha niswaan ihwaaya yimšuun sufuur.* In Bagdad are many women who go around unveiled.

safaara pl. *-aat* embassy.

saafir unveiled, wearing no veil. *binta saafira bass marta titʕajjab.* His daughter goes unveiled but his wife wears a veil.

musaafir pl. *-iin* **1.** traveler. **2.** passenger.

musaafirxaana old-fashioned hotel (esp. an old, dirty one).

s-f-r-j-l

sfarjal (coll.) quince(s).

sfarjala pl. *-aat* quince.

s-f-r-ṭ-a-ṣ

safarṭaas pl. *-aat* a set of separate pans fitted together to carry a hot meal, lunchbox.

s-f-f

sfiifa pl. *sfaayif* **1.** protective bordering. **2.** piping, edging. **3.** molding.

sfuuf a medicinal mixture of ground herbs.

s-f-l

sufli pl. *-iyya* **1.** worthless person, derelict, bum. **2.** ruffian, hooligan, hoodlum.

saafil pl. *safala* **1.** low, lowly, base, mean, despicable. **2.** despicable person.

s-f-n

safiina pl. *sufun* ship, vessel, boat. *safiinat nuuʕ* Noah's ark.

saffaan sailor, man who works on a sailing ship.

s-f-n-j

sfanj (coll.) sponge(s).

sfanja pl. *-aat* a sponge.

s-f-h

tsaffah to behave unrestrainedly, enjoy oneself, have a good time. *raaʕ il-baġdaad ʕatta yitsaffah.* He went to Baghdad to relax and have a good time.

safiih pl. *sufahaaʔ* **1.** foolish, silly, stupid. **2.** intemperate, unrestrained. **3.** shameless.

safaaha **1.** silliness, foolishness, stupidity. **2.** unrestrained conduct, intemperance. **3.** shamelessness, immodesty.

s-q-r

saqar hell, hell-fire. *ˀila saqar!* to hell with him! *yiqbal ma-yiqbal, ˀila saqar.* Whether he agrees or doesn't agree, to hell with him.

s-q-ṭ

s-q-ṭ see *ṣ-q-ṭ*.

s-q-y

siqa (i saqi) = *siga,* which see under *s-g-y*.

saaqa to put water in, to add water to. *l-gahwa θixiina. saaqiiha.* The coffee is thick. Add water to it.

stiqa to draw, derive, obtain. *yistiqi l-ˀaxbaar min maṣaadirha.* He obtains the news from its sources.

saqqa pl. *saqqaaya* water carrier, man who brings water from a river or village well to the houses. || *bint is-saqqa* ladybug, lady beetle, ladybird.

saaqi pl. *suqaat* waiter in a coffee shop.

stisqaaˀ edema, dropsy.

s-q-q

sqaaq pl. *-aat* alley.

sqaaqi pl. *-iyya* **1.** street urchin. **2.** homosexual.

sqaaqiyya pl. *-aat* streetwalker, slut.

s-g-ṭ

siggaaṭa pl. *-aat* (door)bolt.

see also *ṣ-g-ṭ*.

s-g-f

sigaf (u saguf) **1.** to roast (fish) over an open fire. *raḉ-nisguf simač il-yoom.* We're going to roast some fish over an open fire today. **2.** to roof, provide with a roof or ceiling. *sigaf il-ġurfa b-ṭaabuug w-ib-šeelmaan.* He built a roof over the room with bricks and girders.

saggaf to roof, provide with a roof or ceiling. *baačir raḉ-nibdi nsagguf il-beet.* Tomorrow we are going to begin to roof the house.

saguf pl. *sguuf* ceiling.

sagfiyya roofing material.

sigiifa, zgiifa pl. *-aat, siyaagif* **1.** a small hut made of tree branches. **2.** storeroom built on top of a house.

saggaaf pl. *-a* a man who is skilled at cooking fish over an open fire.

masguuf broiled in front of an open fire. *simač mazguuf* broiled fish.

s-g-m

sigam (u sagum) to bother, pester, keep after. *la-tisgum ˀummak. xalliiha tištuġuḷ.* Don't pester your mother. Let her work.

saggam to buy (something, after shopping around for it). *ˀuxuδ hal-miit diinaar w-saggum-lak fadd dukkaan iẓġayyir.* Take this hundred dinars and buy yourself a small shop.

tsaggam to cost, require in exchange. *beeš itsaggam ḉaleek hal-qaaṭ?* How much did that suit cost you?

sugmaan soot.

s-g-y

siga (i sagi) **1.** to water, provide water for. *waddi l-xeel liš-šaṭṭ w-izgiiha.* Take the horses to the river and water them. *l-ḉadiiqa yaabsa. laazim tizgiiha.* The garden's dry. You've got to water it. || *ṣadiiqi sigaani gahuuteen il-yoom.* My friend treated me to two coffees today. **2.** to irrigate. *han-nahar yizgi kull hal-manṭaqa.* This river irrigates all this area. **3.** to temper. *yistawrid fuulaaδ w-yizgii w-ysawwi minna sipringaat.* He imports steel and tempers it and makes springs from it. *l-sipring, ˀiδa ma-mazgi, yinkisir.* If a spring isn't tempered, it will break.

siga pl. *sigyaat* milkskin, hide bag for milk, yoghurt, etc.

saagya pl. *swaagi* irrigation canal, irrigation ditch.

see also *s-q-y*.

s-k-a-r-p-y-n

skaarpiin pl. *aat* women's high-heeled shoes, and also, a pair of high-heeled shoes.

s-k-t

sikat (u sukuut) **1.** to become silent, lapse into silence, shut up. *ˀuskut! ˀinta š-tifham bis-sayyaaraat?* Quiet! What do you know about cars? *ˀuskut lakk, tara ˀamawwtak!* Shut up, you, or I'll kill you. *ma-sikat illa lamma tbarṭal ib-xamsiin diinaar.* He wouldn't shut up until he was bribed with fifty dinars. **2.** to become quiet, quiet down, calm down, subside. *j-jaahil sikat baḉad-ma biča ˀakθar min rubuḉ saaḉa.* The child quieted down after crying more than a quarter of an hour. *lamma l-muḉallim dixal iṣ-ṣaff, kullma skatna.* When the teacher entered the class, we all quieted down. || *la-tiskut-la. ˀiδa δirabak, ˀuδurba.* Don't take it from him. If he hits you, hit him back. *ˀaani ma-askut-la ḉala had-dagga.* I won't forgive him for that dirty trick.

sakkat to silence, quiet, calm. *ˀinṭii diinaar w-sakkta.* Give him a dinar and silence him. *sakkat ij-jaahil b-išwayyat čukleet.* He quieted the child with a little bit of chocolate.

sakta silence, quiet. || *sakta qalbiyya* heart failure.

sukuut quiet, silence. *b-sukuut* quietly, silently, stealthily.

skuuti, pl. *-iyyiin, -iyya* **1.** taciturn, reticent person. **2.** secretive person.

¹s-k-r

sikar (*a sukur*) **1.** to get drunk, become intoxicated. *sikar w-gaam yxarbuṭ ib-ḉačya.* He got drunk and his speech became muddled. **2.** to drink (liquor). *ma-dzawwijata liˀan yiskar.* She didn't marry him because he drinks. *yoomiyya ysikruun ib-hal-baar.* They drink every day in this bar.

sakkar to intoxicate, make drunk. *l-biira ma-tsakkir miθl il-wiski.* Beer doesn't make you drunk the way whiskey does. *sakkiroo w-ˀaxδaw ifluusa.* They got him drunk and took his money.

sakra pl. *-aat* drinking spree, instance of drunkenness.

sakraan pl. *skaara* **1.** drunk, intoxicated. || *sakraan ṭiina* dead drunk. **2.** a drunk, an inebriated person.

sikkiir pl. *-iin* drunkard, habitual drinker.

²s-k-r

*sukkari** sugar, sugary. *maraḍ il-bool is-sukkari* diabetes.

³s-k-r

sukri small grains of baked clay used as an abrasive for cleaning.

s-k-r-t-y-r

sikirteer pl. *-iyya* male secretary.

sikirteera pl. *-aat* female secretary.

s-k-k

sakk (*i sakk*) to mint, coin. *ween ysikkuun ifluusna?* Where do they mint our money?

sikka pl. *sikak* **1.** die, mold. || *ˀinta ġeer sikka sikktak.* I can't figure you out (lit., you're different from your mold). **2.** coined money, coin. *s-sikka maalathum ma-tsawwi sikkatna.* Their coins aren't equal to our coins. **3.** railroad, railroad track. *čaan naayin ḉas-sikka w-siḉaga l-qiṭaar.* He was sleeping on the tracks and the train ran over him. *l-muṭar ġarrag sikkat baġdaad il-baṣra.* The rain flooded the Baghdad-Basra railroad line.

s-k-l-l

sikalla pl. *-aat* scaffold.

skalla pl. *-aat* lumber yard, open storage and marketing area.

s-k-m-l-y

skamli pl. *-iyyaat* chair.

¹s-k-n

sikan (*u sukuun*) **1.** to become still, tranquil, calm, to abate, subside. *baḉad nuṣṣ saaḉa, sikan il-wujaḉ.* After half an hour, the pain subsided. **2.** (*u sukun, sukna*) to reside, dwell, live. *ṣaar-li ˀaskun ib-hal-beet santeen.* I've been living in this house two years. *ˀabuu yiskun ib-baġdaad.* His father resides in Baghdad.

sakkan **1.** to calm, soothe, alleviate. *had-duwa ysakkin il-wujaḉ.* This medicine will alleviate the pain. **2.** to settle, lodge, provide living quarters for. *š-šarika sakkinat ḉummaalha b-ibyuut qariiba minha.* The company settled its workers in houses close to it.

nsikan to be inhabited. *hal-beet ma-yinsikin bii.* This house can't be lived in.

maskan pl. *masaakin* residence, home.

ˀiskaan **1.** settling, settlement. *mašruuḉ ˀiskaan il-ḉašaayir* the project for settling the tribes. **2.** housing, allocation of living quarters. *wizaart il-iskaan* Ministry of Housing.

saakin **1.** tranquil, calm, motionless, still. *l-baḉar il-yoom saakin.* The sea is calm today. || *la-tḉarrik saakin.* Let sleeping dogs lie. **2.** quiet, phlegmatic. *ˀaxuuk fadd waaḉid saakin. yiḉči kulliš qaliil.* Your brother is a quiet one. He talks very little. **3.** unvowelled (of a medial consonant). *ḉaruf saakin* an unvowelled medial consonant. **4.** living, dwelling, residing. *ween saakin hassa?* Where're you living now? **5.** (pl. *sukkaan*) dweller, resident, inhabitant. *sukkaan hal-manṭaqa kullhum ḉarab.* The inhabitants of this district are all Arabs. **6.** (pl. only) population. *sukkaan il-ḉiraaq ˀakθar min sabiḉ malaayiin.* The population of Iraq is more than seven million.

sukkaan **1.** steering mechanism, steering. **2.** steering wheel. **3.** handle bars.

maskuun **1.** inhabited, populated. **2.** haunted. *hal-beet maskuun; bii ˀašbaaḉ.* This house is haunted; there are ghosts in it.

musakkin **1.** pl. *-iin* pacifier, calmer, soother. **2.** (pl. *-aat*) sedative, tranquilizer.

²s-k-n

sikkiin = *siččiin,* which see under *s-č-n.*

³s-k-n

sakin, sikin pl. *-iyya* "second," helper, assistant. *lamma s-saayiq tiḉab is-sikin saaq il-paas.* When the driver got tired the relief driver drove the bus.

s-k-n-j-b-y-l

skanjabiil ginger.

šarbat skanjabiil a non-carbonated soft drink of ginger, sugar and water, sometimes sold as a concentrated syrup.

s-k-n-d-r

skandar Alexander. *l-iskandar* Alexander the Great.

l-iskandariyya Alexandria.

s-l-b

silab (*i salib*) **1.** to rob, steal, plunder, loot. *yaahu l-iymurr, ysilbuu.* Whoever passes by, they rob him. *silbaw kull-ma ʕinda biṭ-ṭariiq.* They stole everything he had along the way. **2.** to bone, cut out the bone. *ʔariid išwayyat laḥam w-ykuun tislib-liyyaaha šgadd-ma tigdar.* I want a little meat and bone it out for me as much as you can.

sallab to rob, steal, plunder, loot. *latsaafir bil-leel tara l-ḥaraamiyya ysallibuuk.* Don't travel by night or the thieves will rob you.

salib **1.** robbing, looting, plundering, pillage. **2.** negation. *ʕalaamat is-salib* minus sign (math.).

*salbi** **1.** negative, minus. *ʔišaara salbiyya* minus sign. **2.** passive. *muqaawama salbiyya* passive resistance.

slaab pl. *-aat* **1.** clothing on a body at the time of death, and also, a derogatory term for any clothing. **2.** useless, worthless thing. *jaaboo-nna muʕallimiin kullhum islaabaat.* They brought some teachers for us that were all worthless.

sallaab pl. *-a* bandit, robber, thief.

ʔusluub pl. *ʔasaaliib* **1.** way, method, procedure. **2.** manner, mode, fashion. **3.** style (esp. of an author).

saalib negative, minus.

masluuba boned, boneless. *laḥma masluuba* a boneless piece of meat.

s-l-b-ḥ

salbuuḥ pl. *slaabiiḥ* worm.

s-l-b-w-y-a

silibooya (coll.) watercolor(s).

silibooyaaya pl. *-aat* un. n. of *silibooya.*

s-l-t

silat (*i salit*) to extract, pull out. *silat xeeṭ min ḥaašyat il-wuṣla w-raaf bii panṭaruuna.* He pulled a thread out of the edge of the cloth and darned his pants with it.

sallat intensive of *silat. la-tsallit ilixyuuṭ maal il-booyinbaaġ.* Don't pull the threads out of the tie.

msallit frayed. *ḥaašyat hač-čaffiyya msallita.* The edge of this handkerchief is frayed.

s-l-ḥ

silaḥ (*a saliḥ*) to drop, put aside. *yiðhar silaḥha lil-qaðiyya.* It seems that he has put the matter aside.

sallaḥ **1.** to arm, provide with weapons. *sallaḥhum w-dazzhum lil-maʕraka.* He armed them and sent them to the battlefield. **2.** to reinforce, strengthen. *laazim insalliḥ il-ʔasaasaat.* We've got to reinforce the foundation.

tsallaḥ to arm oneself. *tsallaḥ ib-musaddas w-xanjar w-raaḥ ʕaleehum.* He armed himself with a pistol and a dagger and went to see them.

nsilaḥ to be dropped, be put aside. *ybayyin masʔalat tarfiiʕi nsilḥat.* It seems that the question of my promotion was laid aside.

slaaḥ pl. *ʔasliḥa* weapon.

musallaḥ **1.** armored. *sayyaara musallaḥa* armored car. **2.** reinforced. *kankari musallaḥ* reinforced concrete.

s-l-s

salis smooth, fluent, easy to read (of a style of writing). *t-taqriir maala salis.* His report is written in a smooth style.

ʔaslas more or most fluent, smooth, etc.

s-l-s-l

silsila pl. *salaasil* **1.** chain (also fig.). *silsilat ijbaal* mountain chain. **2.** series.

tasalsul sequence, succession. *rattib ilkutub ḥasab tasalsul ʔarqaamha.* Stack the books in numerical order. *bit-tasalsul* successively, consecutively.

s-l-ʕ

silʕa pl. *silaʕ* commodity, commercial article.

s-l-f

sallaf to lend, loan, advance. *l-bang iṣṣinaaʕi ysallif ʔaṣḥaab maʕaamil ifluus.* The Industrial Bank lends money to factory owners. *hal-bang ysallif muwaððafiina l-ḥadd il-ʔalif diinaar.* This bank advances its employees up to one thousand dinars.

stilaf to borrow, get a loan, get an advance. *stilafit ʔalif diinaar imnil-bang il-ʕaqaari ḥatta ʔabni beet.* I borrowed a thousand dinars from the Real Estate Bank to build a house. *tigdar tistilif w-tištiri θ-θallaaja.* You can get an advance on your salary and buy the refrigerator.

silfa, sulfa pl. *silaf* loan, advance (of money).

salaf ancestors, forefathers. *naʕla ʕala*

salaf salfaak. ma-ġit-lak la-tsawwi hiiči? Damn you. Didn't I tell you not to do that? || *ˀiδa ma-yrajjiʕ-lak il-ifluus, ˀanʕal salfa salfaa.* If he doesn't return the money to you, I'll raise hell with him.

saalfa, saaluufa see under *s-w-l-f.*

s-l-g

silag (i salig) to boil, scald, to cook in boiling water. *silgat beeδ̣teen w-xallathum ib-jeeb ˀibinha.* She boiled two eggs and put them in her son's pocket. || *min riʕit lil-ˀimtiʕaan iš-šafawi l-muʕallim silagni bil-ˀasˀila.* When I went for the oral examination, the teacher gave me a real hard time.

salig boiling.

salga pl. *-aat* i. n. of *salig.*

silig a kind of chard.

sluugi pl. *-iyya* saluki, a breed of dog similar to the greyhound.

s-l-k

silak (u suluuk) 1. to behave, comport oneself. *ˀiδa tusluk suluuk zeen, tinjaʕ.* If you follow the rules of good behavior, you'll succeed. 2. to get along well, be on good terms. *ma-da-yisluk wiyya ˀabuu.* He's not getting along with his father.

sallak = *silak* 2. *yuʕruf išloon ysallik nafsa wiyya l-muwaδ̣δ̣afiin.* He knows how to get along among the employees.

silk pl. *ˀaslaak* 1. wire. 2. filament (of a light bulb). 3. rayon. 4. corps. *s-silk id-diiploomaasi* the diplomatic corps. *silk it-taʕliim* the teaching profession

*laa-silki** wireless, radio.

silka pl. *-aat* a lightweight woolen fabric worn in summer.

suluuk behavior, deportment, conduct, manners.

s-l-l

sall (i sall) 1. to draw, unsheath. *sall seefa w-ʕayya z-zaʕiim.* He drew his sword and saluted the brigadier. 2. to infect with tuberculosis, cause tuberculosis in. *hiiči manaax ysill iš-šaxuṣ.* This climate gives people tuberculosis. || *ˀibnak ysillni. laa yruuʕ lil-madrasa wala yištuġuḷ.* Your son gives me a pain. He doesn't go to school and he doesn't work.

nsall to catch tuberculosis, become consumptive. *nsall ib-šabaaba.* He got tuberculosis in his youth.

stall to draw, unsheath. *stall seefa w-bida yuδ̣rub biihum.* He drew his sword and began to strike them.

sill tuberculosis, consumption.

salla pl. *slaal* basket. *sallat il-muhmalaat* waste basket. *kurat is-salla* basketball.

silli, silla (coll.) thorn(s).

silliyya pl. *-aat* a thorn.

sillaaya pl. *-aat* 1. thorn. 2. point, nib (of a pen).

masalla pl. *-aat* obelisk.

masluul 1. drawn, unsheathed. *seef masluul* a drawn sword. 2. tubercular, infected with tuberculosis. 3. a person having tuberculosis.

s-l-m

silam (a salaam, salaama) 1. to be safe, unharmed, intact, secure. *bass nuʕbur il-ʕiduud, nislam.* Once we cross the border, we're safe. *ˀiδa triid tislam ʕala ruuʕak, la-timši wiyya hal-ˀašqiyaaˀ.* If you want to be safe, don't run around with this gangster. 2. to escape, get away. *silam imnil-xaṭar.* He escaped from the danger. 3. to pass, get by. *loo bass ˀaslam bil-ˀingiliizi baaqi d-diruus sahla.* If I only pass in English the rest of the courses are easy. *maʕʕad silam. kullna siqaṭna bil-ˀimtiʕaan.* No one made it. All of us failed the exam.

sallam 1. to protect from harm, keep safe, save, preserve. *ˀaḷḷa ysallmak!* God preserve you! (a reply to *šloonak?*). *ˀaḷḷa ysallmak, w-inta šloonak?* God keep you and how are you? *š-ysallma min δoola? kullhum ˀašqiyaaˀiyya.* What will save him from them? They're all gangsters. *ˀaḷḷa sallama; čaan baʕad išwayya yiġrag.* God saved him; he was about to drown. *ˀaḷḷa ysallima; kulliš xooš walad.* God bless him; he's a real good boy. 2. to turn over, hand over, surrender. *sallamit jamiiʕ il-ġaraaδ̣ lil-muwaδ̣δ̣af ij-jidiid.* I turned all the things over to the new employee. *sallam ˀamra l-aḷḷa.* He surrendered his fate to God. *sallam nafsa biš-šurṭa.* He surrendered himself to the police. 3. to deliver to, hand over to, give to. *sallama l-maktuub b-iida.* He delivered the letter to him personally. *sallimni miftaaʕ il-beet.* Give me the house key. *l-baarʕa sallamni xamsiin dinaar.* Yesterday he gave me fifty dinars. 4. to surrender, lay down one's arms. *jiyuuš il-ʕadu kullha sallimat.* All of the enemy forces surrendered. 5. /with *ʕala*/ to greet, salute. *marr w-ma-sallam ʕalayya.* He passed by and didn't say hello to me. *min-itšuufa, sallim-li ʕalee.* When you see him, give him my regards. *nsallim ʕaleekum. la-tinsuun tijuun ʕidna sbuuʕ ij-jaay.* Goodbye. Don't forget to come visit us next week.

ʔaslam to become a Moslem, embrace Islam. *ʔaslam w-ḥajj makka.* He became a Moslem and made a pilgrimage to Mecca.

tsaalam to greet each other, exchange greetings. *tsaalamit wiyyaa l-baarḥa bil-ḥafla.* I exchanged greetings with him yesterday at the party.

stilam **1.** to take delivery of, to receive, obtain, get. *stilamit maktuub il-yoom?* Did you receive a letter today? *raḥ-ʔastilim is-sayyaara baačir.* I will take delivery on the car tomorrow. **2.** to take over, take possession of. *stilam ʔidaarat il-maʕmal.* He took over management of the factory. *l-mulaaḥiḍ ij-jidiid stilam minni.* The new supervisor took over from me.

staslam **1.** to submit, yield, give oneself over, succumb. *ḍall yiḥči wiyyaaha mudda ʔila ʔan staslimat-la.* He kept talking to her for some time, until she gave in to him. **2.** to convert to Islam, become a Moslem. *θneen yahuud staslimaw.* Two Jews became Moslems.

silim peace.

*silmi** **1.** peaceful. *muḍaahara silmiyya* a peaceful demonstration. **2.** pacifist.

sullam pl. *salaalim* scale (mus.).

salaam **1.** soundness, well-being. *b-salaamat raasak, ma-niḥtaj šii.* As long as you're living, we don't need a thing. **2.** peace, peacefulness. *haš-šaʕab muḥibb lis-salaam.* These are peace-loving people. *salaam ʔalla ʕalee; šloon sabiʕ!* God's peace on him; how brave he is! **3.** security, safety. || *s-salaamu ʕaleekum!* Peace be with you (a standard greeting). **4.** (pl. *-aat*) salute. *min ymurr iḍ-ḍaabuṭ, ʔuxuδ-la salaam.* When the officer passes by, give him a salute. **5.** national anthem. *s-salaam ij-jamhuuri* the national anthem of the republic.

¶ *yaa salaam!* a standard exclamation of amazement, surprise, dismay, grief, pity, etc. *yaa salaam, šloon jamaal!* My goodness, what beauty! *was-salaam* that's all, that's final. *ma-ʔaqbal itruuḥ was-salaam.* I don't want you to go and that's final.

salaama **1.** unimpaired state, flawlessness. *laazim nitʔakkid min salaamat il-ġanam imnil-ʔamraaḍ gabuḷ-ma nistawridha.* We must make sure the sheep are free of disease before we import them. *salaamat iδ-δawq* good taste. *salaamat in-niyya* good faith, sincerity, guilelessness. *gaalha b-salaamat niyya.* He said it in good faith. **2.** well-being, welfare. || *salaamtak.* (in reply to a concerned question, roughly:) Thanks for asking. *salaamtak. ma-aku šii.* Thank you, I'm all right. **3.** safety, security. *salaamt il-ʕiraaq titwaqqaf ʕala quwwat jeeša.* The safety of the Iraq depends on the strength of its army. *l-ḥamdilla ʕas-salaama!* Thank goodness you're all right! (said to a returning traveler). *maʕa s-salaama.* Goodbye (a standard farewell).

salaamaat! Greetings! *salaamaat, salaamaat! buqa fikirna ʕindak.* Hello there! We've been thinking about you. || *ʔila hassa salaamaat, laakin baʕad ʕindi mtiḥaaneen.* I'm okay till now, but I've still got two exams.

saliim **1.** safe, secure. **2.** unimpaired, undamaged, unhurt, sound, intact. || *ṣaaġ saliim* safe and sound, in perfect condition. *ṭilaʕ imnil-markab ṣaaġ saliim.* He got off the boat safe and sound. *stilamt ir-raadyo ṣaaġ saliim.* I received the radio in perfect condition. **3.** faultless, flawless. *δooqa saliim.* He has good taste. || *qalba saliim.* He is good-natured. *ṣadiiqi saliim in-niyya.* My friend is sincere.

ʔaslam more or most safe, sound, intact, etc.

ʔislaam **1.** the religion of Islam, the Moslem religion. **2.** followers of Islam, Moslems.

*ʔislaami** Islamic, Moslem. *d-diin il-ʔislaami* The Moslem Religion. *l-markaz il-ʔislaami* The Islamic Center.

saalim **1.** safe, secure. **2.** free. *saalim imnil-amraaḍ il-muʕdiya.* He's free from contagious diseases. **3.** unblemished, flawless, undamaged, intact.

musaalim peaceable, peaceful, peace-loving. *šaʕab musaalim* a peace-loving people.

muslim pl. *-iin* Moslem.

s-l-n-d-r

silindar pl. *-aat* cylinder (of a motor).

[1]*s-l-y*

salla to distract, divert, amuse, entertain. *ma-yuʕruf ʔaḥḥad ihnaa. hamm zeen ʕinda talafizyoon ysallii.* He doesn't know anyone here. It's good that he has a television to amuse him.

tsalla to derive amusement, entertainment, to amuse oneself. *ma-daam ma-ʕindak šuġuḷ, leeš-ma titʕallam fadd liʕba titsalla biiha?* Since you don't have work, why don't you learn some game to keep you amused?

tasliya pl. *-aat* amusement, distraction, diversion, entertainment, pastime.

²*s-l-y*

sillaaya, silliyya, see under *s-l-l.*

s-m-a-w-r

samaawar pl. *-aat* samovar.

s-m-b

sumba pl. *-aat* chisel.

s-m-b-a-d

sumbaada: waraq sumbaada, kaaġad sumbaada sandpaper.

¹*s-m-b-l*

sumbeela: sumbeelt is-sumbeela leap frog.

²*s-m-b-l*

sumbula = *sunbula,* which see under *s-n-b-l.*

s-m-č

simač (coll.) fish. || *da-yiʕči ʕan is-simač bil-mayy.* He's counting his chickens before they hatch.

simča pl. *-aat* a fish.

sammaač pl. *-a* fishmonger.

s-m-ḥ

simaḥ (*a samaaḥ*) to permit, allow, grant permission. *ʔiδa ma-ʕindak biṭaaqa, ma-yismaḥuu-lak tudxul.* If you don't have a ticket, they won't allow you to enter. *minu simaḥ-lak tiṭlaʕ?* Who let you go out? *laa samaḥ aḷḷaa!* God forbid! *ʔismaḥ-li daqiiqa. hassa ʔagul-lak.* Excuse me a minute. I'll tell you right away. *ʔismaḥ-li ʔašraḥ-lak il-mawδuuʕ.* Permit me to explain the matter to you.

saamaḥ to be indulgent, tolerant, generous. *štiri min hal-baggaal. ysaamḥak bis-siʕir ihwaaya.* Buy from that grocer. He gives you very good prices. *saamaḥni diinaar bis-siʕir.* He went down a dinar for me on the price. **2.** to forgive. *raḥ-asaamḥak hal-marra.* I'll forgive you this time.

tsaamaḥ to be tolerant, forbearing, to show gentleness. *tsaamaḥ wiyyaa. haay ʔawwal marra yiġlaṭ.* Be tolerant with him. This is the first time he's done wrong. *yitsaamaḥ ihwaaya b-muʕaamalta lil-muwaδδafiin.* He is very tolerant in his dealings with the employees.

samiḥ generous, magnanimous, liberal. *gaṣṣaabna samiḥ bis-siʕir.* Our butcher is generous about prices.

samaaḥa: samaaḥat il- . . . His Eminence, the . . . (title usually used for religious dignitaries).

masmuuḥ permitted, permissible. *ma-masmuuḥ tisbaḥuun ihnaa.* You're not permitted to swim here.

mitsaamiḥ tolerant, indulgent.

s-m-d

sammad to fertilize, spread manure on. *raḥ-asammid il-ḥadiiqa bir-rabiiʕ.* I'm going to fertilize the garden in the spring.

samaad pl. *ʔasmida* **1.** dung, manure. **2.** fertilizer. *samaad kiimyaawi* chemical fertilizer.

s-m-r

smarr to turn brown. *giʕdat biš-šamis ḥatta yismarr jilidha.* She sat in the sun so her skin would tan.

samaar brownness, brown coloration.

ʔasmar fem. *samra* pl. *sumur* **1.** brown, brown-skinned. *marta šaqra laakin binta samra.* His wife is blonde but his daughter is brunette.

musaamara pl. *-aat* program of social entertainment, show.

s-m-s-m

simsim sesame.

s-m-ṭ

sumaṭ = *ṣumaṭ,* which see under *ṣ-m-ṭ.*

s-m-ʕ

simaʕ (*a samiʕ*) **1.** to hear. *simaʕni ʔaḥči bin-noom.* He heard me talking in my sleep. *simaʕt il-ʔaxbaar?* Did you hear the news? *ma-smaʕit minhum ʔila hassa?* Didn't you hear from them yet? **2.** to listen, pay attention, take heed. *ma-yismaʕ kalaam ʔaḥad.* He won't listen to anybody. *ʔibnak yismaʕ kalaam.* Your son minds what he's told. *δallat tingur ib-raas rajilha ḥatta simaʕ kalaamha.* She kept nagging her husband until he did what she wanted. *ʔismaʕ! ma-ariidak tiji hnaa!* Listen! I don't want you to come here!

sammaʕ to make hear, cause to hear. *ḥičaaha b-ṣooṭ ʕaali ḥatta yisammiʕni.* He said it in a loud voice in order to make me hear him. *da-ysammiʕni ḥači ʕas-sayyaara. ybayyin ma-raaδi ʕanha.* He's hinting about the car. It seems he's dissatisfied with it.

tsammaʕ to listen in, eavesdrop. *yiftarr ʕala kull iš-šuʕab yitsammaʕ ʔaxbaar.* He goes around to all the sections listening in on what is new.

nsimaʕ to be heard. *ʔiḥči ḥeel. ḥissak ma-da-yinsimiʕ.* Speak louder. Your voice can't be heard.

stimaʕ to listen closely, lend one's ear, give ear. *raḥ-nistimiʕ il-xiṭaaba w-nuʕruf iš-da-yṣiir.* We're going to listen closely to his speech and find out what is going on.

samiɛ hearing, sense of hearing. *samɛa θigiil.* He's hard of hearing.

sumɛa reputation, standing, name. *sumuɛta radiiʔ.* His reputation is bad.

samaaɛiyyaat acoustics.

simmaaɛa pl. *-aat* **1.** earphone, earphones, headset. **2.** hearing aid. **3.** (telephone) receiver. **4.** stethoscope.

masmuuɛ audible, perceptible. || *čilimta masmuuɛa. š-ma-yriid yiṣiir.* His word is law. Whatever he wants is done.

mustamiɛ pl. *-iin* **1.** hearer, listener. **2.** auditor (in a class).

s-m-g

summaag sumac (used as seasoning for food).

[1]*s-m-m*

ʔisim, etc., see under *s-m-y.*

[2]*s-m-m*

samm (*i samm*) to poison. *sammoo bis-sijin w-maat.* They poisoned him in prison and he died.

sammam to poison, put poison in. *xalli nsammim il-xubuz ḥatta j-jireediyya yaakluu w-iymuutuun.* Let's poison the bread so the mice will eat it and die.

tsammam to be poisoned. *ʔakal išwayya jibin w-itsammam.* He ate a little cheese and was poisoned.

simm, samm pl. *sumuum* **1.** poison, toxin. **2.** venom.

sumuum: hawa sumuum a hot, dry wind off the desert.

saamm **1.** poisonous, toxic. **2.** venomous.

masmuum poisoned, containing poison, poisonous. *diir baalak minna. huwwa fadd waaḥid masmuum.* Watch out for him. He's poison.

s-m-n

siman (*a simin*) to become fat, plump, stout, corpulent, obese, to gain weight. *šgadd-ma ʔaakul, ma-da-asman.* No matter how much I eat, I don't gain weight.

samman to fatten, make fat. *da-yinṭi d-dijaaj maala fadd nooɛ imnil-akil ysammina.* He's giving his chickens some kind of food to make them fat.

simin **1.** fatness, corpulence, fleshiness. **2.** obesity. **3.** tallow, fat.

simna **1.** fatness, corpulence, fleshiness. **2.** obesity.

simiin **1.** fat, stout, corpulent, plump. *ʔija ɛaleek fadd waaḥid simiin w-iqṣayyir.* A short, fat guy came to see you. **2.** obese. **3.** fatty, rich. *ʔakil simiin* rich food.

samnaan sleek, healthy. *ybaayin ɛaleek samnaah min hawa labnaan.* You look sleek from the Lebanese climate. *samnaan min kuθrat il-ʔakil wir-raaḥa.* You've gained weight from eating a lot and doing nothing.

ʔasman more or most corpulent, etc.

[1]*s-m-w*

sima pl. *-aat* visa.

[2]*s-m-w*

sima pl. *samaawaat* sky. || *l-xaaṭir is-samaawaat, juuz!* For Heavens' sakes, cut it out!

*samaawi** **1.** heavenly, celestial. **2.** sky-blue, azure. *nafnuuf samaawi* a sky-blue dress.

simaaya pl. *-aat* skylight, roof window.

sumuw: ṣaaḥib is-sumuw il-malaki. His Royal Highness (title of a prince).

*saami** lofty, exalted, eminent, sublime, august. *ʔaškur ɛawaaṭfak is-saamiya.* I thank you for your noble sentiments.

s-m-y

samma **1.** to name, designate, call. *š-itsammi haš-šii?* What do you call this thing? **2.** to call, name, give a name to. *samma ʔibna b-isim ʔabuu.* He gave his son his father's name. **3.** to say "*b-ism illaah ir-raḥmaan ir-raḥiim.*" *sammi gabuḷ-ma tinzil lis-sirdaab.* Mention God's name before you go down into the basement. *sammi gabuḷ-ma taakul.* Say grace before you eat.

tsamma to be named, called. *tsamma b-isim jidda.* He is named after his grandfather. *š-tiɛtiqid haaδa laazim yitsamma?* What do you think this should be called?

sami namesake. *ʔaani samiyyak.* I have the same name as you.

ʔisim pl. *ʔasaami, ʔasmaaʔ* **1.** name. *haaδa rijjaal bil-ʔisim bass.* He's a man in name only. *b-ism illaah* in the name of God. *gabuḷ-ma taakul, guul b-ism illaah.* Before you eat, say "In the name of God." *ʔism aḷḷa ɛalee. šloon xooš walad!* God bless him. What a good boy he is! || *baɛadna b-ʔism illaah.* We have just begun. We are barely under way. *ṭ-ṭibiix ma-bii ḥatta wala ʔisim miliḥ.* There isn't even a trace of salt in the rice. **2.** reputation, standing, prestige. *ʔila ʔisim čibiir bis-suug.* He has a big reputation in the market. **3.** (gram.) noun.

*ʔismi** **1.** in name only, nominal. *l-maal il-ʔismi liš-šarika* the nominal capital of the company. **2.** nominal (gram.).

s-n-a

sana, see under *s-n-w.*

s-n-b-l
sunbula pl. *sanaabil* spike, ear (of grain).

s-n-t-m-t-r
santimitir pl. *-aat* centimeter.

s-n-t-y-m
santiim pl. *-aat* centimeter.

s-n-j-b
sinjaab pl. *snaajiib* squirrel.

s-n-ḥ
sinaḥ (*a*) to present itself, offer itself. *ʔiδa tisnaḥ-li l-furṣa, ʔazuurak.* If the opportunity presents itself to me. I'll visit you.

¹s-n-d
sinad (*i sanid*) to prop up, support, provide support for. *ʔisnid is-sabbuura b-hal-ʕamuud.* Prop up the blackboard with this pole. *da-yiḥči b-nifas li-ʔan ʔaku waaḥid ysinda.* He speaks boldly because there's somebody backing him up.

saanad to support, back, assist, help. *saanadhum ib-ḥamlathum il-intixaabiyya.* He supported them in their election campaign.

ʔasnad /with *l-*/ **1.** to entrust to, vest in. *ʔasnidaw ʔila manṣib naaʔib waziir.* They entrusted him with the position of deputy minister. **2.** to incriminate, charge to. *ʔasnidaw it-tuhma ʔila.* They charged the guilt to him.

stinad **1.** to rest one's weight, support one's weight. *ma-agdar ʔaktib ʔiδa ma-astinid ʕala fadd šii ma-yitḥarrak.* I can't write if I don't support myself on something that won't move. **2.** to be supported, based, founded. *hal-maqaal yistinid ʕala iḥṣaaʔaat mawθuuq biiha.* This article is based on trustworthy statistics. **3.** /with *ʕala*/ to use as a basis, rest one's case on, have as evidence. *laazim tistinid ʕala fadd šii gabul-ma ttihma.* You must have something for a basis before you accuse him.

sanad pl. *-aat* **1.** something which can be relied upon, support, backing. **2.** document, deed, legal instrument. **3.** debenture, promissory note. *sanadaat il-qarδ* government bonds.

masnad pl. *masaanid* **1.** support, prop, stay. **2.** back, armrest (of a chair).

²s-n-d
s-sind Sind, a province of West Pakistan. || *banaat s-sind wil-hind.* swallows(?).

sindi (coll.) grapefruit(s).

sindiyya pl. *-aat* grapefruit.

s-n-d-a-n
sindaan pl. *sinaadiin* anvil.

sindaana pl. *-aat, sinaadiin* flower pot.

s-n-s-l
sinisla pl. *snaasil* **1.** chain. **2.** stuffed eggplant.

s-n-ṭ
sinaṭ = *ṣinaṭ*, which see under *ṣ-n-ṭ*.

s-n-g-y
sungi pl. *-iyyaat, snaagi* bayonet.

s-n-g-y-n
sangiin strong, dark. *sawwi č-čaay maali sangiin.* Make my tea strong.

s-n-k
sinak club (suit in cards).

s-n-m
sanaam pl. *-aat* hump (of a camel).

s-l-n-g
sling pl. *-aat* **1.** crane. **2.** sling hoist. **3.** block-and-tackle.

s-n-n
sann (*i sann*) **1.** to sharpen, whet, hone. *da-ysinn il-xanjar.* He is sharpening the dagger. **2.** to enact, establish, pass. *ʔaku ḥtimaal ysinnuun qaanuun yimnaʕuun bii l-uqmaar.* They probably will pass a law prohibiting gambling.

sinn pl. *ʔasnaan* **1.** tooth. *ṭabiib il-ʔasnaan* dentist. **2.** cog, tooth (of a gear wheel). **3.** bedrock. **4.** age. *ma-qibloo bij-jundiyya l-ṣuġur sinna.* They didn't accept him in the army because he was underage.

sunna customary practice, usage. *sunnat in-nabi* the actions and sayings of Mohammed, later established as legally binding.

sinni pl. *sinna* **1.** Sunni, Sunnite, belonging to the orthodox sect of Islam. **2.** a Sunni, a Sunnite.

masann pl. *-aat* whetstone, grindstone.

msannan toothed, notched, jagged.

musinn old, aged, advanced in years. *ʔabuuha rijjaal musinn w-ma-adri ʔayy saaʕa ymuut.* Her father is an old man and he's likely to die at any time.

s-n-w
sana pl. *siniin* year. *sana hijriyya* year of the Moslem calendar, A.H. *sana miilaadiyya* year of the Christian calendar, A.D.

*sanawi** yearly, annual. *waarid sanawi* yearly income.

sanawiyyan annually, each year, per year.

s-h-r
sihar (*a sahar*) to stay awake, go without sleep, stay up at night. *raḥ-anaam hassa ḥatta ʔagdar ʔashar bil-leel.* I'm going to sleep now so I can stay awake tonight. *siharna l-baarḥa lis-saaʕa θlaaθa.* We stayed up last night until three o'clock.

ʕyuuna tilfat min gadd-ma yishar. His eyes were ruined from his staying awake so much.

saahar = *sihar.* *ʔayyaam il-imtiḥaan ʔakθar iṭ-ṭullaab ysaahruun.* Most of the students stay up late during exam time.

sahra pl. *-aat* soiree, evening gathering.

sahraan sleepless.

s-h-l

sihal (*a suhuula*) 1. to become easy, facile, convenient. *min ištiġal wiyyaana, sihlat il-masʔala.* When he worked with us, the problem became easier. 2. (*a ʔishaal*) to purge, relieve of constipation. *štireet duwa mniṣ-ṣaydaliyya yishil il-baṭin.* I bought some medicine from the pharmacy which purges the bowels. 3. (*a sahil*) to move, be relieved, become loose. *sihlat baṭna marrteen il-yoom.* He had two bowel movements today.

sahhal 1. to make easier, to ease, facilitate. *l-muʕallim sahhal il-ʔasʔila hal-marra.* The teacher made the questions easy this time. *hal-makiina tsahhil iš-šuġuḷ ihwaaya.* This machine makes the work a great deal easier. 2. to give a laxative. *ṣaar yoomeen baṭn il-walad ma-ṭilʕat. laazim insahhla.* The boy has been constipated two days. We must give him a laxative.

tsaahal to be indulgent, forbearing, lenient, tolerant, obliging. *l-muʕallim da-yitsaahil wiyyaana.* The teacher is being lenient with us. *tsaahlaw wiyyaaya w-baaʕoo-li s-sayyaara bid-deen.* They were obliging to me and sold me the car on credit.

stashal to consider easy, to deem easy. *la-tistashil il-qaðiyya. raḥ-tiṭlaʕ biiha taʕqiidaat.* Don't consider the matter easy. There will be some complications to it.

sahil easy, facile, convenient. *sahla! ʔay nooʕ imnij-jigaayir triiduun?* Sure, that's easy! What kind of cigarettes do you want?

sahal pl. *suhuul* plain, level ground.

suhuula easiness, facility, convenience. *ma-aku šii b-suhuulat haš-šuġuḷ.* There is nothing as easy as this work. *tʕallam is-siyaaqa b-suhuula.* He learned to drive easily.

ʔashal more or most facile, convenient.

ʔishaal diarrhea.

mushil pl. *-aat* purgative, laxative.

s-h-m

saaham to have a share, to participate, share, take part. *laazim il-kull ysaahmuun b-jamʕ it-tabarruʕaat.* All must participate in collecting donations. *huwwa saaham ib-nuṣṣ raasmaal iš-šarika.* He contributed half the capital of the company.

saham pl. *ʔashum* 1. share, portion, lot. 2. share (of stock). 3. (pl. *sihaam*) arrow. 4. dart.

musaahim pl. *-iin* shareholder, stockholder.

s-h-w

siha (*a sahu*) 1. to be forgetful, neglectful, inattentive. *ma-adri šloon siheet w-ma-xaabarta.* I don't know how I forgot and didn't call him. 2. /with *ʕan*/ to forget, neglect, overlook. *j-jaahil da-yilʕab. la-tisha ʕanna.* The kid is playing. Don't forget about him. *ma-yisha ʕan ʔay šii b-šuġḷa.* He doesn't neglect anything about his work.

sahha to cause to forget. *ðall yiḥči w-sahhaani ʕan il-akil il-ʕan-naar.* He kept talking and made me forget the food that was on the fire.

sahu 1. inattentiveness, inattention, absent-mindedness. 2. negligence, neglectfulness, forgetfulness. 3. mistake, oversight.

sahwan 1. inattentively, absent-mindedly, negligently. 2. inadvertently, by mistake. *ṭubaʕt il-maktuub ʕala waraq xafiif sahwan.* I typed the letter on thin paper by mistake.

s-w-ʔ

saaʔ = *ʔasaaʔ* which see.

ʔasaaʔ to do evil, do harm. *š-ma tsawwii-la zeen, laazim ysiiʔ-lak.* Whatever good you do for him, he always has to do you dirty. || *ʔasaaʔ fahmi.* He misunderstood me. *ʔasaaʔ ið-ðann biyya.* He thought badly of me. *la-tsiiʔ ið-ðann ib-kull waaḥid ma-yittifiq wiyyaak.* Don't have a low opinion of everyone who doesn't agree with you. *š-šurṭa ʔasaaʔat muʕaamalta bis-sijin.* The police mistreated him in prison.

staaʔ to be or become offended, annoyed, disgusted, indignant, displeased. *huwwa staaaʔ min hal-waðiʕ.* He got disgusted with that situation.

suuʔ evil, ill. *suuʔ il-ḥaðð* bad luck, misfortune. *l-suuʔ il-ḥaðð* unfortunately. *suuʔ niyya* evil intent, malice. *b-suuʔ in-niyya* with evil intent, maliciously. *suuʔ il-fahim* misunderstanding. *suuʔ haðum.* indigestion.

sayyiʔ bad, evil, ill. *sayyiʔ il-ḥaðð* unlucky, unfortunate. *sayyiʔ is-sumʕa* of bad reputation. *sayyiʔ iṭ-ṭabuɛ* 1. ill-tempered. 2. ill-mannered. *taġδiya sayyiʔa* malnutrition, poor nourishment.

sayyiʔa pl. *-aat* misdeed, bad deed.

ʔaswaʔ worse, worst.

s-w-a-r

swaar pl. *-aat* bracelet.

s-w-a-r-y

swaari pl. *-iyya* horseman, mounted patrolman.

s-w-p-y-r

suupeer pl. *-aat* (mil.) trench, breastwork.

s-w-t-y-a-n

suutyaan pl. *-aat* brassiere.

s-w-ɛ

saaɛa pl. *-aat* 1. open square, courtyard. 2. open space, park, field. *saaɛat rami* firing range. *saaɛat tanis* tennis court. *saaɛat madrasa* school yard. *ʔalɛaab is-saaɛa* track and field sports.

s-w-d

sawwad to blacken, make black, darken. *d-duxxaan sawwad čaɛb ij-jidir.* The smoke blackened the bottom of the pot. || *sawwad wujih* to show up, expose, make a fool of, shame, discredit, disgrace, dishonor. *sawwad wičči b-hal-iɛčaaya.* He made a fool of me with that remark. *sawwad ʔaḷḷaa wiččak ɛala had-dagga.* May God shame you for this deed.

swadd to be or become black, dark. *l-fuδδa tiswadd bil-ɛajal.* Silver turns dark quickly. || *swadd wičča.* He was disgraced, etc. *swadd wičča; kullhum ɛirfoo čaδδaab.* He's discredited; everyone knows he is a liar.

sawaad 1. blackness, darkness. 2. black clothing, mourning, crepe.

ʔaswad fem. *sooda* pl. *suud* black, dark. *ɛama ʔaswad* total blindness. || *ɛama ʔaswad! muu kisarit rijli!* May you be struck blind! You've just about broken my leg!

s-suudaan the Sudan.

*suudaani** 1. Sudanese. 2. a Sudanese.

miswadda pl. *-aat* 1. rough draft (of a document). 2. galley proof (printing).

s-w-d-n

soodan to make crazy, drive insane. *soodanni ɛaṭ-ṭalab.* He drove me crazy about the request.

tsoodan to be made crazy, insane, to go mad. *nṣaab ib-maraδ ɛaṣabi w-fujʔatan itsoodan.* He got a nervous disease and suddenly went crazy.

swaadiin 1. frenzied madness, insanity. 2. insane behavior.

¹s-w-r

sawwar to enclose, fence in, build a wall or fence around. *laazim itsawwir il-ɛadiiqa ɛatta ma-txušš-ʔilha č-čilaab.* You should fence in the garden so the dogs won't get into it.

suur pl. *ʔaswaar* 1. wall. 2. fence. || *j-jeeš suur il-waṭan.* The army is the bastion of the nation.

²s-w-r

swaar see under *s-w-a-r.*

³s-w-r

swaari see under *s-w-a-r-y.*

s-w-r-b

soorab to see things. *ɛeenak da-tsoorib.* Your eyes are deceiving you. You're seeing things.

s-w-r-y

suurya Syria.

*suuri** 1. Syrian. 2. a Syrian.

s-w-s

sawwas to rot, decay, cause to decay (esp. the teeth). *č-čukleet ysawwis il-isnuun.* Chocolate decays teeth. *sinnak msawwis; laazim ʔašlaɛa.* Your tooth is decayed; I'll have to extract it.

tsawwas pass. of *sawwas. ʔiδa taakul ɛilw ihwaaya, snuunak titsawwas.* If you eat sweets a lot, your teeth will decay.

suus: ɛirg is-suus licorice.

s-w-s-n

sawsan lily of the valley (bot.).

s-w-f

saaf (*u soof*) to become worn, worn down, worn out. *l-burġi saaf. laazim nistaɛmil ġeera.* The screw is worn. We should use another one. *ɛiyuunak saafat min-il-iqraaya.* Your eyes are worn out from reading.

sawwaf to wear, wear down, wear out. *sawwaft il-iklač min gadd-ma tbaddil.* You wore out the clutch from shifting so much.

saaf pl. *suuf* 1. row, file, rank. 2. row, course, layer (as of bricks).

masaafa pl. *-aat* 1. distance, stretch, interval. 2. interval, period (of time).

s-w-q

saaq (*u siyaaqa*) 1. to drive, operate (a vehicle). *tuɛruf itsuuq loori?* Can you drive a truck? 2. to draft, conscript. *saaqoo lij-jundiyya.* They drafted him into the army. 3. to force to go. *saaqoo lil-muɛaakama.* They brought him to trial.

saaq pl. *siiqaan* 1. shank. 2. leg.

saayiq pl. *suwwaaq* 1. driver. 2. chauffeur.

s-w-g

saag (*u soog*) **1.** to drive, herd (animals). *suug iz-zumaaḷ lil-bistaan.* Drive the donkey out to the orchard. || *saagha b-tibinha.* He said it without thinking. **2.** to hit, strike. *saaga b-čillaaq.* He gave him a kick. *saaga b-books waggaɛa.* He hit him and knocked him down. *saaga b-tafla b-wučča.* He spit in his face.

tsawwag to go shopping. *marti titsawwag yoomiyya.* My wife goes shopping every day.

suug pl. *swaag* **1.** marketplace, bazaar. **2.** market. *hal-biḏ̣aaɛa ma-ʔilha suug.* There's no market for these goods.

tiswaag shopping, going to the market. *ɛalee-man it-tiswaag il-yoom?* Whose turn is it to go to the market today?

miswaag **1.** shopping, buying things from the market. *l-miswaag ɛalayya l-yoom. š-tirduun ʔaštiri?* I do the shopping today. What do you want me to buy? **2.** things gotten in the market, supplies, groceries. *raɛ-nuṭbux min yijiib ʔabuuk il-miswaag.* We'll start cooking when your father brings the groceries.

s-w-k

sawwak to brush, scrub (the teeth) with a chewed twig. *ysawwik isnuuna baɛd iṣ-ṣalaa.* He brushes his teeth after prayer.

miswaak pl. *msaawiik* frayed twig used for cleaning the teeth.

s-w-l-f

soolaf to reminisce, to chat, carry on idle conversation, talk. *ḏ̣alleena nsoolif il-nuṣṣ il-leel.* We kept on chatting until midnight. *ʔii, soolif.* Yes, go ahead and tell me.

saaluufa pl. *swaaliif* tale, story, narrative.

saalfa pl. *swaalif* tale, story, narrative.

s-w-m

saam (*u soom*) to quote a price on, to set a price for. *hal-badla beeš saamha ɛaleek il-xayyaaṭ?* What price did the tailor quote you on this suit? *hal-bazzaaz ysuum ġaali.* That yard-goods dealer sets his prices high.

saawam to bargain, haggle with. *ma-aku daaɛi tsaawma. s-siɛir maɛduud.* There's no need to haggle with him. The price is fixed.

s-w-y

yiswa (no perfect form) to be worth, equivalent to, equal to. *hal-iktaab išgadd yiswa?* How much is this book worth? *l-qaḏ̣iyya ma-čaanat tiswa l-iɛraak.* The matter wasn't worth fighting about.

sawwa **1.** to do, to perform, execute, discharge, commit. *š-raɛ-itsawwi hal-leela?* What are you going to do tonight? *gul-li š-itsawwi biiha ɛatta ʔanṭiik-iyyaaha.* Tell me what you'll do with it and I'll give it to you. *sawwoo-la ɛama-liyya.* They performed an operation on him. *ʔiḏa tsawwi muxaalafa, yisɛabuun ʔijaaztak.* If you commit a violation, they'll withdraw your license. *ṭ-ṭullaab msaw-wiin muḏ̣aahara.* The students have staged a demonstration. *sawwa biyya nukta. gal-li ma-aku madrasa l-yoom.* He played a trick on me. He told me there wasn't any school today. *sawwaaha biyya. ʔaxaḏ ifluusi w-inhizam.* He tricked me. He took my money and fled. **2.** to make, to produce, manufacture, fabricate. *sawwi min hal-imqawwaaya ṣanduug.* Make a box out of this cardboard. *hal-maɛmal ysawwi qanaadir.* This factory manufactures shoes. *yaḷḷa ɛaad! sawweetha ṭlaaba.* Come on now! You've made it a complicated thing. *sawwa fitna w-xallaahum yitɛaarkuun.* He stirred up trouble and made them fight. *raɛ-ysawwuun ɛafla b-munaasabat najaaɛa.* They will have a party to celebrate his success. *l-mudiir sawwaani muraaqib ɛaṣ-ṣaff.* The principal made me monitor over the class. *la-tsawwi nafsak kulliš ma-tuɛruf.* Don't act as though you don't know at all.

saawa **1.** to equal, to be equal to, be equivalent to. *θneen w-iθneen ysaawi ʔarbaɛa.* Two plus two equals four. **2.** to level, make level, to smooth, smooth out. *ʔariid ʔasaawi hal-wuṣlat il-gaaɛ.* I want to level this piece of land. **3.** to settle, smooth over, put in order, make up (a dispute, etc.). *saawooha lil-qaḏ̣iyya b-saaɛ w-maɛɛad ɛiraf.* They settled the matter quickly and no one found out. **4.** /with *been*/ to treat alike, be impartial toward. *laazim itsaawi been il-muwaḏ̣ḏ̣afiin.* You've got to treat the employees all alike.

tsaawa **1.** to be equal, equivalent to each other, to come out equal. *r-rijjaal wil-mara tsaawaw ib-naḏ̣ar il-qaanuun.* Man and woman are equal in the eyes of the law. *l-majmuuɛeen tsaawaw.* The two sums came out equal. **2.** to be leveled. *l-gaaɛ baɛadha ma-tsaawat.* The ground is still not leveled.

stuwa **1.** to ripen, mature, be or become ripe. *xalli l-xoox ɛaš-šijar ɛatta yistuwi.* Leave the peaches on the trees until they ripen. **2.** to become well-cooked, done.

l-ʔakil istuwa. taʕaal ʔukul. The food is done. Come and eat. *laḥam il-hooš ma-yistuwi bil-ʕajal.* Beef doesn't cook quickly.

suwa **1.** equal, the same, alike. *kullhum suwa ʕindi.* They're all the same to me. **2.** together, in a body. *xalli nruuḥ suwa.* Let's go together.

taswiya **1.** leveling, smoothing. **2.** settlement, adjustment (of a dispute). *daaʔirt it-taswiya* Office of Land Dispute Settlement.

musaawaaʔ, musaawaat equality, equal rights.

tasaawi equality, equivalence, sameness. *bit-tasaawi* equally. *qassam iš-sugul ʕaleena bit-tasaawi.* He divided the work for us equally.

stiwaaʔ: xaṭṭ il-istiwaaʔ the equator.

*stiwaaʔi** equatorial, tropical. *manṭaqa stiwaaʔiyya* a tropical region.

mistuwi **1.** ripe, mature. **2.** done, cooked.

mustawa level, standard. *mustawa l-baḥar* sea level. *mustawa qtiṣaadi* economic level, standard of living.

s-y-ʔ

saaʔ, sayyiʔ see under *s-w-ʔ*.

s-y-a-h

siyaaha pl. *-aat* list, manifest, invoice.

s-y-b

sayyab to turn loose to wander, to abandon, neglect, forsake. *truuḥ lil-qabuulaat w-itsayyib wulidha biš-šawaariʕ.* She goes to hen parties and leaves her children to run loose in the streets. *saafar il-labnaan w-sayyab ʔahla.* He took off for Lebanon and abandoned his family.

tsayyab to be left to stray, to wander aimlessly, be without a leader. *tsayyibaw baʕad mootat ʔabuuhum.* They split up after their father's death.

saayib stray, abandoned, forsaken, neglected. *člaab saayba* stray dogs.

s-y-b-n-d

seebandi pl. *-iyya* an unscrupulous person, slippery character, double-dealer.

s-y-p-a-y

siipaaya, seepaaya pl. *-aat* **1.** luggage rack (on a car or bicycle). **2.** rack used to hold pots over a cooking fire.

s-y-j

sayyaj to fence in, surround with a fence. *raḥ-insayyij il-ḥadiiqa b-šarak.* We're going to fence in the garden with barbed wire.

siyaaj pl. *-aat* fencing, fence.

s-y-ḥ

saaḥ (i seeḥ) **1.** to flow, run. *l-mayy saaḥ w-ġatta š-šaariʕ.* The water flowed along and covered the street. **2.** *(i siyaaḥa)* to travel, make a tour. *raḥ-insiiḥ ʔawruppa kullha haṣ-ṣeef.* We're going to tour all Europe this summer.

seeḥ flow.

siyaaḥa **1.** traveling, touring, tourism. **2.** (pl. *-aat*) tour, trip.

saayiḥ pl. *siyyaaḥ, suwwaaḥ* **1.** traveler. **2.** tourist.

s-y-d

sayyid pl. *saada* **1.** lord, master. **2.** (a title used in formal speech, approx.:) Mister. *as-sayyid ʕali* Mr. Ali. **3.** (a formal title of address, approx.:) Sir. *sayyidi, il-mulaazim ʔaḥmad yiriid yišuufak.* Sir, Lt. Ahmad wants to see you. **4.** a descendant of the Prophet, and also, the title used in addressing a sayyid.

sayyidiyya pl. *-aat* **1.** (bestowal of the) title of sayyid. **2.** fez with a green band worn by descendants of Mohammed.

sayyida pl. *-aat* **1.** lady. **2.** Mrs.

siyaada mastery, rule, dominion, sovereignty. || *siyaadat ir-raʔiis.* His Excellency the President.

s-y-r

saar (i seer) **1.** /with *ʕala*/ to follow, pursue, maintain. *ma-da-ysiir ʕala xiṭṭa muʕayyana.* He's not following any specific plan of action. **2.** to march (limited mostly to the command:) *ʔila l-ʔamaam, sir!* Forward, march!

sayyar **1.** to order around, to make do one's bidding. *marta tsayyira ʕasab-ma triid.* His wife orders him around however she wants. **2.** /with *ʕala*/ to call on, drop in on. *raḥ-insayyir ʕala jiiraanna bukra.* We're going to drop in on our neighbors tomorrow.

saayar to put up with, go along with, show patience or tolerance toward. *laazim itsaayra. ma-tʕurfa ʕaṣabi?* You should put up with him. Don't you know he's nervous?

seer, siyar pl. *syuur, syuura* **1.** leather strap, band. **2.** strop. **3.** piece of harness. || *ʔiða ma-tidhan is-seer, ma-tḥassil šii.* If you don't bribe someone (lit. oil the harness), you won't get anything.

siira pl. *siyar* behavior, conduct, deportment.

sayyaar **1.** moving about, roving. *l-quwwa s-sayyaara* the roving patrol, the mobile force. **2.** (pl. *-aat*) extension cord. **3.** hose.

sayyaara pl. *-aat* **1.** automobile, car. **2.** vehicle. *sayyaarat ʔisɛaaf* ambulance. *sayyaara p̣uḷman* "Pullman" bus, an air conditioned passenger trailer and tractor.

masiira pl. *-aat* **1.** parade. **2.** march.

tisyaara pl. *-aat* visit.

s-y-s

sayyas to float along, move on water. *r-raggiyya sayyisat biš-šaṭṭ.* The watermelon floated away in the river.

saayas to use extreme tact in handling, to curry favor with. *ʔiδa tsaayis ʔabuuha, tigdar tizzawwajha.* If you suck up to her father, you can marry her.

saayis pl. *siyyaas* stableman, groom.

siyaasa pl. *-aat* **1.** policy. **2.** politics. **3.** diplomacy.

*siyaasi** **1.** political. **2.** diplomatic. **3.** politician. **4.** diplomat, statesman.

s-y-s-y

siisi pl. *-iyyaat* pony, small horse.

s-y-ṭ-r

seeṭar, sayṭar = *ṣeeṭar* which see under *ṣ-y-ṭ-r.*

s-y-f

seef pl. *syuuf* sword, saber, epée.

siif pl. *ʔasyaaf* grain or date warehouse.

s-y-f-w-n

siifoon pl. *-aat* **1.** siphon. **2.** chain-operated toilet flush tank. **3.** a kind of sweet, carbonated beverage.

s-y-q

saayiq, siyaaqa, etc., see under *s-w-q.*

s-y-l

saal (*i seel, sayalaan*) to flow, run, stream. *d-dibis da-ysiil imnit-tanaka.* The molasses is flowing out of the can.

seel pl. *syuul* **1.** flood, inundation. **2.** torrent. || *min yiɛči, yinzil miθl is-seel.* When he talks, he comes out like a torrent.

sayyaal liquid, flowing, fluid. *giir sayyaal* liquid asphalt.

sayalaan gonorrhea.

seelaan date molasses.

saayil, saaʔil **1.** liquid, flowing, fluid. **2.** (pl. *sawaaʔil*) liquid, fluid. **3.** (pl. *-iin*) beggar.

s-y-l-a-n

siilaan Ceylon.

s-y-m

siim pl. *syaama* **1.** wire. **2.** stitches (surgical). **3.** spoke of a wheel. **4.** thin metal rod.

[1]*s-y-n*

siin pl. *-aat* name of the letter *s.*

[2]*s-y-n*

sayyan to make muddy, dirty. *j-jaahil sayyan ihduuma biš-šaariɛ.* The kid got his clothes muddy in the street.

tsayyan to become muddy. *la-tfuut ib-haš-šaariɛ tara titsayyan.* Don't go on that street or you'll get muddy.

syaan muck, mire, mud.

s-y-n-m-a

siinama pl. *-aat* cinema, movie theater. || *l-baarɛa sawwaw ṣadiiqak siinama.* Yesterday they made a laughingstock of your friend.

*siinamaaʔi** cinematic, movie (adj.). *najim siinamaaʔi* movie star. *ruwaaya siinamaaʔi* movie, film story.

Š

š

š- (interrogatory prefix) *š-ṣaar?* what happened? *š-itsawwi?* what are you doing? *š-ismak?* What's your name? *š-biik?* What's (wrong) with you? *š-gadd?* How much? *haaδa š-imɛallma b-ismi?* How does he know my name?

š-ma whatever. *sawwi š-ma yɛijbak.* Do whatever you like.

š-a-x

šaaxa pl. *-aat* child's top with holes in the side to make noise.

š-a-d-y

šaadi pl. *šwaadi* monkey.

š-a-δ-y

šaaδi pl. *šwaaδi* monkey.

š-a-ṣ-y

šaaṣi pl. *-iyyaat* chassis.

š-a-f

šaafa pl. *-aat* suppository.

š-ʔ-m

tšaaʔam **1.** to be pessimistic, have a pessimistic attitude. *la-titšaaʔam. ʔaḷḷa yifrijha.* Don't be pessimistic. God will take care of it. *ʔaani da-ʔatšaaʔam min hal-waḍiɛ.* I'm pessimistic about this situation. **2.** to be superstitious. *yitšaaʔam min šoof il-ibzaaziin is-suud.* He is superstitious about seeing black cats.

šuʔum, šuum bad luck, misfortune.

mašʔuum unlucky, jinxed. *ɛadad*

mašʔuum an unlucky number.

mitšaaʔim **1.** pessimistic. **2.** a pessimist.

š-a-m

š-šaam Damascus or, loosely, Syria.

*šaami** **1.** Damascene, Syrian. **2.** (pl. *-iyyiin, šwaam*) a Damascene, a Syrian.

šaamiyya popcorn.

šaama pl. *-aat* **1.** freckle. **2.** skin blemish.

xaam iš-šaam coarse, unbleached cotton fabric.

š-ʔ-n

šaʔin pl. *šuʔuun* matter, affair, concern, business. *wizaart iš-šuʔuun il-ijtimaaɛiyya.* Ministry of Social Affairs. *b-šaʔin* about, concerning. *ɛičeet wiyya b-šaʔn il-mawḍuuɛ.* I talked to him concerning the subject.

š-a-h

šaah pl. *-aat* **1.** Shah, ruler. **2.** king (in chess).

š-a-h-w-l

šaahuul pl. *šwaahiil* plumb line, plummet, plumb bob.

š-a-h-y-n

šaahiin pl. *šwaahiin* a kind of falcon.

š-a-w-y

šaawi: maṭi šaawi one of a breed of small donkeys.

š-b-a-ṭ

šbaaṭ February.

š-b-b

šabb (*i šabb*) **1.** to become a young man, to adolesce, grow up. *min ṣaar ɛumra ɛašr isniin, šabb fadd marra.* When he became ten, he grew up fast. *maašaḷḷa šabb bil-ɛajal.* By golly, he's sprouted up quickly. **2.** to break out, blaze up, start up (of fire, war, etc.). *n-naar šabbat bil-maxzan.* A fire broke out in the warehouse. **3.** /with *ɛala*/ to jump up on, to climb on top of, mount. *č-čalib šabb ɛalayya.* The dog jumped up on me. *l-iɛṣaan šabb ɛal-faras.* The stallion mounted the mare. **4.** /with *min*/ to jump over. *č-čalib yigdar yšibb min has-siyaaj ib-suhuula.* The dog can jump over this fence easily.

šabbab to breed, cause to mate. *la-tšabbib il-faraṣ illa min iɛṣaan ʔabyaḍ.* Don't breed the mare with anything but a white stallion. *jiib iɛṣaanak ɛatta nšabbiba ɛala faraṣna.* Bring your horse so we can mate it to our mare.

šabb alum.

šabba pl. *-aat* a platform on top of a pole for keeping food, etc. out of reach of prowling animals.

šabaab **1.** youthfulness, youth. **2.** (invar. sing. and pl.) juvenile, adolescent, youth, young person.

šaabb **1.** youthful, young, juvenile. **2.** (pl. *šubbaan*) young man, youth.

š-b-θ

tšabbaθ to be persistent, tenacious, to seek tenaciously. *ḍall mudda yitšabbaθ ɛatta twaḍḍaf.* He kept on trying for some time until he got a job. *ma-ɛidna waḍiifa; ruuɛ tšabbaθ ib-ġeer daaʔira.* We don't have a job; go try in another office. *tšabbaθ ɛala l-waḍiifa laakin ma-ɛaṣṣalha.* He tried hard for the job but he didn't get it. *da-yitšabbaθ ɛala ʔijaazat fatiɛ malha.* He's trying hard to get a license to open a night club.

š-b-č

šibač (*i šabič*) to intertwine, interweave, lace together. *šibač iṣaabɛa w-ṭagṭagha.* He laced his fingers together and cracked his knuckles.

tšaabač to finger wrestle. *la-titšaabač wiyyaa tara huwwa ʔaqwa minnak.* Don't finger wrestle with him because he's stronger than you.

šibač netting, net.

šibča pl. *-aat,* net, piece of netting.

šibbaač pl. *šbaabiič* **1.** window. **2.** grill, grid, latticework. **3.** wicket. **4.** ventilator grill. **5.** a piece of *zlaabya* (a confection which is made in a latticed shape).

mšabbač **1.** latticed, having a latticed or plaited design. **2.** (pl. *-aat*) grill, latticework. **3.** *zlaabya,* a popular confection.

š-b-ɛ

šabaɛ pl. *ʔašbaaɛ* **1.** apparition. **2.** specter, spirit, ghost.

š-b-x

šubax (*u šabux*) to take a large step. *ʔišbux ɛatta ma-titballal rijlak bil-ṃayy.* Take a big step so your foot won't get wet in the water.

šabbax to spread the legs far apart. *šabbux zeen ɛatta tmurr iṣ-ṣaxḷa min jaw-waak.* Spread your legs so the goat can go under you.

šabxa pl. *-aat* giant step, stride.

š-b-r

šibar (*u šabur*) to measure with the span of the hand. *ʔišbur hal-ɛaṣiir w-gul-li šgadd ṭuula.* Measure this mat (with the span of your hand) and tell me how long it is.

šibir pl. *šbaar* a unit of measurement equal to the span of an outstretched hand.

daafᶜaw ᶜan kull šibir imnil-gaaᶜ. They defended every inch of ground.

š-b-ṭ

šabbuuṭ a kind of large fish found in the Tigris and Euphrates rivers.

š-b-ᶜ

šibaᶜ (a šibiᶜ) **1.** to satisfy one's appetite, eat one's fill, to become sated, full. *ma-raᶜ-aguum imnil-ˀakil gabuḷ-ma ˀašbaᶜ.* I'm not going to get up from the table before I get full. **2.** to have enough, have one's fill, become sick and tired. *baᶜad-ma šibaᶜ minha, ṭiradha.* After he satisfied himself with her, he threw her out. **3.** to sate, satisfy, fill. *t-tamur yišbiᶜ il-waaᶜid.* Dates fill you up.

šabbaᶜ to sate, satisfy, fill. *ˀakil hal-maṭᶜam ma-yšabbiᶜ.* This restaurant's food doesn't fill one up. **2.** to satisfy, gratify. *haaδa ṭammaaᶜ; kull ifluus id-dinya ma-tšabbiᶜ ᶜeena.* He's greedy; all the money of the world wouldn't satisfy him. || *daaraw ᶜalee θlaaθathum w-šab-biᶜoo baṣuṭ.* The three of them converged on him and beat him thoroughly.

nšibaᶜ to have enough, have one's fill. *hal-ˀakil kulliš ṭayyib. ma-yinšibiᶜ minna.* This food is very good. You can never get enough of it.

šabᶜaan **1.** sated, satisfied, full. **2.** satiated, fed up, sick and tired. *ˀaani šabᶜaan imnis-siinamaat.* I'm fed up with movies. || *haaδa ᶜeena šabᶜaana. nafsa ma-tidni ᶜala hiiči šii.* He's got everything. He wouldn't care to get such a thing.

ˀišbaaᶜ satiation, saturation, surfeit.

š-b-g

šubag (u šabug) to embrace, hug. *bass nizal imniṭ-ṭiyyaara, šubag ibna.* As soon as he got off of the plane, he embraced his son. *min šifit ᶜali, šubakta. ṣaar-li tlaθ isniin ma-šaayfa.* When I saw Ali, I embraced him. I hadn't seen him for three years.

šabbag to keep hugging, keep embracing. *δall yšabbug w-ybawwis biiha mudda.* He hugged and kissed her for quite a while.

tšaabag to embrace each other. *bass itlaagaw, itšaabgaw.* The moment they met, they embraced.

šabga pl. *-aat* embrace, hug.

š-b-k

šubak = *šubag,* which see under *š-b-g.* (see also *šibač* under *š-b-č*).

štibak to become entangled, involved, engaged, embroiled. *jeešna štibak ib-maᶜraka wiyya l-ᶜadu.* Our forces engaged in battle with the enemy.

šabakiyya pl. *-aat* retina (of the eye).

šibbaak = *šibbaač,* which see under *š-b-č.*

š-b-l

šibil pl. *ˀašbaal* lion cub.

š-b-n-t

šbint dill.

š-b-h

šibah (a šabih) **1.** to resemble, look like, be similar to. *ˀibnak yišbahak kulliš.* Your son resembles you a lot. **2.** *(a šubha)* to cast suspicion upon, bring suspicion to, make suspect. *šibahni min jaab ˀismi bil-maᶜkama.* He cast suspicion on me when he mentioned my name in court.

šabbah **1.** to compare, liken. *yšabbih ᶜabiibta bil-ġazaal.* He compares his darling to a gazelle. **2.** to consider similar or identical, to find a resemblance in. *beeš itšabbih han-nooᶜ imnil-faakiha?* What does this variety of fruit remind you of? *šuuf δaak ir-rijjaal. šabbahta b-axuuk.* Look at that man. I thought he was your brother.

šaabah to resemble, look like, be similar to. *qmaaš sitirti yšaabih is-sarij.* The material of my jacket resembles serge. || *w-ma-šaabah* and the like, and others of the same type. *kull ˀaᶜδaaˀ han-naadi muᶜaamiin, w-ˀaṭṭibaaˀ, w-ma-šaabah.* All the members of this club are lawyers, physicians, and the like.

tšabbah /with *b-*/ to imitate, copy, try to be like. *hal-ibnayya titšabbah bin-niswaan.* That girl copies grown women.

tšaabah to resemble each other, look alike, be similar to each other. *huwwa w-ˀaxuu hwaaya yitšaabhuun.* He and his brother look a lot alike.

nšibah to be or become under suspicion, be suspected. *nšibah li-ˀan daaˀiman yimši wiyya l-mujrim.* He's suspected because he's always hanging around with the criminal.

stibah **1.** to be mistaken, make a mistake. *laazim ištibahit. t-tiffaaᶜ muu halgadd ġaali.* You must be mistaken. Apples aren't that expensive. *štibahit bil-iᶜsaab li-ˀan činit tiᶜči.* I made a mistake on the accounts because you were talking. *l-ᶜafu! štibahit biik.* Sorry! I mistook you for someone else. *štibah biyya w-iᶜtiqad ˀaani najim siinamaaˀi.* He took me for someone else and thought I was a movie star. **2.** /with *b-*/ to suspect, be suspicious about. *š-šurṭa, ʔay waaɛid tištibih bii, taaxδa lil-markaz.* Any one the police suspect, they take to the station.

šibih pl. *ʔašbaah* **1.** resemblance, similarity, likeness. **2.** image. **3.**-like, quasi, semi-, half-. *šibih difaaɛ* halfback (soccer). *šibih rasmi* semi-formal, semi-official. *šibih jaziira* peninsula. *šibih munɛarif* trapezoid (geom.). *šibih muɛayyan* rhomboid (geom.).

šabah pl. *ʔašbaah* **1.** resemblance, similarity, likeness. **2.** image.

šubha pl. *-aat* suspicion. *ʔinta ma-ɛaleek šubha.* You're not under suspicion.

šabiih pl. *ʔašbaah* like, counterpart. *ma-ʔila šabiih bid-dinya.* There's no one like him in the world.

ʔašbah /with *b-*/ more or most similar to. *haay ʔašbah šii bil-xoox.* This is the closest thing to a peach.

tašaabuh resemblance, similarity. *ʔaku tašaabuh beenhum.* There's a resemblance between them.

mašbuuh **1.** under suspicion, suspect, suspicious. *beet mašbuuh* house of ill repute. **2.** (pl. *-iin*) a suspect.

[1]*š-b-w*

šiba imitation gold, brass. *xizzaama šiba* a brass nose ring.

[2]*š-b-w*

šabba to breed, cause to mate. *raɛ-ašabbi l-faraṣ maalti min ʔaɛsan iɛṣaan mawjuud.* I'm going to breed my mare to the best stallion available.

šbuwwa: faɛal išbuwwa, ɛṣaan išbuwwa stud horse. || *yaɛni jaaybiik il-amriika tidrus loo tšiir faɛl išbuwwa.* You think they sent you to America to study or to be a stud?

see also *š-b-b.*

š-t-t

šattat to scatter, disperse, break up, rout. *l-ɛadu šattat šamilhum.* The enemy routed them.

tšattat to be scattered, to disperse. *min ʔijat iš-šurṭa, tšattitaw.* When the police came, they dispersed. *jeeš naapulyoon itšattat ib-ruusya.* Napoleon's army fell apart in Russia.

š-t-l

šital (*i šatil*) **1.** to plant, transplant. *jibit čam hiriš warid w-šitalithum bil-ɛadiiqa.* I got a few flower seedlings and transplanted them in the garden. **2.** to constrain, stay, deter, hobble, confine. *ʔištil iṭ-ṭeer ɛatta ma-yṭiir.* Fasten the bird's wings so he won't fly. *balḷa taɛaal ib-saaɛ. la-tištilni.* Please come right away. Don't leave me here.

šitil pl. *štuul* young plant, seedling.

maštal pl. *mašaatil* nursery, arboretum.

š-t-m

šitam (*i šatim*) to curse, revile, vilify, abuse. *šitamta li-ʔan faššar ɛalayya.* I cussed him out because he talked dirty to me.

šattam intensive of *šitam. tigdar tiɛči bila-ma tšattim.* You can talk without cursing continually.

tšaatam to curse one another, vilify one another. *tšaatmaw w-baɛdeen tbaaṣṭaw.* They threw insults at each other and then got into a fight.

šatma pl. *-aat* insult, vilification.

šattuuma pl. *-aat, štaayim* insult, vilification.

[1]*š-t-w*

šatta **1.** to winter, spend the winter. *yṣayyif biš-šimaal w-yšatti bil-baṣra.* He spend his summers in the North and his winters in Basra. **2.** to put on or wear winter clothing. *ʔašu šatteet bil-ɛajal. d-dinya baɛadha ɛaarra.* It looks like you put on winter clothes too soon. The weather is still hot.

šita pl. *-aayaat* winter.

*šitwi** winter, wintry. *badla šitwiyya* a winter suit.

šitwiyya pl. *-aat* winter, winter time.

mašta pl. *mašaati* winter resort.

[2]*š-t-w*

šita (*u šatu*) to incite, turn loose, sick (a dog). *šita č-čalib ɛala ṣadiiqa.* He sicked the dog on his friend. *štu!* Sick him!

š-j-b

mišjab pl. *mašaajib* gun rack.

š-j-r

šijar (*i šajir, šjaar*) to prepare the baking oven for baking flat bread. *jiib-li ɛaṭab ɛatta ʔašjar it-tannuur.* Bring me some kindling so I can heat up the outdoor oven.

šajjar to plant trees or bushes, to landscape. *šajjiraw iš-šaariɛ ij-jidiid ib-kaalibtooz.* They planted eucalyptus trees along the new street.

šijar (coll.) **1.** tree(s). **2.** bush(es), shrub(s). **3.** squash. **4.** pumpkin(s). *šijar ʔaskala, šijar ʔaɛmar* pumpkin. **5.** dope, dunce, fool, jerk. *la-tizɛal min ɛačya. huwwa fadd waaɛid šijar.* Don't get mad at what he says. He's a simple-minded fellow.

šijra pl. *-aat* **1.** squash. **2.** pumpkin.

3. (pl. *-aat, ˀašjaar*) tree. 4. bush, shrub.

šajara pl. *-aat, ˀašjaar* 1. tree. 2. bush, shrub.

šijraaya pl. *-aat* 1. squash. 2. pumpkin.

mšajjar 1. embellished with trees or bushes, landscaped. 2. having a floral design. *laabsa fistaan imšajjar.* She's wearing a floral print dress.

š-j-ع

šajjaع 1. to encourage, embolden. *šajjaعa عala d-diraasa b-ˀooruppa.* He encouraged him to study in Europe. *kull it-talaamiiδ ˀijaw lis-saaحa حatta yšajjiعuun il-firqa.* All the students came to the field to cheer the team. 2. to support, back, promote. *laazim inšajjiع maṣnuuعaatna l-waṭaniyya.* We should support our domestic products.

tšajjaع to take heart, pluck up courage, be encouraged. *min حičeena wiyyaa, tšajjaع.* When we talked to him, he was encouraged.

šujaaع pl. *šujعaan* 1. brave, courageous, bold, audacious. 2. courageous man.

šajaaعa courage, bravery, valor, boldness, audacity.

ˀašjaع more or most courageous, etc.

š-č-w

šičwa pl. *-aat* a small skin in which cream is shaken to produce butter.

š-ح-ح

šaحح (*i šiححa*) to become scarce, run short, dwindle. *štiri hwaaya min haṣ-ṣaabuun. yiδhar da-yšiحح yoom عan yoom.* Buy a lot of this soap. It appears to be getting scarcer day after day.

šiححa scarcity, paucity, shortage, deficiency.

š-ح-š-ṭ

šaحšaṭ to scrape, scuff, drag along. *da-yimši w-yšaحšiṭ b-inعaala.* He's walking along and scuffing his sandals. *ˀiδa ma-tiqdar itšiil il-guuniyya, šaحšiṭha.* If you can't carry the gunny sack, drag it. || *nijaح najaaح imšaحšaṭ.* He just barely passed.

š-ح-ṭ

šiحaṭ (*a šaحuṭ*) 1. to scrape, scuff, drag along. *da-yimši w-yišحaṭ b-inعaala.* He's walking along and scuffing his sandals. 2. to irritate, cause a lump in (the throat). *n-nuumi l-حaamuδ yišحaṭ il-balعuun.* Lemon puckers the throat.

šaححaṭ to make deficient, make too short. *la-tšaححiṭha. ˀinṭiini عal-ˀaqall itlaθ yaardaat.* Don't make it too short. Give me at least three yards. *hal-wuṣlat il-uqmaaš mšaححiṭa. ma-tṣiir-lak qaaṭ.* This piece of material is too short. It won't make you a suit. *haṭ-ṭamaaṭa tsawwi nuṣṣ kiilu mšaححaṭ.* These tomatoes make barely half a kilo.

šaحṭa irritation, lump (in the throat).

š-ح-f

mašحuuf pl. *mašaaحiif* a kind of long boat, made of wood, or asphalt-covered straw, and propelled by a pole.

š-ح-m

šaححam to lubricate, grease. *baعad-ma šaححamt is-sayyaara, gaamat timši zeen.* After I lubricated the car, it began to run well.

tšaححam pass. of *šaححam.*

šaحam pl. *šuحuum* 1. fat, suet, grease. 2. tallow. *ṣaabuun šaحam* tallow soap.

šaحma pl. *-aat* piece of fat, suet, tallow, or lard. || *šaحmat il-ˀiδin* earlobe.

š-ح-n

šiحan (*a šaحin*) 1. to ship, freight, consign. *raح-nišحan ṭanneen buṣal lil-baṣra.* We're going to ship two tons of onions to Basra. *raح-tišحan ir-raggi bil-qiṭaar loo bil-looriyyaat?* Are you going to ship the watermelons by train or by truck? 2. to charge, load with electricity. *hal-makiina tišحan il-paatriyyaat.* This machine charges batteries.

šaحna pl. *-aat* load, shipment, cargo.

šaaحina pl. *-aat* charger, battery charger.

mašحuun loaded. *loori mašحuun ṭamaaṭa* a truck loaded with tomatoes.

š-x-b-ṭ

šaxbaṭ to scribble, scrawl. *nṭii l-qalam w-xalli yšaxbuṭ عala hal-waraqa.* Give him the pen and let him scribble on this piece of paper.

š-x-x

šaxx (*u šaxx*) to urinate. *l-bazzuuna šaxxat عal-baṭṭaaniyya.* The cat wet on the blanket.

šaxxax to cause to urinate. *šaxxixat ij-jaahil gabuḷ-ma tbaddil-la.* She made the child urinate before she'd change him.

šaxx 1. urinating. 2. urine.

šaxxa pl. *-aat* i. n. of *šaxx.*

šxaax urine.

š-x-r

šixar (*u šaxur*) to snore. *bass-ma xalla raasa عal-umxadda, šixar.* As soon as he put his head on the pillow, he started to snore.

šaxiir, šxiir snoring.

š-x-ṣ

šaxxaṣ to identify, recognize. *عinda quṣur naδar w-ma-yigdar yšaxxiṣ il-waaحid min biƐiid.* He's shortsighted and can't recognize anyone from a distance. **2.** to diagnose. *ṭ-ṭabiib ma-gidar yšaxxiṣ il-maraδ.* The doctor couldn't diagnose the disease.

šaxiṣ pl. *ˀašxaaṣ* person, individual. || *b-šaxṣa* himself, personally, in person. *raaḤ Ɛalee b-šaxṣa w-Ḥiča wiyyaa.* He went to see him personally and talked to him.

*šaxṣi** personal, private. *masˀala saxṣiyya* a private matter.

šaxṣiyyan personally, from a personal viewpoint. *ˀaani šaxṣiyyan ˀafaδδil l-Ɛarag.* I personally prefer arrack.

šaxṣiyya pl. *-aat* **1.** identity. *ma-nuƐruf šaxṣiyyt il-maqtuul.* We don't know the murdered man's identity. **2.** personality. || *Ḥiča Ɛalee Ḥači Ḥaṭṭam šaxṣiita bii.* He gave him a talking to that damaged his ego. **3.** personage, big shot.

tašxiiṣ **1.** identification. **2.** diagnosis.

š-x-ṭ

šixaṭ (*i saxuṭ, šuxuṭ*) **1.** to scratch, mar, make a mark. *šixaṭ šuxṭeen bil-Ḥaayiṭ.* He scratched two marks on the wall. **2.** to cross out, scratch out, strike out. *kitab ič-čilma w-baƐdeen šixaṭha.* He wrote the word and then crossed it out. **3.** to strike (a match). *šixaṭit Ɛuudteen šixxaaṭ w-ma-aku naar.* I struck two matches and got no fire.

šaxxaṭ intensive of *šixaṭ*. *b-iida l-bismaar w-da-yšaxxuṭ bil-baab.* He's got the nail in his hand and he's scratching up the door.

šaxuṭ, šuxuṭ **1.** scratching. **2.** crossing out. **3.** striking (a match). **4.** (pl. *šxuuṭ*) scratch, mark.

šaxṭa pl. *-aat* i.n. of *šaxuṭ* **1, 2,** & **3.**

šixxaaṭ (coll.) match(es), lucifer(s). *Ɛuudat šixxaaṭ* a match.

šixxaaṭa pl. *-aat* **1.** a match. **2.** a box of matches.

mašxuuṭ **1.** scratched, marred, marked, scarred. **2.** slightly crazy, touched in the head.

š-d-d

šadd (*i šadd*) **1.** to tie, fasten, bind. *šadd xeeṭ ib-rijl il-Ɛaṣfuur w-kumaša Ḥatta ma-yṭiir.* He tied a string to the sparrow's leg and held it so it wouldn't fly. *la-tšidd il-išdaad qawi.* Don't tie the bandage tight. *lajjim l-iḤṣaan gabuḷ-ma tšidda bil-Ɛarabaana.* Bridle up the horse before you hitch him up to the cart. **2.** to tie up, tie together, bind together. *xalli θ-θiyaab bil-buqča w-šiddha.* Put the shirts in the sheet and tie it up. **3.** to mount, fasten on, assemble, put together. *šidd il-wiilaat il-giddaamiyya ˀawwal.* Mount the front wheels first. *yigdar yfukk il-panka wuṣla wuṣla w-baƐdeen yšiddha.* He can take apart the fan piece by piece and then put it back together. *šadd-la l-paaysikil ib-nuṣṣ saaƐa.* He put the bicycle together for him in half an hour. || *šidd Ḥeelak w-Ḥaawil itxaḷḷiṣ iš-šuġuḷ.* Gather your strength and try to finish the work. **4.** to stir up, cause trouble between. *bass yƐijba yšiddhum w-iyxalliihum yitbaaṣṭuun.* He just likes to cause trouble between them and make them fight.

šaddad **1.** to strengthen, intensify, make strong, harsh. *maa-daam čiδabit bil-maḤkama, l-Ḥaakim raḤ-yšaddid il-Ɛuquuba Ɛaleek.* Since you lied in court, the judge is going to make your sentence heavier. **2.** to exert pressure, press. *ˀiδa tšaddid Ɛalee, yinṭiik il-ifluus.* If you're firm with him, he'll give you the money.

tšaddad to be harsh, strict, severe, stern. *l-mudiir ij-jidiid da-yitšaddad ihwaaya.* The new principal is getting a lot more strict.

nšadd pass. of *šadd*. *wuṣlat il-makaayin kullha mfakkika. laazim tinšadd bil-maḤall.* The machines arrived completely disassembled. They'll have to be put together in the shop.

štadd **1.** to become hard, harsh, severe, intense. *min wugaƐ θalij biš-šimaal, ištadd il-barid.* When the snow fell in the north, the cold became intense. **2.** to become harder, harsher, more intense, severer. *min yfukka l-banj, raḤ-yištadd il-wujaƐ.* When the anesthetic wears off, the pain will become more severe. **3.** to become aggravated, more critical. *Ɛilnaw il-ˀaḤkaam il-Ɛirfiyya. ybayyin štaddat il-ˀumuur.* They proclaimed martial law. It seems matters have become more critical.

šadd **1.** tying, binding, fastening. **2.** tying up, fastening together. **3.** assembling.

šadda pl. *-aat* **1.** i. n. of *šadd*. **2.** bundle, bunch, pack. *šaddat iqlaam* a bundle of pencils. *šaddat jizar* a bunch of carrots. *šaddat warid* a bouquet of flowers.

šidda **1.** intensity, severity, forcefulness, vehemence, violence. **2.** distress, hardship, adversity.

šadiid strong, powerful, forceful, severe, hard, harsh, violent, vehement, intense. *hal-Ɛummaal ˀiδa ma-ykuun il-waaḤid šadiid wyaahum, ma-yiṭlaƐ šuġuḷ.* If one isn't severe with these workers, no work will get done.

šaddaad, šdaad pl. *-aat* bandage.

ˀašadd more or most forceful, rigorous, intense.

mašadd pl. *-aat* corset.

š-d-r-w-a-n

šadirwaan pl. *-aat* fountain.

š-d-h

šidah (*a šadih*) **1.** to surprise, astonish, astound, amaze. *loon ij-jawhara w-kuburha šidahni.* The color of the diamond and its size amazed me. *jamaalha yišdah.* Her beauty is dazzling. **2.** to distract, preoccupy. *šidahitni w-ma-gidarit ˀaṭbux zeen.* You distracted me and I couldn't cook well. *mašduuh ib-šuġla w-ma-da-yigdar ysaafir.* He's preoccupied with his work and not able to take a trip.

nšidah **1.** to be surprised, astonished, amazed. *min šaaf il-mujawharaat, nšidah.* When he saw the jewelry, he was amazed. **2.** to be distracted, preoccupied. *l-baarḥa nšidahit in-nahaar kulla w-ma-ṣaar-li majaal ˀaxaabrak.* Yesterday, I was preoccupied all day and had no chance to call you.

mašduuh **1.** surprised, astonished, amazed. **2.** distracted, preoccupied. *š-biik mašduuh? ma-da-tismaʕni?* Why are you so distracted? Aren't you listening to me?

š-δ-δ̣

šaδδ (*i šuδuuδ*) **1.** to wander afield, become separated, isolated. *da-tšiδδ ʕan il-mawḍuuʕ w-ma-da-nifham šii.* You're getting off the subject and we can't understand a thing. **2.** to be exceptional, stand out. *yšiδδ ʕan baqiit iṭ-ṭullaab ib-ʕiddat ṣifaat.* He stands out from the rest of the students in several characteristics.

šuδuuδ, šiδuuδ **1.** irregularity, deviation, anomaly. *šiδuuδ jinsi* sexual deviation. **2.** oddness, eccentricity.

šaaδδ **1.** irregular, anomalous, unusual, queer, odd, peculiar, extraordinary, strange, eccentric. *ḥaala šaaδδa* an exceptional situation. *min iṣ-ṣaʕub tinsijim wiyyaa. huwwa fadd waaḥid šaaδδ.* It's difficult to get along with him. He's an eccentric character. **2.** (pl. *šawaaδδ*) exception.

š-δ-r

šaδir (coll.) turquoise.

šaδra pl. *-aat* a turquoise, piece of turquoise.

*ṣaδri** turquoise, turquoise blue. *loon šaδri* turquoise colored.

š-δ-r-w-a-n

šaδirwaan pl. *-aat* fountain.

š-r-b

širab (*a šurub*) **1.** to drink. *yišrab čaay ihwaaya.* He drinks a lot of tea. *la-tqaddim-la biira; tara ma-yišrab.* Don't offer him beer; he doesn't drink. **2.** to smoke. *ʕumra ʕašr isniin w-yišrab jigaayir.* He's ten years old and smokes cigarettes.

šarrab **1.** to make or let drink. *l-walad ma-da-yišrab id-duwa maala. taʕaal šarrba.* The boy isn't drinking his medicine. Come make him drink. *waddi l-xeel lišaṭṭ, šarrubha ṃayy.* Take the horses to the river and water them. **2.** to soak, saturate. *šarrub il-xubuz bil-marag.* Soak the bread in the gravy.

tšarrab to be saturated. *xalli l-xubuz bil-šoorba ˀila ˀan yitšarrab zeen.* Leave the bread in the soup until it's well soaked.

nširab to be drunk. *hal-ṃayy ḥaarr. ma-yinšurub.* This water is hot. It can't be drunk.

šarba pl. *-aat* large clay water jug.

šurba, širba pl. *-aat* drink, draught, sip.

šaraab **1.** wine. **2.** syrup.

šarraab pl. *-iin* heavy drinker, drunkard. || *šarraab jigaayir* chain smoker.

mašrab pl. *mašaarub* cigarette holder.

tašriib bread soaked in boiled meat juices, with meat on top (usually eaten for breakfast).

tašriibaaya a dish made of dried bread and spices boiled in water (usually eaten for breakfast).

šaarib, šaarub pl. *-iin* **1.** drinker. **2.** (pl. *šwaarub*) mustache.

mašruub pl. *-aat* drink, (alcoholic) beverage.

š-r-b-t

šarbat to do hurriedly, carelessly, sloppily. *šloon xaḷḷaṣt iš-šuġuḷ ib-ʕašir daqaayiq? laazim šarbatta.* How did you finish the work in ten minutes? You must have done a sloppy job of it.

šarbat pl. *šaraabit* **1.** sherbet, punch, non-carbonated soft drink. **2.** weak coffee.

š-r-b-k

šarbak to entangle, snarl. *la-tšarbukni b-hal-muškila.* Don't get me into this problem.

tšarbak to become entangled. *rijli tšarbikat bil-ḥabil.* My leg got tangled up in the rope.

š-r-ḥ

širaḥ (*a šariḥ*) **1.** to rip, cut down the

middle, cut lengthwise. *ʔuxuδ il-minšaar w-išraζ hal-looζa.* Take the saw and cut this board lengthwise. **2.** to explain, elucidate, make clear or plain. *l-ʔustaaδ ma-širaζ id-daris zeen.* The professor didn't explain the lesson well.

šarraζ **1.** to cut up, cut in strips. *šarriζha l-hal-looζa.* Cut this board into strips. **2.** to dissect, dismember. *l-yoom raζ-inšarriζ ʔarnab.* Today we're going to dissect a rabbit. *šarriζaw il-mayyit ζatta yšuufuun sabab mootta.* They performed an autopsy on the corpse to find out the cause of his death.

šraζζ to be or become inflamed (of the eye). *bass ʕaad tibči! ʕeenak šraζζat.* Stop crying! Your eyes are all red.

šariζ explanation, elucidation.

širiζ lean. *laζam širiζ* lean meat.

širζa pl. *-aat* slice, piece. *širζat laζam* a piece of meat.

šriiζa pl. *šraayiζ* strip, thin slice.

ʔašraζ fem. *šarζa* pl. *šurζiin, šuruζ* **1.** inflamed, infected (of the eye). **2.** having an eye infection.

tašriiζ dissecting, dissection. *ʕilm it-tašriiζ* anatomy.

š-r-d

širad (*i šarid, šraad*) to run away, flee. *bass šaaf iš-šurṭa, širad.* The moment he saw the police, he ran away. *šaarid imnis-sijin w-da-ydawwruun ʕalee.* He's escaped from prison and they're looking for him. *gaaʕid biṣ-ṣaff w-fikra šaarid.* He is sitting in class but his mind is far away.

šarrad to cause to flee, run away. *šarrad il-ζaramiyya b-iṣyaaζa.* He made the thieves run away with his shouting. *l-ζarub šarridat ihwaaya naas min ibyuuthum.* The war drove a lot of people from their homes. *šarrad ibna gabuḷ-ma tiji š-šurṭa taaxδa.* He sent his son fleeing before the police came to take him.

tšarrad = *širad.* *yitšarrad imnil-madrasa.* He runs away from school.

šarid running away, fleeing.

šarda pl. *-aat* i. n. of *šarid.*

šaarid **1.** running, fleeing, on the lam. **2.** (pl. *-iin*) fugitive, runaway, escapee, deserter.

¹*š-r-r*

šarr (*u šarr*) to hang (on a line). *šurr hal-ihduum il-imballila ʕal-ζabil.* Hang these wet clothes on the line. || *šarroo ʕal-ζabil ib-ζačiihum haaδa.* They exposed him by talking like that.

²*š-r-r*

šarr **1.** evil, wickedness, malice. || *nṭii ʕašr idnaaniir w-itčaffa šarra.* Give him ten dinars and be done with him. *la-tiζči wiyyaa, tara da-ydawwir šarr.* Don't speak to him, because he's looking for trouble.

širriir pl. *ʔašraar* very bad, very evil.

šaraara pl. *-aat* spark.

¹*š-r-s*

šaris **1.** vicious, malicious, ill-tempered. *haš-šurṭi šaris kulliš.* That cop is real mean. **2.** wild, ferocious, fierce. *s-sabiʕ ζaywaan šaris.* The lion is a ferocious animal.

²*š-r-s*

šriis **1.** glue, paste. **2.** a powder which becomes glue or paste when mixed with water.

š-r-ṭ

širaṭ (*u šaruṭ*) to stipulate, to impose as a condition. *širaṭ laazim itkuun ζuṣṣta ʔakθarhum.* He stipulated that his share must be biggest.

šarraṭ to make an incision, cut into, lance. *ʔaxaδ il-muus w-šarraṭ bii l-ζabbaaya.* He took the razor and lanced the boil with it.

šaaraṭ to bet, wager. *ʔašaarṭak raζ-yiṣiir waziir bil-wuzaara j-jidiida.* I bet you he'll be a minister in the new cabinet.

tšaaraṭ to fix mutual conditions, to conclude an agreement. *tšaaraṭ wiyyaahum yaaxuδ xums ir-ribiζ.* He made an agreement with them to take one-fifth of the profits. *tšaaraṭna ʔiδa wuṣal gabḷi, ʔawad-dii lis-siinama.* We made an agreement that if he got there before me, I would take him to the movie.

štiraṭ to stipulate, impose a condition. *štiraṭ ʕaleehum ydizzuun il-biδaaʕa biṭ-ṭiyyaara.* He imposed on them the condition that they send the goods by plane.

šariṭ **1.** pl. *šuruuṭ* condition, precondition, provision, stipulation. *b-šariṭ* on the condition, provided. *ʔaruuζ lis-siinama b-šarṭ tiji wyaay.* I'll go to the movie on condition that you come with me. || *ybiiʕ ir-raggi šarṭ is-siččiin.* He sells the watermelons on the condition that they are good.

šurṭa (coll.) police, policemen, police force.

šurṭi pl. *-iyyiin, šurṭa* policeman.

šariiṭ pl. *ʔašriṭa, šaraaʔiṭ* **1.** ribbon, band, tape, strip. *šariiṭ musajjil* recording tape. **2.** ribbon, medal, decoration.

š-r-ʕ

š-šariʕ the canonical law of Islam. *xilaaf*

iš-šariʕ violation of religious law.

šarʕan legally, in a legal sense. *haaδa šii šarʕan ma-maqbuul.* This sort of thing is legally unacceptable.

*šarʕi** **1.** legal, lawful, legitimate. *faṣla min il-waδiifa muu šarʕi.* Discharging him from his position was illegal. **2.** dealing with religious law. *maḥkama šarʕiyya* religious court.

šarʕiyya lawfulness, legality, legitimacy.

šraaʕ pl. *-aat* sail.

*šraaʕi** sail, sailing, rigged with sails. *markab šraaʕi* sailboat.

š-šariiʕa the Sharia, the canonical law of Islam.

širiiʕa pl. *-aat* an approach to a water hole, a level, flat place beside a body of water.

tašriiʕ legislation.

*tašriiʕi** legislative. *s-sulta t-tašriiʕiyya* the legislative branch.

šaariʕ pl. *šawaariʕ* street. *raas iš-šaariʕ* end of the block, intersection, corner.

mašruuʕ **1.** legal, lawful, legitimate. *ʕamalak muu mašruuʕ.* Your action isn't legal. **2.** acceptable, allowable. *haaδa ʕuδur ġeer mašruuʕ.* That's not an acceptable excuse. **3.** project, undertaking, enterprise.

š-r-f

šarraf **1.** to honor. || *šarrfuuna daayman.* Visit us often (lit., honor us always). **2.** to be more noble, eminent, distinguished, honorable than. *ʔaani ašarrfak w-ašarruf ʕaaʔiltak.* I'm worth more than you and your family.

ʔašraf /with *ʕala*/ **1.** to watch, supervise, oversee *ʔinta ʔišrif ʕaš-šuʕba ʔila ʔan yirjaʕ il-mulaaḥiδ maalkum.* You watch over the section until your superintendent comes back. *yaa muʕaawin yišrif ʕala šuʕbat il-muḥaasaba?* Which assistant supervises the personnel section? **2.** to overlook, be above, command a view of. *ġurufti tišrif ʕaš-šaariʕ.* My room overlooks the street.

tšarraf to be honored, feel honored. *tšarrafna b-maʕriftak.* I'm honored to make your acquaintance.

šaraf **1.** eminence, dignity, nobility, high standing. **2.** honor. *raḥ-insawwi ḥafla ʕala šarafa.* We're going to have a party in his honor. || *biṭaaqat šaraf* invitation for an honored guest.

šariif pl. *ʔašraaf, šurafaaʔ* **1.** distinguished, eminent, illustrious, noble. **2.** honorable, respectable, honest. **3.** sherif, a descendant of Mohammed.

ʔašraf **1.** more or most distinguished, eminent. **2.** more or most honorable, respectable.

tašriifaati pl. *-iyya* usher.

š-r-q

stašraq to become an Oriental, adopt oriental manners. *stašraq w-giδa ʕumra yidrus ʕarabi.* He adopted the Eastern culture and spent his life studying Arabic.

šarq **1.** east. *ʔiiraan itḥidd il-ʕiraaq mniš-šarq.* Iran borders Iraq on the east. **2.** the East, the Orient. *š-šarq il-ʔawsaṭ* The Middle East.

*šarqi** **1.** eastern, easterly. *l-manṭaqa š-šarqiyya* the eastern region. **2.** oriental, eastern. *hduum šarqiyya* oriental clothes. *beet šarqi* a house built around a central patio. *ḥammaam šarqi* eastern style bathroom, Turkish bath.

mustašriq pl. *-iin* a person who has become orientalized.

š-r-g

širag (*u šarig*) **1.** to split, crack. *tigdar tišrug il-xišba bil-faas.* You can split the log with the axe. **2.** to choke, swallow the wrong way. *širag li-ʔan čaan yišrab il-ṃayy ib-surʕa.* He choked because he was drinking the water fast.

šarrag to split, crack repeatedly. *šarrig is-saʕfa w-ṭalliʕ minha ʕuwad irfaaʕ.* Split up the palm leaf and get some thin sticks from it.

šarig pl. *šruug* split, crack, fissure.

šruugi pl. *-iyya, šruug* person from the rural areas of southern Iraq.

š-r-g-w

šargaawi pl. *šraagwa* var. of *šruugi,* which see above.

š-r-g-a-l

širgaaḷ cramp, muscle spasm.

š-r-g-y-ṭ

širgeeṭ cramp, muscle spasm.

š-r-k

širak (*i ʔišraak*) to make a partner, participant, associate, to give a share, include. *la-tširkuuni b-hal-qaδiyya l-ʕawiiṣa.* Don't include me in this complicated matter.

šaarak to enter into partnership, association, participation with, to join, combine, be or become a partner with. *šaarakithum w-ixṣarit.* I went into partnership with them and I lost money.

ʔašrak **1.** = *širak.* **2.** (*širak ib-ʔaḷḷa*) to be a polytheist, hold others equal with God. *lli yišrik ib-ʔaḷḷa yruuḥ lin-naar.* He who holds others equal to God goes to hell.

tšaarak to form a partnership, enter into partnership. *simaʕit raʕ-titšaarak wiyya ṣaaʕib hal-maxzan.* I heard that you're going into partnership with the owner of this store.

štirak **1.** to involve oneself, to participate, take part, join in, collaborate. *štirakit ib-jamʕiyyat il-muʕallimiin.* I became a member of the teachers' association. *ʔašu ma-da-tištirik wiyyaana. l-mawðuuʕ ma-yʕijbak?* I notice you're not joining in with us. The subject doesn't please you? *ṭiyyaaraatna štirkat bil-maʕraka.* Our airplanes took part in the battle. **2.** to subscribe. *jubarni ʔaštirik ib-hal-majalla s-saxiifa.* He forced me to subscribe to this silly magazine.

šarak barbed wire.

šurka partnership, association.

šarika pl. *-aat* company, firm, corporation.

šariik pl. *surakaaʔ, šurkaan* **1.** partner. **2.** confederate, ally, associate. **3.** accomplice.

šaraaka partnership, association.

štiraak **1.** participation, collaboration, sharing, joining. **2.** partnership. **3.** (pl. *-aat*) subscription. **4.** subscription fee, rate. **5.** dues, participation fee.

*stiraaki** **1.** socialist, socialistic. **2.** a socialist.

l-ištiraakiyya socialism.

mušrik pl. *-iin* polytheist.

muštarik pl. *-iin* subscriber.

muštarak joint, combined, collective, common, co-, communal. *baalaġ muštarak* joint communique. *ʕammaam muštarak* communal bath house. *qaasim muštarak* common denominator (math.). *s-suuq il-muštaraka* The Common Market.

š-r-m

širam (*u šarum*) to split, cleave, slit. *t-tirčiyya širmat ʔiðinha.* The earring split her ear.

šarram to do a good job of, do thoroughly, do properly, do up brown. *ʔaani haaða lli ʔaʕurfa. ʔinta ʕuud raʕ-itšarrumha?* That's it as I know it. Now you think you're going to do it up right? *ʕabaali yuʕruf ingiliizi. šarramha! tarjam il-maktuub ġalaṭ.* I thought he knew English. He really did it up brown! He translated the letter wrong. *ʕabaali yiṭlaʕ ʔaʕsan min ʔaxuu. jaa šarramha!* I thought he'd turn out better than his brother. He sure did, by far!

ʔašram fem. *šarma* pl. *šurum, šarmiin* having a harelip.

š-r-m-x

šarmax, šarmuux, etc., var. of *xarmaš, xarmuuš,* etc., which see under *x-r-m-š.*

š-r-n-q

šarnaqa pl. *šaraaniq* cocoon, especially of the silkworm.

šranqa pl. *-aat* **1.** hypodermic syringe, hypo. **2.** shot, injection.

š-r-h

šarih greedy (for food), gluttonous. *š-gadd ma-txallii-la ʔakil, ma-yiktifi. huwwa fadd waaʕid šarih.* No matter how much food you give him, he isn't satisfied. He's greedy.

šaraaha gluttony, greediness for food. *ib-šaraaha* greedily. *yaakul ib-šaraaha.* He eats greedily.

š-r-w

šarwa see *š-r-y.*

š-r-w-a-l

širwaal pl. *-aat, širaawiil* a sort of loose-fitting trousers. *l-akraad yilbasuun širwaal.* The Kurds wear baggy pants.

š-r-y

šira (*i šraaya*) to purchase, buy. *min yaa gaṣṣaab išreet il-laʕam?* From which butcher did you buy the meat? *beeš išreetha?* How much did you buy it for?

štira to purchase, buy. *štira sayyaara jidiida.* He bought a new car. || *yištiri l-ʕarka b-ifluus.* He looks for trouble. *haaða šeeṭaan; yištiriik w-iybiiʕak.* He's a tricky character; he'll take the shirt off your back.

šarwa pl. *-aat* purchase, buy.

šarraay pl. *-a* purchaser, buyer. *bayyaaʕ šarraay* dealer, merchant.

širyaan pl. *šaraayiin* artery.

muštari, mištiri** pl. *-iyya* buyer, purchaser, customer.

l-muštari the planet Jupiter.

mištara pl. *-ayaat* **1.** buying, purchasing, acquisition. **2.** thing purchased, purchased goods.

š-ṣ-ṣ

šuṣṣ pl. *šṣuuṣ* fish hook.

š-ṭ-b

šiṭab (*u šaṭub*) to cross out, mark out, strike out. *šiṭab ʔakθar il-ʔašyaaʔ il-mawjuuda bil-qaaʔima.* He crossed out most of the things on the list.

šaṭṭab intensive of *šiṭab. lizam il-qalam w-gaam yšaṭṭub.* He grabbed the pen and started crossing things out.

šaṭub crossing out.

šaṭba pl. *-aat* i. n. of *šaṭub*.

š-ṭ-ɛ

šaṭiɛ flat, shallow. *maaɛuun šaṭiɛ* a shallow dish.

š-ṭ-ɛ-l-y

šṭaɛli a kind of card game.

š-ṭ-r

šiṭar (*u šaṭir*) to cut into two equal parts. *šiṭar il-laɛma bin-nuṣṣ.* He cut the piece of meat right down the middle.

tšaaṭar to exchange clever or flippant remarks, engage in repartee. *la-titšaaṭar wiyyaa. θneenkum nafs iš-šii.* Don't be smart with him. The two of you are just alike.

šaṭaara **1.** cleverness, shrewdness, cunning, adroitness, skill. **2.** industriousness.

ʔašṭar more or most clever, shrewd, adroit, skillful.

šaaṭir pl. *šuṭṭar* **1.** clever, smart, bright, adroit, skillful. *la-txaaf ɛalee. huwwa kulliš šaaṭir.* Don't worry about him. He's very clever. **2.** industrious, diligent, hard-working. *ṣiir šaaṭir w-xalliṣ šuġlak bil-ɛajal.* Be industrious and finish your work quickly. *kull it-talaamiiδ kaslaaniin. bass ʔibnak šaaṭir.* All of the students are lazy. Your son's the only hard worker.

š-ṭ-r-n-j

šiṭranj **1.** chess. **2.** (pl. *-aat*) chess set.

š-ṭ-ṭ

šaṭṭ pl. *šṭuuṭ* river.

š-ṭ-f

šiṭaf (*u šaṭuf*) **1.** to infatuate, enamor, fill with ardent passion. *šiṭfata. ma-daʔyfakkir ib-ʔaɛɛad ġeerha.* She completely captivated him. He can't think about anyone but her. **2.** to rinse in clean water, rinse off. *ʔaani ʔaṣoobin il-imwaaɛiin w-inta šṭufha.* I'll soap the dishes and you rinse them. **3.** to make ritually clean by dipping three times in water. *ʔiġṣil il-maaɛuun w-šuṭfa. č-čalib ʔakal bii.* Wash the plate and make it ritually clean. The dog ate off it. **4.** to rebuke, belittle, scold, berate. *šiṭfata ġeer šaṭfa.* She gave him a good scolding.

šaṭṭaf to wash the private parts. *l-xaddaama šaṭṭufat ij-jaahil w-baddilat-la.* The maid washed the child's bottom and changed him.

tšaṭṭaf to wash one's private parts. *la-tiṭlaɛ imnil-xalwa gabul-ma titšaṭṭaf.* Don't leave the toilet before you wash yourself.

nšiṭaf to fall madly in love, be madly in love. *š-bil-ɛajal inšiṭafit biiha!* I fell for her right off the bat!

mašṭuuf **1.** madly in love, infatuated, enamored. **2.** rinsed, washed ritually clean.

š-ṭ-n

šeeṭan, etc., see *š-y-ṭ-n*.

š-ṭ-y

šaaṭi pl. *šwaaṭi* flood plain, fields inundated at flood time. || *šaaṭi šabaaṭi, šaaṭi baaṭi* easily, effortlessly. *liɛab bii šaaṭi baaṭi.* He made a fool of him. He beat him without any effort. *liɛbat bii šaaṭi šabaaṭi.* She made a mess out of him.

š-ɛ-b

tšaɛɛab to separate, split, diverge, branch out. *haṭ-ṭariiq baɛdeen raɛ-yitšaɛɛab.* Later on this road will branch out.

šaɛab pl. *šuɛuub* **1.** people, folk. **2.** ethnic group. **3.** nation.

*šaɛbi** popular, folk-. *ʔaġaani šaɛbiyya* folk songs, popular songs. *raʔiis šaɛbi* a popular leader.

šaɛbiyya popularity.

šuɛba pl. *šuɛab* **1.** section, portion, part, division. **2.** department, branch, section.

šaɛbaan Shaban, the eighth month of the Moslem calendar.

š-ɛ-b-θ

šaɛbaθ to disorder, mess up, make a mess of. *š-aku ɛindak da-tšaɛbiθ il-ʔaġraaδ?* Why are you messing up the things? *la-tiɛči giddaama šii. huwwa fadd waaɛid yšaɛbiθ.* Don't say anything in front of him. He's the sort who makes a mess of everything.

š-ɛ-r

šiɛar (*u suɛuur*) **1.** to know, be cognizant. *da-yišɛur ʔan il-kull yɛibbuu.* He knows that everyone likes him. **2.** to realize, notice. *δallaw yiqašmuruun ɛalee w-laa šiɛar.* They kept pulling his leg and he never realized. **3.** to feel, sense. *ṭ-ṭabiib niġaza b-ʔubra w-laa šiɛar biiha.* The doctor poked him with a needle and he never felt it.

šaɛɛar to make aware, conscious. *šaɛɛarta bil-xaṭar w-ɛiraf š-iysawwi.* I awakened him to the danger and he knew what to do.

šaɛar (coll.) **1.** hair(s). || *šaɛar banaat* cotton candy. **2.** fur.

šaɛra pl. *-aat* a hair. || *zeen ɛaṣṣalit diinaar minna. šaɛra min jilid xinziir.* It's good you got a dinar from him. Getting anything from him is like trying to pluck a hog. *l-balam ingiḷab ʔilla šaɛra.* The boat missed turning over by a hair.

*šaʕri** hair, hairy. || *qmaaš šaʕri* raw silk.

šaʕriyya vermicelli.

šiʕir pl. *ʔašʕaar* poetry.

šiʕra pubes, pubic area.

šiʕaar pl. *-aat* **1.** motto, slogan, watchword. **2.** emblem, badge, distinguishing mark, coat-of-arms. **3.** banner.

šiʕiir barley.

šuʕuur **1.** awareness, consciousness. *ġaab ʕan iš-šuʕuur.* He lost consciousness. *šuʕuur bin-naqiṣ* feeling of inferiority. || *fuqad šuʕuura w-ð̣urab ibna siččiina.* He lost his senses and stabbed his son. **2.** sensitivity, sensibility, perceptiveness. *ma-ʕindak šuʕuur.* You have no sensitivity.

šaʕʕaar pl. *-iin, -a* **1.** a male dancer who does female impersonations. **2.** homosexual, fairy, pansy. **3.** procurer, pander, pimp.

mašʕar pubes, pubic area.

mišʕir hirsute, hairy, shaggy. *baʕð̣ il-banaat yiħibbuun ir-rijjaal il-mišʕir.* Some girls like hairy men.

šaaʕir pl. *šuʕaraaʔ* poet.

š-ʕ-ʕ

šaʕʕ (*i šaʕʕ*) to radiate, beam, emit rays or beams. *wujihha yšiʕʕ bij-jamaal.* Her face is radiant with beauty.

šuʕaaʕ, šʕaaʕ pl. *ʔašiʕʕa* **1.** ray, beam. **2.** X-ray. *xan-naaxuð ʔašiʕʕa ṣ-ṣadrak.* Let's take an X-ray of your chest.

š-ʕ-l

šiʕal (*i šaʕil*) **1.** to ignite, light, set fire to. *ʔišʕil išwayya naar. d-dinya baarda.* Light up a little fire. It's cold. *ʔišʕil ʕuudat šixxaaṭ w-baawuʕ ihnaa.* Strike a match and look here. **2.** to turn on (a light). *ʔišʕil ið̣-ð̣uwa gabul-ma txušš.* Turn on the light before you enter. || *l-mudiir šiʕal ʔahalna biš-šuġul.* The director worked us to death.

štiʕal to catch fire, ignite, flare up, blaze, be or become on fire. *tballilat ʕuudt iš-šixxaaṭ w-baʕad ma-tištiʕil.* The match got wet and won't light now. *ð̣allat in-naar tištiʕil il-leel kulla.* The fire kept burning all night. || *ybayyin štiʕlat beenaathum. gaamaw yitṣaayħuun.* It seems like things have gotten hot between them. They've started to shout at each other.

šuʕla pl. *-aat* flame. || *huwwa šuʕla mnin-naar biš-šuġul.* He's a real ball o'fire.

šaaʕuul pl. *šwaaʕiil* fire tender, firekeeper, fireman.

mašʕal pl. *mšaaʕil* fireplace.

mišʕal pl. *mšaaʕil* torch.

š-ʕ-w-ṭ

šaʕwaṭ **1.** to overheat, burn, scorch. *šiil il-ʔakil imnin-naar. muu šaʕwaṭta!* Take the food off the fire. You've burned it! **2.** to harass, torment, bedevil. *šaʕwaṭ ʔumma hwaaya min čaan iṣġayyir.* He gave his mother a lot of trouble when he was small.

tšaʕwaṭ to be burned, scorched. *t-timman itšaʕwaṭ ib-han-naar il-qawiyya.* The rice got burned on that hot fire.

šiʕwaaṭ burning, scorching, overheating. *da-ʔaštam riiħat šiʕwaaṭ.* I smell something burning.

š-ġ-b

šaaġab to make trouble, disturb the peace. *diir baalak minna. tara yšaaġib ʕaleek.* Watch out for him. He'll make trouble for you.

šaġab trouble, strife, discord, dissension, unrest, commotion, controversy.

mušaaġib pl. *-iin* troublemaker, agitator, mischief-maker.

š-ġ-r

šiġar (*a šuġuur*) to be vacant, free, unoccupied. *š-šahar ij-jaay raħ-tišġar waḍiifa. qaddim ʕaleeha.* Next month a position will be open. Apply for it.

šaaġir **1.** free, vacant, unoccupied. *mitʔassifiin. ma-aku mukaan šaaġir.* We're sorry. There's no position open. **2.** (pl. *šawaaġir*) vacancy, opening.

š-ġ-l

šiġaḷ (*i šuġuḷ ʔišġaaḷ*) **1.** to occupy, busy. *kull-ma yzuurni bid-daaʔira, yišġilni b-ħačya w-šuġḷi yitʔaxxar.* Whenever he visits me in the office, he takes up my time talking and my work gets behind. || *ġeebta šiġḷat fikri.* His absence worried me. **2.** to occupy, take up. *d-diraasa šaaġḷa kull wakti.* Studying has taken up all my time. *šiġaḷ waḍiifteen ʔakθar min sana.* He held two jobs for more than a year.

šaġġaḷ **1.** to make or let work. *ma-yjuuz itšaġġiḷ il-masaajiin.* It isn't permitted to make the prisoners work. **2.** to employ, provide employment. *ruuħ ʕalee baačir. balki yšaġġḷak.* Go to him tomorrow. Maybe he'll employ you. **2.** to make work, put to work, put in operation, make run, start. *min ʔašiil iidi, šaġġiḷ is-sayyaara.* When I raise my hand, you start the car. *hal-makiina tištuġuḷ bil-baanziin. ma-tigdar itšaġġiḷha bil-nafuṭ.* This motor runs on gasoline. You can't operate it on kerosene. *šaġġiḷ ir-raadyo. xall-nismaʕ il-ʔaxbaar.* Turn on the radio. Let's hear the news. || *ʔiδa ma-tšaġġiļ il-ƹaṣa ƹaleehum, ma-ydirsuun.* If you don't take a stick to them, they won't study. || *šaġġaļ ʔiida ƹalayya.* He beat me up. **3.** to invest. *šaġġaļ ifluusa bit-tijaara.* He invested his money in commerce.

nšiġaļ to be or become busy, occupied, engrossed, distracted. *waḷḷa, jaani xuṭṭaar w-inšiġaḷit.* Really, I had company and got all tied up.

štiġaļ **1.** to work, to be busy, engaged, occupied. *šgadd ṣaar-lak tištuġuļ ib-had-daaʔira?* How long have you been working in this office? *l-yištuġuļ bis-siyaasa, š-šurṭa daaʔiman waraa.* If anyone's engaged in politics, the police are always after him. **2.** to operate, run, work, be in operation or motion. *tirak is-sayyaara tištuġuļ w-dixal lil-maṭƹam.* He left the car running and went in the restaurant. *har-raadyo yištuġuļ ƹal-paatri.* This radio operates by battery. *ʔašu bass dist iz-zirr, štiġļat il-makiina.* It seems that the minute I pushed the button, the machine started. **3.** to do business, to be in business. *hal-maxzan yištuġuļ xooš šuġuļ.* This shop does a brisk business. *da-yištuġuļ ƹala ḥsaaba.* He's in business for himself. *hal-maṭƹam yištuġuļ il-nuṣṣ il-leel.* This restaurant is open until midnight. *hal-filim baƹda da-yištuġuļ ib-siinama ir-rašiid.* This film is still playing at the Rashid theater.

šuġuļ **1.** work, labor. *sayyaartak yir-raad-ilha šuġuļ ihwaaya.* Your car needs a lot of work. **2.** workmanship. *haz-zuuliyya šuġuļha zeen.* The workmanship on this carpet is good. *has-saaƹa šuġuļ ʔiid.* This watch is hand made. **3.** (pl. *ʔašġaaļ*) work, job, occupation. *ʔaxuuk—ƹinda šuġuļ willa baṭṭaal?* Your brother—has he got a job or is he out of work? *ʔabuuya baƹda biš-šuġuļ.* My father's still at work. **4.** task, chore, thing to be done. *dazzeet ʔibni b-šuġuļ.* I sent my son on an errand. **5.** business, concern. *haaδa muu šuġļak.* That's none of your business. **6.** business, trade.

¶ *waaƹaditni ƹišriin marra w-ma-jeet. haaδa muu šuġuļ.* You made an appointment with me twenty times and didn't show up. That's no way to do things. *ma-ƹindak šuġuļ? haaδa š-iysawwii waziir?* Are you kidding? He'll never make a minister.

šaġļa pl. *-aat* task, chore, something to be done. *ṣaarat ƹindi šaġļa. ma-gdarit ʔaji.* I had some work. I couldn't come. || *haay šloon šaġļa! kull il-maxaazin mƹazzla w-jigaayri xalṣaana.* This is a fine business! All the stores are closed and my cigarettes are all gone.

šaaġuuļ pl. *šwaaġiiļ* hard-working, industrious, diligent. *ƹaamil šaaġuuļ* a hard worker.

mašġuuļ busy, occupied, in use. *ʔaani mašġuul hassa.* I'm busy now. *l-xaṭṭ mašġuuļ.* The line's busy.

š-f-t

šifit pl. *šfuut* tweezers.

š-f-j

šifij pl. *šfuuj* bull water buffalo.

[1]*š-f-r*

šafra pl. *-aat* a chisel-like knife with angled edge at the tip, a skew knife.

[2]*š-f-r*

šafra pl. *-aat* code, cipher.

š-f-ƹ

šifaƹ (*a šafaaƹa*) to put in a good word, intercede, intervene, plead. *hal-marra ma-aku ʔaḥḥad yišfaƹ-lak; raḥ-tinṭirid.* This time there's no one to intercede for you; you're going to be fired.

tšaffaƹ = *šifaƹ*. *ʔiδa nṭiradit, minu raḥ-yitšaffaƹ-lak ƹind il-waziir?* If you get fired, who will plead your case to the minister?

šafiiƹ pl. *šufaƹaaʔ* mediator, intercessor, advocate.

*šaafiƹi** **1.** Shafitic. *l-maδhab iš-šaafiƹi* the Shafiitic school (of Moslem theology). **2.** (pl. *-iin*) Shafiite.

[1]*š-f-f*

šiffa pl. *šfaaf, šfaayif* lip.

[2]*š-f-f*

šaffaaf **1.** thin, flimsy, transparent, translucent. *laabsa ʔatag jawwa fistaanha š-šaffaaf.* She's wearing a slip under her transparent dress. **2.** candid, frank, open. *sadiiqak yiƹjibni. huwwa šaffaaf ihwaaya.* I like your friend. He's very frank.

š-f-q

šifaq (*i ʔišfaaq*) var. of *ʔašfaq.*

ʔašfaq to take pity. *ʔašfaq ƹalee w-ma-ṭallaƹa mniš-šuġuļ.* He took pity on him and didn't put him out of work.

šafaqa pity, compassion, sympathy, kindliness, solicitude, tenderness. *gaḷba ma-bii δarrat šafaqa.* He doesn't have a bit of pity in him.

šafqa pl. *-aat* hat (with a brim).

ʔašfaq more or most compassionate.

š-f-l-ḥ

šifallaḥ a kind of desert bush with red-centered flowers.

š-f-h

*šafahi** = *šafawi**.

š-f-w

*šafawi** oral, spoken.

š-f-y

šifa (*i šifaaʔ*) to recuperate, convalesce, recover, get well, be healed. *loo ma-mistaɛmil had-duwa, ma-čaan šifeet.* If you hadn't used this medicine, you wouldn't have been cured.

šaafa to cure, heal, restore to health. *hawa lubnaan šaafaak.* The Lebanese air cured you.

ʔašfa to provide a cure, to cure, heal, restore to health. *had-duwa ysakkin il-wujaɛ bass ma-yišfi.* This medicine soothes the pain but won't cure. *ʔaḷḷa yišfiik.* May God heal you.

tšaafa = *šifa. l-ɛamd il-ḷḷaa, il-mariið̣ itšaafa.* Thank God, the patient recovered.

štifa to take revenge, receive satisfaction, take it out. *štifeet bii min ṭirdoo, li-ʔan huwwa s-sabab ṭardi.* I got a lot of satisfaction when they fired him, because he's the reason I was fired. *zaffeeta zaffa štifeet minna biiha.* I told him off and got even with him that way.

mustašfa pl. *-ayaat* hospital.

š-q-q

šaqq = *šagg* which see under *š-g-g.*

nšaqq to split off, break away, secede, separate, withdraw. *nšaqqaw ɛan il-ɛizib w-šakkilaw ɛizib ġeera.* They broke with the party and formed a separate party.

šaqq trouble, difficulty, hardship. || *ma-ɛaṣṣalnaaha ʔilla b-šaqq il-ʔanfus.* We didn't get it except by extreme effort.

šiqqa, šuqqa pl. *šuqaq* apartment, flat.

ʔašaqq more or most troublesome, toilsome, tedious, arduous, etc.

šaaqq troublesome, toilsome, tiresome, tedious, arduous, onerous, difficult, hard. || *ɛikama santeen bil-ʔašġaaḷ iš-šaaqqa.* He sentenced him to two years at hard labor.

š-q-l-b

šaqlab = *čaqlab,* which see under *č-q-l-b.*

š-q-l-m-b

šuqlumba = *čuqlumba,* which see under *č-q-l-m-b.*

š-q-y

šaaqa to tease, bait, needle, rib, kid, joke. *la-tšaaqii tara yizɛal bil-ɛajal.* Don't tease him, because he gets mad quickly.

tšaaqa to banter, joke with one another, kid around. *tiqdar tiššaaqa wiyyaa. yiɛijba š-šaqa.* You can kid around with him. He likes kidding.

šaqa badinage, banter, teasing, joking, kidding. *haay kiimya, muu šaqa. laazim tidrus.* This is chemistry, not play. You must study. || *ʔalfeen diinaar muu šaqa.* Two thousand dinars ain't hay.

šaqi pl. *ʔašqiyaaʔ* bandit, highwayman, thug, villain, scoundrel, rogue.

ʔašqiyaaʔ pl. *-iyya* **1.** thug, bully, tough guy. **2.** scoundrel, rogue.

šaqaawa **1.** thuggery, hooliganism. **2.** brutality, savagery.

šaqaayči, šaqqaači pl. *-iyya* joker, clown, tease.

š-g-r

šgarr to become blond. *šaɛarha yišgarr min tilɛab biš-šamis.* Her hair becomes blond when she plays in the sun.

ʔašgar fem. *šagra* pl. *šugur* blond. *šaɛar ʔašgar* blond hair.

š-g-š-g

šagšag to tear, rip repeatedly (see also *š-g-g*). *j-jaahil šagšag il-xariiṭa wuṣla wuṣla.* The child tore the map into little pieces.

tšagšag pass. of *šagšag. l-kitaab itšag-šag. laazim injallida.* The book got torn apart. We should bind it.

[1]*š-g-f*

šigaf (coll.) chip(s), fragment(s), shard(s).

šigfa pl. *-aat* un. n. of *šigaf.*

[2]*š-g-f*

šigaf pl. *-aat* a net on a pole, used to catch birds.

š-g-g

šagg (*u šagg*) **1.** to tear, rip, rend. *mitʔas-sif! šaggeet θoobič.* I'm sorry! I tore your blouse. *baɛad-ma qira l-maktuub, šagga w-δabba.* After he read the letter, he tore it up and threw it away. || *ʔaani ʔargaɛ w-huwwa yšugg.* I set things straight and he makes a shambles. **2.** to dress, clean. *lahhib il-baṭṭa gabuḷ-ma tšuggha.* Singe the duck before you dress it. **3.** to cut through, put through, construct, build (a road or highway). *raɛ-yšugguun šaariɛ ɛaamm ib-hal-manṭiqa.* They're going to cut a public street through this area.

šaggag **1.** to tear to pieces, tear up. *šaggag il-maktuub gabuḷ-ma yiqraa.* He tore up the letter before he read it. **2.** to wear out. *leeš ma-tilbas ġeer qaaṭ? muu šaggagta lil-qaaṭ ij-jidiid!* Why don't you wear a different suit? You've worn out the new suit!

šagg pl. *šguug* rip, tear, slit.

šugga pl. *-aat* half of a butchered animal, a side of meat.

šigga pl. *šgaag* a type of cheap rug.

š-g-n-g

šgannag (coll.) chips, broken pieces (of brick).

šgannaga pl. *-aat* un. n. of *šgannag.*

[1]*š-k-r*

šikar (*u šukur*) to thank, express gratitude to. *ʔaškurkum. haaδa luṭuf minkum.* I thank you. That's nice of you.

tšakkar to be thankful, grateful, to express one's thanks. *ruuḥ itšakkar minna ʕal-hadiyya.* Go thank him for the gift.

šukur 1. gratitude, gratefulness, thankfulness. 2. thanks, acknowledgment. *wajjihoo-la kitaab šukur ʕala našaaṭa.* They sent him a letter of appreciation for his zeal. *l-ḥamdu lil-laah wiš-šukur.* Praise and thanks be to God.

šukran thanks, thank you. *šukran, maadaxxin.* Thanks, I don't smoke.

maškuur meritorious, laudable, praiseworthy, deserving thanks. *haaδa ʕamal maškuur minnak.* That was a laudable thing you did.

mitšakkir grateful, thankful. *ʔiḥna mitšakkriin kulliš.* We're very grateful.

[2]*š-k-r*

šakkar to turn to sugar, become sugar. *d-dibis šakkar.* The date molasses turned to sugar.

šakar sugar. *ruuḥ iš-šakar* saccharine. *šakar daan* sugar bowl.

šakaraat (invar.) sweets, treats, goodies, sugar candy.

šakari: loon šakari light beige, creamy white.

šakarči pl. *-iyya* confectioner, man who makes and sells sweets.

šakarli: gahwa šakarli coffee with sugar.

šukkar a variety of dates.

š-k-r-l-m-a

šakarlama (coll.) a kind of sugar cookie.

šakarlamaaya pl. *-aat* un. n. of *šakarlama.*

š-k-s

šaakas to irritate, antagonize, contradict. *ma-ṣaḥiiḥ itšaakis il-muʕallim.* It isn't proper to contradict the teacher.

šakis ill-tempered, grumpy, unfriendly.

š-k-k

šakk (*u šakk*) 1. to doubt. *ʔašukk ʔan it-tajruba raḥ-tinjaḥ.* I doubt that the experiment is going to succeed. 2. to distrust, suspect. *yšukk ḥatta b-ʔaṣdiqaaʔa.* He suspects even his close friends. 3. to be skeptical, doubtful. *ʔaani ʔašukk. ma-aʕtiqid il-xabar ṣaḥiiḥ.* I'm skeptical. I don't think the information is correct.

šakk pl. *šukuuk* doubt, uncertainty, suspicion, misgiving. *bala šakk* without doubt, certainly. *raḥ-ašuufak bil-ḥafla bala šakk.* I'll see you at the party without fail.

šakkaak skeptical, suspicious, uncertain.

maškuuk doubtful, dubious, uncertain. *haaδa fadd šii maškuuk bii.* This sort of thing is unlikely.

š-k-l

šikal (*i šakil*) to fetter, hobble. *ʔiškil iṭ-ṭeer ḥatta la-yṭiir.* Fetter the bird so he won't fly away.

šakkal 1. to form, fashion, shape, mold, create. *šakkal wizaara jidiida.* He formed a new cabinet. 2. to fasten, affix, pin. *šakkil-li hal-warda b-ṣadri.* Pin this flower on my lapel for me. *šakkil il-čaamulluġ muwaqqatan ib-teel ʔila ʔan noosal lil-garaaj.* Fasten the fender temporarily with wire till we reach the garage. 3. to catch, snag, become caught. *šakkal θoobi bil-bismaar.* My shirt got caught on the nail. *s-saaʕa ma-biiha šii, laakin il-miil da-yšakkil ib-fadd šii.* There's nothing wrong with the watch, but the hand is catching on something. *r-raadyo da-yištuġuḷ išwayya w-iyšakkil.* The radio works a little while and stops. 4. to join. *walaw maakil, šakkil wiyyaana.* Even though you've eaten, join us. *šakkil wiyyaana. hassa nooṣal.* Squeeze in with us. We'll be there in no time. 5. to diversify, vary, variegate, to make assorted, varied. *ʔariid doondirma, bass šakkil-li-yyaaha.* I want some ice cream, but make it several flavors for me. *jiib-li maaʕuun imšakkal.* Bring me an assorted dish.

tšakkal pass. of *šakkal.*

staškal to have doubts about the religious propriety of. *ma-yxalli fluusa bil-bang. yistaškil.* He doesn't put his money in the bank. He feels it might be wrong religiously.

šikil pl. *ʔaškaal, škuul* 1. outward appearance, looks. *ṣadiiqak šloon šikla?* What does your friend look like? *šikla šikl iš-šaadi.* He looks like a monkey. *ʕaab-lak haš-šikil!* Your face is a disgrace! *wilda ġeer škuul. ma-biihum waaعid عilu.* His children sure are ugly. Not a one of them is nice looking. || *qaaṭak ib-šikli.* Your suit looks just like mine. **2.** shape, form, configuration, pattern. *l-uuteel bii baar عala šikil daaʔira b-nuṣṣ il-ġurfa.* The hotel has a bar in the shape of a circle in the middle of the room. **3.** sort, kind, variety, class, type. *عindi ʔaškaal ihwaaya mniθ-θiyaab.* I have many kinds of shirts. *haš-šikil ʔawaadim ma-yuعtamad عaleehum.* That kind of person isn't dependable. || *giddaami yiحči šikil, w-waraaya ġeer šikil.* In my presence he says one thing, and in my absence something else. *haš-šikil* like that, like this, like so, this way. *muu haš-šikil. laazim itraxxi l-burġi ʔawwal.* Not that way. You have to loosen the screw first.

šakli, šikli** **1.** formal, conventional, customary. *haaδa šii šikli, laakin maṭluub.* This is a formality, but it's required. **2.** (pl. *-iyyaat*) formality. *xall nitruk iš-šikliyyaat, w-niji lil-mawδuuع.* Let's dispense with the formalities and come to the point.

škuul pl. *-aat* **1.** looks, appearance. *la-tعayyib عalee. yaعni škuulak ʔaحsan?* Don't ridicule him. Do you think your appearance is better? **2.** example, type. *da-yimši wiyya škuulaat tlaععb in-nafis.* He runs around with sickening types of people.

šikkaala pl. *-aat* clip, clasp, pin.

taškiila pl. *-aat* assortment, selection, variety.

muškila pl. *mašaakil* problem (see also *m-š-k-l*).

š-k-w

šaku = *š-ʔaku,* which see under *ʔ-k-w.*

š-k-y

šika (*i*) **1.** to complain about. *šikaa-li ʔamra.* He complained to me about his situation. **2.** to suffer, have a complaint. *ʔibni yiški min miعidta.* My son is suffering with his stomach.

šakka to make or let complain. *l-mudiir ma-šakkaani.* The director wouldn't let me complain.

tšakka to complain. *la-tibqa tiššakka.* Don't keep on complaining. *ṭ-ṭullaab da-yitšakkuun ihwaaya mnil-imtiحaanaat.* The students are grumbling a lot about the exams.

štika **1.** to suffer, have a complaint. *baعad yištiki min miعidta.* He is still suffering with his stomach. **2.** /with *عala*/ to raise, lodge, file a complaint about. *štikeet عalee عind il-mudarris.* I complained about him to the teacher. *štikeet عalee biš-šurṭa.* I made a complaint against him to the police. **3.** to sue, bring to court. *štika عala š-šarika li-ʔan il-maal ṭilaع bii عeeb.* He sued the company because a defect showed up in the merchandise.

šakwa pl. *šakaawi* **1.** complaint, grievance. **2.** accusation.

šikaaya pl. *-aat* **1.** complaint, grievance. **2.** accusation.

šakiyya, šikiyya pl. *-aat* **1.** complaint, grievance. **2.** accusation.

mištiki complainant, plaintiff.

š-l-b

šilib field rice, rice before being processed for food.

š-l-b-h

tšalbah to climb up, ascend. *l-bazzuuna da-titšalbah عal-حaayiṭ.* The cat's climbing up the wall.

š-l-t

šalta pl. *-aat* pallet, thin mattress.

š-l-t-ġ

šaltaġ to deceive, cheat, lie. *šaltaġ عalee w-axaδ ifluusa.* He tricked him and took his money.

š-l-ح

šallaح **1.** to undress, remove the clothing from the lower part of the body, uncover the legs. *šalliحata w-ġislat rijlee.* She undressed him and washed his legs. **2.** to bare one's legs, disrobe, undress. *šalliحat w-raawatni zruurha.* She lifted her dress and showed me her thighs. *nazzli nafnuufič. muu عeeb tšallحiin biš-šaariع!* Lower your dress. It's shameful to expose yourself on the street! *ʔaxuuk imšallaح. gul-la yidġaṭṭa.* Your brother is indecently exposed. Tell him to cover himself.

tšallaح to undress, disrobe. *sidd iš-šibbaač gabul-ma titšallaح.* Close the window before you undress.

š-l-ع

šilaع (*a šaliع*) **1.** to extract, remove, pull out, take out. *ʔišlaع il-bismaar imnil-حaayiṭ.* Pull the nail out of the wall. *šilعaw iš-šibbaač w-dixlaw il-beet.* They removed the window and entered the house. *raaح il-ṭabiib il-ʔasnaan حatta yišlaع sinna.* He went to the dentist to get his tooth pulled. || *ʔibnič šilaع gaḷbi l-yoom.* Your son gave me a hard time today. *haš-šuġuḷ ṣaعub yišlaع il-gaḷub.* This work is murder. **2.** to leave, depart, go away hurriedly. *ʔaxaδ ġaraaδa w-šilaع.* He took his things and left.

šallaʕ 1. intensive of *šilaʕ*. *šalliʕ čam wuṣlat tamur min hal-ʕallaana.* Dig out some hunks of dates from this basket. *gaaʕid w-yšalliʕ ib-šaʕraata l-biiδ.* He's sitting and plucking his gray hairs. 2. to shed baby teeth. *j-jaahil ma-yibči hwaaya min yibdi yšalliʕ.* The child doesn't cry much when he starts shedding his baby teeth.

tšallaʕ to be pulled out, be removed. *ʔawraaq il-iktaab kullha tšalliʕat.* All the pages of the book were pulled out.

nšilaʕ pass. of *šilaʕ*. || *δall gaaʕid w-ma-nšilaʕ ʔila nuṣṣ il-leel.* He stayed and wouldn't budge till midnight.

šaliʕ 1. pulling out, extracting, removing. 2. leaving hurriedly.

šalʕa i. n. of *šaliʕ*.

š-l-ġ-ṃ

šalġaṃ turnips. *raas šalġam* a turnip.

š-l-f

šilaf (*i šalif*) to eject, expel, get rid of. *buqa bil-waδiifa šahreen w-baʕdeen šilfoo.* He stayed with the job for two months and then they kicked him out. *ʔiʕči wyaa šwayya w-baʕdeen išilfa.* Talk to him a while and then get rid of him.

š-l-g

šilig a cucumber-shaped variety of melon.

š-l-l

šall (*i šall*) to paralyze. *δuraba ʔubra b-rijla w-šallha ʕan il-ʕaraka.* He gave him a shot in his leg and paralyzed it.

nšall to be paralyzed. *baʕad haadiθ is-sayyaara, nšallat iida.* After the auto accident, his hand became paralyzed.

šalal paralysis. *šalal il-ʔaṭfaal* infantile paralysis, polio.

šilla rice cooked to a thick, gummy consistency, usually with gram added to it.

šliil 1. pocket formed with the front of the robe. || *fukk išliilak.* Hold up the front of your robe and form a basket. 2. (pl. *šlaayil*) horse's tail.

šiliila pl. *-aat* a hank of yarn. || *šiliila w-δaayiʕ raasha.* Everything is all fouled up (lit., it's a hank of yarn and the end of it is lost).

šallaal pl. *-aat* waterfall, cataract.

šallaali 1. quick, hurried, sloppy. *la-twaddi hduumak il-hal-ʔuutači. šuġla šallaali.* Don't take your clothes to that presser. His work is hurried and sloppy. 2. quickly, hurriedly. *la-tʕaawil itʕallima ʕaš-šuġuḷ šallaali.* Don't try to teach him the work too quickly.

š-l-m-n

šalman to brag, exaggerate, talk big. *la-tṣaddig bii; yšalmin ihwaaya.* Don't believe him; he brags a lot.

šeelmaan (coll.) 1. girder(s), metal beam(s). 2. blustering, exaggerated talk, bragging. *haaδa kulla šeelmaan.* That's all a lot of talk.

šeelmaana pl. *-aat* girder, steel beam.

šeelmanči pl. *-iyya* braggart, boaster.

š-l-n-f-ṣ

šlunfuṣ pl. *-aat* harridan, hag, shrewish, bitchy woman.

š-l-h

šilah (*a šalih*) to run aground, to hit a snag. *l-balam šilah. laazim injurra.* The boat has run aground. We'll have to pull it off.

šallah to roll up (the sleeves or pants). *šallah irdaana w-xaššaš iida bil-ṗiiṗ.* He rolled up his sleeve and plunged his hand into the barrel.

tšallah 1. to roll up one's sleeves, pants, or robe. *tšallah w-miša bil-ṃayy.* He rolled up his pants and waded into the water. 2. to proceed with vigor. *ʔiδa nitšallah-ilha, nxalliṣha b-saaʕ.* If we plunge right into it, we'll finish it quickly. *tšallah w-xalli nxalliṣ iš-šuġuḷ.* Let's get going and finish the work.

š-l-w-n

šloon 1. how, in what manner, in what way. *ma-yuʕruf išloon yjaawub.* He doesn't know how to answer. 2. how, in what condition, in what state. *šloonak il-yoom?* How are you today? 3. how could it be that, for what reason, why. *šloon idgul-la ma-činit mawjuud ihnaa?* How could you tell him I wasn't here? *šloon ma-šifta li-hassa?* How come you haven't seen him yet? *muu ʕallamtak? šloon ma-tuʕruf ij-jawaab?* Didn't I teach you? What do you mean you don't know the answer? 4. what, what sort of, what kind of, what a. *šloon? ʔinti lli ma-qbalit.* What? You're the one that refused. *šloon muʕaamala haay? huwwa muu čalib.* What kind of treatment is that? He's not a dog. *hassa šloon wiyyaak? ma-tiji wiyyaaya?* Now what's the matter with you? Aren't you coming with me? *ʔadri šloon wujih ylaʕʕib in-nafis ʕalee.* I realize what a sickening face he has. *šloon iʕyuun ʕaleeha! falla!* What gorgeous eyes she has! They're gorgeous!

šloon-ma however, howsoever. *ʔagdar aṣbuġ-lak is-sayyaara sloon-ma triid.* I can paint the car for you any way you want.

š-l-y-k

šilleek (coll.) strawberry(s).

šilleeka pl. *-aat* un. n. of *šilleek*.

š-m-ʔ-z

šmaʔazz to feel disgust, be disgusted. *šmaʔazzat nafsa min hal-ḥayaat.* He got disgusted with that life. *hal-ʔakil tišmiʔizz in-nafis minna.* This food is repulsive.

š-m-t

šammat, to gloat, to rejoice at misfortune. *ʔiδa tinḥibis, raḥ-itšammit biina l-ʕidwaan.* If you go to jail, our enemies will rejoice at our misfortune.

tšammat = *šammat. min xiṣar, kullhum itšammitaw bii.* When he lost, they all gloated over his misfortune.

šamaata malicious joy, gloating.

š-m-r

šumar (*u šamur*) **1.** to toss, cast, throw. *ʔaani ʔašmur il-iglaaṣ w-inta lugfa.* I'll toss the glass and you catch it. *raḥ-aṣʕad foog w-inta šmur-li l-ḥabil.* I'll climb up and you throw me the rope. *ʕayyinoo b-baġdaad bass baʕdeen šumroo l-fadd qarya biʕiida.* They employed him in Baghdad but later sent him off to a distant village. **2.** to go off, roam, range. *šumar biʕiid* He went a long way off. *min iṭlaʕna nṣiid, šmarna biʕiid.* When we went out hunting, we roamed far afield.

šammar to strew, throw around. *ʔibnič, min yirjaʕ imnil-madrasa, yšammur kutba w-ihduuma.* When your son comes in from school, he throws his books and clothes around.

šamra pl. *-aat* **1.** toss, cast, throw. **2.** manner, style, way (esp. of talking). *ʕinda šamra bil-ḥači maaxiδha min ʔabuu.* He has a style of talking that he got from his father.

mašmar pl. *mšaamir* muffler, scarf.

ṣ-m-s

šammas to expose to the sun, lay out in the sun. *šammis ihduumak gabuḷ-ma δδummha.* Lay your clothes out in the sun before you store them.

tšammas to expose oneself to the sun, bask in the sun, sun oneself. *yiʕijbak titšammas il-yoom?* Would you like to get some sun today?

šamis pl. *šmuus* (fem.) sun. || *δuraba š-šamis.* He had a sunstroke. *warid ʕeen iš-šamis* sunflower. *waraq ʕabbaad iš-šamis* litmus paper.

*šamsi** solar, sun-. || *taṣwiir šamsi* picture taken by a professional photographer (as opposed to one taken with a box camera).

šamsiyya pl. *-aat* **1.** umbrella, parasol. **2.** awning.

šamsuqamar sunflower.

š-m-š-m

šamšam to sniff. *šuuf ič-čalib da-yšamšim bil-ġaraaδ.* Look at the dog sniffing at the things.

tšamšam to nose around, snoop. *ʔija yitšamšam il-ʔaxbaar.* He came to sniff out the news.

š-m-ʕ

šammaʕ to wax. *ʔiδa tšammiʕ xeeṭ is-sibḥa, yṣiir ʔaqwa.* If you wax the string of the prayer beads, it'll be strong. || *min šaafni jaay, šammaʕ il-xeeṭ.* When he saw me coming, he ran away.

šamiʕ (coll.) **1.** wax. **2.** candle(s).

šamʕa pl. *-aat, šmuuʕ* **1.** piece of wax. **2.** candle. || *gloob ʔabu sittiin šamʕa* sixty-watt light bulb.

šammaaʕ pl. *-a* maker and seller of candles.

šimmaaʕa pl. *-aat* coat rack, hat rack.

mšammaʕ **1.** waxed. **2.** oilcloth. **3.** (pl. *-aat*) raincoat.

š-m-ʕ-d-a-n

šamiʕdaan pl. *-aat* candlestick, candelabrum.

[1]*š-m-l*

šimal (*i šumuul*) **1.** to include, imply, implicate. *t-tarfiiʕ šimal kull il-muwaδδafiin.* The promotion included all the employees. *t-tuhma ma-tšimlak.* The accusation doesn't include you. || *šimalni b-ʕaṭfa.* He was very kind to me. **2.** to be included among the winners while not winning first place. *l-biṭaaqa maalti ma-ribḥat laakin šimlat.* My ticket didn't win but it did get me something.

štimal /with *ʕala*/ to contain, comprise, include, be made up of. *beetna yištimal ʕala ʔarbaʕ ġuraf w-maṭbax.* Our house consists of four rooms and a kitchen.

šamil **1.** uniting, gathering. *jtimaʕ šamilhum.* They got together, they united, they held a reunion. *jtimaʕ šamilhum baʕad infiṣaal ʕašr isniin.* They had their reunion after a separation of ten years.

šmaal pl. *-aat* the sanitary apparatus worn by women during menstruation.

šaamil comprehensive, exhaustive, detailed. *maqaal šaamil* a detailed article.

muštamal pl. *-aat* a large cottage built

adjacent to a private home for rental purposes or servant quarters.

²š-m-l

šimaal north.

*šimaali** north, northern, northerly. *il-qism iš-šimaali* the north section.

š-m-m

šamm (*i šamm*) to smell, sniff. *šimm hal-warda w-šuuf išloon riiča biiha.* Smell this flower and see what an odor it has.

šammam to make or let smell. *ma-da-yiqbal yšammimni il-warda.* He won't let me smell the flower.

štamm = *šamm. sawwa* *ʕamaliyya b-xašma w-baʕad ma-yištamm zeen.* He had an operation on his nose and since then doesn't smell well.

šamm smelling, sniffing.

šamma pl. *-aat* 1. a smell, a sniff. 2. whiff, slight odor.

šimmaam (coll.) muskmelon(s).

šimmaama pl. *-aat* un. n. of *šimmaam.*

š-n-a-w

šnaaw push-ups. *yaaxuð išnaaw.* He does push-ups.

š-n-t-r

tšantar to behave in a crude, coarse, low-brow or vulgar manner. *l-walad yguum yitšantar min yšuuf banaat.* The boy begins to act up when he sees girls.

mšantir crude, coarse, vulgar, unpolished, ill-bred.

š-n-j

tšannaj to contract, tighten up, stiffen. *ʕaðalaat rijli tšannijat.* My leg muscles have tightened up.

š-n-ʕ

šinaʕ (*a šaniʕ*) to expose to disgrace, notoriety, or unwanted fame. *ʔiða ma-tinṭuuni čuṣṣa, ʔašnaʕkum.* If you don't give me a share, I'll expose you. *ġilaṭit w-git-la rubaʕit miit diinaar w-huwwa šinaʕni.* I goofed and told him I won a hundred dinars and he gave me away.

šaniiʕ repugnant, repulsive, disgusting. *ʕamal šaniiʕ* a disgraceful deed.

ʔašnaʕ more or most repugnant, disgusting, etc.

š-n-q

šinaq (*u šaniq*) to hang. *šinqoo l-fajir.* They hanged him at dawn.

šaniq hanging. *čikmaw ʕalee biš-šaniq.* He was sentenced to death by hanging.

mašnaqa pl. *mašaaniq* gallows, hanging place.

š-n-g

šannag to make (bread dough) into lumps or balls. *šannag il-ʕajiin čatta nuxbuz.* Make the dough into balls so we can bake.

šunga pl. *šunag* a ball of bread dough ready to be rolled out flat to make a loaf.

š-n-n

šann (*i šann*) 1. to launch an attack, make a raid. *l-ʕadu šann čamla qawiyya ʕal-qarya.* The enemy launched a strong campaign against the village. 2. to dilute yoghurt to make a kind of drink. *šinn hal-liban w-xalli bii θalij.* Dilute this yoghurt and put ice in it.

šiniina a kind of drink made of yoghurt diluted with water.

šnaan crude soap made from dried, crushed leaves of a kind of desert bush.

š-n-w

šinu (interrogative pronoun) what? what's this? what do you mean? *šinu haay?* What's this? *tuʕruf šinu lli baqqaani hnaa?* Do you know what made me stay here? *šinu ma-smaʕitni? ʔaani čičeet ib-ṣooṭ ʕaali.* What do you mean you didn't hear me? I spoke in a loud voice.

š-h-b

šihaab pl. *šuhub* meteor, shooting star.

ʔašhab fem. *šahba* pl. *šuhub* light gray, ash-colored.

š-h-d

šihad 1. (*a šuhuud*) to witness, be a witness to. *šuufu, yaa naas! jarr ʕalayya xanjar. šihadtu.* Look, you people! He pulled a knife on me. You're witnesses. 2. (*a šahaada*) to testify, bear witness, give testimony. *la-ddiir baal. rač-ašhad-lak.* Don't worry. I'll testify for you. *tṣawwar, ṣadiiqi šihad ʕalayya bil-mačkama.* Imagine, my friend testified against me in court. *xamis marraat ġilabitni. ʔašhad-lak ʔinta ʔustaað biš-šiṭranj.* Five times you beat me. I can vouch for your being a master at chess. || *šihdu ʕalayya. ʔiða ma-abuṣṭa, čaqqkum.* Mark my words. If I don't beat him up, you can tell everyone. *ʔašhad bil-laah, ʔašhad maa bil-laah* I swear by God. *ʔašhad maa bil-laah xooš walad.* I swear by God he's a good boy. 3. /with *ʕala*/ to sign as a witness. *šihdaw iθneen ʕal-kafaala.* Two signed the bond as witnesses.

šahhad to make or let testify, cause to give testimony. *ʔiða ma-tqurr, rač-ašahhid ʕaleek jamaaʕa.* If you don't confess, I'll have people testify against you.

šaahad to witness, see, watch, observe, view. *l-waziir šaahad ir-ruwaaya w-ʕij-*

bata. The minister watched the play and liked it.

tšaahad 1. to recite the creed of Islam. *muᶜallim id-diin siˀalni ˀatšaahad w-maᶜirafit.* The religion teacher ask me to recite the creed and I didn't know it. 2. (by extension) to be near death. *min šift is-sabiᶜ giddaami, tšaahadit.* When I saw the lion in front of me, I said my last words. *ðall yitšaahad saaᶜa ˀila ˀan maat.* He struggled for life for an hour until he died.

stašhad 1. to die as a martyr, give one's life. *θneen min wilidha stašhidaw bil-maᶜraka.* Two of her children gave their lives in the battle. 2. /with *b-*/ to cite as authority, quote as evidence or support. *b-difaaᶜa, stašhad ib-ᶜiddat ᶜawaadiθ.* In his defense, he cited several incidents. *b-xiṭaaba, stašhad ib-ˀabyaat il-ᶜiddat šuᶜaraaˀ.* In his speech, he quoted the lines of several poets.

šahiid pl. *šuhadaaˀ* martyr.

šahaada pl. *-aat* 1. testimony, witness, evidence, deposition. 2. certificate, certification, affidavit. 3. degree, diploma.

šaahuud pl. *šwaahiid* large bead on the end of a string of prayer beads.

mašhad pl. *mašaahid* 1. scene (of an occurrence). 2. act, scene (in theatre, entertainment).

mušaahada viewing, observing, watching, witnessing.

šaahid pl. *šhuud* witness. || *šaahid ᶜayaan* eye-witness.

š-h-r

šihar (*a šahir*) to make well-known, renowned, famous, notorious. *šiharni w-maxalla ˀaᶜᶜad ma-gal-la.* He exposed me and didn't leave anyone that he didn't tell.

štihar to be or become famous, well-known, famed, celebrated, notorious. *štihar baᶜad-ma nišar iktaaba.* He became famous after he published his book.

šahar pl. *ˀašhur* month. || *šahr il-ᶜasal* honeymoon.

*šahri** monthly, mensal. *l-ištiraak iš-šahri bij-jariida* the monthly subscription rate for the paper. *ˀiijaar šahri* monthly rent.

šahriyya pl. *-aat* monthly payment or salary.

šuhra 1. repute, reputation, renown, fame, famousness. 2. notoriety.

šahiir 1. famous, well-known, celebrated, renowned. *maˀallif šahiir* a famous writer. 2. notorious.

ˀašhar more or most famous, well-known, etc.

mašhuur 1. famous, well-known, renowned, celebrated. *mulaakim mašhuur* a famous boxer. *hal-baṭal mašhuur ib-šajaaᶜta.* That hero's known for his bravery. 2. notorious. *ˀašqiyaaˀ mašhuur* a notorious thug. 3. (pl. *mašaahiir*) a celebrity, a famous person.

š-h-g

šihag (*a šahig*) to hiccup, have the hiccups. *la-tišrab ṃayy min tiðᶜak tara tišhag.* Don't drink water when you laugh or you'll get the hiccups.

šihheega hiccups. *lizmata š-šihheega mudda.* He had the hiccups for a while.

š-h-m

šahim pl. *-iin* noble, gallant, decent, gentlemanly.

šahaama 1. gallantry, gentlemanliness. 2. decency, respectability.

š-h-y

šahha to cause hunger, desire, craving, to whet the appetite, be appetizing. *riiᶜt il-ˀakil itšahhi.* The odor of food whets the appetite.

štiha to wish, desire, crave, have an appetite for. *la-djiib-li ˀakil. ma-aštihi.* Don't bring me any food. I have no appetite. *da-aštihi ˀaklat simač.* I feel like eating fish. *tbayyin mištihi baṣit.* It looks like you're asking for a spanking.

šahwa pl. *-aat* 1. lust, carnal appetite. 2. orgasm.

*šahwaani** 1. lustful, sensuous. 2. debauched, lewd.

šahiyya appetite.

š-w-t

šawwat to kick a ball, shoot. *ˀinta tšawwit kulliš zeen bis-sibaaq.* You kicked well in the game. *šuuf šloon šawwatha liṭ-ṭooba ᶜaali.* Look how high he kicked the ball.

šuut pl. *-aat, šwaata* kick, shot. *ðurab iṭ-ṭooba šuut.* He kicked the ball.

š-w-x-r

šooxar to snore (see also *š-x-r*). *š-biik da-tšooxir? xašmak masduud?* Why are you snoring? Is your nose stopped up?

š-w-r

šaar (*u šoor*) to consult, take counsel with. *šuur ˀabuuk gabuḷ-ma tsaafir.* Consult your father before you leave.

šawwar to have the power to call divine vengeance. *has-sayyid yšawwir.* This descendant of Mohammed has the power to call divine vengeance.

šaawar to whisper to. *šaawurni ɛatta ma-yismaɛ š-itgul-li.* Whisper to me so he won't hear what you tell me.

ˀašaar /with *ɛala*/ to advise, give advice to. *ˀašaar ɛalee ṭ-ṭabiib yaaxuδ mushil.* The doctor advised him to take a laxative.

tšaawar to whisper to each other. *da-yitšaawruun w-ma-da-afham iš-da-yguuluun.* They're whispering to each other and I don't understand what they're saying.

stašaar to ask advice, seek an opinion from. *ma-ysawwi šii ˀiδa ma-yistišiira bil-ˀawwal.* He does nothing without first asking his advice. *ma-aku daaɛi tistašiira. ˀaɛtiqid yittifiq wiyyaak.* There's no need for you to get his opinion. I think he agrees with you.

šuura white, salt-like deposit on lime or concrete in damp places.

mišwaar while, time, interval. *ṣaar-li mišwaar ˀantaδrak.* I've been waiting for you for some time. *ruuɛ fadd mišwaar saaɛa w-taɛaal.* Go away for about an hour and then come.

mašwara counsel, advice, suggestion.

mušaawara **1.** whispering. **2.** (pl. *-aat*) conference, consultation.

ˀišaara pl. *-aat* **1.** signal, sign, indication. **2.** gesture, motion, nod, wink, wave. **3.** mark, indicator.

¶ *ˀišaara laa-silkiyya.* radio message.

stišaara pl. *-aat* advice, recommendation.

*stišaari** advisory. *majlis istišaari* advisory council.

mušaawir pl. *-iin* counselor, adviser, consultant.

mušiir pl. *-iin* field marshal, general of the armies.

mustašaar pl. *-iin* **1.** adviser, counselor. **2.** chancellor.

š-w-r-b-a

šoorba soup, broth.

š-w-š

šawwaš **1.** to muddle, confuse, disturb, upset. *la-tšawwišni; xalli afakkir.* Don't confuse me; let me think. *ˀinta šawwašta hwaaya b-hal-xabar.* You upset him a lot with that news. **2.** /with *ɛala*/ to interfere with, jam. *ˀaku maɛaṭṭat ˀiδaaɛa da-tšawwiš ɛala maɛaṭṭatna.* There's a broadcasting station interfering with our station.

tšawwaš **1.** to be confused, muddled. *ma-adri leeš itšawwašit.* I don't know why I was confused. **2.** to be disturbed, upset, become uneasy, worried. *ɛali ma-rijaɛ li-hassa. fikri tšawwaš ɛalee.* Ali didn't return yet. I'm uneasy about him. *ma-aku daaɛi titšawwaš. huwwa šwayya raɛ-yitˀaxxar.* There's no reason to worry. He'll be a little bit late.

šaaš cheesecloth, gauze.

šaaša pl. *-aat* **1.** piece of muslin. **2.** (movie) screen.

š-w-ṭ

šaaṭ (*u šooṭ*) **1.** (of food) to scorch, burn. *t-timman šaaṭ. laazim in-naar čaanat ɛaalya.* The rice scorched. The fire must have been too high. **2.** to be or become upset, worried, disturbed. *raɛ-agul-lak fadd šii bass la-tšuuṭ.* I'm going to tell you something but don't get upset. *šaaṭat ɛala ˀibinha min simɛat il-xabar.* She got upset about her son when she heard the news.

šawwaṭ **1.** to burn, scorch. *ṭaffi n-naar. šawwaṭt it-timman.* Turn off the fire. You've burned the rice. **2.** to upset, disturb, worry. *raɛ-itšawwuṭa b-hal-xabar. ˀiskut ˀaɛsan-lak.* You'll upset him with this news. It would be better for you to keep quiet.

šooṭ **1.** being or becoming disturbed, anxious, worried. **2.** (pl. *ˀašwaaṭ*) race. **3.** (pl. *-aat*) short circuit, short. *ṣaar šooṭ bil-waayar w-inṭufa δ-δuwa.* There was a short in the wire and the light went off.

šooṭa i. n. of *šooṭ* **1.**

š-w-f

šaaf (*u šoof*) **1.** to see. *laazim ašuuf il-beet gabuḷ-ma aˀajjirha.* I must see the house before I rent it. *šifit hal-filim gabuḷ.* I've seen that film before. *šifta marr min yammna.* I saw him pass by us. *šaayif iš-sawwa biyya?* Did you see what he did to me? *riɛit lil-maɛmal ɛatta ˀašuuf išloon yrakkibuun is-sayyaaraat.* I went to the factory to observe how they assemble cars. *šuuf, da-agul-lak, ˀaani ma-aqbal ib-hiiči siɛir.* Look, I'm telling you, I won't agree to such a price. || *la-tšuufa hiiči. huwwa ˀašṭan min ibliis.* Don't let his looks fool you. He's more clever than a devil. *šifit fariq ɛala had-duwa.* I noticed an improvement with this medicine. *min tidjaadal wiyyaa, yšuuf nafsa yiftihim.* When you argue with him, he sees himself understanding everything. *haaδa yšuuf nafsa ɛala ṭuul.* This guy is always thinking of himself. *ṣadiiqak šaayif nafsa* *hwaaya.* Your friend is very conceited. *l-baarεa šifit ṭeef.* Last night I had a dream. **2.** to experience, go through, sustain, suffer, to find, encounter. *nijaε rağm iṣ-ṣuεuubaat illi šaafha.* He succeeded despite the hardships which he experienced. *muu εajiib yiεči hiiči li-ʔanna ma-šaayif.* It isn't strange that he would talk like that because he's inexperienced. **3.** to find, discover. *da-ašuuf laδδa b-haš-šuğuḷ.* I find pleasure in this work. *šuuf-lak fadd waaεid ysaaεdak.* Find yourself someone to help you. *laazim itšuuf fadd εall il-hal-muškila.* You must find some solution for this problem. **4.** to find out, ascertain, determine. *fuεaṣa ṭ-ṭabiib w-šaaf ma-bii šii.* The doctor examined him and found there was nothing wrong with him. *xaabra w-šuuf š-iyriid.* Phone him and see what he wants. **5.** to think, believe, be of the opinion that. *š-iššuuf? ʔaruuε il-bağdaad loo laaʔ?* What do you think? Should I go to Baghdad or not? *ʔaani ʔašuuf loo dgul-la biiha ʔaεsan.* It seems to me that it would be better if you tell him about it. **6.** to sense, apperceive, feel, to have a hunch, a premonition, a feeling. *ʔaani ʔašuuf taaliiha raε-yijiina ʔiid min wara w-ʔiid min giddaam.* I have a hunch that in the end he'll come to us empty-handed.

šawwaf to cause to see, let see, show. *šawwafni kull kutba.* He showed me all his books. *tigdar itšawwufhum il-kulliyya?* Can you show them the college?

tšaawaf to see each other. *xalli nitšaawaf. muu dğiib fadd marra.* Let's see one another. Don't just disappear altogether.

nšaaf **1.** to be seen. *beeš miltihi? ʔašu ma-da-tinšaaf.* What've you been up to? It seems you haven't been seen around. **2.** to be worth seeing. *hal-filim ma-yinšaaf. ylaεεib in-nafis.* This film isn't worth seeing. It's sickening.

šoof seeing. || *ʔaštiriiha εaš-šoof* I'll buy it on approval.

šoofa pl. *-aat* sight, look, glance.

mašuufa pl. *-aat* mirror, looking glass.

š-w-q

šawwaq to fill with longing, desire, nostalgia. *šawwaqitni εalee. raε-aštirii.* You have made me want it. I'm going to buy it. *har-rasim yšawwuqni l-labnaan.* This drawing makes me long for Lebanon.

štaaq to feel longing, yearning, craving, desire, nostalgia. *štaaqeet il-ʔibni w-δṭar-reet asaafir-la.* I longed to see my son and had to go to him. *ʔaštaaq iδ-δiič il-ayyaam il-εilwa.* I yearn for those pleasant times. *tidri, da-aštaaq-la lil-malεuun.* You know, I miss the rascal.

šooq pl. *ʔašwaaq* longing, desire, craving, yearning.

ʔašwaq more or most desirous, nostalgic, etc.

štiyaaq longing, yearning, craving, desire, nostalgia.

mištaaq longing, yearning, craving, desirous, nostalgic. *mištaaq-lak.* I've been longing for you.

š-w-k

šook (coll.) **1.** thorn(s), spine(s), prickle(s) **2.** thorny bush(es).

šooka pl. *-aat* **1.** un. n. of *šook.* **2.** fork.

šookaaya pl. *-aat* un. n. of *šook.*

š-w-l

šawwaal Shawwal, the tenth month of the Moslem calendar.

š-w-m

šuum var. of *šuʔum,* which see under *š-ʔ-m.*

š-w-m-y-n-a

šoomiina pl. *-aat* **1.** fireplace. **2.** chimney.

š-w-n-d-r

šwandar, šwanδar (coll.) beet(s).

šwandara, šwanδara pl. *-aat* beet.

š-w-h

šawwah to make ugly, to disfigure, deform, deface, distort, mar, mutilate. *j-jidri šawwah wičča.* Smallpox marred his face. *yšawwih il-εaqaayiq.* He distorts the facts. *šawwah sumεat ʔahla b-suluuka.* He debased the reputation of his family by his conduct.

tšawwah pass. of *šawwah. tšawwah wičča bil-εamaliyya.* His face was marred by the operation.

[1]*š-w-y*

šuwa (*i šawi*) to broil, roast, cook (esp. meat). *šuwa l-laεam εal-faεam.* He broiled the meat over the charcoal. || *š-šamis tišwi l-yoom.* The sun's broiling hot today. *šuwatni š-šamis.* I got a sunburn. *l-muεallim šuwaana bil-imtiεaa-naat.* The teacher raked us over the coals in the tests.

nšuwa to be broiled, roasted. *nšuwa l-laεam xooš šawya.* The meat got a good broiling.

mašwi broiled, roasted, cooked. *laεam mašwi* broiled meat.

[2]*š-w-y*

šwayya **1.** a small amount, a little bit, a

few, some. *ʕindi šwayya fluus.* I have a little bit of money. *ʔištiri mnil-baggaaḷ išwayya purṭaqaal.* Buy a few oranges from the grocer. **2.** a short time, a little while. *raḥ-arjaʕ baʕd išwayya.* I'll be back in a little while. *ʔilzam il-baab išwayya ḥatta ʔašidd il-burġi.* Hold the door a minute so I can put the screw in. || *čaan baʕd išwayya tisḥaga s-sayyaara.* The car was just about to hit him. *ʔilla šwayya* almost, very nearly. *ḥaṣṣalitha lis-sayyaara ʔilla šwayya.* I almost got the car. **3.** a little, a little bit, somewhat. *huwwa šwayya mṣaxxin.* He's just a bit feverish. *ʔirjaʕ išwayya ʔila ʔan ʔagul-lak ʔoogaf.* Back up a little until I tell you to stop.

š-y

šii pl. *ʔašyaaʔ* **1.** thing. *šii ʕajiib, ʕabaali ma-ṭumṭur biš-ṣeef.* That's strange. I thought it didn't rain in the summer. *š-šii lli ma-yʕijbak, la-taaxδa.* Whatever you don't want, don't take. *ma-ʕindi šii muhimm.* I don't have anything important. || *baʕδ iš-šii* to a certain extent, a little, somewhat. *ṣiḥḥta tḥassnat baʕδ iš-šii.* His health improved a little. *šii ʕala šii* all in all, on the whole. *šii ʕala šii, huwwa xooš walad.* On the whole, he's a pretty fine fellow. *daris ʔašyaaʔ* general science class. **2.** something. *ġaṭṭi l-ʔakil ib-šii ḥatta la-yitwaṣṣax.* Cover the food with something so that it won't get dirty. *l-yoom ʔabda šii mnin-našaaṭ.* Today he showed some activity. || *ʔaku bii šii.* There's something wrong with it. It has a defect in it.

šwayya see under *š-w-y.*

š-y-ʔ

šaaʔa (*a*) (used in a few phrases, of God) to want, wish, desire. *ʔin šaaʔa ḷḷaah* or *ʔinsaaḷḷa* God willing, it is to be hoped, we hope. *ʔinšaaḷḷa, sant il-luxx inruuḥ il-makka.* God willing, next year we'll go to Mecca. *ʔinšaaḷḷa ma-biik šii.* I hope there's nothing wrong with you. *maa šaaʔa ḷḷaah* or *maašaaḷḷa* (lit.: whatever God intended, used to express:) **1.** a great amount, quantity, or number. *ʕidhum imnil-ġanam maa šaaʔa ḷḷaah.* They have a great number of sheep. *ʕinda fluus maa šaaʔa ḷḷaah.* He has a fabulous amount of money. 2. an exclamation of pleased surprise, approx.: Great! Fine! Wonderful! *maa šaaʔ a ḷḷaah! ṣiḥḥtak zeena il-yoom.* Great! You're in good health today.

š-y-b

šaab (*i šeeb*) **1.** (of hair) to become gray, white. *šaʕra šaab ib-šabaaba.* His hair turned white in his youth. **2.** (of a person) to grow old, become gray-haired. *šaab w-baʕad ma-yigdar yištuġuḷ.* He's grown old and can't work any more. *šaab gabuḷ wakta.* He got old before his time.

šayyab = *šaab. raasa šayyab bil-ʔarbaʕiin.* His hair turned gray at forty. *šayyab imnil-qahar.* He grew old from suffering.

šeeb **1.** grayness of the hair, gray or white hair. **2.** old age.

šeeba pl. *-aat* streak or touch of gray hair.

ʔašyab **1.** more or most aged, old. **2.** more or most gray-haired, gray.

šaayib pl. *šiyyaab* **1.** old, aged. **2.** old man. **3.** king (in card games).

š-y-x

šaax (*i*) **1.** to be or become self-important, pompous, to act like a big shot. *ʔašu min ṣaar mudiir, šaax.* It seems since he became director, it's gone to his head. *šaayix ʕaleehum b-ifluusa.* He lords it over them with his money. **2.** to attain a venerated old age. *min yšiix is-sabiʕ, tiδḥak ʕalee l-waawiyya.* When the lion gets old the jackals laugh at him.

tšayyax = *šaax* **1.** *la-titšayyax ʕaleena. ʔinta minu?* Don't act big with us. Who do you think you are?

šeex pl. *šyuux* **1.** sheikh, chieftain, patriarch, leader, elder (of a tribe). **2.** venerated religious scholar or teacher.

mašyaxa pl. *mašaayix* shiekhdom, territory ruled by a sheikh.

šayxuuxa old age, senility.

š-y-r

šiir **1.** heads (side of a coin). *šiir loo xaṭṭ?* Heads or tails? **2.** (pl. *šyaara*) faucet, spigot, tap.

šiira syrup.

mušiir, etc., see under *š-w-r.*

š-y-r-a-z

šeeraazi: titin šeeraazi a type of tobacco from Persia, especially for use in narghiles.

š-y-r-j

šeeraj sesame oil.

š-y-r-z

seeraz **1.** to sew a border around the edge of (a garment). *ʕid-man raḥ-itšeeriz ʕabaatak?* Who will you have sew the border on your aba? **2.** to stitch together the pages in a book. *hal-iktaab imjallad bass muu mšeeraz.* That book has a binder but it isn't sewn together at the ends.

š-y-r-s

šeeras to put paste or glue on (see also *šriis* under *š-r-s*). *ˀinta šeeris il-ˀawraaq w-aani ˀalzagha.* You put paste on the papers and I'll stick them up.

š-y-š

šaaš (*i šeeš*) to be or become angry, furious. *min simaƐ ˀibna nbuṣat, šaaš w-ṭilaƐ barra.* When he heard that his son had been beaten up, he became furious and went out.

šayyaš to skewer, put on a skewer. *ˀaani ˀaguṣṣ il-laƐam w-inta šayyiša.* I'll cut the meat and you put it on the skewer.

šiiš pl. *šyaaš* **1.** skewer. **2.** metal rod or bar. **3.** knitting needle. || *Ɛali šiiš* turkey (bird).

šiiša pl. *šiyaš* **1.** glass bottle or jar. **2.** globe enclosing the flame of a lantern.

š-y-ṭ-n

šeeṭan to make obnoxiously clever, cause to become a wiseguy, a smart alec. *l-Ɛiiša b-baġdaad šeeṭnata.* Living in Baghdad made him a wise guy.

tšeeṭan to become obnoxiously clever, become a wise guy, a smart alec. *tšeeṭan w-baƐad ma-yingidir Ɛalee.* He became a wise guy and couldn't be controlled any more.

šeeṭana **1.** deviltry, devilishness, mischief. **2.** obnoxious cleverness.

šeeṭan šiiṭaan pl. *šyaaṭiin* **1.** devil, demon, fiend. || *mxaaṭ iš-šiiṭaan* cobweb(s). **2.** rascal, mischief-maker. **3.** wise guy, smart alec, show-off, know-it-all.

ˀašṭan **1.** more or most devilish, fiendish. **2.** more or most mischievous. **3.** more or most clever, sly.

š-y-Ɛ

šaaƐ (*i šeeƐ*) **1.** to spread, diffuse, become widespread. *šaaƐ xabar zawaaja b-surƐa.* The news of his marriage spread quickly. *šaaƐ istiƐmaal it-talafizyoon ib-baġdaad.* The use of television has gotten widespread in Baghdad. **2.** = *ˀašaaƐ*, which see.

šayyaƐ **1.** to spread, divulge, circulate, publicize. *gaamat itšayyiƐ Ɛalee yirtiši.* She started spreading rumors about him taking bribes. **2.** (*šayyaƐ l-ijnaaza*) to pay last respects, to attend a funeral ceremony. *kull ahl il-balda šayyiƐaw ijnaazta.* All the people of the town attended his funeral.

ˀašaaƐ to spread, divulge, circulate, publicize (esp. rumors or gossip). *ˀašaaƐ Ɛaleehum ybiiƐuun tiryaak.* He spread rumors that they sell opium.

tšayyaƐ to become a Shiite, a Shiah, to adopt the Shiitic branch of Islam. *tšayyaƐ Ɛatta binta taaxuδ kull-il-wiriθ.* He became a Shiite so his daughter could get the entire inheritance.

š-šiiƐa the Shiah, the branch of Islam which recognizes Ali as the rightful successor of the prophet Mohammed and does not acknowledge the precepts of the sunna.

*šiiƐi** **1.** Shiitic. **2.** (pl. *šiiƐa*) Shiite, Shiah, adherent of the Shiitic branch of Islam.

*šuyuuƐi** **1.** communist, communistic. *l-mabdaˀ iš-šuyuuƐi* the communist ideology. **2.** a communist.

š-šuyuuƐiyya communism, the communist ideology.

ˀišaaƐa **1.** spreading, circulation (of news). **2.** (pl. *-aat*) rumor, gossip.

tašyiiƐ l-ijnaaza funeral, burial.

š-y-f

šayyaf to slice (fruit or vegetables) lengthwise. *šayyif ir-raggiyya w-qassimha Ɛaleena.* Slice the watermelon and divide it among us.

šiif pl. *šyaaf* slice, piece (of fruit or vegetable).

š-y-l

šaal (*i šeel*) **1.** to lift, raise, elevate, pick up. *šaal il-kursi θ-θigiil ib-fadd ˀiid.* He lifted the heavy chair with one hand. *šaal iṣ-ṣanduug Ɛala δahra w-ṣiƐad li-foog.* He lifted the trunk onto his back and went upstairs. *ma-šaal Ɛeena min Ɛaleeha.* He didn't take his eyes off of her. || *šaayil xašma Ɛan-naas.* He sticks up his nose at everyone. He is conceited. **2.** to carry, convey, transport. *hal-paaṣ yšiil Ɛašir rukkaab.* This bus carries ten passengers. *ˀiδa ma-yidfaƐ ˀujra, ma-raƐ-ašiila.* If he doesn't pay a fare, I won't take him. **3.** to carry on one's person, wear, bear. *yšiil musaddas.* He carries a revolver. *šaayil ifluus wiyyaak?* Do you have any money on you? *l-muqaddam yšiil taaj w-najma.* The lieutenant colonel wears a star and crown. *šaayil hamm. šloon yruuƐ w-yitruk jahhaala waƐƐadhum?* He is burdened with worry. How can he go and leave his children by themselves? || *šaal xaṭiita.* He spoke unjustly about him. He accused him unjustly. **4.** to move, change location, change residence. *jiiraanna raḥ-iyšiiluun il-yoom.* Our neighbors are going to move today. **5.** to take, take away, remove. *jaab kaaree ʔaas w-šaal kull il-meez.* He got four aces and took the whole pot. *l-baanziin yšiil il-lakka mniθ-θoob.* Gasoline will remove the spot from the shirt. || *min simaʕ ʔaani jaay, šaalha.* When he heard I was coming, he beat it. **6.** to take hold, take effect. *j-jidri maali ma-šaal.* My smallpox vaccination didn't take.

šayyal **1.** to load, burden with. *šayyal il-ḥammaal kull ij-jinaṭ.* He loaded the porter with all the suitcases. **2.** to cause to move, change location, change residence. *l-baladiyya šayyilathum min hal-beet.* The city evicted them from this house.

šeela pl. *šiyal* a long head-scarf worn by women.

šayyaal pl. *-aat* (pair of) suspenders.

š-y-l-m-a-n

šeelmaan see *š-l-m-n.*

š-y-m

šayyam to praise for character, virtue, integrity, etc. *šayyim il-imʕeedi w-uxuδ ʕabaata.* Praise the peasant for his virtues and you can take the shirt off his back.

šiima character, integrity, virtue, charity, honor. *ʔahl iš-šiima* people of integrity, charity, honor, etc. *ʔahl iš-šiima ma-ytirkuun jaarhum waḥda ʔiδa ʔaʕʕad ʔiʕtida ʕalee.* People of character don't abandon their neighbor if someone assaults him.

¹*š-y-n*

šeen bad. *ʔaqbala, zeen šeen.* I'll take it, good or bad.

²*š-y-n*

šiin name of the letter *š.*

Ṣ

¹*ṣ-a-j*

ṣaaj pl. *-aat, ṣuuj* a pan or tin used for baking bread or roasting coffee.

²*ṣ-a-j*

ṣaaj = *saaj,* which see under *s-a-j.*

ṣ-a-d

ṣaad name of the letter *ṣ.*

s-a-ġ

ṣaaġ **1.** right, in order, proper, sound (in the expression:) *ṣaaġ saliim* safe and sound, in perfect condition. *rijaʕ min il-ḥarub ṣaaġ saliim.* He returned from the war safe and sound. *stilamit ir-raadyo ṣaaġ saliim.* I received the radio in perfect condition. **2.** pure, unadulterated. *δ-δahab iṣ-ṣaaġ ġaali.* Pure gold is expensive.

ṣ-a-l

ṣaala pl. *-aat* **1.** auditorium, assembly hall. **2.** large room.

ṣ-a-l-w-n

ṣaaloon pl. *-aat* salon, parlor. *ṣaaloon ḥilaaqa* barber shop. *sayyaara ṣaaloon* sedan.

¹*ṣ-b-b*

ṣabb (*u ṣabb*) **1.** to pour, pour out. *ṣubb išwayyat mayy ʕala ʔiidi rajaaʔan.* Pour a little water on my hand please. *ṣubb-li stikaan čaay.* Pour me a cup of tea. *laazim iṣṣubb iš-šoorba bič-čamča.* You'll have to dish up the soup with the ladle. **2.** to pour forth, shed, flow, empty. *šaṭṭ il-ʕarab yṣubb ib-xaliij il-baṣra.* The Shatt Al-Arab empties into the Gulf of Basra. **3.** to pour, mold, cast. *l-ḥaddaad ṣabb rijleen il-qarayoola min iprinj.* The blacksmith cast the legs of the bed out of brass.

ṣabba pl. *-aat* form, casting.

maṣabb pl. *-aat* **1.** outlet, drain. **2.** mouth (of a river).

²*ṣ-b-b*

ṣubbi pl. *ṣubba* a Mandaean, a Sabian.

ṣ-b-ḥ

ṣabbaḥ **1.** to start the day (doing something or in a certain condition or state). *siqna l-leel kulla w-ṣabbaḥna bil-baṣra.* We drove all night and arrived in Basra in the morning. *lli yṣabbuḥ ib-wiččak ma-yšuuf il-xeer.* Anyone who sees you first thing in the morning won't have any luck. *yoomiyya da-aṣabbuḥ ib-wičča.* Every morning I see him. *ṣabbaḥkumullaa bil-xeer.* Good morning.

ʔaṣbaḥ (*i ʔiṣbaaḥ*) to be, become. *ʔaṣbaḥna liʕba b-iidhum.* We've become a plaything in their hands. *ʔaṣbaḥat il-ʔumuur b-ʔiida.* The business is in his hands now. *ʔaṣbaḥ ʕaala ʕal-mujtamaʕ.* He turned out to be a parasite.

ṣubuḥ pl. *ʔaṣbaaḥ* morning. || *yugʕud imniṣ-ṣubuḥ.* He gets up early.

ṣubḥa: yoom iṣ-ṣubḥa the morning after the consummation of a marriage (when gifts are brought to the new couple).

ṣabaaḥ morning (limited to set

phrases). *ṣabaaḥ il-xeer* Good morning. *hala b-haṣ-ṣabaaḥ.* It's nice to see you this morning. || *ṣ-ṣabaaḥ irbaaḥ.* The early bird gets the worm.

*ṣabaaḥi** morning. *d-dawaam iṣ-ṣabaaḥi* the morning session.

ṣubḥiyya pl. *-aat* morning, forenoon.

ṣabbaḥči pl. *-iyya* night watchman who relieves the evening guard (*ʔaġšamči*), and guards from midnight until morning.

ṣ-b-x

ṣabix alkaline. *gaaʕ ṣabxa* alkaline soil.

ṣ-b-r

ṣubar (*u ṣabur*) to be patient, have patience, wait patiently. *ʔiδa tuṣbur, tḥaṣṣilha.* If you have patience, you'll get it. *ṣubar šahar ʕal-ifluus.* He waited a month for the money. *tigdar tuṣbur-li sbuuʕ laax? l-ifluus muu ḥaaδra.* Can you give me another week? The money isn't available now.

ṣṭubar to be patient, have patience. *ṣṭubar išwayya; la-tistaʕjil.* Be a little patient, don't hurry so. *ṣṭubur-li fadd yoomeen w-anṭiik l-ifluus.* Be patient with me just two days and I'll give you the money. *ʔuṣṭubur-li. ʔaani ʔaʕallmak.* Just give me some time. I'll teach you. *ṣṭubur! xall inšuuf šaku hnaa.* Wait! Let's see what's going on here.

ṣabur **1.** patience, forbearance. **2.** a bitter substance made from aloes, applied to the nipples in order to wean an infant, hence: *murr ṣabur* as bitter as aloes.

ṣbuur a kind of kippered fish.

ṣubbeer (coll.) Indian fig(s).

ṣubbeera pl. *-aat* un. n. of *ṣubbeer.*

ṣabbuura pl. *-aat* blackboard.

ṣaabir pl. *ṣwaabir* temple (anat.).

ṣ-b-ṭ

ṣubaṭ (*u ṣabuṭ*) to stay in place, lie down (of hair). *ʔiδa tḥuṭṭ išwayya mayy ʕala šaʕrak, yuṣbuṭ.* If you put a little water on your hair, it'll stay down.

ṣabbaṭ to be still, remain motionless, stay calmly in place. *ʔiδa ma-tṣabbuṭ, ma-agdar ʔazayyinak.* If you don't be still, I can't shave you.

ṣubbaaṭa pl. *-aat* hairnet.

ṣoobaaṭ see *ṣ-w-b-ṭ.*

ṣ-b-ṭ-a-n

ṣabaṭaana pl. *-aat* **1.** barrel. **2.** bore (of a gun).

ṣ-b-ʕ

ʔiṣbiʕ pl. *ʔaṣaabiʕ* **1.** finger. *huwwa ʔila ʔiṣbiʕ bij-jariima.* He has a hand in the crime. || *muu kull iṣaabʕak suwa.* No two people are alike. *min git-la, wučča ṣaar iṣbiʕteen.* When I told him, his face became pale. **2.** toe. **3.** cylinder, stick. *ʔiṣbiʕ diinamiit* stick of dynamite. *ʔaṣaabiʕ jigaayir* empty, rolled cigarette papers.

ṣ-b-ġ

ṣubaġ (*u a ṣubuġ*) **1.** to paint, dye, stain, tint, color. *ṣubaġ beeta loon ʔaxδar.* He painted his house green. *haaδi ṣubġat šaʕarha ʔaṣfar.* She dyed her hair blond. **2.** to black, shine, polish (shoes). *laazim tuṣbuġ qundartak gabuḷ-ma truuḥ lil-ḥafla.* You'd better polish your shoes before you go to the party.

nṣubaġ pass. of *ṣubaġ. l-beet inṣubaġ kulla b-fadd yoom.* The house was all painted in one day.

ṣubuġ pl. *ʔaṣbaaġ* **1.** paint. **2.** dye, coloring. **3.** (shoe) polish.

¶ *raḥ-aruuḥ ʕalee w-aṭayyiḥ ṣubġa.* I'm going to go see him and give him hell.

ṣabbaaġ pl. *-iin, ṣbaabiiġ* **1.** painter. **2.** dyer. **3.** bootblack.

maṣbaġa dye works, dyeing plant.

ṣ-b-n

ṣaabuun, etc., see *ṣ-w-b-n.*

ṣ-b-y

ṣabi, ṣubi pl. *ṣibyaan* youth, lad, boy.

*ṣibyaani** childish, juvenile. *ʔaʕmaal ṣibyaaniyya* childish actions.

ṣ-p-a-n

ṣpaana pl. *-aat, ṣpaayin* wrench, spanner.

ṣ-č-m

ṣačim (coll.) shot, pellet(s), B-B(s). *bunduqiyyat ṣačim* or *tufgat ṣačim* air rifle, pellet gun.

ṣačma pl. *-aat* un. n. of *ṣačim.*

ṣ-ḥ-b

ṣaaḥab **1.** to make friends with, to make up with. *laazim itṣaaḥba li-ʔan ṣ-ṣuuč čaan maalak.* You must make up with him because the fault was yours. **2.** to associate with. *čaan yṣaaḥib jamaaʕa muu min sinna.* He was associating with a group not of his age.

tṣaaḥab to become friends, make up with each other. *tṣaaḥbaw baʕad-ma čaanaw zaʕlaaniin isbuuʕ.* They made up after they'd been mad for a week.

ṣaaḥib pl. *ʔaṣḥaab* **1.** friend, companion, associate. *ʔaṣḥaab in-nabi* the companions of Mohammed. **2.** owner, holder, possessor. *ṣaaḥib maḥall* shop owner. *hiyya ṣaaḥbat ʔaḥla ʕyuun.* She has the prettiest eyes. *ṣaaḥib ij-jalaala* His Majesty. *ṣaaḥib ḥaqq* **1.** rightful owner. 2. the one who is in the right. *ṣaaḥib iz-zamaan* (Shiah) the Mahdi, the last imam who will come to purify Islam. *haaδa ṣaaḥib faḍal ʕalayya.* He has done favors for me. 3. originator, inventor, author. *ṣaaḥib fikra* originator of an idea.

ṣaaḥiba pl. *-aat* fem. of *ṣaaḥib.*

maṣḥuub /with *b-*/ accompanied by, associated with. *maṣḥuub bis-salaama.* Peace be with you. (said on bidding someone good-bye).

ṣ-ḥ-ḥ

ṣaḥḥ (*i a ṣaḥḥa*) 1. to be true, correct, factual, authentic. *ʔiδa ṣaḥḥ il-xabar, qaḍiitak raḥ-tinḥall.* If the news was correct, your case will be solved. 2. (*i a ṣaḥḥ*) /with *l-*/ to come to one, be found by someone. *ṣaḥḥat-li xooš sayyaara w-ma-ʕindi fluus aštiriiha.* I found a good car and don't have the money to buy it. 3. to allow an opportunity, give a chance. *tiʕfiini, waḷḷa ma-yṣaḥḥ-li ʔaji.* Please excuse me, but I don't have the time to come. *yṣiḥḥ-lak itruuḥ wiyyaana baačir?* Will you have a chance to go with us tomorrow? *ʔaani mašġuuḷ ihwaaya, w-ma-yṣaḥḥ-li ʔaḥukk raasi.* I'm awfully busy, and I don't have time to scratch my head.

ṣaḥḥaḥ to correct, grade, mark. *ʔarbaʕ muʕallimiin raḥ-yṣaḥḥiḥuun dafaatir il-imtiḥaan.* Four teachers are going to correct the exam books.

ṣaḥḥ correct, right, proper. *jawaab il-masʔala čaan ṣaḥḥ.* The answer to the question was correct.

ṣiḥḥa 1. health. *šloon ṣiḥḥtak?* How are you? *wizaart iṣ-ṣiḥḥa* Ministry of Health. 2. truth, validity, authenticity, genuineness.

*ṣiḥḥi** 1. wholesome, healthy, healthful. *l-ʔakil bis-sijin muu ṣiḥḥi.* The food in prison isn't wholesome. 2. hygienic, sanitary. *la-tišrab hal-mayy. muu ṣiḥḥi.* Don't drink this water. It isn't sanitary.

ṣaḥiiḥ 1. whole, complete, integral, perfect. 2. proper, correct, right. *zeen git-la gabuḷ ma-truuḥ, haaδa iš-šii ṣ-ṣaḥiiḥ.* It's good that you told him before you left. That was the right thing (to do). 3. true, correct, right, authentic, reliable, credible. *ṣaḥiiḥ? ṣudug raḥ-yiji?* Is that right? He's really coming? *ḥilaf ma-yguul ʔilla ṣ-ṣaḥiiḥ.* He swore he wouldn't speak anything but what was true. *ʔaʕtaqid ʔinta ṣaḥiiḥ, laakin ma-tigdar tiθbitha.* I think you're right, but you can't prove it.

ʔaṣaḥḥ 1. more or most complete, perfect, etc. 2. more or most proper, correct, etc. 3. more or most authentic, reliable, etc.

maṣaḥḥ pl. *-aat* sanatorium.

taṣḥiiḥ correcting, correction.

s-ḥ-r

ṣaḥraaʔ pl. *ṣaḥaari* desert.

*ṣaḥraawi** desert, desolate. *ʔaraaḍi ṣaḥraawiyya* desert lands.

ṣ-ḥ-f

ṣaḥḥaf to bind (a book). *šuġuḷa yṣaḥḥuf iqraaʔiin.* His job is binding Korans.

ṣaḥiifa pl. *ṣaḥaayif* 1. page, leaf (of a book, etc.). || *ṣaḥiifta beeḍa.* He has a clean record. 2. (pl. *ṣuḥuf*) newspaper.

ṣaḥaafa 1. journalism, the newspaper business. 2. the press. *ḥurriyyat iṣ-ṣaḥaafa* freedom of the press.

*ṣuḥufi**, *ṣuḥfi** 1. news, press. *muʔtamar ṣuḥufi* press conference. 2. journalist, newspaperman, reporter.

maṣḥaf pl. *maṣaaḥif* edition, copy (of the Koran).

ṣaḥḥaaf pl. *-a, -iin* bookbinder.

s-ḥ-n

ṣaḥan pl. *ṣuḥuun* 1. plate, saucer. 2. courtyard (of a shrine).

s-ḥ-w

ṣiḥa (*a ṣaḥu*) to regain consciousness, come to, to wake up. *s-sakraan baʕad saaʕteen ma-yiṣḥa.* The drunkard won't wake up for two hours. *ṣiḥa ʕala nafsa w-tirak ir-reesiz.* He came to his senses and quit the races.

ṣaḥḥa 1. to clear up, become clear, bright. *taʕaal šuuf. ṣaḥḥat id-dinya.* Come see. The weather has cleared up. 2. to awaken, rouse, wake up. *baačir ṣaḥḥiini s-saaʕa sabʕa ṣ-ṣubuḥ.* Wake me up tomorrow at seven A.M.

ṣaḥu 1. clearness, brightness (of the weather). 2. clear, bright, sunny weather.

ṣaḥwa consciousness. || *ṣaḥwat ṃoot* a wakeful period between coma and death.

ṣaaḥi 1. clear, bright, sunny. 2. awake, conscious, aware. 3. sober, clear-headed.

ṣ-x-r

saxxar to ask (someone) to do something onerous, to trouble, impose upon. *yṣaxxir il-muwaḍḍafiin yigḍuu-la ʔašġaaḷ xuṣuuṣiyya.* He imposes on the employees to do personal jobs for him. *la-dgul-la wala titʕab. ṣaxxarta w-ma-qibal.* Don't bother to tell him. I've asked him and he wouldn't agree.

tṣaxxar to do a charitable deed, put oneself out to help others. *šloon walad! ʔabad ma-yitṣaxxar.* What kind of boy is he! He never does anything for others.

ṣaxar (coll.) rock(s), stone(s).

ṣaxra pl. *-aat* un. n. of *ṣaxar.*

*ṣaxri** stony, rocky. *ʔaraaḍi ṣaxriyya* rocky land.

ṣuxra pl. *-aat* **1.** imposition, burden, bother, trouble. *ʔagdar ʔaṣaxxrak ṣuxra?* Could I trouble you to do a favor? **2.** corvée, work exacted by the authorities. *min yṣiir fayaḍaan, qisim imnil-ʕummaal yištağluun biṣ-ṣuxra.* When there's a flood, some of the workers work at forced labor.

ṣ-x-r-j

ṣaxraj to be or become overfired, fused. *ṭalliʕ iṭ-ṭaabuug imnil-kuura tara yṣaxrij.* Take the bricks out of the kiln or they'll be overfired.

mṣaxrij overfired, fused bricks. *ʔariid loori ṭaabuug imṣaxrij.* I want a truckload of fused bricks.

s-x-l

ṣaxal pl. *ṣxuul* goat.

ṣaxla pl. *-aat* female goat.

ṣ-x-m

ṣaxxam **1.** to blacken, begrime, besmudge (with soot). *šaal ij-jidir w-ṣaxxam ʔiida.* He lifted the pot and got his hands black. *ṣaxxam ʔaḷḷaa wiččak!* May God blacken your face! Shame on you! **2.** to upbraid, berate, tell off. *min simaʕit da-tiḥči wiyya rajli. ṣaxxamitha w-laṭṭamitha.* When I heard she was talking with my husband, I gave her hell and slapped her around. **3.** to ruin, disgrace, bring shame upon (and by extension, to rape). *ṣaxxumooha w-baʕdeen kitlooha.* They raped her and then killed her.

tṣaxxam to be blackened. *šiil ij-jidir ib-wuṣla ḥatta ma-titṣaxxam iidak.* Lift the pot with a piece of cloth so your hands won't get dirty. *tṣaxxam wučča; ʕirfoo čaḍḍaab.* He's disgraced; they know he's a liar.

ṣxaam soot.

ṣ-x-n

ṣaxxan to be or become feverish, get a fever. *ṣaxxanit il-baarḥa w-ma-gdart aruuḥ lil-madrasa.* I got a fever yesterday and wasn't able to go to school.

ṣuxuuna fever, temperature.

maṣxana, maṣixna pl. *mṣaaxin* large, long-necked copper water container.

ṣ-x-y

ṣixa (*i a ṣaxa, ṣaxaaʔ*) to be or become generous, liberal. *šloon ṣixa yinṭiik xams idnaaniir?* How'd he get so generous as to give you five dinars? *ma-ṣixa yinṭiini s-sayyaara.* He wasn't generous enough to give me the car.

ṣaxxa to make generous, liberal. *ʔaḷḷa ṣaxxaa w-inṭaani l-ifluus.* God made him generous and he gave me the money. *ʔaḷḷa yṣaxxi gaḷbak ʕaleena.* May God soften your heart toward us.

*ṣaxi, ṣixi** generous, liberal. *haaḍa šgadd ṣaxi!* My how generous he is!

ṣ-d-ʔ

ṣadda to rust, oxidize. *l-ḥadiida ṣaddat imnil-mayy.* The piece of iron rusted from the water.

ṣ-d-d

ṣadd (*i ṣadd*) to ward off, deflect, parry, repel, throw back. *ʔilzam id-dirga ḥatta tṣudd ḍarbaat is-seef.* Hold the shield so you can deflect the sword's blows. *jeešna ṣadd hujuum il-ʕadu.* Our army repelled the enemy's attack. *ʔaani ʔaḍrub iṭ-ṭooba w-inta ṣiddha.* I'll hit the ball and you knock it back.

ṣ-d-r

ṣidar (*u ṣuduur*) **1.** to originate, stem, arise, emanate. *l-ʔamur ṣidar min raʔiis ʔarkaan ij-jayš.* The order originated from the Army Chief of Staff. *ma-ʕabaali yiṣdur minnak hiiči ʕamal.* I didn't expect that sort of action from you. **2.** to be issued, be handed down. *sijnoo baʕad-ma ṣidar il-ḥukum ḍidda.* They put him in prison after the sentence was pronounced against him. **3.** to come out, be published. *qaraar il-lujna baʕad ma-ṣidar.* The committee's report hasn't been published yet. *j-jariida ma-raḥ-tiṣdur baačir.* The newspaper won't come out tomorrow. **4.** to be sent out, go out, leave. *l-maktuub ṣidar il-yoom.* The letter went out today.

ṣaddar **1.** to send out, dispatch, forward, send off. *ṣaddarna l-maktuub gabḷ isbuuʕ.* We sent the letter a week ago. **2.** to export. *l-ʕiraaq yṣaddir kammiyya kabiira mnit-tumuur.* Iraq exports a large amount of dates. **3.** to issue, bring out, put out, publish. *l-ḥukuuma ṣaddirat taʕliimaat jidiida l-aṣḥaab il-maṭaaʕim.* The government issued new regulations for restaurant owners. *raḥ-inṣaddir ʕadad xaaṣṣ ib-munaasabat il-ʕiid.* We're going to publish a special edition on the occasion of the holiday.

ṣaadar to sieze, impound, confiscate. *l-ɛukuuma ṣaadrat ʔamlaaka.* The government confiscated his property.

tṣaddar **1.** to be exported. *kull hal-ɛuṇṭa raɛ-titṣaddar.* All this wheat is going to be exported. **2.** to occupy the seat of honor, take the best seat (at a gathering). *haaδa daaʔiman yitṣaddar il-majlis.* He always sits in the best place in the group.

ṣadir pl. *ṣduur* **1.** chest, breast, bosom, bust. || *ɛašr-iryaajiil ma-yoogfuun ib-ṣadra.* Ten men can't stop him. **2.** seat of honor, best seat (at a gathering). *tfaδδal, ʔugɛud bis-ṣadir.* Go ahead, sit in the place of honor. **3.** front seat (of an automobile). *ʔugɛud biṣ-ṣadir, yamm is-saayiq.* Sit in the front seat, next to the driver.

*ṣadri** pectoral, chest. *maraδ ṣadri* chest disease.

ṣadriyya pl. *-aat, ṣadaari* **1.** bib, apron. **2.** laboratory coat.

maṣdar pl. *maṣaadir* **1.** origin, source. *maṣaadir taqriir* reference works of a report. **2.** verbal noun (gram.).

taṣdiir exporting, exportation, export. *ʔijaazat taṣdiir* export license.

muṣaadara seizure, confiscation.

ṣaadir **1.** emanating, originating. **2.** outbound, going out (letters, etc.). || *šuɛbat (il-kutub) iṣ-ṣaadira* out-going mail section, correspondence dispatch office. *kaatib iṣ-ṣaadira* correspondence dispatch clerk. **3.** issued, published, put out.

ṣaadiraat (pl. only) exports.

muṣaddir pl. *-iin* exporter.

maṣduur affected with a pulmonary ailment, consumptive, tubercular.

ṣ-d-ɛ

ṣaddaɛ to trouble, bother, harass. *ṣaddaɛ-naakum ib-haj-jaaya.* I'm afraid we've inconvenienced you by coming now.

tṣaddaɛ pass. of *ṣaddaɛ.* *tṣaddaɛtu hwaaya. niškurkum.* You've been bothered a lot. We thank you.

ṣudaaɛ headache.

ṣ-d-f

ṣidaf (*u ṣidfa*) to happen by chance, occur unexpectedly. *hiiči šii ma-yiṣduf ʔilla marra bis-sana.* This sort of thing doesn't happen more than once a year. *ʔiδa ṣidaf w-šifta gul-la xall yxaaburni.* If it happens that you see him, have him call me.

ṣaadaf **1.** to meet by chance, encounter unexpectedly. *ṣaadaftak marteen il-yoom!* I've run into you twice today! *ṣaadafna ṣuɛuubaat ihwaaya.* We encountered many difficulties. *ma-mṣaadfatni hiiči qaδiyya gabuḷ.* I've never come across such a case before. || *mṣaadif il-xeer!* Good luck! **2.** to coincide with, occur with, be coincident with, to fall on (a certain date). *safara raɛ-yṣaadif yoom zawaaji.* His trip will coincide with the day of my marriage. *l-ɛiid raɛ-yṣaadif yoom ij-jumɛa.* The feast will fall on a Friday. **3.** to happen by chance, occur unexpectedly. *kull-ma ʔariid ʔaṭlaɛ liṣ-ṣeed, yṣaadif muṭar.* Everytime I want to go hunting it rains.

tṣaadaf to happen upon, run into, meet each other unexpectedly. *tṣaadafit wiyyaa bis-suug.* I ran into him in the market.

ṣadaf (coll.) **1.** seashell(s). **2.** mother-of-pearl. **3.** fish scale(s).

ṣadfa pl. *-aat* un. n. of *ṣadaf.*

ṣudfa, ṣidfa pl. *ṣudaf* chance, coincidence, unexpected concurrence. *biṣ-ṣudfa* coincidentally, by chance. *šifta biṣ-ṣudfa.* I saw him by chance.

ṣudfatan coincidentally, by chance, by coincidence. *ṣidfatan huwwa hamm čaan ihnaak.* It so happened that he was there also.

muṣaadafa pl. *-aat* coincidence, unexpected concurrence.

s-d-q

ṣidaq (*i sidiq*) to be truthful, sincere, to tell the truth. *ʔiṣdiqni. minu gal-lak biiha?* Tell me the truth. Who told you about it? *ṭilaɛ ṣaadiq b-iɛčaayta.* He turned out to be telling the truth in his story.

ṣaddaq to consent, assent, approve, endorse, confirm, ratify, certify, substantiate. *l-majlis ṣaddaq il-muɛaahada.* Parliament ratified the treaty. *xalli l-mudiir yṣaddiq ɛariiδtak w-jiibha.* Let the director endorse your application and bring it. *ṣaddaq ɛala kull šii l-gaala.* He agreed to everything he said.

ṣaadaq **1.** to be or become friends with. *š-bil-ɛajal ṣaadaqta?* How'd you make friends with him so fast? **2.** /with *ɛala*/ to approve, confirm, ratify, substantiate, endorse, authenticate, certify. *l-majlis ṣaadaq ɛal-miizaaniyya.* The parliament ratified the budget.

tṣaddaq **1.** pass. of *ṣaddaq.* *l-muɛaahada tṣaddiqat il-yoom.* The treaty was ratified today. **2.** to give alms. *daaʔiman nitṣaddaq*

ℭal-fuqaraaˀ. We always give to the poor.

tṣaadaq to be or become mutual friends, to form a friendship with each other. *šuuf ij-jihaal š-ib-saaℭ tṣaadqaw.* Look at how fast the kids made friends.

ṣadaqa pl. *-aat* **1.** a charitable gift, alms. *sawwiiha ṣadaqa l-ˀaḷḷa.* Do it as a charity for God. || *ˀaṣiir-lak ṣadaaqa.* I'll sacrifice myself for you. I'll do anything for you. *la-tišġiḷ fikrak; baačir indabbur l-ifluus. ˀaṣiir-lak ṣadaqa.* Don't fret yourself; tomorrow we'll get the money. I'll do all I can. **2.** an expression of amazement or astonishment. *ṣadaqa l-ˀaḷḷa, šloon iℭyuun ℭaleeha!* My God, what beautiful eyes she has! *ṣadaqa! gaam yimši!* Glory be! He's started to walk!

ṣadaaqa pl. *-aat* **1.** friendship. **2.** (invar.) friendly, good friends. *ṣaaraw ṣadaaqa wiyyaana.* They became friendly with us.

ṣadiiq pl. *ˀaṣdiqaaˀ, ṣidqaan* friend.

ˀaṣdaq more or most truthful, sincere, honest.

taṣdiiq **1.** belief, faith. **2.** approval, confirmation, ratification, verification, authentication.

musaadaqa consent, agreement, approval, confirmation, ratification, verification, authentication.

ṣaadiq **1.** true, truthful, sincere. **2.** reliable, accurate, genuine.

ṣ-d-g

ṣidag (u ṣudug) **1.** to be truthful, tell the truth. *yuṣdug; ˀaani gitla.* He's right; I told him. **2.** to keep one's promise. *ṣidag wiyyaaya, šuuf ˀamr it-tarfiiℭ!* He kept his word to me. Look, here's the order for promotion!

ṣaddag to consider true, credible, to believe, to trust. *ṣaddag kull čilma l-giltilh iyyaa.* He believed every word I told him. *ṣaddig, ma-ˀaℭruf.* Believe me, I don't know.

tṣaddag to be credible, believable. *ℭčaaytak ma-titṣaddag.* Your story is unbelievable.

ṣudug truth, verity, truthfulness. *ˀaniṣℭak tiℭči ṣ-ṣudug.* I advise you to tell the truth. *ṣudug nijaℭ bil-imtiℭaan?* Is it true that he passed the exam? *ṣudug haaδa ġabi.* He's really stupid. *min ṣudug* actually, really, truly. *ℭabaali da-yitšaaqa. ṭilaℭ ġaalib min ṣudug.* I though he was kidding. He really did win. *ziℭal min ṣudug.* He really got mad. *ṣaayir riyaaδi min ṣudug.* He has become a real athlete.

ṣ-d-m

ṣidam (i ṣadim) to bump, strike, hit, run into. *ṣidamni b-sayyaarta.* He ran into me with his car. || *ṣidmatni hal-ˀakla.* This meal didn't agree with me.

tṣaadam **1.** to collide. *l-qiṭaareen tṣaadmaw ib-waqit-ma čaan δubaab kaθiif.* The two trains collided during a thick fog. **2.** to clash, conflict. *ˀaxuu tṣaadam wiyya l-muℭaasib.* His brother clashed with the accountant.

ṣṭidam **1.** /with *b-*/ to bump into, hit, strike, collide with. *s-sayyaara ṣṭidmat bil-ℭamuud.* The car ran into the pole. **2.** to clash, conflict. *mulaaℭiδna ṣṭidam wiyya l-mudiir ij-jidiid.* Our supervisor clashed with the new director.

ṣadma pl. *-aat* **1.** jolt, shock, blow. **2.** (emotional) shock, blow.

ṣṭidaam collision, crash, impact. *ℭaadiθ iṣṭidaam* a collision, an accident.

s-d-y

tṣadda /with *l-*/ **1.** to oppose, resist, fight against. *bass yintiqid il-waδiℭ ib-xiṭaaba l-kull raℭ-yitṣadduu-la.* As soon as he criticizes the situation in his speech, all will oppose him. **2.** to bar the way of, stand in the path of. *min ymurr min-naa raℭ-yitṣadduu-la w-iybuṣṭuu.* When he passes by here they're going to stand in his way and beat him up.

ṣada pl. *ˀaṣdaaˀ* echo, reverberation.

ṣ-r-a-y

ṣaraay pl. *-aat* **1.** palace. **2.** an office building which serves as the seat of local government. **3.** that section of Baghdad where the ministries are located.

ṣ-r-ℭ

ṣarraℭ to make a statement, make an announcement. *waziir il-xaarijiyya ṣarraℭ ib-ˀašyaaˀ muhimma.* The foreign Minister made an announcement about some important things.

ṣaaraℭ to speak openly, frankly to. *ṣaaraℭni bil-qaδiyya w-ℭirafit kullši.* He spoke frankly to me about the matter and I found out everything. *ṣaaraℭni b-sirra.* He disclosed his secret to me.

tṣaaraℭ to speak frankly, openly, candidly to each other. *bil-ˀaxiir tṣaaraℭna w-waaℭidna riδa ℭan iθ-θaani.* Finally we spoke frankly with each other and each of us was satisfied with the other.

ṣariiℭ **1.** explicit, clear, unambiguous, unequivocal, manifest, plain. **2.** frank, open, candid, sincere.

ṣaraaℭa **1.** clearness, explicity, distinctness. **2.** frankness, openness, candor. *b-ṣaraaḥa* frankly, plainly, candidly, bluntly. *ʔagul-lak ib-ṣaraaḥa, hiyya ma-tḥibbak.* I'll tell you frankly, she doesn't love you.

ṣaraaḥiyya pl. *-aat* water jar, carafe.

taṣriiḥ pl. *-aat, taṣaariiḥ* declaration, statement.

taṣriiḥa: taṣriiḥa gumrugiyya customs declaration.

ṣ-r-x

ṣirax (*a u ṣraax*) to scream, yell, shout, cry out, shriek. *ṣirax ib-kull ḥeela min il-imjabbur jabbar rijla.* He screamed at the top of his lungs when the bonesetter set his leg. *j-jaahil leeš da-yiṣrax?* Why's the kid screaming? **2.** to yell, bellow, roar. *l-ɛariif daaʔiman yiṣrax ɛala j-jinuud ij-jiddad.* The sergeant always yells at the new soldiers. *lamma ṭlabit minna fluus, ṣirax ib-wujhi w-ṭiradni.* When I asked him for money, he shouted in my face and threw me out.

ṣarrax intensive of *ṣirax*. *ṣaar-lak saaɛa tṣarrix. bass ɛaad!* You've been bawling an hour. Knock it off! *δall yṣarrix ʔila ʔan maat.* He kept on screaming till he died.

ṣarix screaming, shouting, yelling.

ṣarxa pl. *-aat* scream, cry, shriek, shout, yell.

ṣaaruux pl. *ṣawaariix* rocket. *ṣaaruux muwajjah* guided missile.

ṣ-r-r

ṣarr (*u ṣarr*) to wrap in a cloth bundle. *ṣarr kull ihduuma w-raaḥ.* He wrapped all his clothes in a bundle and left.

ʔaṣarr **1.** to make up one's mind, resolve, determine. *ʔaṣarr ɛala ʔan yidrus ib-ʔamriika.* He resolved that he would study in America. **2.** to insist, be persistent. *ʔaṣarr yruuḥ wiyyaana.* He insisted on going with us.

ṣurra pl. *-aat, ṣurar* **1.** navel. **2.** belly, soft underside (of a fish). **3.** cloth bundle, packet. **4.** the decorated portion of a quilt not covered by a protective sheet.

ṣ-r-ṣ-r

ṣurṣur pl. *ṣaraaṣir* **1.** cricket. **2.** cockroach.

ṣ-r-ṭ

ṣiraṭ (*u ṣaruṭ*) to gulp down, swallow whole. *šaal il-beeδa w-ṣiraṭha.* He picked up the egg and swallowed it whole.

ṣ-r-ṭ-a-n

ṣaraṭaan pl. *-aat* **1.** lobster. **2.** cancer (med.). **3.** Cancer (astron.). *madaar is-ṣaraṭaan* Tropic of Cancer.

ṣ-r-ɛ

ṣiraɛ (*a ṣariɛ*) to throw down, fell, to get a fall, pin. *ṣiraɛa b-aaxir jawla.* He pinned him in the last round.

ṣaaraɛ to wrestle. *ʔil-man raḥ-itṣaariɛ il-yoom?* Who are you going to wrestle today?

tṣaaraɛ to wrestle each other. *raḥ-yitṣaaraɛ wiyya waaḥid ʔaṭwal minna.* He'll be wrestling with a taller man.

nṣiraɛ pass. of *ṣiraɛ*. *nṣiraɛ marrteen.* He was pinned two times.

ṣaraɛ epilepsy.

ṣarɛa pl. *-aat* an epileptic seizure, a fit.

muṣraɛ pl. *muṣaariɛ* top (child's toy).

muṣaaraɛa wrestling.

muṣaariɛ pl. *iin* wrestler.

ṣ-r-f

ṣiraf (*u ṣaruf*) **1.** to dismiss, send away. *l-muɛallim ṣirafna bil-ɛajal.* The teacher dismissed us quickly. *jaani lil-daaʔira laakin ṣirafta biz-zeeniyya.* He came to the office, but I sent him away with a few pleasantries. || *ṣiraf in-naδar ɛan* to dismiss from one's mind, disregard, pay no attention to. *ṣiraf in-naδar ɛan mašruuɛ is-safra.* He put the plan for the trip out of his mind. *l-ḥukuuma ṣirfat in-naδar ɛan mašruuɛ ij-jisir.* The government dropped the idea of the bridge project. **2.** to spend, pay out, expend. *ṣiraf ihwaaya fluus ib-safirta.* He spent a lot of money on his trip. **3.** to cash. *b-ʔay bang ʔagdar ʔaṣruf hač-čakk?* Which bank can I cash this check in? **4.** to gulp down, swallow whole. *yiṣruf beeδa wiḥda ɛar-riig.* He swallows one egg before breakfast.

ṣarraf **1.** to bring profit, be profitable, be of benefit. *loo yṣarruf, čaan biɛta b-diinaar.* If it had been profitable, I would have sold it for a dinar. *ma-yṣarruf-lak tbiiɛa b-diinaar.* It won't bring you any profit to sell it for a dinar. *ʔaani ma-yṣarruf-li hiiči ḥači.* This sort of talk is of no benefit to me. **2.** to dispose of, liquidate, sell, market. *tigdar itṣarruf il-biδaaɛa b-baġdaad.* You can market the goods in Baghdad. **3.** to change (money). *ʔarjuuk, ṣarruf-li d-diinaar.* Would you please change this dinar for me.

tṣarraf **1.** to act independently, freely, at one's own discretion. *la-tiltizim bit-taɛliimaat. tṣarraf ḥasab iδ-δuruuf.* Don't stick too close to the instructions. Act according to the circumstances. *gul-ilhum iš-ma git-lak. la-titṣarraf ib-keefak.* Tell them what I told you. Don't add anything on your own. *ma-git-lak la-titṣarraf bit-tarjuma?* Didn't I tell you not to render the translation freely? *ma-čaan laazim titṣarraf bil-ifluus.* You weren't supposed to use the money as you wished. *sijnoo li-ʔan tṣarraf ib-maal il-ḥukuuma.* They put him in jail because he misappropriated government property. **2.** to behave, act, conduct oneself, comport oneself. *tṣarraf ib-ṣuura muu laayga.* He behaved in an improper manner. *ma-yuʕruf yitṣarraf.* He doesn't know how to behave.

nṣiraf to be spent. *l-ifluus kullha nṣurfat.* The money's all spent.

ṣirf pure, unadulterated, unmixed. *ḥariir ṣirf* pure silk. *maay ṣirf* plain water. *taʕbiir baġdaadi ṣirf* a pure Baghdadi expression.

ṣarfiyyaat (pl. only) expenses, expenditures, payments.

ṣiriifa pl. *ṣaraayif* hut, shack.

ṣraafa change. *ʕindak iṣraafat diinaar?* Do you have change for a dinar?

ṣarraaf pl. *-iin* **1.** money changer. **2.** spendthrift, big spender.

maṣraf pl. *maṣaariif* **1.** expenditure, expense, cost. **2.** (pl. *maṣaaruf*) bank /in certain formal expressions:/ *maṣraf ḥukuumi* a government bank. *maṣraf ir-raafideen* The Rafidayn Bank. *maṣraf ir-ruhuun* Security Deposit Bank. *maṣraf ziraaʕi* Agricultural Bank.

ʔaṣraf more or most profitable, beneficial, economical. *ʔištiriiha bin-naqdi. ʔaṣraf-lak.* Buy it for cash. It's more economical for you.

taṣarruf pl. *-aat* **1.** action, conduct, behavior, demeanor. **2.** free disposal, right of disposal. *b-taṣarruf* freely, unrestrictedly. *hal-maqaal imtarjam ib-taṣarruf.* This article is translated freely. *taḥat taṣarruf* at the disposal of, under control of. *ḥaṭṭ sayyaarta taḥat taṣarrufi.* He put his car at my disposal. *muṭlaq it-taṣarruf* invested with full power, having unrestricted control.

mutaṣarrif pl. *-iin* governor of a province.

maṣruuf pl. *-aat, maṣaariif* expense, expenditure, cost.

¹*ṣ-r-m*

ṣurmaaya **1.** capital, financial assets. **2.** money.

²*ṣ-r-m*

staṣram to flirt, make passes, chase (girls). *kull yoom yoogaf yamm il-madrasa yistaṣrum ʕal-banaat.* Every day he stands near the school and makes passes at the girls. *čaan da-yistaṣrum yamm is-siinama.* He was trying to make a pick-up near the movie.

ṣurum pl. *ṣraama* (vulgar) rectum.

ṣ-r-m-p-a-r-a

ṣurumpaara pl. *-iyya* **1.** wolf, womanizer, skirt-chaser. **2.** hoodlum, hooligan, ruffian, juvenile delinquent.

ṣ-ṭ-b

maṣṭaba pl. *-aat* bench.

ṣ-ṭ-ḥ

ṣaṭiḥ pl. *ṣṭuuḥ* **1.** (flat) roof. **2.** surface. *ṣaṭḥ il-baḥar* sea level.

*ṣaṭḥi** **1.** external. **2.** superficial. *maʕluumaat ṣaṭḥiyya* superficial knowledge.

ṣ-ṭ-r

ṣiṭar (*u ṣaṭir*) **1.** to chop, hack, cleave, split (esp. with a cleaver). *raḥ-aguṣṣ-lak laḥam baʕad-ma ʔaṣṭur il-lašša.* I'll cut you some meat after I chop up the carcass. **2.** to stun, daze, stupefy. *jamaalha yiṣṭur.* Her beauty dazzles you. *peek waaḥid ṣiṭara.* One drink addled him.

ṣaṭṭar to line up, arrange in a straight line. *ṣaṭṭir l-iglaaṣaat ʕal-meez ḥatta ʔatrusha.* Line up the glasses on the table so I can fill them.

tṣaṭṭar to be lined up, arranged in a straight line. *š-aku tṣaṭṭartu giddaami? ma-turḥuun?* Why are you lined up in front of me? Why don't you leave?

nṣiṭar to be or become stunned, dazed, stupefied. *min simaʕ bil-xabar, nṣiṭar.* When he heard the news he was stupefied.

ṣaṭir pl. *ṣṭuur* **1.** line. **2.** column, row.

ṣaṭra pl. *-aat* a slap on the face.

ṣaaṭuur pl. *ṣwaaṭiir* (meat) cleaver. || *δabbha ʕaṣ-ṣaaṭuur.* He didn't care about the consequences.

ʔuṣṭuura pl. *ʔaṣaaṭiir* legend, fable, myth.

maṣṭar in line, lined up in a row. *ʔoogfu maṣṭar ḥatta ʔaḥsibkum.* Stand in a line until I count you.

maṣṭara pl. *maṣaaṭir* **1.** ruler, straight edge. **2.** clipping, sample (of cloth).

ṣ-ṭ-ʕ

ṣiṭaʕ (*a ṣaṭiʕ*) to shine, gleam, be radiant. *wujihha yiṣṭaʕ nuur.* Her face gleams.

ʔaṣṭaʕ more or most shining, gleaming, radiant.

ṣaaṭiʕ shining, gleaming, glowing,

radiant, brilliant. *nuur iš-šamis ṣaaṭiƐ* The sunlight is bright.

ṣ-ṭ-l

ṣaṭal pl. *-aat, ṣṭuula* bucket, pail.

ṣ-ṭ-w

ṣiṭa (i ṣaṭuw) /with *Ɛala*/ to break into, burglarize. *l-ƹaraamiyya ṣiṭaw Ɛala beeta w-baagaw zuuliyya.* The thieves broke into his house and stole a rug.

ṣaṭwa pl. *-aat* **1.** a burglary. **2.** influence, authority, power.

ṣ-ṭ-w-a-n

ṣṭuwaana pl. *-aat* phonograph record.

ṣ-Ɛ-b

ṣiƐab (a ṣuƐuuba) to be or become difficult, hard, unpleasant. *min tiθlij, is-safar yiṣƐab.* When it snows, traveling becomes difficult. *taƹṣiil waδiifa da-yiṣƐab sana Ɛala sana.* Getting a job is becoming more difficult year after year. *yiṣƐab Ɛalayya ˀatrukhum waƹƹadhum.* It's unpleasant for me to leave them by themselves.

ṣaƐƐab to make difficult, hard. *l-kulliyya ṣaƐƐubat l-imtiƹaan has-sana.* The college has made the exam difficult this year.

tṣaƐƐab to be or become difficult, hard. *laazim nitṣaƐƐab wiyya ṭ-ṭullaab has-sana.* We have to be tough on the students this year. *la-titṣaƐƐab. haaδa xooš siƐir.* Don't be difficult. This is a good price.

staṣƐab to consider difficult, hard. *la-tistaṣƐub ir-rooƹa lid-dukkaan.* Don't make it sound so hard to go to the store.

ṣaƐub difficult, hard, unpleasant. *mtiƹaan ṣaƐub* a difficult exam. *la-tištiri minna. ṣaƐub ihwaaya.* Don't buy from him. He's very hard to deal with.

ṣuƐuuba difficulty, hardship.

ˀaṣƐab more or most difficult, hard, unpleasant.

ṣ-Ɛ-d

ṣiƐad (a ṣuƐuud) **1.** to ascend, rise, go upward. *šwakit yiṣƐad il-baaloon?* What time does the balloon go up? *xall niṣƐad foog.* Let's go up. *siƐr iš-šakar ṣiƐad.* The price of sugar went up. **2.** /sometimes with *Ɛala*/ to climb upon, mount, scale. *ṣiƐad Ɛal-kursi ƹatta yšuuf.* He got up on the chair so he could see. *tigdar tiṣƐad Ɛala haš-šijra?* Can you climb this tree? *ƹṣaani ṣiƐad faraṣkum* My horse mounted your mare.

ṣaƐƐad to cause to rise, ascend, go up, to send up, to take up. *ṣaƐƐid jinuṭti l-gurufti.* Take my bag up to my room.

tṣaaƐad to drift upward, rise, ascend. *d-duxxaan da-yitṣaaƐad min wara t-tall.* The smoke's rising from behind the hill.

nṣiƐad /sometimes with *Ɛala*/ to be ascended, climbed. *haj-jibal ma-yinṣiƐid Ɛalee.* That mountain can't be climbed.

ṣaƐda pl. *-aat* **1.** climbing, ascending. **2.** upward slope, rise, ascent.

maṣƐad pl. *maṣaaƐid* elevator, lift.

ṣaaƐid on the ascent, ascending, rising, climbing. || *haaδa najma ṣaaƐid.* He's coming up in the world (lit., his star is rising). *min-naa w-ṣaaƐid* from here on out, from now on. *min-naa w-ṣaaƐid ma-aku tadxiin bil-ġurfa.* From now on there will be no smoking in the room.

ṣaƐƐaada pl. *-aat* skyrocket (fireworks).

ṣ-Ɛ-q

ṣaaƐiqa pl. *ṣawaaƐiq* bolt of lightning.

ṣ-Ɛ-l-k

ṣaƐluuk pl. *ṣaƐaaliik* **1.** utterly destitute person, pauper. **2.** vagrant, bum.

ṣ-ġ-r

ṣiġar (a ṣuġur) **1.** to be or become small, little. *hal-qaaṭ ṣiġar Ɛalayya.* This suit has gotten too small for me. *ṣiġar ib-Ɛeeni hwaaya min sabb ˀabuu.* He grew a lot smaller in my eyes when he cursed his father.

ṣaġġar **1.** to make smaller. *jeeb haθ-θoob čibiir. tigdar itṣaġġra?* The pocket of this shirt is big. Can you make it smaller? *hal-qanafaat ṣaġġirat il-ġurfa.* These couches made the room smaller. **2.** to reduce, decrease. *ṣaġġrat Ɛumurha santeen.* She reduced her age two years.

tṣaġġar to be made smaller. *han-nafnuuf ma-yitṣaġġar.* This dress can't be made smaller.

staṣġar to consider small, little, insignificant, paltry. *la-tistaẓġira, tara huwwa ˀaqwa minnak.* Don't underestimate him, because he's stronger than you.

ṣuġur **1.** smallness, littleness. *ma-Ɛindi bismaar ib-haṣ-ṣuġur.* I don't have a nail this small. **2.** youth, childhood.

ṣġayyir **1.** small, little. *ġurfa ẓġayyra* a small room. **2.** insignificant, minor, paltry. *mwaδδaf iẓġayyir* a minor official. **3.** young, juvenile, minor. *jiru ẓġayyir* a young puppy.

ˀaṣġar **1.** smaller or smallest. **2.** younger or youngest.

ṣ-ġ-l-m

ṣaġlam (contraction of *ṣaaġ saliim*) safe and sound, in perfect condition.

ṣ-ġ-y

ṣiġa (*i* *ʔiṣġaaʔ*) to heed, listen, pay attention. *laazim tiṣġi lil-muʕallim.* You should pay attention to the teacher.

ṣ-f-ḥ

ṣaafaḥ to shake hands with. *kullna ṣaafaḥna l-waziir.* We all shook hands with the minister.

tṣaffaḥ to leaf through, thumb through. *tṣaffaḥt il-iktaab w-ma-šifit bii šii.* I leafed through the book and didn't see anything in it.

tṣaafaḥ to shake hands with each other. *laazim titṣaafḥuun gabul-ma titlaakmuun.* You have to shake hands before you start fighting.

ṣafuḥ sideways, in a sidewise direction. *j-jinneeb yimši ṣafuḥ.* The crab walks sideways.

ṣafḥa pl. *-aat* **1.** page, leaf (of a book). || *ʔuglub ṣafḥa!* Change the subject! **2.** (pl. *-aat, ṣfaaḥ*) side, face, facet. *ṣafḥa min iṣfaaḥ il-mukaʕʕab loonha faahi.* One of the sides of the cube is light-colored. *yaa ṣafḥa toojʕak?* Which side hurts you? || *ʔaani min ṣafiḥtak.* I'm on your side. *ʕala ṣafḥa* aside, to one side. *jarreeta ʕala ṣafḥa w-ḥičeet wiyyaa.* I took him aside and talked with him. *xalli haš-šuġul ʕala ṣafḥa l-baʕdeen.* Set this work aside for later. **3.** direction, way. *hassa faataw min haṣ-ṣafḥa.* They just went that way. **4.** (pl. *ṣufaaḥ*) ancestor. *naʕla ʕala ṣafḥat ṣafiḥtak!* Damn your ancestors' ancestors! *naʕla ʕaṣ-ṣufaaḥ wir-ruwaaḥ.* A curse upon you and your ancestors.

*ṣafḥaawi** toward the side, sideways.

mṣaffaḥ **1.** plated, armored. **2.** polygonal, many-faceted.

[1]*ṣ-f-r*

ṣufar (*u ṣafur, ṣafiir*) to whistle, make a whistling sound. *l-qiṭaar yuṣfur gabul-ma yitḥarrak.* The train whistles before it moves.

ṣaffar intensive of *ṣifar.* *š-šurṭi ṣaffar-la ḥatta yoogaf.* The policeman whistled at him so he'd stop.

ṣaafira pl. *-aat* whistle.

ṣaffaara pl. *-aat* siren.

[2]*ṣ-f-r*

ṣfarr **1.** to yellow, turn yellow. *bil-xariif, ʔawraaq il-ʔasjaar tiṣfarr w-baʕdeen toogaʕ.* In the fall the leaves of the trees turn yellow and then fall. **2.** (of the face) to become pale, turn pale, pale. *min šaaf is-sabiʕ, xaaf w-iṣfarr wičča.* When he saw the lion, he got scared and his face turned pale.

ṣifir. **1.** brass. **2.** bronze. **3.** copper.

ṣifriyya pl. *-aat* a copper basin built into the floor of a public bath to heat water.

ṣufra **1.** yellowness, yellow. **2.** pallor, paleness (of the face). **3.** vertigo, motion sickness.

ṣafaar **1.** yellowness, yellow. **2.** pallor, paleness. **3.** (pl. *-aat*) egg yolk.

ṣufaar pl. *-aat* egg yolk.

ʔaṣfar fem. *ṣafra* pl. *ṣufur, ṣafriin* **1.** yellow. **2.** pale, pallid, sallow. *wičča ʔaṣfar min širb it-tiryaak.* His face is pale from smoking opium.

ṣaffaar pl. *ṣafafiir, ṣfaafiir* coppersmith.

*ṣafraawi** subject to motion sickness. *ma-arkab biṭ-ṭayyaara liʔanni ṣafraawi.* I don't ride by airplane because I get motion sickness.

[3]*ṣ-f-r*

ṣifir pl. *ṣfaara* zero, nought. || *haaδa ṣifir bil-ḥisaab.* He's a blank in arithmetic.

[4]*ṣ-f-r*

ṣafar Safar, name of the second month of the Moslem year.

ṣ-f-ṣ-f

ṣufṣaaf (coll.) willow(s).

ṣufṣaafa pl. *-aat* un. n. of *ṣufṣaaf.*

ṣ-f-ṭ

ṣufaṭ (*u ṣafuṭ*) **1.** to stack, line up. *ʔuṣfuṭ hal-iktaabeen wiyya δiič il-kutub.* Stack these two books with those books. **2.** to move close together. *ʔuṣfuṭ wiyya ʔaxuuk ḥatta yṣiir mukaan il-ʔuxtak.* Sit close to your brother so there will be room for your sister.

ṣaffaṭ to line up, stack, stack up. *ṣaffaṭ il-kutub ib-har-raazuuna.* Stack the books on this shelf. *ṣaffuṭ l-iglaaṣaat ʕal-meez.* Arrange the glasses on the table. *ṣaffuṭ ihduumak zeen ḥatta la-titʕaqqač.* Pack your clothes well so they won't wrinkle. || *ṣaar-la saaʕa yṣaffuṭ čiδib b-raasi.* He's been telling me lies on top of lies for an hour.

ṣafṭa pl. *-aat* stack, pile.

ṣufaṭ pl. *ṣfaaṭa* small women basket, usually used by women to hold sewing materials.

mṣaffaṭ organized, ordered. *ḥačya*

mṣaffaṭ, bass nuṣṣa čiδib. His talk is well organized, but half of it is lies.

ṣ-f-f

ṣaff (*u ṣaff*) to set in a row or line, line up, align, arrange, array, order. *ṣuff it-talaamiiδ giddaam ġurufti.* Line up the students in front of my office. *ṣaff it-talaamiiδ ṣaffeen.* He lined the pupils up in two lines.

ṣaffaf to arrange, array, set in order. *da-tṣaffuf šaɛarha giddaam il-umraaya.* She is arranging her hair in front of the mirror.

nṣaff to keep close to, hug. *nṣaff bil-ɛaayiṭ ɛatta ysawwi ṭariiq lis-sayyaara.* He hugged the wall in order to make way for the car.

ṣṭaff to form a line or row, line up, fall into formation. *j-jinuud ṣṭaffaw ʔarbaɛa ʔarbaɛa.* The soldiers lined up in columns of four.

ṣaff pl. *ṣfuuf* **1.** row, line, file, column, rank, queue. **2.** grade, form (in school). **3.** course, class. || *δaabuṭ ṣaff* non-commissioned officer. *b-ṣaff* right next to, adjacent to, adjoining. *bil-paaṣ, čaanat ib-ṣaffi bnayya ɛilwa.* On the bus, there was a cute girl right next to me. *ɛuṭṭ il-kursi b-ṣaff il-baab.* Put the chair right by the door.

ṣ-f-q

ṣafqa pl. *-aat* transaction, deal, bargain.

ṣ-f-g

ṣufag (*u ṣafug*) to slap, smack, slam, bang. *ṣufagta b-ɛijil dawwaxta.* I slapped him on the head and made him dizzy. *ṣufag il-baab waraa.* He slammed the door behind him.

ṣaffag to clap, to applaud, clap the hands. *ṣaffug lil-booy ɛatta yiji.* Clap for the waiter to come. *min xallaṣ, ṣaffugoo-la hwaaya.* When he finished, they applauded him a lot.

ṣafga pl. *-aat* **1.** slap, smack, clap. **2.** ovation, round of applause.

ṣ-f-n

ṣufan (*u ṣafun, ṣafna*) to reflect, to ponder, muse, meditate, brood. *ʔuṣfun zeen. š-čaan laabis?* Think carefully. What was he wearing? *ṣufanit saaɛa laakin ʔisma ma-jaa ɛala baali.* I pondered for an hour but his name didn't come to me. *min ʔasʔala, yuṣfun gabuḷ-ma yjaawub.* When I question him, he reflects before he answers. *ʔaani da-aṣfan ɛalee. šloon yičδib ɛalayya?* I'm perplexed about him. How could he lie to me?

ṣaffan to daydream, woolgather. *ma-yigdar yiftihim id-daris li-ʔanna yṣaffun.* He can't understand the lessons because he daydreams.

ṣufna pl. *-aat* a period of daydreaming. *ʔaxδata ṣ-ṣafna w-ma-ftiham iš-gut-la.* A blank look came over him and he didn't understand what I told him.

ṣ-f-w

ṣufa (*a ṣafuw, ṣafaaʔ*) **1.** to be or become clear, unpolluted, limpid, unclouded, pure. *sufat id-dinya w-baɛad ma-aku ɛajaaj.* The weather cleared up and afterward there was no more dust. *baɛad-ma yiṣfa il-ṃayy, ʔišrab minna.* After the water clears, drink some of it. **2.** to remain, be left over. *ʔiδa ʔanṭiikum xamsa xamsa, ma-raɛ-yiṣfaa-li šii.* If I give you each five, nothing will be left for me.

ṣaffa **1.** to make clear, unpolluted, limpid, unclouded, pure, to purify. *yṣaffuun ṃaay iš-šaṭṭ w-iyδixxuu lil-ibyuut.* They purify the river water and pump it to the houses. **2.** to refine. *ween iyṣaffuun nafuṭ hal-manṭiqa?* Where do they refine the oil from this area? **3.** to clear up, settle, straighten out. *laazim itṣaffi šuġlak gabuḷ-ma tsaafir.* You'll have to clear up your work before you leave town. *ṣaffeet iɛsaabak wiyya š-šarika?* Did you settle your account with the company? **4.** to drain, pour off the water. *baɛad-ma tṣaffi t-timman, xalli ɛalee dihin.* After you drain the rice, put some oil on it.

tṣaafa to settle up, become even, reach amiable terms with each other. *ʔiδa ʔanṭiik ɛašr idnaaniir, iykuun tṣaafeena.* If I give you ten dinars, we'll be even. *δaḷḷaw zaɛlaaniin šahar w-baɛdeen itṣaafaw.* They stayed mad for a month and then made up.

ṣṭifa = *tṣaafa. nṭiini fluusi w-inta ruuɛ iṣṭifi wiyyaa.* Give me my money and you go clear it up with him.

maṣfi pl. *maṣaafi* **1.** strainer, filter. **2.** sieve. **3.** colander.

maṣfa pl. *maṣaafi* refinery.

miṣfaa = *maṣfi.*

ʔaṣfa more or most clear, pure, unpolluted.

ṣaafi clear, limpid, pure, unpolluted, unmixed, unadulterated. *s-sima ṣaafya l-yoom.* The sky is clear today. *ṃayy in-nahar ṣaafi.* The river water's clear. *ribiɛ ṣaafi* net profit. || *ʔijat-ta ṣaafya daafya.* He got it with no effort at all.

ṣ-f-y

ṣifa see *w-ṣ-f.*

s-q-r

ṣaqar see *s-q-r.*

ṣ-q-ṭ

ṣiqaṭ (u ṣuquuṭ) **1.** to fall, topple, collapse. *ʔaku ḥtimaal l-wizaara tuṣquṭ.* There's a probability that the cabinet will fall. *yiṣquṭ il-xaaʔin!* Down with the traitor! **2.** to fall, drop, sink down, decline. *ṣiqaṭ ib-naðari min ʕirafit yičðib.* He dropped in my estimation when I discovered he lies. **3.** to fail, flunk. *ṣiqaṭ bil-imtiḥaan marrteen.* He failed the examination twice.

ṣaqqaṭ **1.** to cause to fall, topple, collapse. *ʔiða tlaθ wuzaraaʔ staqaalaw, yṣaqqiṭuun il-wuzaara.* If three ministers resign, they will force the cabinet to fall. || *ṣaqqaṭ ij-jinsiyya ʕan* to deprive of citizenship. || *ṣaqqiṭaw ʕanna j-jinsiyya lamma ʕurfaw ʕanna yitjassas.* They took away his citizenship when they learned he was spying. **2.** to fail, flunk. *l-muʕallim ṣaqqaṭa li-ʔan niqal imnil-yamma.* The teacher flunked him because he copied from the one next to him. **3.** to renounce, give up one's citizenship. *ṣaqqaṭ w-tirak il-balad.* He gave up his citizenship and left the country.

ṣaqaṭ: ṣaqaṭ ʕadiim worthless junk.

maṣqaṭ pl. *maṣaaqiṭ* the place where something falls. *maṣqaṭ ir-raas* birthplace.

ṣaaqiṭ **1.** fallen. **2.** disreputable, notorious. *šaxiṣ ṣaaqiṭ* a disreputable person.

see also *ṣ-g-ṭ*

s-q-ʕ

ṣaqiiʕ **1.** loose-tongued, prattling, garrulous. **2.** foolish, silly. *sloon ṣaqiiʕ! ṣuraf ifluusa w-hassa ma-ʕinda ʔujuur il-madrasa.* How foolish! He spent his money and now he doesn't have tuition for school. *la-tṣiir ṣaqiiʕ. ʔiða tbaṭṭil, tmuut mnij-juuʕ.* Don't be foolish. If you quit, you'll starve.

s-q-l

ṣiqal (u ṣaqil) to smooth, polish, burnish. *ṣiqal iṣ-ṣiiniyya b-jallaafa.* He polished the tray with a scouring pad.

maṣquul **1.** polished, burnished, smoothed. **2.** (coll.) sugar-coated almonds, Jordan almonds.

masquula, pl. *-aat* un. n. of *masquul* **2.**

ṣ-g-r

ṣagur, ṣigar pl. *ṣguur* falcon.

ṣ-g-ṭ

ṣaggaṭ to damage, spoil, wreck, ruin. *l-xayyaaṭ ṣaggaṭ is-sitra maalti.* The tailor ruined my coat. **2.** to cripple, disable. *l-wagʕa mniṣ-ṣatiḥ ṣaggiṭata.* The fall from the roof disabled him.

ṣgaṭṭ to be or become ruined, spoiled, wrecked. *la-tgaṣṣir is-sitra baʕad. raḥ-tiṣgaṭṭ.* Don't shorten the coat any more. It's going to be ruined. *la-tilʕab bil-makiina tara tiṣgaṭṭ.* Don't play with the engine or it'll get broken.

ṣigaṭ (invar.) **1.** broken down, wrecked, ruined, no good, junk. *r-raadyo maalak ṣigaṭ. rajjiʕa.* Your radio's junk. Return it. *šloona bid-diraasa? ṣigaṭ!* How is he at studying? No damn good! **2.** crippled, disabled. *ma-yigdar yištuġul. huwwa ṣigaṭ* He can't work. He is disabled.

see also *ṣ-q-ṭ.*

ṣ-g-ʕ

ṣigaʕ (a ṣagiʕ) to slap on top of the head. *l-ʔumm ṣigʕat ʔibinha min faššar.* The mother slapped her son on top of the head when he talked dirty. || *xušš lil-beet la-tṣigʕak iš-šamis.* Go in the house so you won't get sunstroke.

ṣ-g-l

ṣagla a children's game, similar to jacks, played with pebbles.

¹ṣ-k-k

ṣakk (u ṣakk) **1.** to clench, close tight. *j-jaahil ṣakk rijlee mnil-barid.* The kid closed his legs because of the cold. **2.** to become hard, solid, to harden, set, solidify. *la-tfuut min-naa. l-ičbintu baʕda ma-ṣakk.* Don't go through here. The cement still hasn't hardened. *l-mayy ṣakk bil-iglaaṣ.* The water froze in the glass.

²ṣ-k-k

ṣakk pl. *-aat, ṣkuuk.* check, draft.

¹ṣ-l-b

tṣallab to become hard, solid, firm, rigid. *tṣallubat ʕinda š-šaraayiin w-dixal il-mustašfa.* His arteries hardened and he entered the hospital. *tṣallab ib-mawqifa w-ma-qibal yitfaaham.* He took a rigid position and refused to listen to reason.

ṣalib **1.** hard, firm, rigid. **2.** stubborn, dogged, tenacious.

ṣlubi pl. *ṣluba* nomad, desert dweller.

ṣalaaba **1.** hardness, firmness, rigidity. **2.** stubbornness, obstinacy, doggedness. *b-ṣalaaba* stubbornly, obstinately. *tmassak ib-raʔya ib-ṣalaaba.* He stuck to his opinion stubbornly.

ʔaṣlab 1. more or most hard, firm, rigid. 2. more or most stubborn, tenacious, etc.

taṣallub hardening, hardness. *taṣallub iš-šaraayiin* arteriosclerosis.

²ṣ-l-b

ṣilab (*u ṣalub*) 1. to crucify. *l-maṣiiɛ, ṣilboo ɛaṣ-ṣaliib.* They crucified Christ on the cross. 2. to hang, execute. *ṣilbaw il-qaatil il-fajir.* They hanged the killer at dawn. 3. to keep (someone) waiting. *ṣilabni saaɛa bil-maɛaṭṭa.* He left me stranded at the station for an hour.

ṣaliib pl. *ṣulbaan* cross. || *ṣaliib maɛkuuf* swastika.

ṣaliibi: l-ɛuruub iṣ-ṣaliibiyya The Crusades.

ṣallaab pl. *-a* hangman.

ṣ-l-b-x

ṣalbax to be or become like stone, to petrify, calcify. *t-tunga ṣalbuxat w-baɛad ma-tbarrid ṃayy.* The jar has calcified and won't cool water any more. || *huwwa mṣalbux w-damma θgiil.* He's got a stone face and he's a bore.

ṣaḷbuux pl. *ṣḷaabiix* stone, rock.

ṣ-l-b-w-y-a

ṣulibooya watercolors.

ṣ-l-ɛ

ṣilaɛ (*a ṣalaaɛ*) 1. to be proper, good, right, righteous, pious, godly. *la-ṭṭaffi š-šamɛa l-ɛal-gaḅur. ma-yiṣlaɛ.* Don't put out the candle on the grave. It isn't proper. *haaδa fadd waaɛid ma-yiṣlaɛ. ɛalee ʔalif qaδiyya.* He's a bad guy. He's got a thousand things against him. 2. to be useful, practicable, serviceable, suitable, fit. *šuuf hal-qalam yiṣlaɛ-lak.* See if this pen suits you. *huwwa ma-yiṣlaɛ yṣiir mudiir.* He isn't fit to be director. 3. (*a ʔislaaɛ*) = *ʔaslaɛ* 1. which see.

ṣallaɛ 1. to correct, set in order, adjust, settle. *ṣallaɛ xamsiin daftar min dafaatir il-imtiɛaan.* He corrected fifty of the examination booklets. 2. to repair, fix, mend, restore to usefulness. *ṣallaɛ ir-raadyo loo baɛad?* Did he fix the radio yet? *la-tištiri š-šarba gabuḷ-ma yṣallɛilk-iyyaaha.* Don't buy the clay jug before he patches it for you.

ṣaalaɛ to make peace, become reconciled, reach a settlement or compromise with. *walaw ṣuuča, bass raɛ-aṣaalɛa.* Even though it's his fault, I'll make up with him.

ʔaṣlaɛ 1. to reform, improve, set right, amend, rectify. *laazim niṣliɛ il-ʔawδaaɛ.* We have to improve the conditions. 2. to act as a mediator, bring about peace, agreement, conciliation. *dazzoo ɛatta yiṣliɛ been il-qabiilteen.* They sent him to make peace between the two tribes.

tṣaalaɛ to become reconciled, make peace with each other. *tṣaalɛaw w-ṣaaraw ʔaṣdiqaaʔ marra θaanya.* They made up and became friends again.

ṣṭilaɛ 1. to make peace, become reconciled, reach an agreement or compromise. *ṣṭilɛaw baɛad zaɛal sana.* They made up after not speaking for a year. 2. /with *ɛala*/ to agree upon, accept, adopt. *ṣṭilɛaw ɛala hal-ʔišaara beenaa-thum.* They agreed upon this signal between themselves. 3. to apply, assign. *ṣṭilɛaw ɛaleeha fadd ʔisim ġariib.* They applied a strange name to it.

ṣuluɛ peace, reconciliation, settlement of differences. || *maɛkamt iṣ-ṣulɛ* the lowest criminal court.

ṣalaaɛiyya 1. suitability, fitness, appropriateness, aptness, applicability. 2. usability, usefulness, use, practicability, worth. 3. (pl. *-aat*) full power, authority, jurisdiction.

maṣlaɛa pl. *maṣaaliɛ* 1. benefit, interest, advantage, welfare. 2. government administered agency, department, authority. *maṣlaɛat naql ir-rukkaab* public transit agency. 3. occupation, vocation, profession.

ʔaṣlaɛ 1. more or most pious, virtuous, etc. 2. more or most suitable, fitting, appropriate, etc.

ʔiṣlaaɛ pl. *-aat* reform, correction, improvement, amelioration.

*ʔislaaɛi** reformational, reform. *madrasa ʔiṣlaaɛiyya* reform school, reformatory. *siyaasa ʔiṣlaaɛiyya* policy of reform.

ṣlaaɛ patching material for pottery.

ṣṭilaaɛ pl. *-aat* 1. convention, agreement, practice, usage, thing agreed upon. 2. (gram.) idiom, colloquial expression. 3. technical term. *ṣṭilaaɛ fanni* technical term.

*ṣṭilaaɛi** 1. conventional, agreed upon. 2. (gram.) idiomatic. 3. technical. *taɛbiir iṣṭilaaɛi* technical term.

ṣaaliɛ 1. virtuous, pious, devout, godly. 2. useable, practicable, suitable, appropriate, fitting, fit. *has-sayyaara ma-ṣaalɛa lil-ʔistiɛmaal.* This car isn't serviceable. *ma-ṣaaliɛ lil-xidma l-ɛaskariyya.* He isn't fit for military service. 3. (pl. *ṣawaaliɛ*) benefit, advantage, interest, good.

muṣalliḥ pl. *-iin* 1. repairman, fixer. 2. correcter, grader.

musṭalaḥ 1. generally accepted, agreed upon, conventional, customary. 2. (pl. *-aat*) idiom. 3. technical term.

ṣ-l-x

ṣilax (*a ṣalix*) 1. to skin. *l-gaṣṣaab da-yiṣlax iδ-δibiiḥa.* The butcher's skinning the slaughtered animal. 2. to strike, hit hard. *ṣilxata b-raaždi w-tiflat ib-wičča.* She slapped him hard and spit in his face. 3. to have sexual intercourse with. 4. (*u ṣulux*) to lie, tell lies. *yuṣlux ib-ḥačya hwaaya.* He lies a lot in what he says.

ṣallax to strip, disrobe (someone). *ṭ-ṭabiib ṣallaxa w-ʔaxaδ wazna.* The doctor disrobed him and took his weight.

tṣallax to strip, disrobe, take off one's clothes. *tṣallax w-nizal bil-mayy.* He stripped and went in the water.

ṣulux prevarication, lies.

ṣluux (invar.) stripped, naked, bare, unclothed. *šuuf il-da-ysibḥuun; kullhum ṣluux.* Look at the swimmers; they're all naked.

maṣlax pl. *maṣaalix* slaughterhouse.

muṣlux pl. *maṣaalix* drain.

ṣ-l-ṭ

ṣallaṭ /with *ʕala*/ 1. to set up, put over or above. *ṣalliṭ il-imzammila ʕal-ḥooδ.* Set the faucet over the pool. *ṣallaṭ ʕalee s-seef ʔila ʔan qarr.* He held the sword over him until he confessed. 2. to give power over, set up as overlord. *ʔaḷḷa ṣallaṭ ʕaleehum waaḥid yuʕruf išloon yʕaamilhum.* God put someone in control of them who knows how to treat them. *minu lli ṣallaṭak ʕaleena?* Who set you over us?

tṣallaṭ pass. of *ṣallaṭ*.

ṣulṭa pl. *-aat* 1. power, authority, dominion, influence, jurisdiction. 2. (pl. *-aat*) authority, official agency.

ṣ-l-ʕ

ṣlaʕʕ to be or become bald. *ṣlaʕʕ ib-šabaaba.* He became bald in his youth.

ṣalaʕ baldness.

ṣalʕa pl. *-aat* bald head, bald spot.

ʔaṣlaʕ fem. *ṣalʕa* pl. *ṣuluʕ, ṣalʕiin.* 1. bald, baldheaded. 2. bald person.

ṣ-l-f

ṣalif pl. *-iin* 1. pompous, boorish, rude. 2. boor.

ṣalaafa boorishness, vainglory, rudeness.

ṣ-l-l

ṣall (*i*) to be cold to the touch, to conduct coldness. *l-ḥadiid yṣill biš-šita hwaaya.* Metal is very cold to the touch in the winter.

ṣill pl. *ṣlaal* small snake. *laʔiim miθl iṣ-ṣill; bass yḥibb yʔaδδi n-naas.* He's as mean as a snake; he likes to hurt people. || *ʕumra xamsiin sana w-baʕda miθl iṣ-ṣill.* He is fifty years old and still strong and vigorous.

ṣ-l-w

ṣalla to pray, perform the ritual of prayer. *ʔibni yṣalli w-iyṣuum.* My son prays and fasts. *ṣalleet ṣalaat iṣ-ṣubuḥ w-illa baʕad?* Have you performed the morning prayer yet?

ṣalaa pl. *ṣalawaat* praying, prayer. || *ṣalawaat! l-walad gaam yimši.* My! My! The boy's started to walk.

ṣ-l-y

ṣila (*i ṣali*) 1. to burn, scorch (fig.). *bič-čool iš-šamis tiṣli.* The sun is scorching hot in the desert. *ṣilaana b-hal-ʔasʔila ṣ-ṣaʕba.* He scorched us with these hard questions. 2. to rake, spray with gunfire. *ṣiʕad ʕaj-jibal w-ṣilaahum b-irṣaaṣ ir-raššaaš.* He got up on the mountain and raked them with machine gun fire.

ṣali 1. burning, scorching (fig.). 2. spraying, raking.

ṣalya pl. *-aat* burst, volley.

ṣila see under *w-ṣ-l*.

ṣ-m-t

ṣaamit: filim ṣaamit silent movie.

ṣ-m-x

ṣumax (*u ṣamux*) to endure, last, hold out, remain, survive. *ma-ʕabaali yuṣmux halgadd.* I never thought he'd stick it out so long. *ma-gidar yiṣmux ib-waδiifta j-jidiida.* He couldn't bear to stay in his new position.

ṣmaax pl. *-aat* 1. head, noggin, dome. 2. intellectual, egghead, brain.

ṣ-m-d

ṣumad (*u ṣamid, ṣumuud*) to hold out, stand up defiantly, resist stubbornly. *ʔiδa tṣumduun, itḥaqqiquun maṭaaliibkum.* If you hold on stubbornly, your demands will be met. *ṣumdaw ib-wijh il-ʕadu.* They held out in the face of the enemy.

ṣammad to hoard, lay by, save (money). *da-yṣammid ifluusa ḥatta yištirii-la beet.* He's hoarding his money to buy himself a house.

ṣ-m-ṭ

ṣumaṭ (*u ṣamuṭ*) to scald. *ʔiδa ma-*

tuṣmuṭ il-imwaaƐiin ib-ṃayy Ɛaarr, ma-yruuƐ id-dihin. If you don't scald the dishes in hot water, the grease won't come off. *č-čaay Ɛaarr yiṣmuṭ.* The tea is scalding hot.

ṣimiit (coll.) a type of hard bread, similar to bagels.

ṣimiiṭa pl. *-aat* un. n. of *ṣimiiṭ.*

ṣumaaṭ pl. *-aat* 1. cloth on which food is served. 2. spread, display of food. *ṣ-ṣumaaṭ čaan min-naa l-čaƐb il-ġurfa.* Food was set out from here to the end of the room.

ṣummaaṭa pl. *-aat* pot holder, hot pad.

ṣ-m-ġ

ṣammaġ to put paste or glue on. *ṣammuġ iṣ-ṣuura Ɛatta ʔalzagha bil-iktaab.* Put some glue on the picture so I can paste it in the book.

ṣamuġ pl. *ṣumuuġ* mucilage, glue, paste.

ṣ-m-m

ṣamm (*u ṣamm*) to close, shut. *ṣumm ʔiidak.* Close your hand.

ṣammam 1. to be determined, resolved, to make up one's mind, decide definitely. *sammamit Ɛas-safar.* I made up my mind about traveling. *ṣammamit ʔaruuƐ.* I'm determined to go. 2. to design, plan. *ʔay muhandis ṣammam hal-binaaya?* What engineer designed this building?

ṣamm pl. *ṣmuum* handful. *ṣamm čukleet* a handful of candy.

ṣamiim true, genuine, authentic, through and through. *Ɛiraaqi ṣamiim* a true Iraqi. || *ḍarba biṣ-ṣamiim* a telling blow, effective hit. *min ṣamiim il-galb* wholeheartedly. *ʔaškurak min ṣamiim gaḷbi.* I thank you from the bottom of my heart.

ṣammaam pl. *-aat* valve, stopcock.

taṣmiim design, designing.

ṣ-m-n

ṣammuun (coll.) a kind of bread baked in large, oblong loaves, similar to French bread.

ṣammuuna pl. *-aat* 1. a loaf of *sammuun.* 2. nut (for a bolt or screw). 3. threaded joint in a pipe.

s-n-d-q

ṣanduuq pl. *ṣnaadiiq* place where money is kept, coffer, money box, till. *ʔamiin ṣanduuq* 1. treasurer. 2. cashier. *ṣanduuq tawfiir* postal savings.

ṣ-n-d-q-č

ṣindaqča pl. *-aat* small box, chest, trunk.

ṣ-n-d-g

ṣanduug pl. *ṣnaadiig* 1. box, crate. || *ṣanduug il-wlaayaat* peep-show. *ṣanduug yġanni* gramophone, record player. 2. trunk, chest. 3. trunk (of an automobile).

ṣ-n-d-l

ṣandal 1. sandalwood. 2. (also *ṣindaal* pl. *ṣanaadil*) (pair of) sandals.

ṣ-n-ṭ

ṣinaṭ (*u ṣanṭa*) to be or become silent, quiet, still. *bass-ma dixal il-muƐallim liṣ-ṣaff, kullhum ṣinṭaw.* As soon as the teacher entered the class, they all became silent.

tṣannaṭ to eavesdrop, listen secretly. *ʔiskut. la-tiƐči. ʔaƐtiqid ʔaku waaƐid da-yitṣannaṭ.* Hush. Don't talk. I think there's someone listening in.

ṣanṭa quiet, silence, quietness, stillness. *biṣ-ṣanṭa* quietly, covertly, secretively. *kull il-ʔašyaaʔ ysawwiiha biṣ-ṣanṭa Ɛatta maƐƐad yidri bii.* He does everything quietly so that nobody'll know about it.

ṣanṭaawi quiet, silent, taciturn, close-mouthed. *biṣ-ṣanṭaawi* quietly, silently, covertly, secretively, on the sly. *Ɛaṣṣal Ɛala šuġul biṣ-ṣanṭaawi.* He got a job without letting anyone know.

ṣ-n-ṭ-w-r

ṣanṭuur pl. *ṣanaaṭiir* dulcimer. || *ṭiyyaara ʔumm iṣ-ṣanaaṭiir* kite equipped with a whistling noise maker.

ṣ-n-Ɛ

ṣinaƐ (*a saniƐ*) to manufacture, turn out, produce, make. *hal-maƐmal yiṣnaƐ taayaraat.* This factory manufactures tires.

ṣannaƐ 1. to industrialize. *l-Ɛukuuma raƐ-itṣanniƐ hal-manṭiqa.* The government is going to industrialize this area. 2. to decorate, embellish. *ṣannƐaw il-binaaya lil-Ɛiid.* They decorated the building for the holiday. 3. to apply cosmetics, to make up. *ṣanniƐat nafisha gabuḷ-ma yjuun il-xuṭṭaar.* She made herself up before the guests came.

tṣannaƐ 1. to behave in an artificial, affected, stilted manner. *š-daƐwa titṣannaƐ b-Ɛačyak?* How come you're so affected in your speech? 2. to make oneself up, apply make-up. *ṣaar-lič saaƐa da-titṣannƐiin. ma-txallṣiin Ɛaad!* You've been making up for an hour. Why don't you finish!

ṣtinaƐ to fake, assume, put on, pretend, feign. *ṣtinaƐ il-ibtisaama Ɛatta yixfi xajala.* He faked the smile to hide his embarrassment.

ṣanƐa pl. *-aat, ṣanaayiƐ* **1.** trade, craft, occupation. **2.** technical or artistic skill.
ṣinaaƐa pl. *-aat* industry, manufacturing.
*ṣinaaƐi** industrial, manufacturing. *manṭiqa ṣinaaƐiyya.* an industrial area.
maṣnaƐ pl. *maṣaaniƐ* plant, factory, works.
*ṣṭinaaƐi** artificial, synthetic, imitation. *rijil iṣṭinaaƐiyya* artificial leg. *laastiik iṣṭinaaƐi* synthetic rubber.
ṣaaniƐ pl. *ṣinnaaƐ* **1.** apprentice, helper. **2.** servant. **3.** a student under a mullah.
maṣnuuƐ pl. *-aat* product, manufactured article.
muṣṭanaƐ affected, sham, put-on, phony. *ðiƈkaatha kullha muṣṭanaƐa.* Her laughter is all phony.

ṣ-n-f
ṣannaf **1.** to classify, categorize, sort. *l-ƈukuuma ṣannifat daafƐiin ið-ðaraaʔib ʔila xamis ʔaṣnaaf.* The government classified the taxpayers into five groups. *ṣannif il-biðaaƐa w-xalli Ɛala kull ṣinif siƐir.* Sort the goods and put a price on each category. **2.** /with *Ɛala*/ to ridicule, mock, make fun of. *ðallaw yṣannifuun Ɛalee mudda ʔila ʔan ziƐal.* They kept ridiculing him for some time until he got mad.
ṣinif pl. *ʔaṣnaaf* **1.** kind, sort, type. **2.** genus, species, class, category.
taṣniif **1.** classification, categorization, sorting. **2.** (pl. *-aat*) farce, sham, mockery. *šuğli šloona? taṣniif. kull šii ma-da-asawwi.* How's my work? A farce. I don't do a thing.
mṣannifči pl. *-iyya* joker, buffoon, clown.

ṣ-n-m
ṣanam pl. *ʔaṣnaam* idol, image. || *waaguf miθl iṣ-ṣanam. ma-yitƈarrak.* He's standing like a statue. He isn't moving.

ṣ-n-n
ṣannan to smell of perspiration. *faaniilta ṣanninat imnil-Ɛarag.* His undershirt stank from perspiration.
ṣnaan body odor, odor from the armpits.

ṣ-n-w-b-r
ṣnoobar (coll.) **1.** pine tree(s). **2.** pine nut(s).
ṣnoobara pl. *-aat* un. n. of *ṣnoobar.*

ṣ-h-l
ṣihal (*i ṣihiil*) to neigh, whinny. *l-iƈṣaan da-yiṣhil.* The horse is neighing.

ṣ-h-y-w-n
*ṣahyuuni** **1.** Zionist, Zionistic. **2.** (pl. *-iyyiin, ṣahaani*) a Zionist.
ṣahyuuniyya Zionism.

ṣ-w-b
ṣaab (*i ʔiṣaaba*) **1.** to strike, afflict (principally the evil eye). *l-Ɛeen ṣaabata.* The evil eye fell on him. An evil spell was cast upon him. *ƈaaṭṭa ƈiriz Ɛala ṣadir ʔibinha ƈatta la-tṣiiba l-Ɛeen.* She's put an amulet on her son's chest so the evil eye won't affect him. *ṣaabata b-Ɛeen w-itwajjaƐ.* She gave him the evil eye and he got sick. **2.** = *ʔaṣaab,* which see.
ṣawwab **1.** to aim, point. *ṣawwab il-bunduqiyya Ɛalayya.* He aimed the rifle at me. **2.** to hit (a target), to shoot. *š-šurṭa ṣawwubata b-rijla.* The police shot him in his leg.
ʔaṣaab **1.** to hit (a target). *ma-tṣiib il-hadaf ʔiða ma-tidgarrab išwayya.* You won't hit the target if you don't get a little closer. *l-qanaabul ʔaṣaabat il-hadaf.* The bombs hit the target. **2.** to befall, happen to, fall to the lot of. *šgadd ʔaṣaabak imnil-wiriθ?* How much did you get from the inheritance? *ƈaðða marra yixṭi w-marra yṣiib.* One time his luck misses and one time it holds. *ʔaṣaabata xaṣaara čibiira.* He suffered a great loss. *ʔaṣaaba ğubun.* He got a raw deal. **3.** to strike, attack, afflict. *la-txušš ib-hal-ğurfa. yṣiibak marað.* Don't enter that room. You'll catch a disease. *ʔiða tƐaqqim kullši, mniṣ-ṣaƐub yṣiibak marað.* If you sterilize everything, it'll be difficult for a sickness to strike you. *ʔaṣaabata ntikaasa baƐad il-Ɛamaliyya.* He had a relapse after the operation.
tṣawwab to be hit (by a bullet), to be shot. *tṣawwab w-ʔaxðoo lil-mustašfa.* He got shot and they took him to the hospital.
nṣaab **1.** to be stricken, afflicted, to catch (a disease). *nṣaab bis-sill.* He was stricken by tuberculosis. **2.** to be hit, be shot. *nṣaab ib-ṭalqa b-čitfa l-ʔayman.* He caught a bullet in his right shoulder.
staṣwab to approve, sanction. *staṣwab il-ƈall maali lil-muškila.* He approved of my solution to the problem.
ṣoob (no pl.) **1.** side, bank (of a river). **2.** direction, quarter. **3.** advantage, favor. *min ṣoob* to the advantage of. *has-siƐir zeen w-min ṣoobak.* This price is fair and to your advantage. *ṭabƐan itƈibba, li-ʔan*

yiƐči min ṣoobak. Of course you like him, because he speaks in your favor.

ṣwaab **1.** louse eggs. **2.** (pl. *-aat*) hit, strike, blow. **3.** bullet wound.

ˀaṣwab more or most pertinent, apropos, correct, etc.

ˀiṣaaba pl. *-aat* **1.** score, goal. *madrasatna ġulbathum ib-ˀiṣaabteen.* Our school beat them by two goals. **2.** case, state of being afflicted (by a disease). *ˀaku ˀiṣaaba bij-jidri b-hal-manṭiqa.* There's a case of smallpox in that neighborhood.

muṣiib pertinent, apropos, correct, on the mark, to the point.

muṣiiba pl. *muṣaayib* **1.** tragedy, calamity, disaster, misfortune. *haay ṣudug muṣiiba. l-miskiin kull wilda maataw bil-Ɛaadiθ.* This is a real tragedy. All the poor man's sons died in the accident. **2.** fuss, to-do, ado. *sawweetha muṣiiba Ɛaad!* You've made a big to-do out of it!

maṣyuub pl. *-iin, mṣaawiib* casualty, wounded person.

ṣ-w-b-a

ṣooba pl. *-aat* kerosene heater.

ṣ-w-b-a-ṭ

ṣoobaaṭ pl. *ṣwaabiiṭ* arbor, bower. *ṣoobaaṭ Ɛinab* grape arbor.

ṣ-w-b-n

ṣooban to soap, put soap on. *ṣoobin il-imwaaƐiin w-aani ˀašṭufha.* You soap the dishes and I'll rinse them.

saabuun (coll.) soap.

ṣaabuuna pl. *-aat* **1.** cake of soap. **2.** kneecap. *ṣaabuunat rijil* kneecap.

ṣ-w-p-a

ṣoopa pl. *-aat* kerosene heater.

ṣ-w-t

see *ṣ-w-ṭ*

ṣ-w-č

ṣawwač **1.** to accuse, blame. *luweeš datṣawwični? ˀaani š-Ɛalayya.* Why are you blaming me? I had nothing to do with it. **2.** to convict, find guilty. *l-maƐkama ṣawwičata.* The court found him guilty.

tṣawwač pass. of *ṣawwač. la-txušš lil-ġurfa tara titṣawwač.* Don't enter the room or you'll be blamed.

ṣuuč blame, fault, guilt. *la-δδibb Ɛalayya ṣ-ṣuuč. ˀaani ma-činit mawjuud.* Don't throw the blame onto me. I wasn't there. *ṣuučak. inta lli nṭeeta majaal yiƐči.* It is your fault. You gave him a chance to talk.

muṣwič **1.** at fault, deserving of blame, guilty. **2.** one who is at fault, one who is to blame, guilty party.

ṣ-w-d-a

ṣooda **1.** soda, sodium carbonate. **2.** baking soda, sodium bicarbonate. **3.** soda water. **4.** carbonated beverage.

ṣ-w-r

ṣawwar to represent, depict, portray. *har-rasim iyṣawwir il-Ɛayaat bir-riif il-Ɛiraaqi.* This drawing depicts life in the Iraq countryside.

tṣawwar to conceive, imagine, think. *has-sayyaara muu ġaalya miθil-ma titṣawwar.* This car's not as expensive as you imagine. *titṣawwar yigdar yruuƐ il-ˀooruppa bila muwaafaqat ˀahla?* Do you think he can go to Europe without his family's approval? *haaδa šii ma-yitṣawwara l-Ɛaqil.* That's inconceivable.

ṣuura pl. *ṣuwar* **1.** image, likeness, picture. **2.** photograph. **3.** copy, duplicate. **4.** replica. **5.** sura, chapter or section of the Koran. **6.** way, manner. *Ɛičaaha b-ṣuura jiddiyya.* He said it seriously. *gul-ilh-iyyaa b-ṣuura ma-yizƐal biiha.* Tell it to him in such a way that he won't get mad. *dabbir-li fluus ib-ˀay ṣuura mniṣ-ṣuwar.* Get me some money any way possible. || *b-ṣuura xaaṣṣa* 1. as a special case, as an exception. *qibloo bij-jaamiƐa b-ṣuura xaaṣṣa.* They admitted him to the university as a special case. 2. especially, particularly, in particular. *diir baalak Ɛal-ˀawraaq, w-b-ṣuura xaaṣṣa, makaatiib il-mudiir.* Take good care of the papers, and especially the director's correspondence. *baġdaad Ɛilwa bir-rabiiƐ ib-ṣuura xaaṣṣa.* Baghdad is beautiful in springtime especially. *b-ṣuura Ɛaamma* generally, in general, overall. *b-ṣuura Ɛaamma, l-waδiƐ l-ˀiqtiṣaadi zeen.* In general, the economic situation's good.

taṣwiir **1.** photography. **2.** representation, portrayal, depiction. **3.** (pl. *taṣaawiir*) photograph.

*taṣwiiri** depictive, descriptive.

muṣawwir pl. *-iin* photographer, cameraman.

ṣ-w-ṭ

ṣawwaṭ to vote, cast a ballot. *ma-yƐuqqlak itṣawwiṭ marrteen.* You aren't supposed to vote twice.

ṣooṭ pl. *ˀaṣwaaṭ* **1.** sound, noise. **2.** voice. **3.** vote, ballot. || *iṣ-ṣooṭ* (an oath affirming the truth of what one is saying, approx.:) believe me, so help me. *ṣ-ṣooṭ, walla maa-li ˀay Ɛalaaqa bii.* Take it from me, I swear I have nothing to do with it. *min tihmoo bil-booga, saaƐ iṣ-ṣooṭ w-gaal huwwa bari.*

When they accused him of the theft, he swore he was innocent.

*ṣooṭi**, *ṣawṭi** sonant, sound-, sonic, acoustic, vocal. *xuyuut ṣawṭiyya* vocal chords.

ṣiiṭ **1.** repute, standing, prestige. **2.** fame, renown. *δaayiζ iṣ-ṣiiṭ* famous, celebrated, well-known. *huwwa δaayiζ iṣ-ṣiit bil-fann.* He is famous for his art. *min ġilab, ṭilaζ ṣiiṭa.* After he won, his fame spread.

taṣwiiṭ voting, polling, vote, balloting.

ṣ-w-ṭ-r

ṣooṭari in a daze, oblivious, unaware, inattentive, unheeding, woolgathering, absent-minded. *gaaζid biṣ-ṣaff ṣooṭari w-ma-yidri š-aku ma-aku.* He's sitting in the class not paying attention and doesn't know what's what. *ṣooṭari! leeš da-tdawwir ihnaa? ma-git-lak l-iktaab ihnaak?* Numbskull! Why are you looking here? Didn't I tell you the book was there? *haaδa ṣooṭari. la-tiζtimid ζalee.* He's absent-minded. Don't depend on him.

ṣ-w-ġ

ṣaaġ (*u ṣiyaaġa*) to fashion, form, mold, create. *yaa ṣaayiġ saaġ-lič il-gḷaada?* Which goldsmith fashioned your necklace for you? *ṣaaġ il-marta ζijil δahab.* He had a gold anklet made for his wife.

tṣawwaġ to shop for gifts to take home from a trip. *ʔaζtaaj čam diinaar ʔatṣawwaġ biiha.* I need a few dinars to buy gifts for my homecoming.

ṣooga pl. *-aat* a gift brought back from a journey.

ṣiyaaġa goldsmithing, silversmithing, jewelry making.

ṣaayiġ pl. *ṣiyyaag* goldsmith, silversmith, jeweler.

ṣ-w-f

ṣawwaf to be or become woolly, fuzzy. *min yṣawwuf il-xoox, ykuun laaζig.* When peaches get fuzzy, they're ripe.

ṣuuf pl. *ʔaṣwaaf* wool.

ṣuufa pl. *-aat* piece of wool.

*ṣuufi** **1.** wool, woolen. **2.** wooly.

ṣ-w-f-r

ṣoofar to whistle. *min yimši, loo yṣoofir loo yġanni.* When he walks, he either whistles or sings.

see also *ṣ-f-r*.

ṣ-w-g-r

ṣoogar **1.** to insure, to underwrite. *raζ-aṣoogir il-biδaaζa maalti.* I'm going to insure my goods. **2.** to ensure, assure, guarantee. *nṭiini muhla yoomeen w-aani ʔaṣoogir-lak it-tarfiiζ.* Give me two day's time and I can assure you of the promotion. *wuṣuula l-yoom mṣoogar.* His arrival today is assured.

tṣoogar **1.** to be insured. *ma-aku ζaaja l-baδaayiζ il-ma-tiζtirig titṣoogar.* There's no need for goods which won't catch fire to be insured. **2.** to be ensured, guarantee. *bass yiwaafiq l-mudiir ʔijaazti, titṣoogar.* As soon as the director approves my leave, it'll be guaranteed.

ṣoogarta insurance.

mṣoogar **1.** insured, underwritten. **2.** assured, ensured, guaranteed. *mṣoogar min ʔaji l-baġdaad amurr ζaleekum.* Of course when I come to Baghdad I'll come to see you.

ṣ-w-m

ṣaam (*u ṣoom, ṣiyaam*) to fast, to abstain from food, drink, and sexual intercourse. *ṣaam ζaširt iyyaam bass w-fuṭar.* He fasted for only ten days and stopped.

ṣawwam to cause to fast, make observe the fast. *ʔabuu ṣawwama bass iṭ-ṭabiib faṭṭara.* His father made him fast but the doctor stopped him.

ṣaayim pl. *-iin, ṣiyyaam* **1.** fasting, observing a fast. **2.** faster, person observing a fast.

ṣ-w-m-ζ

ṣawmaζa pl. *ṣawaamiζ* **1.** retreat, haven, hermitage. **2.** monastery.

ṣ-w-n-d

ṣoonda pl. *-aat* hose, rubber tube.

ṣ-w-y

*maṣwi** **1.** thin, frail, skinny. **2.** thin person.

ṣ-y-b

ṣaab, yṣiib see under *ṣ-w-b*.

ṣ-y-t

ṣiit, see *ṣ-w-ṭ*.

ṣ-y-ζ

ṣaaζ (*i ṣiyaaζ*) **1.** to call out, yell, shout. *min δirabta, ṣaaζ "ʔaax!"* When I hit him he yelled "Ouch!" *š-šurṭi ṣaaζ ζalayya min šaafni da-aζbur iš-šaariζ.* The policeman shouted at me when he saw me crossing the street. *la-truuζ lee gabuḷ-ma yṣiiζ ʔismak.* Don't go in to him before he calls your name. **2.** to call, call out to, address. *ṣiζtak miit marra. ʔinta ʔaṭraš?* I called you a hundred times. Are you deaf? *gallat-li "ṣiiζii-li marta."* She told me, "Call his wife for me." *ʔisma kaaδum bass yṣiiζuu ʔabu juwaad.* His name is Kadhum but they call him Abu Juwad. || *ṣaaζ id-daad* to become utterly disgusted, fed up, exasperated. *j-jiiraan saaζaw id-daad min ʔibnak.* The neighbors are thoroughly fed up with your son.

ṣayyaɛ to call or shout repeatedly. *minu da-yṣayyiɛ bid-darub?* Who's shouting out there on the street? || *ṣayyaɛ id-daad* to make utterly disgusted, fed up, exasperated. *ʔibni ṣayyaɛni id-daad ib-kuθrat maṣrafa.* My son has thoroughly exasperated me with his excessive spending.

tṣaayaɛ to shout at one another. *ʔabuuk w-ʔummak da-yitṣaayɛuun. š-aku ɛidhum?* Your father and mother are shouting at each other. What's with them?

ṣeeɛa pl. *-aat* **1.** yell, shout, cry. **2.** scream, shriek, wail.

ṣiyaaɛ **1.** shouting. **2.** screaming, shrieking, wailing.

ṣ-y-x

ṣiix pl. *ṣyaax* **1.** skewer. **2.** rapier.

ṣ-y-d

ṣaad (i ṣeed) **1.** to trap, catch. *l-bazzuuna ṣaadat faara.* The cat caught a mouse. *l-mudiir ṣaadni da-ʔaqra jariida.* The director caught me reading the paper. *ṣaadni b-has-suʔaal.* He trapped me with that question. **2.** to hunt. *raaɛ liš-šimaal yṣiid dibaba.* He went up North to hunt bears. **3.** to hunt down, to bag. *ṣaad ġazaaleen ib-bunduqiiti.* He bagged two gazelles with my rifle. **4.** to fish. *xalli nruuɛ inṣiid simač.* Let's go fishing.

tṣayyad to stalk game, to go hunting. *ṭilaɛ yitṣayyad bil-hoor.* He went out stalking game in the swamp.

nṣaad to be trapped, be caught. *nṣaadeena; jatti š-šurṭa.* We're caught; the police have arrived.

ṣeed **1.** hunting. *bunduqiyyat ṣeed* shotgun. *kull yoom jumɛa yiṭlaɛ liṣ-ṣeed.* Every Friday he goes out hunting. || *waaguf ɛala-rijl iṣ-ṣeed.* He is on pins and needles. **2.** fishing. *ṣeed is-simač* fishing.

ṣeeda pl. *-aat* **1.** bag, catch, thing caught. *ʔilak ɛuṣṣa b-haṣ-ṣeeda.* You have a share in this catch. **2.** find, bargain, rare opportunity. *hiiči sayyaara ma-tiɛṣal kull yoom. haay ṣeeda.* Such a car won't come along every day. This is a real find.

ṣayyaad pl. *-a, -iin* **1.** hunter. **2.** fisherman.

miṣyaada pl. *-aat* **1.** trap, snare. *miṣyaadat faar* mouse trap. **2.** slingshot.

ṣ-y-d-l

ṣaydala pharmacology, pharmacy, apothecary's trade.

ṣaydali pl. *ṣayaadila* pharmacist, druggist.

ṣaydalaaniyya pl. *-aat* female pharmacist.

ṣaydaliyya pl. *-aat* pharmacy, drug store.

ṣ-y-r

ṣaar (i ṣeer) **1.** to become, to come to be, turn out to be. *ʔibinha ṣaar ṭabiib.* Her son became a doctor. *ʔaxuuk ṣaayir ma-yinɛimil.* Your brother has become unbearable. *šaɛra ṣaar ʔabyaḏ.* His hair turned grey. *ṣiir xooš walad w-ruuɛ lil-madrasa.* Be a good boy and go to school. *ʔiḏa yṣiir-la makaan, ʔariida bil-ġurfa.* If a place can be found for it, I want it in the room. *ṣaar il-ʔakil loo baɛad?* Is the food ready yet? *ṣaar ɛaleek diina-areen.* This makes two dinars charged against you. *ṣaarat saaɛa xamsa.* It is five o'clock. *ṣaar waqt il-ʔakil loo baɛad?* It is time to eat yet? *ṣaar waqt iṣ-ṣalaa. xan-nṣalli.* It's time for prayer. Let's pray. *ṣaar mudda ma-šiftak.* I haven't seen you for some time. *raɛ-yṣiir sitt tušhur ma-šaayfak.* It will be six months that I haven't seen you. *ṣaar mudda da-antaḏrak.* I've been waiting for you quite a while. *ṣaar-la yoomeen mariiḏ.* He's been sick two days. *ṣaar-la šahreen bila šuġul.* He's been without a job for two months. *šgadd ṣaar-lak ihnaa?* How long have you been here? || *gabḷ išwayya čaan ihnaa. ween ṣaar?* He was here a bit ago. Where did he get off to? *diir baalak la-yṣiir iṣ-ṣubuġ ɛala hduumak.* Be careful that the paint doesn't get on your clothes. *ṣaar wiyyaaya ḏidda.* He sided with me against him. **2.** to happen, occur, take place. *š-ṣaar bid-daaʔira l-yoom?* What happened at the office today? *ʔiḏa ma-difaɛit-la l-yoom, š-iyṣiir?* If I don't pay him today, what happens? *ʔinta tuɛruf iš-da-yṣiir?* Do you know what's going on? *ṣaarat θawra biš-šimaal.* A revolution took place in the north. *has-sana ma-ṣaar fayaḏaan.* This year there was no flood. *ṭagṭagat il-baab da-tṣiir imnil-hawa.* The banging of the door is happening because of the wind. *l-qaḏiyya raɛ-itṣiir b-hal-kayfiyya.* The matter will be taken care of in this manner. *ṣaarat biyya malarya marrteen.* I had malaria twice. *ʔiḏa txalliiha ɛindi, ma-yṣiir ɛaleeha šii.* If you leave it with me, nothing will happen to it. *š-ṣaar ɛaleek mistaɛjil?* What caused you to be in such a hurry? *ʔaxuuya, ma-ṣaar-la šii b-ɛaadiθ is-sayyaara.* Nothing happened to my brother in the auto accident. **3.** to develop, ensue, follow, result. *š-ṣaar min* *qaḍiitak?* What resulted from that deal of yours? *ṣ-šaar? kulla tuṭlubni diinaar.* What of it? All you have coming from me is a dinar. || *ma-ṣaarat wiyyaak. ma-git-lak la-tilʕab ib-ġaraaḍi?* It left no impression on you. Didn't I tell you not to play with my things? *git-lak miit marra. ma-ṣaarat wiyyaak ʕaad!* I told you a hundred times. It did no good with you then! **4.** to be possible, have a chance of occurrence. *yṣiir ʔaji l-baġdaad w-ma-ašuufkum?* Could it happen that I'd come to Baghdad and not see you? *yṣiir ʔaaxḍ il-qalam?* Can I take the pencil? *ma-yṣiir tidxul bila biṭaaqa.* You can't get in without a ticket. *ma-yṣiir yiqbal hiiči siʕir.* He would never accept such a price. *ma-yṣiir. tkallifni ʔakθar.* Nothing doing. It costs me more. || *ʔarjuuk saaʕid har-rijjaal!—ṣaar.* Please help this man!—O.K. **5.** /with *l-*/ to come to, befall, be the lot of. *ṣaar-la kariš.* He developed a pot-belly. *ʔiḍa tṣiir-lak ḥaaja ʕinda, ma-yʕurfak.* If you should have a need for him, he won't know you. *ṣaar-ilhum sana mitzawwjiin w-ma-ṣaar-ilhum šii.* They've been married a year and they've had no children. **6.** /with *ʕind*/ to fall into the possession of. *ʔanṭiik min itṣiir ʕindi fluus.* I'll give to you when some money comes my way. *hassa šgadd ṣaar ʕindak?* How much do you have now? *ṣaar ʕindak xurda hassa?* Have you gotten any change yet?

maṣiir fate, destiny, lot. *l-lujna jtimʕat ḥatta tqarrir maṣiira.* The committee met to decide his fate. *ma-nidri šloon raḥ-yṣiir maṣiirna.* We don't know how our destiny will turn out. *ḥaqq taqriir il-maṣiir* right of self-determination.

ṣ-y-t

ṣiiṭ see under *ṣ-w-ṭ.*

ṣ-y-ṭ-r

ṣayṭar, ṣeeṭar (*i ṣayṭara*) /with *ʕala*/ **1.** to dominate, control, command. *š-šurṭa ṣayṭirat ʕal-waḍiʕ.* The police took control of the situation. *ma-da-yigdar yṣeeṭir ʕaleehum.* He can't control them. **2.** to master, acquire a command of. *ʔiḍa ma-tiqra hal-iktaabeen, ma-tigdar itṣeeṭir ʕal-mawḍuuʕ.* If you don't read these two books, you can't master the subject.

ṣayṭara **1.** control, command, rule, domination. *ʔila ṣayṭara ʕaleehum.* He has control over them. **2.** mastery, command. *ṣ-ṣayṭara ʕal-luġa l-faransiyya tiḥtaaj wakit.* Mastery of the French language takes time.

ṣ-y-ġ

ṣaaġ (*i ṣiyaaga*) to polish, refine, improve (literary style, etc.). *tigdar itṣiiġ haj-jumla b-ʔusluub ʔaḥsan?* Can you polish this sentence into a better style?

tṣayyaġ to contract a temporary marriage, marry for a limited period. *raaḥ il-ʔiiraan w-itṣayyaġ mara l-muddat baqaaʔa.* He went to Iran and married a woman for the term of his stay.

ṣiiġa **1.** (literary) style, arrangement, wording. **2.** temporary marriage by contract.

ṣiyaaġa, ṣiyyaaġ see *ṣ-w-ġ.*

ṣ-y-f

ṣayyaf **1.** to summer, spend the summer. *has-sana raḥ-aṣayyif b-iswiisra.* This year I'm going to spend the summer in Switzerland. **2.** to wear summer clothing, put on summer clothes. *ḥtarrat id-dinya. raḥ-aṣayyif.* The weather has got hot. I'm going to switch to summer clothes.

ṣṭaaf to take a summer vacation, pass the summer. *raḥ-aṣṭaaf b-iswiisra.* I'm going to take a summer vacation in Switzerland.

ṣeef pl. *ʔaṣyaaf* summer, summertime.

*ṣeefi** summer, summery. *qaaṭ ṣeefi* a summer suit

ṣayfiyya pl. *-aat* summer, summer season.

maṣiif pl. *maṣaayif* summer resort.

ṣṭiyaaf summer vacationing. *mawsim il-iṣṭiyaaf* resort season. *ḥarakat il-iṣṭiyaaf* resort activity.

muṣṭaaf pl. *-iin* summer vacationer.

ṣ-y-m

ṣaayim see *ṣ-w-m.*

ṣ-y-n

ṣ-ṣiin China.

*ṣiini** **1.** Chinese. **2.** a Chinese.

ṣiiniyya pl. *ṣwaani* tray.

ṣ-y-h-w-d

ṣeehuud drought, dry spell, period of low water.

δ̣

δ̣-a-d
δ̣aad name of the letter *δ̣*.

δ̣-ʔ-l
tδ̣aaʔal to diminish, dwindle, wane, decline, decrease. *ṣiḥḥta da-tidδ̣aaʔal yoom ɛala yoom.* His health is getting worse day after day.

δ̣aʔiil small, scanty, meager, sparse, slight. *ḥaṣṣal ɛala ribiḥ δ̣aʔiil min haṣ-ṣafqa.* He realized a very small profit from this transaction.

δ̣-b-b
δ̣abb (*u δ̣abb*) **1.** to gather, bundle, tie together. *δ̣abbaw ġaraaδ̣hum w-xallooha bil-loori.* They bundled their things together and put them on the truck. **2.** to tighten. *δ̣ubb iḥzaamak ḥatta ma-yinzil paṇṭaroonak.* Tighten your belt so your pants won't fall. *δ̣ubb il-burġi b-haddarnafiis.* Tighten the screw with this screwdriver. **3.** to be firm, unyielding, steadfast with or toward. *min yiji yammak, δ̣ubba.* When he comes around, be firm with him. *l-mudiir δ̣abba l-ɛali li-ʔan ma-kammal iš-šuġuḷ.* The director put the screws to Ali because he didn't finish the work. **4.** to take seriously, work hard at. *ʔiδa ma-δ̣δ̣ubb iš-šuġuḷ ma-nistafaad šii.* If you don't take the work seriously, we won't benefit a bit.

nδ̣abb to be tightened. *hal-burġi ma-yinδ̣abb.* The screw can't be tightened.

δ̣abb pl. *δ̣baab* a variety of large lizard.

δ̣abba pl. *-aat* **1.** scolding, talking to. **2.** handful, bunch. *δ̣abbat warid* bunch of flowers.

δ̣ubaab fog, mist.

δ̣-b-r
δ̣abbar to bind, tie up, wrap. *δ̣abbar rijla b-xirga.* He bound up his leg with a rag.

δ̣baara pl. *-aat, ʔaδ̣aabiir* file, dossier.

δ̣-b-δ̣-b
δ̣abδ̣ab to tie up, bundle up, gather up. *δ̣abδ̣ub il-ġaraaδ̣ ib-hal-ḥabil.* Tie the things up with this rope.

tδ̣abδ̣ab pass. of *δ̣abδ̣ab*.

δ̣-b-ṭ
δ̣ubaṭ (*u δ̣abuṭ*) **1.** to control, maintain control over. *l-muɛallim ma-da-yigdar yuδ̣buṭ iṣ-ṣaff.* The teacher can't control the class. *ʔuδ̣buṭ nafsak w-la-tiḥči šii hassa.* Control yourself and don't say anything now. **2.** to observe, check, watch closely. *ʔuδ̣buṭ il-waqit w-šuuf išgadd ʔaṭawwul jawwa l-mayy.* Check the time and see how long I last under water. **3.** to keep track of, keep records of. *ʔuδ̣buṭ kammiyyat il-baanziin illi tistaɛmilha yoomiyya.* Keep track of the amount of gasoline you use daily. *ṭulbat iš-šarika waaḥid yuδ̣buṭ ḥisaabaatha.* The company asked for someone to keep its books. **4.** to set, regulate, adjust. *δ̣ubaṭ saaɛta ɛala saaɛti.* He set his watch by my watch. **5.** to do precisely, exactly, meticulously, accurately. *laazim tuδ̣buṭ il-qiyaas zeen ḥatta nuɛruf išgadd inriid.* You must be precise about measuring so we will know how much we want.

tδ̣abbaṭ to be demanding, greedy (in bargaining). *ʔabuuha qibal yzawwijha bass ʔummha da-tiδ̣δ̣abbaṭ.* Her father agreed to marry her off but her mother is holding out for more dowry. *la-tidδ̣abbaṭ. haaδa xooš siɛir.* Don't be too demanding. This is a good price.

nδ̣ubaṭ pass. of *δ̣ubaṭ*.

δ̣abuṭ **1.** discipline, control, restraint. **2.** observation, checking. **3.** recording. **4.** regulation, adjustment. **5.** exactness, precision, accuracy. *biδ̣-δ̣abuṭ* exactly, precisely, accurately, meticulously. *ʔija saaɛa xamsa biδ̣-δ̣abuṭ.* He came at five o'clock on the dot. **6.** exactly, precisely. *nṭaa xamsiin diinaar δ̣abuṭ.* He gave him fifty dinars exactly.

ʔaδ̣baṭ more or most precise, accurate, exact, correct. || *ɛabaali ɛali čaδδaab. ʔaxuu ṭilaɛ ʔaδ̣baṭ.* I thought Ali was a liar. His brother proved to be even more so.

maδ̣baṭa pl. *maδ̣aabuṭ* petition.

ʔinδ̣ibaaṭ **1.** discipline. *lujnat il-inδ̣ibaaṭ* disciplinary board. **2.** (pl. *-iyya*) military policeman. *jundi nδ̣ibaaṭ* military policeman. *daaʔirt il-inδ̣ibaaṭ* military police headquarters.

δ̣aabuṭ pl. *δ̣ubbaaṭ* officer. *δ̣aabuṭ ṣaff* noncommissioned officer.

maδ̣buuṭ accurate, precise, exact, correct. *ḥačyak kulla maδ̣buuṭ* Everything you say is correct. || *mawaaɛiida ma-maδ̣buuṭa.* He doesn't keep his appointments.

δ̣-b-ɛ
δ̣abuɛ pl. *δ̣baaɛ* hyena.

miδ̣ibɛa: čalba miδ̣ibɛa. **1.** bitch in heat. **2.** ferocious female dog.

ḍ-j-j

ḍajj (u ḍajj) to clamor, shout, raise a hue and cry. *min gaal ʔaku dawaam bukra, kullhum ḍajjaw.* When he said there would be working hours tomorrow, they all raised a ruckus.

ḍajja pl. *-aat* **1.** uproar, din, clamor. **2.** crowd, noisy group.

ḍ-ƈ-k

ḍiƈak (a ḍiƈik) **1.** to laugh. *j-jaahil ḍiƈak min daġdaġta.* The child laughed when I tickled him. **2.** /with *ƈala*/ to mock, ridicule, deride, scorn. *la-tṣaddig biihum. da-yiḍƈakuun ƈaleek.* Don't believe them. They're making fun of you.

ḍaƈƈak to cause to laugh. *ḍaƈƈakna hwaaya b-laṭaayfa.* He made us laugh a lot with his witticisms. *xallaani ʔanšur il-maqaal w-ḍaƈƈak in-naas ƈalayya.* He let me publish the article and made the people laugh at me.

tḍaaƈak to laugh. *gulluu-li ƈala-weeš da-tiḍḍaaƈkuun.* Tell me what you are laughing at. *yidḍaaƈak miθl il-gaƈba.* He laughs like a whore.

nḍiƈak /with *ƈala*/ to be gotten the best of. *haaḍa šiiṭaan. ma-yinḍiƈik ƈalee.* He's a clever rascal. He can't be fooled.

ḍiƈik laughing, laughter. *b-ḍiƈik* in jest, jokingly. *gaalha ḍiƈik. ma-qiṣadha.* He said it jokingly. He didn't mean it. || *ḍiƈik ƈaḍ-ḍiquun* mockery, ridicule, derision.

ḍiƈka pl. *-aat* laugh.

ḍaƈuuk jolly, smiling. *wijih ḍaƈuuk* a pleasant face.

maḍƈaka object of ridicule, laughing-stock.

ḍ-ƈ-l

ḍaƈil **1.** shallow, shoal. **2.** superficial, shallow. *maƈluumaata ḍaƈla.* His knowledge is superficial. **3.** a shallow, a shoal. **4.** frivolous person.

ḍ-ƈ-y

ḍaƈƈa /with *b-*/ to sacrifice, offer up, immolate. *yḍaƈƈi b-kullši min ʔajilha.* He sacrifices everything for her sake.

ḍaƈa (masc.) forenoon. *ḍ-ḍaƈa l-ƈaali* late forenoon.

ḍaƈiyya pl. *ḍaƈaaya* **1.** blood sacrifice. **2.** victim. *raaƈ ḍaƈiyyat il-ġadir wil-xiyaana.* He was a victim of treachery and betrayal.

ʔaḍƈaa: ƈiid il-ʔaḍƈaa a sacrificial feast observed on the tenth day of Zu'lhijja, lasting four days.

ḍaaƈya pl. *ḍawaaƈi* suburb, outlying area. || *sibaaq ḍaaƈya* cross-country foot race.

ḍ-x-x

maḍaxxa pl. *-aat* pump.

ḍ-x-m

ḍaxxam to enlarge, expand, make huge, big, to exaggerate, amplify. *da-ḍḍaxxum il-qaḍiyya bila muujib.* You're blowing the matter up without any reason.

tḍaxxam to be made huge, to swell, expand, distend. *l-kabid maala dḍaxxam.* His liver was distended.

ḍaxim huge, enormous, vast, ample. *binaayat hal-bang ḍaxma.* This bank building is enormous. *yaaxuḍ raatib ḍaxim.* He gets a huge salary.

ʔaḍxam more or most enormous, etc.

taḍaxxum inflation. *taḍaxxum naqdi* inflation (econ.).

ḍ-d-d

ḍaadad to contradict. *kull-ma ʔaguul šii, yḍaadidni.* Everytime I say something, he contradicts me.

tḍaadad to oppose one another. *ʔintu garaayib leeš tidḍaadiduun?* You are relatives. Why are you opposed to each other?

ḍidd pl. *ʔaḍdaad* **1.** opposite, contrast. **2.** adversary, opponent. **3.** antidote, antitoxin. **4.** against. *da-yiƈči ḍiddak bil-gahaawi.* He's talking against you in the coffee shops. *naqla mniš-šuƈba čaan ḍidd raġibti.* His transfer from this section was against my will. **5.** anti-, -proof, impervious to. *ḍidd in-naar* fireproof. *ḍidd il-maay* waterproof. *ḍidd il-kasir* shockproof, unbreakable.

ḍ-r-b

ḍurab, ḍirab (u ḍarub) **1.** to strike, hit, beat. *ḍurab iz-zumaal bil-ƈaṣa.* He hit the donkey with the stick. *ḍuraba b-siččiina b-xaaṣirta.* He stabbed him with a knife in his side. *ḍuraba b-ṭalqa wiƈda w-kitala.* He shot him with one bullet and killed him. || *čaanat il-mumarriḍa ḍḍurba ʔubra kull arbaƈ saaƈaat.* The nurse was giving him a shot every four hours. *ḍrabti θ-θoob maali ʔuuti?* Did you iron my shirt? *ḍurbata š-šamis.* He had a sunstroke. *yiḍrub juluq* He masturbates. *ḍirab dabba w-ma-qibal yiruuƈ.* He got obstinate and refused to go. *ḍurboo ḍeel.* They fired him. *bil-munaaqaša maalta, čaan yuḍrub ihwaaya ʔamθaal.* In his argument, he was quoting a lot of proverbs. *tluumni luweeš ʔaƈči* *hiiči? xalli ʔaḍrub-lak maθal iš-sawwa biyya.* You blame me for saying such a thing? Let me give you an example of what he did to me. *ʔiḍrub čaff, la-truuḥ tiġrag!* Keep paddling or you'll drown! *ʔuḍrubha qaaṭ ṣubuġ laax.* Slap another coat of paint on it. *diir baalak minna; yiḍrub jeeb.* Watch out for him; he picks pockets. *ʔax uuya ḍurab ir-raqm il-qiyaasi bis-sibiḥ.* My brother broke the record in swimming. *raaḥat tistišiir waaḥid yiḍrub bit-taxat ramuḷ.* She went to consult a fellow who practices geomancy. *raḥ-ʔaḍrub raasi muus.* I'm going to shave my head. *ḍurbaw il-ʔakil w-ṭilʕaw.* They bolted down the food and went out. *ṭ-ṭaalib ḍurab id-daris.* The student cut the class. *ween il-muḥaasib? ḍurab il-baab.* Where is the accountant? He just up and left. **2.** to fire, go off. *fuṭraw baʕad-ma ḍurab iṭ-ṭoob.* They ended their fast after the cannon went off. **3.** to multiply. *ʔuḍrub har-raqm ib-xamsa.* Multiply this number by five. **4.** to copulate, fornicate, have sexual intercourse with. **5.** to act severely toward. *l-waziir ḍurab il-mudiir baʕad-ma ʕiraf ʕanna yirtiši.* The minister reassigned the director after he found out that he takes bribes. **6.** to take dishonestly. *ḍurab il-fluus ʕalayya.* He cheated me out of the money.

ḍarrab **1.** to strike repeatedly. *leeš da-dḍarrub ij-jihaal?* Why are you hitting the children? **2.** to breed, cross-breed *l-fallaaḥ ḍarrab il-ġanam maalta wiyya nooʕ aspaani.* The farmer crossed his sheep with a Spanish breed.

ʔaḍrab to go on strike, refuse to work. *l-ʕummaal ʔaḍribaw.* The workers went on strike. *l-masjuuniin ʔaḍribaw ʕan iṭ-ṭaʕaam.* The prisoners went on a hunger strike.

tḍaarab **1.** to exchange blows, hit each other. *tšaatmaw w-baʕdeen idḍaarbaw.* They insulted each other and then exchanged blows. **2.** to conflict, be in disagreement, contradict each other. *ʔaxbaar il-ḥaadiθ idḍaarbat.* Reports of the accident conflicted.

nḍurab to be struck, hit. *nḍurab b-iḥjaara b-raasa.* He got hit on the head by a stone. *z-zariʕ maalhum inḍurab kulla has-sana.* Their crops were all stricken this year. || *buxla, yinḍurab bii l-maθal!* Legends are told about his stinginess! *ṣadiiqi nḍurab ḍeel.* My friend got fired.

ḍṭirab to be or become agitated, upset, disturbed, in a state of turmoil. *ḍṭirabit min simaʕit il-ʔaxbaar.* I became upset when I heard the news. *ybayyin il-ḥaala ḍṭirbat biš-šimaal.* It seems that the situation is in turmoil in the North.

ḍarub **1.** striking, hitting, beating. **2.** multiplication. *jadwal iḍ-ḍarub* the multiplication tables.

ḍarba pl. *-aat* **1.** a blow. **2.** a beating. *ḍarbat iš-šamis* sunstroke.

ḍariiba pl. *ḍaraaʔib* **1.** imposition, excessive requirement. **2.** impost, tax, duty. *ḍariibat id-daxaḷ* income tax.

ḍarraab pl. *-iin: ḍarraab jeeb* pickpocket.

maḍrab pl. *maḍaarib* **1.** camp site, camp. **2.** spot. *maḍrab dihin* a greasy spot, smear, stain.

ʔaḍrab even more so. *hal-muʕallim šadiid laakin il-muʕallim ij-jaay ʔaḍrab minna.* This teacher is strict but the next teacher is much more so than he. *haaḏa yiftihim bass ʔabuu ʔaḍrab minna.* He is knowledgeable but his father is even more so than he. *ʔaxuuk ʔaḍrab min ṣadiiqi bil-laṭaayif.* Your brother is far better than my friend at telling jokes.

ʔiḍraab pl. *-aat* strike.

ḍṭiraab pl. *-aat* trouble, unrest, commotion, tumult, disruption, disturbance.

ḍaarib striking, hitting, beating, etc. || *loon nafnuufha ḍaarib lil-ḥumra.* The color of her dress has a reddish tint.

ḍ-r-ḥ

ḍariiḥ pl. *ḍaraayiḥ* tomb, mausoleum.

ḍ-r-r

ḍarr (*u ḍarr*) to be harmful, noxious, injurious, to harm, impair, damage, injure. *la-taakul ʔakil dihiin tara yḍurrak.* Don't eat greasy food because it's harmful to you. *yḍurr šii ʔiḏa truuḥ waḥdak w-itsawwiiha?* Will it do any harm if you go alone and do it? *ḍarreetni hwaaya b-haš-šarwa.* You caused me a great loss on this purchase.

tḍarrar to suffer, undergo harm, damage, loss. *l-ḥukuuma ʕawwḍat kull-man idḍarrar bil-fayaḍaan.* The government compensated everyone who suffered damage in the flood. *z-zurraaʕ dḍarriraw ihwaaya mnil-ḥaaluub.* The farmers suffered badly from the hail.

nḍarr to be harmed, damaged, injured, impaired. *maḥḥad yinḍarr ib-hal-*

qaanuun ġeer il-fuqaraaʔ. No one will be hurt by this law except the poor. *nð̣arreet ihwaaya b-haš-šaraaka.* I've been hurt badly in this partnership.

ð̣ṭarr **1.** to force, compel, coerce. *ð̣ṭarrooni ʔasawwiiha.* They forced me to do it. **2.** to be forced, compelled, obliged. *ma-čaan ɛindi fluus w-ið̣ṭarreet aruuħ maši.* I had no money and was forced to go on foot.

ð̣arar pl. *ʔað̣raar* **1.** harm, damage, loss. **2.** detriment, disadvantage.

ð̣arra pl. *-aat, ð̣araayir* **1.** an additional wife in a plural marriage. **2.** (pl. *-aat*) an edible gland in the udder of a cow.

ð̣ariir **1.** blind. **2.** blind man.

ð̣aruura pl. *-aat* necessity, need.

*ð̣aruuri** **1.** necessary, imperative, requisite. *l-miliħ ð̣aruuri bil-ʔakil.* Salt is necessary in food. *ð̣aruuri tiji l-yoom.* You must come today. **2.** (pl. *-iyyaat*) necessity, necessary thing.

mað̣arra pl. *-aat, mað̣aarr* harm, damage, detriment, loss, disadvantage.

ʔað̣arr more or most harmful, injurious, etc.

ð̣ṭiraar compulsion, coercion, necessity, exigency. || *ɛind il-ið̣ṭiraar* in case of emergency.

*ð̣ṭiraari** compulsory, necessary, mandatory, obligatory. || *baab xuruuj ið̣ṭiraari* emergency exit.

muð̣irr harmful, injurious, detrimental, noxious.

mað̣ruur harmed, damaged, injured, having suffered loss. *maħħad stafaad. kullna ṭilaɛna mað̣ruuriin.* No one benefited. We all came out short. || *daayin-ni čam diinaar ħatta ʔalɛab wiyyaakum. ʔaani mað̣ruur.* Lend me a few dinars so I can play with you. I'm busted.

ð̣-r-s

ð̣iris pl. *ʔað̣raas* molar, molar tooth.

ð̣-r-ṭ

ð̣iraṭ, ð̣uraṭ (*u ð̣aruṭ, ð̣raaṭ*) to break wind noisily.

ð̣arraṭ **1.** to break wind repeatedly. **2.** to scare, cause to cower, cow. *ṣaaħ ɛalee ṣeeħa waħda ð̣arraṭa biiha.* He shouted at him once and cowed him.

stað̣raṭ to have contempt for, to consider weak, cowardly. *l-muwað̣ð̣afiin stað̣riṭoo lil-mulaaħið̣ min ɛirfoo ð̣aɛiif.* The employees had no respect for the supervisor when they found out he was weak.

ð̣arṭa pl. *-aat* act of breaking wind.

mað̣raṭ pl. *mað̣aariṭ* rectum, anus (vulgar).

ʔað̣raṭ more or most ignoble, lowly, contemptible, etc.

mað̣ruuṭa pl. *-aat* bitch, slut.

mð̣arraṭ pl. *mð̣aarṭa* **1.** low, cowardly, sneaking, mean, ignoble. **2.** ignoble, contemptible person.

ð̣-r-ɛ

tð̣arraɛ /with *l-*/ to implore, beseech, beg. *dð̣arraɛ ir-rabba yxalliṣa min hal-muškila.* He implored his god to deliver him from that problem.

ð̣ariɛ pl. *ð̣ruuɛ* udder.

see also *ð-r-ɛ*.

ð̣-r-f

ð̣aruf pl. *ð̣ruuf* **1.** small leather container, bag, pouch. **2.** envelope. **3.** situation, condition, circumstance. || *b-ð̣aruf* within a period of. *ʔagdar ʔaṣalliħ ir-raadyo b-ð̣aruf saaɛa.* I can fix the radio within an hour.

ð̣-r-g

ð̣irag (*u ð̣arig*) (of a bird or fowl) to defecate, drop excrement. *ð̣irag iṭ-ṭeer ɛala sitirtak.* The bird dropped something on your coat.

ð̣arrag to defecate repeatedly. *d-dijaaj il-leel kulla čaan yð̣arrig ɛal-meez.* The chickens were messing on the table all night long.

ð̣arig pl. *ð̣ruug* bird dropping. *ð̣ruug xiššaaf* bat guano.

ð̣-ɛ-ð̣-ɛ

ð̣aɛð̣aɛ to undermine, weaken, ruin, upset. *ð̣aɛð̣aɛit il-meez min-gadd-ma thizza.* You've weakened the table by shaking it so much. *xallii gaaɛid ib-mukaana. la-ð̣ð̣aɛð̣iɛa.* Leave it sitting where it is. Don't disturb it.

tð̣aɛð̣aɛ to be undermined, weakened. *ṣiħħta dð̣aɛð̣iɛat min širb it-tiryaak.* His health was weakened by smoking opium.

[1]ð̣-ɛ-f

ð̣iɛaf (*a ð̣uɛuf*) **1.** to be or become frail, slim, thin. *ʔiða ma-taakul zeen, tið̣ɛaf.* If you don't eat well, you'll get weak. *čaan simiin laakin ð̣iɛaf haṣ-ṣeef.* He was fat but he lost weight this summer. **2.** to weaken, become weaker, diminish. *markaza bil-ħizib ð̣iɛaf.* His position in the party weakened.

ḍaععaf 1. to make frail, thin, slim. *d-duktoor nṭaani duwa yḍaععuf li-ʔan wazni zaayid.* The doctor gave me a reducing medicine because I was overweight. 2. to weaken, enfeeble, debilitate. *l-ḥarub ḍaععufat jayšna.* The war weakened our army.

ʔaḍعaf = *ḍaععaf. l-ʔaspiriin yiḍعif il-badan.* Aspirin weakens the body.

staḍعaf to consider weak, feeble, to underestimate. *la-tistaḍعifa tara titnaddam.* Don't think of him as weak or you'll be sorry.

ḍaعiif or *ḍiعiif* 1. frail, thin, emaciated. 2. weak, feeble. *ḏaakirta ḍaعiifa.* His memory is poor.

ḍaعfaan weakened, enfeebled, thin, skinny, slim. *ybayyin عaleek ḍaعfaan. ma-da-taakul?* You look thin. Aren't you eating?

ʔaḍعaf more or most delicate, emaciated, feeble, etc.

²*ḍ-ع-f*

ḍaaعaf to double, redouble, multiply, compound. *ʔiḏa dḍaaعif عadad iš-šurṭa, yṣiir ʔamaan bil-balad.* If you double the number of police there'll be safety in the city. *ḍaaعaf θaruuta min ʔassas haš-šarika.* He redoubled his wealth when he formed this company.

tḍaaعaf pass. of *ḍaaعaf. dḍaaعaf عadadhum ib-mudda qaṣiira.* Their number doubled in a short time. *l-ʔalam maala dḍaaعaf min fakka il-banj.* His pain was redoubled when the anesthetic wore off.

ḍiعif pl. *ʔaḍعaaf* 1. double, twice as much. 2. multiple, several times as much. *ribiḥ hal-yoom čaan iθlaθ ʔaḍعaaf ribiḥ il-baarḥa.* Today's profit was three times as much as yesterday's profit.

ḍ-ġ-ṭ

ḍiġaṭ (*u ḍaġiṭ*) /with *عala*/ to exert pressure on, press on, bear down upon. *la-txalli l-išdaad yuḍġuṭ ihwaaya عajjariḥ.* Don't let the bandage press too tightly on the wound. *ḍiġaṭ عalee ḥatta sawwaa-l h-iyyaa.* He pressured him until he did it for him.

ḍaġiṭ pressure. *ḍ-ḍaġṭ ij-jawwi* atmospheric pressure. *ḍaġuṭ damm* blood pressure. *ḍaġuṭ kahrabaaʔi* electric voltage.

maḍġuuṭ compressed. *hawa maḍġuuṭ* compressed air.

ḍ-f-r

ḍufar (*u ḍafur*) 1. to plait, braid. *l-عaruus da-yḍufruun giṣaayibha.* They're plaiting the bride's braids. 2. to catch, grasp, lay one's hands on. *bass ʔaḍufra, ʔaعruf iš-ʔasawwi bii.* Once I catch him, I'll know what to do with him.

ḍafiira pl. *ḍafaayir* adornment on the end of a girl's braid.

ʔiḍfir pl. *ʔaḍaafiir* fingernail, claw, talon.

ḍ-l-ع

ḍiliع pl. *ḍluuع* 1. rib. 2. (pl. *ʔaḍlaaع*) side (of a geometric figure).

ḍilعa pl. *-aat* a cut of meat from the ribs of an animal.

ḍ-l-f

ḍilif pl. *ʔaḍlaaf* cloven hoof.

ḍ-l-l

ḍall (*i u ḍall*) 1. to stay, remain, last. *ḍall saaعa yintaḍrak.* He stayed an hour waiting for you. *ḍull waaguf. balki ymurr.* Stay here. Maybe he'll come by. *šgadd ḍallat ifluus عindak?* How much money do you still have left? *xan-nruuḥ. ma-ḍall wakit.* Let's go. There's no time left. 2. to continue, persist, persevere. *ḍallat tumṭur il-leel kulla.* It kept raining all night. *ʔinta tḍill itšaaġib?* Are you still stirring up trouble?

ḍallal 1. to mislead, misguide, fool, confuse. *ḥaṭṭaw ʔaġṣaan ʔašjaar عad-dabbaabaat ḥatta yḍalliluun il-عadu.* They put tree branches on the tanks to mislead the enemy. 2. to shade, darken, add shadow to. *ḍallil iṣ-ṣuura b-hal-qalam.* Shade the picture with this crayon.

ḍill pl. *ʔaḍlaal* shade, shadow, umbra.

maḍalla pl. *-aat* 1. umbrella, parasol, sunshade. 2. parachute.

maḍalli pl. *-iyyiin* 1. paratrooper. 2. parachutist.

ḍ-l-m

ḍilam (*u ḍulum*) 1. to do wrong or evil, commit outrage, be tyrannical. *hal-mudiir raḥ-yuḍlum ʔakθar imnil-ʔawwal.* This director will be more tyrannical than the first one. 2. to wrong, ill-treat, treat unjustly. *leeš tuḍlumha lil-ibnayya w-itzawwijha l-haš-šaayib?* Why are you being unfair to the girl and marrying her to this old man?

ḍallam to be or become dark, gloomy, to darken. *s-saaعa sitta dḍallum id-dinya.* It gets dark at six o'clock.

tḍallam to complain, make a complaint. *raḥ-yidḍallam عind il-waziir عala qasaawathum.* He's going to complain to the minister about their cruelties.

nḍilam to be wronged, treated unjustly. *nḍilam ihwaaya. l-miskiin ma-msawwi šii.* He was treated very unjustly. The poor guy hasn't done a thing.

ḍlamm to become dark, gloomy, to darken. *ˀijat ʕajja l-baarḥa w-iḍlammat id-dinya minha.* A dust storm came yesterday and the sky grew dark from it.

ḍulum **1.** unfairness, injustice, inequity. **2.** oppression, tyranny.

ˀaḍlam, fem. *ḍalma* pl. *ḍilim* **1.** dark, gloomy, murky. **2.** more or most gloomy, murky, dusky. **3.** more or most unjust, unfair, tyrannical, iniquitous.

maḍlama pl. *maḍaalim* misdeed, wrong, iniquity, outrage, act of injustice.

ḍalaam darkness, gloom, murkiness.

ḍaalim **1.** unjust, unfair, iniquitous, tyrannical. **2.** harsh, severe. **3.** (pl. *ḍullaam*) tyrant, oppressor, evildoer, villain.

maḍluum wronged, maltreated, unjustly treated, tyrannized. *haaḍa maḍluum ib-šuġla.* He's been discriminated against in his job.

muḍlim darkened, lightless. *gurfa múḍilma* darkroom.

ḍ-m-d

ḍammad to dress, bandage. *ruuḥ lil-mustašfa ḥatta yḍammiduu-lak ij-jariḥ.* Go to the hospital so they can bandage the wound for you.

ḍamaad pl. *-aat* bandage.

muḍammid pl. *-iin* hospital attendant who administers minor treatments, male nurse.

ḍ-m-r

ḍumar (*u ḍamur*) **1.** to secrete, keep secret, conceal. *ˀuḍmur ʕadad w-aani ˀaḥizra.* Think of a number and I'll guess what it is. **2.** to harbor, entertain. *tfaadaa. haaḍa da-yiḍmur-lak iš-šarr.* Avoid him. He's holding a grudge against you.

ḍamiir pl. *ḍamaaˀir* **1.** conscience, scruples. **2.** personal pronoun (gram.).

ḍ-m-ḍ-m

ḍamḍam to be secretive, keep things to oneself. *la-dḍamḍum ʕalayya. gul-li kullši.* Don't hide things from me. Tell me everything. *š-ma-tsawwi, ˀummha dḍamḍum ˀilha.* Whatever she does, her mother covers up for her. *da-yḍamḍum b-ifluusa w-ma-yguul l-aḥḥad.* He is hiding his money and doesn't tell anyone.

tḍamḍam to be concealed, be kept secret. *l-qaḍiyya nfuḍḥat w-baʕad ma-tidḍamḍam.* The matter has been disclosed and can't be covered up anymore.

ḍ-m-m

ḍamm (*u ḍamm*) **1.** to be secretive, to keep things to oneself. *ˀiḥči! la-ḍḍumm ʕalayya.* Speak up! Don't hide anything from me. **2.** to hide, conceal, secrete. *j-jaahil ḍamm il-qalam maala b-mukaan ma-nindalla.* The child hid his pencil in a place we wouldn't find. **3.** to put away for safekeeping, to save, to salt away. *la-tuṣruf kull raatbak. ḍumm minna šwayya.* Don't spend all your salary. Put away a little of it. *tigdar idḍumm-li fluusi ʕindak ˀila ˀan ˀarjaʕ?* Could you keep my money for me until I return? **4.** to join, unite, add. *ˀaani ˀaḍumm ṣooti ˀila ṣootak bil-iḥtijaaj.* I'll add my voice to yours in the protest.

nḍamm **1.** to hide oneself. *min šaaf iš-šurṭi jaay, nḍamm.* When he saw the policeman coming, he hid himself. **2.** /with *l-*/ to enter, join. *nḍamm lil-ḥizib biduun muwaafaqat ˀahla.* He joined the political party without his family's consent.

ḍ-m-n

ḍuman (*a ḍamaan*) **1.** to guarantee, ensure, make sure, be certain. *šloon tiḍman ma-yʕiid nafs il-ġalṭa?* How can you be sure that he won't repeat the same mistake? **2.** to contract for the unharvested crop of (an orchard). *ḍuman il-bistaan ib-miiteen diinaar.* He contracted for the orchard for two hundred dinars.

ḍamman to sell the unharvested crop of (an orchard). *ma-aḍammun il-bistaan ib-ˀaqall min miit diinaar.* I won't sell the orchard's crop for less than a hundred dinars.

ḍimin: min ḍimin, b-ḍimin included in, among, belonging to, part of the group of. *min ḍimn il-ˀašyaaˀ il-ḥičaa-li-yyaaha qiṣṣat is-sayyaara.* Among the things he told me was the story about the car. *huwwa min ḍimn ij-jamaaʕa lli ʕtidaw ʕalayya.* He is one of the group who attacked me. *ḍ-ḍariiba daaxla b-ḍimn is-siʕir.* The tax is included in the price.

ḍammaan pl. *-a* landlord, man who owns an orchard and sells the unharvested crop.

ˀaḍman more or most vouchsafed, guaranteed, warranted, safe. *ˀaḍman-lak taaxuḍ wiyyaak ʕašr idnaaniir zaayda.* It's safer for you to take ten dinars extra with you.

ḍ-n-n

ḍann (*u ḍann*) **1.** to think, believe, assume, presume, suppose. *ˀaḍunn raḥ-yooṣal il-yoom min baġdaad.* I think he'll arrive today from Baghdad. **2.** to think capable of, to expect from. *ma-ḍanneetak itxuunni.* I never expected you to betray me. **3.** to be suspicious. *ʔaani ʔaḍunn bii.* I am suspicious of him.

ḍann pl. *ḍunuun* assumption, supposition, view, opinion, idea. || *xaab ḍanni biik.* My opinion of you faltered. I was disappointed in you. *ḥusun iḍ-ḍann* good opinion. *ʔaškurak ʕala ḥusun ḍannak biyya.* I thank you for your good opinion of me. *ʔaġlab iḍ-ḍann, ʔakθar iḍ-ḍann* most probably, most likely. *ʔaġlab iḍ-ḍann raḥ-yintiqil il-ġeer madrasa.* Most probably he will transfer to another school.

ḍ-n-k

ḍinak (*i ḍanak*) to place in straitened, impoverished circumstances. *dafiʕ il-iijaar ḍinakni.* Paying the rent put me in straitened circumstances.

nḍinak to be placed in straitened circumstances. *min štireet il-ḥooš, nḍinakit. fluusi ma-da-tkaffi.* When I bought the house, I put myself in a bind. My money isn't enough.

ḍanak poverty, distress, straits. *ʕaayiš ib-ḍanak.* He's living in poverty.

maḍnuuk in financial straits. *ma-raḥ-agdar adfaʕ qisṭ is-sayyaara haš-šahar. ʔaani maḍnuuk.* I won't be able to pay the car payment this month. I'm in a bind.

ḍ-h-d

ḍṭihad to persecute, oppress, treat unjustly. *stawlaw ʕal-balad w-iḍṭihdaw sukkaana.* They conquered the country and treated its inhabitants unjustly.

ḍ-h-r

ḍihar (*a ḍuhuur*) **1.** to show, appear, emerge, come into view. *baʕad saaʕa, yiḍhar il-gumar.* The moon will appear in an hour. *hassa ḍihrat il-ḥaqiiqa.* Now the truth is out. **2.** to be or become apparent, clear, obvious, evident, manifest. *ḍihar-li baʕdeen fadd waaḥid čaḍḍaab.* It became apparent to me later that he was a liar. *yiḍhar ma-yriid ybiiʕ il-beet.* It seems he doesn't want to sell the house. || *ʕala-ma yiḍhar, ḥasab-ma yiḍhar* according to the evidence, apparently, the way things look. *ʕala-ma yiḍhar, ma-raḥ-yijuun.* Evidently they aren't coming.

ḍahhar to endorse (a check, etc.). *ḍahhir ič-čakk gabuḷ-ma tinṭii.* Endorse the check before you present it.

ʔaḍhar to make visible, make apparent, show, present, demonstrate, bring to light, expose, divulge, disclose, reveal, make known. *b-šahaadta, ʔaḍhar il-ḥaqq.* By his testimony, he revealed the truth.

tḍahhar to be endorsed. *č-čakk, laazim yidḍahhar gabuḷ-ma yinṣuruf.* The check must be endorsed before it can be cashed.

tḍaahar **1.** to demonstrate, stage a public demonstration. *ṭ-ṭullaab idḍaahraw w-ṭaalbaw b-istiqaalat il-waziir.* The students demonstrated and demanded the resignation of the minister. **2.** /with *b-*/ to feign, affect, pretend, simulate. *dḍaahar bil-ḥubb ʔilha.* He pretended to be in love with her.

ḍahar pl. *ḍhuur* **1.** back (anat.). || *ʔija ḍahra.* He reached sexual climax. He had an orgasm. *ṭilaʕ rijjaal. haaḍa ṣudug min ḍahr abuu.* He proved to be a real man. He's really his father's seed. **2.** back, rear, rear side, reverse side. || *ma-yxaaf; il-waziir ib-ḍahra.* He's not afraid; the minister's behind him. **3.** deck. || *ʕala ḍahar il-baaxira* aboard the ship. **4.** backing, support, advocacy. *l-ma-ʕinda ḍahar ma-yḥaṣṣil waḍiifa.* Whoever doesn't have backing can't get a job. **5.** generation. *huwwa mniḍ-ḍahar is-saabiʕ lil-ʔusra l-ḥaakima.* He is from the seventh generation of the ruling family.

ḍuhur pl. *ḍahaari* noon, midday. *raḥ-ašuufa ḍ-ḍuhur.* I'm going to see him at noon. *baʕd iḍ-ḍuhur* afternoon, p.m.

ḍuhriyya noon, noontime.

ḍuhuur **1.** appearance. **2.** visibility, conspicuousness. **3.** ostentation, show, splendor, pomp. *ḥubb iḍ-ḍuhuur* ostentatiousness, love of pomp and splendor.

maḍhar pl. *maḍaahir* **1.** external appearance, looks. **2.** (pl. only) ostentatious displays, status symbols.

muḍaahara pl. *-aat* public demonstration, rally.

ḍaahir visible, distinct, manifest, obvious, conspicuous, clear, evident, apparent. || *ḍ-ḍaahir . . .* apparently, evidently, obviously . . . *ḍ-ḍaahir ṭallag marta.* Evidently he divorced his wife. *ḥasab iḍ-ḍaahir . . .* according to the evidence, the way things look, apparently . . . *ḥasb iḍ-ḍaahir, ma-raḥ-yiji.* Apparently he isn't going to come.

*ḍaahiri** superficial. *ʕamala čaan fadd šii ḍaahiri.* The thing he did was strictly for show.

ḍaahira pl. *ḍawaahiir* phenomenon.

mutaḍaahir pl. *-iin* (public) demonstrator.

ḍ-h-y
ḍaaha to resemble, be like, be comparable to, to match, equal. *jamaalha ma-yḍaahii ˀay jamaal.* He beauty is like no other beauty. *maḥḥad yḍaahii biš-šiʕir.* Nobody can come up to his level in poetry.

ḍ-w-ˀ
ḍuwa, etc. see under *ḍ-w-y.*

ḍ-w-j
ḍaaj (u ḍooj, ḍwaaja) **1.** to become uneasy, upset, annoyed, disturbed, irritated. *la-tjiib ṭaari l-imtiḥaan tara yḍuuj.* Don't bring up the subject of the exam or he'll get upset. *l-muʕallim ḍaaj minna hwaaya.* The teacher got extremely fed up with him. **2.** to become restless, bored. *ḍijit waḥdi bil-ġurfa.* I got bored being alone in the room. *ˀibinkum ḍaaj xooš ḍooja ʕiddna.* Your son got real bored at our place.

ḍawwaj **1.** to upset, bother, disturb, annoy, irritate. *yḍawwij ihwaaya b-kalaama.* He annoys people a lot when he talks. **2.** to bore. *l-baṭaala ḍawwijatni.* The idleness bored me.

tḍawwaj pass. of *ḍawwaj.*

ḍooj **1.** irritation, annoyance. **2.** boredom, restlessness.

ḍooja pl. *-aat* i.n. of *ḍooj.*

ḍwaaja boredom.

ḍawajaan **1.** bothersome, annoying, upsetting. **2.** boring. *haš-šuġul ḍawajaan.* This work is boring.

ḍ-w-g
ḍaag (u ḍoog) **1.** to taste, sample. *ḍaag il-marag w-ma-qibal yaakul.* He tasted the stew and refused to eat. **2.** to taste, experience, undergo, suffer, go through. *ḍaag il-ḥilu wil-murr ib-ḥayaata.* He tasted the sweet and the bitter in his lifetime. *ḍaagat il-murr ib-tarbiita.* She went through hell in raising him.

ḍawwag to give a taste of, let taste. *raḥ-aṭbux w-aḍawwgak iṭ-ṭabux maali.* I'm going to cook and I'll give you a taste of my cooking.

ḍoog **1.** tasting. **2.** experiencing.

ḍooga pl. *-aat* i.n. of *ḍoog.*

see also *ḍ-w-q.*

ḍ-w-y
ḍuwa (i ḍawi) to gleam, beam, radiate, shine. *wujihha yiḍwi miθl il-badir.* Her face shines like the full moon.

ḍawwa **1.** to light, light up, illuminate. *gloob ˀabu miyya yḍawwi l-ġurfa kulliš zeen.* A hundred watt bulb lights the room very well. *ˀišʕil iḍ-ḍuwa, w-ḍawwii-li ṭ-ṭariiq.* Turn on the light and light up the road for me. **2.** to provide light. *ḍawwii-li ḥatta ˀagdar ˀaqra l-quṭʕa.* Give me some light so I can read the sign.

ḍuwa pl. *ḍuwaayaat, ˀaḍwiya* light. *ḍuwa š-šamis* sunlight.

ḍuwi, ḍaawi** bright, lighted, illuminated. *ġurfa ḍwiyya* a bright room. || *ˀugʕud. d-dinya ḍwiyya.* Get up. It's daylight.

ḍ-y-ʕ
ḍaaʕ (i ḍeeʕ) to be lost, get lost. *l-baarḥa ḍaaʕat binta bis-suug.* Yesterday his daughter got lost in the marketplace. *ḍaaʕ miftaaḥ il-qaaṣa.* The key to the safe got lost. *ḍaaʕ ʕalayya l-iḥsaab; ma-adri šgadd ˀaṭulba.* I lost count; I don't know how much he owes me. *leeš ma-qaddamit ʕariiḍa? il-furṣa ḍaaʕat ʕaleek.* Why didn't you submit an application? The opportunity has passed you by.

ḍayyaʕ **1.** to cause to get lost. *ʕabaanna yuʕruf il-beet, laakin fawwatna b-daraabiin w-ḍayyaʕna.* We thought he knew the house, but he sent us through alleys and got us lost. *ḍayyiʕ nafsak fadd saaʕa ḥatta ma-yšuufak.* Make yourself scarce for an hour so he won't see you. **2.** to lose. *ḍayyaʕ saaʕta bis-siinama.* He lost his watch in the movie. *ḍayyaʕ ibna bil-izdiḥaam.* He lost his son in the crowd. **3.** to waste, squander, spend uselessly. *la-dḍayyiʕ waktak bil-liʕib.* Don't waste your time playing. *ḍayyaʕit ʕalayya l-wakit.* You've wasted my time. || *la-dḍayyiʕ il-iḥčaaya. gul-li ˀii loo laa.* Don't beat around the bush. Tell me yes or no. **3.** /with *ʕala*/ to cause to lose, miss. *ḍayyaʕ il-furṣa ʕalayya.* He made me miss the opportunity.

ḍ-y-f
ḍaaf (i ˀiḍaafa) to add, subjoin, annex, attach. *ˀiḍa dḍiif haj-jumla, tinfihim il-qaḍiyya.* If you add this sentence, the matter will be understood.

ḍayyaf **1.** to take in (as a guest), receive hospitably. *ḍayyifoona b-beethum isbuuʕ.* They took us into their house as guests for a week. *ˀiḍa truuḥ ʕaleehum, yḍayyifuuk.* If you go to their house, they treat you like a guest.

staḍyaf to invite to be a guest. *yistiḍiifuun ˀay waaḥid yzuur il-balda.* They invite anyone visiting the city to stay with them.

ḍeef pl. *ḍiyuuf* guest.

δ̣iyaafa **1.** hospitality. **2.** hospitable reception and entertainment.
ʔiδ̣aafa pl. *-aat* addition. *bil-iδ̣aafa* in addition. *bil-iδ̣aafa ʔila δaalik* . . . In addition to that . . . .
*ʔiδ̣aafi** additional, supplementary, auxiliary, extra, secondary. *mablaġ iδ̣aafi* a supplementary amount.
muδ̣iif pl. *muδ̣aayif* hospice, guest house, hostel.
muδ̣ayyifa pl. *-aat* stewardess, hostess.

δ̣-y-q
δ̣ayyaq /with *ℰala*/ to harass, beset, put pressure on. *ʔiδa dδ̣ayyiq ℰalee, yinṭiik il-ifluus.* If you pressure him, he'll give you the money.
δ̣aayaq to vex, annoy, pester, harass, bother, disturb. *da-yδ̣aayiqni ihwaaya b-muxaabaraata.* He's bothering me a lot with his phone calls.
tδ̣aayaq to be or become annoyed, irritated. *yidδ̣aayaq ihwaaya mnizziyaaraat.* He gets very irritated at visits.
δ̣iiq distress, need, want, lack, paucity, poverty. *ℰaayiš ib-δ̣iiq.* He's living in poverty. *ʔagdar asaaℰdak ℰind iδ̣-δ̣iiq.* I can help you in time of need.
maδ̣iiq pl. *maδ̣aayiq* narrow passage, straits. *maδiiq jabalṭaariq* Straits of Gibraltar.

muδ̣aayaqa pl. *-aat* annoyance, disturbance, vexation, irritation, nuisance, harassment.

δ̣-y-g
δ̣aag (*i δ̣iig*) to be or become narrow, straitened, cramped, confining. *ybayyin il-qaaṭ δaag ℰaleek.* It looks like the suit's too small for you. || *δ̣aagat id-dinya bii.* He became depressed (lit., the world became too confining for him). *δaagat il-wasℰa bii.* He became depressed. *ʔiδa δ̣aag xulgič, dδ̣akkiri ʔayyaam ℰirsič.* If you feel sad, remember the days of your wedding.
δ̣ayyag to make narrow, straiten, cramp, tighten. *raℰ-aaxuδ il-panṭaroon lil-xayyaaṭ ℰatta yδ̣ayyiga.* I'm going to take the pants to the tailor so he can make them tighter.
δ̣ayyig **1.** narrow. *šaariℰ δ̣ayyig* a narrow street. **2.** tight, cramped, confining. *sitirti δ̣ayyga ℰalayya. ma-agdar atnaffas.* My jacket is tight on me. I can't breathe. *hal-beet ṣaar δayyig ihwaaya ℰaleena.* This house has gotten too small for us.
ʔaδ̣yag **1.** narrower, narrowest. **2.** more or most confining.

Ṭ

ṭ-a-b-w-r
ṭaabuur pl. *ṭwaabiir* file, queue, line, column (esp. of soldiers).

ṭ-a-b-w-g
ṭaabuug, etc., see *ṭ-b-g*.

ṭ-a-r-y
ṭaari matter, subject, topic (of someone). *la-djiib ṭaariyya. huwwa ma-mawjuud ihnaa.* Don't bring up the subject of him. He's not here. *kull-ma yjiibuun ṭaari ʔibna l-maat, taaxδa l-ℰabra.* Every time they mention his dead son, he bursts into tears. *činna b-ṭaariyyak gabḷ išwayya.* We were just talking about you a moment ago.

ṭ-a-s
ṭaas, ṭaasa, see *ṭ-w-s*.

ṭ-a-g-y
ṭaagiyya, ṭaagya pl. *-aat* skullcap. || *ʔilli yiℰči ṣ-ṣudug ṭaagiita manguuba.* Anybody who tells the truth has got something wrong with him (lit., has a hole in his skullcap).

ṭ-a-w
ṭaawa pl. *-aat* frying pan, skillet.

ṭ-a-w-l-y
ṭaawli **1.** backgammon, tricktrack. **2.** (pl. *-iyyaat*) backgammon set.

ṭ-a-w-w-s
ṭaawuus pl. *ṭawaawiis* peacock.

ṭ-b-b
ṭabb (*u ṭabb*) **1.** to enter, go in. *jeebi ẓġayyir. ʔiidi ma-ṭṭubb bii.* My pocket's too small. My hand won't go in it. *hal-burġi ma-yṭubb biṣ-ṣammuuna.* This bolt won't fit into the nut. *šaal dišdaašta w-ṭabb yxuuδ̣ bil-ṃaay.* He lifted his robe and went wading into the water. *ṭabb ℰaleehum w-šaafhum mašġuuḷiin.* He dropped in on them and found them busy. || *yṭubba maraδ̣!* To hell with him! Plague take him! **2.** to pat, tap lightly. *ṭabb ℰala čitfi w-ibtisam.* He patted my shoulder and smiled. **3.** to slam, dash, bang. *šaala*

w-ṭabba bil-gaaʕ. He picked him up and slammed him on the ground.

ṭabbab **1.** to cause to enter, bring in, take in. *leeš imwagguf ṣadiiqak barra? ṭabbuba lil-beet.* Why are you keeping your friend outside? Bring him in the house. *ṭabbub il-waayar min haz-zuruf.* Insert the wire through this hole. **2.** to treat medically. *ʔaʕsan id-dakaatra ṭab-biboo laakin ma-ṣaarat-la čaara.* The best doctors treated him but there was no cure for him.

tṭabbab pass. of *ṭabbab.*

nṭabb to be entered. *hal-ġurfa ma-yinṭabb.* This room is not to be entered.

ṭibb **1.** medical treatment. **2.** medicine, medical science. *ṭibb il-ʔasnaan* dentistry, dental science.

*ṭibbi** medical. *faḥiṣ ṭibbi* a medical examination.

ṭabiib pl. *ʔaṭibbaaʔ* doctor, physician. *ṭabiib il-ʔasnaan* dentist. *ṭabiib beeṭari* veterinarian.

ṭ-b-j

muṭbij **1.** side-by-side. *tufgat ṣeed muṭibja* double-barreled shotgun. **2.** (pl. *maṭaabij*) a double-tubed flute.

ṭ-b-x

ṭubax, ṭibax (*u ṭabux*) to cook, to prepare. *la-tṭubxiin. raḥ-ajiib ʔakl imnil-maṭʕam.* Don't cook anything. I'll bring some food from the restaurant. *š-ṭaabxa l-yoom?* What have you cooked today? || *xalli ʔaruuḥ gabḷak ʔaṭbuxha lil-qaḍiyya.* Let me go ahead of you and get things ready. *xalli ʔaruuḥ ʔaṭubxa. balki yiqbal yšuufak.* Let me go soften him up. Perhaps he'll agree to see you.

nṭubax to be cooked, prepared. *hal-laḥam ma-yinṭubux ib-saaʕ.* This meat can't be cooked quickly.

ṭabux cooking, cuisine.

ṭabxa pl. *-aat* (cooked) meal, dish, food.

ṭabbaax pl. *-iin* **1.** cook. **2.** (pl. *-aat, maṭaabix*) kitchen stove, range.

ṭibiix cooked rice.

maṭbax, muṭbax pl. *maṭaabix* **1.** kitchen. **2.** kitchen stove.

ṭ-b-r

ṭubar (*u ṭabur*) to hack, chop. *ṭubar raasa bis-seef.* He hacked his head with the sword.

ṭabbar to hack, chop repeatedly or continuously. *ʕima s-siččiina li-ʔan čaan yṭabbur il-xišba biiha.* He dulled the knife because he was chopping up the board with it.

ṭabur hacking, cutting.

ṭabra pl. *-aat* i.n. of *ṭabur.*

ṭubar pl. *ṭbaara* **1.** axe, hatchet. **2.** (pl. *ṭbuur*) small stream.

ṭ-b-š

ṭabbaš to splash, splatter, play (in water). *ʔibnak yiʕijba yṭabbuš bil-mayy.* Your son likes to splash around in the water.

ṭ-b-š-r

ṭabaašiir chalk.

ṭ-b-ṭ-b

ṭabṭab **1.** to pat, tap lightly. *ṭabṭab-ilha lil-bazzuuna ḥatta siktat.* He patted the cat until it kept quiet. **2.** to bounce, dribble. *b-kurat is-salla, laazim itṭabṭub iṭ-ṭooba min timši.* In basketball you have to dribble the ball when you move.

ṭ-b-ʕ

ṭibaʕ, ṭubaʕ (*a ṭabuʕ*) **1.** to print. *ṭibʕaw il-manaašiir ib-maṭbaʕa sirriyya.* They printed the hand bills with a secret press. **2.** to type. *ʔarjuuk, iṭbaʕ-li hal-maktuub.* Please type this letter for me.

ṭabbaʕ **1.** to imprint on, impress on, impart to. *ʔumma ṭabbuʕata ʕala ʔašyaaʔ maḥbuuba hwaaya.* His mother imparted to him many endearing traits. *laazim iṭṭabbuʕuun il-walad b-iṭbaaʕkum.* You have to imprint your characteristics on the boy. **2.** to accustom, condition, train. *ṭabbaʕ zawijta ʕala ḍawqa bil-ʔakil.* He accustomed his wife to his taste in food. *ṭabbaʕ ič-čalib yaakul wiyya l-bazzuuna maalta.* He trained the dog to eat with his cat.

tṭabbaʕ **1.** to be affected, influenced. *rijaʕ muṭṭabbuʕ b-iṭbaaʕ il-ʔawruppiy-yiin.* He came back influenced by European customs. **2.** to be trained, accustomed, conditioned. *l-ġazaal ma-yiṭṭabbaʕ bil-ʕajal.* A gazelle can't be trained easily.

nṭibaʕ **1.** to be printed. *hal-iktaab ween inṭibaʕ?* Where was this book printed? **2.** to be typed. *šuuf il-maktuub nṭibaʕ loo baʕad.* Find out if the letter's been typed or not.

ṭabuʕ **1.** printing, typing. || *taḥt iṭ-ṭabuʕ* being printed or typed, at the press, in press. **2.** disposition, nature, temper, character. **3.** (pl. *ʔaṭbaaʕ*) trait, characteristic, peculiarity. || *biṭ-ṭabuʕ* 1. by nature, naturally. 2. naturally, of course. *biṭ-ṭabuʕ saaʕadni hwaaya li-ʔanna ṣadiiqi.* Naturally he helped me a lot because he's my friend.

ṭabʕan naturally, of course, certainly. *ṭabʕan, ʔaʕurfa.* Of course I know him.

ṭabɛa pl. *-aat* **1.** printing. **2.** edition, issue (of a publication).

ṭabiiɛa pl. *ṭabaayiɛ* **1.** nature, character, constitution. *ṭabiiɛt il-manṭiqa jabaliyya.* The nature of the area is mountainous. **2.** peculiarity, characteristic, trait. *laazim idjuuz min haṭ-ṭabiiɛa.* You should get away from this tendency. **3.** nature. *ṭ-ṭabiiɛa djahhiz il-ḥaywaanaat ib-wasaaʔil id-difaaɛ ɛan-nafis.* Nature provides animals with the means of self-defense.

*ṭabiiɛi** **1.** natural, of nature. *taariix ṭabiiɛi* natural history. **2.** inborn, innate, inherent. **3.** normal, ordinary, usual. *haaδa šii ṭabiiɛi.* That's natural.

ṭabbaaɛ pl. *-iin* printer, typesetter.

maṭbaɛa pl. *maṭaabiɛ* **1.** printing press. **2.** print shop, printing office.

*maṭbaɛi** printing, printer's, typographical. *ġalaṭ maṭbaɛi* a printing error.

ṭaabiɛ pl. *ṭawaabiɛ* (postage, etc.) stamp.

ṭaabiɛa **1.** typing, typewriting. *kaatib ṭaabiɛa* typist. **2.** (pl. *-aat*) typewriter.

maṭbuuɛaat (invar. pl.) **1.** printed matter. **2.** publications.

ṭ-b-q

ṭabbaq **1.** to apply, make applicable. *tiɛtiqid yigidruun yṭabbuquun il-qaanuun ib-hal-manṭiqa?* Do you think they can make the law applicable in this area? **2.** to apply one's knowledge, gain practical experience, to intern. *laazim yṭabbuq ib-fadd madrasa gabuḷ-ma yitxarraj min daar il-muɛallimiin.* He has to practice in a school before he graduates from teacher's college. **3.** to intern. *raḥ-nibdi nṭabbuq mnil-isbuuɛ ij-jaay.* We're going to begin our internship next week.

ṭaabaq **1.** to correlate, compare, contrast. *ṭaabaqit jawaabi wiyyaa w-ṭilɛaw nafs iš-šii.* I compared my answer with his and they came out the same thing. **2.** to correspond, concur, agree, conform with. *ḥčaayta ṭṭaabuq iḥčaaytak.* His story corresponds with your story.

tṭabbaq to be applied. *hal-qaanuun ma-yiṭṭabbaq ib-suhuula.* This law cannot be easily applied.

tṭaabaq **1.** to be compared. *hal-jawaabeen ma-yiṭṭaabquun li-ʔan is-suʔaaleen yixtalfuun.* These two answers can't be compared because the two questions are different. **2.** to compare with one another. *xan-niṭṭaabaq ḥatta nšuuf il-ġalaṭ ween.* Let's compare with each other to see where the mistake is. **3.** to correspond, conform. *hal-muθallaθeen ma-yiṭṭaabquun waaḥid wiyya l-laax.* These two triangles do not correspond with each other.

nṭubaq to be applicable, apply. *l-qaaɛida ma-tinṭubuq ɛala haj-jumla.* The rule doesn't apply to this sentence.

ṭibq: ṣuura ṭibq il-ʔaṣil exact copy, true replica.

ṭabqa pl. *-aat: ṭabqat waraq* a large sheet of paper of a standard size.

ṭabaqa pl. *-aat* **1.** layer, stratum. **2.** class (of society).

taṭbiiq practical experience, practical application, internship.

ṭaabiq pl. *ṭawaabiq* floor, story (of a building).

ṭ-b-g

ṭubag (*u ṭabug*) **1.** to juxtapose, place alongside. *ʔuṭbug haṭ-ṭiriiša wiyya rijl il-kursi ḥatta titḥammal θugul.* Put this slat alongside the leg of the chair so it can bear weight. *ʔuṭbug hal-fardat il-qundara wiyya hal-farda w-šuuf ʔiδa nafs il-qiyaas.* Put this shoe alongside that one and see if they're the same size. *ʔuṭbug hal-looḥaat wiḥda wiyya l-lux w-sawwiiha saguf lil-ġurfa.* Lay these boards one beside the other and make a ceiling for the room. || *ʔinta ʔaxuuya. šloon tuṭbug wiyyaa ɛalayya?* You're my brother. How could you side with him against me? **2.** to close, shut. *ʔuṭbug l-iktaab.* Close the book. *min titlaɛ, ʔuṭbug il-baab rajaaʔan.* When you go out, close the door, please.

ṭabbag **1.** to place a covering, layer over, to cover, superimpose, overspread. *l-gaaɛ kullha mḥaffura. laazim iṭṭabbugha bil-kaaši.* The ground's all dug up. You should cover it with tile. **2.** to fold, make layers of. *ṭabbug il-ihduum zeen gabuḷ-ma txalliiha bij-junṭa.* Fold the clothes well before you put them in the suitcase. **3.** to smother, cover. *ṭabbug id-dijaaj ib-timman.* Fix the chicken smothered in rice. *ɛašaana l-yoom simač mṭabbag.* Our dinner today is fish smothered in rice. **4.** (voice) to be or become hoarse, deep. *ṭabbag ḥissa mnil-bači.* His voice became hoarse from crying.

tṭabbug to be covered. *hal-ġurfa raḥ-tiṭṭabbag ib-kaaši.* This room is going to be laid with tile.

ṭubag, ṭabag pl. *ṭbaag* **1.** a large bamboo basket. **2.** a basketwork tray, usually coated with asphalt.

ṭabug: yoom iṭ-ṭabug the tenth day of Muharram (a day of mourning).

ṭabga **1.** var. of *ṭabqa,* which see under *ṭ-b-q.* **2.** (pl. *-aat*) ferry.

ṭaabuug (coll.) brick(s).

ṭaabuuga pl. *-aat, ṭwaabiig* a brick.

ṭubbaaga pl. *-aat* snap, fastener (on clothing).

muṭbag pl. *mṭaabug* a double-tubed flute.

ṭ-b-l

ṭabbal to make a racket, cause a lot of noise. *šgadd ṭabbal w-ma-faad.* He made so much noise and it served no purpose.

ṭabul pl. *ṭubuul* drum.

ṭabla pl. *-aat* **1.** small table. **2.** ashtray. || *ṭablat il-ˀiδin* eardrum.

ṭabbaal pl. *-a, -iin* drummer.

ṭ-ɛ-l

ṭiɛal (*a ṭaɛil*) to be filling, fill one up. *ṭiɛlatni hal-ˀakla.* This meal bloated me.

nṭiɛal to stuff oneself, eat too much. *ˀakalit ihwaaya w-inṭiɛalit.* I ate a lot and made myself uncomfortable.

ṭɛaal pl. *-aat* spleen.

ṭ-ɛ-l-b

ṭuɛlub pl. *ṭaɛaalib* water moss.

ṭ-ɛ-n

ṭiɛan (*a ṭaɛin*) to mill, grind, pulverize. *ṭɛanna nuṣṣ ṭann ɛunṭa.* We milled a half ton of wheat.

nṭiɛan pass. of *ṭiɛan.*

ṭɛiin flour.

ṭɛiina a thick sauce made from sesame seeds.

ṭaaɛuuna pl. *ṭawaaɛiin: ṭaaɛuuna hawaaˀiyya* windmill.

ṭaɛɛaan pl. *-a* miller.

maṭɛana pl. *maṭaaɛin* **1.** grist mill. **2.** coffee grinder, coffee mill.

ṭ-x-x

ṭaxx (*u ṭaxx*) to bump, strike, hit, touch. *nazzil raasak min itxušš ɛatta la-yṭuxx.* Duck your head when you enter so it won't bump. *ˀiidi toojaɛni. baḷḷa la-tṭuxxha.* My hand hurts. Please don't touch it. *ṭaxxat is-sayyaara b-baab il-garaaj.* The car bumped into the garage door. *s-surɛa zaadat šwayya šwayya ˀila ˀan ṭaxxat bil-miyya.* The speed increased little by little until it reached a hundred. || *ruuɛ ṭuxxa. balki ydaaynak čam diinaar.* Go put the touch on him. Maybe he'll lend you a few dinars.

nṭaxx to be bumped, struck, hit. *raasa nṭaxx bil-baab.* His head got bumped on the door.

ṭaxx bumping, striking, hitting, touching.

ṭaxxa pl. *-aat* i.n. of *ṭaxx.*

ṭ-x-m

ṭaxum pl. *ṭxuuma* set, group. *ṭaxum isnuun* set of false teeth, dentures. || *ṭaxum qanafaat* set of couches (consisting of two couches and four upholstered chairs).

ṭ-r-ˀ

ṭiraˀ (*a*) to come, descend. *hiiči šii ma-yiṭraˀ ɛal-baal.* Such a thing wouldn't come to mind.

ṭaariˀa pl. *ṭawaariˀ* unforeseen event. || *ɛaalat iṭ-ṭawaariˀ* state of emergency.

ṭ-r-a-r

ṭaraar pl. *-aat* shaded veranda facing onto the main patio of an eastern-style house.

ṭ-r-a-m-b-y-l

ṭraambeel see under *ṭ-r-m-b-y-l.*

ṭ-r-b

ṭirab (*u a ṭarab*) **1.** to be delighted, enraptured, filled with joy. *l-baarɛa ṭrabit ihwaaya ɛala ṣooṭ il-muġanniya j-jidiida.* Yesterday I was enraptured by the new singer's voice. **2.** to delight, enrapture. *l-muġaniyya ṭirbat il-kull.* The singer delighted everyone.

ˀaṭrab to delight, fill with joy, enrapture. *l-ġina maala yiṭrib.* His singing fills one with joy.

nṭurab pass. of *ṭurab* **2.**

muṭrib **1.** delightful, charming. **2.** (pl. *-iin*) singer, vocalist.

ṭ-r-b-š

ṭarbuuš pl. *ṭaraabiiš* fez, tarboosh.

ṭ-r-ɛ

ṭiraɛ (*a ṭariɛ*) **1.** to lay flat, spread out, cause to lie down flat. *ṭ-ṭabiib ṭiraɛ ij-jaahil ɛal-meez w-δuraba ˀubra.* The doctor laid the child on the table and gave him a shot. *š-šurṭi ṭiraɛa ɛal-gaaɛ w-dawwara.* The policeman got him down on the ground and searched him. **2.** to subtract. *ˀiṭraɛ iθmaanya mnil-ɛadad.* Subtract eight from the number. **3.** to miscarry, have a miscarriage. *zawijta ṭirɛat.* His wife had a miscarriage.

ṭarraɛ to perform an abortion, cause to have a miscarriage. *ṭarraɛha ṭ-ṭabiib w-maɛɛad dira bii.* The doctor performed an abortion on her and nobody knew about it.

nṭiraɛ to lie down, prostrate oneself. *nṭiraɛit ɛal-ifraaš saaɛteen.* I stretched out on the bed for two hours.

ṭariɛ subtraction.

ṭuruɛ advantage. *nṭeeta daas ṭuruɛ yaḷḷa liɛab wiyyaaya.* I gave him a one game advantage to get him to play with me.

ʔuṭruuḥa pl. *-aat* thesis, dissertation.

maṭruuḥ **1.** laid down, spread out. || *maṭruuḥ ɛala ð̣ahar il-baaxira* loaded on board the ship. *s-siɛir ɛašr idnaaniir lit-ṭann il-waaḥid, maṭruuḥ ɛala ð̣ahr il-baaxira.* The price is ten dinars per single ton, loaded on board the ship. **2.** subtrahend. || *l-maṭruuḥ bii* the minuend.

ṭ-r-d

ṭirad (*u ṭarid*) to drive away, chase away, banish, dismiss, expel, drive out, evict. *ʔuṭrud il-bazzuuna mnil-maṭbax.* Chase the cat out of the kitchen. *xalla l-xaadim ɛinda yoomeen w-baɛdeen ṭirada.* He kept the servant two days and then dismissed him. *ʔiδa tirsib marra lux, yṭurduuk.* If you fail once more, they'll expel you. *ṭirad marta mnil-beet.* He threw his wife out of the house. || *ʔaḷḷa yiṭrud iš-šarr ɛannak.* May God protect you from evil.

ṭaarad to run. *ʔimši ɛala keefak. la-tṭaarid.* Walk slowly. Don't run. || *ṭaarad biš-šiɛir* to play a game of composing lines of poetry. *ṭaaradta biš-šiɛir nuṣṣ saaɛa w-baɛdeen ġilabni.* I matched him in a poetry composing contest for a half hour and then he beat me.

tṭaarad refl. of *ṭaarad*. *xall niṭṭaarad biš-šiɛir.* Let's match lines of poetry.

nṭirad pass. of *ṭirad.*

ṭarid banishment, dismissal, expulsion, eviction.

ṭarda pl. -*aat* i.n. of *ṭarid.*

ṭardi: tanaasub ṭardi* direct proportion (math.).

ṭarraad pl. *-aat* cruiser (warship).

ṭurraada pl. *ṭraariid* dinghy, small row-boat.

ṭ-r-r

ṭarr (*u ṭarr*) **1.** (dawn) to break. *saaɛa beeš yṭurr il-fajir?* What time does dawn break? **2.** to throw. *la-tṭurr iḥjaar ɛal-beet.* Don't throw stones at the house.

ṭurra pl. *-aat* **1.** blaze, mark on an animal's forehead. **2.** heads (of a coin).

ṭ-r-r-h-a-t

ṭurrahaat (invar.) no-good, worthless. *hal-ʔakil ṭurrahaat; ma-yiswa.* This food is lousy; it's not worth anything. *huwwa ṭurrahaat bil-iḥsaab. yiṣquṭ ɛala ṭuul.* He's no good at arithmetic. He continually fails.

ṭ-r-z

ṭarraz to embroider. *tuɛruf itxayyiṭ w-iṭṭarriz zeen.* She knows how to sew and embroider well.

tṭarraz to be embroidered. *hal-iqmaaš θixiin; ma-yiṭṭarraz.* This material is thick; it can't be embroidered.

ṭariz, ṭiraaz (no pl.) type, model, class, sort, kind, variety. *ṭiyyaaraat jeešna min ʔaḥdaθ ṭiraaz.* Our army's planes are the latest type. *haaδa muḥaami mniṭ-ṭiraaz il-ʔawwal.* That lawyer's first class. **2.** style, pattern. *hal-binaaya ɛaṭ-ṭiraaz il-ɛarabi.* This building is in the Arab style.

ṭ-r-z-y-n

ṭaraziina pl. *-aat* self-propelled railroad car.

[1]*ṭ-r-š*

ṭarraš to make deaf, deafen. *ṣooṭ il-makiina da-yṭarriš.* The noise of the machine is deafening.

ṭrašš to be or become deaf. *ṭraššat iδni min haṣ-ṣooṭ.* I've been deafened by this noise.

ṭariš (no pl.) herd (esp. of donkeys).

ʔaṭraš fem. *ṭarša* pl. *ṭuruš, ṭaršiin* **1.** deaf. **2.** deaf person.

ṭaariš pl. *ṭwaariš, ṭraariiš* messenger.

[2]*ṭ-r-š*

ṭurši pickles.

ṭuruščči pl. *-iyya* pickle vendor.

ṭ-r-š-a-n

ṭiršaana dried apricots.

ṭ-r-ṭ-r

ṭarṭuur pl. *ṭaraaṭiir* **1.** braggart, boaster, blowhard. **2.** coward.

ṭ-r-f

tṭarraf to go to extremes, hold a radical position or view. *yiṭṭarraf ihwaaya b-ʔaaraaʔa.* He goes to extremes in his opinions.

ṭaraf pl. *ʔaṭraaf* **1.** extremity, end, tip, edge. **2.** corner (of the eye). **3.** district, zone, region, area.

¶ *min ṭaraf* 1. relative to, concerning, about. *min ṭaraf eeš, xaaḷa?* Concerning what, madam? *ʔaxaaf min ṭaraf l-ifluus.* I figure it's about the money. 2. in favor of, on the side of. *ḥiča hwaaya min ṭarafak.* He spoke a lot in your favor. He spoke warmly of you.

ṭarfa tamarisk.

ṭarfaani endmost, located at the farthest point. *tigdar tugɛud ɛal-kursi ṭ-ṭarfaani.* You can sit on the end chair.

ṭaareef (Jewish usage) not kosher. *laḥam ṭaareef* non-kosher meat.

mutaṭarrif extremist, radical.

ṭ-r-q

tṭarraq to stray, wander, digress. *tṭarraq*

ʔila mawðuuε ma-kaan laazim iybiεθa. He wandered onto a subject he shouldn't have discussed.

staṭraq to pass, go, come. *ʔiða yistaṭriq min-naa, ʔawaggfa.* If he passes by here, I'll stop him.

ṭaraqa pl. *-aat* firecracker.

ṭariiq pl. *ṭuruq* **1.** way. *raε-aaxðak wiy-yaaya bis-sayyaara εatta ddalliini εaṭ-ṭariiq.* I'm going to take you with me in the car so that you can show me the way. *b-ṭariiqak, murr εal-ʔuutači w-jiib θoobi.* On your way, pass by the cleaner's and bring my shirt. *nεiraf εan iṭ-ṭariiq min ṣaadaq haj-jamaaεa.* He turned away from the straight and narrow when he got friendly with that crowd. *ṭilaε εan iṭ-ṭariiq.* He stepped out of line. *sawwu ṭariiq; xall is-sayyaara tfuut.* Make way; let the car pass. *ma-aku ʔay εaqaba b-ṭariiq taqad-dum hal-balad.* There's no obstacle in the way of this country's progress. **2.** road, highway. *ṣaar-ilhum sana yištuġluun ib-haṭ-ṭariiq.* They've been a year working on this road.

ṭariiqa pl. *ṭuruq* **1.** manner, mode, means. **2.** way, method, procedure. **3.** religious brotherhood.

ṭ-r-g

ṭirag (*u ṭarig*) to beat, whip (eggs, etc.). *ʔiṭrug l-liban bil-xaašuuga.* Beat the yogurt with the spoon.

ṭarrag to fold, fold up. *ṭarrig hal-wuṣlat il-uqmaaš.* Fold up this piece of cloth.

b-ṭarig by itself, alone. *ʔaani saakin b-ṭarig ruuεi.* I live alone. *riεt ib-ṭarig ruuεi.* I went by myself. *min maatat marta, biqa b-ṭarig nafsa.* When his wife died, he was left alone. *ṣrafit kull ifluusi w-buqeet ib-ṭarig diinaar.* I spent all my money and was left with only a dinar. *da-yεiiš ib-ṭarig raatba.* He's living on just his salary. *šifitha b-ṭarg il-libaas.* I saw her in just her pants. *huwwa b-ṭarig il-εači; ma-ysawwi šuġuḷ.* He only talks; he doesn't do any work.

ṭirraaga pl. *-aat* egg beater.

ṭ-r-g-ε

ṭargaε to clatter, bang, make noise. *simaεna l-looriyyaat itṭargiε εaj-jisir.* We heard the trucks making a big noise on the bridge.

ṭ-r-m

ṭarma pl. *-aat* porch, veranda.

ṭ-r-m-b

ṭrumba pl. *-aat* **1.** water outlet, hydrant. **2.** faucet.

ṭ-r-m-b-y-l

ṭrumbeel, ṭraambeel pl. *-aat* automobile.

ṭraambeelči pl. *-iyya* driver.

ṭ-r-n-j

ṭrinj (coll.) citron(s).

ṭrinja pl. *-aat* citron.

ṭ-r-h-a-t

ṭurrahaat see under *ṭ-r-r-h-a-t.*

ṭ-r-w

ṭira (*a ṭaraawa*) to be or become fresh, succulent, moist, tender. *ðiif εalee šwayyat mayy εatta yiṭra.* Add a little water to it so it will be fresh.

ṭari soft, tender, succulent, moist, juicy.

ṭaraawa freshness, softness, tenderness.

ʔaṭra more or most tender, succulent, etc.

ṭ-r-y

ṭaari, see *ṭ-a-r-y.*

ṭ-s-s

ṭass (*u ṭass*) **1.** to hit a bump, go over a rough place. *min ṭassat is-sayyaara, raasa dagg bis-saguf.* When the car hit a bump, his head hit the roof. || *ʔiða ma-tidrus zeen, tara ṭṭuss bil-imtiεaan.* If you don't study well, you will mess up on the exam. **2.** to drop in unannounced. *ʔaεtiqid εali bil-beet. xalli nruuε inṭussa.* I believe Ali's at home. Let's go surprise him.

ṭaṣṣa pl. *-aat* bump, rough place in the road.

ṭ-š-t

ṭašit pl. *ṭšuut* **1.** wash basin. **2.** wash tub.

ṭ-š-r

ṭaššar to spill, scatter accidentally. *ṭaššar il-mišmiš kulla bil-gaaε.* He spilled all the apricots on the ground.

tṭaššar to scatter, disperse. *wugaε w-iṭṭašširat kull il-ġaraað minna.* He fell down and all the things scattered away from him. *min šaafaw iš-šurṭa jaayiin, ṭṭašširaw.* When they saw the police coming, they scattered.

ṭ-š-š

ṭašš (*u*) **1.** to scatter, strew around. *ṭušš išwayya šεiir lid-dijaaj.* Throw a little barley to the chickens. **2.** to spill. *diir baalak! la-ṭṭušš il-ṃaay.* Be careful! Don't spill the water. **3.** to spread, disseminate. *ma-čaan laazim iyṭušš il-xabar.* He shouldn't have spread the news all around.

ṭ-ε-m

ṭaεεam **1.** to feed, give food to. *j-jaahil yinraad-la waεεid yiṭaεεima.* The child needs someone to feed him. *jiiraanna ṭaεεmoona simač il-yoom.* Our neighbors brought us over some fish today. **2.** to inoculate, vaccinate. *l-mumarriða ṭaε-*

ع*umat ij-jaahil* ð*idd it-tiifu.* The nurse inoculated the child against typhoid. **3.** to inlay. *ṭa*عع*am il-meez biṣ-ṣadaf.* He inlaid the table with mother-of-pearl.

*staṭ*ع*am* to enjoy, savor, relish the taste of. *ʔaklat il-baar*ح*a, staṭ*ع*amitha hwaaya.* I enjoyed the taste of yesterday's meal a lot.

*ṭa*ع*am, ṭa*ع*um* (no pl.) taste, flavor. || *sawwaaha bila ṭa*ع*am. kull-ma yriid fluus, yiji* ع*alayya.* He's gone too far. Every time he wants money, he comes to me.

*ṭu*ع*um* bait. *ṭalla*ع *diinaar w-raawaa-hiyyaa. ybayyin da-y*ð*ibb-la ṭu*ع*um.* He took out a dinar and showed it to him. It looks like he's throwing out bait to him.

*ṭa*ع*aam* **1.** food, nourishment. **2.** grain.

*maṭ*ع*am* pl. *maṭaa*ع*im* restaurant.

*ṭ-*ع*-n*

*ṭi*ع*an* (*a ṭa*ع*in*) **1.** to stab, transfix, run through. *ṭi*ع*ana bil-xanjar ib-galba.* He stabbed him in his heart with the dagger. **2.** /with *b-*/ to find fault with, discredit, defame. *ma-nigdar niṭ*ع*an ib-*ح*ukma.* We can't find any fault with his judgment. *ma-laazim tiṭ*ع*an bii. huwwa ma-maw-juud.* You shouldn't cut him down. He isn't here.

*ṭa*ع*na* pl. *-aat* **1.** stab, thrust. **2.** stitch.

*ṭaa*ع*uun* pl. *ṭawaa*ع*iin* plague. || *ʔuxu*ð *ṭaa*ع*uunak w-ruu*ح*. jazza*ع*tuuni.* Take your kids and get out. You've made me sick.

*ṭaa*ع*in: ṭaa*ع*in bis-sinn* old, aged, advanced in years.

ṭ-ġ-r

ṭġaar pl. *-aat* a unit of weight equal to 2000 kilograms.

ṭ-ġ-y

ṭiġa (*a i ṭugyaan*) **1.** to overflow, leave its banks. *n-nahar ṭiġa w-ġarrag il-ibsaatiin.* The river overflowed and flooded the orchards. **2.** to be or become tyrannical, despotic, cruel. *min ṣaar raʔiis jamhuur-iyya, ṭiġa.* When he became president, he became a tyrant. **3.** /with ع*ala*/ to dominate, outweigh, overshadow. *jamaalha ṭiġa* ع*ala kull jamaal il-banaat.* Her beauty overshadowed all the girls' beauty.

ʔaṭġa more or most tyrannical, despotic.

ṭaaġi, ṭaaġiya pl. *ṭuġaat* tyrant, despot.

ṭ-f-ʔ

miṭfaʔa, ʔiṭfaaʔi, etc., see *ṭ-f-y.*

*ṭ-f-*ح

*ṭufa*ح (*a ṭafu*ح) **1.** to become full to overflowing. *s-sirdaab ṭufa*ح *ṃayy.* The basement became filled with water. **2.** to overflow, run over, flow over. *ṭufa*ح *il-ṃayy imniṭ-ṭašit.* The water overflowed from the basin.

*ṭṭaafa*ح to overflow, run over, be too full. *j-jidir malyaan ṃaay; da-yiṭṭaafa*ح*.* The cooking pot's full of water; it's overflowing.

ṭ-f-r

ṭufar (*u ṭafur*) **1.** to jump. *har-riyaa*ð*i yuṭfur xamis ʔamtaar.* This athlete jumps five meters. || *ruu*ح*i ṭufrat w-ba*ع*ad ma-at*ح*ammala.* My very being rebelled and I can't stand him any more. || *ʔimši šahar w-la-tuṭfur nahar.* Don't take chances (lit., walk a month but don't jump a river). **2.** /with ع*ala*/ to descend upon, to break into, burglarize. *l-*ح*araami ṭufar* ع*ala beet jiiraanna.* The thief got over the wall into our neighbors' house.

ṭaffar **1.** to jump, bounce repeatedly. *j-jahhaal da-yṭaffuruun* ع*ar-ramuḷ.* The children are jumping in the sand. **2.** to make, let, or help jump. *ṭaffar ṣadiiqa min* ح*aayiṭ il-*ح*adiiqa gabuḷ-ma tiji š-šurṭa.* He helped his friend jump from the garden wall before the police came. **3.** to cause to splash. *ʔi*ð*a* ð*ð*ibb hal-i*ح*jaara bil-*ح*oo*ð*, yṭaffur* ع*aleena hwaaya ṃayy.* If you throw this rock in the pond, it'll splash a lot of water on us. **4.** to skip over, omit, leave out. *ʔiqra ṣaṭir w-ṭaffur ṣaṭir.* Read a line and skip a line. *min qira l-qaaʔima, ṭaffar ʔismi.* When he read the list, he missed my name.

ṭṭaafar to hold a jumping contest, compete with each other in jumping. *xan-niṭṭaafar w-šuuf yaahu l-yuġlub.* Let's have a jumping contest and see who wins.

ṭafur jumping, leaping. || *ṭafr iz-zaana* pole vaulting. *ṭafr il-*ع*arii*ð broad jumping.

ṭafra pl. *-aat* a jump, a leap.

ṭafraan disgusted, fed up, sick and tired.

ṭ-f-f

ṭafiif small, slight, trivial, insignificant. *ʔalam ṭafiif* a slight pain.

ṭ-f-l

ṭṭaffal to intrude, butt in. *la-tiṭṭaffal. ma*حح*ad siʔalak.* Don't intrude. Nobody asked you.

ṭifil pl. *ʔaṭfaal* infant, baby, child.

ṭufuula childhood, infancy.

ṭufayli pl. *-iin* parasite, freeloader, sponger, hanger-on.

ṭ-f-w

ṭufa (*a ṭafu*) to float, rise to the surface. *l-mayyit ṭufa bin-nahar.* The dead man floated in the river.

ṭ-f-y

ṭaffa **1.** to put out, extinguish, smother. *la-tnaam gabuḷ-ma ṭṭaffi n-naar.* Don't go to sleep until you put out the fire. **2.** to turn off, switch off, put out. *la-ṭṭaffi ið̣-ð̣uwa. ʔariid ʔaṭaaliʕ.* Don't turn off the light. I want to study. **3.** to quench. *ʔariid iglaaṣ mayy baarid ḥatta ʔaṭaffi l-ʕaṭaš.* I want a cold glass of water to quench the thirst.

ṭṭaffa pass. of *ṭaffa.*

nṭufa to go out, die down, be extinguished. *ṣaar šooṭ w-inṭufa ð̣-ð̣uwa.* There was a short circuit and the light went out.

miṭfaʔa pl. *maṭaafiʔ* fire extinguisher.

ʔiṭfaaʔi pl. *-iyya* fireman.

ʔiṭfaaʔiyya fire department.

maṭfi turned off, switched off. *ð̣uwa l-gubba maṭfi. laazim maaku ʔaḥḥad biiha.* The light in the room is off. There must not be anyone in it.

ṭ-q-ṣ

ṭaqiṣ weather, climate.

ṭ-q-m

ṭaqum variant of *ṭuxum,* which see under *ṭ-x-m.*

ṭ-g-ṭ-g

ṭagṭag **1.** to make a cracking, snapping, popping noise. *l-ḥaṭab, iða ma-ykuun yaabis, yṭagṭig ihwaaya bin-naar.* If the firewood isn't dry, it crackles and snaps a lot in the fire. || *ṭagṭag ʔiṣaabʕa.* He cracked his knuckles. **2.** to rattle, clatter. *has-sayyaara mčarqiʕa. ṭṭagṭig ihwaaya.* This car is all worn out. It rattles a lot. *snuuni da-ṭṭagṭig imnil-barid.* My teeth are chattering from the cold. *la-ṭṭagṭig. ʔabuuk naayim.* Don't make noise. Your father is sleeping.

ṭagṭaga **1.** cracking, snapping, popping. **2.** clattering, rattling.

ṭigṭaaga pl. *-aat* noisemaker, rattle.

ṭagṭuugiyyaaṭ (pl. only) odds and ends, small things, remnants, scraps.

ṭ-g-ʕ

ṭaggaʕ **1.** to stain, spot, splatter. *j-jaahil ṭaggaʕ ič-čarčaf ib-ḥibir.* The kid stained the tablecloth with ink. *ʕindak iqmaaš ʔabyað̣ mṭaggaʕ ib-ʔaḥmar?* Do you have a white cloth spotted with red? **2.** to become stained, spotted, splotched. *ʔašuu min ġisalit il-uqmaaš, ṭaggaʕ.* It seems when you washed the cloth, the colors ran. **3.** to blanch, pale, show terror. *min simaʕ ḥiss il-madaafiʕ, ṭaggaʕ.* When he heard the noise of the cannons, he blanched.

ṭagʕa pl. *-aat* act of breaking wind.

ṭugʕa pl. *ṭugaʕ* stain, spot, splotch.

ṭuguuʕ, ṭguuʕi **1.** cowardly. *haaða ma-yṣiir jundi. ṭuguuʕ.* He'll never be a soldier. He's chicken. **2.** coward.

ʔaṭgaʕ more or most cowardly.

ṭ-g-g

ṭagg (*u ṭagg*) **1.** to explode, burst. *buṭl iṣ-ṣooda ṭagg w-jiraḥ ʔiidi.* The bottle of soda burst and cut my hand. *ʔabu t-taksi ṭagg ʕinda taayar.* The taxi driver had a tire blow out. *xallaw θalij bit-taabuut ḥatta ma-yṭugg il-mayyit.* They put ice in the coffin so the dead man wouldn't burst. *ya-mʕawwad, xalliini ʔaṭubb ʔawwal. raḥ-iṭṭugg boolti.* For heaven's sake, let me go in first. My bladder's about to pop. || *ʔard aṭlaʕ išwayya barra; ṭaggat ruuḥi hnaa.* I want to go outside for a little bit; I'm fed up in here. **2.** to crack, split, break. *ṭugg-li beeðteen. ʔariid atrayyag.* Break me a couple of eggs. I want to have breakfast. *ṭugg-la buṭil ṣooda!* Open him a bottle of soda pop! || *ṭagg-li ṣuura.* He snapped a picture of me. *j-jundi ṭagg-la salaam lið̣-ð̣aabuṭ.* The soldier gave the officer a snappy salute.

ṭagga pl. *-aat* **1.** sudden noise, crash, bang. **2.** burst, explosion. || *ʕala ṭagga, waagfa ʕala ṭagga* on the verge of exploding. *ma-yindira š-wakit itṣiir il-ʕarka. ʕala ṭagga.* It's not known when the fight'll break out. Any little thing'll do it.

muṭgaaga pl. *-aat* bottle opener.

ṭ-l-b

ṭilab (*u ṭalab*) **1.** to ask for, request, apply for. *ṭ-ṭullaab ṭilbaw imnil-muʕallim ʔan ywaddiihum lil-maṭḥaf.* The students asked the teacher to take them to the museum. *l-ʕummaal ṭilbaw ziyaadat rawaaṭibhum.* The workers asked for an increase in their salaries. *ṭilab ʔiidha w-rufð̣at.* He asked for her hand (in marriage) and she refused. *ʔagdar ʔaṭlub is-sayyaara maattak yoom ij-jumʕa?* Can I borrow your car Friday? **2.** to order. *ṭlabna miit talafiizyoon min ʔamriika.* We ordered a hundred TV sets from America. **3.** to be the creditor of, be owed money by. *niseet išgadd tuṭlubni.* I've forgotten how much I owe you. **4.** to call, telephone, ring up. *ʔuṭlub il-baddaala w-yinṭuuk xaṭṭ.* Ask the switchboard and they'll give you a line. *ʔuṭlub in-najaf w-šuuf š-aku.* Call up Najaf and see what's happening. *minu ṭilabni bit-talafoon?* Who wanted me on the phone?

ṭaalab to make a demand, put forward a claim. *l-ʕummaal da-yṭaalbuun ib-ziyaada.* The workers are asking for a raise. *raḥ-aṭaalba bil-ifluus min yiji.* I'll dun him for the money when he comes.

tṭallab to necessitate, demand, require, exact. *n-najaaḥ yiṭṭallab šuġuḷ ihwaaya.* Success requires a lot of work.

tṭaalab to be argumentative, quarrelsome, make undue demands. *leeš daaʔiman tiṭṭaalab wiyya n-naas?* Why do you always get into fights with people?

nṭilab pass. of *ṭilab.*

ṭalab pl. *-aat* **1.** demand, claim. **2.** request. **3.** application. **4.** demand (econ.).

ṭulba, ṭilba pl. *-aat* request, desire, wish. *ʔili ʕindak ṭilba. tsawwiiha?* I have a favor to ask of you. Would you do it?

ṭalabiyya pl. *-aat* order, commission (com.).

ṭlaaba pl. *ṭlaayib* fuss, to-do, commotion. *sawweet ṭlaaba čbiira ʕala šii ma-yiswa.* You've made a big fuss over something that doesn't matter.

ṭallaab pl. *-a* creditor, lender.

maṭlab pl. *maṭaaliib* demand, claim.

muṭaalaba pl. *-aat* demand, claim. *muṭaalaba b-deen* demand for repayment of a debt.

ṭaalib pl. *ṭullaab* student, pupil.

maṭluub **1.** requested, required, wanted. **2.** due, owed (money, etc.). **3.** indebted. *ʔaani maṭluub-lak.* I'm indebted to you. **4.** (pl. *maṭaaliib*) wish, desire.

ṭ-l-s-m

ṭillisim pl. *ṭalaasim* talisman, charm, amulet. || *maktuuba miθl iṭ-ṭillisim. ma-yinfihim minna šii.* His letter is mystifying. Nothing can be understood from it.

ṭ-l-ʕ

ṭilaʕ (*a ṭalʕa, ṭluuʕ*) **1.** to appear, show, come into view. *raḥ-tiṭlaʕ iš-šamis saaʕa sitta baačir.* The sun will appear at six o'clock tomorrow. *ṭilʕat ḥabbaaya b-iida.* A sore came out on his hand. *ṭilaʕ ʔismak bij-jariida l-yoom.* Your name appeared in the paper today. *ṭilaʕ nafuṭ yamm il-muuṣil.* Oil was discovered near Mosul. *s-sayyaara, ṭilaʕ biiha miit ʕeeb.* A hundred defects showed up in the car. *ṭilʕat-li muškila jidiida.* A new problem has come up for me. *ʔiða ma-ṭilaʕ-la ṣaaḥib, yṣiir maalak.* If an owner doesn't turn up for it, it will be yours. *ṭilʕat-li ij-jaaʔiza l-ʔuula bil-yaanaṣiib.* I got first prize in the lottery. *laazim ʔaaxuð-lak rasm il-laax. haṣ-ṣuura ma-ṭilʕat.* I have to take another picture of you. This photo didn't turn out. *kuumt iθ-θiyaab, ma-yiṭlaʕ minha ġeer θlaaθa zeena.* No more than three good ones will come out of the pile of shirts. *nataaʔij il-imtiḥaan ṭilʕat.* The results of the exam are out. *l-ʔijaaza maaltak ma-tiṭlaʕ hal-yoom.* Your permit won't be issued today. *ʔuturka! haaða ma-yiṭlaʕ šii min waraa.* Leave him! Nothing good will ever come from him. || *min ʔija ʔabuu, ṭilʕat ʕeena w-gaam ysibbna.* When his father came, he got brave and began to insult us. **2.** to come up, sprout, grow forth. *bidat tiṭlaʕ-la snuun.* His teeth have started to come in. *hal-gaaʕ ma-yiṭlaʕ biiha kull zariʕ.* No plant will grow in the land. *makaan ij-jariḥ ma-yiṭlaʕ bii šaʕar.* Hair won't grow on the wound. **3.a.** to come out, go out, get out. *l-iktaab ʕaaṣi b-jeebi. ma-da-yiṭlaʕ.* The book is caught in my pocket. It won't come out. *l-faara ṭilʕat imniz-zaruf.* The mouse came out of the hole. *wugaʕ ib-warṭa ma-yiṭlaʕ minha.* He fell into a mess that he won't get out of. *hassa ṭilaʕ w-yirjaʕ baʕad nuṣṣ saaʕa.* He just went out and he'll be back in a half hour. *ma-tiṭlaʕ ʔilla wiyya ʔaxuuha.* She won't go out except with her brother. *ṭlaʕna liṣ-ṣeed.* We went out hunting. *ʔiṭlaʕ w-la-tiji baʕad!* Get out and don't come back! || *had-darbuuna ma-tiṭlaʕ.* This alley is a dead end. *ṭilaʕ ḥaliib ʔumma min ḥalga.* He was thoroughly exasperated. He took more than he could bear. *ma-ṣaar ʕumra ʕašr isniin ḥatta ṭilaʕ ḥaliib ʔummi min xašmi.* He wasn't ten years old before I'd had all I could take. **b.** to exit, leave, depart. *ṭilaʕit imniš-šarika, hassa da-aštuġuḷ ʕala ḥsaabi.* I left the company and now I'm working on my own. *gaaʕid ib-beetna ṣaar xams isniin w-ma-da-yiṭlaʕ.* He's been living in our house for five years and won't leave. || *ṭilʕat ruuḥa gabuḷ-ma yiji iṭ-ṭabiib.* His soul departed before the doctor came. *ṭilʕat ruuḥi yalla gdarit ʔaḥaṣṣil šuġuḷ.* I almost died before I was able to find work. **4.** to emerge, come out, turn out to be, prove to be. *ṭilaʕ ʔawwal ʕala ṣaffa.* He came out first in his class. *ṭilaʕ naayib min hal-manṭiqa.* He became a representative from that area. *ṭilaʕit xaṣraan diinaar.* I came out a dinar in the hole. *tuʕruf ṣadiiqa ṭilaʕ jaasuus?* Do you know his friend turned out to be a spy? || *ṭilaʕ min ħaqqha.* He was worthy of it. He was able to handle it. *nṭoo šaġla ṣaʕba laakin ṭilaʕ min ħaqqha.* They gave him a hard job, but he managed it. **5.** to look, present an appearance, appear. *ṭilaʕ ħilu bir-rasim.* He looks nice in the picture. *ṭilʕat falla min libsat in-nafnuuf ij-jidiid.* She looked terrific when she put on the new dress. *ʔinta ṭaaliʕ naṣba l-yoom.* You're looking sharp today. *ṭilaʕ ʕala ʔabuu.* He takes after his father. **6.** to overtake, pass, move ahead of. *ʔiṭlaʕa. da-yimši ʕala keefa.* Pass him. He's just poking along. *ʔiṭlaʕ is-sayyaara l-giddaamak ħatta nigdar nisriʕ.* Pass the car in front of you so we can go fast.

ṭallaʕ **1.** to remove, withdraw, take out. *ṭalliʕ ʔiidak min jeebi!* Take your hand out of my pocket! *da-yṭallʕuun ij-juθθa mniš-šaṭṭ.* They're taking the corpse out of the river. || *ʔiδa ma-truuħ lil-madrasa, ʔaṭalliʕ ruuħak.* If you don't go to school, I'll have your hide. *yδawwijuu bid-daaʔira w-bil-leel yṭalliʕ kull darda b-marta.* They give him trouble at the office and at night he takes all his troubles out on his wife. *tiskut loo ʔaji ʔaṭalliʕ kull dard ʔalla biik.* You shut up or I'll come and give you what for. **2.** to obtain, acquire, get. *laazim tṭalliʕ ʔijaazat siyaaqa.* You'll have to get a driving permit. *ṭallaʕ muʕaddal mumtaaz.* He got a fine average. *da-yṭalliʕ diinaar bil-yoom.* He's making a dinar a day. **3.** to put out, stick out. *ṭalliʕ ilsaanak da-ʔafħaṣa.* Stick out your tongue and let me examine it. || *ma-da-aṭalliʕ raas wiyyaa; ʕala ṭuul yuġlubni.* I'm not getting anywhere with him; he always beats me. **4.** to eject, oust, dismiss, expel, evict, throw out. *ṭallʕoo min šuġla.* They dismissed him from his job. *ṭallaʕa mnil-beet li-ʔan ma-difaʕ il-ʔiijaar.* He evicted him from the house because he didn't pay the rent. **5.** to produce, turn out, bring forth, give forth. *hal-makiina tṭalliʕ ʔalif bismaar bid-daqiiqa.* This machine turns out a thousand nails per minute. *had-dawra ṭallʕat ʔaħsan δ̣-δ̣ubbaaṭ.* This class produced the best officers. *makiint is-sayyaara da-tṭalliʕ duxxaan.* The car's motor is giving off smoke. *j-jaahil ṭallaʕ isnuun.* The child has cut his teeth. *mṭalliʕ ħabbaaya b-iida.* He's developed a wart on his hand. *ṭallaʕ-li ħasba jdiida.* He came up with a new problem for me. *la-tṭalliʕ-lak ħijja. ʔinta ma-triid tiji.* Don't make up an excuse for yourself. You just don't want to come. *ṭalliʕ-li in-nisba l-miʔawiyya.* Find the percentage for me. *ṭalliʕ hač-čilma bil-qaamuus.* Look up this word in the dictionary. **6.** to expose, show, uncover, cause to appear. *ṭallaʕ ṣurrta w-šifna biiha wuṣax.* He showed his navel and we saw some lint in it. *ṭallaʕ kull ʕyuuba. ma-xalla šii ma-gaala.* He exposed all of his faults. He didn't leave a thing unsaid. **7.** to make, cause to become. *ʔiδa tinṭi fluus, yṭalliʕuuk naayib.* If you contribute money, they'll make you a representative. *ṭallaʕitni čaδδaab. leeš gilit ʕindi fluus?* You made a liar of me. Why did you say I had money? || *l-ħaakim ṭallaʕa tabriya.* The judge acquitted him.

ṭaalaʕ to read seriously, peruse, study. *daaʔiman yiṭaaliʕ kutub ʔajnabiyya.* He's always studying foreign books.

ʔaṭlaʕ to inform, apprise, notify, tell. *ʔaṭlaʕni ʕala sirra.* He let me in on his secret.

ṭṭilaʕ to study, become acquainted, obtain information. *ṭṭilaʕ ʕala ʔaħdaθ il-ʔasaaliib ib-sinaaʕat il-uqmaaš.* He acquainted himself with the most modern methods of manufacturing cloth.

staṭlaʕ **1.** to scout, reconnoiter. *rijaʕ baʕad-ma staṭlaʕ il-manṭiqa.* He returned after he scouted the area. **2.** to seek information, inquire, find out. *ʔariid astaṭliʕ raʔya ʕan il-mawδ̣uuʕ.* I want to find out his opinion on the case.

ṭaliʕ, ṭuluʕ (no pl.) carbuncle, subcutaneous infection.

ṭalʕa **1.** going out. **2.** excursion, trip. *ʕindak ṭalʕa lis-suug il-yoom?* Are you going to the market today?

ṭilleeʕ pollen of the palm tree.

stiṭlaaʕ **1.** probing, investigation, research. || *ħubb il-istiṭlaaʕ* curiosity. **2.** scouting, exploration, reconnaissance.

mṭalliʕči pl. *-iyya* customs broker or agent.

ṭ-l-q

ṭallaq = *ṭallag,* which see.

ṭalqa pl. *-aat* **1.** bullet. **2.** shot.

ṭ-l-g

ṭilag (*a*) to be in labor. *waddooha lil-mustašfa li-ʔan čaanat tiṭlag.* They took her to the hospital because she was in labor. *ṭallag* **1.** to repudiate, divorce. *ṭallagha baƐad-ma ṣaarat ma-tinƐimil.* He divorced her when she became unbearable. **2.** to get a divorce. *l-baarƐa raaƐaw lil-maƐkama w-ṭalligaw.* Yesterday they went to court and got a divorce.

ṭṭallag to be repudiated, divorced. *simaƐit raƐ-tiṭṭallag.* I heard she's going to be divorced.

ṭalaag pl. *-aat* divorce.

ṭuluuga labor pains, travail. *jattha ṭ-ṭuluuga.* She went into labor.

ṭillaaga pl. *ṭlaaliig* one leaf of a double window or door.

muṭalliga pl. *-aat* divorcee, divorced woman.

ṭ-l-y

ṭila (*i ṭali*) to plate, overlay, coat. *yiṭli l-ixwaašiig ib-fuððа Ɛatta ma-tzanjir.* He plates the spoons with silver so they won't rust.

ṭili pl. *ṭilyaan* lamb, young sheep.

ṭ-m-a-ṭ-a

ṭamaaṭa (coll.) tomato(es)

ṭamaaṭaaya pl. *-aat* tomato.

ṭ-m-ʔ-n

ṭamʔan to calm, pacify, soothe, assure. *ma-qiblat ʔila ʔan ṭamʔanitha Ɛan iš-šarika.* She wouldn't agree until I set her mind at ease about the company.

ṭmaʔann to be calm, tranquil, at ease, relaxed, composed, assured, confident. *ʔiða ma-ʔaṭmaʔinn Ɛala ṣiƐƐtak, ma-aṭlaƐ.* If I don't feel assured about your health, I won't leave.

ṭ-m-Ɛ

ṭumaƐ (*a ṭumuuƐ*) /with *l-* or *b-*/ to aspire to, be ambitious for. *yiṭmaƐ ib-manaaṣib Ɛaalya.* He's aspiring to high positions.

ṭamuuƐ **1.** aspiring, ambitious, striving, eager, craving, avid. **2.** ambitious person. *ṭ-ṭamuuƐ yitqaddam bil-Ɛayaat.* The ambitious person gets ahead in life.

ṭ-m-r

ṭumar (*u ṭamur*) to cover over, bury. *ṭ-ṭiin ṭumar kull id-daayaat.* The mud buried all the seedlings.

ṭ-m-s

ṭumas (*u ṭamus*) **1.** to sink down, bog down, become immersed. *diir baalak la-tuṭmus biṭ-ṭiin.* Be careful not to bog down in the mud. *l-ibduwi ṭumas kulla bir-ramuḷ in-naaƐim.* The Bedouin sank completely into the soft sand. *ʔaani ṭaamus lil-haama biš-šuġuḷ.* I'm buried up to the top of my head in work. *ṭumaṣ bid-deen.* He's up to his neck in debts. *ṭumas b-imtiƐaan waaƐid.* He failed one exam. **2.** to hide, cover up, obscure. *b-tahriijaathum, da-yƐaawluun yṭumsuun il-Ɛaqaayiq.* They're trying to cover up the facts with their commotion.

ṭammas to immerse, plunge, dip, sink, bury. *ṭammus il-imwaaƐiin kullha bil-mayy il-Ɛaarr.* Plunge all the dishes in the hot water. *ṭammus il-xubza bil-marag Ɛatta tingaƐ zeen.* Dip the bread in the stew until it is well soaked. *min činna danisbaƐ, ṭammasni.* When we were swimming, he pulled me under. *ṭammasni bid-deen. kull yoom yištiri šii.* He's buried me in debts. Every day he buys something.

ṭ-m-ṭ-m

ṭamṭam to hide, cover up, conceal. *ṭamṭumaw il-qaðiyya w-ma-wuṣlat liš-šurṭa.* They covered up the story and it didn't get to the police.

ṭ-m-Ɛ

ṭumaƐ (*a tamaƐ*) **1.** to be or become greedy, covetous, avaricious. *la-tiṭmaƐ; ma-daam biiha ribiƐ, biiƐ.* Don't be greedy; since there's profit in it, sell. **2.** to aspire, be ambitious, yearn, long, wish. *yiṭmaƐ yṣiir waziir.* He's anxious to become a minister. *ṭumaƐ bil-manṣab w-sabbab faṣl il-mudiir.* He was avid for the position and brought about the dismissal of the director. *ṭumaƐ biiha w-ʔaxaðha bil-guwwa.* He wanted it and took it by force.

ṭammaƐ to arouse greed, avarice, covetousness, avidity in. *ʔinta da-ṭṭammuƐa b-hal-Ɛači maalak.* You're making him greedy with this talk of yours.

staṭmaƐ to become greedy. *min qibalna bis-siƐir, staṭmaƐ w-gaam yuṭlub ʔakθar.* When we agreed on the price, he became greedy and began to ask for more.

ṭamaƐ greed, greediness, avidity, covetousness, ambitious desire.

ṭammaaƐ greedy, avid, avaricious, desirous. *la-tṣiir ṭammaaƐ. muu ʔaxaðit Ɛuṣṣtak!* Don't be greedy. You've had your share!

ṭ-m-ġ

ṭumaġ (*u ṭamuġ*) to stamp, impress. *ʔuṭmuġ Ɛariiðta w-sajjilha.* Stamp his application and register it.

ṭammaġ to stamp repeatedly or frequently. *šuġla yṭammuġ ṭawaabiƐ makaatib bil-bariid.* His job is cancelling stamps on letters in the post office.

ṭṭammaġ pass. of. *ṭammaġ*. *ʔariid hal-ʔawraaq kullha tiṭṭammaġ ḥaalan.* I want all of these papers stamped immediately.

ṭamġa pl. *-aat* **1.** impression, imprint, stamp. **2.** cancellation stamp. **3.** stamp, rubber stamp. **4.** label, gummed label.

ṭ-m-m

ṭamm (*u ṭamm*) to bury, cover over. *j-jaahil ṭamm il-miḥbas maala bit-tiraab.* The child buried his ring in the dirt.

ṭamma pl. *-aat* city dump.

ṭ-m-n

ṭamman var. of *ṭamʔan,* which see under *ṭ-m-ʔ-n.*

ṭ-n-ṭ-l

ṭanṭal pl. *ṭanaaṭil* **1.** giant. **2.** tall person.

ṭ-n-ṭ-n

ṭanṭan to hum, buzz, drone. *l-bagg yṭanṭin bil-ʔiδin.* Mosquitoes cause a humming noise in the ear.

ṭ-n-n

ṭann pl. *ʔaṭnaan* ton.

ṭ-h-r

ṭahhar **1.** to clean, cleanse, purge, purify, chasten. *l-ḥukuuma j-jidiida raḥ-iṭṭahhir jihaaz il-ḥukuuma mnil-fasaad.* The new government is going to purge the governmental system of corruption. **2.** to circumcise. *d-duktoor ṭahhar il-walad.* The doctor circumcised the boy.

ṭṭahhar pass. of *ṭahhar.*

ṭhuur circumcision.

ṭahaara pl. *ṭahaayir* toilet, lavatory.

ṭaahir **1.** religiously clean, pure. **2.** circumspect, exemplary, faultless. *haaδa waaḥid δimmta ṭaahra.* He is a man of unblemished character.

muṭahhir pl. *-aat* an antiseptic, a disinfectant.

mṭahhirči pl. *-iyya* circumciser.

ṭw-a-r-n-y

ṭwaarni pl. *-iyya* wild pigeon, dove.

ṭ-w-b

ṭoob pl. *ṭwaab* cannon.

ṭooba pl. *-aat, ṭuwab* (rubber) ball.

ṭ-w-x

ṭuwax (*a ṭoox*) to get dark, darken. *loon il-meez min yibas, ṭuwax.* When it dried, the color of the table got darker.

ṭaax (*u*) to become serious, grave. *ṭaaxat il-qaδiyya. jarr musaddas ʕalee.* The matter got out of hand. He pulled a pistol on him. *ṭaaxat ʕaad! kull yoom tiji lil-beet sakraan w-imδayyiʕ fluusak.* That's too much! Every day you come home drunk and with your money all squandered.

ṭawwax **1.** to make dark in color. *loo ṭṭawwix il-loon, tiṭlaʕ ʔaḥla.* If you darken the color, it'll come out better. *ṭawwux-li č-čaay maali.* Make my tea stronger. **2.** to make serious, grave. *bass, ʕaad! muu ṭawwaxitha?* Hold on, there! Haven't you already gone too far?

ṭwaxx to become dark in color, to darken. *šuuf iṣ-ṣubuġ šloon iṭwaxx!* Look how the paint turned dark!

ṭoox **1.** dark, deep. *loon ṭoox* a dark color. *θoob ʔaxδar ṭoox* a dark green shirt. **2.** deep, profound. *beenaatna ṣadaaqa ṭoox.* There's a deep friendship between us.

ʔaṭwax **1.** darker, darkest. **2.** more or most profound.

ṭ-w-d

minṭaad pl. *manaaṭiid* balloon, dirigible, blimp.

ṭ-w-r

ṭṭawwar to evolve, develop. *kullši yiṭṭawwar. ma-yibqa θaabit.* Everything evolves. It doesn't remain still. *l-qaδiyya ṭṭawwurat w-wuṣlat liš-šurṭa.* The matter built up and got to the police.

ṭoor time, period of time. *giδa wiyyaaha fadd ṭoor w-baʕdeen tirakha.* He spent some time with her and then left her.

ʔaṭwaar (invar. pl.): *ġariib il-ʔaṭwaar* eccentric, having strange behavior.

ṭ-w-r-b-y-d

ṭoorbiid pl. *-aat* torpedo.

ṭ-w-z

ṭooz **1.** dust. **2.** powder.

ṭ-w-s

ṭaas pl. *-aat* (pair of) cymbals.

ṭaasa pl. *-aat, ṭuus* drinking bowl, cup.

ṭuusi pl. *-iyyaat* (pair of) cymbals.

ṭaawuus pl. *ṭwaawiis* peacock.

ṭ-w-ṭ

ṭawwaṭ **1.** to blow a horn, honk, toot. *ṭawwuṭ-la ḥatta ywaxxir ʕan is-sayyaara.* Blow the horn at him so he'll get out of the way of the car. **2.** to vaunt, boast, brag. *mqarribhum, li-ʔan yṭawwṭuu-la.* He's a close friend of theirs, because they brag about him. **3.** to broadcast, spread, tell around. *la-dgul-la bil-xabar tara yṭawwuṭ bii.* Don't tell him the news or he will blab it around.

ṭuwwaaṭa pl. *-aat* bulb horn.

ṭ-w-ṭ-ḥ

ṭṭooṭaḥ to stagger, reel, totter. *da-yiṭṭooṭaḥ miθl is-sakraan.* He is tottering like a drunkard.

ṭ-w-ع

ṭaaع (*i ṭaaعa*) to obey, be obedient. *ʔiδa ytiiع ʔabuu, yinṭii š-ma yriid.* If he obeys his father, he gives him whatever he wants.

ṭawwaع to cause to obey, make obedient, discipline. *δ̣all iylaaحighum ḥatta ṭawwaعhum.* He kept after them until he made them obey. *ʔinqul hat-tilmiiδ ib-ṣaffi w-aani ʔaṭawwiع-ilk-iyyaa.* Transfer this student to my class and I'll straighten him out for you. *čaan ʔašqiyaaʔ laakin il-عaskariyya ṭawwعata.* He was a tough guy but the military set him straight.

ṭaawaع to comply with or accede to the wishes of. *nafsi ma-ṭṭaawiعni عal-ġišš.* My nature doesn't allow me to cheat. *nafsa ṭṭaawعa عač-čiδib.* His nature is quite amenable to falsehood.

ṭṭawwaع to volunteer. *lamma ma-ḥaṣṣal šuġul, ṭṭawwaع bij-jeeš.* When he didn't find any work, he volunteered for the army.

nṭaaع to be obeyed. *ʔiδa ykuun qaasi, ma-yinṭaaع.* If he is cruel, he won't be obeyed.

staṭaaع to be able, be in a position to do. *ma-yistiṭiiع yidfaع hal-mablaġ.* He's not able to pay this amount.

ṭaaعa obedience, compliance, submission to.

ṭ-w-f

ṭaaf (*u ṭawaaf*) **1.** to circumambulate, walk around. *ṭaaf il-kaعba θlaθ marraat.* He circumambulated the Kaaba three times. **2.** to tour, wander around, roam all about. *ṭaaf baġdaad kullha.* He wandered all over Baghdad. **3.** (*u ṭoof*) to float. *l-xišab yṭuuf bil-mayy.* Wood floats in water. || *yṭuuf عala bardiyya.* He's very flightly (lit., he'd float on a papyrus twig). **4.** (*u ṭawafaan*) to be or become inundated, flooded. *kull-ma tumṭur, sirdaabna yṭuuf.* Whenever it rains, our basement gets filled with water.

ṭawwaf **1.** to guide, show around. *l-ḥijjaaj da-yintaδ̣ruun fadd waaḥid yṭawwufhum.* The religious pilgrims are waiting for someone to guide them around. **2.** to float, rise, come to the surface. *ʔuṣbur išwayya. hassa raḥ-iṭṭawwuf ṭ-ṭooba.* Wait a minute. The ball will come to the surface now. **3.** to float, cause to float. *yixalluun hawa bil-baaxira il-ġarġaana ḥatta yṭawwufuuna.* They put air in the sunken ship to make it float. **4.** to be or become flooded, inundated. *sidd il-maay. l-ḥadiiqa ṭawwfat.* Cut off the water. The garden's flooded. **5.** to build a wall around. *ṭawwaf il-bistaan ib-ṭiin.* He walled the orchard with mud.

ṭoof, ṭoofa pl. *-aat* mud wall.

ṭawwaafa pl. *-aat* float, buoy.

ṭaayif **1.** wandering, roving, itinerant. **2.** having made a circumambulation (esp. of the Kaaba). **3.** floating. **4.** spare, excess, extra. *ʔaḥtaaj fluus. عindak diinaar ṭaayif?* I need money. Do you have an extra dinar? *hal-muwaδ̣δ̣af ṭaayif w-yimkin yṭalliعuu.* That employee is unneeded and they might get rid of him. *kull waaḥid ʔaxaδ iktaab w-aani biqeet ṭaayif li-ʔan il-kutub xilṣat.* Everyone took a book and I was left out because the books ran out.

ṭaaʔifa pl. *ṭawaaʔif* religious sect, denomination, faction.

*ṭaaʔifi** sectarian, denominational, factional.

mṭawwuf pl. *-iin* pilgrims' guide in Mecca.

ṭ-w-g

ṭawwag to encircle, surround. *j-jinuud ṭawwigoohum w-baعdeen kumšoohum.* The soldiers encircled them and then caught them.

ṭoog pl. *ṭwaag* hoop, large ring.

ṭaag pl. *ṭuug* **1.** arch. **2.** layer, stratum.

ṭaaga pl. *-aat* unit of measure by which fine cloth is sold (approx. three yards).

ṭ-w-l

ṭaal (*u ṭuul*) to last, last long. *ma-aδ̣uuj min had-daris išgadd-ma yṭuul.* I don't get bored with this class, no matter how long it lasts. *ṭaalat ġeebta.* His absence was prolonged. *š-ṣaar min qaδ̣iitak? ʔašu ṭaalat.* What happened to your case? It seems to have become long and drawn out.

ṭuwal (*a ṭuul*) **1.** to be or become long, to lengthen, grow longer. *hal-ḥabil igṣayyir. čammla wuṣilt il-lux ḥatta yiṭwal.* This rope is short. Add another piece to it so it'll be longer. **2.** to become tall, grow tall. *ma-šaa ḷḷaah, ṭuwal bil-عajal!* My goodness gracious, he's sure grown fast!

ṭawwal **1.** to lengthen, elongate, extend, stretch, prolong, protract. *tigdar iṭṭawwil-li l-panṭaroon?* Can you lengthen the pants for me? *da-yṭawwil šaعra.* He's letting his hair grow long. *ʔaḷḷa yṭawwil عumrak.* May God grant you long life. *ṣaar saaعa yiḥči. saluufa gṣayyra ṭaw-walha.* He's been talking for an hour.

He's made a short story long and drawn out. *bass ɛaad, la-ṭṭawwilha!* Okay, don't make a Federal case out of it! || *ṭawwil baalak! raɛ-axalliṣ baɛad daqiiqa.* Hold your horses! I'll be through in a minute. **2.** to make tall, make taller. *hat-tamriin yṭawwil il-waaɛid.* This exercise makes one taller. **3.** to last, endure, continue. *ʔuδbuṭ il-waqit w-šuuf išgadd ʔaṭawwul jawwa l-ṃayy.* Check the time and see how long I last under water. *δijit li-ʔan il-muɛaaδara ṭawwlat saaɛteen.* I became bored because the lecture lasted two hours.

tṭawwal to be lengthened. *hal-irdaan ma-yiṭṭawwal.* This sleeve can't be lengthened.

tṭaawal to be insolent, fresh. *la-tiṭṭaawal ɛalayya, tara aksir xašmak.* Don't be insolent to me, or I'll break your nose.

staṭwal to consider long, too long. *la-tistaṭwil il-mudda. haaδi ɛamaliyya ṣaɛba.* Don't look at the time as being too long. This is a complicated operation.

ṭaala-ma or *ṭaal-ma* while, as long as. *ma-ariid hiiči šii yṣiir bid-daaʔira ṭaal-ma ʔaani mudiir.* I don't want such a thing to take place in the office as long as I'm director. *ṭaala-ma mawjuud, xan-ngul-la.* While he's here, let's tell him.

ṭuul **1.** length. || *hal-panṭaroon bii ṭuul. laazim agaṣṣra.* These pants are a bit too long. I should shorten them. *ʔaxaδni ṭuul w-ɛuruδ.* He took me completely by storm. He overwhelmed me. *ma-nṭaani furṣa ʔaɛči; ʔaxaδni ṭuul w-ɛuruδ.* He didn't give me a chance to speak; just ran up one side and down the other. *xaṭṭ iṭ-ṭuul* geographical longitude, meridian. *b-ṭuul* the same length (or height) as. *ʔariid bismaar ib-ṭuul haaδa.* I want a nail the same length as this. *biṭ-ṭuul* lengthwise. *l-meez yimkin yxušš imnil-baab biṭ-ṭuul.* The table will maybe go through the door lengthwise. *ɛala ṭuul* 1. the whole length, all the way, to the end. *ʔimši ɛala ṭuul iš-šaariɛ.* Go all the way down the street. *ʔaani wiyyaak ɛala ṭuul il-xaṭṭ.* I'm with you all the way down the line. 2. all the time, continually, always, persistently, frequently, often. *huwwa ɛala ṭuul bil-gahwa.* He's always in the coffeeshop. *ʔiδa δδalluun tizzaawruun ɛala ṭuul, yimkin tizzawwajha*. If you keep on visiting with each other frequently, perhaps you will marry her. *zuurna ɛala ṭuul.* Visit us often. **2.** height, tallness, size. **3.** (prep.) all during, throughout. *ṭuul il-leel* all night long. *ṭuul ɛumrak tibqa mjaddi.* All your life you'll be a beggar.

maa-ṭuul as long as, since, being that. *maa-ṭuulak ihnaa, waqqiɛ il-makaatiib.* As long as you're here, sign the letters. *maa-ṭuul il-ʔakil ihwaaya, ʔukul wiyyaana.* Since there's plenty of food, eat with us.

ṭuulaat: š-ṭuulaata! Look at the size of it! *šuuf har-rijjaal iš-ṭuulaata. ʔaɛsanlak ma-titɛaarak wiyyaa.* Look how tall that guy is! It would be better for you not to fight with him. *hal-ɛabil iš-ṭuulaata! ma-yikfi.* Look how short this rope is! It isn't enough.

ṭool pl. *ṭwaal* bolt (of cloth).

ṭoola pl. *-aat* stable.

ṭiila the length, the whole, all. *čaanat itnaam ɛindi ṭiilat hal-mudda.* She was sleeping with me all during this time.

ṭuwiil **1.** long, lengthy. *bismaar ṭuwiil* a long nail. || *ʔiida ṭwiila.* He steals. He has sticky fingers. *lsaana ṭwiil.* He uses vulgar language. He has a dirty mouth. **2.** tall, big. *har-rijjaal išgadd ṭuwiil!* That man's really tall!

ṭwaala (no pl.) an unnecessarily prolonged matter, affair. *haay iṭwaala. ma-tfill ib-yoom ʔaw yoomeen.* It's a long, drawn-out affair. It can't be done in a day or two. *ma-djuuz, ɛaad! muu sawweetha ṭwaala!* Knock it off! You're making a mountain out of a molehill!

ṭuulaani running lengthwise, longitudinal. *fakkaw šaariɛ ṭuulaani jdiid gabuḷ čam sana.* They cut through a new lengthwise street a few years ago.

ʔaṭwal **1.** longer, longest. **2.** taller, tallest.

mustaṭiil pl. *-aat* rectangle.

ṭ-w-y

ṭuwa (*i ṭawi*) to fold, fold up, roll up. *ʔuṭwi l-waraqa ṭawiiteen.* Fold the paper twice. *ʔuṭwi z-zuuliyya w-šiilha.* Roll up the carpet and take it away.

ṭawwa = *ṭuwa. la-tṭawwi l-mqawwaaya.* Don't fold the cardboard.

nṭuwa pass. of *ṭuwa.*

ṭawya, ṭayya pl. *-aat* **1.** fold, pleat. **2.** hem (of a garment).

maṭwa pl. *maṭaawi* a hoop used as a spool for yarn.

ṭ-w-y-r-n-y

ṭweerni pl. *-iyya* wild pigeon, dove.

ṭ-y-b

ṭaab (*i ṭiib*) **1.** to be or become pleasant,

nice, agreeable, enjoyable. *šahr ij-jaay l-hawa yṭiib.* Next month the weather will be nice. *ṭaabat-la l-gaƐda hnaa.* Staying here was pleasant for him. *bila Ɛali ma-ṭṭiib il-gaƐda.* Without Ali the get-together won't be any fun. **2.** (*i ṭeeba*) to heal, become cured, recover. *j-jariƈ baƐda ma-ṭaab.* The wound still hasn't healed. *l-mariiẓ ṭaab min maraẓa.* The patient recovered from his illness. || *š-itƈuṭṭ-ilha w-iṭṭiib?* What can you do about it? Isn't that something? *haay š-itƈuṭṭ-ilha w-iṭṭiib? hal-marra da-yitzawwaj raaqiṣa.* What do you do about this? This time he's marrying a dancer.

ṭayyab **1.** to cure, heal. *ma-aku duktoor yigdar yṭayyiba.* No doctor can cure him. *yimkin had-duwa yṭayybak.* Perhaps this medicine will make you well. **2.** to make delicious, tasty. *ṭ-ṭamaaṭa ṭṭayyib il-ʔakil.* Tomatoes make the meal delicious.

ṭṭayyab to perfume, scent onself. *haak, iṭṭayyab ib-har-riiƈa.* Here, perfume yourself with this scent.

staṭyab to find nice, enjoyable, pleasant, delicious. *ʔaani ʔastaṭyib ṭabuxha.* I enjoy her cooking.

ṭiib goodness. || *Ɛan ṭiib xaaṭir* gladly, with pleasure. *sawwaa-li-yyaaha Ɛan ṭiib xaaṭir.* He did it for me gladly.

ṭayyib **1.** pleasant, enjoyable, agreeable, nice. *hawa ṭayyib* pleasant weather. *ʔaxlaaq ṭayyba* nice manners. **2.** delicious, tasty, good. *laƈam id-dijaaj ṭayyib.* Chicken is tasty. **3.** well, in good health. *ʔumma maatat il-Ɛaam bass ʔabuu ṭayyib.* His mother died last year but his father is well. **4.** (as an answer or comment) fine, good, all right, O.K. *ṭayyib! ʔamurr Ɛaleek min ʔaxalliṣ šuġli.* O.K.! I'll come see you when I finish my work.

ʔaṭyab **1.** more or most pleasant, enjoyable, etc. **2.** more or most tasty, delicious.

ṭ-y-ƈ

ṭaaƈ (*i ṭeeƈ*) **1.** to be or become available. *min iṭṭiiƈ hiiči sayyaara, ʔaxaabrak.* When such a car is available, I'll call you. *l-mišmiš ṭaaƈ bass kulliš ġaali.* Apricots are in season but very expensive. *loo yṭiiƈ b-iidi, ʔasawwi kull-ma triid.* If it were within my power I'd do whatever you want. **2.** to fall, drop. *ṭaaƈ fadd šii mnil-loori.* Something fell out of the truck. **3.** to fall ill, become sick. *ʔabuuhum ṭaaƈ w-mariẓta raƈ-iṭṭawwil.* Their father got sick and his illness will be prolonged.

ṭayyaƈ to drop, allow to fall, cause to fall. *j-jaahil ṭayyaƈ l-iglaaṣ.* The baby dropped the glass. || *ṭayyaƈ ṣubġa.* He blistered him (lit., caused his paint to fall). *raƈ-aruuƈ Ɛalee w-aṭayyiƈ ṣubġa.* I'll go see him and give him hell.

ṭeeƈ falling.

ṭeeƈa pl. *-aat* a fall.

ṭaayiƈ **1.** fallen. **2.** run-down, dilapidated. *beethum ṭaayiƈ w-yriid-la taƐmiir.* Their house is run down and needs renovating. || *ṭaayƈ iṣ-ṣubuġ* ambitionless, listless. *kull wulda dixlaw madrasa bass waaƈid minhum ṭaayiƈ ṣubġa.* All his sons went to school except one of them who has no ambition.

ṭ-y-r

ṭaar (*i ṭayaraan*) **1.** to fly off, fly away, take off. *ṭ-ṭeer ṭaar w-ƈaṭṭ Ɛaš-šijra.* The bird flew off and perched in the tree. *ṭ-ṭayyaara ṭaarat ib-waqit mitʔaxxir.* The airplane took off late. *raƈ-aṭiir is-saaƐa sabƐa min baġdaad.* I'm going to take a plane at seven o'clock from Baghdad. || *lak, di-ṭiir! ʔinta š-jaabak Ɛaš-šiṭranj?* Go on, beat it! What do you know about chess? *ṭaar imnil-faraƈ.* He was overjoyed. *ṭaar Ɛaqla.* He was astounded. **2.** to fly up. *nafnuufha ṭaar min il-hawa w-ṭilƐat izruurha.* Her dress flew up because of the wind and her legs were exposed. **3.** to fly, dash, rush, hurry. *bass git-la ʔabuu rijaƐ, ṭaar lil-beet.* The minute I told him his father had returned, he dashed home. **4.** to fly past, fly away. *š-bil-Ɛajal ṭaar il-wakit!* How fast the time passed! *š-ib-saaƐ ṭaarat fluusi!* How quickly my money went! **4.** to evaporate. *qappuġha l-tanakt il-baanziin tara kulla yṭiir.* Cover up the container of gasoline or it'll all evaporate.

ṭayyar **1.** to cause to fly. *gabbat hawya w-ṭayyirat kullši.* A gust of wind came up suddenly and sent everything flying. *l-hawa ṭayyar nafnuufa.* The wind blew her dress up. || *jamaalha yṭayyir il-Ɛaqil.* Her beauty drives one mad. Her beauty is astounding. **2.** to fly. *ʔaku xooš hawa. xan-nṭayyir ṭayyaaraatna.* There's a good breeze. Let's fly our kites. *l-miṭyarči da-yṭayyir ṭyuura.* The pigeon fancier's flying his pigeons. **3.** to send flying, send packing, boot out. *waziirna, ʔaƐtiqid raƈ-yṭayyiruu.* I think they're going to fire our minister.

ṭṭaayar to fly about, fly in all directions, to diffuse, spread, scatter. *ʔirjaƐ išwayya. š-šaraaraat da-tiṭṭaayar imnin-naar.* Back up a little. Sparks are flying out from the fire.

ṭeer pl. *ṭyuur* **1.** bird. **2.** domestic pigeon.

ṭayyaar pl. *-iin* pilot, aviator, flyer.

ṭayyaara pl. *-aat* **1.** aviatrix, woman pilot. **2.** airplane, aircraft. **3.** kite (toy).

ṭiyyaara pl. *-aat* **1.** airplane, aircraft. **2.** kite (toy).

ṭayaraan **1.** flying, flight. **2.** aviation.

maṭaar pl. *-aat* airport, airfield.

ṭaaʔira pl. *-aat* airplane, aircraft.

mṭayyirči, miṭyarči pl. *-iyya* pigeon fancier, man who raises and trains domesticated pigeons.

ṭ-y-z

ṭiiz buttocks, rump.

ṭ-y-ʕ

ṭayyaʕ = *ṭawwaʕ,* which see under *ṭ-w-ʕ.*

ṭ-y-f

ṭeef pl. *ʔaṭyaaf* vision, apparition, phantasm (in a dream). || *ṭ-ṭeef iš-šamsi* the spectrum (phys.).

ṭ-y-l

ṭiila, mustaṭiil, etc., see under *ṭ-w-l.*

ṭ-y-n

ṭayyan to cover or spatter with mud or clay. *faat bil-bistaan w-ṭayyan rijlee.* He passed through the orchard and got mud on his feet.

tṭayyan to become covered with mud. *wugaʕ biš-šaariʕ w-iṭṭayyinat ihduuma.* He fell down in the street and his clothes got muddy.

ṭiin mud, clay. || *ṭiin xaawa* a white, clay-like substance commonly used to wash the hair. *zaad iṭ-ṭiin balla.* He aggravated the situation. He made things worse.

ṭiina pl. *-aat* a piece of mud or clay.

ṭ-y-y

ṭayya see under *ṭ-w-y.*

ع

ʕ-a-f-r-m

ʕaafarim (an exclamation) well done! good for you! bravo!

ʕ-a-n

ʕaana pl. *-aat* five fils coin. || *raḥ-naaxuδ ʕaanaatna mnil-muḥaasib il-yoom.* We're going to get our pittance from the accountant today.

ʕ-b-a-l

ʕabaal- see under *²b-w-l.*

ʕ-b-b

ʕibb pl. *ʕbuub* front of the *dišdaaša,* above the belt (where objects may be carried), shirt front. || *ma-yinḥaṭṭ bil-ʕibb.* He can't be pushed around. He's no patsy. *da-yiδḥak ib-ʕibba.* He's laughing up his sleeve.

ʕ-b-b-x-a-n

ʕabbaxaana pl. *-aat* (originally powerhouse, now:) a quarter in Baghdad.

ʕ-b-θ

ʕibaθ (*a ʕabaθ*) to cause disorder, confusion, wreak havoc. *fadd ʔaḥḥad ʕibaθ bil-awraaq maalti.* Someone messed up my papers. *j-jeeš dixal il-madiina w-ʕibaθ biiha.* The army entered the city and caused havoc in it. || *š-šurta lizmoo li-ʔan ʕibaθ b-ibnayya ẓǧayyra.* The police picked him up for molesting a little girl.

ʕabbaθ = *ʕibaθ. ma-yigdar ʔilla yʕabbiθ w-yʔaδδi l-ǧeer.* He can't do anything except cause trouble and hurt others.

nʕibaθ pass. of *ʕibaθ. ḥuṭṭha bil-qaaṣa ḥatta ma-yinʕibaθ biiha.* Put them in the safe so that they won't be disturbed.

ʕabaθ in vain, to no avail, uselessly, needlessly. *ṭaʕabi wiyyaa raaḥ ʕabaθ.* My efforts with him were of no avail. *qaddamit ariiδa ʕabaθ.* I submitted an application uselessly. *naṣiiḥtak ʔila ʕabaθ.* Your advice to him is in vain.

ʕ-b-d

ʕibad (*i ʕibaada*) **1.** to worship. *l-majuus yʕibduun in-naar.* The Magians worship fire. **2.** to adore, venerate, worship. *yiʕbid ḥabiibta.* He adores his sweetheart. *yiʕbiduun il-fluus.* They worship money.

ʕabbad to improve, develop (a road), to pave. *l-ḥukuuma da-tʕabbid haṭ-ṭariiq.* The government is improving this road. *l-baladiyya raḥ-itʕabbid kull haṭ-ṭuruq.* The city will pave all these roads.

tʕabbad to devote oneself to God. *r-raahib imsawwii-la mukaan bij-jibal yitʕabbad bii.* The hermit has made himself a place on the mountain in which he devotes himself to worship.

staʕbad to enslave, subjugate. *stawlaw ʕaleehum w-istaʕbidoohum.* They conquered and enslaved them.

ʕabid pl. *ʕabiid* **1.** slave. **2.** Negro.
ʕabda pl. *-aat* **1.** female slave. **2.** Negress.
ʕubuudiyya slavery, serfdom.
ʕabbaad: ʕabbaad iš-šamis sunflower. || *waraq ʕabbaad iš-šamis* litmus paper.
maʕbad pl. *maʕaabid* temple, place of worship.

ʕ-b-r

ʕibar (*u ʕabur, ʕubuur*) to cross. *xal-niʕbur iš-šaariʕ.* Let's cross the street. *raḥ-niʕbur iṣ-ṣoob il-karx.* We'll cross to the Karkh side. *č-čalib ʕubar ʕas-siyaaj w-wugaʕ ʕal-warid.* The dog jumped over the fence and fell on the flowers. || *n-nukta ʕubrat ʕalee.* He fell for the joke. *ma-yuʕbur ʕalee šii.* You can't put anything over on him. *ma-ʕubarit ib-dars il-kiimya.* I didn't pass in chemistry.

ʕabbar **1.** to express, voice, assert, state clearly. *ma-da-agdar aʕabbur ʕan qaṣdi.* I can't express what I mean. **2.** to take across, send across, let across. *š-šurṭi ʕabbar ij-jaahil iš-šaariʕ.* The policeman let the child cross the street. *ʔisʔal ʔabu l-balam. balki yʕabbrak.* Ask the boatman. Maybe he'll take you across. || *ʕabbur-la diinaareen w-ymaššii-lk-iyyaaha.* Slip him two dinars and he'll take care of it for you.

nʕibar to be crossed. *haš-šaṭṭ ʕariiḏ, ma-yinʕubur sibiḥ.* The river is wide. It can't be crossed by swimming.

ʕtubar **1.** to learn a lesson, learn from experience. *ma-ḥtibarit min illi ṣaar b-axuuk?* Didn't you learn a lesson from what happened to your brother? **2.** to consider, regard as. *ʕtubarnaa waaḥid imnil-ʕaaʔila.* We considered him one of the family. *ʔaʕtabra muṭi.* I consider him a jackass. *niʕtubur hal-ʕamal fadd šii xaṭiir.* We regard this act as being serious. *ʕtuburha ṣadaqa l-ʔaḷḷa.* Look at it as a charity for God's sake. **3.** to show regard, to respect, value. *riḥit-la, laakin ma-ʕtubarni.* I went to him, but he didn't show me any consideration.

ʕibir across, over. *ʕibr iš-šaariʕ* across the street.

*ʕibri** **1.** Hebrew, Hebraic. *l-luġa l-ʕibriyya, l-ʕibriyya* the Hebrew language, Hebrew. **2.** a Hebrew.

ʕibri pl. *-iyya* passenger (paying). || *raaḥ ʕibri.* He went as a passenger. He went on public transportation.

ʕibriyya pl. *-aat* female passenger.

ʕabra tears, crying. *lizmata l-ʕabra.* He began to cry. *taaxḏa l-ʕabra.* He bursts into tears.

ʕibra pl. *-aat* a crossing, an act of crossing.

ʕibra pl. *ʕibar* warning, example, lesson, object lesson.

ʕibaara pl. *-aat* sentence, clause, phrase, expression. || *ʕibaara ʕan* actually, really, simply, merely. *l-laasilki ʕibaara ʕan raadyo.* The wireless is simply a radio. *la-ddiir baal. hiyya ʕibaara ʕan xams idnaaniir.* Don't worry. It's only a matter of five dinars.

*ʕibraani** = *ʕibri**.

ʕabbaara pl. *-aat* ferry, ferry boat.

maʕbar pl. *maʕaabir* **1.** crossing, place for crossing. **2.** ford. **3.** ferry landing, dock.

taʕbiir pl. *taʕaabiir* expression, mode of expression, way of putting it. *b-ġeer taʕbiir, b-taʕbiir ʔaaxar* in other words.

ʕtibaar **1.** respect, regard, esteem. || *ʕinda ʕtibaar bis-suug.* He has a good credit rating in the market. **2.** (pl. *-aat*) consideration, regard. || *ʔaxaḏ ib-naḏ̣ar il-iʕtibaar* to take into consideration. *raḥ-yaxḏuun maraḏ̣ak ib-naḏ̣ar il-iʕtibaar.* They'll take your illness into consideration. *b-iʕtibaar* in consideration, considering. *b-iʕtibaar maʕriftak bil-miikaaniik, ʔinta ṣalliḥha.* In consideration of your knowledge of mechanics, you fix it. *b-iʕtibaara* in his capacity as, in the capacity of, as, since. *ʔinta ʔiḥči wiyyaaha b-iʕtibaarak tuʕruf ʔingiliizi.* You talk with her since you know English. *b-iʕtibaara wakiil il-waziir, fitaḥ ij-jisir.* In his capacity as the minister's representative, he opened the bridge.

ʕtibaaran min effective, beginning, starting with. *ʕtibaaran min baačir, laazim niji saaʕa θmaanya.* Beginning tomorrow, we've got to come at eight.

muʕtabar highly regarded, well thought of, much praised. *qmaaš muʕtabar* cloth that is well thought of. *muʕallim muʕtabar* a highly regarded teacher.

ʕ-b-s

ʕabbas to frown, scowl, glower. *ʕabbas min simaʕ il-ifluus tʔaxxrat.* He frowned when he heard the money'd been delayed. *ʕabbas ib-wičči.* He scowled at me.

*ʕabbaasi** Abbaside, belonging to the Abbaside period, an Abbaside.

ʕ-b-q-r

*ʕabqari** pl. *ʕabaaqira* **1.** ingenious, clever, gifted. *qaaʔid ʕabqari* an ingenious leader. *ɛall ɛabqari* an ingenious solution. **2.** genius.

ɛabqariyya ingenuity, genius, cleverness.

ɛ-b-w-l

ɛabaal- see under *b-w-l*.

ɛ-b-y

ɛabba **1.** to stuff, pack. *ɛabbi č-čukleet ib-čiiseen.* Pack the candy into two bags. *šifta yɛabbi šakar ib-jeeba.* I saw him stuffing candy in his pocket. **2.** to fill, pack. *ɛabbi hač-čiis čukleet.* Fill this sack with candy.

ɛaba pl. *ɛibi* aba, a loose, flowing, robe-like outer garment, with arm holes instead of sleeves, worn by men and women.

ɛabaaya pl. *-aat* = *ɛaba*.

ɛ-t-b

ɛitab (*i ɛatab*) to gripe, grumble, complain. *ɛitab ɛala muɛaamaltak ʔila.* He complained about your treatment of him. *da-yiɛtib ihwaaya čeef ma-zirnaa.* He's grumbling a lot because we didn't visit him.

ɛattab to blame, censure. *ʔiδa ṭilaɛ muu zeen, la-tɛattibni.* If it turns out badly, don't blame me. *ʔiδa nhizam imnil-madrasa, ʔaani ma-mɛattab.* If he runs away from school, I'm not to blame.

ɛaatab to scold, upbraid, censure, rebuke. *raɛ-aruuɛ ɛalee w-aɛaatba ɛala hal-ɛamal.* I'm going to see him and scold him for that action.

tɛaatab to find fault with each other. *tɛaatabna šwayya w-baɛdeen kullši giɛad ib-mukaana.* We argued a little and then everything was all right.

ɛatab censure, blame, rebuke.

ɛatba pl. *-aat* sill (window or door).

ɛataba pl. *-aat* shrine, tomb of a holy man. *l-ɛatabaat il-muqaddisa* the holy shrines.

ɛ-t-d

ɛitaad war material, ammunition.

ɛ-t-q

ɛaatiq shoulder. || *ʔaxaδ il-mašruuɛ ɛala ɛaatqa.* He took the project on. *xalliiha ɛala ɛaatqi.* Leave it to me.

ɛ-t-g

ɛitag (*a ɛatig*) to grow old. *saaɛti ɛitgat, laakin baɛadha tištuġuḷ zeen.* My watch has gotten old, but it still works well. *quuṭi kullha ɛitgat.* All my suits have gotten old.

ɛatiig pl. *ɛittag* **1.** old. *sayyaara ɛatiiga* an old car. **2.** obsolete, old-fashioned. *ṭuruq ɛatiiga* old-fashioned methods. || *waawi ɛatiig* a sly old fox.

ʔaɛtag more or most aged. || *laṭaayfa ʔaɛtag imnil-yaxni.* His jokes are old as the hills.

ɛ-t-l

ɛatala pl. *-aat* lever (phys.).

ɛ-t-m

ɛattam to darken, block out. *ɛattimaw il-madiina min simɛaw ɛiss iṭ-ṭiyyaaraat.* They blacked out the city when they heard the noise of airplanes.

taɛtiim blackout.

ɛ-t-h

maɛtuuh **1.** insane, crazy, idiotic. **2.** lunatic, insane person.

ɛ-t-w

ɛitwi pl. *ɛtaawi* a big tom cat.

ɛ-θ-θ

nɛaθθ to become moth-eaten. *la-txalli qaaṭak ib-haṣ-ṣanduug, tara yinɛaθθ.* Don't leave your suit in this trunk or it'll get moths in it.

ɛiθθ (coll.) moth(s).

ɛiθθa pl. *-aat* moth.

maɛθuuθ moth-eaten. *qappuuṭ maɛθuuθ* a moth-eaten overcoat.

ɛ-θ-r

ɛiθar (*i ɛaθir*) **1.** to trip, stumble. *ɛiθar ib-buuri l-mayy w-wugaɛ.* He tripped over the water pipe and fell. **2.** /with *ɛala*/ to come across, hit on, stumble onto. *ɛθarit ɛala xooš qumṣaan ib-fadd maxzan.* I stumbled onto some terrific shirts in a store. **3.** /with *b-*/ to find, run into. *ʔiδa ɛθarit bii, ʔaziffa!* If I run into him, I'll really read him the riot act.

ɛaθθar **1.** to trip, make stumble. *diir baalak ɛal-ɛatba, tara tɛaθθrak.* Watch out for the door sill, or it'll trip you. **2.** to trip up. *tidri ʔinta tɛaθθira b-ʔasʔiltak?* Do you realize you trip him up with your questions?

tɛaθθar **1.** to stumble, trip. *yitɛaθθar ihwaaya min yimši.* He stumbles a lot when he walks. **2.** to stutter, stammer, speak haltingly. *yitɛaθθar ihwaaya b-kalaama.* He stammers a lot in his speech.

ɛaθra stumbling, tripping.

ɛuθuur discovery, detection.

ɛaaθuura something in the way, something underfoot.

ɛ-θ-g

ɛiθig pl. *ɛθuug* bunch, cluster, stalk (of dates, bananas).

ɛ-j-b

ɛijab (*i ɛajib*) to please, delight, appeal to. *l-beet ij-jidiid ɛijabni kulliš.* The new house pleased me very much. *yiɛjibni ʔaruuḥ lis-siinama.* I'd like to go to the movies.

ɛajjab to amaze, astonish, surprise. *mawqifa yɛajjib il-waaḥid.* His attitude is amazing.

tɛajjab to be surprised, amazed, astonished. *tɛajjab min git-la.* He was astonished when I told him. *da-atɛajjab išloon yigdar yištuġuḷ ixmuṣtaɛaš saaɛa!* I'm amazed at how he can work fifteen hours! *luweeš da-titɛajjab? kullši mumkin.* Why are you surprised? Anything is possible.

ɛajab 1. astonishment, amazement. 2. wonder, oddity, strange occurrence. *ɛajab ma-da-ybayyin ihnaa.* It's odd he doesn't show up here. 3. then, in that case. *ɛajab ma-raḥ-yiji?* Then he isn't going to come? || *š-ɛajab* I wonder why. *š-ɛajab ma-ʔija.* I wonder why he didn't come. *ma-siʔalit ɛanni. š-ɛajab.* You didn't ask about me. I wonder why.

ɛajabaa, ɛajaban (approx.:) I wonder, do you suppose. *ɛajabaa raḥ-yinṭuuna ɛuṭla baačir?* Do you think they'll give us a holiday tomorrow? *ɛajaban raḥ-yiqbal?* Do you suppose he's going to accept?

ɛijba sensation, amazing thing, source of amazement.

ɛajiib amazing, remarkable, strange, odd.

ɛajiiba pl. *ɛajaayib* remarkable thing, oddity, curiosity, prodigy, marvel.

ʔaɛjab more or most astonishing, remarkable.

ɛjuuba pl. *ɛajaajiib* = *ɛijba.*

muɛjab admirer. *haaδa muɛjab bir-raaqiṣa.* He's an admirer of the dancer. || *muɛjab ib-nafsa* vain, conceited.

ɛ-j-j

ɛajj (*i ɛajj*) to swarm, teem. *bukra l-maṭaar raḥ-yɛijj bil-musaafiriin.* Tomorrow the airport is going to be packed with travelers.

ɛajjaj to raise the dust. *ʔimši ɛala keefak. la-tɛajjij.* Walk slowly. Don't raise the dust.

ɛajja pl. *-aat* dust storm.

ɛajaaj dust.

ɛ-j-r-f

tɛajraf to be arrogant, haughty. *ṣaarat ɛindak išwayyat ifluus w-gumit titɛajraf ɛan-naas.* You got a little money and then you began to be arrogant toward people.

mitɛajrif arrogant, haughty. *δaabut mitɛajrif* an arrogant officer.

ɛ-j-z

ɛijaz (*a ɛajiz*) 1. to be weak, lack strength, be incapable, unable. *δalleet aliḥḥ ɛalee ʔila ʔan iɛjazit.* I kept insisting on it till I was exhausted. *ɛijaz ɛan dafɛ il-mablaġ w-baaɛaw beeta.* He was incapable of paying the amount and they sold his house. 2. to become sick, become tired. *ɛijazit min ʔakl id-dijaaj.* I've gotten sick of eating chicken.

ɛajjaz 1. to age, grow old. *ɛajjizat w-ma-tigdar tištuġuḷ baɛad.* She has grown old and can't work any more. 2. to weaken, exhaust. *ɛajjazitni b-asʔiltak.* You've exhausted me with your questions.

tɛaajaz to be unwilling, to be unable to bother, to be lazy. *min ʔagul-lak itsawwi šii, la-titɛaajaz.* When I tell you to do something, don't give me a hard time. *yitɛaajaz ysawwi ʔay šii lli ʔaṭulba minna.* He can't be bothered doing anything I ask him.

ɛajiz shortage, deficit.

ɛajiz pl. *ʔaɛjaaz* posterior, rump, backside, buttocks.

ɛajzaan sick and tired, fed up. *ɛajzaan imnid-diraasa* sick and tired of studying.

ɛajuuz pl. *ɛajaza* 1. old, elderly, aged. *mara ɛajuuz* an old woman. 2. old, elderly person, oldster. 3. lazy person, sloth, stick-in-the-mud.

ɛajuuza pl. *-aat, ɛajaayiz* old, elderly, aged woman.

*ɛjuuzi** pl. *-iyya* 1. lazy, slothful, indolent. 2. lazy person.

ɛaajiz weak, feeble, powerless, incapable. *rijjaal ɛaajiz* a feeble man.

muɛjiza pl. *-aat* miracle (esp. those performed by a prophet).

ɛ-j-ɛ-j

ɛajɛaj to stir up dust. *ʔimši ɛala keefak. la-tɛajɛij.* Walk slowly. Don't stir up the dust.

ɛ-j-l

ɛajjal 1. to hurry, rush, speed. *ɛajjil išwayya; ma-buqa wakit.* Hurry up a little bit; there isn't much time left. 2. to hurry, rush, urge, drive. *ma-agdar aktib zeen ʔiδa tɛajjilni.* I can't write well if you rush me.

staɛjal to hurry, rush, be in a hurry.

la-tistaʕjil. ʕidna waqit. Don't hurry. We have time.

ʕijil pl. *ʕjuul* **1.** calf. *laḥam ʕijil* veal. *jilid ʕijil* calfskin. **2.** slap (on the cheek or the back of the neck).

ʕajal: bil-ʕajal in a hurry, quickly, rapidly. *taʕaal ihnaa bil-ʕajal!* Come here, on the double! *gul-la yruuḥ bil-ʕajal.* Tell him to go immediately. *huwwa yidṣaddag bil-ʕajal.* He's easily convinced.

ʕajala haste, hurry. *l-ʕajala mnis-šeeṭaan.* Haste makes waste (lit., is of the devil).

ʕajuul rash, hasty, in a hurry. *ʔiδa ma-tkuun ʕajuul, tigdar itbiiʕha b-siʕir zeen.* If you aren't in too much of a hurry, you can sell it for a good price.

ʔaʕjal quicker, faster.

mistaʕjil in a hurry, hurried. *š-ṣaar ʕindak mistaʕjil?* What are you in such a hurry about?

ʕ-j-m

ʕajami pl. *-iyya* unlearned, unsophisticated, backward person.

ʕajmi, ʕijmi** pl. *ʕajam* Persian, a Persian.

ʕjeemi (invar.) a variety of grape, resembling Tokay.

ʕ-j-n

ʕijan (*i ʕajin*) **1.** to knead (bread dough). *ʔinti ʕijni w-ʔaani ʔaxbuz.* You knead and I'll bake. || *ʔaani ʕaajna w-xaabza.* I know him inside out (lit., I've kneaded him and baked him). **2.** to make dough, mix up dough. *ʕijnat ʕašir kiiluwwaat iṭḥiin.* She made dough from ten kilos of flour.

ʕajjan to become doughy, soft. *šurr il-xubuz ḥatta ma-yʕajjin.* Spread the bread out so it won't turn soft.

ʕajna pl. *-aat* batch of bread dough.

ʕajiin (coll.) bread dough.

ʕajiina pl. *-aat* a piece of dough, ball of dough.

maʕijna pl. *maʕaajin* a large metal bowl usually used to make bread dough.

maʕjuun paste, cream. *maʕjuun ṭamaaṭa* tomato paste. *maʕjuun isnaan* toothpaste.

ʕ-č-l

miʕčaal pl. *mʕaačiil* see under *m-ʕ-č-a-l.*

ʕ-d-d

ʕadd (*i ʕadd*) **1.** to count, reckon, number. *ʕumra sitt isniin w-yigdar iyʕidd lil-miyya.* He's six years old and can count to a hundred. **2.** to consider, think, reckon. *ʔaani ma-aʕidda mniṭ-ṭullaab il-faahmiin.* I don't consider him one of the bright students.

ʕaddad to enumerate, count off. *tigdar itʕaddid ʔasbaab ṣuquuṭ hal-mamlaka?* Can you enumerate the reasons for the fall of this kingdom? *tʕaddad* to multiply, proliferate. *l-ʔasbaab itʕaddidat.* The reasons increased.

stiʕadd **1.** to get ready, prepare oneself. *laazim astiʕidd lil-imtiḥaan.* I must prepare for the exam. **2.** to come to attention. *laazim tistiʕidd min iymurr iδ-δaabuṭ.* You must come to attention when the officer passes by.

ʕidda **1.** several, a number of, many, numerous. *ʕiddat marraat* several times. **2.** legally prescribed period during which a woman may not remarry after being widowed or divorced.

ʕadad pl. *ʔaʕdaad* **1.** number, numeral. **2.** figure, quantity. **3.** number, issue (of a newspaper).

ʕadiid numerous, many. *mašaakil ʕadiida* numerous problems.

tiʕdaad pl. *-aat* count, total.

*ʔiʕdaadi** secondary. *madrasa ʔiʕdaadiyya* secondary school. *šahaada ʔiʕdaadiyya* secondary school degree.

taʕaddud variety, diversity, great number, multitude. || *taʕaddud iz-zawjaat* polygamy.

ʕtidaad confidence, trust, reliance. || *ʕtidaad ib-nafsa* self-confidence, self-reliance.

stiʕdaad **1.** willingness, readiness, preparedness. *ma-ʕindi stiʕdaad ʔaṣruf ʕalee filis waaḥid.* I'm not prepared to spend one fils on him. *ʕindak stiʕdaad tištuġuḷ wiyyaay il-yoom?* Are you willing to work with me today? **2.** preparation, preparedness. *stiʕdaad lil-imtiḥaan* preparation for the examination.

maʕduud limited, few. *ʔaṣdiqaaʔa maʕduudiin* his friends are few.

muʕiddaat (invar. pl.) gear, material, materiel, equipment. *muʕiddaat ḥarbiyya* war material.

mitʕaddid numerous, varied, diverse. *ʔasbaab mitʕaddida* various reasons.

mistiʕidd prepared, ready. *ʔaani ma-mistiʕidd ʔaakul masabba.* I'm not about to take any insults.

ʕ-d-s

ʕadas (coll.) lentil(s).

ʕadasa pl. *-aat* **1.** un. n. of *ʕadas.* **2.** lens.

ع-d-l

عidal **1.** (*i عadil*) /*with been*/ to be impartial toward, not to discriminate between. *ʔiδa yiعdil beenhum, kullhum iyحubbuu.* If he acts impartially toward them, they'll all like him. **2.** (*i عuduul*) to give up, drop, abandon. *عidal عan fikrat is-safar.* He dropped the idea of traveling. **3.** (*a عadil*) to straighten, straighten out, straighten oneself. *šaعra mjaععad. šgadd-ma yحuṭṭ-la dihin, ma-yiعdal.* His hair is kinky. No matter how much oil he puts on, it won't straighten out. || *huwwa miθil δeel ič-čalib. ma-yiعdal.* He's like a dog's tail. He won't straighten out. *l-kurdi walaw yiحči عarabi عišriin sana, luġta ma-tiعdal.* Even if the Kurd speaks Arabic for twenty years, his language won't improve.

عaddal **1.** to straighten, make straight. *عaddal is-siim bič-čaakuuč.* He straightened the wire with the hammer. *عaddil ir-rasim عal-حaayiṭ.* Straighten the picture on the wall. **2.** to smooth, flatten, level. *jaabaw roola tعaddil il-gaaع.* They brought a roller to flatten the ground. **3.** to put in order, straighten out, settle. *ma-عaddal ʔumuura gabuḷ-ma maat.* He didn't get his affairs in order before he died. || *عaddil حačyak. giddaamak ʔaadmi.* Watch your language. There's a gentleman in front of you. **4.** to amend, improve, change, alter. *raح il-حukuuma tعaddi il-qaanuun.* The government is going to amend the law. *l-muعallim عaddal darajta.* The teacher corrected his grade. **5.** to get better, improve. *ʔabuuya عaddal عala hal-hawa.* My father got healthier in this climate. *da-ʔašuufak imعaddil ihwaaya.* I see you're looking a lot healthier.

عaadal **1.** to equal, be equal to, be the equal of. *haj-jundi yعaadil xams ijnuud biš-šajaaعa.* That soldier is equal to five soldiers in bravery. **2.** to find the equivalent, evaluate. *l-wizaara raح-itعaadil šahaadti.* The ministry will evaluate my degree. **3.** to match. *ma-عinda maaniع yعaadilha bil-ifluus حatta yidzawwajha.* He doesn't mind matching her weight in money in order to marry her.

tعaddal **1.** to be straightened. *has-siim ma-yitعaddal ʔilla bič-čaakuuč.* This wire can only be straightened with a hammer. **2.** to straighten oneself, straighten out. *leeš gaaعid ʔaعwaj? tعaddal!* Why are you sitting crooked? Straighten up! **3.** to be smoothed, flattened, leveled. *l-gaaع laazim titعaddal gabuḷ-ma titbaḷḷaṭ.* The ground has to be leveled before it's paved. **4.** to be put in order, be straightened out, be settled. *baعad-ma titعaddal il-ʔumuur, kull waaحid yaaxuδ حaqqa.* After matters are straightened out, everyone will get what's coming to him. **5.** to be changed, amended. *ʔiδa yitعaddal il-qaanuum, yišminna t-tarfiiع.* If the law's amended, we'll be included in the promotions. **6.** to be improved, be bettered. *ṣiححta tعaddlat ib-lubnaan.* His health improved in Lebanon. *l-ʔaحwaal raح-titعaddal, inšaaḷḷa.* Conditions will get better, I hope. *ʔiδa taaxuδ sabعiin bil-imtiحaan titعaddal darajtak.* If you get seventy on the test your grade will improve.

tعaadal **1.** to be equal. *δ̣iif xamsa حatta titعaadal il-muعaadala.* Add five so the equation will be balanced. **2.** to tie, tie each other, be tied. *tعaadlaw il-fariqeen bis-sibaaq.* The two teams tied in the game.

عtidal to be or become moderate, temperate. *raح-yiعtidil il-hawa baعad fadd čam yoom.* The weather will be moderate in a few days. *laazim tiعtidil ib-šurb ij-jigaayir.* You've got to become moderate in smoking cigarettes.

staعdal to straighten out. *dawwir is-sikkaan عal-yimna w-baعdeen istaعdil.* Turn the wheel to the right and then straighten it out. *ʔiδa ʔatraffaع عala xamsiin diinaar, ʔastaعdil tamaam.* If I get a payraise to fifty dinars, I'll be all straightened out.

عadil **1.** straight. *bismaar عadil* a straight nail. *ʔoogaf عadil.* Stand up straight. **2.** straight, vertical, upright, plumb. *šajra عadla* a straight tree. *l-حaayiṭ muu عadla.* The wall's out of plumb. **3.** level, flat, smooth. *gaaع عadla* a level floor. *ʔaraaδ̣i عadla* flat land. *šaariع عadil* a smooth road. **4.** upright, honest, fair, just. || *yimši عadil.* He's honest. *yiحči عadil.* He tells the truth. *kaatib il-عadil* civil servant in the legal system, holding functions of a notary public. **5.** sound, whole, unbroken. *ṭaabuuga عadla.* a whole brick, an unbroken brick. **6.** healthy, hale, alive. *ʔabuu baعda عadil.* His father is still alive.

*عadli** legal, forensic, juristic. *ṭ-ṭibb il-عadli* forensic medicine. || *ṭabiib عadli* coroner.

عidil pl. *عduul* a large pair of bags

slung on either side of a beast of burden.

ʕadiil pl. *ʕudaalaaʔ* the husband of one's wife's sister.

ʕadaala justice, fairness, impartiality.

ʕadliyya justice, jurisprudence. *waziir il-ʕadliyya* Minister of Justice.

ʔaʕdal **1.** more or most just. **2.** straighter, straightest.

taʕdiil pl. *-aat* change, amendment, modification. || *taʕdiil wizaari* cabinet reshuffle.

muʕaadala pl. *-aat* equation (math.).

ʕaadil just, fair, equitable. *ʕaadil ib-ḥukma* just in his decisions. *ʕaadil ib-qisimta* fair in his distribution.

muʕaddal pl. *-aat* (n.) average.

muʕtadil **1.** temperate, moderate. *muʕtadil ib-ṣarf il-fluus* moderate in spending money. **2.** mild, clement. *manaax muʕtadil* mild weather.

ʕ-d-m

ʕidam (i *ʔiʕdaam*) **1.** to spoil, go bad. *l-ʔakil ʕidam w-laazim inδibba.* The food spoiled and we'll have to throw it out. **2.** to ruin, spoil. *l-xayyaaṭ ʕidam il-qaaṭ maali.* The tailor ruined my suit. **3.** to execute. *ʕidmaw ij-jaasuus il-yoom il-fajir.* They executed the spy today at dawn.

ʕadam **1.** nothing, nothingness. **2.** lack of, absence of. *ʕadam it-tadxiin* abstinence from smoking. *ʕadam raġba* lack of desire, lack of interest.

ʕadiim devoid of, without,-less. *ʕadiim iš-šuʕuur* lacking feeling. *ʕadiim iδ-δooq* tasteless. || *ṣaqaṭ ʕadiim* worthless junk. *ʔaštiriiha walaw čaanat ṣaqaṭ ʕadiim.* I'd buy it even if it was junk.

ʔiʕdam execution. *ʕuquubat il-iʕdaam* the death penalty.

maʕduum **1.** ruined, spoiled. *ʔakil maʕduum* spoiled food. **2.** denatured. *kuḥuul maʕduum* denatured alcohol. **3.** executed. **4.** executed person.

ʕ-d-n

maʕdan pl. *maʕaadin* **1.** metal. **2.** mineral. || *jidir maʕdan* enamelware pot. *ʔaθiq bii li-ʔan il-maʕdan maala zeen.* I trust him because he's made of good stuff.

*maʕdani** mineral. *mawaadd maʕdaniyya* mineral substances. *miyaaʔ maʕdaniyya* mineral waters.

ʕ-d-w

ʕida (i *ʕadwa*) to infect. *la-tišrab min iglaaṣa, tara yiʕdiik.* Don't drink from his glass or he'll infect you. *hal-maraδ yiʕdi.* This disease is infectious.

ʕadda to pass, let pass. *š-šurṭi ʕaddaani mnil-baab.* The policeman let me by the door. *š-yʕaddiik ib-hal-izdiḥaam?* How are you going to get through this crowd?

ʕaada **1.** to treat as an enemy, regard as an enemy. *ʔaani ʔaʕaadi kull ʔaʕdaaʔak.* I consider all your enemies as my enemies. **2.** to turn against, fall out with. *ʕaadaani li-ʔan ʔaḥči iṣ-ṣudug.* He turned against me because I tell the truth.

tʕadda **1.** to pass, go by. *ʔaxuuk hassa tʕadda minnaa.* Your brother just now passed by here. **2.** to be insulting, offer insult, give provocation. *ʔinta tʕaddeet ʕalee b-hač-čilma.* You insulted him with that remark. *huwwa tʕadda ʕalayya bil-ʔawwal.* He provoked me in the first place. **3.** to overstep, exceed. *šaqaahum itʕadda l-ḥuduud w-waaḥid gaam ysibb iθ-θaani.* Their teasing went too far and one began to curse the other. **4.** to exceed. *siʕirha ma-yitʕadda l-ʕašr idnaaniir.* Its price won't exceed ten dinars.

tʕaadaw **1.** to be or become hostile to each other, be enemies. *baʕad ij-jidaal, tʕaadaw.* After the argument, they were hostile to each other. **2.** to be or become hostile, inimical. *ʕala-weeš tʕaadeet wiyyaa? sawwaa-lak šii?* Why'd you get mad at him? Did he do anything to you? *min gaal hač-čilma tʕaadaa-la.* When he said this he turned hostile to him.

ʕtida to commit aggression, commit a hostile act, attack. *had-dawla ʕtidat ʕala jiiraanatha.* This nation committed aggression against her neighbor. *ʔiδa tiʕtidi ʕalee yištiki ʕaleek biš-šurṭa.* If you attack him he'll complain to the police about you.

ʕada except, with the exception of. *kullhum ʕada waaḥid* all except one.

ʕadu pl. *ʕaadaaʔ, ʕudwaan* enemy.

ʕadaawa **1.** enmity, hostility, animosity, antagonism. **2.** (invar.) inimical, enemies. *čaanaw ʔaṣdiqaaʔ, w-baʕdeen ṣaaraw ʕadaawa.* They were friends, but later became enemies. *ʔiḥna ʕadaawa wiyyaahum.* We're enemies to them. *huwwa ʕadaawa wiyyaay.* He's an enemy to me.

taʕaddi pl. *-iyyaat* assault, attack, provocation, insult.

ʕtidaaʔ pl. *-aat* attack, assault, aggression.

*muʕdi** contagious, infectious. *maraδ muʕdi* contagious disease.

ɛ-δ-b

ɛaδδab **1.** to torture. *ɛaδδiboo hwaaya ɛatta ɛtiraf.* They tortured him terribly until he confessed. **2.** to torment, pain, afflict. *j-jaahil ʔaδδab ʔuṃṃa ṭuul in-nahaar.* The child tormented his mother all day long. **3.** to punish (of God). *ʔaḷḷa yɛaδδib il-ma-yṣaḷḷuun.* God will punish those who don't pray.

tɛaδδab **1.** to be tortured. *ʔiδa ma-yitɛaδδab, ma-yqurr.* If he isn't tortured, he won't confess. **2.** to suffer, have trouble. *hal-mara tɛaδδibat ihwaaya b-tarbiyat ibinha.* That woman suffered a lot in raising her son. *baaɛ sayyaarta baɛad-ma tɛaδδab biiha.* He sold his car after he'd had a lot of trouble with it.

ɛaδib: ṃayy ɛaδib sweet, fresh water.

ɛaδaab torture.

ɛ-δ-r

ɛiδar (*u ɛuδur*) to excuse. *l-muɛallim ma-yɛuδrak imnil-imtiɛaan ʔiδa ma-djiib taqriir ṭibbi.* The teacher won't excuse you from the exam if you don't bring a medical report. *gul-la "činit mariiδ̣" ɛatta yɛuδrak.* Tell him "I was sick" so he'll excuse you. *ʔiɛdurni; ma-agdar aruuɛ.* I'm sorry; I can't go.

tɛaδδar **1.** to be difficult, impossible. *yitɛaδδar wujuud ʔadawaat has-sayyaara.* It's impossible to find parts for this car. *yitɛaδδar ɛalayya asaaɛdak.* It's impossible for me to help you. **2.** to make excuses, excuse oneself, apologize. *kull-ma aɛizma, yitɛaδδar.* Whenever I invite him to dinner he makes excuses. *muu suuči. luweeš atɛaδδar?* I'm not to blame. Why should I apologize?

ɛtiδar to apologize, excuse onself. *ruuɛ ʔiɛtiδir minna.* Go apologize to him.

ɛuδur pl. *ʔaɛδaar* excuse. *ɛuδur ġeer mašruuɛ* an illegitimate excuse, a poor excuse.

ɛaδra pl. *-aat* virgin.

ɛ-r-b

ɛarrab **1.** to Arabicize, make Arabic. *ɛarrabaw hač-čilma w-sawwaw fiɛil minha.* They Arabicized this word and derived a verb from it. **2.** to translate into Arabic. *minu ɛarrab hal-iktaab?* Who translated this book into Arabic?

tɛarrab to become an Arab, adopt Arab customs, assimilate to the Arabs. *ɛaaš been il qabaaʔil, w-itɛarrab tamaaman.* He lived among the tribes and adopted Arab customs completely.

ɛarab (coll.) Arabs.

*ɛarabi** **1.** (coll. pl. *ɛarab*) **a.** Arab, Arabian. **b.** an Arab. **2.** (invar.) Arabic, the Arabic language. *l-ɛarabiyya* the (classical or literary) Arabic language.

ɛaraba pl. *-aat* **1.** wagon, cart. **2.** car, coach (railroad). || *ɛarabat ʔaṭfaal* baby carriage.

ɛurbi, ɛrubi pl. *ɛurbaan* man from a rural area, tribesman.

ɛuruuba Arabism, pan-Arabism.

ɛarabaana pl. *ɛarabaayin* cart, wagon, horsecart, buggy, carriage.

ɛarabanči pl. *-iyya* driver of an *ɛarabaana.*

ɛ-r-b-d

ɛarbad to shout angrily. *daaʔiman yɛarbid ɛala marta.* He continually raises cain with his wife.

ɛirbiid pl. *ɛaraabiid* a large snake, a male snake.

ɛ-r-b-n

ɛarabuun pl. *ɛaraabiin* deposit, down payment.

ɛ-r-j

ɛiraj (*a ɛaraj*) to limp. *da-yiɛraj li-ʔan rijla maδ̣ruuba.* He is limping because his leg was hurt.

ʔaɛraj fem. *ɛarja* pl. *ɛirij, ɛarjiin* **1.** lame, limping, having a limp. **2.** lame person.

miɛraaj: leelt il-miɛraaj the night of Mohammed's ascension to the seven heavens.

mɛarraj corrugated. *čiinku mɛarraj* corrugated galvanized sheet metal.

ɛ-r-s

ɛarras to get married. *ɛarras ɛala bitt ɛaamma gabuḷ santeen w-lissa ma-jaa ṭifil.* He married his cousin two years ago and still hasn't had a baby.

ɛiris pl. *ʔaɛraas* marriage, wedding. || *ʔabu l-ɛiris* weasel.

ɛaruus, ɛruus pl. *ɛaraayis* bride.

ɛirriis pl. *ɛaraariis* bridegroom.

ɛ-r-š

ɛariš pl. *ɛuruuš* throne.

ɛ-r-ṣ

ɛaraṣa pl. *-aat* a plot of land, a vacant lot, also land and the buildings on it, constituting mortmain endowment (wakf).

ɛ-r-δ̣

ɛiraδ̣ (*a ɛuruδ̣*) to widen, broaden, become wide. *n-nahar, min yiṭlaɛ imnil-balda, yiɛraδ̣.* The river widens when it leaves the city. || *ʔašu kull-ma jaa-lak da-tiɛraδ̣.* It seems you're continually getting fatter. **2.** to show, present, display, exhibit. *raħ-yɛirð̣uun hal-film l-usbuuɛ ij-jaay.* They're going to show this film next week. *ɛirað̣na maṣnuuɛaatna bil-maɛrað̣.* We exhibited our manufactures at the fair. **3.** to submit, turn in, suggest, propose. *haay xooš fikra. raħ-aɛrið̣ha ɛal-mudiir.* That's a good idea. I'll submit it to the director. **4.** to offer. *ʔiɛruð̣ ɛalayya siɛir.* Make me an offer. *ɛirað̣ sayyaarta lil-beeɛ.* He offered his car for sale. *ɛirað̣ sayyaarta ɛalayya b-ʔalif diinaar.* He offered his car to me for a thousand dinars.

ɛarrað̣ **1.** to widen, broaden. *l-ħukuuma raħ-itɛarrið̣ haš-šaariɛ.* The government's going to widen this street. **2.** to expose. *la-tɛarrið̣ nafsak lil-barid.* Don't expose yourself to the cold. *l-mulaazim ɛarrað̣ jinuuda lil-xaṭar.* The lieutenant exposed his troops to danger.

ɛaarað̣ to oppose, object to. *zuɛamaaʔ il-ħizib ɛaarð̣aw siyaasta.* The party bosses opposed his policy.

tɛarrað̣ **1.** to be widened. *š-šaariɛ itɛarrað̣ is-sana l-faatat.* The street was widened last year. **2.** to be exposed, expose oneself. *ṭilaɛ w-itɛarrað̣ lil-barid.* He went out and got exposed to the cold. **3.** /with *b-*/ to annoy, pester, accost, antagonize. *daaʔiman yoogaf biš-šaariɛ w-iytɛarrað̣ bil-banaat.* He's always standing in the street pestering girls. *haað̣a ʔašqiyaaʔ; maħħad yigdar yitɛarrað̣ bii.* He's a tough guy; no one can mess around with him.

tɛaarað̣ **1.** to conflict, be contradictory, be incompatible. *hal-ɛamal yitɛaarað̣ wiyya l-qaanuun.* That action is in conflict with the law. *waqti yitɛaarað̣ wiyya waqtak.* My schedule conflicts with yours. **2.** to get sick, be taken ill, have an attack. *ʔabuu tɛaarað̣ il-baarħa w-jaaboo-la ṭ-ṭabiib.* His father had an attack yesterday and they brought the doctor for him.

nɛirað̣ to be submitted, turned in, proposed. *ṭalabak inɛirað̣ ɛal-lujna.* Your request was submitted to the committee.

ɛtirað̣ **1.** to object, protest, oppose. *maħħað̣ iɛtirað̣ ɛal-iqtiraaħ.* No one objected to the proposal. **2.** to obstruct, block. *ridt axušš bil-binaaya, laakin iš-šurṭi ɛtirað̣ ṭariiqi.* I wanted to enter the building but the policeman blocked the way.

staɛrað̣ **1.** to pass in review. *raħ-tistaɛrið̣ wiyya ij-jinuud willa laa?* Are you going to pass in review with the troops or not? **2.** to review, inspect. *l-qaaʔid staɛrað̣ ij-jinuud.* The commander reviewed the troops.

ɛuruð̣ pl. *ɛuruuð̣* width, breadth. || *bil-ɛuruð̣* across, crosswise, horizontally. *guṣṣ il-xišba bil-ɛuruð̣.* Cut the piece of wood crosswise. *ɛala keefak! ʔašu ʔaxað̣itna ṭuul ɛuruð̣.* Take it easy! You're not giving us a chance.

ɛarð̣: xaṭṭ il-ɛarð̣ degree or parallel of latitude. *saaħat il-ɛarð̣* parade ground. *l-ɛarð̣ wiṭ-ṭalab* supply and demand.

ɛarð̣ honor, good repute. || *naɛla ɛala ɛarð̣ak!* Damn you! (lit., a curse on your honor)

*ɛarð̣aani** transverse, crosswise. *šaariɛ ɛarð̣aani* cross street.

ɛurð̣a target, butt. *ɛurð̣a lis-sabb* a target for curses, exposed to censure. || *bil-ɛurð̣a* (approx.,) help yourself, you're welcome to it (a polite expression when a possession is praised, not expected to be taken literally).

ɛarað̣ pl. *ʔaɛraað̣* symptom, manifestation (of a disease).

ɛariið̣ wide, broad. *šaariɛ ɛariið̣* a wide street.

ɛariið̣a pl. *ɛaraayið̣* application, petition. *kaatib ɛaraayið̣* man who, for a fee, writes applications and official documents.

maɛrað̣ pl. *maɛaarið̣* **1.** showroom, also, used car lot. **2.** exhibition, show. **3.** fair, exposition.

muɛaarað̣a opposition (esp. pol.). *ħizb il-muɛaarað̣a* the opposition party.

taɛaaruð̣ conflict, contradiction.

ɛtiraað̣ objection, protest, rebuttal.

stiɛraað̣ pl. *-aat* parade, review.

stiɛraað̣i: filim istiɛraað̣i* movie musical.

ɛaarið̣ pl. *ɛawaarið̣* an unexpected delay, hindrance, or obstacle.

muɛaarið̣ opponent, antagonist, opposer.

ɛ-r-ð̣-ħ-a-l

ɛarð̣aħaal pl. *-aat* application, petition.

ɛarð̣aħaalči, ɛarð̣aħalči pl. *-iyya* man who sits outside public offices, and for a fee writes out applications.

ɛ-r-f

ɛiraf (*u maɛrifa*) **1.** to know. *ɛirafit kull il-ʔajwiba.* I knew all the answers. *tuɛruf ʔaħħad imnil-mawjuudiin?* Do you know any of those present? *ʔaɛruf išloon aṭalliɛ ifluus minna.* I know how to get money out of him. *yuɛruf yiqra w-yiktib.* He knows how to read and write. *yuɛruf yisbaħ.* He knows how to swim.

maعcad yuعruf lil-raadyo b-gadda. No one knows radios like him. || *huwwa yuعrufni ˀili, muu ġeer šaxuṣ.* He'll come to me, not someone else. *ˀaani ˀaعurfa ˀila. š-aعlayya bil-ġeer?* He's the one I'll deal with. Why should I care about someone else? *ma-tuعruf haaδa šgadd xooš walad.* You can't imagine what a nice guy he is. *yuعruf nafsa. ma-yinġulub biš-šiṭranj.* He's self-confident. He can't be beaten in chess. **2.** to recognize, tell. *tuعruf il-mariiḍ min wičča.* You can tell the sick man by his face. *عirafta min cissa.* I recognized him by his voice. **3.** to see, realize, perceive, acknowledge, concede. *hassa عirafit kull cačya čiδib.* Now I realize all his talk is lies. *ˀinta da-tuعruf iš-da-yṣiir bid-daaˀira?* Are you aware of what's going on in the office? *hassa عirafit fikirti ṣaciiعa?* Now do you admit my idea is right? **4.** to find out, figure out, discover. *baعdeen عirafit minu baag is-saaعa maalti.* Later I found out who stole my watch. *ma-da-agdar ˀaعruf luweeš wugfat il-makiina.* I can't figure out why the motor stopped.

عarraf **1.** to introduce. *ˀariid aعarrfak biz-zuwwaar.* I'd like to introduce you to the visitors. **2.** to define. *tigdar itعarruf-li l-muθallaθ?* Can you define the triangle for me?

tعarraf to be introduced, to meet, to get to know, to get acquainted. *tعarrafit عala waacid ˀamriiki.* I got acquainted with an American. *laazim titعarraf ib-jamaaعa, ˀilhum nufuuḍ.* You've got to get acquainted with any group that has influence.

tعaaraf to become acquainted. *tعaarafna b-fadd munaasaba.* We became acquainted at a celebration. *tعaarafit wiyyaa il-baarca bil-cafla.* I got acquainted with him yesterday at the party.

nعiraf **1.** to be or become known, be discovered. *hassa nعiraf sabab naqla.* Now the reason for his transfer is known. **2.** to be recognized. *caawil yitnakkar laakin inعiraf ib-saaع.* He tried to disguise himself but he was recognized quickly.

عtiraf **1.** to confess, admit, acknowledge, own. *عtiraf bij-jariima b-cuḍuuri.* He confessed to the crime in my presence. *ˀaعtirif haay čaanat ġalṭa minni, laakin ma-ligeet ġeer call.* I admit this was a mistake on my part, but I couldn't find another solution. *ˀaعtirif ˀaani mqaṣṣir ib-caqqak.* I'm afraid I didn't do all I could for you. **2.** /with *b-*/ to recognize, grant recognition to. *ma-čaan laazim niعtirif ib-hal-cukuuma b-surعa.* We shouldn't have recognized this government so quickly.

عuruf **1.** custom, convention, tradition, usage, practice, habit. **2.** (pl. *ˀaعraaf*) crest, comb (of a rooster). || *عurf id-diič* red flower shaped like a cock's comb, cockscomb (?).

*عurfi**: || *l-ˀackaam il-عurfiyya* martial law.

عariif pl. *عurafaaˀ* sergeant. *raˀiis عurafaaˀ* approx.: master sergeant. *naaˀib عariif* approx.: corporal.

ˀaعraf more or most knowledgeable.

maعrifa pl. *maعaarif* **1.** knowledge, learning, information. **2.** acquaintance, conversance.

¶ *waziir il-maعaarif* minister of education.

taعriif pl. *taعaariif* definition.

taعriifa: taعriifa gumrugiyya **1.** tariff. **2.** list of customs duties.

taعaaruf **1.** getting acquainted. *caflat taعaaruf* reception, get-acquainted party. **2.** polite formalities, ceremony.

عtiraaf pl. *-aat* **1.** recognition, acceptance. **2.** confession, admission, acknowledgment.

عaarfa wise man, sage (of a village or tribe).

maعruuf known, well-known. *maعruuf biš-šajaaعa* known for courage. *mulaakim maعruuf* a well-known boxer.

mutaعaaraf customary, usual, common. *š-šii l-mutaعaaraf* the customary thing.

ع-r-q

l-عiraaq Iraq.

*عiraaqi** **1.** Iraqi, from Iraq. **2.** an Iraqi. (see also *ع-r-g*).

ع-r-q-č-y-n

عaraqčiin pl. *-aat* skullcap.

ع-r-q-l

عarqal to complicate, hinder, hamper, obstruct, delay. *qaḍiiti caanat maašya bass ˀinta عarqalitha.* My case was going well but you fouled it up.

tعarqal pass. of *عarqal.* *qaḍiyyat tarfiiعi tعarqilat.* The matter of my promotion was delayed.

عarqala pl. *عaraaqiil* obstacle, hindrance.

ع-r-k

عaarak **1.** to fight, contend with. *yعaa-*

rikhum ʕala ʔaqall šii. He argues with them about the least thing. **2.** to cause to fight, stir up, provoke, incite. *jiib diičak; xalli nʕaarka wiyya diiči.* Bring your cock; let's put it to fight with mine. *yigdar yʕaarikhum b-iččaaya wiḥda.* He can get them fighting with one remark.

tʕaarak to fight one another. *jiiraanna yitʕaarkuun ʕala ṭull.* Our neighbors fight all the time.

ʕarka pl. *-aat* fight, struggle.

maʕraka pl. *maʕaarik* battle, combat.

ʕarraak pl. *-a* fighter, good fighter, scrapper.

mʕaarakči pl. *-iyya* fighter, ruffian, person who picks fights.

ʕ-r-g

ʕirag (*a ʕarig*) to sweat, perspire. *ʕiragit ihwaaya bis-siinama.* I perspired a lot in the movie. || *guṣṣta ma-tiʕrag.* He's not ashamed of anything (lit. his forehead doesn't sweat).

ʕarrag to cause to sweat. *ʕarrag nafsa bil-buxaar.* He got himself all sweaty in the steam.

tʕarrag to sweat freely or copiously. *gabuḷ-ma tiġsil laazim titʕarrag bil-buxaar.* Before you wash you should sweat a lot in the steam. *tġaṭṭa bil-baṭṭaaniyya ḥatta titʕarrag išwayya w-itṭiib.* Cover yourself with the blanket so that you'll sweat a little and get well.

ʕirig pl. *ʕruug* **1.** root. **2.** stem, branch, cutting. **3.** vein. **4.** stock, descent, background, family.

¶ *ʕirg is-suus* licorice root. (*šarbat*) *ʕirg is-suus* a beverage made of licorice. *ʕirg in-nisa* sciatica (med.). *ʕirig tuuθ* a mulberry branch, and by extension, a strong man.

ʕarag **1.** sweat, perspiration. **2.** arrack, liquor.

ʕarga pl. *-aat* a period of sweating.

ʕargaan sweaty. *θiyaab ʕargaana* sweaty clothes.

ʕruug **1.** grain (in wood). **2.** (coll.) a kind of *kabaab,* small hamburgers made of ground meat, flour, parsley, and onions fried in oil.

ʕruugaaya pl. *-aat* un. n. of *ʕruug.* || *xubz iʕruug* bread with pieces of meat, onions, parsley, spices, etc. baked into it.

ʕaragči pl. *-iyya* person who drinks a lot of arrack, hence, a drunkard.

ʕ-r-g-č-y-n

ʕaragčiin pl. *-aat* skullcap.

ʕ-r-w

ʕurwa pl. *ʕraawi* a closed, usually rounded, handle, e.g., of a cup, pitcher, teapot, basket, etc.

ʕ-r-y

ʕarra to undress, disrobe, unclothe. *ʕarri j-jaahil ḥatta yitšammas.* Undress the baby so he can get some sun.

tʕarra to undress oneself, undress. *tʕarra ḥatta yfuḥṣa ṭ-ṭabiib.* He disrobed so the doctor could examine him.

ʕtira to overcome, overwhelm. *ʕtiraa l-xoof.* He was overcome by fear. *ʕtirata nooba ʕaṣabiyya.* He had a nervous breakdown.

ʕaryaan pl. *-iin, ʕraaya* naked, nude, bare, undressed. *niswaan iʕraaya* naked women.

*ʕarri** devoid, bereft. *xabar ʕaari ʕan iṣ-ṣiḥḥa* news devoid of any truth.

ʕaariyya (invar.) loosely, lightly, unsteadily, insecurely. *l-ʕamuud waaguf ʕaariyya.* The pole is standing unsteadily. *rijl il-kursi maḥṭuuṭ ʕaariyya.* The chair leg is insecurely attached. *r-ridin mšakkila bis-sitra ʕaariyya.* The sleeve is attached loosely to the coat. *diir baalak tara l-iglaaṣ maḥṭuuṭ ʕaariyya.* Be careful because the glass is unsteadily settled.

ʕ-z-b

ʕazzab **1.** to be a guest, stay overnight. *ʔiδa truuḥ lin-najaf, ʕazzib ʕind axuuya.* If you go to Najaf, stay with my brother. **2.** to give lodging to, give a place to stay, take in. *raaḥ il-baġdaad w-maḥḥad ʕazzaba.* He went to Baghdad and no one took him in.

ʕizba pl. *-aat* elderly unmarried woman, spinster.

ʕuzuuba bachelorhood.

ʔaʕzab pl. *ʕuzzaab* **1.** unmarried, single. **2.** bachelor.

mʕazzib pl. *maʕaaziib* guest, visitor.

ʕ-z-r-ʔ-y-l

ʕizraʔiil Azrael, the angel of death.

ʕ-z-z

ʕazz (*i ʕazz*) **1.** to cherish, hold dear. *ʔaani ʔaʕizzak ihwaaya.* I hold you very dear. **2.** to pain. *yʕizz ʕaleena tsaafir.* It pains us that you're leaving.

ʕazzaz to strengthen, reinforce. *j-jeeš da-yʕazziz markaza.* The army is fortifying its position.

tʕazzaz to take advantage of devotion. *marta titʕazzaz ʕalee hwaaya.* His wife takes advantage of his devotion.

ʕtazz to be proud, boast, pride oneself.

ʔaani ʔaعtazz ib-kull ṣadiiq muxliṣ. I am proud of every loyal friend.

عizz: ʔayyaam il-عizz the good old days, the days of prosperity. *b-عizz šabaaba* in the prime of his youth.

عaziiz **1.** strong. *suug عaziiz* a strong market. **2.** dear, beloved. *عaziizi* my dear, old buddy.

ʔaعazz dearer or dearest.

maعzuuz beloved, respected, highly regarded. *maعzuuz been ʔahla* beloved by his family. || *maعzuuz il-عeen* dear friend.

ع-z-f

عizaf (i عazif) to play. *tعallam yiعzif عal-kamanja.* He learned to play the violin.

عaazif player, performer (on a musical instrument).

maعzuufa pl. *-aat* piece of music, musical selection.

ع-z-q

عazaqa pl. *-aat* bother, problem, headache.

ع-z-l

عizal (i عazil) **1.** to isolate. *عizloo il-masluuliin imnil-marᵭ il-baaqiin.* They isolated the tuberculosis patients from the rest. **2.** to cull, to sort. *عizalt iṭ-ṭamaaṭa loo baعad?* Have you sorted the tomatoes yet? **3.** to discharge, dismiss, release. *عizloo mnil-waᵭiifa li-ʔan čaan yaaxuᵭ rašwa.* They fired him from the job because he was taking bribes.

عazzal to close, close down, close up. *yoom ij-jumعa l-kull yعazziluun.* On Friday they all close their businesses.

nعizal **1.** pass. of *عizal. hal-mariiᵭ laazim yinعizil willa l-kulla yinṣaabuun.* This patient must be isolated or all will be infected. *ṭ-ṭamaaṭa baعad-ma tinعizil, ʔasعaarha tixtilif.* After the tomatoes are sorted, their prices will vary. *baعad-ma nعizal imnil-waᵭiifa, gaam ybiiع jigaayir.* After he was discharged from his position, he started selling cigarettes. **2.** to separate, part company. *baعad-ma zzawwaj, inعizal عan ʔahla.* After he got married, he separated from his family.

عazil **1.** isolation. *mustašfa عazil* quarantine hospital. **2.** (invar.) culled, discarded. *ṭamaaṭa عazil* culled tomatoes.

عuzla seclusion, privacy, solitude.

ʔaعzal fem. *عazla* pl. *عuzul, عuzzal* defenseless, unarmed.

عaazil insulator, insulating.

nعizaali isolationist.

ع-z-m

عizam (i عazim) to invite. *عizan kull ʔaṣdiqaaʔa عal-عaša.* He invited all his friends to dinner.

عaziima pl. *عazaayim* **1.** invitation. **2.** banquet, dinner party.

ع-z-y

عazza **1.** to comfort, console, offer condolences. *xalli nruuع inعazzii b-wafaat ʔabuu.* Let's go console him about the death of his father. **2.** to charge, blame, upbraid, scold. *ʔard aruuع leeha w-aعazziiha عala čiᵭibha.* I want to go call her to account for her lie. || *ʔaḷḷa yعazziik عala had-dagga haay.* God will punish you for that dirty trick.

tعazza **1.** to be consoled. *tعazza min qibal iṣ-ṣadiiq wil-عadu.* He was consoled by friends and enemies both. **2.** to have trouble, bad luck. *huwwa tعazza biz-zawaaj maala.* He's had a bad time with his marriage.

عaza pl. *عazaayaat, عizyaat* **1.** wake, mourning ceremony. **2.** mourning procession, also a commemorative procession on the anniversary of a man's death.

taعazya pl. *taعaazi* religious ceremony among Shiites observing the marytrdom of Husain.

taعziya pl. *taعaazi* **1.** comfort, consolation. **2.** condolence.

muعazzi consoler, condoler, mourner.

ع-s-r

عassar **1.** to experience difficulty in giving birth. *عassirat ib-ṭifilha il-ʔawwal w-sawwoo-lha عamaliyya.* She had trouble giving birth to her first child and they operated on her. **2.** to experience trouble laying an egg. *d-dijaaja da-titعassir. laazim il-beeᵭa čbiira.* The chicken's having trouble laying. The egg must be too large.

عasir hard. *maay عasir* hard water.

ع-s-k-r

عaskar pl. *عasaakir* army.

*عaskari** military, army—, *ᵭaabuṭ عaskari* army officer.

عaskariyya military service, army.

muعaskar pl. *-aat* army camp, camp.

ع-s-l

عasal honey. || *šahr il-عasal* the honeymoon.

*عasali** honey-colored, amber, brownish. *عyuun عasaliyya* brownish eyes.

maعsuul honeyed. *kalaam maعsuul* sweet talk, honeyed words.

ع-s-y

عasa /with pronominal ending/ may, let, I hope that. *عasaahum ymuutuun.* I hope they die. *ɛasaaha b-kasr ir-rugba.* I hope she breaks her neck. *ṭilaɛ bil-barid w-masimaɛ kalaami. ɛasaa yitmarrað.* He went out in the rain and wouldn't listen to me. I hope he gets sick. *ɛasaak ib-ʔamarr min haay.* I wish you worse than that.

ɛ-š-b

ɛišib grass, pasture.

ɛ-š-r

ɛaašar to be on intimate terms with, associate closely with. *ɛaašarhum mudda laakin šaafhum muu xooš naas.* He associated with them a while but he found they were a bad lot. *ɛaašarha sana w-baɛdeen tirakha.* He lived with her for a year and then left her.

ɛušur pl. *ʔaɛšaar* one tenth, tenth part.

*ɛušri** decimal. *kasir ɛušri* decimal fraction.

ɛašra pl. *-aat* ten.

ɛašiira pl. *ɛašaayir* 1. family, kinfolk, close relatives. 2. tribe, clan. *l-ɛašaayir* the tribes. || *qaanuun il-ɛašaayir* tribal law.

ɛaašuur name for the first Moslem calendar month, Muharram.

ɛišriin twenty.

ɛaašir tenth (ordinal).

ɛ-š-š

ɛaššaš to build a nest, to nest. *l-laglag ɛaššaš ɛal-manaara.* The stork built a nest on the minaret.

ɛišš pl. *ɛšuuš* nest. *ɛišš ɛankabuut* cobweb, spider web.

ɛ-š-ɛ-š

ɛašɛaš = *ɛaššaš.* *ʔakθar iṭ-ṭiyuur itɛašɛiš bir-rabiiɛ.* Most birds build nests in the spring.

ɛ-š-g

ɛišag (*i ɛašig*) to fall passionately in love. *ɛišagha w-idzawwajha.* He fell madly in love with her and married her.

ɛisig love, passion, ardor.

ɛaašig lover.

ɛ-š-y

ɛiša (*i ɛaši*) 1. to be night-blind. *ɛiθar ib-ɛatbat il-baab il-baarɛa bil-leel liʔan yiɛši.* He tripped over the door sill last night because he has night blindness. 2. to be extremely near-sighted. *bass yinzaɛ manaaðra, yguum yiɛši.* He only has to take off his glasses, and he can't see a thing.

ɛašša 1. to give someone a dinner, invite to dinner. *bdaal-ma ɛzamitni ɛala siinama raɛ-aɛaššiik.* In exchange for your inviting me to a movie, I'm going to treat you to dinner. 2. to feed, give someone his supper. *gulii-lha tɛašši ij-jaahil w-itnayyma.* Tell her to give the child supper and put him to bed.

tɛašša to have supper, to dine. *baɛadma titɛašša, xaaburni.* After you have supper, call me.

ɛaša pl. *ɛišyaat* 1. dinner, supper. 2. evening. *ʔašuufak il-ɛaša.* I'll see you this evening.

ɛ-ṣ-b

ɛaṣṣab to wrap the head with a brow band. *l-ʔumm ɛaṣṣubat ibinha l-mariið.* The mother tied a piece of cloth around the forehead of her sick son.

tɛaṣṣab 1. to wrap one's head, wear a headband. *ʔiða ma-titɛaṣṣab, raasha yoojaɛha.* If she doesn't wear a headband, her head hurts. 2. /with *l-*/ to cling fanatically to, support fanatically or obdurately. *yitɛaṣṣibuun il-mabaadiʔ il-ɛizib.* They support the party ideology dogmatically. *yitɛaṣṣab id-diina.* He is fanatic about his religion. 3. to be bigoted, fanatic. *yitɛaṣṣab ihwaaya b-muɛaamalta lil-muwaððafiin.* He's bigoted in his treatment of the employees.

ɛaṣab pl. *ʔaɛṣaab* nerve.

*ɛaṣabi** 1. nervous, neural. *marað ɛaṣabi* a nervous disorder. 2. nervous, high-strung, excitable. *ɛṣaan ɛaṣabi* a nervous horse. 3. mad, angry, irritable, bad-tempered. *šaxiṣ ɛaṣabi* an irritable person.

ɛuṣab plastic. *mišit ɛuṣab* a plastic comb.

ɛuṣba pl. *ɛuṣab* 1. tendon, sinew. 2. headband.

ɛiṣaaba pl. *-aat* gang, band.

ɛṣaaba pl. *-aat* headband.

taɛaṣṣub 1. bigotry, prejudice. 2. fanaticism, ardent zeal.

ɛ-ṣ-d

ɛaṣiida a thick porridge made of flour, oil or butter, and sugar.

ɛ-ṣ-r

ɛiṣar (*i ɛaṣir*) 1. to squeeze, press. *ɛiṣar nuumiyya ɛaamða ɛas-simča.* He squeezed a lemon on the fish. *haaða baxiil ihwaaya. yiɛsir in-nixaala, yṭalliɛ minha dihin.* He's very stingy. He squeezes wheat husks, and gets oil from them. *da-yuɛṣur ihwaaya li-ʔan baṭna qabuð.* He is straining hard because he is constipated. *ɛisar ʔiida b-guwwa.* He clenched his fists. 2. to wring out. *ʔiɛṣir iθ-θoob w-šurra*

Ɛal-ɛabil. Wring out the shirt and hang it on the line.

Ɛaṣṣar intens. of *Ɛiṣar. la-tƐaṣṣir it-ṭamaaṭa b-iidak tara titlaf.* Don't keep squeezing all the tomatoes or they'll spoil.

Ɛaṣir pl. *Ɛuṣuur* 1. age, era, time. *l-Ɛaṣr il-ɛajari* the Stone Age. *l-Ɛaṣr il-ɛaaḏir* the present time. 2. afternoon. *l-Ɛaṣir* in the afternoon.

*Ɛaṣri** modern, recent, contemporary. *majzara Ɛaṣriyya* a modern slaughter-house.

Ɛaṣriyya pl. *-aat* afternoon.

Ɛaṣiir juice.

Ɛṣiir date pulp remaining from date molasses-making, fed to livestock.

Ɛaṣṣaara, Ɛuṣṣaara pl. *-aat* juicer, squeezer, press.

Ɛ-ṣ-ṣ

tƐaaṣaṣ to become caught in penis retentus, to get stuck together. *l-ičlaab yitƐaaṣaṣuun ʔaɛyaanan.* Dogs get stuck together sometimes.

Ɛ-ṣ-Ɛ-ṣ

tƐaaṣƐaṣ = tƐaaṣaṣ.

ƐaṣƐuuṣ pl. *ƐaṣaaƐiiṣ* 1. coccyx. 2. (an insulting term of address, approx.:) jerk.

ƐuṣƐuṣ pl. *ƐṣaaƐiṣ* coccyx.

Ɛ-ṣ-f

Ɛaaṣifa pl. *Ɛawaaṣif* storm.

Ɛ-ṣ-f-r

Ɛiṣfir safflower.

Ɛ-ṣ-f-w-r

Ɛaṣfuur pl. *Ɛaṣaafiir* 1. sparrow. 2. any small bird.

Ɛ-ṣ-m

Ɛaaṣima pl. *-aat* capital city.

maƐṣuum infallible. *ma-aku ʔaɛɛad maƐṣuum imnil-xaṭaʔ.* No one's free of error.

[1]*Ɛ-ṣ-y*

Ɛaṣṣa to become hard and fibrous. *l-fijil Ɛaṣṣa w-ma-yinkaal.* The radishes have gotten hard and can't be eaten.

Ɛaṣa, Ɛuṣṣa, Ɛaṣaaya pl. *Ɛuṣi* 1. stick. 2. blow with a stick.

[2]*Ɛ-ṣ-y*

Ɛiṣa (*i, a Ɛiṣyaan*) to disobey, resist, oppose, defy. *Ɛiṣaw ij-jinuud Ɛaḏ-ḏaabuṭ w-ma-sallmaw islaaɛhum ʔilla bil-guwwa.* The soldiers disobeyed the officer and wouldn't surrender their arms except by force. *min ijjubrak il-ɛukuuma, ma-tigdar tiƐṣi.* When the government compels you, you can't resist. *saafar il-paariis w-Ɛiṣa hnaak.* He went to Paris and stayed there stubbornly. *ʔaxaḏ iṭ-ṭooba j-jaahil w-Ɛiṣa biiha.* The child took the ball and hung on to it. *haš-šaxiṣ ma-tiƐṣa Ɛalee l-qaḏiyya ʔabadan.* That guy never gets stuck with a problem. *Ɛiṣat it-tabbaduura bil-buṭil.* The cork got stuck in the bottle.

staƐṣa 1. to be difficult, hard. *staƐṣat Ɛaleehum il-muškila w-ma-yidruun š-iysawwuun.* The problem was difficult for them and they don't know what to do. 2. to be malignant, incurable. *staƐṣa l-maraḏ.* The disease was incurable.

Ɛiṣyaan pl. *-aat* revolt, rebellion, mutiny.

Ɛaaṣi 1. in revolt, revolting. *Ɛaaṣi Ɛan il-ɛukuuma* in revolt against the government. 2. stuck. *Ɛaaṣi bil-buṭil* stuck in the bottle.

maƐṣiya pl. *maƐaaṣi* disobedience to God, sin.

*mustaƐṣi** incurable. *maraḏ mustaƐṣi* an incurable disease.

Ɛ-ḏ-b

ʔaƐḏab fem. *Ɛaḏba* pl. *Ɛuḏub, Ɛaḏbiin* 1. paralyzed in one hand or arm, having a deformed hand or arm. 2. person with a paralyzed or deformed hand or arm.

Ɛ-ḏ-d

muƐḏad pl. *maƐaaḏid* bracelet.

Ɛuḏud pl. *Ɛuḏuud* stalk of a plant.

Ɛaḏiid pl. *Ɛuḏadaaʔ* backer, supporter.

Ɛ-ḏ-ḏ

Ɛaḏḏ (*a Ɛaḏḏ*) 1. to bite. *ʔibtiƐid Ɛan ič-čalib tara yƐaḏḏak.* Stay away from the dog or he'll bite you. 2. to be sarcastic, biting. *la-tƐaḏḏ ib-ɛačyak.* Don't be caustic in your talk.

Ɛaḏḏa pl. *-aat* bite.

Ɛ-ḏ-Ɛ-ḏ

ƐaḏƐaḏ to chew, to keep biting. *ṭ-ṭifil da-yƐaḏƐaḏ b-iṣibƐi.* The baby is chewing on my finger.

Ɛ-ḏ-l

Ɛaḏala pl. *-aat* muscle.

muƐḏila pl. *-aat* puzzle, enigma, tough problem.

Ɛ-ḏ-m

Ɛaḏḏam 1. to magnify, enlarge. *Ɛaḏḏam il-muškila, w-čaanat baṣiiṭa.* He magnified the problem, but it was really nothing. *š-daƐwa Ɛaḏḏamt il-qaḏiyya!* You really blew the matter up out of all proportion! 2. to become skin and bones, become skinny, waste away. *Ɛaḏḏam jisma mnis-sill.* His body wasted away from tuberculosis.

Ɛaḏum (coll.) bone.

ʕaḏma pl. *-aat* a bone, a piece of bone.

ʕaḏama arrogance, haughtiness. || *junuun il-ʕaḏama* delusions of grandeur.

ʕaḏiim pl. *ʕuḏamaaʔ* 1. great, grand, magnificent. *qaaʕid ʕaḏiim* a great leader. *ʔintiṣaar ʕaḏiim* a great victory. 2. great, wonderful, tremendous. *sayyaara ʕaḏiima* a wonderful car. 3. great person.

ʔaʕḏam greater or greatest.

muʕḏam the majority, most of.

ʕ-ḏ-w

ʕuḏu pl. *ʔaʕḏaaʔ* 1. member, limb, organ (of the body). *ʔaʕḏaaʔ it-tanaasul* reproductive organs, genitals. 2. member (of an organization).

ʕuḏwa pl. *-aat* female member.

ʕuḏwi organic. *kiimyaaʔ ʕuḏwiyya* organic chemistry.

ʕuḏwiyya pl. *-aat* membership.

ʕ-ṭ-b

ʕaṭṭab to char, be scorched. *jurr il-xaawli min yamm in-naar. gaam iyʕaṭṭab.* Pull the towel away from the fire. It's begun to char. || *ʕaṭṭabit imnil-ʕaṭaš.* I became parched from thirst. *haj-jaahil ʕaṭṭab galbi.* That kid has driven me to distraction.

ʕaṭab pl. ʔaʕṭaab damage, defect.

ʕuṭṭaab, ʕiṭṭaab burned or charred cloth. *riiḥat ʕuṭṭaab* smell of something burning.

ʕuṭṭaaba pl. *-aat* a burning cloth, applied to the head to cauterize a head wound or to cure headache.

ʕ-ṭ-r

ʕaṭṭar to perfume, scent. *ʕaṭṭirat šaʕaarha.* She perfumed her hair.

tʕaṭṭar to perfume oneself. *l-ʕaruus da-titʕaṭṭar.* The bride is perfuming herself.

ʕiṭir pl. *ʕuṭuur* perfume, scent, essence.

ʕaṭṭaar dealer in non-perishable foodstuffs (spices, herbs, coffee, tea, soap, nuts —anything except fresh foods).

ʕ-ṭ-r-d

ʕaṭaarid (the planet) Mercury.

ʕ-ṭ-s

ʕiṭas (*a ʕaṭis*) to sneeze. *ʕiṭas lamma baawaʕ biš-šamis.* He sneezed when he looked at the sun.

ʕaṭṭas to sneeze, to sneeze a lot. *da-yʕaṭṭis ihwaaya mnin-našla.* He sneezes a lot because of his cold.

ʕaṭsa pl. *-aat* a sneeze.

ʕ-ṭ-š

ʕiṭaš (*a ʕaṭiš*) to be or become thirsty. *jiib-li swayyat mayy. ʕṭašit.* Bring me a little water. I've gotten thirsty.

ʕaṭṭaš to make thirsty. *l-ʔakil il-maaliḥ yʕaṭṭiš.* Salty food makes one thirsty.

ʕaṭša pl. *-aat* thirst.

ʕaṭšaan 1. thirsty. *ʕaṭšaan ʕala glaaṣ mayy* thirsty for a glass of water. 2. anxious, desirous, craving. *ʕaṭšaan ʕala ʔaxbaar* anxious for news.

mitʕaṭṭiš /with *ʕala* or *l-*/ avid for, craving for. *mitʕaṭṭiš ʕal-mašruub* anxious for a drink. *mitʕaṭṭiš ʕal-ʕilim* avid for knowledge. *mitʕaṭṭiš lid-damm* bloodthirsty.

ʕ-ṭ-ṭ

ʕaṭṭ (*u ʕaṭṭ*) 1. to spread, to permeate, to penetrate. *riiḥt il-buṣal itʕuṭṭ bil-maṭbax.* The odor of onions is permeating the kitchen. 2. to be permeated, penetrated, to be redolent, to reek, to smell. *sayyaartak itʕuṭṭ ib-riiḥt il-baanziin.* Your car's filled with the smell of gasoline. *l-beet itʕuṭṭ bid-duxxaan.* The house is permeated with smoke. *hiyya tʕuṭṭ bir-riiḥa.* She smells of perfume.

ʕ-ṭ-f

ʕiṭaf (*u ʕaṭuf*) to be compassionate, sympathetic. *huwwa yiʕṭuf ʕal-faqiir.* He has compassion for the unfortunate.

staʕṭaf to beseech, implore, plead with. *staʕṭaf il-waziir ʔila ʔan ʕifa ʕanna.* He pleaded with the minister until he pardoned him.

ʕaṭuf compassion, sympathy, mercy.

miʕṭaf pl. *maʕaaṭif* overcoat, topcoat.

ʔaʕṭaf more or most sympathetic, compassionate.

ʕaaṭifa pl. *ʕawaaṭif* emotion, feeling.

*ʕaaṭifi** emotional, sentimental. *qaṣiida ʕaaṭifiyya* an emotional poem. *rijjaal ʕaaṭifi* a sentimental man.

ʕ-ṭ-l

ʕiṭal (*a ʕaṭil*) 1. to tire, become tired. *ʕiṭlat ʔiida mniš-šuġul.* He became tired from the work. *ʕiṭalit imnil-maši.* I got tired walking. || *ʕiṭal ilsaani mnil-ḥači wiyyaa.* I got tired of talking with him. 2. to tire, weary, become sick and tired. *ʕiṭalna min hal-ḥarub.* We've gotten tired of this war. *ʕiṭal imnil-gaʕda.* He got tired of idleness.

ʕaṭṭal 1. to delay, interrupt, hinder, hamper. *la-tʕaṭṭilni. ʔaani mistaʕjil.* Don't delay me. I'm in a hurry. *ʕaṭṭal ʔawraaqi ʕala l-meez maala.* He held up my papers on his desk. *ʕaṭṭilaw iš-šuġul ʕala ḥsaaba.* They suspended the work on account of him. 2. to close up, close down, remain closed. *dawaaʔir il-Çukuuma tÇaṭṭil yoom ij-jumÇa.* Government offices are closed on Fridays. *l-maÇmal imÇaṭṭil ib-sabab il-ʔiδraab.* The factory is closed down because of the strike.

tÇaṭṭal 1. to be late. *ntiδirni bil-baab. ʔaani ma-raç-atÇaṭṭal.* Wait for me by the door. I won't be late. 2. to be stopped, interrupted. *kull iš-šuġuļ w-maṣaalç in-naas itÇaṭṭlat baÇd haθ-θawra.* All business and industry has been interrupted by this revolution. *kull šuġļa maaši; ma-tÇaṭṭlat-la wala qaδiyya.* His work's going well; nothing has been interrupted.

Çuṭla pl. *-aat* 1. holiday. 2. vacation, recess. *Çuṭla rabiiÇiyya* spring vacation.

Çaṭala (invar.) useless, worthless. *walad Çaṭala* a useless boy.

Çaaṭil 1. idle, inactive, unemployed, out-of-work, jobless. *makiina Çaaṭla* an idle machine. *Çummaal Çaaṭliin* idled workers, unemployed workers. 2. worthless, useless. *walad Çaaṭil* a worthless boy. || *muu Çaaṭil* not bad. *šikilha muu Çaaṭil.* She's not bad looking. *sayyaara muu Çaaṭla* not a bad car.

Ç-ṭ-w

tÇaaṭa to deal, to be engaged. *ʔiçna ma-nitÇaaṭa b-hiiči biδaaÇa.* We don't deal in such commodities. *kull ʔahla tÇaaṭuun bit-tijaara.* All his family is engaged in commerce.

staÇṭa to beg, seek alms. *l-umgaddi đa-yistaÇṭi bil-gahwa.* The beggar is begging in the coffeehouse.

Çaṭa pl. *-aayaat* 1. gift, present, reward (from God). *Çaṭa min ʔaḷḷa* a gift from God. 2. giving. || *ma-aku ʔaxiδ w-Çaṭa. s-suug waaguf.* There's no buying and selling. The market's dead. *ʔašu ma-aku ʔaxiδ w-Çaṭa beenaatna.* There doesn't seem to be any give and take between us.

Ç-f-č

Çifač 'Afaq, a city in Diwaniya Province.

*Çifčaawi** 1. from 'Afaq, a native of 'Afaq. 2. crooked, bent, twisted. *Çaṣa Çifčaawiyya* a crooked stick.

Ç-f-r-t

tÇafrat 1. to be a bully, to act tough, to act big. *yitÇafrat Çala l-muwaδδafiin, li-ʔan mitzawwij bitt il-mudiir.* He lords it over the employees because he's married to the director's daughter. 2. to be or become brave, bold. *ʔašu min jaa axuuk tÇafratit.* I see you got brave when your brother came.

Çifriit pl. *Çafaariit* 1. clever, capable. 2. brave, bold. 3. mighty, tough. 4. imp, devil, demon.

Ç-f-s

Çifas (i *Çafis*) = *Çifaṣ.*

Ç-f-ṣ (u *Çafuṣ*) 1. to wrinkle, rumple, crumple. *la-tiÇfiṣ il-waraqa.* Don't crumple the paper. *Çifaṣt iθ-θoob maali.* I wrinkled my shirt. 2. to irritate, anger. *Çifaṣni b-hač-čilma.* He irritated me with that remark.

Çaffaṣ to wrinkle, rumple, crumple. *j-jaahil Çaffaṣ il-iktaab.* The kid wrinkled the pages in the book.

tÇaffaṣ to be or become wrinkled, crumpled. *l-maktuub itÇaffaṣ ib-jeebi.* The letter got crumpled in my pocket.

Çafuṣ (coll.) gall tree(s), and gall-nut(s).

Çafṣa pl. *-aat* un. n. of *Çafuṣ.*

Ç-f-ṭ

Çifaṭ (u *Çafuṭ*) to give a raspberry, to give a Bronx cheer. *kull-ma ʔaçči, yiÇfuṭ.* Everytime I say something, he gives a Bronx cheer. *Çifaṭit-la min gaam yiçči laġwa.* I gave him a Bronx cheer when he started to talk nonsense.

Çafṭa pl. *-aat, Çfaaṭ* Bronx cheer, raspberry. || *jibta b-Çafṭa* I gave him the raspberry. *staqbiloo b-iÇfaaṭ.* They received him with Bronx cheers.

Ç-f-f

Çaff (i *Çiffa, Çafaaf*) 1. to stop, quit, give up, abstain, refrain. *ma-Çaff imnil-boog ʔila ʔan il-çukuuma fuṣlata.* He didn't quit stealing till the government fired him. *min ṣaar Çumra ÇarbaÇiin sana raaç lil-çijj w-Çaff Çan kullši.* When he turned forty he went on the pilgrimage and gave up everything. 2. /with *Çan*/ to leave alone, let alone *ma-tÇiff Çanni! xabbaḷitni.* Leave me alone, will you! You've driven me to distraction.

Çiffa 1. virtuousness, virtue, decency. 2. integrity, honesty, uprightness.

Çafiif 1. virtuous, decent, pure. *mara Çafiifa* a virtuous woman. 2. honest, upright, righteous. *muwaδδaf Çafiif* an honest official.

Ç-f-n

Çaffan 1. to rot, decay, putrefy, spoil. *libb ij-jooz Çaffan.* The nut meats rotted. 2. to be or become moldy, mildewed.

l-xubuz ʕaffan w-δabbeenaa. The bread molded and we threw it out.

ʕafin rotten, decayed, spoiled, moldy, mildewed, musty. *looz ʕafin* a spoiled almond. *beet ʕafin* a musty house.

ʕufuuna rot, decay, mildew, mold.

mʕaffin spoiled, decayed, rotten, putrid, musty, moldy, mildewed. *laḥam mʕaffin* spoiled meat. *jiθθa mʕaffna* a rotted corpse. || *mara mʕaffna* a dirty woman, a smelly woman.

ʕ-f-w

ʕifa (*i ʕafu*) **1.** to forgive, pardon. *ʔiʕfiini hal-marra. baʕad ma-asawwii.* Forgive me this time. I won't do it again. *baʕad-ma ʕtirfaw, ʕifa ʕanhum.* After they confessed, he pardoned them. *rufaq bii l-ḥaakim w-ʕifa ʕanna.* The judge took pity on him and let him off. **2.** to excuse, exempt, free, relieve. *ʕifoo mnil-ʕaskariyya li-ʔan bii sill.* They exempted him from military service because he had tuberculosis. *ʔarjuuk tiʕfiini. ma-agdar aji.* Please excuse me. I can't come. *l-mudarris ʕifaa mnil-imtiḥaan.* The teacher excused him from the examination.

ʕaafa to grant or insure health. *ʔaḷḷa yʕaafiik.* May God grant you good health (to a sick man or someone who has just eaten or drunk).

tʕaafa to recuperate, recover, regain health. *min inšaaḷḷaa, titʕaafa ndizzak il-labnaan.* When, God willing, you regain your health, we'll send you to Lebanon.

ʕafu **1.** pardon, forgiveness. **2.** amnesty. *ʕafu ʕaamm* a general amnesty. || *l-ʕafu* 1. excuse me, pardon me. 2. don't mention it, it's nothing (an answer to *ʔaškurak*).

ʕafwan = *l-ʕafu.*

ʕafya bravo! good! *ʕafya ʕaleek! išloon dabbaritha?* Bravo for you! How did you manage to do it?

ʕaafya pl. *-aat, ʕawaafi* health, good health. || *ʔalif ʕaafya* many thanks. *ʔalif ʕaafya, laakin ma-agdar ʔaakul baʕad.* Many thanks, but I can't eat any more. *hal-keeka sawweetha ʔilak. ʔalif ʕaafya.* I made this cake for you. Eat it in health. *bil-ʕaafya* in health, in good health. *haaδa qaaṭak ij-jidiid? ʔilibsa bil-ʕaafya.* Is this your new suit? Wear it in health. *qaaṭak laṭiif. tgaṭṭiʕa bil-ʕaafya.* Your suit is nice. Wear it out in good health. *bil-ʕaafya, ʔaani šabʕaan. ʔintu ʔuklu.* Thank you, I'm full. But you go ahead and eat. *ʕawaafi* = *ʔalif ʕaafya* (said especially to someone who has just had a bath.)

*maʕfi** exempt. *biḍaaʕa maʕfiyya mnir-ruṣuum il-gumrugiyya* goods exempt from customs duties. *maʕfi mnil-xidma l-ʕaskariyya* exempt from military service.

ʕ-f-y

ʕ-f-y see ʕ-f-w.

ʕ-q-b

ʕiqab (*i ʕaqib*) to follow, succeed. *ʕiqbaw waziir il-maʕaarif is-saabiq waziireen qadiireen.* Two capable ministers succeeded the former minister of education.

ʕaqqab **1.** to follow, follow up, comment. *ʕaqqab ʕala xiṭaab il-waziir ib-taʕliiq laṭiif.* He followed up the minister's speech with a nice comment. *ʕaqqab ʕal-maqaal il-iftitaaḥi ib-maqaal šadiid.* He commented on the editorial in a critical article. **2.** to follow, pursue, trail. *š-šurṭa tʕaqqibaw il-qaatil w-ma-gidraw iylizmuu.* The police followed the killer but they weren't able to catch him. *laazim itʕaqqib muʕaamalat il-paaṣpoort ib-nafsak.* You must follow through the processing of the passport yourself.

ʕaaqab to punish. *l-muʕallim ʕaaqaba li-ʔan ma-kitab darsa.* The teacher punished him because he didn't write his lesson.

tʕaaqab to be punished. *tʕaaqabit ʕala fadd šii ʔaani ma-msawwii ʔabadan.* I was punished for something I never did.

ʕaqaba pl. *-aat* obstacle, difficulty.

ʕuquuba pl. *-aat* punishment, penalty. || *ʕuquubaat ʔiqtiṣaadiyya* economic sanctions. *qaanuun il-ʕuquubaat* penal code.

taʕqiib **1.** comment, criticism. **2.** following, pursuit, following up.

ʕaaqiba pl. *ʕawaaqib* result, consequence.

muʕaqqib an expediter, who for a fee, pushes an application or the like through the bureaucracy.

ʕ-q-č

ʕiqač (*i ʕaqič*) **1.** to wrinkle, crease. *ʕiqačit is-sitra min gaʕdak.* You've wrinkled your suit sitting down. *waxxir ʔiidak. ʕiqačit yaaxt il-qamiiṣ.* Move your hand. You've wrinkled the shirt collar. **2.** to hurt, upset, crush. *ṣadiiqi ʕiqačni hwaaya min ma-daayanni fluus.* My friend crushed me when he wouldn't lend me any money. *ʕiqačit-lak-iyyaa ʕaqča zeena.* I cut him down to size.

ʕaqqač to wrinkle. *minu giʕad ʕas-*

sitra maalti w-ʕaqqačha? Who sat on my coat and wrinkled it?

tʕaqqač to be wrinkled, to wrinkle. *hal-panṭaruun ma-yitʕaqqač ib-suhuula.* These pants don't wrinkle easily.

nʕiqač to be hurt, upset. *nʕiqačit min ʕaaṭ ʕalayya.* I was hurt when he shouted at me.

ʕuqča pl. *ʕuqač* heel (of a shoe).

maʕquuč dejected.

mʕaqqač wrinkled, crumpled. *qaaṭ imʕaqqač* a wrinkled suit. *waraq imʕaqqač* crumpled paper.

ʕ-q-d

ʕiqad (i ʕaqid) **1.** to hold. *raʔiis il-ḥizib ʕiqad jalsa sirriyya lil-lajna l-markaziyya.* The party chief held a secret session of the central committee. *ʕiqdaw ijtimaaʕhum ib-baġdaad.* They held their meeting in Baghdad. *ʕiqdat il-ḥukuuma ttifaaqaat tijaariyya wiyya ʕiddat duwal.* The government concluded trade agreements with several countries. *raḥ-yiji l-qaaḍi saaʕa xamsa yiʕqid il-ʕaqid.* The judge is coming at five to formalize the contract. || *šwakit raḥ-yiʕqid ʕaleeha?* When is he going to sign the marriage contract with her?

ʕaqqad to complicate, make difficult. *leeš itʕaqqid il-muškila?* Why complicate the problem? *ʔinta da-tʕaqqid il-ʔašyaaʔ.* You're complicating things.

tʕaqqad to be or become complicated. *l-ʔumuur tʕaqqidat.* Affairs became complicated.

tʕaaqad **1.** to contract, make a contract. *l-ḥukuuma tʕaaqdat wiyya šarika ʔajnabiyya l-binaaʔ ij-jisir.* The government contracted with a foreign company for building the bridge. **2.** to agree, reach an agreement. *l-baladeen tʕaaqdaw ʕala rafʕ il-ḥawaajiz il-gumrugiyya.* The two countries agreed on lifting the customs barriers.

nʕiqad to be held. *l-muʕtamar raḥ-yinʕiqad bil-usbuuʕ il-qaadim.* The conference will be held next week.

ʕtiqad to believe. *yiʕtiqid bii kulliš.* He believes in him completely. *ʔaʕtiqid huwwa ma-raḥ-yiji l-yoom.* I think he's not going to come today.

ʕaqid pl. *ʕuquud* contract. || *ʕaqd il-qiraan* marriage contract, marriage.

ʕuqda pl. *ʕuqad* quirk, complex, problem. *ʕuqad nafsiyya* personality problems.

ʕaqiid pl. *ʕuqadaaʔ* colonel (mil.).

ʕaqiida pl. *ʕaqaaʔid* **1.** article of faith, tenet, doctrine. **2.** creed, faith, belief. **3.** superstition.

¶ *b-ʕaqiidti* according to my belief.

ʔaʕqad more or most complicated, difficult.

taʕqiid pl. *-aat* complication.

nʕiqaad holding, meeting, convening. *nʕiqaad ij-jalsa* holding the session.

ʕtiqaad pl. *-aat* **1.** belief, faith, trust, confidence, conviction. **2.** tenet, principle of faith.

muʕaqqad complicated, involved, entangled, intricate, difficult. *mawḍuuʕ muʕaqqad* a complicated subject. || *šaxiṣ muʕaqqad* a mixed-up person.

ʕ-q-r

ʕiqaar pl. *-aat* real estate, real property.

ʕiqaari: bang il-ʕiqaari real estate bank, a government supported bank which makes building loans.

ʕaaqir, ʕaaqira sterile, barren (women only). *mara ʕaaqir* a sterile woman.

ʕ-q-f

maʕquuf, etc., = *maʕkuuf,* etc., which see under *ʕ-k-f.*

ʕ-q-l

ʕiqal **1.** to be sensible, to come to one's senses, get some sense. *ʔiʕqal w-ʔismaʕ kalaam abuuk.* Be sensible and listen to what your father says. *ʔibna ʕiqal w-gaam ma-ydawwur imkassiraat.* His son came to his senses and stopped dissipating. **2.** to accept, credit, believe. *hiiči šii ma-yiʕqala ʔasxaf šaxuṣ.* The stupidest person wouldn't believe such a thing.

ʕaqqal to bring someone to his senses. *yiḍhar il-madrasa ʕaqqilata.* It appears that the school has brought him to his senses.

ʕtiqal to intern, to imprison (for political reasons). *l-ḥukuuma ʕtiqlat raʔiis il-ḥizib.* The government jailed the party boss.

ʕaqil mind, intellect, intelligence, reason, sense. || *ma-yitṣawwarha l-ʕaqil.* It's unbelievable. *jamaalha yṭayyir il-ʕaqil.* Her beauty makes one's senses reel. *ʕala gadd ʕaqla* according to his nature, in line with what he is. *daarii ʕala gadd ʕaqla.* Take him for what he is. *kull ʕaqla, b-kull ʕaqla* he's fully convinced, he sincerely believes. *hiyya kull ʕaqilha raḥ-yidzawwajha.* She firmly believes he's going to marry her. *ʔinta kull ʕaqlak ʔaqbal ib-hiiči siʕir?* Do you really believe I will accept such a price?

*ع aqli** mental. *ʔamraaδ ع aqliyya* mental disorders.

ع aqliyya mentality, mental attitude.

ع uqla pl. *-aat* horizontal bar, used in gymnastics.

ع aqlaana, and *maal ع aqlaana* sensible, dignified, serious. *libsa ع aqlaana.* He's moderate in his dress. *laabis ihduum maal ع aqlaana.* He is wearing tasteful, conservative clothes.

ع aaqlaana = *ع aqlaana.*

ʔaع qal more or more sensible.

ع aqiila pl. *-aat* wife, spouse.

maع quul 1. reasonable, sensible, rational. *jawaab maع quul* a reasonable answer. 2. plausible, comprehensible, conceivable. *maع quul yiji w-ma-ygul-li?* Is it conceivable he'd come without telling me? *ع uδur muu maع quul* an implausible excuse.

muع taqal pl. *-aat* 1. concentration camp. 2. internment camp, detention center (for political prisoners).

ع-q-m

ع aqqam to disinfect, sterilize. *ع aqqim iidak gabul-ma tgiis ij-jariح.* Disinfect your hands before you touch the wound. *ʔiδa yع aqqimuun il-ح aliib, yibqa mudda ṭwiila.* If they sterilize the milk, it keeps a long time.

tع aqqam to be sterilized, disinfected. *l-ع ubra tع aqqmat willa baع ad?* Is the needle sterilized yet?

ع aqiim 1. sterile (of men) *zoojha ع aqiim.* Her husband's sterile. 2. useless, futile, ineffectual, ineffective. *ṭuruq ع aqiima* ineffective methods.

mع aqqam sterilized, disinfected. *ʔubra mع aqqama* a sterilized needle. *ح aliib imع aqqam* sterilized milk (heated to a higher temperature and having better keeping properties than pasteurized milk.)

ع-g-b

ع igab (*u ع agub*) to pass. *ع igabtuu lil-maṭع am. ṣaar waraakum.* You passed the restaurant. It's behind you now.

ع aggab to save, leave. *da-tع aggub šii min raatbak willa laa?* Are you saving anything out of your salary or not? *ʔukul w-ع aggub-li šwayya.* Eat and save a little for me.

tع aggab 1. to stay, remain. *tع aggab li-ʔan čaan ع inda šuġul.* He remained behind because he's got work to do. *tع aggab bil-beet.* He stayed at home. 2. to be left over, be saved. *raatbi qaliil. ma-yitع aggab minna šii.* My salary's small. None of it is (ever) left over. *l-ʔakil ṭayyib. ma-yitع aggab minna šii.* The food's good. There's not going to be any of it left over.

tع aagab to pass one another, miss each other. *tع aagabna biṭ-ṭariiq w-ma-šifta.* We passed each other on the way and I didn't see him.

ع ugub after. *ع ugb il-ġada* after lunch. *ع ugb il-muġrub* after sundown. *ع ugub kull il-sawweet-lak-iyyaa, šloon tiحči ع alayya?* After all that I've done for you, how can you talk against me? || *ع ugub baačir* the day after tomorrow. *ʔašuufak ع ugub baačir.* I'll see you day after tomorrow.

ع ugub-ma (conj.) after. *ع ugub-ma xallaṣ ʔakil, tirakna.* After he finished eating, he left us.

ع ugḅa the day after tomorrow.

ع gaab pl. *ع ugbaan* eagle.

ع-g-d

ع igad (*u ع agid*) to knot, tie. *ʔugع ud il-xeeṭ ع ugidteen.* Tie two knots in the string. *ع igad il-ح ableen waaح id bil-laax.* He tied the two ropes together.

ع aggad 1. to knot, tangle. *j-jaahil liع ab bil-kubbaaba w-ع aggad il-xeeṭ.* The baby played with the ball and tangled the yarn. 2. to be or become lumpy, to coagulate. *l-ع ajiin yiع aggid ʔiδa ma-tع ijna zeen.* The dough 'll get lumpy if you don't knead it well. *δiif mayy išwayya šwayya ح atta ma-yع aggid il-liban min tumurda.* Add water gradually so the yoghurt won't get lumpy when you blend it. *l-ibnayya dyuusha tع aggid bil-itlaṭaع aš, w-baع deen tikbar.* The girl's breasts get hard at thirteen, and then enlarge.

tع aggad 1. to be or become tangled, knotted. *ʔuxδ il-xeeṭ imnil-walad gabuḷ-ma yitع aggad.* Take the string away from the boy before it gets tangled.

nع igad to be or become knotted, tied. *l-xeeṭ inع igad; ma-da-yinfakk.* The string has gotten knotted; it won't untie.

ع agid pl. *ع guud* alley, narrow street, side street. || *bil-uع guud* in the street.

ع ugda pl. *ع ugad* 1. knot. 2. knot, lump, swelling, outgrowth. 3. small bundle.

ع-g-r

ع igar (*u ع agir*) to kick (on the leg). *ع igarni min činna da-nilع ab ṭooḅa, w-hassa rijli toojaع ni.* He kicked me while we were playing ball, and now my leg hurts me.

nع igar to be kicked (on the leg). *ma-agdar ʔalع ab baačir li-ʔan inع igarit bis-*

sibaaq il-yoom. I can't play tomorrow, because I got kicked in the game today.

ʕagra pl. *-aat* kick (on the leg).

ʕ-g-r-b

ʕagrab pl. *ʕagaarub* **1.** scorpion. **2.** hand (on a clock or watch). *ʕagrab is-saaʕa* the hour hand. *ʕagrab id-daqaayiq* the minute hand.

ʕ-g-r-g

ʕugrugg (coll.) frog(s).

ʕugrugga pl. *-aat* frog.

ʕ-g-ʕ-g

ʕagʕag pl. *ʕagaaʕig* magpie.

ʕ-g-l

ʕigaḷ (*i ʕagiḷ*) to behave, to be good. *ˀiʕgaḷ tara ˀagul-la l-ˀabuuk.* Behave or I'll tell your father.

ʕaggaḷ to put a headband (and headcloth) on someone. *ˀabuu ʕaggaḷa w-waddaa lis-suug.* His father put a headband and headcloth on him and took him to the market.

tʕaggaḷ to put on one's headband. *tʕaggaḷ w-libas ʕabaata w-ṭilaʕ.* He put on an agal and his aba and went out.

ʕgaaḷ pl. *ʕuguḷ* agal, headband.

ʕaaguul **1.** a low spiny shrub found on waste land and in the desert, camel's-thorn.

ʕ-k-r

ʕakkar to make bumpy or rough, to rut. *l-ʕarabaayin ʕakkirat iš-šaariʕ.* The carts have made the road rough.

tʕakkar to be or become rough, bumpy, or rutted. *š-šaariʕ itʕakkar imnil-looriy-yaat.* The street has gotten rutted from the trucks.

ʕukra pl. *-aat, ʕukar.* **1.** bump, lump, projection. **2.** (pl. *ʕukar*) an irritating or objectionable person, a hard person to deal with, an unpleasant-looking person.

mʕakkar rough, bumpy. *šaariʕ imʕakkar* a bumpy road.

ʕ-k-z

tʕakkaz **1.** to lean, support oneself. *min kisar rijla, gaam yitʕakkaz ib-ʕikkaazteen min yimši.* Since he broke his leg, he's been walking on crutches. *hal-ˀaʕraj yitʕakkaz ʕala ʕikkaaza wiḥda.* This lame man uses one crutch. *ˀiδa txaaf toogaʕ, tʕakkaz biyya.* If you're afraid of falling, hang onto me. **2.** to lean, to depend. *ma-aku ḥaaja titʕakkaz ib-abuuk. ˀiδa ʕindak šuġuḷ, ruuḥ igδii wiḥdak.* There's no need to depend on your father. If you've got something to do, go attend to it by yourself.

ʕikkaaza pl. *-aat* **1.** crutch. **2.** staff, cane.

ʕ-k-s

ʕikas (*i ʕakis*) **1.** to reflect. *l-umraaya tiʕkis iḍ-ḍuwa.* The mirror reflects light. **2.** to reverse. *maḥkamt il-istiinaaf ʕiksat il-qaraar w-barrat il-muttaham.* The Court of Appeals reversed the decision and cleared the accused. **3.** to block, stop. *ʕikas qaḍiyyat tarfiiʕi ḥatta yraffiʕ ˀaxuu.* He blocked my promotion so as to give his brother a raise. *muu kullna nriid inruuḥ lis-siinama. la-tiʕkisha.* Look, all of us want to go to the movies. Don't screw it up.

ʕaakas to oppose, contradict. *yʕaakisni ib-kull iqtiraaḥaati.* He opposes me on all my suggestions. *kullši lli aguula, yʕaaksa.* He contradicts everything I say. **2.** to molest, tease, harass. *la-tʕaaks ij-jaahil. xallii yilʕab.* Don't tease the baby. Let him play. *l-muwaḍḍaf ij-jidiid kullhum yʕaaksuu li-ˀan saxiif.* They all harass the new official because he's stupid.

nʕikas **1.** to be reversed, inverted. *hassa l-ˀumuur inʕiksat. ˀaani l-mudiir hassa.* Now the tables are turned. I'm the director now. **2.** to be blocked, stopped. *qaḍiyyat it-tarfiiʕ nʕiksat.* The promotion was blocked. **3.** to be reflected, be mirrored. *ṣuurti nʕiksat bil-ṃayy.* My image was reflected in the water.

ʕakis **1.** opposite, contrast, contrary, reverse. *huwwa ʕaks abuu.* He's the opposite of his father. *huwwa b-ʕaksak, kulliš δaki.* He's the opposite of you, very smart. || *bil-ʕakis* on the contrary. *bil-ʕakis, sayyaarti ˀaġlab min has-sayyaara.* On the contrary, my car's more expensive than this one. *ˀaani, bil-ʕakis, ˀaḥibb asaaʕdak.* I, on the contrary, would like to help you. (*b-*)*ʕakis-ma* contrary to, opposite of. *b-ʕakis-ma dδinn, haaδa yḥibbak.* Contrary to what you think, he likes you. *sawwa ʕakis-ma gut-la.* He did the opposite of what I told him. **2.** bad luck. **3.** (pl. *ʕkuusa*) photograph.

ʕaksi inverse. *tanaasub ʕaksi* inverse proportion. || *yitnaasab tanaasub ʕaksi wiyya l-ʕumur.* It's inversely proportional to age.

ʕikis pl. *ʕkuus* **1.** elbow, elbow joint. || *ʕikis ġanam* lamb shank. **2.** elbow (plumbing and elec.).

ʕakkaas pl. *-a* photographer.

ʕakkaasa pl. *-aat* camera.

mʕaakas: xišab imʕaakas plywood.

ʕ-k-f

ʕikaf (*u ʕakuf*) to turn, bend. *ruuḥ gubaḷ w-baʕdeen uʕkuf ʕal-yimna.* Go straight ahead and then turn to the right. *ṭ-ṭariiq yuʕkuf ʕal-yimna baʕad masaafat miil.* The road turns to the right after a mile.

ʕakkaf to screw up, twist up. *latʕakkuf wiččak. hassa asawwii-lk-iyyaaha.* Don't twist up your face. I'll do it for you now.

ʕakfa pl. *-aat* turn bend (in a road).

maʕkuuf: ṣaliib maʕkuuf swastika.

ʕ-k-m

ʕakkaam pl. *-a* man who makes all arrangements and leads groups of pilgrims to Mecca.

ʕ-l-b

ʕallab to can, tin. *hal-maʕmal yʕallib mišmiš w-xoox bass.* This factory cans apricots and peaches only.

ʕilba pl. *ʕilab* wooden container, flat and round, used mostly for storing yoghurt. *liban ʕilba* a type of yoghurt, made and stored in an *ʕilba.*

taʕliib canning. *maʕmal taʕliib* canning factory.

muʕallab canned, packaged. *jibin muʕallab* packaged cheese. *fawaakih muʕallaba* canned fruit. *muʕallabaat* canned goods.

ʕilbaa (no pl.) nape, scruff of the neck. *ðirabta ʕijil ʕala ʕilbaata.* I hit him a whack on the back of his neck.

ʕilba (no pl.) **1.** = *ʕilbaa.* **2.** jowl, side of the jaw.

[1]ʕ-l-j

ʕaalaj **1.** to treat (a patient, a disease, or a subject). *ʕaalaja ṭ-ṭabiib muddat isbuuʕeen.* The doctor treated him for two weeks. *yʕaalij in-našla bil-wiski.* He treats a cold with whisky. *laazim itʕaalij il-mawðuuʕ ib-fadd ṣuura maʕquula.* You should treat the subject in a reasonable manner. **2.** to undergo death throes, to be in the last agony. *ma-maat. baʕda da-yʕaalij.* He didn't die. He's still in his last agony.

muʕaalaja pl. *-aat* treatment.

ʕilaaj pl. *-aat* **1.** treatment. **2.** cure.

[2]ʕ-l-j

ʕaliija feedbag.

ʕ-l-č

ʕilač (*i ʕalič*) to chew (gum). *yiʕlič baʕad kull wajbat ʔakil.* He chews gum after every meal.

ʕallač to talk as if chewing gum, to talk from the corner of one's mouth. *har-rijjaal yʕallič ib-ḥačya.* That man distorts his speech.

tʕallač to be or become chewy. *hannooga titʕallač bil-ḥalag.* This nougat becomes chewy in the mouth.

ʕilič gum, chewing gum.

*ʕillaači** chewy. *tamur ʕillaači* chewy dates. *ḥalquum ʕillaači* chewy Turkish delight.

ʕ-l-s

ʕilas (*i ʕalis*) to chew. *ʔiʕlis il-xubza zeen gabuḷ-ma tiblaʕha.* Chew the bread well before you swallow it. *j-jaahil dayiʕlis ib-θooba.* The kid is chewing on his shirt. **2.** to pigeonhole, postpone action indefinitely. *ʔašu ṣaaḥbak ʕilasha lil-qaðiyya.* It seems your friend has decided to forget about the matter.

ʕ-l-f

ʕilaf (*i ʕalif*) to feed. *ʔiʕlif il-xeel gabuḷ-ma ṭalliʕha.* Feed the horses before you take them out.

ʕalaf feed, fodder, provender.

maʕlaf pl. *mʕaalif* manger, feeding trough, feeding place, feeding area. || *yḥaððir il-maʕlaf gabḷ il-iḥṣaan.* He puts the cart before the horse. (lit., he prepares the manger before he has a horse).

ʕ-l-q

ʕilaq (*a ʕaliq*) to stick. *l-fikra ʕilqat ib-ðihni.* The idea stuck in my mind.

ʕallaq to comment, make comments. *maḥḥad ʕallaq ʕal-xiṭaab maala.* Nobody made any comment on his speech.

tʕallaq **1.** to be attached, devoted, fond. *huwwa mitʕallaq ib-ʔumma hwaaya.* He's very attached to his mother. **2.** to depend, be dependent. *duxuuli j-jaamiʕa mitʕalliq ʕal-qabuul.* My entrance into college depends on acceptance. *qaðiiti mitʕalliqa b-qaðiitak.* My case is dependent on your case.

ʕilaaqa pl. *-aat* **1.** relationship, association. **2.** connection, relevance.

taʕliiq remark(s), comment, commentary.

muʕalliq commentator (radio and press).

muʕallaq **1.** suspended, hanging. || *jisir muʕallaq* suspension bridge. **2.** pending, in abeyance, undecided. *qaðiita muʕallaqa.* His case is pending.

ʕ-l-g

ʕilag (*i ʕalig*) to light, ignite, set on fire. *haak iš-šixxaaṭa w-iʕlig il-ḥaṭab.* Take the matches and light the firewood. || *djaadlaw išwaaya w-baعdeen عilgat beenaathum.* They argued a little and then really got mad at each other.

عallag 1. to hang, suspend, attach, fasten. *عallag sitirta bil-bismaar.* He hung his coat on the nail. *عallag ṣuurta yamm ṣuurat ʔabuu.* He hung his picture next to his father's picture. || *ʔiδa tuktilha, yعallguuk.* If you kill her, they'll hang you. 2. to flee, escape, run away. *ʔaxaδ il-ifluus w-عallag.* He took the money and beat it.

عalag (coll.) larva(e) of mosquito.

عalga pl. *-aat* un. n. of *عalag.*

عilga pl. *-aat* tinder, kindling.

عillaaga pl. *-aat* 1. basket. 2. coat hanger.

tiعlaaga pl. *-aat* coat hanger, hanger.

miعlaag pl. *mعaaliig* 1. liver (as food). 2. liver, heart, lungs and windpipe.

ع-l-l

عallal to justify, explain. *š-itعallil عadam raġibta bis-safar?* What reason can you give for his aversion to travel?

tعallal to gather in the evening for socializing. *raح-nitعallal ib-beet ṣadiiqi.* We will spend the evening after dinner at my friend's house.

عilla pl. *-aat* defect, fault, deficiency. || *عilla b-galbak!* Damn you! *عilla b-gaḷub عaduwwak!* Long life to you! || *عala عillaat* /plus pronominal suffix/ at face value, as is. *ʔaxaδ ij-jawaab عala عillaata.* He accepted the answer at face value. *ʔaqbal il-makiina عala عillaatha.* I'll accept the machine as is.

عaliil 1. sick, ill, ailing, weak. 2. sick person.

taعluula pl. *-aat.* 1. a social gathering after the evening meal. 2. the period after the evening meal, when friends normally gather.

ع-l-m

عilam (*a عalim*) to know. *ʔaḷḷa yiعlam šgadd ʔaani aحibbak.* God knows how I love you. || *yiعlam bil-ġeeb.* He's clairvoyant.

عallam 1. to teach, instruct. *huwwa عallamni ʔarkab paaysikil.* He taught me to ride a bike. 2. to mark, designate. *عallim iṣ-ṣanaadiig illi truuح il-baṣra.* Put a mark on the boxes going to Basra.

tعallam to learn, study. *ween tعallamit ifransi?* Where'd you learn French?

staعlam to inquire, ask. *xal-nistaعlim عanna.* Let's inquire about him.

عilim 1. information, knowledge. 2. (pl. *عuluum*) science.

*عilmi** scientific. *ṭariiqa عilmiyya* scientific method.

عalam pl. *ʔaعlaam* 1. flag, banner. 2. dignitary, luminary, authority.

عaalam 1. world. 2. people. 3. (pl. *عillaam, عulama*) religious authority.

*عaalami** world (adj.). *baṭal عaalami* a world champion. *l-maعraδ il-عaalami* the World's Fair.

عallaama (invar.) expert, authority, learned man. *عallaama bir-riyaaδiyyaat* an expert in mathematics.

عalaama pl. *-aat, عalaaʔim* mark. *عalaama faariqa* a distinguishing mark. *عalaama musajjala* registered trade mark. *عalaamat istifihaam* question mark.

maعaalim (pl. only) sights, curiosities.

stiعlaam pl. *-aat* inquiry. *maktab il-istiعlaamaat* information desk.

عaalim pl. *عulamaaʔ* scholar, scientist. *عulamaaʔ id-diin* the religious authorities.

ʔaعlam more or most knowledgeable, learned.

maعluum 1. known, acknowledged, accepted. *šii maعluum* a known fact. || *ma-maعluum* unknown, uncertain, undecided. *baعad ma-maعluum šwakit ʔaruuح.* It's still undecided when I'll go. *ma-maعluum išwakit yiji.* Nobody knows what time he'll come. 2. (an affirmative reply) of course! naturally! certainly! sure! 3. (pl. only) *maعluumaat* data, information.

muعallim teacher, instructor.

mعallim functionary of the Jewish religion, one of whose chief functions is overseeing the slaughtering of animals.

ع-l-n

عilan (*i عalin*) 1. to announce, disclose, declare. *raح-niعlin ʔasmaaʔ il-faaʔiziin bij-jariida wir-raadyo.* We'll announce the winners' names in the newspapers and on the radio. || *hal-balad raح-yiعlin il-حarub عaleena.* That country will declare war on us. 2. to advertise, publicize, proclaim. *عilnaw bij-jariida عan muntajaathum.* They advertised their products in the newspaper.

عalanan openly, overtly, publicly. *gaalha عalanan w-ma-stiحa.* He said it openly and wasn't ashamed.

*عalani** public, open. *mazaad عalani* public auction. *jalsa عalaniyya* open session.

ʔiعlaan pl. *-aat* 1. notice, statement.

lawڝat il-iعlaanaat bulletin board. 2. advertisement, ad.

ع-l-w

عilu, عalwa, etc., see ع-l-y.

ع-l-w-w-a

عalawwaa (exclamation of hope, approx.:) it would be good if, it would be nice if, I wish, I hope. عalawwaa tiji wiyyaaya. Wish you were coming with me!

ع-l-y

عila (a عilu) to rise, ascend. šuuf iṭ-ṭiyyaara da-tiعla. Look at the airplane climbing. šuuf il-binaaya šloon da-tiعla yoom عala yoom. Notice how the building's getting higher every day. kull-ma tiعla darajta, yitkabbar ʔazyad. The higher his position gets, the more supercilious he gets. 2. to rise, get high (sound, in pitch and volume). عissak عila hwaaya. j-jiiraan raڝ-yinzaعjuun. You've raised your voice too much. The neighbors will be annoyed.

عalla 1. to raise. عalli ʔiidak išwayya ڝatta ʔanuuš. Raise your hand a little so I can reach you. عalli ڝissak; ma-da-ʔasmaع. Raise your voice; I can't hear. 2. to render ritually clean by dipping three times in clear water. ʔiġsil il-maaعuun w-عallii. č-čalib ʔakal bii. Wash the dish and make it ritually clean. The dog ate out of it.

tعalla 1. to be raised, lifted, kursi il-ڝallaaq šloon yitعalla? How's the barber's chair raised? 2. to be ritually cleansed. kull hal-imwaaعiin laazim titعalla gabuḷ ma yitxalla biiha ʔakil. All these dishes have to be ritually cleansed before food is put in them.

taعaal. taعaali. taعaalu see t-ع-l and ʔ-j-y.

عilu 1. height. šgadd عilu in-naxḷa? How high is the palm tree? 2. level, volume (of a sound).

عalwa pl. عalaawi 1. a high place. 2. a farmers' market, where farmers and grain merchants bring their goods for wholesale marketing.

عalawči pl. -iyya proprietor of a farmers' market.

عalwa.

عala 1. on, upon, on top of. عal-meez on the table. waaڝid عal-laax one on top of the other. sajjilha عala ڝsaabi. Put it on my bill. || عala عeeni, عala raasi, عala عeeni w-raasi, عal-عeen wir-raas. Gladly, with pleasure. عal-aḷḷa. Not bad (an answer to šloonak?). 2. about, on, concerning. čiča عal-mawðuuع saaعa. He

talked about the subject for an hour. || ʔaani š-aعlayya baعad? What concern of mine is it then? What's it to me then? Why should I care then? عala ڝsaab on account of, on behalf of. hat-tanaqqulaat عala ڝsaab ʔibn il-waziir. These transfers are on behalf of the minister's son. عala šaraf in honor of. عala šaraf ṣadiiqa in his friend's honor. 3. for, over, about. ymuut عat-tiffaaع. He's crazy about apples. maعinda maaniع yuktul عala filis. He wouldn't mind killing for a fils. || la-šukra عala waajib. Don't bother to thank me. عala daqiiqa baعad čaan ʔaġuḷba. With one more minute, I'd have beaten him. 4. against. sajjal šakiyya عalee bil-maڝkama. He filed a complaint against him in court. yičči عaleek ib-ġiyaabak. He talks about you behind your back. yičči عarraayiڝ wij-jaay. He talks everybody down. 5. in accordance with, according to, by. kullši ṣaar عal-maraam. Everything went as desired. kull taṣarrufaata عal-ʔuṣuul. All his actions are as they should be. عala goolak il-qaðiyya xalṣaana bass lissa bayyan šii. By your account the matter's finished, but nothing's appeared so far. || عala ʔan provided that, providing. waafaq yistiriiha عala ʔan yinṭuu taxfiið xamsa bil-miyya. He agreed to buy it providing they gave him a five percent discount. عala kull ڝaal at any rate, anyhow, anyway. عala kull ڝaal, xalninsaaha. At any rate, let's forget it. عala lli = عala ma. عala-ma /plus following verb/ as, according to what, from what. عala-ma dguul, ma-nigdar insawwiiha. From what you say, we can't do it. عala-ma aعruf, ma-aعtiqid il-qaðiyya raڝitṣiir. According to what I know, I don't think that will come about. عala-ma yiðhar evidently, as it appears. عala-ma yiðhar, ma-raڝ-yisawwuuha. Evidently, they're not going to do it.

ʔaعla more or most elevated, etc.

عaali f. and pl. عaalya 1. high, tall, elevated. šijra عaalya a tall tree. mukaan عaali a high place. 2. (by extension) high, inflated. ʔasعaar عaalya high prices. || hat-taajir yuðrub bil-عaali. That merchant charges high prices. ma-aku عaaja tiðrub bil-عaali. yaعni ʔilla tirkub ib-kaadlaak? There's no need to demand the best. Do you have to ride in a Cadillac? 3. high, strong. hawa عaali a high wind. ðaġiṭ عaali high pressure. 4. high. manaaṣib عaalya high positions. ruṭba *ɛaalya* high rank. *darajaat ɛaalya* high grades. || *ð̣-ð̣aɛa l-ɛaali* late forenoon (around 11 a.m.).

ɛaal /invar./ **1.** excellent, first-class, outstanding, of top quality. *qmaaš ɛaal* top quality cloth. || *ɛaal il-ɛaal* the very best, the finest, the highest quality. **2.** (exclamation) excellent! fine! very good!

ɛ-m-b

ɛamḅa (coll.) pickled mangoes, mango pickles.

ɛamḅaaya pl. *-aat* un. n. of *ɛamḅa.*

ɛ-m-b-r

ɛambar, var. of *ɛanbar,* which see under *ɛ-n-b-r.*

ɛ-m-d

ɛammad to baptize, christen. *yuɛanna l-muɛammidaan ɛammad il-masiiɛ.* John the Baptist baptized Christ.

tɛammad **1.** to intend, to do on purpose, to do intentionally. *tɛammad yguulha giddaama.* He intentionally said it in front of him. *tɛammad w-rassab nafsa ɛatta yiṭlaɛ imnil-madrasa.* He acted intentionally to flunk himself to get out of school. **2.** to be baptized. *j-jaahil itɛammad isbuuɛ il-faat.* The baby was baptized last week.

ɛtimad to rely, depend. *ˀagdar ˀaɛtimid ɛalee ib-hal-qað̣iyya.* I can depend on him in this case.

ɛamiid pl. *ɛumadaaˀ* **1.** dean. *ɛamiid il-kulliyya* dean of the college. *ɛamiid is-silk is-siyaasi* dean of the diplomatic corps. **2.** military rank, approx.: general.

ɛamid: ɛan ɛamid on purpose, intentionally, deliberately. *ma-sawwaaha ɛan ɛamid.* He didn't do it on purpose.

ɛamdan intentionally, deliberately. *sawwaaha ɛamdan ɛatta yˀaððiini.* He did it on purpose to hurt me.

*ɛamdi** **1.** intentional, deliberate. *šii ɛamdi* something intentional. **2.** premeditated, willful. *qatil ɛamdi* willful murder.

ɛamuud pl. *ɛawaamiid* **1.** post. **2.** pole (esp. electric or telephone). **3.** (newspaper or magazine) column.

¶ *l-ɛamuud il-faqari* the spinal column.

*ɛamuudi** vertical, perpendicular, upright. *dinga ɛamuudiyya* an upright column. || *ṭiyyaara ɛamuudiyya* helicopter.

ɛtimaad reliance, dependence, confidence, trust. || *l-iɛtimaad ɛan-nafis* self-reliance. *ˀawraaq il-iɛtimaad* credentials (of diplomats).

ɛ-m-r

ɛumar(u) **1.** to thrive, prosper. *ɛumar beetak, inšaaḷḷa.* May your household be prosperous! (said by a guest when leaving. A common answer is: *ˀaḷḷa yɛufð̣ak.* God keep you.) **2.** to be or become populated, built up. *hal-manṭiqa ɛumrat, w-ṣaarat biiha byuut w-madaaris.* This area has been developed, and acquired houses and schools.

ɛammar **1.** to repair, overhaul, restore, refurbish, rebuild. *raɛ-aɛammur il-beet isbuuɛ ij-jaay.* I'm going to have the house repaired next week. *štireet has-sayyaara rxiiṣ, w-ɛammaritha.* I bought this car cheap, and repaired it. **2.** to build up, develop. *l-ɛukuuma binat sadda hnaa w-ɛammrat il-manṭiqa kullha.* The government built a dam here and developed the whole area. **3.** to prepare, arrange, set up. *baḷḷa ma-tɛammir-li n-nargiila?* Would you please fix the narghile for me? *ɛammir-li fadd peek nafiis.* Fix me a real good drink.

tɛammar **1.** to be repaired, rebuilt, renovated. *l-beet itɛammar marteen has-sana.* The house has been fixed twice this year. **2.** to be built. *has-sana hwaaya byuut itɛammrat ib-hal-imɛalla.* A lot of houses have been built in this neighborhood this year. **3.** to be developed, built up. *kull hal-manṭiqa raɛ-titɛammar.* All this area will be developed.

staɛmar **1.** to hold as a colony, exploit. *l-ˀingiliiz staɛmiraw il-hind mudda ṭuwiila.* The British dominated India for a long time. **2.** to make into a colony. *d-duwal il-kubra staɛmirat š-šarq il-ˀawṣat baɛd il-ɛarub.* The Great Powers turned the Middle East into colonies after the war.

ɛumur pl. *ˀaɛmaar* **1.** life, lifetime, life span. || *ɛumri* (a term of endearment, approx.:) dear. *l-ˀaɛmaar ib-ˀiid ˀaḷḷa.* I'll take my chances. **2.** age (of a person).

ɛimaara pl. *-aat* building, edifice, structure.

ɛumraan **1.** development, building. *ɛarakt il-ɛumraan* construction activity. **2.** built-up area.

¶ *ˀuṣṭa ɛumraan* a variety of fresh dates.

*ɛumraani** development, construction. *mašaariiɛ il-ɛumraaniyya* development projects.

ɛammaar pl. *-a* designer, builder.

ɛammaariyya pl. *-aat* a frame of palm

stalks, in which a thorny shrub, *ʕaaguul,* is compressed, and soaked to provide a rudimentary air cooler and humidifier.

ʔaʕmar more or most populous, developed.

miʕmaar builder, contractor, designer.

*miʕmaari** 1. architectural, structural, building. || *muhandis miʕmaari* architect. 2. (pl. *-iyya*) architect.

taʕmiir repair, overhaul. *maḥall taʕmiir sayyaaraat* an auto repair shop.

stiʕmaar 1. colonialism, imperialism. 2. imperialistic exploitation. 3. establishment of imperialistic control.

*stiʕmaari** imperialist, imperialistic. *ʔaġraaḏ istiʕmaariyya* imperialist intentions.

ʕaamir 1. built-up. *manṭiqa ʕaamra* a built-up area. 2. well-stocked, well-furnished. *maktaba ʕaamra* a well-furnished library. *baar ʕaamra* a well-stocked bar. || *jeeba ʕaamir.* He's loaded. He's flush. 3. lively, enjoyable, pleasant. *leela ʕaamra* an enjoyable evening.

mustaʕmir colonialist, imperialist.

mustaʕmara pl. *-aat* colony, settlement.

ʕ-m-š

ʔaʕmaš fem. *ʕamša* pl. *ʕimiš, ʕamšiin* 1. myopic, squint-eyed. 2. myopic or squint-eyed person.

ʕ-m-q

ʕumuq pl. *ʔaʕmaaq* 1. depth, deepness. 2. depth, profoundness, profundity. 3. bottom (of river, sea).

ʕamiiq 1. deep. *nahar ʕamiiq* a deep river. 2. deep, profound. *tafkiir ʕamiiq* profound thought.

ʕ-m-l

ʕimal (*a ʕamal*) to pull a prank, to do something bad. *ʕimal ʕamla čibiira w-ṭardoo mnil-ʕašiira.* He did something very bad and they threw him out of the tribe. *ʕimalha biyya.* He did me a dirty deed. He fouled me up.

ʕammal 1. to work, be effective, give results. *l-baṣuṭ ma-yʕammil bii.* Beating doesn't work with him. 2. to fester, be or become infected. *j-jariḥ ʕammal.* The wound became infected.

ʕaamal 1. to treat, handle, deal with. *ʕaamalni muʕaamala laṭiifa.* He treated me well. 2. to bargain with, haggle with. *ʕaamalta laakin ma-nazzal is-siʕir.* I bargained with him but he didn't lower the price.

tʕaamal 1. to deal, trade. *ʔiḥna ma-nitʕaamal wiyya haš-šarika.* We don't deal with this company. 2. to bargain, haggle. *ṣaaḥib had-dukkaan ʔabadan ma-yitʕaamal.* The owner of this store never bargains.

staʕmal to use, employ, utilize. *štireet šamsiyya bass baʕad ma-staʕmalitha.* I bought an umbrella but I haven't used it yet.

ʕamal 1. work, employment. 2. (pl. *ʔaʕmaal*) act, action. 3. bowel movement.

*ʕamali** practical. *ḥall ʕamali* a practical solution.

ʕamaliyya pl. *-aat* 1. operation, process. 2. operation (med.). || *ġurfat il-ʕamaliyyaat* operating room.

ʕumla pl. *-aat* currency, cash, money.

ʕimla bargaining, haggling.

ʕamiil pl. *ʕumalaaʔ* agent, hireling, lackey. *ʕamiil istiʕmaar* an agent of imperialism.

maʕmiil pl. *maʕaamiil* customer.

ʕumuula pl. *-aat* commission, brokerage.

ʕammaal pl. *-a* bricklayer's helper, builder's helper.

ʕammaala (invar.) 1. bricklayer's helper, builder's helper. 2. road worker.

*ʕummaali** labor (adj.). *nasaaṭ ʕummaali* labor activity.

maʕmal pl. *maʕaamil* factory, mill, plant, works. || *maʕmal il-ʔalbaan* dairy.

muʕaamala 1. behavior, conduct. *muʕaamalta lin-naas ṭayyba.* He treats people well. 2. (pl. *-aat*) business dealings. 3. matter, affair, case.

¶ *bil-muʕaamala* in the works.

stiʕmaal 1. use, usage. 2. operation, handling.

¶ *lastiik istiʕmaal* prophylactic, condom.

ʕaamil pl. *ʕawaamil* 1. factor, element. || *ʕaamil musaaʕid* catalyst (chem.). 2. (pl. *ʕummaal*) laborer, worker.

maʕmuul manufactured, made. || *maʕmuul bii* effective, valid, in force, in effect. *l-qaanuun maʕmuul bii b-jamiiʕ ʔanḥaaʔ il-balad.* The law is effective in all sections of the country.

ʕ-m-l-q

ʕimlaaq pl. *ʕamaaliqa* 1. gigantic, huge. 2. giant.

ʕ-m-m

ʕamm (*i ʕamm*) 1. to be or become general, common, prevalent, to prevail. *b-zaman il-ḥarub l-ġalaaʔ ʕamm ib-kull il-balad.* During the war high prices prevailed in the whole country. 2. to cause trouble, inconvenience. *b-ḏiḥiktak biṣ-ṣaff ʕammeet ʕaleena w-xalleet il-mu-*

εallim yizεal. By your laughter in class you have caused us all trouble and made the teacher mad. *mitʔassif, ʔaani εammeet εaleek w-iεramtak imnir-rawaaε lis-siinama.* I'm sorry I caused you trouble and deprived you of going to the movie.

εammam **1.** to make generally known, to make universally known and applicable. *εammim hal-bayaan εal-imwaδδafiin.* Circulate this notice to the employees. *l-mudiir il-εaamm εammam il-ʔamur εala jamiiε iš-šuεab.* The director general made the order applicable to all the sections. **2.** to put a turban on someone. *εammam ibna w-axaδa wyaa lij-jaamiε.* He put a turban on his son and took him with him to the mosque.

εamm pl. *εmaam, εmuuma.* father's brother, paternal uncle. *ʔibn il-εamm* cousin (on the father's side). *bint il-εamm* female cousin (on the father's side). **2.** (by extension) father-in-law.

εammu (term of address) **1.** = *εammi* my uncle, uncle. **2.** (to a friend or a youngster, approx.:) buddy, pal.

εamma pl. *-aat* paternal aunt.

εumuum **1.** whole, totality, aggregate. *εal-εumuum* on the whole, in general. **2.** *l-εumuum* the public, the people.

*εumuumi** public. *talafoon εumuumi* a public telephone.

εmaama pl. *-aat, εmaayim* turban.

εaamm **1.** public. *r-raʔi l-εaamm* public opinion. **2.** general. *mudiir εaamm* director general.

εaamma the masses, the people. *εaammat in-naas* the populace.

εaammi pl. *εawaamm* **1.** common man, ordinary person, man in the street. **2.** ordinary citizen (without official position).

*εaammi** colloquial. *εiraaqi εaammi* colloquial Iraqi. *l-luġa l-εaammiyya* the colloquial language.

l-εaammiyya colloquial, the colloquial language.

taεmiim circulation, distribution, dissemination.

mεammam turbaned man, i.e., a religious functionary.

ε-m-y

εima (i, a εami) **1.** to go blind. *nṣaab bit-tiraaxooma w-baεdeen εima.* He was attacked by trachoma and later went blind. || *εimat iεyuunha mnil-bači.* She cried her heart out. **2.** to be dulled, become dull. *l-minšaar čaan kulliš εaad, w-staεmalta hwaaya w-εima.* The saw was very sharp, but I used it a lot, and it got dull. **3.** (*i*) to blind. *b-zamaan il-qadiim čaanaw yiεmuun il-mujrimiin.* In olden times they used to blind criminals. *haδ-δuwa l-qawi εima εyuuni l-muddat daqiiqa wiεda.* That strong light blinded me for a minute. **4.** to dull. *j-jaahil εima s-siččiina.* The kid dulled the knife.

nεima to be blinded. *εtirag išwayya bin-ṇaar w-inεimat iεyuuna.* He got burned somewhat in the fire and was blinded.

εima blindness. *εima b-galḅak!* Go to hell! *εima b-ṭiiza!* To hell with him!

ʔaεmi, ʔaεma f. *εamya* pl. *εimi, εimyaan, εimyiin* **1.** blind. *mgaddi ʔaεmi* a blind beggar. **2.** blind person. **3.** dull. *šiččiina εamya* a dull knife.

¶ *haj-jaahil ʔaεmi l-galuḅ. l-madrasa ma-tfiida.* That kid is stupid. School won't do him any good.

ε-n

εan **1.** from, away from, off. *ʔugεud ibεiid εan in-naar.* Sit a long way from the fire. *gaεεid ij-jaahil bil-fayy εan iš-šamis.* Put the baby in the shade away from the sun. *la-tixruj εan il-mawδuuε.* Don't get off the subject. **2.** against, as protection from. *šaayil εiriz εan il-εeen.* He carries a talisman against the evil eye. *laabis manaaδir εan iš-šamis.* He's wearing glasses as protection from the sun. **3.** about, on. *yiεči εannak daaʔiman.* He always talks about you. *qreet maqaal εan hal-mawδuuε.* I read an article on this subject. **4.** for, per. *naaxuδ diinaar εan kull nafar.* We charge a dinar for each person. *laazim tidfaε filseen εan kull yoom ʔiδa ma-trajjiε l-iktaab bil-wakit.* You have to pay 2 fils for each day, if you don't return the book on time. **5.** out of, due to. *gal-lak biiha εan ixlaaṣ.* I told you about it out of sincere concern. *sawwaaha εan raġba.* He did it willingly. **6.** for, in behalf of. *difaεit εanna qisṭ is-sayyaara.* I payed the installment on the car for him. *wazzεaw ifluus εal-fuqaraaʔ εan ruuε il-marεuum.* They distributed money to the poor for the soul of the deceased. **7.** after, on, upon. *yoom εan yoom dayisman.* Day after day he's getting fatter. *sana εan sana da-yṣiir zangiin.* Year after year he gets richer.

¶ *εan ṭariiq* via, by way of, through. *raaε il-baṣra εan ṭariiq il-kuut.* He went to Basra by way of Kut. *tεarrafit εalee ʕan ṭariiq ʕali.* I met him through Ali.

ʕ-n-b

ʕinab (coll.) grape(s).

ʕinbaaya pl. *-aat* grape. || *ʕinab iθ-θaʕlab* black nightshade (bot.).

ʕinnaab (coll.) **1.** jujube(s) (bot.). **2.** (its fruit) jujube(s).

ʕinnaaba pl. *-aat* **1.** un. n. of *ʕinnaab.* **2.** clitoris.

[1]*ʕ-n-b-r*

ʕanbar ambergris. || *ḥuut il-ʕanbar* sperm whale. *timman ʕanbar* a variety of rice of good quality (with a distinctive odor to it).

[2]*ʕ-n-b-r*

ʕanbar pl. *ʕanaabir* warehouse, storehouse.

ʕunbaar pl. *-aat* = *ʕanbar.*

ʕ-n-t-r

ʕantar to become distended, to become erected (of the penis, vulgar).

ʕantar Antar, a heroic historical figure and writer, and by extension, a hero, a strong man.

ʕantiriyya pl. *-aat* boastful promises, boastful threats, big talk.

ʕ-n-t-k

tʕantak to show off, to act up. *la-titʕantak wiyyaaya, tara ʔaʔaδδiik.* Don't get funny with me or you'll be sorry. *l-baarḥa xašš ʕal-mudiir w-itʕantak ib-raasa ʔila ʔan zaʕʕala.* Yesterday he went in to see the director and gave him a hard time until he made him mad. *ʔaani ʔaʕruf luweeš da-yitʕantak ib-raaskum.* I know why he is being critical and acting superior toward you.

ʕantiika pl. *-aat.* **1.** unusual, strange, rare. *warid ʕantiika* rare flowers. *čalib ʕantiika* an unusual dog. **2.** odd, peculiar, eccentric, funny. *walad ʕantiika* a funny guy. **3.** (pl. *-aat, ʕanaatiik*) antique. **4.** old hand, experienced person, wise old man.

ʕ-n-j-r

ʕanjar to beat, beat up. *ʕanjiroo mnil-baṣiṭ.* They beat him black and blue.

tʕanjar to be beaten, beaten up. *tʕanjar ʕanjara zeena.* He really got his lumps.

ʕanjuur (coll.) **1.** small, unripe melon(s). **2.** small, unripe apricot(s).

ʕanjuura pl. *-aat* un. n. of *ʕanjuur.*

ʕunjurra pl. *-aat* lump, swelling (from a blow, esp. on the head).

mʕanjir **1.** hard to get along with. **2.** person who is hard to get along with.

mʕanjar **1.** beaten, beaten up. **2.** person who has been beaten up.

ʕ-n-j-ṣ

ʕinjaaṣ (coll.) plum(s). || *ʕinjaaṣ imyabbis* prune(s).

ʕinjaaṣa pl. *-aat* un. n. of *ʕinjaaṣ.*

ʕ-n-d

ʕaanad **1.** to disobey, resist, oppose. *la-tʕaanid ʔabuuk w-ʔummak.* Don't disobey your father and mother. **2.** to be or become stubborn, to insist. *ʕaanad w-ma-qibal yruuḥ.* He got stubborn and wouldn't go. *ʕaanad ʔilla yruuḥ lis-siinama.* He insisted on going to the movies.

tʕaanad to disagree (stubbornly). *tʕaandaw ʕala fadd šii taafih.* They got stubborn with each other over a trivial thing.

ʕind /before vowel/, *ʕid-* /before cons./ at, near, by, with. *ʕind il-ḥallaaq* at the barber's. *baatat ʕidna.* She stayed overnight with us. || *ʕind il-imtiḥaan, yukram il-marʔ aw yuhaan.* When it comes to the test, you'll come through or catch hell. *ʕind il-ḥaaja, ʕind iδ-δaruura* in case of need, in an emergency. *ʕind il-ḥaaja, ṭalliʕ ifluusak imnil-bang.* If you need to, draw your money out of the bank. *ʔiδa tiḥtaaj ifluus, ʔaani ʕindak.* If you need any money, I'm at your service. **2.** /plus pronominal suffix, signifies possession:/ *ʕindak qalam zaayid?* Do you have an extra pencil? *ma-ʕindi šii muhimm.* I don't have anything important (to say, discuss, bring up, etc.). || *taʕaalu ʕidna baačir.* Come to our place tomorrow. *hassa jeet min ʕidhum.* I just now came from their house. *min ʕind* from, of. *ʔaxaδt il-iktaab min ʕinda.* I got the book from him. *w-haaδa diinaar min ʕindi.* And here's a dinar from me. *haaδa čaan taṣarruf ʔaḥmaq min ʕinda.* That was foolish of him. *min ʕind il-garaayib, yitṣaʕʕab.* When it comes to his relatives, he's real uncooperative.

ʕanuud **1.** stubborn, obstinate, pigheaded **2.** stubborn person.

*ʕnaadi** stubborn, obstinate, pigheaded.

ʕnuudi = *ʕnaadi.*

ʔaʕnad more or most stubborn, obstinate

ʕ-n-z

ʕanz goat(s). || *dees il-ʕanz* a kind of grape, long, sweet, and light green in color.

ʕ-n-ṣ-r

ʕunṣur pl. *ʕanaaṣir* **1.** race, stock, breed,

ethnic origin. **2.** ethnic element. **3.** element (chem. and pol.).

Ɛunṣuriyya racism, ethnic bigotry.

Ɛ-n-f

Ɛaniif fierce, tough, bitter. *muqaawama Ɛaniifa* fierce resistance.

Ɛunf violence, roughness.

Ɛ-n-q

Ɛtinaq to adopt, embrace, take up. *Ɛtinaq id-diin il-ˀislaami.* He adopted the Islamic religion.

Ɛ-n-g

Ɛunig pl. *Ɛnuug* neck.

Ɛ-n-g-d

Ɛanguud pl. *Ɛanaagiid* bunch, cluster (esp. of grapes).

Ɛ-n-k-b-w-t

Ɛankabuut pl. *-aat* spider. *beet il-Ɛankabuut, Ɛišš il-Ɛankabuut* spider web.

Ɛ-n-w

Ɛinnaawa pl. *-aat* (vulgar) clitoris.

Ɛ-n-w-n

Ɛanwan to address. *Ɛanwin il-maktuub ib-ism iš-šarika w-huwwa yooṣal-li.* Address the letter with the company's name and it will reach me.

Ɛinwaan **1.** address. **2.** title. *kalima b-Ɛinwaan . . .* an address entitled. . . . *tabdiil Ɛinwaan* change of (job) title.

Ɛ-n-y

Ɛina (*i Ɛinaaya*) **1.** to concern, interest. *hiiči šii ma-yiƐniik. la-tiddaxxal.* That thing doesn't concern you. Don't interfere. *mašaakilhum ma-tiƐniini; Ɛindi mašaakli l-xaaṣṣa.* Their problems don't interest me; I have my own. *siluuk ˀibni bil-madrasa yiƐniini hwaaya.* My son's behavior in school concerns me greatly. **2.** to mean, to have in mind. *š-tiƐni b-haaδa?* What do you mean by that? *š-tiƐni hač-čilma?* What's this word mean? *ma-yiƐniik ib-hat-taƐliiq.* He didn't have you in mind with that remark. || *yaƐni* 1. that is, in other words, in fact, then. *yaƐni ma-triid tiji wiyyaana.* In other words, you don't want to come with us. *yaƐni, ma-ariidak tiƐči wiyyaa.* In short, I don't want you to talk with him. *yaƐni, guul ma-triid itbiiƐa.* Well then, say you don't want to sell it. 2. (a parenthetical remark, approx.:) then. *šinu, yaƐni? bass ˀili ma-tinṭiini?* What then? I'm the only one you don't give any to? *leeš, yaƐni, ma-jaa?* Why didn't he come then? **3.** (a somewhat noncommital answer, expressing reservations:) so-so, sort of. *yƐijbak haj-jaww?—yaƐni.* Do you like this weather? Well, sort of.

Ɛaana to suffer, bear, endure, undergo. *Ɛaana hwaaya ˀila ˀan txarraj.* He went through a lot before he graduated.

tƐanna to trouble oneself. *la-titƐanna Ɛala muudi.* Don't trouble yourself for my sake.

Ɛtina to take care. *Ɛtini b-qaaṭak ij-jidiid.* Take care of your new suit.

Ɛinaaya **1.** care, caring, taking care of. *Ɛinaaya bil-marδa* caring for patients. **2.** care, pains, carefulness. || *b-Ɛinaaya* carefully. *bala Ɛinaaya* carelessly.

Ɛtinaaˀ care, nursing.

maƐna pl. *maƐaani* sense, meaning. *šinu maƐnaaha?* What's it mean? *b-kull maƐna č-čilma* in every sense of the word. *š-maƐna truuƐ w-ma-dgul-li?* What do you mean going and not telling me? *zaƐalak ma-ˀila maƐna.* There's no reason for your anger.

maƐnawiyyaat morale, spirit.

Ɛ-h-d

tƐahhad **1.** to take on oneself, to guarantee. *ˀatƐahhad-lak bil-ifluus.* I'll guarantee you the money. **2.** to undertake, to bind oneself, to pledge oneself, to obligate oneself. *n-najjaar itƐahhad iyxaḷḷiṣ iš-šuġuḷ ib-yoomeen.* The carpenter undertook to finish the work in two days. **3.** to promise. *tƐahhad-li ma-ysawwiiha.* He promised me he wouldn't do it.

tƐaahad to make a mutual pledge. *tƐaahdaw yibquun ˀaṣdiqaaˀ.* They vowed to remain friends.

Ɛahad **1.** knowledge: || *Ɛahdi bii* to my knowledge, as far as I know. *Ɛahdi bii, ma-ybuug.* To my knowledge, he doesn't steal. **2.** pledge, promise. **3.** time, epoch, era.

¶ *wali l-Ɛahad* the crown prince, heir apparent.

Ɛuhda: Ɛala Ɛuhda in the charge of, under the care of. *raƐ-aaxuδ hal-qaδiyya Ɛala Ɛuhudti.* I'll take this matter on myself. *b-Ɛuhda = Ɛala Ɛuhda. saafar il-mudiir w-xalla kullši b-Ɛuhdat il-muƐaawin maala.* The director went off and left everything in his assistant's charge.

maƐhad pl. *maƐaahid* **1.** (public) institute or institution. **2.** institute.

muƐaahada pl. *-aat* treaty.

taƐahhud promise, pledge, commitment.

mitƐahhid contractor, supplier.

ع-h-r

عaahira pl. *-aat* harlot, prostitute.

ع-w-j

عiwaj (*i عawij*) **1.** to bend, twist. *diir baalak la-tiعwij is-siim.* Be careful not to bend the wire. **2.** to turn off, to turn aside. *fuut išwayya w-baعdeen ʔiعwij عal-yimna.* Go ahead a little way and then bear to the right.

عawwaj to bend, twist. *عawwaj it-teel bič-čillaabteen.* He bent the wire with the pliers.

nعiwaj to be or become bent, twisted. *daععaamiyyat is-sayyaara nعiwjat ib-ح aadiθ il-iṣṭidaam.* The car's bumper got bent in the collision.

عaaj ivory.

*عaaji** **1.** ivory (adj.). *tamaaθiil عaajiyya* ivory statues. **2.** ivory, ivory-like. *عaleeha siiqaan عaajiyya.* She has ivory legs. *snaan عaajiyya* ivory-like teeth.

ʔaعwaj f. *عooja* pl. *عuuj* **1.** bent, crooked, twisted. *bismaar ʔaعwaj* a bent nail. *حalig ʔaعwaj* a twisted mouth. || *ʔugعud ʔaعwaj w-iحči عadil.* Feel at ease but tell the truth. **2.** winding, twisting, tortuous. *ṭariiq ʔaعwaj* a winding road.

ع-w-č

عoočiyya, عuučiyya pl. *-aat* cane, walking stick.

ع-w-d

عaad (*u عauda*) to return, come back. *l-lujna عaadat min jawlatha.* The committee returned from its tour.

عaad (*i ʔiعaada*) **1.** to repeat. *عiid haj-jumla marra θaanya.* Repeat this sentence again. *ma-حufaḏ ič-čilma ʔilla lamma عaadha عiddat marraat.* He didn't memorize the word until he repeated it several times. *la-tعiidha baعad, tara ʔazعal.* Don't do it again, or I'll get mad. || *yaعni kull yoom inعiid w-nuṣqul?* You mean we have to go through this day in and day out? *l-maحkama عaadat in-naḏar bil-qaḏiyya.* The court reconsidered the case. **2.** to return, give back, send back. *عaadaw il-ʔawraaq lil-lujna.* They returned the papers to the committee. *عaadoo lil-waḏiifa.* They sent him back to his regular job.

عawwad to accustom, condition, teach the habit. *عawwidaw ibinhum عan-naḏaafa.* They trained their son to be tidy. *la-tعawwid ilsaanak عal-حači l-waṣix.* Don't get into the habit of using dirty words.

عaawad to revert, resume. *ʔiδa yعaawid, ʔabuṣṭa.* If he does it again, I'll beat him up.

ʔaعaad **1.** to repeat. *ʔaعaad iš-šiعir li-ʔan ma-smaعta.* He repeated the poetry because I didn't hear it. || *l-wizaara raح-itعiid in-naḏar ib-qaḏiita.* The ministry is going to reconsider his case. **2.** to reorganize, revise. *š-šurṭa ʔaعaadat tanḏiim حarakat il-muruur.* The police reorganized the traffic regulations.

tعawwad to get acccustomed to, to accustom oneself. *tعawwad iynaam min wakit.* He got accustomed to going to sleep early.

nعaad **1.** to be returned, to be brought back, to be taken back, to be sent back. *raح-yinعaad il-waḏiifta.* He'll be returned to his job. **2.** to be repeated, to be done over. *l-imtiحaan raح-yinعaad li-ʔan iktišfaw il-ʔasʔila mabyuuga.* The examination will be repeated because they found the questions stolen. *raح-yinعaad ṭabع il-iktaab li-ʔan ʔaku bii sahu.* Typing the letter will be done over because there is a mistake in it.

عtaad to be or become accustomed, used. *laazim tiعtaad عala d-diraasa bil-leel.* You must get used to studying at night.

عuud pl. *ʔaعwaad* **1.** lute. **2.** (an interjection, approx.:) well, then. *عuud min yiji, ʔagul-la.* Well, when he comes, I'll tell him. *du-ruuح hassa, عuud min itrudd ʔanṭiik-iyyaaha.* Go ahead now, and then when you come back I'll give it to you.

عuuda pl. *-aat, عuwad* **1.** splinter. **2.** match, matchstick. *عuudat šixxaaṭ* matchstick.

عuudeen = *عuud* **2.**

عaad **1.** (an exclamation of emphasis used with commands, approx.:) now, mind you, dammit. *bass عaad!* That's enough now! *yeezi عaad!* Quit it, dammit! *la-tθaxxinha عaad!* Don't push your luck too far! *عaad, xalli nruuح!* Dammit, let's go! **2.** (an exclamation of emphasis used in denying or rejecting a statement or proposal, approx.:) but, well, even. *عaad haaδa ʔaحsan walad. ma-ysawwi hiiči šii.* But he's a good boy. He wouldn't do such a thing. *عaad loo yinṭiini milyoon diinaar, ma-abiiع.* Even though he gives me a million dinars, I won't sell. *عaad wala ʔabiiع.* I'll never sell. *عaad muu bil-حeef.* Not on your life.

ʕaada pl. *-aat* **1.** habit, custom, practice. || *l-ʕaada s-sirriyya* masturbation, onanism. *jarat il-ʕaada ʔan yizzaawruun marrteen bil-isbuuʕ.* It became customary for them to visit each other twice a week. *ḥasab il-ʕaada* as usual, according to custom. *raaḥ iyʕayyid jiiraana ḥasab il-ʕaada.* He went to congratulate his neighbors on the feast as is customary. **2.** period, menstruation. || *jattha l-ʕaada.* She got her period.

*ʕaadi** **1.** ordinary, run-of-the-mill, common. *qmaaš ʕaadi* ordinary cloth. **2.** (by extension) cheap, common, vulgar. *fadd waaḥid ʕaadi* a vulgar person.

ʕyaada pl. *-aat* **1.** clinic. **2.** doctor's office.

*ʕtiyaadi** **1.** usual, customary, habitual. *ṭ-ṭariiq il-iʕtiyaadi* the usual way, route. **2.** normal, usual, commonplace. *manðar iʕtiyaadi* a commonplace sight. *šii ʕtiyaadi bil-mustašfa* a common thing in hospitals.

mʕawwad **1.** accustomed, used. *mʕawwad ʕal-ʕiiša bij-jibaal* accustomed to life in the mountains. **2.** (a term of address, often implying a degree of impatience, irritation, or dismay, approx.:) Mac, buster, buddy, man. *mʕawwad, laḥḥig-la. raḥ-yigrag.* Get him, Mac. He's going to drown. *yaa mʕawwad, ʔaani š-aʕlayya?* Look man, what's it to me? *ma-djuuz, yaa mʕawwad! haaða š-imʕarrfa ʔingiliizi?* Knock it off, Mac! What does he know about English? *laa, yaa mʕawwad! š-wakit maat?* No, man! When did he die?

muʕiid **1.** teaching assistant, graduate assistant. **2.** (esp. in the law school) failed in annual examination, person who failed. *ṭilaʕ muʕiid.* He failed his exams.

mitʕawwid used, accustomed. *mitʕawwid yitʔaxxar bil-leel* used to staying out late. *mitʕawwid ʕal-razaala* used to being called on the carpet.

muʕtaad = *mitʕawwid.* || *ḥasb il-muʕtaad* and *kal-muʕtaad* as usual. *xalliṣaw iš-šuġuḷ w-ṭilʕaw iyliʕbuun kura kal-muʕtaad.* They finished the work and went out to play ball as usual.

ع-w-ð

ʕaað (*u ʕiyaað*): *ʔaʕuuðu bil-laah!* (used when something shameful, distasteful, or evil is mentioned or encountered, approx.:) God forbid! Heaven forbid! God save me . . ., God deliver me. . . . *ʔaʕuuðu bil-laah min hal-xilqa!* God save me from this face! *ʔaʕuuðu bil-laah imniṣ-ṣooṭ!* God deliver me from that voice!

ʕuuða pl. *-aat, ʕuwað* **1.** talisman, charm, amulet. **2.** (by extension) something very small. **3.** (an exclamation invoking protection from something dirty, ritually unclean, or distasteful.) *ʕuuða, ʕuuða! la-twaṣṣix ihduumi.* Get away! Don't dirty my clothes. *ʕuuða! šloon xilqa ʕalee!* God forbid! What a face he's got!

ʕiyaað: ʕiyaaðu bil-laah God forbid! God save us! God protect us! *ʕiyaaðu bil-laah min hal-wilid!* God save us from those kids!

taʕwiiða pl. *-aat* talisman, charm, amulet.

ع-w-r

ʕawwar to hurt, to injure. *ʕawwaritni b-hað-ðarba.* You hurt me with this blow. *difaʕa ʕas-siyaaj w-ʕawwara.* He pushed him against the fence and injured him.

ʔaʕaar to lend. *tigdar itʕiirni ktaabak hal-leela?* Can you lend me your book this evening?

tʕawwar to be hurt, get hurt. *wugaʕ imnid-daraj w-itʕawwar.* He fell from the ladder and was hurt.

staʕaar to borrow. *staʕaar minni ʕiddat ʔašyaaʔ w-ma-rajjaʕha.* He borrowed several things from me and didn't return them.

ʕawra pl. *-aat* **1.** genitals, pudendum. **2.** crotch, genital area.

ʕawaara, ʕwaara pl. *-aat* fault, defect.

ʔaʕwar f. *ʕoora* pl. *ʕuur, ʕuuraan, ʕooriin* **1.** one-eyed, blind in one eye. **2.** one-eyed man.

¶ *l-muṣraan il-ʔaʕwar* the vermiform appendix.

ʔiʕaara lending. || *l-ʔiʕaara wit-taʔjiir* lend-lease. *ʔiʕaarat xadamaat* lending the services of personnel.

mustaʕaar false, artificial. *šaʕar mustaʕaar* wig, toupée, hairpiece. || *ʔisim mustaʕaar* pseudonym, assumed name.

ع-w-z

ʕaaz (*u ʔiʕwaaza*) to be needed by, to be lacking. *ʔaani miktifi w-ma-yʕuuzni šii.* I am satisfied and lacking nothing. *has-sayyaara mumtaaza. ma-yʕuuzha ġeer paatri jidiid.* This is an excellent car. It needs only a new battery. *kullši ʕidhum; bass ʕaayizhum talafizyoon.* They have everything but a television set.

ʕtaaz to need, be in need of. *ʔaani ma-miʕtaaz ʔaʕʕad.* I don't need anybody. *ʔiδa tiʕtaaz ifluus, ʔaani ʕaaδir.* If you need money, I'm at your disposal.

ʕaaza need, necessity, exigency.

ʕwaaza extra, in addition, more. *nuṣṣ yaarda ʕwaaza* half a yard more. *gurṣat xubuz iʕwaaza* an extra loaf of bread.

miʕtaaz lacking, in need of. *miʕtaaza taayaraat* in need of tires.

ʕ-w-s-j

ʕoosaj boxthorn, boxthorn plant. *ʕiriš ʕoosaj* boxthorn bush.

ʕ-w-š

ʕawwaš to be or become dispirited, listless. *ʔašu min xalleena il-bilbil bil-qufaṣ, ʕawwaš.* It seems when we put the nightingale in the cage, he drooped visibly. *š-bii ʔabuuk? ʔašu mʕawwiš il-yoom.* What's the matter with your father? He seems down in the mouth today.

ʕ-w-ṣ

ʕiwaṣ (*i ʕawiṣ*) /with *l-ʕeen*/ to squint. *ʕala-weeš da-tiʕwiṣ ʕeenak?* Why are you squinting? *ʕiwaṣ ʕeena w-neešan il-bunduqiyya.* He squinted and aimed the rifle.

ʕawwaṣ = *ʕiwaṣ*. *ma-yigdar yiʕči ʔiδa ma-yiʕawwiṣ iʕyuuna.* He can't talk without squinting his eyes.

ʔaʕwaṣ f. *ʕooṣa* pl. *ʕuuṣ, ʕooṣiin* 1. squinting, squinted. *ʕeena ʕooṣa.* His eye is squinted. 2. person with a narrowed eye, person who squints.

ʕawiiṣ difficult, hard to comprehend, abstruse, obscure. *muškila ʕawiiṣa* a difficult problem.

ʕ-w-δ̣

ʕawwaδ̣ 1. to substitute, replace, take the place. *xalli yruuʕ. ʔaani ʔaʕawwuδ̣ ʕanna.* Let him go. I'll substitute for him. 2. to recompense, compensate. *l-ʕukuuma ʕawwδ̣at il-fallaaʕiin ʕan xaṣaayirhum.* The government compensated the peasants for their losses. *ʔiδa tixṣar, ʔaʕawwuδ̣ak.* If you lose, I'll make it up to you. || *ʔaḷḷa yʕawwuδ̣.* God will provide (an expression of hope for the future, after a loss).

staʕaaδ̣ to replace, exchange, substitute. *tigdar tistaʕiiδ̣ ʕanna b-muwaδ̣δ̣af ʔaaxar.* You can replace him with another employee.

ʕiwaδ̣ compensation, recompense, indemnity.

taʕwiiδ̣ compensation, indemnification, reparation. || *ṭaalab bit-taʕwiiδ̣.* He requested compensation.

ʕ-w-ʕ-y

ʕooʕa (*i*) to crow. *diična yʕooʕi min yismaʕ ʕiss diičkum.* Our rooster crows when he hears your rooster.

ʕ-w-f

ʕaaf (*i ʕeef, ʕeefa*) and *ʕaaf* (*u ʕoof, ʕoofa*) to leave. *yʕuuf sayyaarta gid-daam il-beet.* He leaves his car in front of the house. *ʔiδa tʕiif kutbak ihnaa, tinbaag.* If you leave your books here, they'll get stolen. 2. to desert, abandon. *ṭallag marta w-ʕaaf wilda.* He divorced his wife and deserted his children. 3. /also with *ʕan*/ to leave alone, let alone, let be. *ma-tʕiifni! muu raʕ-itxabḅuḷni!* Let me alone! You're going to drive me to distraction! *ma-tʕuuf ʕanna ʕaad!* Leave him alone, for God's sake! || *ma-tʕuufna! min ʕinda fluus?* Come off it! Who's got any money? *ma-tʕuufna min hal-ʕači!* Spare us that talk!

ʕoofa abandonment, desertion.

ʕeefa = *ʕoofa*.

ʕ-w-q

ʕaaq (*u, i ʔiʕaaqa*) to hinder, prevent. *ma-aku šii yʕuuqni ʕan il-majiiʔ.* Nothing can prevent me from coming.

ʕaayiq pl. *ʕawaayiq* obstacle, stumbling block.

ʕ-w-g

ʕawwag 1. to hinder, delay. *ṣaar-li saaʕa ʔantaδ̣rak. ma-dgul-li šinu lli ʕawwagak?* I've been waiting an hour for you. Why don't you tell me what delayed you? 2. to save, to keep, to leave. *la-tuṣruf raatbak kulla. ʕawwig išwayya minna.* Don't spend all your salary. Save a little of it. *ʔukul w-ʕawwug-li šwayya.* Eat and leave a little bit for me.

tʕawwag 1. to be delayed. *la-tintaδ̣ruuni bil-ʕaša. raʕ-atʕawwag išwayya.* Don't wait dinner for me. I'll be delayed a little while. 2. to be saved, be kept, be left over. *ma-tʕawwag šii mnir-raatib haš-šahar.* Nothing was left over from my salary this month. 3. to stay, remain (behind). *tʕawwag lil-ġada.* He stayed there for lunch.

ʕ-w-l

ʕaal (*u, i ʕool, ʔiʕaala*) to support, provide for. *ʔiδa ymuut ʔabuuhum, minu yʕuulhum?* If their father dies, who'll provide for them?

ʕawwal 1. to rely, depend, count on. *muu ʕawwalna ʕaleek, w-gulna ʔinta tsawwiiha?* Didn't we depend on you and say you would do it? 2. to expect. *ʔinta mʕawwil itḥaṣṣil hiiči daraja?* Did you really expect to get such a grade?

ʕyaal (pl.) **1.** in-laws, especially the husband's family. **2.** dependents. || *ṣaaḥib iʕyaal* supporter of a large family.

ʕaala (invar.) burden, dependent. *ʕaala ʕal-mujtamaʕ* a burden on society.

maʕwal pl. *maʕaawil* pick, pickax, mattock.

ʔiʕaala supporting a family (as an excuse for avoiding military service).

ʕaaʔila pl. *ʕawaaʔil* family.

*ʕaaʔili** family. *qaḍiyya ʕaaʔiliyya* a family matter.

muʕiil provider for a family, sole support of someone (and therefore exempt from military service).

ʕ-w-m

ʕaam: l-ʕaam last year. *l-ʕaam giḍeena ṣ-ṣeef b-ʔawruppa.* Last year we spent the summer in Europe.

ʕaayim floating. *jisir ʕaayim* pontoon bridge.

ʕ-w-n

ʕaan (i ʕawn) to aid, assist, support. *ʔaḷḷa yʕiin il-faqiir.* God helps the poor.

ʕaawan to aid, assist, help. *tigdar itʕaawiini ʔalimm il-ġaraaḍ?* Can you help me gather up the things?

tʕaawan to help each other, cooperate. *loo titʕaawanuun, txallṣuun iš-šuġuḷ b-saaʕ.* If you help each other, you'll finish the work quickly. *leeš ma-titʕaawan wiyyaana?* Why don't you cooperate with us?

staʕaan to seek help. *kull-ma yriid ysawwi šii yistiʕiin biyya.* Whenever he wants to do something, he comes to me for help.

ʕoon **1.** help, assistance, support (in a few expressions:) *ʔaḷḷa ykuun ib-ʕoona.* He'll want divine assistance for that. *jibta ʕoon ṭilaʕ-li firʕoon.* I brought him for support and he turned out a tyrant. He's lucky to go to Europe. **2.** (pl. *ʔaʕwaana*) helper, supporter, henchman. **3.** good fortune, good luck. *ʕoona l-iyruuḥ il-ʔooruppa.*

ʕaana see under *ʕ-a-n.*

muʕaawana aid, assistance, help.

ʔiʕaana pl. *-aat* contribution, aid, donation.

taʕaawun cooperation.

muʕiin: || *ʔaḷḷa l-muʕiin.* God will provide. *yaa ḷḷaa yaa muʕiin!* said when lifting a weight, pushing an object, or otherwise exerting effort, or when in need of divine help.

*taʕaawuni** cooperative. *jamʕiyya taʕaawuniyya* cooperative society.

muʕaawin **1.** assistant. **2.** police lieutenant.

stiʕaana seeking help.

ʕ-w-h

ʕaaha pl. *-aat* defect, handicap.

ʕ-w-y

ʕiwa (i ʕawi) to howl (dog, wolf, jackal). *δ-δiib čaan yiʕwi w-ma-gdarit anaam.* The wolf was howling and I couldn't sleep.

ʕ-w-y-n

ʕuweenaat (pl.) eyeglasses, spectacles.

ʕ-y-b

ʕaab: ʕaab wiččak! ʕaabat hač-čihra! ʕaabat-lak haš-šikil! Damn you! Go to hell!

ʕayyab **1.** to find fault, criticize. *ma-gibal yilbas is-sitra baʕad, li-ʔan ʕayyibaw ʕaleeha.* He wouldn't wear the jacket any more because they criticized it. **2.** to mimic, make fun of. *la-tʕayyib! bass ʔaani ʕarja?* Don't poke fun! Am I the only one with a limp? *šuuf ij-jaahil da-yʕayyib ʕala ʔuxta.* Look at the kid making faces at his sister.

nʕaab to be or become defective. *nʕaabat il-qundara w-ma-tinlibis baʕad.* The shoes became unsuitable for wearing any more.

ʕeeb pl. *ʕyuub* **1.** fault, defect, flaw. **2.** vice, failing, weakness. **3.** sin, disgrace, shame, embarrassment. || *ʕeeb!* For shame! *ʕeeb ʕaleek!* Shame on you!

ʕ-y-θ

ʕaaθ (i ʕeeθ) /with *fasaad*/ to cause havoc, run amuck, ravage. *j-jinuud ʕaaθaw fasaad bil-ʔarḍ.* The soldiers ravaged the countryside.

ʕ-y-d

ʕayyad to celebrate or observe a feast. *raḥ-inʕayyid ib-baġdaad.* We'll celebrate the feast day in Baghdad.

ʕiid pl. *ʔaʕyaad* feast, feast day, holiday. *ʕiid il-istiqlaal* Independence Day. *ʕiid il-čibiir* = *ʕiid il-ʔaḍḥaa* Greater Bairam. *ʕiid iz-zġayyir* = *ʕiid il-fitir* = *ʕiid ramaḍaan* Lesser Bairam. || *l-ʕiid* either of the two major Muslim holy days.

see also *ʕ-w-d.*

ʕ-y-r

ʕaar (i ʕeer) to attach, attribute. *la-tʕiir-la wazin. huwwa fadd waaḥid taafih.* Don't attach any importance to him. He's an insignificant fellow.

ʕayyar to rebuke, reproach, blame, condemn. *da-yʕayyruu b-axuu li-ʔanna jabaan.* They throw his brother up to him because he's a coward. *bintak ʕayyiratni l-baarḥa ʕala libsi.* Your daughter gave me a hard time about my clothes yesterday. **2.** to weigh. *ʕayyir-li kiilu xyaar.* Weigh out a kilo of cucumbers for me.

ʕaar shame, disgrace.

beeʕaar (m. and f.) pl. *-iyya* **1.** shameless, without honor. **2.** shameless person.

ʕaarsizz (m. and f.) pl. *-iyya* = *beeʕaar.*

ʕeer pl. *ʕyuura* penis.

ʕyaar **1.** weight, measure. *ʕyaara naaguṣ.* He gives short weight. **2.** (pl. *-aat*) weight (used on a scale).

ʕ-y-s

ʕiisa Jesus.

ʕ-y-š

ʕaaš (*i ʕeeš*) **1.** to live, be alive. *ʕaaš miit sana.* He lived a hundred years. *zawijta, xaṭiyya, ma-yʕiiš ʔilha.* His wife, poor thing, all her children have died. *ʕaayiš ʕiiša taʕsa.* He's leading a miserable life. **2.** to exist, make a living. *ma-da-nuʕruf imneen da-yʕiiš.* We don't know how he makes his living. *yʕiiš ʕal-boog.* He lives by stealing. **3.** to dwell, reside. *ʕišna b-bağdaad xams isniin, w-sikanna b-beet ičbiir.* We lived in Baghdad five years, in a large house. *l-ʔakraad iyʕiišuun biš-šimaal.* The Kurds live in the North.

¶ *yaʕiiš il-malik!* Long live the King! *ʕaaš min šaafič.* It's real nice to see you again (a standard greeting to someone one hasn't seen for some time).

ʕayyaš to support, provide for. *ʕayyašna sana kaamla.* He helped us with living expenses for a full year. *maat zoojha w-maḥḥad raḥ-yʕayyišha.* Her husband died and no one will take her in.

tʕayyaš to eke out a living, barely make ends meet. *da-yitʕayyaš ib-raatib galiil.* He's barely getting by on a small salary.

nʕaaš /with *b-*/ to be lived in. *hal-qarya ma-yinʕaaš biiha.* It's not possible to live in this town.

ʕiiš life, living. || *ma-aku ʕiiša hnaa.* Things aren't so good here.

maʕaaš salary, pay.

maʕiiša pl. *-aat* life, living.

ʔiʕaaša supply, supplying, provisioning. *ḍaabuṭ ʔiʕaaša* supply officer. *mudiiriyyat il-ʔiʕaaša* quartermaster section, supply directorate.

ʕ-y-ḍ

staʕaaḍ, yistaʕiiḍ see *ʕ-w-ḍ.*

ʕ-y-ṭ

ʕaaṭ (*i ʕeeṭ*) to yell, scream. *ʕaaṭat min šaafat ʔibinha wugaʕ biš-šaṭṭ.* She screamed when she saw her son fall in the river. *kull-ma ʔaḥči wiyyaak, tʕiiṭ ʕalayya.* Whenever I speak with you, you yell at me.

ʕayyaṭ intens. of *ʕaaṭ. l-mara ʕayyṭat min simʕat ʔibinha maat.* The woman screamed when she heard her son died. *ʕalee-man da-tʕayyiṭ?* Who do you think you're shouting at?

tʕaayaṭ to shout at each other, to yell at each other, *ma-aku ḥaaja titʕaayṭuun. xalli nšuuf š-biikum.* There's no need to yell at each other. Let's see what your trouble is. *yoomiyya titʕaayaṭ wiyya j-jiiraan.* Every day she exchanges shouts with the neighbors.

ʕiyaaṭ, ʕyaaṭ shouting, yelling, screaming.

ʕeeṭa pl. *-aat* a shout, a yell, a scream.

ʕ-y-f

ʕaaf (*i*) see *ʕ-w-f.*

ʕ-y-q

ʕayyaq to shout, yell, scream (invective). *bass idgiisha, dguum itʕayyiq ʕaleek.* Just touch her and she begins to shout at you.

ʕayyaaqa pl. *-aat* **1.** bitchy woman, fishwife. **2.** gadabout, woman who neglects her house to roam about and gossip.

ʕaayiq (invar.) = *ʕayyaaqa* **1.**

ʕ-y-q-l

tʕeeqal to be self-important, to give oneself airs, to be picayunish, to be fussy. *ma-aku ḥaaja titʕeeqal; ʔiḏa yʕijbak itruuḥ lis-siinama, yaḷḷa guum.* There's no need to be a prima donna; if you'd like to go to the movies, come on. *ṣadiiqak yitʕeeqal ihwaaya w-šaayif nafsa.* Your friend behaves very haughtily and is conceited. *kull-ma ʔaṭlub minna šii, yguum yitʕeeqal ib-raasi.* Whenever I ask him for something, he gives me a hard time.

ʕ-y-l

ʕaal (*i ʕeel, ʕeela*) **1.** to start, cause, instigate, incite, provoke, stir up. *ʔiḏa tʕiil mara θaanya, taakulha.* If you start trouble again, you'll get it. *l-yʕiil, yinbuṣuṭ.* Whoever starts a fight, gets beat up. **2.** /with *b-* or *ʕala*/ to irritate, anger, provoke, stir up. *ʔinta ʕilit bii b-hač-čilma.* You irritated him with that remark. *buṣaṭṭa li-ʔan ʕaal b-ibni.* I hit him because he provoked my son.

ʕaayil troublemaker, instigator, cause of trouble, the one at fault.

ʕyaal, ʕaaʔila, etc., see *ʕ-w-l.*

ʕ-y-n

ʕayyan **1.** to specify, designate. *ʕayyin-li l-ʔašyaaʔ illi triidha w-aani ʔajiib-ilk-iyyaaha.* Specify the things you want and I'll bring them to you. **2.** to fix, appoint, schedule, stipulate. *ʕayyin-li s-saaʕa w-aani ʔaji ʕal-wakit.* Set me a time and I'll be on time. **3.** to nominate, appoint, assign. *l-ḥukuuma ʕayynata mudiir ziraaʕa.* The government appointed him an agricultural director.

ʕaayan to look, see. *taʕaal ʕaayin ihnaa w-šuuf š-aku!* Come and look over here and see what's going on! *la-tʕaayin ʕaleeha tara hiyya tixjal.* Don't look at her or she'll get embarrassed. *š-aku ʕindak da-tʕaayin ib-jeebi?* What are you doing looking in my pocket? *ʔaani baʕad ma-aʕaayin ib-wičča ʔabadan.* I don't ever want to look at his face again.

tʕayyan **1.** to be appointed, assigned. *tʕayyanit ib-daaʔirt il-bariid.* I got an appointment in the post office department. **2.** to be set, fixed, designated. *mawʕid il-ijtimaaʕ li-hassa ma-tʕayyan.* The date for the meeting hasn't been set yet.

ʕayn pl. *ʔaʕyaan* senator. *majlis il-ʔaʕyaan* senate. || *ʕayn iš-šii* the same thing.

ʕeen pl. *ʕyuun* **1.** eye. || *ʕala ʕeeni w-raasi* gladly, with pleasure (a reply to a request). *huwwa b-ʕeena* he himself personally, none other than he. *minu ṭallaʕ ʕeenak?* Who gave you that impudence? *ʕeeni* my dear, darling, old friend, old buddy. **2.** evil eye, envious eye. *ʕaṭṭaw naʕal ʕal-baab ʕan il-ʕeen.* They put a horseshoe over the door against the evil eye. *yilbas ihduum rixiiṣa ʕan il-ʕeen.* He wears cheap clothes to avoid the envious eye. **3.** spring (of water). **4.** burner. *ṭabbaax ʔabu tlaθ iʕyuun* a three burner stove. **5.** name of the letter *ʕ.*

ʕeena pl. *-aat* mirror.

ʕiina the best, the pick. *ʕiinat iṭ-ṭamaaṭa* the best of the tomatoes.

ʕuweenaat eyeglasses, spectacles.

maʕiin pl. *-aat* rhombus (geom.).

ʕuweenaat (pl.) eyeglasses, spectacles.

taʕyiin **1.** specification, designation. *biduun taʕyiin* at random. **2.** (pl. *-aat*) appointment, assignment.

muʕaayana pl. *-aat* examination (by a doctor).

ʕayaan: šaahid ʕayaan eyewitness.

muʕayyan **1.** fixed, designated, set, prescribed. *waqit muʕayyan* a set time. **2.** nominated, appointed. *muwwaδδaf muʕayyan jidiid* a newly appointed employee. **3.** rhombus (geom.).

(see also *ʕ-w-n*).

Ġ

ġ-a-d

ġaad yonder, over there. *waaguf ġaad ib-δaak iṣ-ṣoob.* He's standing over there on the other bank. || *ruuḥ ġaad! xalliini ʔaštuġuḷ.* Get away! Let me work. *ma-yuʕruf š-aku hnaa. jaay imnil-ġaad.* He doesn't know what's going on here. He's from out-of-town.

ġaadi = *ġaad.*

*ġaadaani** far, distant. *l-iktaab il-ġaadaani* the book on the far end.

ġ-a-z

ġaaz pl. *-aat* gas.

ġ-b-r

ġabbar to become dusty. *hamm id-dinya ġabbarit.* The weather's gotten dusty again.

ġbarr = *ġabbar. d-dinya tiġbarr min iyṣiir hawa.* The weather gets dusty when it's windy.

ġubaar dust.

ʔaġbar f. *ġabra* pl. *ġubur, ġubriin.* **1.** dusty. *yoom ʔaġbar* a dusty day. *dinya ġabra* dusty weather. **2.** dull, slow, not quick-witted, not quick on the uptake. **3.** dull person.

ʔaġbar more or most slow-witted.

ġ-b-š

ġabḅaš to be early, to come, or go, early in the morning. *ʔiδa ma-tġabḅuš, ma-tḥaṣṣil mukaan bil-qiṭaar.* If you don't come at dawn you won't get a seat on the train.

ġubša **1.** early morning. **2.** in the early morning. *raḥ-naaxuδ iṭ-ṭayyaara baačir* *ġubša.* We're going to take the plane tomorrow at dawn.

ġ-b-ṭ

ġubaṭ (*u ġabuṭ*) to envy. *ˀaani ˀaġubṭak ʕala hal-ʕiiša.* I envy you for that life.

ġ-b-n

ġuban (*u ġubun*) to cheat, shortchange, treat unjustly. *l-ḥukuuma ġibnatni b-har-raatib.* The government treated me unfairly with that salary.

ġubun cheating, unfair treatment. || *ˀaṣaaba ġubun.* He got a raw deal. He was treated unfairly.

maġbuun wronged, injured, unfairly treated. *maġbuun bit-tarfiiʕ* wronged as to his raise. || *ḥaqqa maġbuun.* His rights were infringed upon.

ġ-b-y

ġabi pl. *ˀaġbiyaaˀ* **1.** stupid, ignorant, foolish. **2.** stupid person.

ġabaawa ignorance, foolishness, stupidity.

ˀaġba more or most ignorant, foolish, stupid.

ġ-t-r

ġutra pl. *ġutar* headcloth.

ġ-θ-θ

ġaθθ (*u ġaθθ*) to trouble, upset, bother. *gul-li š-biik. minu ġaθθak?* Tell me what's wrong. Who upset you? *la-tġuθθ nafsak ib-taṣliiḥ hal-makiina.* Don't bother yourself with fixing this machine. *loo tġuθθ nafsak bid-diraasa, tinjaḥ.* If you'll stir yourself and study, you'll pass.

nġaθθ to be or become upset, disturbed. *nġaθθ min iḥčaayti.* He got upset at what I said.

ġiθθa bother, nuisance, trouble.

ġaθiiθ **1.** bothersome, pesky. **2.** bothersome person, pest.

ġ-d-d

ġudda pl. *ġudad* gland (zool.).

ġ-d-r

ġidar (*i ġadir*) **1.** to act treacherously toward, to doublecross. *la-tooθiq biihum. ˀaku ḥtimaal yġidruuk.* Don't trust them. They will likely turn on you. **2.** to be unfair to, to wrong. *l-muʕallim ġidarni bit-taṣliiḥ.* The teacher was unfair to me on grading.

ġadiir: ʕiid il-ġadiir annual Shiah feast celebrating the naming of Ali as successor by Mohammed.

ġaddaara pl. *-aat* sub-machine gun, Tommy gun.

ġ-d-y

ġida (*i ġadi*) to become, turn into (in certain expressions:) *širab ḥatta ġida ṭabuḷ.* He drank until his head pounded (lit., he drank until he became a drum). *ġdeet ṃayy imnil-ʕarag.* I got soaking wet with perspiration (lit., I became water).

ġadda **1.** to give lunch, feed. *š-wakit raḥ-itġaddi ij-jahhaal?* When are you going to give the children lunch? **2.** to buy lunch for, treat to lunch. *ˀiδa tsaaʕidni, ˀaġaddiik il-yoom.* If you will help me, I'll treat you to lunch today.

tġadda to have lunch. *ˀimsi tġadda wiyyaay.* Come on and have lunch with me.

ġada pl. *-aayaat, ġidyaat* lunch.

ġ-δ-y

ġaδδa to support, back (with money). *minu da-yġaδδi hal-ḥaraka?* Who's supporting this movement?

dġaδδa to be fed, be nourished, get nourishment. *ṭ-ṭifil yidġaδ̣δ̣a b-ḥaliib ˀumma ˀaḥsan min ḥaliib il-buṭil.* The child is better nourished by his mother's milk than bottled milk. *n-nabaat idġaδδa mnil-ismaad.* The plants get nourishment from fertilizer.

ġiδaaˀ **1.** nourishment, nutriment, food value. **2.** (pl. only) *ˀaġδiya* food, foodstuffs, victuals.

*ġiδaaˀi** nourishing, nutritive, nutritional. *mawaadd ġiδaaˀiyya* nourishing substances.

*muġaδδi** nourishing, nutritious. *ˀakil muġaδδi* nourishing food.

g-r-a-m

ġraam pl. *-aat* gram.

ġ-r-b

ġurab (*u ġuruub*) to set (of the sun). *šwakit raḥ-tuġrub iš-šamis?* What time will the sun set?

tġarrab to go to a foreign country, to emigrate. *ˀubqa b-baġdaad. luweeš itruuḥ tidġarrab?* Stay in Baghdad. Why go and leave the country?

staġrab **1.** to be surprised. *la-tistaġrub ˀiδa smaʕit haaδa ṣaar waziir.* Don't be surprised if you hear he's become a minister. *ˀaani da-astaġrib min taṣarrufa.* I'm surprised by his behavior. **2.** to be frightened, shy. *j-jaahil da-yistaġrub imnil-xuṭṭaar.* The baby's afraid of the guests.

ġarb west. *l-ġarb* the West.

*ġarbi** **1.** western, westerly, west. *hawa ġarbi* a west wind. **2.** occidental, Western, European. *rijjaal ġarbi* a Westerner. **3.** Westerner, European.

ġurba absence from one's homeland.

ġraab pl. *ġirbaan* crow.

ġariib pl. *ġurabaaʔ, ġurba.* **1.** strange, foreign. *walad ġariib* a stranger, a foreigner. **2.** strange, odd, queer. *libis ġariib* strange clothing. || *ġariib iš-šikil* strange-looking. **3.** strange, amazing, astonishing. *quṣṣa ġariiba* an amazing story. **4.** stranger, foreigner, alien, outsider.

ʔaġrab more or most unusual, strange, etc.

l-maġrib **1.** northwest Africa. **2.** Morocco.

muġrub, miġrib **1.** sunset. **2.** sunset, sundown. **3.** at sunset. *xayyamna l-muġrub.* We made camp at sunset.

*maġribi** pl. *maġaariba* **1.** North African. **2.** person from North Africa. **3.** Moroccan, from Morocco. **4.** person from Morocco.

ġ-r-b-l

ġarbal **1.** to sift, sieve. *ġarbil il-ʕunṭa.* Sift the wheat. **2.** to purge, shake up. *ʔaku ʔišaaʕa l-waziir raʕ-yġarbil il-muwaððafiin.* There's a rumor that the minister is going to sift the deadwood from the employees.

ġarbala pl. *-aat* **1.** sifting. **2.** shake-up, purge, reorganization.

ġirbiil, ġarbiil pl. *ġaraabiil* a coarse sieve.

ġ-r-d

ġarrad to sing, twitter. *l-bilbil da-yġarrid.* The nightingale is singing.

ġ-r-z

ġariiza pl. *ġaraaʔiz* instinct, natural impulse.

ġ-r-r

ġarr (*u ġuruur*) to deceive, mislead. *la-yġurrak il-maðhar maala, tara ma-yifham šii.* Don't let his appearance fool you, because he doesn't know a thing.

ġtarr to be or become conceited. *yiġtarr ihwaaya b-nafsa.* He's very taken with himself.

ġurra: ġurrat iš-šahar the first day of the month.

maġruur conceited, vain. *maġruur ib-nafsa* very much taken with himself.

ġ-r-s

ġiras (*i ġaris*) to plant. *ġirsaw ʔašjaar ib-baʕað iš-šawaariʕ.* They planted trees along some of the streets.

ġ-r-š

ġarša pl. *-aat, ġraaš* narghile.

g-r-ð

tġarrað to be biased, prejudiced. *raʔiisi dġarrað wiyyaaya w-ma-raffaʕni.* My boss was prejudiced toward me and didn't promote me. *l-muʕallim idġarrað-la w-ṣiqaṭ bil-imtiʕaan.* The teacher was biased toward him and he failed the exam.

ġarað pl. *ʔaġraað* **1.** intention, design, purpose. || *maa-la ġarað* he doesn't care, he's not concerned. *ruuʕ; š-ma tsawwi, ʔaani maa-li ġarað.* Go ahead; whatever you do, I'm not concerned. **2.** (pl. *ġaraað*) possession, belonging, thing.

ġ-r-ġ-r

tġarġar to gargle. *dġarġar ib-mayy w-miliʕ.* He gargled with water and salt.

ġarġara pl. *-aat* gargle.

g-r-f

ġiraf (*u ġaruf*) **1.** to dip up, ladle, scoop. *nṭiini šii ʔaġruf il-maay bii.* Give me something to dip up the water with. **2.** to paddle (a boat). *haaða yuġruf il-balam kulliš sariiʕ.* He paddles the boat very fast. *ġurafa lil-balam ġarufteen w-ṭayyara.* He paddled the boat two strokes and sent it flying.

ġurfa pl. *ġuraf* room, chamber. || *ġurfat it-tijaara* chamber of commerce.

ġarfa pl. *-aat* **1.** the act of dipping up, a scoop. **2.** a stroke of the paddle.

ġurraafa pl. *-aat, ġiraariif* **1.** scoop. **2.** paddle.

miġrafa pl. *-aat, maġaariif* large spoon, ladle, scoop.

muġraafa pl. *-aat* paddle.

ġ-r-g

ġirag **1.** to sink. *l-baaxira ġirgat ib-ʕaaṣifa.* The boat sank in a storm. **2.** to be immersed, submerged, flooded. *mazraʕti ġirgat imnil-muṭar.* My farm was flooded by the rain. **3.** to go under, be drowned. *fadd walad ġirag biš-šaṭṭ.* A boy drowned in the river. **4.** to be immersed, swamped, snowed under. *ligeeta ġaarig biš-šuġul.* I found him swamped with work. **5.** to be lost, wholly engaged, absorbed. *š-biik ġaarig bit-tafkiir?* What's making you so lost in thought?

ġarrag **1.** to sink, cause to sink. *l-ġawwaaṣa ġarrigat itlaθ bawaaxir.* The submarine sank three ships. **2.** to submerge, immerse, flood. *l-muṭar ġarrag šaariʕna.* The rain flooded our street. *rušš il-gaaʕ bass la-dġarrigha.* Sprinkle the ground but don't flood it. **3.** to drown, cause to drown. *xalli ʔasbaʕ. raaʕ idġarrigni.* Let me swim. You're going to drown me. *hal-mayy qawi. yġarrig.* This water's swift. It'll drown you.

ġargaan **1.** sunk, sunken. **2.** submerged,

flooded. **3.** drowned. **4.** swamped, snowed under.

ġaarig swamped, snowed under. *ġaarig biš-šuġuḷ* swamped with work.

ġ-r-m

ġarram **1.** to fine, impose a fine. *l-ḥaakim ġarrama diinaareen.* The judge fined him two dinars. **2.** to dock, to charge. *l-mudiir ġarrama raatib yoomeen.* The boss docked him two days' pay. *ʔiδa tiksir šii, yġarrimuuk.* If you break anything, they'll charge you for it.

tġarram to be fined, to be docked, to be charged. *dġarram diinaar li-ʔan δabb zibil biš-šaariʕ.* He was fined a dinar because he threw trash in the street.

ġaraam infatuation, love, passion.

*ġaraami** passionate, erotic, amorous, love. *quṣaṣ ġaraamiyya* love stories. *maktuub ġaraami* love letter.

ġaraamiyyaat romance, love. *beenaathum ġaraamiyyaat.* There's a romantic interest between them. || *da-ybiiʕ ġaraamiyyaat ib-raasha.* He's thrusting his affections upon her.

ġaraama pl. *-aat* **1.** fine. **2.** penalty. **3.** charge for breakage.

ġ-r-y

ʔaġra (*i ʔiġraaʔ*) to entice, allure, tempt. *gidar yiġriiha b-ifluusa.* He was able to attract her with his money.

ġira glue.

muġri tempting, enticing, alluring, seductive. *libis muġri* seductive clothing. *ḥalig muġri* a tempting mouth. **2.** attractive, tempting. *raatib muġri* an attractive salary. *šuruuṭ muġriya* attractive conditions. **3.** enviable. *manṣab muġri* an enviable position.

ġ-r-y-q

l-iġriiq the Greeks. *zaman il-iġriiq* the time of the Greeks, the Greek period.

*griiqi** Greek, Grecian. *timθaal iġriiqi* a Greek statue. *falsafa ġriiqiyya* Greek philosophy.

ġ-z-r

ġazzar to be appreciative, to appreciate, to show appreciation. *kull il-ʔakil il-ʔakkalth-iyyaa, ma-da-yġazzir.* All the meals I've fed him, and he isn't appreciative. *š-ma tsawwii-la, ma-yġazzir ib-ʕeena.* Whatever you do for him he doesn't show any appreciation.

ġaziir plentiful, copious, abundant. *muṭar ġaziir* plentiful rainfall. *maʕluumaat ġaziira* a boundless store of information.

ġazaara abundance, profusion. || *b-ġazaara* in abundance. *l-muṭar da-yinzil ib-ġazaara.* The rain is coming down heavily.

g-z-l

ġizal (*i gazil*) to spin. *ġizlat ṣuufat il-xaruuf kullha.* She spun all the sheep's wool.

ġaazal to court, flirt with. *bass itʕarraf ʕaleeha gaam yġaazilha.* As soon as he met her he began courting her.

tġazzal to celebrate in love poems. *dġazzal ib-jamaalha bil-qaṣiida lli hiδamha.* He celebrated her beauty in a poem he wrote. *yidġazzal ib-šiʕra b-kull il-munaasabaat.* He puts amour into his poetry on every occasion.

ġazil **1.** spinning. **2.** yarn, spun thread.

ġazal **1.** flirtation, flirtatiousness, flirtatious remarks. **2.** love poetry, erotic poetry.

*ġazali** amorous, erotic, love. *qaṣiida ġazaliyya* a love poem.

ġazaal pl. *ġizlaan* gazelle.

ġazaala pl. *-aat* female gazelle.

muġzal pl. *maġaazil* a spindle used in wool spinning.

mġeezil: mġeezil ḥaḅa, mġeezil daada a kind of sand spider found in the desert.

ġ-z-w

ġiza (*i ġazu*) to raid, attack, invade. *hal-qabiila raḥ-tiġziihum w-taaxuδ kull-ma ʕidhum.* That tribe will raid them and take all they have. *l-baδaaʔiʕ il-yaabaaniyya raḥ-tiġzi s-suug.* Japanese goods will invade the market.

ġazwa pl. *-aat* raid, attack.

maġza pl. *maġaazi* sense, meaning, import, significance.

ġ-s-l

ġisal (*i ġasil*) **1.** to wash. *ʔiġsil iidak ib-ṃayy ḥaarr.* Wash your hands in hot water. || *ʔaani ġaasil ʔiidi min ʔibni.* I've no hope for my son. *ḥamaata ġislata xooš ġasla.* His mother-in-law gave him a good scolding. **2.** to develop (film, prints). *baḷḷa ʔiġsil il-filim w-raawiini-yyaa.* Please develop the film and show it to me.

ġassal **1.** to wash thoroughly. *ruuḥ ġassil. l-ʔakil ḥaaδir.* Go wash. The food is ready. **2.** to wash (a corpse). *ġassilaw il-mayyit ib-surʕa w-difnoo.* They bathed the corpse quickly and buried it.

ġtisal to perform major ritual ablution (i.e. to wash the whole body after intercourse). *laazim tiġtisil gabuḷ-ma yṭurr il-fajir ḥatta tṣalli.* You must cleanse yourself before dawn breaks in order to pray.

ġasil washing.

ġassaala pl. *-aat* **1.** washerwoman. **2.** washing machine.

maġsal pl. *maġaasil* washbowl, sink.

mġeesil bathhouse for the dead.

ġ-š-š

ġašš (*i ġašš*) **1.** to cheat, act dishonestly. *ma-yinjaḥ ˀiδa ma-yġušš.* He won't pass if he doesn't cheat. **2.** to cheat, swindle. *la-tištiri minna, tara yġuššak.* Don't buy from him or he'll cheat you. **3.** to deceive, fool, take in. *la-dġuššak ihduuma, tara haaδa zangiin.* Don't let his clothes fool you, 'cause he's rich. **4.** adulterate, dilute. *ṣaaḥib il-maṭεam yġišš il-ˀakil maala.* The restaurant owner adulterates his food.

nġašš **1.** to be cheated, taken, swindled. *nġaššeet ib-has-sayyaara.* I got taken on this car. **2.** to be deceived, fooled, taken in. *nġaššeet ib-ḥačya; εabaali haaδa ˀaadmi.* I was fooled by his talk; I thought he was a gentleman. **3.** to be adulterated. *d-dihin yinġišš ib-suhuula.* Oil is easily adulterated.

ġišš cheating, fraud, swindling.

ġaššaaš pl. *-a* cheater, cheat, swindler.

maġšuuš adulterated. *dihin maġšuuš* adulterated oil.

ġ-š-m

ġaššam /with *nafis* or *ruuḥ*/ to feign ignorance, innocence, or inexperience. *naġġha lil-ibnayya w-ġaššam ruuḥa.* He poked the girl and pretended to be innocent. *tuεrufha kulliš zeen. la-dġaššim nafsak.* You know all about it. Don't pretend to be naive.

ġašiim pl. *ġišma, ġuššam* **1.** inexperienced, green, new. *ġašiim bil-maṣlaḥa* new at the business. **2.** greenhorn, bumpkin.

ġ-š-w

tġašša to veil oneself, wear a veil. *bittha sufuur bass hiyya tidġašša.* Her daughter doesn't wear a veil but she veils herself.

ġišaaˀ pl. *ˀaġšiya* membrane. *ġišaaˀ muxaati* mucous membrane. || *ġišaaˀ il-bakaara* hymen, maidenhead.

ġašaawa **1.** filmy covering of the eyes, cataract. **2.** veil.

g-ṣ-b

ġiṣab (*u ġaṣub*) to force, compel, coerce. *la-tuġṣubni. ma-aštihi ˀaakul.* Don't force me. I have no appetite to eat.

nġiṣab to be forced, compelled. *nġiṣabit ˀaruuḥ wiyyaa lis-siinama.* I had to go with him to the movies. *nġiṣab yiftaḥ il-qaaṣa.* He was forced to open the safe.

ġtiṣab to rape, ravish, violate. *baεad-ma ġtiṣabha δ̣ṭarr yidzawwajha.* After he had her he had to marry her.

ġaṣub force, compulsion, coercion. || *bil-ġaṣub* by force, forcibly.

ġaṣban by force, forcibly. || *ġaṣban εalee* and *ġaṣban εanna* against his will, in defiance of him. *raḥ-aštiriiha ġaṣban εaleek.* I'm going to buy it in spite of you. *l-mudiir εayyana ġaṣban εala ˀanfak.* The director appointed him in spite of you.

ġ-ṣ-ṣ

ġaṣṣ (*u ġaṣṣ*) **1.** to choke. *diir baalak, la-dġuṣṣ bis-simač.* Look out you don't choke on the fish. *la-taakul ib-surεa tara dġuṣṣ.* Don't eat fast or you'll choke. **2.** to be or become choked, jammed, packed, congested. *s-siinama ġaṣṣat bin-naas il-baarḥa.* The movie was choked with people yesterday.

ġaṣṣa pl. *-aat* choking spell.

ġ-ṣ-n

ġuṣun pl. *ˀaġṣaan* branch, bough, limb (of a tree).

ġ-δ̣-b

ġiδ̣ab (*a ġaδ̣ab*) to be or become angry, cross, irritated, exasperated, furious. *ˀabuuha yiġδ̣ab εala ˀaqall šii.* Her father gets mad at the least thing.

ˀaġδ̣ab to annoy, exasperate, anger, enrage, infuriate. *ṭ-ṭaalib ˀaġδ̣ab il-muεallim ib-taṣarrufa.* The student angered the teacher with his behavior.

ġaδ̣ab **1.** rage, fury, wrath. *ġaδ̣ab aḷḷa εaleehum. rufεaw il-ˀasεaar bila sabab.* May the wrath of Allah be on them. They raised the prices without any reason. **2.** anger, exasperation, indignation. || *ġaδ̣ab maal ˀaḷḷa* a holy terror, a real menace.

ġaδ̣baan angry, exasperated, furious, infuriated. *ġaδ̣baan εala ˀaxuu* mad at his brother. *ġaδ̣baan minni* mad at me.

ġ-δ̣-r-f

ġuδ̣ruuf pl. *ġaδ̣aariif* cartilage, gristle.

*ġuδ̣ruufi** cartilaginous. *εuδ̣u ġuδ̣ruufi* a cartilaginous organ.

ġ-δ̣-δ̣

ġaδ̣δ̣ (*u ġaδ̣δ̣*) /with *in-naδ̣ar*/ to overlook, ignore, forget. *ˀiδa tidhin ˀiida, yġuδ̣δ̣ in-naδ̣ar εanha.* If you grease his palm, he'll overlook it. *yġuδ̣δ̣ in-naδ̣ar min yšuuf šii muu ṣaḥiiḥ.* He avoids noticing anything not right.

ġ-δ̣-w

tġaaδ̣a /with *εan* or *εala*/ to disregard, ignore, pretend not to see. *huwwa yidġaaδ̣a εan kull il-ˀaġlaaṭ illi ysaw-*

wiiha. He ignores all the mistakes that he makes.

ġ-ṭ-r

ġuṭra pl. *ġuṭar* headcloth.

ġ-ṭ-r-s

tġaṭras to be haughty, arrogant, snobbish, conceited. *haaδa ma-yistaƐiqq iykuun mudiir. yidġatras ihwaaya.* He doesn't deserve to be director. He's extremely arrogant. || *yidġaṭras ib-mašiita.* He has a haughty bearing. He swaggers.

ġ-ṭ-s

ġiṭas (*i ġaṭis*) to sink. *ġiṭas il-maaƐuun bil-Ɛooḏ.* The plate sank in the pool.

ġaṭṭas to dip, plunge, immerse. *ġaṭṭis il-uqmaaš bil-ṃayy Ɛiddat marraat.* Dip the cloth in the water several times.

ġ-ṭ-ṭ

ġaṭṭ (*u gaṭṭ*) to plunge, dive. *ġaṭṭ il-čaƐb in-nahar.* He dived to the bottom of the river. *baawiƐ hal-baṭṭa. hassa raƐ-itġuṭṭ.* Watch this duck. It's about to dive. || *bass-ma xalla raasa Ɛal-imxadda, ġaṭṭ bin-noom.* As soon as he put his head on the pillow, he sank into sleep. **2.** to disappear. *ˀašu gaṭṭeet! ṣaar-inna saaƐteen nintiḏir.* You must have been swallowed up by the earth! We've been waiting two hours. *ġaṭṭ santeen w-maƐƐad dira ween.* He disappeared for two years and no one knew where he was.

ġaṭṭaṭ to plunge, dip, dunk, immerse. *ġaṭṭiṭ il-maaƐuun bil-ṃayy marrteen w-jiiba.* Plunge the plate in the water twice and bring it here. *ˀiδa ma-tfukk yaaxa minni tara ˀaġaṭṭiṭak.* If you don't leave me alone, I'm going to dunk you.

ġaṭṭa pl. *-aat* **1.** dive. **2.** disappearance. || *haay ween hal-ġaṭṭa? ṣaar-inna yoomeen ma-šifnaak.* Where've you been so long? We haven't seen you for two days.

ġ-ṭ-w

ġaṭṭa to cover. *ġaṭṭi j-jidir Ɛatta yfuur il-ṃayy ib-surƐa.* Cover the pot so that the water will boil quickly. *Ɛindak puuleen ˀaačuġ. ġaṭṭiihum.* You've two pieces unguarded. Cover them. || *š-ma tsawwi min naamarbuuṭiyyaat, ˀummha tgaṭṭii-lha.* Whatever mischievous things she does, her mother covers up for her. *xiṭaaba ġaṭṭa Ɛal-kull.* His speech stood out above all the others.

tġaṭṭa **1.** to be or become covered. *dġaṭṭeena bit-turaab min Ɛajaaj il-baarƐa.* We got covered with dust in the dust storm yesterday. **2.** to cover oneself, cover up. *l-baarƐa tġaṭṭeet b-iθlaθ baṭṭaaniyyaat yaḷḷa difeet.* Yesterday I covered up with three blankets before I got warm.

ġaṭa, ġiṭa pl. *ˀaġṭiya* **1.** cover, wrap, wrapper. **2.** covers, bed clothing. **3.** cover, lid.

mġaṭṭa veiled, obscure. *Ɛači mġaṭṭa* veiled talk.

ġ-f-r

ġufar (*u ġafur*) to forgive, grant pardon, remit. *ˀaḷḷa yuġfur-lak ˀiδnuubak.* May God pardon your sins for you.

ġtifar = *ġufar. huwwa ma-ˀaƐtiqid yiġtifir-lak ˀiδa tsawwi šii.* I don't think he'll forgive you if you do anything.

staġfar to seek forgiveness, to ask someone's pardon. *ˀastaġfir ˀaḷḷa.* I ask God's forgiveness.

ġufraan pardon, forgiveness, remission. || *Ɛiid il-ġufraan* Yom Kippur, Day of Atonement.

maġfuur: l-maġfuur lahu the deceased, the late departed (of public figures).

ġ-f-l

ġufal (*u ġaful*) to neglect, ignore, be forgetful, be unmindful. *diir baalak Ɛaj-jaahil. la-tuġfuḷ Ɛanna.* Watch the kid. Don't let your attention off of him.

tġaafal **1.** to overlook, disregard, pretend not to notice. *dġaafalit Ɛanna hal-marra, laakin θaani marra ˀaƐaaqba.* I overlooked it this time, but next time I'll punish him. *ˀaani ˀadri huwwa muhmil, bass da-atġaafal.* I know he is negligent, but I'm pretending not to notice. **2.** to be inattentive. *ˀiδa tidġaafal bid-daris, šloon tifham il-mawḏuuƐ?* If you're inattentive in class, how can you understand the subject? **3.** to be neglectful. *la-tidġaafal biš-šuġuḷ tara yitkawwan Ɛaleek.* Don't be neglectful of your work or it'll pile up on you.

ġaful by surprise, unawares, unprepared, unexpecting. *ˀaxaδni ġaful.* He took me by surprise.

ġafḷa, Ɛala ġafḷa all of a sudden, unawares, unexpectedly. *ṭabbeet Ɛalee Ɛala ġafḷa w-šifta naayim.* I burst in on him unexpectedly and found him sleeping.

ġaflaan unaware, uninformed. *činit ġaflaan Ɛanna.* I wasn't aware of it.

mġaffaḷ **1.** inattentive, absent-minded. **2.** absent-minded person.

ġ-f-w

ġufa (*i ġufa*) to doze off, fall asleep. *bass*

inṭiraḉ ḉal-ufraaš, ġufa. As soon as he lay down on the bed, he was out.

ġaffa to doze, to nod, to nap. *čaan iyġaffi biṣ-ṣaff.* He was dozing in class.

ġaffa pl. *-aat* nap, cat nap, doze.

ġafwa pl. *-aat* = *ġaffa.*

ġ-l-b

ġilab (*u ġalub*) **1.** to win, triumph, be victorious. *ṣaar-la yoomeen yuġḷub bil-uqmaar.* He's been winning at gambling for two days. *fariiq madrasatna ġilab ib-sibaaq kurat il-qadam.* Our school team won the soccer game. **2.** to beat, defeat. *maḉḉad iyġulba bis-sibiḉ.* Nobody beats him at swimming. **3.** to get the better, get the best, to best. *l-bazzaaz ġilabak ib-hal-qaaṭ.* The clothing material dealer got the best of you on this suit.

tġallab to overcome, surmount, master. *b-musaaḉadtak ˀagdar adġallab ḉala jamiiḉ iṣ-ṣuḉuubaat.* With your help, I can overcome all the difficulties.

tġaalab to compete with each other. *ˀibni w-ˀibnak idġaalbaw bir-rikiδ̣ l-baarḉa.* My son and your son raced each other yesterday.

ġilba pl. *-aat* victory.

ˀaġlab the majority, the greater portion, most. || *ḉal-ˀaġlab* mostly, generally, in general. *ḉal-ˀaġlab yiji saaḉa θmaanya.* Usually he comes at eight.

ˀaġlabiyya majority, greater portion.

ġaalub winner, victor.

ġaalib: ḉal-ġaalib mostly, usually, for the most part. *ḉal-ġaalib, yiji l-muġrub.* Mostly, he comes about sunset.

ġaalibiyya majority, greater portion.

maġḷuub beaten, defeated. *l-fariiq il-maġḷuub* the losing team.

mġaaḷab contest, race. || *yaakul ib-surḉa, ḉabaalak il-qaδ̣iyya mġaaḷab.* He eats so fast, you'd think it was a matter of racing.

ġ-l-s

ġallas to feign inattention, to pretend not to hear. *yismaḉ w-iyġallis.* He hears and shows no sign of it. *da-aḉči wyaak. la-dġallis.* I'm talking to you. Don't pretend you didn't hear.

ġ-l-δ̣

ġilaδ̣ (*a ġaliδ̣*) to become thick. *liff čam xeeṭ ḉala hal-ḉabil ḉatta yiġlaδ̣.* Wind some strings around this rope so it'll be thicker.

ġuluδ̣ thickness.

ġaliiδ̣ **1.** thick. *ḉabil ġaliiδ̣* a thick rope. || *l-ˀamḉaaˀ il-ġaliiδ̣a* the large intestine. **2.** deep, rough, gruff. *ṣoot ġaliiδ̣* a deep voice.

ˀaġlaδ̣ thicker or thickest.

ġ-l-ṭ

ġiḷaṭ (*u ġaḷiṭ*) **1.** to make a mistake, commit an error, err, be mistaken. *t-tilmiiδ ġiḷaṭ ib-ḉall il-masˀala.* The student made a mistake in solving the problem. **2.** to be disrespectful, be fresh. *la-tuġḷuṭ, yaa zġayyir, tara ˀabuṣṭak.* Don't get fresh, kid, or I'll smack you. *l-ˀibin ġiḷaṭ ḉala ˀabuu.* The son was impudent to his father.

ġaḷḷaṭ to cause someone to make a mistake. *b-ḉačyak ġaḷḷaṭitni b-ḉall il-masˀala.* With your talk you made me make a mistake in solving the problem.

tġaḷḷaṭ to make mistakes. *yidġaḷḷaṭ ihwaaya bil-qiraaˀa.* He makes lots of mistakes in reading.

ġaḷaṭ wrong, incorrect. *jawaab ġaḷaṭ* a wrong answer.

ġaḷaṭ (coll.) pl. *ˀaġḷaaṭ* error(s), mistake(s).

ġaḷṭa pl. *-aat, ˀaġḷaaṭ* un. n. of *ġaḷaṭ.*

ġaḷṭaan **1.** wrong, mistaken, in error, erring. **2.** erring person.

muġaaḷaṭa pl. *-aat* falsification, distortion.

ġ-l-ġ-l

tġalġal to penetrate, pass through. *dġalġal ib-ṣufuuf il-ḉadu w-ḉiraf kullši.* He penetrated into the enemy lines and found out about everything.

ġ-l-f

ġallaf **1.** to put in a cover, envelope, or case. *ġallif il-iktaab ḉatta ma-yitmazzag.* Put a cover on the book so it won't get worn out. **2.** to wrap, cover. *ġallaf il-paakeet w-dazza bil-bariid.* He wrapped the package and mailed it. *ġallif id-daḉḉaamiyyaat gabuḷ-ma tiṣbuġ is-sayyaara.* Mask the bumpers before you paint the car.

ġilaaf pl. *ˀaġlifa* **1.** covering, wrapper, casing. **2.** cover, book jacket.

ġ-l-g

ġilag (*u ġalig*) **1.** to close, shut. *ˀuġlug il-iktaab w-jiiba li-hnaa.* Close the book and bring it here. **2.** to latch, fasten, secure. *min itsidd il-baab baḷḷa ġlugha.* When you close the door please latch it. *ˀuġlug il-baab bass la-tuqfulha.* Close the door but don't lock it.

ġaḷḷag **1.** to close, shut, fasten, latch. *ġaḷḷig iš-šibaabiič gabuḷ-ma tiṭlaḉ.* Latch the windows before you go out. **2.** to become hoarse. *nnišal il-baarḥa w-gallag ḥissa.* He caught cold yesterday and it made his voice hoarse.

ġalag pl. *ʔaġlaag* latch.

ġ-l-l

ġall (*u ġall*) to nudge, poke. *ṣaaḥbak ma-da-yintibih. ġulla.* Your friend isn't paying attention. Poke him.

staġall **1.** to make a profit, invest profitably, utilize. *l-ḥukuuma da-tistaġill maṣaadir il-balad ib-mašaariiʕ il-ʕumraan.* The government is utilizing the country's resources in the development projects. **2.** to exploit, take advantage of. *staġall baṣaaṭa w-ġašša.* He took advantage of his simplicity and cheated him. *la-titšaarak wiyyaa tara yistaġillak.* Don't go partners with him or he'll take advantage of you.

maġluuḷ: ʔiida maġluuḷa. He's a coward. He won't fight.

ġ-l-w

ġiḷa (*a ġaḷa, ġaḷaaʔ*) to be or become expensive, high priced. *b-ʔayyaam il-ḥarub kullši ġiḷa.* During the war everything became expensive.

ġaḷḷa to raise the price of. *smaʕit raḥ-yġaḷḷuun ʔasʕaar il-ḥubuub.* I heard they're going to raise grain prices.

ġaḷa, ġaḷaaʔ inflation, period of high prices.

ʔaġḷa more or most expensive, costly.

ġaali expensive, high priced. *quuṭ ġaalya* expensive suits. || *binaaʔ il-beet ykallif ġaali.* Building a house costs a lot. *hat-taajir ybiiʕ ġaali.* This merchant charges a lot.

ġ-l-w-n

ġalwan to galvanize. *ʔiδa dġalwan il-ḥadiid, ma-yzanjir.* If you galvanize the metal, it won't rust.

ġ-l-y

ġila (*i ġali, ġalayaan*) **1.** to boil, bubble. *ṭaffi n-naar. l-ṃayy da-yiġli.* Turn off the fire. The water is boiling. **2.** to boil, cause to boil, make boil. *ʔiġli l-ḥaliib gabuḷ-ma tšurba.* Boil the milk before you drink it.

ġaali see *ġ-l-w.*

ġ-m-j

ġammaj, ġumuj, ʔaġmaj, ġamiij = *ġammag,* etc., which see under *ġ-m-g.*

g-m-r

ġumar (*u ġamur*) to flood, inundate. *l-ṃayy ġumar ʔaraaḍiina.* The water covered our lands.

ġaamar **1.** /with *b-*/ to venture, risk. *ġaamarit ib-θaruuti w-ḥaṣṣalit ihwaaya.* I risked my fortune and got a lot back. *ma-ʕinda maaniʕ yġaamir ib-ḥayaata min ʔajl il-ḥizib.* He doesn't mind risking his life for the sake of the party. **2.** to be adventurous, to have adventures. *ġaamar ihwaaya min čaan šabaab.* He was very adventurous when he was a youth.

muġaamara pl. *-aat* adventure.

ġ-m-z

ġumaz (*u ġamuz*) to signal, make a sign, beckon, wink. *ġumaz-la b-ʕeena ḥatta ma-yiḥči.* He winked at him so he wouldn't say anything. *ʔuġmuz ilha. balki tliḥgak.* Give her a come-on. Maybe she'll follow you.

ġamza pl. *-aat* come-on, wink, flirtatious gesture.

ġ-m-s

ġammas to dip, dunk. *da-yġammus il-xubuz bil-marag.* He's dunking the bread in the stew.

ġmuus anything eaten with bread.

ġ-m-ḍ

ġumaḍ (*u ġamuḍ*) to close (of the eye). *l-leel kulla ma-ġumḍat ʕeeni.* My eyes didn't close all night.

ġammaḍ to close, shut. *ġammuḍ ʕeen w-fattiḥ ʕeen min itbawwiʕ bid-darbiin.* Close one eye and open one eye when you look through the telescope.

ġumuuḍ ambiguity, abstruseness.

ġaamiḍ obscure, dark, ambiguous. *sirr ġaamiḍ* deep, dark, hidden secret.

ġummeeḍa children's game similar to blindman's buff.

ġ-m-g

ġammag **1.** to deepen, increase the depth of. *haak il-misḥaa. ġammug in-nugra biiha.* Here's the spade. Deepen the hole with it. **2.** to deepen, darken (color). *ʔiδa triid idġammug loona liθ-θoob, ʔuṣbaġa fadd marrteen lux.* If you want to deepen the color of the shirt, dye it a couple more times. **3.** to go too far, to overstep the bounds. *ġammag wiyyaaya biš-šaqa w-zaʕʕalni.* He went too far in joking with me, and irritated me. *la-dġammug wiyyaa bil-ḥači tara titnaddam.* Don't go too far talking with him or you'll be sorry.

ġumug **1.** depth, deepness. **2.** depth, darkness (of color).

ʔaġmag **1.** deeper or deepest. **2.** darker or darkest (color).

ġamiig **1.** deep. *biir ġamiiga* a deep

well. 2. deep, dark. *loon ġamiig* a dark color.

ġ-m-m

ġamm (u ġamm) to express exasperation with someone by a wave of the hand, as if pushing him away. *min ma-ƹiraf yjaawub, gammata ʔumma.* When he didn't know the answer, his mother waved her hand at him in disgust.

ġtamm to be distressed, be worried. *ġtamm ihwaaya ƹan qaḍiyyat ʔibna.* He worries a lot about his son's situation.

ġamma a gesture of pushing someone away, usually as a result of displeasure.

ġ-m-y

ġima (a i ʔiġmaaʔ) /with *ƹala*/ to overcome. *bil-ḥarr, yiġma ƹalee.* In the heat, he is overcome.

ġ-n-m

ġtinam to seize, take advantage of. *raḥ-ʔaġtinim furṣat wujuud iṭ-ṭabiib ihnaa w-ʔasʔala ƹan ṣiḥḥti.* I'm going to seize the opportunity of the doctor's presence here and ask him about my health.

ġanam pl. *ʔaġnaam* sheep. *laḥm il-ġanam* lamb, mutton. *qaṭiiƹ ġanam* herd of sheep.

ġannaam pl. *-a* 1. sheepherder, shepherd. 2. sheepman, sheep owner.

ġaanim: saalim w-ġaanim safe and sound. *wuṣal saalim w-ġaanim.* He arrived safe and sound.

ġaniima pl. *ġanaayim, ganaaʔim* spoils, booty, loot.

ġ-n-y

ġina (i ġina) to enrich, make rich, make free from want. *ʔaḷḷa yiġniik.* May God enrich you. || *la-yiġniik w-la-yxalliik itgaddi.* He gives you no way out (lit. he won't make you rich and won't let you beg).

ġanna to sing. *minu raḥ-yġanni bil-ḥafla l-yoom?* Who's going to sing at the party today?

tġanna /with *b-*/ to extol, praise, sing the praises of. *l-kull yidġannuun ib-jamaalha.* They all sing the praises of her beauty.

ġtina to become rich. *b-waasṭat ʔabuuha, ġtina hwaaya.* With the influence of her father, he became very rich.

staġna /with *ƹan*/ to spare, dispense with, manage, or do, without. *ʔaani ma-agdar ʔastaġni ƹan il-xaddaama.* I can't get along without the maid.

ġina 1. wealth, riches. 2. singing, song.

*ġani** pl. *ʔaġniyaaʔ* prosperous, well-to-do, wealthy, rich.

*ġinaaʔi** singing, song, vocal. *ḥafla ġinaaʔiyya* song recital, concert of vocal music.

ʔuġniya pl. *-aat, ʔaġaani* song.

ġannuwwa, ġunnuwwa pl. *-aat* song.

muġanni pl. *-iin* singer, vocalist.

muġanniya pl. *-aat* (female) singer, vocalist, songstress, chanteuse.

ġ-w-θ

ʔaġaaθ to help, go to the aid of. *ʔiδa maḥḥad yġiiθhum kullhum ymuutuun.* If no one goes to their aid, they'll all die.

staġaaθ to appeal for help, to seek the aid. *da-yistaġiiθuun biina. xalli nruuḥ insaaƹidhum.* They're calling to us for help. Let's go help them. *bii-man tistaġiiθ? kullhum ƹidwaan.* Whom can you call on for help? They're all enemies.

ġooθ: ṣaaḥ il-ġooθ min ʔiid marta. He's fed up with his wife.

ġ-w-r

ġaar (i ʔiġaara) /with *ƹala*/ to raid, attack, fall upon. *l-qabiila ġaarat ƹal-balda.* The tribe invaded the city.

ġaar (invar.) laurel, bay. *zeet il-ġaar* laurel oil.

ġaar (pl. *-aat*) 1. cave, cavern. 2. burrow, hole (of an animal).

ġaara pl. *-aat* raid, foray, attack, predatory excursion.

maġaara pl. *-aat* cavern, cave, grotto.

ġ-w-r-l-l-a

ġoorilla pl. *-aat* gorilla.

ġ-w-š

ġawwaš to go out of focus, to blur. *raaḥ liṭ-ṭabiib li-ʔan iƹyuuna dġawwiš.* He went to the doctor because his eyes are blurry.

mġawwaš out of focus, blurred, unclear, fuzzy. *ṣuura mġawwiša* a fuzzy picture.

ġ-w-ṣ

ġaaṣ (u ġooṣ) to submerge, dive, plunge. *yigdar yġuuṣ il-čaƹb il-baḥar.* He can dive to the bottom of the sea.

ġawwaaṣ pl. *-iin* diver.

ġawwaaṣa pl. *-aat* submarine.

ġ-w-l

ġuul pl. *ġiilaan* ghoul, demon, giant, ogre.

ġ-w-y

tġaawa to put on airs. *zangiin ihwaaya. luweeš ma-yidġaawa?* He's very rich. Why doesn't he put on airs?

ġuwa snobbishness.

ġ-y-b

ġaab (i ġeeb, ġiyaab, ġeebuuba) 1. to be

absent, be or stay away, absent oneself. *t-tilmiið ġaab ʕan il-madrasa šahreen.* The student was absent from school for two months. **2.** to set, go down. *burdat id-dinya baʕad-ma ġaabat iš-šamis.* It got cold after the sun went down.

¶ *walḷa, ġaabat ʕan baali.* By golly, it slipped my mind. *ġaabat ruuḥa mniṭ-ṭaʕab wil-ḥarr.* He fainted from fatigue and the heat. *s-simač kulla ġaab.* The fish is all soft and old.

ġayyab **1.** to keep away. *mudiir il-madrasa ġayyab iṭ-ṭullaab ʕan il-muðaa-hara.* The school principal kept the students away from the demonstration. *š-ġay-yabak ʕanha?* What kept you away from her?

tġayyab to be absent, be away, stay away. *ʔiða tidġayyab ihwaaya, ma-titʕallam.* If you stay absent a lot you won't learn.

ġtaab to slander. *ʕala ṭuul yiġtaabuun ʔaṣdiqaaʔhum.* They always talk behind their friends' backs.

staġaab = *ġtaab. la-tistiġiiba. xalli yiji w-iḥči giddaama.* Don't talk about him when he isn't here. Let him come and talk in front of him.

ġeeb: l-ġeeb the unknown, the supernatural. *yiʕlam bil-ġeeb.* He's clairvoyant.

ġaaba pl. *-aat* **1.** forest, wood. **2.** jungle.

ġeeba pl. *-aat* absence.

ġiiba slander, harmful talk about someone.

ġiyaab **1.** being away. **2.** (pl. *-aat*) absence.

*ġiyaabi** *ḥukum ġiyaabi* sentencing in absentia. *muḥaakama ġiyaabiyya* trial in absentia.

ġiyaabiyyan in absentia. *ḥukmoo ġiyaabiyyan.* They tried him in absentia.

ġeebuuba unconsciousness, faint, fainting spell.

ġaayib **1.** absent. *ġaayib imnid-daris* absent from class. **2.** person who is absent.

¶ *l-ġaayib* the sum agreed upon in a marriage contract to be paid by a man in case he divorces his wife.

ġ-y-θ

ʔaġaaθ, see *ġ-w-θ*.

ġ-y-r

ġaar (*a ġeera*) **1.** to be jealous. *yġaar min ʔaxuu iẓ-ẓiġayyir.* He's jealous of his little brother. **2.** to be zealous. *yġaar ʕala waṭana.* He's earnestly concerned with his country, he's a zealous patriot. **3.** to be ticklish. *daġdiġa. šuufa yġaar loo laa.* Tickle him and see whether he's ticklish or not.

ġayyar **1.** to change, alter, modify, make different. *la-dġayyir ʔay šii bil-miswadda.* Don't change anything in the draft. || *ʔiða ʔaḷḷaa nṭaa l-ʕaafya raḥ-iyġayyir hawa b-ʔoruppa.* If God grants him good health, he's going to take a change of climate to Europe. *has-sana ġayyiraw išwayya bil-manhaj id-diraasi.* This year they changed a few things in the study program. **2.** to change, exchange, replace. *laazim inġayyir it-taayir.* We've got to change the tire. *ʔiða ma-tʕijbak, iyġayyir-ilk-iyyaaha.* If you don't like it, he'll exchange it for you. **3.** to make jealous. *laabsa nafnuufha j-jidiid; da-dġayyir ṣadiiqatha.* She's wearing her new dress; making her friend jealous.

tġayyar to be replaced. *mudiirna raḥ-yidġayyar iš-šahar ij-jaay.* Our director will be replaced next month.

ġeer **1.** other, another, different. *ġeer θoob* another shirt. *ġeer yoom* another day. *ġeer waaḥid* someone else. **2.** (someone or something) other than, except, else. *da-yitxoorad ʕal-ibnayya b-ifluus ġeera.* He's showing off for the girl with someone else's money. *xalli yiji waaḥid ġeerak yiḥči wiyyaaha.* Let someone besides you come to talk to her. *ma-ʕidkum ġeer il-ʔaqmiša ṣ-ṣuufiyya?* Don't you have anything but wool cloth? *l-ġeer š-aʕlee?* What does he care about anyone else? **3.** (an interrogative used in replying to a question or statement, approx.:) what else but, could it be anything but, wasn't it. *ġeer huwwa raad yʔaððiik?* What else but that he wanted to hurt you? *ġeer min ṭaraf il-ifluus maalti?* Could it be anything else but concerning my money? *ġeer ʔinta ma-qbalit tištiri? huwwa raad ybiiʕ.* Wasn't it you that wouldn't buy? He wanted to sell. *ġeer ʔinta l-gitt-li haay xooš sayyaara w-xal-leetni ʔaštiriiha?* Didn't you yourself tell me this was a good car and let me buy it? || *ṭabʕan! ġeer axuu l-mudiir?* Of course! Isn't his brother the director? **4.** were it not that, except that, but for the fact that. *ġeer il-ḥaakim garaayba, willa čaan inḥikam.* If it weren't for the fact that the judge is related to him, he'd have been found guilty. *ġeer ligeena ṭ-ṭariiq masduud, willa čaan wuṣalna saaʕa xamsa.* If we hadn't found the road closed, we'd have arrived at five. *čaan jaawabt il-ʔasʔila kullha ġeer hiyya muu mnil-iktaab.* I'd've answered all the questions except that they weren't from the book. **5.** (an intensifying particle, approx.:) real, quite a, such a, what a, really, quite, so. *buṣaṭṭa ġeer basṭa!* I gave him a real beating. *nijaḥ ġeer najaaḥ!* What a success he achieved! *haaða ġeer muṭi!* He's a real dope! *binta ġeer ḥilwa!* His daughter's really pretty! **6.** not, non-. *ġeer qaanuuni* illegal, not legal. *ġeer maʕquul* unreasonable, not reasonable.

ġiira jealousy.

taġyiir pl. *-aat* change.

ġ-y-ð̣

ġaað̣ (*i ġaað̣*) to anger, make angry. *la-dgul-la hiiči šii tara dġiið̣a.* Don't tell him such a thing or you'll anger him.

ġtaað̣ to be or become angry, to get mad. *la-tiġtaað̣ minna. huwwa ʔaxuuk.* Don't get angry at him. He's your brother.

ġ-y-m

ġayyam to be or become cloudy, to cloud up. *d-dinya saaʕa dġayyim w-saaʕa tṣaḥḥi.* The sky gets cloudy one hour and then clears up the next. || *š-bii ʔaxuuk? ʔašu wičča mġayyim.* What's with your brother? He seems glum.

ġeem (coll.) cloud(s).

ġeema pl. *ġyuum* cloud.

ġ-y-n

ġeen name of the letter *ġ*.

ġ-y-y

ġaaya pl. *-aat* **1.** object, objective, end, intention, intent, purpose. || *lil-ġaaya* extremely, very. *hal-qaḍiyya muhimma lil-ġaaya.* This matter is extremely important. *ġaaya b-* extremely, extraordinarily. *hiyya ġaaya bij-jimaal.* She is extraordinarily beautiful. *haaða ġaaya bið-ðakaaʔ.* He's extremely intelligent.

F

f-a

faa name of the letter *f*.

f-ʔ-a

fiʔa pl. *-aat* **1.** group, gang, party, faction. **2.** price, denomination. *ṭawaabiʕ fiʔat xams ifluus* five fils stamps.

f-a-t-y

faatya pl. *-aat, fwaati* drawer.

f-a-d

f̈faad heart, chest. || *f̈faada yilzama.* His chest hurts him. *ðiraba b-dafra w-giṭaʕ f̈faada.* He kicked him and hurt him something awful. *ḥčaayta baʕadha tungur b-uf̈faadi.* His remark is still gnawing at my heart. *haš-šuġuḷ dayišlaʕ uf̈faadi.* This work is wearing me out. *la-taakuul raas uf̈faadi.* Don't give me a hard time.

f-a-r

faar pl. *fiiraan* (coll.) mouse (mice). || *ġaab il-qiṭṭ ilʕab yaa faar.* When the cat's away the mice will play.

faara pl. *-aat, fiiraan* **1.** mouse. **2.** any of the muscles of the lamb shank, as meat.

f-a-r-s

faarsi: namil faarsi* a sort of large ant.

f-a-r-g-w-n

faargoon pl. *aat, faraagiin.* railroad car.

f-a-s

faas pl. *-aat, fuus* adze.

f-a-š

*faaši** formal equivalent of *faašisti.*

faašiyya = faašistiyya.

f-a-š-s-t

*faašisti** **1.** fascist, fascistic **2.** a fascist.

faašistiyya fascism.

f-a-ṣ-w-l-y

faaṣuulya (coll.) bean(s).

faaṣuulyaaya pl. *-aat* un. n. of *faaṣuulya.*

faaṣuuliyya (coll.) bean(s).

faaṣuuliyyaaya pl. *-aat* un. n. of *faaṣuuliyya.*

f-a-f-w-n

faafoon aluminum. *ṭaasa faafoon* an aluminum bowl.

f-ʔ-l

tfaaʔal /with *b-*/ **1.** to regard as a good omen, regard as auspicious. *ʔatfaaʔal bil-bilbil.* I always regard the nightingale as a good sign. **2.** to be optimistic. *ʔaani mitfaaʔil ib-haṣ-ṣafqa.* I'm optimistic about this deal. *ʔatfaaʔal-lak bin-najaaḥ.* I predict success for you.

mitfaaʔil optimist.

faal: ||*ʔaxað faal* and *fitaḥ faal.* to tell fortunes, predict the future. *fitaḥ-li faal.* He told my fortune. *nṭii ʕašr ifluus ḥatta yaaxuð-lak faal.* Give him ten fils so he will tell your fortune. *fattaaḥ faal.* fortuneteller. *ruuḥ ib-*

faalak. Go on. Go ahead. Do what you want.

fawwaal pl. *-iin, -a* fortuneteller.

f-a-l

faala pl. *-aat* fish gig, trident.

f-a-l-w-l

faaluul (coll.) wart(s).

faaluula pl. *-aat* un. n. of *faaluula.*

f-a-n-w-s

faanuus pl. *fwaaniis* lantern.

f-a-n-y-l

faaniila **1.** flannel. **2.** (pl. *-aat*) undershirt, tee-shirt. || *faaniila ʔumm ɛillaaga* brief undershirt, sleeveless undershirt.

f-t-t

fatt (*i*) to break. *ʔibnič ma-yinḥimil w-iyfitt il-gaḷuḅ.* Your son is unbearable, and he gets on one's nerves.

fattat to crumble, break into small pieces. *fattit il-xubza w-inṭiiha lil-ɛaṣaafiir.* Crumble the bread and give it to the birds.

tfattat to crumble, disintegrate, break up into fragments. *hal-ikleeča titfattat bil-iid.* These cookies fall apart in the hand. || *ffaadha tfattat imnil-bači.* She cried her heart out.

nfatt to be anguished, be beside oneself. *nfattat ɛala moot ʔabuuha.* She was anguished by her father's death. *nfatt min simaɛ traffaɛit.* He was beside himself when he heard I got promoted. || *nfatt galbi min taṣarrufa.* I was all torn up about his behavior.

ftaat crumbs, pieces. *ftaat xubuz* bread crumbs.

fatiit falling apart, overcooked, cooked to shreds. *laḥam fatiit* overcooked meat.

f-t-ḥ

fitaḥ (*a fatiḥ*) **1.** to open. *fitaḥit buṭil ṣooda jidiid.* I opened a new bottle of soda. || *ʔaḷḷa yiftaḥ-lak.* God bless you (lit. God open the door to riches for you). **2.** (by extension) to open, start. *raḥ-aftaḥ iḥṣaab ib-hal-ḅang.* I'm going to open an account in this bank. *fitaḥ-la maxzan ib-šaariɛ ir-rašiid.* He opened a store on Rashid Street. *fitḥaw šaariɛ jidiid ihnaa.* They opened a new street here. **3.** to open, inaugurate. *raʔiis il-wuzaraaʔ raḥ-yiftaḥ iš-šaariɛ ij-jidiid.* The prime minister will officially open the new street. **4.** to turn on. *fitaḥt ir-raadyo min dixalt il-ġurfa.* I turned on the radio when I entered the room. *fitaḥ il-ṃayy w-xallaa.* He turned on the water and left it on. *ʔiftaḥ ið-ðuwa min itxušš.* Turn on the light when you go in. || *ṭ-ṭurši yiftaḥ iš-šahiyya.* Pickles stimulate the appetite. *nṭiini ʔiidak; xalli ʔaftaḥ-lak faal.* Give me your hand, let me tell your fortune. **5.** to conquer, capture. *l-qaaʔid fitaḥ il-madiina baɛad muqaawama ɛaniifa.* The commander captured the city after a fierce battle.

fattaḥ **1.** to open (something). *la-tfattiḥ ɛeenak ʔila ʔan agullak.* Don't open your eyes till I tell you. *šwakit itfattiḥ kull yoom?* What time do you open each day? || *haaða yfattiḥ bil-liban.* You can't pull the wool over his eyes. **2.** (of flowers) to open, to bloom. *l-warid kulla fattaḥ.* The flowers have all bloomed.

faataḥ to approach, speak to. *raḥ-afaatḥa bil-mawðuuɛ.* I'll bring the subject up with him. *ma-da-aɛruf išloon ʔafaatḥa bil-mawðuuɛ.* I don't know how I'll approach him about the subject.

tfaataḥ to feel out, sound out. *ma-agdar afaatḥa hassa li-ʔan zaɛlaan.* I can't sound him out now since he's mad. *tfaataḥna bil-qaðiyya w-ittifaqna.* We felt each other out on the matter and we agreed.

nfitaḥ to be opened. *šwakit infitaḥ hal-buṭiḷ?* When was this bottle opened? *hal-maxzan šwakit infitaḥ?* When'd this store open?

ftitaḥ to open, inaugurate. *ftitaḥ il-ḥafla b-kalima qaṣiira.* He opened the ceremony with a few words.

staftaḥ to start doing business. *baɛad ma-staftaḥit. ma-ɛindi xurda.* I haven't done any business yet. I haven't got any change.

fatḥa **1.** the vowel point a (gram.). **2.** a card game, roughly similar to rummy.

fattaaḥ: fattaaḥ il-faal fortune teller.

fattaaḥa pl. *-aat* **1.** opener, can opener, bottle opener. **2.** corkscrew.

miftaaḥ pl. *mafaatiiḥ* **1.** key. **2.** opener, can opener, bottle opener.

ʔaftaḥ lighter or lightest (color).

ftitaaḥ opening, inauguration. *ḥaflat il-iftitaaḥ* the opening ceremony.

*ftitaaḥi** opening. *kalima ftitaaḥiyya* opening address. || *maqaal iftitaaḥi* leading article, leader, editorial.

ftitaaḥiyya pl. *-aat* editorial, leader.

stiftaaḥ start, beginning.

faatiḥ **1.** conqueror, victor. **2.** light

(color). *nafnuuf ˀaxḏar faatiḥ* a light green dress.

faatiḥa pl. *fawaatiḥ* a recitation of the opening sura of the Koran. || *l-faatiḥa* name of the first sura of the Koran.

faatḥa pl. *-aat* a commemorative service for a dead man.

maftuuḥ **1.** open, opened. *kitaab maftuuḥ* an open book. **2.** open, open for business. *l-maxzan maftuuḥ.* The store's open. **3.** on. *l-ṃaay maftuuḥ.* The water's on.

mfattiḥ open, opened. *lis-saaʕa šgadd itḏill imfattiḥ?* What hour will you be open to? || *ma-tigdar idġulba. huwwa mfattiḥ bil-liban.* You can't get the best of him. He has eyes in the back of his head (he can see through yoghurt).

f-t-r

fitar (*i fatir*) **1.** to lose interest, cool off. *ḥaḏḏar kullši liz-zawaaj, ˀašu baʕdeen fitar.* He got everything ready for the wedding, but it seems he lost interest after that. *bil-ˀawwal čaan mitḥammis lil-qaḏiyya bass baʕdeen fitar.* At first he was enthusiastic about the matter but later he lost interest. **2.** to measure (by the span of thumb to index finger). *ˀiftir il-meez w-gul-li šgadd ʕurḏa w-ṭuula.* Measure the table with your hand and tell me its width and length.

fattar **1.** to let up, let up on (speed), lower (speed). *fattar is-surʕa min wuṣal lij-jisir.* He let up on the speed when he reached the bridge. *fattir išwayya. ˀaku naas da-yʕubruun iš-šaariʕ.* Slow down a little. There are people crossing the street. **2.** to lower, reduce. *fattir ḥarakat il-faanuus ḥatta ynaam ij-jaahil.* Turn down the lantern wick so the child can sleep. *fattir it-tabbaax; ḥtirag il-ˀakil.* Turn the oven down; the food's gotten burned.

fitir pl. *ftaar* a unit of measurement equal to the span of the extended thumb and index finger.

fatra pl. *-aat* period, spell, while.

faatir tepid, lukewarm. *ṃayy faatir* lukewarm water.

f-t-š

fattaš **1.** to search. *š-šurṭa fattišata w-ʕiθrat ʕala musaddas.* The police searched him and found a pistol. **2.** to inspect, make an inspection. *naḏḏum il-meez. l-mudiir raḥ-yiji yfattiš.* Straighten up the desk. The director is coming to inspect. **3.** to take attendance, check attendance. *kull yoom iṣ-ṣubuḥ, l-muʕallim yfattiš.* Every morning the teacher takes attendance.

taftiiš **1.** search, searching. **2.** inspection. **3.** taking, or checking, attendance.

mufattiš inspector, supervisor.

f-t-q

fatiq pl. *futuuq* hernia, rupture (med.). see also *f-t-g*.

f-t-g

fitag (*i fatig*) **1.** to slit, or split open, a seam, to undo the stitching. *ˀiftig il-guuniyya w-ṭalliʕ išwayya timman.* Split the seam on the gunny sack and take out a little rice. || *fitag-li fatig čibiir.* He really got me into trouble. **2.** to break out, break through (liquids). *l-ṃayy fitag w-ġarrag il-ˀaraaḏi.* The water broke through and flooded the land.

fattag intens. of *fitag*. *fattig il-ikyaas kullha w-inṭiini naamuuna minha.* Open the seam on each of the sacks and give me a sample from it.

tfattag to tear at the seams, split at the seams, be torn. *bass tilbas has-sitra, titfattag.* Just put on this coat, and it will tear.

nfitag **1.** to be split at the seams. *min šaal iida nfitgat sitirta min jawwa l-ˀubuṭ.* When he lifted his arm his coat split a seam under the armpit. **2.** to be broken, ruptured. *s-sadda nfitgat wil-ṃaay ġarrag il-mazaariʕ.* The dam broke and the water flooded the farms.

fatig **1.** split seam. || *fatig riiḥ* hernia. **2.** crack, fissure, break.

f-t-k

fitak (*u fatik*) /with *b-*/ to destroy, annihilate. *ˀahl il-qarya fitkaw bil-ḥaywaanaat ib-hal-manṭiqa.* The villagers have destroyed the animal life in this area. *l-ʕadu fitak biihum.* The enemy annihilated them.

fattaak. **1.** deadly, lethal, murderous. **2.** dangerous person.

f-t-l

fital (*i fatil*) **1.** to twist together. *ˀiftil hal-xeeṭeen ḥatta tṣiiruun ˀaqwa.* Twist these two strings together so they'll be stronger. **2.** to braid, plait. *ˀiftil hal-ixyuuṭ w-sawwiiha ḥabil.* Braid these threads and make a rope out of them.

fatlapiič pl. *-aat* trick, prank.

fitiila pl. *-aat, ftaayil* **1.** wick (of a lamp or candle). **2.** mantle (of a gasoline lantern). **3.** fuse. **4.** rectal suppository.

fattaala pl. *-aat* dust devil, whirlwind.

maftuul: ʕaḍalaat maftuula corded muscles.

f-t-l-k

fatlaka pl. *-aat* a new one, something new, a new twist, a new angle. *ʔabu l-garaaj ṭallaʕ-li fadd fatlaka w-yriid diinaareen baʕad.* The garageman brought out something new on me and wants two more dinars. *triidhum ywaafquun? jiib-ilhum fadd fatlaka.* You want them to give in? Bring up some new angle.

f-t-n

fitan (i fatin) to inform, tell, tattle. *ʔiδa ma-djuuz, tara ʔaftin ʕaleek ʕind il-muʕallim.* If you don't stop it, I'll tell on you to the teacher.

fattan to be in the habit of tattling, informing, to bear tales. *ʔinta šgadd itfattin ʕala ʔaẓdiqaaʔak!* My, how you carry tales on your friends!

fitna 1. tattling, tale bearing. 2. (pl. *-aat, fitan*) an act of tattling. 3. discord, dissension.

fattaan 1. captivating, enchanting, charming, fascinating. *jamaal fattaan* captivating beauty. 2. tattletale, talebearer, informer.

f-t-w

fita (i ʔiftaaʔ) to give a formal legal opinion. *l-ʕaalim id-diini raʕ-yifti biiha.* The religious authority will give a religious opinion on it.

fatwa pl. *fataawi* a formal legal opinion (Islamic law), a formal ruling on a religious matter.

mufti pl. *-iyyin* mufti, official interpreter of Islamic law.

f-j-ʔ

faajaʔ to surprise, take by surprise. *faajaʔta bil-xabar.* I surprised him with the news.

tfaajaʔ to be surprised, be taken by surprise. *tfaajaʔit w-ma-činit ʔadri.* I was taken by surprise and didn't know.

fujʔa, fujʔatan suddenly, unexpectedly. *maat fujʔa.* He died suddenly.

*fujaaʔi** unexpected, sudden. *maraḍ fujaaʔi* an unexpected illness. *ʕarr fujaaʔi* an unexpected heat wave. *hujuum fujaaʔi* a sudden attack.

mufaajaʔa pl. *-aat* surprise. || *mufaajaʔa* by surprise, unexpectedly. *dixal ʕaleena mufaajaʔa.* He came in on us unexpectedly.

mufaajiʔ sudden, unexpected, surprising. *hujuum mufaajiʔ* a sudden attack.

f-j-j

fajj (i fajj) to cut, slice, split, cleave. *fajj raasa bil-ʕuuda.* He split his head open with the stick. *l-baaxira tfijj il-ṃayy min timši.* The ship cuts the water as it goes along.

fijja pl. *fijaj* 1. piece of cloth. 2. small carpet, rug.

f-j-r

fijar (i fajir) to lance, prick. *ma-ariid afjir-lak had-dimbila ʔila ʔan tilʕag.* I don't want to lance that boil for you till it's ready. *ṭ-ṭabiib fijar-li l-buṭbaata.* The doctor opened the blister for me.

fajjar to explode. *š-šurṭa waddaw il-qumbula lič-čool w-fajjirooha.* The police took the bomb to the desert and exploded it.

tfajjar to gush out, spurt forth, erupt, burst out. *šuuf il-ṃayy išloon da-yitfajjar min hal-ʕeen.* Look at how the water is bursting forth from this spring.

nfijar to explode, burst, go off. *δabbaw qumbula ʕas-sayyaara laakin ma-nfijrat.* They threw a bomb at his car but it didn't explode. *d-dimbila nfijrat bil-leel.* The boil burst during the night.

fajir dawn, daybreak.

nfijaar pl. *-aat* explosion.

faajir pl. *fujjaar, fajara.* libertine, debauchee, rake.

faajira pl. *-aat* harlot, loose woman, whore.

f-j-ʕ

fijaʕ (a fajiʕ) to inflict suffering and grief (by bereaving someone). *ʔaḷḷa fijaʕa b-binta.* God took his daughter away.

nfijaʕ to be stricken (with grief, by the death of someone). *nfijaʕit ib-mootat ṣadiiqi.* I was stricken by my friend's death. *nfijaʕ ib-walada.* He was stricken by his son's death.

faajiʕa pl. *fawaajiʕ* calamity, disaster, tragedy.

f-j-l

fijil radish(es).

f-j-w

fajwa pl. *-aat* gap, opening, hole, aperture, breach.

f-č-č

fačč pl. *fčuuč* jaw, jawbone.

f-č-x

fičax (i fačix) to hit (on the head), to injure (the head). *fičax raasa bil-ičmaaġ.* He laid his head open with the club. *fičaxit raasa bil-iʕjaara.* I gashed his head with a rock. *fičaxni w-širad.* He beaned me and ran away.

faččax intens. of *fičax. xaṭiyya, faččixoo j-jahhaal.* Poor guy, the kids plastered him with rocks.

fačxa pl. *-aat* a head wound caused by a blow.

f-ح-š

faaحiša pl. *-aat, fawaaحiš* whore, prostitute.

f-ح-ṣ

fuحaṣ (*a faحiṣ*) to examine, check. *ʔifحaṣ il-kaabreeta; ybayyin biiha wuṣax.* Check the carburetor; it seems to have dirt in it. *d-duktoor fuحaṣni w-gal-li ma-biik šii.* The doctor examined me and told me I was OK.

tfaححaṣ to examine closely, scrutinize. *laazim titfaححaṣ is-sayyaara ʔawwal.* You'd better examine the car carefully first. *da-yitfaححaṣ biiha zeen gabuḷ-ma yištiriiha.* He's scrutinizing it well before he buys it.

nfuحaṣ to be examined. *minu yriid yinfuحiṣ ʔawwal?* Who wants to be examined first?

faحiṣ checkup, examination, physical or medical examination.

f-ح-l

stafحal to become serious, get out of control. *l-ġalaaʔ stafحal wil-حukuuma ma-tuعruf š-itsawwi.* Inflation has gotten out of control and the government doesn't know what to do. *stafحal il-maraδ.* The disease got out of control.

faحal pl. *fحuul* **1.** male. || *ṭilaع faحal عala ʔabuu.* He turned out to be a real man just like his father. *faحl išbuwwa* stud. **2.** (leaf) spring (automobile).

f-ح-m

faححam to char, burn to a crisp. *nisaw il-ʔakil عan-naar ʔila ʔan faححam.* They forgot the food on the fire until it got burned. || *faححamit imnil-عaṭaš.* I'm dried out from thirst.

ʔafحam to dumbfound, strike dumb, astound. *ʔafحamhum ib-xiṭaaba l-mumtaaz.* He dumbfounded them with his excellent speech.

faحam (coll.) charcoal, coal(s).

faحma pl. *-aat* lump of coal, piece of charcoal.

faححaam pl. *-a* coal dealer.

f-ح-w

faحwa essence, main meaning, purport (of a speech, etc.).

f-x-t-y

fuxtiyya pl. *-aat, fuxaati* turtledove.

fuxtaaya pl. *-aat, fuxaati* = *fuxtiyya.*

f-x-j

faxxaj to walk with legs wide apart. *luweeš da-yfaxxij haaδa?* Why's that fellow walking with his legs apart? *ʔiδa tfaxxij, ma-tigdar timši sariiع.* If you splay your legs you can't walk fast.

faaxaj = *faxxaj: yimši w-yfaaxij liʔanna mtahhar.* He walks with his legs spread apart because he's been circumcised.

f-x-δ

fuxuδ pl. *fxaaδ* **1.** thigh. **2.** leg (of meat). **3.** subdivision (of a tribe).

f-x-r

fuxar (*a faxir*) **1.** to be proud, pride oneself. *yifxar b-ibna li-ʔan yinjaع b-imtiyaaz.* He's proud of his son because he passes with flying colors. *ʔaani ʔafxar biik li-ʔannak fadd ṣadiiq muxliṣ w-kariim.* I am proud of you because you are a sincere and generous friend. **2.** to fire, bake. *ʔiδa ma-tfuxruun it-tunag, tmuuع bil-mayy.* If you don't bake the clay jugs, they'll fall apart in water.

faaxar to boast. *حatta loo ṣudug, malaazim itfaaxir il-hal-حadd.* Even though it's true, you shouldn't boast so much.

tfaaxar to boast. *da-yitfaaxruun ibʔajdaadhum illi ṣaaraw itraab.* They are boasting about their ancestors who have become dust.

ftixar to be proud, pride oneself. *ʔiحna niftixir ib-kull waaحid yʔaddi xidma lij-jamعiyya.* We are proud of each one who contributes a service to the association.

faxar **1.** glory, honor, credit. **2.** someone or something to be proud of. *ʔinta faxarna w-kullna niعtazz biik.* You are the object of our pride and we all are proud of you. *tiji عalee bil-baskuut w-itbuṭحa. haaδa muu faxar.* You sneak up on him and throw him. That's no accomplishment.

*faxri** honorary. *raʔiis faxri* honorary chairman.

ʔafxar more or most superb, etc.

mafxara pl. *mafaaxir* someone or something to be proud of.

faaxir superb, magnificent, *ʔakil faaxir* superb food.

f-x-f-x

faxfaxa **1.** luxury, splendor. **2.** ostentation, showiness.

f-x-m

faxxam to praise extravagantly, glorify, build up. *yfaxxim ib-ajdaada.* He makes his ancestors out to have been something special. *da-yfaxxim ihwaaya b-ʔaʕmaal il-ħukuuma.* He's really glorifying the actions of the government.

faxim impressive, stately, magnificent. *qaṣir faxim* a magnificient palace.

faxaama (title of respect for a prime minister) Excellency. *faxaamat raʔiis il-wuzaraaʔ* His Excellency the Prime Minister.

f-d-d

fadd 1. one, a single, the same. *ʔaku fadd ṭariiqa l-ħall hal-muškila.* There's one way to solve this problem. *ʔaku fadd waaħid bass yuʕruf ij-jawaab.* There's only one person who knows the answer. *ʔagdar amawwta b-fadd books.* I can kill him with one punch. *sawweet kull haš-šuġuḷ ib-fadd yoom?* Did you do all this work in one day? *xalleena kull il-ġaraað ib-fadd mukaan.* We put all the things in the same place. *haaða w-ṣadiiqa ylibsuun malaabis fadd šikil.* He and his friend wear the same kind of clothes. *kulla fadd šii bin-nisba ʔili.* It's all the same to me. *fadd marra šifta wiyya bnayya ħilwa.* Once I saw him with a pretty girl. 2. a, an. *ʕindak fadd nuṣṣ diinaar ddaayinni?* Do you have a half dinar to lend me? *tʕarrafit ʕala fadd ʔamriiki il-yoom.* I got acquainted with an American today. *tuʕruf fadd šii ʕan hal-qaḍiyya?* Do you know anything about this matter? *biʕit-la fadd čam ħaaja ʕatiiga.* I sold him a few old things. *ʔagdar ʔaaxuð fadd išwayya min hal-ʕinab?* May I take a few of these grapes? *fadd išwayya w-amurr ʕaleek.* Just a little while and I'll come to your place. 3. one, a real, quite the. *ðoola fadd naas. ma-yinħiči wiyyaahum.* They're some people. You can't talk to them. *haaða fadd balaaʔ. ma-yingidir ʕalee.* He's one smart cookie. You can't get around him. *hal-mwaððaf fadd iẓmaal. la-yħill wala yirbuṭ.* That official's a real jerk. He can't do anything. 4. some, some sort of. *kull-ma agul-la ʕala šii ytalliʕ-li fadd ħijja.* Whenever I tell him anything, he comes up with some sort of excuse. *huwwa yʕiiš ib-fadd qarya maħħad yindallha.* He lives in some village no one can find. *gal-li fadd šii laakin niseeta.* He told me something but I forgot it. *xalli nruuħ il-fadd mukaan w-niskar suwa.* Let's go somewhere and get drunk together. 5. some, a few. *siʔalta w-jaawabni fadd ʔajwiba saxiifa.* I asked him and he gave me some silly answers. *štireet fadd ʔašyaa jidiida il-yoom.* I bought some new things today. *sammaʕni fadd ħači ma-saamʕa gabuḷ.* He let me in on some talk I hadn't heard before. 6. some, about, approximately. *masaafat fadd xamsiin miil* a distance of some fifty miles. *čaanaw fadd ʕišriin waaħid.* There were about twenty people. *ntiðarta fadd nuṣṣ saaʕa w-ma-jaa.* I waited for him about a half hour and he didn't come. 7. simply, only, just. *čaan fadd yiriid yitxalliṣ minnak.* He only wanted to get rid of you. *hamma, fadd yijmaʕ ifluus.* His goal is just to get money. *fadd gul-la b-ismi w-ma-ʕaleek.* Just mention my name to him and you'll have no trouble. *fadd tiðħak ʕala ʔabuu; ybuṣṭak.* Just laugh at his father; he'll hit you. *haaða yiħči fadd ħači. la-tṣaddig bii.* He's just talking. Don't believe him. 8. the minute, as soon as. *fadd wuṣalit, šawwafni l-ġaraað.* The minute I arrived, he showed me the things. *fadd ðakkarta bil-qaḍiyya, sawwaaha.* As soon as I reminded him of the matter, he took care of it. || *muu fadd šii* nothing, no great thing. *taṣliiħ har-raadyo muu fadd šii.* Repairing this radio is nothing.

¶ *fadd marra* 1. might as well. *xoo, fadd marra, guul ʔaani čaððaab.* Well, you might as well say I'm a liar. 2. completely. *sawwa nafsa fadd marra ma-yuʕruf šii.* He pretended not to know anything. *fadd noob* completely. *fadd noob ma-yuʕruf šii.* He really doesn't know anything.

f-d-n

faddaan pl. *fdaadiin* simple, animal-drawn plow.

f-d-y

fida (*i fidaaʔ*) to sacrifice to. *j-jinuud fidaw l-waṭan ib-ʔanfushum.* The soldiers sacrificed themselves to the fatherland. *kullna nifdiik ib-ʔarwaaħna.* We all sacrifice our souls for you.

tfaada to avoid. *ħaawil titfaada l-xaṭar ib-safirtak.* Try to avoid danger on your trip. *ʔaħaawil ʔatfaada š-šaqa.* I try to avoid teasing anyone.

fidaaʔi pl. *iyyiin, -iyya.* 1. fighter who risks his life recklessly. 2. commando, guerrilla, member of the fedayeen.

f-δ-l-k

faδlaka var. of *fatlaka,* which see under *f-t-l-k.*

f-r-a-k

fraak pl. *-aat* full dress, tails.

f-r-j

furaj (*i farij*) dispel, drive away (grief, worries, etc.). *la-tihtamm. ʔaḷḷa yifrijha.* Don't worry. Allah will ease the situation.

farraj to show. *min riꞔit il-baġdaad ꞔammi farrajni ꞔala mukaanaat ihwaaya.* When I went to Baghdad my uncle showed me around many places.

tfarraj to watch, observe. *muu šarṭ tilꞔab. tigdar titfarraj bass.* You don't have to play. You can just watch.

farij pl. *fruuj* pudendum of the female, vulva.

faraj relief from suffering.

furja (no pl.) sight, spectacle. *ʔimšu minnaa! qaabil ꞔidna furja?* Get away from here! Do you think we're holding a sideshow here? *xiliqta ṣaarat furja lin-naas.* His looks were an object of curiosity for the people.

farruuj (coll.) pullet(s).

farruuja pl. *fraariij* pullet.

f-r-j-l

firjaal pl. *faraajiil* compass, dividers.

f-r-č

farrač to brush. *yfarrič isnuuna gabuḷ-ma ynaam.* He brushes his teeth before retiring. *farrič sitirtak. biiha ꞔajaaj ihwaaya.* Brush your coat. There's a lot of dust on it.

firča pl. *firač* brush. *firčat il-buṭiḷ.* 1. brush for cleaning bottles. 2. a plant resembling a bottle brush. || *raꞔ-tilmaꞔ il-qundara min tuδrubha firča.* The shoes will shine when you brush them.

f-r-ꞔ

firaꞔ (*a faraꞔ*) to be glad, happy. *firaꞔit min šifta.* I was pleased when I saw him.

farraꞔ to gladden, make happy, delight. *xabar najaaꞔak farraꞔni hwaaya.* The news of your success delighted me very much.

faraꞔ **1.** happiness, gladness, joy. || *ṭaar imnil-faraꞔ.* He was beside himself with happiness. He jumped for joy. **2.** (pl. *ʔafraaꞔ*) joyous occasion. || *ʔinšaḷḷa, daaʔiman bil-ʔafraaꞔ.* I hope you'll always be happy.

farꞔaan joyful, happy, glad, delighted. *š-biik halgadd farꞔaan?* How come you're so joyful?

f-r-x

farrax to have young ones (of birds). *ṭyuurna farrixaw.* Our birds had a covey of young.

farix pl. *fruux* fledgeling, young bird.

faraxči, farixči pl. *-iyya, iyyiin* a man who likes young boys.

f-r-d

firad (*i farid*) to separate, isolate, segregate. *ʔifrid iṭ-ṭamaaṭa d-duuniyya imniz-zeena.* Separate the bad tomatoes from the good. *ʔifrid id-diič ꞔan id-dijaaj.* Isolate the rooster from the chickens.

nfirad **1.** to withdraw, move away. *la-tinfirid ꞔan ij-jamaaꞔa.* Don't isolate yourself from the group. *raꞔ-anfirid bii w-agul-la.* I will get him alone and tell him.

farid **1.** = *fadd* (which see under *f-d-d*). **2.** (pl. *ʔafraad*) odd, uneven. **3.** odd number.

farda **1.** one part, one of a pair. *fardat qundara* a shoe. *fardat tamur* a date. || *farda w-farda* unmatched. *laabis ijwaariib farda w-farda.* He's wearing unmatched socks. **2.** (pl. *fraad*) heavy cloth sack usually used as a packsaddle on beasts of burden.

*fardi** odd, uneven. *ꞔadad fardi* odd number.

mufrad pl. *-aat* item. || *bil-mufrad* retail. *ma-nbiiꞔ bil-mufrad.* We don't sell retail.

f-r-d-w-s

l-firdoos. Paradise.

f-r-r

farr (*u farr*) **1.** to flee, run off, run away, escape. *tlaθ masaajiin farraw imnis-sijin.* Three prisoners escaped from the prison. **2.** to spin. *farr il-muṣraꞔ w-xallaa ynooꞔir.* He spun the top and made it hum. **3.** to whirl, swing, spin, circle. *farr il-miꞔčaal gabuḷ-ma yiδrub.* He swung the sling before he threw the rock. || *farr b-iida min git-la šii ma-ꞔijaba.* He waved his hand when I told him something he didn't like. *δall yfurr ib-raasa w-ma-yidri š-iysawwi.* He kept shaking his head and didn't know what to do. **4.** to take around, show around, take on a tour. *farrna baġdaad ib-sayyaarta.* He showed us Baghdad in his car. **5.** to greet warmly. *min ṭabbeet ꞔalee, farr biyya.* When I went in to see him, he greeted me warmly.

farrar to show around. *ʔuxuδ ij-jahhaal*

w-farrirhum ib-ḥadiiqt il-ḥaywaanaat. Take the kids and show them around the zoo.

ftarr **1.** to spin, turn. *l-muṣraᶜ baᶜda da-yiftarr.* The top's still spinning. **2.** to wander about. *š-aku ᶜindak tiftarr ihnaa?* What are you doing wandering around here?

farra pl. *-aat* **1.** turn, spin. **2.** circuit, turn, spin, swing. *ʔuxuð-lak fadd farra bis-suug, balki tšuufa.* Take a look around the marketplace, and maybe you'll see him.

firaar flight, escape.

ʔafraar pl. *-iyya* fugitive (esp. from military service).

furraara pl. *-aat* **1.** merry-go-round. **2.** small propeller on a stick played with by children. **3.** a gambling game played with a hexagonal or octagonal stick, differently colored on each side.

mafarr: ma-minha mafarr. It's unavoidable. There's no way out.

f-r-z

faraz (*u fariz*) **1.** to separate, set apart, detach, isolate. *raḥ-nifriz nuṣṣ il-gaaᶜ w-niᶜruðha lil-beeᶜ.* We're going to detach half the lot and offer it for sale. *ʔufruz il-puteeta l-ikbaar.* Separate the large potatoes. **2.** to secrete, excrete, discharge. *l-maraara tifriz maadda ððawwub iš-šiḥuum.* The gall bladder secretes a substance which dissolves fats.

mafraza pl. *-aat* detachment, group, squad.

faariza pl. *fawaariz* comma.

f-r-z-n

farzan **1.** to see clearly, to see details, to see differences, to distinguish things. *naðara ðaᶜiif. ma-yigdar yfarzin.* His eyesight is weak. He can't distinguish things. **2.** to distinguish, tell the difference, see the difference. *ma-yigdar yfarzin baᶜð il-ʔalwaan.* He can't distinguish some colors. *ma-agdar afarzinhum liʔanhum toom.* I can't tell the difference between them because they are twins. *tigdar itfarzan hal-loon min daak?* Can you distinguish this color from that? *hat-toom ma-tigdar itfarzin beenaathum.* You can't tell the difference between these two twins.

tfarzan to be distinguished, be told apart. *hat-toom ma-yitfarzinuun.* Those twins can't be told apart.

f-r-s

faras pl. *ʔafraas* **1.** mare. || *faras il-maaʔ* hippopotamus. **2.** knight (chess).

furuusiyya horsemanship.

fariisa pl. *-aat, faraayis* prey, kill (of a wild animal).

faaris pl. *fursaan, fawaaris* knight.

muftaris predatory. *ḥaywaan muftaris* a beast of prey.

*faarsi** **1.** Persian || *namil faarsi* a sort of large ants. *xaṭṭ faarsi* Farsi script. **2.** a Persian.

faarsi Persian, the Persian language.

f-r-š

furaš (*u faruš*) **1.** to spread, spread out. *ʔufruš haz-zuuliyya b-ġurfat il-xiṭṭaar.* Spread this carpet in the guest room. **2.** to cover. *furšaw il-ġurfa b-izwaali.* They covered the room with carpets. **3.** to make a bed, spread out the bedding, prepare a bed. *furšat il-ʔibinha l-mariið ḥatta ynaam.* She prepared the bed for her sick son so he could sleep.

fraaš pl. *-aat* **1.** mattress, bedding. **2.** bed.

farraaš pl. *-iin* errand boy, handy man, and janitor, in an office or school.

farraaš (coll.) **1.** butterfly (butterflies). **2.** moth(s).

farraaša pl. *-aat* un. n. of *farraaš.*

[1]*f-r-ṣ*

furṣa pl. *furaṣ* **1.** opportunity, chance, auspicious moment. || *ʔintihiz il-furṣa.* Seize the opportunity. **2.** recess (between classes).

[2]*f-r-ṣ*

faraṣ pl. *fruuṣa* mare.

f-r-ð

furað (*u faruð*) **1.** to impose. *l-ḥukuuma raḥ-tufruð ðaraayib ᶜal-ʔaraað iz-ziraᶜiyya.* The government will impose taxes on farm lands. *ma-tigdar tufruð ʔiraadtak ᶜalayya.* You can't force your will on me. **2.** to suppose, assume. *ʔufruð ma-yriid ygul-lak. š-tigdar itsawwi?* Suppose he doesn't want to tell you. What can you do?

ftirað to assume, presuppose. *da-yiftirið ʔašyaaʔ ma-yimkin itṣiir.* He is assuming things which aren't possible.

farið pl. *furuuð* **1.** order, injunction, duty. **2.** any of the five obligatory prayers of the day. **3.** assumption, supposition, hypothesis.

faraðiyya pl. *-aat* theory, hypothesis.

fariiða pl. *faraayið* religious duty, religious obligation.

f-r-ṭ

farraṭ to break the seeds apart. *ʔiksir ir-rummaana w-farriṭha.* Break open the pomegranate and take the seeds out.

tfarraṭ to break apart. *wugᶜat il-*

iglaada w-itfarriṭat. The necklace fell and scattered apart.

faruṭ loose, unpackaged, by the piece, individually. *tbiiʕhum faruṭ loo bil-kooma?* Do you sell them individually or by the pile?

f-r-ʕ

farraʕ **1.** to branch, put out branches. *l-ʔašjaar itfarriʕ bir-rabiiʕ.* The trees grow branches in the spring. **2.** to uncover, bare (the head). *farriʕ ij-jaahil. d-dinya ḥaarra.* Uncover the kid's head. The weather's hot.

tfarraʕ **1.** to branch, branch off, branch out. *n-naxla ma-titfarraʕ.* The palm tree doesn't branch. *n-nahar yitfarraʕ ʔila farʕeen.* The river branches into two streams. *haj-jaadda titfarraʕ minha ʕiddat šawaariʕ.* Several streets branch off from this avenue. **2.** to uncover (one's head), to take off one's hat. *tfarraʕ w-nizaʕ sitirta w-gaam yilʕab.* He uncovered his head and took off his coat and began to play.

fariʕ pl. *fruuʕ* **1.** twig, branch. **2.** branch, branch office.

*farʕi** branch, subsidiary, secondary, tributary, sub-. *šarika farʕiyya* subsidiary company. *daaʔira farʕiyya* branch office. *nahar farʕi* tributary. *lajna farʕiyya* sub-committee.

f-r-ġ

furaġ (*u faruġ*) **1.** to be or become empty. *tanki l-maay furaġ.* The water tank went dry. *δall yiṣruf ifluus ḥatta furaġ jeeba.* He kept on spending money until his pockets were empty. **2.** to be or become vacant. *l-beet furaġ il-baarḥa. triida hassa?* The house was vacated yesterday. Do you want it now? **3.** to be or become free, get done. *ʔasawwi-lk-iyyaaha lamma ʔafraġ.* I'll do it for you when I get free.

farraġ **1.** to empty. *farriġi s-salla; ʔard aruuḥ ʔassawwag.* Empty the basket; I want to go shopping. *farriġ kull ijyuubak.* Empty all your pockets. *farraġ musaddasa b-raasa.* He emptied his pistol into his head. *raaḥ iyfarriġ w-baʕda bil-xalaaʔ.* He went to relieve himself and he's still in the toilet. **2.** to vacate, make empty, evacuate. *farriġoo-lhum il-beet ḥatta yintaqluun.* They vacated the house for them so they could move. **3.** to unload. *farriġaw il-baaxira mnil-ḥimil.* They unloaded the ship of its cargo. *θneenna raḥ-infarriġ il-fargoon.* Two of us will unload the boxcar. **4.** to pour out. *farriġ-li šwayya šoorba.* Pour me out a little soup.

tfarraġ **1.** to be emptied. *laazim ijyuubak kullha titfarraġ gabuḷ-ma yinδurub il-qaaṭ ʔuuti.* Your pockets all have to be emptied before the suit is ironed. **2.** to devote (oneself), apply (oneself). *ʔariidak titfarraġ in-nahaar kulla il-haš-šaġḷa.* I want you to devote the whole day to this job. **3.** to have time. *bass atfarraġ-ilha, ʔaxalliṣha b-saaʕa.* As soon as I have free time for it, I'll finish it in an hour.

farġa pl. *-aat* free time, free period. || *ʕal-farġa* at leisure. *ʔasawwiiha ʕal-farġa.* I'll do it when I get a little free time.

faraaġ pl. *-aat* **1.** void, vacuum, space. **2.** power vacuum, vacuum (pol.). **3.** empty space, emptiness, lack (fig.). *moota tirak faraaġ čibiir.* His death left a great lack. **4.** free time, leisure.

faariġ **1.** empty, void. *jeeb faariġ* an empty pocket. || *ḥači faariġ* empty talk. *fadd waaḥid faariġ* an empty-headed person, an ignorant person. **2.** vacant, unoccupied. *beet faariġ* a vacant house. **3.** free, at leisure, not busy, unoccupied. *ʔiδa faariġ taʕaal ʕaawinni.* If you're free, come and help me.

mafruuġ: ||*mafruuġ minna* finished, settled, a foregone conclusion. *najaaḥa bil-imtiḥaan mafruuġ minna laakin ma-aʕtiqid raḥ-yiṭlaʕ ʔawwal.* His passing is a foregone conclusion but I don't think he'll come out in first place. *ʔidxaal il-mariiδ bil-mustašfa fadd šii mafruuġ minna.* Placing of the sick man in the hospital is a must. *ʔaxiδ il-imtiḥaan iš-šaamil fadd šii mafruuġ minna.* You can't get out of taking the comprehensive exam.

f-r-f-r

farfar to cry one's heart out, to become exhausted from crying. *ʔibnič farfar imnil-bači.* Your son has worn himself out from crying. *ṭabbat ʕaleena tfarfir. ʔaxuuha siḥgata sayyaara.* She came in to us distraught. A car ran over her brother.

f-r-f-w-r

farfuuri china.

f-r-q

firaq (*u fariq*) **1.** to differ, be different. *haaδa muu miθla; yifruq ihwaaya.* That's not the same; it differs quite a bit. **2.** to make a difference. *ma-tufruq ʕindi.* It makes no difference to me. *xoo mtiḥin hassa! š-tufruq?* So take the exam now! What's the difference? *ʔiδa tištiriiha* *mnil-maʕmal raʔsan, tufruq-lak xams idnaaniir.* If you buy it direct from the factory, it will save you five dinars. **3.** to recognize. *ḍaʕfaana hwaaya! ma-firaqtič.* You've gotten very thin. I didn't recognize you.

farraq **1.** to divide: *farriq—tasud.* Divide and rule. **2.** to disperse, scatter. *š-šurṭa farriqat il-mutaḍaahiriin.* The police dispersed the demonstrators. **3.** to distinguish. *halgadd-ma yitšaabhuun ma-agdar afarriq beenhum.* They're so alike I can't distinguish between them. *ma-yigdar iyfarriq il-ʔaḥmar imnil-ʔaxḍar.* He can't distinguish red from green. **4.** to make a difference, to make a saving. *ʔiδa tištiri kullši bij-jumla, yfarriq-lak ihwaaya.* If you buy everything in quantity, it'll make a big difference for you. || *ma-štira s-sayyaara ʔila ʔan farraqha šwayya.* He didn't buy the car until he came down on the price.

tfarraq to disperse, dissolve, break up. *l-muḍaahara tfarriqat.* The demonstration broke up. *l-mutaḍaahiriin itfarriqaw min ʔijaw iš-šurṭa.* The demonstrators dispersed when the police came.

nfiraq to be distinguished. *walaa yinfarquun waaḥid ʕan il-laax.* They can't be distinguished from each other.

ftiraq to split up, to separate. *ḍallaw ʔaṣdiqaaʔ sana w-baʕdeen iftirqaw.* They remained friends for a year and then split up.

fariq pl. *furuuq.* **1.** difference. **2.** difference (math.). **3.** change (esp. one for the better).

firqa pl. *firaq* **1.** team. **2.** band, orchestra. **3.** division (mil.).

fariiq pl. *furaqaaʔ* **1.** team. **2.** lieutenant general.

faariq **1.** distinguishing, distinctive. || *ʕalaama faariqa* trademark, identifying mark. **2.** difference, distinction.

f-r-g

furag (*u farig*) to part (the hair). *ʔuxuδ il-mišit w-ufrug-li šaʕri.* Take the comb and part my hair for me.

farrag to distribute, dispense. *bil-ʕiid yfarriguun ifluus ʕal-fuqaraaʔ.* On the holiday they distribute money to the poor.

farig pl. *fruug* part (in hair).

firga pl. *-aat* act of giving alms to the poor, or of distributing gifts to neighbors.

mafrag pl. *mafaarig* **1.** junction (railroad). **2.** fork, crossroads, highway intersection.

f-r-g-s

fargas **1.** to become blistered. *ʔiidi fargisat immnij-jadif.* My hands got blistered from rowing. **2.** to become inflamed, become infected and swollen. *njiraḥ iṣibʕi w-baʕad-ma ġṣalta bil-maay fargas.* My finger got cut and when I rinsed it in water it became inflamed. *ḥtirag iṣibʕi w-baʕdeen fargas.* My finger got burned and later inflamed.

tfargas = *fargas. tfargisat rijli mnil-qundara.* My feet got swollen and sore from the shoes.

furgaas (coll.) inflammation, infection, swelling, sore(s). *huwwa furgaas ma-yingaas.* He's so sensitive he can't be touched.

furgaasa pl. *-aat, faraagiis* **1.** blister. **2.** un. n. of *furgaas.*

f-r-g-ʕ

fargaʕ to heat clarified butter to boiling. *fargiʕ išwayya dihin lit-timman.* Heat some ghee for the rice.

firgaaʕa boiling clarified butter (for pouring over rice, etc.).

f-r-k

furak (*u farik*) to rub. *la-tufruk ʕeenak tara tiḥmarr.* Don't rub your eye or it'll get red. *ʔufruk iṭ-ṭiina b-iidak w-šuufha šloonha.* Rub the clay between your fingers and see how it is. || *ʔiδa tiḥči zaayid ʔafruk xašmak.* If you talk any more I'll mash your nose.

farrak to rub, massage. *farrkii-li čtaafi; toojaʕni.* Massage my shoulders. They're hurting me. *yeezi tfarrik ib-xašmak!* Stop rubbing your nose!

farka time, time enough. *ʔiδa tinṭiini farka ʔasawwii-lk-iyyaaha.* If you'll just give me enough time, I'll do it for you. *ʔariid ʔaṣalliḥ ir-raadyo bass ma-aku farka.* I want to fix the radio but I don't have time.

f-r-k-y-t

furkeeta pl. *-aat* hair pin, bobby pin. || *dambuus furkeeta* safety pin.

f-r-n

firin pl. *ʔafraan* oven.

firni = *mḥallabi,* a pudding made of milk, rice flour, and sugar.

f-r-n-j

*franji** **1.** European. *hduum ifranjiyya* European clothes. *mirḥaaḍ ifranji* European style toilet. **2.** a European. **3.** (loosely) French. **4.** Frenchman.

f-r-n-g-y

fringi syphilis. || *miliḥ ifringi* Epsom salts.

f-r-h

farih wide, spacious, ample, uncrowded. *ġurfa farha* a spacious room. *wilaaya farha* an uncrowded city.

ʔafrah wider, ampler, more spacious, less crowded.

f-r-w

faru (coll.) (fur(s), pelt(s), skin(s). *qappuuṭ faru* fur coat.

farwa pl. *-aat, fraawi.* **1.** un. n. of *faru.* || *farwat ir-raas* scalp. **2.** a long sheep-skin coat with the wool on the inside.

f-r-y

fira (*i fari*) to break, burst. *ʔifri il-buṭbaaṭa b-isibɛak.* Break the blister with your fingers. *diir baalak. la-tifri l-umraara min itšugg is-simča.* Be careful. Don't break the gall bladder when you clean the fish.

faara to coo (pigeon). *haaδa ḥiss faḥl il-ḥamaam da-yfaari.* That's the sound of the male pigeon cooing.

nfira to be or become broken, to burst. *nfirat il-umraara w-ṣaarat is-simča murra.* The gall bladder got broken and the fish became bitter.

f-r-y-a-d-m

firyaadima (no pl.) orgy, riot, chaotic affair.

f-z-z

fazz (*i fazz*) to be startled, to start. *min xaššeet, gumaz ib-wijhi w-fazzeet.* When I came in, he jumped in front of me and I was startled. *gumzat il-bazzuuna min ɛal-ḥaayiṭ w-fazzeet imnin-noom.* The cat jumped down off the wall and I woke up with a start. **2.** to wake up. *s-saaɛa beeš fazzeet il-baarḥa?* What time did you wake up yesterday?

fazzaz **1.** to startle. *fazzazni b-ɛaṭiṣta.* He startled me with his sneeze. **2.** to wake, wake up, awaken. *fazzazni mnin-noom min wakit.* He woke me up early.

stafazz to agitate, excite, stir up. *ʔinta da-tistifizza b-hiiči ḥači.* You are getting him all worked up with that talk.

stifzaaz pl. *-aat* instigation, agitation, provocation, incitement.

*stifzaazi** inflammatory, rabble-rousing, provocative, incendiary. *ʔaɛmaal istifzaaziyya* inflammatory acts.

f-z-ɛ

fizaɛ (*a faziɛ*) /with *l-*/ to go to someone's aid, to help, go to help someone. *bass itmidd iidak ɛalee, ʔaxuu yifzaɛ-la.* As soon as you lay your hand on him, his brother comes to his aid. *fizɛoo-la fadd fazɛa.* They came to his aid at once.

fazzaɛ to frighten, scare, terrify. *ṣoot il-ʔasad yfazziɛ il-waaḥid.* The lion's roar terrifies a person.

fazɛa group, gang.

fazzaaɛ pl. *-a* rescuer.

f-z-g-a-n

fazgaan silly, light-headed, lame-brained, unreliable. *huwwa fadd waaḥid fazgaan. ma-yidri š-aku b-had-dinya.* He's a dopey guy. He doesn't know what's going on in the world.

f-s-t-a-n

fistaan pl. *fisaatiin* (woman's) dress.

f-s-t-q

fistiq (coll.) pistachio nut(s). || *fistiq ɛabiid* peanut(s).

fistiqa, fistiqaaya pl. *-aat* un. n. of *fistiq.*

fistiqi (invar.) pistachio (color). *loon fistiqi* pistachio colored.

f-s-ḥ

fisaḥ (*a fasiḥ*) to give, allow, provide. *fisaḥit-la l-furṣa marrteen w-ma-stafaad minha.* I gave an opportunity twice and he didn't take advantage of it. *la-tifsaḥ-la l-majaal tara baɛdeen yinkut biik.* Don't give him free rein or he will double-cross you.

nfisaḥ to be given, allowed, provided. *nfisaḥ-li l-majaal ɛiddat marraat aṣiir mudiir w-ma-qbalit.* I was given a chance to be director on several occasions and I didn't accept.

fasḥa room, space, roominess, spaciousness. || *ma-bii fasḥa.* It's not roomy.

f-s-x

fisax, etc., = *fiṣax,* etc. which see under f-ṣ-x.

f-s-d

fisad (*a fasaad*) **1.** to spoil, go bad, become rotten, decayed, putrid. *fisad il-beeδ kulla mnil-ḥarr.* The eggs all spoiled from the heat. **2.** to be or become bad, corrupt, depraved. *ʔiδa yδall yimši wiyya hiiči naas raḥ-yifsad.* If he keeps running around with those people he will turn rotten. **3.** to be or become bad, go to pieces, turn out badly. *l-qaδiyya fisdat ɛaleena.* The affair turned out badly for us.

fassad **1.** to spoil, ruin, corrupt, deprave. *fassidatha ṣadiiqatha.* Her girl friend corrupted her. **2.** to spoil, ruin, mess up. *činna niḥči beenaatna l-mawδuuɛ, w-xašš ɛaleena waaḥid fassad kullši.* We were talking the matter over between us and a guy came over to us and messed it all up.

fasaad depravity, corruption, immorality. || *ydawwur fasaad.* He's depraved.

mafsada place of immorality, place of depravity.

ˀafsad more or most immoral, corrupt, depraved.

faasid pl. *fassaad* **1.** bad, spoiled, rotten, putrid. *beeḍa faasda* a rotten egg. **2.** stale, impure, polluted. *hawa faasid* stale air. **3.** wicked, immoral, depraved. *walad faasid* a bad guy. || *faasid imnil-beeḍa* immoral right from the start.

f-s-r

fassar to explain, interpret. *šloon itfassir hat-tatawwiraat?* How do you explain these developments? *baḷḷa ma-tfassir-li haj-jumla.* Won't you please explain to me what this sentence means. *baʕaḍ il-ˀudabaaˀ il-ˀajaanib fassiraw il-qurˀaan.* Some foreign literary critics interpreted the Koran. **2.** to be able to see well, to have good eyesight (usually negative). *ʕyuuna ḍaʕiifa; ma-tfassir min biʕiid.* His eyes are weak; he can't see anything at a distance. **3.** to break, break up. *ḍirab il-meez ḍarba wiḥda, w-fassara kulla.* He hit the table a single blow and splintered it.

tfassar **1.** to be explained, interpreted. *haaδa š-šiʕir ṣaʕub w-ma-yitfassar.* This poem is difficult and can't be explained. **2.** to be broken up, to be broken to pieces, to be smashed. *ˀiδa txalli l-buṭiḷ ʕala n-naar mudda ṭuwiila, yitfassar.* If you leave the bottle on the fire a long time, it'll get broken.

stafsar to inquire, ask. *stafsar ʕan il-qaḍiyya.* He asked about the matter. *raḥ-astafsir min ʕali.* I'm going to ask Ali. *raḥ-astafsir-lak w-ašuuf šinu l-quṣṣa.* I'm going to inquire for you and find out what the story is.

tafsiir **1.** explanation, interpretation. **2.** (pl. *tafaasiir*) a book intepreting and commenting on the Koran.

mfassir pl. *-iin* interpreter, commentator (esp. on the Koran). || *mfassir il-ˀaḥlaam* oneirocritic, interpreter of dreams.

f-s-l

fisiil (coll.) palm shoot(s), palm seedling(s).

fisiila pl. *-aat, fisaayil* un. n. of *fisiil.*

f-s-w

fisa (*i fasi, fasu*) to break wind noiselessly. *ṣaar wičča ˀaḥmar li-ˀan fisa.* His face became red because he broke wind.

fassa intens. of *fisa.* *ˀiδa taakul ḥummuṣ, itfassi hwaaya.* If you eat peas, you'll be passing a lot of gas.

fasu (coll.) (soundless) breaking wind.

faswa pl. *-aat* un. n. of *fasu.*

f-š-a-f-y-š

fišaafiiš, fašaafiiš (invar.) liver broiled on a skewer.

f-š-x

fišax, etc. = *fičax,* etc., which see under *f-č-x.*

f-š-r

faššar to curse in a vulgar way, to make insulting, off-color remarks. *ma-aku ḥaaja tfaššir ʕalee; wala ḥiča ʕaleek.* There's no need to curse him; he never said anything against you. *ḥalga zafir w-yfaššir ihwaaya.* His mouth is filthy and he curses people a lot. *tiflat ib-wičča li-ˀan faššar ʕaleeha.* She spit in his face because he insulted her.

fšaar profanity, cursing, off-color insults.

faššuura pl. *-aat* off-color word or phrase.

f-š-š

fašš (*i fašš*) **1.** to cause to go down, to deflate. *had-duwa yfišš il-warum.* This medication will reduce the swelling. *fišš ič-čuub gabuḷ-ma tliḥma.* Deflate the tube before you patch it. **2.** to go down, deflate. *n-nuffaaxa nzurfat w-faššat.* The balloon got a hole in it and deflated. **3.** to shrink back, subside, be deflated. *min itṣiiḥ ib-wičča, yfišš.* When you yell in his face, he becomes timid.

f-š-q

fišqi horse manure (when used for fertilizer).

f-š-g

fišag (*i fašig*) to cut in two, split in two, halve. *fišag il-looḥa bil-faas.* He split the board with the adze.

faššag intens. of *fišag.* *faššig ir-raggi w-xallii biṣ-ṣuwaani.* Halve the watermelons and put them on the trays. *faššig il-karab ḥatta nšiʕla.* Split up the palm stems so we can burn them.

fišga pl. *-aat, fišag.* **1.** half, a half (of something). **2.** cartridge, round, bullet.

f-š-l

fišal (*a fašal*) **1.** to fail, be unsuccessful. *fišal bil-imtiḥaan w-baṭṭal.* He failed on the exam and quit. **2.** to be or become embarrassed. *fišalit min majiid li-ˀan raad minni diinaar w-ma-ʕindi.* I was embarrassed by Majid because he wanted to borrow a dinar and I didn't have it.

faššal **1.** to fail, cause to fail. *l-muʕallim*

faššala bil-imtiḥaan. The teacher flunked him in the exam. **2.** to embarrass, ridicule. *ma-laazim itfaššla giddaam in-naas.* You shouldn't embarrass him in front of people. *xalli yiḥči. la-tfaššla.* Let him talk. Don't give him a hard time. *yaa mɛawwad, ʔibδil jahdak. la-tfaššilni.* For gosh sakes, exert yourself. Don't disappoint me.

tfaššal to be embarrassed. *ma-yitfaššal bil-ɛajal.* He's not easily embarrassed. *tara ʔiδa yisʔaluuk, titfaššal.* I tell you, if they ask you, you will be embarrassed.

tfaašal to embarrass each other, to agitate each other. *haay qaδiyya baṣiita ma-tiswa nitfaašal ɛaleeha.* This is a simple matter which isn't worth getting ourselves all in an uproar about.

fašal failure, fiasco.

fašla pl. *-aat* embarrassment, disgrace. || *laazim itsallim ɛalee. fašla.* You must greet him. It's disgraceful not to.

faašil unsuccessful, failing. *muḥaawala faašla* an unsuccessful attempt. || *nidaaʔ faašil* an uncompleted phone call.

f-š-y

fiša (*i faši,*) /with *b-*/ to reveal, let out. *ma-yifši b-ʔay sirr ḥatta loo tbuṣṭa.* He won't reveal any secret even if you beat him.

tfašša to spread. *ʔiδa tfašša l-maraδ, imniṣ-ṣaɛub iṣ-ṣayṭara ɛalee.* If the disease spreads, it'll be hard to control it.

¹f-ṣ-ḥ

faṣiiḥ pure, classical, literary (language). *ɛarabi faṣiiḥ* classical Arabic.

ʔafṣaḥ f. *fuṣḥa* more or most classical, literary. *l-fuṣḥa, l-luga l-fuṣḥa, l-ɛarabiyya l-fuṣḥa* classical Arabic.

²f-ṣ-ḥ

fuṣiḥ: ɛiid il-fuṣiḥ **1.** Easter. **2.** Passover.

f-ṣ-x

fuṣax (*u faṣix*) **1.** to dislocate, put out of joint, sprain. *luwa ʔiidi ḥeel w-fuṣaxha.* He twisted my arm hard and dislocated it. **2.** to dissolve, cancel, void. *fuṣax il-ɛaqid.* He broke the contract. *tɛaarkaw w-fuṣxaw il-xuṭba.* They argued and broke the engagement.

faṣṣax **1.** to tear apart, break apart. *faṣṣax fuxδ il-xaruuf.* He broke the leg of lamb apart. *faṣṣix id-dijaaja lij-jahhaal ḥatta yaakluun.* Split the chicken apart for the children so they can eat. **2.** to take apart, disassemble. *faṣṣax makiint is-sayyaara.* He took the car's motor apart. *faṣṣax il-qanafa ḥatta ydaxxilha bil-ġurfa.* He took the couch apart to get it into the room.

tfaaṣax to split up, to dissolve an association. *δallaw šaraaka sana wiḥda w-baɛdeen itfaaṣxaw.* They remained partners for one year and then split up.

nfuṣax to be dislocated, be put out of joint, be sprained. *δrabta books w-infuṣax iṣibɛi.* I hit him with my fist and my finger got dislocated.

faṣix dislocation, sprain. *mukaan il-faṣix* sprained place.

f-ṣ-d

fuṣad (*u faṣid*) to bleed, perform bloodletting. *ṭ-ṭabiib fuṣad il-ɛirig illi b-rijli.* The doctor took some blood out of the vein in my leg.

f-ṣ-ṣ

fuṣṣ pl. *fṣuuṣ* **1.** stone (of a ring). **2.** lump, chunk, clump, glob. *fuṣṣ miliḥ* lump of salt. *fuṣṣ tamur* chunk of dates.

f-ṣ-l

fuṣal (*i faṣil*) **1.** to separate. *ʔiδa ma-tufṣil il-ɛijil ɛan ʔumma, ma-tḥaṣṣil ḥaliib.* If you don't separate the calf from his mother, you won't get any milk. **2.** to discharge, dismiss, fire. *fuṣloo mnil-waδiifa li-ʔan čaan ybuug.* They fired him from the job because he was stealing. **3.** to ensure a killer's safety by paying the victim's family. *fuṣlaw il-qaatil ib-miit diinaar ḥatta ma-yitɛarriδuu-la.* To ensure the killer's safety they paid the victim's family a hundred dinars so they wouldn't hurt him.

faṣṣal **1.** to cut out, tailor, make to measure. *faṣṣil hal-qaaṭ ɛala qaaṭ axuuya.* Cut this coat like my brother's. *faṣṣalit saaqu ṣuuf ɛind il-xayyaaṭ.* I had a woolen jacket made at the tailor's. **2.** to cut up, cut into sections, cut into pieces. *raḥ-aguṣṣ-lak išwayya laḥam baɛad-ma ʔafaṣṣil il-fuxuδ kulla.* I'll cut you some meat after I cut up all this leg. **2.** to cut up, cut to pieces. *qitala l-ɛaduwwa w-faṣṣala tafṣiil.* He killed his enemy and cut him to pieces.

nfuṣal **1.** to separate oneself, to disassociate oneself, to quit, to leave. *ɛiraf ʔaġlaaṭ il-ḥizib, w-infuṣal minna.* He realized the party's mistakes, and left it. *nfuṣal ɛanhum w-fitaḥ maxzan ɛala bidda.* He disassociated himself from them and opened a shop on his own. **2.** to cut oneself off, isolate onself. *dzawwaj wiḥda ʔajnabiyya w-infuṣal min kull ʔahla w-aṣdiqaaʔa.* He married a foreign girl and cut himself off from all his family and friends. **3.** to be fired, discharged. *nfuṣalit min waδ̣iifti li-ˀan ištirakit ib-muδ̣aaharaat δ̣idd il-ꞓukuuma.* I was sacked from my job because I took part in anti-government demonstrations. **4.** to be suspended. *nfuṣal imnil-madrasa sbuuɛeen.* He was suspended from school for two weeks.

ftiṣal to settle accounts, to settle up. *ˀaani ˀaaxuδ ꞓaqqi w-inta ftiṣil wiyyaa.* I'll take what's mine and you settle up with him.

faṣil **1.** discharge, dismissal. **2.** wergild, money paid by a killer's family to the victim's family to prevent a blood feud. **3.** (pl. *fuṣuul*) chapter. **4.** season. **5.** term, semester.

*faṣli** term, semester. *mtiꞓaan faṣli* semester exam, final exam.

faṣiil, faṣiila pl. *faṣaayil* platoon, squadron.

mafṣal pl. *mafaaṣil* joint. || *mafṣal ˀiid* knuckle. *mafṣal il-guṣba* section of bamboo.

tafṣiil **1.** cut (of a garment). **2.** (pl. *-aat, tafaaṣiil*) detail. || *bit-tafṣiil* in detail.

fṣaal **1.** cutting, cutting out. **2.** cut (of a garment).

f-δ-ˀ

faδaaˀ see under *f-δ̣-w.*

f-δ̣-ꞓ

fuδ̣aꞓ (*a faδ̣iꞓ*) to expose, to disclose or uncover someone's faults or offenses. *j-jariida fuδ̣ꞓathum.* The newspaper exposed them.

ftiδ̣aꞓ to come to light, to be made public. *hal-ꞓaraamiyya ftiδ̣aꞓ ˀamurhum bil-ɛajal.* Those criminals' racket was exposed quickly.

faδ̣iiꞓa pl. *faδ̣aayiꞓ* scandal, disgrace.

f-δ̣-δ̣

faδ̣δ̣ (*u faδ̣δ̣*) **1.** to finish up, conclude. *tigdar itfuδ̣δ̣-li hal-qaδ̣iyya bil-ɛajal, rajaaˀan?* Can you finish this matter up for me quickly, please? *fuδ̣δ̣ni. ˀard aruuꞓ.* Finish my business. I want to go. **2.** to solve, settle. *faδ̣δ̣ il-muškila maalti bil-ɛajal.* He solved my problem quickly.

¶ *faδ̣δ̣ bakaaratha.* He deflowered her.

nfaδ̣δ̣ **1.** to be solved, settled. *hal-qaδ̣iyya ma-tinfaδ̣δ̣ ˀilla ˀiδa tiꞓči wyya l-mudiir.* This problem can't be solved unless you talk with the director. **2.** to be adjourned, concluded, closed. *l-ijtimaaɛ nfaδ̣δ̣ baɛad saaɛteen.* The meeting was adjourned after two hours. *nfaδ̣δ̣at ij-jalsa biduun qaraar.* The session was adjourned without a decision.

ftaδ̣δ̣ (*bakaara*) to deflower. *δ̣ṭarr yidzawwajha li-ˀanna ftaδ̣δ̣ bakaaratha.* He had to marry her because he deflowered her.

fuδ̣δ̣a silver.

*fuδ̣δ̣i** silver, silvery. *ṣiiniyya fuδ̣δ̣iyya* a silver tray. *loon fuδ̣δ̣i* silver color.

f-δ̣-ɛ

faδ̣iiɛ abominable, hideous, repulsive, disgusting, heinous, atrocious, horrid, horrible. *jaraaˀim faδ̣iiɛa* hideous crimes.

ˀafδ̣aɛ more or most hideous, disgusting, horrible.

f-δ̣-l

fuδ̣al (*u faδ̣la*) to be left over, remain. *fuδ̣al ɛindi diinaar waaꞓid.* I only have one dinar left. *baɛad il-ɛaziima, fuδ̣al ˀakil ihwaaya.* After the banquet, a lot of food was left over.

faδ̣δ̣al **1.** to prefer. *ˀafaδ̣δ̣il is-safar bil-qiṭaar ɛala s-safar biṭ-ṭiyyaara.* I prefer traveling by train to traveling by plane. *ˀafaδ̣δ̣il agaddi min ˀan ˀaštuġuḷ gawwaad.* I prefer to beg rather than work as a pimp. **2.** to allow to remain, leave, leave behind, leave over. *baɛad-ma yaakul, yfaδ̣δ̣il ihwaaya.* After he eats, he leaves a lot.

faaδ̣al /with *been*/ to compare. *ˀiδa tfaaδ̣il beenhum, ˀaɛtiqid taaxuδ̣ il-čibiira.* If you compare them, I think you'll take the big one.

tfaδ̣δ̣al **1.** /with *ɛala*/ to honor, favor. *yimkin titfaδ̣δ̣al ɛaleena biz-ziyaara?* Would you be kind enough to honor us with a visit? **2.** (as imperative, approx.:) please, feel free, be my guest, go ahead, come in. *tfaδ̣δ̣al. staɛmil il-qalam maali.* Go ahead. Use my pencil. *l-ˀakil ꞓaaδ̣ir; tfaδ̣δ̣lu.* The food's ready; help yourselves. *tfaδ̣δ̣al, ˀišrab gahwa.* Here, have some coffee. *l-baab mafkuuka; tfaδ̣δ̣al.* The door's open; come on in.

tfaaδ̣al to take liberties, behave incorrectly. *haaδa r-rijjaal tfaaδ̣al biyya.* That man made a pass at me. *ma-laazim titfaaδ̣al b-ifluus ġeerak.* You shouldn't take liberties with other people's money.

faδ̣il pl. *ˀafδ̣aal* favor. *tigdar itsawwi faδ̣il ɛalayya w-jiib-li qamiiṣ wiyyaak?* Could you do a favor for me and bring me a shirt with you? *ṣaaꞓib il-faδ̣il* person who has done one a favor. *min faδ̣lak* please.

faδla pl. *-aat* remainder, residue, rest.

*fuḍuuli** **1.** officious, meddlesome. **2.** busybody, meddler.

faḍiila pl. *faḍaayil* virtue.

ʔafḍal more or most desirable.

ʔafḍaliyya precedence, priority. *hal-mašruuʕ ʔila ʔafḍaliyya ʕala l-kull.* This project takes precedence over all others.

faaḍil **1.** remaining, left. *fluus faaḍla* remaining money. **2.** eminent, distinguished, respected. *rajjaal faaḍil* man of culture and refinement.

f-ḍ-w

faḍaaʔ space, cosmos. || *raaʔid il-faḍaaʔ* astronaut, cosmonaut.

faḍwa pl. *-aat* open space, open area, square.

faaḍi empty, vacant. *mukaan faaḍi* a vacant seat.

f-ṭ-r

fuṭar (*u faṭir*) **1.** to crack. *z-zilzaal fuṭar ḥiiṭaan il-ibyuut.* The earthquake cracked the walls of the houses. **2.** to break one's fast, eat and drink after a fast. *ṣ-ṣaayim fuṭar ʕala šoorba bass.* The faster broke his fast on just soup. || *nṣuum, w-nufṭur ʕala jirriyya.* We work and save and nothing works out (lit., we fast, and then break our fast with catfish).

faṭṭar **1.** intens. of *fuṭar* **1.** *l-mayy l-ḥaarr faṭṭar kull il-ikwaaba.* The hot water cracked all the cups. **2.** to allow someone to break his fast. *ṭ-ṭabiib faṭṭara b-sabab ṣiḥḥta.* The doctor excused him from fasting because of his health.

tfaṭṭar to be cracked, be split, be broken. *ṣabbat il-ičbintu tfaṭṭirat li-ʔan čaan ʔaku nuwa biiha.* The cement form cracked because there were some date pits in it.

nfuṭar = *tfaṭṭar*. *nfuṭar il-maaʕuun ib-hal-wagʕa.* The plate cracked in that fall. || *nfuṭar raasi mnil-wujaʕ.* I had a splitting headache.

faṭir pl. *fṭuur,* crack, split.

fiṭir: ʕiid il-fiṭir Lesser Bairam, feast at the end of Ramadan, breaking the fast.

fiṭra **1.** nature, instinct. *bil-fiṭra* by nature, by instinct, instinctively. *ṭ-ṭifil yḥibb ʔumma bil-fiṭra.* A child loves his mother instinctively. || *ʕal-fiṭra* innocent, unspoiled, untaught, ingenuous. *l-badu baʕadhum ʕal-fiṭra* The Bedouins are still unspoiled. **2.** (pl. *-aat*) an obligation incurred by failing to observe the fast during Ramadan, repaid by fasting or by giving alms.

fṭuur **1.** breaking one's fast at sundown during Ramadan. **2.** (pl. *-aat*) the first meal after the daily fast in Ramadan.

fuṭiir, fṭiir **1.** unleavened. *xubuz fuṭiir.* unleavened bread, also, bread baked before having time to rise. **2.** unripe, green. *raggiyya fuṭiira* an unripe watermelon. **3.** (pl. *fuṭṭar*) foolish, silly, dopey, childish. **4.** dope, jerk.

faṭaara pl. *-aat* nonsense, idiocy, rubbish.

mufṭir pl. *-iin, mufaaṭiir* person who does not observe a fast.

ʔafṭar more or most foolish, childish.

fṭirr (coll.) mushroom(s).

fṭirra pl. *-aat* un. n. of *fṭirr.*

f-ṭ-s

fuṭas (*a faṭis*) (contemptuous) to die. *l-mujrim fuṭas w-ixlaṣna minna.* The criminal died and we were rid of him. || *fuṭasna mniḍ-ḍiḥik.* We nearly died laughing.

faṭṭas to slaughter, slay. *la-titḥaaraš bii tara yfaṭṭisak.* Don't provoke him or he'll slaughter you. || *šifna filim faṭṭasna mniḍ-ḍiḥik.* We saw a film that really slew us.

fuṭiisa pl. *fuṭaayis* dead animal, animal carcass, carrion.

ʔafṭas flat and wide (nose). *xašim ʔafṭas* a flat nose. || *waaḥid ʔafṭas* person with a flat nose.

f-ṭ-f-ṭ

faṭfaṭ **1.** to gurgle, bubble, make a sucking noise. *min yiḥči, yḍill it-tifaal yfaṭfuṭ min ḥalga.* When he talks, the saliva bubbles from his mouth. **2.** to decompose, rot (fish). *l-ḥarr faṭfaṭ is-simač.* The heat decomposed the fish.

mfaṭfuṭ decomposed, rotted. *simač imfaṭfuṭ* rotted fish.

f-ṭ-m

fuṭam (*u faṭum, fiṭaam*) to wean. *raḥ-tufṭum ibinha baʕad čam yoom.* She will wean her son in a few days.

f-ṭ-n

fuṭan (*u faṭin*) /with *ʕala*/ **1.** to be aware of, notice. *haj-jaahil yifṭun ʕala kullši.* That kid notices everything. *ma-da-yifṭun ʕala lli da-aguula.* He isn't aware of what I am talking about. **2.** to recall, remember. *li-hassa yifṭun ʕala zaman il-ḥarb.* He still recalls the time of the war.

faṭṭan to remind. *ʔarjuuk baačir faṭṭinni ʕaleeha.* Please remind me of it tomorrow.

tfaṭṭan to think, to think back, to try to recall. *tfaṭṭan! balki tilgi waaḥid ydaayinni.* Think! Maybe you can find someone to lend me money.

f-ع-ṣ

fuعaṣ (*a faعaṣ*) to dent. *daas عal-laععaaba w-fuعaṣha.* He stepped on the doll and dented it.

faعṣa pl. *-aat* dent.

f-ع-l

fiعal (*a faعil*) to act.

tfaaعal to react, combine. *δ-δahab ma-yitfaaعal wiyya l-ḥaamuδ.* Gold doesn't react with acid.

nfiعal to be or become excited, agitated, upset. *ma-aku daaعi tinfiعil. ʔaani š-gilit?* There's no reason to get excited. What did I say?

fiعil pl. *ʔafعaal* **1.** act, action, deed. **2.** effect, impact. || *bil-fiعil* indeed, in effect, actually, really, sure enough. *bil-fiعil! ʔaḥibbhum kulliš zeen.* Yes indeed! I like them very much. *qarrar yruuḥ, w-bil-fiعil, raaḥ!* He decided to go, and sure enough, he did! *bil-fiعil, raaḥ w-ḥiča wiyyaa w-qibal.* Actually, he went and talked with him and he agreed. **3.** verb (gram.).

fiعlan = *bil-fiعil. w-fiعlan, sajjal w-dixal imtiḥaan.* Actually, he registered and took an exam.

faععaal active. *عuδu faععaal* an active member.

faععaaliyya pl. *-aat* activity, event.

faaعil pl. *-iin* **1.** perpetrator. **2.** (pl. *fawaaعil*) active subject of a verbal clause. || *ʔisim faaعil* active participle.

mafعuul pl. *-aat* **1.** effect, impact. **2.** (pl. *mafaaعiil*) /with *bihi*/ object. || *ʔisim mafعuul* passive participle.

f-f-d

ffaad see under *f-a-d*.

f-q̈-d

fuqad (*i faqid*) to lose. *fuqad saaعta bis-siinama.* He lost his watch in the movie. *ʔay šii txallii bil-mayy yufqud išwayya min wazna.* Anything you put in water loses a little of its weight. || *fuqad šuعuura w-gaam yiḥči miθl il-imxaabiil.* He lost his senses and began talking crazily. *ma-ybaṭṭil iš-šurub ʔila ʔan yifqid.* He doesn't stop drinking till he loses consciousness.

tfaqqad to keep up on, keep up with, keep tabs on, keep in touch with, show concern for. *daaʔiman yitfaqqad ʔaṣdiqaaʔa.* He always shows concern for his friends.

nfuqad to be or become lost. *nfuqad minnak šii bis-suug?* Did you lose anything in the market place?

ftiqad to miss. *ftiqdoo kull ʔaṣdiqaaʔa min saafar.* All his friends missed him when he went away. *ftiqadnaa b-waqit ḥarij.* We missed him at a crucial time.

faqdi: hal-baggaal ybiiع bin-naqdi wil-faqdi. This grocer sells for cash and credit.

faqiid **1.** deceased, dead. **2.** deceased, dead man.

faaqid devoid, destitute, deprived. *faaqid iš-šuعuur, faaqid il-iḥsaas* unconscious.

f-q-r

faqqar to make poor, impoverish. *zawijta faqqirata b-maṣaariifha l-ihwaaya.* His wife made him poor with her large expenditures.

ftiqar /with *l-*/ to need, lack, require, be in need of. *hal-maعmal yiftiqir ʔila عummaal maahriin.* This factory is in need of skilled workers.

faqir: faqir damm anemia.

faqara pl. *-aat* **1.** vertebra. **2.** section, paragraph.

*faqari** spinal, vertebral, *عamuud faqari* spinal column. *ḥaywaan faqari* vertebrate.

fuqur poverty.

faqiir pl. *fuqaraaʔ* **1.** poor, poverty stricken. **2.** quiet, gentle, well-mannered, nice.

ʔafqar poorer, poorest.

f-q-ṭ

faqaṭ only. *ʔariid pakeet waaḥid faqaṭ.* I want only one package. *haj-jisir lis-sayyaaraat faqaṭ.* This bridge is for cars only.

f-q-ع

fuqaaعa pl. *-aat* bubble.

f-q-m

fuqqama pl. *-aat* seal (zool.).

f-q-h

fiqih systematic theology (Islam).

faqiih pl. *fuqahaaʔ* theologian, expert on *fiqih*.

f-g-r

fugar (*u fagir*) to jinx, to bring bad luck. *fugaritni b-ḥačyak w-xalleetni ʔaxṣar.* You put a jinx on me with what you said and made me lose.

fugur (invar.) poor. *kullna fugur w-ma-عidna sayyaaraat.* We are all poor and we don't have cars.

f-g-s

fugas (*u fagis*) **1.** to hatch. *baعad yoomeen w-tufgus il-beeδa.* Two more days and the egg will hatch. **2.** to fall through, fail, fail to work. *qaḍiitak fugsat.* Your case didn't pan out. **3.** to ruin, wreck, mess up. *b-iḥčaayta, fugasha lil-qaḍiyya.* By his remark he threw a monkey wrench into the case. *fugasha ġeer fagsa.* He really messed it up good. || *ʔiδa ma-tinṭiini fluusi ʔafgus ʕeenak w-aaxuδha.* If you don't give me my money, I'll claw your eyes out and take it.

faggas = *fugas. l-beeḍ yfaggis baʕad-ma tnaam ʕalee d-dijaaja.* Eggs hatch after the hen sets on them.

f-k-r

fakkar to reflect, meditate, think over, contemplate, consider. *la-tfakkir. haaδi xooš šarwa.* Don't think it over. This is a good buy. *ʔiδa tfakkir zeen, tigdar itḥill il-masʔala.* If you think hard, you can solve the problem.

ftikar to think, to be of the opinion. *ʔaftikir raḥ-yooṣal bukra.* I think he will arrive tomorrow. *ftikartak tuʕruf ingiliizi.* I had the idea you knew English.

fikir thinking, reflection, meditation, speculation, contemplation. || *yaʕni, š-fikrak? tiddaayan w-ma-tidfaʕ?* Well, what's the big idea? You borrow and don't pay back? *xallii b-fikra. la-tiqtiriḥ šii.* Leave him to his own opinion. Don't suggest anything. *fikra bil-ʕarag wil-uqmaar.* His mind is on liquor and gambling. *la-yḍall fikrak. laazim yooṣal il-yoom.* Don't worry. He has to arrive today. *kull fikri raḥ-ysaaʕidna.* I really believe he will help us.

fikra pl. *-aat, fikir, ʔafkaar.* idea, concept, thought, notion.

*fikri** speculative, mental, requiring thinking. *ʔasʔila fikriyya* questions requiring thought.

mufakkara pl. *-aat* **1.** notebook, datebook. **2.** diary, journal.

f-k-f-k

fakfak to open up. *š-aku ʕiddak da-tfakfuk bij-jinaṭ?* Why are you opening up all the suitcases? || *fakfakha lis-saaʕa wuṣla wuṣla w-ma-gidar yʕammurha.* He took the watch all to pieces and couldn't put it back together.

f-k-k

fakk (*u fakk*) **1.** to open (also fig.). *fakk il-baab w-xašš bil-gubba.* He opened the door and entered the room. *fukk ʕeenak zeen, tara haaδa yġuššak.* Keep your eyes open, or he'll cheat you. *fakk dukkaan biš-šoorja.* He opened a shop in the Shorja district. *ʔay saaʕa yfukk il-maxzan maala?* What time does he open up his store? *fakk iḥsaab bil-bang.* He opened an account in the bank. || *b-iqtiraaḥak haaδa fakkeet-inna fadd baab š-iysiddha baʕad.* With this suggestion of yours, you have started something for us that we can't stop. *l-gaʕda ʕaš-šaṭṭ tfukk il-galub.* Sitting by the river is a relaxing experience (lit., opens up the heart). **2.** to turn on. *fakk il-maay w-fayyaḍha lil-ḥadiiqa.* He turned on the water and flooded the garden. *balla ma-tfukk ir-raadyo?* Would you please turn on the radio? *fukk iḍ-ḍuwa.* Turn on the light. || *fakk ʕalee t-talafoon w-razzala.* He called him on the phone and bawled him out. **3.** to untie, unfasten, undo. *fukk il-ʕugda.* Undo the knot. *fukk il-ḥabil min rijl il-meez.* Untie the rope from the table leg. *fukk sitirtak.* Unbutton your jacket. *fukki d-digam maal θoobič.* Undo the buttons of your blouse. **4.** to pull out, remove, loosen. *fukk il-ibsaamiir yalla tigdar itʕaddil il-meez.* Pull the nails out so you can straighten the table. **5.** to unscrew, loosen. *ʔiδa tfukk hal-burġi, tigdar itšiil il-kaabreeta.* If you unscrew this screw, you can take the carburetor off. **6.** to free, set free, let go, release. *l-mazjuun raḥ-iyfukkuu baačir.* They're going to free the prisoner tomorrow. *lamma šaafaw ma-ʕalee šii, fakkoo.* When they saw he had nothing to do with it, they let him go. *la-tfukka min il-waḍiifa ʔila ʔan yiji l-xalaf maala.* Don't release him from his assignment until his replacement arrives. || *ʔiδa truuḥ w-ma-dgul-la, š-iyfukkak minna.* If you go and don't tell him, nothing will save you from him. *juuz minna; la-tfukk ḥalga.* Leave him alone; don't get him started talking. *ʕinda ʔuxut tfukk il-maṣluub.* He has a sister who is amazingly beautiful (lit., that could release a man condemned to death). *fukkna! haaδa š-imʕallma fransi?* Get off our back! What's he know about French? *fakk yaaxa min* to let go of, get away from, leave alone. *ṣaaḥib il-beet ma-da-yfukk minni yaaxa.* The landlord won't get off my back (lit.—won't let go of my collar). **7.** to divorce. *ʔaʕtiqid raḥ-yfukk marta.* I think he's going to divorce his wife. **8.** to leave, go away. *min yčallib bii wujaʕ ir-raas ma-yfukka ʔabadan.* When he gets a headache, it never goes away. *l-banj fakka.* The anesthetic wore off him.

ˀuxuð hal-ḥabb ḥatta tfukkak iṣ-ṣuxuuna. Take these pills in order to break the fever. **9.** to pay off, pay up, settle up. *fakk ir-rahin ʕala beeta.* He paid off the mortgage on his house. *la-tištiri šii baʕad gabuḷ-ma tfukk idyuunak.* Don't buy anything more before you pay off your debts.

fakkak to take to pieces, take apart, disassemble. *yigdar iyfakkik il-makiina w-iyšiddha min jidiid.* He can tear the machine down and put it back together again.

faakak to separate, break up. *dixal ib-beenaathum w-faakakhum.* He stepped in between them and separated them.

tfaakak to separate, move apart from each other. *ðallaw yitḥaarkuun ʕašir daqaayiq w-baʕdeen itfaakikaw min keef-hum.* They kept on fighting for ten minutes and finally separated by themselves. || *baʕad-ma anṭiik diinaar iykuun itfaakakna.* After I give you a dinar we won't owe each other anything.

nfakk **1.** to open, be opened. *l-baab ma-tinfakk.* The door won't open. **2.** to come out, be removed. *l-burġi ma-yinfakk ib-had-darnafiis.* The screw won't come out with this screwdriver. **3.** to be released, set free, let go. *nfakk imnil-ḥabis il-baarḥa.* He was let out of jail yesterday. *raḥ-yinfakk imnil-waðiifa baačir.* He'll be released from the assignment tomorrow. || *nfakk ib-marta ġeer fakka.* He flew off the handle at his wife. *min git-la, nfakk ʕalayya w-gaam iysayyiḥ nuṣṣ saaʕa.* When I told him, he exploded at me and kept shouting a half hour.

ftakk **1.** to open, be opened. *ˀidfaʕ il-baab ḥeel, balki tiftakk.* Push hard on the door and maybe it will open. **2.** to be released, set free, let go. *š-wakit ˀibnak raḥ-yiftakk imnis-sijin?* When will your son be freed from prison?

fakka pl. *-aat* opening, opportunity, break, chance. *ˀiða ma-tinṭiini fakka, ma-raḥ-agdar axaḷḷiṣ.* If you don't let me alone for a minute, I won't be able to finish.

fkaaka loose, slack. *ḥalga fkaaka.* His mouth is slack. *ḥačya fkaaka.* His speech is sloppy.

mafakka a rest, a moment's peace. *ma-nṭaana mafakka ḥatta ˀaxaðha.* He didn't give us any reprieve until he got it.

mafkuuk loose. *burġi mafkuuk* a loose screw. || *š-bii da-yimši haš-šikil? baraa-ġiyya mafkuuka?* What's wrong with him, walking that way? Is he falling apart?

f-k-h

fukaaha pl. *-aat* joking, fun-making, jesting.

faakiha pl. *fawaakih* fruit.

¹f-l-t

filat (*i falit*) to get loose, come loose, get away, escape. *filat il-ʕaṣfuur min ˀiid ij-jaahil.* The sparrow slipped out of the child's hand. *šidd il-ḥabil zeen ḥatta ma-yiflit.* Tie the rope well so it won't come loose.

fallat **1.** /with *nafsa*/ to get free, break loose. *fallat nafsa min iideen iš-šurṭa.* He wrested himself from the hands of the police. **2.** to let oneself be used sexually.

falta pl. *-aat* **1.** slip, oversight, error. *faltat ilsaan* a slip of the tongue. **2.** freak. **3.** extraordinary, exceptional person.

²f-l-t

flit, fliit insecticide, bug spray.

f-l-t-a-n

filtaan see *flaan* under *f-l-n.*

f-l-j

faalaj paralysis.

f-l-ḥ

filaḥ (*a faliḥ*) **1.** to plow, till, cultivate. *raḥ-yiflaḥ wuṣlat il-gaaʕ maalta.* He is going to cultivate his piece of land. **2.** to prosper, thrive. *l-yiʕtimid ʕala ˀaḷḷa yiflaḥ.* He who depends on Allah prospers.

flaaḥa cultivation, tillage. || *flaaḥa mlaača: ˀaxaðna flaaḥa mlaača.* He didn't give us a chance. *la-taaxuðna flaaḥa mlaača. xalli niḥči!* Don't monopolize everything. Let us talk.

fallaaḥ pl. *-iin, flaaliiḥ* farmer, peasant, fellah.

f-l-z

filizz pl. *-aat* (nonprecious) metal.

f-l-s

fallas **1.** to be or become broke, go broke. *ma-agdar adaaynak—fallasit.* I can't loan you anything—I'm flat broke. **2.** to shell (beans or peas). *fallis il-baagilla w-ḥuṭṭha bij-jidir.* Shell the horse beans and put them in the pot.

staflas to go broke. *staflas w-baaʕ say-yaarta.* He ran out of money and sold his car.

filis pl. *flaas, filsaan* **1.** one fils coin. **2.** (pl. *fluus*) fils, 1/1000 dinar. **3.** (pl. only) *fluus* money. **4.** (fish) scales.

flaas bankruptcy.

miflis pl. *mafaaliis* bankrupt, insolvent, broke. *šarika miflisa* an insolvent company. *ʔaani miflis il-yoom.* I'm broke today.

mfallis = *miflis.*

f-l-s-f

tfalsaf to philosophize. *yitfalsaf ib-ḥačya.* He philosophizes in his talk. *la-titfalsaf ib-raasi.* Don't pretend to be such a philosopher with me. Don't give me any of your guff.

falsafa philosophy.

faylasuuf pl. *falaasifa* philosopher.

f-l-š

fallaš to tear down, demolish. *l-baladiyya fallišat ʔarbaʕ idkaakiin.* The city tore down four shops.

tfallaš 1. to be torn down, demolished. *hal-binaaya raḥ-titfallaš.* This building's going to be torn down. 2. to be dissolved, broken up. *šaraakathum itfallišat.* Their partnership was dissolved.

f-l-ṣ-ṭ-y-n

falaṣṭiin Palestine.

*falaṣṭiini** 1. Palestinian. 2. a Palestinian.

f-l-ṭ-ḥ

mfalṭaḥ flat, flattened. *xašma mfalṭaḥ.* His nose is flattened.

f-l-ʕ

fallaʕ to crack open, split open, cause to split open. *l-ḥarr fallaʕ il-battiix.* The heat caused the melon to crack open.

nfilaʕ to split open, crack open, be split open. *r-rummaan ʔiδa yubqa biš-šijra hwaaya, yinfiliʕ.* If the pomegranate stays on the tree too long it splits.

faliʕ pl. *fluuʕ* crack, split.

f-l-f-l

filfil (coll.) 1. pepper. 2. green pepper(s), hot pepper(s).

filifla pl. *-aat* un. n. of *filfil.*

f-l-q

fallaq to administer the bastinado. *l-mulla fallaqa liʔan ma-xallaṣ waδiifta.* The Mullah switched him on the soles of his feet because he didn't do his homework.

falaqa pl. *-aat* 1. a stickwith a rope on it used to tie the feet for beating. 2. punishment by bastinado. *ʔakal falaqteen il-yoom.* He got two bastinados today.

f-l-k

falak pl. *ʔaflaak* orbit, circuit. *ʕilm il-falak* astronomy.

*falaki** 1. astronomical. 2. astronomer.

filka pl. *-aat* 1. circle, traffic circle. 2. riverboat.

f-l-l

fall (*i fall*) 1 to untie, undo. *fill hal-ʕugudteen il-bil-xeeṭ.* Untie these two knots in the string. *fall iṣ-ṣurra w-ṭallaʕ xaawli minha.* He opened the bundle and pulled a towel out of it. 2. to finish up, take care of. *fallat il-ḥasba b-nuṣṣ saaʕa.* The matter was taken care of in a half hour. *fillha, ʕaad!* Get it over with, for heaven's sake!

falla pl. *-aat* 1. wonderful, amazing, tremendous, terrific. *huwwa falla bir-riyaaδiyyaat.* He's terrific in mathematics. *jamaalha falla.* Her beauty is terrific. 2. loose, unpackaged. *čukleet falla* unpackaged candies.

mafall pl. *-aat* screwdriver.

f-l-m

filim pl. *ʔaflaam* 1. film, roll of film. 2. movie, motion picture, film.

f-l-n

flaan fem. *-a* (used to substitute for an indefinite or unnamed person or thing) so-and-so, such-and-such. *la-tiʕtimid ʕala flaan uw-filtaan; sawwiiha b-nafsak.* Don't depend on this and that person; do it yourself.

*flaani**, *fulaani** (adj. of *flaan*) *l-qaδiyya l-fulaaniyya* such and such a matter. *flaan il-fulaani* John Doe.

f-l-w

filu pl. *flaawa* 1. colt, young horse. 2. young man, young buck.

f-l-w-n-z-a

flawanza var. of *ʔinflawanza.*

f-l-y

falla 1. to delouse, search for lice. *da-tfalli raas ʔibinha.* She is delousing her son's head. 2. to preen (of a bird). *ṭ-ṭeer da-yitfalla biš-šamis.* The bird is sitting in the sun picking and fluffing at its feathers with its beak.

f-l-y-t

fliit insecticide, bug spray.

f-l-y-n

filliin (coll.) cork.

filliina pl. *-aat* a cork.

f-n-j-n

finjaan pl. *fnaajiin* small porcelain cup.

[1]*f-n-d-q*

funduq pl. *fanaadiq* hotel, inn.

[2]*f-n-d-q*

findiq (coll.) variant of *bunduq* which see under *b-n-d-q.*

findiqa pl. *-aat* un. n. of *findiq.*

f-n-r

fanar pl. *-aat* **1.** paper lantern, luminario, chinese lantern. **2.** steel shutter, roll-up shop front.

fanaar pl. *-aat* lighthouse.

f-n-n

tfannan to be inventive, to be versatile, to vary. *hiyya titfannan bil-libis.* She varies her clothes a lot. *marta titfannan biṭ-ṭabux.* His wife is very versatile at cooking.

fann pl. *finuun* **1.** art. || *l-funuun ij-jamiila* the fine arts. *fann it-tajmiil* the art of cosmetics. **2.** (or *finn*) /with pronominal suffix/ just let (him), I dare (him). *finnak itruuħ w-ma-dgul-li.* Just you try to go and not tell me. *finnak itxušš bil-maqbara bil-leel.* I dare you to go into the cemetery at night. *finna yištiki ɛalayya bil-maħkama. waḷḷa ʔakutla.* He better not complain about me to the court. By golly, I'll kill him.

*fanni** **1.** technical. *mawδ̣uuɛ fanni* a technical subject. **2.** artistic. *lawħa fanniyya* an artistic work. **3.** technician.

fannaan artist.

fannaana pl. *-aat* **1.** fem. of *fannaan.* **2.** artiste, night club dancer.

f-n-y

fina (*i fani*) to annihilate, destroy, ruin. *l-ɛadu fina l-madiina ɛan ʔaaxirha.* The enemy destroyed the city completely. **2.** to be consumed, lose oneself. *ʔiħna nitfaana b-ħubb waṭanna.* We are consumed with our love of our nation.

nfina to be annihilated, destroyed, wiped out. *l-firqa nfinat ib-kaamilha bil-maɛraka.* The division was totally wiped out in the battle.

f-h-d

fahad pl. *fuhuud* leopard, panther.

f-h-r-s

fihrass, fihrast pl. *fahaaris* table of contents, index.

f-h-m

fiham (*a fihim*) to understand. *ma-da-agdar afhamak.* I can't understand you.

fahham to make someone understand or see, to instruct, to explain to. *fahhamta maɛna haj-jumla.* I explained the meaning of the sentence to him. *fahhimni š-gal-lak.* Explain to me what he told you.

tfaaham **1.** to communicate with each other. *ma-yiħči ɛarabi. šloon itfaahamtu?* He doesn't speak Arabic. How did you communicate? **2.** to reach an understanding, come to an agreement, come to terms. *xall nigɛud suwa w-nitfaaham.* Let's sit down together and come to an understanding. *čaanaw mitxaarbiin, w-baɛdeen itfaahmaw.* They were on bad terms, but finally they reached an understanding. *haaδa waaħid ma-yitfaaham.* That's one guy who won't listen to you.

nfiham to be understood. *hal-iktaab ma-yinfihim.* This book is incomprehensible.

ftiham **1.** to understand, comprehend. *ftihamta lis-suʔaal?* Did you understand the question? **2.** to be or become aware of something. *hal-muɛallim yiftihim.* That teacher knows what he's doing. *ftihamit šii ɛan il-qaδ̣iyya loo baɛad?* Did you find out anything about the matter yet?

stafham to inquire, ask. *laazim nistafhim ɛan maaδ̣iyya.* We'll have to inquire about his past.

fahim pl. *ʔafhaam* understanding. || *suuʔ fahim* a misunderstanding. *baṭiiʔ il-famin* slow to understand.

fahiim **1.** intelligent. **2.** intelligent person.

ʔafham better or best informed, versed, etc.

tafaahum mutual understanding, mutual agreement, accord.

stifhaam inquiry. || *ɛalaamat istifhaam* question mark.

faahim knowledgeable, competent. *muħaami faahim* a knowledgeable lawyer.

mafhuum **1.** understood. || *šii mafhuum* an accepted fact. **2.** (as a particle) granted, certainly, of course, fine, sure. *mafhuum, bass haaδa muu ɛuδur.* I know, but that's no excuse. **3.** (pl. *mafaahiim*) conception, concept, idea.

¶ *l-mafhuum* it is said, it is reported that. . . . *l-mafhuum ʔinna l-wizaara raħ-tistaqiil.* It's rumored the cabinet will resign.

f-h-w

faahi (invar.) weak, tasteless, flat. *čaay faahi* weak tea. *šarbat faahi* flat-tasting fruit drink. || *ħači faahi* dainty, prissy speech.

fahaawa weakness, tastelessness, flatness.

¹f-w-t

faat (*u foot*) to go, pass. *hassa faat minnaa.* He just went by here. *tigdar itfuut. ma-aku ħaaja ddugg il-baab.* You can come in. There's no need to knock on the door. *fuut lil-beet walaw ʔaani muu hnaak.* Go in the house even if I'm not there. *θ-θaɛlab faat bil-ġaar.* The fox went into the hole. || *ṣiħit bii "fuut."* I yelled at him "Scram." **2.** to pass, go by. *faat wakit taqdiim iṭ-ṭalabaat.* The time for submitting requests has passed. *ˀilbas bil-ɛajal gabul-ma yfuut ɛaleek il-wakit.* Dress quickly before it's too late. *ˀaani ma-yfuut ɛalayya šii. ˀaɛruf š-aku ma-aku.* Nothing gets by me. I know what's happening. *faatatni ġeer foota!* What a chance I missed! *s-sana l-faatat* the past year, the year just passed, last year.

fawwat **1.** to cause to go, cause to pass, put. *fawwit is-siim biz-zuruf.* Insert the wire in the hole. **2.** to cause to go by, cause to pass. *ˀinta fawwatit ɛalayya l-furṣa.* You made me miss the opportunity. **3.** to allow to pass, allow to go by. *bass guul b-ismi w-huwwa yfawwtak.* Just mention my name and he'll let you in. **4.** to let by, let go, overlook. *huwwa ma-yfawwit šii bil-ˀakil.* He doesn't miss anything when he's eating. *raḥ-afawwt-ilk-iyyaaha hal-marra, bass la-tɛiidha.* I'll let it go this time, but don't do it again.

tfaawat to differ, be different. *ˀawqaat majiiˀna da-titfaawat.* Our arrival times differ.

fawaat passing, lapse. || *laazim tooṣal qabil fawaat il-waqit.* You must arrive before it's too late.

tafaawut difference, dissimilarity, contrast.

²*f-w-t*

fuut pl. *-aat, fiitaat* foot (unit of measure).

f-w-j

faaj (*u fooj*) to swim. *tuɛruf itfuuj willa laa?* Do you know how to swim or not?

faawaj to swim with the breast stroke. *ˀiδa triid itɛallma yisbaḥ, xalli yfaawij.* If you want to teach him to swim, let him do the breast stroke.

fooj pl. *ˀafwaaj* regiment (mil.).

fwaaja swimming.

mufaawaja breast stroke.

f-w-ḥ

faaḥ (*u fooḥ*) to spread, diffuse, emanate (odor). *riiḥt il-marag faaḥat min iftaḥta.* The fragrance of the stew came out when you opened it.

fooḥ water left over after rice is boiled in it.

f-w-x

faax (*u foox*) to ease, relax. *l-wujaɛ maal ij-jariḥ ma-faax li-hassa.* The pain from the wound hasn't gone away yet. *ma-fuxit illa lamma sijnoo.* I didn't feel at ease until they imprisoned him.

fawwax to ease, relieve. *hal-marham raḥ-iyfawwix il-wujaɛ.* This ointment will relieve the pain. *fawwaxitni hwaaya b-hal-xabar.* You've relieved me a great deal with this news. *buṣaṭṭa baṣṭa faw-waxit galbi biiha.* I gave him a beating that set my heart at ease.

f-w-d

food see under *f-y-d.*

f-w-r

faar (*u foor*) **1.** to boil, bubble. *sawwi šwayya čaay. l-mayy da-yfuur.* Make a little tea. The water is boiling. **2.** to effervesce, to fizz. *ˀiδa txalli qurṣeen min had-duwa bil-mayy, il-mayy iyguum iyfuur.* If you put two tablets of this medicine in water, the water will start to fizz.

fawwar **1.** to cause to boil, to boil. *fawwir il-ḥaliib gabul-ma tšurba.* Boil the milk before you drink it. **2.** to boil furiously. *r-raadeeta da-tfawwir.* The radiator is boiling over.

tfawwar to be boiled, to be brought to a boil. *l-mayy laazim yitfawwar gabul-ma txalli bii t-timman.* The water has to be boiling before you put the rice in it.

foor, fawr: ɛal-foor at once, immediately, right away, instantly, without delay, promptly, directly. *ˀiδa ma-tsawwiiha ɛal-fawr, yfusluuk.* If you don't do it right away, they'll fire you. *ˀiδa ma-ytumġuun il-ɛariiδa "ɛala l-foor", tit-ɛaṭṭal.* If you don't stamp the application "rush" it'll get delayed.

*fawri** instant, immediate, direct, prompt. *suwar fawriyya* pictures while you wait. *l-wiḥda l-fawriyya* immediate union.

foora, fawra pl. *-aat* a boiling.

fawran at once, right away, immediately, directly. *raḥ-aruuḥ ɛalee fawran w-agul-la.* I'm going over to him right now and tell him. *š-šurṭa ˀijaw il-mukaan il-ḥaadiθ fawran baɛad-ma xaabarnaa-hum.* The police came to the scene of the accident immediately after we called them.

f-w-z

faaz (*u fooz*) to win, triumph, be victorious. *ma-aɛtiqid raḥ-yfuuz ib-hal-ḥamla l-intixaabiyya.* I don't think he will win this election campaign. *ˀay firqa faazat bis-sibaaq?* Which team won the game?

fooz pl. *-aat* victory, triumph, success.

faaˀiz **1.** successful, victorious, triumphant. **2.** victor, winner.

f-w-ṣ

fooṣa pl. *-aat* quarrelsome woman.

f-w-ḍ

fawwaḍ to authorize, empower. *ʔaani fawwaḍta ybiiƐ il-beet.* I authorized him to sell the house.

faawaḍ to negotiate with. *raC-yfaawiḍ iš-šarika Ɛala qaḍiyyat binaaʔ ij-jisir.* He will negotiate with the company about building the bridge.

tfaawaḍ to negotiate. *da-yitfaawaḍuun Ɛala muʔaahada jdiida.* They're negotiating for a new agreement. *dazzaw wafid yitfaawaḍ wiyya l-Cukuuma.* They sent a delegation to negotiate with the government.

fawḍa 1. disorder, confusion, chaos. 2. anarchy.

fawḍawiyya anarchism.

mufawwaḍ pl. *-iin* rank in the police force above sergeant but below lieutenant.

mufawwaḍiyya pl. *-aat* legation.

f-w-ṭ

tfawwaṭ to put on a shawl or scarf. *ma-titlaƐ imnil-beet ʔiδa ma-titfawwaṭ.* She doesn't go out of the house without putting on a long scarf.

fuuṭa pl. *fuwaṭ* woman's head scarf or kerchief.

f-w-q

faaq (*u fooq*) to surpass, excel. *faaq ʔuxuuta bid-diraasa.* He beat his brothers in school studies.

faaq (*i ʔifaaqa*) 1. to awake, wake up. *faaq imnin-noom is-saaƐa sabƐa ṣ-ṣubuC.* He woke up at seven o'clock in the morning. 2. to come to, regain consciousness. *yirraad-la saaƐa Catta yfiiq min ġeebuubta.* He'll need an hour to come out of his unconsciousness.

fawwaq 1. to give preference to, to favor. *l-mudiir fawwaq ibna Ɛala baaqi ṭ-ṭullaab.* The principal set his son above the rest of the students. 2. to consider superior, to prefer. *ʔafawwuq hal-iqmaaš Ɛala δaak.* I rate this material higher than that.

tfawwaq /with *Ɛala*/ to excel, surpass, be superior to. *tfawwaq Ɛala ʔaṣdiqaaʔa bil-luġa l-ingiliiziyya.* He surpasses his friends at English.

fooq 1. above, over. *fooq mustawaak* above your level, over your head. 2. beyond, more than. *fooq ṭaaqti* beyond my authority, outside my jurisdiction. *fooq il-Ɛaada* extraordinary.

f-w-g

foog 1. (adv.) up, upstairs, on top, above. *xall niṣƐad foog.* Let's go upstairs. *ṣaƐƐid il-panṭaruun maalak foog.* Pull your pants up. *ma-aku Caaja tinzil; tigdar tiCči min foog.* No need to come down; you can talk from up there. *tnaggaƐit min foog li-jawwa.* I got wet from top to bottom. *min tiṣbuġ il-Caayit; ʔibdi min foog.* When you paint the wall start from the top. *sajjal ʔismak li-foog.* Sign your name at the top. 2. (prep.) above, over. *ṭ-ṭayyaara ṭaarat foog il-ġeem.* The plane flew above the clouds. *foog il-mulaaCiḍ ʔaku mudiir.* Above the supervisor there's a director. 3. on, on top of. *δibb foog il-ʔakil šwayya miliC.* Sprinkle some salt on top of the food. *waqqiƐ foog iṭ-ṭaabiƐ.* Sign on the stamps. *xalli haj-junṭa foog is-sayyaara.* Put this suitcase on top of the car. 4. beyond, more than. *foog il-miit waaCid ʔijaw.* More than one hundred people came. || *sayyaaraatna ʔasƐaarha min miiteen diinaar w-foog.* The prices of our cars are 200 dinars and up. *foog il-banafsaji* ultraviolet. *l-ʔasiƐƐa l-foog il-banafsaji* ultraviolet rays.

foogaaha in addition to that, furthermore, besides. *rakkabta bis-sayyaara w-foogaaha yriidni ʔašiil ġaraaδa.* I gave him a ride in the car, and on top of that he wants me to carry his stuff. *sawweet kull haaδa, w-foogaaha huwwa zaƐlaan.* I did all that and still he got mad.

*foogaani** higher, upper. *ṭ-ṭaabiq il-foogaani* the upper floor.

[1]*f-w-l*

fuul: raaC fuul. He went at top speed.

[2]*f-w-l*

fawwaal see under *f-ʔ-l*.

f-w-l-a-δ

fuulaaδ steel.

f-w-m

fawwam to soap, suds, lather. *fawwum il-imwaaƐiin biṣ-ṣaabuun w-baƐdeen ʔiġsilhum.* Suds the dishes in the soap and then rinse them.

fuum pl. *fwaama* a sudsing, a soaping, a lathering.

f-w-h

tfawwah /with *b-*/ to pronounce, utter, voice, say. *ʔiδa titfawwah ib-čilma wiCda baƐad, ybuṣṭak.* If you utter one more word, he'll clobber you.

fawha: fawhat Cariiq fire hydrant.

f-y-t

fiita roll-up tape measure (steel or cloth).

f-y-t-a-m-y-n

fiitaamiin pl. *-aat* vitamin.

f-y-t-r
fiitar pl. *-iyya* (automotive) mechanic.
fiitarči pl. *-iyya* = *fiitar.*
f-y-d
faad (*i food, faayda, ˀifaada*) **1.** to benefit, help, be of use, be useful, helpful, beneficial. *hal-iktaab faadni hwaaya bil-ˀimtiḥaan.* This book helped me a lot in the exam. *š-ma tiḥči wyaa ma-yfiid.* No matter what you say to him it doesn't do any good. *xallii ʕindak, tara yfiidak bil-mustaqbal.* Keep it with you because it will be of use to you in the future. **2.** to notify, advise, inform, let know. *tguul ma-ybuug? laʕad xalli ˀafiidak ib-šii.* You say he doesn't steal? Well, let me enlighten you about something.
ˀafaad to inform. *ˀafaadni b-maʕ-luumaat muhimma.* He let me in on some important bits of information.
stifaad (*a, i*) to profit, benefit. *ma-stifaadeet min hal-muʕallim ˀabadan.* I didn't benefit at all from that teacher. *laazim tistifiid min šabaabak.* You should make good use of your youth.
food use, usefulness. benefit. || *haaδa ma-bii food.* He's useless.
ˀafyad more or most useful, beneficial.
ˀifaada pl. *-aat* testimony, statement.
faaˀida, faayda pl. *fawaaˀid* usefulness, benefit, advantage. || *šinu l-faayda?* What's the use? *ma-ard atšaarak li-ˀan haš-šaġḷa ma-biiha faayda.* I don't want to become a partner because there's no profit in this business. *hal-quṣṣa biiha faaˀida ˀilak.* There is a moral in this story for you.
mufiid useful, beneficial, advantageous. *qaamuus mufiid* a useful dictionary.
f-y-r-w-z
fayruuz turquoise.
f-y-z
faayiz = *faayiḍ,* which see under *f-y-ḍ.*
f-y-z-y-a
fiiziya, fiiziyaaˀ physics.
*fiiziyaaˀi** **1.** physical. **2.** physicist.
*fiiziyaawi** = *fiiziyaaˀi.*
f-y-š
fiiša pl. *fiyaš* token, chip, poker chip.
f-y-ḍ
faaḍ (*i fayaḍaan*) to overflow, flow over, run over. *sidd il-mayy. l-ḥooḍ faaḍ.* Turn off the water. The pool's run over. || *ḍall saaʕa yʕaalij w-baʕdeen faaḍat ruuḥa.* He kept struggling with death for an hour and then gave up the ghost.
fayyaḍ = *faaḍ. yeezi ʕaad! muu fayyaḍta lij-jidir.* Hold it, man! You've overflowed the pot.
fayaḍaan pl. *-aat* flood.
faayiḍ usury, interest. || *bil-faayiḍ* on interest. *yinṭi fluus bil-faayiḍ.* He lends money on interest.
f-y-q
faaq, (*i*), see *f-w-q.*
f-y-l
fiil pl. *fyaal* **1.** elephant. **2.** bishop (in chess).
f-y-l-s-f
faylasuuf pl. *falaasif* philosopher. see also *f-l-s-f.*
f-y-n
fiina pl. *fiyan* fez.
f-y-y
fayya to shade, to afford shade. *š-šamis ma-tinḥimil. fayyii-li šwayya ḥatta ˀaštuġuḷ.* The sun is unbearable. Shade me a little so I can work.
fayy **1.** shade, shadow. **2.** (by extension) protection, patronage, benevolence. *ˀiḥna ʕaayšiin ib-fayya.* We are living under his protection.

Q

q-a-b
qaab pl. *-aat* plate, dish.
q-a-b-l-w
qaablo pl. *-owwaat* cable.
q-a-ṣ-a
qaaṣa pl. *-aat* safe, vault.
q-a-f
qaaf name of the letter *q.*
q-a-m-w-s
qaamuus pl. *qawaamiis* dictionary.
q-a-ṭ
qaaṭ see *q-w-ṭ.*
q-a-n-w-n
qaanuun pl. *qawaaniin* **1.** law. || *qaanuun ˀasaasi* constitution. **2.** a musical instrument resembling the zither.
*qaanuuni** legal. || *ġeer qaanuuni* illegal.
qaanuunči pl. *-iyya* one who knows the law, person well versed in the law.

q-a-w-r-m-a
qaawarma, qaawirma chunks of meat fried with tomatoes and onions.
q-a-w-w-š
qaawuuš pl. *qawaawiiš* **1.** ward (in a hospital). **2.** squad bay, bay (in barracks). **3.** large cell (in a prison).
q-a-y-š
qaayiš pl. *-aat, qawaayiš* **1.** leather thong, strap. **2.** strop. **3.** belt. *qaayiš maal il-parawaana* fan belt. **4.** trick, prank.
q-b-a
qaḅa (invar.) **1.** enormous, excessive. *maṣraf qaḅa* an excessive expenditure. **2.** gross, crude, ugly. *sayyaara qaḅa* an ugly car. *ṣooṭ qaḅa* an unpleasant voice.
q-b-b
qubba pl. *qubab* dome. || *sawwa mnil-ɛabba qubba.* He's made a mountain out of a molehill (lit. he made a dome from a seed).
q-b-č
qabač, qabič a kind of partridge.
q-b-ɛ
qabbaɛ: qabbaɛ ʔaḷḷaa wučča! ʔaani ma-gilit hiiči šii. God damn him! I never said such a thing.
qabiiɛ **1.** ugly, repulsive. *šikil qabiiɛ* ugly looks. *wijih qabiiɛ* an ugly face. **2.** shameful, disgraceful, foul, base, mean. *ɛamal qabiiɛ* a dirty deed.
qabaaɛa **1.** ugliness. **2.** shamefulness.
ʔaqbaɛ **1.** uglier, ugliest. **2.** more or most infamous. **3.** fouler, viler.
q-b-r
qabur, maqbara = *gabur, magbara* which see under *g-b-r.*
q-b-r-z
*qibrizi** horse of doubtful lineage, horse which is not pure Arabian.
q-b-r-ṣ
qibriṣ or *qubruṣ* Cyprus.
*qibriṣi** **1.** Cyprian, Cypriote, from Cyprus. **2.** a Cypriote.
q-b-s
qtibas to borrow, adopt. *raaɛ il-ʔameerka w-iqtibas baɛð̣ il-ɛaadaat il-ʔamriikiyya.* He went to America and adopted some American customs. *qtibas il-mawð̣uuɛ min majalla ɛaalamiyya.* He borrowed the topic from an international magazine.
qtibaas quotation, citation (of another's literary work).
q-b-ð̣
qubað̣ (*u qabuð̣*) **1.** to receive, collect. *qubað̣ id-deen maala.* He collected the debt owed him. *š-wakit tuqbuð̣ raatbak?* When do you get your pay? || *ɛizraʔiil yuqbuð̣ il-ʔarwaaɛ.* Azrael gathers souls. *nṭeeta ɛašr idnaaniir w-raɛ-ʔaqbuð̣ min dabaš.* I gave him ten dinars and don't expect to get it back. **2.** /with *ɛala*/ to seize, apprehend, arrest. *š-šurṭa qubð̣at ɛalee.* The police arrested him. **3.** to constipate. *č-čaay yuqbuð̣ il-baṭin.* Tea constipates. **4.** to dispirit, depress. *l-gaɛda wiyyaa tuqbuð̣ ir-ruuɛ.* Sitting with him depresses you. *hal-ġurfa tuqbuð̣ ir-ruuɛ.* This room is too confining.
nqubað̣ **1.** to be or become constipated. *baṭna nqubð̣at min šurb ič-čaay.* He's constipated from drinking tea. **2.** to be or become dispirited, depressed. *nafsi tinqubuð̣ min ʔaɛči wiyyaa.* I'm depressed when I talk with him.
qabuð̣ **1.** apprehension, arrest. || *ʔamur ib-ʔilqaaʔ il-qabuð̣ ɛalee* a warrant for his arrest. **2.** receiving, receipt, collection. **3.** constipation.
¶ *ma-aku qabuð̣.* There's no result. *ʔašuu tizmuṭ w-ma-aku qabuð̣.* You're always bragging but nothing seems to come of it. *la-tkallfa l-haað̣a. kull yabuð̣ ma-aku minna.* Don't ask him. You'll get no results from him.
qabð̣a pl. *-aat* fist, closed hand. *qabð̣at ʔiid* grip.
nqibaað̣ gloom, low spirits, depression.
q-b-ṭ
*qubṭi** pl. *ʔaqbaaṭ* **1.** Copt, Coptic. **2.** a Copt.
q-b-ṭ-a-n
qabṭaan pl. *-iyya* captain (of a ship, etc.).
q-b-ɛ
qubbaɛa pl. *-aat* hat.
q-b-ġ
qabbaġ to cap, cover with a cap. *b-maɛmal iṣ-ṣooda ʔaku makiina tqabbuġ ibṭaala.* In the soda pop factory there's a machine that caps bottles.
tqabbaġ pass. of *qabbaġ.* *kull il-ibṭuula tqabbuġat.* All the bottles have been capped.
qabaġ pl. *-aat* cap, cover, top, lid.
q-b-ġ-l-y
qabaġli: qundara qabaġli a sort of high-heeled slip-on shoe.
q-b-q-b
qubqaab pl. *qabaaqiib, qbaaqiib* (pair of) wooden clogs.
q-b-l
qibal (*a qubuul*) **1.** to accept. *qibal il-hadiyya minni.* He accepted the gift from me. *ʔahla xiṭboo-la ibnayya w-qibalha*

min ġeer šoof. His family betrothed him to a girl and he accepted her without seeing her. *l-ḥukuuma ma-qiblat ʔawraaq iʕtimaad is-safiir.* The government wouldn't accept the credentials of the ambassador. *ʕirḏaw ʕalee waḏiifa zeena w-ma-qibalha.* They offered him a good job but he didn't accept it. *qibal kull il-ḥači il-gut-ilh-iyyaa.* He accepted everything I said to him. *la-tubṣuṭ il-imgaddi. ʔaḷḷa ma-yiqbal.* Don't hit the beggar. God won't accept such a thing. **2.** to acquiesce, agree, consent, assent. *l-maḥkama qassimat il-wiriθ beenaathum, laakin il-ʔaxx ič-čibiir ma-qibal bit-taqsiim.* The court divided the inheritance among them, but the older brother didn't agree to the division. *qibal ʕaš-šuruuṭ il-git-la biiha.* He agreed to the terms I told him about. *qibal yṣiir šariiki.* He agreed to become my partner. || *ʔaani ma-aqbal ib-hiiči beet.* I'm not satisfied with such a house. **3.** to admit. *qiblooni b-kulliyyat iṣ-ṣaydala.* They admitted me to the college of pharmacy.

qabbal to cause to accept. *qabbalh-iyyaa lis-sayyaara b-miiteen diinaar.* He sold him the car for two hundred dinars.

qaabal **1.** to face, be opposite. *wizaaratna tqaabil siinama.* Our ministry is just opposite a theatre. **2.** to meet, receive. *qaabalni b-wujih bašuuš.* He met me with a friendly smile. **3.** to call on. *s-safiir raḥ-iyqaabil waziir il-xaarijiyya l-yoom.* The ambassador's going to call on the foreign minister today. **4.** to meet with, get together with. *laazim aqaabil il-mudiir ʕala hal-muškila.* I'll have to see the director about this problem. **5.** to interview. *l-lujna tqaabil ʕašir ṭullaab kull saaʕa.* The committee interviews ten students every hour. **6.** to return, repay, requite. *qaabal zeeniiti b-muu zeeniyya.* He repaid my good deed with a bad one.

tqabbal to receive, accept. *tqabbal ʔiqtiraaḥi b-raḥaabat ṣadir.* He accepted my suggestion patiently. *ʔaḷḷa yitqabbal duʕaak.* May God accept your prayers.

tqaabal **1.** to meet, encounter. *tqaabalta biš-šaariʕ il-yoom.* I ran into him on the street today. **2.** to meet, get together, have a meeting. *tqaabal wiyya l-mudiir nuṣṣ saaʕa.* He met with the director for a half hour. **3.** to fight, engage in combat. *ḥimat il-maʕraka, w-itqaablaw bis-silaaḥ il-ʔabyaḏ.* The battle got hot and they fought with bayonets. *l-ḥaraami tqaabal wiyya š-šurṭa ʔiḷa ʔan xiḷaṣ irṣaaṣa.* The thief fought with the police until his ammunition ran out.

nqibal to be accepted. *nqibalit bil-kulliyya.* I was accepted by the college. *l-hadiyya ma-nqiblat.* The gift wasn't accepted.

staqbal **1.** to meet, to go to meet. *raḥ-nistaqbala bil-maṭaar.* We're going to meet him at the airport. **2.** to receive. *staqbalni kulliš zeen.* He received me very nicely.

qabil = *gabuḷ* which see under *g-b-l.*

qibla **1.** kiblah, direction Muslims turn to pray (toward the Kaaba). **2.** recess in a mosque indicating the direction of the Kaaba, prayer niche.

qabuul pl. *-aat* an informal party, informal gathering (of either men or women).

qubuul acceptance.

qabiil kind, sort, species. *min hal-qabiil* of this kind, like this, such. *ʕinda ʔašyaaʔ ihwaaya min hal-qabiil.* He has many things of this sort.

qabiila pl. *qabaaʔil* tribe.

qibaala midwifery.

muqaabala pl. *-aat* **1.** encounter, meeting. **2.** interview. **3.** fight, battle.

qbaal demand.

stiqbaal pl. *-aat* reception. *ḥaflat istiqbaal* a reception.

qaabil **1.** appropriate, acceptable, suitable. *hal-qaaṭ qaabil lil-ḥafla?* Is this suit appropriate for the party? *yilbas alwaan muu qaabla.* He wears unsuitable colors. *l-baarḥa šiftak idġušš; haaḏi muu qaabla minnak.* Yesterday I saw you cheating; now that's not acceptable behavior of you. **2.** /as a scathing question/ do you mean to say, do you suppose. *ʔinta ma-da-tsawwi šii. qaabil da-nilʕab ihnaa?* You're not doing anything. You think we just play here? *qaabil ma-raḥ-tumṭur is-sana kullha?* Do you mean it's not going to rain for the whole year? *yaʕni qaabil iyriid yilʕab ib-raasi?* You mean he thinks he can just make a fool out of me? *yaʕni qaabil huwwa ʔaḷḷa?* You mean we should accept him as God? Who does he think he is, God?

qaabila pl. *-aat, qawaabil* midwife.

qaabliyya pl. *-aat* ability, capacity.

maqbuul **1.** accepted. **2.** admitted, accepted (at a school). **3.** acceptable, reasonable. *taṣarrufaat ma-maqbuula* improper conduct.

muqaabil **1.** opposite, facing. *muqaabil lis-siinama* opposite the movie. **2.** equiva-

lent, recompense, remuneration, wages. **3.** interviewer.
mustaqbil pl. *-iin* welcomer, greeter.
mustaqbal future.

q-b-l-n-a-m
qiblanaama pl. *-aat* compass.

q-p-r-ṣ
quprus Cyprus.
*quprusi** **1.** Cyprian, Cypriote. **2.** a Cypriote.

q-p-ṭ
qappaṭ **1.** to be full, filled up. *ma-agdar ʔašrab baʕad. qappaṭit.* I can't drink anymore. I'm filled up. *baʕad fadd raakib w-itqappuṭ is-sayyaara.* One more passenger and the car will be full. **2.** to fill, fill up. *ʔagdar ʔaqappuṭ is-sayyaara b-muddat saaʕa.* I can fill the car in an hour.
qappuuṭ pl. *-aat, qpaapiiṭ* overcoat.

q-p-ġ
qapaġ = *qabaġ* which see under *q-b-ġ*.

q-t-r
qattar to be stingy. *da-yqattir ʕala nafsa ḥatta yijmaʕ fluus is-sayyaara.* He's being stingy with himself so that he can save money for a car.
taqtiir stinginess.

q-t-l
qital, etc. = *kital* which see under [1]*k-t-l*.
qatil murder, killing. || *ḥaadiθ qatil* a murder.
qaatil pl. *-iin, qatala* killer, murderer.

q-t-m
qaatim dark. *loon qaatim* a dark color. *ʔaḥmar qaatim* dark red.

q-č-ġ
qaččaġ to take without cost, cadge, sponge, bum. *da-yqaččiġ jiqaayir imnir-raayiḥ wij-jaay.* He's bumming cigarettes from everyone. *laa, ma-štireeta l-haθ-θoob. qaččaġta min ʕali.* No, I didn't buy this shirt. I took it off Ali.
qačaġ **1.** smuggling. **2.** (invar.) smuggled, contraband. *biðaaʕa qačaġ* smuggled goods. || *miliḥ qačaġ* bootlegged salt. *rikab qačaġ bil-paaṣ.* He rode the bus without paying. **3.** contraband, smuggled goods.
qačaġči pl. *-iyya* smuggler.

q-č-m
ʔaqčam f. *qačma* pl. *qačmiin* pug-nosed. || *sayyaara qačma.* Jeep and other small military vehicles.

q-č-w
qačaawa pl. *-aat* camel litter for females, howdah.

q-ḥ-ḥ
quḥḥ (invar.) pure, unmixed, unadulterated. *ʕarabi quḥḥ* a pure Arab.

q-ḥ-r
qiḥar var. of *qihar* which see under *q-h-r*.

q-ḥ-ṭ
qiḥaṭ (a *qaḥaṭ*) to be scarce. *yaʕni b-kull baġdaad ma-aku tamaaṭa. qaabil qiḥṭat?* You mean in all Baghdad there aren't any tomatoes. Do you mean they're that scarce?
qaḥḥaṭ to withhold, to be stingy. *la-tqaḥḥiṭha ʕaleena. haay ma-tikfi.* Don't be stingy with us. That isn't enough.
qaḥaṭ (invar.) **1.** drought, dryness. **2.** famine. **3.** something scarce. *raawiinayyaaha ʕaad! qaḥaṭ?* Show it to us then! Is it something so precious?

q-d-ḥ
qiddaaḥ (coll.) blossom of citrus tree. *wardat qiddaaḥ* a citrus blossom.
qiddaaḥa pl. *-aat* (= *giddaaḥa, jiddaaḥa*) cigarette lighter.

q-d-r
qidar = *gidar* which see under *g-d-r*.
qaddar **1.** to estimate, evaluate. *š-gadd itqaddir qiimat has-saaʕa?* How much do you estimate the value of this watch to be? *l-ʔustaaδ qaddar-li daraja w-ma-mtiḥanit.* The professor just estimated my grade and I didn't take an exam. **2.** to appreciate, to think highly of. *huwwa ma-yqaddir hiiči nooʕ imnil-hadaaya.* He doesn't appreciate that kind of presents. *kullhum yiḥtarmuu w-yqaddiruu.* They all respect him and think highly of him. **3.** (of God) to ordain, decree. *ʔiδa ʔaḷḷa qaddar w-muṭrat, z-zariʕ ma-ymuut.* If God decides to make it rain, the crops won't die. *ʔiδa—ʔaḷḷa la-yqaddir—mitit, minu yihtamm biina?* If—God forbid—you died, who would care for us?
qadir prestige, regard. || *leelat il-qadir* night of the 26th of Ramadan, celebrating the revealing of the Koran to Mohammed. *qadr il-imkaan, ʕala qadir il-imkaan* as much as possible. *raḥ-aṣbur qadr il-imkaan.* I'll be patient as long as possible. *ʕal-qadir* just right, the right size. *wuṣlat il-uqmaaš čaanat ʕal-qadir.* The piece of cloth was just right. *b-qadir-ma* to the extent that. *b-qadir-ma tsawwi wiyyaa zeen, ysibbak.* To the same extent that you treat him well, he'll insult you.
qadar pl. *ʔaqdaar* divine foreordainment, fate, destiny. || *maat qaδaaʔ w-qadar.* He died of natural causes. *ʔiδa*

ṣaar qadar bis-sayyaara, š-raḥ-insawwi? If something goes wrong with the car, what will we do?

qudra capacity, ability, capability, aptitude. *ʕinda qudra ʕala haš-šuġuḷ iṣ-ṣaʕub.* He has the ability for this difficult work. || *ṭaab ib-qudrat ʔaḷḷa.* He got well by the power of God. *ʕaayiš bil-qudra.* He's living by the will of God.

ʔaqdar more or most capable.

miqdaar pl. *maqaadiir* **1.** period, extent of time. **2.** amount.

taqdiir pl. *-aat* estimate, calculation, valuation. *ʕala ʔaqall taqdiir* at least. *ʕala ʔakθar taqdiir* at most.

qtidaar ability, capability, capacity. *kull man yitbarraʕ ʕala gadd iqtidaara.* Everyone donates according to his means. *ma-ʕindi qtidaar ʔaštiri beet.* I'm not able to buy a house. *saaʕa yaḷḷa yiṭbaʕ saḥiifa. qtidaara halgadd.* It takes him a whole hour to type a page. That's all he's capable of.

muqtadir well to do.

q-d-s

qaddas to hold sacred, venerate, revere. *ʔahl il-qarya yqaddisuun hal-ʕaalim id-diini.* The people of the village venerate this religious authority. || *l-baarḥa kumšoo bid-darbuuna w-qaddisoo.* Yesterday they caught him in the alley and beat him up.

qudus: l-qudus Jerusalem. *ruuḥ il-qudus, r-ruuḥ il-qudus* the Holy Ghost.

qudsiyya holiness, sacredness, sanctity.

quddaas pl. *-aat, qadaadiis* Mass.

qadaasa holiness. *qadaasat il-ḅaaḅa.* His Holiness the Pope.

qiddiis pl. *-iin* saint (Christian).

muqaddas holy, sacred. *l-kitaab il-muqaddas.* The Holy Bible. || *b-muqaddasaati, ma-aʕruf ʕanna šii.* By all the things I hold to be holy, I don't know anything about it.

q-d-ġ

qadaġa bother, trouble, pain-in-the-neck, headache.

q-d-f

qadiifa velvet. || *ʕeer qadiifa* dildo.

q-d-m

qidam = *ʔaqdam* which see.

qaddam **1.** to offer, proffer, tender, extend, present. *qaddimoo-lna keek uw-čaay.* They offered us cake and tea. *qaddamit-la kull musaaʕada mumkina.* I offered him all possible assistance. *qaddam-li hadiyya ḥilwa.* He presented me with a nice gift. *ʔariid aqaddim-lak ṣadiiqi.* I want to present my friend to you. *smaḥ-li aqaddim nafsi.* Let me introduce myself. *qaddam taqriir ʕan ziyaarta lil-maʕmal.* He presented a report on his visit to the factory. **2.** to place (someone) at the head, ahead of. *qaddam ʔibna ʕala baaqi ṭ-ṭullaab.* He placed his son ahead of the rest of the students. *qaddamta ʕala nafsi.* I let him get ahead of me. **3.** to give priority to *la-tqaddim ʔayy šii ʕala haš-šuġuḷ.* Don't give anything priority over this job. **4.** to apply. *qaddam ʕala qabuul bi-θlaθ kulliyyaat.* He applied for admission to three colleges. **5.** to set ahead (a watch). *raḥ-inqaddim saaʕaatna saaʕa waḥda.* We're going to set our watches ahead an hour. **6.** to gain, to be fast (a watch). *saaʕti qaddmat xamis daqaayiq il-yoom.* My watch gained five minutes today.

ʔaqdam to have the audacity to do. *ma-yiqdim ʕala hiiči ʕamal ʔilla l-majnuun.* Nobody would have the audacity for such a deed except a crazy person.

tqaddam **1.** to go forward, advance. *jeešna tqaddam xamis kiilomatraat.* Our army advanced five kilometers. **2.** to progress, make progress. *ṣ-ṣinaaʕa hwaaya tqaddmat.* Industry has progressed a lot. **3.** to be served. *l-ʔakil raḥ-yitqaddam saaʕa xamsa.* The food will be served at five.

staqdam to ask to come, summon. *l-ḥukuuma raḥ-tistaqdim xabiir ʔamriiki bid-dibaaġa.* The government is going to bring in an American expert in tanning.

qidam seniority.

qadam pl. *ʔaqdaam* **1.** foot. *ʔaθar qadam* a footprint. **2.** foot (as a unit of measure).

qadamiyya extra charge by a doctor for a house call.

qadiim pl. *qudamaaʔ* **1.** old, ancient. *ṭ-ṭaariix il-qadiim* ancient history. *ṣadiiq qadiim* an old friend. **2.** former, previous, old. *marta l-qadiima* his former wife. || *min qadiim* from time immemorial. *hal-ʕaaʔila tuskun ib-baġdaad min qadiim.* This family has lived in Baghdad for generations.

ʔaqdam more or most ancient. || *huwwa ʔaqdam minnak ib-had-daaʔira.* He has seniority over you in this office.

ʔaqdamiyya seniority.

qaadim coming, next. *l-isbuuʕ il-qaadim* next week.

muqaddam pl. *-aat* **1.** bow (of a ship). **2.** nose (of an airplane, etc.) **3.** (pl. *-iin*) lieutenant colonel. **4.** (no pl.) portion of the bridal price paid in advance.

muqaddima, muqaddama pl. *-aat* **1.** bow (of a ship), nose (of an airplane). **2.** advance guard, vanguard, van. **3.** foreword, preface, introduction, prologue, preamble. || *gull-li š-itriid. ma-aku ɛaaja lil-muqaddimaat.* Tell me what you want. There's no reason for beating around the bush.

muqaddaman in advance, beforehand, first of all. *difaɛit ɛašr idnaaniir muqaddaman.* I paid ten dinars in advance. *muqaddaman, ʔagul-lak ma-tṣiir.* First of all, I tell you it'll never happen.

mitqaddim in front, ahead. *mitqaddim ɛala jamaaɛta* ahead of his group. *ṭaalib mitqaddim* an advanced student.

q-d-w

qtida to imitate, copy, emulate, follow someone's example. *laazim tiqtiduun bii.* You should follow his example.

qudwa pl. *-aat* model, pattern, example.

q-δ-r

qaδir **1.** dirty, filthy. *maaɛuun qaδir* a filthy plate. **2.** vile, depraved, filthy. **3.** vile person.

ʔaqδar more or most filthy, vile, etc.

qaδaara dirtiness, filthiness, squalor.

qaaδuura pl. *-aat* dirt, filth. *qaaδuuraat* trash, rubbish, garbage.

q-δ-f

qiδaf (i qaδif) **1.** to ejaculate (semen). **2.** to vomit. *nafsa liɛbat w-qiδaf.* He got nauseated and vomited.

qaδiifa pl. *qaδaaʔif* projectile, artillery shell.

qaaδifa: qaaδifat qanaabil bomber (airplane). *qaaδifat lahab* flame thrower.

q-r-ʔ

qira (a qraaya) **1.** to recite, declaim, chant. *minu raɛ-yiqra qurʔaan bir-raadyo l-yoom?* Who is going to recite the Koran on the radio today? *s-saaɛir qira ɛač-čaffiyya w-ingulbat ʔarnab.* The magician recited magic words over the handkerchief and it turned into a rabbit. || *ʔay iktaab yoogaɛ b-iid ɛali baɛad ma-tšuufa. ʔiqra ɛalee s-salaam.* Any book that falls into Ali's hands you won't see again. Kiss it good-by. **2.** to read. *qireet jariidt il-yoom?* Have you read today's paper? *š-imɛarrfak? qaabil tiqra l-mamɛi?* How do you know? Do you mean to tell me you can divine the unknown? **3.** to study. *ʔiδa tiqra zeen, tinjaɛ bil-imtiɛaan.* If you study well, you'll pass the exam.

qarra **1.** to cause to read. *ʔasuu l-muɛallim ma-da-yqarriini.* It seems the teacher doesn't ever ask me to read. **2.** to teach, tutor. *hal-muɛallim iyqarriina ɛsaab.* This teacher teaches us arithmetic. *qarreet ibni druusa.* I helped my son with his lessons.

tqarra to be taught. *hal-mwaaδiiɛ ma-titqarra b-iṣfuuf biiha banaat.* These subjects aren't taught in classes where there are girls.

nqira **1.** to be recited. *l-qaṣiida nqirat loo baɛad?* Has the poem been recited yet? **2.** to be read. *hal-kitaaba ma-tinqiri.* This writing can't be read.

qiraaʔa, qiraaya pl. *-aat* **1.** recitation, recital. **2.** reading.

qraaya pl. *-aat* mourning ceremony (Shiah).

qurʔaan pl. *qraaʔiin* Koran, holy book of the Moslems.

qaari pl. *-iyyiin, qurraaʔ* **1.** reciter. **2.** reader.

q-r-b

qirab = *girab,* which see under *g-r-b.*

qarrab **1.** to cause or allow to come near or get close. *l-ɛaadiθ qarrab been il-ɛaaʔilteen.* The accident brought the two families closer together. **2.** to take as a protégé, take under one's wing, to favor. *l-mudiir ij-jidiid qarrab ɛali ʔila.* The new director took Ali under his wing.

qaarab to come close, get close, approach. *ɛsaabna qaarab il-miit diinaar.* Our account came close to a hundred dinars.

tqarrab **1.** to approach, come or get near, near, come close, get close. *la-titqarrab, tara č-čalib yɛaṣṣak.* Don't get too close or the dog will bite you. *la-titqarrab minni.* Don't come near me. *ʔiδa bardaan, itqarrab yamm in-naar.* If you're cold get close to the fire. *ṣall yitqarrab ɛalayya ʔila ʔan waggaɛni biš-šaṭṭ.* He kept getting closer to me till he knocked me into the river. **2.** /with *ʔila*/ to curry favor with, to seek to gain someone's favor. *šuuf išloon da-yitqarrab lil-mudiir.* Look how he's carrying favor with the boss. *da-yitṣaddaq ɛal-fuqaraaʔ ɛatta yitqarrab il-ʔaḷḷa.* He's giving charity to the poor to endear himself to God.

tqaarab to be or become near each other, approach one another. *nuwwaab il-muɛaaraṣa bidaw yitqaarbuun b-ʔaaraaʔhum wiyya l-ɛukuuma.* The opposition deputies have begun to get close to the government in their opinions.

qtirab to approach, get close. *ṣ-ṣeef qtirab. ḥaðḍir ihduumak.* Summer is getting near. Get your clothes ready. *jeeš il-ʕadu qtirab min mawaaðiʕna.* The enemy army approached our positions.

qurub near, close to. *wuṣal lil-madrasa qurb iḍ-ḍuhur.* He got to the school near noon. || *ma-ʕabaali l-madrasa hal-qurub.* I didn't realize the school was this close. *tiʕtiqid raḥ-yiji b-hal-qurub?* Do you think he'll come in the near future?

qariib 1. near, close, nearby. *qariib imnil-beet* near the house. *qariib ʕas-sayyaara* close to the car. *makaan qariib* a nearby place. 2. about to. *huwwa qariib yṣiir mudiir ʕaamm.* He's about to become director general. 3. (pl. *ʔaqribaaʔ*) relative, relation, kin (by marriage also).

qaraaba relation, relationship, kinship.

qurbaan pl. *qaraabiin* sacrifice.

ʔaqrab more or most near, close, etc. (also fig.).

qurraaba pl. *-aat* carboy, demijohn.

taqriiban roughly, about, approximately, almost, nearly. *raatba miit diinaar taqriiban.* His salary is nearly a hundred dinars.

muqaarib 1. mediocre, borderline. *daraja muqaariba* a borderline grade. 2. almost, close to, approaching. *ʕadadhum čaan muqaarib lil-miyya.* Their number was almost a hundred. *ʔiða ma-ʕindak qaaṭ ʔaswad ʔilbas qaaṭ muqaarib lil-ʔaswad.* If you don't have a black suit, wear a suit that is almost black.

see also *g-r-b.*

q-r-b-a-č

qurbaač, qirbaač pl. *qaraabiič* whip, riding crop, kurbash.

q-r-b-a-z

muqurbaaz pl. *-iyya* cheater, swindler, crook.

q-r-č

qarač (fem.) pl. *qaraayič* 1. loud, brazen, insolent. 2. brazen woman.

q-r-ḥ

qtiraḥ to suggest, recommend. *ʔaqtiriḥ ʕaleek itxaaburni gabuḷ-ma tištiriiha.* I suggest that you call me before you buy it.

qurḥa pl. *quraḥ* ulcer.

qariiḥa genius, talent, gift, faculty.

qtiraaḥ pl. *-aat* suggestion, proposal.

q-r-d

qird pl. *quruud* simian, ape, monkey, chimpanzee.

q-r-d-y-l

qirdeela pl. *-aat* ribbon, hair ribbon, bow.

q-r-r

qarr (*u ʔiqraar*) to confess, admit. *ðallaw iybuṣṭuun bii ḥatta qarr.* They kept beating on him until he confessed.

qarrar 1. to assign, stipulate, approve, decide on. *wizaart il-maʕaarif qarrirat hal-iktaab.* The ministry of education assigned this book. 2. to decide. *qarrarit tiji wyaana willa laa?* Have you decided to come with us or not? 3. to lecture. *baʕad-ma yqarrir il-mudarris id-daris, tṣiir munaaqaša.* After the teacher lectures to the class, there'll be a discussion. *ʔiskut! il-ʔustaað da-yqarrir.* Be quiet! The professor is lecturing. 4. to interrogate, grill, cross-examine. *š-šurṭa ðallat itqarrir bii ʔila ʔan iʕtiraf.* The police kept grilling him until he confessed. *l-maḥkama qarrirat il-masjuun.* The court cross-examined the prisoner.

tqarrar to be decided. *tqarrar naqla lil-baṣra.* It was decided he'd be transferred to Basra.

staqarr 1. to settle down, become settled, take up residence. *ma-da-yistaqirr ib-mukaan.* He won't settle down in one place. 2. to settle, stabilize, become stabilized. *l-waðiʕ staqarr biš-šimaal.* The situation has calmed down in the North. *fikra ma-staqarr ʕala šii baʕad.* His mind hasn't settled on anything yet. His mind isn't made up yet.

qaraar pl. *-aat* decision, resolution. *qaraar il-ḥukum* the sentence, decision of the court.

maqarr pl. *-aat* headquarters, center of operations.

taqriir pl. *taqaariir* (official) report, account. *taqriir il-maṣiir.* self-determination.

ʔiqraar pl. *-aat* confession, admission.

qaarra pl. *-aat* continent.

muqarraraat (pl. only) decisions.

q-r-š

qaaraš 1. to cope, compete, keep up. *ʔiða tiddarrab gabuḷ-ma tilʕab wiyyaa, tiʕtiqid tigdar itqaariš?* If you practice before you play him, do you think you can compete on equal terms? *la-tilʕab wiyyaa ṭaawli tara ma-tigdar itqaariš.* Don't play backgammon with him because you don't have a chance. 2. to bother, pester, plague, annoy, interfere with. *la-tqaarša. xallii yištuġuḷ.* Don't bother him. Let him work. *maḥḥad qaaraša; gaam yibči min keefa.*

No one did a thing to him; he just started crying on his own.

tqaaraš **1.** = *qaaraš* **1.** *ʔaani ma-atqaaraš wiyyaa b-haš-šuġul.* I can't compare with him at this job. **2.** /with *b-*/ to bother, annoy. *la-titqaaraš bii tara ybuṣṭak.* Don't bother him or he'll beat you up.

qiriš pl. *quruuš* piaster. *ṣirafit kull ifluusi; ma-biqa ćindi wala qiriš.* I spent all my money; I don't even have a penny left. *has-sayyaara ma-tiswa qiriš.* This car isn't worth a penny.

qaariš: qaariš waariš hanky panky, funny business.

q-r-ṣ

quruṣ pl. *ʔaqraaṣ* **1.** plate, disk, discus. *rami l-quruṣ* discus throwing. **2.** tablet, lozenge, pastille. *duwa ćala šikil ʔaqraaṣ* medicine in tablet form. **3.** dial (of telephone).

qirraaṣa pl. *-aat* clothespin.

see also *g-r-ṣ*

q-r-ṣ-a-ġ

qurṣaaġ patience, forbearance, endurance.

q-r-ṣ-n

qarṣana piracy.

qurṣaan pl. *qaraaṣina* pirate.

q-r-ć

qurća pl. *qurać* **1.** lot drawing, lottery. *sawwaw qurća.* They drew lots. **2.** conscription, recruitment (by lot). *qurća ćaskariyya* draft, draft call.

q-r-ć-a-n

qurćaan = *qurʔaan* which see under *q-r-ʔ*.

q-r-q

quruq: ćammaam quruq a reserved bathhouse.

q-r-q-r

qarqar to rumble, growl. *baṭni tqarqir. jooćaan.* My stomach is growling. I'm hungry.

qarqara pl. *-aat* growl, rumble (of the stomach).

q-r-q-š

qarqaš **1.** to hit (someone) for money, to demand money from. *ćali ybayyin zangiin il-yoom. xall inruuć inqarqiša.* Ali appears to be rich today. Let's go get some money from him. **2.** to give, to enrich. *yoom il-maaćaaš ʔabuuya yqarqišni b-diinaar.* On payday my father gives me a dinar.

q-r-q-w-z

qaraqooz pl. *-aat* puppet.

q-r-q-w-š

qaraqooš: ćukum qaraqooš arbitrary rule. *šloon tigdar tufṣulni? leeš, maaku qaanuun? qaabil ćukum qaraqooš?* How can you fire me? Isn't there any law? Do you imagine there's anarchy?

q-r-ḍ

qiraḍ (*u qariḍ*) **1.** to kill off, annihilate. *d-diktaatoor qaṣda yuqruḍhum.* The dictator's purpose is to annihilate them. **2.** to talk behind someone's back, to cut down, cut to pieces. *gaaćdiin bil-gahwa yqurḍuun in-naas.* They're sitting in the coffeeshop cutting people to pieces.

qarraḍ to loan, lend, advance (money). *qarriḍni fadd čam diinaar il-baačir.* Lend me a few dinars until tomorrow.

tqarraḍ to borrow. *ʔagdar ʔatqarraḍ nuṣṣ diinaar minnak?* Can I borrow a half dinar from you?

nqiraḍ to become extinct, to die out. *d-daynasoor nqiraḍ.* The dinosaur has become extinct.

qtiraḍ to borrow. *qtiraḍ minni diinaareen w-ma-nṭaani-yyaaha.* He borrowed two dinars from me and didn't give them back to me.

staqraḍ to ask for a loan. *ma-agdar aštiriiha bila-ma ʔastaqriḍ ifluus minna.* I can't buy it unless I ask for money from him.

qariḍ pl. *qruuḍ* loan. *sanad qariḍ* (government) bond.

qurḍa as a loan. *nṭiini miit filis qurḍa* Give me a hundred fils as a loan.

qraaḍa (invar.) worn-out. *r-raadyo maalak ma-yfiid. qraaḍa.* Your radio is no good. It's worn out. *nćaal lit-taqaaćud liʔanna ṣaar iqraaḍa.* He got retired because he became old and worn out.

muqraaḍa pl. *-aat* nail clipper.

munqariḍ extinct. *ćaywaan munqariḍ* an extinct animal.

see also *g-r-ḍ*.

q-r-m

qirma pl. *qiram* pleat.

mqarram pleated. *tannuura mqarrama* a pleated skirt.

see also *g-r-m*.

q-r-m-p-a-r-a

qurumpara pl. *-iyya* pederast, man who commits sodomy with boys.

q-r-m-z

*qirmizi** crimson, carmine, scarlet. *l-ćumma l-qirmiziyya* scarlet fever.

q-r-m-ṭ

qarmaṭ to cut down, cut back, withhold. *qarmiṭoo l-manhaj il-ćafla. laa raćyjiibuun raaqiṣa wala muġanniya.* They

cut down the program for the party. They're not going to bring a dancer or a singer. *nṭiini baᶜad šwayya. la-tqarmuṭha.* Give me a little more. Don't cut down the amount.
see also *g-r-m-ṭ*.

q-r-n
qaaran /with *been*/ to compare. *qaarin been il-luġa il-ˀaspaaniyya wil-luġa il-purtuġaaliyya.* Compare the Spanish language and the Portuguese language.
qarin pl. *quruun* century. *l-quruun il-wusṭa* the Middle Ages.
qaraniyya pl. *-aat* cornea (anat.).
qariina pl. *-aat* formal term for wife.
qiraan: ᶜaqid qiraan marriage contract.
qraan pl. *-aat* term for the twenty fils coin.
muqaarana pl. *-aat* comparison. *bil-muqaarana ṭilᶜaw yitšaabhuun ihwaaya.* In comparison, they turned out to be very similar.

q-r-n-a-b-y-ṭ
qarnaabiiṭ cauliflower.

q-r-n-ṣ
qarnaṣ to scallop, to make a deckle-edge, to pink. *qarnuṣ ᶜaašyat, il-uqmaaš, ᶜatta ma-titsallat il-ixyuuṭ.* Pink the edge of the cloth, so the threads won't come loose. *qarnaṣ ᶜaašyat it-taṣwiir bil-mugaṣṣ.* He scalloped the edge of the photo with scissors.

q-r-n-f-l
qrinfil (coll.) carnation(s).
qrinfila pl. *-aat* u.n. of *qrinfil*.

q-r-w-a-n
qarawaana pl. *-aat, qarawaayin* large round shallow metal serving bowl.

[1]*q-r-y*
qarya pl. *qura* village.
*qurawi** 1. rural, village. *ᶜayaat qurawiyya* village life. 2. villager.

[2]*q-r-y*
qraaya see under *q-r-ˀ*.

q-r-y-w-l
qaryoola pl. *-aat* steel cot. *qaryoola safariyya* folding camp cot.

q-z-a-ṭ-m-a
qazaaṭma a meat and rice dish.

q-z-a-n
qazaan pl. *-aat* kettle, caldron, large metal pot for heating water.

q-z-ᶜ
qazaᶜ: qooz qazaᶜ rainbow.
qazaᶜiyya pl. *-aat* iris (of the eye).

[1]*q-z-z*
qazz (*i qazz*) to be disgusted, nauseated. *nafsi qazzat minna, halgadd-ma waṣix.* I was nauseated by him, he was so dirty.
qazzaz to disgust, nauseate. *manðara yqazziz in-nafis.* The sight of him disgusts you.
tqazzaz to be disgusted, nauseated. *ˀaani tqazzazit minna.* I was disgusted with him.
qazz: duudat il-qazz silkworm.
qazzaaz pl. *-a* silk merchant.

[2]*q-z-z*
qizza pl. *-aat, qizaz* queen, in non-western card games.

q-z-z-l-q-r-ṭ
quzzulqurṭ (exclamation of exasperation, lit., the black wolf, approx.:) Shut up! Drop dead! Go to hell!

q-z-m
qazam, qizim pl. *ˀaqzaam* 1. dwarf, midget, pygmy. 2. little fellow, shrimp.
qazma pl. *-aat* pick, mattock.

q-z-w-y-n
qazwiin: baᶜar qazwiin Caspian Sea.

q-s-s
qiss, qass, qissiis pl. *qissiisiin, qasaawisa qsuus* clergyman, priest, minister, parson, pastor (Christian).

q-s-ṭ
q-s-ṭ, see *q-ṣ-ṭ*.

q-s-m
qisam (*i qisma*) 1. to divide, split. *qisam il-keeka qismeen.* He divided the cake in two. *huwwa qisam il-ġurfa ˀila ġurufteen.* He partitioned the room into two rooms. 2. to destine, foreordain, will. *ˀaḷḷa qisam-la hiiči.* God willed it this way for him.
qisam (*i qasam*) to take an oath, swear. *qisam ib-ˀaḷḷa maa-la ᶜilaaqa bil-mawðuuᶜ.* He swore by God he had nothing to do with the matter.
qassam 1. to divide. *qassim ᶜašra ᶜala θneen.* Divide ten by two. 2. to divide, distribute. *qassam il-ifluus ᶜaleena.* He divided the money among us. 3. /with *ᶜala*/ to play (a stringed instrument). *ᶜilu yqassim ᶜal-ᶜuud.* He plays the lute nicely.
ˀaqsam to swear, take an oath. *ˀaqsam ma-yiᶜči wiyyaak baᶜad.* He swore he wouldn't talk to you any more.
tqassam 1. to be divided. *hal-ᶜadad ma-yitqassam ᶜala θneen.* This number can't be divided by two. *ṭ-ṭullaab tqassmaw ˀila qismeen.* The students were divided into two groups.

tqaasam to divide, divide up. *tqaasmaw il-ifluus.* They split the money.

nqisam to be divided. *j-jayš nqisam ˀila qismeen.* The army was divided into two parts.

qisim pl. *ˀaqsaam* **1.** part, section. **2.** some, part, portion. **3.** section, department.

qisma **1.** dividing, division, distribution, allotment, apportionment. **2.** (math.) division. **3.** (pl. *qisam*) lot, destiny, fate.

qasam pl. *ˀaqsaam* oath.

qasaman I swear! *qasaman bil-ḷḷaa, raḥ-amawwtak ˀiδa ma-tiskut!* By God, I'll kill you if you don't shut up!

qasiima pl. *qasaayim* coupon.

taqsiim **1.** dividing, division, partition, splitting. **2.** distribution, allotment, apportionment. **3.** (pl. *-aat*) division, subdivision. *taqsiimaat ˀidaariyya* administrative divisions. **4.** (elec.) plug with several female sides. **5.** (pl. *taqaasiim*) solo recital (mus.).

qaasim divisor, denominator (math.). *l-qaasim il-muštarak il-ˀaḥδam.* lowest common denominator (lit. highest common denominator).

q-s-w

qisa (*i qaswa, qasaawa*) to be harsh, cruel. *ˀiδa tiqsi b-muḥaamaltak ˀilhum, ykurhuuk.* If you're harsh in your treatment of them, they'll hate you.

qaasa to undergo, suffer, endure, bear, stand. *qaasa hwaaya b-šabaaba.* He suffered a lot in his youth.

qaswa harshness, severity, cruelty, mercilessness.

qasaawa = *qaswa.*

ˀaqsa more or most stern, severe, etc.

*qaasi** **1.** harsh, stern, severe, cruel. *ḥaakim qaasi* a harsh judge.

q-š-l

qišla pl. *qišal* barracks.

q-š-m-r

qašmar (*u qašmara*) **1.** to deceive, fool. *qašmarni w-baaḥ-li saaḥa ma-tištuġuḷ.* He deceived me and sold me a watch that doesn't run. **2.** to joke, chaff, banter, poke fun. *la-tqašmur. yaḥni qaabil sayyaartak ˀaḥsan.* Don't make fun of it. Do you mean to say your car is better? *δallaw yqašmuruun ḥalee w-ma-šiḥar.* They kept pulling his leg and he never realized.

tqašmar to be deceived, fooled. *hal-walad ma-yitqašmar.* This guy can't be fooled.

qašmar pl. *qašaamir, qasaamra* **1.** fool, ass, idiot, jerk. **2.** laughing stock, butt of jokes, person who is not to be taken seriously.

qašmara **1.** deception, fooling. **2.** joking, chaffing, banter, poking fun. **3.** a joke, a laughing stock, a travesty.

qašmiriyyaat (pl. only) **1.** deception, trickery. **2.** joking, banter.

q-ṣ-b

qaṣaba: l-qaṣaba l-hawaaˀiyya the respiratory tract bronchial tubes, windpipe.

q-ṣ-d

qiṣad (*u qaṣid*) **1.** to intend, aim, mean. *ma-qiṣad yzaḥḥlak.* He didn't mean to make you mad. **2.** to mean, try to say. *š-tuqṣud ib-hal-ḥibaara?* What do you mean by that expression?

tqaṣṣad **1.** to decide, set one's mind, make up one's mind. *hat-tilmiiδ mujtahid laakin il-muḥallim tqaṣṣad w-ṣaqqaṭa.* This student is a good one but the teacher had set his mind on failing him. **2.** to mean, try to say. *yitqaṣṣad ib-kull čilma yguulha ḥalayya.* He means every word he says against me.

qtiṣad **1.** to economize, be economical, thrifty. *ma-tigdar tištiri sayyaara ˀiδa ma-tiqtiṣid.* You can't buy a car if you don't economize. **2.** to save. *bdaal-ma ˀarkab paaṣ da-aruuḥ maši lid-daaˀira w-aqtiṣid ḥašr ifluus.* Instead of taking the bus I walk to the office and save ten fils.

qaṣid **1.** intention, intent. **2.** design, purpose. *ḥan qaṣid* intentionally, purposely. *bala qaṣid, ḥan ġeer qaṣid* unintentionally, inadvertently.

qaṣṭani intentionally, on purpose. *sawwaaha qaṣṭani ḥatta yxajjilni.* He did it on purpose to embarrass me.

qaṣiid: beet il-qaṣiid the essence, the gist.

qaṣiida pl. *qasaaˀid* poem, piece of poetry.

maqṣad pl. *maqaasid* **1.** intention, intent. **2.** design, purpose.

qtiṣaad **1.** economization, economy. **2.** economics.

*qtiṣaadi** **1.** saving, thrifty, provident. *marti kulliš iqtiṣaadiyya.* My wife is very thrifty. **2.** economical. *sayyaara qtiṣaadiyya* an economical car. **3.** economic. *l-ḥaala l-iqtiṣaadiyya* the economic situation. **4.** economist, political economist.

q-ṣ-r

qaṣṣar **1.** to shorten, make shorter, curtail. *qaṣṣar ˀaḷḷa b-ḥumrak!* May God shorten your life! **2.** to stint, be sparing. *ma-yqaṣṣir wiyya ʔibna. kull-ma yuṭlub minna yinṭii.* He doesn't stint his son. Anything he asks for he gives him. *ʔinta ma-da-tqaṣṣir wiyyaa. da-tsaaʕda hwaaya.* You aren't sparing anything with him. You're helping him a lot. **3.** to be lax, negligent, neglectful. *qaṣṣarit ma-gut-la ʕaleeha.* You were neglectful not to tell him about it. *laazim čaan tištiriiha; qaṣṣarit.* You should have bought it; you made a mistake. **4.** to lose (time). *saaʕti tqaṣṣir.* My watch loses time. *has-saaʕa tqaṣṣir xamis daqaayiq bil-yoom.* This watch loses five minutes a day.

qtiṣar to be limited, restricted, confined. *raħ-tiqtiṣir ħaflat iz-zawaaj ʕal-ʔaqaarib bass.* The marriage celebration will be restricted to relatives only.

qaṣir pl. *qṣuur* palace, mansion.

quṣur shortness. *quṣur naðar* near-sightedness. *ʕinda quṣur naðar; yiħtaaj manaaðir.* He's near-sighted; he needs glasses.

quṣuur **1.** deficiency, shortcoming, lack. **2.** slackness, laxity, negligence, neglectfulness.

qṣuur change (left after buying something).

qaṣiir **1.** short. *ʕuuda qaṣiira* a short stick. **2.** small, short, low. *rijjaal qaṣiir* a short man. *šijra qasiira* a low tree. *nahaar qaṣiir* a short day.

ʔaqṣar shorter or shortest.

qaaṣir pl. *-iin, quṣṣar* legally minor, underage. || *masħuuq qaaṣir, qaaṣir ʔalwaan* bleaching agent (chem.).

maqṣuura pl. *-aat* box, box seat, loge.

see also *g-ṣ-r.*

q-ṣ-ṣ

qaṣṣ (*u qaṣṣ*) to relate, narrate, tell. *šifta gaaʕid yquṣṣ ʕaleehum iš-šaaf ib-ʔooruppa.* I saw him sitting telling them what he saw in Europe.

qaaṣaṣ to punish. *l-muʕallim qaaṣaṣa liʔan ma-msawwi waðiifta.* The teacher punished him because he didn't do his homework.

qtaṣṣ to avenge, revenge oneself, take vengeance. *laazim ʔaqtaṣṣ minna ʕala had-dagga.* I'll have to get revenge on him for that dirty deed.

quṣṣa, qiṣṣa pl. *qiṣaṣ* story, tale. *šinu quṣṣat axuuk? ybayyin ʕalee zaʕlaan.* What's the story with your brother? He seems mad.

quṣṣaxuun pl. *-iyya* storyteller.

qaṣaaṣ punishment.

q-ṣ-ṭ

qaṣṣaṭ **1.** to distribute, spread out (payments). *ʔiða tqaṣṣiṭ-li qiimt it-talavizyoon kull ʔarbaʕt išhur ʕašir danaaniir, ʔaštiri minnak.* If you spread out the price of the television, ten dinars every four months, I'll buy from you. **2.** to pay in installments. *raħ-aqaṣṣiṭ il-mablaġ ʕala ʔarbaʕ aqṣaaṭ.* I'm going to pay the amount in four installments.

quṣuṭ pl. *ʔaqṣaaṭ* payment. *bil-ʔaqsaaṭ* by installments. *štireenaa bil-ʔaqsaaṭ.* We bought it by installments.

taqṣiiṭ: bit-taqṣiiṭ in installments. *nbiiʕ bit-taqṣiiṭ.* We sell on installment.

q-ṣ-ṭ-n

qaṣṭani see under *q-ṣ-d.*

q-ṣ-ṭ-w-r

qaṣṭoor a kind of cloth, resembling karakul, used for overcoats.

q-ṣ-ʕ

quṣʕa pl. *quṣaʕ* a large bowl or kettle, used for carrying food to the troops, and by extension, an army meal. *wakt il-quṣʕa* chow time. *sinu quṣʕatna l-yoom?* What's for chow today? *l-buuqi da-ydugg il-quṣʕa.* The bugler's playing chow call.

q-ṣ-f

quṣaf (*u qaṣuf*) **1.** to beset, harass, oppress. *ʔaḷḷa yuqṣuf ʕumrak ʕala had-dagga.* Damn you for doing that. **2.** to bomb. *ṭ-ṭayyaaraat quṣfat maʕmaleen bil-madiina.* The airplanes bombed two factories in the city.

nquṣaf to be bombed. *hal-madiina ma-nquṣfat ib-ʔayyaam il-ħarub.* This city didn't get bombed during the war.

q-ṣ-y

ʔaqṣa: ʔila ʔaqṣa ħadd to the extreme limit, to the utmost. *biðal juhda ʔila ʔaqṣa ħadd il-musaaʕadti.* He exerted himself to the utmost limit to help me. *š-šarq il-ʔaqṣa* the Far East.

q-ð-b

qaðiib pl. *quðbaan* **1.** phallus, penis. **2.** wand, rod.

q-ð-w

qaðawiyya pl. *-aat* red fez wrapped with white cloth, worn by Moslem religious functionaries.

q-ð-y

qiða (*i qaðaaʔ*) **1.** to spend, pass. *raħ-yiqði ṣ-ṣeef biš-šimaal.* He'll spend the summer in the north. **2.** /with *ʕala*/ to stamp out, annihilate, eradicate. *had-duwa yiqði ʕala marað il-balhaarizya.*

This medicine will stamp out schistosomiasis. (see also *giδa* under *g-δ-y*)

tqaaδa to deal, reckon. *xalli ysawwi š-ma yriid w-aani baɛdeen atqaaδa wyaa.* Let him do as he pleases and later I'll reckon with him.

qtiδa to necessitate, require. *ʔiδa tiqtiδi l-qaδiyya ɛraak, ʔatɛaarak.* If the matter requires fighting, I'll fight. *ʔuṣruf ɛasab-ma tiqtiδi l-ɛaaja.* Spend as necessity requires. *ma-tiqtiδi tizɛal.* There's no need to get mad. *ʔiδa qtiδa, ʔaji.* If it's necessary, I'll come. *kull-ma yiqtiδii-lak šii, ʔiɛna ɛaaδriin.* Whenever you need something, we're ready.

qaδaaʔ stamping out, eradication. *l-qaδaaʔ ɛal-ʔummiyya* the eradication of illiteracy. **2.** fate. *l-qaδaaʔ wil-qadar* fate and divine decree. **3.** (pl. *ʔaqδiya*) district, sub-province. *qaδaaʔi** judicial. *ṣ-ṣulṭa l-qaδaaʔiyya* judicial branch.

qaδiyya pl. *qaδaaya* **1.** (legal) case, legal affair. **2.** matter, affair. *š-ṣaar min qaδiyyat safarak il-ʔooruppa?* What happened to the plans for your trip to Europe? *raɛ-ašuufak w-ʔagul-lak bil-qaδiyya min ʔawwalha l-taaliiha.* I'll see you and tell you about the story from beginning to end. **3.** question, problem, issue. *šinu qaδiitak? ʔašuu ṭawwalitha.* What's the matter with you? You seem to have taken a long time about it.

qaaδi **1.** mortal, lethal. *δarba qaaδya* a mortal blow. **2.** (pl. *quδaat*) judge of religious law.

see also *g-δ-y*.

q-ṭ-b

quṭub pl. *ʔaqṭaab* pole. *l-quṭb iš-šimaali* the North Pole. *l-quṭb ij-jinuubi* the South Pole. *quṭub saalib* negative pole, cathode. *quṭub muujab* positive pole, anode.

*quṭbi** polar. *l-manṭiqa l-quṭbiyya* the Polar region.

q-ṭ-r

qaṭṭar **1.** to drop, drip, let fall in drops. *tigdar itqaṭṭir ib-ɛeeni fadd qaṭirteen?* Could you drop a couple of eyedrops in my eye? **2.** to distill. *laazim inqaṭṭir il-ṃaay gabuḷ-ma nišraba.* We must distill the water before we drink it. **3.** to line up. *qaṭṭir islaal il-imxaδδar giddaam id-dukkaan ɛatta yšuufuuha n-naas.* Line up the baskets of vegetables in front of the store so that the people will see them.

tqaṭṭar **1.** to be distilled. *l-ṃaay laazim yitqaṭṭar gabuḷ-ma yinšurub.* The water should be distilled before it's drunk. **2.** to be lined up. *l-wulid itqaṭṭiraw bil-baab.* The boys were lined up at the door.

qaṭar pl. *-aat* a line (of things). *leeš waagfiin qaṭar?* Why are you standing in a line?

quṭur pl. *ʔaqṭaar* **1.** region, quarter, area. *ʔaqṭaar id-dinya* the four corners of the world. *haaδa miftarr ʔaqṭaar id-dinya.* This man has toured the countries of the world. **2.** diameter. *nuṣf il-quṭur* radius (of a circle).

qaṭra pl. *-aat* drop (also as a medicine).

qiṭaar pl. *-aat* train.

qaṭṭaara pl. *-aat* dropper, eyedropper.

taqṭiir distilling, distillation.

mqaṭṭar distilled. *ṃaay imqaṭṭar* distilled water.

q-ṭ-ṭ

qaṭṭ (*u qaṭṭ*) to sharpen, point. *quṭṭ il-qalam.* Sharpen the pencil.

nqaṭṭ to be sharpened. *l-qalam nqaṭṭ.* The pencil was sharpened.

miqṭaaṭa pl. *-aat* sharpener, pencil sharpener.

maqṭuuṭ sharpened, sharp. *qalam maqṭuuṭ* a sharp pencil.

q-ṭ-ɛ

qiṭaɛ = *giṭaɛ*, which see under *g-ṭ-ɛ*.

qaaṭaɛ **1.** to boycott. *laazim inqaaṭiɛ il-biδaaɛa l-ʔajnabiyya.* We have to boycott foreign goods. **2.** to interrupt. *la-tqaaṭiɛni min ʔaɛči.* Don't interrupt me when I'm talking. **3.** to trade, exchange (chess) *yqaaṭiɛ ihwaaya b-ʔawwal il-liɛib.* He exchanges a lot in the beginning of the game.

tqaaṭaɛ to trade with each other. *tqaaṭaɛit wiyyaa bil-waziir.* I exchanged queens with him.

qtiṭaɛ to deduct, subtract. *xalli l-muɛaasib yiqtiṭiɛha min raatbi.* Let the accountant take it out of my salary.

staqṭaɛ to deduct. *raɛ-astaqṭiɛ xams idnaaniir min il-ifluus illi tuṭlubni-iyyaaha.* I'll deduct five dinars from the money I owe you.

*qaṭɛi** final, definite. *jawaab qaṭɛi* a definite answer.

qaṭɛiyyan absolutely. *ma-sawweetha qaṭɛiyyan.* I absolutely didn't do it. *ma-ariidak tiɛči wiyyaa qaṭɛiyyan.* I don't want you to talk to him at all.

qiṭɛa pl. *qiṭaɛ* **1.** piece, fragment, lump, chunk. **2.** piece, selection. *qiṭɛa muusiiqiyya* a musical selection. **3.** license plate, number plate. **4.** signboard, shingle.

5. (pl. *-aat, qitaϵ*) plot, piece, lot. *qitϵat il-paaṣaat* bus depot, bus terminal.
qaṭiiϵ pl. *qitϵaan* herd, flock, drove.
qaṭiiϵa pl. *-aat* separation, legal separation.
maqṭaϵ pl. *maqaaṭiϵ* cross-section.
muqaaṭaϵa pl. *-aat* 1. boycott. 2. feudal estate, large land holding.
ˀiqṭaaϵ feudal estate, land held by feudal tenure.
ˀiqṭaaϵi pl. *-iyyiin* feudal landlord, large landholder.
qaaṭiϵ pl. *qawaaṭiϵ* partition, screen, divider.
maqṭuuϵ decided, settled. *siϵir maqṭuuϵ* a fixed price.
see also *g-ṭ-ϵ*.

q-ṭ-m-r
qaṭmar 1. extreme, complete, real. *čaδδaab qaṭmar* a real liar. *šyuuϵi qaṭmar* a confirmed communist. 2. (bot.) double, having more than one row of petals. *paṭuunya qaṭmar* double petunias. *šabbo qaṭmar* double stock, double gillyflower.

q-ṭ-n
qiiṭaan pl. *qyaaṭiin* lace, string, cord.

q-ϵ-d
tqaaϵad to be pensioned off, retire. *ˀaxuuya tqaaϵad is-sana l-faatat.* My brother retired last year.
qiϵda: δu l-qiϵda Zu'lkadah, eleventh month of the Moslem calendar.
qaϵϵaada pl. *-aat* 1. bedpan. 2. potty.
maqϵad pl. *maqaaϵid* 1. seat, chair. 2. seat cushion, pad. 3. backside, seat, buttocks.
taqaaϵud pension, retirement fund. *raḥ-aḥiil nafsi ϵat-taqaaϵud.* I'm going to go on pension.
qaaϵida pl. *qawaaϵid* 1. base, pedestal, support. 2. base (mil.). *qaaϵida jawwiyya* air base. 3. precept, rule, principle. *qawaaϵid il-luġa* grammar. *ḥasb il-qaaϵida* as usual. *ḥasb il-qaaϵida, jaa mitˀaxxir.* As usual, he came late.
see also *g-ϵ-d*.

q-ϵ-r
qaϵar bottom. *qaϵr il-baḥar* bottom of the sea.
muqaϵϵar hollow, dished, concave. *ϵadasa muqaϵϵara* concave lens.

q-ϵ-s
tqaaϵas to be aloof, stand-offish. *saaϵid ˀaṣdiqaaˀak. la-titqaaϵas.* Help your friends. Don't be aloof.

q-f-z
qifaz (*u qafiz*) to jump. *ˀaxuuk yuqfuz ˀaϵla minni.* Your brother jumps higher than I do.
qafiz jumping. *qafz il-ϵaali* high jump. *qafz il-ϵariiḍ* broad jump.
qafza pl. *-aat* jump, leap, spring, bound.

q-f-ṣ
qufaṣ (*u qafaṣ*) to catch. *qufaṣit ṭeer b-iidi.* I caught a bird with my hands. *qufṣoo lil-mujrim ib-beeta.* They captured the criminal at home. *qufaṣta l-ϵali yilϵab ib-kutbak.* I caught Ali playing with your books.
qaffaṣ to fasten, secure. *ˀaani ˀarakkub il-buuriyaat ϵal-ḥaayiṭ w-inta qaffuṣha.* I'll lay the pipes against the wall and you fasten them in place.
nqufaṣ to be caught. *j-jreedi xašš bil-musyaada w-inqufaṣ.* The rat went into the trap and got caught. *ḍall ybuug ġaraaḍ ˀila ˀan nqufaṣ.* He kept on stealing things until he was caught.
qafaṣ, qufaṣ pl. *-aat, qfaaṣ* 1. cage. *l-qafaṣ iṣ-ṣadri* the rib cage, the thorax. *qafaṣ il-ittihaam* (prisoner's) dock. 2. basket, crate (of palm fronds).
qafiiṣ pl. *-aat* (metal) strap, band.

q-f-l
qufal (*u qaful*) to lock. *ˀuqful il-baab baϵad-ma tiṭlaϵ.* Lock the door after you go out.
qaffal to lock up. *qaffalna kull il-abwaab.* We locked up all the doors.
nqufal to be locked. *l-baab ma-da-yinqifil.* The door can't be locked.
quful pl. *qfaal, qfaala.* 1. lock. 2. safety (on a gun).
qaafila pl. *qawaafil* caravan, convoy.

q-f-y
qaffa to rhyme, put into rhyme. *ˀiqra čam beet w-aani ˀaqaffi.* Recite a few lines and I'll put rhymes to them. || *ˀinta muu kull-ma ˀaḥči tqaffii-li?* Every time I speak, why must you interrupt and finish what I'm trying to say?
qaafiya pl. *qawaafi* rhyme.

q-l-a-y
qaḷaay tin (used in tinning copper pots).

q-l-b
qilab (*i qalib*) 1. to change. *čaan loona ˀaḥmar ḥilu laakin qilab.* It used to be a nice red color, but it changed. 2. to go back on one's word, to change one's mind. *gal-li raḥ-ybiiϵ is-sayyaara w-qilab ϵalayya.* He told me he was going to sell the car and then changed his mind on me. *waafaq iybiiϵha b-diinaar w-baϵdeen qilab.* He agreed to sell it for a dinar and

afterwards he went back on his word.

tqallab 1. to fluctuate. *l-ʔasɛaar ma-θaabta. da-titqallab ɛala ṭuul.* Prices are not stable. They are fluctuating all the time. 2. to vary, change, swing. *yitqallab ḥasb iδ-δuruuf.* He changes according to circumstances. *yitqallab wiyya l-hawa.* He swings with the wind.

qlabb 1. to change color. *libast is-sitra čam marra, w-loona qlabb.* I wore the jacket a few times and its color changed. 2. to change. *min šaafni wičča qlabb.* When he saw me his face fell.

qalib, qalb (invar.) 1. bad, counterfeit. *fluus qalb* counterfeit money. 2. inconstant, fickle, variable, changeable. 3. fickle person. 4. insincere. *ḥačya qalb.* His talk is insincere. *ʔaɛmaala qalb.* His actions are insincere.

*qalbi** of the heart, heart. *il-ʔamraaḍ il-qalbiyya* heart diseases.

qalba pl. *-aat* a breach of promise.

qaalab pl. *qawaalib, qwaalib.* 1. form. 2. mold. 3. cake, block. *qaalab ṣaabuun* cake of soap, bar of soap. *qaalab θalij* block of ice. *qaalab tabaašiir* stick of chalk.

taqallub pl. *-aat* fluctuation, change.

nqilaab pl. *-aat* overthrow, coup d'etat.

see also *g-l-b.*

q-l-b-a-l-ġ

qalabaaliġ 1. crowd, throng. 2. commotion.

q-l-d

qallad 1. to copy, ape, imitate. *tigdar itqallid hal-mumaθθil?* Can you imitate this actor? *l-yaabaaniyyiin yuɛrufuun išloon iyqalliduun il-baḍaayiɛ il-ʔajnabiyya.* The Japanese know how to imitate foreign products. 2. /with *ɛala*/ to mock, make fun of. *la-tqallid ɛalee. yaɛni qaabil ʔinta ʔaḥsan?* Don't make fun of him. Do you think you're better? *gaam yqallid ɛalee w-xallaana niḍḥak.* He began to mock him and made us laugh.

tqallad to be imitated. *δiḥikta ma-titqallad.* His laugh can't be imitated.

taqliid pl. *taqaaliid* 1. imitation, copying. 2. convention, custom, usage.

*taqliidi** traditional, customary, usual. *ɛamal taqliidi* routine job.

q-l-ṣ

qallaṣ 1. to contract, draw together. *qallaṣ ɛaḍalaat ʔiida.* He flexed the muscles in his arm. 2. to decrease, cut down. *l-wizaara raḥ-itqalliṣ ɛadad muwaḍḍafiiha.* The ministry will decrease the number of its employees.

tqallaṣ to contract, shrink. *l-ḥadiid yitqallaṣ min tinxufaḍ darajt il-ḥaraara.* Metal contracts as the temperature decreases.

q-ḷ-ṭ-ġ

quḷṭuġ pl. *-aat, qaḷaaṭiġ* overstuffed chair, easy chair.

q-l-ɛ

qilaɛ (*a qaliɛ*) to pull out by the roots, uproot, tear out, extract. *ʔiqlaɛ šijrat il-mišmiš w-izraɛha bil-bistaan.* Pull up the apricot tree and plant it in the orchard. *ṭabiib il-ʔasnaan raḥ-yiqlaɛ sinna.* The dentist will pull his tooth. 2. to quarry. *da-yiqilɛuun ṣ-ṣaxar min hal-manṭiqa.* They're quarrying stone from this area. 3. to budge, move, dislodge. *haaδa min yzuur ʔaḥḥad ma-aku šii yiqlaɛa.* When he visits someone, there's nothing that'll dislodge him.

ngilaɛ to budge, move, be dislodged. *gaaɛid ib-ġurufti ma-da-yinqiliɛ.* He sits in my room and can't be budged. *ʔinqiliɛ min giddaami tara ʔamawwtak.* Get out of here or I'll kill you. || *nqiliɛ, min kull ɛaglak ybiiɛ-lak il-beet?* Come off it! Do you really think he'll sell you the house?

qalɛa pl. *qilaaɛ* 1. castle, fortress. 2. rook, castle (chess).

maqlaɛ pl. *maqaaliɛ* stone quarry.

q-l-f

qaḷaafa pl. *-aat* 1. build, physique. 2. appearance.

q-l-q

qilaq (*a qalaq*) 1. to be or become uneasy, disquieted, apprehensive, anxious, upset, troubled, disturbed. *qilaq ihwaaya ɛala ṣiḥḥat ʔibna.* He was very worried about his son's health. 2. to trouble, worry, alarm, disturb, upset. *hal-ʔaxbaar qilqatni.* This news disturbed me. *ḥamaati da-tiqliq raaḥti.* My mother-in-law is disturbing my rest.

ʔaqlaq = *xilaq* 2. *hal-xabar ʔaqlaqni hwaaya.* That news upset me a lot.

nqilaq = *qilaq* 1. *la-tinqiliq. ma-aku šii ɛal-walad.* Don't worry. There's nothing wrong with the boy.

qalaq anxiety, worry.

q-l-q-l

qalqal = *gaḷgaḷ* which see under *g-l-g-l.*

qalaaqiil (pl. only) 1. things, odds and ends, junk. 2. private parts, genitals. || *haaδa šaayib; qalaaqiila waagɛa.* He's old and falling apart.

q-l-l

qall (*i qall*) to decrease, diminish, to be or become less, littler, smaller, fewer. *fluusna qallat ihwaaya b-sabab is-safra.* Our money dwindled a lot as a result of the trip. *ᶜinda θarwa; ma-tqill ᶜan il-milyoon diinaar.* He has a fortune; not less than a million dinars. *qallat qiimta b-naḏ̣ari.* His worth decreased in my eyes. *qallat qiimta b-ᶜamala haaδa.* He lost some respect because of what he did.

qallal to diminish, lessen, decrease, reduce. *ʔiδa tqallil is-siᶜir itbiiᶜ ihwaaya.* If you'll reduce the price, you'll sell a lot more. *qallil ib-ʔaklak ḥatta yinzil waznak.* Cut down what you eat so your weight will go down. *ʔašu ʔaxuuk qallal min jayyaata leena.* It seems your brother has reduced the frequency of his visits to us.

tqallal to be diminished, lessened, decreased, reduced. *has-siᶜir ma-yitqallal baᶜad ʔakθar min haaδa.* The price can't be reduced any more than that. *ḏ̣-ḏ̣aġit ma-yitqallal baᶜad.* The pressure can't be lowered more.

staqall to be or become independent. *xamis buldaan istaqallat has-sana.* Five countries became independent this year. *baᶜad-ma zzawwaj istaqall ᶜan ʔahla.* After he married he lived independently from his family.

qilla shortage, scarcity, lack. *qillat ʔidraak* lack of understanding, lack of realization. *qillat ḥayaaʔ, qillat ʔadab.* shamelessness, impudence, insolence. *haay qillat ḥayaaʔ minnak. šloon itšattim ʔabuuk?* This is shameless of you. How could you insult your father? || *min qillat il-xeel šaddaw ᶜač-čilaab isruuj.* Any port in a storm (lit., due to the shortage of horses, they saddled the dogs).

qalla: qalla-ma seldom, rarely. *haaδa qalla-ma yinšaaf ib-hal-gahwa.* He is seldom seen in this coffee-shop.

qaliil 1. few. *l-kutub il-muhimma qaliila bil-maktaba.* The important books in the library are few. 2. small, scant, scanty, spare, sparse, meager, insufficient. *haaδa qaliil. ʔariid baᶜad.* This is insufficient. I want more. *fluus il-ᶜindi qaliila. ma-tkaffi.* My money is insufficient. It isn't enough. *yoomiiti qaliila. tigdar itzayyidha?* My daily wage is small. Can you raise it? *haaδa qaliil ib-ḥaqqa. yistaahil ʔazyad.* That's less than his share. He deserves more. || *bil-qaliil* at least. *čaan bil-qaliil git-la ʔaani garaaybak.* You could have at least told him that I'm your relative. *qaliil il-irtifaaᶜ* of low elevation, not very high. *haj-jibal qaliil il-irtifaaᶜ; tigdar tiṣᶜada.* This mountain is of low elevation; you can climb it. *qaliil il-ihtimaam* inattentive. *hal-muwaḏ̣ḏ̣af qaliil il-ihtimaam ib-waajibaata.* This employee is slack in his duties. 3. scarce, rare. *l-ʔaṣdiqaaʔ il-xullaṣ qaliiliin.* Good friends are rare. 4. seldom, rarely, very little. *qaliil yiji hnaa.* He rarely comes here. *qaliil il-ʔadab, qaliil il-ḥaya, qaliil il-ḥayaaʔ* lacking in manners, lacking modesty. *ʔibnak qaliil il-ʔadab.* Your son has no manners. *hiyya qaliilat il-ḥayaaʔ. tfaššir.* She is shameless. She talks dirty.

ʔaqall less, least. *yizᶜal ᶜala ʔaqall šii.* He gets angry at the least little thing. *ʔaqall šii yṣiir bil-walad, ʔinta masʔuul.* If anything happens to the boy, you're responsible. || *ᶜal-ʔaqall* at least. *ʔiδa ma-truuḥ wiyyaay, ᶜal-ʔaqall dalliini.* If you aren't going with me, at least show me how to get there. *ʔaqall-ma* the least that. *ʔaqall-ma ysawwi yiḥči ᶜaleek.* The least he'll do is talk against you. *ʔaqall-ma biihum yimluk ʔalif diinaar.* The least among them has a thousand dinars.

ʔaqallan at least. *ʔaqallan čaan jibit šii lij-jihaal.* At least you could've brought something for the children.

ʔaqallaha at least. *ʔaqallaha čaan štireet-li nafnuuf.* You could have at least bought me a dress.

ʔaqalliyya pl. *-aat* minority.

stiqlaal independence.

mustaqill 1. independent. 2. separate. *beet mustaqill* a separate house.

q-l-m

qallam 1. to trim, prune. *qallim hruuš il-warid.* Trim the rose bushes. 2. to stripe. *qallim wuṣlat il-uqmaaš ib-ʔaḥmar uw-ʔaxḏ̣ar.* Stripe the cloth with red and green.

tqallam 1. to be trimmed, pruned. *l-ihruuš laazim titqallam.* The bushes must be trimmed. 2. to be striped. *hal-iqmaaš, ʔiδa yitqallam, ma-yṣiir ḥilu.* If this cloth were striped, it wouldn't look right.

qalam pl. *qlaam* 1. pen. *qalam ḥibir, qalam paandaan* fountain pen. *qalam ḥibir jaaf* ballpoint pen. *qalam baṣma* pencil, lead pencil. || *ruʔuus ʔaqlaam* notes. 2. stripe, streak, line. 3. section, department. 4. slip, cutting (bot.).

mqallam striped, streaked. *dišdaaša mqallma b-ʔaḥmar* a red-striped robe.

q-m-b-r

qumbura, qambuur, qambuura see under *q-n-b-r*.

q-m-b-l

qumbula, see under *q-n-b-l*.

q-m-č-y

qamči pl. *qmaači* **1.** hose for a narghile. **2.** whip, lash, quirt. **3.** blow with a whip, lash.

q-m-r

qaamar to gamble. *ḥilaf baʕad ma-yqaamir.* He swore he wouldn't gamble any more.

qamar: qamr id-diin a hard, translucent confection made in thin sheets from finely ground apricots.

qamariyya pl. *-aat* arbor, trellis. *qamariyyat ʕinab* grape arbor.

qamarči, qumarči pl. *-iyya* gambler.

qamaara pl. *-aat* private compartment (in a public bathhouse). || *sayyaara qamaara* sedan.

qmaar gambling. *yilʕab uqmaar.* He gambles.

see also *g-m-r*.

q-m-š

qmaaš pl. *-aat, ʔaqmiša* cloth.

q-m-ṣ

qamiiṣ pl. *qumṣaan* **1.** shirt. **2.** white cotton cloth.

q-m-ṣ-l

qamṣala pl. *-aat* jacket, windbreaker.

q-m-m

qumma pl. *qumam* peak, summit, top.

q-n-a-t

qanaat pl. *qanawaat* canal.

q-n-a-ṭ-y

qinnaaṭi candy.

q-n-a-l

qanaal pl. *-aat* canal.

q-n-b-r

qumbura, qunbura pl. *qanaabir* lark (zool.).

qambuur, qanbuur pl. *-iin* hunchback.

qambuura, qanbuura pl. *-aat* hump, hunch. *ʔabu qambuura* hunchback.

q-n-b-l

qumbula, qunbula pl. *qanaabul* **1.** bomb. **2.** shell.

q-n-p

qanapa = *qanafa,* which see under *q-n-f*.

q-n-d

qand rock sugar.

q-n-d-a-ġ

qundaaġ, qindaaġ **1.** very weak tea. **2.** hot water and sugar.

q-n-d-l

qandal **1.** to glow. *haffi lil-faḥam ḥatta yqandil kulla.* Fan the coal until it all glows. **2.** to be or become tipsy, to get a glow on. *širab-la peek waaḥid w-qandal.* He had one drink and became tipsy.

qandiil pl. *qanaadiil* hanging lamp, or light fixture using candles or oil.

mqandil **1.** tipsy, warmed, flushed. *mqandil imniš-šurub* flushed with drink. **2.** short-tempered, hot under the collar. *la-tiḥči wyaa tara huwwa mqandil il-yoom.* Don't talk to him because he is short-tempered today.

q-n-z-a

qanza: qanza wanza (invar.) a trick, a fast one. *waafaq ybiiʕa bass baʕdeen ṭallaʕ-inna qanza wanza.* He agreed to sell it but later he pulled a fast one on us. *jaab-la xooš qanza wanza w-axað minna ðiʕf is-siʕir.* He pulled a real shady trick on him and got double the price from him. *min titʕaamal wiyyaa, yijiib-lak miit qanza wanza.* When you bargain with him, he comes up with a hundred unexpected tricks.

q-n-ṣ-l

qunṣul pl. *qanaaṣil* consul.

*qunṣuli** consular. *ṣulṭa qunṣuliyya* consular authority.

qunṣuliyya pl. *-aat* consulate.

¹*q-n-ṭ-r*

qanṭara pl. *qanaaṭir* **1.** arched bridge, stone bridge. **2.** arch, archway, span.

²*q-n-ṭ-r*

qanṭar to contract, bid. *b-eeš itqanṭir binaaʔ hal-beet?* How much would you contract to build this house for?

qunṭaraat pl. *-aat* contract.

qunṭarči pl. *-iyya* contractor.

q-n-ṭ-w-r

qanṭoor pl. *-aat* wardrobe, movable clothes closet.

q-n-ʕ

qinaʕ (*a qanaaʕa*) **1.** to be or become convinced, persuaded. *š-gadd iḥčeet wiyyaa w-ma-da-yiqnaʕ.* I talked with him so much and he won't become convinced. **2.** (*i ʔiqnaaʕ*) to convince, persuade. *ḥičaa-li l-qiṣṣa w-qinaʕni.* He told me the story and convinced me.

qannaʕ to persuade, convince. *qanniʕta yistuġul wiyyaaya.* I persuaded him to work with me. *gidar yqanniʕha b-ʕašr idnaaniir.* He was able to persuade her with ten dinars.

tqannaع to be persuaded, convinced. *haaδa šloon iعnaadi. ma-yitqannaع.* How stubborn he is. He can't be persuaded.

qtinaع 1. to be or become satisfied, content. *l-mudiir qtinaع bil-عuδur maali.* The principal was satisfied with my excuse. 2. to be or become convinced. *hassa qtinaعit ma-aku عalaaqa beenaathum.* Now I'm convinced there is no relationship between them.

qanaaعa 1. content, contentment. 2. conviction.

qinaaع pl. *ˀaqniعa* mask.

qanuuع frugal, modest, temperate. *ṣiir qanuuع. ˀiqbal ib-har-raatib w-iskut.* Be satisfied. Accept this salary and keep quiet.

q-n-ع-r

tqanعar to put on airs, give oneself airs. *δoola illi yitqanعaruun yguuluun, "banaat iflaan ˀadab-sizziyyaat."* The people who like to show off their erudition say "So and so's daughters are lacking in manners." *la-titqanعar ib-raasi. ˀiδa ma-yعijbak il-waḍiع wir-raatib, baṭṭil.* Don't complain to me. If you don't like the position and the salary, quit.

qanعara putting on airs, giving oneself airs.

q-n-q-y-n

qanaqiina 1. quinine. 2. (pl. *-aat*) unpleasant person, a pill.

q-n-f

qanafa pl. *-aat* couch.

q-n-n

qaanuun see *q-a-n-w-n.*

q-h-r

qihar (*a qahar*) 1. to annoy, irritate, anger, upset. *l-baarḥa ṣadiiqak qiharni hwaaya.* Yesterday your friend annoyed me a lot. *raḥ-araawi paaysikli l-عali w-aqihra.* I'm going to show my bicycle to Ali and make him jealous. 2. to sadden, to grieve. *manδar il-mariiḍ yiqhar.* The sick man is a saddening sight.

nqihar 1. to be or become annoyed, irritated, angry, upset. *la-dgul-la biiha tara yinqihir.* Don't tell him about it or he'll get upset. 2. to be or become saddened, grieved. *nqihar عala ˀibna l-maat bil-ḥariiq.* He became morose over his son who died in the fire.

qahra grief, sorrow.

l-qaahira Cairo.

q-h-q-r

tqahqar to retreat, withdraw. *tqahqaraw ˀamaam il-عadu.* They retreated in front of the enemy.

q-h-w

qahwaaˀi coffee-colored. *ribaaṭ qahwaaˀi* a coffee-colored tie.

maqha pl. *maqaahi* coffee house.

see also *g-h-w.*

q-w-a-n

qawaan (coll.) 1. record(s), phonograph record(s). 2. cartridge case(s), shell(s).

qawaana pl. *-aat* 1. un. n. of *qawaan.* 2. tale, story, strange tale. *haay ṣaarat qawaana. yعijbak tiji wiyyaana loo laa?* You're giving me the same old story. Do you want to go with us or not? 3. fuss, to do. *sawwaa-la qawaana l-baarḥa.* He made a big fuss yesterday. *sawweetha qawaana.* You made a big issue out of it.

q-w-č

qooč a children's game similar to jacks, played with pebbles.

q-w-d

qaad (*u qiyaada*) to lead, command. *ˀayy ḍaabuṭ qaadhum bil-maعraka?* Which officer led them in the battle?

qiyaada 1. leadership, command, control. 2. (pl. *-aat*) command.

qaaˀid pl. *quwwaad* commander, leader.

see also *g-w-d.*

q-w-r-y

quuri pl. *-iyyaat, qwaar* teapot.

q-w-z-ġ

qoozaġ to give someone the shaft, to shaft, to cheat. *baaع-la raadyo ma-yištuġuḷ; qoozaġa bii.* He sold him a radio that doesn't work; he put the shaft to him with it.

tqoozaġ to be given the shaft, be shafted, be cheated.

qaazuuġ pl. *qawaaziiġ* the shaft, the royal shaft, the dirty end of the stick. *ḍiraba qaazuuġ.* He gave him the shaft. *ḍirabni qaazuuġ ib-haš-šarwa.* He gave me the royal shaft on this purchase.

q-w-z-y

quuzi pl. *qwaazi* 1. baby lamb. 2. a dish consisting of rice with roasted mutton on top and sometimes raisins and almonds.

q-w-s

qoos, qaws pl. *ˀaqwaas* 1. bow, longbow. || *qoos qazaḥ* rainbow. 2. arc (geom.). 3. arch, vault (arch.; of a bridge). 4. (*qawseen*) parentheses. *been qawseen* in parentheses.

qawwaas pl. *-iin* 1. guard, doorman, watchman. 2. messenger, porter, handyman (in an office).

q-w-š

qaawuuš, see *q-a-w-w-š.*

q-w-ṭ

qaaṭ pl. *quuṭ* **1.** suit (of clothes). **2.** coat, layer (of paint, etc.). **3.** floor, story, level. *paaṣ ˀabu qaaṭeen* double-decker bus. **4.** time, instance, once. *qaaṭ laax* again, once more.

q-w-ṭ-y

quuṭiyya pl. *qwaaṭi* **1.** tin, tin box, rectangular tin can. **2.** small box.

q-w-ɛ

qaaɛ bottom (of the sea, river, etc.).

qaaɛa pl. *-aat* **1.** hall, large room. *qaaɛat iṭ-ṭaɛaam* dining hall. **2.** auditorium.

[1]*q-w-l*

qaawal to make a deal, strike a bargain with (someone). *qaawalta yjiib il-garaaḍ il-beeti.* I made a deal with him to bring the things to my house.

tqaawal to make a contract. *tqaawalna yjahhizna b-kull iṭ-ṭaabuug in-niḥtaaja.* We made a contract that he'd supply us with all the bricks we need.

qaal: qaal w-qiil gossip, rumors.

qawl pl. *ˀaqwaal* word, promise. *baɛdi ɛala qawli.* I'm still keeping my word.

maqaal, maqaala pl. *-aat* article. *maqaal iftitaaḥi* editorial, leading article.

muqaawala pl. *-aat* contract.

muqaawil pl. *-iin* contractor.

see also *g-w-l.*

[2]*q-w-l*

qoola (invar.) **1.** French cuffs. *θoob ˀabu l-qoola* shirt with French cuffs. **2.** collar.

q-w-m

qaam (*u qiyaam*) to perform, do, carry out, execute. *huwwa xooš ɛaamil; da-yquum ib-waajba.* He's a good worker; he carries out his duties. *yquum ib-ˀaɛmaal muxziya.* He does shameful things.

qaawam **1.** to resist, oppose. *maḥḥad yigdar yqaawma.* No one can stand up against him. **2.** to fight, combat. *l-malaarya ntišrat biṣ-ṣeef w-wazaart iṣ-ṣiḥḥa bidat itqaawumha.* Malaria spread during the summer and the Ministry of Health started to combat it. **3.** to hold up, hold out, last, stand up. *hal-qundara ma-qaawmat šahar.* These shoes didn't last a month. *šgadd-ma tṣiir ṣabuur, ma-tigdar itqaawum wiyya hal-mudiir.* No matter how patient you are, you won't be able to stomach this director. *jeešhum ma-gidar yqaawim ˀakθar min yoomeen.* Their army couldn't stand more than two days.

ˀaqaam **1.** to live, reside, dwell, remain, stay. *raḥ-yqiim b-bağdaad santeen.* He will reside in Baghdad for two years. **2.** to lodge, file (complaint, suit, legal proceedings). *ˀaqaam ɛalee daɛwa bil-maḥkama.* He filed a complaint against him in court.

staqaam **1.** to be or become right, correct, proper, to straighten out. *š-gadd-ma yiḥči ˀabuu wiyyaa, ma-yistiqiim.* No matter how much his father talks to him, he doesn't straighten out. **2.** to remain, endure, keep on. *ma-aɛtiqid hal-ḥaayiṭ raḥ-yistiqiim hwaaya.* I don't believe that this wall will last long. *d-dinya ma-tistiqiim l-aḥḥad.* The world won't stand still for anybody.

*qawmi** **1.** nationalist, nationalistic. **2.** a nationalist.

qawmiyya ethnic pride, ethnic nationalism.

qaama pl. *-aat* a short, broad, double-edged sword. || *ḍaarub qaama.* He's broke. *jeebi ḍaarub qaama.* I'm flat broke.

qawaam greasy. *marag qawaam* greasy stew.

qiyaama resurrection. *ɛiid il-qiyaama* Easter. *yoom il-qiyaama* Judgement Day.

maqaam pl. *-aat* **1.** standing, position, rank, dignity. *ṣaaḥib maqaam* dignitary, holder of a high position. *ṭabɛan ˀaḥtarma. haaḍa b-maqaam ˀabuuya.* Of course I respect him. He is to me like my father. *ˀiḍa ysaafir, minu raḥ-ykuun ib-maqaama?* If he goes away, who will take over his duties? **2.** shrine, sacred place, tomb of a saint. **3.** a style of music with several sub-categories, also a song in this style.

taqwiim pl. *taqaawiim* calendar.

muqaawama resistance. *muqaawama ḍidd il-ˀamraaḍ* resistance to disease. *muqaawama šaɛbiyya* popular resistance, i.e., national guard.

ˀiqaama stay, sojourn. *daaˀirt il-ˀiqaama* Alien Residents' Office. *daftar il-ˀiqaama* temporary residence permit.

stiqaama **1.** straightness. **2.** honesty, integrity, uprightness.

qaaˀim right, upright, erect. *zaawiya qaaˀima* right angle. *qaaˀim iz-zaawiya* right-angled. *muθallaθ qaaˀim iz-zaawiya* right triangle. || *qaaˀim bil-ˀaɛmaal* chargé d'affaires (dipl.).

qaaˀim-maqaam, qayyim-maqaam, qay-maqaam. governor of a sub-province, or *qaḍaaˀ.*

qaa⁹ima pl. *qawaa⁹im* **1.** list, roster, table, schedule. **2.** bill, invoice. **3.** menu, bill of fare.

mustaqiim straight. *xaṭṭ mustaqiim* a straight line.

see also *q-y-m* and *g-w-m*.

q-w-n

qawaan, etc., see under *q-w-a-n*.

q-w-y

quwa (*a quwwa*) **1.** to be or become strong. *kull sana š-šajara tiqwa.* The tree gets stronger every year. *dugg hal-xišibteen ʕaṣ-ṣanduug ʕatta yuqwa.* Nail these two boards onto the crate so it will be strong. **2.** to increase in power, gain ascendency. *hal-waziir bida yiqwa.* That minister has begun to gain power.

qawwa to make strong, strengthen. *l-ʕukuuma qawwat ij-jeeš ib-širaa⁹ iṭ-ṭiyyaaraat.* The government strengthened the army by buying the airplanes. *had-duwa yqawwi l-badan.* This medicine builds up the body.

tqawwa to be or become strong. *jeešna tqawwa hwaaya xilaal il-ʕašr isniin il-⁹axiira.* Our army became much stronger during the last ten years. *da-yitqawwa b-⁹aqaarba.* He derives strength from his relatives.

tqaawa to compete in strength. *la-titqaawa wiyyaaya tara ⁹a⁹aδδiik.* Don't match strength with me or I'll hurt you.

quwwa pl. *-aat* **1.** strength. **2.** power, force. **3.** armed force. *l-quwwa j-jawwiyya* air force. *quwwaat* armed forces, troops. **4.** squad (of police).

qawi pl. *qwaay, ⁹aqwiyaa⁹* **1.** strong, powerful. *rijjaal qawi* a strong man. **2.** firm, solid, hardy, sturdy. *saguf qawi* a sturdy ceiling. *jooza qawwiyya* a tough nut. **3.** intense, violent, vehement. *qaṣiida qawiyya* a strongly-worded poem.

⁹aqwa stronger, strongest.

muqawwi pl. *-iyyaat* tonic, restorative.

mqawwa (coll.) cardboard, corrugated cardboard.

mqawwaaya pl. *-aat* un. n. of *mqawwa*.

q-y-θ-a-r

qiiθaara pl. *-aat* **1.** harp. **2.** lyre. **3.** guitar.

q-y-ʕ

qayyaʕ to fester. *mukaan ij-jariʕ wuram w-itqayyaʕ.* The wound swelled up and festered.

qeeʕ pus.

q-y-d

qayyad **1.** to restrict, limit, confine. *la-tqayyidni. xalliini ⁹aruuʕ w-⁹aji b-keefi.* Don't restrict me. Let me go and come as I wish. **2.** to write, write down, record, list, enter. *qayyid ⁹isma hnaa.* List his name here. *qayyid kull šii lli tbiiʕa bid-daftar.* Enter everything that you sell in the notebook. **3.** to charge, debit. *ma-ʕindi fluus hassa. qayyidha ʕalayya.* I don't have money now. Charge it to me.

tqayyad **1.** to take care, look after, be careful. *tqayyad ʕal-kutub zeen.* Take good care of the book. **2.** to be careful, watch out. *tqayyad ʕali! j-jaahil raʕ-yoogaʕ.* Watch out Ali! The kid's going to fall. *⁹iδa ma-titqayyad ib-⁹aklak titmarraṣ̌.* If you don't watch what you eat, you'll get sick. *huwwa fadd waaʕid xabiiθ. tqayyad minna.* He's a mean one. Be careful of him.

qeed (coll.) **1.** cord(s), band(s), thong(s). **2.** (pl. *quyuud*) tally, count, list, record. **3.** restriction, limitation, reservation. *qibal yrajjiʕha bila qeed wala šarṭ.* He agreed to return it without any reservations. || *š-ma tsawwi b-keefha. ⁹ummha ma-ʕiddha qeed.* Whatever she does is up to her. Her mother has no concern. *beeta da-yiʕtirig wala ʕinda bil-qeed.* His house is burning down and he couldn't care less. *⁹abuu baʕda ʕala qeed il-ʕayaat.* His father is still living.

qeeda pl. *-aat* **1.** un. n. of *qeed* **1.** **2.** razor blade.

taqyiid registering, registration.

q-y-r

qiir = *giir*, which see under *g-y-r*. *yirṣ̌a ma-yirṣ̌a, bil-qiir!* Whether he's satisfied or not, to hell with him.

q-y-r-a-ṭ

qiiraaṭ pl. *-aat* a weight.

q-y-s

qaas (*i qiyaas*) **1.** to measure, take the measurements of. *qiis ṭuul w-ʕurṣ̌ il-ġurfa w-gul-li š-gadd.* Measure the length and width of the room and tell me how much it is. **2.** to weigh, judge, measure. *ma-tigdar itqiis nafsak ib-ġeerak.* You can't judge yourself by someone else. || *w-qiis ʕala δaalik . . .* and along with that . . . , similarly, analogously, along that line also.

nqaas **1.** to be measured. *hal-gaaʕ čibiira. ma-tinqaas bil-sintimitir.* This plot is large. It can't be measured by the centimeter. **2.** to be compared. *haaδa ma-yinqaas ib-haaδa.* This can't be compared with that.

qiyaas pl. *-aat* measure, measurement, dimension.

*qiyaasi**: *raqam qiyaasi* a record (in swimming, racing, etc.).

miqyaas pl. *maqaayiis* **1.** measure, tape measure. **2.** gauge, measuring instrument. *miqyaas in-nahar* stream gauge. *miqyaas il-kahrabaaʔ* electric meter. *miqyaas il-mayy* water meter. **3.** scale (on a map). **4.** standard, criterion.

q-y-ṭ-a-n

qiiṭaan pl. *qyaaṭiin* shoe lace, lacing string.

q-y-l

qaal (*i ʔiqaala*) to dismiss, discharge. *raʔiis ij-jumhuriyya qaal θlaaθ wuzaraaʔ.* The president of the republic dismissed three ministers.

staqaal to resign. *niqam ʕal-waðiʕ w-istaqaal.* He got disgusted at the situation and resigned.

stiqaala pl. *-aat* resignation.

q-y-m

qayyam **1.** to estimate, assess, appraise, value, rate. *beeš itqayyim haz-zuuliyya?* What price would you put on this carpet?

ʔaqaam to attach, assign. *da-tqiim-la wazin ihwaaya.* You attach a heavy value to him.

qiima pl. *qiyam* **1.** price. **2.** value, worth. *ḥačya ma-ʔila kull qiima.* His talk doesn't amount to anything. *xalli yintiqid. šinu qiimta?* Let him criticize. What does he matter? *han-naaʔib ʔila qiimta bil-majlis.* This representative is respected in the senate. **3.** finely ground or chopped meat. **4.** a stew made from chopped meat and peas.

qiyaam, qiyaama see *q-w-m.*

q-y-m-q-a-m

qaymaqaam pl. *-iyya* or *-iin.* governor of a *qaðaaʔ* or sub-province.

qaymaqaamiyya governorship of a *qaðaaʔ.*

q-y-y

tqayya to vomit. *daax w-itqayya.* He got dizzy and vomited.

G

g-a-z

gaaz on edge, edgewise. *waggif ij-jaama gaaz ʕal-meez.* Set the pane of glass on its edge on the table. *nizlat iṭ-ṭayyaara gaaz ʕaṣ-ṣaṭiḥ.* The kite crashed nose-down onto the roof.

g-a-z-g-y-t

gaazgeeta pl. *-aat* gasket.

g-a-z-y-n-w

gaaziino pl. *-owaat, gaaziinaat* night club, casino.

g-b-b

gabb (*u gabb*) **1.** to spring, jump, leap. *bass ntiqad waaḥid minhum, kullhum gaḅḅaw ʕalee.* As soon as he criticized one of them they all jumped on him. || *nṭiini ʔaspiriin. gaḅḅ ʕalayya raasi.* Give me an aspirin. I've got an overwhelming headache. **2.** to come up, spring up. *gaḅḅat hawya w-ṭayyirat il-ʔawraaq.* A breeze came up suddenly and sent the papers flying.

gabbab to raise, stir up. *sidd iš-šibbaak. raḥ-itfuut il-xeel w-itgabbub ʕajaaj.* Close the window. The horses are going to go by and stir up the dust.

gubba pl. *gubab* **1.** room. *štireet beet bii ʔarbaʕ gubab.* I bought a four-room house. **2.** (pl. *gbaab*) dome (of a building), cupola.

g-b-ḥ

gabbaḥ to be unpleasant. *gabbaḥ wiyya kull in-naas. ma-biqa ʕinda ṣadiiq.* He was nasty with everybody. He hasn't a friend left.

tgaabaḥ to be insulting. *ma-ʕindi maaniʕ ʔadgaabaḥ wiyyaa w-asibba.* I don't mind being insulting with him and cursing him.

see also *q-b-ḥ.*

g-b-r

gabur pl. *gbuur* grave, tomb.

magbara pl. *magaabir* cemetery, graveyard.

g-b-g-b

gabgab **1.** to swell. *l-ḥabbaaya gabgubat ihwaaya.* The sore swelled up very much. **2.** to bulge. *sitirtak mgabguba. šaayil šii jawwaaha?* Your jacket is bulging. Are you carrying something under it?

mgabgub **1.** swollen. *ʔiid imgabgub* a swollen hand. **2.** bulging. *ʕilba mgabguba* a bulging can.

g-b-ḷ

gaabaḷ to be or stand opposite. *n-nahaar kulla mgaabuḷ iš-šibbaak w-yitfarraj ʕaš-*

*šaari*c̣. All day he sits facing the window and looking at the street.

tgaabal̟ **1.** to face each other. *la-tdiir* *ðahrak* *ʕalee. dgaabl̟u.* Don't turn your back on him. Face each other. **2.** to get together, team up. *dgaabal̟na* *ʕaleeha* *θneenna w-xallaṣnaaha b-nuṣṣ saaʕa.* Two of us teamed up on it and finished it in a half hour.

gabul̟ **1.** (adv.) previously, formerly, earlier, before. *ma-šaayfa gabul̟.* I haven't seen him before. *ʔaani jeet gabul̟.* I came first. *b-zaman gabul̟, ma-čaan ʔaku sayyaaraat.* In past times, there were no cars. *haaða min ʔahal gabul̟.* He's old-fashioned. He's from a past generation. **2.** (prep.) before. *š-raḥ-insawwi gabl̟ il-ʕaša?* What are we going to do before dinner? *gabul̟-ma* (conj.) before. *gabul̟-ma tguul ʔay šii, xalli ʔaqraa-lak il-maktuub.* Before you say anything, let me read you the letter.

gubal̟ forward, straight ahead. *ʔimši gubal̟ xamis daqaayiq w-tilgi j-jaamiʕ ʕala yamiinak.* Go straight for five minutes and you'll find the mosque on your right.

gbaal̟ in front of, opposite, across from. *gbaal̟ il-beet* in front of the house. *ḥaaṭ rasim marta gbaala w-ybaawiʕ ʕaleeha ṭuul in-nahaar.* He put his wife's picture in front of him and looks at it all day. *ṣaar-lak saaʕa gaaʕid igbaal̟i. šitriid?* You've been sitting opposite me an hour. What do you want? *beet ʕammi ysiknuun igbaal̟na.* My uncle's family lives across the way from us.

gbaal̟a by the job, on a job-rate. *ʔaxaðit haš-šaġl̟a gbaal̟a.* I took this work on a job-rate basis. *ʔiða yaaxðuun iš-šuġul igbaal̟a yḥaṣṣluun ʔakθar.* If they take the work by the job they'll make more.

see also *q-b-l.*

g-b-n

gabban to weigh (with a steelyard). *gabbun ikyaas it-timman w-gul-li šgadd wazinha.* Weigh the sacks of rice and tell me their weight

gubbaan pl. *gubaabiin* **1.** steelyard, large balance scale. **2.** carpenter's level.

g-ḥ-b

tgaḥḥab to sleep around, whore around. *da-dgaḥḥub w-maḥḥad yidri biiha.* She's whoring around and nobody knows about it.

gaḥba pl. *gḥaab* prostitute, whore.

gaḥabči pl. *-iyya* man who frequently patronizes prostitutes.

*gaḥbaawi** **1.** flashy, ostentatious, loud, colorful. *libis gaḥbaawi* flashy clothes. *sayyaara gaḥbaawiyya* a fancy car. **2.** effeminate, sissified, queer. *mašiita gaḥbaawiyya.* His walk is effeminate.

g-ḥ-ḥ

gaḥḥ (*u gaḥḥa*) to cough. *waddii lit-ṭabiib. ʔašu da-yguḥḥ ihwaaya.* Take him to the doctor. He seems to be coughing a lot.

gaḥḥa **1.** coughing, cough. **2.** (pl. *-aat*) a cough.

g-ḥ-f

giḥaf (*a gaḥif*) to walk, trudge, slog (expresses a distaste for walking). *ma-laḥḥagit bil-paaṣ. riḥit agḥaf lil-beet.* I didn't catch the bus. I had to go walking home. *ma-tḥibb tirkab wiyyaana? laʕad ruuḥ igḥaf.* You wouldn't like to ride with us? Then go walk.

gaḥḥaf to dry out, get stale. *liff il-xubuz la-ygaḥḥif.* Wrap up the bread so it won't dry out.

gaḥuf, gaḥif walking, on foot. *ʔijeena lil-madrasa gaḥuf.* We came to school on foot.

giḥif pl. *gḥuuf* **1.** piece of broken pottery, potsherd. **2.** worthless person.

g-ḥ-g-ḥ

gaḥgaḥ to cough. *š-bii ṣadrak? ṣaar-lak saaʕa dgaḥgiḥ.* What's the matter with your chest? You've been coughing for an hour.

g-ʕ-m

giḥam (*a gaḥum*) to overcome, best, beat. *maḥḥad yigḥama biš-šiṭranj.* No one can beat him at chess. *hal-imtiḥaan ṣaʕub. š-yigḥama?* This exam is hard. How can one get through it?

nqiḥam to be overcome, beaten. *l-ʔitfaaʔi ðṭarr yiṭlaʕ imnil-gubba liʔan in-naar ma-tinguḥum.* The fireman had to leave the room because the fire couldn't be brought under control. *haaða fadd waaḥid balaaʔ. ma-yinguḥum.* He's an extraordinary fellow. He can't be beaten.

g-d-ḥ

gidaḥ (*a gadiḥ*) to spark, make sparks. *han-nooʕ imnil-ḥajar ma-yigdaḥ zeen.* This kind of flint doesn't make sparks well.

giddaaḥa pl. *-aat* cigarette lighter.

g-d-d

gadd capable of, equal to. *haaða gadd il-waðiifa.* He's equal to the job. *b-gadd* equal in size, commensurate with, in proportion to. *ʔiδa biik xeer itṣaaraƐ wiyya waaƐid ib-gaddak.* If you're the man you think you are, fight with someone your own size. || *Ɛala gadd* commensurate with, according to, in proportion to. *Ɛidna ʔakil Ɛala gadd il-maƐzuumiin bass.* We've enough food for only those invited. *ʔaƐsan šii w-ʔastar šii waaƐid yuṣruf Ɛala gadd ifluusa.* The best and most proper thing is for one to spend according to the amount of money he has. *haθ-θoob muu Ɛala gaddak.* This shirt isn't your size. *gadd-ma* to the extent that. *min gadd-ma yilgi, ma-xallaana niftihim.* He talked nonsense so much, we couldn't understand him.

šgadd **1.** how much, how many. *šgadd Ɛadadkum biṣ-ṣaff?* How many of you are there in the class? *šgadd itriid Ɛala has-saaƐa?* How much do wou want for this watch? *šgadd ṣaar-lak ib-baġdaad?* How long have you been in Baghdad? **2.** how much, so much, so many. *šgadd gut-la "la-truuƐ," laakin raaƐ.* So many times I told him "Don't go," but he went. *šgadd waṣṣeeta yištiri beeδ̣ w-nisa!* As many times as I told him to buy eggs and he forgot! *šuufa šgadda w-yiƐči kbaar!* Look at his size and he still talks big! *šgadd-ma aƐči wyaa ma-yfiid.* No matter how much I talk to him, it does no good.

šgadduuta how small, how tiny. *šgadduuta w-yiƐči kbaar!* Look how tiny he is and he talks so big! *šuuf has-sayyaara l-ʔajnabiyya šgadduutha!* Look at how tiny this foreign car is!

halgadd so much. *la-tiƐči halgadd.* Don't talk so much. *taqdiirhum ma-čaan halgadd maδ̣buuṭ.* Their estimate wasn't so very correct. *halgadd-ma siman, hduuma ma-gaamat tirham Ɛalee.* He got so fat, his clothes wouldn't fit him.

g-d-r

gidar (*a gadir*) **1.** to be able, to be capable of. *ma-gidar ysaafir il-baarƐa.* He couldn't leave yesterday. *ma-agdar aṣbur.* I can't wait. **2.** to have power, be master. *la ʔabuu wala ʔumma ygidruum Ɛalee.* Neither his father nor his mother can control him. *maƐƐad yigdar-la l-haaδa ġeeri.* No one can handle him but me.

gaddar **1.** to try, measure, fit. *gaddir il-parda Ɛaš-šibbaak.* Measure the curtains to the window. *gaddir hal-qundara, šuufha ʔiδa Ɛala gaddak.* Try on these shoes and see if they're your size. *gaddir il-uqmaaš Ɛalayya.* Fit the cloth to me. *haaδa š-imgaddra yitṣaaraƐ wiyya Ɛali? Ɛali ʔaqwa hwaaya.* How could he possibly wrestle with Ali? Ali is much stronger.

ngidar **1.** /with *Ɛala*/ to be beaten, bested, overcome. *haaδa Ɛifriit. ma-yingidir Ɛalee.* He is very strong. He can't be beaten. **2.** /with *l*/ to be managed. *ʔibnak wakiiƐ. ma-yingidir-la.* Your son is a bad boy. He can't be controlled.

gadar measure, measurement.

gidar pl. *-aat* measure, measuring stick.

gidir pl. *gduur, gduura* small cooking pot.

mugdaar, migdaar pl. *-aat* amount.

see also *q-d-r*.

g-d-m

gaddam **1.** to make or let precede. *ʔuxuδhum bis-sira. la-tgaddim waaƐid Ɛal-laax.* Take them in order. Don't put one ahead of the other. **2.** to move up, move forward, advance. *gaddim il-maaƐuun yammak Ɛatta ma-yoogaƐ il-ʔakil Ɛal-gaaƐ.* Move the dish close to you so that the food won't fall on the floor.

tgaddam to move forward, advance. *la-tidgaddam yamm ič-čalib tara yƐaδ̣δ̣ak.* Don't go near the dog or he'll bite you. *bass tidgaddam! ʔabuṣṭak.* Just take one more step! I'll clobber you.

giddaam in front of. *la-dδibb iz-zibil giddaam il-beet.* Don't throw the trash in front of the house. *nṭaa l-ifluus giddaami.* He gave him the money in my presence.

li-giddaam **1.** to the front, forward. *min itsuuq, baawiƐ li-qiddaam.* When you drive, look to the front. *xall nigƐud li-giddaam.* Let's sit down front. **2.** in advance, beforehand, ahead of time.- *ʔaxaδ Ɛišriin diinaar li-giddaam.* He took twenty dinars in advance. *ʔagul-lak li-giddaam laazim tištiri biṭaaqa.* I'll tell you ahead of time, you have to buy a ticket.

g-d-y

gadda to beg. *kull yoom yugƐud ihnaa w-ygaddi.* He sits here every day and begs. *la-yiġniik wala yxalliik idgaddi.* He won't let you do anything (lit., he won't make you rich and he won't let you beg).

gdaaya begging.

dgiddi = *gdaaya.*

mgaddi pl. *mgaadya* **1.** beggar. **2.** miser, skinflint, tightwad.

g-δ-l

guδla pl. *guδal* forelock.

g-r-a-j

garaaj pl. *-aat* garage.

g-r-b

girab (*a gurub*) **1.** to draw near, approach. *l-ˀimtiḥaan girab. laazim nitḥaððar-la.* The examination is near. We must get ready for it. **2.** (*garaaba*) to be related. *haaða ma-yigrab-li.* He isn't related to me.

garrab **1.** to bring close, to cause or allow to come near or get close. *garrub l-iskamli maalak minni.* Move your chair closer to me. **2.** to approach, get close. *garrab il-ʕiid w-baʕadna ma-mištiriin hduum lij-jihaal.* The holiday is getting close and we still haven't bought clothes for the children.

tgarrab to get close, approach. *la-tidgarrab tara č-čalib yʕaððak.* Don't get too close or the dog will bite you.

tgaarab to approach each other, to get close to each other. *dgaarbaw išwayya šwayya w-baʕdeen itbaaṣṭaw.* They edged closer to each other and then exchanged blows. *ˀaani w-inta raḥ-nitgaarab bir-raatib.* You and I will be close to equal in salary.

stagrab **1.** to find near, regard as near. *ˀadri hal-maḥall ġaali bass istagrabta.* I realize this place is expensive but I figured it was nearer. **2.** to drop in, come by (someone's house). *leeš da-truuḥ lil-beet? stagrub il-yoom w-itġadda wyaana, ma-daam ṣaar wakt il-ˀakil.* Why are you going home? Come on and have dinner with us today, since it's time to eat. *stagrub. l-yoom ʕiddna simač.* Drop by on your way and eat with us. We're having fish today.

gurub **1.** nearness, closeness, proximity. *l-maḥalleen ib-nafs il-gurub minnaa.* Both places are the same distance from here. *ma-ʕabaali beetkum hal-gurub.* I didn't realize your house was so near. || *b-hal-gurub* in the near future. *ˀaʕtiqid raḥ-yiji b-hal-gurub.* I think he is coming soon. **2.** in the vicinity of, near, toward. *ma-jaa ˀilla gurb ið-ðuhur.* He didn't come until almost noon.

girba pl. *girab* **1.** water skin. **2.** water bag made of canvas, desert cooler. **3.** clay water jug.

giriib near, nearby, close. *l-beet giriib.* The house is nearby. *min giriib* up close, from close up. *min giriib loonha ybayyin ˀaḥmar.* Up close its color appears to be red.

graab pl. *-aat* sheath or scabbard (for a knife or sword). *graab musaddis* holster.

garaaba pl. *-aat* **1.** kinship, relationship, relation. **2.** (invar.) related, relatives. *humma garaaba wiyyaana.* They're related to us. *humma garaabatna.* They're our relatives.

garaayib (invar.) relative. *ʕali garaaybi.* Ali is my relative.

grayyib = *giriib. hal garaaj igrayyib. xan-nwaddi s-sayyaara lee.* That garage is near by. Let's take the car to it.

ˀagrab closer, closest.

see also *q-r-b.*

g-r-d

garrad **1.** to hang on, to hold back. *garrad ʕalayya w-ma-xallaani aruuḥ.* He hung on and didn't let me go. **2.** to get in the way, to interfere. *garrad ʕalayya w-ḥiramni mnit-tarfiiʕ.* He got in my way and kept me from being promoted. *b-muxaalaftak lit-taʕliimaat garradit ʕaleena w-ma-nigdar inwagguf is-say-yaara hnaa baʕad.* By your violation of the rules, you loused things up for us and we can't park here anymore.

girid hard luck. *min girda, xaṭiyya, yinfuṣil.* It's his hard luck, poor fellow, to get fired.

garaad (coll.) tick, ticks (zool.).

garaada pl. *-aat* tick (zool.).

magruud pl. *mgaariid* **1.** pitiful, harmless, insignificant. **2.** a pitiful person.

g-r-r

garr (*u garr*) /with *ʕeen*/ to congratulate. *xall inruuḥ ngurr ʕeenha l-ˀumm ʕali. ˀibinha nijaḥ bil-imtiḥaan.* Let's go congratulate Ali's mother. Her son passed the exam.

gurra: gurrat ʕeenak! congratulations! *gurrat ʕeenak! simaʕit ˀibnak ṣaar ṭabiib.* Congratulations! I heard your son became a doctor.

g-r-ṣ

giraṣ (*u gariṣ*) **1.** to pinch. *j-jaahil giraṣ ˀuxta w-xallaaha tibči.* The child pinched his sister and made her cry. **2.** to bite, sting. *girṣata ḥagga.* A bug bit him.

garraṣ intens. of *giraṣ* **1.** *da-ygarriṣ b-ixduudha.* He's pinching her cheeks.

ngiraṣ to be pinched. *ngirṣat ib-rijilha bil-izdiḥaam.* She was pinched on her leg in the crowd.

gurṣa pl. *guraṣ* flat round loaf (of bread).

garṣa pl. *-aat* **1.** pinch. *garṣat barid* a bit of cold, a nip in the air. **2.** bite, sting (of an insect).

gaariṣ pl. *-aat* bedbug(?).

garraaṣa pl. *-aat* clothes pin.
see also *q-r-ṣ*.

g-r-ḏ

giraḏ (*u gariḏ*) **1.** to gnaw, nibble, bite. *l-faara da-tugruḏ sitirtak.* The mouse is gnawing on your jacket. **2.** to smash, mangle. *l-ḥadiida wugʕat ʕala ʔiidi w-girḏat ʔiṣibʕi.* The piece of iron fell on my hand and mashed my finger. **3.** to punch, perforate. *t-tiiti nisa yigruḏ it-tikit maali.* The conductor forgot to punch my ticket. **4.** to gossip, talk behind one's back. *gurḏook il-baarḥa bil-gahwa.* They cut you down behind your back yesterday in the coffee-shop. **5.** to get thick, thicken. *niseet il-murga ʕan-naar w-girḏat.* I left the gravy on the fire and it got thick. *xalli l-gahwa tugruḏ.* Let the coffee get stronger.

garraḏ **1.** to gnaw, nibble. *da-asmaʕ ḥiss il-faar ygarruḏ bil-ihduum.* I hear the mice gnawing on the clothes. **2.** to smash, mangle. *garraḏ ʔasaabʕa kullha bič-čaakuuč.* He smashed all his fingers with the hammer. **3.** to loan, lend, advance (money). *gut-la ygarriḏni fadd diinaar.* I asked him to lend me a dinar.

tgarraḏ **1.** to be gnawed, chewed. *ma-git-lak ʔaku jreediyya hnaa. šuuf sitirti šloon idgarriḏat.* I told you there were mice here. Look how my jacket got gnawed up. **2.** to borrow (money). *raḥ-adgarraḏ-li čam filis minna.* I'm going to borrow some money from him.

ngiraḏ **1.** to be smashed, mangled. *č-čaakuuč wugaʕ ʕala ʔiidi w-isibʕi ingiraḏ.* The hammer fell on my hand and my finger got mashed. **2.** to be or become frayed. *l-ḥabil ʔingiraḏ.* The rope was frayed.

gariḏ pl. *gruuḏ* hole, gnawed place.

mugraaḏa pl. *-aat* nail clipper.
see also *q-r-ḏ*.

g-r-ṭ

giraṭ (*u gariṭ*) **1.** to chew, chew up, to munch, nibble. *z-zumaal giraṭ gišr ir-raggiyya.* The donkey chewed up the watermelon rind. *la-tugruṭ ḥabb iš-šijar, karriza.* Don't chew up the pumpkin seeds, open them up and take the hearts out. *yigruṭ b-isnuuna min ynaam.* He gnashes his teeth in his sleep. || *ṣiḥḥta muu zeena. ybayyin raḥ-yigruṭ il-ḥabil.* His health is bad. It seems he's going to die. **2.** to waste, squander, lose. *wugʕat-la xooš ifluus laakin giratha kullha.* He came into a good sum of money but he went through it all. || *giraṭ raasha l-bitt in-naas.* He was responsible for the girl's death. *giraṭ ifluusi kullha.* He took me for all my money.

garraṭ to munch away, chew away, nibble away. *j-jaahil da-ygarruṭ bil-ixyaar.* The child is munching on the cucumbers.

ngiraṭ to be nibbled, munched. *l-xubuz ngiraṭ.* The bread's been nibbled. *hal-ibnayya šgadd ḥilwa! tingiriṭ.* How pretty this girl is! She looks good enough to eat.

garuṭ **1.** chewing, munching, nibbling. **2.** the sound of munching. **3.** a sort of wild clover.

griiṭ chewing, munching, nibbling.

g-r-ṭ-f

garṭaf to trim, clip. *garṭifaw jnaaḥ iṭ-teer ḥatta ma-yṭiir.* They trimmed the bird's wings so he won't fly away. *l-ḥallaaq garṭaf šaʕri zaayid.* The barber clipped too much off my hair. *ḏallaw ygarṭifuun bil-miizaaniyya ʔila ʔan ma-biqa biiha šii.* They kept trimming the budget till there's no more left of it.

tgarṭaf to be trimmed, clipped. *la-dguṣṣ baʕad. muu šaʕri dgarṭaf!* Don't cut more. My hair has been clipped too much!

mgarṭaf **1.** stingy, tight-fisted, scrimy. **2.** miser, skinflint, tightwad.

g-r-ʕ

garraʕ to scalp, make bald. *la-dguṣṣ šaʕri baʕad. garraʕta r-raasi.* Don't cut any more of my hair. You've made me bald-headed. || *raḥ-ʔanṭii fluusa w-axlaṣ minna. garraʕa r-raasi.* I'm going to give him his money and get rid of him. He pestered me a lot. *š-asawwi? garraʕni ʕaleeha.* What could I do? He kept insisting on it.

graʕʕ to get ringworm. *raasa graʕʕ. laazim nwaddii liṭ-ṭabiib.* He's gotten ringworm. We've got to take him to the doctor.

garaʕ **1.** ringworm. **2.** baldness.

garʕa pl. *-aat* **1.** a bald spot (on the head). **2.** a head infected by ringworm. **3.** mangy head, noggin.

ʔagraʕ fem. *garʕa* pl. *garʕiin* **1.** infected with ringworm, person with ringworm. **2.** bald, bald person. || *l-garʕa tbaahi b-šaʕar ʔuxutha.* The man who lacks something boasts of someone else's (lit., the bald girl brags about her sister's hair).

g-r-f

girif pl. *gruuf* hoof of a butchered animal.

girfa (invar.) **1.** ilk, type (always derogatory). *min nafis il-girfa* of the same type. *ƹala hal-girfa* of that ilk. || *ˀuxuð girfa.* Let's face it, face the facts. **2.** stingy, tight, miserly. *la-tiddaayan minna. haaða fadd waaƹid girfa.* Don't borrow from him. He's a stingy guy.

g-r-g-r

gargari a type of candy, similar to taffy.

g-r-g-š

gargaš to chew, gnaw, munch. *da-ygargiš igšuur raggi.* He's gnawing on watermelon rinds.

g-r-g-ƹ

gargaƹ **1.** to thunder. *da-dgargiƹ w-yimkin raƹ-tumtur.* It's thundering and it might rain. **2.** to shake, rock (fig.). *gargaƹ il-majlis ib-xiṭaaba.* He rocked the parliament with his speech. *huwwa ygargiƹ bil-majlis.* He's a powerful man in the parliament. **3.** to frighten, scare, terrify. *gargaƹa b-hat-tahdiid.* He terrified him with that threat.

tgargaƹ to be scared. *dguul ˀinta sabiƹ? ˀašu dgargaƹit bass ṣaaƹ biik fadd ṣeeƹa.* You claim you're brave? I see that you were scared when he shouted at you only once.

gargaƹa **1.** thundering. **2.** (pl. *garaagiiƹ*) clap of thunder.

garguuƹa pl. *garaagiiƹ* clap of thunder.

g-r-g-f

gargaf to become encrusted. *čaƹab ij-jidir gargaf. ƹukka bij-jallaafa.* The bottom of the pot has a crust formed on it. Scour it with the steel wool. *wičč ij-jaahil imgargif.* The kid's face is crusted with dirt.

g-r-m

giram (*u garum*) to blunt, dull, break. *giram raas is-siččiina.* He blunted the point of the knife.

garram to cripple. *sayyaara ðurbata w-garrmata.* A car hit him and crippled him.

tgarram to be or become crippled. *wugaƹ imniṣ-ṣaṭiƹ w-idgarram.* He fell off the roof and became crippled.

ngiram to be dulled, blunted, broken. *raas is-siččiina ngiram.* The point of the knife was broken off.

girraama (exclamation of surprise or astonishment, approx.:) My God! *girraama šgadd ƹilwa!* My God, how beautiful she is! *girraama ƹala hal-iƹyuun!* My God, those eyes! *gaamat tiƹči. girraama!* She's started to cry. Good God!

mgarram **1.** crippled, lame. *mgarram min ṣuġra.* He's been crippled from childhood. **2.** (pl. *-iin*) cripple. *l-imgarram ma-yigdar yimši.* The cripple can't walk.

g-r-m-ṭ

garmaṭ **1.** =*qarmaṭ* which see under *q-r-m-ṭ*. **2.** to nibble, munch, chew. *ṣ-ṣaxla da dgarmuṭ ib-gišr irraggi.* The goat is munching on the watermelon rinds. || *zawijta garmuṭat ifluusa.* His wife got all his money bit by bit. *garmaṭ kull il-ifluus ˀilli ƹaṣṣalha bil-uqmaar.* He frittered away all the money he won at gambling.

g-r-n

girin pl. *gruun* horn (of an animal). || *ˀabu gruun* 1. cuckold. 2. pimp.

g-r-n-t-y

garanti pl. *-iyyaat* guarantee.

g-r-n-f-l

grunful **1.** clove. **2.** carnation.

g-r-w

garwa, greewa pl. *-aat* hydrocele.

g-z-z

gazz raw silk.

gizza pl. *-aat* nip, playful bite.

giziiz, gizaaz glass.

gazzaaz **1.** tetanus. **2.** (pl. *-a*) silk merchant.

g-z-g-z

gazgaz to gnash one's teeth, grit one's teeth. *min yuƹmaq ƹala ˀibna ygazgiz.* When he gets mad at his son, he gnashes his teeth.

gazguuza pl. *-aat, gazaagiiz.* well proportioned girl with a good figure.

g-z-l

gizal (*i gazil*) to limp, have a stiff leg. *yigzil min yimši.* He limps when he walks.

gazla pl. *-aat* limp, stiff leg.

g-z-w

gazwa pl. *-aat* slingshot.

g-s-b

gassab **1.** to make crisp. *ˀinṭiini-yyaaha w-agassib-ilk-iyyaaha bil-firin.* Give it to me and I'll make it crisp for you in the oven. **2.** to be or become crisp. *xalli l-xubuz ygassib zeen gabuḷ-ma tṭallƹa.* Let the bread get good and crisp before you take it out.

gasib dried dates.

g-s-m

gisam = *qisam* which see under *q-s-m*.

g-s-w

gisa = *qisa* which see under *q-s-w*.

g-š-r

gišar (*u gašir*) to scrape, scratch, pick, chip. *xalli l-ɛabbaaya tṭiib. la-tugšurha.* Let the sore heal. Don't scratch at it. *ʔugšur ij-juṣṣ imniṭ-ṭaabuuga.* Chip the mortar off the brick.

gaššar to peel, pare, shell, skin, scale. *gaššir il-ixyaara gabuḷ-ma tiθrumha.* Peel the cucumber before you chop it up. *gaššir is-simča gabuḷ-ma tšuggha.* Scrape the scales off the fish before you gut it.

tgaššar pass. of *gaššar. l-ixyaara laazim tidgaššar gabul-ma tinθurum.* The cucumber must be peeled before it's cut up.

gišir pl. *gšuur* **1.** peel, rind, skin. **2.** shell. **3.** bark.

gišra dandruff.

gašraat (pl. only) scraps, meat scraps.

ʔagšar fem. *gašra* pl. *-iin* quite a, a real, some. *laaɛuub šiṭranj ʔagšar* quite a chess player. *čaδδaab ʔagšar* a real liar. || *saaɛa gašra* an evil hour. *čaanat saaɛa gašra tɛarrafit ɛalee biiha.* I wish I'd never met him (lit., it was an ill-fated moment in which I met him).

g-š-š

gašš (*u gašš*) **1.** to collect, gather up, pick up. *gušš igṣaagiiṣ il-waraq il-ɛal-gaaɛ.* Sweep up the shreds of paper on the floor. **2.** to skim, take off the top. *gušš il-gišwa gabuḷ-ma tišrab il-ɛaliib.* Skim off the top before you drink the milk. *ʔoozin-li kiilu tamur bass gušš-li min raas iṭ-ṭubag.* Weigh me a kilo of dates but take them off the top of the basket. **3.** to lift, move, budge. *min yruuɛ ib-mukaan ma-aku šii yguššа. yδall in-nahaar kulla.* When he goes someplace, there is nothing that can budge him. He stays all day.

ngašš to leave, take off. *ʔakal w-širab yaḷḷa ngašš.* He ate and drank and then took off.

giššaaya pl. *-aat* small twig.

gšaaš chips, refuse, sweepings.

g-š-ṭ

gišaṭ (*u gašiṭ*) **1.** to scratch, nick, gouge. *ṭ-ṭalqa ğišṭat čitfa.* The bullet grazed his shoulder. *gišaṭ il-meez ib-mukaaneen.* He gouged the table in two places. **2.** to scratch off, scrape off, pick at. *gišaṭ il-ɛabbaaya w-ṭilaɛ id-damm.* He picked at the sore and it bled.

gaššaṭ **1.** to scratch, pick at. *j-jaahil da-ygaššiṭ il-ɛabbaaya.* The kid is picking at the sore. **2.** to peel, flake off. *haṣ-ṣubuġ muu zeen. ygaššiṭ bil-ɛajal.* This paint isn't good. It begins to peel fast.

tgaššaṭ to be peeled off, scraped off. *ṣ-ṣubuġ il-ɛatiig laazim yidgaššaṭ gabul-ma yinṣubuġ il-ɛaayit.* The old paint must be peeled off before you paint the wall.

ngišaṭ to be scratched, nicked. *la-txalli šii ɛal-meez la-yruuɛ yingišiṭ.* Don't put anything on the table or it might get scratched.

gišṭa pl. *-aat* chip, piece (of a dish, etc.).

g-š-w

gišwa pl. *-aat* the thin skin that forms on top of heated milk.

g-š-y

giššaaya, see under *g-š-š*.

g-ṣ-b

guṣab (*u gaṣub*) to cut meat, cut up (a slaughtered animal). *ṣaar-la sana w-baɛda ma-yuɛruf yugṣub.* It's been a year and he still doesn't know how to cut meat. || *la-tištiri min hal-baggaal, tara yugṣub.* Don't buy from that grocer, because he charges an arm and a leg.

guṣab (coll.) reed(s), cane(s).

guṣba pl. *-aat* un. n. of *guṣab*.

gṣaaba the butcher's trade, butchering, meat cutting.

gṣiiba pl. *giṣaayib* pigtail, braid.

gaṣṣaab pl. *-iin, gṣaaṣiib* butcher, meat cutter.

mgaṣṣab embroidered with gold and silver thread, brocaded, trimmed with brocade. *ɛigaal imgaṣṣab* a brocaded head band.

g-ṣ-r

giṣar (*a guṣur*) to be or become short, shorter. *l-ibnayya kubrat w-kull nafaaniifha giṣrat ɛaleeha.* The girl grew and all her dresses are too short for her. *l-leel giṣar ihwaaya b-haš-šahar.* The nights have grown short this month.

gaṣṣar to shorten, make short or shorter. *waddeet il-panṭaruun lil-xayyaaṭ ɛaṭṭa ygaṣṣruu.* I took the pants to the tailor so he could shorten them.

tgaṣṣar to be shortened. *hal-panṭaruun ma-yidgaṣṣar.* These pants can't be shortened.

guṣur shortness, smallness. *ɛali b-guṣr axuu.* Ali is as short as his brother.

ʔagṣar shorter, shortest.

gṣayyir, fem. *gṣayyra* pl. *gṣaar* short. *jumla gṣayyra* a short sentence. *parda gṣayyra* a short curtain.

g-ṣ-ṣ

gaṣṣ (*u gaṣṣ*) to cut, cut off, clip. *diir baalak, la-dguṣṣ ʔiidak bis-siččiin.* Look out, don't cut your hand with the knife.

guṣṣ hal-laحma tlaθ wuṣal. Cut this piece of meat into three pieces. *jiib il-minšaar w-guṣṣ il-xišba.* Bring the saw and saw the piece of wood. *ma-dguṣṣ iðaafrak! ṣaaraw iṭwaal.* Why don't you clip your fingernails! They've gotten long. *ṭ-ṭabiib gaal laazim yguṣṣuun rijla l-yisra.* The doctor said they have to amputate his left leg. *ʔiða ʕiraft itsawwiiha l-haay, ʔaguṣṣha l-ʔiidi!* If you know how to do that, I'll cut off my hand! *ʔiða tiحči čilmat il-luxx, ʔaji ʔaguṣṣa š-šaarbak!* If you say another word, I'll cut your mustache off! *raح-yguṣṣuun šaariع jidiid ihnaa.* They're going to cut a new street through here. *xall inguṣṣ imnil-bistaan حatta yigṣar iṭ-ṭariiq.* Let's cut through the orchard so that it'll be shorter. *ʔiða triid tuعbur iš-šaṭṭ ʕadil, laazim idguṣṣ gaṣṣ.* If you want to cross the river straight, you have to cut diagonally across the current. *l-hawa baarid yguṣṣ.* The wind is cold and cutting. *ṣadiiqak gaṣṣak il-yoom bid-daaʔira.* Your friend cut you down today in the office. *la-tištiri min hal-baggaal tara yguṣṣ.* Don't buy from this grocer, because he overcharges. || *l-yoom gaṣṣeet qaaṭeen.* Today I bought material for two suits. *tigdar idguṣṣ-li biṭaaqa wyaak? ʔaxaaf ma-raح-alaححig ʕal-filim.* Would you buy a ticket for me? I'm afraid I won't be on time for the movie. *ʔiða ma-tbayyið ij-jidir yguum yguṣṣ.* If you don't tin the copper pot, it'll react with what's put in it.

ngaṣṣ to be or become cut. *l-xišba laazim tingaṣṣ minnaa.* The piece of wood must be cut here.

gaṣṣ 1. cutting. || *raggi maalat gaṣṣ is-siččiin* watermelon cut open for inspection. 2. (and *laحam gaṣṣ*) broiled mutton, cut in thin slices and arranged conically on a vertical skewer.

gaṣṣa height, size. *fadd gaṣṣa* the same height. *haṭ-ṭullaab kullhum fadd gaṣṣa.* All these students are the same height.

guṣṣa pl. *guṣaṣ* forehead.

gṣaaṣa diagonally across. *xall nisbaح gṣaaṣa حatta ma-ninحidir.* Let's swim into the current so we won't be swept downstream.

mugaṣ, mugaṣṣ pl. *-aat, mgaaṣa, mugaaṣiiṣ, mgaaṣiiṣ* 1. scissors, shears. 2. tin snips.

g-ṣ-ع

giṣaع (a gaṣiع) 1. to mash, squash, crush. *min šaaf il-gamḷa giṣaعha.* When he saw the louse, he squashed it with his thumbnail. *gaaعid ṣanṭa miθl il-gamla l-magṣuuعa.* He's sitting silent as a squashed louse. 2. to squelch, squash. *giṣaعa b-hal-iččaaya.* He stopped him short by saying that.

gaṣṣaع to crush repeatedly. *ma-ʕinda šuġuḷ bass ygaṣṣiع gamuḷ.* He's got nothing to do but crush lice.

g-ṣ-f

giṣaf (u gaṣuf) 1. to shorten, cut down, cut short. *ʔaḷḷa yugṣuf ʕumrak!* Drop dead (lit., may God cut short your life)! 2. to be or become small. *s-sitra giṣfat ʕaleek.* The jacket has become too small for you.

gaṣṣaf to narrow, cut down. *panṭaruuni ʕariið. gaṣṣfa šwayya.* My pants are too big. Narrow them down a bit.

tgaṣṣaf to be narrowed, cut down. *hal-pantaruun ma-yidgaṣṣaf.* These pants can't be narrowed.

ngiṣaf to be cut short, shortened. *ngiṣaf ʕumrak! ma-tugعud raaحa.* Drop dead! Why don't you be good.

guṣuf narrowness.

giṣiif narrow. *šaariع giṣiif* a narrow street.

g-ṣ-g-ṣ

gaṣgaṣ to cut up, cut to pieces. *gaṣgiṣ il-laحam bis-siččiina.* Cut the meat into pieces with the knife. *j-jaahil b-iida l-mugaṣṣ w-da-ygaṣgiṣ bil-waraq.* The child has the scissors in his hand and is shredding the paper.

tgaṣgaṣ to be cut up, be cut to pieces. *hal-waraq laazim yidgaṣgaṣ.* This paper must be cut up.

gaṣguuṣa pl. *giṣaagiiṣ* piece, shred, scrap.

g-ṣ-y

giṣa (i gaṣi) to harm, hurt. *ʔinta ṣadiiqi. ma-agṣi biik.* You're my friend. I can't hurt you.

g-ð-b

giðab (a gaðub) 1. to seize, catch, find. *š-šurṭi giðaba da-ybuug.* The policeman apprehended him stealing. *giðboo da-yġušš bil-imtiحaan.* They caught him cheating on the exam. 2. to hold, hold on to, hang on to. *ʔigðab raas il-حabil.* Hold the end of the rope. *giðabit-lak makaan yammi bis-siinama.* I saved a place for you near me in the theater. *j-junṭa ma-tigðab kull ihduumi.* The suitcase won't hold all my clothes. *ʔigðab ʔiidak! fluusak raح-tixlaṣ.* Hold it! Your money is about gone.

ngiðab 1. to be seized, caught. *l-حaraami ngiðab bis-sirdaab.* The thief was caught in the basement. **2.** to have a seizure, fit. *xaṭiyya ngiðab bid-daaʔira l-yoom.* The poor guy had a fit in the office today.

mgaððab stiff. *jismi mgaððab; ma-da-agdar ʔatʕarrak.* My body is stiff; I can't move.

g-ð-y

giða (i gaði, giðyaan) **1.** to finish, end, complete. *giðeet ḥaajti b-saaʕa.* I finished my business in an hour. *ʔiða tigðii-li šuġli ʔaaxðak lis-siinama.* If you'll finish my work, I'll take you to the movie. **2.** to spend, pass (time). *giðeena saaʕa b-ḥadiiqt il-ḥaywaanaat.* We spent an hour at the zoo. **3.** to settle, fix, take care of. *tiskut loo ʔaji ʔagðiik.* Shut up or I'll come and fix you good.

gaðða to spend, pass. *gaðða ʔumra bil-ḥiila wis-saxta.* He spent his life playing tricks. *da-nilʕab waraq ḥatta ngaðði wakit.* We're playing cards to pass time.

tgaðða to get along, get by, make do. *laazim nidgaðða ʕala hal-ifluus ʔila raas iš-šahar.* We have to get along on this money until the end of the month.

ngiða **1.** to come to an end, cease, stop. *tingiði. ma-dðall il-ʔumuur hiiči.* It'll come to an end. Things can't go on like this. **2.** to pass, go by, run out. *ngiða n-nahaar w-baʕda ma-jaa.* The day is gone and he hasn't come yet.

gaðyaan finished, done for. *ḥasibta gaðyaana.* He's all worn out.

gaaði finished, done for. *rajul gaaði* an old man. *makiina gaaðya* a worn-out engine.

see also *q-ð-y*.

g-ṭ-ʕ

giṭaʕ (a gaṭiʕ) **1.** to cut, cut off, break off. *l-walad da-yigṭaʕ il-warid.* The boy is picking the roses. *l-hawa giṭaʕ xeeṭ iṭ-ṭiyyaara.* The wind broke the kite string. || *giṭaʕ tikit, giṭaʕ biṭaaqa.* He bought a ticket. *gṭaʕ-li tikit wiyyaak.* Get me a ticket too. *gṭaʕit uffaadi.* You've given me a hard time. **2.** to break off, sever. *l-ʕalaaqaat magṭuuʕa been id-dawilteen.* Relations have been severed between the two countries. **3.** to cut off, interrupt, stop. *ʔiða ma-tidfaʕ il-ifluus, raḥ-nigṭaʕ il-kahrabaaʔ.* If you don't pay the money, we'll cut off the electricity. *giṭʕaw ʕanna l-muxaṣṣaṣaat.* They cut off the allowances to him. *ʔiða ma-ddaawum, yigṭaʕuun raatbak.* If you don't show up at work, they'll cut off your salary. *luwees da-tiḥči ʕalayya? triid tigṭaʕ xubuzti?* Why are you talking about me? Do you want to cut off my livelihood? || *ma-rajjaʕ-li kull il-ifluus. giṭaʕni diinaareen.* He didn't return all the money to me. He short-changed me two dinars. **4.** to block, stop, cut off, intercept. *ḥarrik sayyaartak minnaa; giṭaʕt il-muruur.* Move your car away from here; you've blocked traffic. *j-jeeš giṭaʕ ʕaleena xaṭṭ ir-rajʕa.* The army cut off our return route. *giṭaʕ nafasa nuṣṣ daqiiqa.* He held his breath for half a minute. **5.** to interrupt, break into. *giṭaʕit ʕalayya silsilat ʔafkaari.* You broke into my train of thought. **6.** to conclude, come to agreement on, agree on, settle. *ṣaar-ilna saaʕa nitʕaamal; xall nigṭaʕ is-siʕir.* We've been bargaining for an hour; let's set the price. *ṣadiiqi giṭaʕ mahar w-yimkin yizzawwaj biṣ-ṣeef.* My friend concluded the marriage contract and perhaps will get married this summer. **7.** to cover, traverse. *s-sabbaaḥ giṭaʕ il-masaafa b-daqiiqa w-nuṣṣ.* The swimmer covered the distance in a minute and a half. *giṭaʕ il-masaafa b-iθnaʕaš daqiiqa.* He covered the distance in twelve minutes.

¶ *giṭaʕ il-ʔamal.* He gave up hope. *giṭaʕt il-ʔamal min rajiʕta.* I gave up hope of his returning. *giṭaʕ ʕaqla.* He made up his mind. *yigṭaʕ ʕaqli ma-aruuḥ liš-šuġul.* I've got a good mind not to go to work. *ʕaqla giṭaʕ biiha. baʕad maḥḥad yigdar yibaddil fikra.* His mind is made up. No one can change his idea. *ʕaqli ma-da-yigṭaʕ ib-has-sayyaara.* I've decided not to buy this car.

gaṭṭaʕ **1.** to cut off, break off, pick. *gaṭṭiʕ-li šwayya ʕinab.* Pick me a few grapes. **2.** to break, snap, sever (intens.). *l-walad gaṭṭaʕ il-xeeṭ wuṣla wuṣla.* The boy broke the string into a lot of pieces. **3.** to tear up, wear out. *ma-tilbas ġeer qaaṭ? muu gaṭṭaʕta l-haaða.* Why don't you wear another suit? You've worn that one out.

tgaṭṭaʕ to be or become broken. *hal-xeeṭ yidgaṭṭaʕ ib-suhuula.* This string gets broken easily.

ngiṭaʕ **1.** to break, tear, snap. *la-tḥuṭṭ ihduum ihwaaya; il-ḥabil yingiṭiʕ.* Don't put too many clothes on. The rope will break. **2.** to stop. *ḥuṭṭ had-duwa ʕaj-jariḥ ḥatta yingiṭiʕ id-damm.* Put this medicine on the wound so that it'll stop bleeding. *ngiṭaʕ xamis tiyyaam imnil-*

madrasa. He stopped coming to school for five days.

gaaṭiƐ pl. *gawaaṭiƐ* partition, screen.

mgaṭṭaƐ broken, broken in many places. *filim imgaṭṭaƐ* a much broken reel of film.

see also *q-ṭ-Ɛ*.

g-ṭ-f

giṭaf (*u gaṭuf*) **1.** to duck. *ˀugṭuf raasak; il-baab naaṣi.* Duck your head; the door is low. **2.** to throw, toss. *ˀugṭuf il-iktaab; ˀagdar ˀalugfa.* Throw the book; I can catch it.

gaṭṭaf to throw around. *j-jaahil da-ygaṭṭuf bil-malaaƐiib maalta.* The kid is throwing his toys around.

guṭuf pl. *gṭuuf* butt. *guṭuf jigaara* cigarette butt.

gaṭfa pl. *-aat* throw, toss.

g-ṭ-m

giṭam (*u gaṭum*) **1.** to cut, cut off. *ḍirab il-bazzuuna bil-faasa w-ġiṭam ḍeelha.* He hit the cat with the axe and cut off its tail. **2.** to break, break off. *giṭam il-ixyaara b-iida.* He snapped the cucumber in two in his hand. **3.** to cut short. *giṭam il-quṣṣa liˀan ma-čaan Ɛinda wakit.* He cut the story short because he didn't have time.

gaṭṭam to cut off. *hal-makiina dgaṭṭum ruus id-dijaaj w-itnaḍḍufha.* This machine cuts off the chickens' heads and cleans them.

ngiṭam to be cut off. *nguṭmat ˀiida bil-minšaar il-kahrabaaˀi.* His hand was cut off by the electric saw.

guṭma pl. *guṭam* fragment, piece, shard.

mgaṭṭam **1.** unknown, obscure, without family background. **2.** person with no background.

g-ṭ-n

gaṭṭan to mold, mildew, be or become moldy. *l-xubuz gaṭṭan.* The bread got moldy.

guṭin, guṭun cotton.

gṭiin (coll.) squash, gourd. *gtiin ˀaƈmar* pumpkin.

gṭiina pl. *-aat* un. n. of *gṭiin.*

gaṭṭaan, giṭṭaan a kind of edible fresh-water fish.

g-ṭ-y

giṭa (coll.) sand grouse.

giṭaaya pl. *-aat* un. n. of *giṭa.*

g-Ɛ-d

giƐad (*u guƐuud*) **1.** to sit down, take a seat. *ˀugƐud; stiriiƈ!* Sit down; take a load off your feet! || *tƐaatabna šwayya w-baƐdeen kull šii giƐad ib-mukaana.* We argued for a little while and then everything was straightened out. *ma-tugƐud raaƈa? muu ḍawwajitni!* Why don't you quit it? Haven't you pestered me enough already? *baačir raƈ-agƐud iṣ-ṣubuƈ. Ɛindi šuġul.* I'm going to take the morning off tomorrow. I have something to do. **2.** to sit, be sitting. *ween itƈibb tigƐud?* Where do you want to sit? *giƐadna bil-gahwa nuṣṣ saaƐa nintaḍrak.* We've been sitting in the coffee house a half hour waiting for you. || *hal-qaaṭ giƐad ƈilu Ɛaleek.* This suit fits you well. *loo tuṣbuġ is-sayyaara w-tištirii-lha taayarat, tugƐud.* If you paint the car and buy tires for it, it'll look nice. **3.** to remain, stay, dwell, live. *giƐadna sana wiƈda bil-karx, w-baƐdeen ƈawwalna lil-aƐḍamiyya.* We lived in the Karkh area a year, and then moved to A'dhamiya. *gaaƐdiin bil-karraada.* We live in Karraada. || *zirta yoom waaƈid w-rajjaƐ iz-ziyyaara baƐad šahar, laakin giƐad Ɛal-uffaadi tlaθ-asaabiiƐ.* I visited him for a day, and he returned the visit after a month, but he plagued me for three weeks.

gaƐƐad **1.** to make sit down, make sit, seat. *r-rijjaal gaƐƐadna li-giddaam.* The man seated us down front. *sant il-luxx raƈ-yṣiir Ɛumra sabƐ isniin w-ingaƐƐda bil-madrasa.* Next year he'll be seven years old and we'll enter him in school. || *raˀiis il-wuzaraaˀ gaƐƐada gbaaḷ marta čeef Ɛaaraḍa.* The Prime Minister sent him home because he opposed him. *haṣ-ṣubuġ raƈ-iygaƐƐidha lis-sayyaara.* This paint will make the car look nice. **2.** to wake, wake up, awaken. *gaƐƐidni mnin-noom saaƐa xamsa.* Wake me up at five. *yinraad-li fadd kuub gahwa agaƐƐid raasi bii.* I need a cup of coffee to wake myself up.

tgaaƐad to confer, consult. *tgaaƐadna wiyyaahum w-inƈallat il-muškila.* We conferred with them and the problem was solved.

ngiƐad /with *b-*/ to be lived in, be occupied. *hal-beet Ɛatiig ma-yingiƐid bii.* This house is old. It can't be lived in.

stagƐad to take as a mistress. *stagƐad-la waƈda min čaan bil-baṣra.* He took a mistress when he was in Basra.

gaƐda **1.** sitting. **2.** get together, session. *gaƐdat pookar* a session of poker.

gaaƐid **1.** idle, unemployed. *ˀaxuuk baƐda gaaƐid loo štiġal?* Is your brother still idle or did he get a job? **2.** in the process of, engaged in. *l-makiina gaaɛid tištuġul bil-booš.* The motor's running in neutral.

see also *q-ɛ-d.*

g-f-z

gufaz = *kufaz* which see under *k-f-z.*

g-f-ɛ

gufaɛ (*a gafuɛ*) to peel, to flake. *l-ičbintu gufaɛ imnil-ḥaayiṭ.* The plaster peeled off of the wall.

gaffaɛ to peel, flake. *l-mišag maal ʔiida bida iygaffuɛ liʔan ma-xallaaha dihin wazaliin.* The chapped place on his hand started to peel because he didn't put vaseline on it.

g-f-f

guffa pl. *gufaf* **1.** large basket. **2.** coracle, a round, asphalt covered straw boat.

g-f-g-f

gafgaf to set. *gafgufat id-dijaaja ɛal-beeð kulla w-ma-aku beeða tbayyin.* The hen settled herself over all the eggs and not one is visible.

g-f-y

gufa back, reverse, wrong side. || *ɛala gufa* inside out. *laabis il-ibluuz ɛala gufaa.* He's wearing the sweater inside out. *šurr is-sitra ɛala gufaaha.* Hang out the jacket turned inside out. *yiḥči bil-gufa.* He talks behind one's back. *yiḥči b-gufa n-naas.* He talks behind people's backs.

g-l-a-ṣ

glaaṣ pl. *-aat* glass, drinking cup. *glaaṣ biskit maal doondirma* a cone (for ice cream).

g-l-b

giḷab (*u gaḷub*) **1.** to turn, turn over. *ʔugḷub iṣ-ṣafḥa. ʔard ašuuf ir-rasim.* Turn the page. I want to see the picture. **2.** to turn upside down, turn over. *xall nigḷub is-sanduug. balki l-kitaaba ɛal-čaɛab.* Let's turn the trunk upside down. Perhaps the writing is on the bottom. || *giḷab id-dinya.* He raised heaven and earth. He made a big racket. *leeš gaaḷub xiliqtak?* What's wrong with you? Why the long face? *daax w-giḷab min raasa.* He got dizzy and vomited. **3.** to overturn, upset, topple. *l-bazzuuna giḷbat il-jidir.* The cat upset the pot. **4.** to invert, reverse. *l-xayyaaṭ giḷab il-qoola maalat θoobi.* The tailor turned the collar of my shirt. **5.** to change, switch, alter, convert. *raḥ-iygulbuun il-kahrabaaʔ min dii sii ʔila ʔay sii.* They are going to convert the electricity from D.C. to A.C. *yeezi ɛaad! ʔugḷub ṣafḥa.* That's enough! Change the subject. *luweeš tugḷub il-iḥčaaya? ʔaani ma-gilit hiič.* Why do you twist what's said? I didn't say that. **6.** to tumble, turn somersaults. *haaδa ṭ-ṭeer yugḷub.* This bird turns somersaults. **7.** to change color, run. *hal-uqmaaš, min idġisla, yugḷub.* When you wash this material, the colors run.

gaḷḷab **1.** to turn, turn over. *tigdar idgaḷḷub il-kabaab bič-čaṭal.* You can turn the hamburgers with the fork. **2.** to stir. *baḷḷa gaḷḷub il-marag ḥatta ma-yiḥtirig.* Please stir up the stew so that it won't burn. **3.** to rummage, ransack, rake, poke around. *ṣaar-lak saaɛa dgaḷḷub w-ma-štireet šii.* You've been rummaging around for an hour and haven't bought anything.

tgaḷḷab to be variable, changeable, inconstant, fickle. *la-tṣaddig bii. yidgaḷḷab ihwaaya.* Don't trust him. He's very fickle.

nġiḷab **1.** to turn over. *ngiḷab il-maaɛuun min ʔiida w-wugaɛ il-laḥam.* The plate turned over in his hand and the meat fell. **2.** to change into, turn into, become. *smaɛna fadd rijjaal ngiḷab umrayya.* We heard that a man turned into a woman. **3.** to turn. *čaan ṣadiiqi laakin ingiḷab ɛalayya.* He was my friend but he turned on me.

gaḷub pl. *gḷuub* heart. *ḥičaaha min kull gaḷba.* He said it from the bottom of his heart, he said it wholeheartedly. || *ʔiδa tsaafir, ʔummak yδull gaḷubha ɛaleek.* If you go on a trip, your mother will worry. *ṭallaɛ hal-iḥčaaya min gaḷba.* He made up this talk out of his imagination. *šilaɛ gaḷbi ʔibnak. ʔuxδa.* Your son has pestered me to death. Take him. *ʔakal gaḷbi.* He annoyed me, he got on my nerves. *gaḷbi* my heart, my dear, darling. *niškurič, gaḷbi.* Thank you, dearie.

gaḷba (invar.) **1.** (pants) cuff. **2.** French cuff. **3.** (shirt) collar. **4.** lapels (of a coat.)

magḷuub turned over, inverted. || *bil-magḷuub.* 1. upside down. *mwaggaf il-iglaaṣ bil-magḷuub.* The glass is set upside down. 2. wrong side out. *ʔašuu laabis ijwaariibak bil-magḷuub.* Looks like you're wearing your socks inside out. 3. backwards, wrong way around. *ḥačyak kulla bil-magḷuub. ʔaani lli yḥibb yisaaɛid.* What you say is just the opposite. I'm the one who likes to help. *ṭabb ɛaleena laabis wičča bil-magḷuub.* He came in on us wearing a sour face.

magḷuubi = *bil-magḷuub.*

mugḷaab pl. *mgaaḷub* dump, garbage dump, refuse pile.

see also *q-l-b*.

g-l-j

gullaaj (coll.) flat, disk-shaped capsules that can be filled with a pharmaceutical compound.

gullaaja pl. *-aat* un. n. of *gullaaj*.

g-l-d

gaḷḷad to string. *gaḷḷadti l-baanya willa baɛad?* Did you string up the okra for drying yet?

gḷaada pl. *-aat, gḷaayid* necklace. *gḷaada liilu* a pearl necklace.

g-l-r-y

galari pl. *-iyyaat* gallery (in a theater).

g-l-g

gaḷḷag to dirty, soil.

mgaḷḷag dirtied, befouled, filthy.

g-l-g-l

gaḷgaḷ 1. to move, to shake, wiggle. *gaḷgiḷ il-bismaar ɛatta yinšiliɛ ib-suhuula.* Wiggle the nail so it can be removed easily. 2. to disturb, trouble, harass. *jaab-li fadd xabar, gaḷgaḷ damaaġi bii.* He brought me some news which disturbed me. *ʔibnak ma-yinɛimil. iygaḷgiḷ il-muxx.* Your son is unbearable. He gives you a headache.

tgaḷgaḷ 1. to be moved, shaken, wiggled. *sinni yidgaḷgaḷ. raɛ-ašilɛa.* My tooth is loose. I'm going to pull it. 2. to move. *la-tbiiɛ ġaraaðak wala tidgaḷgaḷ min beetak. haš-šaġḷa muu ʔakiida.* Don't sell your things or move out of your house. That job isn't definite.

gulguli pink (color).

g-l-l

gulla pl. *gulal* 1. cannonball. *rami l-gulla* shotput. 2. Indian club.

giliil, gḷayyil = qaliil which see under *q-l-l*.

g-l-w-b

gḷoob pl. *-aat* light bulb.

g-l-y

giḷa (*i gaḷi*) to fry. *ʔigḷiiha lis-simča.* Fry the fish.

gaḷḷa = giḷa. gaḷḷii-li beeðteen. Fry me two eggs.

tgaḷḷa to fry, be fried. *xalli l-beetinjaan yidgaḷḷa šwayya.* Let the eggplant fry a while. || *l-ɛaṣfuur yitfalla wiṣ-ṣayyaad yitgaḷḷa.* He's enjoying himself and the other guy's stewing in his own juice (lit., the sparrow relaxes and the hunter fries).

g-m-b-ṣ

gambaṣ to squat, hunker down. *j-jaahil gambaṣ ɛala rijlee.* The kid sat on his haunches. *leeš imgambuṣ?* Why are you squatting?

g-m-r

gumar pl. *gmaara* moon.

gamra moonlight. *ɛaayiš ib-gamra w-ribiiɛa. ʔaḷḷa rabba.* He's living the life of Riley. God looks out for him.

gamriyya pl. *-aat* moonlight.

see also *q-m-r*.

g-m-r-g

gamrag 1. to impose a duty or customs tax on. *maʔmuur il-gumrug fattaš ġaraaði w-gamrag bass il-jigaayir.* The customs inspector inspected my things and imposed duty only on the cigarettes. *l-lujna raɛ-idgamrug hal-baðaayiɛ ɛasab qaanuun il-gamaarig.* The committee is going to impose a duty on these goods in accordance with the customs law. 2. to take a portion. *la-traawi r-risuum il-ɛali tara ygamrugha.* Don't show the pictures to Ali or he'll take some of them. 3. to process through customs, put through customs. *ma-tigdar taaxuðha gabuḷ-ma ygamruguuha.* You can't take it before they process it through customs.

tgamrag pass. of *gamrag* 1. *maa-ɛruf iz-zuuliyya š-gadd raɛ-itkallifni ʔilla baɛad-ma tidgamrag.* I won't know how much the rug cost me until it's been taxed by customs.

gumrug pl. *gamaarig* 1. customs duty or tax. 2. customs inspection house.

gumrugi* customs. *taɛliimaat gumrugiyya* customs regulations.

g-m-z

gumaz (*u gamuz*) 1. to jump. *la-tugmuz imniṣ-ṣatiɛ tara tiksir rijlak.* Don't jump from the roof or you'll break your leg. *min saaɛaw ʔisma gumaz w-rikað ib-surɛa.* When they called his name, he jumped up and ran quickly. 2. to bounce. *haṭ-ṭooba tugmuz zeen.* This ball bounces well. 3. to increase, jump, skip. *raatba šloon gumaz min ɛišriin ʔila xamsiin diinaar?* How did his salary jump from twenty to fifty dinars?

gammaz 1. to jump around, bounce up and down. *j-jahhaal da-ygammzuun ɛal-qanafa.* The children are bouncing up and down on the couch. 2. to shift around, switch around. *da-ygammuz min waðiifa l-waδiifa liʔan ʔabuu waziir.* He's shifting from job to job because his father is a minister. **3.** to increase, make increase by jumps. *gammizoo min rutbat ʕariif ʔila mulaazim θaani.* They jumped him from the rank of sergeant to second lieutenant.

ngumaz pass. of *gumaz* **1.** *haṣ-ṣatiḥ yingumuz minna liʔan naasi.* This roof can be jumped from because it's low.

gamza pl. *-aat* **1.** jump. **2.** increase, jump (in wages, rank, etc.) **3.** shift, jump (from job to job).

g-m-ṭ

gumaṭ (*u gamuṭ*) (vulgar) to mate with, to have intercourse with. *d-diič gumaṭ id-dijaaja.* The rooster mated with the hen.

gammaṭ to swaddle. *ʔakθar il-ʔum-mahaat ygammuṭuun ʔaṭfaalhum.* Most mothers swaddle their children.

tgammaṭ to be swaddled. *j-jaahil laazim yidgammaṭ.* The baby has to be swaddled.

gmaaṭ pl. *-aat* swaddling clothes, swaddle.

g-m-ʕ

gumaʕ (*a gamuʕ*) to cause death (by bringing bad luck). *guṣṣta šarr. ʔusbuuʕ wara-ma nwilad, gumaʕ ʔabuu.* He brings bad luck. A week after he was born, he brought death to his father. *ʔagmaʕ ibni, ma-adri.* May I be responsible for my son's death if I know. Honestly, I don't know.

gammaʕ to cut off the stem end. *gammuʕ il-baanya b-has-siččiina.* Cut the stem ends off the okra with this knife.

ngumaʕ pass. of *gumaʕ*. *ngumaʕit! ma-tugʕud raaḥa.* Drop dead! Why don't you be quiet?

gumuʕ pl. *gmuuʕ* **1.** sip. **2.** stem (esp. of an okra pod).

g-m-g-m

gumgum pl. *gmaagum* large copper coffee-pot.

g-m-ḷ

gammaḷ to be or become lice-infested. *ma-tiġsil raasak! muu raḥ-idgammuḷ imnil-wuṣax.* Why don't you take a bath? You're going to become lice-infested from the filth.

gamuḷ (coll.) lice.

gamḷa pl. *-aat* louse.

g-n-b

ginnab hemp.

g-n-b-r

gunubra pl. *gnaabir* lark (zool.).

g-n-ṣ

ginaṣ (*u ganiṣ*) to lie in ambush. *raḥ-yignuṣ lil-baṭṭ ib-hal-mukaan.* He will lie in wait for the ducks right here.

tgannaṣ to lie in wait for, lay for. *šaayil xanjar w-da-yitgannaṣ-la ʕali.* He's carrying a dagger and laying for Ali.

g-n-ṭ-r

ganṭara, guntara = *qanṭara,* which see under *q-n-ṭ-r.*

g-n-f-δ

gunfuδ pl. *ganaafiδ* hedgehog, porcupine.

g-h-w

gahwa **1.** coffee. **2.** (pl. *gahaawi*) a coffee, cup of coffee. **3.** coffeehouse, coffee shop, cafe.

gahwači, gahawči pl. *-iyya* coffeehouse owner, proprietor of a coffeehouse.

g-w-b-a-y-a

guubaaya pl. *-aat* **1.** cold sore. **2.** pimple.

g-w-t-r

gootra (invar.) **1.** undifferentiated, unsorted. *ʔabiiʕa gootra, l-koom ib-miit filis.* I'm selling them as is, a hundred fils per pile. **2.** anarchy, disorder. *šinu, qaabil gootra? ma-aku ḥukuuma?* What, is it the rule of the jungle? Is there no government?

g-w-j-a

gawja (coll.) a kind of large, light-colored plum-like fruit.

gawjaaya pl. *-aat* un. n. of *gawja.*

g-w-d

gawwad to procure, pander, pimp. *l-xaadim maala ygawwid-la.* His servant procures for him. *da-ygawwid ʕaleeha bil-baaraat.* He's pimping for her in the bars.

gwaada **1.** pimping, procurement. **2.** (pl. *-aat*) fee for procurement or pimping.

gawwaad pl. *gwaawiid* pander, pimp, procurer.

gawwaada pl. *-aat* madam, manager of a brothel.

g-w-r

mugwaar pl. *mgaawiir* = *migyaar,* which see under *g-y-r.*

g-w-z

gooz pl. *-aat* **1.** bow, longbow. *gooz kamanja* violin bow. *gooz in-naddaaf* teasing bow used to fluff cotton.

g-w-r-m-m-š

goormamiš pl. *-iyya* crude person, clod, rube, hick. *šloon goormamiš! bass ḥaṭṭaw il-ʔakil ʕal-meez hijam ʕalee.* What a clod! When food is put on the table he attacks it.

g-w-š-r

goošar pl. *gwaašir* **1.** large two-handled basket, woven of palm leaves. **2.** small handle-less basket.

g-w-ʕ

gaaʕ (fem.) pl. *giiʕaan.* **1.** ground, earth. **2.** land. **3.** floor.

gaaʕiyya pl. *-aat* **1.** background (painting). **2.** pot (poker). **3.** ante (poker). **4.** pouch (of a slingshot or sling).

g-w-g

guuga pl. *-aat* rear top part of the head.

g-w-l

gaal (*u gool*) to speak, say, tell. *gaal ma-raḥ-yiji lid-daaʔira l-yoom.* He said he isn't going to come to the office today. *ma-da-afham iš-da-dguul.* I don't understand what you're saying. *ma-yigdar yguul ḥarf il-ʕeen.* He can't pronounce the letter 'ayn. *š-gal-lak?* What did he tell you?

ngaal to be said. *ma-ariid haš-šii yingaal marra lux.* I don't want this thing said again.

gool word, speech, saying, remark. || *haaδa gool w-fiʕil.* He carries out his promises. He's a man of his word.

goola: goolt il-maθal—dawwir, tilgi. As the proverb says—seek and you will find. *gooltak ʔinta—minu ʔabu baačir?* As you say—who knows what tomorrow will bring?

g-w-m

gaam (*u goom*) **1.** to get up, stand up, rise. *gaam ʕala rijla w-bida yimši.* He got up on his feet and started to walk. *gaam min mukaana w-gaʕʕad ʔabuu.* He got up from his place and seated his father. || *lak di-guum! haaδa š-imfahhma bil-kiimya?* Oh, go away! What does he know about chemistry? **2.** to wake up, get up, rise. *šwakit gumit imnin-noom il-baarḥa?* What time did you wake up yesterday? **3.** /with *ʕala*/ to rise against, revolt, rebel against, turn on, attack. *l-ḥaraami gaam ʕala ṣaaḥb il-beet bis-siččiina.* The thief attacked the owner of the house with a knife. *l-qabaaʔil gaamat ʕal-ḥukuuma.* The tribes rose up against the government. *min bida yitḥadda l-ḥaaδriin gaam-la waaḥid w-zaffa xooš zaffa.* When he began challenging the audience a man stood up against him and gave him a piece of his mind. || *gaam ʕalee sinna.* His tooth began bothering him. *beeš gaam ʕaleek il-qaaṭ?* How much did the suit cost you? **4.** to flare up, break out. *l-ḥarub gaamat been il-qabiilteen ʕala šii taafih.* War broke out between the two tribes over a trifling matter. *gaamat θawra biš-šimaal.* A revolt broke out in the North. **5.** to begin, start. *min xaabarta gaam iyʕattibni.* No sooner had I called him than he began upbraiding me. *la-dguum tiḥči ʕalee. huwwa ma-mawjuud.* Don't start talking about him. He isn't here. **6.** to be used up, to be gone. *l-ʔakil gaam ib-xamis daqaaʔiq.* The food was gone in five minutes. *l-yaaxa gaamat; baʕad iθ-θoob ma-yinlibis.* The collar's had it; the shirt can't be worn anymore.

gawwam **1.** to make or cause to rise, make stand up, make get up. *gawwama min mukaana bil-guwwa.* He got him out of his seat by force. **2.** to be or become sexually aroused. *min šaafha mṣallixa, gawwam.* When he saw her nude, he became sexually aroused. **3.** to finish, use up, wear out, ruin. *gawwam yaaxt iθ-θoob hal-gadd-ma ġisala.* He wore out the shirt collar by washing it so much. *gawwam geer is-sayyaara.* He wrecked the car's gearbox.

tgawwam to be made to rise.

goom (invar.) unfriendly, inimical, enemy, enemies. *humma goom.* They're enemies. *ʔaani goom wiyyaa.* I'm an enemy to him.

gaama pl. *-aat* fathom (measure of length, approx. six feet).

gaayim worn out. *yaaxa gaayma* a worn-out collar.

[1]*g-w-n-y*

guuniyya pl. *-aat, gwaani* gunny sack, burlap bag.

[2]*g-w-n-y*

guunya pl. *-aat* = *kuunya,* which see under *k-w-n-y.*

g-y-p-a

giipa pl. *aat* boiled lamb's stomach stuffed with ground lamb, rice, almonds and spices.

g-y-j-l-ġ

geejaluġ pl. *-aat* nightgown.

g-y-r

gayyar **1.** to tar. *ṭabbugaw iṣ-ṣatiḥ w-gayyiroo.* They laid tiles on the roof and put asphalt on it. **2.** to pave. *ʕidna* *makiina tgayyir iš-šawaari*ع. We have a machine that paves streets.

tgayyar 1. to be tarred. *s-sati*ح *laazim yidgayyar* ع*an il-muṭar.* The roof has to be tarred to keep out the rain. 2. to be paved. *ma-nixlaṣ min iṭ-ṭiin* ʔ*illa* ʔ*iδa tgayyar iš-šaari*ع. We won't be rid of the mud unless the street is paved.

giir asphalt, tar. *giir sayyaal.* a naturally liquid type of asphalt, used as waterproofing agent.

migyaar pl. *-aat* a club with a heavy knob of asphalt on the end, used as a blackjack.

g-y-s

gaas (i, u gees) 1. to touch. *bass idgiisa yguum yibči.* The minute you touch him he starts crying. || *l-baar*ح*a gaasni š-šeeṭaan.* I had an emission last night. 2. to blister. *l-qundara gaasat rijli.* The shoe blistered my foot.

ngaas 1. to be touched. *biqa l-*ʔ*akil miθil-ma huwwa. wala ngaas.* The food remained the way it was. It wasn't touched. 2. to be blistered. *rijli ngaasat bil-qundara.* My foot was blistered by the shoe.

g-y-š

gayyaš 1. to wade. *ti*ع*tiqid idgayyiš ib-hal-jadwal?* Do you think you can wade in this creek? 2. to run aground. *l-balam gayyaš.* ʔ*inzil idfa*ع. The boat ran aground. Get out and push. 3. to keep up, to compete, to keep one's head above water. *ma-dgayyiš wiyyaa bil-kiimya.* You can't surpass him in chemistry. *haṣ-ṣaff qawi. ma-agayyiš bii.* This class is tough. I can't keep up. 4. to bag, to sack, to put (dates) in a skin bag. *gayyišaw it-tamur kulla w-dazzoo l-baġdaad.* They put all the dates in skin bags and sent them to Baghdad.

gaayaš to equal, compete with. *ma*حح*ad ygaayiš wiyya haaδa bir-rikiδ.* No one can compete with him in running.

geeš shallow water, shoal, place where one can wade. ʔ*imši, xan-nu*ع*bur. š-šaṭṭ kulla geeš.* Come on, let's go across. The river isn't over your head anywhere. ʔ*inzil bil-mayy w-raawiini l-geeš lu-ween waaṣil.* Get in the water and show me where someone can stand without swimming.

gyaaš = *geeš.*

giiša pl. *giyaš* date container made from a tanned lamb or goat skin, skin bag.

g-y-δ

gayyaδ to put on summer clothes, change to summer dress. *luweeš gayyaδit? d-dinya ba*ع*adha baarda.* Why have you switched to summer clothes? The weather's still cold.

geeδ pl. *-aat* summer, esp. a very hot one.

g-y-w

geewa pl. *-aat* (pair of) cotton slippers, cloth shoes.

g-y-y

gayy money put up by a bridegroom to furnish his bride's new home.

K

k-a

ka- as, in the capacity of. *huwwa, ka-mu*ع*allim, faaxir, bass ka-šurṭi, muu zeen.* He, as a teacher, is great, but as a policeman, no good.

k-a-r

kaar pl. *-aat* vocation, trade, profession, occupation, business. *ra*ح*-*ʔ*atruk in-nijaara li*ʔ*an hal-kaar ma-bii* ع*iiša.* I'm going to quit carpentry because there's no living in this trade. || ʔ*iδa buṣaṭak,* ʔ*aani maa-lii kaar.* If he beats you, it's none of my business.

k-a-r-w-b

kaaruub a large, beetle-like insect.

k-a-r-w-k

kaaruuk pl. *kwaariik* baby cradle.

[1]*k-a-r-y*

kaari curry, curry powder.

[2]*k-a-r-y*

kaaree (in poker) four of a kind.

*k-*ʔ*-s*

*ka*ʔ*s* pl. *ku*ʔ*uus* trophy cup. *madrasatna* ʔ*axδat il-ka*ʔ*s ib-kurat is-salla.* Our school won the trophy cup in basketball.

k-a-s

kaasa pl. *-aat* bowl.

k-a-š-y

kaaši (coll.) tile(s).

kaašiyya pl. *-aat* tile, piece of tiling.

k-a-ġ-d

kaaġad (coll.) paper. *kaaġad sumbaada* sandpaper. || *ba*ع*da bil-kaaġad. ma*حح*ad ista*ع*mala.* It's still brand new (lit., it's

still in the wrappers). No one has used it.
kaaġada pl. *-aat, kwaaġid, kwaaġiid* sheet, piece of paper.

k-a-f
kaaf name of the letter *k*.

k-a-f-w-r
kaafuur camphor.

k-a-k
kaak pl. *-aat* valve, faucet, tap, cock. *kaak buuri d-duuš* the shower faucet. *kaak maal il-buuri l-ʕumuumi* the valve on the main.

k-a-l
kaala pl. *-aat* (pair of) soft, quarterless slipper(s), usually made of felt.

k-a-l-b-t-w-z
kaalibtooz (coll.) eucalyptus.
kaalibtoozaaya pl. *-aat* a eucalyptus tree.

k-a-l-w-š
kaaluuš pl. *-aat, kwaaliiš* **1.** galoshes, rubber overshoes. **2.** a kind of slipper without quarter.

k-a-m-r-a
kaamira pl. *-aat* camera.

k-a-n-w-n
kaanuun: kaanuun ˀawwal December.
kaanuun θaani January.

k-a-h-i
kaahi (coll.) a light, flaky pastry topped with syrup.
kaahiyya pl. *-aat* a piece of *kaahi*.
kaahači pl. -iyya man who makes and sells *kaahi*.

k-a-w-č-w-k
kaawčuuk rubber, caoutchouc.

k-b-b
kubba meatballs made from meat with rice or cracked wheat and spices.
kubbaaya pl. *-aat* un. n. of *kubba*.
kabaab (coll.) meatball(s) broiled on a skewer.
kabaabaaya pl. *-aat* un. n. of *kabaab*.
kababči pl. *-iyya* man who makes and sells *kabaab*.
kabaaba cubeb.
kubbaaba, kabbuuba pl. *-aat* ball of yarn.
see also *č-b-b*.

k-b-d
kabid, kabad pl. *ˀakbaad* liver.

k-b-r
kubar (*a kubur*) to grow, enlarge, become big. *ˀibnak kubar ihwaaya.* Your son's grown a lot. *d-dimbila kubrat ihwaaya. laazim truuḥ lit-ṭabiib.* The sore has become too large. You'd better go to the doctor. *š-daʕwa kubar raasak?* How come you feel so important?
kabbar **1.** to make big, large, to enlarge, magnify, aggrandize, to expand, amplify, extend, widen. *la-tkabbur in-nugra hwaaya.* Don't make the hole too big. *kabbur-li haṣ-ṣuura.* Enlarge this picture for me. *la-tkabbur raasa hal-gadd.* Don't give him such a swelled head. **2.** to praise, glorify (esp. God). *kabbiraw w-ḥimdaw aḷḷa.* They praised and thanked God.
tkabbar **1.** to be enlarged. *haṣ-ṣuura ma-titkabbar.* This picture can't be enlarge. **2.** to be proud, haughty, to feel self-important. *la-titkabbar ʕan-naas.* Don't look down on people.
kubur **1.** size, magnitude, largeness. *ʕindak maaʕuun ib-kubur haaδa?* Do you have a dish of this size? **2.** age. *ˀibni ʕumra sabʕ isniin; ˀibnak iš-kubra?* My son is seven years old; how old is your son? **3.** old age. *δaakirta δuʕfat ib-kubra.* His memory failed in his old age.
kabiir, čibiir pl. *kbaar* (adj.) **1.** big, large. *xall-nigʕud bil-ġurfa č-čibiira.* Let's sit in the big room. **2.** old, aged. *ˀibni č-čibiir duktoor.* My oldest son is a doctor.
ˀakbar **1.** more or most big, large. **2.** more or most old, aged.
kibriyaaˀ arrogance, haughtiness.
kabra: naar kabra ball of fire, human dynamo, an energetic, dynamic, vigorous person. *ibn ij-jiiraan naar kabra.* The neighbor's boy is a real tornado.
mukabbira pl. *-aat* **1.** magnifying glass. **2.** loudspeaker.
mukabbar enlarged, magnified. *sawwii-li nusxa mukabbara min kull ṣuura.* Make me an enlargement of each picture.

k-b-r-t
kibriit sulphur. || *ʕeen kibriit* 1. sulphur spring. 2. a spa in northern Iraq.

k-b-s
kibas (*i kabis*) **1.** to pack, press tightly together. *ykibsuun it-tamur gabuḷ-ma yṣaddruu.* They pack the dates tightly before they export them. **2.** to raid, take by surprise. *š-šurṭa kibsathum ib-hal-beet.* The police raided them in this house. **3.** to spike a ball (in volleyball). *hal-laaʕib yikbis kulliš zeen.* That player spikes the ball very well.
nkibas to be pressed. *t-tamur laazim yinkibis gabuḷ-ma yitʕabba b-iqwaaṭi.* The dates must be pressed before they're packed in crates.

kabiisa: sana kabiisa leap year.

kaabuus pl. *kwaabiis* nightmare, incubus.

makbas pl. *makaabis* packing house (usually for dates).

k-b-s-n

kabsuuna pl. *-aat* **1**. percussion cap. **2**. bullet.

k-b-š

kabiš pl. *kbaaš* ram, male sheep.

k-b-k-b

kaḅkaḅa pomp, ceremony, splendor. *š-daʕwa hal-kaḅkaḅa; qaabil huwwa malik?* Why all this fuss and bother; is he a king?

k-b-n-g

kabang pl. *-aat* roll-up store front, a shutter across the front of a store with no doors. || *baʕad nuṣṣ saaʕa raʕ-innazzil il-kabang.* After half an hour, we'll call it a day.

k-t-b

kitab (*i kitaaba*) to write, to write down, record, inscribe. *ʔiktib ʔasmaaʔ it-talaamiið il-ġaaybiin.* Write down the names of the students who are absent. *kitabit-la maktuub il-baarʕa.* I wrote him a letter yesterday.

kattab to make write. *l-muʕallim kattabna ṣaʕiifteen.* The teacher made us write two pages.

tkaatab **1**. to write to each other, exchange correspondence. *ṣaar-inna sana nitkaatab.* We have kept up a correspondence for a year. **2**. to enter into a written agreement. *tkaatbaw ʕala kull šii gid-daam il-qaaḍi.* They settled a written agreement about everything before the judge. **3**. to join forces. *tkaatbaw wiyya qabiila qawiyya.* They joined forces with a strong tribe.

nkitab pass. of *kitab.* *ʔiða tġiib, ʔismak yinkitib ib-daftar il-ġiyaabaat.* If you are absent, your name will be written down in the absentee log.

kitaab pl. *kutub* **1**. book. **2**. an official correspondence. **3**. business letter.

kitaaba pl. *-aat* writing, handwriting, penmanship.

*kitaabi** clerical. *waḍiifa kitaabiyya* clerical position.

katiiba pl. *kataaʔib* battalion.

maktab pl. *makaatib* **1**. office. **2**. bureau.

maktaba pl. *-aat* **1**. library. *ʔariid ʔaruuʕ adrus bil-maktaba.* I want to go study in the library. **2**. bookstore. *min yaa maktaba štireet hal-iktaab?* From which bookstore did you buy this book? **3**. bookshelf. *n-najjaar raʕ-iysawwii-li maktaba.* The carpenter is going to make me a bookshelf.

kaatib pl. *kuttaab* **1**. writer. **2**. clerk, clerical employee. *kaatib ṭaabiʕa* typist.

maktuub **1**. written, written down, recorded. **2**. fated, foreordained, destined. *maktuub-la yṣiir bii hiiči šii.* It was destined for such a thing to happen to him. **3**. (pl. *makaatiib*) letter, missive, note.

k-t-t

katt (*u*) **1**. (liquid) to pour, gush forth. *l-muṭar da-ykutt il-yoom.* The rain is pouring down today. *l-ṃayy da-ykutt imniṣ-ṣaṭla.* The water is pouring from the bucket. **2**. to express, let forth (an emotion). *katt kull illi b-galba min qahra.* He poured out his heart in his distraction.

k-t-f

kitif, kattaf, etc. = *čattaf,* etc., which see under *č-t-f*.

k-t-k-t

katkat to flow, pour, gush forth. *l-ṃayyaat da-tkatkit imnit-tunag.* The water is pouring out of the jars.

¹k-t-l

kital (*u katil*) **1**. to kill, slay, murder. *kitloo w-ʔaxað ifluusa.* They murdered him and took his money. *ma-ʕidna šuġuḷ. da-nuktil wakit.* We have nothing to do. We're killing time. *kital kull il-fluus bil-iqmaar.* He went through all the money gambling. *kital nafsa ʕala hal-waḍiifa laakin ma-ʕaṣṣalha.* He went all out for this job but he didn't get it. *riiʕt il-balluuʕa tuktil.* The smell from the sewer is killing. **2**. to beat up, whip severely. *j-jaahil kital ʔuxta w-xallaaha tibči.* The kid beat up his sister and made her cry.

kattal /with *b-*/ to slaughter, massacre, butcher. *da-ykattiluun ib-han-naas w-ma-aku.* They're slaughtering those people and there's no end to it.

tkattal pass. of *kattal.* *hwaaya naas raʕ-yitkattluun ib-haθ-θawra.* Many people will be killed in this revolution.

tkaatal to engage in mortal combat, slay each other. *ma-da-nuʕruf ʕala-weeš il-qabaaʔil da-titkaatal.* We don't know why the tribes are killing each other. || *ma-aku ʕaaja titkaatluun. l-maxzan bii saaʕaat kaafya lil-kull.* There's no reason for fighting each other. The store has enough watches for everyone.

nkital pass. of *kital.* *ʔabuuha nkital bil-*

ɛarub. Her father was killed in the war.
kaatil pl. *-iin* killer, murderer.
maktuul pl. *-iin* **1.** murdered. **2.** victim of murder, murdered one.

²k-t-l

kattal to gather (something) into a mass, press into a lump. *xalli mayy ɛaṭ-ṭiin w-kattila.* Put water with the mud and press it into a lump.
tkattal to cluster, clot, agglomerate, gather into a mass. *min itkattilaw, iš-šurṭa farriqathum.* When they massed themselves, the police dispersed them.
kutla pl. *kutal* lump, hunk, clod, clot. || *l-kutla š-šarqiyya* The Eastern Bloc (of nations).

k-t-l-y

kitli pl. *-iyyaat, ktaali, kyaatli* teakettle.

k-t-m

kitam (*i kitmaan*) to conceal, keep secret (something). *ma-yigdar yiktim sirr.* He can't keep a secret.
tkattam to be secretive, keep silent. *yitkattam w-ma-yiɛči šii.* He keeps quiet and won't say a thing. *ma-aku ɛaaja titkattam ib-kull illi tsawwii.* There's no reason to be secretive about everything that you do.
maktuum a variety of fresh dates.

k-t-n

kittaan flax, linen.

k-θ-r

kiθar (*a kuθra*) **1.** to increase, multiply, grow. *ṭullaab madrasatna kiθar ɛadadhum.* The number of students in our school increased. **2.** to be plentiful. *r-raggi yikθar biṣ-ṣeef.* Watermelon becomes plentiful in the summer.
kaθθar **1.** to make more of, to increase, augment, compound, multiply. *hal-kammiyya ma-tikfi. kaθθirha šwayya.* This amount isn't enough. Increase it a little. *ˀaḷḷa ykaθθir min ˀamθaalak.* God should allow more of the likes of you. **2.** to overdo (something), to go to excessive lengths. *ˀisˀala bass. la-tkaθθir wiyyaa.* Just ask him. Don't go to any length with him.
tkaaθar to multiply, grow in number, increase. *l-ˀaraanib titkaaθar ib-surɛa.* Rabbits multiply quickly.
stakθar to consider excessive, regard as too much. *stakθara lis-siɛir.* He thought the price was too much.
kuθur amount. *gul-li š-kuθur itriid w-aani ˀanṭiik.* Tell me how much you want and I'll give it to you.
kuθra, kaθra abundance, copiousness, numerosity, frequency, multiplicity, plurality. *has-sana t-tiffaaɛ mitwaffir ib-kuθra.* This year the apples are available in abundance. *l-kuθra tuǧlub iš-šajaaɛa.* Numbers beat bravery.
ˀakθar more, most. || *ɛal-ˀakθar* most likely, most probably. *šwakit raɛ-itmurr ɛalee? . . . ɛal-akθar baačir iṣ-ṣubuɛ.* When are you going to stop and see him? . . . It'll most likely be tomorrow morning.
ˀakθariyya majority. *l-ˀakθariyya mwaafqiin ɛal-iqtiraaɛ.* The majority are in agreement with the proposal.

k-θ-f

kaθθaf to thicken, condense, concentrate. *ɛidhum makiina tkaθθif il-buxaar.* They have a machine to condense vapor. *ɛaliib mukaθθaf* condensed milk.
kaθaafa **1.** density. *kaθaafat is-sukkaan ib-hal-balad ɛaalya.* The density of population in this country is high. **2.** thickness, solidity, heaviness.
kaθiif pl. *kθaaf* **1.** thick, dense. **2.** heavy, viscous.

k-j-r

kujaraat: čaay kujaraat tea made from zedoary leaves, a red, sour, and aromatic beverage.

k-ɛ-l

kaɛɛal to beautify (eyes) with kohl. *ma-tiṭlaɛ barra ˀiδa ma-tkaɛɛil iɛyuunha.* She won't go out without putting kohl on her eyes. || *jaa ykaɛɛilha w-ɛimaaha.* He was supposed to improve the situation and he made it worse.
tkaɛɛal to beautify one's eyes with kohl. *waagfa giddaam l-umraaya w-datitkaɛɛal.* She's standing in front of the mirror and putting on eye makeup.
kuɛul a preparation of pulverized antimony used as eye cosmetic.
kuɛuul alcohol.
*kuɛuuli** alcoholic.
kɛeela pl. *-aat* thoroughbred mare, horse of the finest breeding.
kɛeelaan a strain of Arabian horses.
makɛala pl. *-aat, makaaɛil* a long-necked jar for kohl.

k-d-ɛ

kidaɛ (*a*) to apply oneself diligently, to work hard. *δall yikdaɛ ˀila ˀan ɛaṣṣal-la šuǧuḷ.* He kept applying himself diligently until he found himself a job.
kaadiɛ **1.** hard-working, diligent. **2.** proletarian.

k-d-d

kadd (*u kadd*) **1.** to work hard, toil, labor,

exert oneself. *ykudd w-ifluusa ytilfuuha wilda.* He works hard and his children waste his money. *ykudd miθl id-daabba w-šuğla ḍaayiʕ.* He works like a mule and his effort is wasted. **2.** to wear, last. *θoob in-naayloon ykudd ihwaaya.* A nylon shirt lasts a long time.

kaaduud pl. *kwaadiid* **1.** hard-working, diligent. **2.** hard worker.

k-d-s

kaddas to pile up, heap up, amass, accumulate. *da-yištiri b-hal-baḍaayiʕ w-iykaddis biiha.* He is buying up those commodities and stockpiling them.

tkaddas pass. of *kaddas. tkaddisat ib-hal-maxzan ʔakθar il-qumṣaan.* Most of the shirts are stocked in this store.

k-d-š

kaddaš (horse) to be or become useless, worthless. *ḥṣaanna kaddaš. raḥ-inbiiʕa.* Our horse has become useless. We'll sell it.

kidiiš pl. *kiddaš* nag, worthless horse. || *l-muwaḍḍaf ij-jidiid kidiiš.* The new employee is a dope.

k-δ-a

kaδa w-kaδa such-and-such, so-and-so. *gaal ʕannak kaδa w-kaδa.* He said such-and-such about you.

k-δ-b

kiδab, etc., = *čiδab,* which see under *č-ḏ-b.*

k-r-b

kirab (*u karub, karaab*) to plow, till. *ʔukrub il-gaaʕ zeen gabuḷ-ma tizraʕha.* Plow up the ground well before you plant it.

karrab **1.** to trim nodules from a palm tree. *yigdar iykarrub in-naxla b-nuṣṣ saaʕa.* He can trim the bumps off a palm tree in a half hour. **2.** to overburden. *da-ykarrubna b-šuğuḷ ihwaaya.* He loads us down with a lot of work. *yidfaʕ-la miit filis bil-yoom w-iykarrub ʕalee ṭuul in-nahaar.* He pays him a hundred fils a day and works him hard all day long.

nkirab pass. of *kirab. l-gaaʕ kullha laazim tinkurub il-yoom.* All of this land must be plowed today.

karaab hard work, toil, drudgery.

karab (coll.) nodules on the trunk of a palm tree from which the fronds grow.

karba pl. *-aat* un. n. of *karab.*

k-r-b-s

karbas to push into an inescapable situation. *karbasni b-has-sayyaara l-muu zeena.* He stuck me with this no-good car.

tkarbas to fall or be pushed into an inescapable situation. *tkarbas il-miḥbas ib-iidi w-ma-da-yiṭlaʕ.* The ring got stuck on my hand and won't come off.

k-r-b-w-n

karboon carbon. *waraq karboon* carbon paper.

k-r-t

karata pl. *-aat* shoehorn.

k-r-t-w-n

kartoon (coll.) thin cardboard, heavy paper.

kartoona pl. *-aat* a sheet of *kartoon.*

k-r-θ

ktiraθ /with *l-*/ to heed, pay attention to, care about, take an interest in. *ʔaani ma-aktiriθ-la. xalli yiḥči š-ma yriid.* I don't care about him. Let him say whatever he wants.

kurraaθ a variety of leek.

kaariθa pl. *kawaariθ* disaster, calamity, catastrophe. *ṣuquuṭ iṭ-ṭiyyaara čaan kaariθa čibiira.* The airplane crash was a terrible disaster.

k-r-x

kirax (*a u karix, kraaxa*) to dredge, clean out (a river, etc.). *l-ḥukumma raḥ-tikrux in-nahar yamm bağdaad.* The government's going to dredge the river near Baghdad.

nkirax pass. of *kirax. n-nahar inkirax is-sana l-faatit.* The river was dredged last year.

karraaxa pl. *-aat* dredge.

k-r-x-a-n

karxaana pl. *-aat, karxaayin* **1.** factory, workshop. **2.** brothel, whorehouse.

karxanči pl. *-iyya* pimp, panderer, procurer.

k-r-d

kurdi **1.** Kurdish. **2.** (pl. *ʔakraad, kurid*) Kurd, person from Kurdistan.

k-r-r

karrar to repeat, reiterate, do again, do repeatedly. *karrir kull čilma ʔaguulha.* Repeat each word I say.

tkarrar to be repeated, to recur. *ʔawaaʕdak hal-ğaḷṭa baʕda ma-titkarrar.* I promise you this error won't recur any more.

mukarrar repeated, reiterated. || *raqam talifoonna xamsa, mukarrar ʔarbaʕa, θneen, waaḥid.* Our phone number is five, four, four, two, one.

k-r-z

karraz to separate the hulls from seeds in the mouth. *riḥna lis-siinama w-karrazna ʕabb ihwaaya.* We went to the movie and ate a lot of seeds.

karaz (coll.) **1.** cherry, cherries. **2.** = *karazaat.*

karza pl. *-aat* cherry.

karazaat generic term for edible nuts.

k-r-s

kurraasa pl. *-aat* **1.** a penmanship book traditionally used to teach school children to write Arabic. **2.** pamphlet, brochure.

kursi pl. *karaasi* **1.** chair. **2.** (and *tamur kursi*) a type of fresh dates.

k-r-s-t-a

karasta (invar.) **1.** the solid material of which anything is constructed, foundation substance. *staʕmilaw xooš karasta b-binaaʔ hal-beet.* They used good materials in building this house. **2.** solid, well-built, soundly constructed. *s-sayyaaraat il-ʔalmaaniyya karasta.* German automobiles are solidly constructed.

k-r-š

kariš pl. *kruuš* pot belly, bay window, paunch. *ṣaar ʕinda kariš min gadd-ma yaakul timman.* He got a pot belly from eating so much rice.

kirša, karša pl. *kiraš* **1.** stomach (of an animal), tripe. **2.** calf (of the leg).

¹k-r-ʕ

kiraʕ = *čarraʕ* which see under *č-r-ʕ.*

²k-r-ʕ

kraaʕ pl. *-iin, -aat, kirʕaan* lower leg and foot of a cow or sheep (esp. as food).

k-r-f

kiraf (*u karuf*) to pick up, scoop up (something) and take it away. *ʔukruf ir-ramuḷ w-δibba bil-loori.* Scoop up the sand and throw it in the truck. *ʔukruf it-tiraaḅ kulla.* Gather up all the dirt and take it out. *jat iš-šurṭa w-kirfathum kullhum.* The police came and picked them all up and took them away.

nkiraf pass. of *kiraf.* *hal-itraab ma-yinkinis; laazim yinkuruf bil-ʔiid.* This dirt can't be swept; it must be gathered up by hand.

karuf **1.** picking up, scooping up and taking away. **2.** in a bunch, as a group. *nbiiʕ il-mišmiš karuf, muu mistanga.* We sell apricots in lots, not singly.

mukraafa pl. *-aat* **1.** scooping device. **2.** dust pan.

k-r-f-t

karfat to shove, force, cram, crowd. *da-ykarfit ij-jahhaal bil-paaṣ w-ma-buqa mukaan.* He's cramming the kids into the bus and there's no room left. *karfitoo bis-sijin.* They threw him in prison.

k-r-f-s

krafus parsley.

¹k-r-k

kirak (*u kuruk*) (fowl) to brood, quit laying, go into lethargy. *dijaajatna raʕ-tukruk baʕad yoomeen.* Our hen will be brooding in two days.

karrak = *kirak.* *dijaajna kulla karrak.* All our chickens quit laying.

²k-r-k

karak pl. *-aat* shovel, scoop.

kaaruuk see under *k-a-r-w-k.*

k-r-k-d-n

karkadann, ʕaywaan il-karkadann rhinoceros.

k-r-k-r

karkar **1.** to laugh noisily, guffaw. *karkar ihwaaya ʕan-nukta maaltak.* He guffawed a lot over your joke. **2.** to giggle. *l-banaat δallaw iykarkiruun.* The girls kept on giggling.

k-r-k-š

karkuuša pl. *karaakiiš* tassel. *ʕindi xaawli bii karaakiiš iṭwiila.* I've got a towel that has long tassels on it.

k-r-k-m

kurkum turmeric.

k-r-m

kiram (*u karam*) to be generous. *ʔaani ma-štireet hal-iktaab. ṣadiiqi kiram-li-yyaa.* I didn't buy this book. My friend gave it to me. *tigdar tikrumni sayyartak muwaqqatan?* Could you lend me your car for a short time?

karram to honor, venerate, treat with deference. *l-ʕarab ykarrimuun iδ-δeef.* The Arabs treat their guests with great deference. *muddat baqaaʔi b-baġdaad karramni w-ʕazzazni kulliš.* During my stay in Baghdad, he was extremely nice to me.

tkarram to show generosity. *tkarram ʕaleena b-raʔyak.* Honor us with your opinion.

karam generosity, magnanimity, liberality, munificence.

karaama **1.** nobility, honor, dignity. **2.** respect, esteem, standing, prestige.

kariim pl. *kuramaaʔ* **1.** generous, munificent, liberal, magnanimous, beneficent. **2.** noble, distinguished, eminent.

ʔakram more or most generous, etc.

ʔikraamiyya pl. *-aat* **1.** bonus. **2.** tangible token of gratitude.

k-r-m-š

karmaš to become wrinkled. *wučča karmaš imnil-kubur.* His face became wrinkled from old age.

k-r-h

kirah (*a karah, kuruh*) to hate, detest, loathe, abhor. *luweeš tikrah abuuk?* Why do you hate your father?

karrah to make hate, cause to hate. *ḍall yδimm it-tadxiin ʔila ʔan karrahniyyaa.* He kept saying bad things about smoking until he made me hate it. *karrah nafsa b-intiqaadaata.* He made himself hated with his criticisms.

ʔakrah to force, compel, coerce. *ʔakrahni ʕala hal-ʕamal.* He forced me into this deed.

tkaarah to hate each other. *čaanaw ʔaṣdiqaaʔ, laakin min šihad ḍidda, tkaarhaw.* They were friends, but since he testified against him, they hate each other.

nkirah pass. of *kirah. nkirah min kull in-naas.* He was hated by everyone.

karaahiyya pl. *-aat* aversion, antipathy, dislike.

kariih loathsome, repugnant, offensive, disgusting, odious.

k-r-w

kura pl. *-aat* ball, globe, sphere. *kurat il-qadam* soccer (game). *l-kura l-ʔarḍiyya* the world globe.

kurawi global, spherical, ball-shaped.

kurayya pl. *-aat* **1.** small ball, globule. **2.** corpuscle.

k-r-y

kira (*i kari*) **1.** to rent, lease, hire out. *hal-maʕall yikri paaysiklaat.* This place rents out bicycles. **2.** to rent, lease, hire. *raʕ-akri paaysikil saaʕa wiʕda.* I will hire a bicycle for one hour. **3.** to dredge, deepen, dig out (a canal, river, etc.) *l-ʕukuuma raʕ-tikri haj-jadwal.* The government will dredge out this canal.

karwa pl. *-aat, karaawi* fare, charge, fee, rent, rental fee.

k-r-y-m

kriim cream, salve, cold cream.

kreema pl. *-aat* a pudding made of milk, eggs, and sugar.

k-z-b-r

kazbar to cause a creepy sensation. *šikilha ykazbur ij-jilid.* Her looks make your skin crawl.

kuzubra coriander.

k-z-z

kazzaaz tetanus.

k-s-b

kisab (*i a kasib*) to win, gain. kisab *ihwaaya bil-pookar il-baarʕa.* He won a lot at poker yesterday.

kassab **1.** = *kisab. ʔibni kassab ihwaaya b-liʕb id-duʕbul.* My son won a lot playing marbles. **2.** to beat, win out over. *liʕab wiyyaana marra wiʕda w-kassabna kullna.* He played with us one time and won all our money.

tkassab to earn a living, work for profit (esp. in a private business). *da-yitkassab ʕala baab ʔaḷḷa.* He is making a living by the grace of God.

ktisab to acquire, obtain, take on. *ktisab il-ʕilim bij-jaamiʕa.* He acquired the knowledge in the university.

kisib gain, profit, winnings. *kisibhum bil-iqmaar čaan išwayya.* Their winnings at gambling were small. *ʔiδa ʔabiiʕha b-miit diinaar, ma-biiha kisib.* If you sell it for a hundred dinars, there won't be a profit in it.

kisba oil cake, meal from vegetables, etc., after they have been dehydrated.

kaasib pl. *kasaba* **1.** winner. **2.** earner, provider. **3.** independent businessman.

k-s-t-n

kastana or *kistaana* (coll.) chestnut(s).

kastanaaya pl. *-aat* chestnut.

k-s-t-y-m

kustiim pl. *-aat* (woman's) attire, outfit, get-up.

k-s-ʕ

kassaʕ to throw out, get rid of, chuck out, bounce. *nṭii l-iktaab w-kassʕa.* Give him the book and get rid of him. *buqa bil-waḍiifa muddat šahar w-baʕdeen kassiʕoo.* He remained in the position for a month and then they sacked him.

tkassaʕ to leave, get out, beat it. *tkassaʕ! ʔiʕma ma-nxaaf minnak.* Scram! We're not afraid of you. *nṭii fluus w-xallii yitkassaʕ.* Give him some money and let him get lost.

ktisaʕ **1.** to overrun, sweep across, spread over. *j-jayš iktisaʕ ij-jaziira.* The army overran the island. *l-maraḍ iktisaʕ ij-junuub kulla.* The disease spread over the whole South. **2.** to flood, inundate, sweep across. *maay il-fayaḍaan iktisaʕ il-wlaaya.* The flood waters swept over the city.

kusaaʕ, maraḍ il-kusaaʕ rickets.

k-s-d

kisad (*a kasaad*) to sell badly, move slowly, find no market. *hal-baḍaayiʕ ʔiδa ma-nbaaεat bil-mawsim, tiksad.* If these goods aren't sold in season, there won't be a market for them.

kassad /with *εala*/ to hurt, injure, damage. *loo-ma tiħči wiyyaaha, čaan da-truuħ wiyyaaya. ʔinta kassadit εalayya.* If you hadn't talked with her, she would have gone with me. You spoiled it for me. *ʔiδa yfattiħ igbaaḷna, raħ-ykassid εaleena.* If he opens up across from us, he will ruin our business.

kasaad **1.** depression, recession, slump, economic stagnation. **2.** slow day. *l-yoom kasaad. ma-biεna kull šii.* There's no business today. We haven't sold a thing.

k-s-r

kisar (*i kasir*) **1.** to break, shatter, fracture. *j-jaahil kisar il-maaεuun.* The child broke the plate. *raħ-iykisruun is-sadda šimaal baġdaad.* They are going to break the levee north of Baghdad. **2.** to break (fig.). *kisar waεda wiyyaaya.* He broke his promise to me. *kisar ir-raqm il-qiyaasi b-rikḍ il-miit matir.* He broke the record in the 100-meter dash. *l-muεallim kisar muεaddali b-had-daraja.* The teacher ruined my average with that grade. || *ħaalta tiksir il-gaḷuḅ.* His situation is heartbreaking. *has-sayyaara kisrat εeeni. baεad ma-aštiri sayyaara mustaεmila ʔabadan.* This car's been a pain in the neck to me. I'll never buy a used car again. *maħħad kisar εeen hal-mulaaħiδ ʔilla l-mudiir ij-jidiid.* No one put the supervisor in his place except the new director. *ma-yiskut ʔilla lamma ʔaksir εeena.* He won't shut up until I take him down a peg. **3.** to defeat, rout. *d-diič maali kisar diič εali.* My rooster defeated Ali's rooster. *wild imħallatna kisraw wild imħallatkum.* The kids in our neighborhood beat up the kids in your neighborhood. **4.** to bankrupt, to break. *ʔiδa yδaḷḷuun ybiiεuun rixiiṣ raħ-iykisruuna.* If they keep on selling cheap they're going to break us. **5.** to break open, cut open. *ʔiksir raggiyya wiħda bass.* Cut only one watermelon.

kassar **1.** to break up. *da-ykassir jooz w-yaakul il-libb.* He is breaking walnuts and eating the meats. *kassir hal-xišab ħatta nšiεla biš-šita.* Cut up this wood so we can burn it during the winter. **2.** to shatter, smash. *δirab il-kuub εal-ħaayiṭ w-kassara.* He threw the cup against the wall and smashed it. **3.** to calculate, figure out. *hassa ʔakassir-ilk-iyyaaha.* Now I'll calculate it for you.

kaasar **1.** to pit against each other, to set against each other. *jiib id-diič maalak ħatta nkaasra wiyya diiči.* Bring your cock so we can fight him with my cock. *biš-šimaal ykaasruun il-qabič.* In the North they pit quail against each other. **2.** to dilute, cut. *ma-agdar ʔašrab il-εarag saada. kaasir-li-yyaa b-ṃayy.* I can't drink arrack straight. Cut it with water for me. *kaasir il-ṃayy ħatta ʔagdar ʔaġsil bii.* Dilute the hot water with some cold water so I can wash with it.

tkassar to be or become broken, shattered, smashed. *l-maaεuun wugaε min ʔiidi w-itkassar. ṣaar miit wuṣla.* The dish fell from my hand and shattered. It's in a hundred pieces. *hal-iglaaṣaat titkassar bil-εajal.* These glasses get broken quickly.

nkisar **1.** to be or become broken. *wugaε il-iglaaṣ w-inkisar.* The glass fell and got broken. *moojt il-ħarr inkisrat.* The heat wave was broken. || *gaḷbi nkisar min šifta yištuġuḷ bil-ħarr.* It broke my heart to see him working in the heat. *nkisar xaaṭri εalee w-inṭeeta diinaar.* I took pity on him and gave him a dinar. *min ʔakal δiič il-basṭa, nkisrat εeena. baεad ma-yilεab bis-sayyaara.* Since he got that beating, he's learned his lesson. He won't play with the car again. *nkisrat εeenak loo ʔaji ʔabusṭak baεad?* Have you had enough or do I have to beat you up again? *ʔadabsizz. ma-tinkisir εeena.* He's got no manners. He can't be shamed. **2.** to be defeated, be destroyed. *nkisar jeeš il-εadu baεad muqaawama qaliila.* The enemy army was defeated after a slight resistance. **3.** to be bankrupted, be broken. *tlat-tujjaar inkisraw haš-šahar.* Three merchants went bankrupt this month.

kasir pl. *ksuur* **1.** break, breach, fracture. *kasir bir-rijil* a fracture of the leg. **2.** fraction (arith.). *kasir εišri* decimal fraction. *yimluk ʔalif diinaar w-iksuur.* He is worth a thousand and some odd dinars. **3.** bankruptcy. *t-taajir ṭilaε kasir.* The merchant went bankrupt.

kasra pl. *-aat* break, breach, fracture.

kisra, kasra pl. *-aat, kisar* piece, fragment, chunk.

kassaar pl. *-iin: kassaar xišab* woodcutter.

kassaara pl. *-aat* **1.** nutcracker. *kassaarat*

jooz walnut cracker. **2.** crusher. *kassaarat saxar* rock crusher.

kaasir predatory. *ḥaywaan kaasir* beast of prey. *ṭeer kaasir* bird of prey.

mkassiraat (pl. only) sins, immoral conduct, loose living. *ʕumra xamsiin sana w-baʕda ydawwur imkassiraat.* He's fifty years old and still leading a wild life.

k-s-s

kuss pl. *ksaasa* **1.** vulva, vagina. **2.** (by extension; vulgar) woman, girl.

k-s-f

kisaf (*i kusuuf*) to be eclipsed. *min tiksif iš-šamis, tiðlamm id-dinya.* When the sun is eclipsed, the sky grows dark.

kassaf to upbraid, berate, tell off, chew out. *raaḥ-la lil-beet w-kassafa.* He went to him at home and berated him.

tkassaf **1.** to be humiliated. *tkassaf giddaam il-mwaððafiin li-ʔan šuġla ṭilaʕ kulla ġalaṭ.* He was humiliated in front of the employees because his work turned out to be all wrong. **2.** to get into trouble, get in a jam. *tkassaf ib-landan. ṣiraf kull ifluusa w-biqa miflis.* He got into trouble in London. He spent all his money and ended up broke. || *lak di-ruuḥ, itkassaf! ʔinta š-imgaddrak tuġlubni biš-šiṭranj?* Aw go on, beat it! How could you beat me in chess?

kasiif **1.** bad, horrible, horrid, terrible. *loon kasiif* a terrible color. *jumla kasiifa* a horrible sentence. **2.** useless, worthless. *waaḥid kasiif* a useless person. *ḥači kasiif* idle talk.

kasaafa pl. *-aat* misery, nightmare, fright. *l-ʕiiša b-hal-qarya kasaafa. laa ʔaku maṭaaʕim w-laa kahrabaaʔ.* Living in this village is misery. There are neither restaurants nor electricity. *š-šuġuḷ ib-had-daaʔira kasaafa.* Working in this office is a nightmare.

kusuuf solar eclipse, eclipse of the sun.

k-s-k-n

kaskan **1.** to be or become angry, irritated, annoyed. *haaða ʕaṣabi; ykaskin bil-ʕajal.* He's irritable; he gets annoyed quickly. **2.** to be or become aroused, excited, get hot. *ykaskin ʕala hal-ḥači.* He gets a charge out of that talk.

kaskiin **1.** strong. *titin kaskiin* strong tobacco. *čaay kaskiin* strong tea. **2.** spicy, hot. *ʔakil kaskiin* spicy food. **3.** sharp. *ḥači kaskiin* sharp words.

k-s-k-y-t

kaskeeta pl. *-aat* cap with a visor.

k-s-l

kassal to make lazy. *jaww il-baṣra ykassil il-waaḥid.* The weather in Basra makes one lazy.

tkaasal to be lazy, sluggish, indolent, become discouraged. *la-titkaasal. xaḷḷiṣ šuġuḷak.* Don't be lazy. Finish your work. *l-masaafa ṭuwiila w-ma-ʕindi sayyaara. tkaasalit.* It's a long way and I don't have a car. I just decided it wasn't worth it.

kasla pl. *-aat* traditional outing, group picnic.

kaslaan pl. *-iin, kasaala* **1.** lazy, indolent. *tilmiið kaslaan* a lazy student. *l-ḥaywaan il-kaslaan, ḥaywaan il-kaslaan* sloth, tree sloth. **2.** lazy person.

ʔaksal more or most indolent, lazy, etc

k-š-t-b-a-n

kuštubaan, kištibaan, kišitbaan pl. *-aat* thimble.

k-š-x

kišax (*a kašxa*) **1.** to show off, be boastful, boast, brag. *kišax ib-sayyaarta j-jidiida.* He showed off with his new car. *la-tikšax ib-raasi. ʔaani ʔaʕurfak šinu ʔinta.* Don't go showing off to me. I know what you are. **2.** /with *b-*/ to waste, squander. *kišax bil-ifluus lli ddaayanha.* He squandered the money he borrowed.

kašxa **1.** showing off, bragging, boasting. *yiḥči kašxa. kull ḥačya bil-malaayiin.* He talks big. Everything is millions with him. *ʕala weeš hal-kašxa? yaʕni maḥḥad ʕinda paaysikil?* Why this showing off? Are you the only one who has a bicycle? **2.** fine, impressive, sharp. *sayyaara kašxa* an impressive car. *beet kašxa* a fine house. *l-yoom ʔinta ṭaaliʕ kašxa b-hal-badla.* Today you are looking sharp in that suit.

kaššaax pl. *-iin, -a* show-off, braggart.

k-š-d

kašiida pl. *kašaayid* fez wrapped with a thick, colored cloth.

k-š-r

kaššar to bare one's teeth. *ʔiða ykaššir il-bazzuun yaʕni ġaðbaan.* If a cat shows its teeth, it means he's mad.

k-š-š

kašš (*i kašš*) **1.** to shoo, shoo away. *kišš id-dijaaj. raḥ-yaakluun it-timman kulla.* Shoo the chickens. They're going to eat all the rice. **2.** (in chess) to check. *raḥ-ʔakišš il-malik.* I'm going to check the king.

nkašš to be shooed, be shooed away. *ð-ðibbaan ma-da-yinkašš. ʔakušša w-yirjaɛ.* The flies can't be shooed away. I shoo them off and they come back. || *ð̣all yiḥči w-ma-nkašš ʔila nuṣṣ il-leel.* He kept talking and didn't leave until midnight.

kišš **1.** shooing, shooing off, shooing away. **2.** checking, check (chess). || *kišš maat* checkmate.

kašša pl. *-aat* a shooing, shooing off, shooing away.

makšuuš checked, in check (chess).

k-š-f

kišaf (*i kašif*) **1.** to uncover, unveil, remove a covering. *kišfat wujha ḥatta tšuuf is-simač zeen.* She uncovered her face to see the fish well. **2.** to disclose, reveal. *ʔarjuuk, ʔikšif-li waraqak.* Show me your cards, please. **3.** /with *ɛala*/ to study, scrutinize, investigate, examine. *l-lujna raḥ-tiji tikšif ɛal-binaaʔ.* The committee is going to come inspect the building. **4.** to examine (medically). *ṭ-ṭabiib kišaf ɛalayya bass ma-liga šii.* The doctor examined me but didn't find anything. **5.** to fade. *hal-iqmaaš yikšif?* Does this cloth fade? *haθ-θoob loona kaašif.* This shirt has faded.

kaššaf to uncover. *la-tnaam imkaššaf, la-truuḥ tubrad.* Don't sleep uncovered or you'll catch cold. *ɛeeb, la-tkaššfiin wujhič biš-šaariɛ!* For shame, don't uncover your face on the street!

tkaššaf to uncover oneself. *ʔiða miḥtarr leeš-ma titkaššaf?* If you're hot why don't you throw off the covers?

tkaašaf to show to each other, reveal to each other. *ma-aku ḥaaja nð̣umm waaḥid ɛal-laax. xan-nitkaašaf w-inšuuf š-itriid.* There's no need to conceal things from each other. Let's be frank with each other and see what you want. *tkaašfu ḥatta nuɛruf minu l-ġaalub.* Show your cards to each other so we'll know who is the winner.

nkišaf to be disclosed, be revealed. *hassa l-ḥaqiiqa nkišfat.* Now the truth is revealed.

ktišaf to discover, find out, detect. *ktišaf jaziira ẓġayyra bil-muḥiiṭ il-hindi.* He discovered a small island in the Indian Ocean.

kašif **1.** inspecting, examining. **2.** (pl. *kušuuf*) (medical) examination, check-up. **3.** inspection, inspection tour.

kaššaaf pl. *-a* scout, boy scout. || *ð̣uwa kaššaaf* **1.** search light. **2.** flare.

ʔaksaf more or most pale, faded, etc.

ktišaaf pl. *-aat* discovery.

stikšaaf **1.** discovery, exploration. **2.** reconnaissance, reconnoitering, scouting. *ṭiyyaarat istikšaaf* a reconnaissance plane.

kaašif **1.** faded. *loon kaašif imnil-ġasil* a color faded by washing. **2.** pale, light. *loon ʔaxð̣ar kaašif* a light green color.

makšuuf uncovered, open, evident. *waraqa makšuufa* a card lying face-up. *pookar makšuuf* stud poker. *ḥači makšuuf* frank talk. *ɛyuub makšuuf* obvious defects. || *ɛal-maksuuf* openly, publicly. *raḥ-aruuḥ ʔaḥči wiyyaa ɛal-makšuuf.* I'm going to go talk with him openly.

muktašif pl. *-iin* explorer, discover.

k-š-k-a

kaška, kaškaa a dish made from cracked wheat, chickpeas, and noodles.

k-š-k-š

kaškaš to shoo, shoo away, scare away. *j-jaahil da-ykaškiš id-dijaaj.* The kid is scaring the chickens away.

kaškaš pleated. *tannuura kaškaš* a pleated skirt.

k-š-k-w-l

kaškuul pl. *-aat* **1.** beggar's bag. **2.** catch-all.

k-š-m-š

kišmiš (coll.) raisin(s).

kišmiša pl. *-aat* un. n. of *kišmiš.*

k-š-n

kušin pl. *-aat, kušnaat* seat, seat cushion (of an automobile).

k-ð̣-ð̣

kað̣ð̣ (*u kað̣ð̣*) **1.** to seize, catch. *ʔurkuð waraa w-kuð̣ð̣a.* Run after him and grab him. **2.** to hold, hold fast to. *kuð̣ð̣ ʔiid ij-jaahil ḥatta ma-yoogaɛ.* Hold onto the kid's hand so he won't fall.

nkað̣ð̣ to be caught, be seized. *ṭ-ṭeer ma-yinkað̣ð̣ bil-ʔiid.* The bird can't be caught with the hand.

ktað̣ð̣ to be overfull, be packed, be chock-full. *ktað̣ð̣at is-siinama bin-naas.* The movie was packed with people.

k-ɛ-b

kaɛɛab to cube. *kaɛɛib har-raqam.* Cube this number.

takɛiibi: j-jað̣r it-takɛiibi cube root (math.).

mukaɛɛab **1.** cube-shaped, cubic. *mitir mukaɛɛab* cubic meter. **2.** cube, cubed.

raqam muqaƐƐab a cubed number. **3.** (pl. *-aat*) blocks, toy blocks.

see also *č-Ɛ-b.*

k-Ɛ-b-r

kaƐbar to crumple up. *kaƐbar il-waraqa w-ðabbha bis-salla.* He crumpled up the paper and threw it into the waste basket. **1.** crumpled, wrinked. *waraq imkaƐbar* crumpled papers. **2.** mis-shapen, gnarled. *raas imkaƐbar* a mis-shapen head.

k-Ɛ-d

kiƐid pl. *kuƐuud* barge, cargo boat (without motor).

k-Ɛ-k

kaƐak (coll.) a type of pretzel-like pastry, sometimes in the form of cookies.

kaƐka pl. *-aat* un. n. of *kaƐak.*

k-Ɛ-k-l

kaƐkuula pl. *-aat* **1.** cowlick, pompadour. **2.** crest (of a bird).

k-f-ʔ

kaafaʔ to reward. *ʔiða tištuġuḷ zeen, ykaafʔak ib-fadd šii.* If you work well, he'll reward you with something.

kufu, kafu **1.** equal, a match. *ma-zawwjooh-iyyaa li-ʔan muu kufu ʔilha.* They didn't marry her to him because he isn't a match for her. **2.** qualified, capable, able, competent. *kufu Ɛala dafƐ il-mablaġ* capable of paying the amount. *haaða muu kufu l-hiiči waḍiifa.* He's not qualified for such a position.

kafiʔ qualified, capable, able, competent. *mwaḍḍaf kafiʔ* a capable employee.

kafaaʔa efficiency, capability, ability, competence.

ʔakfaʔ more or most capable, able, competent, efficient.

k-f-t

kufta a dish composed mainly of meatballs, with spices, tomato sauce, and sometimes rice.

k-f-ɛ

kaafaɛ to combat, to fight against, struggle against. *kaafɛaw il-maraḍ mudda ɛatta qiḍaw Ɛalee.* They struggled with the disease for some time until they conquered it.

kifaaɛ struggle, fight, battle.

k-f-r

kufar (u kufur) to be irreligious, be an infidel, not to believe. *leeš idguul ma-aku ʔaḷḷa? da-tukfur.* Why do you say there's no God? You're blaspheming. *luweeš da-tukfur? ma-txaaf min ʔaḷḷa?* Why are you being so sacrilegious? Have you no respect for God? || *qaabil kufarit jibt isma giddaamak?* Is it so awful I brought up his name in your presence?

kaffar **1.** to atone, make amends, do penance. *wazzaƐ ifluus Ɛal-fuqara ɛatta ykaffur Ɛan ðinuuba.* He gave out money to the poor to atone for his sins. **2.** to curse, to blaspheme. *ḍall ysibb w-ykaffur min ġaḍaba.* He kept cursing and blaspheming in his anger. **3.** to exasperate, madden, infuriate. *ḍall yliɛɛ Ɛalayya ʔila ʔan kaffarni.* He kept insisting until he made me want to curse. *kaffaritni. la-tiɛči Ɛaad!* You're driving me nuts! Can't you shut up! *muu kaffaritni! maɛɛad yiġlaṭ?* Don't give me a hard time! Doesn't anyone else make mistakes?

kuffaara penance, atonement.

kaafir pl. *kafara, kuffaar* infidel, unbeliever, atheist.

k-f-z

kufaz (u kafuz) to mount, cover. *xaruufna kufaz naƐjathum.* Our ram mounted their ewe.

kaffaz intens. of *kufaz.* *haṣ-ṣaxal jaaybii ɛatta ykaffuz ṣaxlaathum.* They've brought this billy goat to breed their female goats.

k-f-f

kaff (u kaff) **1.** to hem, edge. *nafnuufha ṭwiil; raɛ-itkuffa.* Her dress is too long; she's going to hem it. **2.** /with *Ɛan*/ to leave alone, let alone. *kuff Ɛanni. muu ðawwajitni!* Get off my back. You're bothering me!

kaaffa all, all of. *kaaffat ʔahil baġdaad* all the people of Baghdad. *kaaffat iṭ-ṭuḷḷaab* all the students.

k-f-l

kifal (a kafaala) to vouch for, answer for, go bail for, to guarantee, cosign for. *ma-simɛoo-la yitlaƐ liʔan ma-aku waaɛid yikfala.* They didn't permit him to get out because no one would go bail for him. *ʔaani ʔakifla. daayna l-ifluus.* I'll stand good for him. Lend him the money. *l-Ɛaṣfuur kifal iz-zarzuur w-θneenhum ṭayyaara.* The sparrow vouched for the starling and they're both slippery characters (lit., good flyers).

kaffal to ask to be a guarantor, to get as guarantor.

tkaffal to cosign for, guarantee, be a guarantor for, be responsible for. *l-bang ma-ydaayinni l-ifluus ʔilla ʔiða fadd waaɛid itkaffalni.* The bank won't lend me the money unless someone cosigns for me. *ʔinta ʔidfaƐ diinaareen w-aani*

ʔatkaffal il-baaqi. You pay two dinars and I'll be responsible for payment of the rest. *huwwa rajlič muu mitkaffla?* Isn't your husband sponsoring him (acting as surety for him)?

kafaala pl. *-aat* **1.** pledge, deposit, surety, collateral. **2.** bail. *ṭilaƐ imnis-sijin ib-kafaala.* He got out of jail on bail.

kafiil pl. *kufalaaʔ* guarantor, co-signer. *ʔiδa tiddaayan ifluus, ʔil-man raƇ-itkaffil?* If you borrow money, who will you get for a guarantor?

k-f-n

kifan = *čifan,* which see under *č-f-n.*

k-f-y

kifa (*i kifaaya*) to be enough, be sufficient, suffice. *hal-mablaǧ yikfiini šahreen.* This amount will be enough for me for two months. *yikfi Ɛaad titbajjaƇ!* That's enough bragging for now!

kaffa = *kifa. hal-ifluus ma-tkaffiini.* This money won't be enough for me.

ktifa to be content, to content oneself. *l-muƐallim iktifa b-inδaara, w-ma-qaaṣaṣa hal-marra.* The teacher was satisfied with a threat and didn't punish him this time. *ktifeet; ma-agdar aakul baƐad.* I've had enough; I can't eat any more.

kifaaya sufficient amount. *ʔuxuδ kifaaytak imnil-ṃaay wil-baanziin gabuḷ-ma tsaafir.* Take all the water and gas you'll need before you start.

kaafi sufficient, enough, adequate. *tiƐ-tiqid hal-mablaǧ kaafi?* Do you think this amount is enough?

k-k-l-k

kukluk pl. *kakaalik* a kind of game bird resembling the partridge.

k-l-a-š

klaaš pl. *-aat* a sort of quarterless slipper.

k-l-a-w

klaaw pl. *-aat* **1.** cap with no brim or visor. || *laabis klaaw il-xannaas.* He's invisible (lit., he's wearing the devil's cap). *laazim ʔašuufa. qaabil laabis iklaaw il-xannaas?* I should see him. Do you suppose he's made himself invisible? *labbasa klaaw.* He took him. He cheated him. He pulled the wool over his eyes. *ṣaaƇib il-maxzan labbasa xooš klaaw.* The storekeeper really took him to the cleaners. **2.** (pl. only) poppycock, baloney, bull. *la-tihtamm bil-yguuluu. haaδa kullha klaa-waat.* Don't be concerned about what they say. That's all baloney.

klaawči pl. *-iyya* confidence man, con artist.

k-l-b

kalb = *čalib* which see, under *č-l-b.*

k-l-b-č

kalbač to handcuff. *kalbičoo w-axδoo l-markaz iš-šurṭa.* They handcuffed him and took him to the police station. || *kalbičooni b-haš-šuǧuḷ foog kull šuǧḷi.* They saddled me with this job in addition to all my own work.

tkalbač to be handcuffed. *haaδa laazim yitkalbač tara yinhizim.* He has to be handcuffed or he'll escape.

kalabča pl. *-aat* handcuffs.

k-l-b-d-w-n

kalabduun **1.** gold thread. || *šaƐarha ʔaṣfar kalabduun.* Her hair is golden yellow.

k-l-x-a-n

kulxaan pl. *-aat* firepit under a Turkish bath.

kulxanči pl. *-iyya* fireman who stokes the fire in a public bath.

k-l-s

kallas to deflate. *raƇ-ykallisuun ir-riyya maalta.* They're going to deflate his lung.

kils lime.

*kilsi** basic, alkaline. *ʔarḍ kilsiyya* alkaline soil.

[1]k-l-š

kiliiša pl. *-aat, kilaayiš* **1.** engraving, engraved plate. **2.** rubber stamp. **3.** cliché, trite phrase.

[2]k-l-š

kulliš = see under *k-l-l-š.*

k-l-f

kallaf **1.** to cost. *l-qaaṭ šgadd kallafak?* How much did the suit cost you? *qaaṭi kallafni Ɛišriin dinaar.* My suit cost me twenty dinars. **2.** to assign, require, ask, have. *ʔiδa tiƇtaaj šii mnis-suug, ruuƇ ištirii. la-tkallif ʔaƇƇad.* If you need something from the market, go buy it. Don't ask someone else. *da-agul-lak ṣiƇƇti mpančira. kallif ǧeeri ysawwiiha.* I tell you my health's run down. Have somebody else do it. **3.** to bother, trouble, inconvenience. *ʔagdar akallfak ib-šii?* Could I trouble you for something? *la-tkallif nafsak Ɛala muudi.* Don't trouble yourself on my account. *kallafitni ʔalif kulfa l-yoom.* You've imposed on me a thousand times today.

tkallaf **1.** to put oneself out, go to a lot of trouble. *tkallaf ihwaaya l-yoom Ɛala muudi.* He went to a lot of trouble today for my sake. **2.** to be unnatural, affected, pretentious. *yitkallaf ihwaaya b-kalaama.*

He puts on airs with his talk. **3.** /with *ɛala, b-*/ to cost. *hal-beet tkallaf ɛalayya b-ʔalfeen diinaar.* This house cost me 2000 dinars.

kulfa pl. *kulaf* **1.** cost, expense, expenditure, outlay. **2.** assignment, requisition, request, task. **3.** trouble, inconvenience, imposition.

takliif pl. *takaaliif* **1.** cost. *takaaliif il-maɛiiša* the cost of living. **2.** request, task. **3.** imposition, bother.

takalluf mannerisms, airs, affectation, affected behavior.

mukallaf **1.** liable to the draft, eligible for the draft. **2.** person who is eligible for the draft.

mitkallif responsible, concerned, burdened, put out. *ʔiða yriid yruuḥ, ʔaani ma-mitkallif bii.* If he wants to go, it's no skin off my neck. *la-tiji ɛalayya baɛad. ʔaani ma-mitkallif ib-hal-qað̣iyya.* Don't come to me again. I'm not concerned with this matter. || *wal̤la, mitkallif!* You poor overburdened thing! *ṣrafit miit diinaar ib-ʔooruppa? wal̤la mitkallif! ʔaani ṣrafit ʔalif.* You spent a hundred dinars in Europe? You poor guy! I spent a thousand.

[1]*k-l-k*

kallak to trick, deceive, fool. *kallika lij-jaahil w-xallii yiji wiyyaak.* Fool the kid and make him come with you.

kalak pl. *-aat* trick, fast one. *ɛabbar ɛalee fadd kalak w-axaðha minna.* He put one over on him and took it away from him.

kalakči pl. *-iyya* trickster, tricky person, smooth operator.

[2]*k-l-k*

kalak pl. *-aat* raft of inflated skins.

kallaak pl. *-iin* operator of a raft, raftsman.

[1]*k-l-l*

kall (*i u kall*) to be or become tired, fatigued, weary, exhausted. *ð̣alleet atwassal bii ḥatta kalleet.* I kept pleading with him until I was exhausted.

kulla pl. *-aat, kulal* mosquito net.

kalal exhaustion, extreme fatigue.

ʔikliil pl. *ʔakaaliil* wreath, garland.

[2]*k-l-l*

kull **1.** whole, entire, all. *kullna raḥ-inruuḥ.* We're all going. *biqaw ihnaak kull il-yoom.* They stayed there all day. *kull it-talaamiið sawwaw iḍraab.* All the students went on strike. *ʔaani š-b-ʔiidi ɛaleek? huwwa l-kull bil-kull.* What have I got to do for you? He's the one person with authority. **2.** /followed by indefinite noun/ every. *kull tilmiið laazim yiḥð̣ar.* Every student has to be present. *kull waaḥid yuɛruf haaða.* Everyone knows that. *kull šii ṣaar ɛal-maraam.* Everything went well. *kull beeð̣a b-ɛašr ifluus.* The eggs are 10 fils each. || *yaɛni kull yoom inɛiid w-nuṣqul?* You mean we have to go through this day in and day out? *ɛala kull ḥaal, ma-raḥ-nijtimiɛ ʔila ʔan yiji.* At any rate, we're not going to meet until he comes. **3.** (*l-kull*) all of them, every one, everyone. *xabbur il-kull.* Tell everyone. *l-kull inð̣aaf; bass hal-maaɛuun waṣix šwayya.* They're all clean; just this dish is a bit dirty. **4.** /with negative particle/ any, a single, the least. *ma-aɛruf kull šii ɛanna.* I don't know anything about it. *ma-ysawwi kull šii bid-daaʔira.* He doesn't do a single thing in the office. *ma-ʔilak kull filis ɛalayya.* I don't owe you a single penny.

kullši (= *kull šii*) everything.

kull-ma **1.** everything that, all that, whatever. *l-ḥaraami ʔaxað kull-ma ɛindi.* The thief took everything I had. *huwwa ywaafiq kull-ma ʔasawwi.* He agrees to whatever I do. **2.** whenever. *kull-ma axaabra, t-talafoon mašġuul.* Whenever I call him, the phone's busy.

kull-man **1.** everyone who, whoever. *kull-man yištuġul ib-had-daaʔira laazim yjiib šahaada ṣiḥḥiyya.* Everyone who works in this office must bring a health certificate. **2.** everyone. *kull-man yaaxuð ḥaqqa.* Everyone will get his share.

*kulli** entire, complete, overall, comprehensive, complete. *xusuuf kulli* total eclipse. *majmuuɛ kulli* total, sum total.

kullin: ɛala kullin anyway, anyhow, at any rate. *ɛala kullin, ʔariidak tiḥči wiyyaa w-tinsa l-mawð̣uuɛ.* At any rate, I want you to talk to him, and forget the matter.

kulliyya **1.** all, whole, entirety. *kulliyyathum maataw.* All of them died. *kulliitna raḥ-inruuḥ wiyyaak.* All of us will go with you. || *nikar maɛrifti bil-kulliyya.* He denied knowing me entirely. **2.** (pl. *-aat*) college, school (of a university).

kullat- /plus pronominal suffix/ all of. *kullatna* all of us. *kullathum* all of them.

[3]*k-l-l*

kalla pl. *-aat, klaal* **1.** head. **2.** sugar loaf, loaf of sugar.

kallači pl. *-iyya* **1.** seller of sheep heads

and lights. **2.** person who frequents the red-light district.

kallačiyya **1.** former neighborhood in Baghdad where a red-light district was maintained. **2.** (by extension) any red-light district.

k-l-l-š

kulliš (invar.) **1.** very, extremely, highly. *mas?ala kulliš muhimma* a very important question. *has-sayyaara kulliš ġaalya.* This car is very expensive. **2.** very much. *?aɛibbha kulliš.* I like her very much. *l-filim ɛijabni kulliš.* I liked the film very much. *la-tsawwi nafsak kulliš ma-tuɛruf.* Don't make as though you don't know at all. *ɛindi ?amal kulliš yiji baačir.* I have high hopes he'll come tomorrow. *kulliš! mayyit ɛaleeha!* Very much so! He's wild about her!

[1]*k-l-m*

kallam to talk to, speak with. *kallamta biiha w-?aɛtiqid raɛ-yiqbal.* I talked to him about it and I think he will agree.

tkallam to talk, speak. *la-titkallam. xalli l-muɛallim ydarris.* Don't talk. Let the teacher teach.

kalima pl. *-aat* **1.** word. **2.** speech, address.

kalaam **1.** talking, speaking. *kalaam faariġ* idle talk, prattle, nonsense. **2.** words, word, statement, remark. *?iδa tismaɛ kalaam ?abuuk, titwaffaq.* If you listen to what your father says, you will do well. **3.** promise, word, assurance. *nṭaani kalaam bukra ysawwii-li-yyaaha.* He gave me his word he would do it for me tomorrow.

mukaalama pl. *-aat* conversation (especially, on the telephone).

[2]*k-l-m*

kalam kohlrabi(?).

k-l-n

kullin: ɛala kullin see under *k-l-l.*

k-l-y-č

kleeča (coll.) a cookie-like pastry.

kleečaaya pl. *-aat* un. n. of *kleeča.*

k-m

kam = *čam* which see under *č-m.*

k-m-b-r

kumbaar bast, a plant fiber used for making rugs.

k-m-p-y-a-l

kumpiyaala pl. *-aat* promissory note, IOU.

k-m-x

kumax (*u kamux*) to cover with a cloth. *?ukmux iṭ-ṭamaaṭa l-xaδra ɛatta tṣiir ɛamra.* Cover the green tomatoes with a cloth, so they'll turn red.

kammax = *kumax. nazzil ɛarakat iṭ-ṭabbaax w-kammux ij-jidir.* Turn down the stove and cover up the pot with a cloth.

kmaax pl. *-aat* important person, V.I.P., big shot.

k-m-d

kammaada pl. *-aat* compress, pack.

k-m-r

kumar (*u kamur*) to cover. *kumar iṭ-ṭamaaṭa ɛatta tilɛag.* He covered up the tomatoes so they'd ripen.

k-m-š

kumaš (*u kamiš*) **1.** to seize, grasp, grip, clutch. *?ukmuš raas il-ɛabil!* Grab the end of the rope. *kumaš ?iidi w-ma-xallaani ?aδurba.* He grabbed my hand and wouldn't let me hit him. *kumša; baag jizdaani!* Grab him; he stole my wallet! *j-jaahil da-yurkuδ. ruuɛ ukumša.* The baby's running off. Go catch him. *?ukmuš-li mukaan yammak bis-siinama.* Save me a seat next to you in the movies. || *galbi kumašmi.* I got a pain in the chest. *kumašni damaar ib-rijli.* I got a cramp in my leg. **2.** to catch, take hold, take root. *j-jidri maali kumaš.* My smallpox vaccination took. *ybayyin šitl il-warid kumaš.* Looks like the rose bush has taken hold. **3.** to hold, hold back. *la-tukmušni. xalli aruuɛ aɛallma.* Don't hold me. I'll show him. *?ukmuš ?iidak! fluusak raɛ-tixlaṣ.* Hold on! Your money's going to run out. **4.** to contain, hold. *haṣ-ṣanduug ma-yukmuš kull hal-ġaraaδ.* This trunk won't hold all these things.

kammaš to catch, collect, round up. *j-jihaal da-ykammšuun il-ġanam, yɛuṭ-ṭuuha bil-loori.* The boys are catching the sheep and putting them on the truck. *š-šurṭa da-tkammuš kull il-mutaδaahiriin.* The police are picking up all the demonstrators.

nkumaš **1.** to be caught, be seized. *nkumaš gabul-ma yiṭlaɛ imnil-binaaya.* He was caught before he left the building. || *galbi yinkumuš ib-hal-makaan.* I feel cooped up in this place. **2.** to shrink. *hal-uqmaaš yinkimiš min idġisla.* This material shrinks when you wash it.

kamša pl. *-aat* **1.** grasp, grip. **2.** handful.

k-m-ɛ

kamɛa pl. *-aat* sip, taste.

k-m-k-š

kamkaš to grope, feel one's way. *ybayyin ma-da-yšuuf biδ-δalma; šuufa da-ykamkiš.*

Apparently he can't see in the dark; look at him groping about.

tkamkaš = *kamkaš*. *ðall mudda yitkamkaš bið-ðulma ʕatta liga l-baab.* He kept groping in the dark until he found the door.

k-m-l

kimal (*a kamil*) to be finished, done, completed, accomplished. *l-beet raʕ-yikmal baʕad šahar.* The house will be completed in a month. *kull il-ġaraað ir-riditha kimlat.* All the things you wanted are ready. || *ʕali jaa; kimlat is-sibʕa.* Ali is here; it's all set.

kammal to complete, finish, finish up. *kammil haj-jumal ib-kalimaat min ʕindak.* Complete these sentences in your own words. *raʕ-ykammil diraasta b-ʔuruppa.* He will complete his studies in Europe. *kammil šuġlak w-taʕaal.* Finish your work and come on.

tkammal to be completed, finished. *halbeet ma-yitkammal ib-šahar.* This house can't be completed in a month.

kamaal perfection. *ʔalla mawṣuuf bilkamaal.* God is described as perfection.

*kamaali** 1. luxury, luxurious. *ʔašyaaʔ kamaaliyya* luxury items. 2. (pl. only) *kamaaliyyaat* luxuries.

kmaal pl. *-iyya* incomplete, obligated to take a make-up examination. *mtiʕaan l-ikmaal* make-up exam. *ṭilaʕ ikmaal birriyaaðiyyaat.* He ended up having to take a make-up exam in mathematics.

kaamil complete, full. *ʔiða darzan iliqlaam ma-kaamil ma-ʔaaxða.* If the dozen of pencils isn't complete, I won't take them. 2. whole, entire. *staʕmilaw fawj kaamil bil-maʕraka.* They used an entire regiment in the fight. || *b-kaamla* in its entirety. *nisfaw il-madiina b-kaamilha.* They blew up the city completely. *l-qarya b-kaamilha staqbilata.* The whole village received him.

mukammal (invar.) 1. finished, completed. *beet mukammal* a complete house. *muṭbax mukammal* a well-equipped kitchen. 2. perfect, excellent, fine. *saayiq mukammal* an excellent driver. *ṭabbaaxa mukammal* a fine cook. *ʔingiliizi mukammal* perfect English. *ʔibnak ʔadabsizz bass ʔibna mkammal.* Your son has no manners but his son is faultless.

[1]*k-m-m*

kammiyya pl. *-aat* amount, quantity.

[2]*k-m-m*

kammaama pl. *-aat* 1. muzzle. 2. face cover, surgical gauze mask. 3. gas mask.

k-m-n

kammuun cumin, cumin seed.

kamiin 1. ambush. 2. trap. *š-šurṭa nuṣbat-la kamiin.* The police set a trap for him.

k-m-n-j-a

kamanja pl. *-aat* violin, fiddle.

k-n-a-r-y

kanaari canary.

k-n-t-w-r

kantoor pl. *-aat* wardrobe, moveable clothes closet.

k-n-d

kunda pl. *-aat, kunad.* buttocks, bottom.

k-n-z

kinaz (*i kaniz*) to pile up, amass, hoard (money). *da-yiknuz ifluus. ṣaar milyooneer.* He's piling up money. He became a millionaire.

kanz pl. *kunuuz* treasure (especially buried treasure).

k-n-s

kinas (*u kanis*) to sweep. *kinsat il-beet kulla.* She swept the whole house.

nkinas to be swept. *l-baarʕa nkinsat il-gubba. šib-saaʕ wuṣṣaxitha!* The room was swept yesterday. You certainly got it dirty fast!

kannaas pl. *-iin, knaaniis* sweeper, streetsweeper.

kaniisa, kiniisa pl. *kanaayis* church. *raʕ-itruuʕ lil-kaniisa hal-ʔaʕʕad?* Are you going to church this Sunday?

kaanuus pl. *kwaaniis* = *kannaas.*

muknaasa pl. *-aat, mukaaniis* broom. *hal-muknaasa l-ʕatiiga ma-tnaððuf zeen.* This old broom doesn't clean well.

makinsa pl. *mkaanis* = *muknaasa.*

k-n-ġ-r

kanġar and *ʕaywaan il-kanġar* kangaroo.

k-n-k-r-y

kankari, kunkriit concrete.

k-n-y-n

kiniin quinine.

k-h-r-b

kahrab to shock, give a shock. *hal-paanka tkahrubak ʔiða tilʕab biiha.* This fan will give you a shock if you play with it.

tkahrab to get a shock, be given a shock. *tkahrab w-maat.* He got electrocuted.

kahrab 1. amber. 2. made of amber, amber. *sibʕa kahrab* amber worry beads.

kahrabaaʔ electricity. *raʕ-yijurruu-nna kahrabaaʔ il-yoom.* They're going to bring in our electricity today. *ˀabu l-kahrabaaˀ* electrician.

*kahrabaaˀi** 1. electric, electrical. *ˀuuti kahrabaaˀi* an electric iron. 2. electrician.

k-h-l

kahal pl. *kuhuul* 1. middle-aged. 2. middle-aged person. 3. very old, aged. 4. aged person.

k-h-n

tkahhan to predict, foretell, prophesy. *la-taaxuδ kalaama raas. huwwa da-yitkahhan.* Don't take what he says seriously. He's just guessing.

kaahin pl. *kahana* priest, religious leader.

k-w-b

kuub pl. *kwaab* cup.

k-w-p̣

kuup̣a hearts (suit in cards).

k-w-x

kawwax 1. to be or become bent over, stooped, round-shouldered. *jiddi kawwax ib-ˀaaxir ˀawaama.* My grandfather became stooped toward the end of his life. 2. to be worn out, be run down. *kawwax imnil-kubur.* He's run-down from age. *min ṣaar ʕumra ˀarbaʕiin sana, kawwax.* By the time he was forty years old, he was all run down.

kuux pl. *kwaax, kwaaxa* hut, shack.

k-w-d

kaad: bil-kaad hardly, scarcely, not quite. *raatba bil-kaad yikfii.* His salary is hardly enough for him.

k-w-d-a

kooda a tax on livestock, levied at the markets.

k-w-r

kuura pl. *kuwar* 1. forge. 2. kiln, furnace. *kuurat ṭaabuug* brick kiln. *kuurat nuura* lime kiln. || *kuurat zanaabiir* wasp nest.

mkawwar: majmuuʕa mkawwar ṣaar ʕiddna ʕišriin diinaar. All together we've gotten twenty dinars.

k-w-r-s-y

koorsee pl. *-eyaat* corset.

k-w-r-n-y-š

koorniiš pl. *-aat* corniche, road along a river or sea.

k-w-z

kuuz pl. *kwaaz, kwaaza.* clay urn for storing water.

k-w-s

kuus thin, sparse (beard). *liʕiita kuusa.* His beard grows only on his chin.

k-w-s-j

koosaj pl. *kawaasij, kwaasij* shark.

k-w-s-t-m

koostim pl. *-aat* blouse.

k-w-f

l-kuufa Kufa (city in Iraq).

*kuufi** Kufic, Kufi. *kitaaba kuufiyya* Kufic script, Kufic calligraphy.

k-w-k

kawwak 1. to baste, baste together. *l-xayyaaṭ iykawwuk is-sitra gabuḷ-ma yxayyiṭha.* The tailor bastes the jacket together before he sews it. 2. to wind, wind up. *wugfat is-saaʕa. kawwukha.* The watch stopped. Wind it.

kwaaka basting, long stitches.

kuuk spring mechanism, spring drive. *sayyaart ij-jaahil tištuġuḷ ib-kuuk.* The child's car runs by being wound up.

takwiik winding. *burġi takwiik* winding stem. *l-laʕʕaaba tištuġuḷ bit-takwiik.* The toy is spring driven. The toy winds up.

k-w-k-b

kawkab pl. *kawaakib* star. *kawkab siinamaaˀi* movie star. *kawkab sayyaar* planet.

kawkaba pl. *-aat* squadron (mounted police, cavalry, armor).

k-w-k-t-y-l

kookteel cocktail. *ʕaflat kookteel* cocktail party.

k-w-l

kaawli pl. *-iyya, kaawaliyya.* gypsy.

k-w-l-y-r-a

kooleera cholera.

k-w-l-y-s

kuuliis pl. *kawaaliis* coulisse, opening at the side of a stage.

k-w-m

kawwam to heap, pile up, stack up. *kawwam il-ġaraaδ kullha b-nuṣṣ il-ġurfa.* He piled all the things in the center of the room. || *kawwama b-books waaʕid.* He knocked him flat with one punch.

tkawwam to pile up, pile on. *tkawwumaw ʕalee miθil iδ-δibbaan.* They piled on it like flies.

koom pl. *kuwam* heap, pile. *bil-koom* in quantity, in large quantities, wholesale. *l-purtaqaal mawjuud bil-koom il-yoom bis-suug.* There are plenty of oranges at the market today. *l-muʕallim yinṭi darajaat ʕaalya bil-koom.* The teacher gives out good grades left and right. *ybiiʕ bil-koom.* He sells wholesale.

kooma, kuuma pl. *-aat, ˀakwaam* heap, pile, stack.

k-w-n

kaan, čaan (ykuun koon) 1. to be. *l-wafid raʕ-yikuun hinaa baačir.* The delegation will be here tomorrow. *l-baarḥa činit mariiḏ bass il-yoom išwayya ʔaḥsan.* Yesterday I was sick but today I'm a bit better. *ʔadzawwaja š-ma ykuun.* I'll marry him whatever he is. *čaan ʔaku hwaaya naas bil-ḥafla.* There were a lot of people at the party. *čaan ʕindi diinaar waaḥid bass.* I had only one dinar. **2.** (as an auxiliary verb:) **a.** in perfect tense with following imperfect verb, denotes past progressive tense. *činit da-albas qundarti min dagg it-talafoon.* I was putting on my shoes when the phone rang. *wugʕat min čaanat da-tirkab il-paaṣ.* She fell as she was getting on the bus. *čaan da-yaakul min wuṣalna.* He was eating when we arrived. *manaaḏra l-ʕatiiga čaanat da-tsabbib-la wujaʕ raas.* His old glasses were causing him headaches. *čaan ydal-ġum kull-ma yšuufni ʔaṭlaʕ.* He would frown every time he saw me go out. *ma-čaan ysidd iθ-θillaaja baʕad-ma yṭalliʕ minha šii.* He wouldn't close the refrigerator after he took something out of it. *činit adugg kamanja min činit iṣġayyir.* I used to play the violin when I was small. *čaan yḥuṭṭ ihwaaya filfil bil-ʔakil.* He used to put a lot of pepper in the food. *čaanat tirsim zeen.* She used to draw well. **b.** in perfect tense with following active participle, denotes past perfect tense. *lamma wuṣalna lis-siinama, il-filim čaan baadi.* When we got to the theater, the film had started. *čaan baaqii-la yoom yṣiir duktoor.* There was one day remaining for him to become a doctor. *čaanaw imqašmuriini mudda ṭwiila.* They had been making fun of me for a long time. *čaan ḥaaṭṭ il-ifluus ib-jeeba.* He had put the money in his pocket. **c.** (*čaan,* invar., with following verb as result statement of an implied or stated conditional, approx.:) would have, could have, should have. *tidri š-čaan ṣaar loo gaayil-la?* Do you know what would have happened if I'd told him? *loo nkisrat is-sayyaara, š-čaan sawweet?* If the car had broken down, what would you have done? *loo mzayyid diinaar baʕad, čaan biʕit-la s-sayyaara.* If he'd gone up another dinar, I'd have sold him the car. *xoo, čaan adaaynak ʔiḏa čaan ʕindi fluus.* Well, I'd make you a loan if I had any money. *čaan ḏaag il-ʔakil bass maḥḥad ṭilab minna.* He would have tasted the food but no one asked him. *min sabbič, čaan ṣiḥḥti ʕalee š-šurṭi.* When he insulted you, you should have yelled for the policeman.

¶*ykuun* supposedly, presumably, it seems that. *ykuun ʔiḏa yiji l-ʔamriika, yidrus ṭibb.* Supposedly if he comes to America, he will study medicine. *ykuun iṭ-ṭayyaara tooṣal is-saaʕa sitta.* We think the plane will arrive at six o'clock. *ykuun raajʕa lil-baṣra.* She has presumably gone back to Basra. (sometimes expressing hope by the speaker) *ykuun itḥaṣṣil il-waḏiifa.* I hope she gets the job. *ykuun ʕaad yiji w-yaaxuḏ ʔibna!* I sure hope he comes and gets his son! *la-ykuun* (with following imperfect) expresses a strong, negative command, approx., don't let it ever happen that . . .! *la-ykuun tiji l-baġdaad w-ma-tittiṣil biyya.* Don't you come to Baghdad and fail to get in touch with me. *la-ykuun itruuḥuun w-ma-dgulluu-li!* Don't you go and not tell me!

kawwan to produce, create, bring into being, form. *haaḏa kawwan-la ʕiṣaaba.* He formed a gang. *ʔiḏa tibqa muddat šahar, tigdar itkawwin-lak ʔaṣdiqaaʔ.* If you stay a month, you can make yourself some friends.

tkawwan to be formed. *l-muṭar yitkawwan imnil-ġeem.* Rain is formed from clouds.

tkaawan to engage in argument, dispute, controversy. *luweeš titkaawan wiyya j-jiiraan ʕala ṭuul?* Why do you continually fight with the neighbors?

l-kawn, l-koon the world, the universe. *ma-aku miθla bil-kawn.* There's none like it in the world.

l-yakuun the total. *j-jamiʕ il-yakuun* the sum total.

makaan, mukaan pl. *-aat, ʔamaakin, ʔamkina* **1.** place, site, spot, location. *mukaan il-ḥaadiθ* scene of the incident. *b-kull mukaan* everywhere. **2.** place, seat. *twaxxar! hal-mukaan maali.* Move out of the way! This seat is mine. *ġayyir mukaanak. iš-šamis jatti.* Change your seat. The sun has come around. **3.** room, space. *ma-ʔilak mukaan bis-sayyaara.* There's no room for you in the car. *ʔiḏa ʔaku makaan bil-ġurfa, xalli l-ʔaθaaθ bii.* If there is space in the room, put the furniture in it. **4.** place, position, stead. *minu raḥ-yiḥtall makaana ʔiḏa nuqloo?* Who will fill his position if they transfer him? *loo ʔaani b-mukaanak, čaan sawweetha.* If I were in your place, I would have done it. *loo txalli nafsak ib-mukaani, čaan ɛirafit išloon hal-muškila ṣaɛba.* If you put yourself in my place, you would know how difficult this problem is.

makaana pl. *-aat* position, standing, rank, influence, authority. *hal-waziir, makaanta bil-balad maɛruufa.* This minister's standing in the country is well-known. *l-luġa l-ingiliiziyya ʔilha makaanatha.* The English language has considerable importance.

k-w-n-y

kuunya pl. *-aat* **1.** (carpenter's) square. **2.** triangle (drafting).

k-w-y

kuwa (*i kawi*) **1.** to iron, press. *minu raɛ-yikwi qamiiṣak?* Who will press your shirt? **2.** to curl (with a curling iron). *tukwi šaɛarha.* She curls her hair.

makwi pl. *makaawi* pressing shop, cleaner's.

k-w-y-t

l-ikweet Kuwait.

k-w-y-l

kooyil pl. *kooylaat* coil (auto.).

k-y-t

keet: keet w-keet such and such. *gaal ɛanna keet w-keet.* He said such and such about him.

k-y-s

kayyas, kiis, etc. = *čayyas, čiis,* etc. which see under *č-y-s.*

k-y-f

kayyaf **1.** to fit, modify, adjust, adapt. *tigdar itkayyif hal-quṣṣa ɛasab-ma triid.* You can adapt the story however you wish. **2.** to condition. *štireena jihaaz iykayyif il-hawa.* We bought an appliance that conditions the air. **3.** to be amused, pleased, delighted. *j-jaahil kayyaf bil-hadiyya.* The The child was pleased with the gift. **4.** /with *l-*/ to enjoy, take pleasure in. *huwwa ykayyif il-hiiči ɛači.* He enjoys such talk.

tkayyaf to adapt oneself, adjust oneself. *ʔakθar il-ɛaywaanaat titkayyaf ɛasb il-muɛiiṭ.* Most animals adapt themselves according to the environment.

keef **1.** mood, humor, state of mind, frame of mind. *šloon keefak il-yoom?* How do you feel today? **2.** well-being, good humor, high spirits, pleasure, delight. *maa-la keef il-yoom.* He's not feeling well today. *min ɛaṣṣal il-jaaʔiza, ṭaar imnil-keef.* When he won the prize, he jumped with joy. **3.** discretion, option, will. *kull šii ṣaar ɛala keefak.* Everything went the way you wanted it. *ʔiδa ma-triid itruuɛ wiyyaaya, keefak.* If you don't want to go with me, that's up to you. *b-keefak. ʔiδa triid itruuɛ, ʔaani ʔaji wiyyaak.* As you wish. If you want to go, I'll come with you. *suuq ɛala keefak. tigdar itxaḷḷiṣ.* Drive slowly. You can make it. *δallaw yitɛaar-kuun ɛašir daqaayiq w-baɛdeen itfaaki-kaw min keefhum.* They kept on fighting for ten minutes and finally separated by themselves. **4.** (pl. *-aat*) party, celebration. *l-baarɛa čaan ɛiddhum keef.* Yesterday they had a party with singing and dancing.

*keefi** arbitrary. *ɛamal keefi* an arbitrary action. *faṣil keefi* an arbitrary dismissal.

kayfiyya pl. *-aat* manner, mode, fashion.

keefči pl. *-iyya,* good-time Charlie, continuous party goer, party boy.

mukayyifa pl. *-aat* air conditioner.

k-y-k

keek (coll.) cake(s).

keeka pl. *-aat* un. n. of *keek.*

k-y-l

kaal, keela, etc., = *čaal, čeela,* etc., which see under *č-y-l.*

k-y-l-m-t-r

kiilumatir pl. *-aat* **1.** kilometer. **2.** speedometer.

k-y-l-w

keelu pl. *-uwaat* **1.** kilo, kilogram. **2.** (and *keelu kahrabaaʔ*) kilowatt.

kiilu pl. *-uwaat* = *keelu* **1.**

k-y-l-w-n

keeluun pl. *-aat* **1.** large key. **2.** (door) lock.

k-y-m-w-s

keemuus gastric juice.

k-y-m-y-ʔ

kiimya, kiimyaaʔ **1.** chemistry. **2.** alchemy. || *hat-tijaara kiimya.* This trade is a gold mine.

*kiimyaaʔi**, *kiimyaawi** **1.** chemical. *ṣinaaɛa kiimyaaʔiyya* chemical industry. **2.** chemist.

L

[1]*l*

l- (definite article) **the.**

[2]*l*

l- /followed by definite noun/, *ʔil-* /with pronoun suffix/, *-l-* /with pronoun suffix after a verb/ **1.** for. *ʔiδa tšuuf ɛali, gul-la ʔila maktuub ɛindi.* If you see Ali, tell him I've got a letter for him. *ʔilak ɛindi xams idnaaniir.* I owe you five dinars. *ʔariidha n-nafsi.* I want it for myself. *maa-la ʔay mukaan bis-sayyaara.* There's no room for him in the car. *ma-ʔilak ʔay ɛaqq tistaɛmil ġurufti.* You've got no right to use my room. *laazim ʔila sabab.* There must be a reason for it. *ʔaku ɛiddat ʔasbaab il-ṣiquuṭa.* There are many reasons for his failure. *ʔila yoomeen zaɛlaan.* He's been mad two days. *ɛaδδarta lil-marra θ-θaanya w-ma-aɛtiqid yfiid.* I warned him for the second time but I don't think it did any good. **2.** for, to the benefit of, on behalf of, in favor of. *ruuɛ ištiki w-aani ʔašhad-lak.* Go file a complaint and I'll testify for you. *sawweet-ilk-iyyaaha li-ʔannak ṣadiiqi.* I did it for you because you're my friend. *nɛaaz il-jaanib il-ɛukuuma.* He sided with the government. **3.** for, for the purpose of. *hal-ṃayy ma-yiṣlaɛ liš-šurub.* This water isn't suitable for drinking. *has-sayyaara zeena lis-sibaaq.* This car is good for racing. **4.** to (of the dative). *gul-li š-itriid.* Tell me what you want. *jibitha ʔilak.* I brought it to you. *rušš-la miliɛ lil-ʔakil.* Add salt to the food. *tbarraɛ ib-diinaar lil-madrasa.* He donated a dinar to the school. *ma-masmuuɛ-ilhum yaaxδuun il-kutub.* They're not permitted to take the books. *ʔamri l-ʔaḷḷa* My destiny is up to God. **5.** because of, due to, owing to. *l-kuθrat il-muṭar ib-hal-manṭaqa, ma-nigdar nizraɛ ɛunṭa.* Due to the large amount of rain in this area, we can't grow wheat. *ma-sawwoo-la l-ɛamaliyya l-kubur sinna.* They didn't perform the operation on him because of his age. **6.** paraphrases the genitive. *haš-šaadi ma-ʔila δeel.* This monkey has no tail. *hal-marra ʔilak. marrt iθ-θaanya ma-asaamɛak.* This time is gratis. Next time I won't pardon you. **7.** (var. of *ʔila,* which see under *ʔ-l-a*) to, toward (denoting direction or destination). *raɛ-aruuɛ lil-beet.* I'm going to the house. *š-wakit raɛ-tirjaɛ il-baġdaad?* When will you return to Baghdad? **9.** to, up to, until. *lil-yoom ma-aɛruf is-sabab.* To this day I don't know the reason. *ma-šifta li-hassa.* I haven't seen him up to now. *biqeena hnaak il-nuṣṣ il-leel.* We stayed there until midnight. *la-tbaaliġ il-had-daraja.* Don't exaggerate to such an extent. **10.** introduces a post-stated object (see grammar). *ma-yɛibba l-ɛali.* He doesn't like Ali. *ṣaḷḷaɛitha lis-sayyaara.* I've repaired the car. **11.** supports the otherwise unaccented accusative suffix for the purpose of emphasis. *raadni ʔili* or *raadni ʔiliyya.* He wanted *me.* *šiftak ʔilak bil-maɛaṭṭa, muu ʔaxuuk.* I saw you in the station, not your brother.

li-ʔan because. *rajjaɛ ir-raadyo li-ʔan ma-čaan yištuġuḷ.* He returned the radio because it wasn't working.

l-a

laa **1.** no. *laa. ma-ariid ʔaruuɛ.* No. I don't want to go. **2.** there is not, there is no. *laa ʔillaah ʔilla ʔallaa.* There is no god but God. *laa budd (min) . . .* there is no escape from . . ., it is inevitable that . . . . *laa budd yismaɛ il-xabar.* He's bound to hear the news. *laa baʔas* there is no objection, there's nothing wrong. *has-sayyaara laa baʔas biiha, walaw ɛatiiga.* There's nothing wrong with this car, even though it's old. *laa baʔas tiji wyaana.* There's no objection to your coming with us. *laa šakk* there is no doubt, undoubtedly. *laa šakk tuɛruf iš-da-ysawwi.* You undoubtedly know what he's up to. || *laa . . . w-laa . . .* neither . . . nor. . . . *ma-yumluk—laa sayyaara w-laa beet.* He owns nothing—neither a car nor a house. *la-ɛiča wala δiɛak.* He neither spoke nor laughed. **3.** /with shortened vowel and following verb, expressing negative imperative/ don't, don't let it happen that. *la-truuɛ.* Don't go. *la-ykuun itruuɛ w-ma-dgul-li.* You mustn't go and not tell me. *la-yhimmak. ʔaani ɛindak.* Don't let it bother you. I'm with you. *la-yqašmurak, tara ma-ɛinda fluus.* Don't let him fool you, because he doesn't have any money.

*laa-ʔubaali** indifferent.

laa diini irreligious, unreligious, without religion.

laa-silki wireless, radio.

bi-laa = *bila,* which see under *b-l-a.*

wa-laa, w-laa = *wala* **1**, which see under *w-l-a.*

l-a-x

laax var. of *l-ˀaaxar,* which see under *ˀ-x-r.*

l-a-s-t-y-k

laastiik **1.** elastic. **2.** rubber. **3.** (pl. *-aat*) rubber band. **4.** garter. **5.** condom.

l-ˀ-k

malak see under *m-l-k.*

l-a-k-n

laakin but, however. *ˀaani šifta l-axuuk laakin ma-gut-la ɛaleeha.* I saw your brother but I didn't tell him about it. *triid idjaawub laakinnak ma-tuɛruf.* You want to answer but you don't know. *laakin ˀiδa jeet w-ma-lgeetni, xalli xabar ɛind axuuya.* However, if you come and don't find me, leave word with my brother.

l-a-l-n-g-y

laalangi (coll.) tangerine(s).

laalangiyya pl. *-aat* un.n. of *laalangi.*

l-ˀ-m

laaˀam to agree with, be good for, suit. *jaww il-baṣra ma-ylaaˀim ṣiɛɛta.* The weather of Basra doesn't agree with his health.

tlaaˀam **1.** to agree, fit in, go well. *loon il-parda ma-yitlaaˀam wiyya loon il-ɛiiṭaan.* The color of the curtain doesn't go well with the color of the walls. **2.** to get along well, fit in. *ṭallaɛa mniṣ-ṣaff liˀan ma-yitlaaˀam wiyya ṭ-ṭullaab.* He expelled him from the class because he doesn't fit in with the students.

ltiˀam to heal, mend. *j-jariɛ raɛ-yiltiˀim xilaal isbuuɛ.* The wound will heal within a week.

luˀum meanness, wickedness, evil, ignobility.

laˀiim pl. *-iin, luˀamaaˀ* **1.** mean, ignoble, evil, wicked, depraved. **2.** mean, evil person.

laˀaama meanness, ignobility, wickedness, evil.

ˀalˀam more or most ignoble, wicked, etc.

mulaaˀim appropriate, fitting, suitable, proper, favorable. *hal-furṣa mulaaˀima il-mufaataɛta bil-mawδuuɛ.* This is a favorable occasion for approaching him about the matter.

l-ˀ-n

li-ˀan, see under *l-.* See also *ˀan* under *ˀ-n.*

l-b-b

libb (coll.) **1.** core, kernel, meat (of nuts, fruit, etc.). *libb jooz* nut meats. *libb iġraaš* coconut. **2.** prime, best part. *ˀaɛibb ˀibin ˀibni li-ˀan huwwa libb il-libb.* I love my grandson because he's the best of the best.

libba pl. *-aat* un. n. of *libb.*

labba pl. *-aat* kick, blow with the foot. *δurab iṭ-ṭooba labba.* He gave the ball a kick.

see also *l-b-l-b.*

l-b-s

libas (*a libis*) **1.** to put on, to get dressed, clothe oneself. *ˀilbas ihduumak. ṣaar il-wakit.* Put on your clothes. It's time. *yigdar yilbas ib-xamis daqaayiq.* He can dress in five minutes. **2.** to wear, be dressed in. *ɛatta biṣ-ṣeef yilbas qappuuṭ.* Even in the summer he wears an overcoat. || *la-ddiir-la baal; ˀilibsa b-rijlak.* Don't pay him any attention; ignore him.

labbas **1.** to clothe, dress, garb. *labbsi j-jaahil la-yibrad.* Dress the child so he doesn't get cold. **2.** to put on, slip on. *ṣ-ṣaayiġ labbas il-miɛbas b-iṣibɛi.* The jeweler put the ring on my finger. || *labbasa klaaw.* He pulled the wool over his eyes. He duped him. *diir baalak minna haaδa ylabbis klaawaat.* Watch out for him. He'll con you. **3.** to cover. *leeš ma-tlabbis il-qanafa j-jidiida b-wujih?* Why don't you cover the new sofa with a slip cover? **4.** to cover, coat, plate. *ylabbisuun il-ɛadiid bil-fuδδa.* They plate the iron with silver. *hal-miɛbas mlabbas ib-δahab.* This ring is gold plated. **5.** to have sexual intercourse.

tlaabas to be the same size as, to be able to wear each other's clothes. *ˀaani w-ˀuxti nitlaabas.* My sister and I can wear each other's clothes. *lbasit qaaṭ ˀaxuuya li-ˀan ˀaani wiyyaa nitlaabas.* I wore my brother's suit because we're the same size.

nlibas to be worn. *han-nafnuuf ma-yinlibis bil-leel.* This dress isn't worn at night.

ltibas **1.** to become obscure, dubious, ambiguous, equivocal, confusing. *ltibsat ɛalayya l-ˀumuur.* The events have gotten confusing to me. **2.** to mistake, confuse with someone else. *l-ɛafu, iltibasit biik.* Sorry, I mistook you for someone else.

lbaas pl. *-aat, libsaan* 1. (men's) drawers, underpants. 2. pants, panties.

ltibaas confusion, ambiguity, doubt.

mlabbas 1. covered, coated, plated. 2. chunks of candy, bonbons.

malaabis (pl. only) clothes, clothing.

mitlabbis in the act, redhanded. *š-šurṭa lizmoo mitlabbis.* The police caught him in the act.

miltibis confused, mistaken. *laazim inta miltibis.* You must be mistaken.

l-b-ṭ

lubaṭ (*u labuṭ*) to wiggle, wriggle, thrash about. *has-simač taaza w-baعda yilbuṭ.* These fish are fresh and still wiggling.

l-b-l-b

lablab 1. to extract the core, meat, best part from. *lablib ir-raggiyya w-δibb il-igšuur barra.* Take the meat out of the watermelon and throw the rinds outside. 2. to summarize, condense, prepare an extract, make a summary. *min itruuع itwaajih il-mudiir, lablib-la l-qaδiyya b-iعčaayteen.* When you go to see the director, summarize the matter in two sentences for him. *lablabit-la l-mawδuuع w-inṭeeth-iyyaa.* I prepared a concise summary of the subject and gave it to him. 3. to edit, revise, refine, polish. *l-muعarrir lablab il-maqaal w-nišara.* The editor polished up the article and published it.

lablabi boiled chick peas.

lablabaan pl. *-iyya* 1. smooth talker, convincing speaker. *haaδa ġeer laḅlaḅaan. minu yigdar-la?* He's a real talker. Who can get the better of him? 2. talkative person, chatterbox. *haay ġeer laḅlaḅaan. عaligha ma-yoogaf wala daqiiqa.* She's a real chatterbox. Her mouth doesn't stop for a minute.

l-b-n

liban 1. yoghurt, leban, coagulated sour milk. 2. (pl. *ʔalbaan*) milk product, dairy product. *maعmal ʔalbaan* dairy.

libin (coll.) adobe(s), dried mud brick(s).

libna pl. *-aat* 1. un. n. of *libin*. 2. yoghurt, leban.

labbaan pl. *-a* leban vendor.

lubnaan Lebanon.

*lubnaani** 1. Lebanese, from Lebanon. *lahja lubnaaniyya* a Lebanese accent. 2. a Lebanese.

l-b-w

labwa pl. *-aat* lioness.

l-θ-m

laθθam to cover the lower part of the face. *laθθam ibna min gabbat il-عajja.* He covered his son's face when the dust storm came.

tlaθθam to cover the lower part of one's face. *l-عaraami tlaθθam عatta ma-yinعuruf.* The thief masked himself so he wouldn't be recognized.

liθaam pl. *-aat* 1. veil, covering the lower part of the face. 2. mask.

l-j-j

lajj (*i lajj*) to be insistent, persistent. *ʔuṣbur išwayya. la-tlijj.* Be a little patient. Don't be so insistent. *la-tlijj عalee. xallii عala keefa.* Don't nag him. Leave him alone.

lajuuj pl. *-iin* 1. insistent, pestering, bothersome, intrusive. 2. insistent person.

l-j-m

lijam (*i lajim*) 1. to bridle, put the bridle on. *la-tiljim il-iعṣaan gabuḷ-ma twakkla.* Don't bridle the horse before you feed him. 2. to muzzle, silence. *lijam iš-šurṭi ib-xams-idnaaniir.* He muzzled the cop with five dinars.

lajjam = *lijam.*

nlijam to be muzzled, kept quiet, and, by extension, to remain silent. *š-biik nlijamit? ma-tiعči?* Why are you silent? Can't you speak?

ljaam pl. *-aat* 1. bridle. 2. bit, mouthpiece of a bridle.

l-j-n

lujna pl. *lujaan* committee, board, council.

l-č-m

licam (*i lačim*) to hit, strike. *l-walad mṭahhar. diir baalak la-tličma.* The boy's been circumcised. Be careful not to hit him.

nličam to be hit, struck. *la-tilعab wiyya l-wulid la-truuع tinličim.* Don't play with the boys and you won't get hit.

see also *l-k-m.*

l-ع-ع

laعع (*i lعaaع, laعع*) 1. to persist, be persistent, insist. *ʔiδa tliعع ihwaaya b-ʔakl il-عinjaaṣ, yṣiir عindak ishaal.* If you keep on continually eating prunes, you'll get diarrhea. *la-tliعع. ma-agdar ʔaruuع.* Don't be so persistent. I can't go. 2. /with *عala*/ to pester, harass, keep after. *ʔiδa ma-tliعع عalee, ma-yinṭiik ifluusak.* If you don't keep after him, he won't give you your money.

malaعع a pl. *-aat* harassment, pestering, insisting. *baعad il-malaععa xallaani*

ʔastaḉmil sayyaarta. After a lot of pestering he let me use his car.

l-ḉ-d

laḉḉad = *la-ʔaḉḉad,* which see under *ʔ-ḉ-d.*

l-ḉ-s

liḉas (*a laḉis*) to lick. *l-haayša da-tilḉas raas ḉijilha.* The cow is licking her calf's head.

l-ḉ-ð̣

laaḉað̣ 1. to notice, perceive, observe, be aware of. *laaḉað̣it ḉalee ʔay taġayyur?* Have you noticed any change in him? *da-tlaaḉið̣ šloon da-tiṭṭawwar il-ʔašyaaʔ?* Do you see how things are shaping up? 2. to watch, pay attention to. *laaḉð̣a zeen tara ybuug.* Watch him well because he steals.

laḉð̣a pl. *-aat* moment, instant. *ntið̣irni laḉð̣a.* Wait for me a moment. *b-laḉð̣a* in a moment, instantly.

mulaaḉað̣a pl. *-aat* 1. observation, remark, comment. 2. note, post-script (on a letter).

malḉuuð̣ noticeable, noteworthy, remarkable. *taqaddum malḉuuð̣* noticeable progress.

malḉuuð̣a pl. *-aat* 1. observation, remark, comment. 2. note.

mulaaḉið̣ pl. *-iin* superintendent, supervisor (a rank in the Iraqi civil service below that of director).

l-ḉ-f

lḉaaf pl. *liḉif, liḉfaan* quilt, comforter.

l-ḉ-q

liḉaq (*i ʔilḉaaq*) to attach, connect, join, annex, append. *l-ġurfa mulḉaqa b-hal-qaaḉa.* The room is connected to this hall. *liḉqaw mudiiriyyat is-sikak ib-wuzart il-muwaaṣalaat.* They attached the Directorate of Railroads to the Communications Ministry.

ltiḉaq /with *b-*/ to enter, join, enroll in, become a part of. *ʔakθar xirriijiin hal-kulliyya yiltiḉquun ib-xidmat il-ḉukuuma.* Most of the graduates of this college join the government service.

mulḉaq 1. attached, affixed, annexed, appended. *mulḉaq bil-binaaya* attached to the building. *mulḉaq b-hal-qisim* attached to this section. 2. (pl. *malaaḉiq*) attachment, addition. 3. supplement, extra section. 4. appendix. 5. annex. 6. (pl. *-iin*) attaché.

l-ḉ-g

liḉag (*a laḉig*) 1. to follow, trail after. *fadd rijjaal liḉag binti imnil-madrasa.* Some man followed my daughter from the school. 2. to chase, pursue. *š-šurṭi liḉag il-ḉaraami w-lizama.* The policeman chased the thief and caught him. 3. to ripen, become ripe. *kumar iṭ-ṭamaaṭa ḉatta tilḉag.* He covered the tomatoes so they'd ripen. 4. to become ready. *ʔukul-lak išwayyat liban ḉatta yilḉag il-ʔakil.* Have a little yoghurt until the food gets ready. 5. /with *l-*/ to rush to the aid of. *ʔilḉag-li! raḉ-aġrag.* Come help me! I'm about to drown.

laḉḉag 1. to have time for, have a chance to. *ma-alaḉḉig aruuḉ lis-suug w-arjaḉ ib-saaḉa waḉda.* I don't have time to go to the market and back in one hour. *ma-laḉḉagit ḉatta ʔasallim ḉalee. čaan mistaḉjil.* I didn't even have time to greet him. He was in a hurry. 2. /with *b-*/ to catch up with, overtake. *laḉḉagna biihum yamm il-ḉuduud.* We overtook them near the border. *traffaḉit gabḷa laakin baḉad sana laḉḉag biyya.* I was promoted before him but after a year he caught up with me. || *laḉḉig tara l-ʔakil raḉ-yixlaṣ.* Hurry up or the food will be all gone. 3. /with *b-* or *ḉala*/ to be on time for. *ʔið̣a ʔaaxuð̣ iṭ-ṭiyyaara hassa, ʔalaḉḉig ḉala mawḉid il-ijtimaaḉ.* If I take a plane now, I can be on time for the meeting. *xall-naaxuð̣ taksi tara ma-nlaḉḉig biṭ-ṭiyyaara.* Let's take a taxi or we won't catch the plane. 4. to ready, make ready. *raḉ-alaḉḉig-lak il-qaaṭ bit-tlatt iyyaam.* I'll have the suit ready for you in three days. 5. to ripen, make ripe. *hal-ḉarr raḉ-ylaḉḉig it-tamur.* This heat will ripen the dates. 6. to unbalance, cause to be mentally disturbed. *ð̣allaw yitšaaquun w-iyṣannifuun ḉalee ʔila ʔan laḉḉigoo.* They kept poking fun at him and teasing him until they drove him nutty. 6. /with *l-*/ to hammer, pelt. *laḉḉag-la ð̣arba wara ð̣arba, w-laa-nṭaa furṣa yšiil ʔiida.* He threw blow after blow at him, and didn't give him a chance to raise his fist. *laḉḉag-la b-ʔasʔila ḉatta xarbaṭa.* He pelted him with questions until he got him all confused.

tlaḉḉag /with *l-*/ to rush to the aid of. *čaan maat loo ma-yitlaḉḉiguu-la.* He'd have died if they hadn't rushed to his aid.

nliḉag 1. to be followed, pursued. *ʔaftikir inliḉagna.* I think we've been followed. 2. /with *bii*/ to be overtaken, caught. *haað̣a yirkuð̣ kulliš sariiḉ. ʔabad ma-yinliḉig bii.* He runs very fast. He'd never be caught.

laaƸig 1. ready. *l-ˀakil laaƸig loo baƐad?* Is the food ready yet? 2. ripe. *la-tigṭaƐ il-purtaqaal; baƐda ma-laaƸig.* Don't pick the oranges; they aren't ripe yet. || *Ɛaqla laaƸig.* He's got a screw loose. He's a bit crazy.

l-Ƹ-m

liƸam (*a laƸim*) 1. to mend, patch. *l-fiitarči liƸam ič-čuub.* The mechanic patched the tube. 2. to weld, solder. *rijl il-qarayoola nkisrat. laazim tilƸamha.* The leg on the bed broke. You'll have to weld it. 3. to heal. *j-jariƸ liƸam.* The wound healed.

nliƸam pass. of *liƸam.*

laƸam pl. *luƸuum.* meat, flesh.

laƸam pl. *-aat* a piece of meat.

liƸma pl. *-aat* warp (of fabric). || *txayyaṭ il-qaaṭ w-ma-zaad šii mnil-uqmaaš. ṭilƐat sidaaha b-liƸmatha.* The suit was made and no cloth was left over. It came out right on the nose.

*laƸmi** flesh-colored. *laabsa jwaariib loonha laƸmi.* She's wearing flesh-colored hose.

liƸiim 1. welding material. 2. solder.

malƸam healing ointment, salve.

l-Ƹ-n

laƸƸan to compose music. *minu laƸƸan hal-uġniya?* Who wrote the music for this song?

laƸin pl. *ˀalƸaan* song, tune, melody.

mulaƸƸin pl. *-iin* composer (of music).

l-Ƹ-y

liƸya pl. *liƸaaya, liƸa* beard, whiskers. *ṣadiiqi da-yrabbi liƸya.* My friend is growing a beard.

l-x

lux var. of *l-ˀuxra,* which see under *ˀ-x-r.*

l-x-x

laxxa pl. *-aat* crowd, throng (of people). || *s-suug il-yoom laxxa ma-yinṭabb bii.* The market today is crowded. You can't get in.

l-x-m

laxma var. of *lakma,* which see under *l-k-m.*

l-d-ġ

lidaġ (*a ladiġ*) to sting. *lidaġni l-Ɛagrab.* The scorpion stung me.

ladġa pl. *-aat* sting.

l-δ-δ

laδδ (*i laδδa*) to become delightful, pleasant, enjoyable, delicious. *laδδat-li l-Ɛiiša b-baġdaad wala ˀaṭlaƐ minha.* Life in Baghdad is pleasant for me now and I won't ever leave it.

tlaδδaδ /with *b-*/ to enjoy, relish, savor, take delight in. *j-jaahil yitlaδδaδ ib-ˀakl is-saahuun.* The child enjoys eating peanut brittle.

stilaδδ /with *b-*/ to find delightful, take pleasure in, enjoy. *stilaδδeet kulliš b-hal-ˀakla.* I really enjoyed this meal.

laδδa pl. *-aat* 1. delight, joy, bliss, pleasure. || *hal-ˀakil laδδa.* This food is delicious. *simaƐna ˀaxbaar laδδa.* We heard some delightful news. 2. orgasm, climax.

laδiiδ 1. enjoyable, pleasant. *ˀakl id-doondirma laδiiδ.* Eating ice cream is enjoyable. 2. delicious, delightful. *č-čima laδiiδ.* Truffles are delicious.

ˀalaδδ more or most enjoyable, pleasant, delightful, delicious.

l-z-g

lizag (*a lazig*) 1. to adhere, stick, cling. *haṭ-ṭaabiƐ ma-da-yilzag.* This stamp won't stick. *lizag biyya. ma-farragni wala laƸδa.* He stuck to me. He didn't leave me for a minute. 2. to affix, paste, stick. *ˀilzag iṭ-ṭaabiƐ baƐad-ma tiktib il-Ɛinwaan.* Paste the stamp on after you write the address.

lazzag intensive of *lizag. l-Ɛilič ylazzig bil-ˀiid.* Gum really sticks to the hand. *da-yguṣṣ ṣuwar imnil-majalla w-ylazzigha b-daftar.* He cuts pictures out of the magazine and pastes them in a notebook.

tlazzag to be stuck, pasted. *hal-Ƹaayiṭ ma-yitlazzag Ɛalee šii li-ˀan baƐda mballal.* Nothing can be stuck to this wall because it's still wet.

nlizag to be stuck, pasted. *l-Ƹadiid ma-yinlizig Ɛalee šii.* Nothing can be pasted to iron.

lazig adhering, sticking, clinging.

lazga pl. *-aat* 1. i.n. of *lazig.* || *lizag biyya fadd lazga.* He stuck to me like flypaper. 2. stupe, plaster, poultice.

*lazgi** 1. sloppy, slap-dash. *yuδrub bil-Ɛaali w-šuġla lazgi.* He charges high prices and his work is sloppy. 2. (pl. *-iyyaat*) odd job, piecework. *Ɛaayiš bil-lazgiyyaat.* He's making a living at anything he can find.

l-z-m

lizam (*a lazim*) 1. to catch, seize, grab, get hold of. *bass alizma, ˀaziffa xooš zaffa.* When I get hold of him, I'm going to give him hell. *lizmoo w-huwwa da-yinṭi fluus qalb.* They caught him as he was passing counterfeit money. *lizmoo marrteen w-inhizam.* They caught him twice and he got away. *lizam il-qalam w-gaam yšaṭṭub.* He grabbed the pen and started crossing things out. *j-jinuud lizmaw id-darub. ˀay waaḉid ymurr, yfattišuu.* The soldiers seized the road. Anyone who passes, they search. *lizam xooš qunṭaraat.* He hooked a good contract. *ma-lizmaw ḉalee šii.* They didn't get anything on him. **2.** to befall, set upon, descend upon. *lizmatni l-maṭra.* I got caught in the rain. *bass ṭaarat iṭ-ṭiyyaara, lizmata d-dooxa.* As soon as the plane took off, dizziness overcame him. *kull leela tilzama ṣ-ṣuxuuna.* Every night he gets a fever. **3.** to take effect, take hold. *j-jidri maali ma-lizam.* My smallpox vaccination didn't take. **4.** to hold, hold on to, keep a hold on. *rajaaˀan ilzam kutbi ḉatta ˀalbas sitirti.* Please hold my books so I can put on my coat. *j-jaahil laazim iṭ-ṭeer min rijlee.* The kid's holding the bird by its leg. *ˀiδa nhizam bis-sayyaara, ˀaani ˀil-man ˀalzam?* If he runs off with the car, who can I hold responsible? *tḉaṭṭalna li-ˀan lizamna ḉal-ḉaša.* We were late because he kept us for dinner. *ˀilzam haṭ-ṭariiq tooṣal lij-jisir.* Stay on this road and you'll come to the bridge. || *ˀaani laazim galbi. xaaf itkuun il-ˀasˀila ṣaḉba.* I'm very apprehensive. I'm afraid the questions will be hard. **5.** to hold, cling, adhere. *l-ičbintu ma-yilzam zeen liˀan bii ramuḷ ihwaaya.* The cement won't hold well because there is too much sand in it. *wugaḉ iṭ-ṭaabuug kulla li-ˀan il-ičbintu ma-lizam.* All the bricks fell because the cement didn't hold. **6.** to hold, contain, keep in one place. *haṣ-ṣanduug ma-yilzam kull ġaraaδi.* This trunk won't hold all my things. || *ˀilzam iidak!* Hold it! Stop! That's enough! *ˀilzam iidak. intirsat il-ḉillaaga.* Hold it. The basket is full. *ˀilzam iidak. ˀaku jaahil da-ymurr.* Hold up a minute. There's a child coming by. *lizam n-nafis* to control oneself, exercise restraint. *ˀiδa tilzam nafsak fadd šahar, tigdar itbaṭṭil it-tadxiin.* If you control yourself for a month, you can quit smoking. *lizam iḉsaab* to keep count, maintain an accounting. *ˀaani ˀaqra l-ˀarqaam w-inta ˀilzam iḉsaab.* I'll read the numbers and you keep count. *lizam waqit* to time, keep time. *lizamnaa-la waqit min rikaδ̣.* We kept time for him when he ran. *lizam il-miḉda* to calm, settle the stomach. *ˀiδa nafsak da-tilḉab, išrab čaay. yilzam il-miḉda.* If you're nauseated, drink tea. It settles the stomach. *ma-yilzam.* Never mind. It isn't important. *ma-yilzam, ligeet qalami.* Never mind, I found my pen.

lazzam to cause to take hold of. *baḉad-ma yinṭiik daris bis-siyaaqa, ylazzimak is-sukkaan.* After he gives you a driving lesson, he turns the wheel over to you. || *ˀiδa ma-triida l-hal-ḉaamil, lazzma l-baab.* If you don't want this worker, give him the gate.

laazam to hold onto, cling, adhere to, maintain a hold on. *l-maraδ laazama mudda ṭuwiila.* The sickness stayed with him a long time.

tlaazam to grapple with each other. *tšaatmaw w-itlaazmaw, bass iḉna faakak-naahum.* They exchanged insults and grappled with each other, but we separated them.

nlizam to be held. || *rummaanteen ib-fadd iid ma-tinlizam.* You can't do two things at once (lit., two pomegranates can't be held in one hand).

ltizam **1.** to assume responsibility for, to take on as one's own responsibility or duty. *ltizam yidfaḉ kull-ma ṣirfaw ḉalee.* He took the responsibility for paying all they spent on him. *loo ma-yiltizimni, ma-čaan traffaḉit.* If he hadn't been behind me, I wouldn't have been promoted. **2.** to secure a monopoly on, get control of. *ltizam il-bistaan.* He secured a contract on the orchard.

lazma pl. *-aat* grip, handhold, thing to hold on to. || *šgadd-ma tidjaadal wiyyaa, ma-yinṭiik lazma.* No matter how much you argue with him, he won't give you anything you can get your teeth into.

luzuum, lizuum necessity, exigency, need. *ma-aku luzuum tiji. tigdar itxaabur.* There's no need for you to come. You can call. *ḉind il-luzuum* in case of need, as necessary. *ˀaaxuδ imnil-bang ifluus ḉind il-luzuum.* I take money out of the bank as it is necessary. || *maa-li luzuum bii.* I have no concern with it. It isn't important to me. *š-ma yḉijbak, sawwi; ˀaani maa-li lizuum.* Do whatever you like; It's of no concern to me.

*ˀilzaami** compulsory, required. *t-talḉliim ilzaami bil-ḉiraaq.* Education is compulsory in Iraq.

malzam pl. *malaazim* grip, handhold, place to hold on to.

malzama pl. *malaazim* section, signature of a book (printing).

laazim **1.** necessary, requisite, imperative, required, obligatory. *kull jundi laazim* *ʕalee yiṭiiʕ il-ʔawaamir.* Every soldier is required to obey orders. *laazim itruuḥ wiyyaaya.* You have to go with me. *kull waaḥid laazim yṣalli xamis marraat bil-yoom, bass baʕaðhum ma-yṣalluun.* Everyone is supposed to pray five times a day but some of them don't pray. *ma-laazim itsawwi hiiči šii baʕad.* You shouldn't do that any more. *čaan laazim tisʔala.* You should have asked him. || *ma-laazim.* It's not important. Forget it. Never mind. *ma-laazim. ligeet waaḥid.* Never mind. I found one. *ma-laazim! bass ʔinta ʕindak sayyaara?* Forget it! Do you think you're the only one with a car? **2.** (invar.) it must be that. *laazim taṣliiḥ is-sayyaara kallafak ihwaaya.* Repairing the car must have cost you a lot. *laazim hal-igloob maḥruug. baddla.* This bulb must be burned out. Change it.

¶ *b-laazim* in need of. *ʔaani b-laazim ifluus.* I need money. *maa-la laazim.* It's none of his concern. It doesn't concern him. *maa-lak laazim. l-ʕarka beena w-been marta.* It's none of your business. The fight's between him and his wife.

lawaazim (pl. only) necessities, exigencies, requisites.

malzuum **1.** obligated, under obligation. *ʔaani ma-malzuum ʔantaðrak saaʕteen w-ma-tiji.* I'm not obligated to wait for you two hours when you don't come. *ʔiða ṣaar ʕaleek šii, ʔaani ma-malzuum.* If anything happens to you, I'm not responsible.

mulaazim pl. *-iin* lieutenant. *mulaazim ʔawwal* first lieutenant. *mulaazim θaani* second lieutenant.

l-s-s-a

lissa not yet, still not. *lissa bayyan šii.* Nothing has appeared so far.

l-s-n

lsaan pl. *-aat, ʔalsina* **1.** tongue. *ʔisma ʕala raas ilsaani.* His name is on the tip of my tongue. *la-tiḥči wiyyaa. haaða lsaana waṣix.* Don't talk to him. He uses vulgar language. || *šloon lsaan ʕinda.* What a talker he is. *ʔiða tijii b-ilsaan ṭayyib, ywaafuq.* If you approach him in a nice way, he'll agree. **2.** language. **3.** bolt (of a lock).

l-š-š

lašša pl. *-aat, lšaaš* **1.** carcass, animal body dressed for food. **2.** (contemptuous) human carcass, corpse, cadaver, dead body. **3.** (contemptuous) torso, body, physique.

l-š-y

laaša to tease, bait, stir up, encourage to argue. *la-tlaašii. haaða ʔadabsizz.* Don't encourage him. He's got no manners.

tlaaša **1.** to engage in inane, petty argument. *hal-mara titlaaša wiyya ʔay waaḥid.* This woman will argue with anyone. **2.** to disappear, fade away, vanish. *l-ġeem itlaaša b-surʕa baʕd il-muṭar.* The clouds vanished quickly after the rain.

l-ð-m

liðam (*u laðum*) to thread, string. *ʔulðum il-xiraz ib-hal-xeeṭ.* String the beads onto this string. *haak il-ʔubra. ʔulðum biiha xeeṭ.* Here's the needle. Run a thread through it.

laððam to string, string up. *ʔaani ʔagammuʕ il-baanya w-inta laððumha.* I'll take the heads off the okra and you string it up.

malðuum **1.** strung, strung up. **2.** packed closely together, in tight formation. || *malðuum laðum* jam-packed, very crowded. *s-siinama malðuuma laðum bin-naas.* The movie is packed full with people.

l-ṭ-x

liṭax (*u laṭix*) to stain, soil, spatter, spot. *liṭax il-baab ib-ḥibir.* He spattered the door with ink. *liṭax wučča b-ṭiin.* He got his face splotched with mud. **2.** to slam, smash, throw down hard. *šaala w-liṭaxa bil-gaaʕ.* He picked him up and threw him on the ground.

laṭṭax intensive of *liṭax*. *njiraḥ w-laṭṭax θooba bid-damm.* He got wounded and spattered his shirt with blood.

tlaṭṭax to become stained, spattered, spotted. *tlaṭṭixat sitirti bil-booya.* My jacket got spattered by the paint.

laṭxa pl. *-aat* stain, smear, spot.

l-ṭ-š

liṭaš var. of *liṭax*, which see.

l-ṭ-ṭ

laṭṭ (*u laṭṭ*) **1.** to slap. *min faššar ʕaleeha, laṭṭata ʕala ḥalga.* When he insulted her, she slapped him on his mouth. **2.** to slam, bang, throw. *laṭṭeeta bil-gaaʕ marrteen w-ma-nkisar.* I slammed it on the ground twice and it didn't break. *min ʔašuufa, ʔaluṭṭ iḥčaayta b-wičča.* When I see him, I'll make him eat his words.

nlaṭṭ to be slapped. *nlaṭṭ ʕala wučča marrteen.* He was slapped in the face twice.

l-ṭ-ʕ

liṭaʕ (*a laṭiʕ*) to lick, lap up. *l-bazzuuna liṭʕat il-ḥaliib kulla mnil-maaʕuun.* The cat lapped up all the milk from the dish.

laṭṭaƐ to lick repeatedly. *j-jaahil daxxal iṣibƐa bil-imrabba w-gaam iylaṭṭiƐ bii.* The child stuck his finger in the jam and started licking away at it.

nliṭaƐ to be licked. *šiišat l-imrabba nliṭƐat kullha.* The jam jar was licked clean.

laṭƐa pl. *-aat* a lick.

l-ṭ-f

laṭṭaf to make pleasant, enjoyable, nice. *l-muṭar ylaṭṭuf ij-jaww.* The rain makes the weather nice. *laṭṭaf-la s-safar il-ʔooruppa w-iqtinaƐ.* He made travelling to Europe sound pleasant to him, and he decided on it.

laaṭaf to joke with, tease, kid. *da-alaaṭfak. la-tizƐal.* I'm just kidding you. Don't get mad.

tlaṭṭaf 1. to become pleasant, enjoyable, nice. *loo tumṭur, yitlaṭṭaf ij-jaww.* If it rains, the weather will get nice. 2. to be kind, do a favor. *tlaṭṭaf Ɛaleena w-taƐaal zuurna.* Do us the kindness to come and visit us.

tlaaṭaf to joke with each other. *la-tizƐal. da-yitlaaṭaf wiyyaak.* Don't get mad. He's just kidding around with you.

stalṭaf to find pleasant, agreeable, enjoyable, to enjoy, like. *stalṭafit il-ʔakil w-iṭlabit baƐad.* I thought the food was delicious and asked for more.

luṭuf pl. *ʔalṭaaf* kindness, benevolence, friendliness, courtesy, politeness, civility. *ʔaškurak, haaδa luṭuf minnak.* Thank you, that's kind of you. || *b-luṭuf* gently, softly. *Ɛiča b-luṭuf wiyyaaya.* He spoke gently to me.

luṭfan please. *luṭfan ʔagdar ʔastiƐiir qalamak fadd daqiiqa?* Could I please borrow your pencil a moment?

laṭiif pleasant, agreeable, pleasing, enjoyable, nice. *šloon manδar laṭiif!* What a beautiful view! *l-muwaδδaf ij-jidiid šgadd laṭiif w-Ɛabbuub!* How nice and likeable the new employee is! *laṭiif! haaδa xooš jawaab.* Splendid! That's a fine answer. *laṭiif, laṭiif! laƐad ġilabna!* Great, great! So we won!

laṭiifa pl. *laṭaayif* 1. favor, kindness. 2. polite, nice thing to do. *muu laṭiifa minnak itmurr Ɛalee w-ma-tsallim.* It's not a nice thing for you to pass by him and not speak. 3. witticism, quip. *xall-ʔaƐčii-lkum waƐda min laṭaayfa.* Let me tell you one of his witty remarks.

laṭiifči pl. *-iyya* wit, humorist, wag, comic.

ʔalṭaf more or most enjoyable, pleasant, etc.

l-ṭ-l-ṭ

laṭlaṭ to slosh, slop. *la-titris ij-jidir tamaam Ɛatta ma-ylaṭliṭ il-Ɛaliib.* Don't fill the pot completely so the milk won't slosh over.

l-ṭ-m

liṭam (*u laṭim*) to slap, strike with the hand. *min faššar Ɛaleeha, liṭmata Ɛala Ɛalga.* When he talked dirty to her, she slapped him on his mouth. *gaamat tibči w-tulṭum Ɛala ʔibinha l-mayyit.* She began to cry and slap herself over her dead son.

laṭma pl. *-aat* slap, blow with the hand (esp. on the face).

l-Ɛ-b

liƐab (*a liƐib*) 1. to play. *j-jaahil da-yilƐab barra.* The child is playing outside. *liƐbaw kurat il-qadam saaƐa w-nuṣṣ.* They played soccer for an hour and a half. 2. to toy, play around, fool around. *rakkib il-iplakkaat bass la-tilƐab bil-kaabreeta.* Install the spark plugs but don't mess with the carburetor. *la-tilƐab ib-xašmak.* Don't pick at your nose. *haaδa zangiin. yilƐab bil-ifluus.* He's wealthy. He has money to burn. *firqatna liƐbat biihum šaaṭi baaṭi.* Our team played circles around them. *liƐab ib-raasa.* He made a fool of him. *yaƐni qaabil iyriid yilƐab ib-raasi?* You mean he thinks he wants to make a fool of me? *yilƐab il-Ɛableen.* He plays both sides of the fence. *haaδa yilƐab Ɛala miit Ɛabil.* That guy has a hundred angles. 3. to play, wager. *liƐabit diinaareen Ɛala Ɛṣaanak.* I played two dinars on your horse. 4. to act, play, perform. *liƐab door raʔiisi bil-mufaawaδaat.* He played a leading role in the negotiations. 5. to be loose, have play in it, wiggle, move, stir. *sinni da-yilƐab.* My tooth is loose. *haaδa l-Ɛamuud min iddifƐa, yilƐab.* When you push this pole, it moves. *min yiƐči, ʔiδna tilƐab.* When he talks, his ear moves. *l-hawa da-yilƐab il-yoom.* It's windy today. || *Ɛaqla liƐab.* He went crazy. His mind slipped. *nafsa da-tilƐab.* He's nauseated. He's sick at his stomach. *lamma ʔaftarr, nafsi dguum tilƐab.* When I spin around, I begin to get nauseated. *liƐbat nafsi min haš-šuġuḷ.* I got sick of this job.

laƐƐab 1. to make or let play. *ma-da-ylaƐƐibuuni wiyyaahum.* They won't let me play with them. *laƐƐibi j-jaahil ʔila ʔan ʔarjaƐ.* Keep the kid busy until I return. **2.** to wiggle, jiggle, cause to move. *la-tlaʕʕib il-meez. da-ʔaktib.* Don't jiggle the table. I'm writing. *laʕʕab-ilha ċwaajba.* He wiggled his eyebrows at her. || *laʕʕab nafsa.* It nauseated him. It made him sick at his stomach. *loon sayyaartak iylaʕʕib in-nafis.* The color of your car is sickening. *laʕʕab ʔiida* He gave a bribe (lit., waggled his hand). *laʕʕib iidak ċatta asmaċ-lak.* Grease my palm and I'll let you go. *ma-xallaa š-šurṭi ymurr ʔilla baʕad-ma laʕʕab iida.* The cop wouldn't let him pass until he'd come across with a bribe. *laʕʕab muxxa* or *damaaġa.* It addled his brain. *hal-imtiċaan laʕʕab muxxi.* This examination drove me crazy.

laaʕab to play with, play around with. *laaʕibat ʔibinha mudda w-baʕdeen nayyimata.* She played with her son a while and then put him to sleep.

tlaaʕab to toy, play around, meddle, tamper. *t-tujjaar da-yitlaaʕbuun ib-ʔasʕaar il-ċunṭa.* The merchants are meddling with wheat prices. *l-kaatib tlaaʕab bil-iċsaab.* The clerk juggled the accounts.

nliʕab pass. of *liʕab. saaċt it-tanis ma-mxaṭṭiṭa. ma-yinliʕib biiha.* The tennis court is unlined. It can't be played on.

liʕib pl. *ʔalʕaab* **1.** play. *ʔalʕaab riyaaḍiyya* athletics, sports. *ʔalʕaab siċriyya* magic, sleight of hand. *ʔalʕaab suwiidiyya* calisthenics. *ʔalʕaab naariyya* fireworks. **2.** game.

liʕba pl. *-aat, ʔalʕaab* **1.** game. **2.** trick, catch, subterfuge. *leeš da-ybiiʕ sayyaarta b-miit diinaar? laazim haay biiha liʕba.* Why is he selling his car for a hundred dinars? There must be a catch in this somewhere. *hal-qaḍiyya biiha liʕba.* There's something shady about this affair.

*liʕbi** **1.** playful, light-headed, not serious. **2.** tricky, deceitful, untrustworthy. *diir baalak minna, tara haaḍa liʕbi.* Watch out for him, because he's pretty tricky.

laaʕuub pl. *lwaaʕiib* **1.** player, participant in a game. **2.** sportsman.

laʕʕaaba pl. *-aat* doll.

malʕab pl. *malaaʕib* **1.** athletic field. **2.** playground.

malaaʕiib (pl. only) toys, playthings.

liʕbaan: liʕbaan nafis nausea.

laaʕib **1.** playing. **2.** (pl. *-iin*) player, participant in a game. **3.** sportsman.

mlaʕʕab **1.** playful, prankish, waggish. **2.** undependable, unreliable. *šloon mlaʕʕab! ma-tigdar tiʕtimid ʕalee; ygul-lak šii w-ysawwi šii.* What an undependable person! You can't depend on him; he tells you something and does something else. *haaḍa fadd waaċid imlaʕʕab. la-taaxuḍ kalaama miyya bil-miyya.* That guy is always fooling around. Don't take what he says completely.

l-ʕ-d

laʕad **1.** then, so, in that case. *laʕad ma-raċ-tinṭiini l-ifluus il-yoom?* So you're not going to give me the money today? *leeš laʕad ʔaxuuya ʔaxaḍ wuṣla?* Why did my brother get a piece then? *ʔiḍa haaḍa ma-yʕijbak, š-yʕijbak, laʕad?* If this doesn't please you, what will then? *laʕad iš-agul-la ʔiḍa siʔal?* So what do I tell him if he asks? *laʕad ʔabqa ʕašir saaʕaat bila ʔakil?* You mean I should go ten hours without anything to eat? **2.** well? what else? what of it? *xallaṣit šuġlak kulla b-nuṣṣ saaʕa bass? — laʕad?* You finished all your work in just a half hour? — What do you expect? *ṭinṭi bis-sayyaara miit diinaar bass? — laʕad išgadd?!* You'll only give a hundred dinars for the car? — What else?

l-ʕ-l

laʕalla /usually with formal pronominal suffix attached/ perhaps, maybe. *ʔintiḍir išwayya, laʕallahu yiji.* Wait a while and perhaps he'll come.

l-ʕ-l-ʕ

laʕlaʕ to make an irritatingly loud noise. *l-baarċa čaan ṣooṭ ir-raṣṣaaṣ ylaʕliʕ.* Yesterday the sound of the gunfire was terribly noisy.

l-ġ-d

laġġad to grow a double chin, to get fat. *laġġad ʕala hal-ʔakil w-hal-hawa.* He's gotten fat on this food and this climate.

luġud pl. *lġuud* double chin, fold of skin under the chin.

l-ġ-z

laġiz pl. *ʔalġaaz* riddle, puzzle, brainteaser.

l-ġ-m

laġam, luġum pl. *ʔalġaam* (explosive) mine.

l-ġ-m-ṭ

laġmaṭ **1.** to cover, strew, spray, smear. *laġmaṭ ihduuma biṣ-ṣubuġ.* He got his clothes covered with the paint. *laġmuṭ il-ʕajiina biṭ-ṭiċiin ċatta ma-tilzag b-iidak.* Cover the dough with flour so it won't stick to your hands. **2.** to cover up, obscure, hide. *laġmuṭaw il-qaḍiyya ċatta* *ma-yinʕuruf ṣuuč man.* They covered up the affair so it wouldn't be known whose fault it was. **3.** to obscure, blur, make indistinct. *ʔiḥči ʕala keefak w-la-tlaġmuṭ il-iḥčaaya.* Talk slowly and don't mumble the words.

tlaġmaṭ to be blurred, smeared. *l-kitaaba kullha tlaġmuṭat min hal-ḥibir.* The writing all became smeared because of this ink.

l-ġ-w

liġa (i laġuw) **1.** to prattle, chatter, talk incessantly. *min tiftaḥ il-mawḍuuʕ wiyyaa, yilġi hwaaya.* When you bring up the subject to him, he talks on and on endlessly. **2.** *(i ʔilgaaʔ)* to invalidate, abolish, eliminate, do away with. *wizaart il-maʕaarif liġat hal-iktaab.* The Ministry of Education stopped the use of this book. **3.** to cancel. *l-ḥukuuma j-jidiida liġat baʕaḍ il-mašaariiʕ il-qadiima.* The new government cancelled some of the old projects.

tlaaġa to engage in heated discussion, have an argument with each other. *huwwa w-ʔabuu tlaaġaw iṣ-ṣubuḥ.* He and his father argued this morning. *l-baarḥa tlaaġa wiyya marta.* Yesterday he had words with his wife.

nliġa to be nullified, cancelled. *ʔamur naqli nliġa.* My transfer order was cancelled.

luġa pl. *-aat* language.

*luġawi** **1.** linguistic, lexicographic, philological. **2.** a linguist, lexicographer, philologist.

laġwa pl. *-aat* **1.** stir, fuss, uproar, disturbance. **2.** bother, headache, trouble. **3.** argument, heated discussion. **4.** aimless chatter, babbling, nonsense.

*laġwi** **1.** loquacious, talkative, garrulous. **2.** talkative person, chatterbox, prattler.

laġawči, laġwači pl. *-iyya.* talkative person, chatterbox.

l-f-t

lifat (i lfaat): lifat in-naḍar **1.** to call attention, point out. *lifatna naḍarak hal-marra; laakin marrt il-luxx infuṣlak.* This time we warned you; next time we'll fire you. **2.** to catch one's eye, attract attention. *booyinbaaġa lifat naḍari.* His tie caught my eye.

tlaffat to look around, direct one's gaze here and there. *š-aku ʕindak titlaffat? da-tintiḍir waaḥid yiji?* Why are you looking around? Are you waiting for someone to come?

ltifat **1.** to pay attention. *ʔiḏa tiltifit zeen iš-šuġuḷak, titraffaʕ.* If you pay good attention to your work, you'll be promoted. **2.** to turn, turn one's attention. *ltifat ʕalayya w-ḍiḥak.* He looked around at me and laughed.

laafta pl. *laafitaat* sign, signboard (bearing an inscription).

l-f-ḥ

lifaḥ (a lafiḥ) to sear, burn. *hawa s-sumuum yilfaḥ il-wujih.* The dry, hot desert wind burns the face.

l-f-ḍ

lufaḍ (u lafuḍ) to enunciate, articulate, pronounce. *lufaḍha ġalaṭ lič-čilma.* He pronounced the word wrong.

tlaffaḍ = *lufaḍ.* *ʔitlaffaḍ hač-čilma ʕala keefak.* Pronounce this word slowly.

lafuḍ pl. *ʔalfaaḍ* expression, term.

l-f-f

laff (i laff) **1.** to wrap, envelop, cover, swathe. *triid ʔaliff il-qamiiṣ loo taaxḏa hiiči?* Do you want me to wrap up the shirt or will you take it like that? *liff rugubtak ib-hal-wuṣla.* Wrap your neck with this cloth. *liff ij-jaahil ib-qappuuṭak ḥatta yidfa.* Wrap your overcoat around the kid so he'll keep warm. || *š-šurṭa laffat kull il-mutaḍaahiriin ib-looriyeen.* The police bundled all the demonstrators into two trucks. **2.** to roll, wind up, coil, reel. *liff hal-xeeṭ ʕal-bakra.* Roll this string up on the spool. *baḷḷa liff-li fadd jigaara.* Please roll me a cigarette. **3.** to twist together, join, connect. *liff raaseen il-waayar w-sawwii ḥalaqa.* Connect the two ends of the wire and make a ring. **4.** to make off with, abscond with, swipe, steal. *laff il-ifluus kullha.* He swiped all the money. || *huwwa yliffhum kullhum.* He gets the best of all of them.

ltaff **1.** to wind, twist, coil oneself. *ltaffat il-ḥayya ḥawil rugubta.* The snake wrapped itself around his neck. **2.** to intertwine, become tangled, snarled. *ltaffat il-ixyuuṭ w-ma-da-agdar ʔaliffha ʕal-bakra.* The strings got tangled and I can't wind them on the spool.

laff: jigaara laff hand-rolled cigarette.

laffa pl. *-aat* **1.** reel, spool. **2.** roll. **3.** turban. **4.** a sandwich made by rolling up a piece of Arabic bread with filling inside.

lfiifa pl. *lfaayif* a cut of meat from near the backbone of a camel.

laffaaf pl. *-aat* **1.** binding, bandage. **2.** scarf, muffler.

malaffa pl. *-aat* **1.** portfolio, folder. **2.** dossier, file.

l-f-l-f

laflaf **1.** to grab up, snatch up. *huwwa ylaflif kullši yoogaᶜ b-iida.* He grabs up everything that falls into his hands. **2.** to wrap up, bundle up. *laflif nafsak zeen tara d-dinya baarda.* Wrap yourself up well because it's cold.

tlaflaf to wrap oneself up, cover oneself. *tlaflaf gabuḷ-ma tiṭlaᶜ imnil-ᶜammaam.* Wrap yourself up before you leave the bathroom.

lifliif pl. *-iin* **1.** efficient, clever fellow. **2.** opportunist.

l-f-y

lifa (*i*) to spend one's time, hang around, be found. *yoomiyya yilfi bil-gahwa.* He's in the coffeeshop every day. *ṣaar-la sbuuᶜ laafi b-beetna.* He's been at our house for a week. *ˀiδa ma-yᶜibbuuk, luweeš tilfi ᶜleehum?* If they don't like you, why do you go see them?

laffa to cause to spend one's time, allow to spend one's time. *haaδa š-iylaffii bil-beet? n-nahaar kulla yiftarr biš-šawaariᶜ.* What can keep him at home? All day he roams the streets. *loo-ma ᶜamma l-waziir, wala yliffuu yoom ib-had-daaˀira.* If his uncle weren't the minister, they wouldn't let him stay in this office one day. *ˀiδa ˀabuu ṭirada, minu raᶜ-ylaffii?* If his father kicked him out, who'll take him in?

l-q-b

laqab pl. *ˀalqaab* **1.** surname, last name, family name. **2.** honorific or title at the end of one's name.

l-q-l-q

laqlaq to talk nonsense. *haaδa da-ylaqliq. la-tdiir-la baal.* He's just babbling. Don't pay any attention to him.

*liqlaaqi** prattler, babbler.

l-q-m

luqum Turkish delight, a jellylike confection, usually dusted with sugar.

l-q-n

laqqan **1.** to teach, instruct in. *haay minu laqqanak hal-ᶜači?* Who taught you these words? **2.** to prompt. *ma-yigdar yiᶜči ᶜal-masraᶜ ˀiδa ma-ylaqqina waaᶜid.* He can't talk on a stage if someone doesn't prompt him.

mulaqqin pl. *-iin* prompter.

l-g-ṭ

ligaṭ (*u laguṭ*) **1.** to glean, pick out, pick up. *ˀilguṭ il-ᶜaṣu mnit-timman.* Pick the small gravel out of the rice. *la-dguul hiiči ˀašyaaˀ giddaam ij-jaahil, li-ˀan yilguṭ il-ᶜači bil-ᶜajal.* Don't say such things in front of the child, because he picks words up fast. **2.** to pick over. *ṣaar-ilha mudda tilguṭ it-timman.* She's been quite a while picking over the rice. **3.** to sew around the edges, to sew overcast stitches. *baᶜad-ma tilguṭ ᶜaašyat il-panṭaroon, ˀiθniiha.* After you sew the edges of the pants, hem them.

laggaṭ **1.** to pick out, pick up. *laggaṭ il-xiraz il-ᶜumur waᶜda waᶜda.* He picked out the red beads one by one. *š-šurṭa laggiṭat kull il-imgaadya w-xallathum ib-beet xaaṣṣ.* The police gathered up all the beggars and put them in a special house. **2.** to pick over. *baᶜad-ma tlaggṭiin it-timman, ġislii.* After you pick over the rice, wash it.

luguṭ **1.** cracked grain, pieces of grain. **2.** bird food. || *xalleeta yuġḷubni l-yoom ᶜatta ˀaδibb-la lugaṭ w-yilᶜab wiyyaaya baᶜad.* I let him beat me today in order to entice him to play with me again.

lagṭa pl. *-aat* (lucky) find, bargain. *zeen ištireet har-raadyo. čaan xooš lagṭa.* It's good you bought this radio. It was a good bargain.

l-g-f

ligaf (*u laguf*) **1.** to catch, seize, snatch, grab. *šloon-ma tišmur-la ṭ-ṭooba, yilgufha.* However, you throw him the ball, he catches it. *bass ˀalugfa, ˀadammura.* As soon as I catch him, I'll tear him apart. *l-muᶜallim ligafni ˀaᶜči biṣ-ṣaff.* The teacher caught me talking in class. **2.** to breathe laboriously, gasp for breath. *δall yilguf ᶜawaali rubuᶜ saaᶜa gabuḷ-ma ymuut.* He kept gasping for about a quarter hour before he died.

laggaf to keep catching. *hal-pahlawaan raakub ᶜal-paaysikil w-iylagguf ˀarbaᶜ ṭuwab.* That acrobat's riding a bicycle and juggling four balls.

tlaagaf to descend upon, pounce on, jump, catch. *j-jahhaal tlaagfaw is-sakraan bil-iᶜjaar.* The children pounced on the drunkard with rocks. *bass tinzil haθ-θiyaab lis-suug, n-naas yitlaagfooha.* The minute these shirts go on sale in the market, the people will pounce on them.

nligaf to be caught. *ybayyin hal-marra nligafna. š-šurṭa ᶜaaṭaw il-beet.* It looks like this time we're caught. The police have surrounded the house.

l-g-g

lagg (*u lagg*) to lick. *č-čalib da-ylugg*

rijla l-majruuƐa. The dog is licking its wounded leg.

l-g-l-g

laglag pl. *lagaalig* stork.

l-g-m

laggam to cadge, sponge, bum, freeload. *n-nahaar kulla ylaggum b-ibyuut ij-jiyaariin.* All day he bums his meals at the neighbors' houses.

lugma pl. *ligam* bite, mouthful. *xan-nfuut ib-hal-maṭƐam naakul lugma.* Let's go into this restaurant and get a bite to eat.

laggaam pl. *-a* cadger, sponger, free-loader, bum.

l-g-n

ligan pl. *-aat* large metal wash basin.

l-g-w

lagaw a dice game similar to chuck-a-luck.

l-g-y

liga (*i lagi*) **1.** to find. *ligeet diinaar biš-šaariƐ.* I found a dinar on the street. *ligeet-lak xooš sayyaara rixiiṣa.* I found you a good cheap car. **2.** to encounter, meet, run into, come across. *ma-ligeet ṣuƐuuba bil-mawḍuuƐ.* I didn't encounter any difficulty in the matter. *l-ysawwi zeen yilgi zeen.* He who does good reaps good. *beet, w-sayyaara, w-ifluus—ween laagiiha?* A house, a car, and money—where can one come across these things?

lagga **1.** to find, locate. *mumkin itlaggii-la šaġḷa ʔaƐsan min haay?* Could you find him a better job than this? **2.** (of God) to punish. *ʔaḷḷa ylaggiik-iyyaaha b-wul-dak.* May God take it out on you through your children.

laaga **1.** to encounter, meet with. *laageeta l-Ɛali bis-suug.* I ran into Ali in the market. **2.** to meet. *laageena l-xuṭṭaar bil-baab.* We met the guests at the door. *ʔinšaaḷḷa tlaagii kull il-xeer.* I hope that you may meet with only good fortune.

tlagga **1.** to receive. *riƐna nitlaggaa bil-maṭaar.* We went to receive him at the airport. *tlagga! jat-tak iṭ-ṭaabuuga.* Catch! Here comes the brick. **2.** to get, obtain. *naas taakul bid-dijaaj, w-naas titlagga l-Ɛajaaj.* Some people eat chicken, and others get dust. || *ʔinšaaḷḷa titlag-gaaha b-Ɛumrak.* I hope you get your comeuppance sometime in your life.

tlaaga to come together, get together, join each other, meet each other. *xal-nitlaaga bil-masbaƐ is-saaƐa sabƐa.* Let's meet at the beach at seven o'clock. *tlaageet wiyyaa b-daaʔirt il-bariid.* I ran into him in the post office.

nliga **1.** to be found. *hal-buƐayra ma-yinligi biiha simač.* Fish cannot be found in this lake. **2.** to be encountered, be met with. *haaδa ma-yinligi bil-leel.* You never see that guy at night.

ltiga to be available, obtainable, be found. *štiriiha. hiiči sitra ma-tiltigi Ɛala ṭuul.* Buy it. Such a jacket isn't always available. *daaʔiman yiltigi bil-baar.* He can always be found in the bar.

ligya pl. *-aat* find, something found. *mbaarak! haay xooš ligya.* Congratula-tions! That's a good find.

l-k

lak, wilak f. *lič* pl. *lakum* (emphatic par-ticle, approx.:) look, hey you, say. *lak di-walli! š-imgaddrak idġuḷba?* Oh go on! How could you beat him? *lak, ma-git-lak la-tiƐči wiyyaa baƐad?* Look, haven't I told you not to talk with him anymore? *lak ma-Ɛleekum, tara masʔuuliyya.* Look, keep out of it, or you'll get in trouble! *lak šuuf! ʔiδa ma-trajjiƐ-li fluusi, ʔaštiki Ɛaleek.* Look here you! If you don't re-turn my money, I'll sue you. *lak waḷḷa, lli yṭuxxa amawwta.* By God, I'll kill any-one who touches it! *lak, lak, la-tišlaƐ il-warid!* Hey you, don't pick the flowers. *lak xaaṭr aḷḷa, saaƐduuni!* Hey, for the love of God, help me! *lak yaaḅa, haaδa šloon jamaal!* Hey man, that's real beauty!

¹l-k-k

lakk (*u lakk*) **1.** to seal, fasten securely, secure. *lukk il-maktuub Ɛatta maƐƐad yiftaƐa.* Seal the letter so nobody will open it. *š-šurṭa lakkooha lil-qaaṣa.* The police sealed the safe. **2.** to poke in the ribs. *lukka Ɛatta yiltifit Ɛaleek.* Poke him in the ribs so he'll look around at you.

lukk sealing wax.

lakka pl. *-aat* **1.** spot, stain, smudge. **2.** a poke in the ribs.

²l-k-k

lukk a great number, a large, but vague, amount. *lukk marra gut-la w-nisa.* I told him a jillion times and he forgot.

l-k-l-k

laklak **1.** to spatter, spot, stain. *diir baalak. la-tlaklik θoobak.* Be careful. Don't stain your shirt. **2.** to roll, form into a ball or lump. *laklik iṭ-ṭiina w-šiilha.* Roll the piece of mud into a ball and pick it up. **3.** to poke repeatedly in the ribs. *la-tlaklik! da-asmaƐak.* Don't poke at me! I hear you.

lakluuka, luklukka pl. *-aat, lkaaliik* ball, lump, hunk.

l-k-m

likam (*i lakim*) to punch, strike with the fist. *likama ʕala xašma w-waggaʕa.* He punched him on the nose and knocked him down.

laakam to box, engage in a fist fight with. *šifit ḥaywaan il-kanġar ylaakim ṣaaḥba.* I saw a kangaroo boxing with its owner.

lakma pl. *-aat* punch, blow with the fist.

mulaakama boxing, fist fighting.

mulaakim pl. *-iin* boxer, pugilist.

l-l-y

laala to shine, glow, beam, radiate. *hal-ibnayya l-ḥilwa wujihha ylaali.* That pretty girl's face really glows. *jilaf iṣ-ṣiiniyya w-xallaaha tlaali.* He scoured the tray and made it shine.

laala pl. *-aat* lantern, lamp with a candle inside.

l-m-p

lampa pl. *-aat* 1. kerosene lamp. 2. radio tube.

l-m-ḥ

limaḥ (*a lamiḥ*) to glimpse, catch sight of. *lmaḥta da-yiʕbur iš-šaariʕ.* I caught a glimpse of him crossing the street.

lammaḥ to intimate, insinuate, hint, allude, refer. *lammaḥ-li b-raġibta lis-safar il-ʔooruppa.* He hinted to me of his desire to go to Europe.

lamḥa pl. *-aat* glance, quick look. *šifta š-da-ysawwi b-lamḥa wiḥda.* I saw what he was up to in one glance.

malaamiḥ (pl. only) features, outward appearance, looks.

l-m-s

limas (*i lamis*) 1. to touch, feel, handle. *min ilmasit guṣṣta, fazz imnin-noom.* When I touched his forehead, he woke up. 2. to feel, sense, have a hunch. *lmasit ʕinda taʕaṣṣub diini.* I felt that he had religious prejudice.

tlammas to feel, palpate, examine by touch. *tlammas hal-uqmaaš w-šuufa šgadd naaʕim.* Feel this cloth and see how smooth it is.

ltimas 1. to ask, request. *ma-daam il-waziir ṣadiiqak leeš-ma tiltimis minna yʕayyin ibnak.* Since the minister is your friend, why don't you ask him to appoint your son. 2. to make an urgent request, to implore, beseech, beg. *ltimas minna balki yiqbal.* He begged him to accept if he could. *ʔaltamsak tiji titʕašša ʕidna.* Please come have dinner with us.

ltimaas pl. *-aat* 1. request. 2. plea, entreaty.

malmuus 1. touched, felt. 2. tangible, palpable, noticeable. *ʔaku taḥassun malmuus ib-ṣiḥḥta.* There's a noticeable improvement in his health.

l-m-ʕ

limaʕ (*a lamiʕ, lamaʕaan*) to gleam, glisten, shine. *l-miḥbas maalak da-yilmaʕ.* Your ring is shining. *haaδa l-waraq yilmaʕ. ma-yiṣlaḥ lil-makaatiib.* This paper is glossy. It's no good for letters.

lammaʕ to shine, make shine, impart a shine to. *lammiʕ id-digam win-najmaat.* Shine the buttons and the stars. *had-dihin iylammiʕ il-qanaadir.* This polish will make the shoes shine.

lamʕa pl. *-aat* shine, sparkle, gloss, gleam, luster.

lammaaʕ bright, shiny, glistening, sparkling, glossy.

l-m-l-m

lamlam to collect, gather, gather up. *yaḷḷa! lamlim ġaraaδak w-iṭlaʕ!* Come on! Gather up your things and get out!

tlamlam to gather oneself together. *loo titlamlam ib-gaʕidtak, yṣiir-li makaan.* If you don't sit sprawled out, there'll be room.

lamluum gang, bunch (esp. of thieves, etc.). *da-yimši wiyya fadd lamluum ma-biihum xeer.* He runs around with a no-good bunch of riffraff.

l-m-m

lamm (*i lamm*) to collect, gather together, assemble. *limm il-ġaraaδ w-ḥuṭṭha bij-junṭa.* Gather the things and put them in the suitcase. *ṭ-ṭullaab da-ylimmuun tabarruʕaat.* The students are collecting donations. *ṣaar-li sana ʔalimm ifluus ḥatta ʔaštiri paaysikil.* I have been saving money a year to buy a bicycle. *š-šurṭa lammat kull il-mašbuuhiin.* The police rounded up all the suspects. *limm ir-rabuʕ ḥatta nilʕab ṭooba.* Get the gang together so we can play ball. *l-muḥtakir lamm kull iš-šakar il-bis-suug.* The monopolist cornered all the sugar in the market. *l-bazzuuna lammat nafisha w-gumzat ʕaṭ-ṭeer.* The cat drew itself up and pounced on the bird.

nlamm to be collected, gathered. *ṭ-ṭiḥiin ma-yinlam bil-ʔiid.* The flour can't be gathered up by hand.

ltamm to come together, assemble, unite, gather. *ltammaw kullhum yamm mukaan il-ḥaadiθ.* They all gathered near the scene of the accident. *ltammaw ʕalayya ʕišriin waaḥid.* Twenty guys ganged up on me. || *čaanat ʕaayza ltammat.* It was one thing right on top of another. It was more than one could bear. *čaanat ʕaayza ltammat. ṣ-ṣubuʕ beeti ʕtirag, taali ṭallʕooni min šuğli, w-hassa ʕṣaani maat.* It was a chain of catastrophes. This morning my house caught on fire, then they fired me from work, and now my horse died.

lamma pl. *-aat* gathering, assembly, crowd.

malmuum **1.** collected, gathered, assembled. **2.** compact.

l-m-m-a

lamma **1.** when, as, at the time that. *lamma truuʕ lis-suug, la-tinsa tištiri šakar.* When you go to market, don't forget to buy sugar. *la-tiktib ʔilla lamma ʔagul-lak.* Don't write until I tell you. **2.** until, until the time when. *xalliiha ʕindak lamma yiji.* Keep it with you until he comes. **3.** since, whereas. *ma-aku daaʕi tidfaʕ lamma ma-ʕindak ifluus hassa.* There's no need to pay since you don't have any money now.

l-n-g

langa pl. *-aat* **1.** bale (of cotton, etc.). **2.** compartment, section of a container, etc.

l-h-b

lihab (*a lahib*) **1.** to burn, flame, blaze. *l-faanuus da-yilhab. nazzil l-iftiila.* The lantern's blazing. Turn down the wick. **2.** to catch fire, ignite, blaze. *la-tʕuṭṭ naar yamm il-ḅaanziin tara yilhab bil-ʕajal.* Don't put the fire near the gasoline because it catches fire easily.

lahhab to singe, burn. *lahhib il-baṭṭa zeen gabuḷ-ma tšuggha.* Singe the duck well before you dress it.

ltihab **1.** to flame, flare up, burn brightly. *ltihbat in-niiraan bil-maʕmal.* The flames blazed up in the factory. **2.** to become inflamed. *ltihbat il-lawzateen ʕinda.* His tonsils became inflamed.

lahab flare, blaze, flame.

lahba pl. *-aat* flame, blaze.

ʔiltihaab inflammation. *ʔiltihaab il-ʕunjara* tonsilitis. *ʔilthaab il-mafaaṣil* arthritis.

l-h-t

lahaat pl. *-aat* velum, soft palate, rear portion of the roof of the mouth.

l-h-θ

lihaθ (*a lahiθ*) to pant, gasp, be out of breath. *luweeš turkuṣ zaayid w-baʕdeen idguum tilhaθ?* Why do you run so much that you begin to pant?

l-h-s

stalhas **1.** to develop a desire, craving. *la-tinṭi j-jaahil baʕad tara yistalhis.* Don't give the kid any more or he'll get to wanting more and more. *min šaaf ʔaku banaat bil-ʕafla stalhas w-biqa l-nuṣṣ il-leel.* When he saw there were girls at the party he got interested and stayed until midnight.

l-h-g

malhuug eager, avid. *š-biik malhuug? ma-tintiḏir išwayya?* How come you're so eager? Can't you wait a little?

l-h-m

liham (*a lahim*) to devour, gobble up, swallow up. *min ʕaṭṭeena l-akil giddaama, lihámа b-daqiiqa.* When we put the food before him, he devoured it in a minute.

lahma pl. *-aat* bite. *ʔuxuḏ-lak lahma min has-simsim.* Take a bite of this sesame.

lhuum a confection made of ground chickpeas and sugar.

l-h-n

lahhaana, lahaana cabbage.

l-h-y

lahha **1.** to amuse, divert, distract. *lahhi j-jaahil ʔila ʔan yiji ʔabuu.* Entertain the child until his father comes. *t-talafizyoon ylahhi l-waaʕid. n-nahaar yingiḏi wala tʕiss bii.* Television passes one's time. The day goes and you never know it. *lahhaani ʕan šuğli.* He distracted me from my work. *r-riyaaḏa mlahhiita, wala da-yidrus.* Sports have engrossed him, and he won't do any studying. *lahhi š-šurṭi ʕatta ʔaxušš jawwa.* Hold the policeman's attention so I can go in.

tlahha to amuse oneself, pass the time, occupy oneself. *tlahha b-hal-šağḷa ʔila ʔan tilgii-lak ʔaʕsan minha.* Pass the time with this job, until you find something better. *ma-ʕidna fluus ništirii-lak paaysikil jidiid. tlahha b-haaḏa.* We don't have the money to buy you a new bike. Occupy yourself with this one.

ltiha to occupy oneself, devote one's time or attention. *ltihi b-haš-šağḷa ʕatta nšuuf-lak šağḷa ʔaʕsan.* Keep busy with this job until we can find you a better one. *ʔiltiha bil-liʕib w-tirak idruusa.* He spent all his time playing and abandoned his studies. *beeš miltihi hal-ʔayyaam?* What have you been doing these days?

lahu **1.** amusement, fun, entertainment. **2.** diversion, pastime.

malha pl. *malaahi* night club, cabaret.

l-w

loo **1.** if (introducing a conditional or hypothetical clause). *loo saaʕga l-qiṭaar,* *čaan ṣirit masʔuul.* If the train had run over him, you'd have been responsible. *ʔašuuf loo taaxuδ wiyyaak ʔakil, ʔaṣraf-lak.* It seems to me that it would be cheaper for you if you take some food with you. *yaa mƐawwad! loo gaayil-la li-ʔan ma-yidri.* Good Lord! If only you'd told him, because he doesn't know. *leeš difaƐta? loo waagiƐ?* Why did you push him? What if he'd fallen? || *loo maa. . .* if it weren't for . . ., except for the fact that. . . . *loo maa l-qaaṭ ġaali, čaan ištireeta.* If the suit weren't so expensive, I'd have bought it. *loo maa l-muƐallim ʔaxuu, ma-čaan yinjaƐ.* If the teacher weren't his brother, he wouldn't have passed. *loo maa jaay, čaan itrazzalit.* If you hadn't come, I'd have been in a mess. **2.** or. *yaahi ʔaƐsan, sayyaarti loo sayyaartak?* Which is better, my car or your car? || *loo . . . loo . . .* either . . . or . . . . *loo haaδa loo haaδa.* Either this or that. *loo-yiji loo ma-yiji.* Either he'll come or he won't come. *loo baƐad* yet, or not. *xallaṣit loo baƐad?* Have you finished yet?

l-w-b-y

luubya (coll.) cowpea(s), black-eyed pea(s).

luubyaaya pl. *-aat* un. n. of *luubya.*

l-w-θ

lawwaθ to dust, sprinkle dust on. *lawwiθ is-siiniyya biṭ-ṭiƐiin gabuḷ-ma txalli Ɛaleeha l-Ɛajiin.* Dust the tray with flour before you put the dough on it.

lwaaθ fine layer of flour on a pan to prevent sticking.

l-w-Ɛ

laaƐ (*u looƐ*) to hit (a target). *tigdar itluuƐ iš-šijra bil-iƐjaara min hal-mukaan?* Can you hit the tree with the rock from here?

nlaaƐ pass. of *laaƐ. ṭ-ṭeer ma-yinlaaƐ min hal-buƐud.* The bird can't be hit from this distance.

looƐ **1.** hitting (a target). **2.** (coll.) slab(s), sheet(s), plate(s). **3.** board(s), plank(s). **4.** (pl. *lwaaƐ*) plot, patch, section. *qassam Ɛadiiqta ʔila lwaaƐ.* He divided his garden into small plots.

lawƐa, looƐa pl. *-aat, ʔalwaaƐ, lwaaƐ* **1.** board, plank (of wood). **2.** sheet, slab, pane, plate, panel (of glass, etc.). **3.** board, blackboard, slate. **4.** (artist's) canvas. *lawƐa fanniyya* painting.

¶ *lawƐat ʔiƐlaanaat* bulletin board. *l-lawƐa s-suwiidiyya* a program of calisthenics developed in Sweden, Swedish movements. *ʔiδa tkallfa b-šii, yruuƐ lil-looƐa.* If you ask him to do a thing, he goes all the way to help.

laaʔiƐa pl. *lawaaʔiƐ* bill, motion (in parliament).

l-w-Ɛ-g

looƐag to chase, try to catch. *č-čalib da-ylooƐig il-bazzuuna ween-ma truuƐ.* The dog's chasing the cat wherever it goes. *ṣaar-la sbuuƐ imlooƐigni Ɛal-ifluus.* He's been after me for a week for the money.

l-w-x

laax (*u loox*) to make a mess of, mess up, cause to go wrong. *ṣaaƐbak laaxha b-tadaxxula.* Your friend messed it up with his intervention.

lawwax to soil, stain, besmudge, make dirty. *j-jaahil lawwax iida biṭ-ṭiin.* The kid got his hands dirty in the mud.

tlawwax to become soiled, get dirty. *diir baalak la-toogaƐ w-titlawwax ihduumak.* Be careful not to fall or your clothes'll get dirty.

tlaawax to fight with each other. *Ɛali tlaawax wiyya l-muƐallim.* Ali mixed it up with the teacher.

l-w-z

looz **1.** (coll.) almond(s). **2.** (an expression of enthusiastic approval) excellent! splendid! *l-ʔakil mumtaaz! looz!* The food is excellent. Really good! *šloon ibnayya! looz!* What a girl! Wow!

looza pl. *-aat* **1.** almond. **2.** (pl. only) tread. *loozaat taayar* the tread of a tire.

lawza pl. *-aat* tonsil. *l-lawzateen* the tonsils.

l-w-ṣ

laaṣ (*u looṣ*) to make a mess of, mess up. *min čaan yistangi, laaṣ iṭ-ṭamaaṭa kullha.* When he was choosing, he ruined all the tomatoes. *ddaaxal w-laaṣha lil-qaḍiyya.* He interfered and messed up the matter.

lawwaṣ to exaggerate, talk through one's hat. *haaδa da-ylawwiṣ. ma-aku hiiči šii.* He's exaggerating. There's no such thing.

nlaaṣ to be made a mess of, be messed up. *ybayyin il-waḍiƐ inlaaṣ biš-šimaal.* It seems the situation in the north has gotten all messed up.

l-w-f

laaf (*u loof*) to turn, change course, take a different direction. *min tooṣal ir-raas iš-šaariƐ, luuf Ɛal-yimna.* When you get to the end of the block, turn right.

ltaaf to turn, turn around, swing around,

baʕdeen ltaaf ʕalee w-sabba. Then he turned around to him and cursed him.

loofa **1.** turn, curve, change of direction. *haṭ-ṭariiq bii loofaat ihwaaya.* This road's got a lot of curves in it. **2.** detour. *sawwaw biṭ-ṭariiq loofa li-ʔan ʔaku taṣliiḥaat bii.* They made a detour in the road because they're mending it. **3.** way around, way out, expedient. *l-qaðiyya ṣaʕba. laazim inšuuf ʔilha fadd loofa.* The situation is difficult. We'll have to find some way around it.

l-w-q-n-ṭ-a

looqanṭa, laaqunṭa pl. *-aat* restaurant.

l-w-g

laag (u) /with *l-*/ to suit, be fitting for, be just the right thing for. *haaða yluug il-hal-waðiifa.* He's the right man for this position. *l-maawi yluug-lič.* The color blue becomes you. *hal-iθneen waaḥid yluug lil-laax.* These two are made for each other.

l-w-k-s

looks **1.** pl. -aat gasoline lantern, gas mantle lantern. **2.** (invar.) deluxe, of the best quality. *haaða šloon θoob! looks!* What a shirt. Top quality!

l-w-l

luula pl. *luwal* **1.** cylinder, tube, pipe. **2.** large cylindrical pillow.

l-w-l-y

loola (i) to sing a lullaby. *ʔibni ma-ynaam ʔiða ma-tloolii-la ʔumma.* My son won't go to sleep if his mother doesn't sing him a lullaby.

leeluwwa pl. *-aat* lullaby.

l-w-m

laam (u loom) to blame, censure, rebuke, chide, reproach. *la-ddaxxil nafsak tara baʕdeen yluumak.* Don't interfere or later he'll blame you.

lawwam = *laam.* *ḥatta loo ma-tsaaʕida, maḥḥad ylawwimak.* Even if you don't help him, no one will blame you.

tlaawam to blame each other. *ðallaw yitlaawmuun w-maḥḥad ʕiraf ṣuuč-man.* They kept on blaming each other and nobody knew whose fault it was.

nlaam to be blamed, censured, reproached. *l-mudiir ma-yinlaam bii. haaða yistaahil iṭ-ṭarid.* The director can't be blamed for it. This man deserves to be fired. *ma-yinlaam ʕala qasaawta. yistahluun.* He can't be taken to task for his cruelty. They deserve it.

loom blame.

l-w-n

lawwan to color, add color to. *min tirsim il-beet, lawwin il-baab ʔaxðar.* When you draw the house, color the door green.

tlawwan **1.** to be colored. *r-rasim ma-yitlawwan ib-suhuula ʕala han-nooʕ imnil-waraq.* The picture can't be colored easily on this type of paper. **2.** to change colors, shift with the wind, be changeable. *haaða yitlawwan ḥasab ið-ðuruuf.* He shifts his position according to the circumstances.

loon pl. *ʔalwaan* **1.** color, hue, tint, shade, complexion. **2.** kind, sort, variety, species. *qaddimoo-lna ʔalwaan w-ʔaškaal imnil-ʔakil.* They offered us all sorts of food.

talwiin coloring.

mulawwan colored, tinted. *qlaam mulawwana* colored pencils. *filim imlawwan* a color film, color movie.

mitlawwin changeable, inconstant, unreliable, fickle. *haaða waaḥid mitlawwin. la-tiʕtimid ʕalee.* He's changeable. Don't depend on him.

l-w-y

luwa (i luwi) **1.** to bend, flex. *tigdar tilwi haš-šiiš il-ġaliið?* Can you bend this thick rod? **2.** to twist, contort, wrench, warp. *luwa ʔiida w-ʔaxað l-ifluus minna.* He twisted his arm and took the money from him. **3.** to turn aside, avert, hang. *luwa raasa mnil-xajal min il-muʕallim razzala.* He hung his head in embarrassment when the teacher scolded him.

tlawwa to writhe, wriggle, squirm. *l-bazzuuna wugʕat w-gaamat titlawwa mnil-wujaʕ.* The cat fell and began to writhe in pain. *l-ḥayya, min timši, titlawwa.* When the snake moves, he wriggles.

tlaawa to arm wrestle, Indian wrestle. *ʔariid ʔatlaawa wiyya waaḥid ʔiida qawwiyya.* I want to Indian wrestle with someone whose arm is strong.

nluwa to be bent, be flexed. *haš-šiiš ma-yinluwi.* This rod can't be bent.

ltuwa to warp, twist, become bent, crooked, contorted out of shape. *l-looḥa ltuwat imnir-ruṭuuba.* The board warped from the dampness. *rijl ič-čalib iltuwat.* The dog's leg became twisted.

lawi wound, twisted, coiled. *sipringaat lawi* coil springs.

liwaaʔ pl. *ʔalwiya* **1.** province, district. **2.** brigade (mil.). *ʔamiir liwaaʔ* major general.

*malwi** 1. bent, curved, coiled, twisted, spiral, winding. 2. (pl. *malaawi*) twisted metal bracelet.

malwiyya a minaret near Samarra with a spiral path leading up the outside to the top.

miltuwi 1. = *malwi*. 2. tortuous, involved. *la-tiċči b-ṣuura miltawya.* Don't beat around the bush.

l-w-y-š

luweeš, ʔilweeš var. of *leeš*, which see under *l-y-š*.

l-y

lee, leeha, etc. = *ʕalee, ʕaleeha*, etc. See *ʕala* under *ʕ-l-y*.

l-y-t

leet var. of *reet*, which see under *r-y-t*.

l-y-x

laax (*i leex*) to leave in a hurry, depart hurriedly, beat it. *liix gabuḷ-ma ykumšuuk!* Scram before they catch you! *tara min yaaxuð il-ifluus, yliix.* As soon as he gets the money, he'll beat it.

l-y-r-a

leera pl. *-aat* lira.

l-y-s

liisa pl. *-aat* unborn lamb.

l-y-š

leeš, luweeš, ʔilweeš why, for what reason, what for. *leeš ma-tiji wiyyaana?* Why don't you come with us? *ma-ʔadri ʔilweeš.* I don't know why. *luweeš ma-gutt-li l-baarḥa?* Why didn't you tell me yesterday? *sʔalta luweeš ma-xaabar.* I asked him why he didn't phone.

l-y-ṭ

liiṭa pl. *-aat, liyaṭ* thin, flexible stick.

l-y-f

layyaf to scrub with a luffa. *ʔiða ma-tlayyif zeen, ma-yiṭlaʕ il-wuṣax.* If you don't scrub well, the dirt won't come off. *mumkin itlayyif-li šwayya?* Could you scrub me a little?

liif (coll.) bast, plant fiber(s).

liifa pl. *-aat, liyaf* luffa, a pad of plant fibers, commonly used as a scouring pad or bath sponge.

l-y-q

laaq, liyaaqa, etc., = *laag*, etc. which see under *l-w-g*.

l-y-l

leel night, nighttime.

leela pl. *-aat, layaali* 1. night. 2. evening.

*leeli** *layli** night, evening. *madrasa layliyya* night school.

leeliyyan nightly, each night.

l-y-l-w

liilu (coll.) pearl(s).

liiluwwa pl. *-aat* a pearl.

leeluwwa pl. *-aat* lullaby (see also *l-w-l-y*).

l-y-m-w-n

leemuun lemon.

l-y-n

laan (*i liyuuna*) 1. to become soft, pliable, flexible, supple. *jilid hal-qundara qawi laakin iyliin bil-istiʕmaal.* The leather of this shoe is stiff but it'll soften with use. 2. (*i liin*) to soften, become gentle, tender. *galba laan min šaafa yibči.* His heart softened when he saw him cry. 3. to yield, give in. *ʔiða tiḥči wiyyaa b-ilsaan ṭayyib, yliin.* If you talk to him nicely, he'll give in.

layyan to soften, make soft, supple, pliable. *tigdar itlayyinha liṭ-ṭiina b-išwayyit mayy.* You can soften the mud with a little water.

liin tenderness, gentleness, kindness. *ʔiða tiji wiyyaa bil-liin, yiqbal.* If you approach him nicely, he'll agree.

layyin 1. soft, flexible, pliable, pliant, supple, resilient. 2. gentle, tender-hearted.

mulayyin pl. *-aat* 1. softener, softening agent, emollient. 2. mild laxative.

l-y-w-a-n

liiwaan pl. *luwaawiin* a covered, paved area, open to the air, facing on a courtyard.

l-y-y

liyya pl. *-aat* tail (of a fat-tailed sheep, the fat of which is used in cooking).

M

m-a

ma- /negating prefix used with verbs, participles, and prepositions in equational phrases/ not. *ma-ðanneet ʔinnak mašġuuḷ.* I didn't think you were busy. *ma-agdar aji s-saaʕa xamsa.* I can't come at five o'clock. *ʔiða ma-tistaʕjil, ma-raḥ-itxaḷḷiṣ šuġḷak.* If you don't hurry, you won't finish your work. *haay safra ma-titfawwat.* This is a trip that isn't to be passed up. *ʔaani ma-baayit ihnaa gabuḷ.* I haven't spent the night here before. *wildič baʕadhum ma-maakliin.* Your children still haven't eaten. *ˀibni l-iṣġayyir ma-mitzawwij.* My youngest son is not married. *laazim ašuuf-li šiqqa ma-mˀaθθiθa.* I've got to find myself an unfurnished apartment. *laa, ˀaani ma-taʕbaan.* No, I'm not tired. *ma-aku ḥaaja txaabra.* There's no need to phone him. *ma-aku ʕuṭla hal-isbuuʕ.* There isn't any holiday this week. *ṣ-ṣanduug faariġ; ma-bii šii.* The box is empty; there's nothing in it. *hal-fikra, ma-biiha faayda.* There is no advantage to this idea. *hal-uqmaaš, ma-ʕalee ṭalab ihwaaya.* There isn't a lot of demand for this cloth. *ma-ʕindi fluus kaafya.* I don't have enough money.

-ma suffix forming a conjunction from a preposition, interrogative, comparative, and certain other forms (see under first constituent). *xall inxaḷḷiṣ šuġuḷna gábuḷ-ma yiji l-mudiir.* Let's finish our work before the director comes. *sawwiiha šloon-ma triid.* Do it any way you like. *sawwi š-ma yʕijbak.* Do whatever you like. *haaδa ˀaḥsan-ma ʕindak?* Is that the best you've got? *kull-ma ˀašuufa, huwwa sakraan.* Whenever I see him, he's drunk.

m-a-b-y-n

maabeen pl. *-aat* anteroom, entryway, hall.

m-a-č-a

ṃaača pl. *-aat* spade (suit in cards).

m-a-x-w-δ

maaxuuδ pl. *mwaaxiiδ* **1.** club, bludgeon, bat. **2.** a large male sexual organ.

m-a-r-t

maart March.

m-a-r-k-a

maarka pl. *-aat* brand, make. *ˀay maarka has-saaʕa?* What brand of watch is this?

m-a-š

maaš green gram, a leguminous grain plant.

maaša pl. *-aat* **1.** tongs, pincers. **2.** bobby pin, hair pin. **3.** fork (of a bicycle).

m-a-ṣ-w-l

maaṣuul, see *m-w-ṣ-l.*

m-a-ṭ-w-r

maaṭoor pl. *-aat* **1.** motor, engine. **2.** launch, motor boat, motor barge. **3.** motorcycle.

m-a-ṭ-w-r-s-k-l

maaṭoorsikil pl. *-aat* motorcycle.

m-a-ʕ-w-n

maaʕuun pl. *mwaaʕiin* **1.** plate, dish. **2.** (pl. only) dishes, tableware.

m-a-k-w

maaku = *ma-aku,* which see under *ˀ-k-w.*

m-a-k-w-k

maakuuk pl. *mwaakiik* bobbin (of a sewing machine).

m-ˀ-w

miyya pl. *-aat, miyaaya* hundred. *git-lak miit marra, la-tsawwi hiiči!* I've told you a hundred times, don't do that! || *bil-miyya* per cent. *yaaxuδ xamsa bil-miyya dlaala.* He gets a five percent auction fee. *miyya bil-miyya* 1. one hundred percent. 2. totally, completely.

*miˀawi** centigrade. *darajat ḥaraart il-ġurfa θlaaθiin miˀawiyya.* The room temperature is 30° centigrade. || *nisba miˀawiyya* percentage. *ʕiid miˀawi* hundredth anniversary, centennial.

m-a-y

ṃaay var. of *ṃayy,* which see under *m-y-y.*

m-a-y-s

ṃaayis May.

m-a-y-w

maayo pl. *-owaat* woman's bathing suit.

m-t-r

matir, mitir, matra pl. *ˀamtaar, matraat* meter (39.34 inches).

m-t-ʕ

mattaʕ /with *b-*/ to make enjoy. *mattiʕ ʕeenak ib-haj-jamaal.* Feast your eyes upon this beauty.

tmattaʕ /with *b-*/ to enjoy, savor, relish. *tmattaʕ ib-ḥayaatak ma-daamak šabaab.* Enjoy your life while you're still young.

mitʕa temporary marriage for the purpose of sexual gratification.

m-t-n

mitan (a) **1.** to become thick, stout, strong, heavy. *haš-šijra da-timtan sana ʕala sana.* This tree is getting thicker year after year. **2.** (*i*) to dislocate the shoulder. *la-djurr ˀiid il-walad tara tmitna.* Don't tug on the boy's arm or you'll dislocate his shoulder.

matin pl. *mtuun* shoulder.

mitin **1.** thickness, heaviness. **2.** gauge (of wire).

mitiin thick, stout, heavy, strong. *da-yjurr il-balam ib-ḥabil mitiin.* He's pulling the boat with a thick rope.

ˀamtan thicker or thickest, stronger or strongest, etc.

mamtuun having a sprained or dislocated shoulder.

m-θ-l

maθθal **1.** to act, play (a role). *ˀay door yinṭuu, ymaθθila kulliš zeen.* Any role they give him, he plays very well. *ma-yuʕruf* *ymaθθil ˀadwaar hazaliyya.* He doesn't know how to play comedy roles. **2.** to show, demonstrate. *hal-mašaariiع iδ-δaxma tmaθθil ixlaaṣ il-ḥukuuma.* These vast projects show the government's sincerity. **3.** to represent. *minu raḥ-ymaθθil il-wizaara b-hal-lujna?* Who's going to represent the ministry on this committee? **4.** to liken, compare. *ˀamaθθil xašma ib-xarṭuum il-fiil.* I would compare his nose to an elephant's trunk.

mtiθal /with *l-*/ to obey, carry out. *j-jundi yimtiθil lil-ˀawaamir il-ع askariyya.* The soldier obeys military orders.

miθil **1.** like, similar to, just like, the same as. *huwwa fadd xooš walad. ma-aku miθla.* He's a real fine fellow. There's none like him. *laعad miθlak? ˀaṣruf kur-raatbi?* You mean I should be like you? Spend all my salary? *tigdar tiktib ḥarf il-عeen miθli?* Can you write the letter 'ayn the way I do? *ˀašuu miθil ḥissha.* It sounds like her voice. || *bil-miθil* in kind, in the same manner, likewise. *عaamla bil-miθil.* Treat him the same way. **2.** (pl. *ˀamθaal*) similar thing, thing of the same kind. *huwwa w-ˀamθaala.* He and all his kind.

miθil-ma just as, like, the same as. *raḥ-asawwi miθil-ma dguul.* I'll do just as you say.

maθal pl. *ˀamθaal* **1.** proverb, adage. **2.** example. **3.** warning, example, object lesson.

maθalan for example, for instance.

miθaal pl. *ˀamθila* **1.** example. **2.** model, exemplar.

*miθaali** model, exemplary. *ˀabuu muعallim miθaali.* His father is an exemplary teacher.

maθiil equal, match. *ma-ˀila maθiil.* It has no equal. It's incomparable.

timθaal pl. *tamaaθiil* statue.

tamθiil acting.

tamθiiliyya pl. *-aat* play, stage presentation. *tamθiiliyya hazaliyya* a comedy.

mumaθθil pl. *-iin.* **1.** actor, stage performer. **2.** agent, representative.

mumaθθila pl. *-aat* actress.

mumaθθiliyya **1.** agency, representation. **2.** (pl. *-aat*) diplomatic mission.

mumaaθil similar, comparable, corresponding, analogous.

m-θ-n

maθaana pl. *-aat* (urinary) bladder.

m-j-j

majj: mayy majj **1.** hard water, water with high mineral content. **2.** brackish, bad-tasting water.

m-j-d

majjad /with *b-*/ to praise, laud, extol, glorify (esp. God). *l-muwaδδin gabḷ il-fajir ymajjid w-baعdeen ywaδδin.* Before dawn the muezzin praises God and then gives the call to prayer. *daaˀiman ymajjid ib-ˀajdaada.* He's always glorifying his ancestors.

majd splendor, glory.

majiid glorious, illustrious, exalted. *l-qurˀaan il-majiid* the glorious Koran. *wil-qurˀaan il-majiid ma-aعruf.* I swear I don't know.

m-j-r

l-majar Hungary.

*majari** **1.** Hungarian. **2.** a Hungarian.

m-j-n

majjaanan free of charge. *d-duxuul bil-ḥadiiqa majjaanan.* Entrance to the park is free.

maajiina a children's holiday, similar to Halloween, observed during the month of Ramadan.

m-j-w-s

majuus Magi, adherents of Mazdaism.

*majuusi** **1.** Magian. **2.** a Magian.

majuusiyya Mazdaism.

m-ḥ-r

maḥḥaar (coll.) sea shell(s), oyster shell(s), snail shell(s).

maḥḥaara pl. *-aat* un.n. of *maḥḥaar.*

m-ḥ-d

maḥḥad see under *ˀ-ḥ-d.*

m-ḥ-l

maḥal dearth, famine, drought, barrenness.

m-ḥ-l-q-w

maḥlaqoo children's game similar to hopscotch.

m-ḥ-n

maḥḥan to leave stranded. *ˀaxaδ sayyaarti w-maḥḥanni.* He took my car and left me stranded.

mtiḥan **1.** to examine, test. *l-muعallim raḥ-yimtiḥinna bil-ˀingiliizi baačir.* The teacher is going to test us in English tomorrow. **2.** to take an examination. *laazim timtiḥin gabuḷ-ma yiqbaluuk.* You'll have to take an examination before they'll accept you.

miḥna pl. *miḥan* trial, tribulation, ordeal. *marδat ˀabuuya xallatna b-miḥna.* My father's sickness left us under a strain.

mtiḥaan pl. *-aat* examination, test.

m-ḥ-y

miḥa (*i maḥi*) **1.** to erase, rub out, wipe

off. *ˀimḥi hač-čilma w-iktibha marra lux.* Erase this word and write it again. **2.** to wipe out, eradicate, exterminate. *j-jeeš miḥaahum ʕan ˀaaxirhum.* The army wiped them out to the last man.

maḥḥa to erase repeatedly. *l-warqa ṣaarat sooda min gadd-ma ymaḥḥi.* The page turned black from his erasing so much.

nmiḥa to be wiped out, obliterated. *ˀaaθaarhum nmiḥat; maḥḥad yuʕruf š-ṣaar minhum.* Their traces were wiped out; no one knows what happened to them.

maḥḥaaya pl. *-aat* pencil eraser.

mamḥi place where something has been erased. || *ma-yuʕbur ʕalee šii. yiqra l-mamḥi.* Nothing gets past him. He's very clever (lit., reads what's been erased).

m-x-x

muxx pl. *mxaax* **1.** brain. **2.** mind, intelligence. **3.** medulla, marrow.

muxxsizz brainless, senseless. *l-madrasa ma-tfiida. huwwa muxxsizz.* School does him no good. He's brainless.

m-x-ṭ

muxaṭ (*u maxiṭ*) to blow one's nose. *ʕallim ˀibnak yumxuṭ bič-čaffiyya.* Teach your son to blow his nose with a handkerchief.

maxxaṭ **1.** to blow one's nose frequently. *manšuul w-da-ymaxxuṭ ihwaaya.* He's got a cold and he's blowing his nose a lot. **2.** to cause to blow the nose. *maxxiṭat ˀibinha w-misḥat xašma.* She made her son blow and wiped his nose.

maxiṭ blowing the nose.

maxṭa pl. *-aat* i.n. of *maxiṭ.*

muxṭa pl. *-aat* blob of mucus, piece of snot.

mxaaṭ nasal mucus, snot. || *mxaaṭ iš-šeeṭaan* gossamer, cobwebs.

muxṭaan (coll.) pl. *mxaaṭiin* nasal mucus, snot. || *muxṭaan iš-šiiṭaan* cobwebs, gossamer.

muxṭaana pl. *-aat* un. n. of *muxṭaan.*

*muxaaṭi** mucous. *ˀaǧšiya muxaaṭiyya* mucous membranes.

m-x-l-m

maxḷama pl. *-aat* omelette.

m-d-a-l

madaalya pl. *-aat* medal, decoration.

m-d-a-l-y-w-n

madaalyoon pl. *-aat* pendant, locket, medallion.

[1]*m-d-a-m*

madaam, madaama pl. *-aat* madam, lady (polite form of address or term for a non-Arab woman). *laabsa libis ṭaalʕa bii madaama.* She looks like a fashionable foreigner in those clothes she's wearing.

[2]*m-d-a-m*

madaam = *ma-daam,* which see under *d-w-m.*

m-d-ḥ

midaḥ (*a madiḥ*) to commend, praise, laud, extol. *midaḥa b-qaṣiida rannaana.* He praised him in a resounding poem.

nmidaḥ pass. of *midaḥ.*

madiḥ praise.

m-d-d

madd (*i madd*) **1.** to extend, stretch, stretch out. *raḥ-agʕud ihnaa ḥatta ˀagdar ˀamidd rijlayya.* I'll sit here so I can stretch out my legs. *madd-li ˀiida.* He extended his hand to me. **2.** to spread, spread out, lay, lay out. *š-šarika da-tmidd ˀanaabiib nafuṭ minnaa l-baǧdaad.* The company is laying oil pipes from here to Baghdad. **3.** to provide, supply. *gidar yidrus bil-xaarij, li-ˀan ˀabuu čaan ymidda bil-ifluus.* He was able to study abroad because his father was supplying him with money.

maddad **1.** to stretch out, spread out. *maddidoo ʕal-gaaʕ w-dawwraw ijyuuba.* They stretched him out on the ground and went through his pockets. **2.** to extend, distend, elongate, expand. *l-ḥaraara tmaddid il-maʕaadin.* Heat expands metals. **3.** to lengthen, extend, protract, prolong. *raḥ-ˀamaddid ˀijaazti šahar laax.* I am going to extend my leave another month. *maddad-li muddat dafiʕ id-deen šahreen.* He extended the payment time of the debt two months for me.

tmaddad **1.** to be extended, prolonged. *wakt il-imtiḥaan itmaddad ˀila yoom il-xamiis.* The exam time has been put off until Thursday. **2.** to lengthen, expand, distend, extend, stretch, spread. *tirkaw hal-išguug bij-jisir li-ˀan yitmaddad bil-ḥaraara.* They left these cracks in the bridge because it expands in the heat. **3.** to stretch oneself out, sprawl. *l-baarḥa tmaddadit bil-ifraaš w-nimit ihwaaya.* Yesterday I stretched out on the bed and slept quite a while.

mtadd to extend, run, stretch (over a distance). *haṭ-ṭariiq yimtadd min beetna liš-šaṭṭ.* This road extends from our house to the river.

stimadd to draw, derive, get. *yistimidd quuta mnil-ḥizib.* He derives his power from the party.

madd 1. extension, stretching. || *ʕala madd il-baṣar* as far as the eye can see. *ʔaku ʔašjaar ʕala madd il-baṣar.* There are trees as far as the eye can see. 2. lengthening, protraction. || *ʔaani wyaak ʕala madd ʔaḷḷa.* In time I'll show you! 3. tide, flood tide. *has-sifiina ma-raḥ-itruuḥ ʔilla lamma yiji l-madd.* This ship won't depart until the tide comes in.

midda pus, purulent matter.

mudda pl. *mudad* 1. period of time, interval. *b-muddat šahar tʕallam kull šii.* In the period of a month he learned everything. 2. while. *ntiḏ̣arta mudda laakin ma-jaa.* I waited for him a while but he didn't come. *ṣaar-li mudda ṭwiila ma-šaayfak.* It's been a long time since I saw you. 3. limited time, term.

madad pl. *ʔamdaad* advantage, handicap (in a contest, etc.). *nṭiini madad xams amtaar w-atġaalab wiyyaak.* Give me a five-meter handicap and I'll race you.

ʔimdaad pl. *-aat* provision, supply.

maadda pl. *mawaad* 1. material, matter, substance. *mawaad ʔawwaliyya* raw materials. *mawaad ḥarbiyya* war matériel. 2. subject, field of study. *hal-maadda ma-maṭluuba bil-ʔimtiḥaan.* This subject isn't required in the exam. 3. article, paragraph of a legal document). *nḥikam ḥasb il-maadda l-xaamsa mnil-qaanuun.* He was sentenced according to article five of the law.

m-d-n

maddan to civilize, urbanize, refine. *hal-miʕdaan, š-yimaddinhum?* How could these yokels ever be civilized?

tmaddan to become urbanized, civilized, modernized. *l-ʕiraaq itmaddan ihwaaya baʕd il-ḥarub.* Iraq became quite modern after the war. *šuuf ʕali, šloon tmaddan! štira raadyo w-ḥaṭṭ ib-beeta talafoon.* Look how urbanized Ali's gotten! He bought a radio and put a telephone in his house.

madiina pl. *mudun* city, town. || *l-madiina* Medina (city in Saudi Arabia).

*madani** 1. civic, civil, city. *markaz madani* civic center. 2. civilian (as opposed to military). *malaabis madaniyya* civilian clothes. 3. a civilian.

madaniyya civilization.

m-r-ʔ

mara pl. *niswaan* 1. woman. 2. wife.

mrayya pl. *-aat* var. of *mara.*

mariiʔan: ʔukulha haniiʔan mariiʔan Eat it in good health. May you enjoy it.

mruwwa the best virtues of mankind, especially compassion, generosity, and a sense of honor. *hal-gaṣṣaab ybiiʕ ġaali. ma-ʕinda mruwwa.* This butcher charges too much. He has no heart. *ʔahl il-imruwwa jimʕoo-la fluus w-maššoo l-ʔahla.* The kind-hearted people collected money for him and sent him to his family. *mruutak! xaḷḷiṣni min har-rijjaal!* By your honor! Save me from this man! *ʔinta w-mruutak. š-ma tinṭiini, ʔaqbal.* I leave it to your conscience. Whatever you give me, I'll accept.

m-r-a-k-š

maraakiš 1. Marrakech (city in western Morocco). 2. Morocco.

*maraakiši** 1. from or of Marrakech. 2. Moroccan. 3. a native of Marrakech. 4. a Moroccan.

m-r-j-a-n

marjaan, mirjaan coral.

m-r-j-ḥ

tmarjaḥ to swing, pendulate. *xalli j-jaahil yitmarjaḥ ib-hal-marjiiḥa.* Let the child swing in this swing.

marjiiḥa, marjuuḥa pl. *maraajiiḥ* swing.

m-r-x

l-mirriix the planet Mars.

marrax, etc., var. of *marraġ,* etc., which see under *m-r-ġ.*

m-r-d

ṃurad (*u ṃarid*) 1. to crush, squash, mash. *ʕala keefak, ṃuradt iṭ-ṭamaaṭa.* Take it easy, you've crushed the tomatoes. *s-sayyaara daasat ič-čalib w-ṃurdata.* The car ran over the dog and squashed him. *ʔuṃrud iṭ-ṭamaaṭa gabul-ma txalliiha bij-jidir.* Mash the tomatoes before you put them in the pot. *waḷḷaah aṃurdak ʔiḏa tiḥči čilma!* By God, I'll smash you if you say a word! || *l-ḥarr ṃuradni.* The heat took a lot out of me. 2. to waste, squander, fritter away. *ṃurad kull ifluusa bil-uqmaar.* He squandered all his money on gambling.

ṃarrad to smash, crush up. *la-tistangi baʕad. marradt il-ʕinjaaṣ.* Don't choose any more. You've squashed all the plums.

tṃarrad 1. to be crushed, squashed, mashed. *tmarridaw taḥat rijleen in-naas.* They were crushed under the people's feet. || *tṃarrad gaḷbi.* My heart ached (lit., was crushed). *tṃarrad gaḷbi ʕala hal-miskiin.* I was very sorry for that poor fellow. **2.** to be refractory, recalcitrant, unruly, rebellious. *qisim imnij-jeeš itmarrad.* A part of the army rebelled.

nṃurad **1.** to be crushed, squashed. *nṃurad il-xoox kulla.* All the peaches got squashed. || *galbi nṃurad.* My heart ached (lit., was crushed). *galbi nṃurad min simaɛit xabar wafaata.* My heart sank when I heard the news of his death. *nṃuradit bil-imtiħaan.* I did badly in the exam. **2.** to be wasted, squandered, frittered away. *hal-ɛaṣriyya nṃurdat ɛaleena w-ma-sawweena šii.* This afternoon was wasted for us and we didn't do a thing.

ṃarid crushing, squashing, mashing, pulping.

mard var. of *mardaana,* which see under *m-r-d-a-n.*

ṃardi pl. *ṃaraadi* punting pole, long wooden pole used by boatmen.

ṃarda pl. *-aat* i.n. of *ṃarid.*

ṃuriida pulp, mash.

m-r-d-a-n

mardaana man, esp. one possessing the knightly virtues of manliness, chivalrousness, and honor. *hal-xurdafaruuš ybiiɛ ġaraaδ̣ maal zanaana w-maal mardaana.* This variety store sells articles for women and for men. *ʔiδa ma-axaδit ħeefi minnak, ʔaani muu ṃardaana!* If I don't get my revenge on you, I'm not a man! *ṭilaɛ mardaana. ma-xalla ʔaħħad yiɛtidi ɛal-mara.* He proved himself a real man. He didn't let anyone assault the woman. || *dagga mardaana* a gentlemanly, chivalrous, gallant deed. *daggat wiyyaaya dagga mardaana w-ma-daaɛatni bid-deen.* She was very gracious to me and didn't ask me for the debt.

m-r-d-š-w-r

mardašuur pl. *-iyya* **1.** rapacious, grasping, greedy person. **2.** parasite, freeloader.

[1]*m-r-r*

marr (*u marr, muruur*) **1.** to pass, elapse, go by. *marrat ʔayyaam bila-ma nismaɛ minna.* Days passed without us hearing from him. *l-ɛamaliyya marrat ib-salaam.* The operation went well. **2.** to pass, go, come, walk. *kull yoom ɛiddat bawaaxir itmurr imnil-qanaal.* Every day several ships pass through the canal. *gabuḷ išwayya marr min-naa.* A while ago he passed by here. *l-faraaša, b-taṭawwur ħayaatha, tmurr ib-ɛiddat ʔadwaar.* During the development of its life, the butterfly goes through several stages. *ʔaani amurr ɛaleek bil-beet.* I'll drop in on you at home. *marrat ɛalayya ʔayyaam qaasya.* Hard times came my way. *ma-maarra ɛalayya hiiči qaδ̣iyya gabuḷ.* I've never had experience with such a matter before. *ɛariiδ̣ti marrat ɛala ɛiddat ʔašxaaṣ.* My application has gone through several people. *murr-li min tufraġ.* Drop by and see me when you are free.

marrar **1.** to let pass. *haj-jisir ma-ymarriruun ɛalee looriyyaat.* They won't let trucks cross over this bridge. **2.** to pass, cause to pass. *la-tmarrir ʔiidak ɛala šaɛri.* Don't run your hand over my hair.

nmarr to be passed. *haṭ-ṭariiq ma-yinmarr minna.* This road is impassable.

stimarr **1.** to last, endure, continue. *l-muṭar stimarr ɛašir saaɛaat.* The rain continued for ten hours. **2.** to continue, persist, persevere, keep on. *stimirr ɛala diraastak w-tinjaħ bil-imtiħaan.* Go on with your studies and pass the exam.

marr **1.** passing, transit, traversal, coming or going. **2.** (pl. *mraar*) hoe, or tool shaped like a hoe for moving dirt.

marra pl. *-aat* time, instance. *liɛabna pookar marra wiħda.* We played poker once. *git-lak ʔalif marra, la-tsawwi hiiči.* I've told you a thousand times, don't do that. *marra yirkab il-paaṣ w-marra yiji pyaada.* Sometimes he rides the bus and sometimes he comes on foot. || *marra ɛala marra* time after time, continually. *marra mnil-marraat* one of these times, sometime. *marra haaδa, marra δaak.* Sometimes this, sometimes that. || *fadd marra, bil-marra* completely, absolutely, entirely. *ʔaani miflis fadd marra.* I'm completely broke. *ṭilaɛ zmaaḷ fadd marra.* He turned out to be a complete ass. *haaδa fadd marra ma-yiftihim.* He doesn't know at all. *ma-ʔili ɛalaaqa bii bil-marra.* I haven't any connections with him at all. *w-ʔašu fadd marra . . .* and it seemed all at once . . ., and suddenly . . .

muruur **1.** passing, passage. **2.** traffic. *šurṭat il-muruur* traffic police.

mamarr pl. *-aat* passageway, corridor.

maarr pl. *-a* **1.** passer-by. **2.** pedestrian.

[2]*m-r-r*

murr **1.** bitter. *l-gahwa murra. jiib-li šwayya šakar.* The coffee is bitter. Bring me some sugar. *šaaf il-murr, δ̣aag il-murr.* He's experienced hardship. He's had a hard time.

maraara **1.** bitterness. **2.** hardship, difficulty, tribulation. **3.** (pl. *-aat*) gall bladder.

ʔamarr **1.** more or most bitter. **2.** worse,

worst, more or most terrible. || *l-ˀamarreen* (originally, the two worst things, poverty and old age) great hardship, tribulation, difficulty. *qaaseet il-ˀamarreen min ˀiida* I went through terrible hardship because of him.

m-r-s

maaras to pursue, practice (a profession). *maaras mihnat iṭ-ṭibb mudda ṭwiila.* He practiced medicine for a long time.

m-r-ḍ

muraḍ (*a maraḍ*) to become sick. *muraḍ marrteen has-sana.* He got sick twice this year.

marraḍ to make sick. *ˀaklat il-baarḥa marriḍatha.* The food yesterday made her sick.

tmarraḍ to get sick, be made sick. *huwwa ḍaʕiif il-bunya w-yitmarraḍ ib-surʕa.* He has a weak constitution and gets sick easily.

tmaaraḍ to feign illness, malinger. *t-tilmiiδ itmaaraḍ ḥatta ma-yruuḥ lil-madrasa.* The student feigned illness so he wouldn't have to go to school.

maraḍ pl. *ˀamraaḍ* **1.** disease, ailment. **2.** sickness, illness.

marḍa pl. *-aat* bout of sickness, siege of illness.

mariiḍ **1.** sick, ill, ailing. *ʕammi baʕda mariiḍ w-naayim bil-ifraaš.* My uncle's still stick and staying in bed. **2.** (pl. *marḍa*) sick person, patient.

tamriiḍ nursing, caring for the sick.

mumarriḍa pl. *-aat* nurse.

m-r-ġ

marraġ to massage, rub. *ṭulab min ˀibna ymarriġ-la ḍahra.* He asked his son to massage his back for him.

m-r-ġ-l

marġal to roll, roll around. *ḥatta yˀaδδii, marġal šafiqta bit-tiraab.* To hurt him he rolled his hat around in the dirt. *marġal zirr id-dijaaja biṭ-ṭiḥiin gabuḷ-ma ma-ygaḷḷii.* He rolled the chicken leg in flour before he fried it.

tmarġal to wallow, roll around. *č-čalib itmarġal bit-tiraab.* The dog wallowed in the dirt.

m-r-g

ṃarag **1.** gravy. **2.** stew, goulash.

marga pl. *-aat* stew. *margat ispeenaaġ* spinach stew. *margat beetinjaan* eggplant stew.

m-r-g-ṣ

tmargaṣ to mince, move with a mincing gait, move daintily. *yitmargaṣ min yimši. ʕabaalak ibnayya.* He walks with a mincing gait. He looks like a girl.

m-r-m-r

marmar to exasperate, vex. *j-jaahil marmar ˀumma bil-bači maala.* The kid exasperated his mother with his crying.

marmar marble.

m-r-n

marran **1.** to train, drill (someone). *l-muʕallim marranhum ihwaaya gabḷ is-sibaaq.* The teacher drilled them a lot before the game. **2.** to accustom, condition, season, get used. *da-ymarrin nafsa ʕal-kitaaba b-iida l-yisra.* He's accustoming himself to writing with his left hand.

tmarran to exercise, practice, train, rehearse. *laazim titmarran ihwaaya gabuḷ-ma tudxul is-sibaaq.* You've got to practice a lot before you enter the game. *l-mulaakim da-yitmarran saaʕteen kull yoom.* The boxer is training two hours every day. *l-mumaθθiliin da-yitmarrinuun ʕala ˀadwaarhum.* The actors are rehearsing their roles.

marin reasonable, flexible. *tigdar titfaaham wiyyaa. huwwa fadd waaḥid marin.* You can reach an understanding with him. He's a flexible person.

tamriin pl. *-aat, tamaariin* exercise, practice, training.

m-r-w

mruwwa see *m-r-ˀ*.

m-r-y

mraaya pl. *miri,* see under *r-ˀ-y*.

mara, mrayya see under *m-r-ˀ*.

m-r-y-w-l

maryool pl. *-aat* **1.** apron. **2.** smock.

m-z-j

mizaj (*i mazij*) **1.** to mix, blend. *da-ymizjuun šaḥam wiyya z-zeet w-ybiiʕuu.* They're mixing fat with vegetable oil and selling it. **2.** to combine, consolidate. *ma-aku muʕallim il-haṣ-ṣaff. ˀimzij iṣ-ṣaffeen.* There's no teacher for this class. Consolidate the two classes.

mtizaj to mix, mingle. *ˀaani ma-amtizij wiyya hiiči naas.* I don't mingle with that kind of people.

mizaaj pl. *ˀamzija* **1.** temperament, disposition, nature. **2.** frame of mind, mood, humor. **3.** taste, discernment. *haaδa ṣaaḥib mizaaj; ma-ʕinda maaniʕ yuṣruf fluus ˀazyad ʕal-ʕarag iz-zeen.* He has taste; he doesn't mind spending more money for good arrack.

maziij pl. *-aat* **1.** mixture, blend. **2.** compound, combination.

m-z-z
mazza pl. *-aat* appetizers, hors d'oeuvre (when served with alcoholic beverages).
m-z-q
mazzaq to humiliate, degrade, disgrace. *mazziqoo giddaam ˀaṣdiqaaˀa.* They humiliated him in front of his friends.
m-z-g
mizag (*i mazig*) to tear, rip, rend. *l-paaysikil mizag panṭarooni.* The bicycle tore my pants. *mizag warqat id-daftar.* He tore a page of the notebook.
mazzag /with *b-*/ to tear up, tear to bits. *j-jaahil da-ymazzig b-iktaabi.* The kid is tearing my book up.
tmazzag to be or become torn to shreds. *tmazzigat ihduuma mnil-ʕarka.* His clothes were all torn up in the fight.
nmizag to be torn. *tantat is-sayyaara nmizgat.* The convertible car top got torn.
mazig **1.** tearing, ripping, rending. **2.** (pl. *mzuug*) tear, rip, torn place.
mazga pl. *-aat* i.n. of *mazig* **1.**
m-z-l-g
mazlag to make slip. *diir baalak ʕaθθalij tara ymazligak.* Watch out for the ice or it'll make you slip and fall. *l-muʕaami mazlag il-muttaham ib-ˀasˀilta.* The lawyer made the defendant slip with his questions.
tmazlag to slip, slide, be slippery. *l-maaʕuun itmazlag min ˀiidi w-wugaʕ.* The dish slipped from my hand and fell. *ṣ-ṣaabuuna titmazlag bil-iid.* Soap is slippery in the hand.
mizleega pl. *-aat* slick spot, slippery place.
m-z-n
mizna pl. *mizan* rain, shower.
miizaan see *w-z-n.*
m-z-y
maziyya pl. *mazaaya* merit, virtue.
m-z-y-q-a
maziiqa music.
m-s-ˀ
masaaˀ see *m-s-w.*
m-s-t-k-y
mastaki **1.** mastic, resin of the mastic tree. **2.** a confection containing a small amount of mastic.
[1]*m-s-ʕ*
misaʕ (*a masiʕ*) **1.** to wipe, wipe off, clean. *ˀimsaʕ il-meez gabuḷ-ma tʕuṭṭ ʕalee šii.* Wipe off the table before you put anything on it. **2.** to wipe out, rub out, erase. *misʕaw ˀismak min qaaˀimt ittarfiiʕ.* They struck your name off the promotion list. *misaʕ il-ʕaar ʕaaˀilta.* He wiped out the shame on his family.
tmassaʕ **1.** to wipe, cleanse oneself. *l-ˀislaam yitšattifuun wil-masiiʕiyyiin yitmassiʕuun.* The Moslems wash themselves and the Christians wipe themselves. **2.** /with *b-*/ to rub up against. *l-buzzuuna da-yitmassaʕ biyya.* The cat is rubbing up against me.
nmisaʕ to be erased, rubbed out. *l-ʕibir ma-yinmisiʕ bil-missaaʕa.* Ink can't be erased with the eraser.
masiʕ wiping, wiping off, cleaning.
masʕa pl. *-aat* i.n. of *masiʕ.*
massaaʕ pl. *-iin* land surveyor.
missaaʕa pl. *-aat* eraser.
masaaʕa pl. *-aat* **1.** area, surface extent. *masaaʕat daaˀira* area of a circle. **2.** surveying, survey. *mudiiriyyat il-masaaʕa* Directorate of Survey.
l-masiiʕ Christ, the Messiah.
*masiiʕi** **1.** Christian. **2.** a Christian.
masiiʕiyya Christianity.
[2]*m-s-ʕ*
timsaaʕ pl. *tamaasiiʕ* **1.** crocodile. **2.** alligator.
m-s-d
massad to rub, stroke (esp. an animal). *massad-ilha lil-bazzuuna ʕatta hidˀat.* He stroked the cat until it calmed down.
m-s-k
misak (*i mask*) to begin fasting (during Ramadan). *ṣaarat saaʕa xamsa. laazim timsik.* It is five o'clock. You have to start fasting.
ˀamsak = *misak.*
tmassak to cling, adhere, hold fast. *dayitmassak ib-raˀya w-ma-yitnaazal.* He's sticking to his opinion and won't come off it.
mask: mask id-dafaatir book-keeping, accounting.
ˀimsaak **1.** the time of day for beginning the Ramadan fast. **2.** (med.) constipation. *baṭni toojaʕni liˀan ʕindi ˀimsaak.* My stomach hurts me because I'm constipated.
ˀimsaakiyya pl. *-aat* a calendar showing times for sunrise and sunset used for fasting during Ramadan.
mamsak something to hold on to, grip, handhold. || *ma-ʕalee ˀay mamsak.* I can't get anything on him.
mustamsak pl. *-aat* document of proof (e.g. deed, birth certificate, license, etc.).
m-s-k-n
miskiin pl. *masaakiin* poor, wretched, miserable person.

m-s-w

massa to spend the evening. *sabbaʕna b-baġdaad w-masseena bil-baṣra.* In the morning we were in Baghdad and in the evening we were in Basra. *yṣabbuʕ bis-sabb w-ymassi bis-sabb.* He spends the morning and the evening in cursing.

masa, masaaʔ (no pl.) evening. *masaaʔ il-xeer!* Good evening!

*masaaʔi** evening. *jariida masaaʔiyya* an evening newspaper.

ʔumsiyya pl. *-aat* evening.

m-š-š

mašš (*i mašš*) to wipe, wipe off. *mišš il-meez ib-hal-wuṣla.* Wipe the table with this cloth. || *mišš buuzak. ma-aku tarfiiʕaat.* Forget it (lit., wipe your mouth). There aren't any promotions.

m-š-ṭ

maššaṭ to comb. *da-tmaššiṭ šaʕarha jiddaam il-umrayya.* She's combing her hair in front of the mirror. *maššiṭi ṣ-ṣuuf gabul-ma tġizlii.* Comb the wool before you spin it.

tmassaṭ to be combed. *šaʕrak waṣix w-ma-yitmaššaṭ.* Your hair is dirty and can't be combed.

mišiṭ pl. *mšaaṭ, mšaaṭa* 1. comb. 2. clip (of bullets).

m-š-g

maššag to become rough and chapped. *ʔiidi maššigat imnil-barid.* My hands became chapped from the cold.

mišag 1. chapping. 2. chapped skin.

m-š-k-l

maškal to place in a quandary, to cause problems, trouble. *gul-li truuʕ loo laaʔ. la-tmaškilni.* Tell me whether you're going or not. Don't cause me trouble.

tmaškal to have trouble. *štira sayyaara ʕatiiga w-itmaškal biiha.* He bought an old car and had trouble with it.

m-š-m-š

mišmiš (coll.) 1. apricot(s). 2. apricot tree(s).

mišmiša pl. *-aat* 1. apricot. 2. apricot tree.

m-š-y

miša (*i maši*) 1. to walk, go on foot. *j-jaahil bida yimši.* The child has begun to walk. 2. to go. *baačir raʕ-amši lil-mooṣil.* Tomorrow I'm going to go to Mosul. *l-qiṭaar miša saaʕa xamsa.* The train left at five o'clock. 3. to move along, proceed. *ʔimši! la-toogaf ihnaa.* Move along! Don't stand here. *laazim timšuun ʕala xiṭṭa muʕayyana.* You should follow a specific plan. 4. to run around, associate, keep company. *la-timši wiyya s-sarsariyya tara tṣiir miθilhum.* Don't run around with bums or you'll become like them. || *ribaaṭak ma-yimši wiyya hal-qaaṭ.* Your tie doesn't go with this coat. 5. to run, operate, work. *sayyaarti ma-da-timši; yimkin il-baanziin xilaṣ.* My car won't run; maybe it's out of gas. *l-ifluus il-ingiliiziyya ma-timši hnaa.* English money doesn't work here. *l-xaaṭraana ma-timši b-had-daaʔira.* Favoritism doesn't go in this office. *l-ʕiila mišat ʕalee.* The trick worked on him. *mišat baṭnak il-yoom?* Did your bowels move today? 6. to succeed. *mišeet b-imtiʕaan il-kiimya.* I passed the chemistry exam. *haj-jigaayir ij-jidiida mišat; kull in-naas da-yištiruuha.* These new cigarettes went over; all the people are buying them. || *ybayyin qaδiyyat tarfiiʕak ma-raʕ-timši.* It seems that the matter of your promotion isn't going through.

mašša 1. to walk, make or let walk. *xalli nṭalliʕ ij-jaahil barra w-inmašši.* Let's take the child out and walk him. 2. to make or let go, send. *ʔinṭii fluusa w-maššii.* Give him his money and let him go. *raʕ-ymašši ʔibna l-baġdaad.* He's going to send his son to Baghdad. 3. to pass, run. *mašši ʔiidak ʕaleeha w-šuufha šloon naaʕma.* Run your hand across it and see how smooth it is. 4. to advance, further, promote. *kull waaʕid yriid iymašši maṣlaʕta.* Everyone wants to further his own interests. *da-ysawwii-lha diʕaaya lil-biira ʕatta ymaššiiha.* He's running advertising for the beer in order to push it. *mašši š-šuġul; la-tʕaṭṭla.* Get the work going; don't delay it. *maššiini, ya-mʕawwad! ʔaani mistaʕjil.* Hurry up with me, for gosh sakes; I'm in a hurry. || *mašši w-ʕabbi bil-xurij.* Don't take pains. Don't be so fussy (lit., let things go and fill the saddlebags). 5. to allow to advance, to promote, pass. *ma-jaawab zeen bil-ʔimtiʕaan laakin raʕ-ʔamaššii.* He didn't answer very well on the exam but I'm going to pass him. 6. to relieve, loosen (the bowels). *ir-raggi ymašši il-baṭin.* Watermelon relieves the bowels.

maaša to get along with, stay on good terms with, go along with, humor. *ʔiδa triid tidzawwajha, laazim itmaaši ʔabuuha.* If you want to marry her, you'll have to get along with her father. *maašii fadd čam isbuuʕ. huwwa manquul.* Go along with him for a few weeks. He's being transferred.

tmašša to take a walk, to stroll, promenade. *yʕijbak inruuḥ nitmašša šwayya?* Would you like to go for a little stroll?

nmiša pass. of *miša. l-ġurfa malyaana ġaraaḏ ma-yinmiši biiha.* The room is so full of things you can't walk in it.

maši walking.

mašya pl. *-aat* 1. manner of walking, gait, step. 2. trip, journey.

mamša pl. *mamaaši* 1. walkway, passageway, aisle, corridor. 2. footpath, pathway.

maaši 1. walking, going. *jeet maaši mnil-maḥaṭṭa lil-beet.* I came home on foot from the station. 2. (pl. *-iin*) pedestrian. 3. foot soldier, infantryman. 4. *mušaat* (pl. only) infantry.

maašiya pl. *mawaaši* livestock, cattle.

m-ṣ-x

muṣax (*u maṣix*) to upbraid, scold, shame, humiliate. *ʔabuu muṣaxa tamaam.* His father scolded him good and proper. || *muṣax ʔaḥwaala.* He really told him off. He scolded him harshly. *raḥ-ašuufa l-yoom w-ʔamṣux-lak ʔaḥwaala.* I'm going to see him today and tell him off but good.

maṣṣax to make dirty, to soil, stain. *j-jaahil liʕab biṭ-ṭiin w-maṣṣax ihduuma.* The kid played in the mud and got his clothes all dirty. || *yeezi ʕaad! muu maṣṣaxitha!* Enough now! You've already gone too far! *maṣṣax ʔaḥwaala.* He really told him off. He scolded him harshly. *ʕali tʕaarak wiyya saami w-maṣṣax ʔaḥwaala.* Ali had an argument with Sami and really told him off.

tmaṣṣax pass. of *maṣṣax. la-txalli j-jaahil yilʕab biṭ-ṭiin. hduuma tmaṣṣxat.* Don't let the kid play in the mud. His clothes got dirty.

maṣaaxa a humiliating, dirty, unpleasant thing. *š-šuġuḷ ib-hal-maʕmal maṣaaxa.* Working in this factory is an unpleasant thing.

maaṣix flat, tasteless, needing salt. *ʔakil maaṣix* tasteless food. *šgadd-ma axalli miliḥ bii, baʕda maaṣix.* No matter how much salt I add to it, it's still flat.

m-ṣ-r

miṣir, maṣir Egypt.

*miṣri** 1. Egyptian. 2. an Egyptian.

m-ṣ-r-n

muṣraan pl. *mṣaariin* intestine, gut.

m-ṣ-ṣ

maṣṣ (*u maṣṣ*) 1. to suck. *j-jaahil daymuṣṣ ibhaama.* The child is sucking his thumb. 2. to soak up, absorb. *waraq inniššaaf iymuṣṣ il-ḥibir.* Blotter paper soaks up ink. 3. to sip. *ʔiḏa twaṣṣil il-muṣṣaaṣa l-čaʕb il-igḷaaṣ, tigdar itmuṣṣ iš-šarbat kulla.* If you stick a straw to the bottom of the glass, you can sip the whole drink.

nmaṣṣ to be sucked. *hal-ḥabbaaya laazim tinmaṣṣ; ma-tinbiliʕ.* This pill has to be sucked; it can't be swallowed.

mtaṣṣ to soak up, absorb. *ḏibb il-xirga ʕal-ṃayy ḥatta timtaṣṣa.* Throw the rag on the water so it'll soak it up.

maṣṣ 1. sucking, sucking up, soaking up. 2. sipping.

maṣṣa pl. *-aat* i.n. of *maṣṣ.*

muṣṣaaṣa pl. *-aat* 1. sucker, lollipop. 2. drinking straw. 3. something to suck, pacifier.

mamṣuuṣ lean, emaciated, skinny. *šuufa šloon mamṣuuṣ! ʕabaalak ṣaar-la šahr ma-maakil šii.* Look at how skinny he is! As though he's not eaten anything in a month.

m-ṣ-ṭ-b

maṣṭaba, muṣṭaba pl. *maṣaaṭub* bench.

m-ṣ-ṭ-r

maṣṭar to rule, draw straight lines. *maṣṭir id-daftar kulla gabuḷ-ma ddaxxil il-iḥsaab.* Rule off the whole notebook before you enter the amounts.

maṣṭar line, straight line. *ʔoogfu maṣṭar ḥatta ʔaḥsibkum.* Stand in a line so I can count you. *maṣṭara* pl. *maṣaaṭir* 1. ruler, straightedge. 2. sample.

see also *ṣ-ṭ-r.*

m-ṣ-l

maṣṣal to water, salivate. *min šifta yaakul ṭurši, maṣṣal ḥalgi.* When I saw him eating pickles, my mouth watered.

maṣil pl. *ʔamṣaal* 1. serum. 2. plasma.

m-ṣ-l-w

maṣlaawi see under *m-w-ṣ-l.*

m-ṣ-m-ṣ

maṣmaṣ 1. to suck. *lamma xilaṣ il-laḥam, bidaw ymaṣumṣuun bil-iʕḏaam.* When the meat was gone, they started sucking on the bones. 2. (mostly humorous) to kiss. *ḥaṭṭha bis-sayyaara w-bida ymaṣmuṣ biiha.* He got her in the car and started smooching her.

m-ḏ-r-ṭ

tmaḏraṭ (impolite) to make an ass of oneself. *yitmaḏraṭ ib-ḥačya.* He makes an ass of himself when he talks.

see also *ḍ-r-ṭ.*

m-ḍ-ḍ

maḍḍ (*u maḍḍ*) 1. to affect, have an effect, take effect. *ṭ-ṭalqa l-ɛaadiyya ma-tmuḍḍ bit-timsaaɛ.* An ordinary bullet won't have any effect on a crocodile. *l-ɛayya ma-ymuḍḍ biiha is-simm.* Poison won't affect a snake. *l-baṣiṭ ma-ymuḍḍ bii.* Beating doesn't affect him.

ˀamaḍḍ more or most penetrating, effective, trenchant.

maaḍḍ penetrating, effective, trenchant.

m-ḍ-m-ḍ

maḍmaḍ to rinse out (the mouth). *maḍmuḍ ɛalgak ib-had-duwa.* Rinse out your mouth with this medicine.

tmaḍmaḍ to rinse out one's mouth. *tmaḍmaḍ baɛad-ma tfarrič isnuunak.* Rinse out your mouth after you brush your teeth.

m-ḍ-y

muḍa (*i muḍi, maḍi*) 1. to pass, go by, elapse. *muḍat mudda w-ma-difaɛ il-ˀiijaar.* Quite a while passed and he didn't pay the rent. 2. (*i ˀimḍaaˀ*) to sign one's name, affix one's signature. *ˀumḍi b-hal-mukaan bil-ɛariiḍa.* Sign your name in this space on the application.

maḍḍa 1. to pass, spend. *da-nilɛab waraq ɛatta nmaḍḍi waqit.* We're playing cards to kill time. 2. to cause to sign, make sign. *la-tinsa tmaḍḍii gabul-ma tinṭii fluus.* Don't forget to make him sign before you give him any money.

ˀumḍaaˀ pl. *-aat* signature.

maaḍi 1. past, bygone. *s-sana l-maaḍya* last year. 2. past life, history. *haaḍa r-rijjaal maɛruuf maaḍiyya.* This man's past is well-known. *l-maaḍi* 1. the past. *ˀiɛna ma-ɛaleena bil-maaḍi. hassa š-raɛ-insawwi?* We don't care about the past. What will we do now? 2. the past tense.

m-ḍ-y-g

tmaḍyag to behave in an unnatural, affected manner. *yitmaḍyag ib-ɛačya.* He has an affected manner of speaking.

m-ṭ-r

muṭar (*u muṭar*) to rain. *l-baarɛa muṭrat muddat saaɛteen.* Yesterday it rained for two hours.

maṭṭar 1. to rain. *ybayyin raɛ-itmaṭṭir baačir.* It looks like it's going to rain tomorrow. 2. to cause to rain. *balki ˀaḷḷa ymaṭṭirha w-yintiɛiš iz-zariɛ.* Perhaps God will make it rain and the crops will be rejuvenated.

muṭar pl. *ˀamṭaar* rain.

maṭra pl. *-aat* downpour, shower.

maṭṭaara pl. *-aat* canteen, flask.

mumṭir rainy. *jaww mumṭir* rainy weather.

m-ṭ-r-l-w-z

maṭrillooz pl. *-aat* machine gun.

m-ṭ-l

muṭal (*u maṭil*) to throw down (in wrestling). *huwwa ˀakbar minni bass agdar ˀamuṭla.* He's bigger than me but I can throw him down.

maaṭal 1. to wrestle, wrestle with. *maaṭla, w-ˀiḍa tuġlub, taaxuḍ jaaˀiza.* Wrestle him, and if you win, you'll get a prize. 2. to stall, put off. *ḍall šahreen ymaaṭilni gabuḷ-ma yrajjiɛ-li l-ifluus.* He kept putting me off for two months before he returned the money to me.

tmaaṭal to wrestle, wrestle with each other. *šuuf ij-jaahil w-axuu da-yitmaaṭluun ɛaθ-θayyil.* Look at the kid and his brother wrestling on the lawn.

muṭṭaal (coll.) dried dung chips used for fuel.

muṭṭaala pl. *-aat* un. n. of *muṭṭaal.*

mumaaṭala stalling, putting off. *laazim tinṭiini l-ifluus baačir, bila mumaaṭala.* You've got to give me the money tomorrow, without stalling.

m-ṭ-y

maṭṭa 1. to stretch, strain. *la-tmaṭṭi j-jilid zaayid tara yinmizig.* Don't stretch the hide too much or it'll tear. 2. to extend, push out, stick out. *maṭṭa šiffta.* He stuck out his lip.

tmaṭṭa to stretch, extend. *hal-ijwaariib tittmaṭṭa.* These socks are stretchable.

muṭi pl. *mṭaaya* donkey, ass. *la-tṣiir muṭi!* Don't be a jackass!

m-ɛ-a

maɛa (in a few set phrases) with. *maɛa l-ˀasaf* with regrets, regretfully, unfortunately. *maɛa l-ˀasaf, ma-agdar aji.* Unfortunately, I can't come. *maɛa l-ɛilm* with knowledge, knowingly, deliberately, intentionally. *maɛa l-mamnuuniyya* with pleasure, gladly. *maɛa haaḍa* despite that, nevertheless, notwithstanding, even so. *maɛa haaḍa, ma-čaan laazim idgul-la.* Nevertheless, you shouldn't have told him.

m-ɛ-č-a-l

miɛčaal pl. *mɛaačiil* sling, slingshot.

¹*m-ɛ-d*

miɛda pl. *-aat* stomach.

²*m-ε-d*
mεeedi pl. *miεdaan* peasant, yokel, rube, hick.
m-ε-d-n-w-s
maεdanoos a kind of parsley.
m-ε-k-r-w-n-a
maεkaroona macaroni.
m-ε-m-ε
maεmaε to bleat. *haṣ-ṣaxal ymaεmiε ihwaaya.* This billy goat bleats a lot.
m-ε-n
tmaεεan to look closely, check carefully. *tmaεεan bil-qaðiyya gabuḷ-ma tqarrir šii.* Look into the matter carefully before you decide anything.
maaεuun see under *m-a-ε-w-n.*
m-ġ-ṣ
maġaṣ gripes, colic.
m-ġ-ṭ
tmaġġaṭ to stretch, stretch one's limbs. *l-baarḥa ma-naam ihwaaya. da-yiθθaawab w-yitmaġġaṭ.* He didn't sleep much yesterday. He's yawning and stretching.
m-ġ-n-a-ṭ-y-z
miġnaaṭiiz 1. magnetism. 2. (pl. *-aat*) magnet.
m-q-r-n-a
maqarna macaroni.
m-q-l-č
tmaqlač to be strained, act in an unnatural manner. *yitmaqlač ib-ḥačya.* He talks in an unnatural manner.
m-k-r
makkaar cunning, sly, crafty, wily.
m-k-r-f-w-n
mikrafoon pl. *-aat* 1. microphone. 2. loudspeaker, speaker (in a radio, etc.).
m-k-k
makkuuk pl. *-aat* bobbin (of a sewing machine).
maakuuk pl. *mwaakiik* bobbin.
¹*m-k-n*
makkan to enable, put in a position, afford the possibility, make possible. *ṣiḥḥti ma-tmakkinni asaafir.* My health doesn't allow me to travel.
ʔamkan to be possible. *ma-ʔamkanni ʔaji.* It wasn't possible for me to come. *ma-yimkin titraffaε gabuḷ nihaayt is-sana.* It's impossible for you to be promoted before the end of the year. *sawweet kull illi yimkin ʔasawwi.* I did all that I possibly could do. || *yimkin* it's possible, possibly, perhaps, maybe. *yimkin iykuun mawjuud.* Maybe he's there. *yimkin raḥ-tumṭur.* Maybe it'll rain.
tmakkan to be in a position, be able. *ma-atmakkan ʔaji lil-ḥafla.* I can't come to the party.
ʔimkaan 1. power, capacity, capability. *muu b-ʔimkaani ʔasaaεda.* It isn't in my power to help him. *muu b-imkaani asawwiiha.* I'm not in a position to do it. 2. possibility. || *ḥasab il-imkaan, b-* or *εala qadir il-imkaan* as much as possible, as far as possible. *raḥ-amiddak bil-ifluus ḥasab il-imkaan.* I'll provide you with as much money as I can. *raḥ-asaaεdak εala qadir il-imkaan.* I'll help you as much as possible. *εind il-imkaan* when and if possible. *ʔaxaabrak εind il-imkaan.* I'll call you if I have a chance.
ʔimkaaniyya pl. *-aat* possibility. *tbarraε b-aqall min imkaaniita.* He donated less than he could have.
mumkin 1. possible. *haaða šii mumkin.* That's possible. || *ġeer mumkin* impossible. 2. possibly, perhaps, maybe. *mumkin asaafir baačir.* Maybe I'll leave tomorrow.
mitmakkin 1. in a secure position, having everything under control. *b-hal-ḥaraka, raḥ-akuun mitmakkin εaleek.* With this move, I'll have the upper hand on you. 2. well-to-do, well-off, wealthy. *yidrus b-uruppa li-ʔan ʔabuu mitmakkin.* He studies in Europe because his father is well-to-do.
²*m-k-n*
makiina pl. *makaayin* 1. machine. *makiinat maay* water pump. *makiinat ḥilaaqa* razor, shaver. 2. works, movement (of a watch). 3. mill, grist mill. 4. motor, engine.
m-k-y-a-j
mikyaaj 1. make-up. 2. greasepaint.
m-l-j
milaj (i malij) 1. to spread with a trowel. *xalli j-juṣṣ εalee w-ʔimilja.* Put the mortar on it and spread it with a trowel. 2. to mix. *ʔimlij šwayya juṣṣ.* Mix up a little mortar.
maalaj pl. *mwaalij* trowel.
m-l-č
mlaača owner's fee, landlord's share (in share-cropping). *ṣaaḥib il-gaaε yaaxuð rubε il-ḥaaṣil mlaača.* The land owner gets a fourth of the crop for rent.
see also *m-l-k.*
m-l-ḥ
mallaḥ to salt. *baεad-ma tmalliḥ il-beetinjaan, gaḷḷii.* After you salt the eggplant, fry it.
miliḥ pl. *ʔamlaaḥ* salt.

mallaaς pl. *mlaaliiς* sailor, seaman, mariner.

mamlaςa pl. *-aat, mamaaliς* 1. salina, place where salt is obtained. 2. salt shaker, saltcellar.

ʔamlaς fem. *malςa* pl. *miliς* grey, salt-colored. *ribaaṭ ʔamlaς* a gray tie.

ʔamlaς more or most salty.

maaliς salty. *l-murga maalςa l-yoom.* The stew is salty today.

m-l-x

milax (*i malix*) 1. to tear, rip, to tear a piece out of. *l-bazzuuna milxat θoobi.* The cat tore a piece out of my shirt. 2. to hit hard, strike violently. *milaxa b-books kassar snuuna.* He struck him a blow that broke his teeth. 3. to run away, flee. *ʔaxað il-ifluus minna w-milax.* He took the money from him and fled. 4. to exaggerate. *šgadd yimlix ib-ςačya!* He sure does talk big!

mallax 1. to tear up, rip up, tear to shreds. *ςala keefak! mallaxta lil-iktaab.* Take it easy! You've torn up the book. 2. to beat up, give a severe beating to. *ʔibnak, mallixoo mnil-baṣuṭ.* They beat your son to a bloody pulp. 3. to exaggerate. *š-šurṭa ma-ṣaddigat bii li-ʔan ymallix ςala ṭuul.* The police wouldn't believe him because he's always telling wild tales.

tmallax to be torn to shreds, ripped to pieces. *jwaariibha tmallixat imnil-ġasil.* Her stockings became shredded from washing.

tmaalax to have a violent fight, fight with each other. *ςali tmaalax wiyya š-šurṭi.* Ali fought it out with the policeman.

malxiyyaat (pl. only) wild talk, tall tales, nonsense. *ma-txalliina min hal-malxiyyaat?* How about sparing us all that nonsense? *gulnaa-la ʔinto xooš ʔaadmi w-itsaaςid il-aṣdiqaaʔ w-min hal-malxiyyaat.* We told him you're a good guy and help friends and all that line of stuff.

m-l-s

ʔamlas fem. *malsa* pl. *milis, malsiin* smooth, sleek.

m-l-ṣ

milaṣ (*u maliṣ*) 1. to slide, slip. *milaṣ il-miςbas min ʔiṣbiςha.* He slipped the ring off of her finger. || *ʔiskut, tara ʔaji ʔamluṣ rugubtak.* Shut up, or I'll come and take your head off. 2. to sneak off, slip away, escape. *ʔaani ʔalahhi j-jaahil w-inta ʔumluṣ.* I'll amuse the kid and you slip away.

tmallaṣ /with *min*/ to squirm out of, shirk, dodge, evade. *yitmallaṣ imnil-masʔuuliyya ςala ṭuul.* He dodges responsibilities all the time.

nmulaṣ to slide, slip. *l-miςbas nmulaṣ min iṣibςi w-wugaς bil-mayy.* The ring slipped off my finger and fell in the water.

m-l-ṭ

ʔamlaṭ fem. *malṭa* pl. *muluṭ, malṭiin* 1. hairless. 2. hairless person.

m-l-q

tmallaq /with *l-*/ to flatter. *titmallaq ir-rajilha ςatta yištirii-lha hduum.* She flatters her husband so he'll buy clothes for her.

m-l-k

milak (*u muluk*) 1. to possess, own, have, be the owner of. *yimluk giiςaan w-ibyuut.* He owns land and houses. *ma-ʔamluk wala filis.* I don't have even a penny. 2. to dominate, control, be master of. *ʔiða tinṭii diinaareen, timulka biiha.* If you give him two dinars, you can control him with it.

mallak to make the owner of. *l-ςukuuma mallikat il-ςummaal l-ibyuut il-saakniin biiha.* The government deeded the workers the houses they were living in.

tmaalak to control, restrain (an emotion, etc.). *ma-yigdar yitmaalak ʔaςṣaaba.* He can't control his temper.

stamlak. 1. to acquire by purchase, buy. *l-baladiyya stamlikat kull had-dakaakiin.* The municipality bought up all those shops. 2. to take possession of, assume ownership of. *ʔiða tidfaς nuṣṣ qiimt il-beet, tistamlika.* If you pay half the price of the house, you can take possession.

muluk pl. *ʔamlaak* 1. property, possessions, fortune. 2. real estate, landed property. *hal-beet ʔiijaar loo muluk?* Do you rent this house or own it? || *čaanat turguṣ bil-muluk.* She was dancing in the raw.

malik pl. *muluuk* king.

malika pl. *-aat* queen.

malak pl. *malaaʔika* angel.

*malaki** royal, kingly, regal. *ςaras malaki* royal guard.

mulki civil, civilian (as opposed to military). *yilbas mulki.* He wears civilian clothing.

malakiyya monarchy, kingship.

muluukiyya 1. royalty, regality. 2. monarchic rule.

mallaak pl. *-iin, -a* 1. real estate tycoon. 2. landlord, landowner.

mamlaka pl. *mamaalik* kingdom.

maalik: maalik il-ɛaziin heron.

*maaliki** 1. belonging to the Malikite school of Moslem theology. 2. a Maliki.

mamluuk pl. *mamaaliik* white slave, mameluke.

m-l-l

mall (i mall) to be or become tired, bored, impatient, fed up. *malleet min ʔakl id-dijaaj.* I've gotten tired of eating chicken.

mulla pl. *mulaali* tutor, usually an older man who holds classes for children in his home.

mullaaya pl. *-aat* 1. fem. of *mulla.* 2. woman who sings at weddings, funerals, etc.

m-l-y

mila (i mali) 1. to fill. *ʔimli l-qalam ib-ɛibir ʔaxðar.* Fill the pen with green ink. *mila l-ʔakil miliɛ.* He put too much salt in the food. 2. to fill out. *ʔiqra t-taɛlii-maat gabuḷ-ma timli l-istimaara.* Read the instructions before you fill out the application.

malla to dictate. *l-muɛallim mallaana quṣṣa mnil-iktaab.* The teacher dictated a story from the book to us.

ʔamla to dictate. *l-muɛallim ʔamla ɛaleena quṣṣa mnil-iktaab.* The teacher dictated a story from the book to us.

nmila to be filled. *r-raadeeta nmilat ṃayy.* The radiator was filled with water.

mtila to fill up, become full. *j-jidir ʔimtila. ween ʔaɛuṭṭ baqiit it-timman?* The pot is full. Where should I put the rest of the rice?

malyaan full, filled.

ʔimlaaʔ dictation.

m-m-b-a-r

mumbaar large intestine of the lamb, used in making a kind of sausage.

m-m-m

mamma, mammiyya pl. *-att* nipple (for a bottle).

[1]*m-n*

-man (interrogative pronoun suffix) who? whom? whose? (see also *minu* under *m-n-w*). *sayyaarat-man haaði?* Whose car is this? *b-beet-man nimit il-baarɛa?* Whose house did you stay in last night? *ʔil-man triidni ʔanṭi l-maktuub?* Who do you want me to give the letter to? *bii-man itɛarrafit bil-ɛafla?* Who'd you meet at the party? *ɛalee-man da-tiɛči?* Who are you talking about? *min-man ʔaxaðt il-ifluus?* Who'd you get the money from? *har-rasim maal-man?* Whose picture is this?

[2]*m-n*

min /with following vowel, *minn-*/ 1.a. of. *yrabbi ʔanwaaɛ ġariiba mnid-dijaaj.* He raises unusual breeds of chickens. *wiɛda min rijleenaat il-meez gṣayyra.* One of the table legs is too short. *ʔariid wuṣla min hal-uqmaaš.* I want a piece of this cloth. *yoom imnil-ʔayyaam* some day, one of these days. b. of, made of, consisting of. *θoob min ɛariir* a shirt made of silk. *binaa-la beet min ṭiin.* He built himself a house out of mud. *ʔallaf kitaab min quṣaṣ.* He compiled a book of short stories. 2.a. from, away from, out of. *ʔiɛna mnil-ɛiraaq.* We are from Iraq. *nistawrid sayyaaraat imnil-xaarij.* We import cars from abroad. *ṭilaɛ min wara š-šijra.* He came out from behind the tree. *ṭilaɛ mnil-ɛarka ġaaḷub.* He came out of the fight the winner. *ʔišlaɛ tamur min haj-jiha.* Dig out some dates from this side. *s-simča zubgat min ʔiidi.* The fish slipped out of my hand. *haš-šahar giṭɛaw diinaareen min raatbi.* This month they took two dinars out of my salary. *r-riṣaaṣa ṭayyrat wuṣla min xašma.* The bullet blew a piece out of his nose. *qiis il-masaafa min-naa ʔila ʔaaxir il-ġurfa.* Measure the distance from here to the end of the room. *ddaayanit diinaar minna.* I borrowed a dinar from him. || *ʔaani min yammak.* I'm on your side. *s-siɛir min yammak.* The price is in your favor. b. from, since, for. *ʔaɛurfa min gabuḷ.* I know him from a previous time. *min yoom il-ʔimtiɛaan ʔila hassa mariið.* Since the day of the exam until now he's been sick. *ma-šifta min muddat šahar.* I haven't seen him for a month. *da-yištugul ib-had-dukkaan min muddat šahar.* He's been working in this shop for a month. || *taɛaal min wakit.* Come early. c. against, from. *ɛima wičča mnið-ðarba* He protected his face from the blow. *wugaf jawwa š-šijra mnil-muṭar.* He stopped under the tree to avoid the rain. *šaayil šamsiyya mniš-šamis.* He's carrying an umbrella to protect him from the sun. d. through, by. *l-ɛaraami dixal imn iš-šibbaač.* The thief entered through the window. *hal-gadd-ma simiin ma-yxušš mnil-baab.* He's so fat he can't go through the door. *hassa faat min haš-šaariɛ.* He just went up this street. *marr imn il-baab bila-ma yidxul.* He passed by the door without entering. e. than. *sayyaarti ʔaɛsan min sayyaartak.* My car is better than your car. f. by, at, on. *lizama min rijla*

He caught him by the leg. *hazza min čitfa.* He shook him by his shoulder. *šaal ič-čalib min ʔiδna.* He picked the dog up by its ears. **g.** because of, due to, owing to, for. *ma-da-ašuuf imniδ̣-δ̣alaam.* I can't see because of the darkness. *maat mnil-qahar.* He died from sorrow. *tlafta liθ-θoob imnil-ġasil.* You ruined the shirt by washing. *ma-ʕjazit imnil-liʕib?* Aren't you tired of playing? *ḥalga yibas min gadd-ma yiḥči.* His mouth got dry from talking so much. *sawwaaha min ʔajlak.* He did it for your sake. *minn-eeš abuuk yitšakka?* What's your father complaining about? **3.** when. *min yiδ̣ḥak l-kull yismaʕuu.* When he laughs everyone hears him. *la-tsuuq min ʔinta sakraan.* Don't drive when you are drunk. *l-ḥaraami, min ḥuṣroo bil-beet, čayyat imniṣ-ṣaṭiḥ.* When they trapped the thief in the house, he jumped off the roof. **4.** since. *ṣaar šahar min faatat il-mudda.* It's been a month since the time elapsed. *ma-gdarna ništuġuḷ min jaa.* We haven't been able to work since he came.

min-naa = *min ihnaa* from here, from this place.

m-n-č-a-s

minčaasa pl. *mnaačiis* bowl.

m-n-ḥ

minaḥ (*a maniḥ*) to grant, give, award. *minḥoo ʔijaaza nuṣṣ šahar.* They granted him a half a month leave.

minḥa pl. *minaḥ* gift, present, donation, benefaction, grant.

m-n-x

manaax climate, weather.

m-n-ʕ

minaʕ (*a maniʕ*) **1.** to hinder, prevent, stop. *hal-maadda timnaʕ iz-zinjaar.* This material prevents rust. *had-dihin yimnaʕ ṣuquuṭ iš-šaʕar.* This oil stops loss of hair. **2.** to forbid, prohibit. *minʕaw it-tadxiin bis-siinama.* They prohibited smoking in the movie. *l-ḥukuuma minʕata mnis-safar xaarij il-balad.* The government prohibited him from traveling outside the country. *ṭ-ṭabiib minaʕa mnil-ʔakl il-maaliḥ.* The doctor restricted him from salty food.

maanaʕ to be opposed, to put up resistance, act in opposition. *maanaʕ ihwaaya b-duxuul binta lil-madrasa.* He was strongly opposed to his daughter's entering school.

tmannaʕ to refrain, abstain. *tmannaʕ ihwaaya gabuḷ-ma ybiiʕha.* He held off a long time before he sold it.

mtinaʕ /with *min*/ to refrain from, abstain from, stop, cease. *mtinaʕ imnit-tadxiin.* He stopped smoking.

manaaʕa immunity.

mumaanaʕa **1.** opposition. **2.** resistance.

maaniʕ pl. *mawaaniʕ* **1.** hindrance, obstacle, obstruction. *sibaaq qafz il-mawaaniʕ* hurdles race. **2.** preventive, preventative. *maaniʕ liz-zinjaar* rust preventative. *maaniʕ lit-tajammud* anti-freeze. *maaniʕ lir-ruṭuuba* moisture protection. **3.** contraceptive. **4.** objection. *ma-aku maaniʕ tiji wyaana.* There's no objection to your coming with us. *ma-ʕindi maaniʕ.* I don't mind.

mamnuuʕ forbidden, prohibited, banned, interdicted.

m-n-g-n

mangana pl. *-aat* vise.

m-n-l-w-j

manolooj pl. *-aat* **1.** monologue. **2.** (cabaret) act, skit, sketch. **3.** ballad, satirical song.

[1]*m-n-n*

mann (*i mann*) to yearn, be covetous, desire the return. *ʔinṭaani saaʕa w-baʕdeen mann biiha.* He gave me a watch and then wanted it back.

mann: mann is-sima manna.

minniyya pl. *-aat* favor or good deed *w-ḥammalni minniyya.* He helped me with demanding repayment. *ʕaawaani biš-šuġuḷ* the work and imposed an obligation on me. *la-aaxuδ minna šii w-la-ariid minniita.* I don't take anything from him and I don't want to owe him anything.

mamnuun **1.** indebted, obliged, grateful, thankful. *ʔiδa tṣalliḥ ir-raadyo, tsawwiini hwaaya mamnuun.* If you fix the radio, I'll be very much obliged. **2.** gratified, satisfied, pleased. *l-muʕallim ihwaaya mamnuun minnak.* The teacher is very satisfied with you. **3.** (in answer to a request) Gladly! With pleasure! **4.** (as a reply to *ʔaškurak*) You're welcome!

mamnuuniyya **1.** gratefulness, obligation. **2.** pleasure, gladness. *ʔasaaʕdak ib-kull mamnuuniyya.* I'd be most pleased to help you.

mimtann **1.** indebted, obliged, grateful, thankful. *mimtanniin minna liʔanna tbarraʕ ib-mablaġ δ̣axim.* Were grateful to him because he donated a great amount. **2.** gratified, satisfied, pleased. *l-muʕallim mimtann ihwaaya min ibnak.* The teacher is very satisfied with your son.

²m-n-n

mann pl. *mnaan* a measure of weight, approximately 24 kilograms. *sitt ʕugag itsawwi mann. ʔarbaʕ-timnaan itsawwi wazna.* Six huggas equal one mann. Four manns equal one wazna.

m-n-w

minu (interrogative pronoun) who? (see also *man* under *m-n*). *minu ʕallamak ʕas-siyaaqa?* Who taught you driving?

m-n-y

tmanna to wish. *ʔatmanna ʔakuun ib-baġdaad.* I wish I were in Baghdad. *tmanneeta mawjuud ʕatta yšuuf ib-ʕeena.* I wished he was present so he could see with his own eyes. *nitmannaa-lak in-najaaʕ bil-imtiʕaan.* We wish you success on the exam.

mani semen, sperm.

munya pl. *-aat* desire, object of desire, objective, goal. *muniita bil-ʕayaat yṣiir muʕallim.* His goal in life is to become a teacher.

ʔumniyya pl. *ʔamaani* wish, desire, object of desire, goal.

maniyya, miniyya death.

minniyya see under *m-n-n.*

m-n-y-š

mneeš = *min ʔeeš,* which see under *ʔ-y-š.*

m-n-y-n

mneen = *min ween,* which see under *w-y-n.*

m-h-d

mahhad to smooth, level, pave. *ʔabuu mahhad-la ṭ-ṭariiq ʕatta ysawwii waziir.* His father paved the way for him to become a minister.

tmahhad pass. of *mahhad. hassa ṭ-ṭariiq itmahhad. xalli nruuʕ niʕči wyaa.* Now the way is prepared. Let's go talk to him.

mahad pl. *mhuud* cradle, baby's crib.

*tamhiidi** preparatory, preliminary, introductory.

m-h-r

muhar (*u mahir*) to stamp with a personal seal. *xalli yumhur il-ʕariiδa gabuḷ-ma djiibha.* Have him put his seal on the petition before you bring it.

mahar dower, bridal price. || *giṭaʕ il-mahar* to conclude the marriage contract. *giṭaʕna l-mahar il-yoom, laakin raʕ-nizzawwaj baʕad šahreen.* We made the marriage agreement today, but we won't consummate the marriage for two months.

muhur pl. *mhuur, mhaar* **1.** signet, personal seal, stamp used by illiterates as a signature. || *sar-muhur* (Persian, sealed lid) seal, that which secures. *la-tištiri d-duwa ʔiδa ma-ykuun sar-muhur.* Don't buy the medicine if it isn't sealed. **2.** colt, foal.

muhra pl. *-aat* filly.

mahaara skillfulness, adroitness, dexterity, skill, expertness, proficiency, adeptness.

ʔamhar more or most skillful, adroit, proficient, adept, expert.

maahir skillful, adroit, proficient, adept, expert. *zawijta maahra biṭ-ṭabux.* His wife is skillful at cooking.

m-h-r-j-a-n

mahrajaan pl. *-aat* festival, celebration, gala, jamboree.

m-h-l

mihal (*i ʔimhaal*) to allow time, grant a delay. *š-šarika raʕ-timhilni šahar li-ʔan ma-ʕindi fluus.* The company is going to grant me a month's delay because I don't have money.

ʔamhal = *mihal.*

tmahhal to take one's time, proceed slowly and deliberately. *ʔiδa yitmahhal ib-šuġla, kullši yiṭlaʕ zeen.* If he takes his time about his work, everything comes out well.

tmaahal = *tmahhal. la-titmaahal ib-šuġlak tara tinδarr.* Don't be too slow in your work or you'll get in trouble.

mahal slowness, leisureliness. || *ʕala mahlak.* Take your time. Take it easy. *ʔiδa timši ʕala mahlak, ma-tizlag.* If you walk at an easy pace, you won't slip.

muhla pl. *-aat* respite, delay, period of grace.

m-h-m-a

mahmaa **1.** whatever, no matter what. *la-tṣaddig bii mahmaa ygul-lak.* Don't believe him, whatever he tells you. **2.** no matter how much. *raʕ-asawwi haaδa, mahmaa kallaf.* I'm going to do that, no matter what it costs.

m-h-n

mihna pl. *mihan* profession, vocation, occupation, work, trade, business.

*mihani** vocational, trade-. *t-taʕliim il-mihani* vocational education.

m-w

muu (particle of negation) not. *haaδa muu šuġli.* That's not my business. *haaδa muu l-iktaab il-git-lak ʕalee.* This isn't the book that I told you about. *hal-quṣṣa muu saʕiiʕa; la-tṣaddig biiha.* This story isn't true; don't believe it. *ʔabuuya muu bil-beet; baʕda biš-šuġuḷ.* My father isn't at home; he's still at work. *hal-maktuub muu*

ʔilak. This letter isn't for you. *huwwa lli sawwaaha, muu ʔaani.* He's the one who did it, not I. *nṭii fluus, bass muu ʔakθar min ʕašr idnaaniir.* Give him some money, but not more than ten dinars. *ʔariidak itsawwiiha l-yoom, muu baačir.* I want you to do it today, not tomorrow.

m-w-t

maat (u moot) to die, become dead. *maat bis-sakta l-qalbiyya.* He died of a heart attack. *ʔaḥibba l-majiid. ʔamuut ʕalee.* I like Majiid. I would die for him. || *ma-raḥ-itḥaṣṣil ifluusak minna. ybayyin il-xams idnaaniir maatat ʕaleek.* You're not going to collect your money from him. It looks like you're stuck for five dinars. *maat b-iidi d-duušeeš.* I'm stuck with the double six. I can't play the double six.

mawwat to kill. *ðall yuðrub il-bazzuuna bil-ʕaṣa ḥatta mawwatha.* He kept beating the cat with the stick until he killed it. || *ma-aku ḥaaja tmawwit nafsak imniš-šuġuḷ.* There's no reason to kill yourself working. *mawwat nafsa ʕal-waðiifa.* He almost killed himself for the position. *θ-θaʕlab, min yšuuf is-sabiʕ, ymawwit nafsa.* When the fox sees the lion, he plays dead. *l-muʕallim jaab-inna ʔasʔila tmawwit.* The teacher gave us some awfully tough questions.

stamaat to defy death, risk one's life. *j-jinuud istamaataw bil-maʕraka.* The soldiers defied death on the battlefield.

moot 1. death. 2. For shame! Shame on you! *moot! muu ʕeeb itxaaf?* Shame on you! Aren't you ashamed of being afraid?

moota pl. *-aat* death, demise, passing.

mayyit 1. dead, deceased, lifeless, inanimate. 2. (pl. *myaata, moota, ʔamwaat*) dead man, deceased person. || *l-mayyit mayyiti w-aʕurfa.* I know him like the back of my hand (lit., the deceased is mine and I know him).

m-w-j

tmawwaj to rise in waves. *min ykuun hawa ʕaali, ṃayy il-baḥar yitmawwaj.* When there's a strong wind, the sea becomes covered with waves.

mooj (coll.) pl. *ʔamwaaj* 1. seas, billows, breakers. 2. waves. 3. ripples.

mooja, mawja pl. *-aat* 1. sea, billow, breaker. 2. wave. *mawja qaṣiira* short wave (radio). || *mawjat ḥarr* heat wave, hot spell.

m-w-d

muud: ʕala muud 1. on behalf of, for the sake of. *tʕaarak wiyyaahum ʕala muudak.* He fought with them for your sake. 2. about, concerning. *ḥičeet wiyyaa ʕala muud il-ʔiijaar?* Did you talk to him about the rent?

m-w-d-a

mooda pl. *-aat* mode, fashion, style. *ʕal-mooda* in the latest fashion, fashionable. *mzawwij mara ʕal-mooda.* He's married a fashionable lady. *gaaṣṣa šaʕarha ʕal-mooda.* She's cut her hair according to the latest fashion. *hal-ibnayya ṭaalʕa ʕal-mooda.* That girl is dressed fashionably.

m-w-d-y-l

muudeel pl. *-aat* model.

m-w-r-y

moori purple.

m-w-z

mooz (coll.) banana(s).

mooza pl. *-aat* banana.

m-w-s

muus pl. *mwaas, mwaasa* 1. straight razor. 2. razor blade.

m-w-s-y-q

moosiiqa music.

*moosiiqi** 1. musical. *ḥafla moosiiqiyya* concert. 2. (pl. *-iyyiin*) musician.

moosiiqaar pl. *-iyya* musician.

[1]*m-w-ṣ-l*

mooṣal to blow a whistle. *j-jaahil ṣaar-la mudda da-ymooṣil bil-maaṣuul maala.* The kid's been blowing his whistle for quite a while.

maaṣuul pl. *mwaaṣiil* toy whistle, reed whistle.

maaṣuula pl. *-aat* toy whistle, reed whistle.

[2]*m-w-ṣ-l*

l-muuṣil Mosul (province and its principal city in Northern Iraq).

*maṣlaawi** 1. native to Mosul, coming from Mosul. 2. (pl. *mṣaalwa, mwaaṣla*) person from Mosul.

m-w-ع

maaʕ (u mooʕ) to melt, dissolve, become liquefied. *maaʕ iθ-θalij kulla bil-ṃayy.* All the ice melted in the water. *xalli l-ḥabbaaya tmuuʕ ib-ḥalgak.* Let the pill dissolve in your mouth. || *maaʕat ruuḥa.* He fell unconscious. *min šaaf id-damm, maaʕat ruuḥa.* When he saw the blood, he passed out.

mawwaʕ to melt, dissolve, liquefy. *mawwiʕ ir-riṣaaṣ w-ṣubba bil-qaalab.* Melt the lead and pour it in the mold. *mawwiʕ il-miliḥ gabuḷ-ma txallii bij-jidir.* Dissolve the salt before you put it in the pot.

mooƸa 1. pl. *-aat* dissolving, melting, liquefying. 2. unconsciousness. *lizmata il-mooƸa.* Unconsciousness overcame him. *lizmata l-mooƸa mnil-Ƹarr.* He fainted from the heat.

maayiƸ 1. melted, dissolved, liquid. 2. (pl. *-iin*) sissy, softy, pantywaist.

m-w-g

muug pl. *mwaaga* 1. inner corner of the eye. 2. target hole in boys' marble games.

m-w-l

mawwal to finance. *Ƹamma čaan iymawwila Ƹala ṭuul ib-tijaarta.* His uncle was always financing him in his dealings.

maal pl. *ˀamwaal* 1. property, possessions, chattels, goods. 2. wealth, fortune, estate. 3. (a euphemism for the genitals, approx.:) private parts. 4. particle indicating possession or ownership. *ween l-iktaab maali?* Where's my book? *has-sayyaara maalat-man?* Who does this car belong to? 5. for, for the purpose of. *hal-uqmaaš maal iθyaab.* This material is for shirts. *haaδa muu maal muƸallim.* He could never be a teacher. 6. in the realm of, having to do with. *θoob ib-diinaar? maal balaaš.* A shirt for one dinar? That's dirt cheap. *ˀiskut! maal il-wujaƸ.* Shut up! Plague be your lot.

*maali** 1. monetary, financial. 2. fiscal. *sana maaliyya* fiscal year.

maaliyya monetary affairs, finance. *wizaart il-maaliyya* Ministry of Finance.

mitmawwil wealthy, rich, well-to-do. *dzawwajha liˀan ˀabuuha mitmawwil.* He married her because her father is well-to-do.

m-w-n

maan (*u mayaana*) to be a good friend, on close terms. *ˀagdar ˀaṭlub minna haš-šii li-ˀan ˀaani ˀamuun Ƹalee.* I can request such a thing from him because I'm close to him.

mawwan to provision, supply provisions. *raƸ-ymawwinuun iṭ-ṭullaab ib-jamiiƸ-ma yiƸtaajuu min akil.* They're going to provide the students with all the food they need.

tmawwan to store up provisions, provision oneself. *tmawwanna b-kullši lis-safra.* We supplied ourselves with everything for the trip.

muuna 1. provisions, 2. ammunition. 3. nourishment, richness. *haš-šoorba mabiiha muuna.* This soup has no nourishment in it.

mayaana pl. *-aat* 1. close friendship. 2. (invar.) intimate, close. *ṣirna mayaana min ištiğalna suwa.* We became close when we worked together.

m-y-t

mayyit, etc., see *m-w-t.*

m-y-j-n

meejna pl. *-aat, myaajin* a large wooden pestle used to grind grain in a mortar.

m-y-x-a-n

mayxaana, mayxanči = *mayyxaana, mayyxanči,* which see under *m-y-y.*

m-y-d-a-n

miidaan pl. *mayaadiin* 1. square, open place. 2. field (of contest), arena.

miidaanli pl. *-iyya* loafer, idler.

[1]*m-y-z*

mayyaz 1. to consider better. *ˀaani ˀamayyiza Ƹanhum bil-luğa l-ingiliiziyya.* I feel he's better than they are in English. 2. to prefer. *ˀaani ˀamayyiz paariis Ƹala ˀay madiina b-ooruppa.* I prefer Paris above any city in Europe. 3. to distinguish, differentiate. *ma-agdar amayyiz been il-qappuuṭeen. yaahu maalak?* I can't distinguish between the two coats. Which one's yours? 4. to appeal to a higher court. *raƸ-amayyiz id-daƸwa.* I'm going to appeal the case.

tmayyaz to be distinguished, to stand out. *hal-walad yitmayyaz ib-δakaaˀa.* This boy is distinguished by his intelligence.

mtaaz 1. to distinguish oneself, to stand out, be marked. *min činit bil-kulliyya, mtaazeet ib-maƸrifat iθlaθ luğaat.* When I was in college, I distinguished myself by learning three languages. *hal-balda timtaaz ib-naḏaafatha w-ib-šawaariƸha l-waaṣƸa.* This city stands out for its cleanness and its wide streets. 2. /with *Ƹala*/ to excel, surpass, outdo, be better than. *mtaaz Ƹaleena bir-riyaaḏiyyaat.* He surpassed us in mathematics.

miiza pl. *-aat* 1. peculiarity, distinguishing feature, characteristic, essential property. 2. prerogative, priority right. *ˀinta šinu miiztak Ƹanna?* What makes you any better than he?

tamyiiz 1. preference, preferring. 2. differentiation. 3. appeal (jur.). *maƸkamt it-tamyiiz* court of cassation, highest appeal court.

mtiyaaz pl. *-aat* 1. distinction, honor. *nijaƸ b-imtiyaaz.* He passed with distinction. 2. special right, privilege. 3. concession, license, franchise.

mumayyiz pl. *-iin* supervisor, overseer, superintendent.

mumtaaz outstanding, superior, excellent, exceptional, first-rate. *l-ʔakil ib-hal-maṭεam mumtaaz!* The food in this restaurant is excellent!

^{2}*m-y-z*

meez pl. *-aat, myuuza* **1.** table. **2.** desk. **3.** pot (in poker).

m-y-š

miiš a kind of a thin, soft leather.

^{1}*m-y-l*

maal (i meel, mayalaan) **1.** to bend, bend down, lean over. *š-šijra maalat imnil-hawa.* The tree bent in the wind. **2.** to incline, tend, be favorably disposed, have a predilection, liking, or propensity. *n-naas hassa ymiiluun lis-sayyaaraat il-iṣġaar.* People now are more in favor of small cars. *ʔiδa tεaamil ij-jaahil ib-luṭuf, ymiil-lak.* If you treat the child gently, he'll get to like you. **3.** to incline, tend, have a tendency. *loon nafnuufha ymiil lil-ḥumra.* The color of her dress tends toward red.

mayyal **1.** to incline, tip, tilt, bend, bow. *mayyil nafsak išwaaya ḥatta yṣiir raasak bil-fayy.* Bend over a little so that your head will be in the shade. **2.** to make inclined, favorably disposed, sympathetic. *nṭaa lij-jaahil čukleet ḥatta ymayyila ʔila.* He gave the kid some candy to win his favor.

tmaayal to sway, swing. *šuuf il-ibnayya da-titmaayal ib-mašiiha.* Look at the girl swaying as she walks.

stamaal to attract, win over, bring to one's side, to gain favor with, win the affection of. *l-waziir ḥaawal yistimiil baεδ is-siyaasiyyiin.* The minister tried to win over some of the politicians.

meel pl. *miyuul* propensity, disposition, bent, leaning, inclination.

^{2}*m-y-l*

miil pl. *ʔamyaal* mile.

^{3}*m-y-l*

miil pl. *myaala* **1.** Indian club, a heavy wooden weight used in body-building exercises. **2.** stick applicator (for cosmetics). **3.** needle, indicator (of a gauge). **4.** hand (of a watch).

m-y-w-a

meewa fruit.

m-y-n

miina **1.** glaze, glazing. **2.** enamel coating. **3.** face, dial (of a watch or clock).

mayaana see *m-w-n.*

m-y-n-ʔ

miinaaʔ pl. *mawaaniʔ* port, harbor.

^{1}*m-y-y*

ṃayy **1.** water. *ṃayy warid* rose water, and, loosely, any similar perfume made from blossoms. || *dijaaj ṃayy* coot. *xubuz ṃayy* plain bread as opposed to bread with meat, etc., baked into it). **2.** liquid, fluid. **3.** juice. *ṃayy ir-rummaan* pomegranate juice.

*maaʔi** water, aquatic. *ḥaywaanaat maaʔiyya* aquatic animals.

ṃayyxaana pl. *-aat* bar (slightly derogatory).

mayyxanči pl. *-iyya* **1.** bartender, barkeeper. **2.** barfly.

^{2}*m-y-y*

miyya see under *m-ʔ-w.*

N

n-a-r-n-j

naaranj, naarinj (coll.) bitter orange(s).

naaranja pl. *-aat* un. n. of *naaranj.*

n-a-s

naas see *ʔ-n-s.*

n-a-m-r-b-w-ṭ-y-a

naamarbuuṭiyyaat see *r-b-ṭ.*

n-a-m-w-s

naamuus honor, integrity. *ma-εindak naamuus? šloon itxalli martak tixdim ir-riyaajiil?* Haven't you got any honor? How can you let your wife work as a servant to men? *raḥ-axalli l-qaδiyya yamm naamuusak.* I'll leave the matter up to your integrity. *b-naamuusak, ʔaani ṣudug git-lak hiiči?* On your honor, did I really tell you that? *b-naamuusak, ma-yṣiir. xalli ʔaani ʔadfaε.* By your honor, I won't allow it. Let me pay. *w-naamuusak, raḥ-asawwiiha baačir.* I assure you, I'm going to do it tomorrow.

n-a-q-w-ṣ

naaquuṣ pl. *nawaaqiiṣ* (church) bell.

n-a-y

naay pl. *-aat* a kind of flute.

n-b-ʔ

tnabbaʔ to be a prophet, prognosticate, foretell, forecast, predict. *b-maqaala, tnabbaʔ raḥ-itṣiir ḥarub.* In his article, he predicted there was going to be a war.

nubuuˀa pl. *-aat* prediction, prophecy. see also *n b w.*

n-b-b

ˀunbuub, ˀunbuuba pl. *ˀanaabiib* tube. *ˀunbuubat ixtibaar* test tube. *ˀunbuubat maƐjuun isnaan* tube of toothpaste.

n-b-t

nibat (*i nabit*) **1.** to grow. *hal-gaaƐ ma-yinbit biiha ˀay zariƐ.* No crop grows in this land. *ƐirƐaart il-ˀiid, ma-yinbit biiha šaƐar.* Hair won't grow in the palm of the hand. **2.** to stick, become rooted, firmly implanted. *neešin Ɛal-xišba w-δibb is-siččiina Ɛeel Ɛatta tinbit biiha.* Aim at the board and throw the knife hard so that it'll stick in it. *nibat ib-hal-mukaan w-wa-qibal iyruuƐ.* He's gotten rooted in this place and wouldn't think of leaving.

nabbat **1.** to sprout, germinate. *l-bazr iz-ziraƐta sbuuƐ il-faat kulla nabbat.* The seeds I planted last week have all sprouted. **2.** to plant, implant, embed, stick. *tigdar itnabbit is-siččiina bil-Ɛaayiṭ?* Can you stick the knife in the wall?

nabta pl. *nabaataat* plant.

nabaat **1.** plants, vegetation. *Ɛilm in-nabaat* botany. **2.** (pl. *-aat*) plant, vegetable organism. **3.** rock candy.

n-b-Ɛ

nibaƐ (*a nabiƐ*) to bark. *la-txaaf min hač-čalib. huwwa bass yinbaƐ.* Don't be afraid of this dog. He only barks.

tnaabaƐ to bark at each other. *hač-čalbeen ṣaar-ilhum mudda yitnaabƐuun.* Those two dogs have been barking at each other for quite a while.

nabƐa pl. *-aat* a bark, a yelp.

n-b-δ

nibaδ (*i nabiδ*) to reject, spurn with disdain. *kull ˀaẓdiqaaˀa nibδoo b-sabab ˀaxlaaqa.* All his friends rejected him because of his manners.

nubδa pl. *nubaδ* **1.** (printed) article, story, report. **2.** summary, synopsis, abstract.

nabiiδ wine.

manbuuδ pl. *-iin* outcast, pariah, untouchable.

n-b-r

manbar pl. *manaabir* **1.** pulpit. **2.** rostrum, platform, dais.

minbaar pl. *-aat* intestine, gut (used for sausage).

n-b-s

nibas (*i nabis*) to utter, say, speak. *wala nibas ib-čilma.* He didn't even utter one word.

n-b-š

nibaš (*i nabiš*) **1.** to dig up, unearth, disinter. *š-šurṭa nibšat il-gabur w-fuƐṣat il-mayyit.* The police dug up the grave and examined the dead man. **2.** to scratch, poke around, rummage. *d-dijaaja da-tinbiš bit-tiraab.* The chicken's scratching in the dirt. **3.** to stir, stir up. *nibaš il-faƐam Ɛatta yiƐtirig zeen.* He stirred up the coal so that it would burn better.

nabbaš **1.** to keep digging up, keep unearthing. *δ̣all iynabbiš Ɛalayya Ɛatta Ɛaṭṭamni.* He kept digging up things against me until he ruined me. **2.** = *nibaš* **2.** *δ̣all iynabbiš ib-xašma Ɛatta ṭilaƐ id-damm.* He kept picking his nose until it bled. *leeš da-tnabbiš bil-ˀawraaq maalti?* Why are you rummaging through my papers?

ntibaš to go to the grave, be buried (said of someone disliked). *ntibaš w-xilaṣna minna.* He's dead and gone to hell and we're rid of him.

n-b-δ̣

nubaδ̣ (*u nabuδ̣*) to beat, pulsate. *galbi da-yinbuδ̣ ib-surƐa.* My heart's beating fast.

nabuδ̣ **1.** pulsation, beating, throb. **2.** pulse, heartbeat. *jass nabδ̣a ṭ-ṭabiib w-šaaf Ɛinda ṣxuuna.* The doctor felt his pulse and saw he had a fever. || *ˀija yjiss in-nabuδ̣ Ɛatta yuƐruf š-iysawwi.* He came to feel out the situation so he would know what to do.

n-b-Ɛ

nibaƐ (*a nabiƐ*) **1.** to spring, issue, originate, flow. *hal-ṃayy yinbaƐ imnij-jibaal.* This water comes from the mountains. **2.** to appear, burst forth, grow. *bir-ribiiƐ, ˀawraaq il-ˀašjaar tinbaƐ.* In spring, the tree leaves appear.

nabbaƐ **1.** to gush out, pour forth. *δ̣all ˀuƐfur ˀila ˀan iynabbiƐ il-ṃaay.* Keep digging until water gushes out. **2.** to leaf, put forth leaves. *jaa r-ribiiƐ wil-ˀašjaar bidat itnabbiƐ.* Spring has come and the trees have started to leaf.

nabiƐ **1.** spring, source. **2.** growth, shoots.

n-b-ġ

nibaġ (*a nubuuġ*) to become renowned, become an outstanding figure. *nibaġ biš-šiƐir baƐad sinn il-Ɛišriin.* He became an outstanding figure in poetry after the age of twenty.

naabiġa pl. *nawaabiġ* distinguished man, outstanding figure, genius.

n-b-g

nubag (*u nabug*) **1.** to jump up (out of water). *šuuf has-simča nubgat min-naak.* Look at that fish that jumped up over there. *šuuf il-baṭṭa da-dġuṭṭ w-tunbug bil-mayy.* Look at the duck diving under and coming up in the water. **2.** to speak up suddenly, to butt in. *ʔiḥna da-niḥči waḥḥadna. ʔinta luweeš da-tunbug w-idjaawub?* We're talking among ourselves. Why are you butting in and answering?

nabug (coll.) **1.** jujube(s). **2.** jujube tree(s).

nabga pl. *-aat* un. n. of *nabug.*

n-b-l

nabbal to point, sharpen to a point. *nabbil il-ʕuuda ḥatta tigdar tuzruf biiha.* Sharpen the stick so you can poke a hole with it.

nubul nobleness, high-mindedness. *nubla ma-yxallii yiḥči ʕan-naas.* His nobleness keeps him from talking about people.

nabla pl. *-aat* point, tip.

nabiil aristocratic, highborn, patrician, distinguished. *huwwa min ʕaaʔila nabiila.* He's from a distinguished family.

n-b-h

nabbah **1.** to inform, notify, alert. *ma-da-yidri š-da-yṣiir bid-daaʔira. laazim innabbha.* He doesn't know what's happening in the office. We'd better put him wise. **2.** to remind. *la-tinsa tnabbihni ʕala qaḍiitak.* Don't forget to remind me about your matter. *min iyṣiir il-wakit, nabbihni.* When the time comes, remind me.

tnabbah to notice, note, realize, become aware. *ma-yitnabbah ʔilla waaḥid iynabbha.* He won't notice unless someone informs him.

ntibah /with *l-* or *ʕala*/ **1.** to understand, realize, grasp, comprehend. *ma-ntibahit lin-nukta maaltak.* I didn't get your joke. **2.** to pay attention. *ʔiδa tintibih biṣ-ṣaff, tifham id-daris.* If you pay attention in class, you'll understand the lesson. || *ʔintibih ʕala nafsak, tara fluusak raḥ-tixlaṣ.* Come to your senses or your money will be gone.

nabaaha **1.** awareness, alertness. **2.** intelligence.

munabbih **1.** awakening, arousing. *saaʕa munabbiha* alarm clock. **2.** stimulant. *duwa munabbih* a stimulant (medicine). **3.** (pl. *-aat*) stimulant, stimulative agent.

n-b-w

nabi pl. *ʔanbiyaaʔ* prophet. *n-nabi* the Prophet Mohammed.

*nabawi** prophetic, of or pertaining to the Prophet Mohammed.

nubuuwa prophethood.

n-t-j

nitaj (*i natiija*) to result, ensue, arise, be a result (*min* or *ʕan* of, from). *ma-nitaj šii min hal-ijtimaaʕ.* Nothing resulted from that meeting.

ʔantaj to produce, yield, bring forth, make. *ʔiδa tsammid il-gaaʕ zeen, tintij ʔakθar.* If you fertilize the ground well, it'll yield more. *l-ʕiraaq yintij ḥubuub w-tumuur ib-kaθra.* Iraq produces grain and dates in abundance.

stantaj to conclude, infer, deduce, gather. *stantajit min kalaama yḥibb yidrus.* I concluded from his talk that he likes to study. *mneen jibit hal-maʕluumaat? laazim stantajitha mnit-taqriir.* Where did you get this information? You must have deduced it from the report.

natiija pl. *nataaʔij* result, outcome, upshot, consequence. *nataaʔij il-imtiḥaan ma-ṭilʕat li-hassa.* The results of the exam haven't come out yet. *ʔijaw iš-šurṭa. xal-inšuuf in-natiija.* The police have come. Let's see what happens. *haaδa natiijta yruuḥ lil-sijin.* He'll end up going to jail. *n-natiija wyaak? ma-ġit-lak miit marra la-tilʕab ib-ġaraaḍi?* What's going to come of you? Haven't I told you a hundred times not to play with my things? || *bin-natiija* in the end, as a result, consequently, therefore. *bin-natiija, ma-ḥaṣṣalna šii.* In the end, we gained nothing.

ʔintaaj **1.** producing, manufacturing, making. **2.** production. **3.** output.

stintaaj pl. *-aat* inference, conclusion.

naatij result.

mantuuj pl. *-aat* product, creation.

muntij **1.** fruitful, productive, prolific. **2.** (pl. *-iin*) producer, maker, manufacturer.

n-t-r

nitar (*i u natir*) to shout, bark, speak sharply. *min šaafni ʔalʕab bir-raadyo, nitar biyya.* When he saw me playing with the radio, he shouted at me.

natra pl. *-aat* shout.

n-t-š

nitaš (*i natiš*) to snatch, grab away. *fadd*

walad nitaš il-xubuz min ˀiidi. Some boy snatched the bread from my hand.

nnitaš pass. of *nitaš.*

n-t-f

nitaf (*i natif*) **1.** to pluck, pull out, tear out. *nitaf čam riiša mnid-dijaaj.* He plucked some feathers from the chicken. **2.** to strike, hit. *nitafa b-books w-waggaᶓa.* He punched him and knocked him down. || *l-ˀustaað nitafni b-xooš daraja.* The professor fixed me up with a good grade. **3.** to deal harshly with, be stern with. *l-waziir ij-jidiid nitafa lil-mulaaᶜið maalna w-sawwaa kaatib.* The new minister dealt harshly with our supervisor and made him a clerk. *nitafa xooš natfa.* He really told him off.

nattaf to pluck, pull out, tear out. *j-jaahil nattaf ðeel iṭ-ṭeer.* The child pulled out the bird's tail.

tnattaf to be plucked, pulled out. *riiš id-dijaaja yitnattaf ib-suhuula.* The chicken's feathers can be plucked easily.

tnaataf to exchange (blows). *ðallaw yitnaatfuun booksaat saaᶓa zamaan.* They kept on exchanging punches for a whole hour.

nitfa pl. *-aat* pinch, dash, small amount.

mantuuf **1.** plucked. **2.** (pl. *-iin*) rascal, bounder, rogue.

n-t-l

nital (*i natil*) **1.** to jerk, tug at. *ˀintil iṭ-ṭayyaara ᶜatta tiᶓla.* Jerk the kite so it will go up. *ˀiða l-bismaar ma-yinšiliᶓ, ˀinitla ᶜeel.* If the nail won't come out, jerk it hard. **2.** to snag, hook, catch. *nital θooba bil-bismaar.* He snagged his shirt on the nail. **3.** to shock, give an electrical shock. *diir baalak la-ynitlak il-waayar.* Be careful the wire doesn't shock you. **4.** (of fish) to bite, take bait. *la-titᶜarrak tara s-simča da-tintil.* Don't move; the fish is biting.

nattal to jerk hard, tug repeatedly. *šgadd-ma tnattil, ma-yfiid. l-hawa waaguf.* No matter how much you jerk, it won't help. The wind's stopped.

nnital **1.** to become snagged, be caught. *nnitlat ᶓabaata bil-bismaar.* His aba got snagged on the nail. **2.** to be shocked, get a shock. *nnitalit min činit ašidd il-igloob.* I got a shock as I was replacing the bulb.

natla pl. *-aat* **1.** jerk, quick tug, pull. **2.** electrical shock.

nattaala pl. *-aat* small fishhook and line.

n-θ-θ

naθθ (*i naθθ*) to rain lightly, sprinkle, drizzle. *ma-čaan yijri ṃayy ihwaaya biš-šawaariᶓ li-ˀan čaanat itniθθ.* There wasn't much water flowing in the streets because it was just sprinkling.

n-θ-r

niθar (*i naθir*) to scatter, strew, sprinkle. *niθraw warid ᶓalee.* They scattered flowers on him. || *niθrat šaᶓarha w-gaamat turguṣ.* She let her hair down and started dancing.

tnaaθar to be scattered about, be strewn around. *šagg il-imxadda w-itnaaθar ir-riiš minha.* He tore the pillow and the feathers scattered out of it.

nniθar to be strewn, be scattered. *junitti wugᶓat imnis-sayyaara w-kull ġaraaði nniθrat bil-gaaᶓ.* My suitcase fell from the car and all my things got scattered on the ground.

naθir **1.** scattering, strewing about. **2.** prose.

*naθri** **1.** prose, prosaic, in prose. **2.** small, little, insignificant, trifling. *maṣaariif naθriyya* incidental expenses.

naθriyyaat (pl. only) incidentals, sundries, miscellany.

n-θ-y

niθya pl. *nθaaya* female (see also *ˀ-n-θ*).

n-j-b

najaaba nobility, nobleness, high-mindedness.

najiib pl. *-iin, nujabaaˀ* **1.** noble, high-minded. **2.** noble person.

n-j-t

najaat see *n-j-w.*

n-j-ᶜ

nijaᶜ (*a najaaᶜ*) **1.** to succeed, be successful. *nijaᶜ ib-haš-šaġla li-ˀan čaan ᶓinda ṣurmaaya zeena.* He succeeded in this business because he had a good amount of capital. *ṭ-ṭabiib gall-li l-ᶓamaliyya nijᶜat w-baᶓad ma-aku xaṭar ᶓalee.* The doctor told me the operation was a success and that he was no longer in danger. **2.** to pass. *lamma nijaᶜ, abuu hidaa-la saaᶓa.* When he passed, his father presented him with a watch. *ˀibnak nijaᶜ liṣ-ṣaff iθ-θaani.* Your son passed to the second grade.

najjaᶜ to pass, promote. *najjaᶜ ˀibnak biduun istiᶜqaaq.* He passed your son without justification.

najaaᶜ **1.** success. **2.** passing. *darajat najaaᶜ* a passing grade.

n-j-d

stanjad to appeal for aid, seek help. *min ʕaaṣarhum il-ʕadu, stanjidaw biina.* When the enemy encircled them, they appealed to us for aid.

najda pl. *-aat* support, aid, help, assistance. *šurṭat in-najda* police rescue squad.

n-j-r

nijar (*i najir*) to hew, hack, chop. *jiib il-faas w-injira hal-xišba.* Bring the hatchet and chop this piece of wood. || *ʔiltammaw ʕalee w-nijroo xooš najra.* They ganged up on him and gave him a good beating. *muʕallim il-kiimya nijarni b-ṣifir.* The chemistry instructor gave me a zero.

najra pl. *-aat* 1. chopping, hacking. 2. beating.

najjaar pl. *-iin* carpenter.

nijaara, njaara 1. carpentry, the carpenter's trade. *maʕmal nijaara* cabinet shop. 2. wood shavings.

n-j-l

minjal pl. *manaajil* 1. sickle. 2. scythe.

n-j-m

najjam to soar, fly up, rise high. *šuuf iṭ-ṭiyyaara šloon najjmat!* Look how high the kite has soared!

najim pl. *nujuum* 1. star. 2. lucky star, fortune. *najma da-yiṣʕad yoom ʕala yoom.* His lucky star is climbing higher day after day. 3. motion picture star.

najma pl. *-aat* 1. star. 2. asterisk. 3. female motion picture star.

manjam pl. *manaajim* mine (for minerals).

munajjim pl. *-iin* astrologer.

n-j-w

nija (*a najaat*) to escape, be saved, be rescued. *nija mnil-moot b-iʕjuuba.* He escaped death by a miracle.

najja to rescue, deliver, save. *ʔaḷḷa najja mnil-moot.* God saved him from death. *minu yigdar ynajjiik minni?* Who can rescue you from me?

naaja to confide in, entrust a secret to. *yugʕud nuṣṣ il-leel yṣalli w-ynaaji rabba.* He sits half the night praying and confiding in his God.

najaat escape, deliverance, salvation. *kullna hanneenaa b-najaata b-ʕaadiθ iṭ-ṭayyaara.* We all congratulated him on his escape from the plane crash.

n-č-r

načir 1. skittish, wary, timid. *ma-tigdar itʔakkil hal-ʕaṣfuur min ʔiidak li-ʔan načir.* You can't feed this bird from your hand because he's timid. 2. shy, bashful. *la-tṣiir načir. ʔiṭlaʕ ʔugʕud wiyya l-xuṭṭaar.* Don't be shy. Go out and sit with the guests.

n-ʕ-t

niʕat (*a naʕit*) to hew, carve, chisel, sculpture. *niʕat ʔisma ʕala ṣaxra.* He chiseled his name on a rock. *l-fannaan niʕat timθaal ir-raʔiis ij-jamhuuriyya.* The artist sculptured a statue of the president of the republic.

naʕit 1. stonework, stonecutting. 2. sculpturing, sculpture.

naʕʕaat pl. *-a, -iin* 1. stonecutter, stonemason. 2. sculptor.

n-ʕ-r

ntiʕar to commit suicide. *ntiʕar li-ʔan ma-ʕabbata.* He committed suicide because she didn't love him.

n-ʕ-s

naʕis temperamental, moody. *šloon naʕis! la-yitṣaadaq wiyya ʔaʕʕad wala yiʕči šii.* How moody he is! He doesn't make friends with anyone and he doesn't say anything. *ʔibni naʕis. yibči ʕala ṭuul w-ma-yinṭi šii l-ʔaxuu.* My son is temperamental. He cries all the time and doesn't give his brother anything.

nuʕaas copper. *nuʕaas ʔaṣfar* brass.

*nuʕaasi** copper, made of copper. *tamaaθiil nuʕaasiyya* copper statues.

ʔanʕas more or most temperamental, etc.

n-ʕ-l

naʕal (coll.) bee(s).

naʕla pl. *-aat* bee.

n-ʕ-n

niʕna var. of *ʔiʕna* we (see *ʔ-ʕ-n*).

n-ʕ-y

naaʕiya pl. *nawaaʕi* 1. viewpoint, standpoint, aspect, facet. *dirasna l-qaðiyya min jamiiʕ nawaaʕiiha.* We studied the matter in all its aspects. || *min naaʕiya* 1. with regard to, in respect to, as for, concerning, on the part of. *min naaʕiiti, ma-ʕindi maaniʕ.* As for me, I have no objection. 2. on the one hand, for one thing. *min naaʕiya tiʕči ʕalee, w-kull yoom tiṭlaʕ wiyyaa.* On the one hand you talk against him, and then every day you go out with him. 2. subdivision of a subprovince (*qaðaaʔ*) roughly comparable to a precinct or a municipality.

n-x-b

naxxab to make holes in, riddle with holes. *z-zinjaar naxxab it-tanaka.* The rust ate holes in the can. *hač-čiis imnaxxab w-dayoogaɛ minna ṭ-ṭiɛiin.* This bag has holes in it and the flour is falling out of it.

ntixab 1. to select, pick, choose. *kullha b-nafs is-siɛir. ˀintixib yaahu l-tiɛijbak.* They're all the same price. Select any one you like. 2. to elect. *ntixboo raˀiis il-ɛizibhum.* They elected him head of their party.

ntixaab pl. *-aat* 1. election. 2. choice, selection.

*ntixaabi** election. *ɛamla ntixaabiyya* election campaign.

n-x-r

manxar pl. *manaaxir* nostril.

minxaar pl. *manaaxiir* nostril.

n-x-ḷ

nixaḷ u (naxuḷ) to sift. *nixḷat iṭ-ṭiɛiin gabuḷ-ma tɛijna.* She sifted the flour before she made dough from it.

nnixaḷ pass. of *nixaḷ.*

naxaḷ (coll.) date palm(s).

naxḷa pl. *-aat* un. n. of *naxaḷ.*

nxaaḷa 1. the residue left after sifting. 2. bran.

munxul pl. *manaaxil* sifter, sieve.

n-x-w

nixa (i, a naxi) to appeal to the pride of, awaken the sense of honor. *ˀiδa tinxii, ysaaɛdak.* If you arouse his sense of honor, he'll help you.

naxxa = *nixa.*

nnixa pass. of *nixa. šgadd-ma titwassal bii, ma-yinnixi.* No matter how much you beg of him, his sense of honor won't be aroused.

naxwa pride, dignity, sense of honor, self-respect. *haaδa ṣaaɛib naxwa. ˀiδa šaaf mara tiɛtaaj musaaɛada ysaaɛidha.* He's an honorable man. If he saw a woman who needs help, he'd help her.

n-d-b

manduub pl. *-iin* delegate, representative.

n-d-r

nidar (u nudra) to become rare, become scarce. *t-tiffaaɛ yindur ib-hal-mawsim.* Apples get scarce at this season.

tnaddar 1. to be clever, display one's cleverness. *min ma-tuɛruf šii, tiskut; bass min tuɛruf išwayya, titnaddar.* When you don't know anything, you remain silent; but when you know a little, you make yourself look good. *la-titnaddiriin. guumi sawwii-li ˀakil.* Don't act smart. Go make me some food. 2. to be industrious, work diligently. *n-nahaar kulla ma-tištuġuḷ. min yiji rajilha titnaddar.* All day she doesn't work. When her husband comes she makes herself busy.

nadaara 1. cleverness, efficiency. 2. diligence, industriousness.

mindar, mandar pl. *manaadir.* cushion.

naadir 1. rare. *loo maa l-ˀalmaaz naadir, ma-čaan ṣaar ġaali.* If diamonds weren't rare, they wouldn't be expensive. 2. diligent, industrious, able. *martak ˀumm beet naadra.* Your wife is an industrious housekeeper.

naadiran rarely, seldom. *naadiran tumṭur b-haš-šahar.* It rarely rains in this month.

n-d-f

nidaf (i nadif, ndaafa) to tease, fluff (cotton). *nidaf il-guṭin maal id-duwaašig.* He fluffed the mattress cotton.

naddaaf pl. *-iin, ndaadiif* cotton teaser, a man who renovates mattresses by fluffing the cotton in them.

n-d-m

nidam (a nadam, nadaama) to be sorry. *la-tištiriiha tara tindam baɛdeen.* Don't buy it or you'll be sorry later. *nidam ɛala taṣarrufa.* He regretted his behavior.

tnaddam = *nidam. sawweetha w-itnaddamit.* I did it and was sorry.

n-d-h

nidah (a nadih) to call, call to, shout at. *baḷḷa, ma-tindah ˀabuuya min yammak?* Please, would you call to my father from where you are?

nadih calling, calling to.

nadha pl. *-aat* i.n. of *nadih.*

n-d-w

nidaaˀ pl. *-aat* 1. appeal, call, summons. 2. telephone call.

naadi pl. *nawaadi* club, social organization.

n-δ-r

niδar (i niδir) 1. to pledge (a sacrifice) to God. *niδrat xaruuf ˀiδa yṭiib ibinha.* She vowed to sacrifice a sheep if her son got well. 2. *(i ˀinδaar)* to warn, caution, admonish. *hal-marra niδarnaa; marrt il-luxx nfuṣla.* This time we gave him a warning; next time we'll fire him. 3. to notify, give notice, give a warning. *niδroona niṭlaɛ imnil-beet gabuḷ nihaayt iš-šahar.* They gave us notice to vacate the house before the end of the month.

ˀanδar to notify, issue a warning or notice to. *l-ɛukuuma ˀanδirata ˀiδa ma-ysallim, yɛaakmuu ġiyaabiyyan.* The government warned him if he doesn't give up, they'll sentence him in absentia.

nniδar to be warned, cautioned, admonished. *nniδar marrteen w-ma-taab.* He was warned twice and didn't reform.

niδir pl. *nδuur* **1.** sacrificial offering (to God). **2.** vow, solemn pledge.

ˀinδaar pl. *-aat* **1.** admonition **2.** warning. *ṣaffaart il-ˀinδaar* siren. **3.** (military) alert.

n-δ-l

naδil pl. *ˀanδaal* **1.** low, base, depraved. **2.** depraved person.

naδaala lowness, baseness, depravity.

n-r-g-y-l

nargiila pl. *-aat, naraagiil* narghile, hookah, water pipe.

n-r-m-d

nurmaada pl. *-aat* hinge.

n-z-ɛ

nizaɛ (*a, i naziɛ, nizaaɛa*) to empty, drain, clean out. *l-mirɛaaṣ malyaana. laazim injiib waaɛid yinzaɛha.* The septic tank is full. We've got to get someone to empty it.

nazzaaɛ pl. *-iin, nzaaziiɛ* man who empties septic tanks.

n-z-z

nazz (*i nazz*) **1.** to start, jump, twitch. *bass itnuġza, ynizz.* You just poke him and he jumps. **2.** (*i nazz, niziiz*) to seep, ooze, leak. *min iyziid iš-šaṭṭ, l-gaaɛ itnizz.* When the river rises, the ground oozes water.

niziiz seepage.

n-z-ɛ

nizaɛ (*a naziɛ*) **1.** to remove, take off. *nizaɛ qundarta gabuḷ-ma xašš lij-jaamiɛ.* He took off his shoes before he entered the mosque. *nizaɛ jild is-simča.* He skinned the fish. **2.** to disrobe, get undressed. *ˀinzaɛ w-čayyit bil-ṃayy.* Take off your clothes and jump in the water.

nazzaɛ to disrobe, undress, remove the clothes from. *nazzɛata hduuma liṭ-ṭifil w-ġislat-la.* She undressed the child and washed him.

naazaɛ to fight, to contend, dispute with. *naazaɛhum ihwaaya ɛala qaṣiyyat il-gaaɛ.* He fought with them a lot over the land deal.

nnizaɛ to be removed, taken off. *haθ-θoob laazig ib-jildi w-ma-da-yinniziɛ.* This shirt is stuck to my skin and can't be removed.

nazɛa pl. *-aat* inclination, tendency, leaning. || *nazɛa ṭaaˀifiyya* religious prejudice.

manzaɛ pl. *manaaziɛ* dressing room.

n-z-f

naziif bleeding, hemorrhage.

n-z-k

nazaaka **1.** daintiness, delicateness, fragility. **2.** kindness, gentleness, tenderness, compassion.

naazik **1.** dainty, delicate, frail, fragile. *hal-ibnayya šgadd naazka; min ˀaqall šii titˀaδδa!* How delicate this girl is; the least thing can hurt her! **2.** kind, gentle, tender, compassionate.

n-z-l

nizal (*i nuzuul*) **1.** to descend, go down, come down, move down. *ˀintiṣirni; hassa ˀanzil.* Wait for me; I'll come right down. *nizal bil-parašuut.* He parachuted down. *ɛala ġafla bayyan, ɛabaalak nizal imnis-sima.* All of a sudden he appeared as if he descended from the sky. **2.** to get down, get off, alight, dismount, disembark. *b-ˀay mawqif raɛ-tinzil?* Which stop will you get off at? *j-jinuud nizlaw lil-barr ib-nuquuṭeen.* The soldiers went ashore at two points. **3.** to come down, let down, land. *ṭ-ṭiyyaara nizlat gabuḷ saaɛa.* The plane landed an hour ago. **4.** to fall. *hal-manṭiqa, ma-yinzil biiha θalij.* Snow doesn't fall in this area. **5.** to fall, sink, drop, go down. *l-ˀasɛaar nizlat ihwaaya.* Prices have gone down a lot. **6.** to go down, abate, subside, let up. *ˀiidi baɛadha toojaɛni laakin il-waram nizal.* My hand is still hurting me but the swelling went down. *hawa t-taayar nizal.* The air in the tire is low. **7.** to stop over, stay, put up, take lodging. *nizal ɛidna min čaan ib-baġdaad.* He stayed with us when he was in Baghdad. *min intiqlaw il-baġdaad, nizlaw yammna.* When they moved to Baghdad, they took a house near us. **8.** to come, appear, come in season. *r-raggi raɛ-yinzil lis-suuġ isbuuɛ ij-jaay.* Watermelons will come into the market next week. *t-tukki raɛ-yinzil haš-šahar.* Mulberries will come in season this month. **9.** /with *ɛala*/ to fall upon, attack, assault, assail. *nizal ɛalee bis-sabb.* He fell upon him with insults. *l-baarɛa nizal ɛaleena ɛaraami.* Yesterday a thief broke into our house. **10.** to play, put down (a card). *ˀiδa l-billi b-iidak, nizla.* If you have the ace in your hand, play it. ¶ *š-ṣaar? qaabil nizal min-qadrak?*

What's wrong? Do you think it diminished your prestige?

nazzal **1.** to take down, bring down, to put down, let down, lower. *nazzil kull il-karaasi jawwa.* Take all the chairs downstairs. *nazzil ij-jaahil min ʕal-iḥṣaan. raḥ-yoogaʕ.* Take the child down from the horse. He's going to fall. *nazzil raasak ḥatta tigdar iṭṭubb imniš-šibbaač.* Duck your head so you can get through the window. || *ʔaḷḷa nazzal ʕaleehum ġaḏaba.* God sent his wrath down upon them. **2.** to unload. *nazzlu l-karaasi mnil-loori.* Unload the chairs from the truck. || *nazzal lis-suug* to take to market, to put on the market. *raḥ-anazzil il-ḥunṭa lis-suug isbuuʕ ij-jaay.* I'm going to take the wheat to market next week. **3.** to cause to dismount, disembark, get off. *nazzil ir-rukkaab ḥatta nbaddil it-taayar.* Have the passengers get off so we can change the tire. **4.** to land, put ashore (troops). *nazzlaw ʔalif jundi bij-jaziira.* They landed a thousand soldiers on the island. **5.** to lower, decrease, lessen, diminish, reduce. *nazzilaw rutubta min ʕariif ʔila naaʔib ʕariif.* They demoted him from sergeant to corporal. **6.** to take in, put up, lodge, accommodate. *min činna b-baġdaad, nazziloona ʕidhum.* When we were in Baghdad, they put us up at their house.

tnazzal to lower oneself, stoop, condescend. *ma-atnazzal ʔaḥči wiyyaa.* I won't lower myself to talk to him.

tnaazal **1.** to give in, yield, concede. *da-yitmassak ib-raʔya w-ma-yitnaazal.* He's sticking to his opinion and won't give in. **2.** /with *ʕan*/ to relinquish, surrender, give up, waive, forgo, *tnaazal-li ʕan ḥuṣṣta.* He gave up his share to me. *tnaazal ʕan il-ʕarš il-ʔibna.* He gave up the throne to his son. **3.** = *tnazzal.*

nnizal pass. of *nizal. has-sirdaab ma-bii daraj; ma-yinnizil-la.* This basement has no stairs; it can't be gotten down into.

nuzuul **1.** descending, descent. **2.** dismounting, alighting, getting down, off, or out. **3.** landing. **4.** fall, drop.

nzuul **1.** var. of *nuzuul.* **2.** pain, affliction. *ma-titḥarrak? š-biik, nzuul?* Can't you move? Are you crippled or something? *nzuul ʕala gaḷbak! luweeš ḏirabta lil-walad?* Plague take you! Why did you hit the boy? *nzuul, waaḥid ʔawkaḥ imnil-laax!* My God, one's worse than the other! *nzuul! ma-tugʕud raaḥa ʕaad?* Damn it! Can't you let up for just a minute?

manzil pl. *manaazil* inn, hostel.

manzila status, prestige, standing. *ma-buqat-la ʔay manzila.* He had no prestige left.

ʔinzaal pl. *-aat* (military) landing, invasion.

manzuul red-light district.

n-z-h

nazzah to deem or declare honest, respectable, honorable, innocent of guilt. *fadd waaḥid tihama bil-booga bass kull il-muwaḏ̣ḏ̣afiin nazzihoo.* Someone accused him of the theft but all the employees said he was above it. *šloon tigdar itnazzha? l-kull da-yguuluun haaḏa mištirik bil-booga.* How can you say he's above it? Everyone is saying that he took part in the theft. *la-tnazzih nafsak hassa. maḥḥad yiġayyir fikra ʕannak.* Don't claim to be honest now. Nobody will change his idea of you.

tnazzah to enjoy the out-of-doors, to take an outing, go for a stroll. *ṭlaʕna nitnazzah ib-ḥadaayiq baġdaad.* We went out to enjoy ourselves in Baghdad's parks.

nazaaha honesty, purity, righteousness, integrity.

nuzha pl. *-aat* **1.** outing, excursion. **2.** stroll.

naziih pure, blameless, above reproach, respectable. *hal-muwaḏ̣ḏ̣afiin ma-biihum waaḥid naziih.* There's not one of these employees who's above reproach.

muntazah pl. *-aat* recreation ground, park.

n-s-ʔ

nisaaʔ, niswaan (pl.) women.

*nisaaʔi** women's, female. *malaabis nisaaʔiyya* women's apparel.

n-s-b

nisab (*i nasib*) to ascribe, attribute, impute. *nisab beet iš-šiʕir ʔila šaaʕir mašhuur.* He attributed the line of poetry to a famous poet.

nassab to deem or declare more appropriate, suitable, or proper, to recommend. *ʔaani ʔanassib itruuḥ tiḥči wyaa šax-ṣiyyan.* I think it best you go talk with him personally.

naasab **1.** to be appropriate, suitable, fitting, proper. *haaḏa ʕinda diktooraa. ma-ynaasib yinṭuu waḏ̣iifat kaatib.* He has a doctor's degree. It isn't fitting that they give him a position as clerk. *raatba ma-*

ynaasib šuġla. His salary isn't commensurate with his job. || *loo tnaasib, čaan biʕit-lak-iyyaaha b-has-siʕir.* If it were profitable, I would have sold it to you at that price. **2.** to become, befit, behoove. *hal-ḥači ʔabadan ma-ynaasbak.* This kind of talk isn't like you at all. **3.** to become related by marriage to. *da-yriid ynaasibhum li-ʔanhum zanaagiin.* He wants to marry into their family because they're wealthy.

tnaasab **1.** to be related by marriage. *raḥ-nitnaasab wiyya ʕaaʔila mnil-baṣra.* We are going to be related by marriage to a family from Basra. **2.** to be proportionate, match, fit. *quuta ma-titnaasab wiyya ḥajma.* His strength isn't proportionate to his size.

ntisab /with *ʔila*/ to become affiliated, associated with, to join. *ntisab ʔila jamʕiyya xayriyya.* He joined a charitable organization.

nasab pl. *ʔansaab* lineage, ancestry. *nasabhum yirjaʕ lin-nabi.* Their lineage goes back to the Prophet. || *ʔibin ḥasab w-nasab* person from an esteemed old family.

nisba pl. *nisab* **1.** relationship, affinity, connection, link. *ma-aku nisba been šuġuḷ hal-meez w-hal-meez.* There's no comparison between the workmanship in this table and this one. **2.** rate. *nisbat il-moot* death rate. **3.** proportion. *nisbat il-kuḥuul bil-biira qaliila.* The proportion of alcohol in beer is small. *nisba miʔawiyya* percentage.

¶ *bin-nisba ʔila* with regard to, regarding, in connection with, concerning. *bin-nisba ʔili, ma-ʕindi maaniʕ.* As far as I'm concerned, I have no objection.

*nisbi** relative, proportionate, proportional. *ruṭuuba nisbiyya* (relative) humidity.

nisiib pl. *nisbaan* in-law, relative by marriage.

ʔansab more or most suitable, proper, appropriate, etc.

munaasaba **1.** suitability, appropriateness, aptness, fitness. **2.** relationship, affinity. **3.** (pl. *-aat*) relation, reference, relevancy, bearing, pertinence, link, connection. **4.** occasion. *b-munaasabat* on the occasion of. *raḥ-ysawwuun ḥafla b-munaasabat rujuuʕa.* They are going to give a party on the occasion of his return. || *munaasaba yizʕal; ḥačyi kulla ṣudug.* He has nothing to be mad about; all my remarks are true. *bil-munaasaba* by the way, incidentally. *bil-munaasaba, yʕijbak itruuḥ wiyyaana lis-siinama?* Incidentally, would you like to go to the movie with us?

mansuub **1.** ascribed, attributed, imputed. **2.** (water) level. *mansuub mayy in-nahar naazil.* The water level of the river is low.

munaasib suitable, fitting, appropriate, proper. *raḥ-aḥči wyaa b-wakit munaasib.* I'll talk to him at an appropriate time. *siʕir has-sayyaara mnaasib.* The price of this car is reasonable.

n-s-x

nusxa pl. *nusax* transcript, copy. *ʕindak in-nusxa il-ʕarabiyya mnit-taqriir?* Do you have the Arabic copy of the report? *yišbah ʔabuu biḏ-ḏabuṭ; nusxa ṭibq il-ʔaṣil.* He looks exactly like his father; an exact copy of the original.

n-s-r

nisir pl. *nsuur* eagle.

naasuur pl. *nwaasiir* **1.** fistula. **2.** hemorrhoid.

n-s-f

nisaf (*i nasif*) to demolish, blow up, blast to bits. *nisfaw il-maʕmal ib-qumbula muwaqqata.* They blew up the factory with a time bomb. || *ma-buqa šii mnil-ʔakil. nisfoo kulla.* Nothing was left of the food. They demolished it.

nassaf to winnow. *nassif it-timman. bii traab ihwaaya.* Winnow the rice. There's a lot of dirt in it.

nnisaf to be demolished, blown up. *j-jisir ij-jidiid innisaf.* The new bridge was blown up.

n-s-q

nassaq **1.** to dispose, set in proper order, rearrange. *l-mudiir nassaq il-muwaḏḏafiin bid-daaʔira maalta.* The director shuffled the employees in his office. **2.** to let go, fire. *nassiqaw ʕiddat muwaḏḏafiin ib-wizaart iz-ziraaʕa.* They fired several employees in the Agricultural Ministry.

n-s-l

tnaasal to breed, multiply, propagate, reproduce. *l-ʔaraanib, ʔiḏa yxalluuha titnaasil ib-ḥurriyya, yikθar ʕadadha.* If they let rabbits breed freely, their number increases.

nasil progeny, issue, offspring. *taḥdiid in-nasil* birth control.

tanaasul sexual propagation, reproduction, procreation. || *ʔaʕḏaaʔ it-tanaasul* sexual organs, genitals.

n-s-m
nasma pl. *-aat* breeze. *nasmat hawa* a breath of fresh air.
nasiim pl. *nisaam* wind, breeze.
n-s-n-s
nasnaas pl. *nsaaniis* long-tailed monkey.
n-s-w
niswaan women.
n-s-y
nisa (*a nasi, nisyaan*) to forget. *la-tinsa mawƹidna.* Don't forget our date.
nassa to cause to forget. *ðall yiçči wiyyaaya ʔila ʔan nassaani ƹindi jtimaaƹ.* He kept on talking with me till he made me forget I had a meeting.
tnassa to have a craving for strange food (of a pregnant woman). *marti da-titnassa. triid raggi biš-šita.* My wife is craving strange foods. She wants watermelon in the winter.
tnaasa to be or become oblivious to, ignore. *ḥaawil titnaasa l-mawḍuuƹ.* Try to ignore the matter.
nnisa to be forgotten. *kull il-ʔašyaaʔ is-sawweetha nnisat.* Everything I did has been forgotten.
nisyaan forgetfulness. *maraḍ in-nisyaan* amnesia.
n-š-ʔ
nišaʔ (*a nušuuʔ*) to grow up. *nišaʔ ib-biiʔa faqiira.* He grew up in a poor environment.
ʔanšaʔ to found, establish, institute, set up, organize. *l-ḥukuuma ʔanšiʔat maƹaamil ib-ƹiddat ʔalwiya.* The government set up factories in several provinces.
manšaʔ pl. *manaašiʔ* place of origin.
ʔinšaaʔ 1. setting up, establishment, institution, organization. 2. (pl. *-aat*) essay, composition, treatise.
n-š-b
niššaab (coll.) arrow(s).
niššaaba pl. *-aat* arrow.
n-š-t-r
naštar: *ḍurab naštar* to lance, cut open. *ṭ-ṭabiib raḥ-yuḍrub il-ḥabbaaya naštar.* The doctor's going to lance the boil.
n-š-d
nišad (*i našid*) to seek information, inquire, ask. *ma-ƹidna qumṣaan bass tigdar tinšid ib-ðaak id-dukkaan.* We don't have shirts but you can inquire in that store.
naašad to implore, adjure. *l-ḥukuuma naašdat il-ʔahaali ma-ysawwuun muḍaaharaat.* The government appealed to the people not to demonstrate.
nišda pl. *-aat* 1. request for information. *xall niʔal ʔaḥḥad; n-nišda muu ƹeeb.* Let's ask someone; there's nothing wrong with asking. 2. information, answer to a request for information. *ma-yinṭi nišda.* He won't volunteer any information.
n-š-r
nišar (*u našir*) 1. to spread around, publicize, broadcast. *nišar il-iḥčaaya bil-uwlaaya.* He spread the story around town. 2. to publish. *nišar il-quṣṣa b-majalla ʔajnabiyya.* He published the story in a foreign magazine. *j-jariida raḥ-tinšur-la maqaal baačir.* The paper's going to print an article by him tomorrow.
naššar to exorcise evil by burning African rue. *našširat-la ḥatta tuṭrud iš-šarr ƹanna.* She burned African rue to drive evil away from him.
nnišar to be published. *l-iktaab raḥ-yinnišar iš-šahar ij-jaay.* The book will be published next month.
ntišar 1. to spread. *l-maraḍ intišar.* The disease spread. 2. to spread out, scatter. *la-ððalluun mitkattiliin ihnaa. ʔintašru.* Don't stay bunched up here. Spread out.
našra pl. *-aat* 1. announcement, proclamation, notice. 2. (radio) broadcast. 3. publication, periodical.
nšaara sawdust, wood shavings.
minšaar pl. *minaašiir* saw.
naašir pl. *-iin* publisher.
manšuur 1. spread abroad, made public, published. 2. (pl. *manaašiir*) leaflet, pamphlet, circular. 3. extra edition (of a newspaper).
mintišir widespread, current, rife. *l-ʔišaaƹa mintišra bil-wlaaya.* The rumor's widespread in the city.
n-š-z
našaaz 1. dissonance, discord. 2. dissonant, off key. *loo ma-yġanni wiyyaahum ʔaḥsan. ġinaa našaaz.* It'd be better if he didn't sing with them. His singing is off key.
naašiz pl. *nawaašiz* recalcitrant, disobedient. *mara naašiz* a recalcitrant woman, a shrew.
n-š-š
našš (*i našš*) to shoo away, drive away. *d-dijaaj da-yaakul it-timman. nišša.* The chickens are eating the rice. Shoo them away.
n-š-ṭ
nišaṭ (*a našaaṭ, nušuṭ*) to be or become strong or energetic. *ðiif hal-xeeṭeen ƹala*

hal-xeeṭ ɛatta yinšaṭ. Add these two strings to this string so it will be strong.

naššaṭ to invigorate, energize. *d-duuš il-baarid iynaššiṭ ij-jisim.* A cold shower invigorates the body.

tnaššaṭ = nišaṭ. leeš ma-titmašša ɛatta titnaššaṭ. Why don't you walk around so you'll get some energy.

našiṭ **1.** energetic, active, busy, bustling. *hal-walad kulliš našiṭ.* This boy is very energetic. **2.** boisterous, obstreperous, aggressive. *ʔibinkum kulliš našiṭ. l-wilid iyxaafuun minna.* Your son is very aggressive. All the kids are afraid of him.

našiiṭ energetic, active, busy, bustling. *l-muwaδδaf ij-jidiid muu našiiṭ.* The new employee isn't energetic.

našaaṭ energy, enthusiasm.

ʔanšaṭ more or most energetic, active.

n-š-f

nišaf (a našif) to be dry, become dry. *la-tfuut ʔilla lamma tinšaf il-gaaɛ.* Don't go in until the floor dries.

naššaf to dry, make dry, blot dry. *ʔuxuδ il-xaawli w-naššif ij-jaahil.* Take the towel and dry the kid. *l-ɛibir baɛda ma-naašif. naššif il-maktuub gabuḷ-ma tɛuṭṭa biδ-δaruf.* The ink isn't dry yet. Blot the letter before you put it in the envelope.

tnaššaf to dry oneself. *nṭiini l-manšafa da-atnaššaf biiha.* Give me the bath towel so I can dry myself off with it.

niššaaf, niššeef: waraq niššaaf, waraq niššeef blotting paper.

niššaafa pl. *-aat* blotter.

minšafa, manšafa pl. *manaašif* bath towel.

naašif **1.** dry. **2.** hard, tough, stiff.

n-š-l

nišal (i našil) to cause to catch a cold. *l-hawa l-baarid nišalni.* The cold weather gave me a cold. *ʔaani manšuul w-maraɛ-aruuɛ lil-madrasa.* I have a cold and I'm not going to go to school.

nnišal to catch a cold. *nnišalit našla qawiyya.* I caught a bad cold.

našla pl. *-aat* cold, catarrh.

naššaal pl. *-iin* pickpocket.

n-š-m

našmi pl. *nišaama* **1.** helpful, willing to be of service. **2.** helpful person.

n-š-n-š

našnaš to feel unfettered, free, to enjoy oneself. *l-yoom maɛaaš; raɛ-anašniš.* Today is payday; I'll be able to live again. *b-hat-tarfiiɛ, raɛ-anašniš.* With this promotion, I'll be on easy street. *huwwa ynašniš ihwaaya bil-biira.* He really enjoys himself on beer.

n-š-w

ntiša to become intoxicated. *yintiši b-iglaaṣ biira waaɛid.* He gets high on one glass of beer.

našwa intoxication, drunkenness. *širab rubuɛ buṭil ɛarag w-ṣaarat ɛinda našwa.* He drank a quarter of a bottle of arrack and got high. *baɛda b-našwat il-intiṣaar.* He's still drunk with victory.

n-š-y

našša to starch. *gul-lil-mukawwi ynaššii-lak yaaxt il-qamiiṣ.* Tell the cleaner to starch the shirt collar for you.

tnašša to be starched. *haθ-θoob ma-yitnašša.* This shirt can't be starched.

niša starch.

n-ṣ-b

niṣab (u naṣub) **1.** to erect, set up, put up, install, set in place. *raɛ-yniṣbuun timθaal ib-has-saaɛa.* They're going to erect a statue in this square. **2.** to strike a pose. *min tiɛči wyaa, yṭalliɛ ṣadra w-yinṣub miθl id-diič.* When you talk to him he sticks out his chest and poses like a cock. **3.** to look one's best, put one's best foot forward. *ma-yiji lil-ɛafla ʔiδa ma-yunṣub tamaam.* He won't come to the party if he isn't looking his best. **4.** to brag, boast, put on airs. *ma-aku ɛaaja tinṣub ib-raasi.* There's no reason for you to do all this boasting to me. **5.** to set. *ʔunṣub saaɛtak ɛala saaɛti.* Set your watch by mine. **6.** to wind. *ʔunṣub is-saaɛa w-šuuf ʔiδa tištuġuḷ willa laa.* Wind the watch and see if it's working or not.

naṣṣab to appoint, install. *naṣṣuboo b-waδiifa w-huwwa muu gaddha.* They fixed him up with a position and he couldn't handle it.

tnaṣṣab to behave domineeringly, despotically. *ṭilɛat imnil-beet li-ʔan axuuha yitnaṣṣab ɛaleeha.* She left the house because her brother was bossing her around.

ntiṣab to rise up, stand erect.

naṣba pl. *-aat* **1.** posture, position, pose. **2.** bearing, carriage, demeanor. **3.** appearance. *l-yoom inta ṭaaliɛ naṣba.* You're dressed smartly today. **4.** (act of) bragging, boasting, putting on airs. *ɛala man han-naṣba? qaabil ʔiɛna ma-nɛurfič ʔinti minu?* Who are you putting on airs for? Do you think we don't know who you are? **4.** setting, adjustment (of a clock). **5.** winding (a clock).

niṣaab minimum number or amount, quorum.

naṣiib **1.** share, portion. *šgadd naṣiibak min wirθ abuuk?* What's your share of your father's legacy? **2.** lot, fate, destiny. **3.** luck, chance.

yaanaaṣiib pl. *-aat* lottery.

manṣab pl. *manaaṣib* position, post, rank, office.

n-ṣ-ḥ

niṣaḥ **1.** (*a naṣiiḥa, nuṣuḥ*) to advise, counsel, give sincere advice to. *ʔaniṣḥak la-timši wiyya hiiči naas.* I advise you not to run around with such people. *ʔiniṣḥa gabuḷ-ma ysawwi jariima.* Set him straight before he commits a crime. **2.** (*a naṣaaḥa*) to be sincere, to mean well, try to do the right thing. *hal-gaṣṣaab yinṣaḥ ib-muʕaamalta.* That butcher is sincere in his dealings.

naṣiiḥa pl. *naṣaayiḥ* sincere advice.

naaṣiḥ **1.** sincere, well-meaning. **2.** good, beneficial, useful. *haj-jooz ma-bii wiḥda naaṣḥa.* Not one of these walnuts is any good.

n-ṣ-r

niṣar (*u naṣir*) to grant victory to, to allow to triumph. *ʔaḷḷa yinṣur il-ʕarab.* May God make the Arabs victorious.

ntiṣar to triumph, be victorious. *l-ḥulafaaʔ intiṣraw bil-ḥarb.* The allies won the war. *jayšna ntiṣar ʕala jayš il-ʕadu.* Our army triumphed over the enemy's army.

naṣraani pl. *naṣaara* Christian.

naṣraaniyya Christianity.

ʔintiṣaar pl. *-aat* victory, triumph.

[1]*n-ṣ-ṣ*

naṣṣ (*u naṣṣ*) /with *ʕala*/ to stipulate, specify, provide for. *l-qaanuun ynuṣṣ ʕala haš-šii.* The law calls for this.

naṣṣ pl. *nṣuuṣ* **1.** text. *hal-kalima ma-mawjuuda b-naṣṣ il-qaanuun.* This word isn't present in the text of the law. **2.** wording. || *b-naṣṣ* verbatim. *ʔiqraa-li t-taqriir bin-naṣṣ.* Read me the report verbatim.

manaṣṣa pl. *-aat* platform, dais, podium.

[2]*n-ṣ-ṣ*

naṣṣa pl. *-aat* depression, dip, low place. (see also *n-ṣ-y*).

nṣayyiṣ low. *yiktib ʕala meez nṣayyiṣ.* He writes on a low table. || *diir baalak. ʔaani muu ḥaayiṭ inṣayyiṣ.* Watch it. I'm not something to be dismissed easily. *haaδa ḥaayiṭ nṣayyiṣ. yaahu l-yiji yṣayyiḥ ʕalee.* He's a nothing. Everyone shouts at him.

ʔanaṣṣ lower or lowest.

[3]*n-ṣ-ṣ*

nuṣṣ pl. *nṣaaṣ* half. *xaabarni b-nuṣṣ il-leel.* He called me in the middle of the night.

n-ṣ-f

niṣaf (*i ʔinṣaaf*) to be just, act fairly, treat without discrimination. *l-muʕallim ma-niṣaf wiyyaay ib-had-daraja.* The teacher wasn't fair with me on this grade.

naaṣaf = *niṣaf. naaṣaf wiyyaa w-inṭaa kull ḥaqqa.* He was just with him and gave him all he deserved.

niṣif pl. *ʔanṣaaf* half.

*niṣfi** half-, semi-, hemi- (in compounds). *timθaal niṣfi* bust. *šalal niṣfi* hemiplegia.

ʔanṣaf more or most fair, just.

munaaṣafa **1.** fairness, justice, just treatment. **2.** in equal shares, half and half. *qassamna r-ribiḥ munaaṣafa.* We divided the profits fifty-fifty.

ʔinṣaaf justice, fairness.

ʔinṣaafan in all fairness, to be truthful. *ʔinṣaafan, ʕali xooš walad.* In fairness, Ali is a good boy.

munṣif pl. *-iin* **1.** fair, just, righteous. **2.** a righteous man.

n-ṣ-y

niṣa (*a naṣi*) to sink down, become low. *l-ḥaayiṭ da-yinṣa li-ʔan il-gaaʕ muu qawiyya.* The wall is sinking because the ground isn't solid. *ḥisʕhum da-yinṣa. ybayyin raḥ-ynaamuun.* Their voices are getting lower. It seems they're going to sleep.

naṣṣa **1.** to lower. *leeš ḥaaṭṭ ir-rasim ʕaali? naṣṣii šwayya.* Why did you put the picture up so high? Lower it a little. *ʔiδa ma-tnaṣṣi raasak ma-tigdar itxušš.* If you don't duck your head, you can't go in. *naṣṣi ḥissak; j-jihaal naaymiin.* Lower your voice; the children are sleeping. **2.** to squat down, bend down. *naṣṣi šwayya ḥatta ʔašuuf š-aku foog raasak.* Squat down a little so I can see what's on top of your head.

tnaṣṣa to be lowered. *hal-xariiṭa ma-titnaṣṣa li-ʔan laazga bil-ḥaayiṭ.* This map can't be lowered because it is stuck to the wall.

ʔanṣa lower or lowest.

naaṣi low. *diilaab naaṣi* a low cabinet.

nḏ-r

niḏar (*u naḏar*) /with *b-*/ to take under consideration, look into, examine. *l-lujna raḥ-tinḏur bil-mawḏuuʕ.* The committee will look into the matter.

ntiḏar **1.** to expect, anticipate. *ma-ʔantiḏir ʔay ribiḥ min haaḏa.* I don't expect any profit from this. **2.** to await, wait for. *ntiḏirni barra.* Wait for me outside.

stanḏar = *ntiḏar.*

naḏar pl. *ʔanḏaar* **1.** consideration, contemplation, examination, perusal. *l-lujna qarrirat ʔiʕaadt in-naḏar bil-mawḏuuʕ.* The committee decided to resume consideration of the matter. || *ḥaalta ṣ-ṣiḥḥiyya, ʔaxḏooha b-naḏar il-iʕtibaar.* They took his state of health into consideration. *l-qaḏiyya biiha naḏar.* The matter's under consideration. *ʔilfaat naḏar* letter of reprimand. **2.** eyesight, vision. *biʕiid in-naḏar* farsighted. *quṣur naḏar* short-sightedness. || *ḏurab naḏar* to stare. *bass ʕaad tuḏrub naḏar ʕal-banaat!* Stop staring at the girls! **3.** outlook, prospect. **4.** aspect, view. **5.** opinion, point of view. *b-naḏari, haaḏa muu ṣaḥiiḥ.* In my opinion, that's not true. *ʔisʔala; balki ʕinda wujhat naḏar bil-mawḏuuʕ.* Ask him; maybe he has an opinion about the subject.

naḏra pl. *-aat* look, glance.

*naḏari** **1.** optical, visual. **2.** theoretical, hypothetical, speculative. *haaḏa ḥall naḏari lil-muškila.* This is a theoretical solution to the problem.

naḏariyya pl. *-aat* theory, hypothesis.

naḏariyyan theoretically. *naḏariyyan, tigdar itsawwiiha hiiči.* Theoretically, you can do it that way.

naḏiir pl. *nuḏaraaʔ* **1.** similar, like, equal, corresponding, equivalent, comparable. *hal-mara ma-ilha naḏiir.* This woman has no equal.

naḏḏaara pl. *-aat* **1.** (pair of) eyeglasses, spectacles. **2.** (pair of) goggles.

naaḏuur pl. *nuwaaḏiir* **1.** field glasses, binoculars. **2.** telescope, spyglass.

manḏar pl. *manaaḏir* **1.** sight, view, panorama. **2.** scene (of a play).

manḏara pl. *manaaḏir* (pair of) eyeglasses, spectacles. (pair of) goggles.

minḏaar pl. *-aat, manaaḏiir* telescope.

n-ḏ-f

niḏaf (*a naḏaafa*) to be or become clean. *ʔiġsil ʔiidak ʔila ʔan tinḏaf zeen.* Wash your hands until they are very clean.

naḏḏaf to clean, cleanse, make clean. *haṣ-ṣaabuun ynaḏḏuf zeen.* This soap cleans well. *ma-yiṭlaʕ mnid-daaʔira gabul-ma ynaḏḏuf il-meez maala, w-ma-yxalli ʕalee wala warqa.* He won't leave the office before he clears his desk, and he won't leave one paper on it. *l-waziir ij-jidiid raḥ-ynaḏḏuf il-wizaara min ʔamθaal hal-muwaḏḏaf.* The new minister is going to clean up the ministry from the likes of this official.

tnaḏḏaf to be cleaned. *haθ-θoob kulliš waṣix. ma-yitnaḏḏaf.* This shirt is very dirty. It can't be cleaned.

naḏiif clean. *θoob naḏiif* a clean shirt.

ʔanḏaf cleaner or cleanest.

munaḏḏif pl. *-aat* cleanser, cleaning agent.

n-ḏ-m

niḏam (*u naḏum*) to compose (poetry), versify. *š-šaaʕir niḏam qaṣiida raaʔiʕa ʕan taariix baġdaad.* The poet composed a splendid poem about the history of Baghdad.

naḏḏam **1.** to organize, arrange, put in order. *naḏḏum il-faaylaat ḥasab il-ḥuruuf.* Arrange the files in alphabetical order. *ʔiḏa ma-tnaḏḏum il-ġurfa, maḥḥad yʔajjirha.* If you don't straighten up the room, nobody will rent it. **2.** to regulate, adjust, make regular. *ʔiḏa tnaḏḏum waqit ʔaklak, ṣiḥḥtak titḥassan.* If you regulate your meal times, your health will improve. **3.** to put together, make ready, prepare. *naḏḏumaw qawaaʔim ir-rawaatib willa baʕad?* Did they make out the payroll yet?

tnaḏḏam to be organized, arranged, put in order. *hal-faaylaat ma-titnaḏḏam.* These files can't be arranged.

ntiḏam to be well organized, orderly, well arranged. *ʔiḏa tḥuṭṭ il-meez yamm il-baab, il-ġurfa tintiḏum.* If you put the table next to the door, the room will be well arranged. *ma-ntiḏam iš-šuġul ib-had-daaʔira ʔilla baʕad-ma niqlaw ʕali.* The work in this office wasn't well organized until after they transferred Ali.

niḏaam pl. *ʔanḏima* **1.** order, regular arrangement. **2.** system. **3.** statute, law.

*niḏaami** **1.** methodical, orderly, systematic. **2.** regular. *jeeš niḏaami* regular army.

ntiḏaam regularity, orderliness. *b-intiḏaam* regularly, methodically, in an orderly manner, normally. *da-yijiina l-bariid b-intiḏaam.* The mail comes to us regularly. *diraasta da-timši b-intiδaam.* His studies are proceeding normally.

ʔanδam more or most orderly, systematic, well-organized.

naaδum pl. *nawaaδum* barrage, dam.

munaδδama pl. *-aat* organization. *munaδδamat iṭ-ṭullaab il-ʕarab* Arab Student Organization.

muntaδam well-organized, orderly, systematic.

n-ṭ-ʕ

niṭaʕ (*a naṭiʕ*) to butt. *ṣ-ṣaxal niṭaʕ iš-šijra w-inkisrat igruuna.* The goat butted the tree and his horns broke.

tnaaṭaʕ to butt each other. *šuuf δoolak il-ġizlaan da-yitnaaṭʕuun.* Look at those gazelles butting each other.

naṭiʕ butting.

naṭʕa pl. *-aat* i.n. of *naṭiʕ.*

naaṭiʕa pl. *-aat*: *naaṭiʕat is-saʕaab* skyscraper.

n-ṭ-r

niṭar (*u naṭir, nṭaara*) **1.** to stand guard, keep watch. *minu raʕ-yinṭur hal-leela?* Who's going to keep watch tonight? **2.** to await, wait for. *ʔinta xallis šuġlak w-aani ʔaniṭrak ihnaa.* You finish your work and I'll wait for you here.

tnaṭṭar to lie in wait, hide in ambush. *tnaṭṭar-la yamm ij-jisir w-min faat, δuraba b-ṭalqa.* He lay in wait for him near the bridge and when he passed, he shot him.

naaṭuur pl. *nwaaṭiir* watchman, guard.

n-ṭ-ṭ

naṭṭ (*u naṭṭ*) to jump in, butt in. *maʕʕad siʔalak. leeš naṭṭeet min yammak?* No one asked you. Why did you butt in? || *ma-adaaynak loo tnuṭṭ.* I won't make you a loan no matter what you do.

n-ṭ-q

niṭag (*u nuṭuq*) **1.** to speak, utter. *giʕad wiyyaana saaʕa w-ma-niṭaq ib-wala čilma.* He sat with us for an hour and didn't say one word. **2.** to pronounce. *šloon tinṭuq hal-ʕaruf?* How do you pronounce this letter?

naṭṭaq to cause to speak. *ʔaḷḷa naṭṭaqa w-ʕiča ṣ-ṣudug.* Allah moved him to speak and he told the truth.

stanṭaq to question, interrogate, cross-examine. *baʕad-ma stanṭiqoo, ʕirfaw il-quṣṣa.* After they interrogated him, they knew the story.

niṭaaq pl. *-aat, ʔanṭiqa* **1.** scope, range, field, extent, sphere. *la-tixruj ʕan niṭaaq il-mujaadala.* Don't go outside the sphere of the debate. **2.** a wide belt worn by the military.

manṭiq logic.

*manṭiqi** logical.

manṭiqa, manṭaqa pl. *manaaṭiq* **1.** area. **2.** district, zone. || *gaṣṣeet manṭiqteen bil-paaṣ.* I bought a two-zone ticket on the bus. **3.** neighborhood.

naaṭiq **1.** talking, speaking. || *filim naaṭiq* sound film. **2.** spokesman, speaker.

manṭuuq **1.** pronounced, uttered, articulated. **2.** wording, arrangement. **3.** text (of a document).

n-ṭ-y

niṭa (*i naṭi*) **1.** *a.* to give. *nṭeet l-iktaab lil-walad.* I gave the book to the boy. || *nṭiini l-mudiir. ʔard ʔaʕči wyaa.* Give me the boss. I want to talk with him. *huwwa ma-yaaxuδ w-yinṭi. ma-tigdar titfaaham wiyya.* He won't give and take. you can't negotiate with him. **b.** to give up, give away. *ʕali xiṭab bitthum laakin ma-nṭooha.* Ali asked to marry their daughter but they wouldn't give her up. **c.** to afford, allow. *ma-nṭaani majaal ʔaʕči.* He didn't give me a chance to speak. **d.** to grant, permit. *nijʕat il-ʕamaliyya w-ʔaḷḷa nṭaa ʕumur jidiid.* The operation was successful and God granted him a new life. **2.** to offer. *ʔinṭeeta ʔalif diinaar bis-sayyaara w-ma-baaʕ.* I offered him a thousand dinars for the car and he wouldn't sell. **3.** to give off, emit, shed, yield. *l-ʕikis maal il-buuri da-yinṭi mayy.* The elbow of the pipe is leaking water.

nniṭa to be given. *hal-ġaraaδ ma-yṣiir tinniṭi lij-jaahil.* These things shouldn't be given to children. *hiiči ʔašyaaʔ ma-tinniṭi; laazim tinbaaʕ.* Those things aren't to be given away; they should be sold.

n-ʕ-r

niʕar (*a u naʕir*) to whine, scream, roar. *l-loori da-yiṣʕad ij-jibal yinʕur.* The truck's roaring up the mountain. *l-muṣraʕ maali yinʕur zeen.* My top hums nicely.

naaʕuur pl. *nuwaaʕiir* **1.** noria, water wheel. **2.** whistling top.

n-ʕ-j

naʕja pl. *-aat, nʕaaj* ewe, female sheep.

nʕeej: *nʕeej il-mayy* sea gull(s).

n-ʕ-s

niʕas (*a naʕis, naʕsa, nuʕaas*) to become drowsy, sleepy. *da-yitθaawab. ybayyin niʕas.* He's yawning. He must've gotten sleepy.

naʕʕas **1.** = *niʕas. min itṣiir saaʕa tisʕa bil-leel, anaʕʕis.* When it gets nine p.m., I get sleepy. **2.** to cause to be drowsy, sleepy. *hal-jaww ynaʕʕis il-waaʕid.* This weather makes one drowsy.

naʕsaan sleepy, drowsy.

n-ʕ-š

ʔanʕaš to refresh, invigorate, stimulate, arouse, enliven. *hal-hawa yinʕiš il-badan.* This climate invigorates the body.

ntiʕaš **1.** to revive, come to new life, be strengthened. *z-zariʕ ntiʕaš bil-muṭar.* The crops were rejuvenated by the rain. **2.** to be refreshed, invigorated. *ʔuxuδ duuš w-intiʕiš.* Take a shower and refresh yourself.

naʕiš pl. *nʕuuš* bier.

munʕiš refreshing, invigorating, restorative.

[1]*n-ʕ-l*

naʕʕal to shoe, furnish with shoes. *raḥ-ʔanaʕʕil il-iḥṣaan.* I'm going to shoe the horse.

naʕal pl. *-aat* **1.** horseshoe. **2.** sandal. **3.** sole (of a shoe). *naʕal kaamil* full sole. *nuṣṣ naʕal* half sole. *jilid naʕal* a grade of leather used for shoe soles, harness, etc.

naʕalča pl. *-aat* tap, metal plate on a shoe.

nʕaal pl. *-aat, niʕil* (pair of) sandals.

[2]*n-ʕ-l*

niʕal (*a naʕil*) to curse, damn, execrate. *š-sawwa ḥatta tinʕal abuu?* What did he do that you'd curse his father? || *niʕal ʔaṣla w-faṣla.* He really cussed him out (lit., damned his ancestors and his pedigree). *b-haš-šuġuḷ, niʕal salfa salfaaya.* He really gave me hell on this job (lit., cursed the ancestors of my ancestors).

naʕʕal intensive of *niʕal. bass itsawwi šii ma-yʕijba, yguum ynaʕʕil.* Just do something that doesn't please him and he starts cursing up and down.

naʕil cursing.

naʕla pl. *-aat* i.n. of *naʕil. naʕlat ʔaḷḷa ʕaleek!* The curse of God on you!

n-ʕ-m

niʕam (*a nuʕuuma*) **1.** to be or become fine, powdery. *duggha lil-gahwa zeen. balki tinʕam baʕad.* Pound the coffee well. Perhaps it'll become still finer. **2.** to be or become smooth, soft. *staʕmili hadduwa ḥatta jildič yinʕam.* Use this medicine so that your skin will get soft.

naʕʕam **1.** to grind, pulverize, powder. *hal-makiina ma-tnaʕʕim il-gahwa zeen.* This grinder doesn't pulverize the coffee well. *ʔiδa ma-tinčabb, ʔaji anaʕʕim iḍluuʕak.* If you don't shut up, I'll come beat you to a pulp (lit., pulverize your ribs). **2.** to make smooth, soft. *hal-maadda tnaʕʕim il-uqmaaš bil-ġasil.* This stuff'll soften the cloth during washing.

ʔanʕam (of God) to be bountiful, bestow favors. *ʔaḷḷa ʔanʕam ʕalee.* God was good to him. || *ʔaḷḷa yinʕam ʕaleek.* (lit., may God bestow his favor upon you) the standard reply to *naʕiiman.*

tnaʕʕam **1.** to live in luxury, lead a life of ease. *haaδa mitnaʕʕim ib-ḥayaata.* He's lived in luxury during his lifetime. **2.** /with *b-*/ to enjoy. *tnaʕʕam ib-ḥayaatak maa-ṭuul ʕindak ifluus.* Enjoy your life while you still have money.

naʕam **1.** yes, certainly, to be sure. *naʕam, ʔaʕurfa.* Yes, I know him. **2.** yes? what did you say? I beg your pardon? *naʕam? ma-smaʕit iš-gilit.* Pardon? I didn't hear what you said.

niʕma /followed by a noun with definite article/ what a wonderful . . .! such a perfect . . .! *niʕma ṣ-ṣadiiq!* He's truly a fine friend!

niʕma pl. *niʕam* **1.** boon, benefaction, blessing, benefit, grace, kindness. *min niʕmat ʔaḷḷa, ma-miḥtaaj šii.* By the grace of God, I'm not in need of anything. || *ʔibin niʕma* man from a wealthy family. *haaδa ʔibin niʕma; nafsa ma-tidna ʕala šii.* He was born with a silver spoon in his mouth; he isn't hurting for anything. **2.** food.

naʕaam (coll.) ostrich(es).

naʕaama pl. *-aat* ostrich.

naʕiim amenity, comfort, ease, happiness. *haaδa ʕaayiš ib-naʕiim.* He's living comfortably.

naʕiiman a standard polite expression said to someone after a bath or haircut.

naaʕim **1.** pulverized, powdery, fine. *šakar naaʕim* fine sugar. **2.** soft, silky. *hal-iqmaaš naaʕim.* This cloth is soft. **3.** smooth. *n-najjaar randaj il-looḥa w-ṣaarat naaʕma.* The carpenter planed the board and it became smooth. *makiint il-ziyaan il-kahrabaaʔiyya ma-dzayyin naaʕim.* Electric shavers don't shave close. **4.** small, tender (vegetables, etc.). **5.** trim, lean, slim. *rajilha naaʕim li-ʔan ydiir baala ʕala ʔakla.* Her husband is trim because he is careful about what he eats.

n-ع-n-ع
niعnaaع a variety of mint. || *quruṣ niعnaaع* mint candy.

n-ġ-b-š
naġbaš **1.** to dig, search, paw around. *la-tnaġbiš bij-junṭa maalti.* Don't paw through my suitcase. **2.** to dig around, poke around, pry. *ḍall ynaġbuš عalayya ʔila ʔan niqlooni.* He continued to undermine me until they transferred me.

n-ġ-z
niġaz (*u naġiz*) to prick, stick, scratch. *niġazni bil-ubra.* He pricked me with the needle. || *ʔinta عala ṭuul tinġuz ib-عačyak.* You're always making cutting remarks.
naġġaz intensive of *niġaz. baṭṭaaniyyaat iṣ-ṣuuf ir-rixiiṣ itnaġġiz.* Blankets of cheap wool scratch.
tnaġġaz to be pricked, scratched. *min čaan ygaṭṭiع warid, tnaġġzat ʔiida.* When he was picking roses, his hand got pricked.
nniġaz to be pricked. *nniġaz b-iṣibعa marrteen biš-šooka.* He got stuck on his finger two times by the thorn.
niġġeez (coll.) thorn(s).
niġġeeza pl. *-aat* a thorn.

n-ġ-ṣ
naġġaṣ to spoil, disturb, make miserable *naġġaṣ عalayya s-safra w-ma-twannasit.* He spoiled the trip for me and I didn't have a good time. *naġġaṣ عalayya عiišti.* He made life miserable for me.
tnaġġaṣ to be disturbed, feel uneasy, be unable to enjoy oneself. *tnaġġaṣit bil-عafla li-ʔan ʔibni čaan yibči.* I didn't enjoy the ceremony because my son was crying.

n-ġ-ġ
naġġ (*u naġġ*) to poke, jab. *min naġġni, ṣiعit "ʔaax".* When he poked me, I yelled "Ouch".
naġġ poking, jabbing.
naġġa pl. *-aat* poke.

n-ġ-l
naġal pl. *nġuula* illegitimate child, bastard.

n-ġ-m-š
naġmaš to cause a tickling sensation. *n-namla da-tnaġmiš ib-ḍahri.* The ant is making my back itch.

n-ġ-y
naaġa to coo, sing, speak softly. *faعl il-عamaam da-ynaaġi lin-niθya.* The male pigeon is cooing at the female. *l-ʔumm da-tnaaġi l-ʔibinha.* The mother is singing softly to her son.

n-f-θ
naffaaθa, ṭiyyaara naffaaθa jet airplane.

n-f-θ-l-y-n
nafθaliin **1.** naphthalene. **2.** moth balls.

n-f-x
nufax, nifax (*u a nafux*) **1.** to blow up, inflate, fill with air. *ʔunfux ič-čuub عatta nuعruf ʔiδa ynaffis.* Inflate the tube so we can tell whether it leaks. **2.** to blow, puff, breathe on or into. *nufax ič-čaay عatta yubrud.* He blew on the tea so it would cool. **3.** to boast, brag. *la-dṣaddig kull-ma yguul tara yunfax ihwaaya.* Don't believe all he says because he brags a lot. **4.** to hiss, spit. *hal-bazzuuna, min titgarrab yammha, tinfux.* When you come near this cat, it spits.
nnufax **1.** to be blown up, inflated. *šuuf in-nuffaaxa nnufxat bil-عajal!* Look how fast the balloon got inflated! **2.** to become puffed up, filled with pride. *nnufax min ṣaar mudiir.* He's gotten puffed up since he became director.
ntufax to swell, puff up, become bloated, inflated. *j-jiθθa ntufxat w-ṭaafat عal-ṃayy.* The corpse swelled up and floated on the water. *baṭna ntufxat imnil-ʔakil.* His stomach puffed out because of the meal.
nafxa pl. *-aat* blow, puff, breath.
nuffaaxa pl. *-aat* balloon.
naafuux, yaafuux top of the head.
minfaax pl. *manaafiix* bellows.
manfuux puffed up, self-important, conceited. *s-daعwa manfuux hal-gadd?* How come you're so puffed up?

n-f-δ
nifaδ (*i nufuuδ*) /with *min*/ to get through, pass through, penetrate. *š-šibbaač baعda yinfiδ minna hawa.* The window still has air leaking through it.
naffaδ to carry out, execute, accomplish, put into effect, discharge, fulfill. *naffiδaw عukm il-ʔiعdaam bii l-yoom iṣ-ṣubuع.* They carried out the death sentence on him at dawn today.
tnaffaδ pass. of *naffaδ. leeš ʔawaamri ma-da-titnaffaδ?* Why aren't my orders being carried out?
nufuuδ **1.** penetration, permeation, leakage. **2.** influence, authority, prestige.
manfaδ pl. *manaafiδ* opening, vent, outlet.
naafiδ **1.** valid, in effect. **2.** effective, operative.

n-f-r
nufar (*u nafur*) to shy away, stay away,

keep clear. *j-jaahil da-yunfur imniḏ-ḏiyuuf.* The baby's shying away from the guests.

nafar pl. *-aat* **1.** person, individual. *čaanaw msawwiin ʔakil ykaffi miit nafar.* They had prepared enough food for a hundred people. || *čarpaaya ʔumm nafareen* double bed. **2.** (pl. *ʔanfaar*) private, recruit (mil.).

nufra pl. *-aat* aversion, dislike, antipathy.

nafiir: *nafiir ʕaamm* general call to arms, general alarm.

naafuura pl. *-aat, nawaafiir* fountain.

n-f-s

nifas (*i*) to look upon with envy and spoil the possessor's enjoyment of it, to put the evil eye on. *ʔinṭii šwayya mnil-ʔakil gabuḷ-ma ynifsa.* Give him a bit of the food before he ruins it with his envious eyes.

naffas **1.** to leak, let out air. *č-čuub da-ynaffis.* The tube's leaking. **2.** to unburden oneself, relax, take things easy. *ruuħ itwannas w-naffis ʕan nafsak.* Go have a good time and relax.

naafas to compete, vie, fight with. *minu raħ-iynaafsak ʕal-buṭuula?* Who's going to compete with you for the championship?

tnaffas **1.** to breathe, inhale and exhale. *baʕda da-yitnaffas.* He's still breathing. **2.** to take a breather, have a rest break. *ʔariid il-mudiir yiṭlaʕ ħatta atnaffas išwayya.* I wish the director'd go out so I could take a breather.

tnaafas to compete with each other. *ṣaar-ilhum mudda da-yitnaafsuun ʕal-waḏiifa.* They've been competing for the position for some time.

nnifas pass. of *nifas*. *činit ʔatʔammal iħṣaani yuġlub, laakin innifas.* I was expecting my horse would win, but he got the evil eye.

nafis (fem.) pl. *nufuus, ʔanfus* **1.** soul, psyche, id, spirit, subjective tendencies or qualities, nature, essence. *nafsa diniyya.* He's self-indulgent. *jaa min nafsa. maħħad jubara.* He came of his own accord. No one forced him. *ʕilm in-nafis* psychology. **2.** self, personal identity. *laazim tiʕtimid ʕala nafsak.* You've got to depend on yourself. *riħit-la b-nafsi w-ħičeet wiyyaa ʕannak.* I personally went to him and talked to him about you. *b-nafsi, ʔaštiri sayyaara, bass ma-ʕindi fluus.* If it were up to me, I'd buy a car, but I don't have any money. **3.** animate being, living creature, human being, person, individual. *ʔintu čam nafis saakniin ihnaa?* How many of you are there living here? *mudiiriyyat in-nufuus* census bureau. *nufuus il-ʕiraaq sabiʕ malaayiin.* The population of Iraq is seven million. **4.** /followed by a noun in the construct state/ the same, the very same. *haaḏa nafs ir-rijjaal illi šifta l-baarħa.* That's the same man I saw yesterday. *ʔariidha b-nafs il-loon.* I want it in the same color.

*nafsi** psychological, mental. *ħaalta in-nafsiyya muu zeena.* His psychological condition isn't good.

nafas pl. *-aat, ʔanfaas* **1.** breath. **2.** puff (from a cigarette, etc.).

nifsa abed with child, confined to childbed. *ʔummič nifsa. ʔinti sawwi šuġuḷ il-beet.* Your mother is in childbed. You do the housework.

nafiis **1.** precious, valuable, priceless. **2.** magnificent, excellent. *haay šloon igḷaada nafiisa!* What a magnificent necklace!

*nafsaani**: *ʕaalim nafsaani* psychologist.

nifaas **1.** confinement for childbirth. **2.** childbed, puerperium.

nafaasa preciousness, costliness, value.

munaafis pl. *-iin* rival, competitor.

n-f-s-k

nafiska, nafsook covetous, greedy. *šloon nafiska! bass yšuuf čukleet yiriida.* How greedy he is! The minute he sees candy he wants it.

n-f-š

nifaš (*i nafiš*) to puff up, swell out, to ruffle its feathers. *ṭ-ṭeer min yinfiš nafsa, ybayyin čibiir.* When the bird ruffles its feather, it looks big.

naffaš to tease, fluff up. *naffiši ṣ-ṣuuf gabuḷ-ma dġizlii.* Fluff up the wool before you spin it.

nnifaš to become puffed up, self-important. *min ṣaar mudiir, innifaš.* When he became director, he got a swelled head.

ntifaš to ruffle its feathers, to strut, swagger. *d-diič intifaš min šaaf id-dijaaja.* The cock ruffled his feathers when he saw the chicken.

manfuuš disheveled. *ʔašu šaʕrak manfuuš. ma-tmaššiṭ.* I see your hair is disheveled. Why don't you comb it.

n-f-ḏ

nufaḏ (*u nafuḏ*) **1.** to shake, shake out, dust off. *ʔunfuḏ il-parda. biiha ʕajaaj* *ihwaaya.* Shake out the curtain. There's a lot of dust in it. **2.** to shake up, shock. *ʔiδa ma-tnufδa zeen, ma-yitʔaddab.* If you don't shake him up good, he won't behave. **3.** to hit suddenly or unexpectedly. *nufaδta b-books waggaƐta.* I hit him with a punch that knocked him down.

naffaδ to shake out, dust off. *da-ynaffuδuun iz-zuwaali barra.* They're shaking out the carpets outside. *xall-anaffuδ čitfak; Ɛalee traab.* Let me brush off your shoulder; there's dust on it.

ntufaδ to be shaken, upset, shocked. *ntufaδ min simaƐ ibna njiraḥ bil-ḥaadiθ.* He was shaken up when he heard that his son was injured in the accident.

nuffaaδa pl. *-aat* **1.** ashtray. **2.** fit of chills and fever, ague, malaria attack.

nafuδ **1.** shaking. **2.** scolding.

nafδa pl. *-aat* i.n. of *nafuδ.*

n-f-ṭ

nafuṭ petroleum, oil. || *nafuṭ ʔaswad* crude oil. *nafuṭ ʔabyaδ* kerosene.

n-f-Ɛ

nifaƐ (*a nafiƐ*) to benefit, to be useful, beneficial, of use to. *had-duwa hwaaya nifaƐni.* That medicine did me a lot of good. *δumm qisim min ifluusak. yiji yoom tinfaƐak.* Save part of your money. A day will come when it'll be useful to you. *hal-ḥači ma-yinfaƐ.* That talk won't help.

naffaƐ to cause to benefit, gain, profit. *Ɛali naffaƐni miit diinaar.* Ali gained me a hundred dinars.

tnaffaƐ to profit, gain, benefit. *ʔahal hal-wlaaya yitnaffuƐuun ihwaaya mniz-zuwaar.* The people of this city benefit a lot from the visitors.

ntifaƐ = *tnaffaƐ. da-antifiƐ minhum ihwaaya.* I'm benefiting from them a lot.

nafiƐ use, avail, benefit, profit, gain, advantage. *lak, ʔinta ma-biik laa nafiƐ wa-laa dafiƐ.* You're good for nothing and you can't do anything.

*nafƐi** **1.** self-interested, devoted to personal gain. **2.** opportunist, profiteer.

manfaƐa pl. *manaafiƐ* use, avail, benefit, profit, gain, advantage.

ʔanfaƐ more or most useful, beneficial, etc.

naafiƐ useful, beneficial, advantageous, profitable.

n-f-q

naafaq **1.** to play the hypocrite, feign honesty, innocence. *ʔinta šgadd itnaafiq!* You play the hypocrite so much! **2.** to inform, bear tales. *naafaq Ɛalayya Ɛind il-mudiir.* He informed on me to the director.

nafaqa pl. *-aat* **1.** expense, expenditure, outlay. *da-yidrus Ɛala nafaqat il-ḥukuuma.* He's studying at government expense. **2.** alimony. **3.** child support.

nifaaq hypocrisy.

munaafiq pl. *-iin* hypocrite.

n-f-n-w-f

nafnuuf pl. *nafaaniif* (woman's) dress, gown.

n-f-y

nifa (*i nafi*) **1.** to exile, banish, expatriate. *l-ḥukuuma nifata l-qubruṣ.* The government exiled him to Cyprus. **2.** to rebut, deny. *l-ḥukuuma nifat il-xabar bij-jariida.* The government denied the news story in the newspaper.

naafa to contradict, be contrary to. *tṣarrufa ynaafi l-ʔaadaab.* His conduct is contrary to good manners.

tnaafa to contradict each other. *taṣarrufa b-hal-qaδiyya yitnaafa wiyya taṣarrufa b-qaδiyya mušaabiha.* His action in this matter is contrary to his action in a similar matter.

nnifa to be denied. *l-xabar baƐad ma-nnifa.* The news hasn't been denied yet.

nafi negative. *jawaaba čaan kulla bin-nafi.* His answers were all in the negative.

nifaaya pl. *-aat* **1.** castoff, discarded thing. **2.** remnant. **3.** bit, piece, scrap (of dirt, lint, etc.) *ʔaku nifaayaat guṭin Ɛala raasak.* There are some bits of cotton on your head.

manfa pl. *manaafi* **1.** place of exile. **2.** exile, banishment. *buqa bil-manfa Ɛašr isniin gabul-ma yirjaƐ il-waṭana.* He stayed in exile for ten years before he returned to his native land.

n-q-b

naqaaba pl. *-aat* union, guild, association. *naqaabat Ɛummmaal* labor union. *naqaabat il-muḥaamiin il-Ɛiraaqiyyiin* The Iraqi Bar Association.

naqiib pl. *nuqabaaʔ* leader of a union, etc.

manqaba pl. *manaaqib*: *manqaba nabawiyya* A chanting of commendations and praises to the Prophet in poetry.

n-q-d

niqad (*u naqid*) to review, make a critique of. *niqad l-iktaab maali bij-jariida.* He reviewed my book in the newspaper.

naqqad to pay or give cash to. *ʔabuu*

naqqada *ʕašr ifluus.* His father gave him ten fils.

ntiqad to criticize, find fault with. *yintiqidni ʕala ʔay šii.* He criticizes me about any little thing.

naqid 1. criticism, reviewing (literary). 2. (pl. *nuquud*) cash, ready money. 3. pl. only *nuquud* coins.

*naqdi** monetary, pecuniary, cash. *taḏaxxum naqdi* inflation. *hal-baggaal ybiiʕ bin-naqdi bass.* This grocer sells for cash only.

naaqid pl. *nuqqaad* critic, reviewer.

n-q-r

naqqaara pl. *-aat* small metal drum. || *sawwaa-li naqqaara.* He caused me a lot of trouble.

n-q-š

niqaš (*u naqiš*) to carve, engrave, sculpture, chisel *niqaš isma ʕar-raḥla.* He carved his name on the desk.

naqqaš 1. to daub with bright colors, make many-colored. *naqqaš il-beeḏ lil-ḥafla.* He painted the eggs for the party. 2. to decorate, embellish. *ṣaaḥib il-maḥall naqqaš ij-jaamxaana.* The shop owner decorated the show window. || *tiskut loo ʔanaqqiš-lak?* Are you going to shut up or shall I tell you off? 3. to eat a small amount as a courtesy. *walaw šabʕaan, raḥ-anaqqiš wiyyaakum.* Even though I'm full, I'll eat a little bit with you.

naaqaš 1. to debate with, argue with. *ʔaani raʔiisak; la-tnaaqišni.* I'm your boss; don't argue with me. 2. to talk, consult with. *laazim ʔanaaqšak ib-hal-mawḏuuʕ ḥatta ʔanṭiik raʔyi.* I need to discuss this matter with you so I can give you my opinion.

tnaaqaš to argue, debate, discuss with each other. *ʔariid ʔatnaaqaš wiyyaak ʕala fadd nuqṭa muhimma.* I want to discuss an important point with you.

naqiš pl. *nuquuš* 1. engraving, inscription. 2. design, embellishment, decoration. || *jaab naqiš.* 1. He pulled a trick. *jaab naqiš mumtaaz w-ʔaxaḏ ifluusha.* He pulled a clever trick and took her money. 2. He had some luck, he was lucky. *loo ma-yjiib naqiš, ma-čaan ġilabni bit-ṭaawli.* If he had been lucky he wouldn't have beat me in backgammon. *da-yjiib xooš naqiš. b-kull imtiḥaan, yiṭlaʕ ʔawwal.* He's having a streak of luck. He comes out first on every exam.

niqaaš pl. *-aat* controversy, dispute, argument, debate.

minqaaš pl. *manaaqiiš* tweezers.

munaaqaša pl. *-aat* 1. debate, argument. 2. discussion.

n-q-ṣ

naqqaṣ = *naggaṣ*, which see under *n-g-ṣ*.

naqiṣ, naquṣ 1. deficiency, lack, want, shortage, deficit. *l-muḥaasib ʔiktišaf naqiṣ b-iḥsaaba.* The paymaster discovered a shortage in his accounts. *t-taqriir kaamil šaamil. ma-bii ʔay naqiṣ.* The report is complete and comprehensive. It lacks nothing. 2. imperfection, inferiority, defect, shortcoming, failing, fault. *murakkab naquṣ* inferiority complex. *yitṣarraf hiiči liʔanna yišʕur ib-naquṣ.* He behaves that way because he feels inferior.

nuqṣaan shortage, lack.

naqiiṣa pl. *naqaaʔiṣ* 1. deficit, shortage, lack. 2. defect, shortcoming, fault.

munaaqaṣa pl. *-aat* invitation for bids on a contract. *l-ḥukuuma raḥ-tiʕlin munaaqaṣa ʕala binaaʔ jisir.* The government is going to announce an invitation for bids on building a bridge.

naaqiṣ pl. *-iin* 1. inferior, lowly, mean. *huwwa fadd waaḥid ʔadab-sizz w-naaqiṣ.* He's boorish and inferior. 2. (pl. *nawaaqiṣ*) something lacking. *štireet ʕiddat ʔašyaaʔ bass baʕad ʔaku nawaaqiṣ.* I bought several things but there are still some things lacking. *leeš-ma tidzawwajha? bnayya jaahla w-ḥilwa. š-naaqiṣha?* Why don't you marry her? She's young and beautiful. What's wrong with her?

see also *naaguṣ* under *n-g-ṣ*.

n-q-ḏ

niqaḏ (*u naqiḏ*) to cancel, abolish, repeal, revoke, nullify, annul, invalidate, rescind. *maḥkamt il-istiʔnaaf niqḏat il-ḥukum.* The Appeals Court reversed the decision.

naaqaḏ to contradict, be contrary, opposite to, be in conflict, inconsistent with. *yguul šii w-baʕdeen ynaaqiḏ nafsa.* He says something and afterwards contradicts himself.

tnaaqaḏ to contradict each other. *l-da-dguula hassa yitnaaqaḏ wiyya ḥačyak maal il-baarḥa.* What you're saying now is contrary to what you said yesterday.

n-q-ṭ

naqqaṭ 1. to point, put in diacritical marks. *l-ʕarab ma-čaanaw ynaqqiṭuun il-ḥuruuf.* The Arabs didn't used to put dots on the letters of the alphabet. 2. to spot, dot, put in dots. *naqqiṭ haj-jiha bir-rasim ʕatta tbayyin.* Put dots on this side of the diagram so it will show up clearly.

nuqṭa pl. *nuqaṭ* **1.** dot, point, speck, spot. **2.** period. **3.** point, subject, detail, item. **4.** (mil.) post, base, position.

see also *n-g-ṭ.*

n-q-l

niqal (*u naqil*) **1.** to transport, transmit, convey. *jaabaw loori w-niqlaw kull ġaraaðhum.* They brought a truck and moved all their things. **2.** to transfer, shift. *l-mudiir niqala ʔila waðiifa jidiida.* The director transferred him to a new job. || *niqloo-la damm.* They gave him a blood transfusion. **3.** to copy. *niqal ʕalayya bil-imtiʕaan.* He copied from me during the examination. *ʔunqul il-majmuuʕ min il-qawaaʔim ʔila daftar il-iʕsaab.* Copy the total from the bills into the ledger. **4.** to pass on, relate, report. *ʕičeena giddaama w-niqal kull ʕačiina l-ʕali.* We talked in front of him and he related everything we said to Ali. **5.** to relay. *raʕ-yniqluun ʕaflat ġinaaʔ il-maʕaṭṭat baġdaad ʕatta nismaʕa.* They will relay a concert to a Baghdad station so we can hear it. **6.** to spread, communicate. *ð-ðibbaan yunqul ihwaaya ʔamraað.* Flies spread many diseases.

nniqal to be transferred. *ʕali nniqal il-baġdaad.* Ali was transferred to Baghdad.

tnaqqal to rove, roam, travel around. *yʕijba yitnaqqal min balda l-balda.* He likes to move around from town to town. *giða šahar yitnaqqal been ʕawaaṣim ʔawruppa.* He spent a month traveling between the capitals of Europe.

ntiqal **1.** to pass on, be transferred, conveyed. *baʕad moota, mulkiyyat il-beet ntiqlat ʔila ʔibna.* After his death, ownership of the house passed to his son. **2.** to move, change residence. *raʕ-nintiqil min hal-imʕalla.* We're going to move from this neighborhood. **3.** to be spread, communicated. *hal-marað yintiqil bil-ṃaay.* This disease is communicated by water.

naqliyya pl. *-aat* **1.** (usually pl.) transportation, transport, portage. *šarikat naqliyyaat* 1. freight company 2. moving company. *ʔaamir in-naqliyyaat il-ʕaskariyya* Commander of Military Transport. **2.** freight, freight charge, cartage. *ʔaxðaw diinaar naqliyya ʕal-ġaraað.* They charged a dinar freight fee for the stuff.

manqal, manqala pl. *manaaqil* brazier.

naaqil pl. *-iin* carrier, bearer.

naaqila pl. *-aat* transport, transport vessel. *naaqilat nafuṭ* oil tanker.

mutanaqqil, mitnaqqil **1.** mobile. **2.** roving, roaming, itinerant, migrant.

n-q-m

niqam (*i naqma*) to become angry, disgusted, fed up. *niqam ʕal-waðiʕ w-istaqaal.* He got disgusted with the situation and resigned.

ntiqam to take revenge, avenge oneself. *ʔaḷḷa yintiqim minnak.* God will get revenge on you.

niqma, naqma pl. *-aat* affliction, adversity, misfortune.

ntiqaam revenge, vengeance.

naaqim angry, disgusted. *huwwa naaqim ʕaleehum kullhum.* He's disgusted at all of them.

n-q-n-q

naqnaq to mumble to oneself in discontent, to become disgruntled, grumpy, peevish. *la-dguum itnaqniq. hassa ʔarajjiʕ-lak il-qalam.* Don't get grumpy. I'll give the pencil back to you right away.

n-q-h

naqaaha convalescence, recovery. *door in-naqaaha.* convalescent stage.

n-q-w

naqqa to purify, clean, cleanse. *had-duwa ynaqqi d-damm.* This medicine purifies the blood.

naqaawa purity.

naqi **1.** pure, clean. **2.** clear, limpid. *ṃaay naqi* clear water.

n-g-b

nigab (*u nagub*) to pierce, perforate, make a hole in. *nigab il-quuṭiyya bil-bismaar.* He punched a hole in the container with the nail. **2.** to deflower, deprive of virginity. *nigabha w-itwarraṭ biiha.* He deflowered her and got into trouble over it.

naggab intensive of *nigab. naggab ij-jidir w-sawwaa maṣfi.* He punched holes in the pot and made a strainer out of it.

nnigab to be pierced, perforated. *j-jidir nnigab.* The pot's got a hole in it.

nagub, nugub pl. *nguub* **1.** perforation, hole. **2.** (vulgar) anus.

n-g-d

naggad **1.** (of dates) to begin to ripen, show first signs of ripeness. *l-ixlaaḷ naggad w-raʕ-yṣiir ruṭab.* The green dates have begun to ripen and are about to become fresh. **2.** to become mentally unbalanced. *min yiji ṣ-ṣeef, haaða* *ynaggid.* When summer comes, he goes off his rocker.

n-g-r

nigar (*u nagir*) **1.** to peck. *d-diič nigar ij-jaahil ib-ˀiida.* The rooster pecked the boy on his hand. **2.** to pick up, grab off, make off with. *nigarha lij-jaaˀiza l-ˀuula.* He grabbed the first prize. **3.** to tap, beat, drum with the tips of the fingers. *da-yingur ʕad-dumbug nagir xafiif.* He's beating the drum lightly with the tips of his fingers. **4.** to pick at, nag, harass. *ðallat tungur ib-raas rajilha ʕatta simaʕ kalaamha.* She kept nagging her husband until he did what she wanted. || *quṣṣtak tungur b-uffaadi.* Your story makes me very sad. *ʕčaayta ðallat tungur b-uffaadi w-ma-rtaaʕeet ˀilla lamma sabbeeta.* His remark kept bothering me and I couldn't rest until I'd told him off.

naggar to peck repeatedly. *d-dijaaj da-ynaggir biš-šiʕiir.* The chickens are pecking at the barley.

tnaagar to bicker, to quarrel with one another. *ʕali w-ˀuxta yitnaagruun in-nahaar kulla.* Ali and his sister are at each other's throats all day. *jiiraanatna titnaagar wiyya rajilha hwaaya.* The lady next door argues with her husband a lot.

nagra pl. *-aat* **1.** peck. **2.** light blow, tap, rap. *nṭiiha nagra zġayyra bič-čaakuuč.* Give it a little tap with the hammer.

nugra **1.** bickering, wrangling, argument. *ma-da-aʕruf ʕala-weeš han-nugra beenaatkum.* I can't understand why there's this bickering between you. **2.** (pl. *nugar*) hole, pit, cavity. || *raʕ-yʕufruu-la nugra w-ysabbibuun faṣla.* They're going to lay a trap for him and cause him to get fired.

*nugri** **1.** nagging, argumentative. **2.** nagger.

mingaar pl. *mnaagiir* beak, bill (of a bird).

n-g-z

naggaz to jump, hop, leap. *čakkeeta bil-ˀubra w-gaam ynaggiz.* I pricked him with the needle and he began to jump up and down.

naggaaza: *timman naggaaza* a kind of broad-grained rice.

n-g-s

nigas (*a nagaasa*) to become ritually unclean, become impure. *ˀiða č-čalib yaakul bil-maaʕuun, il-maaʕuun yingas.* If the dog eats from the plate, the plate becomes unclean.

naggas **1.** to taint, foul, make dirty. *č-čalib, ˀiða yimši bil-mayy, ynaggsa.* If the dog walks in the water, he makes it dirty. **2.** to foul oneself, soil oneself. *ˀibnič naggas. baddilii-la.* Your son has dirtied his pants. Change him.

tnaggas to become ritually unclean, become impure. *la-timši min-naa tara titnaggas.* Don't walk through here or you'll be made unclean. *ˀatnaggas ˀaʕči wiyya waaʕid miθlak.* I'd be dirtying myself speaking to someone like you.

stangas to consider ritually unclean. *yistangis yišrab b-iglaaṣ ġeera.* He feels it's dirty to drink out of somebody else's glass. *huwwa yistangis imnič-čilaab.* He considers dogs dirty.

nagis **1.** ritually unclean, impure. **2.** dirty, filthy, tainted. *hal-mayy nagis. la-tiġsil bii.* This water is filthy. Don't wash in it. *haaða fadd waaʕid nagis. ma-ˀaθiq bii.* He's a loathsome fellow. I don't trust him.

ˀangas more or most filthy, dirty, etc.

n-g-š

mingaaš pl. *mnaagiiš* **1.** tweezers. **2.** fire tongs.

n-g-ṣ

nigaṣ (*u naguṣ*) **1.** to decrease, diminish, become less. *fluusa nigṣat išwayya.* His money dwindled somewhat. *b-hal-qaðiyya, nigaṣ qadra.* With this affair, his prestige has suffered. **2.** to be lacking, deficient, insufficient, inadequate. *l-muwaaʕiin raʕ-tunguṣ li-ˀan il-xuṭṭaar jaabaw ijhaalhum wiyyaahum.* The dishes won't go around because the guests brought their children with them. **3.** to be missing, absent from, be lacking in. *kull ġaraað il-kubba ʕindi; bass yunguṣni l-kišmiš.* I have all the stuff for the kubba; the raisins are all I'm lacking. *š-yunguṣha? bnayya ʕilwa w-muθaqqafa.* What is lacking in her? She's a nice-looking, educated girl.

naggaṣ **1.** to decrease, diminish, lessen. *l-makiina da-turkuð; naggiṣha.* The engine's racing; slow it down. **2.** reduce, curtail. *š-šarika naggiṣat ʕuṣṣatna hal-marra.* The company reduced our quota this time.

stangaṣ to consider insufficient, deficient, lacking. *rufað iṭ-ṭalab li-ˀan istangaṣ il-kammiyya.* He rejected the order because he considered the quantity insufficient.

ˀangaṣ more or most deficient, lacking,

etc. *l-mayy il-yoom ʔangaṣ min il-baarḥa.* The water is lower today than yesterday.

naaguṣ, naagiṣ deficient, lacking, insufficient, inadequate. *hal-baggaal il-wazin maala naaguṣ.* This grocer's weights are less than they should be. || *taxta naaguṣ.* He's a bit crazy. *la-tṣaddig b-il-yguula, tara huwwa taxta naaguṣ.* Don't take any stock in what he says because his mind has slipped. *ḥači naagiṣ* insults, insulting language. *ma-ataḥammal ḥači naagiṣ min ʔaḥḥad.* I won't take insulting words from anybody.

see also *n-q-ṣ.*

n-g-ð̣

nigað̣ (a nagið̣) to become tired, weary, exhausted. *štiġaḷit bil-ḥadiiqa w-nigað̣it. laazim artaaḥ.* I worked in the garden and got tired. I've got to rest.

naggað̣ to tire, make tired. *rakkað̣ta lil-iḥṣaan ʔila ʔan naggað̣ta.* I ran the horse till I'd tired him out.

nagð̣aan tired, weary, exhausted. *haaða šaayib nagð̣aan; haš-šaġla yinraad-ilha waaḥid qawi.* He's a worn-out old man; this job needs a strong person.

n-g-ṭ

naggaṭ **1.** to spot, dot, dab, speckle, dapple. *ṣubaġ iṣ-ṣanduug ʔabyað̣ w-naggaṭa b-ʔaḥmar.* He painted the box white and speckled it with red. *fistaanha ʔabyað̣ imnaggaṭ ib-ʔaḥmar.* Her dress is white with red polka dots. **2.** to drip, fall in drops. *l-mayy da-ynaggiṭ imnil-ḥanafiyya.* The water is dripping from the faucet. **3.** to drip, let fall in drops. *l-ḥanafiyya da-tnaggiṭ.* The faucet's dripping.

nugṭa pl. *nugaṭ* **1.** spot, dot. **2.** stain. **3.** drop (of liquid). *hal-iglaaṣ ma-bii nugṭat mayy.* This glass doesn't have a drop of water in it.

naaguuṭ **1.** water which has dripped from a porous clay water jug. *naaguuṭ il-ḥibb ṣaafi w-baarid.* The water which has dripped from the water jug is clear and cold. || *ḥasbat iṣ-ṣaruf ʕas-sayyaara ma-tixlas; miθil naaguuṭ il-ḥibb.* The business of spending on the car never ends, like the water that drips from the water jug. **2.** (pl. *nwaagiiṭ*) a small container for collecting droplets from a clay water jug.

see also *n-q-ṭ.*

n-g-ʕ

nigaʕ (a nagiʕ) to soak up moisture, to become thoroughly soaked. *xalli l-ḥummuṣ bil-maay saaʕteen ʔila ʔan yingaʕ zeen.* Put the chickpeas in water for two hours until they're well soaked. *rušš il-gaaʕ ḥatta tingaʕ tamaam.* Sprinkle the ground until it's thoroughly wet.

naggaʕ **1.** to soak, steep. *naggaʕ il-uqmaaš bil-mayy ḥatta yxušš.* He soaked the cloth in water so it would shrink. *ð̣alleet aluuma ʔila ʔan naggaʕta.* I kept blaming him until I got him all worked up. **2.** to cause to sweat, to make nervous, embarrass.

tnaggaʕ to become soaked. *tnaggaʕit bil-muṭar.* I got soaked in the rain.

nguuʕ dried whole apricots.

ʔangaʕ more or most soaked, wet.

naagiʕ soaked, wet.

n-g-n-g

nagnag **1.** to eat a small amount. *walaw šabʕaan, taʕaal nagnig wiyyaana.* Even though you're full, come on and have a bite with us. **2.** = *naqnaq,* which see under *n-q-n-q.*

n-g-y

stanga to pick out, select, choose. *stangi lli yʕijbak.* Pick the one you like.

mistanga picked, chosen, selected. *ṭamaaṭat hal-baggaal mistanga.* This grocer's tomatoes are select. || *ybiiʕ mistanga.* He lets customers pick and choose.

n-k-b

nikab (i nakib) to make unhappy, make miserable, afflict, distress. *l-ḥarub nikbathum. maataw xamsa min wulidhum.* The war caused them great suffering. Five of their sons died. *ʔibni nikabni. štira hwaaya ġaraað̣ bid-deen w-hassa, ma-da-nigdar nsaddid l-ifluus.* My son has caused me a lot of trouble. He bought a lot of things on time and now we can't pay the money.

tnakkab to shoulder, place on one's shoulder. *j-jinuud itnakkibaw is-silaaḥ gabuḷ-ma ymurr waziir id-difaaʕ.* The soldiers shouldered their weapons before the Defense Minister passed.

nnikab pass. of *nikab.* *nnikbaw ib-mootat ʔabuuhum.* They were distressed by the death of their father. *l-miskiin nnikab. kull wilda maataw bil-ḥariiq.* The poor guy has really had troubles. All his sons died in the fire.

nakba pl. *-aat* misfortune, calamity, disaster, catastrophe. *mankuub* pl. *-iin* victim (of a disaster). *mankuubiin l-fayaδaan* the flood victims.

n-k-t

nikat (*u nakit*) **1.** to play a prank, play a trick. *ʕali nikat biyya. galli l-yoom ʕuṭla w-xallaani ma-ʔaruuḥ lil-madrasa.* Ali played a trick on me. He told me today was a day off and caused me not to go to school. **2.** to renege, go back on a promise. *waaʕad yidaayinni fluus w-nikat.* He promised to lend me money and then reneged. *ʔiδa twaaʕid, la-tinkut.* If you make a promise, don't break it. *nikat biyya w-ḥayyarni.* He went back on his word to me and left me all confused. *nikat biyya bil-maḥkama. min jaa yišhad, gaal "ma-aʕurfa."* He double-crossed me in court. When he came to testify he said, "I don't know him."

nakkat **1.** to be witty, crack jokes, tell amusing stories. *δeefna nakkat ihwaaya l-baarḥa.* Our guest told a lot of jokes last night. **2.** /with *ʕala*/ to mock, ridicule, poke fun at. *xalloo bin-nuṣṣ w-gaamaw ynakkituun ʕalee.* They got him in the center and began to poke fun at him.

nnikat to be tricked, duped. *haaδa šiiṭaan; ma-yinnikit bii.* He's a tricky fellow; he can't be humbugged.

nukta pl. *nukat* **1.** joke, witticism, wise-crack, pun. **2.** prank, trick, practical joke.

n-k-θ

nikaθ (*u nakiθ*) **1.** to break, violate (an obligation). *nikaθ il-ʕahad ib-saaʕ.* He broke the pledge right away. **2.** (of moisture) to fall, come down. *baʕadha da-tinkuθ. ybayyin raḥ-tumṭur in-nahaar kulla.* It's still coming down. It looks like it's going to rain all day. **3.** to drip. *ṭabb lil-gubba yinkuθ ʕarag.* He entered the room dripping sweat. **4.** to shake, shake out, wave violently. *ʔinkuθ is-sitra. yjuuz biiha fluus.* Shake the coat. Maybe there are some coins in it.

n-k-ḥ

nikaaḥ marriage, matrimony. *ʕaqd in-nikaaḥ* marriage contract.

n-k-r

nikar (*u nakir*) to deny, disclaim, disavow. *nikar kullši giddaam il-ḥaakim.* He denied everything before the judge. *nikar id-deen ʕalayya.* He denied owing me the debt.

tnakkar to assume a disguise, to mask, disguise oneself. *baṭal ir-ruwaaya tnakkar w-xašš lil-ḥafla.* The hero of the story masked himself and went in to the party.

stankar to denounce, protest, disapprove of. *kullhum stankiraw il-ʕudwaan ʕal-balad.* They all denounced the aggression against the country.

nukraan denial. *nukraan iδ-δaat* self-denial. *nukraan ij-jamiil* ingratitude.

tanakkur disguise.

tanakkuri: *ḥafla tanakkuriyya* masquerade party, costume ball.

mitnakkir disguised. *min lizmata š-šurṭa ṭilaʕ rijjaal mitnakkir ib-zayy mara.* When the police caught him he turned out to be a man disguised as a woman.

n-k-s

nakkas **1.** to lower to half-mast, fly at half-mast. *min maat il-malik, nakkisaw il-ʔaʕlaam.* When the King died, they flew the flags at half-mast. **2.** to bow, hang, bend. *nakkas raasa mnil-xajal.* He bowed his head from shame.

tnakkas pass. of *nakkas. l-ʔaʕlaam raḥ-titnakkas muddat isbuuʕ.* The flags will be flown at half-mast for a week.

ntikas to suffer a relapse. *ṣiḥḥta čaanat da-titḥassan laakin ʔaxaδ barid w-intikas.* His health was improving but he caught a cold and had a relapse. *ntiksat ṣiḥḥta min xarbaṭ bil-ʔakil.* He had a relapse when he didn't follow instructions in his diet.

ntikaasa pl. *-aat* relapse.

n-k-f

stankaf **1.** to look down on, feel too good for, to disdain, scorn. *yistankif yištuġuḷ ib-hal-maṣlaḥa.* He feels that he's above working in this occupation. *yaʕni tistankif tiḥči wiyyaaya?* Do you mean you consider it degrading to talk with me? **2.** /with *ʕan*/ to spurn, reject contemptuously. *jeet ʔaballġa laakin istankaf ʕan it-tabliiġ.* I went to present him with the summons but he contemptuously refused the summons.

nukaaf mumps. *ma-raaḥ lil-madrasa li-ʔan ʕinda nukaaf.* He didn't go to school because he has mumps.

n-k-h

nakha, nukha pl. *-aat* aroma, scent, smell.

¹*n-m-r*

nimir pl. *numuur* **1.** tiger. **2.** leopard.

²*n-m-r*

nammar to number, assign numbers to, put numbers on. *nammur iṣ-ṣafḥaat ḥatta ma-titxarbaṭ.* Number the pages so they won't get mixed up. *numra* pl. *numar* number.

n-m-š

namaš freckles, skin discolorations.

n-m-l

nammal to tingle, prickle, be numb, be asleep. *ˀašu ˀiidi da-tnammil.* I think my hand is asleep.

namil (coll.) ant(s).

namla pl. *-aat* ant.

n-m-n

namuuna, nimuuna pl. *namaayin* sample, specimen.

n-m-n-m

nimnim (coll.) small bead(s). *laabsa glaada nimnim.* She's wearing a necklace of small beads.

nimnima pl. *-aat* small bead.

mnamnam small, diminutive. *š-itsawwi b-hiiči beet čibiir? šuuf-lak beet iṣġayyir imnamnam.* What'll you do with such a big house? Find yourself a small, compact house. *tzawwaj ibnayya ʕilwa mnamnima.* He married a pretty, petite girl.

n-m-w

nima (*a numuw*) to grow, expand. *š-šarika nimat w-ṣaar ˀilha furuuʕ ihwaaya.* The company grew and acquired many branch offices.

namma to cause to grow. *hal-ismaad ynammi il-warid ib-surʕa.* This fertilizer will make the flowers grow fast.

ntima **1.** to become a member. *raʕ-antimi l-hal-ʕizib.* I'm going to join this party. **2.** to trace one's ancestry, to be descended. *yintimi l-ʕaaˀila šariifa.* He is descended from a noble family.

n-m-w-δ-j

numuuδaj pl. *namaaδij* **1.** model. **2.** sample, specimen. **3.** exemplar, example.

*namuuδaji** model, exemplary. *haaδa riyaaḍi namuuδaji.* He's an ideal sportsman.

n-h-b

nihab (*a nahib*) **1.** to steal, plunder, take by force. *waggufoo biṭ-ṭariiq w-nihbaw kull-ma ʕinda.* They stopped him on the road and stole all he had. *la-tištiri min hal-baqqaaḷ tara yinhabak.* Don't buy from this grocer or he'll rob you.

nahhaab pl. *-a* robber. *hat-tijjaar kullhum nahhaaba.* These merchants are all robbers.

n-h-t

nihat (*a nahit*) to pant, gasp, breathe heavily. *ḍall muddat ʕašir daqaayiq yinhat imnir-rikiḍ.* He kept panting for ten minutes after running.

n-h-j

manhaj, minhaaj pl. *manaahij* program, schedule of events.

n-h-d

nahid pl. *nhuud* female breast.

n-h-r

nahar pl. *ˀanhaar* river.

*nahri** river. *s-simač in-nahri ˀaṭyab imnis-simač il-baʕri.* River fish are tastier than ocean fish.

nahaar pl. *-aat* day, daytime, the daylight hours.

*nahaari** day, daytime. *tilmiiδ nahaari* day student. || *ʕafla nahaariyya* matinee.

n-h-z

ntihaz to sieze, take advantage of. *ntihiz il-furṣa w-la-txalliiha tfuutak.* Seize the opportunity and don't let it pass you by.

ntihaazi pl. *-iyyiin* opportunist.

n-h-š

nihaš (*a nahiš*) to mangle, tear to pieces. *č-čilaab iltammat ʕalee w-nihšat ḷaʕma.* The dogs ganged up on him and tore his flesh to pieces.

n-h-g

nihag (*a nahig*) **1.** to bray. *z-zumaal da-yinhag.* The donkey's braying. **2.** to pant. *taʕbaan mnir-rikiḍ. da-yinhag.* He's tired of running. He's panting.

n-h-k

ˀanhak to exhaust, wear out, enervate. *haš-šuġuḷ ˀanhakni.* That work exhausted me.

ntihak to violate, defile, abuse, profane, desecrate. *ntihak ʕurmat ij-jaamiʕ.* He violated the sanctity of the mosque. *ʕibsoo li-ˀanna ntihak ˀaʕraaḍ in-naas.* They jailed him because he desecrated the honor of the people.

n-h-y

niha (*i nahi*) to prohibit, ban, forbid, interdict. *ˀalif marra nheetak imnil-liʕib ihnaa.* I've told you a thousand times not to play here.

ˀanha to bring to an end, terminate, finish, conclude, complete. *la-truuʕ gabuḷ-ma tinhi kull šuġḷak.* Don't go before you finish all your work.

ntiha to come to an end, draw to a close, to be terminated, concluded, finished, done with. *s-sibaaq yintihi s-saaʕa ˀarbaʕa.* The race ends at four o'clock. *kullši beenaathum ntiha.* Everything's all over between them.

nihaaya pl. *-aat* **1.** end. **2.** termination,

conclusion. **3.** outcome, result. || *bin-nihaaya* in the end, finally, at last. *bin-nihaaya, ɛaṣṣal ɛala darajat id-duktoora.* Finally, he obtained his doctoral degree.

laa-nihaaya infinity.

*nihaaʔi** final, last. *mtiɛaan nihaaʔi* final exam.

nihaaʔiyyan. at all, whatsoever. *ma-aku ʔay ɛalaaqa beenaathum nihaaʔiyyaan.* There is no relationship between them at all.

n-w-b

naab (*u niyaaba*) to act as representative, stand in, substitute, act as proxy. *l-waziir ma-gidar yiji. ʔaani ʔanuub ɛanna.* The minister couldn't come. I represent him. *minu ynuub ɛanna min yġiib?* Who substitutes for him when he is absent?

nawwab to appoint as representative, agent, or substitute. *ʔil-man raɛ-ynawwub hal-marra?* Who will he appoint to fill in this time?

tnaawab to take turns, alternate. *ʔiδa titnaawbuun biš-šuġul, ma-ttiɛbuun.* If you take turns at the work, you won't get tired.

nooba pl. *-aat* **1.** turn. *hassa noobat man?* Whose turn is it now? *raɛ-nunṭur il-bistaan bin-nooba.* We're going to guard the orchard by shifts. **2.** time, instance. *xaabartak noobteen laakin ma-čaan ʔaku jawaab.* I called you two times but there was no answer. *han-nooba ʔilak. noobt il-lux ʔabuṣṭak.* This time is for free. Next time I'll bust you. *noobaat yirjaɛ sakraan.* Sometimes he comes back drunk. **3.** fit, spell, attack, paroxysm. *ʔaɛyaanan tilizma nooba ɛaṣabiyya.* Occasionally he has a nervous spell. **4.** swamp fever, malaria.

¶ *fadd nooba* 1. at one time, all at once, in one bunch. *kullkum taɛaalu fadd nooba.* All of you come at the same time. 2. /usually with imperative/ might as well, just go ahead and. *fadd nooba guul kullši ma-yiftihim.* You might as well say he doesn't understand anything. 3. too much, to excess. *sawwaaha fadd nooba. muu ɛaqqi ʔazɛal?* He went too far. Don't I have a right to get mad?

noobači pl. *-iyya* guard, watchman.

niyaaba representation, substitution, deputyship, proxy. || *bin-niyaaba ɛan* in place of, in lieu of. *ʔinta waqqiɛ bin-niyaaba ɛanna.* You sign in his place.

*niyaabi** representative. *ɛukuuma niyaabiyya* representative government.

naaʔib pl. *nuwwaab* **1.** representative. *ʔaxuuya tilaɛ naaʔib min hal-manṭiqa.* My brother become a representative for this district. *majlis in-nuwwaab* house of representatives, lower house of parliament. **2.** vice-. *naaʔib qunṣul* vice-consul. *naaʔib ɛariif* corporal. *naaʔib δaabuṭ* warrant officer.

n-w-ɛ

naaɛ (*u nyaaɛ, manaaɛa*) to give a mournful cry, make a sorrowful sound. *yigluun il-ɛamaam yinuuɛ.* They say that the pigeon gives a mournful cry. *da-tnuuɛ ɛala wulidha l-maataw.* She is mourning for her dead children.

n-w-x

nawwax **1.** to kneel down. *n-naaga nawwuxat bil-ɛajal.* The camel kneeled down quickly. **2.** to make kneel down. *nawwux ij-jimal ɛatta ʔarkab ɛalee.* Make the camel kneel down so I can get on him.

manaax climate, weather.

manaaxa pl. *-aat* parking area for caravans.

n-w-x-δ

nooxδa pl. *-aat* captain of a sailing vessel

n-w-r

nawwar to enlighten. *nawwirna b-ʔaaraaʔak.* Enlighten us with your opinions.

tnawwar to be enlightened. *ʔudxul il-madrasa ɛatta titnawwar bil-ɛilim.* Enter the school so you'll become enlightened by knowledge.

naar pl. *niiraan* **1.** fire. || *l-ʔasɛaar il-yoom naar.* Prices today are unbearable. *ɛyuuna da-tijdaɛ naar imnil-ġaδab.* His eyes are shooting fire from anger. *la-tiɛči wyaa tara ṣaayir naar.* Don't speak to him 'cause he's infuriated. **2.** gunfire.

*naari** fiery, igneous, fire-. *ʔalɛaab naariyya* fireworks. *ʔasliɛa naariyya* firearms.

nuur light, illumination. *l-ġurfa ma-biiha nuur kaafi.* The room doesn't have enough light in it. || *nuur kaššaaf* searchlight.

nuura lime, quicklime.

manaara pl. *manaayir* minaret.

munaawara pl. *-aat* (military) maneuver.

n-w-š

naaš (*u nooš*) to reach, get to. *ma-yigdar iynuuš is-ṣabbuura li-ʔanna qaṣiir.* He can't reach the blackboard because he's short. *l-baṭṭaaniyya naašha mayy. šurrha biš-šamis.* Water has gotten to the blanket.

Hang it out in the sun. || *ʔiδa gaal ysawwiiha, iɛtuburha xalṣaana, li-ʔan haaδa ʔiida tnuuš.* If he said he'd do it, consider it done, because he's a capable fellow.

naawaš to hand, pass. *naawišni l-iktaab ɛatta ʔaxallii ɛar-raff.* Hand me the book so I can put it on the shelf.

tnaawaš 1. to take, seize, grab, take into one's hand. *tnaawaš l-iktaab. ʔiidi tiɛbat.* Take the book. My hand is tired. *tnaawaš is-saaɛa w-δirabni biiha.* He grabbed the clock and hit me with it. 2. to attack, set upon, engage in a skirmish with. *min marr, tnaawšoo ij-jahhaal bil-iɛjaar.* When he passed by, the children attacked him with rocks. *bass xašš lil-ġurfa, tnaawašnaa.* The minute he entered the room, we lit into him.

munaawaša pl. *-aat* hostile encounter, exchange, skirmish.

mnaawišči pl. *-iyya* bricklayer's helper.

n-w-ṭ

nooṭ pl. *nwaaṭ* bank note, bill. *nooṭ ʔabu l-ɛašr idnaaniir* a ten-dinar bill.

nooṭa pl. *-aat* 1. musical note. 2. sheet music. *ma-agdar ʔadugg kamanja bala nooṭa.* I can't play a violin without sheet music.

n-w-ɛ

nawwaɛ to make different, diversify, variegate, add variety to. *ynawwiɛ ib-ʔaɛaadiiθa — marra ʔaxbaar, marra quṣaṣ, marra falsafa.* He inserts variety in his speeches — one time current events, then stories, then philosophy. *loo š-šarika tnawwiɛ il-ɛaajaat it-tištiriiha mnil-xaarij, čaan iyṣiir ɛaleeha qbaal.* If the company diversified the goods that it buys from abroad, there would be a demand for them.

tnawwaɛ pass. of *nawwaɛ. kull-ma titnawwaɛ biδaaɛatna, šuġulna yitɛassan.* The more diversified our goods are, the more our business improves.

nooɛ pl. *ʔanwaaɛ* kind, sort, type, species.

nawɛan-ma somewhat, to a certain degree, in a way. *l-mariiδ nawɛan-ma ʔaɛsan il-yoom.* The patient is somewhat better today.

nawɛiyya pl. *-aat* quality. *l-kammiyya qaliila bass in-nawɛiyya zeena.* The quantity is small but the quality is good.

mutanawwiɛ diversified, different, various. || *mutanawwiɛaat* sundries, miscellany.

n-w-ɛ-r

nooɛar = niɛar, which see under *n-ɛ-r.*

[1]*n-w-g*

naaga pl. *-aat, nuug* female camel.

[2]*n-w-g*

nooga nougat.

n-w-l

nool pl. *ʔanwaal* loom.

n-w-m

naam (a noom, manaam) 1. to sleep. *ʔaani ʔanaam sabiɛ saaɛaat bil-yoom.* I sleep seven hours per night. 2. to retire, go to bed. *ṣaar nuṣṣ il-leel; xalli nruuɛ innaam.* It's midnight; let's go to bed. 3. to lie, lie down. *naam ɛala baṭnak ɛatta ʔamarrix δahrak.* Lie on your stomach so I can massage your back. *ɛuṭṭ dihin ib-šaɛrak ɛatta ynaam.* Put oil on your hair so that it'll stay in place.

nawwam, nayyam 1. to put to bed, put to sleep. *wakkili j-jaahil w-nayyimii.* Feed the child and put him to sleep. *ween raɛ-innayyimhum? ɛidna ġurfat noom waɛda.* Where are we going to bed them down? We have only one bedroom. 2. to make lie down. *had-dihin iynayyim iš-šaɛar.* This cream makes the hair lie down. 3. to hypnotize. *nawwama w-gaam yisʔala ʔasʔila.* He hypnotized him and began asking him questions.

nnaam pass. of *naam. hal-ġurfa baarda; ma-yinnaam biiha.* This room is cold; it can't be slept in.

noom sleeping, sleep. *ġurfat noom* bedroom.

nooma pl. *-aat* i.n. of *noom.*

tanwiim, tanwiim muġnaaṭiisi hypnotism, hypnosis.

munawwim, munawwin muġnaaṭiisi hypnotist.

n-w-m-y

nuumi (coll.), and *nuumi ɛilu* sweet lemon(s), a thin-skinned citrus fruit resembling the orange, but having a yellow skin. || *nuumi ɛaamuδ* lemon(s). *nuumi baṣra* 1. dried lemons imported from Muscat, through the port of Basra. 2. a condiment made from dried lemons.

nuumiyya pl. *-aat* un. n. of *nuumi.*

*nuumaayi**, and *loon nuumaayi* lemon-yellow.

n-w-n

nuun name of the letter *n.*

nuuna pl. *-aat* beauty spot on the forehead, applied artificially by women.

n-w-y

nuwa (i niyya) to intend, propose, plan,

have in mind. *yinwuun yibnuun mustašfa b-hal-manṭiqa.* They plan to build a hospital in this neighborhood.

nuwa (coll.) pit(s), stone(s) (of fruit).

nwaaya pl. *-aat* pit, stone (of a fruit).

*nawawi**, *nuwawi** nuclear, atomic. || *ʔasliḥa nuwawiyya* nuclear weapons.

niyya pl. *-aat* intention, intent, purpose, plan, design, scheme. *ma-čaanat ʕindi niyya ʔaštiriiha bass inta raǧǧabitni ʕaleeha.* I had no intention of buying it but you got me enthusiastic about it. *ʔinta š-niitak? ma-txalliini ʔaštuǧuḷ?* What are you up to? Why don't you let me work? || *ḥusn in-niyya* good intention, good will, sincerity. *sawwaaha b-ḥusun niyya.* He did it with good intentions. *saliim in-niyya* guileless, sincere. *yiʕjibni li-ʔanna šaxuṣ saliim in-niyya.* I like him because he is a sincere person. *suuʔ in-niyya* evil intent, malice, insincerity, deceit.

n-y

nii raw, uncooked. *l-imʕaaliig baʕadha niyya.* The livers are still raw.

n-y-b

naab pl. *ʔanyaab* 1. fang. 2. eye-tooth. 3. tusk.

n-y-č

naač (i neeč) (vulgar) to perform the male role in sexual intercourse.

nayyač to perform the female role in sexual intercourse.

tnaayač to copulate, have sexual intercourse with each other.

neeč copulating, having sexual intercourse.

neeča i.n. of *neeč*.

n-y-ḥ

nyaaḥ see under *n-w-ḥ*.

n-y-š-n

neešan 1. to mark, inscribe, assign an identifying mark to. *neešin iṣ-ṣafḥa ḥatta ma-ððayyiʕha.* Mark the page so you won't lose track of it. 2. to aim, point. *neešan bit-tufga ʕalayya.* He pointed the gun at me. *neešin ʕala markaz id-daaʔira.* Aim at the bull's-eye. 3. to send a gift with a proposal of marriage to. *ʔibn il-waziir neešan ibnayya min garaaybi.* The minister's son sent a gift proposing marriage to one of my relatives. *maʕa l-ʔasaf, bittna mneešna.* Unfortunately, our girl is promised.

niišaan 1. aim. *ʔuxuð niišaan zeen gabuḷ-ma tirmi.* Take good aim before you fire. 2. (pl. *nyaašiin*) mark, sign, identifying character. 3. medal, decoration, badge of honor. 4. a personal gift sent to a girl, the acceptance of which implies consent to marriage.

niišanči pl. *-iyya* marksman, sharpshooter.

¹*n-y-l*

n-niil the Nile.

²*n-y-l*

niil 1. indigo. 2. indigo plant.

*niili** blue, dark blue. *štireet-li qaaṭ niili.* I bought a dark blue suit.

¹*n-y-m*

nayyam to sate oneself with food, to eat one's fill. *l-baarḥa nayyamit zeen bil-ʕaziima.* I really ate my fill at the dinner party yesterday.

²*n-y-m*

nayyam = *nawwam,* which see under *n-w-m*.

n-y-y

niyya, see under *n-w-y* and *n-y*.

H

h-

ha- /plus definite article and noun/ this, this particular. *hal-marra doorak.* This time it's your turn. *har-rasim muu ḥilu.* This painting isn't very pretty.

¹*h-a*

haa 1. (an interjection used in address, approx.:) well, so, yes, okay. *haa ʕali! šloonak il-yoom?* Well Ali! How are you today? *haa ʕammi! š-itriid?* Yes uncle! What can I do for you? *haa haa, kull-man yguul yaa-ruuḥi.* Well, well, everyone looks out for himself. *haa haa! ftihamit.* Oh yeah! Now I understand. 2. (in surprise or amazement) oh? really? what? *haa? dzawwaj w-maḥḥad dira bii?* Oh? He got married and no one knew about it? *haa? maat? laa!* What? He died? Oh, no! 3. (in reply to a half-heard question) huh? what? *haa? waḷḷa ma-adri ween raaḥ.* Huh? Golly, I don't know where he went.

²*h-a*

haa-: *haak,* fem. *haač,* pl. *haakum* here, here you are. *haač diinaar; štirii-lič nafnuuf ḥilu.* Here's a dinar; buy yourself a nice dress. *haak, ʔuxuδha!* Here, take it!

h-a-δ-a

haaδa fem. *haaδi, haay* pl. *δool, δoola, haδool, haδoola* this, this one. *haay marti.* This is my wife. *haδoola wildi.* These are my sons. *ʔuxδ il-laax; haaδa maali.* Take the other one; this one is mine. *ṭabʕan ʔaʕurfa; haaδa ʕammi.* Of course I know him; he's my uncle. *haaδa paaysiklak ṭilaʕ ma-yištuġuḷ.* This bicycle of yours, it turns out, doesn't work. *ṣadiiqi haaδa yguul sayyaartak ma-tiswa.* My friend here says your car's no good. *haδool š-aʕleehum? ʔaani iksarit ij-jaam.* What do these people have to do with it? I broke the glass. *šinu haay? š-da-tsawwi?* What's this? What are you doing? *haay hiyya. la-djiib baʕad.* That's it. Don't bring any more. || *maʕa haaδa* nevertheless, even so. *ʕaṣṣalit-la šuġuḷ zeen w-maʕa haaδa ma-qaabil.* I got him a good job and still he's not satisfied.

h-ʔ-l

haaʔil, see under *h-w-l.*

h-a-y

haay = *haaδi,* which see under *h-a-δ-a.*

h-a-w-n

haawan pl. *hawaawiin* mortar (vessel). || *midfaʕ il-haawan* mortar (weapon).

h-b-b

habb (*i habb*) to blow. *l-hawa, ʔiδa yhibb min haj-jiha, yjiib ʕajaaj.* If the wind blows from this direction, it brings dust.

habb: *habb riiʕ* fem. *habbat riiʕ* pl. *habbiin riiʕ* 1. refreshing, friendly person. 2. capable, willing worker.

h-b-š

habbaš 1. to polish, mill. *raʕ-inhabbiš iš-šilib kulla gabul-ma nbiiʕa.* We're going to polish all the field rice before we sell it. *siʕir it-timman il-imhabbaš diinaar w-nuṣṣ.* The price of polished rice is a dinar and a half. 2. *habbaš* (*ib-ʕačya*) to talk idly, without thought, to chatter, babble, jabber. *da-yhabbiš ib-ʕačya, w-ma-da-yuʕruf iš-da-yguul.* He's talking idly, and he doesn't know what he's saying.

habbaaša pl. *-aat* rice-polishing machine.

h-b-ṭ

hubaṭ (*u habuṭ, hubuuṭ*) to drop, sink, fall downward. *hubṭat darajt il-ʕaraara leelt il-baarʕa.* The temperature went down last night. || *hubaṭ galbi.* My heart sank. *min gal-li bil-qaδiyya, hubaṭ galbi.* When he told me about the thing, my heart sank. *hubaṭit. ʕabaali l-ifluus δaaʕat.* I was scared. I thought the money was gone.

habbaṭ to cause to sink, drop, fall downward. *masiʕ guṣṣat il-mariiδ bil-kuʕuul yhabbuṭ darajt il-ʕaraara.* Rubbing a sick person's forehead with alcohol reduces the fever. || *habbaṭ galba.* He made his heart sink. *ṭilaʕ-li min wara l-baab w-habbaṭ galbi.* He came out from behind the door and scared me.

habuṭ, hubuuṭ dropping, sinking.

habṭa i.n. of *habuṭ. hubaṭ galbi fadd habṭa.* My heart really sank.

hibiiṭ a meat dish prepared and given to the poor as a sacrifice in gratitude for good fortune bestowed by God.

h-b-y

hiba see under *w-h-b.*

h-t-r

stahtar to have little respect, attach little importance. *huwwa yistahtir bil-qawaaniin.* He has little respect for laws.

mistahtir wanton, unrestrained, uninhibited. *l-kull yuʕurfuuha mistahtira. maʕʕad da-yidzawwajha.* Everyone knows she's a bit loose. No one's going to marry her.

h-t-f

hitaf (*i hitaaf*) 1. /with *l-* or *b-*/ to cheer, hail, acclaim, applaud. *j-jamaahiir hitfat liz-zaʕiim min marr min-naa.* The crowds cheered the leader when he passed by here. *hitfaw iθlaθ marraat b-ʕayaat raʔiis ij-jumhuriyya.* They gave three cheers for the life of the president of the republic. 2. /with *δidd*/ to boo, jeer. *min čaan yixṭub gaam waaʕid w-hitaf δidda.* As he was speaking, someone stood up and booed him.

hitaaf pl. *-aat* 1. cheer, shout, hurrah. 2. boo, jeer.

haatif pl. *-iin* caller, shouter, rejoicer.

h-t-k

hitak (*i hatik*) 1. to expose, reveal, bare, disclose. *hitakhum kullhum bij-jariida.* He exposed them all in the newspaper. 2. to disgrace, bring shame to. *j-jaahil hitakna giddaam ij-jiiraan.* The kid disgraced us in front of the neighbors. *hitak ʕarδa.* He disgraced his honor. 3. to ruin. *ʔibinhum ṣarraaf; hitak ʔahla.* Their son is a spendthrift; he ruined his family.

thattak to behave in a disgraceful, shameless manner. *hiyya tithattak ib-*

libisha. She's shameless in her way of dressing.

nhitak 1. to be disgraced. *rigṣat wiyya waaʕid ma-tʕurfa w-inhitkat.* She danced with someone she didn't know and was disgraced. 2. to be ruined. *nhitak; xiṣar kull ifluusa bil-iqmaar.* He was ruined; he lost all his money in gambling.

hatiika pl. *-aat* scandal, disgrace.

mahtuuk 1. exposed, scandalized, shamed, disgraced. 2. ruined, penniless. *šloon adaaynak ifluus? ʔaani mahtuuk.* How could I lend you money? I'm flat broke.

mithattik shameless, dishonorable.

h-j-j

hajj (*i hajj, hajiij*) to flee, run away. *čaan ihnaa, laakin min šaafkum jaayiin, hajj.* He was here, but when he saw you coming, he beat it. *hajj min ʕarr baġdaad.* He escaped from the heat of Baghdad. *raʕ-ahijj min ʔiidak!* I'm going to leave because of the things you do.

hajjaj to cause to flee. *raʕ-ithajjijni ʔiδa tibqa tsawwi hiiči.* You're going to drive me away if you keep on doing that.

hajiij: l-hajiij I'm leaving! I'm getting out of here! *l-hajiij! ma-yinʕaaš ib-hal-beet.* I'm leaving! It's impossible to live in this house.

h-j-r

hijar (*u i hajir*) to abandon, forsake, leave behind, give up. *hijarha l-marta w-idzawwaj wiʕda lux.* He abandoned his wife and married someone else.

haajar to emigrate. *haajar il-ʔamriika.* He emigrated to America.

hijra pl. *-aat* emigration, exodus. || *l-hijra* the Hegira, emigration of the Prophet Mohammed from Mecca to Medina.

*hijri** pertaining to the Hegira. || *sana hijriyya* year in the Moslem era.

mahjar 1. emigration to the Western Hemisphere. 2. the emigrant community, esp. in America. *ʔummha b-libnaan bass ʔabuuha bil-mahjar.* Her mother is in Lebanon but her father is in America.

muhaajir pl. *-iin* 1. emigrant. 2. immigrant.

mahjuur abandoned. *binaaya mahjuura* abandoned building, condemned building.

h-j-ʕ

hijaʕ (*a*) 1. to become calm, still, silent. *ʔibni, š-gadd tibči. ma-tihjaʕ ʕaad?* Son, you're crying so much. Why don't you calm down? 2. to sleep peacefully. *sinni čaan yoojaʕni l-baarʕa. ma-hjaʕit ʔilla qariib iṣ-ṣubuʕ.* My tooth was hurting me yesterday. I didn't get to sleep until almost morning.

h-j-m

hijam (*i hujuum*) 1. /with *ʕala*/ to attack, assault, storm, assail ferociously. *s-sabiʕ hijam ʕaṣ-ṣayyaad.* The lion attacked the hunter. *hijam ʕaleena l-ʕarr fadd marra.* The heat was upon us all at once. 2. (*i hajim*) to destroy. *ʔaḷḷa yihjim ʕumrak! ma-tigʕud raaʕa ʕaad.* God damn you! Why don't you quiet down. || *hijam beeta.* He ruined him (lit., destroyed his house). *hijmat beeti b-hal-maṣraf il-qaba.* She ruined me with that excessive expense.

haajam 1. to attack, assault, assail, charge. *haajmaw il-ʕadu l-fajir.* They attacked the enemy at dawn. 2. to rush, pounce upon. *haajma w-uxδ iṭ-ṭooba minna.* Move in on him and take the ball away from him. 3. to attack, assail, criticize severely. *haajamhum bij-jariida.* He attacked them in the newspaper.

thajjam to assume the offensive, to be aggressive, behave hostilely. *ma-aku ʕaaja tithajjam ʕalee.* There's no reason for you to be so hostile toward him.

nhijam pass. of *hijam.*

hujuum 1. assault, attack, charge. *hujuum muʕaakis* counterattack. 2. forward line, forward positions (in soccer, etc.).

*hujuumi** offensive, aggressive. *xiṭṭa hujuumiyya.* offensive plan.

muhaajim pl. *-iin* 1. attacker, assailant, aggressor. 2. forward (in soccer, etc.).

h-j-n

hajjaana: *šurṭa hajjaana* mounted police, a force which patrols the desert on camels.

h-j-w

hija (*i hijaaʔ*) to satirize, mock, ridicule (esp. in poetry). *haš-šaaʕir yihji kull-man ma-yinṭii fluus.* This poet satirizes everyone who doesn't give him money. *hijaa b-qaṣiida qawiyya.* He made fun of him in a strongly worded poem.

thajja to spell. *šloon tithajja hač-čilma?* How do you spell this word?

hijaaʔ 1. satire, derision, ridicule. 2. alphabet, successive order of letters.

*hijaaʔi** 1. satirical. *qaṣiida hijaaʔiyya* satirical poem. 2. alphabetical.

h-d-ʔ

hidaʔ (*a huduuʔ*) 1. to become calm, calm

down. *j-jaahil biča mudda w-baɛdeen hidaʔ.* The kid cried a while and then calmed down. **2.** to subside, abate, die down, let up. *l-ɛaaṣifa hidʔat.* The storm died down.

haddaʔ to quiet, calm, tranquilize, make still. *ruuḥ haddiʔa. hal-axbaar qilqata.* Go calm him down. That news upset him. *hal-ḥabb yhaddiʔ il-ʔaɛṣaab.* These pills calm the nerves.

huduuʔ tranquility, stillness, quiet, calmness. *yištuġuḷ ib-huduuʔ w-ib-diqqa.* He works quietly and with precision.

ʔahdaʔ more or most tranquil, etc.

haadi calm, still, tranquil, quiet. || *l-muḥiiṭ il-haadi* The Pacific Ocean.

h-d-b

hidib, hadab pl. *ʔahdaab* eyelashes.

h-d-d

hadd (i hadd) **1.** to release, let go of, turn loose, set free. *š-šurṭi hadda baɛad-ma šaaf hawiita.* The policeman released him after seeing his identification. *hidd iidi!* Let go of my hand! *hadd ɛalayya č-čalib.* He turned the dog loose on me. *la-truuḥ lil-ḥadiiqa; č-čalib mahduud.* Don't go in the garden; the dog's been turned loose. **2.** to tear down, wreck, raze. *leeš da-yhidduun hal-ḥaayiṭ?* Why are they wrecking this wall?

haddad to threaten. *haddada ḥatta ywaafiq.* He threatened him so he'd accept. *huwwa haddadni bil-qatil.* He threatened me with death.

nhadd **1.** to be released, get loose. *č-čalib inhadd min ʔiidi.* The dog got loose from me. || *bass simaɛ ṣooṭi bit-talafoon, nhadd ɛalayya fadd hadda.* As soon as he heard my voice on the phone, there came a torrent of abuse at me. **2.** to be destroyed, wrecked. *l-garaaj nhadd bil-ɛaaṣifa.* The garage was wrecked in the storm.

hadda insults, abuse. *nhadd ɛaleena fadd hadda.* There came a torrent of insults at us.

h-d-r-w-j-y-n

hadroojiin hydrogen. *hadroojiini** hydrogen-. *qumbula hadroojiiniyya* hydrogen bomb.

h-d-f

hidaf (i hadif) to aim, endeavor, strive. *l-ḥukuuma tihdif ʔila l-qaḍaaʔ ɛal-ʔummiyya.* The government is aiming at the abolition of illiteracy.

haddaf to shoot (a ball toward the goal in sports). *hal-laaɛib yhaddif mumtaaz.* That player shoots very well.

stahdaf to have as one's aim or goal, to strive for, work toward, reach for. *b-hal-mašruuɛ, il-ḥukuuma tistahdif rafiɛ mustawa l-fallaaḥ.* With this project, the government is striving for an elevation of the farmer's standard.

hadaf pl. *ʔahdaaf* **1.** object, goal, aim, purpose. **2.** target. **3.** goal (in sports).

haddaaf pl. *-iin* good shot, sharpshooter, dead-eye (esp. in sports).

h-d-l

hidal i (hadil) to sag, droop, hang down. *xaalla suutyaan ḥatta ma-tihdil idyuusha.* She's got on a bra so her breasts won't sag. *č-čitif il-yisra maal is-sitra da-yihdil. raḥ-ʔaḥutt-la čattaafiyya.* The left shoulder of the jacket droops. I'm going to put in a shoulder pad.

thaddal to strip to the waist, take off one's shirt. *thaddal w-giɛad biš-šamis.* He stripped to the waist and sat in the sun.

haadil sagging, drooping, hanging down. *š-xaall ib-jeebak? ʔašu haadil.* What have you put in your pocket? It's sagging.

h-d-m

hidam (i hadim) to tear down, raze, wreck, demolish, destroy. *l-baladiyya hidmat čam beet w-sawwat ib-mukaanhum saaḥa.* The city razed several houses and made an open square in their place.

haddam to tear down, raze, demolish, wreck, destroy. *da-yhaddimuun il-ʔuteel w-yibnuun waaḥid ġeera.* They're tearing down the hotel and building another one. *l-ɛarag haddam ṣiḥḥta.* Arrack destroyed his health.

thaddam **1.** pass. of *haddam.* **2.** to fall down, collapse, fall apart. *thaddam il-beet imnil-muṭar.* The house collapsed because of the rain.

nhidam to be demolished, wrecked, ruined. *l-ibnaaya nhidmat bil-ɛaaṣifa.* The building was destroyed by the storm.

hidim, hduum clothes, clothing.

haddaam destructive. *š-šiyuuɛiyya mabdaʔ haddaam.* Communism is a destructive ideology.

h-d-n

hudna pl. *-aat, hudan* armistice, truce.

h-d-h-d

hidhid, hudhud pl. *hadaahid* hoopoe.

h-d-y

hida (i hidaaya) **1.** to lead on the right path. *balki ʔaḷḷa yihdii w-iyjuuz imnil-*

uqmaar. Perhaps God will guide him and he will give up gambling. **2.** (*i ˀihdaaˀ*) to present, give as a gift. *hidaa-la saaᶜa b-munaasabat zawaaja.* He presented him with a watch on the occasion of his marriage.

hadiyya pl. *hadaaya* gift, present.

h-δ-b

haδδab to educate, instruct, edify. *l-madrasa thaδδib ˀabnaaˀna.* School educates our sons.

thaδδab to become educated. *laazim tudxul madrasa ᶜatta tithaδδab.* You have to enter a school to become educated.

h-δ-w-l

haδool see under *h-a-δ-a.*

h-δ-y

hiδa (*i haδi, haδayaan*) to babble, jabber, rave, talk irrationally. *s-sakraan da-yihδi w-ma-yuᶜruf š-da-yguul.* The drunk is talking irrationally and doesn't know what he's saying.

haδayaan drivel, nonsense, jabbering.

h-r-b

hirab (*u harab, huruub*) to flee, run away, escape. *waaᶜid imnil-masaajiin hirab.* One of the prisoners escaped. *hirab imnij-jundiyya.* He deserted from military service.

harrab to smuggle. *harrab kammiyyat ᶜašiiš lil-ᶜiraaq.* He smuggled a quantity of hashish into Iraq.

tharrab /with *min*/ to shirk, evade, dodge, get away from. *leeš titharrab imn-il-masˀuuliyya?* Why do you dodge responsibility?

haarib **1.** fleeing, fugitive, runaway. **2.** (pl. *-iin*) a fugitive, a runaway. **3.** deserter.

muharrib pl. *-iin* smuggler.

h-r-j

hiraj (*i haraj*) to disturb, disrupt, agitate. *naṣṣi ir-raadyo. ᶜissa hiraj il-beet.* Turn down the radio. Its noise has disturbed the whole house.

harraj to talk loudly, shout. *ˀiᶜči yawaaš. la-tharrij.* Speak softly. Don't shout. *haaδa š-jaaba ᶜal-waṭaniyya? bass yharrij.* What does he have to do with nationalism? He just talks loud. *ˀiδa tubqa tharrij ᶜaqiiqtak raᶜ-tinᶜuruf.* If you keep on making a racket, your true nature will be exposed.

haraj commotion, noise, tumult, disorder. || *suug il-haraj* **1.** a marketplace usually used for auctions. 2. (by extension) any place of great confusion.

harja pl. *-aat* noise, racket, commotion, din, clamor.

h-r-s

hiras (*i haris*) to crush, squash, mash. *ᶜala keefak! muu hirast iṭ-ṭamaaṭa!* Take it easy! You're squashing the tomatoes! *s-sayyaara hirsat rijla.* The car crushed his leg.

nhiras to become soft, mushy. *šiil it-tiffaaᶜ min ᶜan-naar. nhiras.* Take the apples off the fire. They've gotten soft.

hariisa a dish consisting of wheat and meat boiled to the consistency of pudding.

h-r-š

hiraš (*i hariš*) to scratch, claw. *dagg jidri w-δall yihriš bii.* He got a smallpox vaccination and kept scratching at it. *č-čalib hiraš rijli.* The dog scratched my leg with his claws.

hiriš pl. *hruuš* plant, bush, vine.

h-r-ṭ-m-a-n

huruṭmaan, hurṭumaan oats.

h-r-f

*harfi** newborn, young. *laᶜm iṭ-ṭili l-harfi yistuwi bil-ᶜajal.* The meat of young lamb cooks quickly.

h-r-m

haram pl. *ˀahraam* pyramid.

h-r-w-l

harwal to jog, trot, run at a medium pace. *xallaana δ̣-δ̣aabuṭ inharwil ib-mukaanna nuṣṣ saaᶜa.* The officer made us run in place for a half hour.

h-r-y

hira (*i hari*) to break open, lacerate. *hira jilda bil-qamči w-gaam yinzil damm.* He lacerated his skin with the whip and he began to bleed. *t-tiizaab hira ˀiida.* The nitric acid burned his hand. || *hira jilda.* He thrashed him soundly. *l-muᶜallim hira jilda bil-ᶜaṣa.* The teacher thrashed him soundly with the stick.

tharra to become worn out, threadbare. *tharrat sitirti mnil-ġasil.* My jacket's gotten worn out from washing.

h-z-ˀ

hizaˀ (*a haziˀ*) to scoff, jeer, laugh, make fun. *yihzaˀ min ˀagul-la ma-tigdar itsawwiiha.* He scoffs when I tell him you can't do it.

stahzaˀ to scoff, jeer, laugh, to consider ridiculous. *la-tistahziˀ b-il-yguula.* Don't scoff at what he says.

h-z-r

hazaar pl. *-aat, bilbil hazaar* nightingale.

h-z-z

hazz (*i hazz*) **1.** to shake, jiggle. *hizz*

iš-šijra ʕatta yoogaʕ it-tukki. Shake the tree so the mulberries will fall. *min hazz čitfa, ʕirafit ma-yihtamm.* When he shrugged his shoulder, I knew he didn't care. **2.** to wave, sway, swing. *l-bazzuuna min tiġδab ithizz δeelha.* When the cat gets mad, it switches its tail. **3.** to rock, jog. *hizzi l-kaaruuk. j-jaahil da-yibči.* Rock the cradle. The kid is crying. **4.** to shake, jiggle, wriggle. *har-raaqiṣa xooš ithizz.* That dancer shakes nicely. *min yjaawub, ma-yiʕči. bass yhizz ib-raasa.* When he answers, he doesn't speak. He just shakes his head. *min yugʕud, yhizz ib-rijla.* When he's sitting down, he jiggles his leg.

nhazz to be shaken, rocked. *min faatat iṭ-ṭiyyaara, nhazzat il-binaaya.* When the plane went by, the building was shaken.

htazz to shake, tremble, quake, quiver. *htazzat il-ibyuut min ṣoot il-madfaʕ.* The houses shook from the noise of the cannon.

hazza pl. *-aat* tremor, shake. || *hazza ʔarδiyya* earthquake.

hizza pl. *-aat, hizaz* a large cloth slung on the shoulder by workmen to carry sand, etc.

htizaaz pl. *-aat* vibration.

h-z-l

hizal (*a hazal*) to joke, banter, speak jokingly. *čaan yihzal min ṭilab minnak il-ifluus.* He was joking when he asked you for the money. *yihzal ib-kull kalaama.* He never talks seriously.

hazal joking. *la-tuʕtubur il-ʔagul-lak-iyyaa fadd šii hazal.* Don't take what I tell you as a joke.

*hazali** funny, comical. *ruwaaya hazal-iyya* a comedy. *muwaθθil hazali* comedian.

mahzala pl. *mahaazil* farce, comedy.

h-z-m

hizam (*i hazim*) to defeat, vanquish. *firqatna hizmathum ib-sibaaqeen.* Our team defeated them in two games.

hazzam **1.** to help or allow to escape. *waggifoo liš-šurṭi liʔan hazzam waaʕid masjuun.* They arrested the policeman because he helped a prisoner escape. **2.** to rout, put to flight, chase away. *l-imtiʕaa-naat il-ihwaaya hazzimata mnil-madrasa.* The numerous examinations drove him away from the school. *leeš gut-la b-has-siʕir? muu hazzamta!* Why did you quote this price to him? You've scared him away!

thazzam **1.** to be evasive, to hedge, temporize. *kull-ma yṭulbuun minna yzuur-hum, yithazzam.* Every time they ask him to visit them, he hedges. **2.** to escape, shrink, stay clear, stay away. *hal-muwaδδaf yδibb iš-šuġuḷ ʕala ġeera w-yithazzam imnil-masʔuuliyya.* This official pushes off work on others and evades responsibility. *δall yithazzam imnil-madrasa ʔila ʔan ṭirdoo.* He kept playing truant from school until they expelled him.

nhizam **1.** to be defeated, vanquished. *baʕad maʕraka qawiyya, nhizam jeeš il-ʕadu.* After a fierce battle, the enemy army was vanquished. **2.** to run away, flee. *j-jaahil nhizam min šaaf ič-čalib.* The child ran away when he saw the dog. **3.** to escape. *nhizam imnis-sijin bil-leel.* He escaped from the jail by night.

haziima pl. *hazaayim* defeat, rout.

hazzaam: *hala bil-hazzaam* (a greeting to a friend one hasn't seen for a long time, approx.:) Hi, stranger!

h-s-t-w

hastaww- /with pronoun suffix/ now, right this moment. *hastawwa ṭilaʕ.* He just this minute went out.

h-s-s-a

hassa **1.** now, right this moment. *ʔariid ifluusi hassa.* I want my money now. *l-matʕaf raʕ-yikuun maftuuʕ min hassa ʔila saaʕa xamsa.* The museum will be open from now until five o'clock. *hassa šloon?* Now what do we do? **2.** right away, in just a moment, soon. *tfaδδal istiriiʕ w-hassa yšuufak iṭ-ṭabiib.* Please have a seat and the doctor will see you in a moment. *hassa yiji w-agul-la.* He'll be coming soon and I'll tell him. **3.** just this moment, just a moment ago. *hassa faat min-naa.* He just now passed by here.

¶ *li-hassa, ʔila hassa* up to now, until this moment. *li-hassa ma-wuṣal.* He hasn't arrived up to now.

[1]*h-š-š*

hašš (*i*) **1.** to shoo, scare away. *hašš iṭ-ṭuyuur imniš-šiʕiir.* He shooed the birds away from the barley. **2.** hush! shush! *hišš! la-tiʕči baʕad.* Hush! Don't say any more.

[2]*h-š-š*

hašš crisp. *hal-ixyaar taaza w-hašš.* These cucumbers are fresh and crisp.

h-š-m

haššam to smash. *ʔahaššim raasak ʔiδa tiʕči baʕad.* I'll smash your head if you say any more.

h-δ-m

hiδam (*u haδum*) **1.** to digest. *had-duwa*

yihð̣um il-ʔakil. This medicine digests the food. **2.** to upset, distress, cause grief to. *hið̣amni hwaaya b-hal-iħčaaya.* He really upset me by that remark.

nhið̣am **1.** to be upset, distressed. *nhið̣amit minna hwaaya liʔan baaʕ is-sayyaara bala ma-ygul-li.* I was very upset by him because he sold the car without telling me. **2.** to be sorry, feel bad, feel regret. *nhið̣am ʕala beeʕat is-sayyaara b-has-siʕir.* He regretted selling the car for that price.

stahð̣am to become upset, distressed. *ħagga l-waaħid yistahð̣um ʔiða ð̣aaʕ-la šii.* A person has a right to get upset if he loses something. *stahð̣amit ʕala ʕali min simaʕit fiṣloo.* I was sorry for Ali when I heard they fired him.

hað̣iima pl. *hað̣aayim* injustice, wrong, outrage. *hað̣iima yzawwjuuha l-hiiči waaħid.* It's a crime they're marrying her off to that guy.

h-ṭ-r

hiṭar (*u haṭir*) to beat, beat up, thrash soundly. *lizmoo b-šaariʕ ʔað̣lam w-hiṭroo zeen.* They caught him in a dark street and beat him up good.

nhiṭar to be beaten, beaten up. *ṣaaħbak nhiṭar xooš haṭra.* Your buddy was beaten up real good.

haṭra pl. *-aat* beating. *ʔakal xooš haṭra mniš-šurṭa.* He took a good beating from the police.

h-f-t

hifat (*i hufuut*) to abate, subside, die down. *bilaʕt il-ħabbaaya w-wujaʕ sinni hifat.* I took the pill and my toothache subsided. *hifat il-waram.* The swelling went down. *la-txalli n-naar tihfit. ðibb-ilha ħaṭab.* Don't let the fire die. Throw some wood on it.

haffat to cause to abate, subside. *ʔariid fadd duwa yhaffit il-wujaʕ.* I want some medicine to relieve the pain.

h-f-f

haff (*i haff*) (interjects the idea of doing something suddenly, quickly, hastily, and with some force) **1.** to hit, strike, slap, smack. *haffa b-iħjaara b-raasa.* He hit him on the head with a rock. *min sabba, haffa b-raašdi.* When he insulted him he slapped him on the side of his head. *haffa b-damġa.* He whacked him on top of the head. **2.** to fire, sack. *l-mudiir ij-jidiid haff nuṣṣ il-muwað̣ð̣afiin w-buqaw bila šuġuḷ.* The new director canned half the employees and they were left without work. **3.** to bolt, gulp down, polish off. *haff dijaaja kaamla w-maaʕuuneen timman.* He downed a whole chicken and two dishes of rice. *yhiff kullši bil-ʔakil.* He'll eat anything. **4.** to seize, grab, snatch. *haff il-ifluus w-inhizam.* He snatched the money and fled. **5.** to have sexual relations with. **6.** to blurt out, come out with. *haffha lil-iħčaaya biduun tafkiir.* He blurted out the remark without thinking.

nhaff to be fired, sacked. *simaʕit mulaaħið̣ ið̣-ð̣aatiyya nhaff.* I heard the personnel supervisor was fired.

h-f-w

hafwa pl. *-aat* slip, lapse, mistake, error. *čaanat hafwa minni w-saamiħni ʕaleeha.* It was a slip on my part and please forgive me for it.

[1]*h-f-y*

haffa to fan. *haffi n-naar ħatta yistiwi l-laħam.* Fan the fire so that the meat will get done. *d-dinya ħaarra. haffi lij-jaahil.* It's hot. Fan the child.

thaffa to fan oneself. *haak mhaffti. thaffa biiha.* Here, take my fan. Fan yourself with it.

mhaffa pl. *-aat, mhaafiif* **1.** hand fan. **2.** manually operated overhead fan.

[2]*h-f-y*

mahfi **1.** famished, starved. **2.** greedy, over-eager.

h-k-l-k

hukluk pl. *hakaalik* a kind of bird similar to the partridge.

h-k-m

thakkam to scoff, mock, jeer, make fun. *la-tithakkam ʕalee. qaabil ʔinta ʔaħsan minna?* Don't make fun of him. Do you think you're better than he is? *la-tithakkam. yiji yoom aġulbak biš-šiṭranj.* Don't laugh. The day'll come when I'll beat you in chess.

[1]*h-l*

hal interrogative particle introducing a question. *hal huwwa baaqi willa laa?* Is he still there or not?

[2]*h-l*

hal- /*ha-* plus definite article/ see *ha-* under *h-*.

h-l-b

hilib light, downy hair.

h-l-s

hilas (*i halis*) **1.** to pluck, pull out. *l-walad hilas kull riiš iṭ-ṭeer.* The boy plucked all the bird's feathers. **2.** to scrape, remove the hair from. *šuġḷa yihlis ijluud* *bil-madbaġa.* His job is to scrape hides in the tannery.

hallas to pluck, pull out. *gaaɛid w-yhallis iš-šaɛar min rijlee.* He's sitting and plucking hair from his legs.

thallas to fall out. *min itmarrað̣, thallas šaɛra kulla.* When he got sick, all his hair fell out.

mahluus **1.** plucked. **2.** hairless, featherless. **3.** broke, penniless. *š-tiddaayan minna? ma-da-tšuufa mahluus?* What can you borrow from him? Don't you see he's been picked clean?

h-l-g-d

halgadd see under *g-d-d.*

h-l-k

hilak (*a halaak*) **1.** to perish, die. *raħ-agɛud išwayya. hilakit imnil-maši.* I'm going to sit down a while. I'm dead from walking. *ʔibinha hilak imnil-bači.* Her son about died from crying. **2.** /with *ɛala*/ to crave, want badly. *hilak ɛal-wað̣iifa.* He wanted the job very much. **3.** (*i halik*) to ruin, destroy, annihilate. *ʔiða ma-dgul-li, ʔahilkak.* If you don't tell me, I'll ruin you. *hilakni l-ħarr.* The heat wilted me. *jaawub, ɛaad! muu hilakitni!* Answer, man! You've made me sick to heath.

stahlak **1.** to wear out. *taayaraat is-sayyaara stahlikat.* The car's tires are worn out. **2.** to consume, use up, exhaust. *s-sayyaara tistahlik banziin ihwaaya.* The car uses a lot of gasoline.

halkaan ruined. *daayin-ni čam diinaar. ʔaani halkaan.* Lend me a few dinars. I'm broke.

mahlaka pl. *mahaalik* dangerous situation, perilous predicament.

tahlika jeopardy, danger, peril.

stihlaak consumption, usage. || *ð̣ariibat istihlaak* consumption tax, a wholesale tax paid on farm produce.

mustahlik pl. *-iin* consumer, buyer, user.

h-l-l

hall (*i hall*) to begin (lunar month). *baačir yhill iš-šahar.* Tomorrow the lunar month begins.

stahall to begin, start. *stahall xiṭaaba b-šukr il-ħaað̣iriin.* He began his speech with thanks to those present.

hilaal (no pl.) **1.** first quarter of the moon, new moon. **2.** crescent, half-moon. || *l-hilaal il-ʔaħmar* The Red Crescent, Middle Eastern branch of the International Red Cross.

h-l-h-l

halhal to make a trilling sound with the voice (on joyous occasions such as weddings). *šuuf hal-mara da-thalhil ib-ɛiris ʔibinha.* Look at that woman trilling at her son's wedding ceremony.

halhuula pl. *halaahil* a burst of trilling.

h-l-w

halaw **1.** hello. *halaw saɛiid. šloonak?* Hello, Sa'id. How are you? **2.** (an expression of enthusiastic approbation, approx.:) great, wow, say, hey. *halaw yaab! ṭallaɛ gooḷ il-laax.* Great, man! He made another goal.

h-l-y-l-j

hleelaj myrobalan, a black fruit from a variety of palm tree.

h-m-a-y-w-n

hamaayuun large bolt, or sheet, of cloth.

h-m-j

hamaji **1.** barbaric, savage. **2.** (pl. *-iyyiin, hamaj*) barbarian, savage.

h-m-z

hamza pl. *-aat* name of the letter *ʔ*, designating the glottal stop.

h-m-s

himas (*i hamis*) to whisper. *himas ib-ʔiðna čam čilma ð̣aħħaka biiha.* He whispered a few words in his ear, which made him laugh.

thaamas to whisper to each other. *š-aku ɛidhum, da-yithaamsuun?* What are they up to, whispering to each other?

hamsa pl. *-aat* whisper.

h-m-š

himaš (*i hamiš*) to seize, grab, take a grip on. *č-čalib himaša min zirra.* The dog seized him by the leg. *la-tihmiš ʔay šii tšuufa ɛal-meez.* Don't grab up anything you see on the table.

hammaš to gesture, gesticulate. *la-thammiš b-iideek! ʔiħči!* Don't wave your hand around! Speak up!

haamiš pl. *hawaamiš* margin, border, space around the edge. || *haaði ħčaaya ɛal-haamiš.* This is an incidental remark.

h-m-l

himal (*i ʔihmaal*) **1.** to neglect. *luweeš da-tihmil waajibaatak?* Why are you neglecting your duties? **2.** to ignore. *ʔiða tihmala, yiskut min keefa.* If you ignore him, he'll shut up of his own accord.

nhimal to be neglected. *j-jihaal inhimlaw. maħħad da-ydaariihum.* The children were neglected. No one is looking after them.

haamil pl. *-iin* neglectful, irresponsible.

muhmil pl. *-iin* neglectful, irresponsible.

muhmal neglected, disregarded. || *sallat il-muhmalaat* wastebasket.

[1]*h-m-m*

hamm (*i hamm*) **1.** to concern, affect, preoccupy. *ṣiḥḥat ʔabuuya thimmni hwaaya.* My father's health concerns me a lot. **2.** to be important, of consequence, to matter. *ma-yhimm. min yiji, agul-la.* It doesn't matter. When he comes I'll tell him. **3.** to make threatening gestures. *sabba w-hamm ʕalee bis-siččiina.* He insulted him and made threatening motions at him with the knife.

nhamm to become distressed, concerned, worried. *min simaʕ ibna ṣiqaṭ, nhamm ihwaaya.* When he heard his son failed, he was very unhappy.

htamm **1.** to worry, be concerned. *xall iyfuṣluuni! minu yihtamm?* Let them fire me! Who cares? *htamm ib-qaḍiitak ihwaaya.* He was very concerned about your case. **2.** to go to great trouble, be very solicitous. *htammaw biina hwaaya w-daaroona.* They went to great lengths on our behalf and took care of us. **3.** to pay attention, to take notice. *la-tihtamm-la. huwwa fadd waaḥid saxiif.* Don't pay any attention to him. He's a foolish fellow.

hamm pl. *humuum* **1.** anxiety, concern, worry. *šaayil hamm. šloon yruuḥ w-yitruk jahhaala waḥḥadhum?* He's burdened with worry. How can he go and leave his children by themselves? **2.** sorrow, grief, distress. *maatat imnil-hamm wil-ḥuzun.* She died from distress and grief. **3.** concern, interest. *kull hamma yṣiir waziir.* His only concern is to become a minister.

himma enthusiasm.

himiim eager, energetic. *majiid kulliš himiim. min itkallfa b-šii yirkuḍ-lak.* Majid is very eager. When you ask him to do something he puts himself out for you.

ʔahamm more or most important.

ʔahammiyya importance, significance, consequence.

htimaam concern, interest.

haamm important, significant, momentous. *raḥ-yilqi xiṭaab haamm bil-muʔtamar.* He will deliver an important speech in the convention.

muhimm important, significant, momentous. *ʕindak šii muhimm?* Do you have anything important to do?

muhimma pl. *-aat* **1.** important thing. **2.** important task, mission.

[2]*h-m-m*

hamm, hammeen, hammeena **1.** also, too, in addition. *ʔinta hamm tidrus ihnaa?* Do you also study here? *ʕali hammeena zaʕlaan minnak.* Ali too is mad at you. *ʔaxaḏ diinaareen w-hammeena yriid baʕad.* He got two dinars and wants more in addition. **2.** again, once more. *hamm gaamat timṭur.* It's started to rain again. *hammeena ḥičeet. ma-git-lak la-tiḥči?* You spoke again. Didn't I tell you not to speak?

h-m-m-a

humma they.

h-n-a

hnaa, hnaana here, in this place. *ma-aku ʔaḥḥad hnaa.* There's no one here. *ʔintiḏirni hnaana.* Wait for me here.

h-n-a-k

hnaak, hnaaka there, in that place. *ma-lgeeta hnaak.* I didn't find him there.

h-n-ʔ

tahniʔa, muhanniʔ, etc., see under *h-n-y*.

h-n-j-l

hanjal **1.** to jump up and down on one foot, to hop on one foot. *tʕawwurat rijla w-gaam yhanjil.* His foot got hurt and he began jumping up and down. *xan-nhanjil lil-madrasa w-inšuuf yaahu yuǧlub.* Let's hop to school on one foot and see who wins. **2.** to bounce. *yhanjil ib-mašiita.* He bounces when he walks.

h-n-d

l-hind India. || *jooz hind* coconut. *tamur hind* tamarind.

*hindi** **1.** Indian. *s-safaara l-hindiyya* the Indian Embassy. **2.** (pl. *hnuud*) an Indian. *hindi ʔaḥmar* American Indian. || *diič hindi* turkey.

h-n-d-r

hindir pl. *-aat* crank handle.

[1]*h-n-d-s*

handas to design, engineer. *minu handas-lak il-beet?* Who designed the house for you?

handasa **1.** (technical) design, engineering. **2.** architecture. **3.** geometry.

muhandis pl. *-iin* **1.** technical designer, engineer. **2.** architect.

[2]*h-n-d-s*

hindis (invar.) pitch black, completely devoid of light. *l-qubba ḏalma hindis.* The room is pitch black.

h-n-ḍ-m

handam to dress up, spruce up, attire

smartly. *ṣaar-la saaʕa yhandim nafsa.* He's spent an hour sprucing up.

thandam to dress oneself smartly. *laazim tithandam gabuḷ-ma tšuufha lil-ibnayya.* You have to get dressed up before you see the girl.

hindaam 1. neatness, tidiness (of attire). 2. appearance, looks.

h-n-d-w-s

hindoos (coll.) Hindu(s).

*hindoosi** Hindu.

h-n-y

hanna 1. to congratulate, felicitate, express good wishes to. *ʔahanniik ʕan-najaaḥ.* Congratulations on your success. *riḥna nhanniihum bil-ʕiid.* We went to give them our best wishes on the occasion of the holiday. 2. to grant happiness, to delight. *ʔaḷḷa yhanniik ib-ʕumrak.* May God grant you happiness in your life. *hannaak ʔaḷḷa* (standard reply to *haniiʔan*) May God grant you happiness.

thanna to take pleasure. *ʔukul ʕala keefak w-ithanna b-ʔaklak.* Eat slowly and enjoy your food.

haniiʔan, haniiʔan mariiʔan (polite expression said to someone who has just eaten, or drunk water) May you enjoy it! May it bring you good health!

tahniya, tahniʔa pl. *tahaani* congratulation, felicitation.

muhanniʔ pl. *-iin* congratulator, well-wisher.

h-w-a-y

hwaaya 1. much, many, numerous. *ʕindi fluus ihwaaya.* I've got a lot of money. *hwaaya naas yzuuruun hal-matḥaf.* Many people visit this museum. 2. too much, excessive. *hal-uqmaaš ihwaaya ʕalayya; raḥ-yzuud minna.* This is too much cloth for me; there will be some of it left over. *ʔiδa taakul ihwaaya, tisman.* If you eat too much, you'll get fat. 3. very, extremely. *ʔaani mamnuun ihwaaya.* I'm very grateful. *hal-binaaya ʕaali hwaaya.* This building is very tall. 4. often, frequently. *yitraddad ihwaaya ʕala hal-maḥall.* He comes back to this spot frequently. 5. for a long time. *δall ybaawiʕ biṣ-ṣuura hwaaya.* He kept looking at the picture a long time.

h-w-j

ʔahwaj fem. *hawja, hooja* pl. *huuj, hoojiin* 1. foolish, rash, thoughtless, harebrained. 2. thoughtless person.

h-w-d

hawwad 1. to abate, subside, calm down, quiet down. *biča mudda w-baʕdeen hawwad.* He cried for a while and then was quiet. *hawwad il-wijaʕ baʕad nuṣṣ saaʕa.* The pain subsided after a half hour. 2. to cause to abate, subside, to soothe, calm, quiet. *hal-ḥabb yhawwid wujaʕ ir-raas.* These pills will relieve a headache.

h-w-d-j

hoodaj pl. *huwaadij* howdah, camel litter.

h-w-r

hawwar to stretch, become too large. *qundarti δallat tikbar bil-istiʕmaal ʔila ʔan hawwrat.* My shoes kept getting larger from use until they got too big.

thawwar 1. to rash, reckless, heedless. *yithawwar ib-kull ʔaʕmaala.* He's rash in everything he does. 2. to speak disrespectfully, to show disrespect. *yithawwar ʕal-muʕallim ʕala ṭuul.* He shows disrespect toward the teacher all the time.

nhaar to collapse, fall down, fall apart. *nhaarat il-ibnaaya ʕaleehum.* The building fell down on them. || *nhaarat ʔaʕṣaaba.* He lost control of himself.

hoor pl. *ʔahwaar* marsh, swamp.

hoora small marsh, bog. || *raaḥat boola b-hoora.* It was all wasted.

h-w-r-n

hoorin pl. *-aat* horn (auto.).

h-w-s

hawwas 1. to chant slogans. *qisim imnil-mutaδaahiriin čaanaw yhawwisuun.* Some of the demonstrators were chanting slogans. 2. to make a commotion, raise an uproar, be noisy. *min gaal-ilhum ʔaku dawaam il-yoom, hawwisaw.* When he told them they had to work today, they raised a ruckus. *ʔaku ʕiris il-yoom w-il-fallaaḥiin da-yhawwisuun.* There is a marriage today and the peasants are being rowdy.

hoosa pl. *-aat* 1. slogan, chant. 2. din, clamor, commotion, uproar.

h-w-š

hooš (coll.) cattle. *laḥam hooš* beef.

haayša pl. *hwaayiš* cow.

h-w-l

hawwal to exaggerate, over-emphasize, magnify. *la-tṣaddig ib-ḥačya ʕala ṭuul. yhawwil kullši.* Don't believe everything he says. He exaggerates everything. *la-thawwil il-qaδiyya l-had-daraja.* Don't magnify the matter to such a degree.

hooḷ (no pl.) family room, rumpus room (where the family lives, as opposed to the parlor, where guests are received).

haala pl. *-aat* 1. halo. 2. nimbus.

haaˀil appalling, stupendous, huge, amazing, enormous. *rtifaaɛ haj-jibal haaˀil.* The height of this mountain is tremendous.

h-w-m

haama pl. *-aat* vertex, crown (of the head).

1*h-w-n*

haan (*u hoon*) **1.** to become easy, simple, facile. *ˀiδa yiji wyaana waaɛid laax, yhuun iš-šuġuḷ.* If one more comes with us, the work will be easy. **2.** (*i ˀihaana*) to humble, abase, humiliate, treat with contempt. *haana giddaam in-naas.* He humiliated him in front of the people. *la-truuɛ ɛalee tara yhiinak.* Don't go see him or he'll humiliate you.

hawwan to make easy, simple, facile. *hal-qaamuus yhawwin ɛalayya d-diraasa.* This dictionary makes studying easier for me.

thaawan to be negligent, careless, lax. *ˀiδa tithaawan ib-šuġḷak, yfuṣluuk.* If you're lax in your work, they'll fire you. *ˀiδa tithaawan ɛala ṭuul, taakulha baɛdeen.* If you take things easy all the time, you'll really catch it later.

nhaan to be humiliated, abased, insulted. *nbuṣat w-inhaan.* He was beaten up and humiliated.

stahaan, stahwan to consider easy, simple, to esteem lightly, underrate, underestimate. *la-tistihiin haš-šaġḷa.* Don't think this job is easy. *la-tistahwin ib-quuta.* Don't take his strength lightly.

hayyin easy, simple, facile. *haš-šuġuḷ hayyin w-ma-bii taɛab.* This work is easy and requires no exertion.

ˀahyan, ˀahwan more or most facile, etc.

mahaana humiliation, degradation, abasement, disgrace.

ˀihaana pl. *-aat* insult.

2*h-w-n*

haawan see under *h-a-w-n*.

h-w-w-a

huwwa he, it. || *haaδa huwwa! xall-yizɛal.* That's the way it is! Let him get mad. *raɛ-ˀazayyid diinaar il-laax w-haaδa huwwa.* I'm going to raise another dinar and that's it. *ween ɛali? maa-huwwa.* Where's Ali? He's not here.

1*h-w-y*

hawwa to ventilate, air. *hawwi l-ġurfa ɛatta yiṭlaɛ il-ɛajaaj.* Air out the room so the dust will go away.

hawa **1.** air. **2.** wind, breeze, draft. *l-hawa šaal nafnuufha.* The wind lifted her dress. *l-yoom id-dinya biiha hawa šwayya.* Today the weather's a little bit windy. **3.** weather, climate. *saafar lis-swiisra ɛatta yġayyir hawa.* He travelled to Switzerland to get a change of climate.

hawya pl. *-aat* gust of wind, breeze.

*hawaaˀi** **1.** air-, pneumatic. *maδaxxa hawaaˀi* air pump. **2.** flighty, capricious, unpredictable. *la-tiɛtamdiin ɛalee biz-zawaaj. haaδa walad hawaaˀi. ybaddil raˀya kull daqiiqa.* Don't depend on him to marry. He's a capricious boy. He changes his mind every minute.

haawya pl. *-aat* pit, chasm, abyss (used figuratively as in:) *wagaɛ bil-haawya.* He fell for the trap.

hiwaaya, huwaaya pl. *-aat* hobby, spare time activity.

haawi pl. *huwaat* amateur, fan.

2*h-w-y*

hawiyya pl. *-aat* **1.** identity. **2.** identification papers.

3*h-w-y*

hwaaya see under *h-w-a-y*.

h-y

hee name of the letter *h*.

h-y-ˀ

hayyaˀ to prepare, make ready, put in readiness. *hayyiˀ mukaan il-ˀarbaɛat ˀašxaaṣ.* Prepare a place for four people.

thayyaˀ to get ready, prepare oneself. *thayyˀu! z-zaɛiim da-yiji.* Get ready! The general's coming.

hayˀa pl. *-aat* **1.** appearance, mien, bearing. **2.** state, condition. **3.** group, organization, association, body. *hayˀat il-ˀumam il-muttaɛida.* The United Nations Organization. *hayˀa diploomaasiyya* diplomatic corps.

h-y-a

hiyya see under *h-y-y-a*.

h-y-b

haab (*a heeba*) to be awed by, stand in awe of. *huwwa ma-yhaab ˀayy waaɛid.* He's not awed by any one. **2.** to respect. *l-muɛallim laazim yhaaba kull ṭaalib.* Every student should respect the teacher. *ˀaani ˀahaab il-qaanuun.* I have a healthy respect for the law.

thayyab to be filled with awe. *min yidxul ɛal-waziir yithayyab ihwaaya.* When he goes in to see the minister he feels great awe.

ˀahyab more or most awesome, venerable, etc.

muhiib awe-inspiring, awesome, venerable.

h-y-j

haaj (*i hiyaaj, hayajaan*) **1.** to be in a state of agitation, turmoil, commotion, excitement. *l-ɛaaṣifa xallat il-baɛar yhiij.* The storm made the sea roll and toss. **2.** to become furious, angry, indignant. *min simaɛ ib-hal-xabar, haaj.* When he heard that news, he exploded.

hayyaj **1.** to provoke, incite, stir up, agitate. *xiṭaaba hayyaj iṭ-ṭullaab.* His speech stirred up the students. **2.** to arouse, excite, awaken. *mašiiha yhayyij.* Her way of walking is provocative.

thayyaj to become agitated, stirred up, excited. *ma-aku ɛaaja tithayyaj w-itṣayyiɛ.* There's no reason for you to get excited and shout. **2.** to become aroused, excited. *ma-yiqra kutub jinsiyya li-ʔan yithayyaj ib-surɛa.* He doesn't read sexy books because he gets excited quickly.

h-y-č

hiiči, hiič **1.** such, this, that, this kind of, that kind of. *šloon timši wiyya hiiči naas?* How could you run around with such people? *šloon tiɛči hiiči? ma-tistiɛi?* How could you say that? Aren't you ashamed? *hiyya hiiči ṣ-ṣadaaqa?* Is that the way friendship is? *min hiiči ma-da-yiɛči wyaaya.* That's why he isn't talking to me. || *ʔaxuuk raaɛ hiič gabuḷ xamis daqaayiq.* Your brother went that way five minutes ago. **2.** so, thus. *ʔirsimha hiiči.* Draw it like this. *bil-ʔawwal ʔamurr ɛalee w-baɛdeen niji ɛaleek. muu hiič?* First I go by his place and then we come to yours. Isn't that it?

h-y-s

hayyas to feel, sense, be aware, cognizant. *rijla mayyta w-ma-yhayyis ʔiδa tinġuzha.* His leg is dead and he doesn't feel if you prick it. *ṭabb lil-beet w-maɛɛad hayyas bii.* He got in the house and no one realized it.

h-y-š

haayša, see under *h-w-š.*

h-y-δ

hayδa Asiatic cholera.

h-y-k-l

haykal **1.** temple, pagan place of worship. **2.** framework. **3.** skeleton. *haykal ɛaδmi* skeleton. **4.** chassis (of an automobile). **5.** shape, looks, appearance.

[1]*h-y-l*

haal (*i*) to pour, strew. *haalaw it-tiraab ɛala gabur il-mayyit.* They threw the dirt onto the dead man's grave.

nhaal to rain down. *nhaalat ɛal-waziir barqiyyaat il-iɛtijaaj.* Telegrams of protest deluged the minister.

[2]*h-y-l*

heel cardamom.

h-y-m

haam (*i heem*) **1.** to roam, wander, rove. *haam bil-barr.* He wandered in the desert. || *nhizam min ʔabuu w-haam ɛala wijha.* He fled from his father and wandered aimlessly about. **2.** (*i hiyaam*) to fall in love. *haam biiha.* He fell in love with her.

hiim pl. *hiyam* crowbar, pry-bar.

heema wilderness, desert.

h-y-n

haan, hayyin, etc., see under *h-w-n.*

h-y-y-a

hiyya she, it. *ʔaani ma-δirabitha; hiyya δirbatni.* I didn't hit her; she hit me. *haay hiyya! loo tiji wyaaya loo ma-aruuɛ.* That's it! Either you come with me or I won't go.

W

w

w **1.** and, plus. *nṭaani l-qalam wil-iktaab.* He gave me the pencil and the book. *taɛaal saaɛa xamsa w-nuṣṣ.* Come at five-thirty. *θneen w-iθneen ysawwi ʔarbaɛ.* Two plus two equals four. **2.** while, as, when. *t-talafoon dagg w-ʔaani bil-ɛammaam.* The telephone rang when I was in the bath. *baagaw il-ifluus minna w-huwwa naayim.* They stole the money from him while he was asleep. **3.** (in an oath or exclamation) by. *w-aḷḷa, ma-adri.* By God, I don't know.

w-ʔilla or else, otherwise. *nṭiini fluusi w-ʔilla ʔaštiki ɛaleek.* Give me my money or I'll sue you.

walaw although, even though. *raɛ-aštiri s-sayyaara, walaw ġaalya.* I'm going to buy the car, although it's expensive.

w-a-ɛ

waaɛa pl. *-aat* oasis.

w-a-w

waaw name of the letter *w*.

w-a-w-y

waawi pl. *-iyya* jackal.

w-a-y-r

waayar pl. *-aat* wire.

w-b-x

wabbax to reprimand, rebuke, censure, scold. *l-muɛallim wabbax iṭ-ṭaalib ɛala kasala.* The teacher reprimanded the student for his laziness.

twabbax pass. of *wabbax*. *twabbax ɛala fadd šii ma-msawwii.* He was scolded for something he hadn't done.

tawbiix reprimand.

w-b-r

wubar camel hair.

w-b-š

ʔawbaaš (pl. only) rabble, riff-raff.

w-t-d

watad pl. *ʔawtaad* stake, peg, pin.

w-t-r

wattar to stretch, draw tight, pull taut, tighten, strain. *la-twattir il-xeeṭ zaayid tara yingiṭiɛ.* Don't stretch the string too tight or it'll break. *wattar ʔiida ɛatta yraawiina ɛaḍalaata.* He tightened his hand in order to show us his muscles.

twattar to become strained, tense. *twattirat il-ɛilaaqaat beenna w-beenhum.* Relations between us and them became strained.

watar pl. *ʔawtaar* **1.** string (of a bow or musical instrument). || *watar ɛassaas* a sensitive area, tender spot, sore spot. *ḍirab ɛala watar ɛassaas; ḍall yḍakkirha b-ʔibinha l-maat bil-ɛarub.* He touched a sore spot; he kept reminding her of her son who died in the war. **2.** hypotenuse (geom.).

mawtuur pl. *-iin* **1.** filled with hate, hostile, malevolent. **2.** vengeful person.

w-θ-q

wiθaq (*a θiqa, wuθuuq*) /with *b-*/ to trust, place confidence in, depend upon, rely on. *wiθaq bii w-inṭaa ifluus.* He trusted him and gave him money. *yooθaq ib-nafsa hwaaya.* He has a lot of self-confidence.

waθθaq to strengthen, make firm, cement, consolidate. *z-zawaaj raɛ-ywaθθiq il-ɛilaaqaat been il-ɛaaʔilteen.* The marriage will cement relations between the two families.

twaθθaq **1.** to be strengthened, consolidated, firmly established. *twaθθiqat il-ɛilaaqaat been hal-baladeen.* Relations have been strengthened between these two countries. **2.** to have confidence, be confident, assured. *twaθθaq loo ʔaɛruf, čaan git-lak.* Rest assured that if I knew, I would have told you.

nwiθaq /with *b*/ to be trusted, be relied on. *haaḍa ma-yinwiθaq bii.* He can't be trusted.

θiqa **1.** trust, confidence, faith. **2.** (pl. *-aat*) reliable, trustworthy. *maṣdar θiqa* a reliable source.

waθiiq firm, solid, strong. *ʔaku ɛilaaqa waθiiqa beeni w-been il-waziir.* There's a firm friendship between me and the minister.

waθiiqa pl. *waθaayiq* **1.** document, certificate, record. **2.** transcript (of school grades).

ʔawθaq **1.** more or most trusting, confident, sure. **2.** more or most firm, strong, solid. **3.** more or most dependable, reliable.

miiθaaq pl. *mawaaθiiq* pact, covenant, treaty, agreement.

waaθiq trusting, confident, certain, sure.

w-θ-n

waθan pl. *ʔawθaan* idol, graven image.

*waθani** pl. *-iyya* **1.** idolater, heathen, pagan. **2.** pagan, idolatrous.

w-j-a-ġ

wjaaġ, ʔoojaaġ pl. *-aat* **1.** hearth, fireplace. **2.** range, cookstove.

w-j-b

wijab (*i wujuub*) to become obligatory, requisite, a duty. *ma-daam ṭaab, wijbat ɛalee ṣ-ṣalaa.* Since he has recovered, it is his duty to pray.

waijab to be very hospitable toward. *min zirithum, wajjibooni hwaaya.* When I visited them, they showed me every possible courtesy.

stawjab to deserve, merit, be worthy of. *l-qaḍiyya ma-tistawjib hat-taɛqiidaat.* The matter doesn't merit these complexities. *j-jariima ma-čaanat tistawjib hiiči ɛukum.* The crime didn't call for such a sentence.

wajba pl. *-aat* **1.** portion, part (of a larger group). *wajba txušš w-wajba tiṭlaɛ. l-qaaɛa malyaana.* A group goes in and a group comes out. The hall's still full. *jaabaw wajbat masaajiin jidiida.* They brought a new shipment of prisoners. **2.** meal, repast.

ʔiijaab: *bil-ʔiijaab* in the affirmative. *jaana jawaab bil-ʔiijaab.* We got an affirmative answer.

waajib **1.** binding, obligatory, necessary,

incumbent. **2.** (pl. *-aat*) duty. **3.** assignment, task.

muujib **1.** positive (elec.). *l-quṭb il-muujib* the positive terminal. **2.** (pl. *-aat*) cause, reason, motive. || *haaδa ma-ʔila muujib.* This is uncalled for.

w-j-d

wujad (*a wujuud*) **1.** to find. *š-šurta wujdat ʔaaθaar ʔaqdaam bil-ḥadiiqa.* The police found footprints in the garden. **2.** to be found, exist. *has-saaʕa ma-yuujad miθilha bid-dinya.* You can't find a watch like this anywhere. *nwujad* to be found. *başmat ʔaṣaabʕak nwujdat ʕal-qaaṣa.* Your fingerprints were found on the safe.

wujdaan conscience. *haaδa ṣaaḥib wujdaan. ma-yiġdur ʔaḥḥad.* He has a conscience. He won't cheat anyone. *b-wujdaanak, ʔaani gilit šii?* Honestly, did I say anything?

waajid much, plenty, a lot of. *ʕiddna ʔakil waajid.* We've got a lot of food.

mawjuud **1.** available, on hand, existent. **2.** present, in attendance, around. *xaabarta, laakin gaaloo-li ma-mawjuud bil-beet.* I called him, but they told me he's not at home. **3.** (pl. *-aat*) stock, supply, store.

w-j-ʕ

wujaʕ (*a wujaʕ*) to pain, hurt. *baṭni da-toojaʕni li-ʔan ʔakalit ihwaaya.* My stomach is hurting me because I ate too much. *raasi da-yoojaʕni.* I have a headache.

wajjaʕ **1.** to hurt, cause pain. *δ-δarba maaltak twajjiʕ.* Your punch hurts a lot. **2.** to make sick, cause to be sick. *la-taaxuδ ḥammaam baarid tara ywajjʕak.* Don't take a cold bath or it'll make you sick.

twajjaʕ to become sick. *la-txalli j-jaahil yilʕab bil-mayy tara yitwajjaʕ.* Don't let the child play in the water or he'll get sick.

wujaʕ pl. *ʔawjaaʕ* **1.** pain, ache. **2.** ailment, sickness, disease. || *wujaʕ! ma-tiskut ʕaad!* Damn it! Why don't you shut up!

wajʕaan pl. *-iin, wjaaʕa* sick, ill.

w-j-n

wajna pl. *-aat* the area of flesh covering the cheekbone just below the eye.

w-j-h

wajjah **1.** to turn, direct, aim, level, point. *wajjihaw madaafiʕhum ʕal-wlaaya.* They trained their artillery on the city. **2.** to direct, give directions to, give orders to. *l-ʔusta wajjah ʕummaala w-bidaw yištaġluun.* The boss gave orders to his workers and they went to work. **3.** to counsel, advise. *ma-aʕruf š-asawwi. wajjihni.* I don't know what to do. Advise me. **4.** to address, direct, send. *ʔariid awajjih suʔaal lir-raʔiis.* I'd like to direct a question to the president. *nwajjih in-nidaaʔ l-kull waṭani yišʕur bil-masʔuuliyya.* We address the call to each patriot who feels the responsibility. *wajjihoo-la ʔilfaat naδar.* They sent him a letter of reprimand. **5.** to display, show, arrange attractively. *ʔiδa twajjih il-ixyaar, yinbaaʕ iṣ-siʕir ʔaʕla.* If you arrange the cucumbers nicely, they'll sell for a higher price.

waajah **1.** to be opposite, facing, across from. *beetna ywaajih il-wizaara.* Our house is directly facing the ministry. **2.** to see personally, have an audience, interview with. *raḥ-awaajh il-mudiir ʕat-tarfiiʕ.* I'm going to see the director about the promotion. **3.** to face, meet, stand up to, counter, withstand. *laazim itwaajih il-muškila b-ṣabur.* You should face the problem with patience.

twajjah **1.** to be directed, aimed, pointed. *l-ʔaδwiya kullha twajjihat ʕal-masraḥ.* All the lights were directed onto the stage. **2.** to turn, head, go. *xan-nitwajjah l-ḥabbaaniyya.* Let's head for Habbaniyya.

twaajah to meet face to face. *twaajahit wiyya l-mudiir.* I met with the director.

ttijah **1.** to turn, head, go. *xamsa min ṭiyyaaraat il-ʕadu ttijhat ʔila mawaaδiʕkum.* Five enemy planes are headed toward your positions. **2.** to lead, go. *haṭ-ṭariiq yittijih ʔila baġdaad.* This road leads to Baghdad.

jiha pl. *-aat* **1.** direction. *b-yaa jiha mišaw?* Which direction did they go? **2.** side. *haj-jiha mnil-binaaya baʕadha ma-maṣbuuġa.* This side of the building isn't painted yet. **3.** point of view, aspect, angle, side. *laazim tidrus il-qaδiyya min kull ij-jihaat.* You have to study the matter from all sides. *min jihti, ʔaani ma-ʕindi maaniʕ.* For my part, I have no objection. *min jiha . . . w-min jiha θaanya . . .* On the one hand . . . and on the other . . . . || *min jihat* about, concerning, with regard to. *ʔariid aḥči wiyyaak min jihat il-waδiifa.* I want to speak to you with regard to the position. **4.** area, section, part, region. *ma-aku ḥayaaya b-haj-jihaat.* There are no snakes in these parts.

wujih, wičč pl. *wujuuh* **1.** face, countenance. || *gal-ilh-iyyaa b-wujha.* He told it to him to his face. He told him about it brazenly. *ḥiča b-wičča.* He talked back to him. *ma-yṣiir tiḥči b-wujh abuuk.* You mustn't talk back to your father. **2.** front, face, façade. **3.** front, front side (of a fabric). || *bluuz ʔabu wiččeen* reversible sweater. **4.** slipcover, upholstery covering. **5.** embroidered pillow cover. **6.** meaning, sense, point. *šinu wujih in-nukta b-hal-quṣṣa maaltak?* What's the point of the joke in this story of yours? **7.** aspect, facet. *biḥaθna l-muškila min kull il-wujuuh.* We studied the problem from all angles.

ʕala wujih one way or the other, in a definite manner. *ḥill il-muškila ʕala wujih. la-titraddad.* Solve the problem one way or the other. Don't vacillate. *sawwiiha ʕala wujih; loo tbiiʕ-ilh-iyyaa, loo tinṭiih-iyyaa.* Do it one way or the other; either sell it to him or give it to him. *ʔaxaδ wujih il-ʕaruusa.* He deflowered the bride. He consummated the marriage.

wujha pl. *-aat* **1.** objective, goal, intention. **2.** destination.

wujhat naḍ̣ar point of view, viewpoint, standpoint.

wajaaha **1.** prestige, eminence, esteem, standing, distinction. **2.** validity, legitimacy, soundness.

wajiih pl. *wujahaaʔ* **1.** notable, eminent, distinguished. **2.** eminent man, notable. **3.** acceptable, sound. *ʔasbaab wajiiha* acceptable reasons.

ʔawjah **1.** more or most eminent, notable, distinguished. **2.** more or most valid, sound, reasonable. **3.** more or most acceptable, proper, correct, suitable.

muwaajaha pl. *-aat* **1.** face to face encounter, meeting. **2.** audience, interview.

ttijaah pl. *-aat* direction, heading, course.

waajiha pl. *-aat* **1.** face, front. **2.** outside. **3.** façade.

w-č-č

wičč var. of *wujih,* which see under *w-j-h.*

w-č-d

waččad to confirm, make sure about, find out for sure. *ma-da-agdar awaččid makaana.* I can't locate him exactly.

twaččad to be confirmed, be corroborated. *l-ʔaxbaar twaččdat.* The news was confirmed.

see also *ʔ-k-d.*

w-č-y

wačča to come to rest, perch, alight, roost. *ṭ-ṭeer ṭaar w-wačča ʕala šijra ʕaalya.* The bird flew up and perched in a high tree. **2.** to dock, berth, tie up. *l-maaṭoor raḥ-ywačči yamm il-balam.* The motor barge is going to dock next to the sailing barge. **3.** to camp, make camp. *l-badu waččaw barra l-iwlaaya.* The Bedouins camped outside the town.

twačča to lean, support oneself. *ma-yigdar yguum ʔiδa ma-yitwačča ʕala šii.* He can't get up if he doesn't support himself on something. *ma-yigdar yimši ʔiδa ma-yitwačča ʕala ʕoočiyya.* He can't walk without leaning on a cane.

see also *t-č-y.*

w-ḥ-d

waḥḥad **1.** to unify, unite, make one. *ḥizibna yriid yiwaḥḥid id-duwal il-ʕarabiyya.* Our party wants to unite the Arab countries. **2.** to standardize. *l-ḥukuuma triid itwaḥḥid il-awzaan.* The government wants to standardize weights.

¶ *waḥḥad ʔallaa* to declare God to be one, proclaim the soleness of God.

twaḥḥad to be unified, united. *juyuuš id-dawilteen itwaḥḥdat.* The armies of the two countries were unified.

ttiḥad to unite, combine, join together, form a union. *d-dawilteen ittiḥdaw.* The two countries united.

ḥida: *ʕala ḥida* alone, apart, separate, detached, isolated. *ḥuṭṭ kull ġaraaδi ʕala ḥida.* Put all my things to one side.

waḥd-, ʕala waḥd- /plus pronominal suffix/ alone, by oneself. *bugeet bil-beet waḥdi.* I stayed in the house by myself.

waḥḥad **1.** alone, by oneself. *riḥit lis-siinama waḥḥdi* I went to the movies alone. *raḥ-itruuḥuun waḥḥadkum?* Are you going by yourselves? || *kull il-ibgaagiil yitʕaamluun. yaʕni bass inta waḥḥad.* All the grocers bargain. In other words, you're the only one who's different. **2.** aside, apart, to one side. *ḥuṭṭ il-beeḍ waḥḥad.* Put the eggs to one side. || *haaδa waḥḥad; ʔiḥna hassa da-niḥči ʕal-imtiḥaan.* That's something else; now we're talking about the exam.

wiḥda **1.** oneness, singleness, unity. *l-wiḥda l-ʕarabiyya* Arab unity. **2.** solitariness, isolation, solitude, loneliness. *l-wiḥda kitlatni hnaa.* I'm dying of loneliness here. **3.** (pl. *-aat*) unit, single group.

wiḥda ḥaskariyya military unit. **4.** (mus.) beat. **5.** fem. of *waaḥid,* which see.

waḥiid **1.** alone. *buqeet waḥiid ṭuul iṇ-ṇahaaṛ.* I was alone all day. **2.** solitary, lonely, lonesome. *ḥaqli ṭaar; biqeet waḥiid b-hal-uwlaaya bala ʔaṣdiqaaʔ.* I went out of my mind; I was lonely in that city without friends. **3.** sole, only, exclusive. *haaδa l-laaḥib il-waḥiid illi ʔabadan ma-xiṣar.* This is the only player who never was defeated. || *haaδa waḥiid il-ʔahla.* He's an only child.

ʔittiḥaad **1.** unity, union, consolidation, amalgamation, merger, fusion. **2.** (pl. *-aat*) union, confederation, league, federation, alliance, association.

waaḥid fem. *wiḥda* **1.** one (numeral). **2.** a person, someone, somebody. *waaḥid siʔal ḥannak.* Someone asked about you. *l-waaḥid ma-yidri ween yruuḥ bil-leel.* One doesn't know where to go at night.

muttaḥid united, combined, consolidated, amalgamated. *l-ʔumam il-muttaḥida* the United Nations.

see also *ʔ-ḥ-d.*

w-ḥ-š

wuḥaš (*i*) to grieve by one's absence, cause to feel lonely. *wuḥašitna b-ġiyaabak.* We missed you a lot.

twaḥḥaš to be or become wild, savage. *la-twaddi d-dibb lil-ġaaba, tara yitwaḥḥaš.* Don't take the bear to the woods, or he'll become wild. *min yitḥaarak, yitwaḥḥaš.* When he fights, he goes wild.

stawḥaš **1.** to feel lonely. *ʔaani ʔastawḥiš ib-hal-beet waḥdi.* I feel lonely in this house by myself. **2.** /with *l-*/ to miss, feel lonely, saddened without. *stawḥašnaa-la min čaan ib-beeruut.* We missed him when he was in Beirut. **3.** /with *min*/ to have an aversion to, feel a distaste for. *ʔibni yistawḥiš imnil-ġariib.* My son has an aversion to strangers.

waḥiš pl. *wuḥuuš* wild animal, wild beast.

waḥša loneliness, forlornness, desolation. || *ʔibni ʔila waḥša. ʔatmanna yiji.* I miss my son. I hope he comes.

*waḥši** wild, untamed. *ḥaywaanaat waḥšiyya* wild animals. *haj-jaahil šloon waḥši!* What a wild kid! || *ʔibni waḥši. ma-yitṣaadaq wiyya n-naas.* My son is shy. He doesn't make friends with people.

waḥšiyya savagery, brutality.

ʔawḥaš **1.** more or most untamed, etc. **2.** more or most savage, ferocious, etc.

muuḥiš desolate, dreary, deserted, forlorn, lonely. *hal-beet ič-čibiir kulliš muuḥiš.* This big house is very lonely. *l-beet ib-manṭiqa muuḥiša.* The house is in a desolate area.

mitwaḥḥiš **1.** wild, untamed, barbarous, barbaric, savage. **2.** (pl. *-iin*) a barbarian, a savage.

w-ḥ-l

waḥal pl. *wuḥuul, ʔawḥaal* slough, morass, mire.

w-x-r

waxxar **1.** to remove, clear away, move aside. *waxxir kutbak išwayya ḥatta yṣiir makaan il-kutbi.* Move your books over a little so there'll be room for my books. *waxxiroo min hal-waδiifa w-xalloo b-waδiifa ʔuxra.* They took him out of this position and put him in another one. **2.** to move aside, get out of the way. *waxxir ḥatta s-sayyaara tfuut.* Get out of the way so the car can pass.

twaxxar to move aside, get out of the way. *twaxxar ḥatta ʔaguṣṣ biṭaaqa.* He moved out of the way so I could get a ticket.

w-d-d

wadd (*i widd, mawadda*) **1.** to like, be fond of, care for. *ʔaani ʔawiddak ikθiir.* I like you a lot. **2.** to want, wish, desire. *ʔawidd ʔaji wiyyaakum.* I would like to come with you.

widd **1.** affection, amity. **2.** wish, desire.

*widdi** friendly, amicable. *l-ḥalaaqaat been id-dawilteen widdiyya.* The relations between the two countries are friendly.

w-d-ḥ

waddaḥ **1.** to bid farewell, say goodbye to. *jeet ʔawaddḥak li-ʔan raḥ-ʔasaafir baačir.* I came to say goodbye to you because I'm going away tomorrow. *laazim inruuḥ lil-maṭaar nwaddḥa.* We should go to the airport to see him off. **2.** to deposit, leave for safekeeping. *waddaḥ ifluusa b-ṣanduug it-tawfiir.* He deposited his money in the postal savings system.

twaadaḥ to bid each other farewell. *taḥaal nitwaadaḥ, li-ʔan iṭ-ṭiyyaara raḥ-iṭṭiir.* Come, let's say goodbye to each other, because the plane is going to leave.

widaaḥ, wadaaḥ farewell, leave-taking, **adieu.**

muwaddiع pl. *-iin* **1.** person saying goodbye. **2.** depositor.

mustawdaع pl. *-aat* warehouse, depot (mil.).

w-d-y

wadda **1.** to convey, transfer, take. *raع-awaddi s-sayyaara lil-garaaj.* I'm going to take the car to the garage. *beetkum ibعiid. š-ywaddiini عlee?* Your house is far away. How will I get to it? || *hal-ʔakil ihwaaya. ween ʔawaddii?* This is a lot of food. Where am I going to put it? **2.** to send. *min idzawwaj, waddeenaa-la hadiyya.* When he got married, we sent him a gift. *waddeet-la xabar willa laa?* Did you send him news or not?

waadi pl. *widyaan* wadi, valley, river valley.

w-δ-n

waδδan to give the call to prayer. *waδδan il-miġrib. xalli nṣalli.* He's given the evening call to prayer. Let's pray.

wδaan pl. *-aat* call to prayer.

muwaδδin pl. *-iin* muezzin, man who calls the people to prayer.

see also *ʔ-δ-n.*

w-r-θ

wuraθ (*a wiriθ*) to inherit. *wuraθ kull hal-ʔamlaak min ʔabuu.* He inherited all this property from his father.

warraθ **1.** to will, leave, bequeath. *ʔabuu ma-warraθa šii li-ʔan ma-yعibba.* His father didn't leave him anything because he didn't like him. *maat miflis w-ma-warraθ l-ibna šii.* He died penniless and left nothing to his son. **2.** to light. *ʔinṭiini šixxaaṭtak عatta ʔawarriθ jigaarti.* Give me your matches so I can light my cigarette. **3.** to be lit, catch fire. *j-jigaara l-imballila ma-twarriθ ib-suhuula.* Wet cigarettes won't light easily. || *ʔašu min simaع il-xabar, warraθ.* When he heard the news, he exploded.

stawraθ to inherit, receive as a legacy. *stawraθ min ʔabuu beeteen.* He inherited two houses from his father.

wiriθ inheritance, legacy.

wariiθ pl. *waraθa* heir, inheritor.

wiraaθa heredity, hereditary transmission.

*wiraaθi** hereditary. *maraδ wiraaθi* a hereditary disease.

miiraaθ pl. *mawaariiθ* inheritance, legacy, heritage.

[1]*w-r-d*

wurad (*i wuruud*) **1.** to drink, take water. *waddi l-xeel liš-šaṭṭ xal-toorid.* Take the horses to the river and let them drink. **2.** to water, take or lead to water. *ṣaar il-miġrib. ruuع ʔooridha lil-xeel.* It's evening. Go water the horses.

nwurad to be watered. *l-xeel nwurdat loo baعad?* Have the horses been watered yet?

stawrad to import. *stawradna kammiyya čibiira mnit-taayaraat.* We imported a large quantity of tires.

wariid pl. *ʔawrida* vein.

mawrid pl. *mawaarid* income, revenue.

ʔiiraad pl. *-aat* revenue, income. || *xaššaw ib-ʔiiraad w-maṣraf. haay baعad š-iyfuδδha?* They've gotten into a fruitless discussion. How'll that ever end?

stiiraad pl. *-aat* import, importation.

waarid pl. *-aat* **1.** revenue, income. **2.** proceeds, return, take. **3.** import.

mustawrid pl. *-iin* importer.

[2]*w-r-d*

warrad **1.** to blossom, be in bloom. *hirš il-igrunful warrad.* The clove plant bloomed. **2.** to make rosy, pink. *š-šamis warridat ixduudha.* The sun made her cheeks rosy. **3.** to become pink, rosy. *warridat ixduudha min hawa labnaan.* Her cheeks grew rosy from the Lebanese climate.

warid (coll.) pl. *ʔawraad* **1.** flower(s), blossom(s), bloom(s). **2.** rose(s). **3.** (exclamation) great! fine! excellent! *warid! عali ṣaar mudiirna.* Great! Ali became our director.

warda pl. *-aat* un. n. of *warid.*

*wardi** pink, rosy, rose-colored.

muwarrad flowered, embellished with flowers. *qmaaš muwarrad* flowered material.

w-r-ṭ

warraṭ to put in an unpleasant situation, get into a bad fix, entangle, embroil, involve. *warraṭitni wiyya l-mudiir. leeš git-la jeet liš-šuġuḷ mitʔaxxir?* You got me into a bad fix with the director. Why did you tell him I came to work late? *ma-aruuع; la-twarriṭni.* I'm not going to go; don't try to get me into something. *warraṭni b-has-sayyaara w-ṭilعat matiswa.* He got me involved with this car and it turned out to be worthless.

twarraṭ to get oneself into a mess, get into trouble, become entangled, involved. *twarraṭit. عabaali ʔaku qiṭaar baعad nuṣṣ il-leel w-tbayyan ma-aku.* I'm in a fix. I thought there was a train after midnight and it turned out there wasn't. *la-tištiri has-sayyaara tara titwarraṭ biiha.* Don't buy this car or you'll get stuck with it.

warṭa, wurṭa pl. *-aat* plight, difficulty, predicament, dilemma, fix, jam. *ʔaxuuya warraṭni hal-wurṭa č-čibiira.* My brother got me into this big mess.

w-r-ɛ

twarraɛ to hesitate, be cautious, take time to think. *min ysawwi šii, ma-yitwarraɛ.* When he does something, he doesn't pause to think. *twarraɛ w-diir baalak.* Size up the situation and be careful.

wariɛ pious, god-fearing, godly. *rajul diini wariɛ* a pious man of God.

w-r-q

warraq **1.** to leaf, put forth leaves. *l-ʔašjaar kullha twarriq bir-ribiiɛ.* All the trees burst into leaf in the spring. **2.** to leaf, thumb. *warriq bil-iktaab. balki tilgi ir-rasim.* Leaf through the book. Maybe you'll find the picture.

waraq (coll.) pl. *ʔawraaq* **1.** foliage, leafage, leaves. **2.** paper. **3.** cards, playing cards. *yilɛab waraq.* He plays cards.

waraqa, warqa pl. *-aat* **1.** leaf. **2.** sheet of paper, piece of paper. **3.** note, paper, document. **4.** banknote.

w-r-g

warag, warga, etc., = *waraq,* etc., which see.

w-r-k

wirik pl. *wruuk* **1.** hip. **2.** buttock.

w-r-m

wuram (*a waram*) to swell up, become swollen. *lidaġa l-ɛagrab w-wurmat iida.* The scorpion stung him and his hand swelled up.

warram **1.** = *wuram. wučča warram min čaan wajɛaan.* His face became swollen when he was sick. **2.** to cause to swell, (and by extension) to bruise, hurt. *buṣaṭa baṣṭa warrama biiha.* He beat him black and blue. *tiskut loo ʔaji ʔawarrmak.* You shut up or I'll come and beat you up. || *warramta biš-šiṭranj.* I beat him badly at chess. *l-muɛallim warramna b-ʔasʔilta ṣ-ṣaɛba.* The teacher tortured us with his hard questions.

twarram to be hurt (esp. figuratively). *twarramit bir-reesiz il-baarɛa. xiṣarit kull ifluusi.* I took a beating at the races yesterday. I lost all my money. *twarramit. kull rooɛa liṭ-ṭabiib tkallif diinaar.* I've had it. Every visit to the doctor costs a dinar.

waram pl. *ʔawraam* **1.** swelling. **2.** swollen place.

w-r-n-y-š

warniiš varnish.

w-r-w-r

warwar pl. *waraawir* pistol, hand gun.

w-r-y

wara **1.** behind, in the rear of, at the back of. *ʔoogaf wara š-šijra ɛan iš-šamis.* Stand behind the tree away from the sun. *taɛaal li-giddaam. leeš waaguf wara l-kull?* Come to the front. Why are you standing behind everyone? || *min wara* **1.** from behind, from the back of. *xašš min wara l-qanafa.* He came out from behind the sofa. **2.** by means of, through, by, because of. *hal-balaawi kullha jattna min waraak.* All these troubles came to us because of you. **2.** to, in, proceeding from, resultant from. *z-zawaaj, ma-waraa ġeer il-mašaakil.* There is nothing to marriage except problems. *hal ɛači ma-waraa natiija.* This talk will lead nowhere. *taɛabak ma-waraa natiija, liʔan ɛayynaw waaɛid.* Your efforts will be useless because they already appointed someone. **3.** after. *ṭabbaw waaɛid wara l-laax.* They came in one after the other. *raɛ-yijuun waraay baɛad saaɛa.* They will come after me in an hour. **3.** behind, in the rear, at the back. *ʔinta ʔugɛud giddaam w-xalli j-jaahil yugɛud wara.* You sit in front and let the kid sit in back. || *li-wara* back, to the rear, backward. *ʔirjaɛ li-wara.* Back up.

wara-ma after. *wara-ma txalliṣ, murr ɛalayya.* After you finish, drop in on me.

warraani rear, back, hind. *d-daɛɛamiyya l-warraaniyya maɛwuuja.* The rear bumper is bent. *rijleen il-ʔarnab il-warraaniyya ʔaṭwal imnil-giddaamiyya.* The rabbit's hind legs are longer than the front ones.

[1]*w-z-r*

wazzar to wrap a loincloth around. *wazzir ij-jaahil gabul-ma yxušš lil-ɛammaam.* Wrap something around the child's waist before he enters the bath.

twazzar to put on or wear a loincloth. *ʔiδa ma-ɛindak čiswa, twazzar w-isbaɛ.* If you don't have a swimming suit, put on a loincloth and go swimming.

wazra, wizra pl. *-aat* loincloth.

[2]*w-z-r*

stawzar to appoint or install as a minister. *raʔiis il-wizaara stawzar iθneen ɛidhum šahaadat duktooraa.* The prime minister appointed as ministers two men with doctorates.

waziir pl. *wuzaraaʔ* minister, cabinet member. *majlis il-wuzaraaʔ* cabinet, council of ministers. *raʔiis il-wuzaraaʔ* prime minister.

wizaara pl. *-aat* **1.** ministry. **2.** cabinet, government. *raʔiis wizaara* prime minister.

*wizaari** **1.** ministerial. **2.** cabinet.

stiizaar installation of a cabinet. *ḥaflat istiizaar* cabinet inauguration ceremony.

[1]*w-z-z*

wazz (*i wazz*) to incite, arouse, stir up, set. *haaδa ma-yitḥaarak. laazim waaḥid wazza.* He never fights. Someone must've incited him. *ḥamaata wazzata wiyya marta w-xallathum yitḥaarkuun.* His mother-in-law got him irritated with his wife and made them fight.

nwazz to be incited, stirred up. *ma-yinwazz bil-ʕajal.* He can't be aroused quickly.

wuzza agitation, inciting.

[2]*w-z-z*

wazz (coll.) goose, geese. *ʔibn il-wazz ʕawwaam.* Like father like son (lit., the goose's son is a swimmer).

wazza pl. *-aat* goose.

w-z-ʕ

wazzaʕ **1.** to distribute, pass out, deal out. *l-waziir wazzaʕ ij-jawaaʔiz ʕal-faaʔiziin.* The minister distributed the awards to the winners. *wazziʕ il-waraq!* Deal the cards! **2.** to deliver. *šuġli ʔawazziʕ bariid ib-hal-manṭaqa.* My job is delivering mail in this area.

twazzaʕ to be distributed. *j-jawaaʔiz raḥ-titwazzaʕ il-yoom.* The awards will be distributed today.

tawziiʕ **1.** distribution. **2.** delivery.

muwazziʕ: *muwazziʕ bariid* mailman, postman.

w-z-n

wuzan (*i, a wazin*) to weigh, weigh out. *wuzan-li l-gaṣṣaab kiilu laḥam.* The butcher weighed out a kilo of meat for me.

waazan **1.** to balance, equilibrate, poise. *tigdar itwaazin il-maṣṭara ʕala raas il-qalam?* Can you balance the ruler on the tip of the pencil? **2.** /with *been*/ to compare, compare with, make a comparison between, weigh against. *waazin been hal-waδ̣iifa w-waδ̣iiftak is-saabqa gabuḷ-ma tintiqil.* Compare this position with your last job before you were transferred. *laazim itwaazin been raatbak w-maṣrafak.* You have to weigh your salary against your expenses.

twaazan to counterbalance each other, be of the same weight. *j-jihateen imnil-maṣṭara ma-da-titwaazan.* The two sides of the ruler don't balance.

nwuzan to be weighed. *la-taaxuδ hač-čiis. baʕad ma-nwuzan.* Don't take this bag. It hasn't been weighed yet.

ttizan to behave in a poised, sedate, dignified manner. *ttizin ib-ḥačyak. ʕeeb ʕaleek!* Be careful what you say. Shame on you!

wazin pl. *ʔawzaan* **1.** weight. *wazin nawʕi* specific gravity. || *la-ddiir-la baal. ma-ʔila kull wazin bid-daaʔira.* Don't pay any attention to him. He carries no weight in the office. **2.** poetic meter. || *ḥamaam ʕala wazin tamaam.* "Pigeon" rhymes with "fine." **3.** conjugation, verb pattern. **4.** weight, weight class (e.g., in boxing).

wazna pl. *-aat* a unit of weight roughly equal to one hundred kilograms.

wazzaan pl. *-a* scale operator.

miizaan pl. *miyaaziin, mawaaziin* **1.** scales, balance. **2.** Libra (astron.).

miizaaniyya pl. *-aat* **1.** balance, equilibrium. **2.** budget. **3.** (tech.) adjustment, setting. **4.** meter, measuring device. *miizaaniit ṃayy* water meter.

muwaazana **1.** balance, equilibrium. **2.** comparison, parallel.

mawzuun **1.** balanced, in equilibrium, evenly poised. **2.** weighed. **3.** metrically balanced (poetry).

w-z-y

waaza **1.** to parallel, be parallel to. *š-šaariʕ ywaazi n-nahar.* The street runs parallel to the river. **2.** to encourage, embolden, urge on. *la-twaaziini tara ʔalʕab ʕašr idnaaniir ʕala hal-iḥṣaan.* Don't push me or I'll play ten dinars on that horse. *waazaani ʕaz-zawaaj w-idzawwajit w-ʔakalitha.* He talked me into marriage and I got married and got myself in a mess.

twaaza **1.** to be parallel. *hal-xaṭṭeen yitwaazuun.* These two lines are parallel. **2.** to become enthusiastic, get excited. *min yšuuf il-waraq, yitwaaza w-yriid yilʕab pookar.* When he sees the cards he becomes excited and wants to play poker. *l-baarḥa twaazeet w-ridt aštiri l-beet ʔilla šwayya.* Yesterday I got all worked up and wanted to buy the house. **3.** to work up one's courage. *fadd yoom raḥ-atwaaza w-abaṭṭil min haš-šuġuḷ.* Some day I'm going to get fed up and quit this job.

mutawaazi **1.** parallel. || *mutawaazi*

l-ʔaḏlaaɛ. parallelogram. **2.** enthusiastic, excited, all worked up.

w-s-ṭ

wassaṭ, wasaṭ see *w-ṣ-ṭ.*

w-s-ɛ

wisaɛ (yoosaɛ, yisaɛ siɛa, wasɛa) to hold, accommodate, have room for, be large enough for. *ṣ-ṣaff yoosaɛ xamsiin talaamiiḏ.* The classroom will hold fifty pupils. *ṣ-ṣaff yisaɛna kullna.* The classroom will hold us all.

wassaɛ **1.** to make roomy, spacious, to enlarge, expand, extend. *raḥ-inwassaɛ il-ḥadiiqa.* We're going to enlarge the garden. **2.** /with *ɛala*/ to be generous toward, to make wealthy. *ʔiḏa ʔaḷḷa ywassiɛ ɛaleena, nigdar ništiri beet.* If God is generous to us, we can buy a house.

twassaɛ **1.** to become wider, more extensive, to expand, grow larger. *ʔašġaalna twassɛat.* Our business has expanded. **2.** to expand, enlarge, expatiate. *ʔiḏa nitwassaɛ ihwaaya bil-mawḏuuɛ, ma-yhuḏmuu.* If we expand on the topic too much, they won't digest it.

ttisaɛ to grow larger, wider, more extensive. *ʔiḏa ttisaɛ iš-šagg, baɛad ma-yinraaf.* If the rip gets wider, it can't be darned any more.

siɛa capacity, holding capacity, volume.

wasɛa spaciousness, roominess. || *ḏaagat il-wasɛa biihum.* They became depressed.

ʔawsaɛ more or most spacious, extensive, etc.

waasiɛ spacious, vast, wide, extensive. *qaaɛa waasɛa* a spacious hall. *ɛindak majaal waasiɛ il-waqt il-imtiḥaan.* You have plenty of time before the exam. *ʔaḷḷa waasiɛ ir-raḥma.* God is abounding in mercy.

mawsuuɛa pl. *-aat* encyclopedia.

w-s-l

twassal /with *b-*/ to plead with, implore, beseech, entreat. *twassal biš-šurṭi yhidda.* He pleaded with the policeman to let him go.

wasiila pl. *wasaaʔil* **1.** means, medium. **2.** device, expedient.

tiwaasiil, twissil imploring, beseeching, begging.

w-s-m

twassam: *twassam bii l-xeer* to see promising signs in someone, have high expectations of someone. *nitwassam bii l-xeer.* We expect him to do great things.

wisaam pl. *ʔawsima* medal, decoration.

wasiim comely, handsome, pretty. *wičča wasiim.* He has a nice-looking face.

mawsim pl. *mawaasim* season, time of the year.

w-s-w-s

waswas **1.** to whisper. *ma-tiḥči ḥeel? luwees da-twaswis ib-ʔiḏna?* Can't you speak up? Why are you whispering in his ear? **2.** to incite to evil, tempt. *ḏalleet itwaswis ʔila ʔan xalleeta yṭallig marta.* You kept talking evil until you made him divorce his wife. **3.** to worry, feel uneasy, be apprehensive. *dazzeet-la l-ifluus b-iid ʔaxuuya l-iṣġayyir, laakin ḏalleet ʔawaswis la-yḏayyiɛha.* I sent the money to him by my little brother, but I kept worrying he might lose it.

w-s-y

waasa to console, comfort. *smaɛit beet saɛiid iḥtirag. xalli nruuḥ inwaasii.* I heard Sa'id's house burned. Let's go comfort him. *xalli-nruuḥ inwaasii ɛala wafaat ʔibna.* Let's go offer condolences to him on the death of his son.

muwaasaat consolation.

w-š-ɛ

wšiiɛa pl. *wšaayiɛ* skein (of string).

w-š-g

waašag **1.** to compare. *waašig hal-booyinbaaġeen w-šuuf ʔiḏa yitšaabhuun.* Compare these two ties and see if they are similar. **2.** to match, go well with. *ḏayyaɛit takk min hal-qundara w-da-ʔadawwur waḥda twaašigha.* I lost one of these shoes and I'm looking for one to match it.

twaašag to match, go together. *ɛindi ɛišriin jooraab laakin ma-biiha θneen titwaašag.* I have twenty socks but there are no two of them that match.

w-š-k

wašak: *ɛala wašak* on the verge of, about to. *l-qaḏiyya ɛala wašak tixlaṣ.* The matter is about to be settled.

w-š-l

waššal **1.** to empty, become empty. *l-ḥibb waššal w-ma-bii gaṭrat ṃayy.* The jug's gone dry and there's not a drop of water in it. || *waššalit w-ma-ɛindi wala filis.* I'm broke and don't have a single cent. **2.** to drain, empty. *ʔuglub it-taanki w-waššila mnil-ṃayy.* Turn the tank over and drain the water out of it. || *hal-maṣraf il-qaba waššalni.* This enormous expense has drained me.

twaššal = *waššal* **1.**

w-š-m
wašim tattoo, tattoo markings.

w-š-y
wuša (*i waši*) to inform, tell. *kitloo li-ʔan wuša biihum.* They killed him because he informed on them.

nwuša passive of *wuša.*

waaši pl. *-iin, wušaat* informer, tattle-tale, stool pigeon.

w-ṣ-x
waṣṣax to dirty, soil, foul. *waṣṣax ʔiida min čaan yilʕab.* He got his hands dirty when he was playing.

twaṣṣax to become dirty. *š-bil-ʕajal twaṣṣax iθ-θoob!* The shirt sure got dirty fast!

wuṣax dirt, filth.

waṣix dirty, filthy, foul. *ruuḥ, ʔiġsil ʔiideek; waṣxa!* Go wash your hands; they're dirty! *la-tiḥči wiyyaa tara lsaana waṣix.* Don't talk with him, because his tongue is filthy.

waṣaaxa dirtiness, filthiness.

w-ṣ-ṭ
waṣṣaṭ to place in the middle, to center. *ʔidfaʕ il-meez išwayya w-waṣṣiṭa bil-ġurfa.* Push the table over a bit and center it in the room. 2. to cause to intercede, have act as agent. *waṣṣaṭit abuuk ʕind il-waziir.* I got your father to intercede with the minister.

twaṣṣaṭ 1. to be in the middle or center of. *twaṣṣaṭ iṣ-ṣaff il-ʔamaami bil-masiira.* He was in the middle of the front row in the procession. 2. to intercede, use one's good offices or influence. *ʔabuuk itwaṣṣaṭ-li bil-qaδiyya.* Your father interceded for me in the matter.

waṣaṭ 1. middle, center. 2. center (of a soccer team). 3. medium, average. *ḥajim waṣaṭ* an average size. *ʔariida ḥajim waṣaṭ.* I want it medium size. 4. intermediate. *laazim nilgi ḥall waṣaṭ lil-muškila.* We've got to find a compromise solution to the problem.

waṣiṭ middle, center.

waṣṭa middle, center.

waṣṭiyya middle, center. || *haay š-jaabha bil-waṣṭiyya? ʔiḥna da-niḥči ʕal-ifluus.* What brought this up? We're talking about money.

*waṣṭaani** 1. middle, central, medial. *ḥuṭṭ il-awraaq ʕar-raff il-waṣṭaani.* Put the papers on the middle shelf. || *ḥaṭṭeenaa waṣṭaani.* We ganged up on him. 2. medium, medium-sized. *ʕindak bismaar waṣṭaani?* Do you have a medium-sized nail?

waṣaaṭa 1. intercession, good offices, recommendation. 2. influence, patronage, favoritism.

ʔawṣaṭ fem. *wuṣṭa* middle, central. *š-šarq il-ʔawṣaṭ* the Middle East.

waaṣṭa pl. *waṣaaʔiṭ* 1. means, medium, mode. *waṣaaʔiṭ in-naqil* means of transportation. 2. (pl. *waṣaayiṭ*) interceder, intermediary, reference, sponsor, patron.

mutawaṣṣiṭ, mitwaṣṣiṭ 1. middle, medium. *mawja mitwaṣṣṭa* medium wave (radio). 2. medial, intermediate. *šahaadat mutawaṣṣiṭa* an intermediate school certificate. 3. central, centrally located. || *l-baḥr il-ʔabyaδ il-mutawaṣṣiṭ.* The Mediterranean Sea. 4. average, mediocre. *darajaatak mutawaṣṣiṭa.* Your grades are mediocre.

w-ṣ-f
wuṣaf (*i waṣuf*) 1. to describe, depict, picture. *wuṣaf il-wlaaya xooš waṣuf.* He gave an excellent description of the town. 2. to credit, praise. *wuṣafa biš-šajaaʕa wil-karam.* He praised him for bravery and generosity. 3. to prescribe (a medicine). *ṭ-ṭabiib wuṣaf-li dihn il-xirwiʕ.* The doctor prescribed castor oil for me.

waṣṣaf to give directions, to explain where something is. *ma-yigdar ywaṣṣuf biduun-ma yʔaššir.* He can't give directions without waving his hands. *ma-aku daaʕi tiji wyaay. waṣṣuf-li.* There's no need to come with me. Just show me where. *tigdar itwaṣṣuf-li ween ṣaayra l-maḥaṭṭa?* Can you tell me where the station is?

nwuṣaf pass. of *wuṣaf.*

ttiṣaf to be marked, characterized, known. *har-rijjaal yittiṣif bil-karam.* This man is known for generosity.

ṣifa pl. *-aat* 1. attribute, trait, quality, characteristic. 2. (gram.) adjective.

waṣfa pl. *-aat* 1. description, depiction. 2. medical prescription.

waṣiifa pl. *waṣaayif* 1. slave woman. 2. servant girl.

muwaaṣafa pl. *-aat* 1. detailed description. 2. explanation. 3. specification.

mustawṣaf pl. *-aat* clinic, dispensary.

w-ṣ-l
wuṣal (*a wuṣuul*) to arrive. *šwakit yooṣal il-qiṭaar?* What time does the train arrive? *l-maktuub wuṣal il-yoom.* The letter got here today. *wuṣal-lak il-maktuub willa laa?* Did you receive the letter or not?

l-mayy wuṣal il-ɛadd il-xaṭar. The water has reached the danger level. *yeezi ɛaad, tara wuṣlat il-ɛaddha.* Take it easy there now, because it's gone far enough. *tbaaɛaθna bil-mawðuuɛ saaɛa laakin ma-wuṣalna l-ʔay natiija.* We deliberated on the matter for an hour but didn't reach any result.

waṣṣal 1. to get, take, bring. *minu raɛ-iywaṣṣil-la l-xabar?* Who is going to give him the news? *la-tiɛči šii giddaama tara haaða ywaṣṣil ɛači lil-mudiir.* Don't say anything in his presence or he'll take what is said to the director. *ðall yzayyid ɛar-raadyo ʔila ʔan waṣṣal siɛra lil-xamsiin diinaar.* He kept bidding on the radio until he brought its price up to fifty dinars. 2. to take, carry, convey. *ʔagdar awaṣṣlak ib-sayyaarti lil-maṭaar.* I can take you in my car to the airport. 3. to reach. *hal-ɛabil ma-ywaṣṣil liš-šibbaač iθ-θaani.* This rope doesn't reach to the other window. *ma-aɛtiqid is-sayyaara raɛ-itwaṣṣil lil-baanziinxaana.* I don't think the car will make it to the filling station.

waaṣal to continue, proceed with, go on with. *staraɛeena šwayya w-baɛdeen waaṣalna s-safar.* We rested a little and then continued the trip. *waaṣla šwayya šwayya ɛatta toofi kull id-deen.* Keep paying him bit by bit until you repay the whole debt.

ʔawṣal to conduct (electricity, heat, etc.). *l-plaatiin yuuṣil il-kahrabaaʔ zeen.* Platinum conducts electricity well.

twaṣṣal 1. to obtain access, get through. *la-txaaf ɛalee. haaða yuɛruf šloon yitwaṣṣal lil-wuzaraaʔ.* Don't worry about him. He knows how to get to the ministers. 2. to attain, arrive, reach. *ma-ɛinda maaniɛ yikðib w-ybuug ɛatta yitwaṣṣal il-ġaayaata.* He doesn't mind lying and stealing in order to achieve his goals.

nwuṣal pass. of *wuṣal. hal-mukaan ma-yinwuṣil-la b-fadd yoom.* This place can't be reached in one day.

ttiṣal 1. to get in touch, make contact. *ttiṣal biyya bit-talifoon gabuḷ yoomeen.* He contacted me by telephone two days ago. *raɛ-attiṣil bii w-agul-la.* I'll get in touch with him and tell him. 2. to join, contact, connect. *baɛr il-ʔabyað mittiṣil bil-baɛr il-ʔaɛmar ɛan ṭariiq qanaat is-siwees.* The Mediterranean Sea is connected to the Red Sea by the Suez Canal. 3. to have a relationship. *ybayyin čaan mittiṣil biiha gabḷ iz-zawaaj.* It seems that he had had a relationship with her before the marriage.

ṣila pl. *-aat* 1. connection, link, tie, bond. 2. relationship. 3. kinship. *ʔilna ṣilat raɛam wiyya hal-ɛaaʔila.* We have a slight family connection with that family.

waṣil pl. *wuṣuulaat* receipt, voucher.

wuṣla pl. *wuṣal* piece, fragment (esp. of cloth).

wuṣuul arrival.

*wuṣuuli** upstart, parvenu, overly ambitious, aspiring person.

muwaaṣalaat (plural only) 1. lines of communication, communications. 2. means of transportation, transportation. *wizaart il-muwaaṣalaat* Ministry of Communications and Transportation.

muuṣil (elec.) conductor.

w-ṣ-w-ṣ

waṣwaṣ to chirp, peep, squeak. *farx il-ɛaṣfuur da-ywaṣwuṣ.* The baby sparrow is cheeping.

w-ṣ-y

waṣṣa. 1. to request, ask, order. *šgadd waṣṣeeta yištiri beeð w-nisa.* How many times I told him to buy eggs and he forgot! *l-mulaaɛið waṣṣaani ʔaṭbaɛ hal-maktuub gabuḷ-ma ʔaṭlaɛ.* The supervisor asked me to type this letter before I leave. 2. to charge, commission. *la-twaṣṣii b-šii tara ma-yjiib-lak-iyyaa.* Don't ask him to get anything because he won't bring it for you. *baɛad ma-ʔawaṣṣiik ɛan hal-qaðiyya.* I won't ask you to take care of this matter any more. 3. /with *ɛala*/ to order, place on order for. *waṣṣeet ɛala pardaat jidiida.* I ordered new curtains. *hassa waṣṣeet-lak ɛala gahwa.* I just ordered you a cup of coffee. 4. /with *b-*/ to enjoin, urge, impress, make incumbent upon. *l-ʔislaam ywaṣṣi bil-ɛišma.* Islam urges propriety. 5. to advise, counsel, recommend. *d-diktoor waṣṣaani ʔaakul bass simač w-dijaaj.* The doctor advised me to eat only fish and chicken. 6. to make a will. *maat w-ma-waṣṣa.* He died and didn't make a will. 7. /with *b-*/ to will, bequeath, leave. *waṣṣa b-kull ifluusa l-marta.* He willed all of his money to his wife.

waṣi pl. *ʔawṣiyaaʔ* 1. guardian. 2. regent.

waṣiyya, wuṣiyya pl. *-aat, waṣayya* 1. request, order. *ʔaani raayiɛ il-baġdaad. ɛindak waṣiyya?* I'm going to Baghdad. Do you have any errands? *min itruuɛ lil-baṣra, wuṣiiti l-waɛiida dzuur ʔaxuuya.*

When you go to Basra, my only request is that you visit my brother. **2.** advice, counsel, recommendation. **3.** will, testament.

tawṣiya pl. *-aat* **1.** (commercial) order, commission. *bit-tawṣiya* to order, on commission. **2.** = *waṣiyya.*

tuuṣaa (invar.) custom made, made to order. *buṣaṭit-lak iyyaa basṭa tuuṣaa.* I beat him up for you just the way you wanted. *qanaadra kullha tuuṣaa li-ʔan rijlee kbaar.* All his shoes are custom made because his feet are big.

w-δ̣-ʔ

twaδ̣δ̣a to perform the ritual ablution before prayer. *yaḷḷa ʔitwaδ̣δ̣a ħatta nruuħ inṣalli.* Hurry up and wash yourself so we can go pray.

wuδ̣uuʔ **1.** ritual cleanliness, purity. **2.** ablution.

w-δ̣-ħ

wuδ̣aħ (*a wuδ̣uuħ*) to become clear, plain, manifest, obvious, evident. *d-daris wuδ̣aħ baʕad-ma staʕmal il-muʕallim ʔamθaal ihwaaya.* The lesson became clear after the teacher used many examples.

waδ̣δ̣aħ to make plain, clear, to explain, elucidate, expound, illustrate. *ṭilbaw minna ywaδ̣δ̣iħ is-suʔaal gabuḷ-ma yjaawbuun.* They asked him to clear up the question before they answered.

twaδ̣δ̣aħ pass. of *waδ̣δ̣aħ.*

ttiδ̣aħ to become clear. *baʕad-ma siʔalhum čam suʔaal, ttiδ̣aħ-la ʔinhum ma-yʕirfuun šii.* After he asked them several questions, it became clear to him that they didn't know anything.

ʔawδ̣aħ more or most clear, plain, etc.

waaδ̣iħ **1.** clear, plain. **2.** obvious, evident, manifest.

w-δ̣-ʕ

wuδ̣aʕ (*a waδ̣iʕ*) to lay, set, put in place. *l-waziir wuδ̣aʕ il-ħajar il-ʔasaasi l-hal-binaaya.* The minister laid the cornerstone for this building. || *wuδ̣aʕ ħadd l-* to put a stop to, cause an end to. *laazim nooδ̣aʕ ħadd lil-ʔašyaaʔ il-datṣiir bid-daaʔira.* We have to put an end to the things that are happening in the office. *wuδ̣aʕ il-yadd ʕala* to sieze, lay hold of. *l-ħukuuma wuδ̣ʕat il-yadd ʕala ʔamlaaka.* The government seized his property.

twaaδ̣aʕ to behave humbly and modestly. *leeš ma-titwaaδ̣aʕ išwayya?* Why don't you be a bit modest? *ma-ʕinda maaniʕ yitwaaδ̣aʕ w-ysallim huwwa bil-awwal.* He has no objection to being humble and saying hello first.

waδ̣iʕ **1.** laying, setting, placing. **2.** (pl. *ʔawδ̣aaʕ*) position, stance, bearing, posture, attitude. **3.** situation, condition, set of circumstances. || *kull yoom yijuun lid-daaʔira mitʔaxxriin. haaδa muu waδ̣iʕ!* Every day they come to the office late. This is no way to do things! *waδ̣ʕiyya* pl. *-aat* **1.** position. **2.** situation.

waδ̣iiʕ pl. *-iin, wuδ̣aʕaaʔ* **1.** lowly, base, vulgar, common. **2.** common, vulgar person.

mawδ̣uuʕ pl. *mawaaδ̣iiʕ* **1.** subject, topic, theme. **2.** matter, affair. **3.** problem, issue, question.

w-δ̣-f

waδ̣δ̣af to appoint to a position, to employ, hire. *l-ħukuuma ma-twaδ̣δ̣uf ʔajaanib.* The government doesn't employ foreigners.

twaδ̣δ̣af to be hired, get a job. *simaʕit ʕali twaδ̣δ̣af ib-daaʔirt il-bariid.* I heard that Ali was hired by the Post Office.

waδ̣iifa pl. *waδ̣aayif* **1.** assignment, task, duty. **2.** homework assignment. **3.** office, position, post, job.

muwaδ̣δ̣af pl. *-iin* appointee, official, employee (esp. of the government).

w-ṭ-ʔ

waṭʔa see under *w-ṭ-y.*

w-ṭ-n

stawṭan to settle in, make a home in, take up residence in. *hal-qabiila haajrat min ij-jinuub w-istawṭinat il-ʕiraaq.* This tribe migrated from the South and settled in Iraq.

waṭan pl. *ʔawṭaan* homeland, fatherland, native country. *ħubb il-waṭan* patriotism.

*waṭani** **1.** indigenous, domestic. *maṣnuuʕaat waṭaniyya* domestic manufactures. **2.** patriotic. **3.** nationalistic. **4.** patriot, nationalist.

waṭaniyya **1.** patriotism. **2.** nationalism (esp. one-country, as opposed to Pan-Arab).

w-ṭ-y

waṭṭa to lower. *waṭṭi ṣootak. da-niqra.* Lower your voice. We're reading.

waṭʔa gravity, seriousness.

wuṭiyya ground, earth, terra firma.

waaṭi low. *l-mayy da-yruuħ lil-gaaʕ il-waaṭya.* The water is flowing into the low ground. *huwa fadd waaħid waaṭi. maħħad yħibba.* He's a low-down character. Nobody likes him.

ʔawṭa lower or lowest.

w-ʕ-d

wuʕad (*i waʕad*) to make a promise, to promise. *wuʕadni b-ṣooġa w-ma-jaab-li.* He promised me a present from his trip and didn't bring it to me.

waaʕad **1.** to make an appointment, set a meeting with. *waaʕadni marrteen w-ma-jaa.* He made an appointment with me twice and didn't come. **2.** to make a promise, to promise. *waaʕadni yinṭiini l-panka min ysaafir.* He promised me he'd give me the fan when he left. **3.** to assure, to state confidently. *ʔaani ʔawaaʕdak hassa, raḥ-ysaafir w-ma-ygull-inna.* I'll tell you for sure now, he'll leave and not tell us. || *ʔawaaʕdak ʔiδa-ma* I assure you that . . . , mark my words that . . . . *ʔawaaʕdak ʔiδa-ma ʕayynoo.* I assure you that they will appoint him. *ʔaani ʔawaaʕdak ʔiδa-ma nikat biina.* I'm sure he'll get us in a mess.

twaʕʕad to threaten. *xaaf minna baʕad-ma twaʕʕada.* He got scared of him after he threatened him.

twaaʕad to make an appointment. *twaaʕadna bil-gahwa.* We agreed to meet in the coffee shop. *xan-nittifiq bil-ʔawwal w-baʕdeen nitwaaʕad ʕal-ijtimaaʕ.* Let's agree first and then we'll set a date for the meeting.

nwuʕad pass. of *wuʕad.*

waʕad pl. *wuʕuud* **1.** promise. **2.** appointed time, appointment.

waʕda term (of a loan).

mawʕid, miiʕaad pl. *mawaaʕiid* **1.** appointment, date, rendezvous. **2.** appointed time, deadline.

mawʕuud **1.** promised. *ʔaani mawʕuud ib-tarfiiʕ.* I have been promised promotion. **2.** booked, scheduled. *ʔaani l-yoom mawʕuud w-ma-agdar aji.* I have an appointment today and can't come.

w-ʕ-r

waʕir rough, rocky, uneven, rugged. *l-ʔaraaδi biš-šimaal waʕra.* The terrain in the north is rugged.

w-ʕ-z

wuʕaz (*i ʔiiʕaaz*) **1.** to give orders, give directions. *l-mudiir wuʕaz-ilhum yibquun wara d-dawaam w-ydirsuun il-qaδiyya.* The boss directed them to stay after hours and study the matter. **2.** to suggest, make a suggestion. *loo ma-tooʕiz-la, ma-čaan sawwa hiiči šii.* If you hadn't put him up to it, he wouldn't have done such a thing.

w-ʕ-δ

wuʕaδ (*i waʕiδ*) to preach, to admonish, exhort. *l-ʔimaam yooʕiδ baʕd iṣ-ṣalaa.* The Imam preaches after the prayer.

ttiʕaδ to learn a lesson, be admonished or warned. *hal-xaṣaara laazim itxalliik tittiʕiδ.* This loss should teach you a lesson.

mawʕiδa pl. *mawaaʕiδ* exhortation, sermon.

waaʕiδ pl. *-iin, wuʕʕaaδ* preacher.

w-ʕ-y

wuʕa (*a waʕi*) **1.** to become aware, pay attention. *ʔiδa ma-tooʕa ʕala zamaanak, tara baʕdeen titnaddam.* If you don't pay attention to what's around you, then later you'll regret it. || *wuʕa ʕala nafsa* It dawned on him that . . . *wuʕa ʕala nafsa w-ʕiraf δoola mṣaadqii ʕala fluusa.* It dawned on him and he knew they befriended him for his money. **2.** to awaken, wake up. *baʕda ma-wuʕa mnin-noom.* He hasn't woken up yet.

waʕʕa to wake, awaken. *ʔarjuuk waʕʕiini s-saaʕa θmaanya.* Please wake me up at eight o'clock.

waʕi consciousness, awareness, wakefulness. *fuqad waʕya.* He fainted.

waaʕi awake, conscious. *δalleet waaʕi lis-saaʕa θinteen iṣ-ṣubuḥ.* I stayed awake until two o'clock in the morning.

w-ġ-f

waġġaf to foam up, froth, make suds. *ṣ-ṣaabuun illi nṭeetni-yyaa ma-ywaġġuf zeen.* The soap that you gave me doesn't suds well.

wagaf foam, froth, suds.

waġfa pl. *-aat* u.n. of *waġaf.*

w-g-w-ġ

wuġwaaġa pl. *-aat* toy noisemaker.

w-f-d

ʔawfad to appoint to a delegation. *l-ḥukuuma ʔawfidata yidrus il-ġalaaʔ ib-hal-manṭiqa.* The government appointed him to study the inflation in this area.

wafid pl. *wufuud* delegation.

w-f-r

waffar **1.** to save, lay by, put by, hoard. *ʔiδa twaffur ifluus kaafya, tigdar tištiri beet.* If you save enough money, you can buy a house. **2.** to save, avoid expenditure of. *l-makiina raḥ-itwaffur ʕaleena hwaaya taʕab w-wakit.* The machine will save us a lot of effort and time.

twaffar to be saved. *raatbi, ma-yitwaffar minna wala filis.* Not a single fils can be saved out of my salary. **2.** to abound, be plentiful, abundant, ample. *s-simač yit-waffar bir-rabiiɛ.* Fish are plentiful in the spring. **3.** to be met, fulfilled. *ʔiδa tuɛbur hal-imtiħaan, š-šuruuṭ titwaffar biik.* If you get by this exam, you will have met the conditions. *ma-qibloo li-ʔan iš-šuruuṭ ma-mitwaffura bii.* They didn't accept him because he didn't fulfill the requirements.

wufra abundance, profusion, plenty. *s-simač mawjuud ib-wufra b-dijla.* Fish are in good supply in the Tigris.

tawfiir saving. *ṣanduuq it-tawfiir* postal savings bank.

w-f-q

waffaq **1.** to allow prosperity, grant success. *ʔiδa ʔaḷḷaa waffaqni, ʔaftaħ maħall ɛala ħsaabi.* If God grants me prosperity, I will open a shop on my own. **2.** /with *been*/ to reconcile, make consistent. *ma-yigdar ywaffiq been iš-šuġuḷ wid-diraasa.* He can't reconcile working with studying.

waafaq **1.** to suit, be agreeable to, be consistent with one's interests. *ma-qibal ybiiɛ li-ʔan is-siɛir ma-waafaqa.* He wouldn't consent to sell because the price did suit him. *l-iħčaaya waafqata hwaaya.* The story pleased him a great deal. **2.** to agree, concur, be of like mind with. *ʔaani ma-awaafqak ib-har-raʔi.* I don't agree with you on this idea. **3.** to agree with, be beneficial for. *ybayyin hawa lubnaan waafaqa.* It seems that the Lebanese weather agrees with him. **4.** to coincide with. *z-zawaaj raħ-iywaafiq yoom il-ɛiid.* The wedding will coincide with the holiday. **5.** to consent, agree, give one's consent. *waafaq yiji wyaay lis-siinama.* He agreed to come with me to the movie. **6.** /with *ɛala*/ to approve, authorize, sanction, ratify. *l-mudiir waafaq ɛal-ʔijaaza.* The director approved the leave.

twaffaq to prosper, be successful. *ṣadiiqi twaffaq ib-haš-šaġḷa, w-sawwa fluus ihwaaya.* My friend prospered in this job and made a lot of money.

twaafaq to agree with each other, to get along together. *ʔibni w-ibnak ma-yitwaafquun abadan.* My son and yours don't get along at all.

ttifaq to agree, reach an agreement. *ma-ttifqaw ɛala ʔay ħall li-hassa.* They've not agreed on any solution yet. *ma-aɛruf kiimya, ʔittifaqna, laakin ʔaɛruf ʔingiliizi.* I don't know chemistry, we agree, but I do know English.

ʔawfaq more or most suitable, appropriate, pleasing, acceptable.

tawfiiq success, prosperity.

muwaafaqa **1.** agreement. **2.** consent, authorization, approval.

ttifaaq pl. *-aat* agreement, treaty. *ttifaaq tijaari* commercial agreement.

ttifaaqiyya pl. *-aat* agreement, pact, treaty.

w-f-y

wufa (*i wufa, wafaaʔ*) **1.** to be loyal, faithful, true. *haaδa ʔabad ma-wufa l-ʔaħħad.* He was never faithful to anyone. **2.** /with *b-*/ to live up to, fulfill, keep, meet, carry out. *wufa b-waɛda.* He kept his promise.

waffa to repay. *li-hassa ma-waffa dyuuna.* He hasn't repaid his debts so far.

twaffa to die, pass away. *ʔabuu twaffa gabuḷ šahar w-xaḷḷaf iθlaθ ytaama.* His father passed away a month ago and left behind three surviving children.

twaafa to settle accounts, settle in full. *haak nuṣṣ diinaar w-hassa twaafeena.* Here's a half-dinar and now we're even.

stawfa to obtain repayment of. *raħ-astawfi l-mablaġ minna.* I'll get back the full amount from him. *ma-aṭulba šii. stawfeet ħaqqi.* He doesn't owe me a thing. I got what was due me.

wufa, wafaaʔ **1.** loyalty, faithfulness, fidelity. **2.** fulfillment, keeping, meeting (of a promise, etc.).

wafaa(t) pl. *wafaayaat* demise, death.

wafi pl. *ʔawfiyaaʔ* loyal, faithful, reliable, true. *ʔinta ṣadiiq wafi.* You're a true friend.

ʔawfa more or most faithful, loyal.

waafi ample, abundant.

w-q-t

waqqat to set. *laazim nigɛud mniṣ-ṣubuħ. la-tinsa twaqqitha lis-saaɛa.* We have to get up early in the morning. Don't forget to set the clock.

waqit pl. *ʔawqaat* **1.** time. *ʔawqaat ymurr ɛaleena w-ʔawqaat bass yxaabur.* At times he comes by to see us and sometimes he just phones. || *šwaqit?* when? what time? *ɛal-waqit* on time, at the proper time. *min waqit* early, ahead of time. *laazim niṭlaɛ iṣ-ṣubuħ min waqit.* We have to leave early in the morning. **2.** period of time, time span. *ʔaani raħ-ʔarkuḍ w-inta ilzam-li waqit.* I'm going to run and you keep time for me.

*waqti** temporary. *haaδa tartiib waqti.* This is a temporary arrangement.

tawqiit 1. setting (of a clock, etc.). 2. reckoning of time, time. *ɛcsab tawqiit baġdaad.* according to Baghdad time.

muwaqqat 1. scheduled, set for a given time. *qumbula muwaqqata* time bomb. 2. effective for a given period of time, temporal, temporary, interim, provisional. *haay tartiibaat muwaqqata.* These are temporary arrangements.

see also w-k-t.

w-q-r

waqqar to respect, honor, treat with reverence. *ɛizmoo w-waqqiroo w-baɛdeen ṭilaɛ muu xooš ʔaadmi.* They invited him and treated him with respect and later he turned out to be a bad sort of person.

waqaar dignity, gravity, dignified conduct.

waquur, waqir dignified, venerable, deserving respect.

ʔawqar more or most dignified, respectable, venerable.

w-q-ɛ

waqqaɛ 1. to sign, affix one's signature to. *l-mudiir waqqaɛ il-maktuub loo baɛad?* Has the director signed the letter yet? 2. to cause to sign, affix a signature. *ʔuxuδ il-ɛariiδa w-waqqiɛhum kullhum.* Take the petition and have them all sign.

waaqaɛ to have sexual intercourse with. *ṭ-ṭabiib minaɛa ywaaqiɛ zawijta muddat šahar.* The doctor forbade him to have sexual intercourse with his wife for a month.

twaqqaɛ to expect, anticipate. *ʔatwaqqaɛ yiji baačir.* I expect him to come tomorrow.

mawqiɛ pl. *mawaaqiɛ* 1. place, location, site. 2. position (mil.).

tawqiiɛ pl. *tawaaqiiɛ* signature.

waaqiɛ: *l-waaqiɛ* the facts, the truth. *ɛčii-li l-waaqiɛ.* Tell me the facts. *l-waaqiɛ, ma-ʔili ɛalaaqa b-hal-mawδuuɛ.* Actually, I have nothing to do with this matter.

*waaqiɛi** real, actual, true. *haay quṣṣa waaqiɛiyya.* This is a true story.

see also *w-g-ɛ.*

w-q-f

waqqaf to detain, hold in custody, arrest. *š-šurṭa waqqifat xamis ṭullaab.* The police detained five students.

twaqqaf 1. to be detained, arrested. *xamis mutaδaahiriin twaqqfaw.* Five demonstrators were arrested. 2. to depend, be dependent, conditional. *titwaqqaf il-qaδiyya ɛala muwaafaqta.* The matter depends on his approval. *baqaaʔa bil-ɛukum mitwaqquf ɛala natiijt il-ʔintixaabaat.* His remaining in power is dependent on the result of the election.

waquf pl. *ʔawqaaf* 1. wakf, religious endowment. 2. unalienable property. || *xalliina nilɛab. qaabil is-saaɛa waquf ɛaleek?* Let us play. Do you think the court is yours alone?

mawqif pl. *mawaaqif* 1. position, stand, opinion, attitude. 2. stopping place, bus stop. 3. detention cell, place of temporary custody.

mawquuf 1. arrested, detained, held in custody. 2. prisoner, person under arrest.

see also *w-g-f.*

w-q-y

twaqqa to protect oneself, be on guard, be wary. *twaqqaa tara yiɛči b-gufaak.* Beware of him because he'll say things behind your back. *titwaqqa minna tara haaδa bii sill.* Protect yourself from him, because he has tuberculosis.

ttiqa 1. = *twaqqa.* 2. to avoid, beware of. *ttiqi š-šarr. la-tiɛči wiyyaa.* Stay out of trouble. Don't talk to him. *ttiqi šarra l-haaδa.* Keep away from that guy. 3. to fear (God). *ttiqi ʔaḷḷa w-la-tsawwi hiiči.* Fear God and don't do that.

*taqi** devout, pious, God-fearing.

ʔatqa more or most devout, pious.

taqwa piety, devoutness, godliness.

w-g-d

moogad pl. *mwaagid* fireplace, hearth (esp. for cooking).

w-g-ɛ

wugaɛ (*a wagiɛ, wuguuɛ*) 1. to fall. *has-sana wugaɛ θalij ihwaaya biš-šimaal.* This year a lot of snow fell in the north. *bass yoogaɛ b-iidi, ʔamawwta.* If only he falls into my hands, I'll murder him. *hiiči ṣayyaara ma-toogaɛ bil-ʔiid kull wakit.* Such a car doesn't come along every time. 2. to fall down, drop. *l-iktaab wugaɛ min ʔiidi.* The book fell from my hand. *ṭiyyaara wugɛat yamm baġdaad.* A plane went down near Baghdad. *šaɛri da-yoogaɛ.* My hair is falling out. 3. /with *ɛala*/ to be humble to, beg the pardon of. *ʔabuuk zaɛlaan ɛaleek. ruuɛ ʔoogaɛ ɛalee w-ṣaalɛa.* Your father is angry at you. Go beg his pardon and make up with him. 4. /with *ɛala* or *l-*/ to fall to, befall, come to, happen to.

wugaʕ-la beet w-ʔalif diinaar. A house and a thousand dinars fell into his lap. **5.** to come in season, ripen, become available. *r-rummaan yoogaʕ bil-xariif.* Pomegranates ripen in the fall. **6.** to fall, pounce. *ʔiltamaw ʕalee w-wugʕaw bii dagg.* They ganged up on him and beat him up. *wugaʕ bid-dijaaj dagg w-xallaṣa kulla.* He dug into the chicken and finished it completely.

¶ *yoogaʕ min qadir* to detract from the standing of, degrade, lower. *yaʕni yoogaʕ min qadrak ʔiδa tnaawišni l-miliḥ?* Do you think it'll degrade you if you pass me the salt?

waggaʕ **1.** to cause to fall. *difaʕni w-waggaʕni ʕal-gaaʕ.* He pushed me and knocked me down on the ground. *waggaʕna ṭiyyaarteen lil-ʕadu.* We downed two enemy planes. *ʔaḷḷa la-ywaggiʕ ʔaḥḥad b-iid haṭ-ṭabiib.* God forbid that anyone should fall into the hands of this doctor. *raḥ-ywaggiʕ nafsa b-warṭa.* He's going to get himself into a jam. **2.** to drop. *l-xaadma waggʕat il-maaʕuun.* The maid dropped the dish.

twaggaʕ to lower, humble, debase oneself. *leeš titwaggaʕ ʕan-naas? ʔiδa š-šuruuṭ mitwaffra biik, ywaḍḍfuuk.* Why do you lower yourself to people? If you meet the qualifications, they'll employ you.

wagiʕ, wuguuʕ falling.

wagʕa pl. *-aat* a fall.

waagiʕ **1.** fallen. **2.** down, down on one's luck. *miskiin ybayyin waagiʕ, ḥatta fluus ʔakil ma-ʕinda.* It seems the poor guy's gone under. He doesn't even have money to eat.

see also *w-q-ʕ*.

w-g-f

wugaf (*a waguf, wuguuf*) **1.** to stop, halt, come to a standstill. *leeš is-sayyaara wugfat?* Why did the car stop? *l-paaṣ ween yoogaf?* Where does the bus stop? *saaʕti wugfat.* My watch stopped. *loo ʔaku fadd šii bir-raadyo loo l-maḥaṭṭa wugfat.* Either there's something wrong with the radio or the station shut down. *ʔoogaf, xalli ʔagul-lak šii.* Wait, let me tell you something. **2.** to stand up, rise, get up. *laazim toogaf min tiḥči wiyya ḍ-ḍaabuṭ.* You must stand up when you talk with the officer. **3.** to stand, take a position, place oneself, post oneself. *ʔoogaf ib-baab id-dukkaan w-intaḍra.* Stand by the door of the shop and wait for him. *ʔoogfu iθneen iθneen.* Stand two by two. || *wugaf ʕala raasi. ma-raaḥ ʔila ʔan xallaṣit.* He stood right over me. He didn't go away until I finished. *kull-ma ʔariid ʔasawwi šii, yoogaf ib-wičči.* Every time I want to do something, he stands in my way. **4.** /with *l-*/ to stand up for, take a position in favor of, back, support. *kull-ma tṣiir ʕindi muškila, yoogaf-li.* Every time I have a problem, he stands up for me. **5.** to come, fall, devolve. *hassa l-qaḍiyya wugfat ʕaleek.* Now the matter is in your hands. *l-muzaayida wugfat ʕalayya b-ʔalif diinaar.* The bidding rested with me at a thousand dinars. *l-beet wugaf ʕalayya b-ʔalif diinaar.* The house fell to me for a thousand dinars. *l-qaḍiyya wugfat ʕala fluus iṭ-ṭawaabiʕ; maḥḥad da-yidfaʕha.* The matter has halted over the money for the stamps; no one is paying it.

waggaf **1.** to stop, halt, bring to a standstill. *wagguf is-sayyaara!* Stop the car! *ʔaku duwa ywagguf in-naziif?* Is there any medicine that can stop the bleeding? *la-txallii yilġi; waggfa ʕind ḥadda.* Don't let him go on talking; put him in his place. **2.** to park. *xalli nwagguf is-sayyaara hnaa.* Let's park the car here. **3.** to cause to stand, to place in an upright position. *wagguf ij-jaahil w-xallii yimši.* Stand the child up and let him walk. *wagguf it-talaamiiδ ḥasb iṭ-ṭuul.* Stand the students up according to height. **4.** to post, position, station, place. *gabuḷ-ma nxušš lil-beet waggaf šurṭi bil-baab il-warraani ḥatta laḥḥad yinhizim.* Before we enter the house put a policeman at the back door so no one can escape.

twaagaf **1.** to reach a stand-off, tie, draw with each other. *liʕabna š-šitranj ṭuul il-leel w-bil-axiir itwaagafna.* We played chess all evening long and in the end we reached a stand-off. **2.** to argue, have a dispute. *twaagafit wiyyaa ʕala diinaar.* I argued with him over a dinar.

nwugaf pass. of *wugaf. hal-kursi mṭaʕṭaʕ. ma-yinwuguf ʕalee.* This chair is wobbly. It can't be stood upon. *š-šamis ḥaarra ma-yinwuguf jawwaaha.* The sun is so hot one can't stand in it.

wagfa pl. *-aat* **1.** stop, halt. **2.** stance, position, posture. **3.** stand, position, stance. *wugaf-li xooš wagfa w-ma-jaaz ʔilla ḥaṣṣal-li t-tarfiiʕ.* He took a strong stand for me and didn't let up until he'd got me the raise. **4.** market place, open square for vendors.

waggaaf pl. *-a* attendant, functionary at a reception or celebration.

waagif **1.** standing, upright, erect. **2.** standing still, motionless, at rest. **3.** (pl. *-iin*) bystander, spectator.

see also *w-q-f*.

[1]*w-g-y*

wuga pl. *-aat* a pad or block of wood put on the head when carrying objects.

[2]*w-g-y*

wgiyya pl. *-aat, wgaaya, ʔawaag* oka, a unit of weight originally, and occasionally now, equal to 1.28 kilograms (approx. 2.75 lbs.), now standardized at one kilogram. || *wgiyya ṣṭanbuul* an Istanbul oka, equal to approx. 320 grams (.7 lb.).

w-k-b

mawkib pl. *mawaakib* (religious) procession, cortege.

w-k-t

wakit time. *ma-ʕindi wakit.* I don't have time. *faat il-wakit.* It's gotten late. *faat il-wakit. laazim iṭ-ṭiyyaara ṭaarat.* It's too late. The plane must have left by now. *š-wakit* what time, when. *šwakit raḥ-yiji?* When's he going to come? *ʕal-wakit* on time, at the appointed time. *jaa ʕal-wakit tamaaman.* He came right on time. *ʕala wakit* early. *wuṣalna ʕala wakit.* We arrived early.

see also *w-q-t*.

w-k-ḥ

wakkaḥ to make insolent, impudent, disrespectful. *jamaaʕta wakkuḥoo w-ṣaar ʔadabsizz.* His gang made a smart aleck out of him and he has no manners anymore.

twakkaḥ to become insolent, impudent, disrespectful. *la-txalli ʔibnak yilʕab wiyya hal-walad tara yitwakkaḥ.* Don't let your son play with this boy or he'll become disrespectful.

stawkaḥ to become insolent, impudent. *min šaaf ʔabuu, stawkaḥ.* When he saw his father, he became bolder.

wakiiḥ pl. *wukkaḥ* **1.** brash, insolent, impudent, bold. *kull wulidha ma-biihum waaḥid wakiiḥ.* Not one of her sons is impudent. **2.** tough, rowdyish, ruffianly. *la-titḥaaraš ib-hal-ibnayya tara ʕidha ʔuxwa wukkaḥ.* Don't make passes at that girl because she has some tough brothers.

wakaaḥa insolence, impudence, boldness. *ʔinta da-tsawwi wakaaḥa hwaaya. raḥ-agul-la l-abuuk.* You're being very naughty. I'm going to tell your father.

ʔawkaḥ more or most brash, insolent, bold.

w-k-d

wakkad var. of *ʔakkad,* which see under *ʔ-k-d.*

w-k-r

wakkar to light, perch, come to rest. *ṭeerna wakkar ʕala ṣaṭiḥkum.* Our pigeon lit on your roof.

w-k-s

wikas (*i wakis*) to reduce the probability of. *wikas qaḏiyyat tarfiiʕi.* He scuttled my chances for promotion.

waksa pl. *-aat* degrading, humiliating, shameful deed.

[1]*w-k-l*

wakkal **1.** to appoint as agent, authorize, empower. *wakkalni ʔabiiʕ il-beet maala.* He authorized me to sell his house. **2.** to engage as counsel. *raḥ-itwakkil muḥaami willa laa?* Will you engage a lawyer or not?

twakkal **1.** to act as counsel. *ma-aku muḥaami yiqbal yitwakkal ʕanna.* There's no lawyer that'll agree to represent him. **2.** /with *ʕala*/ to trust in, put one's confidence in. *twakkal ʕala ʔaḷḷa.* Trust in God.

ttikal to rely, depend, place one's trust. *ʔaani ʔattikil ʕaleek ib-hal-qaḏiyya.* I'm depending on you in this matter.

wakiil pl. *wukalaaʔ* **1.** deputy, vice-*wakiil waziir* deputy minister, undersecretary of a ministry. **2.** agent, representative. || *wakiilak ʔaḷḷa, haaḏa ḥaqqak.* As God is your witness, this is your right.

wakaala pl. *-aat* **1.** power of attorney. **2.** agency. **3.** deputyship, proxy. *waziir bil-wakaala* minister in the interim, acting minister.

[2]*w-k-l*

wakkal var. of *ʔakkal,* which see under *ʔ-k-l.*

w-l-a

wala **1.** (contraction of *w-laa*) and not, nor. *ma-ariid laa haaḏa wala haaḏa.* I don't want this or this. **2.** not even, not so much as. *ma-ʕindi wala filis.* I don't have even a fils. *riḥna liṣ-ṣeed w-maṣidna wala ṭeer.* We went out hunting and didn't bag a single bird. *ma-gidar ydaayinni wala xamsiin filis.* He couldn't lend me even fifty fils. **3.** not at all, never so much as, not in the slightest. *ḏall išgadd yiḥči wala jaawabta.* He kept talking so much and I never answered him at all. *loo-ma* ʕ*amma l-waziir, wala ylaffuu yoom ib-had-daa*ʔ*ira.* If his uncle weren't the minister, they wouldn't let him stay in this office a single day. *wala nibas ib-čilma.* He never even uttered a word.

w-l-d

wilad (*i wilaada*) to give birth, bear a child. *l-baar*ʕ*a, marti wildat bil-mustašfa.* Yesterday, my wife had a baby in the hospital.

wallad to deliver, assist in childbirth. *yaa jidda wallidatha?* Which midwife delivered her? *haj-jidda wallidatna kullna.* This midwife delivered us all. **2.** to generate. *ywalliduun kull il-kahrabaa*ʔ *illi tista*ʕ*mila l-madiina b-hal-ma*ʕ*mal.* They generate all the electricity used by the city in this plant. **3.** to engender, breed, cause. *hal-qaδiyya ra*ʕ*-itwallid nataayij muu zeena.* This affair's going to produce unfavorable results.

twallad to be engendered, caused, occasioned. *ṭ-ṭaa*ʕ*uun yitwallad imnil-faar.* Plague is caused by mice.

twaalad to propagate, reproduce, multiply. *j-jireediyya titwaalad ib-sur*ʕ*a.* Rodents multiply quickly.

nwilad to be born. *nwilad yoom ij-jum*ʕ*a iδ-δuhur.* He was born Friday at noon.

walad pl. *wulid, wilid,* ʔ*awlaad* **1.** son, child, descendant, offspring. **2.** boy. **3.** knave, jack (in cards).

wilaada childbirth, delivery, birth. *taariix il-wilaada* date of birth.

miilaad **1.** birth. **2.** time of birth, birthday, nativity. ʕ*iid miilaad* birthday celebration. || ʕ*iid il-miilaad* Christmas. *qabl il-miilaad* before Christ, B.C.

*miilaadi** **1.** birthday-. **2.** relating to the birth of Christ. **3.** after Christ, A.D. *sanat* ʔ*alf w-tisi*ʕ *miyya w-θmaanya w-xamsiin miilaadi.* the year 1958 A.D.

waalid parent, father. *l-waalideen* one's parents.

waalida pl. *-aat* mother.

mawluud **1.** born. **2.** (pl. *mawaaliid*) private celebration, commemorative ceremony. **3.** (pl. only) members of an age group. *wizaart id-difaa*ʕ *di*ʕ*at mawaaliid sanat* ʔ*alf w-tisi*ʕ *miyya w-*ʔ*arba*ʕ*iin il-xidmat il-*ʕ*alam.* The Ministry of Defense called the 1940 age group to service of the flag.

muwallid pl. *-aat* generator, dynamo.

*w-l-*ʕ

*twalla*ʕ to be or become passionately fond, madly in love. *min šaaf jamaalha w-sima*ʕ ʕ*ačiiha, twalla*ʕ *biiha.* When he saw her beauty and heard her talk, he fell madly in love with her.

*wala*ʕ passion, ardent love or desire. ʕ*inda wala*ʕ *bil-muusiiqa.* He has a passion for music.

*muula*ʕ passionately fond, enamored. *huwwa muula*ʕ *bin-na*ʕ*it.* He's terribly fond of sculpture.

w-l-k

wilak f. *wilič* pl. *wilkum* = *lak* which see under *l-k*.

w-l-l-a

waḷḷa see under ²ʔ*-ḷ-ḷ-a.*

willa = *w-*ʔ*illa,* which see under ¹ʔ*-l-l-a.*

w-l-m

waalam **1.** to suit, fit, match, be appropriate for. *δoola waa*ʕ*id waalam il-laax. θneenhum xara.* Each of them is a good match for the other. They're both scum. **2.** to suit, be agreeable to. ʔ*iδa l-waḍi*ʕ *ma-da-ywaalmak, leeš-ma tistiqiil?* If the situation isn't agreeable to you, why don't you resign? *had-duwa ma-da-ywaalimni.* This medicine doesn't agree with me.

twaalam to get along, go well, fit in with each other. *jiiraanna w-marta ma-yitwaalmuun.* Our neighbor and his wife don't get along with each other.

waliima pl. *walaa*ʔ*im* banquet.

w-l-w

walaw although, even though. *ma-ra*ʕ*-aakul hassa walaw juu*ʕ*aan.* I'm not going to eat now even though I'm hungry.

w-l-y

wila (*i wali*) to catch, corner, gain ascendency over, get the upper hand over, get in one's power. *wuleeta yoom il-ma*ʕ*aaš w-axaδit fluusi minna.* I cornered him on payday and took my money from him. *hal-marra xallaṣit, laakin* ʔ*awliik ġeer marra.* You got away this time, but I'll catch you another time. ʔ*iδa yooli waa*ʕ*id, ma-yhidda.* If he ever gets someone in his power, he won't leave him alone. *δtarreet* ʔ*adfa*ʕ *has-si*ʕ*ir li-*ʔ*an wilaani ġeer wilya.* I had to pay that price because he left me without any choice.

walla **1.** to get out, leave, go away. *jiibii-li wuṣlat xubuz w-istikaan čaay* ʕ*atta* ʔ*awalli.* Bring me a piece of bread and a cup of tea so I can get out of here.

buqaw nuṣṣ saaʕa w-baʕdeen wallaw. They stayed a half hour and then went away. *čaan iylaaʕig il-ibnayya w-gallat-la "leeš ma-twalli?"* He was following the girl and she said to him "Why don't you get lost?" **2.** to appoint as governor, ruler, administrator. *ṣ-ṣulṭaan walla waaʕid min ʔaqribaaʔa ʕal-xilaafa.* The sultan appointed one of his relatives to the caliphate.

twalla to assume control of, to take charge of. *twalla l-ʕukum min čaan ʕumra waaʕid w-ʕišriin sana.* He took over the rule when he was twenty-one years old. *faṣiilna yitwalla l-ʕiraasa hal-leela.* Our platoon is in charge of guard duty tonight.

twalla to follow in succession, come one after the other. *twaalat ʕalee l-maṣaayib.* Misfortunes befell him, one immediately after the other.

nwila to be caught, be cornered. *nwila bil-bistaan min čaan da-yištuğuḷ w-ma-šaayil islaaʕ.* He was cornered in the orchard when he was working, and was unarmed.

stawla to seize control, get control, take possession of. *j-jayš stawla ʕal-ʕukum.* The army seized power. *stawlaw ʕal-madiina.* They captured the city. *stawlat il-ʕukuuma ʕala ʔamlaaka.* The government confiscated his property.

wilya **1.** advantage, opportunity for power, authority, control. || *lizam wilya* to seize the advantage, get the upper hand. *lizam wilya w-raad diinaareen ʕaleeha.* He got the upper hand and wanted two dinars for the thing. *š-daʕwa l-kiilo b-diinaar? haaδi wilya li-ʔan tuʕruf ma-aku ġeer maxzan ihnaa.* What do you mean a dinar per kilo? That's taking advantage just because you know there's no other store here.

wilaaya, wlaaya pl. *-aat* **1.** sovereignty. **2.** state. *l-wilaayaat il-muttaʕida* the United States.

wlaaya pl. *-aat* city, municipality.

ʔawla more or most worthy, deserving.

mawla **1.** master, lord. **2.** /with possessive suffix/ *mawlaaya, mawlaana* a sarcastic form of address. *mawlaana, ʔiδa titlaakam wiyyaaya, ma-tqaawum ʔakθar min jawla waʕda.* My dear sir, if you box with me, you won't last more than one round.

mitwalli **1.** entrusted, in charge, having responsibility. **2.** (pl. *-iyya*) administrator of a religious endowment.

w-m-s

muumis, muumisa pl. *-aat* prostitute.

w-m-ḍ

wamiiḍ **1.** sparkle, twinkle, brightness. **2.** lightning.

w-m-y

ʔooma (yoomi tʔoomi) **1.** to signal, beckon, motion. *ʔoomii-la ʕatta yoogaf.* Signal to him to stop. *ma-yguul šii. bass yoomi b-raasa.* He won't say anything. He just nods his head. **2.** to indicate, point out. *ma-da-ašuufa. ʔoomii-li weena.* I don't see him. Point out where he is for me.

w-n-s

wannas to entertain, amuse, provide entertainment. *hal-filim ywannis ihwaaya.* This movie is very entertaining. *ʔuxuδ ij-jaahil w-wannisa šwayya.* Take the kid and amuse him for a while. *ʔiδa tiji l-bağdaad, ʔawannsak.* If you come to Baghdad, I'll show you a good time.

twannas to be entertained, to enjoy oneself. *twannastu l-baarʕa bil-ʕafla willa laa?* Did you enjoy yourselves yesterday at the party or not?

winsa pleasure, fun.

see also *ʔ-n-s*.

w-n-n

wann (i wann, winiin) to moan, groan. *l-marḍa kullhum da-ywinnuun.* All the sick people are moaning.

wanna pl. *-aat* moan, groan.

w-n-w-n

wanwan to moan, repeatedly or continually. *š-bii da-ywanwin? ʔaku šii yoojʕa?* What's he moaning about? Is something hurting him?

w-h-b

wihab (i) to donate, grant, give, make a gift of. *ṣadiiqa been mudda w-mudda yoohib-la fadd šii.* From time to time his friend makes him a present of something.

hiba pl. *-aat* gift, present, donation. *has-saaʕa huwwa ma-štiraaha. ʔijat-ta hiba.* He didn't buy this watch. It came to him as a gift.

wahhaabi Wahabite, Wahabi.*

mawhiba pl. *mawaahib* talent, gift. *ʕinda mawhiba bir-rasim.* He was a talent for drawing.

mawhuub talented, gifted. *fannaan mawhuub* a talented artist.

w-h-d-n

wahdan **1.** to mislead, lead astray. *ḍall yimdaʕ is-sayyaara ʔila ʔan wahdanni* *w-xallaani ʔaštiriiha.* He kept on praising the car until he misled me and made me buy it. *abuuya wahdanni biz-zawaaj.* My father conned me into marriage. **2.** to confuse. *ʔinta, min ʕičeet, wahdanitni.* When you spoke up, you made me lose track.

twahdan **1.** to be confused. *ʔaani ʕala ṭuul ʔatwahdan bil-imtiʕaan.* I always get mixed up on the exam. **2.** to make a mistake. *la-ykuun titwahdan w-truuʕ il-haṭ-ṭabiib tara ma-yiftihim.* Don't make the mistake of going to this doctor because he doesn't know his business. *ʔišxuṭ hal-ʕibaara. ʔaani twahdanit.* Cross out this phrase. I made a mistake. *la-tištiriiha tara titwahdan biiha.* Don't buy it or you'll get stuck with it.

w-h-s

wahhas to worry, feel uneasy, have doubts. *la-twahhis; ma-aku šii ʕala ʔibnak.* Don't worry; nothing will happen to your son.

waahis, wahis concern, interest, yen, desire. *min ʔagʕud yammha, yṣiir-li waahis.* When I sit near her, I feel desire. *ʔilak waahis itruuʕ lis-siinama?* Are you interested in going to the movies? *ʔibnak waahsa bil-liʕib, muu bid-diraasa.* Your son's interest is in playing, not in studying. *tigdar itsawwii-la waahis yruuʕ wiy-yaana?* Can you talk him into going with us? *b-ʕačyak haaδa, sawweet-li waahis. raʕ-aštiriiha.* With that talk you've given me the urge. I'll buy it.

w-h-m

wahham to confuse, disorient. *ma-ʕiraft il-beet li-ʔan ṣubġa j-jdiid wahhamni.* I didn't recognize the house because its new paint fooled me. *xalliini ʔaʕsib il-ifluus. la-twahhimni.* Let me count the money. Don't confuse me. *ʔaani čint ʔaʕruf ij-jawaab, laakin il-waraay wahhamni.* I knew the answer, but the guy behind me mixed me up.

twahham to make a mistake, get the wrong idea, become confused. *la-ykuun titwahham w-tiqbal il-waδiifa.* Beware of making a mistake and taking the job. *twahhamit w-daxxalit hal-mablaġ b-iʕsaabak.* I made an error and entered this amount in your account. *l-ʕafu. twahhamit biik. ʕabaali ṣadiiqi.* Pardon me. I made a mistake. I thought you were my friend.

ttiham to accuse, charge. *ttiham kull il-muwaδδafiin illi yištuġluun wiyyaa.* He accused all the officials who work with him. *ttihmoo bil-booga.* They accused him of the theft.

waham pl. *ʔawhaam* **1.** delusion, fancy, erroneous impression. **2.** hallucination.

*wahmi** **1.** imaginary. *xaṭṭ il-istiwaaʔ xaṭṭ wahmi.* The equator is an imaginary line. **2.** fictitious. *ṭarzaan šaxiṣ wahmi.* Tarzan is a fictitious person.

wihma pl. *-aat* mistake, error. *rajjiʕ il-ġaraaδ. ṣaarat wihma.* Bring back the things. There's been a mix-up.

wahmaan confused, mixed up, mistaken. *ʔaani ma-ṭlabtak bit-talifoon. ʔinta wahmaan.* I didn't ask for you on the phone. You're mistaken.

ttihaam pl. *-aat* **1.** accusation, charge. **2.** indictment.

muttaham **1.** accused, charged. **2.** indicted.

see also *t-h-m.*

w-h-w-s

wahwas to hesitate, vacillate, feel doubtful, uncertain, unsure. *ʔištiriiha. la-twahwis.* Buy it. Don't be indecisive. *la-twahwis, is-sayyaara ma-biiha šii.* Don't worry, there's nothing wrong with the car.

*wihwaasi** **1.** doubtful, unsure. **2.** (pl. *-iyyiin*) person who is unable to make decisions.

w-h-w-h

twahwah to hesitate, have doubts. *la-titwahwah; loo tiji wiyyaana loo xalliina nruuʕ.* Make up your mind; either go with us or let us go. *š-biik mitwahwih? gulli š-itriid.* Why are you hesitating? Tell me what you want.

w-y-š

weeš see *ʔeeš* under *ʔ-y-š.*

w-y-ṣ

waaṣ (*i weeṣ*) to chirp, peep. *farx id-dijaaja ywiiṣ min yiṭlaʕ imnil-beeδa.* The baby chick chirps when it comes out of the egg.

[1]*w-y-l*

weel distress, woe. || *ʔaweeli ʕalee!* or *weeli ʕalee!* Poor fellow! I'm so sorry for him!

ʔaweelaah! or *ʔaweelaax!* Woe is me! Oh, misery! *ʔaweelaah! šloon ʔagdar aʕiiš bila ʔaṣdiqaaʔ?* Woe is me! How can I ever live without friends?

[2]*w-y-l*

wiil pl. *-aat* wheel.

[3]*w-y-l*

waayil voile, a kind of sheer cloth.

w-y-n

ween where, what place. *ween il-miftaaʕ?*

Where is the key? *ma-adri ween xalleetha.* I don't know where I put it. *ween riḥtu l-baarḥa?* Where did you all go yesterday? *haay weenak? ṣaar isbuuʕ ma-šiftak.* Where have you been? I haven't seen you in a week. *li-ween raayiḥ?* Where are you going? *min ween, mneen* from where? *mneen-lak hal-ifluus?* Where did you get this money? || *haaδa ween w-δaak ween!* This is nothing like that!

ween-ma wherever. *ween-ma yismaʕ ʔaku ḥafla, yruuḥ-ilha.* Wherever he hears there's a party, he goes to it.

w-y-y

wiyya with. *triid tiji wiyyaaya?* Do you want to come with me? *ʔiδa tʕaariḍ hal-iqtiraaḥ, ʔaani wiyyaak.* If you oppose this suggestion, I'm with you. *ma-aku ʔaḥḥad bid-daaʔira, bass ʔaani wiyyaak.* There's no one in the office, just you and I.

Y

[1]*y-a*

yaa **1.** (vocative and exclamatory particle) oh. *yaa ʔibin il-ḥaraam!* You bastard! *yaa naas! šaayfiin hiiči šii?* Hey, people! Have you ever seen such a thing? *yaa ṛaḅḅi, š-raḥ-ʔasawwi?* Oh God! What am I going to do? *θoob ib-rubuʕ diinaar? yaa balaaš!* A shirt for a quarter dinar? That's cheap, man! **2.** (var. of *ʔay* which see also under *ʔ-y*) which, what. *yaa fluus? ma-titṭlubni šii.* What money? I don't owe you anything. *yaa ktaab itriid?* Which book do you want? *min yaa jaamiʕa txarraj?* From which university did he graduate?

ʔáyaa = *yaa* **1.** *ʔáyaa ḥayyaal, š-madriik?* Hey, you sly guy! How'd you know? *ʔáyaa miskiin! tawwa dzawwaj.* Oh, poor guy! He just got married.

yaaḅa, yaaḅ (contraction of *yaa ʔabb*) **1.** oh father, hey dad. *yaaḅa il-ʕaša ḥaaḍir.* Hey, dad! Supper's ready. **2.** hey fella, say pal. *yaaḅa, xalli nruuḥ lis-siinama.* Say, buddy, let's go to the movie. **3.** (general exclamation of approval, astonishment, anguish, etc.) boy, wow, man. *yaaḅa, šloon jamaal haaδa!* Boy, oh boy, what a beauty! *halaw yaab! ṭallaʕ gooḷ il-laax.* Good, good! He scored another goal.

[2]*y-a*

yaa name of the letter *y*.

y-a-b-an

l-yaabaan Japan.

*yaabaani** Japanese.

y-a-x

yaaxa pl. *-aat* **1.** collar (of a garment). **2.** lapel (of a jacket).

y-a-r-da

yaarda pl. *-aat* yard (unit of length).

y-a-z-ġ

yaazuġ **1.** a pity, a shame, too bad. *yaazuġ ʕalee; baʕda šabaab.* It was a sad thing about him. He's still a youngster. *yaazuġ yġulbak. tawwa tʕallam yilʕab.* It's a pity he beat you. He just learned to play. **2.** /with negative/ impossible, unbelievable. *ma-yaazuġ! haaδa wala yigdar yuġlubni biš-šiṭranj.* I don't believe it! He could never beat me at chess. *ma-yaazuġ ʕali ysawwi hiiči; haaδa xooš walad.* I doubt that Ali would do such a thing; he's a good boy.

y-ʔ-s

yiʔas (*a yaʔas, yaʔis*) to despair, give up hope. *la-tiiʔas bil-ʕajal. ḥaawil min jidiid.* Don't give up right away. Try again. *yiʔasit minna; ʔabad ma-yitʕallam.* I've given up hope in him; he'll never learn. *yiʔas imnil-ḥayaat w-kital nafsa.* He lost all hope in life and killed himself.

yaʔʔas to deprive of all hope, to discourage, dissuade. *ma-qibal yirjaʕ ʔilla lamma yaʔʔasta.* He wouldn't agree to return until I gave him no other hope. *ma-tigdar ityaʔʔisni b-suhuula. ʕindi ʔamal qawi.* You can't discourage me easily. I have high hopes.

yaʔas, yaʔis despair, hopelessness. *sinn il-yaʔas* the climacteric.

yaaʔis without hope, desperate.

mayʔuus: *mayʔuus min* lost, hopeless. *ṣiḥḥta mayʔuus minha.* His health is a hopeless case.

y-a-s

yaas privet.

y-a-s-m-y-n

yaasmiin jasmine.

y-a-ġ-d-a-n

yaaġdaan pl. *-aat* oilcan.

y-a-f-w-x

yaafuux top of the head, crown of the head.

y-a-q-w-t

yaaquut (coll.) ruby(ies).

yaaquuta pl. *-aat* ruby.

y-a-n-s-w-n

yaansuun anise, aniseed.

y-a-n-ṣ-b

yaanaṣiib see under *n-ṣ-b.*

y-a-h-w

yaahu fem. *yaahi* pl. *yaahum* (contraction of *yaa huwwa, yaa hiyya, yaa humma*) which, who among them, whoever. *yaahu l-ygul-lak, la-tṣaddig bii.* Whoever tells you, don't believe him. *yaahu minhum sabbak?* Which of them insulted you? || *l-beet maala wil-ifluus fluusa, yaahi maaltak?* The house is his and the money is his money; what concern is it of yours?

y-a-y

yaay pl. *-aat* spring. || *siččiina ʔumm yaay* switch-blade knife.

y-b-s

yibas (a yabis, ybaas) to dry, become dry. *l-ihduum yibsat kullha.* The clothes all got dry. *yibas ʕalga mnil-ʕaṭaš.* His mouth dried up from thirst.

yabbas 1. to make dry, to dry. *haṣ-ṣeef yabbasna baanya hwaaya.* This summer we dried a lot of okra. 2. to stiffen, make hard, rigid. *l-barid yabbasa.* The cold petrified him.

tyabbas to be dried. *l-guṭun laazim yityabbas gabuḷ-ma yinwizin.* The cotton has to be dried before it's weighed.

ʔaybas 1. more or most dessicated, etc. 2. more or most rigid, etc. 3. more or most miserly, etc.

yaabis 1. dry, dried out, arid. *xubuz yaabis* stale bread. *šidd ij-jariʕ maalak; baʕda ma-yaabis.* Bandage your wound; it still hasn't healed. 2. stiff, hard, firm. *la-timsi ʕal-giir; baʕda ma-yaabis.* Don't walk on the asphalt; it hasn't hardened yet. || *haaδa xašma yaabis; la-tsiʔla tara ma-yjaawbak.* He's a snob; don't ask him because he won't answer you. 3. stingy, miserly. *huwwa fadd waaʕid yaabis; ma-yitbarraʕ ib-šii.* He's a stingy person; he wouldn't donate anything.

y-t-m

yattam 1. to deprive of a father. *l-ʕarub yattimat haj-jaahil.* The war left this child fatherless. 2. to orphan, deprive of parents. *ʕaadiθ is-sayyaara yattama min ʔumma w-ʔabuu.* The car accident left him motherless and fatherless.

tyattam to become an orphan, to be deprived of one's father. *tyattam w-ʕumra xams-isniin.* He became an orphan when he was five years old.

yatiim pl. *ytaama, ʔaytaam* 1. fatherless child. 2. orphan.

meetam pl. *mayaatim* orphanage.

y-x-n-y

yaxni a thin stew made of meat, onions and chick-peas. || *simaʕna hal-qiṣṣa miit marra. ṣaarat yaxni.* We've heard this story a hundred times. It's gotten worn out.

y-d-d

yadd (see also *ʔiid* under *ʔ-y-d*) hand. || *ʔila yadd biiha.* He had a hand in it.

yadda pl. *-aat* handle. || *kursi ʔabu yaddaat* armchair.

*yadawi** manual, hand-. *ʕamal yadawi* manual labor. *qumbula yadawiyya* hand grenade.

y-d-g

yadag pl. *-aat* extra, spare, reserve. *ʔuxuδ ispaanteen ʕatta tubqa wiʕda ʕindak yadag ʕala ṭuul.* Take two wrenches so you can always have one as a spare.

y-d-w

yadawi see under *y-d-d.*

y-r-d

yarda pl. *-aat* yard (measure of length).

y-z-d-y

*yaziidi** Yezidi, belonging to the Yezidi religion.

l-yaziidiyya the Yezidi religion, a religion of Kurdistan which includes Devil worship.

y-s-r

yassar to make easy, facilitate. *ʔaḷḷa yyassir ʔumuurak!* May God make things easy for you!

tyassar to be or become available, easy to find. *han-nooʕ imnil-uqmaaš ma-yityassar bis-suug.* This type of cloth is not available in the market.

yusur a kind of semiprecious black stone.

yasaar, yisaar left, left side. *ʔimši gubaḷ w-duur lil-yisaar ib-θaani šaariʕ.* Go straight and turn to the left at the second street.

*yisaari** leftist, left-wing. *ʕinda miyuul yisaariyya.* He has leftist leanings.

*yisraawi** left-handed. *ʔibnak yisraawi.* Your son is left-handed.

ʔaysar more or most easy, etc.

ʔaysar fem. *yisra* left, located to the left. *ʔiida l-yisra maksuura.* His left arm is broken.

maysuur, mityassir available, easy to find.

y-s-w-ع

l-yasuuع Jesus.

*yasuuعi** Jesuit. *l-ʔabaaʔ il-yasuuع-iyyiin.* the Jesuit fathers.

y-š-m-a-ġ

yašmaaġ pl. *yašaamiiġ* a man's headdress or kerchief of white cloth with red or black diamond-shaped embroidery.

y-ṣ-ġ

yaṣṣaġ to outlaw, make unlawful, illegal. *l-ɛukuuma raɛ-ityaṣṣiġ iṣ-ṣeed bir-ribiiع.* The government is going to outlaw hunting in the spring.

yaṣaġ (invar.) unlawful, illegal, prohibited. *yaṣaġ itwaggf is-sayyaara hnaa.* It's forbidden to park the car here. *l-ɛukuuma sawwat iṭ-ṭalعa bil-leel yaṣaġ.* The government made it unlawful to go out at night.

y-q-n

yaqqan to be convinced, sure, certain. *ma-yaqqan ʔilla lamma rawweet-hiyyaa.* He wasn't convinced until I showed it to him. *š-ma-agul-lak, ma-tyaqqin.* No matter what I tell you, you don't believe it.

tyaqqan to ascertain, make sure, assure oneself. *ʔariid atyaqqan zeen gabuḷ-ma ʔaxaabra.* I want to be very sure before I phone him.

yaqiin, عala yaqiin certain, sure, positive. *ʔiδa ʔija l-baġdaad, yaqiin ymurr عaleehum.* If he comes to Baghdad, he'll surely drop in on them. *kuun عala yaqiin ʔaani ma-aɛči b-gufaak.* You can be sure I won't talk behind your back.

y-k-k

yakk one, a single unit (used in set expressions). *kullha yakk ɛasaab عalayya.* It's all the same to me.

y-l-g

yalag pl. *-aat* vest, waistcoat.

y-l-l-a

yaḷḷa see under *ʔ-ḷ-ḷ-a.*

y-m-t-a

yamta When? *ʔaani yamta gut-lak hiiči?* When did I ever tell you that? *yamta dzuurna?* When will you visit us?

yamta-ma whenever, any time. *yamta-ma triid, ʔaani ɛaaḍir.* Whenever you want, I'm ready.

[1]y-m-m

tyammam to resort to sand, to substitute sand for water in ritual ablutions. *ʔiidak majruuعa. ma-tigdar titwaḍḍa. tyammam.* Your hand is cut. You can't wash yourself. Use sand to prepare for prayer.

[2]y-m-m

yamm 1. beside, next to, near. *taعaal ugعud yammi; ʔard agul-lak fadd šii.* Come here and sit next to me; I want to tell you something. *ɛuṭṭha yamm ir-raadyo.* Put it next to the radio. *beetna ṣaayir yamm maɛattat il-qiṭaar.* Our house is near the railroad station. *riɛit yamma fadd saaعa w-iɛčeet wiyyaa.* I went to see him for an hour and talked with him. 2. in the care of, in the hands of. *ʔagdar ʔaxalli saaعti yammak ɛatta ʔasbaɛ?* Can I leave my watch with you so I can swim? *la-ddiir baal. xalliiha yamm ʔaḷḷa.* Don't worry. Leave it in God's hands. *xalliiha yammi.* Leave it to me. || *min yamm* 1. to the advantage of, in the interest of. *ʔiδa binaw jisir hnaa, haay min yammi li-ʔan gaaعi siعirha yziid.* If they build a bridge here, it'll be in my favor because the price of my land will go up. *haay ṣaarat min yammak!* That's a real break for you! 2. on the part of, from the point of view of. *min yammi, ma-عindi maaniع.* For my part, I have no objection.

y-m-n

yimna right, right side. *fuut عal-yimna.* Go to the right.

l-yaman Yemen.

yamani pl. *-iyaat* a kind of slipper.

yamiin pl. *ʔaymaan* oath. *ɛilaf yamiin ma-yilعab uqmaar baعad.* He took an oath he wouldn't gamble any more. *haaδa yamiin, ma-aعruf šii.* I swear I don't know anything.

yamiin right, right side. *fuut bis-šaariع il-عal-yamiin.* Turn into the street on the right.

*yamiini** rightist, right-wing. *haaδa yamiini b-siyaasta.* He's rightist in his politics.

*yamaani** 1. from Yemen, Yemenite. 2. a Yemeni, a Yemenite.

*yimnaawi** right-handed. *nfaḍḍil laa-عuub yimnaawi.* We prefer a right-handed player.

ʔayman fem. *yimna* right, located on the right. *l-ijnaaɛ il-ʔayman maal iṭ-ṭeer maksuur.* The bird's right wing is broken. *عeen il-yimna ḍaعiifa.* The right eye is weak.

y-h-w-d

yahuud (coll.) Jew(s).

*yahuudi** 1. Jewish. 2. Jew.

yahuudiyya Judaism.

y-w-a-š

yawaaš slow, slowly. *nazzil iṣ-ṣanduug yawaaš ḥatta la-titkassar il-imwaaᶜiin.* Let the crate down slowly so the dishes don't get broken. *min faḍlak, ˀiḥči yawaaš. ma-afhamak zeen.* Please speak slowly. I don't understand you very well. *midd iidak yawaaš yawaaš w-ukmuš iṭ-ṭeer.* Extend your hand very slowly and grab the bird. *yawaašak! raḥ-tumrud iṭ-ṭamaaṭa!* Take it easy there! You'll mash the tomatoes!

y-w-ḥ-n

yuuḥanna John.

y-w-d

yood iodine. *tantar yood* tincture of iodine.

y-w-s-f

yuusif Joseph.

y-w-l-l

yawall f. *yawalli* pl. *yawallu* (emphatic particle, approx.:) look, hey you, buddy, mac, man. *yawall, ˀabqa ˀaᶜallim biik w-ma-titᶜallam?* Look, am I going to have to go on teaching you and you won't learn? *yawall, la-tiddaaxal ib-hiiči qaḍaaya!* Look, don't get involved in that sort of thing! *jaa l-imtiḥaan. laazim tidrus, yawall!* The exam's getting close. You'd better study, man!

y-w-m

yoom pl. *ˀayyaam* day. *gḍeena xooš ˀayyaam bil-baṣra.* We spent some wonderful days in Basra. *l-ˀasᶜaar rtifᶜat ihwaaya b-ˀayyaam il-ḥarub.* Prices went up a lot during war time. *banaat hal-yoom yirḥuun lil-madaaris.* The girls nowadays go to schools. || *l-yoom* today. *ma-čaan ihnaa l-yoom.* He wasn't here today.

*yawmi** daily. *jadwal id-dawaam il-yawmi* daily attendance record.

yoomiyya 1. daily, every day. *yoomiyya yxaaburni.* He calls me every day. || *hal-umgaddi yoomiit il-farid yaaxuḍ minni ᶜašr ifluus.* Every single day this beggar gets ten fils from me. 2. (pl. *-aat*) daily wages, day's pay. *ˀaštuġuḷ in-nahaar kulla w-yoomiiti rubuᶜ diinaar.* I work all day and my day's pay is a quarter dinar. *ˀabuuya ma-nṭaani yoomiiti baᶜad.* My father hasn't given me my daily allowance yet.

yoomiyyan daily, every day.

y-w-n-a-n

l-yuunaan Greece.

*yuunaani** Greek.

y-y-a

-yyaa- /particle serving as stem for pronominal suffix, e.g./ *l-qalam maalak baᶜda ᶜinda loo rajjaᶜ-lak-iyyaa?* Does he still have your pencil or did he return it to you?

y-y-z-y

yeezi (invar., an exclamation, approx.:) wait, hold on, that's enough. *yeezi ᶜaad!* Now just one minute!